# WILEY CPA EXAM REVIEW 2008

## Financial Accounting and Reporting

D1717073

O. Ray Whittington, CPA, PhD

Patrick R. Delaney, CPA, PhD

BICENTENNIAL
1807
WILEY
2007
BICENTENNIAL

JOHN WILEY & SONS, INC.

The following items, copyright © by the American Institute of Certified Public Accountants, Inc., are reprinted (or adapted) with permission.

1.  Material from *Uniform CPA Examination Questions and Answers*, 1978 through 2000.

2.  *Information for Uniform CPA Examination Candidates*, Board of Examiners, 2000.

3.  Material from the Certified Internal Auditor Examination, Copyright © 1994 through 1997 by the Institute of Internal Auditors, Inc., are reprinted and/or adapted by permission.

4.  Material from the Certified Management Accountant Examinations, Copyright © 1993 through 1997 by the Institute of Certified Management Accountants re reprinted and/or adapted by permission.

5.  Example financial statements from Industry Audit Guides: *Audits of Colleges and Universities*, *Audits of Voluntary Health and Welfare Organizations*, and *Audits of Providers of Health Care Services*.

6.  Example of Statement of Activity from SOP 78-10.

Reproduction and adaptation of pronouncements, copyright © Financial Accounting Standards Board, Norwalk, Connecticut 06856-5116, with permission.

Reproduction of "Combined Statement of Revenues, Expenditures, and Changes in Fund Balances -- All Governmental Fund Types and Expendable Trust Funds," copyright © Governmental Accounting Standards Board, Norwalk, Connecticut 06856-5116, with permission.

Statement of changes in fund balances for an educational institution from *College and University Business Administration* with permission of the National Association of College and University Business Officers.

# CONTENTS

[1] *As explained in Chapter 1, this book is organized into 14 modules (manageable study units). The numbering of the modules commences with number 7 to correspond with the numbering system used in our two-volume set.*

# PREFACE

**Passing the CPA exam upon your first attempt is possible!** The *Wiley CPA Examination Review* preparation materials provide you with the necessary materials (visit our Web site at www.wiley.com/cpa for more information). It's up to you to add the hard work and commitment. Together we can beat the pass rate on each section of about 40%. All Wiley CPA products are continuously updated to provide you with the most comprehensive and complete knowledge base. Choose your products from the Wiley preparation materials and you can proceed confidently. You can select support materials that are exam-based and user-friendly. You can select products that will help you pass!

**Remaining current is one of the keys to examination success. Here is a list of what's new in this edition of the *Wiley CPA Examination Review Financial Accounting and Reporting* text.**

- The AICPA Content Specification Outlines on Financial Accounting and Reporting for the computerized CPA Examination
- AICPA questions released in 2007
- The new simulation interface
- Coverage of new financial accounting standards, especially

  - Statement of Financial Accounting Standards 157, *Fair Value Measurements*
  - Statement of Financial Accounting Standards 159, *Fair Value Option for Financial Assets and Financial Liabilities—including an amendment of FASB Statement No. 115*

The objective of this work is to provide you with the knowledge to pass the Financial Accounting and Reporting portion of the Uniform Certified Public Accounting (CPA) Exam. The text is divided up into fourteen areas of study called modules. Each module contains written text with discussion, examples, and demonstrations of the key exam concepts. Following each text area, actual American Institute of Certified Public Accountants (AICPA) unofficial questions and answers are presented to test your knowledge. We are indebted to the AICPA for permission to reproduce and adapt examination materials from past examinations. Author constructed questions and simulations are provided for new areas or areas that require updating. All author constructed questions and simulations are modeled after AICPA question formats. The multiple-choice questions are grouped into topical areas, giving candidates a chance to assess their areas of strength and weakness. Selection and inclusion of topical content is based upon current AICPA Content Specification Outlines. Only testable topics are presented. If the CPA exam does not test it, this text does not present it.

The CPA exam is one of the toughest exams you will ever take. It will not be easy. But if you follow our guidelines and focus on your goal, you will be thrilled with what you can accomplish.

Ray Whittington
November 2007

**Don't forget to visit our Web site at www.wiley.com/cpa
for supplements and updates.**

# ABOUT THE AUTHORS

**Ray Whittington**, PhD, CPA, CMA, CIA, is the dean of the College of Commerce at DePaul University. Prior to joining the faculty at DePaul, Professor Whittington was the Director of Accountancy at San Diego State University. From 1989 through 1991, he was the Director of Auditing Research for the American Institute of Certified Public Accountants (AICPA), and he previously was on the audit staff of KPMG. He previously served as a member of the Auditing Standards Board of the AICPA and as a member of the Accounting and Review Services Committee and the Board of Regents of the Institute of Internal Auditors. Professor Whittington has published numerous textbooks, articles, monographs, and continuing education courses.

**Patrick R. Delaney**, deceased, was the dedicated author and editor of the *Wiley CPA Exam Review* books for twenty years. He was the Arthur Andersen LLP Alumni Professor of Accountancy and Department Chair at Northern Illinois University. He received his PhD in Accountancy from the University of Illinois. He had public accounting experience with Arthur Andersen LLP and was coauthor of *GAAP: Interpretation and Application*, also published by John Wiley & Sons, Inc. He served as Vice President and a member of the Illinois CPA Society's Board of Directors, and was Chairman of its Accounting Principles Committee; was a past president of the Rockford Chapter, Institute of Management Accountants; and had served on numerous other professional committees. He was a member of the American Accounting Association, American Institute of Certified Public Accountants, and Institute of Management Accountants. Professor Delaney was published in *The Accounting Review* and was a recipient of the Illinois CPA Society's Outstanding Educator Award, NIU's Excellence in Teaching Award, and Lewis University's Distinguished Alumnus Award. He was involved in NIU's CPA Review Course as director and instructor.

# ABOUT THE CONTRIBUTOR

**Anita L. Feller**, PhD, CPA, is a Lecturer in Accountancy at the University of Illinois at Urbana-Champaign. She is the recipient of the Commerce Council Excellence in Teaching Award. Formerly a staff accountant in the tax department at KPMG Peat Marwick, she teaches courses in financial accounting and applied professional research. Professor Feller also teaches financial and managerial topics in the University of Illinois CPA Review Course.

# 1 BEGINNING YOUR CPA REVIEW PROGRAM

To maximize the efficiency of your review program, begin by studying (not merely reading) this chapter and the next three chapters of this volume. They have been carefully organized and written to provide you with important information to assist you in successfully completing the Financial Accounting and Reporting section of the CPA exam. Beyond providing a comprehensive outline to help you organize the material tested on the Financial Accounting and Reporting section of the exam, Chapter 1 will assist you in organizing a study program to prepare for the Financial Accounting and Reporting portion. Self-discipline is essential.

## GENERAL COMMENTS ON THE EXAMINATION

The Uniform CPA Examination is delivered using computer-based testing (CBT). Computer-based testing has several advantages. You may take the exam one section at a time. As a result, your studies can be focused on that one section, improving your chances for success. In addition, the exam is no longer offered twice a year. During eight months of ever year, you may take the exam on your schedule, six days a week and in the morning or in the afternoon.

Successful completion of the Uniform CPA Examination in Financial Accounting and Reporting is an attainable goal. Keep this point foremost in your mind as you study the first four chapters in this volume and develop your study plan.

### Purpose of the Examination[1]

The Uniform CPA Examination is designed to test the entry-level knowledge and skills necessary to protect the public interest. These knowledge and skills were identified through a Practice Analysis performed in 2000, which served as a basis for the development of the content specifications for the new exam. The skills identified as necessary for the protection of the public interest include

- Analysis—the ability to organize, process, and interpret data to develop options for decision making.
- Judgment—the ability to evaluate options for decision-making and provide an appropriate conclusion.
- Communication—the ability to effectively elicit and/or express information through written or oral means.
- Research—the ability to locate and extract relevant information from available resource materials.

---

[1] More information may be obtained from the AICPA's *Uniform CPA Examination Candidate Bulletin*, which you can find on the AICPA's Web site at www.cpa-exam.org.

- Understanding—the ability to recognize and comprehend the meaning and application of a particular matter.

For the Financial Accounting and Reporting section, the Board of Examiners has provided the following matrix to illustrate the interaction of content and skills:

| Content Specification Outline Areas | Skill Categories | | | | | Content Weights |
|---|---|---|---|---|---|---|
| | Communication | Research | Analysis | Judgment | Understanding | |
| I. Concepts and standards for financial statements | | | | | | 17-23% |
| II. Typical items in financial statements | | | | | | 27-33% |
| II. Specific types of transactions and events | | | | | | 27-33% |
| IV. Accounting and reporting for governmental entities | | | | | | 8-12% |
| V. Accounting and reporting for nongovernmental and not-for-profit organizations | | | | | | 8-12% |
| Skills Weights | 6-16% | 11-21% | 13-23% | 10-20% | 35-45% | |

You should keep these skills foremost in your mind as you prepare and sit for the Financial Accounting and Reporting section.

The CPA examination is one of many screening devices to assure the competence of those licensed to perform the attest function and to render professional accounting services. Other screening devices include educational requirements, ethics examinations, and work experience.

The examination appears to test the material covered in accounting programs of the better business schools. It also appears to be based upon the body of knowledge essential for the practice of public accounting and the auditor of a medium-sized client. Since the examination is primarily a textbook or academic examination, you should plan on taking it as soon as possible after completing your accounting education.

### Examination Content

Guidance concerning topical content of the Financial Accounting and Reporting section of the CPA exam can be found in a document prepared by the Board of Examiners of the AICPA entitled *Uniform CPA Examination—Examination Content Specifications*. We have included the content outlines for Financial Accounting and Reporting in Chapter 5. These outlines should be used as an indication of the topics' relative emphasis on the exam.

The Board's objective in preparing this detailed listing of topics tested on the exam is to help "in assuring the continuing validity and reliability of the Uniform CPA Examination." These outlines are an excellent source of guidance concerning the areas and the emphasis to be given each area on future exams.

They are provided to each candidate in *CPA Candidate Bulletin* which may be downloaded at the AICPA's exam Web site, www.cpa-exam.org.

New accounting and auditing pronouncements, including those in the governmental and not-for-profit areas, are tested in the testing window six months after the pronouncement's *effective* date. If early application is permitted, a pronouncement is tested six months after the *issuance* date; candidates are also responsible for the old pronouncement until it is superseded. The AICPA posts content changes regularly on its Internet site at www.cpa-exam.org.

### Nondisclosure and Computerization of Examination

Beginning May 1996, the Uniform CPA Examination became nondisclosed. For each exam section, candidates are required to agree to a *Statement of Confidentiality,* which states that they will not divulge the nature and content of any exam question. In April of 2004, the CPA exam became computer-based. Candidates take the exam at Prometric sites in the 54 jurisdictions in which the CPA exam is offered. From April 5, 2004, going forward the CPA exam is offered continually during the testing windows shown below.

| Testing Window (Exam Available) | January through February | April through May | July through August | October through November |
|---|---|---|---|---|
| AICPA Review & Update (Exam Unavailable) | March | June | September | December |

One or more exam sections may be taken during any exam window, and the sections may be taken in any desired order. **However, no candidate will be allowed to sit for the same section more than once during any given testing window.** In addition, a candidate must pass all four sections of the CPA exam within a "rolling" eighteen-month period, which begins on the date he or she passes a section. In other words, you must pass the other three sections of the exam within eighteen months of when you pass the first section. If you do not pass all sections within the eighteen-month period, credit for any section(s) passed outside the eighteen-month period will expire and the section(s) must be retaken.

The following table compares the sections of the prior pencil-and-paper exam with the new computer-based exam.

| Pencil-and-Paper Examination up to November 2003 (15.5 hours in 2 days) | Computer-Based Examination commencing April 5, 2004 (14 hours over flexible period of time) |
|---|---|
| Auditing (4.5 hours) | Auditing & Attestation (4.5 hours) |
| Financial Accounting & Reporting (4.5 hours) | Financial Accounting & Reporting (4 hours) |
| Accounting & Reporting (3.5 hours) | Regulation (3 hours) |
| Business Law & Professional Responsibilities (3 hours) | Business Environment & Concepts (2.5 hours) |

### Types of Questions

The computer-based Uniform CPA Examination consists of two basic question formats.

1. Multiple-Choice—questions requiring the selection of one of four responses to a short scenario.
2. Simulations—case studies that are used to assess knowledge and skills in a context approximating that found on the job through the use of realistic scenarios and tasks, and access to normally available and familiar resources.

The multiple-choice questions are much like the ones that have constituted a majority of the CPA examination for years. **And the good news is that these types of questions constitute about 70% of the Financial Accounting and Reporting section.** The simulations are new and information about this type of question is somewhat limited. However, we have attempted in this manual to use the latest available information to design study materials that will make you successful in answering simulation problems. You should refer to the AICPA Web site (www.cpa-exam.org) for the latest information about the format and content of this new type of question.

### Process for Sitting for the Examination

While there are some variations in the process from state to state, the basic process for sitting for the CPA examination may be described as follows:

1. Apply to take the examination (request, complete, and submit an application)
2. Receive your Notice to Schedule (NTS)
3. Schedule your examination(s)
4. Take your examination(s)
5. Receive you score report(s)

### Applying to Take the Examination

The right to practice public accounting as a CPA is governed by individual state statutes. While some rules regarding the practice of public accounting vary from state to state, all State Boards of Accountancy use the Uniform CPA Examination and AICPA advisory grading service as one of the requirements to practice public accounting. Every candidate should contact the applicable State Board of Accountancy to determine the requirements to sit for the exam (e.g., education requirements and fees). For comparisons of requirements for various state boards and those policies that are uniform across jurisdictions, you should refer to the Web site of the National Association of State Boards of Accountancy (NASBA) at www.nasba.org.

A frequent problem candidates encounter is failure to apply by the deadline. **Apply to sit for the examination early. Also, you should use extreme care in filling out the application and mailing required materials to your State Board of Accountancy.** If possible, have a friend review your completed application before mailing with check and other documentation. The name on your application must appear exactly the same as it appears on the identification you plan to use at the testing center. Candidates miss a particular CPA examination window simply because of minor technical details that were overlooked (checks not signed, items not enclosed, question not answered on application, etc.). **Because of the very high volume of applications received in the more populous states, the administrative staff does not have time to call or write to correct minor details and will simply reject your application.**

The various state boards, their Web sites, and telephone numbers are listed on the following page. Be sure to inquire of your state board for specific and current requirements.

It is possible for candidates to sit for the examination at a Prometric site in any state or territory. Candidates desiring to do so should contact the State Board of Accountancy in their home state.

### *Exam Scheduling*

Once you have been cleared to take the exam by the applicable state board, you will receive by mail a Notice to Schedule (NTS) and may then schedule to sit for one or more sections of the exam.

You have the following three options for scheduling your examination:

1. **Visit www.prometric.com/cpa on the Internet**
   This is the easiest and quickest way to schedule an examination appointment (or cancel and reschedule an appointment, if necessary). Simply go to the Web site, select SCHEDULE APPOINTMENT, and follow the directions. It is advised that you print and keep for your records the confirmation number for your appointment.
2. **Call 800-580-9648 (Candidate Services Call Center)**
   Before you call, you must have your NTS in front of you, and have in mind several times, dates, and locations that would work for you. You will not receive written confirmation of your appointment. Be sure to write down the date, time, location, and confirmation number for each of your appointments.
3. **Call your local test center**
   While this method is not recommended, you may call your local test center and schedule appointments. Again, be sure to have your NTS in front of you and write down the date, time, location, and confirmation number for each of your appointments.

You should also be aware that if you have to cancel or reschedule your appointment, you may be subject to a cancellation/rescheduling fee. The AICPA's *Uniform CPA Examination Candidate Bulletin* lists the rescheduling and cancellation fees.

**To assure that you get your desired location and time period it is imperative that you schedule early. To get your first choice of dates, you are advised to schedule at least 45 days in advance. You will not be scheduled for an exam fewer than 5 days before testing.**

## ATTRIBUTES OF EXAMINATION SUCCESS

Your primary objective in preparing for the Financial Accounting and Reporting section is to pass. Other objectives such as learning new and reviewing old material should be considered secondary. The six attributes of examination success discussed below are **essential**. You should study the attributes and work toward achieving/developing each of them **before** taking the examination.

1. **Knowledge of Material**
   Two points are relevant to "knowledge of material" as an attribute of examination success. **First,** there is a distinct difference between being familiar with material and knowing the material. Frequently candidates confuse familiarity with knowledge. Can you remember when you just could not answer an examination question or did poorly on an examination, but maintained to yourself or your instructor that you knew the material? You probably were only familiar with the material. On the CPA examination, familiarity is insufficient; you must know the material. Remember the exam will test your ability to analyze data, make judgments, communicate, perform research, and demonstrate understanding of the material. For example, you may be familiar with the concepts in accounting for leases (SFAS 13), but can you compute the present value of an annuity due under a lease agreement and record entries for the lessee and les-

| | *STATE BOARD WEB ADDRESS* | *TELEPHONE #* |
|---|---|---|
| **AK** | www.commerce.state.ak.us/occ/pcpa.htm | (907) 465-3811 |
| **AL** | www.asbpa.alabama.gov | (334) 242-5700 |
| **AR** | www.state.ar.us/asbpa | (501) 682-1520 |
| **AZ** | www.azaccountancy.gov | (602) 364-0804 |
| **CA** | www.dca.ca.gov/cba | (916) 263-3680 |
| **CO** | www.dora.state.co.us/accountants | (303) 894-7800 |
| **CT** | www.ct.gov/sboa | (860) 509-6179 |
| **DC** | dcra.dc.gov/dcra | (202) 442-4320 |
| **DE** | www.dpr.delaware.gov | (302) 744-4500 |
| **FL** | www.myflorida.com | (850) 487-1395 |
| **GA** | www.sos.state.ga.us/plb/accountancy/ | (478) 207-1400 |
| **GU** | www.guamboa.org | (671) 647-0813 |
| **HI** | www.hawaii.gov/dcca/areas/pvl/boards/accountancy | (808) 586-2696 |
| **IA** | www.state.ia.us/iacc | (515) 281-5910 |
| **ID** | www.isba.idaho.gov | (208) 334-2490 |
| **IL** | www.ilboa.org | (217) 531-0950 |
| **IN** | www.in.gov/pla/bandc/accountancy/ | (317) 234-3040 |
| **KS** | www.ksboa.org | (785) 296-2162 |
| **KY** | cpa.ky.gov | (502) 595-3037 |
| **LA** | www.cpaboard.state.la.us | (504) 566-1244 |
| **MA** | www.mass.gov/reg/boards/pa | (617) 727-1806 |
| **MD** | www.dllr.state.md.us/license/occprof/account.html | (410) 230-6322 |
| **ME** | www.maineprofessionalreg.org | (207) 624-8603 |
| **MI** | www.michigan.gov/accountancy | (517) 241-9249 |
| **MN** | www.boa.state.mn.us | (651) 296-7938 |
| **MO** | pr.mo.gov/accountancy.asp | (573) 751-0012 |
| **MS** | www.msbpa.state.ms.us | (601) 354-7320 |
| **MT** | www.publicaccountant.mt.gov | (406) 841-2389 |
| **NC** | www.nccpaboard.gov | (919) 733-4222 |
| **ND** | www.state.nd.us/ndsba | (800) 532-5904 |
| **NE** | www.nol.org/home/BPA | (402) 471-3595 |
| **NH** | www.nh.gov/accountancy | (603) 271-3286 |
| **NJ** | www.state.nj.us/lps/ca/nonmed.htm | (973) 504-6380 |
| **NM** | www.rld.state.nm.us/b&c/accountancy/index.htm | (505) 841-9108 |
| **NV** | www.nvaccountancy.com/ | (775) 786-0231 |
| **NY** | www.op.nysed.gov/cpa.htm | (518) 474-3817 |
| **OH** | www.acc.ohio.gov/ | (614) 466-4135 |
| **OK** | www.oab.state.ok.us | (405) 521-2397 |
| **OR** | egov.oregon.gov/BOA/ | (503) 378-4181 |
| **PA** | www.dos.state.pa.us/account | (717) 783-1404 |
| **PR** | www.estado.gobierno.pr/contador.htm | (787) 722-4816 |
| **RI** | www.dbr.state.ri.us | (401) 222-3185 |
| **SC** | www.llr.state.sc.us/POL/Accountancy | (803) 896-4770 |
| **SD** | www.state.sd.us/dcr/acountancy | (605) 367-5770 |
| **TN** | www.state.tn.us/commerce/boards/tnsba/index.html | (615) 741-2550 |
| **TX** | www.tsbpa.state.tx.us | (512) 305-7800 |
| **UT** | www.dopl.utah.gov | (801) 530-6396 |
| **VA** | www.boa.virginia.gov | (804) 367-8505 |
| **VI** | www.dlca.gov.vi | (340) 773-4305 |
| **VT** | vtprofessionals.org/opr1/accountants | (802) 828-2837 |
| **WA** | www.cpaboard.wa.gov | (360) 753-2585 |
| **WI** | www.drl.wi.gov/index.htm | (608) 266-5511 |
| **WV** | www.wvboacc.org | (304) 558-3557 |
| **WY** | cpaboard.state.wy.us | (307) 777-7551 |

*NOTE: The publisher does not assume responsibility for errors in the above information. You should request information concerning requirements in your state at least six months in advance of the exam dates.*

sor? Once again, a major concern must be to know the material rather than just being familiar with it. Knowledgeable discussion of the material is required on the CPA examination. **Second,** the Financial Accounting and Reporting exam tests a literally overwhelming amount of material at a rigorous level. From an undergraduate point of view, the CPA examination in Financial Accounting and Reporting includes material from the following courses.

Intermediate Financial (usually two semesters)
Advanced Financial

**Furthermore,** as noted earlier, the CPA exam will test new material, sometimes as early as six months after issuance. In other words, you are not only responsible for material in the above courses, but also for all new developments in each of these areas.

This text contains outlines of accounting topics from FASB pronouncements, financial accounting courses, etc. Return to the original material (e.g., FASB, your accounting textbooks, etc.) only if the outlines do not reinforce material you already know.

2. **Commitment to Exam Preparation**

Your preparation for the CPA exam should begin at least two months prior to the date you plan to schedule your seating for an exam section. If you plan to take more than one section, you should start earlier. Over the course of your preparation, you will experience many peaks and valleys. There will be days when you feel completely prepared and there will also be days when you feel totally overwhelmed. This is not unusual and, in fact, should be expected.

The CPA exam is a very difficult and challenging exam. How many times in your college career did you study months for an exam? Probably not too many. Therefore, candidates need to remain focused on the objective—succeeding on the CPA exam.

Develop a personal study plan so that you are reviewing material daily. Of course, you should schedule an occasional study break to help you relax, but don't schedule too many breaks. Candidates who dedicate themselves to studying have a much greater chance of going through this process only one time. On the other hand, a lack of focus and piecemeal preparation will only extend the process over a number of exam sittings.

3. **Solutions Approach**

The solutions approach is a systematic approach to solving the questions and simulations found on the CPA examination. Many candidates know the material fairly well when they sit for the CPA exam, but they do not know how to take the examination. Candidates generally neither work nor answer problems efficiently in terms of time or grades. The solutions approach permits you to avoid drawing "blanks" on CPA exam problems; using the solutions approach coupled with grading insights (see below) allows you to pick up a sizable number of points on test material with which you are not familiar. Chapter 3 outlines the solutions approach for multiple-choice questions and simulations.

4. **Grading Insights**

Your score on each section of the exam is determined by the sum of points assigned to individual questions and simulation parts. Thus, you must attempt to maximize your points on each individual item.

The multiple-choice questions within each section are organized into three groups which are referred to as testlets. Each multiple-choice testlet is comprised of approximately 30 multiple-choice questions. The multiple-choice testlets vary in overall difficulty A testlet is labeled either "medium difficult" or "difficult" based on its makeup. A "difficult" testlet has a higher percentage of hard questions than a "medium difficult" testlet. Every candidate's first multiple-choice testlet in each section will be a "medium difficult" testlet. If a candidate scores well on the first testlet, he or she will receive a "difficult" second testlet. Candidates that do not perform well on the first testlet receive a second "medium difficult" testlet. Because the scoring procedure takes the difficulty of the testlet into account, candidates are scored fairly regardless of the type of testlets they receive.

Each multiple-choice testlet contains "operational" and "pretest" questions. The operational questions are the only ones that are used to determine your score. Pretest questions are not scored; they are being tested for future use as operational questions. However, you have no way of knowing which questions are operational and which questions are pretest questions. Therefore, you must approach each question as if it will be used to determine your grade.

Simulations include more extensive scenarios and a number of requirements. For example, the requirements may involve calculations, form completion, research, and written communication. The points assigned to the requirements will vary according to their difficulty. Most of the requirements are graded by the computer. Only those that involve written communication are graded manually. The simulations make use of a number of commonly used tools such as spreadsheets and electronic research databases. Therefore, you need to become proficient in the use of these tools to maximize your score on the simulations.

CPA Exam scores are reported on a scale from 0 to 99. The total score is not a percent correct score. It is a combination of scores from the multiple-choice and simulation portions of the exam considering the relative difficulty of the items. A total score of 75 is required to pass each section.

The AICPA includes sample examination questions on its Web site that allow you to get experience with the use of the actual computer tools used on the CPA exam. Also, more experience with computer testing can be obtained by using Wiley CPA Review Practice software.

5. **Examination Strategy**

Prior to sitting for the examination, it is important to develop an examination strategy (i.e., an approach to working efficiently throughout the exam.). Your ability to cope successfully with the 4 hours of examination in Financial Accounting and Reporting can be improved by

a. Recognizing the importance and usefulness of an examination strategy
b. Using Chapter 4, Taking the Examination and previous examination experience to develop a "personal strategy" for the exam
c. Testing your "personal strategy" on example examination questions under conditions similar to those at the test centers (using similar tools and databases and with a time limit)

6. **Examination Confidence**

You need confidence to endure the physical and mental demands of 4 hours of problem solving under tremendous pressure. Examination confidence results from proper preparation for the exam, which includes mastering the first five attributes of examination success. Examination confidence is necessary to enable you to overcome the initial frustration with problems for which you may not be specifically prepared.

This study manual, when properly used, contributes to your examination confidence. Build confidence by completing the questions contained herein.

### *Common Candidate Mistakes*

The CPA Exam is a formidable hurdle in your accounting career. With a pass rate of about 40% on each section, the level of difficulty is obvious. The good news, though, is that about 75% of all candidates (first-time and reexam) sitting for each examination eventually pass. The authors believe that the first-time pass rate could be higher if candidates would be more careful. Eight common mistakes that many candidates make are

1. Failure to understand the exam question requirements
2. Misunderstanding the supporting text of the problem
3. Lack of knowledge of material tested, especially recently issued pronouncements
4. Failure to develop proficiency with computer-based testing and practice tools such as electronic research databases and spreadsheets
5. Inability to apply the solutions approach
6. Lack of an exam strategy (e.g., allocation of time)
7. Sloppiness and logical errors
8. Failure to proofread and edit

These mistakes are not mutually exclusive. Candidates may commit one or more of the above items. Remind yourself that when you decrease the number of common mistakes, you increase your chances of successfully becoming a CPA. Take the time to read carefully the exam question requirements. Do not jump into a quick start, only to later find out that you didn't understand what information the examiners were asking for. Read slowly and carefully. Take time to recall your knowledge. Respond to the question asked. Apply an exam strategy such as allocating your time among all question formats. Do not spend too much time on the multiple-choice testlets, leaving no time to spend on preparing your simulation responses. Upon completion of any written communication requirement, proofread and edit your answer. Use the spell check function of the word processor. Answer questions quickly but precisely, avoid common mistakes, and increase your score.

### PURPOSE AND ORGANIZATION OF THIS REVIEW TEXTBOOK

This book is designed to help you prepare adequately for the Financial Accounting and Reporting examination. There is no easy way to prepare for the successful completion of the CPA Examination; however, through the use of this manual, your approach will be systematic and logical.

The objective of this book is to provide study materials supportive to CPA candidates. While no guarantees are made concerning the success of those using this text, this book promotes efficient preparation by

1. Explaining how to **maximize your score** through analysis of examination grading and illustration of the solutions approach.
2. **Defining areas tested** through the use of the content specification outlines. Note that predictions of future exams are not made. You should prepare yourself for all possible topics rather than gambling on the appearance of certain questions.
3. **Organizing your study program** by comprehensively outlining all of the subject matter tested on the examination in 14 easy-to-use study modules. Each study module is a manageable task which facilitates your exam preparation. Turn to Chapter 5 and peruse the contents to get a feel for the organization of this book.
4. **Providing CPA candidates with previous examination problems** organized by topic (e.g., consolidations, inventory, etc.) Questions have also been developed for new areas and in simulation format.
5. **Explaining the AICPA unofficial answers** to the examination questions included in this text. The AICPA publishes unofficial answers for all questions from exams administered prior to 1996 and for any released questions from exams administered on or after May 1996. However, no explanation is made of the approach that should have been applied to the examination questions to obtain these unofficial answers.

As you read the next few paragraphs which describe the contents of this book, flip through the chapters to gain a general familiarity with the book's organization and contents. Chapters 2, 3, and 4 are to help you maximize your score.

Chapter 2      Examination Grading
Chapter 3      The Solutions Approach
Chapter 4      Taking the Examination

Chapters 2, 3, and 4 contain material that should be kept in mind throughout your study program. Refer back to them frequently. Reread them for a final time just before you sit for the exam.

Chapter 5, Financial Accounting and Reporting, outlines and discusses the coverage of the Financial Accounting and Reporting section of the CPA examination. It also contains the AICPA Content Specification Outlines for all the Financial Accounting and Reporting topics tested in this section of the exam.

Chapter 5 (Financial Accounting and Reporting Modules) contains:

1. AICPA Content Specification Outlines of the material tested on the Financial Accounting and Reporting section of the exam
2. Multiple-choice questions
3. Simulation problems
4. AICPA unofficial answers with the author's explanations for the multiple-choice questions
5. Author's answers to simulation problems

Also included at the end of this text is a complete Sample Financial Accounting and Reporting CPA Examination. The sample exam is included to enable candidates to gain experience in taking a "realistic" exam. While studying the modules, the candidate can become accustomed to concentrating on fairly narrow topics. By working through the sample examination near the end of their study programs, candidates will be better prepared for taking the actual examination. Because some simulations require the use of research materials, it is useful to have the appropriate electronic research database (FASB Financial Accounting Research System or a printed copy of professional standards to complete the sample examination). **Remember that this research material will not be available to answer the multiple-choice questions.**

### Other Textbooks

This text is a comprehensive compilation of study guides and outlines; it should not be necessary to supplement them with accounting textbooks and other materials for most topics. You probably already have some of these texts or earlier editions of them. In such a case, you must make the decision whether to replace them and trade familiarity (including notes therein, etc.), with the cost and inconvenience of obtaining the newer texts containing a more updated presentation.

Before spending time and money acquiring new texts, begin your study program with *CPA EXAMINATION REVIEW: FINANCIAL ACCOUNTING AND REPORTING* to determine your need for supplemental texts.

### Ordering Other Textual Materials

You probably already have intermediate and advanced texts for financial accounting and reporting. If you cannot order desired texts through a local bookstore, write the publisher directly.

If you want to order AICPA materials, locate an AICPA educator member to order your materials, since educators are entitled to a 30% discount and may place Web site or telephone orders.

AICPA (CPA2Biz)
|            |                    |          |                        |
|------------|--------------------|----------|------------------------|
| Telephone  | 888-777-7077       | Address: | Order Department       |
| Web site   | www.CPA2Biz.com    |          | CPA2Biz                |
|            |                    |          | P.O. Box 2209          |
|            |                    |          | Jersey City, NJ 07303-2209 |

A variety of supplemental CPA products are available from John Wiley & Sons, Inc. By using a variety of learning techniques, such as software, computer-based learning, and audio CDs, the candidate is more likely to remain focused during the study process and to retain information for a longer period of time. Visit our Web site at **www.wiley.com/cpa** for other products, supplements, and updates.

### Working CPA Questions

The AICPA Content Outlines, study outlines, etc., will be used to acquire and assimilate the knowledge tested on the examination. This, however, should be only **one-half** of your preparation program. The other half should be spent practicing how to work questions and problems. Some candidates probably spend over 90% of their time reviewing material tested on the CPA exam. Much more time should be allocated to working questions and problems **under exam conditions**. Working examination questions and problems serves two functions. First, it helps you develop a solutions approach as well as solutions that will maximize your score. Second, it provides the best test of your knowledge of the material. At a minimum, candidates should work one of the more complex and difficult problems and simulations (e.g., pensions, statement of cash flows, consolidated financial statement worksheet) in each area or module.

The multiple-choice questions and answers can be used in many ways. First, they may be used as a diagnostic evaluation of your knowledge. For example, before beginning to review deferred taxes you may wish to answer 10 to 15 multiple-choice questions to determine your ability to answer CPA examination questions on deferred taxes. The apparent difficulty of the questions and the correctness of your answers will allow you to determine the necessary breadth and depth of your review. Additionally, exposure to examination questions prior to review and study of the material should provide motivation. You will develop a feel for your level of proficiency and an understanding of the scope and difficulty of past examination questions. Moreover, your review materials will explain concepts encountered in the diagnostic multiple-choice questions.

Second, the multiple-choice questions can be used as a poststudy or postreview evaluation. You should attempt to understand all concepts mentioned (even in incorrect answers) as you answer the questions. Refer to the explanation of the answer for discussion of the alternatives even though you selected the correct response. Thus, you should read the explanation of the unofficial answer unless you completely understand the question and all of the alternative answers.

Third, you may wish to use the multiple-choice questions as a primary study vehicle. This is probably the quickest but least thorough approach in preparing for the exam. Make a sincere effort to understand the question and to select the correct response before referring to the unofficial answer and explanation. In many cases, the explanations will appear inadequate because of your unfamiliarity with the topic. Always refer back to an appropriate study source, such as the outlines and text in this volume, your accounting textbooks, FASB pronouncements, etc.

The multiple-choice questions outnumber the simulations by greater than 10 to 1 in this book. This is similar to the proposed content of the new computer-based examination. One problem with so many multiple-choice questions is that you may overemphasize them. Candidates generally prefer to work multiple-choice questions because they are

1. Shorter and less time-consuming
2. Solvable with less effort
3. Less frustrating than simulations

Another problem with the large number of multiple-choice questions is that you may tend to become overly familiar with the questions. The result may be that you begin reading the facts and assumptions of previously studied questions into the questions on your examination. Guard against this potential problem by reading each multiple-choice question with **extra** care.

Beginning with the introduction of the computer-based examination, the AICPA began testing with simulations. Simulations released by the AICPA, prepared by the authors, and revised from prior CPA exam problems are incorporated in the modules to which they pertain. (See the listing of question material at the beginning of Chapter 5.)

The questions and solutions in this volume provide you with an opportunity to diagnose and correct any exam-taking weaknesses prior to sitting for the examination. Continually analyze your incorrect solutions to determine the cause of the error(s) during your preparation for the exam. Treat each incorrect solution as a mistake that will not be repeated (especially on the examination). Also attempt to generalize your weaknesses so that you may change, reinforce, or develop new approaches to exam preparation and exam taking.

After you have finished reviewing for the Financial Accounting and Reporting section of the exam, work the complete sample exam provided in Appendix A.

## SELF-STUDY PROGRAM

CPA candidates generally find it difficult to organize and to complete their own self-study programs. A major problem is determining **what** and **how** to study. Another major problem is developing the self-discipline to stick to a study program. Relatedly, it is often difficult for CPA candidates to determine how much to study (i.e., determining when they are sufficiently prepared).

The following suggestions will assist you in developing a **systematic, comprehensive,** and **successful** self-study program to help you complete the Financial Accounting and Reporting exam.

Remember that these are only suggestions. You should modify them to suit your personality, available study time, and other constraints. Some of the suggestions may appear trivial, but CPA candidates generally need all the assistance they can get to systemize their study programs.

### Study Facilities and Available Time

Locate study facilities that will be conducive to concentrated study. Factors that you should consider include

1. Noise distraction
2. Interruptions
3. Lighting
4. Availability (e.g., a local library is not available at 5:00 A.M.)
5. Accessibility (e.g., your kitchen table vs. your local library)
6. Desk or table space

You will probably find different study facilities optimal for different times (e.g., your kitchen table during early morning hours and local libraries during early evening hours).

Next review your personal and professional commitments from now until the exam to determine regularly available study time. Formalize a schedule to which you can reasonably commit yourself. At the end of this chapter, you will find a detailed approach to managing your time available for the exam preparation program.

### Self-Evaluation

The *CPA EXAMINATION REVIEW: FINANCIAL ACCOUNTING AND REPORTING* self-study program is partitioned into 14 topics or modules. Since each module is clearly defined and should be studied separately, you have the task of preparing for the Financial Accounting and Reporting section of the CPA exam by tackling 14 manageable tasks. Partitioning the overall project into 14 modules makes preparation psychologically easier, since you sense yourself completing one small step at a time rather than seemingly never completing one or a few large steps.

By completing the following "Preliminary Estimate of Your Knowledge of Subject" inventory, organized by the 14 modules in this program, you will tabulate your strong and weak areas at the beginning of your study program. This will help you budget your limited study time. Note that you should begin studying the material in each module by answering up to 1/4 of the total multiple-choice questions covering that module's topics (see instruction 4.A. in the next section). This "mini-exam" should constitute a diagnostic evaluation as to the amount of review and study you need.

**PRELIMINARY ESTIMATE OF YOUR PRESENT KNOWLEDGE OF SUBJECT***

| No. | Module | Proficient | Fairly proficient | Generally familiar | Not familiar |
|---|---|---|---|---|---|
| 7 | Basic Theory and Financial Reporting | | | | |
| 8 | Inventory | | | | |
| 9 | Fixed Assets | | | | |
| 10 | Monetary Current Assets and Current Liabilities | | | | |
| 11 | Present Value | | | | |
| 12 | Deferred Taxes | | | | |
| 13 | Stockholders' Equity | | | | |
| 14 | Investments | | | | |
| 15 | Statement of Cash Flows | | | | |
| 16 | Business Combinations and Consolidations | | | | |
| 17 | Derivative Instruments and Hedging Activities | | | | |
| 18 | Miscellaneous | | | | |
| 19 | Governmental Accounting | | | | |
| 20 | Not-for-Profit Accounting | | | | |

*The number of modules in this text commences with number 7 to correspond with the numbering system used in our two-volume set.*

### Time Allocation

The study program below entails an average of 80 hours (Step 5. below) of study time. The breakdown of total hours is indicated in the left margin.

[2 1/2 hrs.]   1.   Study Chapters 2-4 in this volume. These chapters are essential to your efficient preparation program. Time estimate includes candidate's review of the examples of the solutions approach in Chapters 2 and 3.

[1/2 hr.]   2.   Begin FINANCIAL ACCOUNTING AND REPORTING by studying Chapter 5.

3.   Study one module at a time. The modules are listed above in the self-evaluation section.

4.   For each module

[14 hrs.]   A.   Work 1/4 of the multiple-choice questions (e.g., if there are 40 multiple-choice questions in a module, you should work every 4th question). Score yourself.
This diagnostic routine will provide you with an index of your proficiency and familiarity with the type and difficulty of questions.
Time estimate: 3 minutes each, not to exceed 1 hour total.

[21 hrs.]   B.   Study the outlines and illustrations. Refer to outlines of authoritative pronouncements per instructions. Also refer to your accounting textbooks and original authoritative pronouncements (this will occur more frequently for topics in which you have a weak background).
Time estimate: 1 hour minimum per module, with more time devoted to topics less familiar to you.

[18 hrs.]   C.   Work the remaining multiple-choice questions. Study the explanations of the multiple-choice questions you missed or had trouble answering.
Time estimate: 3 minutes to answer each question and 2 minutes to study the answer explanation of each question missed.

[8 hrs.]   D.   Work the simulation problems.
Time estimate: 25 minutes for each problem and 10 minutes to study the answer explanations for each item missed.

[10 hrs.]   E.   Under simulated exam conditions, work the simulations in Appendix A.
Time estimate: 45 minutes for each simulation problem, and 20 minutes to review the solution guide for each problem worked.

[6 hrs.]   F.   Work through the sample CPA examination presented at the end of this text. The exam should be taken in one sitting.

Take the examination under simulated exam conditions (i.e., in a strange place with other people present [e.g., your local municipal library or a computer lab]). Apply your solutions approach to each problem and your exam strategy to the overall exam.

You should limit yourself to the time that you will have when taking the actual CPA exam section (4.5 hours for the Financial Accounting and Reporting section). Spend time afterwards grading your work and reviewing your effort. It might be helpful to do this with other CPA candidates. Another person looking over your exam might be more objective and notice things such as clarity of writing assignments, etc.

Time estimate: 5-6 hours to take the exam and review it later.

5. The total suggested time of 80 hours is only an average. Allocation of time will vary candidate by candidate. Time requirements vary due to the diverse backgrounds and abilities of CPA candidates.

Allocate your time so you gain the most proficiency in the least time. Remember that while 80 hours will be required, you should break the overall project down into 14 more manageable tasks. Do not study more than one module during each study session.

### Using Notecards

Below are one candidate's notecards on financial accounting and reporting topics which illustrate how key definitions, formulas, lists, etc. can be summarized on index cards for quick review. Since candidates can take these anywhere they go, they are a very efficient review tool.

| *Business Combinations* |
| --- |
| • *Must use purchase method* |
| • *FMV, differential may have goodwill*<br>  *CNI from date of combination* |

| *Accounting Changes* | *Prospective treat.* | *Restate FS* |
| --- | --- | --- |
| Δ *in estimate* | Y | N |
| Δ *in principle* | N | Y |
| Δ *in reporting entity* | N | Y |

*Prepared by Greg Graber, CPA, former student, Northern Illinois University*

### Level of Proficiency Required

What level of proficiency must you develop with respect to each of the topics to pass the exam? You should work toward a minimum correct rate on the multiple-choice questions of 80%. Working towards these correct rates or higher ones for Financial Accounting and Reporting will allow for a margin.

Warning: Disproportional study time devoted to multiple-choice (relative to simulations) can be disastrous on the exam. You should work a substantial number of simulation problems under exam conditions, even though multiple-choice questions are easier to work and are used to gauge your proficiency. The authors believe that practicing simulation problems will also improve your proficiency on the multiple-choice questions.

### Multiple-Choice Feedback

One of the benefits of working through previous exam questions is that it helps you to identify your weak areas. Once you have graded your answers, your strong areas and weak areas should be clearly evident. Yet, the important point here is that you should not stop at a simple percentage evaluation. The percentage only provides general feedback about your knowledge of the material contained within that particular module. The percentage **does not** give you any specific feedback regarding the concepts which were tested. In order to get this feedback, you should look at the questions missed on an individual basis because this will help you gain a better understanding of **why** you missed the question.

This feedback process has been facilitated by the fact that within each module where the multiple-choice answer key appears, two blank lines have been inserted next to the multiple-choice answers. As you grade the multiple-choice questions, mark those questions which you have missed. However, instead of just marking the questions right and wrong, you should now focus on marking the questions in a manner which identifies **why** you missed the question. As an example, a candidate could mark the questions in the following manner: ✓ for math mistakes, x for conceptual mistakes, and ? for areas which the candidate was unfamiliar with. The candidate should then correct these mistakes by reworking through the marked questions.

The objective of this marking technique is to help you identify your weak areas and thus, the concepts which you should be focusing on. While it is still important for you to get between 75% and 80% correct when working multiple-choice questions, it is more important for you to understand the concepts. This understanding applies to both the questions answered correctly and those answered incorrectly. Remember, questions on the CPA exam will be different from the questions in the book, however, the concepts will be the same. Therefore, your preparation should focus on understanding concepts, not just getting the correct answer.

### Conditional Candidates

If you have received conditional status on the examination, you must concentrate on the remaining section(s). Unfortunately, many candidates do not study after conditioning the exam, relying on luck to get them through the remaining section(s). Conditional candidates will find that material contained in Chapters 1- 4 and the information contained in the appropriate modules will benefit them in preparing for the remaining section(s) of the examination.

## PLANNING FOR THE EXAMINATION

### Overall Strategy

An overriding concern should be an orderly, systematic approach toward both your preparation program and your examination strategy. A major objective should be to avoid any surprises or anything else that would rattle you during the examination. In other words, you want to be in complete control as much as possible. Control is of paramount importance from both positive and negative viewpoints. The presence of control on your part will add to your confidence and your ability to prepare for and take the exam. Moreover, the presence of control will make your preparation program more enjoyable (or at least less distasteful). On the other hand, a lack of organization will result in inefficiency in preparing and taking the examination, with a highly predictable outcome. Likewise, distractions during the examination (e.g., inadequate lodging, long drive) are generally disastrous.

In summary, establishing a systematic, orderly approach to taking the examination is of paramount importance. Follow these six steps:

1. Develop an overall strategy at the beginning of your preparation program (see below)
2. Supplement your overall strategy with outlines of material tested on the Financial Accounting and Reporting exam (see Chapter 5)
3. Supplement your overall strategy with an explicitly stated set of problem-solving procedures—the solutions approach
4. Supplement your overall strategy with an explicitly stated approach to each examination session (see Chapter 4)
5. Evaluate your preparation progress on a regular basis and prepare lists of things "to do" (see Weekly Review of Preparation Program Progress on following page)
6. RELAX: You can pass the exam. About 40 to 45% of the candidates taking a section of the CPA examination pass. But if you take out the individuals that did not adequately prepare, these percentages increase substantially. You will be one of those who pass if you complete an efficient preparation program and execute well (i.e., solutions approach and exam strategy) while taking the exam.

The following outline is designed to provide you with a general framework of the tasks before you. You should tailor the outline to your needs by adding specific items and comments.

A. Preparation Program (refer to Self-Study Program discussed previously)

   1. Obtain and organize study materials
   2. Locate facilities conducive for studying and block out study time
   3. Develop your solutions approach (including solving simulation problems as well as multiple-choice questions)
   4. Prepare an examination strategy
   5. Study the material tested recently and prepare answers to actual exam questions on these topics under examination conditions
   6. Periodically evaluate your progress

B.  Physical Arrangements

   1.  Apply to and obtain acceptance from your state board
   2.  Schedule your testing location and time

C.  Taking the Examination (covered in detail in Chapter 4)

   1.  Become familiar with location of the test center and procedures
   2.  Implement examination strategies and the solutions approach

### Weekly Review of Preparation Program Progress

   The following pages contain a hypothetical weekly review of program progress.  You should prepare a similar progress chart.  This procedure, which takes only about 5 minutes per week, will help you proceed through a more efficient, complete preparation program.

   Make notes of materials and topics

      1.  That you have studied
      2.  That you have completed
      3.  That need additional study

| *Weeks to go* | *Comments on progress, "to do" items, etc.* |
| --- | --- |
| 12 | 1)  Read *Basic Theory and Financial Reporting* Module<br>2)  Made notecards<br>3)  Worked the MC Questions and Simulation Problems, on a sample basis<br>4)  Need to work Simulation Problems using the solutions approach |
| 11 | 1)  Read *Fixed Assets and Stockholders' Equity* Modules<br>2)  Made notecards<br>3)  Read the SFAS and APB outlines that correspond to these topics<br>4)  Briefly looked over the MC for both modules |
| 10 | 1)  Read *Monetary Current Assets and Current Liabilities* Module<br>2)  Made notecards<br>3)  Read the corresponding SFAS/APB outlines<br>4)  Worked the MC Questions and Simulation Problems for Fixed Assets, Stockholders' Equity, and Monetary CA/CL |
| 9 | 1)  Read the *Inventory and Statement of Cash Flows* Modules<br>2)  Made notecards<br>3)  Skimmed the SFAS and APB outlines, taking notes of important areas<br>4)  Worked the MC Questions and Simulation Problems |
| 8 | 1)  Read the *Present Value* Module<br>2)  Made notecards<br>3)  Studied the SFASs and APBs on leases and pensions<br>4)  Completed the MC Questions and Simulation Problems |
| 7 | 1)  Read *Deferred Taxes* Module<br>2)  Made notecards<br>3)  Read the corresponding SFAS and APB outlines<br>4)  Worked the MC Questions and Simulation Problems |

**6**
1) Read the Derivative Instruments and Hedging Activities and Miscellaneous Modules
2) Made notecards
3) Read the corresponding SFAS and APB outlines
4) Worked the MC Questions and Simulation Problems for these modules
5) Confident with these mods; only need a quick review

---

**5**
1) Read Investments Module
2) Made notecards
3) Read the corresponding SFAS and APB outlines
4) Worked the MC Questions and Simulation Problems

---

**4**
1) Read the Business Combinations and Consolidations Module
2) Reviewed consolidations in an advanced accounting textbook
3) Made notecards
4) Worked the MC Questions and Simulation Problems

---

**3**
1) Took Financial Accounting and Reporting Sample Exam

---

**2**
1) Reviewed all prior topics, picking out a few MC for each topic and working them out
2) Did a statement of cash flows

---

**1**
1) Reviewed notecards and SFAS and APB outlines
2) Worked MC from Deferred Taxes and Stockholders' Equity Modules

---

**0**
1) Tried to relax and review topics

---

### Time Management of Your Preparation

As you begin your CPA exam preparation, you obviously realize that there is a large amount of material to cover over the course of the next two to three months. Therefore, it is very important for you to organize your calendar, and maybe even your daily routine, so that you can allocate sufficient time to studying. An organized approach to your preparation is much more effective than a last week cram session. An organized approach also builds up the confidence necessary to succeed on the CPA exam.

An approach which we have already suggested is to develop weekly "to do" lists. This technique helps you to establish intermediate objectives and goals as you progress through your study plan. You can then focus your efforts on small tasks and not feel overwhelmed by the entire process. And as you accomplish these tasks you will see yourself moving one step closer to realizing the overall goal, succeeding on the CPA exam.

Note, however, that the underlying assumption of this approach is that you have found the time during the week to study and thus accomplish the different tasks. Although this is an obvious step, it is still a very important step. Your exam preparation should be of a continuous nature and not one that jumps around the calendar. Therefore, you should strive to find available study time within your daily schedule, which can be utilized on a consistent basis. For example, everyone has certain hours of the day which are already committed for activities such as jobs, classes, and, of course, sleep. There is also going to be the time you spend relaxing because CPA candidates should try to maintain some balance in their lives. Sometimes too much studying can be counterproductive. But there will be some time available to you for studying and working through the questions. Block off this available time and use it only for exam prep. Use the time to accomplish your weekly tasks and to keep yourself committed to the process. After awhile your preparation will develop into a habit and the preparation will not seem as overwhelming as it once did.

---

**NOW IS THE TIME
TO MAKE YOUR COMMITMENT**

# 2 EXAMINATION GRADING

All State Boards of Accountancy use the AICPA advisory grading service. As your grade is to be determined by this process, it is very important that you understand the AICPA grading process and its **implications for your preparation program and for the solution techniques you will use during the examination**.

The AICPA has a full-time staff of CPA examination personnel under the supervision of the AICPA Board of Examiners, which has the responsibility for the CPA examination.

This chapter contains a description of the AICPA grading process, including a determination of the passing standard.

### Setting the Passing Standard of the Uniform CPA Examination

As a part of the development of any licensing process, the passing score on the licensing examination must be established. This passing score must be set to distinguish candidates who are qualified to practice from those who are not. After conducting a number of studies of methods to determine passing scores, the Board of Examiners decided to use candidate-centered methods to set passing scores for the computer-based Uniform CPA Examination. In candidate-centered methods, the focus is on looking at actual candidate answers and making judgments about which sets of answers represent the answers of qualified entry-level CPAs. To make these determinations, the AICPA convened panels of CPAs during 2003 to examine candidate responses and set the passing scores for multiple-choice questions and simulations. The data from these panels provide the basis for the development of question and problem points (relative weightings). **As with the previous pencil-and-paper exam, a passing score on the computer-based examination is 75%.**

### Grading the Examination

Most of the responses on the computer-based CPA examination are objective in nature. Obviously, this includes the responses to the multiple-choice questions. However, it also includes most of the responses to the requirements of simulations. Requirements of simulations include responses involving check boxes, entries into spreadsheets, form completion, graphical responses, drag and drop, and written communications. All of these responses, with the exception of written communications, are computer graded. Therefore, no consideration is given to any comments or explanations outside of the structured responses.

Graders are used to score the responses involving written communication (e.g., a written memorandum). These responses are graded for the quality of the written communication, but not for technical accuracy. However, the response must address the requirement to be graded at all. In other words, they must be on point.

### Multiple-Choice Grading

Financial Accounting and Reporting exams contain three multiple-choice testlets of 30 questions each. **Five of these questions will be pretest questions that will not be considered in the candidate's score.** Also, the possible score on a question and on a testlet will vary based on the difficulty of the questions. The makeup of the second testlet provided to a candidate will be determined based upon the candidate's performance on the first testlet, and the makeup of the third testlet will be determined by the candidate's performance on the first two testlets. Therefore, you should not be discouraged if you get a difficult set of questions; it may merely mean that you performed very well on the previous testlet(s). Also, you will receive more raw points for hard and medium questions than for easy questions.

Your answers to the multiple-choice questions are graded by the computer. Your grade is based on the total number of correct answers weighted by their difficulty (and with no penalty for incorrect answers). As mentioned earlier, 5 of the multiple-choice questions are pretest items that are not included in the candidate's grade.

### Simulation Grading

As indicated previously, the majority of the responses to the simulations will be computer graded. They will typically involve checking a box, selecting a response from a list, or dragging and dropping an answer. The responses involving written communication will be graded for writing skills. These responses are scored based on the following criteria:

1. Organization: structure, ordering of ideas, and linking of one idea to another

   - Overview/thesis statement
   - Unified paragraphs (topic and supporting sentences)
   - Transitions and connectives

2. Development: supporting evidence/information to clarify thoughts

   - Details
   - Definitions
   - Examples
   - Rephrasing

3. Expression: use of standard business English

   - Grammar
   - Punctuation
   - Word usage
   - Capitalization
   - Spelling

**A communication response is not graded for technical accuracy.** However, it must be on point to be graded at all. For example, if the requirement is to write a memorandum to describe the criteria for determining a capital lease, the response must describe criteria although the criteria do not have to be complete or technically accurate. That is, the information must be helpful to the intended user.

As with the multiple-choice questions, a small percentage of the simulation requirements will be pretest items that will not be included in the candidate's grade.

Chapter 3 will provide detailed suggestions on ways that you may use the information about grading to maximize your score.

---

**NOW IS THE TIME
TO MAKE YOUR COMMITMENT**

# 3 THE SOLUTIONS APPROACH

The solutions approach is a systematic problem-solving methodology. The purpose is to assure efficient, complete solutions to CPA exam questions, some of which are complex and confusing relative to most undergraduate accounting questions. This is especially true with regard to the new Simulation type problems. Unfortunately, there appears to be a widespread lack of emphasis on problem-solving techniques in accounting courses. Most accounting books and courses merely provide solutions to specific types of problems. Memorization of these solutions for examinations and preparation of homework problems from examples is "cookbooking." "Cookbooking" is perhaps a necessary step in the learning process, but it is certainly not sufficient training for the complexities of the business world. Professional accountants need to be adaptive to a rapidly changing, complex environment. For example, CPAs have been called on to interpret and issue reports on new concepts such as price controls, energy allocations, and new taxes. These CPAs rely on their problem-solving expertise to understand these problems and to formulate solutions to them.

The steps outlined below are only one of many possible series of solution steps. Admittedly, the procedures suggested are **very** structured; thus, you should adapt the suggestions to your needs. You may find that some steps are occasionally unnecessary, or that certain additional procedures increase your problem-solving efficiency. Whatever the case, substantial time should be allocated to developing an efficient solutions approach before taking the examination. You should develop your solutions approach by working questions and problems.

Note that the steps below relate to any specific question or problem; overall examination strategies are discussed in Chapter 4.

## Multiple-Choice Screen Layout

The following is a computer screenshot that illustrates the manner in which multiple-choice questions will be presented:

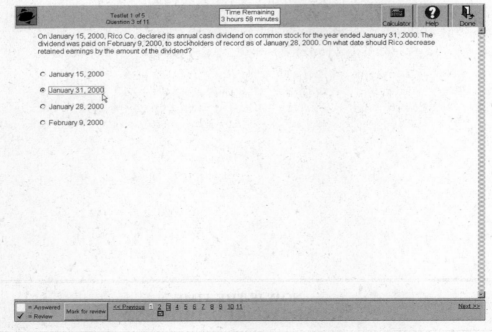

As indicated previously, multiple-choice questions will be presented in three individual testlets of 30 questions. Characteristics of the testlets of multiple-choice questions include the following:

1. You may move freely within a particular testlet from one question to the next or back to previous questions until you click on the "Done" button. Once you have indicated that you have finished the testlet by clicking on the "Done" button, you can never return to that set of questions.
2. The button on the screen will allow you to mark a question for review if you wish to come back to it later.
3. A four-function computer calculator is available as a tool.
4. A time remaining for the entire exam section is shown on the screen.
5. The number of the questions out of the total in the testlet is shown on the screen.
6. The "Help" button will provide you with help in navigating and completing the testlet.

The screenshot above was obtained from the AICPA's tutorial at www.cpa-exam.org. Candidates are urged to complete the tutorial and other example questions on the AICPA's Web site to obtain additional experience with computer-based testing.

### Multiple-Choice Question Solutions Approach Algorithm

1. **Work individual questions in order.**

   a. If a question appears lengthy or difficult, skip it until you can determine that extra time is available. Mark it for review to remind you to return to a question that you have skipped or need to review.

2. **Read the stem of the question without looking at the answers.**

   a. The answers are sometimes misleading and may cause you to misread or misinterpret the question.

3. **Read each question *carefully* to determine the topical area.**

   a. Study the requirements **first** so you know which data are important.
   b. Note keywords and important data.
   c. Identify pertinent information.
   d. Be especially careful to note when the requirement is an **exception** (e.g., "Which of the following is **not** characteristic of variables sampling?").
   e. If a set of data is the basis for two or more questions, read the requirements of each of the questions first before beginning to work the first question (sometimes it is more efficient to work the questions out of order).
   f. Be alert to read questions as they are, not as you would like them to be. You may encounter a familiar looking item; do not jump to the conclusion that you know what the answer is without reading the question completely.

4. **Anticipate the answer before looking at the alternative answers.**

   a. Recall the applicable principle (e.g., the criteria for identification of a capital lease).

5. **Read the answers and select the *best* alternative.**
6. **Click on the correct answer (or your educated guess).**
7. **After completing all of the questions including the ones marked for review, click on the "Done" button to close out the testlet. Remember once you have closed out the testlet you can never return to it.**

### Multiple-Choice Question Solutions Approach Example

A good example of the multiple-choice solutions approach follows, using an actual multiple-choice question from a previous CPA Exam.

*Step 3:*

Topical area?  Bad debt expense

*Step 4A:*

Principle?  Recognize that uncollectible accounts
are debited to the allowance account

Inge Co. determined that the net value of its accounts
receivable at December 31, 2008, based on an aging
of the receivables, was $325,000.  Additional
information is as follows:

| | |
|---|---:|
| Allowance for uncollectible accounts--1/1/08 | $ 30,000 |
| Uncollectible accounts written off during 2008 | 18,000 |
| Uncollectible accounts recovered during 2008 | 2,000 |
| Accounts receivable at 12/31/08 | 350,000 |

For 2008, what would be Inge's uncollectible
accounts expense?

a.  $ 5,000
b.  $11,000
c.  $15,000
d.  $21,000

Currently, all multiple-choice questions are scored based on the number correct, weighted by a  difficulty
rating (i.e., there is no penalty for guessing).  The rationale is that a "good guess" indicates knowledge.  Thus,
you should answer all multiple-choice questions.

### Simulations

Simulations are case-based multiple-part problems designed to

- Test integrated knowledge
- More closely replicate real-world problems
- Assess research, written communication, and other skills

Each simulation will be designed to take from 30 to 50 minutes.

The parts of simulations are separated by computer tabs.  Typically they begin with directions and/or a
situation and continue with various tabs requiring responses and possibly a resource tab.  An example is shown
below.

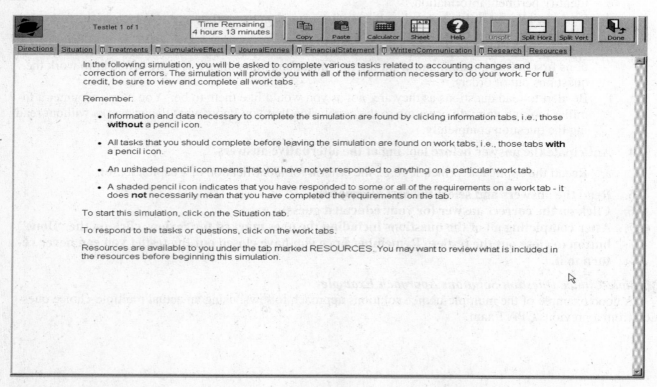

While the tabs without the pencils are informational in nature, the tabs with pencils require a response.

Any of the following types of responses might be required on simulation parts:

- Multiple selection

- Drop-down selection
- Numeric and monetary inputs
- Formula answers
- Check box response
- Enter spreadsheet formulas
- Research results
- Written communications

The screenshot below illustrates a part that requires the candidate to complete a journal entry by selecting from a list of accounts and inputting amounts.

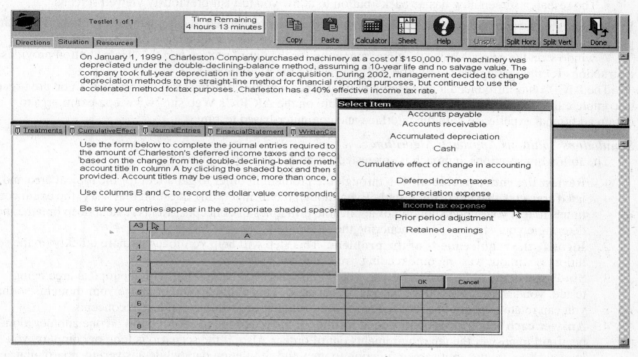

The following screenshot illustrates a part that requires inputting amounts or formulas.

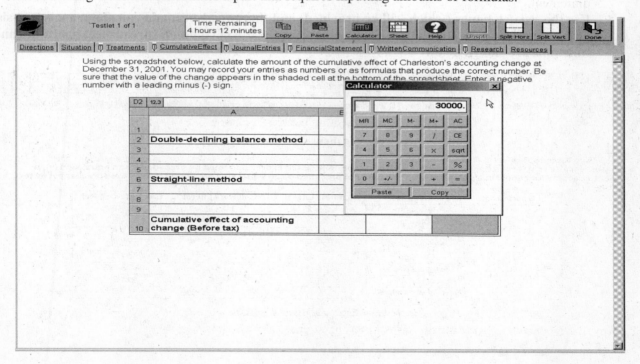

To complete the simulations, candidates are provided with a number of tools, including:

- A four-function computer calculator
- Scratch spreadsheet (The spreadsheet has the wizard functions disabled which means that candidates will have to construct spreadsheet formulas without assistance.)
- The ability to split windows horizontally or vertically to show two tabs on the screen (e.g., you can examine the situation tab in one window and a requirement tab in a second window)
- Access to professional literature databases to answer research requirements
- Copy and paste functions
- A spellchecker to correct written communications
- The research screen now has a "back" button to allow you to visit previously viewed screens

In addition, the resource tab provides other resources that may be needed to complete the problem. For example, a resource tab might contain a present value table for use in answering a lease problem.

A window on the screen shows the time remaining for the entire section and the "Help" button provides instructions for navigating the simulation and completing the requirements.

The AICPA has introduced a new simulation interface which is illustrated in this manual. You are urged to complete the tutorial and other sample tests that are on the AICPA's Web site (www.cpa-exam.org) to obtain additional experience with the interface and computer-based testing.

### Simulations Solutions Approach Algorithm

The following solutions approach is suggested for answering simulations:

1. **Review the entire problem.** Tab through the problem in order to get a feel for the topical area and related concepts that are being tested. Even though the format of the question may vary, the exam continues to test your understanding of applicable principles or concepts. Relax, take a deep breath, and determine your strategy for conquering the simulation.
2. **Identify the requirements of the problem.** This step will help you focus in more quickly on the solution(s) without wasting time reading irrelevant material.
3. **Study the items to be answered.** As you do this and become familiar with the topical area being tested, you should review the concepts of that area. This will help you organize your thoughts so that you can relate logically the requirements of the simulation with the applicable concepts.
4. **Answer each tab requirement one at a time.** If the requirements don't build on one another, don't be afraid to answer the tab requirements out of order. Also, if the scenario is long or complex, you may wish to use the split screen function to view the simulation data while answering a particular requirement.
5. **Use the scratch paper (which will be provided) and the spreadsheet and calculator tools to assist you in answering the simulation. Instructions for the use of common spreadsheet operators and functions are shown below.**

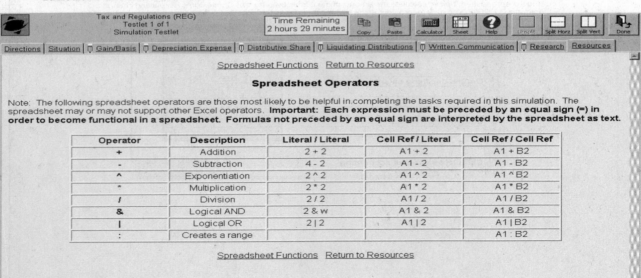

| Function | Description | Syntax | Example |
|---|---|---|---|
| PMT | Returns the payment amount given the present value, specified interest rate, and number of terms | PMT (*Amount, Interest, Terms, TermsPerYear*)<br>Where *Amount* = Present value<br>*Interest* = Interest rate expressed as annual percentage<br>*Terms* = Total number of terms<br>*TermsPerYear* = Number of payments per year | PMT (20000, 6, 120, 12) = 222.05 |
| PRODUCT | Multiplies all the arguments and returns the product | PRODUCT (*value1, value2,...*) | PRODUCT (A1: A9)<br>PRODUCT (1, 2, 3, 5) = 30 |
| PV | Returns the present value of an investment based on the interest rate, number and amount of periodic payments, and future value | PV (*Rate, Nper, Pmt, Fv, Type*)<br>Where *Rate* = Interest per period<br>*Nper* = Number of payment periods<br>*Pmt* = Payment made each period<br>*Fv* = (Optional) Future value<br>*Type* = (Optional) 0 if payment at end of period; 1 if payment at beginning of period | PV(0.005, 60, -100, 0, 1) = 5198.42 |
| SUM | Sums cells | SUM (*value1, value2,...*) | SUM (A1: A9)<br>SUM (9, 13, -4) = 18 |
| ADD | Adds two arguments | ADD (*value1, value2*) | ADD (B3, C4) |
| FV | Returns the future value of an investment based on a present value, periodic payments, and a specified interest rate | FV (*Rate, Nper, Pmt, Pv, Type*)<br>Where *Rate* = interest per period<br>*Nper* = number of payment periods<br>*Pmt* = Payment made each period<br>*Pv* = (Optional) Present value<br>*Type* = (Optional) 0 if payment at end of period; 1 if payment at beginning of period | FV (0.005, 60, -100, 100, 1) = 6877 |
| IF | Returns a value based on a logical value | IF (*value1, value2, value3*)<br>If *value1* is nonzero (True), then *value2* is returned. IF *value1* is zero (False), then *value3* is returned | IF (1>2, 5, 10) = 10 |
| NPER | Returns the number of periods for an investment based on present value, future value, periodic payments, and specified interest rate | NPER (*Rate, Pmt, Pv, Fv, Type*)<br>Where *Rate* = interest per period<br>*Pmt* = Payment made each period<br>*Pv* = (Optional) Present value<br>*Fv* = (Optional) Future value<br>*Type* = (Optional) 0 if payment at end of period; 1 if payment at beginning of period | NPER (0.005, -790, 90000, 0, 1) = 167.72 |

## Research Components of Simulations

All simulations will include a research component. Research components of simulations require candidates to search the professional literature in electronic format and interpret the results. In the Financial Accounting and Reporting section the professional literature database includes

- Statements of Financial Accounting Standards and Interpretations

You may search on a database of the original pronouncements or on a database of the current text. Shown below is a screenshot of the research page for the Financial Accounting and Reporting section of the CPA examination.

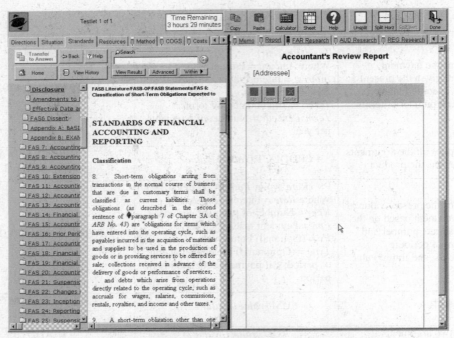

The professional literature may be searched using the table of contents, a keyword search, or a natural language search. **If you use the search function you must spell the term or terms** correctly. In using the table of contents, you simply click on the applicable standards and it expands to the next level of detail. By continuing to drill-down you will get to the topic or professional standard that provides the solution to the requirement.

If possible, it is important to get experience using the FASB Financial Accounting Reporting System to sharpen your research skills. This database is available from the FASB and many colleges and universities have licenses for use in computer labs. In addition, CPA candidates can get a free six-month subscription to the online package of professional literature used in the computerized CPA examination. Other students and recent graduates may subscribe at a special price. Subscriptions are available at www.cpa-exam.org. If that is not available, you should use the printed copy of the professional standards to answer the simulation problems in the manual.

Chapter 5 of this manual contains guidance on how to perform research on the AICPA Professional Standards database.

### Communication Requirements of Simulations

The communications requirements of simulations will involve some real-world writing assignment that a CPA might have to perform, such as a memorandum to a client explaining an accounting issue, or a memorandum to the working papers addressing an accounting issue. The communication should be in your own words. In addition, the communication is not graded for technical accuracy. As long as it is relevant to the topic, the communication is only graded for usefulness to the intended user and writing skills. The following screenshot illustrates a screenshot of a part requiring the composition of a memorandum to a junior accountant.

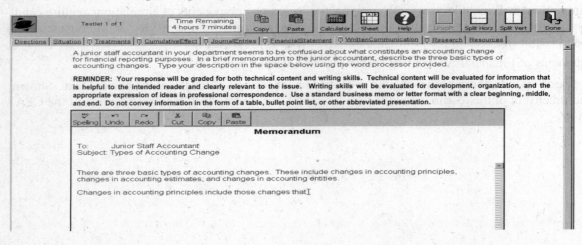

Candidates' writing skills will be graded according to the following criteria:

1. **Coherent organization**

   Candidates should organize their memoranda in a manner that is logical and easy to follow. Jumbled paragraphs and disorderly sentences will only confuse the grader and make his/her job more difficult. The following techniques will help improve written coherence.[1]

   - Use short paragraphs composed of short sentences
   - Indent paragraphs to set off lists, equations, key ideas, etc. when appropriate
   - Maintain coherence **within** paragraphs

     - Use a topic sentence at the beginning of each paragraph
     - Develop and support this topic throughout the rest of the paragraph
     - Present old or given information before discussing new information
     - Discuss ideas in chronological order
     - Use parallel grammatical structure
     - Be consistent in person, verb tense, and number
     - Substitute pronouns or synonyms for previously used keywords
     - Use transitions (e.g., therefore, finally)

   - Maintain coherence **between** paragraphs

     - Repeat keywords from previous paragraph
     - Use transitions

   Candidates are strongly advised to keyword outline their responses **before** writing their communications. This technique helps the candidate to focus on the flow of ideas s/he wants to convey before starting the actual writing task.

2. **Conciseness**

   Candidates should express themselves in as few words as possible. Complex, wordy sentences are hard to understand. Conciseness can be improved using the following guidelines.

   - Write in short sentences
   - Use a simple word instead of a long word if it serves the same purpose
   - Avoid passive constructions (e.g., **was** evalua**ted**)
   - Use words instead of phrases
   - Combine sentences, if possible
   - Avoid empty fillers (e.g., **it is** apparent; **there seems to be**)
   - Avoid multiple negatives (e.g., **no** reason for **not** using)

3. **Clarity**

   Written responses should leave no doubt in the reader's mind as to the meaning intended. Clarity can be improved as follows:

   - Do **not** use abbreviations
   - Use correct terminology
   - Use words with specific and precise meanings
   - Write in short, well-constructed sentences
   - Make sure subjects and verbs agree in number
   - Make sure pronouns and their antecedents agree in number (e.g., the partnership must decide how **it** (not **they**) wants to split profits.)
   - Avoid unclear reference to a pronoun's antecedent (e.g., the comptroller should inform the staff accountant that **he** must compute depreciation.—Who does "he" refer to?)

4. **Use of standard English**

   Spelling, punctuation, and word usage should follow the norm used in most books, newspapers, and magazines. Note the following common mistakes:

   - Confusion of its/it's
     *The firm issued its stock.*
     ***It's** (it is) the stock of that firm.*

---

[1] *Adapted from **Writing for Accountants** by Aletha S. Hendrickson (Cincinnati, OH: Southwestern Publishing Co., 1993) pp. 128-209.*

- Confusion of there/their/they're
  *There will be a dividend declaration.*
  *Their dividend was declared last week.*
  *They're (they are) declaring a dividend.*

- Spelling errors
  *Separate **not** seperate*
  *Receivable **not** recievable*

The word processing software that you will use to write the communication on the exam will likely have a spell check function. Use it.

5. **Appropriateness for the reader**

Candidates will be asked to prepare a communication for a certain reader (e.g., a memorandum for a client). Writing that is appropriate for the reader will take into account the reader's background, knowledge of the subject, interests, and concerns. (When the intended reader is not specified, the candidate should write for a knowledgeable CPA.)

Intended readers may include those who are unfamiliar with most terms and concepts, and who seek financial information because of self-interest (i.e., clients, stockholders). Try the following techniques for these readers:

- Avoid jargon, if possible (i.e., GAAP, etc.)
- Use parenthetical definitions

  - *unearned revenues (advance payments by customers)*
  - *marketable equity securities (short-term investments in stock)*

- Set off definitions as appositives

  *The lag, the time between the receipt and deposit of cash, needs to be shortened.*

- Incorporate a "you" attitude

The requirement of a question may also specify that the response should be directed to professionals who are knowledgeable of most terms and concepts. Employ the following techniques with these readers:

- Use jargon
- Refer to authoritative sources (i.e., FASB pronouncements, SAS)
- Incorporate a "we" attitude

Again, preparing a keyword outline will assist you in meeting many of these requirements. You should also reread each written communication in its entirety. Writing errors are common during the exam, so take your time to proofread and edit your answers. Again, make use of the spell check function of the word processing software if it is available.

### *Methods for Improving Your Writing Skills*

1. **Organization**

Logical organization is very important  Again, this is where the keyword outline helps.

2. **Syntax, grammar, and style**

By the time you sit for the CPA exam, you have at your disposal various grammatical constructs from which you may form sentences. Believe it or not, you know quite a bit of English grammar; if you did not, you would never have made it this far in your studies. So in terms of your grammar, relax! You already know it.

A frequent problem with writing occurs with the syntactic structure of sentences. Although the Board of Examiners does not expect the rhetoric of Cicero, it does expect to read and understand your answer. The way in which the graders will assess writing skills further indicates that they are looking more for writing skills at the micro level (sentence level) than at the macro level (organizational level).

a. Basic syntactic structure (transitive and intransitive action verbs)

Most English sentences are based on this simple dynamic: that someone or something (the subject) does some action (the predicate). These sentences involve action verbs and are grouped in the following categories:

(1)    Subject-Verb

*The AUDITOR WAITED for 3 weeks to get all the confirmations back.*

(2)   Subject-Verb-Direct Object (The object receives the action of the verb.)

> *The ACCOUNTANT CALCULATED an AGING SCHEDULE.*

(3)   Subject-Verb-Indirect Object-Direct Object (The direct object receives the action of the verb, but the indirect object is also affected by this action, though not in the same way as the direct object.)

> *Our CPA GAVE US our INCOME TAX RETURN well before the April 15 deadline.*

b.   Syntactic structure (linking verbs)

Linking verbs are verbs which, rather than expressing action, say something about the subject's state of being.  In sentences with linking verbs, the subject is linked to a work which describes it or renames it.

(1)   Subject-Linking Verb-Nominative (The nominative renames the subject.)

> *In the field of Accounting, the FASB IS the standard-setting BOARD.*

(2)   Subject-Linking Verb-Adjective (The adjective describes the subject.)

> *An amortization SCHEDULE IS always HELPFUL in determining interest payments.*

c.   Subordinate clauses

(1)   Adverbial clauses (subordinating connector + sentence).  These clauses modify the action of the main clause.

> *When a related-party transaction occurs, it must be disclosed in the footnotes to the financial statements.*

(2)   Noun clauses (nominal connectors + sentence).  These clauses function as nouns in the main sentence.

> *In pension accounting, we know that excessive unrecognized gains and losses must be amortized.*

(3)   Adjective clauses [relative pronoun + verb + (object/nominative/adjective)].  These clauses function as noun modifiers.

> *The variance which shows the greatest amount of underapplied overhead is the production volume variance.*

d.   The above are patterns which form basic clauses (both dependent and independent).  In addition, numerous phrases may function as modifiers of the basic sentence elements.

(1)   Prepositional (a preposition + an object)

> *of the FASB*
> *on the data*
> *about a new type of depreciation*

(2)   Verbal

(a)   Verb + ing + a modifier (noun, verb, adverb, prepositional phrase)

i]   Used as an adjective

> *the discount requiring amortization*
> *the option maximizing operating income*

ii]   Used as a noun (gerund)

> *Consolidating the balance sheets of an entity's subsidiaries is difficult and time-consuming.*

(b)   Verb + ed + modifier (noun, adverb, prepositional phrase)

i]   Used as an adjective

> *The method of depreciation used for tax purposes is MACRS.*

(c)   Infinitive (to + verb + object)

i]   Used as a noun

> *The company needs to depreciate that asset over five years.*

4.   **Sentence clarity**

a.   When constructing your sentences, do not separate basic sentence elements with too many phrases.

*The amortization of unrecognized gains and losses falling outside of a predetermined corridor value is another component of pension cost.*

**Better:** *One component of pension cost is the amortization of unrecognized gains and losses which fall outside a predetermined corridor value.*

  b.   Refrain from lumping prepositional and infinitive phrases together.

*The Exposure Draft by the FASB on the accounting for the restructuring of an entity due to troubled debt is very recent.*

**Better:** *Accounting for troubled debt restructuring is the topic of the most recent FASB Exposure Draft.*

  c.   Make sure that your pronouns have a clear and obvious referent.

*When internal auditors perform tests of controls or perform substantive tests of the details of transactions and balances, they serve a special function.*

**Better:** *When performing tests of controls and substantive tests, internal auditors serve a special function.*

  d.   Make sure that any adjectival verbal phrase clearly modifies a noun stated in the sentence.

*To reach this decision, each product's incremental revenue was compared to its incremental costs.*

**Better:** *To reach this decision, we compared each product's incremental revenue with its incremental costs.*

### *Time Requirements for the Solutions Approach*

Many candidates bypass the solutions approach, because they feel it is too time-consuming. Actually, the solutions approach is a time-saver and, more importantly, it helps you prepare better solutions to all questions and simulations.

Without committing yourself to using the solutions approach, try it step-by-step on several questions and simulations. After you conscientiously go through the step-by-step routine a few times, you will begin to adopt and modify aspects of the technique which will benefit you. Subsequent usage will become subconscious and painless. The important point is that you must try the solutions approach several times to accrue any benefits.

In summary, the solutions approach may appear foreign and somewhat cumbersome. At the same time, if you have worked through the material in this chapter, you should have some appreciation for it. Develop the solutions approach by writing down the steps in the solutions approach algorithm at the beginning of this chapter, and keep them before you as you work CPA exam questions and problems. Remember that even though the suggested procedures appear **very structured** and **time-consuming,** integration of these procedures into your own style of problem solving will help improve **your** solutions approach. The next chapter discusses strategies for the overall examination.

---

**NOW IS THE TIME**
**TO MAKE YOUR COMMITMENT**

# 4 TAKING THE EXAMINATION

This chapter is concerned with developing an examination strategy (e.g., how to cope with the environment at the Test Center, time management, etc.).

## EXAMINATION STRATEGIES

Your performance during the examination is final and not subject to revision. While you may sit for the examination again if you are unsuccessful, the majority of your preparation will have to be repeated, requiring substantial, additional amounts of time. Thus, examination strategies (discussed in this chapter) that maximize your exam-taking efficiency are very important.

### Getting "Psyched Up"

The CPA exam is quite challenging and worthy of your best effort. Explicitly develop your own psychological strategy to get yourself "up" for the exam. Pace your study program such that you will be able to operate at peak performance when you are actually taking the exam. Many candidates give up because they have a bad day or encounter a rough problem. A significant advantage of the new computerized exam is that if you have scheduled early in a testing window and do not feel well, you can reschedule your sitting. However, once you start the exam you cannot retake it in the same testing window, so do not leave the exam early. Do the best you can.

### Lodging, Meals, Exercise

If you must travel to the test center, make advance reservations for comfortable lodging convenient to the test center. Do not stay with friends, relatives, etc. Both uninterrupted sleep and total concentration on the exam are a must. Consider the following in making your lodging plans:

1. Proximity to the test center
2. Availability of meals and snacks
3. Recreational facilities

Plan your meal schedule to provide maximum energy and alertness during the day and maximum rest at night. Do not experiment with new foods, drinks, etc., around your scheduled date. Within reasonable limits, observe your normal eating and drinking habits. Recognize that overconsumption of coffee during the exam could lead to a hyperactive state and disaster. Likewise, overindulgence in alcohol to overcome nervousness and to induce sleep the night before might contribute to other difficulties the following morning.

Tenseness should be expected before and during the examination. Rely on a regular exercise program to unwind at the end of the day. As you select your lodging for the examination, try to accommodate your exercise pleasure (e.g., running, swimming, etc.).

To relieve tension or stress while studying, try breathing or stretching exercises. Use these exercises before and during the examination to start and to keep your adrenaline flowing. Remain determined not to have to sit for the section another time.

In summary, the examination is likely to be both rigorous and fatiguing. Expect it and prepare for it by getting in shape, planning methods of relaxation during the exam and in the evening before, and finally, building the confidence and competence to successfully complete the exam.

### Test Center and Procedures

If possible, visit the test center before the examination to assure knowledge of the location. Remember: no surprises. Having a general familiarity with the center will lessen anxiety prior to the examination. Talking to a recent veteran of the examination will give you background for the general examination procedures.  **You must arrive at the test center 30 minutes before your scheduled time.**

Upon completion of check-in at the test location, the candidate

- Is seated at a designated workstation
- Begins the exam after proctor launches the session
- Is monitored by a Test Center Administrator
- Is videotaped

Upon completion of the examination, the candidate

- Signs out
- Collects his/her belongings
- Turns in scratch paper
- Is given a Post Exam Information sheet

If you have any remaining questions regarding examination procedure, call or write your state board or go to Prometric's Web site at www.prometric.com/cpa.

### Allocation of Time

Budget your time.  Time should be carefully allocated in an attempt to maximize points per minute.  While you must develop your own strategy with respect to time allocation, some suggestions may be useful.  First, consider the Financial Accounting and Reporting examination, which is 240 minutes long.  Allocate 5 minutes to reading the instructions.  When you begin the exam you will be given an inventory of the total number of testlets and simulations, including the suggested times.  Budget your time based on this inventory.

Plan on spending about 2 to 2 1/2 minutes working each of the individual multiple-choice questions.  The time allocated to the simulations will vary.  On the Financial and Reporting section you can expect longer simulations with suggested times of about 45 minutes.

### Techniques for Time Management

The Financial Accounting and Reporting section contains three testlets of multiple-choice questions with 30 questions each.  As you complete each testlet keep track of how you performed in relation to the AICPA suggested times.  The Financial and Reporting section will also have two long simulations.  After you finish the multiple-choice testlets, budget your time for the simulations based on your remaining time and the AICPA suggested times.  For example, if you have two hours remaining to complete two simulations that each have the same AICPA suggested time, budget one hour for each simulation.  Remember that you alone control watching your progress towards successfully completing this exam.

### Examination Rules

1. Prior to the start of the examination, you will be required to sign a *Statement of Confidentiality*.
2. You will not be allowed to take any materials with you.  Any reference during the examination to books or other materials or the exchange of information with other persons shall be considered misconduct sufficient to bar you from further participation in the examination.
3. Penalties will be imposed on any candidate who is caught cheating before, during, or after the examination.  These penalties may include expulsion from the examination, denial of applications for future examinations, and civil or criminal penalties.
4. You may not leave the examination with any notes about the examination.

Refer to the brochure *CPA Candidate Bulletin* for other rules.

## CPA EXAM CHECKLIST

**One week before you are scheduled to sit**

___  1.  Look over major topical areas, concentrating on schedule formats and the information flow of the formats.
For example:
Accounting Changes and Error Correction
Income Statement Format
Long-Term Construction Accounting
Inventory Methods
Investments
Lessee-Lessor Accounting
Statement of Cash Flows
Derivatives and Hedging

___  2.  If time permits, work through a few questions in your weakest areas so that techniques/concepts are fresh in your mind.

___  3.  Assemble notecards and key outlines of major topical areas into a manageable "last review" notebook to be taken with you to the exam.

## What to bring

___ 1. *Notice to Schedule (NTS)*—You must bring the proper NTS with you.

___ 2. *Identification*—Bring two valid forms of ID. One must be government issued. The name on the ID must match exactly the name on the NTS. The CPA Candidate bulletin lists valid primary and secondary IDs.

___ 3. *Hotel confirmation*—(if you must travel).

___ 4. *Cash*—Payment for anything by personal check is rarely accepted.

___ 5. *Major credit card*—American Express, Master Card, Visa, etc.

___ 6. *Alarm clock*—This is too important an event to trust to a hotel wake-up call that might be overlooked.

___ 7. *Clothing*—Should be comfortable and layered to suit the possible temperature range in the testing room.

___ 8. *Earplugs*—Even though examinations are being given, there may be constant activity in the testing room (e.g., people walking around, rustling of paper, clicking of keyboards, people coughing, etc.). The use of earplugs may block out some of this distraction and help you concentrate better.

___ 9. *Other*—Any "Last review" materials.

## Evenings before exams

1. Reviewing the evening before the exam could earn you the extra points needed to pass a section. Just keep this last-minute effort in perspective and **do not panic** yourself into staying up all night trying to cover every possible point. This could lead to disaster by sapping your body of the endurance needed to attack questions creatively during the next day.

2. Before taking the Financial Accounting and Reporting section, scan the general schedule formats to imprint the *flow* of information on your mind (e.g., income statement, statement of cash flows, and lease formats, etc.).

3. Read over **key** notecards or the most important outlines on topics in which you feel deficient.

4. Go over mnemonics and acronyms you have developed as study aids. Test yourself by writing out the letters on paper while verbally giving a brief explanation of what the letters stand for.

5. Scan outlines of SFAC 1, 2, 5, 6, 7 and any other notes pertinent to answering conceptual questions to imprint keywords.

6. **Set your alarm and get a good night's rest!** Being well rested will permit you to meet the day's challenge with a fresh burst of creative energy.

## Exam taking strategy

1. Review the AICPA suggested times for the testlets and simulations to plan your time allocation during the exam.

2. Do not spend an excess amount of time on the introductory screens. If you take longer than 10 minutes on these screens, the test session will automatically terminate. If the exam session terminates, it will not be possible to restart the examination and you will have to reapply to take the section.

3. Report equipment/software issues to the test center staff immediately. Do not attempt to correct the problem yourself and do not use examination time thinking about it before reporting it. Remind the test center staff to file a report describing the problem. The test center staff should be able to handle any equipment or software problems. However, if you believe the problem was not handled appropriately, contact NASBA at candidatecare@nasba.org.

4. Report any concerns about test questions to test center staff after you have completed the session. The members of the test center staff know nothing about the CPA Examination content. The test center staff can report the issues to the AICPA. You should also report concerns about the questions in writing to the AICPA (FAX to [609] 671-2922). If possible, the question and testlet numbers should be included in the FAX.

5. In the event of a power outage or incident requiring a restart, the computer clock will stop and you will not lose examination time. Your responses up to the time of the restart will not be lost as responses are saved at frequent intervals throughout the examination.

6. If you have questions about the examination software functions (e.g., the transfer function), you should read the instructions and "Help" tab information. The test center staff is not familiar with the functioning of the examination software and, therefore, will not be able to help you.

7. The crucial technique to use for multiple-choice questions is to read through each question stem **carefully,** noting keywords such as "fair value," "contingent," "other comprehensive income," etc. Then **read each choice** carefully before you start eliminating inappropriate answers. Often the first or second answer may **sound** correct, but a later answer may be more correct. Be discriminating! Reread the question and choose the **best** answer.

8. If you are struggling with questions beyond a minute or two, use the strategy of dividing multiple-choice questions into two categories.

   a. Questions for which you **know** you lack knowledge to answer: Drawing from any responses you have, narrow answers down to as few as possible, then make an **educated guess**.

   b. Questions for which you feel you should be getting the correct answer: Mark the question for review. Your mental block may clear, or you may spot a simple error in logic that will be corrected when you rereview the question.

9. Remember: **Never** change a first impulse answer later unless you are absolutely certain you are right. It is a proven fact that your subconscious often guides you to the correct answer.

10. Begin the simulations, carefully monitoring your time. Read the information and requirement tabs and organize your thoughts around the concepts, mnemonics, acronyms, and buzzwords that are responsive to the requirements. Constantly compare your progress with the time remaining. Fight the urge to **complete** one simulation at the expense of a second one.

11. Remember not to spend time getting a communication requirement technically correct. Communication requirements are not graded for technical accuracy. As long as your communication addresses the issue it will be graded for demonstrated writing skills.

12. Each test may include a simulation requirement or question for which you may feel unprepared. Accept the challenge and go after the points! Draw from all your resources. Ask yourself how GAAP would be applied to similar situations, scan the simulation questions for clues, look for relationships in **all** the available resources given in the problem, try "backing into" the question from another angle, etc. Every simulation (no matter how impossible it may look at first glance) contains some points that are yours for the

taking. Make your best effort. You may be on the right track and not even know it!

13. Make sure that you have completed all requirements of a simulation. Remember the pencil icon will change color when you have answered any of the questions in the tab. It does not indicate that you have answered **ALL** questions.

14. Constantly compare your progress with the time remaining. Never spend excessive amounts of time on one testlet or simulation.

15. The cardinal rule is **never,** but **never,** leave an answer blank.

### After taking the examination

1. Retain the Confirmation of Attendance form issued after the examination because it provides valuable contact information.

2. Report any examination incidents/concerns in writing, even if the issues were already reported to test center staff.

3. If you feel that the circumstances surrounding your test administration prevented you from performing at a level consistent with your knowledge and skills, immediately contact NASBA at candidatecare@nasba.org.

**HAVE YOU MADE YOUR COMMITMENT?**

# 5 FINANCIAL ACCOUNTING AND REPORTING

# INTRODUCTION

This chapter is written to help you review intermediate and advanced accounting (financial accounting) for the Financial Accounting and Reporting section of the exam.  The AICPA Content Specification Outline of financial accounting coverage appears below.

The chapter is organized along the lines of the traditional intermediate and advanced accounting texts. The topics are arranged per the fourteen financial modules (on the previous pages).  The objective is to provide you with the basic concepts, journal entries, and formulas for each topic and subtopic.  Hopefully you will be able to expand, adapt, and apply the basics to specific problem situations as presented in multiple-choice questions and simulations appearing on the CPA exam.  Keep in mind the importance of working questions and simulations under exam conditions as you study the basics set forth in this chapter.  Refer to the multiple-choice questions, problems, and simulation problems on each of the financial accounting topics.

As you work through this chapter, remember that there are many possible series of journal entries and account titles that can be used in accounting for a specific type of economic transaction (e.g., long-term construction contracts).  Reconcile the approach illustrated in the chapter with the approach you studied as an undergraduate per your intermediate or advanced text.

In this chapter, you will be referred frequently to the outlines of authoritative pronouncements at the end of the financial accounting modules in this chapter on the particular topic being discussed.  These outlines can be located easily by referring to the headings identifying the pronouncements which appear at the top of each page at the end of this chapter.  At first consideration, the presentation might appear more comprehensive if the outlines of APB, SFAS, etc., were integrated in this chapter rather than presented separately.  Separate presentation, however, allows separate study of the pronouncements which is particularly beneficial as a last minute review.  Please note that you **do not need to know** the numbers of these pronouncements for the exam.

## *AICPA Content Specification Outline*

The AICPA Content Specification Outline of the coverage of Financial Accounting and Reporting appears below.  This outline was issued by the AICPA, effective for 2005.

## AICPA CONTENT SPECIFICATION OUTLINE:  FINANCIAL ACCOUNTING AND REPORTING

I.  Concepts and Standards for Financial Statements (**17%-23%**)

  A.  Financial Accounting Concepts

    1.  Process by Which Standards Are Set and Roles of Standard-Setting Bodies
    2.  Conceptual Basis for Accounting Standards

  B.  Financial Accounting Standards for Presentation and Disclosure in General-Purpose Financial Statements

    1.  Consolidated and Combined Financial Statements
    2.  Balance Sheet
    3.  Statement(s) of Income, Comprehensive Income, and Changes in Equity Accounts
    4.  Statement of Cash Flows
    5.  Accounting Policies and Other Notes to Financial Statements

  C.  Other Presentations of Financial Data (Financial Statements Prepared in Conformity with Comprehensive Bases of Accounting other than GAAP)

  D.  Financial Statement Analysis

II.  Typical Items: Recognition, Measurement, Valuation, and Presentation in Financial Statements in Conformity with GAAP (**27%-33%**)

  A.  Cash, Cash Equivalents, and Marketable Securities
  B.  Receivables
  C.  Inventories
  D.  Property, Plant, and Equipment
  E.  Investments
  F.  Intangibles and Other Assets
  G.  Payables and Accruals

  H.  Deferred Revenues
  I.  Notes and Bonds Payable
  J.  Other Liabilities
  K.  Equity Accounts
  L.  Revenue, Cost, and Expense Accounts

III.  Specific Types of Transactions and Events: Recognition, Measurement, Valuation, and Presentation in Financial Statements in Conformity with GAAP (**27%-33%**)

  A.  Accounting Changes and Corrections of Errors
  B.  Business Combinations
  C.  Contingent Liabilities and Commitments
  D.  Discontinued Operations
  E.  Earnings Per Share
  F.  Employee Benefits, Including Stock Options
  G.  Extraordinary Items
  H.  Financial Instruments, Including Derivatives
  I.  Foreign Currency Transactions and Translation
  J.  Income Taxes
  K.  Interest Costs
  L.  Interim Financial Reporting
  M.  Leases
  N.  Nonmonetary Transactions
  O.  Related Parties
  P.  Research and Development Costs
  Q.  Segment Reporting
  R.  Subsequent Events

IV.  Accounting and Reporting for Governmental Entities (**8%-12%**)

  A.  Governmental Accounting Concepts

    1.  Measurement Focus and Basis of Accounting

    2. Fund Accounting Concepts and Application

    3. Budgetary Process

B. Format and Content of Governmental Financial Statements

    1. Government-Wide Financial Statements

    2. Governmental Funds Financial Statements

    3. Conversion from Fund to Government-Wide Financial Statements

    4. Proprietary Fund Financial Statements

    5. Fiduciary Fund Financial Statements

    6. Notes to Financial Statements

    7. Required Supplementary Information, Including Management's Discussion and Analysis

    8. Comprehensive Annual Financial Report (CAFR)

C. Financial Reporting Entity Including Blended and Discrete Component Units

D. Typical Items and Specific Types of Transactions and Events: Recognition, Measurement, Valuation, and Presentation in Governmental Entity Financial Statements in Conformity with GAAP

    1. Net Assets

    2. Capital Assets and Infrastructure

    3. Transfers

    4. Other Financing Sources and Uses

    5. Fund Balance

    6. Nonexchange Revenues

    7. Expenditures

    8. Special Items

    9. Encumbrances

E. Accounting and Financial Reporting for Governmental Not-for-Profit Organizations

V. Accounting and Reporting for Nongovernmental Not-for-Profit Organizations (8%-12%)

A. Objectives, Elements, and Formats of Financial Statements

    1. Statement of Financial Position

    2. Statement of Activities

    3. Statement of Cash Flows

    4. Statement of Functional Expenses

B. Typical Items and Specific Types of Transactions and Events: Recognition, Measurement, Valuation, and Presentation in the Financial Statements of Not-for-Profit Organizations in Conformity with GAAP

    1. Revenues and Contributions

    2. Restrictions on Resources

    3. Expenses, Including Depreciation and Functional Expenses

    4. Investments

## PREPARING FOR FINANCIAL ACCOUNTING AND REPORTING

    This section of the exam includes financial accounting theory and its practical application (problem-solving). Candidates can expect to see multiple-choice questions (both concept and computational) and simulations. Therefore, in order to be thoroughly prepared for this section of the exam, candidates will need to master the material covered in Modules 7-20.

    First, candidates' preparation should emphasize an understanding of the basic principles and objectives underlying accounting (e.g., revenue and expense recognition rules, etc.). By focusing in on the key concepts, candidates will be able to develop a solution for whatever question format is tested.

    Candidates should then evaluate their competence by working 10 to 20 multiple-choice questions from each of the Modules (7-20) in this volume. This diagnostic routine will acquaint you with the specific nature of the questions tested on each topic as well as indicate the amount of study required per topic. You should work toward a 75-80% correct response rate as a minimum on each topic.

    Third, work simulations under examination conditions. **This is a critical step that candidates should not overlook.** It is not enough to just work multiple-choice questions. Simulations are more involved and longer than typical problems found on undergraduate accounting examinations. You must develop these skills **before** the examination by applying the "Solutions Approach" described in Chapter 3. Similarly, most CPA candidates have little experience with written communication requirements; undergraduate accounting examinations generally consist of problems. You should write out complete answers to these requirements that are included in the manual. Candidates should also recognize the value of the keyword outline. Practice it while answering examination requirements that involve written communication. Finally, get practice in using databases to research accounting problems. The next section provides some guidance for the research component of the Financial Accounting and Reporting exam.

## RESEARCHING AICPA ACCOUNTING STANDARDS

    Research components of simulations in the Financial Accounting and Reporting section will involve a research database that includes

- Original Pronouncements (i.e., the original text of FASB Statements, APB Opinions, and Interpretations)
- Current Text, the above professional standards organized alphabetically by subject, (e.g., Accounting Changes is contained in Section A06)

Accordingly, there are two ways to cite a particular standard.

1. Using the original standard number (e.g., FAS109, *Accounting for Income Taxes*, paragraph 21.)
2. Using the Current Text Section numbers (e.g., I27.120)

## Database Searching

Searching a database consists of the following five steps:

1. Define the issue. What is the research question to be answered?
2. Select the database to search. Decide which database to search (e.g., the Original Pronouncements).
3. Choose appropriate search technique. Select keywords that will locate the needed information or use the table of contents.
4. Execute the search. Enter the keyword(s) or click on the table of contents item and complete the search.
5. Evaluate the results. Evaluate the research to see if an answer has been found. If not, try a new search.

## Advanced Searches

The advanced search screen allows you to use Boolean concepts to perform more precise searches. Examples of searches that can be performed in the advanced search mode include

1. Containing all these words—Allows you to retrieve sections that contain two or more specified words.
2. Not containing any of these words—Allows you to retrieve sections that do not contain specific words.
3. Containing one or more of these words—Allows you to retrieve sections that contain any one or more of the specified words.
4. Containing these words near each other—Allows you to retrieve sections that contain words near to each other.

The advanced search also allows you to select options for the search. One alternative allows you to retrieve alternative word terms. For example, using this approach with a search on the word "cost" would also retrieve sections containing the word "costing." A synonyms option allows you to retrieve sections that contain words that mean the same as the specified word. You also have the option to only search on the selected sections of the literature.

## BASIC THEORY AND FINANCIAL REPORTING

### A.  Basic Concepts

This module includes the basic financial statements except the Statement of Cash Flows.  It also includes revenue and expense recognition rules, accounting changes, and error correction.  **The relevant accounting pronouncements are indicated in the discussion, complete with cross-references to outlines of the pronouncements at the end of this chapter.**  (Note these outlines appear in the following sequence: ARB, APB, SFAS, and SFAC.  The page headers in the outlines identify the sources of the pronouncements outlined on those pages.)  Turn to each outline as directed and study the outline while reviewing the related journal entries, computations, etc.

### 1.  Basic Accounting Theory

The foundation of financial accounting is generally accepted accounting principles (GAAP).  GAAP is the conventions, rules, and procedures necessary to define accepted practice at a particular time and includes among other items, SFAS, FASB Interpretations, APB Opinions, ARB and SEC releases.  These are the pronouncements to which practitioners look when determining if financial statements fairly present financial position, results of operations, and changes in cash flows.

SAS 69 (AU 411) expanded on the above list and established the hierarchy of GAAP for business enterprises shown below.  If the accountant/auditor cannot find a specified accounting treatment in category (A), s/he would proceed to the next lowest category.

- **Category (A),** officially established accounting principles, consists of Financial Accounting Standards Board (FASB) Statements of Financial Accounting Standards and Interpretations, Accounting Principles Board (APB) Opinions, and AICPA Accounting Research Bulletins.
- **Category (B)** consists of FASB Technical Bulletins and, if cleared by the FASB, AICPA Industry Audit and Accounting Guides and AICPA Statements of Position.
- **Category (C)** consists of AICPA Accounting Standards Executive Committee (AcSEC) Practice Bulletins that have been cleared by the FASB and consensus positions of the FASB Emerging Issues Task Force.
- **Category (D)** includes AICPA accounting interpretations and implementation guides ("Qs and As") published by the FASB staff, and practices that are widely recognized and prevalent either generally or in the industry.

In addition, the above four categories are supplemented by "other accounting literature."

In cases of conflict between the accounting treatment suggested by the categories, the higher category normally prevails over lower categories.  For conflicts within a category the treatment most closely approximating the transaction's economic substance prevails (i.e., substance over form).

Although GAAP is the current basis for financial reporting, it does not constitute a cohesive body of accounting theory.  Generally, SFAS and the other authoritative pronouncements have been the result of a problem-by-problem approach.  The pronouncements have dealt with specific problems as they occur and are not predicated on an underlying body of theory.

Theory can be defined as a coherent set of hypothetical, conceptual, and pragmatic principles forming a general frame of reference for a field of inquiry; thus, accounting theory should be the basic principles of accounting rather than its practice (which GAAP describes or dictates).  Accounting has a definite need for conceptual theoretical structure.  Such a structure is necessary if an authoritative body such as the FASB is to promulgate consistent standards.  A body of accounting theory should be the foundation of the standard-setting process and should provide guidance where no authoritative GAAP exists.

There have been efforts to develop such a frame of reference.  The most recent attempt to develop accounting theory led to the establishment of the Statements of Financial Accounting Concepts (SFAC), of which seven have been issued.  The purpose of this series is "to set forth fundamentals on which financial accounting and reporting standards will be based."  In other words, the SFAC attempt to organize a framework that can serve as a reference point in formulating SFAS.  However, it is important to note that the SFAC do not constitute authoritative GAAP.  They merely serve as a theoretical framework for the development of accounting standards.

***Financial Reporting.***  "Financial reporting includes not only financial statements but also other means of communicating information that relates, directly or indirectly, to the information provided by a business enterprise's accounting system—that is, information about an enterprise's resources, obligations, earnings, etc." (SFAC 1). It is important to note that not all informational needs are met by accounting or financial reporting. The following diagram from SFAC 5 describes the information spectrum.

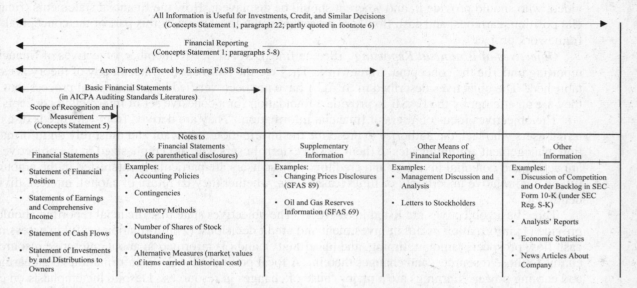

***Components of the Conceptual Framework.*** The components of the conceptual framework for financial accounting and reporting include objectives, qualitative characteristics, elements, recognition, measurement, financial statements, earnings, funds flow, and liquidity. The relationship between these components is illustrated in the following diagram, from *Financial Statements and Other Means of Financial Reporting*, a FASB Invitation to Comment.

In the diagram below, components to the left are more basic and those to the right depend on components to their left. Components are closely related to those above or below them.

**Conceptual Framework
For Financial Accounting and Reporting**

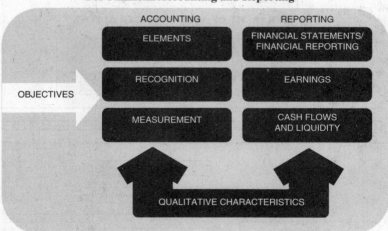

The most basic component of the conceptual framework is the objectives. The objectives underlie the other phases and are derived from the needs of those for whom financial information is intended. The objectives provide a focal point for financial reporting by identifying what types of information are relevant.

The qualitative characteristics also underlie most of the other phases. They are the criteria to be used in choosing and evaluating accounting and reporting policies.

Elements of financial statements are the components from which financial statements are created. They include assets, liabilities, equity, investments by owners, distributions to owners, comprehensive income, revenues, expenses, gains, and losses.

In order to be included in financial statements, an element must meet criteria for recognition and possess an attribute which is relevant and can be reliably measured.

Finally, reporting and display considerations are concerned with what information should be provided, who should provide it, and where it should be displayed.  How the financial statements (financial position, earnings, and cash flow) are presented is the focal point of this part of the conceptual framework project.

**Objectives of Financial Reporting.**  (See outline of SFAC 1.)  Remember, objectives of financial reporting underlie the conceptual framework.  They are the basis upon which a body of theory is established.  The objectives described in SFAC 1 have not been verified by an empirical process, but they are an attempt by the FASB to provide a foundation for a cohesive set of interrelated concepts.

The objectives focus on users of financial information.  They are derived from "the needs of external users who lack the authority to prescribe the information they want and must rely on information management communicates to them."  The external users who are emphasized in the objectives are actual and potential investors and creditors.  These users are particularly interested in the amounts, timing, and relative uncertainty of future cash flows, whether they be return of capital, interest, dividends, etc.

Three basic objectives are listed in SFAC 1.  The objectives state that financial reporting should provide (1) information useful in investment and credit decisions, (2) information useful in assessing cash flow prospects (amount, timing, and uncertainty), and (3) information about enterprise resources, claims to those resources, and changes therein.  A focal point in SFAC 1 is information about earnings and earning power.  Earnings are a major cause of changes in resources.  Despite the emphasis on cash flows, earnings are to be computed on the accrual basis, because accrual accounting "provides a better indication of an enterprise's present and continuing ability to generate favorable cash flows than information limited to the financial effects of cash receipts and payments."

**Qualitative Characteristics.**  (See outline of SFAC 2.)  The qualitative characteristics also underlie the conceptual framework, but in a different way.  While the objectives provide an overall basis, the qualitative characteristics establish criteria for selecting and evaluating accounting alternatives which will meet the objectives.  In other words, information must possess the qualitative characteristics if that information is to fulfill the objectives.

SFAC 2 views these characteristics as a hierarchy of accounting qualities, as represented in the diagram below.

**A HIERARCHY OF ACCOUNTING QUALITIES**

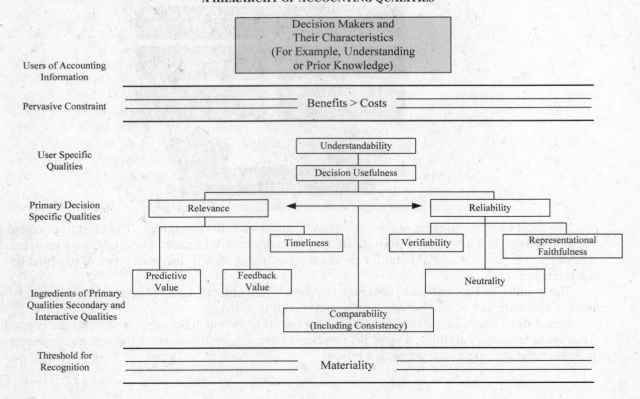

The diagram reveals many important relationships.  At the top and bottom are constraints.  If information falls outside these constraints, it would not be reported although it may possess some qualitative characteristics.  Thus, information is not disclosed if the costs of disclosure outweigh the benefits or if the information is not material enough to influence users.

The first two qualities in the hierarchy (understandability and decision usefulness) are not qualities relating solely to information.  They also depend on qualities of particular decision makers.  The usefulness and understandability of information depends on the knowledge and ability of those using it.  SFAC 1 states that "financial information is a tool, and like most tools, cannot be of direct help to those who are unable or unwilling to use it or who misuse it."

The primary qualities that accounting information should possess are relevance and reliability.  As the chart indicates, each of these is broken down into three components.  Comparability is a secondary quality which interacts with relevance and reliability to enhance usefulness of information.

Accounting information is relevant if it has the "capacity to make a difference" in a decision.  To be relevant in an investment or credit decision, information must help users form predictions about future cash flows (refer to objectives).  This can occur through predictive value (improving capacity to predict) or feedback value (confirmation or correction of prior predictions).  Of course, to be relevant, information must be available before it loses its capacity to affect decisions (timeliness).

Information is reliable if it is reasonably free from error and bias, and faithfully represents what it claims to represent.  Reliability consists of verifiability, representational faithfulness, and neutrality.

The secondary qualities of comparability and consistency become important when assessing cash flows of different enterprises or of the same enterprises over different periods.  Comparability of information enables users to identify similarities in and differences between two enterprises, while consistency (unchanging policies and procedures from period to period) does the same between periods for each enterprise.

**Basic Elements.**  (See outline of SFAC 6.)  Elements of financial statements are the ten basic building blocks from which financial statements are constructed.  These definitions are based upon the objectives of SFAC 1.  They are intended to assure that users will receive decision-useful information about enterprise resources (assets), claims to those resources (liabilities and equity), and changes therein (the other seven elements).  In order to be included in the statements, an item must qualify as an element, meet recognition criteria, and be measurable.

The meaning of financial statement elements depends on the conceptual view of earnings which is adopted.  Two basic views are the asset-liability view and the revenue-expense view.  Under the asset-liability view, earnings are measured by the change (other than investments or withdrawals) in the net economic resources of an enterprise during a period.  Therefore, definitions of assets and liabilities are the key under this view, and definitions of revenues, expenses, gains, and losses are secondary and are based on assets and liabilities.

The revenue-expense view holds that earnings are a measure of an enterprise's effectiveness in using its inputs to obtain and sell outputs.  Thus, definitions of revenues and expenses are basic to this view, and definitions of assets, liabilities, and other elements are derived from revenues and expenses.

The definitions of all ten elements are contained in the outline of SFAC 6.  Let us examine one definition in more detail.  "Assets are probable future economic benefits obtained or controlled by a particular entity as a result of past transactions or events."  This definition is based on the objectives and qualities of SFAC 1 and 2.  The overall thrust of the objectives—predicting and evaluating future cash flows—is reflected in the phrase "probable future economic benefits."  "Control by a particular entity" is crucial if reporting an item as an asset is to have decision usefulness (or relevance).  The quality of reliability is assured by the phrase "as a result of past transactions."  Information is more verifiable, valid, and neutral (the components of reliability) if based on past transactions.  A similar analysis can be applied to liabilities, equity, investments by owners, distributions to owners, comprehensive income, revenues, expenses, gains and losses.

SFAC 6 also defines some other concepts in addition to the ten elements. Especially important among these eleven additional concepts are accrual accounting, realization, recognition, and matching.  Realization and recognition are addressed by the FASB in SFAC 5.  The definition of accrual accounting is important because SFAC 1 stated that accrual accounting should be used since it provides a better indication of future cash flows than the cash basis.  This is true because accrual accounting records transactions with cash consequences (involving future cash flows) as they occur, not when the cash actually moves.  Matching is referred to in most accounting literature as a principle, or fundamental law, of accounting.

   **Recognition and Measurement.**  (See outline of SFAC 5.)  Recognition principles establish criteria concerning when an element should be included in the statements, while measurement principles govern the valuation of those elements.

   SFAC 5 established four fundamental recognition criteria:  definitions, measurability, relevance, and reliability.  If an item meets the definition of an element, can be reliably measured, is capable of making a difference in user decisions, and is verifiable, neutral, and representationally faithful, it should be included in the financial statements.

   Five different attributes are used to measure assets and liabilities in present practice.  These are discussed below in an excerpt from SFAC 5.

a.  *Historical cost (historical proceeds).*  Property, plant, and equipment and most inventories are reported at their historical cost, which is the amount of cash, or its equivalent, paid to acquire an asset, commonly adjusted after acquisition for amortization or other allocations.  Liabilities that involve obligations to provide goods or services to customers are generally reported at historical proceeds, which is the amount of cash, or its equivalent, received when the obligation was incurred and may be adjusted after acquisition for amortization or other allocations.

b.  *Current cost.*  Some inventories are reported at their current (replacement) cost, which is the amount of cash, or its equivalent, that would have to be paid if the same or an equivalent asset were acquired currently.

c.  *Current market value.*  Some investments in marketable securities are reported at their current market value, which is the amount of cash or its equivalent, that could be obtained by selling an asset in orderly liquidation.  Current market value is also generally used for assets expected to be sold at prices lower than previous carrying amounts.  Some liabilities that involve marketable commodities and securities, for example, the obligations of writers of options or sellers of common shares who do not own the underlying commodities or securities, are reported at current market value.  Current market value is sometimes referred to as fair market value.

d.  *Net realizable (settlement) value.*  Short-term receivables and some inventories are reported at their net realizable value, which is the nondiscounted amount of cash, or its equivalent, into which an asset is expected to be converted in due course of business less direct costs, if any, necessary to make that conversion.  Liabilities that involve known or estimated amounts of money payable at unknown future dates, for example, trade payables or warranty obligations, generally are reported at their net settlement value, which is the nondiscounted amount of cash, or its equivalent, expected to be paid to liquidate an obligation in the due course of business, including direct costs, if any, necessary to make that payment.

e.  *Present (or discounted) value of future cash flows.*  Long-term receivables are reported at their present or discounted value (discounted at the implicit or historical rate), which is the present value of future cash inflows into which an asset is expected to be converted in due course of business less present values of cash outflows necessary to obtain those inflows.  Long-term payables are similarly reported at their present or discounted value (discounted at the implicit or historical rate), which is the present or discounted value of future cash outflows expected to be required to satisfy the liability in due course of business.

   SFAC 5 states that each of these attributes is appropriate in different situations and that all five attributes will continue to be used in the future.

   Similarly, SFAC 5 states that nominal units of money will continue to be the measurement unit.  However, if inflation increases to a level where the FASB feels that financial statements become too distorted, another unit (such as units of constant purchasing power) could be adopted.

   SFAC 5 is based on the concept of financial capital maintenance.  Two basic concepts of capital maintenance (financial and physical) can be used to separate return **on** capital (earnings) from return **of** capital (capital recovery).  Remember, any capital which is "used up" during a period must be returned before earnings can be recognized.  In other words, earnings is the amount an entity can distribute to its owners and be as well-off at the end of the year as at the beginning.

   One way "well-offness" can be measured is in terms of financial capital.  This concept of capital maintenance holds that the capital to be maintained is measured by the amount of cash (possibly restated into constant dollars) invested by owners.  Earnings may not be recognized until the dollar investment in net assets, measured in units of money or purchasing power, is returned.  The financial capital maintenance concept is the traditional view which is reflected in most present financial statements.

   An alternative definition of "well-offness" is expressed in terms of physical capital.  This concept holds that the capital to be maintained is the physical productive capacity of the enterprise.  Earnings may not be recognized until the current replacement costs of assets with the same productive capabilities of the assets used up are returned.  The physical capital maintenance concept supports current cost accounting.  Again, the physical productive capacity may be measured in nominal or constant dollars.

A simple example can further clarify the two capital maintenance concepts.  Suppose an enterprise invests $10 in an inventory item.  At year-end, the enterprise sells the item for $15.  In order to replace the item at year-end, they would have to pay $12 rather than $10.  To further simplify, assume the increase in replacement cost is due to specific price changes, and there is no general inflation.

The financial capital concept would maintain that the firm is as well-off once the dollar investment ($10) is returned.  At that point, the financial capital is maintained and the remaining $5 is a return **on** capital, or income.  The physical capital concept maintains that the firm is not as well-off until the physical capacity (a similar inventory item) is returned.  Therefore, the firm must reinvest $12 to be as well-off. Then physical capital is maintained, and only the remaining $3 is a return **on** capital or income.

SFAC 5 also gives specific guidance as to recognition of revenues and gains, and expenses and losses, as indicated below.

| | |
|---|---|
| ***Revenues*** | When realized or realizable (when related assets received or held are readily convertible to known amounts of cash or claims to cash) and earned |
| ***Gains*** | When realized or realizable |
| ***Expenses*** | When economic benefits are consumed in revenue-earning activities, or when future economic benefits are reduced or eliminated |
| ***Losses*** | When future economic benefits are reduced or eliminated |

When economic benefits are consumed during a period, the expense may be recognized by matching (such as cost of goods sold), immediate recognition (such as selling and administrative salaries), or systematic and rational allocation (such as depreciation).

Revenues, expenses, gains, and losses are used to compute **earnings**. Earnings is the extent to which revenues and gains associated with cash-to-cash cycles substantially completed during the period exceed expenses and losses directly or indirectly associated with those cycles.  Earnings adjusted for cumulative accounting adjustments and other nonowner changes in equity (such as foreign currency translation adjustments) is **comprehensive income**.  Per SFAC 5, comprehensive income would reflect all changes in the equity of an entity during a period, except investments by owners and distributions to owners.  SFAS 130, covered in Section D.3. of this module, only goes part way in implementing this concept.

***Cash Flow Information and Present Value.***  (See outline of SFAC 7.)  As discussed earlier, the attributes most often used to measure assets and liabilities include observable marketplace-determined amounts.  These observable marketplace amounts (such as current cost) are generally more reliable and are determined more efficiently than measurements which employ estimates of future cash flows.  However, when observable amounts are unavailable, accountants often turn to estimated cash flows to determine the carrying amount of an asset or liability.  Since those cash flows often occur in one or more future periods, questions arise regarding whether the accounting measurement should reflect the present value or the undiscounted sum of those cash flows.

In February 2000, the FASB issued SFAC 7, *Using Cash Flow Information and Present Value in Accounting Measurements*.  SFAC 7 provides a framework for using future cash flows as the basis of an accounting measurement.  The framework provides general principles governing the use of present value, especially when the amount of future cash flows, their timing, or both, are uncertain.  The framework provided by SFAC 7 also describes the objective of present value in accounting measurements.  Note that SFAC 7 addresses measurement issues, not recognition questions.  SFAC 7 does not specify when fresh-start measurements are appropriate.  Fresh-start measurements are defined by the FASB as measurements in periods following initial recognition that establish a new carrying amount unrelated to previous amounts and accounting conventions.  SFAC 7 applies only to measurements at initial recognition, fresh-start measurements, and amortization techniques based on future cash flows.  SFAC 7 does not apply to measurements based on the amount of cash or other assets paid or received, or on observation of fair values in the marketplace.  If such observations or transactions are present, the measurement would be based on them, not on future cash flows.  The marketplace assessment of present value is already embodied in the transaction price.

The present value formula is a tool used to incorporate the time value of money in a measurement. Thus, it is useful in financial reporting whenever an item is measured using estimated future cash flows. The FASB defines present value as the current measure of an estimated future cash inflow or outflow, discounted at an interest rate for the number of periods between today and the date of the estimated cash flow. The objective of using present value in an accounting measurement is to capture, to the extent possible, the economic difference between sets of future cash flows.

Assets with the same cash flows are distinguished from one another by the timing and uncertainty of those cash flows. Note that an accounting measurement based on undiscounted cash flows would measure assets with the same cash flows at the same amount. For example, an asset with a contractual cash flow of $28,000 due in ten days would be equal to an asset with an *expected* cash flow of $28,000 due in ten years. Present value helps to distinguish between cash flows that might otherwise appear similar. A present value measurement that incorporates the uncertainty in estimated cash flows always provides more relevant information than a measurement based on the undiscounted sum of those cash flows, or a discounted measurement that ignores uncertainty.

To provide relevant information for financial reporting, present value must represent some observable measurement attribute of assets or liabilities. This attribute is fair value. SFAS 157 defines fair value as "the price that would be received to sell an asset or paid to transfer a liability in an orderly transaction between market participants at the measurement date."

**The only objective of present value, when used in accounting measurements at initial recognition and fresh-start measurements, is to estimate fair value.** In the absence of observed transaction prices, accounting measurements at initial recognition and fresh-start measurements should attempt to capture the elements that taken together would comprise a market price if one existed.

Marketplace participants attribute prices to assets and liabilities. In doing so they distinguish the risks and rewards of one asset or liability from those of another. An observed market price encompasses the consensus view of all marketplace participants about an asset's or liability's utility, future cash flows, the uncertainties surrounding those cash flows, and the amount that marketplace participants demand for bearing those uncertainties.

While the expectations of an entity's management are often useful and informative in estimating asset and liability values, the marketplace is the final judge of asset and liability values. An entity is required to pay the market's price when it acquires an asset or settles a liability in a current transaction, regardless of the intentions or expectations of the entity's management. Therefore, for measurements at initial recognition or for fresh-start measurements, fair value provides the most complete and representationally faithful measurement of the economic characteristics of an asset or a liability.

A present value measurement that is able to capture the economic differences between various assets and liabilities would include the following elements according to SFAC 7:

     a.   An estimate of the future cash flow, or in more complex cases, series of future cash flows at different times.
     b.   Expectations about possible variations in the amount or timing of those cash flows.
     c.   The time value of money, represented by the risk-free rate of interest.
     d.   The price for bearing the uncertainty inherent in the asset or liability.
     e.   Other, sometimes unidentifiable factors, including illiquidity and market imperfections.

SFAC 7 contrasts two approaches to computing present value. Either approach may be used to estimate the fair value of an asset or a liability, depending on the circumstances. In the expected cash flow approach only the time value of money, represented by the risk-free rate of interest, is included in the discount rate; the other factors cause adjustments in arriving at risk-adjusted expected cash flows. In a traditional approach to present value, adjustments for factors b. - e. are embedded in the discount rate.

While techniques used to estimate future cash flows and interest rates vary due to situational differences, certain general principles govern any application of present value techniques in measuring assets. These are discussed in the outline of SFAC 7.

Traditionally, accounting applications of present value have used a single set of estimated cash flows and a single interest rate, often described as "the rate commensurate with risk." The traditional approach assumes that a single interest rate convention can reflect all of the expectations about future cash flows and the appropriate risk premium. While the traditional approach may be adequate for some simple measurements, the FASB found that it does not provide the tools needed to address more complex problems. The expected cash flow approach was found to be a more effective measurement tool than the traditional approach in many situations. **The expected cash flow approach** uses all expectations about possible cash flows instead of the single most-likely cash flow. The expected cash flow approach focuses on direct analysis of the cash flows in question and on explicit assumptions about the range of possible estimated cash flows and their respective probabilities.

> *EXAMPLE: A cash flow might be $100, $200, or $300 with probabilities of 10%, 60%, and 30%, respectively. The expected cash flow is $220 ($100 × .1) + ($200 × .6) + ($300 × .3) = $220. However, the traditional approach would choose $200 as the best estimate or most-likely amount.*

When the timing of cash flows is uncertain, the expected cash flow approach allows present value techniques to be utilized. The following example is from SFAC 7.

> *EXAMPLE: A cash flow of $1,000 may be received in one year, two years, or three years with probabilities of 10%, 60%, and 30%, respectively. Notice that the expected present value of $892.36 differs from the traditional notion of a best estimate of $902.73 (the 60% probability). The following shows the computation of expected present value:*

| | | |
|---|---|---|
| Present value of $1,000 in one year at 5% | $952.38 | |
| Probability | 10.00% | $95.24 |
| Present value of $1,000 in two years at 5.25% | $902.73 | |
| Probability | 60.00% | 541.64 |
| Present value of $1,000 in three years at 5.50% | $851.61 | |
| Probability | 30.00% | 255.48 |
| Expected present value | | $892.36 |

An interest rate in a traditional present value computation is unable to reflect any uncertainties in the timing of cash flows. By incorporating a range of possible outcomes (with their respective timing differences), the expected cash flow approach accommodates the use of present value techniques when the timing of cash flows is uncertain.

An estimate of fair value should include an adjustment for risk. The risk adjustment is the price that marketplace participants are able to receive for bearing the uncertainties in cash flows. This assumes that the amount is identifiable, measurable, and significant. Present value measurements occur under conditions of uncertainty. In SFAC 7, the term **uncertainty** refers to the fact that the cash flows used in a present value measurement are estimates, rather than known amounts. Uncertainty has accounting implications because it has economic consequences. Business and individuals routinely enter into transactions based on expectations about uncertain future events. The outcome of those events will place the entity in a financial position that may be better or worse than expected, but until the uncertainties are resolved, the entity is **at risk**.

In common usage, the word **risk** refers to any exposure to uncertainty in which that exposure has potential negative consequences. Risk is a relational concept. A particular risk can only be understood in context. In most situations, marketplace participants are said to be **risk adverse**. They prefer situations with less uncertainty relative to an expected outcome. Marketplace participants seek compensation for accepting uncertainty. This is referred to as a **risk premium**. They demand more compensation (a higher premium) to assume a liability with expected cash flows that are uncertain, than to assume a liability with cash flows of the same expected amount but no uncertainty. This phenomenon can be described with the financial axiom, "the greater the risk, the greater the return." The objective of including uncertainty and risk in accounting measurements is to imitate, to the extent possible, the market's behavior toward assets and liabilities with uncertain cash flows.

If prices for an asset or liability or an essentially similar asset or liability can be observed in the marketplace, there is no need to use present value measurements. The marketplace assessment of present value is already embodied in the price. However, if observed prices are unavailable, present value measurements are often the best available technique with which to estimate what a price would be.

The measurement of liabilities sometimes involves problems different from those encountered in the measurement of assets. Thus, measurement of liabilities may require different techniques in arriving at fair value. Liabilities can be held by individuals who sell their rights differently than they would sell other assets. Liabilities are sometimes settled through assumption by a third party. To estimate the liability's fair value, accountants must estimate the price necessary to pay the third party to assume the liability.

The most relevant measure of a liability always reflects the credit standing of the entity obligated to pay. An entity's credit standing affects the interest rate at which it borrows in the marketplace. The initial proceeds of a loan, therefore, always reflect the entity's credit standing at that time. Likewise, the price at which others buy and sell the entity's loan includes their assessment of the entity's ability to repay. The failure to include changes in credit standing in the measurement of a liability ignores economic differences between liabilities.

Present value techniques are also used in periodic reporting conventions knows collectively as **interest methods of allocation**. Financial statements usually attempt to represent changes in assets and liabilities from one period to the next. In principle, the purpose of all accounting allocations is to report changes in the value, utility, or substance of assets and liabilities over time.

Accounting allocations attempt to relate the change in an asset or liability to some observable real-world phenomenon. An interest method of allocation relates changes in the reported amount with changes in the present value of a set of future cash inflows or outflows. However, allocation methods are only representations. They are not measurements of an asset or liability. The selection of a particular allocation method and the underlying assumptions always involves a degree of arbitrariness. As a result, no allocation method can be demonstrated to be superior to others in all circumstances. The FASB will continue to decide whether to require an interest method of allocation on a project-by-project basis. Refer to the outline of SFAC 7 for further information regarding the interest method of allocation.

2. **Income Determination** (See outlines of SFAC 1, 2, 5, and 6.)

The primary objective of accounting is to measure income. Income is a measure of management's efficiency in combining the factors of production into desired goods and services.

Efficient firms with prospects of increased efficiency (higher profits) have greater access to financial capital and at lower costs. Their stock usually sells at a higher price-earnings ratio than the stock of a company with less enthusiastic prospects. The credit rating of the prospectively efficient company is probably higher than the prospectively less efficient company. Thus, the "cost of capital" will be lower for the company with the brighter outlook (i.e., lower stock dividend yield rates and/or lower interest rates).

The entire process of acquiring the factors of production, processing them, and selling the resulting goods and services produces revenue. The acquisition of raw materials is part of the revenue-producing process, as is providing warranty protection.

Under the accrual basis of accounting, revenue is generally recognized at the point of sale (ARB 43, chap 1A,) or as service is performed. The point of sale is when title passes: generally when seller ships (FOB shipping point) or when buyer receives (FOB destination).

Three exceptions exist to the general revenue recognition rule: during production, at the point where production is complete, and at the point of cash collection. The table below compares the three exceptions with the general revenue recognition rule (point of sale).

| Recognition basis/ source of GAAP | Accounting method | Criteria for use of basis | Reason(s) for departing from sale basis |
|---|---|---|---|
| • **Point of sale** ARB 43 (Ch 1A) | • Transactions approach (sales basis) | • Exchange has taken place<br>• Earnings process is (virtually) complete | |
| • **During production basis ARB 45 and AICPA Contractors Guide** | • Percentage-of-completion | • Long-term construction,* property, or service contract<br>• Dependable estimates of extent of progress and cost to complete<br>• Reasonable assurance of collectibility of contract price | • Availability of evidence of ultimate proceeds<br>• Better measure of periodic income<br>• Avoidance of fluctuations in revenues, expenses, and income |
| • **Completion-of-production basis ARB 43 (Ch 4)** | • Net realizable value | • Immediate marketability at quoted prices<br>• Unit interchangeability<br>• Difficulty of determining costs | • Known or determinable revenues<br>• Inability to determine costs and thereby defer expense recognition until sale |
| • **Cash collection basis APB 10** | • Installment and cost recovery methods | • Absence of a reasonable basis for estimating degree of collectibility | • Level of uncertainty with respect to collection of the receivable precludes recognition of gross profit before cash is received |

*Note that the "completed contract" method for construction contracts is not a departure from the sale basis.*

SOURCE: *Adapted from Henry R. Jaenicke, **Survey of Present Practices in Recognizing Revenues, Expenses, Gains, and Losses**, FASB, 1981.*

Under accrual accounting, expenses are recognized as related revenues are recognized, that is, (product) expenses are matched with revenues. Some (period) expenses, however, cannot be associated with particular revenues. These expenses are recognized as incurred.

(1) Product costs are those which can be associated with particular sales (e.g., cost of sales). Product costs attach to a unit of product and become an expense only when the unit to which they attach is sold. This is known as associating "cause and effect."

(2) Period costs are not particularly or conveniently assignable to a product. They become expenses due to the passage of time by

(a) Immediate recognition if the future benefit cannot be measured (e.g., advertising)

(b) Systematic and rational allocation if benefits are produced in certain future periods (e.g., asset depreciation)

Thus, income is the net effect of inflows of revenue and outflows of expense during a period of time. The period in which revenues and expenses are taken to the income statement (recognized) is determined by the above criteria.

Cash basis accounting, in contrast to accrual basis accounting, recognizes income when cash is received and expenses when cash is disbursed. Cash basis accounting is subject to manipulation (i.e., cash receipts and expenses can be switched from one year to another by management). Another reason for adopting accrual basis accounting is that economic transactions have become more involved and multiperiod. An expenditure for a fixed asset may produce revenue for years and years.

3. **Accruals and Deferrals**

*Accrual*—accrual-basis recognition precedes (leads to) cash receipt/expenditure

Revenue—recognition of revenue earned, but not received
Expense—recognition of expense incurred, but not paid

*Deferral*—cash receipt/expenditure precedes (leads to) accrual-basis recognition

Revenue—postponement of recognition of revenue; cash is received,
  but revenue is not earned
Expense—postponement of recognition of expense; cash is paid,
  but expense is not incurred

A deferral postpones recognition of revenue or expense by placing the amount in liability or asset accounts. Two methods are possible for deferring revenues and expenses depending on whether real or nominal accounts are originally used to record the cash transaction.

### BOOKKEEPING METHODS

#### Deferrals of Expense

| | *Expense method* | | | *Asset method* | | |
|---|---|---|---|---|---|---|
| When paid | Insurance expense | xx | | Prepaid insurance | xx | |
| | Cash | | xx | Cash | | xx |
| Year-end | Prepaid insurance | xx | | Insurance expense | xx | |
| | Insurance expense | | xx | Prepaid insurance | | xx |
| Reverse | Yes | | | No | | |

#### Deferrals of Revenue

| | *Revenue method* | | | *Liability method* | | |
|---|---|---|---|---|---|---|
| When received | Cash | xx | | Cash | xx | |
| | Rent revenue | | xx | Unearned rent | | xx |
| Year-end | Rent revenue | xx | | Unearned rent | xx | |
| | Unearned rent | | xx | Rent revenue | | xx |
| Reverse | Yes | | | No | | |

#### Accruals

| | *Expense* | | | *Revenue* | | |
|---|---|---|---|---|---|---|
| Adjustment | Wages expense | xx | | Interest receivable | xx | |
| | Wages payable | | xx | Interest revenue | | xx |
| Reverse | Yes | | | Yes | | |

Entries are reversed for bookkeeping expediency.  If accruals are reversed, the subsequent cash transaction is reflected in the associated nominal account.  If accruals are not reversed, the subsequent cash transaction must be apportioned between a nominal and real account.

| | |
|---|---|
| Cash | (amount received) |
|    Revenue | (earned in current period) |
|    Revenue receivable | (accrual at last year-end) |

Accruals do not have two methods, but can be complicated by failure to reverse adjusting entries (also true for deferrals initially recorded in nominal accounts).

4.  **Cash to Accrual**

Many smaller companies use the **cash basis** of accounting, where revenues are recorded when cash is received and expenses are recorded when cash is paid (except for purchases of fixed assets, which are capitalized and depreciated).  Often the accountant is called upon to convert cash basis accounting records to the accrual basis.  This type of problem is also found on the CPA examination.

When making journal entries to adjust from the cash basis to the accrual basis, it is important to identify two types of amounts:  the **current balance** in the given account (cash basis) and the **correct balance** in the account (accrual basis).  The journal entries must adjust the account balances from their current amounts to the correct amounts.

It is also important to understand relationships between balance sheet accounts and income statement accounts.  When adjusting a balance sheet account from the cash basis to the accrual basis, the other half of the entry will generally be to the related income statement account.  Thus, when adjusting accounts receivable, the related account is sales; for accounts payable, purchases; for prepaid rent, rent expense; and so on.

For example, assume a company adjusts to the accrual basis every 12/31; during the year, they use the cash basis.  The 12/31/07 balance in accounts receivable, after adjustment, is $17,000.  During 2008, whenever cash is collected, the company debits cash and credits sales.  Therefore, the 12/31/08 balance in accounts receivable **before adjustment** is still $17,000.  Suppose the **correct** 12/31/08 balance in accounts receivable is $28,000.  The necessary entry is

| | | |
|---|---|---|
| Accounts receivable | 11,000 | |
|    Sales | | 11,000 |

This entry not only corrects the accounts receivable account, but also increases sales since unrecorded receivables means that there are also unrecorded sales.  On the other hand, suppose the **correct** 12/31/08 balance of accounts receivable is $12,500.  The necessary entry is

| | | |
|---|---|---|
| Sales | 4,500 | |
|    Accounts receivable | | 4,500 |

Sales is debited because during 2008, $4,500 more cash was collected on account than should be reported as sales.  When cash is received on account the transaction is recorded as a credit to sales, not accounts receivable.  This overstates the sales account.

Some problems do not require journal entries, but instead a computation of accrual amounts from cash basis amounts, as in the example below.

| | 12/31/07 | 12/31/08 | 2008 |
|---|---|---|---|
| *Rent payable* | *$4,000* | *$6,000* | |
| *Prepaid rent* | *8,000* | *4,500* | |
| *Cash paid for rent* | | | *$27,000* |

The rent expense can be computed using either T-accounts or a formula.

T-accounts are shown below.

The use of a formula is illustrated next.

|  |  | Beginning |  | Ending |  | Ending |  | Beginning |  |  |
|---|---|---|---|---|---|---|---|---|---|---|
| Payments | + | prepaid | + | payable | – | prepaid | – | payable | = | Expense |
| $27,000 | + | 8,000 | + | 6,000 | – | 4,500 | – | 4,000 | = | $32,500 |

Formulas for conversion of various income statement amounts from the cash basis to the accrual basis are summarized in the following table.

| Cash basis | | Additions | | Deductions | | Accrual basis |
|---|---|---|---|---|---|---|
| Collections from sales | + | Ending AR (a) / AR written off (b) | – | Beginning AR (c) | = | Sales |
| Collections from other revenues | + | Beginning unearned revenue (d) / Ending revenue receivable (e) | – | Ending unearned revenue (f) / Beginning revenue receivable (g) | = | Other revenues |
| Payments for purchases | + | Beginning inventory (h) / Ending AP (i) | – | Ending inventory (j) / Beginning AP (k) | = | Cost of goods sold |
| Payments for expenses | + | Beginning prepaid expenses (l) / Ending accrued expenses payable (m) | – | Ending prepaid expenses (n) / Beginning accrued expenses payable (o) | = | Operating expenses* |

*Provision must also be made for depreciation expense and similar write-offs and bad debt expense.

(a)  Ending AR and related sales have not yet been recorded
(b)  AR written off reduced AR but did not result in cash collected
(c)  Beginning AR was collected and recorded as sale during the period but was sale of the prior period
(d)  Beginning unearned revenue was collected and recorded as revenue in the prior period but was earned in the current period
(e)  Ending revenue receivable was earned during the period but has not yet been recorded because it has not been collected
(f)  Ending unearned revenue was recorded upon collection as revenue but has not yet been earned
(g)  Beginning revenue receivable was recorded during the current period upon collection as revenue but was earned last period
(h)  Beginning inventory was sold during the period
(i)  Ending AP and related purchases have not yet been recorded
(j)  Ending inventory must be excluded from cost of goods sold
(k)  Beginning AP reflects purchases last period which were not paid for or recorded until the current period
(l)  Beginning prepaid expenses were recorded as expenses when paid in a prior period but are expenses of the current period
(m)  Ending accrued expenses payable have not yet been recorded
(n)  Ending prepaid expenses were recorded as expenses when paid this period but are expenses of future periods
(o)  Beginning accrued expenses payable were recorded currently as expenses when paid but are expenses of the prior period

Since the accrual-basis numbers can be derived with T-accounts, you should not have to memorize the formulas.

## 5.  Installment Sales

Revenue is recognized as cash is collected.  Thus, revenue recognition takes place at the point of cash collection rather than the point of sale.  Installment sales accounting can only be used where "collection of the sale price is not reasonably assured" (APB 10).

Under the installment sales method, gross profit is deferred to future periods and recognized pro-portionately to collection of the receivables.  Installment receivables and deferred gross profit accounts must be kept separate by year, because the gross profit rate usually varies from year to year.

EXAMPLE:

|  |  |  | Collections of | |
|---|---|---|---|---|
| Year | Sales | Cost of sales | Year 1 | Year 3 |
| 1 | 300,000 | 225,000* | 80,000 | -- |
| 2 | -- | -- | 120,000 | -- |
| 3 | 200,000 | 160,000** | 100,000 | 100,000 |

*25% gross profit rate
**20% gross profit rate

| To record sale | Year 1 | Year 2 | Year 3 |
|---|---|---|---|
| Install AR-1 | 300,000 | -- | -- |
| Install AR-3 | -- | -- | 200,000 |
| Install sales | 300,000 | -- | 200,000 |
| **To record cash receipt** | | | |
| Cash | 80,000 | 120,000 | 200,000 |
| Install AR-1 | 80,000 | 120,000 | 100,000 |
| Install AR-3 | -- | -- | 100,000 |
| **To record CGS** | | | |
| Install cost of sales | 225,000 | -- | 160,000 |
| Inventory (or Purchases) | 225,000 | -- | 160,000 |

| To defer gross profit | Year 1 | Year 2 | Year 3 |
|---|---|---|---|
| Install sales | 300,000 | -- | 200,000 |
| Install cost of sales | 225,000 | -- | 160,000 |
| Deferred install GP-1 | 75,000 | -- | -- |
| Deferred install GP-3 | -- | -- | 40,000 |
| **To recognize gross profit** | | | |
| Deferred install GP-1 | 20,000[a] | 30,000[b] | 25,000c |
| Deferred install GP-3 | -- | -- | 20,000d |
| GP realized on install method | 20,000 | 30,000 | 45,000 |

[a](25% × 80,000)          c(25% × 100,000)
[b](25% × 120,000)         d(20% × 100,000)

**Summary of Accounts Used in Installment Sales Accounting**

### BALANCE SHEET

| Cash | | Installment AR—Year 1 | | Installment AR—Year 2 | |
|---|---|---|---|---|---|
| (B) | | Ending balance from year 1 sales | (B) | (A) | (B) |

| Inventory (or Purchases) | | Deferred Gross Profit—Year 1 | | Deferred Gross Profit—Year 2 | |
|---|---|---|---|---|---|
| (C) | | (E) | Ending balance from year 1 installment sales | (E) | (D) |

### INCOME STATEMENT

| Cost of Installment Sales | | Installment Sales | |
|---|---|---|---|
| (C) | (D) | (D) | (A) |

| Realized Gross Profit on Installment Sales | | Income Summary | |
|---|---|---|---|
| (F) | (E) | | (F) |

*Explanation of Journal Entries Made in Year Two*

(A)  To record installment sales
(B)  To record cash collected from year one and year two installment receivables
(C)  To record cost of goods sold (perpetual or periodic)
(D)  To close installment sales and cost of installment sales accounts
(E)  To remove gross profit realized through collections from the deferred gross profit account

   (Gross profit rate for year one × Cash collections from year one receivables)
   (Gross profit rate for year two × Cash collections from year two receivables)

(F)  To close realized gross profit at year-end

6. **Cost Recovery Method**

   The cost recovery method is similar to the installment sales method in that gross profit on the sale is deferred. The difference is that no profit is recognized until the cumulative receipts exceed the cost of the asset sold. For example, in the installment sales example, the entire profit from year one sales ($75,000) would be recognized in year three. Profit on year three sales will be recognized in year four to the extent that in year four cash collections on year three sales exceed the $60,000 ($160,000 cost – $100,000 cash collected) unrecovered cost on year three sales. If interest revenue was to be earned by the seller, it would likewise be deferred until the entire cost was recovered. The cost recovery method is used when the uncertainty of collection is so great that even use of the installment method is precluded.

7. **Franchise Agreements**

   SFAS 45 (see outline) provides that the initial franchise fee be recognized as revenue by the franchiser **only** upon substantial performance of their initial service obligation. The amount and timing of revenue recognized depends upon whether the contract contains bargain purchase agreements, tangible property, and whether the continuing franchise fees are reasonable in relation to future service obligations. Direct franchise costs are deferred until the related revenue is recognized.

8. **Real Estate Transactions**

   Accounting treatment for real estate sales is provided by SFAS 66. Due to the variety of methods of financing real estate transactions, determining when the risks and rewards of ownership have been clearly transferred and when revenue should be recognized becomes very complex.

Profit from real estate sales may be recognized in full, provided the profit is determinable and the earnings process is virtually complete.  Additionally, the following four criteria must be met to recognize profit in full at the point of sale:

1.  A sale is consummated.
2.  The buyer's initial and continuing investments are adequate to demonstrate a commitment to pay for the property.
3.  The seller's receivable is not subject to future subordination.
4.  The seller has transferred to the buyer the usual risks and rewards of ownership in a transaction that is, in substance, a sale and does not have a substantial continuing involvement in the property.

Depending on which combination of criteria is met, the real estate sales will be recorded using one of the following methods:

1.  Deposit
2.  Cost recovery
3.  Installment
4.  Reduced profit
5.  Percentage-of-completion
6.  Full accrual

The deposit and reduced profit methods require explanation.  In accordance with the deposit method, payments received are recorded as a liability until the contract is canceled or a sale is achieved.  Under the reduced profit method, the seller recognizes a portion of profit at the time of sale with the remaining portion recognized in future periods.  Profit recognized at the time of sale is determined by calculating the present value of the buyer's receivable and applying a formula.  The reduced profit recognized at the time of sale is the gross profit less the present value of the receivable as determined above.  The remaining profit is recognized in future periods.  See the outline of SFAS 66.

9. **Software Revenue Recognition**

Statement of Position 97-2 provides guidance on recognizing revenue for software transactions.  Software products that require significant production, modification, or customization should be accounted for using ARB 45, *Long-Term Construction-Type Contracts*.  Software products that do not require significant production, modification, or customization should recognize revenue when all of the following criteria are met:

a.  Persuasive evidence of an arrangement exists.
b.  Delivery has occurred.
c.  Vendor's fee is fixed or determinable.
d.  Collectibility is probable.

The portion of the fee allocated to an element should be recognized using the same list of criteria.

a.  Delivery of an element is considered not to have occurred if other elements essential to the functionality of it are undelivered.
b.  No portion of the fee meets the criterion of collectibility if the portion of the fee allocable to delivered elements is subject to forfeiture, refund, or other concession if undelivered elements are not delivered.

Arrangement that includes multiple elements should allocate the fee to the elements based on vendor-specific objective evidence of fair value, regardless of stated prices in a contract.

a.  Multiple elements

  (1)  Arrangements consisting of multiple software deliverables including

  (a)  Software products
  (b)  Upgrades/enhancements
  (c)  Postcontract customer service (PCS)
  (d)  Services
  (e)  Elements deliverable on a when-and-if-available basis

b.   Vendor-specific objective evidence of fair value

  (1)  Limited to

   (a)  Price charged when the same element is sold separately.
   (b)  Price established by management if not sold separately yet.  It should be probable that the price will not change before being sold separately.

  (2)  Amount allocated to an undelivered element should not be adjusted.  If it is probable that the amount allocated will result in a loss, SFAS 5, *Accounting for Contingencies,* should be followed

c.   Insufficient vendor-specific objective evidence of fair value

  (1)  Defer revenue until whichever one of the following occurs first

   (a)  Sufficient vendor-specific objective evidence does exist
   (b)  All elements have been delivered

  (2)  Exceptions

   (a)  The PCS is the only undelivered element—recognize entire fee ratably
   (b)  Only undelivered element is services that don't require significant production, modification, or customization—recognize the entire fee over the period in which the services will be performed
   (c)  Arrangement is a subscription in substance—recognize entire fee ratably
   (d)  Fee based on the number of copies

d.   Separate accounting for service element of an arrangement is required if both of following criteria met

  (1)  Services not essential to functionality of any other element of the transaction.
  (2)  Services are described in the contract such that total price of the arrangement would be expected to vary as result of inclusion or exclusion of the services.

10. **Sales Basis Criteria for Selected Transactions**

Under GAAP, specific rules have been developed which are stated in the form of conditions which must be met before it is acceptable to recognize profit from "a sale in the ordinary course of business." Unfortunately, these rules represent a patchwork set of criteria for applying the sales basis of revenue recognition.  This patchwork set of criteria contains many inconsistencies either in the results obtained or in the rationale justifying the criteria.  The table below summarizes the criteria which have been devised for applying the sales basis to selected transactions involving the sale of assets.

| *Recognition issue/ source of GAAP* | *Factors to be considered before recognizing revenue on the sale basis* | *Conditions that cause recognition to be delayed beyond time of sale* |
|---|---|---|
| • **Sale with a right of return** SFAS 48 | • Whether economic substance of the transaction is a sale or a financing arrangement<br>• Determination of sales price<br>• Probability of collection of sales price<br>• Seller's future obligations<br>• Predictability of returns | • Sales price not fixed or determinable<br>• Payment excused until product is sold<br>• Payment excused if property stolen or damaged<br>• Buyer without separate economic substance<br>• Seller's obligation to bring about resale of the property<br>• Inability to predict future returns |
| • **Product financing arrangement** SFAS 49 | • Whether risks and rewards of ownership are transferred | • Agreement requires repurchase at specified prices or provides compensation for losses |
| • **Real estate sale** SFAS 66 | • Probability of collection<br>• Seller's continued involvement<br>• Whether economic substance of the transaction is a sale of real estate or another type of transaction such as a service contract | • Inadequate buyer investment in the property<br>• Seller's continuing obligations, such as participation in future losses, responsibility to obtain financing, construct buildings, or initiate or support operations |
| • **Sales-type lease** SFAS 13 | • Transfer of benefits and risks of ownership<br>• Probability of collection<br>• Predictability of future unreimbursable costs | • Inability to meet conditions specified above for real estate sales<br>• Inability to meet specified conditions (four criteria) indicating transfer of benefits and risks of ownership<br>• Collectibility not predictable<br>• Uncertainty about future unreimbursable costs |
| • **Sale of receivables with recourse** SFAS 140 | • Isolation of transferred assets<br>• Right to pledge or exchange transferred assets<br>• Control of receivables | • Transferred assets can be reached by transferor or its creditors<br>• Transferee's inability to pledge or exchange transferred assets<br>• Control of receivables not surrendered due to repurchase or redemption agreement |
| • **Nonmonetary exchange** APB 29 and SFAS 153 | • Transaction has commercial substance | • Fair value not determinable<br>• Exchange transaction to facilitate sales to customers<br>• Transaction lacks commercial substance |
| • **Sale-leaseback transaction** SFAS 13 | • Substance of the transaction<br>• Portion of property leased back<br>• Length of leaseback period | • All sale-leaseback transactions are financing transactions and not sales transactions unless leaseback covers only a small part of the property or is for a short period of time |

*SOURCE: Adapted from Henry R. Jaenicke,* **Survey of Present Practices in Recognizing Revenues, Expenses, Gains, and Losses,** *FASB, 1981.*

## 11.  Research Component

Basic concepts and definitions are found in the Statements of Financial Accounting Concepts (SFACs).  Although the concept statements are not authoritative GAAP, they are the underlying concepts on which the authoritative pronouncements are based.  The earlier pronouncements (ARBs and APB Opinions) address relatively straightforward issues.  As business transactions became increasingly complex, the FASB Statements evolved to address these complex issues.  Therefore, it is essential that you are familiar with earlier accounting standards (ARBs and APB Opinions) and how they relate to later standards.  Specific attention should be given to amended and superseded materials. Amended materials are shown with a black bar beside the text.  Superseded materials are shaded in gray in the FARS database.  Below is a list of the various pronouncements that address revenue recognition issues.

| | |
|---|---|
| Franchising | SFAS 45 |
| Income determination and revenue recognition | ARB 43 |
| Installment method of revenue recognition | APB 10 |
| Nonmonetary exchanges | APB 29 and SFAS 153 |
| Product financing arrangements | SFAS 49 |
| Real estate transactions | SFAS 66 |
| Sale of receivables | SFAS 140 |
| Sales-type leases | SFAS 13 |
| Sales with right of return | SFAS 48 |
| Software revenue recognition | SOP 97-2 |

Keywords for researching basic concepts are shown below.

| | | |
|---|---|---|
| Area franchise | Installment accounting | Sales type lease |
| Bargain purchase | Installment method | Sales value |
| Capital surplus | Net income | Security interest |
| Collectibility | Persuasive evidence arrangement | Seller obligation |
| Collection reasonably assured | Proceeds of sale | Services substantially performed |
| Consummated sale | Product financing | Significant customization |
| Consummation sale | Product financing arrangements | Significant production |
| Continuing franchise fees | Profit loss | Software products |
| Continuing involvement | Profit on transactions | Specified prices resale |
| Culmination of earning process | Reasonable estimate returns | Sponsor purchase |
| Earned surplus | Recognizing revenue software | Sponsor repurchase |
| Fair value determinable | Related transaction purchase | Sponsor sells |
| Financial asset | Repurchase product | Substantial performance |
| Franchise fee revenue | Retained earnings | Substantially identical product |
| Franchisee | Return privilege expired | Transaction completed |
| Franchisor | Revenue recognized | Transfer financial asset |
| Full accrual method | Right of return | Unrealized profit |
| Initial franchise fee | Sales leaseback | Vendor specific evidence |
| Initial services | Sales price | |

**MULTIPLE-CHOICE QUESTIONS (1-70)**

**1.** What are the Statements of Financial Accounting Concepts intended to establish?
  a. Generally accepted accounting principles in financial reporting by business enterprises.
  b. The meaning of "Present fairly in accordance with generally accepted accounting principles."
  c. The objectives and concepts for use in developing standards of financial accounting and reporting.
  d. The hierarchy of sources of generally accepted accounting principles.

**2.** According to the FASB conceptual framework, the objectives of financial reporting for business enterprises are based on
  a. Generally accepted accounting principles.
  b. Reporting on management's stewardship.
  c. The need for conservatism.
  d. The needs of the users of the information.

**3.** According to the FASB conceptual framework, the usefulness of providing information in financial statements is subject to the constraint of
  a. Consistency.
  b. Cost-benefit.
  c. Reliability.
  d. Representational faithfulness.

**4.** During a period when an enterprise is under the direction of a particular management, its financial statements will directly provide information about
  a. Both enterprise performance and management performance.
  b. Management performance but not directly provide information about enterprise performance.
  c. Enterprise performance but not directly provide information about management performance.
  d. Neither enterprise performance nor management performance.

**5.** According to Statements of Financial Accounting Concepts, neutrality is an ingredient of

| | Reliability | Relevance |
|---|---|---|
| a. | Yes | Yes |
| b. | Yes | No |
| c. | No | Yes |
| d. | No | No |

**6.** According to the FASB conceptual framework, which of the following relates to both relevance and reliability?
  a. Comparability.
  b. Feedback value.
  c. Verifiability.
  d. Timeliness.

**7.** According to the FASB conceptual framework, the process of reporting an item in the financial statements of an entity is
  a. Allocation.
  b. Matching.
  c. Realization.
  d. Recognition.

**8.** Under FASB Statement of Financial Accounting Concepts 5, which of the following items would cause earnings to differ from comprehensive income for an enterprise in an industry **not** having specialized accounting principles?
  a. Unrealized loss on investments classified as available-for-sale securities.
  b. Unrealized loss on investments classified as trading securities.
  c. Loss on exchange of similar assets.
  d. Loss on exchange of dissimilar assets.

**9.** Under FASB Statement of Financial Accounting Concepts 5, comprehensive income excludes changes in equity resulting from which of the following?
  a. Loss from discontinued operations.
  b. Prior period error correction.
  c. Dividends paid to stockholders.
  d. Unrealized loss on securities classified as available-for-sale.

**10.** According to the FASB conceptual framework, which of the following situations violates the concept of reliability?
  a. Data on segments having the same expected risks and growth rates are reported to analysts estimating future profits.
  b. Financial statements are issued nine months late.
  c. Management reports to stockholders regularly refer to new projects undertaken, but the financial statements never report project results.
  d. Financial statements include property with a carrying amount increased to management's estimate of market value.

**11.** According to the FASB conceptual framework, which of the following statements conforms to the realization concept?
  a. Equipment depreciation was assigned to a production department and then to product unit costs.
  b. Depreciated equipment was sold in exchange for a note receivable.
  c. Cash was collected on accounts receivable.
  d. Product unit costs were assigned to cost of goods sold when the units were sold.

**12.** What is the underlying concept that supports the immediate recognition of a contingent loss?
  a. Substance over form.
  b. Consistency.
  c. Matching.
  d. Conservatism.

**13.** What is the underlying concept governing the generally accepted accounting principles pertaining to recording gain contingencies?
  a. Conservatism.
  b. Relevance.
  c. Consistency.
  d. Reliability.

**14.** FASB's conceptual framework explains both financial and physical capital maintenance concepts. Which capital maintenance concept is applied to currently reported net income, and which is applied to comprehensive income?

| | Currently reported net income | Comprehensive income |
|---|---|---|
| a. | Financial capital | Physical capital |
| b. | Physical capital | Physical capital |
| c. | Financial capital | Financial capital |
| d. | Physical capital | Financial capital |

**15.** According to the FASB conceptual framework, an entity's revenue may result from
  a.  A decrease in an asset from primary operations.
  b.  An increase in an asset from incidental transactions.
  c.  An increase in a liability from incidental transactions.
  d.  A decrease in a liability from primary operations.

**16.** According to the FASB conceptual framework, which of the following is an essential characteristic of an asset?
  a.  The claims to an asset's benefits are legally enforceable.
  b.  An asset is tangible.
  c.  An asset is obtained at a cost.
  d.  An asset provides future benefits.

**17.** According to the FASB conceptual framework, which of the following attributes would **not** be used to measure inventory?
  a.  Historical cost.
  b.  Replacement cost.
  c.  Net realizable value.
  d.  Present value of future cash flows.

**18.** According to SFAC 7, *Using Cash Flow Information and Present Value in Accounting Measurements*, the most relevant measurement of an entity's liabilities at initial recognition and fresh-start measurements should always reflect
  a.  The expectations of the entity's management.
  b.  Historical cost.
  c.  The credit standing of the entity.
  d.  The single most-likely minimum or maximum possible amount.

**19.** Which of the following is **not** covered by SFAC 7, *Using Cash Flow Information and Present Value in Accounting Measurements*?
  a.  Measurements at initial recognition.
  b.  Interest method of amortization.
  c.  Expected cash flow approach.
  d.  Determining when fresh-start measurements are appropriate.

**20.** In calculating present value in a situation with a range of possible outcomes all discounted using the same interest rate, the expected present value would be
  a.  The most-likely outcome.
  b.  The maximum outcome.
  c.  The minimum outcome.
  d.  The sum of probability-weighted present values.

**21.** A cash flow of $200,000 may be received by Lydia Nickels, Inc. in one year, two years, or three years, with probabilities of 20%, 50%, and 30%, respectively. The rate of interest on default risk-free investments is 5%. The present value factors are

    PV of 1, at 5%, for 1 year is     .95238
    PV of 1, at 5%, for 2 years is    .90703
    PV of 1, at 5%, for 3 years is    .86384

What is the expected present value of Lydia Nickels' cash flow (in whole dollars)?
  a.  $181,406
  b.  $180,628
  c.  $ 90,703
  d.  $ 89,925

**22.** Which of the following statements regarding interest methods of allocations is **not** true?
  a.  The term "interest methods of allocation" refers both to the convention for periodic reporting and to the several approaches to dealing with changes in estimated future cash flows.
  b.  Interest methods of allocation are reporting conventions that use present value techniques in the absence of a fresh-start measurement to compute changes in the carrying amount of an asset or liability from one period to the next.
  c.  Interest methods of allocation are grounded in the notion of current cost.
  d.  Holding gains and losses are generally excluded from allocation systems.

**23.** Which of the following is **not** an objective of using present value in accounting measurements?
  a.  To capture the value of an asset or a liability in the context of a particular entity.
  b.  To estimate fair value.
  c.  To capture the economic difference between sets of future cash flows.
  d.  To capture the elements that taken together would comprise a market price if one existed.

**24.** On December 31, 2007, Brooks Co. decided to end operations and dispose of its assets within three months. At December 31, 2007, the net realizable value of the equipment was below historical cost. What is the appropriate measurement basis for equipment included in Brooks' December 31, 2007 balance sheet?
  a.  Historical cost.
  b.  Current reproduction cost.
  c.  Net realizable value.
  d.  Current replacement cost.

**25.** In the hierarchy of generally accepted accounting principles, APB Opinions have the same authority as AICPA
  a.  Statements of Position.
  b.  Industry Audit and Accounting Guides.
  c.  Issues Papers.
  d.  Accounting Research Bulletins.

**26.** On October 1, 2007, Acme Fuel Co. sold 100,000 gallons of heating oil to Karn Co. at $3 per gallon. Fifty thousand gallons were delivered on December 15, 2007, and the remaining 50,000 gallons were delivered on January 15, 2008. Payment terms were: 50% due on October 1, 2007, 25% due on first delivery, and the remaining 25% due on second delivery. What amount of revenue should Acme recognize from this sale during 2007?
  a.  $ 75,000
  b.  $150,000
  c.  $225,000
  d.  $300,000

**27.** Amar Farms produced 300,000 pounds of cotton during the 2007 season. Amar sells all of its cotton to Brye Co., which has agreed to purchase Amar's entire production at the prevailing market price. Recent legislation assures that the market price will not fall below $.70 per pound during the next two years. Amar's costs of selling and distributing the cotton are immaterial and can be reasonably estimated. Amar reports its inventory at expected exit value. During 2007, Amar sold and delivered to Brye 200,000 pounds at the market price of $.70. Amar sold the remaining 100,000 pounds during 2008 at the market price of $.72. What amount of revenue should Amar recognize in 2007?

- a. $140,000
- b. $144,000
- c. $210,000
- d. $216,000

*30,000 × .72*

**28.** Lin Co., a distributor of machinery, bought a machine from the manufacturer in November 2007 for $10,000. On December 30, 2007, Lin sold this machine to Zee Hardware for $15,000, under the following terms: 2% discount if paid within thirty days, 1% discount if paid after thirty days but within sixty days, or payable in full within ninety days if not paid within the discount periods. However, Zee had the right to return this machine to Lin if Zee was unable to resell the machine before expiration of the ninety-day payment period, in which case Zee's obligation to Lin would be canceled. In Lin's net sales for the year ended December 31, 2007, how much should be included for the sale of this machine to Zee?

- a. $0
- b. $14,700
- c. $14,850
- d. $15,000

**29.** Under a royalty agreement with another company, Wand Co. will pay royalties for the assignment of a patent for three years. The royalties paid should be reported as expense

- a. In the period paid.
- b. In the period incurred.
- c. At the date the royalty agreement began.
- d. At the date the royalty agreement expired.

**30.** Clark Co.'s advertising expense account had a balance of $146,000 at December 31, 2007, before any necessary year-end adjustment relating to the following:

- Included in the $146,000 is the $15,000 cost of printing catalogs for a sales promotional campaign in January 2008.
- Radio advertisements broadcast during December 2007 were billed to Clark on January 2, 2008. Clark paid the $9,000 invoice on January 11, 2008.

What amount should Clark report as advertising expense in its income statement for the year ended December 31, 2007?

- a. $122,000
- b. $131,000
- c. $140,000
- d. $155,000

**31.** An analysis of Thrift Corp.'s unadjusted prepaid expense account at December 31, 2007, revealed the following:

- An opening balance of $1,500 for Thrift's comprehensive insurance policy. Thrift had paid an annual premium of $3,000 on July 1, 2006.
- A $3,200 annual insurance premium payment made July 1, 2007.
- A $2,000 advance rental payment for a warehouse Thrift leased for one year beginning January 1, 2008.

In its December 31, 2007 balance sheet, what amount should Thrift report as prepaid expenses?

- a. $5,200
- b. $3,600
- c. $2,000
- d. $1,600

**32.** Roro, Inc. paid $7,200 to renew its only insurance policy for three years on March 1, 2007, the effective date of the policy. At March 31, 2007, Roro's unadjusted trial balance showed a balance of $300 for prepaid insurance and $7,200 for insurance expense. What amounts should be reported for prepaid insurance and insurance expense in Roro's financial statements for the three months ended March 31, 2007?

| | *Prepaid insurance* | *Insurance expense* |
|---|---|---|
| a. | $7,000 | $300 |
| b. | $7,000 | $500 |
| c. | $7,200 | $300 |
| d. | $7,300 | $200 |

**33.** Aneen's Video Mart sells one- and two-year mail order subscriptions for its video-of-the-month business. Subscriptions are collected in advance and credited to sales. An analysis of the recorded sales activity revealed the following:

| | *2006* | *2007* |
|---|---|---|
| Sales | $420,000 | $500,000 |
| Less cancellations | 20,000 | 30,000 |
| Net sales | $400,000 | $470,000 |
| | | |
| Subscriptions expirations: | | |
| 2006 | $120,000 | |
| 2007 | 155,000 | $130,000 |
| 2008 | 125,000 | 200,000 |
| 2009 | | 140,000 |
| | $400,000 | $470,000 |

In Aneen's December 31, 2007 balance sheet, the balance for unearned subscription revenue should be

- a. $495,000
- b. $470,000
- c. $465,000
- d. $340,000

**34.** Regal Department Store sells gift certificates, redeemable for store merchandise, that expire one year after their issuance. Regal has the following information pertaining to its gift certificates sales and redemptions:

| | |
|---|---|
| Unredeemed at 12/31/06 | $ 75,000 |
| 2007 sales | 250,000 |
| 2007 redemptions of prior year sales | 25,000 |
| 2007 redemptions of current year sales | 175,000 |

Regal's experience indicates that 10% of gift certificates sold will not be redeemed. In its December 31, 2007 balance sheet, what amount should Regal report as unearned revenue?

- a. $125,000
- b. $112,500
- c. $100,000
- d. $ 50,000

**35.** Wren Corp.'s trademark was licensed to Mont Co. for royalties of 15% of sales of the trademarked items. Royalties are payable semiannually on March 15 for sales in July through December of the prior year, and on September 15 for sales in January through June of the same year. Wren received the following royalties from Mont:

|      | *March 15* | *September 15* |
|------|-----------|----------------|
| 2006 | $10,000   | $15,000        |
| 2007 | 12,000    | 17,000         |

Mont estimated that sales of the trademarked items would total $60,000 for July through December 2007. In Wren's 2007 income statement, the royalty revenue should be

- a. $26,000
- b. $29,000
- c. $38,000
- d. $41,000

**36.** In 2006, Super Comics Corp. sold a comic strip to Fantasy, Inc. and will receive royalties of 20% of future revenues associated with the comic strip. At December 31, 2007, Super reported royalties receivable of $75,000 from Fantasy. During 2008, Super received royalty payments of $200,000. Fantasy reported revenues of $1,500,000 in 2008 from the comic strip. In its 2008 income statement, what amount should Super report as royalty revenue?

- a. $125,000
- b. $175,000
- c. $200,000
- d. $300,000

**37.** Rill Co. owns a 20% royalty interest in an oil well. Rill receives royalty payments on January 31 for the oil sold between the previous June 1 and November 30, and on July 31 for oil sold between December 1 and May 31. Production reports show the following oil sales:

| | |
|---|---|
| June 1, 2006 - November 30, 2006 | $300,000 |
| December 1, 2006 - December 31, 2006 | 50,000 |
| December 1, 2006 - May 31, 2007 | 400,000 |
| June 1, 2007 - November 30, 2007 | 325,000 |
| December 1, 2007 - December 31, 2007 | 70,000 |

What amount should Rill report as royalty revenue for 2007?

- a. $140,000
- b. $144,000
- c. $149,000
- d. $159,000

**38.** Decker Company assigns some of its patents to other enterprises under a variety of licensing agreements. In some instances advance royalties are received when the agreements are signed, and in others, royalties are remitted within sixty days after each license year-end. The following data are included in Decker's December 31 balance sheet:

|                     | 2006    | 2007    |
|---------------------|---------|---------|
| Royalties receivable | $90,000 | $85,000 |
| Unearned royalties   | 60,000  | 40,000  |

During 2007 Decker received royalty remittances of $200,000. In its income statement for the year ended December 31, 2007, Decker should report royalty income of

- a. $195,000
- b. $215,000
- c. $220,000
- d. $225,000

**39.** Cooke Company acquires patent rights from other enterprises and pays advance royalties in some cases, and in others, royalties are paid within ninety days after year-end. The following data are included in Cooke's December 31 balance sheets:

|                   | 2006     | 2007     |
|-------------------|----------|----------|
| Prepaid royalties | $55,000  | $45,000  |
| Royalties payable | 80,000   | 75,000   |

During 2007 Cooke remitted royalties of $300,000. In its income statement for the year ended December 31, 2007, Cooke should report royalty expense of

- a. $295,000
- b. $305,000
- c. $310,000
- d. $330,000

**40.** The premium on a three-year insurance policy expiring on December 31, 2009, was paid in total on January 1, 2007. The original payment was initially debited to a prepaid asset account. The appropriate journal entry has been recorded on December 31, 2007. The balance in the prepaid asset account on December 31, 2007, should be

- a. Zero.
- b. The same as it would have been if the original payment had been debited initially to an expense account.
- c. The same as the original payment.
- d. Higher than if the original payment had been debited initially to an expense account.

**41.** On January 1, 2007, Sip Co. signed a five-year contract enabling it to use a patented manufacturing process beginning in 2007. A royalty is payable for each product produced, subject to a minimum annual fee. Any royalties in excess of the minimum will be paid annually. On the contract date, Sip prepaid a sum equal to two years' minimum annual fees. In 2007, only minimum fees were incurred. The royalty prepayment should be reported in Sip's December 31, 2007 financial statements as

- a. An expense only.
- b. A current asset and an expense.
- c. A current asset and noncurrent asset.
- d. A noncurrent asset.

**42.** A retail store received cash and issued gift certificates that are redeemable in merchandise. The gift certificates lapse one year after they are issued. How would the deferred revenue account be affected by each of the following transactions?

|      | *Redemption of certificates* | *Lapse of certificates* |
|------|------------------------------|--------------------------|
| a.   | No effect                    | Decrease                 |
| b.   | Decrease                     | Decrease                 |
| c.   | Decrease                     | No effect                |
| d.   | No effect                    | No effect                |

**43.** Jersey, Inc. is a retailer of home appliances and offers a service contract on each appliance sold. Jersey sells appliances on installment contracts, but all service contracts must be paid in full at the time of sale. Collections received for service contracts should be recorded as an increase in a

- a. Deferred revenue account.
- b. Sales contracts receivable valuation account.
- c. Stockholders' valuation account.
- d. Service revenue account.

**44.** Ward, a consultant, keeps her accounting records on a cash basis. During 2007, Ward collected $200,000 in fees from clients. At December 31, 2006, Ward had accounts receivable of $40,000. At December 31, 2007, Ward had accounts receivable of $60,000, and unearned fees of $5,000. On an accrual basis, what was Ward's service revenue for 2007?

a. $175,000
b. $180,000
c. $215,000
d. $225,000

**45.** Zeta Co. reported sales revenue of $4,600,000 in its income statement for the year ended December 31, 2007. Additional information is as follows:

|  | 12/31/06 | 12/31/07 |
|---|---|---|
| Accounts receivable | $1,000,000 | $1,300,000 |
| Allowance for uncollectible accounts | (60,000) | (110,000) |

Zeta wrote off uncollectible accounts totaling $20,000 during 2007. Under the cash basis of accounting, Zeta would have reported 2007 sales of
a. $4,900,000
b. $4,350,000
c. $4,300,000
d. $4,280,000

**46.** Marr Corp. reported rental revenue of $2,210,000 in its cash basis federal income tax return for the year ended November 30, 2007. Additional information is as follows:

| | |
|---|---|
| Rents receivable—November 30, 2007 | $1,060,000 |
| Rents receivable—November 30, 2006 | 800,000 |
| Uncollectible rents written off during the fiscal year | 30,000 |

Under the accrual basis, Marr should report rental revenue of
a. $1,920,000
b. $1,980,000
c. $2,440,000
d. $2,500,000

**47.** The following information pertains to Eagle Co.'s 2007 sales:

| Cash sales | |
|---|---|
| Gross | $ 80,000 |
| Returns and allowances | 4,000 |
| Credit sales | |
| Gross | 120,000 |
| Discounts | 6,000 |

On January 1, 2007 customers owed Eagle $40,000. On December 31, 2007, customers owed Eagle $30,000. Eagle uses the direct writeoff method for bad debts. No bad debts were recorded in 2007. Under the cash basis of accounting, what amount of net revenue should Eagle report for 2007?
a. $ 76,000
b. $170,000
c. $190,000
d. $200,000

**48.** The following balances were reported by Mall Co. at December 31, 2007 and 2006:

|  | 12/31/07 | 12/31/06 |
|---|---|---|
| Inventory | $260,000 | $290,000 |
| Accounts payable | 75,000 | 50,000 |

Mall paid suppliers $490,000 during the year ended December 31, 2007. What amount should Mall report for cost of goods sold in 2007?
a. $545,000
b. $495,000
c. $485,000
d. $435,000

**49.** Class Corp. maintains its accounting records on the cash basis but restates its financial statements to the accrual method of accounting. Class had $60,000 in cash-basis

pretax income for 2007. The following information pertains to Class's operations for the years ended December 31, 2007 and 2006:

|  | 2007 | 2006 |
|---|---|---|
| Accounts receivable | $40,000 | $20,000 |
| Accounts payable | 15,000 | 30,000 |

Under the accrual method, what amount of income before taxes should Class report in its December 31, 2007 income statement?
a. $25,000
b. $55,000
c. $65,000
d. $95,000

**50.** On February 1, 2007, Tory began a service proprietorship with an initial cash investment of $2,000. The proprietorship provided $5,000 of services in February and received full payment in March. The proprietorship incurred expenses of $3,000 in February, which were paid in April. During March, Tory drew $1,000 against the capital account. In the proprietorship's financial statements for the two months ended March 31, 2007, prepared under the cash basis method of accounting, what amount should be reported as capital?
a. $1,000
b. $3,000
c. $6,000
d. $7,000

**51.** Compared to the accrual basis of accounting, the cash basis of accounting understates income by the net decrease during the accounting period of

|  | Accounts receivable | Accrued expenses |
|---|---|---|
| a. | Yes | Yes |
| b. | Yes | No |
| c. | No | No |
| d. | No | Yes |

**52.** White Co. wants to convert its 2007 financial statements from the accrual basis of accounting to the cash basis. Both supplies inventory and office salaries payable increased between January 1, 2007, and December 31, 2007. To obtain 2007 cash basis net income, how should these increases be added to or deducted from accrual-basis net income?

|  | Supplies inventory | Office salaries payable |
|---|---|---|
| a. | Deducted | Deducted |
| b. | Deducted | Added |
| c. | Added | Deducted |
| d. | Added | Added |

**53.** Before 2007, Droit Co. used the cash basis of accounting. As of December 31, 2007, Droit changed to the accrual basis. Droit cannot determine the beginning balance of supplies inventory. What is the effect of Droit's inability to determine beginning supplies inventory on its 2007 accrual-basis net income and December 31, 2007 accrual-basis owners' equity?

|  | 2007 net income | 12/31/07 owners' equity |
|---|---|---|
| a. | No effect | No effect |
| b. | No effect | Overstated |
| c. | Overstated | No effect |
| d. | Overstated | Overstated |

**54.** Gant Co., which began operations on January 1, 2007, appropriately uses the installment method of accounting. The following information pertains to Gant's operations for the year 2007:

| | |
|---|---:|
| Installment sales | $500,000 |
| Regular sales | 300,000 |
| Cost of installment sales | 250,000 |
| Cost of regular sales | 150,000 |
| General and administrative expenses | 50,000 |
| Collections on installment sales | 100,000 |

In its December 31, 2007 balance sheet, what amount should Gant report as deferred gross profit?
a.   $250,000
b.   $200,000
c.   $160,000
d.   $ 75,000

**55.** Since there is no reasonable basis for estimating the degree of collectibility, Astor Co. uses the installment method of revenue recognition for the following sales:

| | 2007 | 2006 |
|---|---:|---:|
| Sales | $900,000 | $600,000 |
| Collections from: | | |
| 2006 sales | 100,000 | 200,000 |
| 2007 sales | 300,000 | -- |
| Accounts written off: | | |
| 2006 sales | 150,000 | 50,000 |
| 2007 sales | 50,000 | -- |
| Gross profit percentage | 40% | 30% |

What amount should Astor report as deferred gross profit in its December 31, 2007 balance sheet for the 2006 and 2007 sales?
a.   $150,000
b.   $160,000
c.   $225,000
d.   $250,000

**56.** Luge Co., which began operations on January 2, 2007, appropriately uses the installment sales method of accounting. The following information is available for 2007:

| | |
|---|---:|
| Installment accounts receivable, December 31, 2007 | $800,000 |
| Deferred gross profit, December 31, 2007 (before recognition of realized gross profit for 2007) | 560,000 |
| Gross profit on sales | 40% |

For the year ended December 31, 2007, cash collections and realized gross profit on sales should be

| | Cash collections | Realized gross profit |
|---|---|---|
| a. | $400,000 | $320,000 |
| b. | $400,000 | $240,000 |
| c. | $600,000 | $320,000 |
| d. | $600,000 | $240,000 |

**57.** Dolce Co., which began operations on January 1, 2006, appropriately uses the installment method of accounting to record revenues. The following information is available for the years ended December 31, 2006 and 2007:

| | 2006 | 2007 |
|---|---:|---:|
| Sales | $1,000,000 | $2,000,000 |
| Gross profit realized on sales made in: | | |
| 2006 | 150,000 | 90,000 |
| 2007 | -- | 200,000 |
| Gross profit percentages | 30% | 40% |

What amount of installment accounts receivable should Dolce report in its December 31, 2007 balance sheet?

a.   $1,225,000
b.   $1,300,000
c.   $1,700,000
d.   $1,775,000

**58.** On December 31, 2006, Mill Co. sold construction equipment to Drew, Inc. for $1,800,000. The equipment had a carrying amount of $1,200,000. Drew paid $300,000 cash on December 31, 2006, and signed a $1,500,000 note bearing interest at 10%, payable in five annual installments of $300,000. Mill appropriately accounts for the sale under the installment method. On December 31, 2007, Drew paid $300,000 principal and $150,000 interest. For the year ended December 31, 2007, what total amount of revenue should Mill recognize from the construction equipment sale and financing?
a.   $250,000
b.   $150,000
c.   $120,000
d.   $100,000

**59.** On January 2, 2006, Blake Co. sold a used machine to Cooper, Inc. for $900,000, resulting in a gain of $270,000. On that date, Cooper paid $150,000 cash and signed a $750,000 note bearing interest at 10%. The note was payable in three annual installments of $250,000 beginning January 2, 2007. Blake appropriately accounted for the sale under the installment method. Cooper made a timely payment of the first installment on January 2, 2007, of $325,000, which included accrued interest of $75,000. What amount of deferred gross profit should Blake report at December 31, 2007?
a.   $150,000
b.   $172,500
c.   $180,000
d.   $225,000

**60.** For financial statement purposes, the installment method of accounting may be used if the
a.   Collection period extends over more than twelve months.
b.   Installments are due in different years.
c.   Ultimate amount collectible is indeterminate.
d.   Percentage-of-completion method is inappropriate.

**61.** According to the installment method of accounting, gross profit on an installment sale is recognized in income
a.   On the date of sale.
b.   On the date the final cash collection is received.
c.   In proportion to the cash collection.
d.   After cash collections equal to the cost of sales have been received.

**62.** Income recognized using the installment method of accounting generally equals cash collected multiplied by the
a.   Net operating profit percentage.
b.   Net operating profit percentage adjusted for expected uncollectible accounts.
c.   Gross profit percentage.
d.   Gross profit percentage adjusted for expected uncollectible accounts.

**63.** It is proper to recognize revenue prior to the sale of merchandise when

I. The revenue will be reported as an installment sale.
II. The revenue will be reported under the cost recovery method.

    a. I only.
    b. II only.
    c. Both I and II.
    d. Neither I nor II.

**64.** The following information pertains to a sale of real estate by Ryan Co. to Sud Co. on December 31, 2006:

| Carrying amount | | $2,000,000 |
|---|---|---|
| Sales price: | | |
|   Cash | $ 300,000 | |
|   Purchase money mortgage | 2,700,000 | 3,000,000 |

The mortgage is payable in nine annual installments of $300,000 beginning December 31, 2007, plus interest of 10%. The December 31, 2007, installment was paid as scheduled, together with interest of $270,000. Ryan uses the cost recovery method to account for the sale. What amount of income should Ryan recognize in 2007 from the real estate sale and its financing?

    a. $570,000
    b. $370,000
    c. $270,000
    d. $0

**65.** Wren Co. sells equipment on installment contracts. Which of the following statements best justifies Wren's use of the cost recovery method of revenue recognition to account for these installment sales?

    a. The sales contract provides that title to the equipment only passes to the purchaser when all payments have been made.
    b. No cash payments are due until one year from the date of sale.
    c. Sales are subject to a high rate of return.
    d. There is no reasonable basis for estimating collectibility.

**66.** According to the cost recovery method of accounting, gross profit on an installment sale is recognized in income

    a. After cash collections equal to the cost of sales have been received.
    b. In proportion to the cash collections.
    c. On the date the final cash collection is received.
    d. On the date of sale.

**67.** On December 31, 2007, Rice, Inc. authorized Graf to operate as a franchisee for an initial franchise fee of $150,000. Of this amount, $60,000 was received upon signing the agreement and the balance, represented by a note, is due in three annual payments of $30,000 each beginning December 31, 2008. The present value on December 31, 2007, of the three annual payments appropriately discounted is $72,000. According to the agreement, the nonrefundable down payment represents a fair measure of the services already performed by Rice; however, substantial future services are required of Rice. Collectibility of the note is reasonably certain. In Rice's December 31, 2007 balance sheet, unearned franchise fees from Graf's franchise should be reported as

    a. $132,000
    b. $100,000
    c. $ 90,000
    d. $ 72,000

**68.** Each of Potter Pie Co.'s twenty-one new franchisees contracted to pay an initial franchise fee of $30,000. By December 31, 2007, each franchisee had paid a nonrefundable $10,000 fee and signed a note to pay $10,000 principal plus the market rate of interest on December 31, 2008, and December 31, 2009. Experience indicates that one franchisee will default on the additional payments. Services for the initial fee will be performed in 2008. What amount of net unearned franchise fees would Potter report at December 31, 2007?

    a. $400,000
    b. $600,000
    c. $610,000
    d. $630,000

**69.** In which of the following examples of real estate transactions would the seller not transfer the usual risks and rewards of ownership?

I. The buyer can compel the seller to repurchase the property.
II. The seller guarantees the return of the buyer's investment.
III. The seller is required to support operations of the buyer and will be reimbursed on a cost plus 5% basis.

    a. I.
    b. II.
    c. III.
    d. I and II.

**70.** Esker Inc. specializes in real estate transactions other than retail land sales. On January 1, 2007, Esker consummated a sale of property to Kame Ltd. The amount of profit on the sale is determinable and Esker is not obligated to perform any additional activities to earn the profit. Kame's initial and continuing investments were adequate to demonstrate a commitment to pay for the property under SFAS 66. However, Esker's receivable may be subject to future subordination. Esker should account for the sale using the

    a. Deposit method.
    b. Reduced recovery method.
    c. Cost recovery method.
    d. Full accrual method.

**SIMULATION PROBLEMS**

**Simulation Problem 1**          (50 to 60 minutes)

| Situation | | | | | |
|---|---|---|---|---|---|
| | Concepts | Account Classifications | Accrual Basis Worksheet | Communication | Research |

The following information pertains to Baron Flowers, a calendar-year sole proprietorship, which maintained its books on the cash basis during the year.

*Baron Flowers*
**TRIAL BALANCE**
*December 31, 2007*

| | Dr. | Cr. |
|---|---|---|
| Cash | $ 25,600 | |
| Accounts receivable, 12/31/06 | 16,200 | |
| Inventory, 12/31/06 | 62,000 | |
| Furniture & fixtures | 118,200 | |
| Land improvements | 45,000 | |
| Accumulated depreciation, 12/31/06 | | $ 32,400 |
| Accounts payable, 12/31/06 | | 17,000 |
| Baron, Drawings | | |
| Baron, Capital, 12/31/06 | | 124,600 |
| Sales | | 653,000 |
| Purchases | 305,100 | |
| Salaries | 174,000 | |
| Payroll taxes | 12,400 | |
| Insurance | 8,700 | |
| Rent | 34,200 | |
| Utilities | 12,600 | |
| Living expenses | 13,000 | |
| | $827,000 | $827,000 |

Baron has developed plans to expand into the wholesale flower market and is in the process of negotiating a bank loan to finance the expansion. The bank is requesting 2007 financial statements prepared on the accrual basis of accounting from Baron. During the course of a review engagement, Muir, Baron's accountant, obtained the following additional information.

1.    Amounts due from customers totaled $32,000 at December 31, 2007.

2.    An analysis of the above receivables revealed that an allowance for uncollectible accounts of $3,800 should be provided.

3.    Unpaid invoices for flower purchases totaled $30,500 and $17,000, at December 31, 2007, and December 31, 2006, respectively.

4.    The inventory totaled $72,800 based on a physical count of the goods at December 31, 2007. The inventory was priced at cost, which approximates market value.

5.    On May 1, 2007, Baron paid $8,700 to renew its comprehensive insurance coverage for one year. The premium on the previous policy, which expired on April 30, 2007, was $7,800.

6.    On January 2, 2007, Baron entered into a twenty-five-year operating lease for the vacant lot adjacent to Baron's retail store for use as a parking lot. As agreed in the lease, Baron paved and fenced in the lot at a cost of $45,000. The improvements were completed on April 1, 2007, and have an estimated useful life of fifteen years. No provision for depreciation or amortization has been recorded. Depreciation on furniture and fixtures was $12,000 for 2007.

7.    Accrued expenses at December 31, 2006 and 2007, were as follows:

| | 2006 | 2007 |
|---|---|---|
| Utilities | $ 900 | $1,500 |
| Payroll taxes | 1,100 | 1,600 |
| | $2,000 | $3,100 |

8.    Baron is being sued for $400,000. The coverage under the comprehensive insurance policy is limited to $250,000. Baron's attorney believes that an unfavorable outcome is probable and that a reasonable estimate of the settlement is $300,000.

9.    The salaries account includes $4,000 per month paid to the proprietor. Baron also receives $250 per week for living expenses.

| | Concepts | | | | |
|---|---|---|---|---|---|
| Situation | | Account Classifications | Accrual Basis Worksheet | Communication | Research |

In preparing accrual basis financial statements, it is important to understand the sources of generally accepted accounting principles. Match the following description to the appropriate accounting pronouncements.

### Descriptions

A. Official pronouncements of the APB.
B. Sets forth fundamental objectives and concepts that will be used in developing future standards.
C. Primary document of the FASB that establishes GAAP.
D. Provides additional guidance on implementing or applying FASB Standards or Interpretations.
E. Provides guidance on how to account for new and unusual financial transactions that have the potential for creating diversity in financial reporting practices.
F. Represent extensions or modifications of existing standards.

|  | (A) | (B) | (C) | (D) | (E) | (F) |
|---|---|---|---|---|---|---|
| 1. Technical Bulletins | ○ | ○ | ○ | ○ | ○ | ○ |
| 2. Interpretations of the Financial Accounting Standards Board | ○ | ○ | ○ | ○ | ○ | ○ |
| 3. Statement of Financial Accounting Standards | ○ | ○ | ○ | ○ | ○ | ○ |
| 4. EITF Statements | ○ | ○ | ○ | ○ | ○ | ○ |
| 5. Opinions | ○ | ○ | ○ | ○ | ○ | ○ |
| 6. Statement of Financial Accounting Concepts | ○ | ○ | ○ | ○ | ○ | ○ |

| Situation | Concepts | Account Classifications | Accrual Basis Worksheet | Communication | Research |
|---|---|---|---|---|---|

Suppose Baron incorporated and had the following accounts.  Indicate how each of the following is classified on the financial statements.  Below is a list of classifications.

| Balance sheet classification | Income statement classifications |
|---|---|
| A.  Current asset | H.  Revenue |
| B.  Noncurrent asset | I.  Expense |
| C.  Current liability | J.  Contra revenue |
| D.  Noncurrent liability |  |
| E.  Owner's equity |  |
| F.  Contra asset |  |
| G.  Contra equity |  |

|  | Balance sheet classification | | | | | | | Income statement classification | | |
|---|---|---|---|---|---|---|---|---|---|---|
|  | (A) | (B) | (C) | (D) | (E) | (F) | (G) | (H) | (I) | (J) |
| 1. Bonds payable, due in 2017 | ○ | ○ | ○ | ○ | ○ | ○ | ○ | ○ | ○ | ○ |
| 2. Treasury stock | ○ | ○ | ○ | ○ | ○ | ○ | ○ | ○ | ○ | ○ |
| 3. Accounts payable | ○ | ○ | ○ | ○ | ○ | ○ | ○ | ○ | ○ | ○ |
| 4. Sales discounts | ○ | ○ | ○ | ○ | ○ | ○ | ○ | ○ | ○ | ○ |
| 5. Notes payable, due in nine months | ○ | ○ | ○ | ○ | ○ | ○ | ○ | ○ | ○ | ○ |
| 6. Inventory | ○ | ○ | ○ | ○ | ○ | ○ | ○ | ○ | ○ | ○ |
| 7. Accounts receivable | ○ | ○ | ○ | ○ | ○ | ○ | ○ | ○ | ○ | ○ |
| 8. Common stock | ○ | ○ | ○ | ○ | ○ | ○ | ○ | ○ | ○ | ○ |
| 9. Cost of goods sold | ○ | ○ | ○ | ○ | ○ | ○ | ○ | ○ | ○ | ○ |
| 10. Allowance for uncollectible accounts | ○ | ○ | ○ | ○ | ○ | ○ | ○ | ○ | ○ | ○ |

| Situation | Concepts | Account Classifications | Accrual Basis Worksheet | Communication | Research |
|---|---|---|---|---|---|

Using the worksheet below, prepare the adjustments necessary to convert the trial balance of Baron Flowers to the accrual basis of accounting for the year ended December 31, 2007.  Formal journal entries are not required to support your adjustments.  However, use the numbers given with the additional information to cross-reference the postings in the adjustment columns on the worksheet.

*Baron Flowers*
**WORKSHEET TO CONVERT TRIAL BALANCE TO ACCRUAL BASIS**
*December 31, 2007*

| Account title | Cash basis Dr. | Cash basis Cr. | Adjustments Dr. | Adjustments Cr. | Accrual basis* Dr. * | Accrual basis* Cr. * |
|---|---|---|---|---|---|---|
| Cash | 25,600 | | | | | |
| Accounts receivable | 16,200 | | | | | |
| Inventory | 62,000 | | | | | |
| Furniture & fixtures | 118,200 | | | | | |
| Land improvements | 45,000 | | | | | |
| Accumulated depreciation & amortization | | 32,400 | | | | |
| Accounts payable | | 17,000 | | | | |
| Baron, Drawings | | | | | | |
| Baron, Capital | | 124,600 | | | | |
| | | | | | | |
| | | | | | | |
| | | | | | | |
| | | | | | | |
| | | | | | | |
| Sales | | 653,000 | | | | |
| Purchases | 305,100 | | | | | |
| Salaries | 174,000 | | | | | |
| Payroll taxes | 12,400 | | | | | |
| Insurance | 8,700 | | | | | |
| Rent | 34,200 | | | | | |
| Utilities | 12,600 | | | | | |
| Living expenses | 13,000 | | | | | |
| | 827,000 | 827,000 | | | | |

*Completion of these columns is not required.*

| Situation | Concepts | Account Classifications | Accrual Basis Worksheet | Communication | Research |
|---|---|---|---|---|---|

Write a brief memorandum to Baron explaining why the bank would require financial statements prepared on the accrual basis instead of the cash basis.

To:     Mr. Baron Flowers
From:   CPA Candidate
Re:     Accrual-basis financial statements

| Situation | Concepts | Account Classifications | Accrual Basis Worksheet | Communication | Research |
|---|---|---|---|---|---|

Using the FASB Concepts Statements, cut and paste the following definitions into the space provided.

1. Revenue

2. Assets

3. Liability

**Simulation Problem 2**                    (45 to 50 minutes)

| Situation | Concepts | Trial Balance Worksheet | Communication | Research |
|---|---|---|---|---|

The accounts listed below appeared in the December 31 trial balance of Jane Alexander Theater.

| | | |
|---|---:|---:|
| Equipment | 192,000 | |
| Accumulated depreciation equipment | | 60,000 |
| Notes payable | | 90,000 |
| Admissions revenue | | 380,000 |
| Advertising expense | 13,680 | |
| Salaries expense | 57,600 | |
| Interest expense | 1,400 | |

Additional information follows:

1. The equipment has an estimated life of 16 years and a salvage value of $40,000 at the end of that time. (Use straight-line method.)
2. The note payable is a 90-day note given to the bank October 20 and bearing interest at 10%. (Use 360 days for denominator.)
3. In December 2,000 coupon admission books were sold at $25 each. They could be used for admission any time after January 1.
4. Advertising expense paid in advance and included in Advertising Expense, $1,100.
5. Salaries accrued but unpaid, $4,700.

| Concepts | | | | |
|---|---|---|---|---|
| Situation | | Trial Balance Worksheet | Communication | Research |

This question consists of ten items that represent descriptions or definitions of the various elements of the FASB's *Statements of Financial Accounting Concepts*. Select the **best** answer for each item from the terms listed in A – L. A term may be used once, more than once, or not at all.

### Terms

| | | | |
|---|---|---|---|
| A. | Recognition | G. | Gains |
| B. | Comprehensive Income | H. | Net Income |
| C. | Representational Faithfulness | I. | Earnings |
| D. | Revenues | J. | Realization |
| E. | Predictive Value | K. | Replacement Cost |
| F. | Consistency | L. | Current Market Value |

### Concept statement definitions

(A) (B) (C) (D) (E) (F) (G) (H) (I) (J) (K) (L)

1. Component of relevance.

2. Increases in net assets from incidental or peripheral transactions affecting an entity.

3. The process of converting noncash resources and rights into cash or claims to cash.

4. Ingredient of relevance **and** reliability.

5. The process of formally recording an item in the financial statements of an entity after it has met existing criteria and been subject to cost-benefit constraints and materiality thresholds.

6. All changes in net assets of an entity during a period except those resulting from investments by owners and distributions to owners.

7. Inflows or other enhancements of assets of an entity or settlements of its liabilities from delivering or producing goods, rendering services, or other activities that constitute the entity's ongoing operations.

8. The amount of cash, or its equivalent, that could be obtained by selling an asset in orderly liquidation.

9. The quality of information that helps users to increase the likelihood of correctly forecasting the outcome of past or present events.

10. A performance measure concerned primarily with cash-to-cash cycles.

| Situation | Concepts | Trial Balance Worksheet | Communication | Research |
|---|---|---|---|---|

Using the attached Excel file, complete the adjustments, adjusted trial balance, and the income statement columns of the worksheet. For the # column, insert the number of adjustments. Add accounts as needed.

**Jane Alexander Theater**
**December 31, 200X**

| a) | Trial balance | | # | Adjustments | | Adjusted trial balance | | Income statement | |
|---|---|---|---|---|---|---|---|---|---|
| | Debit | Credit | | Debit | Credit | Debit | Credit | Debit | Credit |
| Equipment | 192,000 | | | | | | | | |
| Accumulated depreciation— equipment | | 60,000 | | | | | | | |
| Notes payable | | 90,000 | | | | | | | |
| Admissions revenue | | 380,000 | | | | | | | |
| Advertising expense | 13,680 | | | | | | | | |
| Salaries expense | 57,600 | | | | | | | | |
| Interest expense | 1,400 | | | | | | | | |
| Depreciation expense | | | | | | | | | |
| Interest payable | | | | | | | | | |
| Unearned adm | | | | | | | | | |
| Revenue | | | | | | | | | |
| Prepaid advertising | | | | | | | | | |
| Salaries payable | | | | | | | | | |

| Situation | Concepts | Trial Balance Worksheet | Communication | Research |
|---|---|---|---|---|

Write a brief memorandum to the Director of Jane Alexander Theater explaining to him/her why adjusting and closing entries are necessary.

To:     Ms. Jane Alexander, Theatre Director
From:   CPA Candidate
Re:     Adjusting and closing entries

| |
|---|
| |

| Situation | Concepts | Trial Balance Worksheet | Communication | Research |
|---|---|---|---|---|

Using the FASB Concepts Statements, cut and paste the following definitions into the space provided.

1. Gain

2. Recognition

3. Reliability

---

## Simulation Problem 3                                    (30 to 40 minutes)

| Situation | Concepts | Adjusting Entries | Revenue and Expense Recognition | Communication | Research |
|---|---|---|---|---|---|

Emco is a wholesaler of kitchen appliances to retail dealers. At present, Emco sells to customers on account, with the account receivable due in forty-five days.

| Situation | Concepts | Adjusting Entries | Revenue and Expense Recognition | Communication | Research |
|---|---|---|---|---|---|

SFAC 5 provides guidance on measuring assets and liabilities.  The following measurement methods are available to measure assets and liabilities, as shown in the list below.  Identify the appropriate valuation method for each item.

*Measurement methods*
A.   Historical cost or historical proceeds
B.   Current cost
C.   Current market value
D.   Net realizable value or settlement rate
E.   Present value of future cash flows

| Account | (A) (B) (C) (D) (E) |
|---|---|
| 1. Long-term receivables | O O O O O |
| 2. Available for sale securities | O O O O O |
| 3. Equipment | O O O O O |
| 4. Warranty obligations | O O O O O |
| 5. Short-term payables | O O O O O |
| 6. Accounts receivable | O O O O O |
| 7. Bonds payable, due in ten years | O O O O O |
| 8. Trading securities | O O O O O |

| Situation | Concepts | Adjusting Entries | Revenue and Expense Recognition | Communication | Research |
|---|---|---|---|---|---|

Indicate whether each of the following adjusting entries is an accrual or a deferral type entry.

| | | | *Accrual* | *Deferral* |
|---|---|---|---|---|
| 1. | Depreciation expense | xx | | |
| | Accumulated deprecation | xx | O | O |
| 2. | Interest receivable | xx | | |
| | Interest revenue | xx | O | O |
| 3. | Rent expense | xx | | |
| | Prepaid rent | xx | O | O |
| 4. | Unearned revenue | xx | | |
| | Rent revenue | xx | O | O |
| 5. | Wage expense | xx | | |
| | Wages payable | xx | O | O |

| Situation | Concepts | Adjusting Entries | Revenue and Expense Recognition | Communication | Research |
|---|---|---|---|---|---|

Emco has the following transactions in 2007.  Indicate the amount of revenue or expense recognized in 2007, 2008, and 2009 for each of these items.  You may show expense recognitions in parentheses (xx).

*Amounts to be recognized*
2007     2008     2009

1.  Emco sells $5,000 of goods to a customer, FOB shipping point on 12/30/07.

2.  Emco sells three pieces of equipment on a contract over a three-year period. The sales price of each piece of equipment is $10,000.  Delivery of each piece of equipment is on February 10 of each year.  In 2007, the customer paid a $20,000 down payment, and paid $5,000 per year in 2008 and 2009.  Collectibility is reasonably assured.

3.  In 1/1/07, Emco paid $9,000 for a membership to Wholesalers Association for a two-year membership in the trade association.

| | Amounts to be recognized | | |
|---|---|---|---|
| | 2007 | 2008 | 2009 |

**4.** On 6/1/07, Emco signs a contract for $20,000 for goods to be sold on account. Payment is to be made in two installments of $10,000 each on 12/1/08 and 12/1/09. The goods are delivered on 10/1/07. Collection is reasonably assured, and the goods may not be returned.

**5.** Emco sells goods to a customer on July 1, 2007, for $50,000. If the customer does not sell the goods to retail customers by December 31, 2008, the goods can be returned to Emco. The customer sells the goods to retail customers on October 1, 2008.

| Situation | Concepts | Adjusting Entries | Revenue and Expense Recognition | Communication | Research |
|---|---|---|---|---|---|

Wyatt, CPA, is meeting with Brown, the controller of Emco, a wholesaler, to discuss the accounting issues regarding two unrelated items.

- Emco is considering offering its customers the right to return its products for a full refund within one year of purchase. Emco expects its sales to increase as a result, but is unable to estimate the amount of future returns.
- Brown is aware that Statement of Financial Accounting Standards (SFAS) 106, *Employers' Accounting for Postretirement Benefits other than Pensions*, is effective for years beginning after December 15, 1992. Brown is uncertain about the benefits and beneficiaries covered by this Statement. Brown believes that, regardless of SFAS 106, no estimate of postretirement obligation can be reasonable because it would be based on too many assumptions. For this reason, Brown wishes to continue to account for the postretirement benefits that Emco pays to its retirees on the pay-as-you-go (cash) basis.

Brown has asked Wyatt to write a brief memo to Brown that Brown can use to explain these issues to Emco's president. Write a brief advisory memorandum from Wyatt to Brown to

**1.** Explain the general principle of revenue recognition, the method of revenue recognition when right to return exists, and the impact of offering a right to return on Emco's ability to recognize revenue, if any.

**2.** State the principal benefit covered by SFAS 106 and give an example of other benefits covered by SFAS 106. Explain the reasoning given in SFAS 106 for requiring accruals based on estimates. Indicate the primary recipients of postretirement benefits other than pensions.*

\* *This requirement should not be completed until you have done Module 11D, Present Value: Pensions. A cross-reference in the Module 11 problem material will direct you to return to it.*

To:   Mr. Brown
From: Wyatt, CPA

| Situation | Concepts | Adjusting Entries | Revenue and Expense Recognition | Communication | Research |
|---|---|---|---|---|---|

Using the FASB Concepts Statements, cut and paste the following definitions into the space provided.

**1.** Relevance

**2.** Realizable

**3.** Expense

**4.** Matching

## MULTIPLE-CHOICE ANSWERS[*]

| 1. | c | __ __ | 16. | d | __ __ | 31. | b | __ __ | 46. | d | __ __ | 61. | c | __ __ |
|---|---|---|---|---|---|---|---|---|---|---|---|---|---|---|
| 2. | d | __ __ | 17. | d | __ __ | 32. | b | __ __ | 47. | d | __ __ | 62. | c | __ __ |
| 3. | b | __ __ | 18. | c | __ __ | 33. | c | __ __ | 48. | a | __ __ | 63. | d | __ __ |
| 4. | c | __ __ | 19. | d | __ __ | 34. | d | __ __ | 49. | d | __ __ | 64. | d | __ __ |
| 5. | b | __ __ | 20. | d | __ __ | 35. | a | __ __ | 50. | c | __ __ | 65. | d | __ __ |
| 6. | a | __ __ | 21. | b | __ __ | 36. | d | __ __ | 51. | d | __ __ | 66. | a | __ __ |
| 7. | d | __ __ | 22. | c | __ __ | 37. | c | __ __ | 52. | b | __ __ | 67. | d | __ __ |
| 8. | a | __ __ | 23. | a | __ __ | 38. | b | __ __ | 53. | c | __ __ | 68. | c | __ __ |
| 9. | c | __ __ | 24. | c | __ __ | 39. | b | __ __ | 54. | b | __ __ | 69. | d | __ __ |
| 10. | d | __ __ | 25. | d | __ __ | 40. | b | __ __ | 55. | d | __ __ | 70. | c | __ __ |
| 11. | b | __ __ | 26. | b | __ __ | 41. | b | __ __ | 56. | d | __ __ | | | |
| 12. | d | __ __ | 27. | c | __ __ | 42. | b | __ __ | 57. | c | __ __ | | | |
| 13. | a | __ __ | 28. | a | __ __ | 43. | a | __ __ | 58. | a | __ __ | | | |
| 14. | c | __ __ | 29. | b | __ __ | 44. | c | __ __ | 59. | a | __ __ | 1st: | __/70 = | __% |
| 15. | d | __ __ | 30. | c | __ __ | 45. | d | __ __ | 60. | c | __ __ | 2nd: | __/70 = | __% |

## MULTIPLE-CHOICE ANSWER EXPLANATIONS

### A.1. Basic Accounting Theory

**1.** **(c)** The Statements of Financial Accounting Concepts (SFAC) were issued to establish a framework from which financial accounting and reporting standards could be developed. The SFAC provide the theory behind accounting and reporting and provide guidance when no GAAP exists. The SFAC are not included as GAAP.

**2.** **(d)** Per SFAC 1, the objectives of financial reporting focus on providing present and potential investors with information useful in making investment decisions. Financial statement users do not have the authority to prescribe the data they desire. Therefore, they must rely on external financial reporting to satisfy their information needs, and the objectives must be based on the needs of those users.

**3.** **(b)** The FASB conceptual framework has identified two constraints to the usefulness of providing information in financial statements, cost benefit and materiality. Information is **not** disclosed if the costs of disclosure outweigh the benefits or if the information is not material enough to influence users. Consistency is a secondary quality of accounting information; reliability and relevance are the primary qualities of accounting information; and representational faithfulness is a component of reliability.

**4.** **(c)** Per SFAC 1, the primary focus of financial reporting is to provide information about an enterprise's performance. SFAC 1 states that financial reporting does not directly provide information about the performance of a particular management for the period since actions of past management may also affect the current period earnings. Financial reporting primarily focuses on the enterprise's performance and management performance would only be indirectly illustrated.

**5.** **(b)** SFAC 2 defines neutrality as the quality of information which requires freedom from bias toward a predetermined result. Since unbiased information would always be more reliable than biased information, this quality contributes to reliability. Other components of reliability include verifiability and representational faithfulness. Neutrality is not an ingredient of relevance because relevance refers to the usefulness of information, characterized by its predictive value, feedback value, and timeliness.

**6.** **(a)** Per SFAC 2, comparability is a secondary quality which relates to **both** of the primary qualities of relevance and reliability. Both feedback value and timeliness are described by SFAC 2 as ingredients only of relevance. They are not considered ingredients of reliability. Verifiability is described as an ingredient only of reliability.

**7.** **(d)** Per SFAC 5, recognition is the process of formally recording or incorporating an item into the financial statements as an asset, liability, revenue, expense, or the like. According to SFAC 6, allocation is the process of assigning or distributing an amount according to a plan or formula, matching is the simultaneous recognition of revenues with expenses that are related directly or jointly to the same transactions or events, and realization is the process of converting noncash resources and rights into money.

**8.** **(a)** Per SFAC 5, earnings and comprehensive income have the same broad components—revenues, expenses, gains, and losses—but are not the same because certain classes of gains and losses are excluded from earnings. Changes in market values of investments in marketable equity securities classified as available-for-sale securities are included in comprehensive income, but are excluded from earnings until realized. Answers (b), (c), and (d) are incorrect because they would be included in both earnings and comprehensive income. Note that unrealized gains and losses on marketable equity securities classified as trading securities are included in earnings. This treatment is in accordance with SFAS 115.

**9.** **(c)** Per SFAC 6, comprehensive income includes all changes in equity during a period except those resulting from investments by owners and distributions to owners. Dividends paid to stockholders is a change in equity resulting from a distribution to owners, so it is excluded from comprehensive income. Answers (a), (b), and (d) are all included in comprehensive income because they **are** changes in equity, but are **not** investments by, or distributions to, owners.

*NOTE: Under SFAS 130, prior period error corrections would also be excluded from comprehensive income. This standard addresses*

---

*only the display of unrealized gains (losses) on foreign currency items, available-for-sale marketable securities, and the minimum pension liability adjustment.  Other changes suggested in SFAC 5 and 6 will be addressed in future SFAS.*

**10.   (d)**   Reliability has three subcomponents, as defined in SFAC 2:  neutrality, representational faithfulness, and verifiability.  **Neutrality** means that information should **not** be prepared or reported in such a way as to obtain a predetermined result, and **should** be free from bias.  **Representational faithfulness** is defined as the correspondence between a measure and what it purports to represent.  **Verifiability** means that two or more individuals who are independent of each other would arrive at a similar conclusion based on an examination of the same evidence.  Answer (d) violates verifiability because different individuals would come up with different estimates of market value.  Answer (a) is incorrect because reporting data to analysts does not violate reliability.  Answers (b) and (c) are incorrect because they are examples of violations of relevance, not reliability.  Answer (b) violates the relevance subcomponent of **timeliness,** while answer (c) violates the relevance subcomponent of **feedback value.**

**11.   (b)**   According to SFAC 6, realization is the process of converting noncash resources and rights into money through the sale of assets for cash or claims to cash.  When equipment is sold for a note receivable, money is realized since a note qualifies as a claim to cash.  Answers (a) and (d) relate to cost allocation.  Answer (c) is incorrect because accounts receivable represents a claim to cash.  Realization occurs at the time of sale rather than when cash is collected.

**12.   (d)**   A loss contingency is accrued by a charge to expense if it is reasonably estimable and it is **probable that a liability has been incurred** as of the balance sheet date.  The **cause of the liability must have occurred on or before the date of the financial statements** if the liability is to be accrued, because the intention is to recognize the loss in the same period that the underlying cause took place.  Therefore, some authorities would say that matching is the underlying concept supporting the immediate recognition of a contingent loss.  A larger number, however, would mention conservatism as the more pervasive underlying concept supporting the immediate recognition of these losses.

**13.   (a)**   Conservatism means that when in doubt, accountants should choose the procedure that will be least likely to overstate assets and income.  This concept underlies the GAAP pertaining to recording gain contingencies.  In an effort to not overstate assets or income, gain contingencies are not recorded until they are no longer contingencies, and are disclosed only when probabilities are high that a gain contingency will become reality.

**14.   (c)**   Per SFAC 6, the major difference between financial and physical capital maintenance is related to the effects of price changes on assets held and liabilities owed during a period.  The financial capital concept is applied in current GAAP.  Under this concept, the effects of the price changes described above are considered "holding gains and losses," and are included in computing return on capital.  Comprehensive income, which is described in SFAC 5, is "the change in equity of a business enterprise during a period from transactions and other events and circumstances from nonowner sources."  It is also a measure of return on **finan-**

**cial** capital.  The concept of physical capital maintenance seeks to measure the effects of price changes that are not currently captured under GAAP (e.g., replacement costs of nonmonetary assets).  Under this concept, holding gains and losses are considered "capital maintenance adjustments" which would be included directly in equity and excluded from return on capital.

**15.   (d)**   Per SFAC 6, revenues are inflows of assets or settlements of liabilities, or both, during a period as a result of an entity's major or primary operations.  Two essential characteristics of revenues are that revenues (1) arise from a company's primary earnings activities and (2) are recurring or continuing in nature.  Therefore, answer (d) is correct because it meets the above criteria.  Answers (b) and (c) are incorrect because they result from incidental transactions.  Answer (a) is incorrect because a decrease of an asset is not a revenue.

**16.   (d)**   Per SFAC 6, the common quality shared by all assets is "service potential" or "future economic benefit."  Per SFAC 6, assets commonly have other distinguishing features, such as being legally enforceable, tangible or acquired at a cost.  These features, however, are not essential characteristics of assets.

**17.   (d)**   Per SFAC 5, five different attributes are used to measure assets and liabilities in present practice:  historical cost, current (replacement) cost, current market value, net realizable value, and present value of future cash flows.  Three of these (historical cost, replacement cost, and net realizable value) are used in measuring inventory at lower of cost or market.  Present value of future cash flows is not used to measure inventory.

### Cash Flow Information and Present Value (SFAC 7)

**18.   (c)**   The most relevant measure of a liability always reflects the credit standing of the entity obligated to pay, according to SFAC 7.  Those who hold the entity's obligations as assets incorporate the entity's credit standing in determining the prices they are willing to pay.

**19.   (d)**   SFAC 7 provides a framework for using future cash flows as the basis for accounting measurements at initial recognition or fresh-start measurements and for the interest method of amortization.  **FASB limited SFAC 7 to measurement issues** (how to measure) **and chose not to address recognition questions** (when to measure).  SFAC 7 introduces the expected cash flow approach, which differs from the traditional approach by focusing on explicit assumptions about the range of possible estimated cash flows and their respective probabilities.

**20.   (d)**   The expected cash flow approach uses all expectations about possible cash flows in developing a measurement, rather than just the single most-likely cash flow.  By incorporating a range of possible outcomes (with their respective timing differences), the expected cash flow approach accommodates the use of present value techniques when the timing of cash flows is uncertain.  Thus, the expected cash flow is likely to provide a better estimate of fair value than the minimum, most-likely, or maximum taken alone.  According to SFAC 7, expected present value refers to the sum of probability-weighted present values in a range of estimated cash flows, all discounted using the same interest rate convention.

**21. (b)** The computation of expected present value using a single interest rate is as follows:

| | | |
|---|---:|---:|
| PV of $200,000 in one year at 5% | $190,476 | |
| Probability | 20% | $38,095 |
| PV of $200,000 in two years at 5% | $181,406 | |
| Probability | 50% | 90,703 |
| PV of $200,000 in three years at 5% | $172,768 | |
| Probability | 30% | 51,830 |
| | | $180,628 |

According to SFAC 7, expected present value refers to the sum of probability-weighted present values in a range of estimated cash flows, all discounted using the same interest rate convention.

**22. (c)** Like depreciation and amortization conventions, interest methods are grounded in notions of historical cost, not current cost.

**23. (a)** According to SFAC 7, the objective of using present value in an accounting measurement is to capture, to the extent possible, the economic difference between sets of future cash flows. The objective of present value, when used in accounting measurements at initial recognition and fresh-start measurements, is to estimate fair value. Stated differently, present value should attempt to capture the elements that taken together would comprise a market price, if one existed, that is fair value. Value-in-use and entity-specific measurements attempt to capture the value of an asset or liability in the context of a particular entity. An entity-specific measurement substitutes the entity's assumptions for those that marketplace participants would make.

**24. (c)** SFAS 144 provides guidance on the determination of gain or loss on disposal of a component of a business. According to this guidance, such determination should be based on estimates of the net realizable value of the component. Since Brooks Co. plans to discontinue its entire operations, the appropriate measurement basis for its equipment is net realizable value. Historical cost and current reproduction and replacement costs are not appropriate measurement bases for assets once an entity has decided to discontinue its operations because these amounts do not reflect the entity's probable future benefit, which is a characteristic of assets per SFAC 6.

**25. (d)** Per AU 411, there are four primary levels of authority and an "Other" category in the hierarchy of generally accepted accounting principles. The most authoritative level includes FASB Statements and Interpretations, APB Opinions, and AICPA Accounting Research Bulletins. Statements of Position, Industry Audit and Accounting Guides, and Issues Papers are all sources of support for accounting principles but are lesser in authority.

**A.2. Income Determination**

**26. (b)** Generally, sales revenue is recognized at the date of delivery, because that generally is the time at which a sale has occurred. At that point the two criteria for revenue recognition were met; the revenue is (1) realized or realizable and (2) it is earned (SFAC 6). Therefore, the amount of sales revenue recognized in 2006 is $150,000 (50,000 × $3 = $150,000).

**27. (c)** Per ARB 43, Chapter 4, income generally accrues only at the time of sale, and gains may not be anticipated by reflecting assets at their **current** sales prices. Ex-

ception to this general rule is granted, however, for agricultural products that are homogenous and have an immediate marketability at quoted prices (such as the cotton in this problem). When these inventories are stated at sales prices, they should be reduced by expenditures to be incurred in disposal. Amar Farms should, therefore, recognize revenue on the entire 300,000 pound crop in 2007 at the guaranteed (and prevailing) market price of $.70 per pound. This amounts to $210,000 (300,000 pounds × $.70 per pound = $210,000). Note that the additional $.02 per pound for the cotton sold in 2008 would be recognized in 2008, since its selling price exceeded the current (2007) market price.

**28. (a)** Per SFAS 48, revenue from the sale of a product may be recognized at the time of sale only if **all** of the following conditions are met:

1. The seller's price is fixed or readily determinable.
2. The buyer has paid the seller or is obligated to pay the seller, the obligation not being contingent on resale of the product.
3. The buyer's obligation to the seller remains unchanged in the event of damage or destruction of the product.
4. The buyer is independent from the seller.
5. The seller does not have any significant obligations regarding resale of the product by the buyer.
6. The amount of future returns can be reasonably estimated.

Because the buyer, Zee, has the right to return the machine to the seller, Lin, condition (2) above has not been met. Therefore, the recognition of sales revenue and cost of sales is not allowable for this transaction.

**A.3. Accruals and Deferrals**

**29. (b)** Under accrual accounting, events that change an entity's financial position are recorded in the period in which the events occur. This means revenues are recognized when earned rather than when cash is received, and expenses are recognized when incurred rather than when cash is paid. Therefore, when the royalties are paid, Wand should debit an asset account (prepaid royalties) rather than an expense account. The royalties paid should be reported as expense in the period incurred (by debiting royalty expense and crediting prepaid royalties).

**30. (c)** The balance in the advertising expense account on 12/31/07 before adjustment is $146,000. Since the sales promotional campaign is to be conducted in January, any associated costs are an expense of 2008. Thus, the $15,000 cost of printing catalogs should be removed from the advertising expense account and recorded as a prepaid expense as of 12/31/07. In addition, advertising expense must be increased by the $9,000 cost of December's radio advertisements, which are an expense of 2007 even though they were not billed to Clark or paid until 2008. The $9,000 must be accrued as an expense and a liability at 12/31/07. Therefore, 2007 advertising expense should total $140,000 ($146,000 – $15,000 + $9,000).

**31. (b)** The opening balance in prepaid expenses ($1,500) results from a one-year insurance premium paid on 7/1/06. Since this policy would have expired by 6/30/07, no part of the $1,500 is included in 12/31/07 prepaid expenses. The insurance premium paid on 7/1/07 ($3,200) would be partially expired (6/12) by 12/31/07. The remainder (6/12 ×

$3,200 = $1,600) would be a prepaid expense at year-end. The entire advance rental payment ($2,000) is a prepaid expense at 12/31/07 because it applies to 2008. Therefore, total 12/31/07 prepaid expenses are $3,600.

| Prepaid insurance ($3,200 × 6/12) | $1,600 |
|---|---|
| Prepaid rent | 2,000 |
| Total prepaid expenses | $3,600 |

**32. (b)** Apparently Roro records policy payments as charges to insurance expense and records prepaid insurance at the end of the quarter through an adjusting entry. The unadjusted trial balance amounts at 3/31/07 must represent the final two months of the old policy ($300 of prepaid insurance) and the cost of the new policy ($7,200 of insurance expense). An adjusting entry must be prepared to reflect the correct 3/31/07 balances. Since the new policy has been in force one month (3/1 through 3/31), thirty-five months remain unexpired. Therefore, the balance in prepaid insurance should be $7,000 ($7,200 × 35/36). Insurance expense should include the cost of the last two months of the old policy and the first month of the new policy [$300 + ($7,200 × 1/36) = $500]. Roro's adjusting entry would transfer $6,700 from insurance expense to prepaid insurance to result in the correct balances.

**33. (c)** At 12/31/07, the liability account unearned subscription revenue should have a balance which reflects all unexpired subscriptions. Of the 2006 sales, $125,000 expires during 2008 and would still be a liability at 12/31/07. Of the 2007 sales, $340,000 ($200,000 + $140,000) expires during 2008 and 2009, and therefore is a liability at 12/31/07. Therefore, the total liability is $465,000 ($125,000 + $340,000). This amount would have to be removed from the sales account and recorded as a liability in a 12/31/07 adjusting entry.

**34. (d)** Regal's unredeemed gift certificates at 12/31/06 are $75,000. During 2007, these certificates are either redeemed ($25,000) or expire by 12/31/07 ($75,000 – $25,000 = $50,000). Therefore, none of the $75,000 affects the 12/31/07 unearned revenue amount. During 2007, additional certificates totaling $250,000 were sold. Of this amount, $225,000 is expected to be redeemed in the future [$250,000 – (10% × $250,000)]. Since $175,000 of 2007 certificates were redeemed in 2007, 12/31/07 unearned revenue is $50,000 ($225,000 – $175,000).

**35. (a)** The requirement is to calculate Wren's royalty revenue for 2007. The 3/15/07 royalty receipt ($12,000) would not affect 2007 revenue because this amount pertains to revenues earned for July through December of 2006 and would have been accrued as revenue on 12/31/06. On 9/15/07, Wren received $17,000 in royalties for the first half of 2007. Royalties for the second half of 2007 will not be received until 3/15/08. However, the royalty payment to be received for the second six months (15% × $60,000 = $9,000) has been earned and should be accrued at 12/31/07. Therefore, 2007 royalty revenue is $26,000 ($17,000 + $9,000).

**36. (d)** The agreement states that Super is to receive royalties of 20% of revenues associated with the comic strip. Since Fantasy's 2008 revenues from the strip were $1,500,000, Super's royalty revenue is $300,000 ($1,500,000 × 20%). The other information in the problem about the receivable and cash payments is not needed to compute revenues. Super's 2008 summary entries would be

| Cash | 200,000 | | |
|---|---|---|---|
| Royalties rec. | | 75,000 | |
| Royalty revenue | | 125,000 | ($200,000 – $75,000) |
| Royalties rec. | 175,000 | | |
| Royalty revenue | | 175,000 | ($300,000 – $125,000) |

**37. (c)** Royalty revenues should be recognized when earned, regardless of when the cash is collected. Royalty revenue earned from 12/1/06 to 5/31/07 is $80,000 ($400,000 × 20%). Of this amount, $10,000 ($50,000 × 20%) was earned in December of 2006, so the portion earned in the first five months of 2007 is $70,000 ($80,000 – $10,000). Royalty revenue earned from 6/1/07 to 11/30/07 is $65,000 ($325,000 × 20%). The amount earned from 12/1/07 to 12/31/07, which would be accrued at 12/31, is $14,000 ($70,000 × 20%). Therefore, 2007 royalty revenue is $149,000.

| 1/1/07 - 5/31/07 | $70,000 |
|---|---|
| 6/1/07 - 11/30/07 | 65,000 |
| 12/1/07 - 12/31/07 | 14,000 |
| | $149,000 |

**38. (b)** The requirement is to calculate the amount of royalty income to be recognized in 2007. Cash collected for royalties totaled $200,000 in 2007. However, this amount must be adjusted for changes in the related accounts, as follows:

| 2007 cash received | $200,000 |
|---|---|
| Royalties receivable 12/31/06 | (90,000) |
| Royalties receivable 12/31/07 | 85,000 |
| Unearned royalties 12/31/06 | 60,000 |
| Unearned royalties 12/31/07 | (40,000) |
| Royalty income | $215,000 |

The beginning receivable balance ($90,000) is subtracted because that portion of the cash collected was recognized as revenue last year. The ending receivable balance ($85,000) is added because that amount is 2007 revenue, even though it has not yet been collected. The beginning balance of unearned royalties ($60,000) is added because that amount is assumed to be earned during the year. Finally, the ending balance of unearned royalties ($40,000) is subtracted since this amount was collected, but not earned as revenue, by 12/31/07.

**39. (b)** The requirement is to determine the amount of royalty expense to be recognized in 2007. Cash paid for royalties totaled $300,000 in 2007. However, this amount must be adjusted for changes in the related accounts, as follows:

| 2007 cash paid | $300,000 |
|---|---|
| Royalties payable 12/31/06 | (80,000) |
| Royalties payable 12/31/07 | 75,000 |
| Prepaid royalties 12/31/06 | 55,000 |
| Prepaid royalties 12/31/07 | (45,000) |
| | $305,000 |

The beginning payable balance ($80,000) is subtracted because that portion of the cash paid was recognized as expense during the previous year. The ending payable balance ($75,000) is added because that amount has been accrued as 2007 expense, even though it has not yet been paid. The beginning balance of prepaid royalties ($55,000) is added because that amount is assumed to have expired during the year. Finally, the ending balance of prepaid royalties ($45,000) is subtracted since this amount was paid, but not incurred as an expense, by 12/31/07.

**40.    (b)**    When the insurance policy was initially purchased, the entire balance was debited to a prepaid asset account (i.e., prepaid insurance).  The adjusting entry at December 31, 2007, to recognize the expiration of one year of the policy would be

| Insurance expense | (1/3 of original pymt.) |
|---|---|
| Prepaid insurance | (1/3 of original pymt.) |

After the adjusting entry, the prepaid asset account would contain 2/3 of the original payment.  If the original payment had instead been debited to an expense account (i.e., insurance expense), then the adjusting entry at December 31, 2007 would be

| Prepaid insurance | (2/3 of original pymt.) |
|---|---|
| Insurance expense | (2/3 of original pymt.) |

This alternate approach would also result in 1/3 of the original payment being expensed in 2007 and 2/3 of the original payment being carried forward as a prepaid asset.  Thus, answer (b) is correct.  Answer (a) is incorrect because the premium paid was for a three-year policy, 2/3 of which had not yet expired and would therefore be carried forward in the prepaid asset account.  Answer (c) is incorrect because 1/3 of the original payment was already expensed.  Answer (d) is incorrect because the amount would be the same as it would have been if the original payment had been debited initially to an expense account (as explained for answer (b) above).

**41.    (b)**    Per ARB 43, chap 3A, current assets are identified as resources that are reasonably expected to be realized in cash or sold or **consumed** during the normal operating cycle of the business.  These resources include prepaid expenses such as royalties.  Since the balance remaining in Sip Co.'s royalty prepayment (the payment relating to 2008 royalties) will be consumed within the next year, it should be reported as a current asset.  Additionally, the payment relating to 2007 should be reported as an expense.

**42.    (b)**    At the time the gift certificates were issued, the following entry was made, reflecting the store's future obligation to honor the certificates:

| Cash | xx | |
|---|---|---|
| Deferred revenue | | xx |

Upon redemption of the certificates, the obligation recorded in the deferred revenue account becomes satisfied and the revenue is earned.  Similarly, as the certificates expire, the store is no longer under any obligation to honor the certificates and the deferred revenue should be taken into income.  In both instances, the deferred revenue account must be reduced (debited) to reflect the earning of revenue.  This is done through the following entry:

| Deferred revenue | xx | |
|---|---|---|
| Revenue | | xx |

**43.    (a)**    The revenues from service contracts should be recognized on a pro rata basis over the term of the contract.  This treatment allocates the contract revenues to the period(s) in which they are earned.  Since the sale of a service contract does not culminate in the completion of the earnings process (i.e., does not represent the seller's performance of the contract), payments received for such a contract should be recorded initially in a deferred revenue account.

**A.4.    Cash to Accrual**

**44.    (c)**    The following formula is used to adjust service revenue from the cash basis to the accrual basis:

| Cash fees collected | + | End. AR | − | Beg. AR | + | Beg. unearned fees | − | End. unearned fees | = | Accrual basis service revenue |
|---|---|---|---|---|---|---|---|---|---|---|

$200,000 + $60,000 − $40,000 + 0 − $5,000 = $215,000

As an alternative, T-accounts can be used.

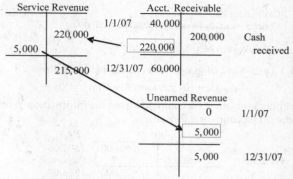

**45.    (d)**    To determine cash basis revenue, the solutions approach is to prepare a T-account for accounts receivable.

| Accounts Receivable | | | |
|---|---|---|---|
| 12/31/06 | 1,000,000 | | |
| Sales | 4,600,000 | 20,000 | Write-offs |
| | | ? | Collections |
| 12/31/07 | 1,300,000 | | |

The missing amount for cash collections is $4,280,000.  Another approach is to use the following formula:

| Sales | + Decrease (− increase) in AR | − Write-offs | = Collections |
|---|---|---|---|
| $4,600,000 | − $300,000 | − $20,000 | = $4,280,000 |

The increase in receivables ($300,000) means that cash collected during the period was less than sales during the period and therefore is deducted from sales revenue.  The write-offs ($20,000) represent recognized sales that will never be collected in cash and therefore must also be deducted to compute collections.

**46.    (d)**    To determine rental revenue, the solutions approach is to prepare a T-account for rents receivable and rent revenues.

| Rent Receivable | | | Rent Revenues | |
|---|---|---|---|---|
| 11/30/06 800,000 | 800,000ª | | 800,000ª | 2,210,000 |
| 1,090,000ᵇ | 30,000ᶜ | | | 1,090,000ᵇ |
| Bal 1,060,000 | 1,060,000 + 30,000 | | | Bal 2,500,000 |

ª  To remove 2006 revenue from the $2,210,000 of cash collected and relieve rent receivable of collections from 2006 receivables.
ᵇ  To recognize unrecorded rent earned including write-offs.
ᶜ  To recognize write-offs.  Debit would be to the allowance account.

**47.    (d)**    Under the cash basis method of accounting, revenue is recognized as it is collected.  Cash sales after returns and allowances totaled $76,000 ($80,000 − $4,000).  Net credit sales for 2007 were $114,000 ($120,000 credit sales − $6,000 discounts).  As made evident by the T-account below, cash collections from credit sales must equal $124,000 ($40,000 + $114,000 − $30,000), since $10,000 in excess of current credit sales was received and reduced Accounts Receivable by this amount.

| Accounts Receivable | | | |
|---|---|---|---|
| Bal. 1/1 | 40,000 | | |
| Net credit sales | 114,000 | ? | Collections |
| Bal. 12/31 | 30,000 | | |

A summary journal entry would be

| | | |
|---|---|---|
| Cash | 124,000 | |
| Sales discounts | 6,000 | |
|     Accounts receivable | | 130,000 |

Total cash basis revenue for 2007 is $200,000 as shown below.

| | |
|---|---|
| Cash sales ($80,000 – $4,000) | $ 76,000 |
| Collections of credit sales [($40,000 + $120,000 – $30,000) – $6,000] | 124,000 |
|     Total cash received | $200,000 |

**48. (a)** Cost of goods sold is computed as follows:

$$\text{Beg. inv.} + \text{Net purchases} - \text{End. inv.} = \text{CGS}$$

Net purchases must be computed from the information given using a T-account or a formula.

```
                        AP
              |    50,000    12/31/06
Payments      |      ?       Purchases
   490,000    |    75,000    12/31/07
```

The missing amount for purchases is $515,000. Another approach is to use the following formula:

| Payments | + | Ending AP | – | Beginning AP | = | Purchases |
|---|---|---|---|---|---|---|
| $490,000 | + | $75,000 | – | $50,000 | = | $515,000 |

This amount can be used to determine cost of goods sold

| | |
|---|---|
| Beg. inventory | $290,000 |
| + Net purchases | 515,000 |
|   Cost of goods available | 805,000 |
| – End. inventory | 260,000 |
|   Cost of goods sold | $545,000 |

**49. (d)** Cash-basis income of $60,000 must be adjusted for changes in accounts receivable and accounts payable to compute accrual income

| | |
|---|---|
| Cash-basis income | $ 60,000 |
| 12/31/04 AR | (20,000) |
| 12/31/05 AR | 40,000 |
| 12/31/04 AP | 30,000 |
| 12/31/05 AP | (15,000) |
| Accrual income | $ 95,000 |

The beginning AR ($20,000) is subtracted because although this amount was **collected in 2007,** it is properly accrued as **2006 revenue.** The ending AR is added because although **not collected in 2007,** it should be accrued as **2007 revenue.** The beginning AP is added because although this amount was **paid in 2007,** it is properly accrued as **2006 expense.** The ending AP is subtracted because although **not paid in 2007,** it should be accrued as **2007 expense.**

**50. (c)** The ending balance in Tory's capital account on either the accrual or cash basis is computed as follows:

| Beginning capital | + | Investments | + | Income | – | Drawings | = | Ending capital |
|---|---|---|---|---|---|---|---|---|

Tory's beginning capital is his initial cash investment of $2,000. No other investments were made. Under the cash basis method of accounting, income is the excess of cash revenues ($5,000) over cash expenses ($0, since the expenses were not paid until after March 31). Therefore, cash basis income is $5,000. Drawings are $1,000. Therefore, ending capital is $6,000 ($2,000 + $0 + $5,000 – $1,000).

**51. (d)** The requirement of this question is to determine if a decrease in accounts receivable and/or a decrease in accrued expenses would result in **cash-basis income** being **lower** than accrual-basis income.

A decrease in the accounts receivable balance would generally mean that cash was collected. In accordance with the cash basis of accounting when cash is received it is recorded as revenue (Dr. Cash, Cr. Revenue). Whereas under the accrual basis the revenue would have recorded when the receivable was recorded (Dr. AR, Cr. Revenue). Thus, a decreased accounts receivable balance would result in increased revenue/income. Therefore, the answer for this account is No.

A decrease in the accrued expenses account would generally mean cash was paid on some expenses. Under the cash basis, when the cash is paid the expense is recorded (Dr. Expense, Cr. Cash). Whereas under the accrual basis the expense would have been recorded when the accrued expense was recorded (Dr. Expense, Cr. Accrued Expense). Thus, a decreased accrued expenses account would result in increased expenses/lower income for the cash basis. Thus, the answer for this account is Yes.

**52. (b)** When a company operates on the accrual basis, supplies are inventoried and expensed as they are used. Under the cash method, however, supplies are expensed as they are paid for. Therefore if White Co. experiences an increase in supplies inventory during the year, this increase must be deducted from accrual income to get to the cash basis, because the cost of the supplies would be expensed at the time of purchase.

Office salaries payable works the opposite way. Under the accrual method, a liability would have been established resulting in additional expense over the amount of cash paid to employees. Under the cash method, no liability is accrued and the unpaid salaries are not expensed. Therefore, the increase must be added to the accrual basis net income.

**53. (c)** Prior to 2007, Droit Co. used the cash basis of accounting. Accordingly, Droit would have expensed all purchases of supplies as incurred. In contrast, under the accrual basis of accounting, the cost of unused supplies at each year-end would have been carried as an asset and, therefore, excluded from the current year's supplies expense. In 2007, the year Droit adopted the accrual basis of accounting, Droit would have inventoried unused supplies at December 31 and excluded those costs from 2007 net income. Since the cost of 2007's beginning balance of supplies was expensed during 2006, even though the supplies were not used until 2007, Droit's inability to determine the beginning supplies inventory would result in an understatement of supplies expense and overstatement of 2007 net income. However, since Droit properly inventoried supplies at December 31, 2007, its cumulative (inception-to-date) supplies expense would be properly stated. Therefore, Droit's inability to determine 2007's beginning supplies expense would have no impact on Droit's December 31, 2007 retained earnings.

**A.5. Installment Sales**

**54. (b)** Under the installment method, gross profit is deferred at the time of sale and is recognized by applying the gross profit rate to subsequent cash collections. At the time of sale, gross profit of $250,000 is deferred ($500,000 installment sales less $250,000 cost of installment sales). The gross profit rate is 50% ($250,000 ÷ $500,000). Since 2007 collections on installment sales were $100,000, gross profit of $50,000 (50% × $100,000) is recognized in 2007. This would decrease the deferred gross profit account to a 12/31/07 balance of $200,000 ($250,000 – $50,000). Note that regular sales, cost of regular sales, and general and administrative expenses do not affect the deferred gross profit account.

**55.   (d)**   Under the installment sales method, gross profit is deferred to future periods and recognized proportionately to collection of the receivables. Therefore, at each year-end, deferred gross profit can be computed by multiplying the gross profit percentage by the accounts receivable balance, as indicated below.

|  | 2007 | 2006 |
|---|---|---|
| Sales | $900,000 | $600,000 |
| 2006 Collections | | (200,000) |
| 2007 Collections | (300,000) | (100,000) |
| 2006 Write-offs | | (50,000) |
| 2007 Write-offs | (50,000) | (150,000) |
| 12/31/07 AR | $550,000 | $100,000 |
| Gross profit % | x   40% | x   30% |
| 12/31/07 Deferred GP | $220,000 | $ 30,000 |

Thus, total deferred gross profit at 12/31/07 is $250,000 ($220,000 + $30,000).

**56.   (d)**   Under the installment sales method, gross profit is deferred to future periods and is recognized proportionately as cash is collected. To determine cash collections in this case, first compute the 2007 installment sales by dividing deferred gross profit by the gross profit percentage ($560,000 ÷ 40% = $1,400,000). Then, the 12/31/07 installment accounts receivable is subtracted to determine cash collections ($1,400,000 – $800,000 = $600,000). Realized gross profit is then computed by multiplying cash collections by the gross profit percentage ($600,000 × 40% = $240,000).

**57.   (c)**   When using the installment method, gross profit realized is computed as indicated below.

Cash collections ×   GP%   =   GP realized

This equation can be rearranged as follows:

GP realized   ÷   GP%   =   Cash collections

Therefore, cash collected to date on 2006 sales is $800,000 [($150,000 + $90,000) ÷ 30%], and on 2007 sales is $500,000 ($200,000 ÷ 40%). Installment accounts receivable at 12/31/07 is computed by subtracting cash collections from the original sales amount.

| Installment AR – 2006 ($1,000,000 – $800,000) | $ 200,000 |
|---|---|
| Installment AR – 2007 ($2,000,000 – $500,000) | 1,500,000 |
| Total 12/31/07 installment AR | $1,700,000 |

**58.   (a)**   The equipment sale is accounted for using the installment method. The gross profit percentage on the sale is 33 1/3% ($600,000 profit ÷ $1,800,000 selling price). Since $300,000 of the sales price is collected in 2007, gross profit of $100,000 is recognized (33 1/3% × $300,000). The **total** revenue recognized is $250,000 ($100,000 gross profit + $150,000 interest revenue).

**59.   (a)**   The machine sale is accounted for using the installment method, where gross profit is deferred and recognized in proportion to cash collected. Initially, the entire $270,000 gain is deferred. In 2006, $150,000 of the sales price was collected, and the gross profit percentage is 30% ($270,000 ÷ $900,000), so gross profit recognized was $45,000 (30% × $150,000). In 2007, $250,000 of the sales price was collected, so gross profit recognized was $75,000 (30% × $250,000). Therefore, at 12/31/07, deferred gross profit is $150,000 ($270,000 – $45,000 – $75,000). As a shortcut, you can compute the 12/31/07 note receivable bal-

ance ($750,000 – $250,000 = $500,000), and multiply by the 30% gross profit percentage (30% × $500,000 = $150,000). Note that the **interest** collected ($75,000) does not affect the computation because it is not a collection of sales price.

**60.   (c)**   Per APB 10, the profit on a sale in the ordinary course of business is considered to be realized at the time of sale unless it is uncertain whether the sale price will be collected. The Board concluded that use of the installment method of accounting is not acceptable unless this uncertainty exists. Answers (a), (b), and (d) are incorrect because they do not involve the element of uncertainty regarding the collectibility of the sale price.

**61.   (c)**   According to the **installment method** of accounting, gross profit on an installment sale is recognized in income in proportion to the cash collection. The cash collected from a given year's sales is multiplied by that year's gross profit percentage to compute the amount of gross profit to be recognized. Answer (a) describes the **point-of-sale** recognition basis, while answer (d) describes the **cost recovery** method. Answer (b) does not describe any recognition basis currently used.

**62.   (c)**   Per APB 10, the installment method of accounting is used when there is a high degree of uncertainty regarding the collectibility of the sale price. Under this method, sales revenues and the related cost of goods sold are recognized in the period of the sale. However, the gross profit is deferred to the periods in which cash is collected. Income recognized in the period of collection is generally computed by multiplying the cash collected by the gross margin percentage. The installment method is based upon deferral of the gross profit, not the net operating profit. APB 10 states that the installment method is generally only applicable when the reporting company is unable to estimate the amount of uncollectible accounts.

**63.   (d)**   Under the installment method (case I) revenue (gross profit) is recognized **after** the sale, in proportion to cash collected. Under the cost recovery method (case II), revenue (gross profit) is again recognized **after** the sale, when cumulative receipts exceed the cost of the asset sold. Therefore, revenue is not recognized prior to the sale of merchandise in either case I or case II.

**A.6.   Cost Recovery Method**

**64.   (d)**   Under the cost recovery method **no profit of any type** is recognized until the cumulative receipts (principal and interest) exceed the cost of the asset sold. This means that the entire gross profit ($3,000,000 – $2,000,000 = $1,000,000) and the 2007 interest received ($270,000) will be deferred until cash collections exceed $2,000,000. Therefore, no income is recognized in 2007.

**65.   (d)**   The **installment method** is used when collection of the selling price is not reasonably assured. However, when the uncertainty of collection is so great that even the use of the installment method is precluded, then the cost recovery method may be used. Having no reasonable basis for estimating collectibility would provide a great enough uncertainty to use the cost recovery method. It is important to note that anytime the installment method is used, some risk of 100% collection exists, but the risk must be extreme before the cost recovery method is employed.

**66.   (a)**   Per APB 10, installment methods of recognizing revenue are appropriate only when "collection of the sale price is not reasonably assured." Under the cost recovery method, gross profit is deferred and recognized only when the cumulative receipts exceed the cost of the asset sold.

### A.7.  Franchise Agreements

**67.   (d)**   Per SFAS 45, Franchise fee revenue is recognized when all material services have been substantially performed by the franchiser.  Substantial performance means the franchiser has performed substantially all of required initial services and has no remaining obligation to refund any cash received.  The $60,000 nonrefundable down payment applies to the initial services already performed by Rice. Therefore, the $60,000 may be recognized as revenue in 2007.  The three remaining $30,000 installments relate to substantial future services to be performed by Rice.  The present value of these payments ($72,000) is recorded as unearned franchise fees and recognized as revenue once substantial performance of the future services has occurred.

| | | |
|---|---|---|
| Cash | 60,000 | |
| Notes receivable | 90,000 | |
| Discount on notes receivable | | 18,000 |
| Franchise revenue | | 60,000 |
| Unearned franchise fees | | 72,000 |

**68.   (c)**   Initial franchise fees are not recognized as revenue until the franchisor makes substantial performance of the required services, and collection is reasonably assured. Since Potter Pie has not yet performed the required services, the initial franchise fee (21 × $30,000 = $630,000) is reported as **unearned franchise fees** at 12/31/06.  The estimated uncollectible amount ($20,000) normally would be recorded as a debit to **bad debt expense** and a credit to **allowance for uncollectible accounts**.  However, since no revenue has yet been recognized, it is inappropriate to record bad debt expense.  Instead, **unearned franchise fees** is debited, because an unearned revenue should not be recorded when, in effect, no related asset has been received.  Therefore, the **net** unearned franchise fees is $610,000 ($630,000 − $20,000).

### A.8.  Real Estate Transactions

**69.   (d)**   Items I and II do not transfer the risks and rewards of ownership to the buyer since both scenarios entitle the buyer to a return of his/her initial investment.  Thus, the risks of ownership still remain with the seller.  The economic substance of such arrangements is that of financing, leasing, or profit-sharing transactions.  Item III transfers the risks and rewards of ownership since the seller will be reimbursed for cost plus a 5% profit on the support provided.  Therefore, the seller is not required to support operations of the property at its **own** risk.

**70.   (c)**   The problem states that the sale has been consummated and that Kame's initial and continuing investments are adequate to demonstrate a commitment to pay for the property.  However, the fact that Esker's receivable is subject to future subordination precludes recognition of the profit in full.  Instead, the cost recovery method must be used to account for the sale.  The deposit method is to be used

1.   Until the sale is consummated, when all activities necessary for closing have been performed.

2.   If the buyer's initial and continuing investments are not adequate to demonstrate a commitment to pay for the property and the seller is not reasonably assured of recovering the cost of the property if the buyer defaults.

The problem states that the sale has been consummated and that Kame's initial and continuing investments are adequate. Therefore, the deposit method will not be used to account for the sale.  The reduced profit method is used only when the initial investment is adequate to demonstrate a commitment to pay for the property but the continuing investments are not.  The continuing investments must also meet certain additional requirements for the reduced profit method to be used.  Since Kame's continuing investments are adequate, the reduced profit method will not be used to account for the sale.  The full accrual method may be used only if profit on the sale is determinable, the earning process is virtually complete, and all of the following:

1.   A sale is consummated.
2.   The buyer's initial and continuing investments are adequate to demonstrate a commitment to pay for the property.
3.   The seller's receivable is not subject to future subordination.
4.   The seller has transferred to the buyer the usual risks and rewards of ownership in a transaction that is, in substance, a sale and does not have a substantial continuing involvement in the property.

## SOLUTIONS TO SIMULATION PROBLEMS

## Simulation Problem 1

| Situation | Concepts | Account Classification | Accrual Basis Worksheet | Communication | Research |
|---|---|---|---|---|---|

(A) (B) (C) (D) (E) (F)

1. Technical Bulletins ○ ○ ○ ● ○ ○
2. Interpretations of the Financial Accounting Standards Board ○ ○ ○ ○ ○ ●
3. Statements of Financial Accounting Standards ○ ○ ● ○ ○ ○
4. EITF Statements ○ ○ ○ ○ ● ○
5. Opinions ● ○ ○ ○ ○ ○
6. Statements of Financial Accounting Concepts ○ ● ○ ○ ○ ○

| Situation | Concepts | Account Classification | Accrual Basis Worksheet | Communication | Research |
|---|---|---|---|---|---|

*Balance sheet classification*      *Income statement classification*

(A) (B) (C) (D) (E) (F) (G)      (H) (I) (J)

1. Bonds payable, due in 2017 — ○ ○ ○ ● ○ ○ ○ — ○ ○ ○
2. Treasury stock — ○ ○ ○ ○ ○ ○ ● — ○ ○ ○
3. Accounts payable — ○ ○ ● ○ ○ ○ ○ — ○ ○ ○
4. Sales discounts — ○ ○ ○ ○ ○ ○ ○ — ○ ○ ●
5. Notes payable, due in nine months — ○ ○ ● ○ ○ ○ ○ — ○ ○ ○
6. Inventory — ● ○ ○ ○ ○ ○ ○ — ○ ○ ○
7. Accounts receivable — ● ○ ○ ○ ○ ○ ○ — ○ ○ ○
8. Common stock — ○ ○ ○ ● ○ ○ ○ — ○ ○ ○
9. Cost of goods sold — ○ ○ ○ ○ ○ ○ ○ — ○ ● ○
10. Allowance for uncollectible accounts — ○ ○ ○ ○ ○ ● ○ — ○ ○ ○

| Situation | Concepts | Account Classification | Accrual Basis Worksheet | Communication | Research |
|---|---|---|---|---|---|

*Baron Flowers*
### WORKSHEET TO CONVERT TRIAL BALANCE TO ACCRUAL BASIS
*December 31, 2007*

| Account title | Cash basis Dr. | Cash basis Cr. | Adjustments Dr. | Adjustments Cr. | Accrual basis* Dr.* | Accrual basis* Cr.* |
|---|---|---|---|---|---|---|
| Cash | 25,600 | | | | 25,600 | |
| Accounts receivable | 16,200 | | (1) 15,800 | | 32,000 | |
| Inventory | 62,000 | | (4) 10,800 | | 72,800 | |
| Furniture & fixtures | 118,200 | | | | 118,200 | |
| Land improvements | 45,000 | | | | 45,000 | |
| Accumulated depreciation & amortization | | 32,400 | | (6) 14,250 | | 46,650 |
| Accounts payable | | 17,000 | | (3) 13,500 | | 30,500 |
| Baron, Drawings | | | (9) 61,000 | | 61,000 | |
| Baron, Capital | | 124,600 | (7) 2,000 | (5) 2,600 | | 125,200 |
| Allowance for uncollectible accounts | | | | (2) 3,800 | | 3,800 |
| Prepaid insurance | | | (5) 2,900 | | 2,900 | |
| Accrued expenses | | | | (7) 3,100 | | 3,100 |
| Estimated liability from lawsuit | | | | (8) 50,000 | | 50,000 |

---
\* *Completion of these columns was not required.*

| Account title` | Cash basis | | Adjustments | | Accrual basis* | |
|---|---|---|---|---|---|---|
| | Dr. | Cr. | Dr. | Cr. | Dr.* | Cr.* |
| Purchases | 305,100 | | (3) 13,500 | | 318,600 | |
| Salaries | 174,000 | | | (9) 48,000 | 126,000 | |
| Payroll taxes | 12,400 | | (7)    500 | | 12,900 | |
| Insurance | 8,700 | | | (5)    300 | 8,400 | |
| Rent | 34,200 | | | | 34,200 | |
| Utilities | 12,600 | | (7)    600 | | 13,200 | |
| Living expenses | 13,000 | | | (9) 13,000 | | |
| Income summary—inventory | | | (4) 62,000 | (4) 72,800 | | 10,800 |
| Uncollectible accounts | | | (2)  3,800 | | 3,800 | |
| Depreciation & amortization | | | (6) 14,250 | | 14,250 | |
| Estimated loss from lawsuit | | | (8) 50,000 | | 50,000 | |
| | 827,000 | 827,000 | 237,150 | 237,150 | 938,850 | 938,850 |

## Explanations of Adjustments

[1]  To convert 2007 sales to accrual basis.
    Accounts receivable balances:
       December 31, 2007                                 $32,000
       December 31, 2006                                  16,200
       Increase in sales                                 $15,800

[2]  To record provision for uncollectible accounts.

[3]  To convert 2007 purchases to accrual basis.
    Accounts payable balances:
       December 31, 2007                                 $30,500
       December 31, 2006                                  17,000
       Increase in purchases                             $13,500

[4]  To record increase in inventory from 12/31/06 to
    12/31/07.
    Inventory balances:
       December 31, 2007                                 $72,800
       December 31, 2006                                  62,000
       Increase in inventory                             $10,800

[5]  To adjust prepaid insurance.
    Prepaid balances:
       December 31, 2007 ($8,700 × 4/12)                 $2,900
       December 31, 2006 ($7,800 × 4/12)                  2,600
       Decrease in insurance expense                     $   300

*  Completion of these columns was not required.

[6]  To record 2007 depreciation and amortization
    expense.
       Cost of leasehold improvement                     $45,000
       Estimated life                                   15 years
       Amortization ($45,000 × 1/15 × 9/12)               2,250
       Depreciation expense on fixtures and equipment    12,000
                                                         $14,250

[7]  To convert expenses to accrual basis.

| | Balances December 31, | | Increase |
|---|---|---|---|
| | 2007 | 2006 | in expenses |
| Utilities | $1,500 | $ 900 | $ 600 |
| Payroll taxes | 1,600 | 1,100 | 500 |
| | $3,100 | $2,000 | $1,100 |

[8]  To record lawsuit liability at 12/31/07.
       Attorney's estimate of probable loss              $300,000
       Amount covered by insurance                        250,000
       Baron's estimated liability                       $ 50,000

[9]  To record Baron's drawings for 2007.
       Salary ($4,000 × 12)                              $48,000
       Living expenses                                    13,000
                                                         $61,000

| Situation | Concepts | Account Classification | Accrual Basis Worksheet | Communication | Research |
|---|---|---|---|---|---|

To:       Mr. Baron Flowers
From:   CPA Candidate
Re:       Accrual-basis financial statements

    You have asked me to explain why the bank would require financial statements prepared on the accrual basis instead of the cash basis. The bank is concerned about your ability to repay the loan. To assess that ability, bank personnel want information about your earnings for the period, total assets, and all claims on those assets. This information about your enterprise's performance and financial position is provided more completely by accrual-basis financial statements than by cash-basis financial statements.

    Under the cash basis, revenues are recognized when received and expenses when paid. Earnings can be manipulated by the timing of cash receipts and disbursements. Accrual basis accounting, while grounded in cash flows, reports transactions and other events with cash consequences at the time the transactions and events occur. Revenues and expenses are reported in the accounting period benefited, not just what the enterprise was able to collect or chose to pay. Therefore, it is understandable why your bank would request accrual-basis financial statements.

    If you have any additional questions, please contact me.

| Situation | Concepts | Account Classification | Accrual Basis Worksheet | Communication | Research |
|---|---|---|---|---|---|

**1. Revenue**

**Revenues**
**CON6, Para 78**

78. Revenues are inflows or other enhancements of assets of an entity or settlements of its liabilities (or a combination of both) from delivering or producing goods, rendering services, or other activities that constitute the entity's ongoing major or central operations.

**2. Assets**

**Assets**
**CON6, Para 25**

25. Assets are probable future economic benefits obtained or controlled by a particular entity as a result of past transactions or events.

**3. Liability**

**Liabilities**
**CON6, Para 35**

35. Liabilities are probable future sacrifices of economic benefits arising from present obligations of a particular entity to transfer assets or provide services to other entities in the future as a result of past transactions or events.

## Simulation Problem 2

| Situation | Concepts | Trial Balance Worksheet | Communication | Research |
|---|---|---|---|---|

_Concept statement definitions_

|  | | (A) | (B) | (C) | (D) | (E) | (F) | (G) | (H) | (I) | (J) | (K) | (L) |
|---|---|---|---|---|---|---|---|---|---|---|---|---|---|
| 1. | Component of relevance. | ○ | ○ | ○ | ○ | ● | ○ | ○ | ○ | ○ | ○ | ○ | ○ |
| 2. | Increases in net assets from incidental or peripheral transactions affecting an entity. | ○ | ○ | ○ | ○ | ○ | ○ | ● | ○ | ○ | ○ | ○ | ○ |
| 3. | The process of converting noncash resources and rights into cash or claims to cash. | ○ | ○ | ○ | ○ | ○ | ○ | ○ | ○ | ○ | ● | ○ | ○ |
| 4. | Ingredient of relevance **and** reliability. | ○ | ○ | ○ | ○ | ○ | ● | ○ | ○ | ○ | ○ | ○ | ○ |
| 5. | The process of formally recording an item in the financial statements of an entity after it has met existing criteria and been subject to cost-benefit constraints and materiality thresholds. | ● | ○ | ○ | ○ | ○ | ○ | ○ | ○ | ○ | ○ | ○ | ○ |
| 6. | All changes in net assets of an entity during a period except those resulting from investments by owners and distributions to owners. | ○ | ● | ○ | ○ | ○ | ○ | ○ | ○ | ○ | ○ | ○ | ○ |
| 7. | Inflows or other enhancements of assets of an entity or settlements of its liabilities from delivering or producing goods, rendering services, or other activities that constitute the entity's ongoing operations. | ○ | ○ | ○ | ● | ○ | ○ | ○ | ○ | ○ | ○ | ○ | ○ |
| 8. | The amount of cash, or its equivalent, that could be obtained by selling an asset in orderly liquidation. | ○ | ○ | ○ | ○ | ○ | ○ | ○ | ○ | ○ | ○ | ○ | ● |
| 9. | The quality of information that helps users to increase the likelihood of correctly forecasting the outcome of past or present events. | ○ | ○ | ○ | ○ | ● | ○ | ○ | ○ | ○ | ○ | ○ | ○ |
| 10. | A performance measure concerned primarily with cash-to-cash cycles. | ○ | ○ | ○ | ○ | ○ | ○ | ○ | ○ | ● | ○ | ○ | ○ |

## Explanation of solutions

1. **(E)** SFAC 5 states that "Relevance is a primary qualitative characteristic. To be relevant, information about an item must have feedback value or predictive value (or both) for users and must be timely."

**2.** **(G)** SFAC 6 states that "Gains are increases in equity (net assets) from peripheral or incidental transactions of an entity and from all other transactions and other events and circumstances affecting the entity except those that result from revenues or investments by owners."

**3.** **(J)** SFAC 5 states that "Revenues and gains are realized when products (goods or services), merchandise, or other assets are exchanged for cash or claims to cash."

**4.** **(F)** SFAC 2 states that "Comparability, including consistency, is a secondary quality that interacts with relevance and reliability to contribute to the usefulness of information."

**5.** **(A)** SFAC 5 states that "Recognition is the process of formally recording or incorporating an item into the financial statements of an entity as an asset, liability, revenue, expense, or the like." SFAC 5 continues the recognition concept by stating, "An item and information about it should meet four fundamental recognition criteria to be recognized and should be recognized when the criteria are met, subject to a cost-benefit constraint and a materiality threshold."

**6.** **(B)** SFAC 5 states that "Comprehensive income is a broad measure of the effects of transactions and other events on an entity, comprising all recognized changes in equity (net assets) of the entity during a period from transactions and other events and circumstances except those resulting from investments by owners and distributions to owners."

**7.** **(D)** SFAC 6 defines revenues as "inflows or other enhancements of assets of an entity or settlements of its liabilities (or a combination of both) from delivering or producing goods, rendering services, or other activities that constitute the entity's ongoing major or central operations."

**8.** **(L)** SFAC 5 defines current market value as "the amount of cash, or its equivalent, that could be obtained by selling an asset in orderly liquidation."

**9.** **(E)** SFAC 2 defines predictive value as "the quality of information that helps users to increase the likelihood of correctly forecasting the outcome of past or present events."

**10.** **(I)** SFAC 5 states that "Earnings is a measure of performance during a period that is concerned primarily with the extent to which asset inflows associated with cash-to-cash cycles substantially completed (or completed) during the period exceed (or are less than) asset outflows associated, directly or indirectly, with the same cycles."

| Situation | Concepts | Trial Balance Worksheet | Communication | Research |
|---|---|---|---|---|

**Jane Alexander Theater**
**December 31, 200X**

| a) | Trial balance | | # | Adjustments | | Adjusted trial balance | | Income statement | |
|---|---|---|---|---|---|---|---|---|---|
| | Debit | Credit | | Debit | Credit | Debit | Credit | Debit | Credit |
| Equipment | 192,000 | | | | | 192,000 | | | |
| Accumulated depreciation—equipment | | 60,000 | 1 | | 9,500 | | 69,500 | | |
| Notes payable | | 90,000 | | | | | 90,000 | | |
| Admissions revenue | | 380,000 | 3 | 50,000 | | | 330,000 | | 330,000 |
| Advertising expense | 13,680 | | 4 | | 1,100 | 12,580 | | 12,580 | |
| Salaries expense | 57,600 | | 5 | 4,700 | | 62,300 | | 62,300 | |
| Interest expense | 1,400 | | 2 | 1,800 | | 3,200 | | 3,200 | |
| Depreciation expense | | | 1 | 9,500 | | 9,500 | | 9,500 | |
| Interest payable | | | 2 | | 1,800 | | 1,800 | | |
| Unearned adm revenue | | | 3 | | 50,000 | | 50,000 | | |
| Prepaid advertising | | | 4 | 1,100 | | 1,100 | | | |
| Salaries payable | | | 5 | | 4,700 | | 4,700 | | |

| Situation | Concepts | Trial Balance Worksheet | Communication | Research |
|---|---|---|---|---|

To: Ms. Jane Alexander, Theater Director
From: CPA Candidate
Re: Adjusting and closing entries

This memorandum summarizes the answers to your questions regarding adjusting and closing entries. The purpose of the balance sheet is to fairly represent the financial position of the firm at a specific point in time. The purpose of an income statement is to fairly present the revenues, expenses, and income over a period of time. Adjusting journal entries are necessary at the end of the period in order to properly report assets, liabilities, owner's equity, revenue, and expenses for the period. Adjusting entries are classified as either accrual- or deferral-type entries. An accrual-type entry records a transaction that have not yet been entered into the accounting records. Deferral-type adjusting entries adjust items that were previously recorded on the books, but are not accurately reflected in the records of the company.

   Closing entries are prepared to transfer the effect of nominal accounts to capital (retained earnings) after the adjusting entries have been recorded and the financial statements prepared.  Closing entries are necessary to reduce the balances in nominal accounts to zero in order to prepare the accounts for the next period's transactions.
   If you have any additional questions, please contact me.

| Situation | Concepts | Trial Balance Worksheet | Communication | Research |
|-----------|----------|-------------------------|---------------|----------|

**1.** Gain

**Gains and Losses**
**CON6, Para 82**

   82.  Gains are increases in equity (net assets) from peripheral or incidental transactions of an entity and from all other transactions and other events and circumstances affecting the entity except those that result from revenues or investments by owners.

**2.** Recognition

**CON5, Para 6**

   6.  Recognition is the process of formally recording or incorporating an item in the financial statements of an entity as an asset, liability, revenue, expense, or the like.  Recognition includes depiction of an item in both words and numbers, with the amount included in the totals of the financial statements.  For an asset or liability, recognition involves recording not only acquisition or incurrence of the item but also later changes in it, including changes that result in removal from the financial statements.

**3.** Reliability

**Reliability**
**CON5, Para 75**

   75.  Reliability is the other primary qualitative characteristic.  To be reliable, information about an item must be representationally faithful, verifiable, and neutral.  To be reliable, information must be sufficiently faithful in its representation of the underlying resource, obligation, or effect of events and sufficiently free of error and bias to be useful to investors, creditors, and others in making decisions.  To be recognized, information about the existence and amount of an asset, liability, or change therein must be reliable.

---

**Simulation Problem 3**

| Situation | Concepts | Adjusting Entries | Revenue and Expense Recognition | Communication | Research |
|-----------|----------|-------------------|---------------------------------|---------------|----------|

| Account | (A) | (B) | (C) | (D) | (E) |
|---------|-----|-----|-----|-----|-----|
| **1.** Long-term receivables | ○ | ○ | ○ | ○ | ● |
| **2.** Available-for-sale securities | ○ | ○ | ● | ○ | ○ |
| **3.** Equipment | ● | ○ | ○ | ○ | ○ |
| **4.** Warranty obligations | ○ | ○ | ○ | ● | ○ |
| **5.** Short-term payables | ● | ○ | ○ | ○ | ○ |
| **6.** Accounts receivable | ○ | ○ | ○ | ● | ○ |
| **7.** Bonds payable, due in ten years | ○ | ○ | ○ | ○ | ● |
| **8.** Trading securities | ○ | ○ | ● | ○ | ○ |

| Situation | Concepts | Adjusting Entries | Revenue and Expense Recognition | Communication | Research |
|---|---|---|---|---|---|

|  |  |  | Accrual | Deferral |  |  |
|---|---|---|---|---|---|---|
| 1. | Depreciation expense | xx |  | ○ | ● |  |
|  | Accumulated deprecation |  | xx |  |  |  |
| 2. | Interest receivable | xx |  | ● | ○ |  |
|  | Interest revenue |  | xx |  |  |  |
| 3. | Rent expense | xx |  | ○ | ● |  |
|  | Prepaid rent |  | xx |  |  |  |
| 4. | Unearned revenue | xx |  | ○ | ● |  |
|  | Rent revenue |  | xx |  |  |  |
| 5. | Wage expense | xx |  | ● | ○ |  |
|  | Wages payable |  | xx |  |  |  |

| Situation | Concepts | Adjusting Entries | Revenue and Expense Recognition | Communication | Research |
|---|---|---|---|---|---|

| | | | | Amounts to be recognized | | |
|---|---|---|---|---|---|
| | | | 2007 | 2008 | 2009 |
| 1. | Emco sells $5,000 of goods to a customer, FOB shipping point on 12/30/07. | | 5,000 | -- | -- |
| 2. | Emco sells three pieces of equipment on a contract over a three-year period. The sales price of each piece of equipment is $10,000. Delivery of each piece of equipment is on February 10 of each year. In 2007, the customer paid a $20,000 down payment, and paid $5,000 per year in 2008 and 2009. Collectibility is reasonably assured. | | 10,000 | 10,000 | 10,000 |
| 3. | In 1/1/07, Emco paid $9,000 for a membership to Wholesalers Association for a two-year membership in the trade association. | | (4,500) | (4,500) | -- |
| 4. | On 6/1/07, Emco signs a contract for $20,000 for goods to be sold on account. Payment is to be made in two installments of $10,000 each on 12/1/08 and 12/1/09. The goods are delivered on 10/1/07. Collection is reasonably assured, and the goods may not be returned. | | 20,000 | -- | -- |
| 5. | Emco sells goods to a customer on July 1, 2007, for $50,000. If the customer does not sell the goods to retail customers by December 31, 2008, the goods can be returned to Emco. The customer sells the goods to retail customers on October 1, 2008. | | -- | 50,000 | -- |

**Explanation of solutions**

**1.** When goods are sold FOB shipping point, title passes at the time the goods are shipped. Therefore, Emco may recognize revenue on 12/30/07 at the time the goods are shipped.

**2.** Revenue is recognized when earned and realizable. This sale is not complete until each piece of equipment is delivered. Therefore, Emco should recognize $10,000 each year as the equipment is delivered, regardless of payment terms.

**3.** Emco should match expenses to the year in which the benefits are received, which is over the two-year period.

**4.** Because Emco delivered the goods in 2007, and collectibility is reasonably assured, Emco should recognize all revenue in 2006.

**5.** Because there is a sale with a right of return, and the buyer may return the merchandise if it is not sold to a retail customer, recognition should be delayed until the right of return has expired.

| Situation | Concepts | Adjusting Entries | Revenue and Expense Recognition | Communication | Research |
|---|---|---|---|---|---|

To:   Mr. Brown
From: Wyatt, CPA

As we discussed, here is a brief overview of the rules for revenue recognition and the accounting for postretirement benefits under Statement of Financial Accounting Standards 106.

1.   Revenue recognition

The revenue recognition principle provides that revenue is recognized when it is realized or realizable and it is earned. Accordingly, revenues from the sale of products ordinarily are recognized at the time of sale. Revenue from sales transactions in which the buyer has a right to return the product are recognized at time of sale only if specified conditions are met. If all these conditions are not met, revenue recognition is postponed until the time when all the requirements are met.

One of the specified conditions for revenue recognition is that the amount of future returns can be reasonably estimated. Since Emco cannot reasonably estimate future returns, Emco should defer recognition of sales revenue and cost of sales until the return privilege has substantially expired or it can reasonably estimate returns, whichever occurs first.

2.   Statement of Financial Accounting Standards 106, *Employers' Accounting for Postretirement Benefits other than Pensions.*

The primary recipients of postretirement benefits other than pensions are retired employees, their beneficiaries, and covered dependents. The principal benefit covered by SFAS 106 is postretirement health care benefits. Examples of other benefits include tuition assistance, legal services, life insurance benefits, day care, and housing subsidies.

SFAS 106 recognizes that estimates of postretirement benefit costs are not precise. However, the statement requires accrual because recording the obligation based on best estimates is superior to implying, by a failure to accrue, that no obligation exists prior to the payment of benefits.

If you have any additional questions about these matters, please contact me.

| Situation | Concepts | Adjusting Entries | Revenue and Expense Recognition | Communication | Research |
|---|---|---|---|---|---|

1.   Relevance

**Relevance**
**CON5, Para 73**

73.  Relevance is a primary qualitative characteristic. To be relevant, information about an item must have feedback value or predictive value (or both) for users and must be timely. 45 Information is relevant if it has the capacity to make a difference in investors', creditors', or other users' decisions. To be recognized, the information conveyed by including an asset, liability, or change therein in the financial statements must be relevant.

2.   Realizable

**Revenues and Gains**
**CON5, Para 83**

83.  Further guidance for recognition of revenues and gains is intended to provide an acceptable level of assurance of the existence and amounts of revenues and gains before they are recognized. Revenues and gains of an enterprise during a period are generally measured by the exchange values of the assets (goods or services) or liabilities involved, and recognition involves consideration of two factors (a) being realized or realizable, and (b) being earned, with sometimes one and sometimes the other being the more important consideration.

  a.   Realized or realizable. Revenues and gains generally are not recognized until realized or realizable. 50 Revenues and gains are realized when products (goods or services), merchandise, or other assets are exchanged for cash or claims to cash. Revenues and gains are realizable when related assets received or held are readily convertible to known amounts of cash or claims to cash. Readily convertible assets have (i) interchangeable (fungible) units and (ii) quoted prices available in an active market that can rapidly absorb the quantity held by the entity without significantly affecting the price.

3.   Expense

**Expenses**
**CON6, Para 80**

80.  Expenses are outflows or other using up of assets or incurrences of liabilities (or a combination of both) from delivering or producing goods, rendering services, or carrying out other activities that constitute the entity's ongoing major or central operations.

**4.** Matching            **CON6, Para 146**

146.  Matching of costs and revenues is simultaneous or combined recognition of the revenues and expenses that result directly and jointly from the same transactions or other events.  In most entities, some transactions or events result simultaneously in both a revenue and one or more expenses.  The revenue and expense(s) are directly related to each other and require recognition at the same time.  In present practice, for example, a sale of product or merchandise involves both revenue (sales revenue) for receipt of cash or a receivable and expense (cost of goods sold) for sacrifice of the product or merchandise sold to customers.  Other examples of expenses that may result from the same transaction and be directly related to sales revenues are transportation to customers, sales commissions, and perhaps certain other selling costs.

## B.  Error Correction

Accountants must be in a position to anticipate, locate, and correct errors in their functions of systems and procedures design, controllership, and attestation.  Errors which are discovered in the same year that they are made are corrected by

1.  Determining the entry that was made
2.  Determining the correct entry
3.  Analyzing increases or decreases needed in affected accounts
4.  Making the correct entry

Errors in classification (e.g., sales expense instead of R&D expense) affect only one period.  Non-systematic errors in adjusting entries (e.g., an error in ending inventory of one period) affect two periods and are known as self-correcting (counterbalancing) errors.  For example, overstating ending inventory of 2007 will overstate the income of 2007 and understate the income of 2008.  Other errors will affect the income of several periods, such as misrecording the cost of a long-lived asset (i.e., depreciation will be misstated for all periods).

The chart below shows four examples of counterbalancing errors.

**ERRORS WHICH WILL SELF-CORRECT AFTER TWO YEARS**
**Omitting Accruals**
*Case #1*

|  | *12/31/07* | *12/31/08* | *1/1/09* |
|---|---|---|---|
| Expense (wages) | Understated | Overstated | Correct |
| Net income | Overstated | Understated | Correct |
| Payable (wages) | Understated | Correct | Correct |
| Retained earnings | Overstated | Correct | Correct |

*Case #2*

| Revenue (interest) | Understated | Overstated | Correct |
|---|---|---|---|
| Net income | Understated | Overstated | Correct |
| Receivable (interest) | Understated | Correct | Correct |
| Retained earnings | Understated | Correct | Correct |

**Omitting Deferrals (Prepaids)**
*Case #3*

| Expense (insurance) | Overstated | Understated | Correct |
|---|---|---|---|
| Net income | Understated | Overstated | Correct |
| Prepaid asset | Understated | Correct | Correct |
| Retained earnings | Understated | Correct | Correct |

*Case #4*

| Revenue (unearned) | Overstated | Understated | Correct |
|---|---|---|---|
| Net income | Overstated | Understated | Correct |
| Liability (un. rev.) | Understated | Correct | Correct |
| Retained earnings | Overstated | Correct | Correct |

Notice that in all four cases the income statement errors have the opposite effect in 2007 and 2008.  Also notice that by the end of 2008 the balance sheet accounts are correct.  Therefore, even if the error is not discovered, the financial statements will be correct by the beginning of the third year.

When an error is discovered in a period subsequent to the period when the error occurred, an entry must be made to correct the accounts as if the error had not been made.  For example, assume the entry to accrue wage expense in the amount of $10,000 is omitted on 12/31/07.  The effects that would be caused by such an omission may be categorized as follows:

|  | *2007* | *2008* | *2009* |
|---|---|---|---|
| Expense | Understated | Overstated | Correct |
| Income | Overstated | Understated | Correct |
| Wages payable | Understated | Correct | Correct |
| Retained earnings | Overstated | Correct | Correct |

If the company follows the policy of reversing adjusting entries for accruals, then correction of the error any time during 2008 will require

| Adjustment to correct error | 10,000 | |
|---|---|---|
| Wage expense | | 10,000 |

The adjustment account, when closed to retained earnings, will correct for the 1/1/08 overstatement in retained earnings due to the overstatement of 2007 income. The credit to wage expense will reduce the expense account for 2008 to an amount equal to 2008 wages.

If the error was discovered in 2009, no entry would be required since the error self-corrects during 2008. The 2009 balances would be the same with or without the error.

The requirements of error analysis questions vary considerably. When asked for the effect of errors, be careful to determine the effect rather than the correction; they are opposite. The effect of revenue overstatement on income is over or plus; therefore, the correction to income is to subtract. Also distinguish between correcting/adjusting entries (which can be made in the accounts to correct the current period) and "worksheet entries" which adjust amounts reported in prior periods (i.e., journal entries are not recorded to correct nominal accounts of prior periods).

SFAS 154 defines accounting errors as errors in recognition, measurement, presentation, or disclosure in the financial statements. An error can occur from mathematical mistakes, mistakes in applying GAAP, or oversight of facts that existed when the financial statements were prepared. A change in accounting principle from non-GAAP to GAAP is a correction of an error.

An error in the financial statements is treated as a prior period adjustment by restating the prior period financial statements. The cumulative effect of the error is reflected in the carrying value of assets and liabilities at the beginning of the first period presented, with an offsetting adjustment to the opening balance in retained earnings for that period. Financial statements for each period are then adjusted to reflect the correction of the period-specific effects of the error.

Footnote disclosures should disclose that the previously issued financial statements were restated, along with a description of the error. In addition, the line item effects of the error and any per share amounts must also be disclosed for each period presented. Footnote disclosures must also indicate the cumulative effect of the change on retained earnings or other components of equity or net assets at the beginning of the earliest period presented.

Other disclosures required by paragraph 26 of APB 9 remain in effect with SFAS 154. The gross effects and net effects from applicable income taxes on the net income of the prior period must be disclosed, as well as the effects on retained earnings and net income for each of the period adjustment must also be disclosed. Once the correction of the error is disclosed, the financial statements of subsequent years do not need to repeat the disclosures.

The example below shows the revision of prior years' financial statements, including the format of the retained earnings statement for the $10,000 wage expense discussed above.

*EXAMPLE: Assume $10,000 of wages were not recorded in Year 1; the error was not discovered until Year 3 after the books were closed for Year 2. The income tax rate was 30%.*

*Income Statement Effects*

|  | Year 1 | Year 2 | Year 3 |
|---|---|---|---|
| Wages expense | − $10,000 | − $10,000 | -0- |
| Income tax expense | + 3,000 | + 3,000 | -0- |
| Net income | + 7,000 | + 7,000 | -0- |

*Comparative Income Statement*
*Issued in Year 3, for Year 2 and Year 3*

|  | Year 2 Restated | Year 3 |
|---|---|---|
| Wages expense | ($ xxxx − 10,000) | $ xxxx |
| Income tax expense | ($ xxx + 3,000) | $ xxxx |
| Net income | ($ xxx + 7,000) | $ xxxx |

*Balance Sheet*

|  | Year 1 | Year 2 | Year 3 |
|---|---|---|---|
| Wages payable | − $10,000 | -0- | -0- |
| Taxes payable | + 3,000 | -0- | -0- |
| Retained earnings | + 7,000 | -0- | -0- |

*Comparative Retained Earnings Statement*
*Issued in Year 3, for year 2 and Year 3*

|  | Year 2 as restated | Year 3 |
|---|---|---|
| Beginning balance | $ xxxx | $ xxxx |
| Prior period adjustment—Understatment of wages expense (net of tax, $3,000) | − 7,000 | -- |
| Retained earnings as adjusted | $ xxxx | $ xxxx |
| Net income as corrected | xxxx | xxxx |
| Dividends | (xxxx) | (xxxx) |
| Ending retained earnings | $ xxxx | $ xxxx |

Inventory errors have an impact on both the balance sheet and the income statement.  Inventory errors include a misstatement of the ending inventory balance, which is followed by a misstatement of the beginning balance for the next period, or an inventory error could be a misstatement of purchases for the period. The analysis of inventory errors in a periodic inventory system is facilitated by setting up a statement of cost of good sold.  The statement of cost of good sold shows the relationship between the inventory and purchases accounts and the impact of incorrect amounts.  The four examples shown below use the statement of cost of goods sold to analyze different inventory errors.  Items that are correct are identified by an "OK," while items that are incorrect are listed as overstated (over) or understated (under).

**INVENTORY ERRORS**

|  | Case #1 (Overstated Inventory Count) | | Case #2 (Understated Inventory Count) | |
|---|---|---|---|---|
|  | 2006 | 2007 | 2006 | 2007 |
| Beginning inventory | OK | Over | OK | Under |
| + Purchases | OK | OK | OK | OK |
| Goods available for sale | OK | Over | OK | Under |
| − Ending inventory* | Over | OK | Under | OK |
| Cost of goods sold | Under | Over | Over | Under |
| Net income | Over | Under | Under | Over |
| Retained earnings | Over | OK | Under | OK |
| Accounts payable | OK | OK | OK | OK |

* Determined by physical count.

| | Case #3 (Overstated Purchases**) | | Case #4 (Understated Purchases***) | |
|---|---|---|---|---|
| | 2005 | 2006 | 2005 | 2006 |
| Beginning inventory | OK | OK | OK | Under |
| + Purchases | Over | Under | Under | Over |
| Goods available for sale | Over | Under | Under | OK |
| − Ending inventory* | OK | OK | Under | OK |
| Cost of goods sold | Over | Under | OK | OK |
| Net income | Under | Over | OK | OK |
| Retained earnings | Under | OK | OK | OK |
| Accounts payable | Over | OK | Under | OK |

   \* *Determined by physical count.*

  \** *Vendor shipped goods FOB destination.  Goods were not received by 12/31, but recorded as purchases and not included in physical inventory count.*

\*** *Vendor shipped goods FOB shipping point prior to 12/31, but not recorded as purchases or included in physical inventory count.*

## Research Component

SFAS 154, issued in May 2005, supersedes APB 20.  It carries forth the guidance in APB 20 for the accounting errors.  Keywords for researching accounting errors are shown below.

| | | |
|---|---|---|
| Correction error | Period-specific effects | Prior period adjustments error |
| Disclosure correction error | Prior period adjustment | Reporting correction error |

## MULTIPLE-CHOICE QUESTIONS (1-14)

**1.** Loeb Corp. frequently borrows from the bank in order to maintain sufficient operating cash. The following loans were at a 12% interest rate, with interest payable at maturity. Loeb repaid each loan on its scheduled maturity date.

| Date of loan | Amount | Maturity date | Term of loan |
|---|---|---|---|
| 11/1/06 | $ 5,000 | 10/31/06 | 1 year |
| 2/1/07 | 15,000 | 7/31/06 | 6 months |
| 5/1/07 | 8,000 | 1/31/07 | 9 months |

Loeb records interest expense when the loans are repaid. As a result, interest expense of $1,500 was recorded in 2007. If no correction is made, by what amount would 2007 interest expense be understated?
- a. $540
- b. $620
- c. $640
- d. $720

**2.** During 2007, Paul Company discovered that the ending inventories reported on its financial statements were incorrect by the following amounts:

| 2005 | $60,000 understated |
|---|---|
| 2006 | 75,000 overstated |

Paul uses the periodic inventory system to ascertain year-end quantities that are converted to dollar amounts using the FIFO cost method. Prior to any adjustments for these errors and ignoring income taxes, Paul's retained earnings at January 1, 2007, would be
- a. Correct.
- b. $ 15,000 overstated.
- c. $ 75,000 overstated.
- d. $135,000 overstated.

**3.** Tack, Inc. reported a retained earnings balance of $150,000 at December 31, 2006. In June 2007, Tack discovered that merchandise costing $40,000 had not been included in inventory in its 2006 financial statements. Tack has a 30% tax rate. What amount should Tack report as adjusted beginning retained earnings in its statement of retained earnings at December 31, 2007?
- a. $190,000
- b. $178,000
- c. $150,000
- d. $122,000

**4.** Conn Co. reported a retained earnings balance of $400,000 at December 31, 2006. In August 2007, Conn determined that insurance premiums of $60,000 for the three-year period beginning January 1, 2006, had been paid and fully expensed in 2006. Conn has a 30% income tax rate. What amount should Conn report as adjusted beginning retained earnings in its 2007 statement of retained earnings?
- a. $420,000
- b. $428,000
- c. $440,000
- d. $442,000

**5.** Lore Co. changed from the cash basis of accounting to the accrual basis of accounting during 2007. The cumulative effect of this change should be reported in Lore's 2007 financial statements as a
- a. Prior period adjustment resulting from the correction of an error.

- b. Prior period adjustment resulting from the change in accounting principle.
- c. Component of income before extraordinary item.
- d. Component of income after extraordinary item.

**6.** Bren Co.'s beginning inventory at January 1, 2007, was understated by $26,000, and its ending inventory was overstated by $52,000. As a result, Bren's cost of goods sold for 2007 was
- a. Understated by $26,000.
- b. Overstated by $26,000.
- c. Understated by $78,000.
- d. Overstated by $78,000.

**7.** On January 2, 2007, Air, Inc. agreed to pay its former president $300,000 under a deferred compensation arrangement. Air should have recorded this expense in 2006 but did not do so. Air's reported income tax expense would have been $70,000 lower in 2006 had it properly accrued this deferred compensation. In its December 31, 2007 financial statements, Air should adjust the beginning balance of its retained earnings by a
- a. $230,000 credit.
- b. $230,000 debit.
- c. $300,000 credit.
- d. $370,000 debit.

**8.** Net income is understated if, in the first year, estimated salvage value is excluded from the depreciation computation when using the

| | Straight-line method | Production or use method |
|---|---|---|
| a. | Yes | No |
| b. | Yes | Yes |
| c. | No | No |
| d. | No | Yes |

**9.** At the end of 2006, Ritzcar Co. failed to accrue sales commissions earned during 2006 but paid in 2007. The error was not repeated in 2007. What was the effect of this error on 2006 ending working capital and on the 2007 ending retained earnings balance?

| | 2006 ending working capital | 2007 ending retained earnings |
|---|---|---|
| a. | Overstated | Overstated |
| b. | No effect | Overstated |
| c. | No effect | No effect |
| d. | Overstated | No effect |

**10.** On December 31, 2007, special insurance costs were incurred and unpaid, but were not recorded. If these insurance costs were related to a particular job order in work in process that was not completed during the period, what is the effect of the omission on accrued liabilities and retained earnings in the December 31, 2007 balance sheet?

| | Accrued liabilities | Retained earnings |
|---|---|---|
| a. | No effect | No effect |
| b. | No effect | Overstated |
| c. | Understated | No effect |
| d. | Understated | Overstated |

**11.** Which of the following errors could result in an overstatement of both current assets and stockholders' equity?
- a. An understatement of accrued sales expenses.
- b. Noncurrent note receivable principal is misclassified as a current asset.

    c.   Annual depreciation on manufacturing machinery is understated.

    d.   Holiday pay expense for administrative employees is misclassified as manufacturing overhead.

**12.** Galaxy Corporation had the following financial statement information:

|  | 2007 | 2006 |
|---|---|---|
| Revenue | $135,000 | $100,000 |
| Expenses | 98,000 | 65,000 |
| Net income | 37,000 | 35,000 |
|  | 12-31-07 | 12-31-06 |
| Total assets | $157,000 | $105,000 |
| Total liabilities | 50,000 | 35,000 |
| Total owners' equity | 107,000 | 70,000 |

Galaxy failed to record $12,000 of accrued wages at the end of 2006. The wages were recorded and paid in January 2007. Assuming that the correct accruals were made on December 31, 2007, what are the corrected balances in the 2006 and 2007 restated financial statements?

|  | 2006 net income | Dec. 31, 2006 total liabilities | Dec. 31, 2007 total owners' equity |
|---|---|---|---|
| a. | $23,000 | $23,000 | $ 95,000 |
| b. | $47,000 | $47,000 | $107,000 |
| c. | $23,000 | $35,000 | $ 95,000 |
| d. | $23,000 | $47,000 | $107,000 |

**13.** Justin Corporation discovered an error in their 2007 financial statements after the statements were issued. This requires that

    a.   The cumulative effect of the error is reported on the 2008 income statement as a cumulative effect of change in accounting principle.

    b.   The cumulative effect of the error is reported in the 2008 beginning balance of each related account.

    c.   The financial statements are restated to reflect the correction of period-specific effects of the error.

    d.   An adjustment to beginning retained earnings in 2008 with a footnote disclosure describing the error.

**14.** During 2008, Kelly Corporation discovered that ending inventory reported in its 2007 financial statements was understated by $10,000. How should Kelly account for this understatement?

    a.   Adjust the beginning inventory balance in 2008 by $10,000.

    b.   Restate the financial statements with corrected balances for all periods presented.

    c.   Adjust the ending balance in the 2008 retained earnings account.

    d.   Make no entry because the error will self-correct.

**SIMULATION PROBLEMS**

**Simulation Problem 1**                                              (55 to 65 minutes)

| Situation | | | | | |
|---|---|---|---|---|---|
| | Effect of Error | Journal Entries | Corrected Financial Statements | Communication | Research |

Cord Corp., a nonpublic enterprise, requires audited financial statements for credit purposes.  After making normal adjusting entries, but before closing the accounting records for the year ended December 31, 2007, Cord's controller prepared the following financial statements for 2007:

*Cord Corp.*
**STATEMENT OF FINANCIAL POSITION**
*December 31, 2007*

*Assets*

| | |
|---|---|
| Cash | $1,225,000 |
| Marketable equity securities | 125,000 |
| Accounts receivable | 460,000 |
| Allowance for doubtful accounts | (55,000) |
| Inventories | 530,000 |
| Property and equipment | 620,000 |
| Accumulated depreciation | (280,000) |
| Total assets | $2,625,000 |

*Liabilities and Stockholders' Equity*

| | |
|---|---|
| Accounts payable and accrued liabilities | $1,685,000 |
| Income tax payable | 110,000 |
| Common stock, $20 par | 300,000 |
| Additional paid-in capital | 75,000 |
| Retained earnings | 455,000 |
| Total liabilities and stockholders' equity | $2,625,000 |

*Cord Corp.*
**STATEMENT OF INCOME**
*For the Year Ended December 31, 2007*

| | |
|---|---|
| Net sales | $1,700,000 |
| Operating expenses: | |
|   Cost of sales | 570,000 |
|   Selling and administrative | 448,000 |
|   Depreciation | 42,000 |
| Total operating expenses | 1,060,000 |
| Income before income tax | 640,000 |
| Income tax expense | 192,000 |
| Net income | $  448,000 |

Cord's tax rate for all income items was 30% for all affected years, and it made estimated tax payments when due.  Cord has been profitable in the past and expects results in the future to be similar to 2007.  During the course of the audit, the following additional information (not considered when the above statements were prepared) was obtained:

1.  The investment portfolio consists of short-term investments, classified as available-for-sale, for which total market value equaled cost at December 31, 2006.  On February 2, 2007, Cord sold one investment with a carrying value of $100,000 for $130,000.  The total of the sale proceeds was credited to the investment account.

2.  At December 31, 2007, the market value of the remaining securities in the portfolio was $142,000.

3.  The $530,000 inventory total, which was based on a physical count at December 31, 2007, was priced at cost.  Subsequently, it was determined that the inventory cost was overstated by $66,000.  At December 31, 2007, the inventory's market value approximated the adjusted cost.

4.  Pollution control devices costing $48,000, which is high in relation to the cost of the original equipment, were installed on December 29, 2006, and were charged to repairs in 2006.

5.  The original equipment referred to in Item 4, which had a remaining useful life of six years on December 20, 2006, is being depreciated by the straight-line method for both financial and tax reporting.

6.  A lawsuit was filed against Cord in October 2007 claiming damages of $250,000.  Cord's legal counsel believes that an unfavorable outcome is probable, and a reasonable estimate of the court's award to the plaintiff is $60,000, which will be paid in 2008 if the case is settled.

7.  Cord determined that its accumulated benefits obligation under the pension plan exceeded the fair value of plan assets by $40,000 at December 31, 2007.  Cord has unrecognized prior service cost of $50,000 at December 31, 2007.  Cord funds the total pension expense each year.

8.  Cord Corp. uses the guidance in SFAS 154 to account for accounting changes.

| Situation | Effect of Error | Journal Entries | Corrected Financial Statements | Communication | Research |
|---|---|---|---|---|---|

Indicate the effects of the inventory overstatement in the 2007 and 2008 financial statements by completing the following table.  Mark each item overstate, understate, or OK.

| | 2007 Effects | | | 2008 Effects | | |
|---|---|---|---|---|---|---|
| | (Overstate) | (Understate) | (OK) | (Overstate) | (Understate) | (OK) |
| Inventory on balance sheet | ○ | ○ | ○ | ○ | ○ | ○ |
| Cost of goods sold | ○ | ○ | ○ | ○ | ○ | ○ |
| Net income | ○ | ○ | ○ | ○ | ○ | ○ |
| Retained earnings | ○ | ○ | ○ | ○ | ○ | ○ |

| Situation | Effect of Error | Journal Entries | Corrected Financial Statements | Communication | Research |
|---|---|---|---|---|---|

Prepare journal entries, without explanations, to record the effects of the foregoing data on Cord's accounting records at December 31, 2007.  Do **not** prepare corrected financial statements for 2007.  The journal entries should be numbered to correspond with the numbers in the additional information.  Include as the last entry any necessary adjustments to the 2007 income tax expense, and support your computations for this entry.

| | Dr. | Cr. |
|---|---|---|
| | | |
| | | |
| | | |
| | | |
| | | |
| | | |

| Situation | Effect of Error | Journal Entries | Corrected Financial Statements | Communication | Research |
|---|---|---|---|---|---|

Complete the following amounts in the corrected financial statements for Cord Corp.

| Cord Corp. STATEMENT OF FINANCIAL POSITION December 31, 2007 | |
|---|---|
| *Assets* | |
| Cash | |
| Marketable equity securities | |
| Accounts receivable | |
| Allowance for doubtful accounts | |
| Inventories | |
| Deferred tax asset | |
| Property and equipment | |
| Accumulated depreciation | |
|     Total assets | |
| *Liabilities and Stockholders' Equity* | |
| Accounts payable and accrued liabilities | |
| Income tax payable | |
| Estimated liability from lawsuit | |
| Pension liability | |
| Common stock, $20 par | |
| Additional paid-in capital | |
| Retained earnings | |
| Other comprehensive income | |
|     Total liabilities and stockholders' equity | |

| Cord Corp.<br>STATEMENT OF INCOME<br>*For the Year Ended December 31, 2007* | |
|---|---|
| Net sales | |
| Operating expenses: | |
|    Cost of sales | |
|    Selling and administrative | |
|    Depreciation | |
|    Pension cost | |
| Total operating expenses | |
| Other income/loss: | |
|    Gain (loss) on marketable securities | |
|    Estimated loss from lawsuit | |
| Income before income tax | |
| Income tax expense | |
| Net income | |

| Situation | Effect of Error | Journal Entries | Corrected Financial Statements | Communication | Research |
|---|---|---|---|---|---|

Rex Bowman, controller of Cord Corporation, would like to know why corrections must be made for the items discovered in the audit.  Write a brief memo explaining the purpose of financial statements and the necessity for error correction to Mr. Bowman.

To:      Mr. Bowman, Controller
From:   CPA Candidate
Re:      Correction of errors

| Situation | Effect of Error | Journal Entries | Corrected Financial Statements | Communication | Research |
|---|---|---|---|---|---|

Use the Financial Accounting Standards to determine how the correction of an accounting error is handled in the financial reporting process.  Cut and paste the appropriate guidance from the professional standards.

---

**Simulation Problem 2**                (50 to 60 minutes)

| Situation | Concepts | Analysis of Error | Error Effects | Communication | Research |
|---|---|---|---|---|---|

The auditors of Cardiff Company have found the following errors in the company's accounting records.  Cardiff Company uses the guidance in FAS 154 in accounting for accounting changes.

| Situation | Concepts | Analysis of Error | Error Effects | Communication | Research |
|---|---|---|---|---|---|

Identify whether each of the following statements is True or False.

| | (T) | (F) |
|---|---|---|
| 1. Accounting errors are reported as adjustments to the end of the year retained earnings in the current year's financial statements. | ○ | ○ |
| 2. A self-correcting error need not be reported as an error if it has corrected itself in the current year. | ○ | ○ |
| 3. A change in depreciation method is treated as an error when adjusting the financial statements for the current year. | ○ | ○ |
| 4. An accounting error is treated as a prior period adjustment. | ○ | ○ |
| 5. A change in the useful lives of assets in calculating depreciation is treated as an accounting error and accumulated depreciation is adjusted to reflect this error. | ○ | ○ |

| Situation | Concepts | Analysis of Error | | Error Effects | Communication | Research |
|-----------|----------|-------------------|--|---------------|---------------|----------|

Indicate how the error will affect the current year's financial statements by choosing an "O" in the column for overstate and "U" in the column for understate.

| | Assets (O) (U) | Liabilities (O) (U) | Retained earnings (O) (U) | Net income (O) (U) | Other comprehensive income (O) (U) |
|--|:--:|:--:|:--:|:--:|:--:|
| 1. Cardiff fails to record a sale on account for $8,000. | ○ ○ | ○ ○ | ○ ○ | ○ ○ | ○ ○ |
| 2. The inventory was miscounted at year-end and overstated by $5,000. | ○ ○ | ○ ○ | ○ ○ | ○ ○ | ○ ○ |
| 3. Cardiff fails to record depreciation expense of $3,500 for the year. | ○ ○ | ○ ○ | ○ ○ | ○ ○ | ○ ○ |
| 4. The company receives a utility bill for $400 on December 29, but fails to record the bill. | ○ ○ | ○ ○ | ○ ○ | ○ ○ | ○ ○ |
| 5. Available-for-sale securities were not marked to market. Later analysis reveals that the securities increased in value by $4,000 as of the end of the current year. Cardiff does not elect the fair value option for any of its available-for-sale securities. | ○ ○ | ○ ○ | ○ ○ | ○ ○ | ○ ○ |
| 6. Cardiff fails to accrue wages of $17,000 at the end of the year. | ○ ○ | ○ ○ | ○ ○ | ○ ○ | ○ ○ |
| 7. Trading securities were not marked to market. Later analysis reveals that the securities declined in value by $8,000 as of the current year. | ○ ○ | ○ ○ | ○ ○ | ○ ○ | ○ ○ |

| Situation | Concepts | Analysis of Error | Error Effects | | Communication | Research |
|-----------|----------|-------------------|---------------|--|---------------|----------|

Calculate the total effect of the errors on the following items:

| Item | Amount | Overstated | Understated |
|------|--------|:--:|:--:|
| Net income | | ○ | ○ |
| Total assets | | ○ | ○ |
| Other comprehensive income | | ○ | ○ |

| Situation | Concepts | Analysis of Error | Error Effects | Communication | | Research |
|-----------|----------|-------------------|---------------|---------------|--|----------|

Write a brief memo to the CEO of Cardiff Company explaining accrual basis accounting and the most common errors that must be corrected before issuing financial statements.

To:    CEO, Cardiff Company
From: CPA Candidate
Re:    Correction of errors

| Situation | Concepts | Analysis of Error | Error Effects | Communication | Research |
|-----------|----------|-------------------|---------------|---------------|----------|

Use the financial accounting standards to answer the following question.  Cut and paste your answer into the space provided.

What is the definition of an accounting error?

| 1. a __ __ | 5. a __ __ | 8. b __ __ | 11. d __ __ | 14. b __ __ |
|---|---|---|---|---|
| 2. c __ __ | 6. c __ __ | 9. d __ __ | 12. d __ __ | |
| 3. b __ __ | 7. b __ __ | 10. c __ __ | 13. c __ __ | 1st: __/14 = __% |
| 4. b __ __ | | | | 2nd: __/14 = __% |

**MULTIPLE-CHOICE ANSWER EXPLANATIONS**

## B.   Error Correction

**1.   (a)**   The correct amount of 2007interest expense is $2,040, as computed below.

| | |
|---|---|
| 11/1/06 note | |
| Interest from 1/1/07 to 10/31/07 | |
| ($5,000 × 12% × 10/12) | $500 |
| 2/1/07 note | |
| Interest from 2/1/07 to 7/31/07 | |
| ($15,000 × 12% × 6/12) | 900 |
| 5/1/07 note | |
| Interest from 5/1/07 to 12/31/07 | |
| ($8,000 × 12% × 8/12) | 640 |
| Total 2007 interest | $2,040 |

Since interest expense of $1,500 was recorded, 2007 interest expense was understated by $540 ($2,040 – $1,500).

**2.   (c)**   The error in understating the 2005 ending inventory would have reversed by 1/1/07 (2005 income understated by $60,000; 2006 income overstated by $60,000). The error in overstating the 2006 ending inventory would **not** have been reversed by 1/1/07. This error overstates both 2006income and the 1/1/07 retained earnings balance by $75,000.

**3.   (b)**   A correction of an error is treated as a prior period adjustment, recorded in the year the error is discovered, and is reported in the financial statements as an adjustment to the beginning balance of retained earnings. The adjustment is reported net of the related tax effect. In this case the net-of-tax effect is $28,000 [$40,000 – ($30% × $40,000)]. This should **increase** beginning retained earnings because the understatement of 12/31/06 inventory would have resulted in an overstatement of cost of goods sold and therefore an understatement of retained earnings. Thus, the adjustment 1/1/07 retained earnings is $178,000 ($150,000 + $28,000). Tack's journal entry to record the adjustment is

| | | |
|---|---|---|
| Inventory | 40,000 | |
| Retained earnings | | 28,000 |
| Taxes payable | | 12,000 |

**4.   (b)**   A correction of an error is treated as a prior period adjustment and is reported in the financial statements as an adjustment to the beginning balance of retained earnings in the year the error is discovered. The adjustment is reported net of the related tax effect. In 2006, insurance expense of $60,000 was recorded. The correct 2006 insurance expense was $20,000 ($60,000 × 1/3). Therefore, before taxes, 1/1/07 retained earnings is understated by $40,000. The net of tax effect is $28,000 [$40,000 – (30% × $40,000)], so the adjusted beginning retained earnings is $428,000 ($400,000 + $28,000).

**5.   (a)**   A change in accounting principle is a change from one **generally accepted** principle to another **generally accepted** principle. A correction of an error is the correction of a mathematical mistake, a mistake in the application of an accounting principle, an oversight or misuse of existing facts, or **a change from an unacceptable principle to a generally accepted one**. Therefore, a switch from the cash basis (unacceptable) to the accrual basis (acceptable) is a correction of an error reported as a prior period adjustment.

**6.   (c)**   The requirement is to determine the effect of inventory errors on cost of goods sold. The effect of the errors on Bren's 2007 cost of goods sold (CGS) is illustrated below.

| | | | |
|---|---|---|---|
| BI | | | |
| + P | – $26,000 | CGS understated | $26,000 |
| GAFS | | | |
| – EI | (+ $52,000) | CGS understated | 52,000 |
| CGS | | CGS understated | $78,000 |

Beginning inventory is the starting point for the CGS computation, so BI errors have a direct effect on CGS. The understatement of BI ($26,000) causes an **understatement** of goods available for sale (GAFS) and thus of CGS. Ending inventory is subtracted in the CGS computation, so EI errors have an inverse effect on CGS. The overstatement of EI ($52,000) means that too much was subtracted in the CGS computation, causing another **understatement** of CGS. Therefore, CGS is understated by a total of $78,000.

**7.   (b)**   The failure to record the $300,000 of deferred compensation expense in 2006 is considered an error. The profession requires that the correction of an error be treated as a prior period adjustment. Thus, the requirement is to determine the retroactive adjustment that should be made to the beginning balance of the retained earnings for 2007 (**including** any income tax effect). The net adjustment to beginning retained earnings would be a debit for $230,000 ($300,000 less the income tax benefit of $70,000).

**8.   (b)**   The depreciable base used to compute depreciation expense under both the straight-line and production methods is equal to cost less estimated salvage value of the asset. Depreciation expense is overstated and net income is, therefore, understated when the estimated salvage value is excluded from the depreciation computation under both of these methods.

**9.   (d)**   The entry Ritzcar should have made to accrue sales commissions earned but unpaid at the end of its 2006 fiscal year is

| | | |
|---|---|---|
| Commission expense | xxx | |
| Commissions payable | | xxx |

Since Commissions payable is a current liability, the 2006 ending working capital is overstated due to Ritzcar's failure to record this entry. Since this error was not repeated at the end of Ritzcar's 2007 fiscal year, the income impact of the 2006 error "self-corrected" during 2007, when Ritzcar recorded both the earned but unpaid 2006 commissions plus the 2007 earned commissions. Therefore, the 2007 ending retained earnings would not be impacted by the error.

**10.   (c)**   A liability is accrued when an obligation to pay or perform services has been incurred. This is the case even if the liability will not be satisfied until a future date. Therefore, accrued liabilities will be understated on the December 31, 2007 balance sheet because the special insurance costs were not recorded. However, there will be no effect on the December 31, 2007 balance of retained earnings because these costs relate to work in process, and work in process does not affect net income currently. Please note that if the special insurance costs related to goods that were sold, cost of goods sold would have been understated that would have caused both net income and retained earnings to be overstated.

**11.   (d)**   The classification of holiday pay expense for administrative employees as manufacturing overhead would result in the capitalization of some or all of these costs as a component of ending inventory, while these costs should be expensed as incurred. This error could overstate ending inventory, a current asset. The overstatement of ending inventory also understates the cost of goods sold (Beginning inventories + Net purchases – Ending inventories = Cost of goods sold), and overstates net income and stockholders' equity. The understatement of accrued sales expenses would not affect current assets. The misclassification of the noncurrent note receivable principal as a current asset would have no impact on stockholders' equity. The understatement of depreciation on **manufacturing** machinery would understate the overhead added to inventories, a current asset.

**12.   (d)**   The entry for the 12/31/06 wage accrual should have been

| Wages expense | 12,000 | |
| Wages payable | | 12,000 |

Failure to accrue wage expense results in an understatement of wage expense and an understatement of wages payable by $12,000 in 2006. As a result, net income and retained earnings are overstated by $12,000 in 2006. The wages were expensed and paid in 2007. Therefore, wage expense for 2007 is overstated, and 2007 net income is understated by $12,000. This is a counterbalancing error, and end retained earnings in 2007 would be correct. Although this is a self-correcting error, SFAS 154 requires that the financial statements are restated with period-specific effects. The restated financial statements are

*Galaxy Corporation*
**RESTATED FINANCIAL STATEMENTS**

| | *2007* | *2006* |
|---|---|---|
| Revenue | $135,000 | $100,000 |
| Expenses | 86,000 | 77,000 |
| Net income | 49,000 | 23,000 |
| | *12-31-07* | *12-31-06* |
| Total assets | $157,000 | $105,000 |
| Total liabilities | 50,000 | 47,000 |
| Total owners' equity | 107,000 | 58,000 |

**13.   (c)**   Per SFAS 154, the financial statements of all periods should be restated and corrections made to reflect any period-specific effects of the error. Answer (a) is incorrect because this is an error, not a change in accounting principle. Answer (b) is incorrect because although the asset accounts may be adjusted to reflect correction of an error, income statement effects must also be disclosed. Answer (d) is incorrect because the financial statements must be restated for all periods presented.

**14.   (b)**   Per SFAS 154, the financial statements must be restated for all periods presented with period-specific effects disclosed. Answer (a) is incorrect because although beginning inventory may be adjusted, prior years' financial statements must also be restated. Answer (c) is incorrect because correcting the balance of ending retained earnings is not sufficient disclosure for error correction. Answer (d) is incorrect because even though it is a self-correcting entry, financial statements must be restated with period-specific effects of the error.

## SOLUTIONS TO SIMULATION PROBLEMS

### Simulation Problem 1

| Situation | Effect of Error | Journal Entries | Corrected Financial Statements | Communication | Research |
|---|---|---|---|---|---|

| | 2007 Effects | | | 2008 Effects | | |
|---|---|---|---|---|---|---|
| | (Overstate) | (Understate) | (OK) | (Overstate) | (Understate) | (OK) |
| Inventory on balance sheet | ● | ○ | ○ | ○ | ○ | ● |
| Cost of goods sold | ○ | ● | ○ | ● | ○ | ○ |
| Net income | ● | ○ | ○ | ○ | ● | ○ |
| Retained earnings | ● | ○ | ○ | ○ | ○ | ● |

| Situation | Effect of Error | Journal Entries | Corrected Financial Statements | Communication | Research |
|---|---|---|---|---|---|

*Cord Corp.*
**ADJUSTING JOURNAL ENTRIES**
*December 31, 2007*
*(Explanations not required)*

| | Dr. | Cr. |
|---|---|---|
| (1) | | |
| Marketable equity securities | $ 30,000 | |
|   Realized gain on sale of marketable equity securities | | $ 30,000 [a] |
| (2) | | |
| Unrealized loss on marketable equity securities (other comprehensive income) | 13,000 | |
|   Adjustment to reduce marketable equity securities to market value | | 13,000 [b] |
| (3) | | |
| Cost of sales | 66,000 | |
|   Inventories | | 66,000 |
| (4) | | |
| Property and equipment | 48,000 | |
|   Income tax payable | | 14,400 [c] |
|   Retained earnings | | 33,600 [c] |
| (5) | | |
| Depreciation | 8,000 | |
|   Accumulated depreciation | | 8,000 [d] |
| (6) | | |
| Estimated loss from lawsuit | 60,000 | |
|   Estimated liability from lawsuit | | 60,000 |
| (7) | | |
| Deferred pension cost | 40,000 | |
|   Additional pension liability | | 40,000 |
| (8) | | |
| Deferred tax asset | 21,900 [i] | |
| Income tax payable | 13,200 [ii] | |
|   Income tax expense | | 35,100 [iii] |

***Supporting Computations for Number 8***

| Corrected total income tax expense for 2007 | | |
|---|---|---|
|       Income before income tax, as reported | | $640,000 |
|     Add adjustment increasing income | | |
|       Realized gain on sale of securities | | 30,000 [1] |
| | | 670,000 |
|     Deduct adjustments decreasing income | | |
|       Increase cost of sales for inventory overstatement | $66,000 | |
|       Depreciation on pollution control devices | 8,000 | 74,000 |
|     Adjusted taxable income before income tax | | $596,000 |

Corrected current portion income tax expense and income taxes payable ($596,000 × 30%)    $178,800

| Deferred income tax benefits—based on following temporary differences: | | |
|---|---|---|
|   Lawsuit expected to be settled in 2008 | $60,000 [6] | |
|   Unrealized loss on short-term marketable equity securities | 13,000 [2] | |
|     Total future deductible amounts | $73,000 | |

| [i] | Deferred tax benefit of future deductible amounts ($73,000 × 30%) | 21,900 |
|---|---|---|
| | Corrected total income tax expense | $156,900 |

| [ii] | Income tax expense as reported (all current, no deferred) | $192,000 |
|---|---|---|
| | Corrected income tax payable and income tax expense | 178,800 |
| | | $ 13,200 |

| [iii] | Income tax expense, as reported | $192,000 |
|---|---|---|
| | Corrected total income tax expense | 156,900 |
| | | $ 35,100 |

**Explanations of Amounts**

[a] Gain on sale of marketable equity securities

| Selling price | $130,000 |
|---|---|
| Cost | 100,000 |
| Gain | $ 30,000 |

[b] Adjustment to reduce marketable equity securities to market value

Marketable equity securities, at cost

| Balance, 2/2/07 as reported | $125,000 |
|---|---|
| Adjustment for recording error | 30,000 |
| Adjusted balance, 12/31/07 | 155,000 |
| Market valuation, 12/31/07 | 142,000 |
| Adjustment required, 12/31/07 | $ 13,000 |

[c] Prior year adjustment for pollution control devices

| Cost of installation, 12/29/06 | $ 48,000 |
|---|---|
| Deduct income tax effect ($48,000 × 30%) | 14,400 |
| Credit adjustment to retained earnings, 1/1/07 | $ 33,600 |

[d] Depreciation for 2007 on pollution control devices

| Cost of the installation on 12/29/06 | $ 48,000 |
|---|---|
| Depreciation for 2007 ($48,000 ÷ 6 years) | $ 8,000 |

| Situation | Effect of Error | Journal Entries | Corrected Financial Statements | Communication | Research |
|---|---|---|---|---|---|

**Cord Corp.**
**STATEMENT OF FINANCIAL POSITION**
*December 31, 2007*

**Assets**

| Cash | $1,225,000 |
|---|---|
| Marketable equity securities | 142,000 |
| Accounts receivable | 460,000 |
| Allowance for doubtful accounts | (55,000) |
| Inventories | 464,000 |
| Deferred tax asset | 21,900 |
| Deferred pension cost | 40,000 |
| Property and equipment | 668,000 |
| Accumulated depreciation | (288,000) |
| Total assets | $2,677,900 |

**Liabilities and Stockholders' Equity**

| Accounts payable and accrued liabilities | $1,685,000 |
|---|---|
| Income tax payable | 111,200 |
| Estimated liability from lawsuit | 60,000 |
| Pension liability | 40,000 |
| Common stock, $20 par | 300,000 |
| Additional paid-in capital | 75,000 |
| Retained earnings | 419,700 |
| Other comprehensive income | (13,000) |
| Total liabilities and stockholders' equity | $2,677,900 |

**Calculation of corrected retained earnings:**

| Previous retained earnings (incorrect) | 455,000 |
|---|---|
| Less: Net income for 2007 (incorrect) | (448,000) |
| Beginning of year retained earnings (correct) | 7,000 |
| Net income (corrected) | 379,100 |
| Prior period adjustment for accounting error in expense pollution control devices in 2006 | 33,600 |
| Corrected retained earnings | 419,700 |

*Cord Corp.*
**STATEMENT OF INCOME**
*For the Year Ended December 31, 2007*

| | |
|---|---:|
| Net sales | $1,700,000 |
| Operating expenses: | |
|     Cost of sales | (636,000) |
|     Selling and administrative | (448,000) |
|     Depreciation | (50,000) |
| Total operating expenses | (1,134,000) |
| Other income/loss: | |
|     Gain (loss) on marketable securities | 30,000 |
|     Estimated loss from lawsuit | (60,000) |
| Income before income tax | 536,000 |
| Income tax expense | (156,900) |
| Net income | 379,100 |

| Situation | Effect of Error | Journal Entries | Corrected Financial Statements | Communication | Research |
|---|---|---|---|---|---|

To:      Mr. Bowman, Controller of Cord Corporation
From:  CPA Candidate
Re:      Correction of errors

    You have requested that I explain why errors in previously issued financial statements must be corrected.  The reliability of the financial reporting process is critical to investors and creditors.  They rely on financial statements to make important decisions which often have significant financial consequences.  Correction of the errors in previously issued financial statements not only corrects the statements of those periods, it also helps ensure that current and future financial statements are not misstated by the errors.  Most accounting errors made in one year automatically correct themselves in future years.  Such errors not only misstate results for one year, they also misstate results for two or more years.

    In order to maintain the integrity of Cord Corporation's financial statements it is imperative that management correct the prior period financial statements for all material errors.

    If you have any further questions or concerns, please contact me.

| Situation | Effect of Error | Journal Entries | Corrected Financial Statements | Communication | Research |
|---|---|---|---|---|---|

**Correction of an Error in Previously Issued Financial Statements**
**FAS 154, Para 25 or Current Text A07.125**

25.  Any error in the financial statements of a prior period discovered subsequent to their issuance shall be reported as a prior-period adjustment by restating the prior-period financial statements.  Restatement requires that

    a.  The cumulative effect of the error on periods prior to those presented shall be reflected in the carrying amounts of assets and liabilities as of the beginning of the first period presented.

    b.  An offsetting adjustment, if any, shall be made to the opening balance of retained earnings (or other appropriate components of equity or net assets in the statement of financial position) for that period.

    c.  Financial statements for each individual prior period presented shall be adjusted to reflect correction of the period-specific effects of the error.

**Simulation Problem 2**

| Situation | Concepts | Analysis of Error | Error Effects | Communication | Research |
|---|---|---|---|---|---|

| | | (T) | (F) |
|---|---|:---:|:---:|
| 1. | Accounting errors are reported as adjustments to the end of the year retained earnings in the current year's financial statements. | ○ | ● |
| 2. | A self-correcting error need not be reported as an error if it has corrected itself in the current year. | ○ | ● |
| 3. | A change in depreciation method is treated as an error when adjusting the financial statements for the current year. | ○ | ● |
| 4. | An accounting error is treated as a prior period adjustment. | ● | ○ |
| 5. | A change in the useful lives of assets in calculating depreciation is treated as an accounting error and accumulated depreciation is adjusted to reflect this error. | ○ | ● |

## Explanation of solutions

**1.** False. Accounting errors require an adjustment to the beginning of the year retained earnings in the current year financial statements.

**2.** False. A self-correcting error would require an adjustment to correct comparative year financial statements. Adjustments to comparative years should be made to reflect retroactive application of the prior period adjustment to the accounts affected.

**3.** False. A change in depreciation method is treated as accumulative effect of change in accounting principle.

**4.** True. Correction of errors involve restatements of prior periods.

**5.** False. A change in the useful lives of an asset is treated on a prospective basis, and depreciation for the current year is calculated based on book value divided by the estimated number of years remaining.

| Situation | Concepts | Assets (O) | (U) | Liabilities (O) | (U) | Retained earnings (O) | (U) | Net income (O) | (U) | Other comprehensive income (O) | (U) |
|---|---|---|---|---|---|---|---|---|---|---|---|
| **1.** Cardiff fails to record a sale on account for $8,000. | | ○ | ● | ○ | ○ | ○ | ● | ○ | ● | ○ | ○ |
| **2.** The inventory was miscounted at year-end and overstated by $5,000. | | ● | ○ | ○ | ○ | ● | ○ | ● | ○ | ○ | ○ |
| **3.** Cardiff fails to record depreciation expense of $3,500 for the year. | | ● | ○ | ○ | ○ | ● | ○ | ● | ○ | ○ | ○ |
| **4.** The company receives a utility bill for $400 on December 29, but fails to record the bill. | | ○ | ○ | ○ | ● | ● | ○ | ● | ○ | ○ | ○ |
| **5.** Available-for-sale securities were not marked to market. Later analysis reveals that the securities increased in value by $4,000 as of the end of the current year. Cardiff does not elect the fair value option for any of its available-for-sale securities. | | ○ | ● | ○ | ○ | ○ | ○ | ○ | ○ | ○ | ● |
| **6.** Cardiff fails to accrue wages of $17,000 at the end of the year. | | ○ | ○ | ○ | ● | ● | ○ | ● | ○ | ○ | ○ |
| **7.** Trading securities were not marked to market. Later analysis reveals that the securities declined in value by $8,000 as of the end of the current year. | | ● | ○ | ○ | ○ | ● | ○ | ● | ○ | ○ | ○ |

## Explanation of solutions

**1.** Cardiff should have debited Accounts Receivable and credited Sales. Therefore, accounts receivable is understated, and retained earnings is understated.

**2.** Cardiff has overstated ending inventory, which understates cost of goods sold. Understating cost of goods sold results in income being overstated for the period. Net income flows into retained earnings, and thus, retained earnings is also overstated in the current period.

**3.** Cardiff should have debited Depreciation Expense and credited Accumulated Depreciation. By not making this entry, depreciation expense is too low, overstating net income, and overstating retained earnings. Accumulated depreciation is also too low, which overstates assets.

**4.** The entry would be to debit Utility Expense and credit Accounts Payable. Failing to make this entry would understate expenses, which results in overstated net income, overstated retained earnings, and understated liabilities.

**5.** The unrealized gain on available-for-sale securities is not recognized in net income, but is recognized as an unrealized gain in other comprehensive income. Failing to mark to market when an available-for-sale security has increased in value would result in understating assets and understating other comprehensive income for the period.

**6.**   The journal entry to accrue wages is to debit Wage Expense and credit Wages Payable.  Failure to accrue wages results in expenses being understated, which in turn, overstates net income and overstates retained earnings for the period.  Failure to accrue wages also results in liabilities being understated.

**7.**   The unrealized gains and losses from trading securities should be included in net income for the period.  Failure to mark to market and recognize the loss would result in assets being overstated, net income being overstated, and retained earnings being overstated for the period.

| Situation | Concepts | Analysis of Error | Error Effects | | Communication | Research |
|-----------|----------|-------------------|---------------|--|---------------|----------|

| *Item* | *Amount* | *Overstated* | *Understated* |
|--------|----------|--------------|---------------|
| Net income | 25,900 | ● | ○ |
| Total assets | 4,500 | ● | ○ |
| Other comprehensive income | 4,000 | ○ | ● |

**Explanation of solutions**

**Net income:**  Under $8,000 from sale, over $5,000 from inventory error, over $3,500 from depreciation expense, over $400 from utility bill, over $17,000 from failure to accrue wages, over $8,000 from failure to record decline in value of trading security.

**Total assets:**  Under $8,000 from failure to record sale on account, over $5,000 from inventory error, over $3,500 from failure to record accumulated depreciation, under $4,000 for failure to mark to market AFS, over $8,000 for failure to mark trading securities to market.

**OCI:**  Understated $4,000 for failure to mark AFS securities to market.

| Situation | Concepts | Analysis of Error | Error Effects | Communication | | Research |
|-----------|----------|-------------------|---------------|---------------|--|----------|

To:       CEO, Cardiff Company
From:    CPA Candidate
Re:       Correction of Errors

The purpose of issuing financial statements is to provide users with reliable financial information to make investment and credit decisions.  Generally accepted accounting principles require companies to use the accrual basis of accounting.  The accrual basis of accounting attempts to measure all economic activity during the period, and record these items as assets, liabilities, owners' equity, revenue, expenses, gains, or losses.  Correct measurement and correct classification of these items is essential to provide investors with accurate and reliable information.

The most common errors that must be corrected prior to issuing financial statements are failing to adjust an existing account for items previously recognized, miscounting inventory, failing to accrue liabilities at the end of the period, and failing to properly classify capitalized or expensed items.  These errors must be corrected to ensure that the values of the assets and liabilities are accurately stated on the balance sheet.  In addition, correcting these errors will also ensure that income and expense for the period is accurately measured and reflected on the income statement.

If I can be of further assistance, please do not hesitate to contact my office.

| Situation | Concepts | Analysis of Error | Error Effects | Communication | Research | |
|-----------|----------|-------------------|---------------|---------------|----------|--|

**FAS 154, Para 2(h) or Current Text A07.408**

h.   Error in previously issued financial statements—an error in recognition, measurement, presentation, or disclosure in financial statements resulting from mathematical mistakes, mistakes in the application of GAAP, or oversight or misuse of facts that existed at the time the financial statements were prepared.  A change from an accounting principle that is not generally accepted to one that is generally accepted is a correction of an error.

## C.  Accounting Changes—SFAS 154

SFAS 154 replaces APB Opinion 20, *Accounting Changes*, and SFAS 3, *Reporting Accounting Changes in Interim Financial Statements*.  It applies to all voluntary changes in accounting principle, as well as changes in accounting principle required by the issuance of new standards that do not include transition provisions.  SFAS 154 changes the treatment for accounting changes.  One significant difference is that changes in accounting principle no longer receive cumulative effect treatment on the income statement of the current year.  Instead, SFAS 154 requires the effect of the change to be applied **retrospectively** (not retroactively) to the earliest period affected in the financial statements.  Additional footnote disclosures are required for the change.  Another important change from APB 20 is that a change in depreciation method is no longer accounted for as a change in accounting principle.  A change in depreciation method is considered a change in accounting principle which is not distinguishable from a change in estimate and is accounted for on a prospective basis.

SFAS 154 requires that once an accounting principle is adopted, it must be used consistently for similar events and transactions.  An entity may change an accounting principle only if it justifies that the alternative method is preferable.

SFAS 154 defines an accounting change as a change in accounting principle, a change in estimate, or a change in the reporting entity.  The correction of an error in previous financial statements is not an accounting change.  The statement further defines two important terms:  restatement and retrospective application.  A restatement is the process of revising previously issued financial statements to correct an error.  A retrospective application is the application of a different accounting principle to previously issued financial statements, as if that principle had always been used.  Retrospective application is required for changes in accounting principle and changes in reporting entity.

1. **Change in Accounting Principle**

    An entity may change accounting principle only if the change is required by a newly issued accounting pronouncement, or if the entity can justify the use of the alternative accounting principle because it is preferable.  A change in accounting principle is accounted for through retrospective application of the new accounting principle to all prior periods, unless it is impracticable to do so.  Retrospective changes require the following:

    1. The cumulative effects of the change are presented in the carrying amounts of assets and liabilities as of **the beginning of the first period presented**.
    2. An offsetting adjustment is made to the opening balance of retained earnings for that period (the beginning of the first period presented).
    3. Financial statements for each individual prior period presented are adjusted to reflect the **period-specific effects** of applying the new accounting principle.

    Only the **direct effects** of the change are recognized.  An example of a direct effect is an adjustment to an inventory balance due to a change in inventory valuation method.  Related changes, such as the effect on deferred taxes or impairment adjustment are also considered direct effects and must be recognized.  **Indirect effects** are any changes to current or future cash flows that result from making a change in accounting principle.  An example of an indirect effect is a change in a profit sharing or royalty payment based on revenue or net income.  Any indirect effects of the change are reported in the period in which the accounting change is made.

    If the cumulative effect of applying the accounting change can be determined but the period-specific effects on all prior periods cannot be determined, the cumulative effect is applied to the carrying amounts of assets and liabilities at the beginning of the earliest period to which it can be applied or calculated.  An offsetting adjustment is then made to the opening balance of retained earnings for that period.

    The following example is adapted from SFAS 154.

    *EXAMPLE: Wagner Corporation began operations on January 1, 2006.  On January 1, 2008, Wagner changes from the weighted-average method of accounting for inventory to the FIFO method.  Wagner provides a profit-sharing plan for its employees.  The bonus or profit-sharing plan allows all employees to share in a 5% bonus based on earnings before income taxes and bonus.  The income tax rate for all periods is 30%.  Assume there are no book/tax differences or deferred taxes.  All taxes and bonuses are accrued at the end of each year on December 31 and paid in January of the following year.*

    *Assume that Wagner's accounting records are adequate to determine the effects of the change in accounting principle for each year.  Ending inventory for the weighted-average and FIFO methods are shown below.*

### Ending Inventory

|  | Weighted-average method | FIFO method |
|---|---|---|
| 12-31-06 | 1,000 | 1,200 |
| 12-31-07 | 2,000 | 2,500 |
| 12-31-08 | 2,400 | 3,200 |

*The income statements for 2006 through 2008 calculated using weighted-average method are shown below.*

### Wagner Corporation
### Income Statements

|  | For the period ending 12-31-08 *(before change)* | For the period ending 12-31-07 *(before change)* | For the period ending 12-31-06 *(before change)* |
|---|---|---|---|
| Sales | $15,000 | $12,000 | $ 8,000 |
| Less: Cost of good sold | (8,900) | (7,000) | (5,000) |
| Gross profit | 6,100 | 5,000 | 3,000 |
| Sales, general & admin. expenses | (3,500) | (3,000) | (2,000) |
| Earnings before bonus and income taxes | 2,600 | 2,000 | 1,000 |
| Bonus compensation expense | (130) | (100) | (50) |
| Earnings before income taxes | 2,470 | 1,900 | 950 |
| Income tax expense | (741) | (570) | (285) |
| Net income | $ 1,729 | $ 1,330 | $ 665 |

*Balance sheets calculated using the weighted-average inventory method before the change to FIFO for 2006-2008 are shown below.*

### Wagner Corporation
### Balance Sheets

|  | Dec. 31, 2008 *(before change)* | Dec. 31, 2007 *(before change)* | Dec. 31, 2006 *(before change)* |
|---|---|---|---|
| Cash | $ 1,900 | $ 1,000 | $ 1,000 |
| Inventory | 2,400 | 2,000 | 1,000 |
| Plant, property, and equipment | 11,000 | 10,000 | 10,000 |
| Total assets | 15,300 | 13,000 | 12,000 |
| Accounts payable | 1,370 | 1,000 | 1,665 |
| Accrued bonus liability | 130 | 100 | 50 |
| Income tax liability | 741 | 570 | 285 |
| Total liabilities | 2,241 | 1,670 | 2,000 |
| Common stock | 500 | 500 | 500 |
| Additional paid-in capital | 8,835 | 8,835 | 8,835 |
| Retained earnings | 3,724 | 1,995 | 665 |
| Total liabilities and owners' equity | $15,300 | $13,000 | $12,000 |

To account for the change in accounting method for inventory, the new accounting method is applied retrospectively. Retrospective application requires that the financial statements are adjusted for the earliest period presented, showing period-specific effects. The period-specific effects for Wagner include the direct effects on inventory, cost of goods sold, income tax expense, and income tax liability for each period. The change in bonus compensation expense and accrued bonus liability are indirect effects and are accounted for in the year of the change, which is the current year, 2008.

To calculate the adjustments in inventory and cost of goods sold for each year, use a T-account. First, calculate the purchases for each year using the weighted-average method.

|  | Inventory (Weighted-average method) |  |  |
|---|---|---|---|
| 1-1-06 | -0- | | |
| Purchases | 6,000 | 5,000 | CGS |
| 12-31-06 | 1,000 | | |
| Purchases | 8,000 | 7,000 | CGS |
| 12-31-07 | 2,000 | | |
| Purchases | 9,300 | 8,900 | CGS |
| 12-31-08 | 2,400 | | |

Then, using the amount of purchases for each period and the information given in the problem for ending inventory using the FIFO method, calculate the adjusted cost of goods sold for each period using the FIFO method.

| | Inventory (Weighted-average method) | | | |
|---|---|---|---|---|
| 1-1-06 | -0- | | | |
| Purchases | 6,000 | 4,800 | | CGS |
| 12-31-06 | 1,200 | | | |
| Purchases | 8,000 | 6,700 | | CGS |
| 12-31-07 | 2,500 | | | |
| Purchases | 9,300 | 8,600 | | CGS |
| 12-31-08 | 3,200 | | | |

After you have calculated the period-specific effects on ending inventory and cost of goods sold, prepare an adjusted income statement for each period.

The adjusted income statement for the period ending December 31, 2006, is shown below.

**Wagner Corporation—Income Statement**
**For the year ending 12-31-06**

| | For the period ending 12-31-06 as originally reported | For the period ending 12-31-06 as adjusted | Effect of the change |
|---|---|---|---|
| Sales | $ 8,000 | $ 8,000 | $   -- |
| Less: Cost of good sold | (5,000) | (4,800) | (200) |
| Gross profit | 3,000 | 3,200 | 200 |
| Sales, general & admin. expenses | (2,000) | 2,000 | -- |
| Earnings before bonus and income taxes | 1,000 | 1,200 | 200 |
| Bonus compensation expense* | (50) | 50* | -- |
| Earnings before income taxes | 950 | 1,150 | 200 |
| Income tax expense | (285) | (345) | (60) |
| Net income | $   665 | $   805 | $   140 |

\*   Bonus expense is an indirect effect of the change; therefore, bonus expense is not adjusted retrospectively. Instead, the indirect effects of the bonus are adjusted in the current year, 2008.

**Wagner Corporation—Income Statement**
**For the year ending 12-31-07**

| | For the period ending 12-31-07 as originally reported | For the period ending 12-31-07 as adjusted | Effect of the change |
|---|---|---|---|
| Sales | $ 12,000 | $ 12,000 | $   -- |
| Less: Cost of good sold | (7,000) | (6,700) | (300) |
| Gross profit | 5,000 | 5,300 | 300 |
| Sales, general & admin. expenses | (3,000) | 3,000 | -- |
| Earnings before bonus and income taxes | 2,000 | 2,300 | 300 |
| Bonus compensation expense* | (100) | (100)* | -- |
| Earnings before income taxes | 1,900 | 2,200 | 300 |
| Income tax expense | (570) | (660) | (90) |
| Net income | $ 1,330 | $ 1,540 | $   210 |

\*   Bonus expense is an indirect effect of the change; therefore, it is adjusted and expensed in the current year, 2008.

**Wagner Corporation—Income Statement**
**For the year ending 12-31-08**

| | For the period ending 12-31-08 current year before adjustment | For the period ending 12-31-08 as adjusted |
|---|---|---|
| Sales | $15,000 | $15,000 |
| Less: Cost of good sold | (8,900) | (8,600) |
| Gross profit | 6,100 | 6,400 |
| Sales, general & admin. expenses | (3,500) | (3,500) |
| Earnings before bonus and income taxes | 2,600 | 2,900 |
| Bonus compensation expense* | (130) | (170)* |
| Earnings before income taxes | 2,470 | 2,730 |
| Income tax expense | (741) | 819 |
| Net income | $ 1,729 | $ 1,911 |

\*   Bonus compensation expense for 2007 is calculated as follows:

| | | | | | |
|---|---|---|---|---|---|
| 2008 | Earnings before bonus and taxes | $2,900 | x | 5% | $145 |
| 2007 | Adjustment to earnings before bonus and taxes | 300 | x | 5% | 15 |
| 2006 | Adjustment to earnings before bonus and taxes | 200 | x | 5% | 10 |
| | Total bonus compensation expense for 2008 | | | | $170 |
| | (adjusted for effects of the accounting change) | | | | |

The adjusted income statements for years 2006 through 2008, resented on a comparative basis are shown below.

**Wagner Corporation**
**Income Statement**

| | For the period ending 12-31-08 | For the period ending 12-31-07 as adjusted | For the period ending 12-31-06 as adjusted |
|---|---|---|---|
| Sales | $15,000 | $12,000 | $ 8,000 |
| Less: Cost of good sold | (8,600) | (6,700) | (4,800) |
| Gross profit | 6,400 | 5,300 | 3,200 |
| Sales, general & admin. expenses | (3,500) | (3,000) | (2,000) |
| Earnings before bonus and income taxes | 2,900 | 2,300 | 1,200 |
| Bonus compensation expense | (170) | (100) | (50) |
| Earnings before income taxes | 2,370 | 2,200 | 1,150 |
| Income tax expense | 819 | (660) | (345) |
| Net income | $ 1,911 | $ 1,540 | $   805 |

The balance sheet is presented on a comparative basis for two years.  Therefore, the assets and liabilities must be retrospectively adjusted for the period-specific effects as of December 31, 2007, the first year presented.  In addition, any previous years' adjustment are shown as an adjustment to retained earnings for the earliest year presented.

**Wagner Corporation—Balance Sheet**
**December 31, 2007**

| | Dec 31, 2007 as originally reported | Dec. 31, 2007 as adjusted |
|---|---|---|
| Cash | $ 1,000 | $ 1,000 |
| Inventory | 2,000 | 2,500 |
| Plant, property, and equipment | 10,000 | 10,000 |
| Total assets | 13,000 | 13,500 |
| Accounts payable | 1,000 | 1,000 |
| Accrued bonus liability | 100 | 100 |
| Income tax liability | 570 | 720* |
| Total liabilities | 1,670 | 1,820 |
| Common stock | 500 | 500 |
| Additional paid-in capital | 8,835 | 8,835 |
| Retained earnings | 1,995 | 2,345** |
| Total liabilities and owners' equity | $13,000 | $13,500 |

\* Tax liability is adjusted for the increase in income tax expense and income tax liability for 2006 and 2007 ($60 in 2006 and $90 in 2007, for a total of $150 increase in income tax liability).

\*\* Retained earnings is adjusted as follows:

| Retained earnings (with adjustments | | |
|---|---|---|
| | 665 | NI 2006, as originally reported |
| | 140 | Adjustment to NI for 2006 |
| | 805 | Bal. in R/E, 12-31-06 adjusted |
| | 1,330 | NI 2007, as originally reported |
| | 210 | Adjustment to NI for 2007 |
| | 2,345 | Bal. in R/E, 12-31-07 after adjustments |
| | 1,911 | Net income in 2008 using FIFO method |
| | 4,256 | Bal. in R/E, 12-31-08 |

The balance sheet for 2008, presented on a comparative basis for two years, is as follows:

**Wagner Corporation**
**Comparative Balance Sheets**

| | Dec. 31, 2008 | Dec. 31, 2007 (as adjusted) |
|---|---|---|
| Cash | $ 1,900 | $ 1,000 |
| Inventory | 3,200 | 2,500 |
| Plant, property, and equipment | 11,000 | 10,000 |
| Total assets | 16,100 | 13,500 |
| Accounts payable | 1,370 | 1,000 |
| Accrued bonus liability | 170* | 100 |
| Income tax liability | 969** | 720** |
| Total liabilities | 2,509 | 1,820 |
| Common stock | 500 | 500 |
| Additional paid-in capital | 8,835 | 8,835 |
| Retained earnings | 4,256 | 2,345** |
| Total liabilities and owners' equity | $16,100 | $13,500 |

\* Bonus liability calculation

Bonus liability will be accrued in 2008 and paid in 2009.  Therefore, the bonus liability at the end of December 31, 2008, is calculated as follows:

| | | | | | |
|---|---|---|---|---|---|
| 2008 | Earnings before bonus and taxes | $2,900 | x | 5% | $145 |
| 2007 | Adjustment to earnings before bonus and taxes | 300 | x | 5% | 15 |
| 2006 | Adjustment to earnings before bonus and taxes | 200 | x | 5% | 10 |
| | Total bonus compensation liability as of 12-31-08 | | | | $170 |
| | (adjusted for effects of the accounting change) | | | | |

\*\* Tax liability calculation

*Because the change in accounting method occurred in 2008, the tax liability resulting from the change will be*
*accrued in 2008 and paid in January, 2009.  The tax liability on the balance sheet is calculated as follows:*

| | | | | | |
|---|---|---|---|---|---|
| 2008 | Earnings before income taxes | $2,730 | x | 30% | $819 |
| 2007 | Adjustment to earnings before income taxes | 300 | x | 30% | 90 |
| 2006 | Adjustment to earnings before income taxes | 200 | x | 30% | 60 |
| | Total tax liability for 2008 | | | | $969 |
| | *(adjusted for effects of the accounting change)* | | | | |

If it is impracticable to determine the cumulative effect to any of the prior periods, the new accounting principle is applied as if the change was made **prospectively** at the earliest date practicable. It is considered impracticable only if one of the three following conditions is met:

1. After making every reasonable effort to apply the new principle to the previous period, the entity is unable to do so
2. Retrospective application requires assumptions about management's intentions in a prior period that cannot be independently substantiated
3. Retrospective application requires significant estimates, and it is impossible to obtain objective information about the estimates

Notes to the financial statements are required for a change in accounting principle.  These include

1. The nature and reason for the change, and explanation as to why the new method is preferable
2. The method of applying the change
3. A description of the prior period information that is retrospectively adjusted
4. The effect of the change on income from continuing operations, net income, and any other affected financial statement line item, and any affected per share amounts for the current period and all periods adjusted retrospectively
5. The cumulative effect of the change on retained earnings or other components of equity or net assets as of the earliest period presented
6. If retrospective application is impracticable, the reason, and a description of how the change was reported
7. A description of the indirect effects of the change, including amounts recognized in the current period, and related per share amounts
8. Unless impracticable, the amounts of indirect effect of the change and the per share amounts for each prior period presented

Disclosures are also required for interim periods.  In the year of the change to the new accounting principle, interim financial statements should disclose the effect of the change on income from continuing operations, net income, and related per share amounts for the postchange interim periods.

Once the change in method is disclosed, financial statements in subsequent periods do not need to repeat the disclosures.

2. **Change in Accounting Estimates**

Changes in accounting estimates are accounted for on a prospective basis.  The financial statements are **not** restated or retrospectively adjusted.  The change is accounted for in the current period and future periods.  If a change in accounting estimate is effected by a change in principle (change in depreciation method), it is treated as a change in estimate.  In cases where an entity effects a change in estimate by changing an accounting principle, the footnote disclosures required by a change in accounting principle apply and must be included in the notes to the financial statements.

An example of a change in estimate effected by a change in accounting principle is a change in depreciation method.

*EXAMPLE:  Gonzalez Corporation acquires equipment on January 1, 2006 for $100,000.  Gonzalez depreciates the equipment using the double-declining balance method.  The equipment has a ten-year life and a $20,000 salvage value. In January, 2008, Gonzalez changes its depreciation method to straight-line.*

*This change in depreciation method is considered a change in estimate effected by a change in accounting principle.  According to SFAS 154, it is accounted for in the current year and future years.*

*Step 1:  Calculate accumulated depreciation and book value at the beginning of the year of the change in depreciation method.*

**Double declining balance method**

*The double-declining rate is* $\frac{1}{10} x\ 2\ =\ 20\%$

| Year | | Book value at beginning of year | Depreciation rate | Depreciation expense |
|------|------|------|------|------|
| 2006 | Year 1 | $100,000 | 20% | $20,000 |
| 2007 | Year 2 | $ 80,000 | 20% | 16,000 |
| Accum. Depr. Jan. 1, 2008 | | | | $36,000 |

*To calculate book value on January 1, 2008:*

| | |
|------|------|
| Historical cost | $100,000 |
| – Accum. depr. | 36,000 |
| Book value 1-1-08 | $ 64,000 |

*Step 2:  Calculate depreciation expense for current year and future years.*

($64,000 BV – $20,000 salvage value) ÷ 8 years remaining life = $5,500 depreciation expense per year

**Journal entry for 2008**

*In 2008 and in future years, the following depreciation entry is recorded:*

| | | |
|------|------|------|
| Depreciation expense | 5,500 | |
| Accumulated depreciation | | 5,500 |

### 3.  Changes in Reporting Entities

Another type of accounting change which may occur is a change in reporting entity.  A change in reporting entity occurs when a change in the structure of the organization is made which results in financial statements that represent a different or changed entity.  Some examples of a change in reporting entity include presenting consolidated statements in place of individual statements, a change in subsidiaries, or a change in the use of the equity method for an investment.

When there is a change in reporting entity, the change is retrospectively applied to the financial statements of all prior periods presented.  Previously issued interim statements are also presented on a retrospective basis.  Footnote disclosures for change in reporting entity include the nature and reason for the change, net income, other comprehensive income, and any related per share amounts for all periods presented.

### 4.  Correction of an Error

A correction of an error in previously issued financial statements requires a prior period adjustment by restating the financial statements.  Prior period adjustments are covered in the previous section of this module.

**TYPES OF ACCOUNTING CHANGES**

| Type of accounting change | Definition | Financial statement treatment | Financial statement disclosure |
|------|------|------|------|
| 1. Change in accounting principle | Change from the use of one generally accepted accounting principle to another generally accepted accounting principle | **Retrospective application:** Report cumulative effect of change in the carrying amounts of assets and liabilities as of the beginning of the first period presented, with an offsetting adjustment to the opening balance of retained earnings for that period.  Financial statements for each period are adjusted to reflect period-specific effects of the change for direct effects. | Disclose the nature and reason for the change; method of applying the change; description of prior period information that is retrospectively adjusted; effect of the change on income from continuing operations, net income, and any other financial statement line item; per share amounts for current period and adjusted periods; and a description of the indirect effects of the change and related per share amounts. |
| 2. Change in estimate | Change of estimated FS amount based on new information or experience | **Prospective:** Report in the period of the change and future periods.  Do not adjust financial statements of previous periods. | Disclose the effect on income from continuing operations, net income, and related per share amounts if the change affects several future periods. |
| 3. Change in reporting entity | Change that results in the financial statements representing a different entity | **Retrospective application:** Report financial statements of all periods to show financial information for the new reporting entity for those periods. | Disclose the type of change and the reasons for the change, the related effects on income before extraordinary items, net income, other comprehensive income, and related per share effects on EPS for all periods presented. |

## MULTIPLE-CHOICE QUESTIONS (1-26)

**1.** On January 1, 2006, Bray Company purchased for $240,000 a machine with a useful life of ten years and no salvage value. The machine was depreciated by the double-declining balance method and the carrying amount of the machine was $153,600 on December 31, 2007. Bray changed retroactively to the straight-line method on January 1, 2008. Bray can justify the change. According to SFAS 154, what should be the depreciation expense on this machine for the year ended December 31, 2008?

- a. $15,360
- b. $19,200
- c. $24,000
- d. $30,720

**Items 2 and 3** are based on the following:

On January 1, 2006, Warren Co. purchased a $600,000 machine, with a five-year useful life and no salvage value. The machine was depreciated by an accelerated method for book and tax purposes. The machine's carrying amount was $240,000 on December 31, 2007. On January 1, 2008, Warren changed retroactively to the straight-line method for financial reporting purposes. Warren can justify the change. Warren's income tax rate is 30%.

**2.** According to SFAS 154, in its 2008 income statement, what amount should Warren report as the cumulative effect of this change?

- a. $120,000
- b. $ 84,000
- c. $ 36,000
- d. $0

**3.** According to SFAS 154, on January 1, 2008, what amount should Warren report as deferred income tax liability as a result of the change?

- a. $120,000
- b. $ 72,000
- c. $ 36,000
- d. $0

**4.** On January 2, 2008, to better reflect the variable use of its only machine, Holly, Inc. elected to change its method of depreciation from the straight-line method to the units of production method. The original cost of the machine on January 2, 2006, was $50,000, and its estimated life was ten years. Holly estimates that the machine's total life is 50,000 machine hours.

Machine hours usage was 8,500 during 2006 and 3,500 during 2007.

Holly's income tax rate is 30%. According to SFAS 154, Holly should report the accounting change in its 2008 financial statements as a(n)

- a. Cumulative effect of a change in accounting principle of $2,000 in its income statement.
- b. Entry for current year depreciation expense on the income statement and treated on a prospective basis.
- c. Cumulative effect of a change in accounting principle of $1,400 in its income statement.
- d. Adjustment to beginning retained earnings of $1,400.

**5.** SFAS 154 specifies that the effects of a change in accounting principle should be recorded on a prospective basis when the change is from the

- a. Cash basis of accounting for vacation pay to the accrual basis.
- b. Straight-line method of depreciation for previously recorded assets to the double-declining balance method.
- c. Presentation of statements of individual companies to their inclusion in consolidated statements.
- d. Completed-contract method of accounting for long-term construction-type contracts to the percentage-of-completion method.

**6.** When a company changes from the straight-line method of depreciation for previously recorded assets to the double-declining balance method, which of the following should be used according to SFAS 154?

| | Cumulative effects of change in accounting principle | Retrospective application |
|---|---|---|
| a. | No | No |
| b. | No | Yes |
| c. | Yes | Yes |
| d. | Yes | No |

**Items 7 and 8** are based on the following:

During 2008, Orca Corp. decided to change from the FIFO method of inventory valuation to the weighted-average method. Inventory balances under each method were as follows:

| | *FIFO* | *Weighted-average* | |
|---|---|---|---|
| January 1, 2008 | $71,000 | $77,000 | 6,000 |
| December 31, 2008 | 79,000 | 83,000 | 4,000 |

Orca's income tax rate is 30%.

**7.** According to SFAS 154, in its 2008 financial statements, what amount should Orca report as the cumulative effect of this accounting change?

- a. $2,800
- b. $4,000
- c. $4,200
- d. $0

**8.** In accordance with SFAS 154, Orca should report the effect of this accounting change as a(n)

- a. Prior period adjustment.
- b. Component of income from continuing operations.
- c. Retrospective application to previous year's financial statements.
- d. Component of income after extraordinary items.

**9.** On January 1, 2008, Roem Corp. changed its inventory method to FIFO from LIFO for both financial and income tax reporting purposes. The change resulted in a $500,000 increase in the January 1, 2008 inventory, which is the only change that could be calculated from the accounting records. Assume that the income tax rate for all years is 30%. According to SFAS 154, retrospective application would result in

- a. An increase in ending inventory in the 2007 balance sheet.
- b. A decrease in ending inventory in the 2008 balance sheet.
- c. A decrease in net income in 2007.

d.  A gain from cumulative effect of change on the income statement in 2008.

**10.** According to SFAS 154, which of the following would receive treatment as a cumulative effect on an accounting change on the income statement?

|    | LIFO to weighted-average | FIFO to weighted-average |
|----|--------------------------|--------------------------|
| a. | Yes | Yes |
| b. | Yes | No |
| c. | No | No |
| d. | No | Yes |

**11.** On August 31, 2008, Harvey Co. decided to change from the FIFO periodic inventory system to the weighted-average periodic inventory system. Harvey is on a calendar year basis. SFAS 154 requires the cumulative effect of the change is determined

a.  As of January 1, 2008.
b.  As of August 31, 2008.
c.  During the eight months ending August 31, 2008, by a weighted-average of the purchases.
d.  As of the earliest period presented if practicable.

**12.** In 2008, Brighton Co. changed from the individual item approach to the aggregate approach in applying the lower of FIFO cost or market to inventories. SFAS 154 requires that the change should be reported in Brighton's financial statements as a

a.  Change in estimate on a prospective basis.
b.  Cumulative effect of change in accounting principle on the current year income statement.
c.  Retrospective application to the earliest period presented if practicable.
d.  Prior period adjustment with a separate disclosure.

**13.** On January 1, 2008, Poe Construction, Inc. changed to the percentage-of-completion method of income recognition for financial statement reporting but not for income tax reporting. Poe can justify this change in accounting principle. As of December 31, 2007, Poe compiled data showing that income under the completed-contract method aggregated $700,000. If the percentage-of-completion method had been used, the accumulated income through December 31, 2007, would have been $880,000. Assuming an income tax rate of 40% for all years, SFAS 154 requires that the cumulative effect of this accounting change to be reported by Poe as

a.  An increase in construction-in-progress for $180,000 in the 2007 balance sheet.
b.  A decrease in the beginning balance of retained earnings for $108,000 in 2008.
c.  A cumulative effect adjustment of $108,000 on the 2008 income statement.
d.  As an increase in ending retained earnings of $180,000 in 2007.

**14.** SFAS 154 requires that the effect of a change in accounting principle that is inseparable from the effect of a change in accounting estimate to be reported

a.  By restating the financial statements of all prior periods presented.
b.  As a correction of an error.
c.  As a component of income from continuing operations, in the period of change and future periods if the change affects both.

d.  As a separate disclosure after income from continuing operations, in the period of change and future periods if the change affects both.

**15.** Which of the following is considered a direct effect of a change in accounting principle according to SFAS 154?

a.  Deferred taxes.
b.  Profit sharing.
c.  Royalty payments.
d.  None of the above.

**16.** Indirect effects from a change in accounting principle should be reported

a.  Retrospectively to the earliest period presented.
b.  As a cumulative change in accounting principle in the current period.
c.  In the period in which the accounting change occurs.
d.  As a prior period adjustment.

**17.** According to SFAS 154, if it is impracticable to determine the cumulative effect of an accounting change to any of the prior periods, the accounting change should be accounted for

a.  As a prior period adjustment.
b.  On a prospective basis.
c.  As a cumulative effect change on the income statement.
d.  As an adjustment to retained earnings in the first period presented.

**18.** According to SFAS 154, if the cumulative effect of applying an accounting change can be determined but the period-specific effects on all periods cannot be determined, the cumulative effect of the change should be applied to

a.  The end balance of retained earnings of the earliest period presented.
b.  Net income of the current year.
c.  Retained earnings of the current year.
d.  The carrying value of the assets and liabilities at the beginning of the earliest period to which it can be applied.

**19.** On January 1, 2004, Taft Co. purchased a patent for $714,000. The patent is being amortized over its remaining legal life of fifteen years expiring on January 1, 2018. During 2007, Taft determined that the economic benefits of the patent would not last longer than ten years from the date of acquisition. What amount should be reported in the balance sheet for the patent, net of accumulated amortization, at December 31, 2007?

a.  $428,400
b.  $489,600
c.  $504,000
d.  $523,600

**20.** On January 1, 2004, Flax Co. purchased a machine for $528,000 and depreciated it by the straight-line method using an estimated useful life of eight years with no salvage value. On January 1, 2007, Flax determined that the machine had a useful life of six years from the date of acquisition and will have a salvage value of $48,000. An accounting change was made in 2007 to reflect these additional data. The accumulated depreciation for this machine should have a balance at December 31, 2007, of

a.  $292,000
b.  $308,000

    c.   $320,000
    d.   $352,000

**21.** How should the effect of a change in accounting estimate be accounted for?

    a.   By restating amounts reported in financial statements of prior periods.
    b.   By reporting pro forma amounts for prior periods.
    c.   As a prior period adjustment to beginning retained earnings.
    d.   In the period of change and future periods if the change affects both.

**22.** During 2007, Krey Co. increased the estimated quantity of copper recoverable from its mine. Krey uses the units of production depletion method. As a result of the change, which of the following should be reported in Krey's 2007 financial statements?

| | Cumulative effect of a change in accounting principle | Pro forma effects of retroactive application of new depletion base |
|---|---|---|
| a. | Yes | Yes |
| b. | Yes | No |
| c. | No | No |
| d. | No | Yes |

**23.** Oak Co. offers a three-year warranty on its products. Oak previously estimated warranty costs to be 2% of sales. Due to a technological advance in production at the beginning of 2007, Oak now believes 1% of sales to be a better estimate of warranty costs. Warranty costs of $80,000 and $96,000 were reported in 2005 and 2006, respectively. Sales for 2007 were $5,000,000. What amount should be disclosed in Oak's 2007 financial statements as warranty expense?

    a.   $ 50,000
    b.   $ 88,000
    c.   $100,000
    d.   $138,000

**24.** For 2006, Pac Co. estimated its two-year equipment warranty costs based on $100 per unit sold in 2006. Experience during 2007 indicated that the estimate should have been based on $110 per unit. The effect of this $10 difference from the estimate is reported

    a.   In 2007 income from continuing operations.
    b.   As an accounting change, net of tax, below 2007 income from continuing operations.
    c.   As an accounting change requiring 2006 financial statements to be restated.
    d.   As a correction of an error requiring 2006 financial statements to be restated.

**25.** A company has included in its consolidated financial statements this year a subsidiary acquired several years ago that was appropriately excluded from consolidation last year. SFAS 154 requires this to be reported as

    a.   An accounting change that should be reported prospectively.
    b.   An accounting change that should be reported retrospectively.
    c.   A correction of an error.
    d.   Neither an accounting change nor a correction of an error.

**26.** According to SFAS 154, which of the following statements is correct regarding accounting changes that result in

financial statements that are, in effect, the statements of a different reporting entity?

    a.   Cumulative-effect adjustments should be reported as separate items on the financial statements pertaining to the year of change.
    b.   No restatements or adjustments are required if the changes involve consolidated methods of accounting for subsidiaries.
    c.   No restatements or adjustments are required if the changes involve the cost or equity methods of accounting for investments.
    d.   The financial statements of all prior periods presented are adjusted retrospectively.

**SIMULATION PROBLEMS**

**Simulation Problem 1**                              (50 to 60 minutes)

| Situation | | | | | |
|---|---|---|---|---|---|
| | Accounting Changes | Calculations | Classification/ Disclosure | Communication | Research |

On January 2, 2008, Quo, Inc. hired Reed to be its controller.  During the year, Reed, working closely with Quo's president and outside accountants, made changes in accounting policies, corrected several errors dating from 2007 and before, and instituted new accounting policies.

Quo's 2008 financial statements will be presented in comparative form with its 2007 financial statements.  In 2008, Quo uses the guidance in SFAS 154 to account for any accounting changes.

| | Accounting Changes | | | | |
|---|---|---|---|---|---|
| Situation | | Calculations | Classification/ Disclosure | Communication | Research |

**Items 1 through 10** represent Quo's transactions.

List A represents possible classifications of these transactions as:  a change in accounting principle, a change in accounting estimate, a correction of an error in previously presented financial statements, or neither an accounting change nor an accounting error.

List B represents the general accounting treatment for these transactions.  These treatments are

- Retrospective application approach—Apply the new accounting principle to all prior periods presented showing the cumulative effect of the change in the carrying value of assets and liabilities at the beginning of the first period presented, and adjust financial statements presented to reflect period-specific effects of the change.
- Retroactive restatement approach—Restate the 2007 financial statements and adjust 2007 beginning retained earnings if the error or change affects a period prior to 2007 financial statements.
- Prospective approach—Report 2008 and future financial statements on the new basis, but do **not** restate 2007 financial statements.

For each item, select one from List A and one from List B.

| *List A (Select one treatment)* | *List B (Select one approach)* |
|---|---|
| A.   Change in accounting principle. | X.   Retrospective application approach. |
| B.   Change in accounting estimate. | Y.   Retroactive restatement approach. |
| C.   Correction of an error in previously presented financial statements. | Z.   Prospective approach. |
| D.   Neither an accounting change nor an accounting error. | |

*Items to be answered*

| | | List A Treatment (A) (B) (C) (D) | List B Approach (X) (Y) (Z) |
|---|---|---|---|
| 1. | Quo manufactures heavy equipment to customer specifications on a contract basis.  On the basis that it is preferable, accounting for these long-term contracts was switched from the completed-contract method to the percentage-of-completion method. | ○ ○ ○ ○ | ○ ○ ○ |
| 2. | As a result of a production breakthrough, Quo determined that manufacturing equipment previously depreciated over fifteen years should be depreciated over twenty years. | ○ ○ ○ ○ | ○ ○ ○ |
| 3. | The equipment that Quo manufactures is sold with a five-year warranty.  Because of a production breakthrough, Quo reduced its computation of warranty costs from 3% of sales to 1% of sales. | ○ ○ ○ ○ | ○ ○ ○ |
| 4. | Quo changed from LIFO to FIFO to account for its finished goods inventory. | ○ ○ ○ ○ | ○ ○ ○ |
| 5. | Quo changed from FIFO to average cost to account for its raw materials and work in process inventories. | ○ ○ ○ ○ | ○ ○ ○ |
| 6. | Quo sells extended service contracts on its products.  Because related services are performed over several years, in 2008 Quo changed from the cash method to the accrual method of recognizing income from these service contracts. | ○ ○ ○ ○ | ○ ○ ○ |

| | | List A Treatment | | | | | List B Approach | | |
|---|---|---|---|---|---|---|---|---|---|
| | | (A) | (B) | (C) | (D) | | (X) | (Y) | (Z) |

7. During 2008, Quo determined that an insurance premium paid and entirely expensed in 2007 was for the period January 1, 2007, through January 1, 2009. ○ ○ ○ ○   ○ ○ ○

8. Quo changed its method of depreciating office equipment from an accelerated method to the straight-line method to more closely reflect costs in later years. ○ ○ ○ ○   ○ ○ ○

9. Quo instituted a pension plan for all employees in 2008 and adopted Statement of Financial Accounting Standards 87, *Employers' Accounting for Pensions.* Quo had not previously had a pension plan. ○ ○ ○ ○   ○ ○ ○

10. During 2008, Quo increased its investment in Worth, Inc. from a 10% interest, purchased in 2007, to 30%, and acquired a seat on Worth's board of directors. As a result of its increased investment, Quo changed its method of accounting for investment in subsidiary from the cost adjusted for fair value method to the equity method. ○ ○ ○ ○   ○ ○ ○

| Situation | Accounting Changes | Calculations | Classification/ Disclosure | Communication | Research |
|---|---|---|---|---|---|

Quo has $500,000 in equipment and machinery that was acquired on January 2, 2006. Quo has been using the double-declining balance method to depreciate the equipment over an estimated 10-year economic life with no salvage. On January 1, 2008, Quo decides to change to the straight-line method with no salvage. Quo has a 40% tax rate.

Calculate the following amounts:

1. Accumulated depreciation as of 12/31/07

2. Depreciation expense for 2008

3. Accumulated depreciation as of 12/31/08

4. Indicate the amount of the accounting change shown net of tax if appropriate

| Situation | Accounting Changes | Calculations | Classification/ Disclosure | Communication | Research |
|---|---|---|---|---|---|

Quo made the following changes in its accounting policies.

• Quo changed its depreciation method for its production machinery from the double-declining balance method to the straight-line method effective January 1, 2008.
• Quo appropriately changed the salvage values used in computing depreciation for its office equipment.
• Quo appropriately changed the specific subsidiaries constituting the group of companies for which consolidated financial statements are presented.

For each of the items that Quo changed, identify whether Quo should show the following by choosing Yes or No in the appropriate columns.

| Change item | Cumulative effect of change in principle in net income of the period of change Yes | No | Pro forma effects of retroactive application for all prior periods presented currently Yes | No | Retrospective application to financial statements of all prior periods presented currently Yes | No |
|---|---|---|---|---|---|---|
| 1. Quo changed its depreciation method for its production machinery from the double-declining balance method to the straight-line method effective January 1, 2008. | ○ | ○ | ○ | ○ | ○ | ○ |
| 2. Quo appropriately changed the salvage values used in computing depreciation for its office equipment. | ○ | ○ | ○ | ○ | ○ | ○ |

| | Cumulative effect of change in principle in net income of the period of change | | Pro forma effects of retroactive application for all prior periods presented currently | | Retrospective application to financial statements of all prior periods presented currently | |
|---|---|---|---|---|---|---|
| *Change item* | *Yes* | *No* | *Yes* | *No* | *Yes* | *No* |
| **3.** Quo appropriately changed the specific subsidiaries constituting the group of companies for which consolidated financial statements are presented. | ○ | ○ | ○ | ○ | ○ | ○ |

| Situation | Accounting Changes | Calculations | Classification/ Disclosure | **Communication** | | Research |
|---|---|---|---|---|---|---|

Write a brief memorandum to the CEO of Quo, Inc. explaining how to account for each of the three changes.

To:      CEO, QUO, Inc.
From:   CPA Candidate
Re:      Changes in accounting

| |
|---|
| |

| Situation | Accounting Changes | Calculations | Classification/ Disclosure | Communication | **Research** |
|---|---|---|---|---|---|

Research each issue as to whether it is considered a change in accounting principle.  Copy the appropriate citation and place in the table below.

| | | |
|---|---|---|
| **1.** | Quo changed its depreciation method for its production machinery from the double-declining balance method to the straight-line method effective January 1, 2008. | |
| **2.** | Quo appropriately changed the salvage values used in computing depreciation for its office equipment. | |
| **3.** | Quo appropriately changed the specific subsidiaries constituting the group of companies for which consolidated financial statements are presented. | |

---

**Simulation Problem 2**                    (45 to 50 minutes)

| Situation | | | | |
|---|---|---|---|---|
| | Accounting Treatment | Accounting Change | Communication | Research |

Falk Co. began operations in January, 2007.  On January 2, 2008, Falk Co. hired a new controller.  During the year, the controller, working closely with Falk's president and outside accountants, made changes in existing accounting policies, instituted new accounting policies, and corrected several errors dating from prior to 2008.

Falk's financial statements for the year ended December 31, 2008, will not be presented in comparative form with its 2007 financial statements.  Falk uses the guidance in SFAS 154 to account for accounting changes in 2008.

List A represents possible classifications of these transactions as a change in accounting principle, a change in accounting estimate, correction of an error in previously presented financial statements, or neither an accounting change nor an error correction.

List B represents the general accounting treatment required for these transactions.  These treatments are

- Retrospective application approach—Apply the new accounting principle to all prior periods presented showing the cumulative effect of the change in the carrying value of assets and liabilities at the beginning of the first period presented, and adjust financial statements presented to reflect period-specific effects of the change.
- Retroactive restatement approach—Adjust 2008 beginning retained earnings if the error or change affects a period prior to 2008.

- Prospective approach—Report 2008 and future financial statements on the new basis, but do not adjust beginning retained earnings or include the cumulative effect of the change in the 2008 income statements.

| *List A—Type of change (Select one)* | *List B—General accounting treatment (Select one)* |
|---|---|
| A. Change in accounting principle. | X. Retroactive application approach. |
| B. Change in accounting estimate. | Y. Retroactive restatement approach. |
| C. Correction of an error in previously presented financial statements. | Z. Prospective approach. |
| D. Neither an accounting change nor an error correction. | |

| Situation | Accounting Treatment | Accounting Change | Communication | Research |
|---|---|---|---|---|

For **Items 1 and 2,** select a classification for each transaction from List A and the general accounting treatment required to report the change from List B.

|  | *List A Type of Change* (A) (B) (C) (D) | *List B Accounting Treatment* (X) (Y) (Z) |
|---|---|---|
| 1. | Falk manufactures customized equipment to customer specifications on a contract basis. Falk changed its method of accounting for these long-term contracts from the completed-contract method to the percentage-of-completion method because Falk is now able to make reasonable estimates of future construction costs. | ○ ○ ○ ○    ○ ○ ○ |
| 2. | Based on improved collection procedures, Falk changed the percentage of credit sales used to determine the allowance for uncollectible accounts from 2% to 1%. | ○ ○ ○ ○    ○ ○ ○ |

| Situation | Accounting Treatment | Accounting Change | Communication | Research |
|---|---|---|---|---|

On January 1, 2008, Falk changed from the average cost method to the FIFO method to account for its inventory. Ending inventory for each method was as follows:

| Year | Average cost | FIFO |
|---|---|---|
| 2007 | $5,000 | $ 7,000 |
| 2008 | $9,000 | $14,000 |

Falk's income statement information calculated by the average cost method was as follows:

**Falk Corporation**
**INCOME STATEMENT**

|  | Before adjustments for the year ending 12-31-08 | Before adjustment for the year ending 12-31-07 |
|---|---|---|
| Sales | $130,000 | $100,000 |
| Cost of goods sold | 90,000 | 70,000 |
| Gross profit | 40,000 | 30,000 |
| Operating expense | 20,000 | 17,000 |
| Earnings before taxes | 20,000 | 13,000 |
| Tax expense | 8,000 | 5,200 |
| Net income | 12,000 | 7,800 |

Assume that Falk has no book/tax differences or deferred taxes. Falk accrues tax expense on December 31 of each year and pays the tax in January of the following year. The income tax rate is 40%.

Prepare an adjusted income statement for 2008 and 2007 after the change to the FIFO inventory method.

**Falk Corporation**
**INCOME STATEMENT**

|  | Adjusted for the year ending 12-31-08 | Adjusted for the year ending 12-31-07 |
|---|---|---|
| Sales | | |
| Cost of goods sold | | |
| Gross profit | | |
| Operating expense | | |
| Earnings before taxes | | |
| Tax expense | | |
| Net income | | |

Indicate the adjusted balances on the December 31 balance sheet for each year.

|  | December 31, 2008 | December 31, 2007 |
|---|---|---|
| Inventory | | |
| Income tax liability | | |
| Retained earnings | | |

| Situation | Accounting Treatment | Accounting Change | Communication | Research |
|---|---|---|---|---|

On January 1, 2008, Falk Co. made the following changes in its accounting policies:

- Changed from the LIFO inventory method to the FIFO inventory method.
- Adopted the straight-line depreciation method for all future machinery acquisitions, but continued to use sum-of-the-years' digits depreciation method for all machinery purchased before 2008.
- Changed from the cash to the accrual basis of accounting for accumulated vacation pay.

Falk prepares two-year comparative financial statements. Write a brief memorandum to the new controller at Falk explaining how these changes should be reported. Specifically, you should address each of the following issues:

1. What type of accounting change is the change from the LIFO to the FIFO inventory costing method? How should Falk report this change in its 2007 comparative financial statements?
2. What type of accounting change is Falk's change from the sum-of-the-years' digits to the straight-line depreciation method for all machinery purchased after 2006? How should Falk report this change?
3. What type of change occurs when recognition of vacation pay expense is changed from the cash basis to the accrual basis? How should Falk report this change?

To:     Controller of Falk Co.
From:   CPA Candidate
Re:     Changes in accounting principle

| Situation | Accounting Treatment | Accounting Change | Communication | Research |
|---|---|---|---|---|

Identify the authoritative literature that governs the accounting treatment of a change from the completed-contract method to the percentage-of-completion method.

**MULTIPLE-CHOICE ANSWERS**

| | | | | | | | | | |
|---|---|---|---|---|---|---|---|---|---|
| 1. b | __ __ | 7. d | __ __ | 13. a | __ __ | 19. b | __ __ | 25. b | __ __ |
| 2. d | __ __ | 8. c | __ __ | 14. c | __ __ | 20. a | __ __ | 26. d | __ __ |
| 3. d | __ __ | 9. a | __ __ | 15. a | __ __ | 21. d | __ __ | | |
| 4. b | __ __ | 10. c | __ __ | 16. c | __ __ | 22. c | __ __ | | |
| 5. b | __ __ | 11. d | __ __ | 17. b | __ __ | 23. a | __ __ | 1st: __/26 = __% |
| 6. a | __ __ | 12. c | __ __ | 18. d | __ __ | 24. a | __ __ | 2nd: __/26 = __% |

**MULTIPLE-CHOICE ANSWER EXPLANATIONS**

## C.1.  Changes in Accounting Principles (SFAS 154)

**1.    (b)**    Per SFAS 154, a change in depreciation method is a change in method that is not distinguishable from a change in estimate, and is accounted for as a change in estimate. The change is reported on a prospective basis in the current year and future years. Book value as of 1/1/08 = $153,600/8 years remaining = $19,200 depreciation expense in 2008.

**2.    (d)**    Zero. Per SFAS 154, a change in depreciation method is a change in method that is not distinguishable from a change in estimate, and is accounted for as a change in estimate. The change is reported on a prospective basis in the current year and future years. A change in depreciation method is no longer given cumulative effect treatment on the income statement.

**3.    (d)**    Zero. Per SFAS 154, a change in depreciation method is a change in method that is not distinguishable from a change in estimate, and is accounted for as a change in estimate. The change is reported on a prospective basis in the current year and future years. Because a change in depreciation method is no longer given cumulative effect treatment on the income statement, there are no deferred income tax liability effects.

**4.    (b)**    Per SFAS 154, a change in depreciation method is a change in method that is not distinguishable from a change in estimate, and is accounted for as a change in estimate. The change is reported on a prospective basis in the current year and future years.

**5.    (b)**    The requirement is to determine which accounting change should be reported on a prospective basis as per SFAS 154. According to SFAS 154, a change in depreciation method is a change in principle that is not distinguishable from a change in estimate, and is accounted for as a change in estimate. The change is reported on a prospective basis in the current year and future years. A change from the cash basis to the accrual basis of accounting is a change from non-GAAP to GAAP accounted for as the correction of an error. A change in reporting entity requires retrospective application to the earliest year presented if practicable. A change in the method of accounting for long-term contracts requires retrospective application to the earliest year presented if practicable.

**6.    (a)**    The requirement is to determine whether a change in depreciation method from straight-line to double-declining balance should be reported as a cumulative effect of a change in accounting principle and receive retrospective application. Per SFAS 154, a change in depreciation method is a change in method that is not distinguishable from a change in estimate, and is accounted for as a change in estimate. The change is reported on a prospective basis in the

current year and future years. Therefore, it does not receive cumulative effect treatment or retrospective treatment.

**7.    (d)**    Per SFAS 154, a change in inventory method no longer receives cumulative effect treatment on the income statement. Instead, the accounting change is given retrospective application to the earliest period presented, if practicable. Therefore, the answer is zero.

**8.    (c)**    Per SFAS 154, a change in inventory method no longer receives cumulative effect treatment on the income statement. Instead, the accounting change is given retrospective application to the earliest period presented, if practicable.

**9.    (a)**    Per SFAS 154, retrospective application requires applying the new principle to the earliest period presented if practicable. Because 2008 beginning inventory is the previous year's ending inventory, the new principle can be applied to the 2007 financial statements. This would result in an increase in ending inventory in the balance sheet for 2007, a decrease in cost of goods sold in 2007, and an increase in the beginning inventory, which would result in a higher cost of goods sold and a lower net income for 2008.

**10.    (c)**    A change in inventory method no longer receives cumulative effect treatment on the income statement. Instead, SFAS 154 requires that the accounting change be given retrospective application to the earliest period presented, if practicable.

**11.    (d)**    Per SFAS 154, retrospective application requires the change to be calculated for the earliest period presented if practicable.

**12.    (c)**    A change in inventory method no longer receives cumulative effect treatment on the income statement. Per SFAS 154, the accounting change is given retrospective application to the earliest period presented, if practicable.

**13.    (a)**    The requirement is to indicate how a change in accounting principle from the completed-contract method to the percentage-of-completion method should be reported. Per SFAS 154, a change in the method of accounting for long-term contracts requires retrospective application to the earliest year practicable. This results in a $180,000 increase in income for 2007. The assets would be adjusted for the earliest period affected, and construction-in-progress would increase by $180,000. Net income for 2007 would increase by $108,000 ($180,000 less 40% tax effects), and the deferred tax liability account would increase in 2007 by $72,000.

**14.    (c)**    Per SFAS 154, the effect of a change in accounting principle which is inseparable from the effect of a change in accounting estimate should be accounted for as a change in accounting estimate. Changes in estimate should be accounted for in the period of change and also in any affected future periods as a component of income from continuing operations. Financial statements are only restated for changes due to an error. Errors include mathematical mistakes, mistakes in applying accounting principles, oversights or misuse of available facts, and changes from unacceptable accounting principles to GAAP. The situation described in this question does not meet the description of an error.

**15.** **(a)** Per SFAS 154, deferred taxes is a direct effect from the change in accounting principle, and its effects should be recorded in the earliest period presented, if practicable. Profit sharing and royalty payments are indirect effects and should be reported in the period of the change.

**16.** **(c)** Per SFAS 154, indirect effects of a change in accounting principle should be reported in the period in which the accounting change occurs. Direct effects are reported retrospectively to the earliest period presented, if practicable. Answers (b) and (d) are incorrect since accounting changes are no longer treated as cumulative effect changes or prior period adjustments.

**17.** **(b)** Per SFAS 154, if it is impracticable to determine the cumulative effect of an accounting change to any of the prior periods, the accounting change should be accounted for on a prospective basis. Answer (a) is incorrect because accounting changes are no longer treated as prior period adjustments. Answer (c) is incorrect because accounting changes are no longer treated as cumulative effect changes on the income statement. Answer (d) is incorrect because the change would not be to retained earnings in the first period presented.

**18.** **(d)** Per SFAS 154, if the cumulative effect of applying an accounting change can be determined, but the period-specific effects on all periods cannot be determined, the cumulative effect of the change should be applied to the carrying value of the assets and liabilities at the beginning of the earliest period to which it can be determined.

### C.2. Change in Accounting Estimates (SFAS 154)

**19.** **(b)** This situation is a change in accounting estimate and should be accounted for currently and prospectively. From 1/1/04 to 12/31/06, patent amortization was recorded using a fifteen-year life. Yearly amortization was $47,600 ($714,000 ÷ 15), accumulated amortization at 12/31/06 was $142,800 ($47,600 × 3), and the book value of the patent at 12/31/06 was $571,200 ($714,000 − $142,800). Beginning in 2007, this book value must be amortized over its remaining useful life of 7 years (10 years − 3 years). Therefore, 2007 amortization is $81,600 ($571,200 ÷ 7) and the 12/31/07 book value is $489,600 ($571,200 − $81,600).

**20.** **(a)** From 1/1/04 to 12/31/06, depreciation was recorded using an eight-year life. Yearly depreciation was $66,000 ($528,000 ÷ 8), and accumulated depreciation at 12/31/06 was $198,000 (3 × $66,000). In 2007, the estimated useful life was changed to six years total with a salvage value of $48,000. Therefore, the 12/31/06 book value ($528,000 − $198,000 = $330,000) is depreciated down to the $48,000 salvage value over a remaining useful life of three years (six years total − three years already recorded). Depreciation expense for 2007 is $94,000 [($330,000 − $48,000) ÷ 3], increasing accumulated depreciation to $292,000 ($198,000 + $94,000).

**21.** **(d)** SFAS 154 states that changes in accounting estimate are to be accounted for in the period of change and in future periods if the change affects both (i.e., **prospectively**). Pro forma amounts are presented for changes in accounting principle accounted for using the **current** (cumulative effect) approach. Answers (a) and (c) are incorrect because they apply to **retroactive**-type changes in principle and error correction, respectively.

**22.** **(c)** SFAS 154 provides examples of items for which estimates are required to prepare financial statements. Recoverable mineral reserves are one of the provided examples. SFAS 154 states that the effect of a change in accounting estimate should be accounted for in (a) the period of change if the change affects that period only, or (b) the period of change and future periods if the change affects both. SFAS 154 further states that a change in an estimate should not be accounted for by restating amounts reported in financial statements of prior periods or by reporting pro forma amounts for prior periods.

**23.** **(a)** A change in estimated warranty costs due to technological advances in production qualifies as a change in accounting estimate. Changes in estimate are treated prospectively; there is no retroactive restatement, and the new estimate is used in current and future years. Therefore, in 2007, Oak should use the new estimate of 1% and report warranty expense of $50,000 ($5,000,000 × 1%).

**24.** **(a)** A change in equipment warranty costs based on additional information obtained through experience qualifies as a change in accounting estimate. Changes in estimate should be accounted for in the period of change as a component of income from continuing operations and in future periods if necessary. Accounting changes reported net of tax below income from continuing operations are cumulative effects of changes in accounting principle. No restatement is required for a change in estimate.

### C.3. Change in Reporting Entity (SFAS 154)

**25.** **(b)** Per SFAS 154, an accounting change that is a change in reporting entity is given retrospective application to the earliest period presented, if practicable. The term "restatement" refers only to correction of errors in previously issued financial statements.

**26.** **(d)** Per SFAS 154, an accounting change that is a change in reporting entity is given retrospective application to the earliest period presented, if practicable. The term "restatement" refers only to correction of errors in previously issued financial statements.

**SOLUTIONS TO SIMULATION PROBLEMS**

**Simulation Problem 1**

| Situation | Accounting Changes | | Calculations | Classification/ Disclosure | Communication | Research |
|---|---|---|---|---|---|---|

|  | List A *Treatment* (A) (B) (C) (D) | List B *Approach* (X) (Y) (Z) |
|---|---|---|

1. Quo manufactures heavy equipment to customer specifications on a contract basis. On the basis that it is preferable, accounting for these long-term contracts was switched from the completed-contract method to the percentage-of-completion method.  **(A) ● ○ ○ ○** — **(X) ● ○ ○**

2. As a result of a production breakthrough, Quo determined that manufacturing equipment previously depreciated over fifteen years should be depreciated over twenty years.  **○ ● ○ ○** — **○ ○ ●**

3. The equipment that Quo manufactures is sold with a five-year warranty. Because of a production breakthrough, Quo reduced its computation of warranty costs from 3% of sales to 1% of sales.  **○ ● ○ ○** — **○ ○ ●**

4. Quo changed from LIFO to FIFO to account for its finished goods inventory.  **● ○ ○ ○** — **● ○ ○**

5. Quo changed from FIFO to average cost to account for its raw materials and work in process inventories.  **● ○ ○ ○** — **● ○ ○**

6. Quo sells extended service contracts on its products. Because related services are performed over several years, in 2008 Quo changed from the cash method to the accrual method of recognizing income from these service contracts.  **○ ○ ● ○** — **○ ● ○**

7. During 2008, Quo determined that an insurance premium paid and entirely expensed in 2007 was for the period January 1, 2007, through January 1, 2009.  **○ ○ ● ○** — **○ ● ○**

8. Quo changed its method of depreciating office equipment from an accelerated method to the straight-line method to more closely reflect costs in later years.  **● ○ ○ ○** — **○ ○ ●**

9. Quo instituted a pension plan for all employees in 2008 and adopted Statement of Financial Accounting Standards 87, *Employers' Accounting for Pensions.* Quo had not previously had a pension plan.  **○ ○ ○ ●** — **○ ○ ●**

10. During 2008, Quo increased its investment in Worth, Inc. from a 10% interest, purchased in 2007, to 30%, and acquired a seat on Worth's board of directors. As a result of its increased investment, Quo changed its method of accounting for investment in subsidiary from the cost adjusted for fair value method to the equity method.  **○ ○ ○ ●** — **○ ● ○**

**Explanation of solutions**

1.  **(A,X)** This situation represents a change in the method of accounting for long-term construction-type contracts and requires retrospective application for all periods presented.

2.  **(B,Z)** This situation is not a change in accounting principle but is a change in an estimate and should be handled prospectively.

3.  **(B,Z)** This situation is a change in an estimate. The change in the percentage of warranty costs is not a change in accounting principle. Changes in estimate are handled prospectively.

4.  **(A,X)** This situation is a change from one acceptable accounting principle to another and requires retrospective application.

5.  **(A,X)** This situation is a change from one acceptable accounting method to another and requires the retrospective application approach.

6.  **(C,Y)** The use of the cash method is considered an error since that method is generally **not** acceptable. The switch to an acceptable method (accrual) is considered the correction of an error and requires the retroactive restatement approach.

7.  **(C,Y)** The write-off of the insurance premium was an error. Since comparative financial statements are prepared, past years must be corrected using the retroactive restatement approach even though this error is self-correcting after two years.

**8.  (A,Z)**  This situation is a change in method which is considered a change in estimate effected by a change in principle.  Per SFAS 154, a change in depreciation method requires prospective application.

**9.  (D,Z)**  Since the company did not previously account for pensions this situation is simply the adoption of an appropriate accounting principle for pensions.  No change in principle occurs.

**10.  (D,Y)**  Quo's increase in ownership interest (10% to 30%) and its acquisition of a seat on Worth's board of directors has given Quo the ability to exercise significant influence in the operating decisions of Worth.  Therefore, according to APB 18, Quo should adopt the equity method to account for its investment in Worth.  The cost adjusted for fair value method is no longer applicable due to the change in Quo's investment in Worth.  However, the change from the cost adjusted for fair value method to the equity method is not a change in accounting principle.  A change in accounting principle occurs when an accounting principle different from the one used previously for reporting purposes is adopted.  For a change to occur, a choice between two or more accounting principles must exist (SFAS 154).  In this case, the change in Quo's situation dictates that the equity method be used to account for the investment.  Quo's current economic situation is clearly different and this necessitates the adoption of a different accounting principle (SFAS 154).  Consequently, this is not an accounting change.  However, APB 18 requires that the investment account be retroactively restated to reflect balances as if the equity method had always been used.

| Situation | Accounting Changes | Calculations | Classification/ Disclosure | Communication | Research |
|---|---|---|---|---|---|
| **1.** Accumulated depreciation as of 12/31/07 | | | | | $180,000 |
| **2.** Depreciation expense for 2008 | | | | | $ 40,000 |
| **3.** Accumulated depreciation as of 12/31/08 | | | | | $220,000 |
| **4.** Indicate the amount of the accounting change shown net of tax if appropriate | | | | | $     0 |

**Explanation of solutions**

**1.**  Before change, Quo used double-declining balance and 10-year life

| | | | | |
|---|---|---|---|---|
| 2006 | 1/10 × 2 × $500,000 book value | = | $100,000 | depreciation expense |
| 2007 | 1/10 × 2 × $400,000 new book value | = | $ 80,000 | depreciation expense |
| | Accumulated depreciation 12/31/07 | | $180,000 | |

**2.**  To calculate depreciation expense for 2008:

| | |
|---|---|
| Historical cost | $500,000 |
| – Accum. depreciation | (180,000) |
| Book value | $320,000 |

($320,000 – $0 salvage) ÷ 8 years remaining life = $40,000 depreciation expense

**3.**  To calculate accumulated depreciation as of 12/31/08:

| | |
|---|---|
| 2006 | $100,000 |
| 2007 | 80,000 |
| 2008 | 40,000 |
| Accum. depr. 12/31/08 | $220,000 |

**4.**  Accounting change net of tax – zero.  SFAS 154 treats changes in depreciation method as a change in estimate effected by a change in method.  Therefore, a change in depreciation is accounted for on a prospective basis.

| Situation | Accounting Changes | Calculations | Classification/ Disclosure | Communication | Research |
|---|---|---|---|---|---|

| | Change item | Cumulative effect of change in principle in net income of the period of change | | Pro forma effects of retroactive application for all prior periods presented currently | | Retrospective application to financial statements of all prior periods presented currently | |
|---|---|---|---|---|---|---|---|
| | | *Yes* | *No* | *Yes* | *No* | *Yes* | *No* |
| **1.** | Quo changed its depreciation method for its production machinery from the double-declining balance method to the straight-line method effective January 1, 2008. | ○ | ● | ○ | ● | ○ | ● |

| Change item | Cumulative effect of change in principle in net income of the period of change | | Pro forma effects of retroactive application for all prior periods presented currently | | Retrospective application to financial statements of all prior periods presented currently | |
|---|---|---|---|---|---|---|
| | *Yes* | *No* | *Yes* | *No* | *Yes* | *No* |
| **2.** Quo appropriately changed the salvage values used in computing depreciation for its office equipment. | ○ | ● | ○ | ● | ○ | ● |
| **3.** Quo appropriately changed the specific subsidiaries constituting the group of companies for which consolidated financial statements are presented. | ○ | ● | ○ | ● | ● | ○ |

**Explanation of solutions**

**1. (N,N,N)** Quo's change in depreciation method is a change in accounting estimate effected by a change in accounting principle. This change would be accounted for on a prospective basis in the current year and future periods.

**2. (N,N,N)** Quo's change in salvage values is a change in accounting estimate. Quo would not report a cumulative effect, nor pro forma effects, nor would prior period financial statements be restated.

**3. (N,N,Y)** Quo's change in the specific subsidiaries constituting the group of companies for which consolidated financial statements are presented is a change in reporting entity. The change in reporting entity requires the change to be retrospectively applied to the financial statements of all prior periods presented to show financial information for the new reporting entity.

| Situation | Accounting Changes | Calculations | Classification/ Disclosure | Communication | Research |
|---|---|---|---|---|---|

To:    CEO, Quo, Inc.
From:  CPA Candidate
Re:    Changes in accounting methods

During 2008, Quo made changes in accounting for certain items. Although these may appear to be similar in nature, for accounting purposes, the changes are handled differently.

First, Quo changed its depreciation method for its production machinery from the double-declining balance method to the straight-line method. This change in depreciation method is considered a change in accounting principle. The change in principle is considered a change in accounting estimate effected by a change in accounting principle. The change in estimate is accounted for on a prospective basis in the current year and future periods. Financial statements of prior periods should not be restated.

The second change made during 2008 was to change the salvage values used in computing depreciation for office equipment. Quo's change in salvage value is a change in estimate and is accounted for on a prospective basis. Quo would not report a cumulative effect, nor pro forma effects, nor would prior period financial statements be restated.

The third change was a change in the specific subsidiaries constituting the group of companies for which Quo prepares consolidated financial statements. This change in subsidiaries constituting the group of companies for which consolidated financial statements are presented is considered a change in reporting entity. The change in reporting entity requires the change to be retrospectively applied to the financial statements of all prior periods presented to show financial information for the new reporting entity.

| Situation | Accounting Changes | Calculations | Classification/ Disclosure | Communication | Research |
|---|---|---|---|---|---|

**1.** Quo changed its depreciation method for its production machinery from the double-declining balance method to the straight-line method effective January 1, 2008.

**FAS 154, Para 20 or Current Text A07.120**

20. Distinguishing between a change in accounting principle and a change in an accounting estimate is sometimes difficult. In some cases, a change in accounting estimate is effected by a change in accounting principle. One example of this type of change is a change in method of depreciation, amortization, or depletion for long-lived, nonfinancial assets (hereinafter referred to as depreciation method). The new depreciation method is adopted in partial or complete recognition of a change in the estimated future benefits inherent in the asset, the pattern of consumption of those benefits, or the information available to the entity about those benefits. The effect of the change in accounting principle, or the method of applying it, may be inseparable from the effect of the change in ac-

counting estimate. Changes of that type often are related to the continuing process of obtaining additional information and revising estimates and, therefore, are considered changes in estimates for purposes of applying this Statement.

**FAS 154, Para 2(e) or Current Text A07.405**

2. The following terms are defined as used in this Statement:

e. Change in accounting estimate effected by a change in accounting principle—a change in accounting estimate that is inseparable from the effect of a related change in accounting principle. An example of a change in estimate effected by a change in principle is a change in the method of depreciation, amortization, or depletion for long-lived, nonfinancial assets.

**2.** Quo appropriately changed the salvage values used in computing depreciation for its office equipment.

**FAS 154, Para 2(d) or Current Text A07.404**

2. The following terms are defined as used in this Statement:

d. Change in accounting estimate—a change that has the effect of adjusting the carrying amount of an existing asset or liability or altering the subsequent accounting for existing or future assets or liabilities. A change in accounting estimate is a necessary consequence of the assessment, in conjunction with the periodic presentation of financial statements, of the present status and expected future benefits and obligations associated with assets and liabilities. Changes in accounting estimates result from new information. Examples of items for which estimates are necessary are uncollectible receivables, inventory obsolescence, service lives and salvage values of depreciable assets, and warranty obligations.

**3.** Quo appropriately changed the specific subsidiaries constituting the group of companies for which consolidated financial statements are presented.

**Change in the Reporting Entity**
**FAS 154, Para 2(f) or Current Text A07.406**

2. The following terms are defined as used in this Statement:

f. Change in the reporting entity—a change that results in financial statements that, in effect, are those of a different reporting entity. A change in the reporting entity is limited mainly to (1) presenting consolidated or combined financial statements in place of financial statements of individual entities, (2) changing specific subsidiaries that make up the group of entities for which consolidated financial statements are presented, and (3) changing the entities included in combined financial statements. Neither a business combination accounted for by the purchase method nor the consolidation of a variable interest entity pursuant to FASB Interpretation No. 46 (revised December 2004), Consolidation of Variable Interest Entities, is a change in reporting entity.

---

## Simulation Problem 2

| Situation | Accounting Treatment | Accounting Change | Communication | Research |
|---|---|---|---|---|

| | List A<br>*Type of Change*<br>(A) (B) (C) (D) | List B<br>*Accounting Treatment*<br>(X) (Y) (Z) |
|---|---|---|
| **1.** Falk manufactures customized equipment to customer specifications on a contract basis. Falk changed its method of accounting for these long-term contracts from the completed-contract method to the percentage-of-completion method because Falk is now able to make reasonable estimates of future construction costs. | ● ○ ○ ○ | ● ○ ○ |
| **2.** Based on improved collection procedures, Falk changed the percentage of credit sales used to determine the allowance for uncollectible accounts from 2% to 1%. | ○ ● ○ ○ | ○ ○ ● |

**Explanation of solutions**

**1. (A,X)** Changing from using the completed-contract method to the percentage-of-completion method is a change in accounting principle per SFAS 154.  Therefore, retrospective application to all periods presented is required.

**2. (B,Z)** The percentage of net credit sales used in determining the amount to be added to the allowance for uncollectible accounts is an estimate made by management.  Changing the percentage is a change in accounting estimate, which is treated prospectively.

| Situation | Accounting Treatment | Accounting Change | Communication | Research |
|-----------|----------------------|-------------------|---------------|----------|

**Falk Corporation**
**INCOME STATEMENT**

|  | Adjusted for the year ending 12-31-08 | Adjusted for the year ending 12-31-07 |
|--|------------------------------------|------------------------------------|
| Sales | $130,000 | $100,000 |
| Cost of goods sold | 87,000 | 68,000 |
| Gross profit | 43,000 | 32,000 |
| Operating expenses | 20,000 | 17,000 |
| Earnings before taxes | 23,000 | 15,000 |
| Income tax expense (40%) | 9,200 | 6,000 |
| Net income | 13,800 | 9,000 |

|  | December 31, 2008 | December 31, 2007 |
|--|-------------------|-------------------|
| Inventory | $14,000 | $7,000 |
| Income tax liability | 10,000 | 6,000 |
| Retained earnings | 16,800 | 9,000 |

**Explanation of solutions:**

To calculate cost of goods sold using FIFO method, you must first calculate purchases using the average cost method. Using T-accounts for analysis, the amounts are as shown below.

*Inventory*
*(Weighted-average method)*

| | | | |
|--|--|--|--|
| 1-1-07 | -0- | | |
| Purchases | 75,000 | 70,000 | CGS |
| 12-31-07 | 5,000 | | |
| Purchases | 94,000 | 90,000 | CGS |
| 12-31-08 | 9,000 | | |

*Inventory*
*(FIFO method)*

| | | | |
|--|--|--|--|
| 1-1-06 | -0- | 68,000 | CGS |
| Purchases | 75,000 | | |
| 12-31-06 | 7,000 | 87,000 | CGS |
| Purchases | 94,000 | | |
| 12-31-07 | 14,000 | | |

Income tax liability for December 31, 2008, is calculated as:

| | |
|--|--|
| 2008 earnings before taxes 23,000 × 40% = | $9,200 |
| 2007 adjustment to earnings before taxes 2,000 × 40% | + 800 |
| Total income tax liability at 12-31-08 | $10,000 |

Retained earnings as of December 31, 2008, is calculated as:

| | |
|--|--|
| Adjusted NI 2007 | $ 9,000 |
| Adjusted NI 2008 | 13,800 |
| Retained earnings 12/31/08 | $22,800 |

| Situation | Accounting Treatment | Accounting Change | Communication | Research |
|---|---|---|---|---|

To:     Controller of Falk Co.
From:   CPA Candidate
Re:     Changes in accounting principle

The appropriate accounting for the accounting changes made by Falk Co. is described below.

A change from the LIFO inventory method to the FIFO inventory method is a change in accounting principle. The company should apply this change retrospectively by adjusting the financial statements of the previous periods presented. Retrospective application requires that the cumulative effect of the change to the new accounting principle is reflected by adjusting the carrying amounts of assets and liabilities as of the beginning of the first period presented. An offsetting adjustment, if any, should be made to the opening balance of retained earnings for that period. Financial statements for each period should also be adjusted to reflect the period-specific effects of applying the new accounting principle. However, only the direct effects of the change should be shown. Notes to the financial statements should disclose the nature of the change, the reason for the change, as well as the effects of the change on income from continuing operations, net income, financial statement line item effects, and any per share amounts for the current period and prior periods.

The company's change to the straight-line depreciation method for all future machinery acquisitions is not a change in accounting principle because the previously recorded assets will continue to be depreciated using the sum-of-the-years' digits method. The nature and justification for the change in depreciation methods should be disclosed in the notes to the 2007 comparative financial statements. The 2006 financial statements are unaffected by the change, but the effects of the change on 2007 income components should be disclosed.

A change from the cash basis of vacation pay expense recognition to the accrual basis is a change from an accounting principle that is not generally accepted to one that is generally accepted. Such a change is considered correction of an error. Falk should restate the 2006 financial statements, including adjustment for the effect on January 1, 2006 retained earnings, for prior-period amounts. Falk Co. should disclose the nature and details of the correction in notes to the 2007 financial statements.

If you have any additional questions, please contact me.

| Situation | Accounting Treatment | Accounting Change | Communication | Research |
|---|---|---|---|---|

**FAS 154, Para 2(c) or Current Text A07.403**

2.   The following terms are defined as used in this Statement:

c.   Change in accounting principle—a change from one generally accepted accounting principle to another generally accepted accounting principle when there are two or more generally accepted accounting principles that apply or when the accounting principle formerly used is no longer generally accepted. A change in the method of applying an accounting principle also is considered a change in accounting principle.

## D.  Financial Statements

### 1.  Income and Retained Earnings Statement Formats

Review the outlines of APB 9, APB 30, SFAS 130, SFAS 144, SFAS 146, SFAS 154, SFAS 157, and SFAS 159 before proceeding.  Income statements may be prepared using a multiple-step or single-step form.  The income (earnings) and comprehensive income statement illustrated below for Totman Company includes separate categories for continuing operations, discontinued operations, and extraordinary items.  SFAS 154 now requires retrospective application for all changes in accounting principle.  Therefore, cumulative effect of change in accounting principle is no longer disclosed as a separate item on the income statement.  The other comprehensive income is required per SFAS 130.  The purpose of these separate categories is to enable users to assess future cash flows.  The Totman Co. statement is a combined statement of income and comprehensive income.

*Totman Company*
**STATEMENT OF EARNINGS AND COMPREHENSIVE INCOME**
*For the Year Ended December 31, 2007*

|  |  |  |  |
|---|---|---:|---:|
|  | Sales |  | $2,677 |
|  | Cost of goods sold |  | 1,489 |
| See | Gross margin on sales |  | 1,188 |
| Note | Operating expenses |  |  |
| #5 |   Selling expenses | $ 220 |  |
| below |   Administrative expenses | 255 | 475 |
|  | Operating income |  | 713 |
|  | Other revenues and gains |  |  |
|  |   Interest revenue | $   5 |  |
|  |   Equity in Huskie Co. earnings | 15 |  |
|  |   Gain on sale of available-for-sale securities | 45 | 65 |
|  | Other expenses and losses |  |  |
|  |   Interest expense | (60) |  |
|  |   Loss from permanent impairment of value of manufacturing facilities | (120) | (180) |
|  | Income from continuing operations before provision for income taxes |  | 598 |
|  | Provision for income taxes |  |  |
|  |   Current | $ 189 |  |
|  |   Deferred | 50 | 239 |
|  | Income from continuing operations |  | 359(a) |
|  | *Discontinued operations:* |  |  |
|  |   Loss from operations of discontinued Division Z, including loss on disposal of $230 | (1,265) |  |
|  |   Income tax benefit | (466) | (799)(b) |
|  | Income (loss) before extraordinary item |  | (440) |
|  |   Extraordinary item:  Loss due to earthquake (less applicable income taxes of $30) |  | (45)(b) |
|  | Net earnings (loss) |  | (485)(a) |
|  | *Other comprehensive income:* |  |  |
|  |   Foreign currency translation adjustments (less applicable income taxes of $6) |  | 26 |
|  |   Unrealized gains on securities: |  |  |
|  |     Unrealized holding gains arising during period (less applicable income taxes of $43) | 179 |  |
|  |     Less:  reclassification adjustment (less applicable income taxes of $10) for gain included in net income | (35) | 144 |
|  |   Other comprehensive income |  | 170 |
|  |   Comprehensive income |  | $(315) |

**Note:**

1.  Assumes a tax rate of 40% on applicable items
2.  (a) indicates where earnings per share (EPS) amounts would be necessary on the face of the IS.  (b) EPS may be shown on the face of the income statement or in the notes.  On the CPA exam, rather than memorizing these, simply calculate an EPS number for all numbers starting with income from continuing operations through net earnings.
3.  Footnote explanations would also be required for many of the above events and transactions.
4.  In the multiple-step format above, the Securities and Exchange Commission (SEC) requires that public companies place impairment losses in operating income instead of under "Other expenses and losses."
5.  This is the format for a multiple-step income statement.  A single-step income statement would differ only for the portion of the statement shown below.  Otherwise, the single-step statement format is the same.

| **Revenues** |  |  |
|---|---:|---:|
| Sales | $2,677 |  |
| Interest | 5 |  |
| Gain on sale of available-for-sale securities | 45 |  |
| Equity in Huskie Co. earnings | 15 |  |
|   Total revenues |  | $2,742 |

*Expenses*

| | |
|---|---:|
| Cost of goods sold | 1,489 |
| Selling expenses | 220 |
| Administrative expenses | 255 |
| Interest expense | 60 |
| Loss from permanent impairment of value of manufacturing facilities | 120 |
| Total expenses | 2,144 |
| Income from continuing operations before provision for income taxes | 598 |

The following chart summarizes the various category definitions and their placement on the income statement and retained earnings statement.  These categories are all discussed in various parts of this module.

### INCOME STATEMENT AND RETAINED EARNINGS STATEMENT CATEGORIES

| Description | Definition | Placement on income statement or retained earnings statement |
|---|---|---|
| **1. Unusual or Infrequent Items** | An unusual or infrequent event considered to be material that does not qualify as extraordinary | Placed as part of income from continuing operations after normal recurring revenues and expenses |
| **2. Discontinued Operations*** | Results from disposal of a business component | Placed as a separate category after income from continuing operations |
| **3. Extraordinary Items*** | An unusual and infrequent nonrecurring event which has material effects | Placed as a separate category after discontinued operations |
| **4. Change in Accounting Principle:** | Change from one generally accepted accounting principle to another | No longer on income statement. **Retrospective application:** Report cumulative effect of change in the carrying amounts of assets and liabilities as of the beginning of the first period presented, with an offsetting adjustment to the opening balance of retained earnings for that period.  Financial statements for each period are adjusted to reflect period-specific effects of the change for direct effects. |
| **5. Correction of an Error** | A correction of a material error from a prior period | Report as prior period adjustment by restating the prior-period financial statements.  Cumulative effect of the error on prior periods is reflected in the carrying value of assets and liabilities at the beginning of the first period, with an offsetting adjustment made to the opening balance of retained earnings for that period.  Financial statements are adjusted to reflect correction of period-specific effects of the error. |

*\* These items are all presented net of applicable income tax effects.*

### 2.   **Unusual or Infrequent Items**

Items that are unusual or infrequent but not both should not be presented as extraordinary items.  However, they are often presented in a separate section in the income statement above income before extraordinary items.  A common example of such items is a "restructuring charge."

A restructuring is a program that is planned and controlled by management and materially changes either (1) the scope of the **business** undertaken by the company, or (2) the manner in which that business is conducted.  Examples include

a.   Sale or termination of a line of business
b.   Closure of business activities in a particular location
c.   Relocation of business activities from one location to another
d.   Changes in management structure, or
e.   Fundamental reorganizations that affect the nature and focus of operations

SFAS 146 deals with accounting for the costs of exit and disposal activities (which include, among other items, restructurings) and provides that a liability for a cost associated with an exit or disposal activity should be recognized and measured initially at fair value in the period in which the liability is incurred.  The fair value is usually determined by determining the present value of the estimate future payments discounted at the credit-adjusted risk-free rate of interest.  In the unusual circumstance when fair value cannot be reasonably estimated, the liability shall be initially recognized in the period in which fair value can be reasonably estimated.  Examples of such liabilities include

    a.   Onetime termination benefits provided to current employees that are involuntarily terminated

    b.   Costs to terminate a contract that is not a capital lease

    c.   Costs to consolidate facilities or relocate employees

The recognition of the liability and expense for onetime termination benefits depends on whether the employees are required to provide services beyond the minimum retention period. If so, the expense is recognized over the period that the services are provided. If they are not required to provide future services, the liability is recognized when the plan is communicated to the employees.

In periods subsequent to initial measurement, changes to the liability shall be measured using the credit-adjusted risk-free rate that was used to measure the liability initially.

Costs associated with an exit or disposal activity that does not involve discontinued operations shall be included in income from continuing operations before income taxes. The footnotes to the financial statements shall provide extensive disclosure of the activities (See outline of SFAS 146).

3.  **Discontinued Operations**

As shown on the Totman Co. income statement, "Discontinued operations" is broken out separately. The "Loss from discontinued operations" includes the loss or income of the component for the period, and the gain or loss on its disposal. Income taxes or tax benefit are deducted from or added to that amount to determine the gain or loss after taxes. To qualify for treatment as discontinued operations the assets must comprise a component of the entity with operations and cash flows that are clearly distinguished, operationally and for financial reporting purposes, from the rest of the entity. A component may be a reportable or operating segment (see the outline of SFAS 131), a reporting unit (see the outline of SFAS 142), a subsidiary, or an asset group.

Many of the assets disposed of as discontinued operations are long-lived assets. Such assets are subject to the requirements of SFAS 144. Accordingly, the component is classified as discontinued operations in the first period that it meets the criteria as being "held for sale":

    a.   Management commits to a plan of disposal

    b.   The assets are available for sale

    c.   An active program to locate a buyer have been initiated

    d.   The sale is probable

    e.   The asset is being actively marketed for sale at a fair price

    f.   It is unlikely that the disposal plan will significantly change

To be reported as discontinued operations, SFAS 144 also requires (1) the operations and cash flows of the component have been (or will be) eliminated from the ongoing operations of the entity as a result of the disposal, and (2) the entity will not have any significant involvement in the operations of the component after disposal.

Long-lived assets classified as "held for sale" are reported at the lower of their carrying amounts or fair values less costs to sell. Therefore, the gain or loss on disposal of discontinued operations is the actual gain or loss if disposal occurs in the same period that the component meets the criteria to be classified as "held for sale" (see the outline of SFAS 144). If the criteria to classify the component as "held for sale" is met in a period before it is disposed of, the amount of the loss (if applicable) on disposal is an estimated loss resulting from the write-down of the group of assets to their estimated fair values. Estimated gains cannot be initially recognized. However, if the component is held for sale over several reporting periods estimated gains can be recognized based on new information but are limited to the amount of losses previously recognized. Thus, the assets can be written up but not above their carrying amounts when they met the criteria as being held for sale.

When "discontinued operations" are disclosed in a comparative income statement, the income statement presented for each previous year must be adjusted retroactively to enhance comparability with the current year's income statement. Accordingly, the revenues, cost of goods sold, and operating expenses (including income taxes) for the discontinued component are removed from the revenues, cost of goods sold, and operating expenses of continuing operations and are netted into one figure, that is, "Income (loss) from operations." The following excerpt from a comparative income statement shows the proper disclosure (2006 figures assumed).

| | *2007* | *2006* |
|---|---|---|
| Discontinued operations: | | |
|   Loss from operations of discontinued Division Z, including loss on disposal | | |
|     in 2007 of $230 | $699 | $990 |
|   Income tax benefit | $466 | $300 |

4.  **Comprehensive Income**

**Reporting.** Comprehensive income is the sum of net earnings (loss) and other comprehensive income. Refer to the outline of SFAS 130. This standard goes part way in implementing the concept of comprehensive income per SFAC 5 and 6. These two concept statements would require reporting all transactions other than those with owners in comprehensive income. However, SFAS 130 leaves prior period adjustments in retained earnings. It requires disclosure of **changes during a period** of the following components of other comprehensive income: unrealized gains and losses on available-for-sale investments and foreign currency items, including any reclassification adjustments and any adjustments necessary to recognize the funding status of pension plans or other postemployment benefits.

This standard allows the management of an enterprise three choices for presenting **other comprehensive income**. These are as follows:

1.  At the bottom of IS, continue from net income to arrive at a comprehensive income figure (illustrated on page 127, or
2.  In a separate statement that starts with net income, (illustrated below), or
3.  In the statement of changes in stockholders' equity illustrated on page 512.

The first two alternatives are preferred by the FASB. If either the second or third one is used, it is necessary to begin with net earnings so that net earnings would be reconciled to comprehensive income as it is in the single statement. The new standard continues the required disclosure of the **accumulated** amounts of these components in the stockholders' equity section of the balance sheet, in a statement of changes in stockholders' equity, or in the notes to financial statements. (See the balance sheet on the following page and the statement of changes in stockholders' equity at the beginning of Module 13.)

**Reclassification adjustments.** As unrealized gains (losses) recorded and reported in other comprehensive income for the current or prior periods are later realized, they are recognized and reported in net income. To avoid double counting it is necessary to reverse the unrealized amounts that have been recognized. Assume that an available-for-sale security was sold April 1, 2007, for a $45 gain. There was $30 of unrealized gain that arose in years prior to 2007 and is in **accumulated other** comprehensive income. The other $15 unrealized gain was reported in the first quarter statements and is part of the $179 reported below under other comprehensive income for 2007.

*Totman Company*
**STATEMENT OF EARNINGS AND COMPREHENSIVE INCOME**
*For the Year Ended December 31, 2007*

| | | |
|---|---|---:|
| Sales | | $2,677 |
| | | |
| Operating income | | 713 |
| Other revenues and gains | | |
| Interest revenue | $    5 | |
| Equity in Huskie Co. earnings | 15 | |
| Gain on sale of available-for-sale securities | 45 | 65 |
| Other expenses and losses | | |
| Interest expense | (60) | |
| Loss from permanent impairment of value of manufacturing facilities | (120) | (180) |
| Income from continuing operations before provision for income taxes | | 598 |
| Provision for income taxes | | |
| Current | $  189 | |
| Deferred | 50 | 239 |
| Income from continuing operations | | 359 |
| | | |
| Net earnings (loss) | | (485) |
| *Other* comprehensive *income:* | | |
| Foreign currency translation adjustments (less applicable income taxes of $6) | | 26 |
| Unrealized gains on securities: | | |
| Unrealized holding gains arising during period (less applicable income taxes of $43) | 179 | |
| Less:  Reclassification adjustment (less applicable income taxes of $10) for gain included in net income | (35) | 144 |
| Other comprehensive income | | 170 |
| Comprehensive income | | $(315) |

The reclassification adjustment to avoid double counting is $45 less a tax effect of $10 or $35 net. Since the $45 was realized in the current period, a realized gain of $45 was reported in the income from continuing operations under other revenues and gains above before provisions for income taxes of $598. The $10 of income tax on the $45 is reported as part of provision for income taxes in the current portion of income tax expense of $189. Recall that all items reported above the provision for income taxes are reported "gross," not the net of tax treatment as in the case of items such as discontinued operations. Also, note the tax effects reported under other comprehensive income are **deferred** since the unrealized components are not recognized for tax purposes until realized.

*Totman Company*
**BALANCE SHEET**
*December 31, 2007*

**Assets**

*Current assets:*

| | | |
|---|---|---|
| Cash and bank deposits: | | |
| Restricted to current bond maturity | $xxx | |
| Unrestricted | xxx | $xxx |
| Short-term investments: | | |
| Marketable securities (Trading) | | xxx |
| Refundable income taxes | | xxx |
| Receivables from affiliates | | xxx |
| Accounts receivable | xxx | |
| Less allowance for doubtful accounts | (xxx) | xxx |
| Notes receivable due in 2008 | | xxx |
| Installment notes due in 2008 | | xxx |
| Interest receivable | | xxx |
| Creditors' accounts with debit balances | | xxx |
| Advances to employees | | xxx |
| Inventories (carried at lower of cost or market by FIFO) | | |
| Finished goods | xxx | |
| Work in process | xxx | |
| Raw materials | xxx | xxx |
| Prepaid expenses: | | |
| Prepaid rent | xxx | |
| Prepaid insurance | xxx | xxx |
| Total current assets | | $xxx |

*Long-term investments:*

| | | |
|---|---|---|
| Investments in marketable securities (available-for-sale) | | xxx |
| Investments in bonds (held-to-maturity) | | xxx |
| Investments in unused land | | xxx |
| Cash surrender value of officers' life insurance policies | | xxx |
| Sinking fund for bond retirement | | xxx |
| Plant expansion fund | | xxx |
| Total long-term investments | | $xxx |

*Property, plant, and equipment:*

| | | |
|---|---|---|
| Land | xxx | |
| Buildings | xxx | |
| Machinery and equipment | xxx | |
| Furniture and fixtures | xxx | |
| Leasehold improvements | xxx | |
| Leased assets | xxx | |
| Less accumulated depreciation and amortization | (xxx) | |
| Total property, plant, and equipment | | $xxx |

*Intangible assets net of amortization:*

| | | |
|---|---|---|
| Goodwill | xxx | |
| Patents | xxx | |
| Trademarks | xxx | |
| Total intangible assets, net | | $xxx |

*Other assets:*

| | | |
|---|---|---|
| Installment notes due after 2008 | xxx | |
| Unamortized bond issue costs | xxx | |
| Equipment to be disposed of | xxx | |
| Total other noncurrent assets | | $xxx |
| Total assets | | $xxx |

**Liabilities and Stockholders' Equity**

*Current liabilities:*

| | | |
|---|---|---|
| Commercial paper and other short-term notes | $xxx | |
| Accounts payable | xxx | |
| Salaries, wages, and commissions | xxx | |
| Taxes withheld from employees | xxx | |
| Income taxes payable | xxx | |
| Dividends payable | xxx | |
| Rent revenue collected in advance | xxx | |
| Other advances from customers | xxx | |
| Current portion of long-term debt | xxx | |
| Current obligations under capital leases | xxx | |
| Deferred tax liability | xxx | |
| Short-term portion of accrued warranty | xxx | |
| Other accrued liabilities | xxx | |
| Total current liabilities | | $xxx |

*Noncurrent liabilities:*

| | | |
|---|---|---|
| Notes payable due after 2008 | xxx | |
| Plus unamortized note premium | xxx | $xxx |
| Long-term bonds: | | |
| 10% debentures due 2018 | xxx | |
| 9-1/2% collateralized obligations maturing serially to 2010 | xxx | |
| 8% convertible subordinated debentures due 2023 | xxx | |
| Less unamortized discounts net of premiums | (xxx) | xxx |
| Accrued pension cost | | xxx |
| Obligations under capital leases | | xxx |
| Deferred tax liability | | xxx |
| Long-term portion of accrued warranty | | xxx |
| Total noncurrent liabilities | | $xxx |
| Total liabilities | | $xxx |

*Capital stock:*

| | | |
|---|---|---|
| $12.50 convertible preferred stock, $100 stated value, 200,000 shares authorized, 175,000 outstanding | xxx | |
| 12% cumulative preferred stock, $100 stated value, callable at $115, 100,000 shares authorized and outstanding | xxx | |
| Common stock, $10 stated value, 500,000 shares authorized, 450,000 issued, 15,000 held in treasury | xxx | |
| Common stock subscribed 10,000 shares | xxx | |
| Less: Subscriptions receivable | (xxx) | xxx |

*Additional paid-in capital:*

| | | |
|---|---|---|
| From 12% cumulative preferred | xxx | |
| From common stock | xxx | |
| From treasury stock transactions | xxx | |
| From stock dividends | xxx | |
| From expiration of stock options | xxx | |
| Warrants outstanding | xxx | xxx |

*Retained earnings:*

| | | |
|---|---|---|
| Appropriated for bond indebtedness | xxx | |
| Free and unappropriated | xxx | xxx |
| Accumulated other comprehensive income: | | xxx* |
| Total stockholders' equity | | $xxx |
| Less: Treasury stock at cost | | (xxx) |
| Total liabilities and stockholders' equity | | $xxx |

*Assumes components thereof are disclosed either in a statement of changes in stockholders' equity or in the notes to FS.

**Balance sheet.**  Accumulated other comprehensive income is reported in the stockholders' equity section of the balance sheet. When an entity has components of other comprehensive income, the total of these is closed to the balance sheet account entitled **accumulated other comprehensive income,** not retained earnings.  In the case above, the other comprehensive income of $170 for the period would need to be closed to accumulated other comprehensive income, not retained earnings as would the ($485) net loss.

5.  **Balance Sheets (Statements of Financial Position)**

Balance sheets or statements of financial position present assets, liabilities, and stockholders' equity.  The balance sheet reports the effect of transactions at a point in time, whereas the statement of earnings (income) and comprehensive income, statement of retained earnings, and statement of cash flows report the effect of transactions over a period of time.

An example of balance sheet classification and presentation is illustrated by the comprehensive balance sheet on the previous page.

Distinction between current and noncurrent assets and liabilities is almost universal.

*Current assets*—"cash and other assets or resources commonly identified as those which are reasonably expected to be realized in cash or sold or consumed during the normal operating cycle of the business."                                               (ARB 43, chap 3A)

*Current liabilities*—"obligations whose liquidation is reasonably expected to require the use of existing resources properly classifiable as current assets or the creation of other current liabilities" (during the normal operating cycle of the business).                     (ARB 43, chap 3A)

Note current assets include those expected to be

   a.  Realized in cash
   b.  Sold
   c.  Consumed

Current liabilities are those expected to

   a.  Use current assets
   b.  Create other current liabilities

The operating cycle is the average time between acquisition of materials and final cash realization. Review the outline of ARB 43, chap 3A.

6.  **Other Financial Statement Concepts**

   a.  **Disclosures.**  Related-party disclosures are covered by SFAS 57 (refer to that outline).  Additional disclosures required for specific situations are specified at the end of most pronouncements (e.g., APB and SFAS).  Study these disclosure requirements by assuming you are a financial analyst analyzing the statements:  "What would you want disclosed?  Note any required disclosures that are not 'common sense.'"  It is not necessary to memorize them for the exam.

   b.  **Accounting policies** must be set forth as the initial footnote to the statements.  Disclosures are required of

   (1)  Accounting principles used when alternatives exist
   (2)  Principles peculiar to a particular industry
   (3)  Unusual or innovative applications of accounting principles

   Turn to the outline of APB 22.

   c.  **Fair value measurements.**  Fair value measurements are required for certain assets and liabilities (investments, derivatives, asset impairments, asset retirement obligations, goodwill, business combinations, troubled debt restructuring).  SFAS 157, issued in September 2006, defines fair value, establishes the framework for measuring fair value, and expands the disclosures for fair value measurements.  Applying the fair value measurement approach involves the following six steps:

   (1)  Identify the asset or liability to be measured.
   (2)  Determine the principal or most  advantageous market (*highest and best use*)
   (3)  Determine the valuation premise (*in-use or in-exchange*)
   (4)  Determine the appropriate valuation technique (*market, income, or cost approach*)

(5)  Obtain inputs for valuation (*Level 1, Level 2, or Level 3*)
(6)  Calculate the fair value of the asset.

SFAS 157 defines fair value as the price that would be received to sell an asset or paid to transfer a liability in an orderly transaction between market participants at the measurement date (at exit price).  An orderly transaction is a transaction that allows for normal marketing activities that are usual and customary.  In other words, it is not a forced transaction or sale.

The fair value measurement assumes that the asset or liability is sold or transferred in either the principal market or the most advantageous market.  The **principal market** is a market in which the greatest volume and level of activity occurs.  The **most advantageous market** maximizes price received for the asset or minimizes the amount paid to transfer the liability. Market participants in the principal or most advantageous market should have the following characteristics:

(1)  Be independent of the reporting entity (not related parties)
(2)  Be knowledgeable
(3)  Able to transact and,
(4)  Willing to transact (i.e. motivated, but not compelled to transact).

This hypothetical price in the principal or most advantageous market should not be adjusted for transaction costs, such as costs to sell.  However, the cost to sell is used to determine which market is the most advantageous.  If location is an attribute of the asset or liability, the price is adjusted for costs necessary to transport the asset or liability to the market.

> EXAMPLE 1: (Adapted from SFAS 157, Appendix A)
>
> Company A is valuing a trading security to fair value at year-end.  The stock is traded on two stock exchanges, the NYSE and NASDAQ.  The price quoted on December 31, 2008, on the NYSE is $50 per share, and the brokerage fees are $4 per share.  The price quoted on the NASDAQ is $48 per share with brokerage fees of $1 per share.
>
> a.  Assume the NYSE is the principal market.  The fair value would be $50 because the FV is the price in the principal market for the asset.
>
> b.  Assume that there is no principal market, and the stock is exchanged equally on both markets.  The fair value would be the price in the most advantageous market.  The NYSE price would allow Company A to receive $46 per share for the stock ($50–$4).  The NASDAQ price would allow company A to receive $47 per share for the stock ($48 – $1 per share).  Therefore, the NASDAQ price would maximize the price received for the asset, and the NASDAQ market would be considered the most advantageous market. The fair value of $48 per share would be the fair value of the stock.  Note that although the selling fees may be used to determine the most advantageous market, selling costs or brokerage fees are NOT used in calculating the fair value.
>
> EXAMPLE 2: (Adapted from SFAS 157, Appendix  A)
>
> Company B is valuing a commodity at year-end.  The commodity is traded on an open-exchange, and the price quoted at December 31, 2008, is $10,000.  Transportation costs to deliver the goods to market are $500.  The fair value of the commodity is $9,500 ($10,000 less the cost to transfer the goods to market of $500).

Fair value measurement also assumes the highest and best use of the asset.  The **highest and best use** will maximize the value of the asset or group of assets.  The use of the asset must be physically possible, legally permissible, and financially feasible at the measurement date.  The highest and best use of the asset is then used to determine the valuation premise used to measure fair value: **in-use** or **in-exchange**.  If the asset provides maximum value by using it with other assets as a group, it is considered an "**in-use**" asset.  The in-use valuation premise is based on the price to sell the asset assuming the asset is used with other assets as a group.  If the asset provides maximum value on a stand-alone basis, the "**in-exchange**" valuation premise is used.  The in-exchange valuation premise bases the fair value on the price that would be received in a current transaction to sell the asset stand-alone.

Three valuation techniques can be used to measure fair value: the market approach, the income approach, and the cost approach.  The **market approach** uses prices and relevant information from market transactions for identical or comparable assets or liabilities.  The **income approach** uses present values techniques to discount cash flows or earnings to present value amounts.  The **cost approach** relies on the current replacement cost to replace the asset with a comparable asset, adjusted for obsolescence.

If a firm changes its valuation technique or approach for measuring fair value, the change is accounted for as a change in accounting estimate and treated on a prospective basis. The disclosure provisions for SFAS 154 for a change in accounting estimate are not required for revisions or changes to valuation techniques used in fair value measurements.

Applying the market approach, income approach, and the cost approach requires gathering information to value the asset or liability. SFAS 157 requires that a fair value hierarchy be used to prioritize the inputs to valuation techniques. The fair value hierarchy is referred to as Level 1, Level 2, and Level 3, with the fair value hierarchy based on the lowest level of input.

Level 1, the lowest level of input, uses quoted prices (unadjusted prices) from active markets for identical assets or liabilities. Quoted prices in active markets provide the most reliable evidence of fair value and should be used whenever available. Examples of Level 1 inputs are stock quotations from the New York Stock Exchange, quotations from dealer markets such as NASDAQ or the market from US Treasury securities, brokered markets wherein brokers match buyers and sellers, and principal-to-principal markets. The fair value of a security measured within Level 1 is the quoted price times the quantity held, and it is not adjusted for the quantity of shares (blockage factor) held.

Level 2 inputs are directly or indirectly observable inputs other than quoted prices of Level 1. Examples of Level 2 inputs include quoted prices for similar assets or liabilities in active markets, quoted prices for identical or similar assets that are in markets where few transaction occur, the prices are not current, or prices vary substantially over time. Level 2 inputs also include observable inputs such as yield curves, bank prime rates, interest rates, volatilities, prepayment speeds, loss severities, credit risks, and default rates.

Level 3 inputs are unobservable inputs. Level 3 inputs may only be used to measure fair value if observable inputs are not available (i.e., there is little market activity for the asset or liability). These unobservable inputs may reflect the reporting entity's own assumptions about the market and are based on the best information available. Example of Level 3 inputs would include pricing a three-year option using the historical volatility on shares, valuing an asset retirement obligation using expected cash flows estimated by the company, or valuing a reporting unit using a firm's financial forecasts for cash flows or earnings.

If an asset is measured at fair value on a recurring basis, disclosures are required in both interim and annual statements that identify the level of hierarchy of the measurements. If Level 3 inputs are used, the total gains or losses for the period (realized and unrealized), the effect of the measurements on earnings for the period, purchases, sales, issuances, and settlements, and any transfers in or out of Level 3 should be disclosed. For annual reports, the valuation techniques used to measure fair value must also be disclosed.

For assets and liabilities measured at fair values on a nonrecurring basis (i.e. impaired assets), disclosures are required for interim and annual reporting periods that identify the fair value measurements used and the reasons for the measurements, the level within the hierarchy, and a description of the inputs used for any Level 3 measurements. For annual periods, disclosures are also required for the valuation techniques used to measure fair value.

d. **The fair value option for reporting financial assets and financial liabilities.** SFAS 159, issued in February 2007, provides that an election can be made to value certain financial assets and financial liabilities at fair value. A financial asset is cash, evidence of an ownership interest in an entity, or a contract that conveys a right to receive cash or another financial instrument or to exchange financial instruments on favorable terms. A financial liability is a contract that imposes an obligation to deliver cash or another financial instrument.

The fair value option applies to all financial assets including available-for-sale, held-to-maturity, and equity method investments. The fair value option also applies to certain financial liabilities, firm commitments that involve financial instruments, written loan commitments, nonfinancial insurance contracts that can be settled by paying a third party, warranties that can be settled by paying a third party, and a host financial instrument that is an embedded nonfinancial derivative instrument separated from a nonfinancial hybrid instrument.

The fair value method does **not** apply to consolidations, pensions, share-based payments, stock options, other postemployment benefits (OPEB), exit or disposal activities, leases, or financial instruments that are a component of equity.

As defined in SFAS 157, the fair value is the price that would be received to sell an asset or paid to transfer a liability in an orderly transaction between market participants at the measurement date.

A company can elect to measure the applicable financial assets or financial liabilities at fair value on the date an eligible item is first recognized, the date the entity enters into a firm commitment, the date financial assets cease to qualify for fair value treatment due to specialized accounting rules (i.e., APB 18 and the equity method). For companies using the equity method of accounting, a company can elect to measure the investment at fair value on the date the percentage of ownership changes and the entity is no longer required to consolidate. For debt modifications, the fair value option can be elected on the date the debt is modified. Once the fair value option is elected, it is irrevocable.

The fair value election can be made on an instrument-by-instrument basis. For example, a company has two available-for-sale securities, Security A and Security B. The company can account for Security A using the rules in SFAS 115 for available-for-sale securities, and it can elect the fair value option and account for Security B at fair value. However, if the fair value option is elected, it must be applied to the entire instrument and not a portion of the instrument. For example, if there are multiple advances to a borrower for a single contract, it must be applied to the entire balance of the contract. If the fair value option is applied to an investment that would normally use the equity method, it must be applied to all debt and equity interests in that entity.

Similarly, if the fair value option is elected for insurance contracts, it must be applied to all claims and obligations for that contract.

If the fair value option is elected, any unrealized gains and losses are reported in earnings for the period. Therefore, any unrealized gains and losses on an available-for-sale security would be reported on the income statement rather than in other comprehensive income. For a held-to-maturity security, the company would no longer use the rules in APB 21 and SFAS 115 to report the investment at amortized cost. Instead, the held-to-maturity security would be marked to fair value at the end of the period, and the resulting unrealized gain or loss would be reported on the income statement. The rules in SFAS 95 remain in effect for classifying items on the statement of cash flows.

Additional financial statement disclosures are required if the fair value option is elected. Two methods are permissible for balance sheet disclosure: (1) present the aggregate fair value and non-fair-value amounts in the same line with amounts measured at fair value parenthetically disclosed, or (2) present two separate line items for fair value and non–fair value carrying amounts.

Additional footnote disclosures are also required if the fair value option is elected. For the balance sheet, the notes to financial statements must include the following:

1. Management's reasons for electing fair value option for each item or group of items.
2. If fair value option is elected for some but not all items
    a. Description of similar items and reason for partial election.
    b. Information to understand how group of similar items relates to individual line items on balance sheet.
3. Information to understand how line items relate to major categories of assets and liabilities presented in SFAS 157 fair value disclosure requirements.
4. Aggregate carrying amount of items included in each line item in balance sheet for any items not eligible for fair value election treatment.
5. Difference between aggregate fair value and aggregate unpaid principal balance of
    a. Loans and long-term receivables using fair value option.
    b. Long-term debt instruments using fair value option.
    c. Aggregate fair value of loans that are 90 days or more past due.
    d. Aggregate fair value of loans in nonaccrual status if interest is recognized separately from changes in fair value.
    e. Difference between aggregate fair value and aggregate unpaid principal balance for loans 90 days or more past due.
6. For investments that would have used equity method, the information required by APB 18 for equity method.

For the income statement, the following items should be disclosed in the notes to the financial statements:

1. Amounts of gains/losses included in earnings for each line item in balance sheet.
2. Description of how interest and dividends are measured and reported on the income statement.
3. For loans and receivables held as assets

    a. Estimated amount of gains/losses in earnings that is attributed to changes in credit risk.
    b. How the gains/losses were determined.

4. For liabilities affected by credit risk

    a. Amount of gains/losses attributable to changes in credit risk.
    b. Qualitative information about reasons for changes.
    c. How gains/losses were determined.

5. Methods and significant assumptions to estimate fair value.

The transition requirements of SFAS 159 provide that at the effective date, a company may elect the fair value option for eligible items. The difference between the carrying value and the fair value of each item is included in a cumulative effect adjustment to the opening balance of retained earnings for the period. Any other balance sheet effects such as amortized deferred costs, fees, premiums, discounts, valuation allowances, or accrued interest must be removed from the balance sheet.

  e. **Development stage enterprise accounting** should be per generally accepted accounting principles. The only additional disclosure required is that cumulative amounts from inception of losses, revenues, expenses, and cash flows should be shown in the income statement and statement of cash flows. Furthermore, the stockholders' equity section of the balance sheet should include cumulative net losses termed "deficit accumulated during development stage." These statements should be identified as those of a development stage enterprise. (More detailed coverage appears in Module 9.)

  f. **Constant dollar accounting.** SFAS 89 encourages, but does not require, a business enterprise that prepares its financial statements in US dollars and in accordance with US generally accepted accounting principles to disclose supplementary information on the effects of changing prices. This statement presents requirements to be followed by enterprises that voluntarily elect to disclose this information.

    Constant dollar accounting is a method of reporting financial statement elements in dollars which have the same purchasing power. This method is often described as accounting in units of current purchasing power.

    Purchasing power indicates the ability of a dollar to command goods and services. If the inflation rate during a given year for a group of items is 10%, then 110 end-of-year dollars are needed to purchase the same group of items which cost $100 at the beginning of the year. Similarly, a machine purchased at the beginning of that year for $1,000 would be presented in a year-end constant dollar balance sheet at a restated cost of $1,100. This represents the basic thrust of constant dollar accounting: the adjustment of historical data (nominal dollars) for changes in the general price level.

    The adjustment of nominal dollar data is facilitated by the use of the Consumer Price Index, which reflects the average change in the retail prices of a wide variety of consumer goods. The adjustment is made by multiplying historical cost by the TO/FROM ratio.

$$\text{Historical cost (nominal dollars)} \times \frac{\text{Price level adjusting to}}{\text{Price level adjusting from}} = \text{Restated historical cost (constant dollar)}$$

For example, an asset was purchased on 12/31/05 for $20,000 and the Consumer Price Index was 100 on 12/31/05 110 on 12/31/06 and 120 on 12/31/07. Restatement for end-of-year balance sheets would be

$$12/31/05 \quad \$20,000 \quad \times \quad \frac{100}{100} \quad = \quad \$20,000$$

$$12/31/06 \quad \$20,000 \quad \times \quad \frac{110}{100} \quad = \quad \$22,000$$

$$12/31/07 \quad \$20,000 \quad \times \quad \frac{120}{100} \quad = \quad \$24,000$$

or

$$\$22,000 \quad \times \quad \frac{120}{110} \quad = \quad \$24,000$$

The preparation of constant dollar financial statements requires the classification of balance sheet items as either monetary or nonmonetary. Items are monetary if their amounts are fixed by statute or contract in terms of numbers of dollars. Examples include cash, accounts and notes receivable, accounts and notes payable, and bonds payable. By contract or statute, these items are already stated in current dollars and require no restatement. Nonmonetary items, on the other hand, do require restatement to current dollars. Inventory, property, plant, and equipment, and unearned service revenue are examples of nonmonetary items. Under some increasingly popular loan arrangements, when the repayment of loan principal is adjusted by an index, the receivable/payable is classified as a nonmonetary item.

The holding of a nonmonetary asset such as land during a period of inflation need not result in a loss of purchasing power because the value of that land can "flow" with the price level (hence, the need for restatement). However, if a monetary asset such as cash is held during a period of inflation with no interest, purchasing power is lost because the cash will be able to purchase less goods and services at year-end than at the beginning of the year. This type of loss is simply called a "purchasing power loss." Holding a monetary liability has the opposite effect. Therefore, if a firm's balance sheet included more monetary liabilities than monetary assets throughout a given year, a purchasing power **gain** would result, since the firm could pay its liabilities using cash which is "worth less" than the cash it borrowed.

A simple example can illustrate both the restatement process and the effect of holding monetary assets. Assume that the Static Company has the following balance sheet at the beginning of period 1:

*Static Co.*
*Beginning of Period 1*
*Consumer Price Index = 100*

| | | | |
|---|---|---|---|
| Cash | $1,000 | Common Stock | $2,000 |
| Land | 1,000 | | |
| | $2,000 | | $2,000 |

Further assume

- Index increases to 110 by the end of year 1
- No transactions have taken place, land and common stock would be restated to end-of-year dollars.
- Cash is still stated at $1,000.
- To have the same level of purchasing power that was present at the beginning of the year, Static Co. should also have cash of $1,100 at year-end. The fact that the company held $1,000 cash throughout the year has resulted in a $100 purchasing power loss. The balance sheet at the end of period 1 would therefore be

*Static Co.*
*End of Period 1*
*Consumer Price Index = 110*

| | | | |
|---|---|---|---|
| Cash | $1,000 | Common Stock | $2,200[b] |
| Land | 1,100[a] | Retained Earnings | (100)[c] |
| | $2,100 | | $2,100 |

[a] $\$1,000 \times \dfrac{110}{100}$  [b] $\$2,000 \times \dfrac{110}{100}$  [c] Purchasing power loss $\$1,000 - \left( \$1,000 \times \dfrac{110}{100} \right)$

What if the entity had acquired equipment costing $1,000 at the beginning of the year by issuing a $1,000 note payable? At the end of the year, under constant dollar accounting, the equipment would be carried at $1,100 and the note payable would be still reported at $1,000. What would the net purchasing power gain (loss) be?  The answer is zero because the ($100) is offset by a $100 gain from holding the note payable.

g.  **Current cost accounting** is a method of valuing and reporting assets, liabilities, revenues, and expenses at their current cost at the balance sheet date or at the date of their use or sale.

It is important to distinguish between constant dollar and current cost accounting.  Constant dollar accounting is concerned only with changes in the unit of measure—from nominal dollars to units of general purchasing power.  Current cost accounting discards historical cost as a reporting model.

Preparation of a current cost income statement requires an understanding of certain basic current cost concepts.  **Current cost income from continuing operations** is sales revenue less expenses on a current cost basis.  **Realized holding gains** (the difference between current cost and historical cost of assets consumed) are then added to arrive at **realized income,** which will always be equal to historical cost net income.  Finally, **unrealized holding gains** (increases in the current cost of assets held throughout the year) are included to result in **current cost net income**.

An example should help clarify these terms.  Bell Co. went into business on 1/1/07.  2007 sales revenue was $200,000 and purchases totaled $150,000.  Inventory with a historical cost of $100,000 was sold when its current cost was $160,000.  Ending inventory (historical cost, $50,000) had a year-end current cost of $80,000.  No other revenue was realized or expenses incurred during 2007.  Historical and current cost income statements for 2007 are presented below.

*Bell Company*
**INCOME STATEMENTS**

| _Historical cost_ | | _Current cost_ | |
|---|---|---|---|
| Sales | $200,000 | Sales | $200,000 |
| Less CGS | (100,000) | Less CGS | (160,000) |
| | | Cur. cost income from cont. oper. | 40,000 |
| | | Realized holding gains (160,000 – 100,000) | 60,000 |
| Net income | $100,000 | Realized income | 100,000 |
| | | Unrealized holding gains (80,000 – 50,000) | 30,000 |
| | | Current cost net income | $130,000 |

2007 journal entries for Bell Company in current cost system would be as follows:

| a) | Inventory | 150,000 | | d) | Cost of goods sold | 160,000 | |
|---|---|---|---|---|---|---|---|
| | Cash | | 150,000 | | Inventory | | 160,000 |
| b) | Inventory | 90,000 | | e) | Realizable holding gain | 90,000 | |
| | Realizable holding gain | | 90,000 | | Realized holding gain | | 60,000 |
| | | | | | Unrealized holding gain | | 30,000 |
| c) | Cash | 200,000 | | | | | |
| | Sales revenue | | 200,000 | | | | |

In general, sales and some expense amounts (salaries, rent, etc.) will be the same under historical and current cost systems.  However, whenever an expense represents the use or consumption of an asset whose current cost has changed since its acquisition (as with the inventory in the Bell Co. example), that expense must be expressed at the current cost of the asset when used.  Realized holding gains are computed by comparing the current cost of assets when used or consumed with their historical cost.  Unrealized holding gains for the period are determined by identifying changes in the current cost of assets held throughout the year (not used or consumed).  Notice that the holding gains do not reflect changes in the general purchasing power.  In other words, the holding gains are not reported net of general inflation when the reporting model is current cost/nominal dollar.

**Current cost/constant dollars.** The relationship measured is current cost, but the measuring unit is restated dollars.  Changes in both the general and specific price levels are separately recorded.

h.  **Risks and uncertainties.**  AICPA Statement of Position 94-6, *Disclosure of Certain Significant Risks and Uncertainties,* requires disclosure in financial statements about the risks and uncertainties existing as of the date of those statements.  The four areas of disclosure are

(1)  Nature of operations

   (a)  Major products/services and principal markets served

(b) Industries operating within and relative importance of each industry, including basis of determination (assets, revenue or earnings).

   NOTE:  *Quantification not required and words such as predominantly, equally, major, or other may be used.*

(2) Use of estimates in preparation of financial statements

(a) This fact must be disclosed by an explanation that management must use estimates
(b) Purpose is to alert users clearly to pervasiveness of estimates

(3) Certain significant estimates

(a) Potential impact of estimates to value assets, liabilities, gains or losses when

   1] Reasonably possible the estimate will change in the near term
   2] Effect of change would be material to financial statements

   NOTE:  *Near term is defined as not to exceed one year from date of financial statements.*

(b) This is not a change in SFAS 5, *Accounting for Contingencies*
(c) Disclosure of factors causing the estimate to be sensitive to change is encouraged, but not required
(d) Materiality is measured by the effect that using a different estimate would have on the financial statements

(4) Current vulnerability due to concentrations

(a) Before issuance of financial statements, management knows that concentrations

   1] Exist at balance sheet date
   2] Make entity vulnerable to risk of near-term severe impact
   3] Reasonably possible events could cause severe impact in near future

   NOTE:  *Severe impact is defined as higher than materiality and would have a significant financially disruptive effect on the normal functioning of the entity.*

(b) Examples are concentrations in

   1] Volume of business transacted with a particular customer, supplier, lender, grantor, or contributor
   2] Revenue from particular products, services, or fund-raising events
   3] Available sources of supply of materials, labor, or services, or of licenses or other rights used in the entity's operations
   4] Market or geographical area in which an entity conducts its operations

(c) Disclose the percentage of labor covered by a collective bargaining agreement and the percentage covered whose agreement expires within one year
(d) Describe for operations outside of home country, the carrying value of net assets and location

7. **Comparative Financial Statements**

The Totman Company balance sheet and income statement illustrated in this module are presented for a single year. Most companies present comparative financial statements. Comparative financial statements present not only the current year's information, but prior periods also. The purpose of comparative financial statements is to enable users to evaluate trends which may reveal information about the company's future performance. The SEC requires that a two-year comparative balance sheet and a three-year comparative income statement and statement of cash flows be presented.

8. **Other Comprehensive Bases of Accounting**

Financial statements may be prepared in conformity with a comprehensive basis of accounting other than generally accepted accounting principles. Other comprehensive bases are illustrated in the chart below.

| Accounting method | Characteristics |
|---|---|
| 1. Cash basis (pure) | Fixed assets would be expensed in the period paid for |
| 2. Income tax bases | |
| • Modified cash basis—hybrid method of IRS | Reflects use of accrual basis for inventories, cost of goods sold, sales, and depreciation if these are significant |
| • Accrual basis—IRS | Use accruals and deferrals with several exceptions (e.g., prepaid income, warranty expense) |
| 3. Prescribed basis by regulatory agency | Determined by regulatory agency |

Guidance for preparing these statements is found in the AICPA publication entitled *Preparing and Reporting on Cash- and Tax-Basis Financial Statements*. When financial statements are prepared on an income tax basis, the financial statements should not simply repeat items and amounts reported in the tax return. Thus, items such as nontaxable municipal interest and the nondeductible portion of travel and entertainment expense should be **fully** reflected in the income statement on the basis used for tax purposes (cash or accrual) with footnote disclosure of the differences between the amounts reported in the income statement and tax return.

9. **Prospective Financial Information**
   - Definitions:
     - Prospective financial information—any financial information about the future
     - Responsible party—person(s), usually management, who are responsible for assumptions underlying the information
     - Users of prospective financial information:
       - General—use of FS by parties with whom responsible party is not negotiating directly
       - Limited use—use of prospective financial information by the responsible party only or by responsible party and third parties with whom responsible party is negotiating directly
     - Financial forecast—prospective FS that present the knowledge and belief of responsible party in terms of expected financial position, results of operations, and cash flows
       - May be prepared for **general or limited** use
       - Monetary amounts are expressed as a single-point estimate of results or range
     - Financial projection—prospective FS that present the knowledge and belief of responsible party, based on one or more **hypothetical** assumptions, the enterprise's financial position, results of operations, and cash flows
       - Assumptions **not necessarily** expected to occur
       - May contain a single-point estimate of results or a range of dollars
       - May be prepared only for **limited** use
   - Reasons for preparation:
     - Needed to obtain external financing
     - Consider change in accounting or operations
     - Prepare budget
   - Process for preparing forecasts and projections may consist of any of the following:
     - Formal system
     - Carrying out a work program that outlines steps followed in preparation
     - Documented procedures, methods, and practices used in preparation
   - Financial forecasts and projections should reflect **a reasonably objective basis** as a result of preparing them:
     - In good faith
     - With due care by qualified personnel
     - In accordance with GAAP
     - With the highest quality information that is reasonably available
     - Using information that is in accordance with plans of the entity
     - Identifying key factors as basis for assumptions
       - Key factors are important matters for which outcomes are expected to depend
     - Using appropriate assumptions
       - Quality of these is crucial
       - **Hypothetical** assumptions used in projections do **not** need to meet a strict reasonableness test; they must, however, be appropriate in light of the purpose of the projection's purpose
     - Providing ways to determine relative effect of variations in main assumptions (i.e., sensitivity analysis)
     - Documenting forecast/projection and process used
     - Providing for comparison of forecast/projection with attained results

- Providing adequate review of the responsible party at appropriate levels of authority in the organization
- Prospective financial statement disclosures include:
  - Summary of significant accounting policies
  - Summary of significant assumptions.

10. **Research Component**

ARB 43 contains the earliest information on accounting standards.  ARB 43, Chapter 2, addresses forms of comparative statements.  Chapter 3 covers working capital definitions, and Chapter 7 addresses capital accounts.  Much of ARB 43 has been superseded by later pronouncements.  APB 9 addresses results of operations, prior period adjustments, and extraordinary items.  Again, much of APB 9 is superseded by APB 20, *Accounting Changes*.  APB 22 provides the accounting rules for disclosing accounting policies.  More recent pronouncements such as SFAS 130, *Reporting Comprehensive Income,* amend or supersede earlier pronouncements.  Likewise, SFAS 144 changed the reporting for discontinued operations.  When you research you should exercise care in looking for amended or superseded materials.  You can often click on the pop-up links and jump links which are cross-referenced to the materials that amend or supersede the paragraph in question.  Often those links will take you directly to the paragraph in a later pronouncement that supersedes or amends the earlier material.  Below is a list of the pronouncements in which you will find information on financial statements and related disclosures.

| | |
|---|---|
| ARB 43, Ch 3A | *Basic Definitions and Accounting* |
| APB 9 | *Results of Operations* |
| APB 22 | *Accounting Policies* |
| APB 30 | *Extraordinary Items, Unusual or Infrequent Items* |
| SFAS 89 | *Changing Prices* |
| SFAS 130 | *Reporting Comprehensive Income* |
| SFAS 131 | *Segment Reporting* |
| SFAS 144 | *Impairment or Disposal of Long-Lived Assets* |
| SFAS 145 | *Technical Corrections and Changes* |
| SFAS 146 | *Exit or Disposal Activities* |
| SFAS 154 | *Accounting Changes* |
| SFAS 157 | *Fair Value Measurements* |
| SFAS 159 | *Fair Value Option* |
| SOP 94-6 | *Disclosure of Significant Risks and Uncertainties* |
| SFAC 5 and 6 | *Basic Concepts and Definitions* |

Keywords for research financial statements and related disclosures are shown below.

| | | |
|---|---|---|
| Accounting policies | Current assets | In-exchange |
| Balance sheet | Current cost purchasing power | Infrequency of occurrence |
| Capital stock | Current liabilities | Interim period information |
| Capital surplus | Disclosure accounting policies | In-use |
| Cash flow estimation | Discontinued operation | Market approach |
| Change in accounting | Disposal activity | Measure impairment loss |
| Change in principle | Disposal of segment | Monetary asset |
| Changes in entity | Earned surplus | Monetary liability |
| Changes in equity | External revenue | Nature products services |
| Changes in estimates | Extraordinary items | Net income period |
| Classifications net income | Fair value hierarchy | Obligations operating cycle |
| Comparative financial statements | Fair value option | Operating cycle |
| Comparative purposes | Financial position | Operating segment |
| Component held for sale | Highest and best use | Other comprehensive income |
| Component of an entity | Impairment loss | Period-specific effects |
| Comprehensive income | Inclusive net income | Principal market |
| Correction of error | Income approach | Prior period adjustments |
| Cost approach | Income statement | Pro forma amounts |

| | | |
|---|---|---|
| Pro forma effects | Recurring operational | Segment item |
| Profit and loss | Reportable segment | Surplus statement |
| Purchasing power gain loss | Results of operations | Translation adjustment |
| Reclassification adjustments | Retroactive adjustment | Unusual nature |
| Reconciliations of totals | Retrospective application | Valuation techniques |
| | | Working capital |

## MULTIPLE-CHOICE QUESTIONS (1-93)

**1.** In Baer Food Co.'s 2007 single-step income statement, the section titled "Revenues" consisted of the following:

| | | |
|---|---|---|
| Net sales revenue | | $187,000 |
| Results from discontinued operations: | | |
|   Loss from discontinued component Z in- | | |
|     cluding loss on disposal of $1,200 | $ 16,400 | |
|     Less tax benefit | 4,000 | (12,400) |
| Interest revenue | | 10,200 |
| Gain on sale of equipment | | 4,700 |
| Extraordinary gain | | 1,500 |
| Total revenues | | $191,000 |

In the revenues section of the 2007 income statement, Baer Food should have reported total revenues of

- a. $216,300
- b. $215,400
- c. $203,700
- d. $201,900

**Items 2 and 3** are based on the following:

Vane Co.'s trial balance of income statement accounts for the year ended December 31, 2008, included the following:

| | Debit | Credit |
|---|---|---|
| Sales | | $575,000 |
| Cost of sales | $240,000 | |
| Administrative expenses | 70,000 | |
| Loss on sale of equipment | 10,000 | |
| Sales commissions | 50,000 | |
| Interest revenue | | 25,000 |
| Freight out | 15,000 | |
| Loss on early retirement of long-term debt | 20,000 | |
| Uncollectible accounts expense | 15,000 | |
| Totals | $420,000 | $600,000 |

*Other information*
Finished goods inventory:

| | |
|---|---|
| January 1, 2008 | $400,000 |
| December 31, 2008 | 360,000 |

Vane's income tax rate is 30%. In Vane's 2008 multiple-step income statement,

**2.** What amount should Vane report as the cost of goods manufactured?

- a. $200,000
- b. $215,000
- c. $280,000
- d. $295,000

**3.** What amount should Vane report as income after income taxes from continuing operations?

- a. $126,000
- b. $129,500
- c. $140,000
- d. $147,000

**4.** Brock Corp. reports operating expenses in two categories: (1) selling, and (2) general and administrative. The adjusted trial balance at December 31, 2007, included the following expense and loss accounts:

| | |
|---|---|
| Accounting and legal fees | $120,000 |
| Advertising | 150,000 |
| Freight-out | 80,000 |
| Interest | 70,000 |
| Loss on sale of long-term investment | 30,000 |
| Officers' salaries | 225,000 |
| Rent for office space | 220,000 |
| Sales salaries and commissions | 140,000 |

One-half of the rented premises is occupied by the sales department.

Brock's total selling expenses for 2007 are

- a. $480,000
- b. $400,000
- c. $370,000
- d. $360,000

**5.** The following costs were incurred by Griff Co., a manufacturer, during 2007:

| | |
|---|---|
| Accounting and legal fees | $ 25,000 |
| Freight-in | 175,000 |
| Freight-out | 160,000 |
| Officers salaries | 150,000 |
| Insurance | 85,000 |
| Sales representatives salaries | 215,000 |

What amount of these costs should be reported as general and administrative expenses for 2007?

- a. $260,000
- b. $550,000
- c. $635,000
- d. $810,000

**6.** Which of the following should be included in general and administrative expenses?

| | Interest | Advertising |
|---|---|---|
| a. | Yes | Yes |
| b. | Yes | No |
| c. | No | Yes |
| d. | No | No |

**7.** In Yew Co.'s 2007 annual report, Yew described its social awareness expenditures during the year as follows:

The Company contributed $250,000 in cash to youth and educational programs. The Company also gave $140,000 to health and human service organizations, of which $80,000 was contributed by employees through payroll deductions. In addition, consistent with the Company's commitment to the environment, the Company spent $100,000 to redesign product packaging.

What amount of the above should be included in Yew's income statement as charitable contributions expense?

- a. $310,000
- b. $390,000
- c. $410,000
- d. $490,000

**8.** During 2007 both Raim Co. and Cane Co. suffered losses due to the flooding of the Mississippi River. Raim is located two miles from the river and sustains flood losses every two to three years. Cane, which has been located fifty miles from the river for the past twenty years, has never before had flood losses. How should the flood losses be reported in each company's 2007 income statement?

| | Raim | Cane |
|---|---|---|
| a. | As a component of income from continuing operations | As an extraordinary item |
| b. | As a component of income from continuing operations | As a component of income from continuing operations |
| c. | As an extraordinary item | As a component of income from continuing operations |
| d. | As an extraordinary item | As an extraordinary item |

9.   Witt Co. incurred the following infrequent losses during 2007:

- $175,000 from a major strike by employees.
- $150,000 from an earthquake (unusual).
- $125,000 from the abandonment of equipment used in the business.

In Witt's 2007 income statement, the total amount of infrequent losses **not** considered extraordinary should be
   a.   $275,000
   b.   $300,000
   c.   $325,000
   d.   $450,000

10.   Kent Co. incurred the following infrequent losses during 2007:

- A $300,000 loss was incurred on disposal of one of four dissimilar factories.
- A major currency devaluation caused a $120,000 exchange loss on an amount remitted by a foreign customer.
- Inventory valued at $190,000 was made worthless by a competitor's unexpected product innovation.

In its 2007 income statement, what amount should Kent report as losses that are **not** considered extraordinary?
   a.   $610,000
   b.   $490,000
   c.   $420,000
   d.   $310,000

11.   Midway Co. had the following transactions during 2007:

- $1,200,000 pretax loss on foreign currency exchange due to a major unexpected devaluation by the foreign government.
- $500,000 pretax loss from discontinued operations of a division.
- $800,000 pretax loss on equipment damaged by a hurricane. This was the first hurricane ever to strike in Midway's area. Midway also received $1,000,000 from its insurance company to replace a building, with a carrying value of $300,000, that had been destroyed by the hurricane.

What amount should Midway report in its 2007 income statement as extraordinary loss before income taxes?
   a.   $  100,000
   b.   $1,300,000
   c.   $1,800,000
   d.   $2,500,000

12.   Ocean Corp.'s comprehensive insurance policy allows its assets to be replaced at current value. The policy has a $50,000 deductible clause. One of Ocean's waterfront warehouses was destroyed in a winter storm. Such storms occur approximately every four years. Ocean incurred $20,000 of costs in dismantling the warehouse and plans to replace it. The following data relate to the warehouse:

| | |
|---|---|
| Current carrying amount | $ 300,000 |
| Replacement cost | 1,100,000 |

What amount of gain should Ocean report as a separate component of income before extraordinary items?
   a.   $1,030,000
   b.   $  780,000
   c.   $  730,000
   d.   $0.

13.   Purl Corporation's income statement for the year ended December 31, 2007, shows the following:

| | |
|---|---|
| Income before income tax and extraordinary item | $900,000 |
| Gain on life insurance coverage—included in the above $900,000 income amount | 100,000 |
| Extraordinary item—loss due to earthquake damage | 300,000 |

Purl's tax rate for 2007 is 40%. How much should be reported as the provision for income tax in Purl's 2007 income statement?
   a.   $200,000
   b.   $240,000
   c.   $320,000
   d.   $360,000

14.   Thorpe Co.'s income statement for the year ended December 31, 2008, reported net income of $74,100. The auditor raised questions about the following amounts that had been included in net income:

| | |
|---|---|
| Unrealized loss on decline in market value of noncurrent in vestments in stock classified as available-for-sale (net of tax) | $(5,400) |
| Gain on early retirement of bonds payable (net of $11,000 tax effect) | 22,000 |
| Adjustment to profits of prior years for errors in depreciation (net of $3,750 tax effect) | (7,500) |
| Loss from fire (net of $7,000 tax effect) | (14,000) |

The loss from the fire was an infrequent but not unusual occurrence in Thorpe's line of business. Thorpe's December 31, 2008 income statement should report net income of
   a.   $65,000
   b.   $66,100
   c.   $81,600
   d.   $87,000

15.   On January 1, 2007, Brecon Co. installed cabinets to display its merchandise in customers' stores. Brecon expects to use these cabinets for five years. Brecon's 2007 multi-step income statement should include
   a.   One-fifth of the cabinet costs in cost of goods sold.
   b.   One-fifth of the cabinet costs in selling, general, and administrative expenses.
   c.   All of the cabinet costs in cost of good sold.
   d.   All of the cabinet costs in selling, general, and administrative expenses.

16.   A material loss should be presented separately as a component of income from continuing operations when it is
   a.   An extraordinary item.
   b.   A discontinued component of the business.
   c.   Unusual in nature and infrequent in occurrence.
   d.   Not unusual in nature but infrequent in occurrence.

17.   During 2007, Peg Construction Co. recognized substantial gains from

- An increase in value of a foreign customer's remittance caused by a major foreign currency revaluation.
- A court-ordered increase in a completed long-term construction contract's price due to design changes.

Should these gains be included in continuing operations or reported as an extraordinary item in Peg's 2007 income statement?

| | Gain from major currency revaluation | Gain from increase in contract's price |
|---|---|---|
| a. | Continuing operations | Continuing operations |
| b. | Extraordinary item | Continuing operations |
| c. | Extraordinary item | Extraordinary item |
| d. | Continuing operations | Extraordinary item |

**18.** An extraordinary item should be reported separately on the income statement as a component of income

| | Net of income taxes | Before discontinued operations of a component of a business |
|---|---|---|
| a. | Yes | Yes |
| b. | Yes | No |
| c. | No | No |
| d. | No | Yes |

**19.** In 2007, hail damaged several of Toncan Co.'s vans. Hailstorms had frequently inflicted similar damage to Toncan's vans. Over the years, Toncan had saved money by not buying hail insurance and either paying for repairs, or selling damaged vans and then replacing them. In 2007, the damaged vans were sold for less than their carrying amount. How should the hail damage cost be reported in Toncan's 2007 financial statements?

a. The actual 2007 hail damage loss as an extraordinary loss, net of income taxes.
b. The actual 2007 hail damage loss in continuing operations, with **no** separate disclosure.
c. The expected average hail damage loss in continuing operations, with **no** separate disclosure.
d. The expected average hail damage loss in continuing operations, with separate disclosure.

**20.** A transaction that is unusual in nature and infrequent in occurrence should be reported separately as a component of income

a. After cumulative effect of accounting changes and before discontinued operations.
b. After cumulative effect of accounting changes and after discontinued operations.
c. Before cumulative effect of accounting changes and before discontinued operations.
d. Before cumulative effect of accounting changes and after discontinued operations.

**21.** In 2007, Teller Co. incurred losses arising from its guilty plea in its first antitrust action, and from a substantial increase in production costs caused when a major supplier's workers went on strike. Which of these losses should be reported as an extraordinary item?

| | Antitrust action | Production costs |
|---|---|---|
| a. | No | No |
| b. | No | Yes |
| c. | Yes | No |
| d. | Yes | Yes |

**22.** In open market transactions, Gold Corp. simultaneously sold its long-term investment in Iron Corp. bonds and purchased its own outstanding bonds. The broker remitted the net cash from the two transactions. Gold's gain on the purchase of its own bonds exceeded its loss on the sale of the Iron bonds. Gold should report the

a. Net effect of the two transactions as an extraordinary gain.
b. Net effect of the two transactions in income before extraordinary items.

c. Effect of its own bond transaction gain in income before extraordinary items, and report the Iron bond transaction as a loss in income before extraordinary items.
d. Effect of its own bond transaction as an extraordinary gain, and report the Iron bond transaction loss in income before extraordinary items.

**23.** Under SFAS 130, *Reporting Comprehensive Income*, corrections of errors are reported in
a. Other comprehensive income.
b. Other income/(expense).
c. Retained earnings.
d. Stockholders' equity

**24.** Service Corp. incurred costs associated with relocating employees in a restructuring of its operations. How should the company account for these costs?
a. Measured at fair value and recognized over the next two years.
b. Measured at fair value and recognized when the liability is incurred.
c. Recognized when the costs are paid.
d. Measured at fair value and treated as a prior period adjustment.

**25.** On January 1, 2007, Deer Corp. met the criteria for discontinuance of a business component. For the period January 1 through October 15, 2007, the component had revenues of $500,000 and expenses of $800,000. The assets of the component were sold on October 15, 2007, at a loss for which no tax benefit is available. In its income statement for the year ended December 31, 2007, how should Deer report the component's operations from January 1 to October 15, 2007?
a. $500,000 and $800,000 should be included with revenues and expenses, respectively, as part of continuing operations.
b. $300,000 should be reported as part of the loss on operations and disposal of a component.
c. $300,000 should be reported as an extraordinary loss.
d. $500,000 should be reported as revenues from operations of a discontinued component.

**26.** Which of the following criteria is not required for a component's results to be classified as discontinued operations?
a. Management must have entered into a sales agreement.
b. The component is available for immediate sale.
c. The operations and cash flows of the component will be eliminated from the operations of the entity as a result of the disposal.
d. The entity will not have any significant continuing involvement in the operations of the component after disposal.

**27.** On November 1, 2007, management of Herron Corporation committed to a plan to dispose of Timms Company, a major subsidiary. The disposal meets the requirements for classification as discontinued operations. The carrying value of Timms Company was $8,000,000 and management estimated the fair value less costs to sell to be $6,500,000. For 2007, Timms Company had a loss of $2,000,000. How much should Herron Corporation present as loss from discontinued operations before the effect of taxes in its income statement for 2007?

   a.  $0
   b.  $1,500,000
   c.  $2,000,000
   d.  $3,500,000

**28.** On December 1, 2007, Greer Co. committed to a plan to dispose of its Hart business component's assets. The disposal meets the requirements to be classified as discontinued operations. On that date, Greer estimated that the loss from the disposition of the assets would be $700,000 and Hart's 2007 operating losses were $200,000. Disregarding income taxes, what net gain (loss) should be reported for discontinued operations in Greer's 2007 income statement?

   a.  $0
   b.  $(200,000)
   c.  $(700,000
   d.  $(900,000)

**29.** A component of Ace, Inc. was discontinued during 2008. Ace's loss on disposal should
   a.  Exclude the associated employee relocation costs.
   b.  Exclude operating losses for the period.
   c.  Include associated employee termination costs.
   d.  Exclude associated lease cancellation costs.

**30.** When a component of a business has been discontinued during the year, this component's operating losses of the current period should be included in the
   a.  Income statement as part of revenues and expenses.
   b.  Income statement as part of the loss on disposal of the discontinued component.
   c.  Income statement as part of the income (loss) from continuing operations.
   d.  Retained earnings statement as a direct decrease in retained earnings.

**31.** When a component of a business has been discontinued during the year, the loss on disposal should
   a.  Include operating losses of the current period.
   b.  Exclude operating losses during the period.
   c.  Be an extraordinary item.
   d.  Be an operating item.

**32.** On January 1, 2008, Shine Co. agreed to sell a business component on March 1, 2008. The gain on the disposal should be
   a.  Presented as an extraordinary gain.
   b.  Presented as an adjustment to retained earnings.
   c.  Netted with the loss from operations of the component as a part of discontinued operations.
   d.  None of the above.

**33.** What is the purpose of reporting comprehensive income?
   a.  To report changes in equity due to transactions with owners.
   b.  To report a measure of overall enterprise performance.
   c.  To replace net income with a better measure.
   d.  To combine income from continuing operations with income from discontinued operations and extraordinary items.

**34.** During 2007, the "other revenues and gains" section of Totman Company's Statement of Earnings and Comprehensive Income contains $5,000 in interest revenue, $15,000 equity in Harpo Co. earnings, and $25,000 gain on sale of available-for-sale securities. Assuming the sale of the securities increased the current portion of income tax expense by $10,000, determine the amount of Totman's reclassification adjustment to other comprehensive income.
   a.  $ 5,000
   b.  $ 2,500
   c.  $35,000
   d.  $15,000

**35.** Which of the following is **not** an acceptable option of reporting other comprehensive income and its components?
   a.  In a separate statement of comprehensive income.
   b.  In a statement of earnings and comprehensive income.
   c.  In the footnotes.
   d.  In a statement of changes in stockholders' equity.

**36.** Accumulated other comprehensive income should be reported on the balance sheet as a component of

| | Retained earnings | Additional paid-in capital |
|---|---|---|
| a. | No | Yes |
| b. | Yes | Yes |
| c. | Yes | No |
| d. | No | No |

**37.** Which of the following changes during a period is not a component of other comprehensive income?
   a.  Unrealized gains or losses as a result of a debt security being transferred from held-to-maturity to available-for-sale.
   b.  Stock dividends issued to shareholders.
   c.  Foreign currency translation adjustments.
   d.  Minimum pension liability adjustments.

**38.** A company buys ten shares of securities at $2,000 each on December 31, 2005. The securities are classified as available for sale. The company does not elect to use the fair value option for reporting its available-for-sale securities. The fair value of the securities increases to $2,500 on December 31, 2006, and to $2,750 on December 31, 2007. On December 31, 2007, the company sells the securities. Assume no dividends are paid and that the company has a tax rate of 30%. What is the amount of the reclassification adjustment for other comprehensive income on December 31, 2007?
   a.  $ 7,500
   b.  $ (7,500)
   c.  $ 5,250
   d.  $ (5,250)

**39.** A company buys ten shares of securities at $1,000 each on January 15, 2007. The securities are classified as available-for-sale. The fair value of the securities increases to $1,250 per share as of December 31, 2007. The company does not elect to use the fair value option for reporting available-for-sale securities. Assume no dividends are paid and that the company has a 30% tax rate. What is the amount of the holding gain arising during the period that is classified in other comprehensive income for the period ending December 31, 2007?
   a.  0
   b.  $7,500

c. $2,500
d. $1,750

**40.** Searles does not elect the fair value option for recording financial assets and liabilities. What amount of comprehensive income should Searles Corporation report on its statement of income and comprehensive income given the following net of tax figures that represent changes during a period?

| | |
|---|---:|
| Pension liability adjustment recognized in OCI | $ (3,000) |
| Unrealized gain on available-for-sale securities | 15,000 |
| Reclassification adjustment, for securities gain included in net income | (2,500) |
| Stock warrants outstanding | 4,000 |
| Net income | 77,000 |

a. $86,500
b. $89,000
c. $89,500
d. $90,500

**41.** If ($2,450) net of tax is the reclassification adjustment included in other comprehensive income in the year the securities are sold, what is the gain (loss) that is included in income from continuing operations before income taxes? Assume a 30% tax rate.
a. $(2,450)
b. $(3,500)
c. $ 2,450
d. $ 3,500

**42.** Which of the following changes during a period is **not** a component of other comprehensive income?
a. Pension liability adjustment for funded status of plan.
b. Treasury stock, at cost.
c. Foreign currency translation adjustment.
d. Reclassification adjustment, for securities gain included in net income.

**43.** Which of the following is true?
a. Separate EPS amounts must be presented for both other comprehensive income and comprehensive income.
b. Separate EPS amounts must be presented for other comprehensive income but not for comprehensive income.
c. Separate EPS amounts must be presented for comprehensive income but not for other comprehensive income.
d. Separate EPS amounts are not required to be presented for either other comprehensive income or comprehensive income.

**44.** Which of the following options for displaying comprehensive income is(are) preferred by FASB?
I. A continuation from net income at the bottom of the income statement.
II. A separate statement that begins with net income.
III. In the statement of changes in stockholders' equity.

a. I.
b. II.
c. II and III.
d. I and II.

**45.** Assume a company does not elect the fair value option in SFAS 159. Which of the following is not classified as other comprehensive income?
a. An adjustment to pension liability to record the funded status of the plan.
b. Subsequent decreases of the fair value of available-for-sale securities that have been previously written down as impaired.
c. Decreases in the fair value of held-to-maturity securities.
d. None of the above.

**46.** When a full set of general-purpose financial statements are presented, comprehensive income and its components should
a. Appear as a part of discontinued operations, extraordinary items, and cumulative effect of a change in accounting principle.
b. Be reported net of related income tax effect, in total and individually.
c. Appear in a supplemental schedule in the notes to the financial statements.
d. Be displayed in a financial statement that has the same prominence as other financial statements.

**Items 47 through 49** are based on the following:

The following trial balance of Mint Corp. at December 31, 2007, has been adjusted except for income tax expense.

| | Dr. | Cr. |
|---|---:|---:|
| Cash | $ 600,000 | |
| Accounts receivable, net | 3,500,000 | |
| Cost in excess of billings on long-term contracts | 1,600,000 | |
| Billings in excess of costs on long-term contracts | | $ 700,000 |
| Prepaid taxes | 450,000 | |
| Property, plant, and equipment, net | 1,480,000 | |
| Note payable—noncurrent | | 1,620,000 |
| Common stock | | 750,000 |
| Additional paid-in capital | | 2,000,000 |
| Retained earnings—unappropriated | | 900,000 |
| Retained earnings—restricted for note payable | | 160,000 |
| Earnings from long-term contracts | | 6,680,000 |
| Costs and expenses | 5,180,000 | |
| | $12,810,000 | $12,810,000 |

Other financial data for the year ended December 31, 2007, are

• Mint uses the percentage-of-completion method to account for long-term construction contracts for financial statement and income tax purposes. All receivables on these contracts are considered to be collectible within twelve months.
• During 2007, estimated tax payments of $450,000 were charged to prepaid taxes. Mint has not recorded income tax expense. There were no temporary or permanent differences, and Mint's tax rate is 30%.

In Mint's December 31, 2007 balance sheet, what amount should be reported as

**47.** Total retained earnings?
a. $1,950,000
b. $2,110,000
c. $2,400,000
d. $2,560,000

**48.** Total noncurrent liabilities?

a.   $1,620,000
b.   $1,780,000
c.   $2,320,000
d.   $2,480,000

**49.** Total current assets?
a.   $5,000,000
b.   $5,450,000
c.   $5,700,000
d.   $6,150,000

**50.** Mirr, Inc. was incorporated on January 1, 2007, with proceeds from the issuance of $750,000 in stock and borrowed funds of $110,000. During the first year of operations, revenues from sales and consulting amounted to $82,000, and operating costs and expenses totaled $64,000. On December 15, Mirr declared a $3,000 cash dividend, payable to stockholders on January 15, 2008. No additional activities affected owners' equity in 2007. Mirr's liabilities increased to $120,000 by December 31, 2007. On Mirr's December 31, 2007 balance sheet, total assets should be reported at
a.   $885,000
b.   $882,000
c.   $878,000
d.   $875,000

**51.** The following changes in Vel Corp.'s account balances occurred during 2007:

|  | Increase |
|---|---|
| Assets | $89,000 |
| Liabilities | 27,000 |
| Capital stock | 60,000 |
| Additional paid-in capital | 6,000 |

Except for a $13,000 dividend payment and the year's earnings, there were no changes in retained earnings for 2007. What was Vel's net income for 2007?
a.   $ 4,000
b.   $ 9,000
c.   $13,000
d.   $17,000

**52.** When preparing a draft of its 2007 balance sheet, Mont, Inc. reported net assets totaling $875,000. Included in the asset section of the balance sheet were the following:

| | |
|---|---|
| Treasury stock of Mont, Inc. at cost, which approximates market value on December 31 | $24,000 |
| Idle machinery | 11,200 |
| Cash surrender value of life insurance on corporate executives | 13,700 |
| Allowance for decline in market value of noncurrent equity investments | 8,400 |

At what amount should Mont's net assets be reported in the December 31, 2007 balance sheet?
a.   $851,000
b.   $850,100
c.   $842,600
d.   $834,500

**53.** In analyzing a company's financial statements, which financial statement would a potential investor primarily use to assess the company's liquidity and financial flexibility?
a.   Balance sheet.
b.   Income statement.
c.   Statement of retained earnings.
d.   Statement of cash flows.

**54.** During 2007, Jones Company engaged in the following transactions:

| | |
|---|---|
| Salary expense to key employees who are also principal owners | $100,000 |
| Sales to affiliated enterprises | 250,000 |

Which of the two transactions would be disclosed as related-party transactions in Jones' 2007 financial statements?
a.   Neither transaction.
b.   The $100,000 transaction only.
c.   The $250,000 transaction only.
d.   Both transactions.

**55.** Dean Co. acquired 100% of Morey Corp. prior to 2007. During 2007, the individual companies included in their financial statements the following:

| | Dean | Morey |
|---|---|---|
| Officers' salaries | $ 75,000 | $50,000 |
| Officers' expenses | 20,000 | 10,000 |
| Loans to officers | 125,000 | 50,000 |
| Intercompany sales | 150,000 | -- |

What amount should be reported as related-party disclosures in the notes to Dean's 2007 consolidated financial statements?
a.   $150,000
b.   $155,000
c.   $175,000
d.   $330,000

**56.** For which type of material related-party transactions does Statement of Financial Accounting Standard 57, *Related-Party Disclosures*, require disclosure?
a.   Only those not reported in the body of the financial statements.
b.   Only those that receive accounting recognition.
c.   Those that contain possible illegal acts.
d.   All those other than compensation arrangements, expense allowances, and other similar items in the ordinary course of business.

**57.** Financial statements shall include disclosures of material transactions between related parties except
a.   Nonmonetary exchanges by affiliates.
b.   Sales of inventory by a subsidiary to its parent.
c.   Expense allowance for executives which exceed normal business practice.
d.   A company's agreement to act as surety for a loan to its chief executive officer.

**58.** Dex Co. has entered into a joint venture with an affiliate to secure access to additional inventory. Under the joint venture agreement, Dex will purchase the output of the venture at prices negotiated on an arm's-length basis. Which of the following is(are) required to be disclosed about the related-party transaction?

I.  The amount due to the affiliate at the balance sheet date.
II. The dollar amount of the purchases during the year.

a.   I only.
b.   II only.
c.   Both I and II.
d.   Neither I nor II.

**59.** What is the purpose of information presented in notes to the financial statements?
a.   To provide disclosures required by generally accepted accounting principles.

b. To correct improper presentation in the financial statements.

c. To provide recognition of amounts **not** included in the totals of the financial statements.

d. To present management's responses to auditor comments.

**60.** Which of the following information should be included in Melay, Inc.'s 2007 summary of significant accounting policies?

a. Property, plant, and equipment is recorded at cost with depreciation computed principally by the straight-line method.

b. During 2007, the Delay component was sold.

c. Business component 2007 sales are Alay $1M, Belay $2M, and Celay $3M.

d. Future common share dividends are expected to approximate 60% of earnings.

**61.** Which of the following information should be disclosed in the summary of significant accounting policies?

a. Refinancing of debt subsequent to the balance sheet date.

b. Guarantees of indebtedness of others.

c. Criteria for determining which investments are treated as cash equivalents.

d. Adequacy of pension plan assets relative to vested benefits.

**62.** According to SFAS 157, fair value of an asset should be based upon

a. The replacement cost of an asset.

b. The price that would be received to sell the asset at the measurement date.

c. The original cost of the asset plus an adjustment for obsolescence.

d. The price that would be paid to acquire the asset.

**63.** Which of the following describes a principal market for establishing fair value of an asset?

a. The market that has the greatest volume and level of activity for the asset.

b. Any broker or dealer market that buys or sells the asset.

c. The most observable market in which the price of the asset is minimized.

d. The market in which the amount received would be maximized.

**64.** Which of the following is true for valuing an asset to fair value?

a. The price of the asset should be adjusted for transaction costs.

b. The fair value of the asset should be adjusted for costs to sell.

c. The fair value price is based upon an entry price to purchase the asset.

d. The price should be adjusted for transportation costs to transport the asset to its principal market.

**65.** According to SFAS 157, which of the following would meet the qualifications as market participants?

a. A liquidation market in which sellers are compelled to sell.

b. A subsidiary of the reporting unit interested in purchasing assets similar to those being valued.

c. An independent entity that is knowledgeable about the asset.

d. A broker or dealer that wishes to establish new market for the asset.

**66.** According to SFAS 157, which of the following is an assumption used in fair value measurements?

a. The asset must be in-use.

b. The asset must be considered in-exchange.

c. The most conservative estimate must be used.

d. The asset is in its highest and best use.

**67.** According to SFAS 157, the fair value at initial recognition is

a. The price paid to acquire the asset.

b. The price paid to acquire the asset less transaction costs.

c. The price paid to transfer or sell the asset.

d. The book value of the asset acquired.

**68.** Which of the following is not a valuation technique used in fair value estimates?

a. Income approach.

b. Residual value approach.

c. Market approach.

d. Cost approach.

**69.** Valuation techniques for fair value that include the Black-Scholes-Merton formula, a binomial model, or discounted cash flows are examples of which valuation technique?

a. Income approach.

b. Market approach.

c. Cost approach.

d. Exit value approach.

**70.** The market approach valuation technique for measuring fair value requires which of the following?

a. Present value of future cash flows.

b. Prices and other relevant information of transactions from identical or comparable assets.

c. The price to replace the service capacity of the asset.

d. The weighted-average of the present value of future cash flows.

**71.** A change in valuation techniques used to measure fair value should be reported as

a. A change in accounting principle with retrospective restatement.

b. An error correction with restatement of the financial statements of previous periods.

c. A change in accounting estimate reported on a prospective basis.

d. An extraordinary item on the current year's income statement.

**72.** According to SFAS 157, which level has the highest priority for valuation inputs?

a. Level 1.

b. Level 2.

c. Level 3.

d. Level 4.

**73.** Which of the following are observable inputs used for fair value measurements?

I. Bank prime rate.

II. Default rates on loans.
III. Financial forecasts.

a. I only.
b. I and II only.
c. I and III only.
d. I, II and III.

**74.** A company that wishes to disclose information about the effect of changing prices in accordance with SFAS 89, *Financial Accounting and Changing Prices*, should report this information in
a. The body of the financial statements.
b. The notes to the financial statements.
c. Supplementary information to the financial statements.
d. Management's report to shareholders.

**75.** Lewis Company was formed on January 1, 2006. Selected balances from the historical cost balance sheet at December 31, 2007, were as follows:

| | |
|---|---|
| Land (purchased in 2006) | $120,000 |
| Investment in nonconvertible bonds (purchased in 2006, and expected to be held to maturity) | 60,000 |
| Long-term debt | 80,000 |

The average Consumer Price Index was 100 for 2006, and 110 for 2007. In a supplementary constant dollar balance sheet (adjusted for changing prices) at December 31, 2007, these selected account balances should be shown at

| | Land | Investment | Long-term debt |
|---|---|---|---|
| a. | $120,000 | $60,000 | $88,000 |
| b. | $120,000 | $66,000 | $88,000 |
| c. | $132,000 | $60,000 | $80,000 |
| d. | $132,000 | $66,000 | $80,000 |

**76.** The following items were among those that appeared on Rubi Co.'s books at the end of 2007:

| | |
|---|---|
| Merchandise inventory | $600,000 |
| Loans to employees | 20,000 |

What amount should Rubi classify as monetary assets in preparing constant dollar financial statements?
a. $0
b. $ 20,000
c. $600,000
d. $620,000

**77.** In its financial statements, Hila Co. discloses supplemental information on the effects of changing prices in accordance with Statement of Financial Accounting Standards 89, *Financial Reporting and Changing Prices*. Hila computed the increase in current cost of inventory as follows:

| | |
|---|---|
| Increase in current cost (nominal dollars) | $15,000 |
| Increase in current cost (constant dollars) | $12,000 |

What amount should Hila disclose as the inflation component of the increase in current cost of inventories?
a. $ 3,000
b. $12,000
c. $15,000
d. $27,000

**78.** When computing purchasing power gain or loss on net monetary items, which of the following accounts is classified as nonmonetary?
a. Advances to unconsolidated subsidiaries.
b. Allowance for uncollectible accounts.

c. Unamortized premium on bonds payable.
d. Accumulated depreciation of equipment.

**79.** During a period of inflation in which a liability account balance remains constant, which of the following occurs?
a. A purchasing power gain, if the item is a nonmonetary liability.
b. A purchasing power gain, if the item is a monetary liability.
c. A purchasing power loss, if the item is a nonmonetary liability.
d. A purchasing power loss, if the item is a monetary liability.

**80.** The following information pertains to each unit of merchandise purchased for resale by Vend Co.:

| *March 1, 2007* | |
|---|---|
| Purchase price | $ 8 |
| Selling price | $12 |
| Price level index | 110 |
| *December 31, 2007* | |
| Replacement cost | $10 |
| Selling price | $15 |
| Price level index | 121 |

Under current cost accounting, what is the amount of Vend's holding gain on each unit of this merchandise?
a. $0
b. $0.80
c. $1.20
d. $2.00

**81.** Kerr Company purchased a machine for $115,000 on January 1, 2007, the company's first day of operations. At the end of the year, the current cost of the machine was $125,000. The machine has no salvage value, a five-year life, and is depreciated by the straight-line method. For the year ended December 31, 2007, the amount of the current cost depreciation expense which would appear in supplementary current cost financial statements is
a. $14,000
b. $23,000
c. $24,000
d. $25,000

**82.** At December 31, 2007, Jannis Corp. owned two assets as follows:

| | Equipment | Inventory |
|---|---|---|
| Current cost | $100,000 | $80,000 |
| Recoverable amount | $ 95,000 | $90,000 |

Jannis voluntarily disclosed supplementary information about current cost at December 31, 2007. In such a disclosure, at what amount would Jannis report total assets?
a. $175,000
b. $180,000
c. $185,000
d. $190,000

**83.** Could current cost financial statements report holding gains for goods sold during the period and holding gains on inventory at the end of the period?

| | Goods sold | Inventory |
|---|---|---|
| a. | Yes | Yes |
| b. | Yes | No |
| c. | No | Yes |
| d. | No | No |

**84.** Manhof Co. prepares supplementary reports on income from continuing operations on a current cost basis in accordance with SFAS 89, *Financial Reporting and Changing Prices.* How should Manhof compute cost of goods sold on a current cost basis?

- a. Number of units sold times average current cost of units during the year.
- b. Number of units sold times current cost of units at year-end.
- c. Number of units sold times current cost of units at the beginning of the year.
- d. Beginning inventory at current cost plus cost of goods purchased less ending inventory at current cost.

**85.** Which of the following are examples of concentrations that create vulnerabilities and therefore would require disclosure of risks and uncertainties?

  I. Market in which an entity conducts its operations.
 II. Available sources of supply of materials used in operations of an entity.
III. Volume of business transacted with a certain contributor.

- a. I and II.
- b. II and III.
- c. I and III.
- d. I, II, and III.

**86.** Which of the following is required to be disclosed regarding the risks and uncertainties that exist?

- a. Factors causing an estimate to be sensitive.
- b. The potential impact of estimates about values of assets and liabilities when it is reasonably possible that the estimate will change in the near future.
- c. The potential impact of estimates about values of assets and liabilities when it is remotely possible that the estimate will change in the near future.
- d. A description of the operations both within and outside of the home country.

**87.** Which of the following accounting bases may be used to prepare financial statements in conformity with a comprehensive basis of accounting other than generally accepted accounting principles?

  I. Basis of accounting used by an entity to file its income tax return.
 II. Cash receipts and disbursements basis of accounting.

- a. I only.
- b. II only.
- c. Both I and II.
- d. Neither I nor II.

**88.** Income tax basis financial statements differ from those prepared under GAAP in that income tax basis financial statements

- a. Do **not** include nontaxable revenues and nondeductible expenses in determining income.
- b. Include detailed information about current and deferred income tax liabilities.
- c. Contain **no** disclosures about capital and operating lease transactions.
- d. Recognize certain revenues and expenses in different reporting periods.

**89.** In financial statements prepared on the income tax basis, how should the nondeductible portion of expenses such as meals and entertainment be reported?

- a. Included in the expense category in the determination of income.
- b. Included in a separate category in the determination of income.
- c. Excluded from the determination of income but included in the determination of retained earnings.
- d. Excluded from the financial statements.

**90.** Which of the following is false?

- a. Prospective financial information may be prepared for general or limited users.
- b. The responsible party is the only limited user.
- c. The financial projection may contain assumptions not necessarily expected to occur.
- d. The financial projection may be expressed as a range of dollars.

**91.** Prospective financial information is defined as

- a. Any financial information about the past, present, or future.
- b. Any financial information about the present or future.
- c. Any financial information about the future related to the day-to-day operations.
- d. Any financial information about the future.

**92.** To achieve a reasonably objective basis, financial forecasts and projections should be prepared

  I. In accordance with GAAP
 II. Using information that is in accordance with the plans of the entity.
III. With due professional care.

- a. I and III.
- b. II and III.
- c. I, II, and III.
- d. I and II.

**93.** Which of the following disclosures should prospective financial statements include?

| | Summary of significant accounting policies | Summary of significant assumptions |
|---|---|---|
| a. | Yes | Yes |
| b. | Yes | No |
| c. | No | Yes |
| d. | No | No |

**SIMULATION PROBLEMS**

**Simulation Problem 1**      (50 to 60 minutes)

| Situation | | | | | |
|---|---|---|---|---|---|
| | Concepts | Financial Statement Classification | Balance Sheet | Communication | Research |

You have been asked to assist the chief accountant of the Stephen King Corporation in the preparation of a balance sheet. Presented below is the balance sheet of Stephen King Corporation for the current year, 2008.

**Stephen King Corporation**
**BALANCE SHEET**
*December 31, 2008*

| | | |
|---|---|---|
| Current assets | | $ 435,000 |
| Investments | | 640,000 |
| Property, plant, and equipment | | 1,720,000 |
| Intangible assets | | 305,000 |
| | | $3,100,000 |
| Current liabilities | $ 330,000 | |
| Long-term liabilities | 1,000,000 | |
| Stockholders' equity | 1,770,000 | |
| | $3,100,000 | |

Consider the following information:

1. The current assets section includes: cash $100,000, accounts receivable $170,000 less $10,000 for allowance for doubtful accounts, inventories $180,000, and unearned revenue $5,000. The cash balance is composed of $114,000, less a bank overdraft of $14,000. Inventories are stated on the lower of FIFO cost or market.
2. The investments section includes: the cash surrender value of a life insurance contract $40,000; investment in common stock, short-term (trading) $80,000 and long-term (available-for-sale) $270,000; and bond sinking fund $250,000. The cost and fair value of investments in common stock are the same.
3. Property, plant, and equipment includes: buildings $1,040,000 less accumulated depreciation $360,000; equipment $450,000 less accumulated depreciation $180,000; land $500,000; and land held for future use $270,000.
4. Intangible assets include: a franchise $165,000; goodwill $100,000; and discount on bonds payable $40,000.
5. Current liabilities include: accounts payable $90,000; notes payable—short term $80,000 and long-term $120,000; and taxes payable $40,000.
6. Long-term liabilities are compose solely of 10% bonds payable due 2016.
7. Stockholders' equity has: preferred stock, no par value, authorized 200,000 shares, issued 70,000 shares for $450,000; and common stock, $1.00 par value, authorized 400,000 shares, issued 100,000 shares at an average price of $10. In addition, the corporation has retained earnings of $320,000.
8. The company's management does not elect to use the fair value option for any of its financial assets or liabilities.

| | Concepts | | | | |
|---|---|---|---|---|---|
| Situation | | Financial Statement Classification | Balance Sheet | Communication | Research |

Identify whether each of the following statements is True or False.

| | | (T) | (F) |
|---|---|---|---|
| 1. | The gain or loss from discontinued operations is placed in a separate category under other income or loss. | ○ | ○ |
| 2. | The gain or loss from infrequent or unusual items is given extraordinary treatment and disclosed on the income statement after discontinued operations. | ○ | ○ |
| 3. | Exit and disposal activities are classified as discontinued operations. | ○ | ○ |
| 4. | A component of a company can be classified as discontinued in the first period that it meets the criteria as being held for sale. | ○ | ○ |
| 5. | A correction of an error is included in the cumulative effect of change in accounting principle on the income statement. | ○ | ○ |
| 6. | Other comprehensive income may be presented at the bottom of the income statement. | ○ | ○ |
| 7. | Separate earnings per share amounts must be presented for both other comprehensive income and comprehensive income. | ○ | ○ |
| 8. | Prospective financial information includes information on the purpose of the statements, assumptions, and significant accounting policies. | ○ | ○ |

| Situation | Concepts | Financial Statement Classification | | Balance Sheet | Communication | Research |
|---|---|---|---|---|---|---|

The outline presented below represents the various classifications suggested by the chief accountant for the balance sheet.

| _Assets_ | _Liabilities_ | _Owner's equity_ | _Other_ |
|---|---|---|---|
| A. Current | G. Current | J. Preferred stock | N. Items excluded from the balance sheet. |
| B. Investments | H. Long-term | K. Common stock | |
| C. Plant and equipment | I. Other liabilities | L. Paid-in capital excess of par | X. Contra valuation account |
| D. Intangibles | | M. Retained earnings | |
| E. Deferred charges | | | |
| F. Other assets | | | |

**Items 1 through 18** represent accounts of the Stephen King Corporation. Determine how each account would be classified from the list above. If the account is a contra or valuation account, mark "X" before the letter. For example: "Allowance for Doubtful Accounts" would be "X–A." An answer may be selected once, more than once, or not at all.

***Items to be answered***

| | | _Assets_ (A-F) | _Liabilities_ (G, H, I) | _Owner's equity_ (J, K, L, M) | _Other_ (N or X) |
|---|---|---|---|---|---|
| 1. | Dividend payable (on King's preferred stock). | | | | |
| 2. | Plant construction in progress by the company. | | | | |
| 3. | Factory building (retired from use and held for sale). | | | | |
| 4. | Land (held for possible future building site). | | | | |
| 5. | Merchandise inventory (held by Stephen King Corporation on consignment). | | | | |
| 6. | Stock dividend distributable (in common stock to common stockholders and to be issued at par). | | | | |
| 7. | Office supplies inventory. | | | | |
| 8. | Sinking fund cash (First National Bank, Trustee). | | | | |
| 9. | Installment sales accounts receivable (average collection period eighteen months). All sales are installment sales. | | | | |
| 10. | Temporary decline in inventory value. | | | | |
| 11. | Advances to officers (indefinite repayment date). | | | | |
| 12. | Estimated warranty costs. The warranty costs are for a one-year warranty on parts and labor. | | | | |
| 13. | Inventory of small tools used in the business. | | | | |
| 14. | Treasury stock under par value method. | | | | |
| 15. | Common stock subscribed (Stephen King Corporation's stock). | | | | |
| 16. | Convertible bonds. | | | | |
| 17. | Securities held as collateral. | | | | |
| 18. | Bank overdraft (only account with bank). | | | | |

| Situation | Concepts | Financial Statement Classification | Balance Sheet | Communication | Research |
|---|---|---|---|---|---|

Complete the corrected balance sheet. To make it a more realistic exam experience use Excel.

| | A | B | C | D | E |
|---|---|---|---|---|---|
| 1 | **Stephen King Corporation** | | | | |
| 2 | **Balance Sheet** | | | | |
| 3 | **December 31, 2008** | | | | |
| 4 | | | | | |
| 5 | Current assets | | | | |
| 6 | Cash | | | | |
| 7 | Trading securities | | | | |
| 8 | Accounts receivable (net of $xxx allowance for doubtful accounts) | | | | |
| 9 | Inventories (lower of FIFO cost or market) | | | | |

| | A | B | C | D | E |
|---|---|---|---|---|---|
| 10 | | | | | |
| 11 | Total current assets | | | | |
| 12 | | | | | |
| 13 | Investments | | | | |
| 14 | Available-for-sale securities | | | | |
| 15 | Bond sinking fund | | | | |
| 16 | Land held for future use | | | | |
| 17 | Cash surrender value of life insurance contract | | | | |
| 18 | | | | | |
| 19 | Total investments | | | | |
| 20 | | | | | |
| 21 | Property, plant, and equipment | | | | |
| 22 | Land | | | | |
| 23 | Buildings (net of accumulated depreciation of $xxx) | | | | |
| 24 | Equipment (net of accumulated depreciation of $xxx) | | | | |
| 25 | | | | | |
| 26 | Total property, plant, and equipment | | | | |
| 27 | | | | | |
| 28 | Intangible assets | | | | |
| 29 | Franchise | | | | |
| 30 | Goodwill | | | | |
| 31 | | | | | |
| 32 | Total intangible assets | | | | |
| 33 | Total assets | | | | |
| 34 | | | | | |
| 35 | Current liabilities: | | | | |
| 36 | Accounts payable | | | | |
| 37 | Notes payable | | | | |
| 38 | Taxes payable | | | | |
| 39 | Bank overdraft | | | | |
| 40 | Unearned revenue | | | | |
| 41 | | | | | |
| 42 | Total current liabilities | | | | |
| 43 | | | | | |
| 44 | Long-term liabilities | | | | |
| 45 | Notes payable | | | | |
| 46 | Bonds payable, 10% due 2015 (less discount of $xxx) | | | | |
| 47 | | | | | |
| 48 | Total long-term liabilities | | | | |
| 49 | Total liabilities | | | | |
| 50 | | | | | |
| 51 | Stockholders' equity | | | | |
| 52 | Paid-in capital | | | | |
| 53 | Preferred stock, no par, authorized xxx shares, issued xxx shares | | | | |
| 54 | Common stock, $1.00 par value, authorized xxx shares, issued xxx shares | | | | |
| 55 | Paid-in capital in excess of par value common | | | | |
| 56 | | | | | |
| 57 | Total paid-in capital | | | | |
| 58 | | | | | |
| 59 | Retained earnings | | | | |
| 60 | | | | | |
| 61 | Total stockholders' equity | | | | |
| 62 | Total liabilities and stockholders' equity | | | | |

| Situation | Concepts | Financial Statement Classification | Balance Sheet | Communication | Research |
|---|---|---|---|---|---|

SFAS 130 requires enterprises to disclose comprehensive income.  Write a memo to the CEO of Stephen King Corporation explaining the following issues related to comprehensive income.

1.   Define comprehensive income, **other** comprehensive income, and **accumulated** other comprehensive income.  You do not need to list specific items of other comprehensive income.

2. How shall comprehensive income be reported in the financial statements?
3. Explain the purpose of reclassification adjustments in measuring comprehensive income.  How should they be
   . reported?
4. What earnings per share disclosures are required for other comprehensive income items and comprehensive income for
   public companies?

To:   CEO, Stephen King Corporation
From: CPA Candidate
Re:   Comprehensive income

```
┌──────────────────────────────────────────────────────────────────────────────────┐
│                                                                                    │
│                                                                                    │
│                                                                                    │
│                                                                                    │
└──────────────────────────────────────────────────────────────────────────────────┘
```

| | | | | | Research |
|---|---|---|---|---|---|
| **Situation** | **Concepts** | **Financial Statement Classification** | **Balance Sheet** | **Communication** | |

Research the professional standards for a description of how items in other comprehensive income are classified.

---

**Simulation Problem 2**                    (50 to 60 minutes)

| Situation | | | | | |
|---|---|---|---|---|---|
| | **Journal Entries** | **Calculations** | **Classification/Disclosures** | **Research** | **Communication** |

Hillside had the following selected account balances as of December 31, 2007.

| | |
|---|---:|
| Accounts receivable | $250,000 |
| Notes receivable | 75,000 |
| Prepaid rent | 168,000 |
| Supplies | 60,000 |
| Inventory | 420,000 |
| Equipment (historical cost) | 640,000 |
| Accounts payable | 176,000 |
| Salaries payable | 15,000 |
| Accumulated depreciation | · 174,000 |

The following information was received from Hillside's accountant.  Adjusting entries have not yet been made.

1. It is estimated that $16,000 of accounts will not be collectible.  A provision for uncollectible accounts has never been
   made by Hillside.
2. Supplies remaining at the end of the year were $37,000.
3. Equipment is depreciated over 20 years with a $60,000 salvage value.
4. Accrued salaries at 12/31/07 were $37,500.
5. The note receivable was signed by the customer on November 1, 2007.  It is a 6-month note with an interest rate of
   12%, with the principle and interest paid at maturity.
6. Rent was paid on August 1, 2007, for 24 months and recorded in a prepaid rent account.
7. Hillside does not elect to use the fair value option for any of its financial assets or liabilities.

| | Journal Entries | | | | |
|---|---|---|---|---|---|
| **Situation** | | **Calculations** | **Classification/Disclosures** | **Research** | **Communication** |

Prepare the adjusting journal entries necessary for each item.  If no entry is necessary, write "no entry."

| | | Calculations | | | |
|---|---|---|---|---|---|
| **Situation** | **Journal Entries** | | **Classification/Disclosures** | **Research** | **Communication** |

Indicate the adjusted balances in the selected accounts after adjusting entries were made on December 31, 2007.

| | |
|---|---|
| Accounts receivable (net) | |
| Notes receivable | |
| Prepaid rent | |
| Supplies | |
| Inventory | |
| Equipment | |
| Accounts payable | |
| Salaries payable | |
| Accumulated depreciation | |

| Situation | Journal Entries | Calculations | Classification/Disclosures | Research | Communication |
|---|---|---|---|---|---|

Hillside Co. is in the process of preparing its financial statements for the year ended December 31, 2008.

**Items 1 through 6** represent various transactions that occurred during 2008.  The following **two** responses are required for each item:

Compute the amount of gain, loss, or adjustment to be reported in Hillside's 2008 financial statements.  Disregard income taxes.  On the CPA exam, a list of numeric answer choices would be provided to select from.

Select from the list below the financial statement category in which the gain, loss, or adjustment should be presented.  A category may be used once, more than once, or not at all.

### Financial Statement Categories

A.  Income from continuing operations.
B.  Extraordinary item.
C.  Cumulative effect of change in accounting principle.
D.  Prior period adjustment to beginning retained earnings.
E.  Separate component of other comprehensive income.

|  | Amount | (A) | (B) | (C) | (D) | (E) |
|---|---|---|---|---|---|---|

1.  On June 30, 2008, after paying the semiannual interest due and recording amortization of bond discount, Hillside redeemed its fifteen-year, 8% $1,000,000 par bonds at 102.  The bonds, which had a carrying amount of $940,000 on January 1, 2008, had originally been issued to yield 10%.  Hillside uses the effective interest method of amortization, and had paid interest and recorded amortization on June 30.  Compute the amount of gain or loss on redemption of the bonds and select the proper financial statement category.    ○ ○ ○ ○ ○

2.  As of January 1, 2008, Hillside decided to change the method of computing depreciation on its sole piece of equipment from the sum-of-the-years' digits method to the straight-line method.  The equipment, acquired in January 2005 for $520,000, had an estimated life of five years and a salvage value of $20,000.  Compute the amount of the depreciation expense for 2008 and select the proper financial statement category, according to FAS 154.    ○ ○ ○ ○ ○

3.  In October 2008, Hillside paid $375,000 to a former employee to settle a lawsuit out of court.  The lawsuit had been filed in 2007, and at December 31, 2007, Hillside recorded a liability from the lawsuit based on legal counsel's estimate that the loss from the lawsuit would be between $250,000 and $750,000.  Compute the amount of gain or loss from settlement of the lawsuit and select the proper financial statement category.    ○ ○ ○ ○ ○

4.  In November 2008, Hillside purchased two marketable securities, I and II, which it bought and held principally to sell in the near term by February 28, 2009.  Relevant data is as follows:

|  | | Fair value | |
|---|---|---|---|
|  | Cost | 12/31/08 | 2/28/09 |
| I | $125,000 | $145,000 | $155,000 |
| II | 235,000 | 205,000 | 230,000 |

  ○ ○ ○ ○ ○

Compute the amount of holding gain or loss at December 31, 2008, and select the proper financial statement category, assuming Hillside classifies the securities as trading securities.

5.  During 2008, Hillside received $1,000,000 from its insurance company to cover losses suffered during a hurricane.  This was the first hurricane ever to strike in Hillside's area.  The hurricane destroyed a warehouse with a carrying amount of $470,000, containing equipment with a carrying amount of $250,000, and inventory with a carrying amount of $535,000 and a fair value of $600,000.  Compute the amount of gain or loss from the financial statement category.    ○ ○ ○ ○ ○

6.  At December 31, 2008, Hillside prepared the following worksheet summarizing the translation of its wholly owned foreign subsidiary's financial statements into dollars.  Hillside purchased the foreign subsidiary for $324,000 on January 2, 2008.  On that date, the carrying amounts of the subsidiary's assets and liabilities equaled their fair values.    ○ ○ ○ ○ ○

|  | Foreign currency amounts | Applicable exchange rates | Dollars |
|---|---|---|---|
| Net assets January 2, 2008 (date of purchase) | 720,000 | $.45 | $324,000 |
| Net income, 2008 | 250,000 | .42 | 105,000 |
| Net assets at December 31, 2008 | 970,000 |  | $429,000 |
| Net assets at December 31, 2008 | 970,000 | .40 | $388,000 |

Compute the amount of the foreign currency translation adjustment and select the proper financial statements category.

| Situation | Journal Entries | Calculations | Classification/Disclosures | Research | Communication |
|---|---|---|---|---|---|

Hillside Company had a loss during the year ended December 31, 2008, that is properly reported as an extraordinary item. On July 1, 2008, Hillside committed itself to a formal plan for sale of a business component that meets the requirements for treatment as discontinued operations. A loss is expected from the proposed sale. Component operating losses were incurred continuously throughout 2008, and were expected to continue until final disposition in 2009. Costs were incurred in 2008 to relocate component employees.

Hillside is also considering changing its method of accounting for inventory from the last-in, first-out (LIFO) method to the average-cost method.

Using the authoritative literature cut and paste your answer to each of the following questions.

1. How should Hillside report the extraordinary item in its income statement?
2. How should Hillside report the effect of the discontinued operations in its 2008 income statement?
3. How should Hillside report the costs that were incurred to relocate employees of the discontinued component?
4. How should Hillside account for the change in inventory method from LIFO to average-cost?
5. What disclosures are required in the financial statements in the year of the change for a change in inventory method?

| Situation | Journal Entries | Calculations | Classification/Disclosures | Research | Communication |
|---|---|---|---|---|---|

Write a memo to the client file answering the following questions:

1. How should Hillside report the extraordinary item in its income statement? Why?
2. How should Hillside report the effect of the discontinued operations in its 2008 income statement?
3. How should Hillside report the costs that were incurred to relocate employees of the discontinued component? Why?

**Do not discuss earnings per share requirements.**

To:   Hillside Company Permanent File
From: CPA Candidate
Re:   Accounting issues related to income statement presentation

---

**Simulation Problem 3**                    (50 to 60 minutes)

| Situation | Classifications | Multistep Income Statement | Retained Earnings Statement | Communication | Research |
|---|---|---|---|---|---|

Presented below is information related to American Horse Company for 2007.

| | |
|---|---|
| Retained earnings balance, January 1, 2007 | $    980,000 |
| Sales for the year | 25,000,000 |
| Cost of goods sold | 17,000,000 |
| Interest revenue | 70,000 |
| Selling and administrative expenses | 4,700,000 |
| Write-off of goodwill (not tax deductible) | 820,000 |
| Income taxes for 2007 | 905,000 |
| Gain on the sale of investments (normal recurring) | 110,000 |
| Loss due to flood damage—extraordinary item (net of tax) | 390,000 |
| Loss on the disposition of the wholesale division | 615,000 |
| Loss on operations of the wholesale division | 200,000 |
| Income tax benefit from discontinued wholesale division | 285,000 |
| Dividends declared on common stock | 250,000 |
| Dividends declared on preferred stock | 70,000 |

American Horse Company decided to discontinue its entire wholesale operations and to retain its manufacturing operations. On September 15, American Horse sold the wholesale operations to Rogers Company.  During 2007, there were 300,000 shares of common stock outstanding all year.

| | Classifications | | | | |
|---|---|---|---|---|---|
| **Situation** | | **Multistep Income Statement** | **Retained Earnings Statement** | **Communication** | **Research** |

The illustrations below represent accounting transactions that affect the recognition of income for an accounting period. Their classification is the subject of this objective format matching question.

For each of the ten illustrations below, select the best classification from those listed A–I below.  A classification may be used once, more than once, or not at all.  Assume SFAS 154 applies to accounting changes.

*Classification*

A.  Change in reporting entity
B.  Correction of an error
C.  Change in accounting principle
D.  Change in estimate
E.  Extraordinary item

F.  Discontinued Operations—Gain or loss from discontinued operations
G.  Not an accounting change
H.  Part of net income before extraordinary items
I.  Discontinued Operations—Gain or loss on disposal

| *Item* | (A) | (B) | (C) | (D) | (E) | (F) | (G) | (H) | (I) |
|---|---|---|---|---|---|---|---|---|---|
| 1.  Newly acquired assets are depreciated using the sum-of-the-years' digits method; previously recorded assets are depreciated using the straight-line method. | O | O | O | O | O | O | O | O | O |
| 2.  Accounting for acquisition of a 100% owned subsidiary. | O | O | O | O | O | O | O | O | O |
| 3.  Reported as a restatement of all periods presented. | O | O | O | O | O | O | O | O | O |
| 4.  Write-down of inventory due to obsolescence. | O | O | O | O | O | O | O | O | O |
| 5.  Gains or losses on the disposal of the net assets of a component are included in this calculation. | O | O | O | O | O | O | O | O | O |
| 6.  Changing from the gross profit method for determining year-end inventory balances to dollar value LIFO. | O | O | O | O | O | O | O | O | O |
| 7.  Accounting for existing construction contracts is changed from completed contract to percentage-of-completion. | O | O | O | O | O | O | O | O | O |
| 8.  The effects of a change in estimate and a change in principle are inseparable for the same event. | O | O | O | O | O | O | O | O | O |
| 9.  The excess of cash paid over the carrying value to extinguish bonds. | O | O | O | O | O | O | O | O | O |
| 10.  Income or loss of the component for the period of disposal included in this calculation. | O | O | O | O | O | O | O | O | O |

| | | **Multistep Income Statement** | | | |
|---|---|---|---|---|---|
| **Situation** | **Classifications** | | **Retained Earnings Statement** | **Communication** | **Research** |

Prepare a multistep income statement.

| American Horse Company INCOME STATEMENT For the Year Ended December 31, 2007 | | |
|---|---|---|
| Sales | | $25,000,000 |
| | | |
| | | |
| | | |
| | | |
| | | |
| | | |
| Net income | | |
| | | |
| Earnings per share | | |
| | | |
| | | |
| | | |
| | | |
| Net income | | |

| Situation | Classifications | Multistep Income Statement | Retained Earnings Statement | Communication | Research |
|---|---|---|---|---|---|

Prepare a retained earnings statement.

| American Horse Company<br>RETAINED EARNINGS STATEMENT<br>For the Year Ended December 31, 2007 | | |
|---|---|---|
| Retained earnings, January 1, 2007 | | $980,000 |
| | | |
| | | |
| | | |
| | | |
| | | |
| | | |
| Retained earnings, December 31, 2007 | | |

| Situation | Classifications | Multistep Income Statement | Retained Earnings Statement | Communication | Research |
|---|---|---|---|---|---|

Write a brief memo to the manager of American Horse explaining the major distinction (1) between revenues and gains, and (2) between expenses and losses.

To:      Manager, American Horse Company
From:   CPA Candidate
Re:      Distinction of income statement items

|  |
|---|
|  |

| Situation | Classifications | Multistep Income Statement | Retained Earnings Statement | Communication | Research |
|---|---|---|---|---|---|

Use the Financial Accounting Standards to research the definition of an extraordinary item.

---

**Simulation Problem 4**                                      (45 to 55 minutes)

| Situation | | | | | |
|---|---|---|---|---|---|
| | Financial Statement Classification | Calculate Net Income | Earnings Per Share | Communication | Research |

Rap Corp. has 100,000 shares of common stock outstanding.  In 2007, the company reports income from continuing operations before taxes of $1,210,000.

Additional transactions not considered in the $1,210,000 are as follows:

1.  In 2007, Rap Corp. sold equipment for $40,000.  The machine had originally cost $80,000 and had accumulated depreciation of $36,000.  The gain or loss is considered ordinary.

2.  The company discontinued operations of one of its subsidiaries during the current year at a loss of $190,000 before taxes.  Assume that this transaction meets the criteria for discontinued operations.  The loss of operations of the discontinued subsidiary was $90,000 before taxes; the loss from disposal of the subsidiary was $100,000 before taxes.

3.  In 2007, the company reviewed its accounts receivable and determined that $26,000 of accounts receivable that had been carried for years appeared unlikely to be collected.

4.  An internal audit discovered that amortization of intangible assets was understated by $35,000 (net of tax) in a prior period.  The amount was charged against retained earnings.

5.  The company sold its only investment in common stock during the year at a gain of $145,000.  The gain is taxed at a total effective rate of 40%.  Assume that the transaction meets the requirements of an extraordinary item.

| Situation | Financial Statement Classification | Calculate Net Income | Earnings Per Share | Communication | Research |
|-----------|-----------------------------------|---------------------|-------------------|---------------|----------|

Select from the list of financial statement categories below the category in which the item should be presented. A financial statement category may be selected once, more than once, or not at all. Assume management does not elect to use the fair value option for any financial assets or liabilities.

### Financial Statement Categories

A. Income from continuing operations, with **no** separate disclosure.
B. Income from continuing operations, with separate disclosure (either on the face of statement or in the notes).
C. Other comprehensive income for the period.
D. Extraordinary items.
E. Separate component of stockholders' equity.
F. None of the above categories include this item.

### Items to be answered

| Item | (A) | (B) | (C) | (D) | (E) | (F) |
|------|-----|-----|-----|-----|-----|-----|
| 1. An increase in the unrealized excess of cost over market value of marketable equity securities classified as trading-type securities. | ○ | ○ | ○ | ○ | ○ | ○ |
| 2. The accumulated amount of the unrealized excess of cost over market value of available-for-sale marketable equity securities. | ○ | ○ | ○ | ○ | ○ | ○ |
| 3. Income from operations of a discontinued component in the component's disposal year. | ○ | ○ | ○ | ○ | ○ | ○ |
| 4. A gain on remeasuring a foreign subsidiary's financial statements from the local currency into the functional currency. | ○ | ○ | ○ | ○ | ○ | ○ |
| 5. A loss on translating a foreign subsidiary's financial statements from the functional local currency into the reporting currency during this period. | ○ | ○ | ○ | ○ | ○ | ○ |
| 6. A loss caused by a major earthquake in an area previously considered to be subject to only minor tremors. | ○ | ○ | ○ | ○ | ○ | ○ |
| 7. The probable receipt of $1,000,000 from a pending lawsuit. | ○ | ○ | ○ | ○ | ○ | ○ |
| 8. The purchase of research and development services. There were **no** other research and development activities. | ○ | ○ | ○ | ○ | ○ | ○ |

| Situation | Financial Statement Classification | Calculate Net Income | Earnings Per Share | Communication | Research |
|-----------|-----------------------------------|---------------------|-------------------|---------------|----------|

Complete the table below for the calculation of net income.

| Rap Corp. INCOME STATEMENT For the Year Ended December 31, 2007 | | | |
|---|---|---|---|
| Income from continuing operations before income tax | | | |
| Income tax | | | |
| Income from continuing operations | | | |
| Discontinued operations: | | | |
| | | | |
| | | | |
| | | | |
| Income before extraordinary item | | | |
| Extraordinary item: | | | |
| | | | |
| Net income | | | |

| Situation | Financial Statement Classification | Calculate Net Income | Earnings Per Share | | Communication | Research |
|---|---|---|---|---|---|---|

Complete the table below for the calculations of earnings per share.

| Rap Corp.<br>EARNINGS STATEMENT<br>For the Year Ended December 31, 2007 | | |
|---|---|---|
| Per share of common stock: | | |
| Income from continuing operations | | |
| Discontinued operations, net of tax | | |
| Income before extraordinary item | | |
| Extraordinary item, net of tax | | |
| Net income | | |

| Situation | Financial Statement Classification | Calculate Net Income | Earnings Per Share | Communication | | Research |
|---|---|---|---|---|---|---|

Write a memo to the controller of Rap explaining the various components of earnings per share that must be disclosed on the income statement and in the notes to the financial statements.

To:      Controller, Rap Corporation
From:   CPA Candidate
Re:      Earnings per share

| Situation | Financial Statement Classification | Calculate Net Income | Earnings Per Share | Communication | Research | |
|---|---|---|---|---|---|---|

Research in the Financial Accounting Standards for a description of the purpose of reporting comprehensive income. Excerpt your answer below.

## MULTIPLE-CHOICE ANSWERS

| | | | | | |
|---|---|---|---|---|---|
| 1.  d __ __ | 18.  b __ __ | 35.  c __ __ | 52.  a __ __ | 69.  a __ __ | 86.  b __ __ |
| 2.  a __ __ | 19.  b __ __ | 36.  d __ __ | 53.  a __ __ | 70.  b __ __ | 87.  c __ __ |
| 3.  a __ __ | 20.  d __ __ | 37.  b __ __ | 54.  c __ __ | 71.  c __ __ | 88.  d __ __ |
| 4.  a __ __ | 21.  c __ __ | 38.  d __ __ | 55.  c __ __ | 72.  a __ __ | 89.  a __ __ |
| 5.  a __ __ | 22.  c __ __ | 39.  d __ __ | 56.  d __ __ | 73.  b __ __ | 90.  b __ __ |
| 6.  d __ __ | 23.  c __ __ | 40.  a __ __ | 57.  b __ __ | 74.  c __ __ | 91.  d __ __ |
| 7.  a __ __ | 24.  b __ __ | 41.  d __ __ | 58.  c __ __ | 75.  c __ __ | 92.  c __ __ |
| 8.  a __ __ | 25.  b __ __ | 42.  b __ __ | 59.  a __ __ | 76.  b __ __ | 93.  a __ __ |
| 9.  b __ __ | 26.  a __ __ | 43.  d __ __ | 60.  a __ __ | 77.  a __ __ | |
| 10.  a __ __ | 27.  d __ __ | 44.  d __ __ | 61.  c __ __ | 78.  d __ __ | |
| 11.  a __ __ | 28.  d __ __ | 45.  c __ __ | 62.  b __ __ | 79.  b __ __ | |
| 12.  c __ __ | 29.  c __ __ | 46.  d __ __ | 63.  a __ __ | 80.  d __ __ | |
| 13.  c __ __ | 30.  b __ __ | 47.  b __ __ | 64.  d __ __ | 81.  c __ __ | |
| 14.  d __ __ | 31.  a __ __ | 48.  a __ __ | 65.  c __ __ | 82.  a __ __ | |
| 15.  b __ __ | 32.  c __ __ | 49.  c __ __ | 66.  c __ __ | 83.  a __ __ | |
| 16.  d __ __ | 33.  b __ __ | 50.  a __ __ | 67.  a __ __ | 84.  a __ __ | 1st:  __/93 = __% |
| 17.  a __ __ | 34.  d __ __ | 51.  b __ __ | 68.  b __ __ | 85.  d __ __ | 2nd:  __/93 = __% |

## MULTIPLE-CHOICE ANSWER EXPLANATIONS

### D.1.  Income and Retained Earnings Statements

**1.  (d)** Baer Food's 2007 revenues should include net sales revenue ($187,000), interest revenue ($10,200), and gain on sale of equipment ($4,700), for a total of $201,900. Discontinued operations (loss of $12,400) and the extraordinary gain ($1,500) are both special items that should be reported as separate components of income, after **income from continuing operations**. Therefore, these items should **not** be included in the revenues section of the income statement (which is placed **before** income from continuing operations).

**2.  (a)** To directly compute cost of goods manufactured (CGM), the formula is

    Beginning work in process
  + Direct materials used
  + Direct labor
  + Factory overhead
  – Ending work in process
    Cost of goods manufactured

However, none of these elements are given in this problem, so CGM must be computed indirectly, using the cost of sales formula

|   | | |
|---|---|---|
| | Beginning finished goods | $400,000 |
| + | Cost of goods manufactured | + CGM |
| – | Ending finished goods | –360,000 |
| | Cost of sales | $240,000 |

Solving for the missing amount, CGM is $200,000.

**3.  (a)** All of the revenues, gains, expenses, and losses given in this problem are components of income from continuing operations. Income before income taxes is $180,000, as computed below.

| | |
|---|---|
| Revenues ($575,000 + $25,000) | $600,000 |
| Expenses and losses ($240,000 + $70,000 + $10,000 + $50,000 + $15,000 + $15,000 + $20,000) | 420,000 |
| Income before income taxes | $180,000 |

To compute income from continuing operations (after taxes), income taxes ($180,000 × 30% = $54,000) must also be deducted ($180,000 – $54,000 = $126,000).

**4.  (a)** The requirement is to compute the amount of expenses to be included in selling expenses for 2007. Advertising ($150,000) and sales salaries and commissions

($140,000) are clearly selling expenses, as is the rent for the office space occupied by the sales department ($220,000 × 1/2 = $110,000). Additionally, freight-out ($80,000) is a selling expense because shipping the goods **from** the point of sale to the customer is the final effort in the selling process. The total selling expense is, therefore, $480,000 ($150,000 + $140,000 + $110,000 + $80,000). The remaining expenses given are general and administrative expenses, except for interest and the loss on sale of long-term investment, which are nonoperating items (other expenses and losses).

**5.  (a)** Operating expenses are usually divided into two categories, **selling expenses** and **general and administrative (G&A) expenses**. Selling expenses are related to the sale of a company's products, while G&A expenses are related to the company's general operations. Therefore, Griff should include the following costs in G&A expense:

| | |
|---|---|
| Accounting and legal fees | $ 25,000 |
| Officers' salaries | 150,000 |
| Insurance | 85,000 |
| G&A expense | $260,000 |

Freight-in ($175,000) is an inventoriable cost which should be reflected in cost of goods sold and ending inventory. Freight-out, the cost of delivering goods to customers ($160,000), is included in selling expenses. Sales representatives salaries ($215,000) is also a selling expense.

**6.  (d)** Interest expense is generally considered to be a nonoperating item and is therefore included in **other expenses and losses**. Operating expenses are usually divided into two categories, **selling expenses** and **general and administrative expenses**. Since advertising expense is directly related to the sale of the company's products, it is included in selling expenses. Therefore, neither of the expenses given are general and administrative expenses.

**7.  (a)** Charitable contributions expense should include all expenses incurred in 2007 by Yew Co. which involve charitable contributions to other entities. The total charitable contributions expense is $310,000, consisting of the $250,000 donated to youth and educational programs and the $60,000 ($140,000 – $80,000) donated to health and human service organizations. The other $80,000 was given to these organizations **by the employees,** with the company merely acting as an agent collecting that amount through payroll deductions and forwarding it on to the organizations. The expenditure for redesigning product packaging ($100,000) would be properly classified as research and development expense.

**8.    (a)**    Per APB 30, extraordinary items are material gains or losses which are both **unusual** in nature and **infrequent** in occurrence. For Raim Co., which sustains flood losses every two to three years, the 2007 flood loss is not infrequent, and should be recognized as a component of income from continuing operations. For Cane Co., the 2007 flood loss is both unusual and infrequent, so it should be recognized as an extraordinary item.

**9.    (b)**    Per APB 30, extraordinary items are material items which are **both unusual** in nature and **infrequent** in occurrence. APB 30 specifically states that the effect of a strike ($175,000) and a gain or loss from sale or abandonment of equipment ($125,000) is **not** considered extraordinary. The loss from the earthquake would be considered unusual and infrequent. Therefore the $150,000 loss is extraordinary, and the total amount of infrequent losses **not** considered extraordinary is $300,000 ($175,000 + $125,000).

**10.    (a)**    Per APB 30, extraordinary items are material items which are **both unusual** in nature and **infrequent** in occurrence. Disposals of plant assets, foreign currency losses, and inventory losses are not considered to be unusual in nature, and thus are not extraordinary. Items that may qualify as extraordinary items include some casualties, expropriations, and prohibitions under a new law. In Kent Co.'s 2007 income statement, losses not considered extraordinary amount to $610,000. The factory disposal ($300,000) is classified as discontinued operations because the operations carried on there are dissimilar from operations carried on at the other factories. The $120,000 foreign currency loss and $190,000 inventory loss are not extraordinary because they are not unusual in nature.

**11.    (a)**    Per APB 30, extraordinary items are material gains or losses which are both **unusual** in nature and **infrequent** in occurrence. Foreign currency losses ($1,200,000) and losses due to discontinued operations ($500,000) are not considered to be unusual in nature and thus are not extraordinary. Items that may qualify as extraordinary include some casualties, expropriations, prohibitions under a new law, and extinguishment of debt. Midway's casualty loss appears to be extraordinary because the hurricane was the first ever to strike in Midway's area. The net pretax loss was $100,000 [$800,000 equipment loss – $700,000 building gain ($1,000,000 – $300,000)].

**12.    (c)**    A gain (loss) must be recognized when a nonmonetary asset is involuntarily converted into monetary assets even if the company reinvests the monetary assets in replacement nonmonetary assets. The gain or loss is the difference between the insurance proceeds ($1,100,000 replacement cost – $50,000 deductible = $1,050,000) and the carrying amount of the assets destroyed or used up as a result of the casualty loss. The warehouse (carrying amount of $300,000) was destroyed, and cash of $20,000 was used to cover removal costs. Therefore, the gain is $730,000 [$1,050,000 – ($300,000 + $20,000)]. It is **not** an extraordi-

nary item because storms similar to the one that destroyed the warehouse occur frequently (every four years).

**13.    (c)**    In this situation, the provision for income tax (income tax expense) will be the amount of the tax liability to the government determined without including the extraordinary loss. This amount is determined by applying the 40% tax rate to pretax accounting income before extraordinary items adjusted for any permanent differences. Accounting income before taxes is $900,000, but that amount includes a gain on life insurance coverage ($100,000). A gain on life insurance coverage is a **permanent** difference because it is included in accounting income but will **never** be included in taxable income. Therefore, the amount of accounting income which will be subject to taxes is $800,000 ($900,000 – $100,000), and the provision for income taxes is $320,000 ($800,000 × 40%). The tax savings from the extraordinary loss ($300,000 × 40% = $120,000) will not affect the provision for income taxes because the extraordinary item must be reported together with its tax effect (extraordinary loss of $180,000; net of tax).

**14.    (d)**    Net income as reported ($74,100) properly included the gain on early retirement of bonds payable ($22,000) and the loss from fire ($14,000). The fact that the gain and loss were reported net of taxes in the income statement was incorrect, but does not cause the net income amount to be in error. However, the other two items should **not** be reported in the income statement at all. An unrealized loss on **noncurrent** investments in stock ($5,400) is reported in other comprehensive income, not in net income. A correction of an error ($7,500) is treated as a prior period adjustment. It is reported in the financial statements as an adjustment to the beginning balance of retained earnings, rather than in the income statement. Since both of these items were subtracted in the computation of reported net income, they must be added back to compute the correct net income of $87,000 ($74,100 + $5,400 + $7,500).

**15.    (b)**    In 2007, Brecon Co. would report one fifth of the cabinet costs as depreciation expense in selling, general, and administrative expenses. Four fifths of the cabinet cost would remain capitalized as fixed assets at the end of 2007. The cabinets are considered fixed assets and not a part of cost of goods sold.

**16.    (d)**    APB 30 states that a material gain or loss that is unusual in nature or infrequent in occurrence, but not both, should be presented as a separate component of income or loss from continuing operations. Both discontinued operations and extraordinary items are reported separately **after** income from continuing operations.

**17.    (a)**    Per APB 30, for an item to qualify as an extraordinary item it must be **both** unusual in nature and infrequent in occurrence. The above criteria must take into account the environment in which the entity operates. An entity with sales in different countries will experience foreign currency revaluations on a regular basis, so a currency revaluation would not be infrequent in occurrence and it is not an extraordinary item. Gains from increases in contract prices are neither infrequent nor unusual, so they cannot qualify as extraordinary items.

**18.    (b)**    Per APB 30, extraordinary items are reported **net of income taxes** as a separate component of income

**after** discontinued operations but before cumulative effect of a change in accounting principle.

**19.    (b)**    Per APB 30, extraordinary items are events and transactions that are distinguished by both their unusual nature and the infrequency of their occurrence. Losses of this type are both common and frequent for Toncan. Per SFAS 5, estimates of the losses would not be presented in the financial statements. No amount is recorded until a loss actually occurs.

**D.2.  Unusual or Infrequent Items**

**20.    (d)**    Per APB 30, a transaction that is unusual in nature and infrequent in occurrence is considered an extraordinary item. An extraordinary item is reported **after** discontinued operations but **before** cumulative effect of accounting changes.

**21.    (c)**    Per APB 30, extraordinary items are events and transactions that are distinguished by both their unusual nature and the infrequency of their occurrence. Teller Co.'s loss arising from its **first** antitrust action meets both of these criteria (particularly since they pleaded guilty) and should therefore be reported as an extraordinary item. The strike against Teller's major supplier, however, should not be reported as an extraordinary item because it is usual in nature but may be expected to recur as a consequence of customary and continuing business activities.

**22.    (c)**    Per APB 30, extraordinary items are material items which are **both unusual** in nature and **infrequent** in occurrence. Therefore, the loss on sale of a bond investment is not extraordinary. In addition, SFAS 145 rescinded SFAS 4 which required gains or losses on extinguishment of debt to be reported as an extraordinary item. Thus, neither item is treated as extraordinary.

**23.    (c)**    SFAS 130 does not completely operationalize the concept of comprehensive income per SFAC 5 and 6 which state all transactions and events other than those with owners should be reported in comprehensive income. Under SFAS 130, corrections of errors shall continue to be reported net of tax in retained earnings as an adjustment of the beginning balance.

**24.    (b)**    SFAS 146 provides that costs of exit activities (including restructuring charges) should be measured and recognized at fair value when they are incurred.

**D.3.  Discontinued Operations**

**25.    (b)**    The operating loss of $300,000 ($500,000 revenues less $800,000 expenses) relates to a discontinued component, so it is part of discontinued operations, **not** continuing operations. It is combined with the loss from disposal on the income statement. **Discontinued operations** is a category distinct from **extraordinary items**.

**26.    (a)**    SFAS 144 includes a number of requirements for disposal of a component to be presented as discontinued operations. However, management is not required to have entered into a sales agreement. It is sufficient if management is committed to a disposal plan that is reasonable. The other items are all required for presentation as discontinued operations.

**27.    (d)**    In discontinued operations, SFAS 144 requires the presentation of the income or loss from operations of the component and the gain or loss on disposal. Since the company met the requirements for "held for sale" status in 2007, the subsidiary should be written down to its fair value less cost to sell. This would result in a loss of $1,500,000 ($8,000,000 carrying amount – $6,500,000 fair value). Therefore, the loss from discontinued operations would be $3,500,000 ($2,000,000 loss from operations + $1,500,000 loss on planned disposal).

**28.    (d)**    According to SFAS 144, the loss from discontinued operations would equal the loss from operations plus the estimated loss from disposal of the component.

**29.    (c)**    SFAS 146 states that costs of termination benefits, lease termination, and consolidating facilities or relocating employees related to a disposal activity that involves discontinued operations should be included in the results of discontinued operations.

**30.    (b)**    The requirement is to determine how a discontinued component's operating losses for the current period should be classified in the financial statements. According to SFAS 144, the "income (loss) from operations" is combined with the loss on disposal.

**31.    (a)**    Per SFAS 144, gains or losses from the operation of a discontinued business component realized for the period are combined with the loss of disposal to determine the loss from discontinued operations.

**32.    (c)**    Per SFAS 144, discontinued operations should include the gain or loss on disposal plus the results of operations during the period.

**D.4.  Comprehensive Income**

**33.    (b)**    Per SFAS 130, the purpose of reporting comprehensive income is to report a measure of overall enterprise performance by displaying all changes in equity of an enterprise that result from recognized transactions and other economic events of the period other than transactions with owners in their capacity as owners. An enterprise should continue to display an amount for net income with equal prominence to the comprehensive income amount displayed.

**34.    (d)**    Once unrealized items recorded and reported in the current or prior period are recognized as realized and reported in net income, it is necessary to reverse them out of other comprehensive income. The reclassification adjustment is to avoid double counting. The reclassification adjustment in this situation is $15,000 ($25,000 gain on AFS securities, net of $10,000 tax).

**35.    (c)**    SFAS 130 allows flexibility in the presentation of comprehensive income in the financial statements. However, the statement should be presented as a primary financial statement. The FASB allows three presentation formats [answer choices (a), (b), and (d)] with a preference for the first two alternatives.

**36.    (d)**    The accumulated balance of other comprehensive income should be reported as a component of equity, separate from retained earnings and additional paid-in capital.

**37.    (b)**    Comprehensive income is defined as the change in equity of a business during a period from transactions of nonowner sources. Stockholders are owners of the corporation or entity, therefore, transactions between the entity and shareholder are not a component of comprehensive income.

**38. (d)** Assuming the fair value option is not used, the calculation of holding gains recognized in other comprehensive income is as follows:

|                    | Before tax | Income tax | Net of tax |
|--------------------|-----------|-----------|-----------|
| Year ended 12/31/06 | $5,000    | $1,500    | $3,500    |
| Year ended 12/31/07 | 2,500     | 750       | 1,750     |
| Total gain          | $7,500    | $2,250    | $5,250    |

The reclassification adjustment should be shown net of tax, so ($5,250) is the adjustment amount. $5,250 had been previously added to other comprehensive income when the gains occurred. The $5,250 needs to be taken out in order to avoid counting the gains twice. The securities have been sold so the gains are now realized and will be part of net income.

**39. (d)** The gain for the period is 10 shares times the increase in fair value, which is $250. This gain of $2,500 must be shown net of tax, so the holding gain is $1,750.

**40. (a)** Per SFAS 130, comprehensive income is computed as follows:

| | | |
|---|---|---|
| Net income | | 77,000 |
| Other comprehensive income net of tax: | | |
| Unrealized gain on securities | 15,000 | |
| Less: Reclassification adjustment | (2,500) | 12,500 |
| Pension liability adjustment | (3,000) | |
| Other comprehensive income | | 9,500 |
| Comprehensive income | | 86,500 |

Notice that stock warrants outstanding are not included as part of comprehensive income.

**41. (d)** If $2,450 (net of tax) is being deducted from other comprehensive income as a reclassification adjustment, $2,450 must be the amount of unrealized gains (net of tax) that have been recognized in other comprehensive income. The realized gains will then be recognized in income from continuing operations before tax. The gains before tax effects are $3,500 ($2,450 ÷ 70%).

**42. (b)** SFAS 130 requires disclosure of changes during a period of the following components of other comprehensive income: unrealized gains and losses on available-for-sale investments and foreign currency items, including any reclassification adjustments, and the pension liability adjustment required to recognize the funded status of the plan. Treasury stock is deducted from stockholders' equity and **not** a component of other comprehensive income.

**43. (d)** Separate EPS calculations are not required for other comprehensive income or comprehensive income according to SFAS 130.

**44. (d)** The FASB prefers that comprehensive income be shown at the bottom of the income statement as a continuation of net income or in a separate statement beginning with net income. Presenting comprehensive income in the statement of changes in stockholders' equity is not a method that is preferred by the FASB.

**45. (c)** If the fair value option is not elected, held-to-maturity securities are reported at amortized cost. Any decreases or increases in fair value are reported neither in net income nor as part of other comprehensive income. Answer (a) and (b) are incorrect because per SFAS 132(R), an adjustment to pension liability to record the funded status of

the plan, and subsequent decreases of the fair value of available-for-sale securities that have been previously written down as impaired are included in other comprehensive income. Answer (d) is incorrect because decreases in the fair value of held-to-maturity securities are not part of other comprehensive income.

**46. (d)** According to SFAS 130, *Reporting Comprehensive Income*, comprehensive income (net income plus other comprehensive income) should be displayed in a financial statement that has the same prominence as other financial statements. Answer (a) is incorrect because the FASB prefers that comprehensive income be displayed either at the bottom of the income statement, continuing from net income to arrive at a comprehensive income figure (equals net income plus other comprehensive income), or in a separate statement of comprehensive income. Answer (b) is incorrect because components of other comprehensive income may be displayed net of related tax effects or before related tax effects with one amount shown for the aggregate income tax effect. Answer (c) is incorrect because comprehensive income can be displayed in the two methods preferred by the FASB (mentioned above) or in the statement of changes in stockholders' equity.

**D.5. Balance Sheets**

**47. (b)** Total retained earnings includes both unappropriated retained earnings and restricted retained earnings. Therefore, before closing entries, total retained earnings is $1,060,000 ($900,000 + $160,000). Before computing 2007 net income, tax expense must be recorded. Earnings ($6,680,000) less costs and expenses ($5,180,000) result in pretax income of $1,500,000. Since the tax rate is 30%, tax expense is $450,000 (30% × $1,500,000). Therefore, an adjustment is necessary to debit **income tax expense** and credit **prepaid taxes** for $450,000. After the adjustment, net income is $1,050,000 ($6,680,000 − $5,180,000 − $450,000). After closing entries, total retained earnings is $2,110,000 ($1,060,000 + $1,050,000).

**48. (a)** The only liabilities included in the trial balance are billings in excess of costs on long-term contracts ($700,000) and note payable-noncurrent ($1,620,000). Only the note is noncurrent. Billings in excess of costs on long-term contracts is similar to unearned revenue and is always reported as a current liability.

**49. (c)** Current assets listed in the trial balance are cash ($600,000), accounts receivable ($3,500,000), cost in excess of billings on long-term contracts ($1,600,000) and prepaid taxes ($450,000). However, income tax expense has not yet been recorded. Earnings ($6,680,000) less costs and expenses ($5,180,000) result in pretax income of $1,500,000. Since the tax rate is 30%, tax expense is $450,000 (30% × $1,500,000). Therefore, an adjustment is necessary to debit **income tax expense** and credit **prepaid taxes** for $450,000. Total current assets, after this adjustment, are $5,700,000.

| | |
|---|---|
| Cash | $ 600,000 |
| Accounts receivable | 3,500,000 |
| Cost in excess of billings | 1,600,000 |
| | $5,700,000 |

**50. (a)** Mirr began operations on 1/1/07 with the following balance sheet elements:

| Assets | = | Liabilities | + | Owners' equity |
|---|---|---|---|---|
| $860,000 | = | $110,000 | + | $750,000 |

During 2007, liabilities increased to $120,000, and owners' equity increased to $765,000 [$750,000 beginning balance + $18,000 net income ($82,000 revenues − $64,000 expenses) − $3,000 dividends declared]. Therefore, 12/31/07 assets must be $885,000.

| Assets | = | Liabilities | + | Owners' equity |
|--------|---|-------------|---|----------------|
| Assets | = | $120,000 | + | $765,000 |
| Assets | = | $885,000 | | |

**51. (b)** The requirement is to determine the net income for 2007 by analyzing changes in the balance sheet. Recall the accounting equation: Assets − Liabilities = Stockholders' equity. By inserting the changes given into this formula, we find an increase of $62,000 exists in the entire stockholders' equity section ($89,000 − $27,000 = $62,000). Stockholders' equity is composed of capital stock, additional paid-in capital and retained earnings. Because increases in the other two balances are given that total $66,000 ($60,000 + $6,000), the retained earnings balance must have decreased by $4,000 ($66,000 − $62,000). When dividends are paid, this reduces retained earnings, while Vel Corp. net income increases the balance of retained earnings. For the equation to balance, the changes in retained earnings account must reduce total stockholders' equity by $4,000. Therefore, if $13,000 in dividends are paid, which reduce retained earnings, and total retained earnings are to be reduced by $4,000, then net income, which increases retained earnings, must be $9,000. This creates the $4,000 difference needed to make the equation balance ($89,000 − $27,000 = $66,000 − $4,000). The following shows the analysis of the retained earnings account:

| | |
|---|---|
| Retained earnings (beg.) | $ xxx |
| Net income (plug) | **9,000** |
| Dividends | ( 13,000) |
| Retained earnings (decrease) | ($ 4,000) |

**52. (a)** Idle machinery ($11,200) and cash surrender value of life insurance ($13,700) are both assets. The allowance for decline in market value of noncurrent marketable equity securities ($8,400) is a contra asset that is properly included in the asset section of the balance sheet (as a deduction). The only item listed which should **not** be included in the asset section of the balance sheet is the treasury stock ($24,000). Although the treasury stock account has a debit balance, it is not an asset; instead, it is reported as a contra equity account. Therefore, the $24,000 must be excluded from the asset section, reducing the net asset amount to $851,000 ($875,000 − $24,000).

**53. (a)** Although the statement of cash flows provides information about liquidity, solvency, and financial flexibility, a potential investor would **primarily** use the balance sheet to assess liquidity and financial flexibility. The balance sheet helps users analyze the company's ability to use current assets to pay current liabilities (liquidity) and the company's ability to alter the amounts and timing of future cash flows to adapt to unexpected needs or to take advantage of opportunities (flexibility).

**D.6.a. Disclosures**

**54. (c)** SFAS 57 requires that financial statements include disclosures of material transactions between related parties. Compensation arrangements in the ordinary course of business, however, are specifically excluded from this disclosure requirement. Therefore, only the $250,000 sale to affiliated enterprises must be disclosed.

**55. (c)** SFAS 57 requires disclosure of material transactions between related parties except: (1) compensation agreements, expense allowances, and other similar items in the ordinary course of business, and (2) transactions which are eliminated in the preparation of consolidated or combined financial statements. The officers' salaries and officers' expenses fall into category (1), while the intercompany sales fall into category (2). Therefore, only the loans to officers ($125,000 + $50,000 = $175,000) are reported as related-party disclosures.

**56. (d)** SFAS 57 requires disclosure of material transactions between related parties except: (1) compensation agreements, expense allowances, and other similar items in the ordinary course of business and (2) transactions eliminated in the preparation of consolidated or combined financial statements.

**57. (b)** SFAS 57 requires disclosure of any material related-party transactions except

1. Compensation agreements, expense allowances, and similar items in the ordinary course of business.
2. Transactions that are eliminated in the preparation of consolidated or combined financial statements.

Since sales of inventory between subsidiary and parent are eliminated in preparing consolidated financial statements, such sales need not be disclosed as a related-party transaction. Nonmonetary exchanges by affiliates are not specifically exempted from disclosure by SFAS 57, and therefore must be disclosed as related-party transactions. SFAS 57 states that compensation arrangements, expense allowances, and similar items in the ordinary course of business need not be disclosed as related-party transactions. However, in this case the allowances are in excess of normal business practice and therefore must be disclosed. Surety and guaranty agreements between related parties are not specifically exempted from disclosure by SFAS 57 and therefore must be disclosed as related-party transactions.

**58. (c)** According to SFAS 57, *Related-Party Disclosures*, disclosures of material transactions shall include (1) nature of relationship(s), (2) description of transaction(s), including those assigned zero or nominal amounts, (3) dollar amounts of transactions for each income statement period and effect of any change in method of establishing terms, and (4) amounts due to/from related parties, including terms and manner of settlement.

**59. (a)** The users of the information are the focus of financial reporting. GAAP requires disclosures in the notes to facilitate the users' understanding of the financial statements. Answer (b) is incorrect because the financial statements should be properly presented in accordance with GAAP; thus no improper presentation should exist. Answer (c) is incorrect because the totals of the financial statements should include all items; thus, no items would be excluded. Answer (d) is incorrect because management's responses to the auditor's comments would be contained in the management letter, which is a separate report typically presented to the audit committee or the board of directors.

**D.6.b. Accounting Policies**

**60. (a)** The requirement is to determine which information should be included in the summary of significant accounting policies. Per APB 22, disclosure of accounting policies should identify and describe the accounting principles followed by the reporting entity and methods of applying those principles. Answer (a) is correct because the method of recording and depreciating assets is an example of such a required disclosure. Answers (b) and (c) are incorrect because both represent detail presented elsewhere in the financial statements. Answer (d) is incorrect because it is an estimate of earnings rather than an accounting policy.

**61.** **(c)** Per APB 22, disclosure of accounting policies should identify and describe the accounting principles followed by the reporting entity and methods of applying those principles. The criteria for determining which investments are treated as cash equivalents is an example of how the entity applies accounting principles. APB 22 states that these disclosures should not duplicate details presented elsewhere as part of the financial statements. Answers (a), (b), and (d) are not disclosures of accounting **policies,** and also would be presented elsewhere in the financial statements.

### D.6.c. Fair Value Measurements

**62.** **(b)** According to SFAS 157, the definition of fair value is the price that would be received to sell an asset in an orderly transaction between market participants at the measurement date. Answer (a) is incorrect because it is an entry price, not an exit price. Answer (c) is incorrect because assets that require to be revalued to fair value should be based on an exit value, not an adjusted historic cost. Answer (d) is incorrect because the price paid to acquire the asset is an entry price, not an exit price.

**63.** **(a)** According to SFAS 157, the principal market is the market in which the reporting entity would sell the asset or transfer the liability with the greatest volume and level of activity for the asset or liability. Answers (b) and (c) are incorrect because they do not meet the definition of principal market. Answer (d) is incorrect because it describes the most advantageous market.

**64.** **(d)** According to SFAS 157, if location is an attribute of the asset, the price in the principal market should be adjusted for costs to transport the asset to its principal or most advantageous market. Answers (a) and (b) are incorrect because prices are not adjusted for transaction costs such as selling costs. Answer (c) is incorrect because fair values are not based upon entry prices to the market.

**65.** **(c)** Market participants are buyers and sellers in the principal market or most advantageous market for the asset or liability. Market participants should be independent, knowledgeable, able to transact for the asset, and willing to transact (i.e., motivated but not compelled to do so). Answer (a) is incorrect because market participants should not be compelled to sell. Answer (b) is incorrect because it is not an independent, unrelated party. Answer (d) is incorrect because the dealer is establishing a new market and is not in the principal market that exists for the asset.

**66.** **(d)** As per SFAS 157, a fair value measurement assumes the highest and best use of the asset that is physically possible, legally permissible, and financially feasible. Answers (a) and (b) are incorrect because to determine the valuation premise, the asset can be classified as either in-use or in-exchange. Answer (c) is incorrect

because for valuation purposes, the highest and best use would maximize the value of the asset.

**67.** **(a)** As per SFAS 157, the fair value at initial recognition is the transaction price that represents the price paid to acquire the asset (an entry price). Answer (b) is incorrect because transaction costs are not included. Answer (c) is incorrect because it is an exit price. Answer (d) is incorrect because it is not a fair value measure.

**68.** **(b)** SFAS 157 outlines three approaches to valuation techniques for fair value: the market approach, the income approach, and the cost approach. There is no technique called the residual value approach.

**69.** **(a)** Per SFAS 157, the income approach uses valuation techniques to convert future amounts to a single present value amount. Therefore, Black-Scholes-Merton, binomial models, or discounted cash flow models are examples of the income approach. Answers (b) and (c) are incorrect because these approaches do not use present value techniques. Answer (d) is incorrect because there is no exit value approach.

**70.** **(b)** Per SFAS 157, the market approach valuation technique uses prices and other relevant information generated by market transactions involving identical or comparable assets or liabilities. Answer (a) is incorrect because it refers to the income approach. Answer (c) is incorrect because it refers to the cost approach. Answer (d) is incorrect because it is not a technique for any of the permissible valuation techniques.

**71.** **(c)** Per SFAS 157, para 20, a change in valuation technique used to measure fair value should be reported as a change in accounting estimate. The change is reported on a prospective basis; however, the disclosures required by SFAS 154 for change in accounting estimate are not required for a change in valuation technique. Answers (a), (b), and (d) are incorrect.

**72.** **(a)** Per SFAS 157, the fair value hierarchy prioritizes the inputs to valuation techniques into three levels: Level 1, Level 2, and Level 3. The highest priority is given to Level 1 inputs, which are quoted prices in active markets for identical assets and liabilities. Answers (b) and (c) are incorrect, because these levels are lower priority than Level 1. Answer (d) is incorrect because there is no Level 4 input.

**73.** **(b)** The bank prime rate and the default rates are both observable inputs. A financial forecast is developed by an entity and is an unobservable input or Level 3 input. Therefore, answers (a), (c), and (d) are incorrect.

### D.6.e. Constant Dollar Accounting

**74.** **(c)** SFAS 89 encourages, but does not require, business enterprises to disclose **supplementary information** on the effects of changing prices. The statement presents requirements to be followed by enterprises that voluntarily elect to disclose this information. Answers (a) and (b) are incorrect because the information is not reported in the body of the financial statements or in the notes to the financial statements. Answer (d) is incorrect because management's report to shareholders identifies management's responsibilities, including responsibilities for the internal control system, and would not include information about changing prices.

**75.   (c)**     The requirement is to determine the amounts to be reported for three balance sheet accounts in a supplementary **constant dollar** balance sheet.  In a constant dollar balance sheet, **nonmonetary** items are restated to the current price level, while monetary items are **not** restated because they are already stated in current dollars.  The investment in bonds and the long-term debt are monetary items since their amounts are fixed by contract in terms of number of dollars.  Therefore, these items are not restated and are reported at $60,000 and $80,000, respectively.  The land, however, is a nonmonetary item and its cost ($120,000) must be restated to current dollars by using the TO/FROM ratio (110/100), resulting in an adjusted amount of $132,000 ($120,000 × 110/100).  Reference to SFAS 89 will provide guidance on monetary/nonmonetary classifications.

**76.   (b)**     According to SFAS 89, "loans to employees" is a monetary asset account since its payment amount is fixed at some point in the future.  Conversely, merchandise inventory is considered a nonmonetary asset account since its value will change based on relative price levels in the future.  The total value of monetary assets is the balance of the loans to employees account, or $20,000.

**77.   (a)**     The increase in current cost (nominal dollars) of $15,000 is the **total** increase in current cost, including any increase caused by inflation.  The effect of changes in the general price level is **not** separated from the effect of changes in specific value.  The increase in current cost (constant dollars) of $12,000 is the increase in current cost after eliminating any increase caused by inflation.  Therefore, the inflation component of the increase in current cost of inventories is $3,000 ($15,000 − $12,000).

**78.   (d)**     The requirement is to determine which item is classified as nonmonetary when computing the purchasing power gain or loss on net monetary items.  SFAS 89 defines a monetary item as one that is fixed or determinable without reference to future prices.  Accumulated depreciation is not a monetary item.  Advances to unconsolidated subsidiaries, allowance for doubtful accounts, and unamortized premium on bonds payable are all monetary items.

**79.   (b)**     Per SFAS 89, a purchasing power gain or loss is the net gain or loss determined by restating in units of constant purchasing power the opening and closing balances of, and transactions in, **monetary** assets and liabilities.  During a period of rising prices, monetary liabilities give rise to purchasing power gains because they will be settled with cash which can be used to purchase relatively fewer goods or services at a future time.

### D.6.f.   Current Cost Accounting

**80.   (d)**     Current cost accounting is a method of valuing and reporting assets, liabilities, revenues, and expenses at their current cost at the balance sheet date or at the date of their use or sale.  A holding gain is recorded as an increase in an item's value.  At December 31, 2007, Vend Co. is holding merchandise which is currently valued at $10 per unit (replacement cost), while the original recorded value of the merchandise was $8 per unit (purchase price).  Therefore, the holding gain is $2 per unit.

**81.   (c)**     The requirement is to calculate the amount of current cost depreciation expense which would appear in supplementary current cost financial statements.  Per SFAS 89, depreciation is to be measured based on the **average** current cost of the asset during the period of use.  The average current cost of this machine during 2007 is $120,000 [($115,000 + $125,000) ÷ 2].  Therefore, 2007 depreciation expense is $24,000 ($120,000 ÷ 5-year useful life).

**82.   (a)**     SFAS 89 requires that current cost for inventories and equipment be measured at the lower of current cost or recoverable amount.  For equipment, recoverable amount ($95,000) is lower than current cost; for inventory, current cost ($80,000) is lower than recoverable amount.  Therefore, the total amount to be reported for these assets is $175,000 ($95,000 + $80,000).

**83.   (a)**     Per SFAS 89, increases or decreases in the current cost of inventory result from the difference between the measures of assets at their entry dates (beginning of year or purchase date) and measures of assets at their exit dates (end of year or date of use/sale).  Based on this definition, holding gains would be reported both when inventory is sold during the year (realized gains), and when inventory is held at the end of the year (unrealized gains).

**84.   (a)**     SFAS 89 illustrates the computation of cost of goods sold under the current cost method.  The current cost of goods sold is computed by multiplying the average cost of units produced or purchased during the year times the number of units sold.

### D.6.g.   Risks and Uncertainites

**85.   (d)**     The market in which an entity conducts its operations, the available sources of supply of materials used in operations of an entity, and the volume of business transacted with a certain contributor are all examples of concentrations that create vulnerabilities that are required to be disclosed per SOP 94-6, *Disclosures of Certain Significant Risks and Uncertainties*.

**86.   (b)**     The potential impact of estimates about values of assets and liabilities when it is reasonably possible that the estimate will change in the near future is a required disclosure regarding significant risks and uncertainties.  Factors causing an estimate to be sensitive is not a required disclosure, only recommended.  The potential impact of estimates about values of assets and liabilities when it is remotely possible that the estimate will change in the near future is not a required disclosure.  It is only a required disclosure if it is reasonably possible that the estimates will change in the near future.  Only a description of operations outside the home country is a required disclosure.

### D.8.   Other Comprehensive Bases of Accounting

**87.   (c)**     Other than generally accepted accounting principles, the only other bases which may be used to prepare financial statements in conformity with a comprehensive basis of accounting are the **cash basis** and a **basis of accounting used to file an income tax return**.

**88.   (d)**     When financial statements are prepared using an income tax basis, two accounting methods can be used:  (1) modified cash basis—hybrid method of IRS and (2) accrual basis—IRS.  The modified cash basis reflects the use of accrual basis for inventories, cost of goods sold, sales, and depreciation, if these are significant. The accrual basis uses accruals and deferrals with several exceptions (e.g., prepaid income, warranty expense). When financial statements are prepared on an income tax basis, the financial statements should not simply repeat items and amounts reported in the tax return. Thus, items such as nontaxable municipal interest and the nondeductible portion of travel and entertainment expense should be fully reflected in the income statement on the basis used for tax purposes, with footnote disclosure of the differences between the amounts reported in the income statements and tax return.

**89.** **(a)** In financial statements prepared on the income tax basis, the nondeductible portion of meals and entertainment expense should be included with the deductible portion as a total amount of travel and entertainment expense. Additionally, the nondeductible portion should be footnoted. Answer (a) is the best answer among the alternatives given, although it does not indicate that a footnote is required. The answer to this question is found in an AICPA practice publication entitled *Preparing and Reporting on Cash- and Tax-basis Financial Statements* that gives guidance to practitioners on preparing financial statements on other comprehensive bases of accounting.

### D.9. Prospective Financial Information

**90.** **(b)** The responsible party is not the only limited user. Third parties with whom the responsible party is negotiating directly are also limited users. Answer (a) is incorrect because prospective financial information may be prepared for general or limited use. Answer (c) is incorrect because it is true that assumptions not necessarily expected to occur may be included in the financial projection. Answer (d) is incorrect because the financial projection may be expressed as a range of dollars.

**91.** **(d)** Prospective financial information is defined as any financial information about the future.

**92.** **(c)** Financial forecasts and projections must be prepared in accordance with GAAP, with the plans of the entity, and with due professional care in order to achieve a reasonably objective basis.

**93.** **(a)** According to the AICPA *Accounting and Auditing Guide*, prospective financial statements include information on the purpose of the statements, assumptions, and significant accounting policies.

**SOLUTIONS TO SIMULATION PROBLEMS**

**Simulation Problem 1**

| Situation | Concepts | Financial Statement Classification | Balance Sheet | Communication | Research |
|---|---|---|---|---|---|

|   |   | (T) | (F) |
|---|---|---|---|
| 1. | The gain or loss from discontinued operations is placed in a separate category under other income or loss. | ○ | ● |
| 2. | The gain or loss from infrequent or unusual items is given extraordinary treatment and disclosed on the income statement after discontinued operations. | ○ | ● |
| 3. | Exit and disposal activities are classified as discontinued operations. | ○ | ● |
| 4. | A component of a company can be classified as discontinued in the first period that it meets the criteria as being held for sale. | ● | ○ |
| 5. | A correction of an error is included in the cumulative effect of change in accounting principle on the income statement. | ○ | ● |
| 6. | Other comprehensive income may be presented at the bottom of the income statement. | ● | ○ |
| 7. | Separate earnings per share amounts must be presented for both other comprehensive income and comprehensive income. | ○ | ● |
| 8. | Prospective financial information includes information on the purpose of the statements, assumptions, and significant accounting policies. | ● | ○ |

**Explanation of solutions**

1. (F) Discontinued operations are placed in a separate category after income from continuing operations and before extraordinary items.

2. (F) An item must be **both** infrequent and unusual to be treated as an extraordinary item.

3. (F) Exit and disposal activities that are not in connection with a component of the entity that qualifies for extraordinary treatment should be reported as unusual or infrequent income/loss in income from continuing operations before income taxes.

4. (T) A component must be classified as discontinued when it meets the criteria.

5. (F) A correction of an error requires restatement of the financial statements.

6. (T) Flexibility is allowed for presentation.

7. (F) Separate EPS amounts are only required for gains/losses from discontinued operations, extraordinary items, and cumulative effect of accounting changes.

8. (T) The notes to prospective financial statements must include those disclosures.

| Situation | Concepts | Financial Statement Classification | Balance Sheet | Communication | Research |
|---|---|---|---|---|---|

|   |   | Assets (A-F) | Liabilities (G, H, I) | Owner's equity (J, K, L, M) | Other (N or X) |
|---|---|---|---|---|---|
| 1. | Dividend payable (on King's preferred stock). | | G | | |
| 2. | Plant construction in progress by the company. | C | | | |
| 3. | Factory building (retired from use and held for sale). | F | | | |
| 4. | Land (held for possible future building site). | B | | | |
| 5. | Merchandise inventory (held by Stephen King Corporation on consignment). | | | | N |
| 6. | Stock dividend distributable (in common stock to common stockholders and to be issued at par). | | | K | |
| 7. | Office supplies inventory. | A | | | |
| 8. | Sinking fund cash (First National Bank, Trustee). | B | | | |
| 9. | Installment sales accounts receivable (average collection period eighteen months). All sales are installment sales. | A | | | |

| | Assets (A-F) | Liabilities (G, H, I) | Owner's equity (J, K, L, M) | Other (N or X) |
|---|---|---|---|---|
| 10.  Temporary decline in inventory value. | | | | N |
| 11.  Advances to officers (indefinite repayment date). | F | | | |
| 12.  Estimated warranty costs. The warranty costs are for a one-year warranty on parts and labor. | | G | | |
| 13.  Inventory of small tools used in the business. | C | | | |
| 14.  Treasury stock under par value method. | | | | X-K |
| 15.  Common stock subscribed (Stephen King Corporation's stock). | | | K | |
| 16.  Convertible bonds. | | H | | |
| 17.  Securities held as collateral. | | | | N |
| 18.  Bank overdraft (only account with bank). | | G | | |

## Explanation of solutions

**1.**  **(G)**  When a corporation declares a cash or property dividend, the amount to be paid becomes a liability of the corporation. The dividends payable amount would be classified as a current liability on the balance sheet. It is important to note that dividends payable represent the amount distributed to stockholders as a return on their investment. Dividends are not expenses.

**2.**  **(C)**  When an item of property, plant, or equipment is being constructed by the company that intends to use it, all of the relevant costs related to the construction should be included in the asset. The asset would be classified as plant and equipment.

**3.**  **(F)**  A factory building that has been retired from use and held for sale should be classified as an **other asset** rather than as property, plant and equipment. The property, plant and equipment account should include only those tangible assets that are being used in operations.

**4.**  **(B)**  Land that is held for speculative or investment purposes should be classified as an investment rather than as property, plant, and equipment. The property, plant, and equipment account should represent only those assets being used in current operations.

**5.**  **(N)**  Consigned inventory is excluded from the balance sheet because it is not owned by King. Consigned inventory represents an arrangement whereby the owner of the goods transfers physical possession to an agent (King). The agent (consignee) will attempt to sell the goods on the owner's behalf. The inventory remains an asset of its owner.

**6.**  **(K)**  A stock dividend distributable represents a dividend to be distributed to shareholders in the form of additional shares of the corporation's stock. Each shareholder will receive a proportional share of additional stock. The declaration of a stock dividend does not result in a liability, as it does not result in any of the corporation's assets being paid. Thus, a stock dividend distributable would be classified as an addition in the stockholders' equity section in the common stock account.

**7.**  **(A)**  Current assets represent cash or other assets that are expected to be used within the operating cycle. Office supplies inventory represents an asset that could be expected to be used within the operating cycle.

**8.**  **(B)**  Generally, a fund is a group of assets set aside for a future nonoperating purpose. A sinking fund contains assets to be used in the future to retire bonds. These assets are generally invested while waiting to be used and are noncurrent.

**9.**  **(A)**  An installment sales accounts receivable results when the corporation makes a sale to a customer and does not receive payment in full on the date of sale. Since this company normally sells on the installment basis, its operating cycle becomes eighteen months. Its receivables are current assets because their average life falls within the operating cycle.

**10.**  **(N)**  Temporary decline in inventory value is a loss and appears on the income statement.

**11.**  **(F)**  Advances to officers are considered nontrade receivables. These types of receivables should be reported separately on the balance sheet as other assets.

**12.**  **(G)**  A warranty is a guarantee made by the seller to the purchaser against defects in the product's quality. Estimated warranty expense for a given period can be estimated as a percentage of sales. The percentage is based on past warranty experience. The estimated warranty cost represents the warranty expenditures in the future for past sales and is a current liability.

**13.**  **(C)**  Property, plant, and equipment consists of items used in the normal operations of a business. The inventory of small tools represents tools **used** in the business and are not for sale.

**14.**  **(X-K)**  Treasury stock is a corporation's own stock which has been issued and reacquired by the corporation. Treasury stock may be accounted for under the cost or par value method. When the par value method is used, treasury stock would be recorded on the balance sheet as a reduction or contra to the common stock account.

**15.**  **(K)**  Common stock subscribed represents stock subscriptions that have not been fully paid. The stock is not considered to be issued until the full price is paid. This account should be classified as an increase in the common stock and it is offset in stockholders' equity by a contra account for the balance of the subscription due.

**16.  (H)** A convertible bond is a bond which may be converted to another form of the corporation's securities during a speci-fied time frame.  A bond is typically classified as a long-term liability on the balance sheet.

**17.  (N)** Corporations do not own securities they hold as collateral.  The corporation will retain the securities only in the event of a default on the receivable the securities are collateralizing.  Thus, the securities are excluded from the balance sheet of King and they appear on the balance sheets of their owners.

**18.  (G)** A bank overdraft occurs when a check is written for a greater amount than the balance in the bank account.  A bank overdraft should be classified as a current liability.  It should not be offset against other cash account balances unless the cash account is in the same bank.

| Situation | Concepts | Financial Statement Classification | Balance Sheet | Communication | Research |
|---|---|---|---|---|---|

| | A | B | C | D | E |
|---|---|---|---|---|---|
| 1 | **Stephen King Corporation** | | | | |
| 2 | **Balance Sheet** | | | | |
| 3 | **December 31, 2008** | | | | |
| 4 | | | | | |
| 5 | Current assets | | | | |
| 6 | Cash | | | | $  114,000 |
| 7 | Trading securities | | | | 80,000 |
| 8 | Accounts receivable (net of $10,000 allowance for doubtful accounts) | | | | 160,000 |
| 9 | Inventories (lower of FIFO cost or market) | | | | 180,000 |
| 10 | | | | | |
| 11 | Total current assets | | | | 534,000 |
| 12 | | | | | |
| 13 | Investments | | | | |
| 14 | Available-for-sale securities | | | | 270,000 |
| 15 | Bond sinking fund | | | | 250,000 |
| 16 | Land held for future use | | | | 270,000 |
| 17 | Cash surrender value of life insurance contract | | | | 40,000 |
| 18 | | | | | |
| 19 | Total investments | | | | 830,000 |
| 20 | | | | | |
| 21 | Property, plant, and equipment | | | | |
| 22 | Land | | | | 500,000 |
| 23 | Buildings (net of accumulated depreciation of $360,000) | | | | 680,000 |
| 24 | Equipment (net of accumulated depreciation of $180,000) | | | | 270,000 |
| 25 | | | | | |
| 26 | Total property, plant, and equipment | | | | 1,450,000 |
| 27 | | | | | |
| 28 | Intangible assets | | | | |
| 29 | Franchise | | | | 165,000 |
| 30 | Goodwill | | | | 100,000 |
| 31 | | | | | |
| 32 | Total intangible assets | | | | 265,000 |
| 33 | Total assets | | | | $3,079,000 |
| 34 | | | | | |
| 35 | Current liabilities: | | | | |
| 36 | Accounts payable | | $90,000 | | |
| 37 | Notes payable | | 80,000 | | |
| 38 | Taxes payable | | 40,000 | | |
| 39 | Bank overdraft | | 14,000 | | |
| 40 | Unearned revenue | | 5,000 | | |
| 41 | | | | | |
| 42 | Total current liabilities | | 229,000 | | |
| 43 | | | | | |
| 44 | Long-term liabilities | | | | |
| 45 | Notes payable | | 120,000 | | |
| 46 | Bonds payable, 10% due 2015 (less discount of $40,000) | | 960,000 | | |
| 47 | | | | | |
| 48 | Total long-term liabilities | | 1,080,000 | | |
| 49 | Total liabilities | | $1,309,000 | | |

| | A | B | C | D | E |
|---|---|---|---|---|---|
| 50 | | | | | |
| 51 | Stockholders' equity | | | | |
| 52 | Paid-in capital | | | | |
| 53 | Preferred stock, no par, authorized 200,000 shares, issued 70,000 shares | | 450,000 | | |
| 54 | Common stock, $1.00 par value, authorized 40,000 shares, issued 100,000 shares | | 100,000 | | |
| 55 | Paid-in capital in excess of par value common | | 900,000 | | |
| 56 | | | | | |
| 57 | Total paid-in capital | | $1,450,000 | | |
| 58 | | | | | |
| 59 | Retained earnings | | 320,000 | | |
| 60 | | | | | |
| 61 | Total stockholders' equity | | 1,770,000 | | |
| 62 | Total liabilities and stockholders' equity | | $3,079,000 | | |

| Situation | Concepts | Financial Statement Classification | Balance Sheet | Communication | Research |
|---|---|---|---|---|---|

To:    CEO, Stephen King Corporation
From: CPA Candidate
Re:    Comprehensive income

As we discussed, you have requested a description of comprehensive income. Comprehensive income, as used in SFAS 130, includes the total of all items of income of which net income is one part. Additional items are called components of other comprehensive income and include revenues, gains, expenses, and losses that are not included in net income under generally accepted accounting principles. Accumulated other comprehensive income represents cumulative amounts which are included in the stockholders' equity section of the balance sheet, whereas other comprehensive income components are single period amounts.

Comprehensive income may be reported in the financial statements under one of three alternatives.

1. At the bottom of the income statement, continuing from net income to arrive at a comprehensive income figure,
2. In a separate comprehensive income statement that starts with net income, or
3. In the statement of changes in stockholders' equity.

All components should be shown net of tax, or a total tax expense may be shown with the detail for each component in the notes.

Reclassification adjustments are necessary to avoid double counting of items recognized as realized in net income of the current period that were recognized as unrealized in other comprehensive income in the current or prior period. The adjustments are shown as additions or subtractions (net of tax) from each item, except for those relating to the minimum pension liability which is shown net of adjustment for the period.

Disclosure of earnings per share is not required for other comprehensive income items or for comprehensive income.

If you have any other questions, please contact me.

| Situation | Concepts | Financial Statement Classification | Balance Sheet | Communication | Research |
|---|---|---|---|---|---|

## Classifications within Other Comprehensive Income
## FAS 130, Para 17 or Current Text C49.111

17. Items included in other comprehensive income shall be classified based on their nature. For example, under existing accounting standards, other comprehensive income shall be classified separately into foreign currency items, minimum pension liability adjustments, and unrealized gains and losses on certain investments in debt and equity securities. Additional classifications or additional items within current classifications may result from future accounting standards.

**Simulation Problem 2**

| Situation | Journal Entries | Calculations | Classification/Disclosures | Research | Communication |
|---|---|---|---|---|---|

| | | | Calculations | Classification/Disclosures | |
|---|---|---|---|---|---|

**1.** Bad debt expense        16,000
     Allowance for uncollectible account        16,000

**2.** Supplies expense        23,000
     Supplies        23,000
     [remaining = 23,000 (60,000 − 37,000)]

**3.** Depreciation expense        29,000
     Accumulated depreciation        29,000
     (640,000 − 60,000) ÷ 20 years = 29,000 per year

**4.** Salary expense        37,500
     Salaries payable        37,500

**5.** Interest receivable        1,500
     Interest income        1,500
     75,000 × 12% × 2/12 = 1,500

**6.** Rent expense        35,000
     Prepaid rent        35,000
     168,000 ÷ 24 mo. = 7,000 per month × 5 months = 35,000

| Situation | Journal Entries | Calculations | Classification/Disclosures | Research | Communication |
|---|---|---|---|---|---|

| | | |
|---|---|---|
| Accounts receivable (net) | 234,000 | (1) |
| Notes receivable | 75,000 | (2) |
| Prepaid rent | 133,000 | (3) |
| Supplies | 37,000 | (4) |
| Inventory | 420,000 | (5) |
| Equipment (historical cost) | 640,000 | (6) |
| Accounts payable | 176,000 | (7) |
| Salaries payable | 52,500 | (8) |
| Accumulated depreciation | 203,000 | (9) |

**Explanation of solutions**

1. $250,000 − $16,000 allowance for uncollectible accounts = $234,000

2. No change. Interest receivable is recorded in a separate account.

3. $168,000 − $35,000 = $133,000

4. Given in the problem.

5. No adjustments were made to inventory.

6. Equipment is at historical cost.

7. No change.

8. $15,000 + $37,500 = $52,500

9. $174,000 + $29,000 = $203,000

| Situation | Journal Entries | Calculations | Classification/Disclosures | Research | Communication |
|---|---|---|---|---|---|

**1. ($73,000, A)** The net carrying amount of the bonds redeemed is determined by adjusting the carrying amount of the bonds at the beginning of the year for any partial year amortization of corresponding premiums or discounts and for any unamortized issue costs. In this example, Hillside would determine its discount amortization by computing the difference between its bond interest expense and its bond interest paid as of June 30, 2008.

$$\underbrace{\left(\substack{\text{Carrying amount of bonds} \\ \text{at beginning of period}} \times \substack{\text{Effective} \\ \text{interest rate}}\right)}_{\text{Bond interest expense}} - \underbrace{\left(\substack{\text{Face value of} \\ \text{bonds}} \times \substack{\text{Stated} \\ \text{interest rate}}\right)}_{\text{Bond interest paid}} = \substack{\text{Amortization} \\ \text{amount}}$$

$$(\$940,000 \times 10\% \times 1/2) - (\$1,000,000 \times 8\% \ 1/2) = \$7,000$$

This amount is added to the carrying amount of the bonds at the beginning of the year to determine the net carrying amount: $\$940,000 + \$7,000 = \$947,000$. This amount is subtracted from the reacquisition price to determine the loss on redemption: $\$1,020,000$ ($\$1,000,000 \times 1.02$) – $\$947,000 = \underline{\$73,000}$. Gains or losses from early redemption of bonds are treated as gains or losses in determining net income. According to SFAS 145, early extinguishment of debt is no longer routinely considered an extraordinary item.

**2. ($50,000, A)** The accounting change is accounted for on a prospective basis. Therefore, it is necessary to calculate the book value of the asset as of the beginning of the year of the change.

| | *SYD* | |
|---|---|---|
| 2005 | $\$500,000 \times 5/15 =$ | $\$166,667$ |
| 2006 | $\$500,000 \times 4/15 =$ | $\$133,333$ |
| 2007 | $\$500,000 \times 3/15 =$ | $\underline{\$100,000}$ |
| | | $\$400,000$ |

On January 1, 2008, the book value is calculated as follows:

| | |
|---|---|
| Historical cost | $\$520,000$ |
| – Accumulated depreciation | $(\underline{400,000})$ |
| Book value 1/1/08 | $\$120,000$ |

Straight-line depreciation for 2008 and future years is calculated as

($\$120,000$ BV – $\$20,000$ salvage value) ÷ 2 years remaining life = $\$50,000$ per year

The depreciation expense would be shown as a part of the calculation of income from continuing operations.

**3. ([$125,000], A)** Since an accrual was made for Hillside's contingent liability in 2007, one must first determine the amount of the liability recorded. SFAS 5 states that if a range of possible losses exists and no amount within the range is more likely than any other amount, an accrual should be made for the minimum amount of the loss, in this case $\$250,000$. As Hillside accrued a $\$250,000$ liability and loss in 2007, the 2008 loss would be $\$125,000$ ($\$250,000 - \$375,000$). Such a loss would be classified under income from continuing operations as it is incurred in conjunction with ordinary operations (amount paid to employee). Such a loss would not be extraordinary as it does not meet the criteria of being both unusual in nature and infrequent in occurrence.

**4. ([$10,000], A)** Trading securities are defined in SFAS 115 as securities that are bought and held principally for the purpose of selling them in the near term. As Hillside purchased these securities to sell in the near term, any unrealized holding gain or loss would appear as income from continuing operations on the income statement. The holding gain or loss from marketable equity securities held in the trading portfolio is computed as of December 31, 2008, by comparing the cost of the securities at the purchase date with the fair market value at the end of the year.

| | *Cost* | *FV (12/31/08* | *Gain (loss)* |
|---|---|---|---|
| I | $\$125,000$ | $\$145,000$ | $\$ 20,000$ |
| II | 235,000 | 205,000 | $(\underline{30,000})$ |
| | | | $\underline{\$(10,000)}$ |

**5. ([$255,000], B)** The amount of gain or loss from the hurricane would be computed by adding the carrying amounts of the assets destroyed and comparing this amount with the amount of insurance recovery. For Hillside, an extraordinary loss would result as follows:

| | |
|---|---|
| Insurance recovery | $\$ \underline{1,000,000}$ |
| Warehouse | 470,000 |
| Equipment | 250,000 |
| Inventory | \underline{535,000} |
| Total carrying value | $\$ \underline{1,255,000}$ |
| Extraordinary loss | $\$(\underline{\ 255,000})$ |

As this hurricane is unusual in that it is not related to the normal activities of the entity and infrequent in occurrence in that it is not expected to occur again in the foreseeable future (this was the first hurricane ever in Hillside's area), the $\$255,000$ loss would be classified as an extraordinary loss.

**6. ($41,000, E)** To compute the translation adjustment for 2008, both the net asset figures in dollars must be compared. The $\$429,000$ represents the translation at the date of purchase plus the translation of net income at a weighted-average exchange rate. The $\$388,000$ represents the net assets at the translated rate at the balance sheet date. The $\$41,000$ difference is the translation adjustment necessary to make the balance sheet balance. This translation adjustment, according to SFAS 52, should not be included in net income, but shall be reported as a separate component of other comprehensive income.

| Situation | Journal Entries | Calculations | Classification/Disclosures | Research | Communication |
|---|---|---|---|---|---|

**1.** How should Hillside report the extraordinary item in its income statement?

**APB30, Para 11 or Current Text I17.102**

11. In the absence of discontinued operations and changes in accounting principles, the following main captions should appear in an income statement if extraordinary items are reported (paragraphs 17-19 of APB Opinion No. 9).

| | |
|---|---|
| Income before extraordinary items 4 | $xxx |
| Extraordinary items | |
|   (less applicable income taxes of ($_____) (Note _____) | xxx |
| Net income | $xxx |

The caption extraordinary items should be used to identify separately the effects of events and transactions, other than the disposal of a segment of a business that meet the criteria for classification as extraordinary as discussed in paragraphs 19-24. Descriptive captions and the amounts for individual extraordinary events or transactions should be presented preferably on the face of the income statement, if practicable; otherwise disclosure in related notes is acceptable. The nature of an extraordinary event or transaction and the principal items entering into the determination of an extraordinary gain or loss should be described. The income taxes applicable to extraordinary items should be disclosed on the face of the income statement; alternatively, disclosure in the related notes is acceptable. The caption net income should replace the three captions shown above if the income statement includes no extraordinary items.

**2.** How should Hillside report the effect of the discontinued operations in its 2008 income statement?

**FAS144, Para 43 or Current Text I14.103**

43. In a period in which a component of an entity either has been disposed of or is classified as held for sale, the income statement of a business enterprise (or statement of activities of a not-for-profit organization) for current periods shall report the results of operations of the component, including any gain or loss recognized in accordance with paragraph 37, in discontinued operations. The results of operations of a component classified as held for sale shall be reported in discontinued operation in the period(s) in which they occur. The results of discontinued operations, less applicable income taxes (benefit), shall be reported as a separate component of income before extraordinary items and the cumulative effect of accounting changes (if applicable). For example, the results of discontinued operations may be reported in the income statement of a business enterprise as follows:

| | |
|---|---|
| Income from continuing operations before income taxes | $xxxx |
| Income taxes | xxxx |
| Income from continuing operations | $xxxx |
| Discontinued operations (Note X) | |
|   Loss from operations of discontinued Component x | |
|     (including loss on disposal of $xxx) | xxxx |
|   Income tax benefit | xxxx |
|   Loss on discontinued operations | xxxx |
| Net income | $xxxx |

A gain or loss recognized on the disposal shall be disclosed either on the face of the income statement or in the notes to the financial statements (paragraph 47(b)).

**3.** How should Hillside report the costs that were incurred to relocate employees of the discontinued component?

**Other Associated Costs**
**FAS146, Para 17 or Current Text L32.117**

17. Other costs associated with an exit or disposal activity include, but are not limited to, costs to consolidate or close facilities and relocate employees. A liability for other costs associated with an exit or disposal activity shall be recognized and measured at its fair value in the period in which the liability is incurred (generally, when goods or services associated with the activity are received). The liability shall not be recognized before it is incurred, even if the costs are incremental to other operating costs and will be incurred as a direct result of a plan.

**Reporting**
**FAS146, Para 18 or Current Text L32.118**

18.  Costs associated with an exit or disposal activity that does not involve discontinued operation shall be included in income from continuing operations before income taxes in the income statement of a business enterprise and in income from continuing operations in the statement of activities of a not-for-profit organization.  If a subtotal such as "income from operations" is presented, it shall include the amounts of those costs. Costs associated with an exit or disposal activity that involves a discontinued operation shall be included in the results of discontinued operations.

**4.** How should Hillside account for the change in inventory method from LIFO to average cost?

**SFAS 154, Para 7 or Current Text A07.106**

7.  An entity shall report a change in accounting principle through retrospective application of the new accounting principle to all prior periods, unless it is impracticable to do so. Retrospective application requires the following:

a.   The cumulative effect of the change to the new accounting prinicple on periods prior to those presented shall be reflected in the carrying amounts of assets and liabilities as of the beginning of the first period presented.

b.   An offsetting adjustment, if any, shall be made to the opening balance of retained earnings (or other appropriate components of equity or net assets in the statement of financial position) for that period.

c.   Financial statements for each individual prior period presented shall be adjusted to reflect the period-specific effects of applying the new accounting principle.

**5.** What disclosures are required in the financial statements in the year of the change?

**SFAS 154, Para 17 or Current Text A07.117**

17.  An entity shall disclose the following in the fiscal period in which a change in accounting principle is made:

a.   The nature of and reason for the change in accounting principle, including an explanation of why the newly adopted accounting principle is preferable.

b.   The method of applying the change, and

1.   A description of the prior-period information that has been retrospectively adjusted, if any.

2.   The effect of the change on income from continuing operations, net income (or other appropriate captions of changes in the applicable net assets or performance indicator), any other affected financial statement line item, and any affected per share amounts for the current period and any prior periods retrospectively adjusted.  Presentation of the effect on financial statement subtotals and totals other than income from continuing operations and net income (or other appropriate captions of changes in the applicable net assets or performance indicator) is not required.

3.   The cumulative effect of the change on retained earnings or other components of equity or net assets in the statement of financial position as of the beginning of the earliest period presented.

4.   If retrospective application to all prior periods (paragraph 7) is impracticable, disclosure of the reasons therefor, and a description of the alternative method used to report the change (paragraphs 8 and 9).

c.   If indirect effects of a change in accounting principle are recognized

1.   A description of the indirect effects of a change in accounting principle, including the amounts that have been recognized in the current period, and the related per-share amounts, if applicable

2.  Unless impracticable, the amount of the total recognized indirect effects of the accounting change and the related per share amounts, if applicable, that are attributable to each prior period presented

Financial statements of subsequent periods need not repeat the disclosures required by this paragraph.  If a change in accounting principle has no material effect in the period of change but is reasonably certain to have a material effect in later periods, the disclosures required by paragraph 17(a) shall be provided whenever the financial statements of the period of change are presented.

| Situation | Journal Entries | Calculations | Classification/Disclosures | Research | Communication |
|---|---|---|---|---|---|

To:      Hillside Company Permanent File
From:  CPA Candidate
Re:      Accounting issues related to income statement presentation
Date:   [*Today's date*]

This memorandum summarizes my research regarding the presentation of certain items in the financial statements of Hillside Company.

Issue 1:   How should Hillside report the extraordinary item in its income statement?

As indicated in APB30, paragraphs 10 and 11, Hillside should report the extraordinary item separately, net of applicable income taxes, below the continuing operations section of the income statement.  Exclusion of extraordinary items from the results of continuing operations is intended to produce a measure of income from continuing operations that is useful in predicting future operating cash flows.

Issue 2:   How should Hillside report the effect of the discontinued operations in its 2008 income statement?

According to FAS144, paragraph 43, Hillside should report the discontinued operations separately in the 2008 income statement immediately below income from continuing operations.  Discontinued operations should be comprised of

• Loss from operations of the discontinued component and the loss on disposal
• Income tax benefit

Issue 3:   How should Hillside report the costs that were incurred to relocate employees of the discontinued component?

According to FAS146, paragraph 8, Hillside should include the costs incurred to relocate employees in the loss on disposal of the discontinued component in its 2008 income statement.  These costs are a direct result of the commitment to dispose of the component.

---

## Simulation Problem 3

| Situation | Classifications | Multistep Income Statement | Retained Earnings Statement | Communication | Research |
|---|---|---|---|---|---|

|  | (A) | (B) | (C) | (D) | (E) | (F) | (G) | (H) | (I) |
|---|---|---|---|---|---|---|---|---|---|
| 1. Newly acquired assets are depreciated using the sum-of-the-years' digits method; previously recorded assets are depreciated using the straight-line method. | ○ | ○ | ○ | ○ | ○ | ○ | ● | ○ | ○ |
| 2. Accounting for the acquisition of a 100% owned subsidiary. | ● | ○ | ○ | ○ | ○ | ○ | ○ | ○ | ○ |
| 3. Reported as a restatement of all periods presented. | ○ | ● | ○ | ○ | ○ | ○ | ○ | ○ | ○ |
| 4. Write-down of inventory due to obsolescence. | ○ | ○ | ○ | ○ | ○ | ○ | ○ | ● | ○ |
| 5. Gains or losses on the disposal of the net assets of a component are included in this calculation. | ○ | ○ | ○ | ○ | ○ | ○ | ○ | ○ | ● |
| 6. Changing from the gross profit method for determining year-end inventory balances to dollar value LIFO. | ○ | ● | ○ | ○ | ○ | ○ | ○ | ○ | ○ |
| 7. Accounting for existing construction contracts is changed from completed contract to percentage-of-completion. | ○ | ○ | ● | ○ | ○ | ○ | ○ | ○ | ○ |

|  | (A) | (B) | (C) | (D) | (E) | (F) | (G) | (H) | (I) |
|---|---|---|---|---|---|---|---|---|---|
| 8. The effects of a change in estimate and a change in principle are inseparable for the same event. | ○ | ○ | ○ | ● | ○ | ○ | ○ | ○ | ○ |
| 9. The excess of cash paid over the carrying value to extinguish bonds. | ○ | ○ | ○ | ○ | ○ | ○ | ○ | ● | ○ |
| 10. Income or loss of the component for the period of disposal included in this calculation. | ○ | ○ | ○ | ○ | ○ | ● | ○ | ○ | ○ |

**Explanation of solutions**

**1.** **(G)** The acquisition of assets does not necessitate that the same method of depreciation be used for the newly acquired assets as for the existing assets. Therefore, no change in accounting principle has occurred because the previously recorded assets will continue to be depreciated using the straight-line method.

**2.** **(A)** Accounting for the acquisition of a 100% owned subsidiary is properly accounted for as a change in reporting entity.

**3.** **(B)** According to SFAS 154, all corrections of errors should be treated as a restatement of the prior period financial statements. This requires prompt recording of the error in the year in which the error was discovered, and reporting the effects of the error in the financial statements as an adjustment to the carrying value of the assets and liabilities as of the beginning of the first period presented with an offsetting adjustment to the opening balance of retained earnings for that period. Financial statements for each individual period are adjusted to reflect the correction of the period-specific effects of the error.

**4.** **(H)** According to APB 30, for an item to qualify as an extraordinary item it must be both unusual in nature and infrequent in occurrence. Clearly, the write-down of inventory due to obsolescence does not qualify for extraordinary treatment; therefore, it should be disclosed separately in the income statement before extraordinary items.

**5.** **(I)** Gains or losses on the disposal of net assets is included in the calculation of gain or loss on disposal of discontinued operations. Therefore, the total gain or loss on disposal should consist of the following two calculations: the net asset gain or loss mentioned above and the income or loss from operations from the measurement date to the disposal date (the phase-out period).

**6.** **(B)** The use of the gross profit method to determine year-end inventory balances is not proper GAAP. Therefore, if a situation such as this existed, it should be treated as a correction of an error.

**7.** **(C)** The change from one generally accepted accounting principle to another is considered a change in accounting principle. Since both the completed contract method and the percentage-of-completion methods are recognized GAAP, the change from one to the other is properly accounted for as a change in accounting principle, and accounted for on a retrospective basis.

**8.** **(D)** According to FAS 154, when it is impossible to determine whether a change in accounting principle or a change in estimate has occurred, the change should be considered as a change in estimate.

**9.** **(H)** Gains or losses on extinguishment of debt are no longer treated as extraordinary items.

**10.** **(F)** Income or loss from operations is properly included in the calculation of the gain or loss on the discontinued operations. Therefore, this calculation includes both the income or loss from operations and the gain or loss on the disposal of net assets. The gain or loss on the disposal should also be disclosed parenthetically or in the notes to the financial statements.

| Situation | Classifications | Multistep Income Statement | Retained Earnings Statement | Communication | Research |
|---|---|---|---|---|---|

| American Horse Company INCOME STATEMENT For the Year Ended December 31, 2007 | | |
|---|---|---|
| Salesz | | $25,000,000 |
| Less cost of goods sold | | (17,000,000) |
| Gross profit | | $ 8,000,000 |
| Less selling and administrative expenses | | (4,700,000) |
| Income from operations | | $ 3,300,000 |
| Other revenue and gains | | |
| Interest revenue | $ 70,000 | |
| Gain on the sale of investments | 110,000 | $180,000 |
| Other expenses and losses | | |
| Write-off of goodwill | | (820,000) |
| Income from continuing operations before income taxes | | $2,660,000 |
| Income taxes | | (905,000) |
| Income from continuing operations | | $1,755,000 |

| | | |
|---|---|---|
| Discontinued operations | | |
| Loss on discontinued wholesale division, including loss on disposal of $200,000 | $815,000 | |
| Income tax benefit | (285,000) | |
| Loss on discontinued operation (net of tax) | | (530,000) |
| Income before extraordinary item | | $1,225,000 |
| Extraordinary loss from flood damage, net of tax | | (390,000) |
| Net income | | $ 835,000 |
| | | |
| Earnings per share | | |
| Income from continuing operations | | $5.62[a] |
| Discontinued operations: | | (1.77) |
| Income before extraordinary item | | 3.85[b] |
| Extraordinary loss (net of tax) | | (1.30) |
| Net income | | $2.55[c] |

$$^a \quad \frac{\$1,755,000 - \$70,000}{300,000 \ shares} = \$5.62$$

$$^b \quad \frac{\$1,225,000 - \$70,000}{300,000 \ shares} = \$3.85$$

$$^c \quad \frac{\$835,000 - \$70,000}{300,000 \ shares} = \$2.55$$

| | | Multistep | Retained Earnings Statement | | |
|---|---|---|---|---|---|
| Situation | Classifications | Income Statement | | Communication | Research |

| *American Horse Company* **RETAINED EARNINGS STATEMENT** *For the Year Ended December 31, 2007* | | |
|---|---|---|
| Retained earnings, January 1, 2007 | | $980,000 |
| Plus net income | | 835,000 |
| | | 1,815,000 |
| Less dividends | $ 70,000 | |
| | 250,000 | (320,000) |
| | | |
| | | |
| | | |
| Retained earnings, December 31, 2007 | | $1,495,000 |

| | | Multistep | Retained Earnings | Communication | |
|---|---|---|---|---|---|
| Situation | Classifications | Income Statement | Statement | | Research |

To:      Manager, American Horse Company
From:    CPA Candidate
Re:      Distinction between income statement items

    This memorandum summarizes the answer to your questions regarding the nature of income statement items. The major distinction between revenues and gains (or expenses and losses) depends on the typical activities of the enterprise. Revenues can occur from a variety of different sources, but these sources constitute the entity's ongoing major or central operations. Gains also can arise from many different sources, but these sources occur from peripheral or incidental transactions of an entity. The same type of distinction is made between an expense and a loss.

    If you have any additional questions, please contact me.

| | | Multistep | Retained Earnings | | Research |
|---|---|---|---|---|---|
| Situation | Classifications | Income Statement | Statement | Communication | |

**APB30, Para 20 or Current Text I17.107 or I17.401**

20. Extraordinary items are events and transactions that are distinguished by their unusual nature and by the infrequency of their occurrence. Thus, both of the following criteria should be met to classify an event or transaction as an extraordinary item.

    a.   Unusual nature—the underlying event or transactions should possess a high degree of abnormality and be of a type clearly unrelated to, or only incidentally related to, the ordinary and typical activities of the entity, taking into account the environment in which the entity operates. (See discussion in paragraph 21.)

  b.   Infrequency of occurrence—the underlying event or transaction should be of a type that would not reasonably be expected to recur in the foreseeable future, taking into account the environment in which the entity operates.  (See discussion in paragraph 22.)

_____

**Simulation Problem 4**

| Situation | Financial Statement Classification | Calculate Net Income | Earnings Per Share | Communication | Research |
|---|---|---|---|---|---|

|  | (A) | (B) | (C) | (D) | (E) | (F) |
|---|---|---|---|---|---|---|
| **1.** An increase in the unrealized excess of cost over market value of marketable equity securities classified as trading-type securities. | ○ | ● | ○ | ○ | ○ | ○ |
| **2.** The accumulated amount of the unrealized excess of cost over market value of available-for-sale marketable equity securities. | ○ | ○ | ○ | ○ | ● | ○ |
| **3.** Income from operations of a discontinued component in the component's disposal year. | ○ | ○ | ○ | ○ | ○ | ● |
| **4.** A gain on remeasuring a foreign subsidiary's financial statements from the local currency into the functional currency. | ○ | ● | ○ | ○ | ○ | ○ |
| **5.** A loss on translating a foreign subsidiary's financial statements from the functional local currency into the reporting currency during this period. | ○ | ○ | ● | ○ | ○ | ○ |
| **6.** A loss caused by a major earthquake in an area previously considered to be subject to only minor tremors. | ○ | ○ | ○ | ● | ○ | ○ |
| **7.** The probable receipt of $1,000,000 from a pending lawsuit. | ○ | ○ | ○ | ○ | ○ | ● |
| **8.** The purchase of research and development services.  There were no other research and development activities. | ○ | ● | ○ | ○ | ○ | ○ |

**Explanation of solutions**

   **1.    (B)** Per SFAS 115, changes in the market value of (trading type) marketable securities shall be included in the determination of income from continuing operations of the period in which the change in market value occurs.

   **2.    (E)** Per SFAS 130, the accumulated changes in the valuation (unrealized excess of cost over market value) of **available-for-sale** marketable equity securities shall be reported as accumulated other comprehensive income.

   **3.    (F)** Per SFAS 144, results of operations of a component that has been or will be discontinued should be reported **separately** as a component of income, after income from continuing operations but before extraordinary items and the cumulative effect of accounting changes.

   **4.    (B)** Per SFAS 52, a foreign subsidiary must **remeasure** its financial statements when its functional currency (the currency of the primary economic environment in which the entity operates) is different from its local currency (the currency currently used by the entity).  The effect of the remeasurement process (gain or loss) should be recognized currently in income.  Aggregate gain or loss for the period should also be disclosed either in the financial statements or in the notes.

   **5.    (C)** Per SFAS 52, when translating a foreign subsidiary's financial statements from functional currency to reporting currency, a translation adjustment will result.  The translation adjustment is not included in net income but is reported as a component of comprehensive income and called other comprehensive income.

   **6.    (D)** Per APB 30, extraordinary items are events and transactions that are **both** unusual and infrequent.  The earthquake in this problem occurred in an area previously considered subject to only minor tremors.  Therefore, the earthquake would be considered an extraordinary event.  Per APB 30, extraordinary items should be shown separately on the income statement, after income from continuing operations.

   **7.    (F)** The question indicates that it is probable that the company will **receive** $1,000,000 from a pending lawsuit.  Thus, the $1,000,000 is a **gain** contingency.  Per SFAS 5, contingencies that may result in **gains** are not reflected in the accounts, as doing so might result in the recognition of revenue before its realization.  Adequate disclosure of the gain contingency should be made, but care should be taken to avoid misleading implications as to the likelihood of realization.

   **8.    (B)** Per SFAS 2, the cost of research and development services performed by others on behalf of the enterprise are included in R&D costs.  R&D costs are charged to expense when incurred and thus are included in income from continuing operations of that period.  In addition, separate disclosure of the total R&D costs for the period should be made either in the financial statements or in the notes.

| Situation | Financial Statement Classification | Calculate Net Income | Earnings Per Share | Communication | Research |
|---|---|---|---|---|---|

### Rap Corp.
### INCOME STATEMENT
#### *For the Year Ended December 31, 2007*

| | | | |
|---|---|---|---|
| Income from continuing operations before income tax | | $1,180,000 | |
| Income tax | | (448,400) | |
| Income from continuing operations | | $ 731,600 | |
| | | | |
| Discontinued operations: | | | |
| Loss from discontinued operations (including loss from disposal of $100,000) | $(190,000) | | |
| Income tax benefit | 72,200 | | |
| Loss from discontinued operations (net of tax) | | 117,800 | |
| Income before extraordinary item | | $ 613,800 | |
| | | | |
| Extraordinary item: | | | |
| Gain on sale of investment | 145,000 | | |
| Less applicable taxes | 58,000 | 87,000 | |
| Net income | | $ 700,800 | |

| Situation | Financial Statement Classification | Calculate Net Income | Earnings Per Share | Communication | Research |
|---|---|---|---|---|---|

### Rap Corp.
### EARNINGS STATEMENT
#### *For the Year Ended December 31, 2007*

| | | | |
|---|---|---|---|
| Per share of common stock: | | | |
| Income from continuing operations | | | $ 7.32 |
| Discontinued operations, net of tax | | | (1.18) |
| Income before extraordinary item | | | 6.14 |
| Extraordinary item, net of tax | | | 0.87 |
| Net income ($762,800/100,000) | | | $ 7.01 |
| | | | |
| | | | |
| | | | |

| Situation | Financial Statement Classification | Calculate Net Income | Earnings Per Share | Communication | Research |
|---|---|---|---|---|---|

To:    Controller, Rap Corporation
From:  CPA Candidate
Re:    Earnings per share

You have requested that I provide a description of the various components of earnings per share that must be disclosed in Rap Corporation's financial statements.  The presentation of earnings per share depends on the capital structure of the company and the types of gains and losses the company presents in its income statement.  Entities with a simple capital structure, with only common stock outstanding, present basic earnings per share for income from continuing operations and for net income on the face of the income statement.  Entities with complex capital structures present both basic and diluted earnings per share amounts for income from continuing operations and for net income on the face of the income statement.

An entity that reports discontinued operations or an extraordinary item should present both basic and diluted per share amounts for those items either on the face of the income statement or in the footnotes to the financial statements.

If you have any further questions, please contact me.

| Situation | Financial Statement Classification | Calculate Net Income | Earnings Per Share | Communication | Research |
|---|---|---|---|---|---|

### FAS130, Para 11 or Current Text C49.107

11. The purpose of reporting comprehensive income is to report a measure of all changes in equity of an enterprise that result from recognized transactions and other economic events of the period other than transactions with owners in their capacity as owners.  Prior to the issuance of this Statement, some of those changes in equity were displayed in a statement that reports the results of operations, while others were included directly in balances within a separate component of equity in a statement of financial position.

# INVENTORY

Inventory is defined in ARB 43 (see outline) as tangible personal property (1) held for sale in the ordinary course of business, (2) in the process of production for such sale, or (3) to be used currently in the production of items for sale.

Inventory is tested on the Financial Accounting and Reporting section of the exam. The primary topics covered by questions on the exam are

1. **Ownership of goods:** the determination of which items are to be included in inventory.
2. **Cost:** the determination of which costs are to be assigned to inventory.
3. **Cost flow assumptions:** the determination of costs assigned to cost of goods sold and inventory under the various cost flow methods.
4. **Valuation:** the determination of how and when inventories should reflect their market values.

ARB 43, chap 4 is the primary authoritative pronouncement regarding the accounting for inventories. You should review the outline before continuing your study of this module.

## A. Determining Inventory and Cost of Goods Sold

The primary basis of accounting for inventories is cost, which includes the cash or other fair value of consideration given in exchange for it. Inventory cost is a function of two variables

1. The number of units included in inventory, and
2. The costs attached to those units

The units to be included in inventory are those which the firm owns; ownership is usually determined by legal title.

The costs to be included in inventory include all costs necessary to prepare the goods for sale. Normal costs for freight-in, handling costs, and normal spoilage are included in inventory. For a manufacturing entity, the cost of inventory includes direct materials, direct labor, and both direct and indirect factory overhead. These costs are then allocated to the work in progress and finished goods inventory account. Per SFAS 151 (effective for fiscal years beginning after June 15, 2005), variable production overhead is allocated to each unit of production based on the actual use of the production facilities. Fixed overhead is allocated based on the normal capacity of the production facilities. The normal capacity of the production facility is the production expected to be achieved over a number of periods or seasons under normal circumstances, taking into account the loss of capacity resulting from planned maintenance. The range of normal capacity will vary based on business and industry-specific factors. The actual level of production may be used if it approximates normal capacity. Unallocated fixed overhead costs are recognized as an expense in the period in which they are incurred. Any abnormal costs for freight-in, handling costs, and spoilage are treated as current period expenses, and are not allocated to inventory.

For a merchandising concern, the costs to be included in inventory include the purchase price of the goods, freight-in, insurance, warehousing, and any other costs incurred in the preparation of these goods for sale. The amount used as a purchase price for the goods will vary depending upon whether the gross or net method is used in the recording of purchases. If the gross method is used to record the purchases, then any subsequent discount taken is shown as purchase discount which is netted against the purchases account in determining cost of goods sold. If the net method is used to record purchases, then any purchase discounts offered are assumed taken and the purchase account reflects the net price. If subsequent to the recording of the purchases the discount is not taken (i.e., payment is tendered after the discount period has elapsed), a purchase discounts lost account is debited. The balance in the purchase discounts lost account does **not** enter into the determination of cost of goods sold; this amount is treated as a period expense. Note that regardless of the method used, purchases are always recorded net of any allowable trade discounts. These are discounts that are allowed to the entity because of its being a wholesaler, a good customer, or merely the fact that the item is on sale at a reduced price. Also note that interest paid to vendors is not included in the cost of inventory.

The determination of cost of goods sold and inventory under each of the cost flow assumptions depends upon the method used to record the inventory: periodic or perpetual.

***Periodic system.*** Inventory is counted periodically and then priced. The ending inventory is usually recorded in the cost of goods sold (CGS) entry.

Ending inventory (EI)                    xx
CGS                                     (plug)
    Beginning inventory (BI)              xx
    Purchases                            xx

CGS = Purchases – (the change in inventory). For example, if ending inventory decreases, all of the purchases and some of the beginning inventory have been sold. If ending inventory increases, not all of the purchases have been sold.

**Perpetual system.** A running total is kept of the units on hand (and possibly their value) by recording all increases and decreases as they occur. When inventory is purchased, the inventory account, rather than purchases, is debited. As inventory is sold, the following entry is recorded.

CGS                                     (cost)
    Inventory                                        (cost)

## B. Inventory Valuation and Cost-Flow Methods

1. Specific identification
2. Weighted-average
3. Simple average
4. Moving average
5. Lower of cost or market
6. Losses on purchase commitments
7. First-in, first-out (FIFO)
8. Last-in, first-out (LIFO)
9. Dollar-value LIFO
10. Gross profit
11. Standard costs
12. Direct costing
13. Market
14. Cost apportionment by relative sales value

### 1. Specific Identification

The seller determines which item is sold. For example, a seller has for sale four identical machines costing $260, $230, $180, and $110. Since the machines are identical, a purchaser will have no preference as to which machine s/he receives when purchased. Note that the seller is able to manipulate income as s/he can sell any machine (and charge the appropriate amount to CGS). Significant dollar value items are frequently accounted for by specific identification. The use of the specific identification method is appropriate when there is a relatively small number of significant dollar value items in inventory.

### 2. Weighted-Average

The seller averages the cost of all items on hand and purchased during the period. The units in ending inventory and units sold (CGS) are costed at this average cost. For example

|  | Cost | Units |  |
|---|---|---|---|
| Beginning inventory | $200 | 100 | ($2.00 unit) |
| Purchase 1 | 315 | 150 | ($2.10 unit) |
| Purchase 2 | 85 | 50 | ($1.70 unit) |
|  | $600 | 300 |  |

Weighted-average cost $600/300 = $2.00 unit

### 3. Simple Average

The seller does not weight the average for units purchased or in beginning inventory (e.g., the above $2.00, $2.10, and $1.70 unit costs would be averaged to $1.93). The method is fairly accurate if all purchases, production runs, and beginning inventory quantities are equal.

### 4. Moving Average

The average cost of goods on hand must be recalculated any time additional inventory is purchased at a unit cost different from the previously calculated average cost of goods on hand. For example

|  | Dollar cost of units on hand | Units on hand | Inventory unit cost |
|---|---|---|---|
| Beginning inventory | $200 | 100 | $2.00 |
| Sale of 50 units @ $2.00 = $100 | 100 | 50 | 2.00 |
| Purchase of 150 units for $320 | 420 | 200 | 2.10 |
| Sale of 50 units @ $2.10 = $105 | 315 | 150 | 2.10 |
| Purchase of 50 units for $109 | 424 | 200 | 2.12 |

Note that sales do not change the unit price because they are taken out of inventory at the average price. Moving average may only be used with perpetual systems which account for changes in value with each change in inventory (and not with perpetual systems only accounting for changes in the number of units).

5.  **Lower of Cost or Market**

"A departure from the cost basis of pricing the inventory is required when the utility of the goods is no longer as great as its cost." (ARB 43, chap 4)

The following steps should be used to apply the lower of cost or market rule given in chapter 4 of ARB 43.

a.  Determine market

Market is replacement cost limited to

(1)  **Ceiling**—which is net realizable value (selling price less selling costs and costs to complete).

(2)  **Floor**—which is net realizable value less normal profit.

Note that if replacement cost is greater than net realizable value, market equals net realizable value. Likewise, market equals net realizable value minus normal profit if replacement cost is less than net realizable value minus normal profit.

b.  Determine cost

Note that the floor and ceiling have nothing to do with cost

c.  Select the lower of cost or market either for each individual item or for inventory as a whole (compute total market and total cost, and select lower)

### LOWER OF COST OR MARKET EXAMPLE

| Item | Cost | Replacement cost | Selling price | Selling cost | Normal profit |
|---|---|---|---|---|---|
| A | $10.50 | $10.25 | $15.00 | $2.50 | $2.50 |
| B | 5.75 | 5.25 | 8.00 | 1.50 | 1.00 |
| C | 4.25 | 4.75 | 5.50 | 1.00 | 1.50 |

| Item | Replacement cost | NRV (ceiling) | NRV-Profit (floor) | Designated market value | Cost | LCM |
|---|---|---|---|---|---|---|
| A | $10.25 | $12.50 | $10.00 | $10.25 | $10.50 | $10.25 |
| B | 5.25 | 6.50 | 5.50 | 5.50 | 5.75 | 5.50 |
| C | 4.75 | 4.50 | 3.00 | 4.50 | 4.25 | 4.25 |

*Item A—Market is replacement cost, $10.25, because it is between the floor ($10.00) and the ceiling ($12.50). Lower of cost or market is $10.25.*

*Item B—Market is limited to the floor, $5.50 ($8.00 – $1.50 – $1.00) because the $5.25 replacement cost is beneath the floor. Lower of cost or market is $5.50.*

*Item C—Market is limited to the ceiling, $4.50 ($5.50 – $1.00) because the $4.75 replacement cost is above the ceiling. Lower of cost or market is $4.25.*

Observations about the ARB 43 rule

(1)  The floor limitation on market prevents recognition of more than normal profit in future periods (if market is less than cost).

(2)  The ceiling limitation on market prevents recognition of a loss in future periods (if market is less than cost).

(3)  Cost or market applied to individual items will always be as low as, and usually lower than, cost or market applied to the inventory as a whole. They will be the same when all items at market or all items at cost are lower.

(4)  Once inventory has been written down there can be no recovery from the write-down until the units are sold. Recall that this differs from marketable securities where recoveries of prior write-downs are required to be taken into the income stream.

Methods of recording the write-down

If market is less than cost at the end of any period, there are two methods available to record the market decline. The entry to establish the ending inventory can be made using the market figure. The difficulty with this procedure is that it forces the loss to be included in the cost of goods sold, thus overstating the cost of goods sold by the amount of the loss. Note that under this method the loss is not separately disclosed.

An alternative treatment is to debit the inventory account for the actual cost (not market) of goods on hand, and then to make the following entry to give separate recognition to the market decline.

Loss due to market decline                    xx
   Inventory                                              xx

6. **Losses on Purchase Commitments**

   Purchase commitments (PC) result from legally enforceable contracts to purchase specific quantities of goods at fixed prices in the future. When there is a decline in market value below the contract price at the balance sheet date and the contracts are noncancellable, an unrealized loss has occurred and, if material, should be recorded in the period of decline.

   | Estimated loss on PC | (excess of PC over mkt.) | |
   |---|---|---|
   | Accrued loss on PC | (excess of PC over mkt.) | |

   If further declines in market value are estimated to occur before delivery is made, the amount of the loss to be accrued should be increased to include this additional decline in market value per SFAS 5. The loss is taken to the income statement; the accrued loss on PC is a liability account and shown on the balance sheet.

   When the goods are subsequently received

   | Purchases | xx | |
   |---|---|---|
   | Accrued loss on PC | xx | |
   | Cash | | xx |

   If a partial or full recovery occurs before the inventory is received, the accrued loss account would be reduced by the amount of the recovery. Likewise, an income statement account, "Recovery on Loss of PC," would be credited.

7. **First-In, First-Out (FIFO)**

   The goods from beginning inventory and the earliest purchases are assumed to be the goods sold first. In a period of rising prices, cost of goods sold is made up of the earlier, lower-priced goods resulting in a larger profit (relative to LIFO). The ending inventory is made up of more recent purchases and thus represents a more current value (relative to LIFO) on the balance sheet. It should be noted that this cost-flow assumption may be used even when it does not match the physical flow of goods. Whenever the FIFO method is used, the results of inventory and cost of goods sold are the same at the end of the period under either a perpetual or a periodic system.

8. **Last-In, First-Out (LIFO)**

   Under this cost-flow method, the most recent purchases are assumed to be the first goods sold; thus, ending inventory is assumed to be composed of the oldest goods. Therefore, the cost of goods sold contains relatively current costs (resulting in the matching of current costs with sales). Again, this cost-flow assumption usually does not parallel the physical flow of goods.

   LIFO is widely adopted because it is acceptable for tax purposes and because in periods of rising prices it reduces tax liability due to the lower reported income (resulting from the higher cost of goods sold). LIFO smooths out fluctuations in the income stream relative to FIFO because it matches current costs with current revenues. A primary disadvantage of LIFO is that it results in large profits if inventory decreases because earlier, lower valued layers are included in the cost of goods sold. This is generally known as a LIFO liquidation. Another disadvantage is the cost involved in maintaining separate LIFO records for each item in inventory. If LIFO is used for tax purposes, it must be used for financial reporting purposes. This is known as the LIFO conformity rule. Under current tax law, inventory layers may be added using the (1) earliest acquisition costs, (2) weighted-average unit cost for the period, or (3) latest acquisition costs. In solving questions on the CPA Exam, use the earliest acquisition costs unless you are instructed to use one of the other alternatives.

   When a company uses LIFO for external reporting purposes and another inventory method for internal purposes, a **LIFO Reserve** account is used to reduce inventory from the internal valuation to the LIFO valuation. LIFO Reserve is a contra account to inventory, and is adjusted up or down at year-end with a corresponding increase or decrease to **Cost of Goods Sold**.

9. **Dollar-Value LIFO**

   Dollar-value LIFO is LIFO applied to **pools** of inventory items rather than to **individual** items. Thus, the cost of keeping inventory records is less under dollar-value LIFO than under unit LIFO. Because the LIFO conformity rule (if LIFO is used for tax, it must also be used for external financial statements) also applies to dollar-value LIFO, companies using dollar-value LIFO define their LIFO pools so as to conform with IRS regulations. Under these regulations, a LIFO pool can contain all of the inventory items for a natural business unit, or a multiple pool approach can be elected whereby a business can group similarly used inventory items into several groups or pools.

The advantage of using inventory pools is that an involuntary liquidation of LIFO layers is less likely to occur because of the increased number of items in the pool (if the level of one item decreases it can be offset by increases in the levels of other items), and because the pools can be adjusted for changes in product composition or product mix.

Like unit LIFO, dollar-value LIFO is a layering method. Unlike unit LIFO, dollar-value LIFO determines increases or decreases in ending inventory in terms of dollars of the same purchasing power rather than in terms of units. Dollar-value LIFO seeks to determine the real dollar change in inventory. Therefore, ending inventory is deflated to base-year cost by dividing ending inventory by the current year's conversion price index and comparing the resulting amount with the beginning inventory, which has also been stated in base-year dollars.

The difference represents the layer which, after conversion, must be added or subtracted to arrive at the appropriate value of ending inventory. Always remember that the individual layers in a dollar-value LIFO inventory are valued as follows:

$$\text{\$ value LIFO} = \frac{\text{Inventory at}}{\text{base-year prices}} \times \frac{\text{Conversion}}{\text{price index}}$$

In applying dollar-value LIFO, manufacturers develop their own indexes while retailers and wholesalers use published figures. In computing the conversion price index, the **double-extension technique** is used, named so because each year the ending inventory is extended at both base-year prices and current-year prices. The index, computed as follows, measures the change in the inventory prices since the base year.

$$\frac{\text{EI at end-of-year prices}}{\text{EI at base-year prices}} = \frac{\text{Conversion}}{\text{price index}}$$

To illustrate the computation of the index, assume that the base-year price of products A and B is $3 and $5, respectively, and at the end of the year, the price of product A is $3.20 and B, $5.75, with 2,000 and 800 units on hand, respectively. The index for the year is 110%, computed as follows:

|  | *EI at end-of-year prices* | ÷ | *EI at base-year prices* | = | *Conversion price index* |
|---|---|---|---|---|---|
| Product A | 2,000 @ $3.20 = $ 6,400 |  | 2,000 @ $3 = $ 6,000 |  |  |
| Product B | 800 @ $5.75 = $ 4,600 |  | 800 @ $5 = $ 4,000 |  |  |
|  | $11,000 |  | $10,000 |  | 1.10 (or 110%) |

Steps in dollar-value LIFO

| *Manufacturers* | *Retailers and wholesalers* |
|---|---|
| 1. Compute the conversion price index | 1. Determine index from appropriate published source |
| 2. Compare BI at base-year prices to EI at base-year prices to determine the | 2. Divide EI by conversion price index to restate to base-year prices |
|    a. New inventory layer added, or<br>   b. Old inventory layer removed (LIFO liquidation) | 3. Same as "2." opposite |
| 3. If there is an increase at base-year prices, value this new layer by multiplying the layer (stated in base-year dollars) by the conversion price index. If there is a decrease at base-year prices, the remaining layers are valued at the index in effect when the layer was first added. | 4. Same as "3." opposite |

For example, assume the following:

|  | *EI at end-of-year prices* | ÷ | *Conversion price index* | = | *EI at base-year prices* |  | *Change as measured in base-year dollars* |
|---|---|---|---|---|---|---|---|
| Year 1 (base) | $100,000 |  | 1.00 |  | $100,000 |  |  |
| Year 2 | 121,000 |  | 1.10 |  | 110,000 | > | $10,000 |
| Year 3 | 150,000 |  | 1.20 |  | 125,000 | > | 15,000 |
| Year 4 | 135,000 |  | 1.25 |  | 108,000 | > | (17,000) |

In both year 2 and year 3, ending inventory in terms of base-year dollars increased 10,000 and 15,000 base-year dollars, respectively. Since layers are added every year that ending inventory at base-year prices is greater than the previous year's ending inventory at base-year prices, the ending inventory for year 3 would be computed as follows:

Ending inventory, Year 3

|  | Base-year prices | × | Index | = | EI at dollar-value LIFO cost |
|---|---|---|---|---|---|
| Year 1 (base) | $100,000 | | 1.00 | | $100,000 |
| Year 2 layer | 10,000 | | 1.10 | | 11,000 |
| Year 3 layer | 15,000 | | 1.20 | | 18,000 |
| Ending inventory | $125,000 | | | | $129,000 |

Note that each layer added is multiplied by the conversion price index in effect when the layer was added. Thus, the year 2 layer is multiplied by the year 2 index of 1.10 and the year 3 layer is multiplied by the year 3 index of 1.20.

In year 4, ending inventory decreased by 17,000 base-year dollars. Therefore, a LIFO liquidation has occurred whereby 17,000 base-year dollars will have to be removed from the previous year's ending inventory. Because LIFO is being used, the liquidation affects the most recently added layer first and then, if necessary, the next most recently added layer(s). Ending inventory in year 4 is composed of

|  | Base-year prices | × | Index | = | EI at dollar-value LIFO cost |
|---|---|---|---|---|---|
| Year 1 (base) | $100,000 | | 1.00 | | $100,000 |
| Year 2 layer | 8,000 | | 1.10 | | 8,800 |
| Ending inventory | $108,000 | | | | $108,800 |

Note that the liquidation of 17,000 base-year dollars in year 4 caused the entire year 3 layer of 15,000 base-year dollars to be liquidated as well as 2,000 base-year dollars from year 2. Also note that the remaining 8,000 base-year dollars in the year 2 layer is still multiplied by the year 2 index of 1.10.

**Link-chain technique.** The computations for application of the double-extension technique can become very arduous even if only a few items exist in the inventory. Also, consider the problems that arise when there is a constant change in the inventory mix or in situations in which the breadth of the inventory is large.

The link-chain method was originally developed for (and limited to) those companies that wanted to use LIFO but, because of a substantial change in product lines over time, were unable to recreate or keep the historical records necessary to make accurate use of the double-extension method.

The link-chain method is the process of developing a single cumulative index. Technological change is allowed for by the method used to calculate each current year index. The index is derived by double extending a representative sample (generally thought to be between 50% and 75% of the dollar value of the pool) at both beginning-of-year prices and end-of-year prices. This annual index is then applied (multiplied) to the previous period's cumulative index to arrive at the new current year cumulative index.

The brief example below illustrates how the links and cumulative index are computed.

| End of period | Ratio of end of period prices to beginning prices* | Cumulative index number** |
|---|---|---|
| 0 | -- | 1.000 |
| 1 | 1.10 | 1.100 |
| 2 | 1.05 | 1.155 |
| 3 | 1.07 | 1.236 |

\* $\frac{End\ of\ period\ prices}{Beginning\ of\ period\ prices}$ = Index number for **this period only**

\*\* Multiply the cumulative index number at the beginning of the period by the ratio computed with the formula shown above.

The ending inventory is divided by the cumulative index number to derive the ending inventory at base period prices. An increase (layer) in base period dollars for the period is priced using the newly derived index number.

10. **Gross Profit**

Ending inventory is estimated by using the gross profit (GP) percentage to convert sales to cost of goods presumed sold. Since ending inventory is only estimated, the gross method is not acceptable for either tax or annual financial reporting purposes. Its major uses are to estimate ending inventory for internal use, for use in interim financial statements, and for establishing the amount of loss due to the destruction of inventory by fire, flood, or other catastrophes.

As an example, suppose the inventory of the Luckless Company has been destroyed by fire and the following information is available from duplicate records stored at a separate facility: beginning inventory of $30,000, purchases for the period of $40,000, sales of $60,000, and an average GP percentage of 25%. The cost of the inventory destroyed is computed as follows:

|   | | |
|---|---|---|
| | Beginning inventory | $30,000 |
| + | Purchases | 40,000 |
| | Goods available | 70,000 |
| − | Cost of goods sold | 45,000* |
| | Inventory destroyed | $25,000 |

*Cost of goods sold is computed as (1) sales of $60,000 − ($60,000 × 25%) or (2) sales of $60,000 × 75%.*

If you need to convert a GP rate on cost to a markup (MU) rate on the selling price, divide the GP rate on cost by 1 **plus** the GP rate on cost, that is, if the GP rate on cost is 50%, then .50/(1 + .50) = 33 1/3% is the MU rate on the selling price. If you need to convert a MU rate on the selling price to a GP rate on cost, divide the MU rate on the selling price by 1 **minus** the MU rate on the selling price, that is, if the MU rate on the selling price is 20%, then .20/(1 − .20) = 25% GP rate on cost. Always be cautious about gross profit rates (on cost or the selling price).

11. **Standard Costs**

Standard costs are predetermined costs in a cost accounting system, generally used for control purposes. Inventory may be costed at standard only if variances are reasonable (i.e., not large). Large debit (unfavorable) variances would indicate inventory (and cost of sales) were undervalued, whereas large credit (favorable) variances would indicate inventory is overvalued.

12. **Direct (Variable) Costing**

Direct costing is not an acceptable method for valuing inventory (ARB 43, chap 4). Direct costing considers only variable costs as product costs and fixed production costs as period costs. In contrast, absorption costing considers both variable and fixed manufacturing costs as product costs.

13. **Market**

Inventory is usually valued at market value when market is lower than cost. However, occasionally, inventory will be valued at market even if it is above cost. This usually occurs with

a. Precious metals with a fixed market value
b. Industries such as meatpacking where costs cannot be allocated and

(1) Quoted market prices exist
(2) Goods are interchangeable (e.g., agricultural commodities)

14. **Cost Apportionment By Relative Sales Value**

Basket purchases and similar situations require cost allocation based on relative value. For example, a developer may spend $400,000 to acquire land, survey, curb and gutter, pave streets, etc. for a subdivision. Due to location and size, the lots may vary in selling price. If the total of all selling prices were $600,000, the developer could cost each lot at 2/3 (400/600; COST/RETAIL ratio) of its selling price.

## C. Items to Include in Inventory

Goods shipped FOB shipping point which are in transit should be included in the inventory of the buyer since title passes to the buyer when the carrier receives the goods. Goods shipped FOB destination should be included in the inventory of the seller until the goods are received by the buyer since title passes to the buyer when the goods are received at their final destination. The more complicated UCC rules concerning transfer of title should be used for the law portion, not the financial accounting and reporting portion, of the exam.

## D. Consignments

Consignors consign their goods to consignees who are sales agents of the consignors. Consigned goods remain the property of the consignor until sold. Therefore, any unsold goods (including a proportionate share of freight costs incurred in shipping the goods to the consignee) must be included in the consignor's inventory.

Consignment sales revenue should be recognized by the consignor when the consignee sells the consigned goods to the ultimate customer. Therefore, no revenue is recognized at the time the consignor ships the goods to the consignee. Note that sales commission made by the consignee would be reported as a selling expense by the consignor and would **not** be netted against the sales revenue recognized by the consignor.  The UCC rules concerning consignments should be used for the law portion, not the financial accounting and reporting portion, of the exam.

**E.  Ratios**

The two ratios below relate to inventory.

1.  **Inventory turnover**—Measures the number of times inventory was sold and reflects inventory order and investment policies

$$\frac{\text{Cost of goods sold}}{\text{Average inventory}}$$

2.  **Number of days' supply in average inventory**—Number of days inventory is held before sale; reflects on efficiency of inventory policies

$$\frac{365}{\text{Inventory turnover}}$$

**F.  Long-Term Construction Contracts**

The outline of ARB 45 should be reviewed before continuing to study long-term construction contracts. This section also reflects the treatment of these contracts in the AICPA's *Construction Contractors Audit and Accounting Guide.*

Long-term contracts are accounted for by two methods:  completed-contract method and percentage-of-completion method.

1.  Completed-contract method—Recognition of contract revenue and profit at contract completion.  All related costs are deferred until completion and then matched to revenues.

2.  Percentage-of-completion—Recognition of contract revenue and profit during construction based on expected total profit and estimated progress towards completion in the current period.  All related costs are recognized in the period in which they occur.

The use of the percentage-of-completion method depends on the ability to make reasonably dependable estimates of contract revenues, contract costs, and the extent of progress toward completion.  For entities which customarily operate under contractual arrangements and for whom contracting represents a significant part of their operations, the **presumption** is that they have the ability to make estimates that are sufficiently dependable to justify the use of the percentage-of-completion method of accounting.

In Statement of Position 81-1, the Accounting Standards Division states that the percentage-of-completion method is **preferable** in circumstances in which reasonably dependable estimates can be made and in which all of the following conditions exist:

• Contracts executed by the parties normally include provisions that clearly specify the enforceable rights regarding goods or services to be provided and received by the parties, the consideration to be exchanged, and the manner and terms of settlement.
• The buyer can be expected to satisfy obligations under the contract.
• The contractor can be expected to perform contractual obligation.

The completed-contract method is **preferable** in circumstances in which estimates cannot meet the criteria for reasonable dependability or one of the above conditions does not exist.

The advantage of percentage-of-completion is periodic recognition of income, and the disadvantage is dependence on estimates.  The advantage of the completed-contract method is that it is based on results, not estimates, and the disadvantage is that current performance is not reflected and income recognition may be irregular.

In practice, various procedures are used to measure the extent of progress toward completion under the percentage-of-completion method, but the most widely used one is **cost-to-cost** which is based on the assumed relationship between a unit of input and productivity.  Under cost-to-cost, either revenue and/or profit to be recognized in the current period can be determined by the following formula.

$$\text{Revenue (profit)} = \left( \frac{\text{Cost to date}}{\substack{\text{Total expected} \\ \text{cost based on} \\ \text{latest estimate}}} \times \substack{\text{Contract price} \\ \text{(Expected profit)}} \right) - \substack{\text{Revenue (profit)} \\ \text{recognized in} \\ \text{previous periods}}$$

It is important to note that revenue and profit are two different terms. Profit is calculated by subtracting construction expenses from revenue. Revenue is the contract price. Therefore, pay particular attention to what item the CPA exam asks you to calculate.

The ledger account titles used in the following discussion are unique to long-term construction contracts. In practice, there are numerous account titles for the same item (e.g., "billings on LT contracts" vs. "partial billings on construction in progress") and various methodologies for journalizing the same transactions (e.g., separate revenue and expense control accounts in lieu of an "income on LT contracts" account). The following example has been simplified to highlight the main concepts.

EXAMPLE: *Assume a 3-year contract at a contract price of $500,000 as well as the following data:*

|                                  | *Year 1*  | *Year 2*  | *Year 3*  |
|----------------------------------|-----------|-----------|-----------|
| Cost incurred this year          | $135,000  | $225,000  | $ 45,000  |
| Prior years' costs               | -0-       | 135,000   | 360,000   |
| Estimated costs to complete      | $315,000  | 40,000    | -0-       |
| Total costs                      | $450,000  | 400,000   | $405,000  |
| Progress billings made during the year | $200,000 | $200,000 | $100,000 |
| Collection of billings each year | $175,000  | $200,000  | $125,000  |

From the above information, the following may be determined.

**Percent of completion** (costs to date/total costs)
Year 1: $135,000/$450,000 = 30%
Year 2: $360,000/$400,000 = 90%
Year 3: $405,000/$405,000 = 100%

|                                           | *Year 1*   | *Year 2*    | *Year 3*   |
|-------------------------------------------|------------|-------------|------------|
| Total revenue                             | $500,000   | $500,000    | $500,000   |
| x Percent of completion                   | × 30%      | × 90%       | × 100%     |
| Total revenue to be recognized by end of year | $150,000 | $450,000 | $500,000 |
| − Revenue recognized in prior periods     | --         | (150,000)   | (450,000)  |
| Current year's revenue (to be recognized) | $150,000   | $300,000    | $ 50,000   |
| Contract price                            | $500,000   | $500,000    | $500,000   |
| − Total estimated costs                   | (450,000)  | (400,000)   | (405,000)  |
| Estimated profit                          | $ 50,000   | $100,000    | $ 95,000   |
| x Percent of completion                   | × 30%      | × 90%       | × 100%     |
| Total profit to be recognized by end of year | $ 15,000 | $ 90,000 | $ 95,000 |
| − Profit recognized in prior periods      | --         | (15,000)    | (90,000)   |
| Current year's profit (to be recognized)  | $ 15,000   | $ 75,000    | $ 5,000    |

|                        |                              | *Percentage-of-completion* |          | *Completed-contract* |          |
|------------------------|------------------------------|----------------------------|----------|----------------------|----------|
| Year 1 Costs           | Construction in progress     | 135,000                    |          | 135,000              |          |
|                        | Cash                         |                            | 135,000  |                      | 135,000  |
| Year 1 Progress billings | Accounts receivable        | 200,000                    |          | 200,000              |          |
|                        | Billings on LT contracts     |                            | 200,000  |                      | 200,000  |
| Year 1 Cash collected  | Cash                         | 175,000                    |          | 175,000              |          |
|                        | Accounts receivable          |                            | 175,000  |                      | 175,000  |
| Year 1 Profit recognition | Construction expenses     | 135,000                    |          | none                 |          |
|                        | Construction in progress     | 15,000                     |          |                      |          |
|                        | Construction revenue         |                            | 150,000  |                      |          |
| Year 2 Costs           | Construction in progress     | 225,000                    |          | 225,000              |          |
|                        | Cash                         |                            | 225,000  |                      | 225,000  |
| Year 2 Progress billings | Accounts receivable        | 200,000                    |          | 200,000              |          |
|                        | Billings on LT contracts     |                            | 200,000  |                      | 200,000  |
| Year 2 Cash collected  | Cash                         | 200,000                    |          | 200,000              |          |
|                        | Accounts receivable          |                            | 200,000  |                      | 200,000  |
| Year 2 Profit recognition | Construction expenses     | 225,000                    |          | none                 |          |
|                        | Construction in progress     | 75,000                     |          |                      |          |
|                        | Construction revenue         |                            | 300,000  |                      |          |

| | | Percentage-of-completion | | Completed-contract | |
|---|---|---|---|---|---|
| Year 3 Costs | Construction in progress | 45,000 | | 45,000 | |
| | Cash | | 45,000 | | 45,000 |
| Year 3 Progress billings | Accounts receivable | 100,000 | | 100,000 | |
| | Billings on LT contracts | | 100,000 | | 100,000 |
| Year 3 Cash collected | Cash | 125,000 | | 125,000 | |
| | Accounts receivable | | 125,000 | | 125,000 |
| Year 3 Profit recognition and closing of special accounts | Construction expenses | 45,000 | | | |
| | Construction in progress | 5,000 | | | |
| | Construction revenue | | 50,000 | | |
| | Billings on LT contracts | 500,000 | | | |
| | Const. in progress | | 500,000 | | |
| | Construction expenses | | | 405,000 | |
| | Const. in progress | | | | 405,000 |
| | Billings on LT contracts | | | 500,000 | |
| | Construction revenue | | | | 500,000 |

The "construction in progress" (CIP) account is a cost accumulation account similar to "work in process" for job-order costing, except that the percentage-of-completion method includes interim profits in the account. The "billings on LT contracts" account is similar to an unearned revenue account. At each financial statement date, the "construction in progress" account should be netted against the "billings on LT contracts" account on a project-by-project basis, resulting in a net current asset and/or a net current liability. Under the percentage-of-completion method in the above example, a net current asset of $50,000 [($135,000 + $15,000 + $225,000 + $75,000) − ($200,000 + $200,000)] would be reported at the end of year 2. A net current liability of $40,000 would result under the completed-contract method [($200,000 + $200,000) − ($135,000 + $225,000)] for the same year.

### SUMMARY OF ACCOUNTS USED IN CONSTRUCTION ACCOUNTING
#### (NO LOSS EXPECTED OR INCURRED)

**Explanation of Journal Entries**

| Both methods | Completed-contract method | Percentage-of-completion method |
|---|---|---|
| (A) To record accumulated costs | (D) To record revenue upon completion and to close billings account | (F) To record recognition of interim revenue and expense |
| (B) To record progress billings | (E) To record expenses upon completion and to close construction in progress account | (G) To close construction-in-progress and billings accounts at project completion |
| (C) To record cash collections | | |

**Balance Sheet Classification***

| Current asset | Current liability |
|---|---|
| Projects where CIP at year-end** > Billings | Projects where billings > CIP at year-end** |
| | Estimated loss on uncompleted contract*** |

  *   Evaluate and classify on a project-by-project basis.

  **   Construction in progress including income (when percentage-of-completion method is used) or loss recognized.

  ***   When recognizing and reporting losses, it is necessary to use a current liability account instead of reducing CIP in those cases in which a contract's billings exceed its accumulated costs.

**Contract losses.** In any year when a **percentage-of-completion** contract has an expected loss on the entire contract, the amount of the loss reported in that year is the total expected loss on the entire contract **plus** all profit previously recognized. For example, if the expected costs yet to be incurred at the end of year two were $147,000, the total expected loss is $7,000 [$500,000 − ($135,000 + $225,000 + $147,000)] and the total loss reported in year two would be $22,000 ($7,000 + $15,000). Similarly, under the **completed-contract** method, total expected losses on the entire contract are recognized as soon as they are estimated. The loss recognized is similar to that for percentage-of-completion except the amount is for the expected loss on the entire contract. In the aforementioned example, the loss to be recognized is only $7,000 (the entire loss on the contract expected in year two) because interim profits have not been recorded. Journal entries and a schedule for profit or loss recognized on the contract under the percentage-of-completion method follow.

| *Journal entry at end of year 2* | *Percentage-of-completion* | | *Completed-contract* |
|---|---|---|---|
| Construction expenses | 227,000* | | |
|    Construction in progress (loss) | | 22,000 | |
|    Construction revenue | | 205,000** | |
| Loss on uncompleted LT contracts | | | 7,000 |
|    Construction in progress (loss) | | | 7,000 |

| * | *Year 2 costs* | | | $225,000 |
|---|---|---|---|---|
| | *Loss attributable to year 3:* | | | |
| |    Year 3 revenue ($500,000 – $150,000 – $205,000) | | $145,000 | |
| |    Year 3 costs (expected) | | 147,000 | 2,000 |
| | Total | | | $227,000 |

** ($360,000/$507,000) (Costs to date/Total estimated costs) = 71% (rounded); (71% × $500,000) – $150,000 = $205,000

### PERCENTAGE-OF-COMPLETION METHOD

| | *Year 1* | *Year 2* | *Year 3* |
|---|---|---|---|
| Contract price: | $ 500,000 | $500,000 | $500,000 |
| Estimated total costs: | | | |
| Costs incurred this year | $ 135,000 | $225,000 | $ 144,000*** |
| Prior year's costs | -- | 135,000 | 360,000 |
| Estimated cost yet to be incurred | 315,000 | 147,000 | -- |
| Estimated total costs for the three-year period, actual for year 3 | $ 450,000 | $507,000 | $504,000 |
| Estimated total income (loss) for three-year period, actual for year 3 | $ 15,000 | $ (7,000) | $ (4,000) |
| Income (loss) on entire contract previously recognized | -- | 15,000 | (7,000) |
| Amount of estimated income (loss) recognized in the current period, actual for year 3 | $ 15,000 | $(22,000) | $ 3,000 |

***Assumed

## G.  Research Component

The authoritative literature for inventory is found primarily in two places in FARS: ARB 43, chapter 4 and ARB 45. ARB 43, chapter 4 is devoted entirely to inventory pricing. Chapter 4 contains the definition of inventory, the significance of inventories, the basis of accounting, cost flows, and application of lower of cost or market. SFAS 151 amends ARB 43, chapter 4, on inventory pricing. ARB 45 focuses on long-term construction contracts and the percentage-of-completion and completed-contract methods. Although the weighted-average, moving average, and gross profit method of accounting for inventory are acceptable methods, few, if any, references are made to these methods in the accounting pronouncements. The only references to methods are first-in first-out, average and last-in first-out. Notice the hyphenation in several of the keywords; typing the keywords with correct hyphenation should produce faster and more accurate results.

Below is a list of keywords.

| | | |
|---|---|---|
| Accumulated costs billings | Expected losses contract | Mark-up inventory |
| Basis consistently applied | Finished goods | Net realizable value |
| Clearly reflects income | Firm purchase commitments | Percentage-of-completion method |
| Completed-contract method | First-in first-out | Physical deterioration |
| Contract costs loss | Held for sale | Raw materials |
| Contracts in process | Inventory obsolescence | Utility of goods |
| Cost or market | Last-in first-out | Work in process |
| Cost principle inventories | Lower of cost or market | |

## MULTIPLE-CHOICE QUESTIONS (1-61)

**1.** The following information applied to Fenn, Inc. for 2007:

| | |
|---|---|
| Merchandise purchased for resale | $400,000 |
| Freight-in | 10,000 |
| Freight-out | 5,000 |
| Purchase returns | 2,000 |

Fenn's 2007 inventoriable cost was

a. $400,000
b. $404,000
c. $408,000
d. $413,000

**2.** On December 28, 2007, Kerr Manufacturing Co. purchased goods costing $50,000. The terms were FOB destination. Some of the costs incurred in connection with the sale and delivery of the goods were as follows:

| | |
|---|---|
| Packaging for shipment | $1,000 |
| Shipping | 1,500 |
| Special handling charges | 2,000 |

These goods were received on December 31, 2007. In Kerr's December 31, 2007 balance sheet, what amount of cost for these goods should be included in inventory?

a. $54,500
b. $53,500
c. $52,000
d. $50,000

**3.** On June 1, 2007, Pitt Corp. sold merchandise with a list price of $5,000 to Burr on account. Pitt allowed trade discounts of 30% and 20%. Credit terms were 2/15, n/40 and the sale was made FOB shipping point. Pitt prepaid $200 of delivery costs for Burr as an accommodation. On June 12, 2007, Pitt received from Burr a remittance in full payment amounting to

a. $2,744
b. $2,940
c. $2,944
d. $3,140

**4.** The following information was taken from Cody Co.'s accounting records for the year ended December 31, 2007:

| | |
|---|---|
| Decrease in raw materials inventory | $ 15,000 |
| Increase in finished goods inventory | 35,000 |
| Raw material purchased | 430,000 |
| Direct labor payroll | 200,000 |
| Factory overhead | 300,000 |
| Freight-out | 45,000 |

There was no work in process inventory at the beginning or end of the year. Cody's 2007 cost of goods sold is

a. $895,000
b. $910,000
c. $950,000
d. $955,000

**5.** The following information pertains to Deal Corp.'s 2007 cost of goods sold:

| | |
|---|---|
| Inventory, 12/31/06 | $ 90,000 |
| 2007 purchases | 124,000 |
| 2007 write-off of obsolete inventory | 34,000 |
| Inventory, 12/31/07 | 30,000 |

The inventory written off became obsolete due to an unexpected and unusual technological advance by a competitor. In its 2007 income statement, what amount should Deal report as cost of goods sold?

a. $218,000
b. $184,000
c. $150,000
d. $124,000

**6.** How should the following costs affect a retailer's inventory?

| | *Freight-in* | *Interest on inventory loan* |
|---|---|---|
| a. | Increase | No effect |
| b. | Increase | Increase |
| c. | No effect | Increase |
| d. | No effect | No effect |

**7.** According to the net method, which of the following items should be included in the cost of inventory?

| | *Freight costs* | *Purchase discounts not taken* |
|---|---|---|
| a. | Yes | No |
| b. | Yes | Yes |
| c. | No | Yes |
| d. | No | No |

**8.** The following information pertained to Azur Co. for the year:

| | |
|---|---|
| Purchases | $102,800 |
| Purchase discounts | 10,280 |
| Freight in | 15,420 |
| Freight out | 5,140 |
| Beginning inventory | 30,840 |
| Ending inventory | 20,560 |

What amount should Azur report as cost of goods sold for the year?

a. $102,800
b. $118,220
c. $123,360
d. $128,500

**9.** When allocating costs to inventory produced for the period, fixed overhead should be based upon

a. The actual amounts of goods produced during the period.
b. The normal capacity of production facilities.
c. The highest production levels in the last three periods.
d. The lowest production level in the last three periods.

**10.** Per SFAS 151, what is considered the normal capacity of production facilities?

a. The average production over the previous five-year period.
b. Actual production for the period.
c. Actual production for the period plus loss of capacity for planned maintenance.
d. A range that may vary based on business and industry-specific factors.

**11.** How should unallocated fixed overhead costs be treated?

a. Allocated to finished goods and cost of goods based on ending balances in the accounts.
b. Allocated to raw materials, work in process, and finished goods, based on the ending balances in the accounts.
c. Recognized as an expense in the period in which they are incurred.

d.   Allocated to work in process, finished goods, and cost of goods sold based on ending balances in the accounts.

**12.** When manufacturing inventory, what is the accounting treatment for abnormal freight-in costs?
a.   Charge to expense for the period.
b.   Charge to the finished goods inventory.
c.   Charge to raw materials inventory.
d.   Allocate to raw materials, work in process, and finished goods.

**13.** On December 15, 2007, Flanagan purchased goods costing $100,000. The terms were FOB shipping point. Costs incurred by Flanagan in connection with the purchase and delivery of the goods were as follows:

| | |
|---|---|
| Normal freight charges | $3,000 |
| Handling costs | 2,000 |
| Insurance on shipment | 500 |
| Abnormal freight charges for express shipping | 1,200 |

The goods were received on December 17, 2007. What is the amount that Flanagan should charge to inventory and to current period expense?

| | Inventory | Current period expense |
|---|---|---|
| a. | $3,000 | $3,700 |
| b. | $5,000 | $1,700 |
| c. | $5,500 | $1,200 |
| d. | $6,700 | $0 |

**14.** Bach Co. adopted the dollar-value LIFO inventory method as of January 1, 2006. A single inventory pool and an internally computed price index are used to compute Bach's LIFO inventory layers. Information about Bach's dollar value inventory follows:

| | Inventory | |
|---|---|---|
| | at base | at dollar |
| Date | year cost | value LIFO |
| 1/1/06 | $90,000 | $90,000 |
| 2006 layer | 20,000 | 30,000 |
| 2007 layer | 40,000 | 80,000 |

What was the price index used to compute Bach's 2007 dollar value LIFO inventory layer?
a.   1.09
b.   1.25
c.   1.33
d.   2.00

**15.** Nest Co. recorded the following inventory information during the month of January:

| | Units | Unit cost | Total cost | Units on hand |
|---|---|---|---|---|
| Balance on 1/1 | 2,000 | $1 | $2,000 | 2,000 |
| Purchased on 1/8 | 1,200 | 3 | 3,600 | 3,200 |
| Sold on 1/23 | 1,800 | | | 1,400 |
| Purchased on 1/28 | 800 | 5 | 4,000 | 2,200 |

Nest uses the LIFO method to cost inventory. What amount should Nest report as inventory on January 31 under each of the following methods of recording inventory?

| | Perpetual | Periodic |
|---|---|---|
| a. | $2,600 | $5,400 |
| b. | $5,400 | $2,600 |
| c. | $2,600 | $2,600 |
| d. | $5,400 | $5,400 |

**16.** The weighted-average for the year inventory cost flow method is applicable to which of the following inventory systems?

| | Periodic | Perpetual |
|---|---|---|
| a. | Yes | Yes |
| b. | Yes | No |
| c. | No | Yes |
| d. | No | No |

**17.** During January 2007, Metro Co., which maintains a perpetual inventory system, recorded the following information pertaining to its inventory:

| | Units | Unit cost | Total cost | Units on hand |
|---|---|---|---|---|
| Balance on 1/1/07 | 1,000 | $1 | $1,000 | 1,000 |
| Purchased on 1/7/07 | 600 | 3 | 1,800 | 1,600 |
| Sold on 1/20/07 | 900 | | | 700 |
| Purchased on 1/25/07 | 400 | 5 | 2,000 | 1,100 |

Under the moving-average method, what amount should Metro report as inventory at January 31, 2007?
a.   $2,640
b.   $3,225
c.   $3,300
d.   $3,900

**18.** Based on a physical inventory taken on December 31, 2007, Chewy Co. determined its chocolate inventory on a FIFO basis at $26,000 with a replacement cost of $20,000. Chewy estimated that, after further processing costs of $12,000, the chocolate could be sold as finished candy bars for $40,000. Chewy's normal profit margin is 10% of sales. Under the lower of cost or market rule, what amount should Chewy report as chocolate inventory in its December 31, 2007 balance sheet?
a.   $28,000
b.   $26,000
c.   $24,000
d.   $20,000

**19.** Reporting inventory at the lower of cost or market is a departure from the accounting principle of
a.   Historical cost.
b.   Consistency.
c.   Conservatism.
d.   Full disclosure.

**20.** The original cost of an inventory item is below both replacement cost and net realizable value. The net realizable value less normal profit margin is below the original cost. Under the lower of cost or market method, the inventory item should be valued at
a.   Replacement cost.
b.   Net realizable value.
c.   Net realizable value less normal profit margin.
d.   Original cost.

**21.** Which of the following statements are correct when a company applying the lower of cost or market method reports its inventory at replacement cost?

I.   The original cost is less than replacement cost.
II.  The net realizable value is greater than replacement cost.

a.   I only.
b.   II only.
c.   Both I and II.
d.   Neither I nor II.

**22.** The original cost of an inventory item is above the replacement cost and the net realizable value. The replacement cost is below the net realizable value less the normal profit margin. As a result, under the lower of cost or market method, the inventory item should be reported at the
   a. Net realizable value.
   b. Net realizable value less the normal profit margin.
   c. Replacement cost.
   d. Original cost.

**23.** On January 1, 2007, Card Corp. signed a three-year noncancelable purchase contract, which allows Card to purchase up to 500,000 units of a computer part annually from Hart Supply Co. at $.10 per unit and guarantees a minimum annual purchase of 100,000 units. During 2007, the part unexpectedly became obsolete. Card had 250,000 units of this inventory at December 31, 2007, and believes these parts can be sold as scrap for $.02 per unit. What amount of probable loss from the purchase commitment should Card report in its 2007 income statement?
   a. $24,000
   b. $20,000
   c. $16,000
   d. $ 8,000

**24.** Thread Co. is selecting its inventory system in preparation for its first year of operations. Thread intends to use either the periodic weighted-average method or the perpetual moving-average method, and to apply the lower of cost or market rule either to individual items or to the total inventory. Inventory prices are expected to generally increase throughout 2007, although a few individual prices will decrease. What inventory system should Thread select if it wants to maximize the inventory carrying amount at December 31, 2007?

|   | Inventory method | Cost or market application |
|---|---|---|
| a. | Perpetual | Total inventory |
| b. | Perpetual | Individual item |
| c. | Periodic | Total inventory |
| d. | Periodic | Individual item |

**25.** Marsh Company had 150 units of product A on hand at January 1, 2007, costing $21 each. Purchases of product A during the month of January were as follows:

|         | Units | Unit cost |
|---------|-------|-----------|
| Jan. 10 | 200   | $22       |
| 18      | 250   | 23        |
| 28      | 100   | 24        |

A physical count on January 31, 2007, shows 250 units of product A on hand. The cost of the inventory at January 31, 2007, under the LIFO method is
   a. $5,850
   b. $5,550
   c. $5,350
   d. $5,250

**26.** During January 2007, Metro Co., which maintains a perpetual inventory system, recorded the following information pertaining to its inventory:

|                      | Units | Unit cost | Total cost | Units on hand |
|----------------------|-------|-----------|------------|---------------|
| Balance on 1/1/07    | 1,000 | $1        | $1,000     | 1,000         |
| Purchased on 1/7/07  | 600   | 3         | 1,800      | 1,600         |
| Sold on 1/20/07      | 900   |           |            | 700           |
| Purchased on 1/25/07 | 400   | 5         | 2,000      | 1,100         |

Under the LIFO method, what amount should Metro report as inventory at January 31, 2007?
   a. $1,300
   b. $2,700
   c. $3,900
   d. $4,100

**27.** Drew Co. uses the average cost inventory method for internal reporting purposes and LIFO for financial statement and income tax reporting. At December 31, 2007, the inventory was $375,000 using average cost and $320,000 using LIFO. The unadjusted credit balance in the LIFO Reserve account on December 31, 2007, was $35,000. What adjusting entry should Drew record to adjust from average cost to LIFO at December 31, 2007?

|    |                    | Debit    | Credit   |
|----|--------------------|----------|----------|
| a. | Cost of goods sold | $55,000  |          |
|    | Inventory          |          | $55,000  |
| b. | Cost of goods sold | $55,000  |          |
|    | LIFO reserve       |          | $55,000  |
| c. | Cost of goods sold | $20,000  |          |
|    | Inventory          |          | $20,000  |
| d. | Cost of goods sold | $20,000  |          |
|    | LIFO reserve       |          | $20,000  |

**28.** A company decided to change its inventory valuation method from FIFO to LIFO in a period of rising prices. What was the result of the change on ending inventory and net income in the year of the change?

|    | Ending inventory | Net income |
|----|------------------|------------|
| a. | Increase         | Increase   |
| b. | Increase         | Decrease   |
| c. | Decrease         | Decrease   |
| d. | Decrease         | Increase   |

**29.** Generally, which inventory costing method approximates most closely the current cost for each of the following?

|    | Cost of goods sold | Ending inventory |
|----|--------------------|------------------|
| a. | LIFO               | FIFO             |
| b. | LIFO               | LIFO             |
| c. | FIFO               | FIFO             |
| d. | FIFO               | LIFO             |

**30.** During periods of rising prices, a perpetual inventory system would result in the same dollar amount of ending inventory as a periodic inventory system under which of the following inventory cost flow methods?

|    | FIFO | LIFO |
|----|------|------|
| a. | Yes  | No   |
| b. | Yes  | Yes  |
| c. | No   | Yes  |
| d. | No   | No   |

**31.** On January 1, 2006, Poe Company adopted the dollar-value LIFO inventory method. Poe's entire inventory constitutes a single pool. Inventory data for 2006 and 2007 are as follows:

| Date     | Inventory at current year cost | Inventory at base year cost | Relevant price index |
|----------|--------------------------------|-----------------------------|----------------------|
| 1/1/06   | $150,000                       | $150,000                    | 1.00                 |
| 12/31/06 | 220,000                        | 200,000                     | 1.10                 |
| 12/31/07 | 276,000                        | 230,000                     | 1.20                 |

Poe's LIFO inventory value at December 31, 2007, is
- a. $230,000
- b. $236,000
- c. $241,000
- d. $246,000

**32.** Brock Co. adopted the dollar-value LIFO inventory method as of January 1, 2006. A single inventory pool and an internally computed price index are used to compute Brock's LIFO inventory layers. Information about Brock's dollar-value inventory follows:

| | Inventory | | |
| Date | At base year cost | At current year cost | At dollar value LIFO |
|---|---|---|---|
| 1/1/06 | $40,000 | $40,000 | $40,000 |
| 2006 layer | 5,000 | 14,000 | 6,000 |
| 12/31/06 | 45,000 | 54,000 | 46,000 |
| 2007 layer | 15,000 | 26,000 | ? |
| 12/31/07 | $60,000 | $80,000 | ? |

What was Brock's dollar-value LIFO inventory at December 31, 2007?
- a. $80,000
- b. $74,000
- c. $66,000
- d. $60,000

**33.** Estimates of price-level changes for specific inventories are required for which of the following inventory methods?
- a. Conventional retail.
- b. Dollar-value LIFO.
- c. Weighted-average cost.
- d. Average cost retail.

**34.** When the double-extension approach to the dollar-value LIFO inventory method is used, the inventory layer added in the current year is multiplied by an index number. Which of the following correctly states how components are used in the calculation of this index number?
- a. In the numerator, the average of the ending inventory at base year cost and at current year cost.
- b. In the numerator, the ending inventory at current year cost, and, in the denominator, the ending inventory at base year cost.
- c. In the numerator, the ending inventory at base year cost, and, the denominator, the ending inventory at current year cost.
- d. In the denominator, the average of the ending inventory at base year cost and at current year cost.

**35.** Jones Wholesalers stocks a changing variety of products. Which inventory costing method will be most likely to give Jones the lowest ending inventory when its product lines are subject to specific price increases?
- a. Specific identification.
- b. Weighted-average.
- c. Dollar-value LIFO.
- d. FIFO periodic.

**36.** Dart Company's accounting records indicated the following information:

| | |
|---|---|
| Inventory, 1/1/07 | $ 500,000 |
| Purchases during 2007 | 2,500,000 |
| Sales during 2007 | 3,200,000 |

A physical inventory taken on December 31, 2007, resulted in an ending inventory of $575,000. Dart's gross profit on sales has remained constant at 25% in recent years. Dart suspects some inventory may have been taken by a new employee. At December 31, 2007, what is the estimated cost of missing inventory?
- a. $ 25,000
- b. $100,000
- c. $175,000
- d. $225,000

**37.** On July 1, 2007, Casa Development Co. purchased a tract of land for $1,200,000. Casa incurred additional cost of $300,000 during the remainder of 2007 in preparing the land for sale. The tract was subdivided into residential lots as follows:

| Lot class | Number of lots | Sales price per lot |
|---|---|---|
| A | 100 | $24,000 |
| B | 100 | 16,000 |
| C | 200 | 10,000 |

Using the relative sales value method, what amount of costs should be allocated to the Class A lots?
- a. $300,000
- b. $375,000
- c. $600,000
- d. $720,000

**38.** Herc Co.'s inventory at December 31, 2007, was $1,500,000 based on a physical count priced at cost, and before any necessary adjustment for the following:

- Merchandise costing $90,000, shipped FOB shipping point from a vendor on December 30, 2007, was received and recorded on January 5, 2008.
- Goods in the shipping area were excluded from inventory although shipment was not made until January 4, 2008. The goods, billed to the customer FOB shipping point on December 30, 2007, had a cost of $120,000.

What amount should Herc report as inventory in its December 31, 2007 balance sheet?
- a. $1,500,000
- b. $1,590,000
- c. $1,620,000
- d. $1,710,000

**39.** Kew Co.'s accounts payable balance at December 31, 2007, was $2,200,000 before considering the following data:

- Goods shipped to Kew FOB shipping point on December 22, 2007, were lost in transit. The invoice cost of $40,000 was not recorded by Kew. On January 7, 2008, Kew filed a $40,000 claim against the common carrier.
- On December 27, 2007, a vendor authorized Kew to return, for full credit, goods shipped and billed at $70,000 on December 3, 2007. The returned goods were shipped by Kew on December 28, 2007. A $70,000 credit memo was received and recorded by Kew on January 5, 2008.
- Goods shipped to Kew FOB destination on December 20, 2007, were received on January 6, 2008. The invoice cost was $50,000.

What amount should Kew report as accounts payable in its December 31, 2007 balance sheet?
- a. $2,170,000
- b. $2,180,000
- c. $2,230,000
- d. $2,280,000

**40.** Lewis Company's usual sales terms are net sixty days, FOB shipping point. Sales, net of returns and allowances, totaled $2,300,000 for the year ended December 31, 2007, before year-end adjustments. Additional data are as follows:

- On December 27, 2007, Lewis authorized a customer to return, for full credit, goods shipped and billed at $50,000 on December 15, 2007. The returned goods were received by Lewis on January 4, 2008, and a $50,000 credit memo was issued and recorded on the same date.
- Goods with an invoice amount of $80,000 were billed and recorded on January 3, 2008. The goods were shipped on December 30, 2007.
- Goods with an invoice amount of $100,000 were billed and recorded on December 30, 2007. The goods were shipped on January 3, 2008.

Lewis' adjusted net sales for 2007 should be
- a. $2,330,000
- b. $2,280,000
- c. $2,250,000
- d. $2,230,000

**41.** On January 1, 2007, Dell, Inc. contracted with the city of Little to provide custom built desks for the city schools. The contract made Dell the city's sole supplier and required Dell to supply no less than 4,000 desks and no more than 5,500 desks per year for two years. In turn, Little agreed to pay a fixed price of $110 per desk. During 2007, Dell produced 5,000 desks for Little. At December 31, 2007, 500 of these desks were segregated from the regular inventory and were accepted and awaiting pickup by Little. Little paid Dell $450,000 during 2007. What amount should Dell recognize as contract revenue in 2007?
- a. $450,000
- b. $495,000
- c. $550,000
- d. $605,000

**42.** On October 20, 2007, Grimm Co. consigned forty freezers to Holden Co. for sale at $1,000 each and paid $800 in transportation costs. On December 30, 2007, Holden reported the sale of ten freezers and remitted $8,500. The remittance was net of the agreed 15% commission. What amount should Grimm recognize as consignment sales revenue for 2007?
- a. $ 7,700
- b. $ 8,500
- c. $ 9,800
- d. $10,000

**43.** The following items were included in Opal Co.'s inventory account at December 31, 2007:

| | |
|---|---|
| Merchandise out on consignment, at sales price, including 40% markup on selling price | $40,000 |
| Goods purchased, in transit, shipped FOB shipping point | 36,000 |
| Goods held on consignment by Opal | 27,000 |

By what amount should Opal's inventory account at December 31, 2007, be reduced?
- a. $103,000
- b. $ 67,000
- c. $ 51,000
- d. $ 43,000

**44.** On December 1, 2007, Alt Department Store received 505 sweaters on consignment from Todd. Todd's cost for

the sweaters was $80 each, and they were priced to sell at $100. Alt's commission on consigned goods is 10%. At December 31, 2007, five sweaters remained. In its December 31, 2007 balance sheet, what amount should Alt report as payable for consigned goods?
- a. $49,000
- b. $45,400
- c. $45,000
- d. $40,400

**45.** Southgate Co. paid the in-transit insurance premium for consignment goods shipped to Hendon Co., the consignee. In addition, Southgate advanced part of the commissions that will be due when Hendon sells the goods. Should Southgate include the in-transit insurance premium and the advanced commissions in inventory costs?

| | Insurance premium | Advanced commissions |
|---|---|---|
| a. | Yes | Yes |
| b. | No | No |
| c. | Yes | No |
| d. | No | Yes |

**46.** Jel Co., a consignee, paid the freight costs for goods shipped from Dale Co., a consignor. These freight costs are to be deducted from Jel's payment to Dale when the consignment goods are sold. Until Jel sells the goods, the freight costs should be included in Jel's
- a. Cost of goods sold.
- b. Freight-out costs.
- c. Selling expenses.
- d. Accounts receivable.

**47.** Heath Co.'s current ratio is 4:1. Which of the following transactions would normally increase its current ratio?
- a. Purchasing inventory on account.
- b. Selling inventory on account.
- c. Collecting an account receivable.
- d. Purchasing machinery for cash.

**48.** During 2007, Rand Co. purchased $960,000 of inventory. The cost of goods sold for 2007 was $900,000, and the ending inventory at December 31, 2007, was $180,000. What was the inventory turnover for 2007?
- a. 6.4
- b. 6.0
- c. 5.3
- d. 5.0

**49.** In a comparison of 2007 to 2006, Neir Co.'s inventory turnover ratio increased substantially although sales and inventory amounts were essentially unchanged. Which of the following statements explains the increased inventory turnover ratio?
- a. Cost of goods sold decreased.
- b. Accounts receivable turnover increased.
- c. Total asset turnover increased.
- d. Gross profit percentage decreased.

**50.** Selected data pertaining to Lore Co. for the calendar year 2007 is as follows:

| | |
|---|---|
| Net cash sales | $ 3,000 |
| Cost of goods sold | 18,000 |
| Inventory at beginning of year | 6,000 |
| Purchases | 24,000 |
| Accounts receivable at beginning of year | 20,000 |
| Accounts receivable at end of year | 22,000 |

Lore would use which of the following to determine the average days' sales in inventory?

|  | Numerator | Denominator |
|---|---|---|
| a. | 365 | Average inventory |
| b. | 365 | Inventory turnover |
| c. | Average inventory | Sales divided by 365 |
| d. | Sales divided by 365 | Inventory turnover |

**51.** Cord Builders, Inc. has consistently used the percentage-of-completion method of accounting for construction-type contracts. During 2006 Cord started work on a $9,000,000 fixed-price construction contract that was completed in 2008. Cord's accounting records disclosed the following:

|  | December 31 | |
|---|---|---|
|  | 2006 | 2007 |
| Cumulative contract costs incurred | $3,900,000 | $6,300,000 |
| Estimated total cost at completion | 7,800,000 | 8,100,000 |

How much income would Cord have recognized on this contract for the year ended December 31, 2007?

- a. $100,000
- b. $300,000
- c. $600,000
- d. $700,000

**52.** State Co. recognizes construction revenue and expenses using the percentage-of-completion method. During 2006, a single long-term project was begun, which continued through 2007. Information on the project follows:

|  | 2006 | 2007 |
|---|---|---|
| Accounts receivable from | | |
| construction contract | $100,000 | $300,000 |
| Construction expenses | 105,000 | 192,000 |
| Construction in progress | 122,000 | 364,000 |
| Partial billings on contract | 100,000 | 420,000 |

Profit recognized from the long-term construction contract in 2007 should be

- a. $ 50,000
- b. $108,000
- c. $128,000
- d. $228,000

**53.** Lake Construction Company has consistently used the percentage-of-completion method of recognizing income. During 2006, Lake entered into a fixed-price contract to construct an office building for $10,000,000. Information relating to the contract is as follows:

|  | At December 31, | |
|---|---|---|
|  | 2006 | 2007 |
| Percentage of completion | 20% | 60% |
| Estimated total cost at completion | $7,500,000 | $8,000,000 |
| Income recognized (cumulative) | 500,000 | 1,200,000 |

Contract costs incurred during 2007 were

- a. $3,200,000
- b. $3,300,000
- c. $3,500,000
- d. $4,800,000

**54.** Hansen Construction, Inc. has consistently used the percentage-of-completion method of recognizing income. During 2007, Hansen started work on a $3,000,000 fixed-price construction contract. The accounting records disclosed the following data for the year ended December 31, 2007:

| Costs incurred | $ 930,000 |
|---|---|
| Estimated cost to complete | 2,170,000 |
| Progress billings | 1,100,000 |
| Collections | 700,000 |

How much loss should Hansen have recognized in 2007?

- a. $230,000
- b. $100,000
- c. $ 30,000
- d. $0

**Items 55 and 56** are based on the following data pertaining to Pell Co.'s construction jobs, which commenced during 2007:

|  | Project 1 | Project 2 |
|---|---|---|
| Contract price | $420,000 | $300,000 |
| Costs incurred during 2007 | 240,000 | 280,000 |
| Estimated costs to complete | 120,000 | 40,000 |
| Billed to customers during 2007 | 150,000 | 270,000 |
| Received from customers during 2007 | 90,000 | 250,000 |

**55.** If Pell used the completed contract method, what amount of gross profit (loss) would Pell report in its 2007 income statement?

- a. $ (20,000)
- b. $ 0
- c. $ 340,000
- d. $ 420,000

**56.** If Pell used the percentage-of-completion method, what amount of gross profit (loss) would Pell report in its 2007 income statement?

- a. $(20,000)
- b. $ 20,000
- c. $ 22,500
- d. $ 40,000

**57.** Which of the following is used in calculating the income recognized in the fourth and final year of a contract accounted for by the percentage-of-completion method?

|  | Actual total costs | Income previously recognized |
|---|---|---|
| a. | Yes | Yes |
| b. | Yes | No |
| c. | No | Yes |
| d. | No | No |

**58.** A company used the percentage-of-completion method of accounting for a five-year construction contract. Which of the following items will the company use to calculate the income recognized in the third year?

|  | Progress billings to date | Income previously recognized |
|---|---|---|
| a. | Yes | No |
| b. | No | Yes |
| c. | No | No |
| d. | Yes | Yes |

**59.** The calculation of the income recognized in the third year of a five-year construction contract accounted for using the percentage-of-completion method includes the ratio of

- a. Total costs incurred to date to total estimated costs.
- b. Total costs incurred to date to total billings to date.
- c. Cost incurred in year three to total estimated costs.
- d. Costs incurred in year three to total billings to date.

**60.** When should an anticipated loss on a long-term contract be recognized under the percentage-of-completion method and the completed-contract method, respectively?

| | *Percentage-of-completion* | *Completed-contract* |
|---|---|---|
| a. | Over life of project | Contract complete |
| b. | Immediately | Contract complete |
| c. | Over life of project | Immediately |
| d. | Immediately | Immediately |

**61.** In accounting for a long-term construction contract using the percentage-of-completion method, the progress billings on contracts account is a

    a.   Contra current asset account.

    b.   Contra noncurrent asset account.

    c.   Noncurrent liability account.

    d.   Revenue account

**SIMULATION PROBLEMS**

**Simulation Problem 1** (50 to 60 minutes)

| Situation | | | | | |
|---|---|---|---|---|---|
| | Concepts | Journal Entries | Calculations | Research | Communication |

A client, Blaedon Co., sells lawn mowers and garden tillers. The garden tillers are purchased from Bestbuilt Tillers and sold to customers without modification. The lawn mowers, however, are purchased from several contractors. Blaedon then makes ongoing design refinements to the mowers before selling them to customers.

The lawn mowers cost $200. Blaedon then makes the design refinements at a cost of $85 per lawn mower. Blaedon stores the lawn mowers in its own warehouse and sells them directly to retailers at a list price of $500. Blaedon uses the FIFO inventory method. Approximately two-thirds of new lawn mower sales involve trade-ins. For each used lawn mower traded in and returned to Blaedon, retailers receive a $40 allowance regardless of whether the trade-in was associated with a sale of a 2007 or 2008 model. Blaedon's net realizable value on a used lawn mower averages $25.

At December 31, 2007, Blaedon's inventory of new lawn mowers includes both 2007 and 2008 models. When the 2008 model was introduced in September 2007, the list price of the remaining 2007 model lawn mowers was reduced below cost. Blaedon is experiencing rising costs.

Blaedon has contacted your firm for advice on how to report the carrying value of inventory, the impact of the decline in value on the 2007 models, and the effects of using the FIFO method on their December 31, 2007 financial statements.

| | Concepts | | | | |
|---|---|---|---|---|---|
| Situation | | Journal Entries | Calculations | Research | Communication |

Indicate whether each of the following is included in the cost of inventory.

| | Included | Not included |
|---|:---:|:---:|
| 1. Merchandise purchased for resale | ○ | ○ |
| 2. Freight out | ○ | ○ |
| 3. Direct materials | ○ | ○ |
| 4. Sales returns | ○ | ○ |
| 5. Packaging for shipment to customer | ○ | ○ |
| 6. Factory overhead | ○ | ○ |
| 7. Interest on inventory loan | ○ | ○ |
| 8. Purchase discounts not taken | ○ | ○ |
| 9. Freight in | ○ | ○ |
| 10. Direct labor | ○ | ○ |

| | | Journal Entries | | | |
|---|---|---|---|---|---|
| Situation | Concepts | | Calculations | Research | Communication |

Assume that Blaedon uses the periodic inventory method for inventories. Prepare the journal entries for each of the following transactions. Blaedon uses the gross method for recording inventory transactions.

1. On January 5, 2007, purchased $17,000 of garden tillers on account from Bestbuilt Tillers, terms 2/10, n/30, FOB destination. Freight charges were $200.

2. On January 10, 2007, returned garden tillers worth $2,000 to Bestbuilt Tillers due to defects.

3. On January 14, 2007, paid for the remaining tillers purchased in **1.**

4. On January 28, 2007, purchased $30,000 of lawn mowers from Lawn Giant, terms 3/10, n/30, FOB shipping point. The freight charges were $820.

5. On February 6, 2007, paid for the lawn mowers purchased in part **4.** from Lawn Giant.

| | | | Calculations | | | |
|---|---|---|---|---|---|---|
| Situation | Concepts | Journal Entries | | | Research | Communication |

Assume that Blaedon had the following information regarding the garden tiller inventory:

| | |
|---|---|
| Purchases | $210,000 |
| Purchase discounts | 38,000 |
| Purchase returns | 17,500 |
| Freight in | 12,100 |
| Freight out | 18,000 |
| Beginning inventory | 42,900 |
| Ending inventory | 34,250 |

Calculate the following items:

1. Goods available for sale
2. Costs of goods sold

| | | | | Research | | |
|---|---|---|---|---|---|---|
| Situation | Concepts | Journal Entries | Calculations | | | Communication |

Research the following issues in the authoritative literature. Insert the appropriate citations to answer each question.

1. What costs should be included in Blaedon's inventory?
2. How should Blaedon report the 2007 inventory that has declined in value below its costs?

| | | | | | Communication |
|---|---|---|---|---|---|
| Situation | Concepts | Journal Entries | Calculations | Research | |

Prepare a memo to your client explaining

- How Blaedon should determine the carrying amounts assigned to its lawn mower inventory for the 2007 and 2008 models.
- Considering only the 2008 model lawn mower, explain in your memo the impact of the FIFO cost flow assumptions in Blaedon's 2007 income statement and balance sheet amounts.

To:       CEO, Blaedon Corp.
From:   CPA Candidate
Re:       Inventory valuation

| |
|---|
| |

---

### Simulation Problem 2            (50 to 60 minutes)

| Situation | | | | | |
|---|---|---|---|---|---|
| | Calculation of Gross Profit | Financial Statement Disclosures | Schedule of Income Taxes | Communication | Research |

London, Inc. began operation of its construction division on October 1, 2006, and entered into contracts for two separate projects. The Beta project contract price was $600,000 and provided for penalties of $10,000 per week for late completion. Although during 2007 the Beta project had been on schedule for timely completion, it was completed four weeks late in August 2008. The Gamma project's original contract price was $800,000. Change orders during 2008 added $40,000 to the original contract price.

The following data pertains to the separate long-term construction projects in progress:

| | Beta | Gamma |
|---|---|---|
| As of September 30, 2007: | | |
| Costs incurred to date | $360,000 | $410,000 |
| Estimated costs to complete | 40,000 | 410,000 |
| Billings | 315,000 | 440,000 |
| Cash collections | 275,000 | 365,000 |
| As of September 30, 2008: | | |
| Costs incurred to date | 450,000 | 720,000 |
| Estimated costs to complete | -- | 180,000 |
| Billings | 560,000 | 710,000 |
| Cash collections | 560,000 | 625,000 |

## Additional information

- London accounts for its long-term construction contracts using the percentage-of-completion method for financial reporting purposes and the completed-contract method for income tax purposes.
- Enacted income tax rates are 25% for 2007 and 30% for future years.
- London's income before income taxes from all divisions, before considering revenues from long-term construction projects, was $300,000 for the year ended September 30, 2007. There were no other temporary or permanent differences.

| Situation | Calculation of Gross Profit | Financial Statement Disclosures | Schedule of Income Taxes | Communication | Research |
|---|---|---|---|---|---|

Prepare a schedule showing London's gross profit (loss) recognized for the years ended September 30, 2007, and 2008, under the percentage-of-completion method.

**London Inc.**
**SCHEDULE OF GROSS PROFIT (LOSS)**

| | Beta | | Gamma |
|---|---|---|---|
| *For the Year Ended September 30, 2007:* | | | |
| Estimated gross profit (loss): | | | |
| Contract price | | | |
| Less total costs | | | |
| Estimated gross profit (loss) | | | |
| Percent complete: | | | |
| Costs incurred to date | | | |
| Total costs | | | |
| Percent complete | | | |
| Gross profit (loss) recognized | | | |
| *For the Year Ended September 30, 2008:* | | | |
| Estimated gross profit (loss): | | | |
| Contract price | | | |
| Less total costs | | | |
| Estimated gross profit (loss) | | | |
| Percent complete: | | | |
| Costs incurred to date | | | |
| Total costs | | | |
| Percent complete | | | |
| Gross profit (loss) recognized | | | |
| Less gross profit (loss) recognized in prior year | | | |
| Gross profit (loss) recognized | | | |

| Situation | Calculation of Gross Profit | Financial Statement Disclosures | Schedule of Income Taxes | Communication | Research |
|---|---|---|---|---|---|

Prepare the following schedule showing London's balances in the following accounts at September 30, 2007, under the percentage-of-completion method:

- Accounts receivable
- Costs and estimated earnings in excess of billings
- Billings in excess of costs and estimated earnings

**London Inc.**
**SCHEDULE OF SELECTED BALANCE SHEET ACCOUNTS**
*September 30, 2007*

| | | |
|---|---|---|
| Accounts receivable | | |
| Costs and estimated earnings in excess of billings: | | |
| Construction in progress | | |
| Less: Billings | | |
| Costs and estimated earnings in excess of billings | | |
| Billings in excess of costs and estimated earnings | | |
| Estimated loss on contract | | |

| Situation | Calculation of Gross Profit | Financial Statement Disclosures | Schedule of Income Taxes | Communication | Research |
|---|---|---|---|---|---|

Prepare the following schedule reconciling London's financial statement income and taxable income for the year ended September 30, 2007, and showing all components of taxes payable and current and deferred income tax expense for the year then ended.  Do not consider estimated tax requirements.[1]

*London Inc.*
**SCHEDULE OF INCOME TAXES PAYABLE AND INCOME TAX EXPENSE**
*September 30, 2007*

| | | |
|---|---|---|
| Financial statement income: | | |
|    From other divisions | | |
|    From Beta project | | |
|    From Gamma project | | |
| Total financial statement income | | |
| Less temporary differences: | | |
|    Beta project income | | |
|    Gamma project loss | | |
| Total taxable income | | |
| Taxes payable | | |
| Deferred tax liability | | |
| Tax expense: | | |
|    Current | | |
|    Deferred | | |

| Situation | Calculation of Gross Profit | Financial Statement Disclosures | Schedule of Income Taxes | Communication | Research |
|---|---|---|---|---|---|

London has recently hired Jim Cauley, a new construction supervisor who has not used the percentage-of-completion method for accounting for long-term construction contracts.  Write a brief memo to Mr. Cauley on the percentage-of-completion method of accounting for long-term construction contracts, explaining the advantages and disadvantages of this method.

To:     Mr. Jim Cauley, Construction Supervisor
From:  CPA Candidate
Re:    Percentage-of-completion method for construction contracts

| Situation | Calculation of Gross Profit | Financial Statement Disclosures | Schedule of Income Taxes | Communication | Research |
|---|---|---|---|---|---|

Using the Original Pronouncements, research the following question.  You may cut and paste your answer into the space provided.

A company is using the completed-contract method for long-term construction contracts.  The company expected the contract will incur a loss.  What disclosures, if any, are necessary if the firm anticipates a loss?

**Simulation Problem 3**                                    (50 to 60 minutes)

| Situation | | | | | |
|---|---|---|---|---|---|
| | Inventory Concepts | Cost Flow Concepts | Schedule of Ending Inventory | Schedule of Cost of Goods Sold | Communication | Research |

York Co. sells one product, which it purchases from various suppliers.  York's trial balance at December 31, 2007, included the following accounts:

---

[1] *This requirement should not be completed until you have done Module 12, Deferred Taxes.  A cross-reference in the Module 12 problem material will direct you to return to it.*

| Sales (33,000 units @ $16) | $528,000 |
|---|---|
| Sales discounts | 7,500 |
| Purchases | 368,900 |
| Purchase discounts | 18,000 |
| Freight-in | 5,000 |
| Freight-out | 11,000 |

York Co.'s inventory purchases during 2007 were as follows:

| | Units | Cost per unit | Total cost |
|---|---|---|---|
| Beginning inventory, January 1 | 8,000 | $8.20 | $ 65,600 |
| Purchases, quarter ended March 31 | 12,000 | 8.25 | 99,000 |
| Purchases, quarter ended June 30 | 15,000 | 7.90 | 118,500 |
| Purchases, quarter ended September 30 | 13,000 | 7.50 | 97,500 |
| Purchases, quarter ended December 31 | 7,000 | 7.70 | 53,900 |
| | 55,000 | | $434,500 |

## Additional information

York's accounting policy is to report inventory in its financial statements at the lower of cost or market, applied to total inventory. Cost is determined under the last-in, first-out (LIFO) method.

York has determined that, at December 31, 2007, the replacement cost of its inventory was $8 per unit and the net realizable value was $8.80 per unit. York's normal profit margin is $1.05 per unit.

| Situation | Inventory Concepts | Cost Flow Concepts | Schedule of Ending Inventory | Schedule of Cost of Goods Sold | Communication | Research |
|---|---|---|---|---|---|---|

**Items 1 through 13** represent True or False statements concerning inventory accounting methods. Indicate whether each statement is true or false by clicking on the appropriate response.

|  | *True* | *False* |
|---|---|---|
| 1. The gross margin method uses historical sales margins to estimate the cost of inventory. | O | O |
| 2. The dollar-value LIFO method preserves old inventory costs by charging current costs to cost of goods sold. | O | O |
| 3. Inventory should be reported at the lower of cost or market and it may be based on the values of individual items, categories, or the total inventory. | O | O |
| 4. A loss on a purchase commitment should be recorded when the contract price is greater than the market and it is anticipated that a loss will occur when the contract is completed. | O | O |
| 5. Under the dollar-value LIFO method, increases and decreases in a layer would be measured based upon the change in the total dollar value of the layer. | O | O |
| 6. The link-chain method uses a cumulative index to value the base cost of ending inventory. | O | O |
| 7. The price index for dollar-value LIFO is a measure of changes in price levels between the current year and the base year. | O | O |
| 8. Under the LIFO method, an inventory liquidation will result in higher profits in a period of rising prices. | O | O |
| 9. A holding gain results from holding an item while the market value experiences a decline. | O | O |
| 10. During a period of rising prices, the LIFO cost flow assumption results in a higher net income as compared to FIFO. | O | O |
| 11. In a period of rising prices, when a company changes from FIFO to LIFO the net income will tend to decline as will working capital. | O | O |
| 12. The use of LIFO for book and tax purposes will result in a lower tax payment in a period of rising prices. | O | O |
| 13. Under the LIFO method, the cost of goods sold balance would be the same whether a perpetual or periodic inventory system is used. | O | O |

| Situation | Inventory Concepts | Cost Flow Concepts | Schedule of Ending Inventory | Schedule of Cost of Goods Sold | Communication | Research |
|---|---|---|---|---|---|---|

Below are statements describing inventory and cost flow methods. Identify which method matches each description by clicking on the correct term and placing it in the space provided. You may use a term once, more than once, or not at all.

<u>*Terms*</u>
Specific identification
Weighted-average
Simple average
Moving average
First-in, first-out
Last-in, first-out
Dollar-value LIFO
Gross profit

<u>*Method*</u>

1. During a period of rising prices, this method results in a higher net income.

2. This method most closely matches the physical flow of inventory.

3. Method that uses historical sales margins to estimate ending inventory.

4. Method that is appropriate when there is a relatively small number of significant dollar value items in inventory.

5. Average cost must be calculated each time additional inventory is purchased.

6. Method that averages the cost of all items on hand and purchased during the period.

7. This method results in the lowest ending inventory in a period of rising prices.

8. Method that uses a price index to measure changes in inventory.

9. If used for tax purposes, this method must also be used for financial reporting purposes.

10. The cost of goods sold balance is the same whether a perpetual or periodic inventory system is used.

| Situation | Inventory Concepts | Cost Flow Concepts | Schedule of Ending Inventory | Schedule of Cost of Goods Sold | Communication | Research |
|---|---|---|---|---|---|---|

**York Co.**
**SUPPORTING SCHEDULE OF ENDING INVENTORY**
*December 31, 2007*

Inventory at cost (LIFO):

| | Units | Cost per unit | Total cost |
|---|---|---|---|
| Beginning inventory, January 1 | | | |
| Purchases, quarter ended March 31 | | | |
| Purchases, quarter ended June 30 | | | |
| Totals | | | |

| Situation | Inventory Concepts | Cost Flow Concepts | Schedule of Ending Inventory | Schedule of Cost of Goods Sold | Communication | Research |
|---|---|---|---|---|---|---|

**York Co.**
**SCHEDULE OF COST OF GOODS SOLD**
*For the Year Ended December 31, 2007*

| | | |
|---|---|---|
| Beginning inventory | | |
| Add: Purchases | | |
| Less: Purchase discounts | | |
| Add: Freight-in | | |
| Goods available for sale | | |
| Less: Ending inventory | | |
| Cost of goods sold | | |

| Situation | Inventory Concepts | Cost Flow Concepts | Schedule of Ending Inventory | Schedule of Cost of Goods Sold | Communication | Research |
|---|---|---|---|---|---|---|

York Co.'s warehouse supervisor, Mr. Binson, has inquired about the accounting for inventory that has declined in value. Write a brief memo explaining to Mr. Binson the rule of lower of cost or market and its application in this situation.

To:      Mr. Binson
From:    CPA Candidate
Re:      Valuation of inventory

| Situation | Inventory Concepts | Cost Flow Concepts | Schedule of Ending Inventory | Schedule of Cost of Goods Sold | Communication | Research |
|---|---|---|---|---|---|---|

Research the Original Pronouncements to answer the following questions:

1. What methods may be used for costing inventories?

2. How is the market value calculated when calculating the lower of cost or market?

## MULTIPLE-CHOICE ANSWERS

| | | | | |
|---|---|---|---|---|
| 1. c __ __ | 14. d __ __ | 27. d __ __ | 40. d __ __ | 53. b __ __ |
| 2. d __ __ | 15. b __ __ | 28. c __ __ | 41. c __ __ | 54. b __ __ |
| 3. c __ __ | 16. b __ __ | 29. a __ __ | 42. d __ __ | 55. a __ __ |
| 4. b __ __ | 17. b __ __ | 30. a __ __ | 43. d __ __ | 56. b __ __ |
| 5. c __ __ | 18. c __ __ | 31. c __ __ | 44. c __ __ | 57. a __ __ |
| 6. a __ __ | 19. a __ __ | 32. c __ __ | 45. c __ __ | 58. b __ __ |
| 7. a __ __ | 20. d __ __ | 33. b __ __ | 46. d __ __ | 59. a __ __ |
| 8. b __ __ | 21. b __ __ | 34. b __ __ | 47. b __ __ | 60. d __ __ |
| 9. b __ __ | 22. b __ __ | 35. c __ __ | 48. b __ __ | 61. a __ __ |
| 10. d __ __ | 23. c __ __ | 36. a __ __ | 49. d __ __ | |
| 11. c __ __ | 24. a __ __ | 37. c __ __ | 50. b __ __ | |
| 12. a __ __ | 25. c __ __ | 38. d __ __ | 51. a __ __ | 1st: __/61 = __% |
| 13. c __ __ | 26. b __ __ | 39. a __ __ | 52. a __ __ | 2nd: __/61 = __% |

## MULTIPLE-CHOICE ANSWER EXPLANATIONS

### A. Determining Inventory and Cost of Goods Sold

**1. (c)** Inventoriable costs include all costs necessary to prepare goods for sale. For a merchandising concern these costs include the purchase price of the goods, freight-in, insurance, warehousing, and any costs necessary to get the goods to the point of sale (except interest on any loans obtained to purchase the goods). In this problem, inventoriable costs total $408,000.

| | |
|---|---|
| Purchase price less returns ($400,000 – $2,000) | $398,000 |
| Freight-in | 10,000 |
| | $408,000 |

Note that freight-out is a **selling expense,** not an inventoriable cost, as the diagram below indicates.

**2. (d)** When the shipping terms are FOB destination, the seller bears **all** costs of transporting the goods to the buyer. Therefore, the seller is responsible for the payment of packaging costs ($1,000), shipping costs ($1,500), and the special handling charges ($2,000). The only amount to be included as the buyer's cost of the inventory purchased is the purchase price ($50,000).

**3. (c)** Purchases are always recorded net of trade discounts. When more than one trade discount is applied to a list price, it is called a chain discount. Chain discounts are applied in steps; each discount applies to the previously discounted price. The cost, net of trade discounts, is $2,800 [$5,000 – (30% × $5,000) = $3,500; and $3,500 – (20% × $3,500) = $2,800]. Payment was made within the discount period, so the net purchase price is $2,744 [$2,800 – (2% × $2,800)]. The remittance from Burr would also include reimbursement of the $200 of delivery costs. Since the terms were FOB shipping point, Burr is responsible for paying this amount, and must reimburse Pitt, who prepaid the freight. Thus, the total remittance is $2,944 ($2,744 + $200).

**4. (b)** Three computations must be performed: raw materials used, cost of goods manufactured, and cost of goods sold.

The decrease in RM inventory is added when computing RM used because RM were used in excess of those purchased. The increase in FG inventory is deducted when computing cost of goods sold because it represents the portion of goods manufactured which were not sold. The freight-out is irrelevant for this question because freight-out is a selling expense and therefore does not affect cost of goods sold.

**5. (c)** To compute cost of goods sold, the solutions approach is to set up a T-account for inventory

| Inventory | | | |
|---|---|---|---|
| 12/31/06 | 90,000 | | |
| Purchases | 124,000 | 34,000 | Write-off |
| | | ? | Cost of goods sold |
| 12/31/07 | 30,000 | | |

Purchases increase inventory, while the write-off and cost of goods sold decrease inventory. Cost of goods sold can be computed as $150,000 using the T-account. An alternate solutions approach is to use the CGS computation

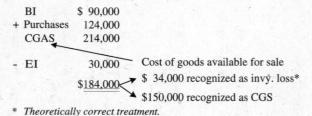

\* *Theoretically correct treatment.*

**6. (a)** Per ARB 43, the cost of inventory should include all expenditures (direct and indirect) incurred to bring an item to its existing condition and location. Freight-in charges are thus appropriately included in inventory costs. Per SFAS 34, interest cost shall not be capitalized for assets that are in use or ready for their intended use in the earnings activities of the enterprise. Thus, interest on an inventory loan should not be included in inventory (it should be expensed as incurred).

**7. (a)** Per ARB 43, the cost of inventory should include all expenditures (direct and indirect) incurred to bring an item to its existing condition and location. Freight charges are thus appropriately included in inventory costs. Under the net purchase method, purchase discounts not taken are recorded in a Purchase Discounts Lost account. When this method is used, purchase discounts lost are considered a financial (i.e., "other") expense, and are thus excluded from the cost of inventory.

**8. (b)** Azur should report cost of goods sold calculated as

Cost of goods sold (CGS) = Beg. Inventory + Net purchases* + Freight in – Ending Inventory

CGS = $ 30,840 + $92,520** + $15,420 – $20,560

CGS = $118,220

Freight out is a selling expense and does not enter the calculation of cost of goods sold.

* *Net purchase = Purchases – Purchase returns and allowances – Purchase discounts*

** ($102,800 – $10,280)

**9. (b)** Per SFAS 151, fixed overhead is allocated based on the normal capacity of the production facilities. Normal capacity is the production expected to be achieved over a number of periods or seasons under normal circumstances, taking into account the loss of capacity resulting from planned maintenance. Answer (a) is incorrect, because the actual amount of production may only be used if it approximates normal capacity. Answers (c) and (d) are incorrect, because SFAS 151 does not specify a formula to calculate normal capacity.

**10. (d)** Per SFAS 151, normal capacity refers to a range in production levels that will vary based on business and industry-specific factors. Normal capacity is the production expected to be achieved over a number of periods or seasons under normal circumstances, taking into account the loss of capacity resulting from planned maintenance. Answer (a) is incorrect because SFAS 151 does not specify a formula for calculating normal capacity. Answers (b) and (c) are incorrect because actual production may only be used if it approximates normal capacity.

**11. (c)** Per SFAS 151, unallocated fixed overhead costs are recognized as an expense in the period in which they are incurred. Prior to SFAS 151, it was acceptable to charge unallocated or underapplied fixed overhead entirely to cost of goods sold, or allocate the underapplied fixed overhead to work in process, finished goods, and cost of goods sold. Therefore, answers (a), (b), and (d) are incorrect according to SFAS 151.

**12. (a)** Per SFAS 151, any abnormal costs for freight, handling costs, and wasted material are required to be treated as current period charges, and not a part of inventory cost. Therefore, answers (b), (c), and (d) are incorrect.

**13. (c)** ARB 43, Chapter 4, provides that inventoriable costs include all costs necessary to prepare goods for sale. For a merchandising concern, these include the purchase price of the goods, freight-in, insurance, warehousing, and any costs necessary to get the goods to the point of sale. SFAS 151 amends ARB 43, Chapter 4, and provides that abnormal freight and handling be charged to expense of the period. Therefore, the normal costs for inventory are $5,500 ($3,000 + $2,000 + $500) and the abnormal freight of $1,200 is charged to current expense of the period.

**B. Inventory Valuation and Cost-Flow Methods**

**14. (d)** Ending inventory at dollar value LIFO is calculated as the base year inventory times the index. Therefore, the index used can be calculated as 2.00 = ($80,000 EI at dollar value LIFO/$40,000 base year cost).

**15. (b)** The inventory valuations are calculated as follows:

Valuations of ending inventory under LIFO perpetual

| | | |
|---|---|---|
| 1,400 units at $1.00 | = | $1,400 |
| 800 units at $5.00 | = | 4,000 |
| Total | | $5,400 |

Value of ending inventory under LIFO periodic

| | | |
|---|---|---|
| 2,000 units at $1.00 | = | $2,000 |
| 200 units at $3.00 | = | 600 |
| Total | | $2,600 |

**B.2. Weighted-Average**

**16. (b)** The requirement is to determine whether the weighted-average inventory method is applicable to a periodic and/or a perpetual inventory system. The weighted-average method computes a weighted-average unit cost of inventory for the entire period and is used with periodic records. The moving-average method requires that a new unit of cost be computed each time new goods are purchased and is used with perpetual records.

**B.4. Moving-Average**

**17. (b)** The moving-average method requires that a new unit cost be computed each time goods are purchased. The new unit cost is used to cost all sales of inventory until the next purchase. After the 1/7/07 purchase, Metro owns 1,600 units (1,000 + 600) at a total cost of $2,800 ($1,000 + $1,800). Therefore, the moving-average unit cost at that time is $1.75 ($2,800 ÷ 1,600 units). After the 1/20/07 sale of 900 units (at a unit of cost of $1.75), Metro owns 700 units at a unit cost of $1.75 (700 × $1.75 = $1,225). The 1/25/07 purchase of 400 units at a total cost of $2,000 increases inventory to its 1/31/07 balance of $3,225 ($1,225 + $2,000). The new unit cost (not required) is $2.93 ($3,225 ÷ 1,100).

**B.5. Lower of Cost or Market**

**18. (c)** ARB 43 requires the use of lower of cost or market (LCM) for financial reporting of inventories. The market value of inventory is defined as the replacement cost (RC), as long as it is less than the ceiling (net realizable value, or NRV) and more than the floor (NRV less a normal profit, or NRV – NP). In this case, the amounts are

| | |
|---|---|
| Ceiling: NRV = $40,000 est. sell. price – $12,000 disp. cost = | $28,000 |
| Floor: NRV – NP = $28,000 – (10% × $40,000) | $24,000 |
| RC: | $20,000 |

Since RC falls below the floor, the floor (NRV – NP) is the designated market value. Once market value is designated, LCM can be determined by simply determining the lower of cost ($26,000) or market ($24,000). Therefore, inventory is reported at $24,000.

**19. (a)** SFAC 5 establishes five different attributes on which assets can be measured. The attribute used should be determined by the nature of the item and the relevance and reliability of the attribute measured. The five attributes are historical cost, current cost, current market value, net realizable value, and present value. Historical cost is defined as the amount of cash, or its equivalent, paid to acquire an asset. Reporting inventory at lower of cost or market is a departure from the historical cost principle as the inventory could potentially be carried at the market value if lower. Although, reporting inventory at lower of cost or market does not create a departure from conservatism as this method carries at inventory the lowest or most conservative value. The use of LCM does not violate the principle of consistency either, as it would be reported on this basis continually. Finally the use of LCM would not violate the principle of full disclosure as its use would be discussed in the footnotes.

**20. (d)** According to ARB 43, inventory is to be valued at the lower of cost or market. Under this method, market is replacement cost provided that replacement cost is lower than net realizable value (ceiling) and higher than net realizable value less the normal profit margin (floor). The question does not specify whether replacement cost is above or below net realizable value, but since the original cost is below **both** of these values, that information is irrelevant.

Either NRV or RC will be designated as the market value of the inventory, and since the original cost is below **both** of these values, the inventory will be valued at its original cost. Answer (c) is incorrect because NRV – NP represents the market floor. Answers (a) and (b) are incorrect because they are both **above** the original cost.

**21. (b)** ARB 43 requires the use of lower of cost or market (LCM) for financial reporting of inventories. The market value of inventory is defined as the replacement cost (RC) as long as it is less than the ceiling (net realizable value, or NRV) and more than the floor (NRV less a normal profit, or NRV – NP). Therefore, if inventory is reported at RC, RC must be less than original cost (meaning statement I is **not** correct), and RC must be less than NRV (meaning statement II **is** correct) and greater than NRV – NP.

**22. (b)** ARB 43 requires the pricing of inventory at market when market value is less than cost. Market value is defined as current replacement cost, subject to a ceiling of net realizable value (NRV) and a floor of net realizable value minus a normal profit margin.

In this situation, replacement cost lies outside of (below) the floor and ceiling limitations. Therefore, NRV less a normal

profit margin (the floor), will be used as the market to determine LCM. Since original cost is greater than market, market will be used to price the inventory for the period.

**B.6. Losses on Purchase Commitments**

**23. (c)** The requirement is to determine the amount of probable loss from the purchase commitment that Card should report in its 2007 income statement. When there is a decline in market value below the contract price at the balance sheet date and the contract is noncancelable, an unrealized loss should be recorded in the period of decline and reported in the income statement. In this case, Card has a contract to purchase a minimum of 100,000 units both in 2008 and 2009 at $.10 per unit. The $20,000 loss (200,000 × $.10) on these obsolete units should be reduced by the amount Card believes is realizable from the sale of these units. Therefore, the loss on **purchase commitment** is $16,000 [$20,000 – (200,000 × .02)]. Additionally, Card Corp. would need to record a loss of $20,000 ($.08 × 250,000) from **inventory obsolescence**.

**24. (a)** To maximize its inventory carrying amount at December 31, 2007, Thread should use the perpetual moving-average method with the lower of cost or market rule applied to the total inventory. First, when using the perpetual moving-average method, the cost of sales throughout the year are determined using the average cost of purchases up to the time of the sale. On the other hand, under the periodic weighted-average method, the cost of each item is the weighted-average of **all** units purchased during the year. During a period of rising prices, the perpetual moving-average method results in a lower cost of goods sold and a higher ending inventory because the cost of items sold throughout the year is the average of the earlier, lower prices. Second, the application of the lower of cost or market rule to the total inventory will result in a higher ending inventory because market values lower than cost are offset against market values higher than cost.

**B.7. & B.8. First-In, First-Out (FIFO), and Last-In, First-Out (LIFO)**

**25. (c)** The requirement is to determine the cost of the 1/31/07 inventory, using the LIFO method. LIFO stands for last-in, first-out; this means that the cost of the units purchased most recently are included in cost of goods sold. Therefore, the 1/31/07 inventory consists of the 250 units that were purchased at the earliest date(s). Thus, the 1/31/07 inventory would consist of the 150 units on hand at 1/1/07 (150 × $21 = $3,150) plus an additional 100 units purchased at the earliest purchase date in January (January 10; 100 × $22 = $2,200). The total value of the inventory at 1/31/07 would be $5,350 ($3,150 + $2,200).

**26. (b)** LIFO stands for last-in, first-out; this means that it is assumed that any units sold are the units most recently purchased. In a perpetual system, LIFO is applied at the time of each sale rather than once a year as in a periodic system. Using LIFO, the 900 units sold on 1/20/07 would consist of the 600 units purchased on 1/7/07 and 300 of the 1,000 units in the 1/1/07 balance. This would leave in inventory 700 units from the 1/1/07 balance. After the 1/25/07 purchase, inventory included those 700 units plus the 400 units purchased on 1/25/07. Therefore, ending inventory is $2,700 [(700 × $1) + (400 × $5)].

**27.   (d)**   When a company uses LIFO for external reporting purposes and another inventory method for internal purposes, a **LIFO Reserve** account is used to reduce inventory from the internal valuation to the LIFO valuation. LIFO Reserve is a contra account to inventory, and is adjusted up or down at year-end with a corresponding increase or decrease to **Cost of Goods Sold**. In this case, the LIFO Reserve account must be adjusted from a balance of $35,000 to a balance of $55,000 ($375,000 – $320,000). Therefore, LIFO Reserve is credited for $20,000 ($55,000 – $35,000) with a corresponding debit to Cost of Goods Sold.

**28.   (c)**   In a change **to** LIFO, no recognition is given to any cumulative effect associated with the change because it is usually not determinable. Thus, the effect on ending inventory and net income is the result solely of current year effects. In a period of rising prices, LIFO will result in a **lower ending inventory** amount than FIFO because the earlier lower costs are assumed to remain in ending inventory. LIFO will also result in a **lower net income** because the more recent higher costs are assigned to cost of goods sold.

**29.   (a)**   The inventory costing method which most closely approximates the current cost for cost of goods sold is LIFO, while the method which more accurately reflects ending inventory is FIFO. Under LIFO, the most recent purchases are assumed to be the first goods sold; thus, cost of goods sold contains relatively current costs. On the other hand, since FIFO assumes that the goods from beginning inventory and the earliest purchases are sold first, the ending inventory is made up of more recent purchases and thus represents a more current value.

**30.   (a)**   Under the FIFO method, the first goods purchased are considered to be the first goods used or sold. Ending inventory is thus made up of the latest (most recent) purchases. Whenever the FIFO method is used, the ending inventory is the same whether a perpetual or periodic system is used. This is true even during periods of rising or falling prices because the inventory flow is always in chronological order. Under the LIFO method, the latest (most recent) purchases are considered to be the first goods used or sold. Ending inventory is thus made up of the first (oldest) purchases. When a periodic method is used, the first/last purchase determination is made only at the end of the year, based upon the actual chronological order of all purchases. When a perpetual method is used, however, the first/last purchase determination is made continuously throughout the year. When inventory levels get low under the perpetual method, early purchase costs will often be assigned to goods sold, a situation that is much less likely to occur in a periodic system. Therefore, in times of either rising or falling prices, LIFO ending inventory is usually different under a periodic system than under a perpetual system.

**B.9.   Dollar-Value LIFO**

**31.   (c)**   When using dollar-value LIFO, the ending inventory at current year cost must first be converted to base year cost. This amount is given at 12/31/07 ($230,000), but it could be computed as follows: $276,000 ÷ 1.20 = $230,000. The next step is to determine the incremental LIFO layers at base year cost. The 1/1/06 (base year) layer is $150,000, the 2006 layer is $50,000 ($200,000 – $150,000), and the 2007 layer is $30,000 ($230,000 – $200,000). Finally, the LIFO

layers are restated using the price index in effect at the time each layer was added.

|            | Base cost |          | Ending inventory at DV LIFO cost |
|------------|-----------|----------|-----------|
| 1/1/06 layer | 150,000 | x 1.00 = | $150,000 |
| 2006 layer | 50,000 | x 1.10 = | 55,000 |
| 2007 layer | 30,000 | x 1.20 = | 36,000 |
|            | $230,000 |          | $241,000 |

**32.   (c)**   When using dollar-value LIFO, the ending inventory at current year cost must first be converted to base year cost. The 12/31/07 inventory at base year cost is given as $60,000. Since the 12/31/06 inventory at base year cost was $45,000 ($40,000 base layer and $5,000 2005 layer), a new layer of $15,000 was added in 2007 ($60,000 – $45,000). This layer must be restated using the 2007 price index. The 2007 price index is computed using the double-extension technique, as illustrated below.

$$\frac{\text{EI at year-end prices}}{\text{EI at base year prices}} = \frac{\$80,000}{\$60,000} = 1.33$$

Therefore, the 12/31/07 inventory using dollar-value LIFO is $66,000 as computed below.

|            | Base cost |          | DV LIFO |
|------------|-----------|----------|---------|
| Base layer | $40,000 |          | $40,000 |
| 2006 layer | 5,000 |          | 6,000 |
| 2007 layer | 15,000 | x 1.33 | 20,000 |
|            |        |          | $66,000 |

**33.   (b)**   The requirement is to determine which inventory method requires estimates of price level changes for specific inventories. In accordance with the dollar-value LIFO method, the ending inventory is first converted to the base year cost so that the incremental layers can be determined. The incremental layers are then restated using the price index which was in effect at the time each of the layers were added to the inventory. Thus, the specific layers of the ending inventory are adjusted to the current price level. Therefore, answer (b) is correct. Answers (a), (c), and (d) are incorrect because these methods do not specifically adjust for price level changes.

**34.   (b)**   The requirement is to determine the appropriate use of ending inventory at current year cost and ending inventory at base year cost in calculating the dollar-value LIFO index. According to ARB 43, chap 4, the index number used to convert the current year's inventory layer is calculated as follows:

$$\text{Index} = \frac{\text{Ending inventory at current year cost}}{\text{Ending inventory at base year cost}}$$

This index indicates the relationship between current and base year prices as a percentage, and when multiplied by the new layer (which is the increase in inventory in base year dollars), it will convert the layer to current dollars.

**35.   (c)**   During periods of rising prices, the inventory costing methods which will give Jones the lowest ending inventory balance are LIFO methods, because inventory items that were purchased at the earliest date (when prices were lower) will remain in inventory and the most recently purchased and more expensive items will be expensed through cost of goods sold. Any FIFO method will produce a higher ending inventory balance during inflation since the items purchased earliest (at lower prices) will be expensed through COGS, while the more expensive items remain in inventory. Answers (a) and (b) are incorrect because neither will give Jones a lower ending inventory balance than dollar-value LIFO, particularly as Jones' inventory changes (because dollar-value LIFO allows the LIFO "layers" to be made up of similar, not necessarily identical, items).

**B.10. Gross Profit**

**36.** **(a)** The gross profit method can be used to estimate the cost of missing inventory. The first step is to compute the cost of goods available for sale.

| | |
|---|---:|
| Beginning inventory | $ 500,000 |
| Purchases | 2,500,000 |
| Cost of goods available for sale | $3,000,000 |

The second step is to estimate cost of goods sold based on the gross profit percentage.

| | |
|---|---:|
| Sales | $3,200,000 |
| Estimated gross profit ($3,200,000 × 25%) | (800,000) |
| Cost of goods sold ($3,200,000 × 75%) | $2,400,000 |

Note that a shortcut is to realize that if gross profit is 25% of sales, cost of goods sold must be 75% of sales. The third step is to compute estimated ending inventory.

| | |
|---|---:|
| Cost of goods available for sale | $ 3,000,000 |
| Estimated cost of goods sold | (2,400,000) |
| Estimated ending inventory | $ 600,000 |

Since the actual count of ending inventory at December 31 was only $575,000, the estimated shortage in inventory is $25,000 ($600,000 − $575,000).

**B.14. Cost Apportionment by Relative Sales Value**

**37.** **(c)** The total cost of acquiring the land and preparing it for sale ($1,200,000 + $300,000 = $1,500,000) should be allocated to the residential lots based on their relative sales value, as computed below.

| Lot class | # of lots | | Sales price | | Total sales value |
|---|---|---|---|---|---|
| A | 100 | × | $24,000 | = | $2,400,000 |
| B | 100 | × | 16,000 | = | 1,600,000 |
| C | 200 | × | 10,000 | = | 2,000,000 |
| | | | | | $6,000,000 |

| Total cost | | Fraction allocated to Class A | | Allocated cost |
|---|---|---|---|---|
| $1,500,000 | × | ($2,400/$6,000) | = | $600,000 |

**C. Items to Include in Inventory**

**38.** **(d)** Before adjustment, the inventory based on a physical count was $1,500,000. The $90,000 of merchandise shipped FOB shipping point by a vendor on 12/30/07 should also be included in Herc's 12/31/07 inventory because Herc, the buyer, owns the goods while in transit under these terms. The goods in the shipping area (cost, $120,000) are also owned by Herc because they were not shipped until 2008 and Herc still retains the risks of ownership until that point. Therefore, 12/31/07 inventory is $1,710,000 ($1,500,000 + $90,000 + $120,000).

**39.** **(a)** Before adjustment, the balance in the Accounts Payable account is $2,200,000. The $40,000 of goods lost in transit from a vendor were shipped FOB **shipping point**. This means the buyer owns the goods while they were in transit; therefore, Kew should record the purchase and accounts payable in 2007. Kew, not the vendor, is ultimately responsible for the lost goods (note that Kew, not the vendor, is suing the common carrier). The $70,000 return that was recorded on 1/5/08 should have been recorded in 2007 when the return was authorized (December 27, 2007). Therefore, Kew should reduce 12/31/07 Accounts Payable by $70,000.

The $50,000 of goods received on 1/6/08 were properly recorded in 2008, since the terms were FOB destination (the buyer does not own the goods until they are physically received). Therefore, no adjustment is necessary for this amount. Kew should report 12/31/07 Accounts Payable at $2,170,000 ($2,200,000 + $40,000 − $70,000).

**40.** **(d)** Net sales is $2,300,000, subject to three possible adjustments. The goods returned ($50,000) should be recorded as a return in 2007, when Lewis authorized the return. Since this return was not recorded until 2008, 2007 sales must be adjusted downward. The goods shipped on 12/30/07 ($80,000) were recorded as a sale in 2008 Since the terms were FOB shipping point, the sale must be recorded in 2007 when the goods were shipped; therefore, 2007 sales must be adjusted upward. The goods shipped on 1/3/08 ($100,000) should not be recorded as a sale until 2008. Since the sale was recorded in 2007, 2007 sales must be adjusted downward. Therefore, adjusted net sales for 2007 should be $2,230,000 ($2,300,000 − $50,000 + $80,000 − $100,000).

**41.** **(c)** Generally, goods are considered sold when legal title to the goods passes to the buyer. In certain situations, however, the transfer of title criteria does not reflect the underlying economics of the situation. In this situation, although transfer of legal title may not have occurred for the 500 segregated desks, the economic substance of the transaction is that the seller no longer retains the risks of ownership. Therefore, all 5,000 desks (including the 500 segregated and accepted desks) are considered sold in 2007, and revenue of $550,000 is recognized (5,000 × $110). Note that the amount of cash collected ($450,000) does not affect the amount of revenue recognized in this case.

**D. Consignments**

**42.** **(d)** A consignor recognizes sales revenue from consignments when the consignee sells the consigned goods to the ultimate customer. Sales commissions earned by the consignee ($10,000 × 15% = $1,500) are reported as a selling expense by the consignor and are **not** netted against sales revenue. Therefore, sales revenue is reported at the total selling price of $10,000 (10 × $1,000). Note that the transportation costs ($800) do not affect sales either; one-fourth (10/40) is reflected in cost of goods sold and three-fourths (30/40) is included in ending inventory.

**43.** **(d)** No adjustment is necessary for the goods in transit ($36,000). The goods were shipped **FOB shipping point,** which means the buyer (Opal) owns the goods while in transit. Therefore, Opal properly included these goods in 12/31/07 inventory. The merchandise **out** on consignment is owned by the consignor (Opal) and should be included in Opal's inventory **at cost** [$40,000 − (40% × $40,000) = $24,000]. Therefore, inventory must be reduced by $16,000 for this item ($40,000 − $24,000). The goods **held** on consignment ($27,000) are owned by the consignor, not Opal; therefore, inventory must be reduced $27,000 for this item. The total reduction in inventory is $43,000 ($16,000 + $27,000).

**44.** **(c)** Alt sold 500 of the consigned sweaters (505 − 5) at $100 each, resulting in total sales of $50,000 (500 × $100). Alt must report a payable to Todd for this amount, less Alt's commission [$50,000 − (10% × $50,000) = $45,000]. Alt does not owe Todd anything for the unsold sweaters until they are sold.

**45. (c)** Inventoriable costs include all costs necessary to prepare goods for sale. These costs include the purchase price or manufacturing cost of the goods, freight, and any other costs necessary to get the goods to the point of sale. The in-transit insurance premium would therefore be included in inventory costs. Commissions paid to the consignee are selling expenses in the period the consigned goods are sold that are not required to ready the goods for sale. These costs, therefore, are not included in inventory.

**46. (d)** In a consignment, the manufacturer or wholesaler is referred to as the consignor and the dealer or retailer is referred to as the consignee. In such an arrangement, title to the goods remains with the consignor until they are sold to a third party. Jel's payment of reimbursable freight costs results in an account receivable from Dale, which Jel will subtract from the sale proceeds it remits to Dale. Answers (a), (b), and (c) are incorrect because the consignee, Jel, generally does not bear any costs associated with the sale of consigned goods.

## E. Ratios

**47. (b)** The formula to compute the current ratio is

$$\text{Current ratio} = \frac{\text{Current assets}}{\text{Current liabilities}}$$

The following entries would be recorded when inventory is sold on account:

| Accounts receivable | } | Sales price |
| Sales | | of merchandise |

| Cost of goods sold | } | Cost of |
| Inventory | | merchandise |

Since the selling price (increase to AR) is normally higher than the cost of the merchandise sold (decrease to merchandise inventory) the sale would normally cause a net increase in current assets, and therefore, a net increase in the current ratio. When the existing current ratio is greater than one, increases of equal amounts to the numerator (inventory, a component of current assets) and denominator (accounts payable, a component of current liabilities) will reduce the ratio. When an account receivable is collected, cash (a current asset) is increased by the same amount that accounts receivable (another current asset) is decreased. Thus, the transaction has no impact on the current ratio. When machinery (a noncurrent asset) is purchased for cash (a current asset), there is a **decrease** in the current ratio.

**48. (b)** The formula for inventory turnover is

$$\frac{\text{Cost of goods sold}}{\text{Average inventory}}$$

Average inventory is equal to beginning inventory plus ending inventory, divided by two. Since beginning inventory is not given, it must be computed using the cost of goods sold relationship

| | Cost of goods sold | $ 900,000 |
| + | Ending inventory | 180,000 |
| | Cost of goods available for sale | $1,080,000 |
| − | Purchases | − 960,000 |
| | Beginning inventory | $ 120,000 |

Therefore, average inventory is $150,000 [($120,000 + $180,000) ÷ 2], and inventory turnover is 6.0 times ($900,000 ÷ 150,000).

**49. (d)** The solutions approach is to create a numerical example that conforms to the facts given in the question. The inventory turnover ratio is calculated as follows:

$$\frac{\text{Cost of goods sold}}{\text{Average inventory}}$$

If we assume that cost of goods sold has increased from 100 to 150 and average inventory has remained unchanged at 50 then the following ratios result:

$$\frac{\text{Cost of goods sold}}{\text{Average inventory}} \quad \frac{100}{50} = 2 \quad \frac{150}{50} = 3$$

Thus, if cost of goods sold increases while inventory remains unchanged, then the inventory turnover ratio will increase.

In addition, we must examine the effects of the increase in cost of goods sold on the gross profit percentage when sales remain constant. Assuming the same facts as above, and sales of $200, we get the following results:

| | | | |
|---|---|---:|---:|
| | Sales | 200 | 200 |
| − | Cost of goods sales | − 100 | − 150 |
| | Gross profit | 100 | 50 |

Thus, as cost of goods sold increases, the gross profit and the gross profit percentage will decrease.
Answer (a) is incorrect because a decrease in cost of goods sold will cause the inventory ratio to increase. Answers (b) and (c) are incorrect because they are not related to inventory turnover.

**50. (b)** Average days' sales in inventory measures the number of days inventory is held before sale; it reflects on efficiency of inventory policies. It is computed using the following formula:

$$\frac{365}{\text{Inventory turnover}}$$

## F. Long-Term Construction Contracts

**51. (a)** The total expected income on the contract at 12/31/07 is $900,000 ($9,000,000 − $8,100,000). The formula for recognizing profit under the percentage-of-completion method is

$$\frac{\text{Cost to date}}{\text{Total expected costs}} \times \text{Expected profit} = \text{Profit recognized to date}$$

$$\frac{\$6,300,000}{\$8,100,000} \times \$900,000 = \$700,000$$

This result is the **total** profit on the contract in 2006 and 2007. The 2006 profit recognized must be subtracted from $700,000 to determine the 2007 profit. At 12/31/06, the total expected income on the contract was $1,200,000 ($9,000,000 − $7,800,000). The income recognized in 2006 was $600,000, as computed below.

$$\frac{\$3,900,000}{\$7,800,000} \times \$1,200,000 = \$600,000$$

Therefore, 2007 income is $700,000 less $600,000, or $100,000.

**52. (a)** Profit to be recognized using the percentage-of-completion method is generally computed as follows:

$$\left(\frac{\text{Cost to date}}{\text{Total expected cost}} \times \text{Expected profit}\right) - \text{Profit recognized in previous periods}$$

Not enough information is given in this problem to perform this computation, so 2007 profit must be computed indirectly. Since only construction expenses and profit are debited to the construction-in-progress (CIP account), 2006 profit must have been $17,000 ($122,000 CIP less $105,000 const. exp.).

Cumulative profit recognized by the end of 2007 must be $67,000 [$364,000 CIP less $297,000 cumulative const. exp. ($105,000 + $192,000)]. Therefore, 2007 profit was $50,000 ($67,000 − $17,000).

| CIP | | |
|---|---|---|
| 2006 Exp. | 105,000 | |
| 2006 Profit | ? | 2006 Profit = $17,000 |
| 2006 End. bal | 122,000 | |
| 2007 Exp. | 192,000 | |
| 2007 Profit | ? | 2007 Profit = $50,000 |
| 2007 End. bal. | 364,000 | |

**53. (b)** Based on the information given, it must be assumed that costs incurred are used to measure the extent of progress toward project completion. At 12/31/06, the proj-ect was 20% complete and total estimated costs were $7,500,000. Therefore, costs incurred as of 12/31/06 were 20% of $7,500,000, or $1,500,000. At 12/31/07, the project was 60% complete and total estimated costs were $8,000,000. Therefore, costs incurred as of 12/31/07 are 60% of $8,000,000 or $4,800,000. The costs incurred during 2007 were $4,800,000 less $1,500,000, or $3,300,000.

**54. (b)** The requirement is to determine the amount of loss to recognize in 2007 on a long-term, fixed-price construction contract. Under both the percentage-of-completion method and the completed-contract method, an expected **loss** on a contract must be recognized in **full** in the period in which the expected loss is discovered. Therefore, Hanson must recognize a loss of $100,000 in 2007.

| | |
|---|---|
| Expected contract revenue | $3,000,000 |
| Expected contract costs ($930,000 + $2,170,000) | 3,100,000 |
| Expected loss | $ (100,000) |

**55. (a)** The expected income on project 1 [$420,000 − ($240,000 + $120,000) = $60,000] is **not** recognized until the project is completed under the completed contract method. However, under the completed contract method, an expected **loss** on a contract must be recognized in full in the period in which it is discovered. Project two has an expected loss of ($20,000) [$300,000 − ($280,000 + $40,000)] which must be recognized immediately in 2007.

**56. (b)** Construction companies that use the percentage-of-completion method in accounting for long-term construction contracts usually recognize gross profit according to the cost-to-cost method.

$$\frac{\text{Costs to date}}{\text{Total estimated costs}} \times \text{Estimated profit} = \text{Gross profit to date}$$

Pell would recognize gross profit of $40,000 on project 1

$$\frac{\$240,000}{\$240,000 + \$120,000} \times [\$420,000 - (\$240,000 + \$120,000)] = \$40,000$$

Note that prior years' gross profit need not be subtracted from $40,000 because the project commenced during 2007. Under both the percentage-of-completion method and the completed-contract method, an expected **loss** must be recognized in full in the period in which the expected loss is discovered. Project two has an expected loss of ($20,000) [$300,000 − ($280,000 + $40,000)] which must be recognized in full in 2007. The net gross profit recognized on the two projects is $20,000 ($40,000 profit less ($20,000) loss).

**57. (a)** In the **final year** of a contract accounted for by the percentage-of-completion method, the percentage of completion is 100%, since costs to date equal total costs.

Therefore, the formula to calculate income to be recognized in the final year is simply

Therefore both **actual total costs** and **income previously recognized** are used in calculating income.

**58. (b)** Under the percentage-of-completion method of accounting for long-term contracts, the cost-to-cost formula is used to compute the amount of income to be recognized in a particular year. The formula to calculate current income is as follows:

$$\left( \frac{\text{Cost to date}}{\text{Total expected cost}} \times \frac{\text{Expected}}{\text{profit}} \right) - \frac{\text{Profit recognized}}{\text{in previous periods}}$$

Progress billings do not impact the amount of income recognized.

**59. (a)** The requirement is to determine the ratio to be used to calculate income in the third year using the percentage-of-completion method. ARB 45 suggests that income be recognized on a cost-to-cost basis when the percentage-of-completion method is used.

$$\left( \frac{\text{Cost to date}}{\text{Total expected cost}} \times \frac{\text{Expected}}{\text{profit}} \right) - \frac{\text{Profit recognized}}{\text{in previous periods}}$$

Answers (b) and (d) are incorrect because billings to date are not used as a basis for recognizing revenues. Answer (c) is incorrect as the cost-to-cost calculation requires a cumulative calculation so changes in expected costs and expected income can be adjusted for; thus, costs incurred in year three would be an incorrect basis for recognition of income.

**60. (d)** Per ARB 45, an anticipated loss on a long-term contract should be recognized immediately under **both** the percentage-of-completion and the completed-contract methods.

**61. (a)** The requirement is to determine the proper classification for the progress billings on contracts account under the percentage-of-completion method. In the construction industry, operating cycles for construction contracts generally exceed one year. Therefore, the predominant practice is to classify all contract-related assets and liabilities as current. On the balance sheet, the Construction in Progress (CIP) account is netted with the contra account, progress billings. If CIP exceeds billings, the excess is reported as a current asset [answer (a)]. If billings exceed CIP, the excess is reported as a current liability. Answers (b) and (c) are incorrect because the accounts related to construction contracts are classified as current. Answer (d) is incorrect because progress billings is not used as a basis for recognizing revenues.

**SOLUTIONS TO SIMULATION PROBLEMS**

**Simulation Problem 1**

| Situation | Concepts | Journal Entries | Calculations | Research | Communication |
|---|---|---|---|---|---|

|  | *Included* | *Not included* |
|---|---|---|
| 1. Merchandise purchased for resale | ● | ○ |
| 2. Freight out | ○ | ● |
| 3. Direct materials | ● | ○ |
| 4. Sales returns | ○ | ● |
| 5. Packaging for shipment to customer | ○ | ● |
| 6. Factory overhead | ● | ○ |
| 7. Interest on inventory loan | ○ | ● |
| 8. Purchase discounts not taken | ○ | ● |
| 9. Freight in | ● | ○ |
| 10. Direct labor | ● | ○ |

**Explanation of solutions**

1. Merchandise purchased for resale is a part of inventory.

2. Freight out is part of selling expense.

3. Direct materials are part of work in process, which is an inventory account for manufacturers.

4. Sales returns are a contra account to sales, and are not part of inventory.

5. Packaging for shipment to customer is part of selling expenses.

6. Factory overhead is part of work in process, which is an inventory account for manufacturing firms.

7. Interest on inventory loan is an operating expense. Per SFAS 34, interest cost should not be capitalized for assets that are in use or ready for their intended use in the earnings activities of the enterprise.

8. Purchase discounts lost are considered a financing expense and are excluded from the cost of inventory.

9. Freight-in is part of getting the goods in place to sell and should be included in inventory.

10. Direct labor is part of work in process, and is an inventory account for manufacturing firms.

| Situation | Concepts | Journal Entries | Calculations | Research | Communication |
|---|---|---|---|---|---|

1. On January 5, 2007, purchased $17,000 of garden tillers on account from Bestbuilt Tillers, terms 2/10, n/30, FOB destination. Freight charges were $200.

| Purchases | 17,000 | |
| Accounts payable | | 17,000 |

2. On January 10, 2007, returned garden tillers worth $2,000 to Bestbuilt Tillers due to defects.

| Accounts payable | 2,000 | |
| Purchase returns | | 2,000 |

3. On January 14, 2007, paid for the remaining tillers purchased in **1**.

| Accounts payable | 15,000 | |
| Purchase discounts | | 300* |
| Cash | | 14,700 |

*15,000 × .02 = 300*

4. On January 28, 2007, purchased $30,000 of lawn mowers from Lawn Giant, terms 3/10, n/30, FOB shipping point. The freight charges were $820.

| Purchases | 30,000 | |
| Freight-in | 820 | |
|     Accounts payable | | 30,820 |

**5.** On February 6, 2007, paid for the lawn mowers purchased in part **4.** from Lawn Giant.

| Accounts payable | 30,000 | |
|     Purchase discounts | | 900 |
|     Cash | | 29,100 |

(This assumes the freight bill is paid separately to the
freight company)

| | | | Calculations | | | |
|---|---|---|---|---|---|---|
| **Situation** | **Concepts** | **Journal Entries** | | | **Research** | **Communication** |

Assume that Blaedon had the following information regarding the garden tiller inventory:

| Purchases | $210,000 |
| Purchase discounts | 38,000 |
| Purchase returns | 17,500 |
| Freight in | 12,100 |
| Freight out | 18,000 |
| Beginning inventory | 42,900 |
| Ending inventory | 34,250 |

Calculate the following items:

**1.** Goods available for sale         209,500

**2.** Costs of goods sold            175,250

**Explanation of solutions**

| Beginning inventory | | 42,900 |
| Purchases | 210,000 | |
| –Purchase discounts | (38,000) | |
| –Purchase returns | (17,500) | |
| Net purchases | 154,500 | |
| +Freight in | 12,100 | |
| | | 166,600 |
| Goods available for sale | | 209,500 |
| –Ending inventory | | (34,250) |
| Cost of goods sold | | 175,250 |

| | | | | Research | |
|---|---|---|---|---|---|
| | | | | | **Communication** |
| **Situation** | **Concepts** | **Journal Entries** | **Calculations** | | |

**1.** What costs should be included in Blaedon's inventory?

**ARB43, Ch. 4, Para 5 (amended by FAS 151, para 2) or Current Text I78.105 and I78.106**
**Statement 3**

The primary basis of accounting for inventories is cost, which has been defined generally as the price paid or consideration given to acquire an asset. As applied to inventories, cost means in principle the sum of the applicable expenditures and charges directly or indirectly incurred in bringing an article to its existing condition and location.

**2.** How should Blaedon report the 2007 inventory that has declined in value below its costs?

**ARB43, Ch. 4, Para 8 or Current Text I78.109**
**Statement 5**

A departure from the cost basis of pricing the inventory is required when the utility of the goods is no longer as great as its cost. Where there is evidence that the utility of goods, in their disposal in the ordinary course of business will be less than cost, whether due to physical deterioration, obsolescence, changes in price levels, or other causes, the difference should be recognized as a loss of the current period. This is generally accomplished by stating such goods at a lower level commonly designated as market.

**ARB43, Ch. 4, Para 9 or Current Text I78.110**
**Statement 6**

As used in the phrase lower of cost or market 4 the term market means current replacement cost (by purchase or by reproduction, as the case may be) except that

(1) Market should not exceed the net realizable value (i.e., estimated selling price in the ordinary course of business less reasonably predictable costs of completion and disposal); and

(2) Market should not be less than net realizable value reduced by an allowance for an approximately normal profit margin.

**Discussion**
**ARB43, Ch. 4, Para 9 or Current Text I78.111**

9. The rule of cost or market, whichever is lower is intended to provide a means of measuring the residual usefulness of an inventory expenditure. The term market is therefore to be interpreted as indicating utility on the inventory date and may be thought of in terms of the equivalent expenditure which would have to be made in the ordinary course at that date to procure corresponding utility. As a general guide, utility is indicated primarily by the current cost of replacement of the goods as they would be obtained by purchase or reproduction. In applying the rule, however, judgment must always be exercised and no loss should be recognized unless the evidence indicates clearly that a loss has been sustained. There are therefore exceptions to such a standard. Replacement or reproduction prices would not be appropriate as a measure of utility when the estimated sales value reduced by the costs of completion and disposal, is lower, in which case the realizable value so determined more appropriately measures utility. Furthermore, where the evidence indicates that cost will be recovered with an approximately normal profit upon sale in the ordinary course of business, no loss should be recognized even though replacement or reproduction costs are lower. This might be true, for example, in the case of production under firm sales contracts at fixed prices, or when a reasonable volume of future orders is assured at stable selling prices.

| Situation | Concepts | Journal Entries | Calculations | Research | Communication |
|---|---|---|---|---|---|

To:      CEO, Blaedon Corp.
From:   CPA Candidate
Re:       Inventory valuation

In our last meeting, you inquired as to the valuation methods used for Blaedon's lawn mower inventory. Normally, inventory is valued by accumulating all necessary and reasonable costs to get the inventory in place for sale to customers. These costs may include design costs, purchase price from contractors, freight-in, and warehousing costs. For its 2008 models, Blaedon should include all these costs in valuing the lawn mower inventory.

However, when the value of inventory is less than its historical cost, then inventory must be written down to net realizable value. For the 2007 model inventory, net realizable value is the current list price reduced by both disposition costs and two-thirds of the difference between the $40 allowance given and the carrying amount assigned to trade-ins. The trade-ins' carrying amount should equal the $25 average net realizable value less the profit margin, if any, assigned to the trade-in mower.

The FIFO method requires that Blaedon assign the costs of the earliest purchased items to cost of goods sold. With rising costs, this would result in matching old, relatively low inventory costs to current revenues. Therefore, net income will be higher than reported using certain other inventory methods.

Using the FIFO method, Blaedon should assign the costs of items most recently purchased to ending inventory. Normally, the carrying amount of Blaedon's FIFO ending inventory would approximate replacement cost. As a result, retained earnings also will be higher than that reported using certain other inventory methods.

If you have any additional questions, please contact me.

**Simulation Problem 2**

| Situation | Calculation of Gross Profit | Financial Statement Disclosures | Schedule of Income Taxes | Communication | Research |
|---|---|---|---|---|---|

### London Inc.
### SCHEDULE OF GROSS PROFIT (LOSS)

|  | Beta | Gamma |
|---|---|---|
| *For the Year Ended September 30, 2007:* | | |
| Estimated gross profit (loss): | | |
|    Contract price | $600,000 | $800,000 |
|    Less total costs | 400,000 | 820,000 |
|    Estimated gross profit (loss) | $200,000 | $ (20,000) |
| Percent complete: | | |
|    Costs incurred to date | $360,000 | $410,000 |
|    Total costs | 400,000 | 820,000 |
|    Percent complete | 90% | 50% |
| Gross profit (loss) recognized | $180,000 | $ (20,000) |
| *For the Year Ended September 30, 2008:* | | |
| Estimated gross profit (loss): | | |
|    Contract price | $560,000 | $840,000 |
|    Less total costs | 450,000 | 900,000 |
|    Estimated gross profit (loss) | $110,000 | $ (60,000) |
| Percent complete: | | |
|    Costs incurred to date | $450,000 | $720,000 |
|    Total costs | 450,000 | 900,000 |
|    Percent complete | 100% | 80% |
| Gross profit (loss) recognized | 110,000 | (60,000) |
| Less gross profit (loss) recognized in prior year | 180,000 | (20,000) |
| Gross profit (loss) recognized | $ (70,000) | $ (40,000) |

| Situation | Calculation of Gross Profit | Financial Statement Disclosures | Schedule of Income Taxes | Communication | Research |
|---|---|---|---|---|---|

### London Inc.
### SCHEDULE OF SELECTED BALANCE SHEET ACCOUNTS
### September 30, 2007

| | | |
|---|---|---|
| Accounts receivable | | $115,000 |
| Costs and estimated earnings in excess of billings: | | |
|    Construction in progress | $540,000 | |
|    Less:  Billings | 315,000 | |
|    Costs and estimated earnings in excess of billings | | 225,000 |
| Billings in excess of costs and estimated earnings | | 30,000 |
| Estimated loss on contract | | 20,000 |

| Situation | Calculation of Gross Profit | Financial Statement Disclosures | Schedule of Income Taxes | Communication | Research |
|---|---|---|---|---|---|

### London Inc.
### SCHEDULE OF INCOME TAXES PAYABLE AND INCOME TAX EXPENSE
### September 30, 2007

| | | |
|---|---|---|
| Financial statement income: | | |
|    From other divisions | | $300,000 |
|    From Beta project | | 180,000 |
|    From Gamma project | | (20,000) |
| Total financial statement income | | $460,000 |
| Less temporary differences: | | |
|    Beta project income | | (180,000) |
|    Gamma project loss | | 20,000 |
| Total taxable income | | $300,000 |
| Taxes payable ($300,000 × 25%) | | $ 75,000 |
| Deferred tax liability ($160,000 × 30%) | | 48,000 |
| Tax expense: | | |
|    Current | $ 75,000 | |
|    Deferred | 48,000 | 123,000 |

**Explanation of solutions**

- This problem consists of three related requirements concerning long-term construction contracts. The candidates must compute gross profit recognized for two years using the percentage-of-completion method, compute balances in various accounts, and reconcile financial statement income and taxable income.
- Using the percentage-of-completion method, gross profit is recognized periodically based on progress toward completion of the project using the following formula.

$$\frac{\text{Costs to date}}{\text{Total estimated costs}} \times \frac{\text{Estimated}}{\text{profit}} = \frac{\text{Gross profit}}{\text{to date}}$$

For the Beta project, London would recognize gross profit of $180,000 the first year.

$$\frac{\$360,000}{(\$360,000 + \$40,000)} \times [\$600,000 - (\$360,000 + \$40,000)] = \$180,000$$

The estimates available at 9/30/07 are used above.

- By the end of the second year, the Beta project is complete and has resulted in actual gross profit of $110,000 ($560,000 revenues less $450,000 costs). Since gross profit of $180,000 was recognized the first year, a loss of $70,000 must be recognized the second year [$110,000 − $180,000 = $(70,000)]. The loss of $70,000 is in effect an adjustment of the excessive gross profit recognized the first year. Instead of restating the prior period, the prior period misstatement is absorbed in the current period, as is appropriate for a change in estimate.
- Under both the percentage-of-completion method and the completed contract method, for financial accounting purposes, an expected **loss** on a contract must be recognized in full in the period in which the expected loss is discovered. At the end of the first year, London has an expected loss on the Gamma contract [$800,000 − ($410,000 + $410,000) = $(20,000)] that must be recognized immediately.
- By the end of the second year, the expected loss on the Gamma contract has increased to $60,000 [$840,000 − ($720,000 + $180,000)]. Since a loss of $20,000 was recognized the first year, an additional loss of $40,000 must be recognized in the second year to bring the cumulative loss recognized up to the new estimate of $60,000.
- Financial Statement Disclosures require the computation of the 9/30/07 balances of accounts receivable, costs and estimated earnings in excess of billings, and billings in excess of costs and estimated earnings. At 10/1/06, the balances in all three accounts were $0 since the construction division began operations on that date.
- **Accounts receivable** is increased by billings

>    Accounts receivable
>        Billings on LT contracts

It is decreased by cash collections

>    Cash
>        Accounts receivable

Therefore, 9/30/07 AR is computed by adding the billings on the two projects ($315,000 + $440,000 = $755,000) and subtracting the collections on the two projects ($275,000 + $365,000 = $640,000). The 9/30/06 balance is $115,000 ($755,000 − $640,000).

- **Construction-in-progress** is debited for costs incurred and profit recognized. **Billings on LT contracts** is credited for billings made. In the balance sheet, the two accounts are netted on a project-by-project basis, resulting in a net current asset and/or a net current liability. At 9/30/07, the costs incurred on the Beta project ($360,000) and the estimated earnings ($180,000 from item two of this solution guide) exceed billings ($315,000) by $225,000.
- On the Gamma project billings ($440,000) exceed costs ($410,000) by $30,000. There is no estimated earnings on this project because it is expected, at 9/30/07, to result in a $20,000 loss (see item 2.2 above). This estimated loss does not affect the excess of billings over costs and estimated earnings because it is reported separately as a current liability.
- Financial statement income consists of income before taxes before considering construction projects ($300,000) plus gross profit from construction contracts [$160,000 from part (a) of the solution], less income tax expense. The **pretax** financial income, therefore, is $460,000 ($300,000 + $160,000). The income not from construction projects will be taxed this year, so current income tax expense is $75,000 ($300,000 × 25%). Because the completed contract method is used for tax purposes, the $160,000 gross profit from construction contracts will not be taxed until future years (note that for **tax** purposes no gross profit or gross **loss** is recognized until completion under the completed contract method). Therefore, deferred tax expense is $48,000 (future enacted rate of 30% times $160,000). Financial statement income is $337,000 [$460,000 − ($75,000 + $48,000)].
- Since the $160,000 gross profit will not be recognized for tax purposes until later years, taxable income is $300,000. To reconcile financial statement income ($337,000 from above) to taxable income, the current and deferred income tax must be added back to compute pretax financial income ($337,000 + $75,000 + $48,000 = $460,000). Then the gross profit not recognized for tax purposes is subtracted to reconcile to taxable income ($460,000 − $160,000 = $300,000).

| Situation | Calculation of Gross Profit | Financial Statement Disclosures | Schedule of Income Taxes | Communication | Research |
|---|---|---|---|---|---|

To:     Mr. Jim Cauley, Construction Supervisor
From:   CPA Candidate
Re:     Percentage-of-completion method for construction contracts

You have requested that I explain the percentage-of-completion method of accounting for contracts. The percentage-of-completion method of accounting recognizes income as work is completed on a project. The amount of income recognized is measured by estimating the amount of work completed to date. Two methods can be used to estimate the percent completed: (1) compare the costs to date to the estimated total costs based on the most recent information, or (2) measure the progress toward completion of the work performed to date.

Income is recognized on the income statement for the percentage of the project that is completed. On the balance sheet a current asset should be recorded for costs and recognized income that has not yet been billed, and a current liability should be recognized for billings in excess of costs. If current estimates indicate that an overall loss on the contract is expected to occur, a provision should be made for the loss on the contract and recognized immediately.

There are two advantages to the percentage-of-completion method. The first advantage is that income is recognized currently as progress is made on the contract. A second advantage is that the status of uncompleted contracts are provided in the financial statements by providing current estimates of the costs and of the progress toward completion. The disadvantage of the percentage-of-completion method is that it relies upon estimates to measure income and costs, and these estimates are subject to uncertainty.

| Situation | Calculation of Gross Profit | Financial Statement Disclosures | Schedule of Income Taxes | Communication | Research |
|---|---|---|---|---|---|

## ARB45, Para 11 or Current Text Co4.108

Although the completed-contract method does not permit the recoding of any income prior to completion, provision should be made for expected losses in accordance with the well established practice of making provision for foreseeable losses. If there is a close relationship between profitable and unprofitable contracts, such as in the case of contracts which are parts of the same project, the group may be treated as a unit in determining the necessity for a provision for losses.

## Simulation Problem 3

| Situation | Inventory Concepts | Cost Flow Concepts | Schedule of Ending Inventory | Schedule of Cost of Goods Sold | Communication | Research |
|---|---|---|---|---|---|---|

|  |  | True | False |
|---|---|---|---|
| 1. | The gross margin method uses historical sales margins to estimate the cost of inventory. | ● | ○ |
| 2. | The dollar-value LIFO method preserves old inventory costs by charging current costs to cost of goods sold. | ● | ○ |
| 3. | Inventory should be reported at the lower of cost or market and it may be based on the values of individual items, categories, or the total inventory. | ● | ○ |
| 4. | A loss on a purchase commitment should be recorded when the contract price is greater than the market and it is anticipated that a loss will occur when the contract is completed. | ● | ○ |
| 5. | Under the dollar-value LIFO method, increases and decreases in a layer would be measured based upon the change in the total dollar value of the layer. | ● | ○ |
| 6. | The link-chain method uses a cumulative index to value the base cost of ending inventory. | ● | ○ |
| 7. | The price index for dollar-value LIFO is a measure of changes in price levels between the current year and the base year. | ● | ○ |
| 8. | Under the LIFO method, an inventory liquidation will result in higher profits in a period of rising prices. | ● | ○ |
| 9. | A holding gain results from holding an item while the market value experiences a decline. | ○ | ● |
| 10. | During a period of rising prices, the LIFO cost flow assumption results in a higher net income as compared to FIFO. | ○ | ● |
| 11. | In a period of rising prices, when a company changes from FIFO to LIFO the net income will tend to decline as will working capital. | ● | ○ |

| | True | False |
|---|:---:|:---:|
| 12. The use of LIFO for book and tax purposes will result in a lower tax payment in a period of rising prices. | ● | ○ |
| 13. Under the LIFO method, the cost of goods sold balance would be the same whether a perpetual or periodic inventory system is used. | ○ | ● |

**Explanation of solutions**

1. **(T)** The gross margin method uses historical margins on sales to estimate the cost of inventory. This method is typically used for interim reporting only because it may not be precise enough for the year-end financial statements.

2. **(T)** The dollar-value LIFO method groups inventory into layers and charges the most recent items to cost of goods sold before using older layers which have older inventory costs.

3. **(T)** Inventory should be carried at the lower of cost or market. In determining the lower of cost or market it may be based on the values of individual items, item categories, or even total inventory.

4. **(T)** When the market price of a contract to purchase goods falls below the contract price and it is foreseeable that the contract will result in a loss, then a loss on the purchase commitment should be recorded.

5. **(T)** The dollar-value LIFO method measures changes in inventory layers based upon the total dollar value change in the layer.

6. **(T)** The link-chain method uses a cumulative index to compute the base cost of inventory. The cumulative index is equal to the current year's prices divided by the prior year's prices, multiplied by the prior year's cumulative index. The link-chain method is only used in limited circumstances.

7. **(T)** A price index provides a measure of the changes in price between base year and the current year. The price index is generally used to compute changes in inventory levels.

8. **(T)** In a period of rising prices, a liquidation of older inventory, which carries lower costs, will result in a decline in the cost of goods sold and higher profits.

9. **(F)** A holding gain results from holding an item while the market value **increases**. Thus, the holding gain would be equal to the current market value less the value on the books.

10. **(F)** During a period of rising prices, the LIFO method will result in higher priced items being charged to cost of goods sold, thus lowering net income. It is the FIFO method which would produce a higher net income because the cost of goods sold would reflect the older or lower cost goods.

11. **(T)** A change from FIFO to LIFO will tend to result in a decrease in net income and working capital. This is because the LIFO method will put the more recent/higher priced items on the income statement (last in) and the older/less expensive goods will be carried in inventory. Thus, net income will be lower due to higher cost of goods sold, and working capital will be lower due to the lower inventory asset balance.

12. **(T)** The LIFO method results in the most recently purchased inventory items being expensed first. In a period of rising prices this would result in a lower net income and thus a lower taxes payable. The IRS allows the use of LIFO for tax only if it is also used for external reporting purposes as well.

13. **(F)** The cost of goods sold would be different because a periodic system will compute the cost of goods sold based on the total goods sold and total purchases for a period, whereas a perpetual one will match each good sold with the most recent purchase on an ongoing basis.

| Situation | Inventory Concepts | Cost Flow Concepts | Schedule of Ending Inventory | Schedule of Cost of Goods Sold | Communication | Research |
|---|---|---|---|---|---|---|

*Method*

1. During a period of rising prices, this method results in a higher net income.  FIFO

2. This method most closely matches the physical flow of inventory.  FIFO

3. Method that uses historical sales margins to estimate ending inventory.  Gross profit method

4. Method that is appropriate when there is a relatively small number of significant dollar value items in inventory.  Specific identification

5. Average cost must be calculated each time additional inventory is purchased.  Moving average

6. Method that averages the cost of all items on hand and purchased during the period.  Weighted-average

7. This method results in the lowest ending inventory in a period of rising prices.  LIFO

| | Method |
|---|---|
| 8. Method that uses a price index to measure changes in inventory. | Dollar value LIFO |
| 9. If used for tax purposes, this method must also be used for financial reporting purposes. | LIFO |
| 10. The cost of goods sold balance is the same whether a perpetual or periodic inventory system is used. | FIFO |

| Situation | Inventory Concepts | Cost Flow Concepts | Schedule of Ending Inventory | Schedule of Cost of Goods Sold | Communication | Research |
|---|---|---|---|---|---|---|

**York Co.**
**SUPPORTING SCHEDULE OF ENDING INVENTORY**
*December 31, 2007*

Inventory at cost (LIFO):

| | Units | Cost per unit | Total cost |
|---|---|---|---|
| Beginning inventory, January 1 | 8,000 | $8.20 | $ 65,600 |
| Purchases, quarter ended March 31 | 12,000 | 8.25 | 99,000 |
| Purchases, quarter ended June 30 | 2,000 | 7.90 | 15,800 |
| | 22,000 | | $180,400 |

| Situation | Inventory Concepts | Cost Flow Concepts | Schedule of Ending Inventory | Schedule of Cost of Goods Sold | Communication | Research |
|---|---|---|---|---|---|---|

**York Co.**
**SCHEDULE OF COST OF GOODS SOLD**
*For the Year Ended December 31, 2007*

| | |
|---|---|
| Beginning inventory | $ 65,600 |
| Add: Purchases | 368,900 |
| Less: Purchase discounts | (18,000) |
| Add: Freight-in | 5,000 |
| Goods available for sale | 421,500 |
| Less: Ending inventory | (176,000) [1] |
| Cost of Goods Sold | $245,500 |

[1] Inventory at market:
  22,000 units @ $8 = $176,000

**Explanation of solutions**

- This problem requires preparation of a cost of goods sold (CGS) schedule with a supporting schedule of ending inventory at lower of cost or market (LCM). York uses the direct method for LCM, which means the LCM amount is used directly in the CGS computation with no separate disclosure of any LCM loss.
- The cost of goods sold schedule can be prepared first, leaving the last two lines (ending inventory and CGS) blank for now. The computation starts with **beginning inventory** plus **cost of goods purchased** equals **cost of goods available for sale** (cost of goods purchased is **purchases** less **purchase discounts** plus **freight-in**). **Freight-out** is a selling expense which does not affect CGS.
- When determining LCM, the market value of inventory is defined as the **replacement cost,** as long as it is less than the ceiling [**net realizable value** (NRV)] and more than the floor (**NRV less a normal profit**).
- There are 22,000 units in ending inventory (55,000 units available less 33,000 units sold). Using LIFO, the earliest units in are assumed to remain in ending inventory. Therefore, ending inventory consists of the 8,000 units from beginning inventory, plus the 12,000 units purchased in the first quarter, plus 2,000 more units from second quarter purchases to get up to the 22,000 unit total. The cost of ending inventory is $180,400 [(8,000 × $8.20) + (12,000 × $8.25) + (2,000 × $7.90)].
- The replacement cost of the inventory is $176,000 (22,000 × $8).
- The ceiling (NRV) is $193,600 (22,000 × $8.80).
- The floor (NRV less a normal profit) is $170,500 [22,000 × ($8.80 – $1.05)].
- Because replacement cost ($176,000) falls between the floor ($170,500) and the ceiling ($193,600), the replacement cost of $176,000 is the designated market value.
- Since the designated market value of $176,000 is less than cost ($180,400), the LCM valuation of ending inventory is $176,000. This amount can be put into the cost of goods sold schedule, resulting in CGS of $245,500.

  Value inventory at LCM
    Market is replacement with limits
      Market must ≤ NRV and
      Market must ≥ NRV – normal profit
    Market is replacement cost in this situation
      Replacement cost ($176,000) falls between above limits
  Inventory reported at market because < cost

| Situation | Inventory Concepts | Cost Flow Concepts | Schedule of Ending Inventory | Schedule of Cost of Goods Sold | Communication | | Research |
|---|---|---|---|---|---|---|---|

To:      Mr. Binson
From:   CPA Candidate
Re:      Valuation of inventory

This memorandum summarizes the rules regarding valuation of inventory. Inventory is normally valued at cost. However, conservatism in accounting requires that assets are not overstated. If inventory becomes damaged, obsolete, or declines in value, it should be revalued to market value using the lower of cost or market method.

In accounting terms, market means current replacement cost, except that

1.   Market should not exceed the net realizable value; and
2.   Market should not be less than net realizable value reduced by an allowance for an estimated normal profit margin.

In this particular situation, since replacement cost ($8 per unit) is less than net realizable value, but greater than net realizable value reduced by a normal profit margin, replacement cost is used as market. The inventory valued at market ($176,000) is lower than inventory valued at cost ($180,400). Therefore, inventory should be reported in the financial statements at market value.

If you have any additional questions, please contact me.

| Situation | Inventory Concepts | Cost Flow Concepts | Schedule of Ending Inventory | Schedule of Cost of Goods Sold | Communication | | Research |
|---|---|---|---|---|---|---|---|

1.   What methods may be used for costing inventories?

**ARB43, Ch. 4, Para 6 or Current Text I78.108**
**Statement 4**

Cost for inventory purposes may be determined under any one of several assumptions as to the flow of cost factors (such as first-in first-out, average, and last-in first-out); the major objective in selecting a method should be to choose the one which, under the circumstances, most clearly reflects periodic income.

6.   The cost to be matched against revenue from a sale may not be the identified cost of the specific item which is sold, especially in cases in which similar goods are purchased at different times and at different prices. While in some lines of business specific lots are clearly identified from the time of purchase through the time of sale and are costed on this basis, ordinarily the identity of goods is lost between the time of acquisition and the time of sale. In any event, if the materials purchased in various lots are identical and interchangeable, the use of identified cost of the various lots may not produce the most useful financial statements. This fact has resulted in the development of general acceptance of several assumptions with respect to the flow of cost factors (such as first-in first-out, average, and last-in first-out) to provide practical bases for the measurement of periodic income.3 In some situations a reversed mark-up procedure of inventory pricing, such as the retail inventory method, may be both practical and appropriate. The business operations in some cases may be such as to make it desirable to apply one of the acceptable methods of determining cost to one portion of the inventory or components thereof and another of the acceptable methods to other portions of the inventory.

2.   How is the market value calculated when calculating the lower of cost or market?

**ARB43, Ch. 4, Para 9 or Current Text I78.111**
**Statement 6**

As used in the phrase lower of cost or market, the term market means current replacement cost (by purchase or by reproduction, as the case may be) except that

(1)   Market should not exceed the net realizable value (i.e., estimated selling price in the ordinary course of business less reasonably predictable costs of completion and disposal); and

(2)   Market should not be less than net realizable value reduced by an allowance for an approximately normal profit margin.

**Discussion**
**ARB43, Ch. 4, Para 9**

9. The rule of cost or market, whichever is lower is intended to provide a means of measuring the residual usefulness of an inventory expenditure. The term market is therefore to be interpreted as indicating utility on the inventory date and may be thought of in terms of the equivalent expenditure which would have to be made in the ordinary course at that date to procure corresponding utility. As a general guide, utility is indicated primarily by the current cost of replacement of the goods as they would be obtained by purchase or reproduction. In applying the rule, however, judgment must always be exercised and no loss should be recognized unless the evidence indicates clearly that a loss has been sustained. There are therefore exceptions to such a standard. Replacement or reproduction prices would not be appropriate as a measure of utility when the estimated sales value reduced by the costs of completion and disposal, is lower, in which case the realizable value so determined more appropriately measures utility. Furthermore, where the evidence indicates that cost will be recovered with an approximately normal profit upon sale in the ordinary course of business, no loss should be recognized even though replacement or reproduction costs are lower. This might be true, for example, in the case of production under firm sales contracts at fixed prices, or when a reasonable volume of future orders is assured at stable selling prices.

# FIXED ASSETS

## A. Acquisition Cost

Fixed assets represent the capitalized amount of expenditures made to acquire tangible property which will be used for a period of more than one year. Their cost, therefore, is deferred to future periods in compliance with the matching principle. Tangible property includes land, buildings, equipment, or any other property that physically exists. All of the costs necessary to get the asset to the work site and to prepare it for use are capitalized, including the cost of negotiations, sales taxes, finders' fees, razing an old building, shipment, installation, preliminary testing, and so forth. When capitalizing such costs it is necessary to associate them with the asset which is being prepared for use. Thus, the cost of razing an old building is added to the cost of acquiring the land on which the building stood. Charges for self-constructed fixed assets include direct materials, direct construction labor, variable overhead, and a fair share of fixed overhead. Assets received through donation should be recorded at FMV with a corresponding credit to revenue; if FMV is not determinable, book value should be used (see outline of SFAS 116). If the entity incurs a liability associated with future retirement of the asset, the fair value (present value) of that obligation should be added to the carrying value of the asset (see outline of SFAS 143).

## B. Capitalization of Interest

SFAS 34 (see outline) requires the capitalization of interest as part of the cost of certain assets. Only assets which require a period of time to be prepared for use qualify for interest capitalization. These include assets constructed for sale produced as discrete projects (e.g., ships) and assets constructed for a firm's own use, whether by the entity itself or by an outsider. For example, a building purchased by an entity **would not** qualify, but one constructed over a period of time **would**. Other assets that do **not** qualify include those in use or ready for use and ones not being used in the earnings activities of a firm (e.g., idle land).

The amount of interest to be capitalized is the amount which could have been avoided if the project had not been undertaken. This amount includes amortization of any discount, premium, or issue costs; but, it shall not exceed the actual interest incurred during the period. The amount of "avoidable" interest is computed as

Average accumulated expenditures during construction     ×     Interest rate     ×     Construction period

The interest rate used is the rate on specific borrowings for the asset, or a weighted-average of other borrowings when a specific rate is not available. Capitalized interest should be compounded. This is usually accomplished by including the interest capitalized in a previous period in the calculation of average accumulated expenditures of subsequent periods. Furthermore, noninterest-bearing payables (e.g., trade payables and accruals) are excluded in determining these expenditures. In practice, both the weighted-average interest rate and the average accumulated expenditures have been computed on the following bases: monthly, quarterly, semiannual, and annual. The interest capitalization period begins when, and continues as long as, all three of the following conditions are met:

1. Expenditures for the asset have been made
2. Activities necessary to get the asset ready for its intended use are in progress
3. Interest cost is being incurred

The period ends when the asset is substantially complete. Brief interruptions and delays do not suspend interest capitalization, while suspension of the activities will. In no case should the amount capitalized exceed the interest actually incurred.

*EXAMPLE: Interest Capitalization*

*Assume the company is constructing an asset which qualifies for interest capitalization. By the beginning of July $3,000,000 had been spent on the asset, and an additional $800,000 was spent during July. The following debt was outstanding for the entire month.*

1. *A loan of $2,000,000, interest of 1% per month, specifically related to the asset.*
2. *A note payable of $1,500,000, interest of 1.5% per month.*
3. *Bonds payable of $1,000,000, interest of 1% per month.*

*The amount of interest to be capitalized is computed below.*

**Average accumulated expenditures** *(for the month of July)*
*($3,000,000 + $3,800,000) ÷ 2 = $3,400,000*

| Avoidable interest | | | Actual interest | | |
|---|---|---|---|---|---|
| $2,000,000 × 1% | = | $20,000 | $2,000,000 × 1% | = | $20,000 |
| 1,400,000 × 1.3%* | = | 18,200 | 1,500,000 × 1.5% | = | 22,500 |
| | | | 1,000,000 × 1% | = | 10,000 |
| $3,400,000 | | $38,200 | $4,500,000 | | $52,500 |

$38,200 \leq $52,500

∴ $38,200 is capitalized

Amount of interest to be capitalized is $38,200

| Asset | 38,200 | |
|---|---|---|
| Interest expense | | 38,200 |

*The average rate on other borrowings is ($22,500 + $10,000) ÷ ($1,500,000 + $1,000,000) = 1.3%. Notice that a specific rate is used to the extent possible and the average rate is used only on any excess. Alternatively, the rate on all debt may be used.*

Interest on expenditures made to acquire land on which a building is to be constructed qualifies for interest capitalization. The capitalization period begins when activities necessary to construct the building commence and ends when the building is substantially complete. Interest so capitalized becomes part of the cost of the building. Thus, it is charged to expense as the building is depreciated.

Frequently, the funds borrowed to finance the construction project are temporarily invested until needed. Per SFAS 62, the interest earned on these funds must be recognized as revenue and may not be offset against the interest expense to be capitalized.

The diagram below outlines the requirements pertaining to capitalization of interest.

**Rationale** for interest capitalization

1. To reflect asset's acquisition cost
2. To match asset's cost with revenue of periods that benefit from its use

## C. Nonmonetary Exchanges

Study the outline of APB 29, FASB Interpretation 30, and SFAS 153. SFAS 153 amends APB 29, and removes the distinction of similar and dissimilar assets. A nonmonetary exchange is a reciprocal transfer wherein the transferor has no substantial continuing involvement in the asset, and the risks and rewards of ownership are transferred.

APB No. 29, Accounting for Nonmonetary Exchanges, does not apply to (1) business combinations, (2) transfers of nonmonetary assets between companies under common control, (3) acquisition of nonmonetary assets or services for the issuance of capital stock, (4) stock issued or received in stock dividends or stock splits, (5) transfer of assets in exchange for equity interests, (6) a pooling of assets in joint undertaking for gas or oil, (7) exchanging part of an operating interest owned for a part of another operating interest owned by another party, and (8) transfers of financial assets within the scope of SFAS 140.

Nonmonetary exchanges are usually recorded using the fair value of the asset exchanged. (See SFAS 157 and Module 7D for definitions of fair value.) If one of the parties could have elected to receive cash instead of the nonmonetary asset, the amount of cash that could have been received is evidence of the fair value of the assets exchanged. If the fair value (FV) of the asset given up cannot be determined, assume it is equal to the fair value of the asset received. Three exceptions exist to the fair value treatment: (1) if fair value is not determinable; (2) if it is an exchange transaction to facilitate sales to customers; or (3) the transaction lacks commercial substance. A transaction has commercial substance if the configuration of cash flows are significantly different as a result of the exchange. The configuration of cash flows includes the risk, timing, and the amount of future cash flows. Cash flows from tax effects are not considered in determining if the transaction has commercial substance. In these three exceptions, the transaction is measured using the recorded amount (book value) of the asset exchanged.

When neither fair values are determinable, the exchange is accounted for at book value, and no gain or loss is recognized. In the other two exceptions, the transaction is measured using the recorded amount (book value) of the exchanged asset, and any losses are recognized. When book values are used, a part of the gain may be recognized when boot is received.

The exchange of nonmonetary assets (such as inventory, property, and equipment) for other nonmonetary assets requires special consideration of two amounts.

1. Gain or loss, if any
2. Fair market value of the nonmonetary assets received

Gain or loss on a nonmonetary exchange is computed as follows:

Fair value of the asset given  –  Book value of the asset given  =  Gain (loss)

The asset received is generally recorded at the fair value of the asset surrendered (or the FV of the asset received if "more clearly evident").  Some exceptions do exist.  Remember, however, that the asset given up will always be removed from the books at book value.

The following rules apply in recording nonmonetary exchanges:

- Losses are always recognized (conservatism).
- Gains are recognized if the exchange is measured at fair value.
- If any of the three conditions for exception to fair value treatment are met, use book value (recorded amount) of the asset exchanged.  If no boot is involved, no gain is recognized.  If boot is given, no gain is recognized, and the new asset is recorded at the book value of the exchanged asset plus the boot given.  If boot is received, a portion of the gain is recognized.

### SUMMARY OF ACCOUNTING FOR INTEREST CAPITALIZATION

> **Capitalization of Interest During Construction**

**Qualifying Assets:**
Capitalize means to include an expenditure in an asset's cost.
Interest costs, when material, incurred in acquiring the following types of assets, shall be capitalized

1. Assets constructed or produced for a firm's own use
   a. Including construction by outside contractors requiring progress payments
2. Assets intended for lease or sale that are produced as discrete projects
   a. For example, ships and real estate developments
3. But **not** on
   a. Routinely produced inventories (e.g., widgets)
   b. Assets ready for their intended use when acquired
   c. Assets not being used nor being readied for use (e.g., idle equipment)
   d. Land, unless it is being developed (e.g., as a plant site, real estate development, etc.).  Then capitalized interest resulting from land expenditure (cash outlay) is added to building.

**When to Capitalize Interest (All three must be met):**
1. Expenditures for asset have been made
2. Activities intended to get asset ready are in progress
3. Interest cost is being incurred

**Applicable Interest (Net of discounts, premiums, and issue costs):**
1. Interest obligations having explicit rates
2. Imputed interest on certain payables/receivables
3. Interest related to capital leases

**How Much Interest Cost Is Capitalized?**

$$\left(\begin{array}{l}\text{Accumulated expenditures beg. of period (C - I - P bal.) +}\\ \text{Accumulated expenditures end of period (C - I - P bal.)}\end{array}\right) \div 2 \times \text{Portion of year} = \text{Weighted-average accumulated expenditures}$$

$$\text{Weighted-average accumulated expenditures} \times \left(\frac{\text{Interest*}}{\text{rate}}\right) = \text{Amount capitalized (cannot exceed total interest incurred)}$$

*\* AICPA questions have given the specific borrowing rate on debt incurred to finance a project and indicated that expenditures were incurred evenly throughout the year.  SFAS 34 requires that the firm's weighted-average borrowing rate be used after the amount of a specific borrowing is exhausted.  Alternatively, only the firm's weighted-average borrowing rate may be used on all expenditures.*

**Qualifications:**
1. Amount of interest to be capitalized cannot exceed total interest costs incurred during the entire reporting period
2. Interest earned on temporarily invested borrowings may not be offset against interest to be capitalized

The chart below summarizes the process involved in accounting for nonmonetary exchanges. Refer to this chart as you work through the following examples.

**ACCOUNTING FOR NONMONETARY EXCHANGES**
**Concepts Summary**

\* *For tax purposes losses are not recognized on exchanges of similar assets; they are adjustments to the asset's basis as are gains*

**FV is not determinable.** When fair value of the asset given up or the asset received is not determinable, book value is used to record the exchanged asset.

> EXAMPLE: *A company trades a machine (cost, $10,000; accumulated depreciation, $3,000) for land. Neither the FV of the machine or the land is determinable.*

| | | |
|---|---|---|
| Land | 7,000 | *(BV given)* |
| Accumulated depreciation | 3,000 | |
| Machine | | 10,000 |

*Since FV is unknown, no gain can be computed, and the asset received is recorded at the BV of the asset given up ($10,000 – $3,000).*

**Loss situations.** Normally, an exchanged asset is valued at fair value of the asset exchanged, or the fair value of the asset received, whichever is more clearly evident. When the fair value is less than the book value, a loss occurs. Because losses are recognized immediately, the treatment in a loss situation is the same for all nonmonetary exchanges, regardless of whether it meets the exception criteria.

### Situation 1. Loss, no boot involved.

> EXAMPLE: *A company trades a machine with a FV of $5,000 (cost, $10,000; accumulated depreciation, $3,000) for land. It is assumed that the transaction has commercial substance and does not meet the exception criteria to fair value measurement.*

| | FV | BV | Gain (loss) |
|---|---|---|---|
| Machine given | $5,000 | $7,000 | $(2,000) |
| Land received | | | |

*The loss (FV – BV) is recognized immediately and the land is recorded at the FV of the machine given up.*

| | | |
|---|---|---|
| Land | 5,000 | *(FV given)* |
| Accumulated depreciation | 3,000 | |
| Loss | 2,000 | |
| Machine | | 10,000 |

*Note that this transaction would be treated the same way if the transaction lacked commercial substance.*

EXAMPLE:  A company trades a machine (cost, $10,000; accumulated depreciation, $3,000) for another machine with a FV of $6,000.  It is assumed that the transaction has commercial substance and does not meet the exception criteria to fair value measurement.

|  | FV | BV | Gain (loss) |
|---|---|---|---|
| Machine given |  | $7,000 | $(1,000) |
| Machine received | $6,000 |  |  |

In this case, the FV of the asset given is unknown.  You can substitute the FV of the asset received for FV given when computing gain/loss.  The fair value of the asset given is implied in this case.

| $6,000 | | $7,000 | | $(1,000) |
|---|---|---|---|---|
| FV given | – | BV given | = | Loss |
| (assumed or implied) | | | | |

| Machine | 6,000 | (FV received) |
|---|---|---|
| Accumulated depreciation | 3,000 | |
| Loss | 1,000 | |
| Machine | | 10,000 |

Again, if the treatment lacked commercial substance, the entries would be the same because of the loss.

## Situation 2.  Loss, boot given.

EXAMPLE:  A company trades a machine with a FV of $6,000 (cost, $10,000; accumulated depreciation, $3,000) and $500 cash for land.  It is assumed that the transaction has commercial substance and does not meet the exception criteria to fair value measurement.

|  | Boot | FV | BV | Gain (loss) |
|---|---|---|---|---|
| Machine given | $500 | $6,000 | $7,000 | $(1,000) |
| Land received |  |  |  |  |

Gain (loss) still equals FV less BV.  Boot given is added to the value of the asset given.

| Land | 6,500 | (FV given + Boot given) |
|---|---|---|
| Accumulated depreciation | 3,000 | |
| Loss | 1,000 | |
| Machine | | 10,000 |
| Cash | | 500 |

Assume the FV of the machine was unknown, but the FV of the land received was known to be $6,000.

|  | Boot | FV | BV | Gain (loss) |
|---|---|---|---|---|
| Machine given | $500 |  | $7,000 | $(1,500) |
| Land received |  | $6,000 |  |  |

To compute gain (loss), you can assume FV given is equal to FV received less boot given ($6,000 – $500).

| $5,500 | | $7,000 | | $(1,500) |
|---|---|---|---|---|
| FV given | – | BV given | = | Loss |
| (assumed) | | | | |

| Land | 6,000 | (FV received) |
|---|---|---|
| Accumulated depreciation | 3,000 | |
| Loss | 1,500 | |
| Machine | | 10,000 |
| Cash | | 500 |

If the transaction lacked commercial substance, the entries would be the same because of the loss.

## Situation 3.  Loss, boot received.

EXAMPLE:  A company trades a machine with a FV of $6,000 (cost, $10,000; accumulated depreciation, $3,000) for land and $500 cash.

|  | Boot | FV | BV | Gain (loss) |
|---|---|---|---|---|
| Machine given |  | $6,000 | $7,000 | $(1,000) |
| Land received | $500 |  |  |  |

Boot received is deducted from the value of the asset given.

| Land | 5,500 | (FV given – Boot received) |
|---|---|---|
| Accumulated depreciation | 3,000 | |
| Cash | 500 | |
| Loss | 1,000 | |
| Machine | | 10,000 |

Now assume the FV of the machine is unknown but the FV of the land received is known to be $6,000.

| | Boot | FV | BV | Gain (loss) |
|---|---|---|---|---|
| Machine given | | | $7,000 | $(500) |
| Land received | $500 | $6,000 | | |

In this case, you can assume FV given is equal to FV received *plus* the boot received ($6,000 + $500).

| $6,500 | | $7,000 | | $(500) |
|---|---|---|---|---|
| FV given (assumed) | – | BV given | = | Loss |

| | | |
|---|---|---|
| Land | 6,000 | (FV received) |
| Accumulated depreciation | 3,000 | |
| Cash | 500 | |
| Loss | 500 | |
| Machine | | 10,000 |

## Gain Situations

### Situation 1.  Gain, fair value measurement.

EXAMPLE:  *A company trades a computer with a FV of $12,000 (cost, $11,000; accumulated depreciation, $4,000) for a building.  The transaction has commercial substance and does not meet any of the exception criteria; therefore the transaction should be valued at fair value.*

| | FV | BV | Gain (loss) |
|---|---|---|---|
| Computer given | $12,000 | $7,000 | $5,000 |
| Building received | | | |

Since the transaction has commercial substance, the earnings process is considered complete and the entire gain is recognized.

| | | |
|---|---|---|
| Building | 12,000 | (FV received) |
| Accumulated depreciation | 4,000 | |
| Computer | | 11,000 |
| Gain | | 5,000 |

If boot had been involved, the accounting would be similar to that illustrated in the loss situation.

### Situation 2.  Gain, transaction lacks commercial substance, no boot involved.

EXAMPLE:  *A company trades equipment with a FV of $12,000 (cost, $11,000; accumulated depreciation, $4,000) for another piece of equipment.  The configuration of cash flows of the asset exchanged does not significantly differ from the cash flows of the new asset.*

| | FV | BV | Gain (loss) |
|---|---|---|---|
| Equipment given | $12,000 | $7,000 | $5,000 |
| Equipment received | | | |

Since this transaction lacks commercial substance, the earnings process is **not** considered complete and no gain is recognized.  The asset received is debited at the book value (**not** fair value) of the asset given.

| | | |
|---|---|---|
| Equipment | 7,000 | (BV given) |
| Accumulated depreciation | 4,000 | |
| Equipment | | 11,000 |

The unrecognized gain of $5,000 will be deferred; it will be recognized as the equipment received is depreciated (lower depreciation results than if FV had been used) and/or sold or disposed of in a subsequent transaction.

### Situation 3.  Gain, transaction lacks commercial substance, boot given.

EXAMPLE:  *A company trades a machine (cost, $10,000; accumulated depreciation, $2,000) and $4,000 in cash for another machine with a FV of $16,000.  The configuration of cash flows of the asset exchanged does not significantly differ from the cash flows of the new asset.*

| | Boot | FV | BV | Gain (loss) |
|---|---|---|---|---|
| Machine given | $4,000 | | $8,000 | $4,000 |
| Machine received | | $16,000 | | |

As in the loss situation, the FV of the asset given can be assumed equal to the FV received less the boot given ($16,000 – $4,000).

| $12,000 | | $8,000 | | $4,000 |
|---|---|---|---|---|
| FV given (assumed) | – | BV given | = | Gain |

Boot given is added to the value of the asset received (in this case, book value).  Gain is still unrecognized.

| | | |
|---|---|---|
| Machine | 12,000 | (BV given + Boot given) |
| Accumulated depreciation | 2,000 | |
| Machine | | 10,000 |
| Cash | | 4,000 |

*Below are alternative ways to calculate the asset received.*

| | | | |
|---|---|---|---|
| FV received | $16,000 | BV given | $ 8,000 |
| Gain deferred | (4,000) | Cash paid | 4,000 |
| | 12,000 | | 12,000 |

## Situation 4.  Gain, transaction lacks commercial substance, boot received.

An exception to nonrecognition of gain on exchange for a transaction lacking commercial substance arises when boot is received in the exchange.  This type earnings process is assumed complete for the portion related to the boot received (i.e., "sale" portion), but is **not** assumed complete for the portion related to the asset received (i.e., "exchange" portion).  Therefore, a gain is recognized only for that portion related to the boot.  Gain recognized is computed as follows:

$$\left(\frac{\text{Boot received}}{\text{Boot received} + \text{FV of asset received}}\right) \times \text{Total gain} = \text{Gain recognized}$$

If the FV of the asset received is not given, it may be determined by subtracting the boot received from the FV of the asset given up.

> *EXAMPLE:  A company trades a machine with a FV of $12,000 (cost, $9,000; accumulated depreciation, $2,000) for a different machine and $2,000 cash.*

| | | Machine | | |
|---|---|---|---|---|
| | Boot received | FV | BV | Gain (loss) |
| Given | | $12,000 | $7,000 | $5,000 |
| Received | $2,000 | ? | ? | |

*Since boot was received, the portion of the gain relating to the boot must be recognized.*

$$\left(\frac{\$2,000}{\$2,000 + \$10,000\ *}\right) \times (\$5,000) = \$833$$

*\*The FV of the asset received ($10,000) was derived by deducting boot received from the FV of the machine given.*

| | | | | |
|---|---|---|---|---|
| $12,000 | | $2,000 | | $10,000 |
| FV given | – | Boot received | = | FV received |
| | | | | (assumed) |

*Thus, only $833 of the gain will be recognized.  The machine received would be recorded at its BV given less boot received, plus gain recognized ($7,000 – $2,000 + $833 = $5,833).  Alternatively this could  be calculated by taking its FV less the gain deferred [$10,000 – ($5,000 gain – $833 gain recognized)].*

| | | | |
|---|---|---|---|
| Cash | 2,000 | | |
| Machine (received) | 5,833 | | |
| Accumulated depreciation | 2,000 | | |
|     Machine (given) | | 9,000 | |
|     Gain | | 833 | |

$$\left(\begin{array}{c}\text{BV given} - \text{Boot received}\\ + \text{Gain recognized}\end{array}\right) \text{ or } \left(\begin{array}{c}\text{FV received} -\\ \text{Gain deferred}\end{array}\right)$$

## D.  Purchase of Groups of Fixed Assets (Basket purchase)

Cost should be allocated based on relative market value.

$$\text{Cost of all assets acquired} \times \frac{\text{Market value of A}}{\text{Market value of all assets acquired}}$$

> *EXAMPLE:  Purchase of Asset 1 with a FMV of $60,000, Asset 2 with a FMV of $120,000, and Asset 3 with a FMV of $20,000 all for $150,000 cash.*

| | FMV | Relative FMV | Total × cost | Allocated = cost |
|---|---|---|---|---|
| Asset 1 | $ 60,000 | 60/200 | $150,000 | $45,000 |
| Asset 2 | 120,000 | 120/200 | 150,000 | 90,000 |
| Asset 3 | 20,000 | 20/200 | 150,000 | 15,000 |
| Total FMV | $200,000 | | | |

*Journalized:*

| | | |
|---|---|---|
| Asset 1 | $45,000 | |
| Asset 2 | 90,000 | |
| Asset 3 | 15,000 | |
|     Cash | | $150,000 |

## E.  Capital vs. Revenue Expenditures

Capital expenditures and revenue expenditures are charges that are incurred after the acquisition cost has been determined and the related fixed asset is in operation.

*Capital expenditures* are not normal, recurring expenses; they benefit the operations of more than one period. The cost of major rearrangements of assets to increase efficiency is an example of a capital expenditure.

*Revenue expenditures* are normal recurring expenditures. However, some expenditures that meet the test for capital expenditures are expensed because they are immaterial (e.g., less than $50).

Expenditures to improve the efficiency or extend the asset life should be capitalized and charged to future periods. A subtle distinction is sometimes made between an improvement in efficiency and an extension of the asset life. Some accountants feel improvements in efficiency should be charged to the asset account, and improvements extending the asset life should be charged to the accumulated depreciation account. The rationale is that improvements extending the asset life will need to be depreciated over an extended period of time, requiring revision of depreciation schedules.

The chart on the following page summarizes the appropriate treatment of expenditures related to fixed assets.

## F. Depreciation

Depreciation is the annual charge to income for asset use during the period. Since depreciation is a noncash expense, it does not provide resources for the replacement of assets. It is simply a means of spreading asset costs to periods in which the assets produce revenue. Essentially, the "depreciation base" is allocated over the asset's useful life in a rational and systematic manner. The meaning of the key terms is as follows:

*Systematic*—Formula or plan
*Rational*—Representational faithfulness (fits with reality)
*Allocation*—Not a process of valuation

The objective is to match asset cost with revenue produced. The depreciation base is cost less salvage value (except for the declining balance method which ignores salvage value). The cost of an asset will include any reasonable cost incurred in bringing an asset to an enterprise and getting it ready for its intended use. The useful life can be limited by

1. Technological change
2. Normal deterioration
3. Physical usage

The first two indicate depreciation is a function of time whereas the third indicates depreciation is a function of the level of activity. Other depreciation methods include inventory, retirement, replacement, group, composite, etc. Depreciation methods based on time are

1. Straight-line (SL)
2. Accelerated
   a. Declining balance (DB)
      (1) Most common is double-declining balance (DDB)
   b. Sum-of-the-years' digits (SYD)

*Straight-line* and *accelerated* depreciation are illustrated by the following example: $10,000 asset, four-year life, $2,000 salvage value.

| Year | Straight line | DDB | SYD |
|------|------|------|------|
| 1 | $2,000 | $5,000 | $3,200 |
| 2 | $2,000 | $2,500 | $2,400 |
| 3 | $2,000 | $ 500* | $1,600 |
| 4 | $2,000 | -- | $ 800 |

Straight-line  $\frac{\$10,000 - \$2,000}{4}$

DDB    Twice the straight-line rate (2 × 25%) times the net book value at beginning of each year, but not below salvage value (salvage value is not deducted for depreciation base).

SYD    4/10**, 3/10, 2/10, 1/10 of ($10,000 – $2,000).

 * $10,000 – ($5,000 + 2,500) = $2,500 Book value at beginning of year three. $2,500 – 2,000 salvage value = $500.

** $\frac{n(n+1)}{2} = \frac{4 \times 5}{2} = 10$

**COSTS SUBSEQUENT TO ACQUISITION OF PROPERTY, PLANT, AND EQUIPMENT**

| Type of expenditure / Characteristics | when incurred | Expense Debit (credit) to asset | Capitalize Debit (credit) to accum. deprec. | Other |
|---|---|---|---|---|
| **1. Additions** | | | | |
| • Extensions, enlargements, or expansions made to an existing asset | | x | | |
| **2. Repairs and maintenance** | | | | |
| **a. Ordinary** | | | | |
| • Recurring, relatively small expenditures | | | | |
|   1. Maintain normal operating condition | x | | | |
|   2. **Do not** add materially to use value | x | | | |
|   3. **Do not** extend useful life | x | | | |
| **b. Extraordinary (major)** | | | | |
| • Not recurring, relatively large expenditures | | | | |
|   1. Primarily increase the quality and/or output of services | | x | | |
|   2. Primarily extend the useful life | | | x | |
| **3. Replacements and improvements** | | | | |
| • Major component of asset is removed and replaced with the same type of component with comparable performance capabilities (replacement) or a different type of component having superior performance capabilities (betterment) | | | | |
| **a. Book value of old component is known** | | | | |
| • Old component amounts | | (x) | | • Recognize any proceeds and loss (or gain) on old asset |
| • New component outlay | | x | x | |
| **b. Book value of old component is not known** | | | | |
| • Primarily increases the use value | | x | | |
| • Primarily extends the useful life | | | x | |
| **4. Reinstallations and rearrangements** | | | | |
| • Provide greater efficiency in production or reduce production costs | | | | |
|   1. Material costs, benefits extend into future accounting periods | | x | | |
|   2. No measurable future benefit | x | | | |

***Physical usage depreciation*** is based on activity (e.g., machine hours) or output (e.g., finished widgets).

$$\text{Annual depreciation} = \frac{\text{Current activity or output}}{\text{Total expected activity or output}} \times \text{Depreciation base}$$

*EXAMPLE: A machine costs $60,000. The machine's total output is expected to be 500,000 units. If 100,000 units are produced in the first year, $12,000 of depreciation would be incurred (100/500 × $60,000).*

Note that physical usage depreciation results in a varying charge (i.e., not constant). Also physical usage depreciation is based on asset activity rather than expiration of time.

Straight-line and accelerated depreciation methods are illustrated by the following graphs:

Accelerated depreciation is justified by

1.   Increased productivity when asset is new
2.   Increasing maintenance charges with age
3.   Risk of obsolescence

Accelerated depreciation methods result in a better matching of costs and revenues when one or more of these factors are present.

***Inventory depreciation*** is a method typically used in situations where there are many low-cost tangible assets, such as hand tools for a manufacturer or utensils for a restaurant. Using this method, an inventory of the assets is taken at the beginning and the end of the year. Valuation of these assets is based on appraisal value. Depreciation is calculated as follows:

$$\text{Annual depreciation} = \text{Beginning inventory} + \text{Cost of acquisitions} - \text{Ending inventory}$$

The inventory method is advantageous in situations involving such small assets because it is not practical to maintain separate depreciation schedules for them. On the other hand, this method is often criticized because it is not systematic and rational.

***Composite (group) depreciation*** averages the service life of a number of property units and depreciates the group as if it were a single unit. The term "group" is used when the assets are similar; "composite" when they are dissimilar. The depreciation rate is the following ratio:

$$\frac{\text{Sum of annual SL depreciation of individual assets}}{\text{Total asset cost}}$$

Thus, composite depreciation is a weighted-average of a group of assets—usually of a similar nature, expected life, etc.

*EXAMPLE: Three types of assets (A, B, and C) are depreciated under the composite method.*

| Asset type | Asset cost | Salvage value | Depreciation base | Useful life (yrs.) | SL annual depreciation |
|---|---|---|---|---|---|
| A | $ 45,000 | $ 15,000 | $ 30,000 | 5 | $ 6,000 |
| B | 90,000 | 50,000 | 40,000 | 4 | 10,000 |
| C | 145,000 | 25,000 | 120,000 | 3 | 40,000 |
|   | $280,000 | $ 90,000 | $190,000 |   | $ 56,000 |

$$\text{Depreciation or composite rate} = \frac{\$56,000}{\$280,000} = 20\%$$

$$\text{Composite life} = 3.39 \text{ years } (\$190,000 \div \$56,000)$$

Note that the composite life is the depreciation base divided by the annual depreciation. Depreciation is recorded until the book value of the composite group is depreciated to the salvage value of the then remaining assets. As assets are retired the composite group salvage value is reduced. Also note that gains and losses are not recognized on disposal (i.e., gains and losses are netted into accumulated depreciation). This latter practice also affects the length of time required to reduce the book value (cost less accumulated depreciation) to the group salvage value. The entry to record a retirement is

| Cash, other consideration | (amount received) | |
|---|---|---|
| Accumulated depreciation | (plug) | |
| Asset | | (original cost) |

***Changes in depreciation.*** Per SFAS 154, a change in depreciation method is a change in accounting estimate effected by a change in accounting principle. Therefore, a change in depreciation method is treated as a change in accounting estimate. Changes in depreciation estimates also include changes in the expected useful life or salvage value. Changes in accounting estimates are accounted for on a prospective basis in the current and future periods. Make the change prospectively from the beginning of the year in which the change in estimate occurs. The procedure for straight-line depreciation is

1. Divide the periods remaining (from the beginning of the year of change) into
2. The remaining depreciation base (i.e., undepreciated cost to date less revised salvage value)

***Fractional year depreciation.*** Many conventions exist for accounting for depreciation for midyear asset acquisitions. They include

1. A whole year's depreciation in year of acquisition and none in year of disposal
2. One-half year's depreciation in year of acquisition and year of disposal
3. Depreciation to nearest whole month in both year of acquisition and year of disposal

CPA exam questions generally specify the convention to be followed.
G. **Disposals and Impairment of Value** (see the outline of SFAS 144)

The entry to record the disposal (sale) of an asset is

| Cash | (amount received) | |
|---|---|---|
| Accumulated depreciation | (old asset) | |
| Old asset | | (cost) |
| Gain or loss | (loss) | (gain) |

Do not forget to record depreciation for disposed assets up to the point of disposal.

*EXAMPLE: Jimco, a manufacturer of sports equipment, purchased a machine for $6,000 on 1/1/03. The machine had an eight-year life, a $600 salvage value, and was depreciated using the straight-line method. Thus, depreciation was charged at a rate of $56.25 per month [($6,000 cost – $600 salvage) ÷ (8 yrs × 12 mos/yr)]. If Jimco sells the asset on 9/1/08 for $3,000, the following entries must be made to record 2008 depreciation and to record the sale:*

| *Depreciation expense* | *450* | |
|---|---|---|
| *Accumulated depreciation* | | *450* |
| *($56.25 × 8 mos)* | | |
| | | |
| *Cash* | *3,000* | |
| *Accumulated depreciation* | *3,825* | |
| *($56.25 × 68 mos)* | | |
| *Equipment* | | *6,000* |
| *Gain on sale of equip.* | | *825* |
| *[$3,000 cash – ($6,000 – $3,825)CV]* | | |

In some cases, assets are intended to be **disposed of** in a future reporting period rather than held for use. Per SFAS 144, if management has adopted such a plan for disposal, a loss is recognized if the fair value minus selling costs (NRV) is less than the recorded carrying value.

Assume that the asset in the above example has not been sold yet. However, management intends to dispose of it in the next year at NRV of $1,500. The entry to record management's intents would be as follows:

| Loss on planned disposition* | 675 | |
|---|---|---|
| Equipment to be disposed of | 1,500 | |
| Accumulated depreciation | 3,825 | |
| Equipment | | 6,000 |

*[($1,500 – ($6,000 – 3,825) CV]

Fixed assets intended for disposal are not subsequently depreciated. The equipment to be disposed of would be classified as other assets on the balance sheet.

**Losses on fixed assets to be disposed of can be recovered** due to changes in the fair value or selling costs associated with the asset. This write-up, however, **cannot** exceed the carrying amount prior to recognition of impairment. If the NRV for this asset increases in the next period, the maximum recovery (gain) that could be recognized is $675.

**Assets that are intended to be held and used** should be tested for impairment. Impairment occurs when the carrying amount of a long-lived asset or asset group exceeds its fair value. However, an impairment loss is recognized only if the carrying amount of the asset is not recoverable.  The carrying value is considered not recoverable if it exceeds the sum of the expected value of the undiscounted cash flows.

The loss on impairment recognized is the difference between the asset's fair value and its carrying value.  SFAS 157 provides guidelines for determining the fair value of an asset.  The principal or most advantageous market for the asset should be used consistent with the asset's highest and best use.  An in-use valuation premise assumes the highest value of the asset is by using it in the business with other assets.  An in-exchange premise assumes that the highest value of the asset is the amount received to sell the asset standalone.

Assume that the asset in the above example is not sold.  A test for impairment indicates that the net undiscounted cash flows from the machine are less than its carrying value.  Thus, the asset is impaired as of 9/1/08.  The machine's actual fair value at this date is $1,400, with **no** salvage value.  Therefore, its carrying value is reduced,

| | | |
|---|---|---|
| Loss on impairment | 775 | |
| [($6,000 – $3,825) CV – $1,400 FV] | | |
|    Accumulated depreciation | | 775 |

and it will continue to be depreciated at $50.00 per month for its remaining useful life ($1,400 ÷ 28 mos = $50.00).  At 12/31/10, when the asset is fully depreciated, Jimco retires it and writes the machine off with the following entry:

| | | |
|---|---|---|
| Accumulated depreciation | 6,000 | |
|    Equipment | | 6,000 |

Note that the entire cost has been depreciated because upon impairment of the asset it was determined that the equipment did not have a salvage value.

When management has alternative courses of action to recover the carrying amount of the assets or a particular course has multiple outcomes in terms of cash flow, SFAS 144 indicates that probability-weighted cash flow approach should be considered.  Subsequent to the impairment loss, the asset is depreciated based on its new carrying value.  **Recoveries of previously recognized impairment losses may not be recognized in subsequent periods.**

### H.  Depletion

Depletion is "depreciation" of natural resources.  The depletion base is the total cost of the property providing the natural resources.  This includes all development costs such as exploring, drilling, excavating, and other preparatory costs.

The depletion base is usually allocated by the ratio of extracted units over the total expected recoverable units.

$$\frac{\text{Units extracted}}{\text{Total expected recoverable units}} \times \text{Depletion base}$$

The unit depletion rate is frequently revised due to the uncertainties surrounding the recovery of natural resources.  The revised unit rate in any year takes the following form:

$$\frac{\text{Orig. cost + Addl. cost incurred – Resid. value – Depletion taken in prev. yrs.}}{\text{Units withdrawn currently + Estimated units recoverable at year-end}}$$

Note that the adjustment is being made prospectively (i.e., the remaining undepleted cost is being expensed over the remaining recoverable units).

Depletion on resources extracted during an accounting period is allocated between inventory and cost of goods sold.

### I.  Insurance

*Loss account for fixed assets.*  When an insured loss occurs, an insurance loss account should be set up and charged for all losses.  These losses include decreases in asset value, earned insurance premiums, etc.  The account should be credited for any payments from the insurance company.  The remainder is closed to revenue and expense summary.

*Coinsurance.*  This area is tested on the Business Environment and Concepts section of the exam.

### J.  Goodwill and Other Intangible Assets (See the outline of SFAS 142)

Intangible assets are nonphysical assets.  Intangible assets normally include only noncurrent intangibles (e.g., accounts receivable are not considered intangibles).  Examples of intangible assets include copyrights, leaseholds, organizational costs, trademarks, franchises, patents, and goodwill.  These intangibles may be categorized according to the following characteristics:

1.  Identifiability.  Separately identifiable or lacking specific identification.
2.  Manner of acquisition.  Acquired singly, in groups, or in business combinations; or developed internally.
3.  Expected period of benefit.  Limited by law or contract, related to human or economic factors, or indefinite or indeterminate duration.
4.  Separability from enterprise.  Rights transferable without title, salable, or inseparable from the entire enterprise.

***Acquisition of intangibles.***  Purchased intangibles should be recorded at cost, which represents the fair value of the intangible at time of acquisition.  Internally developed intangibles are written off as research and development expense; an exception is the cost to register a patent.

***Acquisition of goodwill and allocation to reporting units.***  Goodwill is recorded only when an entire business is purchased.  Purchase of goodwill as part of acquiring a business is discussed in the Investment and Business Combinations and Consolidations modules.

In a business acquisition, the recognized goodwill should be assigned to one or more reporting units.  In essence, the goodwill assigned to a reporting unit is the difference between the fair value of the unit and the value of its individual assets and liabilities.  A reporting unit can be an operating segment (see SFAS 131) or one level below.

> *EXAMPLE:  Allocation of Goodwill to a Reporting Unit*
>
> *Dunn Corporation acquired all of the assets of Yeager Corporation for $12,000,000 cash.  The assets were seen as relating to three different reporting units (operating segments)—Communications, Technology, and Consulting.  The fair value of the Communications reporting unit at the date of acquisition was $4,700,000.  Goodwill associated with the unit would be assigned based on a comparison of its total fair value to the value of its assets and liabilities as shown below.*

**Communications Reporting Unit**
*(In 000s)*

|  | *Fair value* |
| --- | --- |
| Cash | $  200 |
| Accounts receivable | 900 |
| Net Equipment | 2,700 |
| Patents | 1,000 |
| Customer contracts | 700 |
| Current liabilities | (1,100) |
| Fair value of net assets | $4,400 |

> *The amount of goodwill assigned to the reporting unit would be $300,000 ($4,700,000 – $4,400,000), the excess of the fair value of the reporting unit over the value of its net assets.  Goodwill would be assigned to the other two reporting units in a similar manner.*

***Amortization of intangibles.***  Intangible assets that have a definite useful life are amortized by crediting the intangible account directly (ordinarily, contra accounts are not used).

| Amortization expense | xx | |
| --- | --- | --- |
| Intangible asset | | xx |

The method of amortization of intangibles should mirror the pattern that the asset is consumed.  If the pattern cannot be reliably determined, the straight-line basis should be used.  Factors to consider in determining economic life are listed in the outline of SFAS 142.

> *EXAMPLE:  Determination of Useful Life of an Intangible Asset*
>
> *Yeager Communications owns several radio stations and has $5,000,000 recorded as the carrying value of broadcast rights.  The rights have a legal life of 7 more years but may be extended upon appropriate application for an indefinite period.  Since the company has the right and intent to extend the rights indefinitely, the useful life of the asset should be considered indefinite and the rights should not be amortized.*

***Impairment of intangible assets.***  An intangible asset that is amortized should be tested for impairment in accordance with SFAS 144.

An intangible asset that is determined to have an indefinite useful life should not be amortized.  However, it should be reevaluated every reporting period to determine if facts and circumstances have changed creating a limited life and requiring it to be amortized.  Also, such intangible assets should be tested for impairment annually or more frequently if facts and circumstances indicate that impairment may have occurred—see the outline of SFAS 144 for such facts and circumstances.  If the carrying value of the intangible asset exceeds its fair value, an impairment loss should be recorded in the amount of the difference.

*EXAMPLE: Impairment of an Intangible Asset with an Indefinite Life*

> Wilson Company acquired a trademark for a major consumer product several years ago for $50,000. At the time it was expected that the asset had an indefinite life. During its annual impairment test of this asset, the company determined that unexpected competition has entered the market that will significantly reduce the future sales of the product. Based on an analysis of cash flows, the trademark is determined to have a fair market value of $30,000 and is expected to continue to have an indefinite useful life. The $20,000 ($50,000 – $30,000) impairment loss should be recognized as shown below.

| | | |
|---|---|---|
| Impairment loss | 20,000 | |
| Trademark | | 20,000 |

**Impairment of goodwill.** The goodwill assigned to a reporting unit should be tested for impairment on an annual basis and between annual tests in certain circumstances. These circumstances are listed in the outline of SFAS 142. The annual test may be performed any time during the company's fiscal year as long as it is done at the same time every year. Different reporting units may be tested at different times during the year. The test of impairment is a two-step process as described below.

1. Compare the fair value of the reporting unit with its carrying amount. If the carrying amount of the unit exceeds its fair value, the second step is performed. SFAS 157 requires that in determining fair value, a valuation premise should be used that is consistent with the asset's highest and best use. The valuation premise can either be an in-use or an in-exchange premise. An in-use premise is used if the asset is used in a business in combination with other assets, such as a reporting unit.

2. Compare the implied fair value of the reporting unit goodwill with the carrying amount of that goodwill. The implied fair value of goodwill is determined in the same manner as the amount of goodwill recognized in a business combination—see outline of SFAS 141. That is, all assets in the segment are valued in accordance with SFAS 141, and the excess of the fair value of the reporting unit as a whole over the amounts assigned to its assets and liabilities is the implied goodwill. If the implied value of goodwill is less than its carrying amount, goodwill is written down to its implied value and an impairment loss is recognized.

*EXAMPLE: Test of Impairment of Goodwill*

> Dunn Corporation is performing the test of impairment of the Communication reporting unit at 9/30/08. In performing the first step in the test of impairment, the Communication reporting unit is valued through a multiple of earnings approach at $4,450,000. The carrying amount of the unit at 9/30/08 is $4,650,000, requiring the second step to be performed. The fair value of the assets and liabilities are valued as shown below.

**Communications Reporting Unit**
**Estimated Fair Values**
**9/30/08**
*(In 000s)*

| | *Fair value* |
|---|---|
| Cash | $ 150 |
| Accounts receivable | 1,000 |
| Net Equipment | 2,600 |
| Patents | 950 |
| Customer contracts | 800 |
| Current liabilities | (1,100) |
| Fair value of net assets | $4,400 |

The implied value of goodwill is $50,000 ($4,450,000 – $4,400,000) and this is less than the carrying amount of $300,000. Therefore, an impairment of goodwill should be recognized as shown below.

| | | |
|---|---|---|
| Impairment loss | 250,000 | |
| Goodwill-Communications | | 250,000 |

In performing step one of the test, a detailed determination of fair value of a reporting unit may be carried forward from one year to the next if (1) there are no significant changes in the assets and liabilities that make up the reporting unit, (2) the most recent determined fair value exceeded the unit's carrying amount by a significant margin, and (3) based on an analysis of events or circumstances since the last valuation, the likelihood that the carrying amount exceeds fair value is remote.

## K. Reporting on the Costs of Start-up Activities

SOP 98-5 provides guidance on financial reporting of start-up costs, including organization costs. It requires such costs to be expensed as incurred. Start-up costs are defined as one-time activities related to opening a new facility or new class of customer, initiating a new process in an existing facility, or some new operation. In practice, these are referred to as preopening costs, preoperating costs, and organization costs. Routine ongoing efforts to improve existing quality of products, services, or facilities, are not start-up costs.

**L.  Research and Development Costs (SFAS 2)**

SFAS 2 (see outline) require R&D costs to be expensed as incurred except for intangibles or fixed assets purchased from others having alternative future uses. These should be capitalized and amortized over their useful life. Thus, the cost of patents and R&D equipment purchased from third parties may be deferred and amortized over the asset's useful life. Internally developed R&D may not be deferred.

Finally, R&D done under contract for others is not required to be expensed per SFAS 2. The costs incurred would be matched with revenue using the completed-contract or percentage-of-completion method.

**M.  Computer Software Costs**

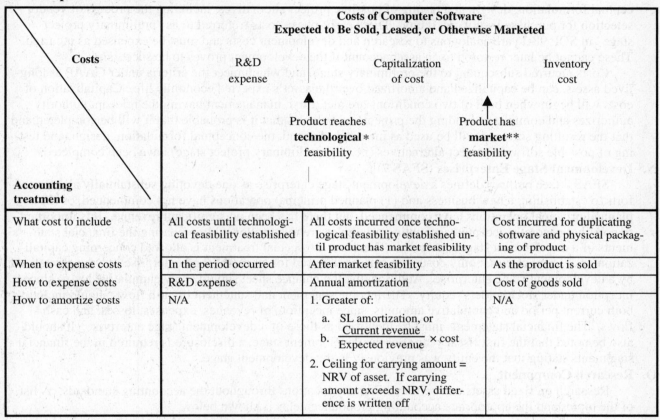

| Costs / Accounting treatment | Costs of Computer Software Expected to Be Sold, Leased, or Otherwise Marketed | | |
|---|---|---|---|
| | R&D expense | Capitalization of cost | Inventory cost |
| | | Product reaches **technological*** feasibility | Product has **market**** feasibility |
| What cost to include | All costs until technological feasibility established | All costs incurred once technological feasibility established until product has market feasibility | Cost incurred for duplicating software and physical packaging of product |
| When to expense costs | In the period occurred | After market feasibility | As the product is sold |
| How to expense costs | R&D expense | Annual amortization | Cost of goods sold |
| How to amortize costs | N/A | 1. Greater of: <br>   a.  SL amortization, or <br>   b.  $\dfrac{\text{Current revenue}}{\text{Expected revenue}} \times \text{cost}$ <br> 2. Ceiling for carrying amount = NRV of asset.  If carrying amount exceeds NRV, difference is written off | N/A |

  \* *Software creation process includes a detail program design.*
 \*\* *Product ready for release to customers.*

**Software developed for sale or lease.** SFAS 86 (see outline) establishes the standards for recording internally developed or purchased computer software costs which are to be either sold, leased, or marketed as an individual product or as part of a process. The costs which are incurred internally to create the software should be expensed as research and development until technological feasibility is established. Thereafter, all costs should be capitalized and reported at the lower of unamortized cost or net realizable value. Capitalization should cease when the software is available for general release to customers.

The annual amortization of capitalized computer software costs will be the greater of the ratio of current revenues to anticipated total revenues or the straight-line amortization which is based on the estimated economic life.

Once the software is available for general release to customers, the inventory costs should include costs for duplicating software and for physically packaging the product. The cost of maintenance and customer support should be charged to expense in the period incurred.

**Software developed for internal use.** SOP 98-1 was developed to provide guidance for internally developed software. Software must meet two criteria to be accounted for as internally developed software. First, the software's specifications must be designed or modified to meet the reporting entity's internal needs, including costs to customize purchased software. Second, during the period in which the software is being developed, there can be no plan or intent to market the software externally, although development of the software can be jointly funded by several entities that each plan to use the software internally.

In order to justify capitalization of related costs, it is necessary for management to conclude that it is probable that the project will be completed and that the software will be used as intended. Absent that level of expectation, costs must be expensed currently as research and development costs are required to be. Entities which historically were engaged in both research and development of software for internal use and for sale to others would have to carefully identify costs with one or the other activity, since the former would (if all conditions are met) be subject to capitalization, while the latter might be expensed as research and development costs until technological feasibility had been demonstrated, per SFAS 86.

Under terms of the standard, cost capitalization commences when an entity has completed the conceptual formulation, design, and testing of possible project alternatives, including the process of vendor selection for purchased software, if any. These early-phase costs (referred to as "preliminary project stage" in SOP 98-1) are analogous to research and development costs and must be expensed as incurred. These cannot be later restored to an asset account if the development proves to be successful.

Costs incurred subsequent to the preliminary stage, and which meet the criteria under GAAP as long-lived assets, can be capitalized and amortized over the asset's expected economic life. Capitalization of costs will begin when both of two conditions are met. First, management having the relevant authority authorizes and commits to funding the project and believes that it is probable that it will be completed and that the resulting software will be used as intended. Second, the conceptual formulation, design, and testing of possible software project alternatives (i.e., the preliminary project stage) have been completed.

## N. Development Stage Enterprises (SFAS 7)

SFAS 7 (see outline) defines a development stage enterprise as one devoting substantially all of its efforts to establishing a new business and (1) planned principal operations have not commenced, or (2) planned principal operations have commenced, but there has been no significant revenue. It is important to note that generally accepted accounting principles are to be followed in preparing the financial statements of a development stage enterprise. Therefore, no special treatment is allowed concerning capitalization or deferral of costs; only costs that may be deferred for an established enterprise may be capitalized by a development stage enterprise. Additionally, the balance sheet should show cumulative losses since inception under stockholders' equity. The income statement and statement of cash flows should include both current period and cumulative amounts, since inception, of revenues, expenses, losses, and cash flows. The financial statements must be identified as those of a development stage enterprise. It should also be noted that the first fiscal year after the development stage, a disclosure is required in the financial statements stating that the entity was previously in the development stage.

## O. Research Component

Research on fixed assets can be found in many locations throughout the accounting standards. A list of the topics and the appropriate accounting pronouncements is shown below.

| | |
|---|---|
| Acquisition cost | SFAS 116 |
| Capitalization of interest | SFAS 34 |
| Disposals and impairment of value | SFAS 144 |
| Fair value measurements | SFAS 157 |
| Goodwill and other intangible assets | SFAS 142 |
| Nonmonetary exchanges of assets | APB 29, FASBI 30, and SFAS 153 |
| Software development for sale or lease | SFAS 86 |
| Software for internal development | SOP 98-1 |
| Start-up activities | SOP 98-5 |
| Changes in depreciation | SFAS 154 |

Keywords for researching in the fixed asset area are shown below.

| | | |
|---|---|---|
| Acquisition cost | Constructed assets | In-use |
| Asset exchange | Contributions received | Indeterminate lives |
| Asset recoverability | Depreciable assets | Intangible assets |
| Asset surrendered | Depreciation | Intangible assets amortization |
| Assigning reporting units | Development stage enterprises | Intangible disclosure |
| Avoided interest | Discontinued operations | Internally developed intangible assets |
| Book value | Disposed of by sale | Long-lived asset |
| Boot | Disposed other than by sale | Lower of carrying amount or fair value |
| Capitalization of interest | Dissimilar assets | Measurement impairment loss |
| Capitalization period | Donated assets | New cost basis |
| Capitalized expenditures | Fair value asset | Nonmonetary asset received |
| Capitalized interest | Fair value determinable | Nonmonetary exchange |
| Capitalized software costs | Future cash flows asset | Nonreciprocal transfer |
| Capitalizing interest | Goodwill | Previously recognized goodwill |
| Carrying amount asset | Goodwill impairment | Recognition impairment loss |
| Classified held-for-sale | Goodwill impairment test | Reporting unit |
| Clearly distinguished operationally | Held and used | Residual value intangible |
| Commercial substance | Held and used assets | Similar assets |
| Computer software costs | Highest and best use | Subject to amortization |
| Computer software leased | Historical cost | Subsequent write-down |
| Computer software marketed | Identifiable assets | Technological feasibility |
| Computer software sold | Impairment loss | Unamortized computer software costs |
| Configuration of cash flows | In-exchange | Undepreciated cost |

**MULTIPLE-CHOICE QUESTIONS (1-81)**

**1.** Merry Co. purchased a machine costing $125,000 for its manufacturing operations and paid shipping costs of $20,000. Merry spent an additional $10,000 testing and preparing the machine for use. What amount should Merry record as the cost of the machine?
- a.   $155,000
- b.   $145,000
- c.   $135,000
- d.   $125,000

**2.** On December 1, 2007, Boyd Co. purchased a $400,000 tract of land for a factory site. Boyd razed an old building on the property and sold the materials it salvaged from the demolition. Boyd incurred additional costs and realized salvage proceeds during December 2007 as follows:

| | |
|---|---|
| Demolition of old building | $50,000 |
| Legal fees for purchase contract and recording ownership | 10,000 |
| Title guarantee insurance | 12,000 |
| Proceeds from sale of salvaged materials | 8,000 |

In its December 31, 2007 balance sheet, Boyd should report a balance in the land account of
- a.   $464,000
- b.   $460,000
- c.   $442,000
- d.   $422,000

**3.** Cole Co. began constructing a building for its own use in January 2007. During 2007, Cole incurred interest of $50,000 on specific construction debt, and $20,000 on other borrowings. Interest computed on the weighted-average amount of accumulated expenditures for the building during 2007 was $40,000. What amount of interest cost should Cole capitalize?
- a.   $20,000
- b.   $40,000
- c.   $50,000
- d.   $70,000

**4.** Clay Company started construction of a new office building on January 1, 2007, and moved into the finished building on July 1, 2008. Of the building's $2,500,000 total cost, $2,000,000 was incurred in 2007 evenly throughout the year. Clay's incremental borrowing rate was 12% throughout 2007, and the total amount of interest incurred by Clay during 2007 was $102,000. What amount should Clay report as capitalized interest at December 31, 2007?
- a.   $102,000
- b.   $120,000
- c.   $150,000
- d.   $240,000

**5.** During 2007, Bay Co. constructed machinery for its own use and for sale to customers. Bank loans financed these assets both during construction and after construction was complete. How much of the interest incurred should be reported as interest expense in the 2007 income statement?

| | Interest incurred for machinery for own use | Interest incurred for machinery held for sale |
|---|---|---|
| a. | All interest incurred | All interest incurred |
| b. | All interest incurred | Interest incurred after completion |
| c. | Interest incurred after completion | Interest incurred after completion |
| d. | Interest incurred after completion | All interest incurred |

**6.** On July 1, 2007, Balt Co. exchanged a truck for twenty-five shares of Ace Corp.'s common stock. On that date, the truck's carrying amount was $2,500, and its fair value was $3,000. Also, the book value of Ace's stock was $60 per share. On December 31, 2007, Ace had 250 shares of common stock outstanding and its book value per share was $50. What amount should Balt report in its December 31, 2007 balance sheet as investment in Ace?
- a.   $3,000
- b.   $2,500
- c.   $1,500
- d.   $1,250

**7.** A nonmonetary exchange is recognized at fair value of the assets exchanged unless
- a.   Exchange has commercial substance.
- b.   Fair value is not determinable.
- c.   The assets are similar in nature.
- d.   The assets are dissimilar.

**8.** In a nonmonetary exchange, which of the following situations will require the asset to be recognized at the recorded value of the asset relinquished?
- a.   A delivery truck exchanged for a delivery van that can deliver four times the quantity of goods to customers.
- b.   The exchanged item is intended to facilitate sales to customers.
- c.   The cash flows from the new asset will be significantly different from cash flows of the exchanged asset.
- d.   The assets are both productive assets.

**9.** For purposes of nonmonetary exchanges, the configuration of cash flows includes which of the following?
- a.   The implicit rate, maturity date of loan, and amount of loan.
- b.   The risk, timing, and amount of cash flows of the assets.
- c.   The entity-specific value of the asset which is equal to the fair value of the asset exchanged.
- d.   The estimated present value of the assets exchanged.

**10.** When determining the commercial substance of the exchange, which of the following items is not considered?
- a.   Cash flow of exchanged asset.
- b.   Cash flow of new asset.
- c.   Cash flow from tax effects on the exchange to avoid taxes.
- d.   Cash flow from potential sale of new equipment at a later date.

**11.** On March 31, 2007, Winn Company traded in an old machine having a carrying amount of $16,800, and paid a cash difference of $6,000 for a new machine having a total cash price of $20,500. The cash flows from the new machine are expected to be significantly different than the cash flows from the old machine. On March 31, 2007, what amount of loss should Winn recognize on this exchange?

- a. $0
- b. $2,300
- c. $3,700
- d. $6,000

**12.** Amble, Inc. exchanged a truck with a carrying amount of $12,000 and a fair value of $20,000 for a truck and $2,500 cash. The cash flows from the new truck are not expected to be significantly different from the cash flows of the old truck. The fair value of the truck received was $17,500. At what amount should Amble record the truck received in the exchange?

- a. $ 7,000
- b. $ 9,500
- c. $10,500
- d. $17,500

**13.** In an exchange of assets that is deemed to lack commercial substance, Transit Co. given up equipment with a fair value equal to the carrying amount of equipment given up. Transit also contributed cash. As a result of the exchange, Transit recognized

- a. A loss equal to the cash given up.
- b. A loss determined by the proportion of cash paid to the total transaction value.
- c. A gain determined by the proportion of cash paid to the total transaction value.
- d. Neither gain **nor** loss.

**14.** May Co. and Sty Co. exchanged nonmonetary assets. The exchange did not result in the expected cash flows of the assets being significantly different for either May or Sty. May paid cash to Sty in connection with the exchange. To the extent that the amount of cash exceeds a proportionate share of the carrying amount of the asset surrendered, a realized gain on the exchange should be recognized by

|     | *May* | *Sty* |
| --- | --- | --- |
| a. | Yes | Yes |
| b. | Yes | No |
| c. | No | Yes |
| d. | No | No |

**15.** Vik Auto and King Clothier exchanged goods, held for resale, with equal fair values. Each will use the other's goods to promote their own products. The retail price of the car that Vik gave up is less than the retail price of the clothes received. Assuming the transaction has commercial substance, what profit should Vik recognize for the non-monetary exchange?

- a. A profit is **not** recognized.
- b. A profit equal to the difference between the retail prices of the clothes received and the car.
- c. A profit equal to the difference between the retail price and the cost of the car.
- d. A profit equal to the difference between the fair value and the cost of the car.

**16.** Yola Co. and Zaro Co. are fuel oil distributors. To facilitate the delivery of oil to their customers, Yola and Zaro exchanged ownership of 1,200 barrels of oil without physically moving the oil. Yola paid Zaro $20,000 to compensate

for a difference in the grade of oil. On the date of the exchange, cost and market values of the oil were as follows:

|  | *Yola Co.* | *Zaro Co.* |
| --- | --- | --- |
| Cost | $100,000 | $126,000 |
| Market values | 130,000 | 150,000 |

In Zaro's income statement, what amount of gain should be reported from the exchange of the oil?

- a. $0
- b. $ 3,200
- c. $20,000
- d. $24,000

**17.** An entity disposes of a nonmonetary asset in a non-reciprocal transfer. A gain or loss should be recognized on the disposition of the asset when the fair value of the asset transferred is determinable and the nonreciprocal transfer is to

|     | *Another entity* | *A stockholder of the entity* |
| --- | --- | --- |
| a. | No | Yes |
| b. | No | No |
| c. | Yes | No |
| d. | Yes | Yes |

**18.** On July 1, 2007, one of Rudd Co.'s delivery vans was destroyed in an accident. On that date, the van's carrying value was $2,500. On July 15, 2007, Rudd received and recorded a $700 invoice for a new engine installed in the van in May 2007, and another $500 invoice for various repairs. In August, Rudd received $3,500 under its insurance policy on the van, which it plans to use to replace the van. What amount should Rudd report as gain (loss) on disposal of the van in its 2007 income statement?

- a. $1,000
- b. $ 300
- c. $0
- d. $ (200)

**19.** Lano Corp.'s forest land was condemned for use as a national park. Compensation for the condemnation exceeded the forest land's carrying amount. Lano purchased similar, but larger, replacement forest land for an amount greater than the condemnation award. As a result of the condemnation and replacement, what is the net effect on the carrying amount of forest land reported in Lano's balance sheet?

- a. The amount is increased by the excess of the replacement forest land's cost over the condemned forest land's carrying amount.
- b. The amount is increased by the excess of the replacement forest land's cost over the condemnation award.
- c. The amount is increased by the excess of the condemnation award over the condemned forest land's carrying amount.
- d. No effect, because the condemned forest land's carrying amount is used as the replacement forest land's carrying amount.

**20.** On July 1, 2007, Town Company purchased for $540,000 a warehouse building and the land on which it is located. The following data were available concerning the property:

|  | *Current appraised value* | *Seller's original cost* |
| --- | --- | --- |
| Land | $200,000 | $140,000 |
| Warehouse building | 300,000 | 280,000 |
|  | $500,000 | $420,000 |

Town should record the land at
- a. $140,000
- b. $180,000
- c. $200,000
- d. $216,000

**21.** During 2007, King Company made the following expenditures relating to its plant building:

| | |
|---|---:|
| Continuing and frequent repairs | $40,000 |
| Repainted the plant building | 10,000 |
| Major improvements to the electrical wiring system | 32,000 |
| Partial replacement of roof tiles | 14,000 |

How much should be charged to repair and maintenance expense in 2007?
- a. $96,000
- b. $82,000
- c. $64,000
- d. $54,000

**22.** On June 18, 2007, Dell Printing Co. incurred the following costs for one of its printing presses:

| | |
|---|---:|
| Purchase of collating and stapling attachment | $84,000 |
| Installation of attachment | 36,000 |
| Replacement parts for overhaul of press | 26,000 |
| Labor and overhead in connection with overhaul | 14,000 |

The overhaul resulted in a significant increase in production. Neither the attachment nor the overhaul increased the estimated useful life of the press. What amount of the above costs should be capitalized?
- a. $0
- b. $84,000
- c. $120,000
- d. $160,000

**23.** A building suffered uninsured fire damage. The damaged portion of the building was refurbished with higher quality materials. The cost and related accumulated depreciation of the damaged portion are identifiable. To account for these events, the owner should
- a. Reduce accumulated depreciation equal to the cost of refurbishing.
- b. Record a loss in the current period equal to the sum of the cost of refurbishing and the carrying amount of the damaged portion of the building.
- c. Capitalize the cost of refurbishing and record a loss in the current period equal to the carrying amount of the damaged portion of the building.
- d. Capitalize the cost of refurbishing by adding the cost to the carrying amount of the building.

**24.** Derby Co. incurred costs to modify its building and to rearrange its production line. As a result, an overall reduction in production costs is expected. However, the modifications did not increase the building's market value, and the rearrangement did not extend the production line's life. Should the building modification costs and the production line rearrangement costs be capitalized?

| | Building modification costs | Production line rearrangement costs |
|---|---|---|
| a. | Yes | No |
| b. | Yes | Yes |
| c. | No | No |
| d. | No | Yes |

**25.** On January 2, 2007, Lem Corp. bought machinery under a contract that required a down payment of $10,000, plus twenty-four monthly payments of $5,000 each, for total cash payments of $130,000. The cash equivalent price of the machinery was $110,000. The machinery has an estimated useful life of ten years and estimated salvage value of $5,000. Lem uses straight-line depreciation. In its 2007 income statement, what amount should Lem report as depreciation for this machinery?
- a. $10,500
- b. $11,000
- c. $12,500
- d. $13,000

**26.** Turtle Co. purchased equipment on January 2, 2005, for $50,000. The equipment had an estimated five-year service life. Turtle's policy for five-year assets is to use the 200% double-declining depreciation method for the first two years of the asset's life, and then switch to the straight-line depreciation method. In its December 31, 2007 balance sheet, what amount should Turtle report as accumulated depreciation for equipment?
- a. $30,000
- b. $38,000
- c. $39,200
- d. $42,000

**27.** Rago Company takes a full year's depreciation expense in the year of an asset's acquisition, and no depreciation expense in the year of disposition. Data relating to one of Rago's depreciable assets at December 31, 2007, are as follows:

| | |
|---|---:|
| Acquisition year | 2004 |
| Cost | $110,000 |
| Residual value | 20,000 |
| Accumulated depreciation | 72,000 |
| Estimated useful life | 5 years |

Using the same depreciation method as used in 2005, 2006, and 2007, how much depreciation expense should Rago record in 2008 for this asset?
- a. $12,000
- b. $18,000
- c. $22,000
- d. $24,000

**28.** On January 2, 2004, Union Co. purchased a machine for $264,000 and depreciated it by the straight-line method using an estimated useful life of eight years with no salvage value. On January 2, 2007, Union determined that the machine had a useful life of six years from the date of acquisition and will have a salvage value of $24,000. An accounting change was made in 2007 to reflect the additional data. The accumulated depreciation for this machine should have a balance at December 31, 2007, of
- a. $176,000
- b. $160,000
- c. $154,000
- d. $146,000

**29.** Weir Co. uses straight-line depreciation for its property, plant, and equipment, which, stated at cost, consisted of the following:

|  | 12/31/07 | 12/31/06 |
|---|---|---|
| Land | $ 25,000 | $ 25,000 |
| Buildings | 195,000 | 195,000 |
| Machinery and equipment | 695,000 | 650,000 |
|  | 915,000 | 870,000 |
| Less accumulated depreciation | 400,000 | 370,000 |
|  | $515,000 | $500,000 |

Weir's depreciation expense for 2007 and 2006 was $55,000 and $50,000, respectively. What amount was debited to accumulated depreciation during 2007 because of property, plant, and equipment retirements?

a. $40,000
b. $25,000
c. $20,000
d. $10,000

**30.** On January 1, 2003, Crater, Inc. purchased equipment having an estimated salvage value equal to 20% of its original cost at the end of a ten-year life. The equipment was sold December 31, 2007, for 50% of its original cost. If the equipment's disposition resulted in a reported loss, which of the following depreciation methods did Crater use?

a. Double-declining balance.
b. Sum-of-the-years' digits.
c. Straight-line.
d. Composite.

**31.** A depreciable asset has an estimated 15% salvage value. At the end of its estimated useful life, the accumulated depreciation would equal the original cost of the asset under which of the following depreciation methods?

|  | Straight-line | Productive output |
|---|---|---|
| a. | Yes | No |
| b. | Yes | Yes |
| c. | No | Yes |
| d. | No | No |

**32.** In which of the following situations is the units-of-production method of depreciation most appropriate?

a. An asset's service potential declines with use.
b. An asset's service potential declines with the passage of time.
c. An asset is subject to rapid obsolescence.
d. An asset incurs increasing repairs and maintenance with use.

**33.** A machine with a five-year estimated useful life and an estimated 10% salvage value was acquired on January 1, 2004. On December 31, 2007, accumulated depreciation, using the sum-of-the-years' digits method, would be

a. (Original cost less salvage value) multiplied by 1/15.
b. (Original cost less salvage value) multiplied by 14/15.
c. Original cost multiplied by 14/15.
d. Original cost multiplied by 1/15.

**34.** Spiro Corp. uses the sum-of-the-years' digits method to depreciate equipment purchased in January 2005 for $20,000. The estimated salvage value of the equipment is $2,000 and the estimated useful life is four years. What should Spiro report as the asset's carrying amount as of December 31, 2007?

a. $1,800
b. $2,000
c. $3,800
d. $4,500

**35.** The graph below depicts three depreciation expense patterns over time.

Which depreciation expense pattern corresponds to the sum-of-the-years' digits method and which corresponds to the double-declining balance method?

|  | Sum-of-the-years' digits | Double-declining balance |
|---|---|---|
| a. | III | II |
| b. | II | I |
| c. | I | III |
| d. | II | III |

**36.** Which of the following uses the straight-line depreciation method?

|  | Group depreciation | Composite depreciation |
|---|---|---|
| a. | No | No |
| b. | Yes | No |
| c. | Yes | Yes |
| d. | No | Yes |

**37.** A company using the composite depreciation method for its fleet of trucks, cars, and campers retired one of its trucks and received cash from a salvage company. The net carrying amount of these composite asset accounts would be decreased by the

a. Cash proceeds received and original cost of the truck.
b. Cash proceeds received.
c. Original cost of the truck less the cash proceeds.
d. Original cost of the truck.

**38.** During 2007, the management of West Inc. decided to dispose of some of its older equipment and machinery. By year-end, December 31, 2007, these assets had not been sold, although the company was negotiating their sale to another company. On the December 31, 2007 balance sheet of West Inc., this equipment and machinery should be reported at

a. Fair value.
b. Carrying amount.
c. The lower of carrying amount or fair value.
d. The lower of carrying amount or fair value less cost to sell.

**39.** At December 31, 2007, Matson Inc. was holding long-lived assets that it intended to sell. The assets do not constitute a separate component of the company. The company appropriately recognized a loss in 2007 related to these assets. On Matson's income statement for the year ended December 31, 2007, this loss should be reported as a(n)

a. Extraordinary item.
b. Component of income from continuing operations before income taxes.
c. Separate component of selling or general and administrative expenses, disclosed net of tax benefit.
d. Component of the gain (loss) from sale of discontinued operations, disclosed net of income taxes.

**40.** Taft Inc. recognized a loss in 2006 related to long-lived assets that it intended to sell. These assets were not sold during 2007, and the company estimated, at December 31, 2007, that the loss recognized in 2006 had been more than recovered. On the December 31, 2007 balance sheet, Taft should report these long-lived assets at their
a. Fair value on December 31, 2006.
b. Fair value less cost to sell on December 31, 2006.
c. Fair value on December 31, 2007.
d. Carrying amount on December 31, 2006.

**41.** Cranston Inc. reported an impairment loss of $150,000 on its income statement for the year ended December 31, 2006. This loss was related to long-lived assets which Cranston intended to use in its operations. On the company's December 31, 2006 balance sheet, Cranston reported these long-lived assets at $920,000 and, as of December 31, 2006, Cranston estimated that these long-lived assets would be used for another five years. On December 31, 2007, Cranston determined that the fair values of its impaired long-lived assets had increased by $25,000 over their fair values at December 31, 2006. On the company's December 31, 2007 balance sheet, what amount should be reported as the carrying amount for these long-lived assets? Assume straight-line depreciation and no salvage value for the impaired assets.
a. $761,000.
b. $736,000.
c. $945,000.
d. $756,000.

**42.** Assets intended to be held and used for productive purposes may suffer from impairment in each of the following circumstances **except**
a. A change in the way the assets are used or physical change in the assets.
b. Asset costs incurred exceed the original amounts planned.
c. Discounted expected future cash flows and interest charges are less than the carrying amount of the assets.
d. A significant adverse change in legal factors that might affect the assets' fair value.

**43.** Synthia, Inc., a clothing manufacturer, purchased a sewing machine for $10,000 on July 1, 2005. The machine had a ten-year life, a $500 salvage value, and was depreciated using the straight-line method. On December 31, 2007, a test for impairment indicates that the undiscounted cash flows from the sewing machine are less than its carrying value. The machine's actual fair value on December 31, 2007 is $3,000. What is Synthia's loss on impairment on December 31, 2007?
a. $6,500
b. $4,750
c. $4,625
d. $4,150

**44.** With regard to impaired assets, the FASB standards provide for

| | Recognition of loss upon impairment | Restoration of previously recognized impairment losses |
|---|---|---|
| a. | Yes | Yes |
| b. | Yes | No |
| c. | No | Yes |
| d. | No | No |

**45.** Scarbrough Company had purchased equipment for $280,000 on January 1, 2004. The equipment had an eight-year useful life and a salvage value of $40,000. Scarbrough depreciated the equipment using the straight-line method. In August 2007, Scarbrough questioned the recoverability of the carrying amount of this equipment. At August 31, 2007, the expected net future cash inflows (undiscounted) related to the continued use and eventual disposal of the equipment total $175,000. The equipment's fair value on August 31, 2007, is $150,000. After any loss on impairment has been recognized, what is the carrying value of Scarbrough's equipment as of August 31, 2007?
a. $175,000
b. $170,000
c. $150,000
d. $130,000

**46.** Under the reporting requirements of SFAS 144, impairment losses for assets to be held and used shall be reported
a. As an extraordinary item.
b. As a component of discontinued operations.
c. As a component of income from continuing operations.
d. As a change in accounting estimate.

**47.** During December 2007, Bubba Inc. determined that there had been a significant decrease in the market value of its equipment used in its manufacturing process. At December 31, 2007, Bubba compiled the information below.

| | |
|---|---|
| Original cost of the equipment | $500,000 |
| Accumulated depreciation | 300,000 |
| Expected net future cash inflows (undiscounted) related to the continued use and eventual disposal of the equipment | 175,000 |
| Fair value of the equipment | 125,000 |

What is the amount of impairment loss that should be reported on Bubba's income statement prepared for the year ended December 31, 2007?
a. $ 75,000
b. $ 25,000
c. $325,000
d. $375,000

**48.** Marjorie, Inc. acquired a machine for $320,000 on August 31, 2004. The machine has a five-year life, a $50,000 salvage value, and was depreciated using the straight-line method. On May 31, 2007, a test for recoverability reveals that the expected net future undiscounted cash inflows related to the continued use and eventual disposal of the machine total $150,000. The machine's actual fair value on May 31, 2007, is $135,000, with no salvage value. Assuming a loss on impairment is recognized May 31, 2007, what is Marjorie's depreciation expense for June 2007?
a. $6,352
b. $5,000
c. $4,500
d. $3,148

**49.** Which of the following statements is(are) correct about the carrying amount of a long-lived asset after an impairment loss has been recognized? Assume the long-lived asset is being held for use in the business and that the asset is depreciable.

  I. The reduced carrying amount of the asset may be increased in subsequent years if the impairment loss has been recovered.

  II. The reduced carrying amount of the asset represents the amount that should be depreciated over the asset's remaining useful life.

    a.  I only.
    b.  II only.
    c.  Both I and II.
    d.  Neither I nor II.

**50.** According to SFAS 144, if a long-lived asset is determined to be impaired, how is the loss calculated?
    a.  Future discounted cash flows less asset's carrying (book) value.
    b.  Future undiscounted cash flows less asset's carrying (book) value.
    c.  Fair value less asset's carrying (book) value.
    d.  Cash outflows needed to obtain cash inflows.

**51.** In accordance with SFAS 144, long-lived assets are required to be reviewed for impairment
    a.  At the balance sheet date, every three years.
    b.  When the asset is fully depreciated.
    c.  When circumstances indicate that the carrying amount of an asset might not be recoverable.
    d.  At the balance sheet date, every year.

**52.** During December 2007, Toni Corp. determined that there had been a significant decrease in the market value of its equipment used in its roofing business. At December 31, 2007, Toni compiled the information below.

| | |
|---|---|
| Original cost of equipment | $800,000 |
| Accumulated depreciation | 450,000 |
| Expected net future cash inflows (undiscounted) related to the continued use and eventual disposal of the equipment | 300,000 |
| Fair value of the equipment | 250,000 |

What is the amount of the impairment loss that should be reported on Toni's income statement prepared for the year ended December 31, 2007?

    a.  $ 50,000
    b.  $100,000
    c.  $150,000
    d.  $200,000

**53.** Miller Company acquired a machine for $420,000 on June 30, 2005. The machine has a seven-year life, no salvage value, and was depreciated using the straight-line method. On August 31, 2007, a test for recoverability reveals that the expected net future undiscounted cash inflows related to the continued use and eventual disposal of the machine total $275,000. The machine's actual fair value on August 31, 2007, is $261,000. Assuming a loss on impairment is recognized August 31, 2007, what is Miller's depreciation expense for September 2007?
    a.  $4,000
    b.  $4,350
    c.  $4,500
    d.  $5,000

**54.** In January 2007, Vorst Co. purchased a mineral mine for $2,640,000 with removable ore estimated at 1,200,000 tons. After it has extracted all the ore, Vorst will be required by law to restore the land to its original condition at an estimated cost of $220,000. The present value of the estimated restoration costs is $180,000. Vorst believes it will be able to sell the property afterwards for $300,000. During 2007, Vorst incurred $360,000 of development costs preparing the mine for production and removed and sold 60,000 tons of ore. In its 2007 income statement, what amount should Vorst report as depletion?
    a.  $135,000
    b.  $144,000
    c.  $150,000
    d.  $159,000

**55.** On December 31, 2006, Byte Co. had capitalized software costs of $600,000 with an economic life of four years. Sales for 2007 were 10% of expected total sales of the software. At December 31, 2007, the software had a net realizable value of $480,000. In its December 31, 2007 balance sheet, what amount should Byte report as net capitalized cost of computer software?
    a.  $432,000
    b.  $450,000
    c.  $480,000
    d.  $540,000

**56.** On January 2, 2007, Judd Co. bought a trademark from Krug Co. for $500,000. Judd retained an independent consultant, who estimated the trademark's remaining life to be fifty years. Its unamortized cost on Krug's accounting records was $380,000. In Judd's December 31, 2007 balance sheet, what amount should be reported as accumulated amortization?
    a.  $ 7,600
    b.  $ 9,500
    c.  $10,000
    d.  $12,500

**57.** On January 2, 2007, Paye Co. purchased Shef Co. at a cost that resulted in recognition of goodwill of $200,000. During the first quarter of 2007, Paye spent an additional $80,000 on expenditures designed to maintain goodwill. In its December 31, 2007 balance sheet, what amount should Paye report as goodwill?
    a.  $180,000
    b.  $200,000
    c.  $252,000
    d.  $280,000

**58.** Northern Airline purchased airline gate rights at Newark International Airport for $2,000,000 with a legal life of five years. However, Northern has the ability and right to extend the rights every ten years for an indefinite period of time. Over what period of time should Northern amortize the gate rights?
    a.  5 years.
    b.  15 years
    c.  40 years.
    d.  The rights should not be amortized.

**59.** On January 2, 2004, Lava, Inc. purchased a patent for a new consumer product for $90,000. At the time of purchase, the patent was valid for fifteen years; however, the patent's useful life was estimated to be only ten years due to the competitive nature of the product. On December 31, 2007, the product was permanently withdrawn from sale under governmental order because of a potential health hazard in the product. What amount should Lava charge against income during 2007, assuming amortization is recorded at the end of each year?

- a.   $ 9,000
- b.   $54,000
- c.   $63,000
- d.   $72,000

**60.** What does SFAS 142 require with respect to accounting for goodwill?

- a.   Goodwill should be amortized over a five-year period.
- b.   Goodwill should be amortized over its expected useful life.
- c.   Goodwill should be recorded and never adjusted.
- d.   Goodwill should be recorded and periodically evaluated for impairment.

**61.** Which of the following statements concerning patents is correct?

- a.   Legal costs incurred to successfully defend an internally developed patent should be capitalized and amortized over the patent's remaining economic life.
- b.   Legal fees and other direct costs incurred in registering a patent should be capitalized and amortized on a straight-line basis over a five-year period.
- c.   Research and development contract services purchased from others and used to develop a patented manufacturing process should be capitalized and amortized over the patent's economic life.
- d.   Research and development costs incurred to develop a patented item should be capitalized and amortized on a straight-line basis over seventeen years.

**62.** Under SFAS 142, goodwill should be tested periodically for impairment

- a.   For the entity as a whole.
- b.   At the subsidiary level.
- c.   At the industry segment level.
- d.   At the operating segment level or one level below.

**63.** On July 12, 2007, Carver, Inc. acquired Jones Company in a business combination. As a result of the combination, the following amounts of goodwill were recorded for each of the three reporting units of the acquired company.

| | |
|---|---|
| Retailing | $30,000 |
| Service | $20,000 |
| Financing | $40,000 |

Near the end of 2007 a new major competitor entered the company's market and Carver was concerned that this might cause a significant decline in the value of goodwill. Accordingly, Carver computed the implied value of the goodwill for the three major reporting units at December 31, 2007 as follows:

| | |
|---|---|
| Retailing | $25,000 |
| Service | $10,000 |
| Financing | $60,000 |

Determine the amount of impairment of goodwill that should be recorded by Carver at December 31, 2007.

- a.   $0

- b.   $10,000
- c.   $15,000
- d.   $25,000

**64.** Sloan Corporation is performing its annual test of the impairment of goodwill for its Financing reporting unit. It has determined that the fair value of the unit exceeds it carrying value. Which of the following is correct concerning this test of impairment?

- a.   Impairment is not indicated and no additional analysis is necessary.
- b.   Goodwill should be written down as impaired.
- c.   The assets and liabilities should be valued to determine if there has been an impairment of goodwill.
- d.   Goodwill should be retested at the entity level.

**65.** Wilson Corporation is performing the test of impairment of its Technology reporting unit at 9/30/07. In the first step of the process, Wilson has valued the unit using a multiple of earnings approach at $2,000,000. The carrying value of the net assets of the Technology unit is $2,100,000. What should Wilson do with this information?

- a.   Record an impairment loss of $100,000.
- b.   Record no impairment loss.
- c.   Value goodwill individually.
- d.   Perform step two of the test of impairment.

**66.** Brunson Corp., a major US winery, begins construction of a new facility in Italy. Following are some of the costs incurred in conjunction with the start-up activities of the new facility:

| | |
|---|---|
| Production equipment | $815,000 |
| Travel costs of salaried employees | 40,000 |
| License fees | 14,000 |
| Training of local employees for production and maintenance operations | 120,000 |
| Advertising costs | 85,200 |

What portion of the organizational costs will be expensed?

- a.   $975,000
- b.   $160,000
- c.   $0
- d.   $139,200

**67.** On January 1, 2007, Kew Corp. incurred organization costs of $24,000. What portion of the organization costs will Kew defer to years subsequent to 2007?

- a.   $23,400
- b.   $19,200
- c.   $ 4,800
- d.   $0

**68.** Which of the following statements is(are) correct regarding the treatment of start-up activities related to the opening of a new facility?

- I. Costs of raising capital should be expensed as incurred.
- II. Costs of acquiring or constructing long-lived assets and getting them ready for their intended use should be expensed as incurred.
- III. Cost of research and development should be expensed as incurred.

- a.   I only.
- b.   III only.
- c.   Both I and III.
- d.   I, II, and III.

**69.** Cody Corp. incurred the following costs during 2007:

| | |
|---|---|
| Design of tools, jigs, molds, and dies involving new technology | $125,000 |
| Modification of the formulation of a process | 160,000 |
| Troubleshooting in connection with breakdowns during commercial production | 100,000 |
| Adaptation of an existing capability to a particular customer's need as part of a continuing commercial activity | 110,000 |

In its 2007 income statement, Cody should report research and development expense of

- a. $125,000
- b. $160,000
- c. $235,000
- d. $285,000

**70.** In 2007, Ball Labs incurred the following costs:

| | |
|---|---|
| Direct costs of doing contract research and development work for the government to be reimbursed by governmental unit | $400,000 |

Research and development costs not included above were

| | |
|---|---|
| Depreciation | $300,000 |
| Salaries | 700,000 |
| Indirect costs appropriately allocated | 200,000 |
| Materials | 180,000 |

What was Ball's total research and development expense in 2007?

- a. $1,080,000
- b. $1,380,000
- c. $1,580,000
- d. $1,780,000

**71.** West, Inc. made the following expenditures relating to Product Y:

- Legal costs to file a patent on Product Y—$10,000. Production of the finished product would not have been undertaken without the patent.
- Special equipment to be used solely for development of Product Y—$60,000. The equipment has no other use and has an estimated useful life of four years.
- Labor and material costs incurred in producing a prototype model—$200,000.
- Cost of testing the prototype—$80,000.

What is the total amount of costs that will be expensed when incurred?

- a. $280,000
- b. $295,000
- c. $340,000
- d. $350,000

**72.** Brill Co. made the following expenditures during 2007:

| | |
|---|---|
| Costs to develop computer software for internal use in Brill's general management information system | $100,000 |
| Costs of market research activities | 75,000 |

What amount of these expenditures should Brill report in its 2007 income statement as research and development expenses?

- a. $175,000
- b. $100,000
- c. $ 75,000
- d. $0

**73.** On January 1, 2007, Jambon purchased equipment for use in developing a new product. Jambon uses the straight-line depreciation method. The equipment could provide benefits over a ten-year period. However, the new product development is expected to take five years, and the equipment can be used only for this project. Jambon's 2007 expense equals

- a. The total cost of the equipment.
- b. One-fifth of the cost of the equipment.
- c. One-tenth of the cost of the equipment.
- d. Zero.

**Items 74 and 75** are based on the following:

During 2007, Pitt Corp. incurred costs to develop and produce a routine, low-risk computer software product, as follows:

| | |
|---|---|
| Completion of detailed program design | $13,000 |
| Costs incurred for coding and testing to establish technological feasibility | 10,000 |
| Other coding costs after establishment of technological feasibility | 24,000 |
| Other testing costs after establishment of technological feasibility | 20,000 |
| Costs of producing product masters for training materials | 15,000 |
| Duplication of computer software and training materials from product masters (1,000 units) | 25,000 |
| Packaging product (500 units) | 9,000 |

**74.** In Pitt's December 31, 2007 balance sheet, what amount should be reported in inventory?

- a. $25,000
- b. $34,000
- c. $40,000
- d. $49,000

**75.** In Pitt's December 31, 2007 balance sheet, what amount should be capitalized as software cost, subject to amortization?

- a. $54,000
- b. $57,000
- c. $59,000
- d. $69,000

**76.** On December 31, 2006, Bit Co. had capitalized costs for a new computer software product with an economic life of five years. Sales for 2007 were 30% of expected total sales of the software. At December 31, 2007, the software had a net realizable value equal to 90% of the capitalized cost. What percentage of the original capitalized cost should be reported as the net amount on Bit's December 31, 2007 balance sheet?

- a. 70%
- b. 72%
- c. 80%
- d. 90%

**77.** Which of the following statements is incorrect regarding internal-use software?

- a. The application and development costs of internal-use software should be amortized on a straight-line basis unless another systematic and rational basis is more representative of its costs.
- b. Internal-use software is considered to be software that is marketed as a separate product or as part of a product or process.
- c. The costs of testing and installing computer hardware should be capitalized as incurred.
- d. The costs of training and application maintenance should be expensed as incurred.

**78.** Which of the following statements is(are) correct regarding the proper accounting treatment for internal-use software costs?

  I. Preliminary costs should be capitalized as incurred.

 II. Application and development costs should be capitalized as incurred.

    a.    I only.

    b.    II only.

    c.    Both I and II.

    d.    Neither I nor II.

**79.** What is the proper accounting treatment for the following stages of internal-use software costs?

| | Preliminary stage costs | Post-implementation costs |
|---|---|---|
| a. | Capitalized as incurred | Capitalized as incurred |
| b. | Expensed as incurred | Capitalized as incurred |
| c. | Capitalized as incurred | Expensed as incurred |
| d. | Expensed as incurred | Expensed as incurred |

**80.** Financial reporting by a development stage enterprise differs from financial reporting for an established operating enterprise in regard to footnote disclosures

    a.    Only.

    b.    And expense recognition principles only.

    c.    And revenue recognition principles only.

    d.    And revenue and expense recognition principles.

**81.** A development stage enterprise

    a.    Issues an income statement that shows only cumulative amounts from the enterprise's inception.

    b.    Issues an income statement that is the same as an established operating enterprise, but does **not** show cumulative amounts from the enterprise's inception as additional information.

    c.    Issues an income statement that is the same as an established operating enterprise, and shows cumulative amounts from the enterprise's inception as additional information.

    d.    Does **not** issue an income statement.

SIMULATION PROBLEMS

**Simulation Problem 1**                 (50 to 60 minutes)

| Situation | | | | | |
|---|---|---|---|---|---|
| | Concepts | Asset Valuation | Depreciation Calculations | Communication | Research |

- Link Co. purchased an office building and the land on which it is located by paying $800,000 cash and assuming an existing mortgage of $200,000. The property is assessed at $960,000 for realty tax purposes, of which 60% is allocated to the building.
- Link leased construction equipment under a seven-year capital lease requiring annual year-end payments of $100,000. Link's incremental borrowing rate is 9%, while the lessor's implicit rate, which is not known to Link, is 8%. Present value factors for an ordinary annuity for seven periods are 5.21 at 8% and 5.04 at 9%. Fair value of the equipment is $515,000.
- Link paid $50,000 and gave a plot of undeveloped land with a carrying amount of $320,000 and a fair value of $450,000 to Club Co. in exchange for a plot of undeveloped land with a fair value of $500,000. The land was carried on Club's books at $350,000. This transaction is considered to lack commercial substance; the configuration of cash flows from the land acquired is not expected to be significantly different from the configuration of cash flows of the land exchanged.

| | Concepts | | | | |
|---|---|---|---|---|---|
| Situation | | Asset Valuation | Depreciation Calculations | Communication | Research |

For **items 1 through 6,** determine for each item whether the expenditure should be capitalized or expensed as a period cost.

| | *Capitalize* | *Expense* |
|---|---|---|
| 1. Freight charges paid for goods held for resale. | O | O |
| 2. In-transit insurance on goods held for resale purchased FOB shipping point. | O | O |
| 3. Interest on note payable for goods held for resale. | O | O |
| 4. Installation of equipment. | O | O |
| 5. Testing of newly purchased equipment. | O | O |
| 6. Cost of current year service contract on equipment. | O | O |

| | | Asset Valuation | | | |
|---|---|---|---|---|---|
| Situation | Concepts | | Depreciation Calculations | Communication | Research |

Calculate the following amounts to be recorded by Link.

*Amount*

1. Building.
2. Leased equipment.
3. Land received from Club on Link's books.
4. Land received from Link on Club's books.

| | | | Depreciation Calculations | | |
|---|---|---|---|---|---|
| Situation | Concepts | Asset Valuation | | Communication | Research |

On January 2, 2006, Link purchased a manufacturing machine for $864,000. The machine has an eight-year estimated life and a $144,000 estimated salvage value. Half expects to manufacture 1,800,000 units over the life of the machine. During 2007, Half manufactured 300,000 units.

Calculate depreciation expense on the manufacturing machine for 2007 for each method listed.

*Amount*

1. Straight-line.
2. Double-declining balance.
3. Sum-of-years' digits.
4. Units of production.

| Situation | Concepts | Asset Valuation | Depreciation Calculations | Communication | Research |
|---|---|---|---|---|---|

Link Co. also rents winter sports equipment to the public. Snowmobiles are depreciated by the double-declining balance method. Before the season began, the estimated lives of several snowmobiles were extended because engines were replaced. Link was given thirty days to pay for the engines. Link gave the old engines to a local mechanic who agreed to provide repairs and maintenance service in the next year equal to the fair value of the engines. Rental skis, poles, and boots are capitalized and depreciated according to the inventory (appraisal) method.

Write a memo to the CEO of Link Co. that explains the following issues:

1.  How should Link account for the purchase of the new engines and the transfer of the old engines to the local mechanic if the old engines' costs are

    a.   Known?
    b.   Unknown?

2.  What are two assumptions underlying use of an accelerated depreciation method?
3.  How should Link calculate the snowmobiles' depreciation?
4.  How should Link calculate and report the costs of the skis, poles, and boots in its balance sheets and income statements?

To:      CEO, Link Co.
From:    CPA Candidate
Re:      Depreciation and sports equipment

| Situation | Concepts | Asset Valuation | Depreciation Calculations | Communication | Research |
|---|---|---|---|---|---|

Research the following issues. Cut and paste the appropriate sections from the professional standards.

1.  **What is the definition of an impaired asset?**

2.  **How is the fair value of an asset determined for impairment purposes?**

3.  **In reporting discontinued operations, how does the accountant determine if the operation qualifies as a component?**

4.  **When there is a gain or loss on an asset that is classified as held-for-sale, where is the gain or loss reported in the financial statements?**

---

**Simulation Problem 2**                                        (50 to 55 minutes)

| Situation | Capitalized Costs | Disposal of Assets | Journal Entry | Balance Sheet Disclosures | Communication | Research |
|---|---|---|---|---|---|---|

Selected accounts included in the property, plant, and equipment section of Carlton Corporation's balance sheet at December 31, 2006, had the following balances:

| | |
|---|---|
| Land | $400,000 |
| Land improvements | 130,000 |
| Buildings | 2,000,000 |
| Machinery and equipment | 800,000 |

During 2007, the following transactions occurred:

1.  A tract of land was acquired for $200,000 as a potential future building site from Alison Corp.
2.  A plant facility consisting of land and building was acquired from Kaufman Company in exchange for 20,000 shares of Carlton's common stock. On the acquisition date, Carlton's stock had a closing market price of $42 per share on a national stock exchange. The plant facility was carried on Kaufman's books at $178,000 for land and $520,000 for the building at the exchange date. Current appraised values for the land and the building, respectively, are $200,000 and $800,000. The building has an expected life of forty years with a $20,000 salvage value.
3.  Items of machinery and equipment were purchased from Apex Equipment at a total cost of $400,000. Additional costs were incurred as follows: freight and unloading, $13,000; installation, $26,000. The equipment has a useful life of ten years with no salvage value.

4. Expenditures totaling $120,000 were made for new parking lots, street, and sidewalks at the corporation's various plant locations. These expenditures had an estimated useful life of fifteen years.
5. Research and development costs were $110,000 for the year.
6. A machine costing $16,000 on January 1, 1999, was scrapped on June 30, 2007. Straight-line depreciation had been recorded on the basis of a 10-year life with no salvage value.
7. A machine was sold for $48,000 on July 1, 2007. Original cost of the machine was $74,000 on January 1, 2004, and it was depreciated on the straight-line basis over an estimated useful life of eight years and a salvage value of $2,000.

| Situation | Capitalized Costs | Disposal of Assets | Journal Entry | Balance Sheet Disclosures | Communication | Research |
|---|---|---|---|---|---|---|

Indicate the capitalized cost of each asset acquired during 2007, and the depreciation expense recorded for each of the acquired items in 2007.

| | *Capitalized cost* | *Depreciation/amortization expense for 2007* |
|---|---|---|
| Land acquired from Alison Corp. | | |
| Land acquired fro Kaufman | | |
| Building acquired from Kaufman | | |
| Machinery and equipment acquired from Apex Equipment | | |
| Land improvements | | |
| Research and development | | |

| Situation | Capitalized Costs | Disposal of Assets | Journal Entry | Balance Sheet Disclosures | Communication | Research |
|---|---|---|---|---|---|---|

Calculate the gain or loss on the disposal of each asset. Place your answer in the appropriate column.

| *Item* | *Amount of gain* | *Amount of loss* |
|---|---|---|
| Scrapped machine on 6/30/07 | | |
| Sale of machine on 7/1/07 | | |

| Situation | Capitalized Costs | Disposal of Assets | Journal Entry | Balance Sheet Disclosures | Communication | Research |
|---|---|---|---|---|---|---|

Prepare the journal entries for the sale of the machine on July 1, 2007. Select your account titles from the following list. Assume depreciation is recorded at the date of disposal for any equipment sold.

Cash
Accumulated depreciation
Equipment
Gain on sale of equipment
Loss on sale of equipment
Depreciation expense

| | *Debit* | *Credit* |
|---|---|---|
| | | |
| | | |
| | | |
| | | |
| | | |
| | | |
| | | |

| Situation | Capitalized Costs | Disposal of Assets | Journal Entry | Balance Sheet Disclosures | Communication | Research |
|---|---|---|---|---|---|---|

Indicate the balances in each of the following accounts as of December 31, 2007. Assume that all depreciation and amortization entries are recorded separately in contra accounts.

|  | Balance as of 12/31/07 |
|---|---|
| Land |  |
| Land improvements |  |
| Buildings |  |
| Equipment and machinery |  |

| Situation | Capitalized Costs | Disposal of Assets | Journal Entry | Balance Sheet Disclosures | Communication | Research |
|---|---|---|---|---|---|---|

Carlton's CEO has contacted you concerning accounting for the impairment of assets. He has presented you with the following list of questions. Prepare a memo to the CEO responding to his questions.

1. Define what is meant by impairment of an operational asset (e.g., equipment).

2. How is the definition of impairment applied in practice? Include in the answer signs or indicators of impairment, loss, determination, and measurement of losses.

3. Describe the accounting and reporting for an impairment loss in current and future periods.

4. How are losses on operational assets that management expects to dispose of measured, accounted for, and reported on the financial statements?

| Situation | Capitalized Costs | Disposal of Assets | Journal Entry | Balance Sheet Disclosures | Communication | Research |
|---|---|---|---|---|---|---|

Research the following accounting issues in the professional literature. You should copy and paste your citation in the space provided.

1. What is meant by impairment of an operational asset?

2. How is the definition of impairment implied in practice?

3. Describe the accounting and reporting for an impairment loss on the income statement in the current period.

4. Describe the information to be disclosed in the notes to the financial statements regarding asset impairment.

5. Describe the accounting for impairment losses on future financial statements.

6. How are losses of operational assets to be sold measured?

---

**Simulation Problem 3**             (45 to 55 minutes)

| Situation | Concepts | Intangible Assets | Expenses Resulting from Intangibles | Goodwill Impairment | Communication | Research |
|---|---|---|---|---|---|---|

During 2007, Broca Co. had the following transactions:

- On January 2, Broca purchased the net assets of Amp Co. for $360,000. The fair value of Amp's identifiable net assets was $172,000. Broca believes that, due to the popularity of Amp's consumer products, the life of the resulting goodwill is unlimited.
- On February 1, Broca purchased a franchise to operate a ferry service from the state government for $60,000 and an annual fee of 1% of ferry revenues. The franchise expires after five years. Broca received $20,000 of ferry revenues in 2007.
- On April 5, Broca was granted a patent that had been applied for by Amp. During 2007, Broca incurred legal costs of $51,000 to register the patent and an additional $85,000 to successfully prosecute a patent infringement suit against a competitor. Broca estimates the patent's economic life to be ten years.

Broca has determined that it is appropriate to amortize these intangibles on the straight-line basis over the maximum period permitted by generally accepted accounting principles, taking a full year's amortization in the year of acquisition.

| Situation | Concepts | Intangible Assets | Expenses Resulting from Intangibles | Goodwill Impairment | Communication | Research |
|---|---|---|---|---|---|---|

Indicate whether each of the following statements is True or False.

|   |   | (T) | (F) |
|---|---|---|---|
| 1. | An intangible asset that is determined to have an indefinite life should be amortized over 40 years. | ○ | ○ |
| 2. | If the carrying value of the intangible asset exceeds its fair value, an impairment loss must be recognized. | ○ | ○ |
| 3. | The impairment test for goodwill must be performed at the end of each fiscal year for each reporting unit. | ○ | ○ |
| 4. | When a company borrows funds to finance a construction project and temporarily invests this cash, the interest expense should be offset against the interest expense to be capitalized. | ○ | ○ |
| 5. | A company may capitalize interest on inventories it regularly produces for resale to customers. | ○ | ○ |
| 6. | Gains are never recognized when similar assets are exchanged. | ○ | ○ |
| 7. | In nonmonetary exchanges, losses are only recognized when cash is received in the transactions. | ○ | ○ |
| 8. | If the fair value of the asset is unknown in a nonmonetary exchange and no gain can be computed, the asset is recorded at the fair market value of the asset given up. | ○ | ○ |
| 9. | A capital expenditure is charged against income over the useful life of the asset. | ○ | ○ |
| 10. | Expenditures to improve the efficiency or extend the useful life of an asset should be capitalized. | ○ | ○ |

| Situation | Concepts | Intangible Assets | Expenses Resulting from Intangibles | Goodwill Impairment | Communication | Research |
|---|---|---|---|---|---|---|

Complete the following schedule for Broca's intangible assets and the related income statement expenses.

**Broca Co.**
**SCHEDULE FOR INTANGIBLE ASSETS AND AMORTIZATION EXPENSE**
**December 31, 2007**

| Item | Valuation *before* adjusting entries | Amortization expense for the year | Valuation on 12/31/07 |
|---|---|---|---|
| Goodwill |  |  |  |
| Franchise (net) |  |  |  |
| Patent (net) |  |  |  |

| Situation | Concepts | Intangible Assets | Expenses Resulting from Intangibles | Goodwill Impairment | Communication | Research |
|---|---|---|---|---|---|---|

Complete the following schedule for Broca's expenses.

**Broca Co.**
**EXPENSES RESULTING FROM INTANGIBLES**
**For the Year Ended December 31, 2007**

| | |
|---|---|
| Amortization: |  |
| Franchise |  |
| Patent |  |
|  |  |
| Franchise fee |  |
| Total expenses |  |

| Situation | Concepts | Intangible Assets | Expenses resulting from intangibles | Goodwill Impairment | Communication | Research |
|---|---|---|---|---|---|---|

Broca Corporation is performing its annual test of the impairment of the goodwill related to its Technology reporting unit. The carrying value of goodwill allocated to the unit is $500,000. Using a multiple of revenue, Broca has determined the fair value of the Technology reporting unit to be $1,700,000 at 12/31/07, and the fair value and carrying value of the assets and liabilities were determined as follows:

|  | *(In 000s)* | |
|---|---|---|
|  | *Carrying value* | *Fair value* |
| Cash | $ 200 | $ 200 |
| Accounts receivable | 250 | 250 |
| Inventory | 350 | 400 |
| Net Equipment | 700 | 700 |
| Patents | 400 | 450 |
| Goodwill | 500 | ? |
| Accounts payable | (200) | (200) |
| Long-term debt | (300) | (300) |
|  | 1,900 | |

1. Calculate the following amounts related to the impairment of goodwill.

   Implied Goodwill              [              ]

   Impairment of Goodwill        [              ]

2. Prepare the related journal entry if there is an impairment of goodwill for the Technology reporting unit.

| | | |
|---|---|---|
| | | |
| | | |

| Situation | Concepts | Intangible Assets | Expenses resulting from intangibles | Goodwill Impairment | Communication | Research |
|---|---|---|---|---|---|---|

Write a brief memo to the CEO of Broca Corporation, explaining the following issues with regard to intangible assets.

1. Describe the characteristics of intangible assets. Discuss the accounting for the purchase or internal development of intangible assets with an indeterminable life, such as goodwill.
2. Over what period should intangible assets be amortized? How should this period be determined?
3. Describe the financial statement disclosure requirements relating to Broca's intangible assets and expenses.

To:     CEO, Broca Corporation
From:   CPA Candidate
Re:     Intangible assets

|  |
|---|
|  |
|  |
|  |

| Situation | Concepts | Intangible Assets | Expenses resulting from intangibles | Goodwill Impairment | Communication | Research |
|---|---|---|---|---|---|---|

Research the following issues. Cut and paste your answer from the professional standards.

1. What assets qualify for capitalization of interest?

2. An asset has been acquired in a nonmonetary exchange that lacks commercial substance. At what amount should this asset be capitalized?

3. At what amount should donated assets be recorded?

## MULTIPLE-CHOICE ANSWERS

| | | | | | |
|---|---|---|---|---|---|
| 1. a __ __ | 18. b __ __ | 35. d __ __ | 52. b __ __ | 69. d __ __ |
| 2. a __ __ | 19. a __ __ | 36. c __ __ | 53. c __ __ | 70. b __ __ |
| 3. b __ __ | 20. d __ __ | 37. b __ __ | 54. b __ __ | 71. c __ __ |
| 4. a __ __ | 21. c __ __ | 38. d __ __ | 55. b __ __ | 72. d __ __ |
| 5. d __ __ | 22. d __ __ | 39. b __ __ | 56. c __ __ | 73. a __ __ |
| 6. a __ __ | 23. c __ __ | 40. d __ __ | 57. b __ __ | 74. b __ __ |
| 7. b __ __ | 24. b __ __ | 41. b __ __ | 58. d __ __ | 75. c __ __ |
| 8. b __ __ | 25. a __ __ | 42. c __ __ | 59. c __ __ | 76. a __ __ |
| 9. b __ __ | 26. b __ __ | 43. c __ __ | 60. d __ __ | 77. b __ __ |
| 10. c __ __ | 27. a __ __ | 44. b __ __ | 61. a __ __ | 78. b __ __ |
| 11. b __ __ | 28. d __ __ | 45. b __ __ | 62. d __ __ | 79. d __ __ |
| 12. c __ __ | 29. b __ __ | 46. c __ __ | 63. c __ __ | 80. a __ __ |
| 13. a __ __ | 30. c __ __ | 47. a __ __ | 64. a __ __ | 81. c __ __ |
| 14. c __ __ | 31. d __ __ | 48. b __ __ | 65. d __ __ | |
| 15. d __ __ | 32. a __ __ | 49. b __ __ | 66. b __ __ | |
| 16. b __ __ | 33. b __ __ | 50. c __ __ | 67. d __ __ | 1st: __/81 = __% |
| 17. d __ __ | 34. c __ __ | 51. c __ __ | 68. b __ __ | 2nd: __/81 = __% |

## MULTIPLE-CHOICE ANSWER EXPLANATIONS

### A. Acquisition Cost

**1.    (a)**   The cost of machinery includes all expenditures incurred in acquiring the asset and preparing it for use. Cost includes the purchase price, freight and handling charges, insurance on the machine while in transit, cost of special foundations, and costs of assembling, installation, and testing. All of the costs given in this problem are properly recorded as the cost of the machine. Therefore the cost to be recorded is $155,000 ($125,000 + $20,000 + $10,000).

**2.    (a)**   Any cost involved in preparing land for its ultimate use (such as a factory site) is considered part of the cost of the land. Before the land can be used as a building site, it must be purchased (involving costs such as purchase price, legal fees, and title insurance) and the old building must be razed (cost of demolition less proceeds from sale of scrap). The total balance in the land account should be $464,000.

| | |
|---|---|
| Purchase price | $400,000 |
| Legal fees | 10,000 |
| Title insurance | 12,000 |
| Net cost of demolition ($50,000 – $8,000) | 42,000 |
| | $464,000 |

### B. Capitalization of Interest

**3.    (b)**   The amount of interest cost which should be capitalized during building construction is the **lower** of **avoidable interest** or **actual interest**. Avoidable interest equals the interest computed on the weighted-average amount of accumulated expenditures on the building ($40,000). Since actual interest is $70,000 ($50,000 + $20,000), the amount capitalized should be $40,000.

**4.    (a)**   The requirement is to calculate the amount of capitalized interest at 12/31/07. The requirements of SFAS 34 for capitalization of interest are met: (1) expenditures for the asset have been made, (2) activities that are necessary to get the asset ready for its intended use are in progress, and (3) interest cost is being incurred. The amount to be capitalized is the lower of avoidable interest or actual interest. Avoidable interest is the average accumulated expenditures multiplied by the appropriate interest rate or rates. Since $2,000,000 was spent on the building evenly throughout the

year, the average accumulated expenditures were $1,000,000 ($2,000,000 ÷ 2) and the avoidable interest was $120,000 ($1,000,000 × 12%). Since actual interest ($102,000) is less than avoidable interest, the actual interest cost is capitalized.

**5.    (d)**   SFAS 34 defines certain assets for which interest costs incurred in their production should be capitalized rather than expensed. Assets which "qualify" for interest capitalization are those constructed or otherwise produced for an enterprise's own use and those intended for sale or lease that are constructed or otherwise produced as **discrete projects**. SFAS 34 further stipulates that the capitalization period shall end when the asset is substantially complete and ready for its intended use. Based upon these criteria, the interest costs associated with the machinery for Bay's own use should be capitalized during the construction period and expensed after completion. Additionally, all costs associated with the machinery held for sale should be expensed because the machinery does not meet the "discrete project" criterion.

### C. Nonmonetary Exchanges

**6.    (a)**   When the investment was acquired, it was recorded at cost—the fair market value of the asset surrendered to acquire it. The July 1 entry was

| | | | |
|---|---|---|---|
| Inv. in Ace stock | 3,000 | | |
| Truck | | 2,500 | |
| Gain on disposal | | 500 | ($3,000 – $2,500) |

The investment would be reported in the 12/31/07 balance sheet at $3,000. The book value of Ace's stock does not affect the amount recorded on Balt's books.

**7.    (b)**   Per SFAS 153, a nonmonetary exchange is recognized at fair value unless the fair value is not determinable, the exchange transaction is to facilitate sales to customers, or the exchange transactions lacks commercial substance. Answer (a) is incorrect, because the exchange must **lack** commercial substance. Answers (c) and (d) are incorrect because SFAS 153 changed APB 29 and there is no longer the distinction of similar or dissimilar assets in nonmonetary exchanges.

**8.    (b)**   Per SFAS 153, a nonmonetary exchange is recognized at fair value unless the fair value is not determinable, the exchange transaction is to facilitate sales to customers, or the exchange transactions lacks commercial substance. Answers (a) and (c) are incorrect; these transactions have commercial substance because there is a significant change in the entity's cash flows as a result of the exchange.

9. **(b)** Per SFAS 153, APB 29, paragraph 21(a) is amended to define that an entity's cash flows are expected to change significantly if the configuration of the cash flows of the asset received differs significantly from the configuration of the cash flows of the asset transferred. The configuration includes the risk, timing, and amount of the cash flows.

10. **(c)** APB 29, paragraph 21(a) (as amended by SFAS 153) provides that a transaction is not given effect for tax purposes unless it serves a legitimate business purpose other than tax avoidance. In assessing the commercial substance of an exchange, tax cash flows arising solely to avoid taxes are not considered. Other cash flows from the nonmonetary exchange are considered.

11. **(b)** The cash price of the new machine represents its fair market value (FMV). The FMV of the old machine can be determined by subtracting the cash portion of the purchase price ($6,000) from the total cost of the new machine: $20,500 – $6,000 = $14,500. Since the book value of the machine ($16,800) exceeds its FMV on the date of the trade-in ($14,500), the difference of $2,300 must be recognized as a loss.

12. **(c)** Because the cash flows of the exchanged assets will not be significantly different, the transaction lacks commercial substances. Therefore, book value is used to record the transition. When the assets are exchanged, boot is received, and a gain results, the exchange is treated as part sale and part exchange. The earnings process is assumed to be complete for the portion relating to the boot received. The gain recognized is computed as follows:

$$\frac{\text{Boot received}}{\text{Boot received} + \text{FMV of assets received}} \times \text{Total gain} = \text{Gain recognized}$$

$$\text{Total Gain} = \underbrace{(17{,}500 + 2{,}500)}_{\substack{\text{Assets received} \\ \text{by Amble}}} - \underbrace{12{,}000}_{\substack{\text{Book value of asset} \\ \text{given up by Beam}}} = 8{,}000$$

The gain recognized would be calculated as follows:

$$\frac{2{,}500}{17{,}500 + 2{,}500} \times 8{,}000 = \$1{,}000 \text{ gain recognized}$$

The asset acquired is recorded at the **book** value of the asset surrendered plus the gain recognized less boot received ($12,000 + $1,000 – $2,500 = $10,500). The journal entry is

| | | |
|---|---|---|
| Truck (new) | 10,500 | |
| Cash | 2,500 | |
|     Truck (old) | | 12,000 |
|     Gain on sale | | 1,000 |

13. **(a)** Per APB 29 if a loss is indicated by the terms of the transaction, the entire loss on the exchange should be recognized. In this case, a loss results because Transit received an asset whose fair value equaled the book value of the asset given up and paid cash. Therefore, Transit gave up more than they given up, the difference being the loss.

14. **(c)** Per SFAS 153, transactions lacking commercial substance are recorded at book value. Per APB 29 when the exchange of nonmonetary assets includes an amount of

monetary consideration, the Board believes that the receiver of monetary consideration has realized a partial gain on the exchange. To determine the partial gain to be recognized, first compute the total gain which is the difference between the fair market value of the nonmonetary asset given up and its book value. Then multiply the ratio of the **monetary** consideration received to the **total** consideration received (i.e., monetary consideration plus the estimated fair market value of the asset received) times the total gain. The result is the realized gain to be recognized. The Board further believes that the entity paying the monetary consideration should **not** recognize any gain until the earnings process is culminated. Note, however, that **all losses** on sales or exchanges are recognized immediately.

15. **(d)** Per APB 29, (as amended by SFAS 153) nonmonetary exchanges of assets that are deemed to have commercial substance are accounted for on the basis of fair values, and both gains and losses recognized. The gain (or loss) for Vik is calculated as the difference between the fair value and cost of the car. Note that the retail/list price of an asset is not always representative of the FMV of the asset. An asset can often be purchased for less than the retail/list price.

16. **(b)** This transaction qualifies as an exception to fair value measurement as per SFAS 153, and should be measured at book value. When these assets are exchanged, in this case inventory, boot is received, and a gain results, the exchange is treated as part sale and part exchange. The earnings process is assumed to be complete for the portion relating to the boot received. The gain recognized is computed as follows:

$$\frac{\text{Boot received}}{\text{Boot received} + \text{FMV of assets received}} \times \text{Total gain} = \text{Gain recognized}$$

$$\text{Total gain} = \underbrace{(130{,}000 + 20{,}000)}_{\substack{\text{Assets received} \\ \text{by Zaro}}} - \underbrace{126{,}000}_{\substack{\text{Book value of asset} \\ \text{given up by Zaro}}} = 24{,}000$$

In this case, it would be calculated as follows:

$$\frac{20{,}000}{(20{,}000 + 130{,}000)} \times 24{,}000 = \$3{,}200$$

17. **(d)** Per APB 29, (as amended by SFAS 153) a transfer of a nonmonetary asset in a nonreciprocal transfer should be recorded at the fair value of the asset transferred, with a gain or loss recognized on the disposition, whether the transfer is made to a stockholder or to another entity.

18. **(b)** A gain (loss) must be recognized when a nonmonetary asset is involuntarily converted into monetary assets even if the company reinvests the monetary assets in replacement nonmonetary assets. The gain or loss is the difference between the insurance proceeds received ($3,500) and the carrying value of the asset destroyed. The unadjusted carrying value ($2,500) must be adjusted for the capital expenditure ($700) which has not yet been recorded. When a major component of an asset like an engine is replaced, the preferred treatment is to take the old component off the books (with a loss recognized) and record the new component. When the book value of the component is unknown (as in this case), the cost of the new component ($700) is simply debited to the accumulated depreciation account. This increases the van's carrying value to $3,200 ($2,500 + $700), which means the gain is $300 ($3,500 –

$3,200). Note that the $500 invoice should be recorded as repairs expense, and therefore does not affect the van's carrying value.

**19. (a)** Per FASB Interpretation 30, involuntary conversions of nonmonetary assets to monetary assets are monetary transactions for which gain or loss shall be recognized even though an enterprise reinvests or is obligated to reinvest the monetary assets in replacement nonmonetary assets. Accordingly, Lano would record the condemnation and replacement of the forest land as two separate transactions. Lano should recognize a gain on the condemnation and subsequently record the replacement land at the total purchase price. The net effect of these events is to increase the amount of forest land on Lano's balance sheet by the excess of the replacement land's cost over the condemned land's carrying amount, as shown below.

### D. Purchase of Groups of Fixed Assets

**20. (d)** The requirement is to determine the amount at which land acquired in a group purchase of fixed assets should be recorded. The total cost ($540,000) of the land and building should be allocated based on their relative fair market value (FMV). Current appraised value is a better indicator of FMV than the seller's original cost. Therefore, the land should be recorded at $216,000.

$$\frac{\text{FMV land}}{\text{Total FMV of assets purchased}} \times \text{Purchase price of group assets}$$

$$\frac{200,000}{500,000} \times 540,000 = \$216,000$$

There is no problem in recording the land at more than its appraised value since value is only an estimate of FMV.

### E. Capital Versus Revenue Expenditures

**21. (c)** The requirement is to calculate the amount to be charged to repair and maintenance expense in 2007. Generally, a cost should be capitalized if it improves the asset and expensed if it merely maintains the asset at its current level. Continuing and frequent repairs ($40,000) should be expensed. Similarly, the cost of repainting the plant building ($10,000) and the cost of partially replacing the roof tiles ($14,000) should be expensed. These are ordinary, regularly occurring expenditures which maintain, rather than improve, the plant building. The work on the electrical wiring system ($32,000) is capitalized instead of expensed since it is a major improvement. Therefore, the total amount expensed is $64,000 ($40,000 + $10,000 + $14,000).

**22. (d)** The cost of the attachment ($84,000) should be capitalized because it is an **addition**. The cost of installing the attachment ($36,000) is also capitalized because this expenditure was required to get the attachment ready for its intended use. The overhaul costs ($26,000 + $14,000 = $40,000) are also capitalized. Even though the overhaul did

not increase useful life, it is a capital expenditure because it increased productivity. The total amount capitalized is $160,000 ($84,000 + $36,000 + $40,000).

**23. (c)** When an entity suffers a casualty loss to an asset, the accounting loss is recorded at the net carrying value of the damaged asset, if known. In this case, the cost and related accumulated depreciation are identifiable. The entity should therefore recognize a loss in the current period equal to the carrying amount of the damaged portion of the building. The refurbishing of the building, which is an economic event separate from the fire damage, should be treated similarly to the purchase of other assets or betterments. The cost of refurbishing the building should therefore be capitalized and depreciated over the shorter of the refurbishment's useful lives or the useful life of the building.

| Loss | xxx | (Plug) |
| Acc. depr. | xxx | |
| Building | | xxx |
| Building | xxx | |
| Cash | | xxx |

Answer (a) is incorrect because in order to reduce the accumulated depreciation account, the useful life of the asset must be extended. In this case, there is no mention of this fact. Answer (d) is incorrect because it fails to recognize the casualty loss and properly remove the cost and accumulated depreciation on the damaged portion of the building from the accounting records.

*NOTE: If the components of the damaged portion are not identifiable, the following entry would be made:*

| Loss | xxx | |
| Cash | | xxx |

**24. (b)** Generally, a cost should be capitalized if it improves the efficiency of the asset or extends its useful life and expensed if it merely maintains the asset at its current level. Since an overall reduction in production costs is expected, efficiency must have been improved by the steps taken by Derby. In this problem, it appears that both the building modification and the production line rearrangement contributed to the improved efficiency in the production process. Therefore, both costs should be capitalized.

### F. Depreciation

**25. (a)** Machinery is recorded at its historical cost, which is measured by the cash or **cash equivalent price** of obtaining the machine and preparing it for use. The journal entry to record this acquisition would be

| Machinery | 110,000 | (cash equiv.) |
| Discount on N.P. | 20,000 | ($130,000 – $110,000) |
| Notes payable | | 120,000 | (24 × $5,000) |
| Cash | | 10,000 | |

The $20,000 discount represents future interest expense (the cost associated with paying for the asset over two years instead of immediately) rather than part of the cost of the machine. Straight-line depreciation for 2007 is computed as follows:

| (Cost – Salvage value) | × | 1/useful life | = | Depr. expense |
| ($110,000 – $5,000) | × | 1/10 | = | $10,500 |

**26. (b)** The formula for 200% double-declining balance (DDB) depreciation is

(Beginning-of-year book value) × DDB rate = Depreciation expense

The DDB rate is two times the straight-line rate (in this case, $1/5 \times 2 = 2/5$ or 40%). Therefore, depreciation for the first two years is

| | | | |
|---|---|---|---|
| 2005: | $50,000 × 40% | = | $20,000 |
| 2006: | ($50,000 – $20,000) × 40% | = | 12,000 |
| | | | $32,000 |

In 2007, Turtle switches to the straight-line method. The book value ($50,000 – $32,000 = $18,000) would be depreciated over the remaining three years (five years less two gone by). Therefore, 2007 depreciation is $6,000 ($18,000 × 1/3) and 12/31/07 accumulated depreciation is $38,000 ($32,000 + $6,000).

**27.   (a)**   The requirement is to calculate the amount of depreciation expense to be recorded in 2008. After three years (2005-2007), accumulated depreciation is $72,000. Therefore, the method that was used was the sum-of-the-years' digits (SYD) method. Using this method, after three years the balance in accumulated depreciation would be 12/15 of the depreciable base (5/15 + 4/15 + 3/15). The depreciable base is the cost ($110,000) less the residual value ($20,000), or $90,000. Thus, using the SYD method, accumulated depreciation at 12/31/07 would be $72,000 ($90,000 × 12/15), which matches the amount given in the problem. 2008 depreciation expense, using the SYD method is $12,000 ($90,000 × 2/15).

**28.   (d)**   From 1/2/04 to 12/31/06, depreciation was recorded using an eight-year life. Yearly depreciation was $33,000 ($264,000 ÷ 8), and accumulated depreciation at 12/31/06 was $99,000 (3 × $33,000). In 2007, the estimated useful life was changed to six years total with a salvage value of $24,000. Therefore, the 12/31/06 book value ($264,000 – $99,000 = $165,000) is depreciated down to the $24,000 salvage value over a remaining useful life of three years (6 years total – 3 years already recorded). The 2007 depreciation expense is $47,000 [($165,000 – $24,000) ÷ 3], increasing accumulated depreciation to $146,000 ($99,000 + $47,000).

**29.   (b)**   The solutions approach is to set up a T-account for **accumulated depreciation** and solve for the unknown.

| Accumulated Depreciation | | | |
|---|---|---|---|
| | | 370,000 | 12/31/06 |
| 2007 retirements | ? | 55,000 | 2007 depr. expense |
| | | 400,000 | 12/31/07 |

The 12/31/06 and 12/31/07 balances were given in the schedule. The 2007 depreciation expense would be recorded by debiting the expense account and crediting accumulated depreciation. The accumulated depreciation would be debited for the property, plant, and equipment retirements. To balance the T-account, the debit must be $25,000. Alternatively, an equation can be used as shown below.

| | | |
|---|---|---|
| $370,000 + $55,000 – X | = | $400,000 |
| 425,000 – X | = | 400,000 |
| X | = | 25,000 |
| | | |
| 370,000 | = | 12/31/06 balance |
| 55,000 | = | 2007 depreciation expense |
| 400,000 | = | 12/31/07 balance |
| X | = | retirements |

**30.   (c)**   After reviewing the different methods, you might realize that the method with the highest carrying amount would result in a loss or

Gain/loss = Proceeds – Carrying amount

$$= 50\% \text{ C} - [\text{C} - 50\% (\text{C} - \text{S})]$$
$$= 50\% \text{ C} - [\text{C} - 50\% (\text{C} - 20\%\text{C})]$$
$$= .5\text{C} - [1.00\text{C} - .5(1.00\text{C} - .2\text{C})]$$
$$= .5\text{C} - [.6\text{C}]$$

Carrying amount > Proceeds

∴ Loss

**31.   (d)**   The formula to compute straight-line depreciation is

$$\frac{\text{Original cost less salvage value}}{\text{Estimated useful life}}$$

The formula to determine depreciation using the productive output method is

$$\frac{\text{Current activity (output)}}{\text{Total expected activity}} \times \text{Original cost less salvage value}$$

Note that both of these methods use cost minus salvage value as the depreciable base of the asset. This means that after all depreciation has been recorded using either method, the net asset will be recorded at salvage value, and accumulated depreciation will equal the original cost minus salvage value.

**32.   (a)**   Depreciation is a method of allocating the cost of an asset in a systematic and rational manner. Since the units-of-production method of depreciation is most appropriate when depreciation is a function of activity, answer (a) is correct. Answer (b) is incorrect because this situation warrants the use of a depreciation method based on the passage of time. Answers (c) and (d) are incorrect because both support the use of an accelerated method of depreciation.

**33.   (b)**   Under the sum-of-the-years' digits (SYD) method, depreciation expense is computed by applying declining fractions to the depreciable cost of the asset. The denominator is the sum of the years in the life of the asset ( 1 + 2 + 3 + 4 + 5 = 15 in this case). Annual depreciation would be computed as follows:

| | | | |
|---|---|---|---|
| 2004 | Original cost less salvage value | x | 5/15 |
| 2005 | Original cost less salvage value | x | 4/15 |
| 2006 | Original cost less salvage value | x | 3/15 |
| 2007 | Original cost less salvage value | x | 2/15 |
| Total | Original cost less salvage value | x | 14/15 |

Accumulated depreciation at December 31, 2007, would be (original cost less salvage value) multiplied by 14/15.

**34.   (c)**   Sum-of-the-years' digits (SYD) depreciation = (Cost less Salvage value) × Applicable fraction.

Where applicable fraction = $\dfrac{\text{Number of years of estimated life remaining as of the beginning of the year}}{\text{SYD}}$

and

$$\text{SYD} = \frac{N(n+1)}{2}$$   Where n = estimated useful life

Calculated as

$$\text{Year 1 (2004)} = \$18,000^* \times \frac{4}{10} = \$7,200$$

$$\text{Year 2 (2005)} = \$18,000^* \times \frac{3}{10} = \$5,400$$

$$\text{Year 3 (2007)} = \$18,000^* \times \frac{2}{10} = \$3,600$$

\* *($20,000 – $2,000)*

On December 31, 2007, the carrying amount of Spiro's asset equals $3,800 (the asset's cost of $20,000 minus accumulated depreciation of $16,200\*\*).

\*\* *($7,200 + $5,400 + $3,600)*

**35. (d)** Line I represents depreciation expense that stays constant over time (i.e., straight-line). Both sum-of-the-years' digits and double-declining balance are accelerated depreciation methods, and hence the depreciation expense for these two methods does not stay constant over time. Line II represents depreciation expense that decreases at a constant rate (i.e., a linear function) and thus would be the pattern of depreciation for sum-of-the-years' digits. Line III represents depreciation expense that decreases at a decreasing rate (i.e., a nonlinear function) and thus would be the pattern of depreciation for the double-declining balance method.

**36. (c)** Composite (group) depreciation averages the service life of a number of property units and depreciates the group as if it were a single unit. The term "group" is used when the assets are similar; the term "composite" is used when they are dissimilar. The mechanical application of both of these methods is identical. The depreciation rate is the following ratio:

$$\frac{\text{Sum of annual SL depreciation of individual assets}}{\text{Total asset cost}}$$

Thus, both group and composite depreciation utilize the straight-line depreciation method.

**37. (b)** The solutions approach is to prepare the journal entry that would be made when an asset is retired under the composite depreciation method.

| | |
|---|---|
| Cash | (cash proceeds) |
| Accumulated depreciation | (plug) |
| Truck | (original cost) |

The net decrease in the carrying amount of the assets is the credit to the asset account less the plug to accumulated depreciation. This amount would be equal to the **cash proceeds received**.

**G. Disposals and Impairment of Value**

**38. (d)** SFAS 144 requires that when management plans to dispose of long-lived assets and limited-lived intangibles, the assets shall be reported at the lower of carrying amount or fair value less cost to sell.

**39. (b)** Per SFAS 144, losses associated with long-lived assets which are to be disposed of are to be reported as a component of income from continuing operations before income taxes for entities preparing income statements. Losses on long-lived assets to be disposed of are neither unusual nor infrequent occurrences. These losses are not part of selling or general and administrative expenses and they are not disclosed net of tax. Discontinued operations result from disposal of a separate business component.

**40. (d)** In 2006, Taft recognized a loss on the long-lived assets that were to be sold and changed the carrying amount of these assets to fair value less cost to sell. In 2007, the assets have still not been sold. The loss recognized has been more than recovered. Per SFAS 144, subsequent revisions in estimates of fair value less cost to sell shall be reported as adjustments of the carrying amount of an asset to be disposed of. However, the carrying amount may not be increased above the carrying amount prior to impairment. The same amount recognized as a loss in 2006 would be recognized as a recovery (gain) in the 2007 income statement.

**41. (b)** According to SFAS 144, the reduced carrying amount of Cranston's assets ($920,000) should be accounted for as their new cost, and this amount should be depreciated over the remaining useful life of five years. Restoration of previously recognized impairment losses is prohibited. Therefore, Cranston should report .80 × $920,000 or $736,000 as the carrying amount of its impaired long-lived assets on its December 31, 2007 balance sheet.

**42. (c)** The requirement is to determine when an asset is impaired. An asset is impaired when the sum of the expected future cash flows is less than the carrying amount of the asset. Per SFAS 144, the expected future cash flows are **not** discounted and do not consider interest charges. Answer (c) refers to one way to measure a loss once it has been determined that an asset has been impaired.

**43. (c)** The loss on impairment is calculated by subtracting the machine's actual fair value from its carrying value at the date of impairment.

| | | | |
|---|---|---|---|
| $10,000 | Initial cost of machine | $10,000 | Cost on 7/1/05 |
| – 500 | Salvage value | – 2,375 | Accumulated depreciation |
| $ 9,500 | Depreciable base | $ 7,625 | Carrying value on 12/31/07 |
| ÷ 10 | Year life | – 3,000 | Actual fair value on 12/31/07 |
| $950 | Depreciation per year | $ 4,625 | Loss on impairment |
| x 2.5 | Years (7/1/05 - 12/31/07) | | |
| $ 2,375 | Accumulated depreciation | | |

**44. (b)** Under SFAS 144, when an asset has been determined to be impaired, it is written down to fair value and loss on impairment is recognized. SFAS 144 specifically states that restoration of previously recognized impairment losses is prohibited.

**45. (b)** According to SFAS 144, a long-lived asset is considered impaired if the future cash flows expected to result from the use of the asset and its eventual disposition are less than the carrying amount of the asset. If deemed impaired, the asset's carrying value is reduced to fair value and a loss on impairment is recognized for the difference (Carrying value – Fair value). In this case, the asset is **not** impaired, as the net cash inflows of $175,000 are greater than the 8/31/07 carrying amount (book value) of $170,000. Therefore, the carrying amount of the asset ($170,000) remains unchanged.

**46. (c)** SFAS 144, states, "an impairment loss for assets to be held and used shall be reported as a component of income from continuing operations before income taxes for entities presenting an income statement and in the statement of activities of a not-for-profit organization. Although there is no requirement to report a subtotal such as "income from operations," entities that present such a subtotal must include the impairment loss in that subtotal.

**47.** **(a)** The undiscounted expected future cash flows ($175,000) are less than the carrying amount of the equipment ($200,000). Therefore, the equipment is deemed impaired. The impairment loss is calculated in the following way:

| | |
|---|---|
| Carrying amount of the equipment on December 31, 2007 | $200,000 |
| Fair value of the equipment on December 31, 2007 | 125,000 |
| Impairment loss reported on 2007 income statement | $ 75,000 |

**48.** **(b)** According to SFAS 144, "after an impairment loss is recognized, the reduced carrying amount of the asset shall be accounted for as its new cost." This new cost (the fair value of the asset at the date of impairment, or $135,000) shall be depreciated over the asset's remaining useful life (twenty-seven months). Therefore, the depreciation expense for June is $5,000 ($135,000 ÷ 27 months × 1 month).

**49.** **(b)** Per SFAS 144, recoveries of impairment losses shall not be recognized.

**50.** **(c)** According to SFAS 144, the loss due to impairment of long-lived assets is measured by deducting the asset's fair value from the carrying (book) value.

**51.** **(c)** SFAS 144 requires long-lived assets and limited lived intangibles to be reviewed for impairment whenever circumstances and situations change such that there is an indication that the carrying amount might not be recoverable. A specific time frame for review of asset impairment, every year or every three years, is not required.

**52.** **(b)** The undiscounted expected future cash flows ($300,000) are less than the carrying amount of the equipment ($350,000). Thus, the equipment is determined to be impaired. The impairment loss is calculated as follows:

| | |
|---|---|
| Carrying value - 12/31/07 | $350,000 |
| Fair value - 12/31/07 | 250,000 |
| Impairment loss reported on 2007 income statement | $100,000 |

**53.** **(c)** According to SFAS 144, after an impairment loss is recognized, the reduced carrying amount of the asset shall be accounted for as its new cost. This new cost (the fair value of the asset at the date of impairment, or $261,000) shall be depreciated over the asset's remaining useful life (58 months). Therefore, the depreciation expense for September is $4,500 ($261,000 ÷ 58 months × 1 month).

**H.   Depletion**

**54.** **(b)** The depletion charge per unit is the **depletion base** (net cost of the resource) divided by the **estimated units of the resource**. Vorst's depletion base is $2,880,000, as computed below.

| | |
|---|---|
| Cost of mine | $2,640,000 |
| Development cost | 360,000 |
| Restoration cost | 180,000 |
| Residual value | (300,000) |
| | $2,880,000 |

Note that the present value of the restoration costs are recorded as required by SFAS 143. The depletion charge is $2.40 per ton ($2,880,000 ÷ 1,200,000 tons). Since 60,000 tons were removed and sold, depletion of $144,000 (60,000

× $2.40) is included in Vorst's 2007 income statement. Note that the amount of depletion included in the income statement depends on the tons **sold**. If more tons were removed than sold, part of the depletion would be included in the cost of ending inventory rather than in the income statement.

**J.   Intangible Assets (SFAS 142)**

**55.** **(b)** The software should be valued at the lower of its unamortized cost or its net realizable value. The software's unamortized cost is $450,000, which is equal to $600,000 – $150,000 ($600,000/4). Answer (c) is incorrect because the software's unamortized cost is less than its net realizable value.

**56.** **(c)** Judd Company would record the trademark at its cost of $500,000. The unamortized cost on the seller's books ($380,000) is irrelevant to the buyer. The trademark has a remaining useful life of fifty years. Therefore, the 2007 amortization expense and 12/31/07 accumulated amortization is $10,000 ($500,000 ÷ 50 years).

**57.** **(b)** SFAS 142 states that a company should record as an asset the cost of intangible assets such as goodwill **acquired from other entities**. SFAS 142 also states that **costs of developing** intangible assets such as goodwill "which are not specifically identifiable, have indeterminate lives, or are inherent in a continuing business and related to an entity as a whole" should be expensed when incurred. Therefore, only the $200,000 (and not the additional $80,000) should be capitalized as goodwill. In accordance with SFAS 142 goodwill should not be amortized.

**58.** **(d)** In determining the useful life of an intangible, SFAS 142 indicates that consideration should be given to the legal, regulatory or contractual life, including rights to extension. Since Northern has the ability and intent to renew the rights indefinitely, the intangible should not be amortized.

**59.** **(c)** Before 2007, Lava would record total amortization of $27,000 [($90,000 × 1/10) × 3 years], resulting in a 12/31/06 carrying amount of $63,000 ($90,000 – $27,000). Since the patent became worthless at 12/31/07 due to government prohibition of the product, the entire carrying amount ($63,000) should be charged against income in 2007 as an impairment loss.

**60.** **(d)** SFAS 142 states that goodwill should not be amortized. Instead, goodwill remains at the amount established at the time of the business combination unless it is determined to be impaired. SFAS 142 requires the testing of goodwill for impairment annually, or more often if events and circumstances indicate that goodwill may be impaired.

**61.** **(a)** Costs incurred in connection with securing a patent, as well as attorney's fees and other unrecovered costs of a successful legal suit to protect the patent, can be capitalized as part of patent costs. Therefore, answer (a) is correct because legal fees and other costs incurred to successfully defend a patent should be amortized along with the acquisition cost over the remaining economic life of the patent. Answer (b) is incorrect because legal fees and other direct costs incurred in registering a patent should be capitalized and amortized on a straight-line basis over its economic life, not five years. Answers (c) and (d) are incorrect because research and development costs related to the development of the product, process or idea that is subsequently patented must be expensed as incurred, not capitalized and amortized.

**62.   (d)**   SFAS 142 requires goodwill to be allocated to reporting units which are operating segments of the business or one level below. Goodwill is also tested for impairment at the level of the reporting unit.

**63.   (c)**   Goodwill impairment is determined at the level of the individual reporting unit. It is the difference between the carrying amount of goodwill and its implied value. The carrying amounts of goodwill of the Retailing and Service reporting units are greater than their implied values. Therefore, an impairment loss should be recognized in the amount of $15,000 ($30,000 + $20,000) – ($25,000 + $10,000).

**64.   (a)**   There are two steps in the test of impairment of goodwill. The first is to compare the carrying value of the reporting unit to its fair value. If the fair value exceeds the carrying value there is no need to perform the second step of valuing the unit's assets and liabilities. Goodwill is never tested at the entity level.

**65.   (d)**   Since the fair value of the reporting unit is less than its carrying amount, the second step in the test should be performed. The assets and liabilities of the unit should be valued and compared to value of the total unit. The implied value of goodwill is the difference. The impairment is equal to the difference between the implied value and the carrying amount of the goodwill.

## K.   Reporting on the Costs of Start-Up Activities

**66.   (b)**   Start-up activities are defined broadly as those onetime activities related to opening a new facility as well as introducing a new product or service and conducting business in a new territory (SOP 98-5). Certain costs that may be incurred in conjunction with start-up activities are not subject to these provisions. These costs include the costs of acquiring long-lived assets such as production equipment, costs of advertising, and license fees, and are not subject to the provisions of SOP 98-5. Answer (b) which includes the costs of training local employees ($120,000) and travel costs of salaried employees ($40,000) is the correct answer.

**67.   (d)**   Organization costs are those incurred in the formation of a corporation. Per SOP 98-5, these costs should be expensed as incurred. The rationale is that uncertainty exists concerning the future benefit of these costs in future years. Thus, they are properly recorded as an expense in 2006.

**68.   (b)**   According to SOP 98-5, the costs of raising capital and the costs of acquiring or constructing long-lived assets and getting them ready for their intended use are not expensed as incurred. Such costs should be accounted for in accordance with other existing authoritative accounting literature. Research and development (R&D) costs are expensed as incurred per SFAS 2.

## L.   Research and Development Costs (SFAS 2)

**69.   (d)**   Research and development (R&D) costs are defined in SFAS 2. SFAS 2 provides detailed lists of examples of activities that would be included in R&D costs and expenses, and that would be excluded from R&D costs and possibly capitalized. Among those items listed as being part

of R&D costs are design of tools, jigs, molds, and dies involving new technology ($125,000) and modification of the formulation of a process ($160,000), for a total R&D expense of $285,000. Included in the items listed in SFAS 2 as **not** being part of R&D costs are troubleshooting breakdowns during production ($100,000), and adaptation of existing capability for a specific customer ($110,000).

**70.   (b)**   Per SFAS 2, all R&D costs must be expensed when incurred. However, R&D costs incurred when performing R&D work under contract for other entities are specifically excluded from the requirements of SFAS 2. Generally such costs are deferred and matched with revenue under the completed-contract or percentage-of-completion method. The other costs listed would all be expensed in 2007. Therefore, Ball's 2007 research and development expense is $1,380,000 ($300,000 + $700,000 + $200,000 + $180,000).

**71.   (c)**   Per SFAS 2, all R&D costs are to be charged to expense when incurred. SFAS 2 specifically includes as R&D costs the cost of designing, constructing, and testing preproduction prototypes, and the cost of R&D equipment (unless it has alternative future uses). Therefore, $340,000 ($60,000 + $200,000 + $80,000) is classified as R&D costs and expensed. The legal costs incurred to obtain a patent ($10,000) are capitalized in the patents account.

**72.   (d)**   In SFAS 2, the FASB excludes from its definitions of research and development expense the acquisition, development, or improvement of a product or process for use in its **selling or administrative activities**. Both costs given in this problem relate to selling or administrative activities, so the expenditures of $175,000 would not be reported as research and development expense.

**73.   (a)**   SFAS 2 requires research and development costs to be expensed as incurred except for fixed assets, intangible assets, or materials purchased that have alternative future uses. Tambon purchased equipment to be used for research and development, but the equipment can only be used for that project. Therefore, the cost of the equipment must be expensed in 2007 as it has no alternative future uses.

## M.   Computer Software Costs (SFAS 86)

**74.   (b)**   Costs incurred in creating a computer software product should be charged to research and development expense when incurred until **technological feasibility** has been established for the product. Technological feasibility is established upon completion of a detailed program design or working model. In this case, $23,000 would be recorded as expense ($13,000 for completion of detailed program design and $10,000 for coding and testing to establish technological feasibility). Costs incurred from the point of technological feasibility until the time when product costs are incurred are capitalized as software costs. In this situation, $59,000 is capitalized as software cost ($24,000 + $20,000 + $15,000). Product costs that can be easily associated with the inventory items are reported as inventory (in this case, $25,000 for duplication of computer software and training materials and $9,000 of packaging costs, for a total of $34,000).

**75.   (c)**   Costs incurred in creating a computer software product should be charged to research and development expense when incurred until **technological feasibility** has been established. Technological feasibility is established upon completion of a detailed program design or working model. In this case, $23,000 would be recorded as expense ($13,000 for completion of detailed program design and $10,000 for coding and testing to establish technological feasibility). Costs incurred from the point of technological feasibility until the time when product costs are incurred are capitalized as software costs. In this situation, $59,000 is capitalized as software cost ($24,000 + $20,000 + $15,000). Product costs that can be easily associated with the inventory items are reported as inventory (in this case, $25,000 for duplication of computer software and training materials and $9,000 of packaging costs, for a total of $34,000).

**76. (a)** Per SFAS 86, the annual amortization of capitalized software costs shall be the greater of

1.  The ratio of the software's current sales to its expected total sales, or
2.  The straight-line method over the economic life of the product.

In this case, the ratio of current to expected total sales is 30% (given). The annual straight-line rate is 20% per year (1 ÷ economic life of five years). The 30% amortization should be recorded in 2007, since it is the higher of the two. The unamortized cost on the 12/31/07 balance sheet should, therefore, be 70% (100% – 30% amortization). Note that SFAS 86 requires that the unamortized cost of capitalized software products must be compared to the net realizable value of those assets at each balance sheet date. Any excess of the amortized cost over the net realizable value must be written off. In this case, the net realizable value (90%) was **above** the unamortized cost (70%), so no additional write-off was required.

**77. (b)** According to SOP 98-1, *Accounting for the Costs of Computer Software Developed or Obtained for Internal Use*, internal-use software is software having the following characteristics: (1) The software is acquired, internally developed, or modified solely to meet the entity's internal needs, and (2) during the software's development or modification, no substantive plan exists to market the software externally.

**78. (b)** Application and development costs create probable future benefit. Therefore, they should be capitalized as incurred. However, preliminary costs are similar to research and development costs and are expensed as incurred, not capitalized.

**79. (d)** Preliminary costs are similar to research and development costs; therefore, they are expensed as incurred. Postimplementation costs such as training are not considered software development costs at all and are expensed as incurred.

### N.  Development Stage Enterprises (SFAS 7)

**80. (a)** Per SFAS 7, a development stage enterprise shall follow the same revenue and expense recognition principles and issue the same basic financial statements as an established operating enterprise, but shall disclose certain additional information. Per SFAS 7, a development stage company shall use the same generally accepted accounting principles that apply to established operating enterprises to govern the recognition of revenue and to determine whether a cost is to be capitalized or expensed as incurred.

**81. (c)** Per SFAS 7, a development stage enterprise shall issue the same basic financial statements as an established operating enterprise, but shall disclose certain additional information. An income statement, in addition to showing amounts of revenues and expenses for each period covered by the income statement, shall include the cumulative amounts from the enterprise's inception.

SOLUTIONS TO SIMULATION PROBLEMS

**Simulation Problem 1**

| Situation | Concepts | Asset Valuation | Depreciation Calculations | Communication | Research |
|---|---|---|---|---|---|

| | | | | *Capitalize* | *Expense* |
|---|---|---|---|---|---|
| 1. | Freight charges paid for goods held for resale. | | | ● | ○ |
| 2. | In-transit insurance on goods held for resale purchased FOB shipping point. | | | ● | ○ |
| 3. | Interest on note payable for goods held for resale. | | | ○ | ● |
| 4. | Installation of equipment. | | | ● | ○ |
| 5. | Testing of newly purchased equipment. | | | ● | ○ |
| 6. | Cost of current year service contract on equipment. | | | ○ | ● |

**Explanation of solutions**

**Items 1 through 6** represent questions concerning expenditures for goods held for resale and equipment and whether these expenditures should be capitalized or expensed as a period cost. The general concept that determines whether expenditures should be product costs and, therefore, capitalized or expensed as period costs is whether or not these expenditures "attach" themselves to the assets of inventory or equipment. Costs that "attach" themselves to assets are those that are directly connected with bringing the goods or equipment to the place of business of the buyer and converting such goods to a salable (inventory) or unusable (equipment) condition.

1. **(C)** Freight charges are directly connected with bringing the goods to the place of business of the buyer.

2. **(C)** Insurance charges are directly connected with bringing the goods to the place of business of the buyer.

3. **(E)** Only interest costs related to continued assets constructed for internal use or assets produced as discrete products for sale or lease should be capitalized. The informational benefit of capitalization does not justify the cost of the accounting for the interest as a product cost.

4. **(C)** Direct cost of bringing the equipment to the buyer.

5. **(C)** Direct cost of converting the equipment to a usable condition.

6. **(E)** Does not relate to bringing the equipment to the buyer or putting it into a usable condition.

| Situation | Concepts | Asset Valuation | Depreciation Calculations | Communication | Research |
|---|---|---|---|---|---|

1.  **($600,000)** Since the land and building were purchased together, the cost of each must be allocated based on the relative market value. The land and building were purchased together for a total cost of $1,000,000 ($800,000 cash + $200,000 mortgage assumption). For property tax purposes, the building is deemed to be 60% of the value of the land and building. Therefore, the cost of the building should be recorded at $600,000 ($1,000,000 × 60%).

2.  **($504,000)** As the lease is classified as a capital lease, Link must record an asset and liability based on the present value of the minimum lease payments. However, the leased assets cannot be recorded at an amount greater than the fair value. To determine the minimum value of the lease payments, Link should discount the future payments using the **lesser** of the lessee's (Link's) incremental borrowing rate (9%) or the lessor's implicit rate if **known** by the lessee. Therefore, since Link does not know the lessor's implicit rate, Link's rate of 9% should be used. The recorded value would be $100,000 × 5.04 = $504,000, which is less than the fair value.

3.  **($370,000)** In recording a nonmonetary exchange, if the transaction lacks commercial substance, the asset received is recorded at the book value of the asset given up plus any boot given when gains and losses are not recognized. The following fact pattern exists for Link:

| | *Boot* | *FV* | *BV* | *Gain (Loss)* |
|---|---|---|---|---|
| Land given | 50,000 | 450,000 | 320,000 | 130,000 |
| Land received | | 500,000 | | |

Link will record the land received from Club at the book value of the land given up plus the boot given ($320,000 + 50,000 = $370,000).

An alternative method to calculate the value to record the land at is to subtract the deferred gain from the fair value of the land received ($500,000 – 130,000 = $370,000).

**4.** **($315,000)** On Club's books the following situation exists:

|  | *Boot* | *FV* | *BV* | *Gain (Loss)* |
|---|---|---|---|---|
| Land given |  | 500,000 | 350,000 | 150,000 |
| Land received | 50,000 | 450,000 |  |  |

An exception to the nonrecognition of gain on similar assets exists when boot is received. The earnings process is considered complete for the portion related to the boot received, but not complete for the portion related to the asset received. A gain is recognized only for the portion related to the boot. The gain is computed as follows:

$$\frac{\text{Boot received}}{\text{Boot received} + \text{FMV of assets received}} \times \text{Total gain} = \text{Gain recognized}$$

$$\frac{50,000}{50,000 + 450,000} \times 150,000 = \$15,000$$

The land received will be recorded at its fair value less the gain deferred.

$$\$450,000 - (150,000 - 15,000) = \$315,000.$$

An alternative method is to record the land received at the book value of the land given less the boot received plus the gain recognized, as follows:

$$\$350,000 - 50,000 + 15,000 = \$315,000.$$

| Situation | Concepts | Asset Valuation | **Depreciation Calculations** | Communication | Research |
|---|---|---|---|---|---|

**1.** **($90,000)** Under the straight-line method of depreciation, the depreciation expense would be calculated as follows:

$$\frac{\text{Cost salvage value}}{\text{Estimated life}} = \frac{\$864,000 - 144,000}{8} = \$90,000$$

Depreciation expense would be $90,000 for all eight years, 2006-2013.

**2.** **($162,000)** The double-declining balance method is calculated by taking two times the straight-line rate times the net book value at the beginning of each year, but not below the salvage value. Furthermore the salvage value is not deducted to arrive at the depreciable base. The calculation would be as follows:

|  | *NBV* |  | *Depreciation expense* |
|---|---|---|---|
| 2006 | $864,000 \times (1/8 \times 2)$ | = | $216,000 |
| 2007 | $(\$864,000 - 216,000) \times (1/8 \times 2)$ | = | $162,000 |

**3.** **($140,000)** Under the sum-of-the-years' digits method, the depreciation expense is calculated as follows:

$$2006 \quad 8 \div \frac{8(8+1)}{2} \times (\$864,000) - \$144,000 = \$160,000$$

$$2007 \quad (7 \div 36) \times (\$864,000 - \$144,000) = \$140,000$$

**4.** **($120,000)** The units of production method is a type of physical usage depreciation that is based on activity. The formula is as follows:

$$\frac{\text{Current activity/output}}{\text{Total expected activity/output}} \times \text{Depreciable base} = \text{Annual depreciation}$$

Depreciation expense for 2007 is calculated as follows:

$$\frac{300,000 \text{ units}}{1,800,000 \text{ units}} \times (\$864,000 - \$144,000) = \$120,000$$

| Situation | Concepts | Asset Valuation | Depreciation Calculations | **Communication** | Research |
|---|---|---|---|---|---|

To:     CEO, Link Co.
From:   CPA Candidate
Re:      Depreciation and sports equipment

     Thank you for your inquiry regarding accounting for snowmobiles and other winter sports equipment used in your business.

     The proper accounting for the purchase of the new snowmobile engines depends on whether the costs of the old engines are known. When the old engines' costs are known, the snowmobiles account is decreased by the old engines' costs and accumulated depreciation is decreased by the accumulated depreciation on the old engines. The net difference between the old engines' carrying amounts and their fair values is recorded as an operating gain or loss. To record the new engines' acquisition, both the snowmobiles account and accounts payable are increased by the new engines' costs.

     If the old engines' costs are unknown, then either the snowmobiles account would be increased or accumulated depreciation would be decreased by the difference between the new engines' costs and the old engines' fair values.

Several assumptions underlie the use of an accelerated depreciation method. The first assumption is that an asset is more productive in the earlier years of its estimated useful life. Therefore, greater depreciation charges in the earlier years would be matched against the greater revenues generated in the earlier years. The second assumption is that repair and maintenance costs are often higher in later periods and an accelerated depreciation method results in a more nearly annual constant total cost over the years of use. Finally, an asset may become obsolete before the end of its originally estimated useful life. The risk associated with estimated long-term cash flows is greater than the risk associated with near-term cash flows. Accelerated depreciation recognizes this condition.

If Link uses double-declining balance depreciation, the accountant should calculate snowmobile depreciation by applying twice the straight-line rate to their carrying amounts. The entry to record depreciation is to debit depreciation expense and credit the accumulated depreciation account. This results in the asset being presented on the statement of financial position at book value.

Under the inventory (appraisal) method, Link should calculate the ending undepreciated cost on the skis, poles, and boots by multiplying the physical quantities of these items on hand by an appraised amount. This ending undepreciated cost is classified as a noncurrent asset. Depreciation included in continuing operations equals the sum of the beginning balance and purchases for the year less ending undepreciated cost.

If you have any questions, please contact my office.

| Situation | Concepts | Asset Valuation | Depreciation Calculations | Communication | Research |
|---|---|---|---|---|---|

**1.** What is the definition of an impaired asset?

**FAS144, Para 7 or Current Text I08.142**

7. For purposes of this Statement, impairment is the condition that exists when the carrying amount of a long-lived asset (asset group) exceeds its fair value. An impairment loss shall be recognized only if the carrying amount of a long-lived asset (asset group) is not recoverable and exceeds its fair value. The carrying amount of a long-lived asset (asset group) is not recoverable if it exceeds the sum of the undiscounted cash flows expected to result from the use and eventual disposition of the asset (asset group). That assessment shall be based on the carrying amount of the asset (asset group) at the date it is tested for recoverability, whether in use (paragraph 19) or under development (paragraph 20). An impairment loss shall be measured as the amount by which the carrying amount of a long-lived asset (asset group) exceeds its fair value.

**2.** How is the fair value of an asset determined for impairment purposes?

**FAS144, Para 22 or Current Text I08.157**

22. The fair value of an asset (liability) is the amount at which that asset (liability) could be bought (incurred) or sold (settled) in a current transaction between willing parties, that is, other than in a forced or liquidation sale. 12 Quoted market prices in active markets are the best evidence of fair value and shall be used as the basis for the measurement, if available. However, in many instances, quoted market prices in active markets will not be available for the long-lived assets (asset groups) covered by this Statement. In those instances, the estimate of fair value shall be based on the best information available, including prices for similar assets (groups) and the results of using other valuation techniques.

**3.** In reporting discontinued operations, how does the accountant determine if the operation qualifies as a component?

**FAS144, Para 41 or Current Text I14.102**

41. For purposes of this Statement, a component of an entity comprises operations and cash flows that can be clearly distinguished, operationally and for financial reporting purposes, from the rest of the entity. A component of an entity may be a reportable segment or an operating segment (as those terms are defined in paragraph 10 of Statement 131), a reporting unit (as that term is defined in Statement 142), a subsidiary, or an asset group (as that term is defined in paragraph 4).

**4.** When there is a gain or loss on an asset that is classified as held-for-sale, where is the gain or loss reported in the financial statements?

**FAS144, Para 45 or Current Text D60.118**

45. A gain or loss recognized for a long-lived asset (disposal group) classified as held for sale that is not a component of an entity shall be included in income from continuing operations before income taxes in the income statement of a business enterprise and in income from continuing operations in the statement of activities of a not-for-profit organization. If a subtotal such as "income from operations" is presented, it shall include the amounts of those gains or losses.

**Simulation Problem 2**

| Situation | Capitalized Costs | | Disposal of Assets | Journal Entry | Balance Sheet Disclosures | Communication | Research |
|---|---|---|---|---|---|---|---|

| | Capitalized cost | Depreciation/amortization expense for 2007 |
|---|---|---|
| Land acquired from Alison Corp. | $200,000 | 0 |
| Land acquired fro Kaufman | 168,000 | 0 |
| Building acquired from Kaufman | 672,000 | 16,300 |
| Machinery and equipment acquired from Apex Equipment | 439,000 | 43,900 |
| Land improvements | 120,000 | 8,000 |
| Research and development | 0 | 0 |

### Explanation of solutions

- Allocation of the land and building for purchase from Kaufman:  FMV = 20,000 shares × $42 per share = $840,000.
- Allocate based on relative fair values.  Therefore, land is $840,000 × $200,000/$1,000,000 = $168,000; Building is $840,000 × $800,000/$1,000,000 = $672,000.  Land is not depreciated. Building is depreciated ($672,000 – $20,000)/40 years = $16,300.
- Items of machinery and equipment should capitalize all costs to get the asset in its intended and useful place.
- Land improvements are depreciated over fifteen years.  $120,000/15 years = $8,000 per year.
- Research and development costs should be expensed as incurred.  They are not capitalized, and they are not depreciated.

| Situation | Capitalized Costs | Disposal of Assets | Journal Entry | Balance Sheet Disclosures | Communication | Research |
|---|---|---|---|---|---|---|

| Item | Amount of gain | Amount of loss |
|---|---|---|
| Scrapped machine on 6/30/07 | | $4,000 |
| Sale of machine on 7/1/07 | $5,500 | |

| Situation | Capitalized Costs | Disposal of Assets | Journal Entry | Balance Sheet Disclosures | Communication | Research |
|---|---|---|---|---|---|---|

| | Debit | Credit |
|---|---|---|
| Depreciation expense | 4,500 | |
| Accumulated depreciation | | 4,500 |
| | | |
| Cash | 48,000 | |
| Accumulated depreciation | 31,500 | |
| Equipment | | 74,000 |
| Gain on sale of equipment | | 5,500 |

| Situation | Capitalized Costs | Disposal of Assets | Journal Entry | Balance Sheet Disclosures | Communication | Research |
|---|---|---|---|---|---|---|

| | Balance as of 12/31/07 |
|---|---|
| Land | 768,000 |
| Land improvements | 250,000 |
| Buildings | 2,672,000 |
| Equipment and machinery | 1,149,000 |

### Explanation of solutions

- Land $400,000 + $200,000 + $168,000 = $768,000
- Land improvements $130,000 + $120,000 = $250,000.
- Buildings $2,000,000 + $672,000 = $2,672,000
- Equipment and machinery $800,000 + New equipment $439,000 – $16,000 scrapped equipment – $74,000 sold equipment = $1,149,000

| Situation | Capitalized Costs | Disposal of Assets | Journal Entry | Balance Sheet Disclosures | Communication | Research |
|-----------|-------------------|--------------------|---------------|---------------------------|---------------|----------|

Below are items to include in your memo to the client.

1. An operational asset is impaired if some or all of the carrying amount of that asset will not be recovered.

2. An asset could be impaired if one or more of the following conditions exists:

   - Significant decrease in market value
   - Change in way the asset is used or physical change in asset
   - Legal factors or change in business climate that might affect asset's fair value or adverse action or assessment by regulator
   - Asset cost incurred greater than planned
   - Operating or cash flow losses from the asset

   If at least one of these conditions exists, a recoverability test shall be performed. Under this test, a loss on operational assets shall be recognized if the expected total net future cash flows are less than the carrying amounts of the assets. Assets should be grouped at lowest level for which there are identifiable cash flows independent of other groupings. Expected net future cash flows are future cash inflows to be generated by the assets less the future cash outflows expected to be necessary to obtain those inflows. Expected future cash flows are not discounted. If the ability to recover the asset is not demonstrated (sum of future cash flows < carrying amount) a loss shall be measured and recorded. The loss is measured as the difference between the fair value of the asset(s) and their carrying amounts.

3. A loss is recognized in the current period by a debit to an impairment loss account and a credit to accumulated depreciation. In future periods, if additional impairment is confirmed, an additional loss shall be recognized. However, recoveries of losses recognized in prior periods are not permitted. Impairment losses are reported in income from continuing operations.

4. In situations in which management has made a decision to dispose of an asset, such asset should be recorded at the lower of the asset's carrying amount or net realizable value (NRV). These assets shall no longer be depreciated. In future periods, recoveries are permitted, but are limited to losses previously recognized on these assets. Losses recognized are reported as part of income from continuing operations. The assets to be disposed of shall be reported under other assets on the company's balance sheet.

| Situation | Capitalized Costs | Disposal of Assets | Journal Entry | Balance Sheet Disclosures | Communication | Research |
|-----------|-------------------|--------------------|---------------|---------------------------|---------------|----------|

1. What is meant by impairment of an operational asset?

**Recognition and Measurement of an Impairment Loss**
**FAS144, Para 7 or Current Text I08.142**

7. For purposes of this Statement, impairment is the condition that exists when the carrying amount of a long-lived asset (asset group) exceeds its fair value. An impairment loss shall be recognized only if the carrying amount of a long-lived asset (asset group) is not recoverable and exceeds its fair value. The carrying amount of a long-lived asset (asset group) is not recoverable if it exceeds the sum of the undiscounted cash flows expected to result from the use and eventual disposition of the asset (asset group). That assessment shall be based on the carrying amount of the asset (asset group) at the date it is tested for recoverability, whether in use (paragraph 19) or under development (paragraph 20). An impairment loss shall be measured as the amount by which the carrying amount of a long-lived asset (asset group) exceeds its fair value.

2. How is the definition of impairment implied in practice?

**When to Test a Long-Lived Asset for Recoverability**
**FAS144, Para 8 or Current Text I08.143**

8. A long-lived asset (asset group) shall be tested for recoverability whenever events or changes in circumstances indicate that its carrying amount may not be recoverable. The following are examples of such events or changes in circumstances:

   a. A significant decrease in the market price of a long-lived asset (asset group).
   b. A significant adverse change in the extent or manner in which a long-lived asset (asset group) is being used or in its physical condition.
   c. A significant adverse change in legal factors or in the busi-

ness climate that could affect the value of a long-lived asset (asset group), including an adverse action or assessment by a regulator.

d. An accumulation of costs significantly in excess of the amount originally expected for the acquisition or construction of a long-lived asset (asset group).

e. A current period operating or cash flow loss combined with a history of operating or cash flow losses or a projection or forecast that demonstrates continuing losses associated with the use of a long-lived asset (asset group).

f. A current expectation that more likely than not, 6 a long-lived asset (asset group) will be sold or otherwise disposed of significantly before the end of its previously estimated useful life.

**3.** Describe the accounting and reporting for an impairment loss on the income statement in the current period.

**Reporting and Disclosure**
**FAS144, Para 25 or Current Text I08.160**

25. An impairment loss recognized for a long-lived asset (asset group) to be held and used shall be included in income from continuing operations before income taxes in the income statement of a business enterprise and in income from continuing operations in the statement of activities of a not-for-profit organization. If a subtotal such as "income from operations" is presented, it shall include the amount of that loss.

**4.** Describe the information to be disclosed in the notes to the financial statements regarding asset impairment.

**FAS144, Para 26 or Current Text I08.161**

26. The following information shall be disclosed in the notes to the financial statements that include the period in which an impairment loss is recognized:

a. A description of the impaired long-lived asset (asset group) and the facts and circumstances leading to the impairment.

b. If not separately presented on the face of the statement, the amount of the impairment loss and the caption in the income statement or the statement of activities that includes that loss.

c. The method or methods for determining fair value (whether based on a quoted market price, prices for similar assets, or another valuation technique).

d. If applicable, the segment in which the impaired long-lived asset (asset group) is reported under FASB Statement No. 131, *Disclosures about Segments of an Enterprise and Related Information.*

**5.** Describe the accounting for impairment losses on future financial statements.

**New Cost Basis**
**FAS144, Para 15 or Current Text I08.150**

15. If an impairment loss is recognized, the adjusted carrying amount of a long-lived asset shall be its new cost basis. For a depreciable long-lived asset, the new costs shall be depreciated (amortized) over the remaining useful life of that asset. Restoration of a previously recognized impairment loss is prohibited.

**6.** How are losses of operational assets to be sold measured?

**Measurement**
**FAS144, Para 34 or Current Text D60.111**

34. A long-lived asset (disposal group) classified as held for sale shall be measured at the lower of its carrying amount or fair value less cost to sell. If the asset (disposal group) is newly acquired, the carrying amount of the asset (disposal group) shall be established based on its fair value less cost to sell at the acquisition date. A long-lived asset shall not be depreciated (amortized) while it is classified as held for sale. Interest and other expenses attributable to the liabilities of a disposal group classified as held for sale shall continue to be accrued.

**Simulation Problem 3**

| Situation | Concepts | Intangible Assets | Expenses Resulting from Intangibles | Goodwill Impairment | Communication | Research |
|---|---|---|---|---|---|---|

|   | (T) | (F) |
|---|---|---|
| **1.** An intangible asset that is determined to have an indefinite life should be amortized over 40 years. | ○ | ● |
| **2.** If the carrying value of the intangible asset exceeds its fair value, an impairment loss must be recognized. | ● | ○ |
| **3.** The impairment test for goodwill must be performed at the end of each fiscal year for each reporting unit. | ○ | ● |
| **4.** When a company borrows funds to finance a construction project and temporarily invests this cash, the interest expense should be offset against the interest expense to be capitalized. | ○ | ● |
| **5.** A company may capitalize interest on inventories it regularly produces for resale to customers. | ○ | ● |
| **6.** Gains are never recognized when similar assets are exchanged. | ○ | ● |
| **7.** In nonmonetary exchanges, losses are only recognized when cash is received in the transactions. | ○ | ● |
| **8.** If the fair value of the asset is unknown in a nonmonetary exchange and no gain can be computed, the asset is recorded at the fair market value of the asset given up. | ○ | ● |
| **9.** A capital expenditure is charged against income over the useful life of the asset. | ● | ○ |
| **10.** Expenditures to improve the efficiency or extend the useful life of an asset should be capitalized. | ● | ○ |

**Explanation of solutions**

**1.** False.  Per FAS 142, intangible assets that have indefinite lives are not amortized.

**2.** True.  The recorded values of intangibles are impaired if they are above fair value.

**3.** False.  The impairment test for goodwill can be performed anytime during the year, but it must be performed at the same time every year.

**4.** False.  Interest earned on temporary investments from borrowed funds used to finance construction projects should be recognized as interest revenue and **not** netted against interest expense during the period.

**5.** False.  A company may not capitalize interest on funds borrowed to finance routinely produced inventory.

**6.** False.  FASB 153 amended APB 29 to require recognition of gain unless the transaction lacks commercial substance.

**7.** False.  Losses on nonmonetary exchanges are recognized.

**8.** False.  In a nonmonetary exchange, if the fair value is unknown and no gain can be computed, the asset is recorded at the book value of the asset given up.

**9.** True.  Capital expenditures are amortized over the useful life of the asset.

**10.** True.  Expenditures to improve capital assets should be capitalized.

| Situation | Concepts | Intangible Assets | Expenses Resulting from Intangibles | Goodwill Impairment | Communication | Research |
|---|---|---|---|---|---|---|

*Broca Co.*
**SCHEDULE FOR INTANGIBLE ASSETS AND AMORTIZATION EXPENSE**
*December 31, 2007*

| *Item* | *Valuation **before** adjusting entries* | | *Amortization expense for the year* | *Valuation on 12/31/07* |
|---|---|---|---|---|
| Goodwill | 188,000 | [1] | -0- | 188,000 |
| Franchise (net) | 60,000 | [2] | 12,000 | 48,000 |
| Patent (net) | 136,000 | [3] | 13,600 | 122,400 |

**Explanation of solutions**

*Broca Co.*
**SUPPORTING CALCULATIONS FOR INTANGIBLES**
*December 31, 2007*

| | | |
|---|---|---|
| Goodwill | | $188,000 [1] |
| Franchise, net of accumulated amortization of $12,000 | | 48,000 [2] |
| Patent, net of accumulated amortization of $13,600 | | 122,400 [3] |

| | | | |
|---|---|---|---|
| [1] | Cash paid | | $360,000 |
| | Value of net assets | | (172,000) |
| | Goodwill | | 188,000 |
| [2] | Franchise | | $60,000 |
| | Amortization over 5 years | | (12,000) |
| | Balance | | $48,000 |
| [3] | Legal costs ($51,000 + $85,000) | | $136,000 |
| | Amortization over 10 years | | (13,600) |
| | Balance | | $122,400 |

[1]  Goodwill calculation

In a purchase, the net assets acquired are recorded at their FMV.  The excess of the cost of the investment ($360,000) over the FMV of the net assets acquired ($172,000) is allocated to goodwill ($360,000 – $172,000 = $188,000).  Intangible assets with an indeterminate or unlimited life, such as this goodwill, are not amortized.  The goodwill is reported in the 12/31/07 balance at its cost.

[2]  Franchise fee

The franchise acquired on 2/1/07 is recorded at its cost of $60,000.  Since Broca amortizes these intangibles on a straight-line basis, and takes a full year's amortization in the year of acquisition, 2007 amortization is $12,000 ($60,000 × 1/5), and the franchise is reported at cost less accumulated amortization at 12/31/07 ($60,000 – $12,000 = $48,000).  In addition to the amortization expense, there is also an annual fee that must be expensed, equal to 1% of ferry revenues.

[3]  Patents are initially recorded at cost of acquisition, which is purchase price for a purchased patent, or legal and other costs of registration ($51,000) for an internally generated patent.  Legal fees incurred in **successfully** defending the patent ($85,000) are also capitalized because such fees help establish the legal right of the holder to any future benefits that will be derived from the patent.  Therefore, this patent is capitalized at a total amount of $136,000 ($51,000 + $85,000).  Since Broca amortizes these intangibles on a straight-line basis and takes a full-year's amortization in the year of acquisition, amortization is $13,600 ($136,000 × 1/10).  The patent is reported at cost less accumulated amortization at 12/31/07 ($136,000 – $13,600 = $122,400).

| Situation | Concepts | Intangible Assets | Expenses Resulting from Intangibles | Goodwill Impairment | Communication | Research |
|---|---|---|---|---|---|---|

**Broca Co.**
**EXPENSES RESULTING FROM INTANGIBLES**
*For the Year Ended December 31, 2007*

| | | |
|---|---|---|
| Amortization: | | |
| Franchise | 12,000 | |
| Patent | 13,600 | |
| | $25,600 | |
| Franchise fee | 200 | |
| ($20,000 × 1%) | | |
| Total expenses | $25,800 | |

| Situation | Concepts | Intangible Assets | Expenses resulting from intangibles | Goodwill Impairment | Communication | Research |
|---|---|---|---|---|---|---|

1. Implied goodwill   $200,000

Impairment of goodwill   $300,000

**Explanation of solutions**

1.  Goodwill acquired through a business combination is the only type of goodwill that is recognized. Such goodwill is not amortized but is tested periodically for impairment. Internally generated goodwill is not recorded. Expenditures to develop, maintain, or enhance goodwill are expensed as incurred.

Since the carrying value of the reporting unit ($1,900,000) exceeds the fair value of the unit ($1,700,000), the second step in the test of impairment should be performed.

The implied value of goodwill is the difference between the fair value of the unit ($1,700,000) and the fair value of its assets and liabilities ($1,500,000). Therefore, the implied value of goodwill is $200,000. Since the carrying value of goodwill is $500,000, there is a $300,000 impairment that must be recognized as shown below.

2.  Journal entry required for goodwill impairment

Impairment loss          $300,000
   Goodwill                          $300,000
*To recognize impairment of goodwill for the Technology*
*reporting unit at 12/31/07.*

| Situation | Concepts | Intangible Assets | Expenses resulting from intangibles | Goodwill Impairment | Communication | Research |
|---|---|---|---|---|---|---|

To:     CEO, Broca Corporation
From:   CPA Candidate
Re:     Intangible assets

This memorandum answers the questions you have regarding intangible assets. The main characteristics of intangible assets are their lack of physical substance, the difficulty of estimating their value, and the high degree of uncertainty regarding their future life. Accounting for intangible assets depends on whether the intangibles have been purchased or developed internally.

Intangible assets purchased from others should be recorded at cost. Then, management should evaluate whether the intangible assets have a finite economic life or an indefinite life. Intangible assets with definite useful lives should be amortized over their estimated useful lives. Estimated useful lives should be determined by consideration of such factors as legal life; provisions for renewal or extensions of contracts; the effects of obsolescence, demand, competition, and other economic factors. Intangible assets with indefinite lives are not amortized. Instead, they are periodically tested for impairment.

The costs of internally developing intangible assets with indeterminable lives are ordinarily not distinguishable from the current costs of operations. Because the costs of internally developed intangibles are not assignable to specific assets, these costs should be expensed immediately.

Your company's financial statements should disclose the amounts assigned to the intangible assets and their gross carrying amounts. The footnotes to the financial statements should disclose (1) the aggregated amount of amortization expense and the estimated amounts for the five succeeding periods; and (2) the weighted-average amortization period, in total and by major class of asset.

If you have any further questions, please contact me.

| Situation | Concepts | Intangible Assets | Expenses resulting from intangibles | Goodwill Impairment | Communication | Research |
|-----------|----------|-------------------|--------------------------------------|----------------------|----------------|----------|
|           |          |                   |                                      |                      |                |          |

**1.** What assets qualify for capitalization of interest?

**Assets Qualifying for Interest Capitalization**
**FAS34, Para 9 or Current Text I67.105**

9.  Subject to the provisions of paragraph 8, interest shall be capitalized for the following types of assets ("qualifying assets"):

a.  Assets that are constructed or otherwise produced for an enterprise's own use (including assets constructed or produced for the enterprise by others for which deposits or progress payments have been made)

b.  Assets intended for sale or lease that are constructed or otherwise produced as discrete projects (e.g., ships or real estate developments).

**2.** An asset has been acquired in a nonmonetary exchange involving dissimilar assets. At what amount should this asset be capitalized?

**APB29, Para 20, as amended by FAS153, Para 2(c) or Current Text N35.107**

A nonmonetary exchange shall be measured based on the recorded amount (after reduction, if appropriate, for an indicated impairment of value) of the nonmonetary asset(s) relinquished, and not on the fair values of the exchanged assets, if any of the following conditions apply:

a.  *Fair Value Not Determinable.* The fair value of neither the asset(s) received nor the asset(s) relinquished is determinable within reasonable limits (paragraph 25).

b.  *Exchange Transaction to Facilitate Sales to Customers.* The transaction is an exchange of a product or property held for sale in the ordinary course of business for a product or property to be sold in the same line of business to facilitate sales to customers other than the parties to the exchange.

c.  *Exchange Transaction That Lacks Commercial Substance.* The transaction lacks commercial substance (paragraph 21).

**3.** At what amount should donated assets be recorded?

**FAS116, Para 8 or Current Text C67.108**

8.  Except as provided in paragraphs 9 and 11, contributions received shall be recognized as revenues or gains in the period received and as assets, decreases of liabilities, or expenses depending on the form of the benefits received. Contributions received shall be measured at their fair values. Contributions received by not-for-profit organizations shall be reported as restricted support or unrestricted support as provided in paragraphs 14-16.

## MONETARY CURRENT ASSETS AND CURRENT LIABILITIES

Chapter 3A of ARB 43 defines current assets and current liabilities. This study module reviews the accounting for current assets (except inventory which is presented in Module 8 and short-term investments which are presented in Module 14). This module also reviews current liabilities.

### A. Cash

Per SFAS 95 (see outline), the definition of cash includes both cash (cash on hand and demand deposits) and cash equivalents (short-term, highly liquid investments). Cash equivalents have to be readily convertible into cash and so near maturity that they carry little risk of changing in value due to interest rate changes. Generally this will include only those investments with original maturities of three months or less from the **date of purchase** by the enterprise. Common examples of cash equivalents include Treasury bills, commercial paper, and money market funds. Unrestricted cash and cash equivalents available for general use are presented as the first current asset.

Cash set aside for special uses is usually disclosed separately. The entry to set up a special fund is

| | | |
|---|---|---|
| Special cash fund | xx | |
| Cash | | xx |

Cash restricted as to use (e.g., not transferable out of a foreign country) should be disclosed separately, but not as a current asset if it cannot be used in the next year (this is true of special funds also).

Imprest (petty) cash funds are generally included in the total cash figure, but unreimbursed expense vouchers are excluded.

### 1. Bank Reconciliations

Bank reconciliations are prepared by bank depositors when they receive their monthly bank statements. The reconciliation is made to determine any required adjustments to the cash balance. Two types of reconciling items are possible.

a. Reconciling items not requiring adjustment on the books (type A)
b. Reconciling items requiring adjustment on the books (type B)

There are three type A reconciling items. They do not require adjusting journal entries.

(1) Outstanding checks
(2) Deposits in transit
(3) Bank errors

All other reconciling items (type B) require adjusting journal entries. Examples of type B reconciling items include

(1) Unrecorded returned nonsufficient funds (NSF) checks
(2) Unrecorded bank charges
(3) Errors in the cash account
(4) Unrecorded bank collections of notes receivable

Two types of formats are used in bank reconciliations.

| *Format 1* | *Format 2* |
|---|---|
| Balance per bank | Balance per bank |
| +(–) A adjustments | +(–) A adjustments |
| Correct cash balance | +(–) B adjustments |
| | Balance per books |
| Balance per books | +(–) B adjustments |
| +(–) B adjustments | Correct cash balance |
| Correct cash balance | |

Type A and B adjustments can be either added or subtracted depending upon the type of format and the nature of the item.

Reconciling items must be analyzed to determine whether they are included in (1) the balance per bank, and/or (2) the balance per books. If they are included in one, but not the other, an adjustment is required. For instance, the $1,800 deposit in transit in the following example is included in the balance per books but not in the balance per bank. Thus, it must be added to the balance per bank to reconcile to the correct cash balance. Deposits in transit do not require an adjusting journal entry. Analyze all reconciling items in this manner, but remember, only journalize type B reconciling items.

### SAMPLE BANK RECONCILIATION (FORMAT 1)

| | |
|---|---:|
| Per bank statement | $ 4,702 |
|    Deposits in transit | 1,800 |
|    Outstanding checks | (1,200) |
|    Bank error | 50 |
| Correct cash balance | |
| | $ 5,352 |
| Per books | $ 5,332 |
|    Service charges | (5) |
|    Note collected by bank | 150 |
|    Customer's NSF check | (170) |
|    Deposit of July 10 recorded as $749 instead of $794 | 45 |
| Correct cash balance | $ 5,352 |

Note that the balance per bank and balance per books each are reconciled directly to the corrected balance.

a.  **Adjusting journal entries**

All of the items in the per books section of a bank reconciliation (type B) require adjusting entries. The entries for the above example appear below.

| | | | | | |
|---|---|---|---|---|---|
| Miscellaneous expense | 5 | | AR | 170 | |
|   Cash | | 5 |   Cash | | 170 |
| Cash | 150 | | Cash | 45 | |
|   Notes receivable | | 150 |   AR (or sales) | | 45 |

b.  **Four-column cash reconciliation**

Unlike the bank reconciliation above, which is as of a specific date, a four-column cash reconciliation, also known as a "proof of cash," reconciles bank and book cash balances over a specified time period. A proof of cash consists of four columns: beginning of the period bank reconciliation, receipts, disbursements, and end-of-the-period bank reconciliation. Thus, the proof of cash cross-foots as well as foots.

### SAMPLE PROOF OF CASH (FORMAT 2)

| | Bank reconciliation June 30, 2007 | Receipts | Disbursements | Bank reconciliation July 31, 2007 |
|---|---:|---:|---:|---:|
| Balance per bank statement | $3,402 | $25,200 | $23,900 | $ 4,702 |
| Deposits in transit | | | | |
|   June 30, 2007 | 1,610 | (1,610) | | |
|   July 31, 2007 | | 1,800 | | 1,800 |
| Outstanding checks | | | | |
|   June 30, 2007 | (450) | | (450) | |
|   July 31, 2007 | | | 1,200 | (1,200) |
| Service charges | | | (5) | 5 |
| Note collected by bank | | (150) | | (150) |
| Customer's NSF check | | | (170) | 170 |
| Deposit of July 10 recorded as | | | | |
|   $749 instead of $794 | | (45) | | (45) |
| Bank error | | | (50) | 50 |
| Balance per books | $4,562 | $25,195 | $24,425 | $ 5,332 |

Note that there are no type B reconciling items in the beginning reconciliation column. This is because the $4,562 has been adjusted when the June bank statement was reconciled. Notice that figures appearing in the center columns have unlike signs if they are adjacent and like signs if they are not adjacent to amounts in the side columns.

The purpose of the proof of cash is to disclose any cash misstatements, such as unrecorded disbursements and receipts within a month, which would not be detected by a bank reconciliation. For example, if the center two columns each required a negative $1,000 to make the top line reconcile with the bottom line, there may be unrecorded receipts and deposits of $1,000.

## B.  Receivables

Accounts receivable should be disclosed in the balance sheet at net realizable value (gross amount less estimated uncollectibles) by source (e.g., trade, officer, etc.). Officer, employee, and affiliate company receivables should be separately disclosed (ARB 43, chap 1A). Unearned interest and finance charges should be deducted from gross receivables (APB 6).

## 1.  Anticipation of Sales Discounts

Cash discounts are generally recognized as expense when cash payment is received within the discount period.  As long as cash discounts to be taken on year-end receivables remain constant from year to year, there is no problem.  If, however, discounts on year-end receivables fluctuate, a year-end allowance can be set up or sales can be recorded net of the discounts.  The entries to record sales at net are shown below in comparison to the sales recorded at gross.

|  |  | *Sales at net* |  |  | *Sales at gross* |  |
|---|---|---|---|---|---|---|
| a. | Sale | AR | (net) | | AR | (gross) |
| | | Sales | (net) | | Sales | (gross) |
| | | | | | | |
| b. | Cash receipt within discount period | Cash | (net) | | Sales disc. | (disc.) |
| | | AR | (net) | | Cash | (net) |
| | | | | | AR | (gross) |
| | | | | | | |
| c. | Cash receipt after discount period | Cash | (gross) | | Cash | (gross) |
| | | AR | (net) | | AR | (gross) |
| | | Disc. not | | | | |
| | | taken | (disc.) | | | |

The rationale for the net method is that sales are recorded at the cash equivalent amount and receivables nearer realizable value.  Note that under both the net and gross methods, sales and accounts receivable are recorded net of trade discounts for the same reason.  If a sales discount allowance method is used, the entry below is made with the gross method entries.  The entry should be reversed.

    Sales discounts                    (expected disc. on year-end AR)
        Allowance for sales disc.                    (expected disc. on year-end AR)

Similarly, when using the "net method," an entry should be made to pick up discounts not expected to be taken on year-end receivables.  Generally, however, these latter adjustments are not made, because they are assumed to be about the same each period.

## 2.  Bad Debts Expense

There are two approaches to bad debts.

- Direct write-off method
- Allowance method

a.  Under the direct write-off method, bad debts are considered expenses in the period in which they are written off.  **Note that this method is not considered acceptable under GAAP,** unless the amounts are immaterial.  The direct write-off method is the method required for tax purposes.

        Bad debts expense           (uncollectible AR)
           AR                            (uncollectible AR)

b.  The allowance method seeks to estimate the amount of uncollectible receivables, and establishes a contra valuation account (allowance for bad debts) for the amount estimated to be uncollectible.  The adjusting entry to set up the allowance is

        Bad debts expense           (estimated)
           Allowance for bad debts               (estimated)

The entry to write off bad debts is

        Allowance for bad debts     (uncollectible AR)
           AR                            (uncollectible AR)

There are two methods to determine the annual charge to bad debts expense.

(1)  Annual sales
(2)  Year-end AR

For example, charging bad debts expense for 1% of annual sales is based on the theory that bad debts are a function of sales; this method emphasizes the income statement.

Charging bad debts on year-end AR is based on the theory that bad debts are a function of AR collections during the period; this method emphasizes the balance sheet.  A bad debts percentage can be applied to total AR or subsets of AR.  Often an aging schedule is prepared for this purpose.  An AR aging schedule classifies AR by their age (e.g., 30, 60, 90, 120, etc., days overdue).

When bad debts expense is estimated as a function of sales, any balance in the allowance account is ignored in making the adjusting entry.  Bad debts expense under this method is simply the total amount computed (i.e., Sales × Percentage). However, when bad debts expense is estimated using outstanding receivables, the expense is the amount needed to adjust the allowance account to the amount computed (i.e., AR × Percentage[s]). Thus, bad debts expense under this method is the amount computed less any credit balance currently in the allowance account (or plus any debit balance).

Net accounts receivable is the balance in accounts receivable less the allowance for bad debts. Also remember that net receivables **do not change** when a specific account is written off since both accounts receivable and the allowance account are reduced by the same amount.

**Methods of Recognizing Bad Debts Expense Concepts Summary**

3. **Pledging and Selling (Factoring) AR**

   Sometimes businesses cannot wait for the cash flow from the normal collection of AR.

   **Pledging of receivables.** Pledging is an agreement where accounts receivable are used as collateral for loans. Generally, the lender has limited rights to inspect the borrower's records to achieve assurance that the receivables do exist. The customers whose accounts have been pledged are not aware of this event, and their payments are still remitted to the original obligee. The pledged accounts merely serve as security to the lender, giving comfort that sufficient assets exist which will generate cash flows adequate in amount and timing to repay the debt. However, the debt is paid by the borrower whether or not the pledged receivables are collected and whether or not the pattern of such collections matches the payments due on the debt.

   **The only accounting issue relating to pledging is that of adequate disclosure.** The accounts receivable, which remain assets of the borrowing entity, continue to be shown as current assets in its financial statements but must be identified as having been pledged. This identification can be accomplished either parenthetically or by footnote disclosures. Similarly, the related debt should be identified as having been secured by the receivables.

   EXAMPLE:  *Proper disclosure for pledged receivables shown parenthetically on the balance sheet*

   | | |
   |---|---:|
   | *Current assets:* | |
   | *Accounts receivable, net of allowance for doubtful accounts of $600,000* | |
   | *($3,500,000 of which has been pledged as collateral for bank loans)* | 8,450,000 |
   | *Current liabilities:* | |
   | *Bank loans payable (secured by pledged accounts receivable)* | 2,700,000 |

   **Factoring of receivables.** This category of financing is the most significant in terms of accounting implications. Factoring traditionally has involved the outright sale of receivables to a financing institution known as a factor. These arrangements involved (1) notification to the customer to forward future payments to the factor and (2) the transfer of receivables **without recourse** which means that the factor assumes the risk of loss from noncollection. Thus, once a factoring arrangement is completed, the entity has no further involvement with the accounts, except for a return of merchandise. In its simplistic form, the receivables are sold and the difference between the cash received and the carrying value is recognized as a gain or loss.

   The classical variety of factoring (i.e., without recourse) provides two financial services to the business: it permits the entity to obtain cash earlier and the risk of bad debts is transferred to the factor. The factor is compensated for each of the services. Interest is charged based on the anticipated length of time between the date the factoring is consummated and the expected collection date of the receivables sold. A fee is charged based upon the factor's anticipated bad debt losses.

*EXAMPLE:  Thirsty Corp., on July 1, 2007, enters into an agreement with Rich Company to sell a group of its receivables **without recourse**.  A total face value of $200,000 of accounts receivable are involved.  The factor will charge 20% interest computed on the weighted-average time to maturity of the receivables of thirty-six days plus a 3% fee.*

*The entries required are as follows:*

| | | |
|---|---:|---:|
| Cash | 190,055 | |
| Interest expense (or prepaid) (200,000 × .20 × 36/365) | 3,945 | |
| Factoring fee (200,000 × .03) | 6,000 | |
| Accounts receivable | | 200,000 |

*The interest expense and factor's fee can be combined into a $9,945 loss on the sale of receivables.*

Merchandise returns will normally be the responsibility of the original vendor, who must then make the appropriate settlement with the factor.  To protect against the possibility of merchandise returns which diminish the total of receivables to be collected, very often a factoring arrangement will **not** advance the full amount of the factored receivables (less any interest and factoring fee deductions).  Rather, the factor will retain a certain fraction of the total proceeds relating to the portion of sales which are anticipated to be returned by customers.  This sum is known as the factor's holdback (due from factor).  When merchandise is returned to the borrower, an entry is made reducing the receivable from the factor.  At the end of the return privilege period, any remaining holdback will become due and payable to the borrower.

*EXAMPLE:  Accounting for the transfer of receivables without recourse*

1. *Thirsty Corp., on July 1, 2007, enters into an agreement with Rich Company to sell a group of its receivables **without recourse**.  A total face value of $200,000 accounts receivable are involved.  The factor will charge 20% interest computed on the weighted-average time to maturity of the receivables of thirty-six days plus a 3% fee.  A 5% holdback will also be retained.*
2. *Thirsty's customers return for credit $4,800 of merchandise.*
3. *The customer return privilege period expires and the remaining holdback is paid to the transferor.*

*The entries required are as follows:*

| | | | |
|---|---|---:|---:|
| 1. | Cash | 180,055 | |
| | Loss on sale of receivables | 9,945* | |
| | Factor's holdback receivable   (200,000 × .05) | 10,000 | |
| | Accounts receivable | | 200,000 |
| | *($3,945 interest expense + $6,000 factoring fee)* | | |
| 2. | Sales returns and allowances | 4,800 | |
| | Factor's holdback receivable | | 4,800 |
| 3. | Cash | 5,200 | |
| | Factor's holdback receivable | | 5,200 |

Factoring does transfer title.  Thus, if there is a **without recourse** provision, the removal of these receivables from the borrower's balance sheet is clearly warranted.

Another variation is known as factoring **with recourse**.  Some entities had such a poor history of uncollectible accounts that factors were only willing to purchase their accounts if a substantial fee were collected to compensate for the risk.  When the company believed that the receivables were of a better quality, a way to avoid excessive factoring fees was to sell these receivables with recourse.  This variation of factoring was really an assignment of receivables with notification to the customers.

In computing the gain or loss to be recognized at the date of the transfer of the receivables, the borrower (transferor) must take into account the anticipated chargebacks from the transferee for bad debts to be incurred.  This action requires an estimate by the transferor, based on past experience.  Adjustments should also be made at the time of sale for the estimated effects of any prepayments by customers (where the receivables are interest-bearing or where cash discounts are available), and for the effects of any defects in the eligibility of the transferred receivables.

*EXAMPLE:  Accounting for the transfer of receivables with recourse*

1. *Thirsty Corp., on July 1, 2007, enters into an agreement with Rich Company to sell a group of its receivables with a face value of $200,000.  Rich Company (the factor) will charge 20% interest computed on the weighted-average time to maturity of the receivables of thirty-six days and a 3% fee.  A 5% holdback will also be retained.*
2. *Generally, 40% of Thirsty's customers take advantage of a 2% cash discount.*
3. *Assume Thirsty Corp. surrenders control of the receivables, per SFAS 140, Thirsty's future obligation is reasonably estimable, and Rich Co. does not have a unilateral ability to require Thirsty to repurchase the receivables.*
4. *The factor accepts the receivables **subject to recourse** for nonpayment.  This means that the transferor has **continuing involvement**.  The recourse obligation has a fair value of $10,000.*

*According to the requirements of SFAS 140, this situation qualifies as a sale. Under this standard, Thirsty must record a liability for the recourse liability due to its continuing involvement with the receivables transferred. It has accepted the obligation for all credit losses and has, in effect, guaranteed the receivables.*

*The entries required to record the sale are*

| | | |
|---|---:|---:|
| *Cash* | *180,055* | |
| *Interest expense* | *3,945* | |
| *Factoring fee* | *6,000* | |
| *Factor's holdback receivable (200,000 × .05)* | *10,000* | |
| *Loss on sale of receivables* | *11,600* | |
| *   Due to factor (200,000 × .40 × .02)* | | *1,600* |
| *   Accounts receivable* | | *200,000* |
| *   Recourse obligation* | | *10,000* |

*Simplified, the entry is*

| | | |
|---|---:|---:|
| *Cash* | *180,055* | |
| *Factor's holdback receivable [(200,000 × .05) – 1,600]* | *8,400* | |
| *Loss on sale of receivables (3,945 + 6,000 + 11,600)* | *21,545* | |
| *   Accounts receivable* | | *200,000* |
| *   Recourse obligation* | | *10,000* |

The accounts receivable are removed from the transferor's books because they have been sold. The loss on sale of receivables is the sum of the interest charged by the factor ($3,945), the factor's fee ($6,000), the expected chargeback for cash discounts to be taken ($1,600), and the fair value of the recourse obligation ($10,000).

Because the transaction resulted in a "sale" rather than a borrowing, the "interest" and "fee" elements relate directly to the sale transaction. Note that in a sale, these components are in essence part of a negotiated price for the receivables. All you need to remember is that in sales transactions, amounts that would ordinarily be income statement amounts are netted together to get the total loss.

If, subsequent to the sale of the receivables, the actual experience relative to the recourse terms differs from the provision made at the time of the sale, a change in an accounting estimate results. It is reflected as an additional gain or loss in the subsequent period. These changes are not corrections of errors or retroactive adjustments.

**Secured borrowings.** If the facts in the example above apply, but the transfer does **not** qualify as a sale, because the transferor does not surrender control of the receivables, the borrower's entry will be

| | | |
|---|---:|---:|
| Cash | 190,055 | |
| Interest expense (or prepaid) | 3,945 | |
| Factoring fee | 6,000 | |
| Factor borrowing payable | | 200,000 |

The accounts receivable remain on the borrower's books. Both the accounts receivable and the factor borrowing payable should be cross-referenced in the balance sheet.

**Transfers of financial assets under SFAS 140.** The FASB uses a financial-components approach for SFAS 140. In doing so, the previous approach that viewed a financial asset as an indivisible unit has become obsolete. **Under the financial component approach, financial assets are now to be viewed as a variety of components with a focus on who controls the components and on whether control has changed with a given transaction.**

The basic accounting problem in this area involves instances of possible continuing involvement through recourse, repurchase agreements, options generated, servicing, and collateral. The issue is whether the transfer has resulted in a sale or a secured borrowing. A sale results, to the extent that consideration other than beneficial interests has been received, when the transferor gives up control.

Under SFAS 140, transfers of financial assets are disaggregated into separate assets and liabilities. Each entity involved in the transaction then

1. Recognizes only the assets controlled and liabilities incurred, and
2. Derecognizes assets where control has been given up or lost and liabilities where extinguishment has occurred.

The chart below summarizes the accounting for the transfer of receivables.

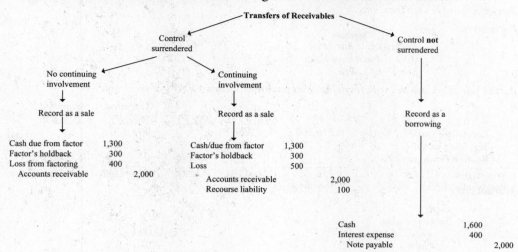

The "factor's holdback" provides a margin of protection against sales discounts, sales returns and allowances, and disputed accounts. It may also be referred to as "Due from factor" or "Receivable from factor." Additionally, when a recourse obligation exists, an amount is included as protection for the transferee against uncollectible accounts.

Control is deemed to have been surrendered by the transferor only if **all** of the following conditions are met:

1. The **assets** transferred are **beyond the reach of the transferor** and its affiliates, its creditors, bankruptcy trustees or other receivers, except for an affiliate that is a qualifying special-purpose entity.

2. The **transferee can pledge or exchange freely** the assets transferred without unreasonable constraints or conditions imposed on its contractual right **or** the holders of beneficial interests in a qualifying special-purpose entity can pledge or exchange those interests freely without unreasonable constraints or conditions imposed on their right.

3. The **transferor has not kept effective control** of the financial assets transferred through a repurchase or redemption agreement that entitles and obligates repurchase or redemption before maturity at a determinable price **or** the ability to unilaterally cause the holder to return specific assets (except for a cleanup call). To meet this condition, the transferor must have received cash or other collateral sufficient at all time to substantially fund repurchase or redemption.

**Interests that continue to be held.** In most cases, the outright transfer of assets and/or liabilities result(s) in changes in control that are obvious from the nature of the transaction. Problems generally occur when there is some sort of continuing involvement by the transferor. Interests that continue to be held include undivided interests for which control has not been given up by the transferor, servicing (mortgages, credit card receivables, etc.) assets and liabilities and beneficial interests in transferred assets to a qualifying special-purpose entity (SPE) in a securitization. In general, the more that the transferor of assets retains an interest, the less likely the transaction will be classified as a sale and the more likely the transaction will be classified as a secured borrowing. The primary reason for this result is that in a sale, the transferor should give up control. If a determination cannot be made between classification as proceeds of a sale or as retained interests, the asset should be classified as proceeds and should be measured at fair value. Interests in transferred assets that are not a part of the proceeds are considered retained interests that are still under the control of the transferor.

Interests that continue to be held are to be measured at their previous carrying value before the transfer through an allocation at the date of sale based on relative fair values of the assets sold and the assets retained. This allocation must be applied to all transfers that have retained interests, regardless of whether or not they qualify as sales. It should be noted that this fair value allocation may result in a relative change in basis unless the fair values are proportionate to their carrying values. Thus, the gain or loss from any sale component could also be affected.

*EXAMPLE: Interests that continue to be held*

*Sale of receivable with servicing*

**Facts given:**

|  |  |
|---|---|
| Receivable's fair value | $16,500 |
| Receivable's book value | 15,000 |
| Servicing asset | 700 |

*Partial sale of receivables with servicing asset retained.  Seller sells 80% of receivables.*

| | FV | 80% FV | 20% FV | Allocated 80% BV | Allocated 20% BV |
|---|---|---|---|---|---|
| Receivables sold | $16,500 | $13,200 | | $11,520 | |
| Servicing asset | 700 | 560 | | 480 | |
| Retained amount (20%) | | | $3,440 | | $3,000 |
| | $17,200 | $13,760 | $3,440 | $12,000 | $3,000 |

**Journal entry**

| | | |
|---|---|---|
| Cash | 13,200 | |
| Servicing asset | 480 | |
| Receivables | | 12,000 |
| Gain | | 1,680 |

*Seller reports retained amount at $3,000.*

The retained interests continue to be the transferor's assets since control of these assets has not been transferred.  They are carried at the allocated book value without recognition of any gain or loss. Thus, the retained interest is considered continuing control over a previous asset (although the form may have changed) and it should not be remeasured at fair value.

**Servicing of financial assets.**  This includes

1.   Collecting payments
2.   Paying taxes and insurance
3.   Monitoring delinquencies
4.   Foreclosing
5.   Investing
6.   Remitting fees
7.   Accounting

Although inherent in transfers of most financial assets, servicing is a distinct asset or liability only when separated contractually from the underlying financial asset.  The servicing asset usually results either from separate purchase or assumption of rights or from securitization with retained servicing. The servicer's obligations are specified in the contract.

Typically, the servicing contract results in an asset since the benefits are more than adequate compensation for the servicing.  The benefits include

1.   Fees
2.   Late charges
3.   Float
4.   Other income

If the above benefits do not provide fair compensation, the contract results in a liability.  With regard to the sale of assets, a servicing liability would reduce the net proceeds and would affect the gain or loss calculation.

The fair value of a servicing contract is based on its value in the market and is not based on the internal cost structure of the servicer.  Thus, the concept of adequate compensation is judged by requirements that would be imposed by a new or outside servicer.  In cases where there are few servicing contracts that are purchased or sold, present value methods may be used for valuation.

In summary, the servicer should classify the components into one of the following categories:

1.   More than adequate—resulting in a recorded asset
2.   Adequate compensation (no asset or liability)
3.   Less than adequate—resulting in a recorded liability

If, under a servicing contract, the transferor transfers assets to a qualifying special purpose entity in a guaranteed mortgage securitization, retains the securities, and classifies them as held-to-maturity debt securities under SFAS 115, the asset or liability can be reported together with the asset being serviced. However, if the entity sells or securitizes with service retained or if the entity purchases or assumes servicing, a servicing asset or liability results. If servicing is retained, the resulting assets are measured by allocating the previous carrying amount between the assets sold and the interests that continue to be held by the transferor based on relative fair values at the date of transfer. The servicing liabilities undertaken, servicing assets purchased, and servicing liabilities assumed are initially measured at fair value.

Specifically, servicing assets or servicing liabilities are to be accounted for separately as follows:

1. Assets are to be reported separately from liabilities. They are not netted.
2. Initially measure servicing assets that continue to be held by the transferor by allocating the carrying amount based on relative fair values at the date of transfer.
3. Initially measure at fair value all purchased assets, assumed liabilities, and liabilities undertaken in a sale or securitization.
4. Account separately for interest-only strips (future interest income from serviced assets that exceed servicing fees).
5. Measure servicing assets and servicing liabilities with one of two methods: amortization method, or fair value method. An election must be made to use the fair value method for each class of servicing assets and servicing liabilities. Once the election is made to value using the fair value method, the election cannot be reversed.
6. Report servicing assets and servicing liabilities on the balance sheet in one of two ways

   a. Display separate line items for amounts valued at fair value and amounts to be measured by amortization method, **or**
   b. Display aggregate amounts for all servicing assets and servicing liabilities, and disclose parenthetically the amount that is measured in fair value that is included in the aggregate amount.

The **amortization method** requires that servicing assets and servicing liabilities are initially recorded at fair value. Assets are then amortized in proportion to and over the period of estimated net servicing income or net servicing loss. At the end of each period, the assets are assessed for impairment or increased obligation based on fair value. Evaluate and measure impairment by stratifying recognized assets based on predominant risk (asset size, type, interest rate, terms, location, date of organization, etc.). Individual stratum should have impairment recognized through a valuation allowance account, and the valuation account is adjusted to reflect needed changes. Excess fair value for a stratum should not be recognized. Liabilities are amortized in proportion to and over the period of net servicing loss. In cases where changes have increased the fair value above the book value, an increased liability and a loss should be recognized.

The **fair value method** requires that servicing assets and servicing liabilities are initially recorded at fair value. The fair value is measured at each reporting date. Changes in fair value are reported in earnings in the period in which the change in fair value occurs.

Required disclosures for **all** servicing assets and servicing liabilities include management's basis for determining its classes, a description of risks, the instruments used to mitigate income statement effect of changes in fair value, and the amount of contractually specified servicing fees, late fees, and ancillary fees for each period on the income statement should be reported.

For servicing assets and liabilities measured at fair value, disclosures must also be provided showing the beginning and end balances, additions, disposals, and changes in fair value inputs or assumptions used, and changes in fair value. A description of the valuation techniques used to estimate fair value, and qualitative and quantitative information about the assumptions used in the model must also be included.

For servicing assets and liabilities that use the amortization method, disclosures must include the beginning and ending balances, additions, disposals, amortization, application of valuation allowance to adjust carrying value, other than temporary impairments, and other changes that affect the balance, as well as a description of the changes. In addition, the fair value at the beginning and end of each period should be disclosed if practicable to estimate the value. A description of the valuation techniques used, assumptions used in the model, and the risk characteristics of the underlying financial assets used for measuring impairment should be disclosed. The activity in the valuation account, including beginning and ending balances, recoveries made, and write-downs charged against the allowance for each period should also be disclosed.

**Securitizations.** Securitization is the transformation of financial assets into securities (asset-backed securities). Various assets including mortgages, credit cards, trade receivables, loans, and leases are grouped and securitized. These groupings of relatively homogeneous assets are then pooled and divided into securities with cash-flows that can be quite different from those of the original assets. With an established market, most of these securities cost less than the alternative use of the assets as collateral for borrowing. Thus, the benefits of most securitizations include lower financing costs, increased liquidity, and lower credit risk.

The transferor (also called issuer or sponsor) forms a securitization mechanism (separate corporation or qualifying special-purpose entity [QSPE]) to buy the assets and to issue the securities. Sometimes, another transfer is made to a trust and the trust issues the securities. These different structures are generally referred to as one-tier or two-tier. The securitization mechanism then generates beneficial interests in the assets or resulting cash flows which are sold. The form of the securities chosen depends on such things as the nature of the assets, income tax considerations, and returns to be received.

Payments by the securitization mechanism are usually classified as **pay-through, pass-through,** or **revolving-period**. In a **pay-through,** cash flows from the assets pay off the debt securities. The assets are essentially collateral. In a **pass-through,** undivided interests are issued and the investors share in the net cash flows. In a **revolving-period,** undivided interests are issued, but until liquidation, the net cash flows are split between buying additional assets and paying off investors.

Various financial components arise from securitizations. Examples include servicing contracts, interest-only strips, retained interests, recourse obligations, options, swaps, and forward contracts. All controlled assets and liabilities must be recognized under SFAS 140.

EXAMPLE:  Sale of loans

**Facts given:**

| | |
|---|---:|
| Loan's fair value | $16,500 |
| Loan's book value | 15,000 |
| Fair value of recourse obligation | (900) |
| Fair value of call option | 800 |
| Fair value of interest rate swap | 700 |

1.  Sale with recourse obligation, call and swap (seller provides floating interest rate return although the basic sale is at fixed interest rate terms).

**Journal entry**

| | | |
|---|---:|---:|
| Cash | 16,500 | |
| Call option | 800 | |
| Interest rate swap | 700 | |
| Loans | | 15,000 |
| Recourse obligation | | 900 |
| Gain | | 2,100 |

2.  Partial sale with recourse obligation, call and swap.  Seller sells 80% of loans.

| | FV | 80% FV | 20% FV | Allocated 80% BV | Allocated 20% BV |
|---|---:|---:|---:|---:|---:|
| Cash | $16,500 | $13,200 | | $12,000 | |
| Call option | 800 | 640 | | | |
| Interest rate swap | 700 | 560 | | | |
| Resource obligation | (900) | (720) | | | |
| Retained amount (20%) | | | $3,420 | | $3,000 |
| | $17,100 | $13,680 | $3,420 | $12,000 | $3,000 |

**Journal entry**

| | | |
|---|---:|---:|
| Cash | 13,200 | |
| Call option | 640 | |
| Interest rate swap | 560 | |
| Loans | | 12,000 |
| Recourse obligation | | 720 |
| Gain | | 1,680 |

Seller reports retained amount at $3,000.

The transferor generally desires for the assets to be taken off the balance sheet. This result can be accomplished if the transaction results in a sale. The key criterion in this case is to be sure that the assets are beyond control of the transferor even in bankruptcy.

**Accounting for collateral.** The treatment depends both on control of the assets and on the liabilities incurred under the collateral agreement. Ordinarily, the transferor should carry the collateral as an asset and the transferee should not record the pledged asset.

If the transferee, however, has control, the secured party should record the asset at fair value and also the liability to return it. The transferor-debtor should reclassify the asset (probably as a receivable) and report it separately in the balance sheet. If the debtor's rights to the collateral are impaired by the transferee's sale or repledge of the collateral, the secured party should recognize the proceeds and also the liability to return the collateral to the extent it hasn't done so.

If the transferor defaults and is not entitled to the return of the collateral, it should be derecognized. If not already recognized, the transferee should record its asset at fair value.

## C. Current Liabilities

"Obligations whose liquidation is reasonably expected to require the use of existing resources properly classifiable as current assets, or the creation of other current liabilities" (ARB 43, chap 3).

1. **Examples of current liabilities** (as they fall within the above definition)

   a. Trade accounts and notes payable

   b. Loan obligations—Including current portions of long-term debt. This is not true if the current portion of long-term debt will not require the use of current assets (e.g., be paid from a sinking fund which is not classified as current).

   c. Short-term obligations expected to be refinanced cannot be reclassified as noncurrent liabilities unless there is both an intent and an ability to refinance. See the outline of SFAS 6.

   d. Dividends payable—Cash dividends are a liability when declared. They cannot be rescinded.

   e. Accrued liabilities—Adjusting entries to reflect the use of goods or services before paying for them. Will pay in future periods even though the expense is incurred in this period (e.g., interest, payroll, rent expenses).

   | | | |
   |---|---|---|
   | Expense account | xx | |
   | Liability (usually current) account | | xx |

   f. Payroll—There are two entries to record payroll. The first records the employee's payment and deductions on behalf of the employee. The second is to record the employer's taxes.

   | | | |
   |---|---|---|
   | Payroll expense | xx (gross pay) | |
   | Payroll payable, cash | | xx (net pay) |
   | Income taxes payable | | xx |
   | FICA taxes payable | | xx |
   | Union dues payable | | xx |
   | Medical insurance payable | | xx |
   | Payroll tax expense | xx | |
   | FICA taxes payable | | xx |
   | Federal unemployment tax payable | | xx |
   | State unemployment tax payable | | xx |

   g. Property taxes. See the outline of ARB 43, chap 10A. Generally, there is a monthly accrual for property taxes over the fiscal period of the taxing authority. If taxes are payable at the end of the tax authority's fiscal period, the monthly accrual would be

   | | | |
   |---|---|---|
   | Property tax expense | xx | |
   | Property tax payable | | xx |

   If the taxes were paid at the beginning of the period, the entry to record the prepayment would be followed by monthly entries to expense the prepayment.

   | | | | | |
   |---|---|---|---|---|
   | Prepaid property taxes | xx | | Property tax expense | xx |
   | Cash | | xx | Prepaid property taxes | xx |

   If taxes are due, but not paid at the beginning of the year, the liability should be recorded and the deferred charge expensed over the fiscal year of the taxing body.

   | | | | | |
   |---|---|---|---|---|
   | Deferred property taxes | xx | | Property tax expense | xx |
   | Property tax payable | | xx | Deferred property taxes | xx |

h.  Bonus arrangements

| Bonus expense | xx | |
|---|---|---|
| Bonus payable | | xx |

Set up equations to describe the terms of the bonus agreement.  The general forms of the equations follow:

$$B = P(NI - B - T)$$
$$T = R(NI - B)$$

| B | = | Bonus |
|---|---|---|
| P | = | Bonus or profit sharing rate (10%) |
| NI | = | Net income ($150,000) |
| T | = | Taxes |
| R | = | Tax rate (40%) |

*EXAMPLE: Work through the above equations using the data in parentheses.*

$$T = .40(150,000 - B)$$
$$T = 60,000 - .4B$$
$$B = .10(150,000 - B - T)$$
$$B = .10(150,000 - B - 60,000 + .4B)$$
$$B = 15,000 - .1B - 6,000 + .04B$$
$$1.06B = 9,000$$
$$B = \$8,491$$

i.  Advances from customers—Record as deferred revenue and recognize as revenue when earned

| Cash | xx | | Deferred revenue | xx | |
|---|---|---|---|---|---|
| Deferred revenue | | xx | Revenue | | xx |

2.  **Contingencies**

a.  **Definitions**—An obligation may be either determinable (fixed) or contingent in accordance with the following definitions.

(1)  **Determinable liabilities**—The amount of cash and time of payment are known and reasonably precise.  Such liabilities are usually evidenced by written contracts but may also arise from implied agreements or imposed legal statutes.  Examples include notes payable and liabilities for various taxes as shown above.

(2)  **Contingent liabilities**—Such obligations **may** exist but are dependent on uncertain future events.  According to SFAS 5 a contingency is defined as an existing condition, situation, or set of circumstances involving uncertainty as to possible gain or loss to an enterprise that will ultimately be resolved when one or more future events occur or fail to occur.

b.  **Recording and disclosing contingencies**—The accounting problems related to contingencies involve the following issues.

(1)  When is it appropriate to record and report the effects of a contingency in the financial statements?  Should the financial impact of the contingency be reported in the period when the contingency is still unresolved or in the period in which the contingency is resolved?

(2)  For contingencies not recorded and reported on the financial statements before they are resolved, what disclosures, if any, are needed in the footnotes to the financial statements?

According to SFAS 5 (see outline), a loss contingency should be accrued if it is **probable** that an asset has been impaired or a liability has been incurred at the balance sheet date **and** the amount of the loss is **reasonably estimable**.  When loss contingencies are accrued, a debit should be made to an expense or to a loss account and a credit should be made to either a liability or to a contra asset account.  Note that to accrue a loss contingency means that the financial effects are reported in the financial statements **before** the contingency is resolved.

When making the decision concerning the accrual of a loss contingency, the term **probable** relates to the likelihood of a future event taking place or failing to take place which would resolve the uncertainty.  However, the likelihood of a future event taking place or failing to take place may not always be judged to be probable.  The likelihood of the future event taking place or failing to take place may instead be judged to be **reasonably possible** or **remote**.  In these last two situations, it is **not** appropriate to accrue the loss contingency as of the balance sheet date, although footnote disclosure may be necessary.  Footnote disclosure will be discussed later in this section.

In addition to being probable, the accrual of a loss contingency also requires that the amount of the loss be **reasonably estimable**. In most situations, a single amount can be estimated, and this represents the loss that is accrued. In other situations, the loss may be estimated in terms of a range, for example, the range of loss may be $100,000 to $500,000. In these situations, the amount of loss to accrue is the best estimate within the range. For example, if the best estimate within the range is $200,000, the loss should be accrued in the amount of $200,000. However, if no number in the range is a better estimate of the loss than any other number in the range, the lower number in the range is accrued as the loss. Thus, $100,000 would be accrued if no other number in the range from $100,000 to $500,000 were a better estimate of the loss than any other number in the range.

c.  **Examples of loss contingencies**—The accounting problems related to contingencies involve the following issues:

- Collectibility of receivables (Bad debts expense/Allowance for uncollectible accounts),
- Obligations related to product warranties and product defects (Warranty expense/ Warranty liability), and
- Premiums offered to customers (Premium expense/Premium liability)

These contingencies are usually accrued because it is **probable** that some receivables will not be collected, that some of the products sold will be defective and may need warranty work, and that some customers will take advantage of premiums offered by the company. In addition, the **amounts** in each case can usually be **estimated** because of past experience with each of these situations.

To illustrate the accrual of a loss contingency, let's focus on a **product warranty** situation. Here are the facts related to the illustration for ABC Company.

| Year | Sales | Actual warranty expenditures | Estimated warranty costs related to dollar sales |
|------|-------|------------------------------|--------------------------------------------------|
| 2007 | $500,000 | $15,000 | Year of sale   4% |
| 2008 | $700,000 | $47,000 | Year after sale 6% |

In 2007, ABC should accrue a loss contingency related to product warranties for $50,000 [$500,000 × (4% + 6%)]. The entry would appear as follows:

| | | |
|---|---|---|
| Warranty expense | 50,000 | |
| Liability for product warranty | | 50,000 |

The **actual** warranty expenditures in 2007 would be recorded in the following manner. (Note that the actual expenditures reduce the liability and have no effect on the expense account.)

| | | |
|---|---|---|
| Liability for product warranty | 15,000 | |
| Cash, parts inventory, etc. | | 15,000 |

ABC's income statement for 2007 would report an expense for $50,000 related to its product warranty, and its December 31, 2007 balance sheet would report a current liability for product warranty of $35,000 ($50,000 – $15,000). In 2008, ABC should accrue a loss contingency related to product warranties for $70,000 [$700,000 × (4% + 6%)]. The entry would appear as follows:

| | | |
|---|---|---|
| Warranty expense | 70,000 | |
| Liability for product warranty | | 70,000 |

The actual warranty expenditures for 2008 would be recorded in the following manner. (Again, note that the actual expenditures only affect the liability account.)

| | | |
|---|---|---|
| Liability for product warranty | 47,000 | |
| Cash, parts inventory, etc. | | 47,000 |

ABC's income statement for 2008 should report an expense related to product warranties of $70,000, and its December 31, 2008 balance sheet should report a current liability for product warranty of $58,000 (the 1/1/08 balance of $35,000 + the 2008 expense of $70,000 less the actual warranty expenditures of $47,000 in 2008).

Another example of accrual of a contingent liability involves companies offering **premiums** (e.g., towels, knives, and other prizes) to promote their products. Such companies often have premium liability for outstanding coupons when it is probable that some of the coupons will be redeemed and the amount can be estimated. The expense should be accrued in the period of sale based on the estimated redemption rate.

| | | |
|---|---|---|
| Premium plan expense | xx | |
|     Premium plan liability | | xx |

As coupons are actually redeemed by customers, the liability is reduced.

| | | |
|---|---|---|
| Premium plan liability | xx | |
|     Premiums | | xx |

Loss contingencies that may be accrued (depending upon whether or not the two conditions of probable and reasonably estimable are satisfied) include the following events.

- Threat of expropriation of assets
- Pending or threatened litigation
- Actual or possible claims and assessments
- Guarantees of indebtedness of others
- Obligations of commercial banks under "Standby letters of credit," and
- Agreements to repurchase receivables (or the related property) that have been sold

**Litigation**—The one event listed above that appears frequently on the exam involves pending litigation. If the loss from litigation is reasonably estimable, and it is probable as of the balance sheet date that the lawsuit will be lost, the loss should be accrued.

To illustrate this point, assume that XYZ Company is presently involved in litigation involving patent infringement that allegedly occurred during 2007. The financial statements for 2007 are being prepared, and XYZ's legal counsel believes it is probable that XYZ will lose the lawsuit and that the damages will be in the range from $500,000 to $800,000 with the most likely amount being $700,000. Based upon XYZ's legal counsel, it should accrue the loss contingency in the following manner at December 31, 2007.

| | | |
|---|---|---|
| Loss from litigation | 700,000 | |
|     Liability from litigation | | 700,000 |

The $700,000 loss from litigation should be reported on XYZ's 2007 income statement, and the liability should be reported on the December 31, 2007 balance sheet.

If XYZ settles the litigation in 2008 by paying damages of $600,000, the following journal entry should be made.

| | | |
|---|---|---|
| Liability from litigation | 700,000 | |
|     Cash | | 600,000 |
|     Recovery of loss from litigation | | 100,000 |

The above entry results in a loss recovery for 2008 because the damages were settled for less than their estimated amount. This situation is not unusual because the loss contingency related to the litigation was based upon an estimate. Note that the loss recovery cannot exceed the estimated loss, which in this case was $700,000. It would be incorrect to revise the 2007 financial statements so that the loss contingency reflected the actual damages of $600,000. When the financial statements for 2007 were issued, the best estimate of loss was $700,000. This estimate is not revised subsequent to the issuance of the 2007 financial statements.

Since loss contingencies involving litigation are only accrued if the conditions of probable and reasonably estimable are present, you should be aware of what is reported if either or both of these conditions are not present. For XYZ's case, suppose that its legal counsel believed it was only **reasonably possible** (not probable) as of the balance sheet date, December 31, 2007, that XYZ would lose its lawsuit. In this situation, it would **not** be appropriate for XYZ to accrue a loss at December 31, 2007. However, because XYZ's legal counsel believes it is reasonably possible to lose the lawsuit, XYZ should disclose this litigation in its footnotes for its 2007 financial statements. The range of loss, noted before as being from $500,000 to $800,000, would also be disclosed in the footnote. In 2008, when the actual damages of $600,000 are known, XYZ would record a loss of this amount and report it on its 2008 income statement.

If XYZ's legal counsel believed that it was **remote** as of December 31, 2007, that the lawsuit would be lost, no accrual or disclosure of the litigation would be necessary.

Loss contingencies that are not accrued or even disclosed in the footnotes include the following events.

- Risk of loss or damage of enterprise property by fire, explosion, or other hazards
- General or unspecified business risks
- Risk of loss from catastrophes assumed by property and casualty insurance companies including reinsurance companies

Losses that result from the above events are recorded and reported in the period when the event occurs that causes the loss. For example, if XYZ's factory is destroyed by fire in 2007, the loss from this event should be recorded and reported in 2007. If the damages from the fire amount to $1,000,000, and XYZ's insurance company reimburses XYZ $800,000, XYZ's loss is $200,000. If XYZ does not insure for fire with an insurance company, XYZ's loss for 2007 would be $1,000,000.

**Compensated absences**—Knowledge of the conditions that must be present in order to accrue a loss contingency is helpful in the accounting for **compensated absences** (vacation, sick leave pay, etc.). According to SFAS 43 (see outline), an employer shall accrue a liability for employees' compensation for future absences if all of the following conditions are met:

- The employer's obligation relating to employees' rights to receive compensation for future absences is attributable to employees' **services already rendered**
- The obligation relates to rights that **vest or accumulate**
- Payment of the compensation is **probable**
- The amount can be reasonably **estimated**

Note that the last two criteria are the general criteria for recognizing a loss contingency per SFAS 5.

To illustrate the accounting for compensated absences, assume MNO Company employees earn two weeks of paid vacation for each year of employment. Unused vacation time can be accumulated and carried forward to succeeding years, and will be paid at the salary level in effect when the vacation is taken. As of December 31, 2007, when John Baker's salary was $600 per week, John Baker had earned eighteen weeks vacation time and had used twelve weeks of accumulated vacation time. At December 31, 2007, MNO should report a liability for John Baker's accumulated vacation time of $3,600 (six weeks of accumulated vacation time times $600 per week). The journal entry at December 31, 2007, would appear as follows (assume previous year's entry was reversed).

| | | |
|---|---|---|
| Salary and wages expense | 3,600 | |
| Accrued liability for compensated absences | | 3,600 |

**Gain contingencies**—The discussion relating to contingencies has focused on the accounting for loss contingencies. On the other hand, contingencies exist that may also result in possible **gains**. According to SFAS 5, contingencies that might result in gains usually are not reflected in the accounts since to do so might be to recognize revenue prior to its realization. This means that any gains that result from gain contingencies should be recorded and reported in the period during which the contingency is resolved. For example, the plaintiff in a lawsuit should not record or report the expected damages to be received until the lawsuit has been decided.

**D. Fair Value Option**

As discussed in Module 7D, SFAS 159 provides that a company can elect the fair value option for reporting financial assets and financial liabilities. The fair value option also applies to firm commitments that would otherwise not be recognized at inception that only involve financial instruments. Nonfinancial insurance contracts and warranties may only be reported at fair value if the obligation can be settled by paying a third party to provide the goods and services.

**E. Ratios**

1. **Solvency**—Measure short-term viability

   a. **Acid-test (quick) ratio**—Measures ability to pay current liabilities from cash and near-cash items

   $$\frac{\text{Cash, Net receivables, Marketable securities}}{\text{Current liabilities}}$$

   b. **Current ratio**—Measures ability to pay current liabilities from cash, near-cash, and cash flow items

$$\frac{\text{Current assets}}{\text{Current liabilities}}$$

2.  **Operational efficiency**—Measures utilization of assets

    a.  **Receivable turnover**—Measures how rapidly cash is collected from credit sales

    $$\frac{\text{Net credit sales}}{\text{Average net receivables}}$$

    b.  **Number of days' sales in average receivables**—Average length of time receivables are outstanding, which reflects credit and collection policies

    $$\frac{365}{\text{Receivable turnover}}$$

    c.  **Inventory turnover**—Indicates how rapidly inventory is sold

    $$\frac{\text{Cost of goods sold}}{\text{Average inventory}}$$

    d.  **Number of days' supply in average inventory**—Measures the number of days inventory is held before sale and therefore reflects the efficiency of the entity's inventory policies

    $$\frac{365}{\text{Inventory turnover}}$$

    e.  **Length of operating cycle**—Measures length of time from purchase of inventory to collection of cash

    $$\begin{array}{c}\text{Number of days'} \\ \text{supply in average} \\ \text{inventory}\end{array} + \begin{array}{c}\text{Number of days'} \\ \text{sales in average} \\ \text{receivables}\end{array}$$

F.  **Research Component**

Basic concepts on current assets and current liabilities are found in ARB 43, Chapter 3. APB 6 amends portions of ARB 43. SFAS 6 addresses the accounting rules for short-term obligations expected to be refinanced. SFAS 5 addresses accounting for contingencies. Careful attention should be given to SFAS 5, as this standard applies to items such as accruals for warranties, lawsuits, expropriation, litigation, and other risk of loss. SFAS 43 addresses compensated absence such as accruals for vacation or sick benefits. The latest pronouncement, SFAS 140, addresses accounting for transfers and servicing of financial assets and extinguishment of liabilities. This chapter provides the more recent rules for factoring or pledging accounts receivable.

A list of keywords for these pronouncements is shown below.

| | | |
|---|---|---|
| Agreement to refinance | Examples loss contingencies | Remote |
| Appropriated retained earnings | Extinguished debt | Retained interests |
| Beneficial interests | Extinguished liability | Rights that vest |
| Benefits of servicing | Fair value retained interests | Sale of financial assets |
| Classification current liabilities | Financial assets | Sale of receivables |
| Collateral | Financial assets exchange | Securitization |
| Collateral pledged | Financial liability | Securitized financial assets |
| Compensation future absences | Loss contingencies | Servicing fees |
| Contingency | Loss contingency | SPE |
| Control transferred assets | Operating cycle | Transferor surrendered control |
| Current assets | Ordinary operations | Transfers financial assets |
| Current liabilities | Primary obligor | Undivided interests |
| Debtor security interest | Probable | Unilateral ability |
| Deduction from receivables | Probable future events | With recourse |
| Derecognize assets | Proceeds | Without recourse |
| Derecognize liability | Reasonably possible | Working capital |
| Estimated loss | Recourse | |
| Estimated or accrued amounts | Refinance obligation | |

**MULTIPLE-CHOICE QUESTIONS (1-111)**

**1.** Burr Company had the following account balances at December 31, 2007:

| | |
|---|---|
| Cash in banks | $2,250,000 |
| Cash on hand | 125,000 |
| Cash legally restricted for additions to plant (expected to be disbursed in 2008) | 1,600,000 |

Cash in banks includes $600,000 of compensating balances against short-term borrowing arrangements. The compensating balances are not legally restricted as to withdrawal by Burr. In the current assets section of Burr's December 31, 2007 balance sheet, total cash should be reported at
- a. $1,775,000
- b. $2,250,000
- c. $2,375,000
- d. $3,975,000

**2.** Ral Corp.'s checkbook balance on December 31, 2007, was $5,000. In addition, Ral held the following items in its safe on that date:

| | |
|---|---|
| Check payable to Ral Corp., dated January 2, 2008, in payment of a sale made in December 2007, not included in December 31 checkbook balance | $2,000 |
| Check payable to Ral Corp., deposited December 15 and included in December 31 checkbook balance, but returned by bank on December 30 stamped "NSF." The check was redeposited on January 2, 2008, and cleared on January 9 | 500 |
| Check drawn on Ral Corp.'s account, payable to a vendor, dated and recorded in Ral's books on December 31 but not mailed until January 10, 2008 | 300 |

The proper amount to be shown as Cash on Ral's balance sheet at December 31, 2007, is
- a. $4,800
- b. $5,300
- c. $6,500
- d. $6,800

**3.** Trans Co. had the following balances at December 31, 2007:

| | |
|---|---|
| Cash in checking account | $ 35,000 |
| Cash in money market account | 75,000 |
| US Treasury bill, purchased 11/1/2007, maturing 1/31/2008 | 350,000 |
| US Treasury bill, purchased 12/1/2007, maturing 3/31/2008 | 400,000 |

Trans's policy is to treat as cash equivalents all highly liquid investments with a maturity of three months or less when purchased. What amount should Trans report as cash and cash equivalents in its December 31, 2007 balance sheet?
- a. $110,000
- b. $385,000
- c. $460,000
- d. $860,000

**4.** On October 31, 2007, Dingo, Inc. had cash accounts at three different banks. One account balance is segregated solely for a November 15, 2007 payment into a bond sinking fund. A second account, used for branch operations, is overdrawn. The third account, used for regular corporate operations, has a positive balance. How should these accounts be reported in Dingo's October 31, 2007 classified balance sheet?
- a. The segregated account should be reported as a noncurrent asset, the regular account should be re-

ported as a current asset, and the overdraft should be reported as a current liability.
- b. The segregated and regular accounts should be reported as current assets, and the overdraft should be reported as a current liability.
- c. The segregated account should be reported as a noncurrent asset, and the regular account should be reported as a current asset net of the overdraft.
- d. The segregated and regular accounts should be reported as current assets net of the overdraft.

**5.** In preparing its August 31, 2007 bank reconciliation, Apex Corp. has available the following information:

| | |
|---|---|
| Balance per bank statement, 8/31/07 | $18,050 |
| Deposit in transit, 8/31/07 | 3,250 |
| Return of customer's check for insufficient funds, 8/31/07 | 600 |
| Outstanding checks, 8/31/07 | 2,750 |
| Bank service charges for August | 100 |

At August 31, 2007, Apex's correct cash balance is
- a. $18,550
- b. $17,950
- c. $17,850
- d. $17,550

**6.** Poe, Inc. had the following bank reconciliation at March 31, 2007:

| | |
|---|---|
| Balance per bank statement, 3/31/07 | $46,500 |
| Add deposit in transit | 10,300 |
| | 56,800 |
| Less outstanding checks | 12,600 |
| Balance per books, 3/31/07 | $44,200 |

Data per bank for the month of April 2007 follow:

| | |
|---|---|
| Deposits | $58,400 |
| Disbursements | 49,700 |

All reconciling items at March 31, 2007, cleared the bank in April. Outstanding checks at April 30, 2007, totaled $7,000. There were no deposits in transit at April 30, 2007. What is the cash balance per books at April 30, 2007?
- a. $48,200
- b. $52,900
- c. $55,200
- d. $58,500

**7.** On the December 31, 2007 balance sheet of Mann Co., the current receivables consisted of the following:

| | |
|---|---|
| Trade accounts receivable | $ 93,000 |
| Allowance for uncollectible accounts | (2,000) |
| Claim against shipper for goods lost in transit (November 2007) | 3,000 |
| Selling price of unsold goods sent by Mann on consignment at 130% of cost (**not** included in Mann's ending inventory) | 26,000 |
| Security deposit on lease of warehouse used for storing some inventories | 30,000 |
| Total | $150,000 |

At December 31, 2007, the correct total of Mann's current net receivables was
- a. $ 94,000
- b. $120,000
- c. $124,000
- d. $150,000

**8.** The following information relates to Jay Co.'s accounts receivable for 2007:

| | |
|---|---:|
| Accounts receivable, 1/1/07 | $ 650,000 |
| Credit sales for 2007 | 2,700,000 |
| Sales returns for 2007 | 75,000 |
| Accounts written off during 2007 | 40,000 |
| Collections from customers during 2007 | 2,150,000 |
| Estimated future sales returns at 12/31/07 | 50,000 |
| Estimated uncollectible accounts at 12/31/07 | 110,000 |

What amount should Jay report for accounts receivable, before allowances for sales returns and uncollectible accounts, at December 31, 2007?

   a.  $1,200,000
   b.  $1,125,000
   c.  $1,085,000
   d.  $ 925,000

**9.** Frame Co. has an 8% note receivable dated June 30, 2005, in the original amount of $150,000. Payments of $50,000 in principal plus accrued interest are due annually on July 1, 2006, 2007, and 2008. In its June 30, 2007 balance sheet, what amount should Frame report as a current asset for interest on the note receivable?

   a.  $0
   b.  $ 4,000
   c.  $ 8,000
   d.  $12,000

**10.** On December 1, 2007, Tigg Mortgage Co. gave Pod Corp. a $200,000, 12% loan. Pod received proceeds of $194,000 after the deduction of a $6,000 nonrefundable loan origination fee. Principal and interest are due in sixty monthly installments of $4,450, beginning January 1, 2008. The repayments yield an effective interest rate of 12% at a present value of $200,000 and 13.4% at a present value of $194,000. Tigg does not elect the fair value option for recording the note to Pod. What amount of accrued interest receivable should Tigg include in its December 31, 2007 balance sheet?

   a.  $4,450
   b.  $2,166
   c.  $2,000
   d.  $0

**11.** On Merf's April 30, 2007 balance sheet a note receivable was reported as a noncurrent asset and its accrued interest for eight months was reported as a current asset. Which of the following terms would fit Merf's note receivable?

   a.  Both principal and interest amounts are payable on August 31, 2007, and August 31, 2008.
   b.  Principal and interest are due December 31, 2007.
   c.  Both principal and interest amounts are payable on December 31, 2007, and December 31, 2008.
   d.  Principal is due August 31, 2008, and interest is due August 31, 2007, and August 31, 2008.

**12.** On August 15, 2007, Benet Co. sold goods for which it received a note bearing the market rate of interest on that date. The four-month note was dated July 15, 2007. Note principal, together with all interest, is due November 15, 2007. Assume Benet did not elect the fair value option for reporting the note. When the note was recorded on August 15, which of the following accounts increased?

   a.  Unearned discount.
   b.  Interest receivable.
   c.  Prepaid interest.
   d.  Interest revenue.

**13.** Delta, Inc. sells to wholesalers on terms of 2/15, net 30. Delta has no cash sales but 50% of Delta's customers take advantage of the discount. Delta uses the gross method of recording sales and trade receivables. An analysis of Delta's trade receivables balances at December 31, 2007, revealed the following:

| Age | | Amount | Collectible |
|---|---|---:|:---:|
| 0 - 15 | days | $100,000 | 100% |
| 16 - 30 | days | 60,000 | 95% |
| 31 - 60 | days | 5,000 | 90% |
| Over 60 days | | 2,500 | $500 |
| | | $167,500 | |

In its December 31, 2007 balance sheet, what amount should Delta report for allowance for discounts?

   a.  $1,000
   b.  $1,620
   c.  $1,675
   d.  $2,000

**14.** Fenn Stores, Inc. had sales of $1,000,000 during December, 2007. Experience has shown that merchandise equaling 7% of sales will be returned within thirty days and an additional 3% will be returned within ninety days. Returned merchandise is readily resalable. In addition, merchandise equaling 15% of sales will be exchanged for merchandise of equal or greater value. What amount should Fenn report for net sales in its income statement for the month of December 2007?

   a.  $900,000
   b.  $850,000
   c.  $780,000
   d.  $750,000

**15.** At January 1, 2007, Jamin Co. had a credit balance of $260,000 in its allowance for uncollectible accounts. Based on past experience, 2% of Jamin's credit sales have been uncollectible. During 2007, Jamin wrote off $325,000 of uncollectible accounts. Credit sales for 2007 were $9,000,000. In its December 31, 2007 balance sheet, what amount should Jamin report as allowance for uncollectible accounts?

   a.  $115,000
   b.  $180,000
   c.  $245,000
   d.  $440,000

**16.** The following accounts were abstracted from Roxy Co.'s unadjusted trial balance at December 31, 2007:

| | Debit | Credit |
|---|---:|---:|
| Accounts receivable | $1,000,000 | |
| Allowance for uncollectible accounts | 8,000 | |
| Net credit sales | | $3,000,000 |

Roxy estimates that 3% of the gross accounts receivable will become uncollectible. After adjustment at December 31, 2007, the allowance for uncollectible accounts should have a credit balance of

   a.  $90,000
   b.  $82,000
   c.  $38,000
   d.  $30,000

**17.** In its December 31 balance sheet, Butler Co. reported trade accounts receivable of $250,000 and related allowance for uncollectible accounts of $20,000. What is the total amount of risk of accounting loss related to Butler's trade accounts receivable, and what amount of that risk is off-balance-sheet risk?

|     | Risk of accounting loss | Off-balance-sheet risk |
|-----|-------------------------|------------------------|
| a.  | $0                      | $0                     |
| b.  | $230,000                | $0                     |
| c.  | $230,000                | $20,000                |
| d.  | $250,000                | $20,000                |

**18.** Inge Co. determined that the net value of its accounts receivable at December 31, 2007, based on an aging of the receivables, was $325,000. Additional information is as follows:

| | |
|---|---|
| Allowance for uncollectible accounts—1/1/07 | $ 30,000 |
| Uncollectible accounts written off during 2007 | 18,000 |
| Uncollectible accounts recovered during 2007 | 2,000 |
| Accounts receivable at 12/31/07 | 350,000 |

For 2007, what would be Inge's uncollectible accounts expense?

   a.  $ 5,000
   b.  $11,000
   c.  $15,000
   d.  $21,000

**19.** The following information pertains to Tara Co.'s accounts receivable at December 31, 2007:

| Days outstanding | Amount | Estimated % uncollectible |
|------------------|--------|---------------------------|
| 0 – 60           | $120,000 | 1% |
| 61 – 120         | 90,000 | 2% |
| Over 120         | 100,000 | 6% |
|                  | $310,000 | |

During 2007, Tara wrote off $7,000 in receivables and recovered $4,000 that had been written off in prior years. Tara's December 31, 2006 allowance for uncollectible accounts was $22,000. Under the aging method, what amount of allowance for uncollectible accounts should Tara report at December 31, 2007?

   a.  $ 9,000
   b.  $10,000
   c.  $13,000
   d.  $19,000

**20.** A method of estimating uncollectible accounts that emphasizes asset valuation rather than income measurement is the allowance method based on

   a.  Aging the receivables.
   b.  Direct write-off.
   c.  Gross sales.
   d.  Credit sales less returns and allowances.

**21.** Which method of recording uncollectible accounts expense is consistent with accrual accounting?

|     | Allowance | Direct write-off |
|-----|-----------|------------------|
| a.  | Yes       | Yes              |
| b.  | Yes       | No               |
| c.  | No        | Yes              |
| d.  | No        | No               |

**22.** When the allowance method of recognizing uncollectible accounts is used, the entry to record the write-off of a specific account

   a.  Decreases both accounts receivable and the allowance for uncollectible accounts.
   b.  Decreases accounts receivable and increases the allowance for uncollectible accounts.
   c.  Increases the allowance for uncollectible accounts and decreases net income.
   d.  Decreases both accounts receivable and net income.

**23.** A company uses the allowance method to recognize uncollectible accounts expense. What is the effect at the time of the collection of an account previously written off on each of the following accounts?

|     | Allowance for uncollectible accounts | Uncollectible accounts expense |
|-----|--------------------------------------|--------------------------------|
| a.  | No effect                            | Decrease                       |
| b.  | Increase                             | Decrease                       |
| c.  | Increase                             | No effect                      |
| d.  | No effect                            | No effect                      |

**24.** Which of the following is a method to generate cash from accounts receivables?

|     | Assignment | Factoring |
|-----|------------|-----------|
| a.  | Yes        | No        |
| b.  | Yes        | Yes       |
| c.  | No         | Yes       |
| d.  | No         | No        |

**25.** Gar Co. factored its receivables. Control was surrendered in the transaction which was on a without recourse basis with Ross Bank. Gar received cash as a result of this transaction, which is best described as a

   a.  Loan from Ross collateralized by Gar's accounts receivable.
   b.  Loan from Ross to be repaid by the proceeds from Gar's accounts receivable.
   c.  Sale of Gar's accounts receivable to Ross, with the risk of uncollectible accounts retained by Gar.
   d.  Sale of Gar's accounts receivable to Ross, with the risk of uncollectible accounts transferred to Ross.

**Items 26 through 28** are based on the following:

Taylored Corp. factored $400,000 of accounts receivable to Rich Corp. on July 1, 2007. Control was surrendered by Taylored. Rich accepted the receivables subject to recourse for nonpayment. Rich assessed a fee of 2% and retains a holdback equal to 5% of the accounts receivable. In addition, Rich charged 15% interest computed on a weighted-average time to maturity of the receivables of forty-one days. The fair value of the recourse obligation is $12,000.

**26.** Taylored will receive and record cash of
   a.  $385,260
   b.  $357,260
   c.  $365,260
   d.  $377,260

**27.** Which of the following statements is correct?
   a.  Rich should record an asset of $8,000 for the recourse obligation.
   b.  Taylored should record a liability and corresponding loss of $12,000 related to the recourse obligation.
   c.  Taylored should record a liability of $12,000, but no loss, related to the recourse obligation.
   d.  No entry for the recourse obligation should be made by Taylored or Rich until the debtor fails to pay.

**28.** Assuming all receivables are collected, Taylored's cost of factoring the receivables would be
   a.  $ 8,000
   b.  $34,740
   c.  $42,740

d.  $14,740

**29.** Which of the following is used to account for probable sales discounts, sales returns, and sales allowances?

|     | Due from factor | Recourse liability |
| --- | --- | --- |
| a.  | Yes | No  |
| b.  | Yes | Yes |
| c.  | No  | Yes |
| d.  | No  | No  |

**30.** Scarbrough Corp. factored $600,000 of accounts receivable to Duff Corp. on October 1, 2007. Control was surrendered by Scarbrough. Duff accepted the receivables subject to recourse for nonpayment. Duff assessed a fee of 3% and retains a holdback equal to 5% of the accounts receivable. In addition, Duff charged 15% interest computed on a weighted-average time to maturity of the receivables of fifty-four days. The fair value of the recourse obligation is $9,000. Scarbrough will receive and record cash of

a.  $529,685
b.  $538,685
c.  $547,685
d.  $556,685

**31.** Synthia Corp. factored $750,000 of accounts receivable to Thomas Company on December 3, 2007. Control was surrendered by Synthia. Thomas accepted the receivables subject to recourse for nonpayment. Thomas assessed a fee of 2% and retains a holdback equal to 4% of the accounts receivable. In addition, Thomas charged 12% interest computed on a weighted-average time to maturity of the receivables of fifty-one days. The fair value of the recourse obligation is $15,000. Assuming all receivables are collected, Synthia's cost of factoring the receivables would be

a.  $12,575
b.  $15,000
c.  $27,575
d.  $42,575

**32.** Bannon Corp. transferred financial assets to Chapman, Inc. The transfer meets the conditions to be accounted for as a sale. As the transferor, Bannon should do each of the following, **except**

a.  Remove all assets sold from the balance sheet.
b.  Record all assets received and liabilities incurred as proceeds from the sale.
c.  Measure the assets received and liabilities incurred at cost.
d.  Recognize any gain or loss on the sale.

**33.** If financial assets are exchanged for cash or other consideration, but the transfer does not meet the criteria for a sale, the transferor and the transferee should account for the transaction as a

|     | Secured borrowing | Pledge of collateral |
| --- | --- | --- |
| a.  | No  | Yes |
| b.  | Yes | Yes |
| c.  | Yes | No  |
| d.  | No  | No  |

**34.** All but one of the following are required before a transfer of receivables can be recorded as a sale.

a.  The transferred receivables are beyond the reach of the transferor and its creditors.
b.  The transferor has not kept effective control over the transferred receivables through a repurchase agreement.
c.  The transferor maintains continuing involvement.
d.  The transferee can pledge or sell the transferred receivables.

**35.** Which of the following is not an objective for each entity accounting for transfers of financial assets?

a.  To derecognize assets when control is gained.
b.  To derecognize liabilities when extinguished.
c.  To recognize liabilities when incurred.
d.  To derecognize assets when control is given up.

**36.** Which of the following is false?

a.  A servicing asset shall be assessed for impairment based on its fair value.
b.  A servicing liability shall be assessed for increased obligation based on its fair value.
c.  An obligation to service financial assets may result in the recognition of a servicing asset or servicing liability.
d.  A servicing asset or liability should be amortized for a period of five years.

**37.** Fusion Corporation uses the amortization method to account for its servicing assets. Which of the following statements is true?

a.  Increases in fair value are reported in other comprehensive income.
b.  Increases in fair value are reported in earnings of the period.
c.  The assets are measured at fair value at the end of each reporting period.
d.  The assets are measured for impairment at the end of each reporting period.

**38.** According to SFAS 156, which of the following statements is true regarding servicing assets and servicing liabilities?

I.  Either the amortization method or the fair value method can be used.
II.  Once the fair value method is elected, the election cannot be reversed.
III.  Changes in fair value are reported in other comprehensive income for the period.

a.  I only.
b.  I and II.
c.  II only.
d.  I and III.

**39.** Binsar Corporation transfers a financial asset but continues to hold an interest in the servicing asset. How should the interest in the servicing asset that continues to be held be measured at the date of the transfer?

a.  At the present value of future cash flows.
b.  At fair value.
c.  By allocating the previous carrying amount between the assets sold and interest that continues to be held based on the relative fair values of the assets.
d.  At net realizable value.

**40.** Which of the following is true?

a. A debtor may not grant a security interest in certain assets to a lender to serve as collateral with recourse.

b. A debtor may not grant a security interest in certain assets to a lender to serve as collateral without recourse.

c. The arrangement of having collateral transferred to a secured party is known as a pledge.

d. Secured parties are never permitted to sell collateral held under a pledge.

**Items 41 through 43** are based on the following:

Company ABC sells loans with a $2,200 fair value and a carrying amount of $2,000. ABC Company obtains an option to purchase similar loans and assumes a recourse obligation to repurchase loans. ABC Company also agrees to provide a floating rate of interest to the transferee company. The fair values are listed.

| _Fair values_ | |
|---|---|
| Cash proceeds | $2,100 |
| Interest rate swap | 140 |
| Call option | 80 |
| Recourse obligation | (120) |

**41.** What is the gain (loss) on the sale?
- a. $ 320
- b. $ 200
- c. $(100)
- d. $ 120

**42.** The journal entry to record the transfer for ABC Company includes
- a. A debit to call option.
- b. A credit to interest rate swap.
- c. A debit to loans.
- d. A credit to cash.

**43.** Assume for this problem that ABC Company agreed to service the loans without explicitly stating the compensation. The fair value of the service is $50. What are the net proceeds received and the gain (loss) on the sale?

| | _Net proceeds received_ | _Gain (loss)_ |
|---|---|---|
| a. | $2,200 | $ 200 |
| b. | $2,250 | $ 250 |
| c. | $2,150 | $ 150 |
| d. | $2,200 | $(250) |

**44.** In accordance with SFAS 140, _Accounting for Transfers and Servicing of Financial Assets and Extinguishments of Liabilities,_ financial assets subject to prepayment should be measured
- a. Like investments in debt securities classified as held-to-maturity.
- b. At cost.
- c. Like investments in debt securities classified as available-for-sale or trading.
- d. At fair value.

**45.** In accordance with SFAS 140, _Accounting for Transfers and Servicing of Financial Assets and Extinguishments of Liabilities,_ all of the following would be disclosed except
- a. Policy for requiring collateral or other security due to repurchase agreements or securities lending transactions.
- b. Cash flows between the securitization special-purpose entity (SPE) and the transferor.

c. Accounting policies for measuring retained interest.

d. Description of assets or liabilities with estimable fair values.

**46.** Taft Inc. borrowed $1,000,000 from Wilson Company on July 2, 2005. As part of the loan agreement, Taft granted Wilson a security interest in land that originally cost $750,000 when it was acquired by Taft in 1998. The land had a fair value of $900,000 on July 2, 2005. In June 2007, Taft defaulted on its loan to Wilson, and the land was transferred to Wilson in full settlement of the debt on June 30. The land had a fair value of $950,000 on June 30, 2007. In accordance with SFAS 140, _Accounting for Transfers and Servicing of Financial Assets and Extinguishments of Liabilities,_ what amount should Wilson record for land on June 30, 2007?
- a. $0.
- b. $750,000.
- c. $900,000.
- d. $950,000.

**47.** Lyle, Inc. is preparing its financial statements for the year ended December 31, 2007. Accounts payable amounted to $360,000 before any necessary year-end adjustment related to the following:

- At December 31, 2007, Lyle has a $50,000 debit balance in its accounts payable to Ross, a supplier, resulting from a $50,000 advance payment for goods to be manufactured to Lyle's specifications.
- Checks in the amount of $100,000 were written to vendors and recorded on December 29, 2007. The checks were mailed on January 5, 2008.

What amount should Lyle report as accounts payable in its December 31, 2007 balance sheet?
- a. $510,000
- b. $410,000
- c. $310,000
- d. $210,000

**48.** Rabb Co. records its purchases at gross amounts but wishes to change to recording purchases net of purchase discounts. Discounts available on purchases recorded from October 1, 2006, to September 30, 2007, totaled $2,000. Of this amount, $200 is still available in the accounts payable balance. The balances in Rabb's accounts as of and for the year ended September 30, 2007, before conversion are

| | |
|---|---|
| Purchases | $100,000 |
| Purchase discounts taken | 800 |
| Accounts payable | 30,000 |

What is Rabb's accounts payable balance as of September 30, 2007, after the conversion?
- a. $29,800
- b. $29,200
- c. $28,800
- d. $28,200

**49.** On March 1, 2006, Fine Co. borrowed $10,000 and signed a two-year note bearing interest at 12% per annum compounded annually. Interest is payable in full at maturity on February 28, 2008. What amount should Fine report as a liability for accrued interest at December 31, 2007?
- a. $0
- b. $1,000
- c. $1,200
- d. $2,320

**50.** On September 1, 2006, Brak Co. borrowed on a $1,350,000 note payable from Federal Bank. The note bears interest at 12% and is payable in three equal annual principal payments of $450,000. On this date, the bank's prime rate was 11%. The first annual payment for interest and principal was made on September 1, 2007. At December 31, 2007, what amount should Brak report as accrued interest payable?

    a. $54,000
    b. $49,500
    c. $36,000
    d. $33,000

**51.** In its 2007 financial statements, Cris Co. reported interest expense of $85,000 in its income statement and cash paid for interest of $68,000 in its cash flow statement. There was no prepaid interest or interest capitalization either at the beginning or end of 2007. Accrued interest at December 31, 2006, was $15,000. What amount should Cris report as accrued interest payable in its December 31, 2007 balance sheet?

    a. $ 2,000
    b. $15,000
    c. $17,000
    d. $32,000

**52.** Ames, Inc. has $500,000 of notes payable due June 15, 2008. Ames signed an agreement on December 1, 2007, to borrow up to $500,000 to refinance the notes payable on a long-term basis with no payments due until 2008. The financing agreement stipulated that borrowings may not exceed 80% of the value of the collateral Ames was providing. At the date of issuance of the December 31, 2007 financial statements, the value of the collateral was $600,000 and is not expected to fall below this amount during 2008. In Ames' December 31, 2007 balance sheet, the obligation for these notes payable should be classified as

| | Short-term | Long-term |
|---|---|---|
| a. | $500,000 | $0 |
| b. | $100,000 | $400,000 |
| c. | $ 20,000 | $480,000 |
| d. | $0 | $500,000 |

**53.** A company issued a short-term note payable with a stated 12% rate of interest to a bank. The bank charged a .5% loan origination fee and remitted the balance to the company. The effective interest rate paid by the company in this transaction would be

    a. Equal to 12.5%.
    b. More than 12.5%.
    c. Less than 12.5%.
    d. Independent of 12.5%.

**54.** Cali, Inc. had a $4,000,000 note payable due on March 15, 2008. On January 28, 2008, before the issuance of its 2007 financial statements, Cali issued long-term bonds in the amount of $4,500,000. Proceeds from the bonds were used to repay the note when it came due. How should Cali classify the note in its December 31, 2008 financial statements?

    a. As a current liability, with separate disclosure of the note refinancing.
    b. As a current liability, with no separate disclosure required.
    c. As a noncurrent liability, with separate disclosure of the note refinancing.
    d. As a noncurrent liability, with no separate disclosure required.

**55.** On December 31, 2007, Largo, Inc. had a $750,000 note payable outstanding, due July 31, 2008. Largo borrowed the money to finance construction of a new plant. Largo planned to refinance the note by issuing long-term bonds. Because Largo temporarily had excess cash, it prepaid $250,000 of the note on January 12, 2008. In February 2008, Largo completed a $1,500,000 bond offering. Largo will use the bond offering proceeds to repay the note payable at its maturity and to pay construction costs during 2008. On March 3, 2008, Largo issued its 2007 financial statements. What amount of the note payable should Largo include in the current liabilities section of its December 31, 2007 balance sheet?

    a. $750,000
    b. $500,000
    c. $250,000
    d. $0

**56.** Rice Co. salaried employees are paid biweekly. Advances made to employees are paid back by payroll deductions. Information relating to salaries follows:

| | 12/31/06 | 12/31/07 |
|---|---|---|
| Employee advances | $24,000 | $ 36,000 |
| Accrued salaries payable | 40,000 | ? |
| Salaries expense during the year | | 420,000 |
| Salaries paid during the year (gross) | | 390,000 |

In Rice's December 31, 2007 balance sheet, accrued salaries payable was

    a. $94,000
    b. $82,000
    c. $70,000
    d. $30,000

**57.** Fay Corp. pays its outside salespersons fixed monthly salaries and commissions on net sales. Sales commissions are computed and paid on a monthly basis (in the month following the month of sale), and the fixed salaries are treated as advances against commissions. However, if the fixed salaries for salespersons exceed their sales commissions earned for a month, such excess is not charged back to them. Pertinent data for the month of March 2007 for the three salespersons are as follows:

| Salesperson | Fixed salary | Net sales | Commission rate |
|---|---|---|---|
| A | $10,000 | $ 200,000 | 4% |
| B | 14,000 | 400,000 | 6% |
| C | 18,000 | 600,000 | 6% |
| Totals | $42,000 | $1,200,000 | |

What amount should Fay accrue for sales commissions payable at March 31, 2007?

    a. $70,000
    b. $68,000
    c. $28,000
    d. $26,000

**58.** Lime Co.'s payroll for the month ended January 31, 2007, is summarized as follows:

| | |
|---|---|
| Total wages | $10,000 |
| Federal income tax withheld | 1,200 |

All wages paid were subject to FICA. FICA tax rates were 7% each for employee and employer. Lime remits payroll taxes on the 15th of the following month. In its financial statements for the month ended January 31, 2007, what amounts should Lime report as total payroll tax liability and as payroll tax expense?

|    | Liability | Expense |
|----|-----------|---------|
| a. | $1,200    | $1,400  |
| b. | $1,900    | $1,400  |
| c. | $1,900    | $ 700   |
| d. | $2,600    | $ 700   |

**59.** Under state law, Acme may pay 3% of eligible gross wages or it may reimburse the state directly for actual unemployment claims. Acme believes that actual unemployment claims will be 2% of eligible gross wages and has chosen to reimburse the state. Eligible gross wages are defined as the first $10,000 of gross wages paid to each employee. Acme had five employees, each of whom earned $20,000 during 2007. In its December 31, 2007 balance sheet, what amount should Acme report as accrued liability for unemployment claims?

    a. $1,000
    b. $1,500
    c. $2,000
    d. $3,000

**60.** Pine Corp. is required to contribute, to an employee stock ownership plan (ESOP), 10% of its income after deduction for this contribution but before income tax. Pine's income before charges for the contribution and income tax was $75,000. The income tax rate is 30%. What amount should be accrued as a contribution to the ESOP?

    a. $7,500
    b. $6,818
    c. $5,250
    d. $4,773

**61.** Able Co. provides an incentive compensation plan under which its president receives a bonus equal to 10% of the corporation's income before income tax but after deduction of the bonus. If the tax rate is 40% and net income after bonus and income tax was $360,000, what was the amount of the bonus?

    a. $36,000
    b. $60,000
    c. $66,000
    d. $90,000

**62.** Ivy Co. operates a retail store. All items are sold subject to a 6% state sales tax, which Ivy collects and records as sales revenue. Ivy files quarterly sales tax returns when due, by the twentieth day following the end of the sales quarter. However, in accordance with state requirements, Ivy remits sales tax collected by the twentieth day of the month following any month such collections exceed $500. Ivy takes these payments as credits on the quarterly sales tax return. The sales taxes paid by Ivy are charged against sales revenue.

Following is a monthly summary appearing in Ivy's first quarter 2007 sales revenue account:

|          | Debit  | Credit   |
|----------|--------|----------|
| January  | $  --  | $10,600  |
| February | 600    | 7,420    |
| March    | --     | 8,480    |
|          | $600   | $26,500  |

In its March 31, 2007 balance sheet, what amount should Ivy report as sales taxes payable?

    a. $  600
    b. $  900

    c. $1,500
    d. $1,590

**63.** Hudson Hotel collects 15% in city sales taxes on room rentals, in addition to a $2 per room, per night, occupancy tax. Sales taxes for each month are due at the end of the following month, and occupancy taxes are due fifteen days after the end of each calendar quarter. On January 3, 2008, Hudson paid its November 2007 sales taxes and its fourth quarter 2007 occupancy taxes. Additional information pertaining to Hudson's operations is

| 2007     | Room rentals | Room nights |
|----------|--------------|-------------|
| October  | $100,000     | 1,100       |
| November | 110,000      | 1,200       |
| December | 150,000      | 1,800       |

What amounts should Hudson report as sales taxes payable and occupancy taxes payable in its December 31, 2007 balance sheet?

|    | Sales taxes | Occupancy taxes |
|----|-------------|-----------------|
| a. | $39,000     | $6,000          |
| b. | $39,000     | $8,200          |
| c. | $54,000     | $6,000          |
| d. | $54,000     | $8,200          |

**64.** On July 1, 2007, Ran County issued realty tax assessments for its fiscal year ended June 30, 2008. On September 1, 2007, Day Co. purchased a warehouse in Ran County. The purchase price was reduced by a credit for accrued realty taxes. Day did not record the entire year's real estate tax obligation, but instead records tax expenses at the end of each month by adjusting prepaid real estate taxes or real estate taxes payable, as appropriate. On November 1, 2007, Day paid the first of two equal installments of $12,000 for realty taxes. What amount of this payment should Day record as a debit to real estate taxes payable?

    a. $ 4,000
    b. $ 8,000
    c. $10,000
    d. $12,000

**65.** Kemp Co. must determine the December 31, 2007 year-end accruals for advertising and rent expenses. A $500 advertising bill was received January 7, 2008, comprising costs of $375 for advertisements in December 2007 issues, and $125 for advertisements in January 2008 issues of the newspaper.

A store lease, effective December 16, 2006, calls for fixed rent of $1,200 per month, payable one month from the effective date and monthly thereafter. In addition, rent equal to 5% of net sales over $300,000 per calendar year is payable on January 31 of the following year. Net sales for 2007 were $550,000.

In its December 31, 2007 balance sheet, Kemp should report accrued liabilities of

    a. $12,875
    b. $13,000
    c. $13,100
    d. $13,475

**66.** On May 1, 2007, Marno County issued property tax assessments for the fiscal year ended June 30, 2008. The first of two equal installments was due on November 1, 2007. On September 1, 2007, Dyur Co. purchased a four-year-old factory in Marno subject to an allowance for accrued taxes. Dyur did not record the entire year's property tax obligation, but instead records tax expenses at the end of each month by adjusting prepaid property taxes or property taxes payable, as appropriate. The recording of the November 1, 2007 payment by Dyur should have been allocated between an increase in prepaid property taxes and a decrease in property taxes payable in which of the following percentages?

| | Increase in pre-paid property taxes | Decrease in property taxes payable |
|---|---|---|
| a. | 66 2/3% | 33 1/3% |
| b. | 0% | 100% |
| c. | 50% | 50% |
| d. | 33 1/3% | 66 2/3% |

*Percentage allocated to*

**67.** Black Co. requires advance payments with special orders for machinery constructed to customer specifications. These advances are nonrefundable. Information for 2007 is as follows:

| | |
|---|---|
| Customer advances—balance 12/31/06 | $118,000 |
| Advances received with orders in 2007 | 184,000 |
| Advances applied to orders shipped in 2007 | 164,000 |
| Advances applicable to orders cancelled in 2007 | 50,000 |

In Black's December 31, 2007 balance sheet, what amount should be reported as a current liability for advances from customer?

a. $0
b. $ 88,000
c. $138,000
d. $148,000

**68.** Marr Co. sells its products in reusable containers. The customer is charged a deposit for each container delivered and receives a refund for each container returned within two years after the year of delivery. Marr accounts for the containers not returned within the time limit as being retired by sale at the deposit amount. Information for 2007 is as follows:

Container deposits at December 31, 2006, from deliveries in

| | | |
|---|---|---|
| 2005 | $150,000 | |
| 2006 | 430,000 | $580,000 |
| Deposits for containers delivered in 2007 | | 780,000 |

Deposits for containers returned in 2007 from deliveries in

| | | |
|---|---|---|
| 2005 | $ 90,000 | |
| 2006 | 250,000 | |
| 2007 | 286,000 | 626,000 |

In Marr's December 31, 2007 balance sheet, the liability for deposits on returnable containers should be

a. $494,000
b. $584,000
c. $674,000
d. $734,000

**69.** Kent Co., a division of National Realty, Inc., maintains escrow accounts and pays real estate taxes for National's mortgage customers. Escrow funds are kept in interest-bearing accounts. Interest, less a 10% service fee, is credited to the mortgagee's account and used to reduce future escrow payments. Additional information follows:

| | |
|---|---|
| Escrow accounts liability, 1/1/07 | $ 700,000 |
| Escrow payments received during 2007 | 1,580,000 |
| Real estate taxes paid during 2007 | 1,720,000 |
| Interest on escrow funds during 2007 | 50,000 |

What amount should Kent report as escrow accounts liability in its December 31, 2007 balance sheet?

a. $510,000

b. $515,000
c. $605,000
d. $610,000

**70.** Cobb Company sells appliance service contracts agreeing to repair appliances for a two-year period. Cobb's past experience is that, of the total dollars spent for repairs on service contracts, 40% is incurred evenly during the first contract year and 60% evenly during the second contract year. Receipts from service contract sales for the two years ended December 31, 2007, are as follows:

| | |
|---|---|
| 2006 | $500,000 |
| 2007 | 600,000 |

Receipts from contracts are credited to unearned service contract revenue. Assume that all contract sales are made evenly during the year. What amount should Cobb report as unearned service contract revenue at December 31, 2007?

a. $360,000
b. $470,000
c. $480,000
d. $630,000

**71.** Toddler Care Co. offers three payment plans on its twelve-month contracts. Information on the three plans and the number of children enrolled in each plan for the September 1, 2007 through August 31, 2008 contract year follows:

| Plan | Initial payment per child | Monthly fees per child | Number of children |
|---|---|---|---|
| #1 | $500 | $ -- | 15 |
| #2 | 200 | 30 | 12 |
| #3 | -- | 50 | 9 |
| | | | 36 |

Toddler received $9,900 of initial payments on September 1, 2007, and $3,240 of monthly fees during the period September 1 through December 31, 2007. In its December 31, 2007 balance sheet, what amount should Toddler report as deferred revenues?

a. $3,300
b. $4,380
c. $6,600
d. $9,900

**72.** A retail store received cash and issued gift certificates that are redeemable in merchandise. The gift certificates lapse one year after they are issued. How would the deferred revenue account be affected by each of the following transactions?

| | Redemption of certificates | Lapse of certificates |
|---|---|---|
| a. | Decrease | No effect |
| b. | Decrease | Decrease |
| c. | No effect | No effect |
| d. | No effect | Decrease |

**73.** On March 31, 2007, Dallas Co. received an advance payment of 60% of the sales price for special-order goods to be manufactured and delivered within five months. At the same time, Dallas subcontracted for production of the special-order goods at a price equal to 40% of the main contract price. What liabilities should be reported in Dallas' March 31, 2007 balance sheet?

|  | Deferred revenues | Payables to subcontractor |
|---|---|---|
| a. | None | None |
| b. | 60% of main contract price | 40% of main contract price |
| c. | 60% of main contract price | None |
| d. | None | 40% of main contract price |

**74.** In June 2007, Northan Retailers sold refundable merchandise coupons. Northan received $10 for each coupon redeemable from July 1 to December 31, 2007, for merchandise with a retail price of $11. At June 30, 2007, how should Northan report these coupon transactions?

    a. Unearned revenues at the merchandise's retail price.
    b. Unearned revenues at the cash received amount.
    c. Revenues at the merchandise's retail price.
    d. Revenues at the cash received amount.

**75.** Delect Co. provides repair services for the AZ195 TV set. Customers prepay the fee on the standard one-year service contract. The 2006 and 2007 contracts were identical, and the number of contracts outstanding was substantially the same at the end of each year. However, Delect's December 31, 2007 deferred revenues' balance on unperformed service contracts was significantly less than the balance at December 31, 2006. Which of the following situations might account for this reduction in the deferred revenue balance?

    a. Most 2007 contracts were signed later in the calendar year than were the 2006 contracts.
    b. Most 2007 contracts were signed earlier in the calendar year than were the 2006 contracts.
    c. The 2007 contract contribution margin was greater than the 2006 contract contribution margin.
    d. The 2007 contribution margin was less than the 2006 contract contribution margin.

**76.** Brad Corp. has unconditional purchase obligations associated with product financing arrangements. These obligations are reported as liabilities on Brad's balance sheet, with the related assets also recognized. In the notes to Brad's financial statements, the aggregate amount of payments for these obligations should be disclosed for each of how many years following the date of the latest balance sheet?

    a. 0
    b. 1
    c. 5
    d. 10

**77.** On January 17, 2007, an explosion occurred at a Sims Co. plant causing extensive property damage to area buildings. Although no claims had yet been asserted against Sims by March 10, 2007, Sims' management and counsel concluded that it is likely that claims will be asserted and that it is reasonably possible Sims will be responsible for damages. Sims' management believed that $1,250,000 would be a reasonable estimate of its liability. Sims' $5,000,000 comprehensive public liability policy has a $250,000 deductible clause. In Sims' December 31, 2006 financial statements, which were issued on March 25, 2007, how should this item be reported?

    a. As an accrued liability of $250,000.
    b. As a footnote disclosure indicating the possible loss of $250,000.

    c. As a footnote disclosure indicating the possible loss of $1,250,000.
    d. No footnote disclosure or accrual is necessary.

**78.** Brite Corp. had the following liabilities at December 31, 2007:

| | |
|---|---|
| Accounts payable | $55,000 |
| Unsecured notes, 8%, due 7/1/08 | 400,000 |
| Accrued expenses | 35,000 |
| Contingent liability | 450,000 |
| Deferred income tax liability | 25,000 |
| Senior bonds, 7%, due 3/31/08 | 1,000,000 |

The contingent liability is an accrual for possible losses on a $1,000,000 lawsuit filed against Brite. Brite's legal counsel expects the suit to be settled in 2009, and has estimated that Brite will be liable for damages in the range of $450,000 to $750,000.

    The deferred income tax liability is not related to an asset for financial reporting and is expected to reverse in 2009.

    What amount should Brite report in its December 31, 2007 balance sheet for current liabilities?

    a. $ 515,000
    b. $ 940,000
    c. $1,490,000
    d. $1,515,000

**79.** On February 5, 2008, an employee filed a $2,000,000 lawsuit against Steel Co. for damages suffered when one of Steel's plants exploded on December 29, 2007. Steel's legal counsel expects the company will lose the lawsuit and estimates the loss to be between $500,000 and $1,000,000. The employee has offered to settle the lawsuit out of court for $900,000, but Steel will not agree to the settlement. In its December 31, 2007 balance sheet, what amount should Steel report as liability from lawsuit?

    a. $2,000,000
    b. $1,000,000
    c. $ 900,000
    d. $ 500,000

**80.** On November 5, 2007, a Dunn Corp. truck was in an accident with an auto driven by Bell. Dunn received notice on January 12, 2008, of a lawsuit for $700,000 damages for personal injuries suffered by Bell. Dunn Corp.'s counsel believes it is probable that Bell will be awarded an estimated amount in the range between $200,000 and $450,000, and that $300,000 is a better estimate of potential liability than any other amount. Dunn's accounting year ends on December 31, and the 2007 financial statements were issued on March 2, 2008. What amount of loss should Dunn accrue at December 31, 2007?

    a. $0
    b. $200,000
    c. $300,000
    d. $450,000

**81.** During 2007, Haft Co. became involved in a tax dispute with the IRS. At December 31, 2007, Haft's tax advisor believed that an unfavorable outcome was probable. A reasonable estimate of additional taxes was $200,000 but could be as much as $300,000. After the 2007 financial statements were issued, Haft received and accepted an IRS settlement offer of $275,000. What amount of accrued liability should Haft have reported in its December 31, 2007 balance sheet?

    a. $200,000
    b. $250,000

   c.   $275,000
   d.   $300,000

**82.** Management can estimate the amount of loss that will occur if a foreign government expropriates some company assets. If expropriation is reasonably possible, a loss contingency should be
   a.   Disclosed but not accrued as a liability.
   b.   Disclosed and accrued as a liability.
   c.   Accrued as a liability but not disclosed.
   d.   Neither accrued as a liability nor disclosed.

**83.** Invern, Inc. has a self-insurance plan. Each year, retained earnings is appropriated for contingencies in an amount equal to insurance premiums saved less recognized losses from lawsuits and other claims. As a result of a 2007 accident, Invern is a defendant in a lawsuit in which it will probably have to pay damages of $190,000. What are the effects of this lawsuit's probable outcome on Invern's 2007 financial statements?
   a.   An increase in expenses and no effect on liabilities.
   b.   An increase in both expenses and liabilities.
   c.   No effect on expenses and an increase in liabilities.
   d.   No effect on either expenses or liabilities.

**84.** In 2006, a personal injury lawsuit was brought against Halsey Co. Based on counsel's estimate, Halsey reported a $50,000 liability in its December 31, 2006 balance sheet. In November 2007, Halsey received a favorable judgment, requiring the plaintiff to reimburse Halsey for expenses of $30,000. The plaintiff has appealed the decision, and Halsey's counsel is unable to predict the outcome of the appeal. In its December 31, 2007 balance sheet, Halsey should report what amounts of asset and liability related to these legal actions?

|   | *Asset* | *Liability* |
|---|---|---|
| a. | $30,000 | $50,000 |
| b. | $30,000 | $0 |
| c. | $0 | $20,000 |
| d. | $0 | $0 |

**85.** During January 2007, Haze Corp. won a litigation award for $15,000 that was tripled to $45,000 to include punitive damages. The defendant, who is financially stable, has appealed only the $30,000 punitive damages. Haze was awarded $50,000 in an unrelated suit it filed, which is being appealed by the defendant. Counsel is unable to estimate the outcome of these appeals. In its 2007 financial statements, Haze should report what amount of pretax gain?
   a.   $15,000
   b.   $45,000
   c.   $50,000
   d.   $95,000

**86.** In May 2003 Caso Co. filed suit against Wayne, Inc. seeking $1,900,000 damages for patent infringement. A court verdict in November 2007 awarded Caso $1,500,000 in damages, but Wayne's appeal is not expected to be decided before 2009. Caso's counsel believes it is probable that Caso will be successful against Wayne for an estimated amount in the range between $800,000 and $1,100,000, with $1,000,000 considered the most likely amount. What amount should Caso record as income from the lawsuit in the year ended December 31, 2007?
   a.   $0
   b.   $ 800,000

   c.   $1,000,000
   d.   $1,500,000

**87.** During 2007, Smith Co. filed suit against West, Inc. seeking damages for patent infringement. At December 31, 2007, Smith's legal counsel believed that it was probable that Smith would be successful against West for an estimated amount in the range of $75,000 to $150,000, with all amounts in the range considered equally likely. In March 2008, Smith was awarded $100,000 and received full payment thereof. In its 2007 financial statements, issued in February 2008 how should this award be reported?
   a.   As a receivable and revenue of $100,000.
   b.   As a receivable and deferred revenue of $100,000.
   c.   As a disclosure of a contingent gain of $100,000.
   d.   As a disclosure of a contingent gain of an undetermined amount in the range of $75,000 to $150,000.

**88.** In 2007, a contract dispute between Dollis Co. and Brooks Co. was submitted to binding arbitration. In 2007, each party's attorney indicated privately that the probable award in Dollis' favor could be reasonably estimated. In 2008, the arbitrator decided in favor of Dollis. When should Dollis and Brooks recognize their respective gain and loss?

|   | *Dollis' gain* | *Brooks' loss* |
|---|---|---|
| a. | 2007 | 2007 |
| b. | 2007 | 2008 |
| c. | 2008 | 2007 |
| d. | 2008 | 2008 |

**89.** Eagle Co. has cosigned the mortgage note on the home of its president, guaranteeing the indebtedness in the event that the president should default. Eagle considers the likelihood of default to be remote. How should the guarantee be treated in Eagle's financial statements?
   a.   Disclosed only.
   b.   Accrued only.
   c.   Accrued and disclosed.
   d.   Neither accrued nor disclosed.

**90.** North Corp. has an employee benefit plan for compensated absences that gives employees 10 paid vacation days and 10 paid sick days. Both vacation and sick days can be carried over indefinitely. Employees can elect to receive payment in lieu of vacation days; however, no payment is given for sick days not taken. At December 31, 2007, North's unadjusted balance of liability for compensated absences was $21,000. North estimated that there were 150 vacation days and 75 sick days available at December 31, 2007. North's employees earn an average of $100 per day. In its December 31, 2007 balance sheet, what amount of liability for compensated absences is North required to report?
   a.   $36,000
   b.   $22,500
   c.   $21,000
   d.   $15,000

**91.** Ross Co. pays all salaried employees on a Monday for the five-day workweek ended the previous Friday. The last payroll recorded for the year ended December 31, 2007, was for the week ended December 25, 2007. The payroll for the week ended January 1, 2008, included regular weekly salaries of $80,000 and vacation pay of $25,000 for vacation time earned in 2007 not taken by December 31, 2007. Ross had accrued a liability of $20,000 for vacation pay at December 31, 2006. In its December 31, 2007 balance sheet, what amount should Ross report as accrued salary and vacation pay?

    a.   $64,000
    b.   $68,000
    c.   $69,000
    d.   $89,000

**92.** Gavin Co. grants all employees two weeks of paid vacation for each full year of employment. Unused vacation time can be accumulated and carried forward to succeeding years and will be paid at the salaries in effect when vacations are taken or when employment is terminated. There was no employee turnover in 2007. Additional information relating to the year ended December 31, 2007, is as follows:

| | |
|---|---|
| Liability for accumulated vacations at 12/31/06 | $35,000 |
| Pre-2006 accrued vacations taken from 1/1/07to | |
|   9/30/07(the authorized period for vacations) | 20,000 |
| Vacations earned for work in 2007 (adjusted to current | |
|   rates) | 30,000 |

Gavin granted a 10% salary increase to all employees on October 1, 2007, its annual salary increase date. For the year ended December 31, 2007, Gavin should report vacation pay expense of

    a.   $45,000
    b.   $33,500
    c.   $31,500
    d.   $30,000

**93.** At December 31, 2007, Taos Co. estimates that its employees have earned vacation pay of $100,000. Employees will receive their vacation pay in 2008. Should Taos accrue a liability at December 31, 2007, if the rights to this compensation accumulated over time or if the rights are vested?

| | Accumulated | Vested |
|---|---|---|
| a. | Yes | No |
| b. | No | No |
| c. | Yes | Yes |
| d. | No | Yes |

**94.** If the payment of employees' compensation for future absences is probable, the amount can be reasonably estimated, and the obligation relates to rights that accumulate, the compensation should be

    a.   Accrued if attributable to employees' services not already rendered.
    b.   Accrued if attributable to employees' services already rendered.
    c.   Accrued if attributable to employees' services whether already rendered or not.
    d.   Recognized when paid.

**95.** During 2007, Gum Co. introduced a new product carrying a two-year warranty against defects. The estimated warranty costs related to dollar sales are 2% within twelve months following the sale and 4% in the second twelve months following the sale. Sales and actual warranty expenditures for the years ended December 31, 2007 and 2008, are as follows:

| | Sales | Actual warranty expenditures |
|---|---|---|
| 2007 | $150,000 | $2,250 |
| 2008 | 250,000 | 7,500 |
| | $400,000 | $9,750 |

What amount should Gum report as estimated warranty liability in its December 31, 2008 balance sheet?

    a.   $ 2,500
    b.   $ 4,250
    c.   $11,250
    d.   $14,250

**96.** Vadis Co. sells appliances that include a three-year warranty. Service calls under the warranty are performed by an independent mechanic under a contract with Vadis. Based on experience, warranty costs are estimated at $30 for each machine sold. When should Vadis recognize these warranty costs?

    a.   Evenly over the life of the warranty.
    b.   When the service calls are performed.
    c.   When payments are made to the mechanic.
    d.   When the machines are sold.

**97.** Lute Corporation sells furnaces that include a three-year warranty. Lute can contract with a third party to provide these warranty services. Lute elects the fair value option in SFAS 159 for reporting financial liabilities. At what amount should Lute record the warranty liability on the balance sheet?

    a.   The cost of expected warranty services.
    b.   The present value of expected warranty costs.
    c.   The fair value of the contract to settle the warranty services.
    d.   The fair value of the contract to settle less the cost to provide services.

**98.** Case Cereal Co. frequently distributes coupons to promote new products. On October 1, 2007, Case mailed 1,000,000 coupons for $.45 off each box of cereal purchased. Case expects 120,000 of these coupons to be redeemed before the December 31, 2007, expiration date. It takes thirty days from the redemption date for Case to receive the coupons from the retailers. Case reimburses the retailers an additional $.05 for each coupon redeemed. As of December 31, 2007, Case had paid retailers $25,000 related to these coupons and had 50,000 coupons on hand that had not been processed for payment. What amount should Case report as a liability for coupons in its December 31, 2007 balance sheet?

    a.   $35,000
    b.   $29,000
    c.   $25,000
    d.   $22,500

**99.** Dunn Trading Stamp Co. records stamp service revenue and provides for the cost of redemptions in the year stamps are sold to licensees. Dunn's past experience indicates that only 80% of the stamps sold to licensees will be redeemed. Dunn's liability for stamp redemptions was $6,000,000 at December 31, 2006. Additional information for 2007 is as follows:

| | |
|---|---|
| Stamp service revenue from stamps sold to licen- | |
|   sees | $4,000,000 |
| Cost of redemptions (stamps sold prior to 1/1/07) | 2,750,000 |

If all the stamps sold in 2007 were presented for redemption in 2008, the redemption cost would be $2,250,000. What amount should Dunn report as a liability for stamp redemptions at December 31, 2007?

    a.   $7,250,000
    b.   $5,500,000
    c.   $5,050,000
    d.   $3,250,000

**Items 100 and 101** are based on the following:

The following trial balance of Trey Co. at December 31, 2007, has been adjusted except for income tax expense.

|  | Dr. | Cr. |
|---|---|---|
| Cash | $ 550,000 | |
| Accounts receivable, net | 1,650,000 | |
| Prepaid taxes | 300,000 | |
| Accounts payable | | $ 120,000 |
| Common stock | | 500,000 |
| Additional paid-in capital | | 680,000 |
| Retained earnings | | 630,000 |
| Foreign currency translation adjustment | 430,000 | |
| Revenues | | 3,600,000 |
| Expenses | 2,600,000 | |
| | $5,530,000 | $5,530,000 |

### Additional information

- During 2007, estimated tax payments of $300,000 were charged to prepaid taxes. Trey has not yet recorded income tax expense. There were no differences between financial statement and income tax income, and Trey's tax rate is 30%.
- Included in accounts receivable is $500,000 due from a customer. Special terms granted to this customer require payment in equal semiannual installments of $125,000 every April 1 and October 1.

**100.** In Trey's December 31, 2007 balance sheet, what amount should be reported as total current assets?
- a. $1,950,000
- b. $2,200,000
- c. $2,250,000
- d. $2,500,000

**101.** In Trey's December 31, 2007 balance sheet, what amount should be reported as total retained earnings?
- a. $1,029,000
- b. $1,200,000
- c. $1,330,000
- d. $1,630,000

**102.** The following is Gold Corp.'s June 30, 2007 trial balance:

| | | |
|---|---|---|
| Cash overdraft | | $ 10,000 |
| Accounts receivable, net | $ 35,000 | |
| Inventory | 58,000 | |
| Prepaid expenses | 12,000 | |
| Land held for resale | 100,000 | |
| Property, plant, and equipment, net | 95,000 | |
| Accounts payable and accrued expenses | | 32,000 |
| Common stock | | 25,000 |
| Additional paid-in capital | | 150,000 |
| Retained earnings | | 83,000 |
| | $300,000 | $300,000 |

### Additional information

- Checks amounting to $30,000 were written to vendors and recorded on June 29, 2007, resulting in a cash overdraft of $10,000. The checks were mailed on July 9, 2007.
- Land held for resale was sold for cash on July 15, 2007.
- Gold issued its financial statements on July 31, 2007.

In its June 30, 2007 balance sheet, what amount should Gold report as current assets?
- a. $225,000
- b. $205,000
- c. $195,000

- d. $125,000

**103. Mill** Co.'s trial balance included the following account balances at December 31, 2007:

| | |
|---|---|
| Accounts payable | $15,000 |
| Bonds payable, due 2008 | 25,000 |
| Discount on bonds payable, due 2008 | 3,000 |
| Dividends payable 1/31/08 | 8,000 |
| Notes payable, due 2009 | 20,000 |

What amount should be included in the current liability section of Mill's December 31, 2007 balance sheet?
- a. $45,000
- b. $51,000
- c. $65,000
- d. $78,000

**Items 104 and 105** are based on the following:

**Rey, Inc.**
**SELECTED FINANCIAL DATA**
*December 31,*

| | 2007 | 2006 |
|---|---|---|
| Cash | $ 170,000 | $ 90,000 |
| Accounts receivable (net) | 450,000 | 400,000 |
| Merchandise inventory | 540,000 | 420,000 |
| Short-term marketable securities | 80,000 | 40,000 |
| Land and building (net) | 1,000,000 | 1,000,000 |
| Mortgage payable—current portion | 60,000 | 50,000 |
| Accounts payable and accrued liabilities | 240,000 | 220,000 |
| Short-term notes payable | 100,000 | 140,000 |

Net credit sales totaled $3,000,000 and $2,000,000 for the years ended December 31, 2007 and 2006, respectively.

**104.** At December 31, 2007, Rey's quick (acid-test) ratio was
- a. 1.50 to 1.
- b. 1.75 to 1.
- c. 2.06 to 1.
- d. 3.10 to 1.

**105.** For 2007, Rey's accounts receivable turnover was
- a. 1.13
- b. 1.50
- c. 6.67
- d. 7.06

**106.** Which of the following ratios is(are) useful in assessing a company's ability to meet currently maturing or short-term obligations?

| | Acid-test ratio | Debt to equity ratio |
|---|---|---|
| a. | No | No |
| b. | No | Yes |
| c. | Yes | Yes |
| d. | Yes | No |

**107.** North Bank is analyzing Belle Corp.'s financial statements for a possible extension of credit. Belle's quick ratio is significantly better than the industry average. Which of the following factors should North consider as a possible limitation of using this ratio when evaluating Belle's creditworthiness?
- a. Fluctuating market prices of short-term investments may adversely affect the ratio.
- b. Increasing market prices for Belle's inventory may adversely affect the ratio.
- c. Belle may need to sell its available-for-sale investments to meet its current obligations.

    d.   Belle may need to liquidate its inventory to meet its long-term obligations.

**108.** On December 30, 2007, Vida Co. had cash of $200,000, a current ratio of 1.5:1 and a quick ratio of .5:1. On December 31, 2007, all cash was used to reduce accounts payable. How did these cash payments affect the ratios?

|     | *Current ratio* | *Quick ratio* |
|-----|-----------------|---------------|
| a.  | Increased       | Decreased     |
| b.  | Increased       | No effect     |
| c.  | Decreased       | Increased     |
| d.  | Decreased       | No effect     |

**109.** Tod Corp. wrote off $100,000 of obsolete inventory at December 31, 2007. The effect of this write-off was to decrease

    a.   Both the current and acid-test ratios.
    b.   Only the current ratio.
    c.   Only the acid-test ratio.
    d.   Neither the current nor the acid-test ratios.

**110.** The following computations were made from Clay Co.'s 2007 books:

| Number of days' sales in inventory | 61 |
|------------------------------------|----|
| Number of days' sales in accounts receivable | 33 |

What was the number of days in Clay's 2007 operating cycle?

    a.   33
    b.   47
    c.   61
    d.   94

**111.** On December 31, 2007, Northpark Co. collected a receivable due from a major customer. Which of the following ratios would be increased by this transaction?

    a.   Inventory turnover ratio.
    b.   Receivable turnover ratio.
    c.   Current ratio.
    d.   Quick ratio.

**SIMULATION PROBLEMS**

**Simulation Problem 1**                    (50 to 60 minutes)

| Instructions | | | | | |
|---|---|---|---|---|---|
| | Concepts | Journal Entries | Reporting Requirements | Communication | Research |

Chester Company has transactions involving current assets and current liabilities.  Complete the various components of the simulation for Chester.

| | Concepts | | | | |
|---|---|---|---|---|---|
| Instructions | | Journal Entries | Reporting Requirements | Communication | Research |

Determine whether each statement is True or False.

|  | (T) | (F) |
|---|---|---|
| 1.  The balance in "factor's holdback" (due from factor) is reported as an expense of the period. | O | O |
| 2.  In a specific assignment of receivables, collections on the assigned accounts are generally remitted to the assignor. | O | O |
| 3.  Factors are banks or finance companies that purchase receivables for a fee and then collect the remittances directly from the selling company. | O | O |
| 4.  A transfer of receivables with recourse may be accounted for as a sale, provided the transferee can require the transferor to repurchase the receivables. | O | O |
| 5.  In a transfer of receivables with recourse accounted for as a borrowing, the difference between the receivables and the total of the factor's holdback plus the proceeds is a financing cost that should be amortized to interest expense over the term of the receivables. | O | O |

| | | Journal Entries | | | |
|---|---|---|---|---|---|
| Instructions | Concepts | | Reporting Requirements | Communication | Research |

The following items relate to the transfer of accounts and notes receivable.  For each item, match the transaction with the appropriate journal entry.  Entries may be used once, more than once, or not at all.

*Journal entries*

| A. | Cash | xxx | | D. | Cash | xxx | |
|---|---|---|---|---|---|---|---|
| | Interest expense | xxx | | | Factor's holdback | xxx | |
| | Liability on discounted NR | | xxx | | Loss on sale of AR | xxx | |
| | Interest revenue | | xxx | | AR | | xxx |

| B. | Cash | xxx | | E. | Parenthetical or note disclosure only. |
|---|---|---|---|---|---|
| | Factor's holdback | xxx | | | |
| | Interest expense (discount) | xxx | | | |
| | Liability on transferred AR | | xxx | | |

| C. | Cash | xxx | | F. | Cash | xxx | |
|---|---|---|---|---|---|---|---|
| | Finance charge | xxx | | | Loss on sale of NR | xxx | |
| | AR assigned | xxx | | | NR | | xxx |
| | Note payable | | xxx | | Interest revenue | | xxx |
| | AR | | xxx | | | | |

|  | (A) | (B) | (C) | (D) | (E) | (F) |
|---|---|---|---|---|---|---|
| 1.  Chester transfers receivables by surrendering control.  Collection is to be made by the purchaser (factor), who assumes risk of loss. | O | O | O | O | O | O |
| 2.  Chester specifically assigns a portion of its receivables as collateral for a loan.  Collections from the assigned receivables will be used to repay the loan and interest. | O | O | O | O | O | O |
| 3.  Chester pledges its receivables as collateral to secure a loan and the debtor collects the proceeds. | O | O | O | O | O | O |
| 4.  Chester sells accounts receivable to a factor in a transaction considered a borrowing. | O | O | O | O | O | O |
| 5.  Chester transfers a note receivable by surrendering control over it.  The transfer was on a without recourse basis. | O | O | O | O | O | O |
| 6.  Chester pledges its accounts receivable as security for a loan. | O | O | O | O | O | O |

| Instructions | Concepts | Journal Entries | Reporting Requirements | Communication | Research |
|---|---|---|---|---|---|

**Items 1 through 6** are based on the following:

Chester Company is preparing its financial statements for the year ended December 31, 2007.

**Items 1 through 6** represent various commitments and contingencies of Chester at December 31, 2007, and events subsequent to December 31, 2007, but prior to the issuance of the 2007 financial statements. For each item, select from the following list the reporting requirement. A reporting requirement may be selected once, more than once, or not at all.

*Reporting requirement*

D.   Disclosure only
A.   Accrual only

B.   Both accrual and disclosure
N.   Neither accrual nor disclosure

| | (D) | (A) | (B) | (N) |
|---|---|---|---|---|
| 1. On December 1, 2007, Chester was awarded damages of $75,000 in a patent infringement suit it brought against a competitor. The defendant did not appeal the verdict, and payment was received in January 2008. | ○ | ○ | ○ | ○ |
| 2. A former employee of Chester has brought a wrongful-dismissal suit against Chester. Chester's lawyers believe the suit to be without merit. | ○ | ○ | ○ | ○ |
| 3. At December 31, 2007, Chester had outstanding purchase orders in the ordinary course of business for purchase of a raw material to be used in its manufacturing process. The market price is currently higher than the purchase price and is not anticipated to change within the next year. | ○ | ○ | ○ | ○ |
| 4. A government contract completed during 2007 is subject to renegotiation. Although Chester estimates that it is reasonably possible that a refund of approximately $200,000 – $300,000 may be required by the government, it does not wish to publicize this possibility. | ○ | ○ | ○ | ○ |
| 5. Chester has been notified by a governmental agency that it will be held responsible for the cleanup of toxic materials at a site where Chester formerly conducted operations. Chester estimates that it is probable that its share of remedial action will be approximately $500,000. | ○ | ○ | ○ | ○ |
| 6. On January 5, 2008, Chester redeemed its outstanding bonds and issued new bonds with a lower rate of interest. The reacquisition price was in excess of the carrying amount of the bonds. | ○ | ○ | ○ | ○ |

| Instructions | Concepts | Journal Entries | Reporting Requirements | Communication | Research |
|---|---|---|---|---|---|

Chester Company has the following contingencies:

- A threat of expropriation exists for one of its manufacturing plants located in a foreign country. Expropriation is deemed to be reasonably possible. Any compensation from the foreign government would be less than the carrying amount of the plant.
- Potential costs exist due to the discovery of a safety hazard related to one of its products. These costs are probable and can be reasonably estimated.
- One of its warehouses located at the base of a mountain could no longer be insured against rock slide losses. No rock slide losses have occurred.

The CEO of Chester would like to know how to account for these items. Write a brief memo to the CEO of Chester explaining the following:

1.   How should Chester report the threat of expropriation of assets? Why?
2.   How should Chester report the potential costs due to the safety hazard? Why?
3.   How should Chester report the noninsurable rock slide risk? Why?

To:      CEO, Chester Company
From:   CPA Candidate
Re:      Contingencies

| Instructions | Concepts | Journal Entries | Reporting Requirements | Communication | Research |
|---|---|---|---|---|---|

Research each of the following questions in the authoritative literature. Insert the solution in the space provided.

1. How should short-term obligations be classified on the balance sheet?

2. Next year, Chester intends to refinance some short-term debt with a long-term note due in five years. What are the criteria to reclassify the short-term debt as long-term?

3. When should the company accrue an estimated loss on a contingency?

4. What is a contingency?

5. Define the three terms used to describe the likelihood of a contingent event occurring.

6. What are the conditions required for Chester to accrue vacation pay for its employees?

7. What are the criteria required to determine if a liability should be removed from the balance sheet?

---

**Simulation Problem 2**                    (50 to 60 minutes)

| Situation | | | | | | | |
|---|---|---|---|---|---|---|---|
| | Concepts | Uncollectible Accounts | Provision for Uncollectible Accounts Expense | Journal Entries | Transfer of Receivables | Communication | Research |

Sigma Co. began operations on January 1, 2006. On December 31, 2006, Sigma provided for uncollectible accounts based on 1% of annual credit sales. On January 1, 2007, Sigma changed its method of determining its allowance for uncollectible accounts by applying certain percentages to the accounts receivable aging as follows:

| Days past invoice date | Percent deemed to be uncollectible |
|---|---|
| 0–30 | 1 |
| 31–90 | 5 |
| 91–180 | 20 |
| Over 180 | 80 |

In addition, Sigma wrote off all accounts receivable that were over one year old.  The following additional information relates to the years ended December 31, 2007, and 2006:

| | 2007 | 2006 |
|---|---|---|
| Credit sales | $3,000,000 | $2,800,000 |
| Collections | 2,915,000 | 2,400,000 |
| Accounts written off | 27,000 | None |
| Recovery of accounts previously written off | 7,000 | None |
| *Days past invoice date at 12/31* | | |
| 0–30 | 300,000 | 250,000 |
| 31–90 | 80,000 | 90,000 |
| 91–180 | 60,000 | 45,000 |
| Over 180 | 25,000 | 15,000 |

| Situation | Concepts | Uncollectible Accounts | Provision for Uncollectible Accounts Expense | Journal Entries | Transfer of Receivables | Communication | Research |
|---|---|---|---|---|---|---|---|

Identify which of the following items are disclosed as cash or cash equivalents on the balance sheet.

| | Cash | Not cash |
|---|---|---|
| 1.  Checking accounts | ○ | ○ |
| 2.  Treasury stock | ○ | ○ |
| 3.  Treasury bills | ○ | ○ |
| 4.  Money market funds | ○ | ○ |
| 5.  Petty cash | ○ | ○ |
| 6.  Trading securities | ○ | ○ |
| 7.  Savings accounts | ○ | ○ |
| 8.  Sinking fund cash | ○ | ○ |
| 9.  Compensating balances against long-term borrowings | ○ | ○ |
| 10.  Cash restricted for new building | ○ | ○ |
| 11.  Postdated check for customers | ○ | ○ |
| 12.  Available-for-sale securities | ○ | ○ |

| Situation | Concepts | Uncollectible Accounts | Provision for Uncollectible Accounts Expense | Journal Entries | Transfer of Receivables | Communication | Research |
|---|---|---|---|---|---|---|---|

Complete the following schedule showing the calculation of the allowance for uncollectible accounts at December 31, 2007.

Schedule to calculate provision and allowance for bad debts

**Sigma Company**
**SCHEDULE OF CALCULATION OF ALLOWANCE FOR UNCOLLECTIBLE ACCOUNTS**
*December 31, 2007*

| | *Amounts of accounts receivable* | *Percentage of uncollectible accounts* | *Estimate of uncollectible accounts* |
|---|---|---|---|
| 0 to 30 days | | | |
| 31 to 90 days | | | |
| 91 to 180 days | | | |
| Over 180 days | | | |
| Total accounts receivable | | | |
| Total allowance for uncollectible accounts | | | |

| Situation | Concepts | Uncollectible Accounts | Provision for Uncollectible Accounts Expense | Journal Entries | Transfer of Receivables | Communication | Research |
|-----------|----------|------------------------|-------|-------|-------|-------|-------|

Complete the following table and calculate the provision for uncollectible accounts expense for 2007.
Computation of 2007 provision

| | |
|---|---|
| Balance December 31, 2006 | |
| Write-offs during 2007 | |
| Recoveries during 2007 | |
| Balance before 2007 provision | |
| Required allowance at December 31, 2007 | |
| 2007 Provision | |

| Situation | Concepts | Uncollectible Accounts | Provision for Uncollectible Accounts Expense | Journal Entries | Transfer of Receivables | Communication | Research |
|-----------|----------|------------------------|-------|-------|-------|-------|-------|

Prepare the journal entries for the write-offs and recoveries for 2007, and for the provision for uncollectible accounts expense at December 31, 2007.

*Write-offs*

| | | |
|---|---|---|
| | | |
| | | |
| | | |
| | | |

*Recoveries*

| | | |
|---|---|---|
| | | |
| | | |
| | | |
| | | |

***Provision for uncollectible accounts expense at December 31, 2007***

| | | |
|---|---|---|
| | | |
| | | |
| | | |
| | | |

| Situation | Concepts | Uncollectible Accounts | Provision for Uncollectible Accounts Expense | Journal Entries | Transfer of Receivables | Communication | Research |
|-----------|----------|------------------------|-------|-------|-------|-------|-------|

Sigma enters into an agreement with First Finance Corporation to sell a group of receivables without recourse. The total face value of the receivables is $150,000. First Finance Corp. will charge 15% interest on the weighted-average time to maturity of the receivables of 45 days plus a 2% fee.

Prepare the journal entry to record the transfer of the receivables.

| | | |
|---|---|---|
| | | |
| | | |
| | | |
| | | |

| Situation | Concepts | Uncollectible Accounts | Provision for Uncollectible Accounts Expense | Journal Entries | Transfer of Receivables | Communication | Research |
|-----------|----------|------------------------|-------|-------|-------|-------|-------|

Write a memo to the CEO of Sigma Company explaining the two methods for estimating uncollectible accounts.

To:     CEO, Sigma Company
From:   CPA Candidate
Re:     Estimating uncollectible accounts

| |
|---|
| |

| | | | | | | | Research |
|---|---|---|---|---|---|---|---|
| Situation | Concepts | Uncollectible Accounts | Provision for Uncollectible Accounts Expense | Journal Entries | Transfer of Receivables | Communication | |

Sigma is planning to obtain cash by transferring some of its accounts receivable to a factor. Research each of the following questions using the Financial Accounting Research System (FARS) database, and paste your answer in the space provided.

1.  With regard to transfers of financial assets, what is the financial components approach?

2.  Describe the criteria for determining when control has been surrendered in a transfer of receivables.

3.  How are transfers of receivables accounted for if one or more of the criteria for determining whether control has been surrendered are not met?

## MULTIPLE-CHOICE ANSWERS

| | | | | | | | | | | | | | | |
|---|---|---|---|---|---|---|---|---|---|---|---|---|---|---|
| 1. c | __ __ | 20. a | __ __ | 39. c | __ __ | 58. d | __ __ | 77. b | __ __ | 96. d | __ __ |
| 2. a | __ __ | 21. b | __ __ | 40. c | __ __ | 59. a | __ __ | 78. c | __ __ | 97. c | __ __ |
| 3. c | __ __ | 22. a | __ __ | 41. b | __ __ | 60. b | __ __ | 79. d | __ __ | 98. a | __ __ |
| 4. a | __ __ | 23. c | __ __ | 42. a | __ __ | 61. b | __ __ | 80. c | __ __ | 99. c | __ __ |
| 5. a | __ __ | 24. b | __ __ | 43. c | __ __ | 62. b | __ __ | 81. a | __ __ | 100. a | __ __ |
| 6. a | __ __ | 25. d | __ __ | 44. c | __ __ | 63. b | __ __ | 82. a | __ __ | 101. c | __ __ |
| 7. a | __ __ | 26. c | __ __ | 45. d | __ __ | 64. b | __ __ | 83. b | __ __ | 102. a | __ __ |
| 8. c | __ __ | 27. b | __ __ | 46. d | __ __ | 65. d | __ __ | 84. d | __ __ | 103. a | __ __ |
| 9. c | __ __ | 28. d | __ __ | 47. a | __ __ | 66. d | __ __ | 85. a | __ __ | 104. b | __ __ |
| 10. c | __ __ | 29. a | __ __ | 48. a | __ __ | 67. b | __ __ | 86. a | __ __ | 105. d | __ __ |
| 11. d | __ __ | 30. b | __ __ | 49. d | __ __ | 68. c | __ __ | 87. d | __ __ | 106. d | __ __ |
| 12. b | __ __ | 31. c | __ __ | 50. c | __ __ | 69. c | __ __ | 88. c | __ __ | 107. a | __ __ |
| 13. a | __ __ | 32. c | __ __ | 51. d | __ __ | 70. d | __ __ | 89. a | __ __ | 108. a | __ __ |
| 14. a | __ __ | 33. b | __ __ | 52. c | __ __ | 71. c | __ __ | 90. d | __ __ | 109. b | __ __ |
| 15. a | __ __ | 34. c | __ __ | 53. b | __ __ | 72. b | __ __ | 91. d | __ __ | 110. d | __ __ |
| 16. d | __ __ | 35. a | __ __ | 54. c | __ __ | 72. c | __ __ | 92. c | __ __ | 111. b | __ |
| 17. b | __ __ | 36. d | __ __ | 55. c | __ __ | 74. b | __ __ | 93. c | __ __ | | |
| 18. b | __ __ | 37. d | __ __ | 56. c | __ __ | 75. b | __ __ | 94. b | __ __ | 1st: __/111 = __% |
| 19. a | __ __ | 38. b | __ __ | 57. c | __ __ | 76. c | __ __ | 95. d | __ __ | 2nd: __/111 = __% |

## MULTIPLE-CHOICE ANSWER EXPLANATIONS

### A. Cash

**1.    (c)**    Cash on hand ($125,000) and cash in banks ($2,250,000) are both reported as cash in the current asset section of the balance sheet because they are both unrestricted and readily available for use. Cash legally restricted for additions to plant ($1,600,000) is not available to meet current operating needs, and therefore should be excluded from current assets. Instead, it should be shown in the long-term asset section of the balance sheet as an investment.

**2.    (a)**    To be classified as cash, the item must be readily available for current needs with no legal restrictions limiting its use. A postdated check is not acceptable for deposit and therefore is not considered cash. Thus, the $2,000 check was correctly excluded from the 12/31 checkbook balance and no adjustment is necessary. An NSF check should not be included in cash until it has been redeposited and has cleared the bank. At 12/31, the NSF check ($500) had not yet been redeposited, so it was incorrectly included in the 12/31 checkbook balance, and an adjustment must be made. The check which was not mailed until 1/10/08 ($300) should not be subtracted from cash until the company gives up physical control of that amount. Therefore, $300 must be added back to the checkbook balance. As a result of these adjustments, the correct cash balance is $4,800 ($5,000 – $500 + $300).

**3.    (c)**    Per SFAS 95, *Statement of Cash Flows*, the definition of cash includes both cash (cash on hand and demand deposits) and cash equivalents (short-term, highly liquid investments). Cash equivalents have to be readily convertible into cash and so near maturity that they carry little risk of changing in value due to interest rate changes. This will include only those investments with original maturities of three months or less from the date of purchase by the enterprise. Common examples of cash equivalents include treasury bills, commercial paper, and money market funds. Trans should report a total of $460,000 ($35,000 + $75,000 + $350,000) on its December 31, 2007 balance sheet. The US treasury bill purchased on 12/1/07 is not included in the

calculation because its original maturity is not within three months or less from the date of purchase.

**4.    (a)**    Cash which is segregated and deposited into a bond sinking fund is presented in a classified balance sheet as a noncurrent asset because its use is restricted. Bank overdrafts are presented as current liabilities, unless other accounts at the **same bank** contain sufficient cash to offset the overdraft. The operating account that has a positive balance, should be presented as a current asset.

### A.1.  Bank Reconciliations

**5.    (a)**    To determine the correct 8/31/07 cash balance, a partial bank reconciliation should be prepared. The balance per bank statement ($18,050) must be adjusted for any items which the bank has not yet recorded and also for any bank errors (none in this problem).

| | |
|---|---|
| Balance per bank statement | $18,050 |
| Deposits in transit | 3,250 |
| Outstanding checks | (2,750) |
| Correct balance | $18,550 |

The deposits in transit and outstanding checks represent transactions that the company has recorded, but the bank has not yet recorded. The insufficient funds check ($600) and bank service charge ($100) are both items which the bank has recorded but the company has not. They would be adjustments to the **book balance**, not the **bank balance**.

**6.    (a)**    The balance per books at 3/31/07 is $44,200. The amount would be increased by cash receipts per books and decreased by cash disbursements per books. Cash receipts per the bank in April were $58,400, but this amount includes the $10,300 in transit at 3/31. Therefore, cash receipts per books in April are $48,100 ($58,400 – $10,300). Cash disbursements per the bank in April were $49,700. This amount includes the 3/31 outstanding checks ($12,600) but does **not** include the 4/30 outstanding checks ($7,000). Therefore, April cash disbursements per books is $44,100 ($49,700 – $12,600 + $7,000). The cash balance per books at 4/30/07 is $48,200 ($44,200 at 3/31/07, plus $48,100 receipts, less $44,100 disbursements). An alternative solutions approach is to first compute the 4/30/07 bank balance

($46,500 + $58,400 − $49,700 = $55,200), and then adjust for outstanding checks ($55,200 − $7,000 = $48,200).

## B. Receivables

**7. (a)** The 12/31/07 current net receivables would include the trade receivables, net of the allowance account ($93,000 − $2,000 = $91,000). The claim against a shipper for goods lost in transit ($3,000) is also a valid receivable at year-end. Therefore, the total current net receivables are $94,000 ($91,000 + $3,000). The **unsold** goods on consignment do not represent a receivable until sold. Therefore, the $26,000 should be removed from receivables and sales and the cost ($26,000 ÷ 130% = $20,000) should be removed from cost of goods sold and reported as ending inventory. The security deposit ($30,000) should be reported as a **long-term** receivable.

**8. (c)** The solutions approach is to set up a T-account for accounts receivable.

|  | AR |  |  |
|---|---|---|---|
| 1/1/07 | 650,000 | | |
| Credit sales | 2,700,000 | 75,000 | Sales returns |
| | | 40,000 | Write-offs |
| | | 2,150,000 | Collections |
| 12/31/07 | 1,085,000 | | |

Credit sales are debited to **AR** and credited to **sales**. Sales returns are debited to **sales returns** and credited to **AR**; write-offs are debited to the **allowance for doubtful accounts** and credited to **AR**; and cash collections are debited to **cash** and credited to **AR**. The estimated future sales returns ($50,000) and estimated uncollectible accounts ($110,000) do not affect the accounts receivable account but are instead recorded in separate allowance accounts. Since the requirement is to determine accounts receivable **before** these allowances, the balance of accounts receivable should include only sales returns and write-offs for 2007.

**9. (c)** Accrued interest receivable at 6/30/07 is interest revenue which has been earned by 6/30/07, but has not yet been received by that date. Interest was last received on 7/1/06; the accrued interest receivable includes interest revenue earned from 7/1/06 through 6/30/07 (a full year). The original balance of the note receivable was $150,000 but the 7/1/06 principal payment of $50,000 reduced this balance to $100,000. Therefore, the 6/30/07 interest receivable is $8,000 ($100,000 × 8%).

**10. (c)** Per SFAS 91, loan origination fees are recognized over the life of the related loan as an adjustment of yield. These fees are recorded as a discount on the note receivable. Therefore, Tigg's 12/1/07 entry is

| Notes receivable | 200,000 | |
|---|---|---|
| Discount on NR | | 6,000 |
| Cash | | 194,000 |

Using the effective interest method, Tigg's 12/31/07 adjusting entry is

| Int. receivable | 2,000 | |
|---|---|---|
| Discount on NR | 166 | |
| Int. revenue | | 2,166 |

The interest receivable is

| Face value | × | Stated rate | × | Time | | |
|---|---|---|---|---|---|---|
| $200,000 | × | 12% | × | 1/12 | = | $2,000 |

The interest revenue is

| Carrying amount | × | Effective rate | × | Time | | |
|---|---|---|---|---|---|---|
| $194,000 | × | 13.4% | × | 1/12 | = | $2,166 |

**11. (d)** A current asset is an asset that can be reasonably expected to be converted into cash, sold or consumed in operations, within a single operating cycle or within a year if more than one cycle is completed each year. A noncurrent asset is an asset that can not be expected to be converted to cash, sold or consumed within a single operating cycle or within one year, whichever is longer. Because accrued interest was reported as a current asset on the 2007 balance sheet, it can be assumed interest will be received on August 31, 2007, since current assets are received within one year. Also, because the note receivable was reported as a noncurrent asset it can be assumed that the principal will not be collected within the next twelve months. Principal that is not due until August 31, 2008, coincides with reporting the note as a noncurrent asset.

**12. (b)** Upon receipt of the interest-bearing note for the sale of goods, Benet would record the following entry:

| Notes receivable | (face value) |
|---|---|
| Interest receivable | (interest from 7/15 to 8/15) |
| Sales | (face + interest) |

Note that the interest that accrued on the note from July 15 to August 15 represents part of the sales price of the merchandise (rather than interest income) because Benet did not hold the note during this period. On November 15, Benet will record the following entry:

| Cash | (Plug) | |
|---|---|---|
| Note receivable | | (face value) |
| Interest revenue | | (interest from 8/15 to 11/15) |
| Interest receivable | | (interest from 7/15 to 8/15) |

### B.1. Anticipation of Sales Discounts

**13. (a)** If material, an allowance for discounts must be reported at year-end in order to match the discounts with the related sales and to report receivables at their collectible amount. At 12/31/07, $100,000 of the accounts receivable have the potential to be discounted by 2% because they are less than fifteen days old (terms 2/15, net 30). Since 50% of the customers are expected to take advantage of the 2% discount, the allowance for discounts should be $1,000 [($100,000 × 50%) × 2%]. None of the other categories require a discount allowance because they are older than the maximum age of fifteen days to receive the 2% discount.

**14. (a)** SFAS 48 requires that when revenue is recognized from sales where a right of return exists, sales revenue must be reduced to reflect estimated returns. In this case, sales of $1,000,000 must be reduced by estimated returns of $100,000 [(7% + 3%) × $1,000,000], resulting in net sales of $900,000. The estimated exchanges (15%) will not result in a future reduction of sales.

### B.2. Bad Debts Expense

**15. (a)** To compute the 12/31/07 allowance for uncollectible accounts, the solutions approach is to set up a T-account for the allowance.

|  | Allowance for U.A. | | |
|---|---|---|---|
| | | 260,000 | 1/1/07 |
| | | 180,000 | Expense (2% × 9,000,000) |
| Write-offs | 325,000 | | |
| | | 115,000 | 12/31/07 |

The 1/1/07 balance is increased by bad debts expense recorded (2% × credit sales of $9,000,000) and decreased by write-offs of specific uncollectible accounts.

**16. (d)** The balance in the allowance for doubtful accounts should reflect the amount of accounts receivable that are estimated to be uncollectible. Since it is estimated that 3% of the gross accounts receivable will become uncollectible, the allowance account should have a 12/31/07 balance of $30,000 (3% × $1,000,000). Note that **bad debt expense** of $38,000 would be recorded for 2007, as indicated below.

| | Allowance | |
|---|---|---|
| Bal. before adj. 8,000 | | |
| | ? | Bad debt expense ($38,000) |
| | 30,000 | 12/31/07 (3% × $1,000,000) |

**17. (b)** The total amount of risk of accounting loss related to Butler's trade accounts receivable is $230,000 ($250,000 trade accounts receivable – $20,000 uncollectible amount). The accounting loss cannot exceed the amount of the account receivable recognized as an asset in the balance sheet ($230,000). Off-balance-sheet risk refers to a potential loss that may exceed the amount recognized as an asset. There is no off-balance-sheet risk in this example.

**18. (b)** The solutions approach is to set up a T-account for the allowance for doubtful accounts.

| | Allowance | | |
|---|---|---|---|
| | | 30,000 | 1/1/07 |
| 2007 Write-offs | 18,000 | 2,000 | 2007 Recoveries |
| | | 14,000 | 12/31/07 Before adj. |
| | | ? | Unc. accts. expense |
| | | 25,000 | 12/31/07 |

In 2007, $18,000 of accounts were written off as uncollectible (debit allowance, credit AR). Also, $2,000 of AR were recovered (debit AR, credit allowance; then, debit cash, credit AR), leaving a balance in the allowance account of $14,000 ($30,000 – $18,000 + $2,000). The desired 12/31/07 balance is $25,000 ($350,000 AR less $325,000 net value per aging schedule). Therefore, to increase the allowance from $14,000 to $25,000, uncollectible accounts expense of $11,000 must be recorded.

**19. (a)** When an aging schedule is used to estimate uncollectibles, the total uncollectibles computed is the amount used for the ending balance in the allowance account. As computed below, the 12/31/07 allowance for uncollectible accounts should be $9,000.

| | | |
|---|---|---|
| $120,000 × 1% | = | $1,200 |
| 90,000 × 2% | = | 1,800 |
| 100,000 × 6% | = | 6,000 |
| | | $9,000 |

The other information given (12/31/06 allowance, write-offs, and recoveries) would be used to determine the bad debt expense adjustment, not the allowance balance. In this case, apparently due to a change in estimate, the bad debt expense adjustment would actually be a credit (to offset the necessary debit to the allowance account).

| | Allowance for U.A. | | |
|---|---|---|---|
| | | 22,000 | 12/31/06 |
| Write-offs | 7,000 | 4,000 | Recoveries |
| | | 19,000 | |
| Adjustment | 10,000 | | |
| | | 9,000 | 12/31/07 |

**20. (a)** The aging of receivables method of estimating uncollectible accounts is based on the theory that bad debts are a function of accounts receivable collections during the period. The aging of receivables method emphasizes reporting accounts receivable at their net realizable value. It is a "balance-sheet" approach, which stresses the collectibility (valuation) of the receivable balance. Once the balance of the allowance account required to reduce net accounts receivable to their realizable value has been computed, bad debts expense is merely the amount needed to adjust the allowance account to the computed balance. Answer (b) is incorrect because under the direct write-off method, bad debts are considered expenses in the period in which they are written off; no consideration is given to the valuation of accounts receivable. Answers (c) and (d) are incorrect because both of these methods are based on the theory that bad debts are a function of sales. Thus, these methods emphasize reporting the bad debts expense amount accurately on the income statement.

**21. (b)** A primary objective of accrual accounting is to record the cash consequences of events that change an entity's financial position in the period in which the events occur. This means recognizing revenues when earned rather than when cash is received, and recognizing expenses when incurred rather than when cash is paid. Expenses are incurred when they help the firm earn revenue. Under the allowance method, uncollectible accounts expense is recognized in the same period as the related revenue. The same credit decisions that enabled the entity to earn revenue caused it to incur uncollectible accounts expense. Therefore, under accrual accounting that expense should be recognized in the same period. On the other hand, when the direct write-off method is used, the uncollectible accounts expense is generally recognized after the period in which the revenue is recognized; after the event (credit decision) which changed financial position. Therefore, the direct write-off method is **not** consistent with accrual accounting.

**22. (a)** When the allowance method for recognizing uncollectible accounts is used, the entry to write off a specific account is

| | | |
|---|---|---|
| Allowance for unc. accts. | xxx | |
| Accts. receivable | | xxx |

Answer (a) is correct because this entry decreases both accounts.

**23. (c)** When an account receivable that was previously written off is collected, two entries must be made. The first entry reverses the write-off and reestablishes the receivable.

| | | |
|---|---|---|
| Accounts receivable | xxx | |
| Allowance for uncollectible accounts | | xxx |

The second entry records the cash receipt.

| | | |
|---|---|---|
| Cash | xxx | |
| Accounts receivable | | xxx |

The credit to the allowance account in the first entry increases its balance. Uncollectible accounts expense, however, is not affected by this transaction.

**B.3. Pledging and Selling AR**

**24. (b)** An **assignment** of accounts receivable is a financing arrangement whereby the owner of the receivables (assignor) obtains a loan from the lender (assignee) by pledging the accounts receivable as collateral. A **factoring**

of accounts receivable is basically a sale of, or borrowing on, the receivables. "Factors" are intermediaries that buy receivables from companies (for a fee) and then collect payments directly from the customers. Thus, both of these are methods of generating cash from accounts receivable.

**25.** **(d)** When receivables are factored and control is surrendered the transaction is treated as a **sale**. Under SFAS 140, a transfer in which control is surrendered will not be treated as a borrowing. The risk of uncollectible accounts is **not** retained by the seller in a sale without recourse.

**26.** **(c)** Taylored will receive the value of the receivables ($400,000), reduced by $20,000 for the amount of the holdback ($400,000 × .05), $8,000 withheld as fee income ($400,000 × .02), and $6,740 withheld as interest expense ($400,000 × .15 × 41/365). Answer (c) is therefore correct ($400,000 – $8,000 – $6,740 – $20,000).

**27.** **(b)** Under SFAS 140, a sale of receivables with recourse is recorded using a financial components approach because the seller has a continuing involvement. Under this approach the seller would reduce receivables, recognize assets obtained and liabilities incurred, and record gain or loss. The entry would be

| | | |
|---|---|---|
| Cash | $365,260 | |
| Factor's holdback | 20,000 | |
| Loss | 26,740* | |
|     Accounts receivable | | $400,000 |
|     Liability under recourse provision | | 12,000 |

\* *($6,740 + $8,000 + $12,000)*

**28.** **(d)** If all receivables are collected, Taylored would eliminate its recourse liability and the corresponding loss. The costs incurred by Taylored would include a fee of $8,000 ($400,000 × .02) and interest expense of $6,740 ($400,000 × .15 × 41/365) for a total of $14,740.

**29.** **(a)** The seller uses a Due from Factor or Factor's Holdback account to account for probable sales discounts, sales returns, and sales allowances. The Recourse liability account is recorded to indicate probable uncollectible accounts.

**30.** **(b)** Scarbrough will receive the value of the receivables ($600,000), reduced by $30,000 for the amount of the holdback ($600,000 × .05), $18,000 withheld as fee income ($600,000 × .03), and $13,315 withheld as interest expense ($600,000 × .15 × 54/365). Answer (b) is therefore correct ($600,000 – $30,000 – $18,000 – $13,315).

**31.** **(c)** If all receivables are collected, Synthia would eliminate its recourse liability and the corresponding loss. The costs incurred by Synthia would include a fee of $15,000 ($750,000 × .02) and interest expense of $12,575 ($750,000 × .12 × 51/365) for a total of $27,575.

**32.** **(c)** According to SFAS 140, the transferor, Bannon, should measure the assets received and liabilities incurred at fair value, not at cost. The transferee, Chapman, should record any assets obtained and liabilities incurred at fair value.

**33.** **(b)** According to SFAS 140, if financial assets are exchanged for cash or other consideration, but the transfer does not meet the criteria to be accounted for as a sale, both the transferor and the transferee should account for the transfer as a secured borrowing and a pledge of collateral.

**34.** **(c)** Under SFAS 140, a sale occurs if the seller surrenders control of the receivables transferred. Control is deemed to have been surrendered by the seller only if all three conditions listed in (a), (b), and (d) are met. Answer (c) is used to determine whether a recourse liability is recorded as part of the sale, not whether a transaction can be recorded as a sale.

**35.** **(a)** To derecognize assets when control is gained is not an objective in accounting for transfers of financial assets. When control is gained, the assets should be recognized. Answer (b) is incorrect because an objective is to derecognize liabilities when extinguished. A liability no longer exists, and it should be removed from the balance sheet. Answer (c) is incorrect because recognizing liabilities when incurred is an objective. Answer (d) is incorrect because derecognizing assets when control is given up is an objective in accounting for transfers of financial assets.

**36.** **(d)** A servicing asset or liability should be amortized in proportion to and over the period of estimated net servicing income or net servicing loss as stated in SFAS 140. Answer (a) is incorrect because a servicing asset shall be assessed for impairment based on its fair value. Answer (b) is incorrect because a servicing liability shall be assessed for increased obligation based on its fair value. Answer (c) is incorrect because an obligation to service financial assets may result in the recognition of a servicing asset or a servicing liability.

**37.** **(d)** Per SFAS 156, the assets must be measured for impairment at the end of each reporting period. Answer (a) is incorrect because increases in fair value are not reported under the amortization method. Answer (a) is also incorrect because when using the fair value method, changes in fair value are reported in earnings, not in other comprehensive income. Answers (b) and (c) are incorrect because these rules refer to the fair value method.

**38.** **(b)** Answer (b) is correct. Per SFAS 156, either the amortization method or the fair value method can be used for servicing assets and servicing liabilities. However, if the fair value method is elected, the election cannot be reversed. Changes in fair value are reported in earnings in the period in which the change occurs.

**39.** **(c)** Per SFAS 156, when a company transfers a financial asset but continues to hold an interest in the servicing asset, the transferor should allocate the previous carrying amount between the assets sold and the interest that continues to be held by the transferor based on their relative fair values. Answers (a), (b), and (d) are incorrect because they represent incorrect values.

**40.** **(c)** The arrangement of having collateral transferred to a secured party is known as a pledge. Answer (a) is incorrect because a debtor may grant a security interest in certain assets to a lender to serve as collateral with recourse. Answer (b) is incorrect because a debtor may grant a security interest in certain assets to a lender to serve as collateral without recourse. Answer (d) is incorrect because secured parties are sometimes permitted to sell collateral held under a pledge.

**41.   (b)**   Net proceeds from the sale are equal to $2,200.

| *Net proceeds* | |
|---|---|
| Cash received | $2,100 |
| Plus: Interest rate swap | 140 |
|     Call option | 80 |
| Less: Recourse obligation | (120) |
| Net proceeds | $2,200 |

The gain is computed as follows:

| | |
|---|---|
| Net proceeds | $2,200 |
| Carrying amount of loans sold | 2,000 |
| Gain on sale | $  200 |

**42.   (a)**   The journal entry to record the transfer for ABC Company is as follows:

| | | |
|---|---|---|
| Cash | 2,100 | |
| Interest rate swap | 140 | |
| Call option | 80 | |
|   Loans | | 2,000 |
|   Recourse obligation | | 120 |
|   Gain on sale | | 200 |

Answer (b) is incorrect because is should be a debit to interest rate swap, not a credit. Answer (c) is incorrect because loans should be credited. It was on ABC Company's books as an asset and must be taken off. Answer (d) is incorrect because cash is being received, so it must be debited.

**43.   (c)**   ABC Company must report a servicing obligation of $50. The calculation of net proceeds is

| | |
|---|---|
| Cash received | $2,100 |
| Plus:   Interest rate swap | 140 |
|     Call option | 80 |
| Less:  Recourse obligation | (120) |
| Servicing obligation | (50) |
| Net proceeds | $2,150 |

The gain is

| | |
|---|---|
| Net proceeds | $2,150 |
| Carrying amount of loans sold | 2,000 |
| Gain on sale | $  150 |

**44.   (c)**   Under SFAS 140, financial assets subject to prepayment should be measured like investments in debt securities classified as available-for-sale or trading.

**45.   (d)**   SFAS 140 requires disclosure of (a), (b), and (c). Answer (d) is the correct answer as disclosure is only required of assets and liabilities with nonestimable fair values.

**46.   (d)**   According to SFAS 140, if the debtor defaults under the terms of the secured contract and is no longer entitled to redeem the pledged asset, it (Taft) shall derecognize the pledged asset, and the secured party (Wilson) shall recognize the collateral as its asset initially measured at fair value.

**C.1.  Examples of Current Liabilities**

**47.   (a)**   Before adjustment, the balance in the Accounts Payable account is $360,000. This amount is net of a $50,000 debit balance in Lyle's account payable to Ross resulting from a $50,000 advance payment for goods to be manufactured to Lyle's specifications. The $50,000 should be reclassified as a current asset, **Advance to Suppliers**. The checks recorded on 12/29/07 incorrectly reduced the accounts payable balance by $100,000. The $100,000 reduction should not have been recorded until the checks were mailed on 1/5/08. The 12/31/07 accounts payable must be increased by $100,000. Therefore, the corrected 12/31/07 accounts payable is $510,000.

| | |
|---|---|
| Unadjusted AP | $360,000 |
| Reclassification of advance | 50,000 |
| Error correction | 100,000 |
| | $510,000 |

**48.   (a)**   When purchases are recorded using the net method, purchases and accounts payable are recorded at an amount net of the cash discounts, and the failure to take advantage of a discount is recorded in a Purchase Discounts Lost account. Therefore, when Rabb changes to the net method, gross accounts payable ($30,000) must be adjusted down to the net amount. Since $200 of discounts are still available in the accounts payable balance, the net accounts payable at 9/30/07 is $29,800 ($30,000 − $200). The journal entry is

| | | |
|---|---|---|
| Purchase discounts lost | 1,000 | |
| Purchase discounts | 800 | |
| Accts. payable | 200 | |
|   Purchases | | 2,000 |

**49.   (d)**   Accrued interest payable at 12/31/07 is interest expense which has been incurred by 12/31/07, but has not yet been paid by that date. The note was issued on 3/1/06 and interest is payable in full at maturity on 2/28/08. Therefore, there is one year and ten months of unpaid interest at 12/31/07 (3/1/06 to 12/31/07). Interest for the first year is $1,200 ($10,000 × 12%). Since interest is compounded annually, the new principal amount for the second year includes the original principal ($10,000) plus the first year's interest ($1,200). Therefore, accrued interest for the ten months ended 12/31/07 is $1,120 ($11,200 × 12% × 10/12), and total accrued interest at 12/31/07 is $2,320 ($1,200 + $1,120).

**50.   (c)**   Accrued interest payable at 12/31/07 is interest expense which has been incurred by 12/31/07, but has not yet been paid by that date. Interest was last paid on 9/1/07; the accrued interest payable includes interest expense incurred from 9/1/07 through 12/31/07 (four months). The original balance of the note payable was $1,350,000 but the 9/1/07 principal payment of $450,000 reduced this balance to $900,000. Therefore, the interest payable at 12/31/07 is $36,000 ($900,000 × 12% × 4/12). The prime rate (11%) does not affect the computation because it is not the stated rate on this note.

**51.   (d)**   The solutions approach is to analyze the interest payable T-account for 2007, assuming all interest payments flow through interest payable.

| Interest Payable | | | |
|---|---|---|---|
| | | 15,000 | 12/31/06 |
| 2007 Int. paid | 68,000 | 85,000 | 2007 Expense |
| | | ? | 12/31/07 |

The beginning interest payable balance ($15,000) is increased by interest expense (debit interest expense, credit interest payable for $85,000) and decreased by interest paid (debit interest payable, credit cash for $68,000), resulting in a 12/31/07 balance of $32,000 ($15,000 + $85,000 − $68,000).

**52.   (c)**   All of the notes are due 6/15/08, and normally the entire amount would be classified as current. However, SFAS 6 states that a short-term obligation can be reclassified as long-term if the enterprise intends to refinance the obligation on a long-term basis **and** the intent is supported by the ability to refinance. Ames demonstrated its ability by entering into a financing agreement before the statements are issued. SFAS 6 further states that the amount to be excluded from current liabilities cannot exceed the amount available for refinancing under the agreement. Ames expects to be able to refinance at least $480,000 (80% × $600,000) of the notes. Therefore, that amount can be classified as long-term, while the remaining $20,000 must be classified as short-term.

**53.   (b)**   The effective rate of interest paid on a note is computed as follows:

$$\text{Effective interest rate} = \frac{\text{Interest paid}}{\text{Cash received}}$$

In this case, let's assume the short-term note payable was in the amount of $100,000. The effective interest rate would be 12.56%.

$$\frac{(100,000 \times .12) + (\$100,000 \times .005)}{\$99,500} = 12.56$$

This is because the loan origination fee increases the interest paid on the note and reduces the net cash received from the note.

**54.   (c)**   The $4,000,000 note payable is due March 15, 2008 and normally would be classified as a current liability in the December 31, 2007 financial statements. However, SFAS 6 states that a short-term obligation can be reclassified as long-term if the enterprise intends to refinance the obligation on a long-term basis and the intent is supported by the ability to refinance. Cali demonstrated its ability to refinance by actually issuing bonds and refinancing the note prior to the issuance of the December 31, 2007 financial statements. Since the proceeds from the bonds exceeded the amount needed to retire the note, the entire $4,000,000 notes payable would be classified as a noncurrent liability, with separate disclosure of the note refinancing required by SFAS 6.

**55.   (c)**   The notes payable ($750,000) are due 7/31/08, and would normally be included in 12/31/07 current liabilities. However, SFAS 6 states that a short-term obligation can be reclassified as long-term if the enterprise intends to refinance the obligation on a long-term basis and the intent is supported by the ability to refinance. Largo demonstrated its ability to refinance by actually issuing $1,500,000 of bonds in February 2008 before the 12/31/07 financial statements were issued on 3/3/08. The bond proceeds will be used to retire the note at maturity. SFAS 6 also states that the amount excluded from current liabilities cannot exceed the amount actually refinanced. Since Largo prepaid $250,000 of the note on 1/12/08 with excess cash, that amount must be included in 12/31/07 current liabilities. Only the remaining $500,000 can be excluded from current liabilities.

**56.   (c)**   A key to solving this problem is understanding that the employee advances do **not** affect the accrued salaries payable. When advances are made to employees, they are a cash payment separate from the payroll function. The advances made, therefore, are not reflected in salaries expense ($420,000) or **gross** salaries paid ($390,000). Therefore, the solutions approach is to analyze the salaries payable T-account for 2007 (disregarding the employee advances).

Salaries Payable

|                |         | 40,000  | 12/31/06          |
|----------------|---------|---------|-------------------|
| 2007 sal. paid | 390,000 | 420,000 | 2006 sal. expense |
|                |         | ?       | 12/31/07          |

The beginning salaries payable balance ($40,000) is increased by salaries expense ($420,000) and decreased by salaries paid ($390,000), resulting in a 12/31/07 balance of $70,000.

**57.   (c)**   No sales commission is due to salesperson A because his commissions earned ($200,000 × 4% = $8,000) are less than his fixed salary ($10,000). Note that the excess of the fixed salary over commissions earned is not charged back against A. Commissions totaling $28,000 are due to salespersons B and C as computed below.

|   | *Commissions earned* | | *Fixed salary paid* | *Commissions payable* |
|---|------------------------|---|------------|------------|
| B | (6% × $400,000) | – | $14,000 | $10,000 |
| C | (6% × $600,000) | – | $18,000 | 18,000 |
|   |                 |   |         | $28,000 |

**58.   (d)**   Lime's payroll tax liability includes amounts withheld from payroll checks [$1,200 of federal income taxes withheld and $700 of the **employees'** share of FICA ($10,000 × 7%)] plus the **employer's** share of FICA (an additional $700). Therefore, the total payroll tax liability is $2,600 ($1,200 + $700 + $700). The amount recorded as payroll tax expense consists only of the employer's share of FICA ($700), since no unemployment taxes are mentioned in the problem.

**59.   (a)**   The contingent unemployment claims liability is both probable and reasonably estimable, so it must be accrued at 12/31/07. Acme's reasonable estimate of its probable liability is 2% of eligible gross wages. Eligible gross wages are the first $10,000 of gross wages paid to each of the five employees (5 × $10,000 = $50,000), so the accrued liability should be $1,000 (2% × $50,000). Note that the 3% rate is not used because Acme has chosen the option to reimburse the state directly, and its best estimate of this liability is based on 2%, not 3%.

**60.   (b)**   To compute the amount of the contribution, the requirements described in the problem must be translated into an equation. The contribution must equal 10% of income **after** deduction of the contribution, but **before** income tax. Therefore, the tax rate (30%) does not enter into the computation. The equation is solved below.

$$
\begin{aligned}
C &= .10 \times (\$75,000 - C) \\
C &= \$7,500 - .10C \\
1.1C &= \$7,500 \\
C &= \$7,500 \div 1.1 \\
C &= \$6,818
\end{aligned}
$$

The amount to be accrued as an expense and liability is $6,818.

**61.   (b)**   If net income **after** bonus and income tax is $360,000, income before taxes can be computed by dividing **$360,000** by **1 minus the tax rate**.

$$\text{Income before taxes} = \frac{\$360,000}{1 - .40} = \underline{\$600,000}$$

The bonus is equal to 10% of income **before** income tax but **after** the bonus. The $600,000 computed above **is** income before tax but after all other expenses including the bonus. Therefore, the bonus must be $60,000 (10% × $600,000). Note that this problem is different from other bonus problems because usually the income before taxes and bonus ($660,000 in this case) is given as the starting point, rather than net income.

**62. (b)** To determine the correct amount for sales revenue, Ivy must divide the total of sales and sales taxes by 100% plus the sales tax percentage (6%) as indicated below.

| Month | Total | | Percentage | | Sales revenue |
|-------|-------|---|-----------|---|--------------|
| Jan. | $10,600 | ÷ | 106% | = | $10,000 |
| Feb. | $7,420 | ÷ | 106% | = | 7,000 |
| March | $8,480 | ÷ | 106% | = | 8,000 |
| Total | | | | | $25,000 |

Sales taxes payable would include all sales taxes collected, less any sales taxes already remitted.

| | |
|---|---|
| January sales taxes ($10,600 – $10,000) | $600 |
| *February sales taxes ($7,420 – $7,000) | 420 |
| March sales taxes ($8,480 – $8,000) | 480 |
| Total | $1,500 |
| Less taxes remitted | 600 |
| Sales taxes payable | $ 900 |

*Note February sales taxes were not remitted since they did not exceed $500.*

**63. (b)** As of 12/31/07 the October sales taxes should have been paid, so there would be no 12/31/07 current liability for those taxes. However, at 12/31/07 sales taxes payable must be reported for the November room rentals as they were not paid until 1/3/08 and the December room rentals [15% × ($110,000 + $150,000) = $39,000]. The fourth quarter occupancy taxes were not paid until 1/3/08, so they would also represent a current liability at 12/31/07 [(1,100 + 1,200 + 1,800) × $2 = $8,200].

**64. (b)** When the warehouse was purchased on 9/1/07, it would be recorded at its total cost before any credit for accrued realty taxes. The offsetting credits would be to **cash** for the net amount paid, and to **real estate taxes payable** for two months' taxes ($12,000 × 2/6 = $4,000). At the end of September and of October, Day would record property tax expense each month as follows:

| | | |
|---|---|---|
| Real estate tax expense | 2,000 | |
|    Real estate taxes payable | | 2,000 |

Therefore, at October 31, Day has a balance of $8,000 in the payable account ($4,000 + $2,000 + $2,000). On 11/1/07, Day would record the semiannual payment as follows:

| | | |
|---|---|---|
| Real estate taxes payable | 8,000 | |
| Prepaid real estate taxes | 4,000 | |
|    Cash | | 12,000 |

The prepaid real estate taxes would then be expensed $2,000 per month at the end of November and December.

**65. (d)** An accrued liability is an expense which has been incurred, but has not been paid. Of the $500 advertising bill, $375 had been incurred as an expense as of 12/31/07 and should be reported as an accrued liability at that time. For the store lease, the fixed portion ($1,200 per month) is payable on the 16th of each month for the preceding month. Therefore, on 12/16/07, rent was paid for the period 11/16/07 to 12/15/07. An additional one-half month's rent expense (1/2 × $1200 = $600) has been incurred but not paid as of 12/31/07. The variable portion of the rent [5% × ($550,000 – $300,000), or $12,500] was incurred during 2007, but will not be paid until 1/31/08. It, too, is an accrued liability at 12/31/07. Total 12/31/07 accrued liabilities are $13,475.

| | |
|---|---|
| Advertising | $ 375 |
| Fixed rent (1/2 × $1,200) | 600 |
| Variable rent [5% × ($550,000 – $300,000)] | 12,500 |
| Total | $13,475 |

**66. (d)** The solutions approach to this problem is to construct a time line documenting the events in the question.

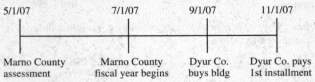

Note that on May 1, 2007, the County has merely determined the amount of property tax owed by each property owner, and no entries would be made by companies subject to property taxes on that date. The fiscal year 2008 taxes are for the period from July 1, 2007, to June 30, 2008. On September 1, 2007, the date on which Dyur purchased the building, two months of the fiscal year had passed, and the property tax expense related to those months was borne by the seller. At October 31, 2007, Dyur would have a liability for four months of property taxes (even though only the months of September and October would have been expensed by Dyur). On November 1, 2007, four months of the fiscal year had passed, and Dyur paid taxes for the first six months of the fiscal year. The entry recorded upon the payment would be

| | |
|---|---|
| Property taxes payable | (four months) |
| Prepaid property taxes | (two months) |
|    Cash | (six months) |

The payment would therefore be allocated as two-sixths (33 1/3%) to an increase in prepaid property taxes and four-sixths (66 2/3%) to a decrease in property taxes payable.

**67. (b)** To determine the 12/31/07 balance of the liability for customer advances, the solutions approach is to set up a T-account for the liability.

| Customer Advances | | | |
|---|---|---|---|
| | | 118,000 | 12/31/06 |
| | | 184,000 | 2007 adv. received |
| 2007 adv. applied | 164,000 | | |
| 2007 cancellations | 50,000 | | |
| | | 88,000 | 12/31/07 |

When advances are received ($184,000), cash is debited and the liability account is credited. When advances are applied to orders shipped ($164,000), the liability account is debited and sales is credited. When an order is cancelled ($50,000), the liability account is debited and a revenue account is credited, since the advance payments are nonrefundable. Thus, the customer advances balance on 12/31/07 is $88,000.

**68. (c)** The solutions approach is to set up a T-account for the liability.

| Liability for Deposits | | | |
|---|---|---|---|
| | | 580,000 | 12/31/06 balance |
| | | 780,000 | 2007 deliveries |
| 2007 returns | 626,000 | | |
| 2007 sales | 60,000 | | |
| | | 674,000 | 12/31/07 balance |

When customers pay the deposit for a container, cash is debited and the liability is credited. Therefore, at 12/31/06 the liability consists of deposits for containers still held by customers from the last two years ($580,000). During 2007, the liability was increased for deposits on containers delivered ($780,000). When containers are returned, the deposits are returned to the customers; in 2007, the liability was debited and cash credited for $626,000. Also, at 12/31/07, some customers still held containers from 2005 ($150,000 − $90,000 = $60,000). The two-year time limit has expired on these, so the company is no longer obligated to return the deposit. The containers are considered sold to the customers, so the liability account is debited and sales credited for $60,000. This results in a 12/31/07 balance of $674,000.

**69.** **(c)** To compute the escrow liability, the solutions approach is to use a T-account.

| | Escrow Liability | | |
|---|---|---|---|
| | | 700,000 | 1/1/07 |
| Taxes paid | 1,720,000 | 1,580,000 | Receipts |
| | | 45,000 | Net interest |
| | | 605,000 | 12/31/07 |

Escrow payments received ($1,580,000) would increase the liability because these amounts are payable to taxing authorities. Taxes paid ($1,720,000) decrease the liability. The net interest credited to the escrow accounts [$50,000 − (10% × $50,000) = $45,000] would increase the liability, resulting in a 12/31/07 balance of $605,000.

**70.** **(d)** All contract sales are made **evenly** during the year. Therefore, the 2006 contracts range from one year expired (if sold on 12/31/06) to two years expired (if sold on 1/1/06), for an average of one and one-half years expired [(2+1)/2]. Similarly, the 2007 contracts range from zero years expired to one year expired, for an average of one-half year expired [(0+1)/2]. The average **unearned** portion of the 2006 contracts is one-half year (two years − one and one-half years), the last half of the second contract year. The amount of unearned revenue related to 2006 contracts is computed as follows:

$$\$500,000 \times 60\% \times 1/2 = \underline{\$150,000}$$

The average **unearned** portion of the 2007 contracts is one and one-half years (two years − one-half year), the last half of the first contract year and all of the second contract year. The amount of unearned revenue related to the 2007 contracts is computed as follows:

| 2007: | $600,000 × 40% × ½ | = | $120,000 |
|---|---|---|---|
| | $600,000 × 60% | = | 360,000 |
| | | | $480,000 |

Therefore, the total unearned revenue is $630,000 ($150,000 + $480,000).

**71.** **(c)** Revenue is earned by Toddler Care Co. as time goes by and care is provided. Therefore, revenue should be recognized on a straight-line basis regardless of the timing of cash receipts. The monthly fees can simply be recognized on a monthly basis, but the initial payment must be deferred and recognized as revenue on a straight-line basis over the twelve-month period. The 12/31/07 deferred revenues are $6,600, as computed below.

| Plan | Initial fees | 2007 revenue (4/12) | 12/31/07 def. rev. (8/12) |
|---|---|---|---|
| 1 | 15 × $500 = $7,500 | $2,500 | $5,000 |
| 2 | 12 × $200 = $2,400 | 800 | 1,600 |
| 3 | $ 0 | 0 | 0 |
| | $9,900 | $3,300 | $6,600 |

Since the total initial payments received are given ($9,900), a shortcut is to multiply that amount by 8/12 ($9,900 × 8/12 = $6,600).

**72.** **(b)** When a company issues gift certificates for cash, the following journal entry is made:

| Cash | (amount of certificate) |
|---|---|
| Deferred revenue | (amount of certificate) |

When the gift certificates are subsequently redeemed, the following journal entry is made:

| Deferred revenue | (amount of certificate) |
|---|---|
| Revenue | (amount of certificate) |

However, if the gift certificates are not redeemed and lapse, the following journal entry is made:

| Deferred revenue | (amount of certificate) |
|---|---|
| Gain on lapse of certificates | (amount of certificate) |

Please note that although different accounts are credited depending on whether the certificates are redeemed or lapse, the Deferred Revenue account is decreased in both cases.

**73.** **(c)** Per SFAC 5, revenues are generally recognized when they are both **realized** or **realizable** and **earned**. Therefore, Dallas Co. should report a liability for deferred revenues equal to the advance payment of 60% of the main contract price. Per SFAC 6, one of three essential characteristics of a liability is that the transaction or other event obligating the entity has already happened. Since the subcontractor had not produced the special-order goods as of March 31, Dallas should not record a liability at that time. Therefore, no payable to the subcontractor would be reported for this activity as of March 31.

**74.** **(b)** At June 30, 2007, Northan Retailers should report the coupon transactions as unearned revenues because the sale of the coupons is not the culmination of the earnings process (i.e., Northan must allow customers to exchange the coupons for merchandise or refund the cost of the coupons at some later date). The unearned revenues should be recorded at the amount of the cash received by debiting cash and crediting an unearned revenue account. The retail price of the merchandise for which coupons may be redeemed does not impact the monetary amount of Northan's liability to its customers, and each coupon redeemed will ultimately result in the recognition of sales of $10, the amount of cash previously received.

**75.** **(b)** The requirement is to determine the situation that might account for the reduction in the deferred revenue balance. When a service contract is purchased by a customer and the fee prepaid, deferred revenue is recognized at the date of payment. Revenue cannot be recorded because revenue has not yet been earned. Revenue is only recorded when services are performed under the contract. The deferred revenue balance is reduced by the **actual** amount of revenue earned when services are performed under the services contract. If more contracts were signed earlier in one year than another year, there is a greater period of time in which to perform actual services. As previously stated, when actual services are performed, the deferred revenue balance is decreased. Therefore, the more actual services that are performed, the greater the reduction in the deferred revenue balance. If more 2007 contracts were signed later in 2007 than 2006, the deferred revenue balance in 2007 would be larger than 2006. There would be less time to perform actual services, therefore less actual revenue would be recognized, creating a larger deferred revenue balance at year-end. There is no contribution margin recognized on service contracts.

**76.   (c)**   Per SFAS 47, the aggregate amount of payments for unconditional purchase obligations that have been recognized on the purchaser's balance sheet shall be disclosed for each of the **five** years following the date of the latest balance sheet presented.

### C.2.   Current Liabilities—Contingencies

**77.   (b)**   Per SFAS 5, a loss contingency should be accrued if it is **probable** that a liability has been incurred at the balance sheet date and the amount of the loss is reasonably estimable. With respect to unfiled claims, the enterprise must consider both the probability that a claim will be filed and the probability of an unfavorable outcome. Although it is probable that claims will be asserted against Sims, it is only **reasonably possible** that the claims will be successful. Therefore, this contingent liability should not be accrued, but should be disclosed. The potential loss to be disclosed is $250,000, since the additional amount above the deductible would be covered by the insurance policy, and therefore is not a loss or liability for Sims.

**78.   (c)**   ARB 43 states that current liabilities are obligations whose liquidation is reasonably expected to require the use of current assets or the creation of other current liabilities. This means that generally, current liabilities are the liabilities that are due within one year of the balance sheet date. Clearly, accounts payable ($55,000) and accrued expenses ($35,000) are current liabilities. Notes payable ($400,000) and bonds payable ($1,000,000) are usually considered to be long-term, but the maturity dates given (7/1/08 and 3/1/08 respectively) indicate they are current liabilities at 12/31/07. The contingent liability ($450,000) and deferred tax liability ($25,000) will not be settled until 2009 and therefore should be classified as long-term at 12/31/07. Thus, the 12/31/07 current liabilities total is $1,490,000 as follows:

| | |
|---|---:|
| Accounts payable | $   55,000 |
| Accrued expenses | 35,000 |
| Unsecured notes 8%—due 7/1/08 | 400,000 |
| Senior bonds 7%—due 3/31/08 | 1,000,000 |
| Total current liabilities | $1,490,000 |

**79.   (d)**   The lawsuit damages must be accrued as a loss contingency in accordance with SFAS 5 because an unfavorable outcome is **probable** and the amount of the loss is **reasonably estimable**. Per FASB Interpretation 14, when a range of possible loss exists, the best estimate within the range is accrued. When no amount within the range is a better estimate than any other amount, the dollar amount at the low end of the range is **accrued** (in this case, $500,000) and the dollar amount of the high end of the range is **disclosed**.

**80.   (c)**   Per SFAS 5, a loss contingency should be accrued if it is **probable** that a liability has been incurred at the balance sheet date and the amount of the loss is **reasonably estimable**. This loss must be accrued because it meets both criteria. Notice that even though the lawsuit was not initiated until 1/12/08, the liability was incurred on 11/5/07 when the accident occurred. FASB Interpretation 14 requires that when some amount within an estimated range is a better estimate than any other amount in the range, that amount is accrued. Therefore, a loss of $300,000 should be

accrued. If no amount within the range is a better estimate than any other amount, the amount at the low end of the range is accrued and the amount at the high end is disclosed.

**81.   (a)**   The additional tax liability must be accrued as a loss contingency in accordance with SFAS 5 because an unfavorable outcome is **probable** and the amount of the loss is **reasonably estimable**. Since $200,000 is the reasonable estimate, that amount should be accrued by debiting Income Tax Expense and crediting Income Tax Payable. The possibility of the liability being as high as $300,000 would be disclosed in the notes. The settlement offer of $275,000 is not accrued at 12/31/07 because prior to financial statement issuance, Haft was unaware of the offer, and $200,000 was the best estimate. In 2008, when the settlement offer was accepted, Haft would record an additional $75,000 of expense and liability.

**82.   (a)**   Per SFAS 5, a loss contingency is accrued if it is **probable** that a liability has been incurred at the balance sheet date and the amount of the loss is reasonably estimable. If no accrual is made for a loss contingency because one or both of the conditions above are not met, disclosure of the contingency shall be made when it is at least **reasonably possible** that a loss was incurred. Therefore, this loss should be disclosed, but not accrued as a liability.

**83.   (b)**   Invern's appropriation of retained earnings for contingencies is merely a reclassification of retained earnings on the balance sheet which tells the readers of the financial statements that such amounts are generally not available to pay dividends. This appropriation has no effect on the income statement. When a loss contingency is probable (as in this instance) **and** reasonably estimable ($190,000 in this instance), SFAS 5 requires accrual of the loss. Therefore, Invern must accrue both a liability and an expense of $190,000. Note that Invern will also reclassify $190,000 of appropriated retained earnings into the "general" retained earnings.

**84.   (d)**   At 12/31/07, Halsey's contingent liability of $50,000 is no longer probable due to the favorable judgment and the inability to predict the outcome of the appeal. Therefore, no liability should be reported in the balance sheet. SFAS 5 states that **gain** contingencies are not reflected in the accounts until realized, so the $30,000 asset is not reported in the 12/31/07 balance sheet, either.

**85.   (a)**   SFAS 5 states that gain contingencies are not recognized in the income statement until realized. As only $15,000 of the litigation awards has been resolved as of December 31, 2007, Haze should report only $15,000 as a gain in its 2007 financial statements.

**86.   (a)**   SFAS 5 states that **gain** contingencies are not reflected in the accounts until realized. Since the case is unresolved at 12/31/07, none of this contingent gain should be recorded as income in 2007. Adequate disclosure should be made of the gain contingency, but care should be taken to avoid misleading implications as to the likelihood of realization.

**87.   (d)**   SFAS 5 states that **gain** contingencies are not reflected in the accounts until realized. Since the case was unresolved at 12/31/07, none of this contingent gain can be recorded as a receivable and/or revenue in 2007. Since the contingency is probable, it should be disclosed along with the 12/31/07 estimate of a range of $75,000 to $150,000. A gain contingency would not be accrued as a receivable. The amount disclosed should be the range because all amounts within the range are considered equally likely.

**88.** **(c)** Per SFAS 5, an estimated loss from a loss contingency shall be accrued by a charge to income if **both** of the following conditions are met:

1. Information available indicates that it is **probable** that an asset has been impaired or a liability has been incurred.
2. The amount of the loss can be **reasonably estimated**.

However, per SFAS 5, gain contingencies are only recognized when a specific event actually occurs, not prior to the event, because to do so would recognize the gain prior to its realization. Therefore, Brooks should recognize the loss in 2007 due to the fact that the event is probable and can be reasonably estimated. Dollis, on the other hand, cannot recognize the gain until 2008, the year they receive the actual award.

**89.** **(a)** Eagle Co. has a contingent liability where the possibility of loss is **remote**. Loss contingencies are accrued when they are **probable** and **reasonably estimable**. All others are disclosed unless remote. However, per SFAS 5, some contingencies, such as guarantees of others' debts, standby letters of credit by banks, and agreements to repurchase receivables, are disclosed even if remote. Eagle's contingent liability is **not** accrued, because it is not probable. It **is** disclosed for two reasons: it is a guarantee of other's debt, and it is a related-party transaction.

**90.** **(d)** SFAS 43 states that accrual of a liability for future vacation pay is required if all the conditions below are met.

1. Obligation arises from employee services already performed.
2. Obligation arises from rights that vest or accumulate.
3. Payment is probable.
4. Amount can be reasonably estimated.

The criteria are met for the vacation pay (150 × $100 = $15,000), so North is required to report a $15,000 liability. The same criteria apply to accrual of a liability for future sick pay, **except** that if sick pay benefits accumulate but do not vest, accrual is **permitted** but not **required** because its payment is contingent upon future employee sickness. Therefore, no liability is **required** for these sick pay benefits (75 × $100 = $7500). Note that the unadjusted balance of the liability account ($21,000) does not affect the computation of the required 12/31/07 liability.

**91.** **(d)** The week ended 1/1/08 included four days in 2007 and one day in 2008. The pay due for this week won't be paid until the following Monday (1/4/08). Therefore, Ross has a liability for four days' accrued salaries at 12/31/07 (4/5 × $80,000 = $64,000). The entire $25,000 of vacation pay is an accrued liability at 12/31/07 because it represents vacation time earned by employees in 2007 but not taken by 12/31/07. Therefore, the total accrued salary and vacation pay is $89,000 ($64,000 + $25,000).

**92.** **(c)** Per SFAS 43, an employer is required to accrue a liability for employees' rights to receive compensation for future absences, such as vacations, when conditions

are met. The Statement does **not**, however, specify how such liabilities are to be measured. Since vacation time is paid by Gavin Co. at the salaries in effect when vacations are taken or when employment is terminated, Gavin adjusts its vacation liability and expense to current salary levels. Gavin's 2007 vacation pay expense consists of vacations earned for work in 2007 (adjusted to current rates) of $30,000 plus the amount necessary to adjust its pre-2007 vacation liability for the 10% salary increase. The amount of this adjustment is equal to 10% of the preexisting liability balance at December 31, 2007 [($35,000 − $20,000) × 10% = $1,500]. Therefore, total vacation pay expense for the period is equal to $31,500 ($30,000 + $1,500).

**93.** **(c)** Per SFAS 43, an employer shall accrue a liability for employees' future absences if **all** of the following conditions are met: (1) the employer's obligation relates to employees' service already rendered, (2) the employees' rights vest **or** accumulate, (3) payment of the compensation is probable, and (4) the amount can be reasonably estimated. All of these conditions are met whether Taos Co.'s employees' rights either accumulate or vest.

**94.** **(b)** SFAS 43 states that accrual of a liability for employees' compensation for future absences is required if all of the conditions below are met.

1. Obligation arises from employee services already performed.
2. Obligation arises from rights that vest or accumulate.
3. Payment is probable.
4. Amount can be reasonably estimated.

**95.** **(d)** The solutions approach is to set up a T-account for warranty liability.

| Warranty Liability | | | |
|---|---|---|---|
| 2007 payments | 2,250 | 9,000 | 2007 exp. (6% × $150,000) |
| 2008 payments | 7,500 | 15,000 | 2008 exp. (6% × $250,000) |
| | | 14,250 | 12/31/08 liability |

Each year warranty expense is estimated at 6% of sales and recorded by debiting the expense account and crediting the liability. As warranty expenditures are made, the liability is debited and cash is credited. Note that the total estimated warranty cost for **both** years (2% + 4% = 6%) is recorded in the year of sale in compliance with the matching principle.

**96.** **(d)** The warranty expense of $30 for each machine sold, although it will be incurred over the three-year warranty period, is directly related to the sales revenue as an integral and inseparable part of the sale and recognized at the time of the sale. The warranty costs make their contribution to revenue in the year of sale by making the product more attractive to the customer. Therefore, in accordance with the matching principle, the warranty costs should be expensed when the machines are sold with a corresponding credit to accrued liability. Answers (a) and (b) are incorrect; this is a sales warranty approach in which the warranty is sold separately from the product. The revenue is recognized on the straight-line basis and they are expensed as incurred. Answer (c) is incorrect because this describes a cash basis method.

**97.** **(c)** SFAS 159 provides that warranty services can be recorded at the fair value only if the contract can be settled by a third party. Therefore, the fair value is considered the settlement amount of the contract.

**98. (a)** Case expects 120,000 coupons to be redeemed at a total cost of $.50 per coupon ($.45 + $.05). Therefore, total expected redemptions are $60,000 (120,000 × $.50). By 12/31/07, $25,000 has been paid on coupon redemptions, so a liability of $35,000 must be established ($60,000 − $25,000). Note that this liability would include both payments due for the 50,000 coupons on hand, and payments due on coupons to be received within the first thirty days after the expiration date.

**99. (c)** Dunn records stamp service revenue and provides for the cost of redemptions in the year stamps are sold. Therefore, Dunn's entries are

| To record sales of stamps | | |
|---|---|---|
| Cash | 4,000,000 | |
| Stamp service revenue | | 4,000,000 |
| To record cost of redemptions | | |
| Liability for stamp reds. | 2,750,000 | |
| Inventory | | 2,750,000 |
| To provide for cost of future redemptions | | |
| Cost of redemptions | 1,800,000 | |
| Liability for stamp reds. | | 1,800,000 |
| (80% × $2,250,000) | | |

The 12/31/07 liability balance is $5,050,000 as shown below.

Liability for Stamp Redemptions

| | | | |
|---|---|---|---|
| | | 6,000,000 | 12/31/06 |
| Redemptions | 2,750,000 | 1,800,000 | Provision for reds. |
| | | 5,050,000 | 12/31/07 |

### Miscellaneous

**100. (a)** Current assets listed in the trial balance are cash ($550,000), accounts receivable ($1,650,000), and prepaid taxes ($300,000). However, part of the AR must be reclassified, and income tax expense has not yet been recorded. Included in AR is $500,000 due from a customer, for which $250,000 is collectible in 2008 (2 × $125,000) and $250,000 is collectible in 2009. The portion collectible in 2008 should be reclassified as a noncurrent asset. Revenues ($3,600,000) less expenses ($2,600,000) result in pretax income of $1,000,000. Since the tax rate is 30%, tax expense is $300,000 (30% × $1,000,000). Therefore, an adjustment is necessary to debit **income tax expense** and credit **prepaid taxes** for $300,000. Total current assets, after reclassification and adjustment, are $1,950,000 [answer (a)] as calculated below.

| | |
|---|---|
| Cash | $ 550,000 |
| AR ($1,650,000 − $250,000) | 1,400,000 |
| Prepaid taxes ($300,000 − $300,000) | -- |
| | $1,950,000 |

**101. (c)** Before closing entries, retained earnings is $630,000. 2007 net income is revenues ($3,600,000) less expenses ($2,600,000) and income tax expense [30% × ($3,600,000 − $2,600,000) = $300,000]. After adjusting for income tax expense, net income is $700,000 [$3,600,000 − ($2,600,000 + $300,000)]. After closing entries, 12/31/07 retained earnings is $1,330,000 ($630,000 + $700,000). The foreign currency translation adjustment ($430,000) does not affect retained earnings; it is reported as a separate component of stockholders' equity.

**102. (a)** Current assets are cash and other assets that are expected to be converted into cash, sold, or consumed either in one year, or in the operating cycle, whichever is longer.

Generally included in this category are cash, temporary investments, short-term receivables, inventories, and prepaid expenses. In this situation, there are two special items. Cash must be adjusted because checks that were not mailed until July 9 were recorded June 29. To compute the correct June 30 cash balance, this $30,000 of checks must be added back to the cash balance, turning the $10,000 overdraft into a $20,000 positive balance [(− $10,000) + $30,000 = $20,000]. Also, land held for resale ($100,000) must be included in current assets because, like inventory, at June 30 it is expected to be sold for cash within the next year. Therefore, June 30 current assets total $225,000.

| | |
|---|---|
| Cash | $20,000 |
| AR, net | 35,000 |
| Inventory | 58,000 |
| Prepaid expenses | 12,000 |
| Land held for resale | 100,000 |
| | $225,000 |

**103. (a)** ARB 43 states that current liabilities are obligations whose liquidation is reasonably expected to require the use of current assets or the creation of other current liabilities. This means that generally, current liabilities are liabilities due within one year of the balance sheet date. Clearly, accounts payable ($15,000) and dividends payable ($8,000) are current liabilities. Generally, bonds payable are a long-term liability; however, since these bonds are due in 2008, they must be reported as a current liability at 12/31/07 ($25,000 fair value less $3,000 discount, or $22,000). Therefore, total current liabilities are $45,000 ($15,000 + $8,000 + $22,000). The notes payable ($20,000) are classified as long-term because they are not due until 2009.

### D. Ratios

**104. (b)** The quick (acid-test) ratio is quick assets (cash, temporary investments in marketable equity securities, and net receivables) divided by current liabilities. The quick ratio measures the ability to pay current liabilities from cash and near-cash items. In this case, quick assets total $700,000 ($170,000 + $450,000 + $80,000) and current liabilities total $400,000 ($60,000 + $240,000 + $100,000), resulting in a quick ratio of 1.75 to 1 ($700,000 ÷ $400,000).

**105. (d)** The formula to compute accounts receivable turnover is

$$\frac{\text{Net credit sales}}{\text{Average accounts receivable}}$$

The average receivable is the sum of the beginning and ending net accounts receivable divided by 2. The 2007 beginning accounts receivable equals the 2006 ending balance in accounts receivable. Average accounts receivable is $425,000 [($450,000 + $400,000) ÷ 2]. Applying the formula, the 2007 accounts receivable turnover is 7.06 times ($3,000,000 ÷ $425,000).

**106. (d)** Ratios that are useful in assessing a company's ability to meet currently maturing or short-term obligations are referred to as solvency ratios. The acid-test ratio is classified as a solvency ratio, and it measures the ability to pay current liabilities from cash and near-cash items. The acid-test ratio is

$$\frac{\text{Cash + Net receivables + Marketable securities}}{\text{Current liabilities}}$$

The debt to equity ratio is a leverage ratio that measures the relative amount of leverage or debt a company has. The debt to equity ratio is

$$\frac{\text{Total liabilities}}{\text{Common stockholders' equity}}$$

Therefore, answer (d) is correct because the acid-test ratio is useful in assessing a company's ability to meet currently maturing or short-term obligations while the debt to equity ratio is not.

**107. (a)** The quick (acid-test) ratio measures the ability to pay current liabilities from cash and near-cash items.

$$\text{Quick ratio} = \frac{\text{Cash, Net receivables, Marketable securities}}{\text{Current liabilities}}$$

Fluctuating market prices of short-term investments may adversely affect Belle's quick ratio and creditworthiness. Inventory and available-for-sale investment items do not affect the quick ratio.

**108. (a)** The solutions approach is to create a numerical example that conforms to the facts given in the question. Assume the following:

$$\text{Current ratio} = \frac{\$900,000}{\$600,000} = 1.5 \text{ to } 1$$

$$\text{Quick ratio} = \frac{\$300,000}{\$600,000} = .5 \text{ to } 1$$

Payments of accounts payable decrease both cash (a current and quick asset) and ac ratios result: counts payable (a current liability). After payment the following

$$\text{Current ratio} = \frac{900 - 200}{600 - 200} = \frac{700}{400} = 1.75 \text{ to } 1$$

$$\text{Quick ratio} = \frac{300 - 200}{600 - 200} = \frac{100}{400} = .25 \text{ to } 1$$

Subtracting equal amounts from the numerator and the denominator of a ratio **greater than one** will **increase** the ratio. Subtracting equal amounts from the numerator and the denominator of a ratio **less than one** will **decrease** the ratio. Therefore, the current ratio will increase while the quick ratio decreases.

**109. (b)** The formula to compute the current ratio is

$$\text{Current ratio} = \frac{\text{Current assets}}{\text{Current liabilities}}$$

The write-off of inventory would decrease current assets and the current ratio. The formula to compute the acid-test (quick) ratio is

$$\text{Acid-test ratio} = \frac{\text{Cash, Net receivables, Marketable securities}}{\text{Current liabilities}}$$

The write-off of inventory has no effect on the acid-test ratio.

**110. (d)** The number of days in the operating cycle measures the length of time from purchase of inventory to collection of cash. The formula is

$$\left(\begin{array}{c}\text{Number of days'}\\\text{sales in inventories}\end{array}\right) + \left(\begin{array}{c}\text{Number of days' sales}\\\text{in accts. receivable}\end{array}\right) = \left(\begin{array}{c}\text{Number of days in}\\\text{operating cycle}\end{array}\right)$$

$$61 \text{ days} \quad + \quad 33 \text{ days} \quad = \quad \underline{94 \text{ days}}$$

Note that the number of days' sales in inventories measures the number of days from the purchase of inventory to the sale of inventory, while the number of days' sales in accounts receivable measures the number of days from the sale of inventory to the collection of cash.

**111. (b)** Collection of a receivable results in an increase in cash and a decrease in the accounts receivable balance. The accounts receivable turnover ratio is computed by dividing net credit sales by the average net accounts receivable balance. Collection of a receivable reduces the average net accounts receivable balance. Thus the receivable turnover ratio increases. Since this transaction does not affect cost of goods sold or inventory, the inventory turnover ratio is unaffected. Neither the current ratio nor the quick ratio is affected by the collection; neither current assets nor quick assets would change as a result of the collection.

**SOLUTIONS TO SIMULATION PROBLEMS**

**Simulation Problem 1**

| | **Concepts** | | | | |
|---|---|---|---|---|---|
| **Instructions** | | **Journal Entries** | **Reporting Requirements** | **Communication** | **Research** |

|   | **(T)** | **(F)** |
|---|---|---|
| 1. The balance in "factor's holdback" (due from factor) is reported as an expense of the period. | ○ | ● |
| 2. In a specific assignment of receivables, collections on the assigned accounts are generally remitted to the assignor. | ● | ○ |
| 3. Factors are banks or finance companies that purchase receivables for a fee and then collect the remittances directly from the selling company. | ○ | ● |
| 4. A transfer of receivables with recourse may be accounted for as a sale, provided the transferee can require the transferor to repurchase the receivables. | ○ | ● |
| 5. In a transfer of receivables with recourse accounted for as a borrowing, the difference between the receivables and the total of the factor's holdback plus the proceeds is a financing cost that should be amortized to interest expense over the term of the receivables. | ● | ○ |

**Explanation of solutions**

1.   **(F)** "Factor's holdback" accounts for the proceeds retained by the factor to cover estimated sales discounts, sales returns, and sales allowances. When all amounts have been collected by the factor, the balance in factor's margin is returned to the seller. Therefore, this account is a receivable reported as a current asset on the balance sheet.

2.   **(T)** A specific assignment of receivables bestows more formal rights upon the assignee (lender) in that the AR do not simply collateralize the loan, but collections on the assigned accounts are actually remitted to the assignor who remits them to the assignee (lender).

3.   **(F)** Once a company sells receivables to a factor it normally has no further involvement with the receivables. The factor usually collects the remittances directly from the **customer**.

4.   **(F)** Per SFAS 140, transfers of receivables in which the transferee can require the transferor to repurchase the receivables may not be considered a sale.

5.   **(T)** The difference between the amount of receivables sold to a factor in a borrowing transaction and the total of the factor's holdback plus the proceeds is recorded in a "Discount on Transferred AR" or interest expense account (see journal entry (B) in part a.). This account represents interest cost and should be recognized over the term of the receivables. If interest expense is debited, an adjusting entry to defer some of the interest as "Discount" would be required if some of the discount pertains to a later period.

| | | **Journal Entries** | | | |
|---|---|---|---|---|---|
| **Instructions** | **Concepts** | | **Reporting Requirements** | **Communication** | **Research** |

|   | **(A)** | **(B)** | **(C)** | **(D)** | **(E)** | **(F)** |
|---|---|---|---|---|---|---|
| 1. Chester transfers receivables by surrendering control. Collection is to be made by the purchaser (factor), who assumes risk of loss. | ○ | ○ | ○ | ● | ○ | ○ |
| 2. Chester specifically assigns a portion of its receivables as collateral for a loan. Collections from the assigned receivables will be used to repay the loan and interest. | ○ | ○ | ● | ○ | ○ | ○ |
| 3. Chester pledges its receivables as collateral to secure a loan and the debtor collects the proceeds. | ○ | ○ | ○ | ○ | ● | ○ |
| 4. Chester sells accounts receivable to a factor in a transaction considered a borrowing. | ○ | ● | ○ | ○ | ○ | ○ |
| 5. Chester transfers a note receivable by surrendering control over it. The transfer was on a without recourse basis. | ○ | ○ | ○ | ○ | ○ | ● |
| 6. Chester pledges its accounts receivable as security for a loan. | ○ | ○ | ○ | ○ | ● | ○ |

**Explanation of solutions**

1.   **(D)** In this transaction, receivables are factored by surrendering control and without recourse. This constitutes an outright sale of the receivables in that title, risk of loss, and rights to future benefits are all transferred. Therefore, a loss on the transaction is recognized.

**2.   (C)** In a specific assignment of receivables, AR assigned are identified by placing them in an AR assigned account. A finance charge is assessed on assignment transactions that are borrowings.

**3.   (E)** When AR are pledged, the receivables serve as collateral for a loan but the proceeds are not remitted to the lender. In this case, the amount of AR pledged is reported at the balance sheet date either parenthetically or in the notes.

**4.   (B)** In this transaction, considered a borrowing, receivables are considered to be factored with recourse. Thus, the transaction is viewed as a loan collateralized by AR and the amount of the proceeds plus the factor's holdback and interest charged should be reported as a liability.

**5.   (F)** A note discounted on which control is surrendered and the terms include without recourse is considered a sales transaction upon which a loss should be recognized. Notes receivable should be credited.

**6.   (E)** A general assignment of receivables is another term for pledging AR, and thus should be disclosed parenthetically or in the notes to the financial statements (no journal entry).

| Instructions | Concepts | Journal Entries | Reporting Requirements | Communication | Research |
|---|---|---|---|---|---|

|  | (D) | (A) | (B) | (N) |
|---|---|---|---|---|
| **1.** On December 1, 2007, Chester was awarded damages of $75,000 in a patent infringement suit it brought against a competitor. The defendant did not appeal the verdict, and payment was received in January 2008. | ○ | ○ | ● | ○ |
| **2.** A former employee of Chester has brought a wrongful-dismissal suit against Chester. Chester's lawyers believe the suit to be without merit. | ○ | ○ | ○ | ● |
| **3.** At December 31, 2007, Chester had outstanding purchase orders in the ordinary course of business for purchase of a raw material to be used in its manufacturing process. The market price is currently higher than the purchase price and is not anticipated to change within the next year. | ○ | ○ | ○ | ● |
| **4.** A government contract completed during 2007 is subject to renegotiation. Although Chester estimates that it is reasonably possible that a refund of approximately $200,000 – $300,000 may be required by the government, it does not wish to publicize this possibility. | ● | ○ | ○ | ○ |
| **5.** Chester has been notified by a governmental agency that it will be held responsible for the cleanup of toxic materials at a site where Chester formerly conducted operations. Chester estimates that it is probable that its share of remedial action will be approximately $500,000. | ○ | ○ | ● | ○ |
| **6.** On January 5, 2008, Chester redeemed its outstanding bonds and issued new bonds with a lower rate of interest. The reacquisition price was in excess of the carrying amount of the bonds. | ● | ○ | ○ | ○ |

**Explanation of solutions**

**1.   (B)** SFAS 5 states "contingencies that might result in gains usually are not reflected in the accounts since to do so might be to recognize revenue prior to its realization." Since this gain contingency was resolved before the issuance of the financial statements, it is handled similar to an ordinary transaction that occurred prior to the year-end and is accrued in the year of its occurrence.

SFAS 5 states "adequate disclosure shall be made of contingencies that might result in gains...."

**2.   (N)** To accrue an estimated loss from a loss contingency it is necessary that it is probable that an asset has been impaired or a liability has been incurred and that the amount of loss can be reasonably estimated. Since Chester's lawyers believe the suit to be without merit, neither condition has been met.

SFAS 5 states "disclosure is also required of some loss contingencies that do not meet 'the accrual requirements mentioned above if' there is a **reasonable possibility** that a loss may be incurred." Again, this condition has not been met.

**3.   (N)** The conditions described in this question would be considered general or unspecified business risks that do not meet the conditions for accrual or disclosure.

**4.   (D)** The words "reasonably possible" require the disclosure of this item. No accrual need be made since the question does not state it is **probable** that an asset has been impaired or a liability incurred and that the amount of loss can be reasonably estimated.

**5.   (B)** The word "probable" and the inclusion of the estimated amount of $500,000 mean that this situation meets the criteria of (1) a probable incurrence of a liability and (2) a reasonable estimate of an amount.

**6.   (D)** SFAS 5 quotes ARB 50 which "required disclosure of a number of situations including...commitments such as those for an obligation to reduce debts." SFAS 5 states "situations of the type described...shall continue to be disclosed in financial statements." Since the entire transaction took place in the next accounting period it does not meet the conditions for an accrual in the current period even though it would be disclosed in a footnote.

| Instructions | Concepts | Journal Entries | Reporting Requirements | Communication | | Research |
|---|---|---|---|---|---|---|

To:　　CEO, Chester Company
From:　CPA Candidate
Re:　　Contingencies

As we discussed, you have requested an explanation of the accounting for certain contingencies. A contingency is a situation with an outcome that depends on the occurrence of a future event. In order to account for a contingency, you must assess the likelihood of the event occurring, and estimate the potential loss. For accounting purposes, a contingency is classified as probable, reasonably possible, or remote.

Chester Company has a threat of expropriation of one of its manufacturing plants located in a foreign country. Because this is only reasonably possible, accrual of a loss is inappropriate. However, the company should disclose the threat in a note to the financial statements. This note should include an estimate of the possible loss or an estimate of the range of the loss.

Chester Company has a potential loss due to the discovery of a safety hazard related to one of its products. Because these costs are probable and can be reasonably estimated, the company should accrue a loss in the income statement and record a liability in the balance sheet. Accrual is required in this situation because (1) it is probable that a liability has been incurred; and (2) the amount of the loss can be reasonably estimated. In addition, the company should separately disclose in a note to the financial statements the nature of this safety hazard.

The third situation, wherein Chester Company cannot insure one of its warehouses against rockslide losses, does not require disclosure. An asset has not been impaired, nor has a liability been incurred. Therefore, disclosure of the uninsured rockslide risk is not required.

If you have any additional questions, please contact me.

| Instructions | Concepts | Journal Entries | Reporting Requirements | Communication | Research |
|---|---|---|---|---|---|

1.　How should short-term obligations be classified on the balance sheet?

**FAS6, Para 8 or Current Text B05.112**

8.　Short-term obligations arising from transactions in the normal course of business that are due in customary terms shall be classified as current liabilities. Those obligations (as described in the second sentence of paragraph 7 of Chapter 3A of ARB No. 43) are "obligations for items which have entered into the operating cycle, such as payables incurred in the acquisition of materials and supplies to be used in the production of goods or in providing services to be offered for sale; collections received in advance of the delivery of goods or performance of services; . . . and debts which arise from operations directly related to the operating cycle, such as accruals for wages, salaries, commissions, rentals, royalties, and income and other taxes."

2.　Next year, Chester intends to refinance some short-term debt with a long-term note due in five years. What are the criteria to reclassify the short-term debt as long-term?

**FAS6, Para 11 or Current Text B05.113**

11.　The enterprise's intent to refinance the short-term obligation on a long-term basis is supported by an ability to consummate the refinancing demonstrated in either of the following ways:

a.　Post-balance-sheet-date issuance of a long-term obligation or equity securities. After the date of an enterprise's balance sheet, but before that balance sheet is issued, a long-term obligation or equity securities have been issued for the purpose of refinancing the short-term obligation on a long-term basis; or

b.　Financing agreement. Before the balance sheet is issued, the enterprise has entered into a financing agreement that clearly permits the enterprise to refinance the short-term obligation on a long-term basis on terms that are readily determinable, and all of the following conditions are met:

(i)　The agreement does not expire within one year (or operating cycle—see paragraph 2) from the date of the enterprise's balance sheet and during that period the agreement is not cancelable by the lender or the prospective lender or investor (and obligations incurred under the agreement are not callable during that period) except for violation of a provision with which compliance is objectively determinable or measurable.

(ii) No violation of any provision in the financing agreement exists at the balance-sheet date and no available information indicates that a violation has occurred thereafter but prior to the issuance of the balance sheet, or, if one exists at the balance-sheet date or has occurred thereafter, a waiver has been obtained.

(iii) The lender or the prospective lender or investor with which the enterprise has entered into the financing agreement is expected to be financially capable of honoring the agreement.

3. When should the company accrue an estimated loss on a contingency?

**FAS5, Para 8 or Current Text C59.105**

8. An estimated loss from a loss contingency (as defined in paragraph 1) shall be accrued by a charge to income if both of the following conditions are met:

a. Information available prior to issuance of the financial statements indicates that it is probable that an asset had been impaired or a liability has been incurred at the date of the financial statements. It is implicit in this condition that it must be probable that one or more future events will occur confirming the fact of the loss.

b. The amount of loss can be reasonably estimated.

4. What is a contingency?

**FAS5, Para 1 or Current Text C59.101**

1. For the purpose of this Statement, a contingency is defined as an existing condition, situation, or set of circumstances involving uncertainty as to possible gain (hereinafter a "gain contingency") or loss (hereinafter a "loss contingency") to an enterprise that will ultimately be resolved when one or more future events occur or fail to occur. Resolution of the uncertainty may confirm the acquisition of an asset or the reduction of a liability or the loss or impairment of an asset or the incurrence of a liability.

5. Define the three terms used to describe the likelihood of a contingent event occurring.

**FAS5, Para 3 or Current Text C59.104**

3. When a loss contingency exists, the likelihood that the future event or events will confirm the loss or impairment of an asset or the incurrence of a liability can range from probably to remote. This Statement uses the terms probable, reasonably possible, and remote to identify three areas within that range, as follows:

a. Probable. The future event or events are likely to occur.

b. Reasonably possible. The chance of the future event or events occurring is more than remote, but less than likely.

c. Remote. The change of the future event or events occurring is slight.

6. What are the conditions required for Chester to accrue vacation pay for its employees?

**FAS43, Para 6 or Current Text C44.104**

6. An employer shall accrue a liability for employees' compensation for future absences if all of the following conditions are met:

a. The employer's obligation relating to employees' rights to receive compensation for future absences is attributable to employees' services already rendered,

b. The obligation relates to rights that vest or accumulate,

c. Payment of the compensation is probable, and

d. The amount can be reasonably estimated.

7.  What are the criteria required to determine if a liability should be removed from the balance sheet?

**FAS140, Para 16 or Current Text L35.103**

16.  A debtor shall derecognize a liability if and only if it has been extinguished. A liability has been extinguished if either of the following conditions is met:

a.  The debtor pays the creditor and is relieved of its obligation for the liability. Paying the creditor includes delivery of cash, other financial assets, goods, or services, or reacquisition by the debtor of its outstanding debt securities whether the securities are canceled or held as so-called treasury bonds.

b.  The debtor is legally released from being the primary obligor under the liability, either judicially or by the creditor.

**Simulation Problem 2**

| | Concepts | | | | | | | |
|---|---|---|---|---|---|---|---|---|
| **Situation** | | **Uncollectible Accounts** | **Provision for Uncollectible Accounts Expense** | **Journal Entries** | **Transfer of Receivables** | **Communication** | **Research** | |

|  | *Cash* | *Not Cash* |
|---|---|---|
| 1.  Checking accounts | ● | ○ |
| 2.  Treasury stock | ○ | ● |
| 3.  Treasury bills | ● | ○ |
| 4.  Money market funds | ● | ○ |
| 5.  Petty cash | ● | ○ |
| 6.  Trading securities | ○ | ● |
| 7.  Savings accounts | ● | ○ |
| 8.  Sinking fund cash | ○ | ● |
| 9.  Compensating balances against long-term borrowings | ○ | ● |
| 10.  Cash restricted for new building | ○ | ● |
| 11.  Postdated check for customers | ○ | ● |
| 12.  Available-for-sale securities | ○ | ● |

| | | Uncollectible Accounts | | | | | |
|---|---|---|---|---|---|---|---|
| **Situation** | **Concepts** | | **Provision for Uncollectible Accounts Expense** | **Journal Entries** | **Transfer of Receivables** | **Communication** | **Research** |

Schedule to calculate provision and allowance for bad debts

*Sigma Company*
**SCHEDULE OF CALCULATION OF ALLOWANCE FOR UNCOLLECTIBLE ACCOUNTS**
*December 31, 2007*

| | *Amounts of accounts receivable* | *Percentage of uncollectible accounts* | *Estimate of uncollectible accounts* |
|---|---|---|---|
| 0 to 30 days | $300,000 | x  1% | $3,000 |
| 31 to 90 days | 80,000 | x  5% | 4,000 |
| 91 to 180 days | 60,000 | x  20% | 12,000 |
| Over 180 days | 25,000 | x  80% | 20,000 |
| Total accounts receivable | $465,000 | | |
| Total allowance for un-collectible accounts | | | $39,000 |

**Explanation of solutions**

1.  This problem consists of two related parts: part a. requires a calculation of the allowance for uncollectible accounts at 12/31/07 using an aging approach, and part b. requires a computation of the 2007 provision for uncollectible accounts (uncollectible accounts expense). The solutions approach is to quickly review the basics of accounting for uncollectible accounts, visualize the solution format, and begin. Some candidates may benefit from preparation of T-accounts (see item 4. below).

2.  When using the aging approach, the **total** uncollectible accounts (in other words, the required ending balance in the allowance account) is estimated by applying a different percentage to the various age categories. The percentage increases as the age of the receivables increases because the older a receivable is, the less likely is its ultimate collection.

2.1. In this case, Sigma estimates that 1% of its receivables in the zero-thirty days age category will prove to be uncollectible. Therefore, of that $300,000 of accounts receivable, it is estimated that $3,000 (1% × $300,000) will be uncollectible. Similar computations are performed for the other age categories, resulting in an estimate that $39,000 of the $465,000 accounts receivable will prove to be uncollectible. This is the required 12/31/07 balance in the allowance account.

3.  When using the aging approach, the first step is to compute the required ending balance in the allowance account (as discussed in items 2. and 2.1 above). The second step is to compute the uncollectible accounts expense necessary to bring the **unadjusted** allowance balance up to the **required** allowance balance.

3.1  The only item affecting the allowance account in 2006 was the recording of uncollectible accounts expense of $28,000 (1% × $2,800,000 credit sales). Therefore, the 1/1/07 balance in this account is $28,000. No adjustment is necessary for the change in the method of estimating this expense (from percent of sales to aging schedule) because any such change is handled prospectively.

*NOTE: Using the aging percents given also results in a $28,000 balance at 1/1/07. Even if the result was different, though, no adjustment is necessary.*

3.2  During 2007, this $28,000 credit balance was decreased by write-offs of $27,000 (debit allowance, credit AR) and increased by $7,000 of recoveries (debit AR, credit allowance; and debit cash, credit AR). Therefore, the 12/31/07 balance in the allowance account, **before adjustment,** is $8,000 ($28,000 − $27,000 + $7,000).

3.3  To increase the allowance account from $8,000 (see 3.2 above) to $39,000 (see 2.1 above), a provision for uncollectible accounts (uncollectible accounts expense) of $31,000 must be recorded for 2007.

4.  Some candidates may benefit from the preparation of T-accounts for the allowance account and accounts receivable. These T-accounts are provided below.

*T-accounts for 2007*

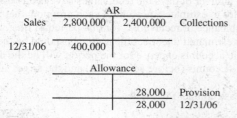

|  | AR |  |  |
|---|---|---|---|
| Sales | 2,800,000 | 2,400,000 | Collections |
| 12/31/06 | 400,000 | | |

|  | Allowance |  |  |
|---|---|---|---|
| | | 28,000 | Provision |
| | | 28,000 | 12/31/06 |

| Situation | Concepts | Uncollectible Accounts | **Provision for Uncollectible Accounts Expense** | Journal Entries | Transfer of Receivables | Communication | Research |
|---|---|---|---|---|---|---|---|

Computation of 2007 provision

| | |
|---|---|
| Balance December 31, 2006 | $28,000 |
| Write-offs during 2007 | (27,000) |
| Recoveries during 2007 | 7,000 |
| Balance before 2007 provision | 8,000 |
| Required allowance at December 31, 2007 | 39,000 |
| 2007 Provision | $31,000 |

| Situation | Concepts | Uncollectible Accounts | Provision for Uncollectible Accounts Expense | **Journal Entries** | Transfer of Receivables | Communication | Research |
|---|---|---|---|---|---|---|---|

*Write-offs*

| | | |
|---|---|---|
| Allowance for uncollectible accounts | 27,000 | |
|     Accounts receivable | | 27,000 |

*Recoveries*

| | | |
|---|---|---|
| Accounts receivable | 7,000 | |
|     Allowance for uncollectible accounts | | 7,000 |
| *To reinstate the account receivable* | | |
| Cash | 7,000 | |
|     Accounts receivable | | 7,000 |
| *To show payment on the account* | | |

*Provision for uncollectible accounts expense at December 31, 2007*

| | | |
|---|---|---|
| Uncollectible accounts expense | 31,000 | |
| Allowance for uncollectible accounts | | 31,000 |

| Situation | Concepts | Uncollectible Accounts | Provision for Uncollectible Accounts Expense | Journal Entries | Transfer of Receivables | Communication | Research |
|---|---|---|---|---|---|---|---|
| Cash | | | 144,226 | | | | |
| Interest expense (150,000 × .15 × 45/365) | | | 2,774 | | | | |
| Factoring fee (2% × 150,000) | | | 3,000 | | | | |
| Accounts receivable | | | | 150,000 | | | |

| Situation | Concepts | Uncollectible Accounts | Provision for Uncollectible Accounts Expense | Journal Entries | Transfer of Receivables | Communication | Research |
|---|---|---|---|---|---|---|---|

To:     CEO, Sigma Company
From:   CPA Candidate
Re:     Estimating uncollectible accounts

This memorandum is designed to answer your questions about the accounting for uncollectible accounts. Under generally accepted accounting principles there are two acceptable methods for estimating uncollectible accounts. One method uses an income statement approach, and the other method uses a balance sheet approach. Either method is acceptable; however, a company should select a method and continue to use the same method.

The income statement (percent-of-credit-sales) approach estimates uncollectible accounts based on credit sales. This approach focuses on income determination by attempting to match uncollectible accounts expense with the revenues generated during the period. A company may use a historical analysis to estimate the percent of credit sales that will not be collected. This percent is multiplied by the credit sales for the period to arrive at uncollectible accounts expense.

The second approach, the aging of accounts receivable method, uses a balance sheet approach to estimate uncollectible accounts. The aging approach groups the accounts receivable by the number of days the receivables have been outstanding. Management then uses historical data or loss experience in the industry to estimate a percent of each grouping that may not be collected. The estimated percent is multiplied by the outstanding balance of receivables for that period of time, and the sum of these estimated uncollectible accounts is totaled. The total of estimated uncollectible accounts should be the ending balance in the allowance for uncollectible accounts. The uncollectible accounts expense for the period will be the difference between the year-end balance in the allowance for uncollectible accounts (before adjustment) and the target number for the allowance account based on the most recent aging schedule.

If you would like assistance in preparing the aging schedule, please contact my office.

| Situation | Concepts | Uncollectible Accounts | Provision for Uncollectible Accounts Expense | Journal Entries | Transfer of Receivables | Communication | Research |
|---|---|---|---|---|---|---|---|

1.  With regard to transfers of financial assets, what is the financial components approach?

**FAS140, Para 7 or Current Text F39.101**

7.  Before FASB Statement No. 125, *Accounting for Transfers and Servicing of Financial Assets and Extinguishments of Liabilities*, accounting standards generally required that a transferor account for financial assets transferred as an inseparable unit that had been either entirely sold or entirely retained. Those standards were difficult to apply and produced inconsistent and arbitrary results. For example, whether a transfer "purported to be a sale" was sufficient to determine whether the transfer was accounted for and reported as a sale of receivables under one accounting standard or as a secured borrowing under another. After studying many of the complex developments that have occurred in financial markets during recent years, the Board concluded that previous approaches that viewed each financial asset as an indivisible unit do not provide an appropriate basis for developing consistent and operational standards for dealing with transfers and servicing of financial assets and extinguishments of liabilities. To address those issues adequately and consistently, the Board decided to adopt as the basis for the Statement a financial-components approach that focuses on control and recognizes that financial assets and liabilities can be divided into a variety of components.

2.  Describe the criteria for determining when control has been surrendered in a transfer of receivables.

**FAS140, Para 9 or Current Text F39.104**

9.  A transfer of financial assets (or all or a portion of a financial asset) in which the transferor surrenders control over those financial assets shall be accounted for as a sale to the extent that consideration other than beneficial interests in the transferred assets is received in exchange.  The transferor has surrendered control over transferred assets if and only if all of the following conditions are met:

a.  The transferred assets have been isolated from the transferor—put presumptively beyond the reach of the transferor and its creditors, even in bankruptcy or other receivership (paragraphs 27 and 28).

b.  Each transferee (or, if the transferee is a qualifying SPE (paragraph 35), each holder of its beneficial interests) has the right to pledge or exchange the assets (or beneficial interests) it received, and no condition both constrains the transferee (or holder) from taking advantage of its right to pledge or exchange and provides more than a trivial benefit to the transferor (paragraphs 29-34).

c.  The transferor does not maintain effective control over the transferred assets through either (1) an agreement that both entitles and obligates the transferor to repurchase or redeem them before their maturity (paragraphs 47-49) or (2) the ability to unilaterally cause the holder to return specific assets, other than through a cleanup call (paragraphs 50-54).

3.  How are transfers of receivables accounted for if one or more of the criteria for determining whether control has been surrendered are not met?

**FAS140, Para 12 or Current Text F39.107**

12.  If a transfer of financial assets in exchange for cash or other consideration (other than beneficial interests in the transferred assets) does not meet the criteria for a sale in paragraph 9, the transferor and transferee shall account for the transfer as a secured borrowing with pledge of collateral (paragraph 15).

# PRESENT VALUE

This module begins by reviewing the basic concepts related to time value of money.  The module then covers four major topics in which time value of money applications are used extensively:  (1) bonds payable and bond investments, (2) debt restructure, (3) pensions, and (4) leases.

## A.  Fundamentals

The concepts of time value of money are essential for successful completion of the CPA exam.  Time value of money concepts are central to capital budgeting, leases, pensions, bonds, and other topics.  You must understand the mechanics as well as the concepts.  After studying the next few pages, work the multiple-choice questions entitled "Fundamentals."  Note that the following abbreviations are used in the text that follows.

> i  =  interest rate
> n  =  number of periods or rents

On the CPA exam, you do not have to know the complex formulas that are used to compute time value of money factors (TVMF).  The factors will be given to you or enough information will be given to you so that you can easily compute them (see A.8. TVMF Applications).  Your main focus of attention should be centered on understanding which TVMF should be used in a given situation.

1. **Future Value (FV) of an Amount** (future value of $1)

   The future value of an amount is the amount that will be available at some point in the future if an amount is deposited today and earns compound interest for "n" periods.  The most common application is savings deposits.  For example, if you deposited $100 today at 10%, you would have $110 [$100 + ($100 × 10%)] at the end of the first year, $121[$100 + ($110 × 10%)] at the end of the second year, etc.  The compounding feature allows you to earn interest on interest.  In the second year of the example you earn $11 interest:  $10 on the original $100 and $1 on the first year's interest of $10.

2. **Present Value (PV) of a Future Amount** (present value of $1)

   The present value of a future amount is the amount you would pay now for an amount to be received "n" periods in the future given an interest rate of "i."  A common application would be the money you would lend today for a noninterest-bearing note receivable in the future.  For example, if you were lending money at 10%, you would lend $100 for a $110 note due in one year or for a $121 note due in two years.

   The present value of $1 is the inverse of the future value of $1.  Thus, given a future value of $1 table, you have a present value of $1 by dividing each value into 1.00.  Look at the present value of $1 and future value of $1 tables on the next page.  The future value of $1 at 10% in five years is 1.611.  Thus, the present value of $1 in five years would be 1.00 ÷ 1.611 which is .621 (check the table).  Conversely, the future value of $1 is found by dividing the present value of $1 into 1.00, that is, 1.00 ÷ .621 = 1.611.

3. **Compounding**

   When interest is compounded more than once a year, two extra steps are needed.  First, **multiply** "n" by the number of times interest is compounded annually.  This will give you the total number of interest periods.  Second, **divide** "i" by the number of times interest is compounded annually.  This will give you the appropriate interest rate for each interest period.  For example, if the 10% was compounded semiannually, the amount of $100 at the end of one year would be $110.25 [$(1.05)^2$] instead of $110.00.  The extra $.25 is 5% of the $5.00 interest earned in the first half of the year.

4. **Future Value of an Ordinary Annuity**

   The future value of an ordinary annuity is the amount available "n" periods in the future as a result of the deposit of an amount (A) at the end of every period 1 through "n."  Compound interest is earned at the rate of "i" on the deposits.  A common application is a bond sinking fund.  A deposit is made at the end of the first period and earns compound interest for n-1 periods (not during the first period, because the deposit is made at the end of the first period).  The next to the last payment earns one period's interest, that is, $n - (n-1) = 1$.  The last payment earns no interest, because it is deposited at the end of the last (nth) period.  Remember that in the FUTURE AMOUNT OF AN ORDINARY ANNUITY TABLE, all of the factors for any "n" row are based on one less interest period than the number of payments.

## TIME VALUE OF MONEY FACTOR (TVMF) TABLES

### Future Value (Amount) of $1

| $n$ | 6% | 8% | 10% | 12% | 15% |
|---|---|---|---|---|---|
| 1 | 1.060 | 1.080 | 1.100 | 1.120 | 1.150 |
| 2 | 1.124 | 1.166 | 1.210 | 1.254 | 1.323 |
| 3 | 1.191 | 1.260 | 1.331 | 1.405 | 1.521 |
| 4 | 1.262 | 1.360 | 1.464 | 1.574 | 1.749 |
| 5 | 1.338 | 1.469 | 1.611 | 1.762 | 2.011 |

### Present Value of $1

| $n$ | 6% | 8% | 10% | 12% | 15% |
|---|---|---|---|---|---|
| 1 | .943 | .926 | .909 | .893 | .870 |
| 2 | .890 | .857 | .826 | .797 | .756 |
| 3 | .840 | .794 | .751 | .712 | .658 |
| 4 | .792 | .735 | .683 | .636 | .572 |
| 5 | .747 | .681 | .621 | .567 | .497 |

### Future Value (Amount) of an Ordinary Annuity of $1

| $n$ | 6% | 8% | 10% | 12% | 15% |
|---|---|---|---|---|---|
| 1 | 1.000 | 1.000 | 1.000 | 1.000 | 1.000 |
| 2 | 2.060 | 2.080 | 2.100 | 2.120 | 2.150 |
| 3 | 3.184 | 3.246 | 3.310 | 3.374 | 3.473 |
| 4 | 4.375 | 4.506 | 4.506 | 4.641 | 4.993 |
| 5 | 5.637 | 5.867 | 6.105 | 6.353 | 6.742 |

### Present Value of an Ordinary Annuity of $1

| $n$ | 6% | 8% | 10% | 12% | 15% |
|---|---|---|---|---|---|
| 1 | .943 | .926 | .909 | .893 | .870 |
| 2 | 1.833 | 1.783 | 1.736 | 1.690 | 1.626 |
| 3 | 2.673 | 2.577 | 2.487 | 2.402 | 2.283 |
| 4 | 3.465 | 3.312 | 3.170 | 3.037 | 2.855 |
| 5 | 4.212 | 3.993 | 3.791 | 3.605 | 3.352 |

## 5.  Present Value of an Ordinary Annuity

The present value of an ordinary annuity is the value today, given a discount rate, of a series of future payments.  A common application is the capitalization of lease payments by either lessors or lessees.  Payments "1" through "n" are assumed to be made at the end of years "1" through "n," and are discounted back to the present.

> EXAMPLE:  Assume a five-year lease of equipment requiring payments of $1,000 at the end of each of the five years, which is to be capitalized.  If the discount rate is 10%, the present value is $3,791 ($1,000 × 3.791).

The behavior of the present value of the lease payment stream over the five-year period is shown below.  Note that the liability (principal amount) grows by interest in the amount of 10% during each period and decreases by $1,000 at the end of each period.

| 0 | 1 | 2 | 3 | 4 | 5 |
|---|---|---|---|---|---|

$3,791 + 380 Int. =   $4,171
                        − 1,000 Pay
                      $3,171 + 320 Int. = $3,491
                                          − 1,000 Pay
                                        $2,491 + 250 Int. =  $2,741
                                                            − 1,000
                                                          $1,741 + 170 Int. =  $1,911
                                                                               − 1,000
                                                                             $ 911 + 91 Int. = $1,002
                                                                                               − 1,000
                                                                                                    2*

\* *Due to rounding*

## 6.  Distinguishing a Future Value of an Annuity from a Present Value of an Annuity

Sometimes confusion arises in distinguishing between the future value (amount) of an annuity and the present value of an annuity.  These two may be distinguished by determining whether the total dollar amount in the problem comes at the beginning (e.g., cost of equipment acquired for leasing) or at the end (e.g., the amount needed to retire bonds) of the series of payments as illustrated below.

Remember: if the total amount comes at the end of the series of payments, it is a **future value** of annuity situation. If the total amount comes at the beginning of the series of payments, it is a **present value** of annuity situation. The total dollar amount may be given in the problem or you may have to compute it; either way, it makes no difference in determining whether a problem involves a present value or future value situation.

Some students feel the need to "convert" all time value of money problems into either present value or future value problems, depending on which they're most comfortable with. This process involves more work and more chance for errors, because an additional TVMF equation must be solved in the conversion. This is inefficient, and unnecessary if you are able to correctly identify between the two initially. Become proficient at determining present value and future value situations, so that you may efficiently select the correct TVMF from the corresponding table. Drawing a timeline for the facts in each problem will help you determine if you need to solve for a present value or a future value.

7. **Annuities Due**

In some cases, the payments or annuities may not conform to the assumptions inherent in the annuity tables. For example, the payments might be made at the beginning of each of the five years instead of at the end of each year. This is an annuity due (annuity in advance) in contrast to an ordinary annuity (annuity in arrears). Both annuity due and ordinary annuity payments are represented by the "x's" in the illustration below.

| Periods | | 1 | 2 | 3 | 4 | 5 |
|---|---|---|---|---|---|---|
| Annuity | | x | x | x | x | x |
| Annuity Due | x | x | x | x | x | |

If the payments in the 5-period lease example above were made at the beginning of the period, the present value of the first payment which is made today is \$1,000 (i.e., the TVMF is 1.00). The remaining 4 payments comprise an ordinary annuity for 4 periods as you can see on the above diagram. Always use time diagrams to analyze application of annuities.

To convert either a future value of an ordinary annuity or the present value of an ordinary annuity factor to an annuity due factor, multiply the ordinary annuity factor times $(1 + i)$. For the above lease example, you would find the present value of an ordinary annuity factor for n = 5 which is 3.993. Then multiply 3.993 by 1.08 to arrive at the annuity due factor, 4.312. The present value of the payments would be \$4,312 (4.312 × \$1,000). Notice that the present value of the annuity due in the above example is \$319 greater than the present value of the ordinary annuity because the payments are moved closer to the present.

8. **TVMF Applications**

The basic formula to use is

$$FV \text{ or } PV = TVMF \times Amount$$

If an annuity is involved, the amount is the periodic payment or deposit; if not, it is a single sum. Note that FV or PV is determined by three variables: time, interest rate, and payment. TVMF represents two variables: time and interest rate. The tables usually have the interest rate on the horizontal axis and time on the vertical axis. The above formula may also be stated as

$$Amount = \frac{FV \text{ or } PV}{TVMF}$$

For example, if we need to accumulate \$12,210 in five years to repay a loan, we could determine the required annual deposit with the above formula. If the savings rate were 10%, we would divide the FV (\$12,210) by the TVMF of the future value of annuity, n=5, i=.10 (6.105) and get \$2,000. Thus,

$2,000 deposited at the end of each of five years earning 10% will result in $12,210. This formula may also be used to find future values of an amount, present values of amounts, and annuities in the same manner.

Another variation of the formula is

$$\text{TVMF} = \frac{\text{FV or PV}}{\text{Amount}}$$

For example, we may be offered a choice between paying $3,312 in cash or $1,000 a year at the end of each of the next four years. We determine the interest rate by dividing the annual payment into the present value of the annuity to obtain the TVMF (3.312) for n=4. We then find the interest rate which has the same or similar TVMF (in this case 8%).

Alternatively, using the above formula, we may know the interest rate but not know the number of payments. Given the TVMF, we can determine "n" by looking in the TVMF table under the known interest rate. Remember the TVMF reflects two variables: time and interest rate.

9. **Notes Receivable and Payable**

Short-term notes receivable and notes payable that arise from transactions with customers and suppliers in the normal course of business and are due in one year are classified as current liabilities. These short-term notes are recorded at their maturity value.

Notes receivable and notes payable due in more than one year (long-term notes) should be recorded at their present values (see outline of APB 21). Upon receipt or issuance of a long-term note, record the net value of the note receivable or payable (i.e., note plus or minus premium or discount) at

1. Cash received or paid

   a. Assumes no other rights or privileges

2. Established exchange price (fair market value) or property or services received or provided

   a. If not determinable, determine present value with imputed interest rate

Record interest revenue (on notes receivable) or interest expense (on notes payable) as the effective rate of interest times the net receivable or payable during the period.

a. **Note exchanged for cash only**—When a note is exchanged for cash and no other rights or privileges are exchanged, the present value of the note is equivalent to the cash exchanged. The cash exchanged, however, may not be equal to the face amount of the note (the amount paid at maturity). When the face amount of a note does not equal its present value, the difference is either a discount or a premium. A discount results when the face of the note exceeds its present value, and a premium results when the present value of the note exceeds its face (see Section B.1. in this module for a more detailed discussion of discounts and premiums).

b. **Note exchanged for cash and unstated rights and privileges**—In the preceding discussion, notes were issued solely for cash, and no other rights or privileges were exchanged. The accounting treatment differs, however, when a note is issued for cash and unstated rights and/or privileges are also exchanged. The cash exchanged for such a note consists of two elements: (1) the present value of the note, and (2) the present value of the unstated right or privilege. Proper accounting for this situation requires that one of the two present values above be determined. Once this is done, the remaining present value is simply the difference between the face amount of the note and the present value that was determined.

For example, on January 1, 2007, Zilch Company borrowed $200,000 from its major customer, Martha Corporation. The borrowing is evidenced by a note payable due in three years. The note is noninterest-bearing. In consideration for the borrowing, Zilch Company agrees to supply Martha Corporation's inventory needs for the loan period at favorable prices. This last feature of the transaction is the unstated right or privilege; that is, the ability of Martha to purchase inventory at less than regular prices.

The present value of the note (assuming it is easier to determine) should be based upon the interest rate Zilch would have to pay in a normal borrowing of $200,000 (i.e., in a transaction that did not include unstated rights or privileges). Assume that Zilch would have to pay interest at 12% in a normal borrowing. The present value of $200,000 discounted for three years at 12% is $142,400 ($200,000 × .712). The difference between the face amount of the note, $200,000, and its present value of $142,400 represents the present value of the unstated right or privilege.  The amount of this present value is $57,600.

The entries below show how both Zilch and Martha should account for this transaction during 2007.

| | *Zilch* | | | | *Martha* | | |
|---|---|---|---|---|---|---|---|
| *1/1/07* | | | | *1/1/07* | | | |
| Cash | 142,400 | | | Note receivable | 200,000 | | |
| Discount on note payable | 57,600 | | | Discount on note receivable | | 57,600 | |
| Note payable | | 200,000 | | Cash | | 142,400 | |
| | | | | | | | |
| Cash | 57,600 | | | Advance payments on inventory | 57,600 | | |
| Deferred revenue | | 57,600 | | Cash | | 57,600 | |
| | | | | | | | |
| *12/31/07* | | | | *12/31/07* | | | |
| Interest expense | 17,088* | | | Discount on note receivable | 17,088 | | |
| Discount on note payable | | 17,088 | | Interest income | | 17,088 | |

\* *$142,400 × .12 = $17,088*

| | *Zilch* | | | | *Martha* | | |
|---|---|---|---|---|---|---|---|
| Deferred revenue | xx | | | Inventory (purchases) | xx | | |
| Sales | | xx | | Advance payments on inventory | | xx | |

The amounts represented by "xx" in the entries above depend upon the amount of goods acquired by Martha during 2007.

On the December 31, 2007 balance sheets of both Zilch and Martha, the above notes should be disclosed in the noncurrent liability (Zilch) and asset (Martha) sections net of the unamortized discount applicable to each note.

c.   **Note exchanged in a noncash transaction**—In addition to notes issued for cash, a note may also be received or issued in a noncash transaction; that is, for goods, property, or services.  The problem created in this situation is how to determine the note's present value in the absence of cash.  One way to solve this problem is to assume that the stated rate or contractual rate stated on the note represents a fair rate of return to the supplier for the use of the related funds.  If the interest rate is presumed to be fair, then the face amount of the note is presumed to equal its present value.  Interest revenue (expense) is computed by multiplying the interest rate stated on the face of the note by the face of the note.  There is no discount or premium to consider because the face of the note is assumed to be equal to its present value.

The assumption that the interest rate on the face of the note is fair is not always valid.  According to APB 21, the assumption is not valid if

1.   The interest rate is not stated (usually, this means the note is noninterest-bearing), or
2.   The stated rate is unreasonable (this refers to both unreasonably low and high rates), or
3.   The stated face amount of the note is materially different from the current cash sales price for the same or similar items, or from the market value of the note at the date of the transaction.

When the interest rate is not fair, the face amount of the note does not equal its present value.  In the absence of cash, the present value of a note is determined according to the following priorities:

1.   First, determine if the goods, property, or services exchanged have a reliable fair market value.  If they do, the fair market value is presumed to be the present value of the note.
2.   If a reliable fair market value does not exist for the goods, property, or services exchanged, then determine if the note has a market value.  If it does, the note's market value is equal to the present value of the note.
3.   Finally, if market values do not exist for either the goods, property, or services or for the note, then an interest rate must be **imputed**.  This imputed interest rate is then used to determine the present value of the note.  The imputed interest rate represents the **debtor's** incremental borrowing rate.

To illustrate the situation where the interest rate on a note is not fair, yet the fair market value of the property exchanged is known, assume the following facts:  Doink Co. sold a building on January 1, 2007, which originally cost $7,000,000 and which had a book value of $4,000,000 for a $14,000,000 (face amount) noninterest-bearing note due in three years.  Since zero interest is not considered to be a fair rate of return, the face amount of Doink's note does not equal its present value.  In Doink's case, the face of its note is $14,000,000.  The present value of the note is the unknown and must be calculated.

To determine the present value of Doink's $14,000,000 noninterest-bearing note, you should first see if the building sold had a reliable fair market value at the date it was sold.  Assume that Doink's building could have sold on January 1, 2007, for $10,000,000 in a straight cash transaction.  Given the information about the building, its fair market value of $10,000,000 on January 1, 2007 represents the note's present value.  Since the face of the note is $14,000,000 and its present value is $10,000,000, the $4,000,000 difference represents the discount.  Doink should record this transaction in the following manner:

| | | |
|---|---:|---:|
| Note receivable | 14,000,000 | |
| Accumulated depreciation | 3,000,000 | |
|    Building | | 7,000,000 |
|    Gain on sale of building | | 6,000,000 |
|    Discount on note receivable | | 4,000,000 |

It is important that you note how the gain is calculated in the entry above.  The gain is the difference between the present value of the note ($10,000,000) and the book value of the property sold ($4,000,000).  The difference between the face amount of the note ($14,000,000) and its present value ($10,000,000) represents the discount of $4,000,000.  This discount should be amortized to interest income using the effective interest method.  However, before this discount can be amortized, the interest rate must be determined.  In situations like this, the interest rate can be determined by reference to present value tables.  In Doink's situation, the present value of the note, $10,000,000, divided by its face amount, $14,000,000, results in the number .714.  This number represents a factor from the present value of $1 table.  Since Doink's note is for 3 periods, the factor .712 in the present value of $1 table is under the 12% interest rate.  Thus, Doink's interest rate is approximately 12%.

If the building sold by Doink did not have a reliable fair market value on January 1, 2007, the next step would be to determine if the note had a market value on that date.

Finally, if the building sold by Doink did not possess a reliable fair market value on January 1, 2007, and the note did not have a market value on that date, the present value of Doink's note would have to be determined by **imputation**.  This means that Doink would determine the present value of its note by reference to the incremental borrowing rate of the company which acquired its building.

The following diagram represents the forementioned relationships and procedures for determining the present value of a note receivable or payable (monetary assets and liabilities) and the amount of a discount/premium.

**ACCOUNTING FOR MONETARY ASSETS AND LIABILITIES WHICH HAVE
MATURITIES GREATER THAN ONE YEAR FROM THE BALANCE SHEET DATE**

### 10. Loan Origination Costs and Fees

Sometimes the lender incurs various loan origination costs when originating or acquiring a loan. According to SFAS 91, the lender shall defer and recognize these costs over the life of the loan only when the costs relate directly to the loan, and would not have been incurred but for the loan. Otherwise, the costs are considered indirect and are charged to expense as incurred.

Sometimes the lender charges the borrower a nonrefundable loan origination fee. According to SFAS 91, both lender and borrower shall defer and recognize the nonrefundable fee over the life of the loan.  The fee is frequently assessed in the form of points, where a point is 1% of the face amount of the loan.

For example, assume that Bannon Bank grants a ten-year loan to VerSteiner, Inc. in the amount of $100,000 with a stated interest rate of 8%.  Payments are due monthly, and are computed to be $1,213.  In addition, Bannon Bank incurs $3,000 of direct loan origination costs (attorney's fees, title insurance, wages of employees' direct work on loan origination), and also charges VerSteiner a 5-point nonrefundable loan origination fee.

Bannon Bank, the lender, has a carrying amount of $98,000.  This reflects the $100,000 face amount of the loan less the $5,000 nonrefundable fee, plus the $3,000 additional investment Bannon Bank incurs to generate the $145,560 total payments from the borrower, VerSteiner.  The effective interest rate is approximately 8.5%.

VerSteiner, the borrower, receives 5% less than the face amount of $100,000, or $95,000, but is still required to pay $1,213 per month under the terms of the loan.  VerSteiner's carrying amount is then $100,000 – $5,000 = $95,000, with an effective interest rate of approximately 9.2%.

*NOTE:  Both the rates can be derived with a financial calculator.  It is not likely that you would be asked to compute these on the CPA exam because the computerized exam provides a simple four-function calculator, and the formula to calculate interest is not included in the spreadsheet formulas.  What you are expected to know is the concept of effective interest.  You also need to know that the loan origination costs are to be added to the principal, by the lender, and any fee charged to the client is deducted from the principal by both parties in calculating the carrying amount.*

11. **Disclosures**

The basic loan situation involves a borrower receiving the face amount of a loan from a lender, with no related discount or premium.  The liability is the face amount, and the effective interest rate is the stated interest rate on the interest-bearing note.  When a note is issued for an amount other than the face of the loan or when a noninterest-bearing note is used, and the rules of APB 21 apply (i.e., the fair value option is not elected) a premium or discount must be recorded for the note.  The discount amount is additional interest over the life of the note; the premium amount is a reduction in interest expense over the life of the loan.  The amount in the discount or premium account is amortized to interest expense over the life of the note using the effective interest rate.

APB 21 requires notes to be reported on the financial statement at their net carrying value.  Discount on notes payable is a liability valuation account (contra account).  It should be reported as a direct reduction from the face amount of the note on the balance sheet.  A premium on the note is reported as an addition to the face amount of the note (adjunct account) on the balance sheet.

In the footnotes to the financial statements, a disclosure must be made for the aggregate amounts of maturities and the sinking fund requirements for all long-term borrowings for each of the five years following the balance sheet date.

12. **Fair Value Option**

As discussed in Module 7D, SFAS 159 provides that a company may elect the fair value option for reporting financial assets and financial liabilities.  If the fair value option is elected for a financial liability, the requirements of APB 21 no longer apply.  Instead, the financial liability is reported at fair value at the end of each reporting period, and the resulting gain or loss is reported in earnings of the period.

13. **Research Component**

The authoritative literature on payables and receivables is found in several locations in FARS: APB 21, SFAS 47, and SFAS 91.  APB 21 addresses the valuation of the note, determining appropriate interest rates, amortization of discounts and premiums, and financial statement presentation of the discount and premium account.  APB 21 applies to all interest payable and interest receivable with the exception of certain items.  APB 21, para 3 specifically excludes receivables and payables arising from transactions with customers in the normal course of business which are due in terms not exceeding one year.  By specifically excluding current receivables and payables in the normal course of business from time value of money calculations, it implies that current receivables and payables are recorded at their face amounts.

SFAS 47 addresses the disclosure of long-term obligations.  The majority of SFAS 47 addresses unconditional purchase obligations; however, it also addresses footnote disclosures for long-term debt.  Specifically SFAS 47, para 10 requires that the combined aggregate amount of maturities and sinking fund requirements for all long-term borrowings be disclosed for each of the five years following the balance sheet date.  SFAS 91 addresses fees and costs associated with originating or acquiring loans, as well as the initial direct costs of leasing (covered in the leasing module).

Because the words "notes receivable" and "notes payable" are used extensively in the FARS database, it is necessary to use more exact vocabulary when researching issues on receivables and payables.  Specifically, there are many synonyms used in accounting practice for long-term debt.  You can narrow your search more quickly if you are familiar with some key terms used by the APB and the FASB in these specific standards.  It is recommended that you read or skim the following paragraphs in the pronouncements to familiarize yourself with the vocabulary terms in this area:

APB 21, para 1, 3, 6, 9, 10, 15, and 16
SFAS 47, para 10
SFAS 91, para 4, 5, 6, 7

Essential keywords for locating items in the research database for notes receivable and payable are shown in the table below.  Notice that the key terms are very specific; this list has been devised by carefully examining the relevant passages to help narrow your search.  You may wish to include the word "note" with other search terms; it will eliminate materials that are not relevant to your search.  For example, if you search for effective interest, you will find over 800 matches.  If you include the term "note" with the terms "effective interest," the search is narrowed to approximately 15 hits, and the database moves directly to APB 21.  In researching origination costs, loan costs, etc., it may be helpful to use the term "fees" in your search.  Also, because this is an exact character string search, notice that long-term is hyphenated in the database, and in this area, they use the term "borrowings" or "obligations" rather than debt.

| | | |
|---|---|---|
| Determining present value | Indirect costs loan | Note issued |
| Direct costs loan | Loan origination fees | Note received |
| Disclosure long-term borrowings | Maturities long-term | Points fees |
| Effective interest note | Noncash transaction note | Present value note |
| Exchange price note | Nonrefundable fees loan | |

## MULTIPLE-CHOICE QUESTIONS (1-22)

**1.** On March 15, 2007, Ashe Corp. adopted a plan to accumulate $1,000,000 by September 1, 2011. Ashe plans to make four equal annual deposits to a fund that will earn interest at 10% compounded annually. Ashe made the first deposit on September 1, 2007. Future value and future amount factors are as follows:

| | |
|---|---|
| Future value of $1 at 10% for 4 periods | 1.46 |
| Future amount of ordinary annuity of $1 at 10% for four periods | 4.64 |
| Future amount of annuity in advance of $1 at 10% for four periods | 5.11 |

Ashe should make four annual deposits (rounded) of
- a. $250,000
- b. $215,500
- c. $195,700
- d. $146,000

**2.** On July 1, 2007, James Rago signed an agreement to operate as a franchisee of Fast Foods, Inc. for an initial franchise fee of $60,000. Of this amount, $20,000 was paid when the agreement was signed and the balance is payable in four equal annual payments of $10,000 beginning July 1, 2008. The agreement provides that the down payment is not refundable and no future services are required of the franchisor. Rago's credit rating indicates that he can borrow money at 14% for a loan of this type. Information on present and future value factors is as follows:

| | |
|---|---|
| Present value of $1 at 14% for four periods | 0.59 |
| Future amount of $1 at 14% for four periods | 1.69 |
| Present value of an ordinary annuity of $1 at 14% for four periods | 2.91 |

Rago should record the acquisition cost of the franchise on July 1, 2007 at
- a. $43,600
- b. $49,100
- c. $60,000
- d. $67,600

**3.** On November 1, 2007, a company purchased a new machine that it does not have to pay for until November 1, 2009. The total payment on November 1, 2009, will include both principal and interest. Assuming interest at a 10% rate, the cost of the machine would be the total payment multiplied by what time value of money concept?
- a. Present value of annuity of $1.
- b. Present value of $1.
- c. Future amount of annuity of $1.
- d. Future amount of $1.

**4.** For which of the following transactions would the use of the present value of an annuity due concept be appropriate in calculating the present value of the asset obtained or liability owed at the date of incurrence?
- a. A capital lease is entered into with the initial lease payment due one month subsequent to the signing of the lease agreement.
- b. A capital lease is entered into with the initial lease payment due upon the signing of the lease agreement.
- c. A ten-year 8% bond is issued on January 2 with interest payable semiannually on July 1 and January 1 yielding 7%.

- d. A ten-year 8% bond is issued on January 2 with interest payable semiannually on July 1 and January 1 yielding 9%.

**5.** Jole Co. lent $10,000 to a major supplier in exchange for a noninterest-bearing note due in three years and a contract to purchase a fixed amount of merchandise from the supplier at a 10% discount from prevailing market prices over the next three years. The market rate for a note of this type is 10%. On issuing the note, Jole should record

| | Discount on note receivable | Deferred charge |
|---|---|---|
| a. | Yes | Yes |
| b. | Yes | No |
| c. | No | Yes |
| d. | No | No |

**6.** On December 30, 2007, Chang Co. sold a machine to Door Co. in exchange for a noninterest-bearing note requiring ten annual payments of $10,000. Door made the first payment on December 30, 2007. The market interest rate for similar notes at date of issuance was 8%. Information on present value factors is as follows:

| Period | Present value of $1 at 8% | Present value of ordinary annuity of $1 at 8% |
|---|---|---|
| 9 | 0.50 | 6.25 |
| 10 | 0.46 | 6.71 |

In its December 31, 2007 balance sheet, what amount should Chang report as note receivable?
- a. $45,000
- b. $46,000
- c. $62,500
- d. $67,100

**Items 7 and 8** are based on the following:

On January 2, 2007, Emme Co. sold equipment with a carrying amount of $480,000 in exchange for a $600,000 noninterest-bearing note due January 2, 2010. There was no established exchange price for the equipment. The prevailing rate of interest for a note of this type at January 2, 2007, was 10%. The present value of $1 at 10% for three periods is 0.75.

**7.** In Emme's 2007 income statement, what amount should be reported as interest income?
- a. $ 9,000
- b. $45,000
- c. $50,000
- d. $60,000

**8.** In Emme's 2007 income statement, what amount should be reported as gain (loss) on sale of machinery?
- a. $(30,000) loss.
- b. $ 30,000 gain.
- c. $120,000 gain.
- d. $270,000 gain.

**9.** On December 31, 2007, Jet Co. received two $10,000 notes receivable from customers in exchange for services rendered. On both notes, interest is calculated on the outstanding balance at the interest rate of 3% compounded annually and payable at maturity. The note from Hart Corp., made under customary trade terms, is due in nine months and the note from Maxx, Inc. is due in five years. The market interest rate for similar notes on December 31, 2007, was 8%. The compound interest factors are as follows:

| | |
|---|---|
| Future value of $1 due in nine months at 3% | 1.0225 |
| Future value of $1 due in five years at 3% | 1.1593 |
| Present value of $1 due in nine months at 8% | .944 |
| Present value of $1 due in five years at 8% | .680 |

At what amounts should these two notes receivable be reported in Jet's December 31, 2007 balance sheet?

| | Hart | Maxx |
|---|---|---|
| a. | $ 9,440 | $6,800 |
| b. | $ 9,652 | $7,820 |
| c. | $10,000 | $6,800 |
| d. | $10,000 | $7,883 |

**10.** Leaf Co. purchased from Oak Co. a $20,000, 8%, five-year note that required five equal annual year-end payments of $5,009. The note was discounted to yield a 9% rate to Leaf. At the date of purchase, Leaf recorded the note at its present value of $19,485. What should be the total interest revenue earned by Leaf over the life of this note?
- a. $5,045
- b. $5,560
- c. $8,000
- d. $9,000

**Items 11 and 12 are based on the following:**

House Publishers offered a contest in which the winner would receive $1,000,000, payable over twenty years. On December 31, 2007, House announced the winner of the contest and signed a note payable to the winner for $1,000,000, payable in $50,000 installments every January 2. Also on December 31, 2007, House purchased an annuity for $418,250 to provide the $950,000 prize monies remaining after the first $50,000 installment, which was paid on January 2, 2008.

**11.** In its December 31, 2007 balance sheet, what amount should House report as note payable—contest winner, net of current portion?
- a. $368,250
- b. $418,250
- c. $900,000
- d. $950,000

**12.** In its 2007 income statement, what should House report as contest prize expense?
- a. $0
- b. $ 418,250
- c. $ 468,250
- d. $1,000,000

**13.** On December 31, 2007, Roth Co. issued a $10,000 face value note payable to Wake Co. in exchange for services rendered to Roth. The note, made at usual trade terms, is due in nine months and bears interest, payable at maturity, at the annual rate of 3%. The market interest rate is 8%. The compound interest factor of $1 due in nine months at 8% is .944. At what amount should the note payable be reported in Roth's December 31, 2007 balance sheet?
- a. $10,300
- b. $10,000
- c. $ 9,652
- d. $ 9,440

**14.** On January 1, 2007, Parke Company borrowed $360,000 from a major customer evidenced by a noninterest-

bearing note due in three years. Parke agreed to supply the customer's inventory needs for the loan period at lower than market price. At the 12% imputed interest rate for this type of loan, the present value of the note is $255,000 at January 1, 2007. What amount of interest expense should be included in Parke's 2007 income statement?
- a. $43,200
- b. $35,000
- c. $30,600
- d. $0

**15.** Pie Co. uses the installment sales method to recognize revenue. Customers pay the installment notes in twenty-four equal monthly amounts, which include 12% interest. What is an installment note's receivable balance six months after the sale?
- a. 75% of the original sales price.
- b. Less than 75% of the original sales price.
- c. The present value of the remaining monthly payments discounted at 12%.
- d. Less than the present value of the remaining monthly payments discounted at 12%.

**16.** On July 1, 2007, a company obtained a two-year 8% note receivable for services rendered. At that time the market rate of interest was 10%. The face amount of the note and the entire amount of the interest are due on June 30, 2009. Interest receivable at December 31, 2007, was
- a. 5% of the face value of the note.
- b. 4% of the face value of the note.
- c. 5% of the July 1, 2007, present value of the amount due June 30, 2009.
- d. 4% of the July 1, 2007, present value of the amount due June 30, 2009.

**17.** Which of the following is reported as interest expense?
- a. Pension cost interest.
- b. Postretirement health care benefits interest.
- c. Imputed interest on noninterest-bearing note.
- d. Interest incurred to finance construction of machinery for own use.

**18.** The discount resulting from the determination of a note payable's present value should be reported on the balance sheet as a(n)
- a. Addition to the face amount of the note.
- b. Deferred charge separate from the note.
- c. Deferred credit separate from the note.
- d. Direct reduction from the face amount of the note.

**19.** In calculating the carrying amount of a loan, the lender adds to the principal

| | Direct loan origination costs incurred by the lender | Loan origination fees charged to the borrower |
|---|---|---|
| a. | Yes | Yes |
| b. | Yes | No |
| c. | No | Yes |
| d. | No | No |

**20.** Duff, Inc. borrowed from Martin Bank under a ten-year loan in the amount of $150,000 with a stated interest rate of 6%. Payments are due monthly, and are computed to be $1,665. Martin Bank incurs $4,000 of direct loan origination costs and $2,000 of indirect loan origination costs. In addition, Martin Bank charges Duff, Inc. a four-point nonrefundable loan origination fee.

Martin Bank, the lender, has a carrying amount of

    a.  $144,000
    b.  $148,000
    c.  $150,000
    d.  $152,000

**21.**  Martin Bank grants a ten-year loan to Duff, Inc. in the amount of $150,000 with a stated interest rate of 6%.  Payments are due monthly, and are computed to be $1,665.  Martin Bank incurs $4,000 of direct loan origination costs and $2,000 of indirect loan origination costs.  In addition, Martin Bank charges Duff, Inc. a four-point nonrefundable loan origination fee.

    Duff, the borrower, has a carrying amount of
    a.  $144,000
    b.  $148,000
    c.  $150,000
    d.  $152,000

**22.**  On December 1, 2007, Money Co. gave Home Co. a $200,000, 11% loan.  Money paid proceeds of $194,000 after the deduction of a $6,000 nonrefundable loan origination fee.  Principal and interest are due in sixty monthly installments of $4,310, beginning January 1, 2008.  The repayments yield an effective interest rate of 11% at a present value of $200,000 and 12.4% at a present value of $194,000.  What amount of income from this loan should Money report in its 2007 income statement?
    a.  $0
    b.  $1,833
    c.  $2,005
    d.  $7,833

**SIMULATION PROBLEMS**

**Simulation Problem 1**                              (60 to 75 minutes)

| Situation | | | | | | |
|---|---|---|---|---|---|---|
| | **Present Value Concepts** | **Long-Term Receivables Disclosure** | **Balance Sheet Disclosure** | **Income Statement Disclosure** | **Research** | **Communication** |

Kern, Inc. had the following long-term receivable account balances at December 31, 2006:

| | |
|---|---|
| Note receivable from the sale of an idle building | $750,000 |
| Note receivable from an officer | 200,000 |

Transactions during 2007 and other information relating to Kern's long-term receivables follow:

- The $750,000 note receivable is dated May 1, 2006, bears interest at 9%, and represents the balance of the consideration Kern received from the sale of its idle building to Able Co.  Principal payments of $250,000 plus interest are due annually beginning May 1, 2007.  Able made its first principal and interest payment on May 1, 2007.  Collection of the remaining note installments is reasonably assured.
- The $200,000 note receivable is dated December 31, 2004, bears interest at 8%, and is due on December 31, 2009.  The note is due from Frank Black, president of Kern, Inc., and is collateralized by 5,000 shares of Kern's common stock.  Interest is payable annually on December 31, and all interest payments were made through December 31, 2007.  The quoted market price of Kern's common stock was $45 per share on December 31, 2007.
- On April 1, 2006, Kern sold a patent to Frey Corp. in exchange for a $100,000 noninterest-bearing note due on April 1, 2009.  There was no established exchange price for the patent, and the note had no ready market.  The prevailing interest rate for this type of note was 10% at April 1, 2007.  The present value of $1 for two periods at 10% is 0.826.  The patent had a carrying amount of $40,000 at January 1, 2007, and the amortization for the year ended December 31, 2007, would have been $8,000.  Kern is reasonably assured of collecting the note receivable from Frey.
- On July 1, 2007, Kern sold a parcel of land to Barr Co. for $400,000 under an installment sale contract.  Barr made a $120,000 cash down payment on July 1, 2007, and signed a four-year 10% note for the $280,000 balance.  The equal annual payments of principal and interest on the note will be $88,332, payable on July 1 of each year from 2008 through 2011.  The fair value of the land at the date of sale was $400,000.  The cost of the land to Kern was $300,000.  Collection of the remaining note installments is reasonably assured.

| | **Present Value Concepts** | | | | | |
|---|---|---|---|---|---|---|
| **Situation** | | **Long-Term Receivables Disclosure** | **Balance Sheet Disclosure** | **Income Statement Disclosure** | **Research** | **Communication** |

Assume that you are the accountant for Kern Corporation and are working on various debt accounting issues.  Use the following responses to define the terms in the table that follows.

*Responses to be selected*

- A.   Effective interest rate × Net receivable or payable balance at the beginning of the period
- B.   Periodic interest is computed on principal balance and interest earned to date
- C.   Represents the debtor's incremental borrowing rate
- D.   Series of payments/receipts which occur at beginning of the period
- E.   The difference between the present value of the note and the cash exchanged when the market rate of interest < rate on note
- F.   Periodic interest is computed based on the principal balance only
- G.   Maturity value of note and interest payments discounted to the present value
- H.   This will result when face rate of the note < yield rate
- I.   The amount which will be available in the future as a result of consecutive payments/receipts at the end of each period—compounded at a specified interest rate
- J.   Series of payments/receipts which are made at the end of the period
- K.   No premium or discount exists

| | (A) | (B) | (C) | (D) | (E) | (F) | (G) | (H) | (I) | (J) | (K) |
|---|---|---|---|---|---|---|---|---|---|---|---|
| 1. Annuity due | O | O | O | O | O | O | O | O | O | O | O |
| 2. Imputed interest rate | O | O | O | O | O | O | O | O | O | O | O |
| 3. Market value of note | O | O | O | O | O | O | O | O | O | O | O |
| 4. Note issued at a discount | O | O | O | O | O | O | O | O | O | O | O |
| 5. Premium on a note | O | O | O | O | O | O | O | O | O | O | O |
| 6. Simple interest method | O | O | O | O | O | O | O | O | O | O | O |
| 7. Interest revenue/expense | O | O | O | O | O | O | O | O | O | O | O |
| 8. Future value of annuity | O | O | O | O | O | O | O | O | O | O | O |
| 9. Face of note equals present value of the note | O | O | O | O | O | O | O | O | O | O | O |

| Situation | Present Value Concepts | Long-Term Receivables Disclosure | Balance Sheet Disclosure | Income Statement Disclosure | Research | Communication |
|---|---|---|---|---|---|---|

Complete the following section of the long-term receivables on the balance sheet.

| Kern, Inc. LONG-TERM RECEIVABLES SECTION OF BALANCE SHEET December 31, 2007 | | |
|---|---|---|
| 9% note receivable from sale of idle building, due in annual installments of $250,000 to May 1, 2009, less current installment | | |
| 8% note receivable from officer, due December 31, 2009, collateralized by 5,000 shares of Kern, Inc. common stock with a fair value of $225,000 | | |
| Noninterest-bearing note from sale of patent, net of 10% imputed interest due April 1, 2009 | | |
| Installment contract receivable, due in annual installments of $88,332 to July 1, 2011, less current installment | | |
| | | |
| Total long-term receivables | | |

| Situation | Present Value Concepts | Long-Term Receivables Disclosure | Balance Sheet Disclosure | Income Statement Disclosure | Research | Communication |
|---|---|---|---|---|---|---|

Complete the following amounts for balance sheet disclosures.

| Kern, Inc. SELECTED BALANCE SHEET ACCOUNTS December 31, 2007 | | |
|---|---|---|
| Current portion of long-term receivables: | | |
| Note receivable from sale of idle building | | |
| Installment contract receivable | | |
| Total | | |
| Accrued interest receivable: | | |
| Note receivable from sale of idle building | | |
| Installment contract receivable | | |
| Total | | |

| Situation | Present Value Concepts | Long-Term Receivables Disclosure | Balance Sheet Disclosure | Income Statement Disclosure | Research | Communication |
|---|---|---|---|---|---|---|

Complete the following schedule showing interest revenue from long-term receivables and gains recognized on the sale of assets to be reported in Kern's 2007 income statement.

| Kern, Inc. INTEREST REVENUE FROM LONG-TERM RECEIVABLES AND GAINS RECOGNIZED ON SALE OF ASSETS For the Year Ended December 31, 2007 | | |
|---|---|---|
| Interest revenue: | | |
| Note receivable from sale of idle building | | |
| Note receivable from sale of patent | | |
| Note receivable from officer | | |
| Installment contract receivable from sale of land | | |
| Total interest revenue | | |
| Gains recognized on sale of assets: | | |
| Patent | | |
| Land | | |
| Total gains recognized | | |

| Situation | Present Value Concepts | Long-Term Receivables Disclosure | Balance Sheet Disclosure | Income Statement Disclosure | Research | Communication |
|---|---|---|---|---|---|---|

For each of the following, find the appropriate paragraph in FARS to answer each question.  Cut and paste the appropriate guidance from professional standards.

1. On July 1, 2007, Kern borrows $100,000 on a noninterest-bearing three-year note and received $85,000 in proceeds.  How should Kern value the note in its July 1, 2007 financial statements?

2. Where is a discount or premium disclosed on the financial statements?

3. How is a discount or premium on a note amortized?

4. What information must a company disclose regarding long-term debt on its financial statements?

5. How does a lender account for loan origination fees?

| Situation | Present Value Concepts | Long-Term Receivables Disclosure | Balance Sheet Disclosure | Income Statement Disclosure | Research | Communication |
|---|---|---|---|---|---|---|

Certain of Kern's notes receivable have a zero interest rate.  Write a memorandum to the audit staff explaining why it is necessary to record zero interest rate notes receivable at their present value.

To:     Audit Staff
From:   CPA Candidate
Re:     Notes receivable

---

**Simulation Problem 2**                              (50 to 60 minutes)

| Situation | Sales Price | Carrying Value | Amortization Table | Gain or Loss | Research | Communication |
|---|---|---|---|---|---|---|

Assume that you are the CPA for Dawson Corporation.  On January 1, 2007, Catrina Corporation sold to Dawson Corporation equipment that originally cost $320,000, with accumulated depreciation of $75,000 for a noninterest-bearing note with a face value of $300,000 due January 1, 2011.  The fair market value of the equipment is readily determinable and the market rate for a note of this type is 6%.  Dawson depreciates equipment over a five-year life with no residual value.

| Situation | Sales Price | Carrying Value | Amortization Table | Gain or Loss | Research | Communication |
|---|---|---|---|---|---|---|

The sales price of the equipment would be calculated as (select the answer from the following list)

   Book value on Catrina's books.
   Cost on Catrina's records.
   Maturity value of the note signed by Dawson.
   Present value of the note at 6% for four periods.
   Future value of the book value at 6% for four periods.

| Situation | Sales Price | Carrying Value | Amortization Table | Gain or Loss | Research | Communication |
|---|---|---|---|---|---|---|

Calculate the carrying value of the note on 1/1/07 on Catrina's books.

*Time value of money factors*

| | |
|---|---|
| FV of $1 for 3 periods | 1.191 |
| FV of $1 for 4 periods | 1.262 |
| FVA of $1 for 3 periods | 3.184 |
| FVA of $1 for 4 periods | 4.375 |
| PV of $1 for 3 periods | .8396 |
| PV of $1 for 4 periods | .7921 |
| PVA of $1 for 3 periods | 2.673 |
| PVA of $1 for 4 periods | 3.465 |
| PVA of $1 due for 3 periods | 2.833 |
| PVA of $1 due for 4 periods | 3.673 |

| Situation | Sales Price | Carrying Value | Amortization Table | Gain or Loss | Research | Communication |
|---|---|---|---|---|---|---|

Prepare an amortization table and calculate the interest income and carrying value of the note for Catrina for the years 2007 and 2008.  Indicate whether the note has a premium or discount by completing the correct columns in the schedule.  (For a more realistic exam experience, complete the problem using a spreadsheet program, such as Excel.)

| Year | Interest income | Premium on note | Discount on note | Carrying value |
|---|---|---|---|---|
| | | | | |
| | | | | |
| | | | | |
| | | | | |
| | | | | |
| | | | | |

| Situation | Sales Price | Carrying Value | Amortization Table | Gain or Loss | Research | Communication |
|---|---|---|---|---|---|---|

Prepare a schedule calculating the gain or loss on Catrina's books for the sale of the fixed asset on 1/1/07.  (For a more realistic exam experience, complete the problem using a spreadsheet program, such as Excel.)

| | | | |
|---|---|---|---|
| Original cost | $320,000 | Proceeds of note | ??? |
| Maturity value note | $300,000 | Premium on note | ??? |
| Accumulated depreciation | $ 75,000 | Discount on note | ??? |
| Interest rate | 6% | | |

| Situation | Sales Price | Carrying Value | Amortization Table | Gain or Loss | Research | Communication |
|---|---|---|---|---|---|---|

Research the professional standards and excerpt the appropriate sections that explain how the equipment should be valued on Dawson's financial statements at date of acquisition.

| Situation | Sales Price | Carrying Value | Amortization Table | Gain or Loss | Research | Communication |
|---|---|---|---|---|---|---|

Write a memo to your client with your recommendations and your rationale for the method of valuing the equipment on the date of acquisition, and any accounting entries that will be necessary for Dawson after the acquisition of the equipment.

To:     CFO, Dawson Corporation
From:   CPA Candidate
Re:     Acquisition of equipment on January 1, 2007

| |
|---|
| |

| 1. c __ __ | 6. c __ __ | 11. b __ __ | 16. b __ __ | 21. a __ __ |
|---|---|---|---|---|
| 2. b __ __ | 7. b __ __ | 12. c __ __ | 17. c __ __ | 22. c __ __ |
| 3. b __ __ | 8. a __ __ | 13. b __ __ | 18. d __ __ | |
| 4. b __ __ | 9. d __ __ | 14. c __ __ | 19. b __ __ | 1st: __/22 = __% |
| 5. a __ __ | 10. b __ __ | 15. c __ __ | 20. b __ __ | 2nd: __/22 = __% |

MULTIPLE-CHOICE ANSWER EXPLANATIONS

## A.  Fundamentals

**1.    (c)**   The desired fund balance on September 1, 2011, ($1,000,000) is a **future amount**. The series of four equal annual deposits is an **annuity in advance,** as illustrated in the diagram below.

D          D          D          D        $1,000,000

9/1/07     9/1/08     9/1/09     9/1/10     9/1/11

This is an annuity in advance, rather than an ordinary annuity, because the last deposit (9/1/10) is made one year prior to the date the future amount is needed. Therefore, these are beginning-of-year payments. The deposit amount is computed by dividing the future amount by the factor for the future amount of an annuity in advance.

$$\$1,000,000 \div 5.11 = \$195,700$$

**2.    (b)**   The requirement is to determine the acquisition cost of a franchise. The cost of this franchise is the down payment of $20,000 plus the present value of the four equal annual payments of $10,000. The annual payments represent an annuity, so the $10,000 annual payment is multiplied by the present value factor of 2.91. Therefore, the franchise cost is $49,100 ($20,000 + $29,100). The journal entry is

| | | |
|---|---|---|
| Franchise | 49,100 | |
| Discount on notes payable | 10,900 | |
|     Notes payable | | 40,000 |
|     Cash | | 20,000 |

**3.    (b)**   The requirement is to determine what time value of money concept would be used to determine the cost of a machine when a payment (principal plus interest) is to be made in two years. Answer (b) is correct because the cost of the machine is to be recorded immediately; therefore, the cost of the present value of a lump-sum payment would be used. Answer (c) is incorrect because a future amount would be used in computing the payment and not the cost of the machine. Also, a lump-sum payment is involved and not an annuity. Answer (d) is incorrect because a future amount would be used in computing the payment and not the cost. Answer (a) is incorrect because a lump-sum payment is involved, not an annuity.

**4.    (b)**   The requirement is the situation which illustrates an annuity due. An annuity due (annuity in advance) is a series of payments where the first payment is made at the beginning of the first period, in contrast to an ordinary annuity (annuity in arrears), in which the first payment is made at the end of the first period. Answer (b) is correct because the initial lease payment is due immediately (at the beginning of the first period). Answers (a), (c), and (d) all illustrate situations in which the first lease or interest payment occurs at the end of the first period. Note that in answers (c) and (d), the stated rate and yield rate of the bonds differ; while this would affect the present value of the bonds, it has

no effect on the classification as an annuity due or an ordinary annuity.

**5.    (a)**   In recording the transaction recognition should be given to both the imputed interest rate and the deferred charge related to the merchandise discount. Answer (b) is incorrect because the deferred charge should also be recognized. Answer (c) is incorrect because a discount on the noninterest-bearing note should also be recognized. Answer (d) is incorrect because both the discount and the deferred charge should be recognized.

### A.9.  Notes Receivable and Payable

**6.    (c)**   If the FMV of the machine and the FMV of the note are not known, the transaction should be recorded at the PV of the note by imputing interest at the prevailing rate (8%) for similar notes. This series of ten payments is an **annuity in advance,** because the first payment is due immediately on 12/30/07. However, the problem requires the amount to be reported for the note receivable on **12/31/07,** after the first payment is received. The remaining nine payments are an ordinary annuity, as illustrated in the diagram below.

PV = ?

                 R1          R2                    R8          R9

12/30/07    12/30/08    12/30/09          12/30/15    12/30/16

In a PV computation, one must look at the first rent to see if it is an ordinary annuity or annuity in advance. If the first rent occurs one period after the computation date, it is an ordinary annuity. Therefore, the PV to be reported for the note receivable at 12/31/07 is $62,500 (10,000 × 6.25).

**7.    (b)**   The $600,000 noninterest-bearing note should be recorded at its present value of $450,000 ($600,000 × .75). The journal entry is

| | | |
|---|---|---|
| Loss on sale of equip. | 30,000 | |
| Note receivable | 600,000 | |
|    Discount on NR | | 150,000 } 450,000 |
|    Equipment (net) | | 480,000 |

At 12/31/07, interest income would be recognized using the effective interest method. Using this method, interest is computing by multiplying the book value of the note ($600,000 – $150,000 = $450,000) by the effective interest rate ($450,000 × 10% = $45,000).

**8.    (a)**   The $600,000 noninterest-bearing note should be recorded at its present value of $450,000 ($600,000 × .75). The journal entry is

| | | |
|---|---|---|
| Loss on sale of equip. | 30,000 | |
| Note receivable | 600,000 | |
|    Discount on NR | | 150,000 } 450,000 |
|    Equipment (net) | | 480,000 |

The loss is recognized because the fair value of the note received ($450,000) is $30,000 less than the carrying amount of the equipment sold ($480,000).

**9. (d)** APB 21 states that receivables bearing an unreasonably low stated interest rate should be recorded at their present value. However, APB 21 does **not** apply to receivables arising through the normal course of business that mature in less than one year. Therefore, the Hart receivable would be recorded at face value ($10,000), since it matures in nine months. The Maxx receivable would be recorded at its present value, since it matures in five years. The Maxx receivable will result in a lump-sum collection of $11,593 ($10,000 × 1.1593), so its present value is $7,883 ($11,593 × .680).

**10. (b)** The total interest revenue earned over the life of the note equals the excess of the cash received over the cash paid to acquire the note. The cash received over the five years is $25,045 (5 receipts of $5,009 each). The cash paid to acquire the $20,000 note was $19,485. Therefore, the total interest revenue is $5,560 ($25,045 − $19,485).

**11. (b)** The $1,000,000 note is payable $50,000 in 2007 (current portion) and $950,000 after 2007 (long-term portion). Per APB 21, this noninterest-bearing long-term note should be recorded at its present value, which can be measured as the amount required to purchase an annuity sufficient to provide the funds to satisfy the obligation. Therefore, the note payable, net of current portion, should be reported at $418,250.

**12. (c)** The contest prize expense must be recognized at the present value of the obligation incurred as a result of the contest. The obligation consists of $50,000 payable in two days, and $950,000 payable over the next nineteen years. The $950,000 long-term portion has a present value of $418,250, as evidenced by the cost of an annuity contract sufficient to satisfy it. Therefore, the total PV of the obligation is $468,250 ($50,000 + $418,250). The journal entry to record the expense is

| | | |
|---|---|---|
| Contest prize expense | $468,250 | |
| Discount on NP | $531,750 | |
| Notes payable | | $1,000,000 |

**13. (b)** APB 21 states that all receivables and payables are subject to present value measurement techniques and interest imputation, if necessary, with certain exceptions. One exception is normal course of business receivables and payables maturing in less than one year. Therefore this note payable, due in nine months at usual trade terms, would be reported at face value ($10,000) rather than at present value ($10,225 × .944 = $9,652).

**14. (c)** The requirement is to determine the amount of interest expense to be recognized in 2007 from a noninterest-bearing note. Parke Company is able to borrow on a noninterest basis because they agree to sell their product at less than the market price. In this type of situation, the note payable is recorded at present value, and the difference between the present value and the cash received is recorded as **unearned sales revenue** (to be recognized when the product is sold at less than market value). The initial journal entry is

| | | |
|---|---|---|
| Cash | 360,000 | |
| Discount on NP | 105,000 | |
| Note payable | | 360,000 } 255,000 |
| Unearned sales revenue | | 105,000 |

When interest expense is recognized at the end of 2007, the effective interest method must be used. Using this method, interest expense is computed by multiplying the book value of the liability ($360,000 − $105,000 = $255,000) by the effective interest rate (12%), resulting in interest expense of $30,600.

**15. (c)** The entry made to record an installment sale (ignoring the cost of sale and inventory) is as follows:

| | |
|---|---|
| Note receivable | (Sale price) |
| Installment sales | (PV of note @ 12%) |
| Discount on notes receivable | (Plug) |

Although the customer would have paid 25% (six out of twenty-four months) of the total payments due under the terms of the installment sale, the **net** carrying value of the note (equal to the principal balance of the note less the unamortized discount) is equal to the present value of the remaining monthly payments discounted at 12%. Under the effective interest method, the carrying value of the note will at all times be equal to the present value of the remaining installment payments, regardless of whether the note is recorded gross or net in Pie Co.'s accounts.

**16. (b)** When a note is issued with a stated rate (8% in this case) below the market rate (10% in this case), the note will be issued at a discount. The entry for the recipient of the note on July 1 would be as follows:

| | | |
|---|---|---|
| Notes receivable | xxx | |
| Disc. on notes rec. | | xxx |
| Service revenue | | xxx |

On December 31, the company must accrue interest on the note. The following entry would be made:

| | |
|---|---|
| Interest receivable | (6 months at stated rate) |
| Disc. on notes rec. | (6 months amortization) |
| Interest revenue | (6 months interest at market rate) |

Note that interest receivable is debited for an amount based upon the **stated** (face) rate of the note. This is because the stated rate will determine the amount of cash interest that will be received upon maturity of the note. Since the bond was held for six months (7/1/07 to 12/31/07) as of 12/31/07, the amount of the receivable would be determined as follows:

$$\frac{\text{Interest}}{\text{receivable}} = \frac{\text{Face value}}{\text{of note}} \times \frac{\text{Stated}}{\text{rate}} \times \frac{\text{Period}}{\text{held}}$$
$$= \text{Face value} \times 8\% \times (6/12 \text{ months})$$
$$= 4\% \times \text{Face value}$$

**17. (c)** When a noninterest-bearing note is issued, APB 21 states that interest must be imputed on the note and amortized to interest expense over the life of the note using the effective interest rate. Answers (a) and (b) are incorrect because interest on pension cost and postretirement health-care benefits is included as a component of future benefit obligation. Answer (d) is incorrect because interest incurred to finance construction of machinery for a company's own use may be capitalized and amortized.

**18. (d)** **Discount on notes payable** is a liability valuation account. It should be reported as a direct reduction from the face amount of the note (contra account). A **pre-**

**mium on notes payable** would be reported as an addition to the face amount of the note. A discount is not recorded as a separate asset because it does not provide any future economic benefit. It is not a deferred credit separate from the note because it is a debit, not a credit, and because it is inseparable from the note. Thus, a discount on notes payable should be reported on the balance sheet as a direct reduction from the face amount of the note.

### A.10.  Lending Activities

**19.    (b)**   In calculating the carrying amount of a loan, loan origination costs are added to the principal by the lender. Any fee charged to the borrower is **deducted** from the principal by both parties (the lender and the borrower) in calculating the carrying amount.

**20.    (b)**   The lender's carrying amount of the loan is calculated by adding the direct loan origination costs to the principal and deducting the loan origination fee charged to the borrower. Indirect loan origination costs are charged to expense as incurred, and are not considered when calculating the carrying amount of the loan. Therefore, Martin Bank has a carrying amount of $148,000 [$150,000 principal plus $4,000 direct loan origination costs minus $6,000 ($150,000 × 0.04) nonrefundable loan origination fee]. The $2,000 indirect loan origination costs are expensed in the period incurred.

**21.    (a)**   Duff, Inc., the borrower, receives 4% less than the face amount of $150,000. Duff's carrying amount is, therefore, $150,000 – $6,000, or $144,000. Loan origination fees charged to the borrower are deducted from the principal in calculating the carrying amount.

*NOTE: Loan origination fees are frequently assessed in the form of points, where a point is 1% of the face amount of the loan.*

**22.    (c)**   Money Co. made a cash outflow of $194,000 for the $200,000 loan Money gave to Home Co. The book value of the loan is $194,000 on Money's books. Money will receive an effective interest rate of 12.4% on its cash outflow. Income from the loan would be calculated by multiplying the book value, times the effective interest rate, and the number of months of the year (in this case just one— December). $194,000 × .124 × 1/12 = $2,004.67. The stated rate is 11% and is not used in the calculation. Money Co. will receive equal monthly installments over the sixty-month life of the loan. Money Co. will effectively earn 12.4% on its initial cash outflow of $194,000, because Home Co. will repay principal for the total loan amount of $200,000.

**SOLUTIONS TO SIMULATION PROBLEMS**

**Simulation Problem 1**

| Situation | Present Value Concepts | Long-Term Receivables Disclosure | Balance Sheet Disclosure | Income Statement Disclosure | Research | Communication |
|---|---|---|---|---|---|---|

| | (A) | (B) | (C) | (D) | (E) | (F) | (G) | (H) | (I) | (J) | (K) |
|---|---|---|---|---|---|---|---|---|---|---|---|
| 1. Annuity due | ○ | ○ | ○ | ● | ○ | ○ | ○ | ○ | ○ | ○ | ○ |
| 2. Imputed interest rate | ○ | ○ | ● | ○ | ○ | ○ | ○ | ○ | ○ | ○ | ○ |
| 3. Market value of note | ○ | ○ | ○ | ○ | ○ | ○ | ● | ○ | ○ | ○ | ○ |
| 4. Note issued at a discount | ○ | ○ | ○ | ○ | ○ | ○ | ○ | ● | ○ | ○ | ○ |
| 5. Premium on a note | ○ | ○ | ○ | ○ | ● | ○ | ○ | ○ | ○ | ○ | ○ |
| 6. Simple interest method | ○ | ○ | ○ | ○ | ○ | ● | ○ | ○ | ○ | ○ | ○ |
| 7. Interest revenue/expense | ● | ○ | ○ | ○ | ○ | ○ | ○ | ○ | ○ | ○ | ○ |
| 8. Future value of annuity | ○ | ○ | ○ | ○ | ○ | ○ | ○ | ○ | ● | ○ | ○ |
| 9. Face of note equals present value of the note | ○ | ○ | ○ | ○ | ○ | ○ | ○ | ○ | ○ | ○ | ● |

**Explanation of solutions**

**1.    (D)** An annuity due (annuity in advance) represents a series of payments made or received at the beginning of the period.

**2.    (C)** An imputed interest rate is used when the rate on a note is not fair and the market value of the items being exchanged is not readily determinable.  An imputed interest rate represents the rate at which the debtor could obtain financing from a different source; this is known as the debtor's incremental borrowing rate.

**3.    (G)** The market value of a note is equal to the maturity value and the interest payments discounted to the present value. The present value represents the amount you would pay now for an amount to be received in the future.  Thus, answer G is the correct response, as the present value equals the current market value of the principal and interest amounts.

**4.    (H)** When a note is exchanged for cash and no other rights or privileges exist, the present value of the note will equal the cash received if the stated rate on the note equals the market yield rate.  However, if the stated rate is less than the market rate, then the note will be issued at a discount to compensate.

**5.    (E)** A premium on a note occurs when the interest rate on a note is greater than the market yield rate.  The market bids up the price of the bond above par until the effective interest rate on the note equals the market yield rate.

**6.    (F)** The simple interest method computes interest based upon the amount of principal only.  Interest is computed as Principal × Interest × Time.  The compound interest method computes interest on principal and any interest earned and not withdrawn.

**7.    (A)** The interest revenue or expense on a note is computed by taking the effective interest rate times the net receivable or payable balance.

**8.    (I)** An annuity is a periodic payment or receipt made in consecutive intervals over time compounded at a stated interest rate.  The future value of an annuity represents the total of the periodic payments and accumulated interest at some point in the future.

**9.    (K)** When a note is exchanged for cash and no other rights or privileges exist, the present value of the note will be equal to the cash exchanged if the stated rate of interest equals the market yield rate.  No premium or discount exists if the stated rate on the note equals the market yield rate.

| Situation | Present Value Concepts | Long-Term Receivables Disclosure | Balance Sheet Disclosure | Income Statement Disclosure | Research | Communication |
|---|---|---|---|---|---|---|

**Kern, Inc.**
**LONG-TERM RECEIVABLES SECTION**
**OF BALANCE SHEET**
*December 31, 2007*

| | | |
|---|---|---|
| 9% note receivable from sale of idle building, due in annual installments of $250,000 to May 1, 2009, less current installment | $250,000 | [1] |
| 8% note receivable from officer, due December 31, 2009, collateralized by 5,000 shares of Kern, Inc. common stock with a fair value of $225,000 | 200,000 | |
| Noninterest-bearing note from sale of patent, net of 10% imputed interest, due April 1, 2009 | 88,795 | [2] |
| Installment contract receivable, due in annual installments of $88,332 to July 1, 2011, less current installment | 219,668 | [3] |
| Total long-term receivables | $758,463 | |

*Explanation of Amounts*
See explanations under Income Statement Disclosure

| Situation | Present Value Concepts | Long-Term Receivables Disclosure | Balance Sheet Disclosure | Income Statement Disclosure | Research | Communication |
|---|---|---|---|---|---|---|

**Kern, Inc.**
**SELECTED BALANCE SHEET ACCOUNTS**
*December 31, 2007*

| | | |
|---|---|---|
| Current portion of long-term receivables: | | |
| Note receivable from sale of idle building | $250,000 | [1] |
| Installment contract receivable | 60,332 | [3] |
| Total | $310,332 | |
| Accrued interest receivable: | | |
| Note receivable from sale of idle building | $30,000 | [4] |
| Installment contract receivable | 14,000 | [5] |
| Total | $44,000 | |

*Explanation of Amounts*
See explanations under Income Statement Disclosure

| Situation | Present Value Concepts | Long-Term Receivables Disclosure | Balance Sheet Disclosure | Income Statement Disclosure | Research | Communication |
|---|---|---|---|---|---|---|

**Kern, Inc.**
**INTEREST REVENUE FROM LONG-TERM RECEIVABLES**
**AND GAINS RECOGNIZED ON SALE OF ASSETS**
*For the Year Ended December 31, 2007*

| | | |
|---|---|---|
| Interest revenue: | | |
| Note receivable from sale of idle building | $52,500 | [6] |
| Note receivable from sale of patent | 6,195 | [2] |
| Note receivable from officer | 16,000 | [7] |
| Installment contract receivable from sale of land | 14,000 | [5] |
| Total interest revenue | $88,695 | |
| Gains recognized on sale of assets: | | |
| Patent | $ 44,600 | [8] |
| Land | 100,000 | [9] |
| Total gains recognized | $144,600 | |

*Explanation of Amounts*

[1]  Long-term portion of 9% note receivable at 12/31/07
| | |
|---|---:|
| Face amount, 5/1/06 | $750,000 |
| Less installment received 5/1/07 | 250,000 |
| Balance, 12/31/07 | 500,000 |
| Less installment due 5/1/08 | 250,000 |
| Long-term portion, 12/31/07 | $250,000 |

[2]  Noninterest-bearing note, net of imputed interest at 12/31/07
| | |
|---|---:|
| Face amount, 4/1/07 | $100,000 |
| Less imputed interest [$100,000 – $82,600 ($100,000 × 0.826)] | 17,400 |
| Balance, 4/1/07 | 82,600 |
| Add interest earned to 12/31/07 [$82,600 × 10% × 9/12] | 6,195 |
| Balance, 12/31/07 | $ 88,795 |

[3]  Long-term portion of installment contract receivable at 12/31/07
| | |
|---|---:|
| Contract selling price, 7/1/07 | $400,000 |
| Less cash down payment | 120,000 |
| Balance, 12/31/07 | 280,000 |
| Less installment due 7/1/08 [$88,332 – $28,000 ($280,000 × 10%)] | 60,332 |
| Long-term portion, 12/31/07 | $219,668 |

[4]  Accrued interest—note receivable, sale of idle building at 12/31/07
| | |
|---|---:|
| Interest accrued from 5/1 to 12/31/07 [$500,000 × 9% × 8/12] | $ 30,000 |

[5]  Accrued interest—installment contract at 12/31/07
| | |
|---|---:|
| Interest accrued from 7/1 to 12/31/07 [$280,000 × 10% × 1/2] | $ 14,000 |

[6]  Interest revenue—note receivable, sale of idle building, for 2007
| | |
|---|---:|
| Interest earned from 1/1/ to 5/1/07 [$750,000 × 9% × 4/12] | $ 22,500 |
| Interest earned from 5/1 to 12/31/07 [$500,000 × 9% × 8/12] | 30,000 |
| Interest revenue | $ 52,500 |

[7]  Interest revenue—note receivable, officer, for 2007
| | |
|---|---:|
| Interest earned 1/1 to 12/31/07 [$200,000 × 8%] | $ 16,000 |

[8]  Gain recognized on sale of patent
| | | |
|---|---:|---:|
| Stated selling price | | $100,000 |
| Less imputed interest | | 17,400  [2] |
| Actual selling price | | 82,600 |
| Less cost of patent (net) | | |
| Carrying value 1/1/07 | $40,000 | 38,000 |
| Less amortization 1/1 to 4/1/07 [$8,000 × 1/4] | 2,000 | 2,000 |
| Gain recognized | | $ 44,600 |

[9]  Gain recognized on sale of land
| | |
|---|---:|
| Selling price | $400,000 |
| Less cost | 300,000 |
| Gain recognized | $100,000 |

| | Present Value Concepts | Long-Term Receivables Disclosure | Balance Sheet Disclosure | Income Statement Disclosure | Research | |
|---|---|---|---|---|---|---|
| **Situation** | | | | | | **Communication** |

**1.** On July 1, 2007, Kern borrows $100,000 on a noninterest-bearing three-year note and received $85,000 in proceeds.  How should Kern value the note in its July 1, 2007 financial statements?

**APB21, Para 11 or Current Text I69.104**

11.  Note exchanged for cash.  When a note is received solely for cash and no other right or privilege is exchanged, it is presumed to have a present value at issuance measured by the cash proceeds exchanged.  If cash and some other rights or privileges are exchanged for a note, the value of the rights or privileges should be given accounting recognition as described in paragraph 7.

**2.** Where is a discount or premium disclosed on the financial statements?

**APB21, Para 16 or Current Text I69.109**

16.  Statement presentation of discount and premium.  The discount or premium resulting from the determination of present value in cash or noncash transactions is not an asset or liability separable from the note which gives rise to it.  Therefore, the discount or premium should be reported in the balance sheet as a direct deduction from or addition to the face amount of the note.  It should not be classified as a deferred charge or deferred credit.  The description of the note should include the effective interest rate; the face amount should also be disclosed in the financial statements or in the notes to the statements.  Amortization of discount or premium should be reported as interest in the statement of income.  Issue costs should be reported in the balance sheet as deferred charges.

**3.** How is a discount or premium on a note amortized?

**APB21, Para 15 or Current Text I69.108**

15. Amortization of discount and premium. With respect to a note which by the provisions of this Opinion requires the imputation of interest, the difference between the present value and the face amount should be treated as discount or premium and amortized as interest expense or income over the life of the note in such a way as to result in a constant rate of interest when applied to the amount outstanding at the beginning of any given period. This is the "interest" method described in and supported by paragraphs 16 and 17 of APB Opinion No. 12, Omnibus Opinion—1967. However, other methods of amortization may be used if the results obtained are not materially different from those which would result from the "interest" method.

**4.** What information must a company disclose regarding long-term debt on its financial statements?

**FAS47, Para 10 or Current Text C32.105**

10. The following information shall be disclosed for each of the five years following the date of the latest balance sheet presented:

    a.  The aggregate amount of payments for unconditional purchase obligations that meet the criteria of paragraph 6 and that have been recognized on the purchaser's balance sheet.

    b.  The combined aggregate amount of maturities and sinking fund requirements for all long-term borrowings.

**5.** How does a lender account for loan origination fees?

**FAS91, Para 5 or Current Text L20.104**

5. Loan origination fees shall be deferred and recognized over the life of the loan as an adjustment of yield (interest income). Likewise, direct loan origination costs defined in paragraph 6 shall be deferred and recognized as a reduction in the yield of the loan except as set forth in paragraph 14 (for a troubled debt restructuring). Loan origination fees and related direct loan origination costs for a given loan shall be offset and only the net amount shall be deferred and amortized. The practice of recognizing a portion of loan origination fees as revenue in a period to offset all or part of the costs of origination shall no longer be acceptable.

| Situation | Present Value Concepts | Long-Term Receivables Disclosure | Balance Sheet Disclosure | Income Statement Disclosure | Research | Communication |
|---|---|---|---|---|---|---|

To:    Audit Staff
From:  CPA Candidate
Re:    Notes receivable

    In performing the audit of Kern, Inc., a staff member noted that certain of Kern's notes receivable bear no interest. Such notes should be recorded at their discounted present value at the time they are acquired. The discount rate used should be the market rate for notes receivable with a similar level of risk. If we do not discount the notes receivable, the notes will be overvalued.

---

**Simulation Problem 2**

| Situation | Sales Price | Carrying Value | Amortization Table | Gain or Loss | Research | Communication |
|---|---|---|---|---|---|---|

PV of $300,000 at 6% for four periods.

    When a note is exchanged for property, goods, and services, the note, the sales price, and the cost of the property should be recorded at the fair value of the property goods, or services at an amount that approximates the market value of the note, whichever is more clearly determinable. Since the value of the property is known, it is assumed that 6% is the appropriate market rate of interest that will equal the value of the property.

| Situation | Sales Price | Carrying Value | Amortization Table | Gain or Loss | Research | Communication |
|-----------|-------------|----------------|--------------------|--------------|----------|----------------|

PV ($300,000) at 6% for four periods = .792 × $300,000 = $237,630

| Situation | Sales Price | Carrying Value | Amortization Table | Gain or Loss | Research | Communication |
|-----------|-------------|----------------|--------------------|--------------|----------|----------------|

Amortization Table (Off in Year 5 due to rounding).

| Year | Interest income | Premium on note | Discount on note | Carrying value |
|------|-----------------|-----------------|------------------|----------------|
| 1/1/2007 | | | $62,370 | $237,630 |
| 12/31/2007 | $14,258 | | 48,112 | 251,888 |
| 12/31/2008 | 15,113 | | 32,999 | 267,001 |
| 12/31/2009 | 16,020 | | 16,979 | 283,021 |
| | | | rounding | |
| 12/31/2010 | 16,981 | | (2) | 300,002 |

| Situation | Sales Price | Carrying Value | Amortization Table | Gain or Loss | Research | Communication |
|-----------|-------------|----------------|--------------------|--------------|----------|----------------|

Catrina—Sale of Equipment

| | |
|---|---|
| Original cost | $320,000 |
| Less:  Accumulated depreciation | (75,000) |
| Book value | $245,000 |
| | |
| Fair market value received | $237,630 |
| Less:  Book value | (245,000) |
| Loss on sale of equipment | $   7,370 |

Since the problem states that the fair market value of the equipment is determinable, it is assumed that the interest rate is fair.  Therefore, the 6% market rate is used to calculate the present value of the note and value the equipment.  The fair value of equipment is $237,630.  Because the fair market value received is less than the book value given up, there is a loss on the sale of the equipment.  The Discount on Note represents interest income that Catrina will earn over the life of the note.

| Situation | Sales Price | Carrying Value | Amortization Table | Gain or Loss | Research | Communication |
|-----------|-------------|----------------|--------------------|--------------|----------|----------------|

**Authoritative Literature**
**APB21, Para 12 or Current Text I69.105**

12.  Note exchanged for property, goods, or service.  When a note is exchanged for property, goods, or service in a bargained transaction entered into at arm's length, there should be a general presumption that the rate of interest stipulated by the parties to the transaction represents fair and adequate compensation to the supplier for the use of the related funds.  That presumption, however, must not permit the form of the transaction to prevail over its economic substance and thus would not apply if (1) interest is not stated, or (2) the stated interest rate is unreasonable (paragraphs 13 and 14), or (3) the stated face amount of the note is materially different from the current cash sales price for the same or similar items or from the market value of the note at the date of the transaction.  In these circumstances, the note, the sales price, and the cost of the property, goods, or service exchanged for the note should be recorded at the fair value of the property, goods, or services or at an amount that reasonably approximates the market value of the note, whichever is the more clearly determinable.  That amount may or may not be the same as its face amount, and any resulting discount or premium should be accounted for as an element of interest over the life of the note (paragraph 15).  In the absence of established exchange prices for the related property, goods, or service or evidence of the market value of the note (paragraph 9), the present value of a note that stipulates either no interest or a rate of interest that is clearly unreasonable should be determined by discounting all future payments on the notes using an imputed rate of interest as described in paragraphs 13 and 14.  This determination should be made at the time the note is issued, assumed, or acquired; any subsequent changes in prevailing interest rates should be ignored.

| Situation | Sales Price | Carrying Value | Amortization Table | Gain or Loss | Research | Communication |
|-----------|-------------|----------------|--------------------|--------------|----------|---------------|

A sample memo follows.

To:　　CFO, Dawson Corporation
From:　CPA Candidate
Re:　　Acquisition of equipment on January 1, 2007
Date:　[*Today's date*]

On January 1, 2007, Dawson Corporation signed a four-year, noninterest-bearing note payable for $300,000 at 6% interest to purchase equipment. We have reviewed this transaction, and we recommend the following accounting treatment.

The Accounting Principles Board Opinion No. 21, paragraph 12 specifies that on the date of acquisition, the equipment should be valued at the fair market value of the equipment or the present value of the note, whichever is more clearly determinable. Using a 6% interest rate, the present value of the note payable was calculated to be $237,600. As 6% reflects the current market rate of interest, and it is a reasonable rate, we can infer that the fair value of the equipment is accurately reflected in this rate. Therefore, Dawson should record the equipment on its balance sheet at $237,630.

The note payable should be recorded at its "face" or maturity value, and a discount on note payable account should be created as a valuation account to correctly record the note at its present value. The amount in the discount account will be amortized using the effective interest method, and a portion will be recognized as interest expense each year during the life of the four-year note. Dawson should calculate interest expense each year by multiplying the carrying value of the note payable times 6%, and the discount on notes payable should be reduced by the amount of interest expense recognized each year. This will, in effect, increase the carrying value of the note each year, until the note reaches its maturity value on January 1, 2011.

Below is an amortization table indicating the amount of interest expense Dawson should record each year on its income statement.

| Year | Interest expense | Discount on note | Carrying value |
|------|------------------|------------------|----------------|
| 1/1/2007 | | $62,370 | $237,630 |
| 12/31/2007 | $14,258 | 48,112 | 251,888 |
| 12/31/2008 | 15,113 | 32,999 | 267,001 |
| 12/31/2009 | 16,020 | 16,979 | 283,021 |
| | | rounding | |
| 12/31/2010 | 16,981 | (2) | 300,002 |

Each year the carrying value of the note must be recalculated as indicated in the above table. As no part of the note payable will be due until January 1, 2011, Dawson should report the note at its carrying value in the long-term liabilities section of the balance sheet until December 31, 2009. On January 1, 2010, Dawson should reclassify the note payable as a current liability because the note will be repaid within twelve months.

Dawson's normal depreciation method for equipment is straight-line method with a five-year life and no residual value. Therefore, each year Dawson should also record depreciation expense on the equipment at the straight-line rate of $47,526 ($237,630 / 5 years). A contra account "accumulated depreciation" should be established for this equipment, and the related accumulated depreciation should be recorded each year. The book value of the equipment (Cost less accumulated depreciation) should be disclosed on the balance sheet under noncurrent assets each year.

If we can be of further assistance or clarify any other issues for you, please contact me at 555-1234.

## B.  Bonds

### 1.   Bonds Payable and Bond Investments

Investment in bonds and bonds payable are discussed together to contrast their treatment.[1]  Bonds generally provide for periodic fixed interest payments at a contract rate of interest.  At issuance, or thereafter, the market rate of interest for the particular type of bond may be above, the same, or below the contract rate.  If the market rate exceeds the contract rate, the book value will be less than the maturity value.  The difference (discount) will make up for the contract rate being below the market rate.

Conversely, when the contract rate exceeds the market rate, the bond will sell for more than maturity value to bring the effective rate to the market rate.  This difference (premium) will make up for the contract rate being above the market rate.  When the contract rate equals the market rate, the bond will sell for the maturity value.

The market value of a bond is equal to the maturity value and interest payments discounted to the present.  You may have to refer to the discussion of time value of money concepts in the previous section before working with the subsequent material.  Finally, when solving bond problems, candidates must be careful when determining the number of months to use in the calculation of interest and discount/premium amortization.  For example, candidates frequently look at a bond issue with an interest date of September 1 and count three months to December 31.  This error is easy to make because candidates focus only on the fact that September is the ninth month instead of also noting whether the date is at the beginning or end of the month.  Candidates should also be aware that bond issues that mature on a single date are called term bonds, and bond issues that mature in installments are called serial bonds.

### 2.   Accounting for Bonds

As discussed in Module 7D, SFAS 159 provides that a company may elect the fair value option for reporting financial assets and financial liabilities.  If the fair value option is elected for a financial liability, the requirements of APB 21 no longer apply.  Instead, the financial liability is reported at fair value at the end of each reporting period, and the resulting gain or loss is reported in earnings of the period.

If an entity does not elect the fair value option, the bond is recorded at its issue price, and the effective interest method is used to amortize any premium or discount on the bond.  The remainder of this module will focus on the pricing of the bond using the effective interest method of amortizing a bond as required by APB 21.

### 3.   Bond Valuation Example

$10,000 in bonds, semiannual interest at 6% contract rate, maturing in six years, and market rate of 5%.

a.   Find present value of maturity value.  Use present value of $1 factor.  Discount $10,000 back 12 periods at 2 1/2% interest (Factor = .7436).  (Semiannual compounding is going to be required to discount the semiannual payments so it is also assumed here.)

$$\$10,000 \quad \times \quad .7436 \quad = \quad \$7,436$$

b.   Find the present value of the annuity of twelve $300 interest payments.  Use present value of an ordinary annuity of $1 factor for twelve periods at 2 1/2% interest (Factor = 10.26).

$$\$300 \quad \times \quad 10.26 \quad = \quad \$3,078$$

c.   Today's value is $10,514 (7,436 + 3,078)

The $514 premium is to be recognized over the life of the bond issue.  It is a reduction of interest expense on the books of the issuer and a reduction of interest revenue on the books of the investor.  Amortization is to be the interest, or present value basis.  (See outline of APB 21.)

The following summarizes when bonds are issued/acquired at a premium or discount:

**ISSUE/ACQUISITION PRICE OF BONDS—PRESENT VALUE OF INTEREST ANNUITY PLUS THE PRESENT VALUE OF THE MATURITY AMOUNT USING THE YIELD OR MARKET RATE**

| *Face amount* | *Premium* | *Discount* |
|---|---|---|
| Yield rate = Face rate | Yield rate < Face rate | Yield rate > Face rate |

---

[1]  *Coverage in this module focuses on a bond's book or carrying value.  Issues concerning FMV, holding gains and losses, and financial statement presentation of bond investments are covered with other marketable debt securities in Module 14, Investments.*

## 4. Journal Entries

The issuer's books will be illustrated at gross (including a premium or discount account) and the investor's books will be illustrated at net (no discount or premium account). The investor may record the bonds either net or gross, but the issuer records at gross. In the past, CPA examination problems and solutions have followed the net method on the books of the investor.

| | | *Issuer* | | | *Investor* | | |
|---|---|---|---|---|---|---|---|
| a. | Issue and | Cash | 10,514 | | Bond invest. | 10,514 | |
| | Acquisition | Bonds pay. | | 10,000 | Cash | | 10,514 |
| | | Bonds prem. | | 514 | | | |
| b. | First int. | Interest exp. | 300 | | Cash | 300 | |
| | payment | Cash | | 300 | Interest rev. | | 300 |
| c. | Premium— | Bond prem. | 37.15* | | Interest rev. | 37.15 | |
| | Amortization | Interest exp. | | 37.15 | Bond invest. | | 37.15* |

\* *Interest receipt (payment) minus effective interest = 300 – 262.85 = 37.15*
*Effective interest = net book value times effective rate = 10,514 × .025 = 262.85*

Entry a. assumes that the bonds are issued on the interest payment date. If bonds are purchased between interest payment dates, the purchaser will also include accrued interest through the purchase date in the total cash paid for the bonds. The payment of this accrued interest on the purchase date will serve to reduce the subsequent receipt of interest income (which covers a time period longer than the time the purchaser held the bond).

Subsequent interest payments are recorded the same as entry b. shown above. The amount of subsequent amortization (entry c. above) changes. Interest to be recorded under the interest method is always computed by

Effective interest rate × Net book value

This formula is true of all applications of the interest method. The effective rate of interest times net book value is the actual interest revenue or expense for the period. The difference between the actual interest and the amount received or paid is the amortization. The amortization table below shows the effective interest amounts and premium amortizations for the first 4 periods.

| Period | 3% cash interest | 2 1/2% effective interest | Decrease in book value | Book value of bonds |
|---|---|---|---|---|
| 0 | | | | $10,514.00 |
| 1 | $300[a] | $262.85[b] | $37.15[c] | 10,476.85[d] |
| 2 | 300 | 261.92 | 38.08 | 10,438.77 |
| 3 | 300 | 260.97 | 39.03 | 10,399.74 |
| 4 | 300 | 259.99 | 40.01 | 10,359.73 |

(a)   3% × $10,000     (c)   $300 – $262.85
(b)   2 1/2% × $10,514.00     (d)   $10,514.00 – $37.15

Since the interest is paid semiannually, interest (including premium amortization) is recorded every six months. The journal entries for periods 2, 3, and 4 are

| | *Issuer* | | | *Investor* | |
|---|---|---|---|---|---|
| Period 2 | Interest expense | 261.92 | Cash | 300.00 | |
| | Bond premium | 38.08 | Interest rev. | | 261.92 |
| | Cash | 300.00 | Bond invest. | | 38.08 |
| Period 3 | Interest expense | 260.97 | Cash | 300.00 | |
| | Bond premium | 39.03 | Interest rev | | 260.97 |
| | Cash | 300.00 | Bond invest. | | 39.03 |
| Period 4 | Interest expense | 259.99 | Cash | 300.00 | |
| | Bond premium | 40.01 | Interest rev. | | 259.99 |
| | Cash | 300.00 | Bond invest | | 40.01 |

Notice that the interest (revenue and expense) decreases over time. This is because the net book value (which is also the present value) is decreasing from the maturity value plus premium to the maturity value. Thus, the effective rate is being multiplied by a smaller amount each six months.

Also, note that the change in interest each period is the prior period's premium amortization times the effective rate. For example, the interest in period 3 is $.95 less than in period 2, and $38.08 of premium was amortized in period 2. The effective rate of 2.5% (every six months) times $38.08 is $.95. Thus, if the interest changes due to the changing level of net book value, the change in interest will be equal to the change in the net book value times the effective rate of interest.

Another complication may arise if the year-end does not coincide with the interest dates. In such a case, an adjusting entry must be made. The proportional share of interest payable or receivable should be recognized along with the amortization of discount or premium. The amortization of discount or premium should be straight-line within the amortization period.

*EXAMPLE: Assume that in the above example, both issuer and investor have reporting periods ending three months after the issuance of the bonds.*

| Entries on the closing date | Issuer | | Investor | |
|---|---|---|---|---|
| | Interest expense     150 | | Interest receivable     150 | |
| | Interest payable | 150 | Interest revenue | 150 |
| | Bond premium     18.57 | | Interest revenue     18.57 | |
| | Interest expense | 18.57 | Bond investment | 18.57 |

Reverse at beginning of new period and make regular entry at next interest payment date.

If bonds are sold (bought) between interest dates, premium/discount amortization must be computed for the period between sale (purchase) date and last (next) interest date. This is accomplished by straight-lining the six-month amount which was calculated using the effective interest method.

*EXAMPLE: The investor sold $5,000 of bonds in the above example, two months after issuance, for $5,250 plus interest.*

1.  The bond premium which must be amortized to the point of sale ($5,000 for two months) is 1/2 × 1/3 × $37.15 or $6.19.

    | Interest revenue     6.19 | |
    |---|---|
    | Investment | 6.19 |

2.  The sale is recorded. The investment account was $5,257 before amortization of $6.19. The cash received would be $5,250 plus $50 interest (1/2 × 1/3 × $300). The loss is a forced figure.

    | Cash     5,300.00 | |
    |---|---|
    | Loss      .81 | |
    | Interest revenue | 50.00 |
    | Investment | 5,250.81 [($10,514.00/2) – $6.19] |

3.  Check the interest revenue recorded ($50.00 – $6.19) to the interest earned: $5,257 × 2 1/2% × 1/3 (which equals $43.81).

Costs incurred in connection with the issuance of bonds (e.g., printing and engraving, accounting and legal fees, and commissions), according to SFAC 6, may be treated two ways. **However,** APB 21 currently allows the treatment of bond issue costs only in one of these ways.

SFAC 6 (see outline) states that the bond issue costs can be treated as either an expense or a reduction of the related bond liability. Bond issue costs are not considered as assets because they provide no future economic benefit. The argument for treating them as a reduction of the related bond liability is that they reduce bond proceeds, thereby increasing the effective interest rate. Thus, they should be accounted for the same as unamortized discounts.

In practice, however, the only acceptable GAAP for bond issue costs is to treat them as deferred charges and amortize them on a straight-line basis over the life of the bond.

5.  **Comparison of Effective Interest and Straight-Line Amortization Methods**

| Method of Amortization | Interest Revenue/Expense | Interest Rate** |
|---|---|---|
| Effective interest method | Changes each period* | Constant each period |
| Straight-line method | Constant each period | Changes each period |

\*  Carrying amount of the bond investment or bonds payable at the beginning of the interest period multiplied times the yield rate
\*\*  Interest revenue/expense for a period divided by the carrying amount of the bond investment or bond liability at the beginning of the interest period

The following table summarizes the various behavior patterns related to the use of the effective interest method:

| Description | Amortization of | |
|---|---|---|
| | Discount | Premium |
| Interest revenue/expense | ↑Increases each period | ↓Decreases each period |
| Amount of amortization | ↑Increases each period | ↑Increases each period |
| Carrying amount of bonds payable/investment in bonds | ↑Increases each period | ↓Decreases each period |

6.  **Convertible Bonds**  (See outlines of APB 14 and SFAS 84)

Bonds are frequently issued with the right to convert the bonds into common stock.  When issued, no value is apportioned to the conversion feature.  Two approaches are possible to account for bond conversions:  valuing the transaction at cost (book value of the bonds), or valuing at market (of the stocks or bonds), whichever is more reliable.  At market, assuming market value exceeds book value, the entries would be

| *Issuer* | | | *Investor* | |
|---|---|---|---|---|
| Loss on redemption | (plug) | | Stock invest | (mkt) |
| Bonds payable | (book value) | | Invest in bonds | (carrying value) |
| Bond premium | (book value) | | Gain on conversion | (plug) |
|    Common stock | | (par) | | |
|    Paid-in excess of par | | (mkt-par) | | |

On the issuer's books, the debit (credit) to the loss (gain) account (ordinary) would be for the difference between the market value of the stock (bonds) and the book value of the bonds.  The conversion is treated as the culmination of an earnings process; thus the loss (gain) should be recognized.  The bonds and the related accounts must be written off, and paid-in excess of par is credited for the excess of the market value of the stock (bonds) over the stock's par value.  On the investor's books, the gain (loss) would also be the difference between the market value the stock (bonds) and the book value of the bonds.  Remember in both cases that the accrued interest and discount or premium amortization must be recorded prior to the conversion.

Conversion under the cost method would result in debits to bonds payable and bond premium (or a credit to bond discount) equal to the book value of the bonds, and credits to common stock and paid-in excess of par equal to the book value.  In practice, conversions are usually recorded at book value.  Note that under this method no gain (loss) is recorded, as no gain (loss) should result from an equity transaction.

To induce conversion, firms sometimes change the original conversion privilege or give additional considerations to the bondholders.  Per SFAS 84 (see outline), the fair market value of these "sweeteners" should be recognized as an expense (ordinary in nature) upon conversion, determined as the excess of the FMV of all securities and consideration transferred over the FMV of the securities issuable per the original conversion terms.

7.  **Debt Issued with Detachable Purchase Warrants**

APB 14 (see outline) requires the proceeds of debt issued with detachable stock purchase warrants to be allocated between the debt and stock warrants based on relative market values.  Example:  units of one bond and one warrant (to buy 10 shares of stock at $50/share) are issued for $1,030.  Thereafter, warrants trade at $40 and the bonds at $960.  The relative market value of the warrants is 4% (40/1,000) and the relative market value of the bonds is 96% (960/1,000).  Thus, $41.20 (.04 × $1,030) of the issue price is assigned to the warrants.

| | | |
|---|---|---|
| Cash | 1,030.00 | |
| Bond discount | 11.20 | |
|    Bonds payable | | 1,000.00 |
|    Paid-in capital—stock warrants | | 41.20 |

If one warrant was subsequently exercised

| | | |
|---|---|---|
| Cash | 500.00 | |
| Paid-in capital—stock warrants | 41.20 | |
|    Common stock | | (par of 10 shs) |
|    Paid-in excess | | (plug) |

Alternatively, the example above could have indicated the market value of the stock (e.g., $54) rather than the market values of the bonds and warrants.  In such a case, one would value the warrants based on the difference between option price and market price, for example, [$54 (market) – $50 (option)] × 10 shares = $40 value for the warrants.

Notice the effect of requiring allocation of the cash received to the stock warrants.  The final effect is to increase interest costs on the bond issue by reducing the premium or increasing the discount.

Note that the allocation to equity shown above is only applicable where the purchase warrants are **detachable**.  In contrast, no allocation is made to equity if the bonds are issued with **nondetachable** stock purchase warrants.  Detachable warrants are often traded separately from the debt and therefore have a readily determinable market value of their own.  The inseparability of nondetachable warrants prevents the determination of a separate market value; therefore, no allocation to equity is permitted by APB 14.

8.  **Extinguishment of Debt** (See outline of APB 26)

Debt is considered extinguished whenever the debtor pays the creditor and is relieved of all obligations relating to the debt.  Typical examples of this are the calling of a bond by the debtor, requiring the bondholder to sell the bond to the issuing corporation at a certain date and stated price, and the open market repurchase of a debt issue.  Refunding of debt (replacement of debt with other debt) is also considered an extinguishment.  However, troubled debt restructures (situations where creditors agree to grant relief to debtors) and debt conversions initiated by the debt holders are not.  Additionally, when the debtor is legally released from being the primary obligor of the debt either judicially or by the creditor, and it is probable the debtor will make no further payments on it, the debt is considered extinguished.

All gains (losses) resulting from the extinguishment of debt should be recognized in the period of extinguishment.  The gain (loss) is the difference between the bond's reacquisition price and its net book value (face value plus [minus] any unamortized premium [discount] and issue costs).  The rule is not affected by the reissuance of debt before or after the refunding.  Furthermore, this rule applies to convertible bonds when reacquired with cash.  The gain or loss is considered an ordinary gain or loss, and is a separate item in net income before extraordinary items.  Because most companies use debt refinancing as a normal risk management tool, early extinguishment of debt is no longer considered an extraordinary item.  If, however, the company can meet the criteria for extraordinary (infrequent in occurrence and unusual in nature), the early extinguishment of debt may be considered for extraordinary treatment.  (See SFAS 145)

|  |  |  |
|---|---|---|
| Loss or gain | xx | xx |
| Bonds payable | xx |  |
| Bond premium | xx |  |
| Unamortized issue costs |  | xx |
| Bond discount |  | xx |
| Cash |  | xx |

9.  **Research Component**

Inasmuch as a bond is a special type of long-term payable, all research from APB 21 covered in Module 11A applies to long-term bonds.  Although APB 21 is titled "Interest on Receivables and Payables," the statement also outlines the presentation of discounts and premiums in the financial statements.  As discussed in the module on present value fundamentals, SFAS 47 addresses the disclosure of long-term obligations in the notes to the financial statements, and SFAS 91 addresses loan origination costs.  These statements also apply to bonds.

Additional materials relevant to bonds are APB 14, APB 26, SFAS 84, and SFAS 145.  APB 14 provides the rules for accounting for convertible debt and debt issued with stock purchase warrants.  APB 26 discusses early extinguishment of debt.  FAS 84 covers the accounting for induced conversions of convertible debt (sweeteners).  The most recent pronouncement that impacts accounting for long-term debt (bonds) is SFAS 145, which no longer allows an early extinguishment of debt to be routinely classified as an extraordinary item on the income statement.  Notice that in extinguishment of debt, the term used in APB 26 is not "carrying value" but "carrying amount."  Note the vocabulary used in extinguishment of debt uses the term "reacquisition price' rather than redemption price or value.

Keywords for researching extinguishment of debt, conversions, and warrants are shown below.

| | | |
|---|---|---|
| Conversion of debt | Extinguishment debt | Net carrying amount |
| Conversion option | Extraordinary unusual transactions | Nondetachable warrant |
| Convertible debt securities | Gains losses extinguishment debt | Reacquisition price |
| Detachable warrant | Induced conversion debt | Value debt securities |

## MULTIPLE-CHOICE QUESTIONS (1-40)

**1.** Hancock Co.'s December 31, 2007 balance sheet contained the following items in the long-term liabilities section:

**Unsecured**

| | |
|---|---|
| 9.375% registered bonds ($25,000 maturing annually beginning in 2011) | $275,000 |
| 11.5% convertible bonds, callable beginning in 2015, due 2027 | 125,000 |

**Secured**

| | |
|---|---|
| 9.875% guaranty security bonds, due 2027 | $275,000 |
| 10.0% commodity backed bonds ($50,000 maturing annually beginning in 2012) | 200,000 |

What are the total amounts of serial bonds and debenture bonds?

| | Serial bonds | Debenture bonds |
|---|---|---|
| a. | $475,000 | $400,000 |
| b. | $475,000 | $125,000 |
| c. | $450,000 | $400,000 |
| d. | $200,000 | $650,000 |

**2.** Blue Corp.'s December 31, 2007 balance sheet contained the following items in the long-term liabilities section:

| | |
|---|---|
| 9 3/4% registered debentures, callable in 2018, due in 2023 | $700,000 |
| 9 1/2% collateral trust bonds, convertible into common stock beginning in 2016, due in 2026 | 600,000 |
| 10% subordinated debentures ($30,000 maturing annually beginning in 2013) | 300,000 |

What is the total amount of Blue's term bonds?
a. $   600,000
b. $   700,000
c. $1,000,000
d. $1,300,000

**3.** Bonds payable issued with scheduled maturities at various dates are called

| | Serial bonds | Term bonds |
|---|---|---|
| a. | No | Yes |
| b. | No | No |
| c. | Yes | No |
| d. | Yes | Yes |

**4.** The following information pertains to Camp Corp.'s issuance of bonds on July 1, 2007:

| | |
|---|---|
| Face amount | $800,000 |
| Term | Ten years |
| Stated interest rate | 6% |
| Interest payment dates | Annually on July 1 |
| Yield | 9% |

| | At 6% | At 9% |
|---|---|---|
| Present value of one for ten periods | 0.558 | 0.422 |
| Future value of one for ten periods | 1.791 | 2.367 |
| Present value of ordinary annuity of one for ten periods | 7.360 | 6.418 |

What should be the issue price for each $1,000 bond?
a. $1,000
b. $   864
c. $   807
d. $   700

**5.** Perk, Inc. issued $500,000, 10% bonds to yield 8%. Bond issuance costs were $10,000. How should Perk calculate the net proceeds to be received from the issuance?

a. Discount the bonds at the stated rate of interest.
b. Discount the bonds at the market rate of interest.
c. Discount the bonds at the stated rate of interest and deduct bond issuance costs.
d. Discount the bonds at the market rate of interest and deduct bond issuance costs.

**6.** The market price of a bond issued at a discount is the present value of its principal amount at the market (effective) rate of interest
a. Less the present value of all future interest payments at the market (effective) rate of interest.
b. Less the present value of all future interest payments at the rate of interest stated on the bond.
c. Plus the present value of all future interest payments at the market (effective) rate of interest.
d. Plus the present value of all future interest payments at the rate of interest stated on the bond.

**7.** On July 1, 2007, Eagle Corp. issued 600 of its 10%, $1,000 bonds at 99 plus accrued interest. The bonds are dated April 1, 2007, and mature on April 1, 2017. Interest is payable semiannually on April 1 and October 1. What amount did Eagle receive from the bond issuance?
a. $579,000
b. $594,000
c. $600,000
d. $609,000

**8.** During 2007, Lake Co. issued 3,000 of its 9%, $1,000 face value bonds at 101 1/2. In connection with the sale of these bonds, Lake paid the following expenses:

| | |
|---|---|
| Promotion costs | $ 20,000 |
| Engraving and printing | 25,000 |
| Underwriters' commissions | 200,000 |

What amount should Lake record as bond issue costs to be amortized over the term of the bonds?
a. $0
b. $220,000
c. $225,000
d. $245,000

**9.** Dixon Co. incurred costs of $3,300 when it issued, on August 31, 2007, five-year debenture bonds dated April 1, 2007. What amount of bond issue expense should Dixon report in its income statement for the year ended December 31, 2007?
a. $   220
b. $   240
c. $   495
d. $3,300

**10.** On November 1, 2007, Mason Corp. issued $800,000 of its ten-year, 8% term bonds dated October 1, 2007. The bonds were sold to yield 10%, with total proceeds of $700,000 plus accrued interest. Interest is paid every April 1 and October 1. What amount should Mason report for interest payable in its December 31, 2007 balance sheet?
a. $17,500
b. $16,000
c. $11,667
d. $10,667

**11.** On July 1, 2007, Day Co. received $103,288 for $100,000 face amount, 12% bonds, a price that yields 10%. Assuming management does not elect the fair value option, interst expense for the six months ended December 31, 2007, should be

a.  $6,197
b.  $6,000
c.  $5,164
d.  $5,000

**12.** On January 2, 2007, West Co. issued 9% bonds in the amount of $500,000, which mature on January 2, 2017.  The bonds were issued for $469,500 to yield 10%.  Interest is payable annually on December 31.  West uses the interest method of amortizing bond discount.  In its June 30, 2007 balance sheet, what amount should West report as bonds payable?
a.  $469,500
b.  $470,475
c.  $471,025
d.  $500,000

**13.** Webb Co. has outstanding a 7%, ten-year $100,000 face-value bond.  The bond was originally sold to yield 6% annual interest.  Webb uses the effective interest rate method to amortize bond premium.  On June 30, 2007, the carrying amount of the outstanding bond was $105,000.  What amount of unamortized premium on bond should Webb report in its June 30, 2008 balance sheet?
a.  $1,050
b.  $3,950
c.  $4,300
d.  $4,500

**14.** For the issuer of a ten-year term bond, the amount of amortization using the interest method would increase each year if the bond was sold at a

|    | Discount | Premium |
|----|----------|---------|
| a. | No | No |
| b. | Yes | Yes |
| c. | No | Yes |
| d. | Yes | No |

**15.** On January 2, 2007, Nast Co. issued 8% bonds with a face amount of $1,000,000 that mature on January 2, 2013.  The bonds were issued to yield 12%, resulting in a discount of $150,000.  Nast incorrectly used the straight-line method instead of the effective interest method to amortize the discount.  How is the carrying amount of the bonds affected by the error?

|    | At December 31, 2007 | At January 2, 2013 |
|----|----------------------|--------------------|
| a. | Overstated | Understated |
| b. | Overstated | No effect |
| c. | Understated | Overstated |
| d. | Understated | No effect |

**16.** The following information relates to noncurrent investments that Fall Corp. placed in trust as required by the underwriter of its bonds:

| | |
|---|---|
| Bond sinking fund balance, 12/31/07 | $ 450,000 |
| 2008 additional investment | 90,000 |
| Dividends on investments | 15,000 |
| Interest revenue | 30,000 |
| Administration costs | 5,000 |
| Carrying amount of bonds payable | 1,025,000 |

What amount should Fall report in its December 31, 2008 balance sheet related to its noncurrent investment for bond sinking fund requirements?
a.  $585,000
b.  $580,000
c.  $575,000

d.  $540,000

**17.** Witt Corp. has outstanding at December 31, 2007, two long-term borrowings with annual sinking fund requirements and maturities as follows:

| | Sinking fund requirements | Maturities |
|---|---|---|
| 2007 | $1,000,000 | $ -- |
| 2008 | 1,500,000 | 2,000,000 |
| 2009 | 1,500,000 | 2,000,000 |
| 2010 | 2,000,000 | 2,500,000 |
| 2011 | 2,000,000 | 3,000,000 |
| | $8,000,000 | $9,500,000 |

In the notes to its December 31, 2007 balance sheet, how should Witt report the above data?
a.  No disclosure is required.
b.  Only sinking fund payments totaling $8,000,000 for the next five years detailed by year need be disclosed.
c.  Only maturities totaling $9,500,000 for the next five years detailed by year need to be disclosed.
d.  The combined aggregate of $17,500,000 of maturities and sinking fund requirements detailed by year should be disclosed.

**18.** On March 1, 2005, a company established a sinking fund in connection with an issue of bonds due in 2017.  At December 31, 2007, the independent trustee held cash in the sinking fund account representing the annual deposits to the fund and the interest earned on those deposits.  How should the sinking fund be reported in the company's balance sheet at December 31, 2007?
a.  The cash in the sinking fund should appear as a current asset.
b.  Only the accumulated deposits should appear as a noncurrent asset.
c.  The entire balance in the sinking fund account should appear as a current asset.
d.  The entire balance in the sinking fund account should appear as a noncurrent asset.

**19.** An issuer of bonds uses a sinking fund for the retirement of the bonds.  Cash was transferred to the sinking fund and subsequently used to purchase investments.  The sinking fund

I. Increases by revenue earned on the investments.
II. Is **not** affected by revenue earned on the investments.
III. Decreases when the investments are purchased.

a.  I only.
b.  I and III.
c.  II and III.
d.  III only.

**20.** On July 2, 2007, Wynn, Inc., purchased as a short-term investment a $1,000,000 face value Kean Co. 8% bond for $910,000 plus accrued interest to yield 10%.  The bonds mature on January 1, 2014, pay interest annually on January 1, and are classified as trading securities.  On December 31, 2007, the bonds had a market value of $945,000.  On February 13, 2008, Wynn sold the bonds for $920,000.  In its December 31, 2007 balance sheet, what amount should Wynn report for short-term investments in trading debt securities?
a.  $910,000
b.  $920,000
c.  $945,000
d.  $950,000

**21.** On July 1, 2007, East Co. purchased as a long-term investment $500,000 face amount, 8% bonds of Rand Corp. for $461,500 to yield 10% per year. The bonds pay interest semiannually on January 1 and July 1. East does not elect the fair value option for reporting these securities. In its December 31, 2007 balance sheet, East should report interest receivable of

    a.   $18,460
    b.   $20,000
    c.   $23,075
    d.   $25,000

**22.** On October 1, 2006, Park Co. purchased 200 of the $1,000 face value, 10% bonds of Ott, Inc., for $220,000, including accrued interest of $5,000. The bonds, which mature on January 1, 2013, pay interest semiannually on January 1 and July 1. Park used the straight-line method of amortization and appropriately classified the bonds as held-to-maturity. On Park's December 31, 2007 balance sheet, the bonds should be reported at

    a.   $215,000
    b.   $214,400
    c.   $214,200
    d.   $212,000

**23.** On July 1, 2007, York Co. purchased as a held-to-maturity investment $1,000,000 of Park, Inc.'s 8% bonds for $946,000, including accrued interest of $40,000. The bonds were purchased to yield 10% interest. The bonds mature on January 1, 2014, and pay interest annually on January 1. York uses the effective interest method of amortization. In its December 31, 2007 balance sheet, what amount should York report as investment in bonds?

    a.   $911,300
    b.   $916,600
    c.   $953,300
    d.   $960,600

**24.** In 2006, Lee Co. acquired, at a premium, Enfield, Inc. ten-year bonds as a long-term investment. At December 31, 2007, Enfield's bonds were quoted at a small discount. Which of the following situations is the most likely cause of the decline in the bonds' market value?

    a.   Enfield issued a stock dividend.
    b.   Enfield is expected to call the bonds at a premium, which is less than Lee's carrying amount.
    c.   Interest rates have declined since Lee purchased the bonds.
    d.   Interest rates have increased since Lee purchased the bonds.

**25.** An investor purchased a bond as a held-to-maturity investment on January 2. Assume the fair value option is not elected for these securities. The investor's carrying value at the end of the first year would be highest if the bond was purchased at a

    a.   Discount and amortized by the straight-line method.
    b.   Discount and amortized by the effective interest method.
    c.   Premium and amortized by the straight-line method.
    d.   Premium and amortized by the effective interest method.

**26.** An investor purchased a bond as a long-term investment on January 1. Annual interest was received on December 31. The investor's interest income for the year would be highest if the bond was purchased at

    a.   Par.
    b.   Face value.
    c.   A discount.
    d.   A premium.

**27.** On March 1, 2007, Clark Co. issued bonds at a discount. Clark incorrectly used the straight-line method instead of the effective interest method to amortize the discount. Clark does not elect the fair value option to report these securities. How were the following amounts, as of December 31, 2007, affected by the error?

| | Bond carrying amount | Retained earnings |
|---|---|---|
| a. | Overstated | Overstated |
| b. | Understated | Understated |
| c. | Overstated | Understated |
| d. | Understated | Overstated |

**28.** Jent Corp. purchased bonds at a discount of $10,000. Subsequently, Jent sold these bonds at a premium of $14,000. During the period that Jent held this investment, amortization of the discount amounted to $2,000. Jent did not elect the fair value option to report these bonds. What amount should Jent report as gain on the sale of bonds?

    a.   $12,000
    b.   $22,000
    c.   $24,000
    d.   $26,000

**29.** On July 1, 2007, after recording interest and amortization, York Co. converted $1,000,000 of its 12% convertible bonds into 50,000 shares of $1 par value common stock. On the conversion date the carrying amount of the bonds was $1,300,000, the market value of the bonds was $1,400,000, and York's common stock was publicly trading at $30 per share. Using the book value method, what amount of additional paid-in capital should York record as a result of the conversion?

    a.   $ 950,000
    b.   $1,250,000
    c.   $1,350,000
    d.   $1,500,000

**30.** On March 31, 2007, Ashley, Inc.'s bondholders exchanged their convertible bonds for common stock. The carrying amount of these bonds on Ashley's books was less than the market value but greater than the par value of the common stock issued. If Ashley used the book value method of accounting for the conversion, which of the following statements correctly states an effect of this conversion?

    a.   Stockholders' equity is increased.
    b.   Additional paid-in capital is decreased.
    c.   Retained earnings is increased.
    d.   An extraordinary loss is recognized.

**Items 31 and 32** are based on the following:

On January 2, 2004, Chard Co. issued ten-year convertible bonds at 105. During 2007, these bonds were converted into common stock having an aggregate par value equal to the total face amount of the bonds. At conversion, the market price of Chard's common stock was 50% above its par value.

**31.** On January 2, 2004, cash proceeds from the issuance of the convertible bonds should be reported as
   a.   Contributed capital for the entire proceeds.
   b.   Contributed capital for the portion of the proceeds attributable to the conversion feature and as a liability for the balance.
   c.   A liability for the face amount of the bonds and contributed capital for the premium over the face amount.
   d.   A liability for the entire proceeds.

**32.** Depending on whether the book value method or the market value method was used, Chard would recognize gains or losses on conversion when using the

|     | Book value method | Market value method |
| --- | --- | --- |
| a. | Either gain or loss | Gain |
| b. | Either gain or loss | Loss |
| c. | Neither gain **nor** loss | Loss |
| d. | Neither gain **nor** loss | Gain |

**33.** On December 30, 2007, Fort, Inc. issued 1,000 of its 8%, ten-year, $1,000 face value bonds with detachable stock warrants at par.  Each bond carried a detachable warrant for one share of Fort's common stock at a specified option price of $25 per share.  Immediately after issuance, the market value of the bonds without the warrants was $1,080,000 and the market value of the warrants was $120,000.  In its December 31, 2007 balance sheet, what amount should Fort report as bonds payable?
   a.   $1,000,000
   b.   $  975,000
   c.   $  900,000
   d.   $  880,000

**34.** On December 31, 2007, Moss Co. issued $1,000,000 of 11% bonds at 109.  Each $1,000 bond was issued with fifty detachable stock warrants, each of which entitled the bondholder to purchase one share of $5 par common stock for $25.  Immediately after issuance, the market value of each warrant was $4.  On December 31, 2007, what amount should Moss record as discount or premium on issuance of bonds?
   a.   $ 40,000 premium.
   b.   $ 90,000 premium.
   c.   $110,000 discount.
   d.   $200,000 discount.

**35.** On March 1, 2007, Evan Corp. issued $500,000 of 10% nonconvertible bonds at 103, due on February 28, 2017. Each $1,000 bond was issued with thirty detachable stock warrants, each of which entitled the holder to purchase, for $50, one share of Evan's $25 par common stock.  On March 1, 2007, the market price of each warrant was $4.  By what amount should the bond issue proceeds increase stockholders' equity?
   a.   $0
   b.   $15,000
   c.   $45,000
   d.   $60,000

**36.** Main Co. issued bonds with detachable common stock warrants.  Only the warrants had a known market value. The sum of the fair value of the warrants and the face amount of the bonds exceeds the cash proceeds.  This excess is reported as
   a.   Discount on bonds payable.

   b.   Premium on bonds payable.
   c.   Common stock subscribed.
   d.   Contributed capital in excess of par—stock warrants.

**37.** When bonds are issued with stock purchase warrants, a portion of the proceeds should be allocated to paid-in capital for bonds issued with

|     | Detachable stock purchase warrants | Nondetachable stock purchase warrants |
| --- | --- | --- |
| a. | No | Yes |
| b. | No | No |
| c. | Yes | No |
| d. | Yes | Yes |

**38.** On June 30, 2007, King Co. had outstanding 9%, $5,000,000 face value bonds maturing on June 30, 2012. Interest was payable semiannually every June 30 and December 31.  On June 30, 2007, after amortization was recorded for the period, the unamortized bond premium and bond issue costs were $30,000 and $50,000, respectively. On that date, King acquired all its outstanding bonds on the open market at 98 and retired them.  At June 30, 2007, what amount should King recognize as gain before income taxes on redemption of bonds?
   a.   $ 20,000
   b.   $ 80,000
   c.   $120,000
   d.   $180,000

**39.** On January 1, 2002, Fox Corp. issued 1,000 of its 10%, $1,000 bonds for $1,040,000.  These bonds were to mature on January 1, 2012 but were callable at 101 any time after December 31, 2005.  Interest was payable semiannually on July 1 and January 1.  On July 1, 2007, Fox called all of the bonds and retired them.  Bond premium was amortized on a straight-line basis.  Before income taxes, Fox's gain or loss in 2007 on this early extinguishment of debt was
   a.   $30,000 gain.
   b.   $12,000 gain.
   c.   $10,000 loss.
   d.   $ 8,000 gain.

**40.** On January 1, 2008, Hart, Inc. redeemed its fifteen-year bonds of $500,000 par value for 102.  They were originally issued on January 1, 1996, at 98 with a maturity date of January 1, 2011.  The bond issue costs relating to this transaction were $20,000.  Hart amortizes discounts, premiums, and bond issue costs using the straight-line method.  What amount of loss should Hart recognize on the redemption of these bonds?
   a.   $16,000
   b.   $12,000
   c.   $10,000
   d.   $0

**SIMULATION PROBLEMS**

**Simulation Problem 1**                         (50 to 60 minutes)

| Situation | | | | | | |
|---|---|---|---|---|---|---|
| | **Concepts** | **Bond Valuation** | **Amortization Schedule** | **Journal Entries** | **Communication** | **Research** |

On January 2, 2007, Parker Co. issued 6% bonds with a face value of $400,000 when the market interest rate was 8%. The bonds are due in ten years, and interest is payable every June 30 and December 31. Parker does not elect the fair value option for reporting its financial liabilities.

| | **Concepts** | | | | | |
|---|---|---|---|---|---|---|
| **Situation** | | **Bond Valuation** | **Amortization Schedule** | **Journal Entries** | **Communication** | **Research** |

Parker Co. $50 par value common stock has always traded above par. During 2007, Parker had several transactions that affected the following balance sheet accounts:

      I.    Bond discounts
     II.   Bond premium
   III.   Bond payable
   IV.   Common stock
    V.   Additional paid-in capital
   VI.   Retained earnings

For each of the following items, determine whether the transaction Increased, Decreased, or had No effect for each of the items in the chart.

| | Bond discounts | Bond premium | Bond payable | Common stock | Additional paid-in capital | Retained earnings |
|---|---|---|---|---|---|---|
| **1.** Parker issued bonds payable with a nominal interest rate that was less than the market rate of interest. | | | | | | |
| **2.** Parker issued convertible bonds, which are common stock equivalents, for an amount in excess of the bonds' face amount. | | | | | | |
| **3.** Parker issued common stock when the convertible bonds described in item **2.** were submitted for conversion. Each $1,000 bond was converted into twenty common shares. The book value method was used for the early conversion. | | | | | | |
| **4.** Parker issued bonds with nondetachable warrants for an amount equal to the face amount of the bonds. The stock warrants do not have a determinable value. | | | | | | |
| **5.** Parker issued bonds, with detachable stock warrants, for an amount equal to the face amount of the bonds. The stock warrants have a determinable value. | | | | | | |
| **6.** Parker redeemed a bond issued at 8% at a discount for an amount that was 102% of face value. | | | | | | |
| **7.** Parker issued bonds payable with a nominal rate of interest that is higher than the market rate. | | | | | | |
| **8.** Parker called a bond that was issued at 105 at a time when the market value of the bond was less than its carrying value. | | | | | | |

| Situation | Concepts | Bond Valuation | Amortization Schedule | Journal Entries | Communication | Research |
|-----------|----------|----------------|----------------------|-----------------|---------------|----------|

Use the following present value and present value annuity tables to calculate the selling price of the bond on January 2, 2007.  Round your final answer to the nearest dollar.

*Present Value Ordinary Annuity of $1*

| Periods | 3% | 4% | 6% | 8% | 12% | 16% |
|---------|-----|-----|-----|-----|------|------|
| 5 periods | 4.5797 | 4.4518 | 4.2124 | 3.9927 | 3.6048 | 3.2743 |
| 10 periods | 8.5302 | 8.1109 | 7.3601 | 6.7101 | 5.6502 | 4.8337 |
| 20 periods | 14.8775 | 13.5903 | 11.4699 | 9.8181 | 7.4694 | 5.9288 |

*Present Value of $1*

| Periods | 3% | 4% | 6% | 8% | 12% | 16% |
|---------|-----|-----|-----|-----|------|------|
| 5 periods | .8626 | .8219 | .7473 | .6806 | .5674 | .4761 |
| 10 periods | .7441 | .6756 | .5584 | .4632 | .3220 | .2267 |
| 20 periods | .5537 | .4564 | .3118 | .2145 | .1037 | .0514 |

Selling price of the bond [                    ]

| Situation | Concepts | Bond Valuation | Amortization Schedule | Journal Entries | Communication | Research |
|-----------|----------|----------------|----------------------|-----------------|---------------|----------|

Prepare the amortization schedule for the bond through December 31, 2007.  Round all numbers to the nearest dollar.

| Date | Interest paid | Interest expense | Amortization of discount | Discount on bond payable | Carrying value of bond payable |
|------|---------------|------------------|--------------------------|--------------------------|--------------------------------|
| 1/2/07 | | | | | |
| 6/30/07 | | | | | |
| 12/31/07 | | | | | |

| Situation | Concepts | Bond Valuation | Amortization Schedule | Journal Entries | Communication | Research |
|-----------|----------|----------------|----------------------|-----------------|---------------|----------|

**1.** Prepare the journal entries for the bond issue on January 2, 2007.

| | | |
|--|--|--|
| | | |
| | | |
| | | |

**2.** Prepare the journal entry for the interest payment on June 30, 2007.

| | | |
|--|--|--|
| | | |
| | | |
| | | |

| Situation | Concepts | Bond Valuation | Amortization Schedule | Journal Entries | Communication | Research |
|-----------|----------|----------------|----------------------|-----------------|---------------|----------|

On June 30, 2004, Parker Co. issued fifteen-year 12% bonds at a premium (effective yield 10%).  On November 30, 2007, Parker transferred both cash and property to the bondholders to extinguish the entire debt.  The fair value of the transferred property equaled its carrying amount.  The fair value of the cash and property transferred exceeded the bonds' carrying amount.

Write a memorandum to the finance manager of Parker that

1. Explains the purpose of the effective interest method and the effect of applying the method in 2004 on Parker's bond premium.

2. States the effect on 2004 interest expense, net income, and the carrying amount of the bonds if Parker had incorrectly adopted the straight-line interest method instead of the effective interest method.

3. Describes how Parker should calculate and report the effects of the November 30, 2007 transaction in its 2007 income statement.  Why is this presentation appropriate? (Ignore income taxes.)

To:   Finance Manager, Parker Co.
From: CPA Candidate
Re:   Accounting for bonds

| Situation | Concepts | Bond Valuation | Amortization Schedule | Journal Entries | Communication | Research |
|---|---|---|---|---|---|---|

Research the professional standards regarding guidance on the appropriate interest rate to use to discount a note payable with an unrealistic rate. Indicate the appropriate source in the box below.

---

**Simulation Problem 2**                                    (50 to 60 minutes)

| Situation | | | | |
|---|---|---|---|---|
| | Concepts | Journal Entries | Communication | Research |

On January 1, 2007, Castle issued $400,000 of 6% bonds. The bonds were issued at 98 and pay interest semiannually on July 1 and December 31 each year.

On September 1, 2007, Castle issued for $530,000 cash, 500 7% five-year nonconvertible bonds dated September 1, 2007. Each $1,000 bond had a detachable stock purchase warrant to purchase 20 shares of $3 par value stock for $10 per share. Immediately after issuance, the warrants had a market value of $45,000, and the bonds were selling at 102 without the warrant.

On January 1, 2003, Castle issued 100 ten-year convertible bonds. Each $1,000 bond is convertible into 20 shares of Castle's $10 par value common stock. The bonds were issued at 105 when the common stock traded for $40 per share. The bonds pay interest annually. On October 1, 2007, half of the bonds were tendered for conversion when the common stock was trading at $62 per share. Castle uses the book value method to account for the conversion. At the time of conversion, the bonds had a carrying value of $104,300. Castle does not elect the fair value option for reporting these financial liabilities.

| Situation | Concepts | Journal Entries | Communication | Research |
|---|---|---|---|---|

Indicate whether each item is True or False.

| | True | False |
|---|---|---|
| 1. Bond issue costs should be treated as deferred charges and amortized over the life of the bond. | O | O |
| 2. Early extinguishment of debt is treated as an extraordinary item. | O | O |
| 3. Losses from extinguishment of debt should be amortized over the remaining life of the debt. | O | O |
| 4. The straight-line method of amortization should be used for bonds due in less than five years. | O | O |
| 5. Bonds that mature on a single date are called serial bonds. | O | O |
| 6. The effective interest is calculated by multiplying the maturity value of the bond by the coupon rate. | O | O |
| 7. A bond premium represents a reduction of interest expense on the books of the issuer. | O | O |
| 8. When the contract or coupon rate is greater than the effective rate, the bonds will sell at a premium. | O | O |

| Situation | Concepts | Journal Entries | Communication | Research |
|---|---|---|---|---|

Prepare the journal entries for the bond transactions during 2007.

**1.** January 1, 2007  Issue bonds

| | | |
|---|---|---|
| | | |
| | | |
| | | |
| | | |
| | | |

**2.** September 1, 2007  Issue bonds with detachable warrants

| | | |
|---|---|---|
| | | |
| | | |
| | | |
| | | |
| | | |

**3.** October 1, 2007  Conversion of bonds

| | | |
|---|---|---|
| | | |
| | | |
| | | |
| | | |
| | | |

| Situation | Concepts | Journal Entries | Communication | | Research |
|---|---|---|---|---|---|

Castle Co. also had 12-year convertible bonds that were issued and dated April 1, 2003.  Each $1,000 bond is convertible at the holder's option into twenty shares of Castle's $25 par value common stock.  The bonds were issued at a premium when the common stock traded at $45 per share.  After payment of interest on April 1, 2007, 30% of the bonds were tendered for conversion when the common stock was trading at $57 per share.  Castle used the book value method to account for the conversion.

Write a brief memo to the controller of Castle Co. answering the following questions relating to the bonds.

**1.** How would the issue price of Castle's convertible bonds be determined?

**2.** How should Castle account for the issuance of the convertible bonds?  Give the rationale for this accounting practice.

**3.** How should Castle account for the conversion of the bonds into common stock?

To:    Controller, Castle Co.
From: CPA Candidate
Re:    Bonds

| |
|---|
| |

| Situation | Concepts | Journal Entries | Communication | Research |
|---|---|---|---|---|

Identify the authoritative literature that explains how to account for the three bond issues in the **Journal Entries** section.  Cut and paste the appropriate paragraph from the accounting literature into the chart below.

**1.** March 1, 2007 issue of bonds   _____

**2.** September 1, 2007 issue of bonds   _____
with warrants

**3.** October 1, 2007 conversion of   _____
bonds

## MULTIPLE-CHOICE ANSWERS

| | | | | | | |
|---|---|---|---|---|---|---|
| 1. a __ __ | 10. b __ __ | 19. a __ __ | 28. b __ __ | 37. c __ __ | | |
| 2. d __ __ | 11. c __ __ | 20. c __ __ | 29. b __ __ | 38. b __ __ | | |
| 3. c __ __ | 12. b __ __ | 21. b __ __ | 30. a __ __ | 39. d __ __ | | |
| 4. c __ __ | 13. c __ __ | 22. d __ __ | 31. d __ __ | 40. a __ __ | | |
| 5. d __ __ | 14. b __ __ | 23. a __ __ | 32. c __ __ | | | |
| 6. c __ __ | 15. b __ __ | 24. d __ __ | 33. c __ __ | | | |
| 7. d __ __ | 16. b __ __ | 25. d __ __ | 34. c __ __ | | | |
| 8. d __ __ | 17. d __ __ | 26. c __ __ | 35. d __ __ | 1st: __/40 = __% | | |
| 9. b __ __ | 18. d __ __ | 27. c __ __ | 36. a __ __ | 2nd: __/40 = __% | | |

## MULTIPLE-CHOICE ANSWER EXPLANATIONS

### B.1.-4.  Bonds

**1.   (a)   Serial** bonds are bond issues that mature in installments (usually on the same date each year over a period of years).  In this case, serial bonds total $475,000 ($275,000 + $200,000).  **Debenture** bonds are bonds that are **not** secured by specifically designated collateral, but rather by the general assets of the corporation.  The unsecured bonds total $400,000 ($275,000 + $125,000).

**2.   (d)   Term bonds** are bond issues that mature on a single date, as opposed to **serial bonds,** which mature in installments.  In this case, the 9 3/4% bonds and the 9 1/2% bonds are term bonds ($700,000 + $600,000 = $1,300,000), while the 10% bonds are serial bonds ($300,000).

**3.   (c)** Serial bonds are bond issues that mature in installments (i.e., on the same date each year over a period of years).  Term bonds, on the other hand, are bond issues that mature on a single date.

**4.   (c)** The issue price of each bond is equal to the present value (PV) of the maturity value plus the PV of the interest annuity.  The PV must be computed using the yield rate (9%).  The computation is

| *Amount* | | *PV factor* | | *PV* |
|---|---|---|---|---|
| $1,000 | × | .422 | = | $422 |
| 60 | × | 6.418 | = | 385 |
| | | | | $807 |

The annuity interest amount above ($60) is the principal ($1,000) times the stated cash rate (6%).

**5.   (d)** The question asks for net proceeds to be received from the issuance.  The market value of a bond is equal to the maturity value and the interest payments discounted at the market rate of interest.  The net proceeds will be the market value of the bond less the bond issuance costs.

**6.   (c)** The market price of a bond issued at any amount (par, premium, or discount) is equal to the present value of all of its future cash flows, discounted at the current market (effective) interest rate.  The market price of a bond issued at a discount is equal to the present value of both its principal and periodic future cash interest payments at the stated (cash) rate of interest, discounted at the current market (effective) rate.

**7.   (d)** To determine the net cash received from the bond issuance, the solutions approach is to prepare the journal entry for the issuance

| | | |
|---|---|---|
| Cash | ? | |
| Discount on BP | 6,000 | |
|    Bonds payable | | 600,000 |
|    Interest expense | | 15,000 |

The bonds were issued at 99 ($600,000 × 99% = $594,000), so the discount is $6,000 ($600,000 − $594,000).  The accrued interest covers the three months from 4/1 to 7/1 ($600,000 × 10% × 3/12 = $15,000).  The cash received includes the $594,000 for the bonds and the $15,000 for the accrued interest, for a total of $609,000.

**8.   (d)** SFAS 91 states that engraving and printing costs, legal and accounting fees, commissions, promotion costs, and other similar costs should be recorded as bond issue costs and amortized over the term of the bonds.  All the costs given are bond issue costs, so the amount reported as bond issue costs is $245,000 ($20,000 + $25,000 + $200,000).

**9.   (b)** Bond issue costs are treated as deferred charges and amortized on a straight-line basis over the life of the bond.  These five-year bonds were issued five months late (4/1/07 to 8/31/07), so they will be outstanding only fifty-five months (60 − 5).  During 2007, the bonds were outstanding for four months (8/31/07 to 12/31/07).  Therefore, the bond issue costs must be amortized for four months out of fifty-five months total, resulting in bond issue expense of $240 ($3,300 × 4/55).

**10.   (b)** Interest payable reported in the 12/31/07 balance sheet would consist of interest due from the bond date (10/1/07) to the year-end (12/31/07); in other words, three months' interest.  The formula for interest payable is

$$\left( \begin{array}{c} \text{Face} \\ \text{value} \end{array} \right) \times \left( \begin{array}{c} \text{Stated} \\ \text{rate} \end{array} \right) \times \left( \begin{array}{c} \text{Time} \\ \text{period} \end{array} \right) = \left( \begin{array}{c} \text{Interest} \\ \text{payable} \end{array} \right)$$

| | | | | | | | |
|---|---|---|---|---|---|---|---|
| $800,000 | × | 8% | × | 3/12 | = | $16,000 | |

This amount would result from two entries.

| *Issuance* | | |
|---|---|---|
| Cash | 705,333 | |
| Discount on BP | 100,000 | |
|    Bonds payable | | 800,000 |
|    Int. payable | | 5,333 |
| | | ($800,000 × 8% × 1/12) |

| *Adjusting entry* | | |
|---|---|---|
| Interest expense | 11,667 | ($700,000 × 10% × 2/12) |
|    Int. payable | | 10,667 |
| | | ($800,000 × 8% × 2/12) |
|    Discount on BP | | 1,000 |

**11.   (c)** A bond premium must be amortized using the interest method or the straight-line method if the results are not materially different.  To use the straight-line method, the amount of time the bonds will be outstanding must be known.  Since this time period is not given, the interest method must be used.  Under the interest method, interest expense is computed as follows:

$$\left(\begin{array}{c}\text{BV of}\\\text{bonds}\end{array}\right) \times \left(\begin{array}{c}\text{Yield}\\\text{rate}\end{array}\right) \times \left(\begin{array}{c}\text{Time}\\\text{period}\end{array}\right) = \left(\begin{array}{c}\text{Interest}\\\text{expense}\end{array}\right)$$

$$\$103,288 \times 10\% \times 6/12 = \$5,164$$

The interest payable at 12/31/07 is $6,000 ($100,000 × 12% × 6/12), so the 12/31/07 journal entry is

| | | |
|---|---|---|
| Interest expense | 5,164 | |
| Premium on BP | 836 | |
| Interest payable | | 6,000 |

**12.   (b)**   Under the effective interest method, interest expense is computed as follows:

$$\left(\begin{array}{c}\text{BV of}\\\text{bonds}\end{array}\right) \times \left(\begin{array}{c}\text{Yield}\\\text{rate}\end{array}\right) \times \left(\begin{array}{c}\text{Time}\\\text{period}\end{array}\right) = \left(\begin{array}{c}\text{Interest}\\\text{expense}\end{array}\right)$$

$$\$469,500 \times 10\% \times 6/12 = \$23,475$$

The cash interest payable is computed below.

$$\left(\begin{array}{c}\text{FV of}\\\text{bonds}\end{array}\right) \times \left(\begin{array}{c}\text{Stated}\\\text{rate}\end{array}\right) \times \left(\begin{array}{c}\text{Time}\\\text{period}\end{array}\right) = \left(\begin{array}{c}\text{Interest}\\\text{payable}\end{array}\right)$$

$$\$500,000 \times 9\% \times 6/12 = \$22,500$$

The bond discount amortization is the difference between these two amounts computed above ($23,475 – $22,500 = $975). This amortization would increase the carrying amount of the bonds to $470,475 ($469,500 original carrying amount + $975 amortization).

**13.   (c)**   Under the effective interest method, interest expense is computed as follows:

$$\left(\begin{array}{c}\text{CA of}\\\text{bonds}\end{array}\right) \times \left(\begin{array}{c}\text{Yield}\\\text{rate}\end{array}\right) \times \left(\begin{array}{c}\text{Time}\\\text{period}\end{array}\right) = \left(\begin{array}{c}\text{Interest}\\\text{expense}\end{array}\right)$$

$$\$105,000 \times 6\% \times 12/12 = \$6,300$$

The cash interest payable is computed as follows:

$$\left(\begin{array}{c}\text{FV of}\\\text{bonds}\end{array}\right) \times \left(\begin{array}{c}\text{Stated}\\\text{rate}\end{array}\right) \times \left(\begin{array}{c}\text{Time}\\\text{period}\end{array}\right) = \left(\begin{array}{c}\text{Cash}\\\text{interest}\end{array}\right)$$

$$\$100,000 \times 7\% \times 12/12 = \$7,000$$

The bond premium amortization is the difference between these two amounts ($7,000 – $6,300 = $700). Therefore, the unamortized premium at 6/30/08 is $4,300 ($5,000 – $700).

**14.   (b)**   The requirement is to determine whether the amount of amortization increases each year using the interest method when a bond is sold either at a discount or premium or both. Using the interest method, interest expense for the period is based on the carrying value of the bond multiplied by the effective rate of interest. Cash interest paid for the period equals the face value of the bond multiplied by the stated rate of interest. The difference between these two resulting figures is the amortization of the discount or premium each period. The solutions approach is to prepare a table for a bond issued at a discount and at a premium and examine the direction of the successive amortization amounts. Consider $100,000 of 8% bonds issued on January 1, 2007, due on January 1, 2014, with interest payable each July 1 and January 1. Investors wish to obtain a yield of 10% on the issue. The amortization for the first two periods is as follows:

| Dates | Credit cash | Debit interest expense | Credit bond discount | Carrying value of bonds |
|---|---|---|---|---|
| 1/1/07 | | | | $92,278 |
| 7/1/07 | $4,000 | $4,614 | $614 | 92,892 |
| 1/1/08 | 4,000 | 4,645 | 645 | 93,537 |

Assume the same facts, except the investors wish to obtain a yield of only 6% on the issue.

| Dates | Credit cash | Debit interest expense | Debit bond premium | Carrying value of bonds |
|---|---|---|---|---|
| 1/1/07 | | | | $108,530 |
| 7/1/07 | $4,000 | $3,256 | $744 | 107,786 |
| 1/1/08 | 4,000 | 3,234 | 766 | 107,020 |

The above tables show that when bonds are sold at either a discount or a premium, the amount of amortization using the interest method will increase each year.

**15.   (b)**   Using the effective interest method, interest expense is computed as the **carrying amount** of the bonds multiplied by the **effective rate** of interest. Cash interest paid equals the **face value** of the bonds multiplied by the **stated rate** of interest. The difference between interest expense and cash interest paid is discount amortization. When bonds are issued at a discount, the carrying amount increases each year, so interest expense increases each year, which causes a larger difference between interest expense and interest paid. Therefore, under the effective interest method, the discount amortization amount increases yearly. Under the straight-line method, discount amortization is constant each period. After one year, the incorrect use of the straight-line method would overstate the carrying amount of the bonds since more discount would have been amortized than under the effective interest method. By the time the bonds mature at 1/2/13, the entire discount would have been amortized under both methods, so the carrying amount would be the same for both methods.

**16.   (b)**   The 12/31/07 bond sinking fund balance ($450,000) was increased by the additional investment ($90,000), dividends ($15,000), and interest ($30,000). It was decreased by administration costs ($5,000), resulting in a 12/31/08 balance of $580,000 ($450,000 + $90,000 + $15,000 + $30,000 – $5,000).

**17.   (d)**   SFAS 47 requires disclosure at the balance sheet date of future payments for sinking fund requirements and maturity amounts of long-term debt during each of the next five years. Therefore, the combined aggregate of $17,500,000 of maturities and sinking fund requirements detailed by year should be disclosed.

**18.   (d)**   Companies sometimes place assets in segregated funds for special needs. These funds may become unavailable for normal operations due to debt covenants or other contractual requirements. Funds segregated for long-term needs, such as the bond sinking fund established in this problem, are reported as investments in the noncurrent section of the balance sheet. When interest is earned on investments held in a bond sinking fund, the following journal entry would be made:

| | | |
|---|---|---|
| Bond sinking fund cash | (revenue earned) | |
| Bond sinking fund revenue | | (revenue earned) |

The debit to the bond sinking fund increases the balance of the fund. The amount credited to bond sinking fund revenue is reported in the "Other Income (Expense)" section of the income statement.

**19.   (a)**   Businesses occasionally accumulate a fund of cash and/or investments for a specific purpose, such as the retirement of bonds in this problem. These funds are referred to as "sinking funds." The sinking fund is increased when periodic additions are made to the fund and when revenue is earned on the investments held in the fund. When cash is used to purchase investments, the components of the fund change (i.e., cash is invested and replaced by bonds or other securities), but the total fund balance is not affected.

**20.   (c)**   Debt and equity securities that are classified as **trading securities** are reported at fair market value, with unrealized gains and losses included in earnings. Therefore, at 12/31/07 Wynn would recognize an unrealized holding gain of $35,000 ($945,000 – $910,000) on the income statement, and report the securities at their fair market value of $945,000. In accordance with SFAS 115, securities classified as trading securities are reported at fair market value on the balance sheet.

**21.   (b)**   Interest **receivable** on an investment in bonds is computed using the basic interest formula

$$\left(\begin{array}{c}\text{Face}\\\text{value}\end{array}\right) \times \left(\begin{array}{c}\text{Stated}\\\text{rate}\end{array}\right) \times \left(\begin{array}{c}\text{Time}\\\text{period}\end{array}\right) = \left(\begin{array}{c}\text{Interest}\\\text{receivable}\end{array}\right)$$

$$\$500,000 \ \times \ \ 8\% \ \ \times \ \ \ 6/12 \ \ = \ \ \ \$20,000$$

Note that interest **revenue** is $23,075 ($461,500 × 10% × 6/12) using the interest method.

**22.   (d)**   The bonds should be recorded at an original cost of $215,000 ($220,000 less accrued interest of $5,000). The premium of $15,000 is amortized using the straight-line method over the period from the 10/1/06 date of purchase to the 1/1/13 maturity date (seventy-five months). By 12/31/07, amortization has been recorded for fifteen months (10/1/06 to 12/31/07), so total amortization is $3,000 ($15,000 × 15/75). Therefore, the bonds should be reported on the 12/31/07 balance sheet at $212,000 ($215,000 – $3,000).

**23.   (a)**   When using the interest method of amortization, interest revenue is computed as follows:

$$\left(\begin{array}{c}\text{BV of}\\\text{bonds}\end{array}\right) \times \left(\begin{array}{c}\text{Yield}\\\text{rate}\end{array}\right) \times \left(\begin{array}{c}\text{Time}\\\text{period}\end{array}\right) = \left(\begin{array}{c}\text{Interest}\\\text{expense}\end{array}\right)$$

$$\$906,000 \ \times \ \ 10\% \ \ \times \ \ \ 6/12 \ \ = \ \ \ \$45,300$$

The initial BV is the total amount paid less the accrued interest ($946,000 – $40,000 = $906,000). The amount of interest receivable for the six months is computed below.

$$\left(\begin{array}{c}\text{FV of}\\\text{bonds}\end{array}\right) \times \left(\begin{array}{c}\text{Stated}\\\text{rate}\end{array}\right) \times \left(\begin{array}{c}\text{Time}\\\text{period}\end{array}\right) = \left(\begin{array}{c}\text{Interest}\\\text{receivable}\end{array}\right)$$

$$\$1,000,000 \ \times \ \ 8\% \ \ \times \ \ \ 6/12 \ \ = \ \ \ \$40,000$$

The discount amortized at 12/31/07 is the difference in these two amounts ($45,300 – $40,000 = $5,300). This increases the book value of the investment to $911,300 ($906,000 + $5,300).

**24.   (d)**   The requirement is to determine the most likely cause of the decline in the bonds' market value. When the bonds were acquired at a premium, they sold above their face value. This meant that the stated rate of the bonds was greater than the market rate of interest on an alternative investment of equal risk. Thus, the investors paid more than the face value to acquire the bonds. However, when bonds are quoted at a discount, the stated rate of the bonds is less than the market rate. Therefore, the market rate of interest has increased since Lee purchased the bonds.

**25.   (d)**   At any point in time, an investor's carrying value of a bond held as a long-term investment is equal to the par value of the bond, plus the amount of the unamortized premium, or less the amount of the unamortized discount. A bond purchased at a premium, thus, has a higher carrying value at any point in time than if it had been purchased at a discount. This is logical since its initial cost is also higher when purchased at a premium.

Having determined that the bond purchased at a premium will result in the highest carrying value, we must now determine which amortization method will result in the higher carrying value at the end of the first year. Under the straight-line method, the periodic amortization is constant; it is computed by dividing the total premium by the number of periods involved. Under the effective interest method, the periodic amortization changes over the term of the bond. A review of amortization tables for bonds issued at a premium will demonstrate that the periodic amortization of the premium is lowest in the first period, but increases over subsequent periods. Therefore, the straight-line method would result in higher amortization of the premium at the end of the first year than under the effective interest method. The higher amortization would result in a smaller unamortized premium and lower, overall carrying value at the end of the first year under the straight-line method than under the effective interest method.

**26.   (c)**   The requirement is to determine the purchase price of a bond which will yield the highest interest income for the investor. If the bond's market rate of interest on the date of acquisition is different than the stated rate, the bonds will sell at a premium or discount. If the market rate of interest is higher than the bond's stated rate, the purchase price will be lower than the face value (i.e., discounted). The discount will be recognized over the life of the investment as an addition to interest income. Annual interest income will equal the cash interest received plus the discount amortization for the year. If the bonds are purchased at par (face value), the interest income will equal the cash interest received. The interest income for a bond purchased at a premium would equal the cash interest received less the premium amortization for the year.

**27.   (c)**   When a company uses the effective interest method to amortize a discount on bonds payable, interest expense (which is based on the carrying value of the bonds) is lower in earlier years when compared to interest expense under the straight-line method. Therefore, the straight-line method results in higher interest expense, lower net income, and **understated** retained earnings. Since more interest expense is recorded under the straight-line method, amortization of the discount on bonds payable will be greater under the straight-line method when compared to the effective-interest method. Therefore, the carrying amount of the bonds under the straight-line method is **overstated**.

**28.   (b)**   The gain on sale of the bond investment is the excess of the selling price over the carrying amount. The selling price was $14,000 **above** face value. The bonds were purchased at a discount of $10,000, but after amortization of $2,000 the carrying amount at the time of sale was $8,000 **below** face value. Therefore, the selling price exceeded the carrying amount by $22,000 ($14,000 premium + $8,000 remaining discount).

## B.5.  Convertible Bonds

**29.  (b)**   Using the book value method, the common stock is recorded at the carrying amount of the converted bonds, less any conversion expenses.  Since there are no conversion expenses in this case, the common stock is recorded at the $1,300,000 carrying amount of the converted bonds.  The par value of the stock issued is $50,000 (50,000 × $1), so additional paid-in capital (APIC) of $1,250,000 ($1,300,000 – $50,000) is recorded.  The entry is

| | | |
|---|---|---|
| Bonds payable | 1,000,000 | |
| Premium on B.P. | 300,000 | |
| Common stock | | 50,000 |
| APIC | | 1,250,000 |

Note that when the book value method is used, FMV are not considered, and no gain or loss is recognized.

**30.  (a)**   Under the book value method, the common stock will be recorded at the book value of the bonds at the date of conversion.  Thus, no gain or loss is recognized on the conversion.  The conversion entry credits common stock and APIC, which increases stockholders' equity.  The amount of additional paid-in capital is the difference between the book value of the bonds and the par value of the stock.  The effect of the conversion would be to increase the APIC.  The conversion has no effect on retained earnings.  No gain or loss is recognized.

**31.  (d)**   Per APB 14, convertible debt securities which may be converted into common stock at the option of the holder, and whose issue price is not significantly greater than face value, should be reported as debt upon issuance for the entire proceeds of the bonds.  This reasoning is based on the inseparability of the debt and the conversion option, and the mutually exclusive options of the holder (i.e., holding either bonds or stock).  Contributed capital would be recorded only upon conversion of the bonds to common stock.

**32.  (c)**   When the **book value method** of accounting for the conversion of bonds into common stock is used, the common stock will be recorded at the book value of the bonds at the date of conversion.  Thus, no gain or loss is recognized on the conversion.  When the **market value method** of accounting for the conversion is used, the following journal entry would be made on the books of the issuer (assuming market value > book value):

| | |
|---|---|
| Loss on redemption | (plug) |
| Bonds payable | (book value) |
| Common stock | (par) |
| APIC-common stock | (mkt.-par) |

The debit to the loss account would be for the difference between the market value of the stock and the book value of the bonds.  The market value method assumes a culmination of the earnings process, and a gain or loss on the conversion may be recognized.  In this case, the market value of the stock exceeds the book value of the bonds, and a loss is recognized.

### B.6.  Debt Issued with Detachable Purchase Warrants

**33.  (c)**   APB 14 states that the proceeds of bonds issued with **detachable** warrants are allocated between the bonds and the warrants based upon their relative FMV at the time of issuance.  In this case, the portion allocated to the bonds is $900,000, calculated as follows:

$$\frac{\$1,080,000}{\$1,080,000 + \$120,000} = 90\%; 90\% \times \$1,000,000 = \$900,000$$

Therefore, the bonds payable are reported at $900,000 (face value $1,000,000 less discount $100,000).

**34.  (c)**   APB 14 states that the proceeds from the issuance of debt with **detachable** stock warrants should be allocated between the debt and equity elements.  1,000 bonds ($1,000,000 ÷ $1,000) were issued with fifty detachable stock warrants each, for a total of 50,000 warrants.  Paid-in capital from stock warrants is $200,000 (50,000 × $4).  Since the bonds and warrants were issued for $1,090,000 ($1,000,000 × 109%), the portion of the proceeds allocated to the bonds is $890,000 ($1,090,000 – $200,000) and the discount is $110,000 ($1,000,000 – $890,000).  Note that if a FMV is given for the **bonds without warrants,** APB 14 states that the proceeds should be allocated between the bonds and warrants based on their relative FMV at the time of issuance.

**35.  (d)**   APB 14 states that the proceeds from the issuance of debt with **detachable** stock warrants should be allocated between the debt and equity elements.  500 bonds ($500,000 ÷ $1,000) were issued with thirty detachable stock warrants each, for a total of 15,000 warrants.  Paid-in capital from stock warrants is $60,000 (15,000 × $4).  Note that if a FMV was given for the **bonds without warrants,** APB 14 states that the proceeds should be allocated between the bonds and warrants based on their relative FMV at the time of issuance.

**36.  (a)**   The solutions approach is to set up the original journal entry on the books of the issuer.  The entry would be made as follows:

| | | |
|---|---|---|
| Cash | (proceeds) | |
| Discount on bonds payable | (plug) | |
| Bonds payable | | (face) |
| APIC—Stock warrants | | (fair value) |

Since the APIC—Stock warrants account is already stated at market value, any remaining difference must be allocated to the **bonds**.  Bonds payable would be credited only at their face (par) value.  Therefore, Discount on bonds payable is debited for the excess of the fair value of the warrants and the face amount of the bonds over cash proceeds.

**37.  (c)**   Bonds issued with stock purchase warrants are, in substance, composed of two elements:  a debt element, and a stockholders' equity element.  Per APB 14, proceeds from bonds issued with **detachable** stock purchase warrants should be allocated between the bonds and the warrants on the basis of their relative fair market values.  Detachable warrants trade separately from the debt; thus, a market value is available.  The amount allocated to the warrants should be accounted for as paid-in capital.  Bonds issued with **nondetachable** stock purchase warrants must be surrendered in order to exercise the warrants.  Since this inseparability prevents the determination of individual market values, no allocation is permitted under APB 14.

### B.7.  Extinguishment of Debt

**38.  (b)**   A gain or loss on redemption of bonds is the difference between the **cash paid** ($5,000,000 × 98% = $4,900,000) and the **net book value of the bonds**.  To compute the net book value, premium or discount and bond issue costs must be considered.  Book value is $4,980,000

($5,000,000 face value, less $50,000 bond issue costs, plus $30,000 premium). Therefore the gain or redemption is $80,000 ($4,980,000 book value less $4,900,000 cash paid).

**39. (d)** The gain on early extinguishment of debt is the excess of the book value of the bonds at the time of retirement over the cash paid ($1,000,000 × 101% = $1,010,000). On 1/1/02, the original balance in the premium account was $40,000 ($1,040,000 – $1,000,000). At 7/1/07, the premium had been amortized for five and one-half years, or eleven six-month periods (1/1/02 to 7/1/07). Since the bond term was ten years, or twenty six-month periods, the total premium amortized was $22,000 ($40,000 × 11/20). Therefore, the unamortized premium was $18,000 ($40,000 – $22,000) and the book value of the bonds was $1,018,000 ($1,000,000 + $18,000). A shortcut approach is to take the 1/1/02 book value ($1,040,000) and subtract the amortization ($22,000) to determine the 7/1/07 book value of $1,018,000. The gain is $8,000 ($1,018,000 book value less $1,010,000 cash paid).

**40. (a)** The total bond discount and bond issue costs were $30,000 at the time of issuance [(.02 × $500,000) + $20,000]. By 1/1/08, twelve years have passed since the bonds were issued on 1/1/96. Since the bonds have a fifteen-year life, 12/15 of the discount and issue costs have been amortized, leaving 3/15 unamortized (3/15 × $30,000 = $6,000). When bonds are retired, the bonds and unamortized premium or discount, and/or issue costs must be removed from the books. In this situation, the difference between the net book value of the bonds ($500,000 – $6,000 = $494,000) and the cash paid ($500,000 × 1.02 = $510,000) is recognized as a loss ($510,000 – $494,000 = $16,000).

**SOLUTIONS TO SIMULATION PROBLEMS**

**Simulation Problem 1**

| Situation | Concepts | | | | | |
|---|---|---|---|---|---|---|
| | Bond Valuation | Amortization Schedule | Journal Entries | Communication | | Research |
| | *Bond discounts* | *Bond premium* | *Bond payable* | *Common stock* | *Additional paid-in capital* | *Retained earnings* |
| 1.  Parker issued bonds payable with a nominal interest rate that was less than the market rate of interest. | Increase | No effect | Increase | No effect | No effect | No effect |
| 2.  Parker issued convertible bonds, which are common stock equivalents, for an amount in excess of the bonds' face amount. | No effect | Increase | Increase | No effect | No effect | No effect |
| 3.  Parker issued common stock when the convertible bonds described in item 2 were submitted for conversion.  Each $1,000 bond was converted into twenty common shares. The book value method was used for the early conversion. | No effect | Decrease | Decrease | Increase | Increase | No effect |
| 4.  Parker issued bonds, with nondetachable warrants for an amount equal to the face amount of the bonds.  The stock warrants do not have a determinable value. | No effect | No effect | Increase | No effect | No effect | No effect |
| 5.  Parker issued bonds, with detachable stock warrants, for an amount equal to the face amount of the bonds.  The stock warrants have a determinable value. | Increase | No effect | Increase | No effect | Increase | No effect |
| 6.  Parker redeemed a bond issued at 8% at a discount for an amount that was 102% of face value. | Decrease | No effect | Decrease | No effect | No effect | Decrease |
| 7.  Parker issued bonds payable with a nominal rate of interest that is higher than the market rate. | No effect | Increase | Increase | No effect | No effect | No effect |
| 8.  Parker called a bond that was issued at 105 at a time when the market value of the bond was less than its carrying value. | No effect | Decrease | Decrease | No effect | No effect | Increase |

**Explanation of solutions**

1.   Since the nominal rate of interest was less than the market rate of interest, the bonds sold at a discount.  In other words, the investors paid less than the face value to acquire the bonds.  The journal entry to record the transaction is

| | |
|---|---|
| Cash | xx |
| Discount on bonds payable | xx |
|     Bonds payable |    xx |

Therefore, the issuance of the bonds would increase both bonds payable and discount on bonds payable.

2.   Per APB 14, convertible debt securities which may be converted into common stock at the option of the holder, and whose issue price is not significantly greater than face value, should be reported as debt upon issuance for the entire proceeds of the bonds.  This reasoning is based on the inseparability of the debt and the conversion option, and the mutually exclusive options of the holder (i.e., holding either bonds or stock).  The journal entry to record the transaction is

| | |
|---|---|
| Cash | xx |
|     Premium on bonds payable |    xx |
|     Bonds payable |    xx |

Therefore, the issuance of the convertible bonds would increase both bonds payable and premium on bonds payable.

**3.** When the book value method of accounting for the conversion of bonds into common stock is used, the common stock will be recorded at the book value of the bonds at the date of conversion. Thus, no gain or loss is recognized on the conversion. The journal entry to record the transaction is

| | | |
|---|---|---|
| Bonds payable | xx | |
| Premium on bonds payable | xx | |
|    Common stock | | xx |
|    Additional paid-in capital | | xx |

Therefore, the conversion of the bonds would decrease bonds payable and premium on bonds payable while increasing common stock and additional paid-in capital.

**4.** Per APB 14, nondetachable warrants are not valued separately from the bond. Therefore, the entry to record the bond is

| | | |
|---|---|---|
| Cash | xx | |
|    Bonds payable | | xx |

**5.** APB 14 states that the proceeds of bonds issued with detachable warrants are allocated between the bonds and the warrants based upon their relative fair market values at the time of issuance. In this case, the bonds, with detachable stock warrants, were issued for an amount equal to the face amount of the bonds. Since part of the proceeds is allocated to the stock warrants, the bonds were issued at a discount. The journal entry to record the transaction is

| | | |
|---|---|---|
| Cash | xx | |
| Discount on bonds payable | xx | |
|    Bonds payable | | xx |
|    Additional paid-in capital—Stock warrants | | xx |

Therefore, the issuance of the bonds, with detachable stock warrants, would increase bonds payable, discount on bonds payable, and additional paid-in capital.

**6.** The bond was sold at a discount. Therefore, when the bond is redeemed, the bonds payable and the discount account must be removed from the records. The net carrying amount is less than the reacquisition price. Therefore, there is a loss on the extinguishment of debt. It will be an ordinary loss on the income statement. The journal entry for the transaction is

| | | |
|---|---|---|
| Bonds payable | xx | |
| Loss on bond | xx | |
|    Discount on bond | | xx |
|    Cash | | xx |

**7.** Since the nominal rate of interest is greater than the market rate, the bonds sold at a premium. In other words, the investors paid more than face value for the bond. The journal entry to record the transaction is

| | | |
|---|---|---|
| Cash | xx | |
|    Bonds payable | | xx |
|    Premium on bond | | xx |

**8.** The net carrying value is greater than the market value of the bond (reacquisition price). Therefore, there is a gain on the redemption of the bond. The journal entry for this transaction is

| | | |
|---|---|---|
| Premium on bonds payable | xx | |
| Bonds payable | xx | |
|    Cash | | xx |
|    Gain on extinguishment of debt | | xx |

| Situation | Concepts | Bond Valuation | Amortization Schedule | Journal Entries | Communication | Research |
|---|---|---|---|---|---|---|

PVA of $12,000 at 4% for 20 periods     +     PV of $400,000 at 4% after 20 periods
      (13.5903 × 12,000)     +     (.4564 × $400,000)
        163,083.60     +     183,560

        =  345,643.60

Rounds to 345,644

| Situation | Concepts | Bond Valuation | Amortization Schedule | Journal Entries | Communication | Research |
|---|---|---|---|---|---|---|

| Date | Interest paid | Interest expense | Amortization of discount | Discount on bond payable | Carrying value of bond payable |
|---|---|---|---|---|---|
| 1/2/07 | 0 | 0 | 0 | 54,356 | 345,644 |
| 6/30/07 | 12,000 | 13,826 | 1,826 | 52,530 | 347,470 |
| 12/31/07 | 12,000 | 13,899 | 1,899 | 50,631 | 349,369 |

1. The discount on bonds is (face – carrying value). The carrying value is $345,644, the issue price. Therefore, the discount account is $54,356 ($400,000 – $345,644).

2. The carrying amount at date of issue is the issue price, $345,644.

3. The cash interest payment is $12,000 and is given in the problem. This represents a semiannual interest rate of 3% ($400,000 × 3% = $12,000).

4. The interest expense is $13,826 ($345,644 × 4%) and is given in the problem.

5. Amortization of discount is interest expense minus cash interest payment ($12,000 – $13,826) = $1,826.

6. The discount is amortized by $1,826. The discount account approaches zero as the bond approaches maturity date. Therefore, the discount on 6/30/07 is $52,530 ($54,356 – $1,826).

7. The new carrying amount on 6/30/07 is $347,470 ($345,644 + $1,826).

8. The cash interest payment is the same the previous period. It is always coupon interest rate times the face of the bond (3% × $400,000) = $12,000.

9. Interest expense is the carrying value times the effective rate. $13,899 = ($347,470 × 4%).

10. Amortization is the difference between the cash payment and the interest expense. $1,899 ($12,000 – $13,899).

11. Discount on bonds is $50,631 ($52,530 – $1,899).

12. Carrying amount is $349,369 ($347,470 + $1,899).

| Situation | Concepts | Bond Valuation | Amortization Schedule | Journal Entries | Communication | Research |
|---|---|---|---|---|---|---|
| 1. January 2, 2007 | Cash | | 345,644 | | | |
| | Discount on bonds payable | | 54,356 | | | |
| | Bonds payable | | | 400,000 | | |
| 2. June 30, 2007 | Interest expense | | 13,826 | | | |
| | Cash | | | 12,000 | | |
| | Discount on bonds payable | | | 1,826 | | |

| Situation | Concepts | Bond Valuation | Amortization Schedule | Journal Entries | Communication | Research |
|---|---|---|---|---|---|---|

To:    Finance Manager, Parker Co.
From: CPA Candidate
Re:    Accounting for bonds

I have researched your issues regarding accounting for bonds. This memorandum provides explanations to your questions relating to the amortization and financial statement disclosures for bonds.

The purpose of the effective interest method is to provide periodic interest expense based on a constant rate over the life of the bonds. The impact of applying the effective interest method on Parker's bond premium in 2004 is to decrease the premium by a lesser amount as compared to using the straight-line method of amortization.

Under the straight-line interest method, the premium is amortized at a constant periodic amount, and in 2004 the premium amortization would have been greater than amortization under the effective interest method. Consequently, for 2004, interest expense would have been understated, net income would have been overstated, and the carrying amount of the bonds would have been understated.

The November 30, 2007 transaction results in an ordinary loss. The loss is equal to the excess of the fair value of the cash and property transferred over the bonds' carrying amount on November 30, 2007. This accounting is appropriate because the transaction involves the early extinguishment of debt.

If you have any additional questions, please contact me.

| Situation | Concepts | Bond Valuation | Amortization Schedule | Journal Entries | Communication | Research |
|---|---|---|---|---|---|---|

**APB 21, Para 13–14 or Current Text I69.106–07.**

13. Determining an appropriate interest rate. The variety of transactions encountered precludes any specific interest rate from being applicable in all circumstances. However, some general guides may be stated. The choice of a rate may be affected by the credit standing of the issuer, restrictive covenants, the collateral, payment and other terms pertaining to the debt, and, if appropriate, the tax consequences to the buyer and seller. The prevailing rates for similar instruments of issuers with similar credit ratings will normally help determine the appropriate interest rate for determining the present value of a specific note at its date of issuance. In any event, the rate used for valuation purposes will normally be

at least equal to the rate at which the debtor can obtain financing of a similar nature from other sources at the date of the transaction.  The objective is to approximate the rate which would have resulted if an independent borrower and an independent lender had negotiated a similar transaction under comparable terms and conditions with the option to pay the cash price upon purchase or to give a note for the amount of the purchase which bears the prevailing rate of interest to maturity.

**APB21, Para 14**

14. The selection of a rate may be affected by many considerations.  For instance, where applicable, the choice of a rate may be influenced by (a) an approximation of the prevailing market rates for the source of credit that would provide a market for sale or assignment of the note; (b) the prime or higher rate for notes which are discounted with banks, giving due weight to the credit standing of the maker; (c) published risks that are traded in open markets; and (e) the current rate charged by investors for first or second mortgage loans on similar property.

---

**Simulation Problem 2**

| Situation | Concepts | Journal Entries | Communication | Research |
|---|---|---|---|---|

Indicate whether each item is True or False.

|  |  | *True* | *False* |
|---|---|---|---|
| 1. | Bond issue costs should be treated as deferred charges and amortized over the life of the bond. | ● | ○ |
| 2. | Early extinguishment of debt is treated as an extraordinary item. | ○ | ● |
| 3. | Losses from extinguishment of debt should be amortized over the remaining life of the debt. | ○ | ● |
| 4. | The straight-line method of amortization should be used for bonds due in less than five years. | ○ | ● |
| 5. | Bonds that mature on a single date are called serial bonds. | ○ | ● |
| 6. | The effective interest is calculated by multiplying the maturity value of the bond by the coupon rate. | ○ | ● |
| 7. | A bond premium represents a reduction of interest expense on the books of the issuer. | ● | ○ |
| 8. | When the contract or coupon rate is greater than the effective rate, the bonds will sell at a premium. | ● | ○ |

**Explanation of solutions.**

1. True.  Bond issue costs are amortized over the bond life.

2. False.  Under SFAS 145, early extinguishment of debt no longer receives routine treatment as an extraordinary item.  It must meet the test for an extraordinary item (infrequent **and** usual) in order to receive extraordinary treatment.

3. False.  Losses shall be recognized in the period of extinguishment.

4. False.  The effective amortization method should be used.

5. False.  Bonds that mature on a single date are called term bonds.

6. False.  The effective interest in calculated by the carrying value times the effective rate.

7. True.  As the premium is amortized, interest expense is decreased.

8. True.  When a bond pays a higher rate than the market, it will sell for a premium.

| Situation | Concepts | Journal Entries | Communication | Research |
|---|---|---|---|---|

1.  January 1, 2007  Issue bonds

| | | |
|---|---|---|
| Cash | 392,000 | |
| Discount on bonds | 8,000 | |
|  |  |  |
| Bonds payable | | 400,000 |
|  |  |  |
|  |  |  |

**2.** September 1, 2007 Issue bonds with detachable warrants

| Cash | 530,000 | |
|---|---|---|
| Discount on bonds | 12,973 | |
| | | |
| Bonds payable | | 500,000 |
| Additional paid-in capital—warrants | | 42,973 |
| | | |

**3.** October 1, 2007 Conversion of bonds

| Bonds payable | 50,000 | |
|---|---|---|
| Premium on bonds payable | 2,150 | |
| | | |
| Common stock | | 10,000 |
| Additional paid-in capital | | 42,150 |
| | | |

| Situation | Concepts | Journal Entries | Communication | Research |
|---|---|---|---|---|

To:     Controller, Castle Co.
From: CPA Candidate
Re:     Accounting for bonds

I have received your note inquiring about the proper accounting for bonds. Below are answers to your specific questions.

The bond issue price would be determined by the expected future cash flows of principal and interest, discounted at the market rate of interest, plus the value of the conversion option at the date of issuance.

Castle should account for the issuance of the convertible bonds by increasing cash for the issue price, increasing bonds payable by the face amount, and increasing premium on bonds payable for the balance. The convertible debt is accounted for solely as debt. The conversion option is not recognized primarily because it is inseparable from the debt, and secondarily because of the practical difficulty of assigning it a value.

Castle should account for the conversion of the bonds into common stock by decreasing both bonds payable and unamortized bond premium by 30%, increasing common stock by $25 for each share issued, and increasing additional paid-in capital by the difference between the three previous amounts.

If we can be of further assistance, please do not hesitate to contact my office.

| Situation | Concepts | Journal Entries | Communication | Research |
|---|---|---|---|---|

The authoritative literature for each of the following transactions is shown below.

**1.** March 1, 2007 issue of bonds

**APB21, Para 16 or Current Text I69.109**

16. Statement presentation of discount and premium. The discount or premium resulting from the determination of present value in cash or noncash transactions is not an asset or liability separable from the note which gives rise to it. Therefore, the discount or premium should be reported in the balance sheet as a direct deduction from or addition to the face amount of the note. It should not be classified as a deferred charge or deferred credit. The description of the note should include the effective interest rate; the face amount should also be disclosed in the financial statements or in the notes to the statements. Amortization of discount or premium should be reported as interest in the statement of income. Issue costs should be reported in the balance sheet as deferred charges.

**2.** September 1, 2007 issue of bonds with warrants

**APB14, Para 16 or Current Text C08.104**

16. The Board is of the opinion that the portion of the proceeds of debt securities issued with detachable stock purchase warrants which is allocable to the warrants should be accounted for as paid-in capital. The allocation should be based on the relative fair values of the two securities at time of issuance. Any resulting discount or premium on the debt securities should be accounted for as such. The same accounting treatment applies to issues of debt securities (issued with detachable warrants) which may be surrendered in settlement of the exercise price of the warrant. However, when stock purchase warrants are not detachable from the debt and the debt se-

curity must be surrendered in order to exercise the warrant, the two securities taken together are substantially equivalent to convertible debt and the accounting specified in paragraph 12 should apply.

**3.**    October 1, 2007 conversion of bonds      **AIN-APB 26, #1 or Current Text D10.501**

In practice, the carrying amount, including any unamortized premium or discount, is credited to the capital accounts upon conversion to reflect the stock issued and no gain or loss is recognized.

## C. Debt Restructure

SFAS 15 (see outline) prescribes accounting for debtors in situations where creditors are compelled to grant relief (i.e., restructure debt) to debtors. Two types of restructure are described. The first is a settlement of the debt at less than the carrying amount and the second is a continuation of the debt with a modification of terms.

SFAS 114 (see outline), as amended by SFAS 118, addresses the accounting by creditors for impairment of certain loans. Impaired loans include all loans that are restructured in a troubled debt restructuring involving a modification of terms.

SFAS 159 provides that an election can be made to value certain financial assets or financial liabilities at fair value. Included in the list of eligible items is modification of debt. If the fair value option is elected, the debt is revalued at fair value and any resulting gain or loss is recognized in earnings for the period. If the fair value option is not elected, then the rules of SFAS 15 apply for the debtor, and the rules of SFAS 114 apply to the creditor. The remainder of this chapter will focus on the rules when the fair value option is **not** elected.

1. **Settlement of Debt**

   a. **Debtors**—If the debt is settled by the exchange of assets, a gain is recognized for the difference between the carrying amount of the debt and the consideration given to extinguish the debt. In accordance with SFAS 145, such gains are no longer extraordinary. If a noncash asset is given, a separate gain or loss is recorded to revalue the noncash asset to FMV as the basis of the noncash asset given. Thus, a two-step process is used: (1) revalue the noncash asset to FMV and (2) determine the restructuring gain. If stock is issued to settle the liability, record the stock at FMV.

   b. **Creditors**

      (1) Assets received in full settlement are recorded at FMV

         (a) Excess of receivable over asset FMV is an ordinary loss
         (b) Subsequently account for the assets as if purchased for cash

*EXAMPLE 1: SETTLEMENT OF DEBT—Debtor company transfers land in full settlement of its loan payable.*

| | |
|---|---|
| Loan payable (5 years remaining) | $90,000 |
| Accrued interest payable on loan | 10,000 |
| Land: | |
|     Book value | 70,000 |
|     Fair value | 80,000 |

| Debtor | | | | Creditor | | |
|---|---|---|---|---|---|---|
| 1. Land | 10,000 | | 1. Land | 80,000 | | |
|   Gain on transfer of | | |   Loss on settlement | 20,000 | | |
|     assets | | 10,000 |     Loan receivable | | 90,000 | |
| 2. Loan payable | 90,000 | |     Interest receivable | | 10,000* | |
|   Interest payable | 10,000 | | | | | |
|     Land | | 80,000 | | | | |
|     Gain on settlement | | | | | | |
|      of debt | | 20,000 | | | | |

\* *If the creditor was a bank or other finance company, this amount would be included as part of Loan receivable.*

2. **Modification of Terms**

   a. **Debtors**

      If the debt is continued with a modification of terms, it is necessary to compare the total future cash flows of the restructured debt (both principal and stated interest) with the prerestructured carrying value. If the total amount of future cash flows is greater than the carrying value, no adjustment is made to the carrying value of the debt; however, a new effective interest rate must be computed. This rate makes the present value of the total future cash flows equal to the present carrying value of debt (principal and accrued interest). If the total future cash flows of the restructured debt are less than the present carrying value, the current debt should be reduced to the amount of the future cash flows and a gain should be recognized. No interest expense would be recognized in subsequent periods because the loan was written down below its carrying value. All payments including those designated as interest would be applied to the principal amount.

If the restructuring consists of part settlement and part modification of payments, first account for the part settlement per the above, and then account for the modification of payments per the above.

b. **Creditors**

Under SFAS 114 a creditor measures impairment based on the present value of expected future cash flows discounted at the loan's effective interest rate. The effective interest rate for a loan restructured in a troubled debt restructuring is based on the original contractual rate, not the rate specified in the restructuring agreement. As a practical expedient, a creditor may measure impairment based on a loan's observable market price, or the fair value of the collateral if the loan is collateral dependent. A loan is collateral dependent if the repayment of the loan is expected to be provided solely by the underlying collateral.

If the measure of the impaired loan is less than the recorded investment in the loan (including accrued interest, net deferred loan fees or costs, and unamortized premium or discount), a creditor shall recognize an impairment by creating a valuation allowance with a corresponding charge to bad debt expense or by adjusting an existing valuation allowance for the impaired loan with a corresponding charge or credit to bad debt expense.

The present value of an impaired loan's expected future cash flows will change from one reporting period to the next because of the passage of time and also may change because of revised estimates in the amount or timing of those cash flows. No guidance is provided on how the creditor should recognize the change in the present value.

The following example of the treatment of modification of terms for creditors demonstrates the accounting for the **debtor** under SFAS 15 and for the **creditor** under SFAS 114.

*EXAMPLE 2: MODIFICATION OF TERMS—GAIN/LOSS RECOGNIZED—Using the previous example with a loan payable of $90,000 and accrued interest payable on the loan of $10,000, assume the interest rate on above loan is 5% and the following modification of terms is made:*

1. *Interest rate is reduced to 4%.*
2. *The accrued interest is forgiven.*
3. *The principal at date of restructure is reduced to $80,000.*

**Debtor**

| Future cash flows (after restructuring): | |
|---|---|
| Principal | $80,000 |
| Interest (5 years × $80,000 × 4%; $3,200 per year) | + 16,000 |
| **Total** cash to be repaid | $96,000 |
| Amount prior to restructure | |
| ($90,000 principal + $10,000 accrued interest) | − 100,000 |
| Gain to be recognized | $ 4,000 |

Analysis of Debtor's Loan Payable Account

| | | | |
|---|---|---|---|
| | | 90,000 | Loan payable before modification of terms |
| Gain | 4,000 | 10,000 | Additional amount payable from accrued interest |
| 4% modified interest payments in years 1-5 | 3,200* 3,200 3,200 3,200 3,200 | 96,000 | Balance after restructure |

\* Note that the $3,200 is recorded as a reduction of principal, not as an interest expense.

**Creditor**

| Present value of future cash flows (after restructuring) discounted at the original effective interest rate of 5% for the 5 years remaining: | |
|---|---|
| Principal ($80,000 × .78353)** | $ 62,682 |
| Interest ($80,000 × 4% × 4.32948)*** | 13,854 |
| Present value of future cash flows | $ 76,536 |
| Recorded investment in loan by creditor | $100,000 |
| Present value of future cash flows after restructuring | 76,536 |
| Impairment loan loss to be recognized by creditor | $ 23,464 |

\*\* PV of 1 for 5 periods at 5%.
\*\*\* PV of ordinary annuity for 5 periods at 5%.

| Debtor (SFAS 15) | | | | Creditor (SFAS 114) | | | |
|---|---|---|---|---|---|---|---|

**Beginning of Year 1**

| Interest payable | 10,000 | | | Bad debt expense | 23,464 | |
|---|---|---|---|---|---|---|
| Loan payable | 4,000 | | | Loan receivable | | 10,000 |
| Loan payable | | 10,000 | | Accrued interest receivable | | 10,000 |
| Gain on restructure of debt | | 4,000 | | Valuation allowance for impaired | | |
| | | | | loans | | 3,464 |

*(The accrued interest is added to the loan payable to arrive at the prerestructure carrying value. The gain reduces the loan payable to the total future cash flows of the restructured debt.)*

*(This entry reduces the principal to $80,000 forgives the accrued interest, and recognizes a loss on impairment.)*

**End of Year 1**

| Loan payable | 3,200 | | | Cash | 3,200 | |
|---|---|---|---|---|---|---|
| Cash | | 3,200 | | Valuation allowance for impaired loans | 627 | |
| | | | | Interest revenue/bad debts expense | | 3,827* |
| | | | | * [($80,000 – $3,464)] × 5% = $3,827 | | |

**End of Year 2**

| Loan payable | 3,200 | | | Cash | 3,200 | |
|---|---|---|---|---|---|---|
| Cash | | 3,200 | | Valuation allowance for impaired loans | 658 | |
| | | | | Interest revenue/bad debts expense | | 3,858* |
| | | | | * [$80,000 – ($3,464 – $627)] × 5% = $3,858 | | |

**End of Year 3**

| Loan payable | 3,200 | | | Cash | 3,200 | |
|---|---|---|---|---|---|---|
| Cash | | 3,200 | | Valuation allowance for impaired loans | 691 | |
| | | | | Interest revenue/bad debts expense | | 3,891* |
| | | | | * [$80,000 – ($3,464 – $627 – $658)] × 5% = $3,891 | | |

**End of Year 4**

| Loan payable | 3,200 | | | Cash | 3,200 | |
|---|---|---|---|---|---|---|
| Cash | | 3,200 | | Valuation allowance for impaired loans | 726 | |
| | | | | Interest revenue/bad debts expense | | 3,926* |
| | | | | * [$80,000 – ($3,464 – $627 – $658 – $691)] × 5% = $3,926 | | |

**End of Year 5**

| Loan payable | 3,200 | | | Cash | 3,200 | |
|---|---|---|---|---|---|---|
| Cash | | 3,200 | | Valuation allowance for impaired loans | 762 | |
| | | | | Interest revenue/bad debts expense | | 3,962* |
| | | | | * [$80,000 – ($3,464 – $627 – $658 – $691 – $726)] × 5% = $3,962 | | |

| Loan payable | 80,000 | | | Cash | 80,000 | |
|---|---|---|---|---|---|---|
| Cash | | 80,000 | | Loan receivable | | 80,000 |

NOTE:  This example does not include any future changes in the amount and timing of future cash flows, due to the complexity of the accounting.

EXAMPLE 3:  MODIFICATION OF TERMS—NO GAIN RECOGNIZED BY DEBTOR—Assume the $90,000 principal is reduced to $85,000.  The interest rate of 5% is reduced to 4%.

| Future cash flows (after restructuring): | |
|---|---|
| Principal | $ 85,000 |
| Interest (5 years × $85,000 × 4%) | 17,000 |
| **Total** cash to be repaid | $102,000 |
| Amount prior to restructure: | |
| ($90,000 principal + $10,000 accrued interest) | – 100,000 |
| Interest expense/revenue to be recognized over 5 years | $ 2,000 |

In Example 3, a new effective interest rate must be computed so that the PV of future payments = $100,000.  A trial and error approach would be used.  For the exam, you need to be prepared to describe this process and the related entries, but you will not have to make such a computation.

**End of Year 1-5**

|  | *Debtor* |  |
|---|---|---|
| Loan payable | xxxx |  |
| Interest expense | xxx |  |
| Cash |  | 3,400 |

**End of Year 5**

|  |  |  |
|---|---|---|
| Loan payable | 85,000 |  |
| Cash |  | 85,000 |

NOTE: *x's equal different amounts each year based on effective interest rate computed.*

**By Creditor**—The creditor would account for the modification in the same way as in the previous example that shows the SFAS 114 approach.  That is, the original effective rate would be used to measure the loss.

To summarize the two basic situations

- **Settlement of debt:** The debtor transfers assets or grants an equity interest to the creditor in full satisfaction of the claim.  Both debtor and creditor account for the fair values of assets transferred and equity interest granted.  A gain or loss is recognized on the asset transferred.  The debtor recognizes a gain and the creditor recognizes a loss for the difference between the recorded value of the debt and the fair values accounted for.

- **Restructuring of the debt:** Under SFAS 15, the terms of the debt are modified in order to reduce or defer cash payments that the debtor is obligated to make to the creditor, but the debt itself is continued.  The debtor accounts for the modification of terms as a reduction in interest expense from the date of restructuring until maturity.  Gains and losses will generally not be recognized unless the total future cash payments specified by the new terms are less than the recorded amount of the debt.  Then the debtor would recognize a gain for the difference.  Under SFAS 114, the creditor accounts for a restructuring using the original effective rate to measure losses.

Refer to the outlines of SFAS 15 and SFAS 114 for the disclosure requirements.

3. **Impairment**

   a. **Debtors**

   The debtor still has a legal obligation to repay the debt, so no entry is made for impairment on the debtor's accounting records.

   b. **Creditors**

   If the creditor determines that, based on current information and events, it is probable that they will be unable to collect all amounts due on an outstanding note receivable, then the note is considered to be impaired.  The criteria for determining uncollectibility of a note should be based on the creditor's normal review procedures.  When a note receivable is considered to be impaired, a loss should be recorded at the time the impairment is discovered.  The loss will be based upon the difference between the current carrying value of the note and the present value of the expected future cash flows from the impaired note, discounted at the loan's contractual rate.

   EXAMPLE 4:  *On January 1, 2007, Spot Corporation issued a $100,000, three-year noninterest-bearing note to yield 10%, to Grover Corporation.  The amortization schedule using the effective interest method for the note is calculated as follows:*

| Date | 10% interest | Carrying value | |
|---|---|---|---|
| 1/1/07 | -- | $ 75,132 | *(present value of 100,000 at 10% for 3 periods, 100,000 × .75132)* |
| 12/31/07 | 7,513 | 82,645 | *(75,132 + 7,513)* |
| 12/31/08 | 8,265 | 90,910 | *(82,645 + 8,265)* |
| 12/31/09 | 9,090 | 100,000 | *(90,910 + 9,090)* |

On December 31, 2007, Spot Co. management determines that it is probable that Grover Co. will be unable to repay the entire note.  It appears as though only $75,000 will be repaid.  Using the effective interest method, the impairment is calculated as follows:

| | |
|---|---|
| Carrying value at 12/31/07 | $82,645 |
| Present value of future receipts | |
| ($75,000, 10%, 2 periods = $75,000 × .82645) | 61,984 |
| Impairment at 12/31/07 | $20,661 |

*The loss due to the impairment of the Grover Co. note will be recorded on Spot Corporation's (the creditor's) books as follows:*

| | | |
|---|---|---|
| Bad debt expense | 20,661 | |
| Allowance for doubtful accounts | | 20,661 |

*The debtor, Grover Co., should not record anything, as it still has a legal obligation to repay the entire $100,000.  The future interest revenue recorded by Spot Co. will be based upon the new carrying value of $61,984.  If there is a significant change in the expected future cash flows, then the impairment should be recalculated and the allowance adjusted accordingly.*

4.  **Research Component**

Four accounting pronouncements address the accounting for debt restructures:  SFAS 15, SFAS 114, SFAS 118, and SFAS 159.  Although the title of SFAS 15 indicates that the standard is for "Accounting for Debtors and Creditors for Troubled Debt Restructuring," portions of the statement have been superseded.  SFAS 15 now addresses only the accounting for debtors.  SFAS 114, issued in May 1993, amends SFAS Statement 15 and details the accounting by creditors for loan impairments.  SFAS 118 amended SFAS 114 by outlining income recognition and disclosures for impaired loans.

When researching impaired loans, it is important that you first distinguish whether you are taking the perspective of the debtor or the creditor.  Using the word debtor or creditor in your search string may help to find the appropriate sites more quickly.  Notice that since 1977, when SFAS 15 was issued, the vocabulary has changed slightly.  More recent pronouncements use the terms "impaired" or "impairment" rather than "troubled debt."  SFAS 159 applies only if the entity elects the fair value option for accounting for a debt modification.

Keywords for researching in this area are shown below.

| | | |
|---|---|---|
| Carrying amount payable | Impairment loan | Restructuring |
| Fair value collateral | Measure impaired loan | Restructuring payables |
| Future cash flows impairment | Modification terms | Troubled debt restructurings |
| Impaired loan | Original contract rate | |

## MULTIPLE-CHOICE QUESTIONS (1-8)

**1.** For a troubled debt restructuring involving only a modification of terms, which of the following items specified by the new terms would be compared to the carrying amount of the debt to determine if the debtor should report a gain on restructuring?

    a.   The total future cash payments.
    b.   The present value of the debt at the original interest rate.
    c.   The present value of the debt at the modified interest rate.
    d.   The amount of future cash payments designated as principal repayments.

**Items 2 and 3** are based on the following:

The following information pertains to the transfer of real estate pursuant to a troubled debt restructuring by Knob Co. to Mene Corp. in full liquidation of Knob's liability to Mene:

| | |
|---|---|
| Carrying amount of liability liquidated | $150,000 |
| Carrying amount of real estate transferred | 100,000 |
| Fair value of real estate transferred | 90,000 |

**2.** What amount should Knob report as a gain (loss) on restructuring of payables?

    a.   $(10,000)
    b.   $0
    c.   $50,000
    d.   $60,000

**3.** What amount should Knob report as a gain (loss) on transfer of real estate?

    a.   $(10,000)
    b.   $0
    c.   $50,000
    d.   $60,000

**4.** On October 15, 2007, Kam Corp. informed Finn Co. that Kam would be unable to repay its $100,000 note due on October 31 to Finn. Finn agreed to accept title to Kam's computer equipment in full settlement of the note. The equipment's carrying value was $80,000 and its fair value was $75,000. Kam's tax rate is 30%. What amounts should Kam report as the gain (loss) on the transfer of assets, and the gain on restructuring of debt?

| | *Transfer gain (loss)* | *Restructuring gain* |
|---|---|---|
| a. | $(5,000) | $25,000 |
| b. | $0 | $30,000 |
| c. | $0 | $20,000 |
| d. | $20,000 | $0 |

**5.** Colt, Inc. is indebted to Kent under an $800,000, 10%, four-year note dated December 31, 2004. Annual interest of $80,000 was paid on December 31, 2005 and 2006. During 2007, Colt experienced financial difficulties and is likely to default unless concessions are made. On December 31, 2007, Kent agreed to restructure the debt as follows:

• Interest of $80,000 for 2007, due December 31, 2007, was made payable December 31, 2008.
• Interest for 2008 was waived.
• The principal amount was reduced to $700,000.

Assume Colt does not elect the fair value option for reporting the debt modification. How much should Colt report as a gain in its income statement for the year ended December 31, 2007?

    a.   $0
    b.   $100,000
    c.   $ 60,000
    d.   $120,000

**6.** Grey Company holds an overdue note receivable of $800,000 plus recorded accrued interest of $64,000. The effective interest rate is 8%. As the result of a court-imposed settlement on December 31, 2007, Grey agreed to the following restructuring arrangement:

• Reduced the principal obligation to $600,000.
• Forgave the $64,000 accrued interest.
• Extended the maturity date to December 31, 2009.
• Annual interest of $40,000 is to be paid to Grey on December 31, 2008 and 2009.

The present value of the interest and principal payments to be received by Grey Company discounted for two years at 8% is $585,734. Grey does not elect the fair value option for reporting the debt modification. On December 31, 2007, Grey would recognize a valuation allowance for impaired loans of

    a.   $ 14,266
    b.   $184,000
    c.   $278,266
    d.   $0

**7.** On December 31, 2005, Marsh Company entered into a debt restructuring agreement with Saxe Company, which was experiencing financial difficulties. Marsh restructured a $100,000 note receivable as follows:

• Reduced the principal obligation to $70,000.
• Forgave $12,000 of accrued interest.
• Extended the maturity date from December 31, 2005 to December 31, 2007.
• Reduced the interest rate from 12% to 8%. Interest is payable annually on December 31, 2006 and 2007.

Present value factors:

| | |
|---|---|
| Single sum, two years @ 8% | .85734 |
| Single sum, two years @ 12% | .79719 |
| Ordinary annuity, two years @ 8% | 1.78326 |
| Ordinary annuity, two years @ 12% | 1.69006 |

In accordance with the agreement, Saxe made payments to Marsh on December 31, 2006 and 2007. Marsh does not elect the fair value option for reporting the modification of debt. How much interest income should Marsh report for the year ended December 31, 2007?

    a.   $0
    b.   $ 5,600
    c.   $ 8,100
    d.   $11,200

**8.** Casey Corp. entered into a troubled debt restructuring agreement with First State Bank. First State agreed to accept land with a carrying amount of $85,000 and a fair value of $120,000 in exchange for a note with a carrying amount of $185,000. What amount should Casey report as a gain from extinguishment of debt in its income statement?

    a.   $0
    b.   $ 35,000
    c.   $ 65,000
    d.   $100,000

**SIMULATION PROBLEM**

**Simulation Problem 1**                              (40 to 50 minutes)

| Situation | | | | | |
|---|---|---|---|---|---|
| | **Present Value** | **Analysis** | **Journal Entries** | **Communication** | **Research** |

Jayson Company has an overdue note receivable from Simpson Corporation for $300,000.  The note was dated January 1, 2005.  It has an annual interest rate of 9%, and interest is paid December 31 of each year.  Simpson paid the interest on the note on December 31, 2005, but Simpson did not pay the interest due in December of 2006.  The current effective rate of interest is 6%.

On January 1, 2007, Jayson agrees to the following restructuring arrangement:

- Reduce the principal to $250,000.
- Forgive the accrued interest.
- Reduce the interest rate to 6%.
- Extend the maturity date of the note to December 31, 2009.

Assume that Jayson does not elect to use the fair value option for reporting the debt modification.

| | **Present Value** | | | | |
|---|---|---|---|---|---|
| **Situation** | | **Analysis** | **Journal Entries** | **Communication** | **Research** |

Calculate the present value of the future cash flows of the restructured note.

| |
|---|
| |

| | | **Analysis** | | | |
|---|---|---|---|---|---|
| **Situation** | **Present Value** | | **Journal Entries** | **Communication** | **Research** |

Calculate the net carrying amount of the prestructured loan.  (For a more realistic exam experience complete this requirement using a spreadsheet program such as Excel.)

| |
|---|
| |

| | | | **Journal Entries** | | |
|---|---|---|---|---|---|
| **Situation** | **Present Value** | **Analysis** | | **Communication** | **Research** |

Prepare the journal entries needed by Jayson for the restructuring of the loan and the interest payment received on December 31, 2007.

January 1, 2007

| | | |
|---|---|---|
| | | |
| | | |
| | | |
| | | |
| | | |
| | | |

December 31, 2007

| | | |
|---|---|---|
| | | |
| | | |
| | | |
| | | |
| | | |

| Situation | Present Value | Analysis | Journal Entries | Communication | Research |
|-----------|---------------|----------|-----------------|---------------|----------|

Write a memo to the CEO of Jayson Company, advising her on the necessary accounting disclosures and the financial statement impact of restructuring the loan from Simpson Corp.

| Situation | Present Value | Analysis | Journal Entries | Communication | Research |
|-----------|---------------|----------|-----------------|---------------|----------|

Using the authoritative literature, determine the interest rate that should be used to calculate the carrying value of the loan after restructuring.  Copy or reference the appropriate literature in the space provided.

| 1. a __ __ | 3. a __ __ | 5. b __ __ | 7. c __ __ | 1st: __/8 = __% |
|---|---|---|---|---|
| 2. d __ __ | 4. a __ __ | 6. a __ __ | 8. c __ __ | 2nd: __/8 = __% |

**MULTIPLE-CHOICE ANSWER EXPLANATIONS**

## C. Debt Restructure

**1.  (a)**   In a restructuring involving only a change in terms, the total future cash payments should be compared to the carrying amount to determine if a gain should be recognized. Answers (b) and (c) are incorrect because the undiscounted future cash flows are compared to the carrying amount. Answer (d) is incorrect because the total amount of future cash flows are compared to the carrying amount.

**2.  (d)**   In this restructure, the debt is retired by the transfer of real estate to the creditor. Per SFAS 15, a gain or loss is recognized on the transfer of real estate, and a gain or loss is recognized on the restructuring. The loss on the transfer of assets is the excess of the real estate's carrying amount over its FMV ($100,000 – $90,000 = $10,000). The restructuring gain is the excess of the carrying amount of the liability over the FMV of the real estate transferred. The restructuring gain is $60,000 ($150,000 – $90,000). The journal entry is

| | | |
|---|---|---|
| Liability | 150,000 | |
| Loss on transfer | 10,000 | |
|   Real estate | | 100,000 |
|   Gain on restructuring | | 60,000 |

**3.  (a)**   In this restructure, the debt is retired by the transfer of real estate to the creditor. Per SFAS 15, a gain or loss is recognized on the transfer of real estate, and a gain or loss is recognized on the restructuring. The loss on the transfer of assets is the excess of the real estate's carrying amount over its FMV ($100,000 – $90,000 = $10,000). The restructuring gain is the excess of the carrying amount of the liability over the FMV of the real estate transferred, net of the related tax effect. The restructuring gain is $60,000 ($150,000 – $90,000). The journal entry is

| | | |
|---|---|---|
| Liability | 150,000 | |
| Loss on transfer | 10,000 | |
|   Real estate | | 100,000 |
|   Gain on restructuring | | 60,000 |

**4.  (a)**   In this restructure, the debt is retired by the transfer of equipment to the creditor. Per SFAS 15, a gain or loss is recognized on the transfer of the equipment, and a gain or loss is recognized on the retirement of the debt. The loss on the transfer of equipment is the excess of the equipment's carrying amount over its fair value ($80,000 – $75,000 = $5,000). The gain on retirement of debt is the excess of the carrying amount of the debt over the fair value of the equipment transferred ($100,000 – $75,000 = $25,000).

**5.  (b)**   The requirement is to determine the amount of gain to be recognized from a troubled debt restructure. According to SFAS 15, if the debt is continued with a modification of terms, a gain is recognized by the debtor if the future cash payments on the debt are less than the carrying value of the debt. For troubled debt restructures, carrying value is defined as the principal amount ($800,000) plus accrued interest ($80,000), or $880,000. The future payments total $780,000 ($700,000 reduced principal and

$80,000 interest). The $100,000 difference ($880,000 – $780,000) is recognized as a restructuring gain.

**6.  (a)**   Under SFAS 114, if the present value of future cash flows is less than the carrying amount of the loan (Principal + Accrued interest) then bad debt expense should be recorded for the total impairment, the accrued interest account should be written off, and the principal balance in the loan receivable account should be reduced to reflect any amounts forgiven. Any remaining balance should be recorded in an allowance account, as follows:

| | | |
|---|---|---|
| Present value of interest and principal payments to be received by Grey Company (as stated in the problem) | | 585,734 |
| Recorded investment by Grey Company ($800,000 principal + $64,000 interest) | | 864,000 |
| Less present value of future cash flows | | (585,734) |
| | | 278,266 |
| | | |
| Bad debt expense | 278,266 | |
|   Loan receivable | | 200,000 |
|   Accrued interest receivable | | 64,000 |
|   Valuation allowance for impaired loans | | 14,266 |

Thus, under SFAS 114, the valuation allowance Grey must recognize is $14,266.

**7.  (c)**   The requirement is to determine the amount of interest revenue to be recorded by Marsh, after a modification of terms type of troubled debt restructure on December 31, 2005.

Under SFAS 114, when a modification of terms results in the present value of future cash flows being less than the carrying amount, then the interest revenue is calculated by using the effective interest method. In this problem the expected future cash flows is determined by discounting the principal and interest at the original effective rate of 12%.

| | | | | |
|---|---|---|---|---|
| 70,000 | × | .79719 | = | 55,803 |
| 5,600 | × | 1.69005 | = | 9,464 |
| Present value of future cash flows | | | | 65,267 |

The interest revenue to be recognized can then be determined using the effective interest method.

| | | |
|---|---|---|
| PV at 12/31/05 | | $65,267 |
| Interest income at 12/31/06 ($65,267 × 12%) | $7,832 | |
| Interest receivable at 12/31/06 (70,000 × 8%) | 5,600 | |
| Increase in carrying value of loan | | 2,232 |
| PV at 12/31/06 | | 67,499 |
| Interest revenue at 12/31/07 (67,499 × 12%) | $8,100 | |

**8.  (c)**   If a debt is settled by the exchange of assets, a restructuring gain is recognized for the difference between the carrying amount of the debt and the fair value of the consideration given to extinguish the debt. If a noncash asset is given, a separate gain or loss is recorded to revalue the nonasset to fair market value as the basis of the noncash asset given. Therefore, a gain of $35,000 ($120,000 – $85,000) will be recorded to revalue the land to fair market value, and a gain of $65,000 ($185,000 – $120,000) will be recorded for the extinguishment of the debt in Casey's income statement.

SOLUTIONS TO SIMULATION PROBLEM

**Simulation Problem 1**

| Situation | Present Value | Analysis | Journal Entries | Communication | Research |
|---|---|---|---|---|---|

PVA ($15,000) at 9%, 3 periods + PV ($250,000) at 9%, 3 periods
2.53130 ($15,000) + .77218 $250,000)
$37,969 + $193,046 = $231,015.

| Situation | Present Value | Analysis | Journal Entries | Communication | Research |
|---|---|---|---|---|---|

| | |
|---|---|
| Prestructure amount | $300,000 |
| + Accrued interest (9% × 300,000) | 27,000 |
| Prestructured loan carrying amount | 327,000 |
| Less PV future cash flows | (231,015) |
| Loss on impairment (Bad debt expense) | $ 95,985 |

| Situation | Present Value | Analysis | Journal Entries | Communication | Research |
|---|---|---|---|---|---|

Journal entries for Jayson Company to record the loan restructure and the interest payment on 12-31-07

| | | |
|---|---|---|
| Bad debt expense | 95,985 | |
| Loan receivable | | 50,000 |
| Interest receivable | | 27,000 |
| Valuation allowance for loan impairment | | 18,985 |
| | | |

| | | |
|---|---|---|
| Cash | 15,000 | |
| Valuation allowance for loan impairment (plug) | 5,791 | |
| Interest income | | 20,791 |
| ($250,000 – $18,985) × 9% = $20,791 interest income | | |

| Situation | Present Value | Analysis | Journal Entries | Communication | Research |
|---|---|---|---|---|---|

Memo to client should contain the following information:

1. This information is based on requirements by SFAS 114 and 118, which require creditors to account for impaired loans.
2. Because Simpson cannot repay on a timely basis, the loan is considered impaired. Since there is a modification in the terms of the agreement, the loan must be written down to present value of the future cash flows that will be collected based on the new loan payment.
3. The interest rate used for discounting is the rate of interest on the original contract.
4. Jayson will need to calculate the prestructure investment in the loan (the carrying amount), which is the face of the loan, accrued interest on the loan, net deferred loan costs, and unamortized premium or discount.
5. This net carrying amount is then compared to the present value of the future cash flows after the restructure, and the difference is considered a loss on the impairment of the loan. The loss on impairment is expensed through the bad debt expense account if a provision has not already been made for the bad debt.
6. An entry should be made to record bad debt expense, reduce the loan receivable to the new restructured amount, and reduce the interest receivable that was accrued and not paid. Any difference will be credited to a valuation allowance for impaired loans, and this amount will be amortized over the life of the loan. Interest revenue will be calculated based on the carrying value of the loan (present value of future cash flows less the valuation allowance) multiplied by the original contract rate before restructure.

| Situation | Present Value | Analysis | Journal Entries | Communication | Research |
|-----------|---------------|----------|-----------------|---------------|----------|

### SFAS 114, Para 14 or Current Text I08.112

14. If a creditor measures an impaired loan using a present value amount, the creditor shall calculate that present value amount based on an estimate of the expected future cash flows of the impaired loan, discounted at the loan's effective interest rate. The effective interest rate of a loan is the rate of return implicit in the loan (i.e., the contractual interest rate adjusted for any net deferred loan fees or costs, premium, or discount existing at the origination or acquisition of the loan.

3. The effective interest rate for a loan restructured in a troubled debt restructuring is based on the original contractual rate, not the rate specified in the restructuring agreement. If the loan's contractual interest rate varies on subsequent changes in an independent factor, such as an index rate (for example, the prime rate, the London offered rate, or the US Treasury bill weekly average), that loan's effective interest rate may be calculated based on the factor as it changes over the life of the loan or may be fixed at the rate in effect at the date the loan meets the impairment criterion in paragraph 9. The creditor's choice shall be applied consistently for all loans whose contractual interest rate varies based on subsequent changes in an independent factor. Projection of changes in the factor should not be made for purposes of determining the effective interest rate or estimating expected future cash flows.

## D.  Pensions

Accounting for pensions involves the use of special terminology.  Mastery of this terminology is essential both to an understanding of problem requirements and to the ability to respond correctly to theory questions.  Review the definitions at the beginning of the outline of SFAS 87 before proceeding with this section of the module.  When you are finished with this section, review the remaining portion of the outline of SFAS 87 and SFAS 158.  Additionally, you should look over the contents of SFAS 88 and SFAS 132(R); SFAS 88 has been tested lightly.  SFAS 132(R) deals solely with employer disclosures about pensions and other postretirement benefits.  It amends Statements 87, 88, and 106.  SFAS 106, which deals with postemployment benefits other than pensions, is modeled very closely after SFAS 87.  Therefore, your knowledge of pensions from SFAS 87, SFAS 132(R), and SFAS 158 should enable you to answer questions on SFAS 106.

In this section the key points covered are as follows:

1. The differences between a defined contribution pension plan and a defined benefit pension plan and the resulting accounting and reporting differences between these two types of plans.
2. The bookkeeping entries made to record an employer's pension expense and the funding of pension cost.
3. The difference between the accumulated benefits actuarial approach and the benefits-years-of-service approach.
4. The calculation and reporting of the additional minimum liability for employers who sponsor defined benefit pension plans.
5. The five elements which, if they all exist, an employer sponsoring a defined benefit pension plan must evaluate for inclusion in its pension expense each year.  These factors are:  (1) service cost, (2) interest cost, (3) actual return on plan assets, (4) amortization of unrecognized prior service cost, and (5) gain or loss.
6. The required disclosures in the financial statements of employers who sponsor pension plans.

### 1.  Employer Sponsor's vs. Plan's Accounting and Reporting

In order to understand the accounting and reporting requirements for pension plans, you must keep in mind that there are two accounting entities involved:  (1) the employer sponsor of the plan, and (2) the pension plan which is usually under the control of a pension trustee.

The employer sponsor reports Pension Expense in its income statement.  In its balance sheet it usually reports a pension liability labeled Accrued/Prepaid Pension Cost (the sum of two accounts, Accrued/Prepaid Pension Cost and Pension Liability, if required) and an Intangible Asset—Deferred Pension Cost (if required).  As discussed later, another entry may be required to accumulated other comprehensive income to report the funding status of the plan.

A separate accounting entity, the pension plan, maintains the following accounts:  Projected Benefit Obligation, Accumulated Benefit Obligation (for reporting purposes only), Vested Benefits (for reporting purposes only), and Plan Assets.  The pension plan pays benefits to the retired employees.

The diagram below shows the relationship of the entities involved in a pension plan, the accounts usually used by each, and the flow of cash.

In addition to the accounts shown in the diagram below, the employer sponsor must also maintain, on a memo basis, accounts for Unrecognized Past Service Cost and Unrecognized Gains and Losses.

You should note as you read the sections below that the projected benefit obligations of the pension plan, the interest on these obligations, the pension plan assets available to meet these obligations, and returns (income) on these plan assets are all economic variables which impact the employer sponsor's yearly calculations of pension expense and its year-end pension liability (or prepaid pension cost).

In the following presentation, key concepts are **boldfaced** to call attention to those terms and phrases that must be clearly understood.

## 2.  An Overview of Employer's Accounting for Pension Plans

Under a **defined contribution plan** the employer agrees to make a defined contribution to a pension plan as determined by the provisions of the plan. Consequently, plan participants will receive at retirement whatever benefits (i.e., payments) the contributions can provide. Accounting for a defined contribution plan is relatively straightforward. Each year the employer records an expense and a related liability for the agreed-upon contribution. Payments are charged against the liability with an offsetting reduction in cash. Additional disclosure requirements include a description of the plan including: employee groups covered, the basis for determining contributions, and the nature and effects of events affecting comparability.

Under a **defined benefit plan** the employer agrees to provide a benefit at retirement that is defined or fixed by a formula. Because the benefits are defined, the employer accepts the risk associated with changes in the variables that determine the amounts needed to meet the obligation to plan participants. These amounts require the use of estimates that may become very complex. However, these estimates are made by actuaries hired by the management of the employer sponsor. They are not made by the sponsoring company's accountants. The remainder of our pension coverage is devoted to a discussion of the issues that arise under this type of plan.

The **accrual accounting objective** for pension costs recognizes the compensation cost of an employee's pension benefits including prior service costs over that employee's service period. Under accrual accounting, pension expense should not be determined on the basis of the employer's cash payout (funding) practices. The **funding of the pension obligation** refers to the amount that the employer contributes to an independent trustee for the pension plan (plans where the fund is under the control of the employer are considered unfunded). Many factors including tax considerations, working capital management, and contractual agreements influence funding decisions. Thus, the amount selected for funding should not govern the determination of the amount to be reported as pension expense under accrual accounting; these events should be distinguished. Although both events can be recorded with one entry, we use two entries to better illustrate this distinction.

| | | |
|---|---|---|
| Pension expense | xxxx | |
|    Accrued/prepaid pension cost | | xxxx |

This adjusting entry is to record the accrued expense. The optional use of the Accrued/Prepaid Pension Cost account simplifies the accounting. If the account has a net debit balance, it is a prepaid asset account. If the account has a net credit balance, it is a liability.

| | | |
|---|---|---|
| Accrued/prepaid pension cost | xxxx | |
|    Cash | | xxxx |

This entry is to record the funding of the pension obligation at the time cash is transferred to the plan's trustee.

The determination of the amounts to be used in the above entries requires the professional expertise of actuaries who assess the benefits to be provided under the pension formula and the characteristics of the employees covered under the plan (e.g., average age). With these factors as given, the actuaries must estimate the values of the variables that will influence the actual amounts to be paid at retirement by making **actuarial assumptions** about factors such as longevity, early retirements, turnover rate, and the rates of return to be earned on invested funds.

The actuarial present value of the obligation determined under the benefits-years-of-service method is referred to as the **projected benefit obligation**. The **accumulated benefit obligation** is the amount computed using the current salary amounts instead of the estimated future salary amounts.

Therefore, if the defined benefit formula is not dependent on the amount of a future salary (say a retiree receives a fixed amount for each month worked), there would be no difference between the two approaches.  If the defined benefit formula is pay-related and salaries are assumed to increase over time, the projected benefit obligation will be a greater amount than the accumulated benefit obligation.

Many of the provisions of SFAS 87 employ the use of amortization procedures that will significantly reduce, over time, the amount of unrecognized pension liability associated with defined benefit plans.  While the FASB conceptually supported immediate recognition of the projected benefit obligation as a balance sheet liability, this position was not adopted in SFAS 87 because it represented too significant a departure from past practices.  SFAS 87 did, however, require a minimum pension liability, which recorded a liability for the difference between the fair value of plan assets and the accumulated benefit obligation.

SFAS 158, issued in September 2006, amended SFAS 87 and requires reporting the funded status of a pension plan.  SFAS 158 requires that both overfunded and underfunded plans must be reported on the balance sheet as either assets or liabilities.  SFAS 158 is effective for all publicly traded companies for all fiscal years ending after December 15, 2006, and for all nonpublicly traded companies for all fiscal years ending after December 15, 2007.

3.  **Funded Status of Pension Plan**

SFAS 158 requires that the funded status of the plan be reported in the balance sheet.  The funded status is the difference between the projected benefit obligation and the fair value of the plan assets at the measurement date.  If the plan is overfunded, a noncurrent asset is recorded on the balance sheet.  If the plan is underfunded, either a current liability, a noncurrent liability, or both are reported on the balance sheet.  Any additional asset or liability not already recognized as pension expense is recognized in other comprehensive income (net of tax).  SFAS 158 also requires that if a plan is amended and either increases or decreases the projected benefit obligation, this amount should be recognized as either a prior service cost or credit.  Prior service costs or credits should be amortized over the future periods of service of the employees expected to receive benefits.

SFAS 158 further requires that all overfunded plans are aggregated and disclosed as a noncurrent asset.  All underfunded plans are aggregated and disclosed as a current liability, noncurrent liability, or both.  In other words, the funding status of plans may NOT be netted (overfunded plans may not be netted with underfunded plans).  SFAS 158 also requires that for fiscal years ending after December 15, 2008, the measurement date for plans is the fiscal year-end, (i.e., balance sheet date) of the entity.  In addition, SFAS 158 amends certain disclosures in notes to the financial statements.  These amended and new disclosures for the notes to the financial statements will be discussed later in this module

This completes the overview of the accounting required by employers for pension plans.  In the next section, the determination of Pension Cost is thoroughly reviewed.  The general term **Pension Cost** is preferred over pension expense because pension cost is included in overhead in the determination of product costs and therefore may be part of inventory in the balance sheet.  When permissible the term "Pension Expense" is used instead because it is simpler and clearer.  The disclosure of the elements included in pension expense is one of the most significant disclosures required by SFAS 132(R) and should be carefully studied.  A comprehensive illustration is presented in Section 5 below.  This illustration integrates the concepts and calculations that have been introduced in the preceding discussions.  Section 4 below is concerned with the additional disclosure requirements that apply.

4.  **Determination of Pension Expense**

The determination of pension expense remains the same for SFAS 87 and SFAS 158.  Pension Expense is a net amount calculated by adding together five factors.  These factors are:  (1) service cost, (2) interest on the projected benefit obligation, (3) expected return on plan assets, (4) amortization of unrecognized prior service cost, and (5) the effect of gains and losses.  Each of these components is discussed below.

a.  **Service cost—Increases pension expense**

**Service cost** is defined as the actuarial present value of benefits attributed by the pension benefit formula to employee service during the current period.  SFAS 87 requires that future salary levels be taken into consideration in this calculation (i.e., the benefits-years-of-service approach).

b. **Interest on projected benefit obligation—Increases expense**

The **interest on the projected benefit obligation** is defined as the increase in the amount of the projected benefit obligation due to the passage of time. Since the pension plan's obligation at the beginning of the year is stated in terms of present value, a provision for interest is required. By the end of the period, the plan's obligation will increase by the amount of interest that would accrue based on the discount (settlement) rate selected. The discount rate selected should be determined by reference to market conditions using such rates as the return on high quality investments or the implicit rate of return in retirement annuities as a basis for comparison. Also, the rate selected must be **explicit** and an unreasonable rate cannot be justified by an argument that the unreasonable rate is **implicitly** valid because of other offsetting actuarial assumptions. The selected discount rate is referred to as the **settlement rate** because it is the rate at which the plan's obligation could be settled.

> EXAMPLE: *Compute the "interest" component of net pension expense for 2007, if the projected benefit obligation was $4,800,000 on January 1, 2007, and the settlement rate is 9%. Answer: Net pension expense for 2007 is increased by $432,000 (9% × $4,800,000) to provide for interest on the projected benefit obligation.*

c. **Actual return on plan assets—Decreases or possibly increases pension expense**

The **actual return on plan assets** is defined as the difference in the fair value of plan assets at the beginning and the end of the period adjusted for contributions made to the plan and benefit payments made by the plan during the period. The formula for determining the actual return is as follows:

Actual return = (End. Bal. of plan assets at fair value – Beg. bal. of plan assets at fair value) + Benefits – Contributions

The **fair value or market value** of plan assets is defined as the price expected in a sales transaction between a willing buyer and seller. **Plan assets** typically include marketable securities and other investments such as real estate that are held in trust for the plan participants. Assets that are under the control of the employer are not considered to be plan assets. In calculating the return on plan assets, considerable leeway has been allowed in measuring the fair value of plan assets.

> EXAMPLE: *Compute the "actual return on plan assets" component of net pension expense, if the fair value of plan assets was $3,100,000 at the beginning of the year and $3,820,000 at year-end. The employer sponsor contributed $450,000 to the plan and the plan paid benefits of $200,000 during the year. Answer: Net pension expense is decreased by $470,000 [($3,820,000 – $3,100,000)] due to the actual return earned on the fair value of plan assets.*

Although the **actual** return on plan assets is measured and disclosed as one of the components of net pension expense, net pension expense will include only an amount equal to the **expected** return on plan assets. This methodology is followed because the difference between the actual return on plan assets and the expected return on plan assets is a canceling adjustment that is included in the gain or loss calculation to be discussed below.

d. **Prior service cost—Increases or possibly decreases pension expense**

**Prior service costs** are retroactive adjustments that are granted to recognize services rendered in previous periods. These costs are caused by either an amendment to an existing plan or the initiation of a new plan where a **retroactive allowance** is made for past services rendered. If, as a result of an amendment to an existing plan, the benefits are increased, then the amount of the plan's projected benefit obligation will increase. The amount of the prior service costs is measured by the increase in the projected benefit obligation caused by the amendment or the initiation of the plan.

While the prior service costs are related to the past, it is assumed that the initiation or amendment of the plan was made with the intent of benefiting the employer's future operations rather than its past operations. Because of this assumption, prior service costs should be amortized over the present and future periods affected. Two methods approved for use in determining the assignment of prior service costs are (1) the expected future years of service method, and (2) the straight-line basis over the average remaining service period of active employees method.

Under the **expected future years of service** method, the total number of employee service years is calculated by grouping employees according to the time remaining to their retirement, based on actuarial assumptions, and multiplying the number in each group by the number of periods remaining to retirement. For example, eight employees expected to work ten years until retirement would contribute eighty expected future years of service to the total. To calculate the amortization of prior service costs for a given year, the number of employee service years applicable to that period is used as the numerator of the fraction and the denominator is the total employee service years based on all the identified groups.  This method produces a declining pattern similar to the amortization applicable to premiums or discounts on serial bonds and the sum-of-the-years' digits method of depreciation.

The **straight-line basis over the average remaining service period** of active employees is a simpler method.  The projected average remaining service period for the affected participants is estimated by the use of a weighted-average method.  For example, ten employees with ten years remaining to retirement, and fifteen employees with twenty years remaining to retirement would have a weighted-average service life of sixteen years computed as follows:  $(10 \times 10 + 15 \times 20)/25$.  In this example, the prior service costs would be amortized and included in pension expense over sixteen years.  Note by including these prior service costs in pension expense, these costs will also be included in the employer's Accrued/Prepaid Pension Cost account over the sixteen years. Thus, the employer will gradually record on its balance sheet the unrecognized liability associated with these prior service costs.

*EXAMPLE:  Compute the "amortization of prior service cost" component of net pension expense for the first three years after an amendment, based on the following facts.  The prior service cost associated with the amendment is determined by the actuaries to be $650,000 (the difference between the projected benefit obligation before and after the amendment).  The employer has 200 employees at the time of the amendment.  It is expected that workers will retire or terminate at the rate of 4% per year, and the employer will use the "expected future years of service" method of amortization.  Answer:  Since the workers will leave at the rate of 8 per year, the denominator of the amortization fraction is computed by summing 200 + 192 + 184 + ... + 8.  This series can be written as 8(25 + 24 + 23 + ... + 1) or 8n(n+1) /2 = 8(25) (26) /2 = 2,600.  The calculations for the first three years and the unamortized balance at year-end are presented in the table below.*

| Year | Amortization fraction | Annual amortization | Unamortized balances |
|---|---|---|---|
| 0 | | | $650,000 |
| 1 | 200/2,600 | $50,000 | 600,000 |
| 2 | 192/2,600 | 48,000 | 552,000 |
| 3 | 184/2,600 | 46,000 | 506,000 |

e.  **Gain or loss—Increases or decreases pension expense**

Net gain or loss is defined as the change in the amount of the projected benefit obligation as well as the change in the value of plan assets (realized and unrealized), resulting from experience being different from that assumed, or from a change in an actuarial assumption.  For this calculation, plan assets are valued at the market-related value, discussed under c. above.

The gain or loss component included in net pension expense consists of two items: (1) the current period difference between the actual and expected return [(Expected rate of return on plan assets) × (Market-related value of plan assets a the beginning of the period)] on plan assets, and (2) amortization of the unrecognized net gain or loss from **previous** periods.  The current  period difference is reported as a component of the current period net pension expense and the unrecognized net gain or loss is subject to amortization.  In the unusual case when a gain or loss arises from an event such as the discontinuation of a business component, the gain or loss should be recognized immediately and associated with the event that was the cause (e.g., discontinued operations) rather than the pension plan.

When the amortization of the cumulative unrecognized net gain or loss from previous periods is required, the procedure is comparable to the amortization of prior service cost and, in general, it requires the use of a systematic method applied on a consistent basis that is dependent on the average remaining service period for active employees.  Unlike past service cost, however, the amount to be amortized is not necessarily the calculated amount of the cumulative unrecognized net gain or loss.  Instead, the minimum amount subject to amortization is determined by the use of a method sometimes referred to as the "corridor" approach.  The minimum amount of the cumulative unrecognized gain or loss required to be amortized is determined by computing, at the beginning of the fiscal year, the excess of the cumulative unrecognized gain or loss over 10% of the greater of the projected benefit obligation or the market-related asset value.  If the cumulative unrecognized gain or loss is equal to or less than the 10% calculated value, no amount need be amortized.

*EXAMPLE:  Compute the "gain or loss" component of net pension expense and the other elements of pension expense based on the following facts:*

*At the beginning of the year the cumulative unrecognized net loss was $500,000, the fair value and market-related value of plan assets was $3,100,000, and the projected benefit obligation was $4,800,000.  The expected return on assets for the year was 9% and the settlement rate was 11%.  The fair value of plan assets at the end of the year was $3,400,000.  There were no contributions to the plan during the year.  The plan made no benefit payments during the year.  Service costs for the year were $400,000.  At the beginning of the year the average remaining service period of active employees was ten years.  There are no other factors to be considered in computing pension expense for the year.*

*Answer:  The elements of net pension expense are calculated as follows:*

| | | |
|---|---:|---|
| Service cost | $400,000 | |
| Interest (.11 × $4,800,000) | 528,000 | |
| Actual return on plan assets | (300,000) | (1) |
| Amortization of unrecognized net loss | 2,000 | (2) |
| Asset gain deferred | 21,000 | (3) |
| Net pension expense | $651,000 | |

*NOTE:  The above components of pension expense are required to be disclosed in the employer sponsor's financial statements.  This would be done in the footnotes to those statements.*

(1)  *$3,400,000 less $3,100,000 less contributions to the plan of $0 plus benefit payments of the plan of $0.*
(2)  *Amortization of unrecognized net loss is calculated as follows:*

| | |
|---|---:|
| "Corridor" 10% × $4,800,000 | $480,000 |
| Cumulative unrecognized net loss at the beginning of the year | 500,000 |
| Excess to be amortized | $ 20,000 |

*Amortization of unrecognized loss is:  $20,000/10 years = $2,000.*

(3)  *The asset gain deferred of $21,000 is calculated as follows:  Actual return on plan assets of $300,000 less expected return on plan assets of $279,000.  The expected return on plan assets is determined by multiplying the expected return on plan assets of 9% times the market-related value of plan assets at the beginning of the year of $3,100,000.  Note that in the above computation of pension expense actual return on assets of $300,000 is included as required by SFAS 87.  However, the expected return on plan assets of $279,000 ($300,000 – $21,000) is the amount that is actually included in pension expense for the year.*

## 5.  Disclosures for Pensions, SFAS 132(R) and SFAS 158

SFAS 158 changed the reporting requirements for the funded status of the pension plans.  As a result, SFAS 158 also amended SFAS 132(R) to reflect those changes.  The required disclosures are as follows:

(1)  A reconciliation schedule of the benefit obligation showing the components separately
(2)  A reconciliation schedule of the fair value of plan assets with the components shown separately
(3)  The funded status of the plans, and the amounts recognized in the balance sheet showing separately the noncurrent assets, current liabilities, and noncurrent liabilities recognized
(4)  Information about plan assets including equity securities and debt securities, a narrative description of investment policies and strategies, a narrative description of the basis used to determine overall expected rate-of-return on assets, disclosure of additional asset categories and information about assets if information is expected to be useful
(5)  For defined benefit pension plans, the accumulated benefit obligation
(6)  The benefits expected to be paid in each of the next five fiscal years and in the aggregate for the five fiscal years thereafter
(7)  The employer's best estimate of contributions expected to be paid to the plan during the rest of the fiscal year
(8)  The net periodic benefit cost recognized with the components shown separately
(9)  The net gain or loss and net prior service cost or credit recognized in other comprehensive income (OCI) for the period, and any reclassification adjustments of OCI (amortization of items) that are recognized in pension cost
(10)  The amounts in accumulated OCI that have not yet been recognized as pension costs, showing separately the net gain or loss, the net prior service cost or credit, and net transition asset or obligation
(11)  On a weighted-average basis, the rates used for the assumed discount rate, rate of compensation increase, and expected long-term rate of return on plan assets, and the assumptions used to determine benefit obligations and net benefit cost

(12) The assumed health care cost trend rate, a description of the pattern of change

(13) The effect a 1-percentage-point increase or decrease would have on the aggregated service and interest cost components and the accumulated postretirement benefit obligation for health-care benefits

(14) The amounts and types of securities of the employer and related parties included in plan assets, the approximate amount of future annual benefits of plan participants covered by insurance contracts issued by employer or related parties, and any significant transactions between the employer or related parties and the plan during the year

(15) Any alternative method used to amortize prior service amounts or unrecognized net gains and losses

(16) Any substantive commitments, such as past practice or history of regular benefit increases used to account for benefit obligation

(17) The cost of providing special or contractual termination benefits recognized during the period and a description of the nature of the event

(18) An explanation of any significant changes in the plan assets or the benefit obligation

(19) The amounts in accumulated OCI expected to be recognized as components of pension cost over the fiscal year-end that follows the most recent balance sheet presented, showing separately net gain or loss, net prior service cost or credit, and net transition asset or obligation

(20) The amount and timing of any plan assets expected to be returned to the employer during the next 12-month period (or operating cycle, if longer) after the most recent balance sheet.

## 6.  Comprehensive Illustration

Schaefer Company has sponsored a noncontributory (i.e., employees make no contributions) defined benefit plan for its 100 employees for several years.  Within this group of 100 employees, it is expected that workers will retire or terminate at the rate of 5 per year for the next twenty years starting January 1, 2008.  Prior to 2008, cumulative pension expense recognized in compliance with SFAS 87 exceeded cumulative contributions by $150,000, resulting in a $150,000 balance sheet liability.  As of January 1, 2008, the company has agreed to an amendment to its plan that includes a retroactive provision to recognize prior service.  To illustrate how the provisions of SFAS 87 should be applied, assumptions about the facts relevant to the pension plan for the years 2007 and 2008 are presented in the tables that follow:

| | *1/1/2007* | *1/1/2008* | *12/31/2008* |
|---|---|---|---|
| Plan assets (at fair value = market-related value) | $400,000 | $ 455,000 | $ 760,500 |
| Accumulated benefit obligation (ABO; 60% vested) | 460,000 | 640,000* | 710,000* |
| Projected benefit obligation | 550,000 | 821,500* | 1,033,650* |
| Unrecognized cumulative gain (loss)—due to unexpected decrease in asset value | -- | (106,000) | ? |
| Prior service cost amendment | -- | 105,000 | ? |
| Accrued pension cost (liability) | (150,000) | ? | ? |

\* *Includes effects of amendment*

| | *12/31/2007* | *12/31/2008* |
|---|---|---|
| Service cost | $117,000 | $130,000 |
| Employer's funding contribution | 125,000 | 260,000 |
| Plan assets (at fair value = market-related value) | 455,000 | 760,500 |
| Accumulated benefit obligation (60% vested) | 620,000 | 710,000 |
| Benefits paid by the plan | -- | -- |
| Unrecognized cumulative gain (loss)—due to unexpected decrease in asset value | (106,000) | (103,729) |
| Rate of return on assets | 9% | 10% |
| Settlement rate | 9% | 10% |

### Schedule of Changes in Plan Assets

|  | 2007 | 2008 |
|---|---|---|
| Plan assets at 12/31 | $455,000 | $760,500 |
| Plan assets at 1/1 | 400,000 | 455,000 |
| Increase in plan assets | 55,000 | 305,500 |
| Add:  Benefits paid | -- | -- |
| Less:  Funding contributions for the year | (125,000) | (260,000) |
| Actual return or (loss) on plan assets | (70,000) | 45,500 |
| Expected return on plan assets |  |  |
| 2007:    9% × $400,000 | 36,000 |  |
| 2008:    10% × $455,000 |  | 45,500 |
| Unrecognized gain (loss) | $(106,000) | $      -- |

## Required:

A.  Prepare a supporting schedule to determine the amounts to be reported as pension expense for 2007 and 2008.  The company has decided to use the "expected future years of service" method to amortize the effects of the amendment made in 2008.

B.  Prepare the journal entries required for 2007 and 2008 with respect to the pension plan including any entry necessary to comply with the **minimum liability** requirement.

C.  Prepare pension worksheets for 2007 and 2008.  Note these worksheets summarize Schaefer's general journal entries and changes in its pension-related accounts.  These worksheets also summarize the changes in the pension plan's accounts, unrecognized prior service cost, and unrecognized gain or loss.  Study these worksheets as they are an excellent tool for pulling together the elements of this comprehensive illustration.[1]

D.  Indicate the pension-related amounts that should appear in the company's financial statements prepared at the end of 2007 and 2008.

E.  Prepare disclosures of the funded status of the plan to the liability shown in the company's balance sheet at 1/1/07, 12/31/07, and 12/31/08.

## Solution

## Part A

### REQUIRED FOOTNOTE DISCLOSURE
#### Pension Expense

| Components of net periodic benefit cost | 12/31/07 | 12/31/08 |
|---|---|---|
| 1.  Service cost | $117,000 | $130,000 |
| 2.  Interest cost on projected benefit obligation | 49,500 | 82,150 |
| 3.  Actual loss or (actual return) on plan assets | 70,000 | (45,500) |
| 4.  Amortization of prior service cost | -- | 10,000 |
| 5.  Deferral of "gain" or (loss) | (106,000) | -- |
| 6.  Loss amortization | -- | 2,271 |
| 7.  Recognized actuarial loss | -- | -- |
| Net periodic benefit cost | $130,500 | $178,921 |

NOTE:  This is one of the required disclosures by SFAS 87, 132(R), and SFAS 158 as discussed above.

## Calculations

1.  **Service cost** is given.

2.  **Interest:**  9% × $550,000 (2007), and 10% × $821,500 (2008).  The settlement rate times PBO.

3.  **Actual return:**  ($70,000) for 2007 and $45,500 (same as expected) for 2008.  Note that in 2007, the $70,000 actual loss on plan assets less the $106,000 unrecognized loss equals the expected return ($36,000).

4.  **Prior service cost amortization:**  Compute the denominator of the fraction for amortization by calculating the sum of the estimated remaining service years by adding $100 + 95 + 90 + ... + 10 + 5$.  This series can be written as $5(20 + 19 + 18 + ... + 2 + 1)$ or $5n(n+1)/2 = 5(20)(21)/2 = 1,050$.  For 2008 the amount is $(100/1,050) × $105,000 = $10,000$.

5.  **Loss:**  The $106,000 unrecognized loss that arose in 2007 is not amortized until 2008, because no unrecognized net gain or loss existed at the **beginning** of the year.  The amortization of the unrecognized net gain or loss should be included as a component of pension expense only if the unrec-

ognized net gain or loss existed as of the **beginning** of the year and the unrecognized gain or loss exceeded the corridor. At 1/1/2008 10% of the greater of the projected benefit obligation ($821,500) or the market-related asset value ($455,000) is equal to $82,150. The **minimum loss** to be amortized is $106,000 − $82,150 or $23,850. The average employee service remaining as of 1/1/2007 assuming a constant work force of 100 and an attrition rate of 5 workers per year is $(100 + 95 + 90 + ... + 10 + 5)/100$ or $1,050/100 = 10.5$ years. The amount of the loss recognized in 2008 is $23,850/10.5 = $2,271. Since actual and expected returns are equal in 2008, no further adjustment is required.

## Part B

The journal entries will include three entries: (1) record pension expense for the period; (2) report the cash paid to fund the plan; and (3) report any pension asset or liability caused by overfunding or underfunding the plan. Below are the journal entries required for Schaefer for the first two entries.

*Journal Entries*

|  | 2007 | | 2008 | |
|---|---|---|---|---|
| Pension expense | 130,500 | | 178,921 | |
|    Accrued/prepaid pension cost | | 130,500 | | 178,921 |
| *To record pension expense* | | | | |
| Accrued/prepaid pension cost | 125,000 | | 260,000 | |
|    Cash | | 125,000 | | 260,000 |
| *To record funding* | | | | |

SFAS 158 requires that the balance sheet reflect the funded status of the plan. The status is determined by comparing the projected benefit obligation to the fair value of the plan assets. The end-of-year projected benefit obligation is calculated as shown below.

|  | 2007 | 2008 |
|---|---|---|
| Projected benefit obligation at beginning of year | $550,000 | $ 821,500 |
| Service cost | 117,000 | 130,000 |
| Interest cost* | 49,500 | 82,150 |
| Benefits paid | 0 | 0 |
| Projected benefit obligation at end of year | $716,500 | $1,033,650 |

   * *The interest cost is determined by multiplying the Settlement rate times the beginning projected benefit obligation. ($49,500 = $550,000 × 9%) ($82,150 = $821,500 × 10%)*

Then the funded status of the plan for the two years may be calculated as follows:

|  | 12/31/2007 | 12/31/2008 |
|---|---|---|
| Projected benefit obligation | $716,500 | $1,033,650 |
| Fair value of plan assets | 455,000 | 760,500 |
| Funded status of plan | $(261,500) | $(273,150) |

Because the plan is underfunded at the end of both years, a liability must be included on the balance sheet equal to the underfunded amount. However, the entity will often already have an accrued/prepaid pension account. To determine the liability adjustment needed, the balance in the accrued/prepaid pension cost must be considered. The balances at 12/31/07 and 12/31/08 are calculated below.

|  | 2007 | 2008 |
|---|---|---|
| Accrued/prepaid pension liability at beginning of year | $(150,000) | $(155,500) |
| Funding contributions | 125,000 | 260,000 |
| Accrual (expense) | (130,500) | (178,921) |
| Accrued/prepaid pension liability at end of year | $(155,500) | $ (74,421) |

Finally, the adjustment to establish to recognize the funding status of the plan for each year is calculated as follows:

|  | 12/31/2007 | 12/31/2008 |
|---|---|---|
| Liability required | $261,500 | $273,150 |
| Accrued/prepaid liability | (155,500) | (74,421) |
| Less: Liability adjustment from prior year | 0 | (106,000) |
| Adjustment to liability | $106,000 | $92,729 |

The journal entry to record the underfunded plan is made to other comprehensive income and shown net of tax.

Assuming a 40% tax rate, the entries for 2007 and 2008 would be

| | | |
|---|---|---|
| 2007 entries | | |
| Other comprehensive income | 106,000 | |
|     Accrued pension cost | | 106,000 |
| Deferred tax asset | 42,400 | |
|     OCI—deferred tax asset | | 42,400 |
| 2008 entries | | |
| Other comprehensive income | 92,729 | |
|     Accrued pension cost | | 92,729 |
| Deferred tax asset | 37,092 | |
|     OCI—deferred tax asset | | 37,092 |

Therefore, in 2007, OCI would decrease by $63,600 net of tax, and in 2008, OCI would decrease $55,637 net of tax.

Similarly, if the pension plan were overfunded, Schaefer would record an adjusting entry to record a noncurrent asset for the amount of the plan that is overfunded.

## Part C

**SCHAEFER COMPANY**
*Pension Worksheet—2007*

| | *Debit (credit)* | | | | | *Debit (credit)* | | | |
|---|---|---|---|---|---|---|---|---|---|
| | *General journal entries* | | | | | *Memo entries* | | | |
| *Items* | *Pension expense* | *Cash* | *Prepaid/ accrued cost* | *Accumulated OCI* | *Deferred tax asset (liab)* | *Projected benefit obligation* | *Plan assets* | *Unrecognized prior service cost* | *Unrecognized net gain or loss* |
| Bal. 1/1/2007 | | | (150,000) | | | (550,000) | 400,000 | | |
| Service cost | 117,000 | | | | | (117,000) | | | |
| Interest cost | 49,500 | | | | | (49,500) | | | |
| Actual loss | 70,000 | | | | | | (70,000) | | |
| Deferred gain (loss) | (106,000) | | | | | | | | 106,000 |
| Contribution | | (125,000) | | | | | 125,000 | | |
| Journal entry for 2007 | 130,500 | (125,000) | (5,500) | | | | | | |
| Over/underfunded adjustment | | | (106,000) | (106,000) | | | | | |
| Def. tax adjustment | | | | 42,400 | 42,400 | | | | |
| Bal. 12/31/2007 | | | (261,500) | (63,600) | 42,400 | (716,500)* | 455,000 | | 106,000 |

*Before plan amendment on 1/1/08*

**SCHAEFER COMPANY**
*Pension Worksheet—2008*

| | *Debit (credit)* | | | | | *Debit (credit)* | | | |
|---|---|---|---|---|---|---|---|---|---|
| | *General journal entries* | | | | | *Memos entries* | | | |
| *Items* | *Pension expense* | *Cash* | *Prepaid/ accrued cost* | *Accumulated OCI* | *Deferred tax asset (liab* | *Projected benefit obligation* | *Plan assets* | *Unrecognized prior service cost* | *Unrecognized net gain or loss* |
| Bal. 1/1/2008 | | | (261,500) | (63,600) | 42,400 | (716,500) | 455,000 | | 106,000 |
| Prior service cost amendment | | | | | | (105,000) | | 105,000 | |
| Service cost | 130,000 | | | | | (130,000) | | | |
| Interest cost | 82,150 | | | | | (82,150) | | | |
| Actual return | (45,500) | | | | | | 45,500 | | |
| Prior service cost amort. | 10,000 | | | | | | | (10,000) | |
| Loss amort. | 2,271 | | | | | | | | (2,271) |
| Contribution | | (260,000) | | | | | 260,000 | | |
| Journal entry for 2008 | 178,921 | (260,000) | 81,079 | | | | | | |
| Over/underfunded adjustment | | | (92,729) | (92,729) | | | | | |
| Def. tax adjustment | | | | 37,092 | 37,092 | | | | |
| Bal. 12/31/2008 | | | (273,150) | (119,237) | 79,492 | (1,033,650) | 760,500 | 95,000 | 103,729 |

## Part D

### Required Footnote Disclosure

| | 12/31/2007 | 12/31/2008 |
|---|---|---|
| **Change in benefit obligation** | | |
| Benefit obligation at beginning of year* | $ 550,000 | $ 716,500* |
| Service cost | 117,000 | 130,000 |
| Interest cost | 49,500 | 82,150 |
| Amendment (prior service cost) | -- | 105,000 |
| Actuarial loss (gain) | -- | -- |
| Benefits paid | -- | -- |
| Benefit obligation at end of year | $ 716,500 | $1,033,650 |

\* *Before effect of plan amendment.*

| | 12/31/2007 | 12/31/2008 |
|---|---|---|
| **Change in plan assets** | | |
| Fair value of plan assets at beginning of year | $ 400,000 | $ 455,000 |
| Actual return (loss) on plan assets | (70,000) | 45,500 |
| Employer contribution | 125,000 | 260,000 |
| Benefits paid | -- | -- |
| Fair value of plan assets at end of year | $ 455,000 | $ 760,500 |
| Funded status | $(261,500) | $ (273,150) |

| | 12/31/2007 | 12/31/2008 |
|---|---|---|
| **Amounts recognized in the statement of financial position (balance sheet) consist of** | | |
| Accrued benefit liability | $(261,500) | $ (273,150) |
| Deferred tax asset | 42,400 | 79,492 |
| Accumulated other comprehensive income | (63,600) | (119,237) |

| | 12/31/2007 | 12/31/2008 |
|---|---|---|
| **Other amounts:** | | |
| Net prior service cost recognized in Accumulated OCI | $    0 | $  10,000 |
| Net prior service cost not recognized in Accumulated OCI | | $  95,000 |

6. **Postretirement Benefits other than Pensions (OPEB)**

SFAS 106 (refer to outline) establishes the standard for employers' accounting for other (than pension) postretirement benefits (OPEB). This standard requires a single method for measuring and recognizing an employer's accumulated postretirement benefit obligation (APBO). It applies to all forms of postretirement benefits, although the most material benefit is usually postretirement health care. It uses the fundamental framework established by SFAS 87 and SFAS 88. To the extent that the promised benefits are similar, the accounting provisions are similar. Only when there is a compelling reason is the accounting different. SFAS 132(R) states the required disclosures for employers with postretirement benefits and pensions.

SFAS 158 also changed the accounting for postretirement benefits similar to the changes made for pensions. SFAS 158 requires that companies disclose the status of overfunded and underfunded postretirement plans on their balance sheets. Refer to coverage earlier in this chapter for applications of SFAS 158 and its related disclosures.

There are, however, some fundamental differences between defined benefit pension plans and postretirement benefits other than pensions. The following list presents these differences.

### Differences between Pensions and Postretirement Health Care Benefits*

| Item | Pensions | Health care benefits |
|---|---|---|
| Funding | Generally funded. | Generally *NOT* funded. |
| Benefit | Well-defined and level dollar amount. | Generally uncapped and great variability. |
| Beneficiary | Retiree (maybe some benefit to surviving spouse). | Retiree, spouse, and other dependents. |
| Benefit payable | Monthly | As needed and used. |
| Predictability | Variables are reasonably predictable. | Utilization difficult to predict. Level of cost varies geographically and fluctuates over time |

\* D. Gerald Searfoss and Naomi Erickson, "The Big Unfunded Liability: Postretirement Health Care Benefits," **Journal of Accountancy**, *November 1988, pp. 28-39.*

SFAS 106 requires accrual accounting and adopts the three primary characteristics of pension accounting: (1) delayed recognition (changes are not recognized immediately, but are subsequently recognized in a gradual and systematic way), (2) reporting net cost (aggregates of various items are reported as one net amount), and (3) offsetting assets and liabilities (assets and liabilities are sometimes shown net).

SFAS 106 distinguishes between the **substantive** plan and **written** plan. Although generally the same, the substantive plan (the one understood as evidenced by past practice or by communication of intended changes) is the basis for the accounting if it differs from the written plan.

OPEBs are considered to be deferred compensation earned in an exchange transaction during the time periods that the employee provides services. The expected cost generally should be attributed in equal amounts (unless the plan attributes a disproportionate share of benefits to early years) over the periods from the employee's hiring date (unless credit for the service is only granted from a later date) to the date that the employee attains full eligibility for all benefits expected to be received. This accrual should be followed even if the employee provides service beyond the date of full eligibility.

The transition obligation, under SFAS 106, is the unrecognized and unfunded APBO (accumulated postretirement benefit obligation) for all of the participants in the plan. This obligation can either (1) be recognized immediately as the effect of an accounting change, subject to certain limitations, or (2) be recognized on a delayed basis over future service periods with disclosure of the unrecognized amount. The delayed recognition has to result in, at least, as rapid a recognition as would have been recognized on a pay-as-you-go basis.

> EXAMPLE: A sample illustration of the basic accounting for OPEB as established by SFAS 106 follows: Firstime Accrual Co. plans to adopt accrual accounting for OPEB as of January 1, 2007. All employees were hired at age 30 and are fully eligible for benefits at age 60. There are no plan assets. This first calculation determines the unrecognized transition obligation (UTO).

**Firstime Accrual**
**December 31, 2006**

| Employee | Age | Years of service | Total years when fully eligible | Expected retirement age | Remaining service to retirement | EPBO | APBO |
|----------|-----|------------------|----------------------------------|-------------------------|----------------------------------|----------|----------|
| A | 35 | 5 | 30 | 60 | 25 | $ 14,000 | $ 2,333 |
| B | 40 | 10 | 30 | 60 | 20 | 22,000 | 7,333 |
| C | 45 | 15 | 30 | 60 | 15 | 30,000 | 15,000 |
| D | 50 | 20 | 30 | 60 | 10 | 38,000 | 25,333 |
| E | 55 | 25 | 30 | 65 | 10 | 46,000 | 38,333 |
| F | 60 | 30 | 30 | 65 | 5 | 54,000 | 54,000 |
| G | 65 | RET | -- | | -- | 46,000 | 46,000 |
| H | 70 | RET | -- | | -- | 38,000 | 38,000 |
| | | | | | 85 | $288,000 | $226,332 |

*Calculations*

1.   EPBO (expected postretirement benefit obligation) is usually determined by an actuary, although it can be calculated if complete data is available.
2.   APBO is calculated using the EPBO. Specifically, it is EPBO × (Years of service/total years when fully eligible)
3.   The unrecognized transition obligation (UTO) is the APBO at 12/31/06 since there are no plan assets to be deducted. The $226,332 can be amortized over the average remaining service to retirement of 14.17 (85/6) years or an optional period of twenty years, if longer. Firstime Accrual selected the twenty-year period of amortization.
4.   Note that Employee F has attained full eligibility for benefits and yet plans to continue working.
5.   Note that the above 2006 table is used in the calculation of the 2007 components of OPEB cost that follows.

After the establishment of UTO, the next step is to determine the benefit cost for the year ended December 31, 2007. This calculation follows the framework established by SFAS 87. The discount rate is assumed to be 10%.

**Firstime Accrual**
**OPEB COST**
**December 31, 2007**

| | | |
|----|-------------------------------------------------|----------|
| 1. | Service Cost | $ 5,000 |
| 2. | Interest Cost | 22,633 |
| 3. | Actual Return on Plan Assets | -- |
| 4. | Gain or Loss | -- |
| 5. | Amortization of Unrecognized Prior Service Cost | -- |
| 6. | Amortization of UTO | 11,317 |
| | Total OPEB Cost | $38,950 |

*Calculations*

1.  *Service cost calculation uses only employees not yet fully eligible for benefits.*

| Employee | 1/1/07 EPBO | Total years when fully eligible | Service cost |
|---|---|---|---|
| A | $14,000 | 30 | $   467 |
| B | 22,000 | 30 | 733 |
| C | 30,000 | 30 | 1,000 |
| D | 38,000 | 30 | 1,267 |
| E | 46,000 | 30 | 1,533 |
| Total service cost | | | $5,000 |

2.  *Interest cost is the 1/1/07 APBO of $226,332 × 10% = $22,633.*
3.  *There are no plan assets so there is no return.*
4.  *There is no gain (loss) since there are no changes yet.*
5.  *There is no unrecognized prior service cost initially.*
6.  *Amortization of UTO is the 1/1/07 UTO of $226,332/20 year optional election = $11,317.*

*Assume that Firstime Accrual makes a year-end cash benefit payment of $20,000.  Firstime Accrual's year-end entry to record other postretirement benefit cost for 2007 would be as follows:*

| | | |
|---|---|---|
| Postretirement benefit cost | 38,950 | |
| Cash | | 20,000 |
| Accrued postretirement benefit cost | | 18,950 |

Required disclosures for a postretirement benefit plan are stated in SFAS 106 and SFAS 132(R). The requirements are the same as the requirements for pensions, which have already been covered in this module.

7.  **Postemployment Benefits** (See the outline of SFAS 112)

Benefits made available to former/inactive employees after employment but before retirement. Examples include continuation of health care and life insurance coverage, severance pay, and disability-related benefits.  Criteria for accrual of these benefits are the same as for compensated absences.

   a.  Obligation relates to **services already provided** by the employee,
   b.  Rights to compensation **vest or accumulate,**
   c.  Payment of obligation is **probable,** and
   d.  Amount to be paid is **reasonably estimable**.

Note that the last two are the general criteria for recognizing a loss contingency per SFAS 5.  If is not possible to reliably estimate benefits, disclosure of that fact is required in the footnotes to the financial statements.

8.  **Deferred Compensation**

Deferred compensation is the payment at a future date for work done in an earlier period(s).  Account for these contracts individually on an accrual basis that reflects the terms of the agreement.  Accrue amounts to be paid in future over the employment period from date agreement is signed to full eligibility date.  The rationale for this treatment is matching.

9.  **Research Component**

SFAS 87, issued in 1985, is effective for all fiscal years beginning after December 15, 1988.  This standard covers the components of pension expense and the accounting rules for pensions, except for the disclosures in notes to the financial statements.  SFAS 88 outlines the rules for curtailments of defined benefit plans and termination benefits.  Other postretirement benefit plans other than pensions are covered by SFAS 106.  The disclosures rules in SFAS 106 have also been revised.

SFAS 112 covers Employers' Accounting for Postemployment Benefits.  Although this title sounds similar to SFAS 106, the two standards cover different topics.  SFAS 106 is for other benefits after an employee retires.  SFAS 112 is for other benefits after an employee resigns or is terminated.

The current rules for disclosures in the notes to the financial statements on pension plans and other postemployment benefits are found in SFAS 132(R).  However, SFAS 132(R) did not change any reporting or disclosure rules in SFAS 112.  An analysis of the vocabulary of these standards reveals subtle similarities in terms; therefore, when researching it is important that you carefully select your keywords and choose the correct standard for the research problem.

Keywords for research for SFAS 87, *Employers' Accounting for Pensions*, are shown below.

| Accumulated benefit obligation | Gains and losses | Rate of return plan assets |
| --- | --- | --- |
| Actual return on assets | Interest cost | Service cost |
| Actuarial present value | Market-related value plan assets | Service cost component |
| Annuity contract | Measurement date minimum liability | Unfunded accumulated benefit |
| Attribution period | Net periodic pension cost |    obligation |
| Benefit formula | Pension benefit formula | Unfunded pension cost |
| Contributory plan | Plan amendments | Unrecognized gain loss |
| Defined benefit plan | Plan curtailment | Unrecognized prior service cost |
| Defined contribution pension plan | Prepaid pension cost | Vested benefit obligation |
| Discount rates assumed | Prior service cost | Vested benefits |
| Expected return plan assets | Projected benefit obligation | Years-of-service approach |

Keywords for research in SFAS 88, *Employers' Accounting for Settlements and Curtailments of Defined Benefit Pension Plans and for Termination Benefits,* are as follows:

| Annuity contract | Curtailment loss | Termination benefits |
| --- | --- | --- |
| Curtailment | Settlement pension | Termination plan |
| Curtailment gain | Settlement pension obligation | Termination services |

Keywords for research in SFAS 106, *Employers' Accounting for Postretirement Benefits other than Pensions,* are shown below.  Notice that the words in SFAS 106 are similar to the words used in SFAS 87 for pensions.  When you research, you should be alert for the subtle differences in wording, and make sure you are in the right pronouncement for the particular type of benefit plan that you are researching.

| Accumulated postretirement | Expected return on plan assets | Per capita claims cost |
| --- | --- | --- |
|    benefit obligation | Full eligibility benefit | Period service cost |
| Actual return plan assets | Gain loss component | Postretirement benefits |
| Amortization of unrecognized | Health care benefits | Service cost |
|    prior service cost | Interest cost | Transition asset |
| Attribution period | Market-related value of plan assets | Transition obligation |
| Benefit formula | Net incurred claims | Unfunded accumulated |
| Credited service period | Net periodic postretirement |    postretirement benefit |
| Expected postretirement |    benefit cost |    obligation |
|    obligation | Participation rights | Unrecognized gain loss |

SFAS 112, *Employers' Accounting for Postemployment Benefits*, only addresses benefits that are **not** covered in SFAS 87, 88, and 106.  SFAS 112 states that if certain conditions are met, SFAS 43 (*Accounting for Compensated Absences*) applies.  Postemployment benefits that do not meet those conditions are accounted for in accordance with SFAS 5 (*Accounting for Contingencies*).  SFAS 112 also amends FASB Statements 5 and 43.

Below are keywords for researching postemployment benefits.

| Accrued postemployment benefits | Postemployment benefits conditions | Postemployment employer |
| --- | --- | --- |
| Postemployment benefits | Postemployment compensated |    liability |
|  |    absences |  |

SFAS 132(R), *Employers' Disclosures about Pensions and Other Postretirement Benefits*, was issued in December 2003 and amends SFAS 87, 88, 106, and 132.  This new standard does not address measurement or recognition issues.  It only addresses the information to be included in the disclosures in the notes to the financial statements for pension and other postretirement benefit plans.

Keywords for this standard are shown below.

| Assumed health care cost trend | Net periodic benefit cost component | Reconciliation fair value plan assets |
| --- | --- | --- |
| Assumptions discount rate | Other comprehensive income | Significant change benefit obligation |
| Effect one-percentage-point | Pension liability | Significant change plan assets |
| Funded status plans | Reconciliation benefit obligation |  |

SFAS 158, *Employers' Accounting for Defined Benefit Pension and Other Postretirement Plans,* is an amendment to FASB Statements 87, 88, 106, and 132(R).  Therefore, these changes should be reflected in those standards as amended.  Some vocabulary has changed as a result of SFAS 158.  For example, the term "unrecognized prior service cost" has been changed to prior service cost or credit to reflect changes to plans that can result in either additional costs or additional credits.  SFAS 158 also eliminates the terms "minimum pension liability" and "additional pension liability."  Instead, SFAS 158 refers to the status of the plan as overfunded and underfunded and requires appropriate entries to recognize pension assets or pension liabilities at year-end.

**MULTIPLE-CHOICE QUESTIONS (1-41)**

**1.**   The following information pertains to Lee Corp.'s defined benefit pension plan for 2007:

| | |
|---|---|
| Service cost | $160,000 |
| Actual and expected gain on plan assets | 35,000 |
| Unexpected loss on plan assets related to a 2007 disposal of a subsidiary | 40,000 |
| Amortization of unrecognized prior service cost | 5,000 |
| Annual interest on pension obligation | 50,000 |

What amount should Lee report as pension cost in its 2007 income statement?

    a.   $250,000
    b.   $220,000
    c.   $210,000
    d.   $180,000

**2.**   Jordon Corporation obtains the following information from its actuary.  All amounts given are **as of** 1/1/07 (beginning of the year).

| | *1/1/07* |
|---|---|
| Projected benefit obligation | $1,530,000 |
| Market-related asset value | 1,650,000 |
| Unrecognized net loss | 235,000 |
| Average remaining service period | 5.5 years |

What amount of unrecognized net loss should be recognized as part of pension cost in 2007?

    a.   $70,000
    b.   $42,727
    c.   $14,909
    d.   $12,727

**3.**   Which of the following disclosures is not required of companies with a defined benefit pension plan?

    a.   A description of the plan.
    b.   The amount of pension expense by component.
    c.   The weighted-average discount rate.
    d.   The estimates of future contributions for the next five years.

**4.**   Bulls Corporation amends its pension plan on 1/1/07.  The following information is available:

| | *1/1/07 amendment* | *1/1/07 after amendment* |
|---|---|---|
| Accumulated benefit obligation | $ 950,000 | $1,425,000 |
| Projected benefit obligation | 1,300,000 | 1,900,000 |

The total amount of unrecognized prior service cost to be amortized over future periods as a result of this amendment is

    a.   $950,000
    b.   $600,000
    c.   $475,000
    d.   $125,000

**5.**   On January 2, 2007, Loch Co. established a noncontributory defined benefit plan covering all employees and contributed $1,000,000 to the plan.  At December 31, 2007, Loch determined that the 2007 service and interest costs on the plan were $620,000.  The expected and the actual rate of return on plan assets for 2007 was 10%.  There are no other components of Loch's pension expense.  What amount should Loch report in its December 31, 2007 balance sheet as prepaid pension cost?

    a.   $280,000
    b.   $380,000
    c.   $480,000
    d.   $620,000

**6.**   Webb Co., a publicly traded company, implemented a defined benefit pension plan for its employees on January 1, 2004.  During 2004 and 2005, Webb's contributions fully funded the plan.  The following data are provided for 2007 and 2006:

| | 2007 *Estimated* | 2006 *Actual* |
|---|---|---|
| Projected benefit obligation, December 31 | $750,000 | $700,000 |
| Accumulated benefit obligation, December 31 | 520,000 | 500,000 |
| Plan assets at fair value, December 31 | 675,000 | 600,000 |
| Projected benefit obligation in excess of plan assets | 75,000 | 100,000 |
| Pension expense | 90,000 | 75,000 |
| Employer's contribution | 90,000 | 50,000 |

What amount should Webb report as a pension liability in its December 31, 2007 balance sheet?

    a.   $ 50,000
    b.   $ 60,000
    c.   $ 75,000
    d.   $100,000

**7.**   Visor Co. maintains a defined benefit pension plan for its employees.  The service cost component of Visor's net periodic pension cost is measured using the

    a.   Unfunded accumulated benefit obligation.
    b.   Unfunded vested benefit obligation.
    c.   Projected benefit obligation.
    d.   Expected return on plan assets.

**8.**   Which of the following components should be included in the calculation of net pension cost recognized for a period by an employer sponsoring a defined benefit pension plan?

| | *Actual return on plan assets, if any* | *Amortization of unrecognized prior service cost, if any* |
|---|---|---|
| a. | No | Yes |
| b. | No | No |
| c. | Yes | No |
| d. | Yes | Yes |

**9.**   Interest cost included in the net pension cost recognized by an employer sponsoring a defined benefit pension plan represents the

    a.   Amortization of the discount on unrecognized prior service costs.
    b.   Increase in the fair value of plan assets due to the passage of time.
    c.   Increase in the projected benefit obligation due to the passage of time.
    d.   Shortage between the expected and actual returns on plan assets.

**10.**   On July 31, 2007, Tern Co. amended its single employee defined benefit pension plan by granting increased benefits for services provided prior to 2007.  This prior service cost will be reflected in the financial statement(s) for

    a.   Years before 2007 only.
    b.   Year 2007 only.
    c.   Year 2007, and years before and following 2007.
    d.   Year 2007, and following years only.

**11.**   Effective January 1, 2007, Flood Co. established a defined benefit pension plan with no retroactive benefits.  The first of the required equal annual contributions was paid on December 31, 2007.  A 10% discount rate was used to calculate service cost and a 10% rate of return was assumed for plan assets. All information on covered employees for 2007 and 2008 is the same. How should the service cost for 2008 compare with 2007, and should the 2007 balance sheet report an accrued or a prepaid pension cost?

|  | Service cost for 2008 compared to 2007 | Pension cost reported on the 2007 balance sheet |
|---|---|---|
| a. | Equal to | Accrued |
| b. | Equal to | Prepaid |
| c. | Greater than | Accrued |
| d. | Greater than | Prepaid |

12. A company that maintains a defined benefit pension plan for its employees reports an unfunded accrued pension cost. This cost represents the amount that the
   a. Cumulative net pension cost accrued exceeds contributions to the plan.
   b. Cumulative net pension cost accrued exceeds the vested benefit obligation.
   c. Vested benefit obligation exceeds plan assets.
   d. Vested benefit obligation exceeds contributions to the plan.

13. The following information pertains to Seda Co.'s pension plan:

| Actuarial estimate of projected benefit obligation at 1/1/07 | $72,000 |
|---|---|
| Assumed discount rate | 10% |
| Service costs for 2007 | 18,000 |
| Pension benefits paid during 2007 | 15,000 |

If **no** change in actuarial estimates occurred during 2007, Seda's projected benefit obligation at December 31, 2007 was
   a. $64,200
   b. $75,000
   c. $79,200
   d. $82,200

14. Which of the following terms includes assumptions concerning projected changes in future compensation when the pension benefit formula is based on future compensation levels (e.g., pay-related and final pay plans)?

|  | Service cost component | Projected benefit obligation | Accumulated benefit obligation |
|---|---|---|---|
| a. | Yes | Yes | Yes |
| b. | Yes | Yes | No |
| c. | No | Yes | No |
| d. | Yes | No | Yes |

15. For a defined benefit pension plan, the discount rate used to calculate the projected benefit obligation is determined by the

|  | Expected return on plan assets | Actual return on plan assets |
|---|---|---|
| a. | Yes | Yes |
| b. | No | No |
| c. | Yes | No |

16. At December 31, 2007, the following information was provided by the Kerr Corp. pension plan administrator:

| Fair value of plan assets | $3,450,000 |
|---|---|
| Accumulated benefit obligation | 4,300,000 |
| Projected benefit obligation | 5,700,000 |

Assume Kerr is a publicly traded company. What is the amount of the pension liability that should be shown on Kerr's December 31, 2007 balance sheet?
   a. $5,700,000
   b. $2,250,000
   c. $1,400,000
   d. $ 850,000

17. Nome Co. sponsors a defined benefit plan covering all employees. Benefits are based on years of service and compensation levels at the time of retirement. Nome determined that, as of September 30, 2007, its accumulated benefit obligation was $380,000, and its plan assets had a $290,000 fair value. The projected benefit obligation on September 30, 2007, was $400,000. In its September 30, 2007 balance sheet, what amount should Nome report as pension liability?
   a. $110,000
   b. $ 90,000
   c. $380,000
   d. $400,000

18. Payne, Inc., a nonpublicly traded company, implemented a defined benefit pension plan for its employees on January 2, 2007. The following data are provided for 2007, as of December 31, 2007:

| Projected benefit obligation | $103,000 |
|---|---|
| Plan assets at fair value | 78,000 |
| Net periodic pension cost | 90,000 |
| Employer's contribution | 70,000 |

What amount should Payne record as pension liability at December 31, 2007?
   a. $0
   b. $25,000
   c. $20,000
   d. $45,000

**Items 19 and 20** are based on the following:

The following data pertains to Hall Co.'s defined-benefit pension plan at December 31, 2007:

| Unfunded projected benefit obligation | $25,000 |
|---|---|
| Unrecognized prior service cost | 12,000 |
| Net periodic pension cost | 8,000 |

Hall made no contributions to the pension plan during 2007.

19. At December 31, 2007, what amount should Hall record as pension liability on the balance sheet?
   a. $ 5,000
   b. $13,000
   c. $17,000
   d. $25,000

20. In its December 31, 2007 statement of stockholders' equity, what amount should Hall report as accumulated other comprehensive income for pension liabilities before tax effects?
   a. $ 5,000
   b. $13,000
   c. $17,000
   d. $25,000

21. According to SFAS 158, an employer sponsoring a defined benefit pension plan must report a liability on the balance sheet equal to
   a. The current year pension cost that was not funded.
   b. The difference between the fair value of plan assets less the accumulated benefit obligation.

c. The difference between the accumulated benefit obligation and the projected benefit obligation.

d. The difference between the fair value of plan assets less the projected benefit obligation.

**22.** Claire, a publicly traded company, has the following defined benefit pension plans with the following information as of December 31, 2007:

|  | *Plan A* | *Plan B* | *Plan C* |
|---|---|---|---|
| Projected benefit obligation | 100,000 | 150,000 | 180,000 |
| Accumulated benefit obligation | 80,000 | 140,000 | 150,000 |
| Fair value of plan assets | 110,000 | 125,000 | 160,000 |

Assume Claire will make no payments within the next 24 months to any pension plan. How should Claire report the pension plans on the December 31, 2007 balance sheet?

a. A noncurrent liability of $35,000.

b. A noncurrent asset of $10,000 and a noncurrent liability of $45,000.

c. A noncurrent liability of $25,000.

d. A noncurrent asset of $30,000 and a noncurrent liability of $25,000.

**23.** Dawson Corporation, a publicly traded company, implemented a defined benefit pension plan for its employees on January 2, 2005. The following data are provided for 2007 and as of December 31, 2007:

| | |
|---|---|
| Projected benefit obligation | $350,000 |
| Accumulated benefit obligation | 320,000 |
| Plan assets at fair value | 362,000 |
| Pension cost for 2007 | 100,000 |
| Employer's contribution for 2007 | 95,000 |

What amount should Dawson report for the pension plan on its December 31, 2007 balance sheet?

a. A current liability of $5,000.

b. No asset or liability.

c. A noncurrent asset of $12,000.

d. A noncurrent asset of $42,000.

**24.** Rose Corporation, a publicly traded company, implemented a defined benefit pension plan for its employees on January 2, 2006. The following data are provided for 2007 and as of December 31, 2007:

| | |
|---|---|
| Projected benefit obligation | $400,000 |
| Accumulated benefit obligation | 360,000 |
| Plan assets at fair value | 362,000 |
| Pension cost for 2007 | 150,000 |
| Pension contribution for 2007 | 150,000 |

Assume that as of January 1, 2007, Rose's pension plan was fully funded, and there were no recorded pension assets or liabilities on the balance sheet. Ignoring tax effects, which of the following entries would be needed to properly record the funding status of Rose's pension plan at December 31, 2007?

a. A debit to noncurrent pension asset of $2,000.

b. A debit to prepaid pension for $150,000.

c. A credit to noncurrent pension liability for $40,000.

d. A debit to other comprehensive income for $38,000.

**25.** Tulip Corporation, a publicly traded company, implemented a defined benefit pension plan for its employees on January 2, 2005. The following data are provided for 2007 and as of December 31, 2007:

| | |
|---|---|
| Projected benefit obligation | $600,000 |
| Accumulated benefit obligation | 550,000 |
| Plan assets at fair value | 520,000 |
| Pension cost for 2007 | 180,000 |
| Pension contribution for 2007 | 150,000 |

Assume that as of January 1, 2007, Tulip's pension plan was fully funded, and there were no recorded pension assets or liabilities on the balance sheet. Assuming a tax rate of 40%, what is the net effect of the required adjustment on accumulated other comprehensive income on December 31, 2007?

a. $90,000 decrease.

b. $108,000 decrease.

c. $36,000 decrease.

d. $0

**26.** On September 1, 2007, Howe Corp. offered special termination benefits to employees who had reached the early retirement age specified in the company's pension plan. The termination benefits consisted of lump-sum and periodic future payments. Additionally, the employees accepting the company offer receive the usual early retirement pension benefits. The offer expired on November 30, 2007. Actual or reasonably estimated amounts at December 31, 2007, relating to the employees accepting the offer are as follows:

- Lump-sum payments totaling $475,000 were made on January 1, 2008.
- Periodic payments of $60,000 annually for three years will begin January 1, 2009. The present value at December 31, 2007, of these payments was $155,000.
- Reduction of accrued pension costs at December 31, 2007, for the terminating employees was $45,000.

In its December 31, 2007 balance sheet, Howe should report a total liability for special termination benefits of

a. $475,000

b. $585,000

c. $630,000

d. $655,000

**27.** SFAS 132 (Revised), *Employers' Disclosures about Pensions and Other Postretirement Benefits*, requires a reconciliation of the beginning and ending balances of the benefit obligation for both defined benefit pension plans and defined postretirement plans. Which of the following items would appear in the schedule related to defined benefit pension plans?

| | *Service cost* | *Benefits paid* |
|---|---|---|
| a. | Yes | No |
| b. | Yes | Yes |
| c. | No | Yes |
| d. | No | No |

**28.** Under the requirements of SFAS 158, a company with a defined benefit pension plan must disclose in the notes to its financial statements

a. A reconciliation of the vested and nonvested benefit obligation of its pension plan with the accumulated benefit obligation.

b. A reconciliation of the accrued or prepaid pension cost reported in its balance sheet with the pension expense reported in its income statement.

c.  A reconciliation of the accumulated benefit obligation of its pension plan with its projected benefit
obligation.
d.  The funded status of its pension plan and the
amounts recognized in the balance sheet showing
separately the noncurrent assets, current liabilities,
and noncurrent liabilities reported.

**29.** SFAS 132 (Revised), *Employers' Disclosures about
Pensions and Other Postretirement Benefits*, requires a
reconciliation of the beginning and ending balances of the
plan assets for both defined pension plans and defined
postretirement plans.  Which of the following items would
appear in the reconciliation schedule related to defined
pension plans?

|     | Benefit payments | Actual return on plan assets |
|-----|------------------|------------------------------|
| a.  | No               | Yes                          |
| b.  | No               | No                           |
| c.  | Yes              | No                           |
| d.  | Yes              | Yes                          |

**30.** Which of the following defined benefit pension plan
disclosures should be made in a company's financial statements?

I.  The amount of net periodic pension cost for the period.
II. The fair value of plan assets.

a.  Both I and II.
b.  I only.
c.  II only.
d.  Neither I nor II.

**31.** According to SFAS 158, which of the following is not a
required disclosure for defined benefit pension plans?

a.  An explanation of a significant change in plan assets if not apparent from other disclosures.
b.  The amount of any unamortized prior service cost
or credit not recognized in the statement of financial position (balance sheet).
c.  The effect of a two-percentage-point increase in
the assumed health care cost trend rate(s).
d.  Reconciliation of beginning and ending balance of
the projected benefit obligation.

**32.** Which of the following rates must be disclosed for defined benefit pension plans?

I.   Assumed discount rate
II.  Expected long-term rate of return on all of the em-
ployer's assets
III. Rate of compensation increase

a.  I and III.
b.  II and III.
c.  I, II, and III.
d.  III only.

**33.** Jan Corp. amended its defined benefit pension plan,
granting a total credit of $100,000 to four employees for
services rendered prior to the plan's adoption.  The employees, A, B, C, and D, are expected to retire from the company
as follows:

A will retire after three years.
B and C will retire after five years.
D will retire after seven years.

What is the amount of prior service cost amortization in the
first year?

a.  $0
b.  $ 5,000
c.  $20,000
d.  $25,000

**34.** The effects of a one-percentage-point increase or decrease in the trend rates for health care costs must be disclosed for which of the following relating to defined benefit
postretirement plans?

I.  The aggregate of the service and interest cost components.
II. The accumulated postretirement benefit obligation.

a.  Both I and II.
b.  I only.
c.  II only.
d.  Neither I nor II.

**35.** According to SFAS 158 and SFAS 132(R), a company
with a defined benefit pension plan must disclose in the
notes to its financial statements all of the following **except**

a.  The funded status of its pension plan with the
amounts recognized in the balance sheet showing
separately the assets, current liabilities, and noncurrent liabilities recognized.
b.  Rates for assumed discount rate, rate of compensation increase, and expected long-term rate of return
on plan assets.
c.  A reconciliation of the accrued or prepaid pension
cost reported in its balance sheet with the pension
expense reported in its income statement.
d.  The recognized amount of the net periodic benefit
cost with the components shown separately.

**36.** The following information pertains to Foster Co.'s defined benefit postretirement plan for the year 2007.

| | |
|---|---|
| Service cost | $120,000 |
| Benefit payment | 55,000 |
| Interest on the accumulated postretirement benefit obligation | 20,000 |
| Unrecognized transition obligation (to be amortized over twenty years) | 200,000 |

Foster Co.'s 2007 net periodic postretirement benefit cost
was

a.  $205,000
b.  $150,000
c.  $ 95,000
d.  $285,000

**37.** Kemp Company provides a defined benefit postretire-
ment plan for its employees.  Kemp adopted the plan on
January 1, 2007, in accordance with the provisions of
SFAS 106, *Employer's Accounting for Postretirement
Benefits other than Pensions*.  Data relating to the pension
plan for 2007 are as follows:

| | |
|---|---|
| Service cost for 2007 | 28,000 |
| Interest on the accumulated postretirement benefit obligation | 5,000 |
| Amortization of the unrecognized transition obligation | 8,000 |

At the end of 2007, Kemp makes a benefit payment of
$10,000 to employees.  In its December 31, 2007 balance
sheet, Kemp should record accrued postretirement benefit
cost of

a.  $35,000
b.  $31,000

    c.   $51,000
    d.   $15,000

**38.** Bounty Co. provides postretirement health care benefits to employees who have completed at least ten years service and are aged fifty-five years or older when retiring. Employees retiring from Bounty have a median age of sixty-two, and no one has worked beyond age sixty-five. Fletcher is hired at forty-eight years old. The attribution period for accruing Bounty's expected postretirement health care benefit obligation to Fletcher is during the period when Fletcher is aged

    a.   48 to 65.
    b.   48 to 58.
    c.   55 to 65.
    d.   55 to 62.

**39.** An employer's obligation for postretirement health benefits that are expected to be provided to or for an employee must be fully accrued by the date the

    a.   Employee is fully eligible for benefits.
    b.   Employee retires.
    c.   Benefits are utilized.
    d.   Benefits are paid.

**40.** Which of the following are correct regarding a transition obligation resulting from the adoption of a defined benefit postretirement plan?

  I.  A transition obligation may be recognized immediately.
 II.  The transition obligation represents the difference between the accumulated postretirement benefit obligation and the fair value of plan assets at the beginning of the year the plan is adopted.
III.  A transition obligation may be amortized on a straight-line basis over a maximum period of twenty years.

    a.   I and II.
    b.   II only.
    c.   I, II, and III.
    d.   II and III.

**41.** Which of the following information should be disclosed by a company providing health care benefits to its retirees?

  I.  The assumed health care cost trend rate used to measure the expected cost of benefits covered by the plan.
 II.  The accumulated postretirement benefit obligation.

    a.   Both I and II.
    b.   I only.
    c.   II only.
    d.   Neither I nor II.

**SIMULATION PROBLEMS**

**Simulation Problem 1**                (25 to 35 minutes)

| Situation | | | | | | |
|---|---|---|---|---|---|---|
| | Concepts | Pension Calculations | Journal Entry | Balance Sheet | Communication | Research |

The following information pertains to Winger Co.'s defined benefit pension plan. The common stock of Winger is publicly traded.

| | |
|---|---|
| Discount rate | 6% |
| Average service life | 12 years |
| *At January 1, 2007:* | |
| Projected benefit obligation | $600,000 |
| Fair value of pension plan assets | 420,000 |
| Accumulated benefit obligation | 380,000 |
| Unrecognized prior service cost | 240,000 |
| *At December 31, 2007:* | |
| Projected benefit obligation | ? |
| Fair value of pension plan assets | 470,200 |

Service cost for 2007 was $80,000. The actual and expected return on assets was 6%. A contribution for pension of $40,000 was made during the year, and $15,000 of benefits were paid. Winger had no prepaid pension or accrued pension liability at December 31, 2006. Winger uses the straight-line method of amortization over the maximum period permitted. Assume no pension benefits are expected to be paid in the next 12 months.

| | Concepts | | | | | |
|---|---|---|---|---|---|---|
| Situation | | Pension Calculations | Journal Entry | Balance Sheet | Communication | Research |

Identify whether each of the following statements is True or False.

|  |  | *True* | *False* |
|---|---|---|---|
| **1.** | A defined contribution plan is a plan where an employer agrees to provide a benefit at retirement defined by a formula. | ○ | ○ |
| **2.** | The present value of the projected benefit obligation is calculated using the benefits years of service method. | ○ | ○ |
| **3.** | Pension liability is calculated by comparing the accumulated benefit obligation with the fair value of plan assets. | ○ | ○ |
| **4.** | A company is required to net overfunded pension plans with underfunded pension plans and report the net amount as either noncurrent asset or noncurrent liability on the balance sheet. | ○ | ○ |
| **5.** | Prior service costs are caused by new individuals entering the plan after the vesting date. | ○ | ○ |
| **6.** | In a defined benefit plan, interest cost represents the increase in the fair value of the plan assets due to the passage of time. | ○ | ○ |
| **7.** | Companies must disclose in the notes to the financial statements the effect that a two percentage point increase in interest costs would have on the aggregate service and interest costs of the accumulated postretirement benefit obligation on health care benefits. | ○ | ○ |
| **8.** | The actual return on plan assets is defined as the difference in the fair value of plan assets at the beginning and the end of the year. | ○ | ○ |

| | | Pension Calculations | | | | |
|---|---|---|---|---|---|---|
| Situation | Concepts | | Journal Entry | Balance Sheet | Communication | Research |

**Part I.**

Calculate the following amounts for Winger's pension cost for 2007.

| | | |
|---|---|---|
| **1.** | _____ | Interest cost |
| **2.** | _____ | Actual return on plan assets |
| **3.** | _____ | Amortization of prior service costs or credits |
| **4.** | _____ | Gain or (Loss) |
| **5.** | _____ | Pension cost for 2007 |
| **6.** | _____ | Projected benefit obligation at December 31, 2007 |

**Part II.**

For the following items determine whether the component Increases or Decreases Winger's unfunded accrued pension liability.

|  | | *Increase* | *Decrease* | *No effect* |
|---|---|:---:|:---:|:---:|
| 1. | Service cost | O | O | O |
| 2. | Interest cost | O | O | O |
| 3. | Actual return on plan assets | O | O | O |
| 4. | Amortization of prior service costs or credits | O | O | O |
| 5. | Gain or loss in 2007 | O | O | O |

| Situation | Concepts | Pension Calculations | Journal Entry | Balance Sheet | Communication | Research |
|---|---|---|---|---|---|---|

Prepare the journal entry to record Winger's pension cost for the period.

| | | |
|---|---|---|
| | | |
| | | |
| | | |

| Situation | Concepts | Pension Calculations | Journal Entry | Balance Sheet | Communication | Research |
|---|---|---|---|---|---|---|

What is the amount of pension assets or liabilities that will be disclosed in each of the following categories on the balance sheet?

1. Current asset _____

2. Noncurrent asset _____

3. Current liability _____

4. Noncurrent liability _____

Winger has no other items that have affected other comprehensive income for the current period or in previous periods. Assuming the tax rate is 30%, what is the amount shown in accumulated other comprehensive income for the period ending December 31, 2007? Indicate whether this amount is a debit or credit.

5. Amount in AOCI _____     Debit     Credit

| Situation | Concepts | Pension Calculations | Journal Entry | Balance Sheet | Communication | Research |
|---|---|---|---|---|---|---|

Winger Co. has just hired a new president, Palmer, and is reviewing its employee benefit plans with the new employee. For current employees, Winger offers a compensation plan for future vacations. Winger also provides postemployment benefits to former or inactive employees.

On the date of Palmer's hire, Palmer entered into a deferred compensation contract with Winger. Palmer is expected to retire in ten years. The contract calls for a payment of $150,000 upon termination of employment following a minimum three-year service period. The contract also provides that interest of 10%, compounded annually, be credited on the amount due each year after the third year.

Mr. Palmer would like to know more about the accounting for postemployment benefits. Write a memo explaining the following issues regarding postemployment benefits:

1. Give an example of postemployment benefits. State the conditions under which Winger is required to accrue liabilities for compensated absences and postemployment benefits. State Winger's disclosure requirements if these conditions, in full or in part, are not met.

2. Describe the general accrual period for amounts to be paid under a deferred compensation contract. State the theoretical rationale for requiring accrual of these liabilities and related expenses.

3. Prepare a schedule of the expense and accrued liability related to Palmer's deferred compensation agreement to be reported in Winger's financial statements for the first four years of the contract.

To:     Mr. Palmer, Winger Company
From:   CPA Candidate
Re:     Postemployment benefits

| Situation | Concepts | Pension Calculations | Journal Entry | Balance Sheet | Communication | Research |
|---|---|---|---|---|---|---|

Winger Company has a single-employer defined benefit pension plan, and a compensation plan for future vacations for its employees.

You have been asked to research the following items and write a memorandum explaining your results.

**1.** Define the interest cost component of net pension cost for a period.

**2.** How should Winger determine its interest cost component of net pension cost for a period?

**3.** Define prior service cost or credits.

**4.** How should Winger account for prior service cost or credits?

**5.** What conditions must be met for Winger to accrue compensation for future vacations?

MULTIPLE-CHOICE ANSWERS

| 1. d | 10. d | 19. d | 28. d | 37. b |
|------|-------|-------|-------|-------|
| 2. d | 11. d | 20. c | 29. d | 38. b |
| 3. d | 12. a | 21. d | 30. a | 39. a |
| 4. b | 13. d | 22. b | 31. c | 40. c |
| 5. c | 14. b | 23. c | 32. a | 41. a |
| 6. c | 15. b | 24. d | 33. c | |
| 7. c | 16. b | 25. a | 34. a | |
| 8. d | 17. a | 26. c | 35. c | 1st: __/41 = __% |
| 9. c | 18. b | 27. b | 36. b | 2nd: __/41 = __% |

MULTIPLE-CHOICE ANSWER EXPLANATIONS

## D.1.-5. Pensions

**1. (d)** Per SFAS 87, the six elements which an employer sponsoring a defined benefit pension plan must include in its net pension cost are service cost, interest cost, actual return on plan assets, amortization of unrecognized prior service cost, deferral of unexpected gain or loss, and amortization of the unrecognized net obligation or unrecognized net asset existing at the date of initial application of SFAS 87. Lee Corp's pension expense is calculated as follows:

| | |
|---|---|
| Service cost | $160,000 |
| Gain (actual and expected) on plan assets | (35,000) |
| Amortization | 5,000 |
| Interest | 50,000 |
| | 180,000 |

Note that per SFAS 87, gains and losses that arise from a single occurrence which is not directly related to the operation of the plan should be reported as part of that occurrence and not as part of the plan's activity. Therefore, the $40,000 unexpected loss on plan assets related to a 2007 disposal of a subsidiary should be reported as part of the "loss on disposal" and not as part of the 2007 pension cost.

**2. (d)** The requirement is to determine the amount of unrecognized net loss to be recognized as a part of pension expense in 2007. Per SFAS 87, the **corridor approach** is to be used to determine gain or loss amortization. Under this approach, only the unrecognized net gain or loss in excess of 10% of the **greater** of the projected benefit obligation (PBO) or the market-related asset value (M-RAV) is amortized. In this case, the M-RAV ($1,650,000) is larger than the PBO ($1,530,000). The corridor is $165,000 (10% × $1,650,000). The unrecognized net loss ($235,000) exceeds the corridor by $70,000 ($235,000 – $165,000). This excess is amortized over the average remaining service period of active employees expected to participate in the plan ($70,000 ÷ 5.5 = $12,727).

**3. (d)** Estimates of future contributions to a defined benefit pension plan are required to be disclosed only for the next fiscal year. Answer (a) is incorrect because a description of the plan is a required disclosure. Answer (b) is incorrect because the amount of pension expense by component is a required disclosure. Answer (c) is incorrect because the weighted-average discount rate is a required disclosure.

**4. (b)** The requirement is to calculate the total amount of unrecognized prior service cost to be amortized over future periods as a result of a pension plan amendment. Prior service cost is the present value of retroactive benefits given to employees for years of service provided before the date of

an amendment to the plan. Per SFAS 87, the cost of these retroactive benefits is measured by the increase in the projected benefit obligation at the date of amendment ($1,900,000 – $1,300,000 = $600,000). This amount will be recognized as expense (amortized) during the service periods of those employees who are expected to receive benefits under the plan.

**5. (c)** Prepaid pension cost is the cumulative excess of the amount funded over the amount recorded as pension expense. In 2007, pension expense is $520,000.

| | |
|---|---|
| Service cost and interest on PBO | $620,000 |
| Actual return on plan assets ($1,000,000 × 10%) | (100,000) |
| Pension expense | $520,000 |

Since 2007 funding was $1,000,000, 12/31/07 prepaid pension cost is $480,000 ($1,000,000 – $520,000).

**6. (c)** As of December 31, 2006, the pension liability for the current year underfunding was $25,000. Before SFAS 158 was issued, the ABO was compared to the fair value of plan assets to determine if there was an additional minimum pension liability that would be reported. As of December 31, 2006, there was no minimum pension liability because the fair value of plan assets, $600,000, was in excess of the ABO of $500,000. Therefore, as of December 31, 2006, there was a pension liability only for the current year's portion of the pension cost that was not funded. In 2007, SFAS 158 applies. SFAS 158 requires the PBO to be compared with the fair value of plan assets, and a liability must be recorded in the balance sheet for the underfunded plan. Therefore, the difference between the PBO and the fair value of the plan assets as of December 31, 2007 ($75,000 minus $675,000) of $75,000 must be reported as a liability on the balance sheet.

**7. (c)** The requirement is to determine how the service cost component of the net periodic pension cost is measured in a defined benefit pension plan. Per SFAS 87 the service cost component recognized shall be determined as "the actuarial present value of benefits attributed by the pension benefit formula to employee service during the period" that is known as the **projected benefit obligation**.

**8. (d)** Per SFAS 87, among the components which should be included in the net pension cost recognized for a period by an employer sponsoring a defined benefit pension plan are **both** actual return on plan assets, if any, and amortization of unrecognized prior service cost, if any.

**9. (c)** Net pension cost (expense) is comprised of six elements. One of these elements is interest on the projected benefit obligation, which is defined as the increase in the amount of the projected benefit obligation due to the passage of time.  Candidates must be careful so as not to confuse "interest cost" with the "actual return" component of net pension cost which is the earnings on the plan assets.  If the latter component is positive, it reduces the net pension cost for the period.

**10.  (d)**   Per SFAS 87 and SFAS 158, "because plan amendments are granted with the expectation that the employer will realize economic benefits in future periods, this Statement ... provides for recognition during the future periods of those employees."  Therefore, the prior service cost will be reflected in the financial statements for 2007 and future years only.

**11.  (d)**   This question addresses the behavior of the components of pension expense over a period of time.  SFAS 87 defines service cost as the actuarial present value of benefits attributed by the pension benefit formula to services rendered by employees during that period.  This problem states that "all information on covered employees for 2007 and 2008 is the same," which indicates that there has been no change in Flood's work force during this two-year period.  The only difference in the service cost for these two years would, therefore, be attributable to differences in the discounting of the benefits.  Each year a group of employees works, the group becomes one year closer to retirement age and to collecting their retirement benefits.  The present value of the benefits earned by employees each year grows as their retirement date grows nearer, because the benefits are discounted over a shorter period of time.  If, for instance, the "average" retirement date for Flood's employees is January 1, 2017, the present value of the benefits for 2008's service will be greater than the present value of 2007 service, because it is discounted eleven years for 2007 versus ten years for 2008.  (This is because every additional year of discounting reduces the present value of the benefits.)  Therefore, the service cost for 2008 will be greater than for 2007.  The problem also states that Flood intends to fund the plan in equal annual installments, and that the discount rate which was used to calculate the service cost is equal to the assumed rate of return on plan assets.  Under these circumstances, to fully fund the pension obligation in equal payments, Flood will contribute an amount which exceeds the pension cost in the first years of the plan and which is less than the pension cost in later years.  The glossary of SFAS 87 defines prepaid pension cost as the cumulative employer contributions in excess of accrued pension cost.  Since 2007's funding would exceed its pension cost, Flood would report a prepaid pension cost on its 2007 balance sheet.  The journal entry to record the funding would be

| | | |
|---|---|---|
| Pension expense | xxx | |
| Prepaid pension cost | xxx | |
| Cash | | xxx |

**12.  (a)**   The requirement is to determine what the "unfunded accrued pension cost" represents.  Per SFAS 87, the unfunded accrued pension cost is a liability recognized when the net periodic pension cost exceeds the amount the employer has contributed to the plan.

**13.  (d)**   The projected benefit obligation is the actuarial present value of the pension obligation at the end of the period.  Since there were no changes in actuarial estimates during the year, the end of period projected benefit obligation is computed as follows:

| | |
|---|---|
| Projected benefit obligation, 1/1/07 | $72,000 |
| Service cost | 18,000 |
| Interest on projected benefit obligation | |
| (10% × $72,000) | 7,200 |
| Benefit payments | (15,000) |
| Pension benefit obligation, 12/31/07 | $82,200 |

Service cost and interest on the projected benefit obligation increase the projected benefit obligation; benefit payments decrease the projected benefit obligation.

**14.  (b)**   The requirement is to determine which of the listed pension terms includes assumptions concerning projected changes in future compensation levels if the pension benefit formula is based on future compensation levels.  Per SFAS 87, the service cost component and the projected benefit obligation reflect projected future compensation levels while the accumulated benefit obligation is measured based on employees' history of service and compensation without an estimate of projected future compensation levels.

**15.  (b)**   Per SFAS 87, the assumed discount rate should reflect the rates at which pension benefits could be effectively settled.  This rate is sometimes referred to as the "settlement rate."  To determine the settlement rate, it is appropriate to look at rates implicit in current prices of annuity contracts that could be used to settle the obligation under the defined benefit plan.  The expected return on plan assets is **not** used to calculate the projected benefit obligation.  The actual return on plan assets is also **not** used to calculate the projected benefit obligation.

**16.  (b)**   SFAS 87, amended by SFAS 158, applies to fiscal year-ends after December 15, 2006, for all publicly traded companies.  SFAS 158 requires that the funding status of the plan be recognized as an asset or liability on the balance sheet.  The difference between Kerr's fair value of plan assets and the projected benefit obligation ($3,450,000 – $5,700,000 = $02,250,000) is the amount of the plan that is underfunded and must be reported as a liability on Kerr's December 31, 2007 balance sheet.

**17.  (a)**   SFAS 158 requires the recognition of a **pension liability** if the projected benefit obligation (PBO) exceeds the FV of the plan assets.  In this case, the excess of the PBO over the FV of plan assets is $110,000 ($400,000 – $290,000).

**18.  (b)**   SFAS 158 requires the reporting of a **pension liability** if the projected benefit obligation (PBO) exceeds the FV of the plan assets.  In this case, the excess of the PBO over the FV of plan assets is $25,000 ($103,000 – $78,000).

**19.  (d)**   SFAS 158 requires that a **pension liability** be reported for the excess of the projected benefit obligation (PBO) over the fair value of the plan assets.  The unfunded projected benefit obligation is this excess.  Therefore, the required liability amount is $25,000.

**20.  (c)**   At December 31, 2007, Hall will record a pension expense of $8,000 and a pension liability of $8,000 for the current year's pension journal entry.  According to SFAS 158, the overfunded or underfunded status of the plan must be recognized on the balance sheet.  Therefore, the unfunded PBO of $25,000 must be recognized as a liability.  An entry must be made to record the adjustment to pension liability for $17,000 (25,000 – 8,000 liability already recorded).  Ignoring the tax effect, the journal entry will include a debit to OCI for $17,000 and a credit to pension liability for $17,000.

**21. (d)** According to SFAS 158, an employer must recognize the overfunded or underfunded status of the pension plan. A liability is reported when the fair value of the plan assets is less than the projected benefit obligation.

**22. (b)** SFAS 158 requires the funded status of the plan to be recognized on the balance sheet. The fair value of plan assets is compared with the projected benefit obligation. Overfunded plans are aggregated and recognized as noncurrent assets on the balance sheet. Underfunded plans are aggregated and recognized as current, noncurrent liabilities, or both. Claire must aggregate Plans B and C, because they are both underfunded. Plan B is underfunded by $25,000 ($125,000 – $150,000), and Plan C is underfunded by $20,000 ($160,000 – $180,000). Because Claire expects to make no payments within the next 12 months, the aggregated underfunded plans are recorded as noncurrent liabilities on the balance sheet. The overfunded amount (Plan A: $110,000 – 100,000) of $10,000 is recognized as a noncurrent asset on the balance sheet. Answer (a) is incorrect because all plans cannot be aggregated. Answers (c) and (d) are incorrect because according to SFAS 158, the accumulated benefit obligation is no longer used to measure the funding status of the plan.

**23. (c)** SFAS 158 requires the funding status of the pension plan to be recorded on the balance sheet. The funding status is determined by comparing the fair value of plan assets to the projected benefit obligation. Dawson's plan assets are $12,000 higher than the projected benefit obligation ($362,000 – 350,000). Therefore, Dawson would be required to report a noncurrent asset of $12,000 on their balance sheet at December 31, 2007. Answer (a) is incorrect because the current liability of $5,000 is part of the journal entry required to record pension cost for the period, and does not reflect the overall funding status of the plan. Answer (b) is incorrect because overfunded or underfunded plans must be recognized on the balance sheet. Answer (d) is incorrect because according to SFAS 158, the accumulated benefit obligation is no longer used to measure the funding status of the plan.

**24. (d)** SFAS 158 requires that the funding status of the pension plan be recorded on the balance sheet. The funding status is determined by comparing the fair value of plan assets to the projected benefit obligation. Because Rose was completely funded as of December 31, 2006, no pension assets or liabilities existed on its balance sheet. The journal entry for 2007 would include a debit to pension cost and a credit to cash for the 2007 pension contribution, which was fully funded for the current year. However, in comparing the PBO and the fair value of plan assets at the end of the year, Rose's pension plan is underfunded by $38,000 ($362,000 – 400,000). Ignoring income tax effects, the entry to record the underfunded plan is to debit other comprehensive income for $38,000 and credit pension liability for $38,000.

**25. (a)** SFAS 158 requires that the funded status of the plan be recognized in the balance sheet. The funding status is determined by comparing the fair value of plan assets to the projected benefit obligation. The pension plan for Rose is underfunded by a total of $180,000 ($520,000 – 600,000). As of December 31, 2007, Rose has recognized a pension liability of $30,000, which is the difference between pension cost for the period and the pension contribution for the period. This $30,000 liability has been recognized as an expense and reduces net income for the period. Because Rose must recognize a $180,000 liability in the balance sheet, an entry must be recorded for the $150,000 needed to increase the pension liability account to the underfunded amount of $180,000. Therefore, the entry to recognize the underfunded portion of the plan would be

| | | |
|---|---|---|
| OCI ($150,000 × 60%) | 90,000 (net of tax) | |
| Deferred tax asset | 60,000 | |
| Pension liability | | 150,000 |

Answer (b) is incorrect because it is necessary to adjust for any existing pension or liability that may exist at year-end. Answers (c) and (d) are incorrect because the accumulated benefit obligation is not used to determine the funded status of the plan.

**26. (c)** Per SFAS 88, when special termination benefits are offered to employees, a loss and liability must be recognized when the employee accepts the offer and the amount can be reasonably estimated. The amount to be recognized shall include any lump-sum payments ($475,000) and the present value of any expected future payments ($155,000). Therefore, the total liability for special termination benefits is $630,000 ($475,000 + $155,000). Note that the reduction of accrued pension costs ($45,000) would reduce the amount of the loss, but would **not** affect the liability. Instead it would be recorded as a reduction of accrued pension costs. The journal entry would be

| | | |
|---|---|---|
| Loss from termination benefits | 585,000 | |
| Accrued pension costs | 45,000 | |
| Liability from termination benefits | | 630,000 |

**27. (b)** The reconciliation schedule for the benefit obligation related to defined benefit pension plans would disclose both the amounts for service cost and benefits paid. Other items that would be disclosed in this reconciliation schedule include (1) interest cost, (2) contributions by plan participants, (3) actuarial gains and losses, (4) plan amendments, (5) divestitures, curtailments, and settlements, and (6) special termination benefits.

**28. (d)** SFAS 158 revised the disclosures required by SFAS 132(R). SFAS 158 requires that the funded status of the pension plans and the amounts be recognized in the balance sheet showing separately the assets, current liabilities, and noncurrent liabilities.

**29. (d)** The reconciliation schedule for the plan assets related to defined benefit pension plans would disclose both the benefit payments and the actual return on plan assets. Other items that would be disclosed in this reconciliation schedule include (1) contributions by the employer, (2) contributions by plan participants, and (3) settlements and divestitures.

**30. (a)** Per SFAS 132 (Revised), an employer sponsoring a defined benefit pension plan must disclose a great deal of information related to the plan. These disclosures include the amount of net periodic pension cost for the period and the fair value of plan assets.

**31. (c)** According to SFAS 158 and SFAS 132(R), the effect of a one-percentage-point increase in the assumed health care cost trend rate(s) is required, not a two-percentage-point increase. An explanation of a significant change in plan assets, if not apparent from other disclosures, is required according to SFAS 132 (Revised). The amount of any unamortized prior service cost or credit not recognized in the statement of financial position (balance sheet) is a required disclosure. Another required disclosure per SFAS 132 (Revised) is a reconciliation of beginning and ending balances of the projected benefit obligation.

**32.  (a)**  According to SFAS 132(R), the assumed discount rate and the rate of compensation increase are both required disclosures. The expected long-term rate of return on all of the employer's assets is not required. The expected long-term rate of return on plan assets is required, however.

**33.  (c)**  There are two methods approved for use in determining the assignment of prior service cost: the expected years of service method, and the straight-line basis over the average remaining service period of active employees method. Under the expected future years of service method, the total number of employee service years is calculated by grouping employees according to the time remaining to their retirement and multiplying the number in each group by the number of periods remaining to retirement. [(1 person × 3) + (2 people × 5) + (1 person × 7) = 20]. To calculate the amortization of prior service costs for a given year, the number of employee service years applicable to that period is used as the numerator of the fraction, and the denominator is the total employee service years based on all the identified groups. (4/20 × $100,000 = $20,000) For the straight-line basis over the average remaining service period method, the total number of service years (calculated above) is divided by the number of employees to find the weighted-average service life of each employee. (20/4 = 5 yrs.) The $100,000 of prior service cost will be amortized over the five years, or at $20,000 ($100,000 ÷ 5 = $20,000) a year.

**34.  (a)**  SFAS 132(R) requires the disclosure of the effects of a one-percentage-point increase or decrease of the trend rates for health care costs on: the aggregate of the service and interest cost components and the accumulated postretirement obligation.

**35.  (c)**  A reconciliation of the accrued or prepaid pension cost reported in its balance sheet with the pension expense reported in its income statement is not required. Answer (a) is incorrect because SFAS 158 requires that the funded status of the pension plan must be reported in the balance sheet as noncurrent assets, current liabilities, and noncurrent liabilities. Answer (b) is also incorrect because rates for assumed discount rate, rate of compensation increase, and expected long-term rate of return on plan assets are also required. Another required disclosure of SFAS 132(R) is the recognized amount of the net periodic benefit cost with the components shown separately.

### D.6.  Postretirement Benefits other than Pensions (OPEB)

**36.  (b)**  Net periodic postretirement benefit cost is a net amount calculated by adding or subtracting six components. Three components present in this problem are combined as follows:

| | |
|---|---|
| Service cost | $120,000 |
| Interest on the accumulated postretirement benefit obligation | 20,000 |
| Amortization of transition obligation ($200,000 ÷ 20 years) | 10,000 |
| Postretirement benefit cost | $150,000 |

Service cost and interest on the accumulated postretirement benefit obligation always increase postretirement benefit cost. Foster Co. has elected to amortize the unrecognized transition obligation over a twenty-year period. Amortization of the $200,000 obligation on the straight-line basis increases postretirement benefit cost by $10,000 per year. The benefit payment represents a cash payment made for benefits by the employer; however, this is not a component of net periodic postretirement benefit cost.

**37.  (b)**  To determine the accrued postretirement benefit cost, the net periodic postretirement benefit cost must first be calculated as follows:

| | |
|---|---|
| Service cost | $28,000 |
| Interest on the accumulated postretirement benefit obligation | 5,000 |
| Amortization of the unrecognized transition obligation | 8,000 |
| Net periodic postretirement benefit cost | $41,000 |

An adjusting entry is required at year-end to record net periodic postretirement benefit cost and the cash benefit payments made to employees. An accrued postretirement benefit cost will be recorded if the net postretirement benefit cost exceeds the cash payments to employees. The journal entry would be

| | | |
|---|---|---|
| Postretirement benefit cost | 41,000 | |
| Cash | | 10,000 |
| Accrued postretirement benefit cost | | 31,000 |

The balance in the accrued postretirement benefit cost account would be $31,000.

**38.  (b)**  The requirement is to determine the attribution period for accruing the expected postretirement health care benefit obligation. In accordance with SFAS 106, the beginning of the attribution period is generally the date of hire, and the end shall be the date of full eligibility. Fletcher's age at the date of hire is forty-eight and the period of eligibility is ten years. Thus, the attribution period is forty-eight to fifty-eight.

**39.  (a)**  SFAS 106 requires an employer's obligation for postretirement benefits expected to be provided to an employee be fully accrued by the full eligibility date of the employee, even if the employee is to render additional service beyond that date.

**40.  (c)**  Per SFAS 106, a transition obligation is measured as the difference between the accumulated postretirement benefit obligation and the fair value of plan assets at the beginning of the fiscal year for which SFAS 106 is adopted. A transition obligation may be recognized immediately in net income of the period of the change, or recognized on a delayed basis as a component of net periodic postretirement benefit cost. If delayed recognition is elected, SFAS 106, states that in general the transition obligation should be amortized on a straight-line basis over the average remaining service period of plan participants. If the average remaining service period is less than twenty years, the employer may elect to use a twenty-year amortization period.

**41.  (a)**  SFAS 106 requires that the employer disclose the amount of the accumulated postretirement benefit obligation. The employer must also disclose the assumed health care cost trend rate used to measure the expected cost of benefits covered by the plan.

**SOLUTIONS TO SIMULATION PROBLEMS**

**Simulation Problem 1**

| Situation | Concepts | Pension Calculations | Journal Entry | Balance Sheet | Communication | Research |
|---|---|---|---|---|---|---|

|  |  | *True* | *False* |
|---|---|---|---|
| 1. | A defined contribution plan is a plan where an employer agrees to provide a benefit at retirement defined by a formula. | ○ | ● |
| 2. | The present value of the projected benefit obligation is calculated using the benefits years of service method. | ● | ○ |
| 3. | Pension liability is calculated by comparing the accumulated benefit obligation with the fair value of plan assets. | ○ | ● |
| 4. | A company is required to net overfunded pension plans with underfunded pension plans and report the net amount as either noncurrent asset or noncurrent liability on the balance sheet. | ○ | ● |
| 5. | Prior service costs are caused by new individuals entering the plan after the vesting date. | ○ | ● |
| 6. | In a defined benefit plan, interest cost represents the increase in the fair value of the plan assets due to the passage of time. | ○ | ● |
| 7. | Companies must disclose in the notes to the financial statements the effects that a two-percentage-point increase in interest costs would have on the aggregate service and interest costs of the accumulated postretirement benefit obligation on health care benefits. | ○ | ● |
| 8. | The actual return on plan assets is defined as the difference in the fair value of plan assets at the beginning and the end of the year. | ○ | ● |

**Explanation of solutions**

**1.** False.  A defined contribution plan is a plan where the employer defines the contribution.  No benefit is promised.  The benefit is provided by a trust that is funded by the defined contribution of the employer.

**2.** True.  The projected benefit obligation is calculated using the benefits years of service method.

**3.** False.  The funded status of the pension plan is calculated by subtracting the projected benefit obligation and the fair value of plan assets at year-end.

**4.** False.  According to SFAS 158, a company may not net the overfunded and underfunded plans.  Overfunded plans must be shown as noncurrent assets on the balance sheet.  Underfunded plans should be shown as current liabilities, noncurrent liabilities, or both.

**5.** False.  Prior service costs are caused by amendments to the plan or initiation of a new plan with a retroactive allowance.

**6.** False.  In a defined benefit plan, the interest cost represents the increase in the projected benefit obligation due to the passage of time.

**7.** False.  Companies must disclose the effect that a one percentage point increase would have on the aggregate service and interest costs of the accumulated postretirement benefit obligation on health care benefits.

**8.** False.  The actual return on plan assets is defined as the difference in the fair value adjusted for contributions made to the plan and benefits paid.

| Situation | Concepts | Pension Calculations | Journal Entry | Balance Sheet | Communication | Research |
|---|---|---|---|---|---|---|

**Part I.**

| 1. | $ 36,000 | Interest cost (PBO at BOY $600,000 × 6% = $36,000) |
|---|---|---|
| 2. | $ 25,200 | Actual return on plan assets (FV of plan assets BOY $420,000 × 6% = $25,200) |
| 3. | $ 20,000 | Amortization of prior service costs or credits ($240,000/12 years = $20,000 per year) |
| 4. | $       0 | Gain or (Loss) (Actual returns = expected returns) |
| 5. | $110,800 | Pension cost for 2007 ($80,000 service cost + $36,000 interest cost − $25,200 ROA + $20,000 amortization of prior service cost = $110,800) |
| 6. | $695,800 | Projected benefit obligation at December 31, 2007 (PBO at BOY $600,000 + Pension Costs $110,800 − Benefits Paid $15,000 = $695,800 PBO at EOY) |

**Part II.**

|  |  | Increase | Decrease | No effect |
|---|---|---|---|---|
| 1. | Service cost | ● | ○ | ○ |
| 2. | Interest cost | ● | ○ | ○ |
| 3. | Actual return on plan assets | ○ | ● | ○ |
| 4. | Amortization of prior service costs or credits | ● | ○ | ○ |
| 5. | Gain or loss in 2007 | ○ | ○ | ● |

**Explanation of solutions**

1. **(I)** Service cost increases pension cost for the period.

2. **(I)** Interest cost increases pension cost for the period.

3. **(D)** Actual return on assets decreases pension costs for the period.

4. **(I)** Amortization of prior service cost increases pension cost for the period.

5. **(N)** Winger had no gain or loss because actual and expected return on assets were the same for 2007.

| Situation | Concepts | Pension Calculations | Journal Entry | Balance Sheet | Communication | Research |
|---|---|---|---|---|---|---|
| Debit pension cost |  |  | 110,800 |  |  |  |
| Credit cash |  |  |  | 40,000 |  |  |
| Credit pension liability |  |  |  | 70,800 |  |  |

| Situation | Concepts | Pension Calculations | Journal Entry | Balance Sheet | Communication | Research |
|---|---|---|---|---|---|---|

What is the amount of pension assets or liabilities that will be disclosed in each of the following categories on the balance sheet?

| 1. | Current asset | 0 |
|---|---|---|
| 2. | Noncurrent asset | 0 |
| 3. | Current liability | 0 |
| 4. | Noncurrent liability | $164,800 |

**Explanation**

The funded status of the plan is determined by comparing the Projected Benefit Obligation at year-end to the fair value of plan assets on December 31, 2007.  The PBO of $695,800 – FV of plan assets of $470,200 = $225,600, which is the amount of the pension plan that is underfunded.  A liability of $225,600 must be recognized on the balance sheet.  A liability of $70,800 exists for the portion of the current year pension cost that was unfunded.  Therefore, the increase in pension liability due to items not recognized in pension costs is $154,800 ($225,600 – $70,800).  This is recognized as a noncurrent liability because Winger does not expect to pay any pension benefits within the next 12 months.

| 5. | Amount in AOCI | $115,360 | **Debit** |
|---|---|---|---|

**Explanation**

The journal entry to record this would be as follows:

| Other comprehensive income | 108,360* |  |
|---|---|---|
| Deferred tax asset | 46,440 |  |
| Pension liability |  | 154,800 |

\*  *$154,800 × 70% = $108,360 (net of tax)*

| Situation | Concepts | Pension Calculations | Journal Entry | Balance Sheet | Communication | Research |
|-----------|----------|----------------------|---------------|---------------|---------------|----------|

To:    Mr. Palmer, Winger Company
From: CPA Candidate
Re:    Postemployment benefits

Thank you for your inquiry regarding accounting for postemployment benefits.  I have analyzed the company's employment agreements, and I have identified the following postemployment benefits that required financial statement presentation.

One postemployment benefit offered by Winger Company is continuation of health care benefits.  The company is required to accrue liabilities for this benefit if all of the following conditions are met:

- The obligation is attributable to employees' services already rendered,
- The employees' rights accumulate or vest,
- Payment is probable, and
- The amount of the benefits can be reasonably estimated.

If an obligation cannot be accrued solely because the amount cannot be reasonably estimated, the financial statements should disclose that fact.

Winger Company also has several deferred compensation contracts.  Estimated amounts to be paid under a deferred compensation contract should be accrued over the period of an employee's active employment from the time the contract is signed to the employee's full eligibility date.  The theoretical rationale for accrual of these obligations is that accrual matches the cost of the benefits to the period in which services are rendered.

Based on the information given to me by your accounting manager, I have prepared the following schedule detailing the company's deferred compensation amounts.

*Winger Co.*
**SCHEDULE OF DEFERRED COMPENSATION AMOUNTS**
*For the Years 2007 through 2010*

| For the year ended | Accrued liability | Deferred compensation expense |
|--------------------|-------------------|-------------------------------|
| 12/31/07 | $ 50,000 | $50,000 [a] |
| 12/31/08 | $100,000 | $50,000 |
| 12/31/09 | $150,000 | $50,000 |
| 12/31/10 | $165,000 | $15,000 [b] |

[a]   $150,000 ÷ 3 (straight-line method)
[b]   $150,000 × 10%

If I can be of further assistance, please do not hesitate to contact me.

| Situation | Concepts | Pension Calculations | Journal Entry | Balance Sheet | Communication | Research |
|-----------|----------|----------------------|---------------|---------------|---------------|----------|

1.    Define the interest cost component of net pension cost for a period.

**FAS87, Para 22 or Current Text P16.116**
**Interest cost**

22.  The interest cost component recognized in a period shall be determined as the increase in the projected benefit obligation due to the passage of time.  Measuring the projected benefit obligation as a present value requires accrual of an interest cost at rates equal to the assumed discount rates.

2.    How should Winger determine its interest cost component of net pension cost for a period?

**FAS87, Para 22 or Current Text P16.116**
**Interest cost**

22.  The interest cost component recognized in a period shall be determined as the increase in the projected benefit obligation due to the passage of time.  Measuring the projected benefit obligation as a present value requires accrual of an interest cost at rates equal to the assumed discount rates.

**3.**   Define prior service cost.

**FAS87, Para 24 or Current Text P16.118**
**Prior service cost**

24.  Plan amendments (including initiation of a plan) often include provisions that grant increased benefits based on services rendered in prior periods.  Because plan amendments are granted with the expectation that the employer will realize economic benefits in future periods, this Statement does not require the cost of providing such retroactive benefits (that is, prior service cost) to be included in net periodic pension cost entirely in the year of the amendment but provides for recognition during the future service period of those employees active at the date of the amendment who are expected to received benefits under the plan.

**FAS87, Para 264 (Glossary) or Current Text P16.451**
**Prior service cost**

The cost of retroactive benefits granted in a plan amendment.  See also Unrecognized prior service cost.

**4.**   How should Winger account for prior service cost?

**FAS87, Para 25 (As amended by SFAS 158)**

25.  A plan amendment that retroactively increases benefits (including benefits that are granted to retirees) increases the projected benefit obligation.  Except as specified in paragraphs 26 and 27, that prior service cost shall be amortized as a component of net periodic pension cost by assigning an equal amount to each future period of service of each employee active at the date of the amendment who is expected to receive benefits under the plan  If all or almost all of a plan's participants are inactive, the cost of retroactive plan amendments affecting benefits of inactive participants shall be amortized based on the remaining life expectancy of those participants instead of based on the remaining service period.  Other comprehensive income is adjusted each period as prior service cost is amortized.

**5.**   What conditions must be met for Winger to accrue compensation for future vacations?

**FAS43, Para 6 or Current Text C44.104**

6.   An employer shall accrue a liability for employees' compensation for future absences if all of the following conditions are met:

   a.  The employer's obligation relating to employees' rights to receive compensation for future absences is attributable to employees' services already rendered,
   b.  The obligation relates to rights that vest or accumulate,
   c.  Payment of the compensation is probable, and
   d.  The amount can be reasonably estimated.

If an employer meets conditions (a), (b), and (c) and does not accrue a liability because condition (d) is not met, that fact shall be disclosed.

## E.  Leases

A lease is a contract between two parties—a lessor and a lessee.  A lease contract gives a lessee rights to use the lessor's property for a specified period of time in return for periodic cash payments (rent) to the lessor.

A major goal in accounting for leases is to recognize the economic substance of the lease agreement over its mere legal form.  For example, many lease agreements are similar to the purchase of an asset financed by the issuance of debt.  The economic substance of a lease agreement generally takes one of two forms:

1. Periodic payments of rent by the lessee for the **use** of the lessor's property
2. Periodic payments similar to an installment purchase by the lessee for the rights to **acquire** the lessor's property in the future (i.e., acquisition of property by financing)

In (1), the risks and rewards of owning the asset remain with the lessor.  Accordingly, the asset is **not** treated as sold by the lessor to the lessee, and remains on the lessor's books.  This form of leasing arrangement is called an **operating lease**.  By contrast, in (2), a lease agreement may transfer many of the risks and rewards of ownership to the lessee.  This form of lease is treated as a sale by the lessor and as a purchase by the lessee.  This concept is clearly stated in SFAS 13 as follows:

> A lease that transfers substantially all of the benefits and risks incident to ownership of property should be accounted for as the acquisition of an asset and the incurrence of an obligation by the lessee and as a sale or financing by the lessor.

When the risks and rewards of ownership are deemed to have been passed from the lessor to the lessee, the lessor will account for the lease as either a **direct financing** or as a **sales-type lease,** and the lessee will account for the lease as a **capital lease**.

To determine whether the risks and rewards of ownership have been transferred to the lessee, **at least one** of the following four criteria must be met:

1. The lease **transfers title** to the lessee
2. The lease contains a **bargain purchase** option
3. The lease **term is 75% or more** of useful life and the lease is not first executed within the last 25% of the original useful life
4. The **present value** of minimum lease payments **is 90% or more** of the net of the **fair market value** of the asset reduced by the investment tax credit (when in effect) retained by the lessor and the lease is not executed in the last 25% of the original useful life

These four criteria apply to both the lessor and to the lessee.  The lessor, however, must meet two additional criteria:

1. **Collectibility** of minimum lease payments is predictable, and
2. There are **no important uncertainties** concerning costs yet to be incurred by the lessor under the lease.

**Both** of the above must be satisfied by the lessor in order for the lessor to treat the lease in substance as an installment sale.

The classification of leases can be summarized as follows:

| | *Lessor* | *Lessee* |
|---|---|---|
| Risks and rewards remain with lessor (no sale and purchase of asset | Operating ———————————— | Operating |
| Risks and rewards transfer to lessee (sale and purchase of asset | Direct financing ———————— / Sales-type | Capital |

## 1.  Study Program for Leases

a. Begin by reviewing the terms peculiar to leases that appear at the beginning of the outline of SFAS 13 in the pronouncement outlines that begin after Module 20.

b.  Review the material in this module so that you will be familiar with the major concepts and applications in the leasing area.

c.  After you have developed a solid base of understanding, you should review the outline of SFAS 13.

d.  The discussion of accounting for leases is structured to follow the lease classification matrix listed above.

### (1) Operating Lease—Lessor/Lessee

An operating lease is any lease not meeting the criteria for a direct financing or sales-type lease in the case of a lessor, or for a capital lease in the case of a lessee.  Under an operating lease, leased assets continue to be carried on the lessor's balance sheet and are depreciated in the normal manner.  These assets, however, are not shown on the lessee's balance sheet since the lessee cannot expect to derive any future economic benefit from the assets beyond the lease term.  Several issues are frequently encountered when dealing with operating leases.  These issues are discussed in the remainder of this section.

### (a) Free rent/uneven payments

Some lease agreements might call for uneven payments or scheduled rent increases over the lease term.  Other agreements might include, as an incentive to the lessee, several months of "free rent" during which the lessee may use the asset without owing rent to the lessor.  In these cases, rental revenue (expense) is still recognized by the lessor (lessee) on a straight-line basis and is prorated over the full term of the lease during which the lessee has possession of the asset.  This is due to the matching principle; if physical usage is relatively the same over the lease term, then an equal amount of benefit is being obtained by both parties to the lease.

*NOTE: Another method to allocate rental revenue (expense) may be used if it better represents the actual physical use of the leased asset.*

When the pattern of actual cash received (paid) as rent is other than straight-line, it will be necessary for both parties to record accruals, or deferrals, depending upon the payment schedule.

|  | | *Accruals* | (or) | *Deferrals* |
|---|---|---|---|---|
| Lessor | -- | Rent receivable | | Unearned rent |
| Lessee | -- | Rent payable | | Prepaid rent |

Numerical Example 1:

### Lease Information

1)  A ten-year lease is initiated on 1/1/07
2)  Payments are $100,000 per year payable January 1 (except for the first year)
3)  Payment for the first year is $50,000, due on 7/1/07

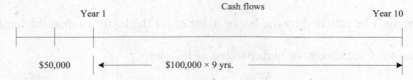

Recognition of revenue/expense:

Actual cash received/paid = (9 years  ×  $100,000) + $50,000 = $950,000 total

Revenue and expense per year = $950,000  ÷  10 years  =  $95,000 per year

| *Journal entries for the lessor* | | | *Journal entries for the lessee* | | |
|---|---|---|---|---|---|
| *Year 1* | | | *Year 1* | | |
| Cash | 50,000 | | Rent expense | 50,000 | |
|     Rent revenue | | 50,000 |     Cash | | 50,000 |
| Rent receivable | 45,000 | | Rent expense | 45,000 | |
|     Rent revenue | | 45,000 |     Rent payable | | 45,000 |
| *Years 2-10* | | | *Years 2-10* | | |
| Cash | 100,000 | | Rent expense | 95,000 | |
|     Rent revenue | | 95,000 | Rent payable | 5,000 (b) | |
|     Rent receivable | | 5,000 (a) |     Cash | | 100,000 |

| Rent Receivable | | (a) | (b) | Rent Payable | |
|---|---|---|---|---|---|
| yr. 1    45,000 | 5,000 | yr. 2 | yr. 2    5,000 | 45,000 | yr. 1 |
| | • | | | • | |
| | • | | | • | |
| | • | yr. 10 | yr. 10 | • | |

### (b) Initial direct costs

The lessor may incur costs in setting up the lease agreement. Such costs might include finder's fees, appraisal fees, document processing fees, negotiation fees, and any costs in closing the transaction. These costs, called initial direct costs, are carried as an asset on the lessor's balance sheet. Initial direct costs are amortized on a straight-line basis to expense over the lease term by the lessor, and are shown net of accumulated amortization on the lessor's balance sheet.

### (c) Lease bonus (fee)

At the inception of the lease, the lessee may pay a nonrefundable lease bonus (fee) to the lessor in order to obtain more favorable leasing terms (e.g., a lease term of three years instead of five years). The lease bonus (fee) would be treated as unearned rent by the lessor and would be amortized to rental revenue on a straight-line basis over the lease term. The lessee would treat the lease bonus (fee) as prepaid rent and would recognize it as rental expense over the lease term on a straight-line basis.

### (d) Security deposits

Some lease agreements may require that the lessee pay the lessor a security deposit at the inception of the lease. Security deposits may be either refundable or nonrefundable. A **refundable** security deposit is treated as a liability by the lessor and as a receivable by the lessee until the deposit is returned to the lessee. A **nonrefundable** security deposit is recorded as unearned revenue by the lessor and as prepaid rent by the lessee until the deposit is considered earned by the lessor (usually at the end of the lease term).

### (e) Leasehold improvements

Frequently, the lessee will make improvements to leased property by constructing new buildings or improving existing structures. The lessee has the right to use these leasehold improvements over the term of the lease; however, these improvements will revert to the lessor at the expiration of the lease. Leasehold improvements are capitalized to "Leasehold Improvements" (a property, plant and equipment account) by the lessee and are amortized over the **shorter** of (1) the remaining lease term, **or** (2) the useful life of the improvement. Improvements made in lieu of rent should be expensed in the period incurred. If the lease contains an option to renew and the likelihood of renewal is uncertain, the leasehold improvement should be written off over the life of the initial lease term or useful life of the improvement, whichever is shorter.

*NOTE: Moveable equipment or office furniture that is not attached to the leased property is **not** considered a leasehold improvement.*

The summary below lists the elements commonly encountered in operating leases.

### *Operating Lease FS Elements*

| | *Lessor* | *Lessee* |
|---|---|---|
| *Balance sheet:* | • Leased asset (net of accumulated depreciation) | • Prepaid rent (including lease bonus/fee and nonrefundable security deposit) |
| | • Rent receivable | • Leasehold improvements (net of accumulated amortization) |
| | • Initial direct costs (net of accumulated amortization) | • Deposit receivable |
| | • Unearned rent (including lease bonus/fee and nonrefundable security deposit) | |
| | • Deposit liability | |
| *Income statement:* | • Rent revenue (including amortization of lease bonus/fee and nonrefundable security deposit) | • Rent expense (including amortization of lease bonus/fee and nonrefundable security deposit) |
| | • Depreciation expense | • Amortization of leasehold improvements |
| | • Amortization of initial direct costs | |
| | • Other maintenance expenses | |

Knowledge of these elements is helpful in answering questions that require a determination of lessor's net income or lessee's total expense in connection with an operating lease.

### (f) Modifications and terminations to capital leases

SFAS 145, issued in April 2002, addresses modifications and terminations to capital leases. A company may modify a capital lease in such a way that it changes the lease to an operating lease. If a capital lease is modified as such, it is treated as a sales-leaseback transaction under the provisions of SFAS 28 or 98. If a company terminates a capital lease, the accounting for the termination depends on whether the lease was a capital lease for real estate or for an asset other than real estate. If the capital lease was for real estate, then the provisions of SFAS 66 apply. The criteria for recognition of gains in SFAS 66 must be met in order for the company to recognize a gain on termination of the lease. However, any loss on the transaction is recognized immediately. If the lease was for assets other than real estate, SFAS 145 applies and the asset and obligation of the lease are removed from the accounts and a gain or loss is recognized for the difference. If the original lessee remains secondarily liable, the guarantee obligation is recognized in accordance with SFAS 140.

### (g) Termination costs

If a lessee terminates an operating lease before the end of its term, the lessee must recognize any termination costs. Termination costs may include a lump-sum payment or payments that continue during the remaining lease term. SFAS 146 requires that such costs are measured and recognized at fair value on the date the agreement is terminated, the entity no longer receives rights to the assets, or the company ceases to use the assets (cease-use date). If the company remains liable for payments after the cease-use date, the fair value of the termination costs is based on the remaining lease rentals reduced by the estimated sublease rentals that could be obtained for the property, even if the entity does not intend to sublease. Termination costs of an operating lease are included in calculating income from continuing operations. If the termination of an operating lease is associated with the exit or disposal of a discontinued operation, these costs are included in the results of discontinued operations. (See outline of SFAS 146.)

## (2) Direct Financing Lease—Lessor

Although most discussions, including SFAS 13, begin with the lessee's accounting for a capital lease, we have chosen to present the lessor's accounting first because the lessor is the party that determines the fixed cash schedule of lease payments that are to be made by the lessee.

A direct financing lease arises when a consumer needs equipment but does not want to purchase the equipment outright, and/or is unable to obtain conventional financing. In this situation, the consumer will turn to a leasing company (e.g., a bank) which will purchase the desired asset from a manufacturer (or dealer) and lease it to the consumer. Direct financing leases apply to leasing companies, as opposed to manufacturers or dealers, because leasing companies purchase the assets solely for leasing, not for resale. Leasing companies are usually involved in financing activities (e.g., banking and insurance), not in the sale of property of the type being leased. The following situation shows when a direct financing lease would arise:

> ABC Company needs new equipment to expand its manufacturing operations but does not have enough capital to purchase the equipment at present. ABC Company employs Universal Leasing Company to purchase the equipment. ABC will lease the asset from Universal. Universal records a direct financing lease.

The relationships in a direct financing lease arrangement are illustrated below.

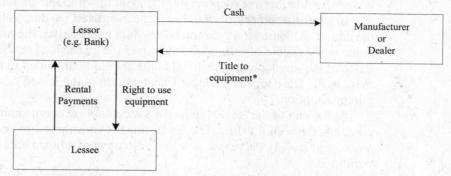

* *Title would stay with the lessor unless criterion (1) or (2) above is met in which case title would pass to the lessee.*

As mentioned, a lease is considered to be a direct financing lease by the **lessor** if at least one of the four criteria applicable to both lessors and lessees is met, and **both** of the additional criteria applicable to lessors is met.

Direct financing leases result in only interest revenue for the lessor.  In essence, no product has been sold by the lessor, so no gain/loss, sales, or cost of sales is recognized from the lease transaction.  Thus the FMV (selling price) of the leased asset equals its cost to the lessor.

The lessor's entry to record the acquisition of title to the asset to be leased is as follows:

| | |
|---|---|
| Asset to be leased | (cost of asset = FMV) |
| Cash | (cash paid) |

At the inception of the lease, the lessor makes the following entry:

| | | |
|---|---|---|
| Lease receivable | xx | |
| Asset to be leased | | xx |
| Unearned interest revenue | | xx |

In effect, the asset is removed from the lessor's books; it will be transferred to the lessee's books if one of the four criteria applicable to lessees is met.  It is possible that the lessee's analysis might result in an operating lease.

In order to calculate the amounts in the entry above, you must first become familiar with several important terms.

(a)  **Minimum lease payments (MLP)**

MLP are the payments that the lessor/lessee is or can be required to make in connection with the leased property.

1.  Rent payments (excluding executory costs and contingent rentals)
2.  Bargain purchase option (if any)
3.  Guaranteed residual value (if any)
4.  Penalty for failure to renew (if any)

Executory costs (e.g., property taxes, insurance, etc.) and contingent rentals are treated as revenues in the period earned.

(b)  **Bargain purchase option (BPO)**

This option allows the lessee to purchase leased property for an amount substantially lower than the expected FMV at the exercise date of the option.

(c)  **Residual value**

Residual value can be unguaranteed or guaranteed.  Some lease contracts require lessees to guarantee residual value to lessors.  The lessee can either buy the leased asset at the end of the lease term for the guaranteed residual value or allow the lessor to sell the leased asset (with the lessee paying any deficiency or receiving any excess over the guaranteed residual value).

***Guaranteed residual value (GRV)*** is considered part of the "minimum lease payment" and is reflected in the lessor's lease receivable account and the lessee's lease payable account.  At the end of the lease term, the receivable and payable on the respective lessor's and lessee's books should be equal to the guaranteed residual value.

Both lessor and lessee consider the guaranteed residual value a final lease payment. The lessee should amortize (depreciate) the asset down to the guaranteed residual value.

***Unguaranteed residual value*** is the estimated residual value of the leased asset at the end of the lease (if a guaranteed residual value exists, the unguaranteed residual value is the excess of estimated value over the guaranteed residual value). The present value of the unguaranteed residual value should be included in the lessor's net investment in the lease unless the lease transfers title to the leased asset or there is a bargain purchase option.

At the end of the lease, the lessor's receivable account should be equal to the unguaranteed residual value. The lessor must review the estimated residual value annually and recognize any decreases as a loss. No upward adjustments of the residual value are permitted.

Now you are ready to calculate the amounts for the lessor's entry using the following formulas:

| **Lease receivable*** ( = gross investment) | = | Total MLP** | + | URV (if any) |
|---|---|---|---|---|
| **Asset to be leased** ( = net investment) ( = FMV or cost of asset) | = | PV of gross investment | | |
| **Unearned interest revenue** | = | Gross investment | − | FMV (or cost) of asset |

\* *The title **Gross investment** is used when there is an unguaranteed residual value because the lower probability of collection of the residual value makes the use of the term **Receivable** undesirable.*

\*\* *Include guaranteed residual value.*

Alternative methods of recording the lease transaction are shown below.

| Lease receivable (gross) | xx | | | Lease receivable (net) | xx | |
|---|---|---|---|---|---|---|
| Asset to be leased | | xx | -or- | Asset to be leased | | xx |
| Unearned interest revenue | | xx | | | | |

We will follow the gross method in our examples for the lessor because it is consistent with SFAS 13 and the questions on the CPA exam.

SFAS 13 specifies additional guidelines when accounting for the lessor.

- The lease receivable should be separated into current and noncurrent components on the lessor's balance sheet.
- Unearned interest revenue must be amortized to produce a constant periodic rate of return on the net investment using the interest method.
- No residual value is assumed to accrue to the value of the lessor if the lease transfers ownership or contains a BPO.
- At the termination of the lease, the balance in the receivable should equal the guaranteed or unguaranteed residual value, assuming title is not transferred and there is no bargain purchase option.

Numerical Example 2:

### *Lease Information*

1) A three-year lease is initiated on 1/1/07 for equipment costing $131,858 with an expected useful life of five years. The FMV of the equipment on 1/1/07 is $131,858.
2) Three annual payments are due to the lessor beginning 12/31/07. The property reverts back to the lessor upon termination of the lease.
3) The guaranteed residual value at the end of year 3 is $10,000.
4) The lessor is to receive a 10% return (implicit rate).
5) Collectivity of minimum lease payments is predictable, and there are no important uncertainties concerning costs yet to be incurred by the lessor under the lease.
6) The cost (FMV) of the asset incurred by the lessor to acquire the asset for leasing is to be recovered through two components: annual rent payments and guaranteed residual value using a discount (implicit) rate of 10%.

7)  The annual rent payment to the lessor is computed as follows:

a)  Find PV of guaranteed residual value

$$\underset{\text{GRV}}{\$10,000} \quad \times \quad .7513 \quad = \quad \$7,513$$

b)  Find PV of annual rent payments

$$\underset{\text{FMV of asset}}{\$131,858} \quad - \quad \$7,513 \quad = \quad \$124,345$$

c)  Find annual rent payment

$$\$124,345 \quad \div \quad \text{PVA}_{n=3;\, i=10\%}$$
$$\$124,345 \quad \div \quad 2.4869 \quad = \quad \$50,000$$

## Lease Classification

This lease is a direct financing lease because criterion 4 (the 90% test) is satisfied.

$$\$124,345 + \$7,513 \geq (.9)(\$131,858)$$

(Since the residual value is guaranteed, the PV of the MLP is 100% of the FMV.)  The two additional criteria for the lessor are satisfied, and FMV equals cost.  If the residual value had been unguaranteed, the 90% test would still have been met because $\$124,345 \geq (.9)\,(\$131,858)$.

## Accounting for Lease

1)  The lease should be recorded at the beginning of year 1 by the lessor.

2)  The lease receivable is calculated as follows:

$$\underset{\$50,000}{\text{(Annual rent payment}} \quad \times \quad \underset{\text{3 yrs.}}{\text{Lease term)}} \quad + \quad \underset{\$10,000}{\text{GRV}} \quad = \quad \$160,000$$

3)  Unearned interest revenue is calculated as follows:

$$\underset{\$160,000}{\text{Lease receivable}} \quad - \quad \underset{\$131,858}{\text{FMV of asset}} \quad = \quad \$28,142$$

4)  Unearned interest is amortized during the lease term using the following amortization schedule:

### AMORTIZATION SCHEDULE

| | | |
|---|---:|---:|
| Carrying value at beg. of yr. 1 ( = PV of gross investment) | | $131,858 |
| Interest revenue (10%) | $ 13,186 | |
| Rent payment | (50,000) | (36,814) |
| Carrying value at beg. of yr. 2 | | 95,044 |
| Interest revenue | 9,504 | |
| Rent payment | (50,000) | (40,496) |
| Carrying value at beg. of yr. 3 | | 54,548 |
| Interest revenue | 5,452 | |
| Rent payment | (50,000) | (44,548) |
| Carrying value at end of yr. 3 ( = residual value) | | 10,000 |

Lease receivable on balance sheet:

| | | | | |
|---|---|---|---|---|
| End of Year 1 | – current portion | = | $40,496 | principal reduction in year 2 |
| | noncurrent portion | = | $54,548 | principal reductions after year 2 |
| End of Year 2 | – current portion | = | $54,548 | principal reduction in the following year (includes residual value) |

*NOTE: As the lease expires, interest revenue decreases and the reduction of principal increases.*

5)  The journal entries for the lessor are shown below.

### JOURNAL ENTRIES FOR THE LESSOR

| *Initial entries (Beg. of Yr. 1)* | | | *End of Year 2* | | |
|---|---|---|---|---|---|
| Equipment for leasing | 131,858 | | Cash | 50,000 | |
| Cash | | 131,858 | Lease receivable | | 50,000 |
| Lease receivable | 160,000 | | Unearned interest | 9,504 | |
| Equipment for leasing | | 131,858 | Interest revenue | | 9,504 |
| Unearned interest | | 28,142 | | | |

| _End of Year 1_ | | | _End of Year 3_ | | |
|---|---|---|---|---|---|
| Cash | 50,000 | | Cash | 50,000 | |
|    Lease receivable | | 50,000 |    Lease receivable | | 50,000 |
| Unearned interest | 13,186 | | Unearned interest | 5,452 | |
|     Interest revenue | | 13,186 |     Interest revenue | | 5,452 |

6)  Assume that when the asset is returned at the end of year 3 the asset has a FMV of only $4,000.  The lessee will need to make a payment of $6,000 ($10,000 − $4,000) because the residual value was guaranteed.  The lessor would make the following entry:

| | | |
|---|---|---|
| Cash | 6,000 | |
| Residual value of equipment | 4,000 | |
|    Lease receivable | | 10,000 |

## (3)  Sales-Type Lease—Lessor

A sales-type lease arises when a manufacturer or dealer leases an asset which otherwise might be sold outright for a profit.  These manufacturers (dealers) use leasing as a way to market their own products (e.g., a car dealership).  The leasing, or financing arrangement, is a means for the manufacturer to sell its products and realize a profit from sales.  (By contrast, direct financing leases serve purely as financing arrangements.)  The following situation shows when a sales-type lease would arise:

ABC Company needs equipment to expand its manufacturing operations.  ABC Company enters into a lease agreement with XYZ Manufacturing, Inc. for the equipment.  XYZ Manufacturing Inc. records a sales-type lease.

The relationships in a sales-type lease arrangement are illustrated below.

\*  *Title stays with lessor and property will be returned to lessor at the end of the lease term unless criterion (1) or (2) above is met.*

Sales-type leases, unlike direct financing leases, result in **both** (1) gross profit (loss) in the period of sales, **and** (2) interest revenue to be earned over the lease term using the effective interest method.  The diagram below compares and contrasts direct financing leases with sales-type leases.

### Direct Financing Lease (Lessor)

### Sales-Type Lease (Lessor)

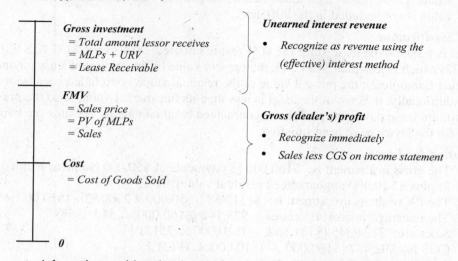

**Gross investment**
= Total amount lessor receives
= MLPs + URV
= Lease Receivable

**FMV**
= Sales price
= PV of MLPs
= Sales

**Cost**
= Cost of Goods Sold

0

***Unearned interest revenue***

• Recognize as revenue using the (effective) interest method

***Gross (dealer's) profit***

• Recognize immediately
• Sales less CGS on income statement

A lease is considered to be a sales-type lease from the viewpoint of the lessor if the criteria mentioned earlier for direct financing leases are satisfied.  However, in the case of a sales-type lease, the FMV of the asset, which is the sales price in the ordinary course of the lessor's business is **greater than** the cost or carrying value of the leased asset.  Because of this difference, a sales-type lease is more complex than a direct financing lease.  The journal entries to record a sales-type are

| | | |
|---|---|---|
| Lease receivable (Gross) | xx | |
| Sales | | xx |
| Unearned interest | | xx |
| CGS | xx | |
| Inventory | | xx |

Note the similarity of these entries to those made for a sale on account.  The differences are "lease receivable" instead of "accounts receivable" and the "unearned interest" for the excess of the receivables over the sales price (present value of future payments).

SFAS 13 specifies additional guidelines unique to sales-type leases.

• The lessor bases the lease payment schedule on the amount the lessee would have paid to purchase the asset outright (i.e., the sales price).  Therefore, sales are equal to the present value of the minimum lease payments.
• The cost of goods sold to be charged against income is equal to the historic cost or carrying value of the leased asset (most likely inventory) **less** the present value of any unguaranteed residual value.
• The difference between the selling price and cost of goods sold is the gross profit (loss) recognized by the lessor at the inception of the lease.
• When accounting for sales-type leases, guaranteed residual value is considered part of sales revenue because the lessor knows the entire asset has been sold.  Unguaranteed residual value, however, is excluded from both sales and cost of sales at its present value because there is less certainty that unguaranteed residual value will be realized.

Numerical Example 3:

### Lease Information

Assume same information as in previous example except

1) The cost of the equipment is $100,000 (either manufactured cost or purchase price paid by dealer).
2) The normal selling price of the equipment is $131,858 which is greater than the $100,000 cost.
3) The residual value is **unguaranteed**.
4) The lease payments are $50,000, the same as computed in the previous example, because the lessor treats an **un**guaranteed residual value in the same way as a guaranteed residual

value.  However, as mentioned below, the present value of the unguaranteed residual value is not included in the 90% test.

## Lease Classification

This is a sales-type lease since the 90% test is satisfied; 90% of the $131,858 FMV = $118,672, which is less than $124,345, the present value of the minimum lease payments (see Numerical Example 2); the present value of the residual value is excluded because it is unguaranteed.  Additionally, the cost of the asset is less than its fair market value (also the present value of the minimum lease payments plus the unguaranteed residual value).  Assume the two additional criteria for the lessor have been satisfied.

## Accounting for Lease

1) The gross investment is:  $160,000 [3 payments of $50,000 (same as Numerical Example 2) plus a $10,000 unguaranteed residual value]

   The PV of gross investment is:  $131,858 [($50,000 × 2.4869) + ($10,000 × .7513)]

   The unearned interest revenue is:  $28,142 ($160,000 − $131,858)

   Sales are:  $124,345 [$131,858 − ($10,000 × .7513)*]

   CGS is:  $92,487 [$100,000 − ($10,000 × .7513)*]

   * Note that there is no effect on gross profit of not including the present value of the unguaranteed residual value in either sales or cost of goods sold.  In both cases, the gross profit is $31,858.  If the residual value were guaranteed, this adjustment would not be made.

2) The entry to record the lease is

| | | |
|---|---|---|
| Lease receivable** | 160,000 | |
| Cost of goods sold | 92,487 | |
|     Sales | | 124,345 |
|     Inventory*** | | 100,000 |
|     Unearned interest | | 28,142 |

   ** On the balance sheet this amount is termed gross investment since it includes an unguaranteed residual value.

   *** Either acquisition cost to dealer or manufacturer's cost of production.

Interest revenue will be recognized at 10% of the outstanding net investment (lease receivable less unearned interest) each period (i.e., interest revenue in year 1 is $131,858 × 10% = $13,186).

At the end of year 1, the following entry(ies) would be made:

| | | |
|---|---|---|
| Cash | 50,000 | |
|     Lease receivable | | 50,000 |
| Unearned interest revenue | 13,186 | |
|     Interest revenue | | 13,186 |

At termination, the lease receivable will have a balance of $10,000 which is the unguaranteed residual value.  Note that the same amortization schedule that appears in Numerical Example 2 above is applicable to this one.  The fact that the residual value is unguaranteed in this example does not affect the amortization schedule because the lessor is projecting that it will get back an asset worth $10,000.  If the asset is returned to the lessor and its fair market value is only $4,000, the following entry is made on the lessor's books:

| | | |
|---|---|---|
| Loss | 6,000 | |
| Residual value of equipment | 4,000 | |
|     Lease receivable | | 10,000 |

Now that we have completed our discussion of lessor's direct financing and sales-type leases, it should be helpful to review the financial statement elements for the lessor, and to preview elements that appear on the lessee's financial statements.  These balance sheet elements are shown below.

***Lessor***

| | *Direct financing lease* | *Sales-type lease* |
|---|---|---|
| Balance sheet: | Lease receivable (current and noncurrent)<br>Initial direct costs (added to net invest-<br>ment causing a new implicit rate of in-<br>terest) | Lease receivable (current and noncurrent) |
| Income statement: | Unearned interest revenue<br>Interest revenue<br>Amortization of initial direct costs | Unearned interest revenue<br>Interest revenue<br>Initial direct costs (expensed immediately)<br>Dealer's profit |

***Lessee***

| | *Capital lease* |
|---|---|
| Balance sheet: | Leased asset (net of accumulated depreciation)<br>Lease obligation (current and noncurrent) |
| Income Statement: | Depreciation expense<br>Interest expense<br>Other maintenance expense |

## (4) Capital Leases—Lessee

When a lessor records a direct financing or sales-type lease, the lessee, in turn, must record a capital lease. Capital leases reflect the transfer of risks and benefits associated with the asset to the lessee. A lease is considered to be a capital lease to the lessee if **any one** of the four criteria of SFAS 13 is satisfied.

1. Transfer of title
2. Bargain purchase
3. 75% of useful life
4. 90% of net FMV

Lease agreements not meeting at least one of the criteria for capital leases are treated as operating leases on the lessee's books. If the lease is classified as a capital lease, the lessee must record an asset and a liability based on the present value of the minimum lease payments as follows:

| | | |
|---|---|---|
| Leased asset | (PV of MLP) | |
|    Lease obligation | | (PV of MLP) |

Note that the above entry reflects recording the transaction "net" (i.e., at present value). If the lease was recorded gross, the lease obligation would be credited for the total amount of the MLP and there would be a debit to "Discount on lease obligation."

| | | |
|---|---|---|
| Leased asset | (PV of MLP) | |
| Discount on lease obligation | (plug) | |
|    Lease obligation | | (gross MLP) |

The gross method is similar to the accounting for deferred payment contracts.

To determine the present value of the MLP, the lessee discounts the future payments using the **lesser** of

1. The lessee's incremental borrowing rate, **or**
2. The lessor's implicit rate if known by the lessee

NOTE: *Using a lower interest rate increases the present value.*

Leased assets, however, should **not** be recorded at an amount greater than the FMV of the asset. If the FMV is less than the PV of the MLP, the lease should be recorded at the FMV and a new implicit interest rate calculated to reflect a constant periodic rate applied to the remaining balance of the obligation.

During the term of the lease, the lessee must use the (effective) interest method to allocate cash paid between interest expense and reduction of the lease obligation. This method is the same as the one used by the lessor as previously described.

Lessees must amortize leased assets recorded on the books under a capital lease. The amortization (depreciation) method used should be consistent with the lessee's normal depreciation policy. The term over which the asset is amortized may differ depending upon which criteria qualified the lease as a capital lease.

1.  If the lease transfers ownership or contains a BPO (criteria 1 or 2), the asset will be amortized over its estimated useful life (since the asset actually becomes the property of the lessee at the end of the lease term and will be used for the remainder of its useful life).
2.  If the 75% of useful life or the 90% test (criteria 3 or 4) is met, the leased asset is amortized over the lease term only (since the property will revert to the lessor at the end of the lease term and will be used for the remainder of its useful life).

The lease term does not extend beyond the date of a bargain purchase option. Lease terms, however, may include the following:

1.  Bargain renewal periods
2.  Periods when the lessor has the option to renew or extend
3.  Periods during which the lessee guarantees the debt of the lessor
4.  Periods in which a material penalty exists for failure to renew

When the lease terminates, the balance in the obligation account should equal the bargain purchase option price or the expected residual value (guaranteed residual value, or salvage value if lower).

Leased assets and obligations should be disclosed as such in the balance sheet. The lease obligation should be separated into both current and noncurrent components.

Numerical Example 4:

### Lease Information

1)  A three-year lease is initiated on 1/1/07 for equipment with an expected useful life of five years. The equipment reverts back to the lessor upon expiration of the lease agreement.
2)  Three payments are due to the lessor in the amount of $50,000 per year **beginning 12/31/07**. An additional sum of $1,000 is to be paid annually by the lessee for insurance.
3)  Lessee guarantees a $10,000 residual value on 12/31/09 to the lessor.
4)  The leased asset is expected to have only a $7,000 salvage value on 12/31/09 despite the $10,000 residual value guarantee; therefore, the asset should be depreciated down to the $7,000 expected residual value.
5)  The lessee's incremental borrowing rate is 10% (same as lessor's implicit rate).
6)  The present value of the lease obligation is

| | | | | | | |
|---|---|---|---|---|---|---|
| PV of guaranteed residual value | = | $10,000 | × | .7513 | = | $ 7,513 |
| PV of annual payments | = | $50,000 | × | 2.4869 | = | 124,345 |
| | | | | | | $131,858 |

Note that since the lessee's incremental borrowing rate is 10% and the residual value is guaranteed, the present value of $131,858 is the same amount used by the lessor in the direct financing lease example (Numerical Example 2) to determine the payments to be made by the lessee. If an incremental borrowing rate different than the lessor's is used and/or the lease contains an unguaranteed residual value, the present value computed by the lessee will differ from the lessor's present value (FMV). These differences account for the fact that many leases are not capitalized by lessees because they don't meet the 90% test.

### Lease Classification

The 90% test is met because the present value of the minimum lease payments ($131,858) is 100% of the FMV of the leased asset.

### Accounting for Lease

1)  Note that executory costs (e.g., insurance, property taxes, etc.) are not included in the present value calculations
2)  The entry to recognize the lease is

| | | | |
|---|---|---|---|
| 1/1/07 | Leased equipment | 131,858 | |
| | Lease obligation | | 131,858 |

3) The entries to record the payments and depreciation are

| | 12/31/07 | | 12/31/08 | | 12/31/09 | |
|---|---|---|---|---|---|---|
| Insurance expense | 1,000 | | 1,000 | | 1,000 | |
| Lease obligation* | 36,814 | | 40,496 | | 44,548 | |
| Interest expense* | 13,186 | | 9,504 | | 5,452 | |
| Cash | | 51,000 | | 51,000 | | 51,000 |
| Depreciation expense** | 41,619 | | 41,619 | | 41,620 | |
| Accumulated depreciation | | 41,619 | | 41,619 | | 41,620*** |

&ast; Refer to the amortization table in the direct financing lease discussion (Numeric Example 2). Note that classification of the lease obligation into current and noncurrent on the lessee's books would parallel classification of the lease receivable on the lessor's books.

&ast;&ast; [($131,858 – 7,000) ÷ 3 years]

&ast;&ast;&ast; Rounding error of $1

4) The 12/31/09 entry to record the guaranteed residual value payment (assuming salvage value = estimated residual value = $7,000) and to clear the lease related accounts from the lessee's books is

| | | |
|---|---|---|
| Lease obligation | 10,000 | |
| Accumulated depreciation | 124,858 | |
| Cash | | 3,000 |
| Leased equipment | | 131,858 |

If the actual residual value were only $5,000, the credit to "cash" would be $5,000 and a $2,000 loss would be recognized by the lessee.

Remember that leased assets are amortized over the lease term unless title transfers or a bargain purchase option exists—then over the useful life of the leased asset. At the end of the lease, the balance of the lease obligation should equal the guaranteed residual value or the bargain purchase option price. To illustrate, consider the example below.

Numerical Example 5:

### Lease Information

1) A three-year lease is initiated on 1/1/07 for equipment with an expected useful life of five years.
2) Three annual $50,000 payments are due the lessor **beginning 1/1/07**.
3) The lessee can exercise a bargain purchase option on 12/31/09 for $10,000. The expected residual value at 12/31/11 is $1,000.
4) The lessee's incremental borrowing rate is 10% (lessor's implicit rate is unknown).

### Lease Classification

Although the lease term is for only 60% of the asset's useful life, the lessee would account for this as a capital lease because it contains a bargain purchase option. Also, the PV of the minimum lease payments is greater than 90% of the FMV of the leased asset.

### Accounting for Lease

1) The present value of the lease obligation is

| | | | | | | |
|---|---|---|---|---|---|---|
| PV of bargain purchase option | = | $10,000 | × | .7513 | = | $ 7,513 |
| PV of annual payments | = | $50,000 | × | 2.7355 | = | 136,775 |
| | | | | | | $144,288 |

2) The following amortization table summarizes the liability amortization:

## AMORTIZATION TABLE

| | | |
|---|---:|---:|
| Carrying value at beg. of yr. 1 | | $144,288 |
| Lease payment | $(50,000) | (50,000) |
| Carrying value at beg. of yr. 1 after first payment | | 94,288 |
| Interest expense | 9,429 | |
| Lease payment | (50,000) | (40,571) |
| Carrying value at beg. of year 2 after second payment | | 53,717 |
| Interest expense | 5,372 | |
| Lease payment | (50,000) | (44,628) |
| Carrying value at beg. of yr. 3 after third payment | | 9,089 |
| Interest expense | 911* | 911 |
| Bargain purchase option | | 10,000 |
| Option payment | (10,000) | (10,000) |
| | | -- |

\* *Rounding error of $2*

NOTE: *This table reflects the fact that the lease is an annuity due with cash payments on 1/1 and interest expense accruals on 12/31; thus, the first payment does not include any interest expense.*

3)  The entry to record the lease is

|       |                  |         |         |
|-------|------------------|---------|---------|
| 1/1/07 | Leased equipment | 144,288 |         |
|        | Lease obligation |         | 144,288 |

4)  The entries to record the payments, interest expense, depreciation (amortization) expense, and the exercise of the bargain purchase are

| | | 2007 | | 2008 | | 2009 | |
|---|---|---:|---:|---:|---:|---:|---:|
| 1/1 | Lease obligation | 50,000 | | 40,571 | | 44,628 | |
| | Accrued interest payable or interest expense* | | | 9,429 | | 5,372 | |
| | Cash | | 50,000 | | 50,000 | | 50,000 |
| 12/31 | Interest expense | 9,429 | | 5,372 | | 911 | |
| | Accrued int. payable | | 9,429 | | 5,372 | | |
| | Lease obligation | | | | | | 911 |
| 12/31 | Depreciation expense** | 28,658 | | 28,658 | | 28,658 | |
| | Accumulated depreciation | | 28,658 | | 28,658 | | 28,658 |
| 12/31 | Lease obligation | | | | | 10,000 | |
| | Cash | | | | | | 10,000 |

\*  *If 12/31 accruals are reversed*
\*\*  *(143,288 ÷ 5 years)*

## 2.  Other Considerations

To supplement the review of lease accounting presented above, the following topics have been selected for further discussion:

a.  Initial direct costs
b.  Sale-leaseback
c.  Disclosure requirements

### a.  Initial direct costs

Initial direct costs are the lessor's costs directly associated with negotiation and consummation of leases.  These costs include commissions, legal fees, credit investigations, document preparation, etc.  In operating leases, initial direct costs are capitalized and subsequently amortized to expense in proportion to the recognition of rental revenue (which is usually straight-line).

Initial direct costs of direct financing and sales-type leases are accounted for differently:
(1) In sales-type leases, charge initial direct costs to operations in the year the sale is recorded;
(2) In direct financing leases add the initial direct costs to the net investment in the lease.  Compute a new effective interest rate that equates the minimum lease payments and any unguaranteed residual value with the combined outlay for the leased asset and initial direct costs.  Finally, the

unearned lease (interest) revenue and the initial direct costs are to be amortized to income over the lease term so that a constant periodic rate is earned on the net investment.

b. **Sale-leaseback**

Sale-leaseback describes a transaction where the owner of property (seller-lessee) sells the property, and then immediately leases all or part of it back from the new owner (buyer-lessor). The important consideration in this type of transaction is the recognition of two separate and distinct economic transactions. It is important, however, to note that there is not a physical transfer of property. First, there is a sale of property, and second, there is a lease agreement for the same property in which the seller is the lessee and the buyer is the lessor. This is illustrated below.

Note that sale-leaseback transactions only affect accounting for the seller-lessee. Buyer-lessor accounting is unaffected.

The accounting treatment from the seller-lessee's point of view will depend upon the degree of rights to use the property retained by the seller-lessee. The degree of rights may be categorized in one of three ways:

1.  Substantially all
2.  Minor
3.  More than minor but less than substantially all

A seller-lessee retains **substantially all** the rights to use the property if the PV of the rental payments is 90% or more of the fair value of the asset sold. This test is based on the criteria used earlier to classify leases. Since the seller-lessee retains use of the asset, this type of sale-leaseback is considered, in substance, a form of financing to the seller-lessee rather than a sale. In this case, any gain on the sale is deferred by the seller-lessee.

| Cash | (selling price) | |
|---|---|---|
| Asset | | (carrying value) |
| Deferred gain | | (excess) |

The asset would be reported on the seller-lessee's balance sheet as follows:

| Leased asset | xx |
|---|---|
| Less: Deferred gain | (xx) |
| | xx |

The net value of the leased asset is the same amount the asset would be if it had not been sold.

If the lease is classified as a capital lease, the deferred gain is amortized over the life of the asset at the same rate as the asset is being depreciated. As deferred gain is amortized, it is charged to depreciation expense.

| Deferred gain | xx | |
|---|---|---|
| Depreciation expense | | xx |

Alternatively, the gain may be recognized as income over the term of the lease.

Although most leases in the "substantially all" category are capital leases, a sale-leaseback occurring in the last 25% of an asset's economic life would be classified as an operating lease.

If the lease is classified as an operating lease, any deferred gain is amortized over the lease term in proportion to the related gross rental charges to expense over the lease term. Amortization in this case is charged to rent expense by the seller-lessee.

| Deferred gain | xx | |
|---|---|---|
| Rent expense | | xx |

The seller-lessee retains only a **minor** portion of rights to use the property when the PV of the rental payments is 10% or less of the fair value of the asset sold. Since the seller-lessee has given up the right to use the asset, the leaseback is considered in substance a sale. Any gain on the sale is recognized in full since the earnings process is considered complete.

| Cash | (selling price) | |
|------|-----------------|---|
| Asset | | (carrying value) |
| Gain | | (excess) |

When only a minor portion of use is retained, the seller-lessee accounts for the lease as an operating lease.

The seller-lessee retains **more than a minor portion but less than substantially all** the rights to use the property when the PV of the rental payments is more than 10% but less than 90% of the fair value of the asset sold. In this situation, gain is recognized only to the extent that it exceeds the PV of the rental payments.

| Cash | (selling price) | |
|------|-----------------|---|
| Asset | | (carrying value) |
| Deferred gain | | (PV of rental payments) |
| Gain | | (excess) |

Recognized gain for capital and operating leases is derived as follows:

1. If the leaseback is classified as an operating lease, recognized gain is the portion of gain that exceeds the PV of the MLP over the lease term. The seller-lessee should use its incremental borrowing rate to compute the PV of the MLP. If the implicit rate of interest in the lease is known and lower, it should be used instead.
2. If the leaseback is classified as a capital lease, recognized gain is the amount of gain that exceeds the recorded amount of the leased asset.

In all cases, the seller-lessee should immediately recognize a loss when the fair value of the property at the time of the leaseback is less than its undepreciated cost (book value). In the example below, the sales price is less than the book value of the property. However, there is no economic loss because the FMV which equals the PV is greater than the book value.

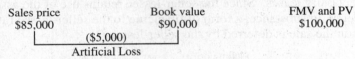

| Sales price | Book value | FMV and PV |
|-------------|------------|------------|
| $85,000 | $90,000 | $100,000 |

      ($5,000)
     Artificial Loss

The artificial loss must be deferred and amortized as an addition to depreciation.

In the chart below, when the leased asset is land only, any amortization should be on a straight-line basis over the lease term, regardless of whether the lease is classified as a capital or operating lease.

The buyer-lessor should account for the transaction as a purchase and a direct financing lease if the agreement meets the criteria of **either** a direct financing lease **or** a sales-type lease. Otherwise, the agreement should be accounted for as a purchase and an operating lease.

To illustrate a sale-leaseback transaction, consider the example below.

Numerical Example 6:

### Lease Information
1) Lessee Corporation sells equipment that has a book value of $80,000 and a fair value of $100,000 to Lessor Corporation, and then immediately leases it back.
2) The sale date is January 1, 2007, and the equipment has a fair value of $100,000 on that date and an estimated useful life of fifteen years.
3) The lease term is fifteen years, noncancelable, and requires equal rental payments of $13,109 at the beginning of each year.
4) Lessee Corp. has the option to renew the lease annually at the same rental payments upon expiration of the original lease.
5) Lessee Corp. has the obligation to pay all executory costs.
6) The annual rental payments provide the lessor with a 12% return on investment.
7) The incremental borrowing rate of Lessee Corp. is 12%.
8) Lessee Corp. depreciates similar equipment on a straight-line basis.

### Lease Classification
Lessee Corp. should classify the agreement as a capital lease since the lease term exceeds 75% of the estimated economic life of the equipment, and because the present value of the lease payments is greater than 90% of the fair value of the equipment. Assuming that collectibility of the lease payments is reasonably predictable and that no important uncertainties exist concerning the amount of unreimbursable costs yet to be incurred by the lessor, Lessor Corp. should classify the transaction as a direct financing lease because the present value of the minimum lease payments is equal to the fair market value of $100,000.

### Accounting for Lease
Lessee Corp. and Lessor Corp. would normally make the following journal entries during the first year:

#### Upon Sale of Equipment on January 1, 2007

| Lessee Corp. | | | Lessor Corp. | | |
|---|---|---|---|---|---|
| Cash | 100,000 | | Equipment | 100,000 | |
| Equipment | | 80,000 | Cash | | 100,000 |
| Unearned profit on | | | Lease receivable | 196,635* | |
| sale-leaseback | | 20,000 | Equipment | | 100,000 |
| Leased equipment | 100,000 | | Unearned interest | | 96,635 |
| Lease obligations | | 100,000 | | | |

* *($13,109 × 15)*

**To Record First Payment on January 1, 2007**

| Lessee Corp. | | | Lessor Corp. | | |
|---|---|---|---|---|---|
| Lease obligations | 13,109 | | Cash | 13,109 | |
| Cash | | 13,109 | Lease receivable | | 13,109 |

**To Record Incurrence and Payment of Executory Costs**

| Lessee Corp. | | | Lessor Corp. |
|---|---|---|---|
| Insurance, taxes, etc. | xxx | | (No entry) |
| Cash (accounts payable) | | xxx | |

**To Record Depreciation Expense on the Equipment, December 31, 2007**

| Lessee Corp. | | | Lessor Corp. |
|---|---|---|---|
| Depreciation expense | 6,667 | | (No entry) |
| Accum. depr.— capital leases | | | |
| ($100,000 ÷ 15) | | 6,667 | |

**To Amortize Profit on Sale-Leaseback by Lessee Corp., December 31, 2007**

| Lessee Corp. | | | Lessor Corp. |
|---|---|---|---|
| Unearned profit on sale-leaseback | 1,333 | | (No entry) |
| Depr. expense | | | |
| ($20,000 ÷ 15) | | 1,333 | |

**To Record Interest for 2005, December 31, 2007**

| Lessee Corp. | | | Lessor Corp |
|---|---|---|---|
| Interest expense | 10,427 | | Unearned interest income  10,427 |
| Accrued interest payable | | 10,427 | Interest income              10,427 |

*(Carrying value $86,891 × .12 = $10,427)*

c. **Disclosure requirements**

The disclosures required of the lessor and lessee are very comprehensive and detailed. In essence, all terms of the leasing arrangement are required (i.e., contingent rentals, subleases, residual values, unearned interest revenue, etc.). For the details see the outline of SFAS 13 (D.5.). There are, however, a couple of generic disclosure requirements. First, a **general description** of the leasing arrangement is required. Second, the minimum future payments to be received (paid) by the lessor (lessee) for each of the **five succeeding fiscal years** should also be disclosed.

### SUMMARY OF KEY PROBLEM SOLUTION POINTS

*(1)  Lessor—direct financing and sales-type leases*

(a) Periodic lease payments (PLP)
  \* *Guaranteed/unguaranteed*
  \*\* *Annuity due or ordinary* = $$\frac{\text{FMV of leased property–PV of RV*/BPO}}{\text{PV of an annuity factor** using the lessor's implicit rate}}$$

(b) Lease payments receivable/Gross investments = (Periodic lease payments × Number of rents) + Residual value/Bar. Pur. Opt.

(c) Unearned interest revenue = Gross investment – PV of PLP, PV of G/U RV, PV of PBO

(d) Net investment = Gross investment – Unearned interest revenue

(e) Gross profit (only for sales-type leases) = Selling price\* – Cost of leased asset sold
  \*(FMV/PV of PLP + G/URV + BPO)

(f) Interest revenue = Carrying value of lease receivable \* ×
  \* (Gross investment – Unearned interest)   Implicit % × Time

Periodic Journal Entries

| | | |
|---|---|---|
| Unearned interest revenue | xxx | |
| Interest revenue | | xxx |
| Cash | xxx | |
| Lease payments receivable | | xxx |

**(2) Lessee—capital lease**

(a) Determine capital lease liability  = (Periodic lease payment [PLP] × Present value factor * ) + (G/URV or BPO × PV of 1.00 factor)

\* *Annuity due or ordinary annuity*

- Use lessee's incremental borrowing %, unless lessor's implicit % is lower and lessee knows it
- PLP is exclusive of executory costs

(b) Leased asset  = Capital lease liability at inception of lease as computed above—PV × MLP [Exception:  where FMV of leased asset < PV of MLP (PLP + GRV or BPO), then leased asset and capital lease liability are recorded at the FMV of leased asset.]

(c) Depreciation (amortization) of leased asset

- Over useful life, regardless of lease term, if either criterion (1) or (2) is met:  title transfer or bargain purchase option.
- Over lease term if criterion (3) or (4) is met: $\geq 75\%$ test or $\geq 90\%$ test

(d) Lease liability =

| | | |
|---|---|---|
| (1) Carrying value at inception of lease | | $xxx |
| (2) Less first payment (usually the first payment is all principal because the lease liability is the PV of an annuity due) | | (xx) |
| (3) Carrying value (CV) | | $xxx |
| (4) Less principal part of second payment [PLP – (CV × interest %)] | | (xxx) |
| (5) Carrying value | | $xxx |
| | | etc. |

(e) CV × % = Interest expense

## Research Component

SFAS 13, *Accounting for Leases,* issued in November 1976, has paragraphs that are amended and superseded by a number of other pronouncements.  The most important amendments and changes to SFAS 13 are found in the following statements:

SFAS 23    *Inception of the Lease*

SFAS 27    *Classification of Renewals or Extensions of Existing Sales-Type or Direct Financing Leases*

SFAS 28    *Accounting for Sales with Leasebacks*

SFAS 29    *Determining Contingent Rentals*

SFAS 91    *Nonrefundable Fees & Costs Associated with Originating or Acquiring Loans and Initial Direct Costs of Leases*

SFAS 98    *Accounting for Leases*

- *Sale-Leaseback Transactions Involving Real Estate*
- *Sales-Type Leases of Real Estate*
- *Definition of the Lease Term*
- *Initial Direct Costs of Direct Financing Leases*

SFAS 145    *Rescission of FASB Statements 4, 44, and 64, Amendment of FASB Statement No. 13, and Technical Corrections*

SFAS 146    *Accounting for Costs Associated with Exit or Disposal Activities*

In addition, a number of issues have also been addressed in the FASB Interpretations (classification of residual value, purchasing assets during the lease term, losses on subleases) and in the FASB Technical Bulletins (interest rates, adjustments of guaranteed residuals, losses on subleases, scheduled rent increases on operating leases, accounting for interest in residual value of leased assets).  The Emerging Issues Task Force has also addressed a variety of issues including SPEs, leveraged leases, revenue recognition issues, and residual values.

The majority of leasing rules are found in SFAS 13 for a typical lease and in SFAS 28 and 98 for sale-leaseback transactions.  There are two recent pronouncements that affect lease accounting. SFAS 145, issued in April 2002, amends SFAS 13 and applies to all financial statements issued on or after May 15, 2002.  SFAS 145 describes the accounting for modifications of a capital lease that give rise to a new agreement that is classified as an operating lease, and treats the modification as a sale-leaseback transaction under the provisions of SFAS 98.  In addition, SFAS 145 addresses the accounting and reporting for subleases, which result in the modification or termination of the capital lease.  SFAS 146 address the costs associated with terminating an operating lease.

Typical research questions may include determining whether a lease is an operating lease or a capital lease or determining which items to include in calculating the minimum lease payments.

Below is a list of keywords used in the various pronouncements.

| | | |
|---|---|---|
| Bargain purchase option | Lease modification | Sales-type lease |
| Capital lease | Leasehold improvement | Substantial rights |
| Costs to terminate | Minimum lease payments | Termination costs |
| Direct financing lease | Modified lease | Termination of agreement |
| Guaranteed residual | New agreement operating lease | Transfer title |
| Initial direct costs | Operating lease | Unguaranteed residual |
| Lease bonus | Sale-leaseback | |

**MULTIPLE-CHOICE QUESTIONS (1-56)**

**1.** Rapp Co. leased a new machine to Lake Co. on January 1, 2007. The lease is an operating lease and expires on January 1, 2012. The annual rental is $90,000. Additionally, on January 1, 2007, Lake paid $50,000 to Rapp as a lease bonus and $25,000 as a security deposit to be refunded upon expiration of the lease. In Rapp's 2007 income statement, the amount of rental revenue should be
   a. $140,000
   b. $125,000
   c. $100,000
   d. $ 90,000

**2.** Wall Co. leased office premises to Fox, Inc. for a five-year term beginning January 2, 2007. Under the terms of the operating lease, rent for the first year is $8,000 and rent for years two through five is $12,500 per annum. However, as an inducement to enter the lease, Wall granted Fox the first six months of the lease rent-free. In its December 31, 2007 income statement, what amount should Wall report as rental income?
   a. $12,000
   b. $11,600
   c. $10,800
   d. $ 8,000

**3.** On January 1, 2007, Wren Co. leased a building to Brill under an operating lease for ten years at $50,000 per year, payable the first day of each lease year. Wren paid $15,000 to a real estate broker as a finder's fee. The building is depreciated $12,000 per year. For 2007, Wren incurred insurance and property tax expense totaling $9,000. Wren's net rental income for 2007 should be
   a. $27,500
   b. $29,000
   c. $35,000
   d. $36,500

**4.** On July 1, 2005, Gee, Inc. leased a delivery truck from Marr Corp. under a three-year operating lease. Total rent for the term of the lease will be $36,000, payable as follows:

12 months at $   500 = $ 6,000
12 months at $   750 =    9,000
12 months at $1,750 =   21,000

All payments were made when due. In Marr's June 30, 2007 balance sheet, the accrued rent receivable should be reported as
   a. $0
   b. $ 9,000
   c. $12,000
   d. $21,000

**5.** On January 1, 2007, Glen Co. leased a building to Dix Corp. under an operating lease for a ten-year term at an annual rental of $50,000. At inception of the lease, Glen received $200,000 covering the first two years' rent of $100,000 and a security deposit of $100,000. This deposit will not be returned to Dix upon expiration of the lease but will be applied to payment of rent for the last two years of the lease. What portion of the $200,000 should be shown as a current and long-term liability, respectively, in Glen's December 31, 2007 balance sheet?

|   | Current liability | Long-term liability |
|---|---|---|
| a. | $0 | $200,000 |
| b. | $ 50,000 | $100,000 |
| c. | $100,000 | $100,000 |
| d. | $100,000 | $ 50,000 |

**6.** As an inducement to enter a lease, Graf Co., a lessor, granted Zep, Inc., a lessee, twelve months of free rent under a five-year operating lease. The lease was effective on January 1, 2007, and provides for monthly rental payments to begin January 1, 2008. Zep made the first rental payment on December 30, 2007. In its 2007 income statement, Graf should report rental revenue in an amount equal to
   a. Zero.
   b. Cash received during 2007.
   c. One-fourth of the total cash to be received over the life of the lease.
   d. One-fifth of the total cash to be received over the life of the lease.

**7.** Quo Co. rented a building to Hava Fast Food. Each month Quo receives a fixed rental amount plus a variable rental amount based on Hava's sales for that month. As sales increase so does the variable rental amount, but at a reduced rate. Which of the following curves reflects the monthly rentals under the agreement?

   a. I
   b. II
   c. III
   d. IV

**8.** As an inducement to enter a lease, Arts, Inc., a lessor, grants Hompson Corp., a lessee, nine months of free rent under a five-year operating lease. The lease is effective on July 1, 2007 and provides for monthly rental of $1,000 to begin April 1, 2008. In Hompson's income statement for the year ended June 30, 2008, rent expense should be reported as
   a. $10,200
   b. $ 9,000
   c. $ 3,000
   d. $ 2,550

**9.** On January 1, 2007, Park Co. signed a ten-year operating lease for office space at $96,000 per year. The lease included a provision for additional rent of 5% of annual company sales in excess of $500,000. Park's sales for the year ended December 31, 2007, were $600,000. Upon execution of the lease, Park paid $24,000 as a bonus for the lease. Park's rent expense for the year ended December 31, 2007, is
   a. $ 98,400
   b. $101,000
   c. $103,400
   d. $125,000

**10.** On July 1, 2007, South Co. entered into a ten-year operating lease for a warehouse facility. The annual minimum lease payments are $100,000. In addition to the base rent,

South pays a monthly allocation of the building's operating expenses, which amounted to $20,000 for the year ended June 30, 2008. In the notes to South's June 30, 2008 financial statements, what amounts of subsequent years' lease payments should be disclosed?

   a. $100,000 per annum for each of the next five years and $500,000 in the aggregate.
   b. $120,000 per annum for each of the next five years and $600,000 in the aggregate.
   c. $100,000 per annum for each of the next five years and $900,000 in the aggregate.
   d. $120,000 per annum for each of the next five years and $1,080,000 in the aggregate.

**11.** On January 1, 2007, Mollat Co. signed a seven-year lease for equipment having a ten-year economic life. The present value of the monthly lease payments equaled 80% of the equipment's fair value. The lease agreement provides for neither a transfer of title to Mollat nor a bargain purchase option. In its 2007 income statement Mollat should report

   a. Rent expense equal to the 2007 lease payments.
   b. Rent expense equal to the 2007 lease payments less interest expense.
   c. Lease amortization equal to one-tenth of the equipment's fair value.
   d. Lease amortization equal to one-seventh of 80% of the equipment's fair value.

**12.** A twenty-year property lease, classified as an operating lease, provides for a 10% increase in annual payments every five years. In the sixth year compared to the fifth year, the lease will cause the following expenses to increase

| | Rent | Interest |
|---|---|---|
| a. | No | Yes |
| b. | Yes | No |
| c. | Yes | Yes |
| d. | No | No |

**13.** On December 1, 2007, Clark Co. leased office space for five years at a monthly rental of $60,000. On the same date, Clark paid the lessor the following amounts:

| | |
|---|---|
| First month's rent | $ 60,000 |
| Last month's rent | 60,000 |
| Security deposit (refundable at lease expiration) | 80,000 |
| Installation of new walls and offices | 360,000 |

What should be Clark's 2007 expense relating to utilization of the office space?

   a. $ 60,000
   b. $ 66,000
   c. $120,000
   d. $140,000

**14.** Star Co. leases a building for its product showroom. The ten-year nonrenewable lease will expire on December 31, 2012. In January 2007, Star redecorated its showroom and made leasehold improvements of $48,000. The estimated useful life of the improvements is eight years. Star uses the straight-line method of amortization. What amount of leasehold improvements, net of amortization, should Star report in its June 30, 2007 balance sheet?

   a. $45,600
   b. $45,000
   c. $44,000
   d. $43,200

**15.** On January 2, 2007, Ral Co. leased land and building from an unrelated lessor for a ten-year term. The lease has a renewal option for an additional ten years, but Ral has not reached a decision with regard to the renewal option. In early January of 2007, Ral completed the following improvements to the property:

| Description | Estimated life | Cost |
|---|---|---|
| Sales office | 10 years | $47,000 |
| Warehouse | 25 years | 75,000 |
| Parking lot | 15 years | 18,000 |

Amortization of leasehold improvements for 2007 should be

   a. $ 7,000
   b. $ 8,900
   c. $12,200
   d. $14,000

**16.** On January 1, 2005, Nobb Corp. signed a twelve-year lease for warehouse space. Nobb has an option to renew the lease for an additional eight-year period on or before January 1, 2009. During January 2007, Nobb made substantial improvements to the warehouse. The cost of these improvements was $540,000, with an estimated useful life of fifteen years. At December 31, 2007, Nobb intended to exercise the renewal option. Nobb has taken a full year's amortization on this leasehold. In Nobb's December 31, 2007 balance sheet, the carrying amount of this leasehold improvement should be

   a. $486,000
   b. $504,000
   c. $510,000
   d. $513,000

**17.** During January 2007, Vail Co. made long-term improvements to a recently leased building. The lease agreement provides for neither a transfer of title to Vail nor a bargain purchase option. The present value of the minimum lease payments equals 85% of the building's market value, and the lease term equals 70% of the building's economic life. Should assets be recognized for the building and the leasehold improvements?

| | Building | Leasehold improvements |
|---|---|---|
| a. | Yes | Yes |
| b. | No | Yes |
| c. | Yes | No |
| d. | No | No |

**18.** A lessee incurred costs to construct office space in a leased warehouse. The estimated useful life of the office is ten years. The remaining term of the nonrenewable lease is fifteen years. The costs should be

   a. Capitalized as leasehold improvements and depreciated over fifteen years.
   b. Capitalized as leasehold improvements and depreciated over ten years.
   c. Capitalized as leasehold improvements and expensed in the year in which the lease expires.
   d. Expensed as incurred.

**19.** Glade Co. leases computer equipment to customers under direct-financing leases. The equipment has no residual value at the end of the lease and the leases do not contain bargain purchase options. Glade wishes to earn 8% interest on a five-year lease of equipment with a fair value of $323,400. The present value of an annuity due of $1 at 8% for five years is 4.312. What is the total amount of interest revenue that Glade will earn over the life of the lease?

a.   $  51,600
b.   $  75,000
c.   $129,360
d.   $139,450

**20.**  On January 1, 2005, JCK Co. signed a contract for an eight-year lease of its equipment with a ten-year life.  The present value of the sixteen equal semiannual payments in advance equaled 85% of the equipment's fair value.  The contract had no provision for JCK, the lessor, to give up legal ownership of the equipment.  Should JCK recognize rent or interest revenue in 2007, and should the revenue recognized in 2007 be the same or smaller than the revenue recognized in 2006?

|   | *2007 revenues recognized* | *2007 amount recognized compared to 2006* |
|---|---|---|
| a. | Rent | The same |
| b. | Rent | Smaller |
| c. | Interest | The same |
| d. | Interest | Smaller |

**21.**  Peg Co. leased equipment from Howe Corp. on July 1, 2007 for an eight-year period expiring June 30, 2015.  Equal payments under the lease are $600,000 and are due on July 1 of each year.  The first payment was made on July 1, 2007.  The rate of interest contemplated by Peg and Howe is 10%.  The cash selling price of the equipment is $3,520,000, and the cost of the equipment on Howe's accounting records is $2,800,000.  The lease is appropriately recorded as a sales-type lease.  What is the amount of profit on the sale and interest revenue that Howe should record for the year ended December 31, 2007?

|   | *Profit on sale* | *Interest revenue* |
|---|---|---|
| a. | $720,000 | $176,000 |
| b. | $720,000 | $146,000 |
| c. | $  45,000 | $176,000 |
| d. | $  45,000 | $146,000 |

**22.**  Howe Co. leased equipment to Kew Corp. on January 2, 2007, for an eight-year period expiring December 31, 2014.  Equal payments under the lease are $600,000 and are due on January 2 of each year.  The first payment was made on January 2, 2007.  The list selling price of the equipment is $3,520,000 and its carrying cost on Howe's books is $2,800,000.  The lease is appropriately accounted for as a sales-type lease.  The present value of the lease payments is $3,300,000.  What amount of profit on the sale should Howe report for the year ended December 31, 2007?
a.   $720,000
b.   $500,000
c.   $  90,000
d.   $0

**23.**  The excess of the fair value of leased property at the inception of the lease over its cost or carrying amount should be classified by the lessor as
a.   Unearned income from a sales-type lease.
b.   Unearned income from a direct-financing lease.
c.   Manufacturer's or dealer's profit from a sales-type lease.
d.   Manufacturer's or dealer's profit from a direct-financing lease.

**24.**  In a lease that is recorded as a sales-type lease by the lessor, interest revenue

a.   Should be recognized in full as revenue at the lease's inception.
b.   Should be recognized over the period of the lease using the straight-line method.
c.   Should be recognized over the period of the lease using the interest method.
d.   Does **not** arise.

**25.**  Lease M does not contain a bargain purchase option, but the lease term is equal to 90% of the estimated economic life of the leased property.  Lease P does not transfer ownership of the property to the lessee at the end of the lease term, but the lease term is equal to 75% of the estimated economic life of the leased property.  How should the lessee classify these leases?

|   | *Lease M* | *Lease P* |
|---|---|---|
| a. | Capital lease | Operating lease |
| b. | Capital lease | Capital lease |
| c. | Operating lease | Capital lease |
| d. | Operating lease | Operating lease |

**26.**  On December 31, 2007, Day Co. leased a new machine from Parr with the following pertinent information:

| | |
|---|---|
| Lease term | 6 years |
| Annual rental payable at beginning of each year | $50,000 |
| Useful life of machine | 8 years |
| Day's incremental borrowing rate | 15% |
| Implicit interest rate in lease (known by Day) | 12% |
| Present value of annuity of 1 in advance for 6 periods at | |
| 12% | 4.61 |
| 15% | 4.35 |

The lease is not renewable, and the machine reverts to Parr at the termination of the lease.  The cost of the machine on Parr's accounting records is $375,500.  At the beginning of the lease term, Day should record a lease liability of
a.   $375,500
b.   $230,500
c.   $217,500
d.   $0

**27.**  On January 1, 2007, Day Corp. entered into a ten-year lease agreement with Ward, Inc. for industrial equipment.  Annual lease payments of $10,000 are payable at the end of each year.  Day knows that the lessor expects a 10% return on the lease.  Day has a 12% incremental borrowing rate.  The equipment is expected to have an estimated useful life of ten years.  In addition, a third party has guaranteed to pay Ward a residual value of $5,000 at the end of the lease.

The present value of an ordinary annuity of $1 at
    12% for ten years is 5.6502
    10% for ten years is 6.1446

The present value of $1 at
    12% for ten years is .3220
    10% for ten years is .3855

In Day's October 31, 2007 balance sheet, the principal amount of the lease obligation was
a.   $63,374
b.   $61,446
c.   $58,112
d.   $56,502

**28.**  Robbins, Inc. leased a machine from Ready Leasing Co.  The lease qualifies as a capital lease and requires ten annual payments of $10,000 beginning immediately.  The lease specifies an interest rate of 12% and a purchase option of $10,000 at the end of the tenth year, even though the machine's estimated value on that date is $20,000. Robbins' incremental borrowing rate is 14%.

The present value of an annuity due of one at
12% for ten years is 6.328
14% for ten years is 5.946

The present value of one at
12% for ten years is .322
14% for ten years is .270

What amount should Robbins record as lease liability at the beginning of the lease term?

- a. $62,160
- b. $64,860
- c. $66,500
- d. $69,720

**29.** Neal Corp. entered into a nine-year capital lease on a warehouse on December 31, 2007. Lease payments of $52,000, which includes real estate taxes of $2,000, are due annually, beginning on December 31, 2008, and every December 31 thereafter. Neal does not know the interest rate implicit in the lease; Neal's incremental borrowing rate is 9%. The rounded present value of an ordinary annuity for nine years at 9% is 5.6. What amount should Neal report as capitalized lease liability at December 31, 2007?

- a. $280,000
- b. $291,200
- c. $450,000
- d. $468,000

**30.** East Company leased a new machine from North Company on May 1, 2007, under a lease with the following information:

| | |
|---|---|
| Lease term | 10 years |
| Annual rental payable at beginning of each lease year | $40,000 |
| Useful life of machine | 12 years |
| Implicit interest rate | 14% |
| Present value of an annuity of one in advance for ten periods at 14% | 5.95 |
| Present value of one for ten periods at 14% | 0.27 |

East has the option to purchase the machine on May 1, 2017 by paying $50,000, which approximates the expected fair value of the machine on the option exercise date. On May 1, 2007, East should record a capitalized lease asset of

- a. $251,500
- b. $238,000
- c. $224,500
- d. $198,000

**31.** On January 1, 2007, Babson, Inc. leased two automobiles for executive use. The lease requires Babson to make five annual payments of $13,000 beginning January 1, 2007. At the end of the lease term, December 31, 2011, Babson guarantees the residual value of the automobiles will total $10,000. The lease qualifies as a capital lease. The interest rate implicit in the lease is 9%. Present value factors for the 9% rate implicit in the lease are as follows:

| | |
|---|---|
| For an annuity due with five payments | 4.240 |
| For an ordinary annuity with five payments | 3.890 |
| Present value of $1 for five periods | 0.650 |

Babson's recorded capital lease liability immediately after the first required payment should be

- a. $48,620
- b. $44,070
- c. $35,620
- d. $31,070

**32.** On December 30, 2007, Rafferty Corp. leased equipment under a capital lease. Annual lease payments of $20,000 are due December 31 for ten years. The equipment's useful life is ten years, and the interest rate implicit in the lease is 10%. The capital lease obligation was recorded on December 30, 2007, at $135,000, and the first lease payment was made on that date. What amount should Rafferty include in current liabilities for this capital lease in its December 31, 2007 balance sheet?

- a. $ 6,500
- b. $ 8,500
- c. $11,500
- d. $20,000

**33.** Oak Co. leased equipment for its entire nine-year useful life, agreeing to pay $50,000 at the start of the lease term on December 31, 2007, and $50,000 annually on each December 31 for the next eight years. The present value on December 31, 2007, of the nine lease payments over the lease term, using the rate implicit in the lease which Oak knows to be 10%, was $316,500. The December 31, 2007 present value of the lease payments using Oak's incremental borrowing rate of 12% was $298,500. Oak made a timely second lease payment. What amount should Oak report as capital lease liability in its December 31, 2008 balance sheet?

- a. $350,000
- b. $243,150
- c. $228,320
- d. $0

**34.** On December 31, 2007, Roe Co. leased a machine from Colt for a five-year period. Equal annual payments under the lease are $105,000 (including $5,000 annual executory costs) and are due on December 31 of each year. The first payment was made on December 31, 2007, and the second payment was made on December 31, 2008. The five lease payments are discounted at 10% over the lease term. The present value of minimum lease payments at the inception of the lease and before the first annual payment was $417,000. The lease is appropriately accounted for as a capital lease by Roe. In its December 31, 2008 balance sheet, Roe should report a lease liability of

- a. $317,000
- b. $315,000
- c. $285,300
- d. $248,700

**35.** In the long-term liabilities section of its balance sheet at December 31, 2007, Mene Co. reported a capital lease obligation of $75,000, net of current portion of $1,364. Payments of $9,000 were made on both January 2, 2008, and January 2, 2009. Mene's incremental borrowing rate on the date of the lease was 11% and the lessor's implicit rate, which was known to Mene, was 10%. In its December 31, 2008 balance sheet, what amount should Mene report as capital lease obligation, net of current portion?

- a. $66,000
- b. $73,500
- c. $73,636
- d. $74,250

**36.** For a capital lease, the amount recorded initially by the lessee as a liability should normally

- a. Exceed the total of the minimum lease payments.

b.  Exceed the present value of the minimum lease payments at the beginning of the lease.
c.  Equal the total of the minimum lease payments.
d.  Equal the present value of the minimum lease payments at the beginning of the lease.

**37.** At the inception of a capital lease, the guaranteed residual value should be

a.  Included as part of minimum lease payments at present value.
b.  Included as part of minimum lease payments at future value.
c.  Included as part of minimum lease payments only to the extent that guaranteed residual value is expected to exceed estimated residual value.
d.  Excluded from minimum lease payments.

**38.** A six-year capital lease entered into on December 31, 2007, specified equal minimum annual lease payments due on December 31 of each year. The first minimum annual lease payment, paid on December 31, 2007, consists of which of the following?

|     | Interest expense | Lease liability |
| --- | --- | --- |
| a.  | Yes | Yes |
| b.  | Yes | No |
| c.  | No | Yes |
| d.  | No | No |

**39.** A six-year capital lease expiring on December 31 specifies equal minimum annual lease payments. Part of this payment represents interest and part represents a reduction in the net lease liability. The portion of the minimum lease payment in the fifth year applicable to the reduction of the net lease liability should be

a.  Less than in the fourth year.
b.  More than in the fourth year.
c.  The same as in the sixth year.
d.  More than in the sixth year.

**40.** A lessee had a ten-year capital lease requiring equal annual payments. The reduction of the lease liability in year two should equal

a.  The current liability shown for the lease at the end of year one.
b.  The current liability shown for the lease at the end of year two.
c.  The reduction of the lease obligation in year one.
d.  One-tenth of the original lease liability.

**41.** On January 2, 2007, Cole Co. signed an eight-year noncancelable lease for a new machine, requiring $15,000 annual payments at the beginning of each year. The machine has a useful life of twelve years, with no salvage value. Title passes to Cole at the lease expiration date. Cole uses straight-line depreciation for all of its plant assets. Aggregate lease payments have a present value on January 2, 2007, of $108,000 based on an appropriate rate of interest. For 2007, Cole should record depreciation (amortization) expense for the leased machine at

a.  $0
b.  $ 9,000
c.  $13,500
d.  $15,000

**42.** On January 2, 2007, Nori Mining Co. (lessee) entered into a five-year lease for drilling equipment. Nori accounted

for the acquisition as a capital lease for $240,000, which includes a $10,000 bargain purchase option. At the end of the lease, Nori expects to exercise the bargain purchase option. Nori estimates that the equipment's fair value will be $20,000 at the end of its eight-year life. Nori regularly uses straight-line depreciation on similar equipment. For the year ended December 31, 2007, what amount should Nori recognize as depreciation expense on the leased asset?

a.  $48,000
b.  $46,000
c.  $30,000
d.  $27,500

**43.** The lessee should amortize the capitalizable cost of the leased asset in a manner consistent with the lessee's normal depreciation policy for owned assets for leases that

|     | Contain a bargain purchase option | Transfer ownership of the property to the lessee by the end of the lease term |
| --- | --- | --- |
| a.  | No | No |
| b.  | No | Yes |
| c.  | Yes | Yes |
| d.  | Yes | No |

**44.** On January 1, 2007, Harrow Co. as lessee signed a five-year noncancelable equipment lease with annual payments of $100,000 beginning December 31, 2007. Harrow treated this transaction as a capital lease. The five lease payments have a present value of $379,000 at January 1, 2007, based on interest of 10%. What amount should Harrow report as interest expense for the year ended December 31, 2007?

a.  $37,900
b.  $27,900
c.  $24,200
d.  $0

**45.** On January 1, 2007, West Co. entered into a ten-year lease for a manufacturing plant. The annual minimum lease payments are $100,000. In the notes to the December 31, 2007 financial statements, what amounts of subsequent years' lease payments should be disclosed?

|     | Amount for appropriate required period | Aggregate amount for the period thereafter |
| --- | --- | --- |
| a.  | $100,000 | $0 |
| b.  | $300,000 | $500,000 |
| c.  | $500,000 | $300,000 |
| d.  | $500,000 | $0 |

**46.** Cott, Inc. prepared an interest amortization table for a five-year lease payable with a bargain purchase option of $2,000, exercisable at the end of the lease. At the end of the five years, the balance in the leases payable column of the spreadsheet was zero. Cott has asked Grant, CPA, to review the spreadsheet to determine the error. Only one error was made on the spreadsheet. Which of the following statements represents the best explanation for this error?

a.  The beginning present value of the lease did **not** include the present value of the bargain purchase option.
b.  Cott subtracted the annual interest amount from the lease payable balance instead of adding it.
c.  The present value of the bargain purchase option was subtracted from the present value of the annual payments.

d.   Cott discounted the annual payments as an ordinary annuity, when the payments actually occurred at the beginning of each period.

**47.** On December 31, 2007, Lane, Inc. sold equipment to Noll, and simultaneously leased it back for twelve years. Pertinent information at this date is as follows:

| | |
|---|---|
| Sales price | $480,000 |
| Carrying amount | 360,000 |
| Estimated remaining economic life | 15 years |

At December 31, 2007, how much should Lane report as deferred gain from the sale of the equipment?
- a.   $0
- b.   $110,000
- c.   $112,000
- d.   $120,000

**48.** The following information pertains to a sale and leaseback of equipment by Mega Co. on December 31, 2007:

| | |
|---|---|
| Sales price | $400,000 |
| Carrying amount | $300,000 |
| Monthly lease payment | $3,250 |
| Present value of lease payments | $36,900 |
| Estimated remaining life | 25 years |
| Lease term | 1 year |
| Implicit rate | 12% |

What amount of deferred gain on the sale should Mega report at December 31, 2007?
- a.   $0
- b.   $ 36,900
- c.   $ 63,100
- d.   $100,000

**49.** On December 31, 2007, Parke Corp. sold Edlow Corp. an airplane with an estimated remaining useful life of ten years. At the same time, Parke leased back the airplane for three years. Additional information is as follows:

| | |
|---|---|
| Sales price | $600,000 |
| Carrying amount of airplane at date of sale | $100,000 |
| Monthly rental under lease | $ 6,330 |
| Interest rate implicit in the lease as computed by Edlow and known by Parke (this rate is lower than the lessee's incremental borrowing rate) | 12% |
| Present value of operating lease rentals ($6,330 for 36 months @ 12%) | $190,581 |

The leaseback is considered an operating lease. In Parke's December 31, 2007 balance sheet, what amount should be included as deferred revenue on this transaction?
- a.   $0
- b.   $190,581
- c.   $309,419
- d.   $500,000

**50.** On June 30, 2007, Lang Co. sold equipment with an estimated useful life of eleven years and immediately leased it back for ten years. The equipment's carrying amount was $450,000; the sale price was $430,000; and the present value of the lease payments, which is equal to the fair value of the equipment, was $465,000. In its June 30, 2007 balance sheet, what amount should Lang report as deferred loss?
- a.   $35,000
- b.   $20,000
- c.   $15,000
- d.   $0

**51.** On January 1, 2007, Hooks Oil Co. sold equipment with a carrying amount of $100,000, and a remaining useful life of ten years, to Maco Drilling for $150,000. Hooks immediately leased the equipment back under a ten-year capital lease with a present value of $150,000 and will depreciate the equipment using the straight-line method. Hooks made the first annual lease payment of $24,412 in December 2007. In Hooks' December 31, 2007 balance sheet, the unearned gain on equipment sale should be
- a.   $50,000
- b.   $45,000
- c.   $25,588
- d.   $0

**52.** In a sale-leaseback transaction, the seller-lessee has retained the property. The gain on the sale should be recognized at the time of the sale-leaseback when the lease is classified as a(n)

| | Capital lease | Operating lease |
|---|---|---|
| a. | Yes | Yes |
| b. | No | No |
| c. | No | Yes |
| d. | Yes | No |

**53.** Able sold its headquarters building at a gain, and simultaneously leased back the building. The lease was reported as a capital lease. At the time of sale, the gain should be reported as
- a.   Operating income.
- b.   An extraordinary item, net of income tax.
- c.   A separate component of stockholders' equity.
- d.   An asset valuation allowance.

**54.** On January 1, 2005, Goliath entered into a five-year operating lease for equipment. In January 2007, Goliath decided that it no longer needs the equipment and terminates the contract by paying a penalty of $3,000. How should Goliath account for the lease termination costs?
- a.   Recognize $3,000 termination cost in 2007 as a loss from continuing operations.
- b.   Recognize $1,000 termination cost each year for the remaining three years of the lease term.
- c.   Recognize the $3,000 termination cost as an extraordinary item in 2007.
- d.   Recognize the $3,000 termination cost as a discontinued operation in 2007.

**55.** In January 2006, Hopper Corp. signed a capital lease for equipment with a term of twenty years. In 2008, Hopper negotiated a modification to a capital lease that resulted in the lease being reclassified as an operating lease. Hopper calculated the company had a gain of $8,000 on the lease modification. Hopper retains all rights to use the property during the remainder of the lease term. How should Hopper account for the lease modification?
- a.   Recognize an $8,000 gain from lease modification during 2008.
- b.   Defer the gain and recognize it over the life of the operating lease.
- c.   Recognize the $8,000 gain as an extraordinary item in 2008.
- d.   Recognize the $8,000 gain as a discontinued operation in 2008.

**56.**  On January 1, 2004, Belkor entered into a 10-year capital lease for equipment.  On December 1, 2007, Belkor terminates the capital lease and incurs a $20,000 loss.  How should Belkor recognize the lease termination on their financial statements?

   a.   Recognize a $20,000 loss in 2007 as a discontinued operation.

   b.   Recognize a $20,000 loss in 2007 as an extraordinary item.

   c.   Recognize a $20,000 loss from continuing operations in 2007.

   d.   Defer recognition of the loss and recognize pro rata over the life of the lease term.

**SIMULATION PROBLEMS**

**Simulation Problem 1**                                    (50 to 60 minutes)

| Situation | | | | | |
|---|---|---|---|---|---|
| | Journal Entries | Concepts | Classification | Communication | Research |

On January 2, 2007, Nesbitt Co. leased equipment from Grant, Inc.  Lease payments are $100,000, payable annually every December 31 for twenty years.  Title to the equipment passes to Nesbitt at the end of the lease term.  The lease is noncancelable.

- The equipment has a $750,000 carrying amount on Grant's books.  Its estimated economic life was twenty-five years on January 2, 2007.
- The rate implicit in the lease, which is known to Nesbitt, is 10%.  Nesbitt's incremental borrowing rate is 12%.
- Nesbitt uses the straight-line method of depreciation.

The rounded present value factors of an ordinary annuity for twenty years are as follows:

| | |
|---|---|
| 12% | 7.5 |
| 10% | 8.5 |

| | Journal Entries | | | | |
|---|---|---|---|---|---|
| Situation | | Concepts | Classification | Communication | Research |

Prepare the necessary journal entries, without explanations, to be recorded by Nesbitt for

1. Entering into the lease on January 2, 2007.

2. Making the lease payment on December 31, 2007.

3. Expenses related to the lease for the year ended December 31, 2007.

| | | Concepts | | | |
|---|---|---|---|---|---|
| Situation | Journal Entries | | Classification | Communication | Research |

The terms listed below refer to lessee and lessor accounting for operating, capital, direct financing, and sales-type leases, as contained in SFAS 13, *Accounting for Leases*.

For each term, select the **best** phrase or description from the answers listed A–Q below.  An answer may be used once, more than once, or not at all.

*Answer list*

A. The substance of this transaction is that it consists of two separate and distinct transactions.
B. Rental payments are recognized on a straight-line basis, even though the lease calls for payments that increase over the term of the lease.
C. Depreciation expense related to the leased asset is reported on the lessee's income statement over the lease term.
D. Sales revenue (the present value of the minimum lease payments) less the carrying amount of the leased asset is reported on the lessor's income statement at the inception of the lease.
E. The rate used by the lessee to determine the present value of the minimum lease payments if the lessee's incremental borrowing rate is less than the lessor's implicit rate.
F. Initial direct costs should be treated as an asset and amortized over the life of the lease on a straight-line basis.
G. The difference between the fair value of the asset leased and the total payments to be received over the lease term.
H. Included in the lessor's gross investment, whether guaranteed or unguaranteed.
I. Interest revenue is the only item reported on the income statement over the lease term.
J. The excess of the sales price over the carrying amount of the leased equipment is considered profit and is included in income over the duration of the lease term.
K. Should be recorded as both an asset and a liability by the lessee when the lease contains a bargain purchase option.
L. Produces a constant periodic rate of return on the net investment.
M. The principal portion of the lease liability which must be paid within the next operating cycle.
N. Produces a desired rate of return which causes the aggregate present value of the minimum lease payments to be equal to the fair value of the leased property.
O. Lessee's right to purchase leased property for an amount substantially lower than the expected FMV at exercise date.
P. Costs, such as appraisal fees, incurred by the lessor in setting up the lease agreement.
Q. A lease agreement which requires the annual payments to be made at the beginning of each period.

| | (A) | (B) | (C) | (D) | (E) | (F) | (G) | (H) | (I) | (J) | (K) | (L) | (M) | (N) | (O) | (P) | (Q) |
|---|---|---|---|---|---|---|---|---|---|---|---|---|---|---|---|---|---|
| 1. Sales-type lease | O | O | O | O | O | O | O | O | O | O | O | O | O | O | O | O | O |
| 2. Direct financing lease | O | O | O | O | O | O | O | O | O | O | O | O | O | O | O | O | O |
| 3. Operating lease—lessee | O | O | O | O | O | O | O | O | O | O | O | O | O | O | O | O | O |
| 4. Operating lease—lessor | O | O | O | O | O | O | O | O | O | O | O | O | O | O | O | O | O |
| 5. Unearned interest revenue | O | O | O | O | O | O | O | O | O | O | O | O | O | O | O | O | O |
| 6. Residual value | O | O | O | O | O | O | O | O | O | O | O | O | O | O | O | O | O |
| 7. Capital lease | O | O | O | O | O | O | O | O | O | O | O | O | O | O | O | O | O |
| 8. Implicit rate | O | O | O | O | O | O | O | O | O | O | O | O | O | O | O | O | O |
| 9. Interest method | O | O | O | O | O | O | O | O | O | O | O | O | O | O | O | O | O |
| 10. Present value of the minimum lease payments | O | O | O | O | O | O | O | O | O | O | O | O | O | O | O | O | O |
| 11. Bargain purchase option | O | O | O | O | O | O | O | O | O | O | O | O | O | O | O | O | O |
| 12. Sale-leaseback | O | O | O | O | O | O | O | O | O | O | O | O | O | O | O | O | O |
| 13. Annuity due | O | O | O | O | O | O | O | O | O | O | O | O | O | O | O | O | O |
| 14. Initial direct costs | O | O | O | O | O | O | O | O | O | O | O | O | O | O | O | O | O |
| 15. Current lease obligation | O | O | O | O | O | O | O | O | O | O | O | O | O | O | O | O | O |

| Situation | Journal Entries | Concepts | Classification | | Communication | Research |
|---|---|---|---|---|---|---|

Nesbitt Co. has the following rental agreements.  You have been asked to advise the accounting treatment for each of these items.

In the space provided, indicate whether each of these agreements is an operating lease or a capital lease.

| | *Operating lease* | *Capital lease* |
|---|---|---|
| 1. Nesbitt rents equipment for three years for $20,000 per year.  The equipment is valued at $200,000.  At the end of the rental term the equipment must be returned to the dealer. | O | O |
| 2. Nesbitt rents equipment for five years for $80,000 per year.  At the end of the rental term Nesbitt can purchase the equipment for $500.  At the date the contract was signed the equipment had a value of $300,000.  At the end of five years, it is expected the equipment will have a value of $42,000. | O | O |
| 3. Nesbitt received six months of free rent on an office building it was leasing for two years.  Rent is normally $1,500 per month. | O | O |
| 4. Nesbitt rents equipment for eight years.  The present value of the lease payments are $80,000.  The market value of the equipment is $90,000 and the useful life of the equipment is ten years. | O | O |
| 5. Nesbitt rents equipment for ten years.  At the end of the lease Nesbitt receives title to the equipment. | O | O |
| 6. Nesbitt rents equipment for seven years.  The life of the equipment is ten years.  The fair value of the equipment is $100,000.  The present value of the minimum lease payments is $85,000. | O | O |

| Situation | Journal Entries | Concepts | Classification | Communication | Research |
|---|---|---|---|---|---|

On December 31, 2007, Nesbitt Co. sold a building for its fair value and leased it back.  The building was sold for more than its carrying amount and a gain was recorded.  Lease payments are due at the end of each month.  Nesbitt accounted for the transaction as a capital lease.  The lease's interest rate was equal to Nesbitt's incremental borrowing rate.

Write a brief memorandum to the CEO of Nesbitt Co. explaining the following:

1.  How should Nesbitt account for the sale portion of the sale-leaseback transaction at December 31, 2007?  Why is this an appropriate method of accounting for this portion of the contract?

2.  How should Nesbitt report the leaseback portion of the sale-leaseback transaction on its December 31, 2008 balance sheet?  How are these reported amounts determined?

To:      CEO, Nesbitt Co.
From:  CPA Candidate
Re:      Sales-Leaseback Transaction

| Situation | Journal Entries | Concepts | Classification | Communication | Research |
|-----------|-----------------|----------|----------------|---------------|----------|

Research the following issues.  Cut and paste your answer from the professional standards.

1.  How are leases disclosed in the balance sheet?

2.  How do we value the liability for termination costs to cancel an operating lease?

3.  What is the minimum lease payment and what items are included in calculating the minimum lease payment?

---

**Simulation Problem 2**                    (50 to 60 minutes)

| Situation | Valuation of Lease | Journal Entries | Amortization Schedule | Financial Statement Disclosures | Communication | Research |
|-----------|--------------------|-----------------|-----------------------|---------------------------------|---------------|----------|

On December 30, 2007, Kelty Corporation signed an agreement to lease equipment for ten years.  The lease payments of $70,000 are due each year on December 30.  Kelty paid its first lease payment immediately after the lease was signed.  The interest rate was 6%.  The fair market value of the leased equipment on December 30, 2007, was $600,000.  At the end of the lease term, Kelty may exercise a bargain purchase option to purchase the equipment for $10,000.  The asset has a useful life of twelve years.  Kelty uses the net method for recording lease obligations.

| Situation | Valuation of Lease | Journal Entries | Amortization Schedule | Financial Statement Disclosures | Communication | Research |
|-----------|--------------------|-----------------|-----------------------|---------------------------------|---------------|----------|

Calculate the lease liability and the value of the leased asset at the time the lease is signed.  (For a more realistic exam experience, complete the problem using a spreadsheet program, such as Excel.)

| Situation | Valuation of Lease | Journal Entries | Amortization Schedule | Financial Statement Disclosures | Communication | Research |
|-----------|--------------------|-----------------|-----------------------|---------------------------------|---------------|----------|

Prepare the journal entry or journal entries to record the lease transactions on December 30, 2007.

|  |  |  |
|--|--|--|
|  |  |  |
|  |  |  |
|  |  |  |

| Situation | Valuation of Lease | Journal Entries | Amortization Schedule | Financial Statement Disclosures | Communication | Research |
|-----------|--------------------|-----------------|-----------------------|---------------------------------|---------------|----------|

Prepare an amortization table for the lease through December 30, 2010.

| Year ending | Interest expense | Lease payment | Amounts applied to carrying value | Carrying value of lease |
|-------------|------------------|---------------|-----------------------------------|-------------------------|
| At signing of note | Not applicable | Not applicable | Not applicable | |
| December 30, 2007 | | | | |
| December 30, 2008 | | | | |
| December 30, 2009 | | | | |
| December 30, 2010 | | | | |

| Situation | Valuation of Lease | Journal Entries | Amortization Schedule | Financial Statement Disclosures | | Communication | Research |
|---|---|---|---|---|---|---|---|

Determine the following amounts to be recognized in the financial statements.

| | |
|---|---|
| Interest expense for 2008 | |
| Interest expense for 2009 | |
| Carrying value of lease on 12/31/09 | |
| Depreciation expense for 2008 | |

| Situation | Valuation of Lease | Journal Entries | Amortization Schedule | Financial Statement Disclosures | Communication | | Research |
|---|---|---|---|---|---|---|---|

The Chief Executive Officer of Kelty is unsure if the company should sign the ten-year lease. Upon discussion of his concerns with the equipment company, the sales agent presented him with two more alternatives to leasing.

1. Purchase the equipment for the retail value of $600,000.

2. Sign a five-year lease and pay rent of $90,000 per year with no option to purchase the equipment later.

Prepare a memo to the CEO of Kelty Corporation discussing the advantages and disadvantages of each of the three alternatives for the equipment, along with your recommendation for the best alternative.

To:    Mr. George Timms
         Chief Executive Officer
         Kelty Corporation
From:  CPA Candidate
Re:    Options for acquisition of equipment

| Situation | Valuation of Lease | Journal Entries | Amortization Schedule | Financial Statement Disclosures | Communication | Research |
|---|---|---|---|---|---|---|

Identify the answers to the following issues by cutting and pasting the appropriate citation to the authoritative literature into the space provided.

1. How should Kelty calculate the amount to record the lease liability on December 30, 2007?

2. How should Kelty calculate amortization expense on the leased equipment?

**Simulation Problem 3**                                    (50 to 60 minutes)

| Situation | | | | | |
|---|---|---|---|---|---|
| | Leasing Concepts | Journal Entries | Interest Expense | Liability Section of Balance Sheet | Communication | Research |

The following information relates to the obligations of Villa Watch Co. as of December 31, 2007:

- Accounts payable for goods and services purchased on open account amounted to $35,000 at December 31, 2007.
- On December 15, 2007, Villa declared a cash dividend of $.05 per common share, payable on January 12, 2008, to shareholders of record as of December 31, 2007. Villa had 1,000,000 shares of common stock issued and outstanding throughout 2007.
- On December 31, 2007, Villa entered into a six-year capital lease on a warehouse and made the first annual lease payment of $100,000. Villa's incremental borrowing rate was 12%, and the interest rate implicit in the lease, which was known to Villa, was 10%. The rounded present value factors for an annuity due for six years are 4.6 at 12% and 4.8 at 10%.
- On July 1, 2007, Villa issued $500,000, 8% bonds for $440,000 to yield 10%. The bonds mature on June 30, 2013, and pay interest annually every June 30. At December 31, 2007, the bonds were trading on the open market at 86 to yield 12%. Villa uses the effective interest method.
- Villa's 2007 pretax financial income was $850,000 and its taxable income was $600,000. The difference is due to $100,000 of permanent differences and $150,000 of temporary differences related to noncurrent assets. At December 31, 2007, Villa had cumulative taxable differences of $300,000 related to noncurrent assets. Villa's effective tax rate is 30%. Villa made no estimated tax payments during the year.

| | Leasing Concepts | | | | |
|---|---|---|---|---|---|
| Situation | | Journal Entries | Interest Expense | Liability Section of Balance Sheet | Communication | Research |

Identify whether each statement is True or False.

|  |  | **(T)** | **(F)** |
|---|---|---|---|
| 1. | Free or uneven lease payments should be recognized by the lessor when the lease payment is received. | ○ | ○ |
| 2. | Initial direct costs are expensed by the lessor when the lease is signed. | ○ | ○ |
| 3. | A refundable security deposit is treated as an asset by the lessor. | ○ | ○ |
| 4. | Leasehold improvements should be amortized over the longer of the remaining lease term or the useful life of the asset. | ○ | ○ |
| 5. | The minimum lease payment includes any penalty for failure to renew. | ○ | ○ |
| 6. | The unguaranteed residual value is considered part of the minimum lease payment for the lessee's liability. | ○ | ○ |
| 7. | If a seller-lessee retains substantially all rights to use the property in a sales-leaseback transaction, the gain on sale is deferred by the seller-lessee. | ○ | ○ |
| 8. | If a capital lease is modified in such a way that it qualifies as an operating lease, it should be treated as a sales-leaseback transaction. | ○ | ○ |

| | | Journal Entries | | | |
|---|---|---|---|---|---|
| Situation | Leasing Concepts | | Interest Expense | Liability Section of Balance Sheet | Communication | Research |

Prepare the journal entries necessary in 2007 for each of the following transactions.

1. Dividend declaration on December 15, 2007

| | | |
|---|---|---|
| | | |
| | | |
| | | |

2. Capital lease agreement and first lease payment on December 31, 2007

| | | |
|---|---|---|
| | | |
| | | |
| | | |

3. Bond issue on July 1, 2007

| | | |
|---|---|---|
| | | |
| | | |
| | | |

**4.** Interest accrual(s) on December 31, 2007

|  |  |  |
|---|---|---|
|  |  |  |
|  |  |  |

| Situation | Leasing Concepts | Journal Entries | Interest Expense | Liability Section of Balance Sheet | Communication | Research |
|---|---|---|---|---|---|---|

Calculate the total interest expense for 2007.

| Interest expense for 2007: | *Amount* |
|---|---|
| Interest on capital lease |  |
| Interest on bonds |  |
| Total interest expense |  |

| Situation | Leasing Concepts | Journal Entries | Interest Expense | Liability Section of Balance Sheet | Communication | Research |
|---|---|---|---|---|---|---|

Complete the following schedule for the liability section of the balance sheet for Villa Watch Company as of December 31, 2007.

*Villa Co.*
**BALANCE SHEET—LIABILITIES SECTION**
*December 31, 2007*

| Accounts payable |  |
|---|---|
| Accrued interest payable |  |
| Income taxes payable |  |
| Dividends payable |  |
| Current portion, long-term debt |  |
| Total current liabilities |  |
| Capital lease payable, less $xxx current portion |  |
| Bonds payable |  |
| Deferred tax liability |  |
| Total liabilities |  |

| Situation | Leasing Concepts | Journal Entries | Interest Expense | Liability Section of Balance Sheet | Communication | Research |
|---|---|---|---|---|---|---|

Villa has the following information regarding contingencies for 2007.

• Contingency information

- Villa has been named a liable party for toxic waste cleanup on its land, and must pay an as-yet-undetermined amount for environmental remediation activities.
- An adjoining landowner, Clear Toothpaste Co., sold its property because of possible toxic contamination of the water supply and resulting potential adverse public reaction toward its product.  Clear sued Villa for damages.  There is a reasonable possibility that Clear will prevail and be awarded between $250,000 and $600,000.
- As a result of comprehensive risk assessment, Villa has discontinued rockslide insurance for its warehouse, which is located at the base of a mountain.  The warehouse has never sustained rockslide damage, and the probability of sustaining future damage is only slight.

Write a brief memo to the CEO of Villa Watch Corporation, explaining how the company should account for each contingency.

To:       CEO, Villa Watch Corp.
From:    CPA Candidate
Re:       Accounting for contingencies

|  |
|---|
|  |

| Situation | Leasing Concepts | Journal Entries | Interest Expense | Liability Section of Balance Sheet | Communication | Research |
|---|---|---|---|---|---|---|

Answer each of the following questions by cutting and pasting the authoritative literature from the FARS database.

1. For how many years must Villa disclose future minimum lease payments?

2. What interest rate is used in calculating the present value of minimum lease payments for the lessee?

3. What are the criteria to determine if a lease is an operating or a capital lease?

## MULTIPLE-CHOICE ANSWERS

| | | | | | | | | | |
|---|---|---|---|---|---|---|---|---|---|
| 1. c | __ __ | 13. b | __ __ | 25. b | __ __ | 37. a | __ __ | 49. b | __ __ |
| 2. c | __ __ | 14. c | __ __ | 26. b | __ __ | 38. c | __ __ | 50. b | __ __ |
| 3. a | __ __ | 15. d | __ __ | 27. b | __ __ | 39. b | __ __ | 51. b | __ __ |
| 4. b | __ __ | 16. b | __ __ | 28. c | __ __ | 40. a | __ __ | 52. b | __ __ |
| 5. b | __ __ | 17. b | __ __ | 29. a | __ __ | 41. b | __ __ | 53. d | __ __ |
| 6. d | __ __ | 18. b | __ __ | 30. b | __ __ | 42. d | __ __ | 54. a | __ __ |
| 7. a | __ __ | 19. a | __ __ | 31. a | __ __ | 43. c | __ __ | 55. b | __ __ |
| 8. a | __ __ | 20. d | __ __ | 32. b | __ __ | 44. a | __ __ | 56. c | __ __ |
| 9. c | __ __ | 21. b | __ __ | 33. b | __ __ | 45. c | __ __ | | |
| 10. c | __ __ | 22. b | __ __ | 34. d | __ __ | 46. a | __ __ | | |
| 11. a | __ __ | 23. c | __ __ | 35. b | __ __ | 47. d | __ __ | 1st: __/56 = __% | |
| 12. d | __ __ | 24. c | __ __ | 36. d | __ __ | 48. a | __ __ | 2nd: __/56 = __% | |

## MULTIPLE-CHOICE ANSWER EXPLANATIONS

### E.1.d.(1)  Operating Leases: Lessor/Lessee

**1.** **(c)** SFAS 13 specifies that, in an operating lease, the lessor should recognize rental revenue on a straight-line basis. This means that the lease bonus ($50,000) should be recorded as unearned revenue on 1/1/07, and recognized as rental revenue over the five-year lease term. Therefore, 2007 rental revenue should be $100,000 [$90,000 + ($50,000 ÷ 5)]. The security deposit ($25,000) does not affect rental revenue. Since it is to be refunded to the lessee upon expiration of the lease, it is recorded as a deposit, a long-term liability when received.

**2.** **(c)** SFAS 13 states that rental revenue on operating leases should be recognized on a straight-line basis unless another method more reasonably reflects the pattern of use given by the lessor. When the pattern of cash flows under the lease agreement is other than straight-line, this will result in the recording of rent receivable or unearned rent. Wall's total rent revenue [(1/2 × $8,000) + (4 × $12,500) = $54,000] should be recognized on a straight-line basis over the five-year lease term ($54,000 × 1/5 = $10,800). Since cash collected in 2007 is only $4,000 (one-half of $8,000, since the first six months are rent-free), Wall would accrue rent receivable and rental revenue of $6,800 ($10,800 – $4,000) at year-end to bring the rental revenue up to $10,800.

**3.** **(a)** Net rental income on an operating lease is equal to rental revenue less related expenses, as computed below.

| | |
|---|---|
| Rental revenue | $50,000 |
| Depreciation expense | (12,000) |
| Executory costs | (9,000) |
| Finder's fee ($15,000 ÷ 10) | (1,500) |
| Net rental income | $27,500 |

The finder's fee ($15,000) is capitalized as a deferred charge at the inception of the lease and amortized over ten years to match the expense to the revenues it enabled the lessor to earn.

**4.** **(b)** SFAS 13 states that for an operating lease, rental revenue should be recognized on a straight-line basis unless another method more reasonably reflects the pattern of use given by the lessor. When the pattern of cash flows under the lease agreement is other than straight-line, this will result in the recording of rent receivable or unearned rent. Gee's total rent revenue ($36,000) should be recognized on a straight-line basis over the thirty-six-month lease, resulting in monthly entries debiting **rent receivable** and crediting **rent revenue** for $1,000. Cash collections will result in

entries debiting **cash** and crediting **rent receivable** for $500 per month for the first twelve months and $750 per month for the second twelve months. Therefore, rent receivable at 6/30/07 is $9,000, as indicated by the T-account below.

| Rent Receivable | | |
|---|---|---|
| Accruals (24 × $1,000) 24,000 | 6,000 | Collections (12 × $500) |
| | 9,000 | Collections (12 × $750) |
| 6/30/07 Balance 9,000 | | |

An alternative way to analyze this problem if Gee records the entry as the customer pays at the beginning of the month. During Year 1, the entry each month will be

| | | |
|---|---|---|
| Cash | 500 | |
| Rent receivable | 500 | |
| Rent revenue | | 1,000 |

During Year 2, the entry each month will be

| | | |
|---|---|---|
| Cash | 750 | |
| Rent receivable | 250 | |
| Rent revenue | | 1,000 |

The Rent receivable account will accrue as follows:

| Rent Receivable | | |
|---|---|---|
| Accruals Year 1 | 6,000 | (500 × 12 mo.) |
| Accruals Year 2 | 3,000 | (250 × 12 mo.) |
| 6/30/07 Balance | 9,000 | |

**5.** **(b)** At 1/1/07, Glen would record as a current liability unearned rent of $50,000, and as a long-term liability unearned rent of $150,000. During 2007, the current portion of unearned rent was earned and would be recognized as revenue. At 12/31/07, the portion of the long-term liability representing the second year's rent ($50,000) would be reclassified as current, leaving as a long-term liability the $100,000 representing the last two years' rent.

**6.** **(d)** SFAS 13 states that rental revenue on operating leases should be recognized on a straight-line basis unless another method more reasonably reflects the pattern of use given by the lessor. When the pattern of cash flows under the lease agreement is other than straight-line, this will result in the recording of rent receivable or unearned rent. Therefore, even though Graf received only one monthly payment in 2007 (1/48 of the total rent to received over the life of the lease), they would accrue as rent receivable and rent revenue an amount sufficient to increase the rent revenue account to a balance equal to one-fifth of the total cash to be received over the five-year life of the lease.

**7.** **(a)** The graph presented in the problem can be interpreted as follows:

Line AB is considered to be fixed rental costs per month. Therefore, answers (c) and (d) are incorrect because lines III and IV do not include the fixed portion of the rental payment, in its graphical representation. The problem states that as the variable rental amount increases, it does so at a decreasing rate. Answer (b) is incorrect because line II is increasing, but at an increasing rate, not a decreasing rate, as line I represents. Therefore, answer (a) is the correct answer because line I is increasing, at a decreasing rate.

**8.    (a)**   SFAS 13 states that rent on operating leases should be expensed on a straight-line basis unless another method is better suited to the particular benefits and costs associated with the lease. In this lease, the lessee must pay rent of $1,000 monthly for five years excluding the first nine months, or fifty-one months (60 – 9). Therefore, total rent expense for the five years is $51,000 (51 × $1,000). Recognizing rent expense on a straight-line basis, rent expense for the first year is $10,200 ($51,000 ÷ 5 years).

**9.    (c)**   SFAS 13 specifies that, in an operating lease, the lessee should recognize rent expense on a straight-line basis unless another method is better suited to the particular lease. Therefore, the lease bonus should be recognized as rent expense on a straight-line basis over the ten-year lease term ($24,000 ÷ 10 = $2,400). However, the contingent rentals, which are based on company sales, shall be expensed in the period to which they relate. Therefore, in 2007, contingent rentals of $5,000 [5% × ($600,000 – $500,000)] should be included in rent expense. Total rent expense is $103,400, as computed below.

| | |
|---|---:|
| Base rental | $ 96,000 |
| Lease bonus ($24,000 ÷ 10) | 2,400 |
| Cont. rental [5% × ($600,000 – $500,000)] | 5,000 |
| | $103,400 |

**10.    (c)**   For operating leases having noncancelable remaining lease terms of more than one year, the lessee must disclose future minimum lease payments in the aggregate and for each of the five succeeding fiscal years. Since the annual **minimum** lease payments are $100,000, South must disclose subsequent years' lease payments of $100,000 per annum for each of the next five years and $900,000 (nine remaining payments × $100,000) in the aggregate.

**11.    (a)**   To qualify for treatment as a capital lease, a lease must meet one or more of the following criteria:

1.    Transfers ownership to lessee.
2.    Contains bargain purchase option.
3.    Lease term is ≥ 75% of the economic life of the leased asset.
4.    Present value of minimum lease payments is ≥ 90% of the FMV of the leased asset.

Since the lease signed by Mollat Company does not meet any of these criteria, it must be classified as an operating lease. For operating leases, the lessee's lease payments are recorded as debits to rent expense. Mollat would report rent expense equal to the 2007 lease payments in its 2007 income statement.

**12.    (d)**   When a leasing agreement is accounted for as an operating lease, the lessor and the lessee recognize rental revenue and rental expense respectively on a straight-line basis unless another systematic and rational basis more clearly reflects the time pattern in which use benefit is given (received) by the respective parties. Per FASB Technical Bulletin 85-3, the straight-lining of uneven lease payments includes scheduled rent increases. Even though the amount of the annual lease payment increases in year six, rental expense would not change. Interest is not an element of revenue (expense) in operating leases.

### E.1.d.(1)(e)    Leasehold Improvements

**13.    (b)**   The first month's rent ($60,000) should be expensed in 2007. The prepayment of the last month's rent (also $60,000) should be deferred and recognized as an expense in November 2012. The security deposit ($80,000) should be recorded as a long-term receivable, since Clark can expect to receive the deposit back at lease end. The installation of new walls and offices ($360,000) is recorded as a leasehold improvement at 12/1/07. At 12/31/07, amortization must be recorded for one month ($360,000 × 1/60 = $6,000). Therefore, 2007 expense is $66,000 ($60,000 + $6,000). The journal entries are

| | | |
|---|---:|---:|
| Rent expense | 60,000 | |
| Prepaid rent | 60,000 | |
| Sec. deposit receivable | 80,000 | |
| Leasehold improvements | 360,000 | |
|    Cash | | 560,000 |
| | | |
| Amortization expense | 6,000 | |
|    Leasehold improvements | | 6,000 |

**14.    (c)**   Leasehold improvements are capitalized and amortized over the shorter of the remaining life of the lease (six years from 1/1/07 to 12/31/12) or the useful life of the improvements (eight years). Therefore, the $48,000 cost is amortized over six years, resulting in annual amortization of $8,000 ($48,000 ÷ 6). For the period 1/1/07 to 6/30/07, amortization is $4,000 ($8,000 × 6/12), so the 6/30/07 net amount for leasehold improvements is $44,000 ($48,000 – $4,000).

**15.    (d)**   Leasehold improvements are properly capitalized and amortized over the shorter of the remaining life of the lease or the useful life of the improvement. If the lease contains an option to renew and the likelihood of renewal is uncertain (as it is in this case), then the remaining life of the lease is based on the initial lease term. In this case, the remaining life of the lease is therefore ten years. Since the estimated lives of all improvements in this case are greater than or equal to ten years, the appropriate amortization period is ten years. The 2007 amortization is thus computed as the total cost of $140,000 ($47,000 + $75,000 + $18,000 = $140,000), divided by ten years, or $14,000. There is no salvage value for leasehold improvements, because the assets revert to the lessor at the end of the lease term. Note that if the renewal of the lease for an additional ten years were considered a certainty, the amortization periods would be as follows: ten years for the sales office (estimated life); twenty years for the warehouse (lease term); and fifteen years for the parking lot (estimated life).

**16.    (b)**    The cost of the leasehold improvements ($540,000) should be amortized over the remaining life of the lease, or over the useful life of the improvements, whichever is **shorter**. The remaining life of the lease should include periods covered by a renewal option **if** it is probable that the option will be exercised. In this case, the remaining life of the lease is eighteen years (12 years of original lease + 8 years in option period – 2 years gone by), and the useful life of the improvements is fifteen years. Therefore, amortization is based on a fifteen-year life ($540,000 ÷ 15 = $36,000). The 12/31/07 carrying amount is $504,000 ($540,000 – $36,000).

**17.    (b)**    Per SFAS 13, a lease should be classified as a capital lease by the lessee if the lease terms meet any one of the following four criteria: (1) the lease transfers ownership of the property to the lessee by the end of the lease term, (2) the lease contains a bargain purchase option, (3) the lease term is greater than or equal to 75% of the economic life of the leased property, or (4) the present value of the minimum lease payments is greater than or equal to 90% of the fair market value of the leased property. In this question, the terms of Vail's lease do not meet any of the four criteria for treatment as a capital lease, so the lease should be accounted for as an operating lease. Vail should therefore **not** recognize the building as an asset. In an operating lease, the lessee should capitalize the cost of the leasehold improvements, recognizing them as assets, and amortize their cost over the shorter of their useful lives or the term of the lease.

**18.    (b)**    Leasehold improvements are properly capitalized and amortized over the remaining life of the lease, or the useful life of the improvements, whichever is shorter. Since the useful life of the office is only ten years and the remaining term of the lease is fifteen years, the cost should be depreciated over the ten-year period.

### E.1.d.(2)    Direct Financing Leases: Lessor

**19.    (a)**    The annual lease payment is $75,000 ($323,400 ÷ 4.312). After five years, total lease payments will be $375,000 (5 × $75,000). The total interest revenue over the life of the lease is the excess of total lease payments over the fair value of the leased asset ($375,000 – $323,400 = $51,600).

**20.    (d)**    This lease qualifies as a direct financing lease; therefore interest revenue will be recognized rather than rent revenue. Had the lease qualified as an operating lease, rent revenue would have been recognized. The lessor's criteria for direct financing classification is as follows:

(1)    The lease transfers ownership to the lessee, at the end of the lease
(2)    The lease contains a bargain purchase option
(3)    The lease term is ≥ 75% of an asset's economic life
(4)    The present value of the minimum lease payments is ≥ 90% of the fair market value of the leased asset.

Note that the question is silent concerning the two additional criteria that apply to lessors: (1) collectibility of minimum lease payments is predictable, and (2) no important uncertainties exist concerning costs yet to be incurred by the lessee. Recall that if one of the four criteria are met, the lease is treated as a capital lease. In this case, since the lease term is for 80% of the asset's economic life, test (3) is met, and the lease is properly treated as a capital lease. In addition,

the amount of interest revenue will be smaller in 2007 than the revenue in 2006. This result occurs because the present value of the minimum lease payments or carrying value of the obligation decreases each year as lease payments are received. As this occurs, the amount of interest revenue on the outstanding amount of the investment will decrease as well. Over the course of time, the investment reduction portion of each level payment increases and the amount of interest declines.

### E.1.d.(3)    Sales-Type Leases: Lessor

**21.    (b)**    This is a sales-type lease, so at the inception of the lease, the lessor would recognize sales of $3,520,000 and cost of goods sold of $2,800,000, resulting in a **profit on sale of $720,000**. In addition, interest revenue is recognized for the period July 1, 2007, to December 31, 2007. The initial net lease payments receivable on 7/1/07 is $3,520,000. The first rental payment received on 7/1/07 consists entirely of principal, reducing the net receivable to $2,920,000 ($3,520,000 – $600,000). Therefore, 2007 **interest revenue for the six months from 7/1/07 to 12/31/07 is $146,000** ($2,920,000 × 10% × 6/12).

**22.    (b)**    This is a sales-type lease, so at the inception of the lease, the lessor would recognize sales of $3,300,000 (the PV of the lease payments), and cost of goods sold of $2,800,000, resulting in profit on the sale of $500,000 ($3,300,000 – $2,800,000). Note that the list selling price of an asset ($3,520,000 in this case) is not always representative of its FMV. An asset can often be purchased for less than its list price.

**23.    (c)**    Per SFAS 13, the excess of the fair value of leased property at the inception of the lease over the lessor's cost is defined as the manufacturer's or dealer's profit. Answer (a) is incorrect because the unearned income from a sales-type lease is defined as the difference between the gross investment in the lease and the sum of the present values of the components of the gross investment. Answer (b) is incorrect because the unearned income from a direct-financing lease is defined as the excess of the gross investment over the cost (also the PV of lease payments) of the leased property. Answer (d) is incorrect because a sales-type lease involves a manufacturer's or dealer's profit while a direct financing lease does not.

**24.    (c)**    Per SFAS 13, revenue is to be recognized for a sales-type lease over the lease term so as to produce a **constant rate** of return on the net investment in the lease. This requires the use of the **interest method**. Per SFAS 13, interest revenue **does** arise in a sales-type lease. Answer (a) is incorrect because the interest is to be earned over the life of the lease, not in full at the lease's inception.

### E.1.d.(4)    Capital Leases: Lessee

**25.    (b)**    SFAS 13 provides criteria for classifying leases as either "capital" or "operating." If **any** of the criteria for classification as a capital lease are met, the lease is classified as such. One of the capital lease criterion is that the lease term is equal to 75% or more of the estimated economic life of the leased property. Thus, both leases M and P should be classified as capital leases.

**26.    (b)**    This is a capital lease for the lessee because the lease term is 75% of the useful life of the machine [6 years =

(75% × 8 years)].  For a capital lease, the lessee records as a **leased asset** and a **lease obligation** the lower of the PV of the minimum lease payments or the FV of the leased asset (not given in this problem).  The PV of the minimum lease payments is computed using the lower of the lessee's incremental borrowing rate (15%) or the implicit rate used by the lessor if known by the lessee (12%).  Since the implicit rate is lower, and known by the lessee, it is used to compute the PV ($50,000 × 4.61 = $230,500).  The cost of the asset on the lessor's books ($375,500) is irrelevant.

**27.** **(b)**  This is a capital lease since the lease term (ten years) is the same as the useful life of the leased asset.  In a capital lease, the lessee records an asset and a liability based on the PV of the minimum lease payments.  The minimum lease payments includes rentals and a guaranteed residual value, **if guaranteed by the lessee**.  In this case the minimum lease payments include only the rentals, since the residual value is guaranteed by a third party.  The minimum lease payments are discounted using the **lower** of the lessee's incremental borrowing rate or the implicit rate used by the lessor, if known.  In this case, the lessee knows the implicit rate is 10%, which is lower than the incremental borrowing rate of 12%.  Thus, the present value or principal amount of the lease obligation is $61,446 ($10,000 × 6.1446) through the first year.  Although accrued interest would be recognized at 10/31/07, the principal amount does not change until 1/1/08.

**28.** **(c)**  The lessee records a capital lease at the present value of the minimum lease payments.  The minimum lease payments includes rental payments and bargain purchase options (among other items).  The $10,000 purchase option is a **bargain** purchase option because it allows the lessor to purchase the leased asset at an amount **less** than its expected fair value.  In accordance with SFAS 13, the lessee computes the present value using its incremental borrowing rate (14%), unless the lessor's implicit rate (12%) is lower and is known by the lessee.  This question indicates that the implicit rate is stated in the lease; therefore it would be known to the lessee.  At the beginning of the lease term, Robbins should record a leased asset and lease liability at $66,500.

| | | | |
|---|---|---|---|
| PV of rentals | ($10,000 × 6.328) | = | $63,280 |
| PV of BPO | ($10,000 × .322) | = | 3,220 |
| PV at 12% | | | $66,500 |

**29.** **(a)**  The annual executory costs (real estate taxes of $2,000) are **not** an expense or liability until incurred; therefore they are excluded from the minimum lease payments and are **not** reflected in the initial lease liability.  The 12/31/07 capital lease liability is recorded at the PV of the minimum lease payments [5.6 × ($52,000 − $2,000) = $280,000].

**30.** **(b)**  The requirement is to determine the amount to be recorded as a capitalized leased asset.  This is a capital lease for the lessee because the lease term exceeds 75% of the economic life of the leased asset (10/12 > 75%).  In a capital lease, the lessee records as an asset and liability the present value (PV) of the minimum lease payments (unless the PV exceeds the asset's FMV, in which case the FMV is recorded).  The minimum lease payments include rentals, and a lessee-guaranteed residual value or a bargain purchase option.  Only rentals apply in this case.  Note that the $50,000 purchase option is not a **bargain** purchase option that the lessee would be compelled to exercise.  A bargain

purchase option is an option to purchase the leased asset at an amount **less** than its expected fair value.  Therefore, the present value of the minimum lease payments is $238,000 ($40,000 × 5.95).

**31.** **(a)**  The initial lease liability at 1/1/07, before the 1/1/07 payment, is the present value of the five rental payments (an **annuity due** since the first payment is made on 1/1/07) plus the present value of the guaranteed residual value.  The computation is below.

| | |
|---|---|
| PV of rentals ($13,000 × 4.240) | $55,120 |
| PV of residual ($10,000 × 0.650) | 6,500 |
| Initial liability | $61,620 |

The 1/1/07 payment consists entirely of principal, bringing the 1/1/07 liability down to $48,620 ($61,620 − $13,000).

**32.** **(b)**  The initial lease obligation at 12/30/07 was $135,000.  The first lease payment was made the same day, and therefore consisted entirely of principal reduction.  After the payment, the lease obligation was $115,000 ($135,000 − $20,000).  This balance will be reported as current (for the portion to be paid in 2008) and long-term (for the portion to be paid beyond 2008).  The next lease payment of $20,000 will be paid 12/31/08, and will consist of both interest ($115,000 × 10% = $11,500) and principal reduction ($20,000 − $11,500 = $8,500).  Thus, the portion of the $115,000 lease obligation to be paid in the next year (and therefore reported as a current liability) is $8,500.  Note that the interest to be paid next year ($11,500) is not a liability at 12/31/07 because it has not yet been incurred.

**33.** **(b)**  This is a capital lease for the lessee because the lease term (nine years) exceeds 75% of the useful life of the machine (also nine years).  For a capital lease, the lessee records as a **leased asset** and a **lease obligation** at the lower of the PV of the minimum lease payments or the FV of the leased asset (not given in this problem).  The PV of the minimum lease payments is computed using the lower of the lessee's incremental borrowing rate (12%) or the implicit rate used by the lessor if known by the lessee (10%).  Since the implicit rate is lower, and known by the lessee, it is used to compute the PV ($316,500).  The initial lease payment ($50,000) is entirely principal because it was made at the inception of the lease.  Therefore, after the 12/31/07 payment, the lease liability is $266,500 ($316,500 − $50,000).  The 12/31/08 payment consists of interest incurred during 2008 ($266,500 × 10% = $26,650) and principal reduction ($50,000 − $26,650 = $23,350).  Therefore, the 12/31/08 capital lease liability is $243,150 ($266,500 − $23,350).

**34.** **(d)**  The initial lease liability at 12/31/07 is $417,000 (the PV of the minimum lease payments).  The annual executory costs ($5,000) are **not** an expense or liability until incurred; therefore, they are excluded from the minimum lease payments and are **not** reflected in the initial lease liability.  The 12/31/07 payment of $105,000 includes $5,000 of executory costs; the remainder ($100,000) is entirely principal since the payment was made at the inception of the lease.  Therefore, after the 12/31/07 payment, the lease liability is $317,000 ($417,000 − $100,000).  The 12/31/08 payment consists of executory costs ($5,000), interest incurred during 2007 ($317,000 × 10% = $31,700), and reduction of principal ($105,000 − $5,000 − $31,700 = $68,300).  Therefore, the 12/31/08 balance sheet should include a lease liability of $248,700 ($317,000 − $68,300).

**35.** **(b)** On 1/2/08, Mene made a lease payment of $9,000, which included payment of the current portion of the lease obligation ($1,364) and interest ($9,000 – $1,364 = $7,636). After this payment, the total lease obligation was $75,000. The 1/2/09 payment would include interest of $7,500 ($75,000 × 10%), and principal of $1,500 ($9,000 – $7,500). This $1,500 amount would represent the current portion of the lease obligation at 12/31/08, so the long-term lease obligation net of the current portion at 12/31/08 is $73,500 ($75,000 – $1,500).

**36.** **(d)** SFAS 13 specifies that if a lease is classified as a capital lease, the lessee must record an asset and a liability, each for an amount equal to the present value of the minimum lease payments at the beginning of the lease.

**37.** **(a)** At the inception of a capital lease, the lessee must record an asset and a liability based on the PV of the minimum lease payments. The minimum lease payments are the payments that lessee is required to make in connection with the leased property, including rent payments, bargain purchase option, and guaranteed residual value. Minimum lease payments (MLP) are recorded at present value. The whole guaranteed residual value is included in MLP.

**38.** **(c)** In a capital lease where the first annual lease payment is made immediately upon signing the lease (annuity due), the first payment consists solely of lease liability reduction, since no time has transpired during which interest expense could be incurred. Subsequent payments include both interest expense and reduction of the liability.

**39.** **(b)** Per SFAS 13, each minimum lease payment shall be allocated between a reduction of the obligation and interest expense so as to produce a constant periodic rate of interest on the remaining balance of the obligation. Since the interest will be computed based upon a **declining** obligation balance, the interest component of each payment will also be declining. The result will be a relatively larger portion of the minimum lease payment allocated to the reduction of the lease obligation in the latter portion of the lease term.

**40.** **(a)** When a leasing agreement is accounted for as capital lease, the lessee recognizes a liability on its books equal to the present value of the minimum lease payments. The liability should be divided between current and noncurrent based upon when each lease payment is due. At the end of year one, the current lease liability should equal the principal portion of the lease payment due in year two. Therefore, when the lease payment is made in year two, the reduction of the lease liability will equal the current liability shown at the end of year one.

**41.** **(b)** This is a capital lease since title passes to Cole, the lessee, at the end of the lease. At the inception of the lease on 1/2/07, the lessee records the PV of the lease payments ($108,000) as an asset and a liability. The asset is depreciated on a straight-line basis over its useful life of twelve years, resulting in a yearly depreciation charge of $9,000 ($108,000 ÷ 12). The asset is depreciated over its useful life rather than over the lease term (eight years) because title transfers to the lessee, allowing the lessee to use the asset for twelve years.

**42.** **(d)** A leased asset acquired in a capital lease should be depreciated over the period of time the lessee expects to use the asset (either the lease term or the useful life, depending on the situation). In this case, Nori expects to use the leased asset for its entire eight-year useful life, due to the expected exercise of the bargain purchase option at the end of the five-year lease term. Therefore, Nori's 2007 depreciation expense is $27,500

$$\frac{(\$240,000 \text{ cost}) - (\$20,000 \text{ salvage})}{8 \text{ years}} = \$27,500$$

**43.** **(c)** The requirement is to determine whether a lessee should amortize the capitalizable cost of a leased asset in a manner consistent with the lessee's normal depreciation policy for owned assets for leases that contained a bargain purchase option and/or transferred ownership at the end of the lease term. Transfer of ownership of the property to the lessee by the end of the lease term and a lease that contains a bargain purchase option are properly classified as capital leases (SFAS 13). Per SFAS 13, if the lease meets either of the above criteria, the asset shall be amortized in a manner consistent with the lessee's normal depreciation policy for owned assets.

**44.** **(a)** At the inception of the lease on 1/1/07, the capitalized liability is $379,000 (the present value of the lease payments). Since the first payment is not due until the **end** of the first year, 2007 interest expense is based on the full initial liability ($379,000 × 10% = $37,900).

**45.** **(c)** SFAS 13, as amended and interpreted, requires the disclosure of future minimum lease payments (MLP) for each of the next five years and the aggregate amount of MLP due after five years. At 12/31/08, eight annual payments of $100,000 each have not yet been paid. Therefore, future MLP are $800,000 (8 × $100,000). The amount for the appropriate required period (five years) is $500,000, while the aggregate amount for the period thereafter is $300,000 ($800,000 – $500,000).

**46.** **(a)** At the end of the lease, the balance in the lease payable column should equal the bargain purchase option price. Failure to include the present value of the bargain purchase option price in the beginning present value of the lease would result in an ending balance in the lease payable column of zero. Both answers (b) and (c) would have resulted in an ending balance of less than zero, while answer (d) would have resulted in an ending balance greater than zero.

**E.2.b. Sale-Leaseback**

**47.** **(d)** According to SFAS 13, sale-leaseback arrangements are treated as though two transactions were a single financing transaction, if the lease qualifies as a capital lease. Any gain or loss on the sale is deferred and amortized over the lease term (if possession reverts to the lessor) or the economic life (if ownership transfers to the lessee). In this case, the lease qualifies as a capital lease because the lease term (twelve years) is 80% of the remaining economic life of the leased property (fifteen years). Therefore, at 12/31/07, all of gain ($480,000 – $360,000 = $120,000) would be deferred and amortized over twelve years. Since the sale took place on 12/31/07, there is no amortization for 2007.

**48.** **(a)** SFAS 13 generally treats a sale-leaseback as a single financing transaction in which any profit on the sale is deferred and amortized by the seller. However, SFAS 28 amends this general rule when either **only a minor part** of the remaining use of the leased asset is retained (case one) or when **more than a minor part but less than substantially all** of the remaining use of the leased asset is retained (case two). Case one occurs when the PV of the lease payments is 10% or less of the FMV of the sale-leaseback property. Case two occurs when the leaseback is more than minor but does **not** meet the criteria of a capital lease. This problem is an example of case one, because the PV of the lease payments ($36,900) is less than 10% of the FMV of the asset (10% × $400,000 = $40,000). SFAS 28 specifies that under these circumstances, the full gain ($400,000 – $300,000 = $100,000) is recognized, and **none is deferred**.

**49. (b)** SFAS 13 generally treats a sale-leaseback as a single financing transaction in which any profit on the sale is deferred and amortized by the seller. However, SFAS 28 amends this general rule when either **only a minor part** of the remaining use of the leased asset is retained (case one or when **more than a minor part but less than substantially all** of the remaining use of the leased asset is retained (case two). Case one occurs when the PV of the lease payments is 10% or less of the FMV of the sale-leaseback property. Case two occurs when the leaseback is more than minor but does **not** meet the criteria of a capital lease. This is an example of case two because while the PV of the lease payments ($190,581) is more than 10% of the FMV of the asset ($600,000), the lease falls into the operating lease category. SFAS 28 specifies that under these circumstances the gain on sale ($600,000 – $100,000 = $500,000) is recognized to the extent that it exceeds the PV of the lease payments ($190,581). The gain reported would be $309,419 ($500,000 – $190,581). The portion of the gain represented by the $190,581 PV of the lease payments is deferred and amortized on a straight-line basis over the life of the lease.

**50. (b)** On a sale-leaseback, generally **losses** are recognized immediately. However, there can be two types of losses in sale-leasebacks. The type that is **recognized immediately** is a **real economic loss,** where the carrying amount of the asset is higher than its FMV. The type that is **deferred** is an **artificial loss** where the sale price ($430,000) is below the carrying amount ($450,000), but the FMV ($465,000) is above the carrying amount ($450,000). The loss in this problem ($450,000 – $430,000 = $20,000) is an artificial loss that must be deferred.

**51. (b)** According to SFAS 13, sale-leaseback transactions are treated as though two transactions were a single financing transaction, if the lease qualifies as a capital lease. Any gain on the sale is deferred and amortized over the lease term (if possession reverts to the lessor) or the economic life (if ownership transfers to the lessee); both are ten years in this case. Since this is a capital lease, the entire gain ($150,000 – $100,000 = $50,000) is deferred at 1/1/07. At 12/31/07, an adjusting entry must be prepared to amortize 1/11 of the unearned gain (1/11 × $50,000 = $5,000), because the lease covers ten years. Therefore, the unearned gain at 12/31/07 is $45,000 ($50,000 – $5,000).

**52. (b)** Per SFAS 28, any profit related to a sale-leaseback transaction in which the seller-lessee retains the property leased (i.e., the seller-lessee retains substantially all of the benefits and risks of the ownership of the property sold), shall be deferred and amortized in proportion to the amortization of the leased asset, if a capital lease. If it is an operating lease, the profit will be deferred in proportion to

the related gross rental charged to expense over the lease term. It is important to note that **losses,** however, are recognized immediately for either a capital or operating lease. Since the gain on the sale should be deferred in either case, no gain is recognized at the time of the sale.

*NOTE: An example of an operating lease in which substantially all of the remaining use of the leased asset is retained by the lessee occurs when the lease term begins within the last 25% of the asset's original useful life.*

**53. (d)** In a sale-leaseback transaction, if the leaseback is recorded as a capital lease and the lessee has retained **substantially all** of the rights to use the property, then any gain on the sale must be deferred and amortized over the life of the property in proportion to the amortization of the leased asset. This deferred gain acts as an asset valuation allowance resulting in the net amount shown for the leased asset being equal to the same carrying value as if the sale and leaseback transaction had not occurred.

**54. (a)** Per SFAS 146, a termination of an operating lease requires that the fair value of the termination costs be recognized as an expense or loss in calculating income from continuing operations in the year the lease was terminated.

**55. (b)** Per SFAS 145, a modification to a capital lease that changes the classification of the lease to an operating lease requires the transaction be accounted for as a sales-leaseback transaction under SFAS 98. Since Hopper retains substantially all rights to use the property (and the property is not within the last 25% of its useful life), the gain will be deferred and recognized over the remaining lease term.

**56. (c)** Per SFAS 145, a loss on a capital lease termination is recognized immediately as a loss from continuing operations.

**SOLUTIONS TO SIMULATION PROBLEMS**

**Simulation Problem 1**

| Situation | Journal Entries | Concepts | Classification | Communication | Research |
|---|---|---|---|---|---|

|  | *Debits* | *Credits* |
|---|---|---|
| **1.** January 2, 2007—to record lease: | | |
| Equipment | 850,000 | |
|    Capital lease liability | | 850,000 |
| **2.** December 31, 2007—to record payment: | | |
| Capital lease liability | 100,000 | |
|    Cash | | 100,000 |
| **3.** December 31, 2007—to record depreciation: | | |
| Depreciation expense | 34,000 | |
|    Accumulated depreciation | | 34,000 |
| Interest expense | 85,000 | |
|    Capital lease liability | | 85,000 |

## Explanation of solutions

**1.** This problem requires preparation of the lessee's journal entries for the first year of a lease. The lease is a capital lease because title passes to the lessee at the end of the lease and the lease term (twenty years) is greater than 75% of the useful life (twenty-five years).

**2.** In a capital lease, the lessee records a **leased asset** and a **lease obligation** at the present value of the minimum lease payments. The lessee's incremental borrowing rate (12%) should be used to determine the present value unless the lessor's implicit rate is lower and is known by the lessee. The lessor's 10% rate is lower and is known by the lessee, so it is used to compute the PV of $850,000 ($100,000 × 8.5).

**3.** The first lease payment on 12/31/07 consists of interest expense incurred during 2007 ($850,000 × 10% = $85,000) and reduction of lease obligation ($100,000 payment – $85,000 interest = $15,000). The $100,000 credit to cash is offset by debits to interest expense ($85,000) and lease obligation ($15,000).

The only other expense related to this lease is depreciation of the leased asset. Leased assets are depreciated over the lease term (twenty years) unless the lease transfers ownership (as this one does) or contains a bargain purchase option. If either of these is present, then the asset is depreciated over the estimated useful life of the asset (twenty-five years). Depreciation expense is cost ($850,000) divided by useful life ($850,000 ÷ 25 years = $34,000). If a salvage value had been given, it would be subtracted from cost before dividing by useful life.

| Situation | Journal Entries | Concepts | Classification | Communication | Research |
|---|---|---|---|---|---|

| | (A) | (B) | (C) | (D) | (E) | (F) | (G) | (H) | (I) | (J) | (K) | (L) | (M) | (N) | (O) | (P) | (Q) |
|---|---|---|---|---|---|---|---|---|---|---|---|---|---|---|---|---|---|
| 1. Sales-type lease | ○ | ○ | ○ | ● | ○ | ○ | ○ | ○ | ○ | ○ | ○ | ○ | ○ | ○ | ○ | ○ | ○ |
| 2. Direct financing lease | ○ | ○ | ○ | ○ | ○ | ○ | ○ | ○ | ● | ○ | ○ | ○ | ○ | ○ | ○ | ○ | ○ |
| 3. Operating lease—lessee | ○ | ● | ○ | ○ | ○ | ○ | ○ | ○ | ○ | ○ | ○ | ○ | ○ | ○ | ○ | ○ | ○ |
| 4. Operating lease—lessor | ○ | ○ | ○ | ○ | ○ | ● | ○ | ○ | ○ | ○ | ○ | ○ | ○ | ○ | ○ | ○ | ○ |
| 5. Unearned interest revenue | ○ | ○ | ○ | ○ | ○ | ○ | ● | ○ | ○ | ○ | ○ | ○ | ○ | ○ | ○ | ○ | ○ |
| 6. Residual value | ○ | ○ | ○ | ○ | ○ | ○ | ○ | ● | ○ | ○ | ○ | ○ | ○ | ○ | ○ | ○ | ○ |
| 7. Capital lease | ○ | ○ | ● | ○ | ○ | ○ | ○ | ○ | ○ | ○ | ○ | ○ | ○ | ○ | ○ | ○ | ○ |
| 8. Implicit rate | ○ | ○ | ○ | ○ | ○ | ○ | ○ | ○ | ○ | ○ | ○ | ○ | ○ | ● | ○ | ○ | ○ |
| 9. Interest method | ○ | ○ | ○ | ○ | ○ | ○ | ○ | ○ | ○ | ○ | ○ | ● | ○ | ○ | ○ | ○ | ○ |
| 10. Present value of the minimum lease payments | ○ | ○ | ○ | ○ | ○ | ○ | ○ | ○ | ○ | ○ | ● | ○ | ○ | ○ | ○ | ○ | ○ |
| 11. Bargain purchase option | ○ | ○ | ○ | ○ | ○ | ○ | ○ | ○ | ○ | ○ | ○ | ○ | ○ | ○ | ● | ○ | ○ |
| 12. Sale-leaseback | ● | ○ | ○ | ○ | ○ | ○ | ○ | ○ | ○ | ○ | ○ | ○ | ○ | ○ | ○ | ○ | ○ |
| 13. Annuity due | ○ | ○ | ○ | ○ | ○ | ○ | ○ | ○ | ○ | ○ | ○ | ○ | ○ | ○ | ○ | ○ | ● |
| 14. Initial direct costs | ○ | ○ | ○ | ○ | ○ | ○ | ○ | ○ | ○ | ○ | ○ | ○ | ○ | ○ | ○ | ● | ○ |
| 15. Current lease obligation | ○ | ○ | ○ | ○ | ○ | ○ | ○ | ○ | ○ | ○ | ○ | ○ | ● | ○ | ○ | ○ | ○ |

| Situation | Journal Entries | Concepts | Classification | | Communication | Research |
|-----------|-----------------|----------|----------------|--|---------------|----------|

1. Nesbitt rents equipment for three years for $20,000 per year. The equipment is valued at $200,000. At the end of the rental term the equipment must be returned to the dealer.

   Operating. Does not meet any of the four criteria.

2. Nesbitt rents equipment for five years for $80,000 per year. At the end of the rental term Nesbitt can purchase the equipment for $500. At the date the contract was signed the equipment had a value of $300,000. At the end of five years, it is expected the equipment will have a value of $42,000.

   Capital lease. The lease has a bargain purchase option.

3. Nesbitt received six months of free rent on an office building it was leasing for two years. Rent is normally $1,500 per month.

   Operating lease. The building is only leased for two years, and it is doubtful that it is greater than 75% of the building's economic life.

4. Nesbitt rents equipment for eight years. The present value of the lease payments are $80,000. The market value of the equipment is $90,000 and the useful life of the equipment is ten years.

   Capital lease. The present value of the lease payments is not greater than 90% of the fair market value of the leased asset; however, the rental term is 80%, which is greater than 75% of the economic life of the asset.

5. Nesbitt rents equipment for ten years. At the end of the lease Nesbitt receives title to the equipment.

   Capital lease. Transfer of title.

6. Nesbitt rents equipment for seven years. The life of the equipment is ten years. The fair value of the equipment is $100,000. The present value of the minimum lease payments is $85,000.

   Operating lease. The lease is not greater than 75% of the economic life of the asset, and the present value of the minimum lease payments is not greater than 90% of the fair market value of the asset.

| Situation | Journal Entries | Concepts | Classification | Communication | | Research |
|-----------|-----------------|----------|----------------|---------------|--|----------|

To:    CEO, Nesbitt Co.
From:  CPA Candidate
Re:    Sales-Leaseback Transaction

    This letter is in response to your questions regarding sales-leaseback transactions. A sales-leaseback transaction is a transaction wherein a company sells an asset and immediately leases it back. Nesbitt should account for the sale portion of the sale-leaseback transaction by increasing cash for the sale price, decreasing property, plant, and equipment for the building's carrying amount, and recording a deferred gain for the excess of the sale price over the building's carrying amount. This accounting is appropriate because Nesbitt still retains substantial ownership rights and obligations pertaining to the building. Since no earning process occurred, this sale-leaseback is not in substance a sale but a financing transaction. Therefore, the gain should be deferred.

    The leased building is included on Nesbitt's December 31, 2007 balance sheet as leased property at its discounted present value on December 31, 2007, less accumulated depreciation, and less unamortized deferred gain on the sale. Its discounted present value at December 31, 2007, represents the future lease payments, discounted at Nesbitt's current borrowing rate.

    The lease obligation on Nesbitt's December 31, 2008 balance sheet equals the building's December 31, 2007 present value less principal repaid in 2008. An amount equal to the principal to be repaid in 2009 should be reported as a current liability. The balance of the obligation should be reported as a noncurrent liability.

    If you have any additional questions, please contact me.

| Situation | Journal Entries | Concepts | Classification | Communication | Research |
|---|---|---|---|---|---|

**1.** How are leases disclosed in the balance sheet?

**FAS13, Para 13 or Current Text L10.106**

13. Assets recorded under capital leases and the accumulated amortization thereon shall be separately identified in the lessee's balance sheet or in footnotes thereto. Likewise, the related obligations shall be separately identified in the balance sheet as obligations under capital leases and shall be subject to the same considerations as other obligations in classifying them with current and noncurrent liabilities in classified balance sheets. Unless the charge to income resulting from amortization of assets recorded under capital leases is included with depreciation expense and the fact that it is so included is disclosed, the amortization charge shall be separately disclosed in the financial statements or footnotes thereto.

**2.** How do we value the liability for termination costs to cancel an operating lease?

**FAS146, Para 16 or Current Text L32.116**

16. A liability for costs that will continue to be incurred under a contract for its remaining term without economic benefit to the entity shall be recognized and measured at its fair value when the entity ceases using the right conveyed by the contract, for example, the right to use a leased property or to receive future goods or services (hereinafter referred to as the cease-use date). If the contract is an operating lease, the fair value of the liability at the cease-use date shall be determined based on the remaining lease rentals, reduced by estimated sublease rentals that could be reasonably obtained for the property, even if the entity does not intend to enter into a sublease. Remaining lease rentals shall not be reduced to an amount less than zero. The provisions of paragraph 6 shall apply in periods subsequent to the cease-use date. (Example 4 of Appendix A illustrates that situation.).

**3.** What is the minimum lease payment and what items are included in calculating the minimum lease payment?

**FAS13, Para 5(j) or Current Text L10.417**

j. *Minimum lease payments.*

i. From the standpoint of the lessee: The payments that the lessee is obligated to make or can be required to make in connection with the lease property. However, a guarantee by the lessee of the lessor's debt and the lessee's obligation to pay (apart from the rental payments) executory costs such as insurance, maintenance, and taxes in connection with the lease property shall be excluded. If the lease contains a bargain purchase option, only the minimum rental payments over the lease term (as defined in paragraph 5(f)) and the payment called for by the bargain purchase option shall be included in the minimum lease payments. Otherwise, minimum lease payments include the following:

(a) The minimum rental payments called for by the lease over the lease term.

(b) Any guarantee by the lessee of the residual value at the expiration of the lease term, whether or not payment of the guarantee constitutes a purchase of the leased property. When the lessor has the right to require the lessee to purchase the property at termination of the lease for a certain or determinable amount, that amount shall be considered a lessee guarantee. When the lessee agrees to make up any deficiency below a stated amount in the lessor's realization of the residual value, the guarantee to be included in the minimum lease payments shall be the stated amount, rather than an estimate of the deficiency to be made up.

(c) Any payment that the lessee must make or can be required to make upon failure to renew or extend the lease at the expiration of the lease term, whether or not the payment would constitute a purchase of the lease property.  In this connection, it should be noted that the definition of lease term in paragraph 5(f) includes "all periods, if any, for which failure to renew the lease imposes a penalty on the lessee in an amount such that renewal appears, at the inception of the lease, to be reasonably assured."  If the lease term has been extended because of that provision, the related penalty shall not be included in minimum lease payments.

ii. From the standpoint of the lessor:  The payments described in (i) above plus any guarantee of the residual value or of rental payments beyond the lease term by a third party unrelated to either the lessee or the lessor, provided the third party is financially capable of discharging the obligations that may arise from the guarantee.

## Simulation Problem 2

| Situation | Valuation of Lease | Journal Entries | Amortization Schedule | Financial Statement Disclosures | Communication | Research |
|---|---|---|---|---|---|---|

Calculate the lease liability and the value of the leased asset at the time the lease is signed.

PVA due ($70,000) at 6% for 10 periods + PV ($10,000) at 6% for 10 periods
7.80169 ($70,000) + .55839 ($10,000)
$551,702

| Situation | Valuation of Lease | Journal Entries | Amortization Schedule | Financial Statement Disclosures | Communication | Research |
|---|---|---|---|---|---|---|

Prepare the journal entry or journal entries to record the lease transactions on December 30, 2007.

| | | |
|---|---|---|
| Leased asset | 551,702 | |
| Obligation under capital lease | | 551,702 |
| Obligation under capital lease | 70,000 | |
| Cash | | 70,000 |

| Situation | Valuation of Lease | Journal Entries | Amortization Schedule | Financial Statement Disclosures | Communication | Research |
|---|---|---|---|---|---|---|

Prepare an amortization table for the lease through December 30, 2010.

| Year ending | Interest expense | Lease payment | Amounts applied to carrying value | Carrying value of lease |
|---|---|---|---|---|
| At signing of note | Not applicable | Not applicable | Not applicable | $551,702 |
| December 30, 2007 | $    0 | $70,000 | $    0 | 481,702 |
| December 30, 2008 | 28,902 | 70,000 | 41,098 | 440,604 |
| December 30, 2009 | 26,436 | 70,000 | 43,564 | 397,040 |
| December 30, 2010 | 23,822 | 70,000 | 46,178 | 350,863 |

| Situation | Valuation of Lease | Journal Entries | Amortization Schedule | Financial Statement Disclosures | Communication | Research |
|---|---|---|---|---|---|---|

| | |
|---|---|
| Interest expense for 2008 | 28,902 |
| Interest expense for 2009 | 26,436 |
| Carrying value of lease on 12/31/09 | 397,040 |
| Depreciation expense for 2008 | 45,975 |

**Explanation of solutions**

Interest expense recognized in 2008

$28,902 (6% × $481,702)

Interest expense recognized in 2009

$26,436 (6% × $440,604)

Carrying value of the lease on December 31, 2009

$397,040 (See table)

Depreciation expense for 2008

$551,702 / 12 years = $45,975
The leased asset is depreciated over the asset's life because there is a bargain purchase option.

| Situation | Valuation of Lease | Journal Entries | Amortization Schedule | Financial Statement Disclosures | Communication | Research |
|-----------|--------------------|-----------------|-----------------------|----------------------------------|---------------|----------|

To:       Mr. George Timms
          Chief Executive Officer
          Kelty Corporation
From:     CPA Candidate
Re:       Options for acquisition of equipment
Date:     [*today's date*]

This memorandum summarizes our views regarding the financial implications of the alternative methods of acquiring the equipment.  As we discussed, you are considering the following three options.

**Capital Lease**

The total cash payments under the capital lease option ($70,000 annual payments for ten years plus a $10,000 bargain purchase option) is $710,000.  In absolute dollars, this appears to be a greater amount than the $600,000 for outright purchase of the equipment.  However, after taking into consideration the time value of money at 6%, the present value of the lease payments and the bargain purchase option is only $551,720.  At the end of the lease term, Kelty will own the equipment.  Since this is a capital lease, the obligation must be recorded.  Increasing the level of debt will increase the firm's debt ratio.

**Purchase**

Although Kelty would receive title to the equipment immediately, Kelty must spend $600,000 cash today to purchase the equipment.  If Kelty uses existing cash, this option would decrease the firm's liquidity.  If the funds are borrowed, it will increase the firm's debt ratio.

**Five-Year Rental Contract**

The five-year rental contract would qualify for operating lease treatment, meaning that Kelty would not record a liability on the balance sheet.  Kelty would recognize rent expense of $100,000 per year.  However, the rental payments are significantly higher than the annual lease payments.  Ignoring present value considerations, the total cash outflow would be $500,000 over five years.  This cash overflow is a significant payment for equipment that the company would not own, as there is no option to purchase the equipment at the end of the rental period.

**Conclusions and Recommendations**

The operating lease is the most costly alternative.  Due to the high rental payments, the company should avoid the operating lease, unless there are extenuating circumstances that preclude the company from acquiring the equipment outright or entering into the ten-year lease agreement.

If Kelty purchases the equipment, it will have a significant cash outflow immediately or an increase in long-term debt to finance the acquisition.  While the lease will also result in a liability, the liability is only $551,702, the present value of the future lease payments.

Considering the time value of money, leasing the equipment for ten years with the option to buy appears to be the most economical alternative.

If you have any questions regarding my recommendations, please contact me.

| Situation | Valuation of Lease | Journal Entries | Amortization Schedule | Financial Statement Disclosures | Communication | Research |
|-----------|-------------------|-----------------|----------------------|-------------------------------|---------------|----------|

**1.** How should Kelty calculate the amount to record the lease liability on December 30, 2007?

**FAS13, Para 10 or Current Text L10.106**

10. The lessee shall record a capital lease as an asset and an obligation at an amount equal to the present value at the beginning of the lease term of minimum lease payments during the lease term, excluding that portion of the payments representing executory costs such as insurance, maintenance, and taxes to be paid by the lessor, together with any profit thereon. However, if the amount so determined exceeds the fair value of the leased property at the inception of the lease, the amount recorded as the asset and obligation shall be the fair value. If the portion of the minimum lease payments representing executory costs, including profit thereon, is not determinable from the provisions of the lease, an estimate of the amount shall be made. The discount rate to be used in determining present value of the minimum lease payments shall be that prescribed for the lessee in paragraph 7(d). (See Appendix C for illustrations.)

**2.** How should Kelty calculate amortization expense on the leased equipment?

**FAS13, Para 11 or Current Text L10.107**

11. Except as provided in paragraphs 25 and 26 with respect to leases involving land, the asset recorded under a capital lease shall be amortized as follows:

a. If the lease meets the criterion of either paragraph 7(a) or 7(b), the asset shall be amortized in a manner consistent with the lessee's normal depreciation policy for owned assets.

b. If the lease does not meet either criterion 7(a) or 7(b), the asset shall be amortized in a manner consistent with the lessee's normal depreciation policy except that the period of amortization shall be the lease term. The asset shall be amortized to its expected value, if any, to the lessee at the end of the lease term. As an example, if the lessee guarantees a residual value at the end of the lease term and has no interest in any excess which might be realized, the expected value of the leased property to him is the amount that can be realized from it up to the amount of the guarantee.

**FAS13, Para 7 or Current Text L10.103**

7. The criteria for classifying leases set forth in this paragraph and in paragraph 8 derive from the concept set forth in paragraph 60. If at its inception (as defined in paragraph 5(b)) a lease meets one or more of the following four criteria, the lease shall be classified as a capital lease by the lessee. Otherwise, it shall be classified as an operating lease. (See Appendix C for an illustration of the application of these criteria.)

a. The lease transfers ownership of the property to the lessee by the end of the lease term (as defined in paragraph 5(f)).

b. The lease contains a bargain purchase option (as defined in paragraph 5(d)).

c. The lease term (as defined in paragraph 5(f)) is equal to 75% or more of the estimated economic life of the leased property (as defined in paragraph 5(g)). However, if the beginning of the lease term falls within the last 25% of the total estimated economic life of the leased property, including earlier years of use, this criterion shall not be used for purposes of classifying the lease.

d. The present value at the beginning of the lease term of the minimum lease payments (as defined in paragraph 5(j)), excluding that portion of the payments representing executory costs such as insurance, maintenance, and taxes to be paid by the lessor, including any profit thereon, equals or exceeds 90% of the excess of the fair value of the leased property (as defined in paragraph 5(c)) to the lessor at the inception of the lease over any related investment tax credit retained by the lessor and expected to be realized by him.  However, if the beginning of the lease term falls within the last 25% of the total estimated economic life of the leased property, including earlier years of use, this criterion shall not be used for purposes of classifying the lease.  A lessor shall compute the present value of the minimum lease payments using the interest rate implicit in the lease (as defined in paragraph 5(k)).  A lessee shall compute the present value of the minimum lease payments using his incremental borrowing rate (as defined in paragraph 5(l)), unless (i) it is practicable for him to learn the implicit rate computed by the lessor and (ii) the implicit rate computed by the lessor is less than the lessee's incremental borrowing rate.  If both of those conditions are met, the lessee shall use the implicit rate.

**Simulation Problem 3**

| Situation | Leasing Concepts | Journal Entries | Interest Expense | Liability Section of Balance Sheet | Communication | Research |
|-----------|------------------|-----------------|------------------|------------------------------------|---------------|----------|

|   |   | *True* | *False* |
|---|---|--------|---------|
| 1. | Free or uneven lease payments should be recognized by the lessor when the lease payment is received. | ○ | ● |
| 2. | Initial direct costs are expensed by the lessor when the lease is signed. | ○ | ● |
| 3. | A refundable security deposit is treated as an asset by the lessor. | ○ | ● |
| 4. | Leasehold improvements should be amortized over the longer of the remaining lease term or the useful life of the asset. | ○ | ● |
| 5. | The minimum lease payment includes any penalty for failure to renew. | ● | ○ |
| 6. | The unguaranteed residual value is considered part of the minimum lease payment for the lessee's liability. | ○ | ● |
| 7. | If a seller-lessee retains substantially all rights to use the property in a sales-leaseback transaction, the gain on sale is deferred by the seller-lessee. | ● | ○ |
| 8. | If a capital lease is modified in such a way that it qualifies as an operating lease, it should be treated as a sales-leaseback transaction. | ● | ○ |

**Explanation of solutions**

1. False.  Free or uneven lease payments received by the lessor should be recognized as revenue on a straight-line basis and prorated over the life of the lease.

2. False.  Initial direct costs should be capitalized and amortized straight-line over the life of the lease.

3. False.  A refundable security deposit is a liability to the lessor and a receivable to the lessee.

4. False.  Leasehold improvements should be amortized over the longer of the remaining lease term or the useful life of the asset.

5. True.  The minimum lease payment includes any penalty.

6. False.  The unguaranteed residual is considered part of the lessor's net investment in lease unless there is a transfer of title or a bargain purchase option.  The unguaranteed residual is not part of the minimum lease payment for the lessee; it is ignored.

7. True.  Gain is deferred in these situations.

8. True.  Sales-leaseback treatment is appropriate.

| Situation | Leasing Concepts | Journal Entries | Interest Expense | Liability Section of Balance Sheet | Communication | Research |
|---|---|---|---|---|---|---|

**1.** December 15, 2007

| Dividends or retained earnings | 50,000 | |
|---|---|---|
| Dividend payable | | 50,000 |

**2.** December 31, 2007

| Leased asset | 480,000 | |
|---|---|---|
| Obligation under capital lease | | 480,000 |

| Lease obligation | 100,000 | |
|---|---|---|
| Cash | | 100,000 |

**3.** July 1, 2007

| Cash | 440,000 | |
|---|---|---|
| Discounts on bonds payable | 60,000 | |
| Bonds payable | | 500,000 |

**4.** Interest expense

| Interest expense (440,000 × 10% × 6/12) | 22,000 | |
|---|---|---|
| Discount on bonds payable | | 2,000 |
| Interest payable (4% × $500,000) | | 20,000 |

*(Interest expense is only needed for the bond because the capital lease was signed on December 31, 2007, and no interest has accrued on the lease for 2007.)*

| Situation | Leasing Concepts | Journal Entries | Interest Expense | Liability Section of Balance Sheet | Communication | Research |
|---|---|---|---|---|---|---|

| Interest expense for 2007: | *Amount* |
|---|---|
| Interest on capital lease | 0 |
| Interest on bonds | 22,000 |
| Total interest expense | 22,000 |

Note there is no interest on the capital lease for 2007 because the lease was signed on December 31, 2007.

| Situation | Leasing Concepts | Journal Entries | Interest Expense | Liability Section of Balance Sheet | Communication | Research |
|---|---|---|---|---|---|---|

*Villa Co.*
**BALANCE SHEET—LIABILITIES SECTION**
*December 31, 2007*

| | | |
|---|---|---|
| Accounts payable | $   35,000 | |
| Accrued interest payable | 20,000 | [2] |
| Income taxes payable | 180,000 | [3] |
| Dividends payable | 50,000 | |
| Current portion, long-term debt | 62,000 | [1] |
| Total current liabilities | 347,000 | |
| Capital lease payable, less $62,000 current portion | 318,000 | [1] |
| Bonds payable | 442,000 | [2] |
| Deferred tax liability | 90,000 | [3] |
| Total liabilities | $1,197,000 | |

| [1] | $100,000 × 4.8 | = | $480,000 |
|---|---|---|---|
| | $480,000 − $100,000 | = | $380,000 |
| | $380,000 × 10% | = | $ 38,000 |
| | $100,000 − $38,000 | = | $ 62,000 |
| | $380,000 − $62,000 | = | $318,000 |
| [2] | 500K × 8% × 1/2 | = | 20K |
| | 440K × 10% × 1/2 | = | 22K |
| | 440 K + (22K − 20K) | = | 442K |
| [3] | 600K × 30% | = | 180K |
| | 300K × 30% | = | 90K |

**Explanation of solutions**

1.  The accounts payable are current because these amounts are typically due in less than one year.

2.  The cash dividends payable are current because they will be paid in the following January. The cash dividends payable is computed as follows:

| Dividend per share | | # outstanding shares | | Dividends payable |
|---|---|---|---|---|
| $.05 | × | 1,000,000 | = | $50,000 |

3.  The lease obligation must be separated into a current and noncurrent portion. The current portion is the amount by which the lease obligation's principal will be reduced in the next year. The carrying value of the lease obligation at 12/31/07 is $380,000 and is computed as follows:

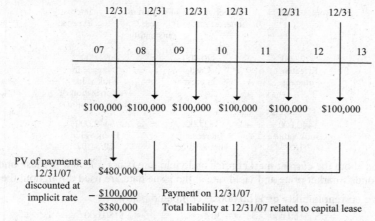

The amount of principal reduction (current liability) for 2008 is $62,000 and is computed as follows:

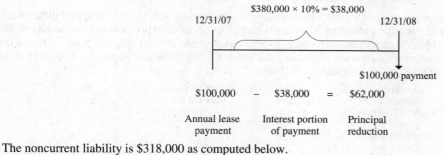

| $100,000 | – | $38,000 | = | $62,000 |
|---|---|---|---|---|
| Annual lease payment | | Interest portion of payment | | Principal reduction |

The noncurrent liability is $318,000 as computed below.

| $380,000 | – | $62,000 | = | $318,000 |
|---|---|---|---|---|
| Capital lease liability | | Current portion of liability | | Noncurrent liability |

Note that because the lessor's implicit rate of 10% is lower than Villa's incremental borrowing rate and Villa is aware of the lessor's implicit rate, it shall be used per SFAS 13.

4.  Accrued interest on the bonds is a current liability. The amount is $20,000 for the six months they are outstanding in 2007 and is computed as follows:

| 6/12 | × 8% | × | $500,000 | = | $20,000 |
|---|---|---|---|---|---|
| Fraction of year outstanding | Contract rate for annual interest | | Face amount of bonds | | Accrued interest |

5.  The bonds payable are all noncurrent because they do not mature until 2013. The carrying amount of the bonds payable is the issue amount of the bonds plus the amortization of the bond discount for six months, or $442,000 and is computed below.

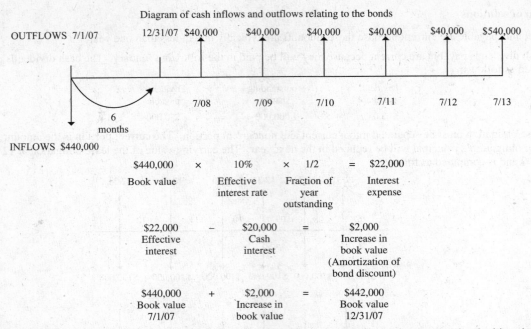

Diagram of cash inflows and outflows relating to the bonds

Note that the information about the current market price and yield rate is not relevant because under the historical cost model per GAAP, the bonds' market price and yield rate at the issue date are used throughout the life of the bond issue.

6.  Income taxes payable is a current liability of $180,000 as computed below.

$$\underset{\substack{\text{Taxable}\\\text{income}}}{\$600,000} \times \underset{\substack{\text{Effective}\\\text{tax rate}}}{30\%} = \underset{\substack{\text{Income taxes}\\\text{payable}}}{\$180,000}$$

7.  Deferred income tax liability is a long-term liability because it relates to noncurrent assets.  Only temporary differences have future taxable or deductible amounts that result in deferred tax liabilities or deferred tax assets.  Current pretax financial income was reduced by the $150,000 temporary difference, a current deductible amount that will result in future taxable amount(s).  The cumulative temporary differences including the $150,000 that arose this period are $300,000.  Therefore, the deferred tax liability is $90,000 and is computed as follows:

$$\underset{\substack{\text{Cumulative}\\\text{taxable differences}\\\text{related to}\\\text{noncurrent assets}}}{\$300,000} \times \underset{\substack{\text{Effective}\\\text{tax rate}}}{30\%} = \underset{\substack{\text{Deferred tax}\\\text{liability}}}{\$90,000}$$

**Other disclosures and information**

Villa should disclose the following information about the capital leases, either in the body of the financial statements or in the notes thereto:

- The gross amount of assets recorded under the capital leases, presented by major classes.  This information may be combined with owned assets.
- Future minimum lease payments as of the balance sheet date, in the aggregate and for each of the five succeeding years.
- A general description of the leasing arrangement, including the existence and terms of renewal, escalation clauses, and restrictions imposed by the lease agreements.

Villa should disclose the following information about the bonds payable, either in the body of the financial statements or in the notes thereto:

- The face amount.
- The nature and terms of the bonds and a discussion of their credit and market risk, cash requirements, and related accounting policies.
- The fair value of the bonds and the method used to estimate their fair value.  The price at which the bonds are trading is the most reasonable estimate of their fair value at December 31, 2007.

| Situation | Leasing Concepts | Journal Entries | Interest Expense | Liability Section of Balance Sheet | Communication | Research |
|---|---|---|---|---|---|---|

To:      CEO, Villa Watch Corp.
From:   CPA Candidate
Re:      Accounting for contingencies

This memorandum is in response to your questions about accounting for contingencies. An accounting contingency is an existing condition, situation, or set of circumstances that possibly could result in a gain or loss to the company. The contingency is resolved at some time in the future when one or more events occur or fail to occur. If a contingency is both probable and reasonably estimable, a loss should be recorded in the current period. However, if a contingency is only reasonably possible or not estimable, only an explanation of the situation is required in the footnotes to the financial statements. If the likelihood of the contingency is remote, then it need not be disclosed. Villa should account for each of its contingencies in a slightly different way because the likelihood of Villa incurring a loss differs in each situation.

For the toxic waste cleanup, a loss has been incurred. In the notes to its financial statements, Villa should disclose the nature of the loss on cleanup and indicate that an estimate of the loss, or range of the loss, cannot be made. No accrual should be made because the loss cannot be reasonably estimated and accrual of an uncertain amount would impair the integrity of the financial statements.

With regard to Clear's claim, it is only reasonably possible, and not probable, that Villa will have to pay. Accordingly, Villa should not accrue the loss. Villa should disclose the existence and nature of Clear's claim in the notes to its financial statements. Disclosure should include an estimate of the potential range of loss.

Regarding the lack of rockslide insurance, no asset has been impaired, and no liability has been incurred. Accordingly, Villa should not accrue a loss. Since the likelihood of a rockslide is remote, disclosure of the uninsured risk, while permitted, is not required.

If further clarification of these contingencies is needed, please contact my office.

| Situation | Leasing Concepts | Journal Entries | Interest Expense | Liability Section of Balance Sheet | Communication | Research |
|---|---|---|---|---|---|---|

**1.** For how many years must Villa disclose future minimum lease payments?

**FAS13, Para 16 or Current Text L10.112**

16. The following information with respect to leases shall be disclosed in the lessee's financial statements or the footnotes thereto (see Appendix D for illustrations).

a. For capital leases

i. The gross amount of assets recorded under capital leases as of the date of each balance sheet presented by major classes according to nature or function. This information may be combined with the comparable information for owned assets.

ii. Future minimum lease payments as of the date of the latest balance sheet presented, in the aggregate and for each of the five succeeding fiscal years, with separate deductions from the total for the amount representing executory costs, including any profit thereon, included in the minimum lease payments and for the amount of the imputed interest necessary to reduce the net minimum lease payments to present value (see paragraph 10).

iii. The total of minimum sublease rentals to be received in the future under noncancelable subleases as of the date of the latest balance sheet presented.

iv. Total contingent rentals (rentals on which the amounts are dependent on some factor other than the passage of time) actually incurred for each period for which an income statement is presented.

b. For operating leases having initial or remaining noncancelable lease terms in excess of one year:

i. Future minimum rental payments required as of the date of the latest balance sheet presented, in the aggregate and for each of the five succeeding fiscal years.

      ii.   The total of minimum rentals to be received in the future under noncancelable subleases as of the date of the latest balance sheet presented.

  c.  For all operating leases, rental expenses for each period for which an income statement is presented, with separate amounts for minimum rentals, contingent rentals, and sublease rentals. Rental payments under leases with terms of a month or less that were not renewed need not be included.

  d.  A general description of the lessee's leasing arrangements including, but not limited to, the following:

      i.   The basis on which contingent rental payments are determined.

      ii.   The existence and terms of renewal or purchase options and escalation clauses.

      iii.   Restrictions imposed by lease agreements, such as those concerning dividends, additional debt, and further leasing.

**2.** What interest rate is used in calculating the present value of minimum lease payments for the lessee?

### FAS13, Para 7 or Current Text L10.103

d.  The present value at the beginning of the lease term of the minimum lease payments (as defined in paragraph 5(j)), excluding that portion of the payments representing executory costs such as insurance, maintenance, and taxes to be paid by the lessor, including any profit thereon, equals or exceeds 90% of the excess of the fair value of the leased property (as defined in paragraph 5(c)) to the lessor at the inception of the lease over any related investment tax credit retained by the lessor and expected to be realized by him. However, if the beginning of the lease term falls within the last 25% of the total estimated economic life of the leased property, including earlier years of use, this criterion shall not be used for purposes of classifying the lease. A lessor shall compute the present value of the minimum lease payments using the interest rate implicit in the lease (as defined in paragraph 5(k)). A lessee shall compute the present value of the minimum lease payments using his incremental borrowing rate (as defined in paragraph 5(1)), unless (i) it is practicable for him to learn the implicit rate computed by the lessor and (ii) the implicit rate computed by the lessor is less than the lessee's incremental borrowing rate. If both of those conditions are met, the lessee shall use the implicit rate.

### FAS13, Para 5 or Current Text L10.412

k.  Interest rate implicit in the lease. The discount rate that, when applied to (i) the minimum lease payments (as defined in paragraph 5(j)), excluding that portion of the payments representing executory costs to be paid by the lessor, together with any profit thereon, and (ii) the unguaranteed residual value (as defined in paragraph 5(i)) accruing to the benefit of the lessor, causes the aggregate present value at the beginning of the lease term to be equal to the fair value of the leased property (as defined in paragraph 5(c)) to the lessor at the inception of the lease, minus any investment tax credit retained by the lessor and expected to be realized by him. (This definition does not necessarily purport to include all factors that a lessor might recognize in determining his rate of return, e.g., see paragraph 44.)

1.  Lessee's incremental borrowing rate. The rate that, at the inception of the lease, the lessee would have incurred to borrow over a similar term the funds necessary to purchase the leased asset.

### FAS13, Para 7 or Current Text L10.103

7.  The criteria for classifying leases set forth in this paragraph and in paragraph 8 derive from the concept as set forth in para-

**3.** What are the criteria to determine if a lease is an operating or a capital lease?

graph 60. If at its inception (as defined in paragraph 5(b)) a lease meets one or more of the following four criteria, the lease shall be classified as a capital lease by the lessee. Otherwise, it shall be classified as an operating lease. (See Appendix C for an illustration of the application of these criteria.)

a. The lease transfers ownership of the property to the lessee by the end of the lease term (as defined in paragraph 5(f)).

b. The lease contains a bargain purchase option (as defined in paragraph 5(d)).

c. The lease term (as defined in paragraph 5(f)) is equal to 75% or more of the estimated economic life of the leased property (as defined in paragraph 5(g)). However, if the beginning of the lease term falls within the last 25% of the total estimated economic life of the leased property, including earlier years of use, this criterion shall not be used for purposes of classifying the lease.

d. The present value at the beginning of the lease term of the minimum lease payments (as defined in paragraph 5(j)), excluding that portion of the payments representing executory costs such as insurance, maintenance, and taxes to be paid by the lessor, including any profit thereon, equals or exceeds 90% of the excess of the fair value of the leased property (as defined in paragraph 5(c)) to the lessor at the inception of the lease over any related investment tax credit retained by the lessor and expected to be realized by him. However, if the beginning of the lease term falls within the last 25% of the total estimated economic life of the leased property, including earlier years of use, this criterion shall not be used for purposes of classifying the lease. A lessor shall compute the present value of the minimum lease payments using the interest rate implicit in the lease (as defined in paragraph 5(k)). A lessee shall compute the present value of the minimum lease payments using his incremental borrowing rate (as defined in paragraph 5(1)), unless (i) it is practicable for him to learn the implicit rate computed by the lessor and (ii) the implicit rate computed by the lessor is less than the lessee's incremental borrowing rate. If both of those conditions are met, the lessee shall use the implicit rate.

## DEFERRED TAXES

SFAS 109, *Accounting for Income Taxes*, requires an asset and liability (balance sheet) approach to recognizing and measuring deferred taxes. To understand the basic concepts of deferred taxes, study this module and the outlines of SFAS 109 and APB 23.

### A.  Overview of Deferred Tax Theory

There are numerous differences between the recognition and measurement of pretax financial (book) income and asset/liability valuation under GAAP and the recognition and measurement of taxable income and asset/liability valuation under the Internal Revenue Code. Because of these differences between the two bodies of promulgated rules, pretax financial (book) income usually differs from taxable income. The amount of Income Tax Expense and the amount of Income Taxes Payable are, therefore, often different amounts.

According to SFAS 109, financial income tax expense (the **current and deferred** tax consequences of **all** events that have been recognized in the financial statements) is charged to Income Tax Expense. Income Tax Expense equals the taxes actually owed (a current tax liability) for the current period plus or minus the change during the current period in amounts payable in the future and in future tax benefits. By using this procedure, any possible income statement or balance sheet distortion that may result from differences in the timing of revenue recognition or expense deductibility and asset or liability valuation between GAAP and the Internal Revenue Code is avoided. The Income Tax Expense reported in the entity's income statement reflects the amount of taxes related to transactions recognized in the financial statements prepared under GAAP for the specific period. The deferred tax asset or liability (the difference between Income Tax Expense and Income Tax Payable) reported in the entity's balance sheet clearly reflects the amount of taxes that the entity has prepaid (an asset) or will have to pay in the future (a liability) because of temporary differences that result from differences in timing of revenue recognition or expense deductibility between GAAP and the Internal Revenue Code.

### B.  Permanent and Temporary Differences Defined

Differences between pretax financial (book) income and taxable income can be divided into two types: temporary differences or permanent differences. SFAS 109 does **not** use the term permanent differences. However, to ease our explanation and your comprehension, the term "permanent difference" will be used in this module, as it is in several intermediate accounting textbooks.

#### 1.  Temporary Differences

SFAS 109 defines a temporary difference as "a difference between the tax basis of an asset or liability and its reported amount in the financial statements that will result in taxable or deductible amounts in future years when the reported amount of the asset or liability is recovered or settled, respectively." This definition of a temporary difference is based on the assumption that assets and liabilities reported on an entity's balance sheet will eventually be recovered or settled at their net reported (book) value. This recovery or settling process will create income statement items (revenues/gains or expenses/losses) as the life of the asset or liability progresses. If the reported financial (book) value of the balance sheet item differs from its tax basis, the correct period for recognition of the related income statement item will differ between the entity's financial statements and the entity's tax return. Thus, from an income statement perspective, a temporary difference occurs when a revenue or expense item: (1) is included in both financial accounting income and taxable income, **and**, (2) is recognized in one period for financial accounting purposes and in another period for income tax purposes because of differences between the promulgated rules of GAAP and the Internal Revenue Code. If such a temporary difference exists, an amount will be recorded and reported as either a deferred tax liability or a deferred tax asset depending upon the relationship between the reported net financial (book) value and the tax basis of the related asset or liability. When the temporary difference reverses, the recorded deferred tax amount is removed from the balance sheet; the amount removed results in an increase or decrease in income tax expense. Some examples of temporary differences are presented below.

a.  **Estimated warranty liability:** Expense recognized in the financial statements when the liability is incurred. Deduction recognized for tax purposes when the work is actually performed.

b.  **Unearned rent (royalty) revenue:** Recognized in the financial statements as a liability when the rent (royalty) is received and as revenue when earned. Recognized as revenue for tax purposes when the cash is received. (Note that the Internal Revenue Code refers to revenue received in advance as "prepaid income," not "unearned revenue.")

c. **Plant assets and accumulated depreciation:** Changes in these assets and the related contra asset are recognized in the financial statements according to depreciation methods acceptable to GAAP. Changes in these assets and the related contra asset are usually recognized for tax purposes according to accelerated methods acceptable to the IRS such as ACRS and MACRS. Note that recovery of these assets occurs as the asset is used in the entity's operations to generate revenue. In essence, a portion of the investment in the asset is being recovered as the product or service is sold.

d. **Donated asset:** According to GAAP, initial valuation in the financial statements of a donated asset is based upon fair market value, and revenue is recognized for the same amount. Depreciation on the asset is computed according to the entity's normal policies. Upon sale of the asset, a gain is recognized for the difference between cash received and net book value. According to the Internal Revenue Code, a donated asset has the same basis for the donee as it did in the donor's hands. Thus, no tax deductions for depreciation are allowed for the asset if the tax basis is zero. When the asset is sold, the entire amount received is a taxable gain.

e. **Involuntary conversion of assets:** According to GAAP (FASB Interpretation 30), a gain (loss) must be recognized when a nonmonetary asset is involuntarily converted into a monetary asset, even though the entity reinvests the monetary assets in replacement nonmonetary assets. The replacement asset is valued at its cost or fair market value on date of acquisition. According to the Internal Revenue Code, no gain is recognized on an involuntary conversion if the amount reinvested in replacement property equals or exceeds the amount realized from the converted property. The tax basis of the replacement asset is valued at its cost less the deferred gain.

f. **Goodwill:** Under GAAP, goodwill is not amortized. The Internal Revenue Code however, mandates an amortization period of fifteen years.

2. **Permanent Differences**

A permanent difference occurs when a revenue or expense item is only included in pretax financial (book) income or in taxable income but will never be included in both. For example, interest income on municipal bonds is included in pretax financial (book) income but is never included in taxable income because it is tax exempt by law. No deferred taxes need to be recognized because no future tax consequences are created. The tax exempt income (or deduction not allowed for taxes) is simply subtracted from (or added to) book income in the book to tax reconciliation. Thus, a permanent difference affects only the current reconciliation of book income to taxable income, and has no effect on the computation of deferred taxes. Some common permanent differences are

a. **State and municipal bond interest income:** included in book income but not included in taxable income.

b. **Life insurance premium expense when the corporation is the beneficiary:** deducted for book income but not for taxable income; proceeds received on such policies result in a book gain but are not taxable.

c. **Federal income tax expense:** deducted for book income but not for taxable income.

d. **Payment of penalty or fine:** deducted for book income but not for taxable income.

e. **Dividend received deduction (DRD):** deducted for taxable income but not for book income.

The example below shows how permanent and temporary differences are used in calculating taxable income, given a corporation's pretax financial (book) income.

*EXAMPLE 1: A corporation has pretax financial accounting (book) income of $146,000 in 2007. Additional information is as follows:*

1. *Municipal bond interest income is $35,000.*
2. *Life insurance premium expense, where the corporation is the beneficiary, per books is $4,000.*
3. *Accelerated depreciation is used for tax purposes, while straight-line is used for books. Tax depreciation is $10,000; book depreciation is $5,000.*
4. *Estimated warranty expense of $500 is accrued for book purposes.*

*Taxable income can be determined as follows:*

| | |
|---|---:|
| Financial (book) income before income taxes | $146,000 |
| Permanent differences | |
|     Life insurance premium | 4,000 |
|     Municipal bond interest | (35,000) |
| Temporary differences | |
|     Amount added to tax accum. depr. and deducted on the tax return > | |
|       Amount added to book accum. deprec. and deprec. exp. | (5,000) |
|     Amount recognized for book estimated warranty | |
|       liability and warranty exp. not recognized on the tax return | 500 |
| Taxable income | $110,500 |

*The above schedule is known as the reconciliation of book income to taxable income. It is similar to the Schedule M-1 of the US Corporate Income Tax Return (Form 1120) except it starts with pretax financial accounting income instead of net income as Schedule M-1 does. Note that the permanent differences only impact the current year (2007 in this case) whereas the temporary differences will have future tax consequences.*

## C. Deferred Tax Assets and Liabilities

SFAS 109 defines a deferred tax asset as the deferred tax consequences attributable to deductible temporary differences and carryforwards. SFAS 109 requires that the deferred tax asset be reduced by a valuation allowance if a portion or all of the deferred tax asset will not be realized in the future. A deferred tax liability is defined as an amount that is recognized for the deferred tax consequence of temporary differences that will result in taxable amounts in future years. SFAS 109, like its predecessor pronouncements, does **not** permit discounting of these deferred tax assets and liabilities.

### 1. Identification and Measurement of Deferred Tax Items

The candidate's ability to work an income tax accounting problem depends upon his/her ability to correctly identify permanent and temporary differences. In order to recognize the tax consequences of a temporary difference, it must be the result of event(s) that have already been recognized in the entity's financial statements for the current or previous years. With regard to a fixed asset, this means that the fixed asset has been acquired before the end of the year for which income taxes are being determined. Thus, planned asset acquisitions for future years cannot result in temporary differences and thereby affect the determination of deferred income taxes.

A **temporary difference** between pretax financial (book) income and taxable income occurs when the tax basis of an asset (or liability) differs from its reported financial statement amount. As shown in *Example 1,* a temporary difference resulting from timing of GAAP recognition vs. timing of recognition for tax purposes can create the need for additions to or subtractions from book income in order to arrive at taxable income. These **additions (taxable amounts)** or **subtractions (deductible amounts)** can occur in the year an asset is acquired or a liability is incurred as well as in future years as the asset is recovered or the liability is settled. The table below presents the various possible relationships between financial statement (book) and tax recognition of revenue and expense and assets and liabilities as well as the nature of the resulting future tax consequences.

| Acctg. income > or < taxable income* | B/S relationships | Temp. differ.** Cur. | Temp. differ.** Fut. | Type of BS tax deferral | Current deferred tax expense effect | Future deferred tax expense effect |
|---|---|---|---|---|---|---|
| | *Assets* | | | | | |
| > | (1) on books > tax return | D | T | Liability | (+) | (−) |
| < | (2) on books < tax return | T | D | Asset | (−) | (+) |
| | *Liabilities* | | | | | |
| < | (3) on books > tax return | T | D | Asset | (−) | (+) |
| | (4) on books < tax return | D | T | Liability | (+) | (−) |

  \* *Relationship in the year the temporary difference originates.*
\*\* *Deductible (D) /Taxable (T)*

For example, a type 1 temporary difference (such as the difference between the financial statement amount and the **zero** tax basis of an asset obtained by a donation) creates a deferred tax liability. If the donated asset is sold for more than its tax basis, recognition of the difference between the asset's financial statement amount and its tax return basis results in a gain for taxable income and either a smaller gain or a loss for book income depending on the amount of book depreciation taken on the asset since it was received by the enterprise. The amount of cash that will be needed to pay the taxes due will be increased because the entire amount of cash received for the donated asset will be reported as gain (taxable amount) on the tax return. A liability is defined in SFAC 6 as "probable future sacrifices of economic benefits arising from present obligations of a particular entity to transfer assets...as a result of past transactions or events." The increase in cash paid out for taxes (a sacrifice of economic benefits) will result when the donated asset (from a past transaction or event) is disposed of; therefore, the future tax impact of the current period difference between financial statement value and tax basis represents a deferred liability. When the liability is recognized, deferred income tax expense is also recognized.

In contrast, a contingent liability recognized in the current period financial statements represents a type 3 temporary difference because a contingent liability has a zero basis for tax accounting. The amount of expense stemming from this contingent liability must be added back to financial (book) income to arrive at taxable income. Therefore, a deferred tax asset is created. When the probable and measurable future event does actually occur, the contingent liability will then represent a loss (deductible amount) on the tax return. Because the tax loss recognized will reduce taxable income and income taxes payable, the amount of cash that will be needed to pay the taxes due will be decreased. Remember, an asset is defined in SFAC 6 as a "probable future economic benefit obtained or controlled by a particular entity as a result of past transactions or events." The reduction of current tax expense and the resulting future decrease in cash paid out for taxes (an economic benefit) will result from the contingent liability (a past transaction or event). Therefore, the future tax impact of the current period difference between the financial statement value and tax basis represents a deferred tax asset in the year the contingency is recognized. Note that the deferred tax expense recorded in this situation is a credit because it represents a current period benefit.

2. **Scheduling and Recording Deferred Tax Amounts**

An entity's total income statement provision for income taxes is the sum of that entity's current and deferred tax amounts. The current tax expense or benefit is defined by SFAS 109 as "the amount of income taxes paid or payable (or refundable) for a year as determined by applying the provisions of the tax law to the taxable income or excess of deductions over revenues for that year." The deferred tax expense or benefit is defined as "the change during the year in an enterprise's deferred tax liabilities or assets." Thus, SFAS 109 requires that current and deferred tax amounts be computed independently.

The deferred tax amount (the future tax consequences of temporary differences) should be recorded in the current financial statements at the amounts that will be paid or recovered based upon tax laws and rates that are already in place and due to be in effect at the date of payment or recovery. These are known as **enacted** tax laws and **enacted** tax rates. In order to comply with SFAS 109, an entity must, therefore, determine when the identified and measured temporary differences will become taxable or deductible. Future **taxable amounts** cause taxable income to be greater than financial (book) income in future periods. They are a result of existing temporary differences and are reported as deferred tax liabilities in the current year. Future **deductible amounts** cause taxable income to be less than financial (book) income in future periods. They are a result of existing temporary differences and are reported as a deferred tax asset in the current year. For illustrative purposes, the following examples show the scheduling of future temporary differences. However, in practice and on the CPA exam, extensive scheduling is generally not necessary unless (1) there is a change in future enacted tax rates or (2) the problem requires the use of a valuation allowance account.

According to SFAS 109, deferred tax liabilities and assets are determined separately for each tax-paying component (an individual entity or group of entities that is consolidated for tax purposes) in each tax jurisdiction. That determination includes the following procedures:

1. Identify the types and amounts of existing temporary differences
2. Identify the nature and amount of each type of operating loss and tax credit carryforward and the remaining length of the carryforward period
3. Measure the total deferred tax liability for taxable temporary differences using the applicable tax rate
4. Measure the total deferred tax asset for deductible temporary differences and operating loss carryforwards using the applicable tax rate
5. Measure deferred tax assets for each type of tax credit carryforward
6. Reduce deferred tax assets by a valuation allowance if, based on the weight of available evidence, it is *more likely than not* (a likelihood of more than 50%) that some portion or all of the

deferred tax assets will not be realized.  The valuation allowance should be sufficient to reduce the deferred tax asset to the amount that is more likely than not to be realized.

7.  Deferred tax assets and liabilities are **not** discounted to reflect their present value

*EXAMPLE 2:  This example shows the **deferred tax accounting in 2007, 2008, and 2009** for the temporary differences included in Example 1 earlier in this module.  Additional details are*

 a. *On 1/1/05 the enterprise acquired a depreciable asset for $30,000 that had an estimated life of six years and is depreciated on a straight-line basis for book purposes.  For tax purposes, the asset is depreciated using the straight-line election under MACRS and qualifies as a three-year asset.*

 b. *The enterprise deducted warranty expense of $500 for book purposes in 2007 that is expected to be deductible for tax purposes in 2008.*

 c. *Taxable income was $110,500 in 2007, $112,000 in 2008, and $113,500 in 2009.*

 d. *The applicable tax rate is 40% for all years affected.*

*The deferred component of income tax expense for 2007 is computed as follows.  First, a schedule of the **temporary depreciation differences** for all affected years is prepared:*

|  | 2005 | 2006 | 2007 | 2008 | 2009 | 2010 |
|---|---|---|---|---|---|---|
| Book depreciation | $ 5,000 | $ 5,000 | $ 5,000 | $5,000 | $5,000 | $5,000 |
| Tax depreciation | 5,000* | 10,000 | 10,000 | 5,000* | -- | -- |
| Temporary difference: | | | | | | |
| No difference | $    0 | | | $    0 | | |
| Book deprec. < Tax deprec. | | $(5,000) | $(5,000) | | | |
| Book deprec. > Tax deprec. | | | | | $5,000 | $5,000 |

 \* Due to MACRS half-year convention

*Then, a schedule of **future taxable (deductible) amounts** is prepared.*

|  | 2008 Taxable (deductible) | 2009 Taxable (deductible) | 2010 Taxable (deductible) | Tax rate | Deferred tax liability (asset) |
|---|---|---|---|---|---|
| Scheduled taxable (deductible) amounts: | | | | | |
| Depreciation differences: | | | | | |
| taxable amounts | | $5,000 | $5000 | 40% | $4,000 Noncurrent |
| Warranty differences: | | | | | |
| deductible amounts | $(500) | | | 40% | $(200) Current |

  The above schedule shows that the future tax benefit (deductible amount) in 2008 of the $500 temporary difference resulting from the Warranty Expense Liability must be recognized automatically as a deferred tax asset in 2007.  The deferred tax asset of $200 ($500 × 40%) should be reported as a current asset at 12/31/07 because the classification of the temporary difference is based on the related asset or liability, in this case a warranty liability that is expected to be satisfied in the next year.  The amount of future taxes payable (deferred tax liability) associated with the total temporary difference of $10,000 resulting from excess depreciation [$5,000 (2007) + $5,000 (2008)] is $4,000 [($5,000 + 5,000) × 40%].  The $4,000 amount is reported as a noncurrent deferred tax liability at 12/31/07, because classification as current or noncurrent is based on the classification of the related asset or liability, in this case a depreciable asset that is noncurrent.

  Once the deferred tax asset and deferred tax liability have been measured at year-end, a journal entry is necessary to adjust the deferred tax account balances to the current year-end amount.  As stated earlier, income tax expense for the year will consist of the taxes currently payable (based on taxable income) plus or minus any change in the deferred tax accounts.

## EQUATION FOR DETERMINING INCOME TAX EXPENSE

$$\text{Income tax expense for financial reporting} = \text{Income tax payable from the tax return} \pm \text{Change in deferred taxes (net)*}$$

 \* *Ending balance of deferred tax liability/asset (net) less beginning balance of deferred tax liability/asset (net)*

NOTES:

1. *Income Tax Expense is the sum of the two numbers on the right side of the equation.  Each of these two numbers is determined directly using independent calculations.  It is not possible to derive Income Tax Expense from pretax financial accounting income adjusted for permanent differences, unless the tax rate is constant for all years affected.*

2. *The $\pm$ refers to whether the change is a credit or additional liability (+) or a debit or additional asset (–).*

3. *Income Tax Payable is the amount of taxes calculated on the corporate tax return.  It is the amount legally owed the government (after credits).*

4. *One deferred tax (net) balance sheet account may be used in practice.  If separate asset and liability accounts are used, the changes in each account would all be netted to determine the deferred tax component of income tax expense.*

*To illustrate, we will use the deferred tax liability computed in Example 2 above and the taxable income derived in Example 1.  Note that prior to adjustment, the deferred tax asset account had a zero balance and the deferred tax liability account had a balance of $2,000 ($5,000 × 40%) that was recognized as a result of the accumulated depreciation temporary difference that originated in 2005.  (Refer to the schedule following the additional information given in Example 2 showing depreciation and the pattern of temporary differences and to the T-account under (c) below.)  To focus on the two components of income tax expense, two entries rather than the typical combined entry will be used.*

| | | |
|---|---|---|
| Income tax expense—current | 44,200 | |
| Income tax payable (a) | | 44,200 |

(a)  *$110,500 taxable income (from Example 1) × 40% = $44,200*

| | | |
|---|---|---|
| Income tax expense—deferred (d) | 1,800 | |
| Deferred tax asset—current (b) | 200 | |
| Deferred tax liability—noncurrent (c) | | 2,000 |

(b)  *$500 × 40% = $200 needed Ending balance; $200 Ending balance – $0 Beginning balance = $200 increase needed in the account*

|  | Deferred Tax Asset |
|---|---|
| Beg. bal. | 0 |
| Increase (b) | 200 |
| End. bal. | 200 |

(c)  *$10,000 × 40% = $4,000 needed Ending balance; $4,000 Ending balance – $2,000 Beginning balance = $2,000 increase needed in the account*

| Deferred Tax Liability | |
|---|---|
| 2,000 | Beg. bal. |
| 2,000 | Increase (c) |
| 4,000 | End. bal. |

(d)  *$2,000 increase in noncurrent deferred tax liability account – $200 increase in current deferred tax asset account = $1,800*

*The bottom of the income statement for 2007 would appear as follows:*

| | | |
|---|---|---|
| Income before income tax | | $146,000 |
| Income tax expense | | |
| Current | $44,200 | |
| Deferred | 1,800 | 46,000 |
| Net income | | $100,000 |

*To determine the deferred component of income tax expense for **2007,** a schedule of future taxable (deductible) amounts is prepared.*

| | 2008 Taxable (deductible) | 2009 Taxable (deductible) | 2010 Taxable (deductible) | Tax rate | Deferred tax liability (asset) |
|---|---|---|---|---|---|
| Scheduled taxable (deductible) amounts: | | | | | |
| Depreciation differences: | | | | | |
| taxable amounts | -0- | $5,000 | $5,000 | 40% | $4,000 Noncurrent |

*The temporary depreciation difference of $10,000 results in future taxes payable (a deferred tax liability) of $4,000 [($5,000 + 5,000) × 40%].  Note that the amount of the deferred tax liability in this example does not change from 2006 to 2007.  The $4,000 amount would be reported as a noncurrent deferred tax liability at 12/31/08, based upon the noncurrent classification of the related depreciable asset.  The $500 warranty expense deducted in 2007 for book purposes is deducted in 2008 for tax purposes.  Therefore, the deferred tax asset related to warranty expense is realized in 2008 and the temporary difference related to warranty expense no longer exists.*

*Once the deferred tax amounts have been measured at year-end, a journal entry is required to adjust the deferred tax account balances to the current year-end amount.  Income tax expense for the year consists of the taxes currently payable plus or minus any change in the deferred tax accounts.  The following journal entries are needed to record income tax expense for 2008:*

| | | |
|---|---|---|
| Income tax expense—current | 44,800 | |
| Income tax payable (a) | | 44,800 |

(a)  *$112,000 taxable income × 40% = $44,800*

| | | |
|---|---|---|
| Income tax expense deferred (c) | 200 | |
| Deferred tax asset current (b) | | 200 |

(b) *The credit to the deferred tax asset is the adjustment necessary to reduce the existing balance to the desired ending balance.*

*Deferred Tax Asset*

| | | | |
|---|---|---|---|
| Beg. bal. | 200 | | |
| | | 200 | Decrease (b) |
| End. bal. | 0 | | |

(c) *Income tax expense—deferred results from the decrease in the deferred tax asset. There is no adjustment to the deferred tax liability account.*

*Deferred Tax Liability*

| | | | |
|---|---|---|---|
| | | 4,000 | Beg. bal. |
| | | 0 | |
| | | 4,000 | End. bal. |

*To determine the deferred component of income tax expense for* **2009** *the following journal entries are required:*

| | | |
|---|---|---|
| Income tax expense—current | 45,400 | |
|     Income tax payable (a) | | 45,400 |

(a) *$113,500 taxable income × 40% = $45,400*

| | | |
|---|---|---|
| Deferred tax liability—noncurrent (b) | 2,000 | |
|     Income tax expense—deferred (c) | | 2,000 |

(b) *The debit to the deferred tax liability is the adjustment necessary to reduce the existing balance to the desired ending balance.*

*Deferred Tax Liability*

| | | | |
|---|---|---|---|
| | | 4,000 | Beg. bal. |
| | 2,000 | | Decrease (b) |
| | | 2,000 | End. bal. |

(c) *Income tax expense—deferred results from the decrease in the deferred tax liability. The deferred tax asset account was closed in 2008 because all temporary differences have reversed.*

*The income tax liability per the tax return in 2009 is higher than total tax expense reported on the income statement since depreciation is not deducted for tax purposes anymore. In effect, the income tax liability in 2009 includes a portion of the tax deferred from 2007-2008 that was recorded as a liability; therefore, the deferred tax liability is reduced in 2009. There is a corresponding decrease in income tax expense—deferred that will reconcile the income tax liability per the tax return to income tax expense on the books.*

| | |
|---|---|
| Income tax expense—current | 45,400 |
| Income tax expense—deferred | (2,000) |
| Income tax expense per income statement | 43,400 |

**Changing tax rates.** The previous examples assumed a constant enacted tax rate of 40%. Under the liability method upon which SFAS 109 is predicated, future taxable or deductible amounts must be measured using enacted tax rates expected to be in effect in the periods such amounts will impact taxable income. Similarly, a deferred tax asset is measured using the applicable enacted tax rate and provisions of the enacted tax law. However, when tax rates change, adjustments to reflect such changes are automatically included in the journal entry amount to increase or decrease the deferred tax accounts to the balances needed to properly reflect balance sheet amounts and to recognize the deferred component of income tax expense. The rate change effect would be included because the amount of the journal entry is determined by comparing the needed balance in deferred taxes at the end of the period which would be based on the newly enacted rates with the balance at the beginning of the period and taking the difference.

*EXAMPLE 3: Assume that in June 2009 a new income tax law is passed which lowers the corporate tax rate to 35% effective January 1, 2010. The entry debiting income tax expense—current and crediting income tax payable for 2009 is identical to that above.*

*However, the debit to the deferred tax liability account is the adjustment necessary to reduce the existing balance to the desired ending balance* **under the new tax rate**.

| | | |
|---|---|---|
| Deferred tax liability—noncurrent | 2,250 | |
|     Income tax expense—deferred | | 2,250 |

*Deferred Tax Liability*

| | | | |
|---|---|---|---|
| | | 4,000 | Beg. bal. |
| | 2,250 | | Decrease |
| | | 1,750 | End. bal. |

*The $1,750 is the necessary balance for the 2010 reversal of the remaining $5,000 at 35%.*

EXAMPLE 4:  *Dart Corporation has the following temporary differences from its first year of operations:*

Treatment in the book<br>to tax reconciliation

1. **Long-term contracts:**

| | | |
|---|---|---|
| Year 1 (Current year): | Book contract income > tax contract income | $300 subtraction |
| Year 2: | Book contract income < tax  contract income | $300 addition |

2. **Accumulated depreciation:**

| | | |
|---|---|---|
| Year 1 (Current year): | Book deprec. < tax deprec. | $1,000 subtraction |
| Year 2: | Book deprec. < tax deprec. | $500 subtraction |
| Year 3: | Book deprec. > tax deprec. | $600 addition |
| Year 4: | Book deprec. > tax deprec. | $400 addition |
| Year 7: | | $500 addition |

3. **Estimated expense liability:**

| | | |
|---|---|---|
| Year 1 (Current year): | Book est. exp./loss > tax deduction | $200 addition |
| Year 7: | Book exp./loss < tax deduction | $200 subtraction |

4. **Rent revenue:**

| | | |
|---|---|---|
| Year 1 (Current year): | Book rev. < tax rev. | $500 addition |
| Year 4: | Book rev. > tax rev. | $200 subtraction |
| Year 7: | Book rev. > tax rev. | $300 subtraction |

5. **Tax rates:**

| | | |
|---|---|---|
| | Current year: | 40% |
| | Years 2-4: | 35% |
| | Years 5-7: | 30% |

*The schedule below combines (1) the pretax accounting income to taxable income reconciliation and (2) the future taxable (deductible) amounts schedule.  Remember that* **taxable amounts** *are added to financial (book) income in the book to tax reconciliation schedule in the future years in which they increase taxable income.* **Deductible amounts** *are subtracted from financial (book) income in the book to tax reconciliation schedule in the future years in which they decrease taxable income.  Taxable income and deferred tax liability (asset) balances for year 1 (the current year) would be determined as follows:*

| | Current year | Future years | | | | |
|---|---|---|---|---|---|---|
| | | Year 2 taxable | Year 3 taxable | Year 4 taxable | Year 7 taxable | Deferred tax liability |
| | *Year 1* | *(deductible)* | *(deductible)* | *(deductible)* | *(deductible)* | *(asset)* |
| Tax rate | 40% | 35% | 35% | 35% | 30% | |
| Pretax accounting income | $1,600 | | | | | |
| Temporary differences: | | | | | | |
| LT contracts | (300) | 300 | | | | $105 Current |
| Accumulated deprec. | (1,000) | (500)* | 600 | 400 | 500 | $325 Noncurrent |
| Estimated expense liability | 200 | | | | (200) | $  (60) Noncurrent |
| Rent revenue | 500 | | | (200) | (300) | $(160) Noncurrent |
| Taxable income | $1,000 | | | | | |
| Income tax payable ($1,000 × 40%) | $  400 | | | | | |

* *Note that in year 2 there is excess tax depreciation as there was in year 1.*

*Income tax expense would be computed as follows:*

$$\text{Income tax expense} = \text{Income taxes payable} \pm \text{Change in deferred taxes (net)}$$

Under SFAS 109, deferred tax assets and liabilities are classified as current or long-term based on the related asset or liability, rather than on the expected timing of the future deductible or taxable amounts.  However, if a deferred tax asset or liability is not related to an asset or liability for financial reporting purposes, it is classified based upon its expected reversal date.  Presented below is a solution for Example 4.

| Temporary difference | Deferred tax asset or liability | Related account | Classification* |
|---|---|---|---|
| LT contracts | $300 × 35% = $105 liability | Const-in-Progress | Current |
| Depreciation | [(500) + 600 + 400] × 35% + $500 × 30% = $325 liability | Accumulated depr. | Noncurrent |
| Est. expense | $200 × 30% = $60 asset | Estimated liability | Noncurrent |
| Rent revenue | $200 × 35% + $300 x 30% = $160 asset | Unearned rent | Noncurrent |

* *Balance sheet disclosure is explained for this example in Section F.3.*

*The journal entries required are as follows:*

| | | |
|---|---|---|
| Income tax expense current | 400 | |
|     Income tax payable | | 400 (a) |

(a)   $1,000 taxable income × 40% = $400

| | | |
|---|---|---|
| Income tax expense deferred (e) | 210 | |
| Deferred tax asset noncurrent (b) | 220 | |
|     Deferred tax liability current (c) | | 105 |
|     Deferred tax liability noncurrent (d) | | 325 |

(b)  $200 × 30% + $200 × 35% + $300 × 30%= $220 needed Ending balance; $220 Ending balance – $0 Beginning balance = $220 increase needed in the account.

| Deferred Tax Asset—Noncurrent | |
|---|---|
| Beg. bal. | -0- |
| Increase (b) | 220 |
| End. bal. | 220 |

(c)  $300 × 35% = $105 Ending balance; $105 Ending balance – $0 Beginning balance = $105 increase needed in the account

| Deferred Tax Liability—Current | |
|---|---|
| -0- | Beg. bal. |
| 105 | Increase (c) |
| 105 | End. bal. |

(d)  $1,000 × 35%  + ($500) × 35% + $500 × 30% = $325 Ending balance; $325 Ending balance –$0 Beginning balance = $325 increase needed in the account.

| Deferred Tax Liability—Noncurrent | |
|---|---|
| -0- | Beg. bal. |
| 325 | Increase (d) |
| 325 | End. bal. |

(e)  $105 increase in current deferred tax liability amount + $325 increase in noncurrent deferred tax liability account – $220 increase in noncurrent deferred tax asset account = $210.

*Note that since this is the firm's first year of operations, there are no beginning balances in the deferred tax accounts. If there were any permanent differences, such differences would affect only the current year as they did in Example 1. In addition, the need for a valuation allowance to reduce the deferred tax asset to its net realizable value would need to be considered.*

***Deferred tax asset valuation allowance.*** SFAS 109 does require that a deferred tax asset be reduced by a valuation allowance if, based on the weight of available evidence, it is more likely than not (a likelihood of more than 50%) that some portion or all of the deferred tax asset will not be realized. All available evidence, both positive and negative, should be considered to determine whether a valuation allowance is needed. The need for a valuation allowance ultimately depends on the existence of sufficient taxable income (necessary to receive the benefit of a future deductible amount) within the carryback/carryforward period, as described in Section E of this module. SFAS 109 provides the following list of possible sources of taxable income; if any one of these sources is sufficient to support a conclusion that a valuation allowance is not necessary, other sources need not be considered.

1.  Possible sources of taxable income

   a.  Future reversals of existing taxable temporary differences
   b.  Future taxable income exclusive of reversing temporary differences and carryforwards
   c.  Taxable income in prior carryback year(s) if carryback is permitted under the tax law
   d.  **Tax-planning strategies** that would, if necessary, be implemented to

   (1)  Accelerate taxable amounts to utilize expiring carryforwards
   (2)  Change the character of taxable or deductible amounts from ordinary income or loss to capital gain or loss
   (3)  Switch from tax-exempt to taxable investments.

SFAS 109 also provides some examples of evidence to be considered when evaluating the need for a valuation allowance. These are summarized in the table below.

1.  Negative evidence—Indicates need for a valuation allowance

   a.  Cumulative losses in recent years
   b.  A history of operating loss or tax credit carryforwards expiring unused
   c.  Losses expected in early future years (by a presently profitable entity)
   d.  Unsettled circumstances that, if unfavorably resolved, would adversely affect future operations and profit levels on a continuing basis in future years
   e.  A carryback/carryforward period that is so brief that it would limit realization of tax benefits if (1) a significant deductible temporary difference is expected to reverse in a single year or (2) the enterprise operates in a traditionally cyclical business.

2.  Positive evidence—Can offset the impact of negative evidence

    a.  Existing contracts or firm sales backlog that will produce more than enough taxable income to realize the deferred tax asset based on existing sales prices and cost structures

    b.  An excess of appreciated asset value over the tax basis of the entity's net assets in an amount sufficient to realize the deferred tax asset

    c.  A strong earnings history exclusive of the loss that created the future deductible amount (tax loss carryforward or deductible temporary difference) coupled with evidence indicating that the loss (for example, an unusual, infrequent, or extraordinary item) is an aberration rather than a continuing condition.

For an example of the recording of a valuation allowance, assume Jeremiah Corporation has determined it has a noncurrent deferred tax asset of $800,000. Note that in the current and prior periods when this asset was recognized, income tax expense was reduced. Based on the weight of available evidence, Jeremiah feels it is more likely than not that $300,000 of this deferred tax asset will not be realized. Jeremiah would prepare the following journal entry:

| | | |
|---|---|---|
| Income tax expense | 300,000 | |
| Allowance to reduce deferred tax asset to expected realizable value | | 300,000 |

The balance sheet presentation is

| | |
|---|---|
| Other Assets (Noncurrent) | |
| Deferred tax asset | $800,000 |
| Less Allowance to reduce deferred tax asset to expected realizable value | (300,000) |
| | $ 500,000 |

At each year-end, the balance on the allowance account is adjusted upward or downward based on the evidence available at that time, resulting in an increase or decrease of income tax expense. For example, if $600,000 was deemed to be the net realizable value at the end of the next year, the following entry would be made:

| | | |
|---|---|---|
| Allowance to reduce deferred tax asset to expected realizable value | 100,000 | |
| Deferred income tax expense | | 100,000 |

## D.  Deferred Tax Related to Business Investments

One additional issue concerns temporary differences from income on long-term investments that are accounted for using the equity method. For these investments a corporation may assume that the temporary difference (the undistributed income since date of acquisition) will ultimately become taxable in the form of a dividend or in the form of a capital gain. Obviously, the tax expense and deferred tax liability recorded when the difference originates will be a function of whichever of these assumptions is made.

To illustrate the application of the requirements of SFAS 109 and APB 23 assume Parent Company owns 70% of the outstanding common stock of Subsidiary Company and 30% of the outstanding common stock of Investee Company. Additional data for Subsidiary and Investee Companies for the year 2007 are as follows:

| | *Investee Co* | *Subsidiary Co* |
|---|---|---|
| Net income | $50,000 | $100,000 |
| Dividends paid | 20,000 | 60,000 |

## 1.  Income Tax Effects from Investee Co.

The pretax accounting income of Parent Company will include equity in Investee income equal to $15,000 ($50,000 × 30%). Parent's taxable income, however, will include dividend income of $6,000 ($20,000 × 30%), and a dividends received deduction of 80% of the $6,000, or $4,800, will also be allowed for the dividends received. This 80% dividends received deduction is a permanent difference between pretax accounting and taxable income and is allowed for dividends received from domestic corporations in which the ownership percentage is less than 80% and equal to or greater than 20%. The originating temporary difference results from Parent's equity ($9,000) in Investee's undistributed income of $30,000 ($50,000 – $20,000). The amount by which the deferred tax liability account would increase in 2007 depends upon the expectations of Parent Co. as to the manner in which the $9,000 of undistributed income will be received. If the expectation of receipt is via dividends, then the temporary difference is 20% of $9,000 because 80% of the expected dividend will be excluded from taxable income when received. This temporary difference in 2007 of $1,800, multiplied by the tax rate, will give the amount of the increase in the deferred tax liability. If the expectation of receipt, however, is through future sale of the investment, then the temporary difference is $9,000, and the change in the deferred tax liability is the capital gains rate (currently the same as ordinary rate) times the $9,000.

The entries below illustrate these alternatives. A tax rate of 34% is used for both ordinary income and capital gains. Note that the amounts in the entries below relate only to Investee Company's incremental impact upon Parent Company's tax accounts.

| | Expectations for undistributed income | |
| --- | --- | --- |
| | Dividends | Capital gains |
| Income tax expense | 1,020 | 3,468 |
| Deferred taxes (net) | 612[b] | 3,060[c] |
| Income taxes payable | 408[a] | 408[a] |

[a]Computation of income taxes payable

| | |
| --- | --- |
| Dividend income—30% ($20,000) | $6,000 |
| Less: 80% dividends received deduction | (4,800) |
| Amount included in Parent's taxable income | $1,200 |
| Tax liability—34% ($1,200) | $   408 |

[b]Computation of deferred tax liability (dividend assumption)

| | |
| --- | --- |
| Temporary difference—Parent's share of undistributed income— 30% ($30,000) | $ 9,000 |
| Less: 80% dividends received deduction | (7,200) |
| Originating temporary difference | $1,800 |
| Deferred tax liability—34% ($1,800) | $   612 |

[c]Computation of deferred tax liability (capital gain assumption)

| | |
| --- | --- |
| Temporary difference—Parent's share of undistributed income— 30% ($30,000) | $9,000 |
| Deferred tax liability—34% ($9,000) | $3,060 |

## 2.   Income Tax Effects from Subsidiary Co.

The pretax accounting income of Parent will also include equity in Subsidiary income of $70,000 (70% of $100,000). Note also that this $70,000 will be included in pretax consolidated income if Parent and Subsidiary consolidate. For tax purposes, Parent and Subsidiary cannot file a consolidated tax return because the minimum level of control (80%) is not present. Consequently, the taxable income of Parent will include dividend income of $42,000 (70% of $60,000) and there will be an 80% dividends received deduction of $33,600. The temporary difference results from Parent's equity ($28,000) in Subsidiary's undistributed earnings of $40,000 ($100,000 − $60,000). Remember that the undistributed income of Subsidiary has been recognized for book purposes, but only distributed income (dividends) has been included in taxable income. The amount of the deferred tax liability in 2007 depends upon the expectations of Parent Company as to the manner in which this $28,000 of undistributed income will be received in the future. The same expectations can exist as previously discussed for Parent's equity in Investee's undistributed earnings (i.e., through future dividend distributions or capital gains). Determination of the amounts and the accounts affected for these two assumptions would be similar. The diagram below illustrates the accounting and income tax treatment of the undistributed investee/subsidiary earnings by corporate investors under different levels of ownership.

**SUMMARY OF TEMPORARY DIFFERENCES OF INVESTEES AND SUBSIDIARIES**

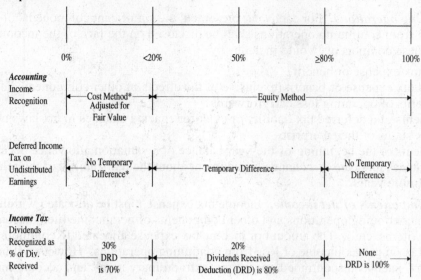

**Recognition of Temporary Differences**

* Both pretax financial accounting and taxable income would include only dividends declared by the investee. If evidence indicates that significant influence exists at an ownership level less than 20%, a temporary difference would be recognized.

## E. Loss Carryforwards and Carrybacks

Operating losses of a particular period can be carried back to the two immediate past periods' income resulting in a refund. Losses still remaining after carrybacks may also be carried forward for twenty years to offset income if income arises in any of those twenty years. Companies may at the time of the loss elect to use only the carryforward provision.

*Loss carrybacks* occur when losses in the current period are carried back to periods in which there was income. Loss carrybacks result in tax refunds in the loss period and thus should be recognized in the year of the loss. The entry to record the benefit is

| | | |
|---|---|---|
| Tax refund receivable | (based on tax credit due to loss) | |
|     Tax loss benefit (income tax expense) | | (same) |

The tax loss benefit account would be closed to revenue and expense summary in the year of the loss.

*Tax loss carryforwards* are recognized in the year the loss occurs. Under SFAS 109, the benefit of a loss carryforward is **always** recognized as a deferred tax asset which may be reduced by a valuation allowance if necessary. For example, assume Caleb Corporation has a loss carryforward of $300,000 which could result in future tax savings of $120,000 (40% × $300,000). Caleb feels that based on the weight of available evidence it is more likely than not that $50,000 of these savings will not be realized. Caleb's entries to record the benefit and the valuation allowance are

| | | |
|---|---|---|
| Deferred tax asset | 120,000 | |
|     Tax loss benefit (income tax expense) | | 120,000 |
| Tax loss benefit (income tax expense) | 50,000 | |
|     Allowance to reduce deferred tax asset to expected realizable | | |
|       value | | 50,000 |

## *Income statement presentation*

The income statement for the year in which both a loss carryback and carryforward are realized would appear as follows:

| | | |
|---|---|---|
| Loss before income taxes | | $ (xx) |
| Less: | | |
|     Benefit from operating loss carryback | xx | |
|     Benefit from operating loss carryforward | <u>xx</u> | <u>xx</u> |
| Net loss | | $ <u>(xx)</u> |

## F.  Financial Statement Presentation of Income Tax

1.  Income Statement

    ***Continuing operations.***  For each year presented, the significant components of income tax expense arising from continuing operations shall be disclosed on the face of the income statement or in the notes.  These components would include

    a.  Current tax expense or benefit
    b.  Deferred tax expense or benefit (exclusive of the effects of other components listed below)
    c.  The benefits of operating loss carryforwards
    d.  Adjustments of a deferred tax liability or asset for enacted changes in tax laws or rates or a change in the tax status of the enterprise
    e.  Adjustments of the beginning-of-the-year balance of a valuation allowance because of a change in circumstances that causes a change in judgment about the realizability of the related deferred tax asset in future years.

    ***Other components of net income.***  Income tax expense must be allocated within an accounting period between continuing operations and other components of net income (i.e., discontinued operations, extraordinary items, etc.).  The amount of income tax expense allocated to continuing operations is equal to the tax on pretax income or loss from continuing operations.  However, if net income includes "special items" such as discontinued operations, extraordinary items, and accounting changes, the amount of income tax expense allocated to continuing operations must consider these items.  The amount allocated to an item other than continuing operations (e.g., discontinued operations, extraordinary items, and accounting changes) is equal to the incremental effect on income taxes resulting from that item.

    > EXAMPLE:  Alco Co. has income from continuing operations of $2,000,000, an extraordinary gain of $450,000, and no permanent or temporary differences.  The current tax rate is 34%.  Total income tax expense is $833,000 ($2,450,000 × 34%).  This amount will first be allocated to income from continuing operations, and the remainder (incremental tax consequences attributable to the remaining components of net income) will be allocated to the extraordinary gain.

    | | |
    |---|---:|
    | Total income tax expense | $ 833,000 |
    | Tax consequences associated with income from continuing operations ($2,000,000 × 34%) | 680,000 |
    | Remainder to extraordinary gain | $ 153,000 |

    The bottom of the income statement would appear as follows:

    | | |
    |---|---:|
    | Income from continuing operations | $2,000,000 |
    | Income tax expense | 680,000 |
    | Income before extraordinary item | $1,320,000 |
    | Extraordinary gain (net of $153,000 tax) | 297,000 |
    | Net income | $1,617,000 |

    > EXAMPLE:  Benjamin Corporation's ordinary loss from continuing operations is $1,000.  Benjamin also has an extraordinary gain of $1,800 that is a capital gain for tax purposes.  The tax rate is 40% on ordinary income and 30% on capital gains.  Income taxes currently payable are $240 [($1,800 – $1,000) × 30%].  Since the effect of the $1,000 loss was to offset a capital gain, the benefit allocated to continuing operations is $300 (30% × $1,000) rather than $400 (40% × $1,000).  The incremental tax expense allocated to the extraordinary gain is $540 (difference between the $300 tax benefit and the $240 total tax expense).

    ***Other comprehensive income.***  Components of other comprehensive income may be displayed net of related deferred tax effects or before related deferred tax effects with one amount shown for the aggregate income tax effect (with detail shown in notes).  Refer to Module 7D for more information regarding comprehensive income.

2.  Retained Earnings

    Any income tax effects associated with adjustments of the opening balance of retained earnings for a **special type** change in accounting principle or correction of an error are to be charged or credited directly to retained earnings.  The income tax effects of other stockholders' equity items (e.g., cumulative translation adjustment) are charged or credited to stockholders' equity.

3.  Balance Sheet

    The classification of deferred tax liabilities and assets is a two-stage process.  First, all deferred tax liabilities and assets are classified as current or noncurrent.  Deferred tax liabilities and assets are classified as current or long-term based on the related asset or liability.  A deferred tax liability or asset is related to an asset or liability if reduction of the asset or liability will cause the temporary difference to reverse. If the deferred tax liability or asset is **not** related to any asset or liability for financial reporting purposes (such as a deferred tax asset caused by a loss carryforward), it is classified based on the timing of its expected reversal or utilization date. Once classification has been determined, all current amounts are netted to get a net current asset or liability and the noncurrent amounts are likewise netted to obtain a net noncurrent amount.

This process is illustrated in Example 4 that appeared earlier in this module. In Example 4, the only current deferred tax asset/liability is the $105 current liability. Thus the net current amount is a $105 liability. The other amounts are netted to find the net noncurrent amount. In this case the net noncurrent amount is a $105 liability ($325 – $220).

If an allowance account has been recognized for a deferred tax asset, it would be deducted from the related deferred tax asset before the netting process described above is done. If the allowance account balance relates to a deferred tax asset that is classified partially as current and partially as noncurrent, the allowance balance should be allocated between them in the ratio of each asset balance to the total asset balance.

Note that if a tax refund receivable results from a loss carryback in the current period, this element would not be included in the netting process; only deferred tax assets and liabilities are netted.

### G.  Treatment of Selected Temporary Differences

On the following page we have summarized the treatment of selected temporary differences from the period of origination to the period of reversal.

### H.  Research Component

SFAS 109 addresses most research questions on deferred taxes. An important concept is that SFAS 109 uses the asset/liability method in recognizing deferred taxes. The most likely research questions are defining temporary differences, identifying the tax rates used to calculate deferred taxes, classifying items as current or noncurrent, and the use of valuation accounts. SFAS 109 defines temporary differences and lists examples. An important point is that the statement does not define the term "permanent differences," nor does it use this term in the standard.

Although the accounting rules are contained in the body of the standard, Appendix A of SFAS 109 explains the rationale for SFAS 109 and may be helpful in understanding the accounting rules for deferred taxes. Appendix B provides additional discussion of the standard and numerical examples on how to apply the rules. Appendix C is background information on APB Opinion 11 and the revision process of the standard on accounting for income taxes. Appendix D contains the amendments to other FASB Standards. FASB Interpretations, or FASB Technical Bulletins that reference or impact deferred tax issues such as intraperiod tax allocation for interim reporting, effects of deferred taxes on accounting for leases, and effects on prior period adjustments. The STATUS portion on the first page of SFAS 109 provides a comprehensive list of all standards, interpretations, and bulletins that have been amended, changed, or superseded by SFAS 109. Refer to this list before citing any other standard that discusses deferred taxes to ensure that a paragraph was not superseded or amended. Appendix E of SFAS 109 contains the glossary of terms used in the standard.

Keywords for researching the most important issues in deferred taxes are shown below.

| | | |
|---|---|---|
| Carrybacks | Deferred tax consequences | Income taxes currently payable |
| Carryforwards | Deferred tax expense | Negative evidence |
| Change tax rates | Deferred tax liability | Positive evidence |
| Current tax expense | Enacted tax rates | Taxable income |
| Deductible temporary differences | Future deductible amount(s) | Taxable temporary differences |
| Deferred tax asset | Future taxable amount(s) | Valuation allowance tax |
| Deferred tax benefit | Income tax expense | |

# TREATMENT OF SELECTED TEMPORARY DIFFERENCES

| | Book value | | Tax basis | | Previous and current reconciliations of book income to tax income | Future years(s) reconciliation of book income to tax income | Deferred consequence* |
|---|---|---|---|---|---|---|---|
| **a. Estimated liability under warranties** | 56,000 | Less | — | = | 56,000 addition(s) | 56,000 subtraction(s) | Asset (3) |
| **b. Unearned rent (royalty) revenue received (liability)** | 40,000 | Less | — | = | 40,000 addition(s) | 40,000 subtraction(s) | Asset (3) |
| **c. Long-term contracts:** | | | | | | | |
| Construction in process (asset) | 1,125,000 | Less | 1,000,000 | = | 125,000 subtraction | 125,000 addition | Liability (1) |
| **d. Plant assets and accumulated depreciation:** | | | | | | | |
| Equipment (asset) | 50,000 | Less | 50,000 | | | | |
| Accumulated depreciation (contra asset) | 10,000 | Less | 18,500 | | | | |
| End of period basis | 40,000 | Less | 31,500 | = | 8,500 subtraction(s) | 8,500 addition(s) | Liability (1) |
| **e. Donated assets:** | | | | | | | |
| *Year of acquisition:* | | | | | | | |
| Machinery (asset) | 90,000 | Less | — | = | Not included because donat. recorded in S/E | See deprec. below | Liability (1) |
| *Depreciation:* | | | | | | | |
| Machinery (asset) | 90,000 | Less | 90,000 | | | | |
| Accumulated depreciation (contra asset) | 18,000 | Less | — | | | | |
| End of period basis | 72,000 | Less | 90,000 | = | 18,000 addition(s) | 18,000 addition(s) | Reduction of liability |
| *Sale of asset:* | | | | | | | |
| Cash received | 80,000 | Less | 80,000 | | | | |
| Basis of asset | 72,000 | Less | 80,000 | | | | |
| Gain (revenue) | 8,000 | Less | 80,000 | = | 72,000 subtraction(s) | 72,000 addition | Reduction of liability |
| **f. Replacement asset for involuntarily converted asset:** | | | | | | | |
| *Year of acquisition:* | | | | | | | |
| Building (asset) | 280,000 | Less | 280,000 | | | | |
| Deferred gain from involuntary conversion | —** | Less | (110,000) | | | | |
| Initial basis of asset | 280,000 | | 170,000 | = | 110,000 subtraction | | Liability (1) |
| *Depreciation:* | | | | | | | |
| Building (asset) | 280,000 | Less | 170,000 | | | | |
| Accumulated depreciation (contra asset) | (14,000) | Less | (28,900) | | | | |
| End of period basis | 266,000 | | 141,100 | = | 14,900 subtraction | | Liability (1) |
| *Sale of replacement asset:* | | | | | | | |
| Cash received | 270,000 | Less | 270,000 | | | | |
| Basis of asset | (266,000) | Less | (141,100) | | | | |
| Gain (revenue) | 4,000 | | 128,900 | = | | 124,900 addition | Reduction of liability |

* The numbers in parenthesis refer to the relationships presented on page 481.

** The $110,000 gain was recognized in the financial statements in the period the involuntary conversion occurred.

**MULTIPLE-CHOICE QUESTIONS (1-41)**

**1.** Justification for the method of determining periodic deferred tax expense is based on the concept of
a. Matching of periodic expense to periodic revenue.
b. Objectivity in the calculation of periodic expense.
c. Recognition of assets and liabilities.
d. Consistency of tax expense measurements with actual tax planning strategies.

**2.** Among the items reported on Cord, Inc.'s income statement for the year ended December 31, 2007, were the following:

| | |
|---|---|
| Payment of penalty | $ 5,000 |
| Insurance premium on life of an officer with Cord as owner and beneficiary | 10,000 |

Temporary differences amount to
a.   $0
b.   $ 5,000
c.   $10,000
d.   $15,000

**3.** Caleb Corporation has three financial statement elements for which the December 31, 2007, book value is different than the December 31, 2007, tax basis

| | Book value | Tax basis | Difference |
|---|---|---|---|
| Equipment | $200,000 | $120,000 | $80,000 |
| Prepaid officers insurance policy | 75,000 | 0 | 75,000 |
| Warranty liability | 50,000 | 0 | 50,000 |

As a result of these differences, future taxable amounts are
a.   $ 50,000
b.   $ 80,000
c.   $155,000
d.   $205,000

**4.** Temporary differences arise when revenues are taxable

| | After they are recognized in financial income | Before they are recognized in financial income |
|---|---|---|
| a. | Yes | Yes |
| b. | Yes | No |
| c. | No | No |
| d. | No | Yes |

**5.** Which of the following differences would result in future taxable amounts?
a. Expenses or losses that are deductible after they are recognized in financial income.
b. Revenues or gains that are taxable before they are recognized in financial income.
c. Expenses or losses that are deductible before they are recognized in financial income.
d. Revenues or gains that are recognized in financial income but are never included in taxable income.

**6.** Dunn Co.'s 2007 income statement reported $90,000 income before provision for income taxes. To compute the provision for federal income taxes, the following 2007 data are provided:

| | |
|---|---|
| Rent received in advance | $16,000 |
| Income from exempt municipal bonds | 20,000 |
| Depreciation deducted for income tax purposes in excess of depreciation reported for financial statements purposes | 10,000 |
| Enacted corporate income tax rate | 30% |

If the alternative minimum tax provisions are ignored, what amount of current federal income tax liability should be reported in Dunn's December 31, 2007 balance sheet?
a. $18,000
b. $22,800
c. $25,800
d. $28,800

**7.** Pine Corp.'s books showed pretax income of $800,000 for the year ended December 31, 2007. In the computation of federal income taxes, the following data were considered:

| | |
|---|---|
| Gain on an involuntary conversion | $350,000 |
| (Pine has elected to replace the property within the statutory period using total proceeds.) | |
| Depreciation deducted for the tax purposes in excess of depreciation deducted for book purposes | 50,000 |
| Federal estimated tax payments, 2007 | 70,000 |
| Enacted federal tax rates, 2007 | 30% |

What amount should Pine report as its current federal income tax liability on its December 31, 2007 balance sheet?
a. $ 50,000
b. $ 65,000
c. $120,000
d. $135,000

**8.** For the year ended December 31, 2007, Tyre Co. reported pretax financial statement income of $750,000. Its taxable income was $650,000. The difference is due to accelerated depreciation for income tax purposes. Tyre's effective income tax rate is 30%, and Tyre made estimated tax payments during 2007 of $90,000. What amount should Tyre report as current income tax expense for 2007?
a. $105,000
b. $135,000
c. $195,000
d. $225,000

**9.** Tower Corp. began operations on January 1, 2006. For financial reporting, Tower recognizes revenues from all sales under the accrual method. However, in its income tax returns, Tower reports qualifying sales under the installment method. Tower's gross profit on these installment sales under each method was as follows:

| Year | Accrual method | Installment method |
|---|---|---|
| 2006 | $1,600,000 | $ 600,000 |
| 2007 | 2,600,000 | 1,400,000 |

The income tax rate is 30% for 2006 and future years. There are no other temporary or permanent differences. In its December 31, 2007 balance sheet, what amount should Tower report as a liability for deferred income taxes?
a. $840,000
b. $660,000
c. $600,000
d. $360,000

**10.** On June 30, 2007, Ank Corp. prepaid a $19,000 premium on an annual insurance policy. The premium payment was a tax deductible expense in Ank's 2007 cash basis tax return. The accrual basis income statement will report a $9,500 insurance expense in 2007 and 2008.

Ank's income tax rate is 30% in 2007 and 25% thereafter. In Ank's December 31, 2007 balance sheet, what amount related to the insurance should be reported as a deferred income tax liability?
a. $5,700

b.   $4,750
c.   $2,850
d.   $2,375

**11.** Mill, which began operations on January 1, 2005, recognizes income from long-term construction contracts under the percentage-of-completion method in its financial statements and under the completed-contract method for income tax reporting. Income under each method follows:

| Year | Completed-contract | Percentage-of-completion |
|------|--------------------|--------------------------|
| 2005 | $    -- | $300,000 |
| 2006 | 400,000 | 600,000 |
| 2007 | 700,000 | 850,000 |

The income tax rate was 30% for 2005 through 2007. For years after 2007, the enacted tax rate is 25%. There are no other temporary differences. Mill should report in its December 31, 2007 balance sheet a deferred income tax liability of

a.   $ 87,500
b.   $105,000
c.   $162,500
d.   $195,000

**Items 12 and 13** are based on the following:

Zeff Co. prepared the following reconciliation of its pretax financial statement income to taxable income for the year ended December 31, 2007, its first year of operations:

| | |
|---|---|
| Pretax financial income | $160,000 |
| Nontaxable interest received on municipal securities | (5,000) |
| Long-term loss accrual in excess of deductible amount | 10,000 |
| Depreciation in excess of financial statement amount | (25,000) |
| Taxable income | $140,000 |

Zeff's tax rate for 2007 is 40%.

**12.** In its 2007 income statement, what amount should Zeff report as income tax expense—current portion?

a.   $52,000
b.   $56,000
c.   $62,000
d.   $64,000

**13.** In its December 31, 2007 balance sheet, what should Zeff report as deferred income tax liability?

a.   $2,000
b.   $4,000
c.   $6,000
d.   $8,000

**14.** West Corp. leased a building and received the $36,000 annual rental payment on June 15, 2007. The beginning of the lease was July 1, 2007. Rental income is taxable when received. West's tax rates are 30% for 2007 and 40% thereafter. West had no other permanent or temporary differences. West determined that no valuation allowance was needed. What amount of deferred tax asset should West report in its December 31, 2007 balance sheet?

a.   $ 5,400
b.   $ 7,200
c.   $10,800
d.   $14,400

**15.** Black Co., organized on January 2, 2007, had pretax accounting income of $500,000 and taxable income of $800,000 for the year ended December 31, 2007. The only temporary difference is accrued product warranty costs that are expected to be paid as follows:

| | |
|---|---|
| 2008 | $100,000 |
| 2009 | 50,000 |
| 2010 | 50,000 |
| 2011 | 100,000 |

Black has never had any net operating losses (book or tax) and does not expect any in the future. There were no temporary differences in prior years. The enacted income tax rates are 35% for 2007, 30% for 2008 through 2010, and 25% for 2011. In Black's December 31, 2007 balance sheet, the deferred income tax asset should be

a.   $ 60,000
b.   $ 70,000
c.   $ 85,000
d.   $105,000

**16.** A temporary difference that would result in a deferred tax liability is

a.   Interest revenue on municipal bonds.
b.   Accrual of warranty expense.
c.   Excess of tax depreciation over financial accounting depreciation.
d.   Subscriptions received in advance.

**17.** Orleans Co., a cash-basis taxpayer, prepares accrual basis financial statements. In its 2008 balance sheet, Orleans' deferred income tax liabilities increased compared to 2007. Which of the following changes would cause this increase in deferred income tax liabilities?

I.   An increase in prepaid insurance.
II.  An increase in rent receivable.
III. An increase in warranty obligations.

a.   I only.
b.   I and II.
c.   II and III.
d.   III only.

**18.** At the end of year one, Cody Co. reported a profit on a partially completed construction contract by applying the percentage-of-completion method. By the end of year two, the total estimated profit on the contract at completion in year three had been drastically reduced from the amount estimated at the end of year one. Consequently, in year two, a loss equal to one-half of the year one profit was recognized. Cody used the completed-contract method for income tax purposes and had no other contracts. The year two balance sheet should include a deferred tax

| | Asset | Liability |
|---|-------|-----------|
| a. | Yes | Yes |
| b. | No | Yes |
| c. | Yes | No |
| d. | No | No |

**19.** A deferred tax liability is computed using

a.   The current tax laws, regardless of expected or enacted future tax laws.
b.   Expected future tax laws, regardless of whether those expected laws have been enacted.
c.   Current tax laws, unless enacted future tax laws are different.
d.   Either current or expected future tax laws, regardless of whether those expected laws have been enacted.

**20.** For the year ended December 31, 2007, Grim Co.'s pretax financial statement income was $200,000 and its taxable income was $150,000.  The difference is due to the following:

| | |
|---|---|
| Interest on municipal bonds | $70,000 |
| Premium expense on keyman life insurance | (20,000) |
| Total | $50,000 |

Grim's enacted income tax rate is 30%.  In its 2007 income statement, what amount should Grim report as current provision for income tax expense?

a. $45,000
b. $51,000
c. $60,000
d. $66,000

**Items 21 and 22** are based on the following:

Venus Corp.'s worksheet for calculating current and deferred income taxes for 2007 follows:

| | *2007* | *2008* | *2009* |
|---|---|---|---|
| Pretax income | $1,400 | | |
| Temporary differences: | | | |
| Depreciation | (800) | $(1,200) | $2,000 |
| Warranty costs | 400 | (100) | (300) |
| Taxable income | $1,000 | | |
| | | | |
| Enacted rate | 30% | 30% | 25% |
| | | | |
| Deferred tax accounts | | | |
| | | *Asset* | *Liability* |
| Current | | $ (30)ᵃ | |
| Noncurrent (before netting) | | $ (75)ᵇ | $ 140ᶜ |

ᵃ  *[($100) × 30%]*
ᵇ  *[($300) × 25%]*
ᶜ  *[($1,200) × 30%] + [$2,000 × 25%]*

Venus had no prior deferred tax balances.  In its 2007 income statement, what amount should Venus report as

21. Current income tax expense?
    a. $420
    b. $350
    c. $300
    d. $0

22. Deferred income tax expense?
    a. $350
    b. $300
    c. $120
    d. $ 35

23.  Shear, Inc. began operations in 2007.  Included in Shear's 2007 financial statements were bad debt expenses of $1,400 and profit from an installment sale of $2,600.  For tax purposes, the bad debts will be deducted and the profit from the installment sale will be recognized in 2008.  The enacted tax rates are 30% in 2007 and 25% in 2008.  In its 2007 income statement, what amount should Shear report as deferred income tax expense?
    a. $300
    b. $360
    c. $650
    d. $780

24.  Quinn Co. reported a net deferred tax asset of $9,000 in its December 31, 2006 balance sheet.  For 2007, Quinn reported pretax financial statement income of $300,000.  Temporary differences of $100,000 resulted in taxable income of $200,000 for 2007.  At December 31, 2007, Quinn had cumulative taxable differences of $70,000.  Quinn's effective income tax rate is 30%.  In its December 31, 2007,

income statement, what should Quinn report as deferred income tax expense?
    a. $12,000
    b. $21,000
    c. $30,000
    d. $60,000

25.  Rein Inc. reported deferred tax assets and deferred tax liabilities at the end of 2006 and at the end of 2007.  For the year ended 2007, Rein should report deferred income tax expense or benefit equal to the
    a. Decrease in the deferred tax assets.
    b. Increase in the deferred tax liabilities.
    c. Amount of the current tax liability plus the sum of the net changes in deferred tax assets and deferred tax liabilities.
    d. Sum of the net changes in deferred tax assets and deferred tax liabilities.

26.  On its December 31, 2007 balance sheet, Shin Co. had income taxes payable of $13,000 and a current deferred tax asset of $20,000 before determining the need for a valuation account.  Shin had reported a current deferred tax asset of $15,000 at December 31, 2006.  No estimated tax payments were made during 2007.  At December 31, 2007, Shin determined that it was more likely than not that 10% of the deferred tax asset would not be realized.  In its 2007 income statement, what amount should Shin report as total income tax expense?
    a. $ 8,000
    b. $ 8,500
    c. $10,000
    d. $13,000

27.   Under current generally accepted accounting principles, which approach is used to determine income tax expense?
    a. Asset and liability approach.
    b. A "with and without" approach.
    c. Net of tax approach.
    d. Periodic expense approach.

28.  Bart, Inc., a newly organized corporation, uses the equity method of accounting for its 30% investment in Rex Co.'s common stock.  During 2007, Rex paid dividends of $300,000 and reported earnings of $900,000.  In addition

• The dividends received from Rex are eligible for the 80% dividends received deductions.
• All the undistributed earnings of Rex will be distributed in future years.
• There are no other temporary differences.
• Bart's 2007 income tax rate is 30%.
• The enacted income tax rate after 2007 is 25%.

In Bart's December 31, 2007 balance sheet, the deferred income tax liability should be
    a. $10,800
    b. $ 9,000
    c. $ 5,400
    d. $ 4,500

29.  Leer Corp.'s pretax income in 2007 was $100,000.  The temporary differences between amounts reported in the financial statements and the tax return are as follows:

• Depreciation in the financial statements was $8,000 more than tax depreciation.

- The equity method of accounting resulted in financial statement income of $35,000. A $25,000 dividend was received during the year, which is eligible for the 80% dividends received deduction.

Leer's effective income tax rate was 30% in 2007. In its 2007 income statement, Leer should report a current provision for income taxes of
- a. $26,400
- b. $23,400
- c. $21,900
- d. $18,600

**30.** Dix, Inc., a calendar-year corporation, reported the following operating income (loss) before income tax for its first three years of operations:

| 2005 | $100,000 |
|------|----------|
| 2006 | (200,000) |
| 2007 | 400,000 |

There are no permanent or temporary differences between operating income (loss) for financial and income tax reporting purposes. When filing its 2006 tax return, Dix did not elect to forego the carryback of its loss for 2006. Assume a 40% tax rate for all years. What amount should Dix report as its income tax liability at December 31, 2007?
- a. $160,000
- b. $120,000
- c. $ 80,000
- d. $ 60,000

**31.** Town, a calendar-year corporation incorporated in January 2005, experienced a $600,000 net operating loss (NOL) in 2007 due to a prolonged strike. Town never had a strike in the past that significantly affected its income and does not expect such a strike in the future. Additionally, there is no other negative evidence concerning future operating income. For the years 2005-2007, Town reported a taxable income in each year, and a total of $450,000 for the two years. Assume that: (1) there is no difference between pretax accounting income and taxable income for all years, (2) the income tax rate is 40% for all years, (3) the NOL will be carried back to the profit years 2005-2007 to the extent of $450,000, and $150,000 will be carried forward to future periods. In its 2007 income statement, what amount should Town report as the reduction of loss due to NOL carryback and carryforward?
- a. $240,000
- b. $180,000
- c. $270,000
- d. $360,000

**32.** Bishop Corporation began operations in 2005 and had operating losses of $200,000 in 2005 and $150,000 in 2006. For the year ended December 31, 2007, Bishop had pretax book income of $300,000. For the three-year period 2005 to 2007, assume an income tax rate of 40% and no permanent or temporary differences between book and taxable income. Because Bishop began operations in 2005, the entire amount of deferred tax assets recognized in 2005 and 2007 were offset with amounts added to the allowance account. In Bishop's 2007 income statement, how much should be reported as current income tax expense?
- a. $0
- b. $ 40,000
- c. $ 60,000
- d. $120,000

**33.** Mobe Co. reported the following operating income (loss) for its first three years of operations:

| 2005 | $ 300,000 |
|------|-----------|
| 2006 | (700,000) |
| 2007 | 1,200,000 |

For each year, there were no deferred income taxes, and Mobe's effective income tax rate was 30%. In its 2006 income tax return, Mobe elected to carry back the maximum amount of loss possible. Additionally, there was more negative evidence than positive evidence concerning profitability for Mobe in 2007. In its 2007 income statement, what amount should Mobe report as total income tax expense?
- a. $120,000
- b. $150,000
- c. $240,000
- d. $360,000

**34.** In 2007, Rand, Inc. reported for financial statement purposes the following items, which were not included in taxable income:

| Installment gain to be collected equally in 2008 through 2010 | $1,500,000 |
|---|---|
| Estimated future warranty costs to be paid equally in 2008 through 2010 | 2,100,000 |

There were no temporary differences in prior years. Rand's enacted tax rates are 30% for 2007 and 25% for 2008 through 2010.

In Rand's December 31, 2007 balance sheet, what amounts of the deferred tax asset should be classified as current and noncurrent?

| | Current | Noncurrent |
|---|---|---|
| a. | $60,000 | $100,000 |
| b. | $60,000 | $120,000 |
| c. | $50,000 | $100,000 |
| d. | $50,000 | $120,000 |

**35.** Thorn Co. applies Statement of Financial Accounting Standards 109, *Accounting for Income Taxes*. At the end of 2007, the tax effects of temporary differences were as follows:

| | Deferred tax assets (liabilities) | Related asset classification |
|---|---|---|
| Accelerated tax depreciation | $(75,000) | Noncurrent asset |
| Additional costs in inventory for tax purposes | 25,000 | Current asset |
| | $(50,000) | |

A valuation allowance was not considered necessary. Thorn anticipates that $10,000 of the deferred tax liability will reverse in 2008. In Thorn's December 31, 2007 balance sheet, what amount should Thorn report as noncurrent deferred tax liability?
- a. $40,000
- b. $50,000
- c. $65,000
- d. $75,000

**36.** Because Jab Co. uses different methods to depreciate equipment for financial statement and income tax purposes, Jab has temporary differences that will reverse during the next year and add to taxable income. Deferred income taxes that are based on these temporary differences should be classified in Jab's balance sheet as a

a. Contra account to current assets.
b. Contra account to noncurrent assets.
c. Current liability.
d. Noncurrent liability.

**37.** At the most recent year-end, a company had a deferred income tax liability arising from accelerated depreciation that exceeded a deferred income tax asset relating to rent received in advance which is expected to reverse in the next year. Which of the following should be reported in the company's most recent year-end balance sheet?

a. The excess of the deferred income tax liability over the deferred income tax asset as a noncurrent liability.
b. The excess of the deferred income tax liability over the deferred income tax asset as a current liability.
c. The deferred income tax liability as a noncurrent liability.
d. The deferred income tax liability as a current liability.

**38.** On December 31, 2007, Oak Co. recognized a receivable for taxes paid in prior years and refundable through the carryback of all of its 2007 operating loss. Also, Oak had a 2007 deferred tax liability derived from the temporary difference between tax and financial statement depreciation, which reverses over the period 2008–2012. The amount of this tax liability is less than the amount of the tax asset. Which of the following 2007 balance sheet sections should report tax-related items?

 I. Current assets.
 II. Current liabilities.
III. Noncurrent liabilities.

a. I only.
b. I and III.
c. I, II, and III.
d. II and III.

**39.** The amount of income tax applicable to transactions that are not reported in the continuing operations section of the income statement is computed

a. By multiplying the item by the effective income tax rate.
b. As the difference between the tax computed based on taxable income without including the item and the tax computed based on taxable income including the item.
c. As the difference between the tax computed on the item based on the amount used for financial reporting and the amount used in computing taxable income.
d. By multiplying the item by the difference between the effective income tax rate and the statutory income tax rate.

**40.** No net deferred tax asset (i.e., deferred tax asset net of related valuation allowance) was recognized in the 2006 financial statements by the Chaise Company when a loss from discontinued operations was carried forward for tax purposes because it was more likely than not that none of this deferred tax asset would be realized. Chaise had no temporary differences. The tax benefit of the loss carried forward reduced current taxes payable on 2007 continuing operations. The 2007 income statement would include the tax benefit from the loss brought forward in

a. Income from continuing operations.
b. Gain or loss from discontinued operations.
c. Extraordinary gains.
d. Cumulative effect of accounting changes.

**41.** Which of the following statements is correct regarding the provision for income taxes in the financial statements of a sole proprietorship?

a. The provision for income taxes should be based on business income using individual tax rates.
b. The provision for income taxes should be based on business income using corporate tax rates.
c. The provision for income taxes should be based on the proprietor's total taxable income, allocated to the proprietorship at the percentage that business income bears to the proprietor's total income.
d. No provision for income taxes is required.

SIMULATION PROBLEMS

**Simulation Problem 1**　　　　　　　　　　　　　　(40 to 50 minutes)

| Directions | | | | | |
|---|---|---|---|---|---|
| | Situation | Tax Calculations | Tax Differences | Deferred Tax Classification | Research |

In the following simulation you are asked to complete several tasks related to deferred taxes. The tasks are identified by the tabs shown above.

| | Situation | | | | |
|---|---|---|---|---|---|
| Directions | | Tax Calculations | Tax Differences | Deferred Tax Classification | Research |

The following partially completed worksheet contain Lane Co.'s reconciliation between financial statement income and taxable income for the three years ended April 30, 2007, and additional information.

*Lane Co.*
**INCOME TAX WORKSHEET**
*For the Three Years Ended April 30, 2007*

| | April 30, 2005 | April 30, 2006 | April 30, 2007 |
|---|---|---|---|
| Pretax financial income | $900,000 | $1,000,000 | $1,200,000 |
| Permanent differences | 100,000 | 100,000 | 100,000 |
| Temporary differences | 200,000 | 100,000 | 150,000 |
| Taxable income | $600,000 | $ 800,000 | $ 950,000 |
| Cumulative temporary differences (future taxable amounts) | $200,000 | $ (2) | $ 450,000 |
| Tax rate | 20% | 25% | 30% |
| Deferred tax liability | $ 40,000 | $ 75,000 | $ (4) |
| Deferred tax expense | $ -- | $ (3) | $ -- |
| Current tax expense | $ (1) | $ -- | $ -- |

The tax rate changes were enacted at the beginning of each tax year and were not known to Lane at the end of the prior year.

| | | Tax Calculations | | | |
|---|---|---|---|---|---|
| Directions | Situation | | Tax Differences | Deferred Tax Classification | Research |

**Items 1 through 4** represent amounts omitted from the worksheet. For each item, determine the amount omitted from the worksheet. Select the amount from the following list. An answer may be used once, more than once, or not at all.

*Amount*

| | | | |
|---|---|---|---|
| A. | $ 25,000 | H. | $135,000 |
| B. | $ 35,000 | I. | $140,000 |
| C. | $ 45,000 | J. | $160,000 |
| D. | $ 75,000 | K. | $180,000 |
| E. | $100,000 | L. | $200,000 |
| F. | $112,500 | M. | $300,000 |
| G. | $120,000 | N. | $400,000 |

| *Specific audit objective* | (A) (B) (C) (D) (E) (F) (G) (H) (I) (J) (K) (L) (M) (N) |
|---|---|
| 1. Current tax expense for the year ended April 30, 2005. | ○ ○ ○ ○ ○ ○ ○ ○ ○ ○ ○ ○ ○ ○ |
| 2. Cumulative temporary differences at April 30, 2006. | ○ ○ ○ ○ ○ ○ ○ ○ ○ ○ ○ ○ ○ ○ |
| 3. Deferred tax expense for the year ended April 30, 2006. | ○ ○ ○ ○ ○ ○ ○ ○ ○ ○ ○ ○ ○ ○ |
| 4. Deferred tax liability at April 30, 2007. | ○ ○ ○ ○ ○ ○ ○ ○ ○ ○ ○ ○ ○ ○ |

| | | | Tax Differences | | |
|---|---|---|---|---|---|
| Directions | Situation | Tax Calculations | | Deferred Tax Classification | Research |

**Items 1 through 7** describe circumstances resulting in differences between financial statement income and taxable income. For each numbered item, determine whether the difference is

*List*

A. A temporary difference resulting in a deferred tax asset.
B. A temporary difference resulting in a deferred tax liability.
C. A permanent difference.

Indicate the classification of each item.  An answer may be selected once, more than once, or not at all.

| | A<br>Temporary difference<br>DTA | B<br>Temporary difference<br>DTL | C<br>Permanent difference |
|---|---|---|---|
| 1. For plant assets, the depreciation expense deducted for tax purposes is in excess of the depreciation expense used for financial reporting purposes. | ○ | ○ | ○ |
| 2. A landlord collects some rents in advance. Rents received are taxable in the period in which they are received. | ○ | ○ | ○ |
| 3. Interest is received on an investment in tax-exempt municipal obligations. | ○ | ○ | ○ |
| 4. Costs of guarantees and warranties are estimated and accrued for financial reporting purposes. | ○ | ○ | ○ |
| 5. Life insurance proceeds are collected on the death of a key officer. | ○ | ○ | ○ |
| 6. Bad debts are estimated and expensed on the income statement.  No bad debts were charged to the allowance account and written off during the year. | ○ | ○ | ○ |
| 7. Goodwill is deducted on the tax return. | ○ | ○ | ○ |

| Directions | Situation | Tax Calculations | Tax Differences | Deferred Tax Classification | Research |
|---|---|---|---|---|---|

Identify whether each item would create a deferred tax asset or a deferred tax liability, and whether each item would be classified as current or noncurrent.

| | *Deferred tax asset* | *Deferred tax liability* | *Current* | *Noncurrent* |
|---|---|---|---|---|
| 1. Tax depreciation in excess of book depreciation | ○ | ○ | ○ | ○ |
| 2. Bad debts expense in excess of actual write-offs | ○ | ○ | ○ | ○ |
| 3. Rent collected in advance for next 12 months | ○ | ○ | ○ | ○ |

| Directions | Situation | Tax Calculations | Tax Differences | Deferred Tax Classification | Research |
|---|---|---|---|---|---|

The CEO of Lane Corporation has contacted you regarding questions she has about deferred taxes.  She has requested that you research a list of questions in the authoritative literature, copy the relevant paragraphs, and fax her a copy of the results for her review.  Below is her list of questions.

1. What are the objectives of accounting for income taxes?
2. What is a temporary difference?
3. How are deferred taxes presented in the financial statements?
4. What tax rate is used to calculate deferred taxes?
5. What components of income tax expense that relate to continuing operations must be included in the notes to the financial statements?

**Simulation Problem 2**       (50 to 60 minutes)

| Directions | | | | | | | | |
|---|---|---|---|---|---|---|---|---|
| | Situation | Temporary and Permanent Differences | Deferred Tax Schedule | Calculate Taxable Income | Journal Entries | Disclosures | Communication | Research |

In the following simulation you are asked to complete several tasks related to deferred taxes. The tasks are identified by the tabs shown above.

| | Situation | | | | | | | |
|---|---|---|---|---|---|---|---|---|
| Directions | | Temporary and Permanent Differences | Deferred Tax Schedule | Calculate Taxable Income | Journal Entries | Disclosures | Communication | Research |

Jasco Corporation is in its first year of operations. The company has pretax income of $400,000. The company has the following items recorded in its records. No estimated tax payments were made during 2007.

| | |
|---|---|
| Premiums on life insurance of key officer | $10,000 |
| Depreciation on tax return in excess of book depreciation | 12,000 |
| Interest on municipal bonds | 5,300 |
| Warranty expense | 4,000 |
| Actual warranty repairs | 3,250 |
| Bad debt expense | 1,400 |
| Beginning balance in allowance for uncollectible accounts | 0 |
| End balance for allowance for uncollectible accounts | 800 |
| Rent received in advance from clients that will be recognized evenly over the next three years | 24,000 |
| Tax rate for 2007 and future years | 40% |

| | | Temporary and Permanent Differences | | | | | | |
|---|---|---|---|---|---|---|---|---|
| Directions | Situation | | Deferred Tax Schedule | Calculate Taxable Income | Journal Entries | Disclosures | Communication | Research |

Identify for Jasco which of the following items create temporary differences and which create permanent differences.

| | *Temporary* | *Permanent* |
|---|---|---|
| Premiums on life insurance of key officer | O | O |
| Depreciation | O | O |
| Interest on municipal bonds | O | O |
| Warranties | O | O |
| Bad debts | O | O |
| Rent received in advance from clients | O | O |

| | | | Deferred Tax Schedule | | | | | |
|---|---|---|---|---|---|---|---|---|
| Directions | Situation | Temporary and Permanent Differences | | Calculate Taxable Income | Journal Entries | Disclosures | Communication | Research |

Prepare the following schedule for the deferred tax amounts for the year. Choose items from the following list:

*Items*

| | |
|---|---|
| Premium on life insurance | Warranties |
| Depreciation | Bad debts |
| Interest on municipal bonds | Rent received |

| Item | Difference between taxable amount and income statement amount | Classification: Deferred tax asset Deferred tax liability | Current or noncurrent | Deferred tax amount |
|---|---|---|---|---|
| | | | | |
| | | | | |
| | | | | |
| | | | | |
| | | | | |

| Directions | Situation | Temporary and Permanent Differences | Deferred Tax Schedule | Calculate Taxable Income | Journal Entries | Disclosures | Communication | Research |
|---|---|---|---|---|---|---|---|---|

Complete the following table to calculate taxable income. If no adjustment is needed for a particular item enter 0 as your calculation.

| | |
|---|---|
| Pretax financial income | |
| Premiums on life insurance of key officer | |
| Interest on municipal bonds | |
| Depreciation for tax in excess of book depreciation | |
| Adjustment for warranties | |
| Adjustment for bad debts | |
| Adjustment for rent received in advance | |
| | |
| Taxable income | |

| Directions | Situation | Temporary and Permanent Differences | Deferred Tax Schedule | Calculate Taxable Income | Journal Entries | Disclosures | Communication | Research |
|---|---|---|---|---|---|---|---|---|

Prepare the journal entries to record tax expense for 2007. Select your account titles from the following list:

Deferred tax asset—Current
Deferred tax asset—Noncurrent
Deferred tax liability—Current
Deferred tax liability—Noncurrent
Income tax expense
Income taxes payable
Prepaid income taxes

| Account title | Debit | Credit |
|---|---|---|
| | | |
| | | |
| | | |
| | | |
| | | |
| | | |
| | | |

| Directions | Situation | Temporary and Permanent Differences | Deferred Tax Schedule | Calculate Taxable Income | Journal Entries | Disclosures | Communication | Research |
|---|---|---|---|---|---|---|---|---|

Using the appropriate netting procedures, indicate the amounts that will be shown in which of the following classifications on the balance sheet.

| | |
|---|---|
| Deferred tax asset—Current | |
| Deferred tax asset—Noncurrent | |
| Deferred tax liability—Current | |
| Deferred tax liability—Noncurrent | |

| Directions | Situation | Temporary and Permanent Differences | Deferred Tax Schedule | Calculate Taxable Income | Journal Entries | Disclosures | Communication | Research |
|---|---|---|---|---|---|---|---|---|

Chris Green, CPA, is auditing Jasco Co.'s 2007 financial statements. The controller, Dunn, has provided Green with the following information relating to income taxes:

- Dunn has prepared a schedule of all differences between financial statement and income tax return income. Dunn believes that as a result of pending legislation, the enacted tax rate at December 31, 2007, will be increased for 2007. Dunn is uncertain which differences to include and which rates to apply in computing deferred taxes under SFAS 109. Dunn has requested an overview of SFAS 109 from Green.

**Required:**

Prepare a brief memo to Dunn from Green

- Identifying the objectives of accounting for income taxes,
- Defining temporary differences,
- Explaining how to measure deferred tax assets and liabilities, and
- Explaining how to measure deferred income tax expense or benefit.

To:    Mr. Dunn
From:  Mr. Green, CPA
Re:    Accounting for income taxes

| | | | | | | | | | Research |
|---|---|---|---|---|---|---|---|---|---|
| | | **Temporary and Permanent Differences** | **Deferred Tax Schedule** | **Calculate Taxable Income** | **Journal Entries** | | | | |
| **Directions** | **Situation** | | | | | **Disclosures** | **Communication** | | |

Using the authoritative literature from the FASB Original Pronouncements, cut and paste the appropriate paragraph that provides the definition for deferred tax expense.

| | | | | | | | | | |
|---|---|---|---|---|---|---|---|---|---|
| 1. c __ __ | 10. d __ __ | 19. c __ __ | 28. b __ __ | 37. c __ __ |
| 2. a __ __ | 11. c __ __ | 20. a __ __ | 29. b __ __ | 38. b __ __ |
| 3. b __ __ | 12. b __ __ | 21. c __ __ | 30. b __ __ | 39. b __ __ |
| 4. a __ __ | 13. c __ __ | 22. d __ __ | 31. a __ __ | 40. a __ __ |
| 5. c __ __ | 14. c __ __ | 23. c __ __ | 32. a __ __ | 41. d __ __ |
| 6. b __ __ | 15. c __ __ | 24. c __ __ | 33. c __ __ | |
| 7. a __ __ | 16. c __ __ | 25. d __ __ | 34. c __ __ | |
| 8. c __ __ | 17. b __ __ | 26. c __ __ | 35. d __ __ | 1st: __/41 = __% |
| 9. b __ __ | 18. b __ __ | 27. a __ __ | 36. d __ __ | 2nd: __/41 = __% |

## MULTIPLE-CHOICE ANSWER EXPLANATIONS

### A. Overview of Deferred Tax Theory

**1. (c)** SFAS 109 states that the objective of accounting for income taxes is to recognize the amount of current and deferred taxes payable or refundable at the date of the financial statements. The standard further states that this objective is implemented through recognition of deferred tax liabilities or assets. Deferred tax expense results from changes in deferred tax assets and liabilities.

### B. Permanent and Temporary Differences Defined

**2. (a) Temporary** differences are differences between taxable income and accounting income which originate in one period and reverse in one or more subsequent periods. The payment of a penalty ($5,000) and insurance premiums where the corporation is the beneficiary ($10,000) are **not** temporary differences because they never reverse. These are examples of **permanent** differences, which are items that either enter into accounting income but never into taxable income (such as these two items), or enter into taxable income but never into accounting income.

**3. (b)** The officer insurance policy difference ($75,000) is a permanent difference which does not result in future taxable or deductible amounts. The warranty difference ($50,000) is a temporary difference, but it results in future **deductible** amounts in future years when tax warranty expense exceeds book warranty expense. However, the equipment difference ($80,000) is a temporary difference that results in future taxable amounts in future years when tax depreciation is less than book depreciation.

**4. (a)** SFAS 109 cites examples of temporary differences. Among these examples are revenues which are taxable both before and after they are recognized in financial income. Note that emphasis is placed on the difference between book and tax, not the chronological order of the reporting.

**5. (c)** Expenses or losses that are deductible before they are recognized in financial income would result in future taxable amounts. For example, the cost of an asset may have been deducted for tax purposes faster than it was depreciated for financial reporting. In future years, tax depreciation will be less than financial accounting depreciation, meaning future taxable income will exceed future financial accounting income. Answers (a) and (b) are temporary differences that would result in future deductible amounts. Answer (d) is a permanent difference that does not result in either future taxable or future deductible amounts.

### C. Deferred Tax Assets and Liabilities

**6. (b)** To determine the current federal tax liability, **book** income ($90,000) must be adjusted for any temporary or permanent differences to determine **taxable** income.

| | |
|---|---|
| Book income | $90,000 |
| Rent received in advance | 16,000 |
| Municipal interest | (20,000) |
| Excess tax depreciation | (10,000) |
| Taxable income | $76,000 |

Rent received in advance (temporary difference) is added to book income because rent is taxable when received, but is not recognized as book revenue until earned. Municipal interest (permanent difference) is subtracted from book income because it is excluded from taxable income. The excess tax depreciation (temporary difference) is subtracted because this excess amount is an additional tax deduction beyond accounting depreciation. The current tax liability is computed by multiplying taxable income by the tax rate ($76,000 × 30% = $22,800).

**7. (a)** The **current** federal income tax liability is based on **taxable** income, which is computed in the "book to tax reconciliation" below.

| | |
|---|---|
| Accounting income | $ 800,000 |
| Nontaxable gain | (350,000) |
| Excess tax depreciation | (50,000) |
| Taxable income | $ 400,000 |

The gain on involuntary conversion was included in accounting income but is deferred for tax purposes. Depreciation deducted for tax purposes in excess of book depreciation also causes taxable income to be less than accounting income. Taxes payable before considering estimated tax payments is $120,000 ($400,000 × 30%). Since tax payments of $70,000 have already been made, the 12/31/07 current federal income tax liability is $50,000 ($120,000 – $70,000).

**8. (c)** SFAS 109 states that income tax expense must be reported in two components: the amount currently payable (current portion) and the tax effects of temporary differences (deferred portion). The current portion is computed by multiplying taxable income by the current enacted tax rate ($650,000 × 30% = $195,000). The deferred portion is $30,000 ($100,000 temporary difference × 30%). The estimated tax payments ($90,000) do not affect the amount of tax expense, although the payments would decrease taxes payable.

**9. (b)** Over the two years, accounting income on the accrual basis is $4,200,000 ($1,600,000 + $2,600,000) and taxable income using the installment method is $2,000,000 ($600,000 + $1,400,000). This results in future taxable amounts at 12/31/07 of $2,200,000 ($4,200,000 – $2,000,000). Therefore, at 12/31/07, Tower should report a deferred tax liability of $660,000 ($2,200,000 × 30%).

**10.   (d)**   For accounting purposes, prepaid insurance is $9,500 at 12/31/07. For tax purposes, there was no prepaid insurance at 12/31/07, since the entire amount was deducted on the 2007 tax return. Therefore, the temporary difference is $9,500. This temporary difference will result in a future taxable amount in 2008, when the tax rate is 25%. Therefore, at 12/31/07, a deferred tax liability of $2,375 (25% × $9,500) must be reported.

**11.   (c)**   Mill's total accounting income using percentage-of-completion ($300,000 + $600,000 + $850,000 = $1,750,000) will eventually be subject to federal income taxes. However, by 12/31/07, only $1,100,000 of income ($400,000 + $700,000) has been reported as taxable income using the completed-contract method. The amount of accounting income which has not yet been taxed ($1,750,000 – $1,100,000 = $650,000 temporary difference) will be taxed eventually when the related contracts are completed. The resulting future taxable amounts will all be taxed after 2007 when the enacted tax rate is 25%. Therefore, the 12/31/07 deferred tax liability is $162,500 ($650,000 × 25%). To record the liability, the following entries would be made each year:

**2005**

| | | |
|---|---|---|
| Income tax expense—deferred | 90,000 | |
| Deferred tax liability | | 90,000 |

**2006**

| | | |
|---|---|---|
| Income tax expense—deferred | 60,000 | |
| Deferred tax liability | | 60,000 |

**2007**

| | | |
|---|---|---|
| Income tax expense—deferred | 12,500 | |
| Deferred tax liability | | 12,500 |

The total in the deferred tax liability account on 12/31/07 should be $162,500. Therefore, the entry in 2007 is the amount needed to correctly state the deferred tax liability account. Since $150,000 was already accrued in the deferred tax liability account in 2005 and 2006, the entry for 2007 is $162,500 – $150,000.

**12.   (b)**   SFAS 109 states that income tax expense must be reported in two components: the amount currently payable (current portion) and the tax effects of temporary differences (deferred portion). The amount currently payable, or current income tax expense, is computed by multiplying taxable income by the current enacted tax rate ($140,000 × 40% = $56,000).

**13.   (c)**   The deferred tax liability reported at 12/31/07 results from future taxable (and possibly deductible) amounts which exist as a result of past transactions, multiplied by the appropriate tax rate. The nontaxable interest received on municipal securities ($5,000) is a **permanent** difference that does **not** result in future taxable or deductible amounts. SFAS 109 requires the netting of current deferred tax assets and liabilities, and noncurrent deferred tax assets and liabilities. The future deductible amount ($10,000) resulting from a loss accrual results in a **long-term** deferred tax asset of $4,000 ($10,000 × 40%) because it is related to a **long-term** loss accrual. The future taxable amount ($25,000) caused by depreciation results in a **long-term** deferred tax liability of $10,000 ($25,000 × 40%) because it is related to a **long-term** asset (property, plant, and equip-

ment). Since these are both long-term, they are netted and a long-term deferred tax liability of $6,000 is reported in the balance sheet ($10,000 liability less $4,000 asset).

**14.   (b)**   At 12/31/07, unearned rent for financial accounting purposes is $18,000 ($36,000 × 6/12). The amount of rent revenue recognized on the income statement is six of twelve months (36,000 × 6/12) = 18,000. Rental income on the tax return is $36,000 because rental income is taxed when received. Therefore, the timing difference is $18,000 ($36,000 – $18,000 = $18,000) giving rise to a deferred tax asset on the balance sheet of $18,000 × 40% = $7,200. The deferred tax asset to be recorded is measured using the future enacted tax rate of 40% in accordance with SFAS 109.

**15.   (c)**   Under SFAS 109, a deferred tax asset is recognized for all deductible temporary differences. The computation of the deferred tax asset for Black Co. arising from the accrued product warranty costs of $300,000 is shown below.

| | _2008_ | _2009_ | _2010_ | _2011_ | _Total_ |
|---|---|---|---|---|---|
| Future deductible amounts | $100,000 | $50,000 | $50,000 | $100,000 | $300,000 |
| Tax rate | 30% | 30% | 30% | 25% | |
| Deferred tax asset | $30,000 | $15,000 | $15,000 | $25,000 | $85,000 |

Thus, the total deferred tax asset at the end of 2007 is $85,000.

**16.   (c)**   An excess of tax depreciation over financial accounting depreciation results in future taxable amounts and, therefore, a deferred tax liability. Answer (a) is an example of a permanent difference that does not result in future taxable or deductible amounts. Answers (b) and (d) are examples of temporary differences that result in future deductible amounts and a possible deferred tax asset.

**17.   (b)**   The increase in prepaid insurance in 2008 creates a deductible amount for income tax reporting purposes for the insurance paid; however, for financial reporting purposes the expense is not recognized until years subsequent to 2008. As a result, net taxable income for future years is increased, thus, the deferred income tax liability increases. The increase in rent receivable in 2008 also increases the deferred tax liability. For income tax purposes, rents are not included in income until received (i.e., years subsequent to 2008). However, the amount of the receivable is earned and recognized in the income statement in 2008. The increase in warranty obligations results in warranty expense for 2008 and will provide future deductible amounts, because under the IRC, a deduction for warranty cost is not permitted until such cost is incurred. Future deductible amounts lead to deferred tax assets.

**18.   (b)**   Per SFAS 109, a deferred tax liability is recognized for temporary differences that will result in **net** taxable amounts (taxable income exceeds book income) in future years. Although Cody Co. has recognized a loss (per books) in year two of the construction contract, the contract is still profitable over the three years. Therefore, in year three when the contract is completed, Cody will recognize the total profit on its tax return, and only a portion of the profit will be recorded in its income statement. Thus, the contract will result in a taxable amount in year three and a deferred tax liability exists. Note that this liability was recorded at the end of year 1 and reduced by one-half at the end of year two due to the change in estimated profit. Answers (a) and (c) are incorrect because no deferred tax asset is created. Answer (d) is incorrect because Cody will include a deferred tax liability on its balance sheet.

**19.** **(c)** Per SFAS 109, a deferred tax liability is recognized for the amount of taxes payable in **future** years as a result of the deferred tax consequences (as measured by the provisions of **enacted** tax laws) of events recognized in the financial statements in the current or preceding years.

**20.** **(a)** SFAS 109 states that income tax provision (expense) must be reported in two components: the amount currently payable (current portion) and the tax effects of temporary differences (deferred portion). The current portion is computed by multiplying taxable income by the current enacted tax rate ($150,000 × 30% = $45,000). Note that in this case, the deferred portion is $0, because both differences are permanent differences, which do not result in a deferred tax liability. Therefore, the current provision for income taxes should be reported at $45,000. It is important to note that if temporary differences did exist the tax effects would have been included in the tax expense for the current period.

**21.** **(c)** SFAS 109 states that income tax expense must be reported in two components: the amount currently payable (current portion) and the tax effects of temporary differences (deferred portion). The amount currently payable, or current income tax expense, is computed by multiplying taxable income by the current enacted tax rate ($1,000 × 30% = $300).

**22.** **(d)** SFAS 109 states that income tax expense must be reported on the IS in two components: the amount currently payable (current portion) and the tax effects of temporary differences (deferred portion). Note that scheduling is required in this question because the tax rates are not the same in all future years. The worksheet indicates two temporary differences: depreciation and warranty costs. The scheduling contained in the worksheet shows that these two temporary differences will result in a deferred tax asset of $105 ($30 + $75) and deferred tax liability of $140. The liability has the effect of increasing 2007 tax expense while the asset has the effect of decreasing 2007 tax expense. The net effect is deferred income tax expense of $35 for 2007 [$140 – ($30 + $75)].

**Not required:**

The balance sheet presentation would show a current deferred tax asset of $30 and a noncurrent deferred tax liability of $65 ($140 – $75).

**23.** **(a)** The deferred portion of income tax expense can be computed by determining the tax effect of the two temporary differences. The installment sale profit results in a future taxable amount in 2008 of $2,600, and the bad debt expense results in a future deductible amount of $1,400. The deferred tax consequences of these temporary differences will be measured by Shear in 2007 using the enacted tax rate expected to apply to taxable income in the year the deferred amounts are expected to be settled. The following journal entry is necessary to record the deferred tax liability related to the installment sale:

| | | |
|---|---|---|
| Deferred tax expense | 650 | |
|    Deferred tax liability | | 650 |
|    [$2,600 × .25] | | |

To record the deferred tax asset related to the bad debt expense, the following journal entry is required:

| | | |
|---|---|---|
| Deferred tax asset | 350 | |
|    Deferred tax expense | | 350 |
|    [$1,400 × .25] | | |

The amount of deferred tax expense to be reported by Shear in its 2007 income statement is $300 ($650 – $350). Note that one journal entry could have been used. Using two entries more clearly shows the opposite effect of an asset versus a liability on deferred tax expense.

**24.** **(c)** SFAS 109 states that income tax expense must be reported in two components: the amount currently payable (current portion) and the tax effects of temporary differences (deferred portion). The current portion is computed by multiplying taxable income by the current enacted tax rate ($200,000 × 30% = $60,000). The deferred portion is $30,000 ($100,000 temporary difference × 30%). An alternative computation for the deferred portion is shown below.

| | | |
|---|---|---|
| DT asset at 12/31/07 | $    0 | |
| DT asset at 12/31/06 | 9,000 | |
|    Decrease in DT asset | | $ 9,000 |
| DT liability at 12/31/07 ($70,000 × 30%) | $21,000 | |
| DT liability at 12/31/06 | 0 | |
|    Increase in DT liability | | 21,000 |
| Deferred portion of tax expense | | $30,000 |

**25.** **(d)** SFAS 109 defines the deferred income tax expense or benefit as the net change during the year in an enterprise's deferred tax liabilities or assets. The deferred income tax expense or benefit must consider the net effect of changes (both increases and decreases) in both deferred tax assets and deferred tax liabilities. The decrease in deferred tax assets alone or the increase in deferred tax liabilities alone will not be equal to the deferred income tax expense. The amount of income tax liability (current portion which comes off the tax return) plus the sum of the net changes in deferred tax assets and deferred tax liabilities is the total amount of income tax expense or benefit for the year. The question asks only for the deferred portion.

**26.** **(c)** From 12/31/06 to 12/31/07, the deferred tax asset increased by $5,000 (from $15,000 to $20,000). Income taxes payable at 12/31/07 are $13,000. Based on this information, the following journal entries can be recreated.

| | | |
|---|---|---|
| Income tax expense—current | 13,000 | |
|    Income tax payable | | 13,000 |
| Deferred tax asset | 5,000 | |
|    Income tax expense—deferred | | 5,000 |

An additional entry would be prepared by Shin to record an allowance to reduce the deferred tax asset to its realizable value (10% × $20,000 = $2,000).

| | | |
|---|---|---|
| Income tax expense—deferred | 2,000 | |
|    Allowance to reduce deferred | | |
|      tax asset to realizable value | | 2,000 |

Based on these three entries, total 2007 income tax expense is $10,000 ($13,000 – $5,000 + $2,000).

**27.** **(a)** SFAS 109, *Accounting for Income Taxes,* specifies that income tax expense is the sum of income taxes currently payable or refundable and the deferred tax expense or benefit which is the change during the year in an enterprise's deferred tax liabilities and assets.  This method is more commonly called the asset and liability approach.

### D.  Deferred Tax Related to Business Investments

**28.  (b)**   The deferred income tax liability is the result of the undistributed earnings of an equity investee, which are expected to be distributed as dividends in future periods.  For accounting purposes, investment revenue is $270,000 ($900,000 × 30%).  For tax purposes, dividend revenue is $90,000 ($300,000 × 30%), which will be partially offset by the 80% dividends received deduction.  Because of this 80% deduction, the difference ($270,000 − $90,000 = $180,000) is partially a permanent difference (80% × $180,000 = $144,000 which will never be subject to taxes) and partially a temporary difference (20% × $180,000 = $36,000 which will be taxable in future years).  This future taxable amount of $36,000 will become taxable after 2007, when the expected tax rate is 25%.  Therefore, the deferred tax liability is $9,000 (25% × $36,000).  The entry to record the liability is as follows:

| | | |
|---|---|---|
| Income tax expense—deferred | 9,000 | |
| Deferred tax liability | | 9,000 |

**29.  (b)**   The **current** provision for income taxes is computed by multiplying taxable income on the Form 1120 by the current tax rate.  Since taxable income is not given, pretax book income must be adjusted to compute taxable income.

| | |
|---|---|
| Pretax book income | $100,000 |
| Excess book depreciation | 8,000 |
| Excess book investment revenue | |
| [$35,000 − (20% × $25,000)] | (30,000) |
| Taxable income | $78,000 |

Excess book depreciation is added because it causes book income to be lower than taxable income.  For book purposes, investment revenue of $35,000 was recognized using the equity method; for tax purposes, net dividend revenue of $5,000 was recognized [$25,000 − (80% × $25,000)].  The excess book revenue ($35,000 − $5,000 = $30,000) is deducted to compute taxable income.  Therefore, the **current** provision for income taxes is $23,400 ($78,000 × 30%).

### E.  Loss Carryforwards and Carrybacks

**30.  (b)**   Dix did **not** elect to forego the loss carryback, so $100,000 of the $200,000 loss will be carried back to offset 2005 income, resulting in a tax refund of $40,000 (40% × $100,000).  The remaining $100,000 of the 2006 loss will be carried forward to offset part of 2007 income.  Thus, the income tax **liability** at 12/31/07 will be $120,000 [40% × ($400,000 − $100,000)].

**31.  (a)**   The requirement is to determine the amount to be reported in 2007 as the reduction of loss due to NOL carryback and carryforward (i.e., benefit [negative tax expense] on the face of the IS).  Per SFAS 109, a deferred tax liability or asset is recognized for all temporary differences, operating losses, and tax credit carryforwards.

#### Income Tax Return Analysis

| | 2005-2006 | 2007 |
|---|---|---|
| Inc (loss) | 450,000 | $(600,000) |
| Carryback | (450,000) | 450,000 |
| Unused NOL | | $150,000 |

Town can thus recognize tax benefits from both the NOL carryback and carryforward.  Town may carryback $450,000

of the NOL which will provide a tax benefit of $180,000 ($450,000 × .40).  The journal entry to recognize the loss carryback would be as follows:

| | | |
|---|---|---|
| Tax refund receivable | 180,000 | |
| Benefit due to loss carryback | | 180,000 |

The additional $150,000 NOL can be carried forward to future periods to provide a benefit of $60,000 ($150,000 × .40).  The following journal entry reflects the loss carryforward:

| | | |
|---|---|---|
| Deferred tax asset | 60,000 | |
| Benefit due to loss carryforward | | 60,000 |

Therefore, the reduction of the loss due to NOL carryback and carryforward is $240,000.  Note that an allowance for nonrealization of the deferred tax asset is not necessary because the information given about the strike indicates that it is not more likely than not that part of the deferred tax asset may not be recognized.

The carryback and carryforward would be shown in the income statement as follows:

| | | |
|---|---|---|
| Loss before income taxes | | $(600,000) |
| Less: | | |
| Benefit from operating loss carryback | $180,000 | |
| Benefit from operating loss carryforward | 60,000 | 240,000 |
| Net loss | | $(360,000) |

**32.  (a)**   The requirement is to determine the amount of 2007 current income tax expense (or income taxes payable from tax return) to be reported in the income statement.  For tax purposes, loss carryforwards should not be recognized until they are actually realized.

#### Income Tax Return Analysis

| | 2005 | 2006 | 2007 |
|---|---|---|---|
| Income or loss | $(200,000) | $(150,000) | $300,000 |
| Carryforward | 200,000 | 100,000 | (300,000) |
| Unused Carryforward | 0 | $ 50,000 | 0 |

Bishop would recognize, in the income statement, income tax expense of $0 as the loss carryforward fully offsets the 2007 income.

**Not required:**

The deferred tax component for 2007 would be as follows:

Balance in the deferred tax asset and allowance accounts at 1/1/07

| | Deferred Tax Asset | | Allow for Reduction, etc. | |
|---|---|---|---|---|
| 12/31/05 | 80,000 | | 80,000 | 12/31/05 |
| 12/31/06 | 60,000 | | 60,000 | 12/31/06 |
| 12/31/06 balance | 140,000 | | 140,000 | 12/31/06 balance |

The deferred tax entry for 2007 would be

| | | |
|---|---|---|
| Allow for reduction, etc. | 140,000 | |
| Deferred tax asset | | 120,000 |
| Income tax expense—deferred | | 20,000 |

The bottom of the income statement would be

| | | |
|---|---|---|
| Income before taxes | | $300,000 |
| Income tax expense or benefit | | |
| Current | | 0 |
| Deferred **benefit** | | 20,000 |
| Net income | | $320,000 |

**33.   (c)**   Per SFAS 109, a deferred tax liability or asset is recognized for all temporary differences and operating loss carryforwards. In 2006, Mobe would prepare the following entries:

| | | |
|---|---|---|
| Tax refund receivable ($300,000 × 30%) | 90,000 | |
| Deferred tax asset ($400,000 × 30%) | 120,000 | |
|   Tax loss benefit (income tax expense) | | 210,000 |
| Tax loss benefit (income tax expense) | 120,000 | |
|   Allowance to reduce deferred tax asset to realizable value | | 120,000 |

The tax refund receivable results from carrying $300,000 of the 2006 loss **back** to offset 2005 taxable income. The deferred tax asset results from the potential **carryforward** of the remaining $400,000 loss ($700,000 – $300,000). However, the inconsistent performance of the company (profitable operations in the first year, loss in the second year) coupled with the lack of positive evidence concerning future operations indicate that at the end of 2006 it is more likely than not that none of the deferred tax asset will be realized. Therefore, Mobe must establish a valuation allowance to reduce this asset to its expected realizable value. In 2007, the entries are

| | | |
|---|---|---|
| Income tax expense ($1,200,000 × 30%) | 360,000 | |
|   Deferred tax asset | | 120,000 |
|   Income taxes payable [(($1,200,000 – $400,000) × 30%] | | 240,000 |
| Allowance to reduce deferred tax asset to realizable value | 120,000 | |
|   Benefit due to loss carryforward (income tax expense) | | 120,000 |

**Income taxes payable** is 2007 income of $1,200,000 less the $400,000 loss carryforward, times 30%. Total income tax expense for 2007 is $240,000 ($360,000 – $120,000). Note that if the facts had indicated positive evidence following 2006 for 2007 operations, the allowance account would not have been recognized and 2007 expense would have been $360,000.

## F.  Financial Statement Presentation of Income Tax

**34.   (c)**   The warranty temporary difference results in future deductible amounts of $700,000 per year in 2008 through 2010 ($2,100,000 ÷ 3). The installment temporary difference results in future taxable amounts of $500,000 per year in 2008 through 2010 ($1,500,000 ÷ 3). The portions of the resulting deferred tax asset and deferred tax liability that will be netted to find the amount of the current asset/current liability to be presented on the BS are shown below.

| | |
|---|---|
| Deferred tax asset: | |
|   $(700,000) × 25% = | $(175,000) |
| Deferred tax liability: | |
|   $500,000 × 25% = | <u>125,000</u> |
| Current deferred tax asset (CDTA) shown on BS | $ <u>(50,000)</u> |

The noncurrent deferred tax asset is $100,000 [25% × ($2,100,000 – $1,500,000)] – $50,000 CDTA.

**35.   (d)**   Per SFAS 109, deferred tax liabilities and assets are classified as current or noncurrent based on the classification of the related asset or liability for financial reporting. The deferred tax liability resulting from accelerated tax depreciation should be considered noncurrent because the related asset is classified as noncurrent. The deferred tax asset resulting from additional costs in inventory for tax purposes is classified as current because the related asset is classified

as current. Therefore, Thorn would report a **noncurrent deferred tax liability** of **$75,000**.

**36.   (d)**   Deferred tax liabilities and assets are classified as current or noncurrent based on the related asset or liability. A deferred tax liability or asset is considered to be related to an asset or liability if reduction of the asset or liability will cause the temporary difference to reverse. If the deferred tax liability or asset is **not** related to any asset or liability, then it is classified based on the timing of its expected reversal or utilization date. This deferred tax liability is related to equipment, which is noncurrent, so the deferred tax liability should also be classified as a noncurrent liability. Deferred taxes are always classified as assets or liabilities, rather than as contra accounts.

**37.   (c)**   Deferred tax assets and liabilities are classified as current or noncurrent based on the classification of the related asset or liability for financial reporting. Therefore, a deferred tax liability relating to depreciation of a fixed asset would be noncurrent in nature. The deferred tax asset relating to rent received in advance that is expected to reverse in the following year would be classified as current. No netting of net current amounts and net noncurrent amounts can occur.

**38.   (b)**   Per SFAS 109, a **deferred** tax liability or asset should be classified in two categories (the current amount and the noncurrent amount) on the balance sheet based on the classification of the related asset or liability for financial reporting. The receivable for taxes paid in prior years and refundable through the carryback of the 2007 operating loss is **not** considered a **deferred** tax asset. A current asset should be reported on the balance sheet for the amount of the refund due to Oak Co. Note that if there was a current deferred tax liability it would not be netted with the refund receivable. However, a current deferred tax asset would be so netted. A noncurrent deferred tax liability should be reported on the balance sheet for temporary differences related to depreciation of fixed assets.

**39.   (b)**   Per SFAS 109, income tax expense must be associated with (i.e., allocated among) income from continuing operations, discontinued operations, extraordinary items, cumulative effect of an accounting change, and prior period adjustments. The tax effect to be associated with any of the special items (other than income from continuing operations) is computed by determining the income tax on overall taxable income and comparing it with the income tax on continuing operations. If more than one special item exists, the difference between tax on ordinary operations and tax on overall taxable income must be allocated proportionately among the special items.

**40.   (a)**   Per SFAS 109, the tax benefit of an operating loss carryforward or carryback shall be reported in the same manner as the **source of income (loss) in the current year**. Thus, in 2007, the tax benefit shall be reported under income from continuing operations.

**41.   (d)**   Sole proprietorships do not pay any income taxes as the tax items related to a sole proprietorship flow through to the owner's tax return. Because the sole proprietorship is not a taxable entity, no provision for income taxes would be included in the financial statements of the sole proprietorship. Although answer (a) illustrates the correct formula for calculating the taxes payable related to a sole proprietorship's operations, it is an incorrect response because the tax provision would not be shown on the sole proprietorship's financial statements since it flows through to the owner and is a liability of the owner. The income tax expense would be calculated using the owner's tax rates, as it is the owner's personal liability, not the entity's. The proprietorship would have **no** provision for income taxes on its books. The entire income tax liability is the personal responsibility of the owner.

**SOLUTIONS TO SIMULATION PROBLEMS**

**Simulation Problem 1**

| | | Tax Calculations | Tax Differences | Deferred Tax Classification | Research |
|---|---|---|---|---|---|
| Directions | Situation | | | | |

| *Specific audit objective* | (A) | (B) | (C) | (D) | (E) | (F) | (G) | (H) | (I) | (J) | (K) | (L) | (M) | (N) |
|---|---|---|---|---|---|---|---|---|---|---|---|---|---|---|
| 1. Current tax expense for the year ended April 30, 2005. | ○ | ○ | ○ | ○ | ○ | ○ | ● | ○ | ○ | ○ | ○ | ○ | ○ | ○ |
| 2. Cumulative temporary differences at April 30, 2006. | ○ | ○ | ○ | ○ | ○ | ○ | ○ | ○ | ○ | ○ | ○ | ○ | ● | ○ |
| 3. Deferred tax expense for the year ended April 30, 2006. | ○ | ● | ○ | ○ | ○ | ○ | ○ | ○ | ○ | ○ | ○ | ○ | ○ | ○ |
| 4. Deferred tax liability at April 30, 2007. | ○ | ○ | ○ | ○ | ○ | ○ | ○ | ● | ○ | ○ | ○ | ○ | ○ | ○ |

**Explanation of solutions**

**1.   (G)**  Current tax expense for FY 2005 is equal to taxable income (Form 1120) of $600,000 times 20% or $120,000.

**2.   (M)**  The $100,000 temporary difference for FY 2006 is deducted from pretax financial income to arrive at taxable income.  Therefore, cumulative temporary differences or future taxable amounts are increased.  Thus, $300,000 ($200,000 + $100,000) will be added to pretax financial income in future reversal years.

**3.   (B)**  Deferred tax expense is equal to the increased rate on future taxable amounts outstanding at the beginning of FY 2006 plus the amount related to the $100,000 of temporary differences that originated in FY 2006.  Thus, deferred tax expense is equal to $35,000 [$200,000 × (.25 – .20) + $100,000 × .25].  The entry is

| | | |
|---|---|---|
| Deferred tax expense | 35,000 | |
| Deferred tax liability | | 35,000 |

**4.   (H)**  In FY 2007 cumulative temporary differences (future taxable amounts) increased by $150,000.  The deferred tax liability account for three years is shown below.

| Deferred Tax Liability | |
|---|---|
| 40,000 | *2005* <br> (200,000 × .20) |
| 10,000 <br> 25,000 | *2006* <br> [200,000 × (.25 – .20)] <br> (100,000 × .25) |
| 15,000 <br> 45,000 | *2007* <br> [300,000 × (.30 – .25)] <br> (150,000 × .30) |
| | Bal. 135,000 |

The $135,000 is equal to the cumulative temporary differences of $450,000 ×.30.

| | | | Tax Differences | | |
|---|---|---|---|---|---|
| Directions | Situation | Tax Calculations | | Deferred Tax Classification | Research |

| | | A <br> *Temporary difference DTA* | B <br> *Temporary difference DTL* | C <br> *Permanent difference* |
|---|---|---|---|---|
| 1. | For plant assets, the depreciation expense deducted for tax purposes is in excess of the depreciation expense used for financial reporting purposes. | ○ | ● | ○ |
| 2. | A landlord collects some rents in advance. Rents received are taxable in the period in which they are received. | ● | ○ | ○ |
| 3. | Interest is received on an investment in tax-exempt municipal obligations. | ○ | ○ | ● |
| 4. | Costs of guarantees and warranties are estimated and accrued for financial reporting purposes. | ● | ○ | ○ |
| 5. | Life insurance proceeds are collected on the death of a key officer. | ○ | ○ | ● |

| | | A<br>*Temporary difference<br>DTA* | B<br>*Temporary difference<br>DTL* | C<br>*Permanent difference* |
|---|---|:---:|:---:|:---:|
| **6.** | Bad debts are estimated and expensed on the income statement. No bad debts were charged to the allowance account and written off during the year. | ● | ○ | ○ |
| **7.** | Goodwill is deducted on the tax return. | ○ | ○ | ● |

### Explanation of solutions

**1. (B)** In cases in which tax depreciation is greater than accounting (book) depreciation, taxable income will be less than accounting income and a deferred tax liability results. The reason is that in future years tax depreciation will be less than book depreciation and taxable income will be greater than book income. This will result in future cash flows for the income tax liability shown on the Form 1120 exceeding those that would occur based on pretax accounting income. Thus a deferred tax liability will result. The entry is

| Deferred income tax expense | xx | |
|---|---|---|
| Deferred tax liability | | xx |

In the reversal year, the entry would be

| Deferred tax liability | xx | |
|---|---|---|
| Deferred tax expense | | xx |

**2. (A)** Taxable income will exceed pretax accounting (book) income in the year in which the rents are received. In effect, income taxes on the portion of the rent that is unearned for financial reporting under GAAP must be prepaid under the Internal Revenue Code. Thus, a deferred tax asset would result because in future years when the rent received in advance is earned, no taxes will be payable on the amount earned, because the taxes were paid in the year rent was received. The entry is

| Deferred tax asset | xx | |
|---|---|---|
| Deferred tax expense | | xx |

**3. (C)** Interest earned on a tax-exempt municipal obligation is a permanent difference. The interest is deducted in the year received from pretax accounting income to arrive at taxable income. However, it will never be reported as income on the firm's Form 1120. Therefore, such a difference does not result in deferred income taxes.

**4. (A)** Costs of guarantees and warranties are not deductible under the Internal Revenue Code until incurred. Under SFAS 5, however, they are estimated and recorded as an expense (loss) and a liability in the period of sale. In effect, income taxes are prepaid because in later years a benefit is received when these costs are incurred and deducted on the tax return. The entry in the origination year is

| Deferred tax asset | xx | |
|---|---|---|
| Deferred tax expense | | xx |

The entry when the warranty costs are deducted is

| Deferred tax expense | xx | |
|---|---|---|
| Deferred tax asset | | xx |

**5. (C)** life insurance proceeds are not taxable under the Internal Revenue Code. This gives rise to a permanent difference.

**6. (A)** The Internal Revenue Code requires the direct write-off method for bad debts. Therefore, bad debts cannot be deducted until the debt becomes uncollectible and is written off. Since no deduction is allowed in the current year, this leads to a future deductible amount and is a deferred tax asset.

**7. (C)** Goodwill is no longer amortized for GAAP. However, goodwill is deducted for tax purposes. Therefore, goodwill gives rise to a permanent difference.

| Directions | Situation | Tax Calculations | Tax Differences | Deferred Tax Classification | | Research |
|---|---|---|---|---|---|---|

| | | *Deferred tax asset* | *Deferred tax liability* | *Current* | *Noncurrent* |
|---|---|:---:|:---:|:---:|:---:|
| **1.** | Tax depreciation in excess of book depreciation | ○ | ● | ○ | ● |
| **2.** | Bad debts expense in excess of actual write-offs | ● | ○ | ● | ○ |
| **3.** | Rent collected in advance for next 12 months | ● | ○ | ● | ○ |

| Directions | Situation | Tax Calculations | Tax Differences | Deferred Tax Classification | Research |
|---|---|---|---|---|---|

**1.** What are the objectives of accounting for income taxes?

**Objectives and Basic Principles**
**FAS109, Para 6 or Current Text I27.105**

6. One objective of accounting for income taxes is to recognize the amount of taxes payable or refundable for the current year. A second objective is to recognize deferred tax liabilities and assets for the future tax consequences of events that have been recognized in an enterprise's financial statements or tax returns.

**FAS109, Para 7 or Current Text I27.106**

7. Ideally, the second objective might be stated more specifically to recognize the expected future tax consequences of events that have been recognized in the financial statements or tax returns. However, that objective is realistically constrained because (a) the tax payment or refund that results from a particular tax return is a joint result of all the items included in that return, (b) taxes that will be paid or refunded in future years are the result of events of the current or prior years and events of future years, and (c) information available about the future is limited. As a result, attribution of taxes to individual items and events is arbitrary and except in the simplest situations, requires estimates and approximations.

**2.** What is a temporary difference?

**Temporary Differences**
**FAS109, Para 10 or Current Text I27.109**

10. Income taxes currently payable for a particular year usually include the tax consequences of most events that are recognized in the financial statements for that year. However, because tax laws and financial accounting standards differ in their recognition and measurement of assets, liabilities, equity, revenues, expenses, gains, and losses, differences arise between

a. The amount of taxable income and pretax financial income for a year.
b. The tax bases of assets or liabilities and their reported amounts in financial statements.

**FAS109, Para 13 or Current Text I27.112**

13. This Statement refers collectively to the types of differences illustrated by those eight examples and to the ones described in paragraph 15 as temporary differences. Temporary differences that will result in taxable amounts in future years when the related asset or liability is recovered or settled are often referred to in this Statement as taxable temporary differences (examples a., b., and c., in paragraph 11 are taxable temporary differences). Likewise, temporary differences that will result in deductible amounts in future years are often referred to as deductible temporary differences (examples b., c., f., and g., in paragraph 11 are deductible temporary differences). Business combinations accounted for by the purchase method (example h.) may give rise to both taxable and deductible temporary differences.

**FAS109, Appendix A., Para 289 or Current Text I27.404**
**Temporary difference**

A difference between the tax basis of an asset or liability and its reported amount in the financial statements that will result in taxable or deductible amounts in future years when the reported amount of the asset or liability is recovered or settled, respectively. Paragraph 11 cites 8 examples of temporary differences. Some temporary differences cannot be identified with a particular asset or liability for financial reporting (paragraph 15), but those temporary differences (a) result from events that have been recognized in the financial statements and (b) will result in taxable or deductible amounts in future years based on provisions of the tax law. Some events recognized in financial statements do not have tax consequences. Certain revenues are exempt from taxation and certain expenses are not deductible. Events that do not have tax consequences do not give rise to temporary differences.

3. How are deferred taxes presented in the financial statements?

**Financial Statement Presentation**
**FAS109, Para 41 or Current Text I27.140**

41. In a classified statement of financial position, an enterprise shall separate deferred tax liabilities and assets into a current amount and a noncurrent amount. Deferred tax liabilities and assets shall be classified as current or noncurrent based on the classification of the related asset or liability for financial reporting. A deferred tax liability or asset that is not related to an asset or liability for financial reporting (paragraph 15), including deferred tax assets related to carryforwards, shall be classified according to the expected reversal date of the temporary difference pursuant to FASB Statement No. 37, *Balance Sheet Classification of Deferred Income Taxes*. The valuation allowance for a particular tax jurisdiction shall be allocated between current and noncurrent deferred tax assets for that tax jurisdiction on a pro rata basis.

**FAS109, Para 42 or Current Text I27.141**

42. For a particular tax-paying component of an enterprise and within a particular tax jurisdiction, (a) all current deferred tax liabilities and assets shall be offset and presented as a single amount and (b) all noncurrent deferred tax liabilities and assets shall be offset and presented as a single amount. However, an enterprise shall not offset deferred tax liabilities and assets attributable to different tax paying components of the enterprise or to different tax jurisdictions.

4. What tax rate is used to calculate deferred taxes?

**FAS109, Para 18 or Current Text I27.117**

18. The objective is to measure a deferred tax liability or asset using the enacted tax rate(s) expected to apply to taxable income in the periods in which the deferred tax liability or asset is expected to be settled or realized. Under current US federal tax law, if taxable income exceeds a specified amount, all taxable income is taxed, in substance, at a single flat tax rate. That tax rate shall be used for measurement of a deferred tax liability or asset by enterprises for which graduated tax rates are not a significant factor. Enterprises for which graduated tax rates are a significant factor shall measure a deferred tax liability or asset using the average graduated tax rate applicable to the amount of estimated annual taxable income in the periods in which the deferred tax liability or asset is estimated to be settled or realized (paragraph 236). Other provisions of enacted tax laws should be considered when determining the tax rate to apply to certain types of temporary differences and carryforwards (for example, the tax law may provide for different tax rates on ordinary income and capital gains). If there is a phased-in change in tax rates, determination of the applicable tax rate requires knowledge about when deferred tax liabilities and assets will be settled and realized.

**An Enacted Change in Tax Laws or Rates**
**FAS109, Para 27 or Current Text I27.126**

27. Deferred tax liabilities and assets shall be adjusted for the effect of a change in tax laws or rates. The effects shall be included in income from continuing operations for the period that includes the enactment date.

5. What components of income tax expense that relate to continuing operations must be included in the notes to the financial statements?

**FAS109, Para 45 or Current Text I27.144**

45. The significant components of income tax expense attributable to continuing operations for each year presented shall be disclosed

in the financial statements or notes thereto. Those components would include, for example

a. Current tax expense or benefit
b. Deferred tax expense or benefit (exclusive of the effects of other components listed below)
c. Investment tax credits
d. Government grants (to the extent recognized as a reduction of income tax expense)
e. The benefits of operating loss carryforwards
f. Tax expense that results from allocating certain tax benefits either directly to contributed capital or to reduce goodwill to other noncurrent intangible assets of an acquired entity.
g. Adjustments of a deferred tax liability or asset for enacted changes in tax laws or rates or a change in the tax status of the enterprise.
h. Adjustments of the beginning-of-the-year balance of a valuation allowance because of a change in circumstances that causes a change in judgment about the realizability of the related deferred tax asset in future years.

## Simulation Problem 2

| Directions | Situation | Temporary and Permanent Differences | Deferred Tax Schedule | Calculate Taxable Income | Journal Entries | Disclosures | Communication | Research |
|---|---|---|---|---|---|---|---|---|

|  | Temporary | Permanent |
|---|---|---|
| Premiums on life insurance of key officer | ○ | ● |
| Depreciation | ● | ○ |
| Interest on municipal bonds | ○ | ● |
| Warranties | ● | ○ |
| Bad debts | ● | ○ |
| Rent received in advance from clients | ● | ○ |

| Directions | Situation | Temporary and Permanent Differences | Deferred Tax Schedule | Calculate Taxable Income | Journal Entries | Disclosures | Communication | Research |
|---|---|---|---|---|---|---|---|---|

| Item | Difference between taxable amount and income statement amount | Classification: Deferred tax asset Deferred tax liability | Current or noncurrent | Deferred tax amount |
|---|---|---|---|---|
| Depreciation | 12,000 | Deferred tax liability | Noncurrent | 4,800 |
| Warranties | 750 | Deferred tax asset | Current | 300 |
| Bad debts | 800 | Deferred tax asset | Current | 320 |
| Rent received | 8,000 | Deferred tax asset | Current | 3,200 |
| Rent received | 16,000 | Deferred tax asset | Noncurrent | 6,400 |

## Explanation of solutions

The adjustment to warranties is the difference between warranty expense deducted on the income statement and the actual warranty work performed during the period ($4,000 − $3,250 = $750). The adjustment to bad debt is the difference between bad debt expense subtracted on the balance sheet, and the actual bad debts written off during the period ($1,400 − $600 = $800). Note that rent received is taxable in the period received, and for deferred tax purposes, it must be fragmented into two components, current and noncurrent.

| Directions | Situation | Temporary and Permanent Differences | Deferred Tax Schedule | Calculate Taxable Income | Journal Entries | Disclosures | Communication | Research |
|---|---|---|---|---|---|---|---|---|

| Pretax financial income | $400,000 |
|---|---|
| Premiums on life insurance of key officer | 10,000 |
| Interest on municipal bonds | (5,300) |
| Depreciation for tax in excess of book depreciation | (12,000) |
| Adjustment for warranties | 750 |
| Adjustment for bad debts | 800 |
| Adjustment for rent received in advance | 24,000 |
| | |
| Taxable income | 418,250 |

| Directions | Situation | Temporary and Permanent Differences | Deferred Tax Schedule | Calculate Taxable Income | Journal Entries | Disclosures | Communication | Research |
|---|---|---|---|---|---|---|---|---|

| Account title | Debit | Credit |
|---|---|---|
| Deferred tax asset—Current | 3,820 | |
| Deferred tax asset—Noncurrent | 6,400 | |
| Tax expense | 161,880 | |
| Deferred tax liability—Noncurrent | | 4,800 |
| Income taxes payable | | 167,300 |
| | | |
| | | |

### Explanation of solutions

The total for deferred tax asset—current can be found by adding the current items in the deferred tax schedule in one of the previous simulation tasks.

| Directions | Situation | Temporary and Permanent Differences | Deferred Tax Schedule | Calculate Taxable Income | Journal Entries | Disclosures | Communication | Research |
|---|---|---|---|---|---|---|---|---|

| Deferred tax asset—Current | 3,820 |
|---|---|
| Deferred tax asset—Noncurrent | 1,600 |
| Deferred tax liability—Current | 0 |
| Deferred tax liability—Noncurrent | 0 |
| | |

### Explanation of solutions

The netting rules for deferred taxes require that current assets be netted against current deferred tax liabilities. Noncurrent deferred tax assets are netted against noncurrent deferred tax liabilities. Using the journal entries from the previous task, we find that total current deferred tax assets are $3,820. There are no current deferred tax liabilities. Netting noncurrent deferred tax assets and liabilities ($6,400 – $4,800) = $1,600 disclosed on the balance sheet as a noncurrent deferred tax asset.

| Directions | Situation | Temporary and Permanent Differences | Deferred Tax Schedule | Calculate Taxable Income | Journal Entries | Disclosures | Communication | Research |
|---|---|---|---|---|---|---|---|---|

To:   Mr. Dunn
From: Mr. Green, CPA
Re:   Accounting for income taxes

You have requested that I provide a brief overview of accounting for income taxes in accordance with SFAS 109. The objectives of accounting for income taxes are to recognize (1) the amount of taxes payable or refundable for the current year, and (2) deferred tax liabilities and assets for the estimated future tax consequences of temporary differences and carryforwards. Temporary differences are differences between the tax basis of assets or liabilities and their reported amounts in the financial statements that will result in taxable or deductible amounts in future years.

Deferred tax assets and liabilities are measured based on the provisions of enacted tax law; the effects of future changes in the tax laws or rates are not anticipated. The measurement of deferred tax assets is reduced, if necessary, by a valuation allowance to reflect the net asset amount that is more likely than not to be realized.  Deferred income tax expense or benefit is measured as the change during the year in an enterprise's deferred tax liabilities and assets.

   If you have any other questions, please contact me.

| Directions | Situation | Temporary and Permanent Differences | Deferred Tax Schedule | Calculate Taxable Income | Journal Entries | Disclosures | Communication | Research |
|---|---|---|---|---|---|---|---|---|

## FAS109, Para 16

16. An enterprise shall recognize a deferred tax liability or asset for all temporary differences and operating loss and tax credit carryforwards in accordance with the provisions of paragraph 17.  Deferred tax expense or benefit is the change during the year in an enterprise's deferred tax liabilities and assets.  For deferred tax liabilities and assets acquired in a purchase business combination during the year, it is the change since the combination date.  Total income tax expense or benefit for the year is the sum of deferred tax expense or benefit and income taxes currently payable or refundable.

## STOCKHOLDERS' EQUITY

Stockholders' equity is the residual of assets minus liabilities (i.e., net assets). Due to the number of fraudulent manipulations involving stocks, many states have legislated accounting for stockholders' equity transactions, and they are controlled to some degree (e.g., conditions under which dividends may be paid).

Common stockholders' equity consists of two major categories: contributed capital and retained earnings. Retained earnings are either appropriated or unappropriated. Paid-in consists of paid-in excess and legal capital. Legal capital is the par or stated value of stock. An outline of stockholders' equity follows:

- Contributed capital

  - Paid-in (e.g., common and preferred stock)

    - Legal—par, stated, no par
    - Paid-in capital in excess of par or stated value
    - Paid-in capital from other transactions

      - Treasury stock
      - Retirement of stock
      - Stock dividends recorded at market
      - Stock warrants detachable from bonds
      - Lapse of stock purchase warrants
      - Conversion of convertible bonds
      - Any other gain on the company's own stock transactions

- Retained earnings

  - Appropriated
  - Unappropriated

- Accumulated other comprehensive income
- Contra stockholders' equity item (deducted after contributed capital, retained earnings, and accumulated other comprehensive income above are totaled)

  - Treasury stock (cost method)

When significant changes occur in stockholders' equity accounts, enterprises are required to disclose them. Most companies satisfy this requirement by issuing a statement of changes in stockholders' equity (illustrated below). These statements show changes in the number of shares (not included due to space limits) as well as dollars between balance sheet dates. The statement of changes in stockholders' equity may also be used to report comprehensive income per SFAS 130 (see the second column in the following statement). This is the FASB's least preferable means of disclosing it. See Module 7D, page 361.

Disclosure requirements concerning information about an entity's capital structure is covered in SFAS 129 (see outline).

*Northern Corporation*
**STATEMENT OF CHANGES IN STOCKHOLDERS' EQUITY**
*For the Year Ended December 31, 2007*

| | Common stock | Comprehensive income | Retained earnings | Accumulated other comprehensive income | Total |
|---|---|---|---|---|---|
| Balances, January 1, 2007 | $1,500,000 | | $213,675 | $ (3,450) | $1,710,225 |
| Comprehensive income | | | | | |
| Net income | | $63,250 | 63,250 | | |
| Other comprehensive income: | | | | | |
| Foreign currency translation adjustments, net of tax | | 8,000 | | | |
| Unrealized gains on securities: | | | | | |
| Unrealized holding gains arising during period, net of tax | | 13,000 | | | |
| Less: reclassification adjustment, net of tax, for gain included in net income | | (4,000) | | | |
| Other comprehensive income | | 7,000 | | 17,000 | |
| Comprehensive income | | 80,250 | | | 80,250 |
| Proceeds from issuance of shares | 200,000 | | | | 200,000 |
| Dividends paid | -- | | (24,825) | | (24,825) |
| Balances, December 31, 2007 | $1,700,000 | | $252,100 | $13,550 | $1,965,650 |

## A. Common Stock

The entry to record the issuance of common stock is

| | |
|---|---|
| Cash | (amount received) |
|     Common stock | (par or stated value) |
|     Paid-in capital in excess of par | (forced) |

If stock is sold for less than par, a discount account is debited.

Very little stock is issued at a discount because of the resulting potential liability to the original purchaser for the difference between the issue price (when less than par) and par which in many states is legal capital. This liability has been avoided by the use of stated value and no par stock, but is mainly avoided by establishing par values below market.

Control accounts are occasionally used to control unissued stock. At authorization

| | |
|---|---|
| Unissued common stock | (total par or stated value) |
|     Common stock authorized | (same) |

At issuance

| | |
|---|---|
| Cash | (cash received) |
|     Unissued common stock | (par or stated value) |
|     Paid-in capital in excess of par | (forced) |

The credit balance in the authorized account is the total available for issuance. The debit balance in the unissued account is the amount not issued. Thus, authorized (cr) – unissued (dr) = issued (cr). The unissued account is an offset account to the authorized account.

No-par stock is occasionally issued (i.e., no par or stated value exists). All of the proceeds from issuance of no-par stock are credited to "common stock."

| | |
|---|---|
| Legal expenses | (FMV) |
| Assets | (FMV) |
|     Common stock | (par) |
|     Paid-in capital in excess of par | (forced) |

Costs of registering and issuing common stock are generally netted against the proceeds (i.e., reduce "paid-in capital in excess of par"). An alternative method is to consider stock issue costs an organizational cost.

## B. Preferred Stock

As implied, preferred stock has preferential rights: most commonly the right to receive dividends prior to common stockholders. Generally the dividend payout is specified (e.g., 7% of par). Additional possible features are

1. Participating—share with common stockholders in dividend distributions after both preferred and common stockholders receive a specified level of dividend payment

   a. Participation with common stockholders in dividends is usually specified in terms of a percentage of legal capital. For example, 7% preferred receive 7% of their par value in dividends before common stockholders receive dividends. Fully participating preferred would receive the same percentage dividend as common stockholders if the common stockholders received over a 7% (of par value) dividend.

2. Cumulative—dividends not paid in any year (dividends in arrears) must be made up before distributions can be made to common stockholders

   a. However, dividends in arrears are not a liability until declared. They should be disclosed parenthetically or in the footnotes.

3. Convertible—preferred stockholders have an option of exchanging their stock for common stock at a specified ratio

   a. Conversion is usually accounted for at book value

| | |
|---|---|
| Preferred stock | (par converted) |
| Preferred paid in accounts | (related balances) |
|     Common stock | (par) |
|     Paid-in capital in excess of par | (forced) |

   b. If market value is used, common stock and paid-in excess are credited for the market value, usually resulting in a large debit to retained earnings. (Plug figure in the journal entry.)

4.  Callable—the corporation has the option to repurchase the preferred stock at a specified price

    a.  If called, no gain or loss is recognized on the income statement. Gains are taken to a paid-in capital account; losses are charged to retained earnings.

    | | |
    |---|---|
    | Preferred stock | (par) |
    | Preferred paid in accounts | (related balances) |
    | Retained earnings | (if dr. needed) |
    |   Cash | (amount paid) |
    |   Paid-in capital from preferred retirement | (if cr. needed) |

Any of the above features present in a preferred stock issuance should be disclosed parenthetically in the balance sheet next to the account title.

SFAS 150, *Accounting for Certain Financial Instruments with Characteristics of Both Liabilities and Equity*, requires that any financial instrument that imposes an obligation on the issuer to transfer assets or issue equity shares be classified as a liability. Therefore, mandatorily redeemable preferred stock must be classified as liabilities on the balance sheet.

## C.  Stock Subscriptions

Stock (common/preferred) can be subscribed by investors. A receivable is established and "stock subscribed" credited. When the total subscription price is received, the stock (common/preferred) is issued.

At subscription

| | |
|---|---|
| Cash | (any cash received) |
| Subscription receivable | (balance) |
|   Common stock subscribed | (par) |
|   Paid-in capital in excess of par | (subscription price > par) |

Cash receipt and issuance

| | |
|---|---|
| Cash | (balance) |
|   Subscriptions receivable | (balance) |
| Common stock subscribed | (par) |
|   Common stock* | (par) |

\* *Unissued common stock, if unissued and authorized accounts are being used.*

Upon default of subscription agreements, depending on the agreement, the amount paid to date may be

1.  Returned to subscriber
2.  Kept by company
3.  Held to cover any losses on resale and balance returned

If returned

| | |
|---|---|
| Common stock subscribed | (par) |
| Paid-in capital in excess of par | (subscription price > par) |
|   Cash | (any cash received) |
|   Subscriptions receivable | (balance) |

If kept by the company, no cash would be paid and "paid-in from subscription default" credited instead of cash.

If held to cover any losses on resale, a "refundable subscription deposit" liability would be credited instead of cash. If the stock were resold at less than the original subscription price, the difference would be debited to "refundable subscription deposit."

| | |
|---|---|
| Cash | (payment) |
| Refundable subscription deposit | (forced) |
|   Stock | (par) |
|   Paid-in capital in excess of par | (amount from original sale) |

The balance in the refundable subscription account would be paid (possibly in an equivalent number of shares) to the original subscriber.

## D.  Treasury Stock Transactions

A firm's own stock repurchased on the open market is known as treasury stock. Treasury stock is **not** an asset, as a firm may not own shares of itself. Instead it is treated as a reduction of stockholders' equity. There are two methods of accounting for treasury stock: cost and par value.

1. **Cost Method**

   Under the **cost method,** treasury stock is debited for the cost of treasury stock. Any gain (loss) is recognized at the point of resale. However, such gains (losses) are not included in the determination of periodic income. Gains are credited to "paid-in capital from treasury stock transactions." Losses should be charged first to "paid-in capital from treasury stock (TS) transactions" or "paid-in capital from stock retirement" to the extent that either of these exists for that class of stock. The remainder of any loss is to be charged to retained earnings. In essence a one-transaction viewpoint is used, as the firm is treated as a middle "person" for the transfer of stock between two shareholders.

2. **Par Value Method**

   Under the **par value** method, all capital balances associated with the treasury shares are removed upon acquisition. Any excess of treasury stock cost over par value is accounted for by charging "paid-in capital from common stock" for the amount in excess of par received when the shares were originally issued. Any excess of the cost of acquiring the treasury stock over the original issue cost is charged to retained earnings. If treasury stock is acquired at a cost equal to or less than the original issue cost, "paid-in capital from common stock" is charged (debited) for the original amount in excess of par and "paid-in capital from treasury stock" is credited for the difference between the original issue price and the cost to acquire the treasury stock. When the treasury stock is resold, it is treated as a typical issuance, with the excess of selling price over par credited to "paid-in capital from common stock." Note that the par value method takes on a two-transaction viewpoint. The purchase is treated as a "retirement" of the shares, while the subsequent sale of the shares is treated as a "new" issue.

   *EXAMPLE:  100 shares ($50 par) are originally sold at $60, reacquired at $70, and subsequently resold at $75.*

| *Cost method* | | | *Par value method* | | |
|---|---|---|---|---|---|
| *Treasury stock* | *7,000* | | *Treasury stock* | *5,000* | |
| *Cash* | | *7,000* | *Paid-in capital—common stock* | *1,000* | |
| | | | *Retained earnings* | *1,000* | |
| | | | *Cash* | | *7,000* |
| *Cash* | *7,500* | | *Cash* | *7,500* | |
| *Treasury stock* | | *7,000* | *Treasury stock* | | *5,000* |
| *Paid-in capital—* | | | *Paid-in capital—common* | | |
| *treasury stock* | | *500* | *stock* | | *2,500* |

   *If the shares had been resold at $65:*

| *Cost method* | | | *Par value method* | | |
|---|---|---|---|---|---|
| *Cash* | *6,500* | | *Cash* | *6,500* | |
| *Retained earnings** | *500* | | *Treasury stock* | | *5,000* |
| *Treasury stock* | | *7,000* | *Paid-in capital—common stock* | | *1,500* |

   \* *"Paid-in capital—treasury stock" or "paid-in capital—retired stock" of that issue would be debited first to the extent it exists.*

   Note that total stockholders' equity is not affected by the method selected; only the allocation among the equity accounts is different.

E. **Retirement of Stock**

   Formal retirement or constructive retirement (purchase with no intent of reissue) of stock is handled very similarly to treasury stock. When formally retired

| Common stock | xx | |
|---|---|---|
| Paid-in capital in excess of par* | xx | |
| Retained earnings* | xx | |
| Treasury stock* | | xx |

   \* *Assuming a loss on the retirement of treasury stock*

1. "Paid-in capital from treasury stock transactions" may be debited to the extent it exists
2. A pro rata portion of all paid-in capital existing for that issue (e.g., if 2% of an issue is retired, up to 2% of all existing paid-in capital for that issue may be debited)

   Alternatively, the entire or any portion of the loss may be debited to retained earnings. Any gains are credited to a "paid-in capital from retirement" account.

F. **Dividends**

1. At the date of declaration, an entry is made to record the dividend liability.

| Retained earnings (dividends) | xx | |
|---|---|---|
| Dividends payable | | xx |

2.  No entry is made at the date of record.  Those owning stock at the date of record will be paid the previously declared dividends.

    a.  The stockholder records consist of

        (1)  General ledger account
        (2)  Subsidiary ledger

            (a)  Contains names and addresses of stockholders

        (3)  Stock certificate book

    b.  Outside services:  usually banks

        (1)  Transfer agent issues new certificates, canceling old, and maintains stockholder ledger
        (2)  Registrar validates new certificates and controls against overissuance
        (3)  Functions are now becoming combined

3.  At the payment date, the liability is paid.

    | | | |
    |---|---|---|
    | Dividends payable | xx | |
    | Cash | | xx |

4.  Property dividends are accounted for as cash dividends.  They are recorded at FMV of the asset transferred with a gain (loss) recognized on the difference between the asset's BV and FMV at disposition (see APB 29).

5.  Liquidation dividends (dividends based on other than earnings) are a return of capital to stockholders and should be so disclosed.  Paid-in capital is usually debited rather than retained earnings.  Common stock cannot be debited because it is the legal capital which can only be eliminated upon corporate dissolution.

6.  Scrip dividends are issuance of promises to pay dividends in the future (and may bear interest) instead of cash.

    | | | |
    |---|---|---|
    | Retained earnings | xx | |
    | Scrip dividends payable | | xx |

    Scrip dividends are a liability which is extinguished by payment.

    | | | |
    |---|---|---|
    | Scrip dividends payable | xx | |
    | Interest expense (maybe) | xx | |
    | Cash | | xx |

7.  Unlike cash and property dividends, stock dividends are not a liability when declared.  They can be rescinded, as nothing is actually being distributed to stockholders except more stock certificates.  Current assets are not used to "pay" the dividend.

    a.  After stock dividends, shareholders continue to own the same proportion of the corporation.
    b.  At declaration

        | | |
        |---|---|
        | Retained earnings | (FMV of shares) |
        | Stock dividend distributable | (par) |
        | Paid-in capital in excess of par | (plug) |

    c.  At issuance

        | | | |
        |---|---|---|
        | Stock dividend distributable | xx | |
        | Common stock | | xx |

    d.  Charge retained earnings for FMV of stock dividend if less than 20%-25% increase in stock outstanding; charge RE for **par value** of stock dividend if greater than 20-25% increase in stock outstanding.

        (1)  Not required if closely held company

## G.  Stock Splits

Stock splits change the number of shares outstanding and the par value per share.  Par value is reduced in proportion to the increase in the number of shares.  The total par value outstanding does not change and no charge is made to retained earnings.  If legal requirements preclude changing the par or stated value, charge retained earnings only for the par or stated value issued.

**STOCK DIVIDENDS AND SPLITS:  SUMMARY OF EFFECTS**

| | Total S.E. | Par value per share | Total par outstanding | RE | Legal capital | Additional paid-in capital | No. of shares outstanding |
|---|---|---|---|---|---|---|---|
| Stock dividend < 20-25% of shares outstanding | N/C | N/C | + | Decrease by market value of shares issued | + | + | + |
| Stock split effected in form of dividend > 20 – 25% of shares outstanding | N/C | N/C | + | Decrease by par value of shares issued | + | N/C | + |
| Stock split | N/C | Decrease proportionately | N/C | N/C | N/C | N/C | + |

*N/C = No Change*
*+ = Increase*
*Prepared by Professor John R. Simon, Northern Illinois University*

## H. Appropriations of Retained Earnings (Reserves)

An entry to appropriate retained earnings restricts the amount of retained earnings that is available for dividends.

```
RE (or Unappropriated RE)                        xx
     Reserve for RE (or Appropriated RE)          xx
```

It is important to note, however, that the restriction of retained earnings does not necessarily provide cash for any intended purpose.  The purpose is to show that **assets** in the amount of the appropriation are not available for dividends.  SFAS 5 requires that when a reserve is no longer needed it must be returned directly to unappropriated retained earnings by reversing the entry that created it.

## I. Share-Based Payments

SFAS 123 Revised, *Share-Based Payment*, was issued in December, 2004.  It is a revision of SFAS 123, Accounting for Stock-Based Compensation, and supersedes APB 25.

SFAS 123(R) applies to all share-based payment transactions wherein an entity acquires goods or services by issuing shares, share options, or other equity instruments.  It also applies to transactions with an employee or supplier wherein the entity incurs a liability that is based on the price of the entity's shares or that will be settled using equity shares.

There are two important distinctions for applying the rules in SFAS 123(R).

* Is the share-based payment to employees or nonemployees?
* Is the share-based payment considered equity or a liability?

**Share-based payments to nonemployees.**  Share-based payments to nonemployees for goods and services are measured at the fair value of the equity instruments or the fair value of the goods and services, whichever is more reliable.  EITF No. 96-18 specifies criteria for determining the measurement date for share-based payments to nonemployees.

**Share-based payments to employees.**  Share-based payments to employees are measured based on the fair-value-based method.  The costs of services are measured at the grant-date fair value of the equity instruments issued, or the fair value of the liability incurred.  Employee service cost is based on fair value net of any amount the employee pays or is obligated to pay for the instrument.

The fair value of an equity share option is measured based on the observable market price of an option with the same or similar terms and conditions, or it can be estimated using an option-pricing model.  If it is not possible to estimate fair value at grant-date, the compensation cost is measured using the intrinsic value at the end of each reporting period, and final compensation cost is measured at the settlement date.

Compensation cost for share-based employee compensation classified as equity is amortized straight-line over the requisite service period.  The **requisite service period** is the period in which the employee is required to provide services, which is often the vesting period.  The **service inception date** is the beginning of the requisite service period.  SFAS 123(R) requires firms to estimate the number of forfeitures.  No compensation cost is recognized if an employee forfeits shares because a service  or performance condition is not met.  However, if an employee renders the requisite service and the share option expires or is unexercised, previously recognized compensation cost is not reversed.

Although SFAS 150 specifically excludes transactions covered by the original SFAS 123, the new SFAS 123(R) provides that SFAS 150 will apply in determining whether certain financial instruments in share-based payments are treated as liabilities.  Puttable shares are considered liabilities if the repurchase feature allows the employee to avoid bearing the risks and rewards for a reasonable period (six months or more).

The measurement date for liability instruments is the settlement date; therefore, share-based payments are remeasured at the end of each reporting period. Compensation cost is the change in fair value of the instrument for each reporting period.

| Share-Based Payments | | |
|---|---|---|
| | Classified as Equity | Classified as Liability |
| When to measure | Grant-date fair value of equity instrument | Each reporting period. Final measurement on settlement date. |
| How to measure | Observable market price of option with same or similar terms OR Estimate using options pricing model OR Intrinsic value at end of each reporting period if no market price or estimate (net of amounts that employee must pay) | Fair value of liability incurred |
| How to allocate compensation expense | Straight-line over requisite service period | Straight-line over requisite service period |

## J.   Accounting Entries for the Share-Based Payments to Employees

### 1.   Share-based payments classified as equity

If an option-pricing model (such as Black-Scholes model) is used, the options pricing model should consider the following variables:

a.   Current price of the underlying stock
b.   Exercise price of the option
c.   Expected life of the option
d.   Expected volatility of the underlying stock
e.   Expected dividends on the stock
f.   Risk-free interest rate during the expected option term

The resulting fair value shall be applied to the number of options expected to vest (based on the grant date estimate) or the total number of options issued.

To illustrate the recognition and measurement of stock compensation expense, suppose ABC Corporation (a public company) establishes an employee stock option plan on January 1, 2008. The plan allows its employees to acquire 10,000 shares of its $1 par value common stock at $52 per share, when the market price is also $52. The options may not be exercised until five years from the grant date. The grant-date fair value of an option with similar terms and conditions is $8.62.

*Accounting for Stock Based Compensation*
*Calculation of Compensation Cost*

| | |
|---|---|
| Fair Value of Option at grant-date | $  8.62 |
| Times number of options | 10,000 |
| Deferred comp. expense | $86,200 |

The journal entry to recognize the deferred compensation expense in Year 1 is shown below.

| | | |
|---|---|---|
| Deferred comp. expense | 86,200 | |
| Stock options outstanding | | 86,200 |

During each of the next five years which is the requisite service period, compensation expense is recognizes as follows:

| | | |
|---|---|---|
| Compensation expense | 17,240 | |
| Deferred comp. expense | | 17,240 |

When the option is exercised, cash is received and stock is issued as reflected in the following entry (assume exercise after the five-year period):

| | | |
|---|---|---|
| Cash | 52,000 | (option price) |
| Stock options outstanding | 86,200 | |
|     Common stock | 10,000 | (par) |
|     Additional paid-in capital | 128,200 | (plug) |

If modifications are made to a shared-based payment plan, the incremental compensation cost is measured by comparing the fair value of the modified plan with the fair value of the plan immediately before the modification.

Deferred compensation is presented in the balance sheet by subtracting the balance in the deferred compensation account from stock options outstanding in the paid-in capital section of owners' equity to indicate the net contributed services on any date.

2. **Share-based payments classified as liabilities.**

When a share-based payment is treated as a liability, it is measured at the fair value of the liability incurred. The measurement date is the date of settlement. Therefore, the liability is remeasured at the end of each reporting period until the date of settlement. Compensation cost for each period is based on the change in fair value of the instrument for each reporting period. If the requisite service period has not been completed, the compensation cost recognized is equal to the percentage of the requisite service that has been rendered as of that date.

An example of share-based payment classified as a liability is a stock appreciation right. Stock appreciation rights (SAR) allow employees to receive stock or cash equal in amount to the difference between the market value and some predetermined amount per share for a certain number of shares. SARs allow employees to receive share appreciation without having to make a cash outlay as is common in stock option plans.

For financial reporting purposes, compensation expense is the excess of market value over a predetermined amount. Compensation expense is recorded in each period prior to exercise based on the excess of market value at the end of each period over a predetermined amount. Compensation expense is adjusted up or down as the market value of the stock changes before the measurement date (which is the exercise date). Therefore, compensation expense could be credited if the stock's market value drops from one period to the next.

*EXAMPLE: Assume a company grants 100 SAR, payable in cash, to an employee on 1/1/08. The predetermined amount for the SAR plan is $50 per right, and the market value of the stock is $55 on 12/31/08, $53 on 12/31/09, and $61 on 12/31/10. Compensation expense recorded in each year would be*

*Total expense – Exp. previously accrued = Current expense*

| | | | | | |
|---|---|---|---|---|---|
| 2008 | 100 ($55 – $50) | = | $ 500 – $ 0 | = | $ 500 |
| 2009 | 100 ($53 – $50) | = | $ 300 – $500 | = | $ (200) |
| 2010 | 100 ($61 – $50) | = | $1,100 – $300 | = | $ 800 |

*The total expense recognized over the three-year period is $1,100 [100($61 – $50)]. Journal entries would be*

| 2008 and 2010 | | 2009 | |
|---|---|---|---|
| *Compensation expense* | *$500/$800* | *Liability under SAR plan* | *$200* |
|     *Liability under SAR plan* | *$500/$800* |     *Compensation expense* | *$200* |

*[If the SAR were to be redeemed in common stock, Stock Rights Outstanding (a paid-in capital account) would replace the liability account in the above entries.]*

*The above example assumes no service or vesting period, which is the period of time until the SAR become exercisable. If the above plan had a two-year service period, 50% of the total expense would be recognized at the end of the first year, and 100% at the end of the second year and thereafter until exercised. The compensation would be accrued as follows:*

| | | | | | | |
|---|---|---|---|---|---|---|
| 2008 | $ (500) | (50%) | = | $ 250 – $ 0 | = | $250 |
| 2009 | $ (300) | (100%) | = | $ 300 – $250 | = | $ 50 |
| 2010 | $(1,100) | (100%) | = | $1,100 – $300 | = | $800 |

3. **Disclosures**

Excess tax benefits are recognized as additional paid in capital. Cash retained as a result of excess tax benefits are presented in the statement of cash flows as a cash inflow from financing activities (not as a reduction of taxes paid). Diluted earnings per share is based on the actual number of options or shares granted and not yet forfeited, unless the shares are antidilutive. If equity share options are outstanding for only a part of a period, the shares are weighted to reflect the portion of time outstanding.

Disclosures for share-based payments should include the following:

- The nature and terms of arrangements during the period and potential effects on shareholders
- The effect of compensation cost from share-based arrangements on the income statement
- The method of estimating the fair value of goods or services received, or fair value of the equity instruments granted during the period
- The cash flow effects from share-based payments

## K. Basic Earnings Per Share

CPA candidates must be able to compute both basic and diluted earnings per share (EPS). In addition to the computations, candidates should also understand the presentation and disclosure requirements. Only public entities (those who trade their stock on the major stock exchanges and over the counter) are required to present earnings per share. Nonpublic companies often choose to present such information, but they are not required to do so. Before continuing, it is recommended that candidates read the outline of SFAS 128, *Earnings Per Share,* in the back of the FARE section.

The objective of EPS is to measure the performance of an entity over the reporting period. Required presentation calls for a **basic** EPS in all situations and a **diluted** EPS in those situations where an entity's capital structure includes potential dilutive securities. Basic and dilutive (when applicable) earnings per share amounts must be presented on the face of the income statement for two elements.

1. Income from continuing operations **and**
2. Net income

In those situations where an entity also reports discontinued operations, extraordinary items, and/or cumulative effects of an accounting change in principle, the entity **may report** EPS on the face of the income statement or disclose such information in the footnotes to the financial statements. Note that the only required EPS presentations are for income from continuing operations and net income. All other presentations of EPS are optional.

Public corporations begin by computing **basic** earnings per share. In this calculation, only those shares of common stock **outstanding** are included. Any **potential** issuance of securities is **ignored**. The computational formula is as follows:

$$\text{Basic EPS} = \frac{\text{Net income available to common stockholders}}{\text{Weighted-average number of common shares \textbf{outstanding}}}$$

The **numerator** (net income available to common stockholders) for EPS on **net income** is computed by taking the **net income** and **subtracting**

1. The dividends **declared** in the period on the **noncumulative preferred stock** (whether paid or not) **and**
2. The dividends **accumulated** for the period on the **cumulative preferred stock** (whether or not declared).

The **numerator** (net income available to common stockholder1s) for EPS on **net income from continuing operations** is computed by taking the **net income** and subtracting any net income or adding any net loss from the following:

- Discontinued operations
- Extraordinary items
- Cumulative effect of a change in accounting principle.

The net income from continuing operations is then adjusted by subtracting the preferred stock dividends as described in points number 1. and 2. above.

The following example will illustrate the application of this formula:

| *Numerator information* | | *Denominator information* | |
|---|---|---|---|
| a. Net income | $100,000 | a. Common shares outstanding | |
| b. Extraordinary loss | | 1/1/07 | 100,000 |
| (net of tax) | 30,000 | b. Shares issued for cash 4/1 | 20,000 |
| c. 6% preferred stock, | | c. Shares issued in 10% stock | |
| $100 par, 1,000 shares | | dividend declared in July | 12,000 |
| issued and outstanding | | d. Shares of treasury stock | |
| ($100,000 × .06) | 6,000 | purchased 10/1 | 10,000 |

Earnings per common share:

On income from continuing operations $= \dfrac{\$130,000 - 6,000}{\text{Common shares outstanding}}$

Our net income $= \dfrac{\$100,000 - 6,000}{\text{Common shares outstanding}}$

When calculating the amount of the numerator, the claims of senior securities (i.e., preferred stock) should be deducted to arrive at the earnings attributable to common shareholders. In the example, the preferred stock is cumulative. Thus, regardless of whether or not the board of directors declares a preferred dividend, holders of the preferred stock have a claim of $6,000 (1,000 shares × $6 per share) against 2007 earnings. Therefore, $6,000 is deducted from the numerator to arrive at the net income attributable to common shareholders. Note that this $6,000 would have been **deducted for noncumulative preferred only if a dividend of this amount had been declared**. Cumulative preferred stock dividends are always deducted whether or not declared.

The numerator of the EPS calculation covers a particular time period such as a month, a quarter, or a year. It is, therefore, consistent to calculate the average number of common shares which were outstanding during this same time period. The calculation below in Table I illustrates the determination of weighted-average common shares outstanding. Note that for stock dividends the number of shares is adjusted retroactively for the shares which were outstanding prior to the stock dividend. Since the stock dividend was issued **after** the issuance of additional shares for cash on 4/1, the shareholders of those additional shares and the shareholders of the shares outstanding at the beginning of the year will receive the stock dividend. However, if the stock dividend had been issued **before** the issuance of additional shares of stock for cash on 4/1, only the shareholders who own the shares outstanding at the beginning of the period would have received the stock dividend. Stock splits are handled in an identical fashion.

*TABLE 1*

| *Dates* | *Number common shares outstanding* | *Months outstanding* | *Fraction of year* | *Shares × Fraction of year* |
|---|---|---|---|---|
| 1/1 to 4/1 | 100,000 + 10% (100,000) = 110,000 | 3 | ¼ | 27,500 |
| 4/1 to 10/1 | 110,000 + 20,000 + 10% (20,000) = 132,000 | 6 | ½ | 66,000 |
| 10/1 to 12/31 | 132,000 – 10,000 = 122,000 | 3 | ¼ | 30,500 |
| | Weighted-average of common shares outstanding | | | 124,000 |

In the weighted-average computation, if common shares are issued in a business combination during the year, the common shares are weighted from the date of issuance. Other complications in the weighted-average calculation are posed by actual conversions of debt and preferred stock to common during the year and by exercise of warrants and options. These situations are introduced in the example presented with diluted earnings per share in the next section.

To complete the basic EPS example, the weighted-average number of common shares determined in Table I is divided into the income elements previously computed to arrive at the following:

Earnings per common share

On income from continuing operations $\dfrac{\$130,000 - 6,000}{124,000 \text{ common shares}} = \$1,000$

On net income $\dfrac{\$100,000 - 6,000}{124,000 \text{ common shares}} = \$ \ .76$

The above EPS numbers should be presented on the face of the income statement. Reporting a $.24 loss per share due to the extraordinary item is optional.

## L. Diluted Earnings Per Share

Diluted EPS measures the performance of the entity over the reporting period (same as basic EPS) while also taking into account the effect of all dilutive potential common shares that were outstanding during the period. The only difference in the computation of diluted and basic EPS is that the denominator of the diluted EPS computation is increased to include the number of additional common shares that would have been outstanding if the dilutive potential common shares had been issued. In addition, the numerator is adjusted to add back any convertible preferred dividends, the after-tax amount of interest recognized in the period associated with any convertible debt, and any other changes in income (loss) that would result from the assumed conversion of the potential common shares. Diluted EPS should be based on the security holder's most advantageous conversion rate or exercise price. Similar to basic EPS, all antidilutive securities are disregarded.

The following two independent examples will illustrate the procedures necessary to calculate basic and diluted EPS. For both examples, assume net income is $50,000, and the weighted-average of common shares outstanding is 10,000.

In the first example, assume the following additional information with respect to the capital structure:

1.  4% nonconvertible, cumulative preferred stock, par $100, 1,000 shares issued and outstanding the entire year
2.  Options and warrants to purchase 1,000 shares of common stock at $8 per share. The average market price of common stock during the year was $10 and the closing market price was $12 per share. The options and warrants were outstanding all year.

Diluted EPS must be computed because of the presence of the options and warrants. The preferred stock is not convertible; therefore, it is not a potentially dilutive security.

The first step in the solution of this problem is the determination of the basic EPS. This calculation appears as follows:

$$\frac{\text{Net income} - \text{Preferred dividends}}{\text{Weighted-average of common shares}} = \frac{\$50,000 - 4,000}{10,000 \text{ shares}} = \$4.60$$

Note that preferred dividends are deducted to arrive at net income applicable to common stock. When preferred stock is cumulative, this deduction is made whether or not dividends have been declared.

The calculation of diluted EPS is based upon outstanding common stock and all dilutive common shares that were outstanding during the period. In the example, the options and warrants are the only potentially dilutive security. Options and warrants are considered to be common stock equivalents at all times. Consequently, the only question that must be resolved is whether or not the options and warrants are dilutive. This question is resolved by comparing the average market price per common share of $10 with the exercise price of $8. If the average market price is > the exercise price, the effect of assuming the exercise of options and warrants is dilutive. However, if the average market price is ≤ the exercise price, the effect of assuming the exercise of options and warrants would be antidilutive (i.e., EPS would stay the same or increase). In the example, the options and warrants are dilutive ($10 > $8).

The method used to determine the dilutive effects of options and warrants is called the **treasury stock method**.

In the example above, all of the options and warrants are assumed to be exercised at the beginning of the year (the options and warrants were outstanding the entire year) and the cash received is used to reacquire shares (treasury stock) at the average market price. The computation below illustrates the "treasury stock" method.

| | |
|---|---:|
| Proceeds from assumed exercise of options and warrants (1,000 shares × $8) | <u>$8,000</u> |
| Number of shares issued | 1,000 |
| Number of shares reacquired ($8,000 ÷ $10) | <u>800</u> |
| Number of shares assumed issued and not reacquired | <u>200</u>* |

\* *An alternative approach that can be used to calculate this number for diluted EPS is demonstrated below.*

$$\frac{Average\ market\ price - Exercise\ price}{Average\ market\ price} \quad \times \quad Number\ of\ shares\ under\ options/warrants \quad = \quad Shares\ not\ reacquired$$

$$\frac{\$10-8}{\$10} \quad \times \quad 1{,}000\ shares \quad = \quad 200\ shares$$

Diluted EPS can now be calculated, as follows, including the effects of applying the "treasury stock" method.

$$\frac{Net\ income - Preferred\ dividends}{\substack{Weighted\text{-}average\ of\ common\ shares \\ outstanding + Number\ of\ shares\ not\ acquired \\ with\ proceeds\ from\ options\ and\ warrants}} = \frac{\$50{,}000 - 4{,}000}{10{,}000 + 200\ shares} = \$4.51$$

Note the incremental effects of the treasury stock method; there was no effect on the numerator of the EPS calculation while there were 200 shares added to the denominator. Note also that the options and warrants are dilutive. EPS is reduced from $4.60 to $4.51.

Table II summarizes the calculations made for the first example involving diluted EPS.

TABLE II

| | Basic EPS | | Diluted EPS | |
|---|---|---|---|---|
| *Items* | *Numerator* | *Denominator* | *Numerator* | *Denominator* |
| Net income | $50,000 | | $50,000 | |
| Preferred div. | (4,000) | | (4,000) | |
| Common shares out-standing | | 10,000 shs. | | 10,000 shs. |
| Options and warrants | | | | 200 |
| Totals | $46,000 ÷ | 10,000 shs. | $46,000 ÷ | 10,200 shs. |
| EPS | | $4.60 | | $4.51 |

For the second example, assume the following additional information about the capital structure (net income of $50,000 and common shares of 10,000 as in previous example).

1. 8% convertible debt, 200 bonds each convertible into 40 common shares. The bonds were outstanding the entire year. The average AA corporate bond yield was 10% at the date the bonds were issued. The income tax rate is 40%. The bonds were issued at par ($1,000 per bond). No bonds were converted during the year.

2. 4% convertible, cumulative preferred stock, par $100, 1,000 shares issued and outstanding. Each preferred share is convertible into 2 common shares. The preferred stock was outstanding the entire year, and the average AA corporate bond yield at the date the preferred stock was issued was 10%. The preferred stock was issued at par. No preferred stock was converted during the year.

The capital structure is complex in this example because of the presence of the two convertible securities. The first step in the solution of this example is the calculation of basic EPS based upon weighted-average of common shares outstanding. This EPS is the same as it was for the first example (i.e., $4.60). The next step is the computation of diluted EPS. The diluted EPS computation will include the convertible preferred stock if it is dilutive.

To determine the dilutive effect of the preferred stock, an assumption (called the **if converted method**) is made that all of the preferred stock is converted at the earliest date that it could have occurred during the year. In this example, the date would be January 1. The effects of this assumption are twofold. One, if the preferred stock is converted, there will be no preferred dividend of $4,000 for the year; and, two, there will be an additional 2,000 shares of common stock outstanding during the year (the conversion rate is 2 common for 1 preferred). EPS is computed, as follows, reflecting these two assumptions.

$$\frac{Net\ income}{\substack{Weighted\text{-}average\ of\ common\ shares \\ outstanding + Shares\ issued\ upon\ conversion \\ of\ preferred\ stock}} = \frac{\$50{,}000}{10{,}000 + 2{,}000\ shares} = \$4.17$$

The convertible preferred stock is dilutive because it reduced EPS from $4.60 to $4.17.

In the example, the convertible bonds are assumed to have been converted at the beginning of the year. The effects of this assumption are twofold. One, if the bonds are converted, there will be no interest expense of $16,000 (8% × $200,000 face value); and, two, there will be an additional 8,000 shares (200 bonds × 40 shares) of common stock outstanding during the year. One note of caution, however, must be mentioned; namely, the effect of not having $16,000 of interest expense will increase income, but it will also increase tax expense. Consequently, the net effect of not having interest expense is $9,600 [$16,000 – (40% × $16,000)]. Diluted EPS is computed, as follows, reflecting the dilutive preferred stock and the effects noted above for the convertible bonds:

$$\frac{\text{Net income + Interest expense (net of tax)}}{\substack{\text{Weighted-average of common shares} \\ \text{outstanding + Shares issued upon conversion} \\ \text{of preferred and conversion of bonds}}} = \frac{\$50,000 + 9,600}{10,000 + 2,000 + 8,000 \text{ shares}} = \$2.98$$

The convertible debt is dilutive. Both the convertible bonds and preferred stock reduced EPS from $4.60 to $2.98. Table III summarizes the computations made for the second example.

The income statement disclosures for EPS, as a result of the second example, would be as follows:

|  |  |
|---|---|
| Earnings per common share (see Note X) | $4.60 |
| Earnings per common share assuming dilution | 2.98 |

Note X would state the assumptions made in determining both basic and diluted EPS numbers.

### TABLE III

| Items | Basic EPS Numerator | Basic EPS Denominator | Diluted EPS Numerator | Diluted EPS Denominator |
|---|---|---|---|---|
| Net income | $50,000 |  | $50,000 |  |
| Preferred div. | (4,000) |  |  |  |
| Common shares outstanding |  | 10,000 shs. |  | 10,000 shs. |
| Conversion of preferred |  |  |  | 2,000 |
| Conversion of bonds |  |  | 9,600 | 8,000 |
| Totals | $46,000 | ÷ 10,000 shs. | $59,600 | ÷ 20,000 shs. |
| EPS | $4.60 |  | $2.98 |  |

In the two examples, all of the potentially dilutive securities were outstanding the entire year and no conversions or exercises were made during the year. If a potentially dilutive security was not outstanding the entire year, then the numerator and denominator effects would have to be "time-weighted." For instance, suppose the convertible bonds in the second example were issued during the current year on July 1. If all other facts remain unchanged, diluted EPS would be computed as follows:

$$\frac{\text{Net income + Interest expense (net of tax)}}{\substack{\text{Weighted-average of common shares} \\ \text{outstanding + Shares issued upon conversion} \\ \text{of preferred and conversion of bonds}}} = \frac{\$50,000 + 1/2\,(9,600)}{10,000 + 2,000 + \frac{1}{2}(8,000)} = \$3.43$$

The convertible debt is dilutive whether or not it is outstanding the entire year or for part of a year.

If actual conversions or exercises take place during a period, the common shares issued will be outstanding from their date of issuance and, therefore, will be in the weighted-average of common shares outstanding. These shares are then weighted from their respective times of issuance. For example, assume that all the bonds in the second example are converted on July 1 into 8,000 common shares. Several important effects should be noted, as follows:

1.  The weighted-average of common shares outstanding will be increased by (8,000)(.5) or 4,000. Income will increase $4,800 net of tax, because the bonds are no longer outstanding.
2.  The "if converted" method is applied to the period January 1 to July 1 because it was during this period that the bonds were potentially dilutive. The interest expense, net of tax, of $4,800 is added to the income, and 4,000 shares (.5 of 8,000) are added to the denominator.
3.  Interestingly, the net effect of items 1 and 2 is the same for the period whether these dilutive bonds were outstanding the entire period or converted during the period.

It should also be noted that when convertible debt is issued for a premium or discount, the interest expense net of taxes must be computed after giving effect to premium/discount amortization.

The benchmark used to determine if including individual securities decreases income is income from continuing operations unless an enterprise has no discontinued operations. In that case income before extraordinary items or cumulative effect would be the benchmark number.

**Contingent issuances of common stock.** Also mentioned are **contingent issuances** of common stock (e.g., stock subscriptions). If shares are to be issued in the future with no restrictions on issuance other than the passage of time, they are to be considered issued and treated as outstanding in the computation of dilutive EPS (SFAS 128). Other issuances that are dependent upon certain conditions being met are to be evaluated in a different respect. SFAS 128 uses as examples the maintenance of current earnings levels and the attainment of specified earnings increases. If the contingency is to merely maintain the earnings levels currently being attained, then the shares are considered outstanding for the entire period and considered in the computation of dilutive EPS if the effect is dilutive. If the requirement is to increase earnings over a period of time, the diluted EPS computation shall include those shares that would be issued based on the assumption that current amount of earnings will remain unchanged, if the effect is dilutive.

**EPS on comprehensive income and other comprehensive income components.** EPS numbers below net income are not required per SFAS 130 for comprehensive income components.

## M. Corporate Bankruptcy

The going concern assumption is one of the basic principles underlying the primary financial statements (balance sheet, income statement and statement of cash flows). However, this assumption of continued existence is threatened in corporations that are in severe financial trouble. A range of alternative actions is available to a company before it enters bankruptcy, such as seeking extensions on due dates of debt, restructuring its debt, or allowing a court-appointed trustee to manage the corporation. These prebankruptcy options are presented in the following modules:

> Creditor's agreements—Module 27, Bankruptcy
> Troubled debt restructurings—Module 11, Present Value, Section C

Bankruptcy is the final legal act for a company. In bankruptcy, the accounting and financial reporting must present the information necessary for the liquidation of the business. The **Statement of Affairs** is prepared to present the current market values of the assets and the status of the various categories of the equity interests of the corporation.

The accountant must provide a prioritization of the creditors' claims against the net assets of the corporation. The legal rights of each creditor are determined by the terms of the credit agreement it has with the company and by the National Bankruptcy Act.

The **Statement of Affairs** classifies assets in the following order of priority (highest to lowest):

1. Assets pledged with fully secured creditors—assets having a fair valuation equal to or greater than the debts for which they serve as collateral
2. Assets pledged with partially secured creditors—assets having a fair valuation less than their associated debts
3. Free assets—uncommitted assets available for remaining equity interests

The equity interests are classified in the following order (highest to lowest):

1. Preferred claims—these claims have priority as specified in the Bankruptcy Act
2. Fully secured creditors—these are claims which should be fully covered with the realizations from the assets pledged to the claims
3. Partially secured creditors—these are claims which may not be fully covered by the realizations of the pledged assets for these claims; the amount of the uncovered claims goes to the unsecured creditors category
4. Unsecured creditors—these are claims that have no priority and do not have any collateral claims to any specific assets
5. Stockholders' equity—this represents any residual claim

The historical cost valuation principles used in a balance sheet assume a going concern assumption. As a business enters bankruptcy, the liquidation values of the assets become the most relevant measures. In addition, anticipated costs of liquidation should be recognized. The Statement of Affairs begins with the present book values of the company's assets in order to articulate with the balance sheet. After relating the projected proceeds from the liquidation of the assets to the various equity interests, the statement concludes with the estimated dollar amount of unsecured claims that cannot be paid (estimated deficiency).

> EXAMPLE: The Vann Corporation's balance sheet for December 31, 2007, is shown below. The corporation is entering bankruptcy and expects to incur $8,000 of costs for the liquidation process. The estimated current values of the assets are determined and the various equity claims are prioritized. The Statement of Affairs for Vann Corporation is presented on the following page.

**The Vann Corporation**
**BALANCE SHEET**
*December 31, 2007*

*Assets*

| | |
|---|---|
| Cash | $ 1,500 |
| Marketable securities | 10,000 |
| Accounts receivable (net) | 18,000 |
| Merchandise inventory | 41,000 |
| Prepaid expenses | 2,000 |
| Land | 6,000 |
| Building (net of depreciation) | 65,000 |
| Machinery (net of depreciation) | 21,000 |
| Goodwill | 10,000 |
| | $174,500 |

*Equities*

| | |
|---|---|
| Accounts payable | $ 30,000 |
| Notes payable | 37,000 |
| Accrued wages | 6,500 |
| Mortgages payable | 45,000 |
| Capital stock ($10 par) | 100,000 |
| Retained earnings (deficit) | (44,000) |
| | $174,500 |

## N. Reorganizations

Chapter 11 of the Bankruptcy Reform Act of 1978 allows legal protection from creditors to provide time for a bankrupt corporation to return its operations to a profitable level. SOP 90-7 provides guidance for financial reporting during Chapter 11 reorganizations. The SOP requires the balance sheet, income statement, and statement of cash flows to distinguish events and transactions related with the reorganization from those related to ongoing operations. Liabilities should be reported at expected amounts per the plan on the balance sheet. Liabilities should be classified as unsecured or secured liabilities before reorganization and liabilities incurred after the filing date for Chapter 11. Transactions directly related to the reorganization should be reported separately on the income statement in the period incurred, and disclosure should be made of any anticipated changes in common stock or common stock equivalents. Cash flows related to the reorganization should be reported separately from those related to regular operations. At confirmation of the plan of reorganization, an entity may be considered a new entity for reporting purposes if the reorganization value of assets before confirmation is less than liabilities incurred after petition for Chapter 11 and voting shareholders before confirmation receive less than 50% of the voting shares of the emerging entity. If the entity does not qualify as a new entity, the reorganization should be accounted for as troubled debt restructuring which is discussed in Module 11C.

## O. Quasi Reorganization (ARB 43, Chapter 7A)

The purpose of a quasi reorganization is to allow companies to avoid formal bankruptcy proceedings through an informal proceeding. The procedure is applicable for a situation where a going concern exists except for overvalued assets and a possible deficit. The overvalued assets result in high depreciation charges and losses or lower net income. The deficit precludes payment of dividends.

The procedure is applicable during a period of declining price levels (normally associated with decreased economic activity), such as the 1930s.

The procedures involve

1. Proper authorization including that from stockholders and creditors where required
2. Revaluation of assets to current values
3. Elimination of any deficit by charging paid-in capital

   a. First, capital surplus
   b. Second, capital stock

To write down assets: here the adjustments are taken directly to retained earnings. An alternative is to use an intermediary account such as "adjustment account" which would later be closed to retained earnings.

| | | |
|---|---|---|
| Retained earnings | (write-down) | |
| Assets | | (write-down) |

## The Vann Corporation
### STATEMENT OF AFFAIRS
#### December 31, 2007

**ASSETS**

| Book values | | Estimated current values | Amount available to unsecured claims |
|---|---|---|---|
| | (1) Assets Pledged with Fully Secured Creditors: | | |
| $ 6,000 | Land | $12,000 | |
| 65,000 | Building | 41,000 | |
| | | $53,000 | |
| | Less Mortgages Payable | 45,000 | $ 8,000 |
| | (2) Assets Pledged with Partially Secured Creditors: | | |
| 10,000 | Marketable Securities | $12,000 | |
| | Notes Payable | 37,000 | |
| | (3) Free Assets | | |
| 1,500 | Cash | 1,500 | |
| 18,000 | Accounts Receivable (net) | 14,000 | |
| 41,000 | Merchandise Inventory | 22,500 | |
| 2,000 | Prepaid Expenses | 0 | |
| 21,000 | Machinery | 13,200 | |
| 10,000 | Goodwill | 0 | 51,200 |
| | Estimated amount available | | 59,200 |
| | Less: creditors with priority | | (14,500) |
| | Net Estimated amount available to unsecured creditors (81 cents on the dollar) | | 44,700 |
| | Estimated deficiency to unsecured creditors | | 10,300 |
| $ 174,500 | | | $55,000 |

**EQUITIES**

| Book values | | | Amount unsecured |
|---|---|---|---|
| | (1) Creditors with Priority | | |
| 0 | Estimated Liquidation Expenses (accounting, legal and other costs of liquidation process) | $ 8,000 | |
| 6,500 | Accrued Wages | 6,500 | |
| | | $14,500 | |
| | (2) Fully Secured Creditors | | |
| 45,000 | Mortgages Payable | 45,000 | |
| | (3) Partially Secured Creditors | | |
| 37,000 | Notes Payable | 37,000 | |
| | Less Marketable Securities | 12,000 | 25,000 |
| | (4) Unsecured Creditors | | |
| 30,000 | Accounts Payable | | 30,000 |
| | (5) Stockholders' Equity | | |
| 100,000 | Capital Stock | | |
| (44,000) | Retained Earnings (deficit) | | |
| $ 174,500 | | | $55,000 |

To eliminate the deficit

| Paid-in capital | (deficit) | |
|---|---|---|
| Retained earnings | | (deficit) |

In many cases, paid-in capital in excess of par value will be insufficient, and the par or stated value of the capital stock must be reduced to eliminate the deficit.

| Existing paid-in capital | (amount on the books) | |
|---|---|---|
| Capital stock | (total reduction in par) | |
| Retained earnings | | (deficit) |
| Paid-in capital from | | |
| quasi reorganization | | (forced figure) |

The paid-in capital arises from reducing the par or stated value from, for example, $100 to $50 rather than to $59.415. The $59.415 would come from dividing the shares outstanding into the retained earnings deficit.

ARB 46 requires retained earnings to be dated for ten years (less than ten years justified under exceptional circumstances) after a quasi reorganization takes place. Disclosure similar to "since quasi reorganization of June 30, 2001," would be appropriate.

## P.  Stock Rights

Generally, before additional stock is offered to the public, stock rights are issued to existing shareholders to prevent involuntary dilution of their voting rights (e.g., the preemptive privilege). The stock rights, evidenced by warrants, indicate the number and price at which the shares may be purchased. At issuance, the issuer makes only a memorandum entry. Upon exercise, the following entry is made:

| Cash | (proceeds) | |
|---|---|---|
| Common stock | | (par) |
| Paid-in capital | | (plug) |

Information relating to stock rights outstanding must be disclosed. Detachable stock rights issued with preferred stock are treated like those on bonds (see Module 11, Section B.6.). Treatment of stock rights by recipients is discussed in Module 14, Section F.

## Q.  Employee Stock Ownership Plan (ESOP)

An employee stock ownership plan (ESOP) is a qualified stock bonus plan designed to invest primarily in qualifying employer securities, including stock and other marketable obligations. In some instances, the ESOP will borrow funds from a bank or other lender in order to acquire shares of the employer's stock. If such an obligation of the ESOP is guaranteed by the employer (assumption by the employer of the ESOP's debt), it should be recorded as a liability in the employer's financial statements. The offsetting debit to the liability should be accounted for as a reduction of shareholders' equity. Shareholders' equity will increase symmetrically with the reduction of the liability as the ESOP makes payments on the debt. Assets held by an ESOP should not be included in the employer's financial statements, because such assets are owned by the employees, not the employer. Additionally, the employer should charge to compensation expense the amount the employer contributed or committed to be contributed to an ESOP with respect to a given year. This is done regardless of whether or not the ESOP has borrowed funds.

## R.  Ratios

The following ratios use stockholders' equity components in their calculations:

1.  **Dividend payout**—measures percentage of earnings distributed as dividends

$$\frac{\text{Dividends per share}}{\text{Earnings per share}}$$

2.  **Book value of common stock** (at a point in time)—not a meaningful measure because assets are carried at historical costs

$$\frac{\text{Common stockholders' equity}}{\text{Shares outstanding}}$$

3.  **Rate of return on common stockholders' equity**—measures the return earned on the stockholders' investment in the firm

$$\frac{\text{Net income available to common stockholders}}{\text{Common stockholders' equity}}$$

4.  **Debt to equity**—shows creditors the corporation's ability to sustain losses

$$\frac{\text{Total debt (all liabilities)}}{\text{Stockholders' equity}}$$

## S.  Research Component

Stockholders' equity includes a variety of transactions and accounts that have been addressed in many different accounting pronouncements.  From a historical perspective, as the equity transactions have become more creative, additional pronouncements were passed to address the issues created by these more complex financial transactions.

A brief list of topics and the related pronouncements are shown below.

| | |
|---|---|
| Capital structure disclosures | SFAS 129 |
| Comprehensive income | SFAS 130 |
| Conversion of convertible bonds | SFAS 84 |
| Earnings per share | SFAS 128 |
| Financial instruments with characteristics of both debt and equity | SFAS 150 |
| Property dividends | APB 29 |
| Stock dividends and stock splits | ARB 43, CH 7B |
| Stock options | SFAS 123(R) |
| Stock warrants, detachable from bonds | APB 14 |
| Treasury stock | ARB 43, CH 1B; APB 6 |

The most effective way to research in such a broad topic area is to focus your keywords on the particular topic of research.  Note that in some of the older literature, keywords in the authoritative literature may not be the same words that we would see today in the newer standards.

Research keywords are shown organized into various categories as shown below.

Basic stockholders equity definitions and issues

| | | |
|---|---|---|
| Appropriation retained earnings | Earned surplus | Undistributed profits |
| Capital stock | Retained earnings | |
| Capital surplus | Retained income | |

Stock dividends, stock splits, property dividends, treasury stock

| | | |
|---|---|---|
| Gains on sales treasury stock | Sales of treasury stock | Stock retirement |
| Nonmonetary asset transfer | Stock dividend | Stock split-up |
| Nonreciprocal transfer to owners | Stock purchased | Treasury stock |
| Recipient stock dividend | Stock retired | |

Earnings per share

| | | |
|---|---|---|
| Antidilutive effect | Denominator EPS | Reverse treasury stock method |
| Basic EPS | Diluted EPS | Treasury stock method |
| Contingent issuable shares | Dilutive potential shares | Warrants EPS |
| Contingently issuable shares EPS | If-converted method | Weighted-average common shares |
| Conversion rate EPS | Numerator EPS | |
| Convertible securities | Options EPS | |

Capital structure disclosures

| | | |
|---|---|---|
| Dividend liquidation preferences | Per-share amounts | Redeemable stock |
| Information about securities | Redeemable preferred stock | |

Stock options, stock warrants, conversion of bonds

| | | |
|---|---|---|
| Black-Scholes | Grand date option | Restricted stock |
| Compensation cost option | Intrinsic value method | Service inception date |
| Compensatory plans | Measurement date option | Service period |
| Employee stock option | Measuring compensation | Share-based payments |
| Employee stock purchase plan | Noncompensatory plans | Stock-based compensation |
| Expected volatility | Nonvested stock options | Vested employee options |
| Fair value method | Option pricing model | Volatility |
| Fixed award | Requisite service period | |

Comprehensive income

| | | |
|---|---|---|
| Classified items income | Display of income | Reclassification adjustments |
| Comprehensive income | Other comprehensive income | |

**1.** East Co. issued 1,000 shares of its $5 par common stock to Howe as compensation for 1,000 hours of legal services performed. Howe usually bills $160 per hour for legal services. On the date of issuance, the stock was trading on a public exchange at $140 per share. By what amount should the additional paid-in capital account increase as a result of this transaction?

    a.  $135,000
    b.  $140,000
    c.  $155,000
    d.  $160,000

**2.** On July 1, 2007, Cove Corp., a closely held corporation, issued 6% bonds with a maturity value of $60,000, together with 1,000 shares of its $5 par value common stock, for a combined cash amount of $110,000. The market value of Cove's stock cannot be ascertained. If the bonds were issued separately, they would have sold for $40,000 on an 8% yield to maturity basis. What amount should Cove report for additional paid-in capital on the issuance of the stock?

    a.  $75,000
    b.  $65,000
    c.  $55,000
    d.  $45,000

**3.** Beck Corp. issued 200,000 shares of common stock when it began operations in 2005 and issued an additional 100,000 shares in 2006. Beck also issued preferred stock convertible to 100,000 shares of common stock. In 2007, Beck purchased 75,000 shares of its common stock and held it in Treasury. At December 31, 2007, how many shares of Beck's common stock were outstanding?

    a.  400,000
    b.  325,000
    c.  300,000
    d.  225,000

**4.** A corporation was organized in January 2007 with authorized capital of $10 par value common stock. On February 1, 2007, shares were issued at par for cash. On March 1, 2007, the corporation's attorney accepted 5,000 shares of the common stock in settlement for legal services with a fair value of $60,000. Additional paid-in capital would increase on

| | February 1, 2007 | March 1, 2007 |
|---|---|---|
| a. | Yes | No |
| b. | Yes | Yes |
| c. | No | No |
| d. | No | Yes |

**5.** On April 1, 2007, Hyde Corp., a newly formed company, had the following stock issued and outstanding:

- Common stock, no par, $1 stated value, 20,000 shares originally issued for $30 per share.
- Preferred stock, $10 par value, 6,000 shares originally issued for $50 per share.

Hyde's April 1, 2007 statement of stockholders' equity should report

| | Common stock | Preferred stock | Additional paid-in capital |
|---|---|---|---|
| a. | $ 20,000 | $ 60,000 | $820,000 |
| b. | $ 20,000 | $300,000 | $580,000 |
| c. | $600,000 | $300,000 | $0 |
| d. | $600,000 | $ 60,000 | $240,000 |

**6.** On March 1, 2007, Rya Corp. issued 1,000 shares of its $20 par value common stock and 2,000 shares of its $20 par value convertible preferred stock for a total of $80,000. At this date, Rya's common stock was selling for $36 per share, and the convertible preferred stock was selling for $27 per share. What amount of the proceeds should be allocated to Rya's convertible preferred stock?

    a.  $60,000
    b.  $54,000
    c.  $48,000
    d.  $44,000

**7.** During 2005, Brad Co. issued 5,000 shares of $100 par convertible preferred stock for $110 per share. One share of preferred stock can be converted into three shares of Brad's $25 par common stock at the option of the preferred shareholder. On December 31, 2007, when the market value of the common stock was $40 per share, all of the preferred stock was converted. What amount should Brad credit to Common Stock and to Additional Paid-in Capital— Common Stock as a result of the conversion?

| | Common stock | Additional paid-in capital |
|---|---|---|
| a. | $375,000 | $175,000 |
| b. | $375,000 | $225,000 |
| c. | $500,000 | $ 50,000 |
| d. | $600,000 | $0 |

**8.** Quoit, Inc. issued preferred stock with detachable common stock warrants. The issue price exceeded the sum of the warrants' fair value and the preferred stock's par value. The preferred stock's fair value was not determinable. What amount should be assigned to the warrants outstanding?

    a.  Total proceeds.
    b.  Excess of proceeds over the par value of the preferred stock.
    c.  The proportion of the proceeds that the warrants' fair value bears to the preferred stock's par value.
    d.  The fair value of the warrants.

**9.** Blue Co. issued preferred stock with detachable common stock warrants at a price that exceeded both the par value and the market value of the preferred stock. At the time the warrants are exercised, Blue's total stockholders' equity is increased by the

| | Cash received upon exercise of the warrants | Carrying amount of warrants |
|---|---|---|
| a. | Yes | No |
| b. | Yes | Yes |
| c. | No | No |
| d. | No | Yes |

**10.** When collectibility is reasonably assured, the excess of the subscription price over the stated value of the no par common stock subscribed should be recorded as

    a.  No par common stock.
    b.  Additional paid-in capital when the subscription is recorded.

c.   Additional paid-in capital when the subscription is collected.

d.   Additional paid-in capital when the common stock is issued.

**11.** On December 1, 2007, shares of authorized common stock were issued on a subscription basis at a price in excess of par value. A total of 20% of the subscription price of each share was collected as a down payment on December 1, 2007, with the remaining 80% of the subscription price of each share due in 2008. Collectibility was reasonably assured. At December 31, 2007, the stockholders' equity section of the balance sheet would report additional paid-in capital for the excess of the subscription price over the par value of the shares of common stock subscribed and

a.   Common stock issued for 20% of the par value of the shares of common stock subscribed.

b.   Common stock issued for the par value of the shares of common stock subscribed.

c.   Common stock subscribed for 80% of the par value of the shares of common stock subscribed.

d.   Common stock subscribed for the par value of the shares of common stock subscribed.

**12.** In 2006, Seda Corp. acquired 6,000 shares of its $1 par value common stock at $36 per share. During 2007, Seda issued 3,000 of these shares at $50 per share. Seda uses the cost method to account for its treasury stock transactions. What accounts and amounts should Seda credit in 2007 to record the issuance of the 3,000 shares?

| | Treasury stock | Additional paid-in capital | Retained earnings | Common stock |
|---|---|---|---|---|
| a. | | $102,000 | $42,000 | $6,000 |
| b. | | $144,000 | | $6,000 |
| c. | $108,000 | $ 42,000 | | |
| d. | $108,000 | | $42,000 | |

**13.** At December 31, 2006, Rama Corp. had 20,000 shares of $1 par value treasury stock that had been acquired in 2006 at $12 per share. In May 2007, Rama issued 15,000 of these treasury shares at $10 per share. The cost method is used to record treasury stock transactions. Rama is located in a state where laws relating to acquisition of treasury stock restrict the availability of retained earnings for declaration of dividends. At December 31, 2007, what amount should Rama show in notes to financial statements as a restriction of retained earnings as a result of its treasury stock transactions?

a.   $ 5,000

b.   $10,000

c.   $60,000

d.   $90,000

**14.** United, Inc.'s unadjusted current assets section and stockholders' equity section of its December 31, 2007 balance sheet are as follows:

**Current assets**

| | |
|---|---|
| Cash | $   60,000 |
| Investments in trading securities (including $300,000 of United, Inc. common stock) | 400,000 |
| Trade accounts receivable | 340,000 |
| Inventories | 148,000 |
| Total | $ 948,000 |

**Stockholders' equity**

| | |
|---|---|
| Common stock | $2,224,000 |
| Retained earnings (deficit) | (224,000) |
| Total | $2,000,000 |

The investments and inventories are reported at their costs, which approximate market values.

In its 2007 statement of stockholders' equity, United's total amount of equity at December 31, 2007, is

a.   $2,224,000

b.   $2,000,000

c.   $1,924,000

d.   $1,700,000

**15.** Cyan Corp. issued 20,000 shares of $5 par common stock at $10 per share. On December 31, 2006, Cyan's retained earnings were $300,000. In March 2007, Cyan reacquired 5,000 shares of its common stock at $20 per share. In June 2007, Cyan sold 1,000 of these shares to its corporate officers for $25 per share. Cyan uses the cost method to record treasury stock. Net income for the year ended December 31, 2007, was $60,000. At December 31, 2007, what amount should Cyan report as retained earnings?

a.   $360,000

b.   $365,000

c.   $375,000

d.   $380,000

**16.** Victor Corporation was organized on January 2, 2007, with 100,000 authorized shares of $10 par value common stock. During 2007 Victor had the following capital transactions:

January 5—issued 75,000 shares at $14 per share.

December 27—purchased 5,000 shares at $11 per share.

Victor used the par value method to record the purchase of the treasury shares. What would be the balance in the paid-in capital from treasury stock account at December 31, 2007?

a.   $0

b.   $ 5,000

c.   $15,000

d.   $20,000

**17.** On incorporation, Dee Inc. issued common stock at a price in excess of its par value. No other stock transactions occurred except treasury stock was acquired for an amount exceeding this issue price. If Dee uses the par value method of accounting for treasury stock appropriate for retired stock, what is the effect of the acquisition on the following?

| | Net common stock | Additional paid-in capital | Retained earnings |
|---|---|---|---|
| a. | No effect | Decrease | No effect |
| b. | Decrease | Decrease | Decrease |
| c. | Decrease | No effect | Decrease |
| d. | No effect | Decrease | Decrease |

**18.** Posy Corp. acquired treasury shares at an amount greater than their par value, but less than their original issue price. Compared to the cost method of accounting for treasury stock, does the par value method report a greater amount for additional paid-in capital and a greater amount for retained earnings?

| | Additional paid-in capital | Retained earnings |
|---|---|---|
| a. | Yes | Yes |
| b. | Yes | No |
| c. | No | No |
| d. | No | Yes |

**19.** In 2005, Rona Corp. issued 5,000 shares of $10 par value common stock for $100 per share. In 2007, Rona reacquired 2,000 of its shares at $150 per share from the estate of one of its deceased officers and immediately canceled these 2,000 shares. Rona uses the cost method in accounting for its treasury stock transactions. In connection with the retirement of these 2,000 shares, Rona should debit

| | Additional paid-in capital | Retained earnings |
|---|---|---|
| a. | $ 20,000 | $280,000 |
| b. | $100,000 | $180,000 |
| c. | $180,000 | $100,000 |
| d. | $280,000 | $0 |

20. The following accounts were among those reported on Luna Corp.'s balance sheet at December 31, 2006:

| | |
|---|---|
| Available-for-sale securities (market value $140,000) | $ 80,000 |
| Preferred stock, $20 par value, 20,000 shares issued and outstanding | 400,000 |
| Additional paid-in capital on preferred stock | 30,000 |
| Retained earnings | 900,000 |

On January 20, 2007, Luna exchanged all of the available-for-sale securities for 5,000 shares of Luna's preferred stock. Market values at the date of the exchange were $150,000 for the available-for-sale securities and $30 per share for the preferred stock. The 5,000 shares of preferred stock were retired immediately after the exchange. Which of the following journal entries should Luna record in connection with this transaction?

| | | Debit | Credit |
|---|---|---|---|
| a. | Preferred stock | 100,000 | |
| | Additional paid-in capital on preferred stock | 7,500 | |
| | Retained earnings | 42,500 | |
| | Available-for-sale securities | | 80,000 |
| | Gain on exchange of securities | | 70,000 |
| b. | Preferred stock | 100,000 | |
| | Additional paid-in capital on preferred stock | 30,000 | |
| | Available-for-sale securities | | 80,000 |
| | Additional paid-in capital from retirement of preferred stock | | 50,000 |
| c. | Preferred stock | 150,000 | |
| | Available-for-sale securities | | 80,000 |
| | Additional paid-in capital on preferred stock | | 70,000 |
| d. | Preferred stock | 150,000 | |
| | Available-for-sale securities | | 80,000 |
| | Gain on exchange of securities | | 70,000 |

21. On December 31, 2007, Pack Corp.'s board of directors canceled 50,000 shares of $2.50 par value common stock held in treasury at an average cost of $13 per share. Before recording the cancellation of the treasury stock, Pack had the following balances in its stockholders' equity accounts:

| | |
|---|---|
| Common stock | $540,000 |
| Additional paid-in capital | 750,000 |
| Retained earnings | 900,000 |

| | |
|---|---|
| Treasury stock, at cost | 650,000 |

In its balance sheet at December 31, 2007, Pack should report a common stock balance of

a. $0
b. $250,000
c. $415,000
d. $540,000

22. In 2006, Fogg, Inc. issued $10 par value common stock for $25 per share. No other common stock transactions occurred until March 31, 2008, when Fogg acquired some of the issued shares for $20 per share and retired them. Which of the following statements correctly states an effect of this acquisition and retirement?

a. 2008 net income is decreased.
b. 2008 net income is increased.
c. Additional paid-in capital is decreased.
d. Retained earnings is increased.

23. Plack Co. purchased 10,000 shares (2% ownership) of Ty Corp. on February 14, 2007. Plack received a stock dividend of 2,000 shares on April 30, 2007, when the market value per share was $35. Ty paid a cash dividend of $2 per share on December 15, 2007. In its 2007 income statement, what amount should Plack report as dividend income?

a. $20,000
b. $24,000
c. $90,000
d. $94,000

24. Arp Corp.'s outstanding capital stock at December 15, 2007, consisted of the following:

• 30,000 shares of 5% cumulative preferred stock, par value $10 per share, fully participating as to dividends. No dividends were in arrears.
• 200,000 shares of common stock, par value $1 per share.

On December 15, 2007, Arp declared dividends of $100,000. What was the amount of dividends payable to Arp's common stockholders?

a. $10,000
b. $34,000
c. $40,000
d. $47,500

25. At December 31, 2006 and 2007, Apex Co. had 3,000 shares of $100 par, 5% cumulative preferred stock outstanding. No dividends were in arrears as of December 31, 2005. Apex did not declare a dividend during 2006. During 2007, Apex paid a cash dividend of $10,000 on its preferred stock. Apex should report dividends in arrears in its 2007 financial statements as a(n)

a. Accrued liability of $15,000.
b. Disclosure of $15,000.
c. Accrued liability of $20,000.
d. Disclosure of $20,000.

26. East Corp., a calendar-year company, had sufficient retained earnings in 2007 as a basis for dividends, but was temporarily short of cash. East declared a dividend of $100,000 on April 1, 2007, and issued promissory notes to its stockholders in lieu of cash. The notes, which were dated April 1, 2007, had a maturity date of March 31, 2008, and a 10% interest rate. How should East account for the scrip dividend and related interest?

a. Debit retained earnings for $110,000 on April 1, 2007.
b. Debit retained earnings for $110,000 on March 31, 2008.
c. Debit retained earnings for $100,000 on April 1, 2007, and debit interest expense for $10,000 on March 31, 2008.
d. Debit retained earnings for $100,000 on April 1, 2007, and debit interest expense for $7,500 on December 31, 2007.

**27.** On January 2, 2007, Lake Mining Co.'s board of directors declared a cash dividend of $400,000 to stockholders of record on January 18, 2007, payable on February 10, 2007. The dividend is permissible under law in Lake's state of incorporation. Selected data from Lake's December 31, 2006 balance sheet are as follows:

| | |
|---|---|
| Accumulated depletion | $100,000 |
| Capital stock | 500,000 |
| Additional paid-in capital | 150,000 |
| Retained earnings | 300,000 |

The $400,000 dividend includes a liquidating dividend of
a. $0
b. $100,000
c. $150,000
d. $300,000

**28.** On June 27, 2007, Brite Co. distributed to its common stockholders 100,000 outstanding common shares of its investment in Quik, Inc., an unrelated party. The carrying amount on Brite's books of Quik's $1 par common stock was $2 per share. Immediately after the distribution, the market price of Quik's stock was $2.50 per share. In its income statement for the year ended June 30, 2007, what amount should Brite report as gain before income taxes on disposal of the stock?
a. $250,000
b. $200,000
c. $ 50,000
d. $0

**29.** On December 1, 2007, Nilo Corp. declared a property dividend of marketable securities to be distributed on December 31, 2007, to stockholders of record on December 15, 2007. On December 1, 2007, the trading securities had a carrying amount of $60,000 and a fair value of $78,000. What is the effect of this property dividend on Nilo's 2007 retained earnings, after all nominal accounts are closed?
a. $0.
b. $18,000 increase.
c. $60,000 decrease.
d. $78,000 decrease.

**30.** Long Co. had 100,000 shares of common stock issued and outstanding at January 1, 2007. During 2007, Long took the following actions:

| | | |
|---|---|---|
| March 15 | — | Declared a 2-for-1 stock split, when the fair value of the stock was $80 per share. |
| December 15 | — | Declared a $.50 per share cash dividend. |

In Long's statement of stockholders' equity for 2007, what amount should Long report as dividends?
a. $ 50,000
b. $100,000
c. $850,000

d. $950,000

**31.** A company declared a cash dividend on its common stock on December 15, 2007, payable on January 12, 2008. How would this dividend affect stockholders' equity on the following dates?

| | December 15, 2007 | December 31, 2007 | January 12, 2008 |
|---|---|---|---|
| a. | Decrease | No effect | Decrease |
| b. | Decrease | No effect | No effect |
| c. | No effect | Decrease | No effect |
| d. | No effect | No effect | Decrease |

**32.** Ole Corp. declared and paid a liquidating dividend of $100,000. This distribution resulted in a decrease in Ole's

| | Paid-in capital | Retained earnings |
|---|---|---|
| a. | No | No |
| b. | Yes | Yes |
| c. | No | Yes |
| d. | Yes | No |

**33.** Instead of the usual cash dividend, Evie Corp. declared and distributed a property dividend from its overstocked merchandise. The excess of the merchandise's carrying amount over its market value should be
a. Ignored.
b. Reported as a separately disclosed reduction of retained earnings.
c. Reported as an extraordinary loss, net of income taxes.
d. Reported as a reduction in income before extraordinary items.

**34.** The following stock dividends were declared and distributed by Sol Corp.:

| Percentage of common share outstanding at declaration date | Fair value | Par value |
|---|---|---|
| 10 | $15,000 | $10,000 |
| 28 | 40,000 | 30,800 |

What aggregate amount should be debited to retained earnings for these stock dividends?
a. $40,800
b. $45,800
c. $50,000
d. $55,000

**35.** Ray Corp. declared a 5% stock dividend on its 10,000 issued and outstanding shares of $2 par value common stock, which had a fair value of $5 per share before the stock dividend was declared. This stock dividend was distributed sixty days after the declaration date. By what amount did Ray's current liabilities increase as a result of the stock dividend declaration?
a. $0
b. $ 500
c. $1,000
d. $2,500

**36.** How would total stockholders' equity be affected by the declaration of each of the following?

| | Stock dividend | Stock split |
|---|---|---|
| a. | No effect | Increase |
| b. | Decrease | Decrease |
| c. | Decrease | No effect |
| d. | No effect | No effect |

**37.** On July 1, 2007, Bart Corporation has 200,000 shares of $10 par common stock outstanding and the market price of the stock is $12 per share. On the same date, Bart declared a 1-for-2 reverse stock split. The par of the stock was increased from $10 to $20 and one new $20 par share was issued for each two $10 par shares outstanding. Immediately before the 1-for-2 reverse stock split, Bart's additional paid-in capital was $450,000. What should be the balance in Bart's additional paid-in capital account immediately after the reverse stock split is effected?

   a.   $0
   b.   $450,000
   c.   $650,000
   d.   $850,000

**38.** How would a stock split in which the par value per share decreases in proportion to the number of additional shares issued affect each of the following?

| | Additional paid-in capital | Retained earnings |
|---|---|---|
| a. | Increase | No effect |
| b. | No effect | No effect |
| c. | No effect | Decrease |
| d. | Increase | Decrease |

**39.** At December 31, 2006, Eagle Corp. reported $1,750,000 of appropriated retained earnings for the construction of a new office building, which was completed in 2007 at a total cost of $1,500,000. In 2007, Eagle appropriated $1,200,000 of retained earnings for the construction of a new plant. Also, $2,000,000 of cash was restricted for the retirement of bonds due in 2008. In its 2007 balance sheet, Eagle should report what amount of appropriated retained earnings?

   a.   $1,200,000
   b.   $1,450,000
   c.   $2,950,000
   d.   $3,200,000

**40.** The following information pertains to Meg Corp.:

- Dividends on its 1,000 shares of 6%, $10 par value cumulative preferred stock have not been declared or paid for three years.
- Treasury stock that cost $15,000 was reissued for $8,000.

What amount of retained earnings should be appropriated as a result of these items?

   a.   $0
   b.   $1,800
   c.   $7,000
   d.   $8,800

**41.** A retained earnings appropriation can be used to

   a.   Absorb a fire loss when a company is self-insured.
   b.   Provide for a contingent loss that is probable and reasonably estimable.
   c.   Smooth periodic income.
   d.   Restrict earnings available for dividends.

**42.** On January 1, 2008, Doro Corp. granted an employee an option to purchase 3,000 shares of Doro's $5 par value common stock at $20 per share. The option became exercisable on December 31, 2009, after the employee completed two years of service. The option was exercised on January 10, 2010. The market prices of Doro's stock and stock options were as follows:

| Date | Market price of stock | Market price of similar stock option |
|---|---|---|
| January 1, 2008 | $30 | $8 |
| December 31, 2009 | 50 | 9 |
| January 10, 2010 | 45 | 11 |

For 2008, Doro should recognize compensation expense under SFAS 123(R) of

   a.   $45,000
   b.   $30,000
   c.   $15,000
   d.   $12,000

**43.** In connection with a stock option plan for the benefit of key employees, Ward Corp. intends to distribute treasury shares when the options are exercised. These shares were bought in 2007 at $42 per share. On January 1, 2008, Ward granted stock options for 10,000 shares at $38 per share as additional compensation for services to be rendered over the next three years. The options are exercisable during a four-year period beginning January 1, 2011, by grantees still employed by Ward. Market price of Ward's stock was $47 per share at the grant date. The fair value of a similar stock option with the same terms was $12 at the grant date. No stock options were terminated during 2008. In Ward's December 31, 2008 income statement, what amount should be reported as compensation expense pertaining to the options under SFAS 123(R)?

   a.   $90,000
   b.   $40,000
   c.   $30,000
   d.   $0

**Items 44 and 45 are based on the following:**

On January 2, 2008, Kine Co. granted Morgan, its president, compensatory stock options to buy 1,000 shares of Kine's $10 par common stock. The options call for a price of $20 per share and are exercisable for three years following the grant date. Morgan exercised the options on December 31, 2008. The market price of the stock was $50 on January 2, 2008, and $70 on December 31, 2008. The fair value of a similar stock option with the same terms was $28 on the grant date.

**44.** What is compensation expense for 2008 for the share-based payments under SFAS 123(R)?

   a.   $ 9,333
   b.   $10,000
   c.   $20,000
   d.   $28,000

**45.** By what net amount should stockholders' equity increase as a result of the grant and exercise of the options under SFAS 123(R)?

   a.   $20,000
   b.   $30,000
   c.   $50,000
   d.   $70,000

**46.** On January 2, 2008, Morey Corp. granted Dean, its president, 20,000 stock appreciation rights for past services. Those rights are exercisable immediately and expire on January 1, 2011. On exercise, Dean is entitled to receive cash for the excess of the stock's market price on the exercise date over the market price on the grant date. Dean did not exercise any of the rights during 2008. The market price of Morey's stock was $30 on January 2, 2008, and $45 on December 31, 2008. As a result of the stock appreciation rights, Morey should recognize compensation expense for 2008 of

a. $0
b. $100,000
c. $300,000
d. $600,000

**47.** Wall Corp.'s employee stock purchase plan specifies the following:

- For every $1 withheld from employees' wages for the purchase of Wall's common stock, Wall contributes $2.
- The stock is purchased from Wall's treasury stock at market price on the date of purchase.

The following information pertains to the plan's 2008 transactions:

| | |
|---|---|
| Employee withholdings for the year | $ 350,000 |
| Market value of 150,000 shares issued | 1,050,000 |
| Carrying amount of treasury stock issued (cost) | 900,000 |

Before payroll taxes, what amount should Wall recognize as expense in 2008 under SFAS 123(R) for the stock purchase plan?

a. $1,050,000
b. $ 900,000
c. $ 700,000
d. $ 550,000

**48.** In accounting for stock-based compensation under SFAS 123(R), what interest rate is used to discount both the exercise price of the option and the future dividend stream?

a. The firm's known incremental borrowing rate.
b. The current market rate that firms in that particular industry use to discount cash flows.
c. The risk-free interest rate.
d. Any rate that firms can justify as being reasonable.

**49.** In what circumstances is compensation expense immediately recognized, under SFAS 123(R)?

a. In all circumstances.
b. In circumstances when the options are exercisable within two years for services rendered over the next two years.
c. In circumstances when options are granted for prior service, and the options are immediately exercisable.
d. In no circumstances is compensation expense immediately recognized.

**50.** Compensation cost for a share-based payment to employees that is classified as a liability is measured as

a. The change in fair value of the instrument for each reporting period.
b. The total fair value at grant date.
c. The present value of cash payments due over the life of the grant.
d. The actual cash outlay for the period.

**51.** What is the measurement date for a share-based payment to employees that is classified as a liability?

a. The service inception date.
b. The grant date.
c. The settlement date.
d. The end of the reporting period.

**52.** Shafer Corporation (a nonpublic company) established an employee stock option plan on January 1, 2008. The plan allows its employees to acquire 20,000 shares of its $5 par value common stock at $70 per share, when the market price is $75. The options may not be exercised until five years from the grant date. The risk-free interest rate is 6%, and the stock is expected to pay dividends of $3 annually. The fair value of a similar option at the grant date is $6.40. What is the amount of deferred compensation expense that should be recorded in year one under SFAS 123(R)?

a. $ 20,000
b. $ 25,000
c. $100,000
d. $128,000

**53.** Galaxy has a tax benefit and cash retained of $20,000 as a result of share-based payments to employees. How is this tax benefit disclosed in the financial statements?

a. As a component of other comprehensive income.
b. As a prior period adjustment.
c. As a current liability on the balance sheet.
d. As a cash inflow from financing activities on the statement of cash flows.

**54.** On July 1, 2008, Jordan Corp. granted employees share-based payments in the form of compensatory stock options. How should Jordan account for the outstanding options in calculating earnings per share for 2008 if the options are not antidilutive?

a. Include the options in the denominator of basic and diluted earnings per share for the entire year.
b. Include the options in the denominator of diluted earnings per share for the entire year.
c. Include the options in the denominator of diluted earnings per share weighted by number of months outstanding.
d. Ignore the options in the calculation of diluted earnings per share.

**55.** At December 31, 2007 and 2006, Gow Corp. had 100,000 shares of common stock and 10,000 shares of 5%, $100 par value cumulative preferred stock outstanding. No dividends were declared on either the preferred or common stock in 2007 or 2006. Net income for 2007 was $1,000,000. For 2007, basic earnings per share amounted to

a. $10.00
b. $ 9.50
c. $ 9.00
d. $ 5.00

**56.** Ute Co. had the following capital structure during 2006 and 2007:

| | |
|---|---|
| Preferred stock, $10 par, 4% cumulative, 25,000 shares issued and outstanding | $ 250,000 |
| Common stock, $5 par, 200,000 shares issued and outstanding | 1,000,000 |

Ute reported net income of $500,000 for the year ended December 31, 2007. Ute paid no preferred dividends during 2006 and paid $16,000 in preferred dividends during 2007. In its December 31, 2007 income statement, what amount should Ute report as basic earnings per share?

a. $2.42
b. $2.45
c. $2.48
d. $2.50

**57.** The following information pertains to Jet Corp.'s outstanding stock for 2007:

| Common stock, $5 par value | |
| --- | --- |
| Shares outstanding, 1/1/07 | 20,000 |
| 2-for-1 stock split, 4/1/07 | 20,000 |
| Shares issued, 7/1/07 | 10,000 |
| **Preferred stock, $10 par value, 5% cumulative** | |
| Shares outstanding, 1/1/07 | 4,000 |

What are the number of shares Jet should use to calculate 2007 basic earnings per share?

- a. 40,000
- b. 45,000
- c. 50,000
- d. 54,000

**58.** Timp, Inc. had the following common stock balances and transactions during 2007

| 1/1/07 | Common stock outstanding | 30,000 |
| --- | --- | --- |
| 2/1/07 | Issued a 10% common stock dividend | 3,000 |
| 7/1/07 | Issued common stock for cash | 8,000 |
| 12/31/07 | Common stock outstanding | 41,000 |

What were Timp's 2007 weighted-average shares outstanding?

- a. 30,000
- b. 34,000
- c. 36,750
- d. 37,000

**59.** Strauch Co. has one class of common stock outstanding and no other securities that are potentially convertible into common stock. During 2006, 100,000 shares of common stock were outstanding. In 2007, two distributions of additional common shares occurred: On April 1, 20,000 shares of treasury stock were sold, and on July 1, a 2-for-1 stock split was issued. Net income was $410,000 in 2007 and $350,000 in 2006. What amounts should Strauch report as basic earnings per share in its 2007 and 2006 comparative income statements?

| | 2007 | 2006 |
| --- | --- | --- |
| a. | $1.78 | $3.50 |
| b. | $1.78 | $1.75 |
| c. | $2.34 | $1.75 |
| d. | $2.34 | $3.50 |

**60.** Earnings per share data must be reported on the income statement for

| | Cumulative effect of a change in accounting principle | Extraordinary items |
| --- | --- | --- |
| a. | Yes | No |
| b. | No | No |
| c. | No | Yes |
| d. | Yes | Yes |

**61.** On January 31, 2008, Pack, Inc. split its common stock 2 for 1, and Young, Inc. issued a 5% stock dividend. Both companies issued their December 31, 2007 financial statements on March 1, 2008. Should Pack's 2007, basic earnings per share (BEPS) take into consideration the stock split, and should Young's 2007 BEPS take into consideration the stock dividend?

| | Pack's 2007 BEPS | Young's 2007 BEPS |
| --- | --- | --- |
| a. | Yes | No |
| b. | No | No |
| c. | Yes | Yes |
| d. | No | Yes |

**62.** Mann, Inc. had 300,000 shares of common stock issued and outstanding at December 31, 2006. On July 1, 2007, an additional 50,000 shares of common stock were issued for cash. Mann also had unexercised stock options to purchase 40,000 shares of common stock at $15 per share outstanding at the beginning and end of 2007. The average market price of Mann's common stock was $20 during 2007. What is the number of shares that should be used in computing diluted earnings per share for the year ended December 31, 2007?

- a. 325,000
- b. 335,000
- c. 360,000
- d. 365,000

**63.** Peters Corp.'s capital structure was as follows:

| | December 31 | |
| --- | --- | --- |
| | 2006 | 2007 |
| Outstanding shares of stock: | | |
| Common | 110,000 | 110,000 |
| Convertible preferred | 10,000 | 10,000 |

During 2007, Peters paid dividends of $3.00 per share on its preferred stock. The preferred shares are convertible into 20,000 shares of common stock and are considered common stock equivalents. Net income for 2007 was $850,000. Assume that the income tax rate is 30%. The diluted earnings per share for 2007 is

- a. $6.31
- b. $6.54
- c. $7.08
- d. $7.45

**64.** Cox Corporation had 1,200,000 shares of common stock outstanding on January 1 and December 31, 2007. In connection with the acquisition of a subsidiary company in June 2006, Cox is required to issue 50,000 additional shares of its common stock on July 1, 2008, to the former owners of the subsidiary. Cox paid $200,000 in preferred stock dividends in 2007, and reported net income of $3,400,000 for the year. Cox's diluted earnings per share for 2007 should be

- a. $2.83
- b. $2.72
- c. $2.67
- d. $2.56

**65.** On June 30, 2006, Lomond, Inc. issued twenty $10,000, 7% bonds at par. Each bond was convertible into 200 shares of common stock. On January 1, 2007, 10,000 shares of common stock were outstanding. The bondholders converted all the bonds on July 1, 2007. The following amounts were reported in Lomond's income statement for the year ended December 31, 2007:

| Revenues | $977,000 |
| --- | --- |
| Operating expenses | 920,000 |
| Interest on bonds | 7,000 |
| Income before income tax | 50,000 |
| Income tax at 30% | 15,000 |
| Net income | $ 35,000 |

What is Lomond's 2007 diluted earnings per share?

- a. $2.50
- b. $2.85
- c. $2.92
- d. $3.50

**66.** West Co. had earnings per share of $15.00 for 2007 before considering the effects of any convertible securities.

No conversion or exercise of convertible securities occurred during 2007. However, possible conversion of convertible bonds, not considered common stock equivalents, would have reduced earnings per share by $0.75. The effect of possible exercise of common stock options would have increased earnings per share by $0.10. What amount should West report as diluted earnings per share for 2007?

    a.    $14.25
    b.    $14.35
    c.    $15.00
    d.    $15.10

**67.** In determining diluted earnings per share, dividends on nonconvertible cumulative preferred stock should be

    a.    Disregarded.
    b.    Added back to net income whether declared or not.
    c.    Deducted from net income only if declared.
    d.    Deducted from net income whether declared or not.

**68.** The if-converted method of computing earnings per share data assumes conversion of convertible securities as of the

    a.    Beginning of the earliest period reported (or at time of issuance, if later).
    b.    Beginning of the earliest period reported (regardless of time of issuance).
    c.    Middle of the earliest period reported (regardless of time of issuance).
    d.    Ending of the earliest period reported (regardless of time of issuance).

**69.** In determining earnings per share, interest expense, net of applicable income taxes, on convertible debt that is dilutive should be

    a.    Added back to weighted-average common shares outstanding for diluted earnings per share.
    b.    Added back to net income for diluted earnings per share.
    c.    Deducted from net income for diluted earnings per share.
    d.    Deducted from weighted-average common shares outstanding for diluted earnings per share.

**70.** For contingent issue agreements requiring passage of time or earnings threshold that is met, before issuing stock, these should be

| | Included in basic earnings per share | Included in computing diluted earnings per share |
|---|---|---|
| a. | No | No |
| b. | No | Yes |
| c. | Yes | No |
| d. | Yes | Yes |

**71.** Kent Co. filed a voluntary bankruptcy petition on August 15, 2007, and the statement of affairs reflects the following amounts:

| | Book value | Estimated current value |
|---|---|---|
| *Assets* | | |
| Assets pledged with fully secured creditors | $ 300,000 | $370,000 |
| Assets pledged with partially secured creditors | 180,000 | 120,000 |
| Free assets | 420,000 | 320,000 |
| | $ 900,000 | $810,000 |

| *Liabilities* | |
|---|---|
| Liabilities with priority | $ 70,000 |
| Fully secured creditors | 260,000 |
| Partially secured creditors | 200,000 |
| Unsecured creditors | 540,000 |
| | $1,070,000 |

Assume that the assets are converted to cash at the estimated current values and the business is liquidated. What amount of cash will be available to pay unsecured nonpriority claims?

    a.    $240,000
    b.    $280,000
    c.    $320,000
    d.    $360,000

**72.** Seco Corp. was forced into bankruptcy and is in the process of liquidating assets and paying claims. Unsecured claims will be paid at the rate of 40 cents on the dollar. Hale holds a $30,000 noninterest-bearing note receivable from Seco collateralized by an asset with a book value of $35,000 and a liquidation value of $5,000. The amount to be realized by Hale on this note is

    a.    $ 5,000
    b.    $12,000
    c.    $15,000
    d.    $17,000

**73.** Kamy Corp. is in liquidation under Chapter 7 of the Federal Bankruptcy Code. The bankruptcy trustee has established a new set of books for the bankruptcy estate. After assuming custody of the estate, the trustee discovered an unrecorded invoice of $1,000 for machinery repairs performed before the bankruptcy filing. In addition, a truck with a carrying amount of $20,000 was sold for $12,000 cash. This truck was bought and paid for in the year before the bankruptcy. What amount should be debited to estate equity as a result of these transactions?

    a.    $0
    b.    $1,000
    c.    $8,000
    d.    $9,000

**74.** On December 30, 2007, Hale Corp. paid $400,000 cash and issued 80,000 shares of its $1 par value common stock to its unsecured creditors on a pro rata basis pursuant to a reorganization plan under Chapter 11 of the bankruptcy statutes. Hale owed these unsecured creditors a total of $1,200,000. Hale's common stock was trading at $1.25 per share on December 30, 2007. As a result of this transaction, Hale's total stockholders' equity had a net increase of

    a.    $1,200,000
    b.    $ 800,000
    c.    $ 100,000
    d.    $ 80,000

**75.** The primary purpose of a quasi reorganization is to give a corporation the opportunity to

    a.    Obtain relief from its creditors.
    b.    Revalue understated assets to their fair values.
    c.    Eliminate a deficit in retained earnings.
    d.    Distribute the stock of a newly created subsidiary to its stockholders in exchange for part of their stock in the corporation.

**76.** When a company goes through a quasi reorganization, its balance sheet carrying amounts are stated at

    a.    Original cost.

b.  Original book value.
c.  Replacement value.
d.  Fair value.

**77.** The stockholders' equity section of Brown Co.'s December 31, 2007 balance sheet consisted of the following:

Common stock, $30 par, 10,000 shares au-
  thorized and outstanding               $300,000
Additional paid-in capital                150,000
Retained earnings (deficit)             (210,000)

On January 2, 2008, Brown put into effect a stockholder-approved quasi reorganization by reducing the par value of the stock to $5 and eliminating the deficit against additional paid-in capital. Immediately after the quasi reorganization, what amount should Brown report as additional paid-in capital?

    a.  $ (60,000)
    b.  $150,000
    c.  $190,000
    d.  $400,000

**78.** On July 1, 2007, Vail Corp. issued rights to stockholders to subscribe to additional shares of its common stock. One right was issued for each share owned. A stockholder could purchase one additional share for 10 rights plus $15 cash. The rights expired on September 30, 2007. On July 1, 2007, the market price of a share with the right attached was $40, while the market price of one right alone was $2. Vail's stockholders' equity on June 30, 2007, comprised the following:

Common stock, $25 par value, 4,000 shares
  issued and outstanding               $100,000
Additional paid-in capital                60,000
Retained earnings                    80,000

By what amount should Vail's retained earnings decrease as a result of issuance of the stock rights on July 1, 2007?

    a.  $0
    b.  $ 5,000
    c.  $ 8,000
    d.  $10,000

**79.** In September 2005, West Corp. made a dividend distribution of one right for each of its 120,000 shares of outstanding common stock. Each right was exercisable for the purchase of 1/100 of a share of West's $50 variable rate preferred stock at an exercise price of $80 per share. On March 20, 2007, none of the rights had been exercised, and West redeemed them by paying each stockholder $0.10 per right. As a result of this redemption, West's stockholders' equity was reduced by

    a.  $ 120
    b.  $ 2,400
    c.  $12,000
    d.  $36,000

**80.** On November 2, 2007, Finsbury, Inc. issued warrants to its stockholders giving them the right to purchase additional $20 par value common shares at a price of $30. The stockholders exercised all warrants on March 1, 2008. The shares had market prices of $33, $35, and $40 on November 2, 2007; December 31, 2007; and March 1, 2008, respectively. What were the effects of the warrants on Finsbury's additional paid-in capital and net income?

| | Additional paid-in capital | Net income |
|---|---|---|
| a. | Increased in 2008 | No effect |
| b. | Increased in 2007 | No effect |
| c. | Increased in 2008 | Decreased in 2007 and 2008 |
| d. | Increased in 2007 | Decreased in 2007 and 2008 |

**81.** A company issued rights to its existing shareholders to purchase, for $30 per share, unissued shares of $15 par value common stock. Additional paid-in capital will be credited when the

| | Rights are issued | Rights lapse |
|---|---|---|
| a. | Yes | No |
| b. | No | No |
| c. | No | Yes |
| d. | Yes | Yes |

**Items 82 and 83** are based on the following:

On January 1, 2007, Fay Corporation established an employee stock ownership plan (ESOP). Selected transactions relating to the ESOP during 2007 were as follows:

- On April 1, 2007, Fay contributed $30,000 cash and 3,000 shares of its $10 par common stock to the ESOP. On this date the market price of the stock was $18 a share.
- On October 1, 2007, the ESOP borrowed $100,000 from Union National Bank and acquired 5,000 shares of Fay's common stock in the open market at $17 a share. The note is for one year, bears interest at 10%, and is guaranteed by Fay.
- On December 15, 2007, the ESOP distributed 6,000 shares of Fay common stock to employees of Fay in accordance with the plan formula.

**82.** In its 2007 income statement, how much should Fay report as compensation expense relating to the ESOP?

    a.  $184,000
    b.  $120,000
    c.  $ 84,000
    d.  $ 60,000

**83.** In Fay's December 31, 2007 balance sheet, how much should be reported as a reduction of shareholders' equity and as an endorsed note payable in respect of the ESOP?

| | Reduction of shareholders' equity | Endorsed note payable |
|---|---|---|
| a. | $0 | $0 |
| b. | $0 | $100,000 |
| c. | $100,000 | $0 |
| d. | $100,000 | $100,000 |

**84.** Zinc Co.'s adjusted trial balance at December 31, 2007, includes the following account balances:

| | |
|---|---|
| Common stock, $3 par | $600,000 |
| Additional paid-in capital | 800,000 |
| Treasury stock, at cost | 50,000 |
| Net unrealized loss on available-for-sale securities | 20,000 |
| Retained earnings: appropriated for uninsured earthquake losses | 150,000 |
| Retained earnings: unappropriated | 200,000 |

What amount should Zinc report as total stockholders' equity in its December 31, 2007 balance sheet?

    a.  $1,680,000
    b.  $1,720,000
    c.  $1,780,000
    d.  $1,820,000

**85.** Rudd Corp. had 700,000 shares of common stock authorized and 300,000 shares outstanding at December 31, 2006. The following events occurred during 2007:

| | |
|---|---|
| January 31 | Declared 10% stock dividend |
| June 30 | Purchased 100,000 shares |
| August 1 | Reissued 50,000 shares |
| November 30 | Declared 2-for-1 stock split |

At December 31, 2007, how many shares of common stock did Rudd have outstanding?
- a.   560,000
- b.   600,000
- c.   630,000
- d.   660,000

**86.** Nest Co. issued 100,000 shares of common stock. Of these, 5,000 were held as treasury stock at December 31, 2006. During 2007, transactions involving Nest's common stock were as follows:

| | |
|---|---|
| May 3 | 1,000 shares of treasury stock were sold. |
| August 6 | 10,000 shares of previously unissued stock were sold. |
| November 18 | A 2-for-1 stock split took effect. |

Laws in Nest's state of incorporation protect treasury stock from dilution. At December 31, 2007, how many shares of Nest's common stock were issued and outstanding?

| | Shares | |
|---|---|---|
| | Issued | Outstanding |
| a. | 220,000 | 212,000 |
| b. | 220,000 | 216,000 |
| c. | 222,000 | 214,000 |
| d. | 222,000 | 218,000 |

**87.** The following information pertains to Ali Corp. as of and for the year ended December 31, 2007:

| | |
|---|---|
| Liabilities | $ 60,000 |
| Stockholders' equity | $500,000 |
| Shares of common stock issued and outstanding | 10,000 |
| Net income | $ 30,000 |

During 2007, Ali's officers exercised stock options for 1,000 shares of stock at an option price of $8 per share. What was the effect of exercising the stock options?
- a.   Debt to equity ratio decreased to 12%.
- b.   Earnings per share increased by $0.33.
- c.   Asset turnover increased to 5.4%.
- d.   No ratios were affected.

**88.** Selected information for Irvington Company is as follows:

| | December 31 | |
|---|---|---|
| | 2006 | 2007 |
| Preferred stock, 8%, par $100, non-convertible, noncumulative | $125,000 | $125,000 |
| Common stock | 300,000 | 400,000 |
| Retained earnings | 75,000 | 185,000 |
| Dividends paid on preferred stock for year ended | 10,000 | 10,000 |
| Net income for year ended | 60,000 | 120,000 |

Irvington's return on common stockholders' equity, rounded to the nearest percentage point, for 2007 is
- a.   17%
- b.   19%
- c.   23%
- d.   25%

**89.** Hoyt Corp.'s current balance sheet reports the following stockholders' equity:

| | |
|---|---|
| 5% cumulative preferred stock, par value $100 per share; 2,500 shares issued and outstanding | $250,000 |
| Common stock, par value $3.50 per share; 100,000 shares issued and outstanding | 350,000 |
| Additional paid-in capital in excess of par value of common stock | 125,000 |
| Retained earnings | 300,000 |

Dividends in arrears on the preferred stock amount to $25,000. If Hoyt were to be liquidated, the preferred stockholders would receive par value plus a premium of $50,000. The book value per share of common stock is
- a.   $7.75
- b.   $7.50
- c.   $7.25
- d.   $7.00

**90.** Grid Corp. acquired some of its own common shares at a price greater than both their par value and original issue price but less than their book value. Grid uses the cost method of accounting for treasury stock. What is the impact of this acquisition on total stockholders' equity and the book value per common share?

| | Total stockholders' equity | Book value per share |
|---|---|---|
| a. | Increase | Increase |
| b. | Increase | Decrease |
| c. | Decrease | Increase |
| d. | Decrease | Decrease |

**91.** How are dividends per share for common stock used in the calculation of the following?

| | Dividend per share payout ratio | Earnings per share |
|---|---|---|
| a. | Numerator | Numerator |
| b. | Numerator | Not used |
| c. | Denominator | Not used |
| d. | Denominator | Denominator |

**SIMULATION PROBLEMS**

**Simulation Problem 1**                                    (40 to 50 minutes)

| Situation | | | | | |
|---|---|---|---|---|---|
| | Concepts | Statement of Retained Earnings | Financial Statement Disclosures | Research | Communication |

Min Co. is a publicly held company whose shares are traded in the over-the-counter market. The stockholders' equity accounts at December 31, 2006, had the following balances:

| | |
|---|---|
| Preferred stock, $100 par value, 6% cumulative; 5,000 shares authorized; 2,000 issued and outstanding | $200,000 |
| Common stock, $1 par value, 150,000 shares authorized; 100,000 issued and outstanding | 100,000 |
| Additional paid-in capital | 800,000 |
| Retained earnings | 1,586,000 |
| Total stockholders' equity | $2,686,000 |

Transactions during 2007 and other information relating to the stockholders' equity accounts were as follows:

- February 1, 2007—Issued 13,000 shares of common stock to Ram Co. in exchange for land. On the date issued, the stock had a market price of $11 per share. The land had a carrying value on Ram's books of $135,000, and an assessed value for property taxes of $90,000.

- March 1, 2007—Purchased 5,000 shares of its own common stock to be held as treasury stock for $14 per share. Min uses the cost method to account for treasury stock. Transactions in treasury stock are legal in Min's state of incorporation.

- May 10, 2007—Declared a property dividend of marketable securities held by Min to common shareholders. The securities had a carrying value of $600,000; fair value on relevant dates were

| | |
|---|---|
| Date of declaration (May 10, 2007) | $720,000 |
| Date of record (May 25, 2007) | 758,000 |
| Date of distribution (June 1, 2007) | 736,000 |

- October 1, 2007—Reissued 2,000 shares of treasury stock for $16 per share.

- November 4, 2007—Declared a cash dividend of $1.50 per share to all common shareholders of record November 15, 2007. The dividend was paid on November 25, 2007.

- December 20, 2007—Declared the required annual cash dividend on preferred stock for 2007. The dividend was paid on January 5, 2008.

- January 16, 2008—Before closing the accounting records for 2007, Min became aware that no amortization had been recorded for 2006 for a patent purchased on July 1, 2006. Amortization expense was properly recorded in 2007. The patent was properly capitalized at $320,000 and had an estimated useful life of eight years when purchased. Min's income tax rate is 30%. The appropriate correcting entry was recorded on the same day.

- Adjusted net income for 2007 was $838,000.

| | Concepts | | | | |
|---|---|---|---|---|---|
| Situation | | Statement of Retained Earnings | Financial Statement Disclosures | Research | Communication |

**Items 1 through 10** require the candidate to select the best response from the responses to be selected.

*Responses to be selected*

A. Contains no potentially dilutive securities
B. A form of compensation which allows employees to receive stock or cash for the difference between the stated value and the market value
C. Legal or contractual restrictions on the number of shares an employee may own
D. Issuance of additional shares in order to reduce the market value
E. Purchase by the corporation of its own stock
F. The value of treasury shares are recorded at cost of acquisition
G. A dividend paid which is considered a return of the shareholders' investment
H. Actions by the board of directors to disclose amounts not available for dividends
I. The balance of the treasury stock account reflects the par value
J. A form of compensation which allows employees to purchase shares at a specified price
K. A dividend issued in the form of a note payable
L. A stock transaction resulting in a reduced number of shares outstanding and a higher market value
M. Assumes convertible securities were converted at the beginning of the period

|  | (A) | (B) | (C) | (D) | (E) | (F) | (G) | (H) | (I) | (J) | (K) | (L) | (M) |
|---|---|---|---|---|---|---|---|---|---|---|---|---|---|
| 1. Par value method | O | O | O | O | O | O | O | O | O | O | O | O | O |
| 2. Appropriations of retained earnings | O | O | O | O | O | O | O | O | O | O | O | O | O |
| 3. Stock split | O | O | O | O | O | O | O | O | O | O | O | O | O |
| 4. Simple capital structure | O | O | O | O | O | O | O | O | O | O | O | O | O |
| 5. If-converted method | O | O | O | O | O | O | O | O | O | O | O | O | O |
| 6. Scrip dividend | O | O | O | O | O | O | O | O | O | O | O | O | O |
| 7. Stock appreciation rights | O | O | O | O | O | O | O | O | O | O | O | O | O |
| 8. Stock option | O | O | O | O | O | O | O | O | O | O | O | O | O |
| 9. Liquidating dividend | O | O | O | O | O | O | O | O | O | O | O | O | O |
| 10. Treasury stock | O | O | O | O | O | O | O | O | O | O | O | O | O |

| Situation | Concepts | Statement of Retained Earnings | Financial Statement Disclosures | Research | Communication |
|---|---|---|---|---|---|

Calculate the amounts to be reported on Min's 2007 statement of retained earnings.

|  | *Amount* |
|---|---|
| 1. Prior period adjustment | _____ |
| 2. Preferred dividends | _____ |
| 3. Common dividends—cash | _____ |
| 4. Common dividends—property | _____ |

| Situation | Concepts | Statement of Retained Earnings | Financial Statement Disclosures | Research | Communication |
|---|---|---|---|---|---|

Calculate the following amounts to be reported on Min's statement of stockholders' equity at December 31, 2007.

|  | *Amount* |
|---|---|
| 1. Number of common shares issued at December 31, 2007 | _____ |
| 2. Amount of common stock issued | _____ |
| 3. Additional paid-in capital, including treasury stock transactions | _____ |
| 4. Treasury stock | _____ |

**Items 5 and 6** represent other financial information for 2006 and 2007.

|  | *Amount* |
|---|---|
| 5. Book value per share at December 31, 2006, before prior period adjustment | _____ |
| 6. Numerator used in calculation of 2007 earnings per share for the year | _____ |

| Situation | Concepts | Statement of Retained Earnings | Financial Statement Disclosures | Research | Communication |
|---|---|---|---|---|---|

You have been asked to find the appropriate authoritative literature on the following questions. Insert the appropriate citation from the authoritative accounting literature.

1. A company issues a small stock dividend. At what amount should the stock dividend be recorded?

2. A company issues a property dividend. How should the property dividend be valued?

3. A company appropriates retained earnings for a loss contingency. How should this be disclosed in the financial statements?

| | | | | | Communication |
|---|---|---|---|---|---|
| **Situation** | **Concepts** | **Statement of Retained Earnings** | **Financial Statement Disclosures** | **Research** | |

Kay Smith, the CEO of Min Co., has asked you to explain the difference between common stock and cumulative preferred stock. Write a memorandum to Kay describing the difference between these two types of financial instruments.

To:     Ms. Kay Smith, CEO, Min Co.
From:   CPA Candidate
Re:     Preferred and Common Stock

---

**Simulation Problem 2**                                    (50 to 60 minutes)

| **Situation** | | | | | | |
|---|---|---|---|---|---|---|
| | **Analysis of Transactions** | **Balance Sheet Disclosures** | **Calculation Basic EPS** | **Calculation Diluted EPS** | **Communication** | **Research** |

M Corporation was incorporated in 2006. During 2006, the company issued 100,000 shares of $1 par value common stock for $27 per share. During 2007, the company had the following transactions.

| | |
|---|---|
| 1/2/07 | Issued 10,000 shares of $100 par value cumulative preferred stock at par. The preferred stock was convertible into five shares of common stock and had a dividend rate of 6%. |
| 3/1/07 | Issued 3,000 shares of common stock for legal service performed. The value of the legal services was $100,000. The stock was actively traded on a stock exchange and valued on 3/1/07 at $32 per share. |
| 7/1/07 | Issued 40,000 shares of common stock for $42 per share. |
| 10/1/07 | Repurchased 16,000 shares of treasury stock for $34 per share. M Corp. uses the cost method to account for treasury shares. |
| 12/1/07 | Sold 3,000 shares of treasury stock for $29 per share. |
| 12/30/07 | Declared and paid a dividend of $0.20 per share on common stock and a 6% dividend on the preferred stock. |

During 2006, M Corporation had net income of $250,000 and paid dividends of $28,000. During 2007 M Corporation had net income of $380,000.

| | **Analysis of Transactions** | | | | | |
|---|---|---|---|---|---|---|
| **Situation** | | **Balance Sheet Disclosures** | **Calculation Basic EPS** | **Calculation Diluted EPS** | **Communication** | **Research** |

Indicate the impact that the transactions for M Company have on its owner equity accounts. Place the appropriate amounts in the table below. If an amount is negative, show the amount in parentheses.

| Date | Transaction | Preferred stock | APIC – Preferred stock | Common stock | APIC – Common stock | Retained earnings | Treasury stock | APIC – Treasury stock |
|---|---|---|---|---|---|---|---|---|
| 1/2/07 | Issue preferred stock at par | | | | | | | |
| 3/1/07 | Issue common stock for services | | | | | | | |
| 7/1/07 | Issue common stock for cash | | | | | | | |
| 10/1/07 | Repurchase treasury stock | | | | | | | |
| 12/1/07 | Sell treasury stock | | | | | | | |
| 12/30/07 | Declare and pay dividends | | | | | | | |

| | | **Balance Sheet Disclosures** | | | | |
|---|---|---|---|---|---|---|
| **Situation** | **Analysis of Transactions** | | **Calculation Basic EPS** | **Calculation Diluted EPS** | **Communication** | **Research** |

Prepare the stockholders' equity section of the balance sheet by completing the following schedule.

| Owners' equity: | |
|---|---|
| Preferred stock | |
| Common stock | |
| Additional paid-in capital preferred stock | |
| Additional paid-in capital common stock | |
| Additional paid-in capital treasury stock | |
| Retained earnings | |
| Treasury stock | |
| Other comprehensive income | |
| Total owners' equity | |

| Situation | Analysis of Transactions | Balance Sheet Disclosures | Calculation Basic EPS | Calculation Diluted EPS | Communication | Research |
|---|---|---|---|---|---|---|

Calculate basic earnings per share.  Show the components of your solution in the following table:

| Numerator | |
|---|---|
| Denominator | |
| Basic earnings per share | |

| Situation | Analysis of Transactions | Balance Sheet Disclosures | Calculation Basic EPS | Calculation Diluted EPS | Communication | Research |
|---|---|---|---|---|---|---|

Calculate diluted earnings per share.  Show the components of your solution in the following table:

| Numerator | |
|---|---|
| Denominator | |
| Diluted earnings per share | |

| Situation | Analysis of Transactions | Balance Sheet Disclosures | Calculation Basic EPS | Calculation Diluted EPS | Communication | Research |
|---|---|---|---|---|---|---|

Mr. Fenton, the CEO of M Corporation, does not understand the purpose of earnings per share.  He has contacted you for information regarding the reasons for calculating earnings per share and why there are two forms of earnings per share.  Write a brief memo to Mr. Fenton explaining the purpose of earnings per share and the difference between basic earnings per share and diluted earnings per share.

To:       Mr. Fenton, CEO, M Corporation
From:    CPA Candidate
Re:       Earnings per share

| Situation | Analysis of Transactions | Balance Sheet Disclosures | Calculation Basic EPS | Calculation Diluted EPS | Communication | Research |
|---|---|---|---|---|---|---|

Research the professional standards to obtain the appropriate section to answer the following question:

When treasury shares are sold for more than purchased, how is it recorded on the financial statements?

---

**Simulation Problem 3**                    (50 to 60 minutes)

| Situation | | | | | | |
|---|---|---|---|---|---|---|
| | Concepts | Journal Entries | Retained Earnings | Stockholders' Equity Section of Balance Sheet | Communication | Research |

Field Co.'s stockholders' equity account balances at December 31, 2006, were as follows:

| Common stock | $ 800,000 |
|---|---|
| Additional paid-in capital | 1,600,000 |
| Retained earnings | 1,845,000 |

The following 2007 transactions and other information relate to the stockholders' equity accounts:

- Field had 400,000 authorized shares of $5 par common stock, of which 160,000 shares were issued and outstanding.
- On March 5, 2007, Field acquired 5,000 shares of its common stock for $10 per share to hold as treasury stock. The shares were originally issued at $15 per share. Field uses the cost method to account for treasury stock. Treasury stock is permitted in Field's state of incorporation.
- On July 15, 2007, Field declared and distributed a property dividend of inventory. The inventory had a $75,000 carrying value and a $60,000 fair market value.
- On January 2, 2004, Field granted stock options to employees to purchase 20,000 shares of Field's common stock at $18 per share, which was the market price on that date. The options may be exercised within a three-year period beginning January 2, 2007. The measurement date is the same as the grant date. On October 1, 2007, employees exercised all 20,000 options when the market value of the stock was $25 per share. Field issued new shares to settle the transaction. The stock options were accounted for in accordance with APB 25, which was in effect at the time.
- Field's net income for 2007 was $240,000.

| Situation | Concepts | Journal Entries | Retained Earnings | Stockholders' Equity Section of Balance Sheet | Communication | Research |
|---|---|---|---|---|---|---|

Identify whether each of the following statements is True or False.

|  |  | *True* | *False* |
|---|---|---|---|
| 1. | Mandatorily redeemable preferred stock is classified as owners' equity and is disclosed after common stock. | O | O |
| 2. | Property dividends are valued at the book value of the property. | O | O |
| 3. | When a company makes a liquidating dividend, it debits the common stock account. | O | O |
| 4. | Scrip dividends are a liability on the date of declaration. | O | O |
| 5. | Stock dividends of 40% of the outstanding shares of stock are valued at fair market value on the date of declaration. | O | O |
| 6. | If a company has cumulative preferred stock, all dividends in arrears must be subtracted from net income in the numerator of basic earnings per share. | O | O |
| 7. | Cash dividends become a liability to the corporation when declared. | O | O |
| 8. | Stock issued for services should be recorded at the fair market value of the services rendered if that value is greater than the fair market value of the stock traded on the exchange. | O | O |

| Situation | Concepts | Journal Entries | Retained Earnings | Stockholders' Equity Section of Balance Sheet | Communication | Research |
|---|---|---|---|---|---|---|

Prepare journal entries for the following transactions in 2007.

1. Treasury stock purchased on March 5, 2007

|  |  |  |
|---|---|---|
|  |  |  |
|  |  |  |

2. Declaration and distribution of a property dividend on July 15, 2007

|  |  |  |
|---|---|---|
|  |  |  |
|  |  |  |

|  |  |  |
|---|---|---|
|  |  |  |
|  |  |  |

3. Issue of common stock on October 1, 2007.

|  |  |  |
|---|---|---|
|  |  |  |
|  |  |  |
|  |  |  |

| Situation | Concepts | Journal Entries | **Retained Earnings** | Stockholders' Equity Section of Balance Sheet | Communication | Research |
|-----------|----------|-----------------|----------------|-----------------------------------------------|---------------|----------|

Complete the following schedule for retained earnings for Field Company.

*Field Company*
**STATEMENT OF RETAINED EARNINGS**
*for the Year ending December 31, 2007*

| | |
|---|---|
| Beginning retained earnings, 1-1-07 | |
| Net income | |
| Dividends | |
| End retained earnings, 12-31-07 | |

| Situation | Concepts | Journal Entries | Retained Earnings | **Stockholders' Equity Section of Balance Sheet** | Communication | Research |
|-----------|----------|-----------------|-------------------|---------------------------------------------------|---------------|----------|

*Field Company*
**STOCKHOLDERS' EQUITY SECTION OF BALANCE SHEET**
*December 31, 2007*

| | |
|---|---|
| Common stock | |
| Additional paid-in capital | |
| Retained earnings | |
| Treasury stock | |
| Accumulated other comprehensive income | |
| Total stockholders' equity | |

| Situation | Concepts | Journal Entries | Retained Earnings | Stockholders' Equity Section of Balance Sheet | **Communication** | Research |
|-----------|----------|-----------------|-------------------|-----------------------------------------------|---------------|----------|

The CEO of Field Company has inquired about calculating earnings per share. Write a brief memo explaining basic and diluted earnings per share.

To:      CEO, Field Company
From:   CPA Candidate
Re:      Earnings per share

|  |
|--|
|  |

| Situation | Concepts | Journal Entries | Retained Earnings | Stockholders' Equity Section of Balance Sheet | Communication | **Research** |
|-----------|----------|-----------------|-------------------|-----------------------------------------------|---------------|----------|

Answer the following questions using the Financial Accounting Research System (FARS) database. Cut and paste your answer from the authoritative literature.

1.  How is diluted earnings per share calculated?

2.  What is the purpose of reporting comprehensive income?

3.  A company has available-for-sale securities and recognizes an unrealized holding gain in year 1. In year 2, the company sells these securities. How should this affect other comprehensive income on the financial statements?

## MULTIPLE-CHOICE ANSWERS

| | | | | | |
|---|---|---|---|---|---|
| 1. a __ __ | 20. a __ __ | 39. a __ __ | 58. d __ __ | 77. c __ __ | |
| 2. b __ __ | 21. c __ __ | 40. a __ __ | 59. b __ __ | 78. a __ __ | |
| 3. d __ __ | 22. c __ __ | 41. d __ __ | 60. b __ __ | 79. c __ __ | |
| 4. d __ __ | 23. b __ __ | 42. d __ __ | 61. c __ __ | 80. a __ __ | |
| 5. a __ __ | 24. c __ __ | 43. b __ __ | 62. b __ __ | 81. b __ __ | |
| 6. c __ __ | 25. d __ __ | 44. d __ __ | 63. b __ __ | 82. c __ __ | |
| 7. a __ __ | 26. d __ __ | 45. a __ __ | 64. d __ __ | 83. d __ __ | |
| 8. d __ __ | 27. b __ __ | 46. c __ __ | 65. b __ __ | 84. a __ __ | |
| 9. a __ __ | 28. c __ __ | 47. c __ __ | 66. a __ __ | 85. a __ __ | |
| 10. b __ __ | 29. c __ __ | 48. c __ __ | 67. d __ __ | 86. a __ __ | |
| 11. d __ __ | 30. b __ __ | 49. c __ __ | 68. a __ __ | 87. a __ __ | |
| 12. c __ __ | 31. b __ __ | 50. a __ __ | 69. b __ __ | 88. c __ __ | |
| 13. c __ __ | 32. d __ __ | 51. c __ __ | 70. b __ __ | 89. d __ __ | |
| 14. d __ __ | 33. d __ __ | 52. d __ __ | 71. d __ __ | 90. c __ __ | |
| 15. a __ __ | 34. b __ __ | 53. d __ __ | 72. c __ __ | 91. b __ __ | |
| 16. c __ __ | 35. a __ __ | 54. c __ __ | 73. d __ __ | | |
| 17. b __ __ | 36. d __ __ | 55. b __ __ | 74. b __ __ | 1st: __/91 = __% | |
| 18. c __ __ | 37. b __ __ | 56. b __ __ | 75. c __ __ | 2nd: __/91 = __% | |
| 19. c __ __ | 38. b __ __ | 57. b __ __ | 76. d __ __ | | |

## MULTIPLE-CHOICE ANSWER EXPLANATIONS

### A.  Common Stock

**1.     (a)**   When stock is issued for services, the transaction should be recorded at either the FMV of the stock issued or the FMV of the services received, whichever is more clearly determinable.  The FMV of stock traded on a public exchange is a more objective, reliable measure than a normal billing rate for legal services, which is likely to be negotiable.  If the transaction is valued at $140 per share, legal expense would be debited for $140,000 (1,000 × $140), common stock would be credited for the par value of $5,000 (1,000 × $5), and additional paid-in capital would be credited for the difference ($140,000 − $5,000 = $135,000).

**2.     (b)**   When stock is issued in combination with other securities (lump sum sales), the proceeds can be allocated by the **proportional method** or by the **incremental method**.  If the FMV of each class of securities is determinable, the proceeds should be allocated to each class of securities based on their relative FMV.  In the instances where the FMV of all classes of securities is not determinable, the incremental method should be used.  The market value of the securities is used as a basis for those classes that are known, and the remainder of the lump sum is allocated to the class for which the market value is not known.  In this problem, the FMV of the stock is unknown.  As such, the incremental method must be used as follows:

| | |
|---|---|
| Lump sum receipt | $110,000 |
| FMV of bonds | 40,000 |
| Balance allocated to common stock | $ 70,000 |

As the par value of the common stock is $5,000 (1,000 shares × $5), $65,000 ($70,000 − $5,000) should be reported as additional paid-in capital on the issuance of the stock.

**3.     (d)**   The number of common shares outstanding is equal to the issued shares less treasury shares.  Beck Corp. had 300,000 shares outstanding at 1/1/07.  The purchase of treasury shares in 2007 reduced the number of shares outstanding to 225,000 (300,000 − 75,000).  The preferred stock convertible into 100,000 shares of common stock is recorded as preferred stock until it is **converted** by the stockholder.

**4.     (d)**   On February 1, 2007, when shares were issued at par for cash, the following journal entry would have been made:

| | | |
|---|---|---|
| Cash | (cash received) | |
| Common stock | | (par) |

On March 1, 2007, however, the issuance of 5,000 shares in settlement for legal services rendered would have been recorded as follows:

| | | |
|---|---|---|
| Legal fees | 60,000 | |
| Common stock ($10 × 5,000 shares) | | 50,000 |
| Addl. paid-in capital | | 10,000 |

Per APB 29, stock issued for services (i.e., in a nonmonetary transaction) should be recorded at the fair market value of those services (in this case $60,000).

### B.  Preferred Stock

**5.     (a)**   When the common stock was issued, it was recorded at stated value with the excess recorded as additional paid-in capital.

| | | |
|---|---|---|
| Cash | 600,000 | |
| Common stock | | 20,000 |
| Addl. paid-in capital | | 580,000 |

The preferred stock was recorded at par value with the excess credited to additional paid-in capital.

| | | |
|---|---|---|
| Cash | 300,000 | |
| Preferred stock | | 60,000 |
| Addl. paid-in capital | | 240,000 |

Therefore, at 4/1/07, the balances are common stock ($20,000), preferred stock ($60,000), and additional paid-in capital ($580,000 + $240,000 = $820,000).

**6.     (c)**   In a lump-sum issuance of common and preferred stock, the proceeds ($80,000) are generally allocated based on the relative fair market values of the securities issued.  The FMV of the convertible preferred stock is $54,000 ($27 × 2,000) and the FMV of the common stock is $36,000 ($36 × 1,000).  The proceeds are allocated as follows:

| Convertible preferred | $\dfrac{\$54,000}{\$90,000}$ | × | $80,000 | = | $48,000 |
|---|---|---|---|---|---|
| Common | $\dfrac{\$36,000}{\$90,000}$ | × | $80,000 | = | $32,000 |

**7. (a)** All 5,000 shares of convertible preferred stock were converted to common stock at a rate of 3 shares of common for every share of preferred. Therefore, 15,000 shares of common stock were issued (5,000 × 3). The common stock account is credited for the par value of these shares (15,000 × $25 = $375,000). APIC – CS ($550,000 – $375,000 = $175,000) is credited for the difference between the carrying amount of the preferred stock (5,000 × $110 = $550,000) and the par value of the common stock. The journal entry is

| Preferred stock | 500,000 | |
| APIC-PS | 50,000 | |
| Common stock | | 375,000 |
| APIC-CS | | 175,000 |

Note that the $40 market value of the common stock is ignored. The book value method must be used for conversion of preferred stock, so no gains or losses can be recognized.

**8. (d)** Per APB 14, when an issuance of debt, or in this case preferred stock, contains detachable common stock warrants the total proceeds from the sale should be allocated to both the preferred stock and the detachable stock warrants. This treatment arises due to the separability of the stock and the detachable warrants. The allocation of the proceeds is based on the relative fair values of both the stock and the warrants at the time of the issuance. However, in instances where only one of the fair values is known, the known fair value will be used to allocate proceeds to the security in which the fair value is determinable. The remainder is then allocated to the security for which the fair value is unknown. Therefore, because only the fair value of the warrants is known, answer (d) is correct. Answers (a) and (b) are incorrect because fair market value is used to allocate proceeds to the warrants, not the total proceeds or excess proceeds over par value. Answer (c) is incorrect because proceeds are allocated in proportion to both fair values, if determinable, not the fair market value and par value.

**9. (a)** When the preferred stock and detachable warrants are issued, the following journal entry is made:

| Cash | (cash received) |
| Preferred stock | (par value) |
| APIC—preferred stock | (FMV of preferred stock – par value) |
| APIC—stock warrants | (plug) |

When the stock warrants are exercised, the following journal entry is made:

| Cash | (cash received) |
| APIC—stock warrants | (original amount credited) |
| Common stock | (par value) |
| APIC—common stock | (plug) |

Therefore, stockholders' equity is increased by the cash received upon the exercise of the common stock warrants. The carrying amount of the warrants increased total stockholders' equity when the preferred stock was issued, not when the warrants were issued.

## C. Stock Subscriptions

**10. (b)** When no par common stock is sold on a subscription basis at a price above the stock's stated value, the stock is not issued until the full subscription price is received. The journal entry on the subscription contract date would be

| Cash | (amount received—if any) |
| Subscription receivable | (balance due) |
| Common stock subscribed | (stated value) |
| Additional paid-in capital | (plug) |

The journal entry on the date the balance of the subscription is collected and the common stock issued would be

| Cash | (balance due) |
| Common stock subscribed | (stated value) |
| Common stock | (stated value) |
| Subscription receivable | (balance due) |

Additional paid-in capital increases on the date that the stock is subscribed, not paid for or issued.

**11. (d)** When stock is sold on a subscription basis, the full price of the stock is not received initially, and the stock is not issued until the full subscription price is received. On the subscription contract date of December 1, 2007, the journal entry would be

| Cash | (amount received) |
| Subscriptions receivable | (balance due) |
| Common stock subscribed | (par) |
| Additional paid-in capital | (plug) |

## D. Treasury Stock Transactions

**12. (c)** Under the cost method, the treasury stock account is debited for the cost of the shares acquired. If the treasury shares are reissued at a price in excess of the acquisition cost, the excess is credited to an account titled Paid-in Capital from Treasury Stock. This question refers to it as Additional Paid-in Capital because typically companies do not segregate the two accounts on the balance sheet for reporting purposes. If the treasury shares are reissued at less than the acquisition cost, the deficiency is treated first as a reduction to any paid-in capital related to previous reissuances or retirements of treasury stock of the same class. If the balance in Paid-in Capital from Treasury Stock is not sufficient to absorb the deficiency, the remainder is recorded as a reduction of retained earnings. As the shares in this question were reissued at a price in excess of the acquisition price, the following journal entry would be made at the time of reissue:

| Cash (3,000 × $50) | 150,000 | |
| Treasury stock (3,000 × $36) | | 108,000 |
| Additional paid-in capital ($150,000 – $108,000) | | 42,000 |

**13. (c)** The entry that Rama made on acquisition of treasury stock was as follows using the **cost method:**

| Treasury stock (20,000 × $12) | 240,000 | |
| Cash | | 240,000 |

When some of the shares are later reissued, the entry is

| Cash (15,000 × $10) | 150,000 | |
| Retained earnings | 30,000 | |
| Treasury stock (15,000 × $12) | | 180,000 |

It is assumed there was no balance in APIC—Treasury stock prior to this entry. If the problem had stated there was a credit balance, APIC—Treasury stock would be debited before retained earnings to the extent a credit balance existed in APIC—Treasury stock. SFAS 5 requires disclosure when retained earnings are legally restricted. In this case, the net treasury stock account balance is $60,000 ($240,000 – $180,000), and this is the amount of retained earnings that must be disclosed as legally restricted.

**14. (d)** The unadjusted stockholders' equity section shows a total of $2,000,000. However, analysis of the current asset section reveals that United has incorrectly classified $300,000 of treasury stock as a current asset. Although this account has a debit balance, it is **not an asset**. Treasury stock should be reported as a reduction of stockholders' equity. Therefore, total equity at 12/31/07 should be $1,700,000 ($2,000,000 – $300,000).

**15. (a)** Under the cost method, when treasury stock is acquired, **treasury stock** is debited and **cash** is credited for the cost.

| | | |
|---|---|---|
| Treasury stock | 100,000 | |
| Cash | | 100,000 |

When the treasury stock is resold at an amount above cost, **cash** is debited for the proceeds, **treasury stock** is credited at cost, and the difference is credited to **additional paid-in capital—treasury stock**.

| | | |
|---|---|---|
| Cash | 25,000 | |
| Treasury stock | | 20,000 |
| APIC—TS | | 5,000 |

Neither of these two transactions affect **retained earnings**. Therefore, 12/31/07 retained earnings consists of the 12/31/06 balance ($300,000) plus 2007 net income ($60,000), or $360,000.

**16. (c)** The requirement is to determine the balance in the paid-in capital from treasury stock account at 12/31/07. Using the par value method, treasury stock is debited for par value (5,000 × $10, or $50,000) when purchased. Any excess over par from the original issuance (5,000 × $4, or $20,000) is removed from the appropriate paid-in capital account. In effect, the total original issuance price (5,000 × $14, or $70,000) is charged to the two accounts. Any difference between the original issue price ($70,000) and the cost of the treasury stock (5,000 × $11, or $55,000) is credited to paid-in capital from treasury stock, as illustrated below.

| | | | |
|---|---|---|---|
| Treasury stock | 50,000 | | (5,000 × $10) |
| APIC | 20,000 | | (5,000 × $ 4) |
| Cash | | 55,000 | (5,000 × $11) |
| PIC—Treasury stock | | 15,000 | ($70,000 – $55,000) |

**17. (b)** When Dee Inc. issued common stock at a price in excess of its par value, the following journal entry was made:

| | |
|---|---|
| Cash | (Cash received) |
| Common stock | (Par) |
| Additional paid-in capital | (Excess of cash capital received over par) |

When Dee Inc. acquires treasury stock using the par method for an amount exceeding the issue price the following journal entry is made:

| | |
|---|---|
| Treasury stock | (Par) |
| Additional paid-in capital | (Excess of original issue price over par) |
| Retained earnings | (Excess of acquisition price over issue price) |
| Cash | (Cash paid) |

**Net** common stock decreases by the par value of treasury stock acquired. Additional paid-in capital decreases by the excess of the original issue price over the par value. Retained earnings decreases by the excess of the acquisition price over the original issue price.

**18. (c)** In this case, the par value method does not report a greater amount for additional paid-in capital or retained earnings than the cost method. The entries for an acquisition of treasury shares at greater than par but less than the original issue price are as follows:

| Cost method | | | Par value method | | |
|---|---|---|---|---|---|
| Treasury stock | xxx | | Treasury stock | xxx | |
| Cash | | xxx | PIC in excess of par | xxx | |
| | | | Cash | | xxx |
| | | | PIC from treasury stock | | xxx |

Since under the par value method the original paid-in capital in excess of par must be removed from the accounts upon reacquisition, the par value method actually reports a decrease in additional paid-in capital. On the other hand, under the cost method no change in additional paid-in capital is recorded. There is no change in retained earnings under either method.

**E. Retirement of Stock**

**19. (c)** When accounting for the retirement of stock, common stock and additional paid-in capital are removed from the books based on the original issuance of the stock. Cash is credited for the cost of the shares. Any difference is debited to **retained earnings** or credited to **paid-in capital from retirement**. The entry in this case is

| | | |
|---|---|---|
| Common stock | 20,000 | (2,000 × $10) |
| APIC | 180,000 | (2,000 × $90) |
| Retained earnings | 100,000 | (2,000 × $50) |
| Cash | | 300,000 |

Therefore, APIC should be debited for $180,000 and retained earnings should be debited for $100,000.

**20. (a)** In this problem, Luna Corp. is exchanging its available-for-sale securities (AFS) for its preferred stock (i.e., they are retiring some of their preferred stock by exchanging AFS). Upon disposition of the AFS, a gain of $70,000, which is the difference between the carrying amount ($80,000) and the FMV ($150,000), must be recognized. Upon retirement of the stock, the preferred stock is debited for the $100,000 par amount (5,000 shares × $20 par). The additional paid-in capital (APIC) is debited for $7,500, which is 1/4 of the original APIC (i.e., 5,000 of the 20,000 shares were retired). The remainder of the FMV of the preferred stock ($42,500 = $150,000 – $100,000 – $7,500) is debited to retained earnings.

**21. (c)** When accounting for the retirement of treasury stock that was initially recorded using the cost method, common stock and additional paid-in capital are removed from the books based on the original issuance of the stock. Treasury stock is credited for the cost of the shares acquired. Any difference is debited to retained earnings or credited to paid-in capital from retirement. In this problem, common stock should be debited for $125,000 (50,000 shares × $2.50), and the common stock balance at December 31, 2007, is $415,000 ($540,000 – $125,000).

**22. (c)** The requirement is to determine which of the statements correctly identifies an effect of the acquisition and retirement of common stock. The entry to record the retirement of common stock appears as follows:

| | | |
|---|---|---|
| Common stock (par) | xxx | |
| Additional paid-in capital | xxx | |
| Retained earnings | xxx | |
|     Cash | | xxx |

Additional paid-in capital is debited to the extent it exists. In this case, based on the original issuance, the additional paid-in capital (APIC) balance was $15 per share on the shares retired. When stock is repurchased, if the APIC balance is depleted to zero, retained earnings must also be debited. In this case, retained earnings would not be needed, however. Common stock would be debited for $10 per share and additional paid-in capital would be debited for $10 a share. Excess APIC remains, so retained earnings are not needed to retire the stock. When common stock is repurchased and retired, additional paid-in capital decreases. When common stock is retired, net income is never affected; only stockholders' equity balances are affected. If retained earnings are needed to retire stock, the account decreases, not increases.

## F. Dividends

**23. (b)** Since this is an investment accounted for on the cost basis, the dividend income should be the amount of cash dividends received. Since Plack Co. had 12,000 shares at the time the cash dividend was paid, the total amount of cash dividends received is $24,000 (12,000 × $2.00).

**24. (c)** When preferred stock is participating, there may be different agreements as to how the participation feature is to be executed. However, in the absence of any specific agreement, the following procedure should be used:

After the preferred stock is allocated its current year dividend, the common stock will receive a "like" percentage of par value outstanding. If there are remaining declared dividends, this amount should be shared by both the preferred and common stock in proportion to the par value dollars outstanding of each stock as follows:

Current year's dividend:

| | | |
|---|---|---|
| Preferred, 5% of $300,000 | | |
|   (30,000 shares × $10 Par) | $15,000 | |
| Common, 5% of $200,000 | | |
|   (200,000 shares × $1 Par) | 10,000 | $ 25,000 |
| Amount available for participation | | |
|   ($100,000 – $25,000) | | $ 75,000 |
| Par value of stock that is to participate | | |
|   ($300,000 + $200,000) | | $500,000 |

Proportional share of participating dividend:

| | | | | | |
|---|---|---|---|---|---|
| Preferred | $\dfrac{\$300,000}{\$500,000}$ | × | 75,000 | = | $ 45,000 |
| Common | $\dfrac{\$200,000}{\$500,000}$ | × | 75,000 | = | $ 30,000 |

Thus, the dividends payable to common shareholders is $40,000 ($10,000 + $30,000).

**25. (d)** For **cumulative** preferred stock, dividends not paid in **any** year will accumulate and must be paid in a later year before any dividends can be paid to common stock-

holders. The unpaid prior year dividends are called "dividends in arrears." The balance of dividends in arrears should be disclosed in the financial statements rather than accrued, as they are not considered a liability until they are declared. Dividends in arrears at 12/31/07 total $20,000, as computed below.

| | | | |
|---|---|---|---|
| 2006 | $300,000 × 5% | = | $15,000 |
| 2007 | $300,000 × 5% | = | 15,000 |
| Total cumulative preferred dividends | | | $30,000 |
| Less 2007 dividend payment | | | (10,000) |
| Balance of dividends in arrears | | | $20,000 |

Answer (c) is incorrect because dividends in arrears are not considered to be a liability until they are declared. They should be disclosed parenthetically or in the notes to the financial statements. Answer (b) is incorrect because the total dividends amount needs to reflect both the 2006 and 2007 unpaid dividends since it is cumulative preferred stock. Answer (a) is incorrect because the dividends in arrears would not be considered a liability until they are declared and the $15,000 amount is the incorrect balance as discussed above.

**26. (d)** The interest is not an expense or liability until incurred, thus, none of it is recorded on April 1. The April 1 entry would be

| | | |
|---|---|---|
| Retained earnings | 100,000 | |
|   Scrip dividends payable | | 100,000 |

By December 31 (the year-end for this calendar-year company), nine months' interest had been incurred, which would not be paid until the maturity date of 3/31/08. The $7,500 of interest expense ($100,000 × 10% × 9/12) must be accrued at 12/31/07 with the following entry:

| | | |
|---|---|---|
| Interest expense | 7,500 | |
|   Interest payable | | 7,500 |

**27. (b)** Dividends that are based on funds other than retained earnings are considered to be liquidating dividends. The cash dividend declared of $400,000 is first assumed to be a return **on** capital for the distribution of the retained earnings balance of $300,000. The excess $400,000 dividend – $300,000 RE = $100,000 is considered to be a return **of** capital or a liquidating dividend rather than a return **on** capital. Note that the amount of liquidating dividend also equals the balance in accumulated depletion. Companies in the extractive industries may pay dividends equal to the accumulated income **and** depletion.

**28. (c)** Per APB 29, a transfer of a nonmonetary asset to a stockholder or to another entity in a nonreciprocal transfer should be recorded at the fair value of the asset transferred, and a gain or loss should be recognized on the disposition of the asset. The fair value of the nonmonetary asset distributed is measured by the amount that would be realized in an outright sale at or near the time of distribution. In this case, a gain should be recognized for the difference between the fair value of $2.50 per share and the carrying amount of $2 per share, or a total gain of $50,000 [100,000 × ($2.50 – $2.00)].

**29. (c)** Per APB 29, a transfer of a nonmonetary asset to a stockholder or to another entity in a nonreciprocal transfer should be recorded at the fair market value of the asset transferred, and a gain or loss should be recognized on the disposition of the asset. At the date of declaration, Nilo records

| Trading securities | 18,000 | |
| Gain on disposition of securities | | 18,000 |
| Retained earnings (dividends) | 78,000 | |
| Property dividends payable | | 78,000 |

At the date of distribution, Nilo records

| Property dividends payable | 78,000 | |
| Trading securities | | 78,000 |

After all nominal accounts are closed, the effect on retained earnings from the above entries would be $60,000 ($78,000 debit to retained earnings less $18,000 credit to retained earnings when the "gain on disposition" account is closed out).

**30. (b)** A stock split is **not** a dividend. Stock splits change the number of shares outstanding and the par value per share. Par value per share is reduced in proportion to the increase in the number of shares. Therefore, the total par value outstanding does not change, and no journal entry is required. The only dividend to be reported in Long's 2007 statement of stockholders' equity is the 12/15 cash dividend. The stock split increased the number of shares outstanding to 200,000 (100,000 × 2), so the amount of the cash dividend is $100,000 (200,000 × $.50).

**31. (b)** The requirement is to determine the effect of a cash dividend on stockholders' equity at the three dates listed. On the date of declaration, December 15, 2007, the following entry should be made:

| Retained earnings | xxx | |
| Dividends payable | | xxx |

Thus, at December 15, 2007, stockholders' equity is reduced due to the debit to retained earnings. On December 31, 2007, there is no effect on stockholders' equity because an entry would not be recorded. On January 12, 2008, the following entry would be made:

| Dividends payable | xxx | |
| Cash | | xxx |

The net effect of this entry is to decrease assets and liabilities by an equal amount. Thus, stockholders' equity (or net assets) would be unaffected.

**32. (d)** Any dividend not based on earnings must be a reduction of corporate paid-in capital and, to that extent, it is a liquidating dividend. The following journal entries would be made for this situation:

At date of declaration:

| Additional paid-in capital | 100,000 | |
| Dividends payable | | 100,000 |

At date of payment:

| Dividends payable | 100,000 | |
| Cash | | 100,000 |

Thus, a liquidating dividend would decrease Ole's paid-in capital, not its retained earnings.

**33. (d)** A property dividend is a nonreciprocal transfer of nonmonetary assets between an enterprise and its owners. APB 29 requires that "nonreciprocal transfers of nonmonetary assets to a stockholder or another entity shall be recorded at the fair value of the asset transferred. Additionally, a gain or loss shall be recognized on the disposition of the asset." Accordingly, Evie Corp. should record the following journal entries to reflect the property dividend:

At the date of declaration:

| Loss on decline in inventory value (Carrying amount – Market value) | xxx | |
| Merchandise inventory | | xxx |
| Retained earnings (market value) | xxx | |
| Property dividends payable | | xxx |

At the date of distribution:

| Property dividends payable | xxx | |
| Merchandise inventory | | xxx |

The loss recorded in the above journal entry does not qualify as unusual and infrequent, thus it is not an extraordinary item. The loss should be reported as a reduction in income before extraordinary items.

**34. (b)** The requirement is to determine the amount to be debited to retained earnings for these stock dividends. Per ARB 43, chap 7B, the issuance of a stock dividend less than **20-25%** (a "small" stock dividend) requires that the **market value** of the stock be transferred from retained earnings, and a dividend greater than **20-25%** (a "large" stock dividend) requires the **par value** of the stock to be transferred from retained earnings. Thus, a 10% stock dividend is considered to be "small" and should be transferred from retained earnings at the FMV of $15,000. A 28% stock dividend is considered to be "large" and should be transferred at the par value of $30,800. The aggregate amount to be transferred from retained earnings is $45,800.

**35. (a)** When the stock dividend is less than 20-25% of the common shares outstanding at the time of the declaration, generally accepted accounting principles require that the FMV of the stock issued be transferred from retained earnings. At the date of declaration, the following entry would be made:

| Retained earnings (Stock dividends declared) (.05 × 10,000 shares × $5) | 2,500 | |
| Common stock dividend distributable (.05 × 10,000 × $2) | | 1,000 |
| Additional paid-in capital (plug) | | 1,500 |

Note from the entry above that no asset or liability has been affected. The entry merely reflects a reclassification within the equity accounts. When a balance sheet is prepared between the dates of declaration and distribution, the common stock dividend distributable should be shown in the stockholders' equity section as an addition to capital stock.

**G. Stock Splits**

**36. (d)** ARB 43, chap 7, defines a stock dividend as an issuance by a corporation of its own common shares to its common shareholders without consideration...to give the recipient shareholders evidence of a part of their respective interests in accumulated corporate earnings without distribution of cash or other property. A stock split is defined as an issuance by a corporation of common shares to its common shareholders without consideration...prompted mainly by a desire to increase the number of outstanding shares for the purpose of effecting a reduction in their unit market price and, thereby, of obtaining wider distribution and improved marketability of the shares. Thus, neither of these transactions results in a transfer of assets among the shareholders and the corporation. While the allocation of stockholders' equity among the various accounts (retained earnings, common stock, and additional paid-in capital) will change, the **total** stockholders' equity is **not** affected.

**37. (b)** The requirement is to determine the balance of additional paid-in capital immediately after a reverse stock split. Stock splits change the number of shares outstanding and the par value per share, but the total par value outstanding does not change. Stock splits do not affect any account balances, including additional paid-in capital. Therefore, the balance of additional paid-in capital remains at $450,000.

**38. (b)** A stock split does not affect either the balance of the additional paid-in capital or the retained earnings accounts. The number of shares outstanding and the par value per share merely change in proportion to each other. When this occurs, only a memorandum entry is made.

## H. Appropriations of Retained Earnings (Reserves)

**39. (a)** The requirement is to determine the amount of appropriated retained earnings Eagle should report in its 2007 balance sheet. The entry to record the appropriation of retained earnings in 2007 for the construction of a new plant is as follows:

| | | |
|---|---|---|
| RE (or Unappropriated RE) | $1,200,000 | |
| RE Appropriated for plant expansion | | $1,200,000 |

The cash restricted for the retirement of bonds due in 2007 should **not** be reported as an appropriation of retained earnings because the facts in the question do not indicate that appropriation was made by management. SFAS 5 requires that when an appropriation is no longer needed, it must be returned directly to unappropriated retained earnings by reversing the entry that created it. Therefore, when the office building was completed in 2007, the following entry was made:

| | | |
|---|---|---|
| RE Appropriated for plant expansion | $1,750,000 | |
| RE (or Unappropriated RE) | | $1,750,000 |

The total cost to complete the building has no effect on appropriated retained earnings.

**40. (a)** Retained earnings are typically appropriated due to legal requirements, contractual requirements, or through the discretion of the board of directors. Dividends in arrears are not considered a liability to the company, and retained earnings would not be appropriated for this amount. In many cases, retained earnings must be appropriated for an amount equal to the cost of treasury stock acquired. However, this appropriation would be removed upon reissuance of the treasury stock.

**41. (d)** SFAS 5, states that appropriations of retained earnings are not prohibited provided that the appropriation is clearly identified as such in the stockholders' equity section of the balance sheet. Costs or losses cannot be charged to an appropriation of retained earnings. A contingent loss that is probable and reasonably estimable should be accrued as a loss and liability under the guidance of SFAS 5.

## I.1. Stock Options

**42. (d)** Under SFAS 123(R), employee compensation expense as the result of a stock option plan is calculated as the fair value of the equity instrument **at the date of grant** times the number of option shares.

3,000 shares × $8 fair value of option = $24,000

The total compensation expense must be recognized over the requisite service period for which the option plan represents compensation. If not otherwise specified, the required

service period (two years) is assumed to be the period benefited. Therefore, 2008 compensation expense is $12,000 ($24,000 ÷ 2). Note that compensation expense is not affected by changes in the market value of the stock after the measurement date.

**43. (b)** Under SFAS 123(R), total compensation expense as a result of a stock option plan is calculated as the fair value of the equity instruments at the date of grant times the number of options.

10,000 options × $12 fair value of option = $120,000

The total compensation expense must be recognized over the requisite service period for which the option plan represents compensation. Therefore, 2008 compensation expense is $40,000 ($120,000 ÷ 3 years). Note that the cost of treasury stock distributed in an option plan does not determine compensation expense.

**44. (d)** The fair value of the stock option at date of grant was $28 ($28 × 1,000 shares = $28,000). The entire amount is recognized because the options are exercisable immediately for three years after the grant date.

**45. (a)** The net increase in stockholders' equity (SE) as a result of the grant and exercise of the options is equal to the increase in cash (1,000 shares × $20 option price = $20,000). The journal entry to record the options has no effect on SE because a SE account will be credited while a contra SE account will be debited as follows:

| | | |
|---|---|---|
| Deferred compensation | 28,000 | |
|    Paid-in capital stock options | | 28,000 |
| (1000 shares × $28 per option) | | |

The entry to recognize compensation expense has no effect on SE because the debit decreases SE while the credit increases SE by reducing the contra account as follows:

| | | |
|---|---|---|
| Compensation expense | 28,000 | |
|    Deferred compensation | | 28,000 |

The only entry which does affect SE is the entry for the exercise of the options, which decreases SE by $28,000 while increasing it by $48,000 (a net increase of $20,000).

| | | |
|---|---|---|
| Cash (1,000 × $20) | 20,000 | |
| Paid-in capital stock options (1,000 × $28) | 28,000 | |
|    Common stock (1,000 × $10) | | 10,000 |
|    Paid-in capital in × of PV (plug) | | 38,000 |

Thus, the net increase in stockholders' equity is $20,000.

## I.2. Stock Appreciation Rights

**46. (c)** The 20,000 stock appreciation rights (SAR) each entitle the holder to receive cash equal to the excess of the market price of the stock on the exercise date over the market price on the grant date ($30). Since these SAR are payment for past services and are exercisable immediately, there is no required service period. Therefore, the expense computed at 12/31/08 does **not** have to be allocated to more than one period. At 12/31/08, compensation expense is measured based on the excess of the 12/31/08 market price ($45) over the predetermined price ($30), resulting in compensation expense of $300,000 [20,000 ($45 − $30)]. Note that **if** Dean were **required** to work three years **before** the SAR could be exercised, the expense would be allocated over the three years of required service ($300,000 × 1/3 = $100,000).

## J.  Stock Compensation under SFAS 123

**47.   (c)**   Per SFAS 123(R), when accounting for stock compensation plans, total compensation expense is computed as the excess of the fair value of the equity instrument over the amount contributed by employees. In this case, the fair value of the 150,000 shares issued in 2008 is $1,050,000, and the employees' contributions for these shares is $350,000. Therefore, Wall should recognize $700,000 ($1,050,000 – $350,000) as expense in 2008 for the stock compensation plan.

**48.   (c)**   According to SFAS 123(R), *Share-Based Payment*, the rate of interest used to discount both the exercise price and dividends is the risk-free interest rate.

**49.   (c)**   If the stock options are for past services, as indicated when the options are immediately exercisable by the holders, compensation cost must be fully expensed at the grant date. Answer (a) is incorrect because usually deferred compensation expense is recognized. Answer (b) is incorrect because deferred compensation expense is recognized when service has not yet been provided. Answer (d) is incorrect because when options are provided for prior service compensation expense must immediately be recognized.

**50.   (a)**   Compensation cost for a share-based payment to employees that is classified as a liability is measured by the change in fair value of the instrument for each reporting period.

**51.   (c)**   Per SFAS 123(R), the final measurement date is the settlement date for share-based payments to employees classified as liabilities.

**52.   (d)**   Accounting for stock-based compensation using the fair value method under SFAS 123(R) is as follows:

| | |
|---|---:|
| Fair value of option at grant date | 6.40 |
| Times # of options | × 20,000 |
| Deferred compensation expense | $128,000 |

**53.   (d)**   Cash retained as a result of excess tax benefits in connection with share-based payments to employees should be recognized as a cash inflow from financing activities in the statement of cash flows.

**54.   (c)**   Per SFAS 123(R), the options should be included in the denominator of diluted earnings per share unless the shares are antidilutive. If the equity share options are outstanding for only a part of a period, the shares are weighted to reflect the period of time outstanding.

## K.  Basic Earnings Per Share

**55.   (b)**   The formula for basic earnings per share (BEPS) is

$$\frac{\$1,000,000 \text{ net income} - \$50,000 \text{ preferred dividends}}{200,000 \text{ common shares outstanding}} = \$9.50$$

In calculating the numerator, the claims of preferred shareholders against 2007 earnings should be deducted to arrive at the 2007 earnings attributable to common shareholders. This amount is 50,000 (5% × $100 × 10,000 shares). The $50,000 preferred dividends in arrears is not deducted to compute the numerator in determining 2007 BEPS. This is because the $50,000 dividends in arrears is a claim of preferred shareholders against 2006 earnings and would reduce 2006 BEPS.

**56.   (b)**   The formula for basic earnings per share (BEPS) is

$$\frac{\$500,000 \text{ net income} - 10,000 \text{ preferred dividends}}{200,000 \text{ common shares outstanding}} = \$2.45$$

In calculating the numerator, the claims of preferred shareholders against 2007 earnings should be deducted to arrive at the 2007 earnings attributable to common shareholders. This amount is $10,000 ($250,000 × 4%). During 2006, the BEPS numerator would have been reduced by $10,000 even though no preferred dividends were declared, because the cumulative feature means that $10,000 of 2006 earnings are reserved for, and will ultimately be paid to, preferred stockholders. In 2007, the 2006 dividends in arrears are paid, as well as $6,000 of the $10,000 2007 preferred dividend. Even though only $6,000 is paid, the entire $10,000 is subtracted for reasons explained above.

**57.   (b)**   SFAS 128 states that for EPS purposes, shares of stock issued as a result of stock dividends or splits should be considered outstanding for the entire period in which they were issued. Therefore, both the original 20,000 shares and the additional 20,000 issued in the 4/1 stock split are treated as outstanding for the entire year (20,000 × 2 = 40,000). The 7/1 issuance of 10,000 shares results in a weighted-average of 5,000 shares (10,000 × 6/12) because the shares were outstanding for only six months during the year. Therefore, Jet should use 45,000 shares (40,000 + 5,000) to calculate EPS.

**58.   (d)**   The computation of weighted-average shares outstanding is

| *Date* | *# of shares* | | *Fraction* | | *WA* |
|---|---|---|---|---|---|
| 1/1 | 30,000 | × | 12/12 | = | 30,000 |
| 2/1 | 3,000 | × | 12/12 | = | 3,000 |
| 7/1 | 8,000 | × | 6/12 | = | 4,000 |
| | | | | | 37,000 |

The 3,000 shares issued as a result of a stock dividend are weighted at 12/12 instead of 11/12 because for EPS purposes stock dividends are treated as if they occurred at the beginning of the year.

**59.   (b)**   The formula for computing BEPS for a simple capital structure is

$$\frac{\text{Net income} - \text{Applicable pref. stock dividends}}{\text{Weighted-average \# of common shares outstanding}}$$

Net income is $410,000 and $350,000 in 2007 and 2006, respectively, and there are no preferred dividends. The weighted-average number of common shares outstanding must be computed for 2007. Stock dividends and stock splits are handled retroactively for comparability. The 2007 computation is

| *Dates* | *Number of Shares* | *Fraction* | *WA* |
|---|---|---|---|
| 1/1 to 3/31 | 100,000 × 2 = 200,000 | 3/12 | 50,000 |
| 4/1 to 6/30 | (100,000 + 20,000) × 2 = 240,000 | 3/12 | 60,000 |
| 7/1 to 12/31 | 120,000 × 2 = 240,000 | 6/12 | 120,000 |
| | | | 230,000 |

The 2006 weighted-average of 100,000 is retroactively restated to 200,000 for comparability. Therefore, the BEPS amounts are

| *2007* | | *2006* | |
|---|---|---|---|
| $\frac{\$410,000}{230,000} = \$1.78$ | | $\frac{\$350,000}{200,000} = \$1.75$ | |

**60.** **(b)** Per SFAS 128, earnings per share must be shown on the face of the income statement for income from continuing operations and net income. Discontinued operations, extraordinary items, and cumulative effect of change in accounting principle may be shown on the income statement or in the notes.

**61.** **(c)** Per SFAS 128, if the number of common shares outstanding increases as a result of a stock dividend or stock split or decreases as a result of a reverse split, the computations of EPS should give retroactive recognition for all periods presented. If these events take place after the close of the period but before completion of the financial report, the per share computations should be based on the new number of shares. Note that when per share computations reflect such changes in the number of shares after the close of the period, this fact should be disclosed.

## L. Diluted Earnings Per Share

**62.** **(b)** The requirement is to determine the number of shares that should be used in computing 2007 diluted earnings per share. The first step is to compute the weighted-average number of common shares outstanding. 300,000 shares were outstanding the entire year, and 50,000 more shares were outstanding for six months, resulting in a weighted-average of 325,000 [300,000 + (50,000 × 6/12)]. Second, the stock options increase the number of shares used in the computation **only** if they are dilutive. The stock options are dilutive because the exercise price is less than the market value. Thus, the denominator effect of the options must be computed. This is done using the **treasury stock method,** as illustrated below.

| | |
|---|---:|
| Assumed proceeds (40,000 × $15) | $600,000 |
| Shares issued | 40,000 |
| Shares reacquired ($600,000 ÷ $20) | (30,000) |
| Shares issued, not reacquired | 10,000 |

Therefore, the number of shares used for computing diluted earnings per share is 335,000 (325,000 + 10,000).

**63.** **(b)** Diluted earnings per share is based on common stock and all dilutive potential common shares. To determine if a security is dilutive, EPS, including the effect of the dilutive security, must be compared to the basic EPS. In this case, basic EPS is $7.45.

$$\frac{850,000 \text{ (NI)} - 30,000 \text{ (pref. div.)}}{110,000 \text{ shares}} = \$7.45$$

The effect of the convertible preferred stock is to increase the numerator by $30,000 ($3.00 dividend per share × 10,000 shares) for the amount of the preferred dividends that would not be paid (assuming conversion) and increase the denominator by 20,000 shares. This security is dilutive because it decreases the EPS from $7.45 to $6.54.

$$\frac{850,000 - 30,000 + 30,000}{110,000 + 20,000} = \$6.54$$

If the EPS increases due to the inclusion of a security, that security is antidilutive and should not be included.

**64.** **(d)** The requirement is to compute the diluted earnings per share for 2007. Therefore, **all** potential common shares that **reduce** current EPS must be included in the computation. The formula for diluted EPS is

$$\frac{\text{Net income available to common shareholders}}{\text{Weighted-average common shares outstanding}}$$

The net income available to common shareholders is $3,200,000. This is the net income of $3,400,000 less the preferred stock dividend of $200,000. The weighted-average common shares outstanding is 1,250,000. This is computed as the actual common shares outstanding for the full year of 1,200,000 plus the contingent common shares of 50,000 that were outstanding for the full year because the contingency was incurred in 2005. Thus,

$$\text{Diluted EPS} = \frac{\$3,200,000}{1,250,000} = \$2.56$$

**65.** **(b)** The effect of convertible bonds is included in diluted EPS under the if converted method, if they are dilutive. The bonds are dilutive as shown below.

$$\text{Basic EPS} = \frac{\$35,000}{(1/2)\,10,000 + (1/2)\,14,000} = \$2.92$$

$$\begin{array}{l}\text{Incremental}\\\text{per share effect}\end{array} = \frac{(7\% \times \$10,000) - 30\% (7\% \times \$10,000)}{200 \text{ shares per bond}} = \frac{\$490}{200} = \$2.45$$

Since $2.45 < $2.92, the bonds are dilutive. Under the if converted method, the assumption is made that the bonds were converted at the beginning of the current year (1/1) or later in the current year if the bonds were issued during the current year. In this case, conversion is assumed for the first six months of 2007 only because the bonds were actually converted on July 1. Under their assumed conversion, the numerator would increase because bond interest expense would not have been incurred for the first six months of the year [1/2 ($14,000 – 30% × $14,000) = $4,900]. The denominator would increase because the 4,000 shares (20 × 200) would have been outstanding for the first six months of the year (4,000 × 6/12 = 2,000). Therefore, diluted EPS is $2.85.

$$\frac{\$35,000 + \$4,900}{12,000 + 2,000} = \frac{\$39,900}{14,000} = \$2.85$$

**66.** **(a)** Diluted EPS takes into account the effect of all dilutive potential common shares that were outstanding during the period. Thus, the possible conversion of convertible bonds would be included because they are dilutive (i.e., EPS would be reduced), but the possible exercise of common stock options would not be included because they are antidilutive (i.e., EPS would be increased). Diluted EPS = $15.00 – $.75 = $14.25.

**67.** **(d)** The requirement is to determine the treatment of nonconvertible cumulative preferred dividends in determining diluted EPS. Per SFAS 128, dividends on nonconvertible cumulative preferred shares should be deducted from net income whether an actual liability exists or not. This is because cumulative preferred stock owners must receive any dividends in arrears before future dividend distributions can be made to common stockholders.

**68.** **(a)** Per SFAS 128, the if converted method of computing earnings per share assumes that convertible securities are converted at the beginning of the earliest period reported or, if later, at the time of issuance.

**69.** **(b)** Per SFAS 128, if convertible securities are deemed to be dilutive, then interest expense should be added back to net income when computing diluted earnings per share.

**70.** **(b)** Per SFAS 128, the effect of contingent issue agreements are not included in basic earnings per share.

They are included in diluted earnings per share if the contingency is met.

## M.  Corporate Bankruptcy

**71.  (d)**  The total cash available to pay **all** unsecured claims, including priority claims, is the cash obtained from free assets ($320,000) and any excess cash available from assets pledged with fully secured creditors after they are used to satisfy those claims ($370,000 – $260,000 = $110,000). Therefore, total cash available is $430,000 ($320,000 + $110,000). After paying priority claims, $360,000 will remain to pay all unsecured nonpriority claims ($430,000 – $70,000).

**72.  (c)**  Bankruptcy law requires that the claims of secured creditors be satisfied before any unsecured claims are paid. Hale is a secured creditor in the amount of $5,000 (the liquidation value of the collateral). The remainder of Hale's claim ($30,000 – $5,000 = $25,000) is an unsecured claim, because it is not secured by any collateral. Therefore, Hale will receive a total of $15,000 on this note: $5,000 received in full as a secured creditor, and $10,000 received as an unsecured creditor ($25,000 × $.40).

**73.  (d)**  A bankruptcy trustee may establish a new set of accounting records to maintain accountability for the bankruptcy estate. Once the trustee assumes custody of the estate, the trustee will enter any unrecorded assets or liabilities in the estate equity account. Any gains or losses and liquidation expenses incurred will also be recorded. In the Kamy Corp. bankruptcy, both the $8,000 loss on sale of the truck ($20,000 carrying value – $12,000 cash selling price) and the $1,000 unrecorded liability would be debited to the estate equity account as follows:

| | | |
|---|---|---|
| Estate equity | 1,000 | |
|    Accounts payable | | 1,000 |
| Cash | 12,000 | |
| Estate equity | 8,000 | |
|    Truck | | 20,000 |

## N.  Reorganizations

**74.  (b)**  The requirement is to determine the net increase in total stockholders' equity as a result of the payments to unsecured creditors pursuant to a reorganization plan under Chapter 11. The net increase in stockholders' equity can be determined as follows:

| | |
|---|---|
| Fair value of liabilities owed to unsecured | |
|   creditors | $1,200,000 |
| Cash paid | (400,000) |
| Common stock issued (80,000 × $1.25) | (100,000) |
| Gain on settlement of debt | $ 700,000 |

The gain on the settlement of debt would be included in the income statement and closed to retained earnings. The net increase in stockholders' equity would equal $800,000 ($700,000 gain + $100,000 FMV of stock issued).

## O.  Quasi Reorganization

**75.  (c)**  Although assets are often revalued to fair value during a quasi reorganization, the **primary** purpose of a quasi reorganization is to eliminate a deficit in retained earnings so that dividends may be paid without waiting years to eliminate the deficit through future earnings. A quasi reorganization does not directly allow a corporation to obtain relief from creditors or result in a distribution of stock.

**76.  (d)**  Per ARB 43, chap 7A, in certain instances an entity may elect to restate its assets, capital stock, and surplus through a readjustment (or "quasi reorganization") and thus avail itself of permission to relieve its future income account or earned surplus account of charges which would otherwise be made there against. In such instances, the entity should present a **fair (value)** balance sheet as of the date of the reorganization.

**77.  (c)**  A quasi reorganization generally involves (1) revaluing assets, (2) reducing par, and (3) writing the deficit off against additional paid-in capital. In this case, no mention is made of the first step, revaluing assets. The second step, reducing par, results in a decrease to **common stock** and an increase to **additional paid-in capital** of $250,000 [10,000 × ($30 – $5)]. The third step, writing off the deficit, increases **retained earnings** by $210,000 (creating a $0 balance) and decrease **additional paid-in capital** by the same amount. Immediately after the quasi reorganization, Brown should report additional paid-in capital of $190,000 ($150,000 + $250,000 – $210,000).

## P.  Stock Rights

**78.  (a)**  When a corporation issues rights to its stockholders, it only makes a memorandum entry. If rights are later exercised, the corporation would make the following entry:

| | | |
|---|---|---|
| Cash | xxx | |
|    Common stock | | xxx |
|    Additional paid-in capital | | xxx |

**79.  (c)**  The only time a journal entry is recorded for the issuance and exercise of stock rights is on the date of exercise. At the date of issuance, only a memorandum entry is recorded. The redemption of the rights issued to the shareholders should be treated like a dividend. Accordingly, retained earnings will be decreased by the amount paid to the shareholders (120,000 × $0.10 = $12,000).

**80.  (a)**  The requirement is to determine the effects of the stock warrants on the additional paid-in capital account and on net income. When a corporation issues stock warrants to its stockholders it only makes a memorandum entry. Then, when the warrants are exercised, the following entry is made:

| | | |
|---|---|---|
| Cash | xxx | |
|    Common stock | | xxx |
|    Additional paid-in capital | | xxx |

Net income is not affected by the exercise of stock warrants because the transaction represents a process of raising capital and is not related to the earnings process. Additional paid-in capital is not affected until the exercise date in 2007.

**81.  (b)**  Note that the only time an entry related to the issuance and exercise of stock rights, which affects the equity accounts of a corporation, is recorded is on the date of exercise. At the date of issuance, only a memorandum entry is recorded, and on the date of the rights lapsing, no entry is recorded which would affect the company's equity accounts. Thus, the correct answer is (b): the additional paid-in capital account would not be credited at the time the rights are issued or at the date on which the rights lapse.

## Q.  Employee Stock Ownership Plan (ESOP)

**82. (c)** Per SOP 76-3, the amount contributed or committed to be contributed to an employee stock ownership plan (ESOP) in a given year should be the measure of the amount to be charged to expense by the employer. Therefore, Fay should record 2007 compensation expense of $84,000 [contribution of $30,000 cash and common stock with a FMV of $54,000 (3,000 × $18)].

**83. (d)** Per SOP 76-3, an obligation of an Employee Stock Ownership Plan (ESOP) should be recorded as a liability in the financial statements of the employer when the obligation is covered by either a guarantee of the employer or a commitment by the employer to make future contributions to the ESOP sufficient to meet the debt service requirements. Therefore, the note payable of $100,000 (which is guaranteed by Fay) should be reported in Fay's 12/31/07 balance sheet. The SOP also states that the offsetting debit to the employer's liability should be reported as a reduction of stockholders' equity. Therefore, Fay should also report $100,000 as a reduction of stockholders' equity.

### Stockholders' Equity:  Comprehensive

**84. (a)** All of the accounts given are stockholders' equity accounts. Total stockholders' equity is computed below.

| | | |
|---|---|---|
| Paid-in capital | | $ 600,000 |
| Common stock | | 800,000 |
| Addl. paid-in capital | | 1,400,000 |
| Retained earinings | | |
| Appropriated | $150,000 | |
| Unappropriated | 200,000 | 350,000 |
| | | 1,750,000 |
| Accumulated other comprehensive income | | |
| Unrealized loss on available-for-sale securities | | (20,000) |
| Less:  Treasury stock | | (50,000) |
| | | $1,680,000 |

Both **treasury stock** and **net unrealized loss on available-for-sale securities** are contra stockholders' equity accounts.

**85. (a)** The number of shares outstanding is equal to the issued shares less treasury shares. The table below shows the effects of each of the stock transactions on the common shares outstanding.

| | *Outstanding shares* |
|---|---|
| 1/1/07 | 300,000 |
| 1/31/07 declaration of 10% stock dividend | 30,000 |
| 6/30/07 purchase of TS | (100,000) |
| 8/1/07 sale of TS | 50,000 |
| Subtotal | 280,000 |
| 11/30/07 stock split | × 2 |
| 12/31/07 | 560,000 |

**86. (a)** Shares issued and outstanding are computed below.

| | *Issued* | *Outstanding* |
|---|---|---|
| 12/31/06 | 100,000 | 95,000 |
| 5/3/07 | | 1,000 |
| 8/6/07 | 10,000 | 10,000 |
| Subtotal | 110,000 | 106,000 |
| 11/18/07 | 110,000 | 106,000 |
| 12/31/07 | 220,000 | 212,000 |

At 12/31/06, shares issued were 100,000 and outstanding 95,000 (100,000 issued less 5,000 treasury). The reissuance of treasury stock does not increase shares issued, but does increase shares outstanding by 1,000 to 96,000 (100,000

issued less 4,000 treasury). The issuance of previously unissued stock on 8/6/07 increases both issued and outstanding shares by 10,000, bringing the totals to 110,000 issued and 106,000 outstanding prior to the stock split. Since treasury stock is protected from dilution, shares issued, treasury shares, and outstanding shares are all doubled by the stock split.

## R.  Ratios

**87. (a)** The requirement is to determine the effect on Ali Corp. of exercising the stock options. First, the debt to equity ratio is calculated as follows:

$$\text{Debt to equity} = \frac{\text{Total liabilities}}{\text{Common stockholders' equity}}$$

The figures given in the problem reflect the account balances **after** the exercise of the stock options. Thus, Ali's debt to equity ratio after the exercise is

$$\frac{\$60,000}{\$500,000} = 12\%$$

When the options were exercised, total stockholders' equity would have increased by the amount of the option price as follows:

| Common stock | ↑ | by par value × 1,000 shares |
|---|---|---|
| Paid-in capital | ↑ | by (option price-par) × 1,000 shares |

Note that the information given is incomplete as to whether compensation was recorded under the stock option plan. However, even if compensation were recorded, the entries are made only to accounts that impact stockholders' equity, and the net effect is no change. Thus, the only change is an increase resulting from the exercise of the options. Since common stockholders' equity increased, the denominator of the debt to equity ratio also increased. As the denominator becomes larger and the numerator remains constant, the quotient becomes smaller. Therefore, the debt to equity ratio must have **decreased** to its current level of 12%. Answer (b) is incorrect because earnings per share decreased by $0.33. Answer (c) is incorrect because not enough information is given to calculate the asset turnover. Answer (d) is incorrect because the debt to equity ratio, rate of return on common stock, earnings per share, price earnings ratio, and book value per share were all affected by exercising the stock options.

**88. (c)** The requirement is to determine Irvington's return on common stockholders' equity for 2007, which is computed by dividing net income available to common stockholders (net income less preferred dividends) by average common stockholders' equity

$$\frac{\$120,000 - \$10,000}{(\$375,000 + \$585,000) / 2} = 23\%$$

**89. (d)** The requirement is to determine the book value per common share. The book value per common share is the amount each share would receive if the company were liquidated. The book value per common share is calculated as follows:

|                                  | *Preferred* | *Common* |
|----------------------------------|------------|----------|
| Preferred stock, 5%              | $250,000   |          |
| Common stock                     |            | $350,000 |
| APIC in excess of par value of common stock |  | 125,000 |
| Retained earnings:               |            |          |
|    Dividends in arrears | 25,000 |        |
|    Liquidation premium | 50,000 |         |
| Remainder to common (Plug)       |            | 225,000  |
|    Totals         | $325,000   | $700,000 |
| Shares outstanding               |            | 100,000  |
| Book value per share             |            | $  7.00  |

Note that when calculating the remainder to common, total stockholders' equity before the liquidation must be equal to the amount after the assumed liquidation.

**90.   (c)**   Under the cost method, treasury stock is debited for the cost of the treasury stock, thus decreasing total stockholders' equity.  However, the book value per share will increase due to the acquisition of the treasury stock. Book value per share is calculated by dividing common stockholders' equity by the shares outstanding.  An example will help illustrate.

$$\frac{\text{Stockholders' equity}}{\text{Common stock (30,000 shares)}}$$

| $5 par                   | $150,000 |
|--------------------------|----------|
| Additional paid-in capital | 550,000 |
| Retained earnings        | 250,000  |
|                          | $950,000 |

$$\text{Book value per share} = \frac{\$950,000}{30,000} = \$31.67$$

Per the facts in the question, treasury stock was acquired at more than par and original issue price, but less than book value per share.  Therefore, the acquisition price must be greater than $23.33 per share (700,000 ÷ 30,000) and less than $31.67 per share.

Let's say 1,000 shares of treasury stock were acquired at $27.00 per share.

$$\text{Book value per share} = \frac{\$950,000 - (1,000 \times \$27)}{30,000 - 1,000}$$
$$= \frac{923,000}{29,000}$$
$$= \$31.83$$

The book value per share increased after the acquisition of the treasury stock.

**91.   (b)**   Dividends per share is used in the numerator of the dividend payout ratio as shown below.

$$\frac{\text{Dividend}}{\text{payout ratio}} = \frac{\text{Dividends per share}}{\text{Earnings per share}}$$

However, dividends per share are not used in the calculation of earnings per share.

$$\frac{\text{Earnings}}{\text{per share}} = \frac{\text{Net income} - \text{Preferred dividends}}{\text{Weighted-average number of shares outstanding}}$$

**SOLUTIONS TO SIMULATION PROBLEMS**

**Simulation Problem 1**

| | Concepts | Statement of Retained Earnings | Financial Statement Disclosures | | Research | Communication |
|---|---|---|---|---|---|---|
| Situation | | | | | | |

| | (A) | (B) | (C) | (D) | (E) | (F) | (G) | (H) | (I) | (J) | (K) | (L) | (M) |
|---|---|---|---|---|---|---|---|---|---|---|---|---|---|
| 1. Par value method | ○ | ○ | ○ | ○ | ○ | ○ | ○ | ○ | ● | ○ | ○ | ○ | ○ |
| 2. Appropriations of retained earnings | ○ | ○ | ○ | ○ | ○ | ○ | ○ | ● | ○ | ○ | ○ | ○ | ○ |
| 3. Stock split | ○ | ○ | ○ | ● | ○ | ○ | ○ | ○ | ○ | ○ | ○ | ○ | ○ |
| 4. Simple capital structure | ● | ○ | ○ | ○ | ○ | ○ | ○ | ○ | ○ | ○ | ○ | ○ | ○ |
| 5. If-converted method | ○ | ○ | ○ | ○ | ○ | ○ | ○ | ○ | ○ | ○ | ○ | ○ | ● |
| 6. Scrip dividend | ○ | ○ | ○ | ○ | ○ | ○ | ○ | ○ | ○ | ○ | ● | ○ | ○ |
| 7. Stock appreciation rights | ○ | ● | ○ | ○ | ○ | ○ | ○ | ○ | ○ | ○ | ○ | ○ | ○ |
| 8. Stock option | ○ | ○ | ○ | ○ | ○ | ○ | ○ | ○ | ○ | ● | ○ | ○ | ○ |
| 9. Liquidating dividend | ○ | ○ | ○ | ○ | ○ | ○ | ● | ○ | ○ | ○ | ○ | ○ | ○ |
| 10. Treasury stock | ○ | ○ | ○ | ○ | ● | ○ | ○ | ○ | ○ | ○ | ○ | ○ | ○ |

**Explanation of solutions**

**1.** **(I)** In accordance with the par value method, treasury shares are recorded at par value by debiting treasury stock when acquired. Any additional paid-in capital from the original issue of the acquired shares is also debited, cash is credited, and either additional paid-in capital—treasury stock is credited or retained earnings are debited for the difference between cash and the other two debits previously mentioned.

**2.** **(H)** Appropriations of retained earnings are actions by the board of directors to disclose amounts not available for dividends.

**3.** **(D)** A stock split changes the number of shares outstanding and the par value per share. The purpose of a stock split is to reduce the market price per share.

**4.** **(A)** A simple capital structure for a corporation exists if there are no potentially dilutive securities.

**5.** **(M)** The if-converted method for convertible securities assumes that the securities were converted at the later of the beginning of the period or the date of issue. The method thus increases the weighted-average number of shares in the denominator of the EPS equation. Since the method assumes conversion at the beginning of the period, no preferred dividends or interest would be considered to have been paid.

**6.** **(K)** A scrip dividend is a dividend issued by the corporation in the form of a note payable.

**7.** **(B)** A stock appreciation right allows an employee to receive the excess of the market value of the stock over a preestablished value in the form of cash, shares of stock, or both on the exercise date.

**8.** **(J)** A stock option is a form of compensation given to employees which allows them to purchase shares of stock at a specified price.

**9.** **(G)** A dividend paid to shareholders in excess of the retained earnings balance which is considered to be a return of capital and a liquidating dividend.

**10.** **(E)** When a corporation purchases its own stock in the market, the stock is termed treasury stock. Treasury stock is not an asset as a corporation cannot invest in itself. Treasury stock is recorded in a contra equity account.

| Situation | Concepts | Statement of Retained Earnings | Financial Statement Disclosures | Research | Communication |
|---|---|---|---|---|---|
| | | | | | |

This problem is a collection of miscellaneous stockholders' equity problems. The candidate should start the problem by scanning the required information to determine the amounts to be calculated. While scanning, the candidate should recognize that some of the required items are related, such as number 2 (preferred dividends) in the Statement of Retained Earnings, and numbers 1,2,4 and 6 in the Financial Statement Disclosures. These relationships require that the candidate label each answer, so that it will be possible to quickly find that answer when it is used in a subsequent problem.

Unlike many previous exam problems, the order of the information concerning the transactions does not coincide with the order of the required answers. This arrangement makes it necessary to read the required amount and then hunt for the transaction information needed to calculate that required amount.

**1.** **($14,000)** Prior period adjustment is the term generally applied to corrections of errors of prior periods. In this problem no amortization had been recorded in a prior year—an error. Since this is not a self-correcting error, it still existed in 2008. The calculation is cost ($320,000) ÷ useful life (eight years) for 1/2 year (purchased July 1).  Prior period adjustments are disclosed net of tax (30%).  $320,000/8 × 1/2 × (1 – .3) = $14,000.

**2.    ($12,000)**  Preferred dividends are 6% and cumulative.  They were declared during 2007 and paid in 2008.  The declaration is sufficient to record and recognize the dividends legally; they do not have to be paid in the current year to be recognized during that time period.  These dividends will be used in the numerator in question 20 when calculating the 2007 EPS.  Since these dividends are cumulative, they would be used in the calculation of EPS even if they had not been declared.  The amount of preferred dividends is derived by multiplying the par value of the stock by its rate.  6% × $200,000 par = $12,000 dividends.

**3.    ($165,000)**  Common dividends—cash is calculated by the formula:  Common shares outstanding × Dividend per share.  In this problem the number of shares outstanding is affected by the beginning shares (100,000), shares issued (13,000), and treasury shares purchased and sold (5,000 purchased, 2,000 sold) prior to the dividend date of November 4.  100,000 + 13,000 – 5,000 + 2,000 = 110,000 shares outstanding × dividend rate $1.50 = $165,000.

**4.    ($720,000)**  Common dividends—property differs from cash dividends because the property may be carried in the accounts at an amount which does not equal its fair value (cash is always at its fair value).  Management intends to distribute the property at its fair value, therefore it is necessary to bring the property to fair value on the date management is legally forced to distribute it (the declaration date).  Value fluctuations beyond that date are irrelevant.

| Situation | Concepts | Statement of Retained Earnings | Financial Statement Disclosures | Research | Communication |
|---|---|---|---|---|---|

**1.    (113,000)**  The number of shares issued differs from the number of shares outstanding which was used in question 3 under Calculations.  Shares issued include those outstanding as well as those held in the treasury.  Shares outstanding from question 3 above, 110,000 plus 3,000 treasury shares = 113,000 shares.

**2.    ($113,000)**  Amount of common stock issued—This question takes the answer from question 1 above (113,000 shares) and multiplies that figure by the par value of each share, $1.

**3.    ($934,000)**  The additional paid-in capital, including treasury stock transactions, is derived by adding the beginning balance ($800,000) to the excess ($10) of issue price ($11) over par value ($1) for the shares issued (13,000) to acquire land on February 1, 2007.  In addition, the sale of the treasury stock (2,000 shares) at an amount ($16) greater than cost ($14) gives rise to a nonoperating gain that cannot be included in net income since it was both not related to operations and is a transaction in the company's own stock.  $800,000 + (13,000 × $10) + [2,000 × (16-14)] = $934,000.

**4.    ($42,000)**  Treasury stock—Since Min Co. follows the cost method of accounting for treasury stock, this answer is derived by multiplying the shares of treasury stock (3,000) by their cost ($14).  3,000 × $14 = $42,000.

**5.    ($24.86)**  Book value per share is a concept that relates common stockholders' equity to shares of common stock.  The "per share" referred to is always the **common** shares unless the problem states some other type of shares.  In this case it is to be calculated before the prior period adjustment.  It is necessary to subtract preferred stock's total liquidating value ($100 × 2,000 sh = $200,000) from total stockholders' equity ($2,686,000) to obtain common stockholders' equity.  In this problem no liquidating value is given, so par value is used.  The resulting amount ($2,686,000 – $200,000 = $2,486,000) is divided by the common shares outstanding (100,000) to obtain book value per share ($24.86).  ($2,686,000 – $200,000) ÷ 100,000 = $24.86.

**6.    ($826,000)**  The formula for calculating earnings per share is (NI – Preferred dividends) ÷ Wtd.-avg. shares outstanding.  The numerator is income available to common stockholders.  The problem states that adjusted net income for 2007 was $838,000.  The word "adjusted" tells the candidate that net income includes all information concerning transactions in the problem and need not be changed in any way.  Preferred dividends ($12,000) were calculated in question 2 under Calculations.  $838,000 – $12,000 = $826,000.

| Situation | Concepts | Statement of Retained Earnings | Financial Statement Disclosures | Research | Communication |
|---|---|---|---|---|---|

**1.**  A company issues a small stock dividend.  At what amount should the stock dividend be recorded?

**As to the Issuer**
**ARB43, Ch. 7B, Para 10 or Current Text C20.103**
**Stock dividends**

10.  As has been previously stated, a stock dividend does not, in fact, give rise to any change whatsoever in either the corporation's assets or its respective shareholders' proportionate interests therein.  However, it cannot fail to be recognized that, merely as a consequence of the expressed purpose of the transaction and its characterization as a dividend in related notices to shareholders and the public at large, many recipients of stock dividends look upon them as distributions of corporate earnings and usually in an amount equivalent to the fair value of the additional shares received.  Furthermore, it is to be presumed that such views of recipients are ma-

terially strengthened in those instances, which are by far the most numerous, where the issuances are so small in comparison with the shares previously outstanding that they do not have any apparent effect upon the share market price and, consequently, the market value of the shares previously held remains substantially unchanged. The committee therefore believes that where theses circumstances exist the corporation should in the public interest account for the transaction by transferring from earned surplus to the category of permanent capitalization (represented by the capital stock and capital surplus accounts) an amount equal to the fair value of the additional shares issued. Unless this is done, the amount of earnings which the shareholder may believe to have been distributed to him will be left except to the extent otherwise dictated by legal requirements, in earned surplus subject to possible further similar stock issuance or cash distributions.

**2.** A company issues a property dividend. How should the property dividend be valued?

**APB29, Para 18 or Current Text C11.101**

18. The Board concludes that in general accounting for nonmonetary transactions should be based on the fair values of the assets (or services) involved which is the same basis as that used in monetary transactions. Thus, the cost of a nonmonetary asset acquired in exchange for another nonmonetary asset is the fair value of the asset surrendered to obtain it, and a gain or loss should be recognized on the exchange. The fair value of the asset received should be used to measure the cost if it is more clearly evident than the fair value of the asset surrendered. Similarly, a nonmonetary asset received in a nonreciprocal transfer should be recorded at the fair value of the asset received. A transfer of a nonmonetary asset to a stockholder or to another entity in a nonreciprocal transfer should be recorded at the fair value of the asset transferred, and a gain or loss should be recognized on the disposition of the asset. The fair value of an entity's own stock reacquired may be a more clearly evident measure of the fair value of the asset distributed in a nonreciprocal transfer if the transaction involves distribution of a nonmonetary asset to eliminate a disproportionate part of owners' interests (that is, to acquire stock for the treasury or for retirement).

**3.** A company appropriates retained earnings for a loss contingency. How should this be disclosed in the financial statements?

**Appropriation of Retained Earnings**
**FAS5, Para 15 or Current Text C59.117 or R70.103**

15. Some enterprises have classified a portion of retained earnings as "appropriated" for loss contingencies. In some cases, the appropriation has been shown outside the stockholders' equity section of the balance sheet. Appropriation of retained earnings is not prohibited by this Statement provided that it is shown within the stockholders' equity section of the balance sheet and is clearly identified as an appropriation of retained earnings. Costs or losses shall not be charged to an appropriation of retained earnings, and no part of the appropriation shall be transferred to income.

| Situation | Concepts | Statement of Retained Earnings | Financial Statement Disclosures | Research | Communication |
| --- | --- | --- | --- | --- | --- |

To: Ms. Kay Smith, CEO, Min Co.
From: CPA Candidate
Re: Preferred and common stock

You have requested that I provide a description of the differences between common stock and cumulative preferred stock. While both of these types of financial instruments reflect an ownership interest in the company, preferred stock is closer to a debt instrument in that the holders are entitled to their stated dividend before any distributions are made to common stockholders. This is true with respect to the current dividend as well as any dividends unpaid from prior years. In addition, preferred stockholders have preference over common stockholders when the company is liquidated. While preferred stockholders are limited to their stated dividend rate, common stockholder's dividends are limited only by the earnings of the company.

If you have any other questions, please contact me.

## Simulation Problem 2

| Situation | Analysis of Transactions | Balance Sheet Disclosures | Calculation Basic EPS | Calculation Diluted EPS | Communication | Research |
|---|---|---|---|---|---|---|

| Date | Transaction | Preferred stock | APIC— preferred stock | Common stock | APIC— common stock | Retained earnings | Treasury stock | APIC— treasury stock |
|---|---|---|---|---|---|---|---|---|
| 1/2/07 | Issue preferred stock at par | 1,000,000 | | | | | | |
| 3/1/07 | Issue common stock for services | | | 3,000 | 93,000 | | | |
| 7/1/07 | Issue common stock for cash | | | 40,000 | 1,640,000 | | | |
| 10/1/07 | Repurchase treasury stock | | | | | | 544,000 | |
| 12/1/07 | Sell treasury stock | | | | | (15,000) | (102,000) | |
| 12/30/07 | Declare and pay dividends | | | | | (86,000) | | |

### Explanation of solutions

- Preferred stock 10,000 × $100 = $1,000,000
- Value of services = Fair value of stock which is more reliable since stock is traded on the open market. 3,000 shares × $32 per share = $96,000
- Common stock: 40,000 shares of common stock × $1 par = $40,000 to common stock account; $40,000 × 41 = $1,640,000 to APIC.
- Treasury stock is recorded at cost. 16,000 shares × $34 per share = $544,000
- Treasury stock is reduced by the cost paid 3,000 × $34 per share = $102,000. There is a $5 per share loss on the treasury shares which is debited to retained earnings 3,000 shares × $5 = $15,000
- Dividends to preferred shareholders = 10,000 × $100 par = $1,000,000 × 6% = $60,000 preferred dividends
- Dividends to common shareholders. Number of common shares outstanding equals 100,000 shares + 3,000 shares issued + 40,000 shares issued – 16,000 treasury shares purchased + 3,000 treasury shares reissued = 130,000 outstanding shares × $0.20 = $26,000. Therefore, total dividend is $86,000

| Situation | Analysis of Transactions | Balance Sheet Disclosures | Calculation Basic EPS | Calculation Diluted EPS | Communication | Research |
|---|---|---|---|---|---|---|

| Owners' equity: | |
|---|---|
| Preferred stock | 1,000,000 |
| Common stock | 143,000 |
| Additional paid-in capital preferred stock | 0 |
| Additional paid-in capital common stock | 4,333,000 |
| Additional paid-in capital treasury stock | 0 |
| Retained earnings | 501,000 |
| Treasury stock | (442,000) |
| Other comprehensive income | 0 |
| Total owners' equity | 5,535,000 |

### Explanation of solutions

- Preferred stock: Issued at par. 10,000 shares × $100 = $1,000,000
- Common stock: $100,000 + $3,000 + $40,000 = $143,000
- Additional paid-in capital—Common stock: $2,600,000 + $93,000 + $1,640,000 = $4,333,000
- Retained earnings: $250,000 – $28,000 = $222,000 at end of 2005
- Retained earnings for 2006: $222,000 – $15,000 – $86,000 + $380,000 = $501,000
- Treasury stock: $544,000 – $102,000 = $442,000

| Situation | Analysis of Transactions | Balance Sheet Disclosures | Calculation Basic EPS | Calculation Diluted EPS | Communication | Research |
|---|---|---|---|---|---|---|

| Numerator | 320,000 |
|---|---|
| Denominator | 118,750 |
| Basic earnings per share | 2.6947 |

**Explanation of solutions**

Numerator:  $380,000 net income – $60,000 in preferred dividends = $320,000.  Denominator – Weighted-average common shares.

| Date | # shares | Time outstanding | WACS |
|------|----------|------------------|------|
| 1/1 | 100,000 | 12/12 | 100,000 |
| 3/1 | 3,000 | 10/12 | 2,500 |
| 7/1 | 40,000 | 6/12 | 20,000 |
| 10/1 | (16,000) treasury shares | 3/12 | (4,000) |
| 12/1 | 3,000 treasury shares sold | 1/12 | 250 |
| | Total WACS outstanding | | 118,750 |

| Situation | Analysis of Transactions | Balance Sheet Disclosures | Calculation Basic EPS | Calculation Diluted EPS | Communication | Research |
|-----------|--------------------------|---------------------------|-----------------------|-------------------------|---------------|----------|

| Numerator | 380,000 |
|-----------|---------|
| Denominator | 168,750 |
| Diluted earnings per share | 2.2519 |

WACS outstanding:  Basic EPS 118,750 + Convertible preferred (10,000 shares preferred × 5 shares common) 50,000 = 168,750

| Situation | Analysis of Transactions | Balance Sheet Disclosures | Calculation Basic EPS | Calculation Diluted EPS | Communication | Research |
|-----------|--------------------------|---------------------------|-----------------------|-------------------------|---------------|----------|

To:      Mr. Fenton, CEO, M Corporation
From:    CPA Candidate
Re:      Earnings per share

As you requested, I have prepared this memorandum to answer your questions about earnings per share.  The objective of earnings per share is to measure the performance of an entity over a reporting period.  There are two computations for earnings per share:  basic and diluted.  Basic earnings per share is computed by dividing the income available to common stockholders by the weighted-average number of common shares outstanding for the period.  Shares issued and reacquired during the period are weighted for the period of time they were outstanding.  Diluted earnings per share is another measure of performance; however, diluted earnings per share gives the effect of all potentially dilutive common shares that were outstanding during the period.  Hence, diluted earnings per share will be less than basic earnings per share.

If you have any other questions, please contact me.

| Situation | Analysis of Transactions | Balance Sheet Disclosures | Calculation Basic EPS | Calculation Diluted EPS | Communication | Research |
|-----------|--------------------------|---------------------------|-----------------------|-------------------------|---------------|----------|

**APB6, Para 12 or Current Text C23.103**

12.  The Board considers that the following accounting practices, in addition to the accounting practices indicated in Chapter 1B, are acceptable, and that they appear to be more in accord with current developments in practice:

    a.  When a corporation's stock is retired, or purchased for constructive retirement (with or without an intention to retire the stock formally in accordance with applicable laws)

        i.  An excess of purchase price over par or stated value may be allowed between capital surplus and retained earnings.  The portion of the excess allocated to capital surplus should be limited to the sum of (a) all capital surplus arising from previous retirements and net "gains" on sales of treasury stock of the same issue, and (b) the pro rata portion of capital surplus paid in, voluntary transfers of retained earnings, capitalization of stock dividends, etc., on the same issue.  For this purpose, any remaining capital surplus applicable to issues fully retired (formal or constructive) is deemed to be applicable pro rata to shares of common stock.  Alternatively, the excess may be charged entirely to retained earnings in recognition of the fact that a corporation can always capitalize or allocate retained earnings for such purposes.

        ii.  An excess of par or stated value over purchase price should be credited to capital surplus.

    b.  When a corporation's stock is acquired for purposes other than retirement (formal or constructive), or when ultimate disposition has not yet been decided, the cost of acquired stock may be shown separately as a deduction from the total of capital stock, capital surplus, and retained earnings, or may be accorded the accounting treatment appropriate for retired stock, or in some circumstances may be shown as an asset in accordance with paragraph 4 of Chapter 1A of ARB43.  "Gains" on sales of treasury stock not previously accounted for as constructively retired should be credited to capital surplus; "losses" may be charged to capital surplus to the extent that previous net "gains" from sales or retirements of the same class of stock are included therein, otherwise to retained earnings.

**Simulation Problem 3**

| Situation | Concepts | Journal Entries | Retained Earnings | Stockholders' Equity Section of Balance Sheet | Communication | Research |
|---|---|---|---|---|---|---|

|  | *True* | *False* |
|---|---|---|
| 1. Mandatorily redeemable preferred stock is classified as owners' equity and is disclosed after common stock. | ○ | ● |
| 2. Property dividends are valued at the book value of the property. | ○ | ● |
| 3. When a company makes a liquidating dividend, it debits the common stock account. | ○ | ● |
| 4. Scrip dividends are a liability on the date of declaration. | ● | ○ |
| 5. Stock dividends of 40% of the outstanding shares of stock are valued at fair market value on the date of declaration. | ○ | ● |
| 6. If a company has cumulative preferred stock, all dividends in arrears must be subtracted from net income in the numerator of basic earnings per share. | ○ | ● |
| 7. Cash dividends become a liability to the corporation when declared. | ● | ○ |
| 8. Stock issued for services should be recorded at the fair market value of the services rendered if that value is greater than the fair market value of the stock traded on the exchange. | ○ | ● |

**Explanation of solutions**

1. False. Per FAS 150, mandatorily redeemable preferred is classified as a liability on the balance sheet.

2. False. Property dividends are valued at fair market value of the property at the date of declaration.

3. False. When a company makes a liquidating dividend, a company usually debits additional paid-in capital rather than retained earnings. Common stock cannot be debited because it is considered legal capital which is only eliminated upon the dissolution of the corporation.

4. True. All dividends are liabilities on the dates declared.

5. False. Large stock dividends are recorded at par. A stock dividend of 40% of the shares outstanding is considered a large stock dividend.

6. False. If a company has cumulative preferred stock, only the current year dividends in arrears are subtracted from net income in the numerator of basic earnings per share.

7. True. All dividends are liabilities on the dates declared.

8. False. The more objective measurement of the value of the goods or services exchanged for stock is the fair market value of the stock if the stock is traded on a stock exchange.

| Situation | Concepts | Journal Entries | Retained Earnings | Stockholders' Equity Section of Balance Sheet | Communication | Research |
|---|---|---|---|---|---|---|

1. Treasury stock purchased on March 5, 2007

| | | |
|---|---|---|
| Treasury stock | 50,000 | |
| Cash | | 50,000 |

(5,000 shares at $10 per share)

2. Declaration and distribution of a property dividend on July 15, 2007

| | | |
|---|---|---|
| Loss on inventory | 15,000 | |
| Inventory | | 15,000 |
| Retained earnings | 60,000 | |
| Inventory | | 60,000 |

**3.** Issue of common stock on October 1, 2007.

| Cash | 360,000 | |
|---|---|---|
| Common stock (20,000 × $5) | | 100,000 (par) |
| Additional paid-in capital | | 260,000 (plug) |

(20,000 shares × $18 exercise price)

| Situation | Concepts | Journal Entries | Retained Earnings | Stockholders' Equity Section of Balance Sheet | Communications | Research |
|---|---|---|---|---|---|---|

**Field Company**
**STATEMENT OF RETAINED EARNINGS**
*For the Year ending December 31, 2007*

| Beginning retained earnings, 1-1-07 | 1,845,000 |
|---|---|
| Net income | 240,000 |
| Dividends | (80,000) |
| End retained earnings, 12-31-07 | 2,025,000 |

| Situation | Concepts | Journal Entries | Retained Earnings | Stockholders' Equity Section of Balance Sheet | Communication | Research |
|---|---|---|---|---|---|---|

**Field Company**
**STOCKHOLDERS' EQUITY SECTION OF BALANCE SHEET**
*December 31, 2007*

| Common Stock [1] | 900,000 |
|---|---|
| Additional paid-in capital [2] | 1,860,000 |
| Retained earnings | 2,025,000 |
| Treasury stock | (50,000) |
| Accumulated other comprehensive income | 0 |
| Total stockholders' equity | 4,735,000 |

[1] Shares issued: 160,000 + 20,000 = 180,000 × $5 = $900,000
[2] Additional paid-in capital $1,600,000 + [20,000 × ($18 − 5)] = $1,860,000 (1,600,000 + 260,000)

**Explanation of solutions**

To prepare the stockholders' equity section of Field's December 31, 2007 balance sheet, certain computations need to be made first.

1.  The common stock authorized does not change throughout the problem; it is 400,000 shares. The number of shares outstanding increases by the 20,000 shares issued when the stock options were exercised. The balance in the common stock account is the number of shares issued times the par value of the common stock (180,000 × $5 = $900,000).

2.  The treasury stock is accounted for by the cost method, which means the treasury stock is recorded at cost (5,000 shares × $10 = $50,000). The journal entry for the treasury stock is

    | Treasury stock | 50,000 | |
    |---|---|---|
    | Cash | | 50,000 |

3.  The information given indicates that the intrinsic value method of APB 25 is used. This option is granted and exercised **before** SFAS 123(R) was in effect. Compensation cost is zero and no entry is made until the options are recognized. Additional paid-in capital is the amount of money received for stock above the par value. The exercise or option price of the stock options exercised was $18 per share. The $13 per share paid above the par value of the stock needs to be added to the additional paid-in capital account, so $260,000 ($13 × 20,000 shares) should be added to the beginning balance of $1,600,000 for a total of $1,860,000 in the additional paid-in capital account.

4.  The formula for retained earnings is

    Beginning balance
    Add:    Net income
    Less:   Dividends
    Ending balance

    The amount of the dividends is the fair market value of the property distributed, which is $60,000 in this case. A $15,000 loss is recognized from the property dividend for the difference between the $75,000 carrying value and market value of the inventory. However, this loss would already be included in 2007 net income. Retained earnings is calculated as follows:

    | Beginning balance | $1,845,000 |
    |---|---|
    | Add: Net income | 240,000 |
    | Less: Dividend | (60,000) |
    | Ending balance | $2,025,000 |

| Situation | Concepts | Journal Entries | Retained Earnings | Stockholders' Equity Section of Balance Sheet | Communication | Research |
|---|---|---|---|---|---|---|

To:     CEO, Field Company
From:   CPA Candidate
Re:     Earnings per share

This memorandum explains the presentation of basic and diluted earnings per share. A company is required to calculate earnings per share and disclose this information on the bottom of the income statement for each year presented. If a company has a simple capital structure with no convertible securities or common stock equivalents, the company presents only basic earnings per share. However, if a company has a complex capital structure with convertible securities or common stock equivalents, a second calculation for diluted earnings per share must be made. In the case of companies with complex capital structures, both basic and diluted earnings per share must be disclosed on the face of the income statement.

Basic earnings per share is based on income available for common stockholders divided by the weighted-average number of outstanding shares. Income available to common stockholders is net income less preferred dividends declared. Preferred dividends on cumulative preferred stock are deducted from net income. However, preferred dividends on noncumulative preferred stock are deducted for the current year only if declared.

Diluted earnings per share is basic earnings per share adjusted for the effects of dilutive securities. Dilutive securities include options, warrants, convertible bonds, and preferred stock. The adjustments include positive numerator adjustments for bond interest (net of tax), and preferred dividends. The positive denominator adjustments are for dilutive shares that would be issued upon conversion of convertible securities and from applying the treasury stock method for dilutive options and warrants.

If you need assistance with calculating earnings per share, please contact my office.

| Situation | Concepts | Journal Entries | Retained Earnings | Stockholders' Equity Section of Balance Sheet | Communication | Research |
|---|---|---|---|---|---|---|

**1.** How is diluted earnings per share calculated?

**FAS128, Para 11 or Current Text E11.106**

11. The objective of diluted EPS is consistent with that of basic EPS—to measure the performance of an entity over the reporting period—while giving effect to all dilutive potential common shares that were outstanding during the period. The computation of diluted EPS is similar to the computation of basic EPS except that the denominator is increased to include the number of additional common shares that would have been outstanding if the dilutive potential common shares had been issued. In addition, in computing the dilutive effect of convertible securities, the numerator is adjusted to add back (a) any convertible preferred dividends, and (b) the after-tax amount of interest recognized in the period associated with any convertible debt. The numerator also is adjusted for any other changes in income or loss that would result from the assumed conversion of those potential common shares, such as profit-sharing expenses. Similar adjustments also may be necessary for certain contracts that provide issuer or holder with a choice between settlement methods.

**FAS128, Para 12 or Current Text E11.107**

12. Diluted EPS shall be based on the most advantageous conversion rate or exercise price from the standpoint of the security holder. Previously reported diluted EPS data shall not be retroactively adjusted for subsequent conversions or subsequent changes in the market price of the common stock.

**2.** What is the purpose of reporting comprehensive income?

**Purpose of Reporting Comprehensive Income**
**FAS130, Para 11 or Current Text C49.107**

11. The purpose of reporting comprehensive income is to report a measure of all changes in equity of an enterprise that result from recognized transactions and other economic events of the period other than transactions with owners in their capacity as owners. Prior to the issuance of this Statement, some of those changes in equity were displayed in a statement that reports the results of operations, while others were included directly in balances within a separate component of equity in a statement of financial position.

**FAS130, Para 12 (not referenced in Current Text)**

12. If used with related disclosures and other information in the financial statements, the information provided by reporting comprehensive income should assist investors, creditors, and others in assessing an enterprise's activities and the timing and magnitude of an enterprise's future cash flows.

**3.** A company has available-for-sale securities and recognizes an unrealized holding gain in year 1. In year 2, the company sells these securities. How should this affect other comprehensive income on the financial statements?

**Reclassification adjustments**
**FAS130, Para 18 or Current Text C49.112**

18. Adjustments shall be made to avoid double counting in comprehensive income items that are displayed as part of net income for a period that also had been displayed as part of other comprehensive income in that period or earlier periods. For example, gains on investment securities that were realized and included in net income of the current period that also had been included in other comprehensive income as unrealized holding gains in the period in which they arose must be deducted through other comprehensive income of the period in which they are included in net income to avoid including them in comprehensive income twice. Those adjustments are referred to in this Statement as reclassification adjustments.

# INVESTMENTS

## Introduction

Investments in debt and equity securities are accounted for using SFAS 115, APB 18, or SFAS 159. The accounting treatment for investments is different depending upon the percentage of ownership, the classification of the security, and the election of the fair value option for reporting financial assets. This module will begin by covering the rules of SFAS 115 for trading, available-for-sale, and held-to-maturity securities. Then the equity method of accounting and the rules of APB 18 for investments where significant influence exists will be covered. After you understand the reporting rules of SFAS 115 and APB 18, the newer rules of SFAS 159, the fair value option, will be discussed.

## A. Concepts of Accounting and Investment Percentage

1. **Debt securities** are covered by SFAS 115 (see outline), *Accounting for Certain Investments in Debt and Equity Securities*, which defines debt securities as "any security representing a creditor relationship with an enterprise." This includes corporate debt, convertible bonds, US Treasury and municipal securities, redeemable preferred stock, commercial paper, and other secured debt instruments. Excluded are unsecured trade receivables and consumer loans and notes receivable because they are not normally traded on organized exchanges and because of cost/benefit considerations. SFAS 115 requires that investments in debt securities be classified into three categories: trading securities, available-for-sale securities, and held-to-maturity securities. Debt securities are discussed in Section B of this module and also in Module 11, Section B.

2. **Equity securities** include ownership interests (common, preferred, and other capital stock), rights to acquire ownership interests (rights, warrants, call options), and rights to dispose of ownership interests (put options). The accounting rules for investments in the common stock of another corporation are generally based on the percentage of the voting stock obtained.

   a. Investments of less than 20% of the outstanding stock

   In most cases, "small" investments in marketable equity securities are classified into two categories as specified by SFAS 115: trading securities and available-for-sale securities. Discussion of these smaller investments is presented in Section B.

   b. Investments between 20% and 50% of the outstanding stock

   At 20% or more ownership, the investor is presumed to be able to significantly influence the operating or financial decisions of the investee. Most investments in this range will result in significant influence; however, the 20% level is just a guide. FASB Interpretation 35 presents several examples in which an investor owning between 20% and 50% may not be able to exercise influence over the investee. An example of this situation is when the majority ownership is concentrated among a small group of investors who ignore the views of the minority investor. Additional examples are included in the summary of Interpretation 35, page 895. The equity method of accounting is used for investments resulting in significant influence. Investments where significant influence does exist are discussed in Section C.

   c. Investments of more than 50% of the outstanding stock

   At more than 50% ownership, the investor has control because of its majority ownership of the voting stock. Most of these investments will require the preparation of consolidated financial statements. Consolidations are discussed in Module 16.

3. Securities are originally recorded at cost, including any broker's fees, taxes, etc.; this amount is the best estimate of fair value at acquisition. Cost equals the cash paid or, in noncash transactions, the fair value of either the securities received or the resources sacrificed, whichever is more clearly determinable. The fair value of debt securities equals the present value of their future cash inflows. The present value is calculated using the current market rate of interest for similar instruments with similar risk. Any accrued interest is accounted for separately. The fair value of equity securities to be marked to market must be readily determinable from quotes obtainable from a securities exchange registered with the SEC or from the over-the-counter market. Investments which are considered to be nontradeable or investments which do not have determinable market values should be carried at cost and adjusted only for permanent declines in value.

   The exhibit below illustrates the major concepts of accounting for investments in equity securities.

**PERCENTAGE OF OUTSTANDING VOTING STOCK ACQUIRED**

Several exceptions to these general concepts exist. These exceptions are noted in the following discussions.

**B.   Investments in Which Significant Influence Does *Not* Exist**

Investments which do not confer significant influence over the operating or financial decisions of the investee consist of all debt securities and generally all small (less than 20%) investments in equity securities. SFAS 115 dictates that such investments be segregated into held-to-maturity securities (debt securities only), trading securities, and available-for-sale securities; the appropriateness of the classification should be reviewed at each reporting date.

1.   **Held-to-Maturity Securities (amortized cost)**

This category includes only debt securities and requires the positive intent and ability to hold the securities to maturity (not simply an absence of intent to sell). Held-to-maturity securities are carried at amortized cost (acquisition cost adjusted for amortization of premium or discount) using effective interest method; thus, unrealized holding gains and losses are not reported. However, realized gains and losses are included in earnings, as are interest income and premium and discount amortization. These securities are classified on the balance sheet as current or noncurrent on an individual basis, and on the statement of cash flows as investing activities.

In rare instances, the investor company's intent to hold a security to maturity may change without casting doubt on its intent to hold other debt securities to maturity. The circumstances must be nonrecurring and unforeseeable, such as the continuing deterioration of the issuer's credit. Premature sale of held-to-maturity securities may be considered as maturities if either of the following conditions are met:

a.   The sale occurs so close to the maturity date that interest rate risk is virtually eliminated, or

b.   The sale occurs after at least 85% of the principal has been collected.

Investments in held-to-maturity securities are accounted for under the cost method, which requires that they be carried at amortized cost (acquisition cost adjusted for amortization of premium or discount). Coverage of accounting for these appears under bond investments in Module 11B.

2.   **Trading Securities (mark-to-market)**

Debt and equity securities purchased and held principally for the purpose of generating gains on current resale are classified as trading securities. Trading securities are accounted for according to the cost adjusted for fair value (mark-to-market) method, under which the carrying amount is adjusted at financial statement dates for subsequent changes in fair value (i.e., they are carried at market value). (See Module 7D for a discussion of SFAS 157 and fair value measurements.) Trading securities are generally held by brokers, bankers, and other financial institutions which engage in active buying and selling activities. Both unrealized and realized gains and losses are included in income. However, to the extent that realized gains/losses have been previously reported as unrealized, only changes in the current period shall be reported as realized in the period of sale. Other components of earnings include dividend and interest revenue. Dividends on equity securities are recognized as income when declared by the investee. However, if dividends received exceed cumulative earnings since acquisition, the excess is accounted for as a liquidating dividend. Trading securities are reported on the balance sheet as current assets and on the statement of cash flows as operating activities.

Debt securities reported at fair value require special accounting treatment. The securities are to be carried at market value while interest and amortization are to be calculated using the effective interest method. Therefore, any unrealized gain or loss is actually the difference between fair value and amortized cost, that is, the adjustment equals the change in fair value during the period, plus premium amortization (decrease in book value) or minus discount amortization (increase in book value). Both the interest revenue and the unrealized holding gain/loss are included in current earnings. An example of accounting for trading debt securities is presented in the comprehensive example at the end of Section B.

3.   **Available-for-Sale Securities (mark-to-market)**

Available-for-sale securities include debt and equity securities not categorized as either held-to-maturity securities or trading securities. For example, a company such as a manufacturing firm may purchase securities to make use of idle cash. These securities are not actively traded, nor will they necessarily be held to maturity. Included in earnings are realized gains and losses (which include previously unrealized holding gains and losses) and dividend and interest income. Available-for-sale securities are accounted for according to the cost adjusted for fair value (mark-to-market) method, under which the carrying amount is adjusted at financial statement dates for subsequent changes in fair value (i.e., they are carried at market value).

Unrealized gains and losses on available-for-sale debt and equity securities are calculated in the same manner as those on trading securities. These gains and losses, however, are not recognized in income of the period. Instead, the changes in fair value during a period (unrealized gains/losses) are reported as other comprehensive income (see Module 7D), and the accumulated unrealized gain/loss on marketable securities account is presented as accumulated other comprehensive income in stockholders' equity. The following chart summarizes the three categories of marketable securities and the accounting treatment of each.

**ACCOUNTING AND REPORTING OF MARKETABLE DEBT AND EQUITY SECURITIES**

| *Category* | *Definition* | *How the security is reported on the balance sheet* | *How unrealized holding gains and losses are reported on the income statement** | *How realized gains and losses are reported on the income statement* |
|---|---|---|---|---|
| **Trading (trading securities)** | **Debt and equity** securities bought and held principally for the purpose of selling them in the near term | Reported at fair market value and grouped with current assets on the balance sheet | Unrealized gains and losses are included in earnings in the period they occur | Realized gains and losses not already recognized as unrealized components are recognized |
| **Available-for-sale** | **Debt and equity** securities not classified as trading or held-to-maturity | Reported at fair market value and may be classified as current or noncurrent | Unrealized gains and losses for a period are excluded from earnings and reported as other comprehensive income (If decline is "other than temporary" then recognized in earnings) | Realized gains and losses are recognized (which include unrealized holding gains and losses recognized previously as unrealized) |
| **Held-to-maturity** | **Debt** securities that the organization has the positive intent and ability to hold to the maturity date | Reported at amortized cost and may be classified as current or noncurrent | Unrealized gains and losses are excluded from earnings (unless decline is "other than temporary") | Realized gains and losses are recognized in accordance with amortized cost method |

\*   *Or on the statement where items of other comprehensive income are reported.*

The fair value of a debt security minus its amortized cost represents the correct unrealized gain or loss for this security in the accumulated other comprehensive income account at year-end. The adjusting entry for this account at the end of the period will equal the difference between the account's balance before adjustment and the cumulative unrealized gain or loss on the debt and equity securities at the end of the period.

Available-for-sale securities are classified on the balance sheet as current or noncurrent on an individual basis based on management's intent concerning the holding period and appear on the statement of cash flows as investing activities.

**Comprehensive Example**

On 1/01/07, when interest rates were 12%, STC Corporation purchased the following securities:

| Security description | Acquisition cost |
|---|---|
| • Shaner Enterprise ten-year, 10%, $1,000 face value bonds (STC Corp. intends to hold the bond until it matures) | $ 887 |
| • Harmony Corporation five-year, 14%, $5,000 face value bond (STC Corp. expects that interest rates will fall and the bond will be sold at a profit) | $5,360 |
| • 100 shares Keswick Corporation common stock (STC anticipates that the price of the stock will rise 10%, at which time the stock will be sold) | $2,200 |
| • 150 shares Rusell Inc. common stock (STC has no immediate plans to sell this stock) | $5,600 |

The Shaner bond must be classified as held-to-maturity and carried at amortized cost since management has the ability and intent to hold the investment to the maturity date. The Harmony and Keswick securities are classified as trading securities because STC intends to hold these investments for only a short period of time expressly to realize a quick profit. The Rusell, Inc. stock is classified as available-for-sale because STC has not expressed an intent to hold the stock for current resale. The Harmony, Keswick, and Rusell investments are all carried at fair market value.

At the end of 2007, the fair values of the Keswick and Rusell stock are $2,700 and $5,190, respectively. Interest rates have fallen to 10%, boosting the value of the Harmony bond to $5,634. Interest income, premium amortization, and unrealized gain on this bond are calculated as

| Date | 14% Cash interest | 12% Effective interest | Premium amortization | Carrying value | Fair value | Unrealized gain (loss) |
|---|---|---|---|---|---|---|
| 1/01/07 | | | | $5,360 | $5,360 | |
| 12/31/07 | $700 | $643 | $57 | 5,303 | 5,634 | $331 |

Note that the unrealized gain ($331) equals the increase in fair value ($274) plus the premium amortization ($57).

Interest income and discount/premium amortization must be recorded for the bonds in any of the three portfolios. Both the Harmony and Shaner bonds were purchased to yield 12%. The adjusting journal entries required at 12/31/07 are

| | | |
|---|---|---|
| Interest receivable | 100 | |
| Investment in Shaner bond—held-to-maturity | 6 | |
|    Interest income ($887 × 12%) | | 106 |
| | | |
| Interest receivable | 700 | |
|    Investment in Harmony securities—trading | | 57 |
|    Interest income | | 643 |

On 12/31/07 after the two adjusting entries above are posted, the carrying values and fair market values are

| | 12/31/07 Carrying amount | 12/31/07 Fair market value |
|---|---|---|
| Held-to-maturity: | | |
|   Shaner bond | $ 893 | NA |
| Trading: | | |
|   Harmony bond | 5,303 | $5,634 |
|   Keswick stock | 2,200 | 2,700 |
| Available-for-sale: | | |
|   Rusell stock | 5,600 | 5,190 |

At this time, the adjusting journal valuation entries are made for the trading and the available-for-sale portfolios of securities, as follows:

| | | |
|---|---|---|
| Investment in Harmony securities—trading | 331 | |
|   Unrealized gain on holding debt securities | | |
|    (income statement) | | 331 |
| | | |
| Investment in Keswick securities—trading | 500 | |
|   Unrealized gain on holding equity securities | | |
|    (income statement) | | |
|     ($2,700 FMV − $2,200 CV) | | 500 |
| | | |
| Unrealized loss on Rusell securities—available-for-sale | | |
|  (other comprehensive income account) | 410 | |
|   Investment in Rusell securities—available-for-sale | | |
|    ($5,600 CV − $5,190 FMV) | | 410 |

The unrealized holding gain on trading securities is a nominal account which is closed to income at 12/31/07. The unrealized loss on available-for-sale securities is closed out to the "accumulated other comprehensive income" account at year-end, which is presented in the stockholders' equity section of the 12/31/07 balance sheet. **It is important to note that the increases and decreases in market value recorded above may alternatively be recorded in a separate fair value adjustment account (contra asset account).** If a fair value adjustment account is used to carry the holding gains and losses, then the fair value adjustment account and the investment account would be netted for presentation purposes. The carrying amount of the Shaner bond at 12/31/07 is $893 ($887 + $6).

Now assume that in July 2008, 75 of the 150 shares of Rusell stock were sold for $30 per share. The entry to record the sale is

| | | |
|---|---|---|
| Cash ($30 × 75) | 2,250 | |
| Loss on sale of securities | 550 | |
|     Investment in Rusell securities—available-for-sale* | | 2,595 |
|     Reclassification adjustment of unrealized loss on | | |
|       Rusell securities—available-for-sale | | 205 |

\* *Carrying value = $5,190 ($5,600 – 410) market value on books ÷ 150 shares = $34.60/share.*
*$2,595 = $34.60 × 75 shares*

The loss on sale of securities equals the initial acquisition cost of the securities less the sales price. Because the Rusell securities are classified as available-for-sale, the proportionate amount of unrealized holding gains or losses ($205 = ½ × $410) which had accumulated in the stockholders' equity account would be reclassified and becomes part of the realized loss for inclusion in earnings of the period of the sale. Note that the accumulated other comprehensive income account in stockholders' equity is a "holding account" for the difference between the initial acquisition cost of the available-for-sale security and its current fair market value at the balance sheet date. No other holding gains or losses beyond the $410 holding loss recognized on December 31, 2007, had accumulated since December 31, 2007. When the available-for-sale security is sold, the amount of the previously recognized unrealized holding gain or loss is reclassified and becomes part of the realized gain or loss on the sale of available-for-sale securities. The realized gain or loss on the sale is then the difference between the selling price and the initial acquisition cost ($550 = $2,250 – $2,800 acquisition cost of 75 shares).

In September 2008, Keswick Corp. declared a 10% stock dividend. Stock dividends should not be reflected in income. The stock's current carrying value of $2,700 should be allocated to the additional shares received from the dividend. Since STC holds 100 shares, the dividend will be 10 shares, resulting in a total of 110 shares. After the dividend, the 110 shares will each have a carrying value of $24.55 ($2,700 ÷ 110) which will be adjusted to market at the end of the reporting period.

STC Corporation periodically reviews its intent to hold or actively trade its securities. At 12/31/08, when interest rates are 8%, STC decides that it will hold the Harmony bond indefinitely. Because this bond was originally classified as trading, it must be transferred to available-for-sale. Market value on this date is $5,773. The entries to record interest income and to transfer the bond are

| | | |
|---|---|---|
| Interest receivable | 700 | |
|     Investment in Harmony securities—trading | | 64 |
|     Interest income | | 636 |
| Investment in Harmony securities—trading | 204 | |
|     Unrealized gain on holding debt securities | | 204 |
| Investment in Harmony securities—available-for-sale | 5,773 | |
|     Investment in Harmony securities—trading | | 5,773 |

The holding gain of $204 ($5,773 FMV 12/08 – $5,634 FMV 12/07 plus premium amortization of $64) is recognized in current earnings, and the value recorded in the available-for-sale portfolio reflects the market value of $5,773 at the transfer date. Note that from this point forward any holding gains or losses should be recognized as other comprehensive income and included in accumulated other comprehensive income in stockholders' equity in accordance with the available-for-sale classification.

Also on 12/31/08, STC sold its held-for-trading Keswick stock for $32 per share. This transaction was recorded as follows:

| | | |
|---|---|---|
| Cash ($32 × 110 shares) | 3,520 | |
|     Investment in Keswick securities—trading | | 2,700 |
|     Gain on sale of securities | | 820 |

On 12/31/08, STC also recorded the appropriate entries for amortization of the Shaner bond ($7 discount amortization and $107 interest income) and to adjust the Rusell stock to its current fair value of $29 per share.

Finally, on 12/31/08 STC discovered that Shaner Enterprise is experiencing financial difficulty due to mismanagement, and the full amount of the bond will not be collected. This impairment would be considered other than temporary, so the investment in Shaner Enterprise bonds must be reduced to its current fair value of $500. The realized loss of $400 ($900 12/31/08 current carrying value – $500 FMV) is reported in earnings, and no write-up will be allowed if a recovery is made at a later date.

To summarize STC Corporation's marketable securities transactions for 2007 and 2008, T-accounts for each security are shown below, followed by earnings information relating to the investments.

| Harmony Bond—Trading | | | | | Harmony Bond—Available-for-Sale | | |
|---|---|---|---|---|---|---|---|
| 1/01/07 Acquisition | 5,360 | 57 | 12/31/07 Amort. | | 12/31/08 Transfer | 5,773 | |
| 12/31/07 Adj. to FMV | 331 | 64 | 12/31/08 Amort. | | | | |
| 12/31/08 Adj. To FMV | 204 | 5,773 | 12/31/08 Transfer | | | | |
| Bal. 12/31/08 | 0 | | | | Bal. 12/31/08 | 5,773 | |

| Shaner Bond—Held-to-Maturity | | | | Keswick Stock—Trading | | |
|---|---|---|---|---|---|---|
| 1/01/07 Acquisition | 887 | | | 1/01/07 Acquisition | | |
| 12/31/07 Amort. | 6 | | | (100 shares) | 2,200 | |
| 12/31/08 Amort. | 7 | $400 12/31/08 Write-down | | 12/31/07 Adj. to FMV | 500 | |
| Bal. 12/31/08 | 500 | | | (9/07 Stock div.—10 shares) | | 2,700  12/31/08 Sale |
| | | | | Bal. 12/31/08 | 0 | |

| Rusell Stock—Available-for-Sale | | | |
|---|---|---|---|
| 1/01/07 Acquisition | | | |
| (150 shares) | 5,600 | 410 | 12/31/07 Adj. to FMV |
| | | 2,595 | 7/08 Sale (75 shares) |
| | | 420 | 12/31/08 Adj. to FMV |
| Bal. 12/31/08 | 2,175 | | |

| Year | Transaction | Income/Gain | Loss | Net earnings | Other comprehensive income |
|---|---|---|---|---|---|
| 2007 | Harmony adj. to FMV | $ 331 | | | |
| | Keswick adj. to FMV | 500 | | | |
| | Interest on Shaner bond | 106 | | | |
| | Interest on Harmony bond | 643 | | | |
| | Rusell adj. to FMV | | | | $(410) |
| | 2007 total | $1,580 | | $1,580 | (410) |
| 2008 | Write-down of Shaner bond | | $(400) | | |
| | Sale of one-half of Rusell securities | | (550) | | $ 205 |
| | Gain on Keswick securities | $ 820 | | | |
| | Harmony adj. to FMV | 203 | | | |
| | Interest on Shaner bond | 107 | | | |
| | Interest on Harmony bond | 636 | | | |
| | Rusell adj. to FMV | | | | (420) |
| | 2008 total | $1,766 | $(950) | $ 816 | $(215) |

4.  **Transfers between Categories**

SFAS 115 requires that the classification of securities be reviewed at each balance sheet date. Although a reclassification should be rare, a company may deem it necessary to transfer a security from one category to another. Such transfers are accounted for at fair value, taking into consideration any unrealized holding gains or losses. For example, when a security is transferred **from** trading securities, any recognized unrealized gain or loss as of the date of transfer should not be reversed. On the other hand, in a transfer **to** trading securities, unrealized holding gains and losses are recognized immediately. Held-to-maturity securities reclassified **to** available-for-sale securities must be restated to fair value; any unrealized holding gain or loss that results is reported as accumulated other comprehensive income in stockholders' equity. However, transfers **from** held-to-maturity should be rare. Unrealized holding gain or loss on securities transferred **to** held-to-maturity from available-for-sale is also reported as accumulated other comprehensive income in stockholders' equity, but this gain or loss is then amortized over the remaining life of the security as an adjustment to yield. The treatment of securities transfers is summarized in the chart below.

*Securities transferred to:*

|  |  | Held-to-maturity | Available-for-sale | Trading |
|---|---|---|---|---|
| *Securities transferred from:* | **Held-to-maturity** |  | Report unrealized G/L as accumulated other comprehensive income in SE | Recognize unrealized G/L immediately |
|  | **Available-for-sale** | Report unrealized G/L as accumulated other comprehensive income in SE & amortize the gain or loss over remaining life of security |  | Recognize unrealized G/L immediately |
|  | **Trading** | Do not reverse unrealized G/L previously recognized in income | Do not reverse unrealized G/L previously recognized in income |  |

## 5.   Income Statement Presentation

Since held-to-maturity and available-for-sale securities are held for some length of time, these securities may become impaired at some point. If the decline in value is other than temporary, then the impaired security must be written down to fair value and the realized loss included in earnings. Any subsequent recovery would not be recognized in earnings unless realized through sale of the security. An other than temporary impairment cannot occur in the context of trading securities because holding gains and losses are recognized in current earnings without limitation.

SFAS 115 does not change the method of recognition of cash dividends or interest income on debt and equity securities. Thus, cash dividends or interest income should be included in the current period's income. The method of recognition for stock dividends is also not affected by SFAS 115; stock dividends should not be reflected in income. Additional shares received from a stock dividend should be added to the original shares and the per share value should be calculated upon the original shares' carrying value. At the end of the period the carrying value of the stock is adjusted to the fair value, and any unrealized holding gain or loss is recorded.

Additionally, SFAS 115 requires that realized and **unrealized** gains and losses on trading securities be included in the current period's earnings. Only realized gains and losses on sales of available-for-sale and held-to-maturity securities should be included in earnings. Unrealized gains (losses) on available-for-sale securities are reported as other comprehensive income in one of three ways (see Module 7D). Finally, amortization of any unrealized holding gain or loss on securities transferred to held-to-maturity from available-for-sale is included in income.

## C.   Investments Where Significant Influence *Does* Exist

APB 18 requires the use of the **equity method** when accounting for investments which give the investor the ability to exercise significant influence over the operating and financial policies of the investee. APB 18 assumes that ownership of 20% or more of the outstanding stock will result in that ability. Exceptions to the use of the equity method (i.e., the cost adjusted for fair value method) are related to an assessment of the investor's level of influence over the investee. The cost adjusted for fair value method in SFAS 115 should be used if an investment of more than 20% is judged to be temporary, if the investment is in a company operating in a foreign country which has severe restrictions on the operations of companies and on the transfer of monies to outside the country, and for other investments of more than 20% that do not result in significant influence. There may be unusual circumstances in which a less than 20% investor may have significant influence over the investee, in which case the equity method must be used to account for the investment.

*1.   Cost adjusted for fair value method*—The cost adjusted for fair value and the equity methods differ in the treatment of the investment account and in the recognition of earnings from the investment. The cost adjusted for fair value method first records the cost of the investment in the investment account. Income is recognized for dividends distributed from income of the investee earned since the date the investor acquired the stock. Any dividends distributed by the investee which exceed earnings since the acquisition date are classified as return of capital and recorded as a reduction of the investment account. Under the cost adjusted for fair value method, equity securities must be adjusted for subsequent changes in market value, and the unrealized holding gain or loss on equity securities for the period equals the current fair value minus the previous period's fair value on the books.

   2.   *Equity method*—The equity method also begins with recording the cost of the investment in the investment account but the two methods differ from this point on. A basic concept of the equity method is the reciprocal relationship formed between the investment account on the investor's books and the book values of the net assets on the investee's books. As changes in the investee's net assets occur (e.g., earnings, dividends, etc.), the investor will recognize in the investment account the percentage of ownership share of those changes.

   Another aspect of the equity method is the computation and accounting for the difference between the cost of the investment and the book value of the acquired asset share at the investment date. The abundance of advanced accounting texts currently in print use an assortment of terms to describe the characteristics of this concept. For purposes of uniformity, the following boldfaced terms shall be used throughout this module.

**Differential:**     The difference between the cost of the investment and the underlying book value of the net assets of the investee. This difference can be either positive or negative, as follows:

   1.   **Excess of Cost over Book Value,** which is generally attributable to

   a.   **Excess of fair value over book value,** when the fair values of the investee's assets are greater than their book values, and

   b.   **Goodwill,** when the investee has high earnings potential for which the investor has paid more than the fair values of the other net assets

   2.   **Excess of Book Value over Cost,** which is generally attributable to

   a.   **Excess of book value over fair value,** when the book values of the net assets of the investee are greater than their fair values, and

   b.   **Excess of fair value over cost,** when the cost of the investment is less than even the fair values of the investee's net assets. Some authors term this "negative goodwill."

If the differential is related to assets with finite useful lives, it will be amortized to the investment account. In accordance with SFAS 142, goodwill will not be amortized; it will be written down if the investment is determined to be impaired.

> EXAMPLE: *A Company purchased 20 shares of B Company's 100 shares of common stock outstanding for $25,000. The book value of B's total net worth (i.e., stockholders' equity) at the date of the investment was $120,000. Any excess of cost over book value is due to equipment that has a ten-year remaining useful life.*
>
> | | | |
> |---|---:|---:|
> | Investment cost | | $ 25,000 |
> | Book value of B Company | $120,000 | |
> | Percentage owned | 20% | |
> | Investor's share | | 24,000 |
> | Excess of cost over book value (due to equipment) | | $ 1,000 |
>
> *Amortization over forty years*
> *$1,000 ÷ 10 years = $100*

Under the equity method, the Income from Investment account is a parallel income statement account to the Investment in Stock balance sheet account. These two accounts should include all the income recognition and amortization resulting from the investment. Note that under the equity method, dividends received from the investee are a reduction in the Investment balance sheet account and are **not** part of the Income from Investment account.

Alternative levels of recording the results of intercompany transactions and amortization in both the investment and investment income accounts are used in accounting practice. The alternatives are presented below.

   1.   *Cost adjusted for fair value method*—No intercompany transactions or amortization are recognized in either the investment account or investment income account under this method.

   2.   *"Partial" equity*—Includes recognition of percentage share of income or loss, dividends, and any changes in the investment percentage. This method is often used for investments that will be consolidated. Thus, amortization and other adjustments are made on the worksheets, not in the investment account.

3. **"Full" equity**—In addition to the factors above, this level includes any necessary amortization or write-off of the differential between the investment cost and book value of the investment. This level also recognizes the effects of any intercompany transactions (e.g., inventory, fixed assets, and bonds) between the investor and investee corporations. APB 18 requires that all unconsolidated investments be reported in the financial statements using the "full" equity method.

*EXTENDED EXAMPLE: Assume the same facts for A Company and B Company as stated above. In addition, B Company earned $10,000 income for the year and paid $6,000 in dividends. There were no intercompany transactions. If A Company does **not** have significant influence over B Company, the investment would be accounted for by the cost adjusted for fair value method. If A Company can significantly influence B Company, the equity method is used to account for and report the investment. The appropriate entries are*

|  | Cost adjusted for fair value method | | | Equity method | | |
|---|---|---|---|---|---|---|
| 1. | To record purchase of 20% interest | | | | | |
|  | Investment in stock of B | 25,000 | | Investment in stock of B | 25,000 | |
|  |   Cash | | 25,000 |   Cash | | 25,000 |
| 2. | To record percentage of share of investee's reported income | | | | | |
|  | No entry | | | Investment in stock of B | 2,000 | |
|  | | | |   Income from investment | | |
|  | | | |   (20% × $10,000) | | 2,000 |
| 3. | To record percentage share of dividend received as distribution of income | | | | | |
|  | Cash | 1,200 | | Cash | 1,200 | |
|  |   Dividend income from | | |   Investment in stock of B | | 1,200 |
|  |   investment (20% × $6,000) | | 1,200 | | | |
| 4. | To record amortization of equipment in accordance with APB 18 | | | | | |
|  | No entry (no differential amortization under this method) | | | Income from investment | 100 | |
|  | | | |   Investment in stock of B | | 100 |

The differences in the account balances under the equity method vs. the cost adjusted for fair value method reflect the different income recognition processes and underlying asset valuation concepts of the two methods. The investment account balance under the cost adjusted for fair value method remains at the investment cost of $25,000 (although subsequent changes in fair value would require that the investment account be adjusted to market value), while under the equity method, the investment balance increases to $26,700. The $700 difference is the investor's share of the increase in the investee's undistributed earnings less the investor's amortization of the differential (excess of cost over the book value of the investment).

The amount of the investment income to be recognized by the investor also depends upon the length of time during the year the investment is owned. For example, assume that A Company acquired the 20% interest on July 1, 2007, and B Company earned $10,000 of income ratably over the period from January 1 to December 31, 2007. The entry to record A Company's percentage share of B Company's income for the period of July 1 to December 31, 2007, would be

| Cost adjusted for fair value method | | Equity method | | |
|---|---|---|---|---|
| No entry | | Investment in stock of B | 1,000 | |
| | | Income from investment | | 1,000 |
| | | (20% × $10,000 × 6/12) | | |

The receipt of the $1,200 dividends after the acquisition date would require additional analysis since the $1,200 dividend received is greater than the investor's share of the investee's income ($1,000) since acquisition. The difference of $200 ($1,200 – $1,000) is a return of capital under the cost adjusted for fair value method, and is recorded as follows:

| Cost adjusted for fair value method | | | Equity method | | |
|---|---|---|---|---|---|
| Cash | 1,200 | | Cash | 1,200 | |
|   Dividend income from investment | | 1,000 |   Investment in stock of B | | 1,200 |
|   Investment in stock of B | | 200 | | | |

The amortization of equipment will also be prorated to the time period the investment was held.

3. **Changes to or from the equity method**—when an investor changes from the cost adjusted for fair value to the equity method, the investment account must be adjusted retroactively and prior years' income and retained earnings must be retroactively restated. A change to the equity method would be made if an investor made additional purchases of stock and, for the first time, is able to exercise significant influence over the operating and financial decisions of the investee. Remember that APB 18 states that investments

of 20% or more of the investee's outstanding stock carry the "presumption" that the investor has the ability to exercise significant influence.  Therefore, in most cases, when an investment of less than 20% increases to more than 20%, the investor will retroactively change from the cost adjusted for fair value method to the equity method.

The retroactive change to the equity method requires a prior period adjustment for the difference in the investment account and retained earnings account between the amounts that were recognized in prior periods under the cost adjusted for fair value method and the amounts that would have been recognized if the equity method had been used.  In the full-year investment example on the previous page where A Company had a $25,000 balance in its Investment in B account under the cost adjusted for fair value method and $26,700 under the equity method, if A changed from the cost to the equity method because of its increased influence over B, the change entry would be

| | | |
|---|---|---|
| Investment in B Company | 700 | |
| Retained earnings | | 700 |
| ($775 = $2,000 – $1,200 – $25) | | |

In addition, any balance in the Unrealized holding gain or loss account must be reversed.  Assume that the fair value of the B Company stock had increased from $25,000 to $27,000 as of the end of the year of acquisition.  The investment account would have been debited for $2,000 and the Unrealized gain on MES account credited for $2,000 to bring the carrying value of the stock up to its market value.  Upon retroactive change to the equity method, the following reversing entry would be made:

| | | |
|---|---|---|
| Unrealized gain on MES | 2,000 | |
| Investment in stock of B | | 2,000 |

If the change is made at any time point other than the beginning of the fiscal period, the change entry would also include an adjustment to the period's Income from investment account to record the difference between the cost adjusted for fair value and equity methods handling of the investor's share of the investee's income for the current period.

When an investor discontinues using the equity method because of an inability to influence the investee's financial and operating policies, no retroactive restatement is allowed.  An example of this would be a disposal of stock resulting in a decrease in the percentage of stock owned from more than 20% to less than 20%.  The earnings or losses that relate to the shares retained by the investor that were previously recognized by the investor should remain as a part of the carrying amount.  However, if dividends received by the investor in subsequent periods exceed the investor's share of the investee's earnings for such periods, the excess should be accounted for as a return of capital and recorded as a reduction in the investment carrying amount.

A T-account is used to exhibit the major changes in the Investment in stock account under the equity method.

| Investment in Stock | |
|---|---|
| Original cost of investment | Percentage share of investee's losses since acquisition |
| Percentage share of investee's income since acquisition | Percentage share of dividends received |
| Amortization of excess of book value over cost | Amortization of excess of cost over book value |
| Increase above "significant influence" ownership— retroactive adjustment for change to equity | Disposal or sales of investment in stock |

In addition to the above, several adjustments may be added if the "full equity" method is used.  This method eliminates the effects of intercompany profits from transactions such as sales of inventory between the investor and investee corporations.  This method is rarely required on the exam but candidates should briefly review these additions in association with the discussion of the elimination entries required for consolidated working papers presented later in this module.

| Investment in Stock (continued) | |
|---|---|
| Realized portion of intercompany profit from last period confirmed this period | Elimination of unrealized portion of intercompany profit transactions from current period |

## D.  Equity Method and Deferred Income Taxes

Recognition of deferred taxes may be required when the equity method is used.  The difference between the income recognized using the equity method and the dividends received from the investee represents a temporary difference for which interperiod allocation is necessary.  Note that companies are allowed to exclude 80% of the dividend income from domestic investees.  If an investor owns 80% or more of the investee's stock, the dividend exclusion is increased to 100% (i.e., no taxes are due on investee dividend distributions). The dividend exclusion (dividends received deduction) is a permanent difference.

A discussion of deferred income taxes arising from equity method investments and several examples are provided in Module 12, Deferred Taxes.

### E. The Fair Value Option

SFAS 159, issued in February 2007, allows an entity to value its securities at fair value. A firm can elect the fair value option on an instrument-by-instrument basis. If the firm elects the fair value option for reporting available-for-sale or held-to-maturity securities, the security is revalued to fair value and any gain or loss is recorded in earnings for the period. Likewise, if the fair value option is elected for instruments that would otherwise be reported using the rules of APB 18 (equity method), the securities are revalued to fair value. Any gain or loss is recorded in earnings for the period. If the fair value option is elected for instruments that would normally use the equity method, it must be applied to all interests in that entity (i.e., both debt and equity instruments would be valued at fair value).

The fair value option can be elected on the date an investment is first recognized, or when the investment no longer qualifies for fair value treatment under SFAS 115 or APB 18. For example, if Company A has a trading security in Company B stock and acquires more than 20% of Company B, the rules of APB 18 (equity method of reporting) would normally be applied. However, if the fair value option is elected, Company A is no longer required to use the equity method, but instead values the security at year-end at fair value. Any unrealized gain or loss is recognized in earnings for the period.

The rules of SFAS 95 continue to apply for determining the classification of a purchase or sale of security on the statement of cash flows. Additional disclosures in the notes to the financial statements are required if the fair value option is elected. Refer to the outline of SFAS 159 for these disclosures.

### F. Stock Dividends and Splits

Stock dividends and stock splits are not recorded as income. The recipient continues to own the same proportion of the investee as before the stock split or dividend. The investor should make a memo entry to record the receipt of the additional shares and recompute the per share cost of the stock.

### G. Stock Rights

Investors in common stock occasionally receive stock rights to purchase additional common stock below the existing market price. The investee company has probably issued the stock rights to satisfy the investor's preemptive right to maintain an existing level of ownership of the investee. It is possible to waive these preemptive rights in some jurisdictions.

Rights are issued below the existing market price to encourage the exercise of the rights (i.e., the investor's use thereof resulting in acquisitions of additional shares of stock). The rights are separable, having their own markets, and should be accounted for separately from the investment in common stock. The rights represent a possible dilution of investor ownership and should be recorded by allocating the cost of the stock between the market value of the rights and the market value of the stock. This is accomplished by multiplying the following ratio by the cost basis of the stock:

$$\frac{\text{Market value of right}}{\text{Market value of right} + \text{Market value of stock}}$$

The following entry is made to record the receipt of the rights:

| | | |
|---|---|---|
| Investment in stock rights | xx | |
|    Investment in common stock | | xx |

The rights can be sold or exercised. The entry for exercise is

| | | |
|---|---|---|
| Investment in common stock | xx | |
|    Investment in stock rights | | xx |
|    Cash | | xx |

If the stock rights lapse

| | | |
|---|---|---|
| Loss on expiration of stock rights | xx | |
|    Investment in stock rights | | xx |

*EXAMPLE: A Company acquired 1,000 shares of common stock in B Company for $12,000. A Company subsequently received two stock rights for every share owned in B Company. Four rights and $12 are required to purchase one new share of common stock. At the date of issuance the market value of the stock rights and the common stock is $5 and $20, respectively. The entry to record the receipt of the rights is as follows:*

| | | |
|---|---|---|
| *Investment in stock rights* | *4,000* | |
|    *Investment in common stock* | | *4,000* |

*The $4,000 above was computed as follows:*

| | | |
|---|---|---|
| Total market value of rights | 2,000 rights × $ 5 = | $10,000 |
| Total market value of shares | 1,000 shares × $20 = | $20,000 |
| Combined market value | | $30,000 |

Cost allocated to stock rights $\dfrac{\$10,000}{\$30,000} \times \$12,000 = \$4,000$

Cost allocated to common stock $\dfrac{\$20,000}{\$30,000} \times \$12,000 = \$8,000$

*Note that $2 ($4,000 ÷ 2,000 rights) of cost is assigned to each stock right and $8 ($8,000 ÷ 1,000 shares) of cost to each share of stock.*

*If A uses 800 rights to purchase 200 additional shares of stock, the following entry would be made to record the transaction.*

| | | |
|---|---|---|
| Investment in common stock | 4,000 | |
|    Investment in stock rights | | 1,600* |
|    Cash | | 2,400** |

\* (800 rights × $2/right)
\*\* (200 shares × $12/share)

*If 1,000 stock rights are sold outright for $5 per right, the following entry would be made to record the transaction.*

| | | |
|---|---|---|
| Cash | 5,000* | |
|    Investment in stock rights | | 2,000** |
|    Gain on sale of rights | | 3,000 |

\* (1,000 rights × $5/right)
\*\* (1,000 rights × $2/right)

*If the 200 remaining stock rights are permitted to expire, the following entry would be made:*

| | | |
|---|---|---|
| Loss on expiration of stock rights | 400* | |
|    Investment in stock rights | | 400* |

\* (200 rights × $2/right)

*The journal entries above can be summarized as follows:*

| Investment in common stock | | | | | Investment in stock rights | | |
|---|---|---|---|---|---|---|---|
| Purchase, 1,000 shares @ $12 | 12,000 | $ 4,000 | ← Cost allocated to stock rights → | | 4,000 | | |
| | | | | | | 1,600 | Exercise of 800 rights |
| Purchase, 200 shares by exercise of rights | 4,000 | | | | | 2,000 | Sale of 1,000 rights |
| | | | | | | 400 | Expiration of 200 rights |
| | 12,000 | | | | | -- | |

## H.  Cash Surrender Value of Life Insurance

The cash surrender value of life insurance policies represents a noncurrent investment when the company is the beneficiary (rather than insured employees).  The entry to record insurance premiums that increase cash surrender value is

| | | |
|---|---|---|
| Insurance expense | (plug) | |
| Cash surrender value | (increase in CSV) | |
|    Cash | | (total premium) |

Cash surrender value remains a noncurrent asset unless the company plans to cash in the policy within the next period.

During the first few years of a policy, no cash surrender value may attach to the policy.  During this period, the entire insurance premium would be expense.  In addition, any dividends received from the life insurance policy are not recorded as revenue, but instead are offset against insurance expense.

## I.  Research Component

The research for investments can be found primarily in APB 18 and SFAS 115.  It should be noted, however, that when SFAS 115 was released, the pronouncement for reporting comprehensive income did not exist.  Therefore, SFAS 130 amends SFAS 115 and outlines which investment transactions affect comprehensive income.  Specifically, SFAS 130 changed the wording of "separate component of shareholders' equity" to "other comprehensive income."  SFAS 135 also made several technical corrections to SFAS 115.

Keyword for researching investments are shown below.

| | | |
|---|---|---|
| Asset-liability management | Fair value investment | Other comprehensive income loss |
| Available-for-sale | Fair value option | Readily determinable fair value |
| Carrying amount investment | Fair value security | Security maturity date |
| Cash flows securities | 50% or less | Shares of investee |
| Classified securities | Held-to-maturity | Significant influence |
| Change intent | Increase in ownership investee | Trading |
| Debt equity securities | Intent indefinite period | Transfer between categories |
| Decline in fair value | Intercompany profits | Unrealized holding gains |
| Disclosure securities | Interest income | Unrealized holding losses |
| Dividend income | Investments equity securities | Voting privileges |
| Enterprise disclose | Loss temporary decline | |
| Equity method investment | Other comprehensive income gain | |

## MULTIPLE-CHOICE QUESTIONS (1-59)

**1.** Puff Co. acquired 40% of Straw, Inc.'s voting common stock on January 2, 2008, for $400,000. The carrying amount of Straw's net assets at the purchase date totaled $900,000. Fair values equaled carrying amounts for all items except equipment, for which fair values exceeded carrying amounts by $100.000. The equipment has a five-year life. During 2008, Straw reported net income of $150,000. What amount of income from this investment should Puff report in its 2008 income statement if Puff uses the equity method to account for the investment?

a. $40,000
b. $52,000
c. $56,000
d. $60,000

**2.** On April 1, 2007, Saxe, Inc. purchased $200,000 face value, 9% US Treasury Notes for $198,500, including accrued interest of $4,500. The notes mature July 1, 2008, and pay interest semiannually on January 1 and July 1. Saxe uses the straight-line method of amortization and intends to hold the notes to maturity. Saxe does not elect the fair value option for recording the securities. In its October 31, 2007 balance sheet, the carrying amount of this investment should be

a. $194,000
b. $196,800
c. $197,200
d. $199,000

**3.** Kale Co. purchased bonds at a discount on the open market as an investment and intends to hold these bonds to maturity. Kale uses the reporting requirements of SFAS 115. Kale should account for these bonds at

a. Cost.
b. Amortized cost.
c. Fair value.
d. Lower of cost or market.

**4.** For a marketable debt securities portfolio classified as held-to-maturity, which of the following amounts should be included in the period's net income, assuming the rules of SFAS 115 apply?

I. Unrealized temporary losses during the period.
II. Realized gains during the period.
III. Changes in the valuation allowance during the period.

a. III only.
b. II only.
c. I and II.
d. I, II, and III.

**5.** Bing Corporation purchased bonds at a discount on the open market as an investment and intends to hold these bonds to maturity. Assume that Bing elects the reporting rules in SFAS 159. Bing should account for these bonds at

a. Cost.
b. Amortized cost.
c. Fair value.
d. Lower of cost or market.

**6.** For a marketable debt securities portfolio classified as held-to-maturity, which of the following amounts should be included in the period's net income, assuming the company elects the fair value option of reporting all of its financial instruments in the portfolio?

I. Unrealized temporary losses during the period.
II. Realized gains during the period.
III. Changes in the valuation allowance during the period.
IV. Unrealized gains during the period.

a. I only
b. I and II
c. I and III.
d. I, II, and IV.

**Items 7 and 8** are based on the following:

The following data pertains to Tyne Co.'s investments in marketable equity securities:

|  | | Market value | |
| --- | --- | --- | --- |
|  | Cost | 12/31/07 | 12/31/06 |
| Trading | $150,000 | $155,000 | $100,000 |
| Available-for-sale | 150,000 | 130,000 | 120,000 |

**7.** What amount should Tyne report as unrealized holding gain in its 2007 income statement, assuming Tyne uses SFAS 115 to report its investments?

a. $50,000
b. $55,000
c. $60,000
d. $65,000

**8.** Assume Tyne uses SFAS 115 to report investments. What amount should Tyne report as net unrealized loss on marketable equity securities at December 31, 2007, in accumulated other comprehensive income in stockholders' equity?

a. $0
b. $10,000
c. $15,000
d. $20,000

**9.** Reed Insurance Co. began operations on January 1, 2007. The following information pertains to Reed's December 31, 2007 portfolio of marketable equity securities:

|  | Trading securities | Available-for-sale securities |
| --- | --- | --- |
| Aggregate cost | $360,000 | $550,000 |
| Aggregate market value | 320,000 | 450,000 |
| Aggregate lower of cost or market value applied to each security in the portfolio | 304,000 | 420,000 |

Reed uses the provisions of SFAS 115 and does not elect the fair value option of SFAS 159. If the market declines are judged to be temporary, what amounts should Reed report as a loss on these securities in its December 31, 2007 income statement?

|  | Trading securities | Available-for-sale securities |
| --- | --- | --- |
| a. | $40,000 | $0 |
| b. | $0 | $100,000 |
| c. | $40,000 | $100,000 |
| d. | $56,000 | $130,000 |

**10.** Stone accounts for available-for-sale securities as required by SFAS 115. Information regarding Stone Co.'s portfolio of available-for-sale securities is as follows:

| Aggregate cost as of 12/31/07 | $170,000 |
| --- | --- |
| Unrealized gains as of 12/31/07 | 4,000 |
| Unrealized losses as of 12/31/07 | 26,000 |
| Net realized gains during 2007 | 30,000 |

At December 31, 2006, Stone reported an unrealized loss of $1,500 in other comprehensive income to reduce these securities to market. Under the accumulated other comprehensive income in stockholders' equity section of its December 31, 2007 balance sheet, what amount should Stone report?

  a.  $26,000
  b.  $22,000
  c.  $20,500
  d.  $0

**11.** Data regarding Ball Corp.'s available-for-sale securities follow:

| | Cost | Market value |
|---|---|---|
| December 31, 2006 | $150,000 | $130,000 |
| December 31, 2007 | 150,000 | 160,000 |

Differences between cost and market values are considered temporary. Ball uses SFAS 115 to account for available-for-sale securities. The effect on Ball's 2007 other comprehensive income would be

  a.  $30,000
  b.  $20,000
  c.  $10,000
  d.  $0

**12.** Alton Co. began operations on January 1, 2008. The following information pertains to Alton's December 31, 2008 portfolio of marketable equity securities:

| | Trading securities | Available-for-sale securities |
|---|---|---|
| Aggregate cost | $360,000 | $550,000 |
| Aggregate market value | 320,000 | 450,000 |
| Aggregate lower of cost or market value applied to each security in the portfolio | 304,000 | 420,000 |

Alton uses the provisions of SFAS 159 and elects the fair value option for all financial instruments. If the market declines are judged to be temporary, what amounts should Alton report as a loss on these securities in its December 31, 2008 income statement?

| | Trading securities | Available-for-sale securities |
|---|---|---|
| a. | $40,000 | $0 |
| b. | $0 | $100,000 |
| c. | $40,000 | $100,000 |
| d. | $56,000 | $130,000 |

**13.** Information regarding Shelton Co.'s portfolio of available-for-sale securities is as follows:

| | |
|---|---|
| Aggregate cost as of 12/31/08 | $150,000 |
| Unrealized gains as of 12/31/08 | 14,000 |
| Unrealized losses as of 12/31/08 | 26,000 |
| Net realized gains during 2008 | 30,000 |

Shelton elects to use the fair value option for reporting all available-for-sale securities in accordance with SFAS 159. At December 31, 2008, what total amount should Shelton report on its income statement?

  a.  $ 4,000 gain
  b.  $18,000 gain
  c.  $30,000 gain
  d.  $44,000 gain

**14.** Data regarding Shannon Corp.'s available-for-sale securities follow:

| | Cost | Market value |
|---|---|---|
| December 31, 2008 | $150,000 | $130,000 |
| December 31, 2009 | 150,000 | 160,000 |

Differences between cost and market values are considered temporary. Shannon elects to use the fair value option for

reporting all available-for-sale securities. The effect of accounting for available-for-sale securities on other comprehensive income would be

  a.  $30,000
  b.  $20,000
  c.  $10,000
  d.  $0

**15.** Antonio Corp. has a portfolio of marketable equity securities that it does not intend to sell in the near term. Antonio elects the fair value option for reporting its financial assets in accordance with SFAS 159. How should Antonio classify these securities, and how should it report unrealized gains and losses?

| | Classify as | Report as a |
|---|---|---|
| a. | Trading securities | Component of income from continuing operations |
| b. | Available-for-sale securities | Separate component of other comprehensive income |
| c. | Trading securities | Separate component of other comprehensive income |
| d. | Available-for-sale securities | Component of income from continuing operations |

**16.** During 2007, Rex Company purchased marketable equity securities as a short-term investment. These securities are classified as available-for-sale. Rex uses SFAS 115 to account for available-for-sale securities. The cost and market value at December 31, 2007, were as follows:

| Security | Cost | Market value |
|---|---|---|
| A—100 shares | $ 2,800 | $ 3,400 |
| B—1,000 shares | 17,000 | 15,300 |
| C—2,000 shares | 31,500 | 29,500 |
| | $51,300 | $48,200 |

Rex sold 1,000 shares of Company B stock on January 31, 2008, for $15 per share, incurring $1,500 in brokerage commission and taxes. On the sale, Rex should report a realized loss of

  a.  $ 300
  b.  $1,800
  c.  $2,000
  d.  $3,500

**17.** Cap Corp. reported accrued investment interest receivable of $38,000 and $46,500 at January 1 and December 31, 2007, respectively. During 2007, cash collections from the investments included the following:

| | |
|---|---|
| Capital gains distributions | $145,000 |
| Interest | 152,000 |

What amount should Cap report as interest revenue from investments for 2007?

  a.  $160,500
  b.  $153,500
  c.  $152,000
  d.  $143,500

**18.** Nola has a portfolio of marketable equity securities that it does not intend to sell in the near term. Assume that Nola accounts for these securities using SFAS 115. How should Nola classify these securities, and how should it report unrealized gains and losses from these securities?

|    | Classify as | Report as a |
|----|-------------|-------------|
| a. | Trading securities | Component of income from continuing operations |
| b. | Available-for-sale securities | Separate component of other comprehensive income |
| c. | Trading securities | Separate component of other comprehensive income |
| d. | Available-for-sale securities | Component of income from continuing operations |

**19.** On December 29, 2007, BJ Co. sold a marketable equity security that had been purchased on January 4, 2006. BJ owned no other marketable equity security. An unrealized loss was reported in 2006 as other comprehensive income. A realized gain was reported in the 2007 income statement. Was the marketable equity security classified as available-for-sale and did its 2006 market price decline exceed its 2007 market price recovery?

|    | Available-for-sale | 2006 market price decline exceeded 2007 market recovery |
|----|--------------------|---------------------------------------------------------|
| a. | Yes | Yes |
| b. | Yes | No |
| c. | No | Yes |
| d. | No | No |

**20.** On January 10, 2007, Box, Inc. purchased marketable equity securities of Knox, Inc. and Scot, Inc., neither of which Box could significantly influence. Box classified both securities as available-for-sale. At December 31, 2007, the cost of each investment was greater than its fair market value. The loss on the Knox investment was considered other-than-temporary and that on Scot was considered temporary. How should Box report the effects of these investing activities in its 2007 income statement, assuming Box uses SFAS 115 to account for these securities?

I.   Excess of cost of Knox stock over its market value.
II.  Excess of cost of Scot stock over its market value.

a.  An unrealized loss equal to I plus II.
b.  An unrealized loss equal to I only.
c.  A realized loss equal to I only.
d.  No income statement effect.

**21.** On both December 31, 2006, and December 31, 2007, Kopp Co.'s only marketable equity security had the same market value, which was below cost. Kopp considered the decline in value to be temporary in 2006 but other than temporary in 2007. At the end of both years the security was classified as a noncurrent asset. Kopp considers the investment to be available-for-sale. Assume that Kipp uses SFAS 115 to account for its available-for-sale securities. What should be the effects of the determination that the decline was other than temporary on Kopp's 2007 net noncurrent assets and net income?

a.  No effect on both net noncurrent assets and net income.
b.  No effect on net noncurrent assets and decrease in net income.
c.  Decrease in net noncurrent assets and **no** effect on net income.
d.  Decrease in both net noncurrent assets and net income.

**22.** For the last ten years, Woody Co. has owned cumulative preferred stock issued by Hadley, Inc. During 2007, Hadley declared and paid both the 2007 dividend and the 2006 dividend in arrears. How should Woody report the 2006 dividend in arrears that was received in 2007?

a.  As a reduction in cumulative preferred dividends receivable.
b.  As a retroactive change of the prior period financial statements.
c.  Include, net of income taxes, after 2007 income from continuing operations.
d.  Include in 2007 income from continuing operations.

**Items 23 and 24** are based on the following:

Deed Co. owns 2% of Beck Cosmetic Retailers. A property dividend by Beck consisted of merchandise with a fair value lower than the listed retail price. Deed in turn gave the merchandise to its employees as a holiday bonus.

**23.** How should Deed report the receipt and distribution of the merchandise in its income statement?

a.  At fair value for both dividend revenue and employee compensation expense.
b.  At listed retail price for both dividend revenue and employee compensation expense.
c.  At fair value for dividend revenue and listed retail price for employee compensation expense.
d.  By disclosure only.

**24.** How should Deed report the receipt and distribution of the merchandise in its statement of cash flows?

a.  As both an inflow and outflow for operating activities.
b.  As both an inflow and outflow for investing activities.
c.  As an inflow for investing activities and outflow for operating activities.
d.  As a noncash activity.

**25.** Pal Corp.'s 2007 dividend revenue included only part of the dividends received from its Ima Corp. investment. Pal Corp. has an investment in Ima Corp. that it intends to hold indefinitely. The balance of the dividend reduced Pal's carrying amount for its Ima investment. This reflects the fact that Pal accounts for its Ima investment

a.  As an available-for-sale investment, and only a portion of Ima's 2007 dividends represent earnings after Pal's acquisition.
b.  As an available-for-sale investment and its carrying amount exceeded the proportionate share of Ima's market value.
c.  As an equity investment, and Ima incurred a loss in 2007.
d.  As an equity investment, and its carrying amount exceeded the proportionate share of Ima's market value.

**26.** In its financial statements, Pare, Inc. uses the cost method of accounting for its 15% ownership of Sabe Co. At December 31, 2007, Pare has a receivable from Sabe. How should the receivable be reported in Pare's December 31, 2007 balance sheet?

a.  The total receivable should be reported separately.
b.  The total receivable should be included as part of the investment in Sabe, without separate disclosure.

c.   85% of the receivable should be reported separately, with the balance offset against Sabe's payable to Pare.

d.   The total receivable should be offset against Sabe's
payable to Pare, without separate disclosure.

**Items 27 and 28** are based on the following:

Sun Corp. had investments in marketable debt securities costing $650,000 that were classified as available-for-
sale.  On June 30, 2007, Sun decided to hold the investments
to maturity and accordingly reclassified them to the held-to-
maturity category on that date.  The investments' market
value was $575,000 at December 31, 2006, $530,000 at
June 30, 2007, and $490,000 at December 31, 2007.  Sun
does not elect the fair value option to account for these
investments.

**27.**  What amount of loss from investments should Sun report in its 2007 income statement?

a.   $  45,000
b.   $  85,000
c.   $120,000
d.   $0

**28.**  What amount should Sun report as net unrealized loss
on marketable debt securities in its 2007 statement of stockholders' equity?

a.   $  40,000
b.   $  45,000
c.   $160,000
d.   $120,000

**29.**  A marketable debt security is transferred from
available-for-sale to held-to-maturity securities.  At the
transfer date, the security's carrying amount exceeds its
market value.  Assume SFAS 115 is used to report this security.  What amount is used at the transfer date to record the
security in the held-to-maturity portfolio?

a.   Market value, regardless of whether the decline in
market value below cost is considered permanent
or temporary.

b.   Market value, only if the decline in market value
below cost is considered permanent.

c.   Cost, if the decline in market value below cost is
considered temporary.

d.   Cost, regardless of whether the decline in market
value below cost is considered permanent or temporary.

**Items 30 and 31** are based on the following:

Jill Corp. had investments in marketable debt securities purchased on January 1, 2007, for $650,000 that were classified
as trading securities and accounted for using SFAS 115.
On June 30, 2008, Jill decided to hold the investments to
maturity and accordingly reclassified them to the held-to-
maturity category on that date.  The investments' market
value was $575,000 at December 31, 2007, $530,000 at
June 30, 2008, and $490,000 at December 31, 2008.  Jill
elects the fair value option for reporting these held-to-
maturity securities.

**30.**  What amount of loss from investments should Jill
report in its 2008 income statement?

a.   $  40,000
b.   $  85,000
c.   $160,000
d.   $0

**31.**  What amount should Jill report as net unrealized loss on
marketable debt securities in other comprehensive income in
its 2008 statement of stockholders' equity?

a.   $0
b.   $  40,000
c.   $  45,000
d.   $120,000

**Items 32 through 34** are based on the following:

Grant, Inc. acquired 30% of South Co.'s voting stock
for $200,000 on January 2, 2006.  Grant's 30% interest in
South gave Grant the ability to exercise significant influence
over South's operating and financial policies.  During 2006,
South earned $80,000 and paid dividends of $50,000.  South
reported earnings of $100,000 for the six months ended
June 30, 2007, and $200,000 for the year ended Decem-
ber 31, 2007.  On July 1, 2007, Grant sold half of its stock in
South for $150,000 cash.  South paid dividends of $60,000
on October 1, 2007.  Grant does not elect the fair value
option to report this investment.

**32.**  Before income taxes, what amount should Grant include in its 2006 income statement as a result of the investment?

a.   $15,000
b.   $24,000
c.   $50,000
d.   $80,000

**33.**  In Grant's December 31, 2006 balance sheet, what
should be the carrying amount of this investment?

a.   $200,000
b.   $209,000
c.   $224,000
d.   $230,000

**34.**  In its 2007 income statement, what amount should
Grant report as gain from the sale of half of its investment?

a.   $24,500
b.   $30,500
c.   $35,000
d.   $45,500

**35.**  Moss Corp. owns 20% of Dubro Corp.'s preferred stock
and 80% of its common stock.  Dubro's stock outstanding at
December 31, 2007, is as follows:

| | |
|---|---|
| 10% cumulative preferred stock | $100,000 |
| Common stock | 700,000 |

Dubro reported net income of $60,000 for the year ended
December 31, 2007.  Assume that Moss does not elect the
fair value option to report the investment in Dubro.  What
amount should Moss record as equity in earnings of Dubro
for the year ended December 31, 2007?

a.   $42,000
b.   $48,000
c.   $48,400
d.   $50,000

**36.**  Sage, Inc. bought 40% of Adams Corp.'s outstanding
common stock on January 2, 2007, for $400,000.  The car-
rying amount of Adams' net assets at the purchase date totaled $900,000.  Fair values and carrying amounts were the
same for all items except for plant and inventory, for which
fair values exceeded their carrying amounts by $90,000 and
$10,000, respectively.  The plant has an eighteen-year life.
All inventory was sold during 2007.  During 2007, Adams

reported net income of $120,000 and paid a $20,000 cash dividend. Assume that Sage uses the reporting requirements of APB 18 to account for this investment. What amount should Sage report in its income statement from its investment in Adams for the year ended December 31, 2007?

- a. $48,000
- b. $42,000
- c. $36,000
- d. $32,000

**37.** Pear Co.'s income statement for the year ended December 31, 2007, as prepared by Pear's controller, reported income before taxes of $125,000. The auditor questioned the following amounts that had been included in income before taxes:

| | |
|---|---|
| Unrealized gain on available-for-sale investment | $40,000 |
| Equity in earnings of Cinn Co. | 20,000 |
| Dividends received from Cinn | 8,000 |
| Adjustments to profits of prior years for arith- | |
|   metical errors in depreciation | (35,000) |

Pear owns 40% of Cinn's common stock. Pear accounts for its investment in Cinn in accordance with the requirements of APB 18. Pear's December 31, 2007 income statement should report income before taxes of

- a. $ 85,000
- b. $117,000
- c. $112,000
- d. $152,000

**38.** On January 2, 2007, Saxe Company purchased 20% of Lex Corporation's common stock for $150,000. Saxe Corporation intends to hold the stock indefinitely. This investment did not give Saxe the ability to exercise significant influence over Lex. During 2007 Lex reported net income of $175,000 and paid cash dividends of $100,000 on its common stock. There was no change in the market value of the common stock during the year. The balance in Saxe's investment in Lex Corporation account at December 31, 2007 should be

- a. $130,000
- b. $150,000
- c. $165,000
- d. $185,000

**39.** On January 2, 2007, Well Co. purchased 10% of Rea, Inc.'s outstanding common shares for $400,000. Well is the largest single shareholder in Rea, and Well's officers are a majority on Rea's board of directors. Rea reported net income of $500,000 for 2007, and paid dividends of $150,000. Well does not elect the fair value option to report its investment in Rea. In its December 31, 2007 balance sheet, what amount should Well report as investment in Rea?

- a. $450,000
- b. $435,000
- c. $400,000
- d. $385,000

**40.** On January 2, 2007, Kean Co. purchased a 30% interest in Pod Co. for $250,000. On this date, Pod's stockholders' equity was $500,000. The carrying amounts of Pod's identifiable net assets approximated their fair values, except for land whose fair value exceeded its carrying amount by $200,000. Pod reported net income of $100,000 for 2007, and paid no dividends. Kean accounts for this investment using the equity method. In its December 31, 2007 balance sheet, what amount should Kean report as investment in subsidiary?

- a. $210,000
- b. $220,000
- c. $270,000
- d. $280,000

**41.** On January 1, 2007, Mega Corp. acquired 10% of the outstanding voting stock of Penny, Inc. On January 2, 2008, Mega gained the ability to exercise significant influence over financial and operating control of Penny by acquiring an additional 20% of Penny's outstanding stock. The two purchases were made at prices proportionate to the value assigned to Penny's net assets, which equaled their carrying amounts. Mega does not elect the fair value option to report its investment in Penny. For the years ended December 31, 2007 and 2008, Penny reported the following:

| | 2007 | 2008 |
|---|---|---|
| Dividends paid | $200,000 | $300,000 |
| Net income | 600,000 | 650,000 |

In 2008, what amounts should Mega report as current year investment income and as an adjustment, before income taxes, to 2007 investment income?

| | 2008 investment income | Adjustment to 2007 investment income |
|---|---|---|
| a. | $195,000 | $160,000 |
| b. | $195,000 | $100,000 |
| c. | $195,000 | $ 40,000 |
| d. | $105,000 | $ 40,000 |

**42.** Pare, Inc. purchased 10% of Tot Co.'s 100,000 outstanding shares of common stock on January 2, 2007, for $50,000. On December 31, 2007, Pare purchased an additional 20,000 shares of Tot for $150,000. There was no goodwill as a result of either acquisition, and Tot had not issued any additional stock during 2007. Tot reported earnings of $300,000 for 2007. Pare does not elect the fair value option to report its investment in Tot. What amount should Pare report in its December 31, 2007 balance sheet as investment in Tot?

- a. $170,000
- b. $200,000
- c. $230,000
- d. $290,000

**43.** When the equity method is used to account for investments in common stock, which of the following affects the investor's reported investment income?

| | Equipment amortization related to purchase | Cash dividends from investee |
|---|---|---|
| a. | Yes | Yes |
| b. | No | Yes |
| c. | No | No |
| d. | Yes | No |

**44.** Park Co. uses the equity method to account for its January 1, 2007 purchase of Tun Inc.'s common stock. On January 1, 2007, the fair values of Tun's FIFO inventory and land exceeded their carrying amounts. How do these excesses of fair values over carrying amounts affect Park's reported equity in Tun's 2007 earnings?

| | Inventory excess | Land excess |
|---|---|---|
| a. | Decrease | Decrease |
| b. | Decrease | No effect |
| c. | Increase | Increase |
| d. | Increase | No effect |

**45.** An investor in common stock received dividends in excess of the investor's share of investee's earnings subsequent to the date of the investment. How will the investor's investment account be affected by those dividends for each of the following investments?

|     | Available-for-sale securities | Equity method investment |
| --- | --- | --- |
| a. | No effect | No effect |
| b. | Decrease | No effect |
| c. | No effect | Decrease |
| d. | Decrease | Decrease |

**46.** Peel Co. received a cash dividend from a common stock investment. Should Peel report an increase in the investment account if it has classified the stock as available-for-sale or uses the equity method of accounting?

|     | Available-for-sale | Equity |
| --- | --- | --- |
| a. | No | No |
| b. | Yes | Yes |
| c. | Yes | No |
| d. | No | Yes |

**47.** On January 1, 2007, Point, Inc. purchased 10% of Iona Co.'s common stock. Point purchased additional shares bringing its ownership up to 40% of Iona's common stock outstanding on August 1, 2007. During October 2007, Iona declared and paid a cash dividend on all of its outstanding common stock. Point uses the equity method to account for its investment in Iona. How much income from the Iona investment should Point's 2007 income statement report?

- a. 10% of Iona's income for January 1 to July 31, 2007, plus 40% of Iona's income for August 1 to December 31, 2007.
- b. 40% of Iona's income for August 1 to December 31, 2007 only.
- c. 40% of Iona's 2007 income.
- d. Amount equal to dividends received from Iona.

**48.** In its financial statements, Pulham Corp. uses the equity method of accounting for its 30% ownership of Angles Corp. At December 31, 2007, Pulham has a receivable from Angles. How should the receivable be reported in Pulham's 2007 financial statements?

- a. None of the receivable should be reported, but the entire receivable should be offset against Angles' payable to Pulham.
- b. 70% of the receivable should be separately reported, with the balance offset against 30% of Angles' payable to Pulham.
- c. The total receivable should be disclosed separately.
- d. The total receivable should be included as part of the investment in Angles, without separate disclosure.

**49.** Wood Co. owns 2,000 shares of Arlo, Inc.'s 20,000 shares of $100 par, 6% cumulative, nonparticipating preferred stock and 1,000 shares (2%) of Arlo's common stock. During 2007, Arlo declared and paid dividends of $240,000 on preferred stock. No dividends had been declared or paid during 2006. In addition, Wood received a 5% common stock dividend from Arlo when the quoted market price of Arlo's common stock was $10 per share. What amount should Wood report as dividend income in its 2007 income statement?

- a. $12,000
- b. $12,500
- c. $24,000
- d. $24,500

**50.** Stock dividends on common stock should be recorded at their fair market value by the investor when the related investment is accounted for under which of the following methods?

|     | Cost | Equity | Fair value |
| --- | --- | --- | --- |
| a. | Yes | Yes | Yes |
| b. | Yes | No | No |
| c. | No | Yes | Yes |
| d. | No | No | No |

**51.** On March 4, 2007, Evan Co. purchased 1,000 shares of LVC common stock at $80 per share. On September 26, 2007, Evan received 1,000 stock rights to purchase an additional 1,000 shares at $90 per share. The stock rights had an expiration date of February 1, 2008. On September 30, 2007, LVC's common stock had a market value, ex-rights, of $95 per share and the stock rights had a market value of $5 each. What amount should Evan report on its September 30, 2007 balance sheet as the cost of its investment in stock rights?

- a. $ 4,000
- b. $ 5,000
- c. $10,000
- d. $15,000

**52.** On January 3, 2005, Falk Co. purchased 500 shares of Milo Corp. common stock for $36,000. On December 2, 2007, Falk received 500 stock rights from Milo. Each right entitles the holder to acquire one share of stock for $85. The market price of Milo's stock was $100 a share immediately before the rights were issued, and $90 a share immediately after the rights were issued. Falk sold its rights on December 3, 2007, for $10 a right. Falk's gain from the sale of the rights is

- a. $0
- b. $1,000
- c. $1,400
- d. $5,000

**53.** In 2004, Chain, Inc. purchased a $1,000,000 life insurance policy on its president, of which Chain is the beneficiary. Information regarding the policy for the year ended December 31, 2007, follows:

| | |
| --- | --- |
| Cash surrender value, 1/1/07 | $ 87,000 |
| Cash surrender value, 12/31/07 | 108,000 |
| Annual advance premium paid 1/1/07 | 40,000 |

During 2007, dividends of $6,000 were applied to increase the cash surrender value of the policy. What amount should Chain report as life insurance expense for 2007?

- a. $40,000
- b. $25,000
- c. $19,000
- d. $13,000

**54.** An increase in the cash surrender value of a life insurance policy owned by a company would be recorded by

- a. Decreasing annual insurance expense.
- b. Increasing investment income.
- c. Recording a memorandum entry only.
- d. Decreasing a deferred charge.

**55.** Upon the death of an officer, Jung Co. received the proceeds of a life insurance policy held by Jung on the officer. The proceeds were not taxable. The policy's cash surrender value had been recorded on Jung's books at the time of payment. What amount of revenue should Jung report in its statements?

    a.   Proceeds received.
    b.   Proceeds received less cash surrender value.
    c.   Proceeds received plus cash surrender value.
    d.   None.

**Items 56 through 58** are based on the following data:

Lake Corporation's accounting records showed the following investments at January 1, 2007:

| | |
|---|---|
| Common stock: | |
|   Kar Corp. (1,000 shares) | $ 10,000 |
|   Aub Corp. (5,000 shares) | 100,000 |
| | |
| Real estate: | |
|   Parking lot (leased to Day Co.) | 300,000 |
| | |
| Other: | |
|   Trademark (at cost, less accumulated | |
|     amortization) | 25,000 |
| Total investments | $435,000 |

Lake owns 1% of Kar and 30% of Aub. Lake's directors constitute a majority of Aub's directors. The Day lease, which commenced on January 1, 2005, is for ten years, at an annual rental of $48,000. In addition, on January 1, 2005, Day paid a nonrefundable deposit of $50,000, as well as a security deposit of $8,000 to be refunded upon expiration of the lease. The trademark was licensed to Barr Co. for royalties of 10% of sales of the trademarked items. Royalties are payable semiannually on March 1 (for sales in July through December of the prior year), and on September 1 (for sales in January through June of the same year).

During the year ended December 31, 2007, Lake received cash dividends of $1,000 from Kar, and $15,000 from Aub, whose 2007 net incomes were $75,000 and $150,000, respectively. Lake also received $48,000 rent from Day in 2007 and the following royalties from Barr:

| | *March 1* | *September 1* |
|---|---|---|
| 2006 | $3,000 | $5,000 |
| 2007 | 4,000 | 7,000 |

Barr estimated that sales of the trademarked items would total $20,000 for the last half of 2007.

**56.** In Lake's 2007 income statement, how much should be reported for dividend revenue?

    a.  $16,000
    b.  $ 2,400
    c.  $ 1,000
    d.  $   150

**57.** In Lake's 2007 income statement, how much should be reported for royalty revenue?

    a.  $14,000
    b.  $13,000
    c.  $11,000
    d.  $ 9,000

**58.** In Lake's 2007 income statement, how much should be reported for rental revenue?

    a.  $43,000
    b.  $48,000
    c.  $53,000
    d.  $53,800

**59.** Band Co. uses the equity method to account for its investment in Guard, Inc. common stock. How should Band record a 2% stock dividend received from Guard?

    a.   As dividend revenue at Guard's carrying value of the stock.
    b.   As dividend revenue at the market value of the stock.
    c.   As a reduction in the total cost of Guard stock owned.
    d.   As a memorandum entry reducing the unit cost of all Guard stock owned.

**SIMULATION PROBLEMS**

**Simulation Problem 1**                    (50 to 60 minutes)

| Situation | | | | | |
|---|---|---|---|---|---|
| | Concepts | Accounting Treatment | Financial Statement Disclosures | Research | Communication |

The following information pertains to Dayle, Inc.'s portfolio of marketable investments for the year ended December 31, 2007:

| | Cost | Fair value 12/31/06 | 2007 activity Purchases | Sales | Fair value 12/31/07 |
|---|---|---|---|---|---|
| *Held-to-maturity securities* | | | | | |
| Security ABC | | | $100,000 | | $95,000 |
| *Trading securities* | | | | | |
| Security DEF | $150,000 | $160,000 | | | 155,000 |
| *Available-for-sale securities* | | | | | |
| Security GHI | 190,000 | 165,000 | | | |
| Security JKL | 170,000 | 175,000 | | $175,000 | 160,000 |

Security ABC was purchased at par. All declines in fair value are considered to be temporary. Dayle does not elect the fair value option for any of its financial assets.

| | Concepts | | | | |
|---|---|---|---|---|---|
| Situation | | Accounting Treatment | Financial Statement Disclosures | Research | Communication |

The following questions relate to investments in debt securities and in equity securities that do not involve significant influence. For each item, match the accounting treatment with the appropriate concept. Concepts may be used once, more than once, or not at all. Assume the fair value option is not elected.

*Concept*

A.  Available-for-sale securities
B.  Valuation allowance
C.  Transfer from trading to available-for-sale
D.  Held-to-maturity securities
E.  Permanent impairment
F.  Other-than-temporary securities
G.  Amortization of differential
H.  Trading securities
I.  Transfer from available-for-sale to held-to-maturity

*Accounting treatment*

| | (A) | (B) | (C) | (D) | (E) | (F) | (G) | (H) | (I) |
|---|---|---|---|---|---|---|---|---|---|
| 1. Cash flows from purchases and sales of these securities are reported as an operating activity on the statement of cash flows. | O | O | O | O | O | O | O | O | O |
| 2. Include unrealized holding gains/losses in earnings of current period. | O | O | O | O | O | O | O | O | O |
| 3. Amortize unrealized holding gain/loss over life of security. | O | O | O | O | O | O | O | O | O |
| 4. Report at amortized cost. | O | O | O | O | O | O | O | O | O |
| 5. Report unrealized holding gains/losses as other comprehensive income and close to accumulated other comprehensive income, a separate component of stockholders' equity. | O | O | O | O | O | O | O | O | O |
| 6. Classify as a current asset. | O | O | O | O | O | O | O | O | O |
| 7. Subsequent recovery not recognized unless realized. | O | O | O | O | O | O | O | O | O |

| | | Accounting Treatment | | | |
|---|---|---|---|---|---|
| Situation | Concepts | | Financial Statement Disclosures | Research | Communication |

Determine whether each statement is True or False.

| | *True* | *False* |
|---|---|---|
| 1. Held-to-maturity securities are classified as current or noncurrent on an individual basis. | O | O |
| 2. For trading securities, some realized gains/losses are excluded from earnings. | O | O |
| 3. A premature sale of held-to-maturity securities may be considered maturity if at least 80% of the principal has already been collected. | O | O |
| 4. Dividends received on available-for-sale securities decrease the investment account. | O | O |
| 5. A company that owns more than 50% of the outstanding shares of stock of another company must use the fair value method. | O | O |

| Situation | Concepts | Accounting Treatment | Financial Statement Disclosures | | Research | Communication |
|---|---|---|---|---|---|---|

For the following questions, choose from the answer list below.

*Answer List*

| A. $0 | D. $ 15,000 | G. $100,000 | J. $160,000 |
|---|---|---|---|
| B. $ 5,000 | E. $ 25,000 | H. $150,000 | K. $170,000 |
| C. $ 10,000 | F. $ 95,000 | I. $155,000 | |

**Items 1 through 6** describe amounts to be reported in Dayle's 2007 financial statements. For each item, select from the following list the correct numerical response. An amount may be selected once, more than once, or not at all. Ignore income tax considerations.

*Amount*

|  | (A) | (B) | (C) | (D) | (E) | (F) | (G) | (H) | (I) | (J) | (K) |
|---|---|---|---|---|---|---|---|---|---|---|---|
| 1. Carrying amount of security ABC at December 31, 2007. | O | O | O | O | O | O | O | O | O | O | O |
| 2. Carrying amount of security DEF at December 31, 2007. | O | O | O | O | O | O | O | O | O | O | O |
| 3. Carrying amount of security JKL at December 31, 2007. | O | O | O | O | O | O | O | O | O | O | O |

**Items 4 through 6** require a second response. For each item, indicate whether a gain or a loss is to be reported.

| | *Amount* | | | | | | | | | | | *Gain* | *Loss* |
|---|---|---|---|---|---|---|---|---|---|---|---|---|---|
| | (A) | (B) | (C) | (D) | (E) | (F) | (G) | (H) | (I) | (J) | (K) | | |
| 4. Recognized gain or loss on sale of security GHI. | O | O | O | O | O | O | O | O | O | O | O | O | O |
| 5. Unrealized gain or loss to be reported in 2007 net income. | O | O | O | O | O | O | O | O | O | O | O | O | O |
| 6. Unrealized gain or loss to be reported at December 31, 2007, as a separate component of stockholders' equity entitled "accumulated other comprehensive income." | O | O | O | O | O | O | O | O | O | O | O | O | O |

| Situation | Concepts | Accounting Treatment | Financial Statement Disclosures | Research | | Communication |
|---|---|---|---|---|---|---|

Suppose that Dayle has two portfolios of marketable equity securities. One is classified as available-for-sale and the other is classified as trading securities. Dayle does not have the ability to exercise significant influence over any of the companies in either portfolio. Some securities from each portfolio were sold during the year. One of the securities in the trading securities portfolio was reclassified to the available-for-sale securities portfolio when its market value was less than cost. At the beginning and end of the year, the aggregate cost of each portfolio exceeded its aggregate market value by different amounts. Assume that Dayle does not elect the fair value option for reporting its financial assets.

Research the following issues. Cut and paste the appropriate authoritative literature.

1. How should Dayle report the effects of unrealized gains and losses during the year from each portfolio?

2. How should Dayle account for the security that was reclassified from the trading securities portfolio to the available-for-sale securities portfolio?

3. How should Dayle report the investments in each portfolio in its balance sheet as of the end of the period?

| Situation | Concepts | Accounting Treatment | Financial Statement Disclosures | Research | Communication |
|---|---|---|---|---|---|

Prepare a memo for the client file answering the questions that you researched.

1. How should Dayle report the effects of unrealized gains and losses during the year from each portfolio?

2. How should Dayle account for the security that was reclassified from the trading securities portfolio to the available-for-sale securities portfolio?

3. How should Dayle report the investments in each portfolio in its balance sheet as of the end of the period? Why?

To:  Dayle Inc. Permanent File
From: CPA Candidate
Re:  Accounting issues related to marketable securities

---

**Simulation Problem 2**     (50 to 60 minutes)

| Situation | | | | | |
|---|---|---|---|---|---|
| | **Classification of Securities** | **Journal Entries** | **Financial Statement Disclosures** | **Communication** | **Research** |

Harold Johnson, an investor in Acme Co., asked you for advice on the propriety of Acme's financial reporting for two of its investments. Assume that Acme does not elect the fair value option for reporting its financial assets and liabilities. You obtained the following information related to the investments from Acme's December 31, 2007 financial statements:

- 20% ownership interest in Kern Co., represented by 200,000 shares of outstanding common stock purchased on January 2, 2007, for $600,000.
- 20% ownership interest in Wand Co., represented by 20,000 shares of outstanding common stock purchased on January 2, 2007, for $300,000.
- On January 2, 2007, the carrying values of the acquired shares of both investments equaled their purchase price.
- Kern reported earnings of $400,000 for the year ended December 31, 2007, and declared and paid dividends of $100,000 during 2007.
- Wand reported earnings of $350,000 for the year ended December 31, 2007, and declared and paid dividends of $60,000 during 2007.
- On December 31, 2007, Kern's and Wand's common stock were trading over-the-counter at $18 and $20 per share, respectively.
- The investment in Kern is accounted for using the equity method.
- The investment in Wand is accounted for as available-for-sale securities.

You recalculated the amounts reported in Acme's December 31, 2007 financial statements, and determined that they were correct. Stressing that the information available in the financial statements was limited, you advised Johnson that, assuming Acme properly applied generally accepted accounting principles, Acme may have appropriately used two different methods to account for its investments in Kern and Wand, even though the investments represent equal ownership interests.

| | **Classification of Securities** | | | | |
|---|---|---|---|---|---|
| **Situation** | | **Journal Entries** | **Financial Statement Disclosures** | **Communication** | **Research** |

**Items 1 through 4** are based on the following:

Acme Co. purchased various securities during 2007 to be classified as held-to-maturity securities, trading securities, or available-for-sale securities.

**Items 1 through 4** describe various securities purchased by Acme. For each item, select from the following list the appropriate category for each security. A category may be used once, more than once, or not at all.

<u>Categories</u>
H. Held-to-maturity
T. Trading
A. Available-for-sale

<u>Category</u>
**(H) (T) (A)**

1. Debt securities bought and held for the purpose of selling in the near term. ○ ○ ○

2. US Treasury bonds that Acme has both the positive intent and the ability to hold to maturity. ○ ○ ○

3. $3 million debt security bought and held for the purpose of selling in three years to finance payment of Acme's $2 million long-term note payable when it matures. ○ ○ ○

4. Convertible preferred stock that Acme does not intend to sell in the near term. ○ ○ ○

| Situation | Classification of Securities | Journal Entries | Financial Statement Disclosures | Communication | Research |
|---|---|---|---|---|---|

1. Prepare the journal entry for Acme's investment in Kern Co. on January 2, 2007.

2. Prepare the journal entry for the dividends received from Kern in 2007.

3. Prepare the journal entry required for Kern's reported income for the year ending on December 31, 2007.

| Situation | Classification of Securities | Journal Entries | Financial Statement Disclosures | Communication | Research |
|---|---|---|---|---|---|

Identify the following amounts on Acme's financial statements.

| | |
|---|---|
| Carrying value of Kern investment | |
| Carrying value of Wand investment | |
| Income on Income Statement | |
|    Kern investment | |
|    Wand investment | |
| Other comprehensive income | |
|    Kern investment | |
|    Wand investment | |

| Situation | Classification of Securities | Journal Entries | Financial Statement Disclosures | Communication | Research |
|---|---|---|---|---|---|

Prepare a detailed memorandum to Mr. Johnson supporting your conclusion that, under generally accepted accounting principles, Acme may have appropriately used two different methods to account for its investments representing equal ownership interests.

To:       Mr. Harold Johnson
From:   CPA Candidate
Re:       Acme Co. Investments in Kern Co. and Wand Co.

| Situation | Classification of Securities | Journal Entries | Financial Statement Disclosures | Communication | Research |
|---|---|---|---|---|---|

Research the following accounting issues. Cut and paste the appropriate guidance from the professional standards.

1. What is a trading security?

2. A company sells available-for-sale securities. Where is this transaction found on the statement of cash flows?

3. A company has dividend income from available-for-sale securities. Where is this dividend income found on the financial statements?

---

**Simulation Problem 3**                    (50 to 60 minutes)

| Situation | | | | | | |
|---|---|---|---|---|---|---|
| | Concepts | Available for Sale Securities | Long-Term Marketable Equity Securities | Investment Income | Communication | Research |

At December 31, 2006, Poe Corp. properly reported as available-for-sale securities the following marketable equity securities:

| | Cost | Fair value |
|---|---|---|
| Axe Corp., 1,000 shares, $2.40 convertible preferred stock | $ 40,000 | $ 42,000 |
| Purl, Inc., 6,000 shares of common stock | 60,000 | 66,000 |
| Day Co., 2,000 shares of common stock | 55,000 | 40,000 |
| Total available-for-sale securities | $155,000 | $148,000 |

On January 2, 2007, Poe purchased 100,000 shares of Scott Corp. common stock for $1,700,000, representing 30% of Scott's outstanding common stock and an underlying equity of $1,400,000 in Scott's net assets on January 2.  Poe had no other financial transactions with Scott during 2007.  As a result of Poe's 30% ownership of Scott, Poe has the ability to exercise significant influence over Scott's financial and operating policies.

During 2007, Poe disposed of the following securities:

- January 18—sold 2,500 shares of Purl for $13 per share.
- June 1—sold 500 shares of Day, after a 10% stock dividend was received, for $21 per share.
- October 1—converted 500 shares of Axe's preferred stock into 1,500 shares of Axe's common stock, when the market price was $60 per share for the preferred stock and $21 per share for the common stock.

The following 2007 dividend information pertains to stock owned by Poe:

- February 14—Day issued a 10% stock dividend, when the market price of Day's common stock was $22 per share.
- April 5 and October 5—Axe paid dividends of $1.20 per share on its $2.40 preferred stock, to stockholders of record on March 9 and September 9, respectively.  Axe did not pay dividends on its common stock during 2007.
- June 30—Purl paid a $1.00 per share dividend on its common stock.
- March 1, June 1, September 1, and December 1 —Scott paid quarterly dividends of $0.50 per share on each of these dates.  Scott's net income for the year ended December 31, 2007, was $1,200,000.

At December 31, 2007, Poe's management intended to hold Scott's stock on a long-term basis.  The remaining investments were considered temporary.  Market prices per share of the marketable equity securities were as follows:

|  | At December 31 | |
|---|---|---|
|  | *2007* | *2006* |
| Axe Corp.—preferred | $56 | $42 |
| Axe Corp.—common | 20 | 18 |
| Purl, Inc.—common | 11 | 11 |
| Day Co.—common | 22 | 20 |
| Scott Corp.—common | 16 | 18 |

All of the foregoing stocks are listed on major stock exchanges.  Declines in market value from cost would not be considered permanent.  Poe does not elect the fair value option for reporting its financial assets and liabilities.

| Situation | Concepts | Available-for-Sale Securities | Long-Term Marketable Equity Securities | Investment Income | Communication | Research |
|---|---|---|---|---|---|---|

Identify whether each of the following statements is True or False.  Assume the fair value option is not elected.

|  | *True* | *False* |
|---|---|---|
| 1. Unrealized gains from trading securities are reported in other comprehensive income. | ○ | ○ |
| 2. Investments in stocks and bonds may be classified as trading securities, available-for-sale securities, and held-to-maturity securities. | ○ | ○ |
| 3. X Company has significant influence over Y Company and owns 35% of the voting stock of Y Company.  x Company must use the equity method of accounting for the investment in Y Company. | ○ | ○ |
| 4. Unrealized gains and losses from available-for-sale securities that result from the change in fair value during the period should be reported as other comprehensive income. | ○ | ○ |
| 5. The temporary unrealized gain or loss from held-to-maturity securities must be reported in income for the current period. | ○ | ○ |
| 6. If a security is transferred from available-for-sale to trading securities classification, unrealized holding gains and losses are recognized immediately in the income statement. | ○ | ○ |
| 7. The equity method of accounting requires a company to include the percent of income of the investee in the investor company's net income for the period. | ○ | ○ |
| 8. The equity method of accounting requires that a company adjust the cost of the investee to fair value at the end of each period. | ○ | ○ |
| 9. A company that receives stock dividends records income equal to the fair value of the stock on the date the dividend is declared. | ○ | ○ |
| 10. Held-to-maturity securities are carried at amortized cost using the effective interest method. | ○ | ○ |

| | | | | Investment Income | Communication | Research |
|---|---|---|---|---|---|---|

Complete the following schedule for the available-for-sale securities of Poe Corp. as of December 31, 2007.

**Poe Corp.**
**SCHEDULE OF AVAILABLE-FOR-SALE**
**SECURITIES**
*December 31, 2007*

| | Number of shares | Cost | Beginning carrying amount at market | Ending market price per share | Market value | Cumulative gain or (loss) | Unrealized gain or (loss) in 2007 |
|---|---|---|---|---|---|---|---|
| Axe—preferred | | | | | | | |
| Axe—common | | | | | | | |
| Purl—common | | | | | | | |
| Day—common | | | | | | | |
| | | | | | | | |

| Situation | Concepts | Available-for-Sale Securities | Long-Term Marketable Equity Securities | Investment Income | Communication | Research |
|---|---|---|---|---|---|---|

Prepare the following schedule for the long-term marketable equity securities for Poe Corp. as of December 31, 2007.

**Poe Corp.**
**SCHEDULE OF LONG-TERM MARKETABLE**
**EQUITY SECURITIES**
*December 31, 2007*

| Scott Corp.—100,000 shares of common stock: | |
|---|---|
| Cost: | |
| Acquisition price | |
| Increase in equity during 2007: | |
| Poe's interest in Scott's income | |
| Less: | |
| Dividends received | |
| Net increase in equity | |
| Carrying amount of Poe Corp.'s investment in Scott | |

| Situation | Concepts | Available-for-Sale Securities | Long-Term Marketable Equity Securities | Investment Income | Communication | Research |
|---|---|---|---|---|---|---|

Complete the following schedule outlining the income for Poe Corp. for the year ended December 31, 2007.

**Poe Corp.**
**SCHEDULE OF INVESTMENT INCOME**
*For the Year Ended December 31, 2007*

| Dividends: | |
|---|---|
| Axe Corp.—preferred | |
| Purl, Inc.—common | |
| Total dividend revenue | |
| Gains on marketable equity securities: | |
| Realized gain/(loss) on sale of securities: | |
| Purl, Inc.—common | |
| Day Co.—common | |
| Net realized gain on sale of securities | |
| Equity in income of Scott Corp.: | |
| Total investment income | |

| Situation | Concepts | Available-for-Sale Securities | Long-Term Marketable Equity Securities | Investment Income | Communication | |
|---|---|---|---|---|---|---|
| | | | | | | Research |

Write a brief memo to the CEO of Poe Corp. explaining the equity method of accounting for investments in other companies.

To:     CEO, Poe Corp.
From:   CPA Candidate
Re:     Equity method of accounting

| Situation | Concepts | Available-for-Sale Securities | Long-Term Marketable Equity Securities | Investment Income | Communication | Research |
|---|---|---|---|---|---|---|

Use the FARs research database to answer the following questions.  Cut and paste the results.

1. When a company owns between 20% and 50% of the outstanding stock of another company and uses the equity method of accounting, how is income from the investee disclosed?

2. What are the three classifications for investment in debt and equity securities?

3. When a security is removed from the trading category, should the earnings previously recorded be reversed?  (Assume the fair value option is not elected.)

## MULTIPLE-CHOICE ANSWERS

| | | | | | | | | | |
|---|---|---|---|---|---|---|---|---|---|
| 1. b __ __ | 14. d __ __ | 27. d __ __ | 40. d __ __ | 53. c __ __ |
| 2. b __ __ | 15. d __ __ | 28. d __ __ | 41. c __ __ | 54. a __ __ |
| 3. b __ __ | 16. d __ __ | 29. a __ __ | 42. c __ __ | 55. b __ __ |
| 4. b __ __ | 17. a __ __ | 30. b __ __ | 43. d __ __ | 56. c __ __ |
| 5. c __ __ | 18. b __ __ | 31. a __ __ | 44. b __ __ | 57. d __ __ |
| 6. d __ __ | 19. b __ __ | 32. b __ __ | 45. d __ __ | 58. c __ __ |
| 7. b __ __ | 20. c __ __ | 33. b __ __ | 46. a __ __ | 59. d __ __ |
| 8. d __ __ | 21. b __ __ | 34. b __ __ | 47. a __ __ | |
| 9. a __ __ | 22. d __ __ | 35. a __ __ | 48. c __ __ | |
| 10. b __ __ | 23. a __ __ | 36. b __ __ | 49. c __ __ | |
| 11. a __ __ | 24. d __ __ | 37. c __ __ | 50. d __ __ | |
| 12. c __ __ | 25. a __ __ | 38. b __ __ | 51. a __ __ | 1st: __/59= __% |
| 13. b __ __ | 26. a __ __ | 39. b __ __ | 52. c __ __ | 2nd: __/59= __% |

## MULTIPLE-CHOICE ANSWER EXPLANATIONS

### A.   Concepts of Accounting and Investment Percentage

**1.   (b)**   The investment should be accounted for on the equity basis and the calculation of Puff's income from the investment is shown below.

| | |
|---|---|
| Straw's net income | $150,000 |
| | × 40% |
| Puff's share of Straw's net income | $ 60,000 |
| Less: Puff's depreciation of excess value of equipment | |
| Excess cost | $100,000 |
| | × 40% |
| Puff's share | $ 40,000 |
| Remaining useful life | ÷ 5 |
| Puff's share of excess depreciation for 2008 | (8,000) |
| Income from investment on the equity basis | $ 52,000 |

### B.1.   No Significant Influence:  Held-to-Maturity

**2.   (b)**   Per SFAS 115, held-to-maturity securities are to be carried at amortized cost. Therefore, the investment is recorded on 4/1/07 at its cost of $194,000 ($198,500 less accrued interest of $4,500). The carrying amount is calculated as cost plus amortized discount, which at 10/31/07 is $196,800 [$194,000 + ($6,000 × 7/15)].

**3.   (b)**   Per SFAS 115, **held-to-maturity** securities, which include only debt securities, are reported on the balance sheet at **amortized cost** without adjustment to fair value. If the investment in bonds had been classified as trading or available-for-sale, answer (c) would be correct. **Trading** securities are reported at **fair value** with holding gains or losses flowing through the income statements. **Available-for-sale** securities are reported at **fair value** with holding gains or losses reported as a component of other comprehensive income. Cost and lower of cost or market are not used as reporting bases for bond investments.

**4.   (b)**   Per SFAS 115, held-to-maturity securities are carried at cost, so unrealized holding gains and losses are not reported. However, realized gains and losses on held-to-maturity securities should always be included in the income statement of the appropriate period. No valuation allowance exists for any marketable debt or equity securities. Realized gains for the period are the only item listed that is included in that period's net income.

**5.   (c)**   SFAS 159 provides that a company may elect to value held-to-maturity securities at fair value. Any increase or decrease in value is reported as a gain or loss and included in earnings for the period. Answer (a) is incorrect because bonds are recorded at cost, but reported at amortized cost at year-end according to SFAS 115. Answer (b) is incorrect because Bing elected the fair value option. Answer (d) is incorrect because investments are not recorded at lower of cost or market.

**6.   (d)**   SFAS 159 provides that a company may elect to value held-to-maturity securities at fair value. Any increase or decrease in value, whether realized or unrealized, is reported in earnings for the period. Therefore, I, II, and IV should be reported in earnings if the fair value option of reporting is elected. Changes in the valuation allowance are not relevant because when an election is made to use the fair value option, any related allowance accounts are removed from the balance sheet.

### B.2.   No Significant Influence:  Trading

**7.   (b)**   Debt and equity securities that are classified as **trading securities** are reported at fair value with unrealized gains and losses included in earnings. During 2007, Tyne had an unrealized holding gain of $55,000 ($155,000 – $100,000) on its trading securities. The unrealized holding gain on **available-for-sale** securities ($130,000 – $120,000 = $10,000) is excluded from earnings and reported as other comprehensive income.

**8.   (d)**   The requirement is to determine the accumulated other comprehensive income to be reported in the December 31, 2007 statement of stockholders' equity. Unrealized gains and losses on **trading securities** are included in earnings. Unrealized gains and losses on **available-for-sale** securities are excluded from earnings and reported as accumulated other comprehensive income in a separate component of shareholders' equity. This amount is the net unrealized loss on available-for-sale securities at 12/31/07 is $20,000 ($150,000 – $130,000).

**9.   (a)**   SFAS 115 states that unrealized holding gains and losses for trading securities are to be reported in earnings. On the other hand, this statement also states that unrealized gains or losses on available-for-sale securities should be excluded from earnings and reported as other comprehensive income. Therefore, only the $40,000 ($360,000 –

$320,000) unrealized loss on trading securities is included in income.

### B.3. No Significant Influence: Available-for-Sale

**10. (b)** Available-for-sale securities are reported at market value on the balance sheet. At 12/31/07, Stone has incurred gross unrealized gains of $4,000 and gross unrealized losses of $26,000 on its available-for-sale securities. Therefore, at 12/31/07, the net unrealized loss is $22,000 ($26,000 – $4,000). Stone would have to increase the balance in accumulated other comprehensive income from $1,500 to $22,000 at 12/31/07.

**11. (a)** SFAS 115, as amended by SFAS 130, dictates that unrealized holding gains and losses on available-for-sale securities be reported as other comprehensive income. At 12/31/06, available-for-sale securities would have been reported in the balance sheet at their fair value of $130,000, with a corresponding unrealized loss of $20,000. At 12/31/07, the fair value of these securities is $160,000. Therefore, an unrealized gain of $30,000 ($160,000 – $130,000) would result in other comprehensive income of $30,000 as **accumulated** other comprehensive income.

**12. (c)** The provisions of SFAS 115 apply to trading securities, and a $40,000 loss is recorded on the income statement for the loss on trading securities. SFAS 159 provides that an election can be made to value available-for-sale securities at fair value. Therefore, the available-for-sale securities are valued at fair value, and the loss is reported on the income statement.

**13. (b)** SFAS 159 allows a company to elect the fair value option for reporting available-for-sale securities. If the fair value option is elected, realized and unrealized gains and losses from available-for-sale securities are included in earnings of the period. Therefore, the net gain of $18,000 ($14,000 unrealized gains + $30,000 realized gains – $26,000 unrealized losses) is reported on the income statement for the period.

**14. (d)** If Shannon elects the fair value option for reporting available-for-sale securities, any unrealized gains or losses are recorded in earnings for the period. In 2008, Shannon would report a loss on the income statement of $20,000, and the available-for-sale securities would be carried on the balance sheet at the market value of $130,000. On December 31, 2009, the securities would be valued at $160,000 and an unrealized gain of $30,000 ($160,000 – $130,000) would be recognized on the 2009 income statement. Therefore, under the provisions of SFAS 159, there would be no entry to other comprehensive income for available-for-sale securities.

**15. (d)** SFAS 115 requires marketable equity securities that are not intended to be sold in the near future to be classified as available-for-sale securities. SFAS 159 allows a company to elect to record an available-for-sale security at its fair value, and any unrealized gains or losses may be recognized as a component of income from continuing operations on the income statement. Answer (a) is incorrect because Antonio does not intend to sell the asset in the near future; therefore, it cannot be classified as a trading security. Answer (b) is incorrect because when the fair value option is elected, the unrealized gain or loss is reported in earnings, not in other comprehensive income. Answer (c) is incorrect

because the securities are not classified as trading and the gain is not recognized in OCI.

**16. (d)** In accordance with SFAS 115, the securities purchased by Rex are classified as available-for-sale securities and accounted for at fair value. At 12/31/07, the fair value of security B was $15,300; an unrealized loss of $1,700 resulted in other comprehensive income in that amount. At 1/31/08, the stock was sold when its fair value was $15,000 and the following entry would have been made:

| | | |
|---|---|---|
| Cash (net) | 13,500 | |
| Loss on sale of stock | 3,500 | |
| Investment in Security B | | 15,300 |
| Unrealized loss on Sec. B. | | 1,700 |

The unrealized loss of $1,700 on Security B is a credit. It would be netted with unrealized gains and/or losses recognized in 2008. The effect is to offset the $1,700 loss recognized in 2007 that was closed to other comprehensive income, net retained earnings, thus avoiding double counting.

**17. (a)** The capital gains distribution ($145,000) would not be reported as interest revenue. The solutions approach is to set up a T-account for interest receivable.

| Interest Receivable | | | |
|---|---|---|---|
| Beg. bal. | 38,000 | | |
| Int. rev. | ? | 152,000 | Int. collected |
| End. bal. | 46,500 | | |

Beginning and ending balances are given in the question. Interest receivable would be credited for cash collections to reduce the receivable.

| | | |
|---|---|---|
| Cash | 152,000 | |
| Interest receivable | | 152,000 |

Interest receivable would be debited for interest revenue.

| | | |
|---|---|---|
| Interest receivable | xxx | |
| Interest revenue | | xxx |

Solve for interest revenue ($46,500 + $152,000 – $38,000 = $160,500).

**18. (b)** In accordance with SFAS 115, marketable equity securities (MES) are classified as either trading (held for current resale) or available-for-sale (if not categorized as trading). Since Nola does not intend to sell these securities in the near term, they should be classified as available-for-sale. SFAS 115 requires MES to be carried at market value. The unrealized gains or losses of available-for-sale MES are reported as a separate component of other comprehensive income. It is important to note that unrealized gains or losses on **trading** securities would be reported as a component of income from continuing operations on the income statement. Thus, answer (b) is correct because the securities would be classified as available-for-sale and unrealized gains and losses from these securities would be reported as other comprehensive income.

**19. (b)** Per SFAS 115, unrealized losses on available-for-sale securities are reported as a separate component of other comprehensive income, while unrealized gains and losses on trading securities are recognized in income and unrealized gains and losses on held-to-maturity securities are ignored. Thus, this security is classified as available-for-sale. A realized gain will be reported only if the security was sold for a price in excess of its cost. Therefore, the 2006 price decline was **less than** the 2007 price recovery. For example, assume that the investment was purchased for

$1,000 on 1/07/06. At 12/31/06, its market value was $800, and on 12/29/07 its market value was $1,200. The following entries would have been made:

| 1/07/06 | Investment | 1,000 | |
| | Cash | | 1,000 |
| 12/31/06 | Unrealized loss | 200 | |
| | Investment | | 200 |
| 12/29/07 | Cash | 1,200 | |
| | Investment | | 800 |
| | Unrealized loss | | 200 |
| | **Gain on sale of securities** | | **200** |

**20. (c)** The requirement is to determine how the losses on the securities classified as available-for-sale should be reported. In accordance with SFAS 115, a decline in market value of a security, which is considered to be **other-than-temporary,** should be reported on the income statement in the current period. A decline in market value, which is considered to be **temporary,** would be recorded as an unrealized loss, and recognized as other comprehensive income. Therefore, answer (c) is correct as the loss on the Knox stock is considered to be other-than-temporary and it would be reported on the income statement. Answer (a) is incorrect because the unrealized loss on the Scot stock would be reported as other comprehensive income. Answer (b) is incorrect because the loss on the Knox stock is considered to be a realized loss as it is other-than-temporary. Answer (d) is incorrect because the other-than-temporary decline in Knox stock results in a realized loss that is reported on the income statement.

**21. (b)** Per SFAS 115, the carrying amount of a marketable equity security classified as available-for-sale shall be the fair market value and the unrealized holding gain or loss should be reported as other comprehensive income. In 2006 when the value declined, the portfolio was reported at market with an unrealized holding loss recorded as other comprehensive income. In 2007, the decline is considered to be other than temporary. Thus, the security must be written down to market and a realized loss recognized. However, since there is no actual change in value, in 2007 the security will be reported at the same amount (cost – write-down of asset) as in 2006. Therefore, there is no effect on **net** noncurrent assets in 2007. However, net income will be affected because a realized loss is recorded on the income statement. Note that the unrealized loss account charged to other comprehensive income in 2006 would be credited and the realized loss account would be debited for the same amount. The allowance accounts will be closed against each other because the new basis after the write-down will equal the lower FMV amount. Answer (a) is incorrect because net income is affected. Note that if the decline was merely temporary, there would be no net income effect because temporary declines in value of noncurrent portfolios are reported as other comprehensive income, rather than net income. Answer (c) is incorrect because there is no net decrease in noncurrent assets, but there is a net income effect. Answer (d) is incorrect because only net income decreases.

**22. (d)** Dividends in arrears are not a receivable to the cumulative preferred stockholder until the issuing corporation's board of directors formally declares the dividend. In this case, Hadley, Inc. did not declare the 2006 dividends in arrears until 2007. At the 2007 dividend declaration date, Woody Co. records dividends receivable and dividend income. Dividend income is included in income from continuing operations.

**23. (a)** Per APB 29, a nonmonetary asset (the merchandise in this case) received in a nonreciprocal transfer should be recorded at the fair value of the asset received. Additionally, the transfer of a nonmonetary asset to a stockholder or other entity (Deed's employees in this case) should be recorded at the fair value of the asset received.

**24. (d)** Per SFAS 95, noncash transactions should be excluded from the statement of cash flows to better achieve the statement's objectives. However, SFAS 95 requires that information about noncash investing and financing transactions be reported in related disclosures.

**25. (a)** Per SFAS 115, an investor carries an investment in the stock of an investee at market, and recognizes as income dividends received that are distributed from the net accumulated earnings of the investee **since the date of acquisition** by the investor. Dividends received in excess of earnings subsequent to the date of investment are considered to be return of investment or a liquidating dividend and are recorded as reductions of the cost of the investment. Therefore, Pal Corp.'s accounting treatment of the dividend it received from Ima Corp. indicates that Pal is accounting for the securities under SFAS 115 as an available-for-sale investment in Ima. Answer (b) is incorrect because Ima's market value does not impact Pal's treatment of dividends received. Answers (c) and (d) are incorrect because all dividends received are treated as reductions in an investee's carrying value under the equity method.

**26. (a)** Intercompany receivables and payables are not eliminated unless consolidated financial statements are prepared. Since Pare only has a 15% interest in Sabe, consolidated financial statements would not be prepared. Thus, on the 12/31/07 balance sheet, Pare should separately report the total amount of the receivable.

### B.4. No Significant Influence: Transfers

**27. (d)** The requirement is to determine the amount of loss on investments to be reported in Sun's 2007 income statement. SFAS 115 requires this transfer to be accounted for at fair market value and any holding gains or losses on securities that are transferred to held-to-maturity from available-for-sale be reported as accumulated other comprehensive income. This amount is then amortized over the remaining life of the security as an adjustment to yield. Since cost is greater than market value by $75,000 at 12/31/06 ($650,000 cost – $575,000 fair market value), the following entry would be recorded:

| Unrealized loss | 75,000 | |
| Marketable debt securities | | 75,000 |

Then on June 30, 2007, when Sun decides to hold the investments to maturity, an additional $45,000 will be recorded in the valuation account ($575,000 value on books – $530,000 FMV) to reflect the change in FMV. The following entry would be recorded:

| Unrealized loss | 45,000 | |
| Marketable debt securities | | 45,000 |

Each year the unrealized loss would be reported as other comprehensive income that would be closed to "accumulated other comprehensive income."

**28. (d)** Per SFAS 115, when a security is transferred to held-to-maturity from available-for-sale the unrealized holding gain or loss continues to be reported as a separate component of stockholders' equity. Held-to-maturity securities are carried at amortized cost, and any unrealized holding gains or losses are not reported. Thus, the balance in the "accumulated other comprehensive income" in stockholders' equity on the 2007 statement of stockholders' equity would be $120,000 ($75,000 amount reported at 12/31/06 plus the $45,000 amount reported at June 30, 2007). The $120,000 will be amortized over the remaining life of the security as an adjustment to yield. The additional decline in value from 6/30/07 to 12/31/07 would not be reported, as held-to-maturity securities do not report unrealized losses.

**29. (a)** SFAS 115, states that "the transfer of a security between categories of investments shall be accounted for at fair value." If fair value is less than the security's carrying amount at the date of transfer, it is irrelevant whether the decline is temporary or permanent.

**30. (b)** SFAS 159 provides that an election can be made to use the fair value option when financial assets cease to qualify for fair value treatment due to specialized accounting rules. On June 30, 2008, the trading securities were reclassified to the held-to-maturity category, and an election was made to report them at fair value. On June 30, 2008, the held-to-maturity securities were valued at $530,000, and Jill would recognize a loss of $45,000 ($575,000 – $530,000). At December 31, 2008, the securities declined in value an additional $40,000. Therefore, the total loss recognized in 2008 was $85,000 ($45,000 + $40,000). Answer (a) is incorrect because the entire amount of loss in fair value should be recognized in 2008. Answer (c) is incorrect because the loss from January 1, 2007 to December 31, 2007, would have been recognized in 2007 because it was classified as a trading security. Answer (d) is incorrect because if the fair value option is elected, unrealized gains and losses are recognized in the current year's earnings.

**31. (a)** Jill would recognize the unrealized loss on trading securities in the income statement. On June 30, 2008, when the securities were classified as held-to-maturity, Jill elected the fair value option for reporting the investment. Therefore, any unrealized gain or loss on the held-to-maturity securities would be reported in earnings for the period. An unrealized gain or a temporary loss on available-for-sale securities would be reported in other comprehensive income only if the fair value option were not elected. Held-to-maturity securities would be valued at amortized cost if the fair value option of reporting were not elected. Therefore, answers (b), (c), and (d) are incorrect because Jill elects the fair value option on the held-to-maturity securities.

### C. Investment Where Significant Influence Does Exist

**32. (b)** This investment should be accounted for using the equity method since Grant owns a 30% interest and can exercise significant influence over South. Grant's share of South's 2006 earnings (30% × $80,000 = $24,000) would be recognized as investment revenue under the equity method. If there was any excess of cost over book value of assets with finite useful lives, resulting from the purchase of the investment, it would be amortized, reducing investment revenue. However, not enough information was given to determine if there was an excess. The dividends received by Grant (30% × $50,000 = $15,000) do not affect investment revenue using the equity method; they are recorded as a reduction of the investment account.

**33. (b)** The equity method is used because Grant owns a 30% interest and can exercise significant influence. Under this method, the investment account is increased by Grant's equity in South's earnings (30% × $80,000 = $24,000) and is decreased by Grant's dividends received from South (30% × $50,000 = $15,000). This results in a 12/31/06 carrying amount for the investment of $209,000, as indicated in the T-account below.

| | Investment in South | | |
|---|---|---|---|
| 1/2/06 | 200,000 | | |
| Equity in earnings | 24,000 | 15,000 | Dividends |
| 12/31/06 | 209,000 | | |

**34. (b)** The equity method is used because Grant owns a 30% interest and can exercise significant influence. Under this method, the investment account is increased by Grant's equity in South's earnings (30% × $80,000 = $24,000 in 2006; 30% × $100,000 = $30,000 for first six months of 2007) and is decreased by Grant's dividends received from South (30% × $50,000 = $15,000 in 2007; none in first six months of 2007). This results in a 7/1/07 carrying amount of $239,000, as indicated in the T-account below.

| | Investment in South | | |
|---|---|---|---|
| 1/2/06 | 200,000 | | |
| Equity in earnings | 24,000 | 15,000 | Dividends |
| Equity in earnings | 30,000 | | |
| 7/1/07 | 239,000 | | |

The gain on sale is the excess of the proceeds ($150,000) over the carrying amount of the shares sold (1/2 × $239,000 = $119,500), or $30,500 ($150,000 – $119,500).

**35. (a)** An investor's share of the income of a company in which it holds a 20% or greater investment is referred to as the investor's equity in earnings of the investee. Per APB 18, the investor's share of the investee's earnings should be computed after deducting the investee's cumulative preferred dividends (whether declared or not). In this case, the income available to common stockholders is $50,000 [$60,000 income – (10% × $100,000 total pref. div.)], so Moss Corp.'s equity in earnings is $40,000 (80% ownership × $50,000). Since $40,000 is not one of the answer choices, apparently the candidate is expected to include the preferred dividend revenue of $2,000 [20% ownership × ($100,000 × 10% total pref. div.)] on the income statement in the equity in earnings line item. Although preferred dividends are usually classified separately, answer (a) is the best answer given. The answer, therefore, is $42,000.

| Equity in earnings | $40,000 |
|---|---|
| Dividend revenue | 2,000 |
| | $42,000 |

**36. (b)** Sage paid $400,000 for its 40% investment in Adams when Adams' net assets had a carrying amount of $900,000. Therefore, the book value Sage purchased is $360,000 (40% × $900,000), resulting in an excess of cost over book value of $40,000 ($400,000 – $360,000). This excess must be attributed to specific assets of Adams; any amount not attributed to specific assets is attributed to goodwill. In this case, the excess is attributed to plant assets (40% × $90,000 = $36,000) and inventory (40% × $10,000 = $4,000). The portion attributed to plant assets is amortized over eighteen years, while the portion attributed to inventory is expensed immediately (since all inventory was sold during 2007). Therefore, Sage's investment income is $42,000, as computed below.

| | |
|---|---:|
| Share of income (40% × $120,000) | $48,000 |
| Excess amortization [($36,000/18) + $4,000] | (6,000) |
| | $42,000 |

**37. (c)** The unrealized gain on the available-for-sale securities is improperly included in Pear's $125,000 income before taxes. Per SFAS 115, unrealized holding gains and losses on available-for-sale securities are reported as a separate component of stockholders' equity. The equity in Cinn's earnings is properly included in Pear Co.'s pretax income. However, the dividends from Cinn are also improperly included in income because under the equity method, dividends received are a reduction of the investment account rather than dividend revenue. The adjustments to profits of prior years for arithmetic errors in depreciation ($35,000) should be recorded as a retroactive adjustment to beginning retained earnings and should **not** have been deducted when computing 2007 income before taxes. Therefore, 2007 income before taxes should be $112,000 as computed below.

| | |
|---|---:|
| Tentative income | $125,000 |
| Unrealized holding gain | (40,000) |
| Dividends received | (8,000) |
| Prior period adjustment | 35,000 |
| Correct income | $112,000 |

**38. (b)** The equity method is to be used when the investor owns 20% or more of the investee's voting stock, unless there is evidence that the investor does **not** have the ability to exercise significant influence over the investee. Since this is the case, Saxe must carry the stock at market in the available-for-sale category. Under this method, dividends received are to be recognized as income to the investor, and the investment account is unaffected. Also, under this method, the investor's share of the investee's net income is not recognized. Any changes in the market value of the stock would be reflected in the book value of the stock with a corresponding amount in a separate account in stockholders' equity. As there has been no change in the market value, the investment account would still have a balance of $150,000 at 12/31/07. Note that the dividends received by Saxe were distributed from Lex's net accumulated earnings since the date of acquisition by Saxe. However, if dividends received had been in excess of earnings subsequent to the investment date, they are considered a return of capital and would be recorded as a reduction in the investment account.

**39. (b)** Ownership of less than 20% leads to the presumption of **no substantial influence** unless evidence to the contrary exists. Well's position as Rea's largest single shareholder and the presence of Well's officers as a **majority** of Rea's board of directors constitute evidence that Well **does have significant influence** despite less than 20% ownership. Therefore, the equity method is used. The investment account had a beginning balance of $400,000 (purchase price). This amount is increased by Well's equity in Rea's earnings (10% ownership × $500,000 income = $50,000) and decreased by Well's dividends received from Rea (10% share × $150,000 total div. = $15,000), resulting in a balance of $435,000 (see T-account below).

| | Investment in Rea | | |
|---|---:|---:|---|
| 1/2/07 | 400,000 | | |
| Equity in earnings | 50,000 | 15,000 | Dividends |
| 12/31/07 | 435,000 | | |

**40. (d)** The investment should have been originally recorded at the $250,000 purchase price. This amount would be increased by Kean's share of Pod's earnings (30% × $100,000 = $30,000), decreased by the amortization of excess of cost over book value, and decreased by dividends received by Kean (none in this case). The book value Kean purchased is $150,000 (30% × $500,000), resulting in an excess of cost over book value of $100,000 ($250,000 – $150,000). This excess must be attributed to the specific assets of Pod that have a fair value greater than their book value; any amount not attributed to specific assets is attributed to goodwill. In this case, the excess would be attributed first to land (30% × $200,000 = $60,000) and the remainder to goodwill ($100,000 – $60,000 = $40,000). The portion attributed to land and goodwill should not be amortized. Therefore, Kean's 12/31/07 balance of the investment in subsidiary is $280,000 as computed below.

| | |
|---|---:|
| Original cost | $250,000 |
| Share of income (30% × $100,000) | 30,000 |
| | $280,000 |

**41. (c)** APB 18 states that when an investment that has been accounted for using another method qualifies for the use of the equity method due to a change in ownership level (such as from 10% to 30%), the change to the equity method should be reported **retroactively**. At the date of the change (1/2/08), the **investment** account and **retained earnings** are adjusted as if the equity method had been used all along, and the results of operations in prior years are restated to reflect the equity method. In 2008, use of the equity method results in recognition of investment income of $195,000 (30% × $650,000 investee income). 2007 investment income must be restated from the previously reported dividend income (10% × $200,000 = $20,000) to equity method income (10% × $600,000 = $60,000), an adjustment of $40,000 ($60,000 – $20,000 = $40,000).

**42. (c)** The requirement is to determine the balance in the December 31, 2007, investment account. APB 18 states that when an investment that has been accounted for using another method qualifies for the use of the equity method due to a change in ownership level (in this case, from 10% to 30%), the change to the equity method should be applied retroactively. At the date of the change (12/31/07), the accounts are adjusted as if the equity method had been used all along. If the equity method had been used beginning at 1/2/07, Pare would have recorded its share of Tot's earnings (10% × $300,000 = $30,000) as investment revenue and as an increase in the investment account. Therefore, at 12/31/07, Pare's investment in Tot would be reported at $230,000.

| | Investment in Tot | |
|---|---:|---|
| 1/2/07 purchase | 50,000 | |
| 12/31/07 purchase | 150,000 | |
| Equity in earnings | 30,000 | |
| | 230,000 | |

**43. (d)** Under the equity method, a reciprocal relationship is formed between the investment account on the investor's books and the book values of the net assets on the investee's books. As changes in the investee's net assets occur (earnings, dividends, etc.), the investor will recognize the percentage of ownership share of that change in the investment account. Therefore, cash dividends from the investee will be recorded in the investment account, not the investment income account. The entry includes a debit to cash and a credit to the investment account. Another aspect of the equity method is the amortization of the equipment related to the purchase. The investment income account and the investment in stock account should include all the income recognitions and amortizations resulting from the investment. The entry to record the equipment amortization is a debit to Investment income and a credit to Investment in stock.

**44.** (**b**)   When the equity method is used, APB 18 requires the investor to amortize any portion of the excess of fair values over carrying amounts (differential) that relates to depreciable or amortizable assets held by the investee. Amortization of the differential results in a reduction of the investment account and a reduction in the equity of the investee's earnings. For inventory, an excess of FMV over cost, FIFO cost in this case, has the same effect on the investment account and equity in investee earnings in the period in which the goods are sold. Therefore, the portion of the differential that relates to inventory would decrease Park's reported equity in Tun's earnings, and answers (c) and (d) are incorrect. Land is not a depreciable asset, so there would be no amortization of the differential related to land, and answer (a) is incorrect.

**45.** (**d**)   Dividends received in excess of earnings subsequent to the date of investment are considered a return of investment and are recorded as reductions of cost of the investment. Additionally, per APB 18, under the equity method, "dividends received from an investee reduce the carrying amount of the investment."

**46.** (**a**)   The requirement is to determine the effects of a cash dividend on an investors investment account, accounted for both as an available-for-sale security, and under the equity method. Dividends received on available-for-sale securities are to be recognized as income to the investor and the investment account is unaffected. If the dividends received are in excess of earnings to date, then they would be considered a return of the investment and would result in a reduction of the investment account. Under the equity method, the receipt of cash dividends reduces the carrying value of the investment. Therefore, answer (a) is correct as the receipt of a cash dividend would not result in an increase in the investment account under either method.

**47.** (**a**)   The requirement is to determine the amount of investment income to be reported in the 2007 income statement. APB 18 states that when an investment which has been accounted for using a different method qualifies for the use of the equity method, due to a change in ownership level (such as 10% to 40%), then the change to the equity method should be reported **retroactively**. At the date of the change, the investment account and the retained earnings account are adjusted as if the equity method had been used all along. Therefore answer (a) is correct as Point owned 10% of Iona's stock from January 1 to July 31, 2007, and 40% of Iona's stock from August 1 to December 31, 2007. Answers (b) and (c) are incorrect because income should be recognized under the equity method according to the percentage of ownership existing during each of the periods. Answer (d) is incorrect because when Iona reports its earn-

ings to Point, Point will record its share of the revenue. When Point receives the dividends, (which may be in a different period than Point recognized its share of Iona's income), the carrying amount of the investment will be reduced by the amount received. Therefore, the income recognized does not usually equal the dividends received.

**48.** (**c**)   APB 18 requires the use of the equity method when accounting for investments in which the investor has the ability to exercise significant influence over the operating and financial policies of the investee. APB 18 generally assumes that ownership of 20% or more of the outstanding common stock demonstrates this ability. In this case, Pulham Corp. owns 30% of Angles and properly uses the equity method. Under the equity method intercompany profits and losses are eliminated. However, receivables and payables are not eliminated as they are in the case of consolidated financial statements. On the December 31, 2007 balance sheet, Pulham should separately disclose the total amount of the receivable. Additionally, this receivable should be shown separately from other receivables.

### E. Stock Dividends and Splits

**49.** (**c**)   Arlo's annual preferred stock dividend is $120,000 ($2,000,000 × 6%). The $240,000 dividend paid includes $120,000 dividends in arrears from 2006 and $120,000 for 2007. Therefore, Wood would receive **$24,000 of cash dividends** ($200,000 × 6% × 2) which would be reported as **dividend income** in 2007 (preferred dividends in arrears are not recognized as income until declared). No dividend income is recognized when an investor receives a proportional **stock** dividend, because the investor continues to own the same proportion of the investee as before the stock dividend, and the investee has not distributed any assets to the investor.

**50.** (**d**)   Regardless of the accounting method used, no dividend revenue is recognized when an investor receives a proportional **stock** dividend, because the investor continues to own the same proportion of the investee as before the stock dividend. In addition, the investee has not distributed any assets to the investor. Therefore, **no entry** is prepared to record the receipt of a stock dividend. The investor simply makes a memo entry to record the additional number of shares owned, while leaving the balance in the investment account unchanged. The balance is then spread over the total number of shares (previous holdings + stock dividend) to determine the new per share cost of the stock.

### F. Stock Rights

**51.** (**a**)   When stock rights are received, the cost of the investment (1,000 × $80 = $80,000) is allocated between the stock and the rights based on the relative fair market value of each, as calculated below.

| | | | |
|---|---|---|---|
| FMV of stock | 1,000 × $95 | = | $ 95,000 |
| FMV of rights | 1,000 × $ 5 | = | 5,000 |
| Total FMV | | | $100,000 |

The cost allocated to the stock is $76,000 ($80,000 × 95/100) and the cost allocated to the rights is $4,000 ($80,000 × 5/100).

**52.** (**c**)   When the rights are received, the cost of the investment ($36,000) is allocated between the stock and the rights based on their relative fair market values, calculated below.

| FMV of stock | 500 × $90 | = | $45,000 |
|---|---|---|---|
| FMV of rights | 500 × $10 | = | 5,000 |
| Total FMV | | | $50,000 |

The cost allocated to the stock is $32,400 ($45,000/$50,000, or 90%, of $36,000) and to the rights is $3,600 ($5,000/$50,000, or 10%, of $36,000). The net proceeds from the sale of the rights is $5,000 (500 × $10), so the gain on the sale of the rights is $1,400 ($5,000 – $3,600).

### G. Cash Surrender Value of Life Insurance

**53.** **(c)** The cash surrender value (CSV) of the life insurance policy increased by $21,000 during 2007 ($108,000 – $87,000). Therefore, part of the premium paid is not expense but a payment to increase the CSV. The formula to compute insurance expense is

| Cash paid | – | (Ending CSV – Beginning CSV) | – | Cash divs. received |
|---|---|---|---|---|
| $40,000 | – | ($108,000 – $87,000) | – | $0 = $19,000 |

The dividends in this problem are **not** cash dividends received. They are dividends that the insurance company applied to increase the CSV. They are not separately considered in the formula above because the effect of the dividends is reflected in the increase in CSV, which **is** included in the formula. 2007 journal entries are presented below.

| | | |
|---|---|---|
| Cash surr. value | $15,000 | ($21,000 – $6,000) |
| Ins. expense | 25,000 | |
|    Cash | | $40,000 |
| Cash surr. value | $ 6,000 | |
|    Ins. expense | | $ 6,000 |

**54.** **(a)** When a company insures the lives of employees and names itself the beneficiary, the cash surrender value of the policies is considered an asset. During the first few years of a policy, no cash surrender value may accrue. If no increase in cash surrender value (CSV) occurs, the journal entry to record a premium paid would be

| | | |
|---|---|---|
| Insurance expense | xxx | |
|    Cash | | xxx |

However, if cash surrender value increases, part of the cash paid is recorded as an increase in the CSV. The entry is

| | | |
|---|---|---|
| Insurance expense | xx | |
| Cash surrender value | xx | |
|    Cash | | xxx |

Therefore, the increase in CSV decreases insurance expense because the same amount of cash paid must be allocated between the two accounts. The increase in CSV does **not** affect investment income or deferred charges.

**55.** **(b)** When a company insures the lives of employees and names itself as the beneficiary, the cash surrender value (CSV) of the policy is considered an asset. Premiums paid are debited to CSV for the increase in CSV that year and to insurance expense for the excess of cash paid over increase in CSV. Upon the death of the insured employee, the company recognizes a gain for the excess of proceeds received over CSV.

### Miscellaneous

**56.** **(c)** In determining the amount which should be reported in Lake's 2007 income statement as dividend revenue, the first step is to determine what method should be used in accounting for Lake's investments. Per APB 18, the Board concluded that the equity method of accounting for an investment in common stock should be followed by an investor whose investment in common stock gives it the abil-ity to exercise significant influence over the operating and financial policies of an investee even though the investor may hold 50% or less of the voting stock. Ability to exercise that influence may be indicated in several ways, such as representation on the board of directors. Another important consideration is the extent of ownership by an investor. The Board concluded that an investment of 20% or more of the voting stock of an investee should lead to a presumption, in the absence of evidence to the contrary, that an investor has the ability to exercise significant influence over an investee. Conversely, an investment of less than 20% of the voting stock of an investee should lead to a presumption that an investor does **not** have the ability to exercise significant influence unless such ability can be demonstrated. Lake's 30% ownership of Aub and its representation on Aub's board of directors clearly indicate that the investment in Aub should be accounted for using the equity method. Lake's 1% ownership in Kar and lack of evidence in this problem that Lake has "significant influence" over Kar indicate that this investment should be accounted for using the cost adjusted for fair value method, in accordance with SFAS 115. Per APB 18, when the **equity** method is used, dividends received from an investee reduce the carrying amount of the investment (i.e., are **not** reported as dividend revenue). Per APB 18, however, the investor recognizes dividends received from investees as **income** under the **cost adjusted for fair value** method. Therefore, the $1,000 of cash dividends from Kar would be reported as dividend revenue by Lake, while the $15,000 of cash dividends from Aub would reduce the carrying amount of Lake's investment in Aub.

**57.** **(d)** Lake's royalty revenue results from the licensing of their trademark to Barr Co. Lake receives royalties of 10% of Barr's sales of trademarked items. To determine royalty revenue for 2007, it must first be realized that the royalty payment on September 1, 2007, is for sales in January through June of 2007. This royalty payment of $7,000 is the first portion of royalty revenue for 2007. The second portion of royalty revenue is for Barr's sales of trademarked items for July through December of 2007. This second portion consists of 10% of Barr's estimated sales of trademarked items for the last half of 2007. Royalty revenue for the second half of 2007 is then $2,000 (10% × $20,000). Therefore, answer (d) is correct because royalty revenue would be $9,000 for 2007 and is comprised of the $7,000 royalty payment received on September 1, 2007, plus 10% of estimated sales for months July through December.

**58.** **(c)** Lake receives rental revenue from leasing a parking lot to Day Co. The annual rental payment made by Day Co. to Lake is $48,000. However, Day Co. also paid a nonrefundable deposit of $50,000 on January 1, 2005. This $50,000 deposit, since it is nonrefundable, is considered unearned revenue that must be recognized over the life of the lease on a straight-line basis. Therefore, in addition to the $48,000 annual rental payment, $5,000 ($50,000 ÷ 10 years) of the nonrefundable deposit will be recognized as rental revenue in 2007. Thus, answer (c) is correct because $53,000 will be recognized as rental revenue in 2007. Note that the $8,000 security deposit will not be revenue because it is to be refunded at the end of the lease period. It is deferred in its entirety and recorded as a long-term liability. Only a nonrefundable deposit would be recognized as rental revenue over the life of the lease.

**59. (d)** Stock dividends are not income to the recipient, but rather, are an adjustment of the per share basis of the investment. Answer (c) is incorrect because no change in the total investment cost is made when an investor receives stock dividends. Answer (d) is correct because some companies make a memorandum journal entry to note the receipt of the stock dividend and the adjustment of the per share basis of the investment.

**SOLUTIONS TO SIMULATION PROBLEMS**

**Simulation Problem 1**

| Situation | Concepts | Accounting Treatment | Financial Statement Disclosures | Research | Communication |
|-----------|----------|---------------------|--------------------------------|----------|---------------|

*Accounting treatment*

| | (A) | (B) | (C) | (D) | (E) | (F) | (G) | (H) | (I) |
|---|---|---|---|---|---|---|---|---|---|
| 1. Cash flows from purchases and sales of these securities are reported as an operating activity on the statement of cash flows. | ○ | ○ | ○ | ○ | ○ | ○ | ○ | ● | ○ |
| 2. Include unrealized holding gains/losses in earnings of current period. | ○ | ○ | ○ | ○ | ○ | ○ | ○ | ● | ○ |
| 3. Amortize unrealized holding gain/loss over life of security. | ○ | ○ | ○ | ○ | ○ | ○ | ○ | ○ | ● |
| 4. Report at amortized cost. | ○ | ○ | ○ | ● | ○ | ○ | ○ | ○ | ○ |
| 5. Report unrealized holding gains/losses as other comprehensive income and close to accumulated other comprehensive income, a separate component of stockholders' equity. | ● | ○ | ○ | ○ | ○ | ○ | ○ | ○ | ○ |
| 6. Classify as a current asset. | ○ | ○ | ○ | ○ | ○ | ○ | ○ | ● | ○ |
| 7. Subsequent recovery not recognized unless realized. | ○ | ○ | ○ | ○ | ● | ○ | ○ | ○ | ○ |

**Explanation of solutions**

1.  **(H)** SFAS 115 dictates that purchases and sales of trading portfolio securities be classified as operating activities on the statement of cash flows due to the short-term, profit-seeking nature of the investment. In contrast, available-for-sale and held-to-maturity securities are classified as investing activities.

2.  **(H)** Unrealized holding gains and losses on trading securities are included in income of the period.

3.  **(I)** Unrealized holding gains and losses on securities transferred to held-to-maturity from available-for-sale are reported as a separate component of stockholders' equity (accumulated other comprehensive income) and amortized over the remaining life of the security.

4.  **(D)** Held-to-maturity securities are carried at amortized cost.

5.  **(A)** Unrealized holding gains and losses on available-for-sale securities are reported as other comprehensive income, whereas those on trading securities are included in income and those on held-to-maturity securities are not reported.

6.  **(H)** Trading securities appear on the balance sheet as current assets.

7.  **(E)** When a decline in value of a security is deemed to be other than temporary, the impaired security is written down to fair value. Any subsequent recovery may not be recognized in earnings unless realized through sale of the security.

| Situation | Concepts | Accounting Treatment | Financial Statement Disclosures | Research | Communication |
|-----------|----------|---------------------|--------------------------------|----------|---------------|

| | True | False |
|---|---|---|
| 1. Held-to-maturity securities are classified as current or noncurrent on an individual basis. | ● | ○ |
| 2. For trading securities, some realized gains/losses are excluded from earnings. | ● | ○ |
| 3. A premature sale of held-to-maturity securities may be considered maturity if at least 80% of the principal has already been collected. | ○ | ● |
| 4. Dividends received on available-for-sale securities decrease the investment account. | ○ | ● |
| 5. A company that owns more than 50% of the outstanding shares of stock of another company must use the fair value method. | ○ | ● |

**Explanation of solutions**

1.  **(T)** Held-to-maturity securities are classified as current or noncurrent according to how soon they will mature, (i.e., a security maturing within one year is classified as current, while one with a more distant maturity date is considered noncurrent).

2.  **(T)** Some unrealized holding gains and losses on trading securities could have already been included in income as unrealized components. Thus, to recognize them again upon realization would result in an erroneous doubling of the actual gain/loss.

3.  **(F)** Premature sale of held-to-maturity securities are considered at maturity if either (1) the sale occurs so close to maturity that interest rate risk is virtually eliminated, or (2) the sale occurs after at least 85% of the principal has been collected.

**4.** **(F)** Dividends received on available-for-sale securities are treated as dividend income on the income statement.

**5.** **(F)** A company that owns more than 50% of the outstanding shares of stock should use the equity method and prepare consolidated financial statements (assuming the company exercises control).

| Situation | Concepts | Accounting Treatment | Financial Statement Disclosures | | Research | Communication |
|---|---|---|---|---|---|---|

*Amount*

|  | (A) | (B) | (C) | (D) | (E) | (F) | (G) | (H) | (I) | (J) | (K) |
|---|---|---|---|---|---|---|---|---|---|---|---|
| 1. Carrying amount of security ABC at December 31, 2007. | ○ | ○ | ○ | ○ | ○ | ○ | ● | ○ | ○ | ○ | ○ |
| 2. Carrying amount of security DEF at December 31, 2007. | ○ | ○ | ○ | ○ | ○ | ○ | ○ | ○ | ● | ○ | ○ |
| 3. Carrying amount of security JKL at December 31, 2007. | ○ | ○ | ○ | ○ | ○ | ○ | ○ | ○ | ○ | ● | ○ |

*Amount*                                                            *Gain*   *Loss*

|  | (A) | (B) | (C) | (D) | (E) | (F) | (G) | (H) | (I) | (J) | (K) | Gain | Loss |
|---|---|---|---|---|---|---|---|---|---|---|---|---|---|
| 4. Recognized gain or loss on sale of security GHI. | ○ | ○ | ○ | ● | ○ | ○ | ○ | ○ | ○ | ○ | ○ | ○ | ● |
| 5. Unrealized gain or loss to be reported in 2007 net income. | ○ | ● | ○ | ○ | ○ | ○ | ○ | ○ | ○ | ○ | ○ | ○ | ● |
| 6. Unrealized gain or loss to be reported at December 31, 2007, as a separate component of stockholders' equity entitled "accumulated other comprehensive income." | ○ | ○ | ● | ○ | ○ | ○ | ○ | ○ | ○ | ○ | ○ | ○ | ● |

## Explanation of solutions

**1.** **(G; $100,000)** SFAS 115 states that held-to-maturity securities "shall be . . .measured at amortized cost." Since this debt security was purchased at par, there is neither a discount nor a premium to amortize, therefore amortized cost equals par or $100,000. Ignore fair value.

**2.** **(I; $155,000)** SFAS 115 states "Investments in . . .securities that are not classified as held-to-maturity and that have readily determinable fair values shall be . . .measured at fair value." $155,000 is fair value.

**3.** **(J; $160,000)** Same answer as question 6. Since security JKL is not a debt security classified as held-to-maturity and since it has a readily determinable fair value it "shall be . . .measured at fair value."

**4.** **(D, L)** Recognized gains and losses on the sale of available-for-sale securities are measured as the difference between original cost ($190,000) and the selling price of the securities ($175,000). The unrealized loss that existed in accumulated other comprehensive income in the equity section prior to the sale ($25,000) will be reversed as a credit to unrealized loss and that reversal will be reported as other comprehensive income and closed to accumulated other comprehensive income that is reported in the equity section of the balance sheet (see question 10 below). The journal entry to record the sale would be

| | | |
|---|---|---|
| Cash | 175,000 | |
| Realized loss on sale of A-F-S securities | 15,000 | |
| A-F-S securities | | 165,000 |
| Unrealized loss on A-F-S securities | | 25,000 |

**5.** **(B, L)** The only unrealized gains or losses on securities reported in the net income relate to value changes in trading securities. In this case the value of the JKL securities has decreased from $160,000 to $155,000.

**6.** **(C, L)** The 1/1/07 balance of the unrealized gain or loss on A-F-S securities reported in the equity section was $20,000, the difference between the 1/1/07 $25,000 unrealized loss of GHI ($190,000 – $165,000) and the 1/1/07 $5,000 unrealized gain of JKL ($175,000 – $170,000). The changes during the year were (1) the $25,000 reversal (credit) of the unrealized loss of GHI when it was sold and (2) the $15,000 loss ($175,000 – $160,000) in value during the year of JKL. The Other Comprehensive Income account would appear as follows:

Other Comprehensive Income

| | | |
|---|---|---|
| Beg. bal. | -- | |
| 12/31/07 JKL | 15,000 | 12/31/07 Reverse GHI  25,000 |
| Close to Accumulated Other Comprehensive Income | 10,000 | |

The Accumulated Other Comprehensive Income account would appear as follows:

Accumulated Other Comprehensive Income

| | | |
|---|---|---|
| 1/1/07 | 20,000 | |
| | | 12/31/07  Close from Other Comprehensive Income |
| 12/31/07 Balance | 10,000 | |

| Situation | Concepts | Accounting Treatment | Financial Statement Disclosures | Research | Communication |
|-----------|----------|----------------------|----------------------------------|----------|----------------|

**1.** How should Dayle report the effects of unrealized losses and gains during the year from each portfolio?

**FAS115, Para 13 (as amended) or Current Text I80.110**

13. Unrealized **holding gains and losses** for trading securities shall be included in earnings. Unrealized holding gains and losses for available-for-sale securities (including those classified as current assets) shall be excluded from earnings and reported [FAS115, ¶13] in other comprehensive income [as required in Section C49, "Comprehensive Income: Financial Statement Presentation,"] [FAS130, ¶33(a)] until realized except as indicated in the following sentence. All or a portion of the unrealized holding gain or loss of an available-for-sale security that is designated as being hedged in a fair value hedge shall be recognized in earnings during the period of the hedge, pursuant to paragraph .119 of Section D50. [FAS133, ¶534(b)] Paragraph .135 of Section 127, "Income Taxes," provides guidance on reporting the tax effects of unrealized holding gains and losses reported in [FAS115, ¶13] other comprehensive income. [FAS130, ¶33(a)] [Refer to paragraph .1001 for an EITF Issue that provides interpretive guidance on this paragraph.]

**2.** How should Dayle account for the security that was reclassified from the trading securities portfolio to the available-for-sale securities portfolio?

**FAS115, Para 15 or Current Text I80.114**

15. The transfer of a security between categories of investments shall be accounted for at fair value. At the date of the transfer, the security's unrealized holding gain or loss shall be accounted for as follows:

    a. For a security transferred from the trading category, the unrealized holding gain or loss at the date of the transfer will have already been recognized in earnings and shall not be reversed.

**3.** How should Dayle report investments in each portfolio in its balance sheet as of the end of the period?

**Financial Statement Presentation**
**FAS115, Para 17 as altered by FAS 135 Para 4(t)(2) or Current Text I80.116**

17. An enterprise that presents a classified statement of financial position shall report individual held-to-maturity securities, individual available-for-sale securities, and individual trading securities as either current or noncurrent, as appropriate, under the provisions of ARB No. 43, Chapter 3A, "Working Capital—Current Assets and Current Liabilities."

**ARB43, Ch. 3A, Para 4 and 5**

4. For accounting purposes, the term *current assets* is used to designate cash and other assets or resources commonly identified as those which are reasonably expected to be realized in cash or sold or consumed during the normal operating cycle of the business. Thus the term comprehends in general such reserves as (a) cash available for current operations and items which are the equivalent of cash; (b) inventories of merchandise, raw materials, goods in process, finished goods, operating supplies, and ordinary maintenance material and parts; (c) trade accounts, notes, and acceptances receivable; (d) receivables from officers, employees, affiliates, and others, if collectible in the ordinary course of business within a year; (e) installment or deferred accounts and notes receivable if they conform generally to normal trade practices and terms within the business; (f) marketable securities representing the investment of cash available for current operations; and (g) prepaid expenses such as insurance, interest, rents, taxes, unused royalties, current paid advertising service not yet received, and operating supplies. Prepaid expenses are not current assets in the sense that they will be converted into cash but in the sense that, if not paid in advance, they would require the use of current assets during the operating cycle.

5. The ordinary operations of a business involve a circulation of capital within the current asset group. Cash is expended for materials, finished parts, operating supplies, labor, and other factory services, and such expenditures are accumulated as inventory cost. Inventory costs, upon sale of the products to which such costs attach, are converted into trade receivables and ultimately into cash again. The average time intervening between the acquisition of materials or services entering this process and the final cash realization constitutes an *operating cycle*. A one-year time period is to be used as a basis for the segregation of current assets in cases where there are several operating cycles occurring within a year. However, where the period of the operating cycle is more than twelve months, as in, for instance the tobacco, distillery, and lumber businesses, the longer period should be used. Where a particular business has no clearly defined operating cycle, the one-year rule should govern.

| Situation | Concepts | Accounting Treatment | Financial Statement Disclosures | Research | Communication |
|-----------|----------|----------------------|----------------------------------|----------|---------------|

To:     Dayle Inc. Permanent File
From:  CPA Candidate
Re:     Accounting issues related to marketable securities
Date:   [*Today's date*]

This memorandum summarizes my research regarding the accounting for marketable securities by Dayle, Inc.

Issue 1:  How should Dayle report the effects of unrealized gains and losses during the year for each portfolio?

Guidance for accounting for unrealized gains and losses on securities is contained in paragraph 13 of FAS115, as amended by FAS130. For investments classified as trading securities, the unrealized holding gains and losses should be included in earnings. The unrealized gains and losses of investments classified as available-for-sale securities should be excluded from earnings and reported in other comprehensive income.

Issue 2:  How should Dayle account for the security that was reclassified from the trading securities portfolio to the available-for-sale securities portfolio?

According to FAS115, paragraph 15, the transfer of a security between portfolios should be effected at the fair value of the security on the date of transfer. Because the transfer in question was from the trading portfolio to the available-for-sale portfolio, the loss has already been taken to earnings and should not be reversed.

Issue 3:  How should Dayle present the investments in each portfolio in its balance sheet at the end of the period?

FAS115, paragraph 17, indicates that the firm should report individual available-for-sale and trading securities as current or noncurrent under the provisions of ARB43.

ARB43, Ch. 3A, Paras 4 and 5 state that the term current assets is used to designate cash and other assets or resources commonly identified as those which are reasonably expected to be realized in cash or sold or consumed during the normal operating cycle of the business or one year whichever is longer. Therefore, securities that are available to meet current cash needs should be classified as current; other investments should be classified as noncurrent.

If you have any additional questions, please contact me.

---

**Simulation Problem 2**

| Situation | Classification of Securities | Journal Entries | Financial Statement Disclosures | Communication | Research |
|-----------|------------------------------|-----------------|----------------------------------|---------------|----------|

*Category*

|   |   | (H) | (T) | (A) |
|---|---|-----|-----|-----|
| **1.** | Debt securities bought and held for the purpose of selling in the near term. | ○ | ● | ○ |
| **2.** | US Treasury bonds that Acme has both the positive intent and the ability to hold to maturity. | ● | ○ | ○ |
| **3.** | $3 million debt security bought and held for the purpose of selling in three years to finance payment of Acme's $2 million long-term note payable when it matures. | ○ | ○ | ● |
| **4.** | Convertible preferred stock that Acme does not intend to sell in the near term. | ○ | ○ | ● |

**Explanation of solutions**

**1.**    **(T)** Trading. SFAS 115 states that "securities that are bought and held principally for the purpose of selling them in the near term (thus held for only a short period of time) shall be classified as **trading securities**."

**2.**    **(H)** Held-to-maturity. SFAS 115 states that "investments in debt securities shall be classified as **held-to-maturity** and measured at amortized cost...only if the reporting enterprise has the positive intent and ability to hold those securities to maturity." Both conditions are met in this case.

**3.**    **(A)** Available-for-sale. The company does not have the "positive intent . . .to hold this debt security to maturity," therefore the security cannot be classified as held-to-maturity. Also, since it will be sold beyond the "near term," it cannot be classified as "trading." SFAS 115 states that "investments not classified as trading (nor as held-to-maturity securities) shall be classified as **available-for-sale securities**."

**4.**    **(A)** Available-for-sale. Since this security is neither a debt security nor a security that will be sold in the near term, it is classified as available-for-sale.

| Situation | Classification of Securities | Journal Entries | Financial Statement Disclosures | Communication | Research |
|---|---|---|---|---|---|

**1.** Prepare the journal entry for the investment in Kern Co. on January 2, 2007.

| | | |
|---|---|---|
| Investment in Kern | 600,000 | |
|     Cash | | 600,000 |

**2.** Prepare the journal entry for the dividends received from Kern in 2007.

| | | |
|---|---|---|
| Cash | 20,000 | |
|     Investment in Kern | | 20,000 |
|     [100,000 × 20% = 20,000] | | |

**3.** Prepare the journal entry required for Kern's reported income for the year ending December 31, 2007.

| | | |
|---|---|---|
| Investment in Kern | 80,000 | |
|     Income from Kern | | 80,000 |
|     [400,000 × 20% = 80,000] | | |

| Situation | Classification of Securities | Journal Entries | Financial Statement Disclosures | Communication | Research |
|---|---|---|---|---|---|

Identify the following amounts on Acme's financial statements.

| | |
|---|---|
| Carrying value of Kern investment | $660,000 |
| Carrying value of Wand investment | $400,000 |
| | |
| Income on Income Statement | |
|     Kern investment | $ 80,000 |
|     Wand investment | $ 12,000 |
| Other comprehensive income | |
|     Kern investment | $ -- |
|     Wand investment | $100,000 |

**Explanation of solutions**

Carrying value of Kern.

### Kern

**Balance sheet**–Acme reported its investment in Kern at a carrying amount of $660,000

> *Calculations*:
>
> Equity in earnings = $80,000 ($400,000 × 20%)
>
> Dividend rec'd = $20,000 ($100,000 × 20%)
>
> Carrying amount = $600,000 + $80,000 – $20,000 = $660,000

Carrying value of Wand.

### Wand

**Balance sheet**–Acme reported its investment in Wand at a fair value of $400,000

> *Calculation*:
>
> 20,000 shares × $20 per share = $400,000

## Income Statement Amounts

Income from Kern        $400,000 × 20% = $80,000

Income from Wand        $12,000 dividend income

Dividend income $12,000

*Calculation*:

$60,000 × 20% = $12,000

## Other Comprehensive Income

Kern Investment         $0

Wand investment         Unrealized gain $100,000

*Calculation*:

$400,000 – $300,000 = $100,000

| Situation | Classification of Securities | Journal Entries | Financial Statement Disclosures | Communication | Research |
|---|---|---|---|---|---|

To:     Mr. Harold Johnson
From:   CPA Candidate
Re:     Acme Co. Investments in Kern Co. and Wand Co.

The purpose of this memorandum is to explain to you the reasoning behind our belief that although Acme's investment in Wand and Kern represents equal ownership interests of 20%, the use of different accounting methods may be appropriate under generally accepted accounting principles.

Under generally accepted accounting principles, Acme must use the equity method to account for an investment if Acme's ownership interest allows it to exercise significant influence over the investee company. Generally, an investor is presumed to be able to exercise significant influence when it has an ownership interest of 20% or more, and is presumed to be unable to exercise significant influence when it has an ownership interest of less than 20%. However, either presumption may be overcome by predominant evidence to the contrary. The determination of whether an investor can exercise significant influence is not always clear and often requires judgment in light of such factors as an investor's representation on the investee's board of directors, participation in policymaking activities, and/or the extent of ownership as compared to that investee's other shareholders.

Acme used the equity method to account for its investment in Kern which indicates that its 20% ownership interest allowed it to exercise significant influence over Kern's operating and financial policies.

Acme accounted for its investment in Wand as available-for-sale securities. Despite its 20% ownership interest, there was evidence that Acme could not exercise significant influence over Wand's operating and financial policies. Hence, Acme did not use the equity method to account for its investment in Wand.

If you have any other questions, please contact me.

| Situation | Classification of Securities | Journal Entries | Financial Statement Disclosures | Communication | Research |
|---|---|---|---|---|---|

**1.** What is a trading security?

**FAS115, Para 12a or Current Text I80.109**

12. Investments in debt securities that are not classified as held-to-maturity and equity securities that have readily determinable fair values shall be classified in one of the following categories and measured at fair value in the statement of financial position:

a. Trading securities. Securities that are bought and held principally for the purpose of selling them in the near term (thus held for only a short period of time) shall be classified as trading securities. Trading generally reflects active and frequent buying and selling, and trading securities are generally used with the objective of generating profits on short-term differences in price. Mortgage-backed securities that are held-for-sale in conjunction with mortgage banking activities, as described in FASB Statement No. 65, *Accounting for Certain Mortgage Banking Activities*, shall be classified as trading securities. (Other mortgage-backed securities not held-for-sale in conjunction with mortgage banking activities shall be classified based on the criteria in this paragraph and paragraph 7.)

      b. Available-for-sale securities. Investments not classified as trading securities (nor as held-to-maturity securities) shall be classified as available-for-sale securities.

**2.** A company sells available-for-sale securities. Where is this transaction found on the statement of cash flows?

**FAS115, Para 18 or Current Text I80.117**

18. Cash flows from purchases, sales, and maturities of available-for-sale securities and held-to-maturity securities shall be classified as cash flows from investing activities and reported gross for each security classification in the statement of cash flows. Cash flows from purchases, sales, and maturities of trading securities shall be classified as cash flows from operating activities.

**3.** A company has dividend income from available-for-sale securities. Where is this dividend income found on the financial statements?

**FAS115, Para 14 or Current Text I80.111**

14. Dividend and interest income, including amortization of the premium and discount arising at acquisition, for all three categories of investments in securities shall continue to be included in earnings. This Statement does not affect the methods used for recognizing and measuring the amount of dividend and interest income. Realized gains and losses for securities classified as either available-for-sale or held-to-maturity also shall continue to be reported in earnings.

---

## Simulation Problem 3

| Situation | Concepts | Available-for-Sale Securities | Long-Term Marketable Equity Securities | Investment Income | Communication | Research |
|---|---|---|---|---|---|---|

Identify whether each of the following statements is True or False.

| | True | False |
|---|---|---|
| **1.** Unrealized gains from trading securities are reported in other comprehensive income. | ○ | ● |
| **2.** Investments in stocks and bonds may be classified as trading securities, available-for-sale securities, and held-to-maturity securities. | ○ | ● |
| **3.** X Company has significant influence over Y Company and owns 35% of the voting stock of Y Company. X Company must use the equity method of accounting for the investment in Y Company. | ● | ○ |
| **4.** Unrealized gains and losses from available-for-sale securities that result from the change in fair value during the period should be reported as other comprehensive income. | ● | ○ |
| **5.** The temporary unrealized gain or loss from held-to-maturity securities must be reported in income for the current period. | ○ | ● |
| **6.** If a security is transferred from available-for-sale to trading securities classification, unrealized holding gains and losses are recognized immediately in the income statement. | ● | ○ |
| **7.** The equity method of accounting requires a company to include the percent of income of the investee in the investor company's net income for the period. | ● | ○ |
| **8.** The equity method of accounting requires that a company adjust the cost of the investee to fair value at the end of each period. | ○ | ● |
| **9.** A company that receives stock dividends records income equal to the fair value of the stock on the date the dividend is declared. | ○ | ● |
| **10.** Held-to-maturity securities are carried at amortized cost using the effective interest method. | ● | ○ |

### Explanation of solutions

**1.** False. Unrealized gains from trading securities are reported in income for the period.

**2.** False. Stocks cannot be classified as held-to-maturity because they have no maturity date.

**3.** True. The equity method is required when an investor exercises significant influence over the investee.

**4.** True. Unrealized gains and losses are reported as other comprehensive income.

**5.** False. The temporary unrealized gain from held-to-maturity securities is excluded from earnings; instead, the held-to-maturities are reported at amortized cost.

**6.** True.  Unrealized gains or losses are recognized when transferred.

**7.** True.  The investor recognizes its share of income as earned.

**8.** False.  In the equity method, the investor does not revalue the stock to fair value.  The equity method requires that the investor record the percentage share of net income and percentage share of dividends of the investee.

**9.** False.  Stock dividends require a memo entry to show receipt of additional shares of stock.  The company then recomputes the cost per share based upon the new number of shares.

**10.** True.  Held-to-maturity securities are carried at amortized cost.

| Situation | Concepts | Available-for-Sale Securities | Long-Term Marketable Equity Securities | Investment Income | Communication | Research |
|---|---|---|---|---|---|---|

Complete the following schedule for the available-for-sale securities of Poe Corp. as of December 31, 2007.

*Poe Corp.*
**SCHEDULE OF AVAILABLE-FOR-SALE**
**SECURITIES**
*December 31, 2007*

| | Number of shares | Cost | Beginning carrying amount at market | Ending market price per share | Market value | Cumulative gain or (loss) | Unrealized gain or (loss) in 2007 |
|---|---|---|---|---|---|---|---|
| Axe—preferred | 500 | $ 20,000 | $ 21,000 | $56 | $ 28,000 | $ 8,000 | $ 7,000 |
| Axe—common | 1,500 | 20,000 | 21,000 | 20 | 30,000 | 10,000 | 9,000 |
| Purl—common | 3,500 | 35,000 | 38,500 | 11 | 38,500 | 3,500 | -- |
| Day—common | 1,700 | 42,500 | 30,900 | 22 | 37,400 | (5,100) | 6,500 |
| | | $117,500 | $111,400 | | $133,900 | $16,400 | $22,500 |

| Situation | Concepts | Available-for-Sale Securities | Long-Term Marketable Equity Securities | Investment Income | Communication | Research |
|---|---|---|---|---|---|---|

Prepare the following schedule for the long-term marketable equity securities for Poe Corp. as of December 31, 2007.

*Poe Corp.*
**SCHEDULE OF LONG-TERM MARKETABLE**
**EQUITY SECURITIES**
*December 31, 2007*

| Scott Corp.—100,000 shares of common stock: | |
|---|---|
| Cost: | |
| Acquisition price | $1,700,000 |
| Increase in equity during 2007: | |
| Poe's interest in Scott's income | $ 360,000 |
| Less: | |
| Dividends received | 200,000 |
| Net increase in equity | 160,000 |
| Carrying amount of Poe Corp.'s investment in Scott | $1,860,000 |

| Situation | Concepts | Available-for-Sale Securities | Long-Term Marketable Equity Securities | Investment Income | Communication | Research |
|---|---|---|---|---|---|---|

Complete the following schedule outlining the income for Poe Corp. for the year ended December 31, 2007.

*Poe Corp.*
**SCHEDULE OF INVESTMENT INCOME**
*For the Year Ended December 31, 2007*

| | |
|---|---|
| Dividends: | |
| Axe Corp.—preferred (1,000 shares × $2.40 per share) | $2,400 |
| Purl, Inc.—common (3,500 shares × $1.00 per share) | 3,500 |
| Total dividend revenue | $5,900 |
| Gains on marketable equity securities:                         [1] | |
| Realized gain/(loss) on sale of securities: | |
| Purl, Inc.—common ($13 – $10 = $3 × 2,500 shares | $7,500 |
| Day Co.—common ($55,000/2,000 shares × 110%, or cost per share of $25 – $21 selling price per share = $4 loss per share × 500 shares sold) | (2,000) |
| Net realized gain on sale of securities | 5,500 |
| Equity in income of Scott Corp.: | |
| Poe's 30% interest in Scott's net income of $1,200,000 | 360,000 |
| Total investment income | $371,400 |

### Explanation of amount

[1]   Unrealized gains (losses) on available-for-sale securities are excluded from investment income and thus are excluded from Poe's schedule of investment income. They are reported as other comprehensive income.

### Explanation of calculations and problem solving

1.   This problem consists of three related requirements concerning a company's investments in marketable equity securities.

1.1   A schedule of Poe's available-for-sale securities at 12/31/07 must be prepared. This schedule should include columns for cost, market, and unrealized gain or loss.

1.2   A schedule to show the carrying amount of Poe's long-term investments accounted for by the equity method at 12/31/07 is required.

1.3   Finally, a schedule showing all revenues, gains, and losses for 2007 relating to Poe's investments must be prepared.

1.4   The solutions approach for problems of this type in which the requirements are interrelated is to prepare time lines for each security and proceed through the given information making computations and notations on the appropriate time line. Labeling of computations by requirement helps to organize your data. For example, if a computation or number relates to requirement c., it can be labeled "c." Using this approach, the candidate will be solving a part of two to three requirements as each security is covered, but not necessarily in the same order as given on the exam. After working through all the information given, the formal required schedules can be prepared.

2.   At 12/31/06, Poe owned 1,000 shares of Axe preferred with a fair value of $42,000 ($42/share). At 10/1/07, Poe converted 500 shares of Axe preferred into 1,500 shares of Axe common. The preferred fair value is allocated to the common since half of the preferred $21,000 was surrendered to acquire it. The remaining preferred is still carried at $21,000 ($42 × 500 shares). At year-end, the preferred is reported at $28,000 ($56 FV/sh × 500 sh) and the common stock is reported at $30,000 ($20 FV/sh × 1,500 sh). See time line after 2.1.

2:1   Dividend revenue received on the Axe preferred stock should be included in Poe's income statement. The Axe preferred stock paid a $1.20 dividend on 1,000 shares twice during the year, for a total of $2,400. Note that the second dividend was received on October 5, after 500 shares of preferred were converted. However, the dividend was received for all 1,000 shares, since the date of record was September 9.

3.   Poe owned 6,000 shares of Purl common that originally cost $60,000 ($10/sh) and had a fair value of $66,000 ($11/sh) at 12/31/07. 2,500 of these shares were sold. The 3,500 still held have a carrying value of $38,500 (3,500 sh × $11). See time line after 3.2.

3.1  On 1/18/07, Poe sold 2,500 shares of Purl common for $32,500 (2,500 sh × $13) when the carrying value (fair value) was $27,500 (2,500 sh × $11). Since unrealized gains/losses on available-for-sale securities are not recognized in income the gain on the sale is $7,500 ($32,500 – $25,000).

3.2  Dividend income received on the Purl common stock should also be included in Poe's income statement. A $1.00 per share dividend was received on the Purl common stock (3,500 shares × $1.00 per share or $3,500).

4.   At 1/1/07, Poe owned 2,000 shares of Day common that cost $55,000 and had a fair value of $40,000. Day issued a 10% stock dividend on February 14 when the stock's fair value was $44,000 (2,000 × $22), which gave Poe an additional 200 shares (2,000 × 10%) at no additional cost. Therefore, the 2,200 shares had an adjusted cost of $25 per share ($55,000 ÷ 2,200). The adjusted carrying value per share was $18.18 ($40,000 ÷ 2,200 shs). The stock dividend is not reflected in income. Poe sold 500 shares on June 1. The 1,700 still held have a cost of $42,500 (1,700 × $25), a carrying value of $30,900 (1,700 × $18.18) and a fair value of $37,400 (1,700 × $22). See time line after 4.1.

4.1  The Day stock sold for $10,500 (500 × $21) and had a cost of $12,500 (500 × $25). Thus, a $2,000 loss was realized on the sale of Day common and should be included in Poe's income statement.

5.   Poe intends to hold the Scott stock as a long-term investment. Since Poe owns 30% of the voting stock and can exercise significant influence over Scott, the use of the equity method is appropriate.

5.1  The original cost of the investment was $1,700,000. The excess of investment cost ($1,700,000) over the book value of the net assets purchased ($1,400,000) is $300,000. This amount is not amortized, in accordance with SFAS 142.

5.2  The investment account is also reduced by dividends received when the equity method is used. Scott paid quarterly dividends of $.50 a share, or a total of $50,000 each quarter to Poe (100,000 × $.50). Therefore, Poe received a total of $200,000 in dividends (4 × $50,000) from Scott. See time line after 5.3.

| | | |
|---|---|---|
| Cash | 200,000 | |
|     Investment in Scott | | 200,000 |

Note that the dividend received from Scott is not recognized as income under the equity method.

5.3  Using the equity method, the investment account is increased by the investor's share of investee earnings 30% × $1,200,000 = $360,000).

| | | |
|---|---|---|
| Investment in Scott | 360,000 | |
|     Investment revenue | | 360,000 |

| | | | | Communication | |
|---|---|---|---|---|---|
| Situation | Concepts | Available-for-Sale Securities | Long-Term Marketable Equity Securities | Investment Income | Research |

To:    CEO, Poe Corp.
From:  CPA Candidate
Re:    Equity method of accounting

This memorandum is designed to explain the equity method of accounting for an investment. When a company owns stock in another company and can exercise significant influence over the operating and financial policies of that company, the equity method of accounting should be used. Generally, ownership between 20 and 50% of the outstanding stock of another company will result in the investor having significant influence over the investee.

The equity method requires that the investor recognize its percentage share of income or loss and dividends received for a period. The full equity method may also require that a company amortize the difference between the investment cost and book value of the investment.  In addition, the full equity method requires that the effects of inter-company transactions be eliminated.  If you have an investment that you believe qualifies for treatment under the equity method, please contact my office.  We will be glad to assist you with the accounting for your investments.

| Situation | Concepts | Available-for-Sale Securities | Long-Term Marketable Equity Securities | Investment Income | Communication | Research |
|---|---|---|---|---|---|---|

**1.** When a company owns between 20% and 50% of the outstanding stock of another company and uses the equity method of accounting, how is income from the investee disclosed?

**APB18, Para 19 or Current Text I82.109**

c.  The investment(s) in common stock should be shown in the balance sheet of an investor as a single amount, and the investor's share of earnings or losses of an investee(s) should ordinarily be shown in the income statement as a single amount except for the extraordinary items as specified in (d) below.

**2.** What are the three classifications for investment in debt and equity securities?

**FAS115, Para 6 or Current Text I80.103**

6.  At acquisition, an enterprise shall classify debt and equity securities into one of three categories:  held-to-maturity, available-for-sale, or trading.  At each reporting date, the appropriateness of the classification shall be reassessed.

**3.** When a security is removed from the trading category, should the earnings previously recorded be reversed?

**FAS115, Para 15 or Current Text I80.114**

a.  For a security transferred from the trading category, the unrealized holding gain or loss at the date of the transfer will have already been recognized in earnings and shall not be reversed.

# STATEMENT OF CASH FLOWS

A. **Objectives of the Statement of Cash Flows** (See outline of SFAS 95 also)

The primary purposes of this statement are to provide information about an entity's cash receipts and cash payments and to disclose information about the financing and investing activities of an entity. This statement should help the users of the statement assess: (1) an entity's ability to generate positive future cash flows; (2) an entity's ability to meet its obligations and pay dividends; (3) the reasons for differences between income and associated cash receipts and payments; and (4) the cash and noncash aspects of an entity's investing and financing transactions.

In order to facilitate the users in making those assessments, a statement of cash flows shall report cash receipts and cash payments of an entity's operations, its investing transactions, and its financing transactions. A separate schedule accompanying the statement should also report the effects of investing and financing transactions that **do not affect cash**.

The statement of cash flows is required to be prepared based on changes during the period in cash and cash equivalents. Cash equivalents include short-term, highly liquid investments that (1) are readily convertible to known amounts of cash and (2) are so near their maturity (original maturity of three months or less from **date of purchase** by the enterprise) that they present negligible risk of changes in value because of changes in interest rates. Treasury bills, commercial paper, and money market funds are all examples of cash equivalents.

B. **Statement of Cash Flows Classification**

Cash receipts and cash payments are to be classified into operating, financing, and investing activities.

Operating activities include delivering or producing goods for sale and providing services. Operating activities include all transactions that are **not** investing and financing activities. More specifically, cash flows from operations should not include cash flows from transactions whose effects are included in income but are investing and financing activities. For example, a gain (loss) on extinguishment of debt should properly be classified as a financing activity, and a gain (loss) from disposal of property should be classified as an investing activity.

Investing activities include the acquisition and disposition of long-term productive assets or securities that are not considered cash equivalents. Investing activities also include the lending of money and collection on loans.

Financing activities include obtaining resources from owners and returning the investment. Also included is obtaining resources from creditors and repaying the amount borrowed.

The FASB has listed the following as examples of classifications of transactions.

## ACTIVITIES REPORTED ON THE STATEMENT OF CASH FLOWS

| *Description of the activity* | *Positive cash flow* | *Negative cash flow* |
|---|---|---|
| **Operating activities (direct method):** | | |
| • Cash received from customers | xx | |
| • Cash received from interest | xx | |
| • Cash received from dividends | xx | |
| • Cash received from sales of securities classified as trading | xx | |
| • Cash paid to suppliers | | xx |
| • Cash paid for operating expenses | | xx |
| • Cash paid for interest | | xx |
| • Cash paid for income taxes | | xx |
| • Cash paid for securities classified as trading | | xx |
| **Investing activities:** | | |
| • Proceeds from sales of property, plant, and equipment | xx | |
| • Proceeds from sales of investments in stocks (available for sale) and bonds (available for sale) | xx | |
| • Proceeds from the sale or redemption of investments in bonds classified as held to maturity | xx | |
| • Proceeds from collection of loans (principal only) | xx | |
| • Proceeds from selling components of the company | xx | |
| • Acquisition of property, plant, and equipment (capital expenditures) | | xx |
| • Acquisition of investments in stocks and bonds (available for sale or held to maturity) | | xx |
| • Making loans to other entities | | xx |
| • Acquiring other businesses | | xx |

| _Description of the activity_ | _Positive cash flow_ | _Negative cash flow_ |
|---|---|---|
| **Financing activities:** | | |
| • Proceeds from issuing common and preferred stock | xx | |
| • Proceeds from reissuing treasury stock | xx | |
| • Proceeds from issuing short-term debt | xx | |
| • Proceeds from issuing long-term debt | xx | |
| • Paying cash dividends | | xx |
| • Repurchasing common stock (treasury stock) | | xx |
| • Repaying short-term loans (principal only) | | xx |
| • Repaying long-term loans, including capital lease obligations (principal only) | | xx |

**Noncash investing and financing activities**

- Acquiring an asset through a capital lease
- Conversion of debt to equity
- Exchange of noncash assets or liabilities for other noncash assets or liabilities
- Issuance of stock to acquire assets

Note that noncash investing and financing activities should be excluded from the statement itself. These transactions involve no cash inflows and outflows, but they have a significant effect on the prospective cash flows of a company. Therefore, they must be distinguished from activities that involved cash receipts and payments and must be reported in a separate schedule or in the footnotes to the financial statements.

In the statement, the inflows and outflows for each category (operating, investing, and financing) should be shown separately, and the **net** cash flows (the difference between the inflows and outflows) should be reported.

## C. Direct or Indirect Presentation in Reporting Operating Activities

The FASB decided that the preferable method of presenting net cash flows from operating activities is by **directly** showing major classes of operating cash receipts and payments. However, the **indirect (reconciliation) method** is also permitted. When the direct method is used, it is also necessary to present a separate accompanying schedule showing the indirect method. The **direct method** is discussed first, followed by a discussion of the **indirect method**.

Under the direct approach, cash flow elements of operating activities are derived from the accrual basis components of net income. In converting to the cash basis, accounts that should be analyzed under operating activities are those which are debited or credited when recording transactions that affect the income statement. These transactions include transactions with outsiders and adjusting entries. For example, these accounts include sales, cost of sales, operating expenses, and tax expense, as well as assets and liabilities which are related to them, such as accounts receivable, inventory, accounts payable, accrued expenses, and prepaid expenses. Note that interest expense and interest revenue are included within operating activities. Formulas for conversion of various income statement amounts from the accrual basis to the cash basis are summarized in the following table:

| _Accrual basis_ | | _Additions_ | | _Deductions_ | | _Cash basis_ |
|---|---|---|---|---|---|---|
| Net sales | + | Beginning AR | – | $\left(\begin{array}{l}\text{Ending AR}\\ \text{AR written off}\end{array}\right)$ | = | Cash received from customers |
| Cost of goods sold | + | $\left(\begin{array}{l}\text{Ending inventory}\\ \text{Beginning AP}\end{array}\right)$ | – | $\left(\begin{array}{l}\text{Depreciation and amortization}^*\\ \text{Beginning inventory}\\ \text{Ending AP}\end{array}\right)$ | = | Cash paid to suppliers |
| Operating expenses | + | $\left(\begin{array}{l}\text{Ending prepaid expenses}\\ \text{Beginning accrued}\\ \text{expenses payable}\end{array}\right)$ | – | $\left(\begin{array}{l}\text{Depreciation and amortization}\\ \text{Beginning prepaid expenses}\\ \text{Ending accrued expenses payable}\end{array}\right)$ | = | Cash paid for operating expenses |

\* _Applies to a manufacturing entity_

A T-account analysis method may be used instead of the above formulas to determine cash received and cash paid. T-account analysis provides a quick, systematic way to accumulate the information needed to prepare the statement.

The direct approach would be presented in the statement of cash flows as follows:

*Cash flows from operating activities*

| | | |
|---|---:|---:|
| Cash received from dividends | $   500 | |
| Cash received from interest | 1,000 | |
| Cash received from sale of goods | 9,000 | |
| Cash provided by operating activities | | $10,500 |
| Cash paid to suppliers | 5,000 | |
| Cash paid for operating expenses | 500 | |
| Cash paid for interest | 500 | |
| Cash paid for taxes | 500 | |
| Cash disbursed from operating activities | | 6,500 |
| Net cash flows from operating activities | | $ 4,000 |

The other way of reporting net cash flows from operations is known as the **indirect method**. This is done by starting with income from continuing operations and adjusting for changes in operating related accounts (e.g., inventory and accounts payable) and noncash expenses, revenues, losses, and gains.

Noncash items that were subtracted in determining income must be added back in determining net cash flows from operations. Each of these noncash items is a charge against income but does not decrease cash.

Items to be added back include depreciation, amortization of intangibles, amortization of discount on bonds payable, bad debt expense, and any increase in the deferred tax liability. Note each of these items is charged against income but does not decrease cash.

Noncash items that were added in determining income must be subtracted from net income in determining net cash flows from operations. Each of these noncash items is an increase to income but does not increase cash.

Items to be deducted from income include decreases in the deferred tax liability and amortization of the premium on bonds payable.

Finally, gains (losses) on fixed assets require adjustment, since the cash received is not measured by the gain (loss), that is, a fixed asset with a book value of $10, sold for $15 in cash, provides $15 in cash but is reported as only a $5 gain on the income statement. The $15 is shown as a separate item on the cash flow statement under investing activities and the $5 gain is subtracted from income. Losses on asset disposals are added back to income.

When preparing the cash flows from operating activities section of a Statement of Cash Flows under the indirect method, reconstructing journal entries may help in determining if an item should be added or subtracted to net income.

For example, if accounts receivable increased by $20,000 over the year, the journal entry that would result in an increase to accounts receivable would be

```
Accounts receivable        xx
   Sales                          xx
```

This entry results in an increase to net income (through sales), but cash is not affected. Therefore, the amount of the increase is deducted from net income in determining cash flows from operating activities.

If accounts payable decreased by $35,000, the entry for a decrease in accounts payable would be

```
Accounts payable        xx
   Cash                       xx
```

Since the corresponding credit results in a decrease to cash, the amount of this decrease should be deducted from net income in determining cash flows from operating activities.

When the **indirect** method is used, SFAS 95 permits, but does not require, separate disclosure of cash flows related to extraordinary items and discontinued operations. If an entity chooses to disclose this information, disclosure must be consistent for all periods affected. Extraordinary items, if disclosed, should be added to (or subtracted from) operating activities (adjustment to net income) at the gross amount, not the net-of-tax amount. Under either method, the extraordinary item should be included in financing or investing activities, whichever is appropriate.

The direct and indirect approaches will both be illustrated throughout the remainder of this module.

**ADJUSTMENTS TO NET INCOME FOR INDIRECT METHOD**

| *Add to net income* | *Deduct from net income* |
|---|---|
| **Decreases in:** | **Increases in:** |
| Accounts receivable (net) | Accounts receivable (net) |
| Inventories | Inventories |
| Prepaid expenses | Prepaid expenses |
| Deferred tax asset | Deferred tax asset |
| **Increases in:** | **Decreases in:** |
| Accounts payable | Accounts payable |
| Income taxes payable | Income taxes payable |
| Deferred tax liability | Deferred tax liability |
| Interest payable | Interest payable |
| Other accrued payables | Other accrued payables |
| Unearned revenue | Unearned revenue |

**Other items:**

- Losses from disposals of property, plant, and equipment and available-for-sale investments
- Depreciation expense
- Amortization expense related to intangible assets and bond discounts
- Bad debts expense (if adjustment for accounts receivable is based upon the gross, not the net, change in accounts receivable)
- Losses from early extinguishments of debt

**Other items:**

- Gains from disposals of property, plant and equipment and available-for-sale investments
- Undistributed income from equity method investments (equity income less the cash dividends received during the period)
- Amortization of a bond premium
- Gains from early extinguishments of debt

## D.  Example of Statement of Cash Flows

The following information pertains to the Haner Company at December 31, 2007.  Comparative balance sheets for 2006 and 2007 are as follows:

|  | *2007* | *2006* | *Net change* |
|---|---|---|---|
| Cash | $ 9,000 | $ 8,000 | $ 1,000 |
| Treasury bills | 4,000 | 3,000 | 1,000 |
| Accounts receivable | 4,000 | 5,000 | (1,000) |
| Inventory | 1,000 | 2,000 | (1,000) |
| Prepaid insurance | 2,000 | 3,000 | (1,000) |
| Investment in Simba Co. (held-for-trading) | 15,000 | 15,000 | -- |
| Market increase adjustment (trading) | 3,000 | -- | 3,000 |
| Investment in ABC Co. (available-for-sale) | 15,400 | 22,000 | (6,600) |
| Market decrease adjustment (available-for-sale) | (3,500) | -- | (3,500) |
| Fixed assets | 22,000 | 17,000 | 5,000 |
| Accumulated depreciation | (5,000) | (4,000) | (1,000) |
| Deferred tax asset | 1,400 | -- | 1,400 |
|  | $68,300 | $71,000 | $(2,700) |
| Accounts payable | $ 4,000 | $ 7,000 | $(3,000) |
| Income tax payable | 3,000 | 1,000 | 2,000 |
| Deferred tax liability | 6,360 | 3,000 | 3,360 |
| Bonds payable | 5,000 | 10,000 | (5,000) |
| Common stock | 20,000 | 20,000 | -- |
| Accumulated other comprehensive income |  |  |  |
| Unrealized loss on available-for-sale securities (net of tax) | (2,100) | -- | (2,100) |
| Retained earnings | 32,040 | 30,000 | 2,040 |
|  | $68,300 | $71,000 | $(2,700) |

**Income Statement** for 2007 is as follows:

| | | |
|---|---|---|
| Net sales | | $50,000 |
| Cost of goods sold | | (20,000) |
| Gross profit | | 30,000 |
| Operating expenses | | (17,000) |
| Income from operations | | 13,000 |
| Other revenue and gains | $5,000 | |
| Other expenses and losses | (2,560) | 2,440 |
| Income before extraordinary item and income taxes | | 15,440 |
| Income tax expense: | | |
| Current portion | 5,000 | |
| Deferred portion | 3,360 | 8,360 |
| Net income | | $7,080 |

**Statement of Comprehensive Income** for 2007 is as follows:

| | | |
|---|---|---|
| Net income | | $7,080 |
| Other comprehensive income | | |
| Unrealized loss on available-for-sale securities, (net of tax of $2,000) | ($3,000) | |
| Less: | | |
| Reclassification on sale of available-for-sale securities, (net of tax of $600) | (900) | (2,100) |
| Comprehensive income | | $4,980 |

Additional information includes

- Treasury bills have a maturity of less than three months from date of purchase
- Fixed assets costing $5,000 with a book value of $2,000 were sold for $4,000
- Three-year insurance policy was purchased in 2005
- At 12/31/07, available-for-sale investments with a book value of $6,600 at 12/31/06 and $5,100 at 12/31/07 sold for $5,100.
- Additional bonds were issued on 12/31/07 for $4,000. There was no premium or discount.
- Bonds with a book value of $9,000 were retired on 12/31/07.
- Other revenue and gains include a $3,000 unrealized gain recognized for trading securities
- Other expenses and losses consist of $1,060 interest paid and $1,500 realized loss on available-for-sale securities
- Changes in investments:
  - No changes in fair value of the investments occurred prior to 2007
  - There were no sales or purchases of trading securities during 2007
  - The tax rate is 40%

1. **Procedural Steps**

   a.  The first step is to calculate the change in cash and cash equivalents.

   | | 2007 | 2006 | Change |
   |---|---|---|---|
   | Cash | $9,000 | $8,000 | +$1,000 |
   | Treasury bills | 4,000 | 3,000 | + 1,000 |
   | Net change in cash and cash equivalents | | | +$2,000 |

   b.  Calculate net cash flows from operating activities

   (1) Indirect approach

   | | | |
   |---|---|---|
   | Net income | $ 7,080 | |
   | Decrease in accounts receivable | 1,000 | (a) |
   | Decrease in inventory | 1,000 | (b) |
   | Decrease in prepaid insurance | 1,000 | (c) |
   | Decrease in accounts payable | (3,000) | (d) |
   | Increase in income tax payable | 2,000 | (e) |
   | Increase in deferred tax liability | 3,360 | (f) |
   | Unrealized gain on trading securities | (3,000) | (g) |
   | Realized loss on available-for-sale securities | 1,500 | (h) |
   | Gain on sale of fixed assets | (2,000) | (i) |
   | Depreciation expense | 4,000 | (j) |
   | Net cash flows from operating activities | | $12,940 |

   Reconstructing journal entries may serve to explain the effect on net income of an increase or decrease of a particular account.

   (a) **Accounts receivable.** For accounts receivable to decrease, the journal entry must have been

   | | | |
   |---|---|---|
   | Cash | xx | |
   | Accounts receivable | | xx |

Cash increased as a result of the collection of accounts receivable. The $1,000 decrease in accounts receivable should be added to net income.

| | | |
|---|---|---|
| Cost of goods sold | xx | |
|     Inventory | | xx |

(b) **Inventory.** For inventory to decrease, the entry must have been

Expenses (CGS) increased without an additional cash outlay for inventory, so the $1,000 decrease is added back to net income.

(c) **Prepaid insurance.** For prepaid insurance to decrease, the entry must have been

| | | |
|---|---|---|
| Insurance expense | xx | |
|     Prepaid insurance | | xx |

Because expenses increased without a corresponding cash outlay, the $1,000 decrease in prepaid insurance should be added to net income.

(d) **Accounts payable.** For accounts payable to decrease, the entry must have been

| | | |
|---|---|---|
| Accounts payable | xx | |
|     Cash | | xx |

The entry involves a cash outlay, so the $3,000 decrease in accounts payable is deducted from net income.

(e) **Income tax payable.** For income tax payable to increase, the entry must have been

| | | |
|---|---|---|
| Income tax expense | xx | |
|     Income tax payable | | xx |

Expenses increased without an actual cash outlay; therefore the $2,000 increase in the liability is added back to net income.

(f) **Deferred tax liability.** For deferred tax liability to increase, the entry must have been

| | | |
|---|---|---|
| Income tax expense | xx | |
|     Deferred tax liability | | xx |

Expenses increased without an actual cash outlay; therefore the $3,360 increase in the liability, which is a noncash expense, is added back to net income.

(g) **Unrealized gain on trading securities.** The entry to record the unrealized gain on trading securities would have been

| | | |
|---|---|---|
| Investment in Simba Co.—held-for-trading | 3,000 | |
|     Unrealized holding gain | | 3,000 |

Since unrealized gains on trading securities are recognized as income but do not involve a cash inflow, such gains must be subtracted from net income.

(h) **Realized loss on available-for-sale securities.** When $5,100 stock in ABC Co. was sold, the previously unrealized loss of $1,500 ($5,100 FMV at 12/31/07 – $6,600 FMV at 12/31/06) which arose in 2007 became realized. The entry to record the sale would have been

| | | |
|---|---|---|
| Cash | 5,100 | |
| Realized loss | 1,500 | |
|     Available for sale | | 6,600 |

Because the realized loss does not involve any cash outflow, it must be added back to net income. Note that a $1,500 unrealized loss would have been recognized in financial statements prepared during 2007. The entry to remove this amount from the other comprehensive income account entitled "Unrealized loss on available-for-sale securities account" and the tax effect is

| | | |
|---|---|---|
| Adjustment to market (available-for-sale securities) | 1,500 | |
| Deferred tax benefit—unrealized loss | 600 | |
|     Unrealized loss on available-for-sale securities | | 1,500 |
|     Deferred tax asset | | 600 |

Since an unrealized loss on AFS securities of $3,500 was recognized during 2007 (from 2006 to 2007), a $5,000 decline in FMV must have occurred in 2007, as shown below. The deferred tax asset of $1,400 came from recognizing the future benefit of the unrealized loss of $3,500. The entry was

| Deferred tax asset | 1,400 | |
|---|---|---|
| Deferred tax expense (benefit) | | 1,400 |

| Available-for-Sale Securities | | | Market Adjustment (Available-for-Sale Securities) | | |
|---|---|---|---|---|---|
| 2006 Bal. | 22,000 | | | | -- 2006 Bal. |
| | | 6,600 Sale | Sale | 1,500 | 5,000 2007 Unreal. loss |
| 2007 Bal. | 15,400 | | | | 3,500 2007 Bal. |

| Unrealized Loss on AFS Securities | | | Deferred Tax Benefit— Unrealized Loss | | |
|---|---|---|---|---|---|
| 2006 Bal. | -- | 1,500 Realized upon sale | Sale | 600 | -- |
| Unreal. Loss recog. During year | 5,000 | 3,500 Closing entry | Closing entry | 1,400 | 2,000 2007 adj. |
| 2007 Bal. | -- | | 2007 Bal. | | -- |

| Deferred Tax Asset | | | Accumulated Other Comprehensive Income | | |
|---|---|---|---|---|---|
| 2006 Bal. | -- | 600 Sale | | | |
| 2007 Adj. | 2,000 | | Closing entry | 3,500 | 1,400 Closing entry |
| 2007 Bal. | 1,400 | | 2007 Bal. | | 2,100 |

Because unrealized gains/losses on available-for-sale securities do not affect cash flows, no adjustment for this change is necessary on the statement of cash flows.

(i) **Gain on sale of fixed assets.** The entry to record the sale would have been

| | | |
|---|---|---|
| Cash | 4,000 | |
| Accumulated depreciation | 3,000 | |
| Gain on sale | | 2,000 |
| Asset | | 5,000 |

The total amount of cash received in payment for the asset, not just the amount of the gain, represents the cash inflow. Since cash inflow from the sale (including the amount of the gain) appears in the investing section, the gain should be subtracted from net income.

(j) **Depreciation expense.** The entry to record depreciation is

| | | |
|---|---|---|
| Depreciation expense | 4,000 | |
| Accumulated depreciation | | 4,000 |

Because expenses increased without a corresponding cash outlay, the amount recorded for depreciation expense should be added to net income. In this case, the increase in accumulated depreciation must take into consideration the accumulated depreciation removed with the sale of the asset.

| AD | | |
|---|---|---|
| AD of sold asset | 3,000* | 4,000 Beg. bal. |
| | | 4,000 Depreciation (plug) |
| | | 5,000 End. bal. |

\* *$5,000 Cost – $2,000 book value*

(2) Direct approach

| | | |
|---|---|---|
| Cash received from customers | | $51,000 (a) |
| Cash provided by operating activities | | |
| Cash paid to suppliers | 22,000 (b) | |
| Cash paid for operating expenses | 12,000 (c) | |
| Cash paid for interest | 1,060 (d) | |
| Cash paid for income taxes | 3,000 (e) | |
| Cash disbursed for operating activities | | 38,060 |
| Net cash flows from operating activities | | $12,940 |

(a) **Cash received from customers.** Net sales + Beginning AR – Ending AR = Cash received from customers ($50,000 + $5,000 – $4,000 = $51,000). Cash received from customers also may be calculated by analyzing T-accounts.

| Accounts Receivable | | |
|---|---|---|
| Beg. bal. | 5,000 | |
| Sales | 50,000 | 51,000 Cash collected |
| End. bal. | 4,000 | |

(b) **Cash paid to suppliers.** Cost of goods sold + Beginning AP – Ending AP + Ending inventory – Beginning inventory = Cash paid to suppliers ($20,000 + $7,000 – $4,000 +

$1,000 – $2,000 = $22,000). This is a two-account analysis. The amount for cash paid to suppliers equals the debit to accounts payable, but to solve for that amount, you must first determine purchases. To calculate purchases you must analyze the inventory account.

Step 1.  Calculate purchases

| | Inventory | | |
|---|---|---|---|
| Beg. bal. | 2,000 | | |
| Purchases | 19,000 | 20,000 | CGS |
| End. bal. | 1,000 | | |

Step 2.  Calculate cash payments to suppliers

| | Accounts Payable | | |
|---|---|---|---|
| Cash paid to suppliers | 22,000 | 7,000 | Beg. bal. |
| | | 19,000 | Purchases |
| | | 4,000 | End. bal. |

Note that the $2,000 difference between the $20,000 CGS (accrual-basis amount) and the $22,000 cash payments made to suppliers (cash-basis amount) equals the difference between the $1,000 decrease in inventory and the $3,000 decrease in accounts payable when the indirect method is used. However, under the indirect method the difference is deducted from net income. This is because when the direct method is used, expenses such as CGS are examined as **outflows** of cash, whereas when the indirect method is used, net income (revenue-expenses, including CGS) is treated as a net cash **inflow**.

(c) **Cash paid for operating expenses.** Operating expenses + Ending prepaid expenses – Beginning prepaid expenses – Depreciation expense (and other noncash operating expenses) = Cash paid for operating expenses ($17,000 + $2,000 – $3,000 – $4,000 = $12,000). The two accounts in this problem that relate to operating expenses are accumulated depreciation and prepaid insurance.

| | Prepaid Insurance | | | | | Accumulated Depreciation | | |
|---|---|---|---|---|---|---|---|---|
| Beg. bal. | 3,000 | | | | | | 4,000 | Beg. bal. |
| | | 1,000 | Insurance expense | AD of sold asset | 3,000 | | 4,000 | Depreciation expense |
| End. bal. | 2,000 | | | | | | 5,000 | End. bal. |

Since neither the expiration of prepaid insurance nor depreciation expense required a cash outlay, cash basis operating expenses are accrual expenses of $17,000 less depreciation ($4,000) and insurance expense ($1,000), or $12,000.

(d) **Cash paid for interest.** No analysis needed; amount was given in problem

(e) **Cash paid for income taxes.** Current portion of income tax expense + Beginning income tax payable – Ending income tax payable = Cash paid for income taxes ($5,000 + $1,000 – $3,000 = $3,000). The journal entry for income tax expense is

| | | |
|---|---|---|
| Income tax expense—current | 5,000 | |
| Income tax expense—deferred | 3,360 | |
| Income tax payable (current portion) | | 5,000 |
| Deferred tax liability | | 1,360 |

Therefore, taxes paid are $3,000, as shown in the T-account below.

| | Income Tax Payable | | |
|---|---|---|---|
| | | 1,000 | Beg. bal. |
| Income taxes paid | 3,000 | 5,000 | Current portion |
| | | 3,000 | End. bal. |

c.  Analyze other accounts and determine whether the change is a cash inflow or outflow and whether it is a financing, an investing, or a noncash investing and financing activity.

(1) Investments in ABC Co. decreased by $5,100 when this portion was sold (cash inflow, investing activity). The entry to record the sale was

| | | |
|---|---|---|
| Cash | 5,100 | |
| Investment in ABC Co.—available-for-sale | | 5,100 |

(2) Fixed assets increased by $5,000 after $5,000 of assets were sold for $4,000 (cash inflow, investing activity). Thus, $10,000 of fixed assets were purchased (cash outflow, investing activity).

Fixed Assets

| | | | |
|---|---|---|---|
| Beg. bal. | $17,000 | | |
| Purchase of new assets | 10,000 | 5,000 | Sold asset |
| End. bal. | 22,000 | | |

(3) Bonds payable increased by $4,000 when additional bonds were issued (cash inflow, financing activity).

(4) Bonds payable decreased by $9,000 when they were retired (cash outflow, financing activity). The entry to record the retirement of debt was

| | | |
|---|---|---|
| Bonds payable | 9,000 | |
| Cash | | 9,000 |

(5) Common stock had no change.

(6) Retained earnings increased $2,040 after net income of $7,080, indicating a dividend of $5,040 (cash outflow, financing activity).

Retained Earnings

| | | | |
|---|---|---|---|
| | | 30,000 | Beg. bal. |
| Cash dividend | 5,040 | 7,080 | Net income |
| | | 32,040 | End. bal. |

d. Prepare formal statement

**Haner Company**
**STATEMENT OF CASH FLOWS**
*For the Year Ended December 31, 2007*

| | | |
|---|---|---|
| *Cash flows from operating activities:* | | |
| Cash received from customers | $51,000 | |
| Cash provided by operating activities | | $51,000 |
| Cash paid to suppliers | 22,000 | |
| Cash paid for operating expenses | 12,000 | |
| Cash paid for income taxes | 3,000 | |
| Cash paid for interest expense | 1,060 | |
| Cash disbursed for operating activities | | 38,060 |
| Net cash flows from operating activities | | $12,940 |
| | | |
| *Cash flows from investing activities:* | | |
| Proceeds from sale of investments | $5,100 | |
| Proceeds from sale of fixed assets | 4,000 | |
| Acquisition of fixed assets | (10,000) | |
| Net cash used by investing activities | | (900) |
| | | |
| *Cash flows from financing activities:* | | |
| Proceeds from sale of bonds | $4,000 | |
| Repayment of long-term debt | (9,000) | |
| Dividends paid | (5,040) | |
| Net cash used by financing activities | | (10,040) |
| Net increase in cash and cash equivalents | | $ 2,000 |
| Cash and cash equivalents at beginning of year | | 11,000 |
| Cash and cash equivalents at end of year | | $13,000 |

**Reconciliation of net income to cash provided by operating activities:**
[This schedule would include the amounts from D.1.b.(1) (near the beginning of this example) starting with "net income" and ending with Net cash flows from operating activities of $13,040.]

**Disclosure of accounting policy:**
For purposes of the statement of cash flows, the Company considers all highly liquid debt instruments purchased with a maturity of three months or less to be cash equivalents.

Note that if the reconciliation approach for operating activities had been shown in the body of the statement instead of the direct approach, an additional schedule showing interest paid and income taxes paid would be necessary.

### E.  Capital Leases

In the period an entity enters into a capital lease, a noncash financing and investing activity in the amount of the present value of the minimum lease payments is reported following the cash flow statement. As payments are made by the lessee, the principal reduction component is reported as a cash outflow under financing activities.  The interest component is reported in the operating activities section under the direct method.  Under the indirect method, interest paid must be disclosed as supplementary information.

### F.  Research Component

SFAS 95 was effective for fiscal years ending after July 15, 1988.  Typical research issues may involve determining the cash equivalents of the enterprise; classifying items as either operating, investing, or financing activities; and identifying significant noncash transactions.  Note that SFAS 95, para 33 specifically prohibits reporting cash flow per share information on the statement of cash flows.  Note also that SFAS 115, *Accounting for Certain Investments in Debt and Equity Securities*, was issued after the standard on the statement of cash flows; therefore, the treatment of trading and available-for-sale securities is found in SFAS 115, para 18.

The most significant amendments to SFAS 95 are SFAS 102 and SFAS 145.  SFAS 102, para 5 provides that a statement of cash flows is not required to be provided by defined benefit pension plans or other employee benefit plans that present financial information in accordance with SFAS 35.  SFAS 102 also provides that certain investment companies may be exempted from the requirement to provide a cash flow statement if certain conditions are met.  SFAS 145, para 9, issued in April 2003, made technical corrections to SFAS 95.

Below are keywords for researching issues on the statement of cash flows.  Note that in some paragraphs in FARS, the work "transaction" or "transactions" (rather than "activity") is used to discuss whether an item is included in the operating, investing, or financing section of the statement of cash flows.

| | |
|---|---|
| Cash equivalents | Noncash activities |
| Financing activities | Noncash transactions |
| Financing transactions | Operating activities |
| Investing activities | Operating transactions |
| Investing transactions | Reconciliation of net income |

**MULTIPLE-CHOICE QUESTIONS (1-37)**

**1.** At December 31, 2007, Kale Co. had the following balances in the accounts it maintains at First State Bank:

| | |
|---|---|
| Checking account #101 | $175,000 |
| Checking account #201 | (10,000) |
| Money market account | 25,000 |
| 90-day certificate of deposit, due 2/28/08 | 50,000 |
| 180-day certificate of deposit, due 3/15/08 | 80,000 |

Kale classifies investments with original maturities of three months or less as cash equivalents. In its December 31, 2007 balance sheet, what amount should Kale report as cash and cash equivalents?

    a. $190,000
    b. $200,000
    c. $240,000
    d. $320,000

**2.** The primary purpose of a statement of cash flows is to provide relevant information about
    a. Differences between net income and associated cash receipts and disbursements.
    b. An enterprise's ability to generate future positive net cash flows.
    c. The cash receipts and cash disbursements of an enterprise during a period.
    d. An enterprise's ability to meet cash operating needs.

**3.** Mend Co. purchased a three-month US Treasury bill. Mend's policy is to treat as cash equivalents all highly liquid investments with an original maturity of three months or less when purchased. How should this purchase be reported in Mend's statement of cash flows?
    a. As an outflow from operating activities.
    b. As an outflow from investing activities.
    c. As an outflow from financing activities.
    d. Not reported.

**4.** Alp, Inc. had the following activities during 2007:

- Acquired 2,000 shares of stock in Maybel, Inc. for $26,000. Alp intends to hold the stock as a long-term investment.
- Sold an investment in Rate Motors for $35,000 when the carrying value was $33,000.
- Acquired a $50,000, four-year certificate of deposit from a bank. (During the year, interest of $3,750 was paid to Alp.)
- Collected dividends of $1,200 on stock investments.

In Alp's 2007 statement of cash flows, net cash used in investing activities should be
    a. $37,250
    b. $38,050
    c. $39,800
    d. $41,000

**5.** In 2007, a tornado completely destroyed a building belonging to Holland Corp. The building cost $100,000 and had accumulated depreciation of $48,000 at the time of the loss. Holland received a cash settlement from the insurance company and reported an extraordinary loss of $21,000. In Holland's 2007 cash flow statement, the net change reported in the cash flows from investing activities section should be a
    a. $10,000 increase.
    b. $21,000 decrease.

    c. $31,000 increase.
    d. $52,000 decrease.

**6.** In a statement of cash flows, if used equipment is sold at a gain, the amount shown as a cash inflow from investing activities equals the carrying amount of the equipment
    a. Plus the gain.
    b. Plus the gain and less the amount of tax attributable to the gain.
    c. Plus both the gain and the amount of tax attributable to the gain.
    d. With **no** addition or subtraction.

**7.** On September 1, 2007, Canary Co. sold used equipment for a cash amount equaling its carrying amount for both book and tax purposes. On September 15, 2007, Canary replaced the equipment by paying cash and signing a note payable for new equipment. The cash paid for the new equipment exceeded the cash received for the old equipment. How should these equipment transactions be reported in Canary's 2007 statement of cash flows?
    a. Cash outflow equal to the cash paid less the cash received.
    b. Cash outflow equal to the cash paid and note payable less the cash received.
    c. Cash inflow equal to the cash received and a cash outflow equal to the cash paid and note payable.
    d. Cash inflow equal to the cash received and a cash outflow equal to the cash paid.

**Items 8 and 9** are based on the following:

A company acquired a building, paying a portion of the purchase price in cash and issuing a mortgage note payable to the seller for the balance.

**8.** In a statement of cash flows, what amount is included in investing activities for the above transaction?
    a. Cash payment.
    b. Acquisition price.
    c. Zero.
    d. Mortgage amount.

**9.** In a statement of cash flows, what amount is included in financing activities for the above transaction?
    a. Cash payment.
    b. Acquisition price.
    c. Zero.
    d. Mortgage amount.

**10.** Fara Co. reported bonds payable of $47,000 at December 31, 2006, and $50,000 at December 31, 2007. During 2007, Fara issued $20,000 of bonds payable in exchange for equipment. There was no amortization of bond premium or discount during the year. What amount should Fara report in its 2007 statement of cash flows for redemption of bonds payable?
    a. $ 3,000
    b. $17,000
    c. $20,000
    d. $23,000

**Items 11 and 12** are based on the following:

In preparing its cash flow statement for the year ended December 31, 2007, Reve Co. collected the following data:

| | |
|---|---|
| Gain on sale of equipment | $ (6,000) |
| Proceeds from sale of equipment | 10,000 |
| Purchase of A.S., Inc. bonds (par value $200,000) | (180,000) |
| Amortization of bond discount | 2,000 |
| Dividends declared | (45,000) |
| Dividends paid | (38,000) |
| Proceeds from sale of treasury stock (carrying amount $65,000) | 75,000 |

In its December 31, 2007 statement of cash flows,

**11.** What amount should Reve report as net cash used in investing activities?

    a.  $170,000
    b.  $176,000
    c.  $188,000
    d.  $194,000

**12.** What amount should Reve report as net cash provided by financing activities?

    a.  $20,000
    b.  $27,000
    c.  $30,000
    d.  $37,000

**13.** On July 1, 2007, Dewey Co. signed a twenty-year building lease that it reported as a capital lease. Dewey paid the monthly lease payments when due. How should Dewey report the effect of the lease payments in the financing activities section of its 2007 statement of cash flows?

    a.  An inflow equal to the present value of future lease payments at July 1, 2007, less 2007 principal and interest payments.
    b.  An outflow equal to the 2007 principal and interest payments on the lease.
    c.  An outflow equal to the 2007 principal payments only.
    d.  The lease payments should **not** be reported in the financing activities section.

**14.** Which of the following should be reported when preparing a statement of cash flows?

| | Conversion of long-term debt to common stock | Conversion of preferred stock |
|---|---|---|
| a. | No | No |
| b. | No | Yes |
| c. | Yes | Yes |
| d. | Yes | No |

**15.** Which of the following information should be disclosed as supplemental information in the statement of cash flows?

| | Cash flow per share | Conversion of debt to equity |
|---|---|---|
| a. | Yes | Yes |
| b. | Yes | No |
| c. | No | Yes |
| d. | No | No |

**16.** Which of the following is **not** disclosed on the statement of cash flows when prepared under the direct method, either on the face of the statement or in a separate schedule?

    a.  The major classes of gross cash receipts and gross cash payments.
    b.  The amount of income taxes paid.
    c.  A reconciliation of net income to net cash flow from operations.
    d.  A reconciliation of ending retained earnings to net cash flow from operations.

**Items 17 through 21** are based on the following:

Flax Corp. uses the direct method to prepare its statement of cash flows. Flax's trial balances at December 31, 2007 and 2006 are as follows:

| | December 31 2007 | 2006 |
|---|---|---|
| **Debits** | | |
| Cash | $ 35,000 | $ 32,000 |
| Accounts receivable | 33,000 | 30,000 |
| Inventory | 31,000 | 47,000 |
| Property, plant, & equipment | 100,000 | 95,000 |
| Unamortized bond discount | 4,500 | 5,000 |
| Cost of goods sold | 250,000 | 380,000 |
| Selling expenses | 141,500 | 172,000 |
| General and administrative expenses | 137,000 | 151,300 |
| Interest expense | 4,300 | 2,600 |
| Income tax expense | 20,400 | 61,200 |
| | $756,700 | $976,100 |
| **Credits** | | |
| Allowance for uncollectible accounts | $ 1,300 | $ 1,100 |
| Accumulated depreciation | 16,500 | 15,000 |
| Trade accounts payable | 25,000 | 17,500 |
| Income taxes payable | 21,000 | 27,100 |
| Deferred income taxes | 5,300 | 4,600 |
| 8% callable bonds payable | 45,000 | 20,000 |
| Common stock | 50,000 | 40,000 |
| Additional paid-in capital | 9,100 | 7,500 |
| Retained earnings | 44,700 | 64,600 |
| Sales | 538,800 | 778,700 |
| | $756,700 | $976,100 |

- Flax purchased $5,000 in equipment during 2007.
- Flax allocated one third of its depreciation expense to selling expenses and the remainder to general and administrative expenses. There were no write-offs of accounts receivable during 2007.

What amounts should Flax report in its statement of cash flows for the year ended December 31, 2007, for the following:

**17.** Cash collected from customers?

    a.  $541,800
    b.  $541,600
    c.  $536,000
    d.  $535,800

**18.** Cash paid for goods to be sold?

    a.  $258,500
    b.  $257,500
    c.  $242,500
    d.  $226,500

**19.** Cash paid for interest?

    a.  $4,800
    b.  $4,300
    c.  $3,800
    d.  $1,700

**20.** Cash paid for income taxes?

    a.  $25,800
    b.  $20,400
    c.  $19,700
    d.  $15,000

**21.** Cash paid for selling expenses?

    a.  $142,000
    b.  $141,500
    c.  $141,000
    d.  $140,000

**22.** In a statement of cash flows, which of the following would increase reported cash flows from operating activities using the direct method? (Ignore income tax considerations.)
- a. Dividends received from investments.
- b. Gain on sale of equipment.
- c. Gain on early retirement of bonds.
- d. Change from straight-line to accelerated depreciation.

**23.** A company's wages payable increased from the beginning to the end of the year. In the company's statement of cash flows in which the operating activities section is prepared under the direct method, the cash paid for wages would be
- a. Salary expense plus wages payable at the beginning of the year.
- b. Salary expense plus the increase in wages payable from the beginning to the end of the year.
- c. Salary expense less the increase in wages payable from the beginning to the end of the year.
- d. The same as salary expense.

**24.** Metro, Inc. reported net income of $150,000 for 2007. Changes occurred in several balance sheet accounts during 2007 as follows:

| | |
|---|---|
| Investment in Videogold, Inc. stock, carried on the equity basis | $5,500 increase |
| Accumulated depreciation, caused by major repair to projection equipment | 2,100 decrease |
| Premium on bonds payable | 1,400 decrease |
| Deferred income tax liability (long-term) | 1,800 increase |

In Metro's 2007 cash flow statement, the reported net cash provided by operating activities should be
- a. $150,400
- b. $148,300
- c. $144,900
- d. $142,800

**25.** Lino Co.'s worksheet for the preparation of its 2007 statement of cash flows included the following:

| | December 31 | January 1 |
|---|---|---|
| Accounts receivable | $29,000 | $23,000 |
| Allowance for uncollectible accounts | 1,000 | 800 |
| Prepaid rent expense | 8,200 | 12,400 |
| Accounts payable | 22,400 | 19,400 |

Lino's 2007 net income is $150,000. What amount should Lino include as net cash provided by operating activities in the statement of cash flows?
- a. $151,400
- b. $151,000
- c. $148,600
- d. $145,400

**26.** In a statement of cash flows (using indirect approach for operating activities) an increase in inventories should be presented as a(n)
- a. Outflow of cash.
- b. Inflow and outflow of cash.
- c. Addition to net income.
- d. Deduction from net income.

**27.** How should a gain from the sale of used equipment for cash be reported in a statement of cash flows using the indirect method?
- a. In investment activities as a reduction of the cash inflow from the sale.

- b. In investment activities as a cash outflow.
- c. In operating activities as a deduction from income.
- d. In operating activities as an addition to income.

**28.** Would the following be added back to net income when reporting operating activities' cash flows by the indirect method?

| | Excess of treasury stock acquisition cost over sales proceeds (cost method) | Bond discount amortization |
|---|---|---|
| a. | Yes | Yes |
| b. | No | No |
| c. | No | Yes |
| d. | Yes | No |

**29.** Which of the following should **not** be disclosed in an enterprise's statement of cash flows prepared using the indirect method?
- a. Interest paid, net of amounts capitalized.
- b. Income taxes paid.
- c. Cash flow per share.
- d. Dividends paid on preferred stock.

**Items 30 through 32** are based on the following:

The differences in Beal Inc.'s balance sheet accounts at December 31, 2007 and 2006, are presented below.

| | Increase (Decrease) |
|---|---|
| **Assets** | |
| Cash and cash equivalents | $ 120,000 |
| Available-for-sale securities | 300,000 |
| Accounts receivable, net | -- |
| Inventory | 80,000 |
| Long-term investments | (100,000) |
| Plant assets | 700,000 |
| Accumulated depreciation | -- |
| | $1,100,000 |
| **Liabilities and Stockholders' Equity** | |
| Accounts payable and accrued liabilities | $ (5,000) |
| Dividends payable | 160,000 |
| Short-term bank debt | 325,000 |
| Long-term debt | 110,000 |
| Common stock, $10 par | 100,000 |
| Additional paid-in capital | 120,000 |
| Retained earnings | 290,000 |
| | $1,100,000 |

The following additional information relates to 2007:

- Net income was $790,000.
- Cash dividends of $500,000 were declared.
- Building costing $600,000 and having a carrying amount of $350,000 was sold for $350,000.
- Equipment costing $110,000 was acquired through issuance of long-term debt.
- A long-term investment was sold for $135,000. There were no other transactions affecting long-term investments.
- 10,000 shares of common stock were issued for $22 a share.

In Beal's 2007 statement of cash flows,

**30.** Net cash provided by operating activities was
- a. $1,160,000
- b. $1,040,000
- c. $ 920,000
- d. $ 705,000

**31.** Net cash used in investing activities was
- a. $1,005,000

b. $1,190,000
c. $1,275,000
d. $1,600,000

**32.** Net cash provided by financing activities was
   a. $  20,000
   b. $  45,000
   c. $150,000
   d. $205,000

**Items 33 through 36** relate to data to be reported in the statement of cash flows of Debbie Dress Shops, Inc. based on the following information:

**Debbie Dress Shops, Inc.**
**BALANCE SHEETS**

| | December 31 | |
| --- | --- | --- |
| | 2007 | 2006 |
| **Assets** | | |
| Current assets: | | |
| Cash | $ 300,000 | $ 200,000 |
| Accounts receivable—net | 840,000 | 580,000 |
| Merchandise inventory | 660,000 | 420,000 |
| Prepaid expenses | 100,000 | 50,000 |
| Total current assets | 1,900,000 | 1,250,000 |
| Long-term investments | 80,000 | -- |
| Land, buildings, and fixtures | 1,130,000 | 600,000 |
| Less accumulated depreciation | 110,000 | 50,000 |
| | 1,020,000 | 550,000 |
| Total assets | $3,000,000 | $1,800,000 |
| **Equities** | | |
| Current liabilities: | | |
| Accounts payable | $ 530,000 | $ 440,000 |
| Accrued expenses | 140,000 | 130,000 |
| Dividends payable | 70,000 | -- |
| Total current liabilities | 740,000 | 570,000 |
| Note payable—due 2009 | 500,000 | -- |
| Stockholders' equity: | | |
| Common stock | 1,200,000 | 900,000 |
| Retained earnings | 560,000 | 330,000 |
| | 1,760,000 | 1,230,000 |
| Total liabilities and stock-holders' equity | $3,000,000 | $1,800,000 |

**Debbie Dress Shops, Inc.**
**INCOME STATEMENTS**

| | Year ended December 31 | |
| --- | --- | --- |
| | 2007 | 2006 |
| Net credit sales | $6,400,000 | $4,000,000 |
| Cost of goods sold | 5,000,000 | 3,200,000 |
| Gross profit | 1,400,000 | 800,000 |
| Expenses (including income taxes) | 1,000,000 | 520,000 |
| Net income | $ 400,000 | $ 280,000 |

Additional information available included the following:

- All accounts receivable and accounts payable related to trade merchandise. Accounts payable are recorded net and always are paid to take all of the discount allowed. The allowance for doubtful accounts at the end of 2007 was the same as at the end of 2006; no receivables were charged against the allowance during 2007.
- The proceeds from the note payable were used to finance a new store building. Capital stock was sold to provide additional working capital.

**33.** Cash collected during 2007 from accounts receivable amounted to
   a. $5,560,000
   b. $5,840,000

c. $6,140,000
d. $6,400,000

**34.** Cash payments during 2007 on accounts payable to suppliers amounted to
   a. $4,670,000
   b. $4,910,000
   c. $5,000,000
   d. $5,150,000

**35.** Net cash provided by financing activities for 2007 totaled
   a. $140,000
   b. $300,000
   c. $500,000
   d. $700,000

**36.** Net cash used in investing activities during 2007 was
   a. $  80,000
   b. $530,000
   c. $610,000
   d. $660,000

**37.** Bee Co. uses the direct write-off method to account for uncollectible accounts receivable. During an accounting period, Bee's cash collections from customers equal sales adjusted for the addition or deduction of the following amounts:

| | Accounts written off | Increase in accounts receivable balance |
| --- | --- | --- |
| a. | Deduction | Deduction |
| b. | Addition | Deduction |
| c. | Deduction | Addition |
| d. | Addition | Addition |

SIMULATION PROBLEMS

**Simulation Problem 1**                              (50 to 60 minutes)

| Situation | | | | |
|---|---|---|---|---|
| | Concepts—<br>Direct Method | Statement of Cash Flows—<br>Indirect Method | Communication | Research |

The following is a condensed trial balance of Probe Co., a publicly held company, after adjustments for income tax expense.

*Probe Co.*
**CONDENSED TRIAL BALANCE**

| | 12/31/07<br>Balances<br>Dr. (Cr.) | 12/31/06<br>Balances<br>Dr. (Cr.) | Net<br>change<br>Dr. (Cr.) |
|---|---|---|---|
| Cash | $ 484,000 | $ 817,000 | $(333,000) |
| Accounts receivable, net | 670,000 | 610,000 | 60,000 |
| Property, plant, and equipment | 1,070,000 | 995,000 | 75,000 |
| Accumulated depreciation | (345,000) | (280,000) | (65,000) |
| Dividends payable | (25,000) | (10,000) | (15,000) |
| Income taxes payable | (60,000) | (150,000) | 90,000 |
| Deferred income tax liability | (63,000) | (42,000) | (21,000) |
| Bonds payable | (500,000) | (1,000,000) | 500,000 |
| Unamortized premium on bonds | (71,000) | (150,000) | 79,000 |
| Common stock | (350,000) | (150,000) | (200,000) |
| Additional paid-in capital | (430,000) | (375,000) | (55,000) |
| Retained earnings | (185,000) | (265,000) | 80,000 |
| Sales | (2,420,000) | | |
| Cost of sales | 1,863,000 | | |
| Selling and administrative expenses | 220,000 | | |
| Interest income | (14,000) | | |
| Interest expense | 46,000 | | |
| Depreciation | 88,000 | | |
| Loss on sale of equipment | 7,000 | | |
| Gain on extinguishment of bonds | (90,000) | | |
| Income tax expense | 105,000 | | |
| | $           0 | $           0 | $300,000 |

*Additional information*

- During 2007 equipment with an original cost of $50,000 was sold for cash, and equipment costing $125,000 was purchased.
- On January 1, 2007, bonds with a par value of $500,000 and related premium of $75,000 were redeemed. The $1,000 face value, 10% par bonds had been issued on January 1, 1998, to yield 8%. Interest is payable annually every December 31 through 2017.
- Probe's tax payments during 2007 were debited to Income Taxes Payable. Probe recorded a deferred income tax liability of $42,000 based on temporary differences of $120,000 and an enacted tax rate of 35% at December 31, 2006; prior to 2006 there were no temporary differences. Probe's 2007 financial statement income before income taxes was greater than its 2007 taxable income, due entirely to temporary differences, by $60,000. Probe's cumulative net taxable temporary differences at December 31, 2007, were $180,000. Probe's enacted tax rate for the current and future years is 35%.
- 60,000 shares of common stock, $2.50 par, were outstanding on December 31, 2006. Probe issued an additional 80,000 shares on April 1, 2007.
- There were no changes to retained earnings other than dividends declared.

| | Concepts—<br>Direct Method | | | |
|---|---|---|---|---|
| Situation | | Statement of Cash Flows—<br>Indirect Method | Communication | Research |

Below is a list of accounts and transactions. Prepare the outline of a statement of cash flows using the **direct method** by placing the appropriate items in the correct location on the statement of cash flows. Indicate whether each item selected for use in the statement of cash flows would be a cash inflow or a cash outflow.

| | | |
|---|---|---|
| Amortization of patents | Dividends received on trading securities | Issue of common stock |
| Borrow on long-term note payable | Gain on sale of land | Loss on sale of equipment |
| Cash collected on account | Increase in accounts receivable | Net income |
| Cash paid for inventory | Increase in dividends payable | Payment of dividend |
| Cash paid for supplies | Increase in inventories | Purchase of held-to-maturity securities |
| Cash sales | Increase in taxes payable | Purchase of treasury stock |
| Decrease in accounts payable | Interest accrued at December 31 | Redemption of bonds |
| Decrease in prepaid expenses | Interest expense | Sale of land |
| Depreciation expense | Interest paid on note | Taxes paid |

**Probe Co.**
**STATEMENT OF CASH FLOWS**
*For the Year Ending 12/31/07*

| | Cash Inflow or Cash Outflow |
|---|---|
| **From Operating Activities** | |
| | |
| | |
| | |
| | |
| | |
| | |
| | |
| | |
| | |
| | |
| **From Investing Activities** | |
| | |
| | |
| | |
| | |
| | |
| | |
| | |
| | |
| | |
| | |
| **From Financing Activities** | |
| | |
| | |
| | |
| | |
| | |
| | |
| | |
| | |
| | |

| Situation | Concepts—Direct Method | Statement of Cash Flows—Indirect Method | Communication | Research |
|---|---|---|---|---|

Prepare a statement of cash flows using the **indirect method**. Select the titles and the numbers from the lists provided. You may use a number more than once, if necessary. You should also enter the following amounts:

- Subtotals for each class of activity.
- Net Change in cash for the year.
- Reconciliation to cash amounts

Complete the following statement of cash flows using the **indirect method**. (Select from titles and amounts from the tables that follow.)

| Probe Co. STATEMENT OF CASH FLOWS For the Year Ending 12/31/07 | |
|---|---|
| | Cash Source (Use) |
| **From Operating Activities** | |
| | |
| | |
| | |
| | |
| | |
| | |
| | |
| | |
| | |
| | |
| **From Investing Activities** | |
| | |
| | |
| | |
| | |
| | |
| | |
| **From Financing Activities** | |
| | |
| | |
| | |
| | |
| | |

### Titles

| | | |
|---|---|---|
| Increase in accounts receivable | Decrease in bonds payable | Net income |
| Decrease in accounts receivable | Issue bonds | Net loss |
| Increase in property, plant, equipment | Redeem bonds | Taxes paid |
| Decrease in property, plant, equipment | Increase in unamortized premium on bonds | Interest paid |
| Purchase of equipment | Decrease in unamortized premium on bonds | Cash collections from customers |
| Sale of equipment | Gain on sale of bonds | Cash paid for expenses |
| Loss on sale of equipment | Increase in common stock | Net cash flows from operating activities |
| Increase in accumulated depreciation | Decrease in common stock | Net cash flows from investing activities |
| Decrease in accumulated depreciation | Issue common stock | Net cash flows from financing activities |
| Increase in income taxes payable | Repurchase common stock | Other significant noncash transactions |
| Decrease in income taxes payable | Increase in additional paid-in capital | Net increase in cash |
| Increase in deferred income tax liability | Decrease in additional paid-in capital | Net decrease in cash |
| Decrease in deferred income tax liability | Increase in retained earnings | Cash at beginning of year |
| Increase in bonds payable | Decrease in retained earnings | Cash at end of year |

### Amounts

| | | | | |
|---|---|---|---|---|
| 4,000 | 46,000 | 88,000 | 255,000 | 610,000 |
| 7,000 | 50,000 | 90,000 | 300,000 | 670,000 |
| 10,000 | 55,000 | 95,000 | 333,000 | 780,000 |
| 13,000 | 60,000 | 120,000 | 350,000 | 817,000 |
| 14,000 | 63,000 | 125,000 | 410,000 | 1,000,000 |
| 15,000 | 65,000 | 150,000 | 484,000 | 2,360,000 |
| 20,000 | 74,000 | 174,000 | 485,000 | 2,420,000 |
| 21,000 | 75,000 | 185,000 | 500,000 | 2,480,000 |
| 23,000 | 79,000 | 195,000 | 515,000 | 3,030,000 |
| 25,000 | 80,000 | 200,000 | 575,000 | |
| 42,000 | 85,000 | 240,000 | 590,000 | |

| | Communication | | |
|---|---|---|---|
| Situation | Concepts—<br>Direct Method | Statement of Cash Flows—<br>Indirect Method | Research |

The CEO of Probe would like to know what effect, if any, each of the following seven items have upon the preparation of a cash flow statement, assuming **direct** presentation is used to present cash flows from operations.

1. Accounts receivable—trade
2. Inventory
3. Depreciation
4. Deferred tax liability from interperiod allocation
5. Issuance of long-term debt in payment for a building
6. Payoff of current portion of debt
7. Sale of fixed asset resulting in a loss

Write a brief memorandum explaining how these items would be disclosed on the statement of cash flows.

To:     CEO, Probe Co.
From:   CPA Candidate
Re:     Statement of Cash Flows

| | | | Research |
|---|---|---|---|
| Situation | Concepts—<br>Direct Method | Statement of Cash Flows—<br>Indirect Method | Communication |

Suppose Probe had the following transactions. Research each item and select the appropriate paragraph from the authoritative literature that indicates how the item is disclosed on the statement of cash flows. Assume Probe uses the indirect method.

1. On February 2, 2007, Probe purchased 10,000 shares of stock of Stone Corporation. Stone Corporation paid a dividend of $2 per share to Probe on November 5, 2007. Probe's management believes it will hold the stock of Stone for at least 2 years.
2. Probe purchased new equipment for $100,000.
3. On June 1, 2007, Probe repurchased 4,000 shares of its own stock for $20 per share and immediately retired the shares.

---

**Simulation Problem 2**                (50 to 60 minutes)

| Situation | | | | |
|---|---|---|---|---|
| | Concepts | Calculations | Communication | Research |

The following is a condensed trial balance of Probe Co., a publicly held company, after adjustments for income tax expense.

*Probe Co.*
**CONDENSED TRIAL BALANCE**

| | 12/31/07<br>Balances<br>Dr. (Cr.) | 12/31/06<br>Balances<br>Dr. (Cr.) | Net<br>change<br>Dr. (Cr.) |
|---|---|---|---|
| Cash | $ 484,000 | $ 817,000 | $(333,000) |
| Accounts receivable, net | 670,000 | 610,000 | 60,000 |
| Property, plant, and equipment | 1,070,000 | 995,000 | 75,000 |
| Accumulated depreciation | (345,000) | (280,000) | (65,000) |
| Dividends payable | (25,000) | (10,000) | (15,000) |
| Income taxes payable | (60,000) | (150,000) | 90,000 |
| Deferred income tax liability | (63,000) | (42,000) | (21,000) |
| Bonds payable | (500,000) | (1,000,000) | 500,000 |
| Unamortized premium on bonds | (71,000) | (150,000) | 79,000 |
| Common stock | (350,000) | (150,000) | (200,000) |
| Additional paid-in capital | (430,000) | (375,000) | (55,000) |
| Retained earnings | (185,000) | (265,000) | 80,000 |

| | 12/31/07 Balances Dr. (Cr.) | 12/31/06 Balances Dr. (Cr.) | Net change Dr. (Cr.) |
|---|---|---|---|
| Sales | (2,420,000) | | |
| Cost of sales | 1,863,000 | | |
| Selling and administrative expenses | 220,000 | | |
| Interest income | (14,000) | | |
| Interest expense | 46,000 | | |
| Depreciation | 88,000 | | |
| Loss on sale of equipment | 7,000 | | |
| Gain on extinguishment of bonds | (90,000) | | |
| Income tax expense | 105,000 | | |
| | $_____0 | $_____0 | $300,000 |

### Additional information

- During 2007 equipment with an original cost of $50,000 was sold for cash, and equipment costing $125,000 was purchased.
- On January 1, 2007, bonds with a par value of $500,000 and related premium of $75,000 were redeemed. The $1,000 face value, 10% par bonds had been issued on January 1, 1998, to yield 8%. Interest is payable annually every December 31 through 2017.
- Probe's tax payments during 2007 were debited to Income Taxes Payable. Probe recorded a deferred income tax liability of $42,000 based on temporary differences of $120,000 and an enacted tax rate of 35% at December 31, 2006; prior to 2006 there were no temporary differences. Probe's 2007 financial statement income before income taxes was greater than its 2007 taxable income, due entirely to temporary differences, by $60,000. Probe's cumulative net taxable temporary differences at December 31, 2007, were $180,000. Probe's enacted tax rate for the current and future years is 35%.
- 60,000 shares of common stock, $2.50 par, were outstanding on December 31, 2006. Probe issued an additional 80,000 shares on April 1, 2007.
- There were no changes to retained earnings other than dividends declared.

| | Concepts | | | |
|---|---|---|---|---|
| **Situation** | | **Calculations** | **Communication** | **Research** |

Indicate whether each of the following should be classified as an operating, investing, or financing activity on the statement of cash flows.

| | | Operating | Investing | Financing |
|---|---|---|---|---|
| 1. | Payment for inventory | O | O | O |
| 2. | Payment of dividend | O | O | O |
| 3. | Cash received from sale of equipment | O | O | O |
| 4. | Cash sales | O | O | O |
| 5. | Issuance of stock to investors | O | O | O |
| 6. | Payment of utility bill | O | O | O |
| 7. | Payment of interest on long-term note payable | O | O | O |
| 8. | Purchase of treasury stock | O | O | O |

| | | Calculations | | |
|---|---|---|---|---|
| **Situation** | **Concepts** | | **Communication** | **Research** |

For each transaction in **items 1 through 7**

- Determine the amount to be reported in Probe's 2007 statement of cash flows prepared using the **direct method**.
- Select from the list the appropriate classification of the item on the statement of cash flows.
- Indicate whether the item is a cash inflow or cash outflow.

Calculate the amount, and select the classification and direction from the items shown below.

**Classification of Activity**

Operating
Investing
Financing
Supplementary information
Not reported on Probe's statement of cash flows

**Direction of Cash Flow**

Inflow
Outflow

|  | Amount | Classification of Activity | Direction of Cash Flow |
|---|---|---|---|

1. Cash paid for income taxes

2. Cash paid for interest

3. Redemption of bonds payable

4. Issuance of common stock

5. Cash dividends paid

6. Proceeds from sale of equipment

7. Cash collections from customers

| | | | Communication | |
|---|---|---|---|---|
| **Situation** | **Concepts** | **Calculations** | | **Research** |

The CEO of Probe has several questions related to the statement of cash flows. Write a brief memorandum to her, answering her two questions as shown below.

1. What are the objectives of the statement of cash flows?

2. What are the two types of transactions that would be disclosed in a separate schedule in the statement of cash flows although they do not affect cash during the report period?

To:     CEO, Probe Co.
From:   CPA Candidate
Re:     Statement of Cash Flows

| | | | | Research |
|---|---|---|---|---|
| **Situation** | **Concepts** | **Calculations** | **Communication** | |

Suppose Probe had the following transactions. Research each item and select the appropriate paragraph from the authoritative literature that indicates how the item is disclosed on the statement of cash flows. Assume Probe uses the indirect method.

1. Probe exchanged a delivery vehicle with a historical cost of $70,000 and a book value of $40,000 for a new forklift.

2. Probe pays $10,000 interest on long-term note payable.

3. Probe has 1,000 convertible bonds with a $100 par value that can be converted to 200 shares of $1 par common stock. During the year, the bondholders converted the bonds to shares of common stock.

| | | | | | |
|---|---|---|---|---|---|
| 1. c __ __ | 9. c __ __ | 17. d __ __ | 25. a __ __ | 33. c __ __ |
| 2. c __ __ | 10. b __ __ | 18. d __ __ | 26. d __ __ | 34. d __ __ |
| 3. d __ __ | 11. a __ __ | 19. c __ __ | 27. c __ __ | 35. d __ __ |
| 4. d __ __ | 12. d __ __ | 20. a __ __ | 28. c __ __ | 36. c __ __ |
| 5. c __ __ | 13. c __ __ | 21. c __ __ | 29. c __ __ | 37. a __ __ |
| 6. a __ __ | 14. c __ __ | 22. a __ __ | 30. c __ __ | |
| 7. d __ __ | 15. c __ __ | 23. c __ __ | 31. a __ __ | 1st: __/37 = __% |
| 8. a __ __ | 16. d __ __ | 24. c __ __ | 32. d __ __ | 2nd: __/37 = __% |

**MULTIPLE-CHOICE ANSWER EXPLANATIONS**

### A. Objectives of the Statement of Cash Flows

**1. (c)** The 12/31/07 cash and cash equivalents balance is $240,000, as computed below.

| | |
|---|---|
| Checking account #101 | $175,000 |
| Checking account #201 | (10,000) |
| Money market account | 25,000 |
| 90-day CD | 50,000 |
| Total cash and cash equivalents | $240,000 |

Bank overdrafts (like account #201) are normally reported as a current liability. However, when available cash is present in another account **in the same bank,** as in this case, offsetting is required. The money market account of $25,000 and the 90-day CD of $50,000 are considered cash equivalents because they had original maturities of three months or less. The 180-day CD of $80,000 is excluded because its original maturity was more than three months.

**2. (c)** Per SFAS 95, the **primary** purpose of a statement of cash flows is to provide relevant information about the enterprise's cash receipts and cash payments during a period. Answers (a), (b), and (d) are incorrect because, although they represent uses of the statement of cash flows, they are not the primary use.

**3. (d)** The statement of cash flows is required to be prepared based on inflows and outflows of cash and cash equivalents during the period. The purchase of a cash equivalent using cash is **not** an outflow of cash and cash equivalents; it is merely a change in the composition of cash and cash equivalents. Cash has decreased and cash equivalents have increased, but total cash and cash equivalents is unchanged. Therefore this purchase is **not** reported in the statement of cash flows.

### B. Statement of Cash Flows Classification

**4. (d)** Investing activities include all cash flows involving **assets,** other than operating items. The investing activities are

| | |
|---|---|
| Purchase of inv. in stock | $(26,000) |
| Sale of inv. in stock | 35,000 |
| Acquisition of CD | (50,000) |
| Net cash used | (41,000) |

The gain on sale of investment in Rate Motors ($35,000 – $33,000 = $2,000), the interest earned ($3,750), and dividends earned ($1,200) are all operating items. Note that the sale of investment is reported in the investing section at the cash inflow amount ($35,000), not at the carrying value of the investment ($33,000). If the CD had been for three months instead of four years, it would be part of "Cash and Cash equivalents" and would not be shown under investing activities.

**5. (c)** The building which was destroyed had a book value of $52,000 ($100,000 – $48,000). The cash settlement from the insurance company resulted in a loss of $21,000. Therefore, the cash inflow from this investing activity must be $31,000 as shown below.

| Proceeds | – | Book value | = | Loss |
|---|---|---|---|---|
| ? | – | $52,000 | = | ($21,000) |
| $31,000 | – | $52,000 | = | ($21,000) |

Note that the $21,000 extraordinary loss must be before any income tax effect because SFAS 95 requires that any tax effect be left in operating activities.

**6. (a)** The cash inflow from the sale of equipment is the carrying amount plus the gain. Answers (b) and (c) are incorrect because the tax attributable to the gain is a cash outflow in the operating activities section of the statement of cash flows. Note that when using the indirect method, the gain is deducted from operating activities, as to not double count the gain.

**7. (d)** The requirement is to determine how the equipment transactions should be reported in the statement of cash flows. Per SFAS 95, companies are required to report the gross amounts of cash receipts and cash payments, rather than net amounts. Therefore, the gross cash inflow from the sale of equipment and the gross outflow for the payment of new equipment should be reported. Answer (a) is incorrect because both gross inflow and outflow should be reported, rather than reporting the net cash flow from the transaction. Answer (b) is incorrect because gross cash flows, not net, are reported and because a note payable is not reported since the transaction results in no actual inflow or outflow in the period in which the payable occurs. This noncash activity would be reported in a separate schedule or in the footnotes. Noncash transactions commonly recognized in a separate schedule in the financial statements include: conversion of debt to equity and acquisition of assets by assuming liabilities, including lease obligations. Answer (c) is incorrect because the note payable is not reported on the statement of cash flows; rather it is shown in a separate schedule.

**8. (a)** Per SFAS 95, payments at the time of purchase or soon before or after purchase to acquire property, plant, and equipment and other productive assets are categorized as cash outflows for investing activities. Generally, these payments only include advance payments, down payments, or payments made at the time of purchase or soon before or after purchase. Therefore, only the cash payment is considered a cash outflow for investing activities.

**9. (c)** Per SFAS 95, noncash investing and financing activities include acquiring assets by assuming directly related liabilities, such as purchasing a building by incurring a mortgage to the seller. This type of transaction does not involve the flow of cash. Therefore, cash flows for financing activities related to this transaction would be zero. Note that the cash down payment would be reported as a cash outflow for **investing** activities. The amount of the mortgage payment would be included in the noncash activities at the bottom of the statement of cash flows.

**10.**   **(b)**    To determine the cash paid for redemption of bonds payable, the solutions approach is to set up a T-account for bonds payable.

| | Bonds Payable | |
|---|---|---|
| | 47,000 | 12/31/06 |
| Bonds redeemed    ? | 20,000 | Bonds issued |
| | 50,000 | 12/31/07 |

The amount of bonds redeemed can be computed as $17,000. ($47,000 + $20,000 − $50,000 = $17,000)

**11.**   **(a)**    Investing activities include all cash flows involving **assets** other than operating items. The investing activities are

| | |
|---|---|
| Proceeds from sale of equipment | $ 10,000 |
| Purchase of A.S., Inc. bonds | (180,000) |
| Net cash used in investing activities | $(170,000) |

The gain on sale of equipment ($6,000) and amortization of bond discount ($2,000) are net income adjustments in the operating section, while dividends paid ($38,000) and proceeds from sale of treasury stock ($75,000) are financing items. The excess of dividends declared over dividends paid is a noncash financing activity.

**12.**   **(d)**    Financing activities include all cash flows involving **liabilities and owners' equity** other than operating items. The financing activities are

| | |
|---|---|
| Dividends paid | $(38,000) |
| Proceeds from sale of treasury stock | 75,000 |
| Net cash provided by financing activities | $ 37,000 |

The excess of dividends declared over dividends paid is a **noncash** financing activity. The gain on sale of equipment ($6,000) and amortization of bond discount ($2,000) are net income adjustments in the operating section, while the proceeds from sale of equipment ($10,000) and purchase of A.S., Inc. bonds ($180,000) are investing items.

**13.**   **(c)**    Financing activities include the repayment of debt principal or, as in this case, the payment of the capital lease obligation. Thus, the cash outflow is equal to the 2007 rincipal payments only. The interest on the capital lease is classified as an operating cash outflow.

**14.**   **(c)**    According to SFAS 95, information about all investing and financing activities of an enterprise during a period that affect recognized assets and liabilities but that do not affect cash receipts or cash payments in the period should be reported in a supplemental schedule to the financial statements. This schedule includes all noncash investing and financing activities for the period. The conversion of long-term debt into common stock does not have any effect on cash flow, and it also results in a reduction of liabilities and an increase in stockholders' equity. Therefore, the conversion of long-term debt into common stock should be reported as a noncash financing activity in the supplemental schedule. FAS 150 requires that mandatorily redeemable preferred stock be classified as a liability. On the date the preferred stock is redeemable, it is considered li-

ability. Therefore, when the preferred stock is converted into common stock, the conversion should be reported as a noncash financing activity in the supplemental schedule.

**15.**   **(c)**    Noncash investing and financing activities are reported as supplemental information to the statement of cash flows because while they do not affect cash in the current year, they may have a significant effect on the prospective cash flows of the company. Therefore, conversion of debt to equity is disclosed as supplemental information to the statement of cash flows. However, SFAS 95 specifies that cash flow per share should **not** be reported on the statement of cash flows because it may be misleading and may be incorrectly used as a measure of profitability.

## C.    Direct or Indirect Presentation in Reporting Operating Activities

**16.**   **(d)**    Under either the direct method or indirect method, the major classes of gross cash receipts and gross cash payments must be reported in the statement of cash flows. Under the direct method, the amount of income taxes paid is one of the components of net cash flows from operating activities; under the indirect method, it is a required supplemental disclosure. A reconciliation of net income to net cash flow from operations is a required supplemental disclosure under the direct method, and is included in the body of the statement under the indirect method. Only a reconciliation of ending retained earnings to net cash flow from operations is **not** required under either method.

**17.**   **(d)**    Cash collected from customers can be computed using either a formula or a T-account. The formula is

| Sales | [End AR | − | (Beg AR | − | Write-offs)] | = | Collections |
|---|---|---|---|---|---|---|---|
| $538,800 | [$33,000 | − | ($30,000 | − | $0)  ] | = | $535,800 |

In the formula above, sales is adjusted for the **change in AR, exclusive of write-offs,** because write-offs represent sales (and AR) which will never be collected in cash. In this problem, there were no write-offs, so it must be assumed that the change in the allowance account results solely from bad debt expense (no write-offs). Since there are no write-offs, the increase in AR ($33,000 − $30,000 = $3,000) is subtracted from sales because those sales increased AR instead of cash. The T-account solution is below.

| | Accounts Receivable | | |
|---|---|---|---|
| 12/31/06 | 30,000 | | |
| Sales | 538,800 | 0 | Write-offs |
| | | ? | Collections = 535,800 |
| 12/31/07 | 33,000 | | |

**18.**   **(d)**    Cash paid for goods to be sold can be computed using either a formula or T-accounts. The formula is

| CGS | + | (End. inv. − Beg. inv.) | − | (End. AP − Beg. AP) | − | Cash paid |
|---|---|---|---|---|---|---|
| $250,000 | + | ($31,000 − $47,000) | − | ($25,000 − $17,500) | − | Cash paid |
| $250,000 | − | $16,000 | − | $75,000 | − | $226,500 |

The decrease in inventory ($16,000) is subtracted from CGS because that portion of CGS resulted from a use of inventory purchased in prior years, rather than from a cash payment. The increase in AP is subtracted because that portion of CGS was not paid this year. Using T-accounts, first purchases are computed using the inventory account, then payments are computed using the accounts payable account.

Inventory

| 12/31/06 | 47,000 | | |
|---|---|---|---|
| Purchases | ? | 250,000 | CGS |
| 12/31/07 | 31,000 | | |

1. Purchases = $234,000

Accounts Payable

| | | 17,500 | 12/31/06 |
|---|---|---|---|
| Payments | ? | 234,000 | Purchases |
| | | 25,000 | 12/31/07 |

2. Payments = $226,500

**19. (c)** The trial balance does **not** include prepaid interest or interest payable, both of which would affect the computation of cash paid for interest. In the absence of those accounts, cash paid for interest is equal to interest expense plus (minus) bond premium (discount) amortization.

| Interest expense | – | Discount amortization | = | Cash paid |
|---|---|---|---|---|
| $4,300 | – | ($5,000 – $4,500) | = | $3,800 |

Flax's 2007 entry to record interest expense was

| Interest expense | 4,300 | |
|---|---|---|
| Cash | | 3,800 |
| Discount on bonds payable | | 500 |

**20. (a)** Cash paid for income taxes can be computed using the following formula:

$$\text{Inc. tax expense} - \left(\text{End. inc. tax payable} - \text{Beg. inc. tax payable}\right) - \left(\text{End. def. tax liability} - \text{Beg. def. tax liability}\right) = \text{Cash paid for inc. tax}$$

| $20,400 | – | ($21,000 – $27,000) | – | ($5,300 – $4,600) | = | Cash paid |
|---|---|---|---|---|---|---|
| $20,400 | + | $6,100 | – | $700 | = | $25,800 |

The decrease in income taxes payable is added to income tax expense because cash was used to decrease the liability as well as to pay tax expense. The increase in the deferred tax liability is deducted from income tax expense because that portion of tax expense was deferred (not paid in cash). Flax's summary journal entry to record income taxes for 2008 is

| Inc. tax expense | 20,400 | |
|---|---|---|
| Inc. tax payable | 6,100 | |
| Cash | | 25,800 |
| Deferred taxes | | 700 |

**21. (c)** In general, cash paid for selling expenses is affected by prepaid selling expenses, accrued selling expenses, depreciation and/or amortization expense, and possibly bad debts expense. In this case, there are no prepaid or accrued selling expenses in the trial balances, and bad debts expense is apparently included in general and administrative expenses (see discussion below). Therefore, cash paid for selling expenses is $141,000 ($141,500 selling expenses less $500 depreciation expense). Total depreciation expense can be determined from the change in the accumulated depreciation account ($16,500 – $15,000 = $1,500), and 1/3 of that amount is selling expense (1/3 × $1,500 = $500). Note that bad debt expense ($1,300 – $1,100 = $200) must be included in general and administrative expenses, because the answer obtained by assuming it is part of selling expenses ($141,000 – $200 = $140,800) is not given as one of the four choices.

**22. (a)** Per SFAS 95, businesses are encouraged to use the direct method of reporting operating activities under which major classes of cash receipts and cash payments are shown. The minimum cash flows to be disclosed under this method are cash collected from customers, interest and divi-

dends received, cash paid to employees and suppliers, income taxes paid, and interest paid.

**23. (c)** In a statement of cash flows in which the operating activities section is prepared using the direct method, the cash paid for wages would be equal to the accrual-basis salary expense, plus/minus any decrease/increase in the wages payable account. (The logic is essentially the same as an accrual-basis to cash-basis adjustment.)

**24. (c)** Net income was $150,000. Three of the four items given are net income adjustments (the major repair to projection equipment [$2,100] is a cash outflow under investing activities), resulting in net cash provided by operating activities of $144,900.

| Net income | $150,000 |
|---|---|
| Equity method income | (5,500) |
| Premium amortization | (1,400) |
| Increase in def. tax liability | 1,800 |
| Cash provided by operating activities | $144,900 |

When equity method income is recorded, the offsetting debit is to the investment account, not cash; when premium on bonds payable is amortized, the credit to interest expense is offset by a debit to the premium account, not cash. Therefore, both of these items **increase** income without increasing cash, and must be **deducted** as a net income adjustment. For the deferred tax items, when income tax expense is debited, the offsetting credit is to deferred tax liability, not cash. Therefore, this item **decreases** net income without decreasing cash, and it must be **added back** as a net income adjustment. Note that there should normally be depreciation expense as a net income adjustment, but it is not given.

**25. (a)** Based only on the items given, net cash provided by operating activities is $151,400, as computed below.

| Net income | $150,000 |
|---|---|
| Increase in net AR | |
| [($29,000 – 1,000) – ($23,000 – 800)] | (5,800) |
| Decrease in prepaid rent ($12,400 – $8,200) | 4,200 |
| Increase in AP ($22,400 – $19,400) | 3,000 |
| Cash provided by ops. | $151,400 |

The increase in net AR is deducted from net income because it indicates that cash collected is less than sales revenue. The decrease in prepaid rent is added because it reflects rent expense that was **not** a cash payment, but an allocation of previously recorded prepaid rent. Finally, the increase in AP is added because it also represents an expense (cost of goods sold) that was not yet paid.

**26. (d)** The objective of a statement of cash flows is to explain what caused the change in the cash balance. The first step in this process is to determine cash provided by operations. When presenting cash from operating activities under the indirect approach, net income must be adjusted for changes in current assets other than cash and in current liabilities. These adjustments are required because items that resulted from noncash events must be removed from accrual-based income. For example, when inventory increases during the period, inventory sold is less than inventory purchased. Considering only the increase in the inventory account, cost of goods sold on an accrual basis is less than it would have been if cash basis were being used. In converting to the cash basis, the increase in inventory must be subtracted from net income to arrive at cash from operations. Answer (a) is incorrect because even though an increase in inventories requires an outflow of cash, inventories are shown as adjustments to net income under the indirect method. Answer (b) is incorrect because changes in inventories are shown as adjustments to net income under the indirect method. Answer (c) is incorrect because an increase in an inventory would be a deduction from net income, not an addition.

**27. (c)** When using the indirect method for reporting net cash flows from operations, you start with net income from continuing operations and adjust for changes in operating related accounts (i.e., inventory, accounts payable) and non-cash expenses, revenues, gains and losses. The proceeds from the sale of equipment is reported as an inflow in the investing section of the statement of cash flows, at its gross amount. This gross amount includes the gain. Therefore, to avoid double counting and to properly classify cash inflows, the gain is subtracted from net income to show the proper cash balance from operating activities.

**28. (c)** Under the indirect method of reporting cash flows from operations, income from continuing operations is adjusted for changes in operating related accounts and non-cash expenses, revenues, losses, and gains. Noncash items that were subtracted in determining income must be added back in. This would include amortization of bond discount, as it is a charge against income but does not decrease cash. The excess of treasury stock acquisition cost over sales proceeds would not be added back to net income. Under the cost method, this loss would not be included in net income but would be charged back to a paid-in capital account or retained earnings. The acquisition and sale of treasury stock, furthermore, would be financing activities.

**29. (c)** SFAS 95 specifies that cash flow per share should **not** be reported on the statement of cash flows because it may be misleading and may be incorrectly used as a measure of profitability. Answers (a) and (b) are incorrect because, when the indirect method is used, separate disclosure is required for **interest paid** (net of amounts capitalized) and **income taxes paid**. Answer (d) is incorrect because, regardless of the method used, **dividends paid** on preferred stock are reported as a **financing activity**.

**D. Example of Statement of Cash Flows**

**30. (c)** Net cash provided by operating activities can be computed by using either the **direct** or **indirect** approach. In this case, there is not enough information to use the direct approach. In the indirect approach, net income is adjusted for noncash items, as shown below.

| | |
|---|---:|
| Net income | $790,000 |
| Gain on sale of LT investment | (35,000) |
| Increase in inventory | (80,000) |
| Depreciation expense | 250,000 |
| Decrease in AP and accrued liabs. | (5,000) |
| | $920,000 |

The additional information indicates that a LT investment was sold for $135,000. The listing of accounts shows a decrease in LT investments of $100,000. The gain on sale ($135,000 – $100,000 = $35,000) is deducted because the total cash effect of this transaction ($135,000) will be reported as an investing activity. Two of the working capital accounts that changed are related to net income. The increase in inventory ($80,000) is deducted because cash was used to increase inventory. The decrease in accounts payable and accrued liabilities is deducted because cash was

used to pay these liabilities. The increase of $300,000 for Available-for-Sale Securities is an investing activity. The only other information or account given which affects net income is accumulated depreciation. Although this account did not show any net decrease or increase during 2006, we know it was decreased by $250,000 when the building was sold ($600,000 cost less $350,000 carrying amount equals $250,000 accumulated depreciation). Therefore, depreciation expense of $250,000 must have increased the accumulated depreciation account to result in a net effect for the year of $0. Depreciation expense is added because it is a noncash expense.

An alternative method of computing net cash provided by operating activities is to back into the answer after determining cash used in investing activities and cash provided by financing activities.

| | |
|---|---:|
| Cash provided by Operating Activities | $ ? |
| Cash used in Investing Activities | (1,005,000) |
| Cash provided by Financing Activities | 205,000 |
| Net increase in Cash | $ 120,000 |

The problem tells us that cash and cash equivalents increased by $120,000. Therefore, cash provided by operating activities is $920,000 ($920,000 – $1,005,000 + $205,000 = $120,000).

**31. (a)** **Investing** activities include all cash flows involving **assets,** other than operating items. **Financing** activities include all cash flows involving **liabilities and equity,** other than operating items. The common stock issued is a financing activity. In this case, the changes in the inventory and accumulated depreciation accounts are operating items. The cash flows involving the other assets, listed below, are investing activities

| | |
|---|---:|
| Purchase of AFS Securities | $ (300,000) |
| Sale of LT investments | 135,000 |
| Sale of plant assets | 350,000 |
| Purchase of plant assets | (1,190,000) |
| | $(1,005,000) |

The amounts above were given, except for the purchase of plant assets, the amount of which can be determined from the following T-account:

| | Plant Assets | | |
|---|---:|---:|---|
| Cost of equip. acquired | 110,000 | 600,000 | Cost of |
| Cost of plant assets purchased | ? | | bldg. sold |
| Net increase | 700,000 | | |

The equipment acquired through issuance of LT debt is a **noncash** investing and financing activity so it does not affect net **cash** used in investing activities.

**32. (d)** **Financing** activities include all cash flows involving **liabilities and equity,** other than operating items. **Investing** activities include all cash flows involving **assets,** other than operating items. In this case, the change in the **accounts payable and accrued liabilities** account is an operating item. The part of the change in **retained earnings** caused by net income ($790,000) is also an operating item. The cash flows involving the other liability and equity accounts, listed below, are financing activities.

| | |
|---|---:|
| Payment of dividends ($500,000 – $160,000) | $(340,000) |
| Issuance of ST debt | 325,000 |
| Issuance of common stock (10,000 × $22) | 220,000 |
| | $205,000 |

The problem states that $500,000 of dividends were **declared,** and this is confirmed by the change in the retained earnings account ($790,000 net income – $500,000 dividends declared = $290,000 net increase). However, since dividends payable increased by $160,000, only $340,000 of dividends were **paid** ($500,000 – $160,000). The issuance of common stock (10,000 shares × $22 per share = $220,000) is confirmed by the increases in the **common stock** and **additional paid-in capital** accounts ($100,000 + $120,000 = $220,000). The issuance of LT debt for equipment ($110,000) is a **noncash** financing and investing activity, so it does not affect net **cash** provided by financing activities. Note that the answers to the three related questions can be verified by comparing them to the increase in cash and cash equivalents ($120,000) given in the problem.

| | |
|---|---:|
| Cash provided by oper. acts. | $ 920,000 |
| Cash used in inv. acts. | (1,005,000) |
| Cash provided by fin. acts. | 205,000 |
| Increase in cash and cash equivalents | $ 120,000 |

**33.  (c)**  The requirement is to calculate the amount of cash collected during 2007 from accounts receivable. The solutions approach is to prepare a T-account for accounts receivable. The allowance account has no effect on this analysis, because the problem states that the balance in this account has not changed and no accounts receivable were written off. Net credit sales are the only debit to accounts receivable because all accounts receivable relate to trade merchandise. In the T-account below, you must solve for the missing credit to determine that $6,140,000 was collected on account during 2007.

| AR—Net | | | |
|---|---|---|---|
| 12/31/06 balance | 580,000 | ? | 2007 Collections |
| 2007 net credit sales | 6,400,000 | | |
| 12/31/07 balance | 840,000 | | |

*NOTE: Based on the information given in this problem, no bad debt expense was recorded during 2007. However unrealistic this assumption might be, it is important to simply work with the information as given.*

**34.  (d)**  The requirement is to calculate the amount of cash payments during 2007 on accounts payable. The solutions approach is to visualize the accounts payable T-account.

| Accounts Payable | | | |
|---|---|---|---|
| | | 440,000 | 12/31/06 |
| Payments | ? | ? | Purchases |
| | | 530,000 | 12/31/07 |

It is apparent that to determine payments to suppliers, purchases of trade merchandise must first be computed. The cost of goods sold statement can be used to compute purchases.

| | | |
|---|---|---:|
| Beginning inventory | $ | 420,000 |
| + Purchases | + | ? |
| – Ending inventory | – | 660,000 |
| Cost of goods sold | | $5,000,000 |

Purchases = $5,000,000 – ($420,000 – $660,000)
= $5,240,000

Finally, the purchases are entered into the accounts payable T-account, and payments to suppliers of $5,150,000 can be plugged in.

| Accounts Payable | | | |
|---|---|---|---|
| | | 440,000 | 12/31/06 |
| Payments | 5,150,000 | 5,240,000 | Purchases |
| | | 530,000 | 12/31/07 |

**35.  (d)**  The requirement is to determine net cash flows provided by financing activities in 2007. The solutions ap-

proach is to work through the comparative balance sheets noting increases and decreases in liability accounts other than those related to operations and increases or decreases in stockholders' equity accounts. The additional information given must be considered in connection with these changes. Notice the note payable was issued for cash and the proceeds were used to purchase a building. Cash inflows from financing activities include proceeds from long-term borrowing, and issuance of capital stock.

| | |
|---|---:|
| Proceeds from long-term note | $500,000 |
| Proceeds from issuance of common stock | 300,000 |
| | $800,000 |

To determine the amount of dividends paid, it is necessary to analyze both the retained earnings and the dividends payable accounts.

| Dividends Payable | | | | Retained Earnings | | |
|---|---|---|---|---|---|---|
| | | -- | 12/31/06 | | 330,000 | 12/31/06 |
| Dividends paid | ? | ? | Dividends declared | ? | 400,000 | Net income |
| | | 70,000 | 12/31/07 | | 560,000 | 12/31/07 |

Dividends declared = $330,000 + 400,000 – 560,000 = $170,000
Dividends paid    = $0 + 170,000 – 70,000 = $100,000

Net cash flows provided by financing activities is $700,000 ($800,000 – $100,000).

**36.  (c)**  The requirement is to compute the cash used in investing activities during 2007. The two assets other than those related to operations shown on the balance sheet (long-term investments and land, building, and fixtures) have increased from 12/31/06 to 12/31/07, indicating cash purchases since the additional information does not suggest any other means of acquisition. Therefore, cash outflows from investing activities include $80,000 for long-term investments and $530,000 ($1,130,000 – $600,000) for land, building, and fixtures. Notice that the building was purchased for $500,000, so fixtures or land must have been acquired for $30,000.

**37.  (a)**  The solutions approach is to set up T-accounts for the related accounts.

| Sales | | AR | |
|---|---|---|---|
| | Sales | Beg. Bal. | Collections |
| | | Sales | Write-offs |
| | | End. Bal. | |

Sales are debited to AR and credited to sales; collections are debited to cash and credited to AR. Under the direct write-off method, write-offs of customer accounts are debited to bad debts expense, and credited to AR. To adjust sales to cash collections from customers, Bee must subtract the increase in accounts receivable (because Bee has not yet received cash for the sales remaining in AR). Bee must also subtract the accounts written off, because these sales have not resulted in cash receipts (and probably never will).

## SOLUTIONS TO SIMULATION PROBLEMS

### Simulation Problem 1

| Situation | Concepts—<br>Direct Method | Statement of Cash Flows–<br>Indirect Method | Communication | Research |
|---|---|---|---|---|

#### Probe Co.
#### STATEMENT OF CASH FLOWS
*For the Year Ending 12/31/07*

| | Cash Inflow or Cash Outflow |
|---|---|
| **From Operating Activities** | |
| Cash paid for inventory | Outflow |
| Cash paid for supplies | Outflow |
| Cash collected on account | Inflow |
| Cash sales | Inflow |
| Dividends received on trading securities | Inflow |
| Interest paid on note | Outflow |
| Taxes paid | Outflow |
| | |
| **From Investing Activities** | |
| Purchase of held-to-maturity securities | Outflow |
| Sale of land | Inflow |
| | |
| **From Financing Activities** | |
| Borrow on long-term note payable | Inflow |
| Issue of common stock | Inflow |
| Payment of dividend | Outflow |
| Purchase of treasury stock | Outflow |
| Redemption of bonds | Outflow |

| Situation | Concepts—<br>Direct Method | Statement of Cash Flows–<br>Indirect Method | Communication | Research |
|---|---|---|---|---|

#### Probe Co.
#### STATEMENT OF CASH FLOWS
*For the Year Ending 12/31/07*

| | Cash Source (Use) |
|---|---|
| **From Operating Activities** | |
| Net income | 195,000 |
| Loss on sale of equipment | 7,000 |
| Gain on extinguishments of bonds | (90,000) |
| Depreciation Expense | 88,000 |
| Increase in Account Receivable | (60,000) |
| Decrease in Income Tax Payable | (90,000) |
| Increase in Deferred Tax Liability | 21,000 |
| Amortization of Premium on Bond | (4,000) |
| Net cash flows from operating activities | 67,000 |
| | |
| **From Investing Activities** | |
| Sale of equipment | 20,000 |
| Purchase of equipment | (125,000) |
| | |
| Net cash flow from investing activities | (105,000) |
| | |
| **From Financing Activities** | |
| Redeem bonds | (485,000) |
| Issue common stock | 255,000 |
| Pay dividends | (65,000) |
| Net cash flows from financing activities | (295,000) |
| Net decrease in cash | (333,000) |
| Cash at beginning of year | 817,000 |
| Cash at end of year | 484,000 |

| | | | Communication | |
|---|---|---|---|---|
| Situation | Concepts—Direct Method | Statement of Cash Flows—Indirect Method | | Research |

To:         CEO, Probe Co.
From:     CPA Candidate
Re:         Statement of Cash Flows

This memorandum is in response to your questions regarding the statement of cash flows. The effects and procedural considerations of the seven account balances (transactions) that you had questions about are summarized below.

**1.**    Accounts receivable—trade are generated as a result of credit sales. A balance in accounts receivable—trade represents sales (a part of operating earnings) not represented by cash. An increase in the accounts receivable—trade balance indicates that the actual cash generated is equal to sales as reported on the earnings statement less the increase in accounts receivable—trade balance. Conversely, a net decrease in the accounts receivable—trade balance would have to be added to sales as reported on the earnings statement to arrive at cash generated from sales. In the preparation of a statement of cash flows the increase (decrease) in this account balance between two periods is subtracted from (or added to) net sales to arrive at cash received from customers for sales.

**2.**    Inventory is a component part of cost of goods sold. The net change in inventory balances affects the cash used to purchase inventory. An increase in ending inventory over beginning inventory increases the cash used to purchase inventory because cash was presumed to be used to increase the inventory balance. Therefore, when there is an increase in inventory balances, the cash to purchase inventory is the cost of goods sold as shown in the current earnings statement plus the increase in inventory balance.

A similar analysis leads to the conclusion that a decrease in inventory gives rise to a reduction in the cash used to purchase inventory.

**3.**    Depreciation represents a systematic allocation of the cost of a fixed asset to the accounting periods benefited by the asset. The process of recognizing depreciation does not affect cash. Accordingly, cash paid for operating expenses is determined by deducting depreciation expense from total operating expenses and adjusting the operating expenses for prepaid expenses.

**4.**    Deferred income taxes are the difference between income taxes matched against earnings and the actual amount paid or payable for the period. If the balance of the deferred tax liability account, for example, increases between two periods, the amount of income taxes paid was less than the indicated income tax expense. Conversely, if deferred liability tax account decreases, the amount paid was greater than the amount of income tax expense. Although the change in the deferred tax liability account is included in the indirect approach, the direct approach is not affected by the change. To determine the cash paid for taxes under the direct presentation, the **current** portion of income tax expense is adjusted for the increase or decrease in the income tax payable account.

**5.**    The purchase of a building by issuing long-term debt obviously does not require a cash outlay. However, this noncash activity should be reported in a separate schedule as a noncash financing and investing activity.

**6.**    The payment of the current portion of debt represents a cash outflow from financing activities.

**7.**    The total proceeds from the sale of the fixed asset should be shown as an inflow from investing activities. This transaction would not be reflected under operating activities when the **direct** presentation is used.

If you have any further questions, please contact my office.

| | | | | Research |
|---|---|---|---|---|
| Situation | Concepts—Direct Method | Statement of Cash Flows—Indirect Method | Communication | |

**1.**    On February 2, 2007, Probe purchased 10,000 shares of stock of Stone Corporation. Stone **Corporation** paid a dividend of $2 per share to Probe on November 5, 2007. Probe's management believes it will hold the stock of Stone for at least 2 years.

**Definition**
**FAS115, Para 18 or Current Text I80.117**

18. Cash flows from purchases, sales, and maturities of available-for-sale securities and held-to-maturity securities shall be classified as cash flows from investing activities and reported gross for each security classification in the statement of cash flows. Cash flows from purchases, sales, and maturities of trading securities shall be classified as cash flows from operating activities.

**FAS95, Para 22 or Current Text C25.120**

22. Cash inflows from operating activities are

a.    Cash receipts from sales of goods or services, including receipts from collection or sale of accounts and both short- and long-term notes receivable from customers arising from those sales

b. Cash receipts from returns on loans, other debt instruments of other entities, and equity securities—interest and dividends

c. All other cash receipts that do not stem from transactions defined as investing or financing activities, such as amounts received to settle lawsuits; proceeds of insurance settlements except for those that are directly related to investing or financing activities, such as from destruction of a building, and refunds from suppliers.

**2.** Probe purchased new equipment for $100,000.

**FAS95, Para 16 (c) or Current Text C25.114**

16. Cash inflows from investing activities are

a. Receipts from collections or sales of loans made by the enterprise and of other entities' debt instruments (other than cash equivalents) that were purchased by the enterprise

b. Receipts from sales of equity instruments of other enterprises and from returns of investment in those instruments

c. Receipts from sales of property, plant, and equipment and other productive assets.

**3.** On June 1, 2007, Probe repurchased 4,000 shares of its own stock for $20 per share and immediately retired the shares.

**FAS95, Para 20 or Current Text C25.118**

20. Cash outflows for financing activities are

a. Payment of dividends or other distributions to owners, including outlays to reacquire the enterprise's equity instruments

b. Repayments of amounts borrowed

c. Other principal payments to creditors who have extended long-term credit.

---

## Simulation Problem 2

| | Concepts | | | | |
| --- | --- | --- | --- | --- | --- |
| Situation | | Calculations | Communication | Research | |

Indicate whether each of the following should be classified as an operating, investing, or financing activity on the statement of cash flows.

| | | *Operating* | *Investing* | *Financing* |
| --- | --- | --- | --- | --- |
| **1.** | Payment for inventory | ● | ○ | ○ |
| **2.** | Payment of dividend | ○ | ○ | ● |
| **3.** | Cash received from sale of equipment | ○ | ● | ○ |
| **4.** | Cash sales | ● | ○ | |
| **5.** | Issuance of stock to investors | ○ | ○ | ● |
| **6.** | Payment of utility bill | ● | ○ | ○ |
| **7.** | Payment of interest on long-term note payable | ● | ○ | ○ |
| **8.** | Purchase of treasury stock | ○ | ○ | ● |

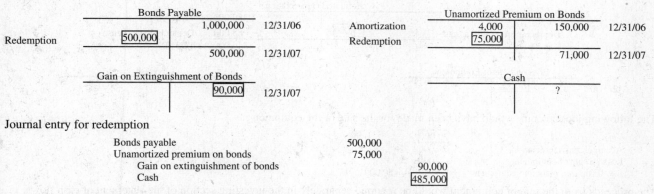

| Item | Amount | Classification on Statement of Cash Flows | Cash Inflow/Cash Outflow |
|---|---|---|---|
| 1. Cash paid for income taxes | 174,000 | Operating Activity | Outflow |
| 2. Cash paid for interest | 50,000 | Operating Activity | Outflow |
| 3. Redemption of bonds payable | 485,000 | Financing Activity | Outflow |
| 4. Issuance of common stock | 255,000 | Financing Activity | Inflow |
| 5. Cash dividends paid | 65,000 | Financing Activity | Outflow |
| 6. Proceeds from sale of equipment | 20,000 | Investing | Inflow |
| 7. Cash collections from customers | 2,360,000 | Operating Activity | Inflow |

**Explanation of solutions**

**1.    ($174,000, O)**  The payments for income taxes during the year were debited to the income taxes payable account.  To arrive at the amount of payments, a T-account can be used as follows:

```
                    Income Taxes Payable
                               |  150,000    12/31/06
            Payments  174,000  |   84,000    Income Tax Accrual
                               |   60,000    12/31/07
```

Note that the deferred tax liability account increased by 21,000 (120,000 × 35%).  Therefore, the entry for tax expense for 2007 would have been

```
Tax Expense                           105,000
    Deferred Tax Liability                         21,000
    Taxes Payable                                  84,000
```

Using the direct method, the payment of taxes would appear in the operating section of the cash flow statement.

**2.    ($50,000, O)**  Interest paid on the bonds in 2007 would be $50,000 ($500,000 × 10%).  Alternatively, the $46,000 plus the $4,000 premium amortization (see explanation for the next item below) also results in $50,000 as the amount paid for interest. The amount paid for interest would be included in the operating activities section of the cash flow statements if the direct method is used.  (Note:  The amount of cash paid for interest would be reported separately as supplementary information for a statement of cash flows using the indirect method.)

**3.    ($485,000, F)**  Through the following T-account analyses, a journal entry for the redemption of the bonds payable can be determined:

```
              Bonds Payable                              Unamortized Premium on Bonds
                       | 1,000,000  12/31/06   Amortization    4,000  | 150,000   12/31/06
Redemption  500,000    |                       Redemption     75,000  |
                       |   500,000  12/31/07                           |  71,000   12/31/07

    Gain on Extinguishment of Bonds                            Cash
                       |   90,000   12/31/07                           |    ?
```

Journal entry for redemption

```
Bonds payable                         500,000
Unamortized premium on bonds           75,000
    Gain on extinguishment of bonds               90,000
    Cash                                         485,000
```

This amount paid for the redemption of the bonds would be separately reported in the financing section on the statement of cash flows prepared using the indirect method.  Financing activities include obtaining resources from owners and returning the investment, as well as obtaining resources from creditors and **repaying the amounts borrowed**.

**4.    ($255,000, F)**  An additional 80,000 shares of $2.50 par value common stock were issued during 2007.  The following T-accounts depict the changes in the common stock and additional paid-in capital accounts:

```
              Common Stock
                       |  150,000   12/31/06
                       |  200,000   Issuance      (80,000 × $2.50)
                       |  350,000   12/31/07
```

| | Additional Paid-in Capital | | |
|---|---|---|---|
| | | 375,000 | 12/31/06 |
| | | 55,000 | Issuance |
| | | 430,000 | 12/31/07 |

The journal entry for the issuance of the stock would have been

| Cash | 255,000 | |
|---|---|---|
| Common stock | | 200,000 |
| Additional paid-in capital | | 55,000 |

This amount received for the issuance of the common stock would be reported separately in the financing section of the statement of cash flows prepared using the indirect method. Financing activities include **obtaining resources from owners** and returning the investment, as well as obtaining resources from creditors and repaying the amounts borrowed.

**5.** **($65,000, F)** The problem states that there were no changes to retained earnings during the year other than dividends declared. Therefore, the following T-account analyses depict the dividend activity during the year:

| | Retained Earnings | | |
|---|---|---|---|
| | | 265,000 | 12/31/06 |
| Dividends declared | 80,000 | | |
| | | 185,000 | 12/31/07 |

| | Dividends Payable | | | | Cash | |
|---|---|---|---|---|---|---|
| | | 10,000 | 12/31/06 | | | ? |
| Dividends paid | ? | 80,000 | Accrual during 2007 | | | |
| | | 25,000 | 12/31/07 | | | |

The following journal entry would have been made:

| Retained earnings | 80,000 | |
|---|---|---|
| Dividends payable | | 80,000 |
| Dividends payable | 65,000 | |
| Cash | | 65,000 |

This amount paid for the dividends would be reported separately in the financing section of the statement of cash flows prepared using the indirect method. Financing activities include obtaining resources from owners and **returning the investment,** as well as obtaining resources from creditors and repaying the amounts borrowed.

**6.** **($20,000, I)** The following T-account analyses depict the sale of the equipment during 2007:

| | Property, Plant and Equipment | | |
|---|---|---|---|
| 12/31/06 | 995,000 | | |
| | | 50,000 | Sale |
| Purchase | 125,000 | | |
| 12/31/07 | 1,070,000 | | |

| | Accumulated Depreciation | | |
|---|---|---|---|
| | | 280,000 | 12/31/06 |
| Depreciation on sold asset | 23,000 | 88,000 | Depreciation expense |
| | | 345,000 | 12/31/07 |

| | Loss on Sale of Equipment | | | Cash | |
|---|---|---|---|---|---|
| 12/31/07 | 7,000 | | | ? | |

The following journal entry would have been made for the sale of the equipment:

| Cash | 20,000 | |
|---|---|---|
| Accumulated depreciation | 23,000 | |
| Loss on sale of equipment | 7,000 | |
| Property, plant and equipment | | 50,000 |

The proceeds from the sale of equipment would be reported separately in the investing section of the statement of cash flows. Included in the investing section are the acquisition and disposition of long-term productive assets or securities (not considered cash equivalents), as well as the lending of money and collection of loans.

**7.** The following T-account analysis depicts the cash received from customers. Assume all sales are made on account.

| | Accounts Receivable | | |
|---|---|---|---|
| 12/31/06 | 610,000 | | |
| Sale on Account | 2,420,000 | | |
| | | 2,360,000 | Collections on account |
| 12/31/07 | 670,000 | | |

Therefore, the cash collections on account were 610,000 + 2,420,000 − 670,000 = 2,360,000.

| | | | Communication | |
|---|---|---|---|---|
| Situation | Concepts | Calculations | | Research |

To:     CEO, Probe Co.
From:   CPA Candidate
Re:     Statement of Cash Flows

This memorandum is in response to your questions regarding the statement of cash flows. The objective of the statement of cash flows is to provide information about cash receipts and payments from operating, investing, and financing activities. This information helps users assess the company's ability to generate future net cash flows, to meet obligations, and to pay dividends. The statement also helps users assess the differences between income and associated cash receipts and payments.

Companies sometimes make significant noncash transactions. Investing and financing activities that do not involve cash receipts and payments during the period should be excluded from the cash flow statement and reported in a separate schedule. Transactions that would be classified as significant noncash financing and investing activities would include the following:

1.  Purchase of assets by the issuance of capital stock or debt
2.  Purchase of assets by a trade or a reduction in another asset
3.  Reduction of a liability by the issuance of capital stock
4.  Reduction of a liability by incurrence of another liability (refinancing)
5.  Reduction in a liability by repayment with an asset, resulting in a reduction in an asset

If you have any transactions that you cannot classify, please contact my office for further assistance.

| | | | | Research |
|---|---|---|---|---|
| Situation | Concepts | Calculations | Communication | |

**1.** Probe exchanged a delivery vehicle with an historical cost of $70,000 and a book value of $40,000 for a new forklift.

**FAS95, Para 32 or Current Text C25.134**

32. Information about all investing and financing activities of an enterprise during a period that affect recognized assets or liabilities but that do not result in cash receipts or cash payments in the period shall be reported in related disclosures. Those disclosures may be either narrative or summarized in a schedule, and they shall clearly relate the cash and noncash aspects of transactions involving similar items. Examples of noncash investing and financing transactions are converting debt to equity; acquiring assets by assuming directly related liabilities, such as purchasing a building by incurring a mortgage to the seller; obtaining an asset by entering into a capital lease; and exchanging noncash assets or liabilities for other noncash assets or liabilities. Some transactions are part cash and part noncash; only the cash portion shall be reported in the statement of cash flows.

**2.** Probe pays $10,000 interest on long-term note payable.

**FAS95, Para 23 (d) or Current Text C25.121**

23. Cash outflows for operating activities are

   a.  Cash payments to acquire materials for manufacture or goods for resale, including principal payments on accounts and both short- and long-term notes payable to suppliers for those materials or goods
   b.  Cash payments to other suppliers and employees for other goods and services
   c.  Cash payments to governments for taxes, duties, fines, and other fees or penalties
   d.  Cash payments to lenders and other creditors for interest
   e.  All other cash payments that do not stem from transactions defined as investing or financing activities, such as payments to settle lawsuits, cash contributions to charities, and cash refunds to customers.

**3.** Probe has 1,000 convertible bonds with a $100 par value that can be converted to 200 shares of $1 par common stock. During the year, the bondholders converted the bonds to shares of common stock.

**FAS95, Para 32 or Current Text C25.134**

32. Information about all investing and financing activities of an enterprise during a period that affect recognized assets or liabilities but that do not result in cash receipts or cash payments in the period shall be reported in related disclosures. Those disclosures may be either narrative or summarized in a schedule, and they shall clearly relate the cash and noncash aspects of transactions involving similar items. Examples of noncash investing and financing transactions are converting debt to equity; acquiring assets by assuming directly related liabilities, such as purchasing a building by incurring a mortgage to the seller; obtaining an asset by entering into a capital lease; and exchanging noncash assets or liabilities for other noncash assets or liabilities. Some transactions are part cash and part noncash; only the cash portion shall be reported in the statement of cash flows.

## BUSINESS COMBINATIONS AND CONSOLIDATIONS

Many companies expand their operations by acquiring other businesses. The acquiring company may be seeking diversification of its business, a more stable supply of raw materials for its production, an increase in the range of products or services it offers, or any one of many other business reasons. The accounting issues of business combinations begin with properly recording and reporting the economic events of the date of business combination. Accounting subsequent to the combination is dependent on the alternatives selected at the combination date. Thus, as you study this section, you should fully understand how the combination is first recorded and reported before proceeding to events occurring after the combination date.

From a legal perspective, business combinations are classified into three categories as follows:

1. **Merger**—One company acquires the assets and liabilities of one or more other companies in exchange for stock, cash, or other consideration. The acquiring company continues to exist as a separate legal entity, but the acquired company ceases to exist as a separate legal entity, its stock is cancelled, and its books are closed. The separate assets and liabilities are recorded on the acquiring firm's books. (A Corp. + B Corp. = A Corp.)

2. **Statutory Consolidation**—A new firm is formed to issue stock in exchange for the stock of two or more combining or consolidating companies. The acquired firms normally cease to continue as separate legal entities; therefore, the new (acquiring) firm will record the separate assets and liabilities of the acquired firms. (A Corp. + B Corp. = C Corp.)

3. **Acquisition**—A company acquires a majority (> 50%) of the common stock of another company and each company continues its legal existence. The acquiring company (parent) will record an "Investment in Acquired Company's Stock" in the combination entry. (A Corp. + B Corp. = Consolidated Financial Statements of A and B)

Mergers and statutory consolidations require 100% ownership of the acquired company but the acquisition business combination requires only a majority ownership of the outstanding stock. In addition, by maintaining the separate legal existence of the acquired company (B Corp.) and not canceling its stock, the parent company (A Corp.) can retain greater flexibility in raising additional capital by using B Corp. shares as collateral for a loan or through the issuance of new shares of B Corp.

Financial statements for combinations which are in the legal forms of mergers and statutory consolidations are prepared in the normal accounting process since all assets and liabilities are recorded on just one set of books. Accounting for an **acquisition,** however, results in an investment account on the acquiring company's books while the assets and liabilities are still recorded and shown on the books of the acquired company. Financial reporting for this type of combination generally requires the bringing together, or **accounting consolidation,** of the accounts from these two sets of books to prepare financial reports for the economic entity now formed between the parent and subsidiary companies. This process is explained in detail in Section F. of this module.

## A. Accounting for the Combination

Regardless of the legal form (merger, statutory consolidation, acquisition), there is only one accounting method that currently can be applied to any business combination—the purchase method. The FASB in Statement of Financial Accounting Standards 141, *Business Combinations,* eliminated the other method that was used to account for business combinations—pooling of interest accounting. Both methods are described below because combinations that occurred on or before June 30, 2001, and accounted for under the pooling method will continue to be accounted for in that fashion.

### 1. Purchase Accounting

Purchase accounting for a combination is similar to the accounting treatment used in the acquisition of any asset group. The fair market value of the consideration (cash, stock, debt securities, etc.) given by the acquiring firm is used as the valuation basis of the combination. The assets and liabilities of the acquired firm are revalued to their respective fair market values at the combination date. (See Module 7D for a discussion of SFAS 157 and fair value measurements.) Any difference between the value of the consideration given and the fair market values of the net assets obtained is normally recorded as goodwill. When the fair market values of the net assets exceed the acquisition cost, the excess first is used to reduce the carrying value of noncurrent, nonfinancial assets. If such assets are reduced to zero, any additional amount is recognized as an extraordinary gain. The financial statements of the acquiring company reflect the combined operations from the date of combination.

2.  **The Pooling Method**

The pooling method assumes a combining of stockholders' interests. The basis of valuation in pooling is the book value of the net assets on the books of the acquired company. Therefore, goodwill may **not** be created at the date of combination in a pooling combination. The financial statements of the acquiring company will include a restatement of all prior years presented to include the operations and financial position of the pooled companies for all years presented.

B.  **A Company and B Company—Date of Combination**

A presentation of the date of combination entries for the purchase method will be made in the next two sections of this module. We will be using a comprehensive example for these sections and the remaining parts of the discussion on consolidation accounting. The following balance sheets of A Company and B Company provide the foundation for further discussion. As you study the remainder of this module, be sure you understand how the numbers are derived.

*A Company and B Company*
**BALANCE SHEETS 1/1/07**
*(Immediately Before Combination)*

| Assets | A Company | B Company |
| --- | --- | --- |
| Cash | $ 30,900 | $ 37,400 |
| Accounts receivable | 34,200 | 9,100 |
| Inventories | 22,900 | 16,100 |
| Equipment | 200,000 | 50,000 |
| Less:  Accumulated depreciation | (21,000) | (10,000) |
| Patents | -- | 10,000 |
| Total assets | $267,000 | $112,600 |
| **Liabilities and Equity** | | |
| Accounts payable | $  4,000 | $  6,600 |
| Bonds payable | 100,000 | -- |
| Capital stock ($10 par) | 100,000 | 50,000 |
| Additional paid-in capital | 15,000 | 15,000 |
| Retained earnings | 48,000 | 41,000 |
| Total liabilities and equity | $267,000 | $112,600 |

The concept of book value of the investment is a basic principle of accounting for business combinations and will be used in many different computations. Note that the book value of the net assets of B Company may be computed by two different methods.

1.  Subtract the book value of the liabilities from the book values of the assets, or

$$\$112,600 - \$6,600 = \$106,000$$

2.  Add the book values of the components of B Company stockholders' equity

$$\$50,000 + \$15,000 + \$41,000 = \$106,000$$

C.  **Date of Combination—Purchase Accounting**

Purchase accounting uses fair market values of the net assets as the valuation basis for the combination. The difference between the value of the consideration given by the acquiring firm and the **book value** of the net assets obtained is the excess of cost over book value, or excess of book value over cost (referred to here as differential) of the net assets obtained. As discussed earlier, this differential has two components, as follows:

1.  An amount representing an adjustment of the book values of the net assets up (or down) to their respective fair market values, and
2.  An amount representing goodwill, or reduction in the carrying value of noncurrent, nonfinancial assets

In determining the components of the assets acquired, intangible assets that arise from contractual or legal rights or can be disposed of separate from the entity should be recognized as assets apart from goodwill. Examples include trademarks, customer contracts, leases, patents, computer software, licensing agreements, and internet domain names.

Assume that our Company A purchased **all** the net assets of B Company. At the date of combination, the fair values of all the assets and liabilities were determined by appraisal, as follows:

| B Company item | Book value (BV) | Fair market value (FMV) | Difference between BV and FMV |
|---|---|---|---|
| Cash | $ 37,400 | $ 37,400 | $    -- |
| Accounts rec. (net) | 9,100 | 9,100 | -- |
| Inventories | 16,100 | 17,100 | 1,000 |
| Equipment (net) | 40,000 | 48,000 | 8,000 |
| Patents | 10,000 | 13,000 | 3,000 |
| Accounts payable | (6,600) | (6,600) | -- |
| Totals | $106,000 | $118,000 | $12,000 |

The $12,000 is the difference between the book value and fair market values of B Company and is one component of the differential.  Goodwill, the other component of the differential, is the difference between the cost of the investment and the FMV of the net assets.  Goodwill may be positive or negative.

Four different cases displaying a range of total acquisition costs are presented below.  The form of consideration paid to B Company by A Company is assumed to be cash but, under purchase accounting, it could be stock, cash, debentures, or any other form of payment.

The allocation of the difference between cost and book value is a two-step process.  First, the assets and liabilities must be valued at their respective fair market values and then any remainder is allocated to goodwill (or a reduction in the carrying value of certain assets).  Note that the differential may be positive or negative and that the net assets could have fair market values less than book values.

|  | Case A | Case B | Case C | Case D |
|---|---|---|---|---|
| Consideration paid | $134,000 | $118,000 | $106,000 | $100,000 |
| Notes: | (> FMV) | (= FMV) | (< FMV) | (< FMV) |
|  | (> BV) | (> BV) | (= BV) | (< BV) |

**Step 1.  Compute the Differential**

|  | Case A | Case B | Case C | Case D |
|---|---|---|---|---|
| Book value | $106,000 | $106,000 | $106,000 | $106,000 |
| Investment cost | 134,000 | 118,000 | 106,000 | 100,000 |
| Differential | $ 28,000 | $ 12,000 | $    -- | $ (6,000) |

**Step 2.  Allocation of Differential**

a. Revaluation of net assets to fair market value

|  | Case A | Case B | Case C | Case D |
|---|---|---|---|---|
| FMV, net assets | $118,000 | $118,000 | $118,000 | $118,000 |
| Less BV | 106,000 | 106,000 | 106,000 | 106,000 |
| Portion to net assets | $ 12,000 | $ 12,000 | $ 12,000 | $ 12,000 |

b. Remainder (Excess of cost greater than fair value, or fair value greater than cost)

|  | Case A | Case B | Case C | Case D |
|---|---|---|---|---|
| FMV, net assets | $118,000 | $118,000 | $118,000 | $118,000 |
| Less investment cost | 134,000 | 118,000 | 106,000 | 100,000 |
| Goodwill | $ 16,000 | $    -- |  |  |
| Amount to reduce carrying value of net assets |  |  | $ (12,000) | $ (18,000) |

**Step 3.  Accounting for Goodwill and the Excess of Fair Value Greater Than Cost**

SFAS 141 assumes the excess of cost greater than fair values of acquired assets and liabilities is goodwill (Case A).  Goodwill is accounted for in accordance with SFAS 142.  If the fair value of the assets and liabilities is **greater than** the investment cost (Cases C and D), then SFAS 141 requires this excess to be proportionally applied to reduce the assigned values of the noncurrent assets acquired, except financial assets (other than investments accounted for on the equity basis), assets to be disposed of by sale, deferred tax assets, and prepaid assets related to pensions or other postretirement benefit plans.  If such assets are reduced to zero value, any remaining excess of fair value over cost should be recognized as an **extraordinary gain**.

Reallocations are required in Cases C and D because the fair values of the net assets are greater than costs, as follows:

| | Item | Assigned values of noncurrent assets acquired | Proportion | Excess of fair value over cost | Reallocation | New assigned value |
|---|---|---|---|---|---|---|
| Case C: | Equipment | $48,000 | $48,000/$61,000 | ($12,000) | $ (9,443) | $38,557 |
| | Patents | $13,000 | $13,000/$61,000 | ($12,000) | $ (2,557) | $10,443 |
| | | $61,000 | | | $(12,000) | |
| Case D: | Equipment | $48,000 | $48,000/$61,000 | ($18,000) | $(14,164) | $33,836 |
| | Patents | $13,000 | $13,000/$61,000 | ($18,000) | $ (3,836) | $ 9,164 |
| | | $61,000 | | | $(18,000) | |

Date of combination entries on A Company's books for a purchase-merger are

| | Case A | Case B | Case C | Case D |
|---|---|---|---|---|
| Cash | 37,400 | 37,400 | 37,400 | 37,400 |
| AR | 9,100 | 9,100 | 9,100 | 9,100 |
| Inventories | 17,100 | 17,100 | 17,100 | 17,100 |
| Equipment (net) | 48,000 | 48,000 | 38,557 | 33,836 |
| Patents | 13,000 | 13,000 | 10,443 | 9,164 |
| Goodwill | 16,000 | -- | -- | -- |
| AP | | 6,600 | 6,600 | 6,600 | 6,600 |
| Cash | | 134,000 | 118,000 | 106,000 | 100,000 |

B Company would close its books and cease to operate as a separate entity.

If B Company maintained its separate legal status, the combination would be accounted for as a 100% acquisition. The date of combination entries on A Company's books for each of the four cases would be

| | Case A | Case B | Case C | Case D |
|---|---|---|---|---|
| Investment in B Company | 134,000 | 118,000 | 106,000 | 100,000 |
| Cash | | 134,000 | 118,000 | 106,000 | 100,000 |

Consolidated financial statements would normally be prepared when acquisitions of more than 50% of outstanding stock are made. Consolidated statements are discussed later in this module.

Some candidates find that using value lines to display the features of purchase accounting helps to sort out the various concepts. Value lines are provided below for Cases A and D. You might want to do the value lines for Cases B and C.

**CASE A**

| | | | | |
|---|---|---|---|---|
| | Cost | $134,000 | (2b) | Remainder (Excess of cost > FMV) |
| | | | | Goodwill = $16,000 |
| (1) Differential = $28,000 (Excess of Cost > BV) | FMV | $118,000 | | |
| | BV | $106,000 | (2a) | Revalue net assets to FMV $12,000 |

**CASE D**

| | | | | |
|---|---|---|---|---|
| | FMV | $118,000 | (2a) Revalue net assets to FMV $12,000 | (2b) Remainder (Excess of FMV > Cost) ($18,000) |
| (1) Differential = <$6,000> (Excess of BV > Cost) | BV | $106,000 | | |
| | Cost | $100,000 | | |

## D.  Purchase Combination Entries Reviewed

The following table provides a review of the combination entries of the surviving or investing firm for the three legal forms of combination (merger, consolidation, and acquisition) for which stock is given. The legal form is primarily dependent on whether the combined company, Company B in our examples, retains a separate, legal existence or transfers its assets and liabilities to Company A and cancels any remaining stock of Company B. The items in the parentheses are valuation bases or the company source for determining the dollar amount for the entry.

| Legal form | Accounting |
|---|---|
| 1. Merger | Assets (FMV of B) |
| (A Co. + B Co. = A Co.) | Liabilities (FMV of B) |
| | Capital stock (Co. A) |
| | APIC (Co. A) |

| *Legal form* | *Accounting* |
|---|---|
| 2. Statutory Consolidation | Assets (FMV of both A and B) |
| (A Co. + B Co. = C Co.) | Liabilities (FMV of A and B) |
| | Capital stock (Co. C) |
| | APIC (Co. C) |
| 3. Acquisition | Investment in B (FMV) |
| (A Co. + B Co. = Consolidated | Capital stock (Co. A) |
| statements of A and B) | APIC (Co. A) |

## E.  Consolidated Financial Statements

An acquisition of more than 50% of the outstanding voting stock will normally require the preparation of consolidated financial statements.  The complete consolidation process is presented in the next section of this module.  The investment account will be eliminated in the consolidation working papers and will be replaced with the specific assets and liabilities of the investee corporation.  Consolidation is generally required for investments of more than 50% of the outstanding voting stock except when

1.  The control is likely to be temporary.
2.  Control is not held by the majority owner.

    a.  The investee is in legal reorganization or bankruptcy.
    b.  The investee operates in a foreign country which has severe restrictions on the financial transactions of its business firms or is subject to material political or economic uncertainty that casts significant doubt on the parent's ability to control the subsidiary.

In these limited cases, the investment will be reported as a long-term investment in an unconsolidated subsidiary on the investor's balance sheet with its balance determined by using the cost method unless the parent can demonstrate that it has significant influence in which case the equity method shall be used.

In certain instances control over an entity may be achieved through arrangements that do not involve voting interests.  Special rules apply, as set forth in FASB Interpretation 46, to variable interest entities (often special-purpose entities) in which control is achieved based on contractual, ownership, or other pecuniary interests that change with changes in the entity's net asset value.  An entity is a variable interest entity subject to consolidation if by design either of the following conditions exist:

1.  The total equity investment at risk is not sufficient to permit the entity to finance its activities without additional subordinated financial support from other parties (i.e., the equity investment at risk is not greater then the expected losses of the entity).
2.  As a group the holders of the equity investment at risk lack any one of the following three characteristics of a controlling financial interest:

    a.  The direct or indirect ability to make decisions about an entity's activities through voting rights or similar rights.
    b.  The obligation to absorb the expected losses of the entity if they occur.
    c.  The right to receive the expected residual returns of the entity if they occur.

The determination of whether an entity is a variable interest entity is made on the date the investor becomes involved and is not reconsidered unless there is a change in the nature of the entity or the relationship of the investors (e.g., a change in the contractual arrangements).

An equity investment of less than 10% of total assets generally should be considered to be insufficient to fund the entity's operations unless there is clear evidence to the contrary, such as evidence that it can get financing for its activities without additional subordinated financial support.  Some entities may require an equity interest greater than 10% of total assets to finance their activities, especially if they engage in high-risk activities.

Thus, entities with less than 10% equity are generally considered to be a variable interest entity for purposes of consolidation unless there is definitive evidence that they can fund their activities.  Entities with 10% or more equity may or may not be considered variable interest entities depending on the circumstances.

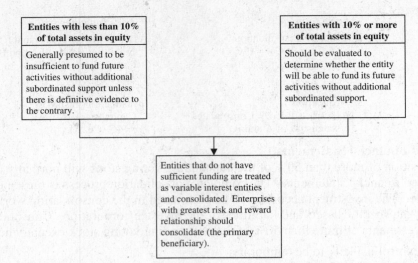

| Entities with less than 10% of total assets in equity | Entities with 10% or more of total assets in equity |
|---|---|
| Generally presumed to be insufficient to fund future activities without additional subordinated support unless there is definitive evidence to the contrary. | Should be evaluated to determine whether the entity will be able to fund its future activities without additional subordinated support. |

Entities that do not have sufficient funding are treated as variable interest entities and consolidated. Enterprises with greatest risk and reward relationship should consolidate (the primary beneficiary).

A variable interest entity should be consolidated by the enterprise that will absorb a majority of the entity's expected losses if they occur, receive a majority of the entity's expected residual returns if they occur, or both. This enterprise is referred to as the primary beneficiary.

In addition to consolidation, the primary beneficiary should disclose: (1) the nature, purpose, size, and activities of the variable interest entity, (2) the carrying amount and classification of consolidated assets that are collateral for the variable interest entity's obligations, and (3) lack of recourse if creditors of a consolidated variable interest entity have no recourse to the general credit of the primary beneficiary. An enterprise that holds a significant variable interest in a variable interest entity that is not the primary beneficiary should disclose: (1) the nature of its involvement with the variable interest entity and when involvement began, (2) the nature, purpose, size, and activities of the variable interest entity, and (3) the enterprise's maximum exposure to loss as a result of its involvement with the variable interest entity.

The concept of consolidated statements is that the resources of two or more companies are under the control of the parent company. Consolidated statements are prepared as if the group of legal entities were one economic entity group. Consolidated statements are presumed to be more meaningful for management, owners, and creditors of the parent company and they are required for fair presentation of the financially-related companies. Individual company statements should continue to be prepared for minority ownership and creditors of the subsidiary companies.

The accounting principles used to record and report events for a single legal entity are also applicable to a consolidated economic entity of two or more companies. The concept of the reporting entity is expanded to include more than one company, but all other accounting principles are applied in the same way as for an individual company. The consolidation process eliminates reciprocal items that are shown on both the parent's and subsidiary's books. These eliminations are necessary to avoid double-counting the same items which would misstate the financials of the combined economic entity.

Consolidated financial statements are prepared from worksheets which begin with the trial balances of the parent and subsidiary companies. Eliminating worksheet entries are made to reflect the two separate companies' results of operations and financial position as one combined economic entity. The entire consolidation process takes place **only on a worksheet;** no consolidation elimination entries are ever recorded on either the parent's or subsidiary's books.

Consolidated balance sheets are typically prepared at the date of combination to determine the initial financial position of the economic entity. Any intercompany accounts between the parent and subsidiary must be eliminated against each other. In addition, the "Investment in subsidiary's stock" account from the parent's books will be eliminated against the reciprocal accounts of the subsidiary's stockholders' equity. The remaining accounts are then combined to prepare the consolidated balance sheet. The preparation of consolidated statements after the date of combination becomes a little more complex because the parent's and subsidiary's income statements may include reciprocal intercompany accounts which must be eliminated. The next section of the module will present an example of the preparation of a consolidated balance sheet at the date of combination for both purchase and pooling accounting. You should carefully review the date of combination consolidation process before proceeding to the preparation of consolidation statements subsequent to combination.

**F. Date of Combination Consolidated Balance Sheet—Purchase Accounting**

This example uses the numbers from the A Company and B Company presented at the beginning of Section B of this module. The discussion in the preceding sections assumed a 100% combination in which the parent acquired control of all the subsidiary's stock or net assets. For the remainder of the module, we will assume that the parent company (A Company) acquired a 90% interest in the net assets of the subsidiary company (B Company). The remaining 10% of the outstanding stock is held by third-party investors referred to as the **minority interest,** or noncontrolling interest. In the illustrated problem, you will be able to review the determination of how minority interest is computed and disclosed on the consolidated financial statements. Note that only the "acquisition" legal form leads to the preparation of consolidated statements and includes less than 100% business combinations.

The assumptions for this illustration are

1. On January 1, 2007, A Company acquires a 90% interest in B Company in exchange for 5,400 shares of $10 par value stock having a total market value of $120,600.
2. The purchase method of accounting is used for the combination.

The workpaper for a consolidated balance sheet at the date of acquisition is presented below. The first two columns are the trial balances from the books of A Company and B Company immediately following the acquisition.

1. **Investment Entry on A Company's Books**

The entry to record the 90% purchase-acquisition on A Company's books was

| | | |
|---|---|---|
| Investment in Stock of B Company | 120,600 | |
| Capital Stock | | 54,000 |
| Additional Paid-in Capital | | 66,600 |

*To record the issuance of 5,400 shares of $10 par value stock to acquire a 90% interest in B Company.*

Although common stock is used for the consideration in our example, A Company could have used debentures, cash, or any other form of consideration acceptable to B Company's stockholders to make the purchase combination.

**A COMPANY AND B COMPANY CONSOLIDATED WORKING PAPERS**
*For Date of Combination - 1/1/07*

Purchase accounting
90% Interest

| | A Company | B Company | Adjustments and eliminations Debit | Adjustments and eliminations Credit | Minority interest | Consolidated balances |
|---|---|---|---|---|---|---|
| Balance sheet 1/1/07 | | | | | | |
| Cash | 30,900 | 37,400 | | | | 68,300 |
| Accounts receivable | 34,200 | 9,100 | | | | 43,300 |
| Inventories | 22,900 | 16,100 | (b) 900 | | | 39,900 |
| Equipment | 200,000 | 50,000 | (b) 9,000 | | | 259,000 |
| Accumulated depreciation | (21,000) | (10,000) | | (b) 1,800 | | (32,800) |
| Investment in stock of B Company | 120,600 | | | (a) 120,600 | | |
| Difference between cost and book value | | | (a) 25,200 | (b) 25,200 | | |
| Excess of cost over fair value (goodwill) | | | (b) 14,400 | | | 14,400 |
| Patents | | 10,000 | (b) 2,700 | | | 12,700 |
| Total assets | 387,600 | 112,600 | | | | 404,800 |
| Accounts payable | 4,000 | 6,600 | | | | 10,600 |
| Bonds payable | 100,000 | | | | | 100,000 |
| Capital stock | 154,000 | 50,000 | (a) 45,000 | | 5,000 | 154,000 |
| Additional paid-in capital | 81,600 | 15,000 | (a) 13,500 | | 1,500 | 81,600 |
| Retained earnings | 48,000 | 41,000 | (a) 36,900 | | 4,100 | 48,000 |
| Minority interest | | | | | 10,600 | 10,600 |
| Total liabilities and equity | 387,600 | 112,600 | 147,600 | 147,600 | | 404,800 |

2. **Difference between Investment Cost and Book Value**

The difference between the investment cost and the parent company's equity in the net assets of the subsidiary is computed as follows:

|                                         |          |          |
|-----------------------------------------|----------|----------|
| Investment cost                         |          | $120,600 |
| – Book value % at date of combination   |          |          |
| B Company's:                            |          |          |
| Capital stock                           | $ 50,000 |          |
| Additional paid-in capital              | 15,000   |          |
| Retained earnings                       | 41,000   |          |
| Total                                   | $106,000 |          |
| Parent's share of ownership             | × 90%    |          |
| Parent's share of book value            |          | 95,400   |
| Excess of cost over book value          |          | $ 25,200 |

This difference is due to several undervalued assets and to unrecorded goodwill. The allocation procedure is similar to that shown on page 646 for a 100% purchase; however, in this case, the parent company obtained a 90% interest and thus will recognize 90% of the difference between the fair market values and book values of the subsidiary's assets, not 100%. The allocation is presented as

| Item | Book value (BV) | Fair market value (FMV) | Difference between BV and FMV | Ownership percentage | Percentage share of difference between BV and FMV |
|------|----------------|-------------------------|------------------------------|----------------------|---------------------------------------------------|
| Cash | $ 37,400 | $ 37,400 | $     -- | | |
| Accounts receivable (net) | 9,100 | 9,100 | -- | | |
| Inventories | 16,100 | 17,100 | 1,000 | 90% | $    900 |
| Equipment | 50,000 | 60,000 | 10,000 | 90% | 9,000 |
| Accumulated depreciation | (10,000) | (12,000) | (2,000) | 90% | (1,800) |
| Patents | 10,000 | 13,000 | 3,000 | 90% | 2,700 |
| Accounts payable | (6,600) | (6,600) | -- | | |
| Total | $106,000 | $118,000 | $12,000 | | $10,800 |

| | |
|---|---|
| Amount of difference between cost and book value share allocated to revaluation of net assets | $10,800 |
| Total differential | 25,200 |
| Remainder allocated to goodwill | $14,400 |

The equipment has a book value of $40,000 ($50,000 less 20% depreciation of $10,000). An appraisal concluded with a judgment that the equipment's replacement cost was $60,000 less 20% accumulated depreciation of $12,000 resulting in a net fair value of $48,000.

3. **Elimination Entries on Workpaper**

The basic reciprocal accounts are the investment in subsidiary account on the parent's books and the subsidiary's stockholder equity accounts. Only the parent's share of the subsidiary's accounts may be eliminated as reciprocal accounts. The remaining 10% portion is allocated to the minority interest. The entries below include documentation showing the company source for the information. Those aids will help you trace the numbers. The workpaper entry to eliminate the basic reciprocal accounts is

| | | | |
|---|---|---|---|
| (a) | Capital stock—B Co. | 45,000 | |
| | Additional paid-in capital—B Co. | 13,500 | |
| | Retained earnings—B Co. | 36,900* | |
| | Differential | 25,200 | |
| | Investment in stock of B Co.—A Co. | | 120,600 |

* ($36,900 = 90% × $41,000)

Note that only 90% of B Company's stockholders' equity accounts are eliminated. Also, an account called "Differential" is debited in the workpaper entry. The differential account is a temporary account to record the difference between the cost of the investment in B Company from the parent's books and the book value of the parent's interest (90% in our case) from the subsidiary's books.

The next step is to allocate the differential to the specific accounts by making the following workpaper entry:

| | | | |
|---|---|---|---|
| (b) | Inventories | 900 | |
| | Equipment | 9,000 | |
| | Patents | 2,700 | |
| | Goodwill | 14,400 | |
| | Accumulated depreciation | | 1,800 |
| | Differential | | 25,200 |

This entry reflects the allocations prepared in Step 2 and recognizes the parent's share of the asset revaluations.

The minority interest column is the 10% interest of B Company's net assets owned by outside, third parties. Minority interest must be disclosed because 100% of the book values of B Company are included in the consolidated statements although A Company controls only 90% of the net assets. An alternative method to "prove" minority interest is to multiply the net assets of the subsidiary by the minority interest share, as follows:

$$\text{Stockholders equity of B company} \quad \text{Minority interest \%}$$
$$\$106,000 \quad \times \quad 10\% \quad = \$10,600$$

The $10,600 would be reported on the credit side of the consolidated balance sheet between liabilities and stockholders' equity.

The principle used to prepare the consolidated balance sheet is called the **parent company concept**. This is the method used most often on the CPA exam and also used in virtually all actual cases of consolidations of less than wholly owned subsidiaries. An alternative approach is known as the **entity concept**. The two differ in the amount of the asset revaluations recognized on the consolidated balance sheet. Under the parent company concept, just the parent's share of the revaluation is shown and the minority interest is reported at its share of the subsidiary's book value. If the entity concept were used, the net assets of B Company would be included in the consolidated balance sheet at 100% of their fair values at the date of acquisition and minority interest would be reported at its share of the fair value of the subsidiary. In our example, minority interest under the entity concept would have been

$$\text{Total fair market value of net assets of B Company} \quad \text{Minority interest}$$
$$\$118,000 \quad \times \quad 10\% \quad = \$11,800$$

Our example does not include any other intercompany accounts as of the date of combination. If any existed, they would be eliminated to fairly present the consolidated entity. Several examples of other reciprocal accounts will be shown later in this module for the preparation of consolidated financial statements subsequent to the date of acquisition.

## G. Consolidated Financial Statements subsequent to Acquisition

The concepts used to prepare subsequent consolidated statements are essentially the same as used to prepare the consolidated balance sheet at the acquisition date. The income statement and statement of retained earnings are added to reflect the results of operations since the acquisition date for a purchase. Furthermore, some additional reciprocal accounts may have to be eliminated because of intercompany transactions between the parent and subsidiary corporations. Please note that the financial statements of a consolidated entity are prepared using the same accounting principles that would be employed by a single, unconsolidated enterprise. The only difference is that some reciprocal accounts appearing on both companies' books must be eliminated against each other before the two corporations may be presented as one consolidated economic entity. Your review should concentrate on the accounts and amounts appearing on the consolidated statements (amounts in the last column of the worksheet). This "end-result" focus will help provide the understanding of why certain elimination entries are necessary.

An expanded version of the consolidated worksheet is necessary if the income statement and retained earnings statement must also be prepared. A comprehensive format often called "the three statement layout" is an integrated vertical array of the income statement, the retained earnings statement, and the balance sheet. The net income of the period is carried to the retained earnings statement and the ending retained earnings are carried down to the balance sheet. If you are required to prepare just the consolidated balance sheet, then eliminating entries involving nominal accounts (income statement accounts and "Dividends declared" account) would be made directly against the ending balance of retained earnings presented on the balance sheet.

The following discussion assumes the parent is using the partial equity method to account for the majority investment. Some firms may use the cost method during the period to record investment income because it requires fewer book adjustments to the investment account. In cases where the cost method is used during the period, one approach is to adjust the investment and investment income accounts to the equity method through an entry on the workpaper and the consolidation process may then be continued. Assuming that an income statement and retained earnings statement are being prepared in addition to the balance sheet, the general form of this restatement from cost to equity entry is made on the workpapers.

| | |
|---|---|
| Dividend income (for income recognized using cost method) | xx |
| Investment in sub (% of undistributed income of sub) | xx |
|      Equity in subsidiary's income (for income recognized using equity method) |     xx |

Additional workpaper restatement entries would be required to recognize the equity income in prior periods if the investment were owned for more than one period and to recognize the amortizations of any differential for all periods the investment was held. After these entries are made, the investment and equity in subsidiary's income accounts would be stated at equity and the consolidation process may continue. It is important to note that the formal consolidated statements will be the same regardless of the method used by the parent to account for the investment on its books. The concept of measurement used in the preparation of the consolidated statements is equivalent to the full equity method and the elimination process will result in statements presented under that concept.

## H. Intercompany Transactions and Profit Confirmation

Three general types of intercompany transactions may occur between the parent and subsidiary companies. Intercompany transactions require special handling because the profit or loss from these events must be properly presented on the consolidated financial statements. The three types of intercompany transactions are: intercompany sales of merchandise, transactions in fixed assets, and intercompany debt/equity transactions. These events may generate "unrealized profit" (also referred to as unconfirmed profit) which is a profit or gain shown in the trial balance from one of the company's books, but should not be shown in the consolidated financial statements. Intercompany bond transactions may require recognition of a gain or loss on the consolidated financials which is not in the trial balances of either the parent or subsidiary companies.

### 1. Intercompany Inventory Transactions

Unrealized profit in ending inventory arises through intercompany sales above cost that are not resold to third parties prior to year-end. Thus, the profit on the selling corporation's books is overstated, because an arm's-length transaction has not yet taken place. The inventory is overstated on the purchaser's books for the amount of the unrealized intercompany profit. An exhibit of the relationships is shown below.

Companies A and B are two separate legal entities and will each record the sale or purchase of goods. From a consolidated or economic entity viewpoint, however, the intercompany transaction is a transfer of assets which cannot result in revenue recognition until these goods are sold to a third party. Assuming a sale from Company A to Company B (a "downstream" intercompany sale), the sale income of Company A cannot be recognized until the goods are sold to third parties by Company B. In addition, the ending inventory of Company B is overstated by the amount of profit in the inventory acquired from Company A. Once intercompany sales have been sold to third parties, the earning process has been verified by an arm's-length transaction with third parties. Thus, recognition of previously unrecognized profit must be made at that time.

### 2. Intercompany Fixed Asset Transactions

Unrealized profits on fixed assets arise through intercompany sales of fixed assets above undepreciated cost. From a consolidated viewpoint, the transaction represents the internal transfer of assets and no gain (loss) should be recognized. Therefore, any gain (loss) must be eliminated and the carrying value of the transferred asset must be returned to its initial book value basis. In subsequent periods, in the case of an intercompany gain, depreciation expense is overstated, because an overvalued asset is being depreciated on the books of the company showing the asset. This overstatement of depreciation must also be eliminated in the consolidation process. In essence, the company that acquired the intercompany asset is including the intercompany gain (loss) in its depreciation expense.

### 3. Intercompany Bond Transactions

When one consolidated company buys bonds of another consolidated company, there are several reciprocal items to eliminate: investment in bonds and bonds payable, interest income and interest expense, and interest payable and interest receivable. Intercompany gains and losses **cannot** arise from direct intercompany bond purchases.  The book value would be the same on both books and the interest accounts would be reciprocal.  Note that APB 21 does not require the use of the effective interest method for debt transactions between parent and subsidiary companies.  Straight-line amortizations of premiums or discounts are sometimes used in these instances.

Gains and losses on intercompany bond holdings occur when

a.  Already outstanding bonds of the parent (subsidiary) are purchased by a subsidiary (parent),
b.  From a third party, and
c.  For an amount different from the carrying value of the issuer.

From a consolidated viewpoint, these bonds are viewed as retired.  However, the bonds are still recorded as liabilities on the issuer's separate books and as investment in bonds on the purchasing corporation's books.  The eliminating entry is to recognize the imputed gain (loss) on the consolidated "retirement of debt" in the year of intercompany bond purchase.  As indicated in SFAS 145, gains on early extinguishment of debt are no longer routinely considered extraordinary.

## I.  Example of Subsequent Consolidated Financial Statements

The following information extends the basic example of A Company and B Company begun earlier in this module.  The example illustrates the major consolidation concepts and procedures most likely to appear on the exam.

On January 1, 2007, A Company acquired 90% of the stock of B Company in exchange for 5,400 shares of $10 par value stock having a total market value of $120,600.  The purchase method of accounting must be used for the combination.

On January 1, 2007, B Company's assets and liabilities had the following book and fair values.

|  | Book value | Fair value |
|---|---|---|
| Cash | $ 37,400 | $ 37,400 |
| Accounts receivable (net) | 9,100 | 9,100 |
| Inventories | 16,100 | 17,100 |
| Equipment | 50,000 | 60,000 |
| Accumulated depreciation | (10,000) | (12,000) |
| Patents | 10,000 | 13,000 |
| Accounts payable | (6,600) | (6,600) |
|  | $106,000 | $118,000 |

Financial statement data of the two companies as of December 31, 2007 (the end of the first year after combination) are presented below.

During 2007, A Company sold merchandise to B Company that originally cost A Company $15,000 and the sale was made for $20,000.  On December 31, 2007, B Company's inventory included merchandise purchased from A Company at a cost to B Company of $12,000.

Also during 2007, A Company acquired $18,000 of merchandise from B Company.  B Company uses a normal markup of 25% above its cost.  A Company's ending inventory includes $10,000 of the merchandise acquired from B Company.

B Company reduced its intercompany account payable to A Company to a balance of $4,000 as of December 31, 2007, by making a payment of $1,000 on December 30.  This $1,000 payment was still in transit on December 31, 2007.

On January 2, 2007, B Company acquired equipment from A Company for $7,000.  The equipment was originally purchased by A Company for $5,000 and had a book value of $4,000 at the date of sale to B Company.  The equipment had an estimated remaining life of four years as of January 2, 2007.

On December 31, 2007, B Company purchased for $44,000, 50% of the $100,000 of outstanding bonds issued by A Company to third parties.  The bonds mature on December 31, 2014 and were originally issued at par.  The bonds pay interest annually on December 31 of each year and the interest was paid to the prior investor immediately before B Company's purchase of the bonds.

The consolidated worksheet for the preparation of consolidated financial statements as of December 31, 2007, is presented below.

The investment account balance at the statement date should be reconciled to ensure the parent company made the proper entries under the method of accounting used to account for the investment.  As noted earlier, A Company is using the partial equity method, without amortizations.  The amortizations of the excess of cost over book value will be recognized only on the worksheets.  This method is the one typically followed on the CPA exam; however, be sure you determine the method used in the exam problem—do not assume! The "proof" of the investment account of A Company is

| Investment in Stock of B Company | | | |
|---|---|---|---|
| Original cost | 120,600 | | |
| % of B Company's income (90% × $9,400) | 8,460 | 3,600 | % of B Company's dividends declared (90% × $4,000) |
| Bal. 12/31/07 | 125,460 | | |

Any errors will require correcting entries before the consolidation process is continued. Correcting entries will be posted to the books of the appropriate company; eliminating entries are **not** posted to either company's books.

The difference between the investment cost and the book value of the net assets acquired was determined and allocated in the preparation of the date of combination consolidated statements presented on page 649. For purposes of brevity, that process will not be duplicated here since the same computations are used in preparing financial statements for as long as the investment is owned.

## A COMPANY AND B COMPANY CONSOLIDATED WORKING PAPERS
### Year Ended December 31, 2007

Purchase accounting
90% Owned
Subsequent, partial equity

| | A Company | B Company | Adjustments and eliminations Debit | | Adjustments and eliminations Credit | | Minority interest | Consolidated balances |
|---|---|---|---|---|---|---|---|---|
| **Income statement for year ended 12/31/07** | | | | | | | | |
| Sales | 750,000 | 420,000 | (a) | 38,000 | | | | 1,132,000 |
| Cost of sales | 581,000 | 266,000 | (b) | 5,000 | (a) | 38,000 | | 814,900 |
| | | | (i) | 900 | | | | |
| Gross margin | 169,000 | 154,000 | | | | | | 317,100 |
| Depreciation and interest expense | 28,400 | 16,200 | (i) | 1,800 | (d) | 750 | | 45,650 |
| Other operating expenses | 117,000 | 128,400 | (i) | 270 | | | | 245,670 |
| Net income from operations | 23,600 | 9,400 | | | | | | 25,780 |
| Gain on sale of equipment | 3,000 | | (d) | 3,000 | | | | |
| Gain on bonds | | | | | (e) | 6,000 | | 6,000 |
| Equity in subsidiary's income | 8,460 | | (f) | 8,460 | | | | |
| Minority income (.10 × $7,400) | | | | | | | 740 | (740) |
| Net income | 35,060 | 9,400 | | 57,430 | | 44,750 | 740 | 31,040 |
| **Statement of retained earnings for year ended 12/31/07** | | | | | | | | |
| 1/1/07 Retained earnings | | | | | | | | |
| A Company | 48,000 | | | | | | | 48,000 |
| B Company | | 41,000 | (g) | 36,900 | | | 4,100 | |
| Add net income (from above) | 35,060 | 9,400 | | 57,430 | | 44,750 | 740 | 31,040 |
| Total | 83,060 | 50,400 | | | | | 4,840 | 79,040 |
| Deduct dividends | 15,000 | 4,000 | | | (f) | 3,600 | 400 | 15,000 |
| Balance December 31, 2007 | 68,060 | 46,400 | | 94,330 | | 48,350 | 4,440 | 64,040 |
| **Balance sheet 12/31/07** | | | | | | | | |
| Cash | 45,300 | 6,400 | (l) | 1,000 | | | | 52,700 |
| Accounts receivable (net) | 43,700 | 12,100 | | | (l) | 1,000 | | 50,800 |
| | | | | | (c) | 4,000 | | |
| Inventories | 38,300 | 20,750 | (h) | 900 | (b) | 5,000 | | 54,050 |
| | | | | | (i) | 900 | | |
| Equipment | 195,000 | 57,000 | (h) | 9,000 | (d) | 2,000 | | 259,000 |
| Accumulated depreciation | (35,200) | (18,900) | | | (d) | 250 | | (57,950) |
| | | | | | (h) | 1,800 | | |
| | | | | | (i) | 1,800 | | |
| Investment in stock of B Company | 125,460 | | | | (f) | 4,860 | | |
| | | | | | (g) | 120,600 | | |
| Differential | | | (g) | 25,200 | (h) | 25,200 | | |
| Goodwill | | | (h) | 14,400 | | | | 14,400 |
| Investment in bonds of A Company | | 44,000 | | | (e) | 44,000 | | |
| Patents | | 9,000 | (h) | 2,700 | (i) | 270 | | 11,430 |
| Total assets | 412,560 | 130,350 | | | | | | 384,430 |

| | A Company | B Company | Adjustments and eliminations Debit | Adjustments and eliminations Credit | Minority interest | Consolidated balances |
|---|---|---|---|---|---|---|
| Accounts payable | 8,900 | 18,950 | (c) 4,000 | | | 23,850 |
| Bonds payable | 100,000 | | (e) 50,000 | | | 50,000 |
| Capital stock | 154,000 | 50,000 | (g) 45,000 | | 5,000 | 154,000 |
| Additional paid-in capital | 81,600 | 15,000 | (g) 13,500 | | 1,500 | 81,600 |
| Retained earnings (from above) | 68,060 | 46,400 | 94,330 | 48,350 | 4,440 | 64,040 |
| Minority interest | | | | | 10,940 | 10,940 |
| Total liabilities and equity | 412,560 | 130,350 | 260,030 | 260,030 | | 384,430 |

The following adjusting and eliminating entries will be required to prepare consolidated financials as of December 31, 2007. Note that a consolidated income statement is required and, therefore, the nominal accounts are still "open." The number or letter in parentheses to the left of the entry corresponds to the key used on the worksheet.

Step 1. Complete the transaction for any intercompany items in transit at the end of the year.

(a)  Cash                                                                            1,000
        Accounts receivable                                                          1,000

This **adjusting** entry will now properly present the financial positions of both companies and the consolidation process may be continued.

Step 2. Prepare the eliminating entries.

(a)  Sales                                                                           38,000
        Cost of goods sold                                                          38,000

Total intercompany sales of $38,000 include $20,000 in a downstream transaction from A Company to B Company and $18,000 in an upstream transaction from B Company to A Company.

(b)  Cost of goods sold                                                              5,000
        Inventories                                                                 5,000

The ending inventories are overstated because of the unrealized profit from the intercompany sales. The debit to cost of goods sold is required because a decrease in ending inventory will increase cost of goods sold to be deducted on the income statement. Supporting computations for the entry are

| | In ending inventory of A Company | In ending inventory of B Company |
|---|---|---|
| Intercompany sales not resold, at selling price | $10,000 | $12,000 |
| Cost basis of remaining intercompany merchandise company merchandise | | |
| From B to A (÷125%) | (8,000) | |
| From A to B (÷133 1/3%) | | (9,000) |
| Unrealized profit | $ 2,000 | $ 3,000 |

When preparing consolidated workpapers for 2008 (the next fiscal period), an additional eliminating entry will be required if the goods in 2007's ending inventory are sold to outsiders during 2008. The additional entry will recognize the profit for 2008 that was eliminated as unrealized in 2007. This entry is necessary since the entry at the end of 2007 was made only on the worksheet. The 2008 entry will be

Retained earnings—B Comp. (1/1/08)                                                   200
Retained earnings—A Comp. (1/1/08)                                                   4,800
        Cost of goods sold (2008)                                                   5,000

The $200 debit to B's 1/1/08 retained earnings is for the minority interest's share of the unrealized profit on the 2007 upstream sale.

(c)  Accounts payable                                                                4,000
        Accounts receivable                                                         4,000

This eliminates the remaining intercompany receivable/payable owed **by** B Company to A Company. This eliminating entry is necessary to avoid overstating the consolidated entity's balance sheet.  The receivable/payable is not extinguished and B Company must still transfer $4,000 to A Company in the future.

|  |  |  |  |
|---|---|---:|---:|
| (d) | Gain on sale of equipment | 3,000 |  |
|  | Equipment |  | 2,000 |
|  | Accumulated depreciation |  | 250 |
|  | Depreciation expense |  | 750 |

Eliminates the gain on the intercompany sale of the equipment, eliminates the overstatement of equipment, and removes the excess depreciation taken on the gain.  Supporting computations for the entry are

|  | Cost | At date of intercompany sale accum. depr. | 2007 depreciation expense | End-of-period accum. depr. |
|---|---:|---:|---:|---:|
| Original cost (to seller-A Co.) | $ 5,000 | $(1,000) | $1,000 | $(2,000) |
| New cost (to buyer-B Co.) | 7,000 | -- | 1,750 | (1,750) |
| Difference | $(2,000) |  | $ (750) | $ 250 |

If the intercompany sale had not occurred, A Company would have depreciated the remaining book value of $4,000 over the estimated remaining life of four years.  However, since B Company's acquisition price ($7,000) was more than A Company's book value in the asset ($4,000), the depreciation recorded on the books of B Company will include part of the intercompany unrealized profit.  The equipment must be reflected on the consolidated statements at the original cost to the consolidated entity.  Therefore, the "write-up" of $2,000 in the equipment, the excess depreciation of $750, and the gain of $3,000 must be eliminated and the ending balance of accumulated depreciation must be shown at what it would have been if the intercompany equipment transaction had not occurred.  In future periods, a retained earnings account will be used instead of the gain account; however, the other concepts will be extended to include the additional periods.

|  |  |  |  |
|---|---|---:|---:|
| (e) | Bonds payable | 50,000 |  |
|  | Investment in bonds of A Company |  | 44,000 |
|  | Gain on extinguishment of debt |  | 6,000 |

This entry eliminates the book value of A Company's debt against the bond investment account of B Company.  To the consolidated entity, this transaction must be shown as a retirement of debt even though A Company has the outstanding intercompany debt to B Company.  In future periods, B Company will amortize the discount, thereby bringing the investment account up to par value and a retained earnings account will be used in the eliminating entry instead of the gain account.

|  |  |  |  |
|---|---|---:|---:|
| (f) | Equity in subsidiary's income—A Co. | 8,460 |  |
|  | Dividends declared—B Co. |  | 3,600 |
|  | Investment in stock of B Company |  | 4,860 |

This elimination entry adjusts the investment account back to its balance at the beginning of the period and also eliminates the income from subsidiary account.

|  |  |  |  |
|---|---|---:|---:|
| (g) | Capital stock—B Co. | 45,000 |  |
|  | Additional paid-in capital—B Co. | 13,500 |  |
|  | Retained earnings—B Co. | 36,900 |  |
|  | Differential | 25,200 |  |
|  | Investment in stock of B Co.—A Co. |  | 120,600 |

This entry eliminates 90% of B Company's stockholders' equity at the beginning of the year, 1/1/07.  Note that the changes **during** the year were eliminated in entry (f) above.  The differential account reflects the excess of investment cost greater than the book value of the assets acquired.

|  |  |  |  |
|---|---|---:|---:|
| (h) | Inventories | 900 |  |
|  | Equipment | 9,000 |  |
|  | Patents | 2,700 |  |
|  | Goodwill | 14,400 |  |
|  | Accumulated depreciation |  | 1,800 |
|  | Differential |  | 25,200 |

This entry allocates the differential (excess of investment cost over the book values of the assets acquired).  Note that this entry is the same as the allocation entry made to prepare consolidated financial statements for January 1, 2007, the date of acquisition.

(i)  Cost of goods sold                                                          900
     Depreciation expense                                                      1,800
     Other operating expenses—Patent amortization                               270
          Inventories                                                                              900
          Accumulated depreciation                                                               1,800
          Patents                                                                                   270

This elimination entry amortizes the revaluations to fair market value made in entry (h).  The inventory has been sold and therefore becomes part of the cost of goods sold.  Other assets including goodwill were evaluated for impairment and determined to be unimpaired.  The remaining revaluation will be amortized as follows:

| | Amortization revaluation | Annual period | Amortization |
|---|---|---|---|
| Equipment (net) | $ 7,200 | 4 years | $1,800 |
| Patents | 2,700 | 10 years | 270 |

The amortizations will continue to be made on future worksheets.  For example, at the end of the next year (2008), the amortization entry (i) would be as follows:

Retained earnings—A Co. (1/1/07)                                      2,970
Depreciation expense                                                  1,800
Other operating expenses—Patent amortization                          270
     Inventories                                                                           900
     Accumulated depreciation                                                            3,600
     Patents                                                                               540

The initial debit of $4,410 to retained earnings is an aggregation of the prior period's charges to income statement accounts ($900 + $1,800 + $270).  During subsequent years, some authors prefer reducing the allocated amounts in entry (h) for prior period's charges.  In this case, the amortization entry in future periods would reflect just that period's amortizations.

This extended example has assumed the purchase method was used to account for the combination of A Company and B Company.  As a result, the consolidated financial statements will include the parent company's share of the revaluations to fair market values of the subsidiary's net assets.  A pooling, however, is based on book values.  No differential exists in pooling accounting and, thus, entry (g) above would be different while entries (h) and (i) would not be made for a pooling.  All other eliminating entries would be the same.  The basic elimination entry (g) for a pooling, using the equity method of accounting for the investment, would be

Capital stock—B Co.                               45,000
Additional paid-in capital—B Co.                  13,500
Retained earnings—B Co.                           36,900
     Investment in stock of B Company                             95,400

## J.  Minority Interest

The parent company often acquires less than 100% (but more than 50%) of the subsidiary's outstanding stock.  Under either the purchase or pooling method the consolidated financial statements will include all of the assets, liabilities, revenues, and expenses of these less than wholly owned subsidiaries.  The percentage of the stock not owned by the parent company represents the minority interest's share of the net assets of the subsidiary.  Minority interest will be a line item deduction on the income statement for its portion of the subsidiary's income and, under the parent company concept, will be shown on the consolidated balance sheet after long-term debt but before stockholders' equity.  The following procedures apply to cases of less than wholly owned subsidiaries.

1.  Only the parent's share of the subsidiary's shareholders' equity is eliminated in the basic eliminating entry.  The minority interest's share is presented separately.
2.  The entire amount of intercompany reciprocal items is eliminated.  For example, all receivables/payables and sales/cost of sales with a 90% subsidiary are eliminated.
3.  For intercompany transactions in inventory and fixed assets, the possible effect on minority interest depends on whether the original transaction affected the subsidiary's income statement.  Mi-

nority interest is adjusted only for upstream intercompany transactions (i.e., when the subsidiary is the selling entity). In this case, the minority interest is adjusted for its percentage ownership of the common stock of the subsidiary. The minority interest is **not** adjusted for unrealized profits on downstream sales. The effects of downstream transactions are confined solely to the parent's (i.e., controlling) ownership interests.

The minority interest's share of the subsidiary's income is shown as a deduction on the consolidated income statement since 100% of the subsidiary's revenues and expenses are combined although the parent company owns less than a 100% interest. The minority interest receives only its percentage share of the subsidiary's income that has been earned in transactions with external third parties. For our example, the minority interest deduction on the income statement is computed as follows:

| | |
|---|---|
| B Company's reported income | $ 9,400 |
| Less: Unrealized profit on an upstream inventory sale | (2,000) |
| B Company's income for consolidated financial purposes | $ 7,400 |
| Minority interest share | 10% |
| Minority interest on income statement | $ 740 |

The minority interest's share of the net assets of B Company is shown on the consolidated balance sheet between liabilities and controlling interest's equity. The computation for the minority interest shown in the balance sheet for our example is

| | | | | |
|---|---|---|---|---|
| B Company's capital stock, 12/31/07 | | | $50,000 | |
| Minority interest share | | | 10% | $ 5,000 |
| B Company's additional paid-in capital, 12/31/07 | | | $15,000 | |
| Minority interest share | | | 10% | 1,500 |
| B Company's retained earnings, 1/1/07 | $41,000 | | | |
| Minority interest share | 10% | 4,100 | | |
| B Company's 2007 income for consolidated purposes | $ 7,400 | | | |
| Minority interest share | 10% | 740 | | |
| B Company's dividends during 2007 | $ 4,000 | | | |
| Minority interest share | 10% | (400) | | 4,440 |
| Total minority interest, 12/31/07 | | | | $10,940 |

The remainder of the consolidation process is just worksheet techniques, as follows:

1. Take all income items across horizontally and foot the adjustments, minority interest, and consolidated columns down to the net income line.
2. Take the amounts on the net income line (on income statement) in the adjustments, minority interest, and consolidated balances columns **down to** retained earnings items across the consolidated balances column. Foot and crossfoot the retained earnings statement.
3. Take the amounts of ending retained earnings in each of the four columns down to the ending retained earnings line in the balance sheet. Foot the minority interest column and place its total in the consolidated balances column. Take all the balance sheet items across to consolidated balances column.

## K. Subsequent Consolidated Balance Sheet Only

Consolidation exam problems sometimes require only the consolidated balance sheet. In this case, the effects of all the income statement account balances would have been closed to the retained earnings accounts. You should carefully review the adjustments and eliminations that were made noting that the nominal accounts (income statement accounts and dividends declared account) would be replaced with the account "Retained Earnings." Thus, elimination entry (a) would not be required; entry (b) would be

| | | |
|---|---|---|
| (b) Retained earnings | 5,000 | |
| Inventories | | 5,000 |

Retained earnings would be substituted for the nominal accounts in all other eliminating entries. A shortcut alternative to eliminating entries (f) and (g) is to use the ending balance of B Company's retained earnings as follows:

| | | | |
|---|---|---:|---:|
| (f & g) | Capital stock—B Co. | 45,000 | |
| | Additional paid-in capital—B Co. | 13,500 | |
| | *Retained earnings—B Co. | 41,760 | |
| | Differential | 25,200 | |
| | Investment in stock of B Co.—A Co. | | 125,460 |

* ($41,760 = 90% × $46,400 ending balance of B Company's retained earnings)

A worksheet for just the consolidated balance sheet is presented below.  The adjusting and eliminating entries are keyed to the entries and entry explanations for the three-statement layout presented earlier. Several elimination entries have been combined and are shown as (f/g) or (h/i).  Note that the final consolidated balance sheet amounts are the same when only the balance sheet is being prepared as well as when all three statements are being prepared.

## L.  Consolidated Net Income and Consolidated Retained Earnings

In some cases, you may be asked just to determine the Consolidated Net Income (CNI) of the parent and subsidiary companies.  A shorter, analytical approach may be used instead of the worksheet method. An analytical definition of CNI is exhibited for our example above.

If the "full" equity method had been used to account for the investment, all the adjustments to the parent company's income (see above) would have been reflected in the "Equity in Subsidiary's Income" account on the parent company's books.  Under the "partial" equity method, only the equity accrual of $8,460 is shown in the Equity in Subsidiary's Income account.  All other adjustments are made only on the consolidated worksheet.

### A COMPANY AND B COMPANY CONSOLIDATED WORKING PAPERS
### CONSOLIDATED BALANCE SHEET ONLY
#### December 31, 2007

Purchase accounting
90% Owned
Subsequent, partial equity

| Assets | A Company | B Company | Adjustments and eliminations Debit | | Adjustments and eliminations Credit | | Minority interest | Consolidated balances |
|---|---:|---:|---|---:|---|---:|---:|---:|
| Cash | 45,300 | 6,400 | (l) | 1,000 | | | | 52,700 |
| Accounts receivable (net) | 43,700 | 12,100 | | | (l) | 1,000 | | 50,800 |
| | | | | | (c) | 4,000 | | |
| Inventories | 38,300 | 20,750 | (h/i) | 900 | (b) | 5,000 | | 54,050 |
| | | | | | (h/i) | 900 | | |
| Equipment | 195,000 | 57,000 | (h/i) | 9,000 | (d) | 2,000 | | 259,000 |
| Accumulated depreciation | (35,200) | (18,900) | | | (d) | 250 | | (57,950) |
| | | | | | (h/i) | 3,600 | | |
| Investment in stock of B Company | 125,460 | | | | (f/g) | 125,460 | | |
| Differential | | | (f/g) | 25,200 | (h/i) | 25,200 | | |
| Goodwill | | | (h/i) | 14,400 | | | | 14,400 |
| Investment in bonds of A Company | | 44,000 | | | (e) | 44,000 | | |
| Patents | | 9,000 | (h/i) | 2,430 | | | | 11,430 |
| Total | 412,560 | 130,350 | | | | | | 384,430 |
| **Liabilities and Stockholders' Equity** | | | | | | | | |
| Accounts payable | 8,900 | 18,950 | (c) | 4,000 | | | | 23,850 |
| Bonds payable | 100,000 | | (e) | 50,000 | | | | 50,000 |
| Capital stock | 154,000 | 50,000 | (f/g) | 45,000 | | | 5,000 | 154,000 |
| Additional paid-in capital | 81,600 | 15,000 | (f/g) | 13,500 | | | 1,500 | 81,600 |
| Retained earnings | 68,060 | 46,400 | (b) | 5,000 | (e) | 6,000 | 4,400 | 64,040 |
| | | | (d) | 2,250 | | | | |
| | | | (f/g) | 41,760 | | | | |
| | | | (h/i) | 2,970 | | | | |
| Minority interest | | | | | | | 10,940 | 10,940 |
| Total | 412,560 | 130,350 | | 217,410 | | 217,410 | | 384,430 |

The computation of CNI for the purchase method is

| | |
|---|---:|
| Parent company's net income from **independent** operations | $26,600 |
| ± Parent company's share of subsidiary's equity income (loss) (equity accrual) | |
|     (90% × $9,400—reported income of B Co.) | +8,460 |
| ± Period's amortization of difference between cost and book value ($900—inventories | |
|     $1,800—equip.; $270—patent) | –2,970 |
| – Parent company's share of **unrealized** profit on intercompany transactions | |
|     ($3,000—merchandise sale of A to B; $1,800—90% of sale of goods from B to A; | |
|     $3,000—sale of equipment) | –7,800 |
| + Parent company's share of **realized** profit on intercompany transactions | |
|     ($6,000—bonds; $750—from elimination of excessive depr. on equip. sale from A to B) | +  6,750 |
| CNI (purchase method) | $31,040 |

Consolidated Retained Earnings (CRE) under the purchase method may be determined once CNI is found. An analytical definition of CRE for our example is

| | |
|---|---:|
| Parent company's beginning retained earnings (1/1/07) | $48,000 |
| + Consolidated net income for period | +31,040 |
| – Parent company's dividends to its shareholders (NOTE:  subsidiary's dividends to | |
|     outside parties are a component of minority interest, not CRE) | –15,000 |
| CRE (purchase method) | $64,040 |

Make special note that under the "full" equity method of accounting, consolidated retained earnings will equal the retained earnings of the parent company. This is true because consolidated retained earnings under the full equity method equals beginning of the year consolidated retained earnings plus consolidated net income (which is identical to parent company net income), minus dividends declared during the year by the parent company only.

## M. Changes in Ownership

Changes in the level of ownership of subsidiaries frequently occur through purchase or sale of the subsidiary's stock by the parent or changes in the sub's shares outstanding. If the subsidiary changes the number of shares outstanding (for example, through treasury stock transactions), the transaction may require an entry on the parent's books to maintain the parent's reciprocity in the net assets of the subsidiary.

For example, if the subsidiary, through treasury stock transactions, increases the relative book value owned by the parent, the increase must be recorded to maintain reciprocity between the investment account on the parent's accounting records and its equivalent stockholders' equity accounts in the subsidiary's books.

| | | |
|---|---|---|
| Investment in subsidiary | xx | |
|     Paid-in capital | | xx |

On the other hand, if the subsidiary's treasury stock transactions decrease the parent's equity

| | | |
|---|---|---|
| Paid-in capital | xx | |
|     Investment in subsidiary | | xx |

When the parent's share of ownership increases through a purchase of additional stock, simply debit investment and credit cash for cost. A problem occurs with consolidated income statements when the change in ownership takes place in mid-period. Consolidated statements should be prepared based on the ending ownership level. For example, assume that A Company increased its ownership of B Company from 90% to 95% on October 1, 2007. The investment was acquired at book value of $5,452.50 [5% × ($50,000 CS + $15,000 APIC + $44,050 RE at 10-1-07)]. If the subsidiary earned its income of $9,400 evenly over the year, the consolidated net income should reflect a net of

| | | | | | | | |
|---|---|---:|---|---|---|---|---:|
| 90% | × | $9,400 | × | 12/12 | = | | $8,460.00 |
| + 5% | × | $9,400 | × | 3/12 | = | | 117.50 |
| 95% | | | | | | | $8,577.50 |

The interim stock purchase will result in a new account being shown on the consolidated income statement. The account is **Purchased Preacquisition Earnings** which represents the percentage of the subsidiary's earnings earned, in this case, on the 5% stock interest from January 1, 2007, to October 1, 2007. The basic eliminating entries would be based on the 95% ownership as follows:

| | | |
|---|---|---|
| Equity in subsidiary's income—A Co. | 8,577.50 | |
| Dividends declared—B Co. | | 3,600.00 |
| Investment in stock of B Company | | 4,977.50 |
| Capital stock—B Co. | 47,500.00 | |
| Additional paid-in capital—B Co. | 14,250.00 | |
| Retained earnings—B Co. | 38,750.00* | |
| Purchased preacquisition earnings | 352.50** | |
| Differential | 25,200.00 | |
| Investment in stock of B Co.—A Co. | | 126,052.50 |

| | | | |
|---|---|---|---|
| * 95% × $41,000 beginning 2007 balance | = | $38,950 | |
| Less preacquisition dividend of 5% × $4,000 | = | $   (200) | |
| Retained earnings available, as adjusted | = | $38,750 | |
| ** $352.50 = 5% × $9,400 × 9/12) | | | |

Purchased Preacquisition Earnings is shown as a deduction along with Minority Interest to arrive at Consolidated Net Income. You should note that purchased preacquisition earnings are used only with interim acquisitions under the purchase accounting method.

## N. Combined Financial Statements

Combined financial statements is the term used to describe financial statements prepared for companies that are owned by the same parent company or individual. These statements are often prepared when several subsidiaries of a common parent are not consolidated. Combined financial statements are prepared by combining all of the separate companies' financial statement classifications. Intercompany transactions, balances, and profit (loss) should be eliminated in the same way as in consolidated statements.

## O. Push-Down Accounting

"Push-down accounting" describes the method used to prepare the separate financial statements for significant, very large subsidiaries that are either wholly owned or substantially owned ($\geq$ 90%). For publicly traded companies, the SEC requires a one-time adjustment under the purchase method to revalue the subsidiary's assets and liabilities to fair value, and this entry is made directly on the books of the subsidiary.

Push-down accounting requires the subsidiary to record an entry revaluing all assets and liabilities with a balancing entry to a revaluation capital account. The revaluation capital account will be eliminated in consolidation against the investment in subsidiary account. Push-down accounting will have no effect on the presentation of the consolidated financial statements or the separate financial statements of the parent company. However, the subsidiary's financial statements would be reported at fair value rather than historical cost. Advocates of push-down accounting believe that a change of ownership through a purchase-combination justifies the use of a new basis for the acquired entity. Thus, the new basis should be pushed down or directly recorded on the acquired entity's books.

## P. Research Component

ARB 51, *Consolidated Financial Statements*, was the first pronouncement addressing consolidated financial statements. Portions of ARB 51 are still in effect. These paragraphs include the purpose of consolidated statements, general consolidation procedure, minority interest, stock dividends of subsidiary, combined statements, intercompany transactions, and parent company statements. APB Opinion 16, which originally covered business combinations, has completely been superseded by SFAS 141. SFAS 141 eliminates the pooling method and addresses more recent issues involved with business combinations. SFAS 142 addresses goodwill and other intangible assets after the date of acquisition.

Below is a list of keywords for searching business combination issues.

| | | |
|---|---|---|
| Acquired research and development | Contractual-legal criterion | Intercompany profit or loss |
| Acquiring entity | Controlling interest | Legal rights |
| Allocate cost assets | Costs registering securities | Minority interest |
| Allocating cost asset | Date of acquisition | Noncontrolling interest |
| Asset apart from goodwill | Derecognized | Obtains control |
| Assigning amounts to assets | Disclosure financial statement | Parent-company |
| Business combinations | Fair value exchanged | Purchase method |
| Combined entity notes to financial statements | Financial assets | Reportable segment |
| Combined financial statements | Goodwill | Reporting unit |
| Commonly controlled companies | Initial measurement | Rights transferable or separable |
| Consolidated financial statements | Initial recognition | Separability criterion |
| Consolidation purposes | Intangible asset class | Stock dividends subsidiary |
| Contingency | Intangible assets acquired | Subsequent accounting acquisition |
| Contingent consideration | Intangible assets subject to amortization | |
| Contractual rights | Intercompany balances | |

**MULTIPLE-CHOICE QUESTIONS (1-66)**

**1.** On April 1, 2007, Dart Co. paid $620,000 for all the issued and outstanding common stock of Wall Corp. The recorded assets and liabilities of Wall Corp. on April 1, 2007, follow:

| | |
|---|---|
| Cash | $ 60,000 |
| Inventory | 180,000 |
| Property and equipment (net of accumulated depreciation of $220,000) | 320,000 |
| Goodwill | 100,000 |
| Liabilities | (120,000) |
| Net assets | $ 540,000 |

On April 1, 2007, Wall's inventory had a fair value of $150,000, and the property and equipment (net) had a fair value of $380,000. What is the amount of goodwill resulting from the business combination?
a. $150,000
b. $120,000
c. $ 50,000
d. $ 20,000

**2.** A business combination is accounted for as a purchase. Which of the following expenses related to the business combination should be included, in total, in the determination of net income of the combined corporation for the period in which the expenses are incurred?

| | Fees of finders and consultants | Registration fees for equity securities issued |
|---|---|---|
| a. | Yes | Yes |
| b. | Yes | No |
| c. | No | Yes |
| d. | No | No |

**3.** On August 31, 2007, Wood Corp. issued 100,000 shares of its $20 par value common stock for the net assets of Pine, Inc., in a business combination accounted for by the purchase method. The market value of Wood's common stock on August 31 was $36 per share. Wood paid a fee of $160,000 to the consultant who arranged this acquisition. Costs of registering and issuing the equity securities amounted to $80,000. No goodwill was involved in the purchase. What amount should Wood capitalize as the cost of acquiring Pine's net assets?
a. $3,600,000
b. $3,680,000
c. $3,760,000
d. $3,840,000

**Items 4 and 5** are based on the following:

On December 31, 2007, Saxe Corporation was merged into Poe Corporation. In the business combination, Poe issued 200,000 shares of its $10 par common stock, with a market price of $18 a share, for all of Saxe's common stock. The stockholders' equity section of each company's balance sheet immediately before the combination was

| | Poe | Saxe |
|---|---|---|
| Common stock | 3,000,000 | $1,500,000 |
| Additional paid-in capital | 1,300,000 | 150,000 |
| Retained earnings | 2,500,000 | 850,000 |
| | $6,800,000 | $2,500,000 |

**4.** In the December 31, 2007 consolidated balance sheet, additional paid-in capital should be reported at
a. $ 950,000
b. $1,300,000
c. $1,450,000

d. $2,900,000

**5.** In the December 31, 2007 consolidated balance sheet, common stock should be reported at
a. $3,000,000
b. $3,500,000
c. $4,000,000
d. $5,000,000

**6.** On January 1, 2008, Neal Co. issued 100,000 shares of its $10 par value common stock in exchange for all of Frey Inc.'s outstanding stock. The fair value of Neal's common stock on December 31, 2007, was $19 per share. The carrying amounts and fair values of Frey's assets and liabilities on December 31, 2007, were as follows:

| | Carrying amount | Fair value |
|---|---|---|
| Cash | $ 240,000 | $ 240,000 |
| Receivables | 270,000 | 270,000 |
| Inventory | 435,000 | 405,000 |
| Property, plant, and equipment | 1,305,000 | 1,440,000 |
| Liabilities | (525,000) | (525,000) |
| Net assets | $1,725,000 | $1,830,000 |

What is the amount of goodwill resulting from the business combination?
a. $175,000
b. $105,000
c. $ 70,000
d. $0

**7.** Consolidated financial statements are typically prepared when one company has a controlling financial interest in another **unless**
a. The subsidiary is a finance company.
b. The fiscal year-ends of the two companies are more than three months apart.
c. Such control is likely to be temporary.
d. The two companies are in unrelated industries, such as manufacturing and real estate.

**8.** With respect to business combinations, SFAS 141 provides that
a. The pooling of interests method must be used for all combinations.
b. The pooling of interests method may be used only when specific requirements are met.
c. The purchase method must be used for all combinations.
d. The purchase method may be used only when specific requirements are met.

**9.** A business combination is accounted for appropriately as a purchase. Which of the following should be deducted in determining the combined corporation's net income for the current period?

| | Direct costs of acquisition | General expenses related to acquisition |
|---|---|---|
| a. | Yes | No |
| b. | Yes | Yes |
| c. | No | Yes |
| d. | No | No |

**10.** PDX Corp. acquired 100% of the outstanding common stock of Sea Corp. in a purchase transaction. The cost of the acquisition exceeded the fair value of the identifiable assets and assumed liabilities. The general guidelines for assigning amounts to the inventories acquired provide for

a. Raw materials to be valued at original cost.
b. Work in process to be valued at the estimated selling prices of finished goods, less both costs to complete and costs of disposal.
c. Finished goods to be valued at replacement cost.
d. Finished goods to be valued at estimated selling prices, less both costs of disposal and a reasonable profit allowance.

**11.** In accounting for a business combination, which of the following intangibles should not be recognized as an asset apart from goodwill?
a. Trademarks.
b. Lease agreements.
c. Employee quality.
d. Patents.

**12.** With respect to the allocation of the cost of a business acquisition, SFAS 141 requires
a. Cost to be allocated to the assets based on their carrying values.
b. Cost to be allocated based on fair values.
c. Cost to be allocated based on original costs.
d. None of the above.

**Items 13 through 17** are based on the following:

On January 1, 2007, Polk Corp. and Strass Corp. had condensed balance sheets as follows:

|  | Polk | Strass |
|---|---|---|
| Current assets | $ 70,000 | $20,000 |
| Noncurrent assets | 90,000 | 40,000 |
| Total assets. | $160,000 | $60,000 |
| Current liabilities | $ 30,000 | $10,000 |
| Long-term debt | 50,000 | -- |
| Stockholders' equity | 80,000 | 50,000 |
| Total liabilities and stockholders' equity | $160,000 | $60,000 |

On January 2, 2007, Polk borrowed $60,000 and used the proceeds to purchase 90% of the outstanding common shares of Strass. This debt is payable in ten equal annual principal payments, plus interest, beginning December 30, 2007. The excess cost of the investment over Strass' book value of acquired net assets should be allocated 60% to inventory and 40% to goodwill.

On Polk's January 2, 2007 consolidated balance sheet,

**13.** Current assets should be
a. $99,000
b. $96,000
c. $90,000
d. $79,000

**14.** Noncurrent assets should be
a. $130,000
b. $134,000
c. $136,000
d. $140,000

**15.** Current liabilities should be
a. $50,000
b. $46,000
c. $40,000
d. $30,000

**16.** Noncurrent liabilities including minority interests should be
a. $115,000
b. $109,000

c. $104,000
d. $ 55,000

**17.** Stockholders' equity should be
a. $ 80,000
b. $ 85,000
c. $ 90,000
d. $130,000

**18.** On November 30, 2007, Parlor, Inc. purchased for cash at $15 per share all 250,000 shares of the outstanding common stock of Shaw Co. At November 30, 2007, Shaw's balance sheet showed a carrying amount of net assets of $3,000,000. At that date, the fair value of Shaw's property, plant and equipment exceeded its carrying amount by $400,000. In its November 30, 2007 consolidated balance sheet, what amount should Parlor report as goodwill?
a. $750,000
b. $400,000
c. $350,000
d. $0

**19.** A subsidiary, acquired for cash in a business combination, owned inventories with a market value greater than the book value as of the date of combination. A consolidated balance sheet prepared immediately after the acquisition would include this difference as part of
a. Deferred credits.
b. Goodwill.
c. Inventories.
d. Retained earnings.

**20.** Company J acquired all of the outstanding common stock of Company K in exchange for cash. The acquisition price exceeds the fair value of net assets acquired. How should Company J determine the amounts to be reported for the plant and equipment and long-term debt acquired from Company K?

|  | Plant and equipment | Long-term debt |
|---|---|---|
| a. | K's carrying amount | K's carrying amount |
| b. | K's carrying amount | Fair value |
| c. | Fair value | K's carrying amount |
| d. | Fair value | Fair value |

**21.** In a business combination accounted for as a purchase, the appraised values of the identifiable assets acquired exceeded the acquisition price. How should the excess appraised value be reported?
a. As negative goodwill.
b. As additional paid-in capital.
c. As a reduction of the values assigned to certain assets and an extraordinary gain for any unallocated portion.
d. As positive goodwill.

**22.** Wright Corp. has several subsidiaries that are included in its consolidated financial statements. In its December 31, 2007 trial balance, Wright had the following intercompany balances before eliminations:

|  | Debit | Credit |
|---|---|---|
| Current receivable due from Main Co. | $ 32,000 | |
| Noncurrent receivable from Main | 114,000 | |
| Cash advance to Corn Corp. | 6,000 | |
| Cash advance from King Co. | | $ 15,000 |
| Intercompany payable to King | | 101,000 |

In its December 31, 2007 consolidated balance sheet, what amount should Wright report as intercompany receivables?

a.  $152,000
b.  $146,000
c.  $ 36,000
d.  $0

**23.** Shep Co. has a receivable from its parent, Pep Co. Should this receivable be separately reported in Shep's balance sheet and in Pep's consolidated balance sheet?

| | Shep's balance sheet | Pep's consolidated balance sheet |
|---|---|---|
| a. | Yes | No |
| b. | Yes | Yes |
| c. | No | No |
| d. | No | Yes |

**Items 24 through 27** are based on the following:

Selected information from the separate and consolidated balance sheets and income statements of Pard, Inc. and its subsidiary, Spin Co., as of December 31, 2007, and for the year then ended is as follows:

| | Pard | Spin | Consolidated |
|---|---|---|---|
| **Balance sheet accounts** | | | |
| Accounts receivable | $ 26,000 | $ 19,000 | $ 39,000 |
| Inventory | 30,000 | 25,000 | 52,000 |
| Investment in Spin | 67,000 | -- | -- |
| Goodwill | -- | -- | 30,000 |
| Minority interest | -- | -- | 10,000 |
| Stockholders' equity | 154,000 | 50,000 | 154,000 |
| **Income statement accounts** | | | |
| Revenues | $200,000 | $140,000 | $308,000 |
| Cost of goods sold | 150,000 | 110,000 | 231,000 |
| Gross profit | 50,000 | 30,000 | 77,000 |
| Equity in earnings of Spin | 11,000 | -- | -- |
| Net income | 36,000 | 20,000 | 40,000 |

*Additional information*

• During 2007, Pard sold goods to Spin at the same markup on cost that Pard uses for all sales. At December 31, 2007, Spin had not paid for all of these goods and still held 37.5% of them in inventory.
• Pard acquired its interest in Spin on January 2, 2007.

**24.** What was the amount of intercompany sales from Pard to Spin during 2007?
a.  $ 3,000
b.  $ 6,000
c.  $29,000
d.  $32,000

**25.** At December 31, 2007, what was the amount of Spin's payable to Pard for intercompany sales?
a.  $ 3,000
b.  $ 6,000
c.  $29,000
d.  $32,000

**26.** In Pard's consolidated balance sheet, what was the carrying amount of the inventory that Spin purchased from Pard?
a.  $ 3,000
b.  $ 6,000
c.  $ 9,000
d.  $12,000

**27.** What is the percent of minority interest ownership in Spin?
a.  10%
b.  20%
c.  25%

d.  45%

**28.** On January 1, 2007, Owen Corp. purchased all of Sharp Corp.'s common stock for $1,200,000. On that date, the fair values of Sharp's assets and liabilities equaled their carrying amounts of $1,320,000 and $320,000, respectively. During 2007, Sharp paid cash dividends of $20,000.

Selected information from the separate balance sheets and income statements of Owen and Sharp as of December 31, 2007, and for the year then ended follows:

| | Owen | Sharp |
|---|---|---|
| **Balance sheet accounts** | | |
| Investment in subsidiary | $1,320,000 | -- |
| Retained earnings | 1,240,000 | 560,000 |
| Total stockholders' equity | 2,620,000 | 1,120,000 |
| **Income statement accounts** | | |
| Operating income | 420,000 | 200,000 |
| Equity in earnings of Sharp | 140,000 | -- |
| Net income | 400,000 | 140,000 |

In Owen's December 31, 2007 consolidated balance sheet, what amount should be reported as total retained earnings?
a.  $1,240,000
b.  $1,360,000
c.  $1,380,000
d.  $1,800,000

**29.** When a parent-subsidiary relationship exists, consolidated financial statements are prepared in recognition of the accounting concept of
a.  Reliability.
b.  Materiality.
c.  Legal entity.
d.  Economic entity.

**30.** A subsidiary was acquired for cash in a business combination on January 1, 2007. The purchase price exceeded the fair value of identifiable net assets. The acquired company owned equipment with a market value in excess of the carrying amount as of the date of combination. A consolidated balance sheet prepared on December 31, 2007, would
a.  Report the unamortized portion of the excess of the market value over the carrying amount of the equipment as part of goodwill.
b.  Report the unamortized portion of the excess of the market value over the carrying amount of the equipment as part of plant and equipment.
c.  Report the excess of the market value over the carrying amount of the equipment as part of plant and equipment.
d.  Not report the excess of the market value over the carrying amount of the equipment because it would be expensed as incurred.

**31.** Pride, Inc. owns 80% of Simba, Inc.'s outstanding common stock. Simba, in turn, owns 10% of Pride's outstanding common stock. What percentage of the common stock cash dividends declared by the individual companies should be reported as dividends declared in the consolidated financial statements?

| | Dividends declared by Pride | Dividends declared by Simba |
|---|---|---|
| a. | 90% | 0% |
| b. | 90% | 20% |
| c. | 100% | 0% |
| d. | 100% | 20% |

**32.** It is generally presumed that an entity is a variable interest entity subject to consolidation if its equity is
   a. Less than 50% of total assets.
   b. Less than 25% of total assets.
   c. Less than 10% of total assets.
   d. Less than 10% of total liabilities.

**33.** Morton Inc., Gilman Co., and Willis Corporation established a special-purpose entity (SPE) to perform leasing activities for the three corporations. If at the time of formation the SPE is determined to be a variable interest entity subject to consolidation, which of the corporations should consolidate the SPE?
   a. The corporation with the largest interest in the entity.
   b. The corporation that will absorb a majority of the expected losses if they occur.
   c. The corporation that has the most voting equity interest.
   d. Each corporation should consolidate one-third of the SPE.

**34.** The determination of whether an interest holder must consolidate a variable interest entity is made
   a. Each reporting period.
   b. When the interest holder initially gets involved with the variable interest entity.
   c. Every time the cash flows of the variable interest entity change.
   d. Interests in variable interest entities are never consolidated.

**35.** Matt Co. included a foreign subsidiary in its 2007 consolidated financial statements. The subsidiary was acquired in 2004 and was excluded from previous consolidations. The change was caused by the elimination of foreign exchange controls. Including the subsidiary in the 2007 consolidated financial statements results in an accounting change that should be reported
   a. By footnote disclosure only.
   b. Currently and prospectively.
   c. Currently with footnote disclosure of pro forma effects of retroactive application.
   d. By restating the financial statements of all prior periods presented.

**36.** On June 30, 2007, Purl Corp. issued 150,000 shares of its $20 par common stock for which it received all of Scott Corp.'s common stock. The fair value of the common stock issued is equal to the book value of Scott Corp.'s net assets. Both corporations continued to operate as separate businesses, maintaining accounting records with years ending December 31. Net income from separate company operations and dividends paid were

| | Purl | Scott |
|---|---|---|
| **Net income** | | |
| Six months ended 6/30/07 | $750,000 | $225,000 |
| Six months ended 12/31/07 | 825,000 | 375,000 |
| **Dividends paid** | | |
| March 25, 2007 | 950,000 | -- |
| November 15, 2007 | -- | 300,000 |

On December 31, 2007, Scott held in its inventory merchandise acquired from Purl on December 1, 2007, for $150,000, which included a $45,000 markup. In the 2007 consolidated income statement, net income should be reported at
   a. $1,650,000

   b. $1,905,000
   c. $1,950,000
   d. $2,130,000

**37.** On June 30, 2007, Pane Corp. exchanged 150,000 shares of its $20 par value common stock for all of Sky Corp.'s common stock. At that date, the fair value of Pane's common stock issued was equal to the book value of Sky's net assets. Both corporations continued to operate as separate businesses, maintaining accounting records with years ending December 31. Information from separate company operations follows:

| | Pane | Sky |
|---|---|---|
| Retained earnings— | | |
| 12/31/06 | $3,200,000 | $925,000 |
| Net income—six months | | |
| ended 6/30/07 | 800,000 | 275,000 |
| Dividends paid—3/25/07 | 750,000 | -- |

What amount of retained earnings would Pane report in its June 30, 2007 consolidated balance sheet?
   a. $5,200,000
   b. $4,450,000
   c. $3,525,000
   d. $3,250,000

**Items 38 and 39** are based on the following:

Scroll, Inc., a wholly owned subsidiary of Pirn, Inc., began operations on January 1, 2007. The following information is from the condensed 2007 income statements of Pirn and Scroll:

| | Pirn | Scroll |
|---|---|---|
| Sales to Scroll | $100,000 | $ -- |
| Sales to others | 400,000 | 300,000 |
| | 500,000 | 300,000 |
| Cost of goods sold: | | |
| Acquired from Pirn | -- | 80,000 |
| Acquired from others | 350,000 | 190,000 |
| Gross profit | 150,000 | 30,000 |
| Depreciation | 40,000 | 10,000 |
| Other expenses | 60,000 | 15,000 |
| Income from operations | 50,000 | 5,000 |
| Gain on sale of equipment to Scroll | 12,000 | -- |
| Income before income taxes | $ 62,000 | $ 5,000 |

*Additional information*

- Sales by Pirn to Scroll are made on the same terms as those made to third parties.
- Equipment purchased by Scroll from Pirn for $36,000 on January 1, 2007, is depreciated using the straight-line method over four years.

**38.** In Pirn's December 31, 2007, consolidating worksheet, how much intercompany profit should be eliminated from Scroll's inventory?
   a. $30,000
   b. $20,000
   c. $10,000
   d. $ 6,000

**39.** What amount should be reported as depreciation expense in Pirn's 2006 consolidated income statement?
   a. $50,000
   b. $47,000
   c. $44,000
   d. $41,000

**40.** Clark Co. had the following transactions with affiliated parties during 2007:

- Sales of $60,000 to Dean, Inc., with $20,000 gross profit. Dean had $15,000 of this inventory on hand at year-end. Clark owns a 15% interest in Dean and does not exert significant influence.
- Purchases of raw materials totaling $240,000 from Kent Corp., a wholly owned subsidiary. Kent's gross profit on the sale was $48,000. Clark had $60,000 of this inventory remaining on December 31, 2007.

Before eliminating entries, Clark had consolidated current assets of $320,000. What amount should Clark report in its December 31, 2007 consolidated balance sheet for current assets?

    a.  $320,000
    b.  $317,000
    c.  $308,000
    d.  $303,000

**41.** Parker Corp. owns 80% of Smith Inc.'s common stock. During 2007, Parker sold Smith $250,000 of inventory on the same terms as sales made to third parties. Smith sold all of the inventory purchased from Parker in 2007. The following information pertains to Smith and Parker's sales for 2007:

|              | Parker       | Smith     |
|--------------|--------------|-----------|
| Sales        | $1,000,000   | $700,000  |
| Cost of sales| 400,000      | 350,000   |
|              | $ 600,000    | $350,000  |

What amount should Parker report as cost of sales in its 2007 consolidated income statement?

    a.  $750,000
    b.  $680,000
    c.  $500,000
    d.  $430,000

**42.** Selected information from the separate and consolidated balance sheets and income statements of Pare, Inc. and its subsidiary, Shel Co., as of December 31, 2007, and for the year then ended is as follows:

|                             | Pare      | Shel      | Consolidated |
|-----------------------------|-----------|-----------|--------------|
| **Balance sheet accounts**  |           |           |              |
| Accounts receivable         | $ 52,000  | $ 38,000  | $ 78,000     |
| Inventory                   | 60,000    | 50,000    | 104,000      |
| **Income statement accounts** |         |           |              |
| Revenues                    | $400,000  | $280,000  | $616,000     |
| Cost of goods sold          | 300,000   | 220,000   | 462,000      |
| Gross profit                | $100,000  | $ 60,000  | $154,000     |

*Additional information*:

During 2007, Pare sold goods to Shel at the same markup on cost that Pare uses for all sales.

In Pare's consolidating worksheet, what amount of unrealized intercompany profit was eliminated?

    a.  $ 6,000
    b.  $12,000
    c.  $58,000
    d.  $64,000

**43.** During 2007, Pard Corp. sold goods to its 80%-owned subsidiary, Seed Corp. At December 31, 2007, one-half of these goods were included in Seed's ending inventory. Reported 2007 selling expenses were $1,100,000 and $400,000 for Pard and Seed, respectively. Pard's selling expenses included $50,000 in freight-out costs for goods sold to Seed. What amount of selling expenses should be reported in Pard's 2007 consolidated income statement?

    a.  $1,500,000
    b.  $1,480,000
    c.  $1,475,000
    d.  $1,450,000

**44.** On January 1, 2007, Poe Corp. sold a machine for $900,000 to Saxe Corp., its wholly owned subsidiary. Poe paid $1,100,000 for this machine, which had accumulated depreciation of $250,000. Poe estimated a $100,000 salvage value and depreciated the machine on the straight-line method over twenty years, a policy which Saxe continued. In Poe's December 31, 2007 consolidated balance sheet, this machine should be included in cost and accumulated depreciation as

|     | Cost        | Accumulated depreciation |
|-----|-------------|--------------------------|
| a.  | $1,100,000  | $300,000                 |
| b.  | $1,100,000  | $290,000                 |
| c.  | $ 900,000   | $ 40,000                 |
| d.  | $ 850,000   | $ 42,500                 |

**45.** Wagner, a holder of a $1,000,000 Palmer, Inc. bond, collected the interest due on March 31, 2007, and then sold the bond to Seal, Inc. for $975,000. On that date, Palmer, a 75% owner of Seal, had a $1,075,000 carrying amount for this bond. What was the effect of Seal's purchase of Palmer's bond on the retained earnings and minority interest amounts reported in Palmer's March 31, 2007 consolidated balance sheet?

|     | Retained earnings   | Minority interest    |
|-----|---------------------|----------------------|
| a.  | $100,000 increase   | $0                   |
| b.  | $ 75,000 increase   | $ 25,000 increase    |
| c.  | $0                  | $ 25,000 increase    |
| d.  | $0                  | $100,000 increase    |

**46.** Sun, Inc. is a wholly owned subsidiary of Patton, Inc. On June 1, 2007, Patton declared and paid a $1 per share cash dividend to stockholders of record on May 15, 2007. On May 1, 2007, Sun bought 10,000 shares of Patton's common stock for $700,000 on the open market, when the book value per share was $30. What amount of gain should Patton report from this transaction in its consolidated income statement for the year ended December 31, 2007?

    a.  $0
    b.  $390,000
    c.  $400,000
    d.  $410,000

**47.** Perez, Inc. owns 80% of Senior, Inc. During 2007, Perez sold goods with a 40% gross profit to Senior. Senior sold all of these goods in 2006. For 2007 consolidated financial statements, how should the summation of Perez and Senior income statement items be adjusted?

    a.  Sales and cost of goods sold should be reduced by the intercompany sales.
    b.  Sales and cost of goods sold should be reduced by 80% of the intercompany sales.
    c.  Net income should be reduced by 80% of the gross profit on intercompany sales.
    d.  No adjustment is necessary.

**48.** Water Co. owns 80% of the outstanding common stock of Fire Co. On December 31, 2007, Fire sold equipment to Water at a price in excess of Fire's carrying amount, but less than its original cost. On a consolidated balance sheet at

December 31, 2007, the carrying amount of the equipment should be reported at

a. Water's original cost.
b. Fire's original cost.
c. Water's original cost less Fire's recorded gain.
d. Water's original cost less 80% of Fire's recorded gain.

**49.** Port, Inc. owns 100% of Salem, Inc. On January 1, 2007, Port sold Salem delivery equipment at a gain. Port had owned the equipment for two years and used a five-year straight-line depreciation rate with no residual value. Salem is using a three-year straight-line depreciation rate with no residual value for the equipment. In the consolidated income statement, Salem's recorded depreciation expense on the equipment for 2007 will be decreased by

a. 20% of the gain on sale.
b. 33 1/3% of the gain on sale.
c. 50% of the gain on sale.
d. 100% of the gain on sale.

**50.** P Co. purchased term bonds at a premium on the open market. These bonds represented 20% of the outstanding class of bonds issued at a discount by S Co., P's wholly owned subsidiary. P intends to hold the bonds until maturity. In a consolidated balance sheet, the difference between the bond carrying amounts in the two companies would

a. Decrease retained earnings.
b. Increase retained earnings.
c. Be reported as a deferred debit to be amortized over the remaining life of the bonds.
d. Be reported as a deferred credit to be amortized over the remaining life of the bonds.

**51.** Eltro Company acquired a 70% interest in the Samson Company in 2006. For the years ended December 31, 2007 and 2008, Samson reported net income of $80,000 and $90,000, respectively. During 2007, Samson sold merchandise to Eltro for $10,000 at a profit of $2,000. The merchandise was later resold by Eltro to outsiders for $15,000 during 2008. For consolidation purposes what is the minority interest's share of Samson's net income for 2007 and 2008 respectively?

a. $23,400 and $27,600.
b. $24,000 and $27,000.
c. $24,600 and $26,400.
d. $26,000 and $25,000.

**Items 52 and 53** are based on the following:

On January 1, 2007, Ritt Corp. purchased 80% of Shaw Corp.'s $10 par common stock for $975,000. On this date, the carrying amount of Shaw's net assets was $1,000,000. The fair values of Shaw's identifiable assets and liabilities were the same as their carrying amounts except for plant assets (net) that were $100,000 in excess of the carrying amount. For the year ended December 31, 2007, Shaw had net income of $190,000 and paid cash dividends totaling $125,000.

**52.** In the January 1, 2007 consolidated balance sheet, goodwill should be reported at

a. $0
b. $ 75,000
c. $ 95,000
d. $175,000

**53.** In the December 31, 2007 consolidated balance sheet, minority interest should be reported at

a. $200,000
b. $213,000
c. $220,000
d. $233,000

**Items 54 through 56** are based on the following:

On January 2, 2008, Pare Co. purchased 75% of Kidd Co.'s outstanding common stock. Selected balance sheet data at December 31, 2008, is as follows:

|  | Pare | Kidd |
|---|---|---|
| Total assets | $420,000 | $180,000 |
| Liabilities | $120,000 | $ 60,000 |
| Common stock | 100,000 | 50,000 |
| Retained earnings | 200,000 | 70,000 |
|  | $420,000 | $180,000 |

During 2008 Pare and Kidd paid cash dividends of $25,000 and $5,000, respectively, to their shareholders. There were no other intercompany transactions.

**54.** In its December 31, 2008 consolidated statement of retained earnings, what amount should Pare report as dividends paid?

a. $ 5,000
b. $25,000
c. $26,250
d. $30,000

**55.** In Pare's December 31, 2008 consolidated balance sheet, what amount should be reported as minority interest in net assets?

a. $0
b. $ 30,000
c. $ 45,000
d. $105,000

**56.** In its December 31, 2008 consolidated balance sheet, what amount should Pare report as common stock?

a. $ 50,000
b. $100,000
c. $137,500
d. $150,000

**57.** On September 1, 2006, Phillips, Inc. issued common stock in exchange for 20% of Sago, Inc.'s outstanding common stock. On July 1, 2007, Phillips issued common stock for an additional 75% of Sago's outstanding common stock. Sago continues in existence as Phillips' subsidiary. How much of Sago's 2007 net income should be reported as accruing to Phillips?

a. 20% of Sago's net income to June 30 and all of Sago's net income from July 1 to December 31.
b. 20% of Sago's net income to June 30 and 95% of Sago's net income from July 1 to December 31.
c. 95% of Sago's net income.
d. All of Sago's net income.

**58.** Mr. & Mrs. Dart own a majority of the outstanding capital stock of Wall Corp., Black Co., and West, Inc. During 2007, Wall advanced cash to Black and West in the amount of $50,000 and $80,000, respectively. West advanced $70,000 in cash to Black. At December 31, 2007, none of the advances was repaid. In the combined December 31, 2007 balance sheet of these companies, what amount would be reported as receivables from affiliates?

a. $200,000
b. $130,000
c. $ 60,000
d. $0

**59.** Selected data for two subsidiaries of Dunn Corp. taken from December 31, 2007 preclosing trial balances are as follows:

| | Banks Co. debit | Lamm Co. credit |
|---|---|---|
| Shipments to Banks | $ -- | $150,000 |
| Shipments from Lamm | 200,000 | -- |
| Intercompany inventory profit on total shipments | -- | 50,000 |

Additional data relating to the December 31, 2007 inventory are as follows:

| | | |
|---|---|---|
| Inventory acquired from outside parties | $175,000 | $250,000 |
| Inventory acquired from Lamm | 60,000 | -- |

At December 31, 2007, the inventory reported on the combined balance sheet of the two subsidiaries should be
a. $425,000
b. $435,000
c. $470,000
d. $485,000

**60.** Ahm Corp. owns 90% of Bee Corp.'s common stock and 80% of Cee Corp.'s common stock. The remaining common shares of Bee and Cee are owned by their respective employees. Bee sells exclusively to Cee, Cee buys exclusively from Bee, and Cee sells exclusively to unrelated companies. Selected 2007 information for Bee and Cee follows:

| | Bee Corp. | Cee Corp. |
|---|---|---|
| Sales | $130,000 | $91,000 |
| Cost of sales | 100,000 | 65,000 |
| Beginning inventory | None | None |
| Ending inventory | None | 65,000 |

What amount should be reported as gross profit in Bee and Cee's combined income statement for the year ended December 31, 2007?
a. $26,000
b. $41,000
c. $47,800
d. $56,000

**61.** The following information pertains to shipments of merchandise from Home Office to Branch during 2007:

| | |
|---|---|
| Home Office's cost of merchandise | $160,000 |
| Intracompany billing | 200,000 |
| Sales by Branch | 250,000 |
| Unsold merchandise at Branch on December 31, 2007 | 20,000 |

In the combined income statement of Home Office and Branch for the year ended December 31, 2007, what amount of the above transactions should be included in sales?
a. $250,000
b. $230,000
c. $200,000
d. $180,000

**62.** Mr. and Mrs. Gasson own 100% of the common stock of Able Corp. and 90% of the common stock of Baker Corp. Able previously paid $4,000 for the remaining 10% interest in Baker. The condensed December 31, 2007 balance sheets of Able and Baker are as follows:

| | Able | Baker |
|---|---|---|
| Assets | $600,000 | $60,000 |
| Liabilities | $200,000 | $30,000 |
| Common stock | 100,000 | 20,000 |
| Retained earnings | 300,000 | 10,000 |
| | $600,000 | $60,000 |

In a combined balance sheet of the two corporations at December 31, 2007, what amount should be reported as total stockholders' equity?
a. $430,000
b. $426,000
c. $403,000
d. $400,000

**63.** Mr. Cord owns four corporations. Combined financial statements are being prepared for these corporations, which have intercompany loans of $200,000 and intercompany profits of $500,000. What amount of these intercompany loans and profits should be included in the combined financial statements?

| | Intercompany Loans | Profits |
|---|---|---|
| a. | $200,000 | $0 |
| b. | $200,000 | $500,000 |
| c. | $0 | $0 |
| d. | $0 | $500,000 |

**64.** Combined statements may be used to present the results of operations of

| | Companies under common management | Commonly controlled companies |
|---|---|---|
| a. | No | Yes |
| b. | Yes | No |
| c. | No | No |
| d. | Yes | Yes |

**65.** Which of the following items should be treated in the same manner in both combined financial statements and consolidated statements?

| | Income taxes | Minority interest |
|---|---|---|
| a. | No | No |
| b. | No | Yes |
| c. | Yes | Yes |
| d. | Yes | No |

**66.** Which of the following items should be treated in the same manner in both combined financial statements and consolidated statements?

| | Different fiscal periods | Foreign operations |
|---|---|---|
| a. | No | No |
| b. | No | Yes |
| c. | Yes | Yes |
| d. | Yes | No |

SIMULATION PROBLEMS

**Simulation Problem 1**                                    (50 to 60 minutes)

| Situation | | | | | |
|---|---|---|---|---|---|
| | **Concepts** | **Journal Entries** | **Financial Statement Amounts** | **Communication** | **Research** |

Presented below are selected amounts from the separate unconsolidated financial statements of Poe Corp. and its 90%-owned subsidiary, Shaw Co., at December 31, 2007. Additional information follows:

| | *Poe* | *Shaw* |
|---|---|---|
| ***Selected income statement amounts*** | | |
| Sales | $710,000 | $530,000 |
| Cost of goods sold | 490,000 | 370,000 |
| Gain on sale of equipment | -- | 21,000 |
| Earnings from investment in subsidiary | 61,000 | -- |
| Interest expense | -- | 16,000 |
| Depreciation | 25,000 | 20,000 |
| ***Selected balance sheet amounts*** | | |
| Cash | $ 50,000 | $ 15,000 |
| Inventories | 229,000 | 150,000 |
| Equipment | 440,000 | 360,000 |
| Accumulated depreciation | (200,000) | (120,000) |
| Investment in Shaw | 189,000 | -- |
| Investment in bonds | 100,000 | -- |
| Discount on bonds | (9,000) | -- |
| Bonds payable | -- | (200,000) |
| Common stock | (100,000) | (10,000) |
| Additional paid-in capital | (250,000) | (40,000) |
| Retained earnings | (402,000) | (140,000) |
| ***Selected statement of retained earnings amounts*** | | |
| Beginning balance, December 31, 2006 | $272,000 | $100,000 |
| Net income | 210,000 | 70,000 |
| Dividends paid | 80,000 | 30,000 |

**Additional information**

- On January 2, 2007, Poe, Inc. purchased 90% of Shaw Co.'s 100,000 outstanding common stock for cash of $155,000. On that date, Shaw's stockholders' equity equaled $150,000 and the fair values of Shaw's identifiable assets and liabilities equaled their carrying amounts. Poe has accounted for the acquisition as a purchase.
- On September 4, 2007, Shaw paid cash dividends of $30,000.
- On December 31, 2007, Poe recorded its equity in Shaw's earnings.

| | Concepts | | | | |
|---|---|---|---|---|---|
| **Situation** | | **Journal Entries** | **Financial Statement Amounts** | **Communication** | **Research** |

**Items 1 through 12** below refer to accounts that may or may not be included in Poe and Shaw's consolidated financial statements. The list below refers to the various possibilities of those amounts to be reported in Poe's consolidated financial statements for the year ended December 31, 2007. Consider all transactions stated in items 1 through 4 in determining your answer. Ignore income tax considerations.

*Responses to be selected*

A. Sum of amounts on Poe and Shaw's separate unconsolidated financial statements
B. Less than the sum of amounts on Poe and Shaw's separate unconsolidated financial statements but not the same as the amount on either
C. Same as amount for Poe only
D. Same as amount for Shaw only
E. Eliminated entirely in consolidation
F. Shown in consolidated financial statements but not in separate unconsolidated financial statements
G. Neither in consolidated nor in separate unconsolidated financial statements

(A) (B) (C) (D) (E) (F) (G)

**1.** Cash             ○ ○ ○ ○ ○ ○ ○

**2.** Equipment        ○ ○ ○ ○ ○ ○ ○

**3.** Investment in subsidiary    ○ ○ ○ ○ ○ ○ ○

|                                 | (A) | (B) | (C) | (D) | (E) | (F) | (G) |
|---------------------------------|-----|-----|-----|-----|-----|-----|-----|
| 4. Bonds payable                | O   | O   | O   | O   | O   | O   | O   |
| 5. Minority interest            | O   | O   | O   | O   | O   | O   | O   |
| 6. Common stock                 | O   | O   | O   | O   | O   | O   | O   |
| 7. Beginning retained earnings  | O   | O   | O   | O   | O   | O   | O   |
| 8. Dividends paid               | O   | O   | O   | O   | O   | O   | O   |
| 9. Gain on retirement of bonds  | O   | O   | O   | O   | O   | O   | O   |
| 10. Cost of goods sold          | O   | O   | O   | O   | O   | O   | O   |
| 11. Interest expense            | O   | O   | O   | O   | O   | O   | O   |
| 12. Depreciation expense        | O   | O   | O   | O   | O   | O   | O   |

| Situation | Concepts | Journal Entries | Financial Statement Amounts | Communication | Research |
|-----------|----------|-----------------|-----------------------------|---------------|----------|

**Items 1 through 3** below represent transactions between Poe and Shaw during 2007. Prepare the eliminating entries in general journal format for each of these transactions.

1. On January 3, 2007, Shaw sold equipment with an original cost of $30,000 and a carrying value of $15,000 to Poe for $36,000. The equipment had a remaining life of three years and was depreciated using the straight-line method by both companies.

|  |  |  |
|--|--|--|
|  |  |  |
|  |  |  |
|  |  |  |
|  |  |  |

2. During 2007, Shaw sold merchandise to Poe for $60,000, which included a profit of $20,000. At December 31, 2007, half of this merchandise remained in Poe's inventory.

|  |  |  |
|--|--|--|
|  |  |  |
|  |  |  |

3. On December 31, 2007, Poe paid $91,000 to purchase 50% of the outstanding bonds issued by Shaw. The bonds mature on December 31, 2012, and were originally issued at par. The bonds pay interest annually on December 31 of each year, and the interest was paid to the prior investor immediately before Poe's purchase of the bonds.

|  |  |  |
|--|--|--|
|  |  |  |
|  |  |  |
|  |  |  |
|  |  |  |

| Situation | Concepts | Journal Entries | Financial Statement Amounts | Communication | Research |
|-----------|----------|-----------------|-----------------------------|---------------|----------|

Calculate the amounts that will appear on Poe's consolidated financial statement on December 31, 2007.

1. Cash
2. Goodwill
3. Equipment
4. Common stock
5. Investment in Shaw
6. Dividends
7. Bonds payable

| Situation | Concepts | Journal Entries | Financial Statement Amounts | Communication | Research |
|---|---|---|---|---|---|

Write a brief memo to the CEO of Poe Corporation explaining the various accounting methods for investments in other company's stock and the rationale for consolidated financial statements.

To:      CEO, Poe Corporation
From:   CPA Candidate
Re:      Consolidated Financial Statements

| Situation | Concepts | Journal Entries | Financial Statement Amounts | Communication | Research |
|---|---|---|---|---|---|

Research the following issues. Cut and paste the appropriate sections of professional standards.

1. What method of accounting is used to record a business combination?

2. In a business combination, what is the definition of goodwill?

3. What are the conditions in which a new intangible asset can be recognized in a business combination?

---

**Simulation Problem 2**                                   (45 to 55 minutes)

| Situation | Concepts | Consolidation at Date of Acquisition | Intercompany Transactions & Eliminations | Consolidation at Year-End | Communication | Research |
|---|---|---|---|---|---|---|

On January 1, 2007, Arcelia Corporation acquired Gavino corporation by purchasing 100% of the stock of Gavino in exchange for 20,000 shares of Arcelia stock. On the date of acquisition Arcelia stock traded for $18 per share on the stock exchange.

The book values of each company on January 1, 2007, are shown below.

|  | Arcelia Corp. | Gavino Corp. |
|---|---|---|
| Current assets | $320,000 | 70,000 |
| Noncurrent assets | 640,000 | 380,000 |
| Current liabilities | 210,000 | 50,000 |
| Noncurrent liabilities | 150,000 | 90,000 |
| Owners' equity | 600,000 | 310,000 |

**Additional information**

- The fair market value of Gavino's inventory is $10,000 higher than the book value.
- During 2007, the following transactions occurred:

1. Arcelia sold inventory to Gavino for $50,000 on account. The normal profit on sales for Arcelia is 40%. At December 31, 2007, Gavino had 20% of the goods remaining in ending inventory. At December 31, 2007, Gavino had not paid Arcelia for $8,000 of the inventory.

2. On October 1, 2007, Gavino Corp. sold equipment to Arcelia for $24,000. The equipment was purchased by Gavino on 1/1/04 for $60,000 and was depreciated straight-line over five years with no salvage value. Arcelia depreciated the new equipment over three years with no salvage value.

- During 2007, Arcelia did not make entries to record the income of Gavino.
- At December 31, 2007, totals from the preclosing trial balances of both firms are as follows:

**Arcelia Corporation & Subsidiaries**
**UNADJUSTED TRIAL BALANCE**
*December 31, 2007*

|  | Arcelia Corp. | Gavino Corp. |
|---|---|---|
| Revenues | 1,000,000 | 400,000 |
| Expenses | 780,000 | 335,000 |
| Current assets | 400,000 | 110,000 |
| Noncurrent assets | 1,260,000 | 420,000 |
| Current liabilities | 300,000 | 70,000 |
| Noncurrent liabilities | 180,000 | 85,000 |
| Owners' equity | 960,000 | 310,000 |

| Situation | Concepts | Consolidation at Date of Acquisition | Intercompany Transactions & Eliminations | Consolidation at Year-End | Communication | Research |
|---|---|---|---|---|---|---|

Answer True or False to each of the following questions by checking the correct box.

| | | *True* | *False* |
|---|---|---|---|
| **1.** | A company can use either the purchase or the pooling method for business combinations. | O | O |
| **2.** | Total revenues for a consolidated entity are calculated by adding the total revenue of the parent for the year and the total revenue of the subsidiary from the date of acquisition. | O | O |
| **3.** | Goodwill is amortized over a period of forty years. | O | O |
| **4.** | Goodwill is classified and included with other intangible assets for purposes of measuring impairment. | O | O |
| **5.** | Intangible assets with indefinite lives are not amortized. | O | O |
| **6.** | The stockholder equity accounts in the consolidated balance sheet are those of the parent company. | O | O |
| **7.** | The effect of unrealized profits and sales between the parent company and its subsidiaries is classified as an intercompany transaction and must be eliminated. | O | O |
| **8.** | A newly identified intangible asset must meet the contractual legal criterion to be recognized as an intangible asset at the time of consolidation. | O | O |

| Situation | Concepts | Consolidation at Date of Acquisition | Intercompany Transactions & Eliminations | Consolidation at Year-End | Communication | Research |
|---|---|---|---|---|---|---|

Calculate each of the following balance sheet amounts for Arcelia Corporation immediately following the acquisition of Gavino.

| | |
|---|---|
| Total current assets | |
| Total noncurrent assets | |
| Total current liabilities | |
| Total noncurrent liabilities | |
| Total owners' equity | |

| Situation | Concepts | Consolidation at Date of Acquisition | Intercompany Transactions & Eliminations | Consolidation at Year-End | Communication | Research |
|---|---|---|---|---|---|---|

Below is a consolidation worksheet dated December 31, 2007 (before closing the books of Arcelia and Gavino). Prepare the following worksheet with working paper eliminations and entries.

*Arcelia Corporation*
**CONSOLIDATION WORKSHEET**
*December 31, 2007*

| | Arcelia Corp, | Gavino Corp. | Elimination entries | | End balance |
|---|---|---|---|---|---|
| | | | Debit | Credit | |
| Revenues | 1,000,000 | 400,000 | | | |
| Expenses | 780,000 | 335,000 | | | |
| Current assets | 400,000 | 110,000 | | | |
| Noncurrent assets | 1,260,000 | 420,000 | | | |
| Current liabilities | 300,000 | 70,000 | | | |
| Noncurrent liabilities | 180,000 | 85,000 | | | |
| Owners' equity | 960,000 | 310,000 | | | |

| Situation | Concepts | Consolidation at Date of Acquisition | Intercompany Transactions & Eliminations | Consolidation at Year-End | Communication | Research |
|---|---|---|---|---|---|---|

Indicate the balances of each of the following that will be found on the 2007 financial statements after all consolidation entries have been made and the books have been closed.

*Arcelia Corporation & Subsidiaries*
**CONSOLIDATED BALANCES**
*December 31, 2007*

| | |
|---|---|
| Total revenues | |
| Total expenses | |
| Total current assets | |
| Total noncurrent assets | |
| Total current liabilities | |
| Total noncurrent liabilities | |
| Total owners' equity | |

| Situation | Concepts | Consolidation at Date of Acquisition | Intercompany Transactions & Eliminations | Consolidation at Year-End | Communication | Research |
|---|---|---|---|---|---|---|

The CEO of Arcelia has inquired as to why the purchase price of Gavino could exceed the book value of the assets. Explain the valuation methods for acquiring the firm, the concept of goodwill, and how assets of the newly acquired subsidiary are recorded on the financial statements. Explain the calculation of goodwill and whether subsequent entries are necessary in accounting for goodwill.

To: CEO, Arcelia Corporation
From: CPA Candidate
Re: Valuation of acquired firm

| Situation | Concepts | Consolidation at Date of Acquisition | Intercompany Transactions & Eliminations | Consolidation at Year-End | Communication | Research |
|---|---|---|---|---|---|---|

What is an intercompany transaction and how should it be treated for financial reporting purposes?

---

**Simulation Problem 3**                          (10 to 20 minutes)

| Situation | Financial Statement Amounts |
|---|---|

On January 2, 2007, Purl Co. purchased 90% of Strand Co.'s outstanding common stock at a purchase price that was in excess of Strand's stockholders' equity. On that date, the fair value of Strand's assets and liabilities equaled their carrying amounts. Purl has accounted for the acquisition as a purchase. Transactions during 2007 were as follows:

- On February 15, 2007, Strand sold equipment to Purl at a price higher than the equipment's carrying amount. The equipment has a remaining life of three years and was depreciated using the straight-line method by both companies.
- During 2007, Purl sold merchandise to Strand under the same terms it offered to third parties. At December 31, 2007, one-third of this merchandise remained in Strand's inventory.
- On November 15, 2007, both Purl and Strand paid cash dividends to their respective stockholders.
- On December 31, 2007, Purl recorded its equity in Strand's earnings.

| Financial Statement Amounts | |
|---|---|
| Situation | |

**Items 1 through 10** relate to accounts that may or may not be included in Purl and Strand's consolidated financial statements. The list below refers to the possible ways those accounts may be reported in Purl's consolidated financial statements for the year ended December 31, 2007. An answer may be selected once, more than once, or not at all.

<u>Responses to be selected</u>

A.  Sum of the amounts on Purl and Strand's separate unconsolidated financial statements
B.  Less than the sum of the amounts on Purl and Strand's separate unconsolidated financial statements, but not the same as the amount on either separate unconsolidated financial statement
C.  Same as the amount for Purl only
D.  Same as the amount for Strand only
E.  Eliminated entirely in consolidation
F.  Shown in the consolidated financial statements but not in the separate unconsolidated financial statements

|  | (A) | (B) | (C) | (D) | (E) | (F) |
|---|---|---|---|---|---|---|
| 1. Cash | ○ | ○ | ○ | ○ | ○ | ○ |
| 2. Equipment | ○ | ○ | ○ | ○ | ○ | ○ |
| 3. Investment in subsidiary | ○ | ○ | ○ | ○ | ○ | ○ |
| 4. Minority interest | ○ | ○ | ○ | ○ | ○ | ○ |
| 5. Common stock | ○ | ○ | ○ | ○ | ○ | ○ |
| 6. Beginning retained earnings | ○ | ○ | ○ | ○ | ○ | ○ |
| 7. Dividends paid | ○ | ○ | ○ | ○ | ○ | ○ |
| 8. Cost of goods sold | ○ | ○ | ○ | ○ | ○ | ○ |
| 9. Interest expense | ○ | ○ | ○ | ○ | ○ | ○ |
| 10. Depreciation expense | ○ | ○ | ○ | ○ | ○ | ○ |

## MULTIPLE-CHOICE ANSWERS

| | | | | |
|---|---|---|---|---|
| 1. a __ __ | 15. b __ __ | 29. d __ __ | 43. d __ __ | 57. b __ __ |
| 2. d __ __ | 16. b __ __ | 30. b __ __ | 44. a __ __ | 58. d __ __ |
| 3. c __ __ | 17. a __ __ | 31. a __ __ | 45. a __ __ | 59. c __ __ |
| 4. d __ __ | 18. c __ __ | 32. c __ __ | 46. a __ __ | 60. b __ __ |
| 5. d __ __ | 19. c __ __ | 33. b __ __ | 47. a __ __ | 61. a __ __ |
| 6. c __ __ | 20. d __ __ | 34. b __ __ | 48. c __ __ | 62. b __ __ |
| 7. c __ __ | 21. c __ __ | 35. d __ __ | 49. b __ __ | 63. c __ __ |
| 8. c __ __ | 22. d __ __ | 36. b __ __ | 50. a __ __ | 64. d __ __ |
| 9. c __ __ | 23. a __ __ | 37. d __ __ | 51. a __ __ | 65. c __ __ |
| 10. d __ __ | 24. d __ __ | 38. d __ __ | 52. c __ __ | 66. c __ __ |
| 11. c __ __ | 25. b __ __ | 39. b __ __ | 53. b __ __ | |
| 12. b __ __ | 26. c __ __ | 40. c __ __ | 54. b __ __ | |
| 13. a __ __ | 27. b __ __ | 41. c __ __ | 55. b __ __ | 1st: __/66 = __% |
| 14. c __ __ | 28. a __ __ | 42. a __ __ | 56. b __ __ | 2nd: __/66 = __% |

## MULTIPLE-CHOICE ANSWER EXPLANATIONS

### A. Accounting for the Combination, and Sections B. – D.

**1.** **(a)** In a purchase, the net assets of the acquired firm are recorded at their FMV. The excess of the cost of the investment over the FMV of the net assets acquired is allocated to goodwill. The cost of the investment is $620,000, and the FMV of the net assets acquired, **excluding goodwill,** is $470,000, as computed below.

| | FMV |
|---|---|
| Cash | 60,000 |
| Inventory (BV = $180,000) | 150,000 |
| Prop. and equip. (BV = $320,000) | 380,000 |
| Liabilities | (120,000) |
| Total FMV | 470,000 |

Therefore, the amount allocated to goodwill is $150,000 ($620,000 – $470,000).

**2.** **(d)** Both finders' fees and registration fees are included in calculating the cost of the investment. They are not expensed in the year incurred. Answers (a) and (b) are incorrect because finders fees are included in the cost of the investment and not expensed in the year incurred. Registration fees for equity securities are a reduction in the issue price of the securities.

**3.** **(c)** In a business combination accounted for as a purchase, the fair market value of the net assets is used as the valuation basis for the combination. In this case, the net assets of the subsidiary have an implied fair market value of $3,600,000 which is the value of the common stock issued to Pine's shareholders (100,000 shares × $36). Also, per SFAS 141, the direct cost of acquisition should be included as part of the cost of a company acquired, and the cost of registering equity securities should be a reduction of the issue price of the securities (i.e., additional paid-in capital) in a business combination accounted for by the purchase method. Thus, the $160,000 paid for a consultant who arranged the acquisition should also be capitalized, and the $80,000 cost for registering and issuing the equity securities should be treated as a reduction of additional paid-in capital. The total amount to be capitalized is $3,760,000 ($3,600,000 + $160,000).

**4.** **(d)** In a business combination accounted for as a purchase, the fair market value of the net assets is used as the valuation basis for the combination. In this case, the net assets of the subsidiary have an implied fair market value of $3,600,000 which is the value of the common stock issued to Saxe's shareholders (200,000 × $18). Since $3,600,000 is the basis for recording this purchase, the common stock issued is recorded at $2,000,000 (200,000 shares × $10 par value per share) and additional paid-in capital is recorded at $1,600,000 ($3,600,000 – $2,000,000). Therefore, in the 12/31/07 consolidated balance sheet, additional paid-in capital should be reported at $2,900,000 ($1,300,000 + $1,600,000).

**5.** **(d)** In a business combination, the common stock account of the combined entity is the number of shares outstanding multiplied by the par value of the stock. The total common stock account of the combined entity is equal to $5,000,000, the $3,000,000 originally outstanding plus the total par value of the stock issued, $2,000,000 (200,000 × $10).

**6.** **(c)** In a business combination accounted for as a purchase, the fair market value of the net assets is used as the valuation basis for the combination. In this case, Frey's assets have an implied fair market value of $1,900,000 which is the market value of the common stock issue (100,000 shares × $19). The value assigned to goodwill is $70,000, which is the value of the stock minus the fair value of Frey's identifiable assets ($1,900,000 – $1,830,000).

**7.** **(c)** Per ARB 51, a subsidiary should not be consolidated when control is likely to be temporary. SFAS 94 requires consolidation of all majority-owned subsidiaries regardless of the industry or business of the subsidiary. ARB 51 states that a difference in fiscal periods of a parent and a subsidiary does not of itself justify the exclusion of the subsidiary from consolidation.

**8.** **(c)** SFAS 141 requires the use of the purchase method for all business combinations initiated after June 30, 2001. The pooling of interests method, which was allowed previously under certain circumstances, is only used for firms acquired in a transaction qualified for pooling treatment prior to 6/30/01.

**9.** **(c)** Per SFAS 141, the direct costs of acquisition should be included as part of the cost of a company acquired in a business combination accounted for by the purchase method. General expenses related to the acquisition, however, are deducted as incurred in determining the combined corporation's net income for the current period.

**10.** **(d)** The requirement is to select the correct general guideline for assigning amounts to inventories under the purchase method. Per SFAS 141, finished goods inventories should be valued at estimated selling prices less the costs of disposal and a reasonable profit allowance for the selling effort of the acquiring corporation. Raw materials should be valued at current replacement costs, not original cost. Work in process should be valued at the estimated selling prices of finished goods less the costs to complete, the costs of disposal, **and** a reasonable profit allowance.

**11.** **(c)** SFAS 141 requires intangibles to be recognized as assets apart from goodwill if they arise from contractual or legal rights, regardless of whether those rights are transferable or separable from the acquired entity or from other rights and obligations. If an intangible asset does not arise from contractual or other legal rights, it shall be recognized as an asset apart from goodwill only if it is separable (i.e., capable of being sold, transferred, or licensed). Trademarks, lease agreements, and patents all arise from contractual or legal rights. Employee quality does not and is not separable.

**12.** **(b)** SFAS 141 requires the use of the purchase method for all business combinations. In applying the purchase method, the acquisition cost is allocated to acquired assets and liabilities based on their fair values. Any excess of cost over the fair value of net assets is allocated to goodwill.

### F. Date of Combination Consolidated Balance Sheet—Purchase Accounting

**13.** **(a)** In the consolidated balance sheet, the parent company's "investment in subsidiary" account should be eliminated and replaced by the net assets of the subsidiary. Under the purchase method, the assets of the acquired firm are recorded at their FMV. The cost of the investment is $60,000 and the book value of the acquired net assets is $45,000 (90% × $50,000), so the excess of cost over book value is $15,000 ($60,000 – $45,000). 60% of this excess is allocated to inventory because its FMV exceeds its cost (60% × $15,000 = $9,000). Therefore, current assets should be reported at $99,000.

| | |
|---|---|
| Current assets—Polk | $70,000 |
| Current assets—Strass | 20,000 |
| Excess allocated to inventory | 9,000 |
| Total | $99,000 |

**14.** **(c)** In the consolidated balance sheet, the parent company's "investment in subsidiary" account should be eliminated and replaced by the net assets of the subsidiary. Under the purchase method, the assets of the acquired firm are recorded at their FMV. The cost of the investment is $60,000 and the book value of the acquired net assets is $45,000 (90% × $50,000) the excess of cost over book value is $15,000 ($60,000 – $45,000). 40% of this excess is allocated to goodwill (40% × $15,000 = $6,000). Therefore, noncurrent assets should be reported at $136,000.

| | |
|---|---|
| Noncurrent assets—Polk | $90,000 |
| Noncurrent assets—Strass | 40,000 |
| Excess allocated to goodwill | 6,000 |
| Total | $136,000 |

**15.** **(b)** In the consolidated balance sheet, the parent company's "investment in subsidiary" account should be eliminated and replaced by the assets and liabilities of the subsidiary. Therefore, the consolidated balance sheet should include the current liabilities of both companies, plus the current portion of the debt incurred on 1/2/07 ($60,000 ÷ 10 = $6,000). Thus, current liabilities should be reported at $46,000 as computed below.

| | |
|---|---|
| Current liabilities—Polk | $30,000 |
| Current liabilities—Strass | 10,000 |
| Current portion of new debt | 6,000 |
| Total | $46,000 |

**16.** **(b)** In the consolidated balance sheet, the parent company's "investment in subsidiary" account should be eliminated and replaced by the assets and liabilities of the subsidiary. Therefore, the consolidated balance sheet should include the noncurrent liabilities of both companies, plus the noncurrent portion of the debt incurred on 1/2/07 ($60,000 – $6,000 = $54,000), plus the minority interest in the subsidiary ($50,000 × 10% = $5,000).

| | |
|---|---|
| Noncurrent liabilities—Polk | $ 50,000 |
| Noncurrent liabilities—Strass | 0 |
| Noncurrent portion of new debt | 54,000 |
| Minority interest | 5,000 |
| Total | $109,000 |

**17.** **(a)** In the consolidated balance sheet, neither the parent company's investment account nor the subsidiary's stockholders' equity is reported. These amounts are eliminated in the same journal entry that records the excess of cost over book value. The portion of the subsidiary's stockholders' equity that is **not** eliminated is reported as minority interest in the noncurrent liabilities section of the consolidated balance sheet. Therefore, the parent's stockholders' equity ($80,000) equals the consolidated stockholders' equity. Note that once the candidate has completed items 14 through 18, the answers can be checked using the balance sheet equation.

| Current assets | + | Non-current assets | = | Current liabilities | + | Non-current liabilities | + | Stock-holders' equity |
|---|---|---|---|---|---|---|---|---|
| $99,000 | + | $136,000 | = | $46,000 | + | $109,000 | + | $80,000 |

**18.** **(c)** In a purchase, the net assets of the acquired firm are recorded at their FMV. The excess of the cost of the investment over the FMV of the net assets acquired is allocated to goodwill. The cost of this investment is $3,750,000 (250,000 shares × $15), and the FMV of the net assets acquired, **excluding goodwill** is $3,400,000 ($3,000,000 + $400,000). Therefore, the amount allocated to goodwill is $350,000 ($3,750,000 – $3,400,000).

**19.** **(c)** The assets acquired would be revalued to their fair market value. The inventory account would then include the difference between the market value and book value. Answer (a) is incorrect because a deferred credit is never recorded. Answer (b) is incorrect because goodwill represents the excess of cost over fair market value. Answer (d) is incorrect because the retained earnings account is not affected by this transaction when purchase accounting is used.

**20.** **(d)** SFAS 141 states that, in general, all assets and liabilities (including plant and equipment and long-term debt) should be reported at fair value. Answer (a) is incorrect because it describes the treatment accorded to plant and equipment when a combination is accounted for as a pooling of interests.

**21.** **(c)** When the appraised values of the identifiable assets acquired in a **purchase** combination exceed the acquisition price, the difference is referred to as negative goodwill. SFAS 141 requires negative goodwill to be allocated against noncurrent assets acquired, excluding marketable securities, in proportion to their fair values. If the noncurrent assets are reduced to zero and some negative goodwill remains unallocated, the excess should be reported on the balance sheet as an extraordinary gain. Answer (a) is incorrect because the excess is not **reported** as negative goodwill. Answer (b) is incorrect because APIC is not affected by this excess. Answer (d) is incorrect because **positive** goodwill results from an excess of acquisition price over appraised value of identifiable assets, not vice versa.

## G. Consolidated Financial Statements subsequent to Acquisition

**22.   (d)**   Consolidated statements are prepared as if the parent and subsidiaries were one economic entity. From the point of view of the consolidated entity, any intercompany receivables or payables from parent to subsidiary or vice versa are **not** payable to or receivable from any **outside** company. In other words, the consolidated entity does not have a receivable or payable. Therefore, all of Wright's intercompany receivables, payables and advances are eliminated. None are reported as intercompany receivables.

**23.   (a)**   When a subsidiary prepares separate financial statements, intercompany receivables (and payables) should be reported in the balance sheet as a separate line item. When consolidated financial statements are prepared by the parent company, all intercompany receivables (and payables) should be eliminated to avoid overstating assets and liabilities.

**24.   (d)**   Pard's separate revenues are $200,000, and Spin's separate revenues are $140,000, resulting in a total of $340,000 ($200,000 + $140,000). Since the consolidated income statement shows sales of only $308,000, intercompany sales of $32,000 ($340,000 – $308,000) from Pard to Spin must have been eliminated during consolidation.

**25.   (b)**   Pard's separate accounts receivable is $26,000, and Spin's separate accounts receivable is $19,000, resulting in a total of $45,000 ($26,000 + $19,000). Since the consolidated balance sheet shows accounts receivable of only $39,000, intercompany receivables of $6,000 ($45,000 – $39,000) must have been eliminated during consolidation. Since Pard sold goods to Spin that Spin had not fully paid for by 12/31/07, the eliminated receivable must be Pard's receivable from Spin. Therefore, Spin's 12/31/07 payable to Pard is also $6,000.

**26.   (c)**   Pard's intercompany sales to Spin totaled $32,000 during 2007. Therefore, Spin recorded a purchase of inventory of $32,000. At 12/31/07, Spin still held 37.5% of these goods in inventory; in Spin's books, this inventory was carried at $12,000 (37.5% × $32,000). In the consolidated balance sheet, the intercompany profit would be eliminated, and this inventory would be carried at Pard's original cost. Pard's sales to Spin were at the same markup on cost that Pard uses for all sales. In Pard's income statement, cost of sales is 75% of sales ($150,000 ÷ $200,000). Therefore, Pard's original cost for the $12,000 of goods in Spin's inventory is $9,000 (75% × $12,000).

**27.   (b)**   The percentage of the subsidiary's stockholders' equity not owned by the parent company represents the mi-

nority interest's share of the net assets of the subsidiary. In the 12/31/07 consolidated balance sheet, minority interest is $10,000. At the same date, Spin's stockholders' equity is $50,000. Therefore, the percent of minority interest ownership is 20% ($10,000 ÷ $50,000).

**28.   (a)**   When the equity method of accounting is used the parent company's retained earnings will be equal to the consolidated retained earnings balance. It can be determined that the equity method is being followed because the account "Equity in earnings of Sharp" appears in the parent's income statement. In addition it is important to note that the balance sheet accounts presented are dated as of the end of the year; therefore, the parent company's retained earnings of $1,240,000, should already include **all** income statement balance account adjustments. Thus, no additional income amounts will need to be added to the $1,240,000 retained earnings balance, in order to determine the total retained earnings balance.

**29.   (d)**   The requirement is to determine which accounting concept relates to the preparation of consolidated financial statements. Answer (d) is correct because when a parent-subsidiary relationship exists, the financial statements of each separate entity are brought together, or consolidated. When financial statements represent a consolidated entity, the concept of economic entity applies. Answer (a) is incorrect because reliability is a concept that applies to all financial statements, not just consolidated financial statements. Reliability, as identified in SFAC 2, is a primary quality that makes accounting information useful for decision making. This quality should be found in all statements. Answer (b) is incorrect because the concept of materiality applies to all financial statements, not just consolidated financial statements. The concept of materiality, as applied to financial statements, deals with the impact an item in the financial statements will have on a user's decision-making process, when studying the financial statements. Answer (c) is incorrect because the concept of legal entity refers to the form or type of combination that takes place between entities (i.e., mergers, consolidations or acquisitions), not the basis on which financial statements are prepared.

**30.   (b)**   The purchase method is used to account for this situation because the subsidiary was acquired for cash. SFAS 141 states that, in general, all assets and liabilities (including equipment) should be reported at market value. The excess of the equipment's market value over its carrying amount is allocated to the equipment and amortized over the equipment's useful life. The unamortized portion of the excess of the market value over the carrying amount of the equipment is then reported as part of plant and equipment. Only the unamortized portion of the excess of the acquisition cost over the market value of the net identifiable assets acquired is reported as goodwill. The excess of the market value over the carrying amount of the equipment is capitalized and subsequently amortized over the equipment's useful life, **not** expensed as incurred.

**31.   (a)**   When two companies own stock in each other, a reciprocal ownership relationship exists. In this case, Pride (the parent) owns 80% of Simba (the sub), and Simba owns 10% of Pride. When Pride declares a cash dividend, 90% of it is distributed to outside parties and 10% goes to Simba. Because Simba is part of the consolidated entity, its 10% share of Pride's dividend is eliminated when determining consolidated dividends declared. Thus, only 90% of dividends declared by Pride will be reported in the consolidated financial statements. When Simba declares a dividend, 80% of the dividend is distributed to Pride (the parent), and 20% is distributed to outside parties (the noncontrolling interest of Simba stock). The 80% share to Pride is eliminated when determining consolidated dividends declared because it represents an intercompany transaction. The remaining 20% to the noncontrolling interest is likewise not included in consolidated dividends declared because, from the parent company's point of view, subsidiary dividends do not represent dividends of the consolidated entity and must be eliminated.

**32. (c)** Per FASB Interpretation 46, it is presumed that an entity with equity of less than total assets does not have sufficient funding to finance its activities unless there is definitive evidence to the contrary (e.g., a source of outside financing).

**33. (b)** Per FASB Interpretation 46, a variable interest entity should be consolidated by the enterprise that will absorb the majority of the entity's expected losses if they occur, or receive the majority of the residual returns if they occur, or both.

**34. (b)** Per FASB Interpretation 46, the determination of whether an entity is a variable interest entity and which enterprise should consolidate that entity is made at the time the enterprise initially gets involved with the variable interest entity. The determination does not change unless there is a fundamental change in the nature of the entity or the relationship between the interest holders.

**35. (d)** FAS 154 states that accounting changes that result in financial statements that are, in effect, financial statements of a different reporting entity (such as presenting consolidated statements in place of statements of individual companies) should be reported by restating the financial statements of all prior periods presented so that the resulting restated prior periods' statements on a consolidated basis are the same as if the subsidiary had been consolidated since it was acquired.

**36. (b)** In a purchase, the consolidated financial statements reflect the combined operations of the parent and subsidiary **from the date of combination**. Earnings of the subsidiary prior to the combination are **not** included with the parent's income. The parent's 2007 income is $1,575,000 ($750,000 + $825,000), while the subsidiary's income after the combination is $375,000 for a total of $1,950,000 ($1,575,000 + $375,000). The unrealized inventory profit of $45,000 must be eliminated, because from a consolidated viewpoint, revenue cannot be recognized until these goods are sold to a third party (i.e., a sale has not yet occurred). Therefore, 2007 consolidated net income is $1,905,000 ($1,950,000 − $45,000). Note that the net income amounts given are from **separate company operations,** so no elimination of equity earnings or dividend income is necessary.

**37. (d)** In a business combination accounted for as a purchase, the FMV of net assets is used as the valuation basis for the combination. The investment is recorded at the fair value of the net assets, common stock is recorded at par value (150,000 × $20 = $3,000,000), and any difference is recorded as APIC. The subsidiary's retained earnings are **not** recorded in a purchase. Therefore, 6/30/07 consolidated

retained earnings is equal to Pane's separate 6/30/07 retained earnings $3,250,000 ($3,200,000 + $800,000 − $750,000).

## H. Intercompany Transactions and Profit Confirmation

**38. (d)** Unrealized profit in ending inventory arises when intercompany sales are made at prices above cost and the merchandise is not resold to third parties prior to year-end. The profit is unrealized because the inventory has not yet been sold outside of the consolidated entity. In this case, Pirn sold goods to Scroll for $100,000, which would become Scroll's cost. However, Scroll's cost of goods sold includes only $80,000 of goods acquired from Pirn. Therefore, $20,000 of original $100,000 remains in Scroll's ending inventory. Since Pirn's gross profit rate is 30% ($150,000 ÷ $500,000), the gross profit Pirn recognized on the original $20,000 sale was $6,000 (30% × $20,000). This intercompany profit must be eliminated on the consolidating worksheet.

**39. (b)** When computing consolidated income, the objective is to restate the accounts as if the intercompany transactions had not occurred. When Scroll recorded depreciation, it included depreciation on the asset purchased from Pirn for $36,000. Since Pirn recorded a $12,000 gain when it sold the asset to Scroll, Pirn's book value at the time of sale must have been $24,000. Therefore, consolidated depreciation expense should be based on $24,000 rather than on $36,000. Depreciation expense for 2007 must be decreased by $3,000 ($12,000 excess ÷ 4 years). Depreciation expense in Pirn's 2007 consolidated income statement should therefore be $47,000, as computed below.

| | |
|---|---|
| Pirn's recorded depr. | $40,000 |
| Scroll's recorded depr. | 10,000 |
| Less adjustment ($12,000 ÷ 4) | (3,000) |
| | $47,000 |

**40. (c)** Unrealized profit in ending inventory arises when intercompany sales are made at prices above cost and the merchandise is not resold to third parties prior to year-end. The profit is unrealized because the inventory has not yet been sold outside of the consolidated entity. In this case, there is no unrealized profit on the sales to Dean because the consolidated statements would not include Dean, and the equity method is not applicable. (Clark owns only 15% of Dean). However, there is unrealized profit on the materials sold by Kent, a wholly owned subsidiary, to Clark. $60,000 of the $240,000 of materials sold by Kent to Clark remains in ending inventory. The gross profit Kent recognized on this $60,000 of materials at the time of sale was $12,000 ($48,000 ÷ $240,000 = 20% gross profit rate; 20% × $60,000 = $12,000). For the consolidated entity, this $12,000 gross profit has not been earned and must be eliminated. Therefore, consolidated current assets should be $308,000 ($320,000 − $12,000).

**41. (c)** When preparing the consolidated income statement, the objective is to restate the accounts as if the intercompany transactions had not occurred. As a result of the intercompany sale, Parker has recorded $250,000 of sales and Smith has recorded $250,000 cost of sales which should be eliminated (note that Parker's **cost of sales** on the original sale is the amount left in consolidated cost of sales, and Smith's **sales** when the goods were sold to outside parties is the amount left in consolidated sales). Therefore, Parker should report $500,000 as cost of sales in the 2007 consolidated income statement ($400,000 + $350,000 – $250,000).

**42.  (a)**    Pare's separate gross profit is $100,000, and Shel's separate gross profit is $60,000, resulting in a total of $160,000. Since the consolidated income statement shows gross profit of only $154,000, unrealized intercompany profit of $6,000 ($160,000 – $154,000) must have been eliminated.

**43.  (d)**    The requirement is to determine the amount of **selling** expenses to be reported in Pard's 2007 consolidated income statement. Pard's selling expenses for 2007 include $50,000 in freight-out costs for goods sold to Seed, its subsidiary. This $50,000 becomes part of Seed's inventory because it is a cost directly associated with bringing the goods to a salable condition. One half of the goods sold to Seed by Pard remained in Seed's inventory at the end of 2007. Therefore, one half of the $50,000 ($25,000) flowed out as part of cost of goods sold, and one half remains in ending inventory. Thus, none of the $50,000 represents a selling expense for the consolidated entity, and $1,450,000 ($1,100,000 + $400,000 – $50,000) should be reported as selling expenses in the consolidated income statement.

**44.  (a)**    When preparing consolidated financial statements, the objective is to restate the accounts as if the intercompany transactions had not occurred. Therefore, the 2007 gain on sale of machine of $50,000 [$900,000 – ($1,100,000 – $250,000)] must be eliminated, since the consolidated entity has not realized any gain. In effect, the machine must be reflected on the consolidated balance sheet at 1/1/07 at Poe's cost of $1,100,000, and accumulated depreciation of $250,000, instead of at a new "cost" of $900,000. For consolidated statement purposes, 2007 depreciation is based on the original amounts [($1,100,000 – $100,000) × 1/20 = $50,000]. Therefore, in the 12/31/07 **consolidated** balance sheet, the machine is shown at a cost of $1,100,000 less accumulated depreciation of $300,000 ($250,000 + $50,000).

**45.  (a)**    When Seal purchased the bonds from Wagner, the bonds were viewed as retired from a consolidated viewpoint since there is no longer any obligation to an outside party. Therefore, the consolidated entity would recognize a $100,000 gain ($1,075,000 carrying amount – $975,000 cash paid), which would increase consolidated retained earnings. This transaction has no effect on minority interest, since the subsidiary (Seal) has merely exchanged one asset for another (cash for investment in bonds).

**46.  (a)**    The requirement is to determine the amount of gain to be reported on the consolidated income statement when a wholly owned subsidiary purchases parent company stock. A parent company reports no gain or loss when a wholly owned subsidiary purchases its common stock. In effect, the consolidated entity is purchasing treasury stock when the purchase is made, and gains are not recognized on treasury stock transactions. The dividends paid by the parent to the subsidiary also do not affect income because such intercompany transactions are eliminated when consolidated financial statements are prepared. Therefore, $0 gain should be reported by the consolidated entity.

**47.  (a)**    When computing consolidated income, the objective is to restate the accounts as if the intercompany transaction had not occurred. As a result of the intercom-

pany sale, sales and cost of goods sold are overstated and an eliminating entry is needed to reduce these accounts by the intercompany sale. Answer (b) is incorrect because sales and cost of goods sold need to be reduced by the entire amount of the intercompany sale in order to arrive at their proper consolidated amounts. Answer (c) is incorrect because net income is not effected by the intercompany sale. Sales and cost of goods sold are overstated by the same amount; thus, net income is correct for consolidated purposes. Answer (d) is incorrect because an adjustment is necessary.

**48.  (c)**    The key to this problem is that the equipment must be revalued at Fire's carrying amount (Fire's original cost less accumulated depreciation) in the consolidation process. Assume the following potential scenario:

Fire buys a piece of equipment on 12/31/07 for $1,000. At 12/31/07, the equipment was depreciated $200, and Fire's carrying value is $800 ($1,000 – $200). On 12/31/07, Fire sells the equipment to Water for $900. Water's original cost is therefore $900, and Fire will record a $100 gain that must be eliminated. After consolidation, the equipment is reported at $800, Fire's carrying value. Fire's carrying value is also equal to Water's original cost ($900) less Fire's recorded gain ($100). Answer (a) is incorrect because Water's original cost includes an unrealized gain that must be eliminated. Answer (b) is incorrect because revaluing the equipment at Fire's original cost would not take into consideration the depreciation already recorded by Fire. Answer (d) is incorrect because the entire gain, not 80% of the gain, must be eliminated.

**49.  (b)**    The requirement is to determine by how much depreciation will be reduced. Use the solutions approach and set up a simple numerical example.

> Port's original cost = $1,000
> Depreciation per yr = $200
> Selling price = $810

If Port sells equipment for $810, they recognize a $210 gain on the sale (selling price of $810 – carrying value of the equipment $600). Salem, Inc. will now depreciate the equipment on their books at $810, the price that they paid. Because the gain was not realized with an entity outside of the consolidated entity, it must be eliminated. In the consolidated financial statements, equipment will be reported at its original carrying value, the gain on the sale will be removed and depreciation expense must be recorded at Port, Inc. original amount ($200), not the amount of depreciation that Salem, Inc. records. Salem would record depreciation of $270 (810/3). Therefore, depreciation must be reduced by $70 on the consolidated financial statements to reflect the original depreciation recorded by Port. Depreciation is reduced by $70, which as shown by the example, is 33 1/3% of the gain ($70/$210).

**50.  (a)**    This question is silent as to which year consolidated financial statements are being prepared. However, answer (a) is correct for either the year of acquisition or a subsequent year. If financial statements were being prepared for the current year the loss would be reported as an ordinary loss on the income statement. P Co. acquired the 20% interest in S Company bonds and incurred a loss on them. This loss would be carried through to the consolidated balance sheet as a decrease in retained earnings. In subsequent years, the unamortized portion of the loss would also decrease retained earnings.

## J.   Minority Interest

**51.   (a)**   Without the intercompany transaction, the minority interest income from Samson in 2007 would be $24,000 (30% of $80,000). In 2008 the minority interest income would be $27,000 (30% of $90,000). On the consolidated statements in 2007 the $2,000 intercompany profit will be eliminated, because from a consolidated viewpoint an arm's-length transaction has not occurred with third parties. The elimination entry will be to credit inventory (which is in effect on the books of Eltro) for $2,000 and debits will be made of $1,400 to majority interest income and $600 to minority interest income. In 2008 when Eltro sells the inventory to outsiders, the $2,000 profit has effectively been earned. In 2008 an entry will be made on the consolidated books to effectively recognize this profit and allocate it to the majority and minority interest. Thus, the 2007 minority interest income will be reduced by $600 and 2008 minority interest income increased by $600.

|  | 2007 |  | 2008 |
|---|---|---|---|
| MI % of profit | $24,000 | MI % of profit | $27,000 |
| Elim. of inter- |  | Recognition |  |
| company profit | – 600 | of profit | 600 |
| MI income | $23,400 |  | $27,600 |

**52.   (c)**   The cost of this investment is $975,000. Ritt purchased 80% of the identifiable net assets of Shaw, which have a fair value of $1,100,000 ($1,000,000 + $100,000). Thus, Ritt purchased net assets with a fair value of $880,000 (80% × $1,100,000). The excess amount paid ($975,000 – $880,000 = $95,000) is allocated to goodwill.

**53.   (b)**   The percentage of the subsidiary's stockholders' equity not owned by the parent company represents the minority interest's share of the net assets of the subsidiary. The minority interest is based on **book** value, to remove the minority shareholders' portion of reported equity from the financial statements (parent company concept). At 12/31/07, the subsidiary's stockholders' equity at book value is $1,065,000, as computed below.

| | |
|---|---|
| 1/1/07 net assets (stockholders' equity) | $1,000,000 |
| 2007 net income | 190,000 |
| 2007 dividends | (125,000) |
| 12/31/07 net assets (stockholders' equity) | $1,065,000 |

Since the parent's share is 80%, the minority interest is 20% of $1,065,000, or $213,000.

**54.   (b)**   Pare paid cash dividends of $25,000 and Kidd, the 75%-owned subsidiary, paid cash dividends of $5,000. The dividends paid by Pare are all payments to owners of the consolidated company and are reported as dividends paid in the consolidated statement of retained earnings. The $5,000 dividend paid by Kidd is paid 75% to Pare, and 25% to outside parties (the noncontrolling interest in Kidd's stock). The 75% share to Pare is eliminated when determining consolidated dividends declared because it is an intracompany transaction. The remaining 25% to the noncontrolling interest is likewise not included in consolidated dividends declared because, from the parent company's point of view, subsidiary dividends do not represent dividends of the consolidated entity.

**55.   (b)**   The portion of the subsidiary's stockholders' equity **not** owned by the parent company represents the mi-

nority interest's share of the net assets of the subsidiary. At 12/31/08, the subsidiary's stockholders' equity is $120,000 ($50,000 common stock + $70,000 retained earnings). Since the parent's share is 75%, the minority interest is 25% of $120,000, or $30,000.

**56.   (b)**   In the consolidated balance sheet, neither the parent company's investment account nor the subsidiary's stockholders' equity is reported. These amounts are eliminated in the same journal entry that records the excess of cost over book value. The portion of the subsidiary's stockholders' equity that is **not** eliminated is reported as minority interest. Therefore, the amount reported as common stock in the 12/31/08 consolidated balance sheet consists solely of Pare's common stock ($100,000). Kidd's common stock ($50,000) is eliminated along with the rest of its stockholders' equity.

## M.   Changes in Ownership

**57.   (b)**   The requirement is to determine how much of Sago's 2007 net income should be reported as accruing to Phillips. Under a purchase, consolidated net income reflects the parent's net income to the date of combination and both entities' income after the combination. Phillips, Inc. can only recognize the net income of Sago, based on their 20% interest, up to the date of combination. However, after the date of combination they will recognize 95% of Sago's net income, their new ownership interest.

## N.   Combined Financial Statements

**58.   (d)**   **Combined financial statements** are financial statements prepared for companies that are owned by the same parent company or individual. Combined financial statements are prepared by combining all the companies' financial statement classifications. Intercompany transactions and profits should be eliminated in the same way as for consolidated statements (ARB 51). Therefore, **none** of the intercompany receivables should be included in the combined financial statements.

**59.   (c)**   The inventory reported on the 12/31/07 combined balance sheet should reflect the **original cost** to the companies of any inventory on hand (ARB 51). The inventory on hand that was acquired from outside parties should be reported at its cost ($175,000 + $250,000 = $425,000). The Banks inventory on hand that was acquired from Lamm must be restated back to the cost Lamm originally paid when it was purchased from outside parties. This must be done to eliminate intercompany profits. During 2007, Lamm shipped inventory that originally cost $150,000 to Banks at a billing price of $200,000. Therefore, the original cost is 75% of Banks' carrying amount. Therefore, the correct inventory amount is $470,000 [$175,000 + $250,000 + ($60,000 × 75%)].

**60.   (b)**   Combined financial statements are prepared for companies that are owned by the same parent company or individual but are not consolidated. These statements are prepared by combining the separate companies' financial statement classifications. Intercompany transactions, balances, and profit (loss) should be eliminated. Therefore, to determine the gross profit in Bee and Cee's combined income statement, the intercompany profit resulting from Bee's sales to Cee should be eliminated. Cee sold to outsiders 50% ($65,000/$130,000) of the inventory purchased from Bee. The cost of sales to the combined entity is thus 50% of the $100,000 cost of sales reported by Bee. Gross profit of the combined entity amounts to $41,000, equal to $91,000 of sales to unrelated companies less $50,000 cost of sales.

**61.** **(a)** When computing sales to be reported in the combined income statement, the objective is to restate the accounts as if the intercompany transaction had not occurred. Assuming that there were no sales between Home Office and Branch, the correct amount of sales to be included in the combined income statement is the $250,000 sold by Branch to unrelated customers.

**62.** **(b)** Combined financial statements is the term used to describe financial statements prepared for companies that are owned by the same parent company or individual. Combined financial statements are prepared by combining all of the subsidiaries' financial statement classifications. Intercompany transactions should be eliminated in the same way as for consolidated statements. Combining the stockholders' equity accounts of Able and Baker results in a total of $430,000 ($100,000 + $20,000 + $300,000 + $10,000). The intercompany balances (Investment in Baker, $4,000; and Common Stock, $4,000) must be eliminated, which reduces combined stockholders' equity to $426,000 ($430,000 – $4,000). If these amounts were not eliminated, the combined balance sheet would overstate both assets and equity by $4,000.

**63.** **(c)** **Combined financial statements** are financial statements prepared for companies that are owned by the same parent company or individual. Combined financial statements are prepared by combining all the companies' financial statement classifications. Intercompany transactions and profits should be eliminated in the same way as for consolidated statements (ARB 51). Therefore, **none** of the intercompany loans or profits should be included in the combined financial statements.

**64.** **(d)** Per ARB 51, combined statements may be used to present the financial position and results of operations of commonly controlled companies, companies under common management, and of a group of unconsolidated subsidiaries.

**65.** **(c)** Per ARB 51, where combined statements are prepared for a group of related companies, intercompany transactions and profit and losses should be eliminated. Matters such as minority interests, income taxes, foreign operations, or different fiscal periods should be treated in the same manner for both combined financial statements and consolidated statements.

**66.** **(c)** Per ARB 51, where combined statements are prepared for a group of related companies, if there are any problems in connection with such matters as minority interests, foreign operations, different fiscal periods, or income taxes, they should be treated in the same manner as in consolidated statements.

## SOLUTIONS TO SIMULATION PROBLEMS

### Simulation Problem 1

| Situation | Concepts | Journal Entries | Financial Statement Amounts | Communication | Research |
|---|---|---|---|---|---|

**(A) (B) (C) (D) (E) (F) (G)**

|   |   | (A) | (B) | (C) | (D) | (E) | (F) | (G) |
|---|---|---|---|---|---|---|---|---|
| 1. | Cash | ● | ○ | ○ | ○ | ○ | ○ | ○ |
| 2. | Equipment | ○ | ● | ○ | ○ | ○ | ○ | ○ |
| 3. | Investment in subsidiary | ○ | ○ | ○ | ○ | ● | ○ | ○ |
| 4. | Bonds payable | ○ | ● | ○ | ○ | ○ | ○ | ○ |
| 5. | Minority interest | ○ | ○ | ○ | ○ | ○ | ● | ○ |
| 6. | Common stock | ○ | ○ | ● | ○ | ○ | ○ | ○ |
| 7. | Beginning retained earnings | ○ | ○ | ● | ○ | ○ | ○ | ○ |
| 8. | Dividends paid | ○ | ○ | ● | ○ | ○ | ○ | ○ |
| 9. | Gain on retirement of bonds | ○ | ○ | ○ | ○ | ○ | ● | ○ |
| 10. | Cost of goods sold | ○ | ● | ○ | ○ | ○ | ○ | ○ |
| 11. | Interest expense | ○ | ○ | ○ | ● | ○ | ○ | ○ |
| 12. | Depreciation expense | ○ | ● | ○ | ○ | ○ | ○ | ○ |

### Explanation of solutions

**1.** **(A)** Consolidated statements are prepared as if the parent and subsidiaries are one economic entity. Therefore, cash is included in the consolidated balance sheet at their full amounts regardless of the percentage ownership held by the parent.

**2.** **(B)** When preparing consolidated financial statements, the objective is to restate the accounts as if the intercompany transaction had not occurred. Therefore, on the consolidated balance sheet the equipment needs to be stated at its original cost to Shaw. The three balance sheets would show the sold equipment at December 31, 2007, as follows:

**BALANCE SHEET**
*12/31/07*

|   | *Poe* | *Shaw* | *Consolidated* |
|---|---|---|---|
| Equipment | $36,000 | $0 | $30,000 |

**3.** **(E)** In the consolidated balance sheet, the parent company's "Investment in subsidiary" should be eliminated completely and replaced by the net assets of the subsidiary.

**4.** **(B)** When Poe purchased the bonds from an investor outside the consolidated entity, the bonds are viewed as retired from a consolidated viewpoint since there is no longer any obligation to an outside party. Therefore, the consolidated balance sheet will show the bonds payable at $100,000.

**5.** **(F)** The percentage of the subsidiary's stockholders' equity not owned by the parent company represents the minority interest's share of the net assets of the subsidiary. This amount is only reported in the consolidated balance sheet in the noncurrent liabilities.

**6.** **(C)** In the consolidated balance sheet the subsidiary's common stock is not reported. Therefore, the parent's common stock equals the consolidated common stock.

**7.** **(C)** In the consolidated balance sheet, the subsidiary's beginning retained earnings is not reported. Therefore, the parent's beginning retained earnings equals the consolidated beginning retained earnings.

**8.** **(C)** The dividends paid by the subsidiary are eliminated in the consolidated financial statements. Ninety percent of the dividends paid are eliminated along with the "Investment in subsidiary" elimination. The remaining 10% is reflected in "Minority Interest." Therefore, only the parent's dividends paid are included on the consolidated financial statements.

**9.** **(F)** When Poe purchased the bonds from an investor outside the consolidated entity, the bonds are viewed as retired from a consolidated viewpoint since there is no longer any obligation to an outside party. Therefore, the consolidated entity would recognize a gain of $9,000 ($100,000 carrying value of the bonds – $91,000 purchase price) on the retirement of the debt. Since the bonds are still outstanding in relation to Shaw, no gain would be recognized on Shaw's unconsolidated income statement.

**10.** **(B)** When preparing the consolidated income statement, the objective is to restate the accounts as if the intercompany transactions had not occurred. As a result of the intercompany sale, Poe has recorded cost of sales of $30,000 and Shaw has recorded cost of sales of $40,000. The actual cost of sales to third parties outside the consolidated entity is $20,000 (1/2 of the merchandise Poe sold to third parties at the original cost of the merchandise purchased by Shaw).

**11. (D)** The requirement is to determine how the interest expense is to be reported in Poe's consolidated financial statements for December 31, 2007. As the Shaw bonds were held by an unaffiliated party for the entire period, the entire interest expense amount recorded by Shaw relates to payments outside the consolidated entity. Thus, the entire portion on Shaw's books should be included in the 12/31/07 consolidated financial statements. Therefore, answer D is correct.

**12. (B)** When preparing consolidated financial statements, the objective is to restate the accounts as if the intercompany transactions had not occurred. As a result of the sale of the equipment, Poe recorded depreciation expense of $12,000 ($36,000 ÷ 3 years). For consolidated purposes, depreciation must be computed based on the cost of the asset to the consolidated entity, which is the cost ($30,000) of the asset to Shaw. Therefore, depreciation expense should be $5,000 ($30,000 ÷ 6 yrs.) on the consolidated income statement.

| Situation | Concepts | Journal Entries | Financial Statement Amounts | Communication | Research |
|---|---|---|---|---|---|

**1.**

| | | | |
|---|---|---|---|
| Gain on equipment | 21,000 | | |
|      Accumulated depreciation | | 15,000 | |
|      Equipment | | 6,000 | |
| Accumulated depreciation | 7,000 | | |
|      Depreciation expense | | 7,000 | |

**2.**

| | | |
|---|---|---|
| Sales | 60,000 | |
|      Cost of goods sold | | 50,000 |
|      Ending inventory | | 10,000 |

**3.**

| | | |
|---|---|---|
| Bonds payable | 100,000 | |
| Discount on bonds | 9,000 | |
|      Gain on retirement of bonds | | 9,000 |
|      Investment in bonds | | 100,000 |

**Explanation of solutions**

**1. ($14,000)** When preparing consolidated financial statements, the objective is to restate the accounts as if the intercompany transactions had not occurred. Therefore, the 2007 gain on sale of equipment of $21,000 ($36,000 – $15,000) must be eliminated, since the consolidated entity has not realized any gain. In addition, for consolidated statement purposes, 2007 depreciation is based on the original cost of the equipment to Shaw. This elimination entry can be made in two separate entries. The first entry eliminated the gain, and restores the accumulated depreciation and equipment accounts as if the intercompany sale were never made. The second entry adjusts the current year depreciation expense to the amount that would have been recorded if the sale were never made. New depreciation is $36,000 ÷ 3 years = $12,000 for Poe. Shaw's depreciation was book value $15,000 ÷ 3 years = $5,000 per year. Therefore, depreciation expense must be adjusted by $12,000 – $5,000 = $7,000.

**2. ($10,000)** Unrealized profit in ending inventory arises when intercompany sales are made at prices above cost and the merchandise is not resold to third parties prior to year-end. The profit is unrealized because the inventory has not yet been sold outside the consolidated entity. In this case, one half of the merchandise was left in Poe's inventory at year-end. For the consolidated entity, one half of the $20,000 profit has not been earned and must be eliminated.

**3. ($9,000)** When Poe purchased the bonds from an investor outside the consolidated entity, the bonds are viewed as retired from a consolidated viewpoint since there is no longer any obligation to an outside party. Therefore, the consolidated entity would recognize an ordinary gain of $9,000 ($100,000 carrying value of the bonds – $91,000 purchase price) on the retirement of the debt.

| Situation | Concepts | Journal Entries | Financial Statement Amounts | Communication | Research |
|---|---|---|---|---|---|

Calculate the amounts that will appear on Poe's consolidated financial statement in December 31, 2007.

1. Cash                 $ 65,000

2. Goodwill           $ 20,000

3. Equipment         $794,000

4. Common stock     $100,000

5. Investment in Shaw    $ 0

6. Dividends           $ 80,000

7. Bonds payable      $100,000

**Explanation of solution**

1. $50,000 + $15,000 = $65,000

2. ($20,000)  The goodwill from Poe's 90% purchase of Shaw can be determined as follows:

   | | |
   |---|---|
   | $155,000 | Purchase price |
   | 135,000 | Fair value ($150,000 × 90%) |
   | $ 20,000 | Goodwill |

3. $440,000 + $360,000 – $6,000 = $794,000

4. $100,000, common stock of parent

5. The investment in Shaw account is eliminated

6. Dividends paid of the subsidiary are eliminated

7. $100,000. $200,000 bonds payable – $100,000 bonds payable eliminated

| Situation | Concepts | Journal Entries | Financial Statement Amounts | Communication | Research |
|---|---|---|---|---|---|

To:   CEO, Poe Corporation
From: CPA Candidate
Re:   Consolidated Financial Statements

This memorandum was prepared to answer your questions about investments in other companies. A company may invest in another corporation by purchasing stock of that corporation. If the investment is less than 20% of the outstanding shares of stock, the fair value method of accounting is used. Under this method, the investment is recorded at the price paid for the stock, and value of the investment is adjusted to fair value at the end of each accounting period.

If a company purchases between 20 and 50% of the stock of another corporation, the acquiring company is assumed to have significant influence over the other company. In these instances, the equity method of accounting is used. The company includes its proportionate share of net income of the acquired company by increasing the investment account. Similarly, the company decreases its investment account by the amount of dividends paid by the investee.

If a company purchases greater than 50% of the voting shares of stock of another corporation and can exercise control, then consolidated financial statements must be prepared. These consolidated statements reflect the consolidated operating results, cash flows, and financial position as if a parent company and its subsidiaries are a single entity.

Consolidated financial statements are required because they better reflect the operating results, financial status, and central management ties that bind the company into a single economic and financial unit. These consolidated financial statements are representationally more faithful and fair because they are not biased and do not exclude or net data. Consolidated financial statements are also more comparable with information about other economic entities regardless of the company's legal framework. Finally, consolidated financial statements are more complete and relevant for investors and other parties basing decisions on the data.

If you have any further questions on consolidated financial statements, please do not hesitate to call me.

| Situation | Concepts | Journal Entries | Financial Statement Amounts | Communication | Research |
|---|---|---|---|---|---|

1. What method of accounting is used to record a business combination?

   **FAS141, Para 13 or Current Text B51.112**

   13. All business combinations in the scope of this Statement shall be accounted for using the purchase method as described in this Statement and other pronouncements (refer to paragraph A3 of Appendix A).

2. In a business combination, what is the definition of goodwill?

   **FAS141, Para 43 or Current Text B51.156**

   43. The excess of the cost of an acquired entity over the net of the amounts assigned to assets acquired and liabilities assumed shall be recognized as an asset referred to as goodwill. An acquired intangible asset that does not meet the criteria in paragraph 39 shall be included in the amount recognized as goodwill.

3. What are the conditions in which a new intangible asset can be recognized in a business combination?

**FAS141, Para 39 or Current Text B51.138**

39. An intangible asset shall be recognized as an asset apart from goodwill if it arises from contractual or other legal rights (regardless of whether those rights are transferable or separable from the acquired entity or from other rights and obligations). If an intangible asset does not arise from contractual or other legal rights, it shall be recognized as an asset apart from goodwill only if it is separable, that is, it is capable of being separated or divided from the acquired entity and sold, transferred, licensed, rented, or exchanged (regardless of whether there is an intent to do so). For purposes of this Statement, however, an intangible asset that cannot be sold, transferred, licensed, rented, or exchanged individually is considered separable if it can be sold, transferred, licensed, rented, or exchanged in combination with a related contract, asset, or liability. For purposes of this Statement, an assembled workforce shall not be recognized as an intangible asset apart from goodwill. Appendix A provides additional guidance relating to the recognition of acquired intangible assets apart from goodwill, including an illustrative list of intangible assets that meet the recognition criteria in this paragraph.

---

**Simulation Problem 2**

| Situation | Concepts | Consolidation at Date of Acquisition | Intercompany Transactions & Eliminations | Consolidation at Year-End | Communication | Research |
|---|---|---|---|---|---|---|

|   |   | *True* | *False* |
|---|---|:---:|:---:|
| **1.** | A company can use either the purchase or the pooling method for business combinations. | ○ | ● |
| **2.** | Total revenues for a consolidated entity are calculated by adding the total revenue of the parent for the year and the total revenue of the subsidiary from the date of acquisition. | ● | ○ |
| **3.** | Goodwill is amortized over a period of forty years. | ○ | ● |
| **4.** | Goodwill is classified and included with other intangible assets for purposes of measuring impairment. | ○ | ● |
| **5.** | Intangible assets with indefinite lives are not amortized. | ● | ○ |
| **6.** | The stockholder equity accounts in the consolidated balance sheet are those of the parent company. | ● | ○ |
| **7.** | The effect of unrealized profits and sales between the parent company and its subsidiaries is classified as an intercompany transaction and must be eliminated. | ● | ○ |
| **8.** | A newly identified intangible asset must meet the contractual legal criterion to be recognized as an intangible asset at the time of consolidation. | ○ | ● |

| Situation | Concepts | Consolidation at Date of Acquisition | Intercompany Transactions & Eliminations | Consolidation at Year-End | Communication | Research |
|---|---|---|---|---|---|---|

| Total current assets | $400,000 |
|---|---|
| Total noncurrent assets | 1,060,000 |
| Total current liabilities | 260,000 |
| Total noncurrent liabilities | 240,000 |
| Total owners' equity | 960,000 |

**Explanation of solutions**

**Current assets:** $320,000 parent + $70,000 book value subsidiary + $10,000 inventory write-up = $400,000

**Noncurrent assets:** $640,000 parent + $380,000 book value subsidiary + $40,000 goodwill = $1,060,000

**Total current liabilities:** $210,000 parent + $50,000 subsidiary = $260,000

**Noncurrent liabilities:** $150,000 + $90,000 = $240,000

**Total owners' equity:** $600,000 parent + $360,000 new stock of parent issued in acquisition = $960,000

| Situation | Concepts | Consolidation at Date of Acquisition | Intercompany Transactions & Eliminations | Consolidation at Year-End | Communication | Research |
|---|---|---|---|---|---|---|

### Arcelia Corporation
### CONSOLIDATION WORKSHEET
#### December 31, 2007

| | Arcelia Corp, | Gavino Corp. | | Elimination entries Debt | Credit | | End balance |
|---|---|---|---|---|---|---|---|
| Revenues & gains | 1,000,000 | 400,000 | (c) | 50,000 | | | 1,341,000 |
| | | | (e) | 9,000 | | | |
| Expenses | 780,000 | 335,000 | (f) | 1,000 | 46,000 | (c) | 1,070,000 |
| Current assets | 400,000 | 110,000 | (b) | 10,000 | 4,000 | (c) | 508,000 |
| | | | | | 8,000 | (d) | |
| Noncurrent assets | 1,260,000 | 420,000 | (b) | 40,000 | 360,000 | (a) | 1,350,000 |
| | | | (e) | 36,000 | 45,000 | (e) | |
| | | | | | 1,000 | (f) | |
| | | | (a) | 50,000 | 50,000 | (b) | |
| Current liabilities | 300,000 | 70,000 | (d) | 8,000 | | | 362,000 |
| Noncurrent liabilities | 180,000 | 85,000 | | | | | 265,000 |
| Owners' equity | 960,000 | 310,000 | (a) | 310,000 | | | 960,000 |

## Elimination entries in journal entry form

a.  Eliminate subsidiary equity accounts

| | | |
|---|---|---|
| Common stock & APIC | 310,000 | |
| Difference | 50,000 | |
| Investment in Gavino | | 360,000 |

b.  To record asset write-up and goodwill.  Goodwill = Purchase price $360,000 – FMV of net identifiable assets $320,000 ($460,000 – $140,000) = $40,000 goodwill.

| | | |
|---|---|---|
| Inventory | 10,000 | |
| Goodwill | 40,000 | |
| Difference | | 50,000 |

c.  Eliminate profits from inventory not sold.  80% of inventory sold; therefore, cost of goods sold should be 80% × $30,000 = $24,000.  Ending inventory is carried on Gavino's books at $10,000.  Ending inventory should be 20% × $30,000 cost to manufacture = $6,000.

| | | |
|---|---|---|
| Sales | 50,000 | |
| Cost of goods sold | | 46,000 |
| Ending inventory | | 4,000 |

d.  Eliminate intercompany receivable and payable

| | | |
|---|---|---|
| Accounts payable | 8,000 | |
| Accounts receivable | | 8,000 |

e.  Eliminate sale of equipment

| | | |
|---|---|---|
| Gain on sale of equipment | 9,000 | |
| Equipment | 36,000 | |
| Accumulated depreciation | | 45,000 |

f.  Restore depreciation expense as if equipment had not been sold.  Normally Gavino depreciates equipment $60,000/5 years = $12,000 per year.  Equipment sold on 10/1/07; therefore, Gavino recorded depreciation of 3/4 × $12,000 = $9,000.  Arcelia's cost is $24,000 and depreciation is recorded straight-line over 3 years = $8,000 per year.  However, Arcelia depreciated equipment 3/12 months = $2,000 per year.  Total depreciation by both firms = $11,000.  Total depreciation if asset not sold = $12,000.  Therefore, an additional $1,000 depreciation must be recorded.

| | | |
|---|---|---|
| Depreciation expense | 1,000 | |
| Accumulated depreciation | | 1,000 |

| Situation | Concepts | Consolidation at Date of Acquisition | Intercompany Transactions & Eliminations | Consolidation at Year-End | Communication | Research |
|---|---|---|---|---|---|---|

Ending balances on financial statements, 2007

*Arcelia Corporation & Subsidiaries*
**CONSOLIDATED BALANCES**
*December 31, 2007*

| | |
|---|---|
| Total revenues | $1,341,000 |
| Total expenses | 1,070,000 |
| Total current assets | 508,000 |
| Total noncurrent assets | 1,350,000 |
| Total current liabilities | 362,000 |
| Total noncurrent liabilities | 265,000 |
| Total owners' equity | 1,231,000 |

| Situation | Concepts | Consolidation at Date of Acquisition | Intercompany Transactions & Eliminations | Consolidation at Year-End | Communication | Research |
|---|---|---|---|---|---|---|

To:     CEO, Arcelia Corporation
From:  CPA Candidate
Re:     Valuation of acquired firm

This memorandum was prepared to answer your questions about business combinations. When a company acquires another firm, the assets are appraised and revalued to fair value. Any new assets which meet the legal contractual criterion or the separability criterion are also valued at fair value and recorded as assets on the acquiring firm's financial statements. If the amount paid for the acquired firm exceeds the fair market value of net identifiable assets (assets minus liabilities), the amount in excess of the fair value is allocated to goodwill.

Goodwill is assigned to reporting units of the firm and it is not amortized. However, goodwill must be tested each year for impairment. If it is deemed that goodwill is impaired, an entry should be recorded to recognize a loss and write goodwill down to its new value. There are two steps to the impairment test. The first step compares the fair value of a reporting unit with its carrying amount including goodwill. If the carrying amount of the reporting unit exceeds its fair value, the second step of the goodwill impairment test is performed to measure the impairment loss. The second step involves a comparison of the implied fair value of reporting unit goodwill with the carrying amount of the goodwill. If the carrying amount of the reporting unit goodwill exceeds the implied fair value of that goodwill, an impairment loss is recognized. After a goodwill impairment loss is recognized, the carrying amount of the goodwill is adjusted for the loss. Once a loss is recognized, subsequent reversal of the impairment loss is not allowed.

| Situation | Concepts | Consolidation at Date of Acquisition | Intercompany Transactions & Eliminations | Consolidation at Year-End | Communication | Research |
|---|---|---|---|---|---|---|

What is an intercompany transaction and how should it be treated for financial reporting purposes?

**ARB51, Para 6 or Current Text C51.109**

6. In the preparation of consolidated statements, intercompany balances and transactions should be eliminated. This includes intercompany open account balances, security holdings, sales and purchases, interest, dividends, etc. As consolidated statements are based on the assumption that they represent the financial position and operating results of a single business enterprise, such statements should not include gain or loss on transactions among the companies in the group. Accordingly, any intercompany profit or loss on assets remaining within the group should be eliminated; the concept usually applied for this purpose is gross profit or loss. (See also paragraph 17.)

---

**Simulation Problem 3**

| Situation | Financial Statement Amounts |
|---|---|

|  | (A) | (B) | (C) | (D) | (E) | (F) |
|---|---|---|---|---|---|---|
| 1. Cash | ● | ○ | ○ | ○ | ○ | ○ |
| 2. Equipment | ○ | ● | ○ | ○ | ○ | ○ |
| 3. Investment in subsidiary | ○ | ○ | ○ | ○ | ● | ○ |

|     |                             | (A) | (B) | (C) | (D) | (E) | (F) |
| --- | --------------------------- | --- | --- | --- | --- | --- | --- |
| 4.  | Minority interest           |  ○  |  ○  |  ○  |  ○  |  ○  |  ●  |
| 5.  | Common stock                |  ○  |  ○  |  ●  |  ○  |  ○  |  ○  |
| 6.  | Beginning retained earnings |  ○  |  ○  |  ●  |  ○  |  ○  |  ○  |
| 7.  | Dividends paid              |  ○  |  ○  |  ●  |  ○  |  ○  |  ○  |
| 8.  | Cost of goods sold          |  ○  |  ●  |  ○  |  ○  |  ○  |  ○  |
| 9.  | Interest expense            |  ●  |  ○  |  ○  |  ○  |  ○  |  ○  |
| 10. | Depreciation expense        |  ○  |  ●  |  ○  |  ○  |  ○  |  ○  |

## Explanation of solutions

**1.**    **(A)** The total of cash on each entity's books equals the total for the consolidated entity.

**2.**    **(B)** The amount shown for equipment on the consolidated balance sheet is less than the sum of the amounts on Purl's and Strand's unconsolidated balance sheets because on an upstream intercompany transaction the parent's share (90%) of the gain would be eliminated. The equipment now on the parent's books would be reduced on the worksheet by subtracting 90% of the gain not realized through depreciation from equipment.

**3.**    **(E)** The investment in subsidiary would be eliminated in the process of consolidation in the same entry in which the subsidiary's equity accounts are eliminated.

**4.**    **(F)** Minority interest is presented only in the consolidated balance sheet.

**5.**    **(C)** Only Purl's common stock would be included in the consolidated balance sheet. All of Strand's common stock would be eliminated. Ten percent would be included in minority interest.

**6.**    **(C)** Beginning retained earnings would be the same as Purl's. Under the purchase method none of the acquiree's (Strand's) retained earnings is carried forward in recording the business combination.

**7.**    **(C)** Dividends paid would include only the parent's. The dividends of the subsidiary are all eliminated in consolidation.

**8.**    **(B)** Cost of goods would be less than the sum of that of Purl and Strand because intercompany profit would be eliminated from cost of goods sold. The amount eliminated would be 100% of the intercompany profit on two-thirds of the downstream sale from Purl to Strand.

**9.**    **(A)** No information is given to indicate that there is any intercompany interest-bearing debt. Thus, the amount included for interest expense in the consolidated financial statements would be the sum of the two entities.

**10.**   **(B)** Depreciation expense would be less on the consolidated financial statements than the sum of depreciation in each firm's unconsolidated financial statements because the part relating to the intercompany profit on equipment sold upstream would be eliminated in consolidation.

## DERIVATIVE INSTRUMENTS AND HEDGING ACTIVITIES

### A.  Foreign Currency Transactions

A foreign currency transaction, according to SFAS 52, is a transaction ". . .denominated in a currency other than the entity's functional currency." Denominated means that the balance is fixed in terms of the number of units of a foreign currency regardless of changes in the exchange rate. When a US company purchases or sells goods or services (or borrows or lends money) to a foreign entity, and the transaction is denominated in foreign currency units, the US company has a foreign currency transaction in which the US dollar is the functional currency. In these situations, the US company has "crossed currencies" and directly assumes the risk of fluctuating foreign exchange rates of the foreign currency units. This exposed foreign currency risk may lead to recognition of foreign exchange transaction gains or losses in the income statement of the US company, as defined in SFAS 52. If the US company pays or receives US dollars in import and export transactions, the risk resulting from fluctuating foreign exchange rates is borne by the foreign supplier or customer, and there is no need to apply the procedures outlined in SFAS 52 to the transaction reported in US dollars on the US company's books.

The following example illustrates the terminology and procedures applicable to the translation of foreign currency transactions. Assume that US Company, an exporter, sells merchandise to a customer in Germany on December 1, 2007, for 10,000 euros (€). Receipt of €10,000 is due on January 31, 2008, and US Company prepares financial statements on December 31, 2007. At the transaction date (December 1, 2007), the spot rate for immediate exchange of foreign currencies indicates that €1 is equivalent to $.90. This quotation is referred to as a direct quotation since the exchange rate is stated in terms of a direct translation of the currency in which the debt is measured. To find the US dollar equivalent of this transaction, simply multiply the foreign currency amount, €10,000, by $.90 to get $9,000. Occasionally, spot rates are quoted indirectly (e.g., $1 is equivalent to €1.1111). In the example used, since $1 is equivalent to €1.1111, the foreign currency amount would be divided by €1.1111 to get the US dollar amount of $9,000 (assuming the calculation is performed using four decimal places and rounded to the nearest dollar).

At December 1, 2007, the foreign currency transaction should be recorded by US Company in the following manner:

| | | |
|---|---|---|
| Accounts receivable (€) | 9,000 | |
| Sales | | 9,000 |

The accounts receivable and sales are measured in US dollars at the transaction date using the spot rate at the time of the transaction. While the accounts receivable is measured and reported in US dollars, the receivable is also denominated or fixed in euros. This characteristic can result in foreign exchange transaction gains or losses if the spot rate for euros changes between the transaction date and the date the transaction is settled.

If financial statements are prepared between the transaction date and the settlement date, the FASB requires that receivables and liabilities denominated in a currency other than the functional currency be restated to reflect the spot rates in existence at the balance sheet date. Assume that, on December 31, 2007, the spot rate for euros is €1 = $.93. This means that €10,000 are worth $9,300, and that the accounts receivable denominated in euros are increased by $300. The following journal entry should be recorded as of December 31, 2007:

| | | |
|---|---|---|
| Accounts receivable (€) | 300 | |
| Foreign currency transaction gain | | 300 |

Note that the sales account, which was credited on the transaction date for $9,000, is not affected by changes in the spot rate. This treatment exemplifies the "two-transaction" viewpoint adopted by the FASB. In other words, making the sale is the result of an operating decision, while bearing the risk of fluctuating spot rates is the result of an investment decision. Therefore, the amount determined as sales revenue at the transaction date should not be altered because of an investment decision to wait until January 31, 2008, for payment of the account. The risk of a foreign exchange transaction loss can be avoided either by demanding immediate payment on December 1 or by entering into a forward exchange contract to hedge the exposed asset (accounts receivable). The fact that US Company in the example did not act in either of these two ways is reflected by the required recognition of foreign currency transaction gains or losses on this type of transaction. These gains or losses are reported on US Company's income statement as financial (nonoperating) items in the period during which the exchange rates changed.

It is also important to note that reporting transaction gains or losses before the transaction is settled results in reporting unrealized gains or losses. This represents an exception to the conventional realization principle which normally applies. This practice also results in a temporary difference between pretax accounting income and taxable income because foreign exchange transaction gains and losses do not enter into the determination of taxable income until the year they are realized. Thus, the recognition of foreign currency transaction gains and losses on unsettled foreign currency transactions results in deferred tax assets/liabilities (depending on whether the temporary differences result in future taxable or future deductible amounts).

To complete the previous illustration, assume that on January 31, 2008, the foreign currency transaction is settled when the spot rate is €1 = $.91. Note that the account receivable is still valued at $9,300 at this point. The receipt of euros and their conversion into dollars should be journalized as follows:

| | | |
|---|---|---|
| Foreign currency (€) | 9,100 | |
| Foreign currency transaction loss | 200 | |
|     Accounts receivable (€) | | 9,300 |
| Cash | 9,100 | |
|     Foreign currency (€) | | 9,100 |

The net effect of this foreign currency transaction was the receipt of $9,100 from a sale which was measured originally at $9,000. This realized net foreign currency transaction gain of $100 is reported on the income statements of more than one period—a $300 gain in 2007 and a $200 loss in 2008.

The financial statement disclosures required by SFAS 52 include the following:

1.  Aggregate transaction gain (loss) that is included in the entity's net income
2.  Significant rate changes subsequent to the date of the financial statements including effects on unsettled foreign currency transactions

## B. Derivative Instruments and Hedging Activities

Hedging activities and the use of derivative instruments has increased dramatically in the past few years. This increase has raised the concern that inconsistent and/or improper accounting treatment could occur, even in the case of identical hedging/derivative activities. As a result, in June 1998 the FASB issued Statement of Financial Accounting Standards 133, *Accounting for Derivative Instruments and Hedging Activities*. SFAS 137 was issued in June 1999. It delayed the required implementation of SFAS 133 for one year. SFAS 138 was issued in June 2001 and amends several of the specific applications of SFAS 133. SFAS 149, issued in April 2004, and SFAS 155, issued in February 2006, further amend SFAS 133.

The term "financial instruments and other contracts" is used frequently in SFAS 133. Financial instruments include cash, accounts/notes receivable, accounts/notes payable, bonds, common stock, preferred stock, stock options, foreign currency forward contracts, futures contracts, various financial swaps, etc. Other contracts which are also considered financial instruments meet the following two criteria: (1) the contract imposes a contractual obligation on one party (to the contract) to deliver cash or another financial instrument to the second party, or to exchange financial instruments on potentially unfavorable terms with the second party; (2) the contract conveys a contractual right to the second party to receive cash or another financial instrument from the first party, or to exchange financial instruments on favorable terms with the first party. A glossary of derivative-related terms is presented at the end of this section.

It is from this universe of financial instruments and other contracts that a subset is identified that qualifies as derivative instruments. Derivative instruments are so called because they derive their value as a financial instrument from something outside the instrument itself. For example, a call option to purchase an exchange-traded stock would qualify as a derivative instrument. The value of the call option can only be determined by the market price of the related stock. For example, a call option allows the holder to purchase 1,000 shares of stock at $50 per share, but no determination can be made as to the value of the call option until the stock price is determined. If the market value of the stock is $58 per share, the value of the call option is easily determined to be $8,000 (1,000 shares × [$58 − $50]). In SFAS terminology, the stock price is called the "underlying," the rate or price that exists outside the derivative instrument that is used to determine the value of the derivative instrument. The 1,000 shares of stock is known as the "notional amount," that is the number of units related to the derivative instrument. Both of these terms are important for two reasons: (1) their existence is a necessary condition for determining whether or not a financial instrument or other contract is a derivative instrument; (2) they are determining factors in calculating the "settlement amount" of a derivative instrument. All of these terms are discussed in more detail later in this section, but this basic understanding of derivative instruments may be helpful in working through the remaining definitions, explanations, and examples.

1.  **Foundation Principles for SFAS 133**—The basic principles driving the structure of SFAS 133 are

    a.  **Fair value measurement.** Derivative instruments meet the definition of assets and liabilities (probable future economic benefits or sacrifices of future economic benefits resulting from past transactions or events). As such they should be reported on an entity's financial statements. The most relevant measure for reporting financial instruments is "fair value." SFAS 157 defines fair value as "the price that would be received to sell an asset or paid to transfer a liability in an orderly transaction between market participants at the measurement date." As a corollary to this principle, gains and losses that result from the change in the fair value of derivative instruments are **not** assets and liabilities. Therefore, gains and losses should not be reported on the balance sheet but rather should either appear in comprehensive income or be reported in current earnings. The details for reporting gains and losses appear in a subsequent section.

    b.  **Hedging.** Certain derivative instruments will qualify under the definition of hedging instruments. Those that qualify will be accounted for using hedge accounting, which generally provides for matching the recognition of gains and losses of the hedging instrument and the hedged asset or liability. (More details about hedge accounting are provided in a later section.) Three kinds of hedges have been defined in the standard.

        (1) Fair value hedge—A hedge of the exposure to changes in the fair value of (a) a recognized asset or liability, or (b) an unrecognized firm commitment.
        (2) Cash flow hedge—A hedge of the exposure to variability in the cash flows of (a) a recognized asset or liability, or (b) a forecasted transaction.
        (3) Foreign currency hedge—A hedge of the foreign currency exposure of (a) an unrecognized firm commitment, (b) an available-for-sale security, (c) a forecasted transaction, or (d) a net investment in a foreign operation.

        If a derivative instrument does not qualify as a hedging instrument under one of the three categories shown above, then its gains or losses must be reported and recognized in current earnings.

2.  **Definition of a Derivative Instrument**—SFAS 133 identifies three distinguishing characteristics of a derivative instrument, **all** of which must be present for a financial instrument or other contract to be considered a derivative instrument.

    a.  The financial instrument or other contract must contain (a) one or more **underlyings,** and (b) one or more **notional amounts** (or payment provisions or both). An underlying is any financial or physical variable that has either observable changes or objectively verifiable changes. Therefore, underlyings would include traditional financial measures such as commodity prices, interest rates, exchange rates, or indexes related to any of these items. More broadly, measures such as an entity's credit rating, rainfall, or temperature changes would also meet the definition of an underlying.

        Notional amounts are the "number of currency or other units" specified in the financial instrument or other contract. In the case of options, this could include bushels of wheat, shares of stock, etc. The settlement amount of a financial instrument or other contract is calculated using the underlying(s) and notional amount(s) in some combination. Computation of the settlement amount may be as simple as multiplying the fair value of a stock times a specified number of shares. On the other hand, calculation of the settlement amount may require a very complex calculation, involving ratios, stepwise variables, and other leveraging techniques.

        *NOTE: The term "notional amount" is sometimes used interchangeably with "settlement amount." Watch to determine if the context in which the term is used is calling for a number of units (notional amount), or a dollar value (settlement amount).*

    b.  The financial instrument or other contract requires no initial net investment or an initial net investment that is smaller than would be required for other types of contracts that would be expected to have a similar response to changes in market factors. Many derivative instruments require no net investment or simply a premium as compensation for the time value of money. Futures contracts may require the establishment of a margin account with a balance equal to a small percentage (2 - 3%) of the value of the contract. A call option on a foreign currency contract would again only cost a small fraction of the value of the contract. These are typical contracts that would meet this definition and would be included in the definition of derivative instruments.

c.   The terms of the financial instrument or other contract do one of the following with regard to settlement:

(1)  Require or permit net settlement, either within the contract or by a means outside the contract. Net settlement means that a contract can be settled through the payment of cash rather than the exchange of the specific assets referenced in the contract. This type of settlement typically occurs with a currency swap or an interest rate swap. This definition may have some unanticipated consequences. For example, a contract with a liquidating damages clause for nonperformance, the amount of which is determined by an underlying, would meet this criterion. This is a prime example of the breadth of the definition of a derivative instrument for the purposes of SFAS 133.

(2)  Provide for the delivery of an asset that puts the recipient in a position not substantially different from net settlement. This might include a futures contract where one party to the contract delivers an asset, but a "market mechanism" exists (such as an exchange) so that the asset can be readily converted to cash. Convertibility to cash requires an active market and is a determining factor in whether or not a financial instrument or other contract will be treated as a derivative instrument.

3.  **Inclusions in and Exclusions from Derivative Instruments**

The following table provides a list of those financial instruments and other contracts that meet the definition of derivative instruments and must be accounted for using SFAS 133, and those that are not required to be accounted for under SFAS 133, either because they do not meet the definition of derivative instruments or because they are specifically excluded from treatment.

Interest rate swaps are one of the most commonly used derivative instruments in business. The following discussion first describes an interest rate swap and then shows how it meets the definition of a derivative instrument. In a common example, two parties may agree to swap interest payments on debt. Usually this occurs when one party (Company F) has issued fixed-rate debt and believes that interest rates are going to drop, while a second party (Company V) has issued variable-rate debt and believes that interest rates are going to rise. In this case, both companies would be interested in exchanging interest payments since both believe that their interest expense would decrease as a result of the swap. Variable-rate interest may be determined by any number of indices (e.g., London Interbank Offered Rate [LIBOR], S&P 500 index, some fixed relationship to T-bill rates, AAA corporate bonds, etc.).

In this example, the notional amount is defined as the principal portion of the debt, which would be the same for both the fixed and variable rate debt. The underlying is the index that determines the variable interest rate, for example, six-month LIBOR. There is no initial net investment required for this contract since the first payment will not occur until the first interest date arrives, and net settlement can be achieved through the payment of interest and principal at the maturity date. Therefore, all three of the criteria for a derivative instrument are present, and SFAS 133 controls the accounting that must be used for this interest rate swap. Similar examples could be developed for the other financial instruments listed in the "included" column below.

| *Included* | *Excluded* |
|---|---|
| • Options to purchase (call) or sell (put) exchange-traded securities | • Normal purchases and sales (does not exclude "take or pay" contracts with little or no initial net investment and products that are readily convertible to cash) |
| • Futures contracts | • Equity securities |
| • Interest rate swaps | • Debt securities |
| • Currency swaps | • Regular-way (three-day settlement) security trades (this exclusion applies to "to be announced" and "when issued" trades) |
| • Swaptions (an option on a swap) | • Leases |
| • Credit indexed contracts | • Mortgage-backed securities |
| • Interest rate caps/floors/collars | • Employee stock options |
| | • Royalty agreements and other contracts tied to sales volumes |
| | • Variable annuity contracts |
| | • Adjustable rate loans |
| | • Guaranteed investment contracts |
| | • Nonexchanged traded contracts tied to physical variables |
| | • Derivatives that serve as impediments to sales accounting (e.g., guaranteed residual value in a leasing arrangement) |

4. **Embedded Derivative Instruments and Bifurcation**

Financial instruments and other contracts may contain features which, if they stood alone, would meet the definition of a derivative instrument. These financial instruments and other contracts are known as "hybrid instruments." This means that there is a basic contract, known as the "host contract," that has an embedded derivative instrument. In these circumstances, the embedded derivative instrument may have to be separated from the host contract, a process known as bifurcation, and treated as if it were a stand-alone instrument. In this case, the host contract (excluding the embedded derivative) would be accounted for in the normal manner (as if it had never contained the embedded derivative), and the now stand-alone derivative instrument would be accounted for using SFAS 133.

Three criteria are used to determine if bifurcation must occur. **All** criteria must be met.

a.  The embedded derivative meets the definition of a derivative instrument for the purposes of applying SFAS 133.

b.  The hybrid instrument is **not** regularly recorded at fair value, with changes reported in current earnings as they occur under other GAAP. If the hybrid instrument is regularly recorded at fair value, then there is no need to bifurcate the embedded derivative since the same end result is being accomplished already.

c.  The economic characteristics and risks of the embedded derivative instrument are **not** "clearly and closely related" to the economic characteristics and risks of the host contract.

Below are listed a number of hybrid instruments that would normally require bifurcation under SFAS 133.

1.  A bond payable with an interest rate based on the S&P 500 index.

2.  An equity instrument (stock) with a call option, allowing the issuing company to buy back the stock.

3.  An equity instrument with a put option, requiring the issuing company to buy back the stock at the request of the holder.

4.  A loan agreement that permits the debtor to pay off the loan prior to its maturity with the loan payoff penalty based on the short-term T-bill rates.

5.  Loans with term-extending options whose values are based on the prime rate at the time of the extension.

6.  Convertible debt (from the investor's viewpoint)

It should be clear from the brief list shown above that many existing financial instruments that did not require any special accounting treatment prior to SFAS 133 will now be viewed as financial instruments with embedded derivative instruments.

d.  SFAS 155, issued in February 2006, amends SFAS 133. SFAS 155 allows the holder of a hybrid instrument normally requiring bifurcation to make an election **not** to bifurcate the instrument. Instead, the entire instrument is valued at fair value. This election is irrevocable and is made on an instrument-by-instrument basis. Changes in fair value of the hybrid instruments are recognized each year in earnings. If a company elects to use fair value measurement on selected hybrid instruments, the balance sheet disclosure may be presented in one of two ways: (a) as separate line items for the fair value and non–fair value instruments on the balance sheet, or (b) as an aggregate amount of all hybrid instruments with the amount of the hybrid instruments at fair value shown in parentheses.

When a company initially adopts SFAS 155, the difference between the total carrying amount of the components of the bifurcated hybrid financial instruments and the fair value of the combined hybrid financial instruments is recognized as a cumulative effect adjustment to the beginning balance of retained earnings of the period. Prior periods are not restated. The gross gains and losses of the cumulative effect of the adjustment should be disclosed in the notes to the financial statements. SFAS 155 does not apply to hedging instruments.

e.  SFAS 159, issued in February 2007, also amends SFAS 133. SFAS 159 provides that the fair value option may be applied to host financial instruments resulting from separation of an embedded nonfinancial derivative instrument from a nonfinancial hybrid instrument. If the fair value option is elected, the disclosure rules for SFAS 159 apply.

5. **Hedging Instruments—General Criteria**

Two primary criteria must be met in order for a derivative instrument to qualify as a hedging instrument.

a. Sufficient documentation must be provided at the beginning of the process to identify at a minimum (1) the objective and strategy of the hedge, (2) the hedging instrument and the hedged item, and (3) how the effectiveness (see below) of the hedge will be assessed on an ongoing basis.

b. The hedge must be "highly effective" throughout its life. Effectiveness is measured by analyzing the hedging instrument's (the derivative instrument) ability to generate changes in fair value that offset the changes in value of the hedged item. At a minimum, its effectiveness will be measured every three months and whenever earnings or financial statements are reported. A "highly effective" hedge has been interpreted to mean that "the cumulative change in the value of the hedging instrument should be between 80 and 125% of the inverse cumulative changes in the fair value or cash flows of the hedged item." (This is a reuse of the definition of "high correlation" from SFAS 80. SFAS 133 does not provide any specific definition for "highly effective," so this definition has been offered as a surrogate.) The method used to assess effectiveness must be used throughout the hedge period and must be consistent with the approach used for managing risk. Similar hedges should usually be assessed for effectiveness in a similar manner unless a different method can be justified. (Even though a hedging instrument may meet the criterion for being highly effective, it may not eliminate variations in reported earnings, because to the extent that a hedging instrument is not 100% effective, the difference in net loss or gain in each period must be reported in current earnings.)

6. **Fair Value Hedges**

A fair value hedge is the use of a derivative instrument to hedge the exposure to changes in the fair value of an asset or a liability.

a. **Specific criteria.** The hedged asset/liability must meet certain criteria in order to qualify as a fair value hedge. The hedged item must be either all or a specific portion (e.g., a percentage, a contractual cash flow) of a recognized asset/liability or an unrecognized firm commitment. Both of these situations arise frequently in foreign currency transactions. For example, a company may enter into a firm commitment with a foreign supplier to purchase a piece of equipment, the price of which is denominated in a foreign currency and both the delivery date and the payment date are in the future. The company may decide to hedge the commitment to pay for the equipment in a foreign currency in order to protect itself from currency fluctuations between the firm commitment date and the payment date. For the period between the firm commitment date and the delivery date, the company will be hedging against an unrecognized firm commitment. For the period between the delivery date and the payment date, the company is hedging against a recognized liability. (See Section 9 of this module for the accounting associated with this example.) For an unrecognized firm commitment to qualify it must be (1) binding on both parties, (2) specific with respect to all significant terms, and (3) contain a nonperformance clause that makes performance probable.

b. **Accounting for a fair value hedge.** Under SFAS 133, gains and losses on the hedged asset/liability and the hedging instrument will be recognized in current earnings.

> EXAMPLE: On 10/1/06, Dover Corp. purchases 20 shares of Porter, Inc. stock at $40. The securities are classified as available-for-sale. The market price moves to $45 by the end of the year. Assume Dover does not elect the fair value option to report its shares of Porter stock. In order to protect itself from a possible decline in the stock value of its available-for-sale security, Dover purchases an at-the-money put option for $300 on 12/31/06. The put option gives Dover the right, but not the obligation, to sell 200 shares of Porter stock at $45 per share, and the option expires on 12/31/08. Dover designates the hedge as a fair value hedge because it is hedging changes in the security's fair value. The fair value of an option is made up of two components, the time value and the intrinsic value. At the time of purchase, the time value is the purchase price of the options and the intrinsic value is $0 (because the option was purchased at-the-money. Over the life of the option, the time value will drop to $0. This is due to the fact that time value relates to the ability to exercise the option over a specified period of time. As the option moves toward the expiration date, the perceived value of the time value portion of the option will decrease as a function of the time value of money (TVM) issues and other market forces. The time value will generally decrease over the life of the option, but not necessarily in a linear fashion. The intrinsic value will vary based on the difference between the current stock price vs. the stock price on the date the option was purchased. As shown in the table below, the intrinsic value of the option increases from $0 to $200 between 12/31/06 and 12/31/07 because the stock price has dropped by $1 (× 200 shares), and the hedge has been effective for that same amount. As can be seen by analyzing the two components of the put option, the market is the primary driver of the value that

*should be assigned to the option. As is often the case, the intrinsic value of the option is considered to be a "highly effective" hedge against changes in the stock price, while the time value is ineffective and is reflected in current earnings. Additional information is provided below.*

| Item | 1/1/06 | 12/31/06 | 12/31/07 | 12/31/08 |
|---|---|---|---|---|
| Porter stock price | $40 | $ 45 | $ 44 | $ 42 |
| Put option | | | | |
| Time value | | $300 | $160 | $0 |
| Intrinsic value | | $ 0 | $200 | $600 |
| | | | (200 × $1) | (200 × $3) |

**1/1/06**

1. Available-for-sale securities .................... 8,000
   Cash .................................................. 8,000
   *Record the purchase of Porter stock (200 × $40).*

**12/31/06**

2. Available-for-sale securities .................... 1,000
   Other comprehensive income .................. 1,000
   *Record the unrealized gain on Porter stock (accounting prior to the hedge in accordance with SFAS 115). (200 × $5 valuation increase from holding gain to market value)*

3. Put option ........................................... 300
   Cash .................................................. 300
   *Record the purchase of at-the-money put option.*

**12/31/07**

4. Put option ........................................... 200
   Gain on hedge activity .......................... 200
   *Record the increase in the intrinsic value (fair value) of the option.*

5. Loss on hedge activity ........................... 200
   Available-for-sale securities .................. 200
   *Record the decrease in the fair value of the securities (accounting after the hedge is established) $200 = 200 shares × $1 holding loss.*

   Note that the $200 gain on hedge activity from the put option is balanced effectively against the $200 loss on hedge activity from the hedged available-for-sale security. SFAS 133 amends SFAS 115 to require that the portion of the unrealized holding gain or loss on an available-for-sale security that is designated as a hedged item in a fair value hedge be recognized in earnings during the period of the hedge. This is why the $200 holding loss on the available-for-sale securities is recognized in the period's earnings.

6. Loss on hedge activity ........................... 140
   Put option .......................................... 140
   *Record the loss related to the time value of the option.  $140 = $300 – $160*

**12/31/08**

7. Put option ........................................... 400
   Gain on hedge activity .......................... 400
   *Record the increase in the intrinsic value of the put option.*

8. Loss on hedge activity ........................... 400
   Available-for-sale securities .................. 400
   *To record the decrease in the fair value of the securities (accounting after the hedge is established); $400 = 200 shares × $2 holding loss on available-for-sale securities.*

9. Loss on hedge activity ........................... 160
   Put option .......................................... 160
   *Record the loss related to the time value of the option.  $140 = $300 – $160*

10. Cash .................................................. 9,000
    Put option .......................................... 600
    Available-for-sale securities .................. 8,400
    *Record the exercise of the put option (sell the 200 shares of stock @ $45) and close out the put option investment.*

11. Other comprehensive income .................. 1,000
    Gain on Porter stock ............................ 1,000
    *To reclassify the unrealized holding gain recognized in entry 2., from other comprehensive income to earnings, because the securities were sold.*

## 7. Cash Flow Hedges

Cash flow hedges use derivative instruments to hedge the exposure to variability in expected future cash flows.

   a. **Specific criteria.** Additional criteria must be met in order to qualify as a cash flow hedge. The primary criterion is that the hedged asset/liability and the hedging instrument must be "linked."

Linking is established if the basis (the specified rate or index) for the change in cash flows is the same for the hedged asset/liability and the hedging instrument. Cash flows do not have to be identical, but they must meet the highly effective threshold discussed above. In addition, if the hedged asset/liability is a **forecasted transaction,** it must be considered **probable,** based on appropriate facts and circumstances (i.e., past history). Also, if the forecasted hedged asset/liability is a series of transactions, they must "share the same risk exposure." Purchases of a particular product from the same supplier over a period of time would meet this requirement.

b. **Accounting for a cash flow hedge.** Under SFAS 133, for the hedging instrument (1) the effective portion is reported in other comprehensive income, and (2) the ineffective portion and/or excluded components are reported on a cumulative basis to reflect the lesser of (1) the cumulative gain/loss on the derivative since the creation of the hedge, or (2) the cumulative gain/loss from the change in expected cash flows from the hedged instrument since the creation of the hedge.

The above amounts need to be adjusted to reflect any reclassification of other comprehensive income to current earnings. This will occur when the hedged asset/liability affects earnings (e.g., when hedged inventory is sold and the cost of inventory passes through to cost of goods sold).

> *EXAMPLE: A commercial bakery believes that wheat prices may increase over the next few months. To protect itself against this risk, the bakery purchases call options on wheat futures to hedge the price risk of their forecasted inventory purchases. If wheat prices increase, the profit on the purchased call options will offset the higher price the bakery must pay for the wheat. If wheat prices decline, the bakery will lose the premium it paid for the call options, but can then buy the wheat at the lower price. On June 1, 2007, the bakery pays a premium of $350 to purchase a September 30, 2007 call for 1,000 bushels of wheat at the futures price of $16.60 per bushel. The call option is considered a cash flow hedge because the designated risk that is being hedged is the risk of changes in the cash flows relating to changes in the purchase price of the wheat. On September 30, the bakery settles its call options and purchases wheat on the open market. Pertinent wheat prices are shown below.*

| | | |
|---|---|---|
| Spot price (June 1) | | $16.50 |
| Futures price (as of June 1 for September 30) | | $16.60 |
| Spot price (September 30) | | $17.30 |

**June 1**

| | | | |
|---|---|---|---|
| 1. | Call option | 350 | |
| | Cash | | 350 |

*Record the purchase of the call option.*

**September 30**

| | | | |
|---|---|---|---|
| 2. | Loss on hedge activity | 350 | |
| | Call option | 350 | 350 |

*Record the expiration (change in time value) of the call option.*

| | | | |
|---|---|---|---|
| 3. | Call option | 700 | |
| | Other comprehensive income | 700 | 700 |

*Record the increase in intrinsic value of the call option.*
*$700 = {1,000 bushels × [$17.30 (the spot price per bushel on September 30) – $16.60 (the futures price as of June 1 for September 30)]}*

| | | | |
|---|---|---|---|
| 4. | Cash | 700 | |
| | Call option | | 700 |

*Record the cash settlement of the call option.*

| | | | |
|---|---|---|---|
| 5. | Inventory | 17,300 | |
| | Cash | | 17,300 |

*Record the purchase of the wheat at the spot price. $17,300 = 1,000 bushels × $17.30*

8. **Foreign Currency Hedges**

Foreign currency denominated assets/liabilities that arise in the course of normal business are often hedged with offsetting forward exchange contracts. This process, in effect, creates a natural hedge. Normal accounting rules (i.e., SFAS 52) apply, and the FASB decided not to change this accounting treatment in the implementation of SFAS 133. SFAS 133 does specify hedge accounting in four areas related to foreign currency hedges. The application of hedge accounting is generally more restrictive under SFAS 133 than it was under SFAS 52. The four foreign currency hedges under SFAS 133 are discussed below.

a. **Unrecognized firm commitment.** Either a derivative instrument or a nonderivative financial instrument (such as a receivable in a foreign currency) can be designated as a hedge of an unrecognized firm commitment attributable to changes in foreign currency exchange rates. If the requirements for a fair value hedge are met, then this hedging arrangement can be accounted for as a **fair value hedge,** discussed above.

b. **Available-for-sale securities.** Prior to SFAS 133, a firm commitment to purchase a trading security and several transactions related to held-to-maturity securities were permitted to use hedging accounting under certain conditions. SFAS 133 has eliminated the use of hedge accounting for both trading and held-to-maturity securities (in many cases hedge accounting wasn't required anyway) and limited the use of hedge accounting to transactions for securities designated as available-for-sale. Derivative instruments can be used to hedge debt or equity available-for-sale securities. However, equity securities must meet two additional criteria.

(1) They cannot be traded on an exchange denominated in the investor's functional currency.
(2) Dividends must be denominated in the same foreign currency as is expected to be received on the sale of the security.

If the above criteria are met, hedging instruments related to available-for-sale securities can be accounted for as **fair value hedges,** discussed above.

c. **Foreign currency denominated forecasted transactions.** This is an expansion in the permitted use of hedge accounting under SFAS 133. Only derivative instruments can be designated as hedges of foreign currency denominated forecasted transactions. A forecasted export sale with the price denominated in a foreign currency might qualify for this type of hedge treatment. Forecasted transactions are distinguished from firm commitments (discussed in a. above) because the timing of the cash flows remains uncertain. This additional complexity results in hedging instruments related to foreign currency denominated forecasted transactions being accounted for as cash flow hedges, discussed above. Hedge accounting is permissible for transactions between unrelated parties, and under special circumstances (not discussed here) for intercompany transactions.

d. **Net investments in foreign operations.** The accounting for net investments in foreign operations has not changed from the SFAS 52 rules, except that the hedging instrument has to meet the new "effective" criterion. The change in the fair value of the hedging derivative is recorded in other comprehensive income which is then closed to the accumulated other comprehensive income account in the equity section of the balance sheet.

### Hedge Accounting under SFAS 133

| *Attribute* | *Fair Value* | *Type of Hedge—SFAS 133* *Cash Flow* | *Foreign Currency (FC)* |
|---|---|---|---|
| Types of hedging instruments permitted | Derivatives | Derivatives | Derivatives or nonderivatives depending on the type of hedge |
| Balance sheet valuation of hedging instrument | Fair value | Fair value | Fair value |
| Recognition of gain or loss on changes in value of hedging instrument | Currently in earnings | Effective portion currently as a component of other comprehensive income (OCI) and reclassified to earnings in future period(s) that forecasted transaction affects earnings | **FC denominated firm commitment** Currently in earnings **Available-for-sale security (AFS)** Currently in earnings |
| | | Ineffective portion currently in earnings | **Forecasted FC transaction** Same as cash flow hedge **Net investment in a foreign operation** OCI as part of the cumulative translation adjustment to the extent it is effective as a hedge |
| Recognition of gain or loss on changes in the fair value of the hedged item | Currently in earnings | Not applicable; these hedges are not associated with recognized assets or liabilities | **FC denominated firm commitment** Currently in earnings **Available-for-sale security (AFS)** Currently in earnings **Forecasted FC transaction** Not applicable; same as cash flow hedge |

## 9. Forward Exchange Contracts

It was stated previously that foreign currency transaction gains and losses on assets and liabilities which are denominated in a currency other than the functional currency can be hedged if a US company enters into a forward exchange contract. The following example shows how a forward exchange contract can be used as a hedge, first against a firm commitment and then, following delivery date, as a hedge against a recognized liability. The general rule for estimating the fair value of forward exchange contracts is to use the forward exchange rate for the remaining term of the contract.

> *EXAMPLE: Baker Simon, Inc. enters into a firm commitment with Dempsey Ing., Inc. of Germany, on October 1, 2006, to purchase a computerized robotic system for €6,000,000. The system will be delivered on March 1, 2007, with payment due sixty days after delivery (April 30, 2007). Baker Simon, Inc. decides to hedge this foreign currency firm commitment and enters into a forward exchange contract on the firm commitment date to receive €6,000,000 on the payment date. The applicable exchange rates are shown in the table below.*

| Date | Spot rates | Forward rates for April 30, 2006 |
|---|---|---|
| October 1, 2006 | €1 = $.90 | €1 = $ .91 |
| December 31, 2006 | €1 = $.92 | €1 = $ .94 |
| March 1, 2007 | €1 = $.92 | €1 = $.935 |
| April 30, 2007 | €1 = $.96 | |

The following example separately presents both the forward contract receivable and the dollars payable liability in order to show all aspects of the forward contract. For financial reporting purposes, most companies present just the net fair value of the forward contract, which would be the difference between the current value of the forward contract receivable and the dollars payable accounts.

The transactions which reflect the forward exchange contract, the firm commitment and the acquisition of the asset and retirement of the related liability appear as follows:

### Forward contract entries

(1)  10/1/06 (forward rate for 4/30/07
€1 = $.91)

| | | |
|---|---|---|
| Forward contract receivable (€) | 5,460,000 | |
| Dollars payable | | 5,460,000 |

This entry recognizes the existence of the forward exchange contract using the gross method. Under the net method, this entry would not appear at all, since the fair value of the forward contract is zero when the contract is initiated. The amount is calculated using the 10/1/06 forward rate for 4/30/07 (€6,000,000 × $.91 = $5,460,000). Note that the **net** fair value of the forward exchange contact on 10/1/06 is zero because there is an exact amount offset of the forward contract receivable with the dollars payable liability.

(2)  12/31/06 (forward rate for 4/30/06
€1 = $.94)

| | | |
|---|---|---|
| Forward contract receivable (€) | 180,000 | |
| Gain on hedge activity | | 180,000 |

€6,000,000 × ($ .94 – $ .91) = $180,000. The dollar values for this entry reflect, among other things, the change in the forward rate from 10/1/06 to 12/31/06. However, the actual amount recorded as gain or loss (gain in this case) will be determined by all market factors.

(4)  3/1/07 (forward rate for 4/30/07
€1 = $.935)

| | | |
|---|---|---|
| Loss on hedge activity | 30,000 | |
| Forward contract receivable (€) | | 30,000 |

€6,000,000 × ($ .935 – $ .94) = $30,000. These entries again will be driven by market factors, and they are calculated the same way as entries (2) and (3) above. Notice that the decline in the forward rate from 12/31/06 to 3/1/07 resulted in a loss against the forward contract receivable and a gain against the firm commitment.

### Hedge against firm commitment entries

(3)  12/31/06

| | | |
|---|---|---|
| Loss on hedge activity | 180,000 | |
| Firm commitment | | 180,000 |

The dollar values for this entry are identical to entry (2), reflecting the fact that the hedge is highly effective (100%) and also the fact that the market recognizes the same factors in this transaction as for entry (2). This entry reflects the first use of the firm commitment account, a temporary liability account pending the receipt of the asset against which the firm commitment has been hedged.

(5)  3/1/07

| | | |
|---|---|---|
| Firm commitment | 30,000 | |
| Gain on hedge activity | | 30,000 |

(6)  3/1/07 (spot rate €1 = $.92)

| | | |
|---|---|---|
| Equipment | 5,370,000 | |
| Firm commitment | 150,000 | |
| Accounts payable (€) | | 5,520,000 |

This entry records the receipt of the equipment (recorded at fair value determined on a discounted net present value basis), the elimination of the temporary liability account (firm commitment), and the recognition of the payable, calculated using the spot rate on the date of receipt (€6,000,000 × $.92 = $5,520,000).

(7)  4/30/07 (spot rate €1 = $.96))

| | | |
|---|---|---|
| Forward contract receivable (€) | 150,000 | |
| Gain on forward contract | | 150,000 |

(8)  4/30/07

| | | |
|---|---|---|
| Transaction loss | 240,000 | |
| Accounts payable (€) | | 240,000 |

The gain or loss (gain in this case) on the forward contract is calculated using the change in the forward to the spot rate from 3/1/07 to 4/30/07 [€6,000,000 × ($..96 – $.935) = $150,000]

The transaction loss related to the accounts payable reflects only the change in the spot rates and ignores the accrual of interest. [€6,000,000 × ($.96 – $.92) = $180,000]

(9)   4/30/07

| | | |
|---|---|---|
| Dollars payable | 5,460,000 | |
|    Cash | | 5,460,000 |
| Foreign currency units (€) | 5,760,000 | |
|    Forward contract receivable (€) | | 5,760,000 |

This entry reflects the settlement of the forward contract at the 10/1/06 contracted forward rate (€6,000,000 × $.91 = $5,460,000) and the receipt of foreign currency units valued at the spot rate (€6,000,000 × $.96 = $5,760,000).

(10)

| | | |
|---|---|---|
| Accounts payable (€) | 5,760,000 | |
|    Foreign currency units | | 5,760,000 |

This entry reflects the use of the foreign currency units to settle the account payable.

In the case of using a forward exchange contract to speculate in a specific foreign currency, the general rule to estimate the fair value of the forward contract is to use the forward exchange rate for the remainder of the term of the forward contract.

10. **Disclosures**

Disclosures related to financial instruments, both derivative and nonderivative, that are used as hedging instruments must include the following information: (1) objectives and the strategies for achieving them, (2) context to understand the instrument, (3) risk management policies, and (4) a list of hedged instruments. These disclosures have to be separated by type of hedge and reported every time a complete set of financial statements is issued. In addition, disclosure requirements exist for derivative instruments that are not designated as hedging instruments.

11. **Fair Value and Concentration of Credit Risk Disclosures of Financial Instruments other than Derivatives**

SFAS 107, as amended by SFAS 133, requires disclosure of fair values of financial instruments for which it is practicable to estimate fair value (see outline of SFAS 107). This requirement pertains to both asset and liability financial instruments, whether recognized in the balance sheet or not.

A sample footnote is provided below. Additionally, a summary of SFAS 107 is presented in the following chart.

SFAS 107 requires disclosure of concentrations of credit risk. Credit risk is the risk that a loss will occur because parties to the instrument do not perform as expected. Such concentrations exist when a number of an entity's financial instruments are associated with similar activities and economic characteristics that could be affected by changes in similar conditions (e.g., an entity whose principal activity is to supply parts to one type of industry).

---

**Lenaburg, Inc.**
**Notes to Financial Statements**
*FAIR VALUE OF FINANCIAL INSTRUMENTS HELD OR ISSUED FOR PURPOSES*
*OTHER THAN TRADING (in thousands)*

|  | December 31, 2007 | |
|---|---|---|
|  | *Carrying amount* | *Fair value* |
| **Assets** | | |
| Cash and cash equivalents | 32,656 | 32,656 |
| Long-term investments | 12,719 | 14,682 |
| **Liabilities** | | |
| Short-term debt | 3,223 | 3,223 |
| Long-term debt | 150,000 | 182,500 |

*FAIR VALUE OF FINANCIAL INSTRUMENTS HELD FOR TRADING PURPOSES (in thousands)*

|  | December 31, 2007 | |
|---|---|---|
|  | *Carrying amount* | *Fair value* |
| **Assets** | | |
| Short-term investments | 4,074 | 4,074 |

Cash and cash equivalents—The carrying amount of cash and cash equivalents approximates fair value due to their short-term maturities.

Long-term investments—The fair value is estimated based on quoted market prices for these or similar investments.

Short-term investments—The Company holds US Treasury notes and highly liquid investments for trading purposes. The carrying value of these instruments approximates fair value.

Short- and long-term debt—The fair value of short- and long-term debt is estimated using quoted market prices for the same or similar instruments or on the current rates offered to the Company for debt of equivalent remaining maturities.

**Summary of Disclosure Standards for Financial Instruments other than Derivatives**

| SFAS | *Pertains to* | *Required disclosures* |
|---|---|---|
| 107 | Financial Instruments (Assets and Liabilities), Whether on Balance Sheet or Not | • Fair value, when practicable to estimate<br>• Information pertinent to estimating fair value (carrying value, effective interest rate, maturity) if not practicable to estimate, and reasons for impracticability of estimation<br>• Distinguish between instruments held or issued for trading purposes and instruments held or issued for purposes other than trading<br>• Do not net or aggregate fair values of derivative financial instruments with fair values of nonderivative financial instruments or with fair values of other derivative financial instruments |
| | Financial Instruments with Concentrations of Credit Risk | • Information about similar activity, region, or economic characteristics<br>• Maximum potential accounting loss<br>• Information about collateral or security requirements |

## C. Research Component

SFAS 52 contains the accounting rules for foreign currency transactions. SFAS 133 contains the accounting rules for derivative instruments and hedging transactions. SFAS 138 and 149 amended SFAS 133. Therefore, when you research, you should be alert for jump links that will indicate amended materials.

A list of research terms is shown below.

| | | |
|---|---|---|
| At the money | Financial instrument | Insurance contracts |
| Bifurcation | Firm commitment hedge | Intrinsic value |
| Call option | Forecasted transaction hedge | LIBOR |
| Cash flow hedge | Foreign currency derivative | Net settlement |
| Changes in fair value | Foreign currency hedge | Notional amounts |
| Derivative instrument | Forward contract | Out of the money |
| Designation as hedged item | Forward exchange contract | Payment provision hedge |
| Discount forward contract | Futures contract | Premium forward contract |
| Embedded derivative | Hedged item | Put option |
| Embedded derivative instruments | Hybrid instrument | Regular way securities trades |
| Fair value financial instruments | Impediments to sales accounting | Swaption |
| Fair value hedge | In the money | Transaction gain or loss |
| Financial guarantee contracts | Initial net investment | Underlyings |

## Glossary

SFAS 133 defines a number of important terms which are used to describe various derivative instruments and hedging relationships. These include the following:

**At the money.** An at-the-money option is one in which the price of the underlying is equal to the strike or exercise price.

**Bifurcation.** The process of separating an embedded derivative from its host contract. This process is necessary so that hybrid instruments (a financial instrument or other contract that contains an embedded derivative) can be separated into their component parts, each being accounted for using the appropriate valuation techniques.

**Call option.** An American call option provides the holder the right to acquire an underlying at an exercise or strike price, anytime during the option term. A premium is paid by the holder for the right to benefit from the appreciation in the underlying.

**Derivative instruments.** In SFAS 133, derivative instruments are defined by their three distinguishing characteristics. Specifically, derivative instruments are financial instruments or other contracts that have

1. One or more underlyings and one or more notional amounts (or payment provisions or both);
2. No initial net investment or a smaller net investment than required for contracts expected to have a similar response to market changes; and
3. Terms that require or permit

   a. Net settlement
   b. Net settlement by means outside the contract

    c.   Delivery of an asset that results in a position substantially the same as net settlement

**Discount or premium on a forward contract.**  The foreign currency amount of the contact multiplied by the difference between the contracted forward rate and the spot rate at the date of inception of the contract.

**Embedded derivative.**  A feature on a financial instrument or other contract, which if the feature stood alone, would meet the definition of a derivative.

**Fair value.**  Defined as the amount at which the asset or liability could be bought or settled in an arm's-length transaction; measured by reference to market prices or estimated by net present value of future cash flows, options pricing models, or by other techniques.

**Financial instrument.**  Financial instruments include cash, accounts/notes receivable, accounts/notes payable, bonds, common stock, preferred stock, stock options, foreign currency forward contracts, futures contracts, various financial swaps, etc.  Other contracts which are also considered financial instruments meet the following two criteria:  (1) the contract imposes a contractual obligation on one party (to the contract) to deliver cash or another financial instrument to the second party or to exchange potentially unfavorable terms with the second party; (2) the contract conveys a contractual right to the second party to receive cash or another financial instrument from the first party or to exchange financial instruments on favorable terms with the first party.

**Firm commitment.**  An agreement with an unrelated party, binding on both, usually legally enforceable, specifying all significant terms and including a disincentive for nonperformance sufficient to make performance likely.

**Forecasted transaction.**  A transaction expected to occur for which there is no firm commitment, and thus, which gives the entity no present rights or obligations.  Under SFAS 133, forecasted transactions can be hedged and special hedge accounting can be applied.

**Foreign currency transactions.**  Transactions whose terms are denominated in a currency other than the entity's functional currency.  Foreign currency transactions arise when an enterprise (1) buys or sells on credit goods or services whose prices are denominated in foreign currency, (2) borrows or lends funds and the amounts payable or receivable are denominated in foreign currency, (3) is a party to an unperformed forward exchange contract, or (4) for other reasons, acquires or disposes of assets, or incurs or settles liabilities denominated in foreign currency.

**Forward contract.**  A forward contract is an agreement between two parties to buy and sell a specific quantity of a commodity, foreign currency, or financial instrument at an agreed-upon price, with delivery and/or settlement at a designated future date.  Because a forward contract is not formally regulated by an organized exchange, each party to the contract is subject to the default of the other party.

**Forward exchange contract.**  An agreement to exchange at a specified future date currencies of different countries at a specified rate (forward rate).

**Futures contract.**  A futures contract is a forward-based contract to make or take delivery of a designated financial instrument, foreign currency, or commodity during a designated period, at a specified price or yield. The contract frequently has provisions for cash settlement.  A futures contract is traded on a regulated exchange and, therefore, involves less credit risk than a forward contract.

**In the money.**  A call option is in the money if the price of the underlying is greater than the strike or exercise price of the underlying.

**Initial net investment.**  A derivative instrument is one where the initial net investment is zero or is less than the notional amount (possibly plus a premium or minus a discount).  This characteristic refers to the relative amount of investment.  Derivative instruments allow the opportunity to take part in the rate or price change without owning the asset or owing the liability.  If an amount approximating the notional amount must be invested or received, it is not a derivative instrument.  The two basic forms of derivative instruments are futures contracts and options.  The futures contract involves little or no initial net investment.  Settlement is usually near the delivery date.  Call options, when purchased, require a premium payment that is less than the cost of purchasing the equivalent number of shares.  Even though this distinguishing characteristic is the result of only one of the parties, it determines the application for both.

**Intrinsic value.**  With regard to call (put) options, it is the larger of zero or the spread between the stock (exercise) price and the exercise (stock) price.

**LIBOR.**  London Interbank Offer Rate.  A widely used measure of average interest rates at a point in time.

**Net settlements.**  To qualify as derivative instruments, one of the following settlement criteria must be met:

1.  No delivery of an asset equal to the notional amount is required. For example, an interest rate swap does not involve delivery of the instrument in which the notional amount is expressed.
2.  Delivery of an asset equal to the notional amount is required of one of the parties, but an exchange (or other market mechanism, institutional arrangement or side agreement) facilitates net settlement. For example, a call option has this attribute.
3.  Delivery by one of the parties of an asset equal to the notional amount is required but the asset is either readily convertible to cash (as with a contract for the delivery of a marketable equity security), or is required but that asset is itself a derivative instrument (as is the case for a swaption [an option on a swap]).

This characteristic means that the derivative instrument can be settled by a net delivery of assets (the medium of exchange does not have to be cash). Contract terms based on changes in the price or rate of the notional that implicitly or explicitly require or permit net settlement qualify. Situations where one of the parties can liquidate their net investment or be relieved of the contract rights or obligations without significant transaction costs because of a market arrangement (broadly interpreted) or where the delivered asset can be readily converted to cash also meet the requirements for net settlement. It is assumed that an exchange traded security is readily converted to cash. Thus, commodity-based contracts for gold, oil, wheat, etc. are now included under this standard. The convertible to cash condition requires an active market and consideration of interchangeability and transaction volume. Determining if delivery of a financial asset or liability equal to the notional amount is a derivative instrument may depend upon whether it is readily convertible into cash. Different accounting will result if the notional is not readily converted to cash. Using the notional as collateral does not necessarily mean it is readily convertible to cash.

**Notional amount.** The notional amount (or payment provision) is the referenced associated asset or liability. A notional amount is commonly a number of units such as shares of stock, principal amount, face value, stated value, basis points, barrels of oil, etc. It may be that amount plus a premium or minus a discount. The interaction of the price or rate (underlying) with the referenced associated asset or liability (notional amount) determines whether settlement is required and, if so, the amount.

**Out of the money.** A call option is out of the money if the strike or exercise price is greater than the price of the underlying. A put option is out of the money if the price of the underlying is greater than the strike or exercise price.

**Put option.** An American put option provides the holder the right to sell the underlying at an exercise or strike price, anytime during the option term. A gain accrues to the holder as the market price of the underlying falls below the strike price.

**Swap.** A swap is a forward-based contract or agreement generally between two counterparties to exchange streams of cash flows over a specified period in the future.

**Swaption.** A swaption is an option on a swap that provides the holder with the right to enter into a swap at a specified future date at specified terms (freestanding option on a swap) or to extend or terminate the life of an existing swap (embedded option on a swap). These derivatives have characteristics of an option and an interest rate swap.

**Time value.** The difference between an option's price and its intrinsic value.

**Transaction gain or loss.** Transaction gains or losses result from a change in exchange rates between the functional currency and the currency in which a foreign currency transaction is denominated. They represent an increase or decrease in (a) the actual functional currency cash flows realized upon settlement of foreign currency transactions, and (b) the expected functional currency cash flows on unsettled foreign currency transactions.

**Underlyings.** An underlying is commonly a specified price or rate such as a stock price, interest rate, currency rate, commodity price, or a related index. However, any variable (financial or physical) with (1) observable changes or (2) objectively verifiable changes such as a credit rating, insurance index, climatic or geological condition (temperature, rainfall) qualifies. Unless it is specifically excluded, a contract based on any qualifying variable is accounted for under SFAS 133 if it has the distinguishing characteristics stated above.

**MULTIPLE-CHOICE QUESTIONS (1-50)**

**1.** On September 1, 2007, Bain Corp. received an order for equipment from a foreign customer for 300,000 local currency units (LCU) when the US dollar equivalent was $96,000. Bain shipped the equipment on October 15, 2007, and billed the customer for 300,000 LCU when the US dollar equivalent was $100,000. Bain received the customer's remittance in full on November 16, 2007, and sold the 300,000 LCU for $105,000. In its income statement for the year ended December 31, 2007, Bain should report as part of net income a foreign exchange transaction gain of

    a.   $0
    b.   $4,000
    c.   $5,000
    d.   $9,000

**2.** On September 1, 2007, Cano & Co., a US corporation, sold merchandise to a foreign firm for 250,000 Botswana pula. Terms of the sale require payment in pula on February 1, 2008. On September 1, 2007, the spot exchange rate was $.20 per pula. At December 31, 2007, Cano's year-end, the spot rate was $.19, but the rate increased to $.22 by February 1, 2008, when payment was received. How much should Cano report as foreign exchange transaction gain or loss as part of 2008 income?

    a.   $0.
    b.   $2,500 loss.
    c.   $5,000 gain.
    d.   $7,500 gain.

**3.** Lindy, a US corporation, bought inventory items from a supplier in Argentina on November 5, 2006, for 100,000 Argentine pesos, when the spot rate was $.4295. At Lindy's December 31, 2006 year-end, the spot rate was $.4245. On January 15, 2007, Lindy bought 100,000 pesos at the spot rate of $.4345 and paid the invoice. How much should Lindy report as part of net income for 2006 and 2007 as foreign exchange transaction gain or loss?

| | 2006 | 2007 |
|---|---|---|
| a. | $ 500 | $(1,000) |
| b. | $0 | $ (500) |
| c. | $ (500) | $0 |
| d. | $(1,000) | $ 500 |

**4.** Hunt Co. purchased merchandise for £300,000 from a vendor in London on November 30, 2007. Payment in British pounds was due on January 30, 2008. The exchange rates to purchase one pound were as follows:

| | November 30, 2007 | December 31, 2007 |
|---|---|---|
| Spot-rate | $1.65 | $1.62 |
| 30-day rate | 1.64 | 1.59 |
| 60-day rate | 1.63 | 1.56 |

In its December 31, 2007, income statement, what amount should Hunt report as foreign exchange transaction gain as part of net income?

    a.   $12,000
    b.   $ 9,000
    c.   $ 6,000
    d.   $0

**5.** Ball Corp. had the following foreign currency transactions during 2007:

- Merchandise was purchased from a foreign supplier on January 20, 2007, for the US dollar equivalent of $90,000. The invoice was paid on March 20, 2007, at the US dollar equivalent of $96,000.
- On July 1, 2007, Ball borrowed the US dollar equivalent of $500,000 evidenced by a note that was payable in the lender's local currency on July 1, 2009. On December 31, 2007, the US dollar equivalents of the principal amount and accrued interest were $520,000 and $26,000, respectively. Interest on the note is 10% per annum.

In Ball's 2007 income statement, what amount should be included as foreign exchange transaction loss as part of net income?

    a.   $0
    b.   $ 6,000
    c.   $21,000
    d.   $27,000

**6.** On November 30, 2007, Tyrola Publishing Company, located in Colorado, executed a contract with Ernest Blyton, an author from Canada, providing for payment of 10% royalties on Canadian sales of Blyton's book. Payment is to be made in Canadian dollars each January 10 for the previous year's sales. Canadian sales of the book for the year ended December 31, 2007, totaled $50,000 Canadian. Tyrola paid Blyton his 2007 royalties on January 10, 2007. Tyrola's 2007 financial statements were issued on February 1, 2008. Spot rates for Canadian dollars were as follows:

| | |
|---|---|
| November 30, 2006 | $.87 |
| January 1, 2007 | $.88 |
| December 31, 2007 | $.89 |
| January 10, 2008 | $.90 |

How much should Tyrola accrue for royalties payable at December 31, 2007?

    a.   $4,350
    b.   $4,425
    c.   $4,450
    d.   $4,500

**7.** Shore Co. records its transactions in US dollars. A sale of goods resulted in a receivable denominated in Japanese yen, and a purchase of goods resulted in a payable denominated in euros. Shore recorded a foreign exchange transaction gain on collection of the receivable and an exchange transaction loss on settlement of the payable. The exchange rates are expressed as so many units of foreign currency to one dollar. Did the number of foreign currency units exchangeable for a dollar increase or decrease between the contract and settlement dates?

| | Yen exchangeable for $1 | Euros exchangeable for $1 |
|---|---|---|
| a. | Increase | Increase |
| b. | Decrease | Decrease |
| c. | Decrease | Increase |
| d. | Increase | Decrease |

**8.** On October 1, 2007, Mild Co., a US company, purchased machinery from Grund, a German company, with payment due on April 1, 2008. If Mild's 2007 operating income included no foreign exchange transaction gain or loss, then the transaction could have

    a.   Resulted in an extraordinary gain.
    b.   Been denominated in US dollars.
    c.   Caused a foreign currency gain to be reported as a contra account against machinery.

d.   Caused a foreign currency translation gain to be reported as other comprehensive income.

9.   On October 1, 2007, Velec Co., a US company, contracted to purchase foreign goods requiring payment in Qatari rials, one month after their receipt at Velec's factory. Title to the goods passed on December 15, 2007. The goods were still in transit on December 31, 2007. Exchange rates were one dollar to twenty-two rials, twenty rials, and twenty-one rials on October 1, December 15, and December 31, 2007, respectively. Velec should account for the exchange rate fluctuation in 2007 as
   a.   A loss included in net income before extraordinary items.
   b.   A gain included in net income before extraordinary items.
   c.   An extraordinary gain.
   d.   An extraordinary loss.

10.   Derivatives are financial instruments that derive their value from changes in a benchmark based on any of the following except
   a.   Stock prices.
   b.   Mortgage and currency rates.
   c.   Commodity prices.
   d.   Discounts on accounts receivable.

11.   Derivative instruments are financial instruments or other contracts that must contain
   a.   One or more underlyings, **or** one or more notional amounts.
   b.   No initial net investment or smaller net investment than required for similar response contacts.
   c.   Terms that do not require or permit net settlement or delivery of an asset.
   d.   All of the above.

12.   The basic purpose of derivative financial instruments is to manage some kind of risk such as all of the following except
   a.   Stock price movements.
   b.   Interest rate variations.
   c.   Currency fluctuations.
   d.   Uncollectibility of accounts receivables.

13.   Which of the following statements is(are) true regarding derivative financial instruments?

   I.   Derivative financial instruments should be measured at fair value and reported in the balance sheet as assets or liabilities.
   II.   Gains and losses on derivative instruments not designated as hedging activities should be reported and recognized in earnings in the period of the change in fair value.

   a.   I only.
   b.   II only.
   c.   Both I and II.
   d.   Neither I nor II.

14.   Which of the following is an underlying, according to SFAS 133?
   a.   A credit rating.
   b.   A security price.
   c.   An average daily temperature.
   d.   All of the above could be underlyings.

15.   If the price of the underlying is greater than the strike or exercise price of the underlying, the call option is
   a.   At the money.
   b.   In the money.
   c.   On the money.
   d.   Out of the money.

16.   Which of the following is **not** a distinguishing characteristic of a derivative instrument?
   a.   Terms that require or permit net settlement.
   b.   Must be "highly effective" throughout its life.
   c.   No initial net investment.
   d.   One or more underlyings and notional amounts.

17.   An example of a notional amount is
   a.   Number of barrels of oil.
   b.   Interest rates.
   c.   Currency swaps.
   d.   Stock prices.

18.   Disclosures related to financial instruments, both derivative and nonderivative, used as hedging instruments must include
   a.   A list of hedged instruments.
   b.   Maximum potential accounting loss.
   c.   Objectives and strategies for achieving them.
   d.   Only a. and c.

19.   Which of the following financial instruments or other contracts is not specifically excluded from the definition of derivative instruments in SFAS 133?
   a.   Leases.
   b.   Call (put) option.
   c.   Adjustable rate loans.
   d.   Equity securities.

20.   Which of the following is **not** a derivative instrument?
   a.   Futures contracts.
   b.   Credit indexed contracts.
   c.   Interest rate swaps.
   d.   Variable annuity contracts.

21.   Which of the following criteria must be met for bifurcation to occur?
   a.   The embedded derivative meets the definition of a derivative instrument.
   b.   The hybrid instrument is regularly recorded at fair value.
   c.   Economic characteristics and risks of the embedded instrument are "clearly and closely" related to those of the host contract.
   d.   All of the above.

22.   Financial instruments sometimes contain features that separately meet the definition of a derivative instrument. These features are classified as
   a.   Swaptions.
   b.   Notional amounts.
   c.   Embedded derivative instruments.
   d.   Underlyings.

23.   The process of bifurcation
   a.   Protects an entity from loss by entering into a transaction.
   b.   Includes entering into agreements between two counterparties to exchange cash flows over specified period of time in the future.

   c.   Is the interaction of the price or rate with an associated asset or liability.

   d.   Separates an embedded derivative from its host contract.

**24.** Alvarez Corporation has two hybrid financial instruments. According to SFAS 155, how can Alvarez account for these instruments?

   a.   Alvarez must bifurcate all hybrid financial instruments and record the components separately.

   b.   Alvarez can elect to not disclose the financial instruments on the balance sheet.

   c.   Alvarez can elect not to bifurcate the hybrid instruments on an instrument by instrument basis.

   d.   Alvarez can make an election that requires all hybrid financial instruments not to be bifurcated.

**25.** According to SFAS 155, when a company elects not to bifurcate a hybrid financial instrument, the entire hybrid instrument should be valued at

   a.   Fair value.

   b.   Net present value.

   c.   Net realizable value.

   d.   Book value.

**26.** When an election is made not to bifurcate a hybrid financial instrument, how should this be disclosed on the financial statements?

  I.   As separate line items for the fair value and non–fair value instruments on the balance sheet.

  II.   As an aggregate amount of all hybrid instruments with the amount of the hybrid instruments at fair value shown in parentheses.

  III   As a footnote disclosure.

   a.   I only.

   b.   II and III only.

   c.   III only.

   d.   I and II only.

**27.** If a company elects not to bifurcate a hybrid financial instrument and records the entire instrument at fair value, which of the following is true?

   a.   No changes in value are recorded until the hybrid instrument is sold.

   b.   Changes in fair value of the hybrid instrument are recognized each year in other comprehensive income.

   c.   Changes in fair value of the hybrid instrument are recognized each year in earnings.

   d.   Changes in fair value of the hybrid instrument are recognized each year by recognizing a cumulative effect adjustment to the beginning balance of retained earnings for the period.

**28.** Hedge accounting is permitted for all of the following types of hedges except

   a.   Trading securities.

   b.   Unrecognized firm commitments.

   c.   Available-for-sale securities.

   d.   Net investments in foreign operations.

**29.** Which of the following is a general criterion for a hedging instrument?

   a.   Sufficient documentation must be provided at the beginning of the process.

   b.   Must be "highly effective" only in the first year of the hedge's life.

   c.   Must contain a nonperformance clause that makes performance probable.

   d.   Must contain one or more underlyings.

**30.** For an unrecognized firm commitment to qualify as a hedged item it must

   a.   Be binding on both parties.

   b.   Be specific with respect to all significant terms.

   c.   Contain a nonperformance clause that makes performance probable.

   d.   All of the above.

**31.** A hedge of the exposure to changes in the fair value of a recognized asset or liability, or an unrecognized firm commitment, is classified as a

   a.   Fair value hedge.

   b.   Cash flow hedge.

   c.   Foreign currency hedge.

   d.   Underlying.

**32.** Gains and losses on the hedged asset/liability and the hedged instrument for a fair value hedge will be recognized

   a.   In current earnings.

   b.   In other comprehensive income.

   c.   On a cumulative basis from the change in expected cash flows from the hedged instrument.

   d.   On the balance sheet either as an asset or a liability.

**33.** Gains and losses of the effective portion of a hedging instrument will be recognized in current earnings in each reporting period for which of the following?

| | Fair value hedge | Cash flow hedge |
|---|---|---|
| a. | Yes | No |
| b. | Yes | Yes |
| c. | No | No |
| d. | No | Yes |

**34.** Which of the following risks are inherent in an interest rate swap agreement?

  I.   The risk of exchanging a lower interest rate for a higher interest rate.

  II.   The risk of nonperformance by the counterparty to the agreement.

   a.   I only.

   b.   II only.

   c.   Both I and II.

   d.   Neither I nor II.

**35.** According to SFAS 133, which of the following meet the definition of assets and/or liabilities?

| | Derivative instruments | G/L on the fair value of derivatives |
|---|---|---|
| a. | Yes | No |
| b. | No | Yes |
| c. | Yes | Yes |
| d. | No | No |

**36.** Which of the following is **not** a type of foreign currency hedge?

   a.   A forecasted transaction.

   b.   An available-for-sale security.

   c.   A recognized asset or liability.

d. An unrecognized firm commitment.

**37.** Which of the following foreign currency transactions is not accounted for using hedge accounting?
   a. Available-for-sale securities.
   b. Unrecognized firm commitments.
   c. Net investments in foreign operations.
   d. Foreign currency denominated forecasted transactions.

**Items 38 through 41** are based on the following:

On December 12, 2007, Imp Co. entered into three forward exchange contracts, each to purchase 100,000 euros in ninety days. The relevant exchange rates are as follows:

|  | Spot rate | Forward rate (for March 12, 2008) |
|---|---|---|
| November 30, 2007 | $.87 | $.89 |
| December 12, 2007 | .88 | .90 |
| December 31, 2007 | .92 | .93 |

**38.** Imp entered into the first forward contract to hedge a purchase of inventory in November 2007, payable in March 2008. At December 31, 2007, what amount of foreign currency transaction gain from this forward contract should Imp include in net income?
   a. $0
   b. $ 3,000
   c. $ 5,000
   d. $10,000

**39.** At December 31, 2007, what amount of foreign currency transaction loss should Imp include in income from the revaluation of the Accounts Payable of 100,000 euros incurred as a result of the purchase of inventory at November 30, 2007, payable in March 2008?
   a. $0
   b. $3,000
   c. $4,000
   d. $5,000

**40.** Imp entered into the second forward contract to hedge a commitment to purchase equipment being manufactured to Imp's specifications. The expected delivery date is March 2008 at which time settlement is due to the manufacturer. The hedge qualifies as a fair value hedge. At December 31, 2007, what amount of foreign currency transaction gain from this forward contract should Imp include in net income?
   a. $0
   b. $ 3,000
   c. $ 5,000
   d. $10,000

**41.** Imp entered into the third forward contract for speculation. At December 31, 2007, what amount of foreign currency transaction gain from this forward contract should Imp include in net income?
   a. $0
   b. $ 3,000
   c. $ 5,000
   d. $10,000

**42.** The risk of an accounting loss from a financial instrument due to possible failure of another party to perform according to terms of the contract is known as
   a. Off-balance-sheet risk.
   b. Market risk.

c. Credit risk.
   d. Investment risk.

**43.** Examples of financial instruments with off-balance-sheet risk include all of the following except
   a. Outstanding loan commitments written.
   b. Recourse obligations on receivables.
   c. Warranty obligations
   d. Futures contracts.

**44.** Off-balance-sheet risk of accounting loss does not result from
   a. Financial instruments recognized as assets entailing conditional rights that result in a loss greater than the amount recognized in the balance sheet.
   b. Financial instruments not recognized as either assets or liabilities yet still expose the entity to risk of accounting loss.
   c. Financial instruments recognized as assets or liabilities where the amount recognized reflects the risk of accounting loss to the entity.
   d. Financial instruments recognized as liabilities that result in an ultimate obligation that is greater than the amount recognized in the balance sheet.

**45.** If it is **not** practicable for an entity to estimate the fair value of a financial instrument, which of the following should be disclosed?

 I. Information pertinent to estimating the fair value of the financial instrument.
 II. The reasons it is not practicable to estimate fair value.

   a. I only.
   b. II only.
   c. Both I and II.
   d. Neither I nor II.

**46.** Disclosure requirements for financial instruments include
   a. Method(s) and significant assumptions used in estimating fair value.
   b. Distinction between financial instruments held or issued for trading purposes and purposes other than trading.
   c. A note containing a summary table cross-referencing the location of other financial instruments disclosed in another area of the financial statements.
   d. All of the above should be disclosed.

**47.** Disclosure of credit risk of financial instruments with off-balance-sheet risk does **not** have to include
   a. The amount of accounting loss the entity would incur should any party to the financial instrument fail to perform.
   b. The entity's policy of requiring collateral or security.
   c. The class of financial instruments held.
   d. The specific names of the parties associated with the financial instrument.

**48.** Disclosure of information about significant concentrations of credit risk is required for
   a. All financial instruments.
   b. Financial instruments with off-balance-sheet credit risk only.

   c.   Financial instruments with off-balance-sheet market risk only.

   d.   Financial instruments with off-balance-sheet risk of accounting loss only.

**49.** Kline Bank has large amounts of notes receivable from companies with high debt-to-equity ratios as a result of buy-out transactions.  Kline is contemplating the following disclosures for the notes receivable in its year-end financial statements:

I.   Information about shared activity, region, or economic characteristic.

II.  A brief description of collateral supporting these financial instruments.

Which of the above disclosures are required under GAAP?

   a.   I only.

   b.   II only.

   c.   Neither I nor II.

   d.   Both I and II.

**50.** Whether recognized or unrecognized in an entity's financial statements, disclosure of the fair values of the entity's financial instruments is required when

   a.   It is practicable to estimate those values.

   b.   The entity maintains accurate cost records.

   c.   Aggregated fair values are material to the entity.

   d.   Individual fair values are material to the entity.

## SIMULATION PROBLEMS

### Simulation Problem 1                                    (50 to 60 minutes)

| Situation | | | | | |
|---|---|---|---|---|---|
| | **Terminology** | **Concepts** | **Applicability of SFAS 133** | **Communication** | **Research** |

Riley Corp. has entered into several derivative contracts in order to manage its risk exposure. Riley Corp. has adopted SFAS 133, *Accounting for Derivative Instruments and Hedging Activities.*

| | **Terminology** | | | | |
|---|---|---|---|---|---|
| **Situation** | | **Concepts** | **Applicability of SFAS 133** | **Communication** | **Research** |

Select the **best** answer for each item from the terms listed in A-L.  No term should be used more than once.

### Answer List

A.   A hedge of the exposure to changes in the fair value of a recognized asset or liability or an unrecognized firm commitment.

B.   A hedge of the exposure to variability in the cash flows of a forecasted transaction or a recognized asset or liability.

C.   A hedge of the foreign currency exposure of an unrecognized firm commitment, an available-for-sale security, a forecasted transaction, or a net investment in a foreign operation.

D.   Financial instruments that contain features which, if they stood alone, would meet the definition of a derivative instrument.

E.   Two or more separate derivatives traded as a set.

F.   Commonly a specified price or rate such as a stock price, interest rate, currency rate, commodity price, or a related index.

G.   A legally enforceable, binding agreement with an unrelated party, specifying all significant terms and including a disincentive for nonperformance sufficient to make performance likely.

H.   The referenced associated asset or liability, commonly a number of units.

I.   The difference between an option's price and its intrinsic value.

J.   A transaction expected to occur for which there is no firm commitment, which gives the entity no present rights or obligations.

K.   With regard to put options, it is the larger of zero or the spread between the exercise price and the stock price.

L.   Agreement between two parties to buy and sell a specific quantity of a commodity, foreign currency, or financial instrument at an agreed-upon price, with delivery and/or settlement at a designated future date.

|  | (A) | (B) | (C) | (D) | (E) | (F) | (G) | (H) | (I) | (J) | (K) | (L) |
|---|---|---|---|---|---|---|---|---|---|---|---|---|
| 1. Forward contract | O | O | O | O | O | O | O | O | O | O | O | O |
| 2. Forecasted transaction | O | O | O | O | O | O | O | O | O | O | O | O |
| 3. Firm commitment | O | O | O | O | O | O | O | O | O | O | O | O |
| 4. Embedded derivative | O | O | O | O | O | O | O | O | O | O | O | O |
| 5. Intrinsic value | O | O | O | O | O | O | O | O | O | O | O | O |
| 6. Underlying | O | O | O | O | O | O | O | O | O | O | O | O |
| 7. Notional amount | O | O | O | O | O | O | O | O | O | O | O | O |
| 8. Cash flow hedge | O | O | O | O | O | O | O | O | O | O | O | O |
| 9. Fair value hedge | O | O | O | O | O | O | O | O | O | O | O | O |
| 10. Foreign currency hedge | O | O | O | O | O | O | O | O | O | O | O | O |

| | | **Concepts** | | | |
|---|---|---|---|---|---|
| **Situation** | **Terminology** | | **Applicability of SFAS 133** | **Communication** | **Research** |

Select the **best** answer for each item from the terms listed in A-E.  All terms should be used once.

### Answer List

A.   Granted special hedge accounting treatment

B.   Resulting gains or losses are taken into current earnings in the period in which they arise.

C.   Two currencies other than a functional currency expected to move relative to an entity's functional currency.

D.   A hedge against an exposed asset position created by having an account in a denomination other than the functional currency.

E.   The difference between the futures rate and the spot rate at the date of a forward contract.

|   | (A) | (B) | (C) | (D) | (E) |
|---|-----|-----|-----|-----|-----|
| 1. Tandem currencies | ○ | ○ | ○ | ○ | ○ |
| 2. Discount or premium | ○ | ○ | ○ | ○ | ○ |
| 3. Ineffective portion of a hedge | ○ | ○ | ○ | ○ | ○ |
| 4. Effective portion of a hedge | ○ | ○ | ○ | ○ | ○ |
| 5. Forward contract | ○ | ○ | ○ | ○ | ○ |

| Situation | Terminology | Concepts | Applicability of SFAS 133 | Communication | Research |
|-----------|-------------|----------|---------------------------|---------------|----------|

This question consists of 14 items that represent financial instruments and other contracts that may be included in or excluded from the requirements of SFAS 133, *Accounting for Derivative Instruments and Hedging Activities.*

For the following items, determine if they are (I) included under the requirement of SFAS 133, or (E) excluded from SFAS 133 treatment.

I.   Item meets the definition of a derivative instrument and must be accounted for using SFAS 133.
E.   Item is not required to be accounted for under SFAS 133, either because it does not meet the definition of derivative instrument or because the item is specifically excluded from SFAS 133 treatment.

|   | (I) | (E) |
|---|-----|-----|
| 1. Leases | ○ | ○ |
| 2. Guaranteed investment contracts | ○ | ○ |
| 3. Futures contracts | ○ | ○ |
| 4. Equity securities | ○ | ○ |
| 5. Credit indexed contracts | ○ | ○ |
| 6. Mortgage-backed securities | ○ | ○ |
| 7. Debt securities | ○ | ○ |
| 8. Interest rate caps | ○ | ○ |
| 9. Swaptions | ○ | ○ |
| 10. Employee stock options | ○ | ○ |
| 11. Options to purchase or sell exchange-traded securities | ○ | ○ |
| 12. Variable annuity contracts | ○ | ○ |
| 13. Adjustable rate loans | ○ | ○ |
| 14. Interest rate swaps | ○ | ○ |

| Situation | Terminology | Concepts | Applicability of SFAS 133 | Communication | Research |
|-----------|-------------|----------|---------------------------|---------------|----------|

Write a brief memorandum to the CEO of Riley Corp. explaining the required disclosures related to the company's financial instruments (SFAS 133).

To:     CEO, Riley Corporation
From:   CPA Candidate
Re:     Financial Instrument Disclosures

| Situation | Terminology | Concepts | Applicability of SFAS 133 | Communication | Research |
|-----------|-------------|----------|---------------------------|---------------|----------|

Research the following issues. Cut and paste the appropriate sections from the professional standards.

1. What is a derivative instrument?
2. A company has a foreign currency fair value hedge. Where is the gain or loss reported in the financial statements?
3. Where is the effective portion of a gain or loss on a cash flow hedge reported on the financial statements?

---

**Simulation Problem 2**                    (50 to 60 minutes)

| Situation | | | | | | |
|-----------|------------|-------------------|------------------|--------------|-------------|----------|
| | **Terminology** | **Journal Entries** | **Foreign Currency Transaction Gains/Losses** | **Financial Statement Disclosures** | **Communication** | **Research** |

Logan Corporation markets their products internationally. The company buys and sells goods in Great Britain, France, and Germany. Although Logan's functional currency is the US dollar, the transactions are denominated in the currencies for each country as shown in the table below.

| Country | Currency |
|---------|----------|
| Great Britain | £ |
| France | € |
| Germany | € |

The spot rates for various dates throughout the year are shown below.

| Date | US $ per £1 | US $ per €1 |
|------|-------------|-------------|
| January 1, 2007 | 1.786 | 1.258 |
| March 1, 2007 | 1.869 | 1.249 |
| April 15, 2007 | 1.791 | 1.197 |
| November 10, 2007 | 1.857 | 1.290 |
| December 1, 2007 | 1.911 | 1.329 |
| December 20, 2007 | 1.945 | 1.333 |
| December 31, 2007 | 1.927 | 1.364 |
| January 15, 2008 | 1.869 | 1.311 |
| Average daily rate, 2007 | 1.886 | 1.279 |

| | **Terminology** | | | | | |
|-----------|------------|-------------------|------------------|--------------|-------------|----------|
| **Situation** | | **Journal Entries** | **Foreign Currency Transaction Gains/Losses** | **Financial Statement Disclosures** | **Communication** | **Research** |

Select the **best** answer for each item from the terms listed in A-O. No answer should be used more than once.

*Answer List*

A. An agreement with an unrelated party, binding on both, usually legally enforceable, specifying all significant terms and including a disincentive for nonperformance sufficient to make performance likely.
B. A call option where the price of the underlying is greater than the strike or exercise price of the underlying.
C. A feature on a financial instrument or other contract, which if the feature stood alone, would meet the definition of a derivative.
D. A forward-based contract or agreement generally between two counterparties to exchange streams of cash flows over a specified period in the future.
E. With regard to call options, it is the larger of zero or the spread between the stock price and the exercise price.
F. Provides the holder the right to acquire an underlying at an exercise or stock price, anytime during the option term.
G. An agreement between the two parties to buy and sell a specific quantity of a commodity, foreign currency, or financial instrument at an agreed-upon price, with delivery and/or settlement at a designated future date.
H. A call option where the strike or exercise price is greater than the price of the underlying.
I. The process of separating an embedded derivative from its host contract.
J. The referenced associated asset or liability, commonly a number of units.
K. A specified price or rate such as a stock price, interest rate, or commodity price.
L. An option where the price of the underlying is equal to the strike or exercise price.
M. The difference between an option's price and its intrinsic value.
N. Provides the holder the right to sell the underlying at an exercise or strike price, anytime during the option term.
O. A forward-based contract to make or take delivery of a designated financial instrument, foreign currency, or commodity during a designated period, at a specified price or yield.

|  | (A) | (B) | (C) | (D) | (E) | (F) | (G) | (H) | (I) | (J) | (K) | (L) | (M) | (N) | (O) |
|---|---|---|---|---|---|---|---|---|---|---|---|---|---|---|---|
| 1. At the money | O | O | O | O | O | O | O | O | O | O | O | O | O | O | O |
| 2. Bifurcation | O | O | O | O | O | O | O | O | O | O | O | O | O | O | O |
| 3. Call option | O | O | O | O | O | O | O | O | O | O | O | O | O | O | O |
| 4. Embedded derivative | O | O | O | O | O | O | O | O | O | O | O | O | O | O | O |
| 5. Forward contract | O | O | O | O | O | O | O | O | O | O | O | O | O | O | O |
| 6. Futures contract | O | O | O | O | O | O | O | O | O | O | O | O | O | O | O |
| 7. In the money | O | O | O | O | O | O | O | O | O | O | O | O | O | O | O |
| 8. Notional amount | O | O | O | O | O | O | O | O | O | O | O | O | O | O | O |
| 9. Out of the money | O | O | O | O | O | O | O | O | O | O | O | O | O | O | O |
| 10. Put option | O | O | O | O | O | O | O | O | O | O | O | O | O | O | O |
| 11. Swap | O | O | O | O | O | O | O | O | O | O | O | O | O | O | O |
| 12. Underlying | O | O | O | O | O | O | O | O | O | O | O | O | O | O | O |

| Situation | Terminology | Journal Entries | Foreign Currency Transaction Gains/Losses | Financial Statement Disclosures | Communication | Research |
|---|---|---|---|---|---|---|

The following transactions are denominated in each country's local currency.

On March 1, 2007, Logan sells goods on account to Lexington Corporation, located in London, for £370,000. The account is due in 60 days. Lexington pays the full balance due on April 15, 2007.

On November 10, 2007, Logan purchases supplies from Dietmar Corporation in Germany for €190,000. On December 1, 2007, Logan pays Dietmar for the supplies.

On December 20, 2007, Logan sells goods on account to Cordier Corporation in France for €250,000. Cordier pays for the goods on January 15, 2008.

**1.** Prepare the journal entry for the sale of goods to Lexington on March 1.

**2.** Prepare the journal entry on April 15, 2007, when Lexington pays for the goods.

**3.** Prepare the journal entry for the purchase of supplies from Dietmar Corporation on November 10, 2007.

**4.** Prepare the journal entry for the payment to Dietmar on December 1, 2007.

**5.** Prepare the journal entry for the sale of goods to Cordier Corporation.

**6.** Prepare any entries necessary on December 31, 2007, with regard to the foreign currency transactions with Lexington, Dietmar, and Cordier Corporation.

**7.** Prepare the journal entry for Cordier's payment of goods on January 15, 2008.

| Situation | Terminology | Journal Entries | Foreign Currency Transaction Gains/Losses | Financial Statement Disclosures | Communication | Research |
|-----------|-------------|-----------------|-------------------------------------------|---------------------------------|---------------|----------|

Prepare the following schedule outlining the foreign currency transaction gains and losses for 2007 and 2008 for Logan Corporation.

**Logan Corporation**
**SCHEDULE OF FOREIGN CURRENCY TRANSACTION GAIN/LOSSES**
*For the years 2007 and 2008*

|  | 2007 gain/(loss) | 2008 gain/(loss) |
|--|------------------|------------------|
| Lexington Corporation |  |  |
| Dietmar Corporation |  |  |
| Cordier Corporation |  |  |
| Total FC gain/(loss) |  |  |

| Situation | Terminology | Journal Entries | Foreign Currency Transaction Gains/Losses | Financial Statement Disclosures | Communication | Research |
|-----------|-------------|-----------------|-------------------------------------------|---------------------------------|---------------|----------|

Indicate from the list below where the foreign currency transaction gain or loss in 2007 will be disclosed on the financial statements.

> A.   Extraordinary gain/loss
> B.   Other gain/loss
> C.   Other comprehensive income
> D.   Revenue
> E.   Expense

**(A) (B) (C) (D) (E)**

1.  Foreign currency transaction gain/loss for 2007 will be disclosed where on the financial statement?   ○  ○  ○  ○  ○

| Situation | Terminology | Journal Entries | Foreign Currency Transaction Gains/Losses | Financial Statement Disclosures | Communication | Research |
|-----------|-------------|-----------------|-------------------------------------------|---------------------------------|---------------|----------|

Logan Corporation is the holder of several hybrid instruments.  Logan has adopted SFAS 133, *Accounting for Derivative Instruments and Hedging Activities.*

Write a brief memo to the CEO of Logan Corporation answering the following questions:

1.   What is a hybrid instrument?

2.   What is bifurcation?

3.   Identify the three criteria used to determine if bifurcation must occur.

4.   List three examples of hybrid instruments that would require bifurcation under SFAS 133.

To:     CEO, Logan Corporation
From:  CPA Candidate
Re:     Hybrid Financial Instruments

| Situation | Terminology | Journal Entries | Foreign Currency Transaction Gains/Losses | Financial Statement Disclosures | Communication | Research |
|-----------|-------------|-----------------|-------------------------------------------|---------------------------------|---------------|----------|

Research the professional standards and provide excerpts that answer the following questions.

1.   What is the definition of functional currency?

2.   Sometimes foreign currency receivables or payables have not been settled by year-end.  At what amount should these transactions be disclosed in the balance sheet?

3.   At what exchange rate should a foreign currency transaction be recorded?

### MULTIPLE-CHOICE ANSWERS

| | | | | | |
|---|---|---|---|---|---|
| 1. c __ __ | 12. d __ __ | 23. d __ __ | 34. c __ __ | 45. c __ __ | |
| 2. d __ __ | 13. c __ __ | 24. c __ __ | 35. a __ __ | 46. d __ __ | |
| 3. a __ __ | 14. d __ __ | 25. a __ __ | 36. c __ __ | 47. d __ __ | |
| 4. b __ __ | 15. b __ __ | 26. d __ __ | 37. c __ __ | 48. a __ __ | |
| 5. d __ __ | 16. b __ __ | 27. c __ __ | 38. b __ __ | 49. d __ __ | |
| 6. c __ __ | 17. a __ __ | 28. a __ __ | 39. d __ __ | 50. a __ __ | |
| 7. b __ __ | 18. a __ __ | 29. a __ __ | 40. b __ __ | | |
| 8. b __ __ | 19. b __ __ | 30. d __ __ | 41. b __ __ | | |
| 9. b __ __ | 20. d __ __ | 31. a __ __ | 42. c __ __ | | |
| 10. d __ __ | 21. a __ __ | 32. a __ __ | 43. c __ __ | 1st: __/50 = __% | |
| 11. b __ __ | 22. c __ __ | 33. a __ __ | 44. c __ __ | 2nd: __/50 = __% | |

### MULTIPLE-CHOICE ANSWER EXPLANATIONS

### A.  Foreign Currency Transactions

**1.  (c)**  When the **sale is made** on 10/15/07, Bain would record a receivable and sales at $100,000, the US dollar equivalent on that date.

| | | |
|---|---|---|
| Accounts receivable | 100,000 | |
| Sales | | 100,000 |

On 11/16/07, Bain receives foreign currency worth $105,000. Since the receivable was recorded at $100,000, a $5,000 gain must be recorded.

| | | |
|---|---|---|
| Foreign currency | 105,000 | |
| Accounts receivable | | 100,000 |
| Foreign exchange transaction gain | | 5,000 |

The US dollar equivalent when the order was received on 9/1/07 ($96,000) is not used to compute the gain because no entry is recorded on this date. The receipt and acceptance of a purchase order from a customer is an executory commitment which is not generally recorded.

**2.  (d)**  On 9/1/07, Cano obtained a receivable which will be collected in a foreign currency. SFAS 52 states that a gain (loss) will result if the exchange rate on the settlement date is different from the rate existing on the transaction date. A gain (loss) must be recognized at any intervening balance sheet dates, if necessary. Therefore, Cano would recognize a $2,500 foreign exchange transaction loss in its **2007** income statement since a change in the exchange rate reduced the receivable (in US dollars) from $50,000 on 9/1/07 (250,000 × $.20) to $47,500 on 12/31/07 (250,000 × $.19). In 2008, a foreign exchange transaction gain of $7,500 is recognized because the receivable (in US dollars) increased from $47,500 on 12/31/07 to $55,000 when received (250,000 × $.22) on February 1, 2008.

**3.  (a)**  A transaction has occurred in which settlement will be made in Argentine pesos. Since Lindy's functional currency is the US dollar, a foreign exchange transaction gain (loss) will result if the spot rate on the settlement date is different than the rate on the transaction date (SFAS 52). A provision must be made at any intervening year-end date if there has been a rate change. Thus, in 2006, a $500 foreign exchange transaction gain [100,000 × ($.4295 – $.4245)] would be recognized, while in 2007 a $1,000 foreign exchange transaction loss [100,000 × ($.4245 – $.4345)] would be recognized.

**4.  (b)**  A purchase has been made for which payment will be made in British pounds. A foreign exchange transaction gain or loss will result if the spot rate on the settle-

ment date is different from the rate used on the transaction date. SFAS 52 states that a gain or loss must also be recorded at any intervening balance sheet date if there has been a rate change. Thus, at 12/31/07 a foreign exchange transaction gain of $9,000 is recognized [300,000 × ($1.65 – $1.62)] as the foreign currency payable is reduced from $495,000 (300,000 × $1.65) to $486,000 (300,000 × $1.62). The thirty-day and sixty-day rates would affect Hunt only if the company had entered into forward contracts.

**5.  (d)**  On 1/20/07, Ball would record purchases and accounts payable at $90,000. When the account was paid, the equivalent of $96,000 was required to liquidate the $90,000 liability, resulting in a foreign exchange transaction loss of $6,000. SFAS 52 requires that foreign exchange transaction gains (losses) also be recognized at intervening balance sheet dates. The note payable originally recorded at $500,000 was equivalent to a liability of $520,000 at the balance sheet date, resulting in a 2007 loss of $20,000. The interest payable of $25,000 ($500,000 × 10% × 6/12) was equivalent to a liability of $26,000 at year-end, resulting in an additional 2007 loss of $1,000. Therefore, the total 2007 foreign exchange transaction loss is $27,000 ($6,000 + $20,000 + $1,000).

**6.  (c)**  The requirement is to determine the amount that Tyrola should accrue for royalties payable, 12/31/07. This situation is a foreign currency transaction in which settlement is denominated in other than a company's functional currency (SFAS 52). In this case the functional currency is the US dollar because it is the currency of the primary economic environment in which the Colorado firm operates. Note that in this royalty agreement, 12/31/07 is the point at which the amount due to the author (50,000 Canadian dollars × 10% = 5,000 Canadian dollars) is determined. Royalty expense is measured and the related liability is denominated at 12/31/07. The year-end accrual would be

.89 (10% × 50,000 Canadian dollars) = $4,450.

On January 10, 2008, Tyrola will have to purchase 5,000 Canadian dollars for payment to the Canadian author. The amount of US dollars required to accomplish this will depend on the spot rate on January 10 ($.90 in this case). The number of US dollars required to satisfy the obligation will be $50 greater [($.90 – .89) × 5,000 Canadian dollars]. This will result in a $50 foreign exchange transaction loss which would be included in 2008 net income.

**7.  (b)**  In the case of the receivable denominated in Japanese yen, a foreign exchange transaction gain was recorded on the collection of the receivable. This means that more yen was received than was recorded in the receivable account. For that to happen the rate of yen exchangeable for a dollar would have had to decrease, requiring more yen to be paid at the settlement date for the same amount of dollars at the contract date. On the other hand, there was a foreign exchange transaction loss on the payable denominated in euros. This means that at the settlement date Shore Co. had to pay more euros than were recorded in the payable account. For this to occur the rate of euros exchangeable for a dollar would have had to decrease, requiring more euros to be paid at the settlement date for the same amount of dollars at the contract date.

**8.  (b)**    Per SFAS 52, a transaction that is denominated in a currency other than the entity's functional currency, which is payable at a fixed amount at a later date, may result in an increased or decreased amount payable because of a change in the exchange rate. This increase/decrease would be classified as a foreign exchange transaction gain/loss, and would be included as a component of income. The gain/loss would not be considered extraordinary.

**9.  (b)**    The requirement is to determine how Velec should account for the exchange rate fluctuation in 2007. A foreign currency transaction, according to SFAS 52, is a transaction denominated in a currency other than the entity's functional currency. Denominated means that the balance is fixed in terms of the number of units of a foreign currency, regardless of changes in the exchange rate. When a US company buys or sells to an unrelated foreign company, and the US company agrees either to pay for goods or receive payment for the goods in foreign currency units, this is a foreign currency transaction from the point of view of the US company (the functional currency is the US dollar). In these situations, the US company has "crossed currencies" and directly assumes the risk of fluctuating foreign exchange rates of the foreign currency units. As exchange rates fluctuate, a company will record an ordinary gain or loss on their income statement, **not** an extraordinary gain or loss. Velec has an accounts payable denominated in a foreign currency (Quatari rials) as of December 15, the date the title to the goods passes to Velec. As the value of the rial per dollar rises above twenty rials per dollar, Velec Co. will have to come up with less dollars to pay off the payable, as of December 31, 2007, than they would have on December 15, 2007. This creates a foreign exchange transaction gain. As shown numerically, if 4000 rials are assumed as being payable, on December 15 you would need $200 (4000/20) to pay off the payable. However, on December 31, $190 would be needed (4000/21). The difference between $200 and $190 represents the gain. A foreign exchange transaction gain should be included in net income, not a loss.

### B.1.-2.   Derivative Instruments and Hedging Activities

**10.  (d)**    Derivatives are financial instruments that derive their value from changes in a benchmark based on stock prices, interest rates, mortgage rates, currency rates, commodity prices, or some other agreed-upon base. Discounts on accounts receivable are not the basis of a benchmark for a derivative financial instrument.

**11.  (b)**    Derivative instruments must contain one or more underlyings **and** one or more notional amounts. Derivative instruments do contain terms that require or permit net settlement or delivery of an asset.

**12.  (d)**    Derivative financial instruments are contracts that are supposed to protect or hedge one or more of the parties from adverse movement in the underlying base. Answer (d) is correct because it does not fit the definition of a financial instrument. Risk of uncollectable accounts can be managed by effective credit policies.

**13.  (c)**    Derivative instruments meet the definition of assets and liabilities. As such they should be reported on the entity's financial statements. The most relevant measure for reporting financial instruments is fair value. Thus, statement I is true. If a derivative instrument does not qualify as a hedging instrument, then its gains or losses must be reported and recognized in current earnings. Thus, statement II is also true.

**14.  (d)**    All of the above meet the basic definition of an underlying, which is any financial or physical variable that has either observable changes or objectively verifiable changes.

**15.  (b)**    A call option is in the money if the price of the underlying is greater than the strike or exercise price of the underlying. An at-the-money option is one in which the price of the underlying is equal to the strike or exercise price. A call option is out of the money if the strike or exercise price is greater than the price of the underlying.

**16.  (b)**    Under SFAS 133, derivative instruments contain

1.  One or more underlyings and one or more notional amounts
2.  No initial net investment or smaller net investment than required for contracts with an expected similar response to market changes, and
3.  Terms that require or permit net settlement, net settlement by means outside the contract, and delivery of an asset that is substantially the same as net settlement.

**17.  (a)**    Notional amounts are the referenced associated asset or liability that are commonly a number of units such as barrels of oil. Answers (b) and (d) are incorrect because they are examples of underlyings. Answer (c) is incorrect because it is an example of a derivative instrument.

**18.  (d)**    Disclosures related to financial instruments that are used as hedging instruments must include the following information:

1.  Objectives and strategies for achieving them.
2.  Context to understand the instrument.
3.  Risk management policies.
4.  A list of hedged instruments.

Disclosure of the maximum potential accounting loss is only required for financial instruments with concentrations of credit risk.

### B.3.   Inclusions in and Exclusions from Derivative Instruments

**19.  (b)**    Only call (put) options are included in the definition of derivative financial instruments. Leases are excluded because they require a payment equal to the value of the right to use the property. Equity securities and adjustable rate loans are excluded because they require an initial net investment equivalent to the fair value.

**20.    (d)**    Futures contracts, credit indexed contracts, and interest rate swaps are all included in derivative instruments.

**B.4.   Embedded Derivative Instruments and Bifurcation**

**21.    (a)**    The hybrid instrument is **not** recorded at fair value.  Economic characteristics and risks of the embedded instrument are **not** "clearly and closely" related to those of the host contract.  For purposes of applying SFAS 133, the embedded derivative must meet the definition of a derivative instrument.

**22.    (c)**    An embedded derivative is a feature of a financial instrument or other contract, which if the feature stood alone, would meet the definition of a derivative.

**23.    (d)**    Bifurcation is the process of separating an embedded derivative from its host contract.  This process is necessary so that hybrid instruments can be separated into their component parts, each being accounted for using the appropriate valuation techniques.

**24.    (c)**    Per SFAS 155, Alvarez can elect not to bifurcate the hybrid instrument, and this election can be made on an instrument by instrument basis.  Answer (a) is incorrect because SFAS 140 required all hybrid financial instruments to be bifurcated and the components valued separately.  Answer (b) is incorrect because hybrid financial instruments must be disclosed.  Answer (d) is incorrect because the hybrid financial instruments can be selected on an instrument by instrument basis.

**25.    (a)**    Per SFAS 155, if a company elects not to bifurcate a hybrid financial instrument, the entire instrument is valued at fair value.  Answers (b), (c), and (d) are incorrect because these valuation models are incorrect.

**26.    (d)**    Per SFAS 155, the balance sheet disclosure may be presented in one of two ways: as a separate line item for the fair value and non–fair value instruments on the balance sheet, or as an aggregate amount of all hybrid instruments with the amount of the hybrid instruments at fair value shown in parentheses.  Answers (a), (b), and (c) are incorrect because two disclosures are permissible on the balance sheet.

**27.    (c)**    Per SFAS 155, if a company elects not to bifurcate a hybrid financial instrument, the entire instrument is recorded at fair value.  Changes in fair value each year are recognized in earnings for the period.  Answer (a) is incorrect because changes in fair value must be recognized.  Answer (b) is incorrect because the changes are not recognized in other comprehensive income.  Answer (d) is incorrect, because an adjustment is only made to beginning retained earnings in the year that a company initially adopts SFAS 155.

**B.5.-8   Hedging Instruments**

**28.    (a)**    According to SFAS 133, hedge accounting is permitted for four types of hedges.

1.   Unrecognized firm commitments.
2.   Available-for-sale securities.
3.   Foreign currency denominated hedge forecasted transactions.
4.   Net investments in foreign operations.

Trading securities is not one of the four types.

**29.    (a)**    The general criteria for a hedging instrument are that sufficient documentation must be provided at the beginning of the process and the hedge must be "highly effective" throughout its life.

**30.    (d)**    For an unrecognized firm commitment to qualify as a hedged item it must

1.   Be binding on both parties.
2.   Be specific with respect to all significant items including quantity to be exchanged, the fixed price, and the timing of the transaction.
3.   Contain a nonperformance clause that makes performance probable.

**31.    (a)**    A fair value hedge is a hedge of the exposure to changes in the fair value of a recognized asset or liability or firm commitment.  Two other types of hedges are cash flow and foreign currency hedges.  An underlying is commonly a specified price or rate.

**32.    (a)**    Under SFAS 133, gains and losses of a fair value hedge will be recognized in current earnings.  The effective portion of a cash flow hedge is reported in other comprehensive income and the ineffective portion is reported on a cumulative basis to reflect the lessor of the cumulative gain/loss on the derivative or the cumulative gain/loss from the change in expected cash flows from the hedged instrument.  Gains and losses from a change in the fair value of derivative instruments are not assets and liabilities and should not be reported on the balance sheet.

**33.    (a)**    Fair value hedges will recognize gains and losses for the effective portion of the hedging instrument in each reporting period.  Cash flow hedges will recognize gains and losses for the effect portion of the hedging instrument in other comprehensive income.

**34.    (c)**    An interest rate swap agreement involves the exchange of cash flows determined by various interest rates.  Fluctuations in interest rates after the agreement is entered into may result in the risk of exchanging a lower interest rate for a higher interest rate.  Financial instruments, including swaps, also bear credit risk or the risk that a counterparty to the agreement will not perform as expected.

**35.    (a)**    One of the basic principles that supports SFAS 133 is that derivatives do meet the definition of assets/ liabilities and, therefore, should be recognized and reported as such on the financial statements.  In contrast, gains and losses that result from the change in the fair value of derivatives are not assets/liabilities and should either appear in other comprehensive income or be reported in current earnings.

**36.    (c)**    The four foreign currency hedges under SFAS 133 are an unrecognized firm commitment, an available-for-sale security, a foreign currency denominated forecasted transaction, and a net investment in foreign operations.  A hedge of a recognized asset or liability is a fair value hedge or cash flow hedge, not a foreign currency hedge.

**37.    (c)**    SFAS 52 remains in effect for hedges of net investments in foreign operations.  The hedged net investment is viewed as a single asset.  The provisions for recognizing the gain or loss on the hedged asset/liability and the hedging instrument in SFAS 133 do not apply to the hedges of net investments in foreign operations.

## B.9. Forward Exchange Contracts

**38. (b)** SFAS 133 requires fair market valuation for forward exchange contracts. Each period this is accomplished by marking the forward exchange contract to market using the forward rate at the FS date. At 12/31/07 the forward rate is $.93. The difference between $.93 and $.90, the forward rate on the date the contracts were entered into, times 100,000 euros is $3,000, the forward exchange gain. The entry would be as follows:

| | | |
|---|---|---|
| Forward contract receivable | 3,000 | |
| Forward contract gain | | 3,000 |

The $3,000 forward exchange contract gain would be included in 2007 net income.

**39. (d)** The accounting for gains and losses from foreign currency transactions is prescribed by SFAS 52 which requires a revaluation of exposed net assets and liabilities denominated in foreign currency units at the current spot rate. At 12/31/07 there is a foreign exchange transaction loss of $5,000 [($.92 − .87) × 100,000 euros]. Note that accounts payable was created on 11/30/07. The entry to record the loss is as follows:

| | | |
|---|---|---|
| Foreign exchange loss | 5,000 | |
| Accounts payable | | 5,000 |

The loss would be reported in 2007 net income.

**40. (b)** Hedges involving firm purchase commitments are treated in the same manner as a forward exchange contract that was entered into to hedge an exposure of a liability.

| | | |
|---|---|---|
| Forward contract receivable | 3,000 | |
| Forward contract gain | | 3,000 |
| *To revalue forward contract using forward rates* | | |
| Foreign exchange loss | 3,000 | |
| Firm purchase commitment | | 3,000 |
| *To recognize loss on firm commitment* | | |

Note that this hedge is 100% effective because the gain on the forward contract and the loss on the firm purchase commitment offset each other, net.

**41. (b)** Using a forward exchange contract to speculate would result in a gain or loss each period FS are prepared. The contract would be revalued each reporting period using the forward rate. The gain or loss calculated would be reported in net income. The journal entry would be as follows:

| | | |
|---|---|---|
| Forward contract receivable | 3,000 | |
| Forward contract gain | | 3,000 |

## B.11. Fair Value and Credit Risk Disclosures

**42. (c)** Per SFAS 105, credit risk is the risk of accounting loss from a financial instrument due to possible failure of another party to perform according to the terms of the contract. Off-balance-sheet risk is the possible amount of loss from an instrument that is not reflected on the balance sheet. Market risk is the risk that future changes in market prices may make a financial instrument less valuable.

**43. (c)** The value of derivative financial instruments is typically derived from the value of an underlying asset or is tied to an index. As the price of the underlying asset changes, the price of the derivative changes. Outstanding loan commitments written, recourse obligations on receivables, and futures contracts are all tied to an asset account. Warranty obligations are the result of the sale of goods.

**44. (c)** Off-balance-sheet risk is the possible amount of loss from an instrument that is not reflected on the balance sheet because a loss has not yet occurred or because the item is not recognized as an asset or liability. If the amount recognized on the balance sheet reflects the accounting loss to the entity, then there is no off-balance-sheet risk to consider.

**45. (c)** According to SFAS 107, if it is not practicable for an entity to estimate the fair value of a financial instrument, (1) information pertinent to estimating fair value **and** (2) the reasons why it is not practicable to estimate fair value should be disclosed.

**46. (d)** SFAS 107 requires the following disclosures:

- Method(s) and significant assumptions used in estimating fair value.
- A distinction between financial instruments held or issued for trading purposes and purposes other than trading.
- Information pertinent to estimating the fair value of a financial instrument if it is not practicable for the entity to estimate and the reason why estimation is not practicable.
- Derivative financial instruments may not be combined, aggregated, or netted with nonderivative or other derivative financial instruments.
- If financial instruments are disclosed in more than one area in the financial statements, one note must contain a summary table cross-referencing the location of the other instruments.

**47. (d)** SFAS 107 requires the following disclosures about credit risk for financial instruments with off-balance-sheet credit risk:

- The amount of accounting loss the entity would incur should any party to the financial instrument fail to perform according to the terms of the contract and the collateral, if any, is of no value.
- The class of financial instruments held.
- Categorization between instruments held for trading purposes and purposes other than trading.

**48. (a)** Concentrations of credit risk exist when an entity has a business activity, economic characteristic, or location that is common to most of its financial instruments. SFAS 105 requires disclosure of information about significant concentrations of credit risk for **all** financial instruments.

**49. (d)** Since many of Kline Bank's debtors have high debt-to-equity ratios, this group of debtors has a similar economic characteristic, and thus, would be considered a concentration of credit risk to Kline Bank. SFAS 107 requires that with concentrations of credit risk, the entity disclose the following:

1. Information about the shared activity, region, or economic characteristic of the group.
2. Amount of accounting loss that the entity would incur as a result of the concentrated parties' failure to perform according to the terms of the contracts.
3. Information regarding entity's policy of requiring collateral.

**50. (a)** SFAS 107, *Disclosures about Fair Value of Financial Instruments*, requires entities to disclose the fair market value of financial instruments, both assets and liabilities whether recognized or not recognized in the statement of financial position, for which it is practicable to estimate fair value. Pertinent descriptive information as to the fair value of the instrument is to be disclosed if an estimate of fair value cannot be made without incurring excessive costs.

## SOLUTIONS TO SIMULATION PROBLEMS

### Simulation Problem 1

| | Situation | Terminology | Concepts | Applicability of SFAS 133 | Communication | Research |
|---|---|---|---|---|---|---|

| | | (A) | (B) | (C) | (D) | (E) | (F) | (G) | (H) | (I) | (J) | (K) | (L) |
|---|---|---|---|---|---|---|---|---|---|---|---|---|---|
| 1. | Forward contract | O | O | O | O | O | O | O | O | O | O | O | ● |
| 2. | Forecasted transaction | O | O | O | O | O | O | O | O | O | ● | O | O |
| 3. | Firm commitment | O | O | O | O | O | O | ● | O | O | O | O | O |
| 4. | Embedded derivative | O | O | O | ● | O | O | O | O | O | O | O | O |
| 5. | Intrinsic value | O | O | O | O | O | O | O | O | O | O | ● | O |
| 6. | Underlying | O | O | O | O | O | ● | O | O | O | O | O | O |
| 7. | Notional amount | O | O | O | O | O | O | O | ● | O | O | O | O |
| 8. | Cash flow hedge | O | ● | O | O | O | O | O | O | O | O | O | O |
| 9. | Fair value hedge | ● | O | O | O | O | O | O | O | O | O | O | O |
| 10. | Foreign currency hedge | O | O | ● | O | O | O | O | O | O | O | O | O |

### Explanation of solutions

**1.** **(L)** Agreement for purchase and sale of a specified quantity of a commodity, foreign currency, or financial instrument at an agreed-upon price, with future delivery and/or settlement at a designated future date.

**2.** **(J)** A transaction expected to occur for which there is no firm commitment, which gives the entity no present rights or obligations.

**3.** **(G)** A legally enforceable, binding agreement with an unrelated party, specifying all significant terms and including a disincentive for nonperformance sufficient to make performance likely.

**4.** **(D)** Financial instruments that contain features which, if they stood alone, would meet the definition of a derivative instrument.

**5.** **(K)** With regard to put options, it is the larger of zero or the spread between the exercise price and the stock price.

**6.** **(F)** Commonly a specified price or rate such as a stock price, interest rate, currency rate, commodity price, or a related index.

**7.** **(H)** The referenced associated asset or liability, commonly a number of units.

**8.** **(B)** A hedge of the exposure to variability in the cash flows of a forecasted transaction or a recognized asset or liability.

**9.** **(A)** A hedge of the exposure to changes in the fair value of a recognized asset or liability or an unrecognized firm commitment.

**10.** **(C)** A hedge of the foreign currency exposure of an unrecognized firm commitment, an available-for-sale security, a forecasted transaction, or a net investment in a foreign operation.

| | Situation | Terminology | Concepts | Applicability of SFAS 133 | Communication | Research |
|---|---|---|---|---|---|---|

| | | (A) | (B) | (C) | (D) | (E) |
|---|---|---|---|---|---|---|
| 1. | Tandem currencies | O | O | ● | O | O |
| 2. | Discount or premium | O | O | O | O | ● |
| 3. | Ineffective portion of a hedge | O | ● | O | O | O |
| 4. | Effective portion of a hedge | ● | O | O | O | O |
| 5. | Forward contract | O | O | O | ● | O |

### Explanation of solutions

**1.** **(C)** Tandem currencies are two currencies other than a functional currency expected to move in tandem with each other relative to an entity's functional currency.

**2.** **(E)** A discount or premium is the difference between the futures rate and the spot rate at the date of a forward contract.

3.   **(B)** The ineffective portion of a hedge has resulting gains or losses taken into income in the period in which they arise.

4.   **(A)** The effective portion of a hedge is given special hedge accounting treatment. The evaluation of effectiveness is done no less than every three months. A highly effective hedge will have a value change ranging from roughly .8 to 1.2 times the variability of the cash flows being hedged.

5.   **(D)** A forward contract is a hedge against an exposed asset position created by having an account in a denomination other than the functional currency.

| Situation | Terminology | Concepts | Applicability of SFAS 133 | | Communication | Research |
|---|---|---|---|---|---|---|
| | | | **(I)** | **(E)** | | |
| 1. Leases | | | ○ | ● | | |
| 2. Guaranteed investment contracts | | | ○ | ● | | |
| 3. Futures contracts | | | ● | ○ | | |
| 4. Equity securities | | | ○ | ● | | |
| 5. Credit indexed contracts | | | ● | ○ | | |
| 6. Mortgage-backed securities | | | ○ | ● | | |
| 7. Debt securities | | | ○ | ● | | |
| 8. Interest rate caps | | | ● | ○ | | |
| 9. Swaptions | | | ● | ○ | | |
| 10. Employee stock options | | | ○ | ● | | |
| 11. Options to purchase or sell exchange-traded securities | | | ● | ○ | | |
| 12. Variable annuity contracts | | | ○ | ● | | |
| 13. Adjustable rate loans | | | ○ | ● | | |
| 14. Interest rate swaps | | | ● | ○ | | |

**Explanation of solutions**

1.   **(E)** Leases are excluded from SFAS 133 treatment.
2.   **(E)** Guaranteed investment contracts are not required to be accounted for under SFAS 133.
3.   **(I)** Futures contracts must be accounted for using SFAS 133.
4.   **(E)** Equity securities do not fall under the requirements of SFAS 133.
5.   **(I)** Credit indexed contracts are required to be accounted for under SFAS 133.
6.   **(E)** Mortgage-backed securities are excluded from SFAS 133 treatment.
7.   **(E)** Debt securities are not required to be accounted for using SFAS 133.
8.   **(I)** Interest rate caps must be accounted for using SFAS 133.
9.   **(I)** Swaptions meet the definition of a derivative instrument and must be accounted for using SFAS 133.
10.  **(E)** Employee stock options are excluded from SFAS 133 treatment.
11.  **(I)** Options to purchase (call) or sell (put) exchange-traded securities are included under SFAS 133 requirements.
12.  **(E)** Variable annuity contracts do not fall under the requirements of SFAS 133.
13.  **(E)** Adjustable rate loans are not required to be accounted for under SFAS 133.
14.  **(I)** Interest rate swaps must be accounted for using SFAS 133.

| Situation | Terminology | Concepts | Applicability of SFAS 133 | Communication | Research |
|---|---|---|---|---|---|

To:     CEO, Riley Corporation
From:   CPA Candidate
Re:     Financial Instrument Disclosures

Thank you for your inquiry regarding financial statement disclosures under SFAS 133. According to SFAS 133, an entity that holds or issues derivative or nonderivative financial instruments that are used as hedging instruments is required to disclose its objectives for holding or issuing those instruments as well as its strategies for achieving those objectives.

The context needed to understand the instruments must also be disclosed. In addition, the entity must disclose its risk management policies and a list of hedged instruments. These disclosures must be separated by type of hedge. Finally, entities must make these financial instrument disclosures for every reporting period for which a complete set of financial statements is issued.

If you have further questions, please contact my office.

| Situation | Terminology | Concepts | Applicability of SFAS 133 | Communication | Research |
|---|---|---|---|---|---|

**1.** What is a derivative instrument?

**FAS133, Para 6 or Current Text D50.103**

6. A derivative instrument is a financial instrument or other contract with all three of the following characteristics:

a. It has (1) one or more underlyings and (2) one or more notional amounts or payment provisions or both. Those terms determine the amount of the settlement or settlements, and, in some cases, whether or not a settlement is required.

b. It requires no initial net investment or an initial net investment that is smaller than would be required for other types of contracts that would be expected to have a similar response to changes in market factors.

c. Its terms require or permit net settlement, it can readily be settled net by a means outside the contract, or it provides for delivery of an asset that puts the recipient in a position not substantially different from net settlement.

**2.** A company has a foreign currency fair value hedge. Where is the gain or loss reported in the financial statements?

**FAS133, Para 39 or Current Text D50.136**

39. Gains and losses on a qualifying foreign currency fair value hedge shall be accounted for as specified in paragraphs 22-27. The gain or loss on a nonderivative hedging instrument attributable to foreign currency risk is the foreign currency transaction gain or loss as determined under Statement 52. That foreign currency transaction gain or loss shall be recognized currently in earnings along with the change in the carrying amount of the hedged firm commitment.

**3.** Where is the effective portion of a gain or loss on a cash flow hedge reported on the financial statements?

**FAS133, Para 30 or Current Text D50.127**

30. The effective portion of the gain or loss on a derivative designated as a cash flow hedge is reported in other comprehensive income, and the ineffective portion is reported in earnings. More specifically, a qualifying cash flow hedge shall be accounted for as follows:

a. If an entity's defined risk management strategy for a particular hedging relationship excludes a specific component of the gain or loss, or related cash flows, on the hedging derivative from the assessment of hedge effectiveness (as discussed in paragraph 63 in Section 2 of Appendix A), that excluded component of the gain or loss shall be recognized currently in earnings. For example, if the effectiveness of a hedge with an option contract is assessed based on changes in the option's intrinsic value, the changes in the option's time value would be recognized in earnings. Time value is equal to the fair value of the option less its intrinsic value.

b. Accumulated other comprehensive income associated with the hedged transaction shall be adjusted to a balance that reflects the lesser of the following (in absolute amounts):

(1) The cumulative gain or loss on the derivative from inception of the hedge less (a) the excluded component discussed in paragraph 30(a) above and (b) the derivative's gains or losses previously reclassified from accumulated other comprehensive income into earnings pursuant to paragraph 31.

(2) The portion of the cumulative gain or loss on the derivative necessary to offset the cumulative change in expected future cash flows on the hedged transaction from inception of the hedge less the derivative's gains or losses previously reclassified from accumulated other comprehensive income into earnings pursuant to paragraph 31.

That adjustment of accumulated other comprehensive income shall incorporate recognition in other comprehensive income of part or all of the gain or loss on the hedging derivative, as necessary.

c. A gain or loss shall be recognized in earnings, as necessary, for any remaining gain or loss on the hedging derivative or to adjust other comprehensive income to the balance specified in paragraph 30(b) above.

## Simulation Problem 2

| Situation | Terminology | Journal Entries | Foreign Currency Transaction Gains/Losses | Financial Statement Disclosures | Communication | Research |
|---|---|---|---|---|---|---|

|  | (A) | (B) | (C) | (D) | (E) | (F) | (G) | (H) | (I) | (J) | (K) | (L) | (M) | (N) | (O) |
|---|---|---|---|---|---|---|---|---|---|---|---|---|---|---|---|
| 1. At the money | ○ | ○ | ○ | ○ | ○ | ○ | ○ | ○ | ○ | ○ | ○ | ● | ○ | ○ | ○ |
| 2. Bifurcation | ○ | ○ | ○ | ○ | ○ | ○ | ○ | ○ | ● | ○ | ○ | ○ | ○ | ○ | ○ |
| 3. Call option | ○ | ○ | ○ | ○ | ○ | ● | ○ | ○ | ○ | ○ | ○ | ○ | ○ | ○ | ○ |
| 4. Embedded derivative | ○ | ○ | ● | ○ | ○ | ○ | ○ | ○ | ○ | ○ | ○ | ○ | ○ | ○ | ○ |
| 5. Forward contract | ○ | ○ | ○ | ○ | ○ | ○ | ● | ○ | ○ | ○ | ○ | ○ | ○ | ○ | ○ |
| 6. Futures contract | ○ | ○ | ○ | ○ | ○ | ○ | ○ | ○ | ○ | ○ | ○ | ○ | ○ | ○ | ● |
| 7. In the money | ○ | ● | ○ | ○ | ○ | ○ | ○ | ○ | ○ | ○ | ○ | ○ | ○ | ○ | ○ |
| 8. Notional amount | ○ | ○ | ○ | ○ | ○ | ○ | ○ | ○ | ○ | ● | ○ | ○ | ○ | ○ | ○ |
| 9. Out of the money | ○ | ○ | ○ | ○ | ○ | ○ | ● | ○ | ○ | ○ | ○ | ○ | ○ | ○ | ○ |
| 10. Put option | ○ | ○ | ○ | ○ | ○ | ○ | ○ | ○ | ○ | ○ | ○ | ○ | ● | ○ | ○ |
| 11. Swap | ○ | ○ | ○ | ● | ○ | ○ | ○ | ○ | ○ | ○ | ○ | ○ | ○ | ○ | ○ |
| 12. Underlying | ○ | ○ | ○ | ○ | ○ | ○ | ○ | ○ | ○ | ○ | ● | ○ | ○ | ○ | ○ |

**Explanation of solutions**

1. **(L)** An at-the-money option is one in which the price of the underlying is equal to the strike or exercise price.

2. **(I)** Bifurcation is the process of separating an embedded derivative from its host contract. This process is necessary so that hybrid instruments (a financial instrument or other contract that contains an embedded derivative) can be separated into their component parts, each being accounted for using the appropriate valuation techniques.

3. **(F)** An American call option provides the holder the right to acquire an underlying at an exercise or strike price anytime during the option term. A premium is paid by the holder for the right to benefit from the appreciation in the underlying.

4. **(C)** An embedded derivative is a feature on a financial instrument or other contract which, if the feature stood alone, would meet the definition of a derivative.

5. **(G)** A forward contract is an agreement between two parties to buy and sell a specific quantity of a commodity, foreign currency, or financial instrument at an agreed-upon price, with delivery and/or settlement at a designated future date. Because a forward contract is not formally regulated by an organized exchange, each party to the contract is subject to the default of the other party.

6. **(O)** A futures contract is a forward-based contract to make or take delivery of a designated financial instrument, foreign currency, or commodity during a designated period, at a specified price or yield. The contract frequently has provisions for cash settlement. A future contract is traded on a regulated exchange and, therefore, involves less credit risk than a forward contract.

7. **(B)** A call option is in the money if the price of the underlying is greater than the strike or exercise price of the underlying.

**8.   (J)**  The notional amount (or payment provision) is the referenced associated asset or liability.  A notional amount is commonly a number of units such as shares of stock, principal amount, face value, stated value, basis points, barrels of oil, etc.  It may be that amount plus a premium or minus a discount.  The interaction of the price or rate (underlying) with the referenced associated asset or liability (notional amount) determines whether settlement is required and, if so, the amount.

**9.   (H)**  A call option is out of the money if the strike or exercise price is greater than the price of the underlying.  A put option is out of the money if the price of the underlying is greater than the strike or exercise option.

**10.   (N)**  An American put option provides the holder the right to sell the underlying at an exercise or strike price, anytime during the option term.  A gain accrues to the holder as the market price of the underlying falls below the strike price.

**11.   (D)**  A swap is a forward-based contract or agreement generally between two counterparties to exchange streams of cash flows over a specified period in the future.

**12.   (K)**  An underlying is commonly a specified price or rate such as a stock price, interest rate, currency rate, commodity price, or a related index.  However, any variable (financial or physical) with (1) observable changes or (2) objectively verifiable changes such as a credit rating, insurance index, climatic or geological condition (temperature, rainfall) qualifies.  Unless it is specifically excluded, a contract based on any qualifying variable is accounted for under SFAS 133 if it has the distinguishing characteristics stated above.

| Situation | Terminology | Journal Entries | | Foreign Currency Transaction Gains/Losses | Financial Statement Disclosures | Communication | Research |
|---|---|---|---|---|---|---|---|
| **1.** | Accounts receivable (£) | 691,530 | | | | | |
| | Sales | | | 691,530 | | | |

370,000£ × 1.869 = $691,530

| | | | | | | | |
|---|---|---|---|---|---|---|---|
| **2.** | Cash | 662,670 | | | | | |
| | Loss on FC transaction | 28,860 | | | | | |
| | Accounts receivable (£) | | | 691,530 | | | |

370,000£ × 1.791 = $662,670

| | | | | | | | |
|---|---|---|---|---|---|---|---|
| **3.** | Supplies | 245,100 | | | | | |
| | Accounts payable (€) | | | 245,100 | | | |

190,000€ × 1.290 = $245,100

| | | | | | | | |
|---|---|---|---|---|---|---|---|
| **4.** | Accounts payable (€) | 245,100 | | | | | |
| | Loss on FC transaction | 7,410 | | | | | |
| | Cash | | | 252,510 | | | |

190,000€ × 1.329 = $252,510

| | | | | | | | |
|---|---|---|---|---|---|---|---|
| **5.** | Accounts receivable (€) | 333,250 | | | | | |
| | Sales | | | 333,250 | | | |

250,000€ × 1.333 = $333,250

| | | | | | | | |
|---|---|---|---|---|---|---|---|
| **6.** | Accounts receivable (€) | 7,750 | | | | | |
| | Gain on FC transaction | | | 7,750 | | | |

Adjust to spot rate on balance sheet date
250,000€ × (1.364 − 1.333) = $7,750 gain

| | | | | | | | |
|---|---|---|---|---|---|---|---|
| **7.** | Cash | 327,750 | | | | | |
| | Loss on FC transaction | 13,250 | | | | | |
| | Accounts receivable (€) | | | 341,000 | | | |

250,000€ × 1.311 = $327,750
Original A/R of $333,250 + 7,750 gain = $341,000 balance in A/R as of 12/31/07
Loss is $341,000 − 327,750 = $13,250

**Explanation of solutions**

Foreign currency transactions are recorded at the spot rate on the date of the transaction.  When the account is settled in the foreign currency, the currency is exchanged at the spot rate on the date of settlement, and any gain or loss is recognized as a transaction gain/loss.

If the account is outstanding at the balance sheet date, the account receivable or payable is adjusted to the spot rate on the balance sheet date and the gain/loss from foreign currency transaction is recognized as other income for the period.

| Situation | Terminology | Journal Entries | Foreign Currency Transaction Gains/Losses | Financial Statement Disclosures | Communication | Research |
|---|---|---|---|---|---|---|

Prepare the following schedule outlining the foreign currency transaction gains and losses for 2007 and 2008 for Logan Corporation.

*Logan Corporation*
**SCHEDULE OF FOREIGN CURRENCY TRANSACTION GAIN/LOSSES**
*For the years 2007 and 2008*

| | 2007 gain/(loss) | 2008 gain/(loss) |
|---|---|---|
| Lexington Corporation | (28,860) | 0 |
| Dietmar Corporation | (7410) | 0 |
| Cordier Corporation | 7,750 | (13,250) |
| Total FC gain/(loss) | (28,520) | (13,250) |

| Situation | Terminology | Journal Entries | Foreign Currency Transaction Gains/Losses | Financial Statement Disclosures | Communication | Research |
|---|---|---|---|---|---|---|

Indicate from the list below where the foreign currency transaction gain or loss in 2007 will be disclosed on the financial statements.

- A. Extraordinary gain/loss
- B. Other gain/loss
- C. Other comprehensive income
- D. Revenue
- E. Expense

**(A) (B) (C) (D) (E)**

**1.** Foreign currency transaction gain/loss for 2007 will be disclosed where on the financial statement?　○ ● ○ ○ ○

| Situation | Terminology | Journal Entries | Foreign Currency Transaction Gains/Losses | Financial Statement Disclosures | Communication | Research |
|---|---|---|---|---|---|---|

To:　CEO, Logan Corporation
From:　CPA Candidate
Re:　Hybrid Financial Instruments

　　This memorandum provides a definition of a number of terms related to derivatives, which will help you understand the accounting for financial instruments.

　　A hybrid instrument is a financial instrument or other contract containing a feature that, if it stood alone, would meet the definition of a derivative instrument. This feature is known as an embedded derivative instrument. There is a basic contract in a hybrid instrument that is called the host contract that has the embedded derivative instrument.

　　Bifurcation is the process of separating the embedded derivative instrument from its host contract. The embedded derivative instrument should then be treated as if it were a stand-alone instrument, and accounted for using SFAS 133. The host contract (excluding the embedded derivative) should be accounted for in the normal manner, as if it had never contained the embedded derivative.

　　Bifurcation must occur if, and only if, all of the following three criteria are met. First, the embedded derivative instrument must meet the definition of a derivative instrument for the purposes of applying SFAS 133. Second, the hybrid instrument must not be regularly reported at fair value, with changes in its fair value being reported in current earnings. Finally, the economic characteristics and risks of the embedded derivative must not be clearly and closely related to the economic characteristics and risks of the host contract.

　　Examples of hybrid instruments that would require bifurcation under SFAS 133 include the following:

- A bond payable with an interest rate based on the S&P 500 Index.
- An equity instrument with a call option, allowing the issuing company to buy back the stock.
- Loans with term-extending options whose values are based on the prime rate at the time of the extension.

　　If you have further questions or need additional assistance with hybrid instruments, please contact my office.

| Situation | Terminology | Journal Entries | Foreign Currency Transaction Gains/Losses | Financial Statement Disclosures | Communication | Research |
|-----------|-------------|-----------------|-------------------------------------------|---------------------------------|---------------|----------|

1.  What is the definition of functional currency?

**FAS52, Para 57 or Current Text F60.104**

5. The assets, liabilities, and operations of a foreign entity shall be measured using the functional currency of that entity. An entity's functional currency is the currency of the primary economic environment in which the entity operates; normally, that is the currency of the environment in which an entity primarily generates and expends cash. Appendix A provides guidance for determination of the functional currency. The economic factors cited in Appendix A, and possibly others, should be considered both individually and collectively when determining the functional currency.

2.  Sometimes foreign currency receivables or payables have not been settled by year-end. At what amount should these transactions be disclosed in the balance sheet?

**FAS52, Para 16 or Current Text F60.123**

16. For other than forward exchange contracts (paragraphs 17-19), the following shall apply to all foreign currency transactions of an enterprise and its investees:

a.  At the date the transaction is recognized, each asset, liability, revenue, expense, gain, or loss arising from the transaction shall be measured and recorded in the functional currency of the recording entity by use of the exchange rate in effect at that date (paragraphs 26-28).

b.  At each balance sheet date, recorded balances that are denominated in a currency other than the functional currency of the recording entity shall be adjusted to reflect the current exchange rate.

3.  At what exchange rate should a foreign currency transaction be recorded?

**FAS52, Para 27 or Current Text F60.137**

27. The exchange rates to be used for translation of foreign currency transactions and foreign currency statements are as follows:

a.  Foreign Currency Transactions—The applicable rate at which a particular transaction could be settled at the transaction date shall be used to translate and record the transaction. At a subsequent balance sheet date, the current rate is that rate at which the related receivable or payable could be settled at that date.

## MISCELLANEOUS

### A.  Personal Financial Statements[1]

Personal financial statements may be prepared for an individual, husband and wife, or family.  Personal financial statements (PFS) consist of

1. Statement of financial condition—presents estimated current values of assets, estimated current amounts of liabilities, estimated income taxes, and net worth at a specified date
2. Statement of changes in net worth—presents main sources of increases (decreases) in net worth over the time period included by the statement of changes in net worth.

Assets and liabilities, including changes therein, should be recognized using the accrual basis of accounting.  Assets and liabilities should be listed by order of liquidity and maturity, not a current/noncurrent basis.

In PFS, **assets** should be presented at their estimated current value.  This is an amount at which the item could be exchanged assuming both parties are well informed, neither party is compelled to buy or sell, and material disposal costs are deducted to arrive at current values.  **Liabilities** should be presented at the lesser of the discounted amount of cash to be paid or the current cash settlement amount.  Income taxes payable should include unpaid income taxes as of the date of the statement of financial condition.  Also, PFS should include the **estimated income tax** on the difference between the current value (amount) of assets (liabilities) and their respective tax bases as if they had been realized or liquidated.  The table below summarizes the methods of determining "estimated current values" for assets and "estimated current amounts" for liabilities.

Business interests which comprise a large portion of a person's total assets should be shown separately from other investments.  An investment in a separate entity which is marketable as a going concern (e.g., closely held corporation) should be presented as one amount for its fair value.  If the investment is a limited business activity, not conducted in a separate business entity, separate asset and liability amounts should be shown (e.g., investment in real estate and related mortgage).  Of course, only the person's beneficial interest in the investment is included in their PFS.

| Assets and liabilities | Discounted cash flow | Market price | Appraised value | Other |
|---|---|---|---|---|
| • Receivables | x | | | |
| • Marketable securities | | x | | |
| • Options | | x | | |
| • Investment in life insurance | | | | Cash value less outstanding loans |
| • Investment in closely held business | x | | x | Liquidation value, multiple of earnings, reproduction value, adjustment of book value or cost |
| • Real estate | x | | x | Sales of similar property |
| • Intangible assets | x | | | |
| • Future interests (nonforfeitable rights) | x | | | |
| • Payables and other liabilities | x | | | Discharge amount if lower than discounted amount |
| • Noncancelable commitments | x | | | |
| • Income taxes payable | | | | Unpaid income tax for completed tax years and estimated income tax for elapsed portion of current tax year to date of financial statements |
| • Estimated income tax on difference between current values of assets and current amounts of liabilities and their respective tax bases | | | | Computed as if current value of assets and liabilities had been respectively realized or liquidated considering applicable tax laws and regulations, recapture provisions and carryovers |

---

[1]  *The source of GAAP for personal financial statements is AICPA Statement of Position 82-1 which has been summarized in this module.  (These are not outlined in this text.)  At the current time this statement is not listed as a potential research source in the table of specification on the CPA exam.*

**MULTIPLE-CHOICE QUESTIONS (1-17)**

**1.** Green, a calendar-year taxpayer, is preparing a personal statement of financial condition as of April 30, 2007. Green's 2006 income tax liability was paid in full on April 15, 2007. Green's tax on income earned between January and April 2007 is estimated at $20,000. In addition, $40,000 is estimated for income tax on the differences between the estimated current values and current amounts of Green's assets and liabilities and their tax bases at April 30, 2007. No withholdings or payments have been made towards the 2007 income tax liability. In Green's April 30, 2007 statement of financial condition, what amount should be reported, between liabilities and net worth, as estimated income taxes?

  a. $0
  b. $20,000
  c. $40,000
  d. $60,000

**2.** On December 31, 2007, Shane is a fully vested participant in a company-sponsored pension plan. According to the plan's administrator, Shane has at that date the nonforfeitable right to receive a lump sum of $100,000 on December 28, 2008. The discounted amount of $100,000 is $90,000 at December 31, 2007. The right is not contingent on Shane's life expectancy and requires no future performance on Shane's part. In Shane's December 31, 2007, personal statement of financial condition, the vested interest in the pension plan should be reported at

  a. $0
  b. $ 90,000
  c. $ 95,000
  d. $100,000

**3.** The following information pertains to marketable equity securities owned by Kent:

| Stock | Fair value at December 31, 2008 | 2007 | Cost in 2006 |
|---|---|---|---|
| City Mfg., Inc. | $95,500 | $93,000 | $89,900 |
| Tri Corp. | 3,400 | 5,600 | 3,600 |
| Zee, Inc. | | 10,300 | 15,000 |

The Zee stock was sold in January 2008 for $10,200. In Kent's personal statement of financial condition at December 31, 2008, what amount should be reported for marketable equity securities?

  a. $93,300
  b. $93,500
  c. $94,100
  d. $98,900

**4.** Clint owns 50% of Vohl Corp.'s common stock. Clint paid $20,000 for this stock in 2004. At December 31, 2007, Clint's 50% stock ownership in Vohl had a fair value of $180,000. Vohl's cumulative net income and cash dividends declared for the five years ended December 31, 2007, were $300,000 and $40,000, respectively. In Clint's personal statement of financial condition at December 31, 2007, what amount should be shown as the investment in Vohl?

  a. $ 20,000
  b. $150,000
  c. $170,000
  d. $180,000

**5.** Jen has been employed by Komp, Inc. since February 1, 2005. Jen is covered by Komp's Section 401(k) deferred

compensation plan. Jen's contributions have been 10% of salaries. Komp has made matching contributions of 5%. Jen's salaries were $21,000 in 2005, $23,000 in 2006, and $26,000 in 2007. Employer contributions vest after an employee completes three years of continuous employment. The balance in Jen's 401(k) account was $11,900 at December 31, 2007, which included earnings of $1,200 on Jen's contributions. What amount should be reported for Jen's vested interest in the 401(k) plan in Jen's December 31, 2007 personal statement of financial condition?

  a. $11,900
  b. $ 8,200
  c. $ 7,000
  d. $ 1,200

**6.** The following information pertains to an insurance policy that Barton owns on his life:

| | |
|---|---|
| Face amount | $100,000 |
| Accumulated premiums paid up to December 31, 2008 | 8,000 |
| Cash value at December 31, 2008 | 12,000 |
| Policy loan | 3,000 |

In Barton's personal statement of financial condition at December 31, 2008, what amount should be reported for the investment in life insurance?

  a. $97,000
  b. $12,000
  c. $ 9,000
  d. $ 8,000

**7.** Ely had the following personal investments at December 31, 2007:

- Realty held as a limited business activity not conducted in a separate business entity. Mortgage payments were made with funds from sources unrelated to the realty. The cost of this realty was $500,000, and the related mortgage payable was $100,000 at December 31, 2007.
- Sole proprietorship marketable as a going concern. Its cost was $900,000, and it had related accounts payable of $80,000 at December 31, 2007.

The costs of both investments equal estimated current values. The balances of liabilities equal their estimated current amounts.

How should the foregoing information be reported in Ely's statement of financial condition at December 31, 2007?

| | | Assets | Liabilities |
|---|---|---|---|
| a. | Investment in real estate | $ 400,000 | |
| | Investment in sole proprietorship | 820,000 | |
| b. | Investment in real estate | $ 500,000 | |
| | Investment in sole proprietorship | 820,000 | |
| | Mortgage payable | | $100,000 |
| c. | Investment in real estate | $ 500,000 | |
| | Investment in sole proprietorship | 900,000 | |
| | Mortgage payable | | $100,000 |
| | Accounts payable | | 80,000 |
| d. | Investments | $1,400,000 | |
| | Accounts and mortgage payable | | $180,000 |

**8.** At December 31, 2007, Ryan had the following noncancelable personal commitments:

| | |
|---|---|
| Pledge to be paid to County Welfare Home thirty days after volunteers paint the walls and ceiling of the Home's recreation room | $ 5,000 |
| Pledge to be paid to City Hospital on the recovery of Ryan's comatose sister | $25,000 |

What amount should be included in liabilities in Ryan's personal statement of financial condition at December 31, 2007?

a. $0
b. $ 5,000
c. $25,000
d. $30,000

**9.** The estimated current values of Lane's personal assets at December 31, 2007, totaled $1,000,000, with tax bases aggregating $600,000. Included in these assets was a vested interest in a deferred profit-sharing plan with a current value of $80,000 and a tax basis of $70,000. The estimated current amounts of Lane's personal liabilities equaled their tax bases at December 31, 2007. Lane's 2006 effective income tax rate was 30%. In Lane's personal statement of financial condition at December 31, 2007, what amount should be provided for estimated income taxes relating to the excess of current values over tax bases?

a. $120,000
b. $117,000
c. $ 3,000
d. $0

**10.** Shea, a calendar-year taxpayer, is preparing a personal statement of financial condition as of April 30, 2007. Shea's 2006 income tax liability was paid in full on April 15, 2007. Shea's tax on income earned from January through April 2007 is estimated at $30,000. In addition, $25,000 is estimated for income tax on the differences between the estimated current values of Shea's assets and the current amounts of liabilities and their tax bases at April 30, 2007. No withholdings or payments have been made towards the 2007 income tax liability. In Shea's statement of financial condition at April 30, 2007, what is the total of the amount or amounts that should be reported for income taxes?

a. $0
b. $25,000
c. $30,000
d. $55,000

**11.** The following information pertains to Smith's personal assets and liabilities at December 31, 2007:

| | Historical cost | Estimated current values | Estimated current amounts |
|---|---|---|---|
| Assets | $500,000 | $900,000 | |
| Liabilities | 100,000 | | $80,000 |

Smith's 2007 income tax rate was 30%. In Smith's personal statement of financial condition at December 31, 2007, what amount should be reported as Smith's net worth?

a. $294,000
b. $420,000
c. $694,000
d. $820,000

**12.** Personal financial statements usually consist of
a. A statement of net worth and a statement of changes in net worth.

b. A statement of net worth, an income statement, and a statement of changes in net worth.
c. A statement of financial condition and a statement of changes in net worth.
d. A statement of financial condition, a statement of changes in net worth, and a statement of cash flows.

**13.** Personal financial statements should report assets and liabilities at
a. Estimated current values at the date of the financial statements and, as additional information, at historical cost.
b. Estimated current values at the date of the financial statements.
c. Historical cost and, as additional information, at estimated current values at the date of the financial statements.
d. Historical cost.

**14.** A business interest that constitutes a large part of an individual's total assets should be presented in a personal statement of financial condition as
a. A separate listing of the individual assets and liabilities at cost.
b. Separate line items of both total assets and total liabilities at cost.
c. A single amount equal to the proprietorship equity.
d. A single amount equal to the estimated current value of the business interest.

**15.** Smith owns several works of art. At what amount should these artworks be reported in Smith's personal financial statements?
a. Original cost.
b. Insured amount.
c. Smith's estimate.
d. Appraised value.

**16.** For the purpose of estimating income taxes to be reported in personal financial statements, assets and liabilities measured at their tax bases should be compared to assets and liabilities measured at their

| | Assets | Liabilities |
|---|---|---|
| a. | Estimated current value | Estimated current amount |
| b. | Historical cost | Historical cost |
| c. | Estimated current value | Historical cost |
| d. | Historical cost | Estimated current amount |

**17.** In personal financial statements, how should estimated income taxes on the excess of the estimated current values of assets over their tax bases be reported in the statement of financial condition?
a. As liabilities.
b. As deductions from the related assets.
c. Between liabilities and net worth.
d. In a footnote disclosure only.

## MULTIPLE-CHOICE ANSWERS

| | | | | |
|---|---|---|---|---|
| 1. c __ __ | 5. b __ __ | 9. a __ __ | 13. b __ __ | 17. c __ __ |
| 2. b __ __ | 6. c __ __ | 10. d __ __ | 14. d __ __ | |
| 3. d __ __ | 7. b __ __ | 11. c __ __ | 15. d __ __ | 1st: __/17 = __% |
| 4. d __ __ | 8. a __ __ | 12. c __ __ | 16. a __ __ | 2nd: __/17 = __% |

## MULTIPLE-CHOICE ANSWER EXPLANATIONS

### A. Personal Financial Statements

**1.** **(c)** Only the estimated amount of income taxes on the differences between the estimated current values and current amounts of assets and liabilities is presented between liabilities and net worth. Answer (a) is incorrect because the $40,000 estimated income taxes on the differences between the estimated current values and current amounts of assets and liabilities is presented between liabilities and net worth. Answer (b) is incorrect because the $20,000 current tax liability would be presented as a liability. Answer (d) is incorrect because the $20,000 current tax liability would be presented as a liability while the $40,000 amount would be presented between liabilities and net worth.

**2.** **(b)** In a personal statement of financial condition, assets are generally presented at estimated current values. Depending on the nature of the asset, current value can be estimated using fair market value, net realizable value, discounted cash flow, or appraised value. AICPA Statement of Position 82-1 specifies that a future interest that is nonforfeitable should be valued using discounted cash flow. Therefore, the interest in the pension plan should be valued at $90,000.

**3.** **(d)** Per SOP 82-1, assets are generally presented at their estimated current values on personal financial statements. For Kent's December 31, 2008 personal statement of financial condition, the current values of the marketable equity securities held as of that date should be used. Thus, Kent should report $98,900 ($95,500 + $3,400) for marketable equity securities.

**4.** **(d)** Per SOP 82-1, assets are generally presented at their estimated current values. Depending on the nature of the asset, current value can be estimated using fair market value (FMV), net realizable value, discounted cash flow, or appraised value. In this problem, the fair value of the stock ($180,000) is known and should be shown as the investment in Vohl. Note that the net income and dividends have nothing to do with the amount shown as the investment in Vohl, and this information is irrelevant.

**5.** **(b)** This problem requires that we determine Jen's vested interest in the 401(k) plan to be reported in her December 31, 2007 personal statement of financial condition. The problem states that employer contributions vest after an employee completes three years of service. As Jen has not completed three years of service as of December 31, 2007, none of the employer's contributions have vested. Thus, the problem is to determine Jen's contributions and the earnings on **her** contributions as follows:

| | |
|---|---|
| 2005 contributions | 2,100 |
| 2006 contributions | 2,300 |
| 2007 contributions | 2,600 |
| | 7,000 |
| Earnings on above contributions | 1,200 |
| Jen's vested interest | 8,200 |

**6.** **(c)** SOP 82-1 states that assets are generally presented at their estimated current values in personal financial statements. Specifically, investments in life insurance are to be valued at their cash surrender value less outstanding loans on the policy. Therefore, the investment should be reported at $9,000 ($12,000 cash value – $3,000 outstanding loan).

**7.** **(b)** Per SOP 82-1, when investments in a limited business activity are not conducted in a separate business entity, separate asset and liability amounts of the investment should be shown on the statement of financial condition. Thus, the realty (asset) and the mortgage (liability) should be reported separately at $500,000 and $100,000, respectively (their estimated current values). An investment in a separate entity that is marketable as a going concern (e.g., closely held corporation) should be presented as one amount. Thus, the $80,000 in accounts payable should be netted against the current value of $900,000 to report a net investment of $820,000.

**8.** **(a)** Per SOP 82-1, noncancelable personal commitments should be reported at their discounted cash flow. A commitment must have all of the following attributes: (1) are for fixed or determinable amounts; (2) are not contingent on others' life expectancies or occurrence of a particular event (e.g., disability/death); and (3) do not require future performance of service by others. As the pledge to County Welfare Home is contingent upon the volunteers painting the walls and ceiling and the pledge to City Hospital is contingent upon the recovery of Ryan's comatose sister, both liabilities should be excluded from Ryan's personal statement of financial condition at December 31, 2007.

**9.** **(a)** Per SOP 82-1, estimated taxes that would be paid if all the assets were converted to cash and all the liabilities were paid should be included with the liabilities. Thus, $120,000 [($1,000,000 – $600,000) × .30] should be provided for estimated income taxes relating to the excess of current values over tax bases.

**10.** **(d)** A personal statement of financial condition presents estimated current values of assets and liabilities, estimated income taxes, and estimated net worth at a specified date. Income taxes payable should include unpaid income taxes for completed tax years, the estimated tax for the elapsed portion of the current year, and the estimated income tax on the difference between the current value of assets and the current amounts of liabilities and their respective tax bases. Thus, the amount to be reported on Shea's statement of financial condition for income taxes is $55,000, equal to the sum of $30,000 tax on income earned from January through April and $25,000 estimated income tax on the difference between the current value and tax bases of assets and liabilities.

**11.** **(c)** Per SOP 82-1, assets are generally presented at their estimated current values on personal financial statements. Therefore, the assets should be reported at their fair value of $900,000, rather than at their cost of $500,000.  SOP 82-1 also states that liabilities are presented at the lesser of the discounted amount of cash to be paid, or the current cash settlement amount.  Therefore, the liabilities should be reported at $80,000.  Estimated taxes that would be paid if all the assets were converted to cash and all the liabilities were paid should be included with the liabilities.  Thus, 126,000 [(820,000 – 400,000) × .30] should be provided for estimated income taxes relating to the excess of current values over tax bases.  Smith's net worth should be reported as $694,000 ($900,000 – $80,000 – $126,000).

**12.  (c)**    Per SOP 82-1, personal financial statements consist of (1) a statement of financial condition and (2) a statement of changes in net worth.

**13.  (b)**    Per SOP 82-1, a personal financial statement presents the estimated current values of assets and liabilities. Additional information at historical cost is not required.

**14.  (d)**    Per SOP 82-1, business interests that constitute a large part of a person's total assets should be shown separately from other investments.  The estimated **current value** of an investment in a separate entity, such as a closely held corporation, a partnership, or a sole proprietorship, should be shown in **one amount** as an investment if the entity is marketable as a going concern.

**15.  (d)**    Per SOP 82-1, assets are generally presented at their estimated current values in a personal statement of financial condition.  Depending on the nature of the asset, current value can be estimated using fair market value, net realizable value, discounted cash flow, or appraised value. The best estimate of the fair value of art is the appraised value.

**16.  (a)**    In personal financial statements assets should be stated at their estimated current values and liabilities should be stated at the lower of the discounted value of their future cash payments or their current cash settlement amounts in accordance with SOP 82-1.  These current amounts will differ from their tax bases and will give rise to **unrealized** tax gains and losses.  A provision for estimated income taxes on these unrealized amounts should be incorporated into personal financial statements because when the unrealized gains and losses are realized, the related income taxes will have to be either paid or received.

**17.  (c)**    SOP 82-1 specifically addresses the presentation of estimated income taxes on the excess of the estimated current values of assets over their tax bases in the statement of financial condition.  This statement requires that the estimated income taxes should be presented between liabilities and net worth in the statement of financial condition.

## B.  Interim Reporting

The term interim reporting is used to describe financial reporting for periods of less than one year, generally quarterly financial statements.  The primary purposes of interim reporting are to provide information which is more timely than is available in annual reports, and to highlight business turning points which could be "buried" in annual reports.

There are two basic conceptual approaches to interim reporting:  the **discrete view** and the **integral view**.

**Discrete view**—Each interim period is a separate accounting period; interim period must stand on its own; same principles and procedures as for annual reports; no special accruals or deferrals.

**Integral view**—Each interim period is an integral part of an annual period; expectations for annual period must be reflected in interim reports; special accruals, deferrals, and allocations utilized.

APB 28 (see outline) adopted the **integral view**.

APB 28 consists of two parts.  Part one does not require issuance of interim financial statements, but does prescribe accounting standards to be used in preparing such statements.  Part two sets forth minimum disclosures to be included in interim financial reports.

The table below summarizes the accounting standards set forth in part one of APB 28.

| *Income statement item* | *General rule* | *Exceptions* |
|---|---|---|
| **Revenues** | Same basis as annual reports | None |
| **Cost of goods sold** | Same basis as annual reports | 1. Gross profit method may be used to estimate CGS and ending inventory for each interim period<br>2. Liquidation of LIFO base-period inventory, if expected to be replaced by year-end, is charged to CGS at its estimated replacement cost<br>3. Temporary declines in inventory market value need not be recognized<br>4. Planned manufacturing variances should be deferred if expected to be absorbed by year-end |
| **All other costs and expenses** | Same basis as annual reports | Expenditures which **clearly benefit** more than one interim period may be allocated among periods benefited (e.g., annual repairs, property taxes). |
| **Income taxes** | (Year-to-date income x Estimated annual effective tax rate) – (Expense recognized in previous quarters) | None |
| **Discontinued operations** | Recognized in interim period as incurred | None |
| **Extraordinary items** | Recognized in interim period as incurred. Materiality is evaluated based on expected annual results | None |
| **Change in accounting principle** | Retrospective application. Cumulative effect of change reflected in the carrying amounts of assets and liabilities as of the first period presented with offsetting adjustment to retained earnings for that period. Financial statements are adjusted for period-specific effects of the change. | None |

The disclosures required in part two of APB 28 are summarized in the pronouncement outline of ABP 28 and SFAS 148.  A key disclosure item for interim reporting is the seasonal nature of the firm's operations.  This disclosure helps prevent misleading inferences and predictions about annual results.

APB 28 as interpreted by FASB Interpretation 18 requires that income tax expense be estimated each period using an estimated annual effective tax rate (see FASB Interpretation 18).  The example below illustrates the application of this requirement.

| Qtr | (a)<br>Quarterly income<br>before<br>income taxes | (b)<br>Year-to-date<br>income before<br>income taxes | (c)<br>Estimated<br>annual effective<br>tax rate | (d) = (b) x (c)<br>Year-to-date<br>income tax<br>expense | (e)<br>Previous<br>quarter's<br>expense | (f) = (d) – (e)<br>Current<br>quarter's<br>expense |
|---|---|---|---|---|---|---|
| 1 | $100,000 | $100,000 | 30% | $ 30,000 | $     0 | $ 30,000 |
| 2 | 150,000 | 250,000 | 32% | 80,000 | 30,000 | 50,000 |
| 3 | 300,000 | 550,000 | 36% | 198,000 | 80,000 | 118,000 |
| 4 | 200,000 | 750,000 | 35% | 262,500 | 198,000 | 64,500 |

In the above chart, columns (a) and (c) are assumed to be given.  Column (b) is obtained by accumulating column (a) figures.  Column (e) is either the preceding quarter's entry in column (d) or the **cumulative** total of previous quarters in column (f).

## Research Component

The research on interim reporting is found predominantly in APB 28.  However, for FASB statements that have changed certain accounting rules, such as SFAS 109 on deferred taxes, SFAS 141 on business combinations, and SFAS 123 and 148 on accounting for stock-based compensation, changes to interim reporting rules for specific areas can be found in the related FASB statement.  A general search using the term "interim" should locate the updated rules for specific areas.

Keywords for research are shown below.

Costs and expenses interim            Interim reporting

Costs interim periods                 Inventory interim

Costs of goods sold interim periods   Seasonal variations

Interim period

**MULTIPLE-CHOICE QUESTIONS (1-16)**

**1.** On January 1, 2007, Builder Associates entered into a $1,000,000 long-term, fixed-price contract to construct a factory building for Manufacturing Company. Builder accounts for this contract under the percentage-of-completion, and estimated costs at completion at the end of each quarter for 2007 were as follows:

| Quarter | Estimated percentage-of-completion | Estimated costs at completion |
|---------|-----------------------------------|-------------------------------|
| 1 | 10% | $750,000 |
| 2* | 10% | $750,000 |
| 3 | 25% | $960,000 |
| 4* | 25% | $960,000 |

*No work performed in the 2nd and 4th quarters.

What amounts should be reported by Builder as "Income on Construction Contract" in its quarterly income statements based on the above information?

| | Gain (loss) for the three months ended | | | |
|---|---|---|---|---|
| | 3/31/07 | 6/30/07 | 9/30/07 | 12/31/07 |
| a. | $0 | $0 | $0 | $10,000 |
| b. | $25,000 | $0 | $(15,000) | $0 |
| c. | $25,000 | $0 | $0 | $0 |
| d. | $25,000 | $0 | $ 6,000 | $0 |

**2.** Kell Corp.'s $95,000 net income for the quarter ended September 30, 2007, included the following after-tax items:

- A $60,000 extraordinary gain, realized on April 30, 2007, was allocated equally to the second, third, and fourth quarters of 2007.
- A $16,000 cumulative-effect loss resulting from a change in inventory valuation method was recognized on August 2, 2007.

In addition, Kell paid $48,000 on February 1, 2007, for 2007 calendar-year property taxes. Of this amount, $12,000 was allocated to the third quarter of 2007.

For the quarter ended September 30, 2007, Kell should report net income of

- a. $ 91,000
- b. $103,000
- c. $111,000
- d. $115,000

**3.** Vilo Corp. has estimated that total depreciation expense for the year ending December 31, 2007, will amount to $60,000, and that 2007 year-end bonuses to employees will total $120,000. In Vilo's interim income statement for the six months ended June 30, 2007, what is the total amount of expense relating to these two items that should be reported?

- a. $0
- b. $ 30,000
- c. $ 90,000
- d. $180,000

**4.** On June 30, 2007, Mill Corp. incurred a $100,000 net loss from disposal of a business segment. Also, on June 30, 2007, Mill paid $40,000 for property taxes assessed for the calendar year 2007. What amount of the foregoing items should be included in the determination of Mill's net income or loss for the six-month interim period ended June 30, 2007?

- a. $140,000
- b. $120,000
- c. $ 90,000
- d. $ 70,000

**5.** During the first quarter of 2007, Tech Co. had income before taxes of $200,000, and its effective income tax rate was 15%. Tech's 2006 effective annual income tax rate was 30%, but Tech expects its 2007 effective annual income tax rate to be 25%. In its first quarter interim income statement, what amount of income tax expense should Tech report?

- a. $0
- b. $30,000
- c. $50,000
- d. $60,000

**6.** Bailey Company, a calendar-year corporation, has the following income before income tax provision and estimated effective annual income tax rates for the first three quarters of 2007:

| Quarter | Income before income tax provision | Estimated effective annual tax rate at end of quarter |
|---------|-----------------------------------|------------------------------------------------------|
| First | $60,000 | 40% |
| Second | 70,000 | 40% |
| Third | 40,000 | 45% |

Bailey's income tax provision in its interim income statement for the third quarter should be

- a. $18,000
- b. $24,500
- c. $25,500
- d. $76,500

**7.** Advertising costs may be accrued or deferred to provide an appropriate expense in each period for

| | Interim financial reporting | Year-end financial reporting |
|---|---|---|
| a. | Yes | No |
| b. | Yes | Yes |
| c. | No | No |
| d. | No | Yes |

**8.** A planned volume variance in the first quarter, which is expected to be absorbed by the end of the fiscal period, ordinarily should be deferred at the end of the first quarter if it is

| | Favorable | Unfavorable |
|---|---|---|
| a. | Yes | No |
| b. | No | Yes |
| c. | No | No |
| d. | Yes | Yes |

**9.** Due to a decline in market price in the second quarter, Petal Co. incurred an inventory loss. The market price is expected to return to previous levels by the end of the year. At the end of the year the decline had not reversed. When should the loss be reported in Petal's interim income statements?

- a. Ratably over the second, third, and fourth quarters.
- b. Ratably over the third and fourth quarters.
- c. In the second quarter only.
- d. In the fourth quarter only.

**10.** An inventory loss from a market price decline occurred in the first quarter. The loss was not expected to be restored in the fiscal year. However, in the third quarter the inventory had a market price recovery that exceeded the market decline that occurred in the first quarter. For interim financial reporting, the dollar amount of net inventory should

- a. Decrease in the first quarter by the amount of the market price decline and increase in the third quarter by the amount of the market price recovery.

b.   Decrease in the first quarter by the amount of the market price decline and increase in the third quarter by the amount of decrease in the first quarter.

c.   Not be affected in the first quarter and increase in the third quarter by the amount of the market price recovery that exceeded the amount of the market price decline.

d.   Not be affected in either the first quarter or the third quarter.

**11.** For external reporting purposes, it is appropriate to use estimated gross profit rates to determine the cost of goods sold for

|    | Interim financial reporting | Year-end financial reporting |
|----|----|----|
| a. | Yes | Yes |
| b. | Yes | No |
| c. | No | Yes |
| d. | No | No |

**12.** For interim financial reporting, the computation of a company's second quarter provision for income taxes uses an effective tax rate expected to be applicable for the full fiscal year.  The effective tax rate should reflect anticipated

|    | Foreign tax rates | Available tax planning alternatives |
|----|----|----|
| a. | No | Yes |
| b. | No | No |
| c. | Yes | No |
| d. | Yes | Yes |

**13.** For interim financial reporting, a company's income tax provision for the second quarter of 2007 should be determined using the

a.   Effective tax rate expected to be applicable for the full year of 2007 as estimated at the end of the first quarter of 2007.

b.   Effective tax rate expected to be applicable for the full year of 2007 as estimated at the end of the second quarter of 2007.

c.   Effective tax rate expected to be applicable for second quarter of 2007.

d.   Statutory tax rate for 2007.

**14.** APB 28, *Interim Financial Reporting,* concluded that interim financial reporting should be viewed primarily in which of the following ways?

a.   As useful only if activity is spread evenly throughout the year.

b.   As if the interim period were an annual accounting period.

c.   As reporting for an integral part of an annual period.

d.   As reporting under a comprehensive basis of accounting other than GAAP.

**15.** Conceptually, interim financial statements can be described as emphasizing

a.   Timeliness over reliability.

b.   Reliability over relevance.

c.   Relevance over comparability.

d.   Comparability over neutrality.

**16.** Wilson Corp. experienced a $50,000 decline in the market value of its inventory in the first quarter of its fiscal year.

Wilson had expected this decline to reverse in the third quarter, and in fact, the third quarter recovery exceeded the previous decline by $10,000.  Wilson's inventory did not experience any other declines in market value during the fiscal year.  What amounts of loss and/or gain should Wilson report in its interim financial statements for the first and third quarters?

|    | First quarter | Third quarter |
|----|----|----|
| a. | $0 | $0 |
| b. | $0 | $10,000 gain |
| c. | $50,000 loss | $50,000 gain |
| d. | $50,000 loss | $60,000 gain |

## MULTIPLE-CHOICE ANSWERS

| | | | | |
|---|---|---|---|---|
| 1. b __ . | 5. c __ __ | 9. d __ __ | 13. b __ __ | 16. a __ __ |
| 2. a .. __ | 6. b __ __ | 10. b __ __ | 14. c __ __ | |
| 3. c __ __ | 7. b __ __ | 11. b __ __ | 15. a __ __ | 1st: __/16 = __% |
| 4. b __ __ | 8. d __ __ | 12. d __ __ | | 2nd: __/16 = __% |

## MULTIPLE-CHOICE ANSWER EXPLANATIONS

### B. Interim Reporting

**1. (b)** The requirement is to compute the income to be recognized in quarterly (interim) financial statements on a construction contract using the percentage-of-completion method. The solutions approach is to compute the income on the contract at the end of each quarter by (1) applying the estimated percentage-of-completion to the total estimated income to be recognized on the contract, and (2) subtracting the income recognized in preceding quarters to arrive at the income for the latest quarter. In the second and fourth quarters there was no work done on the contract and no change in the total estimated cost of completion. In quarter three the estimated costs of completion are revised upward. Since the cumulative income to date is less than income recognized in the first quarter, it is necessary to recognize a loss in the third quarter. The loss is handled as a change in accounting estimate rather than restating the first quarter.

> *Quarter 1:*
> 10% ($1,000,000 – $750,000) = $25,000 income recognized
>
> *Quarter 2:*
> -0-
>
> *Quarter 3:*
> 25% ($1,000,000 – $960,000) = $10,000 income earned to date
>
> $10,000 income to date – $25,000 income recognized in previous periods = $(15,000) loss for quarter
>
> *Quarter 4:*
> -0-

**2. (a)** Per APB 28, extraordinary items, gains or losses from disposal of a segment of a business, and unusual or infrequently occurring items should not be prorated over the balance of the fiscal year. Thus, the $20,000 ($60,000 ÷ 3) extraordinary gain that was allocated to the third quarter should be subtracted from net income as it actually occurred in the second quarter. Consistent with the view that all accounting changes should be made effective as of the beginning of the fiscal period, the cumulative effect of the accounting change on retained earnings is computed at the beginning of the fiscal year and reported in the first interim period's income statement. If a cumulative-effect type change is made during an interim period subsequent to the first one, the prior interim reports must be restated as if the changes had been effective as of the first day of the fiscal year. Thus, the $16,000 cumulative-effect loss should not be recognized in the third quarter. The prior interim reports should be restated and the $16,000 loss should be added back to income of the third quarter to correct the income to be reported for the quarter. Property taxes should be allocated among the applicable quarters. As Kell Corp. properly allocated their property taxes, no adjustment to income is needed. Kell should report $91,000 ($95,000 – $20,000 + $16,000) as net income for the quarter ended September 30, 2007.

**3. (c)** Per APB 28, a cost charged to expense in an annual period should be allocated among the interim periods which clearly benefit from the expense through the use of accruals and/or deferrals. Both yearly bonuses and the use of an asset (depreciation expense) benefit the entire year. The expense for the **six month** interim statement should be ($60,000 + $120,000) ÷ 2 = $90,000.

**4. (b)** APB 28 states that revenues and gains should be recognized in interim reports on the same basis as used in annual reports. At June 30, 2007, Mill Corp. would report the entire $100,000 loss on the disposal of its business segment since the loss was incurred during the interim period. APB 28 also states that a cost charged to an expense in an annual period should be allocated among the interim periods that clearly benefit from the expense through the use of accruals and/or deferrals. Since the $40,000 property tax payment relates to the entire 2007 calendar year, $20,000 of the payment would be reported as an expense at June 30, 2007, while the remaining $20,000 would be reported as a prepaid expense.

**5. (c)** APB 28 states that the tax provision for an interim period is the tax for the year to date (estimated effective rate for the year times year-to-date income) less the total tax provisions reported for previous interim periods. In this case, the requirement is to calculate the tax provision for the first quarter interim income statement. The tax expense is $50,000 ($200,000 × 25%).

**6. (b)** The requirement is to calculate Bailey's income tax provision (expense) in its interim income statement for the third quarter. APB 28 states that the tax provision for an interim period is the tax for the year-to-date (estimated effective rate for the year times year-to-date income) less the total tax provisions reported for previous interim periods.

| | |
|---|---|
| Year-to-date tax (45%)($170,000) | $76,500 |
| Previously reported tax (40% × $130,000) | 52,000 |
| Third quarter tax provision | $24,500 |

**7. (b)** Per APB 28, advertising costs may be deferred within a fiscal year if the benefits clearly extend beyond the interim period that the expense was paid. Also, advertising costs may be accrued and assigned to interim periods in relation to sales. Year-end accruals and deferrals of costs are also considered appropriate accounting treatment. Note, however, that deferral in year-end reporting is permitted only if the advertising has not been run in the media.

**8. (d)** Per APB 28, a planned volume variance that is expected to be absorbed by the end of the fiscal year should be deferred at interim reporting dates.

**9. (d)** The requirement is to determine when the inventory loss should be reported. Per APB 28, inventory losses from market declines should not be deferred beyond the interim period in which the loss occurs. However, if the market decline is considered to be **temporary** and will be recovered by year-end, no loss needs to be recognized. A loss will be recognized in the fourth quarter only. In the second quarter the loss is considered temporary, therefore no loss is recognized. However, in the fourth quarter, when the decline does not reverse, it is deemed permanent and recognized in the fourth quarter. Losses are recognized in the period in which they occur, not ratably over several periods. Only expenses that benefit several periods (i.e., repairs and maintenance) are recognized ratably. The loss is not recorded in a period of temporary decline, only when the decline is considered to be permanent.

**10.  (b)**    Per APB 28, a decline in inventory market price, expected to be other than temporary, should be recognized in the period of decline. A subsequent recovery of market value should be recognized as a cost recovery in the period of increase, but **never** above original cost. The decline should be recognized when it occurs in the first quarter. The subsequent recovery should be recognized when it occurs in the third quarter. The subsequent recovery cannot exceed the amount of decline. A nontemporary decline should be shown in the quarter of price decrease.

**11.  (b)**    The requirement is to determine the appropriateness of estimated gross profit rates in determining cost of goods sold for interim and year-end external financial reporting purposes. The use of estimated gross profit rates to determine the cost of goods sold for an interim period is appropriate per APB 28. The method of estimation used and any significant adjustments that result from reconciliations with the annual physical inventory should be disclosed. An estimation of cost of goods sold is not allowable for year-end financial reporting per APB 43. (The actual cost of the goods sold must be determined by the use of a cost flow assumption that most clearly reflects periodic income.) Thus, an estimated cost of goods sold figure may be used for interim but not year-end statements.

**12.  (d)**    Per APB 28, "the effective tax rate should reflect anticipated investment tax credits, foreign tax rates, percentage depletion, capital gains rates, and other available tax planning alternatives."

**13.  (b)**    The requirement is to determine what tax rate should be used to calculate the income tax provision for interim reporting. Per APB 28, each interim period is considered to be an integral part of the annual period. Therefore, expectations for the annual period must be reflected in the interim report. The income tax expense should be calculated using the estimated annual effective tax rate. The estimated tax rate should be updated as of the end of each interim period (here, as of the second quarter). The statutory tax rate is only a part of the effective tax. The effective tax rate includes the statutory tax rate and a variety of other items.

**14.  (c)**    APB 28 adopted the **integral view,** which holds that each interim period is an integral part of an annual period, must reflect expectations for the annual period, and must utilize special accruals, deferrals, and allocations.

**15.  (a)**    The primary purposes of interim reporting are to provide information which is more **timely** than is available in annual reports and to highlight business turning points which could be "buried" in annual reports. This emphasis on timeliness comes at the expense of **reliability**. Accounting information pertaining to shorter periods may require more arbitrary allocations, and may not be as verifiable or representationally faithful as information contained in annual reports. Interim reports are generally more relevant and less reliable. Interim financial statements should not be any more or less comparable than annual reports.

**16.  (a)**    According to APB 28, *Interim Financial Reporting*, temporary declines in inventory market values are not recognized. Only declines that are apparently permanent or other than temporary need to be recognized. In this case, Wilson expected the decline to reverse in the third quarter; therefore, the decline is temporary and no loss would be recorded in the first quarter. Because no loss was recorded for the decline, no gain will be recognized in the third quarter for the recovery of the $50,000 decline. Also, assuming that the inventory was valued at cost at the beginning of the fiscal year, no gain will be recorded for the recovery excess of $10,000 since inventory may not be valued at an amount in excess of cost.

## C.   Segment Reporting

SFAS 131 (see outline) sets forth financial reporting standards for segment reporting, the disclosure of information about different components of an enterprise's operations as well as information related to the enterprise's products and services, its geographic areas, and its major customers.

The purpose of segment disclosure is to assist investors and lenders in assessing the future potential of an enterprise.  Consolidated statements give the user the overall view (results of operations, financial position, cash flows).  However, trends, opportunities, risk factors, etc., can get lost when data for a diversified company are merged into consolidated statements. Additionally, most intersegment transactions that are eliminated from consolidated financial information are included in segment information.

The approach used in SFAS 131 is a "management approach," meaning it is based on the way management organizes segments internally to make operating decisions and assess performance.  Companies can segment their financial information by products or services, by geography, by legal entity, or by type of customer.  The management approach facilitates consistent descriptions of an enterprise for both internal and external reporting and, in general, provides that external financial reporting closely conforms to internal reporting.

SFAS 131 does not apply to not-for-profit organizations or nonpublic enterprises.

### Operating Segments

In SFAS 131, an **operating segment** is defined as

*A component of an enterprise engaged in business activity for which it may earn revenues and incur expenses, about which separate financial information is available that is evaluated regularly by the chief operating decision makers in deciding how to allocate resources and in assessing performance.*

A segment is significant (reportable) if it satisfies **at least one** of the following three 10% tests:

**Revenues**—Segment revenue (including intersegment revenue) is 10% or more of combined segment revenue (including intersegment revenue)
**Operating profit or loss**—The absolute amount of segment profit or loss is 10% or more of the **greater,** in absolute amount, of combined profit of segments reporting profit, or combined loss of segments reporting loss
**Segment assets**—Segment assets are 10% or more of total segment assets

Operating profit or loss is unaffiliated revenue and intersegment revenue, less **all** operating expenses as defined by the chief operating decision maker to evaluate the performance of the segments.  Since segment revenue includes **intersegment sales, transfer pricing** becomes an issue.  FASB requires companies to use the same transfer prices for segment reporting purposes as are used internally.  Since most segments are **profit centers,** internal transfer prices generally reflect market prices.

Common costs are operating expenses incurred by the enterprise for the benefit of more than one operating segment.  These costs should only be allocated to a segment for external reporting purposes if they are included in the measure of the segments profit or loss that is used internally by the chief operating decision maker.

Similarly, only those assets that are included internally in the measure of the segment's assets used to make operating decisions shall be reported as assets of the segment in external financial reports.

Interperiod comparability must be considered in conjunction with the results of the 10% tests.  If a segment fails to meet the tests, but has satisfied the tests in the past and is expected to in the future, it should be considered reportable in the current year for the sake of comparability.  Similarly, if a segment which rarely passes the tests does so in the current year as the result of an unusual event, that segment may be excluded to preserve comparability.

There are some limitations to the number of segments which are to be reported.  There must be enough segments separately reported so that at least 75% of unaffiliated revenues are shown by reportable segments (75% test).  If the 75% test is not satisfied, additional segments must be designated as reportable until the test is satisfied.  Also, the number of reportable segments should not be so large (ten is a rule of thumb) as to make the information less useful.

The following example illustrates the three 10% tests (revenues, operating profit or loss, and identifiable assets) and the 75% test:

| Segment | Unaffiliated revenue | Intersegment revenue | Total revenue | Operating profit (loss) | Segment assets |
|---------|---------------------|---------------------|---------------|------------------------|----------------|
| A | $   90 | $ 90 | $  180 | $ 20 | $ 70 |
| B | 120 | | 120 | 10 | 50 |
| C | 110 | 20 | 130 | (40) | 90 |
| D | 200 | | 200 | 0 | 140 |
| E | 330 | 110 | 440 | (100) | 230 |
| F | 380 | | 380 | 60 | 260 |
| Total | $1,230 | $220 | $1,450 | $ (50) | $840 |

**Revenues test:**  (10%)($1,450) = $145

> Reportable segments:  A, D, E, F

**Operating profit or loss test:**  (10%)($140) = $14

> Reportable segments:  A, C, E, F

*NOTE:  Operating loss ($140) is greater than operating profit, $90*

**Segment assets test:**  (10%)($840) = $84

> Reportable segments:  C, D, E, F

**Reportable segments:**  Those segments which pass **at least one** of the 10% tests.  Segments A, C, D, E, and F are reportable in this example.

**75% test:**  (75%)($1,230) = $922.50

Segments A, C, D, E, and F have total unaffiliated revenue of $1,110, which is greater than $922.50. The 75% test is satisfied; no additional segments need be reported.

Certain other factors must be considered when identifying reportable segments.  An enterprise may consider aggregating two or more operating segments if they have similar economic characteristics and if the segments are similar in each of the following areas:

1. The nature of the products and services
2. The nature of the production processes
3. The type of customer for their products and services
4. The methods used to distribute their products or provide their services
5. The nature of the regulatory environment

Aggregation can occur prior to performing the 10% tests if the enterprise desires.

Additionally, the enterprise may combine information on operating segments that do not meet any of the 10% tests to produce a reportable segment, but only if the segments meet a majority of the aggregation criteria presented above.  It should be noted that information about operating segments that do not meet any of the 10% thresholds may still be disclosed separately, rather than as an aggregated total.

**Segment Disclosures**

SFAS 131 requires several disclosures regarding the enterprise's reportable segments.  They include

1. **General information**—An explanation of how management identified the enterprise's reportable segments, including whether operating segments have been aggregated.  Additionally, a description of the types of products and services from which each reportable segment derives its revenues.

2. **Certain information about reported segment profit and loss, segment assets, and the basis of measurement**—The enterprise shall disclose the following about each reportable segment if the specified amounts are reviewed by the chief operating decision maker:

   a. Revenues from external customers
   b. Intersegment revenues
   c. Interest revenue and expense (reported separately unless majority of segment's revenues are from interest and management relies primarily on net interest revenue to assess performance)
   d. Depreciation, depletion, and amortization expense
   e. Unusual items, extraordinary items
   f. Equity in the net income of investees accounted for by the equity method
   g. Income tax expense or benefit
   h. Significant noncash items

Also, the basis of measurement for these items must be disclosed, including differences in measurement practices between a segment and the complete entity and differences in measurement practices in a segment between periods.

3. **Reconciliations**—The enterprise will need to reconcile the segment amounts disclosed to the corresponding enterprise amounts.

4. **Interim period information**—Although the interim disclosures are not as extensive as in the annual financial report, certain segment disclosures are required in interim financial reports.

## Restatement of Previously Reported Segment Information

Segment reporting is required on a comparative basis. Therefore, the information must be restated to preserve comparability whenever the enterprise has changed the structure of its internal organization in a manner that causes a change to its reportable segments. The enterprise must explicitly disclose that it has restated the segment information of earlier periods.

## Enterprise-Wide Disclosures about Products and Services, Geographic Areas, and Major Customers

The enterprise-wide disclosures are required for all enterprises, even those that have a single reportable segment. Disclosures need to be provided only if not provided as part of the segment information. Disclosures are required regardless of whether the information is used in making operating decisions.

**Products and services.** Revenue from external customers for each product and service shall be reported by the enterprise, unless it is impractical to do so.

**Geographic areas.** An enterprise shall report revenues from external customers and long-lived assets attributable to its domestic operations and **foreign operations,** unless it is impractical to do so. If revenues or assets of an individual foreign country are material, then these amounts should be separately disclosed. In addition, the enterprise's basis for attributing revenue to individual countries shall be disclosed.

**Major customers.** Certain disclosures are made concerning major customers if the following 10% test is met. If 10% or more of **consolidated revenue** comes from a **single** external customer, the enterprise must disclose this fact in addition to the amount of such revenues, and the identity of the segment or segments making the sales. (A group of customers under common control, such as subsidiaries of a parent, is regarded as a single customer. Similarly, the various agencies of a government are considered to be a single customer.)

## Research Component

SFAS 131, issued June 1997, uses a management approach to segment and enterprise reporting. Although, SFAS 135 amends SFAS 131, these amendments are technical corrections and rewording of sentences for clarification purposes. A careful analysis of the vocabulary used in the standards is slightly different than most individuals would use in discussion. For example, we may use the term "total revenue" whereas the standard uses the term "combined revenue." Instead of using the word "tests," the standard refers to them as "quantitative thresholds." Although these differences seem trivial, they will affect your ability to find the material using a keyword search.

Below is a list of keywords that are useful in researching SFAS 131. If you add the word "segment" or "segments" to your search string, it may significantly reduce the number of irrelevant paragraphs.

| | | |
|---|---|---|
| Aggregation segments | Enterprise disclosure | Management approach |
| Combined assets segments | External revenue segments | Operating segment |
| Combined profit segments | Geographic areas | Products services segment |
| Combined revenue operating segments | Geographic information | Reportable segment |
| Enterprise disclose | Major customer | Single reportable segment |

**Flowchart for Identifying Reportable Operating Segments***

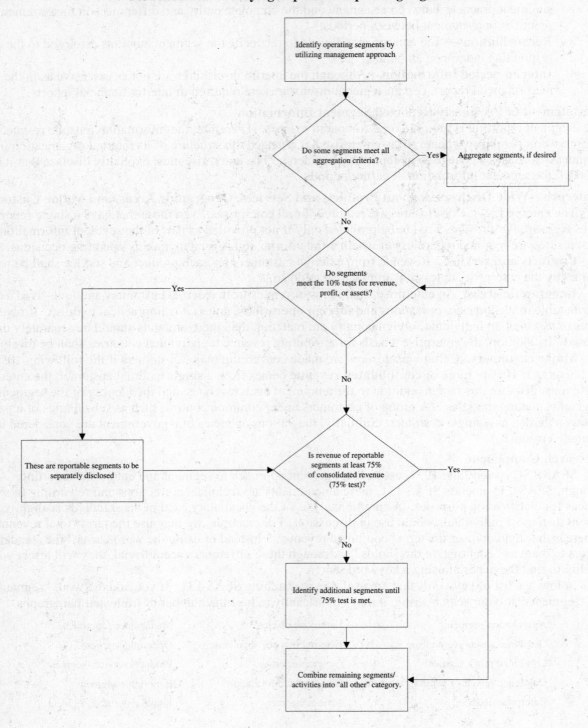

**MULTIPLE-CHOICE QUESTIONS (1-11)**

**1.** Correy Corp. and its divisions (each is an operating segment) are engaged solely in manufacturing operations. The following data (consistent with prior years' data) pertain to the operations conducted for the year ended December 31, 2007:

| *(Industry operating segment)* | *Total revenue* | *Operating profit* | *Identifiable assets at 12/31/07* |
|---|---|---|---|
| A | $10,000,000 | $1,750,000 | $20,000,000 |
| B | 8,000,000 | 1,400,000 | 17,500,000 |
| C | 6,000,000 | 1,200,000 | 12,500,000 |
| D | 3,000,000 | 550,000 | 7,500,000 |
| E | 4,250,000 | 675,000 | 7,000,000 |
| F | 1,500,000 | 225,000 | 3,000,000 |
| | $32,750,000 | $5,800,000 | $67,500,000 |

In its segment information for 2007, how many reportable segments does Correy have?

  a. Three.
  b. Four.
  c. Five.
  d. Six.

**2.** The following information pertains to Aria Corp. and its operating segments for the year ended December 31, 2007:

| | |
|---|---|
| Sales to unaffiliated customers | $2,000,000 |
| Intersegment sales of products similar to those sold to unaffiliated customers | 600,000 |
| Interest earned on loans to other industry segments | 40,000 |

Aria and all of its divisions are engaged solely in manufacturing operations and evaluates divisional performance based on controllable contribution. Aria has a reportable segment if that segment's revenue exceeds

  a. $264,000
  b. $260,000
  c. $204,000
  d. $200,000

**Items 3 and 4** are based on the following:

Grum Corp., a publicly owned corporation, is subject to the requirements for segment reporting. In its income statement for the year ended December 31, 2007, Grum reported revenues of $50,000,000, operating expenses of $47,000,000, and net income of $3,000,000. Operating expenses include payroll costs of $15,000,000. Grum's combined identifiable assets of all industry segments at December 31, 2007, were $40,000,000. Reported revenues include $30,000,000 of sales to external customers.

**3.** In its 2007 financial statements, Grum should disclose major customer data if sales to any single customer amount to at least

  a. $ 300,000
  b. $1,500,000
  c. $4,000,000
  d. $5,000,000

**4.** External revenue reported by operating segments must be at least

  a. $22,500,000
  b. $15,000,000
  c. $12,500,000
  d. $37,500,000

**5.** Enterprise-wide disclosures include disclosures about

| | *Geographic areas* | *Allocated costs* |
|---|---|---|
| a. | Yes | Yes |
| b. | Yes | No |
| c. | No | Yes |
| d. | No | No |

**6.** Enterprise-wide disclosures are required by publicly held companies with

| | *Only one reportable segment* | *More than one reportable segment* |
|---|---|---|
| a. | Yes | Yes |
| b. | Yes | No |
| c. | No | Yes |
| d. | No | No |

**7.** An enterprise must disclose all of the following about each reportable segment if the amounts are used by the chief operating decision maker, except

  a. Depreciation expense.
  b. Allocated expenses.
  c. Interest expense.
  d. Income tax expense.

**8.** In financial reporting for segments of a business, an enterprise shall disclose all of the following except

  a. Types of products and services from which each reportable segment derives its revenues.
  b. The title of the chief operating decision maker of each reportable segment.
  c. Factors used to identify the enterprises reportable segments.
  d. The basis of measurement of segment profit or loss and segment assets.

**9.** In financial reporting for segments of a business enterprise, segment data may be aggregated

  a. Before performing the 10% tests if a majority of the aggregation criteria are met.
  b. If the segments do not meet the 10% tests but meet all of the aggregation criteria.
  c. Before performing the 10% tests if all of the aggregation criteria are met.
  d. If any one of the aggregation criteria are met.

**10.** The method used to determine what information to report for business segments is referred to as the

  a. Segment approach.
  b. Operating approach.
  c. Enterprise approach.
  d. Management approach.

**11.** Taylor Corp., a publicly owned corporation, assesses performance and makes operating decisions using the following information for its reportable segments:

| | |
|---|---|
| Total revenues | $768,000 |
| Total profit and loss | 40,600 |

Included in the total profit and loss are intersegment profits of $6,100. In addition, Taylor has $500 of common costs for its reportable segments that are not allocated in reports used internally. For purposes of segment reporting, Taylor should report segment profit of

  a. $35,000
  b. $34,500
  c. $41,100
  d. $40,600

**SIMULATION PROBLEMS**

**Simulation Problem 1**                                    (50 to 60 minutes)

| Situation | | | | | | |
|---|---|---|---|---|---|---|
| | **Income Test** | **Revenue Test** | **Asset Test** | **Reportable Segments** | **Segment Reporting Test** | **Research** | **Communication** |

Caslow Co. is a new manufacturing company located in the United States, with divisions that operate in Spain, Turkey, and Thailand.

Each division has several reporting units that report its activities and financial information to the chief operating decision maker.  Below is a list of the units and information for each unit of the three divisions.  All amounts are in thousands.

| Division | Reporting unit | Total revenue | Total income | Total assets | External revenue | Affiliated revenue |
|---|---|---|---|---|---|---|
| Spain | A | $100,000 | $20,000 | $260,000 | $60,000 | $40,000 |
| | B | 45,000 | 6,000 | 110,000 | 20,000 | 25,000 |
| Turkey | C | 85,000 | 19,000 | 120,000 | 50,000 | 35,000 |
| | D | 65,000 | 11,000 | 150,000 | 50,000 | 15,000 |
| | E | 25,000 | 5,000 | 60,000 | 25,000 | 0 |
| Thailand | F | 38,000 | 7,000 | 90,000 | 30,000 | 8,000 |
| | G | 120,000 | 39,000 | 290,000 | 50,000 | 70,000 |

| | Income Test | | | | | |
|---|---|---|---|---|---|---|
| Situation | | **Revenue Test** | **Asset Test** | **Reportable Segments** | **Segment Reporting Test** | **Research** | **Communication** |

Identify which reporting units meet the income threshold to be a reportable segment.

| | Division | Reporting unit | Income threshold |
|---|---|---|---|
| 1. | Spain | A | ○ |
| 2. | | B | ○ |
| 3. | Turkey | C | ○ |
| 4. | | D | ○ |
| 5. | | E | ○ |
| 6. | Thailand | F | ○ |
| 7. | | G | ○ |

| | | Revenue Test | | | | |
|---|---|---|---|---|---|---|
| Situation | **Income Test** | | **Asset Test** | **Reportable Segments** | **Segment Reporting Test** | **Research** | **Communication** |

Identify which reporting units meet the revenue threshold to be a reportable segment.

| | Division | Reporting unit | Revenue threshold |
|---|---|---|---|
| 1. | Spain | A | ○ |
| 2. | | B | ○ |
| 3. | Turkey | C | ○ |
| 4. | | D | ○ |
| 5. | | E | ○ |
| 6. | Thailand | F | ○ |
| 7. | | G | ○ |

| | | | Asset Test | | | |
|---|---|---|---|---|---|---|
| Situation | **Income Test** | **Revenue Test** | | **Reportable Segments** | **Segment Reporting Test** | **Research** | **Communication** |

Identify which reporting units meet the asset threshold to be a reportable segment.

|     | Division | Reporting unit | Asset threshold |
|-----|----------|----------------|-----------------|
| 1.  | Spain    | A              | ○               |
| 2.  |          | B              | ○               |
| 3.  | Turkey   | C              | ○               |
| 4.  |          | D              | ○               |
| 5.  |          | E              | ○               |
| 6.  | Thailand | F              | ○               |
| 7.  |          | G              | ○               |

| Situation | Income Test | Revenue Test | Asset Test | Reportable Segments | Segment Reporting Test | Research | Communication |
|-----------|-------------|--------------|------------|---------------------|------------------------|----------|---------------|

Which segments are reportable?

|     | Division | Reporting unit | Reportable segment |
|-----|----------|----------------|--------------------|
| 1.  | Spain    | A              | ○                  |
| 2.  |          | B              | ○                  |
| 3.  | Turkey   | C              | ○                  |
| 4.  |          | D              | ○                  |
| 5.  |          | E              | ○                  |
| 6.  | Thailand | F              | ○                  |
| 7.  |          | G              | ○                  |

| Situation | Income Test | Revenue Test | Asset Test | Reportable Segments | Segment Reporting Test | Research | Communication |
|-----------|-------------|--------------|------------|---------------------|------------------------|----------|---------------|

Complete the following schedule to determine if enough segments have been reported.

| | |
|---|---|
| Total external revenues | |
| × percent | |
| Amount of unaffiliated revenue that must be reported | |
| Amount of unaffiliated revenue reported | |

1. Indicate whether enough segments have been reported.   Yes ○   No ○

| Situation | Income Test | Revenue Test | Asset Test | Reportable Segments | Segment Reporting Test | Research | Communication |
|-----------|-------------|--------------|------------|---------------------|------------------------|----------|---------------|

Using the authoritative literature, answer each of the following questions by cutting and pasting the appropriate citation from FARS in the space provided.

1. What is the definition of an operating segment?

2. What are the three tests that determine if a company must report information about an operating segment?

3. What types of geographic information should a company report if practical?

| Situation | Income Test | Revenue Test | Asset Test | Reportable Segments | Segment Reporting Test | Research | Communication |
|-----------|-------------|--------------|------------|---------------------|------------------------|----------|---------------|

Using the results of your research, prepare a memo to the client explaining the requirements of segment reporting.

**Simulation Problem 2**                              (40 to 50 minutes)

| Situation | | | | | | |
|---|---|---|---|---|---|---|
| | Concepts | Segment Tests | Reportable Segments | Disclosures | Communication | Research |

Barnet Co. has distinct operating units in its operations.  Each of these components of the business reports its activities and its financial information to the chief operating decision maker.  The company has no foreign operations, sales, or major individual customers.  Below is information provided by Barnet's operating units (in millions).

| Reporting unit | Total revenue | External revenue | Affiliated revenue | Income | Assets |
|---|---|---|---|---|---|
| A | 4,200 | 3,000 | 1,200 | 1,200 | 15,900 |
| B | 500 | 200 | 300 | (300) | 6,700 |
| C | 800 | 650 | 150 | 250 | 4,420 |
| D | 1,400 | 800 | 600 | 510 | 7,800 |
| E | 2,300 | 1,200 | 1,100 | (900) | 6,500 |
| F | 5,000 | 4,000 | 1,000 | 2,600 | 28,600 |

| | Concepts | | | | | |
|---|---|---|---|---|---|---|
| Situation | | Segment Tests | Reportable Segments | Disclosures | Communication | Research |

Indicate whether each of the following statements is True or False.

| Statement | True | False |
|---|---|---|
| 1. The method used for reporting segment information is the asset-liability approach. | O | O |
| 2. If management judges that an operating segment is reportable in 2006 and is of continuing significance, information about that segment should be reported in 2007 even if it does not meet the requirements for reportability in 2007. | O | O |
| 3. An enterprise must report separate information about an operating segment if its assets are 10% or more of the combined assets of all operating segments. | O | O |
| 4. An enterprise must report separately the costs and expenses incurred by each segment. | O | O |
| 5. One of the requirements of segment reporting is to report cash flows for each reportable segment. | O | O |
| 6. An enterprise must report the interest revenue for each reportable segment if this information is normally reviewed by the chief operating decision maker. | O | O |

| | | Segment Tests | | | | |
|---|---|---|---|---|---|---|
| Situation | Concepts | | Reportable Segments | Disclosures | Communication | Research |

Identify which of the segments meets the quantitative threshold for revenues, profits/losses, and assets.

| | Reporting unit | Revenue threshold | Profits/losses threshold | Asset threshold |
|---|---|---|---|---|
| 1. | A | O | O | O |
| 2. | B | O | O | O |
| 3. | C | O | O | O |
| 4. | D | O | O | O |
| 5. | E | O | O | O |
| 6. | F | O | O | O |

| | | | Reportable Segments | | | |
|---|---|---|---|---|---|---|
| Situation | Concepts | Segment Tests | | Disclosures | Communication | Research |

Which segments are reportable?

| | Reporting unit | Reportable segment |
|---|---|---|
| 1. | A | O |
| 2. | B | O |
| 3. | C | O |
| 4. | D | O |
| 5. | E | O |
| 6. | F | O |

| Situation | Concepts | Segment Tests | Reportable Segments | Disclosures | | Communication | Research |
|-----------|----------|---------------|---------------------|-------------|---|---------------|----------|

Answer each of the following questions related to disclosure of segment information.

*Amount*

1. What is the amount of external revenue that must be included from all reportable segments in order to meet the segment reporting requirements?

_____

2. Based on your evaluation of reportable segments, have enough segments been reported?  (Yes or No)

*Yes*  ○   *No*  ○

| Situation | Concepts | Segment Tests | Reportable Segments | Disclosures | Communication | Research |
|-----------|----------|---------------|---------------------|-------------|---------------|----------|

Barnet Company's CEO has contacted you and would like information on segment reporting.  He has asked the following questions:

1. What is the purpose of segment disclosure?

2. Define operating segments and describe the approach used to identify operating segments.

3. What tests should Barnet apply in determining its reportable segments?

Write a memo to Barnet's CEO responding to each of his questions.

To:      CEO, Barnet Co.
From:  CPA Candidate
Re:      Segment reporting

| | |
|---|---|
| | |

| Situation | Concepts | Segment Tests | Reportable Segments | Disclosures | Communication | Research |
|-----------|----------|---------------|---------------------|-------------|---------------|----------|

Identify the types of information that an enterprise should report in its segment reporting.

**MULTIPLE-CHOICE ANSWERS**

| 1. c __ __ | 4. a __ __ | 7. b __ __ | 9. c __ __ | 11. d __ __ |
|---|---|---|---|---|
| 2. b __ __ | 5. b __ __ | 8. b __ __ | 10. d __ __ | 1st: __/11 = __% |
| 3. d __ __ | 6. a __ __ | | | 2nd: __/11 = __% |

**MULTIPLE-CHOICE ANSWER EXPLANATIONS**

## C. Segment Reporting

**1.** **(c)**   A division is a reportable segment if it is significant. A division is significant if it satisfies at least **one** of
the three 10% tests:

  1.  **Revenue** is 10% or more of the combined segment
      revenue (including intersegment revenue).
  2.  **Operating profit** (loss) is 10% or more of the
      greater of the **absolute** combined segment profit or
      loss.
  3.  **Identifiable assets** are 10% or more of the com-
      bined segment identifiable assets.

Industry A, B, C, and E pass the revenue and operating
profit tests, but A, B, C, D, and E all pass the identifiable
assets test. Since a division only has to pass one of the three
10% tests to be considered a reportable segment, Corey
Corp. has five reportable segments.

**2.** **(b)**   SFAS 131 requires that selected data for a segment be reported separately if one of three criteria is met.
One of these criteria is met when a segment's revenue is
greater than or equal to 10% of the combined revenues of all
industry segments. Combined revenue includes sales to
unaffiliated customers and intersegment sales or transfers.
Thus, Aria has a reportable segment if that segment's revenues exceed $260,000 [($2,000,000 + $600,000) × 10%].
The $40,000 interest would not be included in combined
revenue because it is not controllable at the division level.

**3.** **(d)**   Per SFAS 131, if 10% or more of the revenue of
an enterprise is derived from sales to any single customer,
that fact and the amount of revenue from each customer
shall be disclosed. In this problem, Grum reported revenues
of $50,000,000 and thus should disclose major customer
data if sales to any single customer amount to $5,000,000
($50,000,000 × 10%).

**4.** **(a)**   Per SFAS 131, there must be enough segments
reported so that at least 75% of unaffiliated revenues is
shown by reportable segments (75% test). Sales to external
customers total $30,000,000 so external revenues reported
by operating segments must be at least $22,500,000
($30,000,000 × 75%).

**5.** **(b)**   Per SFAS 131, enterprise-wide disclosures about
products and services, geographic areas, and major customers are required for all enterprises.

**6.** **(a)**   Per SFAS 131, enterprise-wide disclosures are to
be reported by all public business enterprises, including
those with a single reportable segment because the criteria
for splitting the enterprise into reportable segments are not
met.

**7.** **(b)**   Per SFAS 131, the enterprise shall disclose the
following about each reportable segment if the specified
amounts are reviewed by the chief operating decision maker:

  a.  Revenues from external customers
  b.  Intrasegment revenues

  c.  Interest revenue and expense (reported separately
      unless majority of segment's revenues are from
      interest and management relies primarily on net
      interest revenue to assess performance)
  d.  Depreciation, depletion, and amortization expense
  e.  Unusual items, extraordinary items
  f.  Equity in the net income of investees accounted for
      by the equity method
  g.  Income tax expense or benefit
  h.  Significant noncash items

Allocated expenses are not specifically included as a required disclosure.

**8.** **(b)**   Per SFAS 131, an enterprise shall disclose general information, including factors used to identify reportable segments and the types of products and services from
which each reportable segment derives its revenues. SFAS
131 states that an enterprise shall disclose certain information about reported segment profit and loss, assets, and basis
of measurement. SFAS 131 does not require disclosures
about the term chief operating decision maker and specifically states that this term identifies a function, not necessarily a manager with a specific title.

**9.** **(c)**   Per SFAS 131, two or more operating segments
may be aggregated into a single operating segment if all of
the aggregation criteria are met or if after performing the
10% test a majority of the aggregation criteria are met.

**10.** **(d)**   Per SFAS 131, the method chosen for determining what information to report is referred to as the management approach.

**11.** **(d)**   Per SFAS 131, an enterprise shall report a measure of profit and loss based on the measure reported to the
chief operating decision maker for purposes of making decisions. The information used by management includes intersegment profits and should be included, but common
costs are not allocated to the segments when assessing performance and should not be included.

**SOLUTIONS TO SIMULATION PROBLEMS**

**Simulation Problem 1**

| Situation | Income Test | Revenue Test | Asset Test | Reportable Segments | Segment Reporting Test | Research | Communication |
|-----------|-------------|--------------|------------|---------------------|------------------------|----------|---------------|

Total income = $107,000

$107,000 × 10% = $10,700

Identify which reporting units meet the income threshold to be a reportable segment.

|    | *Division* | *Reporting unit* | *Income threshold* |
|----|-----------|------------------|--------------------|
| 1. | Spain     | A                | ●                  |
| 2. |           | B                | ○                  |
| 3. | Turkey    | C                | ●                  |
| 4. |           | D                | ●                  |
| 5. |           | E                | ○                  |
| 6. | Thailand  | F                | ○                  |
| 7. |           | G                | ●                  |

| Situation | Income Test | Revenue Test | Asset Test | Reportable Segments | Segment Reporting Test | Research | Communication |
|-----------|-------------|--------------|------------|---------------------|------------------------|----------|---------------|

Total revenue = $478,000

$478,000 × 10% = $47,800

Identify which reporting units meet the revenue threshold to be a reportable segment.

|    | *Division* | *Reporting unit* | *Revenue threshold* |
|----|-----------|------------------|---------------------|
| 1. | Spain     | A                | ●                   |
| 2. |           | B                | ○                   |
| 3. | Turkey    | C                | ●                   |
| 4. |           | D                | ●                   |
| 5. |           | E                | ○                   |
| 6. | Thailand  | F                | ○                   |
| 7. |           | G                | ●                   |

| Situation | Income Test | Revenue Test | Asset Test | Reportable Segments | Segment Reporting Test | Research | Communication |
|-----------|-------------|--------------|------------|---------------------|------------------------|----------|---------------|

Total assets = $1,060,000

$1,060,000 × 10% = $106,000

Identify which reporting units meet the asset threshold to be a reportable segment.

|    | *Division* | *Reporting unit* | *Asset threshold* |
|----|-----------|------------------|-------------------|
| 1. | Spain     | A                | ●                 |
| 2. |           | B                | ●                 |
| 3. | Turkey    | C                | ●                 |
| 4. |           | D                | ●                 |
| 5. |           | E                | ○                 |
| 6. | Thailand  | F                | ○                 |
| 7. |           | G                | ●                 |

| Situation | Income Test | Revenue Test | Asset Test | Reportable Segments | Segment Reporting Test | Research | Communication |
|---|---|---|---|---|---|---|---|

Which segments are reportable?

| | Division | Reporting unit | Reportable segment |
|---|---|---|---|
| **1.** | Spain | A | ● |
| **2.** | | B | ● |
| **3.** | Turkey | C | ● |
| **4.** | | D | ● |
| **5.** | | E | ○ |
| **6.** | Thailand | F | ○ |
| **7.** | | G | ● |

| Situation | Income Test | Revenue Test | Asset Test | Reportable Segments | Segment Reporting Test | Research | Communication |
|---|---|---|---|---|---|---|---|

Complete the following schedule to determine if enough segments have been reported.

| | |
|---|---|
| Total external revenues | $285,000 |
| × percent | 75% |
| Amount of unaffiliated revenue that must be reported | $213,750 |
| Amount of unaffiliated revenue reported | $230,000 |

                                                                       *Yes*      *No*

1. Indicate whether enough segments have been reported.                        ●      ○

**Explanation of solution**

1. Yes, because we have reported $230,000 of unaffiliated (external) revenue from A, B, C, D, and G, and the reported unaffiliated revenue is greater than $213,750.

| Situation | Income Test | Revenue Test | Asset Test | Reportable Segments | Segment Reporting Test | Research | Communication |
|---|---|---|---|---|---|---|---|

1. What is the definition of an operating segment?

**Definition**
**FAS131, Para 10 or Current Text S30.109**

10. An operating segment is a component of an enterprise

     a. That engages in business activities from which it may earn revenues and incur expenses (including revenues and expenses relating to transactions with other components of the same enterprise),

     b. Whose operating results are regularly reviewed by the enterprise's chief operating decision maker to make decisions about resources to be allocated to the segment and assess its performance, and

     c. For which discrete financial information is available.

An operating segment may engage in business activities for which is has yet to earn revenues, for example, start-up operations may be operating segments before earning revenues.

2. What are the three tests that determine if a company must report information about an operating segment?

**Quantitative Thresholds**
**FAS131, Para 18 or Current Text S30.117**

18. An enterprise shall report separately information about an operating segment that meets any of the following quantitative thresholds:

     a. Its reported revenue, including both sales to external customers and intersegment sales or transfers, is 10% or more of the combined revenue, internal and external, of all reported operating segments.

    b.   The absolute amount of its reported profit or loss is 10% or more of the greater, in absolute amount, of (1) the combined reported profit of all operating segments that did not report a loss, or (2) the combined reported loss of all operating segments that did report a loss.

    c.   Its assets are 10% or more of the combined assets of all operating segments.

Information about operating segments that do not meet any of the quantitative thresholds may be disclosed separately.

**3.** What types of geographic information should a company report if practical?

### Information about Geographic Areas
### FAS131, Para 38 or Current Text S30.137

38.  An enterprise shall report the following geographic information unless it is impracticable to do so:

    a.   Revenues from external customers (1) attributed to the enterprise's country of domicile, and (2) attributed to all foreign countries in total from which the enterprise derives revenues.  If revenues from external customers attributed to an individual foreign country are material, those revenues shall be disclosed separately.  An enterprise shall disclose the basis for attributing revenues from external customers to individual countries.

    b.   Long-lived assets other than financial instruments, long-term customer relationships of a financial institution, mortgage and other servicing rights, deferred policy acquisition costs, and deferred tax assets (1) located in the enterprise's country of domicile, and (2) located in all foreign countries in total in which the enterprise holds assets.  If assets in an individual foreign country are material, those assets shall be disclosed separately.

The amounts reported shall be based on the financial information that is used to produce the general-purpose financial statements.  If providing the geographic information is impracticable, that fact shall be disclosed.  An enterprise may wish to provide, in addition to the information required by this paragraph, subtotals of geographic information about groups of countries.

| Situation | Income Test | Revenue Test | Asset Test | Reportable Segments | Segment Reporting Test | Research | Communication |
|-----------|-------------|--------------|------------|---------------------|------------------------|----------|---------------|

### Key points in the memo to the client

1.  Segment disclosures assist in analyzing and understanding financial statements by permitting better assessment of past performance and future prospects.  Disaggregated information provides more precise details of the uncertainties surrounding the timing and the amount of expected cash flows, because the various segments may have different rates of profitability, degrees and types of risk, opportunities for growth, and future capital demands.

2.  An operating segment is a component of an enterprise engaged in business activity for which it may earn revenues and incur expenses about which separate financial information is prepared and evaluated by the chief operating decision makers to assess performance and allocate resources.

    The approach used to identify segments is referred to as the management approach, meaning it is based on the way management organizes segments internally to make operating decisions and assess performance.  The management approach will provide that external descriptions of an enterprise are consistent with internal descriptions and that external reporting will more closely conform to internal reporting used by management.

3.  Caslow should have reported a segment that satisfies one or more of the following tests:

- The segment's revenue, including both sales to unaffiliated customers and intersegment sales or transfers, is 10% or more of the combined revenue of all Caslow's segments.
- The segment's absolute amount of operating profit or loss is 10% or more of the greater in absolute amount of

    • The combined operating profits of all segments with operating profits, or
    • The combined operating losses of all segments with operating losses.

- The segment's identifiable assets are 10% or more of the combined identifiable assts of all segments.

4. If the company operates in an environment where they collect discrete information on separate divisions or units, Caslow needs to organize their accounting system to collect information on revenues based on whether items are sold to outside parties (unaffiliated revenue) or to other units within the company (affiliated revenues or intersegment revenues). If the company already prepares operating profit/loss statements for each division or unit, they should aggregate that information in order to perform the required test to determine which units qualify as an operating segment. They should also identify how many assets are assigned or utilized by each unit in order to comply with the asset threshold test.

5. Caslow should provide enterprise-wide disclosures regarding products and services, as well as information about geographic areas. If practical, Caslow should report revenues from external customers attributed to the United States and attributed to the other three foreign countries. Caslow should also disclose long-lived assets, deferred policy acquisition costs, and deferred tax assets in the United States and in foreign countries, as well as total assets in each foreign country, if material.

6. Caslow should also report information regarding reliance on major customers if sales to a single customer amount to 10% or more of Caslow's revenues.

---

**Simulation Problem 2**

| Situation | Concepts | Segment Tests | Reportable Segments | Disclosures | Communication | Research |
|---|---|---|---|---|---|---|

| | Statement | True | False |
|---|---|---|---|
| 1. | The method used for reporting segment information is the asset-liability approach. | ○ | ● |
| 2. | If management judges that an operating segment is reportable in 2006 and is of continuing significance, information about that segment should be reported in 2007 even if it does not meet the requirements for reportability in 2007. | ● | ○ |
| 3. | An enterprise must report separate information about an operating segment if its assets are 10% or more of the combined assets of all operating segments. | ● | ○ |
| 4. | An enterprise must report separately the costs and expenses incurred by each segment. | ○ | ● |
| 5. | One of the requirements of segment reporting is to report cash flows for each reportable segment. | ○ | ● |
| 6. | An enterprise must report the interest revenue for each reportable segment if this information is normally reviewed by the chief operating decision maker. | ● | ○ |

| Situation | Concepts | Segment Tests | Reportable Segments | Disclosures | Communication | Research |
|---|---|---|---|---|---|---|

| | Reporting unit | Revenue threshold | Profits/losses threshold | Asset threshold |
|---|---|---|---|---|
| 1. | A | ● | ● | ● |
| 2. | B | ○ | ○ | ○ |
| 3. | C | ○ | ○ | ○ |
| 4. | D | ○ | ● | ● |
| 5. | E | ● | ● | ○ |
| 6. | F | ● | ● | ● |

**Explanation of solutions**

**Revenue threshold:** Total revenues $14,200 \times 10\% = \$1,420$. Segment should be reported if it exceeds this revenue amount.

**Income threshold:** Total profit = $4,560. Total loss = $1,200. Segment should be reported if the profit/loss in absolute value is greater than 10% of $4,560 (the larger amount of profit or loss), $456.

**Asset threshold:** Total assets $69,920 \times 10\% = \$6,992$. Segment should be reported if it exceeds this asset amount.

| Situation | Concepts | Segment Tests | Reportable Segments | Disclosures | Communication | Research |
|---|---|---|---|---|---|---|

|   | *Reporting unit* | *Reportable segment* |
|---|---|---|
| **1.** | A | ● |
| **2.** | B | ○ |
| **3.** | C | ○ |
| **4.** | D | ● |
| **5.** | E | ● |
| **6.** | F | ● |

### Explanation of solutions

Segment is reportable if it meets any **one** of the three threshold tests in previous question.

A meets all tests.

B and C do not meet any of the tests.

D meets income and asset test.

E meets revenue and income/loss test.

F meets all three tests.

| Situation | Concepts | Segment Tests | Reportable Segments | Disclosures | Communication | Research |
|---|---|---|---|---|---|---|

| | | *Amount* |
|---|---|---|
| **1.** What is the amount of external revenue that must be included from all reportable segments in order to meet the segment reporting requirements? | | $10,650 |

| | *Yes* | *No* |
|---|---|---|
| **2.** Based on your evaluation of reportable segments, have enough segments been reported?  (Yes or No) | ○ | ● |

### Explanation of solutions

Threshold for reporting revenue:  Total external revenue reported must be at least 75% total consolidated revenues.  75% × Total consolidated revenue of $14,200 = $10,650.  Based on reporting only segments A, D, E, and F, there is only $9,000 of external revenue reported.  Therefore, there are not enough segments reported for Barnet.  Barnet should aggregate segments and include additional segments until the total of external revenue of reportable segments is at least $10,650.

| Situation | Concepts | Segment Tests | Reportable Segments | Disclosures | Communication | Research |
|---|---|---|---|---|---|---|

To:     CEO, Barnet Co.
From:   CPA Candidate
Re:     Segment reporting

I am pleased to respond to your questions about segment reporting.  Segment disclosures assist in analyzing and understanding financial statements by permitting better assessment of past performance and future prospects.  Disaggregated information provides more precise details of the uncertainties surrounding the timing and the amount of expected cash flows, because various segments may have different rates of profitability, degrees and types of risk, opportunities for growth, and future capital demands.

An operating segment is a component of an enterprise engaged in business activity for which it may earn revenues and incur expenses, and for which separate financial information is prepared and evaluated by the chief operating decision makers to assess performance and allocate resources.

The approach used to identify segments is referred to as the management approach, meaning it is based on the way management organizes segments internally to make operating decisions and assess performance.  The management approach will help ensure that external descriptions of an enterprise are consistent with internal descriptions, and that external reporting will more closely conform to internal reporting used by management.

Barnet should report information about segments that satisfy one or more of the following tests:

- The segment's revenue, including both sales to unaffiliated customers and intersegment sales or transfers, is 10% or more of the combined revenue of all Barnet's segments.
- The segment's absolute amount of miserating profit or loss is 10% or more of the greater in absolute amount of

- The combined operating profits of all segments with operating profits, or
- The combined operating losses of all segments with operating losses.

- The segment's identifiable assets are 10% or more of the combined identifiable assets of all segments.

| Situation | Concepts | Segment Tests | Reportable Segments | Disclosures | Communication | Research |
|---|---|---|---|---|---|---|

**1.** Identify the types of information that an enterprise should report in its segment reporting.

**FAS131, Para 27 or Current Text S30.126**
Information about Profit or Loss and Assets

27. An enterprise shall report a measure of profit or loss and total assets for each reportable segment. An enterprise also shall disclose the following about each reportable segment if the specified amounts are included in the measure of segment profit or loss reviewed by the chief operating decision maker:

a. Revenues from external customers
b. Revenues from transactions with other operating segments of the same enterprise
c. Interest revenue
d. Interest expense
e. Depreciation, depletion, and amortization expense
f. Unusual items as described in paragraph 26 of APB Opinion No. 30, *Reporting the Results of Operations— Reporting the Effects of Disposal of a Segment of a Business, and Extraordinary, Unusual and Infrequently Occurring Events and Transactions*
g. Equity in the net income of investees accounted for by the equity method
h. Income tax expense or benefit
i. Extraordinary items
j. Significant noncash items other than depreciation, depletion, and amortization expense

An enterprise shall report interest revenue separately from interest expense for each reportable segment unless a majority of the segment's revenues are from interest and the chief operating decision maker relies primarily on net interest revenue to assess the performance of the segment and make decisions about resources to be allocated to the segment. In that situation, an enterprise may report that segment's interest revenue net of its interest expense and disclose that it has done so.

## D. Partnership Accounting

There are no authoritative pronouncements concerning the accounting for partnerships; thus, all of the principles described below have evolved through accounting practice.

Partnership accounting typically is tested through a few multiple-choice questions on the Financial Accounting and Reporting Exam. Occasionally, the material is tested through a problem.

### 1. Partnership Formation

The partnership is a separate **accounting entity** (not to be confused with a separate legal entity), and therefore its assets and liabilities should remain separate and distinct from the individual partner's personal assets and liabilities.

Thus, all assets contributed to the partnership are recorded by the partnership at their **fair market values**. All liabilities assumed by the partnership are recorded at their **present values**.

Upon formation, the amount credited to each partner's capital account is the difference between the fair market value of the assets contributed and the present value of the liabilities assumed from that partner. The capital accounts represent the residual equity of the partnership. The capital account of each partner reflects all of the activity of an individual partner: contributions, withdrawals, and the distributive share of net income (loss). In some cases, a **drawing** account is used as a clearing account for each partner's transactions with only the net effect of each period's activity shown in the capital account.

> EXAMPLE: *Partnership Formation*
>
> *A and B form a partnership. A contributes cash of $50,000, while B contributed land with a fair market value of $50,000 and the partnership assumes a liability on the land of $25,000.*
> *The entry to record the formation of the partnership is*

| | | |
|---|---|---|
| Cash | 50,000 | |
| Land | 50,000 | |
| Liabilities | | 25,000 |
| A Capital | | 50,000 |
| B Capital | | 25,000 |

### 2. Allocation of Partnership Income (Loss)

The partners should have a written agreement (articles of copartnership) specifying the manner in which partnership income (loss) is to be distributed. Note that in the absence of a predetermined agreement, the profit and loss (P&L) is divided equally among the partners.

It is important to remember that P&L should **not** be distributed using a ratio based on the partners' capital balances unless this is the ratio specified in the articles of copartnership. A number of issues arise which complicate the allocation of partnership income (loss).

a. Partners may receive interest on their capital balances. If so, it must be determined what will constitute the capital balance (e.g., the year-end amount or some type of weighted-average).

b. Some of the partners may receive a salary.

c. Some of the partners may receive a bonus on distributable net income. If so, you need to determine if the bonus should be computed before or after salary and interest allocations.

d. A formula needs to be determined for allocating the remaining income. The formula agreed upon is usually termed the **residual, remainder**, or **profit (loss) sharing ratio**.

e. Finally, the partners should decide upon how income is to be allocated if net income is insufficient to cover partners' salaries, bonuses, and interest allocations. These allocations are usually made even if the effect is to create a negative remainder. This remainder is usually allocated in accordance with the profit (loss) ratio. However, it is important to note that partners may choose to allocate losses (or a negative remainder) in a different manner than income.

> EXAMPLE: *Partnership P&L Distribution*
>
> *Partners receive 5% interest on beginning capital balances*
> *Partner B receives a $6,000 salary*
> *Partner C receives a 10% bonus after interest and salaries*
> *The P&L ratios are A — 50%, B — 30%, C — 20%*

*Assuming partnership net income of $18,250, the following distribution schedule would be prepared:*

|  | A | B | C | Total |
|---|---|---|---|---|
| P&L ratio | 50% | 30% | 20% | |
| Beginning capital balance | 30,000 | 10,000 | 5,000 | 45,000 |
| Net income | | | | (18,250) |
| 5% interest | 1,500 | 500 | 250 | 2,250 |
| Salary | | 6,000 | | 6,000 |
| Bonus | | | 1,000* | 1,000 |
| Distribution of residual | 4,500 | 2,700 | 1,800 | 9,000 |
| Total | 6,000 | 9,200 | 3,050 | -- |
| Ending capital balances | 36,000 | 19,200 | 8,050 | |

\* ($18,250 – $8,250) × .10 = $1,000

Note that if the interest, salary, and bonus allocation had exceeded net income, the excess would have been deducted on the distribution schedule in the P&L ratio.

### 3. Partnership Dissolution (Changes in Ownership)

Partnership dissolution occurs whenever there is a change in ownership (e.g., the addition of a new partner, or the retirement or death of an existing partner). This is not to be confused with partnership liquidation, which is the winding up of partnership affairs and termination of the business. Under dissolution the partnership business continues, but under different ownership.

When partnership dissolution occurs a new accounting entity results. The partnership should first adjust its records so that all accounts are properly stated at the date of dissolution. After the income (loss) has been properly allocated to the existing partners' capital accounts, all assets and liabilities should be adjusted to their fair market value and their present values, respectively. The latter step is performed because the dissolution results in a new accounting entity.

After all adjustments have been made, the accounting for dissolution depends on the type of transaction that caused the dissolution. These transactions can be broken down into two types:

- Transactions between the partnership and a partner (e.g., a new partner contributes assets, or a retiring partner withdraws assets)
- Transactions between partners (e.g., a new partner purchases an interest from one or more existing partners, or a retiring partner sells his/her interest to one or more existing partners)

#### a. Transactions between a partner and the partnership

##### (1) Admission of a new partner

When a new partner is admitted to the partnership essentially three cases can result. The new partner can invest assets into the partnership and receive a capital balance

- (a) Equal to his/her purchase price
- (b) Greater than his/her purchase price
- (c) Less than his/her purchase price

If the new partner's capital balance is equal to the assets invested, then the entry debits the asset(s) contributed and credits the new partner's capital account for the fair value of the asset(s) contributed.

If the new partner's capital balance is not equal to the assets invested [as in situation (b) and (c) above], then either the bonus or goodwill method must be used to account for the difference.

**Bonus method**—The old partnership capital plus the new partner's asset contribution is equal to the new partnership capital. The new partner's capital is allocated his purchase share (e.g., 40%) and the old partner's capital accounts are adjusted as if they had been paid (or as if they paid) a bonus. The adjustment to the old partners' capital accounts is made in accordance with their profit (loss) sharing ratio.

The bonus method implies that the old partners either received a bonus from the new partner, or they paid a bonus to the new partner. As a result the old partners' capital accounts are either debited to reflect a bonus paid, or credited to reflect a bonus received. The new partner's capital account is **never** equal to the amount of assets contributed in a case where the bonus method is used.

**Goodwill method**—The old partnership capital plus the new partner's asset contribution is **not** equal to the new partnership capital. This is because goodwill is recorded on the partnership books for the difference between the total identifiable assets of the partnership (not including goodwill) and the deemed value of the partnership entity (which includes goodwill). Under the goodwill method, valuation of the new partnership is the objective.

How the value of the partnership is determined depends on whether the book value acquired is greater or less than the asset(s) invested. If the book value acquired is less than the asset(s) invested, the value is determined based upon the new partner's contribution, and goodwill is allocated to the old partners' accounts. If the book value acquired is greater than the asset(s) contributed, the value is based upon the existing capital accounts, and goodwill is attributed to the new partner.

The decision as to whether the bonus or goodwill method should be used rests with the partners involved. In other words, the bonus and goodwill methods are alternative solutions to the same problem.

*EXAMPLE:  Partnership Dissolution—Bonus Method*

*Total old capital for ABC Partnership is $60,000.*

| Partner | A | B | C |
|---|---|---|---|
| Capital | $10,000 | $20,000 | $30,000 |
| P&L Ratio | 40% | 40% | 20% |

**Case 1**

*D is admitted to the partnership and is given a 20% interest in the capital in return for a cash contribution of $30,000.*

| | | |
|---|---|---|
| Cash | 30,000 | |
| D Capital | | 18,000 |
| A Capital | | 4,800 |
| B Capital | | 4,800 |
| C Capital | | 2,400 |

*The total partnership capital to be shown on the books is $90,000 ($60,000 + $30,000) of which D is entitled to a 20% interest, or a capital balance of $18,000. The remaining $12,000 is treated as a bonus to the old partners and is allocated to their capital accounts in accordance with their P&L ratio.*

**Case 2**

*D is admitted to the partnership and is given a 20% interest in the capital in return for a cash contribution of $10,000.*

| | | |
|---|---|---|
| Cash | 10,000 | |
| A Capital | 1,600 | |
| B Capital | 1,600 | |
| C Capital | 800 | |
| D Capital | | 14,000 |

*The total partnership capital to be shown on the books is $70,000 ($60,000 + $10,000) of which D is entitled to a 20% interest, or a capital balance of $14,000. The difference of $4,000 ($10,000 – $14,000) is allocated to the old partners' accounts as if they had paid a bonus to the new partner.*

*EXAMPLE:  Partnership Dissolution—Goodwill Method*

*Use the same original data as given above.*

**Case 1**

*D is admitted to the partnership and is given a 20% interest in the capital in return for a cash contribution of $20,000. The partners elect to record goodwill. The book value acquired [($60,000 + $20,000) × 20% = $16,000] is less than the asset contributed.*

*The value of the partnership is determined based upon the contribution of the new partner. In this case it is assumed that the partnership value is $100,000 ($20,000/20%). The resulting goodwill is $20,000 ($100,000 – $80,000). The $80,000 represents the total current capital, exclusive of goodwill, $60,000 of which is attributable to the old partners and $20,000 of which is attributable to the new partner.*

| | | |
|---|---|---|
| Goodwill | 20,000 | |
| A Capital | | 8,000 |
| B Capital | | 8,000 |
| C Capital | | 4,000 |
| Cash | 20,000 | |
| D Capital | | 20,000 |

*Goodwill was allocated to the old partners in their P&L ratio. Also note that the capital balance of D represents 20% of the total capital of the partnership.*

**Case 2**

*D is admitted to the partnership and is given a 20% interest in the capital in return for a cash contribution of $10,000. The partners elect to record goodwill. The book value acquired [($60,000 + $10,000) × 20% = $14,000] is greater than the asset contributed.*

*The partnership value is based upon the capital accounts of the existing partners.  Because D is entitled to a 20% interest, the $60,000 capital of the old partners must represent 80% of the capital.  This means that the total value of the partnership is $75,000 ($60,000/80%).  D's total contribution consists of the $10,000 in cash and $5,000 of goodwill.  The goodwill is determined as the difference between the cash contribution and the 20% of the partnership capital.*

| | | |
|---|---|---|
| Cash | 10,000 | |
| Goodwill | 5,000 | |
| D Capital | | 15,000 |

*Note that in this last case no adjustment is made to the capital accounts of partners A, B, and C.*

The table below summarizes the bonus and goodwill situations discussed above:

| **When to Apply Bonus Method** | **When to Apply Goodwill Method** |
|---|---|
| New         Old        New Partner's<br>Partnership = Partners' +     Asset<br>Capital     Capital     Investment | New          Old        New Partner's<br>Partnership > Partners' +     Asset<br>Capital      Capital      Investment |
| **Which Partner(s) Receive Bonus**<br>• *New Partner*<br> New Partner's    New Partner's<br> Capital Credit > Asset Investment<br>(The difference represents the bonus.) | **Which Partner(s) Goodwill Is Recognized**<br>• *New Partner's Goodwill*<br> New Partner's     New Partner's<br> Capital Credit > Asset Investment<br>(The difference represents goodwill.) |
| • *Old Partners*<br> New Partner's    New Partner's<br> Capital Credit < Asset Investment<br>(The difference represents the bonus allocated<br>to old partners in their P&L Ratio.) | • *Old Partners' Goodwill*<br> New Partner's     New Partner's<br> Capital Credit = Asset Investment<br>(Goodwill is allocated to old partners in<br>their P & L Ratio.) |

## (2)  Partner death or withdrawal

The death or withdrawal of a partner is treated in much the same manner as the admission of a new partner.  However, there is no new capital account to be recorded; we are dealing only with the capital accounts of the original partners.  Either the bonus or goodwill method may be used.  The key thing to remember in regard to a partner's withdrawal from the partnership is that the withdrawing partner's capital account must be adjusted to the amount that the withdrawing partner is expected to receive.

*EXAMPLE:  Partner Withdrawal*

*Assume the same partnership data as given for the ABC partnership earlier.*

*Case 1*

*Assume that A withdraws from the partnership after reaching an agreement with partners B & C that would pay him $16,000.  The remaining partners elect not to record goodwill.*

| | | |
|---|---|---|
| B Capital | 4,000 | |
| C Capital | 2,000 | |
| A Capital | | 6,000 |
| A Capital | 16,000 | |
| Cash | | 16,000 |

*The $6,000 bonus is determined as the difference between the current balance of A's capital account and the amount of his buyout agreement.  This "bonus" is then allocated between the remaining partners' capital accounts in proportion to their P&L ratios.*

*Case 2*

*Assume again that A withdraws from the partnership pursuant to the same agreement except that this time the partners elect to record goodwill.*

*The first step is to determine the amount of goodwill to be recorded.  In this case we know that A's capital account must have a balance of $16,000, the agreed buyout payment he is to receive.  In order to accomplish this, the total partnership assets must be increased by some amount of which $6,000 represents 40%, A's P&L ratio.  Therefore, the amount of goodwill to be recorded is $15,000 ($6,000/40%).*

| | | |
|---|---|---|
| Goodwill | 15,000 | |
| A Capital | | 6,000 |
| B Capital | | 6,000 |
| C Capital | | 3,000 |
| A Capital | 16,000 | |
| Cash | | 16,000 |

*Note that in this case all of the partners' capital accounts are adjusted to record the goodwill in accordance with their P&L ratios.*

b.   **Transactions between partners**

The sale of a partnership interest is a transaction only between the partners.  Thus, the treatment accorded the transaction is determined by the partners involved.

There are two means of dealing with such a transaction.  The first is to simply transfer a portion of the existing partners' capital to a new capital account for the buying partner.

*EXAMPLE:  Sale of a Partnership Interest—No Goodwill Recorded*

*Assume the following for the AB partnership:*

| Partner | A | B |
|---------|------|------|
| Capital | $50,000 | $50,000 |
| P&L Ratio | 60% | 40% |

**Case 1**

*Assume that C wishes to enter the partnership by buying 50% of the partnership interest from both A and B for a total of $80,000.  It is important to note that the $80,000 is being paid to the individual partners and **not** to the partnership.  Thus, we are only concerned with the proper adjustment between the capital accounts, **not** the recording of the cash.  This approach ignores the price that C paid for the partnership interest.*

| | | |
|---|---|---|
| A Capital | 25,000 | |
| B Capital | 25,000 | |
| C Capital | | 50,000 |

The other method available for recording a transaction between partners involves the recording of implied goodwill.

*EXAMPLE:  Sale of Partnership Interest—Recording Goodwill*

*Assume the same facts presented above for the sale of the partnership interest except that in this case the partners elect to record goodwill.*

**Case 1**

*Assuming that C paid $80,000 for a 50% interest in the partnership the implied value of the partnership assets is $160,000 ($80,000/50%).  Because total capital prior to the purchase is only $100,000, the amount of goodwill that must be recorded is $60,000.  The goodwill is allocated to the prior partners' accounts in proportion to their P&L ratios.  Note that this entry is made **before** an adjustment is made to reflect C's admission to the partnership.*

| | | |
|---|---|---|
| Goodwill | 60,000 | |
| A Capital | | 36,000 |
| B Capital | | 24,000 |

Now we can record the sale of the partnership interest to C. The capital balance of A is now $86,000 ($50,000 + $36,000) while the capital balance of B is $74,000 ($50,000 + $24,000).  Recall that C is to receive 50% of each balance.

| | | |
|---|---|---|
| A Capital | 43,000 | |
| B Capital | 37,000 | |
| C Capital | | 80,000 |

Notice that in this situation the capital balance of C after the purchase is equal to the amount of the purchase price.  Again no entry is made to record the receipt of cash because the cash goes directly to the individual partners, A and B.

## 4.  Partnership Liquidation

A liquidation is the winding up of the partnership business. That is, it sells all of its noncash assets, pays its liabilities, and makes a final liquidating distribution to the remaining partners.

There are four basic steps to a partnership liquidation.

1.   Any operating income or loss up to the date of the liquidation should be computed and allocated to the partners' capital accounts on the basis of their P&L ratio.
2.   All noncash assets are sold and converted to cash.  The gain (loss) realized on the sale of such assets is allocated to the partners' capital accounts on the basis of their P&L ratio.
3.   Any creditors' claims, including liquidation expenses or anticipated future claims, are satisfied through the payment or reserve of cash.
4.   The remaining unreserved cash is distributed to the remaining partners in accordance with the balance in their capital accounts.  Note that this is **not** necessarily the P&L ratio.

Two factors that may complicate the liquidation process are the existence of loans or advances between the partnership and one or more of the partners, or the creation of a deficit in a partner's capital account because of the allocation of a loss.  When loans exist between the partnership and a partner, the capital account and the loan(s) are combined to give a net amount. This is often referred to as the right of offset. When a deficit exists, the amount of the deficit is allocated to the remaining solvent partners' capital accounts on the basis of their relative P&L ratio. Note here that if the partner with the capital deficit is personally solvent, he has a liability to the remaining partners for the amount of the deficit.

There are two topics that appear with regularity on the CPA examination in regard to the liquidation of a partnership. They are the statement of partnership liquidation and the determination of a "safe payment" in an installment liquidation.

a.   **Statement of partnership liquidation**

The statement of partnership liquidation shows in detail all of the transactions associated with the liquidation of the partnership. It should be noted here that the liquidation of a partnership can take one of two forms: simple or installment. A simple liquidation (illustrated below) is one in which all of the assets are sold in bulk and all of the creditors' claims are satisfied before a single liquidating distribution is made to the partners. Because the assets are sold in bulk there is a tendency to realize greater losses than if the assets were sold over a period of time. As a result, many partnerships liquidate on an installment basis. In an installment liquidation the assets are sold over a period of time and the cash is distributed to the partners as it becomes available.

> EXAMPLE:  Statement of Partnership Liquidation—Simple Liquidation
>
> Assume the following:
>
> The capital balances are as given below.
> The P&L ratio is 5:3:2 for A, B, and C, respectively.

**STATEMENT OF PARTNERSHIP LIQUIDATION**

| | Cash | Other assets | Liabilities | A (50%) | B (30%) | C (20%) |
|---|---|---|---|---|---|---|
| | | | | | *Capital* | |
| Balances | 5,000 | 75,000 | 45,000 | 12,000 | 17,000 | 6,000 |
| Sale of assets ($20,000 loss) | 40,000 | (60,000) | | (10,000) | (6,000) | (4,000) |
| | 45,000 | 15,000 | 45,000 | 2,000 | 11,000 | 2,000 |
| Payment of liabilities | (45,000) | | (45,000) | | | |
| | 0 | 15,000 | 0 | 2,000 | 11,000 | 2,000 |
| Sale of assets ($5,000 loss) | 10,000 | (15,000) | | (2,500) | (1,500) | (1,000) |
| | 10,000 | 0 | 0 | (500) | 9,500 | 1,000 |
| Distribution of A's deficit | | | | 500 | (300) | (200) |
| | 10,000 | 0 | 0 | 0 | 9,200 | 800 |
| Final distribution of cash | (10,000) | | | | (9,200) | (800) |

> Notice that after the noncash assets have been sold and the creditors satisfied, a $500 deficit remains in A's capital account. The deficit is allocated to the remaining solvent partners on the basis of their relative P&L ratios, in this case, 3:2. A is liable to the partnership for the $500. If A is personally solvent and repays the $500, then $300 will go to B and $200 will go to C.

If in the above example there had been liquidation expenses or loans between the partnership and partners, these would have to be recognized in the statement prior to any distribution to partners. A loan receivable from or payable to a partner is simply offset to (closed against) that partner's capital account.

b.   **Installment method of cash distribution**

There are two keys to preparing a statement of partnership liquidation under the installment method: the determination of the available cash balance at any given point in time and the determination of which partner(s) is(are) to receive the payment of that cash. The reason that the cash is not distributed in accordance with the P&L ratio is twofold: first, the final cash distribution is based upon the balance in each partner's capital account, **not** the P&L ratio, and second, there will be situations, as illustrated in the previous example, where one or more partners will have deficit balances in their capital accounts. If this is the case, they should **never** receive a cash distribution, even if the deficit does not arise until late in the liquidation process.

The determination of the available cash balance is generally very straightforward. The beginning cash balance (cash on hand at the start of the liquidation process) is adjusted for the cash receipts from receivables, sale of noncash assets, payment to creditors, and liquidation expenses incurred. A situation may occur where a certain amount of cash is to be reserved for payment of future liabilities that may arise. If this is the case, this cash should be treated as an escrowed, or restricted, asset which makes it unavailable for current distribution to the partners.

The determination of which partner(s) is(are) to receive the available cash is somewhat more difficult.  There are a number of ways to make this computation, all of which are equally correct in the eyes of the examiners.  This determination can be made at the beginning of the liquidation process or at the time of each payment.  In making this determination there are two key assumptions that must be made:  (1) the individual partners are assumed to be personally insolvent, and (2) the remaining noncash assets are deemed to be worthless (thus creating a maximum possible amount of loss).

One method of determining the amount of the "safe payment" is the use of an Installment Cash Distribution Schedule.  This schedule is prepared by determining the amount of loss required to eliminate each partner's capital account.  As noted above, all of the remaining noncash assets are to be considered worthless at the time a safe payment is determined.  Thus, if we determine the amount of loss required to eliminate each partner's capital balance, we can determine the order in which the partners should receive the cash payments.

When preparing this schedule it is important to make sure that the proper capital balance is used.  The capital balance used **must** be inclusive of any loans or advances between the partnership and partners.  Thus, the capital balance at the beginning of the liquidation process is increased by any amount owed to the partner by the partnership, and decreased by any amount owed to the partnership by the partner.

*EXAMPLE:  Schedule of Possible Losses and Installment Cash Distribution*

*Assume the same data as used for the previous example.*

### SCHEDULE OF POSSIBLE LOSSES

| | *Total* | *A (50%)* | *B (30%)* | *C (20%)* |
|---|---|---|---|---|
| *Net capital balances* | *$35,000* | *$12,000* | *$17,000* | *$6,000* |
| *Loss to eliminate A* | *24,000* | *(12,000)* | *(7,200)* | *(4,800)* |
| | | *0* | *$ 9,800* | *$1,200* |
| *Additional loss to eliminate C* | *3,000\** | | *(1,800)* | *(1,200)* |
| | | | *8,000* | *0* |
| *Additional loss to eliminate B* | *8,000* | | *(8,000)* | |
| | *$35,000* | | *0* | |

\* *Allocated 60:40*

The total capital balance of $35,000 indicates that if the noncash assets are sold for $35,000 less than their book value, then none of the partners will receive a cash distribution.  The purpose of this schedule is to determine how much of a loss each partner's capital account can withstand based on that partner's P&L ratio.  In this example A's capital would be eliminated if the partnership incurred a $24,000 ($12,000/50%) loss, B's would be eliminated by a $56,667 ($17,000/30%) loss, and C's by a $30,000 ($6,000/20%) loss.  A is assumed to be eliminated first because it would take the smallest amount of loss to eliminate his account.  Once A is eliminated as a partner, the P&L ratios change to reflect the relative P&L ratio of the remaining partners, in this case B and C.  Based on the remaining capital balances and the relative P&L ratio, it would take a $16,333 ($9,800/60%) loss to eliminate B and a $3,000 ($1,200/40%) loss to eliminate C.  Now that C is eliminated B will share all of the profits and losses as a sole partner (i.e., 100%).  It will now take an $8,000 loss to eliminate B's capital.  The resulting installment cash distribution schedule would appear as follows (this schedule assumes that all creditors have already received full payment; thus, the cash amount represents available cash):*

### INSTALLMENT CASH DISTRIBUTION SCHEDULE

| *Partner* | | *A* | *B* | *C* |
|---|---|---|---|---|
| *First* | *$ 8,000* | | *100%* | |
| *Next* | *3,000* | | *60%* | *40%* |
| *Next* | *24,000* | *50%* | *30%* | *20%* |
| *Any other* | | *50%* | *30%* | *20%* |

While the example shown in section 4.a. was not an installment liquidation, the Installment Cash Distribution Schedule shown above could still be used to determine how the available cash of $10,000 is to be distributed.  This is illustrated below.*

| *Partner* | | *A* | *B* | *C* |
|---|---|---|---|---|
| *First* | *$ 8,000* | | *$8,000* | |
| *Next* | *2,000* | | *1,200* | *$800* |
| *Total* | *$10,000* | *--* | *$9,200* | *$800* |

It is important to note that this method is acceptable for most purposes; however, a CPA exam problem may require the "safe payment" approach where the amount of the safe payment is computed at a specific point in time.

5.  **Incorporation of a Partnership**

The incorporation of a partnership results in the formation of a new accounting (and legal) entity. This means that the partnership must adjust its records up to the date of incorporation. First, the partnership closes its books and recognizes any income or loss up to the date of incorporation. Second, the books of the partnership are adjusted to reflect the fair market value of the partnership assets and the present value of partnership liabilities. A corresponding adjustment is made to the capital accounts in accordance with the partners' P&L ratio. Third, common stock is distributed to the partners in accordance with the amounts in their capital accounts. Note that the entries to record the receipt of stock by the corporation are different depending upon whether the corporation retains the partnership books or establishes new books.

Retention of the partnership books means that the issuance of common stock results in the closing of the partners' capital accounts with credits going to common stock and additional paid-in capital.

Establishing new books means that the assets and liabilities are closed out and the difference between their net value and the value of the corporate stock is debited to an asset "capital stock from corporation." This account is then credited and the partners' capital accounts debited to record the distribution of stock.

6.  **Research Component**

Because there are no authoritative pronouncements in the accounting standards for partnerships, research in the partnership area is limited to the concepts statements that apply for all for-profit entities. You should be prepared to answer conceptual questions on typical accounting concepts such as revenue recognition, matching, valuation, allocation, and other accrual basis accounting concepts that are applicable to all business entities.

**MULTIPLE-CHOICE QUESTIONS (1-23)**

**1.** Roberts and Smith drafted a partnership agreement that lists the following assets contributed at the partnership's formation:

|  | Contributed by | |
|---|---|---|
|  | Roberts | Smith |
| Cash | $20,000 | $30,000 |
| Inventory | -- | 15,000 |
| Building | -- | 40,000 |
| Furniture & equipment | 15,000 | -- |

The building is subject to a mortgage of $10,000, which the partnership has assumed.  The partnership agreement also specifies that profits and losses are to be distributed evenly.  What amounts should be recorded as capital for Roberts and Smith at the formation of the partnership?

|  | Roberts | Smith |
|---|---|---|
| a. | $35,000 | $85,000 |
| b. | $35,000 | $75,000 |
| c. | $55,000 | $55,000 |
| d. | $60,000 | $60,000 |

**2.** On April 30, 2007, Algee, Belger, and Ceda formed a partnership by combining their separate business proprietorships.  Algee contributed cash of $50,000.  Belger contributed property with a $36,000 carrying amount, a $40,000 original cost, and $80,000 fair value.  The partnership accepted responsibility for the $35,000 mortgage attached to the property.  Ceda contributed equipment with a $30,000 carrying amount, a $75,000 original cost, and $55,000 fair value.  The partnership agreement specifies that profits and losses are to be shared equally but is silent regarding capital contributions.  Which partner has the largest April 30, 2007 capital account balance?

a. Algee.
b. Belger.
c. Ceda.
d. All capital account balances are equal.

**3.** Abel and Carr formed a partnership and agreed to divide initial capital equally, even though Abel contributed $100,000 and Carr contributed $84,000 in identifiable assets.  Under the bonus approach to adjust the capital accounts, Carr's unidentifiable asset should be debited for

a. $46,000
b. $16,000
c. $ 8,000
d. $0

**4.** When property other than cash is invested in a partnership, at what amount should the noncash property be credited to the contributing partner's capital account?

a. Fair value at the date of contribution.
b. Contributing partner's original cost.
c. Assessed valuation for property tax purposes.
d. Contributing partner's tax basis.

**5.** Red and White formed a partnership in 2007.  The partnership agreement provides for annual salary allowances of $55,000 for Red and $45,000 for White.  The partners share profits equally and losses in a 60/40 ratio.  The partnership had earnings of $80,000 for 2007 before any allowance to partners.  What amount of these earnings should be credited to each partner's capital account?

|  | Red | White |
|---|---|---|
| a. | $40,000 | $40,000 |

| b. | $43,000 | $37,000 |
| c. | $44,000 | $36,000 |
| d. | $45,000 | $35,000 |

**6.** Fox, Greg, and Howe are partners with average capital balances during 2006 of $120,000, $60,000, and $40,000, respectively.  Partners receive 10% interest on their average capital balances.  After deducting salaries of $30,000 to Fox and $20,000 to Howe, the residual profit or loss is divided equally.  In 2007 the partnership sustained a $33,000 loss before interest and salaries to partners.  By what amount should Fox's capital account change?

a. $ 7,000 increase.
b. $11,000 decrease.
c. $35,000 decrease.
d. $42,000 increase.

**7.** The partnership agreement of Axel, Berg & Cobb provides for the year-end allocation of net income in the following order:

- First, Axel is to receive 10% of net income up to $100,000 and 20% over $100,000.
- Second, Berg and Cobb each are to receive 5% of the remaining income over $150,000.
- The balance of income is to be allocated equally among the three partners.

The partnership's 2007 net income was $250,000 before any allocations to partners.  What amount should be allocated to Axel?

a. $101,000
b. $103,000
c. $108,000
d. $110,000

**8.** The partnership agreement of Reid and Simm provides that interest at 10% per year is to be credited to each partner on the basis of weighted-average capital balances.  A summary of Simm's capital account for the year ended December 31, 2007, is as follows:

| Balance, January 1 | $140,000 |
|---|---|
| Additional investment, July 1 | 40,000 |
| Withdrawal, August 1 | (15,000) |
| Balance, December 31 | 165,000 |

What amount of interest should be credited to Simm's capital account for 2007?

a. $15,250
b. $15,375
c. $16,500
d. $17,250

**9.** The Flat and Iron partnership agreement provides for Flat to receive a 20% bonus on profits before the bonus.  Remaining profits and losses are divided between Flat and Iron in the ratio of 2:3, respectively.  Which partner has a greater advantage when the partnership has a profit or when it has a loss?

|  | Profit | Loss |
|---|---|---|
| a. | Flat | Iron |
| b. | Flat | Flat |
| c. | Iron | Flat |
| d. | Iron | Iron |

**10.** Blau and Rubi are partners who share profits and losses in the ratio of 6:4, respectively.  On May 1, 2007, their respective capital accounts were as follows:

Blau                         $60,000
Rubi                          50,000

On that date, Lind was admitted as a partner with a one-third interest in capital and profits for an investment of $40,000. The new partnership began with total capital of $150,000. Immediately after Lind's admission, Blau's capital should be
    a.   $50,000
    b.   $54,000
    c.   $56,667
    d.   $60,000

**11.** Kern and Pate are partners with capital balances of $60,000 and $20,000, respectively. Profits and losses are divided in the ratio of 60:40. Kern and Pate decided to form a new partnership with Grant, who invested land valued at $15,000 for a 20% capital interest in the new partnership. Grant's cost of the land was $12,000. The partnership elected to use the bonus method to record the admission of Grant into the partnership. Grant's capital account should be credited for
    a.   $12,000
    b.   $15,000
    c.   $16,000
    d.   $19,000

**12.** Dunn and Grey are partners with capital account balances of $60,000 and $90,000, respectively. They agree to admit Zorn as a partner with a one-third interest in capital and profits, for an investment of $100,000, after revaluing the assets of Dunn and Grey. Goodwill to the original partners should be
    a.   $0
    b.   $33,333
    c.   $50,000
    d.   $66,667

**Items 13 and 14** are based on the following:

The following condensed balance sheet is presented for the partnership of Alfa and Beda, who share profits and losses in the ratio of 60:40, respectively:

Cash                      $ 45,000
Other assets               625,000
Beda, loan                  30,000
                          $700,000
Accounts payable          $120,000
Alfa, capital              348,000
Beda, capital              232,000
                          $700,000

**13.** The assets and liabilities are fairly valued on the balance sheet. Alfa and Beda decide to admit Capp as a new partner with 20% interest. No goodwill or bonus is to be recorded. What amount should Capp contribute in cash or other assets?
    a.   $110,000
    b.   $116,000
    c.   $140,000
    d.   $145,000

**14.** Instead of admitting a new partner, Alfa and Beda decide to liquidate the partnership. If the other assets are sold for $500,000, what amount of the available cash should be distributed to Alfa?
    a.   $255,000
    b.   $273,000
    c.   $327,000
    d.   $348,000

**15.** In the Adel-Brick partnership, Adel and Brick had a capital ratio of 3:1 and a profit and loss ratio of 2:1, respectively. The bonus method was used to record Colter's admittance as a new partner. What ratio would be used to allocate, to Adel and Brick, the excess of Colter's contribution over the amount credited to Colter's capital account?
    a.   Adel and Brick's new relative capital ratio.
    b.   Adel and Brick's new relative profit and loss ratio.
    c.   Adel and Brick's old capital ratio.
    d.   Adel and Brick's old profit and loss ratio.

**Items 16 and 17** are based on the following:

On June 30, 2007, the condensed balance sheet for the partnership of Eddy, Fox, and Grimm, together with their respective profit and loss sharing percentages were as follows:

Assets, net of liabilities          $320,000
Eddy, capital (50%)                  $160,000
Fox, capital (30%)                     96,000
Grimm, capital (20%)                   64,000
                                     $320,000

**16.** Eddy decided to retire from the partnership and by mutual agreement is to be paid $180,000 out of partnership funds for his interest. Total goodwill implicit in the agreement is to be recorded. After Eddy's retirement, what are the capital balances of the other partners?

|    | *Fox* | *Grimm* |
|----|----|----|
| a. | $ 84,000 | $56,000 |
| b. | $102,000 | $68,000 |
| c. | $108,000 | $72,000 |
| d. | $120,000 | $80,000 |

**17.** Assume instead that Eddy remains in the partnership and that Hamm is admitted as a new partner with a 25% interest in the capital of the new partnership for a cash payment of $140,000. Total goodwill implicit in the transaction is to be recorded. Immediately after admission of Hamm, Eddy's capital account balance should be
    a.   $280,000
    b.   $210,000
    c.   $160,000
    d.   $140,000

**18.** On June 30, 2007, the balance sheet for the partnership of Coll, Maduro, and Prieto, together with their respective profit and loss ratios, were as follows:

Assets, at cost             $180,000
Coll, loan                   $ 9,000
Coll, capital (20%)           42,000
Maduro, capital (20%)         39,000
Prieto, capital (60%)         90,000
Total                       $180,000

Coll has decided to retire from the partnership. By mutual agreement, the assets are to be adjusted to their fair value of $216,000 at June 30, 2007. It was agreed that the partnership would pay Coll $61,200 cash for Coll's partnership interest, including Coll's loan which is to be repaid in full. No goodwill is to be recorded. After Coll's retirement, what is the balance of Maduro's capital account?
    a.   $36,450
    b.   $39,000
    c.   $45,450
    d.   $46,200

**19.** Allen retired from the partnership of Allen, Beck, and Chale. Allen's cash settlement from the partnership was based on new goodwill determined at the date of retirement plus the carrying amount of the other net assets. As a consequence of the settlement, the capital accounts of Beck and Chale were decreased. In accounting for Allen's withdrawal, the partnership could have used the

| | Bonus method | Goodwill method |
|---|---|---|
| a. | No | Yes |
| b. | No | No |
| c. | Yes | Yes |
| d. | Yes | No |

**20.** When Mill retired from the partnership of Mill, Yale, and Lear, the final settlement of Mill's interest exceeded Mill's capital balance. Under the bonus method, the excess

a. Was recorded as goodwill.
b. Was recorded as an expense.
c. Reduced the capital balances of Yale and Lear.
d. Had **no** effect on the capital balances of Yale and Lear.

**21.** The following condensed balance sheet is presented for the partnership of Smith and Jones, who share profits and losses in the ratio of 60:40, respectively:

| | |
|---|---|
| Other assets | $450,000 |
| Smith, loan | 20,000 |
| | $470,000 |
| Accounts payable | $120,000 |
| Smith, capital | 195,000 |
| Jones, capital | 155,000 |
| | $470,000 |

The partners have decided to liquidate the partnership. If the other assets are sold for $385,000, what amount of the available cash should be distributed to Smith?

a. $136,000
b. $156,000
c. $159,000
d. $195,000

**22.** On January 1, 2007, the partners of Cobb, Davis, and Eddy, who share profits and losses in the ratio of 5:3:2, respectively, decided to liquidate their partnership. On this date the partnership condensed balance sheet was as follows:

| *Assets* | |
|---|---|
| Cash | $ 50,000 |
| Other assets | 250,000 |
| | $300,000 |

| *Liabilities and Capital* | |
|---|---|
| Liabilities | $ 60,000 |
| Cobb, capital | 80,000 |
| Davis, capital | 90,000 |
| Eddy, capital | 70,000 |
| | $300,000 |

On January 15, 2007, the first cash sale of other assets with a carrying amount of $150,000 realized $120,000. Safe installment payments to the partners were made the same date. How much cash should be distributed to each partner?

| | Cobb | Davis | Eddy |
|---|---|---|---|
| a. | $15,000 | $51,000 | $44,000 |
| b. | $40,000 | $45,000 | $35,000 |
| c. | $55,000 | $33,000 | $22,000 |
| d. | $60,000 | $36,000 | $24,000 |

**23.** Jay & Kay partnership's balance sheet at December 31, 2007, reported the following:

| | |
|---|---|
| Total assets | $100,000 |
| Total liabilities | 20,000 |

| | |
|---|---|
| Jay, capital | 40,000 |
| Kay, capital | 40,000 |

On January 2, 2008, Jay and Kay dissolved their partnership and transferred all assets and liabilities to a newly formed corporation. At the date of incorporation, the fair value of the net assets was $12,000 more than the carrying amount on the partnership's books, of which $7,000 was assigned to tangible assets and $5,000 was assigned to goodwill. Jay and Kay were each issued 5,000 shares of the corporation's $1 par value common stock. Immediately following incorporation, additional paid-in capital in excess of par should be credited for

a. $68,000
b. $70,000
c. $77,000
d. $82,000

**SIMULATION PROBLEMS**

**Simulation Problem 1**                                    (45 to 55 minutes)

| Situation | | | | |
|---|---|---|---|---|
| | Liquidation Schedule | Schedule of Safe Payments | Incorporation of Partnership | Communication |

On January 1, 2007, the partners of Dove, Eagle, and Falcon who share profits and losses in the ratio of 5:3:2, respectively decided to liquidate their partnership. On this date, the partnership's condensed balance sheet was as follows:

| *Assets* | |
|---|---|
| Cash | $80,000 |
| Note receivable—(loan to Eagle) | 20,000 |
| Plant, property, and equipment | 300,000 |
| | 400,000 |
| | |
| *Liabilities and Capital* | |
| Liabilities | 120,000 |
| Dove, capital | 150,000 |
| Eagle, capital | 70,000 |
| Falcon, capital | 60,000 |

On January 30, 2007, the first cash sale of other assets with a carrying amount of $120,000 was sold for $150,000. On February 5, 2007, the remaining assets were sold for $100,000.

| | Liquidation Schedule | | | |
|---|---|---|---|---|
| Situation | | Schedule of Safe Payments | Incorporation of Partnership | Communication |

Prepare a Schedule of Partnership Liquidation for the partnership. Indicate the cash distribution to each partner. (For a more realistic exam experience, prepare the schedule using a spreadsheet program such as Excel.)

*Partnership of Dove, Eagle, and Falcon*
**SCHEDULE OF PARTNERSHIP LIQUIDATION**
*February 5, 2007*

| | *Cash* | *Notes receivable* | *Plant, property, and equip.* | *Liabilities* | *Dove* | *Eagle* | *Falcon* |
|---|---|---|---|---|---|---|---|
| Balances | | | | | | | |
| Partner loans | | | | | | | |
| Sale of assets, Jan. 30 | | | | | | | |
| Sale of assets, Feb. 5 | | | | | | | |
| Payment of liabilities | | | | | | | |
| Amount distributed to each partner | | | | | | | |

| | | Schedule of Safe Payments | | |
|---|---|---|---|---|
| Situation | Liquidation Schedule | | Incorporation of Partnership | Communication |

Suppose that on January 30, 2007, the first cash sale of other assets was sold for $180,000. The carrying value of the assets sold was $160,000.

Prepare a schedule of safe payments for the partnership after the sale on January 30, 2007.

*Partnership of Dove, Eagle, and Falcon*
**SCHEDULE OF SAFE PAYMENTS**
*January 30, 2007*

| | *Cash* | *Notes receivable* | *Plant, property, and equip.* | *Liabilities* | *Dove* | *Eagle* | *Falcon* |
|---|---|---|---|---|---|---|---|
| Balances | | | | | | | |
| Partner loans | | | | | | | |
| Sale of assets, Jan. 30 | | | | | | | |
| Subtotal | | | | | | | |
| Payment of liabilities | | | | | | | |
| Subtotal | | | | | | | |
| Assume total loss on other assets | | | | | | | |
| Amount distributed to each partner | | | | | | | |

| Situation | Liquidation Schedule | Schedule of Safe Payments | Incorporation of Partnership | |
|---|---|---|---|---|
| | | | | Communication |

Suppose that rather than liquidate the partnership, the partners choose to incorporate the partnership on January 30, 2007. After adjusting the partnership's books to fair value, the capital balances of the partners are as follows:

| | |
|---|---|
| Dove | $175,000 |
| Eagle | $ 65,000 |
| Falcon | $ 70,000 |

The new company, Canary Corp., is incorporated in the state of Delaware with 300,000 authorized shares of $2 par value common stock. The corporation retains the partnership's books and closes the partners' capital accounts. Dove receives 50,000 shares of stock, Eagle receives 30,000 shares of stock, and Falcon receives 20,000 shares of stock.

Prepare the journal entry to record the incorporation of the partnership.

| | | | | Communication |
|---|---|---|---|---|
| Situation | Liquidation Schedule | Schedule of Safe Payments | Incorporation of Partnership | |

Write a memo to the partners explaining the difference between a liquidation schedule and a schedule of safe payments.

To:    Mr. Dove, Mr. Eagle, and Mr. Falcon
From: CPA Candidate
Re:    Liquidation and safe payment schedules

---

**Simulation Problem 2**                              (45 to 55 minutes)

| Situation | | | | | |
|---|---|---|---|---|---|
| | Journal Entries | Allocation of Income | Admission of New Partner | Partnership Liquidation | Communication |

On January 2, 2007, Alkire and Higdon drafted a partnership agreement to create a new partnership. The following items were contributed by each of the partners:

| | Alkire | Higdon |
|---|---|---|
| Cash | $40,000 | $60,000 |
| Inventory | | 10,000 |
| Building | | 180,000 |
| Equipment | 60,000 | |

The building is subject to a mortgage of $50,000 which the partnership has assumed. The partnership agreement specifies that each partner receives 10% interest on his beginning capital balance. Alkire receives an annual salary of $15,000; Higdon receives an annual salary of $20,000. The residual profit or loss is divided using a 2:3 ratio with 2 parts assigned to Alkire and 3 parts assigned to Higdon.

During 2007 the partnership had income of $185,000. Assume there were no drawings during 2007.

| | Journal Entries | | | | |
|---|---|---|---|---|---|
| Situation | | Allocation of Income | Admission of New Partner | Partnership Liquidation | Communication |

Record the journal entry for each partner's contribution to the partnership.

- Journal entry for Alkire's contribution
- Journal entry for Higdon's contribution

| | | Allocation of Income | | | |
|---|---|---|---|---|---|
| Situation | Journal Entries | | Admission of New Partner | Partnership Liquidation | Communication |

Complete the following schedule showing the allocation of partnership income for each partner.

| | Alkire | Higdon |
|---|---|---|
| Beginning capital balance | | |
| Interest on capital balance | | |
| Annual salary | | |
| Remainder | | |
| Ending capital balance | | |

| Situation | Journal Entries | Allocation of Income | Admission of New Partner | Partnership Liquidation | Communication |
|---|---|---|---|---|---|

On January 1, 2008, Alkire and Higdon decide to admit a new partner, Zukoski, for a 1/6 interest in the firm for $175,000. The bonus method is used to record the admission of the new partner.  After admitting the new partner, the partnership agreement is amended as follows:

Each partner receives 10% interest on his beginning capital balance.  Each partner receives an annual salary of $20,000.  The residual profit or loss is divided in a ratio of 30% to Alkire, 50% to Higdon, and 20% to Zukoski.

Record the entry for admission of Zukoski to the partnership.

| Situation | Journal Entries | Allocation of Income | Admission of New Partner | Partnership Liquidation | Communication |
|---|---|---|---|---|---|

Assume that on 12/31/09, the partnership is dissolved.  On that date, after closing the books, the following information is available:

| | |
|---|---|
| Cash | $160,000 |
| Loan to Higdon | 50,000 |
| Other assets | 700,000 |
| Liabilities | 110,000 |
| Capital, Alkire | 200,000 |
| Capital, Higdon | 400,000 |
| Capital, Zukoski | 200,000 |

Other information necessary for the liquidation is as follows:

During the month of January 2010, assets with a book value of $180,000 were sold for $210,000.

Prepare a schedule of safe payments as of January 31, 2010.

### Partnership of Alkire, Higdon, and Zukoski
### SCHEDULE OF SAFE PAYMENTS
#### January 31, 2010

| | Cash | Notes receivable | Plant, property, and equip. | Liabilities | Alkire | Higdon | Zukoski |
|---|---|---|---|---|---|---|---|
| Balances | $160,000 | $50,000 | $700,000 | $110,000 | $200,000 | $400,000 | $200,000 |
| Partner loans | | | | | | | |
| Sale of assets, Jan. | | | | | | | |
| Payment of liabilities | | | | | | | |
| Loss on other assets | | | | | | | |
| Safe payment to partners | | | | | | | |

| Situation | Journal Entries | Allocation of Income | Admission of New Partner | Partnership Liquidation | Communication |
|---|---|---|---|---|---|

When the partnership was admitting Zukoski, the existing partners Alkire and Higdon did not understand the accounting methods used to admit a new partner.  Write a brief memo explaining to Mr. Alkire and Mr. Higdon the bonus method for accounting for the admission of Zukoski to the partnership.

To:      Mr. Alkire
          Mr. Higdon
From:  CPA Candidate
Re:      Admission of new partner

MULTIPLE-CHOICE ANSWERS

| | | | | |
|---|---|---|---|---|
| 1.  b  __ __ | 6.  a  __ __ | 11.  d  __ __ | 16.  c  __ __ | 21.  a  __ __ |
| 2.  c  __ __ | 7.  c  __ __ | 12.  c  __ __ | 17.  b  __ __ | 22.  a  __ __ |
| 3.  d  __ __ | 8.  b  __ __ | 13.  d  __ __ | 18.  c  __ __ | 23.  d  __ __ |
| 4.  a  __ __ | 9.  b  __ __ | 14.  b  __ __ | 19.  d  __ __ | 1st:  __/23 = __% |
| 5.  b  __ __ | 10.  b  __ __ | 15.  d  __ __ | 20.  c  __ __ | 2nd:  __/23 = __% |

MULTIPLE-CHOICE ANSWER EXPLANATIONS

## D.1.  Partnership Formation

**1.  (b)**   The requirement is to determine the amounts to be recorded as capital for Roberts and Smith at the formation of the partnership.  Unless otherwise agreed upon by the partners, individual capital accounts should be credited for the fair market value (on the date of contribution) of the net assets contributed by that partner.  It is necessary to assume that the amounts listed are fair market values.  The amount of net assets that Roberts contributed is $35,000 ($20,000 + $15,000).  The fair market value of the net assets Smith contributed is $75,000 ($30,000 + $15,000 + $40,000 – $10,000).  The partners' profit and loss sharing ratio does not affect the initial recording of the capital accounts.

**2.  (c)**   The requirement is to determine which partner has the largest capital account balance.  Use the solutions approach to solve the problem.

| | *Algee* | *Belger* | *Ceda* |
|---|---|---|---|
| Partner contribution | 50,000 | 80,000 | 55,000 |
| Less:  Liabilities assumed by the partnership | 0 | (35,000) | 0 |
| Ending capital balance | $50,000 | $45,000 | $55,000 |

Each partner values his contribution to the partnership at its fair market value.  The fair market value becomes the partner's balance in his capital account and is basis to the partnership under generally accepted accounting principles.  Any liabilities assumed by the partnership, reduces the partners' capital balance by the amount assumed.

**3.  (d)**   Under the bonus method, unidentifiable assets (i.e., goodwill) are not recognized.  The total resulting capital is the FMV of the tangible investments of the partners.  Thus, there would be no unidentifiable assets recognized by the creation of this new partnership.

**4.  (a)**   Noncash assets contributed to an entity should be recorded at fair market value at the date of contribution.  The creation of a new entity creates a new accountability for these assets.  The partner's original cost relates to a previous accountability.  The assessed valuation and the tax basis may differ from fair market value.

## D.2.  Allocation of Partnership Income (Loss)

**5.  (b)**   Credits to partners' capital accounts are based upon earnings after allowance for interest, salary and bonus.  The earnings before any allowance of $80,000 is reduced by the salary allowances of $100,000 and results in a loss of $20,000.  The $20,000 loss is then distributed to the partners in relation to their profit and loss ratios as follows:

| | *Red* | *White* | *Total* |
|---|---|---|---|
| Profit before allowance | | | $ 80,000 |
| Salary allowances | $55,000 | $45,000 | (100,000) |
| Loss after allowances 60/40 | (12,000) | (8,000) | (20,000) |
| Earnings credited to partners | $43,000 | $37,000 | $ 80,000 |

It is important to note that the losses are distributed 60/40 while profits are shared equally.

**6.  (a)**   When dividing the partnership loss of $33,000, first interest and salaries are allocated to the partners, **increasing** their capital balances.  This allocation of interest and salaries will also increase the amount of loss.  This increased loss amount would then be allocated to the partners, **decreasing** their capital accounts.  The computations are shown below.

| | *Fox* | *Greg* | *Howe* |
|---|---|---|---|
| Interest allowance (10% of avg. cap. balances) | $12,000 | $ 6,000 | $ 4,000 |
| Salaries | 30,000 | | 20,000 |
| Residual* ($105,000 ÷ 3) | (35,000) | (35,000) | (35,000) |
| Increase (decrease) in cap. account | $ 7,000 | $(29,000) | $(11,000) |

Thus, Fox's account increases by $7,000.

*The residual loss of $105,000 is the loss resulting after the interest and salary allowances are deducted [$33,000 loss – ($12,000 + $6,000 + $4,000) – ($30,000 + $20,000)].*

**7.  (c)**   The distribution of the partnership net income of $250,000 occurs in three steps as follows:

| *Step* | | *Axel* | *Berg* | *Cobb* |
|---|---|---|---|---|
| 1. | Axel:  10% of first $100,000, 20% over $100,000 | $ 10,000 30,000 | | |
| 2. | Berg & Cobb:  5% of remaining income over $150,000 [($250,000 – $10,000 – $30,000 – $150,000) × .05] | | $ 3,000 | $ 3,000 |
| 3. | Remaining allocated equally: [($250,000 – $10,000 – $30,000 – $3,000 – $3,000) × 1/3] | 68,000 | 68,000 | 68,000 |
| | Totals | $108,000 | $71,000 | $71,000 |

Thus, $108,000 would be distributed to Axel.

**8.  (b)**   We must first determine Simm's weighted-average capital balance for 2007 as follows:

| *Capital bal.* | × | *# of months/12* | = | *Weighted-avg.* |
|---|---|---|---|---|
| 140,000 | × | 6/12 | = | $ 70,000 |
| 180,000 | × | 1/12 | = | 15,000 |
| 165,000 | × | 5/12 | = | 68,750 |
| | | | | $153,750 |

The problem states that interest of 10% per year is to be credited to each partner's capital account, and 10% of Simm's weighted-average capital balance of $153,750 is $15,375.

**9.  (b)**   In both the case of a profit or a loss, Flat will have a greater advantage. When there is a profit, Flat will obtain a 20% bonus on profits before the bonus, and also take 40% of the profit after the bonus. Iron on the other hand, will only receive 60% of the profit after the bonus. The following example illustrates this:

|  | Flat | Iron | Profit |
|---|---|---|---|
| P & L ratio | 40% | 60% | 1,000 |
| 20% Bonus | 200 | 0 | (200) |
|  |  |  | 800 |
| Share in profit | 320 | 480 |  |
| Total distribution | 520 | 480 |  |

In the case of a loss, it can easily be seen that since Flat has a smaller percentage share in the loss that he has a greater advantage.

### D.3.a.(1)  Admission of a New Partner

**10.  (b)**   The requirement is to calculate the balances in the capital accounts of a partnership after the admission of a new partner. In this case, the new partner is investing $40,000 for a 1/3 interest in the new total capital of $150,000. No goodwill is recorded because the new capital ($150,000) equals the total of the old capital ($110,000) and Carter's investment ($40,000). However, a bonus of $10,000 is being credited to the new partner's capital account because his interest (1/3 of $150,000, or $50,000) exceeds his investment ($40,000). The bonus to the new partner is charged to the old partners in their profit and loss ratios as shown below.

| | |
|---|---|
| Blau [60,000 – 3/5 (10,000)] | $54,000 |
| Rubi [50,000 – 2/5 (10,000)] | 46,000 |
| Lind (150,000 ÷ 3) | 50,000 |
| | $150,000 |

**11.  (d)**   The requirement is to determine the balance in the new partner's capital account after admission using the bonus method. In this case, Grant is investing land with a FMV of $15,000 for a 1/5 interest in the new total capital of $95,000. Using the bonus method, the new capital $95,000 equals the total of the old capital plus Grant's investment ($60,000 + $20,000 + $15,000). Thus, a bonus of $4,000 is being credited to Grant's capital account because his interest (1/5 of $95,000, or $19,000) exceeds his investment ($15,000). The bonus to the new partner is charged to the old partners' capital accounts in their profit and loss ratios.

**12.  (c)**   The requirement is to determine the amount of goodwill implied by Zorn's investment. Zorn is investing $100,000 for a 1/3 interest in the partnership. Therefore, $100,000 represents 1/3 of the value of the equity of the new partnership ($100,000 ÷ 1/3 = $300,000). The tangible portion of the equity is $250,000 ($60,000 + $90,000 + $100,000). Thus, the total implied goodwill is $50,000 ($300,000 – $250,000).

**13.  (d)**   If no goodwill or bonus is to be recorded, the formula to determine the necessary contribution is

| Partnership interest of new partner | × | ( Capital bal. of existing + partners | Amount to be contributed ) | = | Amount to be contributed |
|---|---|---|---|---|---|

$$20\% \times (\$580,000 + x) = x$$
$$\$116,000 + .2x = x$$
$$\$116,000 = .8x$$
$$\$145,000 = x$$

An alternative computation is to divide the old partner's capital ($580,000) by their interest after the new partner's admission. The result is the total capital after admission ($580,000 ÷ 80% = $725,000). To compute the new partner's contribution, the old partners' capital can be subtracted from total capital ($725,000 – $580,000 = $145,000), or total capital can be multiplied by 20% (20% × $725,000 = $145,000).

**14.  (b)**   To determine the amount of cash distributed during liquidation, the solutions approach is to prepare an abbreviated statement of partnership liquidation. In a partnership liquidation, cash is distributed based on the capital balances of the partners **after** adjusting them for any income (loss) to the date of liquidation and any loans or advances between the partners and the partnership. The abbreviated statement follows:

|  | Alfa | Beda | Total |
|---|---|---|---|
| Beg. capital balance | $348,000 | $232,000 | $580,000 |
| Adj. for loans |  | (30,000) | (30,000) |
| Adj. for loss on sale |  |  |  |
| of assets* (60-40) | (75,000) | (50,000) | (125,000) |
| Adj. capital balance | $273,000 | 152,000 | $425,000 |

*($500,000 – $625,000)*

Note that the total cash available also equals $425,000.

| | |
|---|---|
| Beginning cash | $ 45,000 |
| Proceeds from sale | 500,000 |
| Payment of AP | (120,000) |
| | $425,000 |

Therefore, Alfa can receive $273,000 in cash in full liquidation of his capital balance.

**15.  (d)**   The bonus method implies that the old partners either received a bonus from the new partner, or they paid a bonus to the new partner. In this case, Colter, the new partner, contributed an amount in excess of the amount credited to Colter's capital account. Accordingly, the excess should be treated as a bonus to Adel and Brick. This bonus should be treated as an adjustment to the old partners' capital accounts and should be allocated by using Adel and Brick's old profit and loss ratio.

### D.3.a.(2)  Partner Death or Withdrawal

**16.  (c)**   Eddy is to be paid $180,000 for his 50% interest in the partnership. This implies that the net assets of the partnership are worth $360,000 ($180,000 ÷ 50%). Since the net assets are currently reported at $320,000, implied goodwill is $40,000 ($360,000 – $320,000). When goodwill is recorded, the goodwill account is debited and the partners' capital accounts are credited for their share of the goodwill. Therefore, the capital balances of Fox and Grimm are $108,000 and $72,000, as computed below.

|  | Fox | Grimm |
|---|---|---|
| Previous capital balance | $96,000 | $64,000 |
| Share of goodwill |  |  |
| Fox (30% × $40,000) | 12,000 |  |
| Grimm (20% × $40,000) | -- | 8,000 |
| New capital balance | $108,000 | $72,000 |

**17.  (b)**   Hamm will pay $140,000 for a 25% interest in the partnership. This implies that the net assets of the partnership, including the new investment, are worth $560,000

($140,000 ÷ 25%).  Net assets are currently reported at $320,000, and Hamm's cash payment of $140,000 brings that total up to $460,000.  Therefore, implied goodwill is $100,000 [$560,000 – ($320,000 + $140,000)].  When goodwill is recorded, the goodwill account is debited and the partners' capital accounts are credited for their share of goodwill.  Therefore, Eddy's capital balance ($160,000) is increased by his share of the goodwill (50% × $100,000 = $50,000), to result in a balance of $210,000 ($160,000 + $50,000).

**18.  (c)**  The requirement is to determine the balance in Maduro's capital account after Coll's retirement.  When a partner withdraws from a partnership a determination of the fair market value of the entity must be made.  Since it is stated in the problem that the withdrawing partner is selling his interest to the partnership and that no goodwill is to be recorded, the bonus method must be employed after re-statement of assets to FMV.  The capital accounts after re-statement to FMV would be

> Coll
> [$42,000 + 20%($216,000 – $180,000)] = $ 49,200
>
> Maduro
> [$39,000 + 20%($216,000 – $180,000)] = $ 46,200
>
> Prieto
> [$90,000 + 60%($216,000 – $180,000)] = $111,600

The bonus paid to Coll is the difference between the cash paid to him for his partnership interest and the balance of that interest plus his loan balance.

> Bonus = [$61,200 – ($49,200 + $9,000)] = $3,000

Maduro's capital account would be reduced by his propor-tionate share of the bonus, based on the profit and loss ratio of the remaining partners [20%/(20% + 60%) = 25%].

> Maduro's capital [$46,200 – 25% ($3,000)] = $45,450.

**19.  (d)**  Under both the bonus and goodwill methods, the assets of the partnership must first be restated to their fair market value.  Then, the withdrawing partner's capital ac-count must be adjusted to the amount that the withdrawing partner is expected to receive.  When the bonus method is used, no new goodwill is recorded.  Instead, the existing partners' capital accounts are reduced by the amount neces-sary to increase the withdrawing partner's capital to the amount s/he is to be paid.  When the goodwill method is used, new goodwill is recorded, and each partner's capital account is increased accordingly.  Therefore, the bonus method results in a **decrease** of existing partners' capital accounts, while the goodwill method results in an **increase** of existing partners' capital accounts.

**20.  (c)**  Under the bonus method, adjustments are made only among partner's capital accounts (no goodwill is re-corded on the partnership books).  Since Mill's partnership interest exceeded the amount of Mill's capital balance, the excess interest would reduce the capital balances of Yale and Lear.  Only under the goodwill method can the excess interest be recorded as goodwill.  Under no circumstances should the excess partnership interest be recorded as an ex-pense.

### D.4.  Partnership Liquidation

**21.  (a)**  This situation represents a simple liquidation since all assets are distributed at one point in time rather than in installments.  In a simple liquidation all of the non-

cash assets are sold and the proceeds from their sale are compared to their book value to compute the gain or loss.  The gain or loss on the assets is then distributed to the part-ners' accounts before any of the cash is distributed.  The partner loan should not be considered a noncash asset for the purpose of determining gain or loss, thus, Smith is responsi-ble to the partnership for the repayment of the entire amount of the loan.  The repayment of the loan reduces that partner's (Smith) distribution as follows:

| Partner balances before liquidation | Smith | Jones | Total |
|---|---|---|---|
| Loan (debit) | $(20,000) | | $(20,000) |
| Capital (credit) | 195,000 | $155,000 | 350,000 |
| Net balances | $175,000 | $155,000 | $330,000 |
| Loss on sale of other assets (450 – 385) | 39,000 | 26,000 | (65,000) |
| Cash available for partners | $136,000 | $129,000 | $265,000 |
| Cash available for credits | | | 120,000 |
| Total cash from sale of noncash assets | | | $385,000 |

**22.  (a)**  A schedule of safe payments must be prepared to determine the amount of cash to be distributed to each partner at January 15, 2007.  The first cash sale of other assets with a total book value of $150,000 realized $120,000 in cash, resulting in a $30,000 loss.  This loss is allocated among the partners based upon their profit and loss ratios.  The schedule is completed based upon the assumption that the remaining other assets are totally worthless, and their book values are distributed to the partners as losses, based upon the partners' profit and loss ratios.  The cash payments to each partner can be found at the bottom of the schedule.

| | Cash | O/A | Liab. |
|---|---|---|---|
| Beginning | $ 50 | $ 250 | $ 60 |
| Sale of assets | +120 | −150 | -- |
| | 170 | 100 | 60 |
| Dist. to creditors | −60 | -- | −60 |
| | 110 | 100 | 0 |
| Disposal of other assets | -- | −100 | -- |
| Dist. to partners | −110 | -- | -- |
| | 0 | 0 | 0 |

| | Capital | | |
|---|---|---|---|
| | C | D | E |
| Beginning | $80,000 | $90,000 | $70,000 |
| Sale of assets | −15,000 | −9,000 | −6,000 |
| | 65,000 | 81,000 | 64,000 |
| Disposal of other assets | −50,000 | −30,000 | −20,000 |
| | 15,000 | 51,000 | 44,000 |
| Dist. to partners | −15,000 | −51,000 | −44,000 |
| | 0 | 0 | 0 |

Thus, the cash should be distributed as follows: $15,000 to Cobb, $51,000 to Davis, and $44,000 to Eddy.

### D.5.  Incorporation of a Partnership

**23.  (d)**  When a partnership incorporates, assets and liabilities must be revalued to their fair market values on the date of incorporation.  In this case, the net assets have a fair market value of $92,000 ($80,000 + $12,000) and the amount to be credited to Additional Paid-in Capital is $82,000 ($92,000 – $10,000 par value).

**SOLUTIONS TO SIMULATION PROBLEMS**

**Simulation Problem 1**

| Situation | Liquidation Schedule | Schedule of Safe Payments | Incorporation of Partnership | Communication |
|---|---|---|---|---|

**Steps in Preparing Partnership Liquidation Schedule**

1. Net out loans to partners.
2. Sale of assets on January 30: FMV received minus book value given up = Gain/Loss on sale of assets $150,000 – $120,000 = $30,000 gain. Allocate gain as follows: Dove 50% × $30,000 = $15,000; Eagle $30,000 × 30% = $9,000; Falcon $30,000 × 20% = $6,000.
3. Sale of assets on February 5: $100,000 received – $180,000 carrying value = $80,000 loss. Allocate as follows: Dove $80,000 × 50% = $40,000 loss; Eagle $80,000 × 30% = $24,000 loss; Falcon $80,000 × 20% = $16,000 loss.
4. Pay liabilities $120,000.
5. Amount to distribute to partners: Dove = $125,000; Eagle = $35,000; Falcon = $50,000.

*Partnership of Dove, Eagle, and Falcon*
**SCHEDULE OF PARTNERSHIP LIQUIDATION**
*February 5, 2007*

| | Cash | Notes receivable | Plant, property, and equip. | Liabilities | Dove | Eagle | Falcon |
|---|---|---|---|---|---|---|---|
| Balances | $80,000 | $20,000 | $300,000 | $120,000 | $150,000 | $70,000 | $60,000 |
| Partner loans | | (20,000) | | | | (20,000) | |
| Sale of assets, Jan. 30 | 150,000 | | (120,000) | | 15,000 | 9,000 | 6,000 |
| Sale of assets, Feb. 5 | 100,000 | | (180,000) | | (40,000) | (24,000) | (16,000) |
| Payment of liabilities | (120,000) | | | (120,000) | | | |
| Amount distributed to each partner | $210,000 | $     -- | $     -- | $     -- | $125,000 | $35,000 | $50,000 |

| Situation | Liquidation Schedule | Schedule of Safe Payments | Incorporation of Partnership | Communication |
|---|---|---|---|---|

*Partnership of Dove, Eagle, and Falcon*
**SCHEDULE OF SAFE PAYMENTS**
*January 30, 2007*

| | Cash | Notes receivable | Plant, property, and equip. | Liabilities | Dove | Eagle | Falcon |
|---|---|---|---|---|---|---|---|
| Balances | 80,000 | 20,000 | 300,000 | 120,000 | 150,000 | 70,000 | 60,000 |
| Partner loans | | (20,000) | | | | (20,000) | |
| Sale of assets, Jan. 30 | 180,000 | | (160,000) | | 10,000 | 6,000 | 4,000 |
| Subtotal | 260,000 | 0 | 140,000 | 120,000 | 160,000 | 56,000 | 64,000 |
| Payment of liabilities | (120,000) | | | (120,000) | 0 | 0 | 0 |
| Subtotal | 140,000 | | (140,000) | 0 | 160,000 | 56,000 | 64,000 |
| Assume total loss on other assets | | | 140,000 | | (70,000) | (42,000) | (28,000) |
| Amount distributed to each partner | 140,000 | | | | 90,000 | 14,000 | 36,000 |

**Explanation of solutions**

Steps in the schedule of safe payments

1. Net out loans to partners.
2. Sale of assets results in a $20,000 gain which is allocated on a 5:3:2 basis.

   • Dove receives 50% × $20,000 = $10,000
   • Eagle receives 30% × $20,000 = $6,000
   • Falcon receives 20% × $20,000 = $4,000

3. Pay liabilities with cash.
4. Assume a total loss on other assets of $140,000.

   • Dove receives 50% × $140,000 of loss = $70,000 loss
   • Eagle receives 30% × $140,000 = $42,000 loss
   • Falcon receives 20% × $140,000 = $28,000 loss

5. Safe payment is made based on balances in the capital accounts.

| Situation | Liquidation Schedule | Schedule of Safe Payments | Incorporation of Partnership | Communication |
|---|---|---|---|---|

| | | | |
|---|---|---|---|
| Dove, capital | 175,000 | | |
| Eagle, capital | 65,000 | | |
| Falcon, capital | 70,000 | | |
| Common stock | | 200,000 | |
| Additional paid-in capital | | 110,000 | |

| | | | Communication |
|---|---|---|---|
| Situation | Liquidation Schedule | Schedule of Safe Payments | Incorporation of Partnership |

To:    Mr. Dove, Mr. Eagle, and Mr. Falcon
From:  CPA Candidate
Re:    Liquidation and safe payment schedules

This memorandum is designed to describe the difference between a liquidation schedule and a schedule of safe payment. A liquidation schedule is prepared to calculate the amount of cash to be distributed to each partner upon complete liquidation of the partnership. First, the assets are sold, and any gain or loss is recognized on the sale of assets. Each partner's account is adjusted for the gain or loss based on his/her profit/loss sharing ratio. Then, the liabilities are paid with cash, and the remaining cash is distributed to the partners.

A schedule of safe payment is prepared when partners desire a distribution before all of the partnership assets are sold, and the partnership is completely liquidated. First, some of the assets are sold, and the resulting gain or loss is recorded in each partner's capital account based on the profit/loss sharing ratio of each partner. The existing cash and cash proceeds from the sale of assets are used to pay all liabilities. Then, it is assumed that the remaining assets will be a total loss. This assumed loss is recorded in each partner's capital account, based on the profit/loss sharing ratio of each partner. The remaining cash is then distributed to the partners based on the ending capital balance in each account.

In either situation, if the partners have loans to or from the partnership, these loans are netted against the partner's capital account as the first step in the liquidation or safe payment schedule. For example, if a partner has a loan from the partnership for $10,000, the note receivable of the partnership is reduced by $10,000 and the partner's capital account is reduced by $10,000. Similarly, if a partner has loaned money to the partnership, the note payable account is reduced, and the partner's capital account is increased.

If you need assistance with preparing one of these schedules, please contact my office.

---

## Simulation Problem 2

| | Journal Entries | | | | |
|---|---|---|---|---|---|
| Situation | | Allocation of Income | Admission of New Partner | Partnership Liquidation | Communication |

Journal entry for Alkire's contribution

| | | |
|---|---|---|
| Cash | 40,000 | |
| Equipment | 60,000 | |
| Capital, Alkire | | 100,000 |

Journal entry for Higdon's contribution

| | | |
|---|---|---|
| Cash | 60,000 | |
| Inventory | 10,000 | |
| Building | 180,000 | |
| Note payable | | 50,000 |
| Capital, Higdon | | 200,000 |

| | | Allocation of Income | | | |
|---|---|---|---|---|---|
| Situation | Journal Entries | | Admission of New Partner | Partnership Liquidation | Communication |

| | Alkire | Higdon |
|---|---|---|
| Beginning capital balance | $100,000 | $200,000 |
| Interest on capital balance | 10,000 | 20,000 |
| Annual salary | 15,000 | 20,000 |
| Remainder | 48,000 | 72,000 |
| Ending capital balance | $173,000 | $312,000 |

**Explanation of solution**

Each partner receives 10% on beginning capital balance. Each partner receives his respective income ($15,000 to Alkire and $20,000 to Higdon). The amount distributed thus far is $65,000. The remainder to be distributed is $120,000 (185,000 – 30,000 – 35,000). Two-fifths of this remainder 2/5 × 120,000 = 48,000 is allocated to Alkire; 3/5 × $120,000 = 72,000 is allocated to Higdon. The total income allocated to Alkire is $73,000; total income allocated to Higdon is $112,000.

| Situation | Journal Entries | Allocation of Income | Admission of New Partner | Partnership Liquidation | Communication |
|---|---|---|---|---|---|

Entry for admission of Zukoski to the partnership

| | | |
|---|---|---|
| Cash | 175,000 | |
|  Capital, Zukoski | | 110,000 |
|  Capital, Alkire | | 26,000 |
|  Capital, Higdon | | 39,000 |

**Explanation of solution**

The book value of the partnership after the income distribution in 2007 was $485,000 (A = $173,000 and B = $312,000). After Zukoski's contribution, the value of the partnership is $485,000 + $175,000 = $660,000. A one-sixth interest in the partnership is $660,000 × 1/6 = $110,000. Using the bonus method, we calculate a bonus of $175,000 – $110,000 = $65,000. Using the 2:3 profit sharing ratio, the amount allocated to Alkire is 2/5 × $65,000 = $26,000; the amount allocated to Higdon is 3/5 × $65,000 = $39,000.

| Situation | Journal Entries | Allocation of Income | Admission of New Partner | Partnership Liquidation | Communication |
|---|---|---|---|---|---|

*Partnership of Alkire, Higdon, and Zukoski*
**SCHEDULE OF SAFE PAYMENTS**
*January 31, 2010*

| | Cash | Notes receivable | Plant, property, and equip. | Liabilities | Alkire | Higdon | Zukoski |
|---|---|---|---|---|---|---|---|
| Balances | $160,000 | $50,000 | $700,000 | $110,000 | $200,000 | $400,000 | $200,000 |
| Partner loans | | (50,000) | | | | (50,000) | |
| Sale of assets, Jan. (1) | 210,000 | | (180,000) | | 9,000 | 15,000 | (6,000) |
| Payment of liabilities | (110,000) | | | (110,000) | | | |
| Loss on other assets | | | (520,000) | | (156,000) | (260,000) | (104,000) |
| Safe payment to partners | $260,000 | | | | 53,000 | 105,000 | 102,000 |

**Explanation of solution**

(1) The sale of assets produced a $30,000 dividend gain, which is distributed to the partners based on the new profit sharing ratio: 30% to Alkire (9,000), 50% to Higdon (15,000), and 20% to Zukoski (6,000). Liabilities are paid. A total loss is assumed on other assets and the assumed loss of $520,000 is distributed 30% to Alkire (156,000), 50% to Higdon (260,000), and 20% to Zukoski (104,000).

| Situation | Journal Entries | Allocation of Income | Admission of New Partner | Partnership Liquidation | Communication |
|---|---|---|---|---|---|

To: Mr. Alkire
   Mr. Higdon
From: CPA Candidate
Re: Admission of new partner

This memorandum is designed to answer your questions regarding the admission of a new partner. When a partnership admits a new partner to the partnership, two situations can occur. If the new partner invests assets equal to the capital balance received, the new partner's capital account will be credited for that amount. However, if the amount invested is not equal to the capital balance received, the partnership must select an accounting method to calculate the new capital balances. The partnership may choose either the bonus method or the goodwill method.

The bonus method records the new partnership's capital by first calculating the new partnership's book value. The new book value is calculated by adding the old partnership capital plus the new partner's asset contribution. The new partner is then allocated his percentage of the share of purchased capital by taking his ownership percentage times the new book value of the firm. The old partner accounts are adjusted as if they had been paid a bonus (or in some cases, as if they had given a bonus to the new partner). The old partner accounts are adjusted based on their profit-loss sharing ratio.

In your case, Mr. Zukoski paid more than the partnership share allocated to him. This implies that the old partners received a bonus from the new partner, Mr. Zukoski. Prior to Zukoski's admission, the book value of the partnership was $485,000. After admitting Zukoski, the book value increased by $175,000 (the amount invested by Zukoski) to $660,000.

Mr. Zukoski would receive a 1/6 interest in the new capital balance of $660,000, and his capital account would be credited for $110,000.  The bonus of $65,000 ($175,000 – $110,000) would be allocated to the existing partners based on their 2:3 profit/loss sharing ratio.  Therefore, Alkire's capital balance would increase by $26,000, and Higdon's capital balance would increase by $39,000.

If you have any questions concerning these issues, please contact me.

## E.  Foreign Currency Translation

### 1.  Objective of Foreign Currency Translation

The rules for the translation of foreign currency into US dollars apply to two major areas.

a.  Foreign currency transactions which are denominated in other than a company's functional currency (e.g., exports, imports, loans), and

b.  Foreign currency financial statements of branches, divisions, subsidiaries, and other investees which are incorporated with the financial statements of a US company by combination, consolidation, or the equity method

The objectives of translation are

a.  To provide information relative to the expected economic effects of rate changes on an enterprise's cash flows and equity, and

b.  To provide information in consolidated statements relative to the financial results and relationships of each individual foreign consolidated entity as reflected by the functional currency of each reporting entity

The first objective influences the rules for the translation of foreign currency transactions, while both objectives influence the rules for the translation of foreign currency financial statements.  After working through this module, read through the outline of SFAS 52.

### 2.  Translation of Foreign Currency Statements

Assume that a US company has a 100% owned subsidiary in France.  The subsidiary's operations consist of leasing space in an office building.  Its balance sheet at December 31, 2007, and its income statement for 2007 are presented below.

**French Company**
**BALANCE SHEET**
*December 31, 2007*

| Assets | Euros | Liabilities and Owners' Equity | Euros |
|---|---|---|---|
| Cash | 60 | Accounts payable | 100 |
| Accounts receivable (net) | 100 | Mortgage payable | 200 |
| Land | 200 | Common stock | 100 |
| Building | 500 | Retained earnings | 360 |
| Less accumulated depr. | (100) | Total liabilities and | |
| Total assets | €760 | Owners' equity | €760 |

**French Company**
**INCOME STATEMENT**
*For Year Ended December 31, 2007*

| | |
|---|---|
| Revenues | €260 |
| Operating Expenses (excluding depreciation expense) | 140 |
| Depreciation expense | 20 |
| Net Income | €100 |

In addition to the information above, the following data are also needed for the translation process:

1.  Transactions involving land, building, mortgage payable, and common stock all occurred in 2005.

2.  No dividends were paid during the period 2005-2007.

3.  Exchange rates for various dates follow.

   €1 =  $.90 in 2005
   €1 =  $1.05 at beginning of 2007
   €1 =  $1.12 at end of 2007
   €1 =  $1.10 weighted-average for 2007

If the US company wants to present consolidated financial statements which include the results of its French subsidiary, the financial statements of the French company must be translated into US dollars.  However, before this can be accomplished, the management of the US company must determine the functional currency of its French subsidiary.  SFAS 52 defines an entity's functional currency as ". . .the currency of the primary economic environment in which the entity operates; normally, that is the currency of the environment in which an entity primarily generates and expends cash."  The decision concerning the functional currency is important because, once determined, it should be used consistently, unless it is clear that economic facts and circumstances have changed.  The selection of the functional currency depends upon an evaluation of several factors.  These factors include the following:

1.  Cash flows—Do the foreign entity's cash flows directly affect the parent's cash flows and are they immediately available for remittance to the parent?
2.  Sales prices—Are the foreign entity's sales prices responsive to exchange rate changes and to international competition?
3.  Sales markets—Is the foreign entity's sales market the parent's country or are sales denominated in the parent's currency?
4.  Expenses—Are the foreign entity's expenses incurred in the parent's country?
5.  Financing—Is the foreign entity's financing primarily from the parent or is it denominated in the parent's currency?
6.  Intercompany transactions—Is there a high volume of intercompany transactions between the parent and foreign entity?

If the answers to the questions above are predominantly yes, the functional currency would be the reporting currency of the parent (i.e., the US dollar).  On the other hand, if the answers to the questions were predominantly no, the functional currency would be the foreign currency.  In the example described previously, the euro would be the functional currency if the answers were no.  Note that the functional currency does not necessarily have to be the local currency of the foreign country when the answers to the questions are negative.  In other words, it is possible for a foreign currency other than the euro to be the functional currency of our French company.  For example, Swiss francs or British pounds could be the functional currency for the French company if one of these currencies is the currency of the primary economic environment in which the entity operates.  However, assume these other possibilities are not alternatives in the example mentioned previously.

If the circumstances indicate the euro to be the functional currency, SFAS 52 mandates that the current rate method be used for translation of the foreign currency financial statements.  The rules for applying the current rate method are

1.  All assets and liabilities are translated using the current rate at the balance sheet date.
2.  All revenues and expenses are translated at the rates in effect when these items are recognized during the period.  Due to practical considerations, however, weighted-average rates can be used to translate revenues and expenses which were incurred throughout the year.
3.  Owners' equity accounts are translated using historical exchange rates.
4.  Dividends are translated at the historic rate on the date of declaration.
5.  The translation adjustment for the period is reported as other comprehensive income under one of several acceptable reporting alternatives and the parent company's share of the accumulated amount is reported as accumulated other comprehensive income in the stockholders' equity section of the consolidated balance sheet.

This current rate method is illustrated below for the French financial statements shown previously.

**Current Rate Method**

*French Company*
**BALANCE SHEET**
*December 31, 2007*
*(Euro is Functional Currency)*

|  | Euros | Exchange rates | US dollars |
|---|---|---|---|
| **Assets** | | | |
| Cash | 60 | 1.12 | 67.20 |
| Accounts receivable (net) | 100 | 1.12 | 112.00 |
| Land | 200 | 1.12 | 224.00 |
| Building (net) | 400 | 1.12 | 448.00 |
| Totals | €760 | | $851.20 |
| **Liabilities and Owners' Equity** | | | |
| Accounts payable | 100 | 1.12 | 112.00 |
| Mortgage payable | 200 | 1.12 | 224.00 |
| Common stock | 100 | .90 | 90.00 |
| Retained earnings, 12/31/07 | 360 | see income statement | 352.00 |
| Translation adjustment (gain) | | | 73.20 (plug) |
| Totals | €760 | | $851.20 |

**French Company**
**COMBINED INCOME AND RETAINED EARNINGS STATEMENT**
*For the Year Ending December 31, 2007*

|  | Euros | Exchange rates | US dollars |
|---|---|---|---|
| Revenues | 260 | 1.10 | $ 286 |
| Operating expenses (excluding €20 of depreciation expense) | (140) | 1.10 | (154) |
| Depreciation expense | (20) | 1.10 | (22) |
| Net income | 100 | | 110 |
| **Retained earnings calculation:** | | | |
| Retained earnings at 1/1/07 | 260 | | 242* |
| Net income | 100 | | 110 |
| Retained earnings at 12/31/07 | €360 | | $352 |

> \* The US dollar amount of retained earnings results from applying weighted-average exchange rates to translate revenues and expenses during the period 2005 through 2007.  Retained earnings cannot be translated using a single exchange rate.  The beginning retained earnings would be taken from the prior period's translated financial statements.

The translation adjustments result from translating all assets and liabilities at the current rate, while owners' equity is translated using historical rates.  Common stock was issued in 2005 when the exchange rate was €1 = $.90.  The beginning balance of retained earnings for 2007 was accumulated during the period 2005 through 2006.  The new balance in ending retained earnings is placed on the balance sheet, and the translation adjustment is a plug figure to bring the balance sheet back into balance.  In this situation, there is a translation gain of $73.20 that is credited to other comprehensive income.

You can use a trial balance technique as shown below.  Translate all balance sheet and income statement items as indicated in the rules for the current rate method.  The foreign currency translation gain/loss is the amount that will bring the trial balance back into balance.

**French Company**
**TRIAL BALANCE**
*December 31, 2007*

|  | Euros DR | Euros CR | Exchange rates | US dollars DR | US dollars CR |
|---|---|---|---|---|---|
| Cash | 60 | | 1.12 | 67.20 | |
| Accounts rec. (net) | 100 | | 1.12 | 112.00 | |
| Land | 200 | | 1.12 | 224.00 | |
| Building (net) | 400 | | 1.12 | 448.00 | |
| Accounts payable | | 100 | 1.12 | | 112.00 |
| Mortgage payable | | 200 | 1.12 | | 224.00 |
| Common stock | | 100 | .90 | | 90.00 |
| Retained earnings 1/1/07 | | 260 | | | 242.00 |
| Revenues | | 260 | 1.10 | | 286.00 |
| Expenses | 140 | | 1.10 | 154.00 | |
| Depreciation exp. | 20 | | 1.10 | 22.00 | |
| Totals | €920 | €920 | | $1027.20 | $954.00 |
| Translation adjustment (gain) | | | | | 73.20 |
| Totals | | | | $1027.20 | $1027.20 |

The previous illustration of the current rate technique assumed the euro to be the functional currency.  Assume, however, that the circumstances were evaluated by the US company, and the US dollar was chosen as the functional currency.  Under this alternative, SFAS 52 requires the foreign currency financial statements to be remeasured into US dollars.  According to SFAS 52, the ". . .remeasurement process is intended to produce the same result as if the entity's books of record had been maintained in the functional currency."  If the US dollar is the functional currency, the remeasurement of foreign currency financial statements into US dollars results in a remeasurement gain or loss that is included in the subsidiary's income for the period.  The remeasurement process begins by classifying assets and liabilities as either monetary or nonmonetary items and then applying the appropriate exchange rate depending on whether the item is monetary or nonmonetary.

The following rules apply to the remeasurement process:

1. Monetary assets and monetary liabilities are remeasured using the current rate at the balance sheet date.
2. Nonmonetary assets and liabilities (e.g., land, building) which have historical cost balances are remeasured using historical exchange rates at the date the item entered the subsidiary.
3. Owners' equity accounts such as common stock and additional paid in capital are translated using historic rates.
4. Dividends is translated at the historic rate at the date of declaration
5. Retained earnings is brought forward from the translated statement of the previous year.
6. Revenues and most expenses that occur during a period are remeasured, for practical purposes, using the weighted-average exchange rate for the period.  However, revenues and expenses that represent allocations of historical balances (e.g. depreciation) are remeasured using the same historical exchange rates as used for those items on the balance sheet.
7. The remeasurement loss is reported on the consolidated income statement.  The loss is the result of a remeasurement process which assumes that the US dollar is the functional currency.
8. The calculation of the remeasurement loss is the result of the rules employed in the remeasurement process.  In mechanical terms, the remeasurement loss is the amount needed to make the debits equal the credits in the French company's US dollar trial balance.

The remeasurement process is illustrated below for the French subsidiary.

**Remeasurement Method**

### French Company
### BALANCE SHEET
### December 31, 2007
### (US dollar is Functional Currency)

| Assets | (Classification) | Euros | Exchange rates | US dollars |
|---|---|---|---|---|
|  |  | 60 |  |  |
| Cash | (Monetary) | 100 | 1.12 | 67.20 |
| Accounts receivable (net) | (Monetary) | 200 | 1.12 | 112.00 |
| Land | (Nonmonetary) | 400 | .90 | 180.00 |
| Building (net) | (Nonmonetary) | €760 | .90 | 360.00 |
| Totals |  |  |  | $719.20 |
| **Liabilities and Owners' Equity** |  |  |  |  |
| Accounts payable | (Monetary) | 100 | 1.12 | 112.00 |
| Mortgage payable | (Monetary) | 200 | 1.12 | 224.00 |
| Common stock |  | 100 | .90 | 90.00 |
| Retained earnings, 12/31/07 |  | 360 |  | 293.20 (plug) (A) |
| Totals |  | €760 |  | $719.20 |

The end retained earnings number is a plug figure to bring the balance sheet back into balance (**A**). This number is then used as end retained earnings in the statement of retained earnings to calculate net income after the remeasurement gain or loss (**B**).  The remeasurement gain or loss (**C**) is the plug figure needed on the income statement to arrive at the calculated net income figure (**B**).

### French Company
### COMBINED INCOME AND RETAINED EARNINGS STATEMENT
### For the Year Ending December 31, 2007

| | Euros | Exchange rates | US dollars | |
|---|---|---|---|---|
| Revenues | 260 | 1.10 | 286.00 | |
| Expenses (exclusive of depreciation) | (140) | 1.10 | (154.00) | |
| Depreciation | (20) | .90 | (18.00) | |
| Earnings before remeasurement loss | | | 114.00 | |
| Remeasurement loss | -- | -- | (40.80) | (plug) (**C**) |
| Net income (loss) | 100 | | 73.20 | (Taken from R/E Stmt) |
| **Calculation of retained earnings, net** | | | | |
| **Income and measurement loss:** | | | | |
| Retained earnings at 1/1/07 | 260 | | 220* | (given in problem) |
| Net income | | | 73.20 | (plug) (**B**) |
| Retained earnings at 12/31/07 | €360 | | $293.20 | (plug from balance sheet) |

* Retained earnings of $220 includes remeasured income from the period 2005 through 2006, which includes remeasurement losses applicable to those years due to the strengthening of the euro compared to the US dollar.  Beginning retained earnings were taken from the prior period's financial statements.

An easier way to calculate the foreign currency translation gain or loss is to use the trial balance approach. The remeasurement gain/loss is the amount needed to bring the trial balance back into balance. The trial balance approach is shown below.

*French Company*
**TRIAL BALANCE**
*December 31, 2007*

| | Euro DR | Euro CR | Exchange rates | US dollars DR | US dollars CR | |
|---|---|---|---|---|---|---|
| Cash | 60 | | 1.12 | 67.20 | | |
| Accounts rec. (net) | 100 | | 1.12 | 112.00 | | |
| Land | 200 | | .90 | 180.00 | | |
| Building (net) | 400 | | .90 | 360.00 | | |
| Accounts payable | | 100 | 1.12 | | 112.00 | |
| Mortgage payable | | 200 | 1.12 | | 224.00 | |
| Common stock | | 100 | .90 | | 90.00 | |
| Retained earnings 1/1/07 | | 260 | | | 220* | (given in problem) |
| Revenues | | 260 | 1.10 | | 286.00 | |
| Expenses | 140 | | 1.10 | 154.00 | | |
| Depreciation exp. | 20 | | .90 | 18.00 | | |
| Totals | €920 | €920 | | $891.20 | $932.00 | |
| Remeasurement loss | | | | 40.80 | -- | (plug) |
| Totals | | | | $932.00 | $932.00 | |

The significant points to remember about the French illustration are summarized below.

1.  Before foreign currency financial statements can be translated into US dollars, a decision must be made regarding the functional currency.

2.  If the functional currency is the foreign currency, the current rate method is used to translate to US dollars. All assets and liabilities are translated using the current rate at the balance sheet date. Owners' equity is translated using historical rates while revenues (and gains) and expenses (and losses) are translated at the rates in existence during the period when the transactions occurred. A weighted-average rate can be used for items occurring numerous times throughout the period. The translation adjustments (debit or credit) which result from the application of these rules are reported as a separate item in owners' equity in the consolidated balance sheet of the US parent.

3.  If the functional currency is the reporting currency (the US dollar), the foreign currency financial statements are remeasured into US dollars. All foreign currency balances are restated to US dollars using either historical or current exchange rates. Foreign currency balances which reflect prices from past transactions (e.g., inventories carried at cost, prepaid insurance, property, plant, and equipment, etc.) are remeasured using historical rates while foreign currency balances which reflect prices from current transactions (e.g., inventories and trading and available-for-sale securities carried at market, etc.) are remeasured using the current rate. Monetary assets and liabilities are remeasured using the current rate. (Deferred taxes are remeasured using the current rate.) Remeasurement gains/losses that result from the remeasurement process are reported on the consolidated income statement under "Other Income (Expense)."

The above summary can be arranged in tabular form as shown below.

| Functional currency | Functional currency determinants | Translation method | Reporting |
|---|---|---|---|
| Local currency of foreign company | a. Operations not integrated with parent's operations<br>b. Buying and selling activities primarily in local currency<br>c. Cash flows not immediately available for remittance to parent | Current Rate (All assets/ liabilities translated using current rate; revenues/expenses use weighted-average rate; equity accounts use historical rates) | Translation adjustments are reported as other comprehensive income under one of several acceptable reporting alternatives and as accumulated other comprehensive income in the equity section of consolidated balance sheet. Analysis of changes in accumulated translation adjustments disclosed via footnote |
| US Dollar | a. Operations integrated with parent's operations<br>b. Buying and selling activities primarily in US and/or US dollars<br>c. Cash flows immediately available for remittance to parent | Remeasurement (Monetary assets/ liabilities use current rate; historical cost balances use historical rates; revenues/ expenses use weighted-average rates and historical rates, the latter for allocations such as depr. exp.). | Remeasurement gain/loss is reported on the consolidated income statement. |

A few comments concerning the translation of foreign currency financial statements in highly inflationary economies should be made. If the cumulative inflation rate is $\geq 100\%$ over a three-year period in a foreign country, the foreign currency statements of a company located in that country are remeasured into the reporting currency (i.e., the US dollar). In other words, it is assumed the US dollar is the functional currency. The following flowchart summarizes the requirements of SFAS 52 with respect to foreign currency financial statements.

**FOREIGN CURRENCY FINANCIAL STATEMENTS**

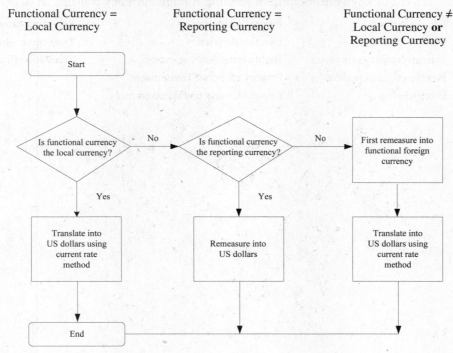

3. **Glossary**

**Foreign Currency Statements**

Financial statements that employ as the unit of measure a functional currency that is not the reporting currency of the enterprise.

**Foreign Currency Translation**

The process of expressing in the reporting currency of the enterprise those amounts that are denominated or measured in a different currency.

**Functional Currency**

An entity's functional currency is the currency of the primary economic environment in which the entity operates; normally, that is the currency of the environment in which an entity primarily generates and expends cash.

**Local Currency**

The currency of a particular country being referred to.

**Remeasurement**

If an entity's books and records are not kept in its functional currency, remeasurement into the functional currency is required. Monetary balances are translated using the current exchange rate and nonmonetary balances are translated using historical exchange rates. If the US dollar is the functional currency, remeasurement into the reporting currency (the US dollar) makes translation unnecessary.

**Reporting Currency**

The currency in which an enterprise prepares its financial statements.

**Translation Adjustments**

Translation adjustments result from the process of translating financial statements from the entity's functional currency into the reporting currency.

4. **Research Component**

SFAS 52 addresses the issues related to translation of financial statements. Notice that Appendix A outlines the considerations in determining the functional currency. Appendix B outlines the application of the remeasurement process and identifies accounts to be remeasured using historical exchange rates. Note that SFAS 52 was issued in December 1982; therefore, SFAS 52 does not contain any information regarding the inclusion of the translation gain or loss in other comprehensive income. The new rules for including a translation gain in other comprehensive income can be found in SFAS 130, *Reporting Comprehensive Income*.

Below is a list of keywords helpful in locating foreign currency translation issues.

| | | |
|---|---|---|
| Exchange rate | Foreign operations | Reporting currency |
| Foreign currency | Functional currency | Translation adjustment(s) |
| Foreign currency statements | Highly inflationary economy | Translation financial statement |
| Foreign currency translation | Primary economic environment | |
| Foreign entity | Remeasurement functional currency | |

## MULTIPLE-CHOICE QUESTIONS (1-9)

**1.** Certain balance sheet accounts of a foreign subsidiary of Rowan, Inc., at December 31, 2007, have been translated into US dollars as follows:

|  | Translated at | |
|---|---|---|
|  | *Current rates* | *Historical rates* |
| Note receivable, long-term | $240,000 | $200,000 |
| Prepaid rent | 85,000 | 80,000 |
| Patent | 150,000 | 170,000 |
|  | $475,000 | $450,000 |

The subsidiary's functional currency is the currency of the country in which it is located. What total amount should be included in Rowan's December 31, 2007 consolidated balance sheet for the above accounts?

- a. $450,000
- b. $455,000
- c. $475,000
- d. $495,000

**2.** A wholly owned subsidiary of Ward, Inc. has certain expense accounts for the year ended December 31, 2007, stated in local currency units (LCU) as follows:

|  | *LCU* |
|---|---|
| Depreciation of equipment (related assets were purchased January 1, 2005) | 120,000 |
| Provision for doubtful accounts | 80,000 |
| Rent | 200,000 |

The exchange rates at various dates are as follows:

|  | *Dollar equivalent of 1 LCU* |
|---|---|
| December 31, 2007 | $.40 |
| Average for year ended 12/31/07 | .44 |
| January 1, 2005 | .50 |

Assume that the LCU is the subsidiary's functional currency and that the charges to the expense accounts occurred approximately evenly during the year. What total dollar amount should be included in Ward's 2007 consolidated income statement to reflect these expenses?

- a. $160,000
- b. $168,000
- c. $176,000
- d. $183,200

**3.** Which of the following should be reported as a stockholders' equity account?

- a. Discount on convertible bonds.
- b. Premium on convertible bonds.
- c. Cumulative foreign exchange translation loss.
- d. Organization costs.

**4.** A foreign subsidiary's functional currency is its local currency, which has not experienced significant inflation. The weighted-average exchange rate for the current year would be the appropriate exchange rate for translating

|  | *Sales to customers* | *Wages expense* |
|---|---|---|
| a. | No | No |
| b. | Yes | Yes |
| c. | No | Yes |
| d. | Yes | No |

**5.** The functional currency of Nash, Inc.'s subsidiary is the French franc. Nash borrowed French francs as a partial hedge of its investment in the subsidiary. In preparing consolidated financial statements, Nash's translation loss on its investment in the subsidiary exceeded its exchange gain on

the borrowing. How should the effects of the loss and gain be reported in Nash's consolidated financial statements?

- a. The translation loss less the exchange gain is reported as other comprehensive income.
- b. The translation loss less the exchange gain is reported in net income.
- c. The translation loss is reported as other comprehensive income and the exchange gain is reported in net income.
- d. The translation loss is reported in net income and the exchange gain is reported as other comprehensive income.

**6.** A balance arising from the translation or remeasurement of a subsidiary's foreign currency financial statements is reported in the consolidated income statement when the subsidiary's functional currency is the

|  | *Foreign currency* | *US dollar* |
|---|---|---|
| a. | No | No |
| b. | No | Yes |
| c. | Yes | No |
| d. | Yes | Yes |

**7.** When remeasuring foreign currency financial statements into the functional currency, which of the following items would be remeasured using historical exchange rate?

- a. Inventories carried at cost.
- b. Marketable equity securities reported at market values.
- c. Bonds payable.
- d. Accrued liabilities.

**8.** Park Co.'s wholly owned subsidiary, Schnell Corp., maintains its accounting records in German marks. Because all of Schnell's branch offices are in Switzerland, its functional currency is the Swiss franc. Remeasurement of Schnell's 2007 financial statements resulted in a $7,600 gain, and translation of its financial statements resulted in an $8,100 gain. What amount should Park report as a foreign exchange gain as net income in its income statement for the year ended December 31, 2007?

- a. $0
- b. $ 7,600
- c. $ 8,100
- d. $15,700

**9.** In preparing consolidated financial statements of a US parent company with a foreign subsidiary, the foreign subsidiary's functional currency is the currency

- a. In which the subsidiary maintains its accounting records.
- b. Of the country in which the subsidiary is located.
- c. Of the country in which the parent is located.
- d. Of the environment in which the subsidiary primarily generates and expends cash.

**SIMULATION PROBLEMS**

**Simulation Problem 1**                         (45 to 55 minutes)

| Situation | | | | | | |
|---|---|---|---|---|---|---|
| | Concepts | Translation of Income Statement | Translation of Retained Earnings Statement | Translation of Balance Sheet | Communication | Research |

Your client, Jay, Inc., prepares consolidated financial statements, which include two subsidiaries, Jay Co. of Australia (Jay A), and Jay Co. of France (Jay F).  Jay A operates with US dollars, but maintains its financial statements in Australian dollars.  Jay F operates primarily with euros and maintains its financial statements in euros.

Your client has asked for assistance with translating the financial statements of Jay F into US dollars.  Below are the financial statements of Jay F in euros.

**Jay F**
**INCOME STATEMENT**
*For the year ended December 31, 2007*

| | In euros |
|---|---|
| Revenue | 650,000 |
| Cost of goods sold | (390,000) |
| Gross profit | 260,000 |
| Sales expense | (50,000) |
| General and administrative expense | (110,000) |
| Depreciation expense | (15,000) |
| Net income | 85,000 |

**Jay F**
**STATEMENT OF RETAINED EARNINGS**
*For the year ended December 31, 2007*

| | In euros |
|---|---|
| Beginning retained earnings, 1/1/07 | 140,000 |
| Add: Net income | 85,000 |
| Less: Dividends | 0 |
| End retained earnings, 12/3/07 | 225,000 |

**Jay F**
**BALANCE SHEET**
*December 31, 2007*

| | In euros |
|---|---|
| Assets: | |
| Cash | 18,000 |
| Accounts receivable | 42,000 |
| Inventory | 137,000 |
| Land | 120,000 |
| Building | 250,000 |
| Less: Accumulated depreciation | (30,000) |
| Total assets | 537,000 |
| | |
| Liabilities: | |
| Accounts payable | 49,000 |
| Note payable, due 12-5-2013 | 100,000 |
| Common stock | 50,000 |
| Additional paid-in capital | 113,000 |
| Retained earnings | 225,000 |
| | |
| Total liabilities and owners' equity | 537,000 |

*Additional information*

Jay F began operations on January 2, 2005.  All outstanding stock was issued on January 2, 2005.  Jay F earned the following income since the company began operations.  No dividends have been paid to date.

| Year | Income |
|---|---|
| 2005 | 60,000 |
| 2006 | 80,000 |

The exchange rates are as follows:

| Date | Dollars per euro |
|---|---|
| January 2, 2005 | 1.10 |
| January 1, 2007 | 1.24 |
| December 31, 2007 | 1.36 |
| Weighted-average rate 2005 | 1.15 |
| Weighted-average rate for 2006 | 1.18 |
| Weighted-average rate for 2007 | 1.31 |

| Situation | Concepts | Translation of Income Statement | Translation of Retained Earnings Statement | Translation of Balance Sheet | Communication | Research |
|---|---|---|---|---|---|---|

**Items 1 through 9** are based on the following:

A foreign subsidiary's trial balance is translated from its functional currency to the functional currency of the parent.

For each item determine which date the exchange rate from Table A should be used for the translation.  The subsidiary's functional currency is its **local** currency.

**TABLE A**

| | Event | Date |
|---|---|---|
| A. | Company begins | 12/31/05 |
| B. | Beginning of current year | 1/1/07 |
| C. | 1st quarter | 4/1/07 |
| D. | 2nd quarter | 7/1/07 |
| E. | 3rd quarter | 10/1/07 |
| F. | Year-end | 12/31/07 |
| G. | 1st quarter | 4/1/08 |
| H. | Year average | |
| I. | Average since acquisition | |
| J. | No translation rate used | |

Indicate the correct exchange rate by placing an x in the table in the appropriate box.

| | A 12/31/05 | B 1/1/07 | C 4/1/07 | D 7/1/07 | E 10/1/07 | F 12/31/07 | G 4/1/08 | H Year average | I Average since acquisition | J No translation rate used |
|---|---|---|---|---|---|---|---|---|---|---|
| **1.** Cash | | | | | | | | | | |
| **2.** Inventory that had been purchased evenly throughout the year | | | | | | | | | | |
| **3.** Account payable for equipment purchased on 4/1/07 | | | | | | | | | | |
| **4.** Cost of goods sold | | | | | | | | | | |
| **5.** Sales | | | | | | | | | | |
| **6.** Dividends declared on 10/1/07 | | | | | | | | | | |
| **7.** Dividends declared in (**6**) were paid 1/2/08 | | | | | | | | | | |
| **8.** Retained earnings | | | | | | | | | | |
| **9.** Common stock | | | | | | | | | | |

| Situation | Concepts | Translation of Income Statement | Translation of Retained Earnings Statement | Translation of Balance Sheet | Communication | Research |
|---|---|---|---|---|---|---|

Complete the following table for the foreign currency translation into US dollars for Jay F.

**Jay F**
**INCOME STATEMENT**
*For the year ended December 31, 2007*

| | In euros | Exchange rate | US dollars |
|---|---|---|---|
| Revenue | 650,000 | | |
| Cost of goods sold | (390,000) | | |
| Gross profit | 260,000 | | |
| Sales expense | (50,000) | | |
| General and administrative expense | (110,000) | | |
| Depreciation expense | (15,000) | | |
| Net income | 85,000 | | |

| Situation | Concepts | Translation of Income Statement | Translation of Retained Earnings Statement | Translation of Balance Sheet | Communication | Research |
|-----------|----------|--------------------------------|-------------------------------------------|-----------------------------|---------------|----------|

Complete the following table to translate the retained earnings of Jay F into US dollars.

### Jay F
### STATEMENT OF RETAINED EARNINGS
#### For the year ended December 31, 2007

|  | In euros | Exchange rate | US dollars |
|--|----------|---------------|------------|
| Beginning retained earnings, 1/1/07 |  |  |  |
| 2005 net income | 60,000 |  |  |
| 2006 net income | 80,000 |  |  |
| Net income for 2007 | 85,000 |  |  |
| Less: Dividends | 0 |  |  |
| End retained earnings, 12/31/07 | 225,000 |  |  |

| Situation | Concepts | Translation of Income Statement | Translation of Retained Earnings Statement | Translation of Balance Sheet | Communication | Research |
|-----------|----------|--------------------------------|-------------------------------------------|-----------------------------|---------------|----------|

Complete the following table to translate the balance sheet accounts of Jay F into US dollars.

### Jay F
### BALANCE SHEET
#### December 31, 2007

|  | In euros | Exchange rate | Translation into US dollars |
|--|----------|---------------|------------------------------|
| Assets: |  |  |  |
| Cash | 18,000 |  |  |
| Accounts receivable | 42,000 |  |  |
| Inventory | 137,000 |  |  |
| Land | 120,000 |  |  |
| Building | 250,000 |  |  |
| Less: Accumulated depreciation | (30,000) |  |  |
| Total assets | 537,000 |  |  |
|  |  |  |  |
| Liabilities: |  |  |  |
| Accounts payable | 49,000 |  |  |
| Note payable, due 12-5-2013 | 100,000 |  |  |
| Common stock | 50,000 |  |  |
| Additional paid in capital | 113,000 |  |  |
| Retained earnings | 225,000 |  |  |
| Other comprehensive income (foreign currency translation adjustment) | -0- |  |  |
| Total liabilities and owners' equity | 537,000 |  |  |

| Situation | Concepts | Translation of Income Statement | Translation of Retained Earnings Statement | Translation of Balance Sheet | Communication | Research |
|-----------|----------|--------------------------------|-------------------------------------------|-----------------------------|---------------|----------|

Write a memorandum to the CEO of Jay F Co. Explain the objectives of translating the company's subsidiary financial statements.

To:    CEO, Jay F Co.
From: CPA Candidate
Re:    Translating foreign subsidiary financial statements

| | | | | | | Research |
|---|---|---|---|---|---|---|
| Situation | Concepts | Translation of Income Statement | Translation of Retained Earnings Statement | Translation of Balance Sheet | Communication | |

Research each of the following issues using the authoritative literature, and cut and paste paragraph(s) that address the issue.

1. What are the objectives of translating a foreign subsidiary's financial statements?

2. How are gains and losses arising from remeasuring Jay A subsidiary's financial statements reported on Jay Inc.'s consolidated financial statements?

3. How are gains and losses arising from translating Jay F subsidiary's financial statements measured and reported in Jay Inc. consolidated financial statements?

4. The financial accounting standards identify several economic indicators that are to be considered both individually and collectively in determining the functional currency for a consolidated subsidiary. List three of those indicators.

5. What exchange rate is used to incorporate Jay F's assets, liabilities, revenues, and expenses in Jay Inc.'s consolidated financial statements on 12/31/07?

## MULTIPLE-CHOICE ANSWERS

| | | | | | |
|---|---|---|---|---|---|
| 1.  c  __ __ | 4.  b  __ __ | 6.  b  __ __ | 8.  b  __ __ | | |
| 2.  c  __ __ | 5.  a  __ __ | 7.  a  __ __ | 9.  d  __ __ | 1st:  __/9 = __% | |
| 3.  c  __ __ | | | | 2nd:  __/9 = __% | |

## MULTIPLE-CHOICE ANSWER EXPLANATIONS

### E.2.  Translation of Foreign Currency Statements

**1.   (c)**   When the **functional currency** of a foreign subsidiary is the **foreign currency,** asset and liability accounts are **translated** using the **current** exchange rate (the rate of translation in effect at the balance sheet date).  Therefore, these accounts should be included in the balance sheet at $475,000.  Note that if the **functional currency** was the **US dollar,** balance sheet accounts would be **remeasured** using a combination of **historical and current rates**.

**2.   (c)**   The requirement is to determine the total amount of various expenses incurred by a foreign subsidiary which should be reported in the 2007 consolidated income statement.  SFAS 52 states that if the foreign currency is the functional currency of the subsidiary, the **current rate** method should be used to translate the financial statements.  In this method, revenues and expenses are translated at the rates in effect at the time these items were recognized during the period.  Because translation at the date the revenues and expenses were recognized is generally deemed impractical, SFAS 52 allows that an appropriate weighted-average rate may be used to translate these items.  This results in a translated expense of $176,000 [($120,000 + $80,000 + $200,000) × .44].

**3.   (c)**   The requirement is to determine which item is reported in the stockholders' equity section.  According to SFAS 52 and 130, accumulated gains and losses on certain foreign currency transactions should be reported as a component of stockholders' equity entitled other comprehensive income.  Answers (a), (b), and (d) are incorrect because these items are reported on the balance sheet in the assets and liabilities sections and are amortized over their respective lives.

**4.   (b)**   SFAS 52 mandates the current rate method for the translation of foreign currency financial statements when a foreign subsidiary's functional currency is its local currency.  Using the current rate method, revenue and expenses should be translated into US dollars at the weighted-average rate for the current year.  Thus, both sales to customers and wages expense should be translated at the weighted-average rate.

**5.   (a)**   According to SFAS 52 and SFAS 130, translation adjustments resulting from the translation of foreign currency statements should be reported separately as components of other comprehensive income, accumulated other comprehensive income,  and stockholders' equity.  Additionally, gains and losses on certain foreign currency transactions should also be reported similarly.  Those gains and losses which should be excluded from net income and instead reported as components of other comprehensive income and of accumulated other comprehensive income in stockholders' equity include foreign currency transactions designated as economic hedges of a net investment in a foreign entity.  Thus, both the translation loss and the exchange gain are to be reported as other comprehensive income and

accumulated other comprehensive income in the stockholders' equity section of the balance sheet.  Because the translation loss on the investment exceeds the exchange gain on the borrowing, the translation loss less the exchange gain is the amount to be reported as separate components of other comprehensive income and accumulated other comprehensive income equity in the consolidated financial statements.

**6.   (b)**   Per SFAS 52, **translation** adjustments result from translating an entity's financial statements into the reporting currency.  Such adjustments, which result when the entity's functional currency is the **foreign currency,** should not be included in net income.  Instead, such adjustments should be reported as other comprehensive income and accumulated other comprehensive income in the stockholders' equity section of the balance sheet.  If the functional currency is the **reporting currency** (US dollar), a **remeasurement** process takes place, with the resulting gain or loss included in net income.

**7.   (a)**   The requirement is to determine which item would be remeasured using historical exchange rates when foreign currency financial statements are being remeasured into the functional currency.  Per SFAS 52, when an entity's books are not maintained in the functional currency, it is necessary to use historical exchange rates in the remeasurement process of certain accounts.  Among the accounts listed is inventories carried at cost.  Only marketable equity securities reported at **cost** would be remeasured using historical exchange rates.  Bonds payable and accrued liabilities would be remeasured at the current rate.

**8.   (b)**   Schnell's accounting records are kept in German marks, and its functional currency is the Swiss franc.  Before Schnell's financial statements can be consolidated with Park's financial statements, they must be remeasured from German marks to Swiss francs, and then translated from Swiss francs to US dollars.  As a result of these restatements, there is a remeasurement gain of $7,600, and a credit translation adjustment of $8,100.  SFAS 52 states that a remeasurement gain or loss is included in net income, but a translation adjustment is **not**.  Therefore, Park would report a foreign exchange gain of $7,600 in its 2007 income statement.

**9.   (d)**   SFAS 52, *Foreign Currency Translation*, defines an entity's functional currency as the currency of the primary economic environment in which the entity operates; normally, that is the currency of the environment in which an entity primarily generates and expends cash.

**SOLUTIONS TO SIMULATION PROBLEMS**

**Simulation Problem 1**

| Situation | Concepts | Translation of Income Statement | | Translation of Retained Earnings Statement | | Translation of Balance Sheet | | Communication | Research |
|---|---|---|---|---|---|---|---|---|---|
| | | A | B | C | D | E | F | G | H | I | J |
| | | *12/31/05* | *1/1/07* | *4/1/07* | *7/1/07* | *10/1/07* | *12/31/07* | *4/1/08* | *Year average* | *Average since acquisition* | *No translation rate used* |
| 1. Cash | | | | | | | x | | | | |
| 2. Inventory that had been purchased evenly throughout the year | | | | | | | x | | | | |
| 3. Account payable for equipment purchased on 4/1/07 | | | | | | | x | | | | |
| 4. Cost of goods sold | | | | | | | | | x | | |
| 5. Sales | | | | | | | | | x | | |
| 6. Dividends declared on 10/1/07 | | | | | | x | | | | | |
| 7. Dividends declared in (6) were paid 1/2/08 | | | | | | | x | | | | |
| 8. Retained earnings | | | | | | | | | | | x |
| 9. Common stock | | x | | | | | | | | | |

**Explanation of solutions**

1.   (**F**)  Assets are valued at the current rate at year-end.

2.   (**F**)  Assets are valued at the current rate at year-end.

3.   (**F**)  Liabilities are valued at the current rate at year-end.

4.   (**H**)  Expense accounts are valued at the average rate for the current year of business.

5.   (**H**)  Revenue accounts are valued at the average rate for the current year of business.

6.   (**E**)  Dividends are valued at the rate of the date of declaration.

7.   (**F**)  Liabilities (dividends payable) are valued at the current rate at year-end.

8.   (**J**)  The retained earnings are carried over from 1/1/07 with the translated net income added and translated dividends subtracted.

9.   (**A**)  Common stock is valued at the historical rate when it was issued.

| Situation | Concepts | Translation of Income Statement | Translation of Retained Earnings Statement | Translation of Balance Sheet | Communication | Research |
|---|---|---|---|---|---|---|

Complete the following table for the foreign currency translation into US dollars for Jay F.

**Jay F**
**INCOME STATEMENT**
*For the year ended December 31, 2007*

| | In euros | Exchange rate | US dollars |
|---|---|---|---|
| Revenue | 650,000 | 1.31 | $ 851,500 |
| Cost of goods sold | (390,000) | 1.31 | (510,000) |
| Gross profit | 260,000 | 1.31 | 340,600 |
| Sales expense | (50,000) | 1.31 | (65,500) |
| General and administrative expense | (110,000) | 1.31 | (144,100) |
| Depreciation expense | (15,000) | 1.31 | (19,650) |
| Net income | 85,000 | 1.31 | $ 111,350 |

| Situation | Concepts | Translation of Income Statement | Translation of Retained Earnings Statement | Translation of Balance Sheet | Communication | Research |
|-----------|----------|--------------------------------|-------------------------------------------|------------------------------|---------------|----------|

Complete the following table to translate the retained earnings of Jay F into US dollars.

### Jay F
### STATEMENT OF RETAINED EARNINGS
#### For the year ended December 31, 2007

|  | In euros | Exchange rate | US dollars |
|--|----------|---------------|------------|
| Beginning retained earnings, 1/1/07 |  |  |  |
|     2005 net income | 60,000 | 1.15 | $ 69,000 |
|     2006 net income | 80,000 | 1.18 | 94,400 |
| Net income for 2007 | 85,000 | 1.31 | 111,350 |
| Less: Dividends | 0 |  |  |
| End retained earnings, 12/31/07 | 225,000 |  | $274,750 |

| Situation | Concepts | Translation of Income Statement | Translation of Retained Earnings Statement | Translation of Balance Sheet | Communication | Research |
|-----------|----------|--------------------------------|-------------------------------------------|------------------------------|---------------|----------|

Complete the following table to translate the balance sheet accounts of Jay F into US dollars.

### Jay F
### BALANCE SHEET
#### December 31, 2007

|  | In euros | Exchange rate | Translation into US dollars |
|--|----------|---------------|------------------------------|
| Assets: |  |  |  |
|     Cash | 18,000 | 1.36 | $24,480 |
|     Accounts receivable | 42,000 | 1.36 | 57,120 |
|     Inventory | 137,000 | 1.36 | 186,320 |
|     Land | 120,000 | 1.36 | 163,200 |
|     Building | 250,000 | 1.36 | 340,000 |
|     Less: Accumulated depreciation | (30,000) | 1.36 | (40,800) |
|     Total assets | 537,000 |  | $730,320 |
|  |  |  |  |
| Liabilities: |  |  |  |
|     Accounts payable | 49,000 | 1.36 | $66,640 |
|     Note payable, due 12-5-2013 | 100,000 | 1.36 | 136,000 |
|     Common stock | 50,000 | 1.10 | 55,000 |
|     Additional paid in capital | 113,000 | 1.10 | 124,300 |
|     Retained earnings | 225,000 |  | 274,750 |
| Other comprehensive income (foreign currency translation adjustment) | -0- |  | 73,630 |
|     Total liabilities and owners' equity | 537,000 |  | $730,320 |

**Explanation of solutions**

For Jay F, the functional currency is the foreign currency (euros).

Therefore, the current rate method is used.

The following rules apply to the current rate method:

- Assets and liabilities—use current rate at balance sheet date
- Revenues and expenses—use weighted-average rate (or rate at time of exchange if known)
- Owners' equity—use historical rates
- Dividends—use historical rates

Because Jay F's retained earnings is from three years, each year must be translated at the appropriate rate. The weighted-average rate is used for each year.

The translation gain is the plug figure to bring the balance sheet into balance, and is reported as "other comprehensive income" in the owners' equity section of the balance sheet.

Total assets = $730,320

Total liabilities + Owners' equity **before** translation adjustment = $656,690

Translation adjustment = $730,320 − 656,690 = $73,630.

| Situation | Concepts | Translation of Income Statement | Translation of Retained Earnings Statement | Translation of Balance Sheet | Communication | Research |
|---|---|---|---|---|---|---|

To:      CEO, Jay Co.
From:   CPA Candidate
Re:      Translating foreign subsidiary financial statements

     You have asked us to explain the objectives of translating your company's foreign subsidiary's financial statements. The primary reason for translation is to allow the consolidation of the financial statements of Jay Co. with its foreign subsidiary. In addition, translation provides users information about the effects of currency rate changes on the consolidated company's financial statements.

     If you have additional questions, please contact us.

| Situation | Concepts | Translation of Income Statement | Translation of Retained Earnings Statement | Translation of Balance Sheet | Communication | Research |
|---|---|---|---|---|---|---|

**1.** What are the objectives of translating a foreign subsidiary's financial statements?

**Objectives of Translation**
**FAS52, Para 4 or Current Text F60.103**

4. Financial statements are intended to present information in financial terms about the performance, financial position, and cash flows of an enterprise. For this purpose, the financial statements of separate entities within an enterprise, which may exist and operate in different economic and currency environments, are consolidated and presented as though they were the financial statements of a single enterprise. Because it is not possible to combine, add, or subtract measurements expressed in different currencies, it is necessary to translate into a single reporting currency those assets, liabilities, revenues, expenses, gains, and losses that are measured or denominated in a foreign currency. However, the unity presented by such translation does not alter the underlying significance of the results and relationships of the constituent parts of the enterprise. It is only through the effective operation of its constituent parts that the enterprise as a whole is able to achieve its purpose. Accordingly, the translation of the financial statements of each component entity of an enterprise should accomplish the following objectives:

    a.  Provide information that is generally compatible with the expected economic effects of a rate change on an enterprise's cash flows and equity.

    b.  Reflect in consolidated statements the financial results and relationships of the individual consolidated entities as measured in their functional currencies in conformity with US generally accepted accounting principles.

**FAS52, Para 10 or Current Text F60.115**

10. If an entity's books of record are not maintained in its functional currency, remeasurement into the functional currency is required. That remeasurement is required before translation into the reporting currency. If a foreign entity's functional currency is the reporting currency, remeasurement into the reporting currency obviates translation. The remeasurement process is intended to produce the same results as if the entity's books of record had been maintained in the functional currency. The remeasurement of and subsequent accounting for transactions denominated in a currency other than the functional currency shall be in accordance with the requirements of this Statement (paragraphs 15 and 16). Appendix B provides guidance for remeasurement into the functional currency.

**FAS52, Para 15 or Current Text F60.122**

15. Foreign currency transactions are transactions denominated in a currency other than the entity's functional currency. Foreign currency transactions may produce receivables or payables that are fixed in terms of the amount of foreign currency that will be re-

**2.** How are gains and losses arising from remeasuring Jay A subsidiary's financial statements reported on Jay Inc.'s consolidated financial statements?

ceived or paid.  A change in exchange rates between the functional currency and the currency in which a transaction is denominated increases or decreases the expected amount of functional currency cash flows upon settlement of the transaction.  That increase or decrease in expected functional currency cash flows is a foreign currency transaction gain or loss that generally shall be included in determining net income for the period in which the exchange rate changes.  Likewise, a transaction gain or loss (measured from the transaction date or the most recent intervening balance sheet date, whichever is later) realized upon settlement of a foreign currency transaction generally shall be included in determining net income for the period in which the transaction is settled.  The exceptions to this requirement for inclusion in net income of transaction gains and losses are set forth in paragraphs 20 and 21 and pertain to certain intercompany transactions and to transactions that are designated as, and effective as, economic hedges of net investments and foreign currency commitments.

**3.**  How are gains and losses arising from translating Jay F subsidiary's financial statements measured and reported in Jay Inc. consolidated financial statements?

**Translation of Foreign Currency Statements**
**FAS52, Para 12 or Current Text F60.118**

12.  All elements of financial statements shall be translated by using a current exchange rate.  For assets and liabilities, the exchange rate at the balance sheet date shall be used.  For revenues, expenses, gains, and losses, the exchange rate at the dates on which those elements are recognized shall be used.   Because translation at the exchange rates at the dates the numerous revenues, expenses, gains, and losses are recognized is generally impractical, an appropriately weighted-average exchange rate for the period may be used to translate those elements.

**FAS135, Para 4(1) or Current Text F60.134**

1.  FASB Statement 52, *Foreign Currency Translation*.

(1)  In paragraph 24, a separate component of equity in the  second sentence and that separate component of equity in the last sentence are replaced by other comprehensive income (effectively amended by FASB Statement 130, *Reporting Comprehensive Income*).

**FAS52, Para 41 or Current Text F60.109**

41.  The Board has developed, with significant input from its task force and other advisors, the following general guidance on indicators of facts to be considered in identifying the functional currency.  In those instances in which the indicators are mixed and the functional currency is not obvious, management's judgment will be required in order to determine the functional currency that most faithfully portrays the economic results of the entity's operations and thereby best achieves the objectives of foreign currency translation set forth in paragraph 4.  Management is in the best position to obtain the pertinent facts and weigh their relative importance in determining the functional currency for each operation.  It is important to recognize that management's judgment is essential and paramount in this determination, provided only that it is not contradicted by the facts.

**4.**  The financial accounting standards identify several economic indicators that are to be considered both individually and collectively in determining the functional currency for a consolidated subsidiary.  List three of those indicators.

**FAS52, Para 42 or Current Text F60.110**

42.  The salient economic factors set forth below, and possibly others, should be considered both individually and collectively when determining the functional currency.

    a.    Cash flow indicators

        (1)  Foreign currency—Cash flows related to the foreign entity's individual assets and liabilities are primarily in the foreign currency and do not directly impact the parent company's cash flows.

        (2)  Parent's currency—Cash flows related to the foreign entity's individual assets and liabilities directly im-

pact the parent's cash flows on a current basis and are readily available for remittance to the parent company.

b. Sales price indicators

(1) Foreign currency—Sales prices for the foreign entity's products are not primarily responsive in a short-term basis to changes in exchange rates but are determined more by local competition or local government regulation.

(2) Parent's currency—Sales prices for the foreign entity's products are primarily responsive on a short-term basis to changes in exchange rates; for example, sales prices are determined more by worldwide competition or by international prices.

c. Sales market indicators

(1) Foreign currency—There is an active local sales market for the foreign entity's products, although there also might be significant amounts of exports.

(2) Parent's currency—The sales market is mostly in the parent's country or sales contracts are denominated in the parent's currency.

d. Expense indicators

(1) Foreign currency—Labor, materials, and other costs for the foreign entity's products or services are primarily local costs, even though there also might be imports from other countries.

(2) Parent's currency—Labor, materials, and other costs for the foreign entity's products or services, on a continuing basis, are primarily costs for components obtained from the country in which the parent company is located.

e. Financing indicators

(1) Foreign currency—Financing is primarily denominated in foreign currency, and funds generated by the foreign entity's operations are sufficient to service existing and normally expected debt obligations.

(2) Parent's currency—Financing is primarily from the parent or other dollar-denominated obligations, or funds generated by the foreign entity's operations are not sufficient to service existing and normally expected debt obligations without the infusion of additional funds from the parent company. Infusion of additional funds from the parent company for expansion is not a factor, provided funds generated by the foreign entity's expanded operations are expected to be sufficient to service that additional financing.

f. Intercompany transactions and arrangements indicators

(1) Foreign currency—There is a low volume of intercompany transactions and there is not an extensive interrelationship between the operations of the foreign entity and the parent company. However, the foreign entity's operations may rely on the parent's or affiliates' competitive advantages, such as patents and trademarks.

(2) Parent's currency—There is a high volume of intercompany transactions and there is an extensive interrelationship between the operations of the foreign entity and the parent company. Additionally, the parent's currency generally would be the functional currency if the foreign entity is a device or shell corporation for holding investments, obligations, intangible

**5.** What exchange rate is used to incorporate Jay
F's assets, liabilities, revenues, and expenses
in Jay Inc.'s consolidated financial statements
on 12/31/07?

assets, etc., that could readily be carried on the parent's or an affiliate's books.

**Translation of Foreign Currency Statements
FAS52, Para 12 or Current Text F60.118**

12.  All elements of financial statements shall be translated by using
a current exchange rate.  For assets and liabilities, the exchange rate
at the balance sheet date shall be used.  For revenues, expenses,
gains, and losses, the exchange rate at the dates on which those
elements are recognized shall be used.   Because translation at the
exchange rates at the dates the numerous revenues, expenses, gains,
and losses are recognized is generally impractical, an appropriately
weighted-average exchange rate for the period may be used to
translate those elements.

# GOVERNMENTAL (STATE AND LOCAL) ACCOUNTING

Governmental accounting has many similarities to commercial accounting.  For example, governmental accounting uses the double-entry system, journals, ledgers, trial balances, financial statements, internal control, etc.  Differences arise due to the objectives and environment of government.  The major differences include

1.   The absence of a profit motive, except for governmental enterprises, such as utilities
2.   A legal emphasis that involves restrictions both in the raising and spending of revenues
3.   An inability to "match" revenues with expenditures, as revenues are often provided by persons other than those receiving the services
4.   An emphasis on accountability or stewardship of resources entrusted to public officials
5.   The use of fund accounting and reporting, as well as government-wide reporting
6.   The recording of the budget in some funds
7.   The use of modified accrual accounting rather than full accrual accounting in some funds

As mentioned earlier, the Governmental Accounting Standards Board (GASB) has the authority to establish standards of financial reporting for all units of state and local government.  The GASB was created in 1984 and replaced the National Council on Governmental Accounting (NCGA).  Current pronouncements (level "A" GAAP) are reflected in the *Codification of Governmental Accounting and Financial Reporting Standards*, issued by the GASB each year.  Level "B" GAAP are contained in the AICPA Audit and Accounting Guide, *Audits of State and Local Governmental Units*, issued each year.  To date, the GASB has issued (as of this writing) 39 Statements, 6 Interpretations, and 2 Concepts Statements.  The GASB has authority under the AICPA Ethics Rule 203, *Accounting Principles*.

## A.  The Government Reporting Model

GASB 34 provides requirements that constitute the minimum required to be in compliance with GAAP.  These requirements for **general-purpose** governmental units (states, municipalities, counties) are

- Management's Discussion and Analysis (MD&A) (Required Supplementary Information)
- Government-Wide Financial Statements
    Statement of Net Assets
    Statement of Activities
- Fund Financial Statements
    Governmental Funds
        Balance Sheet
        Statement of Revenues, Expenditures, and Changes in Fund Balances
    Proprietary Funds
        Statement of Net Assets (or Balance Sheet)
        Statement of Revenues, Expenses, and Changes in Fund Net Assets (or Fund Equity)
        Statement of Cash Flows
    Fiduciary Funds
        Statement of Fiduciary Net Assets
        Statement of Changes in Fiduciary Net Assets
- Notes to the Financial Statements
- Required Supplementary Information (RSI) other than Management's Discussion and Analysis
    Schedule of Funding Progress (for Entities Reporting Pension Trust Funds)
    Schedule of Employer Contributions (for Entities Reporting Pension Trust Funds)
    Budgetary Comparison Schedules
    Information about Infrastructure Assets (for Entities Reported Using the Modified Approach)
    Claims Development Information When the Government Sponsors a Public Entity Risk Pool

In addition, general-purpose governments may choose to provide certain **other supplementary information,** including combining statements for nonmajor funds.  If a government wishes to prepare a complete **Comprehensive Annual Financial Report (CAFR),** three major sections would be included.  First, an **introductory section** (unaudited) would include a letter of transmittal, organization chart, and list of principal officials.  Second, a **financial section** would be prepared, including an auditor's report, the required information, and other supplementary information listed above.  Finally, a **statistical section** would include a number of schedules such as net assets by component, changes in net assets, revenue capacity, debt capacity, and demographic and economic statistics.

**Special-purpose governments** include park districts, tollway authorities, school districts, and sanitation districts. GASB has categorized special-purpose governments as those that are engaged in governmental activities, business-type activities, fiduciary activities, and both governmental and business-type activities. Special-purpose governments that are engaged in governmental activities and have more than one program and special-purpose governments that are engaged in both governmental and business-type activities must prepare both the government-wide and fund financial statements. Special-purpose governments that are engaged in a single governmental activity (such as a cemetery district) may combine the government-wide and fund financial statements or use other methods allowed by GASB. Special-purpose governments that are engaged in only business-type activities or fiduciary activities are not required to prepare the government-wide statements, but only prepare the proprietary or fiduciary fund statements. All governments must include the MD&A, Notes, and RSI.

Public colleges and universities and other governmental not-for-profit organizations may choose to report as special-purpose governments engaged in only business-type activities, engaged in only governmental activities, or engaged in both governmental and business-type activities.

**B.  The Reporting Entity**

The GASB carefully defines the **reporting entity** in an effort to ensure that all boards, commissions, agencies, etc. that are under the control of the reporting entity are included. A **primary government** is either (1) a state government, (2) a general-purpose local government, or (3) a special-purpose local government that has a separately elected governing body, is legally separate, and is fiscally independent of other state or local governments. A **component unit** is a legally separate organization for which the elected officials of a primary government are financially accountable, or for which the nature and significance of their relationships with a primary government is such that omission would cause the primary government's financial statements to be misleading.

Most component units are reported, in the government-wide financial statements, in a separate column or columns to the right of the information related to the primary government (**discretely presented**). Component units whose activities are so closely tied to the primary government as to be indistinguishable should be **blended** with the primary government figures. Thus, the **primary government** and several additional **component units** may be combined to constitute the **reporting entity**.

GASB 39, *Determining Whether Certain Organizations Are Component Units*, requires that a fundraising foundation and similar organization whose primary purpose is to raise or hold significant resources for the benefit of a specific governmental unit should be reported as a component unit of that government.

**C.  Management's Discussion and Analysis**

The **Management's Discussion and Analysis (MD&A)** provides, in plain English terms, an overview of the government's financial activities. This section is to provide a comparison of the current year results with the results of the prior year, with emphasis on the prior year. Included will be

- A brief discussion of the financial statements
- Condensed financial information from the government-wide financial statements and individual fund statements
- An analysis of significant variations between the original budget, final budget, and actual results for the year
- A description of significant capital asset and long-term debt activity for the year
- A discussion by governments that use the modified approach to report infrastructure assets regarding the condition of these capital assets and changes from the prior year
- A description of any known facts, decisions, or conditions that would have a significant effect on the government's financial position or results of operations.

MD&A is considered to be Required Supplementary Information (RSI). The nature of RSI is described in Section G. Only items required by GASB are included.

**D.  Government-Wide Financial Statements**

The **government-wide** statements include the Statement of Net Assets and the Statement of Activities, both of which are reproduced in this module. The government-wide statements are prepared on the economic resources measurement focus and accrual basis of accounting. All activities of the primary government are included, with the exception of fiduciary activities, as well as discretely presented component units.

The **Statement of Net Assets** is a type of balance sheet, except that the form, "Assets – Liabilities = Net assets" is used. Full accrual accounting is to be used, including the recording and depreciation of fixed assets, including infrastructure. Note that "net assets" is broken down into three categories: (1) invested in capital assets, net of related debt, (2) restricted, and (3) unrestricted. The term "invested in capital assets, net of related debt" is computed by taking the value of capital (fixed) assets, less accumulated depreciation, less the debt associated with the acquisition of the capital assets. The term "restricted," as defined by GASB means "(a) externally imposed by creditors (such as through debt covenants), grantors, contributors, or laws or regulations of other governments, and (b) imposed by law through constitutional provisions or enabling legislation." Unrestricted net assets is a "plug" figure, computed by taking the total net assets and subtracting the invested in capital assets, net of related debt and the restricted net assets.

Note also that the columns are separated into (1) governmental activities, (2) business-type activities, (3) total primary government, and (4) component units. Governmental activities are those that are financed primarily through taxes and other nonexchange transactions. Business-type activities are those normally financed through user charges. The terms "primary government" and "component units" are described above. If a government has more component units than can be displayed effectively in the Statement of Net Assets, then the detail of each component unit should be disclosed in the notes to the financial statements.

The **Statement of Activities** reports revenues and expenses, on the full accrual basis. This is a consolidated statement except that interfund transactions are not eliminated, when those transactions are between governmental and business-type activities, and between the primary government and discretely presented component units. Expenses are reported by function. Revenues are also reported on the accrual basis and may be exchange revenues or nonexchange revenues. **Exchange revenues** are reported when goods or services are transferred for payment of (approximately) equal value, as is true for business enterprises. **Nonexchange revenues** are reported in accord with Section I below.

Program revenues, those that are directly associated with the functional expense categories, are deducted to arrive at the net expense or revenue. Note that program revenues include (1) charges for services, (2) operating grants and contributions, and (3) capital grants and contributions, although program revenues are not limited to the three categories. Examples of program revenue would be the fees charged for park operations under "culture and recreation," and fines and forfeits. Charges for services are deducted from the function which creates the revenues. Grants and contributions (both operating and capital) are reported in the function to which their use is restricted. The net expense or revenue is broken out between governmental activities, business-type activities, and component units, the same as in the Statement of Net Assets. General revenues are deducted from the net expenses to obtain net revenues. General revenues include all taxes levied by the reporting government and other nonexchange revenues not restricted to a particular program. After that, separate additions or deductions are made for special items, extraordinary items, and transfers (between categories). If a government had contributions to term and permanent endowments and contributions to permanent fund principal, these would also be shown after general revenues. Finally, the net assets at the beginning and end of the year are reconciled. (This is called an "all-inclusive activity" statement.)

**Extraordinary items** are those that are both unusual in nature and infrequent in occurrence (the same as for business enterprises). **Special items** (a new GASB category) are those events within the control of management that are either unusual in nature or infrequent in occurrence. An example of a special item would be the gain on sale of park land.

Alternatively, the internal balances could be reported on separate lines as assets and liabilities. A notation would need to be added to inform the reader that the "Total" column is adjusted for those amounts.

*Sample City*
**STATEMENT OF NET ASSETS**
*December 31, 2005*

| | Governmental activities | Business-type activities | Total | Component units |
|---|---|---|---|---|
| | *Primary government* | | | |
| **Assets** | | | | |
| Cash and cash equivalents | $ 13,597,899 | $ 10,279,143 | $ 23,877,042 | $ 303,935 |
| Investments | 27,365,221 | -- | 27,365,221 | 7,428,952 |
| Receivables (net) | 12,833,132 | 3,609,615 | 16,442,747 | 4,042,290 |
| Internal balances | 175,000 | (175,000) | -- | -- |
| Inventories | 322,149 | 126,674 | 448,823 | 83,697 |
| Capital assets, net (Note 1) | 170,022,760 | 151,388,751 | 321,411,511 | 37,744,786 |
| Total assets | 224,316,161 | 165,229,183 | 389,545,344 | 49,603,660 |
| **Liabilities** | | | | |
| Accounts payable | 6,783,310 | 751,430 | 7,534,740 | 1,803,332 |
| Deferred revenue | 1,435,599 | -- | 1,435,599 | 38,911 |
| Noncurrent liabilities (Note 2): | | | | |
| Due within one year | 9,236,000 | 4,426,286 | 113,662,286 | 1,426,639 |
| Due in more than one year | 83,302,378 | 74,482,273 | 157,784,651 | 27,106,151 |
| Total liabilities | 100,757,287 | 79,659,989 | 180,417,276 | 30,375,033 |
| **Net assets** | | | | |
| Invested in capital assets, net of related debt | 103,711,386 | 73,088,574 | 176,799,960 | 15,906,392 |
| Restricted for: | | | | |
| Capital projects | 11,705,864 | -- | 11,705,864 | 492,445 |
| Debt service | 3,020,708 | 1,451,996 | 4,472,704 | -- |
| Community development projects | 4,811,043 | -- | 4,811,043 | -- |
| Other purposes | 3,214,302 | -- | 3,214,302 | -- |
| Unrestricted (deficit) | (2,904,429) | 11,028,624 | 8,124,195 | 2,829,790 |
| Total net assets | $123,558,874 | $ 85,569,194 | $209,128,068 | $19,228,627 |

*Net assets restricted for capital projects* includes approximately $13 million of capital debt for which the proceeds have not yet been used to construct capital assets.

SOURCE: GASB 34, page 201.

All governments are required to report those expenses that are directly associated with each function on the appropriate line. If a government chooses to allocate some indirect expenses to functions, separate columns should show the direct, indirect, and total costs charged to each function. Direct expenses include depreciation that can be directly charged. Depreciation expense that serves all functions may be allocated as an indirect expense or charged to general government or as unallocated depreciation expense. Depreciation expense for general **infrastructure assets** (roads, bridges, storm sewers, etc.) should not be allocated but shown as an expense of that function that normally is used for capital outlay (public works, for example) or as a separate line. Interest on long-term debt would be included in direct expenses if the interest is due to a single function. Most interest, however, cannot be identified with a single function and should be shown in a separate line. Interest is capitalized for business-type activities but not for governmental activities.

A government may choose to use a **modified approach for recording charges for infrastructure assets** rather than charge depreciation. Under the modified approach, if a government meets certain criteria for maintaining its infrastructure, expenditures to extend service life would be reported as expenses in lieu of depreciation. A fixed asset management system must be in place that meets certain criteria, and extensive disclosures are required.

**Sample City**
**STATEMENT OF ACTIVITIES**
*For the Year Ended December 31, 2005*

> The detail presented for government activities represents the *minimum* requirement. Governments are encouraged to provide more details—for example, police, fire, EMS, and inspections—rather than simply "public safety."

| Functions/Programs | Expenses | Program revenues: Charges for services | Program revenues: Operating grants and Contributions | Program revenues: Capital grants and contributions | Net (expense) revenue: Primary government Governmental activities | Net (expense) revenue: Primary government Business-type activities | Net (expense) revenue: Primary government Total | Component units |
|---|---|---|---|---|---|---|---|---|
| **Primary government** | | | | | | | | |
| **Governmental activities:** | | | | | | | | |
| General government | $ 9,571,410 | $ 3,146,915 | $ 843,617 | $ — | $ (5,580,878) | $ — | $ (5,580,878) | $ — |
| Public safety | 34,844,749 | 1,198,855 | 1,307,693 | 62,300 | (32,275,901) | — | (32,275,901) | — |
| Public works | 10,128,538 | 850,000 | — | 2,252,615 | (7,025,923) | — | (7,025,923) | — |
| Engineering services | 1,299,645 | 704,793 | — | — | (594,852) | — | (594,852) | — |
| Health and sanitation | 6,738,672 | 5,612,267 | 575,000 | — | (551,405) | — | (551,405) | — |
| Cemetery | 735,866 | 212,496 | — | — | (523,370) | — | (523,370) | — |
| Culture and recreation | 11,532,350 | 3,995,199 | 2,450,000 | — | (5,087,151) | — | (5,087,151) | — |
| Community development | 2,994,389 | — | — | 2,580,000 | (414,389) | — | (414,389) | — |
| Education (payment to school district) | 21,893,273 | — | — | — | (21,893,273) | — | (21,893,273) | — |
| Interest on long-term debt | 6,068,121 | — | — | — | (6,068,121) | — | (6,068,121) | — |
| Total governmental activities | 105,807,013 | 15,720,525 | 5,176,310 | 4,894,915 | (80,015,263) | — | (80,015,263) | — |
| **Business-type activities:** | | | | | | | | |
| Water | 3,595,733 | 4,159,350 | — | 1,159,909 | — | 1,723,526 | 1,723,526 | — |
| Sewer | 4,912,853 | 7,170,533 | — | 486,010 | — | 2,743,690 | 2,743,690 | — |
| Parking facilities | 2,796,283 | 1,344,087 | — | — | — | (1,452,196) | (1,452,196) | — |
| Total business-type activities | 11,304,869 | 12,673,970 | — | 1,645,919 | — | 3,015,020 | 3,015,020 | — |
| Total primary government | $117,111,882 | $28,394,495 | $5,176,310 | $6,540,834 | (80,015,263) | 3,015,020 | (77,000,243) | — |
| **Component units** | | | | | | | | |
| Landfill | $ 3,382,157 | $ 3,857,858 | $ — | $ 11,397 | | | | 487,098 |
| Public school system | 31,186,498 | 705,765 | 3,937,083 | — | | | | (26,543,650) |
| Total component units | $ 34,568,655 | $ 4,563,623 | $3,937,083 | $ 11,397 | | | | (26,056,552) |
| **General revenues:** | | | | | | | | |
| Taxes: | | | | | | | | |
| Property taxes, levied for general purposes | | | | | 51,693,573 | — | 51,693,573 | — |
| Property taxes, levied for debt service | | | | | 4,726,244 | — | 4,726,244 | — |
| Franchise taxes | | | | | 4,055,505 | — | 4,055,505 | — |
| Public service taxes | | | | | 8,969,887 | — | 8,969,887 | — |
| Payment from Sample City | | | | | | | | 21,893,273 |
| Grants and contributions not restricted to specific programs | | | | | 1,457,820 | — | 1,457,820 | 6,461,708 |
| Investment earnings | | | | | 1,958,144 | 601,349 | 2,559,493 | 881,763 |
| Miscellaneous | | | | | 884,907 | 104,925 | 989,832 | 22,464 |
| Special item—gain on sale of park land | | | | | 2,653,488 | — | 2,653,488 | — |
| Transfers | | | | | 501,409 | (501,409) | — | — |
| Total general revenues, special items, and transfers | | | | | 76,900,977 | 204,865 | 77,105,842 | 29,259,208 |
| Change in net assets | | | | | (3,114,286) | 3,219,885 | 105,599 | 3,202,656 |
| Net assets—beginning | | | | | 126,673,160 | 82,349,309 | 209,022,469 | 16,025,971 |
| Net assets—ending | | | | | $123,558,874 | $85,569,194 | $209,128,068 | $19,228,627 |

*SOURCE: GASB 34, pp. 208-9.*

### E.  Fund Financial Statements

In addition to government-wide statements, GASB 34 requires a number of fund financial statements. Most governments use fund accounting internally and prepare the government-wide statements with worksheet adjustments from this fund accounting base.  A fund is defined by the GASB as

> A fiscal and accounting entity with a self-balancing set of accounts recording cash and other financial resources, together with all related liabilities and residual equities and balances, and changes therein, which are segregated for the purpose of carrying on specific activities or attaining certain objectives in accordance with special regulations, restrictions, or limitations.

GASB now has 11 fund types, which are classified into three general categories.

| *Governmental funds* | *Proprietary funds* | *Fiduciary funds* |
|---|---|---|
| (1) General | (6) Internal service | (8) Agency |
| (2) Special revenue | (7) Enterprise | (9) Pension and other employee |
| (3) Debt service | | benefit trust funds |
| (4) Capital projects | | (10) Investment trust funds |
| (5) Permanent | | (11) Private-purpose trust funds |

Fund financial statements are presented separately for the governmental, proprietary, and fiduciary fund categories.  Each government has only one general fund; each other fund type may have any number of individual funds, although GASB encourages having as few funds as possible.  Fixed assets and long-term debt are not reported in the fund financial statements, only in the government-wide financial statements.

The fund financial statements for the governmental and enterprise fund categories report **major funds,** not all funds.  The general fund is always a major fund.  Other funds must be considered major when both of the following conditions exist: (1) total assets, liabilities, revenues, expenditures/expenses of that individual governmental or enterprise fund constitute 10% of the governmental or enterprise category **and** (2) total assets, liabilities, revenues, expenditures/expenses are 5% of the total of the governmental and enterprise category combined.  In addition, a government may choose to call any fund major if it feels that reporting that fund would be useful.[1]  In governmental and enterprise fund statements, the nonmajor funds are aggregated and reported as a single column.  Combining statements for nonmajor funds are shown as "Other supplementary information" later in the financial section of CAFR.  Internal service funds are reported in a single column on the proprietary fund statements.

Fiduciary fund financial statements report a separate column for fund type (agency, pension and other employee benefit trust, investment trust, and private purpose).  If separate reports are not available for each pension trust fund, then the notes must disclose this information.  If separate reports are available, then the notes must disclose how readers can obtain those reports.

A reconciliation between the information presented in the governmental fund financial statements and the governmental activities column of the government-wide financial statements is required either at the bottom of the fund financial statements or in a schedule immediately following the fund financial statements.  Explanations should either accompany the reconciliation or be in the notes.

**Governmental funds** focus on the current financial resources raised and expended to carry out general government purposes.  Governmental funds include the general, special revenue, debt service, capital projects, and permanent funds.  The **General fund** accounts for all financial resources except those required to be accounted for in another fund. The general fund includes expenditures for general government, public safety, culture and recreation, public works and engineering, and other activities not set aside in other funds.  **Special revenue funds** account for specific revenue sources that are legally restricted to expenditure for specified current purposes.  An example would include a motor fuel tax limited by law to highway and street construction and repair.  **Debt service funds** account for the accumulation of resources

---

[1] *The determination of whether or not a fund is major or nonmajor can be illustrated by the HUD Programs Fund, shown in the governmental funds statements as a major fund.  The first step is to determine whether or not the HUD Programs Fund is 10% of the governmental funds assets ($7,504,765/51,705,690 = 14.5%), liabilities ($6,428,389/16,812,584 = 38.3%), revenues ($2,731,473/97,482,467 = 2.80%), or expenditures ($2,954,389/121,332,470 = 2.44%).  The first (10%) criterion is met for assets and liabilities but not for revenues and expenditures.  As a result, the 5% test will be applied for assets and liabilities only.  See the statements for governmental and proprietary funds.  The assets do not qualify [$7,504,765/(51,705,690 + 165,404,18) = 3.45%].  However, the liabilities do exceed 5% [$6,428,389/(16,812,584 + 79,834,989) = 6.65%].  Thus, the HUD Programs Fund must be shown as a major fund.*

for, and the payment of, general long-term debt and interest. **Capital projects funds** account for financial resources to be used for the acquisition or construction of major capital facilities, other than those financed by proprietary funds or trust funds. **Permanent funds** are used to report resources that are legally restricted to the extent that only earnings, and not principal, may be used to support government programs.

Two governmental fund financial statements are required: (1) **Balance Sheet** and (2) **Statement of Revenues, Expenditures, and Changes in Fund Balances**. Both of these are illustrated in this module. Governmental fund financial statements are prepared on the current financial resources measurement focus and modified accrual basis of accounting (see Section H., "Measurement Focus and Basis of Accounting"). Note in the Balance Sheet that fund balances are broken down between "reserved" and "unreserved." In fund accounting terminology, a reservation of fund balance represents a commitment that makes that portion unavailable for appropriation. Examples include encumbrances, inventories, and amounts set aside equal to long-term assets in governmental funds. Unreserved fund balance is the amount that is available for appropriation. Note in the Statement of Revenues, Expenditures, and Changes in Fund Balances that revenues are reported by source, expenditures are reported by character (current, debt service, capital outlay) and then by function (general government, public safety, etc.). The category "other financing sources and uses" includes transfers between funds and proceeds from the sale of long-term debt and proceeds from the sale of fixed assets. Special and extraordinary items are reported in this statement in the same manner as in the government-wide Statement of Activities, and a reconciliation between the beginning and ending fund balance completes the statement. Interest related to fixed assets is **not** capitalized.

**Proprietary funds** focus on total economic resources, income determination, and cash flow presentation. Proprietary funds include internal service funds (which are considered governmental activities in the government-wide statements) and enterprise funds (which are considered business-type activities in the government-wide statements). **Internal service funds** report any activity that provides goods or services to other funds of the primary government on a cost-reimbursement basis. Examples might include print shops, motor pools, and self-insurance activities. Internal service funds may incidentally provide services to other governments on a cost-reimbursement basis. **Enterprise funds** may be used to provide goods or services to external users for a fee. Enterprise funds must be used if (1) the activity is financed with debt that is secured solely by a pledge of the net revenues from fees and charges of that activity, (2) laws or regulations require that the activity's cost of providing services be recovered with fees and charges, rather than from taxes or similar revenues, or (3) the pricing policies of the activity establish fees and charges designed to cover its costs including capital costs (e.g., depreciation and debt service). Examples of enterprise funds would include water utilities, airports, and swimming pools.

Statements required for proprietary funds include (1) **Statement of Net Assets (or Balance Sheet)**, (2) **Statement of Revenues, Expenses, and Changes in Net Assets (or Fund Equity)**, and (3) **Statement of Cash Flows**. These statements are all included in this module. Note that the Statement of Net Assets is prepared in the same "Assets – Liabilities = Net Assets" format as the Statement of Net Assets in the government-wide statements. GASB permits the more traditional balance sheet format, "Assets = Liabilities + Fund Equity" for this proprietary funds statement. The net asset category has the same breakdown as the government-wide statement of net assets, "invested in capital assets, net of related debt," "restricted," and "unrestricted." Note also that the internal service funds are shown separately to the right as a fund type, with all internal service funds grouped together. A classified format, with current and noncurrent assets and liabilities shown separately, is required by GASB.

The Statement of Revenues, Expenses, and Changes in Fund Net Assets is an all-inclusive operating statement, with a reconciliation of the beginning and ending fund net assets as the last item. Major enterprise funds are shown, along with a total of all enterprise fund activity, and the total of internal service funds is shown separately. GASB requires an operating income figure, with operating revenues and expenses shown separately from nonoperating revenues and expenses. Capital contributions, transfers, extraordinary items, and special items are to be shown after the nonoperating revenues and expenses. GASB requires that depreciation be shown separately as an operating expense and that interest be shown as a nonoperating expense. Interest related to fixed assets is capitalized.

Sample City
BALANCE SHEET
GOVERNMENTAL FUNDS
December 31, 2005

| | General | HUD programs | Community redevelopment | Route 7 construction | Other governmental funds | Total governmental funds |
|---|---|---|---|---|---|---|
| **Assets** | | | | | | |
| Cash and cash equivalents | $3,418,485 | $1,236,523 | $ -- | $ -- | $ 5,606,792 | $ 10,261,800 |
| Investments | -- | -- | 13,262,695 | 10,467,037 | 3,485,252 | 27,214,984 |
| Receivables, net | 3,644,561 | 2,953,438 | 353,340 | 11,000 | 10,221 | 6,972,560 |
| Due from other funds | 1,370,757 | -- | -- | -- | -- | 1,370,757 |
| Receivables from other governments | -- | 119,059 | -- | -- | 1,596,038 | 1,715,097 |
| Liens receivable | 791,926 | 3,195,745 | -- | -- | -- | 3,987,671 |
| Inventories | 182,821 | -- | -- | -- | -- | 182,821 |
| Total assets | $9,408,550 | $7,504,765 | $13,616,035 | $10,478,037 | $10,698,303 | $51,705,690 |
| **Liabilities and fund balances** | | | | | | |
| Liabilities | | | | | | |
| Accounts payable | $3,408,680 | $129,975 | $ 190,548 | $1,104,632 | $1,074,831 | $ 5,908,666 |
| Due to other funds | -- | 25,369 | -- | -- | -- | 25,369 |
| Payable to other governments | 94,074 | -- | -- | -- | -- | 94,074 |
| Deferred revenue | 4,250,430 | 6,273,045 | 250,000 | 11,000 | -- | 10,784,475 |
| Total liabilities | 7,753,184 | 6,428,389 | 440,548 | 1,115,632 | 1,074,831 | 16,812,584 |
| Fund balances | | | | | | |
| Reserved for: | | | | | | |
| Inventories | 182,821 | | | | | 182,821 |
| Liens receivables | 791,926 | | | | | 791,926 |
| Encumbrances | 40,292 | 41,034 | 119,314 | 5,792,587 | 1,814,122 | 7,807,349 |
| Debt service | | | | | 3,832,062 | 3,832,062 |
| Other purposes | | | | | 1,405,300 | 1,405,300 |
| Unreserved, reported in: | | | | | | |
| General fund | 640,327 | | | | | 640,327 |
| Special revenue funds | | 1,035,342 | | | 1,330,718 | 2,366,060 |
| Capital projects funds | | | 13,056,173 | 3,569,818 | 1,241,270 | 17,867,261 |
| Total fund balances | 1,655,366 | 1,076,376 | 13,175,487 | 9,362,405 | 9,623,472 | 34,893,106 |
| Total liabilities and fund balances | $9,408,550 | $7,504,765 | $13,616,035 | $10,478,037 | $10,698,303 | $51,705,690 |

"Designations" of unreserved fund balances may be displayed or disclosed in the notes.

Amounts reported for governmental activities in the statement of net assets are different because:

Capital assets used in governmental activities are not financial resources and therefore are not reported in the funds.    161,082,708

Other long-term assets are not available to pay for current-period expenditures and therefore are deferred in the funds.    9,348,876

Internal service funds are used by management to charge the costs of certain activities, such as insurance and telecommunications, to individual funds. The assets and liabilities of the internal service funds are included in governmental activities in the statement of net assets.    2,994,691

Long-term liabilities, including bonds payable, are not due and payable in the current period and therefore are not reported in the funds.    (84,760,507)

Net assets of governmental activities    $123,558,874

SOURCE: GASB 34, pp. 220-1.

**Sample City**

## STATEMENT OF REVENUES, EXPENDITURES, AND CHANGES IN FUND BALANCES
### GOVERNMENTAL FUNDS
*For the Year Ended December 31, 2005*

| | General | HUD programs | Community redevelopment | Route 7 construction | Other governmental funds | Total governmental funds |
|---|---|---|---|---|---|---|
| **Revenues** | | | | | | |
| Property taxes | $51,173,436 | $ -- | $ -- | $ -- | $ 4,680,192 | $ 55,853,628 |
| Franchise taxes | 4,055,505 | -- | -- | -- | -- | 4,055,505 |
| Public service taxes | 8,969,887 | -- | -- | -- | -- | 8,969,887 |
| Fees and fines | 606,946 | -- | -- | -- | -- | 606,946 |
| Licenses and permits | 2,287,794 | -- | -- | -- | -- | 2,287,794 |
| Intergovernmental | 6,119,938 | 2,578,191 | -- | -- | 2,830,916 | 11,529,045 |
| Charges for services | 11,374,460 | -- | -- | -- | 30,708 | 11,405,168 |
| Investment earnings | 552,325 | 87,106 | 549,489 | 270,161 | 364,330 | 1,823,411 |
| Miscellaneous | 881,874 | 66,176 | -- | 2,939 | 94 | 951,083 |
| Total Revenues | 86,022,165 | 2,731,473 | 549,489 | 273,100 | 7,906,240 | 97,482,467 |
| **Expenditures** | | | | | | |
| Current | | | | | | |
| General government | 8,630,835 | -- | 417,814 | 16,700 | 121,052 | 9,186,401 |
| Public safety | 33,729,623 | -- | -- | -- | -- | 33,729,623 |
| Public works | 4,975,775 | -- | -- | -- | 3,721,542 | 8,697,317 |
| Engineering services | 1,299,645 | -- | -- | -- | -- | 1,299,645 |
| Health and sanitation | 6,070,032 | -- | -- | -- | -- | 6,070,032 |
| Cemetery | 706,305 | -- | -- | -- | -- | 706,305 |
| Culture and recreation | 11,411,685 | -- | -- | -- | -- | 11,411,685 |
| Community development | -- | 2,954,389 | -- | -- | -- | 2,954,389 |
| Education—payment to school district | 21,893,273 | -- | -- | -- | -- | 21,893,273 |
| Debt service | | | | | | |
| Principal | -- | -- | -- | -- | 3,450,000 | 3,450,000 |
| Interest and other charges | -- | -- | -- | -- | 5,215,151 | 5,215,151 |
| Capital outlay | -- | -- | 2,246,671 | 11,281,769 | 3,190,209 | 16,718,649 |
| Total expenditures | 88,717,173 | 2,954,389 | 2,664,485 | 11,298,469 | 15,697,954 | 121,332,470 |
| Excess (deficiency) of revenues over expenditures | (2,695,008) | (222,916) | (2,114,996) | (11,025,369) | (7,791,714) | (23,850,003) |
| **Other Financing Sources (Uses)** | | | | | | |
| Proceeds of refunding bonds | -- | -- | -- | -- | 38,045,000 | 38,045,000 |
| Proceeds of long-term capital-related debt | -- | -- | 17,529,560 | -- | 1,300,000 | 18,829,560 |
| Payment to bond refunding escrow agent | -- | -- | -- | -- | (37,284,144) | (37,284,144) |
| Transfers in | 129,323 | -- | -- | -- | 5,551,187 | 5,680,510 |
| Transfers out | (2,163,759) | (348,046) | (2,273,187) | -- | (219,076) | (5,004,068) |
| Total other financing sources and uses | (2,034,436) | (348,046) | 15,256,373 | -- | 7,392,967 | 20,266,858 |
| **Special Item** | | | | | | |
| Proceeds from sale of park land | 3,476,488 | -- | -- | -- | -- | 3,476,488 |
| Net change in fund balances | (1,252,956) | (570,962) | 13,141,377 | (11,025,369) | (398,747) | (106,657) |
| Fund balances—beginning | 2,908,322 | 1,647,338 | 34,110 | 20,387,774 | 10,022,219 | 34,999,763 |
| Fund balances—ending | $ 1,655,366 | $1,076,376 | $13,175,487 | $ 9,362,405 | $ 9,623,472 | $ 34,893,106 |

*SOURCE: GASB 34, pp. 222-3*

The Statement of Cash Flows is prepared in accord with the requirements of GASB 9, as modified by GASB 34, and contains several major differences from the familiar business cash flow statement required by FASB. First, only the direct method is acceptable, and a reconciliation is required. Second, the reconciliation is from operating income to net cash provided by operating activities, not from net income as required by FASB. Third, GASB has four categories instead of the three required by FASB. These are operating, noncapital financing, capital and related financing, and investing. Fourth, cash receipts from interest are classified as investing, not operating activities. Fifth, cash payments for interest are classified as financing (either noncapital or capital and related), not as operating activities. Finally, purchases of capital assets (resources provided by financing activities) are considered financing, not investing, activities.

*Sample City*
**STATEMENT OF NET ASSETS**
**PROPRIETARY FUNDS**
*December 31, 2005*

> This statement illustrates the "net assets" format; the "balance sheet" format also is permitted. Classification of assets and liabilities is required in either case.

| | Business-type activities—enterprise funds | | | Governmental activities—internal service funds |
|---|---|---|---|---|
| | Water and sewer | Parking facilities | Totals | |
| **Assets** | | | | |
| *Current assets:* | | | | |
| Cash and cash equivalents | $ 8,416,653 | $  369,168 | $  8,785,821 | $ 3,336,099 |
| Investments | -- | -- | -- | 150,237 |
| Receivables, net | 3,564,586 | 3,535 | 3,568,121 | 157,804 |
| Due from other governments | 41,494 | -- | 41,494 | -- |
| Inventories | 126,674 | -- | 126,674 | 139,328 |
| Total current assets | 12,149,407 | 372,703 | 12,522,110 | 3,783,468 |
| *Noncurrent assets:* | | | | |
| Restricted cash and cash equivalents | -- | 1,493,322 | 1,493,322 | -- |
| Capital assets: | | | | |
| Land | 813,513 | 3,021,637 | 3,835,150 | -- |
| Distribution and collection systems | 39,504,183 | -- | 39,504,183 | -- |
| Buildings and equipment | 106,135,666 | 23,029,166 | 129,164,832 | 14,721,786 |
| Less accumulated depreciation | (15,328,911) | (5,786,503) | (21,115,414) | (5,781,734) |
| Total noncurrent assets | 131,124,451 | 21,757,622 | 152,882,073 | 8,940,052 |
| Total assets | 143,273,858 | 22,130,325 | 165,404,183 | 12,723,520 |
| **Liabilities** | | | | |
| *Current liabilities:* | | | | |
| Accounts payable | 447,427 | 304,003 | 751,430 | 780,570 |
| Due to other funds | 175,000 | -- | 175,000 | 1,170,388 |
| Compensated absences | 112,850 | 8,827 | 121,677 | 237,690 |
| Claims and judgments | -- | -- | -- | 1,687,975 |
| Bonds, notes, and loans payable | 3,944,609 | 360,000 | 4,304,609 | 249,306 |
| Total current liabilities | 4,679,886 | 672,830 | 5,352,716 | 4,125,929 |
| *Noncurrent liabilities:* | | | | |
| Compensated absences | 451,399 | 35,306 | 486,705 | -- |
| Claims and judgments | -- | -- | -- | 5,602,900 |
| Bonds, notes, and loans payable | 54,451,549 | 19,544,019 | 73,995,568 | -- |
| Total noncurrent liabilities | 54,902,948 | 19,579,325 | 74,482,273 | 5,602,900 |
| Total liabilities | 59,582,834 | 20,252,155 | 79,834,989 | 9,728,829 |
| **Net Assets** | | | | |
| Invested in capital assets, net of related debt | 72,728,293 | 360,281 | 73,088,574 | 8,690,746 |
| Restricted for debt service | -- | 1,451,996 | 1,451,996 | -- |
| Unrestricted | 10,962,731 | 65,893 | 11,028,624 | (5,696,055) |
| Total net assets | $ 83,691,024 | $ 1,878,170 | $ 85,569,194 | $ 2,994,691 |

*SOURCE: GASB 34, page 227.*

**Fiduciary fund** financial statements provide information, based on the economic resources measurement focus and accrual accounting, on resources held and used by governments for the benefit of individuals and entities other than the government. Fiduciary fund statements are the Statement of Fiduciary Net Assets and the Statement of Changes in Fiduciary Net Assets. Unlike the statements for the governmental and enterprise fund categories, fiduciary fund statements report totals for each of the four fund types.  The fund types are (1) pension (and other employee benefit) trust funds, (2) investment trust funds, (3) private-purpose trust funds, and (4) agency funds.  However, each individual pension or employee benefit trust fund report must be reported in the notes if separate reports have not been issued.  If separate reports have been issued, the notes to the financial statement must indicate how the reader might obtain such reports.

**Pension (and other employee benefit) trust funds** account for funds held in trust for the payment of employee retirement and other benefits.  These trust funds exist when the government is the trustee for the pension plan.  Accounting for these plans is covered by GASB 25, 43, and 50.  **Investment trust funds** are used to report the external portions of investment pools, when the reporting government is trustee.  **Private-purpose trust funds** should be used to report all other trust arrangements where the principal and income benefit individuals, private organizations, and other governments.  An example would be a fund to report scholarship funds contributed by individuals and businesses, by a public school system.  Finally, **agency funds** report resources held by the reporting government in a purely custodial capacity.  Agency funds report only assets and liabilities and are not included in the Statement of Changes in Fiduciary Net Assets.

*Sample City*
**STATEMENT OF REVENUES, EXPENSES, AND CHANGES IN FUND NET ASSETS**
**PROPRIETARY FUNDS**
*For the Year Ended December 31, 2005*

| | Business-type activities—enterprise funds | | | Governmental activities—internal service funds |
| --- | --- | --- | --- | --- |
| | Water and sewer | Parking facilities | Totals | |
| *Operating revenues:* | | | | |
| Charges for service | $11,329,883 | $1,340,261 | $12,670,144 | $15,256,164 |
| Miscellaneous | -- | 3,826 | 3,826 | 1,066,761 |
| Total operating revenues | 11,329,883 | 1,344,087 | 12,673,970 | 16,322,925 |
| *Operating expenses:* | | | | |
| Personal services | 3,400,559 | 762,348 | 4,162,907 | 4,157,156 |
| Contractual services | 344,422 | 96,032 | 440,454 | 584,396 |
| Utilities | 754,107 | 100,726 | 854,833 | 214,812 |
| Repairs and maintenance | 747,315 | 64,617 | 811,932 | 1,960,490 |
| Other supplies and expenses | 498,213 | 17,119 | 515,332 | 234,445 |
| Insurance claims and expenses | -- | -- | -- | 8,004,286 |
| Depreciation | 1,163,140 | 542,049 | 1,705,189 | 1,707,872 |
| Total operating expenses | 6,907,756 | 1,582,891 | 8,490,647 | 16,863,457 |
| Operating income (loss) | 4,422,127 | (238,804) | 4,183,323 | (540,532) |
| *Nonoperating revenues (expenses):* | | | | |
| Interest and investment revenue | 454,793 | 146,556 | 601,349 | 134,733 |
| Miscellaneous revenue | -- | 104,925 | 104,925 | 20,855 |
| Interest expense | (1,600,830) | (1,166,546) | (2,767,376) | (41,616) |
| Miscellaneous expense | -- | (46,846) | (46,846) | (176,003) |
| Total nonoperating revenues (expenses) | (1,146,037) | (961,911) | (2,107,948) | (62,031) |
| Income (loss) before contributions and transfers | 3,276,090 | (1,200,715) | 2,075,375 | (602,563) |
| Capital contributions | 1,645,919 | -- | 1,645,919 | 18,788 |
| Transfers out | (290,000) | (211,409) | (501,409) | (175,033) |
| Change in net assets | 4,632,009 | (1,412,124) | 3,219,885 | (758,808) |
| Total net assets—beginning | 79,059,015 | 3,290,294 | 82,349,309 | 3,753,499 |
| Total net assets—ending | $83,691,024 | $1,878,170 | $85,569,194 | $ 2,994,691 |

SOURCE:  GASB 34, page 229.

The statements required for fiduciary funds are the **Statement of Fiduciary Net Assets** and **Statement of Changes in Fiduciary Net Assets**.  Examples of these statements are reflected in this module.  The Statement of Fiduciary Net Assets is prepared in the form "Assets – Liabilities = Net Assets."  Columns are included for each fund type.  The Statement of Changes in Fiduciary Net Assets uses the terms "additions" and "deductions" instead of revenues and expenses, but the additions and deductions are computed on the full accrual basis.  This, like all other GASB operating statements, is an "all-inclusive" statement with a reconciliation of the beginning and ending net assets at the bottom of the statement.  Note that agency funds have only assets and liabilities and are not reported in the Statement of Changes in Fiduciary Net Assets.

**Sample City**
**STATEMENT OF CASH FLOWS**
**PROPRIETARY FUNDS**
*For the Year Ended December 31, 2005*

| | Business-type activities—enterprise funds | | | Governmental activities—internal service funds |
| --- | --- | --- | --- | --- |
| | Water and sewer | Parking facilities | Totals | |
| **Cash flows from operating activities** | | | | |
| Receipts from customers | $11,400,200 | $ 1,345,292 | $12,745,492 | $15,326,343 |
| Payments to suppliers | (2,725,349) | (365,137) | (3,090,486) | (2,812,238) |
| Payments to employees | (3,360,055) | (750,828) | (4,110,883) | (4,209,688) |
| Internal activity—payments to other funds | (1,296,768) | — | (1,296,768) | (1,296,768) |
| Claims paid | — | — | — | (8,482,451) |
| Other receipts (payments) | (2,325,483) | — | (2,325,483) | 1,061,118 |
| Net cash provided by operating activities | 1,692,545 | 229,327 | 1,921,872 | 883,084 |
| **Cash flows from noncapital financing activities** | | | | |
| Operating subsidies and transfers to other funds | (290,000) | (211,409) | (501,409) | (175,033) |
| **Cash flows from capital and related financing activities** | | | | |
| Proceeds from capital debt | 4,041,322 | 8,660,778 | 12,702,100 | — |
| Capital contributions | 1,645,919 | — | 1,645,919 | — |
| Purchases of capital assets | (4,194,035) | (144,716) | (4,338,751) | (400,086) |
| Principal paid on capital debt | (2,178,491) | (8,895,000) | (11,073,491) | (954,137) |
| Interest paid on capital debt | (1,479,708) | (1,166,546) | (2,646,254) | 41,616 |
| Other receipts (payments) | — | 19,174 | 19,174 | 131,416 |
| Net cash (used) by capital and related financing activities | (2,164,993) | (1,526,310) | (3,691,303) | (1,264,423) |
| **Cash flows from investing activities** | | | | |
| Proceeds from sales and maturities of investments | — | — | — | 15,684 |
| Interest and dividends | 454,793 | 143,747 | 598,540 | 129,550 |
| Net cash provided by investing activities | 454,793 | 143,747 | 598,540 | 145,234 |
| Net (decrease) in cash and cash equivalents | (307,655) | (1,364,645) | (1,672,300) | (411,138) |
| Balances—beginning of the year | 8,724,308 | 3,227,135 | 11,951,443 | 3,747,237 |
| Balances—end of the year | $ 8,416,653 | $ 1,862,490 | $10,279,143 | $ 3,336,099 |
| **Reconciliation of operating income (loss) to net cash provided (used) by operating activities** | | | | |
| Operating income (loss) | $ 4,422,127 | $ (238,804) | $ 4,183,323 | $ (540,532) |
| Adjustments to reconcile operating income to net cash provided (used) by operating activities: | | | | |
| Depreciation expense | 1,163,140 | 542,049 | 1,705,189 | 1,707,872 |
| Change in assets and liabilities: | | | | |
| Receivables, net | 653,264 | 1,205 | 654,469 | 31,941 |
| Inventories | 2,829 | — | 2,829 | 39,790 |
| Accounts and other payables | (297,446) | (86,643) | (384,089) | 475,212 |
| Accrued expenses | (4,251,369) | (11,520) | (4,239,849) | (831,199) |
| Net cash provided by operating activities | $ 1,692,545 | $ 229,327 | $ 1,921,872 | $ 883,084 |

*SOURCE: GASB 34, pp. 230–231*

## F.  Notes to the Financial Statements

Note disclosure requirements are found in the GASB *Codification* Section 2300 and in GASB Statements 34, 38, and 40.  Some of the major disclosures are a summary of accounting policies, a description of the reporting entity, disclosures on cash and investments (including securitization), fixed assets, long-term debt, pensions, commitments and contingencies, information on exceeding the budget at the legal level of control, disclosures of individual funds with deficit fund balances, and risks related to deposits and investments.  Some disclosures brought about by GASB 34 include a description of the government-wide statements, the policy for capitalizing fixed assets and estimating useful lives, segment information for enterprise funds, and the policy for recording infrastructure, including the use of the modified approach, if applicable.

## G.  Required Supplementary Information (RSI) other than MD&A

GASB requires four types of information that should be included immediately after the notes to the financial statements.  These four items, along with MD & A (see Section C) are considered Required Supplementary Information (RSI).  RSI is information presented outside the basic financial statements.  While RSI is not covered in the audit opinion, omission of RSI, incomplete RSI, or misleading RSI requires a comment by the auditor.  However, an auditor may not modify the report on the basic financial statements as a result of problems discovered related to RSI.

The four types of information are (1) two pension schedules, (2) schedules when the government sponsors a public entity risk pool, (3) budgetary comparison schedules, and (4) certain schedules when using the modified approach for reporting infrastructure.  The pension schedules include a **Schedule of Funding Progress** and a **Schedule of Employer Contributions**.  These statements are required when a government reports a defined benefit pension plan.  The Schedule of Funding Progress provides actuarial information regarding the actuarial value of assets, the actuarial accrued liability, and the unfunded actuarial liability, if any.  The Schedule of Employer Contributions reflects the amount contributed compared with the amount required to be contributed.

The second type of schedule required when the government is sponsor of a public entity risk pool provides revenue and claims development information.

*Sample City*
**STATEMENT OF FIDUCIARY NET ASSETS**
**FIDUCIARY FUNDS**
*December 31, 2005*

|  | Employee retirement plan | Private-purpose trusts | Agency funds |
|---|---|---|---|
| **Assets** | | | |
| Cash and cash equivalents | $      1,973 | $ 1,250 | $ 44,889 |
| Receivables: | | | |
| Interest and dividends | 508,475 | 760 | -- |
| Other receivables | 6,826 | -- | 183,161 |
| Total receivables | 515,301 | 760 | 183,161 |
| Investments, at fair value: | | | |
| US government obligations | 13,056,037 | 80,000 | -- |
| Municipal bonds | 6,528,019 | -- | -- |
| Corporate bonds | 16,320,047 | -- | -- |
| Corporate stocks | 26,112,075 | -- | -- |
| Other investments | 3,264,009 | -- | -- |
| Total investments | 65,280,187 | 80,000 | -- |
| Total assets | 65,797,461 | 82,010 | $228,050 |
| **Liabilities** | | | |
| Accounts payable | -- | 1,234 | -- |
| Refunds payable and others | 1,358 | -- | 228,050 |
| Total liabilities | 1,358 | 1,234 | $228,050 |
| **Net Assets** | | | |
| Held in trust for pension benefits and other purposes | $65,796,103 | $80,776 | |

*SOURCE:  GASB 34, page 235.*

*Sample City*
**STATEMENT OF CHANGES IN FIDUCIARY NET ASSETS**
**FIDUCIARY FUNDS**
*For the Year Ended December 31, 2005*

|  | Employee retirement plan | Private-purpose trusts |
|---|---|---|
| *Additions* | | |
| Contributions: | | |
| Employer | $ 2,721,341 | $ -- |
| Plan members | 1,421,233 | -- |
| Total contributions | 4,142,574 | -- |
| Investment earnings: | | |
| Net (decrease) in fair value of investments | (272,522) | -- |
| Interest | 2,460,871 | 4,560 |
| Dividends | 1,445,273 | -- |
| Total investment earnings | 3,633,622 | 4,560 |
| Less investment expense | 216,428 | -- |
| Net investment earnings | 3,417,194 | 4,560 |
| Total additions | 7,559,768 | 4,560 |
| *Deductions* | | |
| Benefits | 2,453,047 | 3,800 |
| Refunds of contributions | 464,691 | -- |
| Administrative expenses | 87,532 | 678 |
| Total deductions | 3,005,270 | 4,478 |
| Change in net assets | 4,554,498 | 82 |
| Net assets—beginning of the year | 61,241,605 | 80,694 |
| Net assets—end of the year | $65,796,103 | $80,776 |

SOURCE:   *GASB 34, pages 235-6.*

The third type of information is to provide **budgetary comparison schedules** for the general fund and all major special revenue funds for which an annual budget has been passed by the governmental unit. Prior accounting principles required this as one of the general-purpose financial statements. Current GAAP permits, but does not require, this schedule to be shown as a basic statement. If the government has significant budgetary perspective differences that result in it not being able to present budgetary comparison information for its general fund and major special revenue funds, the government must present a budget comparison schedule based on the structure of its legally adopted budget. These schedules include the original budget, the final budget, and the actual revenues and expenditures computed on the budgetary basis. A variance column may or may not be used. The format may be that of the original budget document or in the format, terminology, and classifications in the Statement of Revenues, Expenditures, and Changes in Fund Balances. Information must be provided, either in this schedule or in notes to the RSI, which provides a reconciliation from the budgetary basis to GAAP. An example of a Budget—Actual Statement is included below.

*Sample City*
**STATEMENT OF REVENUES, EXPENDITURES, AND CHANGES IN FUND BALANCES—**
**BUDGET AND ACTUAL**
**GENERAL FUND**
*For the Year Ended December 31, 2005*

|  | Budgeted amounts | | Actual amounts |
|---|---|---|---|
|  | *Original* | *Final* | *(budgetary basis)* |
| *Revenues* | | | |
| Property taxes | $52,017,833 | $51,853,018 | $51,173,436 |
| Other taxes—franchise and public service | 12,841,209 | 12,836,024 | 13,025,392 |
| Fees and fines | 718,800 | 718,800 | 606,946 |
| Licenses and permits | 2,126,600 | 2,126,600 | 2,287,794 |
| Intergovernmental | 6,905,898 | 6,571,360 | 6,119,938 |
| Charges for services | 12,392,972 | 11,202,150 | 11,374,460 |
| Interest | 1,501,945 | 550,000 | 552,325 |
| Miscellaneous | 3,024,292 | 1,220,991 | 881,874 |
| Total revenues | 91,043,549 | 87,078,943 | 86,022,165 |

| | Budgeted amounts | | Actual amounts |
| | Original | Final | (*budgetary basis*) |
|---|---|---|---|
| **Expenditures** | | | |
| Current | | | |
| General government (including contingencies and miscellaneous) | 11,837,534 | 9,468,155 | 8,621,500 |
| Public safety | 33,050,966 | 33,983,706 | 33,799,709 |
| Public works | 5,215,630 | 5,025,848 | 4,993,187 |
| Engineering services | 1,296,275 | 1,296,990 | 1,296,990 |
| Health and sanitation | 5,756,250 | 6,174,653 | 6,174,653 |
| Cemetery | 724,500 | 724,500 | 706,305 |
| Culture and recreation | 11,059,140 | 11,368,070 | 11,289,146 |
| Education—payment to school district | 22,000,000 | 22,000,000 | 21,893,273 |
| Total expenditures | 90,940,295 | 90,041,922 | 88,774,763 |
| Excess (deficiency) of revenues over expenditures | 103,254 | (2,962,979) | (2,752,598) |
| **Other Financing Sources (Uses)** | | | |
| Transfers in | 939,525 | 130,000 | 129,323 |
| Transfers out | (2,970,256) | (2,163,759) | (2,163,759) |
| Total other financing sources and uses | (2,030,731) | (2,033,759) | (2,034,436) |
| **Special Item** | | | |
| Proceeds from sale of park land | 1,355,250 | 3,500,000 | 3,476,488 |
| Net change in fund balance | (572,227) | (1,496,738) | (1,310,546) |
| Fund balances—beginning | 3,528,750 | 2,742,799 | 2,742,799 |
| Fund balances—ending | $ 2,956,523 | $ 1,246,061 | $ 1,432,253 |

SOURCE: GASB 34, pages 272-273. Budget to GAAP Reconciliation Omitted.

The fourth type of information is presented only when the government is using the **modified approach for reporting infrastructure**. Governments have the option of not depreciating their infrastructure assets if they adopt the "modified" approach for recording infrastructure. Two requirements must be met to adopt this approach. First, the government must manage the eligible infrastructure assets using an asset management system that has certain characteristics. These characteristics include (1) keeping an up-to-date inventory of infrastructure assets, (2) performing condition assessments of eligible infrastructure assets, summarizing the results using a measurement scale, and (3) estimating the costs each year to preserve the infrastructure assets at the condition level established and disclosed by the government. Second, the government must document that the infrastructure assets have been preserved at the condition level prescribed by the government. Two schedules are required: (1) a schedule reflecting the condition of the government's infrastructure, and (2) a comparison of the needed and actual expenditures to maintain the government's infrastructure. Certain disclosures are needed to provide explanations, in notes to the RSI.

An example is provided to illustrate the difference between the "depreciation approach" and the "modified approach" to record infrastructure. Assume a government had $1,000,000 in ordinary maintenance expenses, $2,000,000 in expenditures to extend the life of existing infrastructure, and $3,000,000 in expenditures to add to or improve existing infrastructure. Depreciation (if recorded) amounted to $2,500,000. If the "depreciation approach" were used, $3,500,000 would be charged to expense ($1,000,000 + $2,500,000). If the modified approach were used, the amount charged to expense would be $3,000,000 ($1,000,000 + $2,000,000). In both cases, the $1,000,000 would be charged to expense, and the $3,000,000 would be capitalized. Under the "modified approach," the $2,000,000 in expenditures to extend the life of infrastructure is substituted for depreciation expense.

## H. Measurement Focus and Basis of Accounting (MFBA)

GASB Standards require two methods of accounting, each used in certain parts of the financial statements. These are described in terms of measurement focus and basis of accounting. The first is the **economic resources measurement focus and accrual basis of accounting**. This method is similar to accounting for business enterprises. The objective is to measure all of the economic resources available to the governmental entity, including fixed assets and subtracting long-term debt. Full accrual accounting is used, where revenues are recognized when earned and expenses are recognized when incurred. Fixed assets are recorded and depreciated. The economic resources measurement focus and accrual basis of accounting is used for the government-wide statements, the proprietary fund statements, and the fiduciary fund statements.

The second is the **current financial resources measurement focus and modified accrual basis of accounting**. The objective is to measure only the current financial resources available to the governmental entity. As a result fixed assets are not accounted for nor is long-term debt. Modified accrual accounting is used. Under modified accrual accounting, revenues are recognized when measurable and available to finance expenditures of the current period. Property taxes may be considered "available" when collected within sixty days of the end of the fiscal year. The recognition of expenditures (not expenses) is modified in the following way. First, expenditures may be recorded for current items (salaries, supplies), capital outlays (purchase of a police car, construction expenditures), or debt service (matured interest, matured principal). Second, payment of principal and interest on long-term indebtedness, including bonds, notes, capital leases, compensated absences, claims and judgments, pensions, special termination benefits, and landfill closure and postclosure care are recorded when due, rather than accrued. However, a government may accrue an additional amount if it has provided financial resources to a debt service fund for payment of liabilities that will mature early in the following period (not more than a month). Otherwise expenditures are accrued and reported as fund liabilities. The current financial resources measurement focus and modified accrual basis of accounting are used in the governmental fund financial statements and will be illustrated later.

I.  **Accounting by Governments for Certain Events and Transactions**

1.  **Accounting for nonexchange transactions.** The previous section indicated that, under the accrual basis of accounting, revenues are recognized when earned. Revenues include **exchange transactions**, in which goods or services of equal or approximately equal values are exchanged, and **nonexchange transactions.** GASB indicates that revenues from exchange transactions are to be recognized in accord with generally accepted accounting principles as those principles have evolved over the years and provides no special guidance. However, GASB 33, *Accounting and Financial Reporting for Nonexchange Transactions*, defines nonexchange transactions as transactions "in which a government gives (or receives) value without directly receiving (or giving) equal value in exchange." GASB 33 is written under the presumption that an entity is following full accrual accounting. When governmental fund financial statements are issued, modified accrual accounting "modifies" the provisions of GASB 33 to require that resources must be measurable and available to finance the expenditures of the current period, as described in Section H. above.

    GASB 33 classifies nonexchange transactions into four categories, and revenue recognition depends upon the category. The categories are: (1) derived tax revenues, (2) imposed nonexchange revenues, (3) government-mandated nonexchange transactions, and (4) voluntary nonexchange transactions. For the government-wide financial statements, revenue from nonexchange transactions is considered to be an increase in unrestricted net assets unless the revenue is restricted by the grantor, donor, or legislation. For example, a hotel-motel tax may have to be used, by legislation, for promotion of tourism. Purpose restrictions do not affect the timing of revenue recognition.

    In order for a receivable and revenue to be recognized, four types of **eligibility requirements** must be met. First is the **required characteristics of the recipients**. The recipient of resources must have the characteristics required by the provider. For example, the recipient of certain state funds allocated for road repairs may have to be either a county government, a municipality, or a township. Second, **time requirements** must be met, if a provider specifies that resources must be expended in a certain future period. For example, if a state indicates that funds are appropriated for water system improvements for the fiscal year ended June 30, 2004, then neither a receivable nor revenue would be recognized by the local governments receiving the funds until that fiscal year. In the absence of specified time requirements, a receivable and revenue would be recognized when a promise is unconditional. Third, certain grants from one government to another cannot be provided until the receiving government has expended the funds. This is a condition the GASB calls a **reimbursement**. Reimbursement grant revenues are recognized only when expenditures are recognized. Finally, resources pledged that have a **contingency** attached are not to be recognized until that contingency is removed.

    **Derived tax revenues** result from taxes assessed by governments on exchange transactions. Examples include sales taxes, income taxes, and motor fuel taxes. Receivables and revenues are to be recognized when the underlying transaction (the sale, the income, etc.) takes place. For example, under accrual accounting, if a state imposed a sales tax of 6%, the state would record a revenue of $6 when a merchant recorded a sale of $100. If resources are received before the underlying transaction takes place, then the asset would be offset by deferred revenues, a liability.

    **Imposed nonexchange transactions** are taxes and other assessments by governments that are not derived from underlying transactions. Examples include property taxes, special assessments, and fines and forfeits. Assets from imposed nonexchange transactions should be recognized when an enforceable legal claim exists, or when the resources are received, whichever occurs first. In the case of property taxes, this would normally be specified in the enabling legislation, such as the lien or assessment date. Revenues for property taxes should be recognized, net of estimated refunds and estimated uncollectible taxes, in the period for which the taxes are levied, regardless of when the enforcement date or collection date might be. All other imposed nonexchange transactions should be recognized as revenues at the same time as the assets, or as soon as use is first permitted. On the modified accrual basis, property taxes may not be recognized unless collected within sixty days after the end of a fiscal year.

**Government-mandated nonexchange transactions** exist when the providing government, such as the federal government or a state government, requires the receiving government to expend funds for a specific purpose. For example, a state may require school districts to "mainstream" certain children by including them in regular classes and also to provide additional assistance in the form of extra aides. Funding for this purpose would be considered to be a government-mandated nonexchange transaction. Receiving governments should recognize assets and revenues when all eligibility requirements have been met.

**Voluntary nonexchange transactions** include grants and entitlements from one government to another where the providing government does not impose specific requirements upon the receiving government. For example, a state provides a grant for new technology for school districts but does not require those school districts to accept the grant or utilize that technology. Even though the use of the grant is restricted, it is a voluntary nonexchange transaction. It also includes voluntary contributions from individuals and other entities to governments. An example of this type of transaction would be the gift of funds from an individual to a school district or a college. Voluntary nonexchange transactions may or may not have purpose restrictions. The recognition of assets and revenues would be when all eligibility requirements have been met, the same as government-mandated nonexchange transactions.

If after a revenue has been recognized by a governmental entity (in a later fiscal year), those funds must be returned to the provider, then the recipient government must record an expense and liability (or reduction of cash). If there is a difference in the provider government's and recipient government's fiscal year, then the provider's fiscal year would govern for purposes of determining eligibility requirements. If the providing government, a state, has a biennial fiscal year, then half of the grant would be recognized by the recipient government in each of the providing government's two fiscal years.

2. **Accounting for intangible assets.** GASB 51 describes the accounting for intangible assets and allows only **identifiable** intangible assets to be recognized as capital assets in the statement of net assets (at historical cost). Costs related to internally generated intangibles (e.g., proprietary software systems) may begin to be capitalized when

   a. The government's specific **objective** for the project and the proposed **service capacity** has been determined,
   b. The **feasibility** of completing the project has been demonstrated, and
   c. The government's **intention** to complete or to continue the development of the asset has been demonstrated.

   Intangible assets should be amortized over their useful lives. An intangible asset that has no legal, contractual, regulatory, technological, or other factors limiting its useful life should be considered to have an indefinite useful life and should not be amortized unless its useful life is later determined to be no longer indefinite.

3. **Sales and pledges of receivables and future revenues.** In some situations a state or local government may decide to sell receivables or future revenues (e.g., future tobacco settlement receipts, or delinquent tax receivables). GASB 48 provides guidance for accounting for such transactions. Specifically, this statement provides criteria for determining when the assets have been sold and should be removed from the government's financial statements as opposed to treating the transaction as a collateralized loan.

   GASB 48 establishes that a transaction is a collateralized borrowing unless the government both transfers the receivables or future revenues and has no continued involvement with them. Circumstances that would indicate continued involvement and prevent accounting for the transaction as a sale include

- The government or the buyer can cancel the sale.
- The government can limit the buyer's ability to subsequently sell or pledge the receivables or future revenue.
- The government has access to the receivables, future revenues, or the cash collected from them.
- The government can substitute for or reacquire specific receivables without the buyer's consent.
- The government is actively involved in the future generation of sold revenues (e.g., the revenues are the product of goods or services provided by the government).

Receivables that meet the requirements for sale should be removed from the assets of the selling government's financial statements. The difference between the carrying value of the receivables and the funds received is reported as a gain or loss on accrual-basis financial statements or as revenue in modified-accrual-basis financial statements. In a sale of future revenue, the government generally reports the proceeds as deferred revenue and recognizes the revenue over the life of the sales agreement.

If the transaction does not meet the requirements of a sale, it is accounted for as a collateralized loan. The proceeds represent a liability that is repaid as the receivables or revenues are collected.

4. **Accounting for pollution remediation obligations.** GASB 49 establishes rules for accounting for estimated obligations for pollution remediation. A government must estimate its expected outlays for pollution remediation if it knows a site is polluted and any of the following recognition triggers occur:

- Pollution poses an imminent danger to the public or environment and the government has little or no discretion to avoid fixing the problem.
- The government has violated a pollution prevention-related permit or license.
- A regulator (e.g., the EPA) has identified the government as responsible or potentially responsible for cleaning up pollution or paying some of the cost of the cleanup.
- The government is named in a lawsuit to compel it to address the pollution.
- The government begins or legally obligates itself to begin cleanup or postcleanup activities.

Liabilities and expenses are estimated using an "expected cash flows" measurement technique.

## J. Budgetary Accounting for the General and Special Revenue Funds

The GASB, in one of its basic principles, states

1. An annual budget(s) should be adopted by every governmental unit.
2. The accounting system should provide the basis for appropriate budgetary control.
3. A common terminology and classification should be used consistently throughout the budget, the accounts, and the financial reports of each fund.

In accordance with the principle above, budgets should be prepared for each of the fund types used by governmental units. This directive, by itself, does not differentiate governmental from commercial enterprises. What is different, however, is the inclusion of budgetary accounts in the formal accounting system for the general and major special revenue funds. Inclusion of the budgetary accounts facilitates a budget-actual comparison in Required Supplementary Information or as a basic financial statement. The budget-actual comparison is required for the general fund and all major special revenue funds that have a legally adopted annual budget. Budgetary accounts are generally used in those funds for which the budget-actual comparison is made. As a result, CPA examination questions always assume budgetary accounts for the general fund and sometimes, but not always, assume budgetary accounts for special revenue funds.

Budgetary accounts (Estimated Revenues, Appropriations, Estimated Other Financing Sources, Estimated Other Financing Uses, Budgetary Fund Balance) are incorporated into governmental accounting systems to provide legislative control over revenues and other resource inflows and expenditures and other resource outflows. Recording the budget also provides an assessment of management's stewardship by facilitating a comparison of budget vs. actual. The journal entries that follow illustrate the budgetary accounts used by the general and special revenue funds.

Upon adoption of the estimated revenues and appropriations budgets (at the beginning of the period), the following entry is made and posted to the general ledger:

| | |
|---|---|
| Estimated Revenues Control[2] (individual items are posted to subsidiary ledger) | 1,000,000 (anticipated resources/revenues) |
| Appropriations Control (individual items are posted to subsidiary ledger) | 980,000 (anticipated expenditures/liabilities) |
| Budgetary Fund Balance | 20,000 (surplus is anticipated) |

Budgetary Fund Balance is a budgetary account. This budgetary entry is reversed at year-end.

As actual resource inflows and outflows occur during the year, they are recorded in Revenues and Expenditures accounts, and the detail is posted to the revenues and expenditures subsidiary ledgers to facilitate budget vs. actual comparisons. To prevent the overspending of an item in the appropriations budget, an additional budgetary account is maintained during the year. This budgetary account is called Encumbrances. When goods or services are ordered, appropriations (specific items in the subsidiary ledger) are encumbered (restricted) with the following entry:

| | |
|---|---|
| Encumbrances Control (detail posted to subsidiary ledger) | 5,000 (cost estimate) |
| Budgetary Fund Balance—Reserved for Encumbrances | 5,000 (cost estimate) |

Budgetary Fund Balance—Reserved for Encumbrances is also a budgetary account. When the debit in the entry is posted, the amount that can still be obligated or expended for an individual budget line item is reduced. Thereafter, when the goods or services ordered are received, the encumbrance entry is reversed and the actual resource outflow (expenditures) is recorded.

| | |
|---|---|
| Budgetary Fund Balance—Reserved for Encumbrances | 5,000 |
| Encumbrances Control (detail posted to subsidiary ledger) | 5,000 |
| Expenditures Control (detail posted to subsidiary ledger) | 5,200 (actual cost) |
| Accounts Payable | 5,200 (actual cost) |

The Encumbrances account does not represent an expenditure; it is a budgetary account which represents the estimated cost of goods or services which have yet to be received. In effect, the recording of encumbrances represents the recording of executory contracts, which is essential to prevent overspending of an appropriation (normally, an illegal act). Likewise, the account "Budgetary Fund Balance—Reserved for Encumbrances" is not a liability account; it is a budgetary account. If encumbrances are outstanding at the end of a period, that account is closed to the Fund Balance—Reserved for Encumbrances, which is reported in the fund balance section of the balance sheet (similar to an appropriation of retained earnings on a corporation's balance sheet).

At the end of the year, the following closing entries would be recorded, assuming actual revenues for the year totaled $1,005,000, actual expenditures for the year were $950,000, and encumbrances outstanding at year-end were $10,000:

| | | | |
|---|---|---|---|
| 1. | Budgetary Fund Balance | 20,000 | |
| | Appropriations Control | 980,000 | |
| | Estimated Revenues Control | | 1,000,000 |
| | *To reverse the budgetary entry and close the budgetary accounts* | | |
| 2. | Revenues Control | 1,005,000 | |
| | Expenditures Control | | 950,000 |
| | Encumbrances Control | | 10,000 |
| | Fund Balance—Unreserved | | 45,000 |
| | *If Expenditures and Encumbrances had exceeded Revenues, Fund Balance—* | | |
| | *Unreserved, an equity account, would have been debited in this closing entry.* | | |
| 3. | Budgetary Fund Balance—Reserved for Encumbrances | 10,000 | |
| | Fund Balance—Reserved for Encumbrances | | 10,000 |

Fund Balance—Unreserved and Fund Balance—Reserved for Encumbrances are balance sheet equity accounts.

## K.  Expenditure Classification for Governmental Funds

**Expenditure classification.** The GASB *Codification* includes guidelines for the classification of governmental fund expenditure data as set forth in GASB Statement 1. Both internal and external management control benefit from multiple classification of expenditures. In addition, multiple classifications prove important from an accountability standpoint. This classification system provides assistance in aggregating data and performing data analysis. Internal evaluations, external reporting, and intergovern-

---

[2] *Throughout this module "Control" has been used in the journal entries. However, to avoid redundancy, "Control" has not been used in this text.*

mental comparisons can be enhanced by this multiple classification system.  The following chart describes each expenditure classification with examples.

| *Classification* | *Description* | *Examples* |
|---|---|---|
| Function (or program) | • Provides information on the overall purposes or objectives of expenditures<br>• Represents a major service or area of responsibility | Highways and streets<br>Health and welfare<br>Education<br>General government<br>Public safety |
| Organization unit (department) | • Grouped according to the government's organizational structure<br>• The responsibility for a department is fixed | Police department<br>Fire department<br>Parks and recreational department<br>Personnel department<br>City clerk |
| Activity | • Specific and distinguishable line of work performed by an organizational unit as part of one of its functions or programs<br>• More meaningful if the performance of each activity is fixed | Police protection function<br>Subactivities:<br>   Police administration<br>   Crime control and investigation<br>   Traffic control<br>   Police training<br>   Support services |
| Character | • Classifies expenditures by the fiscal period benefited | Current expenditures<br>Capital outlays<br>Debt service |
| Object | • Classified according to the types of items purchased or services obtained | Personal services<br>Supplies<br>Rent<br>Utilities<br>Buildings |

The Statement of Revenues, Expenditures, and Changes in Fund Balances (see page 803) generally reports expenditures by function within character classifications.  Budgets often report expenditures by object class at the departmental level.

## L.  Accounting for the General Fund

The general fund is the most significant governmental fund.  It accounts for all transactions not accounted for in any other fund.  Revenues come from many sources (taxes, licenses and permits, fines and forfeits, charges for services, etc.), and the expenditures cover the major functions of government (public safety, highways and streets, education, etc.).  The illustration below presents an overview of the general fund account structure.

**GENERAL FUND ACCOUNT STRUCTURE**

*Real Accounts*
Current Assets (DR)
Current Liabilities (CR)
Fund Balance (Fund Equity) (CR)
    Reserved (Encumbrances, Inventories, etc.)
   Unreserved
     Designated
     Undesignated

| *Nominal Accounts* | *Budgetary Accounts* |
|---|---|
| Revenues Control (CR) | Estimated Revenues Control (DR) |
| Other Financing Sources Control (CR) | Estimated Other Financing |
|   (Transfers In) |   Sources Control (DR) |
|   (Bond Issue Proceeds) | |
|   (Sale of Capital Assets) | |
| Expenditures Control (DR) | Appropriations Control (CR) |
| | Encumbrances Control (DR) |
| Other Financing Uses Control (DR) | Estimated Other Financing |
|   (Transfers Out) |   Uses Control (CR) |
| | Budgetary Fund Balance (DR) (CR) |
| | Budgetary Fund Balance—Reserved |
| |   for Encumbrances (CR) |

The following represents an accounting cycle problem for the general fund.  Some of these entries have been illustrated previously.

a.  Adoption of a budget where estimated revenues exceed appropriations and planned transfers by $10,000. (First year of existence for this governmental unit.)

| | | |
|---|---|---|
| Estimated Revenues Control (detail posted to subsidiary ledger) | 300,000 | |
|     Appropriations Control (detail posted to subsidiary ledger) | | 240,000 |
|     Estimated Other Financing Uses Control | | 50,000 |
|     Budgetary Fund Balance | | 10,000 |

b.  Transfers to a debt service fund (for general long-term debt payments) amount to $50,000.

| | | |
|---|---|---|
| Other Financing Uses—Transfers Out | 50,000 | |
|     Due to Debt Service Fund | | 50,000 |

According to the GASB, transfers should be recognized in the accounting period in which the interfund receivable and payable arises. The account "Other Financing Uses—Transfers Out" is a temporary/nominal account that is compared with the budgetary account "Estimated Other Financing Uses." The account "Due to—Fund" is a current liability. Note that the debt service fund would record a receivable as follows:

***Debt Service***

| | | |
|---|---|---|
| Due from General Fund | 50,000 | |
|     Other Financing Sources—Transfers In | | 50,000 |

The "Transfers" accounts are closed at the end of the year. It is important to note that the account "Transfers Out" is not an expenditure account, but is an Other Financing Use, and that the account "Transfers In" is not a revenue account, but is an Other Financing Source. (See the combined statement of revenues, expenditures, and changes in fund balance shown previously.) There is a complete discussion of interfund transactions and transfers later in this module (Section T).

c.  The property tax levy is recorded as revenues, under the modified accrual basis, in the year for which the tax levy is enacted by the governmental unit, if collections will be in time to finance expenditures of the current period. The tax bills amount to $250,000, and $20,000 is estimated to be uncollectible.

| | | |
|---|---|---|
| Property Taxes Receivable—Current | 250,000 | |
|     Allowance for Uncollectible Taxes—Current | | 20,000 |
|     Revenues Control | | 230,000 |

Under the modified accrual basis, revenues should be recorded in the period in which they are both measurable and available. The GASB requires that property taxes be recognized as a revenue if the taxes are

1.  Available—collected by year-end or soon enough to pay liabilities of the current period (no more than sixty days after the end of the fiscal year)
2.  To finance the budget of the current period

To the extent the modified accrual criteria for recognition are not met, the property tax levy would be recorded with a credit to Deferred Revenues, a liability, instead of Revenues.

If cash is needed to pay for expenditures before the property tax receivables are collected, it is not uncommon for governmental units to borrow on tax anticipation notes. The receivable serves as security for this loan and, as taxes are collected, the anticipation warrants are liquidated (i.e., Tax Anticipation Notes Payable is debited).

Note, also, the treatment of the allowance for uncollectible accounts. Expendable funds account for resource inflows (revenues) and resource outflows (expenditures). Expenses are not recorded. The Allowance for Uncollectible Accounts represents an estimated reduction in a resource inflow and, accordingly, revenues are recorded net of estimated uncollectible taxes.

d.  Revenues from fines, licenses, and permits amount to $40,000.

| | | |
|---|---|---|
| Cash | 40,000 | |
|     Revenues Control (detail posted) | | 40,000 |

Resource inflows from fines, licenses, permits, etc. are usually not measurable until the cash is collected. Sometimes, it is possible to measure the potential resource inflow; however, because the availability is questionable, revenues are recorded when cash is collected.

e.  The state owes the city $25,000 for the city's share of the state sales tax. The amount has not been received at year-end, but it is expected within the first few months of the next fiscal year (in time to pay the liabilities as of the current fiscal year).

| State Sales Tax Receivable | 25,000 | |
| Revenues Control (detail posted) | | 25,000 |

Sales taxes, income taxes, etc. may be accrued before collection by a governmental unit, if collection is anticipated in time to pay for current year expenditures. Other firm commitments from the state or other governmental units for grants, etc. are also recorded.

f.   Incurred liabilities for salaries, repairs, utilities, rent, and other regularly occurring items for $200,000.

| Expenditures Control (detail posted) | 200,000 | |
| Accounts Payable | | 200,000 |

Note that all resource outflows authorized in the appropriations budget are debited to Expenditures. It makes no difference whether the outflow is for a fire truck or for rent. Remember, expendable funds do not have a capital maintenance objective. Also, note that the encumbrance accounts were not used in this example. There is usually no need to encumber appropriations for items that occur regularly, and which possess a highly predictable amount (e.g., salaries, rent, etc.). It should be pointed out, however, that there is no hard and fast rule for when to use encumbrances, and encumbrance policies do vary tremendously (i.e., from every expenditure being encumbered to virtually no expenditures being encumbered).

g.   Ordered one police car; estimated cost is $17,000. One month later, ordered second police car; estimated cost is $16,500.

| Encumbrances Control | 17,000 | |
| Budgetary Fund Balance—Reserved for Encumbrances | | 17,000 |
| Encumbrances Control | 16,500 | |
| Budgetary Fund Balance—Reserved for Encumbrances | | 16,500 |

Recording encumbrances prevents overspending line-item appropriations. In the case of the police cars, assume the appropriations budget authorized $34,000 for police vehicles. After the first police car was ordered, the unencumbered appropriation for police vehicles was reduced to $17,000. This placed a dollar limit on what could be spent on the second car.

h.   Police car ordered first was received; actual cost is $16,800.

| Budgetary Fund Balance—Reserved for Encumbrances | 17,000 | |
| Encumbrances Control | | 17,000 |
| Expenditures Control | 16,800 | |
| Accounts Payable | | 16,800 |

i.   Property tax collections amounted to $233,000, payments to other funds amounted to $50,000 (see item b.), and payments of vouchers were $190,000.

| Cash | 233,000 | |
| Property Taxes Receivable—Current | | 233,000 |
| Due to Debt Service Fund | 50,000 | |
| Cash | | 50,000 |
| Accounts Payable | 190,000 | |
| Cash | | 190,000 |
| Allowance for Uncollectible Taxes—Current | 3,000 | |
| Revenues Control | | 3,000 |

The last entry above is required because the Allowance for Uncollectible Taxes—Current was overstated. Note that the estimate was $20,000 in entry c. above. Tax revenues were estimated to be $230,000. Since property tax collections exceeded $230,000 for the current year, an increase in revenues is required.

j.   Recorded $5,000 inventory of materials and supplies, reduced the allowance for uncollectible property taxes to $10,000, and reclassified uncollected property taxes to delinquent accounts.

| | | |
|---|---|---|
| Materials and Supplies Inventory[3] | 5,000 | |
|     Fund Balance—Reserved for Inventory of Materials and Supplies | | 5,000 |
| Allowance for Uncollectible Taxes—Current | 7,000 | |
|     Revenues Control | | 7,000 |
| Property Taxes Receivable—Delinquent | 17,000 | |
| Allowance for Uncollectible Taxes—Current | 10,000 | |
|     Allowance for Uncollectible Taxes—Delinquent | | 10,000 |
|     Property Taxes Receivable—Current | | 17,000 |

One of the reasons for recording the inventory of materials and supplies is to inform the preparers of the budget that items purchased during the year and charged to expenditures (item f.) are still unused. The account "Fund Balance—Reserved for Inventory of Materials and Supplies" is a reservation of Fund Balance. In this respect, it is similar to "Fund Balance—Reserved for Encumbrances."

The second entry adjusts the estimate of uncollectible property taxes to $10,000. This is the result of collecting more property taxes than anticipated (see entries made in c. and i. above) and of an estimate that $7,000 will now be collected.

The third entry reclassifies property taxes receivable from current to delinquent at the end of the year. Generally, interest and penalty charges accrue on the unpaid taxes from the date they become delinquent. If these items have accrued at the end of a fiscal period, they would be recorded in the following way:

| | | |
|---|---|---|
| Interest and Penalties Receivable on Delinquent Taxes | xx | |
|     Allowance for Uncollectible Interest and Penalties | | xx |
|     Revenues Control | | xx |

k.  Appropriate closing entries are made.

| | | |
|---|---|---|
| Budgetary Fund Balance | 10,000 | |
| Appropriations Control | 240,000 | |
| Estimated Other Financing Uses Control | 50,000 | |
|     Estimated Revenues Control | | 300,000 |
| Revenues | 305,000 | |
|     Expenditures Control | | 216,800 |
|     Encumbrances Control | | 16,500 |
|     Other Financing Uses—Transfers Out | | 50,000 |
|     Fund Balance—Unreserved | | 21,700 |
| Budgetary Fund Balance—Reserved for Encumbrances | 16,500 | |
|     Fund Balance—Reserved for Encumbrances | | 16,500 |

**Financial statements.** Under the GASB *Codification*, individual fund statements should not be prepared that simply repeat information found in the basic or combining statements but may be prepared to present individual fund budgetary comparisons (not needed for the general or major special revenue funds), to present prior year comparative data, or to present more detailed information than is found in the basic or combining statements.

The balance sheet below would represent the general fund portion of the governmental funds balance sheet. Note the following points from the balance sheet:

1.  The total fund balance (equity) is $43,200, but only $21,700 is unreserved. This $21,700 represents the appropriable component of total fund balance (i.e., the amount that can be used next period to help finance a deficit budget). The $21,700 represents unreserved net liquid resources.

2.  The reason for crediting "Fund Balance—Reserved for Inventory of Materials and Supplies" in item j. previously should now be more meaningful. The inventory of materials and supplies is not a liquid resource that can be used to finance future expenditures. Consequently, if this asset is disclosed, it must be disclosed via a fund restriction.

3.  The "Fund Balance—Reserved for Encumbrances" which is disclosed on the balance sheet relates to the second police car that was ordered but not delivered at year-end. When the car is received in the next period, the following journal entries could be made, assuming the actual cost is $16,600:

---

[3]  *The illustration covers the "purchases method" for materials and supplies. The "consumption method" is not covered in this illustration. Consult an advanced or governmental text for coverage of the latter method.*

| | | |
|---|---|---|
| Expenditures—Prior Year | 16,500 | |
| Expenditures Control | 100 | |
|     Accounts Payable | | 16,600 |
| | | |
| Fund Balance—Reserved for Encumbrances | 16,500 | |
|     Expenditures—Prior Year | | 16,500 |

The police car would not be recorded in the general fund as a fixed asset; rather it would be displayed as a fixed asset in the government-wide Statement of Net Assets.

*City of X*
**GENERAL FUND**
**BALANCE SHEET**
*At June 30, 2005*

| *Assets* | | | *Liabilities and Fund Equity* | | |
|---|---|---|---|---|---|
| Cash | | $33,000 | *Liabilities:* | | |
| Property Taxes Receivable—Delinquent | $17,000 | |   Accounts Payable | | $26,800 |
|   Less: Allowance for Uncollectible | | | *Fund Equity:* | | |
|     Taxes—Delinquent | 10,000 | 7,000 |   Reserved for Inventory of Materials | | |
| State Sales Tax Receivable | | 25,000 |     and Supplies | $ 5,000 | |
| Inventory of Materials and Supplies | | 5,000 |   Reserved for Encumbrances | 16,500 | |
| | | |   Unreserved Fund Balance | 21,700 | |
| | | |     Total Fund Equity | | $43,200 |
| Total Assets | | $70,000 | Total Liabilities and Fund Equity | | $70,000 |

The following would be the general fund portion of the Budgetary Comparison Schedule:

*City of X*
**BUDGETARY COMPARISON SCHEDULE**
**GENERAL FUND**
*For the Year Ended June 30, 2005*

| | Budgeted amounts | | Actual amounts | Variances with final budget |
|---|---|---|---|---|
| | *Original* | *Final* | *(Budgetary basis)* | *positive (negative)* |
| Budgetary Fund Balance, July 1, 2004 | -- | -- | -- | -- |
| Resources (Inflows) | $300,000 | $300,000 | $305,000 | $ 5,000 |
| Amounts Available for Appropriation | 300,000 | 300,000 | 305,000 | 5,000 |
| Charges to Appropriations (Outflows) | 240,000 | 240,000 | 233,300 | 6,700 |
| Transfers to Other Funds | 50,000 | 50,000 | 50,000 | -- |
| Total Charges to Appropriations | 290,000 | 290,000 | 283,300 | 6,700 |
| Budgetary Fund Balance, June 30, 2005 | $ 10,000 | $ 10,000 | $ 21,700 | $11,700 |

The Budgetary Comparison Schedule is included in Required Supplementary Information (RSI), presented after the notes to the basic statements. The format may be in accord with the budget or in accord with the Statement of Revenues, Expenditures, and Changes in Fund Balances (see page 803). The Budgetary Fund Balance may or may not be the same as the Unreserved Fund Balance reported in the Balance Sheet for the General Fund. (In this example, it is the same.)

One additional point needs to be covered before going to special revenue funds; that is, how to account for the inventory of materials and supplies in the second or any subsequent year. Accordingly, assume that at the end of the second year, $4,000 of materials and supplies were unused. The adjusting entry would appear as follows:

| | | |
|---|---|---|
| Fund Balance—Reserved for Inventory of Materials and Supplies | 1,000 | |
|     Materials and Supplies Inventory | | 1,000 |

This entry, when posted, will result in a balance of $4,000 in the inventory and reserve accounts. Note the entry at the end of the first year established a $5,000 balance in these accounts. Thereafter, the inventory and reserve accounts are adjusted upward or downward to whatever the balance is at the end of the year.[4]

## M. Accounting for Special Revenue Funds

Special revenue funds account for earmarked revenue as opposed to the many revenue sources that are accounted for in the general fund. The earmarked revenue is then used to finance various authorized expenditures. For example, a city might place its share of the state's gasoline tax revenues into a State Gasoline Tax Fund, which could then be used to maintain streets. Note that a governmental unit has some

---

[4] *Again, this entry illustrates the "purchases method" of accounting for inventories. Consult a governmental or advanced text for illustration of the "consumption method."*

discretion in terms of how many special revenue funds it creates. Sometimes separate funds are required by law or grant requirements. Many federal and state grants are reported in special revenue funds.

The accounting for special revenue funds parallels that of the general fund. One type of transaction that often takes place in a special revenue fund is a "reimbursement" grant from a federal or state government. **GASB Statement 33** lists reimbursement grant requirements as one of the conditions that must be satisfied before a revenue can be recognized, either for accrual or modified accrual accounting. With a reimbursement grant, the granting government will not provide resources unless the receiving government provides evidence that an appropriate expenditure has taken place; **GASB 33** requires that the expenditure must be recognized prior to a revenue being recognized.

For example, assume a municipality with a calendar fiscal year receives a grant award on November 1, 2005, in the amount of $30,000. No entry would be recorded (either a receivable or revenue) until the expenditure takes place.

Assume the expenditure takes place on March 1, 2006. The entries would be (for accrual accounting)

| | | |
|---|---|---|
| Expenditures Control | 30,000 | |
| Cash | | 30,000 |
| Grants Receivable | 30,000 | |
| Revenues Control—Grants | | 30,000 |

Assume cash is received on April 1, 2006; the entry would be

| | | |
|---|---|---|
| Cash | 30,000 | |
| Grants Receivable | | 30,000 |

The budgetary comparison schedule in RSI must include "major" special revenue funds for which annual budgets have been legally adopted.

## N. Accounting for Capital Projects Funds

Capital projects funds account for the acquisition and use of resources for the construction or purchase of major, long-lived fixed assets, except for those that are financed by internal service, enterprise, and trust funds. Resources for construction or purchase normally come from the issuance of general long-term debt, from government grants (federal, state, and local), and from interfund transfers.

Project budgets for estimated resources and expenditures must be approved before the project can begin. However, unlike the budgets of general and special revenue funds, an annual budget for capital projects funds may not be legally adopted and need not be recorded formally in the accounts.

The following transactions illustrate the entries encountered in a capital projects fund:

a. City Council approved the construction of a new city hall at an estimated cost of $10,000,000. General obligation long-term serial bonds were authorized for issuance in the face amount of $10,000,000. (No entries are required.)

b. $10,000,000 in 8% general obligation serial bonds were issued for $10,100,000. Assume that the premium is transferred to a debt service fund for the eventual payment of the debt. (Premiums and discounts in governmental funds are not amortized in the fund financial statements.)

| | | |
|---|---|---|
| Cash | 10,100,000 | |
| Other Financing Sources—Proceeds of Bonds | | 10,100,000 |
| Other Financing Uses—Transfers Out | 100,000 | |
| Cash | | 100,000 |

Note the credit to Proceeds of Bonds. This is an Other Financing Source on the operating statement, whereas the Transfers Out is an Other Financing Use. Both accounts are temporary accounts that are closed to Unreserved Fund Balance at year-end.

The transfer requires an entry in the debt service fund.

***Debt Service Fund***

| | | |
|---|---|---|
| Cash | 100,000 | |
| Other Financing Sources—Transfer In | | 100,000 |

This entry will be explained in more detail later.

c. The bond issue proceeds are temporarily invested in a Certificate of Deposit (CD) and earn $50,000. The earnings are authorized to be sent to the debt service fund for the payment of bonds.

**Capital Projects Fund**

| | | |
|---|---|---|
| Investment in CD | 10,000,000 | |
|    Cash | | 10,000,000 |
| | | |
| Cash | 50,000 | |
|    Revenues—Interest | | 50,000 |

**Debt Service Fund**

| | | | | |
|---|---|---|---|---|
| Other financing uses— | | | Cash | 50,000 | |
|   Transfers out | 50,000 | |   Other financing sources— | |
|     Cash | | 50,000 |     Transfers in | 50,000 |

d.   The lowest bid, $9,800,000, is accepted from a general contractor.

| | | |
|---|---|---|
| Encumbrances Control | 9,800,000 | |
|    Fund Balance—Reserved for Encumbrances[5] | | 9,800,000 |

e.   $2,000,000 of the temporary investments are liquidated.

| | | |
|---|---|---|
| Cash | 2,000,000 | |
|    Investment in CD | | 2,000,000 |

f.   Progress billings due to the general contractor for work performed amount to $2,000,000. The contract allows 10% of the billings to be retained until final inspection and approval of the building. The contractor was paid $1,800,000.

| | | |
|---|---|---|
| Fund Balance—Reserved for Encumbrances | 2,000,000 | |
|    Encumbrances Control | | 2,000,000 |
| | | |
| Expenditures—Construction | 2,000,000 | |
|    Contracts Payable | | 2,000,000 |
| | | |
| Contracts Payable | 2,000,000 | |
|    Cash | | 1,800,000 |
|    Contracts Payable—Retained Percentage | | 200,000 |

The account "Contracts Payable—Retained Percentage" is a liability account. Note, also, that the fixed asset is not recorded in the capital projects fund because this fund is expendable and does not have a capital maintenance objective.

g.   Interest accrued on a CD at the end of the year amounted to $40,000. This was authorized to be sent to the debt service fund for the payment of debt.

**Capital Projects Fund**

| | | |
|---|---|---|
| Interest Receivable | 40,000 | |
|    Revenues—Interest | | 40,000 |

**Debt Service Fund**

| | | | | |
|---|---|---|---|---|
| Other Financing Uses— | | | Due from Other Funds | 40,000 | |
|   Transfers Out | 40,000 | |   Other Financing Sources— | |
|     Due to Other Funds | | 40,000 |     Transfers In | 40,000 |

The interest is recognized because it is measurable and will soon be available to finance debt service fund expenditures.

h.   Closing entries for the capital projects fund would appear as follows:

(1)

| | | |
|---|---|---|
| Revenues—Interest | 90,000 | |
| Other Financing Sources—Proceeds of Bonds | 10,100,000 | |
|    Fund Balance—Unreserved | | 10,190,000 |

(2)

| | | |
|---|---|---|
| Fund Balance—Unreserved | 9,800,000 | |
|    Encumbrances Control | | 7,800,000 |
|    Expenditures—Construction | | 2,000,000 |

(3)

| | | |
|---|---|---|
| Fund Balance—Unreserved | 190,000 | |
|    Other Financing Uses—Transfers Out | | 190,000 |

The GASB requires that the totals for "major" capital projects funds appear in the balance sheet and the Statement of Revenues, Expenditures, and Changes in Fund Balances, for governmental funds. Combining statements are required in the CAFR for nonmajor capital projects funds along with other nonmajor governmental funds.

A "stand-alone" Statement of Revenues, Expenditures, and Changes in Fund Balances appears for the capital projects fund example.

---

[5]   *Since an annual budget is not assumed in this example, the credit is taken directly to the fund equity account.*

**City of X**
*Capital Projects Fund*
**STATEMENT OF REVENUES, EXPENDITURES, AND CHANGES
IN FUND BALANCES**
*Year Ended June 30, 2005*

| | | |
|---|---|---|
| *Revenues:* | | |
| Interest on Temporary Investments | | $    90,000 |
| *Expenditures:* | | |
| ·   Construction of City Hall | | 2,000,000 |
| Excess of Expenditures over Revenues | | (1,910,000) |
| *Other Financing Sources and Uses:* | | |
| Proceeds of General Obligation Bonds | $10,100,000 | |
| Transfer to Debt Service Fund | (190,000) | 9,910,000 |
| Excess of Revenues and Other Financing Sources over | | |
| Expenditures and Other Financing Uses | | 8,000,000 |
| Fund Balance—Beginning of Year | | -- |
| Fund Balance—End of Year | | $8,000,000 |

At the beginning of the second year, the following entry would be made to reestablish the Encumbrances balance:

| | | |
|---|---|---|
| Encumbrances Control | 7,800,000 | |
| Fund Balance—Unreserved | | 7,800,000 |

The purpose of this entry is to permit the recording of expenditures in the normal manner (i.e., reverse the encumbrances before recording the expenditures).

When the city hall project is finished, the capital projects fund should be terminated. Assuming there are no cost overruns, the excess cash left in the fund upon project completion must be transferred to some other fund, normally a debt service fund. This entry is described along with other interfund transactions and transfers in Section S.

**Impairment of capital assets**. In accordance with GASB 42, governments must evaluate prominent events or changes in circumstances affecting capital assets to determine whether impairment of the assets has occurred. Such events include evidence of physical damage, enactment or approval of laws or regulations, changes in environmental factors, technological changes or evidence of obsolescence, changes in the manner or duration of use of the asset, or construction stoppage. The asset is considered impaired if (a) the decline in service utility of the asset is large in magnitude, and (b) the event or change in circumstance is outside the normal life cycle of the capital asset (e.g., unexpected).

Impaired capital assets that are no longer used by the government should be reported at the lower of carrying value or fair value. Impairment losses on capital assets that will continue to be used by the government should be measured using the method that best reflects the asset's diminished service utility. As an example, if the asset is damaged, the loss should be measured at an estimate of the cost to restore the capital asset (the restoration approach). If the asset is affected by changes in environmental factors or obsolescence, the impairment should be measured using an approach that compares the service units provided by the asset before and after the impairment (the service units approach). If the asset is affected by a change in the manner or duration of use, the loss generally should be measured using the service units approach or the depreciated replacement cost approach which quantifies the cost of the service currently provided by the capital asset and converts that cost to historical cost.

Any insurance recovery associated with events or changes in circumstances resulting in impairment of a capital asset should be netted against the impairment loss.

**O. Debt Service Funds**

Debt service funds usually handle the repayment of general obligation long-term debt and interest. This type of debt is secured by the good faith and taxing power of the governmental unit. Repayment of internal service and enterprise long-term debt is accounted for in those individual funds. Consequently, debt service funds are normally established as the result of issuing general obligation bonds for capital projects. The bond liability to be extinguished is not recorded in the debt service fund until it matures. General long-term debt is reported only in the government-wide financial statements.

Assume the City of X authorizes a debt service fund for the general obligation serial bonds issued to finance the city hall project. The debt service fund is also authorized to pay the 8% interest on the $10,000,000 of debt on December 31 and June 30. The fiscal year-end is June 30. Note that the debt service fund has received resources from the general and capital projects funds. Transactions showing recognition and receipt of these resources were illustrated in the discussions of the general and capital projects funds. They are repeated below as follows:

| | | | | | |
|---|---|---|---:|---:|---|
| (1) | Due from General Fund | | 50,000 | | (Transaction b. |
| | Other Financing Sources—Transfers In | | | 50,000 | in Section L.) |
| (2) | Cash | | 50,000 | | (Transaction i. |
| | Due from General Fund | | | 50,000 | in Section L.) |
| (3) | Cash | | 100,000 | | (Transaction b. |
| | Other Financing Sources—Transfers In | | | 100,000 | in Section N.) |
| (4) | Cash | | 50,000 | | (Transaction c. |
| | Other Financing Sources—Transfers In | | | 50,000 | in Section N.) |
| (5) | Due from Capital Projects Fund | | 40,000 | | (Transaction g. |
| | Other Financing Sources—Transfers In | | | 40,000 | in Section N.) |

Assume the bonds were issued on July 1. In addition, assume that $250,000 of the bonds mature each six months, starting June 30.

    a.   The property tax levy contains $870,000 portion allocable to the debt service fund. $20,000 of this amount is estimated to be uncollectible.

| | | |
|---|---:|---:|
| Property Taxes Receivable—Current | 870,000 | |
|     Allowance for Uncollectible Taxes—Current | | 20,000 |
|     Revenues—Property Taxes | | 850,000 |

    b.   $840,000 of property taxes are collected during the year. The remainder of the property taxes is reclassified as delinquent.

| | | |
|---|---:|---:|
| Cash | 840,000 | |
|     Property Taxes Receivable—Current | | 840,000 |
| | | |
| Property Taxes Receivable—Delinquent | 30,000 | |
| Allowance for Uncollectible Taxes—Current | 20,000 | |
|     Property Taxes Receivable—Current | | 30,000 |
|     Allowance for Uncollectible Taxes—Delinquent | | 20,000 |

    c.   The semiannual interest is paid on December 31 and June 30. The following entries are made on December 31:

| | | |
|---|---:|---:|
| Expenditures—Interest | 400,000 | |
|     Matured Interest Payable | | 400,000 |
| | | |
| Matured Interest Payable | 400,000 | |
|     Cash | | 400,000 |

The following entries are made on June 30:

| | | |
|---|---:|---:|
| Expenditures—Interest | 400,000 | |
|     Matured Interest Payable | | 400,000 |
| | | |
| Matured Interest Payable | 400,000 | |
|     Cash | | 400,000 |

Note that if interest were paid on dates other than December 31 and June 30, interest would not be accrued to the end of the fiscal year.

    d.   On June 30, the first $250,000 principal payment became due, and $200,000 was paid. The following entries would be made in the debt service fund:

| | | |
|---|---:|---:|
| Expenditures—Principal | 250,000 | |
|     Matured Bonds Payable | | 250,000 |
| | | |
| Matured Bonds Payable | 200,000 | |
|     Cash | | 200,000 |

If a bank were used as the fiscal agent, cash would first be transferred to a "Cash with Fiscal Agent" account, and payment would then be made from that account.

    e.   Appropriate closing entries are made based upon all information presented.

| | | |
|---|---:|---:|
| Revenues—Property Taxes | 850,000 | |
| Other Financing Sources—Transfers In | 240,000 | |
|     Expenditures—Interest | | 800,000 |
|     Expenditures—Principal | | 250,000 |
|     Fund Balance—Reserved for Debt Service | | 40,000 |

The balance sheet for the debt service fund would appear as follows:

*City of X*
**DEBT SERVICE FUND**
**BALANCE SHEET**
*June 30, 2005*

| Assets | | Liabilities and Fund Equity | |
|---|---|---|---|
| Cash | $40,000 | *Liabilities*: | |
| Due from Capital Projects Fund | 40,000 | Matured Bonds Payable | $50,000 |
| Property taxes receivable—Delinquent (net of | | *Fund Equity*: | |
| $20,000 allowance for uncollectible taxes) | 10,000 | Fund Balance—Reserved for Debt Service | 40,000 |
| Total Assets | $90,000 | Total Liabilities and Fund Equity | $90,000 |

Under modified accrual accounting, expenditures for principal and interest are generally not accrued but recorded when due. GASB 36 provides that if resources are available at year-end and payment is to be made within one month after year-end, an accrual may be made, if a debt service fund is used.

## P. Permanent Funds

A fifth category of governmental funds, introduced by GASB 34, is the **permanent fund** type. Permanent funds account for nonexpendable funds provided and held for some governmental purpose. The income from those investments will be recorded as revenues and expenditures.

A common example would be a cemetery perpetual care fund. Assume a local citizen was concerned about the deplorable condition of the city cemetery and on January 2, 2005, contributed $500,000 with the stipulation that the funds be invested and held; the income is to be used for the purpose of maintaining the city cemetery. On January 2, the cash was received and invested.

| | | |
|---|---|---|
| Cash | 500,000 | |
| Revenues—Additions to Permanent Endowments | | 500,000 |
| Investments | 500,000 | |
| Cash | | 500,000 |

During 2005, $30,000 was earned on the investment, and $25,000 was expended.

| | | |
|---|---|---|
| Cash (and/or interest receivable) | 30,000 | |
| Revenues—Investment Income | | 30,000 |
| Expenditures | 25,000 | |
| Cash (or Accounts Payable) | | 25,000 |

## Q. Accounting for Special Assessments

GASB 6, *Accounting and Reporting for Special Assessments,* outlines the accounting and financial reporting for special assessments. Special assessments are levied for projects to be paid primarily by the property owners who benefited (for example, a street lighting or sidewalk project).

Under GASB 6, the accounting for special assessment capital projects depends on the liability of the governmental unit for the special assessment debt. If the governmental unit is not obligated in any way for the debt, the special assessment activities will be accounted for in an agency fund. However, if the governmental unit is either **primarily** or **potentially liable** for the debt, the accounting will take place as if it were any other capital improvement and financing transaction. Construction activities will be recorded in a capital projects fund and debt principal and interest activities would be recorded in a debt service fund.

## R. Accounting for Proprietary Funds

**Internal service funds** are established to account for the provision of goods and services by one department of the government to other departments within the government, generally on a cost-reimbursement basis. Uses of internal service fund services are budgeted through the budgets of the user departments. Internal service funds are normally established for the following types of activities: central garages, motor pools, central printing and duplicating, stores departments, self-insurance, etc. **Enterprise funds,** on the other hand, account for activities for which the government provides goods and services that are (1) rendered primarily to the general public, (2) financed substantially or entirely through user charges, and (3) intended to be self-supporting. Enterprise funds are usually established for public utilities, airports, toll roads and bridges, transit systems, golf courses, solid waste landfills, etc.

Proprietary funds use the accrual basis of accounting and are nonexpendable; capital is to be maintained. Revenues and expenses are recorded generally as they would be in commercial enterprises. Fixed assets are recorded in proprietary funds, and depreciation expense is deducted from revenues. These funds also report their own long-term liabilities. The GASB has provided a special rule regarding the use of FASB pronouncements in enterprise funds of state and local government. That rule has two parts.

1.   Enterprise funds should follow FASB pronouncements issued prior to November 30, 1989, unless those FASB pronouncements conflict with GASB pronouncements.

2.   Enterprise funds may or may not follow FASB pronouncements issued after November 30, 1989, that do not conflict with GASB pronouncements.  The decision regarding whether or not to follow such FASB pronouncements must be applied consistently to all FASB pronouncements, and the choice must be disclosed.

An example of a FASB pronouncement that does conflict would be SFAS 35 regarding pensions, which has different conclusions than GASB reached in its pension standards.

When proprietary funds are initially established, a contribution or advance is usually received from the general fund.  A contribution is a transfer and would be recorded by the internal service or enterprise fund as follows:

| Cash | xx | |
|------|----|----|
|    Capital Contributions | | xx |

The Capital Contributions account is a separate category in the statement of Revenues, Expenses, and Changes in Net Assets.  On the other hand, an advance from the general fund is a long-term loan and would be recorded by an internal service or enterprise fund as follows:

| Cash | xx | |
|------|----|----|
|    Advance from General Fund | | xx |

The advance is a long-term liability on the proprietary fund's balance sheet.  It is a long-term asset on the general fund's balance sheet, which requires a reservation of Fund Balance.

Accounting entries for proprietary funds are similar to those for business enterprises.  "Operating Revenues—Charges for Services" is a common operating revenue account for both internal service and enterprise funds.  As indicated earlier, revenues and expenses are recognized on the full accrual basis and are classified as operating and nonoperating.  Some features that distinguish the accounting for proprietary funds are

1.   Long-term debt is recorded directly in internal service and enterprise funds.  Revenue bonds are those that are backed only by the revenues of the proprietary activity.  However, revenue bonds with general obligation backing and general obligation bonds that are to be paid with revenues of the proprietary activities are also recorded in the proprietary funds.

2.   Interest on long-term debt is accrued as an expense, unlike interest on general long-term debt (see debt service funds).  Premiums and discounts on debt issuances, as well as debt issue costs, are recorded with the debt and amortized over the life of the bonds.

3.   Fixed assets are capitalized and depreciated, using one of the generally accepted methods used by business enterprises.  Interest during construction is capitalized.

4.   Revenues, expenses, capital contributions, and transfers are closed out to net assets at year-end.  Three categories of net assets exist, as indicated earlier: (a) invested in capital assets, net of related debt, (b) restricted, and (c) unrestricted.  These are the same asset categories as are used in the government-wide Statement of Net Assets.

5.   Net assets—invested in capital assets, net of related debt, would be the net of fixed assets, less accumulated depreciation, less any long-term debt issued to finance capital assets.  Net assets—restricted would offset, for example, any resources held for future debt service in accord with bond indenture requirements.

6.   A special problem exists with self-insurance funds, which are often classified as internal service funds.[6]  Governments transfer resources from other funds to self-insurance funds, from which claims are paid.  To the extent that the transfers do not exceed the actuarially determined liability of the government, they are recorded as expenditures or expenses.  Any transfers in addition to the actuarially determined liability are classified as transfers.

7.   Another special problem exists with municipal waste landfills, which are often classified as enterprise funds.  Many of the solid waste landfills in the US are operated by local governmental units.  The problem which arises in accounting for municipal landfills is that most revenue is earned early in the useful life of the landfill, as various persons and organizations pay to dispose of waste; conversely, a significant portion of the costs, termed closure and postclosure care costs as defined by

---

[6]   *GASB requires that, if self-insurance is to be recorded in a single fund, that fund must be an internal service or the general fund.*

US Government regulations, occur up to twenty to thirty years later. The GASB requires that these future costs be estimated and charged against periodic revenues on a "units of production" basis according to the amount of landfill capacity consumed during each period. If a municipal waste landfill is operated as an enterprise fund, expenses and liabilities are accounted for on a full accrual basis and recorded directly in the enterprise fund. If the municipal waste landfill is operated through a governmental fund, the expenditure and fund liability would be limited to the amount that will be paid with currently available resources, and the remaining liability would be reported in the government-wide statements.

CPA exam questions sometimes portray a situation, such as a federal government grant for bus purchases, and ask candidates to provide accounting treatment for when the transaction is recorded in a governmental fund (record a revenue if expended, defer revenue if not), and for when the transaction is recorded in a proprietary fund (record as capital contributions). When uncertain, candidates should generally recall business accounting principles to record the proprietary fund transaction.

## S.  Accounting for Fiduciary Funds

Fiduciary funds (trust and agency) account for resources invested or to be expended for the benefit of other governments, private organizations, or individuals. (Resources held and invested for the benefit of the reporting government are classified as permanent funds, a governmental fund category.) Included in the fiduciary fund category are pension (and other employee benefit) trust funds, investment trust funds, private-purpose trust funds, and agency funds.

**Pension (and other employee benefit) trust funds** are maintained when the governmental unit is trustee for the pension (or other employee benefit) plan. In addition, many state governments operate statewide Public Employee Retirement Systems (PERS) for local governments, teachers, university employees, judges, etc. These PERS are normally a part of the state government reporting entity. Full accrual accounting is used for pension trust funds, and investments are reported at fair value. Pension trust funds are required to have two statements and two schedules (included as required supplementary information; see the contents of the CAFR). The pension trust funds are included in the (1) Statement of Fiduciary Net Assets and the (2) Statement of Changes in Fiduciary Net Assets. The two RSI schedules are the (1) Schedule of Funding Progress (which illustrates actuarial status) and the (2) Schedule of Employer Contributions. Accounting for pension plans by government employers is covered by GASBS 27 and 50. Accounting by pension plans is covered by GASBS 25 and 50.

Government pension plans do not include the accrued actuarial liability in the statement of fiduciary net assets. Rather, the actuarial liability is reported in the schedule of funding progress and in the notes. Extensive note disclosures are required, both for the PERS and for the government as employer, whether or not it is trustee of the pension plan.

The above requirements relate to **defined benefit** pension plans. Under **defined contribution** plans, the government is liable only for the required contributions not made.

Employer accounting for defined benefit plans is the same, regardless of whether or not the government is the trustee for the pension plan. Expenditures (or expenses) are charged in the appropriate funds (especially the general, special revenue, and enterprise funds) in an amount equal to the amount provided to the pension plan. The pension trust fund (or statewide PERS) would record those contributions as additions. Other additions for the pension trust fund would include employee contributions, investment income, and gains in the market value of investments. Deductions would include retirement benefit payments, disability payments, refunds to terminated (nonvested) employees, and losses in the market value of investments.

Statewide PERS may be **agency** defined benefit, **cost-sharing** defined benefit, or defined contribution. **Agency** plans maintain separate balances for each participating government so that it is possible to determine its unfunded actuarial liability (or assets in excess of accrued actuarial benefits). **Cost-sharing** plans normally compute balances on a statewide basis only; it is not the responsibility of each participating government to fund its own liability.

A final use for pension trust funds is IRS Sec. 457 Deferred Compensation Plans (tax-deferred annuities for government employees). In many cases, these plans will not be recorded. However, when the plan meets the criteria for inclusion in a government financial statement, GASB 34 requires that a pension trust fund be used.

The financial reporting framework for **postretirement benefits other than pensions** under GASB 45 is similar to the reporting for pensions under GASB 27. Employers are required to measure and disclose the amount for annual other post employment benefits (OPEB) cost on the accrual basis. Annual OPEB cost is equal to the employer's annual required contribution to the plan with certain adjustments if the OPEB obligation is under- or overfunded. This is essentially the same as the accounting required by commercial enterprises under SFAS 106 (See Module 11). However, GASB 45 allows an alternative simplified measurement method for employers with fewer than 100 total plan members.

A government may decide to provide **voluntary termination benefits,** such as early-retirement incentives to its employees. They may also provide **involuntary termination benefits,** such as severance pay. In governmental financial statements prepared on the accrual basis, governments should recognize a liability and expense for voluntary termination benefits when the offer has been accepted by the employees and the amount of liability can be estimated. For involuntary termination benefits, the liability should be recognized when the plan has been approved and communicated to the employees and the amount of the liability can be estimated. GASB 47 provides that the liability for termination benefits should be measured at the present value of the expected future benefit payments. In financial statements prepared on the modified accrual basis, the liability and expenditures for termination benefits should be recognized to the extent the liabilities are normally expected to be liquidated with expendable available financial resources.

**Investment trust funds** are required when a government sponsors an external investment pool; for example, when a county sponsors an investment pool for all cities, school districts, and other governments within its borders. The **external portion** of investment pools are to be reported (by the county) in a manner similar to pension trust funds. Statements of Net Fiduciary Assets and of Changes in Fiduciary Net Assets are required. Statements of Cash Flows are not required.

**Private-purpose trust funds** represent all other trust arrangements under which principal and income benefit other governments, private organizations, or individuals. Private-purpose trust funds may be **nonexpendable** or **expendable**. A nonexpendable trust fund is one in which the principal cannot be expended but which provide that income may be expended for some agreed-upon purpose. Sometimes, this is called an endowment. For example, a donor gives $500,000 to a city with instructions that the principal be invested permanently and that the income be used to provide scholarships for low-income children to attend a private, not-for-profit day care program. The receipt and investment of the gift would be recorded as

| | | |
|---|---|---|
| Cash | 500,000 | |
|    Additions—Contributions | | 500,000 |
| Investments | 500,000 | |
|    Cash | | 500,000 |

Assume $30,000 is received in investment income and expended.

| | | |
|---|---|---|
| Cash | 30,000 | |
|    Additions—Investment Income | | 30,000 |
| Deductions—Awarding of Scholarships | 30,000 | |
|    Cash | | 30,000 |

Expendable private-purpose trust funds are accounted for in the same manner, except that the principal as well as investment income may be expended. For example, a donor may give $10,000 to a school district with instructions that each year $2,000 plus investment income be awarded to the top student in the senior class, as a scholarship.

Another use of private-purpose trust funds, in some cases, is for **escheat property**. Escheat property is property taken over by a government, usually state government, when the property is abandoned and the legal owners cannot be found. GASB 37 concluded that escheat property generally is recorded in the governmental or proprietary fund to which the property ultimately escheats (e.g., an educational fund). A liability is recorded for estimated amounts to potential claimants. A private-purpose trust fund is used when resources are held for individuals, private organizations, or another government.

**Agency funds** are used to account for activities where the government is acting as an agent for others. Agency funds have only assets and liabilities; no fund equity, revenue, or expenditure accounts are used. The GASB requires the use of agency funds for special assessments where the government is not liable in any way for the debt.

Another common use of agency funds is to account for property taxes. Property taxes are usually remitted to a county treasurer who places the monies in a county Tax Agency Fund. The taxes are held until such time as they are remitted to each of the other local governments located within the county. Often, a fee is charged, which decreases the amount that is distributed to the other local governments and increases the amount that is distributed to the County General Fund.

## T.  Reporting Interfund Activity

Under GASB 34, interfund activity is shown between individual funds in fund financial statements and between business-type and governmental-type activities in the government-wide financial statements. GASB provides for two major types of interfund activity, each with two subtypes.

1. Reciprocal interfund activity

    a.  Interfund loan and advances

    b.  Interfund services provided and used

2. Nonreciprocal interfund activity

    a.  Interfund transfers

    b.  Interfund reimbursements

**Interfund loans and advances** are transactions in which one fund provides resources with a requirement for repayment. Short-term loans are recorded with "Due from" and "Due to" accounts. For example, if an enterprise fund made a short-term loan to the general fund, the entry would be

| *Enterprise Fund* | | | *General Fund* | | |
|---|---|---|---|---|---|
| Due from General Fund | 100,000 | | Cash | 100,000 | |
|   Cash | | 100,000 |   Due to Enterprise Fund | | 100,000 |

Long-term interfund receivables and payables use the terms "Advance to" and "Advance from." If a governmental fund makes a long-term loan to another fund, it is necessary to reserve fund balances, as the resources are not "available" for expenditure. For example, assume the general fund advances $50,000 to an internal service fund. The entries would be

| *General Fund* | | | *Internal Service Fund* | | |
|---|---|---|---|---|---|
| Advance to Internal Service | | | Cash | 50,000 | |
|   Fund | 50,000 | |   Advance from General Fund | | 50,000 |
|     Cash | | 50,000 | | | |
| Fund Balance—Unreserved | 50,000 | | | | |
|   Fund Balance—Reserved for | | | | | |
|     Long-Term Advances | | 50,000 | | | |

Loans and advances to and from component units are to be separately identified in the government-wide financial statements.

**Interfund services provided and used** represent transactions in which sales and purchases of goods and services between funds are made at prices approximating their external exchange price. Examples would include the sale of water from an enterprise fund to the general fund, the provision of services by an internal service fund to a governmental fund, a payment in lieu of taxes from an enterprise fund to the general fund (where payment is approximately equal to services provided), and the payment of a retirement fund contribution from the general fund to a pension trust fund. Revenues (or additions) are recognized by one fund, and an expenditure or expense is recorded by another fund. As a result, the operating statements will include these revenues and expenditures/expenses. For example, assume an internal services fund provides $30,000 in service to the general fund.

| *Internal Service Fund* | | | *General Fund* | | |
|---|---|---|---|---|---|
| Due from General Fund | 30,000 | | Expenditures Control | 30,000 | |
|   Operating Revenues— | | |   Due to Internal Service Fund | | 30,000 |
|     Charges for Services | | 30,000 | | | |

Prior to GASB 34, these were known as quasi-external transactions.

**Interfund transfers** are nonreciprocal transfers between funds, where payment is not expected. Examples would include an annual subsidy from an enterprise fund to the general fund or an annual transfer from the general fund to a debt service fund. To illustrate the latter in the amount of $300,000

| *General Fund* | | | *Debt Service Fund* | | |
|---|---|---|---|---|---|
| Other Financing Uses—Transfer | | | Cash | 300,000 | |
|   to Debt Service Fund | 300,000 | |   Other Financing Sources— | | |
|     Cash | | 300,000 |     Transfer from General Fund | | 300,000 |

Transfers are reported as "Other Financing Sources/Uses" in the governmental fund operating statements.

**Interfund reimbursements** are repayments from funds responsible for expenditures or expenses to those funds that initially paid for them. For example, assume the general fund paid an enterprise fund for a consultant's fee that was initially paid by the enterprise fund and charged to expense.

| General Fund | | | Enterprise Fund | | |
|---|---|---|---|---|---|
| Expenditures Control | 50,000 | | Cash | 50,000 | |
| Cash | | 50,000 | Consultant Fee Expense | | 50,000 |

## U. Accounting for Investments

GASB's rules for investment accounting are contained in Statement 31, *Accounting and Financial Reporting for Certain Investments and for External Investment Pools.* GASB 31 provides that investments in debt securities and in equity securities with determinable fair values be reported at fair value. Changes in fair value should be reported as a part of operations, using modified accrual or accrual accounting, as appropriate. No distinction is to be made on the face of the financial statements between realized and unrealized gains and losses, although disclosure may be made of realized gains in the notes. Investment income should be reported in the fund for which investments are held, when investments are pooled.

## V. Conversion from Fund Financial Statements to Government-Wide Financial Statements

Most state and local governments will keep their books on a fund basis in order to facilitate the preparation of fund financial statements and to prepare the budget-actual schedule as a part of RSI. This will mean that governments will record transactions on the modified accrual basis for governmental funds and on the accrual basis for proprietary and fiduciary funds. Many governments will make changes, on a worksheet basis, in order to prepare the government-wide financial statements. The following are the major changes that will be necessary to convert from governmental fund statements to the governmental activities portion of the government-wide statements.

### 1. General fixed assets

When general fixed assets are acquired through governmental funds, the account expenditures is debited. Governmental funds do not record fixed assets. It will be necessary to eliminate the expenditure accounts in the governmental funds and record fixed assets. These fixed assets will increase the net assets of the governmental activities. Assuming the amount is $10 million the entry would be

| | | |
|---|---|---|
| Fixed Assets (Land, Buildings, Equipment, etc.) | 10,000,000 | |
| Expenditures Control | | 10,000,000 |

In addition, a depreciation charge will be required for the equipment.

### 2. Issuance of general long-term debt

When general long-term debt is issued, governmental funds credit Proceeds of Debt, which is an Other Financing Source. Also, premiums and discounts are not amortized but simply add to or deduct from the amount of resources available. It will be necessary to eliminate those entries and record the debt as a liability, to be shown as a reduction of net assets in the governmental activities column of the Statement of Net Assets. Moreover, any premium or discount must be associated with the liability and amortized over the life of the bonds. The worksheet entry to convert the sale of bonds from governmental fund accounting to government-wide statements, assuming a sale of $5 million at par, would be

| | | |
|---|---|---|
| Other Financing Sources—Proceeds of Bonds | 5,000,000 | |
| Bonds Payable | | 5,000,000 |

### 3. Debt service payments

When making principal payments on long-term debt, governmental funds debit expenditures. Those expenditures will need to be eliminated and replaced with a debit to the debt principal when preparing the government-wide statements. In addition, governmental funds do not accrue interest payable but record expenditures on the maturity date. Accrual of interest payable will be required for the government-wide statements, including adjustments for amortization of premiums and discounts. The worksheet entry to convert a $100,000 principal payment from governmental fund accounting to government-wide statements would be

| | | |
|---|---|---|
| Bonds Payable | 100,000 | |
| Expenditures—Principal | | 100,000 |

### 4. Adjustment of revenue recognition

Governmental funds recognize revenues only when measurable and available to finance expenditures of the current period. In the case of property taxes, revenues cannot be recognized if those revenues will be collected more than sixty days after the end of the fiscal year. When preparing the government-wide financial statements, some adjustments will be required to recognize all revenues, net of uncollectible receivables, in accord with revenue accounting for exchange and nonexchange transactions, as described earlier in this module. Assume a government levied $10 million in property taxes for the year 2005 with 2% uncollectible.  The amount to be recognized on the government-wide statements is $9,800,000.  Assume that during 2005 and the first sixty days of 2006, $9,600,000 had been and was expected to be collected, limiting the amount reported as revenues in the governmental funds Statement of Revenues, Expenditures, and Changes in Fund Balances to $9,600,000.  The $200,000 would have been shown as a deferred revenue (liability) in the Governmental Funds Balance Sheet.  The worksheet entry would be

| | | |
|---|---|---|
| Deferred Revenues | 200,000 | |
| Revenues Control | | 200,000 |

5.  **Accrual of expenses**

Under modified accrual accounting, expenditures are recorded for items that are current, capital outlay, and debt service.  As indicated earlier, adjustments must be made to reduce expenditures for capital outlay payments and debt service principal payments.  In addition, adjustments must be made to record the noncurrent portion of certain liabilities (claims and judgments, compensated absences, etc.).  These worksheet entries would debit expenses and credit liabilities.

6.  **Other**

Some governments use the purchases method to record governmental fund inventories, and these must be changed to the consumption method when using accrual accounting.  Other governments do not record and amortize certain prepaid items, such as prepaid insurance and prepaid rent.  Adjustments must also be made for these items.

7.  **Reclassifications**

Fund financial statements are presented separately for governmental, proprietary, and fiduciary fund categories.  Government-wide financial statements have columns for governmental activities, business-type activities, and component units.  In order to make the transition from fund financial statements, the fiduciary funds will be eliminated.  Internal service funds, which are proprietary funds, are to be classified as governmental activities in the government-wide statements.  Discretely presented component units, which are not presented at all in the fund financial statements, will be added when preparing the government-wide financial statements.

## W.  College and University Accounting—Public (Governmental)—GASB 35

GASB 35, *Basic Financial Statements—and Management's Discussion and Analysis—for Public Colleges and Universities,* becomes effective in three phases for public institutions that are not component units of another reporting entity based on total revenues in the first fiscal year ending after June 15, 1999.

- Institutions with total annual revenues of $100 million or more—for periods beginning after June 15, 2001.
- Institutions with total annual revenues of $10 million or more but less than $100 million—for periods beginning after June 15, 2002.
- Institutions with annual revenues of less than $10 million—for periods beginning after June 15, 2003.

These are the same dates as required for state and local governments outlined in GASB 34.  As is true for state and local governments, retroactive adoption of infrastructure reporting is deferred a few years.  Public colleges that are component units of other reporting entities (states, for example) must adopt the provisions of GASB 35 at the same time as their primary government.

GASB 35 requires that public colleges follow the standards for special purpose governments outlined in GASB 34.  This means that public colleges may choose to use the guidance for special purpose governments engaged in (1) only business-type activities, (2) engaged in only governmental activities, or (3) engaged in both governmental and business-type activities.

Public colleges that choose to report as special purpose governments that are engaged in only governmental activities or in governmental and business-type activities are required to follow the reporting model presented earlier in this module for state and local governments.  This model requires (1) a Management's Discussion and Analysis (MD&A), (2) Government-Wide Financial Statements, (3) Fund Financial Statements, (4) Notes to the Financial Statements, and (5) Required Supplementary Information (CRSI) other than MD&A.

While a number of community colleges may choose to report in the manner described in the previous paragraph, most public colleges and universities will choose to report as special entities engaged only in **business-type** activities.  In this case, proprietary fund statements only are required.  These institutions will report (1) an MD&A, (2) a Statement of Net Assets, (3) a Statement of Revenues, Expenses, and Changes in Net Assets, (4) a Statement of Cash Flows, and (5) Required Supplementary Information other than MD&A. Public colleges reporting in this format present statements using the **economic resources measurement focus and the accrual basis of accounting**.

The **Statement of Net Assets** (as illustrated) may be presented in the format: Assets – Liabilities = Net Assets. Alternatively, a balance sheet format (Assets = Liabilities + Net Assets) may be presented. In either case, a classified statement must be presented, distinguishing between current and long-term assets and between current and long-term liabilities. As is the case for state and local governments, net assets must be segregated between (1) invested in capital assets, net of related debt, (2) restricted, and (3) unrestricted. Restricted net assets should show major categories of restrictions. It is **not** permissible to show designations of unrestricted net assets.

The **Statement of Revenues, Expenses, and Changes in Net Assets** is reported in an "all-inclusive" format that reconciles to the ending total net assets. GASB requires that revenues be reported by major source and that a distinction be made between operating and nonoperating revenues and expenses. The general format is

|   |   |
|---|---|
|   | Operating Revenues |
| – | Operating Expenses |
| = | Operating Income (Loss) |
| ± | Nonoperating Revenues and Expenses |
| = | Income Before Other Revenues, Expenses Gains, Losses, and Transfers |
| ± | Capital Contributions, Additions to Permanent and Term Endowments, Special and Extraordinary Items, and Transfers |
| = | Increase (Decrease) in Net Assets |
| + | Net Assets, Beginning of Period |
| = | Net Assets, End of Period |

GASB Statement 35 requires that state appropriations for operating purposes be shown as a nonoperating revenue. State appropriations for capital outlay are shown separately as capital appropriation. Capital grants and gifts, additions to permanent endowments, extraordinary items, and special items are also displayed separately.

The **Statement of Cash Flows** is prepared using the GASB format described earlier in this module. The direct method must be used, along with a reconciliation between net operating income (loss) and net cash provided (used) by operating activities. Four categories are used: (1) operating activities, (2) noncapital financing activities, (3) capital and related financing activities, and (4) investing activities. Note that interest paid is classified as a (capital or noncapital) financing activity and interest received is classified as cash flows from investing activities.

GASB Statement 35 requires that cash flows from state appropriations for operations be reported as cash flows from noncapital financing activities. It also requires that cash flows from state appropriations for construction be reported as cash flows from capital and related financing activities.

*ABC University*
**STATEMENT OF NET ASSETS**
*June 30, 2005*

|   | Primary institution | Component unit hospital |
|---|---|---|
| **Assets** | | |
| Current assets: | | |
| Cash and cash equivalents | $ 4,571,218 | $ 977,694 |
| Short-term investments | 15,278,981 | 2,248,884 |
| Accounts receivable, net | 6,412,520 | 9,529,196 |
| Inventories | 585,874 | 1,268,045 |
| Deposit with bond trustee | 4,254,341 | -- |
| Notes and mortgages receivable, net | 359,175 | -- |
| Other assets | 432,263 | 426,427 |
| Total current assets | $31,894,372 | $14,450,246 |

| | *Primary institution* | *Component unit hospital* |
|---|---|---|
| *Noncurrent assets:* | | |
| Restricted cash and cash equivalents | 24,200 | 18,500 |
| Endowment investments | 21,548,723 | -- |
| Notes and mortgages receivable, net | 2,035,323 | -- |
| Other long-term investments | -- | 6,441,710 |
| Investments in real estate | 6,426,555 | -- |
| Capital assets, net | 158,977,329 | 32,602,940 |
| Total noncurrent assets | 189,012,130 | 39,063,150 |
| Total assets | $220,906,502 | $53,513,396 |
| **Liabilities** | | |
| *Current liabilities:* | | |
| Accounts payable and accrued liabilities | 4,897,470 | 2,911,419 |
| Deferred revenue | 3,070,213 | -- |
| Long-term liabilities—current portion | 4,082,486 | 989,321 |
| Total current liabilities | $12,050,169 | $3,900,740 |
| *Noncurrent liabilities:* | | |
| Deposits | 1,124,128 | -- |
| Deferred revenue | 1,500,000 | -- |
| Long-term liabilities | 31,611,427 | 2,194,236 |
| Total noncurrent liabilities | 34,235,555 | 2,194,236 |
| Total liabilities | $46,285,724 | $6,094,976 |
| **Net Assets** | | |
| Invested in capital assets, net of related debt | $126,861,400 | $32,199,938 |
| *Restricted for:* | | |
| Nonexpendable: | | |
| Scholarships and fellowships | 10,839,473 | -- |
| Research | 3,767,564 | 2,286,865 |
| Expendable: | | |
| Scholarships and fellowships | 2,803,756 | -- |
| Research | 5,202,732 | -- |
| Instructional department uses | 938,571 | -- |
| Loans | 2,417,101 | -- |
| Capital projects | 4,952,101 | 913,758 |
| Debt service | 4,254,341 | 152,947 |
| Other | 403,632 | -- |
| Unrestricted | 12,180,107 | 11,864,912 |
| Total net assets | $174,620,778 | $47,418,420 |

SOURCE:  GASB 35, page 27.

**ABC University**
**STATEMENT OF REVENUES, EXPENSES, AND CHANGES IN NET ASSETS**
*For the Year Ended June 30, 2005*

> Operating expense may be displayed using either object or functional classification.

| | *Primary institution* | *Component unit hospital* |
|---|---|---|
| **Revenues** | | |
| *Operating revenues:* | | |
| Student tuition and fees (net of scholarship allowances of $3,214,454) | $ 36,913,194 | $          -- |
| Patient services (net of charity care of $5,114,352) | -- | 46,296,957 |
| Federal grants and contracts | 10,614,660 | -- |
| State and local grants and contracts | 3,036,953 | 7,475,987 |
| Nongovernmental grants and contracts | 873,740 | -- |
| Sales and services of educational departments | 19,802 | -- |
| Auxiliary enterprises: | | |
| Residential life (net of scholarship allowances of $428,641) | 28,079,274 | -- |
| Bookstore (net of scholarship allowances of $166,279) | 9,092,363 | -- |
| Other operating revenues | 143,357 | 421,571 |
| Total operating revenues | 88,773,343 | 54,194,515 |

| | Primary institution | Component unit hospital |
|---|---|---|
| ***Expenses*** | | |
| *Operating expenses:* | | |
| Salaries: | | |
| Faculty (physicians for the hospital) | 34,829,499 | 16,703,805 |
| Exempt staff | 29,597,676 | 8,209,882 |
| Nonexempt wages | 5,913,762 | 2,065,267 |
| Benefits | 18,486,559 | 7,752,067 |
| Scholarships and fellowships | 3,809,374 | -- |
| Utilities | 16,463,492 | 9,121,352 |
| Supplies and other services | 12,451,064 | 7,342,009 |
| Depreciation | 6,847,377 | 2,976,212 |
| Total operating expenses | 128,398,803 | 54,170,594 |
| Operating income (loss) | (39,625,460) | 23,921 |
| ***Nonoperating Revenues (Expenses)*** | | |
| State appropriations | 39,760,508 | -- |
| Gifts | 1,822,442 | -- |
| Investment income (net of investment expense of $87,316 for the primary institution and $19,823 for the hospital) | 2,182,921 | 495,594 |
| Interest on capital asset—related debt | (1,330,126) | (34,538) |
| Other nonoperating revenues | 313,001 | 321,449 |
| Net operating revenues | 42,748,746 | 782,505 |
| Income before other revenues, expenses, gains, or losses | 3,123,286 | 806,426 |
| Capital appropriations | 2,075,750 | -- |
| Capital grants and gifts | 690,813 | 711,619 |
| Additions to permanent endowments | 85,203 | -- |
| Increase in net assets | 5,975,052 | 1,518,045 |
| ***Net Assets*** | | |
| Net assets—beginning of year | 168,645,726 | 45,900,375 |
| Net assets—end of year | $174,620,778 | $47,418,420 |
| *SOURCE: GASB 35, page 28.* | | |

GASB Statement 39 provides guidance relating to whether or not certain legally separate tax-exempt entities are to be reported in the financial statements of governments. These provisions are especially important to public colleges and universities, many of which have legally separate foundations. GASB Statement 39 will result in many of these foundations being reported as discretely presented component units in public college and university financial statements. All three of the following criteria must be met before these foundations are included:

1. The economic resources received or held by the separate organization are entirely or almost entirely for the benefit of the primary government, its component units, or its constituents.
2. The primary government or its component units is entitled to, or has the ability to otherwise access a majority of the economic resources received or held by the separate organization.
3. The economic resources received or held by an individual organization that the specific primary government is entitled to, or has the ability to otherwise access are significant to that primary government.

*ABC University*
**STATEMENT OF CASH FLOWS**
*For the Year Ended June 30, 2005*

| The direct method of reporting cash flows is required. | | |
|---|---|---|
| | Primary institution | Component unit hospital |
| ***Cash Flows from Operating Activities*** | | |
| Tuition and fees | $ 33,628,945 | $      -- |
| Research grants and contracts | 13,884,747 | -- |
| Payments from insurance and patients | -- | 18,582,530 |
| Medicaid and Medicare | -- | 31,640,524 |
| Payments to suppliers | (28,175,500) | (13,084,643) |
| Payments to employees | (87,233,881) | (32,988,044) |
| Loans issued to students and employees | (384,628) | -- |
| Collection of loans to students and employees | 291,642 | -- |
| Auxiliary enterprise charges: | | |
| Residence halls | 26,327,644 | -- |
| Bookstore | 8,463,939 | -- |
| Other receipts (payments) | 1,415,502 | (997,502) |
| Net cash provided (used) by operating activities | (31,781,590) | 3,152,865 |

| | Primary institution | Component unit hospital |
|---|---|---|
| **Cash Flows from Noncapital Financing Activities** | | |
| State appropriations | 39,388,534 | -- |
| Gifts and grants received for other than capital purposes: | | |
| Private gifts for endowment purposes | 85,203 | -- |
| Net cash flows provided by noncapital financing activities | 39,473,737 | -- |
| **Cash Flows from Capital and Related Financing Activities** | | |
| Proceeds from capital debt | 4,125,000 | -- |
| Capital appropriations | 1,918,750 | -- |
| Capital grants and gifts received | 640,813 | 711,619 |
| Proceeds from sale of capital assets | 22,335 | 5,066 |
| Purchases of capital assets | (8,420,247) | (1,950,410) |
| Principal paid on capital debt and lease | (3,788,102) | (134,095) |
| Interest paid on capital debt and lease | (1,330,126) | (34,538) |
| Net cash used by capital and related financing activities | (6,831,577) | (1,402,358) |
| **Cash Flows from Investing Activities** | | |
| Proceeds from sales and maturities of investments | 16,741,252 | 2,843,124 |
| Interest on investments | 2,111,597 | 70,501 |
| Purchase of investments | (17,680,113) | (4,546,278) |
| Net cash provided (used) by investing activities | 1,172,736 | (1,632,653) |
| Net increase in cash | 2,033,306 | 117,854 |
| Cash—beginning of year | 2,562,112 | 878,340 |
| Cash—end of year | $ 4,595,418 | $ 996,194 |
| *Reconciliation of net operating revenues (expenses) to net cash provided (used) by operating activities:* | | |
| Operating income (loss) | $(39,625,460) | $ 23,921 |
| Adjustments to reconcile net income (loss) to net cash provided (used) by operating activities: | | |
| Depreciation expense | 6,847,377 | 2,976,212 |
| Change in assets and liabilities: | | |
| Receivables, net | 1,295,704 | 330,414 |
| Inventories | 37,284 | (160,922) |
| Deposit with bond trustee | 67,115 | -- |
| Other assets | (136,229) | 75,456 |
| Accounts payable | (323,989) | (75,973) |
| Deferred revenue | 217,630 | -- |
| Deposits held for others | (299,428) | -- |
| Compensated absences | 138,406 | (16,243) |
| Net cash provided (used) by operating activities | $(31,781,590) | $3,152,865 |

---

NOTE: *The required information about noncash investing, capital, and financing activities is not illustrated.*

---

SOURCE: *GASB 35, pages 29-30.*

**MULTIPLE-CHOICE QUESTIONS (1-116)**

**1.** Which of the following statements about the statistical section of the Comprehensive Annual Financial Report (CAFR) of a governmental unit is true?

    a. Statistical tables may **not** cover more than two fiscal years.

    b. Statistical tables may **not** include nonaccounting information.

    c. The statistical section is **not** part of the basic financial statements.

    d. The statistical section is an integral part of the basic financial statements.

**2.** What is the basic criterion used to determine the reporting entity for a governmental unit?

    a. Special financing arrangement.

    b. Geographic boundaries.

    c. Scope of public services.

    d. Financial accountability.

**3.** South City School District has a separately elected governing body that administers the public school system. The district's budget is subject to the approval of the city council. The district's financial activity should be reported in the City's financial statements by

    a. Blending only.

    b. Discrete presentation.

    c. Inclusion as a footnote only.

    d. Either blending or inclusion as a footnote.

**4.** Marta City's school district is a legally separate entity, but two of its seven board members are also city council members and the district is financially dependent on the city. The school district should be reported as a

    a. Blended unit.

    b. Discrete presentation.

    c. Note disclosure.

    d. Primary government.

**5.** Darien Village adopted the provision of GASB 34, *Basic Financial Statements—and Management's Discussion and Analysis—for State and Local Governments*, for its financial statements issued for 2005. As of December 31, 2005, Darien determined that it had spent $5,000,000 on infrastructure assets since the village was incorporated in 1980, and that infrastructure had an expected life of fifty years. These infrastructure assets consist primarily of roads and bridges that were financed with general long-term debt. Darien decided to use the modified approach for reporting its infrastructure assets on its government-wide financial statements for 2005. During 2005, Darien spent $250,000 maintaining and preserving its roads and bridges, and $500,000 to extend the life of existing infrastructure. On the statement of net assets at December 31, 2005, what amount should Darien report for infrastructure under the governmental activities column?

    a. $5,000,000

    b. $0

    c. $4,900,000

    d. $5,500,000

**6.** Hunt Community Development Agency (HCDA), a financially independent authority, provides loans to commercial businesses operating in Hunt County. This year, HCDA made loans totaling $500,000. How should HCDA classify the disbursements of loans on the cash flow statement?

    a. Operating activities.

    b. Noncapital financing activities.

    c. Capital and related financing activities.

    d. Investing activities.

**7.** The statement of activities of the government-wide financial statements is designed primarily to provide information to assess which of the following?

    a. Operational accountability.

    b. Financial accountability.

    c. Fiscal accountability.

    d. Functional accountability.

**Items 8 and 9** are based on the following:

As of December 31, 2007, Fullerton City compiled the information below for its capital assets, exclusive of infrastructure assets.

| | |
|---|---|
| Cost of capital assets financed with general obligation debt and tax revenues | $3,500,000 |
| Accumulated depreciation on the capital assets | 750,000 |
| Outstanding debt related to the capital assets | 1,250,000 |

**8.** On the government-wide statement of net assets at December 31, 2007, under the governmental activities column, what amount should be reported for capital assets?

    a. $3,500,000

    b. $1,500,000

    c. $2,250,000

    d. $2,750,000

**9.** On the government-wide statement of net assets at December 31, 2007, under the governmental activities column, the information related to capital assets should be reported in the net assets section at which of the following amounts?

    a. $3,500,000

    b. $1,500,000

    c. $2,250,000

    d. $2,750,000

**10.** In accordance with GASB 34, *Basic Financial Statements—and Management's Discussion and Analysis—for State and Local Governments*, which of the following statements is correct about the accounting for infrastructure assets using the modified approach?

    I. Depreciation expense on the infrastructure assets should be reported on the government-wide statement of activities, under the governmental activities column.

    II. Certain information about infrastructure assets reported using the modified approach is required supplementary information in the annual report.

    a. I only.

    b. II only.

    c. Both I and II.

    d. Neither I nor II.

**11.** In accordance with GASB 34, *Basic Financial Statements—and Management's Discussion and Analysis—for State and Local Governments*, depreciation expense would be reported on which of the following financial statements?

    I. The government-wide statement of activities.

    II. The statement of revenues, expenses, and changes in fund net assets prepared for proprietary funds.

a. I only.
b. II only.
c. Both I and II.
d. Neither I nor II.

**12.** In accordance with GASB 34, *Basic Financial Statements—and Management's Discussion and Analysis—for State and Local Governments*, governments should prepare

a. Combined financial statements, using the modified accrual basis of accounting and the flow of economic resources.
b. Combined financial statements, using the accrual basis of accounting and the flow of financial resources.
c. Government-wide financial statements, using the accrual basis of accounting and the flow of financial resources.
d. Government-wide financial statements, using the accrual basis of accounting and the flow of economic resources.

**13.** In accordance with GASB 34, *Basic Financial Statements—and Management's Discussion and Analysis—for State and Local Governments*, which of the following statements is true?

I. Infrastructure assets do not need to be reported on the government-wide statement of net assets if the government decides to use the modified approach in its accounting for infrastructure.
II. Component units are reported on the financial statements for governmental funds.

a. I only.
b. II only.
c. Both I and II.
d. Neither I nor II.

**14.** Fund accounting is used by governmental units with resources that must be

a. Composed of cash or cash equivalents.
b. Incorporated into combined or combining financial statements.
c. Segregated for the purpose of carrying on specific activities or attaining certain objectives.
d. Segregated physically according to various objectives.

**15.** Dogwood City's water enterprise fund received interest of $10,000 on long-term investments. How should this amount be reported on the Statement of Cash Flows?

a. Operating activities.
b. Noncapital financing activities.
c. Capital and related financing activities.
d. Investing activities.

**16.** The primary authoritative body for determining the measurement focus and basis of accounting standards for governmental fund operating statements is the

a. Governmental Accounting Standards Board (GASB).
b. National Council on Governmental Accounting (NCGA).
c. Governmental Accounting and Auditing Committee of the AICPA (GAAC).
d. Financial Accounting Standards Board (FASB).

**17.** Which event(s) should be included in a statement of cash flows for a governmental entity?

I. Cash inflow from issuing bonds to finance city hall construction.
II. Cash outflow from a city utility representing payments in lieu of property taxes.

a. I only.
b. II only.
c. Both I and II.
d. Neither I nor II.

**18.** The following transactions were among those reported by Corfe City's electric utility enterprise fund for 2007:

| | |
|---|---|
| Capital contributed by subdividers | $ 900,000 |
| Cash received from customer households | 2,700,000 |
| Proceeds from sale of revenue bonds | 4,500,000 |

In the electric utility enterprise fund's statement of cash flows for the year ended December 31, 2007, what amount should be reported as cash flows from capital and related financing activities?

a. $4,500,000
b. $5,400,000
c. $7,200,000
d. $8,100,000

**19.** For which of the following governmental entities that use proprietary fund accounting should a statement of cash flows be presented?

| | *Tollway authorities* | *Governmental utilities* |
|---|---|---|
| a. | No | No |
| b. | No | Yes |
| c. | Yes | Yes |
| d. | Yes | No |

**20.** In accordance with GASB 34, *Basic Financial Statements—and Management's Discussion and Analysis—for State and Local Governments*, which of the following financial statements should be prepared for proprietary funds?

a. Statement of revenues, expenditures, and changes in fund balances.
b. Statement of activities.
c. Statement of changes in proprietary net assets.
d. Statement of cash flows.

**21.** In accordance with GASB 34, *Basic Financial Statements—and Management's Discussion and Analysis—for State and Local Governments*, which of the following statements is correct about the information reported on the balance sheet prepared for the governmental funds?

I. The focus is on reporting major funds, with all nonmajor funds aggregated and reported in a single column.
II. Fund balances are reported in two amounts—restricted and unrestricted.

a. I only.
b. II only.
c. Both I and II.
d. Neither I nor II.

**22.** In accordance with GASB 34, *Basic Financial Statements—and Management's Discussion and Analysis—for State and Local Governments*, which of the following statements is correct about the information reported on the statement of net assets for the proprietary funds?

I. Assets and liabilities are classified into current and noncurrent classifications.
II. All activities of internal service funds are aggregated and reported in a single column.

    a.  I only.
    b.  II only.
    c.  Both I and II.
    d.  Neither I nor II.

**23.** In accordance with GASB 34, *Basic Financial Statements—and Management's Discussion and Analysis—for State and Local Governments*, which of the following financial statements is prepared using the accrual basis of accounting and the economic resources measurement focus?

I. The statement of net assets for proprietary funds.
II. The statement of revenues, expenditures, and changes in fund balances for the governmental funds.

    a.  I only.
    b.  II only.
    c.  Both I and II.
    d.  Neither I nor II.

**24.** In accordance with GASB 34, *Basic Financial Statements—and Management's Discussion and Analysis—for State and Local Governments*, agency funds are reported on which of the following financial statements?

I. Statement of fiduciary net assets.
II. Statement of changes in fiduciary net assets.

    a.  I only.
    b.  II only.
    c.  Both I and II.
    d.  Neither I nor II.

**25.** In accordance with GASB 34, *Basic Financial Statements—and Management's Discussion and Analysis—for State and Local Governments*, private-purpose trust funds are reported on which of the following financial statements?

I. Government-wide statement of net assets.
II. Statement of changes in fiduciary net assets.

    a.  I only.
    b.  II only.
    c.  Both I and II.
    d.  Neither I nor II.

**26.** In accordance with GASB 34, *Basic Financial Statements—and Management's Discussion and Analysis—for State and Local Governments*, which fund type(s) is(are) reported on the statement of cash flows?
    a.  Governmental and fiduciary fund types.
    b.  Governmental and proprietary fund types.
    c.  Fiduciary and proprietary fund types.
    d.  Proprietary fund type only.

**27.** In accordance with GASB 34, *Basic Financial Statements—and Management's Discussion and Analysis—for State and Local Governments*, which of the following statements is(are) true regarding the statement of cash flows?

I. The statement of cash flows is a government-wide financial statement.
II. The statement of cash flows reports cash flows from three activities—operating, investing, and financing.

    a.  I only.
    b.  II only.
    c.  Both I and II.
    d.  Neither I nor II.

**28.** In accordance with GASB 34, *Basic Financial Statements—and Management's Discussion and Analysis—for State and Local Governments*, a reconciliation must be shown of the items that cause the difference between (1) the total of the fund balances that appears on the balance sheet for the governmental funds and (2) the total net assets that are disclosed for governmental activities on the government-wide statement of net assets. Which of the following items would be disclosed in this reconciliation?

I. Capital assets used in governmental activities.
II. The assets and liabilities of internal service funds included in governmental activities.

    a.  I only.
    b.  II only.
    c.  Both I and II.
    d.  Neither I nor II.

**29.** In accordance with GASB 34, *Basic Financial Statements—and Management's Discussion and Analysis—for State and Local Governments*, a reconciliation must be shown of the items that cause the difference between (1) the net change in fund balances for the governmental funds on the statement of revenues, expenditures, and changes in fund balances, and (2) the change in net assets of governmental activities on the statement of activities. Which of the following items would be disclosed in this reconciliation?

I. Revenues and expenses of internal service funds that were reported in proprietary funds.
II. The amount by which capital outlays exceeded depreciation expense for the period.

    a.  I only.
    b.  II only.
    c.  Both I and II.
    d.  Neither I nor II.

**30.** In accordance with GASB 34, *Basic Financial Statements—and Management's Discussion and Analysis—for State and Local Governments*, what measurement focus should be used for the preparation of the following financial statements?

| | Statement of changes in fiduciary net assets | Government-wide statement of net assets |
|---|---|---|
| a. | Financial resources | Economic resources |
| b. | Economic resources | Financial resources |
| c. | Economic resources | Economic resources |
| d. | Financial resources | Financial resources |

**31.** In accordance with GASB 34, *Basic Financial Statements—and Management's Discussion and Analysis—for State and Local Governments*, which of the following statement is(are) true?

I. Pension trust funds are reported on the statement of changes in fiduciary net assets.
II. Retained earnings is reported in the net assets section of the statement of net assets for proprietary funds.

    a.  I only.
    b.  II only.
    c.  Both I and II.
    d.  Neither I nor II.

**32.** In accordance with GASB 34, *Basic Financial Statements—and Management's Discussion and Analysis—for State and Local Governments*, which of the following statements is correct concerning the statement of cash flows prepared for proprietary funds?

    a. The statement format is the same as that of a business enterprise's statement of cash flows.

    b. Cash flows from capital financing activities are reported separately from cash flows from noncapital financing activities.

    c. Cash flows from operating activities may not be reported using the direct method.

    d. Cash received from interest revenue and cash paid for interest expense are both reported as operating activities.

**33.** For governmental fund reporting, which item is considered the primary measurement focus?

    a. Income determination.

    b. Flows and balances of current financial resources.

    c. Capital maintenance.

    d. Cash flows and balances.

**34.** Which of the following funds of a governmental unit recognizes revenues in the accounting period in which they become available and measurable?

| | General fund | Enterprise fund |
|---|---|---|
| a. | Yes | No |
| b. | No | Yes |
| c. | Yes | Yes |
| d. | No | No |

**35.** Property taxes and fines represent which of the following classes of nonexchange transactions for governmental units?

    a. Derived tax revenues.

    b. Imposed nonexchange revenues.

    c. Government-mandated nonexchange transactions.

    d. Voluntary nonexchange transactions.

**36.** In accordance with GASB 33, *Accounting and Financial Reporting for Nonexchange Transactions*, which of the following transactions would qualify as a nonexchange transaction in the City of Geneva?

    a. The water utility (enterprise) fund billed the general fund for water usage.

    b. Property taxes were levied by the general fund.

    c. The motor pool (internal service) fund billed other departments for services rendered.

    d. The general fund sold police cars for their estimated residual value.

**Items 37 and 38** are based on the following:

The general fund of Elizabeth City received a $100,000 grant from the state to be used for retraining its police force in modern crime-fighting methods. The state recently passed legislation that requires retraining for all police departments in the state. The grant was received in cash on June 15, 2007, and was used for retraining seminars during July 2007. The state mandated that the grant be spent in the fiscal year ending June 30, 2008. Elizabeth's fiscal year ends on June 30. Answer each of the questions below based upon the guidance provided by GASB 33, *Accounting and Financial Reporting for Nonexchange Transactions*.

**37.** What account should be credited in the general fund on the date the grant was received?

    a. Restricted revenue.

    b. Deferred revenue.

    c. Revenue.

    d. Unreserved fund balance.

**38.** The grant from the state is an example of what type of nonexchange transaction?

    a. Government-mandated.

    b. Imposed.

    c. Voluntary.

    d. Derived.

**Items 39 and 40** are based on the following:

The merchants of Eldorado City collect a sales tax of 5% on retail sales. The sales taxes are remitted by retailers to the state and distributed by the state to the various governmental units that are within the boundaries of Eldorado City. During the month of June 2007, the state received $50,000 of sales taxes from merchants in Eldorado. As of June 30, 2007, none of the sales taxes had been remitted to Eldorado or to any of the other governments that were within the boundaries of Eldorado. However, Eldorado estimated that its share of the sales taxes would be received in early July 2007, and would be used to pay for expenditures incurred during the year ended June 30, 2007. Eldorado's fiscal year ends on June 30. Answer both of the questions below using the guidance provided in GASB 33, *Accounting and Financial Reporting for Nonexchange Transactions*.

**39.** From the perspective of Eldorado City, the sales taxes are an example of what type of nonexchange transaction?

    a. Imposed.

    b. Voluntary.

    c. Derived.

    d. Government-mandated

**40.** On the statement of revenues, expenditures, and changes in fund balance for the year ended June 30, 2007, how should the general fund of Eldorado report its share of the sales taxes that will be received in July 2007?

    a. Deferred revenue.

    b. Restricted revenue.

    c. Revenue.

    d. Unreserved fund balance.

**41.** On July 1, 2007, the general fund of Sun City levied property taxes for the fiscal year ending June 30, 2008. According to GASB 33, *Accounting and Financial Reporting for Nonexchange Transactions*, property taxes are an example of what type of nonexchange transaction?

    a. Voluntary.

    b. Government-mandated.

    c. Imposed.

    d. Derived.

**42.** For the year ended December 31, 2007, the general fund of Karsten City levied property taxes of $1,000,000. The city estimated that $10,000 of the levy would not be collectible. By December 31, 2007, the city had collected $850,0000 of property taxes and expected to collect the remainder of the taxes as follows:

    • $100,000 by March 1, 2008

    • $ 40,000 during the remainder of 2008

In accordance with GASB 33, *Accounting and Reporting for Nonexchange Transactions*, how much property tax revenue should be reported by the general fund on the statement of revenues, expenditures, and changes in fund balances prepared for the year ended December 31, 2007?

- a. $   850,000
- b. $   950,000
- c. $   990,000
- d. $1,000,000

**43.** For the year ended December 31, 2007, the general fund of Ward Village reported revenues from the following sources on the statement of revenues, expenditures, and changes in fund balances:

| | |
|---|---|
| Sales taxes | $ 25,000 |
| Property taxes | 125,000 |
| Income taxes | 15,000 |
| Fines | 10,000 |

In accordance with GASB 33, *Accounting and Reporting for Nonexchange Transactions*, what is the amount of revenues that came from imposed nonexchange transactions?

- a. $175,000
- b. $150,000
- c. $140,000
- d. $135,000

**44.** In December 2007, the general fund of Millard City received $25,000 from the state as an advance on the city's portion of sales tax revenues, and it received $20,000 from property owners for property taxes to be levied in 2008. The advance payment of sales taxes represented the amount that the state collected in 2007 that would have been distributed to Millard in the early part of 2008. Millard used the advance to pay for expenditures incurred by the general fund in 2007. The cash received from property owners for property taxes to be levied in 2008 will be used to pay for expenditures incurred in 2008. In accordance with GASB 33, *Accounting and Reporting for Nonexchange Transactions*, what amount of revenue from these transactions should be reported by Millard's general fund on the statement of revenues, expenditures, and changes in fund balances for the year ended December 31, 2007?

- a. $25,000
- b. $20,000
- c. $0
- d. $45,000

**45.** In accordance with GASB 33, *Accounting and Reporting for Nonexchange Transactions*, which of the following revenues results from taxes assessed by a government on exchange transactions (a derived tax revenue)?

- a. Property tax revenues.
- b. Fines and forfeits.
- c. Motor fuel taxes.
- d. Unrestricted government grants.

**46.** In accordance with GASB 33, *Accounting and Reporting for Nonexchange Transactions*, which of the following revenues results from taxes and other assessments imposed by governments that are not derived from underlying transactions?

- a. Income taxes.
- b. Sales taxes.
- c. Motor fuel taxes.
- d. Fines and forfeits.

**47.** Devon County is developing its own software system to maintain property tax records. Which of the following is not required for Devon to begin capitalizing the software costs?

- a. Devon has established the objective for the project and the proposed scope of the software system.
- b. Devon has established the feasibility of creating the software system.
- c. Devon has established an accurate budget for the software system.
- d. Devon has established its intention to complete or continue developing the system.

**48.** The State of Texas is scheduled to receive a substantial amount of revenues as a part of a tobacco settlement. The revenues for the next five years have been sold to a commercial business for $5,000,000. Assuming that Texas has no involvement with the future revenues, how should it account for this transaction?

- a. Recognize $5,000,000 of revenue at the date of the transaction.
- b. Recognize $5,000,000 in liability to the commercial business.
- c. Recognize $5,000,000 in deferred revenue and recognize the revenue over a five-year period.
- d. Recognize the difference between the cash received and the amount of future revenues sold as an expense.

**Items 49 and 50** are based on the following:

Ridge Township's governing body adopted its general fund budget for the year ended July 31, 2007, comprised of Estimated Revenues of $100,000 and Appropriations of $80,000. Ridge formally integrates its budget into the accounting records.

**49.** To record the appropriations of $80,000, Ridge should

- a. Credit Appropriations Control.
- b. Debit Appropriations Control.
- c. Credit Estimated Expenditures Control.
- d. Debit Estimated Expenditures Control.

**50.** To record the $20,000 budgeted excess of estimated revenues over appropriations, Ridge should

- a. Credit Estimated Excess Revenues Control.
- b. Debit Estimated Excess Revenues Control.
- c. Credit Budgetary Fund Balance.
- d. Debit Budgetary Fund Balance.

**51.** For the budgetary year ending December 31, 2007, Maple City's general fund expects the following inflows of resources:

| | |
|---|---|
| Property Taxes, Licenses, and Fines | $9,000,000 |
| Proceeds of Debt Issue | 5,000,000 |
| Interfund Transfers for Debt Service | 1,000,000 |

In the budgetary entry, what amount should Maple record for estimated revenues?

- a. $  9,000,000
- b. $10,000,000
- c. $14,000,000
- d. $15,000,000

**52.** In 2007, New City issued purchase orders and contracts of $850,000 that were chargeable against 2007 budgeted appropriations of $1,000,000. The journal entry to record the issuance of the purchase orders and contracts should include a

a.   Credit to Vouchers Payable of $1,000,000.
b.   Credit to Budgetary Fund Balance—Reserved for Encumbrances of $850,000.
c.   Debit to Expenditures of $1,000,000.
d.   Debit to Appropriations of $850,000.

**53.** During its fiscal year ended June 30, 2007, Cliff City issued purchase orders totaling $5,000,000, which were properly charged to Encumbrances at that time. Cliff received goods and related invoices at the encumbered amounts totaling $4,500,000 before year-end. The remaining goods of $500,000 were not received until after year-end. Cliff paid $4,200,000 of the invoices received during the year. What amount of Cliff's encumbrances were outstanding at June 30, 2007?
a.   $0
b.   $300,000
c.   $500,000
d.   $800,000

**54.** Elm City issued a purchase order for supplies with an estimated cost of $5,000. When the supplies were received, the accompanying invoice indicated an actual price of $4,950. What amount should Elm debit (credit) to Budgetary Fund Balance—Reserved for Encumbrances after the supplies and invoice were received?
a.   $   (50)
b.   $    50
c.   $4,950
d.   $5,000

**55.** A budgetary fund balance reserved for encumbrances in excess of a balance of encumbrances indicates
a.   An excess of vouchers payable over encumbrances.
b.   An excess of purchase orders over invoices received.
c.   An excess of appropriations over encumbrances.
d.   A recording error.

**56.** Encumbrances outstanding at year-end in a state's general fund should be reported as a
a.   Liability in the general fund.
b.   Fund balance reserve in the general fund.
c.   Liability in the General Long-Term Debt Account Group.
d.   Fund balance designation in the general fund.

**57.** When Rolan County adopted its budget for the year ending June 30, 2007, $20,000,000 was recorded for Estimated Revenues Control. Actual revenues for the year ended June 30, 2007, amounted to $17,000,000. In closing the budgetary accounts at June 30, 2007,
a.   Revenues Control should be debited for $3,000,000.
b.   Estimated Revenues Control should be debited for $3,000,000.
c.   Revenues Control should be credited for $20,000,000.
d.   Estimated Revenues Control should be credited for $20,000,000.

**58.** The budget of a governmental unit, for which the appropriations exceed the estimated revenues, was adopted and recorded in the general ledger at the beginning of the year. During the year, expenditures and encumbrances were less than appropriations, whereas revenues equaled estimated revenues. The Budgetary Fund Balance account is

a.   Credited at the beginning of the year and debited at the end of the year.
b.   Credited at the beginning of the year and **not** changed at the end of the year.
c.   Debited at the beginning of the year and credited at the end of the year.
d.   Debited at the beginning of the year and **not** changed at the end of the year.

**59.** The following information pertains to Park Township's general fund at December 31, 2007:

| | |
|---|---|
| Total assets, including $200,000 of cash | $1,000,000 |
| Total liabilities | 600,000 |
| Fund balance—Reserved for encumbrances | 100,000 |

Appropriations do not lapse at year-end. At December 31, 2007, what amount should Park report as unreserved fund balance in its general fund balance sheet?
a.   $200,000
b.   $300,000
c.   $400,000
d.   $500,000

**60.** The following information pertains to Pine City's general fund for 2007:

| | |
|---|---|
| Appropriations Control | $6,500,000 |
| Expenditures Control | 5,000,000 |
| Other Financing Sources Control | 1,500,000 |
| Other Financing Uses Control | 2,000,000 |
| Revenues Control | 8,000,000 |

After Pine's general fund accounts were closed at the end of 2007, the fund balance increased by
a.   $3,000,000
b.   $2,500,000
c.   $1,500,000
d.   $1,000,000

**61.** Cedar City issues $1,000,000, 6% revenue bonds at par on April 1 to build a new water line for the water enterprise fund. Interest is payable every six months. What amount of interest expense should be reported for the year ended December 31?
a.   $0
b.   $30,000
c.   $45,000
d.   $60,000

**62.** The expenditure element "salaries and wages" is an example of which type of classification?
a.   Object.
b.   Program.
c.   Function.
d.   Activity.

**Items 63 and 64** are based on the following information for Oak City for the calendar year 2007:

| | |
|---|---|
| Collections during 2007 | $500,000 |
| Expected collections during the first sixty days of 2008 | 100,000 |
| Expected collections during the balance of 2008 | 60,000 |
| Expected collections during January 2009 | 30,000 |
| Estimated to be uncollectible | 10,000 |
| Total levy | $700,000 |

**63.** What amount should Oak City report for 2007 property tax revenues in the Statement of Revenues, Expenditures, and Changes in Fund Balances prepared for governmental funds?

a. $700,000
b. $690,000
c. $600,000
d. $500,000

**64.** What amount should Oak City report for 2007 property tax revenues in the government-wide Statement of Activities?
    a. $700,000
    b. $690,000
    c. $600,000
    d. $500,000

**65.** Which of the following transactions is an expenditure of a governmental unit's general fund?
    a. Contribution of enterprise fund capital by the general fund.
    b. Transfer from the general fund to a capital projects fund.
    c. Operating subsidy transfer from the general fund to an enterprise fund.
    d. Routine employer contributions from the general fund to a pension trust fund.

**66.** During the year, a city's electric utility, which is operated as an enterprise fund, rendered billings for electricity supplied to the general fund. Which of the following accounts should be debited by the general fund?
    a. Appropriations.
    b. Expenditures
    c. Due to Electric Utility Enterprise Fund.
    d. Transfers.

**67.** Which of the following fund types used by a government most likely would have a Fund Balance—Reserved for Inventory of Supplies?
    a. General.
    b. Internal service.
    c. Enterprise.
    d. Debt service.

**68.** The following revenues were among those reported by Ariba Township in 2007:

| | |
|---|---:|
| Net rental revenue (after depreciation) from a parking garage owned by Ariba | $ 40,000 |
| Interest earned on investments held for employees' retirement benefits | 100,000 |
| Property taxes | 6,000,000 |

What amount of the foregoing revenues should be accounted for in Ariba's governmental-type funds?
    a. $6,140,000
    b. $6,100,000
    c. $6,040,000
    d. $6,000,000

**Items 69 through 70** are based on the following:

The general fund of Cliff Township acquired two police cars at the beginning of January 2007, at a total cost of $40,000. The cars are expected to last for four years and have a $10,000 residual value. Straight-line depreciation is used. Cliff adopted the provisions of GASB 34, *Basic Financial Statements—and Management's Discussion and Analysis—for State and Local Governments,* for its financial statements issued for 2007.

**69.** On the balance sheet for the governmental funds at December 31, 2007, the police cars will be reported under assets in the general fund column at which of the following amounts?
    a. $40,000
    b. $32,500
    c. $0
    d. $22,500

**70.** On the government-wide statement of net assets at December 31, 2007, the police cars will be reported under assets in the governmental activities column at which of the following amounts?
    a. $40,000
    b. $32,500
    c. $0
    d. $22,500

**71.** On the statement of revenues, expenditures, and changes in fund balances prepared for the governmental funds for the year ended December 31, 2007, the police cars will be reported as
    a. Expenditures of $40,000.
    b. Expense of $7,500.
    c. Expenditures of $7,500.
    d. Expense of $40,000.

**Items 72 through 75** are based on the following:

The City of Vicksburg adopted the provisions of GASB 34, *Basic Financial Statements—and Management's Discussion and Analysis—for State and Local Governments*, for its financial statements issued for the year ended December 31, 2007. During the year ended December 31, 2007, the general fund of Vicksburg has the following selected transactions:

- Acquired police cars for $75,000 in January 2007. The cars have an estimated five-year useful life and a $15,000 salvage value. The City uses the straight-line method to depreciate all of its capital assets.
- Transferred $30,000 to the pension trust fund. The amount represented the employer's contribution.
- Levied property taxes in the amount of $800,000. Two percent of the levy was not expected to be collected. At December 31, 2007, $750,000 of the property taxes were collected, but the remainder was not expected to be collected within sixty days after the end of 2007.
- Received $100,000 of sales tax revenues from the state and was owed another $25,000 by the state for sales taxes collected in 2007 that will not be remitted to Vicksburg until mid-March 2008. The sales taxes expected to be received in March will be used to pay for expenditures incurred in 2008.

**72.** On the statement of revenues, expenditures, and changes in fund balances prepared for the governmental funds for the year ended December 31, 2007, what amount should be reported for expenditures in Vicksburg's general fund related to the acquisition of police cars and to the pension transfer?
    a. $ 42,000
    b. $105,000
    c. $ 75,000
    d. $ 30,000

**73.** On the statement of revenues, expenditures, and changes in fund balances prepared for the governmental funds for the year ended December 31, 2007, what amount should be reported for revenues in Vicksburg's general fund related to property taxes and sales taxes?

- a. $884,000
- b. $909,000
- c. $850,000
- d. $875,000

**74.** On the government-wide statement of activities prepared for the year ended December 31, 2007, what amount should be reported for expenses for governmental activities related to the acquisition of the police cars and to the pension transfer?

- a. $ 42,000
- b. $105,000
- c. $ 75,000
- d. $ 30,000

**75.** On the government-wide statement of activities prepared for the year ended December 31, 2007, what amount should be reported for revenues from governmental activities related to the property taxes and the sales taxes?

- a. $884,000
- b. $909,000
- c. $850,000
- d. $875,000

**76.** In November 2007, Maple Township received an unexpected state grant of $100,000 to finance the purchase of school buses, and an additional grant of $5,000 was received for bus maintenance and operations. According to the terms of the grant, the State reimbursed Maple Township for $60,000 for the purchase of school buses and an additional $5,000 for bus maintenance during the year ended June 30, 2008. The remaining $40,000 of the capital grant is expected to be spent during the next fiscal year June 30, 2009. Maple's school bus system is appropriately accounted for in a special revenue fund. In connection with the grants for the purchase of school buses and bus maintenance, what amount should be reported as grant revenues for the year ending June 30, 2008, when using modified accrual accounting?

- a. $ 5,000
- b. $ 60,000
- c. $ 65,000
- d. $100,000

**77.** Lake County received the following proceeds that are legally restricted to expenditure for specified purposes:

| | |
|---|---|
| Levies on affected property owners to install sidewalks | $500,000 |
| Gasoline taxes to finance road repairs | 900,000 |

What amount should be accounted for in Lake's special revenue funds?

- a. $1,400,000
- b. $ 900,000
- c. $ 500,000
- d. $0

**78.** Should a major special revenue fund with a legally adopted budget maintain its accounts on an accrual basis and integrate budgetary accounts into its accounting system?

| | Maintain on accrual basis | Integrate budgetary accounts |
|---|---|---|
| a. | Yes | Yes |
| b. | Yes | No |
| c. | No | Yes |
| d. | No | No |

**79.** In 2007, Menton City received $5,000,000 of bond proceeds to be used for capital projects. Of this amount, $1,000,000 was expended in 2007. Expenditures for the $4,000,000 balance were expected to be incurred in 2008. These bond proceeds should be recorded in capital projects funds for

- a. $5,000,000 in 2007.
- b. $5,000,000 in 2008.
- c. $1,000,000 in 2007 and $4,000,000 in 2008.
- d. $1,000,000 in 2007 and in the general fund for $4,000,000 in 2007.

**80.** Financing for the renovation of Fir City's municipal park, begun and completed during 2007, came from the following sources:

| | |
|---|---|
| Grant from state government | $400,000 |
| Proceeds from general obligation bond issue | 500,000 |
| Transfer from Fir's general fund | 100,000 |

In its 2007 capital projects fund operating statement, Fir should report these amounts as

| | Revenues | Other financing sources |
|---|---|---|
| a. | $1,000,000 | $0 |
| b. | $ 900,000 | $ 100,000 |
| c. | $ 400,000 | $ 600,000 |
| d. | $0 | $1,000,000 |

**81.** An impaired capital asset that is no longer used by a government should be reported in the financial statements at

- a. Historical cost.
- b. Historical cost adjusted for depreciation.
- c. The lower of carrying value or fair value.
- d. Fair value.

**82.** A government should recognized the impairment of a capital asset when events or circumstances indicate that there is a significant decline in service utility and

- a. The asset is not in service.
- b. The event or circumstance is outside the normal life cycle of the asset.
- c. The asset is not covered by insurance.
- d. The asset is not fully depreciated.

**83.** In which of the following fund types of a city government are revenues and expenditures recognized on the same basis of accounting as the general fund?

- a. Pension trust.
- b. Internal service.
- c. Enterprise.
- d. Debt service.

**84.** Japes City issued $1,000,000 general obligation bonds at 101 to build a new city hall. As part of the bond issue, the city also paid a $500 underwriter fee and $2,000 in debt issue costs. What amount should Japes City report as other financing sources?

- a. $1,010,000
- b. $1,008,000
- c. $1,007,500
- d. $1,000,000

**85.** Dale City is accumulating financial resources that are legally restricted to payments of general long-term debt principal and interest maturing in future years. At December 31, 2007, $5,000,000 has been accumulated for principal payments and $300,000 has been accumulated for interest payments. These restricted funds should be accounted for in the

| | Debt service fund | General fund |
|---|---|---|
| a. | $0 | $5,300,000 |
| b. | $ 300,000 | $5,000,000 |
| c. | $5,000,000 | $ 300,000 |
| d. | $5,300,000 | $0 |

**86.** On April 1, 2007, Oak County incurred the following expenditures in issuing long-term bonds:

| Issue costs | $400,000 |
|---|---|
| Debt insurance | 90,000 |

Oak County has established a debt service fund for the payment of interest and principal of its long-term bonds. Assuming Oak County's fiscal year ends of June 30, what amount of issue costs and debt insurance costs should be reported as an asset on the governmental funds' balance sheet at June 30, 2007?

- a. $0
- b. $ 90,000
- c. $400,000
- d. $490,000

**87.** Receipts from a special tax levy to retire and pay interest on general obligation bonds should be recorded in which fund?

- a. General.
- b. Capital projects.
- c. Debt service.
- d. Special revenue.

**88.** Wood City, which is legally obligated to maintain a debt service fund, issued the following general obligation bonds on July 1, 2007:

| Term of bonds | 10 years |
|---|---|
| Face amount | $1,000,000 |
| Issue price | 101 |
| Stated interest rate | 6% |

Interest is payable January 1 and July 1. What amount of bond premium should be amortized in Wood's debt service fund for the year ended December 31, 2007?

- a. $1,000
- b. $ 500
- c. $ 250
- d. $0

**89.** The debt service fund of a governmental unit is used to account for the accumulation of resources for, and the payment of, principal and interest in connection with a

| | Trust fund | Proprietary fund |
|---|---|---|
| a. | No | No |
| b. | No | Yes |
| c. | Yes | Yes |
| d. | Yes | No |

**90.** Tott City's serial bonds are serviced through a debt service fund with cash provided by the general fund. In a debt service fund's statements, how are cash receipts and cash payments reported?

| | Cash receipts | Cash payments |
|---|---|---|
| a. | Revenues | Expenditures |
| b. | Revenues | Other Financing Use |
| c. | Other Financing Source | Expenditures |
| d. | Other Financing Source | Other Financing Use |

**91.** On March 2, 2007, Finch City issued ten-year general obligation bonds at face amount, with interest payable March 1 and September 1. The proceeds were to be used to finance the construction of a civic center over the period April 1, 2007, to March 31, 2008. During the fiscal year ended June 30, 2007, no resources had been provided to the debt service fund for the payment of principal and interest.

On June 30, 2007, Finch's debt service fund should include interest payable on the general obligation bonds for

- a. 0 months.
- b. Three months.
- c. Four months.
- d. Six months.

**92.** Fish Road property owners in Sea County are responsible for special assessment debt that arose from a storm sewer project. If the property owners default, Sea has no obligation regarding debt service, although it does bill property owners for assessments and uses the monies it collects to pay debt holders. What fund type should Sea use to account for these collection and servicing activities?

- a. Agency.
- b. Debt service.
- c. Investment trust funds.
- d. Capital projects.

**93.** Cy City's Municipal Solid Waste Landfill Enterprise Fund was established when a new landfill was opened January 3, 2007. The landfill is expected to reach capacity and close December 31, 2025. Cy's 2007 expenses would include a portion of which of the year 2026 expected disbursements?

I. Cost of a final cover to be applied to the landfill.
II. Cost of equipment to be installed to monitor methane gas buildup.

- a. I only.
- b. II only.
- c. Both I and II.
- d. Neither I nor II.

**94.** Chase City uses an internal service fund for its central motor pool. The assets and liabilities account balances for this fund that are not eliminated normally should be reported in the government-wide statement of net assets as

- a. Governmental activities.
- b. Business-type activities.
- c. Fiduciary activities.
- d. Note disclosures only.

**95.** The billings for transportation services provided to other governmental units are recorded by an internal service fund as

- a. Transportation appropriations.
- b. Operating revenues.
- c. Interfund exchanges.
- d. Intergovernmental transfers.

**96.** The following information for the year ended June 30, 2007, pertains to a proprietary fund established by Burwood Village in connection with Burwood's public parking facilities:

| Receipts from users of parking facilities | $400,000 |
|---|---|
| Expenditures | |
| Parking meters | 210,000 |
| Salaries and other cash expenses | 90,000 |
| Depreciation of parking meters | 70,000 |

For the year ended June 30, 2007, this proprietary fund should report net income of

a. $0
b. $  30,000
c. $100,000
d. $240,000

**97.** A state government had the following activities:

I. State-operated lottery        $10,000,000
II. State-operated hospital        3,000,000

Which of the above activities should be accounted for in an enterprise fund?

a. Neither I nor II.
b. I only.
c. II only.
d. Both I and II.

**98.** For governmental units, depreciation expense on assets acquired with capital grants externally restricted for capital acquisitions should be reported in which type of fund?

|  | Governmental fund | Proprietary fund |
|---|---|---|
| a. | Yes | No |
| b. | Yes | Yes |
| c. | No | No |
| d. | No | Yes |

**99.** An enterprise fund would be used when the governing body requires that

I. Accounting for the financing of an agency's services to other government departments be on a cost-reimbursement basis.
II. User charges cover the costs of general public services.
III. Net income information be reported for an activity.

a. I only.
b. I and II.
c. I and III.
d. II and III.

**100.** The following transactions were among those reported by Cliff County's water and sewer enterprise fund for 2007:

| | |
|---|---|
| Proceeds from sale of revenue bonds | $5,000,000 |
| Cash received from customer households | 3,000,000 |
| Capital contributed by subdividers | 1,000,000 |

In the water and sewer enterprise fund's statement of cash flows for the year ended December 31, 2007, what amount should be reported as cash flows from capital and related financing activities?

a. $9,000,000
b. $8,000,000
c. $6,000,000
d. $5,000,000

**101.** The orientation of accounting and reporting for all proprietary funds of governmental units is

a. Income determination.
b. Project.
c. Flow of funds.
d. Program.

**Items 102 through 104** are based on the following:

Rock County has acquired equipment through a non-cancelable lease-purchase agreement dated December 31, 2007. This agreement requires no down payment and the following minimum lease payments:

| December 31 | Principal | Interest | Total |
|---|---|---|---|
| 2008 | $50,000 | $15,000 | $65,000 |
| 2009 | 50,000 | 10,000 | 60,000 |
| 2010 | 50,000 | 5,000 | 55,000 |

**102.** What account should be debited for $150,000 in the general fund at inception of the lease if the equipment is a general fixed asset and Rock does **not** use a capital projects fund?

a. Other Financing Uses Control.
b. Equipment.
c. Expenditures Control.
d. Memorandum entry only.

**103.** If the equipment is used in enterprise fund operations and the lease payments are to be financed with enterprise fund revenues, what account should be debited for $150,000 in the enterprise fund at the inception of the lease?

a. Expenses Control.
b. Expenditures Control.
c. Other Financing Sources Control.
d. Equipment.

**104.** If the equipment is used in internal service fund operations and the lease payments are financed with internal service fund revenues, what account or accounts should be debited in the internal service fund for the December 31, 2007 lease payment of $65,000?

| | | |
|---|---|---|
| a. | Expenditures Control | $65,000 |
| b. | Expenses Control | $65,000 |
| c. | Capital Lease Payable | $50,000 |
| | Expenses Control | 15,000 |
| d. | Expenditures Control | $50,000 |
| | Expenses Control | 15,000 |

**105.** Hill City's water utility fund held the following investments in US Treasury securities at June 30, 2007:

| Investment | Date purchased | Maturity date | Carrying amount |
|---|---|---|---|
| Three-month T-bill | 5/31/07 | 7/31/07 | $30,000 |
| Three-year T-note | 6/15/04 | 8/31/07 | 50,000 |
| Five-year T-note | 10/1/03 | 9/30/08 | 100,000 |

In the fund's balance sheet, what amount of these investments should be reported as cash and cash equivalents at June 30, 2007?

a. $0
b. $  30,000
c. $  80,000
d. $180,000

**106.** The following fund types used by Green Township had total assets at June 30, 2007, as follows:

| | |
|---|---|
| Agency funds | $  300,000 |
| Debt service funds | 1,000,000 |

Total fiduciary fund assets amount to

a. $0
b. $  300,000
c. $1,000,000
d. $1,300,000

**107.** Grove County collects property taxes levied within its boundaries and receives a 1% fee for administering these collections on behalf of the municipalities located in the county. In 2007, Grove collected $1,000,000 for its municipalities and remitted $990,000 to them after deducting fees of $10,000. In the initial recording of the 1% fee, Grove's agency fund should credit

   a.   Net Assets—Agency Fund, $10,000.
   b.   Fees Earned—Agency Fund, $10,000.
   c.   Due to Grove County General Fund, $10,000.
   d.   Revenues Control, $10,000.

**Items 108 and 109** are based on the following:

Elm City contributes to and administers a single-employer defined benefit pension plan on behalf of its covered employees. The plan is accounted for in a pension trust fund. For the year ended December 31, 2007, employer contributions to the pension trust fund amounted to $11,000.

**108.** What account should be credited in the pension trust fund to record the 2007 employer contribution of $11,000?
   a.   Additions.
   b.   Other Financing Sources Control.
   c.   Due from Special Revenue Fund.
   d.   Pension Benefit Obligation.

**109.** To record the 2007 pension contribution of $11,000, what debit is required in the governmental-type fund used in connection with employer pension contributions?
   a.   Other Financing Uses Control.
   b.   Expenditures Control.
   c.   Expenses Control.
   d.   Due to Pension Trust Fund.

**110.** In accordance with GASB 34, *Basic Financial Statements—and Management's Discussion and Analysis—for State and Local Governments*, what types of interfund transactions are included in the amount reported for transfers on the government-wide statement of activities?

  I.   Yearly operating subsidies from the general fund to an enterprise fund.
  II.   Billings from an enterprise fund to an internal service fund for services rendered.

   a.   I only.
   b.   II only.
   c.   Both I and II.
   d.   Neither I nor II.

**111.** Jamestown adopted the provisions of GASB 34, *Basic Financial Statements—and Management's Discussion and Analysis—for State and Local Governments*, for its financial statements issued for the year ended December 31, 2007. During the year ended December 31, 2007, Jamestown had the following selected transactions:

- The general fund made a $100,000 advance to an internal service fund. The internal service fund will repay the advance in 2008.
- The water utility enterprise fund billed the general fund $25,000 for water usage.
- The general fund transferred $30,000 to a debt service fund to pay interest on general obligation bonds.

On Jamestown's government-wide statement of activities for the year ended December 31, 2007, what amount should be reported for transfers?
   a.   $125,000
   b.   $ 55,000
   c.   $0
   d.   $130,000

**112.** The town of Harrisville adopted the provisions of GASB 34, *Basic Financial Statements—and Management's Discussion and Analysis—for State and Local Governments*, for its financial statements issued for the year ended December 31, 2007. During the year ended December 31, 2007, Harrisville had the following selected transactions:

- The general fund made a permanent transfer of $100,000 to an enterprise fund. The enterprise fund used the amount transferred to acquire capital assets.
- The general fund transferred $1,000,000 to a capital projects fund for the town's portion of the cost for the renovation of the town hall.
- The general fund was reimbursed $5,000 by an enterprise fund for expenses paid by the general fund that were properly charged as operating expenses of the enterprise fund.

On Harrisville's government-wide statement of activities for the year ended December 31, 2007, what amount should be reported as transfers?
   a.   $   100,000
   b.   $1,100,000
   c.   $1,005,000
   d.   $   105,000

**113.** In accordance with GASB 35, a public college or university that chooses to report only business-type activities should present only the financial statements required for
   a.   Enterprise funds.
   b.   Government funds.
   c.   Internal service funds.
   d.   Enterprise and internal service funds.

**114.** In accordance with GASB 35, a public college or university that chooses to report both governmental and business-type activities should report

| | *Fund financial statements* | *Government-wide financial statements* |
|---|---|---|
| a. | No | Yes |
| b. | Yes | No |
| c. | Yes | Yes |
| d. | No | No |

**115.** A public college had tuition and fees of $20,000,000. Scholarships, for which no services were required, amounted to $1,000,000. Employee discounts, which were provided in exchange for services, amounted to $2,000,000. The amount to be reported as net tuition and fees by the public college would be
   a.   $20,000,000.
   b.   $19,000,000.
   c.   $18,000,000.
   d.   $17,000,000.

**116.** Which of the following is true regarding the Statement of Revenues, Expenses, and Changes in Net Assets for a public college choosing to report as a special-purpose entity engaged in business-type activities only?
   a.   State appropriations should be reported as nonoperating income.
   b.   An operating income figure must be displayed.
   c.   Both contributions for plant and for endowment purposes must be reported separately after both operating and nonoperating revenues and expenses.
   d.   All of the above.

## MULTIPLE-CHOICE ANSWERS

| | | | | | | | | | |
|---|---|---|---|---|---|---|---|---|---|
| 1. c | __ __ | 27. d | __ __ | 53. c | __ __ | 79. a | __ __ | 105. c | __ __ |
| 2. d | __ __ | 28. c | __ __ | 54. d | __ __ | 80. c | __ __ | 106. b | __ __ |
| 3. b | __ __ | 29. c | __ __ | 55. d | __ __ | 81. c | __ __ | 107. c | __ __ |
| 4. b | __ __ | 30. c | __ __ | 56. b | __ __ | 82. b | __ __ | 108. a | __ __ |
| 5. a | __ __ | 31. a | __ __ | 57. d | __ __ | 83. d | __ __ | 109. b | __ __ |
| 6. a | __ __ | 32. b | __ __ | 58. c | __ __ | 84. a | __ __ | 110. a | __ __ |
| 7. a | __ __ | 33. b | __ __ | 59. b | __ __ | 85. d | __ __ | 111. c | __ __ |
| 8. d | __ __ | 34. a | __ __ | 60. b | __ __ | 86. a | __ __ | 112. a | __ __ |
| 9. b | __ __ | 35. b | __ __ | 61. c | __ __ | 87. c | __ __ | 113. a | __ __ |
| 10. b | __ __ | 36. b | __ __ | 62. a | __ __ | 88. d | __ __ | 114. c | __ __ |
| 11. c | __ __ | 37. b | __ __ | 63. c | __ __ | 89. a | __ __ | 115. b | __ __ |
| 12. d | __ __ | 38. a | __ __ | 64. b | __ __ | 90. c | __ __ | 116. d | __ __ |
| 13. d | __ __ | 39. c | __ __ | 65. d | __ __ | 91. a | __ __ | | |
| 14. c | __ __ | 40. c | __ __ | 66. b | __ __ | 92. a | __ __ | | |
| 15. d | __ __ | 41. c | __ __ | 67. a | __ __ | 93. c | __ __ | | |
| 16. a | __ __ | 42. b | __ __ | 68. d | __ __ | 94. a | __ __ | | |
| 17. b | __ __ | 43. d | __ __ | 69. c | __ __ | 95. b | __ __ | | |
| 18. b | __ __ | 44. a | __ __ | 70. b | __ __ | 96. d | __ __ | | |
| 19. c | __ __ | 45. c | __ __ | 71. a | __ __ | 97. d | __ __ | | |
| 20. d | __ __ | 46. d | __ __ | 72. b | __ __ | 98. d | __ __ | | |
| 21. a | __ __ | 47. c | __ __ | 73. c | __ __ | 99. d | __ __ | | |
| 22. c | __ __ | 48. c | __ __ | 74. a | __ __ | 100. c | __ __ | | |
| 23. a | __ __ | 49. a | __ __ | 75. b | __ __ | 101. a | __ __ | | |
| 24. a | __ __ | 50. c | __ __ | 76. c | __ __ | 102. c | __ __ | | |
| 25. b | __ __ | 51. a | __ __ | 77. b | __ __ | 103. d | __ __ | 1st: __/116 = __% |
| 26. d | __ __ | 52. b | __ __ | 78. c | __ __ | 104. c | __ __ | 2nd: __/116 = __% |

## MULTIPLE-CHOICE ANSWER EXPLANATIONS

### B. The Reporting Entity

**1.** **(c)** GASB 34 indicates that the basic financial statements include only the government-wide statements, the fund statements, and the notes to the financial statements.

**2.** **(d)** The concept underlying the definition of the financial reporting entity is that elected officials are accountable to their constituents for their actions. Accordingly, the financial reporting entity consists of (1) the primary government, (2) organizations for which the primary government is **financially accountable,** and (3) other organizations for which the nature and significance of their relationship with the primary government is such that exclusion would cause the reporting entity's financial statements to be misleading or incomplete. Thus, the basic criterion used to determine the reporting entity is financial accountability.

**3.** **(b)** The requirement is to determine how the school district's financial activity should be reported. The school district is a component unit, which means it is a legally separate organization for which the elected officials of a primary government are financially accountable. Component units can be presented either discretely or blended. If the component unit is so closely tied to the primary government that the activities seem to be indistinguishable, the presentation should be blended. The school district's budget requires separate approval of the city council, so it is not indistinguishable. In addition, the school board members are independently elected. The activities of the component unit are distinguishable from the primary government, and therefore should be shown discretely.

**4.** **(b)** The requirement is to determine how the school district should be reported. A component unit is a legally

separate organization for which the elected officials of a primary government are financially accountable. The school district is a component unit, which can be presented either discretely or blended. The unit is blended if the activities of the unit are so closely tied to the primary government as to be indistinguishable. Even though two of the district's members are city council members, the activities of the school district are distinct from the primary government and should be presented discretely.

### D. Government-Wide Financial Statements

**5.** **(a)** In accordance with GASB 34, state and local governments are required to report infrastructure assets on the government-wide statement of net assets. However, GASB 34 does not require infrastructure assets to be depreciated. GASB 34 permits governments to use a modified approach in its accounting for infrastructure assets. The modified approach results in the government reporting expense for the maintenance costs related to infrastructure assets (on the government-wide statement of activities) and in its reporting no depreciation expense, if certain conditions are met by the government as specified in GASB 34. Therefore, on the statement of net assets for Darien Village at December 31, 2005, infrastructure assets would be reported at $5,000,000 without any reduction for accumulated depreciation.

**6.** **(a)** GASB 9, para 19, indicates that "cash flows from operating activities include transactions of certain loan programs." These include "program loan" programs that are undertaken to fulfill a governmental responsibility, such as the loan program mentioned in this problem.

**7.** **(a)** GASB 34, para 296, (part of the basis of conclusions) indicates that "The Board concluded that a government's basic financial statements should provide operational accountability information for the government as a whole, including information about the cost of services, operating results, and financial position."

**8.   (d)**   In accordance with GASB 34, capital assets, exclusive of infrastructure assets, are reported on the government-wide statement of net assets at cost less accumulated depreciation. In the case involving Fullerton City, the amount reported under assets is $2,750,000, computed by subtracting $750,000 of accumulated depreciation from the $3,500,000 cost of the capital assets.

**9.   (b)**   In the net assets section of the government-wide statement of net assets, GASB 34 requires that the amount invested in capital assets be reported net of related debt. In the case of Fullerton City, the amount reported would be $1,500,000, computed by subtracting $1,250,000 from $2,750,000, the amount reported for capital assets in the asset section of the statement of net assets.

**10.   (b)**   In accordance with GASB 34, depreciation expense on infrastructure assets is not required if the government chooses the modified approach. Under the modified approach, infrastructure assets are reported on the government-wide statement of net assets at their cost without reduction for accumulated depreciation. On the government-wide statement of activities, the cost to extend the life of the infrastructure assets is reported as an expense, and certain information about infrastructure assets is disclosed as required supplementary information.

**11.   (c)**   According to GASB 34, the government-wide statement of activities should be prepared using the accrual basis of accounting and the flow of economic resources measurement focus. As a result, capital assets are reported as assets and depreciated over their useful lives, and depreciation expense should be reported on the statement of activities. The statement of revenues, expenses, and changes in fund net assets prepared for the proprietary funds is also prepared using the accrual basis of accounting and the flow of economic resources measurement focus. Therefore, capital assets are depreciated over their useful lives, and depreciation expense is reported on the statement of revenues, expenses, and changes in fund net assets.

**12.   (d)**   According to GASB 34, governments should prepare government-wide financial statements based upon the accrual basis of accounting and the economic resources measurement focus. In addition to the government-wide financial statements, governments are also required to report financial statements for governmental funds, proprietary funds, and fiduciary funds. The financial statements for governmental funds are based upon the modified accrual basis and the financial resources measurement focus, while the financial statements for proprietary and fiduciary funds are based upon the accrual basis of accounting and the flow of economic resources measurement focus.

**13.   (d)**   According to GASB 34, infrastructure assets are required to be reported on the government-wide statement of net assets. The use of the modified approach for infrastructure assets means that these assets are not depreciated if certain conditions are satisfied. However, infrastructure assets are reported on the statement of net assets, even if they are not depreciated. According to GASB 34, component units are reported on the entity-wide financial state-

ments. They are not reported on the financial statements of the governmental funds.

**E.   Fund Financial Statements**

**14.   (c)**   A fund is defined as a fiscal and accounting entity with a self balancing set of accounts. These funds record cash and other financial resources, together with all related liabilities and residual equities or balances, and changes therein, **and are segregated for the purpose of carrying on specific activities or attaining certain objectives** in accordance with special regulations, restrictions, or limitations.

**15.   (d)**   GASB 9, para 27, indicates that cash flows from investing activities includes interest received as returns on investments. The candidate should note that this is different from SFAS 95, which classifies interest on investments as cash flows from operating activities.

**16.   (a)**   The Governmental Accounting Standards Board (GASB) has the authority to establish standards of financial reporting for all units of state and local government. Upon its formation in 1984, GASB adopted the past pronouncements of its predecessor organization, the National Council on Governmental Accounting (NCGA), and guidelines in the AICPA *Audits of State and Local Governmental Units*, which the GASB later modified. The FASB sets standards for profit-seeking businesses, and not governmental units.

**17.   (b)**   The requirement is to determine which event(s) should be included in a statement of cash flows for a government entity. Governmental funds do not have a statement of cash flows because they are accounted for on the modified accrual basis. A statement of cash flows is included for proprietary funds because they are accounted for on the accrual basis. The cash inflow from issuing bonds to finance city hall construction is accounted for in the governmental funds. The cash outflow from a city utility representing payments in lieu of property taxes is accounted for in the proprietary funds.

**18.   (b)**   Cash flows from sale of revenue bonds and capital contributed by subdividers are classified as cash flows from capital and related financing activities. Both the $4,500,000 proceeds from sale of revenue bonds and $900,000 capital contributed by subdividers would be reported as cash flows from capital and related financing activities. Cash flows from customer households are operating cash flows.

**19.   (c)**   The statement of cash flows is applicable to proprietary funds and governmental entities that use proprietary fund accounting, including public benefit corporations and authorities, governmental utilities, and governmental hospitals. PERS (Public Employee Retirement Systems) and pension trust funds are exempt from this requirement.

**20.   (d)**   In accordance with GASB 34, there are three financial statements that should be prepared for proprietary funds. The financial statements for proprietary funds include

1.   The statement of net assets
2.   The statement of revenues, expenses, and changes in fund net assets
3.   The statement of cash flows

**21.** **(a)** In accordance with GASB 34, the focus of fund financial statements is on major and nonmajor funds, not on fund types. On the balance sheet for the governmental funds, the general fund is always reported as a major fund, while other funds are evaluated as major or nonmajor based upon criteria specified in GASB 34. A separate column is required for each major fund, while all nonmajor funds are aggregated in a single column. On the balance sheet for the governmental funds, fund balances are reported in two categories—reserved and unreserved. The terms restricted and unrestricted are not used on the balance sheet for the governmental funds.

**22.** **(c)** In accordance with GASB 34, the statement of net assets for proprietary funds should (1) report assets and liabilities in current and noncurrent classifications, and (2) report all the activities of internal service funds in a single column.

**23.** **(a)** According to GASB 34, the financial statements of proprietary funds should be based upon the accrual basis of accounting and the economic resources measurement focus. Therefore, the statement of net assets for proprietary funds is prepared on the accrual basis and the economic resources measurement focus. On the other hand, the financial statements prepared for governmental funds should be based upon the modified accrual basis of accounting and the financial resources measurement focus. Therefore, the statement of revenues, expenditures, and changes in fund balances prepared for governmental funds is not prepared on the accrual basis and the economic resources measurement focus.

**24.** **(a)** According to GASB 34, two financial statements should be prepared for fiduciary funds—the statement of fiduciary net assets and the statement of changes in fiduciary net assets. Fiduciary funds include pension trust, investment trust, private-purpose trust, and agency funds. Agency funds should be reported on the statement of fiduciary net assets, but not on the statement of changes in fiduciary net assets. Since agency funds report only assets and liabilities, they are reported on the statement of fiduciary net assets, but they are not reported on the statement of changes in fiduciary net assets.

**25.** **(b)** According to GASB 34, private-purpose trust funds are fiduciary funds that should be reported on two fiduciary fund financial statements: (1) the statement of fiduciary net assets and (2) the statement of changes in fiduciary net assets. Therefore, private-purpose trust funds are reported on the statement of changes in fiduciary net assets. According to GASB 34, the government-wide statement of net assets discloses information about governmental activities, business-type activities, and component units. Fiduciary activities are not disclosed on the government-wide financial statements. This means that private-purpose trust funds would not be reported on the statement of net assets for governmental and business-type activities.

**26.** **(d)** According to GASB 34, the statement of cash flows is prepared only for the proprietary funds. The statement of cash flows is not a government-wide financial statement. Therefore, governmental and fiduciary fund types are not reported on the statement of cash flows.

**27.** **(d)** According to GASB 34, the statement of cash flows is prepared only for the proprietary funds. The statement of cash flows is not a government-wide financial statement. The format of the statement of cash flows consists of four sections. The sections include cash flows from (1) operating activities, (2) noncapital financing activities, (3) capital and related financing activities, and (4) investing activities. This format for the statement of cash flows is different from the format used by business enterprises that discloses operating, investing, and financing activities.

**28.** **(c)** According to GASB 34, the balance sheet prepared for the governmental funds is based on the modified accrual basis of accounting and financial resources measurement focus. However, the government-wide statement of net assets is prepared based on the accrual basis of accounting and the economic resources measurement focus. The differences between these two financial statements result in a difference between the amount reported for net assets for governmental activities on the statement of net assets and the amount reported for fund balances on the balance sheet for the governmental funds. GASB 34 requires that the reasons for this difference be reported in a reconciliation schedule. One of the reasons for the difference is the acquisition of capital assets by governmental funds during the year. These capital assets do not appear under assets on the balance sheet of the governmental funds because they are recorded as expenditures using the modified accrual basis of accounting and the financial resources measurement focus. Therefore, the acquisition of capital assets has the effect of reducing the fund balances of governmental funds on the balance sheet. However, capital assets are reported as assets on the government-wide statement of net assets. Capital assets acquired by governmental funds are reported on this statement as assets under governmental activities. Therefore, total net assets related to governmental activities are not affected on the statement of net assets when capital assets are acquired. Accordingly, capital assets used in governmental activities are items that are reported in the schedule that reconciles the net assets of governmental activities with the fund balances of the governmental funds. The assets and liabilities of internal service funds are additional items that cause a difference between the fund balances of the government funds and the net assets of governmental activities. The reason that the assets and liabilities of internal service funds cause a difference is that they are included with governmental activities on the statement of net assets, thereby causing net assets of governmental activities to increase. However, internal service fund assets and liabilities are not reported in the governmental fund financial statements; rather, they are included in the proprietary fund financial statements. Therefore, the fund balances of the governmental funds do not include these items. Accordingly, the assets and liabilities of internal service funds are reported in the schedule that reconciles the net assets of governmental activities with the fund balances of the governmental funds.

**29.** **(c)** According to GASB 34, the statement of revenues, expenditures, and changes in fund balances prepared for the governmental funds is prepared using the modified accrual basis of accounting and the financial resources measurement focus. However, the government-wide statement of activities is prepared using the accrual basis of accounting and the economic resources measurement focus. The differences between these two financial statements result in a difference between the amount reported for the change in net assets for governmental activities on the statement of activities, and the amount reported for the net change in fund balances on the statement of revenues, expenditures, and changes in fund balances for the governmental funds. GASB 34 requires that the reasons for this difference be reported in a reconciliation schedule. One of the reasons for the difference is capital assets that were acquired by governmental funds during the year. On the statement of revenues, expenditures, and changes in fund balances, capital assets are reported as expenditures, using the modified accrual basis of accounting and the financial resources measurement focus. However, capital assets acquired by governmental funds are reported as assets and are depreciated on the government-wide statement of activities. Therefore, the difference between capital expenditures and depreciation expense is reported as a reconciling item. On the other hand, the revenues and expenses of internal service funds are additional items that cause a difference between the net change in the fund balances reported on the statement of revenues, expenditures, and changes in fund balances of the governmental funds and the change in the net assets of governmental activities reported on the statement of activities. The reason that the revenues and expenses of internal service funds cause a difference is that they are included with governmental activities on the statement of activities, thereby causing the net change in fund balances of governmental activities to increase. However, internal service fund revenues and expenses are not reported in the governmental fund financial statements; rather, they are included in the proprietary fund financial statements. Therefore, the net change in fund balances of the governmental funds do not include internal service fund revenues and expenses. Accordingly, the revenues and expenses of internal service funds should be reported in the schedule that reconciles the change in net assets of governmental activities with the net change in the fund balances of the governmental funds.

**30.    (c)**    According to GASB 34, the accrual basis of accounting and the economic resources measurement focus are concepts that go together. This means that financial statements prepared using the accrual basis also are based upon the economic resources measurement focus. Both the government-wide statement of net assets and the statement of changes in fiduciary net assets are prepared using the accrual basis of accounting and the economic resources measurement focus. The only financial statements that use the financial resources measurement focus are those prepared for governmental funds—the balance sheet and the statement of revenues, expenditures, and changes in fund balances.

**31.    (a)**    According to GASB 34, pension trust funds are fiduciary funds that are reported on the statement of changes in fiduciary net assets. On the statement of net assets for proprietary funds, net assets are disclosed in three classifications: (1) invested in capital assets, net of related debt, (2) restricted, and (3) unrestricted. Retained earnings is not disclosed on the statement of net assets for proprietary funds; the term "net assets" is used as the equity account.

**32.    (b)**    According to GASB 34, the statement of cash flows is prepared for proprietary funds. The statement format is not the same as that for business enterprises. The format for the statement of cash flows for proprietary funds contains four sections: (1) cash flows from operating activities, (2) cash flows from noncapital financing activities, (3)

cash flows from capital and related financing activities, and (4) cash flows from investing activities. The cash flows from operating activities can be presented using either the direct method or the indirect method. Cash paid for interest is not reported in the operating activities section. It would be disclosed either in the noncapital financing activities' section or the capital and related financing activities' section, depending upon where the debt that caused the interest payments was reported. Interest revenue received in cash is not reported in the operating activities' section. It is reported in the investing activities' section because this is where the investments were reported that resulted in the interest revenue.

## H. Measurement Focus and Basis of Accounting

**33.    (b)**    The governmental fund measurement focus is on determination of current financial position (sources, uses, and balances of financial resources), rather than upon income determination.

**34.    (a)**    Governmental fund revenues should be recognized in the accounting period in which they become available and measurable. Governmental funds include the general fund, special revenue funds, capital projects funds, debt service funds, and permanent funds. Proprietary fund revenues should be recognized in the accounting period in which they are earned and become measurable. Proprietary funds include the enterprise and internal service funds. As the question requires the funds in which revenue is recognized in the period it becomes available and measurable, this would include the general fund but not the enterprise fund.

## I. Accounting by Governments for Certain Events and Transactions

**35.    (b)**    GASB 33, para 7, indicates that "imposed nonexchange revenues result from assessments by governments on nongovernmental entities, including individuals, other than assessments on nonexchange transactions. Examples include property (ad valorem) taxes; fines and penalties...."

**36.    (b)**    The levy of property taxes is a nonexchange transaction. GASB 33 defines nonexchange transactions as transactions "in which a government gives (or receives) value without directly receiving (or giving) equal value in exchange." Exchange transactions are transactions "in which each party receives and gives up essentially equal values." In the case of a property tax levy, the government is receiving value, the right to receive payments from property owners, without directly giving equal value in return. The government services that are financed from a property tax levy are not provided to individual taxpayers in proportion to the amount of property taxes that are paid. The other answers are incorrect because they are examples of exchange transactions.

**37.    (b)**    Deferred revenue should be credited upon receipt of the grant. According to the guidance provided in GASB 33, cash received from government-mandated grants should be reported as deferred revenue when cash is received prior to all eligibility requirements being met. A time restriction is one example of eligibility requirements not being met before the end of the fiscal period. Note that, if there was no time restriction placed on the government-mandated grant by the state, Elizabeth City would have reported revenue for the year ended June 30, 2007.

**38.** (**a**)  According to the guidance provided in GASB 33, the grant from the state is an example of a government-mandated type of nonexchange transaction. Government-mandated nonexchange transactions exists when the providing government, such as a state government, requires the receiving government to expend the funds for a specific purpose.

**39.** (**c**)  According to the guidance provided by GASB 33, sales tax revenues are an example of a derived tax revenue. Derived tax revenues result from taxes assessed by government on exchange transactions. In the case of sales taxes, exchange transactions between merchants and consumers provide the basis for the collection of the sales tax revenues.

**40.** (**c**)  The general fund of Eldorado should report the sales taxes to be received in July 2007 as revenue for the year ended June 30, 2007. Under the modified accrual measurement focus, the sales taxes should be reported as revenue for the year ended June 30, 2007 because the sales taxes are available to finance expenditures made in the year ended June 30, 2007.

**41.** (**c**)  According to the guidance provided by GASB 33, property tax revenues are an example of an imposed tax revenue. Imposed revenues result from taxes and other assessments imposed by governments that are not derived from underlying transactions.

**42.** (**b**)  In accordance with GASB 33, the modified accrual basis of accounting should be used for recording and reporting property tax revenues for the general fund on the statement of revenues, expenditures, and changes in fund balances. Under the modified accrual basis of accounting, revenues are recognized in the period when they are both measurable and available to pay for expenditures incurred during the current fiscal period. With respect to property tax revenues, "available" means collected during the year and within the first sixty days after the end of the year. For the general fund of Karsten City, the property taxes collected in 2007 of $850,000 as well as the $100,000 expected to be collected by March 1 of 2008 would be added to get the property tax revenues recognized in 2007. The sum of $950,000 of property tax revenues would be reported by the general fund on the statement of revenues, expenditures, and changes in fund balances for the year ended December 31, 2007. The journal entries to record the property tax levy and collections for 2007 appear below.

| | | |
|---|---:|---:|
| Property taxes receivable—Current | 1,000,000 | |
| Property tax revenues ($850,000 + 100,000) | | 950,000 |
| Deferred revenues (report as a liability on the balance sheet) | | 40,000 |
| Allowance for estimated uncollectible property taxes—Current | | 10,000 |
| Cash | 850,000 | |
| Property taxes receivable—Current | | 850,000 |

The deferred revenue account of $40,000 represents the property taxes expected to be collected after March 1, 2008. Because the taxes are expected to be collected after sixty days from the end of 2007, the taxes are not considered available to pay for expenditures incurred in 2007. This is the reason for crediting deferred revenue in 2007.

**43.** (**d**)  In accordance with GASB 33, imposed nonexchange transactions include taxes and other assessments derived from underlying transactions. Examples include property taxes, special assessments, and fines and forfeits. For the general fund of Ward Village, imposed nonexchange transactions would include property tax revenues of $125,000 and fines of $10,000. Sales taxes and income taxes would be classified as derived tax revenues.

**44.** (**a**)  In accordance with GASB 33, the modified accrual basis of accounting should be used for recording and reporting revenues reported by the general fund on the Statement of Revenues, Expenditures, and Changes in Fund Balances. The modified accrual basis of accounting for revenues results in revenues being recognized in the period in which they are both measurable and available to pay for expenditures incurred during the current fiscal period. The sales tax advance of $25,000 should be reported as revenue in 2007 because it was available to pay for expenditures incurred by the general fund in 2007. On the other hand, the cash received from property owners of $20,000 should not be reported as revenue in 2007 because the money cannot be used to pay for expenditures incurred by the general fund in 2007. The property taxes received in December 2007 should be reported as deferred revenue on the December 31, 2007 balance sheet for the general fund. Deferred revenue would appear under the liabilities classification. The entry to record both of the cash receipts in the general fund in December 2007 appears below.

| | | |
|---|---:|---:|
| Cash | 45,000 | |
| Sales tax revenues | | 25,000 |
| Deferred revenue | | 20,000 |

**45.** (**c**)  According to GASB 33, revenues that result from taxes assessed by government on exchange transactions are classified as derived tax revenues. Examples of derived tax revenue include sales taxes, income taxes, and motor fuel taxes. Property tax revenues and fines and forfeits are examples of revenues that come from imposed nonexchange transactions. Imposed nonexchange transactions are taxes and other assessments imposed by governments that are not derived from underlying transactions. Unrestricted government grants are an example of voluntary nonexchange transactions. This category includes grants and entitlements from one government to another where the providing government does not impose certain requirements on the receiving government.

**46.** (**d**)  According to GASB 33, revenues that result from taxes and other assessments imposed by governments that are not derived from underlying transactions are categorized as imposed nonexchange transactions. Examples include property taxes, special assessments, and fines and forfeits. Income taxes, sales taxes, and motor fuel taxes are examples of derived tax revenues. Derived tax revenues result from taxes assessed by government on exchange transactions.

**47.** (**c**)  The requirement is to identify the item that is not a requirement for a government to start capitalizing software costs. GASB 51 establishes three requirements to begin capitalizing the cost of an internally generated intangible asset: (1) the government must determine the objective and the service capacity of the project, (2) the government must establish the feasibility of the project, and (3) the government must establish its intention to complete or continue the project. There is no specific requirement in GASB 51 to have developed an accurate budget for the project. Therefore, answer (c) is correct.

**48.   (c)**   The requirement is to identify the item that correctly describes the proper accounting for the transfer of future revenue. Answer (c) is correct because GASB 48 states that a sale of future revenue should be recorded as deferred revenue and recognized over the life of the agreement.

## J.  Budgetary Accounting for the General and Special Revenue Funds

**49.   (a)**   To record the budget, Ridge would make the following journal entry:

| | | |
|---|---|---|
| Estimated Revenues Control | 100,000 | |
| Appropriations Control | | 80,000 |
| Budgetary Fund Balance | | 20,000 |

Therefore, as the Appropriations account is credited for the anticipated expenditures.

**50.   (c)**   To record the budget, Ridge would make the following journal entry:

| | | |
|---|---|---|
| Estimated Revenues Control | 100,000 | |
| Appropriations Control | | 80,000 |
| Budgetary Fund Balance | | 20,000 |

Therefore, the Budgetary Fund Balance account is credited for the anticipated surplus of revenues over expenditures.

**51.   (a)**   Revenues to the general fund are defined as "increases in fund financial resources other than from interfund transfers and debt issue proceeds." Transfers to a fund and debt issue proceeds received by a fund are classified as other financing sources of the fund. Therefore, in Maple's budgetary entry, estimated revenues would be debited for the $9,000,000 expected from property taxes, licenses, and fines. The Estimated Other Financing Sources account would be debited for the $6,000,000, consisting of the debt issue proceeds and the interfund transfers.

**52.   (b)**   Assuming that encumbrance accounting is utilized by the city, the journal entry to record the issuance of purchase orders and contracts is a debit to Encumbrances Control and a credit to Budgetary Fund Balance—Reserved for Encumbrances for the amount of the purchase order or estimated cost of the contracts.

**53.   (c)**   As Cliff approves and issues its purchase orders, the purchase order amount ($5,000,000) is recorded in the Encumbrances Control account. As the goods are received, the related purchase order amount of these goods (i.e., the amount that was originally recorded, $4,500,000) is removed from the Encumbrances Control account. Therefore, at year-end, the amount of outstanding encumbrances is $500,000. Keep in mind that the actual invoice amount is not the amount removed from the Encumbrances Control account. The invoice amount will be vouchered and charged to Expenditures Control.

**54.   (d)**   When Elm issued its purchase order, the following journal entry would have been made to encumber the amount:

| | | |
|---|---|---|
| Encumbrances Control | 5,000 | |
| Budgetary Fund Balance—Reserved for Encumbrances | | 5,000 |

When the supplies were received the following journal entries would have been made:

| | | |
|---|---|---|
| Budgetary Fund Balance—Reserved for Encumbrances | 5,000 | |
| Encumbrances Control | | 5,000 |
| Expenditures Control | 4,950 | |
| Vouchers Payable | | 4,950 |

**55.   (d)**   When purchase orders for goods or services are approved and issued, the Encumbrances Control account is debited and the Budgetary Fund Balance—Reserved for Encumbrances is credited for the amount of the purchase orders. As goods are received or services are rendered the above encumbrance entry is reversed. Thus, the amount left in each would be zero. Note that the same amount is initially recorded in each of the accounts (i.e., the debit equals the credit). The same amount is also relieved from both accounts. A Budgetary Fund Balance—Reserved for Encumbrances in excess of a balance in the Encumbrances Control account indicates there has been a recording error.

**56.   (b)**   Encumbrances outstanding at year-end represent the estimated amount of the expenditures that could result if unperformed contracts in process at year-end are computed. Encumbrances outstanding at year-end are not expenditures or liabilities. Where appropriations do not lapse at year-end, encumbrances outstanding at year-end should be reported as reservations of fund balance for the subsequent year expenditures. Where appropriations lapse at year-end, the governmental unit may honor the contracts in progress at year-end or cancel them. If the governmental unit intends to honor them, the encumbrances outstanding at year-end should be disclosed by reservation of fund balance.

**57.   (d)**   When closing entries are made for a governmental unit, Estimated Revenues Control is credited for the same amount that it was debited for in the beginning of the period budget/entry. Also, Revenues Control is debited in the amount of recorded revenue for the year. In this case, Estimated Revenues Control would be credited for $20,000,000 and Revenues Control would be debited for $17,000,000 to close the books. Revenues Control and Estimated Revenues Control are not netted in the closing entry.

**58.   (c)**   The Budgetary Fund Balance account is debited upon budget adoption when the appropriations exceed the estimated revenues. The following entry is made when the budget is adopted:

| | | |
|---|---|---|
| Estimated Revenues Control | xx | |
| Budgetary Fund Balance | xx | |
| Appropriations Control | | xx |

At the end of the year, the budgetary accounts must be closed out. The budgetary closing entry is simply a reverse of the adoption entry.

| | | |
|---|---|---|
| Appropriations Control | xx | |
| Estimated Revenues Control | | xx |
| Budgetary Fund Balance | | xx |

The Budgetary Fund Balance is debited at the beginning of the year when appropriations exceed the estimated revenues. An entry must be made to close the Budgetary Fund Balance account at the end of the year. Note that any differences between the budgetary revenues and appropriations and the actual revenues and expenditures and encumbrances do not affect the **Budgetary** Fund Balance account. They would, however, affect the Unreserved Fund Balance account when the operations accounts are closed out.

**59. (b)** The $100,000 balance in the Fund Balance—Reserved for Encumbrances account indicates that there were open purchase orders at year-end. Since the appropriations do not lapse at year-end, the Fund Balance—Reserved for Encumbrances account will not be closed but will be reported as a separate line item in the fund balance section of the balance sheet. The term "reserve" indicates that the funds are not available for expenditure. Therefore, the $100,000 cannot be included in the unreserved fund balance amount. Therefore, the amount of the Unreserved Fund Balance in the 2005 balance sheet would be $300,000 ($1,000,000 – $600,000 – $100,000).

**60. (b)** The closing of the general fund accounts is done by closing the budgetary accounts against each other and the actual revenue, expenditure and other accounts to the Unreserved Fund Balance. This is done most easily by reversing the beginning of the year budget entry in one entry and then using a separate entry to close the actual accounts to fund balance. The following entry would therefore be made to close the actual accounts to obtain the amount of increase in the fund balance:

| General Fund | | |
|---|---|---|
| Other Financing Sources Control | 1,500,000 | |
| Revenues Control | 8,000,000 | |
| Expenditures Control | | 5,000,000 |
| Other Financing Uses Control | | 2,000,000 |
| Fund Balance—Unreserved | | 2,500,000 |

The Appropriations account would be closed in the reversal of the budget entry and has no effect on fund balance.

**61. (c)** GASB 34, para 92, indicates that proprietary funds (including enterprise funds) are to use accrual accounting. Paragraph 93 indicates that FASB pronouncements issued on or before November 30, 1989, are to be followed unless superceded by a GASB pronouncement. Accrual accounting recognizes interest revenue over time; in this case, interest revenue would be $1,000,000 × .06 × 9/12 = $45,000.

### K. Expenditure Classification for Governmental Funds

**62. (a)** Expenditure classification by object is based upon the type of items purchased or services obtained. Examples of "Current Operations" object of expenditure classifications are personal services, supplies, and other services and charges. Salaries are an example of classification by object. Function or program classifications provide information regarding the overall purpose or objectives of expenditures (i.e., police protection, sanitation, highways and streets, etc.). Activity classification provides data for calculating expenditures per unit of activity (i.e., street resurfacing).

### L. Accounting for the General Fund

**63. (c)** "When a property tax assessment is made, it is to finance the budget of a particular period, and the revenue produced from any property tax assessment should be recognized in the fiscal period for which it was levied, provided the 'available' criteria are met. 'Available' means then due, or past due and receivable within the current period, and collected within the current period or expected to be collected soon enough thereafter to pay liabilities of the current period. Such time thereafter shall not exceed sixty days." This is how property tax revenues are reported on the Statement of Revenues, Expenditures, and Changes in Fund Bal-

ances for governmental funds. Therefore, both the collections during 2007 of $500,000 and the expected collections during the first sixty days of 2008 of $100,000 would be reported as property tax revenues for 2007. Remember that the estimated uncollectible amounts are not reported on the operating statement as an offset to revenues, but rather are reported as a contra asset account. The governmental unit, in calculating the amount of the levy, factors in what has historically been uncollectible, so that the revenues in effect have already been adjusted.

**64. (b)** Under GASB Statement 33, imposed nonexchange revenues, including property taxes, should be recorded in the year for which budgeted. In this case, the amount would be $690,000, the total levy less the estimated uncollectible amount.

**65. (d)** Interfund services provided and used are transactions that would be treated as revenues or expenditures/expenses if they involved organizations external to the government (i.e., **routine employer contributions from a general fund to a pension trust fund,** internal service fund billings to departments, enterprise funds billing for services provided to the general fund). The proper accounting for interfund services provided and used is to treat them as revenues in the fund providing the goods or services and **as expenditures/ expenses in the fund receiving the goods or services,** exactly as if the transactions involved parties external to the government. Thus, answer (d) is correct because the general fund should record an expenditure for routine employer contributions to the pension trust fund. Answer (a) is incorrect because the contribution of enterprise fund capital by the general fund should be recorded in the general fund as a transfer. Answers (b) and (c) are incorrect because routine transfers between funds should also be recorded as transfers.

**66. (b)** Interfund services provided and used are treated as revenues or expenditures/expenses if they involved organizations external to the government (i.e., a city's electric utility providing electricity to the general fund, internal service fund billings to departments, routine employer contributions from a general fund to a pension trust fund). The proper accounting for interfund services provided and used transactions is to treat them as revenues in the fund providing the goods or services and as expenditures/expenses in the fund receiving the goods or services, exactly as if the transactions involved parties external to the government. The general fund should recognize an expenditure for the amount billed by the city's electric utility.

**67. (a)** The internal service fund and the enterprise fund use the accrual basis of accounting and both report net assets, not fund balances. Net assets are reported in the following manner: (1) invested in capital assets, net of related debt, (2) restricted, and (3) unrestricted. The capital projects fund does not keep an inventory of supplies and therefore would not have a Fund Balance—Reserved for Inventory of Supplies. The general fund does maintain an inventory of supplies and would therefore have a Fund Balance—Reserved for Inventory of Supplies.

**68. (d)** The $6,000,000 in property taxes would be accounted for in Ariba's general fund, which is a governmental fund. The $40,000 of net rental revenue (after depreciation) from a parking garage would be accounted for in an enterprise fund, which is a proprietary fund. An enterprise fund provides products or services to the public, such as the use of the parking garage. The $100,000 interest earned on investments held for employees' retirement benefits would be included in a trust fund (more than likely a pension trust fund).

**69.  (c)**   In accordance with GASB 34, the balance sheet prepared for the governmental funds should be based on the current financial resources measurement focus and the modified accrual basis of accounting. This means that capital assets, such as police cars, are not reported on the balance sheet for governmental funds. Instead, the police cars are reported as expenditures on the statement of revenues, expenditures, and changes in fund balances for the year ended December 31, 2007.

**70.  (b)**   In accordance with GASB 34, the government-wide statement of net assets is prepared using the economic resources measurement focus and the full accrual basis of accounting. In the column for governmental activities, the police cars would be reported at $32,500. This amount is the original cost of $40,000 less accumulated depreciation of $7,500. The use of full accrual accounting means that the police cars are depreciated. The depreciation expense is reported on the government-wide statement of activities. Depreciation expense would be $7,500, computed by taking $40,000 less the salvage value of $10,000, and dividing by the useful life of four years.

**71.  (a)**   GASB 34 requires use of the current financial resources measurement focus and the modified accrual basis of accounting for governmental funds. On the statement of revenues, expenditures, and changes in fund balances prepared for 2007 for the governmental funds, the acquisition of the police cars is reported as expenditures of $40,000.

**72.  (b)**   According to GASB 34, the statement of revenues, expenditures, and changes in fund balances prepared for governmental funds is based upon the modified accrual basis of accounting and the financial resources measurement focus. On the statement of revenues, expenditures, and changes in fund balances, the acquisition of police cars is reported as expenditures of $75,000. The $30,000 payment by the general fund to the pension trust fund is reported as an interfund services provided and used transaction. On the statement of revenues, expenditures, and changes in fund balances, the $30,000 should be reported as expenditures. Therefore, the acquisition of the police cars and the pension transfer result in $105,000 of expenditures being reported on the statement of revenues, expenditures, and changes in fund balances for the governmental funds.

**73.  (c)**   According to GASB 34, the statement of revenues, expenditures, and changes in fund balances prepared for governmental funds is based upon the modified accrual basis of accounting and the financial resources measurement focus. On the statement of revenues, expenditures, and changes in fund balances, the revenue from property taxes should be reported at $750,000. The levy of $800,000 less the 2% that was not expected to be collected results in $784,000, of which $750,000 was collected in 2007. Because the remaining $34,000 was not expected to be collected within sixty days of the end of 2007, the $34,000 is not considered available in 2007, and, therefore, it is not reported as revenue in 2007. At December 31, 2007, the

$34,000 should be reported as deferred revenue on the balance sheet prepared for the governmental funds. Deferred revenues are reported as liabilities on this balance sheet. On the other hand, sales tax revenues for 2007 would be $100,000. The amount of sales taxes that are expected to be received in mid-March of 2008 is not considered available in 2007, and should not be included in revenues on the statement of revenues, expenditures, and changes in fund balances prepared for the governmental funds for the year ended December 31, 2007. Therefore, property tax revenues and sales tax revenues for 2007 would be reported at $850,000.

**74.  (a)**   According to GASB 34, the government-wide statement of activities should be prepared based upon the accrual basis of accounting and the economic resources measurement focus. The statement of activities reports governmental activities, business-type activities, and component units. For the police cars that were purchased in 2007, this means that depreciation expense of $12,000 would be reported under governmental activities. The police cars would be reported as assets on the government-wide statement of net assets, and the depreciation expense for 2007 would be computed by dividing five years into $75,000 less the salvage value of $15,000. The transfer to the pension trust fund would be reported under governmental activities as an expense of $30,000. The transfer is accounted for as an interfund services provided and used transaction in 2007. This means that the transfer would be reported in expenses under governmental activities for the year ended December 31, 2007. Therefore, $42,000 of expenses result from the acquisition of the police cars and the pension transfer in 2007. These expenses would be reported on the government-wide statement of activities for 2007.

**75.  (b)**   According to GASB 34, the government-wide statement of activities should be prepared based upon the accrual basis of accounting and the economic resources measurement focus. The statement of activities reports governmental activities, business-type activities, and component units. For 2007, property tax revenues should be reported at the full amount of the levy of $800,000 less the 2% that was not expected to be collected. This means that $784,000 would be reported for property tax revenues in 2007. The $34,000 of property taxes that were not collected in 2007 are reported as revenues in 2007 because the statement of activities is based upon accrual accounting. For 2007, sales tax revenues should be reported at $125,000. Sales tax revenues reported for 2006 include the $100,000 collected during 2007 as well as the $25,000 that will be collected in mid-March of 2008. The $25,000 of sales taxes that will be collected in mid-March 2008 are reported as revenues in 2007 on the statement of activities because the sales taxes were collected by the state in 2007. Therefore, the accrual basis of accounting mandates that the $25,000 be reported as revenue under governmental activities in 2007. Therefore, for the year ended December 31, 2007, a total of $909,000 of revenues are reported for property taxes ($784,000) and sales taxes ($125,000) on the government-wide statement of activities.

**M.  Accounting for Special Revenue Funds**

**76.  (c)**   According to GASB 33, the grant received by Maple Township is an example of a voluntary nonexchange transaction in which the providing State government imposes purpose restrictions on the grant to Maple Township. Under modified accrual accounting, grant revenue should be recognized when it is both measurable and available. Applying these criteria to the grant, revenues should be recognized in the period that Maple received reimbursement from the state for the purchase of buses ($60,000) and for bus maintenance ($5,000). It is at the point of reimbursement that the grant becomes available.

**77. (b)** Special revenue funds are used to account for the proceeds of specific revenue sources (other than expendable trusts or for major capital projects) that are legally restricted to expenditures for specified purposes. Thus, the gasoline taxes to finance road repairs should be accounted for in a special revenue fund. The levies to property owners to install sidewalks would be recorded either in an agency fund (if special assessment debt is not backed by the government) or by a debt service fund (if the debt is backed by the government).

**78. (c)** A major special revenue fund is a governmental fund and therefore uses the modified accrual basis of accounting, not the accrual basis. Budgetary accounts should be used in the general fund and special revenue fund.

**N. Accounting for Capital Projects Funds**

**79. (a)** The objective of a capital projects fund is to account for the financial resources to be used for the acquisition or construction of major capital facilities. The inflow of bond proceeds should be accounted for in the year received, regardless of when the bond proceeds are expended. Therefore, the $5,000,000 of bond proceeds should be recorded in the capital projects fund in 2007, the year received. They should be treated as an "other financing source" in the operating statement of the fund. Note that the servicing of the debt will be accounted for in the debt service fund.

**80. (c)** Grants received by the capital projects fund from another governmental unit are considered revenues of the capital projects fund. Also, taxes or other revenues raised specifically for the capital projects fund are recorded as revenues of the fund. However, proceeds of debt issues should be recorded as proceeds of bonds/long-term debt and should be reported as an other financing source in the operating statement. Similarly, resources transferred to the capital projects fund generally from the general or special revenue fund are recorded as transfers in and reported in the other financing sources section of the operating statement. Thus, Fir should report only the $400,000 from the grant as a revenue. The $600,000 consisting of the bond issue proceeds and general fund transfer should be reported as other financing sources.

**81. (c)** The requirement is to identify how an impaired capital asset that is no longer used by a government should be reported in the financial statements. The correct answer is (c). GASB 42 indicates that the asset should be reported at the lower of carrying value or fair value. Answers (a) and (b) are incorrect because they are often elements of the carrying value of the asset. Answer (d) is incorrect because the required valuation is the lower of carrying value or fair value.

**82. (b)** The requirement is to identify when impairment of a capital asset should be recognized. The correct answer

is (b). GASB 42 states that impairment of a capital asset should be recognized when an event or change in circumstance causes a decline in service utility of the asset, and (1) the decline is large in magnitude and (2) the event or change in circumstance is outside the normal life cycle of the capital asset.

**O. Debt Service Funds**

**83. (d)** Governmental fund revenues and expenditures should be recognized on the modified accrual basis. Governmental funds include the general fund, special revenue funds, capital projects funds, debt service funds, and permanent funds. Proprietary fund revenues and expenses should be recognized on the accrual basis. Proprietary funds include enterprise funds and internal service funds. Fiduciary fund additions and deductions should be recognized on the accrual basis. Pension trust funds should be accounted for on the accrual basis.

**84. (a)** GASB 37, para 16, indicates that proceeds of long-term issues not recorded as fund liabilities should be reported as other financing sources in governmental funds. In addition, general long-term debt issue premiums should also be reported as other financing sources. Paragraph 87 of GASB 34 indicates that debt issue costs, including underwriter fees, should be reported as expenditures.

**85. (d)** Debt service funds are to account for the accumulation of resources for and payment of, general long-term debt principal and interest. The general fund does not account for resources restricted for payment of general long-term debt principal and interest.

**86. (a)** According to GASB 34, the balance sheet prepared for governmental funds is prepared using the modified accrual basis of accounting and the flow of financial resources measurement focus. Under the modified accrual basis of accounting and the financial resources measurement focus, the bond issue costs of $400,000 and the debt insurance costs of $90,000 should be charged to expenditures in the debt service fund on June 30, 2007. This means that none of the costs will be reported as an asset on the governmental funds' balance sheet prepared at June 30, 2007.

**87. (c)** The requirement is to determine which fund should record receipts from a special tax levy to retire and pay interest on general obligation bonds. The correct answer is (c) because the debt service fund usually handles the repayment of general obligation long-term debt interest. A levy allocable to the debt service fund is recorded in the fund. Answer (a) is incorrect because levies for the purpose of paying interest do not get recorded in the general fund. The general fund records levies that do not have a specific purpose. Answer (b) is incorrect because capital projects funds are for construction or the purchase of fixed assets. Answer (d) is incorrect because special revenue funds are for earmarked revenue that is not to pay interest on general obligation debt.

**88. (d)** The bond premium amount is usually deemed to be another financing source in a governmental fund and is recorded as such when the bonds are sold. The premium is not capitalized and amortized.

**89. (a)** The GASB classifies three types of funds used in governmental accounting: governmental, proprietary, and fiduciary. Debt service funds are used to accumulate resources to pay general long-term debt of governmental funds. The debt service fund is not used in connection with either a trust fund or a proprietary fund.

**90.   (c)**   Cash received in the debt service fund from the general fund for debt service is recorded as a transfer. Cash payments of principal and interest on the debt are then recorded as expenditures in the debt service fund. The following entries would be made in the debt service fund:

| | | |
|---|---|---|
| Cash | xx | |
|    Transfers In—General Fund | | xx |
| | | |
| Expenditures—Principal | xx | |
| Expenditures—Interest | xx | |
|    Cash (Payable) | | xx |

**91.   (a)**   Interest on the general obligation bonds is payable on March 1 and September 1. The debt service fund accounts for the accumulation of cash to pay the interest and principal on general obligation bonds. However, interest on the bonds is not recorded until it is legally payable. On June 30, 2007, no interest is legally payable, so there would be no accrual of interest to be paid as of that date.

### Q. Accounting for Special Assessments

**92.   (a)**   The debt service transactions of a special assessment issue for which the government is not obligated in any manner should be reported in an agency fund, rather than a debt service fund. The government's duties are limited to acting as an agent for the assessed property owners and the bondholders.

### R. Accounting for Proprietary Funds

**93.   (c)**   Municipal solid waste landfills that use proprietary accounting (i.e., enterprise fund) should recognize as expense (and liability) a portion of the estimated total cost of closure and post closure in each period that the landfill accepts solid waste. Estimated total costs should be assigned to periods based on use rather than on the passage of time, using a formula based on the percentage of capacity used each period. Because Cy City's landfill operates as an enterprise fund, the city's 2007 expenses should include a portion of the year 2026 expected disbursements for both the final cover (I) and cost of equipment to monitor methane gas buildup (II).

**94.   (a)**   GASB 34, para 13, clearly states that, in the government-wide statements, governmental activities normally include transactions that are reported in governmental and internal service funds.

**95.   (b)**   Internal service funds account for activities that produce goods or services to be provided to other departments or governmental units on a cost reimbursement basis. Internal service funds also use the full accrual method of accounting. When the governmental units are billed, the internal service fund would record the following entry:

| | | |
|---|---|---|
| Billings to Departments | xx | |
|    Operating Revenues | | xx |

**96.   (d)**   A proprietary fund is created to account for goods or services the governmental unit provides to benefit the general public. It uses the accrual basis of accounting and the flow of economic resources measurement focus (i.e., capital maintenance is an objective). Fixed assets and depreciation expense on them are recorded in such funds. Therefore, the $210,000 expenditure for the parking meters would be capitalized and shown net of accumulated depreciation on Burwood's June 30, 2007 balance sheet. Burwood's net income for the year ending June 30, 2007, would be $240,000 calculated as

| | |
|---|---|
| Receipts from users | $400,000 |
| Expenses | |
|    Depreciation—Parking meters | (70,000) |
|    Salaries and other | (90,000) |
|    Net income | $240,000 |

**97.   (d)**   Enterprise funds are used to account for operations that are financed and operated in a manner similar to private business enterprises—where the intent of the government is that costs of providing goods or services to the general public on a continuing basis be financed or recovered primarily through user charges; or where the government has decided that periodic determination of net income is appropriate for accountability purposes. Accordingly, revenues from lotteries need to be matched with related expenses for prizes. Thus, lotteries should be accounted for in a fund type that uses full accrual accounting, most commonly an enterprise fund. In addition, the GASB *Codification*, Section H05, requires that hospitals be reported as a single enterprise fund when they are included as part of another government's reporting entity.

**98.   (d)**   Depreciation of general fixed assets should **not** be recorded in the accounts of governmental funds. Depreciation of fixed assets accounted for in a proprietary fund should be recorded in the accounts of that fund. The determination of recording depreciation expense in a governmental unit's fund does not change as a result of the funding source used to acquire the asset.

**99.   (d)**   An enterprise fund is used to account for operations where the intent of the governing body is to finance the cost of the operations through user charges or where the governing body has decided revenue, expenses, and net income information is necessary. A fund that accounts for the financing of an agency's services to other government departments on a cost-reimbursement basis is an internal service fund.

**100.   (c)**   Cash flows from sale of revenue bonds and capital contributed by subdividers are classified as cash flows from capital and related financing activities. Both the $5,000,000 proceeds from sale of revenue bonds and $1,000,000 capital contributed by subdividers would be reported as cash flows from capital and related financing activities. Cash flows from customer households are operating cash flows.

**101.   (a)**   Proprietary funds are used to account for a government's ongoing organizations and activities that are similar to those often found in the private sector. The generally accepted accounting principles here are those applicable to similar businesses in the private sector; and the measurement focus is on **determination of net income,** financial position, and cash flows.

**102.   (c)**   As described in the GASB *Codification*, the aggregate lease liability is recorded as an expenditure and an "Other Financing Source" in the general fund. Therefore, Expenditures Control is debited. Answer (b) is incorrect because capital assets are not reported in the general fund. Answer (d) is incorrect because an entry needs to be recorded and posted on the books when equipment is acquired through noncancelable lease-purchase agreement. A memorandum entry is not sufficient. Answer (a) is incorrect because "Other Financing Uses" account is used for transfers out of a fund.

**103. (d)** The enterprise fund is a proprietary fund and all assets and liabilities of proprietary funds are accounted for and reported in their respective funds. Therefore, transactions for enterprise fund capital leases are accounted for and reported entirely within the enterprise fund. Equipment would be debited for $150,000 in the enterprise fund.

**104. (c)** All assets and liabilities of proprietary funds are accounted for and reported in their respective funds. The entry to establish the capital lease in the internal service fund would include a debit to Equipment for $150,000 and a credit to Capital Lease Payable for $150,000. Using general business accounting, the entry to make the December 31, 2007 payment of $65,000 would debit Capital Lease Payable for the principal of $50,000 and Expenses Control for the interest of $15,000, and credit Cash for $65,000. The internal service fund is nonexpendable and **expenses** (**not** expenditures) are recognized on the full accrual basis. Expenses should only be debited for the interest of $15,000, not for the principal of $50,000.

**105. (c)** Per the GASB *Codification*, cash includes both cash and cash equivalents. Cash equivalents are highly liquid investments readily convertible into cash, usually maturing within three months (ninety days) or less from the date the entity **purchased** the security. Maturity is not measured from the original issuance date. Therefore, in this question, the three-month treasury bill would be included in cash and cash equivalents as well as the three-year treasury note. The three-year treasury note was purchased on 6/15/07 and matures 8/31/07. Therefore, it will be held less than ninety days. The correct answer is (c), $80,000 ($30,000 + $50,000).

**S. Accounting for Fiduciary Funds**

**106. (b)** Fiduciary funds are used to account for assets held by a governmental unit in a trustee capacity or as an agent for individuals, private organizations, other governmental units, and/or other funds. They include investment trust, private-purpose trust, pension trust, and agency funds. Therefore, the total fiduciary fund assets of Green Township at June 30, 2007, is $300,000. The debt service fund is a governmental-type fund.

**107. (c)** Fiduciary funds (i.e., agency funds and trust funds) are used to account for assets held by a governmental unit in a trustee capacity or as an agent for individuals, private organizations, other governmental units, and/or other funds. The entry to record the 1% fee and the disbursement to the municipalities would be as follows:

| | | |
|---|---|---|
| Due to Various Municipalities | 1,000,000 | |
| Due to Grove County | | 10,000 |
| General Fund Cash | | 990,000 |

Note that the general fund would make the following entry:

| | | |
|---|---|---|
| Due from Agency Fund | xxx | |
| Revenue from Tax Collec. Serv. | | xxx |

Agency funds have only assets and liabilities as accounts and do not record revenues, expenditures, or transfers. In addition, agency funds do not have net assets.

**108. (a)** The entry to record the 2007 employer contribution in the Pension Trust Fund consists of a debit to Cash (or a "Due From" account) and a credit to Additions—Employer Contributions, both for $11,000. The GASB *Codification* classifies this contribution as an interfund services provided and used transaction that would be treated as an addition if it involved organizations external to the governmental unit. Therefore, the GASB states that it should be accounted for as an addition for the pension trust fund. Answer (b) is incorrect because Other Financing Sources include transfers to a fund which are recurring, routine transfers from one fund to another. The employer contribution is not a transfer. Answer (c) is incorrect because "Due From" is a debit account and the question asks for the credit account. Answer (d) is incorrect because Pension Benefit Obligation is the actuarial present value of credited projected benefits. It measures the present value of pension benefits adjusted for the effects of projected salary increases and any step-rate benefits estimated to be payable in the future as a result of employer service to date. The employer contribution is not included in this definition.

**109. (b)** The employer pension contribution is an interfund services provided and used transaction, one that would be treated as an addition, revenue, expense, or expenditure if it involved organizations external to the governmental unit. In this case, the entry for the governmental-type fund would include a debit to Expenditures Control for $11,000 and a credit to Cash (or a "Due To" account) for $11,000. Answer (a) is incorrect because Other Financing Uses include transfers out of a fund, which are routine recurring transfers of resources from one fund to another. Consequently, the employer contribution does not fall under the category of an Other Financing Use. Answer (c) is incorrect because governmental funds use modified accrual accounting and report expenditures, not expenses. Answer (d) is incorrect because Due To Pension Trust Fund could be the credit entry, and not the debit entry asked for in the question.

**T. Reporting Interfund Activity**

**110. (a)** On the government-wide statement of activities, transfers are reported between government activities and business-type activities. The business-type activities include the activities of enterprise funds, while the governmental activities include those of governmental funds and internal service funds. Transfers that are made to establish enterprise funds as well as yearly transfers to help subsidize enterprise funds are both reported as transfers, according to the guidance provided by GASB 34. On the other hand, billings by an enterprise fund to an internal service fund for services rendered are not reported as transfers on the statement of activities. This transition is a quasi-external transaction that should be reported on the statement of activities as an expense of governmental activities and as an operating revenue for business-type activities. The revenues and expenses of internal service funds are reported as governmental activities on the government-wide statement of activities.

**111. (c)** According to GASB 34, the amount reported for transfers on the government-wide statement of activities represents transfers between governmental activities and business-type activities. Examples of transfers would be permanent transfers from governmental activities to business-type activities in order to establish enterprise funds and annual transfers from governmental activities to help subsidize enterprise fund activities. The activities of internal service funds are included with governmental activities, while the activities of enterprise funds are reported under business-type activities. The $100,000 advance to an internal service fund constitutes a loan, and the general fund asset and internal service fund liability that result would be eliminated in preparing the government-wide statement of net assets. Therefore, the advance would not be reported in transfers on the statement of activities. The $25,000 billing by the enterprise fund to the general fund is recorded as a quasi-external transaction. Under governmental activities, $25,000 would be included in expenses, while, under business-type activities, the $25,000 would be reported as revenues. Therefore, the quasi-external transaction would not be reported in transfers. Finally, the $30,000 transferred by the general fund to a debt service fund is recorded as a transfer in by the debt service fund and as a transfer out by the general fund. However, because both of these funds are reported in governmental activities, the transfer in and transfer out are eliminated in preparing the statement of activities and are not reported in the governmental activities column on the statement of activities. Therefore, the general fund transfer to the debt service fund would not be reported as a transfer on the statement of activities.

**112. (a)** According to GASB 34, transfers are reported on the government-wide statement of activities. For transfers to be reported, they must be between governmental activities and business-type activities. Governmental activities include the activities of internal service funds, while business-type activities include the activities of enterprise funds. Two kinds of transfers that are reported on the statement of activities include (1) permanent transfers either from governmental activities to business-type activities or from business-type activities to governmental activities and (2) recurring transfers from governmental activities to business-type activities or from business-type activities to governmental activities. Permanent transfers are typically made once, while the recurring transfers are typically made annually. The $100,000 transfer from the general fund to an enterprise fund would be reported as a transfer on the statement of activities because it is an example of a permanent transfer. The $1,000,000 transfer from the general fund to a capital project fund is a transfer made within governmental activities and, therefore, would not be disclosed as a transfer on the statement of activities. The $5,000 reimbursement from the enterprise fund to the general fund is not reported as a transfer on the statement of activities. The effect of this transaction is to increase expenses under business-type activities and to decrease expenses under governmental activities.

## W. College and University Accounting—Public (Governmental)—GASB 35

**113. (a)** According to GASB 35, public colleges and universities that choose to report only business-type activities should present only the financial statements required for enterprise funds.

**114. (c)** According to GASB 35, public colleges and universities that choose to report both governmental and business-type activities should report both government-wide and fund financial statements.

**115. (b)** Both public and private colleges report tuition and fee income net of the amount provided for scholarships, for which no services are provided. On the other hand, scholarships provided in exchange for services are reported as an expense and are not deducted from revenues. As a result, the net tuition and fees would be the $20,000,000 less the $1,000,000 scholarships provided, not in exchange for services, or $19,000,000.

**116. (d)** GASB Statement 35 provides that public colleges may choose to report as special-purpose entities engaged in business-type activities. GASB Statement 34 requires that special-purpose entities engaged only in business-type activities should prepare the statements required for enterprises funds, including a Statement of Revenues, Expenses, and Changes in Net Assets. One requirement for that statement is that an operating income figure must be displayed (answer b). GASB Statement 34 also indicates that contributions for plant and endowment purposes are not recorded as revenues but in separate categories; GASB Statement 35 illustrations show those items listed after revenues and expenses (answer c). GASB Statement 35 specifically requires that state appropriations must be reported as nonoperating income (answer a). Since answers (a), (b), and (c) are correct, answer (d) is the choice.

## NOT-FOR-PROFIT ACCOUNTING

Nonprofit[1] organizations provide socially desirable services without the intention of realizing a profit. Nonprofit organizations are financed by user charges, contributions from donors and/or foundations, investment income, and government grants. The nature and extent of support depends upon the type of nonprofit organization.

As mentioned in the introduction to Module 19, nonprofit organizations are either in the private sector (nongovernmental) or in the public sector (governmental). Examples of private sector nonprofits would be private colleges (University of Chicago), private sector health care entities operated by religious or other nonprofit organizations, voluntary health and welfare organizations, and various "other" nonprofits, such as performing arts companies. Examples of government nonprofits would be public colleges (Northern Illinois University), government hospitals, and government museums. Private sector nonprofit organizations have GAAP set primarily by the FASB; governmental nonprofit organizations have GAAP set primarily by the GASB.

In June of 1993, the FASB issued SFAS 116, *Accounting for Contributions Received and Contributions Made,* and SFAS 117, *Financial Statements of Not-for-Profit Organizations.* These standards are applicable to private sector not-for-profit organizations of all types. This module presents GAAP for private sector nonprofits under SFAS 116 and 117. The AICPA has developed two *Audit Guides* that correspond and add to the new FASB principles: (1) Not-for-Profit Organizations, and (2) Health Care Organizations. The *Not-for-Profit Guide* applies only to private sector not-for-profits. The *Health Care Guide* applies to all health care entities, private for-profit, private not-for-profit, and governmental.

Governmental nonprofits are not permitted to follow SFAS 116 and 117. (The definition of a government is provided in the introductory section of Module 19.) As applied to colleges, health care entities, and other not-for-profit organizations, that guidance has been outlined through different pronouncements.

First, in November 1999, the GASB issued Statement 35, *Basic Financial Statements—and Management's Discussion and Analysis—for Public Colleges and Universities.* GASB 35 permits public colleges to report as special-purpose entities engaged in governmental or business-type activities, or both. Most four-year institutions are expected to report as special-purpose entities engaged only in business-type activities. Some community colleges may choose to report as special-purpose entities engaged in governmental activities due to the extent of state and local government tax support. The provisions of GASB 35 are outlined in Module 19.

Second, GASB 34 indicates that hospitals and other health care providers may be considered special-purpose entities that may be engaged in either governmental or business-type activities, or both. Most health care organizations will choose to report as special-purpose entities that are engaged in business-type activities. As a result, proprietary fund statements will be required for those health care entities. The AICPA Audit and Accounting Guide, *Health Care Organizations*, contains guidance for both private sector and governmental health care organizations; both are presented in this module.

Third, other governmental not-for-profit organizations (essentially governmental voluntary health and welfare and "other" not-for-profit organizations) also may be considered special-purpose entities that may be engaged in either governmental or business-type activities, or both. However, GASB 34 specifically permits these organizations that were using the "AICPA Not-for-Profit Model" upon adoption of GASB 34 to report as special-purpose entities engaged in business-type activities. These entities will present proprietary fund statements. The AICPA Audit and Accounting Guide, *Not-for-Profit Organizations*, applies only to private sector organizations and these principles are contained in this module; governmental not-for-profits are less significant and are not illustrated in this module.

The first section of this module presents the FASB and AICPA standards for all nongovernmental nonprofits, including private sector colleges, universities, and health care entities. The second section presents standards that apply primarily to private colleges and universities. The third and fourth sections present standards for health care entities; first for private sector health care entities; next for governmental health care entities. Module 19 presents standards for public colleges and universities.

## A.  FASB and AICPA Standards for Private Sector Nonprofits

SFAS 116, *Accounting for Contributions Received and Contributions Made,* and SFAS 117, *Financial Statements of Not-for-Profit Organizations,* apply to private sector nonprofits subject to FASB guidance; they do not apply to governmental nonprofits subject to GASB guidance.

---

[1] *The terms not-for-profit and nonprofit are used interchangeably here and in practice.*

More recently, FASB issued Statement 124, *Accounting for Certain Investments Held by Not-for-Profit Organizations*. This statement requires fair value accounting for most equity and debt investments by not-for-profit organizations and requires reporting of realized and unrealized gains and losses directly in the Statement of Activities.

Most recently, FASB issued Statement 136, *Transfers of Assets to a Not-for-Profit Organization or Charitable Trust That Raises or Holds Contributions for Others*. This statement provides guidance regarding proper reporting by foundations and similar not-for-profits when funds are raised for others, as described in 1.n. and o. below.

The FASB guidance is intended to eliminate the differences in accounting and reporting standards that existed previously between four types of not-for-profit organizations. While some differences exist, for example, in functional categories reported, private sector nonprofit colleges and universities, health care entities, voluntary health and welfare organizations, and "other" organizations follow the basic guidance in the FASB standards; some differences between health care entities and other private sector not-for-profits will be illustrated later. The section lists a number of basic requirements, illustrates financial statements, and presents a few journal entries as required by SFAS 116, 117, 124, and 136. All illustrations are for a general nongovernmental not-for-profit organization, but remember that the principles apply to all four types (colleges and universities, health care organizations, voluntary health and welfare organizations, and "other" not-for-profit organizations).

1. **Important Features of the FASB Guidance**

   a.  The standards apply to **all** nongovernmental nonprofit organizations, except those that operate for the direct economic benefit of members (such as mutual insurance companies). General FASB standards, unless specifically prohibited by those standards or do not apply because of their nature (capital stock, etc.) or unless modified by these standards, are presumed to apply.

   b.  Net assets are divided into three classes: unrestricted, temporarily restricted, and permanently restricted. Fund classifications are not reported, unless the information can be shown as subdivisions of the three major classes. To be restricted, resources must be restricted by donors or grantors; internally designated resources are unrestricted. Only contributed resources may be restricted.

   c.  Permanently restricted resources include (1) certain assets, such as artwork, etc. that must be maintained or used in a certain way, and (2) endowments, which represent resources that must be invested permanently with income to be used for either restricted or unrestricted purposes, and (3) land, when that land must be held in perpetuity.

   d.  Temporarily restricted resources include unexpended resources that are to be used for a particular purpose, at a time in the future, or are to be invested for a period of time (a term endowment). Temporarily restricted resources might also be used for the acquisition or receipt of a gift of plant and would represent the undepreciated amount. As the plant is depreciated, the amount depreciated would be reclassified from temporarily restricted net assets to unrestricted net assets and shown as a deduction from unrestricted revenues, gains, and other support on the statement of activities. Alternatively, plant may be initially recorded as unrestricted.

   e.  Unrestricted resources include all other resources including unrestricted contributions, the net amount from providing services, unrestricted income from investments, etc. Resources are presumed to be unrestricted, unless evidence exists that donor-imposed restrictions exist. As mentioned above, undepreciated plant may be included as unrestricted or temporarily restricted.

   f.  Statements required are (1) Statement of Financial Position, (2) Statement of Activities, and (3) Statement of Cash Flows. Certain note disclosures are also required and others recommended. In addition, voluntary health and welfare organizations are required to report a Statement of Functional Expenses that show expenses by function and by natural classifications.

   g.  The Statement of Financial Position reports assets, liabilities, and net assets. Organization-wide totals must be provided for assets, liabilities and net assets, and net assets must be broken down between unrestricted, temporarily restricted, and permanently restricted.

   h.  The Statement of Activities reports revenues, expenses, gains, losses, and reclassifications (between classes of net assets). Organization-wide totals must be provided. Separate revenues, expenses, gains, losses, and reclassifications for each class may or may not be reported, but the changes in net assets for each class must be reported.

   i.  Revenues, expenses, gains, and losses are reported on the full accrual basis. A revenue is presumed to be unrestricted unless donor-imposed restrictions apply, either permanent or temporary.

A presumption is made, in the absence of contrary information, that a given expense would use restricted resources first, rather than unrestricted resources. Revenues and expenses should be reported at gross amounts; gains and losses are often reported net. Investment gains and losses may be reported net.

j.  Unconditional contributions are to be recorded as assets (contributions receivable) and as revenues (contribution revenue). However, a donor-imposed **condition** causes a not-for-profit organization to not recognize either a receivable or a revenue. A donor-imposed condition specifies a future or uncertain event whose occurrence or failure to occur gives the promisor a right of return of the assets transferred or releases the promisor from its obligation to transfer the assets promised. For example, a not-for-profit organization receives a pledge from a donor that she will transfer $1,000,000 if matching funds can be raised within a year. The $1,000,000 would not be recognized as a revenue until the possibility of raising the matching funds is reasonably certain.

k.  Multiyear contributions receivable would be recorded at the present value of the future collections. Moneys to be collected in future years would be presumed to be temporarily restricted revenues (based on time restrictions) and then reclassified in the year of receipt. The difference between the previously recorded temporarily restricted revenue at present value amounts and the current value would be recorded as contribution revenue, not interest. **All** contributions are to be recorded at fair market value as of the date of the contribution.

l.  Organizations making the contributions, including businesses and other nonprofits, would recognize contribution expense using the same rules as followed by the receiving organization.

m.  Contributions are to be distinguished from exchange revenues. The *Not-for-Profit Guide* indicates criteria that indicate when an increase in net assets is a contribution and when it is an exchange revenue; the most important rule is that if nothing is given by the not-for-profit organization in exchange in a transaction, that transaction would be considered a contribution. Contributions are recognized as additions to any of the net asset classifications. Exchange revenues (tuition, membership dues, charges for services, etc.) are increases in unrestricted net assets and are recognized in accordance with GAAP as applied to business enterprises.

n.  SFAS 136 requires that when a not-for-profit organization (such as a foundation) is an **intermediary** or an **agent** for the transfer of assets to another not-for-profit organization, that intermediary or agent would not recognize a contribution. Unless the intermediary or agent not-for-profit organization is granted **variance power** to redirect the resources, or unless it is financially interrelated, the receipt of resources would be offset with the recognition of a liability to the recipient organization. If variance power exists, the recipient organization would recognize contribution revenue.

o.  SFAS 136 also requires that the recipient organization recognize a revenue when the intermediary or agent recognizes a liability. When the intermediary or agent and the beneficiary are **financially interrelated,** the intermediary or agent would recognize contribution revenue; the beneficiary would recognize its interest in the net assets of the intermediary or agent.

p.  Expenses are to be reported by function either in the statements or in the notes. The FASB does not prescribe functional classifications but does describe functions as program and supporting. Major program classifications should be shown. Supporting activities include management and general, fund raising, and membership development. Other classifications may be included, such as operating income, but are not required, except for health care entities. All expenses are reported as decreases in unrestricted net assets.

q.  Plant is recorded, as mentioned above, either as temporarily restricted or unrestricted, and depreciated. Depreciation is to be charged for exhaustible fixed assets.

r.  An entity may or may not capitalize "collections." "Collections" are works of art, historical treasures, and similar assets if those assets meet all of the following conditions:

(1) They are held for public exhibition, education, or research in furtherance of public service rather than financial gain;
(2) They are protected, kept encumbered, cared for, and preserved;
(3) They are subject to an organizational policy that requires the proceeds from sales of collection items to be used to acquire other items for collections.

If collections are not capitalized, revenues (contributions) would not be recognized for donated collections. Extensive note disclosure regarding accessions, disposals, etc. are required.

s.	Investments in all debt securities and investments in equity securities that have readily determinable fair values (except equity securities accounted for under the equity method and investments in consolidated subsidiaries) are to be reported at fair value in the Statement of Net Assets.  Unlike SFAS 115 for business enterprises, all unrealized gains and losses are to be reflected in the Statement of Activities along with realized gains and losses, in the appropriate net asset class.

t.	Contributed services, when recognized, are recognized as both revenue and expense.  However, contributed services should be recognized only when the services:  (1) create or enhance nonfinancial assets, or (2) require specialized skills, are provided by individuals possessing those skills, and would typically be purchased if not provided by donation.

u.	All expenses are reported as unrestricted.  Expenses using resources that are temporarily restricted, including depreciation of plant, would be matched by a reclassification of resources from temporarily restricted to unrestricted net assets.

v.	The "Reclassification" category of the Statement of Activities is unique.  Sometimes "Reclassifications" are called "Net Assets Released from Restrictions."  Reclassifications generally include (1) satisfaction of program restrictions (a purpose restriction by a donor), (2) satisfaction of equipment acquisition restrictions (depreciation of assets classified as temporarily restricted), (3) satisfaction of time restrictions (donor actual or implied restrictions as to when funds be used), and (4) expiration of term endowment.

w.	Cash Flow statements are required for nonprofit organizations.  The three FASB categories (operating, investing, and financing) are to be used.  As is true for business organizations, either the direct or indirect method may be used.  The indirect method, or reconciliation schedule for the direct method, will reconcile the change in **total** net assets to the net cash used by operating activities.  Restricted contributions for long term purposes (endowments, plant, future program purposes, etc.) are reported as financing activities.

x.	Note disclosures are required for all items required for generally accepted accounting principles that are relevant to nonprofit organizations.  In addition, specific requirements of SFAS 117 include (1) policy disclosures related to choices related to restricted contributions received and expended in the same period, and to the recording of plant as temporarily restricted or unrestricted, and (2) more detailed information regarding the nature of temporarily and permanently restricted resources.

y.	The FASB specifically encourages note disclosures on (1) detail of the reclassification, (2) detail of investments and (3) breakdown of expenses by function and natural classifications (except for Voluntary Health and Welfare Organizations, which must include this information in a Statement of Functional Expenses).

z.	The *Not-for-Profit Guide* provides guidance for **split-interest agreements,** such as charitable lead trusts and charitable remainder trusts.  Split-interest agreements represent arrangements whereby both a donor (or beneficiary) and a not-for-profit organization receive benefits, often at different times in a multiyear arrangement.  Specific rules exist for each type of split-interest agreement.  The general rule is that the not-for-profit will record revenues in an amount equal to the present value of anticipated receipts.

aa.	FASB requires that fund-raising expenses be reported either on the face of the financial statements or in the notes.  AICPA Statement of Position 98-2 indicates that when an activity, such as a mailing, might involve fund-raising and either program or management and general activities, it is presumed to be fund-raising unless three criteria exist.  Those criteria are

(1)	**Purpose.**  The activity has more than one purpose, as evidenced by whether compensation or fees for performing the activity are based strictly on the amount raised or on the performance of some program and/or management and general activity.

(2)	**Audience.**  If the audience is selected on the basis of its likelihood to contribute to the not-for-profit, this criterion is not met.

(3)	**Content.**  In order for this criterion to be met, the mailing or event must include a call to action other than raising money.  For example, a mailing from the American Cancer Society might call for recipients to have regular check-ups, to exercise, to eat the right kinds of food, etc.

2.  **Illustrative Financial Statements**

The FASB requires three financial statements for nongovernmental, not-for-profit organizations, including (1) Statement of Financial Position, (2) Statement of Activities, and (3) Statement of Cash Flows. Voluntary health and welfare organizations (such as the American Red Cross, a mental health association, or a Big Brothers/Big Sisters organization) are required to prepare a fourth statement, a Statement of Functional Expenses. The first three of these statements are described and illustrated below.

a.  **Statement of Financial Position.** A Balance Sheet or Statement of Financial Position must show total assets, total liabilities, and total net assets. Net assets must be broken down between those that are unrestricted, temporarily restricted, and permanently restricted. Assets and liabilities may be classified or reported in order of liquidity and payment date. Assets restricted for long-term purposes must be reported separately from those that are not. The comparative format illustrated is optional; entities may report only balances for one year. Contributions receivable are to be reported at the present value of future receipts. Investments in securities with determinable fair values are to be reported at fair value. The following reflects one of the permissible formats in SFAS 117:

*Not-for-Profit Organization*
**STATEMENTS OF FINANCIAL POSITION**
*June 30, 20X1 and 20X0*
(in thousands)

|                                                    | 20X1 | 20X0 |
|----------------------------------------------------|------:|------:|
| *Assets*                                           |       |       |
| Cash and cash equivalents                          | $     75 | $    460 |
| Accounts and interest receivable                   | 2,130 | 1,670 |
| Inventories and prepaid expenses                   | 610 | 1,000 |
| Contributions receivable                           | 3,025 | 2,700 |
| Short-term investments                             | 1,400 | 1,000 |
| Assets restricted to investment in land, buildings, and equipment | 5,210 | 4,560 |
| Land, buildings, and equipment                     | 61,700 | 63,590 |
| Long-term investments                              | 218,070 | 203,500 |
|    Total assets                     | $292,220 | $278,480 |
|                                                    |       |       |
| *Liabilities and net assets*                       |       |       |
| Accounts payable                                   | $  2,570 | $  1,050 |
| Refundable advance                                 |       | 650 |
| Grants payable                                     | 875 | 1,300 |
| Notes payable                                      |       | 1,140 |
| Annuity obligations                                | 1,685 | 1,700 |
| Long-term debt                                     | 5,500 | 6,500 |
|    Total liabilities                | 10,630 | 12,340 |
|                                                    | 20X1 | 20X0 |
| *Net assets*                                       |       |       |
| Unrestricted                                       | 115,228 | 103,670 |
| Temporarily restricted                             | 24,342 | 25,470 |
| Permanently restricted                             | 142,020 | 137,000 |
|    Total net assets                 | 281,590 | 266,140 |
|    Total liabilities and net assets | $292,220 | $278,480 |

SOURCE: *SFAS 117, page 56*

b.  **Statement of Activities.** Note the following from the example Statement of Activities:

(1) Contributions, income on long-term investments, and net unrealized and realized gains on long-term investments may increase unrestricted, temporarily restricted, and permanently restricted net assets. All of these revenue sources increase unrestricted net assets unless restricted by donors.

(2) Fees increase unrestricted net assets. All exchange revenues increase unrestricted net assets. Exchange revenues include admissions charges, fees, and membership dues.

(3) Net unrealized gains are shown together with realized gains and investments. FASB prohibits displaying net unrealized and realized gains separately.

(4) All expenses decrease unrestricted net assets. (Losses, such as the actuarial loss, may decrease restricted net assets.)

(5) At some point net assets are released from restrictions (reclassified) from temporarily restricted to unrestricted net assets. This might be for satisfaction of program restrictions, satisfaction of equipment acquisition restrictions, expiration of time restrictions, or expiration of term endowments. Note that when net assets are released from restrictions, temporarily restricted net assets decrease and unrestricted net assets increase.

(6) Expenses are broken down between programs (A, B, C) and supporting (management and general, fund-raising). While the FASB does not require these functional breakdowns, the FASB does have two requirements.

(a) Expenses must be reported by function in the notes if not in this statement, and
(b) Fund-raising expenses must be disclosed in the notes, if not in this statement.

The FASB permits other formats. For example, some entities prepare two statements.

(a) Statement of Revenues, Expenses, and Changes in Unrestricted Net Assets, and
(b) Statement of Changes in Net Assets.

Regardless of the format used, the change in net assets must be reported, by net asset class and in total.

**Not-for-Profit Organization**
**STATEMENT OF ACTIVITIES**
*Year Ended June 30, 20X1*
(in thousands)

| | Unrestricted | Temporarily restricted | Permanently restricted | Total |
|---|---|---|---|---|
| Revenues, gains, and other support: | | | | |
| Contributions | $  8,640 | $  8,110 | $   280 | $ 17,030 |
| Fees | 5,400 | | | 5,400 |
| Income on long-term investments | 5,600 | 2,580 | 120 | 8,300 |
| Other investment income | 850 | | | 850 |
| Net unrealized and realized gains on long-term investments | 8,228 | 2,952 | 4,620 | 15,800 |
| Other | 150 | | | 150 |
| Net assets released from restrictions: | | | | |
| Satisfaction of program restrictions | 11,990 | (11,990) | | |
| Satisfaction of equipment acquisition restrictions | 1,500 | (1,500) | | |
| Expiration of time restrictions | 1,250 | (1,250) | | |
| Total revenues, gains, and other support | 43,608 | (1,098) | 5,020 | 47,530 |
| Expenses and losses: | | | | |
| Program A | 13,100 | | | 13,100 |
| Program B | 8,540 | | | 8,540 |
| Program C | 5,760 | | | 5,760 |
| Management and general | 2,420 | | | 2,420 |
| Fund raising | 2,150 | | | 2,150 |
| Total expenses | 31,970 | | | 31,970 |
| Fire loss | 80 | | | 80 |
| Actuarial loss on annuity obligations | | 30 | | 30 |
| Total expenses and losses | 32,050 | 30 | | 32,080 |
| Change in net assets | 11,558 | (1,128) | 5,020 | 15,450 |
| Net assets at beginning of year | 103,670 | 25,470 | 137,000 | 266,140 |
| Net assets at end of year | $115,228 | $24,342 | $142,020 | $281,590 |

*SOURCE:  SFAS 117, page 59.*

c. **Statement of Cash Flows.** In general, the FASB rules for cash flow statements, required by FASB Statement 95, apply to not-for-profit organizations. Note that GASB rules, illustrated in Module 19, do not apply. The only major difference is that cash receipts for contributions restricted for long-term purposes are classified as financing activities.

**Not-for-Profit Organization**
**STATEMENT OF CASH FLOWS**
***Year Ended June 30, 20X1***
(in thousands)

*Cash flows from operating activities:*

| | |
|---|---:|
| Cash received from service recipients | $ 5,220 |
| Cash received from contributors | 8,030 |
| Cash collected on contributions receivable | 2,615 |
| Interest and dividends received | 8,570 |
| Miscellaneous receipts | 150 |
| Interest paid | (382) |
| Cash paid to employees and suppliers | (23,808) |
| Grants paid | (425) |
| Net cash used by operating activities | (30) |

*Cash flows from investing activities:*

| | |
|---|---:|
| Insurance proceeds from fire loss on building | 250 |
| Purchase of equipment | (1,500) |
| Proceeds from sale of investments | 76,100 |
| Purchase of investments | (74,900) |
| Net cash used by investing activities | (50) |

*Cash flows from financing activities:*

| | |
|---|---:|
| Proceeds from contributions restricted for: | |
|   Investment in endowment | 200 |
|   Investment in term endowment | 70 |
|   Investment in plant | 1,210 |
|   Investment subject to annuity agreements | 200 |
| | 1,680 |
| Other financing activities: | |
|   Interest and dividends restricted for reinvestment | 300 |
|   Payments of annuity obligations | (145) |
|   Payments on notes payable | (1,140) |
|   Payments on long-term debt | (1,000) |
| | (1,985) |
| Net cash used by financing activities | (305) |
| Net decrease in cash and cash equivalents | (385) |
| Cash and cash equivalents at beginning of year | 460 |
| Cash and cash equivalents at end of year | $ 75 |

*Reconciliation of change in net assets to net cash used by operating activities:*

| | |
|---|---:|
| Change in net assets | $ 15,450 |

*Adjustments to reconcile change in net assets to net cash used by operating activities:*

| | |
|---|---:|
| Depreciation | 3,200 |
| Fire loss | 80 |
| Actuarial loss on annuity obligations | 30 |
| Increase in accounts and interest receivable | (460) |
| Decrease in inventories and prepaid expenses | 390 |
| Increase in contributions receivable | (325) |
| Increase in accounts payable | 1,520 |
| Decrease in refundable advance | (650) |
| Decrease in grants payable | (425) |
| Contributions restricted for long-term investment | (2,740) |
| Interest and dividends restricted for long-term investment | (300) |
| Net unrealized and realized gains on long-term investments | (15,800) |
| Net cash used by operating activities | $ (30) |

*Supplemental data for noncash investing and financing activities:*

| | |
|---|---:|
| Gifts of equipment | $140 |
| Gift of paid-up life insurance, cash surrender value | $80 |

*SOURCE: SFAS 117, pages 64-65.*

3. **Illustrative Transactions**

    a.  Unrestricted revenues and expenses.

Under FASB guidance, full accrual accounting is used. A look at the Statement of Activities indicates that revenues might include contributions, fees, investment income, and realized and unrealized gains on investments. Expenses must be reported as unrestricted and reported by function, either in the statements or in the notes.

Assume the following unrestricted revenues:

| | | |
|---|---|---|
| Cash | 1,000,000 | |
| Contributions Receivable | 200,000 | |
| Accounts Receivable | 100,000 | |
| Interest Receivable | 50,000 | |
| Contributions—Unrestricted | | 700,000 |
| Fees—Unrestricted | | 300,000 |
| Income on Long-Term Investments—Unrestricted | | 350,000 |

Income earned from investments can be unrestricted, temporarily restricted, or permanently restricted depending on the wishes of the donor. If the donor does not specify, the investment income is unrestricted, even if the investment principal itself is permanently restricted.

Assume the following expenses, reported by function:

| | | |
|---|---|---|
| Program A Expense | 400,000 | |
| Program B Expense | 300,000 | |
| Program C Expense | 200,000 | |
| Management and General Expense | 100,000 | |
| Fund Raising Expense | 200,000 | |
| Cash | | 900,000 |
| Accounts Payable | | 300,000 |

b.  Purpose restrictions—temporarily restricted resources

Temporarily restricted resources are generally restricted by purpose, by time, and for the acquisition of plant. Assume that in 20X0 a donor gives $100,000 in cash for cancer research and that the funds are expended in 20X1. In 20X0, the following entry would be made:

| | | |
|---|---|---|
| Cash | 100,000 | |
| Contributions—Temporarily Restricted | | 100,000 |

At the end of 20X0 the $100,000 would be a part of the net assets of the temporarily restricted net asset class. In 20X1, the following entries would be made, assuming the funds are expended for cancer research.

| | | |
|---|---|---|
| Program A Expense (Research) | 100,000 | |
| Cash | | 100,000 |
| Reclassifications from Temporarily Restricted Net Assets— | | |
| Satisfaction of Program Restrictions | 100,000 | |
| Reclassifications to Unrestricted Net Assets—Satisfaction of | | |
| Program Restrictions | | 100,000 |

Note that the assets are released from restriction by the expense, by conducting the research. Looking at the example statement of activities, the $100,000 would be included as a part of the $11,990,000 in program reclassifications.

c.  Time restrictions—temporarily restricted resources

If a donor makes a contribution and indicates that the contribution should be used in a future period, that contribution would be recorded as a revenue in the temporarily restricted net asset class and then transferred to the unrestricted net asset class in the time period specified by the donor. In the absence of other information, if a pledge is made, the schedule of anticipated receipts would determine when the net assets are reclassified. Assume a $100,000 pledge in late 20X0, intended to be used by the nonprofit organization in 20X1; the entry in 20X0 would be

| | | |
|---|---|---|
| Pledges receivable | 100,000 | |
| Contributions—Temporarily Restricted | | 100,000 |

At the end of 20X0, the $100,000 would be reflected in the net assets of the temporarily restricted in class. In 20X1, the following entries would be made:

| | | |
|---|---|---|
| Cash | 100,000 | |
| Pledges receivable | | 100,000 |
| Reclassifications from Temporarily Restricted Net Assets— | | |
| Satisfaction of Time Restrictions | 100,000 | |
| Reclassifications to Unrestricted Net Assets—Satisfaction of | | |
| Time Restrictions | | 100,000 |

The $100,000 above would be a part of the $1,250,000 in reclassifications for satisfaction of time restrictions in the statement of activities. Note that time, not an expense, determines when the asset is released from restrictions. In the special case of multiyear pledges, the present value of the future payments should be recorded as a revenue in the year of the pledge. In future years, the increase in the present value, due to the passage of time, is to be recorded as contribution revenue, not interest.

Finally, note that a time restriction might be explicit or implicit. An explicit time restriction would occur when a donor states specifically that the funds are for a certain year (this might be printed on pledge cards). An implicit time restriction reflects the provision that cash must be received from a donor during an accounting period, or the pledge will be assumed to carry a time restriction. The idea is that, if a donor wished a nonprofit to spend the money this year, the donor would have contributed the cash.

d.  Plant acquisition restrictions—temporarily restricted resources

Sometimes donors give moneys restricted for the acquisition of plant, often in connection with a fund drive. The resources, whether in the form of pledges, cash, or investments, would be held in the temporarily restricted net asset class until expended. When expended, the nonprofit organization has a choice of two options: (1) reclassify the resources to the unrestricted class and record the entire plant as unrestricted, or (2) record the plant as temporarily restricted and reclassify to unrestricted in accordance with the depreciation schedule. Under the first option, assume that a donor gives $50,000 to a nonprofit organization in 20X0 for the purchase of equipment. The equipment is purchased in 20X1. The following entry would be made in the temporarily restricted class in 20X0:

| | | |
|---|---|---|
| Cash | 50,000 | |
|    Contributions | | 50,000 |

In 20X1, the following entries would be made:

| | | |
|---|---|---|
| Equipment | 50,000 | |
|    Cash | | 50,000 |
| Reclassifications from Temporarily Restricted Net Assets— | | |
|   Satisfaction of Equipment Acquisition Restrictions | 50,000 | |
|    Reclassification to Unrestricted Net Assets—Satisfaction of | | |
|     Equipment Acquisition Restrictions | | 50,000 |

The equipment would then be depreciated as a charge to expense in the unrestricted class as would be normal in business accounting. Remember that depreciation may be allocated to functional categories. Assume a ten-year life and that the equipment was purchased at the beginning of the year and that the equipment was used solely for Program A.

| | | |
|---|---|---|
| Program A Expense | 5,000 | |
|    Accumulated Depreciation—Equipment | | 5,000 |

The above alternative has normally been used in the CPA Examination. When this is the case, the problem often states that, "the Not-for-Profit Organization implies no restriction on the acquisition of fixed assets."

The second alternative is to record the equipment as an increase in temporarily restricted net assets and reclassify it over time. The entries are illustrated below. Assume the contribution was received but unexpended in 20X0.

| | | |
|---|---|---|
| Cash | 50,000 | |
|    Contributions—Temporarily Restricted | | 50,000 |

Assume the equipment was acquired early in 20X1.

| | | |
|---|---|---|
| Equipment | 50,000 | |
|    Cash | | 50,000 |

Note that the $50,000 remains in temporarily restricted net assets. At the end of 20X1, the depreciation entry is made, and $5,000 is reclassified.

| | | |
|---|---|---|
| Program A Expense | 5,000 | |
|    Accumulated Depreciation—Equipment | | 5,000 |
| Reclassification from Temporarily Restricted Net Assets— | | |
|   Satisfaction of Equipment Acquisition Restrictions | 5,000 | |
|    Reclassification to Unrestricted Net Assets—Satisfaction of | | |
|     Equipment Acquisition Restrictions | | 5,000 |

Note that, using the first alternative, at the end of 20X1, the net asset balance of $45,000 would be in the unrestricted net asset class; in the second alternative, the $45,000 net asset balance would be in the temporarily restricted net asset class.

e. Permanently restricted resources

Resources in the permanently restricted class are held permanently. An example would be an endowment, where a donor makes a contribution with the instructions that the amount be permanently invested. The income might be unrestricted or restricted for a particular activity or program. Assume that in 20X1 a donor gave $100,000 for the purpose of creating an endowment. An entry would be made in the permanently restricted class (this would be part of the $280,000 shown in the Statement of Activities).

| | | |
|---|---|---|
| Cash | 100,000 | |
|     Contributions—Permanently Restricted | | 100,000 |

Note that revenues can be recorded in any of the three net asset classes but that expenses are recorded only in the unrestricted class. Note also that the expiration of restrictions is recorded by reclassifications.

**B. College and University Accounting—Private Sector Institutions**

Private colleges and universities are subject to the same guidance as other not-for-profit organizations that are included under the *Not-for-Profit Guide*. However, a few comments that specifically impact colleges and universities are in order.

1. Student tuition and fees are reported net of those scholarships and fellowships that are provided not in return for compensation. For example, a scholarship provided by an institution based on grades, entering ACT or SAT, etc., would be debited to a revenue deduction account.

| | | |
|---|---|---|
| Cash | 8,000 | |
| Revenue Deduction—Student Scholarships | 2,000 | |
|     Revenue—Student Tuition and Fees | | 10,000 |

2. Student graduate assistantships and other amounts given as tuition remissions (for example for full-time employees) that are given in return for services provided to the institution are charged as expenses, to the department and function where the services are provided. For example, assume the services were provided to the Biology Department.

| | | |
|---|---|---|
| Cash | 8,000 | |
| Expense—Instruction (Biology Department) | 2,000 | |
|     Revenue—Student Tuition and Fees | | 10,000 |

3. The AICPA *Not-for-Profit Guide* specifically states that operation and maintenance of physical plant is not to be reported as a functional expense. Those costs, including depreciation, are to be allocated to other functions.

4. The *Not-for-Profit Guide* does not include examples of financial statements for colleges and universities, or other not-for-profit organizations. The illustrative statement of activities for an educational institution is taken from the *Financial Accounting and Reporting Manual for Higher Education* published by the National Association of College and University Business Officers. Many other formats are possible, as long as the changes in net assets are shown separately for unrestricted, temporarily restricted, and permanently restricted net assets. Note that all expenses are reported as decreases in unrestricted net assets; losses may be reported as decreases in any of the net asset classes.

**Educational Institution**
**ILLUSTRATIVE STATEMENT OF ACTIVITIES**
*Multicolumn Format*

|  | Unrestricted | Temporarily Restricted | Permanently Restricted | Total |
|---|---|---|---|---|
| *Revenues and gains:* | | | | |
| Tuition and fees | $xxx | -- | -- | $xxx |
| Contributions | xxx | $xxx | $xxx | xxx |
| Contracts and other exchange transactions | xxx | -- | -- | xxx |
| Investment income on life income and annuity agreements | -- | xxx | -- | xxx |
| Investment income on endowment | xxx | xxx | xxx | xxx |
| Other investment income | xxx | xxx | xxx | xxx |
| Net realized gains on endowment | xxx | xxx | xxx | xxx |
| Net realized gains on other investments | xxx | xxx | xxx | xxx |
| Sales and services of auxiliary enterprises | xxx | -- | -- | xxx |
| Total revenues and gains | xxx | xxx | xxx | xxx |
| Net assets released from restrictions | xxx | (xxx) | -- | -- |
| Total revenues and gains and other support | xxx | xxx | xxx | xxx |
| *Expenses and losses:* | | | | |
| Educational and general: | | | | |
| Instruction | xxx | -- | -- | xxx |
| Research | xxx | -- | -- | xxx |
| Public service | xxx | -- | -- | xxx |
| Academic support | xxx | -- | -- | xxx |
| Student services | xxx | -- | -- | xxx |
| Institutional support | xxx | -- | -- | xxx |
| Total educational and general expenses | xxx | -- | -- | xxx |
| Auxiliary enterprises | xxx | -- | -- | xxx |
| Total expenses | xxx | -- | -- | xxx |
| Fire loss | xxx | -- | -- | xxx |
| Payments to life income beneficiaries | -- | xxx | -- | xxx |
| Actuarial loss on annuity obligations | xxx | -- | -- | xxx |
| Total expenses and losses | xxx | -- | -- | xxx |
| Increase (decrease) in net assets | xxx | xxx | xxx | xxx |
| Net assets at beginning of year | xxx | xxx | xxx | xxx |
| Net assets at end of year | $xxx | $xxx | $xxx | $xxx |

SOURCE: *National Association of College and University Business Officers,* **Financial Accounting and Reporting Manual for Higher Education**, *Chapter 500, as modified with the exclusion of Operation and Maintenance of Physical Plant and Scholarships and Fellowships as functional expenses.*

## C. Health Care Organization Accounting—Private Sector

The AICPA has issued an AICPA Audit and Accounting Guide, *Health Care Organizations*. This *Guide* applies both to private sector and governmental health care organizations; separate illustrative statements are presented for each. This section of the module presents private sector health care principles, first by indicating the unique features (beyond part A of this module) that apply and second by presenting illustrative statements. A few of the major features are as follows:

1. Requirements of the *Guide* apply to clinics, medical group practices, individual practice associations, individual practitioners, emergency care facilities, laboratories, surgery centers, other ambulatory care organizations, continuing care retirement communities, health maintenance organizations, home health agencies, hospitals, nursing homes, and rehabilitation centers. Sometimes, a fine line is drawn between those organizations that are considered health care entities and those that are considered voluntary health and welfare organizations, which are not covered by this *Guide*. The distinction is made by the source of revenues, not by the services provided. A nonprofit organization providing health care service in return for payment (an exchange transaction) by the recipient of the service, by a third-party payor, or a government program would be considered a health care organization. A nonprofit organization providing health care service funded primarily by voluntary contributions (from persons or organizations not receiving the service) would be considered a voluntary health and welfare organization.

2. Health care organizations may be not-for-profit, investor owned, or governmental. When possible, accounting and reporting for all types should be similar.

3. Financial statements include a balance sheet, a statement of operations, a statement of changes in net assets, a cash flow statement, and notes to the financial statements.

4. The statement of operations should include a performance indicator, such as operating income, revenues over expenses, etc. The *Guide* specifically indicates that the following must be reported separately from (underneath) that performance indicator (this is a partial list):

   a. Equity transfers involving other entities that control the reporting entity, are controlled by the reporting entity, or are under the common control of the reporting entity.
   b. Receipt of restricted contributions.
   c. Contributions of (and assets released from donor restrictions related to) long-lived assets.
   d. Unrealized gains and losses on investments not restricted by donors or by law, except for those investments classified as trading securities.
   e. Investment returns restricted by donors or by law.
   f. Other items that are required by GAAP to be reported separately (such as extraordinary items, the effect of discontinued operations, accounting changes).

5. Note disclosure must indicate the policies adopted by the entity to determine what is and what is not included in the performance indicator.

6. Patient service revenue is to be reported on the accrual basis net of adjustments for contractual and other adjustments in the operating statement. Provisions recognizing contractual adjustments and other adjustments (for example, hospital employee discounts) are deducted from gross patient revenue to determine **net patient** revenue. Significant revenue under capitation agreements (revenues from third party payors based on number of employees to be covered, etc. instead of services performed) is to be reported separately. Note disclosure should indicate the methods of revenue recognition and description of the types and amounts of contractual adjustments.

7. Patient service revenue does not include charity care. Management's policy for providing charity care and the level of charity care provided should be disclosed in the notes.

8. "Other revenues, gains, and losses" (included in operative revenues) include items such as

   a. Investment income
   b. Fees from educational programs
   c. Proceeds from sale of cafeteria meals
   d. Proceeds from gift shop, parking lot revenue, etc.

9. As is true for other not-for-profit organizations, contributions restricted to long-term purposes (plant acquisition, endowment, term endowment, etc.) would not be reported in the Statement of Operations (as unrestricted revenue) but would be reported in the Statement of Changes in Net Assets as a revenue increasing temporarily restricted or permanently restricted net assets, as appropriate.

10. Expenses are decreases in unrestricted net assets. Expenses may be reported by either natural (salaries, supplies, etc.) or functional classification. Not-for-profit health care entities must disclose expenses in the notes by function if functional classification is not presented on the operating statement. Functional classifications should be based on full cost allocations. Unlike organizations subject to the *Not-for-Profit Guide,* health care organizations may report depreciation, interest, and bad debt expense along with functional categories.

11. Health care organizations, except for continuing care retirement communities, are to present a classified balance sheet, with current assets and current liabilities shown separately. Continuing care retirement communities may sequence assets in terms of nearness to cash and liabilities in accordance with the maturity date.

Two statements are presented for a private sector not-for-profit hospital, both taken from the *Guide.* The statement of operations is presented with one line shown for "excess of revenues over expenses." This is the performance indicator. Note the separation of items above and below that line. Also note the presentation separately for depreciation, interest, and provision for bad debts. In addition, note that the net assets released from restrictions includes separate amounts for those net assets released for operations and those released for other items. The statement of changes in net assets presents the other changes required by SFAS 116 and 117.

*Sample Not-for-Profit Hospital*
**STATEMENTS OF OPERATIONS**
*Years Ended December 31, 20X7 and 20X6*
(in thousands)

|  | 20X7 | 20X6 |
|---|---|---|
| *Unrestricted revenues, gains and other support:* | | |
| Net patient service revenue | $85,156 | $78,942 |
| Premium revenue | 11,150 | 10,950 |
| Other revenue | 2,601 | 5,212 |
| Net assets released from restrictions used for operations | 300 | -- |
| Total revenues, gains and other support | 99,207 | 95,104 |
| *Expenses:* | | |
| Operating expenses | 88,521 | 80,585 |
| Depreciation and amortization | 4,782 | 4,280 |
| Interest | 1,752 | 1,825 |
| Provision for bad debts | 1,000 | 1,300 |
| Other | 2,000 | 1,300 |
| Total expenses | 98,055 | 89,290 |
| Operating income | 1,152 | 5,814 |
| *Other income:* | | |
| Investment income | 3,900 | 3,025 |
| Excess of revenues over expenses | 5,052 | 8,839 |
| Change in net unrealized gains and losses on other than trading securities | 300 | 375 |
| Net assets released from restrictions used for purchase of property and equipment | 200 | |
| Change in interest in net assets of Sample Hospital Foundation | 283 | 536 |
| Transfers to parent | (688) | (3,051) |
| Increase in unrestricted net assets, before extraordinary item | 5,147 | 6,699 |
| Extraordinary loss from extinguishment of debt | (500) | -- |
| Increase in unrestricted net assets | $ 4,647 | $ 6,699 |

*See accompanying notes to financial statements.*

SOURCE: AICPA Audit and Accounting Guide, **Health Care Organizations.**

*Sample Not-for-Profit Hospital*
**STATEMENTS OF CHANGES IN NET ASSETS**
*Years Ended December 31, 20X7 and 20X6*
(in thousands)

|  | 20X7 | 20X6 |
|---|---|---|
| *Unrestricted net assets:* | | |
| Excess of revenues over expenses | $ 5,052 | $ 8,839 |
| Net unrealized gains on investments, other than trading securities | 300 | 375 |
| Change in interest in net assets of Sample Hospital Foundation | 283 | 536 |
| Transfers to parent | (688) | (3,051) |
| Net assets released from restrictions used for purchase of property and equipment | 200 | -- |
| Increase in unrestricted net assets before extraordinary item | 5,147 | 6,699 |
| Extraordinary loss from extinguishment of debt | (500) | -- |
| Increase in unrestricted net assets | 4,647 | 6,699 |
| *Temporarily restricted net assets:* | | |
| Contributions for charity care | 140 | 996 |
| Net realized and unrealized gains on investments | 5 | 8 |
| Net assets released from restrictions | (500) | -- |
| Increase (decrease) in temporarily restricted net assets | (355) | 1,004 |
| *Permanently restricted net assets:* | | |
| Contributions for endowment funds | 50 | 411 |
| Net realized and unrealized gains on investments | 5 | 2 |
| Increase in permanently restricted net assets | 55 | 413 |
| Increase in net assets | 4,347 | 8,116 |
| Net assets, beginning of year | 72,202 | 64,086 |
| Net assets, end of year | $76,549 | $72,202 |

*See accompanying notes to financial statements.*

SOURCE: AICPA Audit and Accounting Guide, **Health Care Organizations.**

**D.  Health Care Organization Accounting—Governmental**

Governmental health care organizations, as mentioned earlier, are not allowed to use the principles established in SFAS 116 and 117 for not-for-profit organizations.  The AICPA *Health Care Guide,* however, attempts to present accounting and reporting principles allowed by the GASB in as close a fashion as possible to private sector health care entities.  A few major observations should be noted.

1.  Governmental health care organizations are permitted by GASB 34 to report as special-purpose entities engaged in governmental or business-type activities, or both.  Most will choose to report as special-purpose entities engaged in business-type activities.

2.  Governmental health care organizations reporting as special-purpose entities engaged in business-type activities will prepare the statements required for proprietary funds.  These are the (a) Balance Sheets, (b) Statement of Revenues, Expenses, and Changes in Net Assets, and (c) Statement of Cash Flows

3.  GASB principles must be followed in the separate reports of governmental health care organizations.  For example, net assets are to be categorized as (a) invested in capital assets, net of related debt; (b) restricted, and (c) unrestricted.  The GASB cash flow format should be used.  Refer to the proprietary fund example statements in Module 19.

4.  To the extent possible, AICPA *Health Care Guide* principles should also be followed.  For example, the items listed above in Section C.4. should be reported below the performance indicator, net patient revenue should be calculated in the same manner as described in C.6. above and should not include charity care cases (see above).

**MULTIPLE-CHOICE QUESTIONS (1-83)**

**1.** A statement of functional expenses is required for which one of the following private nonprofit organizations?
   a. Colleges.
   b. Hospitals.
   c. Voluntary health and welfare organizations.
   d. Performing arts organizations.

**2.** The statement of financial position (balance sheet) for Founders Library, a private nonprofit organization, should report separate dollar amounts for the library's net assets according to which of the following classifications?
   a. Unrestricted and permanently restricted.
   b. Temporarily restricted and permanently restricted.
   c. Unrestricted and temporarily restricted.
   d. Unrestricted, temporarily restricted, and permanently restricted.

**3.** Chicago Museum, a private nonprofit organization, has both regular and term endowments. On the museum's statement of financial position (balance sheet), how should the net assets of each type of endowment be reported?

|   | *Term endowments* | *Regular endowments* |
|---|---|---|
| a. | Temporarily restricted | Permanently restricted |
| b. | Permanently restricted | Permanently restricted |
| c. | Unrestricted | Temporarily restricted |
| d. | Temporarily restricted | Temporarily restricted |

**4.** Kerry College, a private not-for-profit college, received $25,000 from Ms. Mary Smith on April 30, 2006. Ms. Smith stipulated that her contribution be used to support faculty research during the fiscal year beginning on July 1, 2006. On July 15, 2006, administrators of Kerry awarded research grants totaling $25,000 to several faculty in accordance with the wishes of Ms. Smith. For the year ended June 30, 2006, Kerry College should report the $25,000 contribution as
   a. Temporarily restricted revenues on the statement of activities.
   b. Unrestricted revenue on the statement of activities.
   c. Temporarily restricted deferred revenue on the statement of activities.
   d. An increase in fund balance on the statement of financial position.

**5.** Good Hope, a private not-for-profit voluntary health and welfare organization, received a cash donation of $500,000 from Mr. Charles Peobody on November 15, 2006. Mr. Peobody directed that his donation be used to acquire equipment for the organization. Good Hope used the donation to acquire equipment costing $500,000 in January of 2007. For the year ended December 31, 2006, Good Hope should report the $500,000 contribution on its
   a. Statement of activities as unrestricted revenue.
   b. Statement of financial position as temporarily restricted deferred revenue.
   c. Statement of financial position as unrestricted deferred revenue.
   d. Statement of activities as temporarily restricted revenue.

**6.** On the statement of activities for a private not-for-profit performing arts center, expenses should be deducted from
  I. Unrestricted revenues.
  II. Temporarily restricted revenues.
  III. Permanently restricted revenues.

   a. I, II, and III.
   b. Both I and II.
   c. I only.
   d. II only.

**7.** Albert University, a private not-for-profit university, had the following cash inflows during the year ended June 30, 2006:
  I. $500,000 from students for tuition.
  II. $300,000 from a donor who stipulated that the money be invested indefinitely.
  III. $100,000 from a donor who stipulated that the money be spent in accordance with the wishes of Albert's governing board.

On Albert University's statement of cash flows for the year ended June 30, 2006, what amount of these cash flows should be reported as operating activities?
   a. $900,000
   b. $400,000
   c. $800,000
   d. $600,000

**8.** Gamma Pi, a private nonprofit fraternal organization, should prepare a statement of financial position and which of the following financial statements?
  I. Statement of activities.
  II. Statement of changes in fund balances.
  III. Statement of cash flows.

   a. I, II, and III.
   b. III only.
   c. II and III.
   d. I and III.

**9.** Save the Planet, a private nonprofit research organization, received a $500,000 contribution from Ms. Susan Clark. Ms. Clark stipulated that her donation be used to purchase new computer equipment for Save the Planet's research staff. The contribution was received in August of 2006, and the computers were acquired in January of 2007. For the year ended December 31, 2006, the $500,000 contribution should be reported by Save the Planet on its
   a. Statement of activities as unrestricted revenue.
   b. Statement of activities as deferred revenue.
   c. Statement of activities as temporarily restricted revenue.
   d. Statement of financial position as deferred revenue.

**10.** United Ways, a private not-for-profit voluntary health and welfare organization, received a contribution of $10,000 from a donor in 2006. The donor did not specify any use restrictions on the contribution; however, the donor specified that the donation should not be used until 2007. The governing board of United Ways spent the contribution in 2007 for fund-raising expenses. For the year ended December 31, 2006, United Ways should report the contribution on its
   a. Statement of financial position as deferred revenue.
   b. Statement of activities as unrestricted revenue.
   c. Statement of financial position as an increase in fund balance.
   d. Statement of activities as temporarily restricted revenue.

**11.** The statement of cash flows for a private not-for-profit hospital should report cash flows according to which of the following classifications?

   I. Operating activities.
   II. Investing activities.
   III. Financing activities.

     a.    I, II, and III.
     b.    II and III.
     c.    I only.
     d.    I and III.

**12.** Pharm, a nongovernmental not-for-profit organization, is preparing its year-end financial statements. Which of the following statements is required?
     a.    Statement of changes in financial position.
     b.    Statement of cash flows.
     c.    Statement of changes in fund balance.
     d.    Statement of revenue, expenses and changes in fund balance.

**13.** Stanton College, a not-for-profit organization, received a building with no donor stipulations as to its use. Stanton does not have an accounting policy implying a time restriction on donated fixed assets. What type of net assets should be increased when the building is received?

   I. Unrestricted.
   II. Temporarily restricted.
   III. Permanently restricted.

     a.    I only.
     b.    II only.
     c.    III only.
     d.    II or III.

**14.** Sea Lion Park, a private not-for-profit zoological society, received contributions restricted for research totaling $50,000 in 2006. None of the contributions were spent on research in 2006. In 2007, $35,000 of the contributions were used to support the research activities of the society. The net effect on the statement of activities for the year ended December 31, 2007, for Sea Lion Park would be a
     a.    $15,000 increase in temporarily restricted net assets.
     b.    $35,000 decrease in temporarily restricted net assets.
     c.    $35,000 increase in unrestricted net assets.
     d.    $35,000 decrease in unrestricted net assets.

**15.** Clara Hospital, a private not-for-profit hospital, earned $250,000 of gift shop revenues and spent $50,000 on research during the year ended December 31, 2006. The $50,000 spent on research was part of a $75,000 contribution received during December of 2005 from a donor who stipulated that the donation be used for medical research. Assume none of the gift shop revenues were spent in 2006. For the year ended December 31, 2006, what was the increase in unrestricted net assets from the events occurring during 2006?
     a.    $300,000
     b.    $200,000
     c.    $250,000
     d.    $275,000

**16.** Which of the following transactions of a private not-for-profit voluntary health and welfare organization would increase temporarily restricted net assets on the statement of activities for the year ended June 30, 2006?

   I. Received a contribution of $10,000 from a donor on May 15, 2006, who stipulated that the donation not be spent until August of 2006.
   II. Spent $25,000 for fund-raising on June 20, 2006. The amount expended came from a $25,000 contribution on March 12, 2006. The donor stipulated that the contribution be used for fund-raising activities.

     a.    Both I and II.
     b.    Neither I nor II.
     c.    I only.
     d.    II only.

**17.** Catherine College, a private not-for-profit college, received the following contributions during 2006:

   I. $5,000,000 from alumni for construction of a new wing on the science building to be constructed in 2006.
   II. $1,000,000 from a donor who stipulated that the contribution be invested indefinitely and that the earnings be used for scholarships. As of December 31, 2006, earnings from investments amounted to $50,000.

For the year ended December 31, 2006, what amount of these contributions should be reported as temporarily restricted revenues on the statement of activities?
     a.    $     50,000
     b.    $5,050,000
     c.    $5,000,000
     d.    $6,050,000

**18.** On December 31, 2006, Hope Haven, a private not-for-profit voluntary health and welfare organization, received a pledge from a donor who stipulated that $1,000 would be given to the organization each year for the next five years, starting on December 31, 2007. Present value factors at 6% for five periods are presented below.

| | |
|---|---|
| Present value of an ordinary annuity for 5 periods at 6% | 4.21236 |
| Present value of an annuity due for 5 periods at 6% | 4.46511 |

For the year ended December 31, 2006, Hope Haven should report, on its statement of activities,
     a.    Unrestricted revenues of $5,000.
     b.    Temporarily restricted revenues of $4,465.
     c.    Unrestricted revenues of $4,465.
     d.    Temporarily restricted revenues of $4,212.

**19.** For Guiding Light, a nongovernmental nonprofit religious organization, net assets that can be expended in accordance with the wishes of the governing board of the organization should be reported as

   I. Unrestricted.
   II. Temporarily restricted.
   III. Permanently restricted.

     a.    I only.
     b.    Both I and II.
     c.    I, II, and III.
     d.    Either I or II.

**20.** The Jackson Foundation, a private not-for-profit organization, had the following cash contributions and expenditures in 2007:

Unrestricted cash contributions of $500,000.
Cash contributions of $200,000 restricted by the donor to the acquisition of property.
Cash expenditures of $200,000 to acquire property with the donation in the above item.

Jackson's statement of cash flows should include which of the following amounts?

| | Operating activities | Investing activities | Financing activities |
|---|---|---|---|
| a. | $700,000 | $(200,000) | $0 |
| b. | $500,000 | $0 | $0 |
| c. | $500,000 | $(200,000) | $200,000 |
| d. | $0 | $ 500,000 | $200,000 |

**21.** United Hope, a private not-for-profit voluntary health and welfare organization, received the following contributions in 2007:

I. $500 from donors who stipulated that the money not be spent until 2008.
II. $1,000 from donors who stipulated that the contributions be used for the acquisition of equipment, none of which was acquired in 2006.

Which of the above events increased temporarily restricted net assets for the year ending December 31, 2007?
- a. I only.
- b. Both I and II.
- c. II only.
- d. Neither I nor II.

**22.** A statement of financial position (balance sheet), which reports unrestricted, temporarily restricted, and permanently restricted net assets, is required for which one of the following organizations?

I. A public university.
II. A private, not-for-profit hospital.

- a. Both I and II.
- b. I only.
- c. Neither I nor II.
- d. II only.

**23.** A storm broke glass windows in the building of Lea Meditators, a not-for-profit religious organization. A member of Lea's congregation, a professional glazier, replaced the windows at no charge. In Lea's statement of activities, the breakage and replacement of the windows should
- a. Not be reported.
- b. Be reported by note disclosure only.
- c. Be reported as an increase in both expenses and contributions.
- d. Be reported as an increase in both net assets and contributions.

**24.** SFAS 117, *Financial Statements of Not-for-Profit Organizations,* focuses on
- a. Basic information for the organization as a whole.
- b. Standardization of funds nomenclature.
- c. Inherent differences of not-for-profit organizations that impact reporting presentations.
- d. Distinctions between current fund and noncurrent fund presentations.

**25.** On December 30, 2007, Leigh Museum, a not-for-profit organization, received a $7,000,000 donation of Day Co. shares with donor-stipulated requirements as follows:

Shares valued at $5,000,000 are to be sold, with the proceeds used to erect a public viewing building.
Shares valued at $2,000,000 are to be retained, with the dividends used to support current operations.

As a consequence of the receipt of the Day shares, how much should Leigh report as temporarily restricted net assets on its 2007 statement of financial position (balance sheet)?
- a. $0
- b. $2,000,000
- c. $5,000,000
- d. $7,000,000

**26.** The Jones family lost its home in a fire. On December 25, 2007, a philanthropist sent money to the Amer Benevolent Society, a not-for-profit organization, to purchase furniture for the Jones family. During January 2008, Amer purchased this furniture for the Jones family. How should Amer report the receipt of the money in its 2007 financial statements?
- a. As an unrestricted contribution.
- b. As a temporarily restricted contribution.
- c. As a permanently restricted contribution.
- d. As a liability.

**27.** If the Pel Museum, a not-for-profit organization, received a contribution of historical artifacts, it need **not** recognize the contribution if the artifacts are to be sold and the proceeds used to
- a. Support general museum activities.
- b. Acquire other items for collections.
- c. Repair existing collections.
- d. Purchase buildings to house collections.

**28.** A large not-for-profit organization's statement of activities should report the net change for net assets that are

| | Unrestricted | Permanently restricted |
|---|---|---|
| a. | Yes | Yes |
| b. | Yes | No |
| c. | No | No |
| d. | No | Yes |

**29.** Which of the following classifications is required for reporting of expenses by all not-for-profit organizations?
- a. Natural classification in the statement of activities or notes to the financial statements.
- b. Functional classification in the statement of activities or notes to the financial statements.
- c. Functional classification in the statement of activities and natural classification in a matrix format in a separate statement.
- d. Functional classification in the statement of activities and natural classification in the notes to the financial statements.

**30.** Rosary Botanical Gardens, a private not-for-profit organization, established a $500,000 quasi endowment on September 1, 2007. On the garden's statement of financial position at December 31, 2007, the assets in this quasi endowment should be included in which of the following classifications?
- a. Temporarily restricted net assets.
- b. Unrestricted net assets.
- c. Permanently restricted net assets.
- d. Either temporarily or permanently restricted net assets, depending on the expected term of the quasi endowment.

**31.** During 2007, an alumnus of Smith College, a private not-for-profit college, transferred $100,000 to the college with the stipulation that it be spent for library acquisitions.

However, the alumnus specified that none of the cash transferred could be spent until the college had matched the entire amount transferred with donations from other alumni by December 31, 2008. As of December 31, 2007, the college had received matching cash donations of only $5,000 from other alumni, and the college estimated that it was reasonably possible that it would not reach the goal of $100,000 by December 31, 2008. If the funds are not matched by December 31, 2008, the cash will be returned to the alumnus. On the college's statement of financial position at December 31, 2007, the cash transfer of $100,000 would be included in the amount reported for

    a.   Liabilities.
    b.   Unrestricted net assets.
    c.   Temporarily restricted net assets.
    d.   Permanently restricted net assets.

**32.** During the year ended December 31, 2007, a not-for-profit performing arts entity received the following donor-restricted contribution and investment income:

   I.  Cash contribution of $100,000 to be permanently invested.
  II.  Cash dividends and interest of $6,000 to be used for the acquisition of theater equipment.

As a result of these cash receipts, the statement of cash flows for the year ended December 31, 2007, would report an increase of

    a.   $106,000 from operating activities.
    b.   $106,000 from financing activities.
    c.   $6,000 from operating activities and an increase of $100,000 from financing activities.
    d.   $100,000 from operating activities and an increase of $6,000 from financing activities.

**33.** Which of the following private, nonprofit entities is required to report expenses both by function and by natural classification?

    a.   Hospitals.
    b.   Colleges and universities.
    c.   Voluntary health and welfare organizations.
    d.   Performing arts organizations.

**34.** On December 5, 2007, Jones Heating and Air Conditioning Service repaired the heating system in the building occupied by Good Hope, a private not-for-profit voluntary health and welfare organization. An invoice for $1,500 was received by Good Hope for the repairs on December 15, 2007. On December 30, 2007, Jones notified Good Hope that the invoice was canceled and that the repairs were being donated without charge. For the year ended December 31, 2007, how should Good Hope report these contributed services?

    a.   Only in the notes to the financial statements.
    b.   No disclosure is required either in the financial statements or in the notes.
    c.   As an increase in unrestricted revenues and as an increase in expenses on the statements of activities.
    d.   As an increase in temporarily restricted net assets on the statement of activities.

**35.** During the year ended December 31, 2007, the James Community Foundation, a private not-for-profit organization, received the following contributed services:

   I.  Anderson & Anderson, attorneys-at-law, contributed their services which involved advice related to the foundation's regular endowments.
  II.  Senior citizens participated in a telethon to raise money for a new music building.

Which of these contributed services should be included in unrestricted revenues, gains, and other support on James Community Foundation's statement of activities for the year ended December 31, 2007?

    a.   Both I and II.
    b.   Neither I nor II.
    c.   II only.
    d.   I only.

**36.** Child Care Centers, Inc., a not-for-profit organization, receives revenue from various sources during the year to support its day care centers. The following cash amounts were received during 2007:

   $2,000 restricted by the donor to be used for meals for the children.
   $1,500 received for subscriptions to a monthly child-care magazine with a fair market value to subscribers of $1,000.
   $10,000 to be used only upon completion of a new playroom that was only 50% complete at December 31, 2007.

What amount should Child Care Centers record as contribution revenue in its 2007 Statement of Activities?

    a.   $  2,000
    b.   $  2,500
    c.   $10,000
    d.   $11,000

**37.** On December 20, 2007, United Appeal, a private not-for-profit voluntary health and welfare organization, received a donation of computer equipment valued at $25,000 from a local computer retailer. The equipment is expected to have a useful life of three years. The donor placed no restrictions on how long the computer equipment was to be used, and United has an accounting policy that does not imply a time restriction on gifts of long-lived assets. On United's statement of activities prepared for the year ended December 31, 2007, the donation of computer equipment should be reported

    a.   As an increase in temporarily restricted net assets.
    b.   Only in the notes to the financial statements.
    c.   As an increase in unrestricted net assets.
    d.   As either an increase in temporarily restricted net assets or as an increase in unrestricted net assets.

**38.** On December 30, 2007, the Board of Trustees of Henry Museum, a private not-for-profit organization, designated $4,000,000 of unrestricted net assets for the construction of an addition to its building. What effect does this designation have on the museum's unrestricted and temporarily restricted net assets which are reported on the statement of financial position (balance sheet) at December 31, 2007?

|   | Unrestricted net assets | Temporarily restricted net assets |
|---|---|---|
| a. | No effect | Increase |
| b. | Decrease | Increase |
| c. | Decrease | No effect |
| d. | No effect | No effect |

**39.** Darlin Hospital, a private not-for-profit hospital, had the following cash receipts for the year ended December 31, 2007:

| | |
|---|---|
| Patient service revenue | $300,000 |
| Gift shop revenue | 25,000 |
| Interest revenue restricted by donor stipulation for acquisition of equipment | 50,000 |

As a result of these cash receipts, the hospital's statement of cash flows for the year ended December 31, 2007, would report an increase in operating activities of

   a.   $325,000
   b.   $375,000
   c.   $350,000
   d.   $300,000

**40.** For a private, not-for-profit organization, when is a donor's conditional promise to give considered to be unconditional?

   a.   When the condition is partially met.
   b.   When the possibility that the condition will not be met is remote.
   c.   When the conditional promise is made.
   d.   When cash or other assets promised are received.

**41.** A not-for-profit organization receives $150 from a donor. The donor receives two tickets to a theater show and an acknowledgment in the theater program. The tickets have a fair market value of $100. What amount is recorded as contribution revenue?

   a.   $0
   b.   $ 50
   c.   $100
   d.   $150

**42.** On November 30, 2006, Justin Barlow, an alumnus of Murry School, a private, not-for-profit high school, contributed $15,000, with the stipulation that the donation be used for faculty travel expenses during 2007. During 2007, Murry spent all of the donation in accordance with Mr. Barlow's wishes. For the year ended December 31, 2007, what was the effect of the donation on unrestricted and temporarily restricted net assets?

| | Unrestricted net assets | Temporarily restricted net assets |
|---|---|---|
| a. | Increase | Decrease |
| b. | No effect | Decrease |
| c. | Increase | No effect |
| d. | No effect | No effect |

**43.** A private not-for-profit voluntary health and welfare organization received a cash donation in 2006 that contained a donor-imposed restriction that stipulated that the donation could not be spent until 2007. The voluntary health and welfare organization spent the donation in 2007 on fundraising activities. On the statement of activities prepared for the year ended December 31, 2007, the expiration of the time restriction would result in reporting a(n)

   a.   Increase in temporarily restricted net assets.
   b.   Reclassification that decreased temporarily restricted net assets.
   c.   Increase in unrestricted net assets.
   d.   Expense that decreased temporarily restricted net assets.

**44.** According to SFAS 117, which prescribes the financial statements of not-for-profit organizations, reporting reclassifications is caused by which of the following?

  I. Expiration of donor-imposed conditions.
  II. Expiration of donor-imposed restrictions.

   a.   I only.
   b.   Both I and II.
   c.   II only.
   d.   Neither I nor II.

**45.** Which of the following transactions would result in an increase in unrestricted net assets for the year ended December 31, 2007?

  I. A private, not-for-profit hospital earned interest on investments that were board-designated.
  II. A private, not-for-profit voluntary health and welfare organization received unconditional promises to give (pledges) which will not be received until the beginning of 2008. The donors placed no restrictions on their donations.

   a.   Both I and II.
   b.   I only.
   c.   II only.
   d.   Neither I nor II.

**46.** Benevolent Society, a private not-for-profit organization, should recognize contributed services on its statement of activities if which of the following conditions is(are) met?

  I. The contributed services create or enhance nonfinancial assets.
  II. The contributed services require specialized skills, are provided by individuals possessing those skills, and would typically need to be purchased if not provided by donation.

   a.   Both I and II.
   b.   Neither I nor II.
   c.   I only.
   d.   Either I or II.

**47.** During 2005, Margaret Billingsley, a prominent art collector, donated several items in her collection to the Darwin Museum, a private, not-for-profit organization. Ms. Billingsley stipulated that her contribution be shown to the public, that it should be preserved, and not be sold. Darwin's accounting policy is to capitalize all donations of art, historical treasures, and similar items. On the date of donation, what was the effect of Ms. Billingsley's donation on Darwin's financial statements?

   a.   Temporarily restricted net assets increased.
   b.   Reclassifications caused a simultaneous increase in permanently restricted net assets and a decrease in temporarily restricted net assets.
   c.   There was no effect on any class of Darwin's net assets.
   d.   Permanently restricted net assets increased.

**48.** Which of the following transactions or events would cause an increase in unrestricted net assets for the year ended December 31, 2007?

  I. A private not-for-profit voluntary health and welfare organization spent a restricted donation that was received in 2006. In accordance with the donor's wishes, the donation was spent on public health education during 2007.

II. During 2007, a private, not-for-profit college earned dividends and interest on term endowments. Donors placed no restrictions on the earnings of term endowments. The governing board of the college intends to use this investment income to fund undergraduate scholarships for 2008.

    a.   II only.
    b.   I only.
    c.   Neither I nor II.
    d.   Both I and II.

**49.** Mary Egbart promised Columbus College, a private, not-for-profit college, that she would provide 80% of the funds needed to construct a new performing arts center, if the college could get the remaining 20% of the funds needed from other donors by July 1, 2008. The promise was made in 2007. At December 31, 2007, the governing board of the college had received donations from other donors for approximately 15% of the cost of the new center and believed that the probability of not getting the remaining 5% of the necessary funds was remote. For the year ended December 31, 2007, Ms. Egbart's promise would

    a.   Be reported as an increase in permanently restricted net assets on the statement of activities.
    b.   Not be reported on the statement of activities.
    c.   Be reported as an increase in deferred support on the statement of financial position.
    d.   Be reported as an increase in temporarily restricted net assets on the statement of activities.

**50.** A private, not-for-profit hospital adopted SFAS 124, *Accounting for Certain Investments Held by Not-for-Profit Organizations*. For the year ended December 31, 2007, how should the hospital report its investments in debt securities that are classified as current assets and noncurrent assets on its statement of financial position (balance sheet)?

|     | Debt securities in current assets | Debt securities in noncurrent assets |
| --- | --- | --- |
| a. | Fair value | Amortized cost |
| b. | Amortized cost | Fair value |
| c. | Fair value | Fair value |
| d. | Amortized cost | Amortized cost |

**51.** The governing board of Crestfallen, a private not-for-profit voluntary health and welfare organization, acquired equity securities of BMZ Company at a cost of $35,000 on May 1, 2007. The governing board used unrestricted net assets to acquire this investment, and it intends to use the income from its investment in BMZ, as well as other investments, to acquire much needed computer equipment for the organization. The investment in the equity securities of BMZ Company, which is listed on a national stock exchange, represents less than a 1% interest in the company. On November 15, 2007, Crestfallen received $1,000 of dividends from BMZ, and the fair value of the BMZ equity securities was $42,000 on December 31, 2007. Assume Crestfallen adopted SFAS 124, *Accounting for Certain Investments Held by Not-for-Profit Organizations*. As a result of Crestfallen's investment in BMZ Company, the statement of activities for the year ended December 31, 2007 would report an increase of

    a.   $8,000 in unrestricted net assets.
    b.   $8,000 in temporarily restricted net assets.

    c.   $1,000 in unrestricted net assets.
    d.   $7,000 in unrestricted net assets.

**52.** Jazz Planners, a private not-for-profit performing arts organization, has donor-restricted permanent endowment funds which include investments in equity securities. These equity securities all have readily determinable fair values because they are all traded on national security exchanges. Most of the equity investments represent between 1% and 3% of the common stock of the investee companies; however, a few of Jazz Planner's investments permit the organization significant influence over the operating and financing policies of the investee companies. Jazz Planner's adopted SFAS 124, *Accounting for Certain Investments Held by Not-for-Profit Organizations*. How should the organization report these equity securities on its statement of financial position (balance sheet)?

|     | Equity securities: 1% to 3% ownership | Equity securities: significant influence |
| --- | --- | --- |
| a. | Fair value | Fair value |
| b. | Fair value | Use equity method |
| c. | Lower of cost or market | Fair value |
| d. | Fair value | Lower of cost or market |

**53.** Rose Smith made a cash donation for a specific purpose in December 2007, to United Ways, a nongovernmental, nonprofit organization that raises contributions for others. Assume United Ways was (1) not granted variance power by Rose Smith over her donation and (2) the beneficiaries of the donation are not financially related to United Ways. According to SFAS 136, *Transfer of Assets to a Not-for-Profit Organization or Charitable Trust That Raises or Holds Contributions for Others*, how should United Ways account for Rose's cash donation?

    a.   As an increase in contribution revenue.
    b.   As an increase in liabilities.
    c.   As either an increase in contribution revenue or liabilities.
    d.   As neither an increase in contribution revenue nor liabilities.

**54.** World-Wide Helpers Foundation, a nonprofit entity, received a cash donation in 2007 from Herold Smith. World-Wide Helpers Foundation is controlled by World-Wide Helpers, a nonprofit entity that raises resources for others. The resources of World-Wide Helpers Foundation are used for the benefit of World-Wide Helpers. World-Wide Helpers and its foundation have adopted SFAS 136, *Transfer of Assets to a Not-for-Profit Organization or Charitable Trust That Raises or Holds Contributions for Others*, for its 2007 financial statements. How should World-Wide Helpers Foundation account for the cash donation?

    a.   As an increase in contribution revenues.
    b.   As an increase in liabilities.
    c.   As either an increase in contribution revenue or liabilities.
    d.   As neither an increase in contribution revenue or liabilities.

**55.** In accordance with SFAS 136, *Transfer of Assets to a Not-for-Profit Organization or Charitable Trust That Raises or Holds Contributions for Others*, a cash donation from a resource provider should be reported as contribution revenue by a recipient organization when which of the following exists?

    a. The recipient organization and beneficiary are **not** financially interrelated.

    b. The resource provider does **not** allow the recipient organization to use the donation for beneficiaries other than those specified by the resource provider.

    c. The resource provider does **not** grant variance power to the recipient organization to redirect the donation to other beneficiaries.

    d. The resource provider grants variance power to the recipient organization to redirect the donation to other beneficiaries.

**56.** Peter Smith made a cash donation in January 2007, to World-Wide Helpers, a nongovernmental, nonprofit organization that raises contributions for others. Peter specified the beneficiaries for his contribution, but provided variance power to World-Wide Helpers to use the donation for beneficiaries not specified by Peter. According to SFAS 136, *Transfer of Assets to a Not-for-Profit Organization or Charitable Trust That Raises or Holds Contributions for Others*, how should World-Wide Helpers account for Peter's cash donation?

    a. As an increase in contribution revenue.

    b. As an increase in liabilities.

    c. As either an increase in contribution revenue or liabilities.

    d. As neither an increase in contribution revenue nor liabilities.

**57.** The Taft family lost its home in a flood in October 2005. In November of 2007, Mary Wilson donated cash to Goodbody Benevolent Society to purchase furniture for the Taft family. In December 2007, Goodbody purchased this furniture for the Taft family. Goodbody has adopted SFAS 136, *Transfer of Assets to a Not-for-Profit Organization or Charitable Trust That Raises or Holds Contributions for Others*. How should Goodbody report the receipt of the cash donation in its 2007 financial statements?

    a. As an unrestricted contribution.

    b. As a temporarily restricted contribution.

    c. As a liability.

    d. As either a liability or as a temporarily restricted contribution.

**58.** An arrangement where a donor makes an initial gift to a trust or directly to the not-for-profit organization, in which the not-for-profit organization has a beneficial interest but is not the sole beneficiary is known as a

    a. Donor-imposed condition.

    b. Donor-imposed restriction.

    c. Share-the-wealth agreement.

    d. Split-interest agreement.

**59.** Under which of the following cases should joint costs be allocated between fund-raising and the appropriate program or management and general function?

    a. An appeal for funds accompanied by a statement of the mission of the not-for-profit entity.

    b. An appeal for funds accompanied by a brochure explaining why funds are needed and how they will be used.

    c. An organization seeks the involvement of the public in the attainment of their missions by telling people what they should do about particular issues in addition to fund-raising appeals.

    d. An appeal for funds and education materials sent to a person based on his/her presumed ability to provide financial support.

**60.** Which of the following are considered to be capital additions in the statement of activity of a not-for-profit organization?

  I. Nonexpendable gifts, grants, and bequests restricted by donors to endowment funds.

  II. Legally restricted investment income on investments held in endowment funds that must be added to the principal.

  III. Donor-restricted gifts for program or supporting services.

    a. I, II, and III.

    b. I and III only.

    c. I and II only.

    d. III only.

**61.** Depending on the extent of discretion that the not-for-profit recipient has over the use or subsequent disposition of the assets, gifts in kind may be treated as

| | Agency transactions | Contributions |
|---|---|---|
| a. | No | No |
| b. | No | Yes |
| c. | Yes | Yes |
| d. | Yes | No |

**62.** A not-for-profit organization receives an asset for which they have little or no discretion over the use of the asset. The organization should report the asset as a(n)

    a. Contribution.

    b. Agency transaction.

    c. Exchange.

    d. Conditional transfer.

**63.** Elizabeth Hospital, a nonprofit hospital affiliated with a religious group, should prepare which of the following financial statements?

| | Statement of changes in net assets | Statement of operations |
|---|---|---|
| a. | Yes | No |
| b. | No | Yes |
| c. | Yes | Yes |
| d. | No | No |

**64.** Williams Hospital, a nonprofit hospital affiliated with a religious group, reported the following information for the year ended December 31, 2007:

| | |
|---|---|
| Gross patient service revenue at the hospital's full established rates | $980,000 |
| Bad debts expense | 10,000 |
| Contractual adjustments with third-party payors | 100,000 |
| Allowance for discounts to hospital employees | 15,000 |

On the hospital's statement of operations for the year ended December 31, 2007, what amount should be reported as net patient service revenue?

    a. $865,000

    b. $880,000

    c. $855,000

    d. $955,000

**65.** For private sector health care organizations, which of the following is included in patient service revenue?
- a. Contractual adjustments.
- b. Charity care.
- c. Significant revenue under capitation agreements (premium revenue).
- d. Unrestricted contributions.

**66.** Which of the following is **not** covered by the AICPA Audit and Accounting Guide, *Health Care Organizations*?
- a. Nursing homes.
- b. Home health agencies.
- c. Hospitals.
- d. Voluntary health and welfare organizations.

**67.** Which of the following can be included in the performance indicator on the statement of operations for private sector health care organizations?
- a. Extraordinary items.
- b. Premium revenue from capitation agreements.
- c. Equity transfers.
- d. Contributions of long-lived assets.

**68.** If private not-for-profit health care entities do not use this expense classification on the operating statement, they must provide it in the notes.
- a. Natural.
- b. Character.
- c. Functional.
- d. Object.

**69.** When functional classifications are used by private sector health care organizations, they should be based on
- a. Net present value.
- b. Full cost allocations.
- c. Percentage allocations.
- d. Resale value.

**70.** Which of the following would be acceptable as a performance indicator on a private sector health care entity's statement of operations?
- a. Increase in unrestricted net assets.
- b. Net income.
- c. Increase in net assets.
- d. Excess of revenues over expenses.

**71.** How is charity care accounted for on the financial statements of a not-for-profit private sector health care organization?
- a. As patient service revenue.
- b. As bad debt expense.
- c. As a separate component of revenue.
- d. Not included on the financial statements.

**72.** How are nonrefundable advance fees representing payments for future services to be accounted for by nonprofit continuing care retirement communities?
- a. As revenue.
- b. As a liability.
- c. As other financing sources.
- d. In a trust fund.

**73.** Kash Hospital, a private sector, not-for-profit organization, has gross patient service revenues of $750,000, charity care of $75,000, amounts disallowed by third-party payors of $63,000, and donor-unrestricted contributions of $110,000. What is the amount of net patient service revenue?

- a. $687,000
- b. $722,000
- c. $785,000
- d. $797,000

**74.** James Hospital, a nonprofit hospital affiliated with a private university, provided $200,000 of charity care for patients during the year ended December 31, 2007. The hospital should report this charity care
- a. As net patient service revenue of $200,000 on the statement of operations.
- b. As net patient service revenue of $200,000 and as an operating expense of $200,000 on the statement of operations.
- c. As accounts receivable of $200,000 on the balance sheet at December 31, 2007.
- d. Only in the notes to the financial statements for 2007.

**75.** Michael Hospital, a nonprofit hospital affiliated with a private university, reported the following information for the year ended December 31, 2007:

| | |
|---|---|
| Cash contributions received from donors for capital additions to be acquired in 2008 | $150,000 |
| Proceeds from sales at hospital gift shop and snack bar | 75,000 |
| Dividend revenue not restricted by donors or by law | 25,000 |

Using the information provided, what amount should be reported as "other revenue and gains" on the hospital's statement of operations for the year ended December 31, 2007?
- a. $ 25,000
- b. $ 75,000
- c. $100,000
- d. $250,000

**76.** Swathmore Hospital, a nonprofit hospital affiliated with Swathmore University, received the following cash contributions from donors during the year ended December 31, 2006:

| | |
|---|---|
| Contributions restricted by donors for research | $ 50,000 |
| Contributions restricted by donors for capital acquisitions | 250,000 |

Neither of the contributions was spent during 2006; however, during 2007, the hospital spent the entire $50,000 contribution on research and the entire $250,000 contribution on a capital asset that was placed into service during the year. The hospital has adopted an accounting policy that does not imply a time restriction on gifts of long-lived assets. On the hospital's statement of operations for the year ended December 31, 2007, what total amount should be reported for "net assets released from restrictions?"
- a. $ 50,000
- b. $300,000
- c. $250,000
- d. $0

**77.** The governing board of Smithson Hospital, a nonprofit hospital affiliated with a religious organization, acquired 100 BMI Company bonds for $103,000 on June 30, 2007. The bonds pay interest on June 30 and December 30. On December 31, 2007, interest of $3,000 was received from BMI, and the fair value of the BMI bonds was $105,000. The governing board acquired the BMI bonds with cash which was unrestricted, and it classified the bonds as trading securities at December 31, 2007, since it intends to sell all of the bonds in January 2008.  As a result of the investment in BMI bonds, what amount should be included in revenue, gains, and other support on the statement of operations for the year ended December 31, 2007?

    a.   $0
    b.   $3,000
    c.   $2,000
    d.   $5,000

**78.**  On the statement of operations for a nonprofit, nongovernmental hospital, which of the items below is included in the amount reported for "revenue and gains over expenses and losses" (the performance indicator)?

  I.  Unrealized loss on other than trading securities.  The securities are included in unrestricted net assets.
  II.  Contribution received from a donor that cannot be used until next year.

    a.   I only.
    b.   II only.
    c.   Both I and II.
    d.   Neither I nor II.

**79.**  Tucker Hospital, a nonprofit hospital affiliated with Tucker University, received a donation of medical supplies during the year ended December 31, 2007.  The supplies cost the vendor $10,000 and had a selling price of $15,000 on the date they were donated.  The vendor did not place any restrictions on how the supplies were to be used.  During 2007, all of the donated medical supplies were used.  On the hospital's statement of operations for the year ended December 31, 2007, how should the donation be reported?

    a.   The donation should be included in both revenue and operating expenses in the amount of $10,000.
    b.   The donation should be excluded from the statement of operations.
    c.   The donation should be included in both revenue and operating expenses in the amount of $15,000.
    d.   The donation should be included in revenue in the amount of $15,000 and in operating expenses in the amount of $10,000.

**80.**  Wilson Hospital, a nonprofit hospital affiliated with Wilson College, had the following cash receipts for the year ended December 31, 2007:

| | |
|---|---:|
| Collections of health care receivables | $750,000 |
| Contribution from donor to establish a term | |
|   endowment | 250,000 |
| Tuition from nursing school | 50,000 |
| Dividends received from investments in permanent endowment | 80,000 |

The dividends received are restricted by the donor for hospital building improvements.  No improvements were made during 2007.  On the hospital's statement of cash flows for the year ended December 31, 2007, what amount of these cash receipts would be included in the amount reported for net cash provided (used) by operating activities?

    a.   $ 880,000
    b.   $ 800,000
    c.   $1,050,000
    d.   $ 750,000

**81.**  Which of the following financial statements of a private, nonprofit hospital reports the changes in unrestricted, temporarily restricted, and permanently restricted net assets for a time period?

| | *Balance sheet* | *Statement of operations* |
|---|---|---|
| a. | Yes | Yes |
| b. | Yes | No |
| c. | No | Yes |
| d. | No | No |

**82.**  Unrealized gains on investments which are permanently restricted as to use by donors are reported by a private, nonprofit hospital on the

    a.   Statement of operations.
    b.   Statement of cash flows.
    c.   Statement of changes in net assets.
    d.   Statement of operations and statement of cash flows.

**83.**  The statement of operations for a private, nonprofit hospital should include a performance indicator that indicates the results of operations for a period.  Which of the following items would be included in a hospital's performance indicator reported on the statement of operations?

  I.  Proceeds from sales of cafeteria meals and guest trays to employees, medical staff, and visitors.
  II.  Net assets released from restrictions used for operating expenses.

    a.   I only.
    b.   Both I and II.
    c.   II only.
    d.   Neither I nor II.

## MULTIPLE-CHOICE ANSWERS

| | | | | | | | | | |
|---|---|---|---|---|---|---|---|---|---|
| 1. c | | 19. a | | 37. c | | 55. d | | 73. a | |
| 2. d | | 20. c | | 38. d | | 56. a | | 74. d | |
| 3. a | | 21. b | | 39. a | | 57. c | | 75. c | |
| 4. a | | 22. d | | 40. b | | 58. d | | 76. b | |
| 5. d | | 23. c | | 41. b | | 59. c | | 77. d | |
| 6. c | | 24. a | | 42. b | | 60. c | | 78. d | |
| 7. d | | 25. c | | 43. b | | 61. c | | 79. c | |
| 8. d | | 26. d | | 44. c | | 62. b | | 80. b | |
| 9. c | | 27. b | | 45. b | | 63. c | | 81. d | |
| 10. d | | 28. a | | 46. d | | 64. a | | 82. c | |
| 11. a | | 29. b | | 47. d | | 65. a | | 83. b | |
| 12. b | | 30. b | | 48. a | | 66. d | | | |
| 13. a | | 31. a | | 49. d | | 67. b | | | |
| 14. b | | 32. b | | 50. c | | 68. c | | | |
| 15. c | | 33. c | | 51. a | | 69. b | | | |
| 16. c | | 34. c | | 52. b | | 70. d | | | |
| 17. b | | 35. d | | 53. b | | 71. d | | 1st: __/83 = __% | |
| 18. d | | 36. b | | 54. a | | 72. b | | 2nd: __/83 = __% | |

## MULTIPLE-CHOICE ANSWER EXPLANATIONS

### A.  FASB and AICPA Standards for Private Sector Nonprofits

**1.    (c)**    According to SFAS 117, a statement of functional expenses is required for voluntary health and welfare organizations.  Other private nonprofit organizations are encouraged to disclose this information, but they are not required to.

**2.    (d)**    According to SFAS 117, a statement of financial position for a nongovernmental nonprofit entity, like a library, should report net assets according to whether the net assets are unrestricted, temporarily restricted, or permanently restricted.

**3.    (a)**    According to SFAS 117, the net assets of term endowments should be reported as temporarily restricted, while the net assets of regular endowments should be reported as permanently restricted.  The net assets of term endowments are temporarily restricted because the donor of a term endowment stipulates that the endowment last only a specific number of years.  Donors of regular endowments intend that these endowments last indefinitely; hence, the net assets are permanently restricted.

**4.    (a)**    According to SFAS 116, contributions are reported as revenue in the year received even though there are donor-imposed use or time restrictions on the donation.  Since Ms. Smith's donation was use and time restricted, the donation should be reported as a temporarily restricted revenue on the statement of activities for the year ended June 30, 2006.  This reporting is in accordance with SFAS 117.

**5.    (d)**    According to SFAS 116, contributions are reported as revenue in the year received even though there are donor-imposed use or time restrictions on the contribution.  Since Mr. Peobody's contribution was use restricted, the contribution would be reported as temporarily restricted revenue on the statement of activities for the year ended December 31, 2006.  This reporting is in accordance with SFAS 117.

**6.    (c)**    According to SFAS 117, all expenses are reported as unrestricted on the statement of activities.  This

means that expenses are deducted only from unrestricted revenues.

**7.    (d)**    In accordance with SFAS 117, nongovernmental not-for-profit organizations are required to report a statement of cash flows.  On this statement, cash flows are reported using the classifications of operating, investing, and financing activities.  Cash flows related to revenues and expenses that are unrestricted should be reported in the operating activities section.  The cash inflows from both tuition ($500,000) and the unrestricted contribution ($100,000) are both unrestricted and should be reported as operating activities.  Restricted contributions for long-term purposes, like the $300,000 endowment, are reported as financing activities on the statement of cash flows.

**8.    (d)**    According to SFAS 117, nongovernmental, not-for-profit entities should prepare the following financial statements:

1.  Statement of financial position
2.  Statement of activities
3.  Statement of cash flows

In addition, a voluntary health and welfare organization should also prepare a statement of functional expenses.

**9.    (c)**    According to SFAS 116, donor restricted contributions should be reported as revenue in the period received.  According to SFAS 117, donor restricted contributions which are restricted according to use should be reported as either temporarily restricted revenues or as permanently restricted revenues, depending on the restriction.  In the case of Save the Planet, the restriction is temporary, not permanent.  Therefore, Ms. Clark's contribution should be reported as temporarily restricted revenue on the statement of activities for the year ended December 31, 2006.

**10.    (d)**    According to SFAS 116, donor restricted contributions are revenues in the year the contribution is made, not in the year the contribution is spent.  According to SFAS 117, contributions that are restricted temporarily should be reported on the statement of activities as temporarily restricted revenues.

**11.   (a)**   According to SFAS 117, the statement of cash flows for a nongovernmental not-for-profit entity should report its cash flows from operating, investing, and financing activities.

**12.   (b)**   SFAS 117, para 6, indicates that "a complete set of financial statements of not-for-profit organization shall include a statement of financial position as of the end of the reporting period, a statement of activities and a statement of cash flows for the reporting period, and accompanying notes to financial statements."

**13.   (a)**   SFAS 116, para 16, states

*Gifts of long-lived assets received without stipulations about how long the donated asset must be used shall be reported as restricted support if it is an organization's accounting policy to imply a time restriction that expires over the useful life of the donated assets...In the absence of that policy and other donor-imposed restrictions on use of the asset, gifts of long-lived assets shall be reported as unrestricted support.*

**14.   (b)**   For the year ended December 31, 2006, the contributions received for research would be reported on the statement of activities as an increase of $50,000 in temporarily restricted net assets. According to SFAS 116, contributions received from outside donors for use in research are reported as temporarily restricted net assets. For the year ended December 21, 2007, a reclassification of net assets would be reported on the statement of activities. A reclassification of $35,000 would be reported as both a decrease in temporarily restricted net assets and an increase in unrestricted net assets. In addition, research expense of $35,000 would be reported as a decrease in unrestricted net assets on the statement of activities for the year ended December 31, 2007. Therefore, as a result of the transactions in 2007, there was a decrease of $35,000 in temporarily restricted net assets and no effect on unrestricted net assets (the $35,000 reclassification to unrestricted net assets is offset by a $35,000 increase in research expense).

**15.   (c)**   Unrestricted net assets increased $250,000 for the year ended December 31, 2006. According to SFAS 117, the $50,000 spent on research during 2006 would be reclassified (added) to unrestricted net assets when the money was spent for research. The $50,000 addition to unrestricted revenues, gains, and other support would be accompanied by a $50,000 reclassification (deduction) from temporarily restricted revenues. The expenses of $50,000 for research are deducted from unrestricted revenues, etc., which include the $50,000 reclassification. Therefore, the net effect on unrestricted net assets of spending $50,000 on research is zero. The $250,000 of gift shop revenue is unrestricted revenue because the governing board has control of this revenue.

**16.   (c)**   According to SFAS 116, contributions should be reported as revenue in the period of contribution, even though a donor has placed a time or use restriction on the contribution. According to SFAS 117, the $10,000 and the $25,000 contributions should be reported as temporarily restricted revenues on the statement of activities for the year ended June 30, 2006. When the $25,000 is spent on fund-raising, a reclassification of $25,000 should be reported as a deduction from temporarily restricted revenues. This $25,000 deduction results in a net increase in temporarily restricted net assets of $10,000 on the statement of activities for the year ended June 30, 2006. The deduction of $25,000

from temporarily restricted revenues also results in an increase in unrestricted revenues, gains, and other support of $25,000. According to SFAS 117, expenses can only be deducted from unrestricted revenues on the statement of activities. Therefore, the fund-raising expenses of $25,000 will be deducted from unrestricted revenues, gains, and other support that includes the $25,000 reclassification from temporarily restricted revenues. Alternatively, SFAS 117 also permits temporarily restricted revenues to be reported as unrestricted revenues in the year the resources are received. This alternative is allowed only for the amount of temporarily restricted revenues that are spent during the year. In the situation presented, $25,000 would be disclosed as both an unrestricted revenue and expense for 2006. There would be no need for a reclassification; however, the answer would not change because temporarily restricted net assets increase $10,000 as a result of the contribution that was not spent in 2006.

**17.   (b)**   According to SFAS 116, contributions should be reported as revenues in the period received, even though donors have placed time or use restrictions on the contributions. According to SFAS 117, the $5,000,000 contribution from alumni for a new wing for the science building should be reported as a temporarily restricted revenue on the statement of activities for the year ended December 31, 2006. Also, the $50,000 of earnings related to the investments should also be reported as temporarily restricted revenues on the statement of activities for the year ended December 31, 2006. The $1,000,000 contribution from the donor, who stipulated that the contribution be invested indefinitely, should be reported as a permanently restricted revenue on the statement of activities for the year ended December 31, 2006.

**18.   (d)**   According to SFAS 116, a multiyear pledge should be reported at its present value. According to SFAS 117, if there is a time restriction on the pledge, the pledge should be reported as a temporarily restricted revenue in the year the pledge is given. In Hope Haven's situation, the pledge should be reported as temporarily restricted revenue in 2006. The pledge should be reported at its present value. This amount is calculated by using the present value of an ordinary annuity factor for five periods at 6% ($1,000 × 4.21236 = $4,212 rounded).

**19.   (a)**   According to SFAS 117, net assets under the control of the governing board are reported as unrestricted net assets.

**20.   (c)**   The requirement is to determine how to report three cash flows on the statement of cash flows for a nongovernmental, nonprofit entity, the Jackson Foundation. According to the guidance provided in SFAS 117, the $500,000 cash inflow from unrestricted contributions should be reported as an increase in the operating activities section. The $200,000 cash inflow restricted for the acquisition of property should be reported as an increase in the financing activities section, while the use of the $200,000 to acquire property should be shown as a decrease in the investing activities section.

**21.   (b)**   According to SFAS 116, contributions are reported as revenue in the year received, whether the donors place time or use restrictions on the resources. According to SFAS 117, net assets should be disclosed according to whether they are unrestricted, temporarily restricted, and permanently restricted. Both of the events listed would increase temporarily restricted net assets for the year ending December 31, 2007.

**22. (d)**   SFAS 117 requires a statement of financial position which reports unrestricted, temporarily restricted, and permanently restricted net assets for nongovernmental, not-for-profit organizations. Therefore, the statement of financial position is required for a private, not-for-profit hospital, but not for a public university, which is supported by government.

**23. (c)**   Per SFAS 116, contributed services which would be purchased if not donated, and which require performance by a specialist, shall be recorded as an increase in both expenses and contributions. In this case, the requirements of SFAS 116 are met since the window needs to be replaced and the work is performed by a professional glazier (specialist).

**24. (a)**   SFAS 117 establishes standards for general-purpose external financial statements. This statement focuses on the basic information of the organization as a whole so as to enhance the relevance, understandability, and comparability of the financial statements by the external users. Thus, answer (a) is correct since the overall objective is the enhancement of the basic information, while answers (b), (c), and (d) address factors that are taken into consideration to achieve the objective.

**25. (c)**   SFAS 117 requires classification of an organization's net assets and its revenues, expenses, gains, and losses based on the existence or absence of donor-imposed restrictions. It requires that the amount for **each** of three classes of net assets—permanently restricted, temporarily restricted, and unrestricted—be displayed in a statement of financial position and that the amounts of change in each of those classes of net assets be displayed in a statement of activities.

A temporary restriction is a donor-imposed restriction that permits the donee organization to use up or expend the donated assets as specified; it is satisfied either by the passage of time or by actions of the organizations involved. Accordingly, the $5,000,000 contribution of Day Co. shares represents temporarily restricted net assets until the shares are sold and the proceeds used to erect a public viewing building. The $2,000,000 contribution of Day Co. shares represents permanently restricted net assets because the shares are to be retained permanently.

**26. (d)**   A liability (not revenue) is recorded when the reporting entity acts as an agent or trustee. A recipient of assets who is an agent or trustee has little or no discretion in determining how the assets transferred will be used. The receipt of cash to purchase furniture specifically for the Jones family would constitute a "transfer" of assets. Upon receipt of the asset (cash), the Amer Benevolent society must expend (i.e., purchase furniture) the contribution to comply with the restrictions of the donor. Answer (a) is incorrect because the donee restricted the use of the contribution. Answer (c) is incorrect because a permanent restriction stipulates that the resources be maintained permanently (but permits the donee organization to expend part or all of the income or other economic benefits derived from the donated assets).

**27. (b)**   Per SFAS 116, an entity need not recognize the contributions of works of art and historical artifacts if the collection is held for public exhibition rather than financial profit, cared for and preserved, and, if sold, the proceeds are used to acquire other items for collections.

**28. (a)**   A Statement of Activities reports revenues, expenses, gains, losses, and reclassifications. Resources are divided into three classes: unrestricted, temporarily restricted, and permanently restricted. Separate revenues, expenses, gains, losses, and reclassifications for each class may or may not be reported, but the change in net assets for each class **must** be reported.

**29. (b)**   The requirement is to determine what classification is required to report expenses of all not-for-profit organizations. All not-for-profit organizations must classify expenses according to their function in either the financial statement or in the notes to the financial statements.

**30. (b)**   Quasi endowment funds are established by the governing board of an organization using unrestricted net assets. Therefore, the assets in the quasi endowment would be included in the unrestricted net assets category.

**31. (a)**   According to SFAS 116, a transfer of assets with a conditional promise to contribute them shall be accounted for as a refundable advance until the conditions have been substantially met. The conditions have been substantially met when the possibility that they will not be met is remote. In this question, the chance that the condition will not be met is reasonably possible, which is a higher level of doubt than remote and thus results in reporting the cash transfer as a liability at December 31, 2007.

**32. (b)**   According to SFAS 117, the receipt of cash from a donor to establish a permanent endowment should be reported as a financing activity on the statement of cash flows. This same paragraph also states that receipts from investment income that by donor stipulation are restricted for the purposes of acquiring plant, equipment, and other long-lived assets should also be reported as a financing activity.

**33. (c)**   According to SFAS 117, voluntary health and welfare organizations should provide a statement of functional expenses. This statement reports expenses by both function (program and supporting) and by their natural classification (salaries expense, depreciation expense, etc.).

**34. (c)**   According to SFAS 116, donations of services are recognized on the statement of activities if either of the following two conditions are met: (1) the services create or enhance a nonfinancial asset, or (2) the services require specialized skills, are provided by individuals possessing those skills, and would typically need to be purchased if not provided by donation. The services provided by Jones Heating and Air Conditioning would clearly meet the second criterion. Good Hope would record the invoice in the following manner:

| | | |
|---|---|---|
| Supporting Expenses | 1,500 | |
| Accounts Payable | | 1,500 |

Upon notification that the invoice was canceled, Good Hope would make the following journal entry:

| | | |
|---|---|---|
| Accounts Payable | 1,500 | |
| Unrestricted Revenues | | 1,500 |

Therefore, the net effect of the contributed services is an increase in expenses and an increase in unrestricted revenues.

**35.   (d)**   According to SFAS 116, donations of services are recognized on the statement of activities if either of the following conditions are met: (1) the services create or enhance a nonfinancial asset, or (2) the services require specialized skills, are provided by individuals possessing those skills, and would typically need to be purchased if not provided by donation. The services of Anderson and Anderson, attorneys-at-law, clearly meet criterion 2 and should be reported as unrestricted revenues on James' statement of activities. However, the services provided by the senior citizens do not meet either criterion, and should not be reported on the foundation's statement of activities.

**36.   (b)**   The requirement is to determine what amount should be reported as contribution revenue in the 2007 statement of activities. The $2,000 restricted for meals is considered contribution revenue even though it is restricted. The amount received over the fair market value of the subscriptions is considered to be contribution revenue, which is $500 ($1,500 – $1,000). The $10,000 to be used upon completion of a new playroom is not part of 2007 revenue contribution because a condition, completion of a new playroom, has not been fulfilled. The money is only available upon completion, and the building is not complete in 2007. What is included in contribution revenue is $2,500 ($2,000 + $500).

**37.   (c)**   According to SFAS 116, gifts of long-lived assets should be reported as unrestricted support if the organization has an accounting policy which does not imply a time restriction on such gifts.

**38.   (d)**   The designation of unrestricted net assets by the board of Henry Museum for the building addition does not change the classification of the net assets which were designated. The assets designated were unrestricted before the designation, and they remain unrestricted after the designation.

**39.   (a)**   Cash flows from operating activities would include both the cash received from patient service revenue of $300,000 and the cash received from gift shop sales of $25,000. According to SFAS 117, cash received from investment income that is restricted by donors for the acquisition of long-lived fixed assets should be reported as financing activities.

**40.   (b)**   According to SFAS 116, a conditional promise to give is considered unconditional if the possibility that the condition will not be met is remote.

**41.   (b)**   The requirement is to determine how much of the $150 from a donor in exchange for theater tickets and an acknowledgment is considered contribution revenue. Contribution revenue is the amount given above the fair market value. The amount given, $150, is $50 more than fair market value of the tickets, which is $100.

**42.   (b)**   The use of the cash donation for faculty travel in 2007 is reported as a reclassification on the high school's statement of activities for 2007. Reclassifications are reported on the statement of activities as "net assets released from restrictions." Net assets released from restrictions of $15,000 are reported as a negative amount for temporarily restricted

net assets in 2007, while net assets released from restrictions of $15,000 are reported as a positive amount for unrestricted net assets for 2007. However, the $15,000 of travel expense is reported on the statement of activities as an expense for 2007. According to SFAS 117, all expenses are reported on the statement of activities as decreases in unrestricted net assets. This means that the use of the donation for faculty travel had no effect on unrestricted net assets in 2007. Note that, when the donation was received in 2006, temporarily restricted net assets increased by $15,000 on the statement of activities prepared for 2006.

**43.   (b)**   According to SFAS 117, expiration of donor-imposed restrictions that simultaneously increase one class of net assets and decrease another should be reported as reclassifications on the statement of activities. Reclassifications are reported as "net assets released from restrictions." When the time restriction on the donation expired in 2007, unrestricted net assets increased while temporarily restricted net assets decreased. The spending of the donation on fund-raising should be reported as an expense, which, according to SFAS 117, is a deduction from unrestricted net assets. Therefore, the net effect of the reclassification and the use of the donation is zero on unrestricted net assets. However, the reclassification decreased temporarily restricted net assets for 2007.

**44.   (c)**   According to SFAS 117, reclassifications result from expirations of donor-imposed restrictions. The donor-imposed restrictions may be either time or purpose related. When a donor-imposed condition is satisfied, the conditional promise to give assets becomes unconditional, and there is an increase in the appropriate classification of net assets, depending on the restrictions placed upon the assets by the donors. However, this increase is reported as either revenue or support at the time the promise becomes unconditional.

**45.   (b)**   Interest earned on board-designated investments is reported as unrestricted revenue. When the governing board of a not-for-profit organization places limitations on assets, they are designating the use of unrestricted net assets. Therefore, income earned on board-designated investments represents an increase in unrestricted net assets. Unconditional promises to give are reported in the period the pledges are made, not in the period of cash collection. However, since the contributions will not be received until 2006, the contributions should be reported as an increase in temporarily restricted net assets on the statement of activities for 2007 because of this time restriction.

**46.   (d)**   According to SFAS 116, contributed services should be recognized if either of the following conditions is met: (1) the services create or enhance nonfinancial assets, or (2) the services require specialized skills, are provided by individuals possessing those skills, and would typically need to be purchased if not provided by donation.

**47.   (d)**   According to SFAS 117, donations of works of art for which the donor stipulated a specified purpose and which are to be preserved and not be sold, represent permanently restricted net assets. Since the museum's policy is to capitalize all donations of art, Ms. Billingsley's donation would be reported as an increase in permanently restricted net assets on the statement of activities.

**48.   (a)**   The restricted donation of the voluntary health and welfare organization is reported as a reclassification on the statement of activities for 2007.  The net effect of the re-classification and the recognition of the expense is zero.  The reclassification resulting from the expiration of the donor-imposed restriction increases unrestricted net assets; however, the expense resulting from using the funds for public health education is subtracted from this increase, causing no effect on unrestricted net assets.  The interest and dividends earned on the term endowments are unrestricted, and should be reported as an increase in unrestricted revenue for 2007.  Since no expenses have been incurred from the use of the investment income for 2007, the net effect is an increase in unrestricted net assets for 2007.

**49.   (d)**     According to SFAS 116, a conditional promise to give is considered unconditional if the possibility that the condition will not be met is remote.  At December 31, 2007, Ms. Egbart's promise would be considered unconditional.  This means that the college should report the funds that Ms. Egbart promised as an increase in temporarily restricted net assets on its statement of activities prepared for the year ended December 31, 2007.

**50.   (c)**     According to SFAS 124, all investments in debt securities should be measured at fair value in the statement of financial position.

**51.   (a)**     According to SFAS 124, the investment in BMZ is covered by the standard, since the standard does not apply to investments in equity securities which are accounted for under the equity method or are consolidated.  Since Crestfallen owns less than 1% of BMZ Company, the equity method cannot be used to account for the investment.  Therefore, the provisions of paragraph 7 apply to the investment in BMZ.

According to SFAS 124, investments in equity securities with readily determinable market values should be reported at fair value in the statement of financial position.  In order to report BMZ's equity securities at their market value of $42,000, a gain of $7,000 should be recognized on the statement of activities.  This gain represents an increase in unrestricted net assets, since the gain is related to an investment made by the governing board with unrestricted net assets.  In addition, the dividends of $1,000 would also be reported as an increase in unrestricted net assets, since the dividends were earned on unrestricted net assets.  Therefore, the investment in BMZ would result in an $8,000 increase in unrestricted net assets on the statement of activities prepared for the year ended December 31, 2007.

**52.   (b)**     According to SFAS 124, investments in equity securities that are accounted for under the equity method are not covered by the standard.  Therefore, Jazz Planners' investments that permit it to have significant influence over the operating and financing policies of the investee companies should be reported on the statement of financial position using the equity method.  On the other hand, the investments that represent 1% to 3% ownership interests would be covered by SFAS 124.  According to of SFAS 124, these investments in equity securities should be reported on the statement of financial position at fair value.

**53.   (b)**     According to SFAS 136, when a resource provider transfers assets to a nonprofit entity and (1) does not grant the recipient organization variance power and (2) the recipient organization and the beneficiaries are not financially interrelated, the recipient entity should record an in-

crease in assets and liabilities as a result of the donation.  In the case at hand, United Ways is the recipient entity that should record the cash donation by increasing both assets and liabilities.

**54.   (a)**     According to SFAS 136, when the recipient organization and the beneficiary are financially interrelated organizations, and the resources held by the recipient organization must be used for the benefit of the beneficiary, the recipient entity should account for the asset transfer as an increase in assets and as an increase in contribution revenue.  In the case at hand, World-Wide Helpers Foundation is the recipient entity that should record the asset transfer by increasing cash and increasing contribution revenue.

**55.   (d)**     According to SFAS 136, a contribution from a resource provider is reported as contribution revenue if (1) the recipient organization is granted variance power by the resource provider or (2) the recipient organization and the beneficiary are financially interrelated organizations.  In the case at hand, answer (d) is correct because the resource provider granted variance power to the recipient organization.  Answers (b) and (c) are incorrect because the resource provider designates the beneficiaries and does not grant the recipient organization the ability to redirect the donation to other than the specified beneficiaries.  For both situations (b) and (c), the recipient organization should record the donation by increasing both assets and liabilities.  Answer (a) is incorrect because contribution revenue is reported by a recipient organization if the recipient organization and the beneficiary are financially interrelated.  If they are not financially interrelated, the recipient organization should report the donation as an increase in assets and an increase in liabilities.

**56.   (a)**     According to SFAS 136, when the resource provider provides variance power over transferred assets, the recipient entity should account for the assets donated as an increase in assets and an increase in contribution revenue.  Variance power means the ability of the recipient organization to redirect the resources transferred to it by a resource provider.  In case at hand, World-Wide Helpers is the recipient entity that should record the cash donation by increasing both assets and contribution revenue.

**57.   (c)**     According to SFAS 136, a recipient organization that receives a contribution from a resource provider is required to report the contribution as an asset and a liability unless one of two condition exist (1) the recipient organization is granted variance power to redirect the resources, or (2) the recipient organization and the beneficiary are financially interrelated organizations.  Since Mary Wilson did not grant variance power to Goodbody to redirect her donation to other flood victims, and the Taft family and Goodbody are not financially interrelated organizations, the cash donation should be reported as a liability in Goodbody's 2007 financial statements.

**58.   (d)**     According to the AICPA Audit and Accounting Guide, *Not-for-Profit Organizations*,

*Under a split-interest agreement, a donor makes an initial gift to a trust or directly to the not-for-profit organization, in which the not-for-profit organization has a beneficial interest but is not the sole beneficiary....The assets are invested and administered by the organization, a trustee, or a fiscal agent, and distributions are made to a beneficiary or beneficiaries during the term of the agreement.  At the end of the agreement's term, the remaining assets covered by the agreement are distributed to or retained by either the not-for-profit organization or another beneficiary or beneficiaries.*

**59.** **(c)**   According to the Not-for-Profit Guide, all joint costs of informational materials or activities that include a fund-raising appeal should be reported as fund-raising expense unless an appeal is designed to motivate its audience to action other than providing financial support. Answer (c) is the only alternative that requires both other action and financial support.

**60.** **(c)**   According to the Not-for-Profit Guide, capital additions include nonexpendable gifts restricted to endowment, plant, or loan funds and the legally restricted investment income on investments in such funds. Donor-restricted gifts for programs or supporting services are not capital additions.

**61.** **(c)**   According to the Not-for-Profit Guide, gifts in kind are noncash assets received by not-for-profit organizations from resource providers. These gifts in kind are reported as agency transactions or as contributions depending on the extent of discretion that the not-for-profit recipient has over the use or subsequent disposition of the assets.

**62.** **(b)**   According to the Not-for-Profit Guide, when a not-for-profit organization has little or no discretion over the use of the asset, the transaction is an agency transaction.

## C.  Health Care Organization Accounting—Private Sector

**63.** **(c)**   According to the AICPA Audit and Accounting Guide, *Health Care Organizations*, the basic financial statements for a hospital include a balance sheet, a statement of operations, a statement of changes in net assets, and a statement of cash flows. Accordingly, Elizabeth Hospital should prepare both a statement of changes in net assets as well as a statement of operations.

**64.** **(a)**   According to the AICPA Audit and Accounting Guide, *Health Care Organizations*, the provision for contractual adjustments and discounts is recognized on the accrual basis and deducted from gross patient service revenue to determine net patient revenue. Bad debts expense is reported as an operating expense, not as a contra to gross patient service revenue. Accordingly, net patient service revenue for 2005 is $865,000. This amount is determined by subtracting the contractual adjustments of $100,000 and the discounts of $15,000 from gross patient service revenue of $980,000.

**65.** **(a)**   Patient service revenue is to be reported net of adjustments for contractual and other adjustments in the operating statement. Provisions recognizing contractual adjustments and other adjustments are recorded on an accrual basis and deducted from gross service revenue to determine net service revenue.

**66.** **(d)**   Voluntary health and welfare organizations are categorized as not-for-profit, nonbusiness-oriented organizations that are covered by the AICPA Audit and Accounting Guide, *Not-for-Profit Organizations*. Nursing home, home health agencies, and hospitals are all considered health care entities and are covered in the AICPA Audit and Accounting Guide, *Health Care Organizations*.

**67.** **(b)**   The AICPA Audit and Accounting Guide, *Health Care Organizations* lists the items that must be reported separately from the performance indicator. Among these are extraordinary items (and other items required by GAAP to be reported separately), equity transfers, receipt of restricted contributions, contributions of long-lived assets, restricted investment returns, and unrealized gains/losses of unrestricted investments (except trading securities). Premium revenue is included in the performance indicator.

**68.** **(c)**   The AICPA Audit and Accounting Guide, *Health Care Organizations* states that expenses may be reported on the face of the financial statements using either a natural classification or functional presentation. Not-for-profit organizations that report using a natural classification of expenses are required to disclose expenses by functional classification in the notes.

**69.** **(b)**   Functional classifications should be based on full cost allocations. Health care organizations may report depreciation, interest, and bad debts along with functions.

**70.** **(d)**   The performance indicator should report the results of operations. However, it should not include such items as extraordinary items, unrealized gains and losses on nontrading securities, and contributions of long-lived assets. Increase in unrestricted net assets and increase in net assets include these items and so cannot be performance indicators. Net income is a term associated with for-profit enterprises and so is not used by health care entities.

**71.** **(d)**   According to the AICPA Audit and Accounting Guide, *Health Care Organizations*,

*Charity care represents health care services that are provided but are never expected to result in cash flows. As a result, charity care does not qualify for recognition as receivables or revenue in the financial statements. Distinguishing charity care from bad-debt expense requires the exercise of judgment. Charity care is provided to a patient with demonstrated inability to pay. Each organization establishes its own criteria for charity care consistent with its mission statement and financial ability. Only the portion of a patient's account that meets the organization's charity care criteria is recognized as charity. Although it is not necessary for the entity to make this determination upon admission or registration of an individual, at some point the entity must determine that the individual meets the established criteria for charity care.*

Therefore, charity care is not included on the financial statements.

**72.** **(b)**   According to the AICPA Audit and Accounting Guide, *Health Care Organizations*, "Under provisions of continuing-care contracts entered into by a CCRC and residents, nonrefundable advance fees represent payment for future services and should be accounted for as deferred revenue." Deferred revenue is classified as a liability.

**73.** **(a)**   Patient service revenue is to be reported net of contractual adjustments. Contractual adjustments are the difference between revenue at established rates and the amounts realizable from third-party payors under contractual agreements. Charity care is not part of patient service revenue, and donor contributions are reported separately. Therefore,

|   | | |
|---|---|---|
|   | Gross patient service revenue | $750,000 |
| − | Contractual adjustments | − 63,000 |
| = | Net patient service revenue | $687,000 |

**74.** **(d)** According to the AICPA Audit and Accounting Guide, *Health Care Organizations*, charity care does not qualify for recognition as receivables or revenue in the financial statements. According to the AICPA Audit and Accounting Guide, *Health Care Organizations,* management's policy for providing charity care, as well as the level of charity care provided, should be disclosed in the financial statements. Such disclosure generally is made in the notes to the financial statement and is measured based on the providers' rates, costs, units of service, or other statistical measure.

**75.** **(c)** According to the AICPA Audit and Accounting Guide, *Health Care Organizations*, a hospital's other revenue, gains, and losses are derived from services other than providing health care services or coverage to patients. Other revenue, gains, and losses typically include interest and dividends that are unrestricted as well as proceeds from sales at gift shops and snack bars. Cash contributions from donors that are restricted to the acquisition of capital assets during 2008 are not reported on the statement of operations for 2007. The capital contribution should be reported on the statement of changes in net assets for the year ended December 31, 2007, as an increase in temporarily restricted net assets. Therefore, the amount that Michael should report as other revenue and gains on its statement of operations for 2007 is $100,000.

**76.** **(b)** According to the AICPA Audit and Accounting Guide, *Health Care Organizations*, expirations of donor restrictions on temporarily restricted net assets should be reported on the statement of operations as net assets released from restrictions. On Swathmore's statement of operations for 2007, the use of the $50,000 contribution for research in 2007 should be reported as "net assets released from restrictions." This amount should be included in revenues, gains, and other support on the statement of operations, and it is also included in the "performance indicator" reported on the statement of operations. The use of the $250,000 contribution to acquire a capital asset placed into service during 2007 is also reported as "net assets released from restrictions" on the 2007 statement of operations. This results because the hospital adopted an accounting policy that did not imply a time restriction on gifts of long-lived assets. However, this amount is reported after the performance indicator on the statement of operations. Accordingly, the total amount reported as net assets released from restrictions on the 2007 statement of operations is $300,000.

**77.** **(d)** According to the AICPA Audit and Accounting Guide, *Health Care Organizations*, unrealized gains on trading securities should be included as part of the amount reported for revenue, gains, and other support on the statement of operations. These unrealized gains are included in the performance indicator. Likewise, unrestricted revenues from interest and dividends are included as part of the amount reported for revenue, gains, and other support on the statement of operations. Therefore, Smithson Hospital should report both the $3,000 of interest revenue and the $2,000 unrealized holding gain ($105,000 less $103,000) in the amount reported for revenue, gains, and other support on its statement of operations for the year ended December 31, 2007.

**78.** **(d)** According to the AICPA Audit and Accounting Guide, *Health Care Organizations*, unrealized gains and losses from other than trading securities, which are not restricted by donors, are reported after the performance indicator on the statement of operations. Therefore, the unrealized loss in item I is reported on the statement of operations, but it is not included in the amount reported for revenue and gains over expenses and losses, the performance indicator. The donor contribution that cannot be used until next year is not reported on the statement of operations. The contribution represents an increase in temporarily restricted net assets and is reported on the statement of changes in net assets.

**79.** **(c)** According to the AICPA Audit and Accounting Guide, *Health Care Organizations*, a donation of noncash assets should be reported at fair value and reported as an increase in the appropriate net asset class. If there are no donor-imposed restrictions on the donation, the donation increases unrestricted net assets on the statement of operations. More specifically, the donation is included in the amount reported for revenue, gains, and other support if the donation is used for the operations of the hospital. The use of the donation in the operations of the hospital is reported as part of the operations expenses for the period. The donation of medical supplies to Tucker Hospital should be reported as both a revenue and as an operating expense in the amount of $15,000 on the statement of operations for the year ended December 31, 2007.

**80.** **(b)** The cash flows from revenues, gains, and other support, which are reported on the hospital's statement of operations, would be included in the net cash provided (used) by operating activities on the statement of cash flows. Both net patient service revenue and tuition revenue are included in the amount reported for revenue, gains, and other support on the hospital's statement of operations. Accordingly, cash received from patient service revenue and from tuition revenue are both included in the amount reported for cash flows from operating activities. The cash received for the term endowment as well as the cash received from dividends would not be included in the amount reported for net cash provided (used) by operating activities. Both of these cash receipts would be reported as increases in cash flows provided by financing activities. According to SFAS 117, cash contributions that are donor-restricted for long-term purposes are reported as financing activities on the statement of cash flows. In addition, the AICPA Audit and Accounting Guide, *Health Care Organizations*, states that cash received for long-term purposes, for example, the cash received for the term endowment and the building improvements, is not reported as a current asset. So that the statement of cash flows will reconcile with the change in cash and cash equivalents reported as current assets on the balance sheet, an amount equal to the cash received for the two financing activities is included in the amount reported for cash flows from investing activities. For Wilson Hospital, this would mean that $330,000, the sum of the $250,000 for the term endowment and the $80,000 of restricted dividends, is reported as a negative amount in the investing activities' section of the statement of cash flows. Note that both of these amounts are reported as investing activities whether the cash was spent this period or in subsequent period(s).

**81.** **(d)** The statement of changes in net assets reports the changes in the hospital's unrestricted, temporarily restricted, and permanently restricted net assets for a time period. The statement of operations discloses only the changes in unrestricted net assets for a time period, while the balance sheet discloses the amounts of unrestricted, temporarily restricted, and permanently restricted net assets as of a specific date. Therefore, neither the balance sheet nor the statement of operations discloses the changes in unrestricted, temporarily restricted, and permanently restricted net assets for a time period.

**82.  (c)**   According to the AICPA Audit and Accounting Guide, *Health Care Organizations*, investment returns not restricted by donors are reported on the statement of operations. The statement of operations explains the change in the hospital's unrestricted net assets for a period. Consequently, investment returns that are permanently restricted would not be reported on the statement of operations. Investment returns that are realized in cash are reported on the statement of cash flows. However, investment returns that are not realized in cash are not reported on the statement of cash flows. Investment returns, whether realized or unrealized, that are restricted by donors are reported on the statement of changes in net assets. Unrealized gains on investments that are permanently restricted represent investment returns which would be reported as an increase in permanently restricted net assets on the statement of changes in net assets.

**83.  (b)**   The AICPA Audit and Accounting Guide, *Health Care Organizations,* lists proceeds from sales of cafeteria meals and guest trays to employees, medical staff, and visitors as one of the items reported as other revenue on the statement of operations. Other revenue is included in the performance indicator on the statement of operations. Net assets released from restrictions are also reported in the performance indicator if the net assets are used for operating expenses.

# ARB, APB, AND FASB PRONOUNCEMENTS

## Study Program for the Accounting Pronouncements

Outlines of the unsuperseded official accounting pronouncements are presented in chronological order in this chapter. Effective dates of pronouncements are omitted unless they are a current implementation problem. You should

1. Study through the outlines as you are referred to them in the modules in this chapter
   a. On the exam it is not necessary to know the pronouncement numbers
   b. The outlines presume some prior study of the topics covered by the pronouncements
   c. Note that additional comments have been added to some outlines, relating to the rationale or justification for these standards
2. **Required disclosures.** It is not necessary to memorize all the required disclosures. A good approach is to take the position of a financial analyst: What data would you want to know? Utilizing this approach, you only have to memorize any exceptions (i.e., items you would not normally think a financial analyst would be interested in).

## References to FASB Materials

Each of the outlines in the last part of this chapter is referenced to the section where it is found in the FASB *Accounting Standards—Current Texts: General/ Industry Standards*, John Wiley & Sons, Inc. These references appear in parentheses right after the original pronouncement reference in the heading of each pronouncement outlined. When using either the FASB's Current Text or Original Pronouncements to supplement your study, be sure you have a recent edition (not more than two years old). If your study of intermediate accounting has been recent (within the last two years) or, if longer and you purchase a new intermediate text, it is not likely that you will need them.

In studying the outlines, you might notice that parts of some pronouncements have not been outlined. The reason some sections of the pronouncements are excluded from the outlines is that they have never been tested on the exam. Also, outlines for very specialized pronouncements (e.g., SFAS 50, *Financial Reporting in the Record and Music Industry*) are not included in this manual. Several others are outlined more generally. Only those FASB Interpretations and Technical Bulletins having widespread applicability are included in this chapter. They are set apart with solid lines **only** to distinguish them from the SFAS.

## ACCOUNTING RESEARCH BULLETINS

### ARB 43—Chapter 1A (A31, B50, C08, C23, R36, R70, R75)[1] Rules Adopted by Membership

Four rules recommended by the Committee on Cooperation with Stock Exchanges in 1934. The last rule is from another 1934 Institute committee.

1. Profit is realized at the point of sale unless collection is not reasonably assured.
2. Capital (paid-in) surplus should not be charged with losses or expenses, except in quasi reorganizations.
3. Receivables from officers, employees, and affiliates must be separately disclosed.
4. Par value of stock issued for assets cannot be used to value the assets if some of the stock is subsequently donated back to the corporation.

### Chapter 1B (C23) Profits or Losses on Treasury Stock  (Revised by APB 6)

Profits on treasury stock are not income and should be reflected in capital surplus.

### Chapter 2A (F43) Comparative Financial Statements  (Cross-referenced to APB 20)

Comparative statements enhance the usefulness of financial statements and should be presented.

### Chapter 3A (B05, I78) Current Assets and Current Liabilities

(Amended by APB 6, 21 and SFAS 6)

Chapter 3A contains the definitions and examples of current assets and liabilities.

A. **Current assets** are "cash and other assets or resources commonly identified as those which are reasonably expected to be (1) realized in cash, (2) sold, or (3) consumed during the ordinary operating cycle of the business."
   1. Cash available for current operations
   2. Inventories
   3. Trade receivables

---

[1] *The references in parentheses are from the* **FASB Accounting Standards—Current Texts: Volumes 1 and 2,** *John Wiley & Sons, Inc. These are included only for facilitating the use of the Current Texts for candidates who have access to them.*

4. Other receivables collectible in one year
5. Installment, deferred accounts, and notes receivable
6. Prepaid expenses

**B. Current liabilities** are "obligations whose liquidation is reasonably expected to require the use of existing resources properly classifiable as current assets or the creation of other current liabilities during the ordinary operating cycle of the business."

1. Trade payables
2. Collections received in advance of services
3. Accruals of expenses
4. Other liabilities coming due in one year
5. Note that liabilities not using current assets for liquidation are not current liabilities (e.g., bonds being repaid from a sinking fund)

**C. Operating cycle** is "average time intervening between the acquisition of materials or services entering this process and the final cash realization."

## Chapter 4 (I78) Inventory Pricing (see also SFAS 151)
Contains 10 statements outlining inventory valuation

1. Inventory consists of tangible personal property
   a. Held for sale in ordinary course of business
   b. In process of production for such sale
   c. To be currently consumed in the production of such goods
2. Major objective of inventory valuation is proper income determination
   a. Matching of costs and revenues
3. Primary basis is cost. Cost includes all reasonable and necessary costs of preparing inventory for sale. These costs would include expenditures to bring inventory to existing condition and location.
   a. Direct or variable costing is not acceptable (use absorption costing)
4. Cost may be determined under any flow assumption. Use method which most clearly reflects income.
5. Departure from cost to market required when utility of goods, in their disposal in the ordinary course of business, is not as great as cost.
   a. Write-down recognized as a loss of the current period
   b. Use of lower of cost or market method more fairly reflects income of the period than would the cost method
   c. Results in a more realistic estimate of future cash flows to be realized from the assets
   d. Supported by doctrine of conservatism
6. Market means current replacement cost subject to
   a. Market should not exceed net realizable value (sales price less selling and completion costs)
   b. Market should not be less than net realizable value less normal profit
7. Lower of cost or market may be applied to individual items or the inventory as a whole. Use method that most clearly reflects income.
8. Basis for stating inventories and changes therein should be consistent and disclosed.
9. Inventories may be stated above cost in exceptional cases
   a. No basis for cost allocation (e.g., meatpacking)
   b. Disposal assured and price known (e.g., precious metals)
10. Purchase commitment loss should be recognized in the same manner as inventory losses.

## Chapter 7A (Q15) Quasi Reorganization
Describes what is permitted before and after quasi reorganization.

**A. Procedure in readjustment**
1. A clear report should be made to shareholders to obtain consent for the proposed restatements of assets and shareholders' equity.
2. Write-down of assets should not go below fair value.
3. If potential losses exist, provide for maximum probable loss.
4. When determined, amounts should be written off first to retained earnings and then to capital surplus.

**B. Procedure after readjustment**
1. After readjustment, accounting should be similar to that appropriate for a new company
2. A new, dated retained earnings account should be created
   a. Dated for ten years to indicate when the reorganization occurred.

## Chapter 7B (C20, Q15) Stock Dividends and Stock Splits

A. **Dividend**—evidence given to shareholders of their share of accumulated earnings that are going to be retained in the business

B. **Split**—stock issued to increase number of outstanding shares to reduce market price and/or to obtain a wider distribution of ownership

C. To the recipient, splits and dividends are not income. Dividends and splits take nothing from the property of the corporation and add nothing to the property of the recipient.
   1. Upon receipt of stock dividend or split, recipient should reallocate cost of shares previously held to all shares held.

D. Issuer of a stock dividend (issuance is small in relation to shares outstanding and consequently has no apparent effect on market price) should capitalize retained earnings equal to the fair market value of shares issued.
   1. Unless retained earnings are capitalized, retained earnings thought to be distributed by the recipient will be available for subsequent distribution.
   2. Issuances less than 20-25% of previously outstanding shares are dividends. Issuances greater than 20-25% of previously outstanding shares are splits.
   3. Where stock dividend is so large it may materially affect price (a split effected in the form of a dividend), no capitalization is necessary other than that required by law.
      a. Some jurisdictions require that the par value of splits be capitalized (i.e., changes in par value are not permitted).
   4. For closely held corporations, there is no need to capitalize retained earnings other than to meet legal requirements.

## Chapter 10A (T10) Real and Personal Property Taxes

Accounting for personal and real property taxes which vary in time of determination and collection from state to state

A. In practice, the dates below have been used to apportion taxes between accounting periods.
   1. Assessment date
   2. Beginning of fiscal period of taxing authority
   3. End of fiscal period of taxing authority
   4. Lien date
   5. Date of tax levy
   6. Date tax is payable
   7. Date tax is delinquent
   8. Period appearing on tax bill

B. The most acceptable basis is a monthly accrual on the taxpayer's books during the fiscal period of the taxing authority.
   1. At year-end, the books will show the appropriate prepayment or accrual.
   2. An accrued liability, whether known or estimated, should be shown as a current liability.
   3. On income statement, property taxes may be charged to operating expense, deducted separately from income, prorated among accounts to which they apply, or combined with other taxes (but not with income taxes).

## Chapter 13B (C47) Stock Option Compensation Plans (Also see APB 25 and SFAS 123)

Cost of services received for compensation paid in stock options should be included in operations.

A. Compensation may arise when the corporation agrees to issue common stock to an employee at a stated price.
   1. Other options may result in employee obligations such as continued employment.

B. Stock options do not result in compensation if
   1. Stock options are offered at a reasonable amount to raise capital
   2. Stock options are offered at a reasonable amount to induce wider holdings by employees

C. Date of grant should be used for measurement
   1. Considering the date of grant as a contract, it is the date value is determined
   2. Date of grant is date corporation foregoes alternative use
   3. Adoption date and grantee's disposition date are not relevant

**D.** Compensation cost should be spread over the period of service covered by the option contract.
  1. Cash and compensation are equal to consideration for the stock when exercised (amount credited to stock and paid-in capital).
**E.** Disclosure should be made annually of
  1. Number of shares under option
  2. Option price
  3. Number of shares exercisable
  4. Number of shares and price of options exercised

## ARB 45 (Co4) Long-Term Construction Contracts
Discusses accounting for multiple-period projects
**A.** The percentage-of-completion method recognizes income as work progresses.
  1. Recognized income based upon a percentage of estimated total income
     a. (Incurred costs to date)/(Total expected costs) known as cost-to-cost measure
     b. Other measure of progress based on work performed (e.g., engineering or architectural estimate)
  2. Costs, for percentage-of-completion estimate, might exclude materials and subcontracts, especially in the early stages of a contract.
     a. Avoids overstating the percentage-of-completion
  3. If a loss is estimated on the contract, the **entire loss** should be recognized currently.
  4. Contracts should be separated into net assets and net liabilities.
     a. Current assets include costs and income (loss) in excess of billings.
     b. Current liabilities include billings in excess of costs and income (loss).
     c. Contracts should not be offset on the balance sheet.
  5. Advantages of percentage-of-completion are periodic recognition of income and reflection of the status of the contract.
     a. Results in appropriate matching of costs and revenues
     b. Avoids distortions in income from year to year and thus provides more relevant information to financial statement users
  6. The principal disadvantage is the reliance on estimates.
  7. The percentage-of-completion method is required when total costs and percent of completion can be reasonably estimated.
**B.** The completed-contract method recognizes income when the contract is complete.
  1. General and administrative expenses can be allocated to contracts.
     a. Not necessary if many projects are in process
     b. No excessive deferring of costs
  2. Provision should be made for **entire amount of any expected loss** prior to job completion.
     a. That is, losses are recognized immediately in their entirety—conservative treatment
  3. An excess of accumulated costs over related billings is a current asset. An excess of accumulated billings over related costs is a liability (current in most cases).
     a. Balance sheet accounts are determined as in A.4., except no income is included
     b. Recognized losses in B.2. reduce accumulated costs.
  4. The advantage of the completed-contract method is that it is based on final results, and its primary disadvantage is that it does not reflect current performance.
     a. Overall, the completed-contract method represents a conservative approach.

## ARB 51 (B50, C20, C51, R70) Consolidated Financial Statements (Also see SFAS 141)
 (Amended by SFAS 94)
**A.** Consolidated statements present financial statements of a parent and subsidiaries, as if the group were a single company for the benefit of the parent's stockholders and creditors.
  1. **Substance** (effectively a single entity) takes precedence over **legal form** (legally separate entities).
  2. Consolidated financial statements result in **more meaningful presentation of financial position and operating results** than if separate statements were presented for the parent and subsidiary.
**B.** The general condition for consolidation is over 50% ownership of subsidiaries.
  1. Theoretical condition is **control** of the subsidiaries.
     a. This is generally implicit in greater than 50% ownership.

2. Subsidiaries that are a temporary investment (in reorganization, in bankruptcy, etc.) should not be consolidated.
3. Large indebtedness to bondholders should not preclude consolidation.

---

**FASB INTERPRETATION NO. 46 CONSOLIDATION OF VARIABLE INTEREST ENTITIES**
Variable interest entities are entities that must be consolidated because they do not have sufficient funding to finance their future activities without the infusion of additional subordinated investment. Entities are presumed to be variable interest entities subject to consolidation if their equity is less than ten percent of total assets. To avoid consolidation of such entities, definitive evidence must be provided that they can fund their future activities without additional subordinated investment. Entities with equity of ten percent or more of total assets may also be a variable interest entity if it appears that the entity will not be able to fund its activities without obtaining additional subordinated investment. A variable interest entity is consolidated by the primary beneficiary, which is the enterprise that is obligated to fund the majority of the variable interest entity's expected losses if they occur, or will receive the majority of the residual returns if they occur, or both.

---

C. A difference in fiscal periods should not preclude consolidation.
  1. Differences of three months are acceptable if one discloses material intervening events.
  2. Differences in excess of three months should be consolidated on the basis of interim statements of the subsidiary.
D. Consolidation policy should be disclosed by headings or footnotes.
E. Intercompany balances and transactions should be eliminated in consolidated statements.
  1. Intercompany gains and losses on assets remaining in the group should be eliminated (eliminate entire gross profit or loss even on transactions with minority interest subsidiaries).
F. Retained earnings of subsidiaries at the acquisition date should not appear in the consolidated statements.
G. When a parent purchases a subsidiary in several blocks of stock, the subsidiary's retained earnings should be determined by the step method (apply equity method to subsidiary retroactively).
H. When a subsidiary is purchased in midyear, subsidiary operations may be included in the consolidated income statement for the year and then the operating results prior to acquisition would be deducted.
  1. As an alternative for a subsidiary purchased in midyear, postacquisition operations can be included in the consolidated income statement.
  2. For midyear disposals, omit operations from the consolidated income statement and include equity in subsidiary's operations up to disposal date as a separate item in the income statement.

*NOTE: F. through H. pertain only to acquisitions accounted for as purchases per APB 16.*

I. Sometimes combined, as distinguished from consolidated, financial statements are appropriate for commonly owned companies and are prepared when consolidated statements are not appropriate.

## ACCOUNTING PRINCIPLES BOARD OPINIONS

### APB 6 (B05, C23, D40, I60) Status of Accounting Research Bulletins
A. ARB 43, Chapter 1B Treasury Stock
  1. An excess of purchase price of treasury stock, purchased for retirement or constructive retirement, over par or stated value may be allocated between paid-in capital and retained earnings.
    a. The charge to paid-in capital is limited to all paid-in capital from treasury stock transactions and retirements of the same issue and a pro rata portion of all other paid-in capital of that issue.
    b. Also, paid-in capital applicable to fully retired issues may be charged.
  2. Alternatively, losses may be charged entirely to retained earnings.
  3. All gains on retirement of treasury stock go to paid-in capital.
  4. When the decision to retire treasury stock has not been made, the cost of such is a contra shareholders' equity item. Losses may only be charged to paid-in capital from treasury transactions and retirements of the same issue.
  5. Some state laws prescribe accounting for treasury stock. The laws are to be followed where they are at variance with this APB. Disclose all statutory requirements concerning treasury stock such as dividend restrictions.

**B.** ARB 43, Chapter 3A   Current Assets and Liabilities
Unearned interest, finance charges, etc. included in receivables should be deducted from the related receivable.

**C.** ARB 43, Chapter 7B   Stock Dividends and Splits
States "the shareholder has no income solely as a result of the fact that the corporation has income," but does not preclude use of the equity method.

## APB 9 (I17, C08) Reporting the Results of Operations

**A.** Designates a new format for income statement in which all normal operating items would be presented at the top of the income statement resulting in "net income before extraordinary items."
   1. "Net income before extraordinary items" is followed by extraordinary items resulting in "net income."

**B.** "Prior period adjustments" are excluded from the income statement and constitute adjustments of beginning retained earnings disclosed at the top of the retained earnings statement. (See SFAS 16.)
   1. Beginning retained earnings are adjusted by "prior period adjustments" resulting in "restated beginning retained earnings."
   2. "Restated retained earnings" is then adjusted for net income and dividends which results in ending retained earnings.

**C.** Prior period adjustments should be disclosed in the period of adjustment.
   1. The effect on each prior period presented should be disclosed including restated income taxes.
   2. Disclosure in subsequent periods is not normally required.
   3. Historical summary data should also be restated and disclosed in the period of adjustment.

**D.** The APB also reaffirmed earlier positions that the following should not affect determination of net income:
   1. Transactions in the company's own stock
   2. Transfers to or from retained earnings
   3. Quasi reorganization adjustments

## APB 10 (A35, B10, C16, I24, I25, I28, R75) Omnibus Opinion—1966

**A.** ARB 43, Chapter 3B   Working Capital
   1. Offsetting of liabilities and assets in the balance sheet is not acceptable unless a right of offset exists.
   2. Most government securities are not designed to be prepayment of taxes and thus may not be offset against tax liabilities. Only where an explicit prepayment exists may an offset be used.

---

FASB INTERPRETATION NO. 39   OFFSETTING OF AMOUNTS RELATED TO CERTAIN CONTRACTS

    A right of setoff exists when all of the following conditions are met: (a) each of the two parties to a contract owes the other determinable amounts, (b) the reporting entity has the right to set off the amount owed with the amount owed by the other entity, (c) the reporting entity intends to set off, and (d) the right of setoff is enforceable at law.

---

**B.** Installment method of accounting
Revenues should be recognized at the point of sale unless receivables are in doubt. The installment or cost recovery method may be used.

## APB 12 (C08, C38, D40, I69, V18) Omnibus Opinion—1967

**A.** Allowance or contra accounts (allowance for bad debts, accumulated depreciation, etc.) should be deducted from assets or groups of assets with appropriate disclosure.

**B.** Disclosure of depreciable assets should include
   1. Depreciation expense for the period
   2. Balances of major classes of depreciable assets by nature or function
   3. Accumulated depreciation either by major class or in total
   4. Description of method(s) of depreciation by major classes of assets

**C.** Changes in the separate shareholder equity accounts in addition to retained earnings and changes in number of equity securities must be disclosed in the year of change
   1. In separate statements
   2. Or the financial statements
   3. Or the notes

## APB 14 (D10, C08) Convertible Debt and Debt Issued with Stock Warrants

**A.** Convertible debt constitutes securities which are convertible into common stock of the user or affiliate. Terms generally include
   1. Lower interest rate than on ordinary debt
   2. Initial conversion price greater than the common price at time of issuance
   3. A conversion price which does not decrease except to protect against dilution

**B.** While there are arguments to account for the debt and equity characteristics separately, the APB has concluded no proceeds of a convertible issue should be attributed to the conversion factor.
   1. Primary **reasons** are
      a. The inseparability of the debt and conversion features
      b. The practical difficulties of valuing the conversion feature

**C.** When debt is issued with detachable purchase warrants, the debt and warrants generally trade separately and should be treated separately.
   1. The allocation of proceeds should be based on relative market value at date of issuance.
   2. Any resulting debt discount or premium should be accounted for as such.

**D.** Separate valuation of debt and warrants is applicable where the debt may be used as consideration when exercising the warrants. Separate valuation is **not** acceptable where the debt must be tendered to exercise the warrants (i.e., the warrants are, in essence, nondetachable).

## APB 18 (I82) The Equity Method for Investments

**A.** The equity method should be used for corporate joint ventures.

**B.** The equity method should be applied to investments where less than 50% ownership is held but the investor **can exercise significant influence over operating and financing policies of the investee**.
   1. Twenty percent (20%) or more ownership should lead to presumption of substantial influence, unless there is evidence to the contrary.
   2. Conversely, less than 20% ownership leads to the presumption of no substantial influence unless there is evidence to the contrary.
   3. The 20% test should be based on voting stock outstanding and disregard common stock equivalents.
   4. The following procedures should be used in applying the equity method:
      a. Intercompany profits should be eliminated.
      b. Difference between cost and book value of net assets acquired should be accounted for per SFAS 141 and 142.
      c. The investment account and investor's share of investee income should be presented as single amounts in investor statements with the exception of d. below.
      d. Investor's share of discontinued operations, extraordinary items, cumulative effects of accounting changes, and prior period adjustments of investee should be so presented in statements of investor.
      e. Investee capital transactions should be accounted for as are subsidiary capital transactions in consolidated statements.
      f. Gains on sale of investment are the difference between selling price and carrying value of investment.
      g. When investee and investor fiscal periods do not coincide, use most recent investee statement and have consistent time lag.
      h. Losses, not temporary in nature, of investment value should be recognized by investor.
      i. Investor's share of investee loss should not be recorded once investment account is written to zero. Subsequent income should be recognized after losses not recognized are made up.
      j. Investor's share of investee's earnings should be computed after deducting investee's cumulative preferred dividends whether declared or not.
      k. If an investor's holding falls below 20%, discontinue applying the equity method but make no retroactive adjustment.

l.  When an investor's holding increases from a level less than 20% to a level equal to or greater than 20%, the investment account and retained earnings of the investor should be adjusted retroactively to reflect balances as if the equity account had been used.  This is accounted for like a prior period adjustment.

5.  Statements of investors applying the equity method should disclose
   a.  Investees and percentages held
      (1)  Accounting policies followed
      (2)  Treatment of goodwill, if any
   b.  Aggregate market value of investment (not for subsidiaries)
   c.  When investments are material to investor, summarized information of assets, liabilities, and results of operations of investee may be necessary
   d.  Conversion of securities, exercise of warrants, or issuances of investee's common stock which significantly affects investor's share of investee's income

---

FASB INTERPRETATION NO. 35  CRITERIA FOR APPLYING THE EQUITY METHOD OF ACCOUNTING FOR INVESTMENTS IN COMMON STOCK.  Interprets APB 18.

Investors owning between 20 and 50 percent of an investee may **not** be able to exercise significant influence over the investee's operating and financial policies.  The presumption of significant influence stands until overcome by evidence to the contrary, such as:  (1) opposition by the investee, (2) agreements under which the investor surrenders shareholder rights, (3) majority ownership by a small group of shareholders, (4) inability to obtain desired information from the investee, (5) inability to obtain representation on investee board of directors, etc.  Whether contrary evidence is sufficient to negate the presumption of significant influence is a matter of judgment requiring a careful evaluation of all pertinent facts and circumstances, in some cases over an extended period of time.  Application of this interpretation resulting in changes to or from the equity method shall be treated per APB 18, paras 19l and 19m.

---

FASB INTERPRETATION NO. 1  ACCOUNTING CHANGES RELATED TO THE COST OF INVENTORY

Changes in the cost composition of inventory is an accounting change and must conform to APB 20, including justification for the change.  Preferably should be based on financial reporting objectives rather than tax-related benefits.

---

## APB 21 (I69) Interest on Receivables and Payables

Accounting for receivables and payables whose face value does not approximate their present value

A.  Applies to receivables and payables except
   1.  Normal course of business receivables and payables maturing in less than one year
   2.  Amounts not requiring repayment in the future (will be applied to future purchases or sales)
   3.  Security deposits and retainages
   4.  Customary transactions of those whose primary business is lending money
   5.  Transactions where interest rates are tax affected or legally prescribed (e.g., municipal bonds and tax settlements)
   6.  Parent-subsidiary transactions
   7.  Estimates of contractual obligations such as warranties

B.  Notes exchanged for cash are recorded at their present value.  Present value equals the cash paid/received.  If face value of note ≠ cash paid/received, difference is a discount/premium.
   1.  If **unstated rights or privileges** are exchanged in issuance of note for cash, adjust cash payment to obtain present value of the note and unstated rights.

C.  Notes exchanged for **goods or services** in arm's-length transaction are recorded at face amount (presumption that face amount = present value).
   1.  Presumption not valid if note is
      a.  Noninterest-bearing
      b.  Stated interest rate is unreasonable
      c.  Face amount of the note differs materially from sales price of goods or services

2. When presumption not valid, record note at fair value of goods or services
   a. Compute **implicit** rate (rate that discounts the future value [face of note plus cash interest, if any] to fair value of goods and services) for interest expense/revenue recognition
3. When no established market price for goods and services exists, record note at its fair market value.
   a. Compute **implicit** rate (rate that discounts the future value [face of note plus cash interest, if any] to fair [present] value of note) for interest expense/revenue recognition
4. When no fair market value exists for either the goods and services or the note, record note at approximation of market value.
   a. Use **imputed** rate to compute present value of (and discount on) note.
   b. Imputed rate should approximate the rate an independent borrower and lender would negotiate in a similar transaction. Consider
      (1) Credit standing of issuer
      (2) Restrictive covenants
      (3) Collateral
      (4) Payment and other terms
      (5) Tax consequences to buyer and seller
      (6) Market rate for sale or assignment
      (7) Prime rate
      (8) Published rates of similar bonds
      (9) Current rates charged for mortgages on similar property
D. Discount or premium should be amortized by the interest method (constant rate of interest on the amount outstanding).
   1. Other methods (e.g., straight-line) may be used if the results are not materially different from those of the interest method.
E. Discount or premium should be netted with the related asset or liability and **not** shown as separate asset or liability.
   1. Issue costs should be reported as deferred charges.

## APB 22 (A10) Disclosure of Accounting Policies

A. Accounting policies can affect reported results significantly and the usefulness of the financial statements depends on the user's understanding of the accounting policies adopted by the reporting entity. Disclosure of accounting policies are
   1. Essential to users
   2. Integral part of financial statements
   3. Required for one or more financial statements
   4. Required for not-for-profit entities
   5. Not required for unaudited interim statements
      a. If no change in accounting policy has occurred
B. Disclosure should include accounting principles and methods of applying them if material to reported amounts.
   1. Generally, disclosure pertinent to principles involving recognition of revenue and expense
   2. Specifically, disclosure pertinent to
      a. Selection from existing alternatives
      b. Principles peculiar to a particular industry
      c. Unusual or innovative applications
   3. Examples
      a. Consolidation method
      b. Depreciation method
      c. Amortization of intangibles
      d. Inventory pricing
      e. R&D references amended by SFAS 2
      f. Translation of foreign currencies
      g. Long-term contract accounting
      h. Franchising and leasing activities
   4. Accounting policy disclosure should not duplicate disclosures elsewhere in the statements.

C. Particularly useful is a separate **Summary of Significant Accounting Policies** either preceding or as the initial note.

## APB 23 (I25, I42, and B17) Accounting for Income Taxes—Special Areas
(Amended by SFAS 109)
A. Undistributed earnings of domestic subsidiaries
1. Inclusion of undistributed earnings in pretax accounting income of parent (either through consolidation or equity method) results in temporary difference.
a. Tax effect may be based on assumptions such as
(1) Earnings would be distributed currently as dividends or
(2) Earnings would be distributed in form of capital gain.
B. Foreign subsidiaries are not required to accrue deferred taxes for undistributed earnings if sufficient evidence exists that subsidiary would reinvest the undistributed earnings indefinitely or remit them tax free.

## APB 25 (C47) Accounting for Stock Issued to Employees—Superseded by SFAS 123(R)

FASB INTERPRETATION NO. 28 ACCOUNTING FOR STOCK APPRECIATION RIGHTS AND OTHER VARIABLE STOCK OPTION OR AWARD PLANS
Changes in the market value of stock between the date of the grant and the measurement date (the date both the number of shares and the option price are known) are adjustments to compensation expense in the period the market value of the stock changes.

## APB 26 (D14) Early Extinguishment of Debt
(Amended by SFAS 84 and SFAS 145)
A. Definitions
1. **Net carrying amount.** "Amount due at maturity, adjusted for unamortized premium, discount, and cost of issuance."
2. **Reacquisition price.** "Amount paid on extinguishment, including a call premium and miscellaneous costs of reacquisition."
3. **Refunding.** Replacement of debt with other debt
B. Retirement is usually achieved by use of liquid assets.
1. Currently in existence
2. From sale of equity securities
3. From sale of debt securities
C. A **difference** between **reacquisition price** and **net carrying amount** of the extinguished debt should be recognized in the year of extinguishment as a separate item.
1. Gains and losses should not be amortized to future years.
2. Gains and losses are ordinary.

## APB 28 (I73) Interim Financial Reporting
(Amended by SFAS 3, FASB Interpretation 18)
## PART I Application of GAAP to Interim Periods
A. APB faced basic question about interim periods
1. Are interim periods basic accounting periods?
2. Are interim periods integral parts of the annual period?
B. The APB decided interim periods are an **integral part of an annual period**.
1. Certain GAAP must be modified for interim reporting to better relate the interim period to the annual period.
C. Revenue should be recognized on the same basis as for the annual period.
D. Costs directly associated with revenue should be reported as in annual periods with the following **exceptions:**
1. Estimated gross profit rates may be used to estimate inventory. Disclose method used and significant adjustments to reconcile to later physical inventory.
2. When LIFO base period inventories are liquidated during the interim period but are expected to be replaced by the end of the annual period, cost of sales should be priced at replacement costs rather than at base period costs.

3.   Declines in inventory market values, unless temporary, should be recognized.  Subsequent recovery of market value should be recognized as a cost recovery in the subsequent period.
4.   Unanticipated and unplanned standard cost variances should be recognized in the respective interim period.

E.   The objective of reporting all other costs is to obtain fair measure of operations for the annual period. These expenses include
1.   Direct expenditures—salaries
2.   Accruals—vacation pay
3.   Amortization of deferrals—insurance

F.   These costs should be applied in interim statements as follows:
1.   Charge to income as incurred, or based on time expiration, benefit received, etc.  Follow procedures used in annual reports.
2.   Items not identified with specific period are charged as incurred.
3.   No arbitrary assignment.
4.   Gains and losses of any interim period that would not be deferred at year-end cannot be deferred in the interim period.
5.   Costs frequently subjected to year-end adjustments should be anticipated in the interim periods.
   a.   Inventory shrinkage
   b.   Allowance for uncollectibles, quantity discounts
   c.   Discretionary year-end bonuses

G.   Seasonal variations in above items require disclosure and one may add twelve-month reports ending at the interim date for current and preceding years.

H.   The best estimate of the annual tax rate should be used to provide taxes on a year-to-date basis.
1.   The best estimate should take investment credits, capital gains, etc. into account, but not extraordinary items.
2.   Tax effects of losses in early portion of the year should not be recognized unless realization in subsequent interim periods is assured beyond a reasonable doubt (e.g., an established pattern of loss in early periods).
   a.   When tax effects of losses in early periods are not recognized, no taxes should be accrued in later periods until loss credit has been used.

I.   Extraordinary items should be disclosed separately and recognized in the interim period in which they occur.
1.   The materiality of extraordinary items should be determined in relation to expected annual income.
2.   Effects of disposals of a component of a business are not extraordinary items, but should be disclosed separately.
3.   Extraordinary items should **not** be prorated over remainder of the year.
4.   Contingencies should be disclosed in the same manner as required in annual reports.

J.   Each interim report should disclose any change in accounting principle from
1.   Comparable period of prior year
2.   Preceding periods of current year
3.   Prior annual report

K.   Reporting these changes
1.   SFAS 154 should be applied.
2.   A change in accounting estimate (including effect on estimated tax rate) should be accounted for in period of change and disclosed in subsequent periods if material.
3.   Changes in principle should be given retrospective application.  Financial statements are retrospectively adjusted showing the effects of the change on the carrying amounts of assets and liabilities for the earliest period presented, with an adjustment to beginning retained earnings for that period.  Period-specific effects of the change should be shown for all direct effects of the change.

**PART II Required Interim Disclosures by Publicly Traded Companies**

A.   Minimum disclosure includes
1.   Sales, provision for taxes, extraordinary items, cumulative effect of principle changes, and net income
2.   BEPS and DEPS
3.   Seasonal revenue, costs, and expenses
4.   Significant changes in estimates of taxes

5. Disposal of a business component and extraordinary items
6. Contingent items
7. Changes in accounting principles and estimates
8. Significant changes in financial position
9. Reportable operating segments
   a. External revenues
   b. Intersegment revenues
   c. Segment profit/loss
   d. Total assets (if material change from last annual report)
   e. Description of changes from last annual report in method of determining segments or measurement of segment profit/loss
   f. Reconciliation of total of reportable segments' profit/loss to corresponding enterprise amount
**B.** When **summarized interim data** are reported regularly, the above should be reported for the
1. Current quarter
2. Current year-to-date or last twelve months with comparable data for the preceding year
**C.** If fourth quarter data are not separately reported, disclose in annual report
1. Disposal of business component
2. Extraordinary, unusual, and infrequent items
3. Aggregate year-end adjustments
**D.** The APB encourages interim disclosure of financial position and funds flow data.
1. If not disclosed, significant changes therein should be disclosed.

---

## FASB INTERPRETATION NO. 18  ACCOUNTING FOR INCOME TAXES IN INTERIM PERIODS
Tax on income from continuing operations for an interim period is based on estimated annual effective rate, which reflects anticipated tax planning alternatives. Expense of interim period is (Year-to-date income) x (Estimated rate) less (Expense recognized in prior interim periods). Tax effect of special items (below continuing operations) computed as they occur.

---

## APB 29 (N35, C11) Accounting for Nonmonetary Transactions (see SFAS 153)
**A.** Definitions
1. **Monetary assets and liabilities.** "Assets and liabilities whose amounts are fixed in terms of units of currency by contract or otherwise. Examples are cash, short- or long-term accounts and notes receivable in cash, and short- or long-term accounts and notes payable in cash."
2. **Nonmonetary assets and liabilities.** "Assets and liabilities other than monetary ones. Examples are inventories; investments in common stocks; property, plant and equipment; and liabilities for rent collected in advance."
3. **Exchange.** "A reciprocal transfer between an enterprise and another entity that results in the enterprise's acquiring assets or services or satisfying liabilities by surrendering other assets or services or incurring other obligations. A reciprocal transfer of a nonmonetary asset shall be deemed an exchange only if the transferor has no substantial continuing involvement in the transferred asset such that the usual risks and rewards of ownership of the asset are transferred."
4. **Nonreciprocal transfer.** "Transfer of assets or services in one direction, either from an enterprise to its owners (whether or not in exchange for their ownership interests) or another entity or from owners or another entity to enterprise. An entity's reacquisition of its outstanding stock is an example of a nonreciprocal transfer."
5. **Productive assets.** "Assets held for or used in the production of goods or services by the enterprise. Productive assets include an investment in another entity if the investment is accounted for by the equity method but exclude an investment not accounted for by that method."
**B.** APB 29 does **not** apply to
1. Business combinations
2. Transfer of nonmonetary assets between companies under common control
3. Acquisition of nonmonetary assets with capital stock of an enterprise
4. Stock dividends and splits, issued or received
5. A transfer of assets for an equity interest
6. A transfer of a financial asset under SFAS 140

**C.** APB 29 does apply to
   1. Nonreciprocal transfers with owners. Examples are distributions to stockholders
     a. Dividends
     b. To redeem capital stock
     c. In liquidation
     d. To settle rescission of a business combination
   2. Nonreciprocal transfer with other than owners. Examples are
     a. Contribution to charitable institutions
     b. Contribution of land by governmental unit to a business
   3. Nonmonetary exchange

**D.** Nonmonetary transactions should generally be accounted for as are monetary transactions.
   1. Cost of a nonmonetary asset is the fair value of the asset surrendered to obtain it.
     a. The difference between fair value and book value is a gain or loss.
     b. Fair value of asset received, if clearer than that of asset given, should value transaction.
   2. Recorded (book) value shall be used for exchanges in which
     a. Fair value is not determinable
     b. Exchange transaction is to facilitate sales to customers
     c. Exchange transaction lacks commercial substance
   3. A nonmonetary transaction has commercial substance if the entity's future cash flows are expected to significantly change as a result of the exchange. Tax cash flows that arise solely because the tax business purpose is based on achieving a specified financial reporting result are not considered in cash flows.

**E.** If a nonmonetary exchange, which is recorded at book value, contains boot received, the portion of the gain recognized should be limited to the ratio [Boot ÷ (Boot received + FMV of asset received)] times the gain.
   1. Firm paying boot should not recognize gain.

**F.** Liquidation distributions to owners should **not** be accounted for at fair value if a gain results (loss may be recognized).
   1. Use historical cost
   2. Other nonreciprocal distributions to owners should be accounted for at fair value if fair value
     a. Is objectively measurable
     b. Would be clearly realizable if sold

**G.** Fair value should be determined in accordance with SFAS 157, *Fair Value Measurements*
   1. If one party could elect to receive cash instead of monetary asset, the amount of cash is evidence of fair value

**H.** Nonmonetary transaction disclosures should include
   1. Nature of the transactions
   2. Basis of accounting
   3. Gains and losses recognized

---

**FASB INTERPRETATION NO. 30 ACCOUNTING FOR INVOLUNTARY CONVERSIONS OF NONMONETARY ASSETS TO MONETARY ASSETS**
   When involuntary conversions of nonmonetary assets (e.g., fixed assets) to monetary assets (e.g., insurance proceeds) occur, the difference between the assets' cost and the monetary assets received should be reported as a gain or loss. If an unknown amount of monetary assets are to be received in a later period, gain (loss) is estimated per SFAS 5. Could be extraordinary per APB 30.

---

### APB 30 (E09, I13, I17, I22) Reporting the Results of Operations
(Amended by SFAS 144)
**A.** Extraordinary items are **both** unusual and infrequent.
   1. **Unusual nature.** "The underlying event or transaction should possess a high degree of abnormality and be of a type clearly unrelated to, or only incidentally related to, the ordinary and typical activities of the entity, taking into account the environment in which the entity operates."
     a. Special characteristics of the entity
       (1) Type and scope of operations

(2) Lines of business

(3) Operating policies

2. **Infrequency of occurrence.** "The underlying event or transaction should be of a type that would not reasonably be expected to recur in the foreseeable future, taking into account the environment in which the entity operates."

3. Example of extraordinary presentation

| | |
|---|---|
| Income before extraordinary items ...................................................... | $xxx |
| Extraordinary items (less applicable income taxes of $___) (Note ___) . | xxx |
| Net income.................................................................................... | $xxx |

4. Examples of gains and losses that are **not** generally extraordinary
   a. Write-downs or write-offs of receivables, inventories, R&D, etc.
   b. Translation of foreign exchange including major devaluations
   c. Disposal of a component of a business
   d. Sale of productive assets
   e. Effects of strikes
   f. Accruals on long-term contracts

5. Extraordinary items should be classified separately if material on an individual basis.

6. Gains or losses that are unusual **or** infrequent but not both should be disclosed separately (but not net of tax) in the income statement or notes.

## STATEMENTS OF FINANCIAL ACCOUNTING STANDARDS

### SFAS 2 (Co2, R50) Accounting for Research and Development Costs (R&D)

A. Establishes accounting standards for R&D costs with objective of reducing alternative practices. In summary, all R&D costs are expensed except intangible assets purchased from others and tangible assets that have alternative future uses (which are capitalized and depreciated or amortized as R&D expense).

1. SFAS 2 specifies
   a. R&D activities
   b. Elements of R&D costs
   c. Accounting for R&D costs
   d. Required disclosures for R&D

2. SFAS 2 does not cover
   a. R&D conducted for others under contract
   b. Activities unique to extractive industries

B. R&D activities

1. Research is "planned search or critical investigation aimed at discovery of new knowledge with the hope that such knowledge will be useful in developing a new product or service or a new process or technique in bringing about a significant improvement to an existing product or process."

2. Development is "the translation of research findings or other knowledge into a plan or design for a new product or process or for a significant improvement to an existing product or process whether intended for sale or use."

3. R&D examples
   a. Laboratory research to discover new knowledge
      (1) Seeking applications for new research findings
   b. Formulation and design of product alternatives
      (1) Testing for product alternatives
      (2) Modification of products or processes
   c. Preproduction prototypes and models
      (1) Tools, dies, etc. for new technology
      (2) Pilot plants not capable of commercial production
   d. Engineering activity until product is ready for manufacture

4. Exclusions from R&D
   a. Engineering during an early phase of commercial production
   b. Quality control for commercial production
   c. Troubleshooting during commercial production breakdowns
   d. Routine, ongoing efforts to improve products

    e.  Adaptation of existing capability for a specific customer or other requirements
    f.  Seasonal design changes to products
    g.  Routine design of tools, dies, etc.
    h.  Design, construction, startup, etc. of equipment except that used solely for R&D
    i.  Legal work for patents or litigation
    j.  Items a. - h. above are normally expensed but not as R&D; i. is capitalized

**C.** Elements of R&D costs
  1.  Materials, equipment, and facilities
    a.  If acquired for a specific R&D project and have no alternative use
    b.  If there are alternative uses, costs should be capitalized
      (1)  Charge to R&D as these materials, etc., are used
  2.  Salaries, wages, and related costs
  3.  Intangibles purchased from others are treated as materials, etc. in 1. above
    a.  If capitalized, amortization is covered by APB 17
  4.  R&D services **performed by others**
  5.  A reasonable allocation of indirect costs
    a.  Exclude general and administrative costs not clearly related to R&D

**D.** Accounting for R&D
  1.  Expense R&D as incurred

**E.** Disclosure required on face of IS or notes
  1.  Total R&D expensed per period

**SFAS 5 (C59, I50, In6, R70) Accounting for Contingencies** (Supersedes Chapter 6, ARB 43, ARB 50)
**A.** Contingency is "an existing condition, situation, or set of circumstances involving uncertainty as to possible gain (loss) to an enterprise that will ultimately be resolved when one or more future events occur or fail to occur."
  1.  Definitions
    a.  Probable—future events are likely to occur
    b.  Reasonably possible—chance of occurrence is more than remote, but less than likely
    c.  Remote—chance of occurrence is slight
  2.  Loss contingency examples
    a.  Receivable collection
    b.  Product warranty obligations
    c.  Risk of property losses by fire, explosion, etc.
    d.  Asset expropriation threat
    e.  Pending, threatened, etc., litigation
    f.  Actual or possible claims and assessments
    g.  Catastrophe losses faced by insurance companies
    h.  Guarantees of indebtedness of others
    i.  Banks' obligations under "standby letters of credit"
    j.  Agreements to repurchase receivables, related property, etc. that have been sold

**B.** Estimated loss from contingencies shall be accrued and charged to income when
  1.  It is probable (at balance sheet date) that an asset has been impaired or liability incurred
  2.  **And** the amount of loss can be reasonably estimated
    a.  Difference between estimate recorded and actual amount determined in subsequent period is a change in accounting estimate

**C.** Loss contingency disclosures
  1.  Nature and amount of material items
  2.  Nonaccrued loss contingencies for which a reasonable possibility of loss exists
    a.  Disclose nature of contingency
    b.  Estimate possible range of loss
      (1)  Or state estimate cannot be made
  3.  If a loss contingency develops after year-end, but before statements are issued, disclosure of the nature of the contingency and amount may be necessary.
    a.  If a year-end contingency results in a loss before issuance of the statements, disclosure (possibly pro forma amounts) may be necessary.

4. Disclose nature and amount of the following loss contingencies (even if remote)
   a. Guarantees of others' debts
   b. Standby letters of credit by banks
   c. Agreements to repurchase receivables
**D.** General, unspecified risks are not contingencies.
**E.** Appropriation of RE for contingencies shown within shareholders' equity is not prohibited.
   1. Cannot be shown outside shareholders' equity
   2. Contingency costs and losses cannot be charged to appropriation.
**F.** Gain contingency accounting
   1. Normally not reflected in accounts until realized.
   2. Adequate disclosure should be made without misleading implications of likelihood of realization.
**G.** Rationale for accounting for contingencies per SFAS 5
   1. Reflects **conservatism**—recognize losses immediately (if probable and reasonably estimable), but recognize gains only when realized.
   2. Results in better matching—contingent losses are recognized in time period of origin.

---

## FASB INTERPRETATION NO. 14  REASONABLE ESTIMATION OF THE AMOUNT OF LOSS

A range of the amount of a loss is sufficient to meet the criteria of SFAS 5 that the amount of loss be "subject to reasonable estimate." When one amount in the range is a better estimate, use it; otherwise, use the minimum of the range and disclose range.

---

## STATEMENTS OF POSITION NO. 96-1  ENVIRONMENTAL REMEDIATION LIABILITIES

This SOP includes accounting guidance, preceded by a very detailed description of relevant laws, remediation laws, remediation provisions and other pertinent information, useful to auditors as well as clients. Auditing guidance is limited to recitation of SFAS 5 concerns about reasonable estimation of loss accruals.

Accounting guidance includes the following provisions:

**A.** Interprets SFAS 5 in the context of environmental obligations (e.g., threshold for accrual of liability, etc.) and sets "benchmarks" for recognition.
**B.** Benchmarks for accrual and evaluation of estimated liability (stages which are deemed to be important to ascertaining the existence and amount of the liability) are
   1. Identification and verification of an entity as a potentially responsible party (PRP), since the proposal stipulated that accrual should be based on premise that expected costs will be borne by only the "participating potentially responsible parties" and that the "recalcitrant, unproven and unidentified" PRP will not contribute to costs of remediation
   2. Receipt of unilateral administrative order
   3. Participation, as a PRP, in the remedial investigation/feasibility study (RI/FS)
   4. Completion of the feasibility study
   5. Issuance of the Record of Decision (ROD)
   6. Remedial design through operation and maintenance, including postremediation monitoring
**C.** The amount of liability is affected by
   1. The entity's allocable share of liability for a specified site; and
   2. Its share of the amounts related to the site that will not be paid by the other PRP or the government
**D.** Costs to be included in the accrued liability are
   1. Incremental direct costs of the remediation effort itself; and
      a. Fees to outside law firms for work related to the remediation effort
      b. Costs relating to completing the RI/FS
      c. Fees to outside consulting and engineering firms for site investigations and development of remedial action plans and remedial actions
      d. Costs of contractors performing remedial actions
      e. Government oversight costs and past costs
      f. Cost of machinery and equipment dedicated to the remedial actions that do not have an alternative use
      g. Assessments by a PRP group covering costs incurred by the group in dealing with a site

    h.   Costs of operation and maintenance of the remedial action, including costs of postremediation monitoring required by the remedial action plan

  2.  Costs of compensation and benefits for employees directly involved in the remediation effort

  3.  Costs are to be estimated based on existing laws and technologies, and not discounted to present value unless timing of cash payments is fixed or reliably determinable

---

## SFAS 6 (B05) Classification of Short-Term Obligations Expected to Be Refinanced
(Modifies para 8 of Chapter 3A, ARB 43)

**A.**  Short-term obligations shall be classified as a current liability unless

  1.  Enterprise intends to refinance the obligation on a long-term basis

  2.  AND the intent is supported by ability to refinance

    a.   Post-balance-sheet issuance of long-term debt or equity securities, or

    b.   Financing agreement that clearly permits refinancing on a long-term basis

      (1)  Does not expire or is not callable for one year

      (2)  No violation of the agreement exists at the balance sheet date or has occurred to date

  3.  The amount of the short-term obligation excluded from current liability status should not exceed the

    a.   Net proceeds of debt or securities issued

    b.   Net amounts available under refinancing agreements

      (1)  The enterprise must intend to exercise the financing agreement when the short-term obligation becomes due.

  4.  Refinancing of short-term obligations is a FS **classification** issue, **not** a **recognition** and **measurement** issue.

---

### FASB INTERPRETATION NO. 8  CLASSIFICATION OF A SHORT-TERM OBLIGATION REPAID PRIOR TO BEING REPLACED BY A LONG-TERM SECURITY

    Short-term obligations that are repaid after the balance sheet date but **before** funds are obtained from long-term financing are to be classified as current liabilities at the balance sheet date.

*EXAMPLES:*

    *In situation 1 below, the obligation will be classified as a noncurrent liability at the balance sheet date. Why? Proceeds from refinancing were obtained **prior** to the due date of the obligation.*

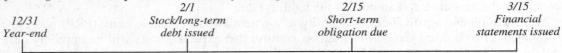

| 12/31 | 2/1 | 2/15 | 3/15 |
|---|---|---|---|
| Year-end | Stock/long-term debt issued | Short-term obligation due | Financial statements issued |

*Situation 1:*  Classify obligation due 2/15 as noncurrent liability at balance sheet date.

    *In situation 2 below, the short-term obligation will be classified as a current liability. Why? Proceeds from the issuance of stock or long-term debt were not obtained until **after** the due date of the short-term obligation. Therefore, current assets must have been used to pay the short-term obligation.*

| 12/31 | 2/1 | 2/15 | 2/15 |
|---|---|---|---|
| Year-end | Short-term obligation due | Stock/long-term debt issued | Financial statements issued |

*Situation 2:*  Classify obligation due 2/1 as current liability at balance sheet date

---

## SFAS 7 (De4) Accounting and Reporting by Development Stage Companies

**A.**  A company, division, component, etc., is in the development stage if

  1.  Substantially all efforts are devoted toward establishing the business, or

  2.  Principal operations are underway but have not produced significant revenues

**B.**  Example activities of development stage companies

  1.  Financial planning

  2.  Raising capital

  3.  Exploring or developing natural resources

  4.  R&D

  5.  Establishing sources of supply

  6.  Acquiring property, plant, equipment, etc.

  7.  Personnel recruitment and training

8. Developing markets
9. Production start-up
C. No special accounting standards apply to development stage companies.
  1. Report revenue in the income statement as in normal operations
  2. Expense costs as one would for a company in normal operations
  3. Capitalize costs as one would for a company in normal operations
     a. Determine cost recoverability within entity for which statements are being prepared
D. Development stage company statements include
  1. A balance sheet with cumulative net losses termed "deficit accumulated during development stage"
  2. An income statement with revenues and expenses for both current period and cumulative expenses and revenues from the inception of the development stage
  3. A statement of cash flows for both current period and cumulative amounts from inception
  4. Statement of owner's investment including
     a. Dates of issuance and number of shares, warrants, etc.
     b. Dollar amounts must be assigned to each issuance
        (1) Dollar amounts must be assigned for noncash consideration
     c. Dollar amounts received for each issuance or basis for valuing noncash consideration
  5. Identification of statements as those of a development stage company
  6. During the first period of normal operations, notes to statements should disclose that company was, but is no longer, in the development stage

## SFAS 13 (L10, C51) Accounting for Leases

(Supersedes APB 5, 7, 27, 31, and para 15 of APB 18; paras 18 and 23 amended by SFAS 91)
(The outline below is based on the comprehensive restatement as of January 1990 which includes SFAS 17 [rescinded by SFAS 91], 22, 23, 26, 27, 28, and 29 and Interpretations 19, 21, 23, 24, 26, and 27.)

Applies to agreements for use of property, plant, and equipment, but not natural resources and not for licensing agreements such as patents and copyrights.

The major issue in accounting for leases is whether the benefits and risks incident to ownership have been transferred from lessor to lessee. If so, the lessor treats the lease as a sale or financing transaction and the lessee treats it as a purchase. Otherwise, the lease is accounted for as a rental agreement. These different treatments recognize the **substance** of a transaction rather than its **form;** that is, what is legally a lease may be effectively the same as or similar to an installment purchase by the lessee and a sale or financing transaction by the lessor.

The following terms are given specific definitions for the purpose of SFAS 13:

**Bargain purchase option**—A provision allowing the lessee the option of purchasing the leased property for an amount that is sufficiently lower than the expected fair value of the property at the date the option becomes exercisable. Exercise of the option must appear reasonably assured at the inception of the lease.

**Contingent rentals**—Rentals that represent the increases or decreases in lease payments which result from changes in the factors on which the lease payments are based occurring subsequent to the inception of the lease.

**Estimated economic life of lease property**—The estimated remaining time which the property is expected to be economically usable by one or more users, with normal maintenance and repairs, for its intended purpose at the inception of the lease. This estimated time period should not be limited by the lease term.

**Estimated residual value of leased property**—The estimated fair value of the leased property at the end of the lease term.

**Executory costs**—Those costs such as insurance, maintenance, and taxes incurred for leased property, whether paid by the lessor or lessee. Amounts paid by a lessee in consideration for a guarantee from an unrelated third party of the residual value are also executory costs. If executory costs are paid by the lessor, any lessor's profit on those costs is considered the same as executory costs.

**Fair value of leased property**—The price that would be received to sell the property in an orderly transaction between market participants at the measurement date.

When the lessor is a **manufacturer or dealer,** the fair value of the property at the inception of the lease will ordinarily be its normal selling price net of volume or trade discounts.

When the lessor is not a **manufacturer or dealer,** the fair value of the property at the inception of the lease will ordinarily be its costs net of volume or trade discounts.

**Implicit interest rate**—The discount rate that, when applied to the minimum lease payments, excluding that portion of the payments representing executory costs to be paid by the lessor, together with any profit thereon, and the unguaranteed residual value accruing to the benefit of the lessor, causes the aggregate present value at the beginning of the lease term to be equal to the fair value of the leased property to the lessor at the inception of the lease.

**Inception of the lease**—The date of the written lease agreement or commitment (if earlier) wherein all principal provisions are fixed and no principal provisions remain to be negotiated.

**Incremental borrowing rate**—The rate that, at the inception of the lease, the lessee would have incurred to borrow over a similar term (i.e., a loan term equal to the lease term) the funds necessary to purchase the leased asset.

**Initial direct costs**—(See outline of SFAS 91)

**Lease term**—The fixed, noncancelable term of the lease plus all renewal terms when renewal is reasonably assured.

*NOTE: The lease term should not extend beyond the date of a bargain purchase option.*

**Minimum lease payments**—For the **lessee:** The payments that the lessee is or can be required to make in connection with the leased property. Contingent rental guarantees by the lessee of the lessor's debt, and the lessee's obligation to pay executory costs are excluded from minimum lease payments. If the lease contains a bargain purchase option, only the minimum rental payments over the lease term and the payment called for in the bargain purchase option are included in minimum lease payments. Otherwise, minimum lease payments include the following:

1. The minimum rental payments called for by the lease over the lease term
2. Any guarantee of residual value at the expiration of the lease term made by the lessee (or any party related to the lessee), whether or not the guarantee payment constitutes a purchase of the leased property. When the lessor has the right to require the lessee to purchase the property at termination of the lease for a certain or determinable amount, that amount shall be considered a lessee guarantee. When the lessee agrees to make up any deficiency below a stated amount in the lessor's realization of the residual value, the guarantee to be included in the MLP is the stated amount rather than an estimate of the deficiency to be made up.
3. Any payment that the lessee must or can be required to make upon **failure to renew or extend** the lease at the expiration of the lease term, whether or not the payment would constitute a purchase of the leased property

For the **lessor:** The payments described above plus any guarantee of the residual value or of the rental payments beyond the lease term by a third party unrelated to either the lessee or lessor (provided the third party is financially capable of discharging the guaranteed obligation).

**Unguaranteed residual value**—the estimated residual value of the leased property exclusive of any portion guaranteed by the lessee, by any party related to the lessee, or any party unrelated to the lessee. If the guarantor is related to the lessor, the residual value shall be considered as unguaranteed.

A. Classification of leases by lessees. Leases that meet one or more of the following criteria are accounted for as capital leases; all other leases are accounted for as operating leases:
   1. Lease transfers ownership (title) to lessee during lease term.
   2. Lease contains a bargain purchase option.
   3. Lease term is 75% or more of economic useful life of property.
   4. Present value of minimum lease payments equals 90% or more of FMV of the leased property.
      a. Present value is computed with lessee's incremental borrowing rate, unless lessor's implicit rate is known and is less than lessee's incremental rate (then use lessor's implicit rate).
      b. FMV is cash selling price for sales-type lease; lessor's cost for direct financing of lease. (If not recently purchased, estimate FMV)

   *NOTE: 3. and 4. do not apply if lease begins in last 25% of asset's life.*

B. Classification of leases by lessors
   1. Sales-type leases provide for a manufacturer or dealer profit (i.e., FMV of leased property is greater than lessor cost or carrying value).
      a. Sales-type leases must meet one of the four criteria for lessee capital leases (A.1. to A.4. above) and **both** of the following two criteria:
         (1) Collectibility is reasonably predictable, and

       (2) No important uncertainties regarding costs to be incurred by lessor exist, such as unusual guarantees of performance. Note estimation of executory expense such as insurance, maintenance, etc., is not considered.

   2. Direct financing leases must meet same criteria as sales-type leases (just above) but do not include a manufacturer's or dealer's profit.

   3. Operating leases are all other leases that have not been classified as sales-type, direct financing, or leveraged.

**C.** Lease classification is determined at the inception of the lease.

   1. If changes in the lease are subsequently made which change the classification, the lease generally should be considered a new agreement and reclassified and accounted for as a new lease. Exercise of renewal options, etc., are not changes in the lease. However, if the terms of a capital lease are modified such that it should be reclassified as an operating lease, the lessee should account for it under the sale-leaseback provisions of SFAS 98

   2. Changes in estimates (e.g., economic life or residual value) or other circumstances (e.g., default) do not result in a new agreement but accounts should be adjusted and gains or losses recognized.

   3. An important goal of SFAS 13 was to achieve **symmetry** in lease accounting (i.e., an operating lease for the lessee will be an operating lease for the lessor) and likewise for capital leases.

**D.** Accounting and reporting by lessees

   1. Record capital leases as an asset and liability

     a. Leased asset shall not be recorded in excess of FMV. If the present value of the lease payments is greater than the FMV, the leased asset and related liability are recorded at FMV and the effective interest rate is thereby increased.

     b. Recognize interest expense using the effective interest method.

     c. If there is a transfer of ownership or a bargain purchase option, the asset's depreciation/amortization period is its economic life. Otherwise, depreciate/amortize assets to the expected residual value at the end of the lease term.

   2. Rent on operating leases should be expensed on a straight-line basis unless another method is better suited to the particular benefits and costs associated with the lease.

   3. Contingent rentals are reported as rent expense in the period incurred.

   4. Disclosures by lessees include

     a. General description of leasing arrangement including

       (1) Basis of computing contingent payments

       (2) Existence and terms of renewal or purchase options and escalation clauses

       (3) Restrictions imposed by the lease agreement such as limitations on dividends and further leasing arrangements

     b. Capital lease requirements

       (1) Usual current/noncurrent classifications

       (2) Depreciation/amortization should be separately disclosed

       (3) Future minimum lease payments in the aggregate and for each of the five succeeding fiscal years with separate deductions being made to show the amounts representing executory cost and interest

       (4) Total minimum sublease rentals to be received in the future under noncancelable subleases

       (5) Total contingent rental actually incurred for each period for which an income statement is presented

     c. Operating leases which have initial or remaining noncancelable term > 1 year

       (1) Future minimum lease payments in the aggregate and for each of the five succeeding fiscal years

       (2) Total minimum sublease rentals to be received in the future under noncancelable subleases

       (3) All operating leases—rent expense of each IS period

         (a) Present separate amounts for minimum rentals, contingent rentals, and sublease rentals

         (b) Rental payments for leases with a term of a month or less may be excluded

**E.** Accounting and reporting by lessors

1. Sales-type leases
   a. Lease receivable is charged for the gross investment in the lease (the total net minimum lease payments plus the unguaranteed residual value). Sales is credited for the present value of the minimum lease payments.
   b. Cost of sales is the carrying value of the leased asset plus any initial direct costs less the present value of the unguaranteed residual value. Note that in a sales-type lease, initial direct costs are deducted in full in the period when the sale is recorded. Unearned Interest Income is credited for the difference between the gross investment and the sales price.
   c. Recognize interest revenue using the effective interest method
   d. At the end of the lease term, the balance in the receivable account should equal the amount of residual value guaranteed, if any.
   e. Contingent rental payments are reported as income in the period earned.

2. Direct financing leases
   a. Accounting is similar to sales-type lease except that no manufacturer's or dealer's profit is recognized.
   b. Lease receivable is charged for the gross investment in the lease, the asset account is credited for the net investment in the lease (cost to be acquired for purpose of leasing) and the difference is recorded as unearned income.
   c. Initial direct costs are recorded in a separate account. A new effective interest rate is computed that equates the minimum lease payments and any unguaranteed residual value with the combined outlay for the leased asset and initial direct costs. The initial direct costs and unearned lease revenue are both amortized so as to produce a constant rate of return over the life of the lease.
   d. The remaining requirements are the same as those for the sales-type lease.

3. Operating leases
   a. Leased property is to be included with or near PP&E on the BS, and lessor's normal depreciation policies should be applied.
   b. Rental revenue should be recognized on a straight-line basis unless another method is better suited to the particular benefits and costs associated with the lease.
   c. Initial direct costs should be deferred and allocated over the lease term in proportion to the recognition of rental revenue.

**F.** Related-party leases shall be accounted for as unrelated-party leases except when terms have been significantly affected by relationship.

**G.** Sale-leasebacks

1. Legally two separate transactions
2. Lessee (seller) accounts for the gain (loss) as follows:
   a. Loss (when FMV < Book value) on the sale should be recognized immediately.
   b. Gain treatment
      (1) Seller relinquishes the right to substantially all of the remaining use of the property sold (PV of reasonable rentals ≤ 10% of fair value of asset sold)—then separate transactions, and entire gain is recognized.
      (2) Seller retains more than a minor part, but less than substantially all of the remaining use (PV of reasonable rentals are > 10% but < 90% of fair value of asset sold)—then gain on sale is recognized to the extent of the excess of gain over the present value of minimum lease payments (operating) or the recorded amount of the leased asset (capital).
      (3) Seller retains right to substantially all of the remaining use—then entire gain on sale is deferred.
   c. If the gain is deferred and lease is accounted for as
      (1) Capital lease—defer and amortize gain over lease term using same method and life used for depreciating/amortizing cost of leased asset
         (a) Deferral and amortization of the gain are required because the sale and leaseback are components of a single transaction and are interdependent.
      (2) Operating lease—recognize gain on straight-line basis
         (a) Treat as a reduction of rent expense.
3. Lessor records as a purchase of asset to be leased and as a direct financing or operating lease

## FASB TECHNICAL BULLETIN 85-3 ACCOUNTING FOR OPERATING LEASES WITH SCHEDULED RENT INCREASES

SFAS 13 requires lessees or lessors to recognize rent expense or rental income for an operating lease on a straight-line basis. Certain operating lease agreements specify scheduled rent increases over the lease term. The effects of these scheduled rent increases, which are included in minimum lease payments under SFAS 13, should also be recognized by lessors and lessees on a straight-line basis over the lease term.

## SFAS 15 (D22) Accounting by Debtors and Creditors for Troubled Debt Restructurings
(Superseded by SFAS 114 with regard to creditors)

A.  Troubled debt restructurings occur when a creditor is compelled to grant relief to a debtor due to the debtor's inability to service the debt. This SFAS prescribes accounting for such debt restructurings if
 1.  By creditor-debtor agreement
 2.  Imposed by a court
 3.  Result of repossessions and foreclosures
 4.  But not changes in lease agreements
   a.  Nor legal actions to collect receivables
   b.  Nor quasi reorganizations
B.  If a **debtor** transfers assets to settle fully a payable, recognize a gain on restructuring equal to the book value of the payable less FMV of assets transferred.
 1.  Use fair value measurements as outlined by SFAS 157.
 2.  The difference between set FMV and carrying value of the assets transferred is a gain or loss in disposition of assets per APB 30.
C.  If a **debtor** issues an equity interest to settle fully a payable, account for equity issued at FMV.
 1.  Excess of carrying value of payable over equity FMV is a gain on restructuring.
D.  A **debtor** having the terms of troubled debt modified should account for the restructure prospectively (i.e., no adjustment of the payable).
 1.  Recompute the new effective rate of interest based on the new terms
   a.  Total cash payments to be paid, less carrying value of payable is the interest
   b.  Amortize the payable by the interest method (APB 21) using the new interest rate
 2.  Exception is if restructured terms require total cash payments (including interest) which are less than the carrying value of the payable, write down the payable to the total cash to be paid
   a.  Include contingent payments in calculation; this precludes recognizing a gain currently and interest expense later
   b.  Recognize gain on the write-down
   c.  All future cash payments reduce the payable (i.e., no interest expense is recognized)
E.  If restructured by partial settlement (assets and/or equity issuance) and modified terms
 1.  First account for asset and/or equity issuance per above
 2.  Then account for modified terms per above
F.  Related matters
 1.  A repossession or foreclosure is accounted for per the above.
 2.  Contingent payments on restructured debt shall be recognized per SFAS 5 (i.e., its payment is probable and subject to reasonable estimate).
 3.  Legal fees on debt restructuring involving equity issuance reduce the amounts credited to the equity accounts.
   a.  All other direct costs of debt restructuring reduce gain or are expenses of the period if there is no gain.
G.  Disclosures by **debtors**
 1.  Description of major changes in debt of each restructuring
 2.  Aggregate gain on debt restructuring and related tax effect
 3.  Aggregate net gain (loss) on asset transfers due to restructuring
 4.  EPS amount of aggregate gain on restructuring net of tax effect

## SFAS 16 (A35, C59, I16, I17, and I73) Prior Period Adjustments
(Supersedes paras 23 and 24 of APB 9)
(Amends inconsistent references to APB 9 in APB 20, 30, and SFAS 5)
A.  All P&L items are included in the determination of net income except the correction of an error in statements of a prior period.
   1.  Account for and report as a prior period adjustment to beginning retained earnings
B.  An exception exists for interim reporting regarding certain adjustments relating to prior interim periods of the current year.
   1.  These "adjustments" (affecting prior interim periods of the current fiscal year) are settlements or adjustments of
      a.  Litigation or similar claims
      b.  Income taxes
      c.  Renegotiation proceedings
      d.  Utility revenue per the rate-making process
   2.  These "adjustments" must also
      a.  Be material to operating income, trends in income, etc.
      b.  All or part of the adjustment is specifically identified with specified prior interim periods of the current fiscal year.
      c.  Not subject to reasonable estimation prior to the current interim period (e.g., new retroactive tax legislation)

## SFAS 34 (I67, I69) Capitalization of Interest Cost
(Paras 8 and 9 amended by SFAS 42)  (Paras 9, 10, and 20 amended by SFAS 58)
A.  Interest costs, when material, incurred in acquiring the following types of assets, shall be capitalized:
   1.  Assets constructed or produced for a firm's own use
      a.  Including construction by others requiring progress payments
   2.  Assets intended for lease or sale that are produced as discrete projects
      a.  For example, ships and real estate developments
   3.  But not on
      a.  Routinely produced inventories
      b.  Assets ready for their intended use
      c.  Assets not being used nor being readied for use
      d.  Land, unless it is being developed (e.g., as a plant site, real estate development, etc.)
   4.  The objective of interest capitalization is to
      a.  Reflect the acquisition cost of assets
      b.  Match costs to revenues in the period benefited
   5.  Capitalized interest shall be treated as any other asset cost for depreciation and other purposes.
   6.  Required interest cost disclosures
      a.  Total interest cost incurred
      b.  Interest capitalized, if any
B.  Amount of interest to be capitalized
   1.  Conceptually, the interest that would have been avoided if the expenditures had not been made
   2.  Based on the average accumulated expenditures on the asset for the period
      a.  Includes payment of cash, transfer of other assets, and incurring interest-bearing liabilities
      b.  Reasonable approximations are permitted
   3.  Use the interest rates incurred during period
      a.  First, the rates on specific new borrowings for the asset
      b.  Second, a weighted-average of other borrowings
         (1)  Use judgment to identify borrowings
   4.  Interest cost capitalized in any period cannot exceed interest cost incurred in that period.
      a.  On a consolidated basis for consolidated statements
      b.  On an individual company basis for individual company statements
   5.  Capitalized interest should be compounded.
C.  Interest capitalization period
   1.  Begins when all the following three conditions are present:
      a.  Asset expenditures have been made

      b.   Activities to ready asset for intended use are in progress
         (1)  Includes planning stages
      c.   Interest cost is being incurred
   2.  If activities to ready asset for intended use cease, interest capitalization ceases
      a.   Not for brief interruptions that are externally imposed
   3.  Capitalization period ends when asset is substantially complete
      a.   For assets completed in parts, interest capitalization on a part of the asset ends when that part is complete
      b.   Capitalize all interest on assets required to be completed in entirety until entire project is finished
   4.  Interest capitalization continues if capitalized interest raises cost above market values
      a.   Apply impairment accounting per SFAS 144

## SFAS 43 (C44) Accounting for Compensated Absences

**A.** This statement addresses the accounting for future sick pay benefits, holidays, vacation benefits, and other like compensated absences.

**B.** Accrual of a liability for future compensated absences is required if **all** of the conditions listed below exist.
   1.  Obligation of employer to compensate employees arises from services already performed
   2.  Obligation arises from vesting or accumulation of rights
   3.  Probable payment of compensation
   4.  Amount can be reasonably estimated

**C.** Above criteria require accrual of a liability for vacation benefits; however, other compensated absences typically may not require accrual of a liability.
   1.  In spite of the above criteria, accrual of a liability is not required for accumulating nonvesting rights to receive sick pay benefits because amounts are typically not large enough to justify cost.

## SFAS 45 (Fr3) Accounting for Franchise Fee Revenue

**A.** Definitions
   1.  **Franchisee**—Party who has been granted business rights
   2.  **Franchisor**—Party who grants business rights
   3.  **Area franchise**—Agreement transferring franchise rights within a geographical area permitting the opening of a number of franchise outlets
   4.  **Continuing franchise fee**—Consideration for continuing rights granted by the agreement (general or specific) during its life
   5.  **Franchise agreement**—Essential criteria
      a.   Contractual relation between franchisee and franchisor
      b.   Purpose is distribution of a product, service, or entire business concept
      c.   Resources contributed by both franchisor and franchisee in establishing and maintaining the franchise
      d.   Outline of specific marketing practices to be followed
      e.   Creation of an establishment that will require and support the full-time business activity of the franchisee
      f.   Both franchisee and franchisor have a common public identity
   6.  **Initial franchise fee**—Consideration for establishing the relationship and providing some initial services
   7.  **Initial services**—Variety of services and advice (e.g., site selection, financing and engineering services, advertising assistance, training of personnel, manuals for operations, administration and recordkeeping, bookkeeping and advisory services, quality control programs)

**B.** Franchise fee revenue from individual sales shall be recognized when all material services or conditions relating to the sale have been substantially performed or satisfied by the franchisor.
   1.  Substantial performance means
      a.   Franchisor has no remaining obligation or intent to refund money or forgive unpaid debt
      b.   Substantially all initial services have been performed
      c.   No other material conditions or obligations exist
   2.  If large initial franchise fee is required and continuing franchise fees are small in relation to future services, then portion of initial franchise fee shall be deferred and amortized over life of franchise.

C. Continuing franchise fees shall be reported as revenue as fees are earned and become receivable from the franchise. Related costs shall be expensed as incurred.
D. Direct franchise costs shall be deferred until related revenue is recognized.
   1. These costs should not exceed anticipated revenue less estimated additional related costs.
E. Disclosure of all significant commitments and obligations that have not yet been substantially performed are required
   1. Notes to the FS should disclose whether the installment or cost recovery method is used.
   2. Initial franchise fees shall be segregated from other franchise fee revenue if significant.

## SFAS 47 (C32) Disclosure of Long-Term Obligations
A. This statement requires that firm disclose
   1. Commitments under unconditional purchase obligations that are associated with suppliers (financing arrangements)
   2. Future payments on long-term borrowings
B. **Unconditional purchase obligations** are obligations to transfer funds in the future for fixed or minimum amounts of goods or services at fixed or minimum prices.
C. Unconditional purchase obligations that have all the following characteristics must be disclosed; they are not recorded on the balance sheet.
   1. Is noncancelable or cancelable only
      a. Upon occurrence of a remote contingency, or
      b. With permission of another party, or
      c. If a replacement agreement is signed between same parties, or
      d. Upon penalty payment such that continuation appears reasonably assured
   2. Was negotiated as part of arranging financing for the facilities that will provide the contracted goods
   3. Has a remaining term greater than one year
D. Disclosure of those unconditional purchase obligations **not recorded** on the balance sheet shall include
   1. Nature and term of obligation
   2. Amount of fixed and determinable portion of obligation as of most recent BS in aggregate and if determinable for each of next five years
   3. Description of any variable elements of the obligation
   4. Amounts purchased under the obligation(s) for each year an income statement is presented
   5. Encourages disclosing imputed interest to reduce the obligation to present value using
      a. Effective interest rate, or if unknown
      b. Purchaser's incremental borrowing rate at date obligation was entered into
E. This statement **does not change** the accounting for obligations that **are recorded on the balance sheet,** nor does it suggest that disclosure is a substitute for accounting recognition. For **recorded** obligations, the following information should be disclosed for each of the next five years:
   1. Aggregate amount of payments for unconditional obligations that meet criteria for balance sheet recognition
   2. Combined aggregate amount of maturities and sinking fund requirements for all long-term borrowings

## SFAS 48 (R75) Revenue Recognition When Right of Return Exists
(Extracts from AICPA Statement of Position [SOP] 75-1)
A. Specifies accounting for sales in which a product may be returned for refund, credit applied to amounts owed, or in exchange for other products.
   1. Right is specified by contract or is a matter of existing practice.
   2. Right may be exercised by ultimate customer or party who resells product to others.
   3. Not applicable to service revenue, real estate or lease transactions, or return of defective goods
B. Recognize revenue from right of return sales only if all of the following conditions are met:
   1. Price is substantially fixed or determinable at date of sale.
   2. Buyer has paid or is unconditionally obligated to pay.
   3. Obligation is not changed by theft, destruction, or damage of product.
   4. Buyer has "economic substance" apart from seller (i.e., sale is not with a party established mainly for purpose of recognizing sales revenue).
   5. Seller has no significant obligation for performance to directly cause resale of product.
   6. Amount of future returns can be reasonably estimated.

**C.** If all of the conditions in B. above are met, record sales and cost of sales **and**
1. Reduce sales revenue and cost of sales to reflect estimated returns
2. Accrue expected costs or losses in accordance with SFAS 5

**D.** If any condition in B. above is not met, do not recognize sales and cost of sales until either
1. All conditions are subsequently met, or
2. Return privilege has substantially expired

**E.** Factors which may impair ability to make a reasonable estimate of returns include
1. Susceptibility of product to significant external factors (e.g., obsolescence or changes in demand)
2. Long period of return privilege
3. Absence of experience with similar products or inability to apply such experience due to changing circumstances (e.g., marketing policies or customer relationships)
4. Absence of large volume of similar transactions

## SFAS 52 (F60) Foreign Currency Translation
(Supersedes SFAS 8, SFAS 20, and FASB Interpretations 15 and 17)

**A.** Primary objectives of foreign currency translation
1. Should provide information disclosing effects of rate changes on enterprise cash flows and equity
2. Should also provide information in consolidated statements as to financial results and relationships of individual consolidated entities measured in their respective functional currencies in accordance with US GAAP

**B.** **Functional currency** is the currency of the primary economic environment in which a foreign entity operates (i.e., the environment in which the entity generates and spends cash).
1. A foreign entity's assets, liabilities, revenues, expenses, gains, and losses shall be measured in that entity's functional currency.
2. The functional currency could be the currency of the country in which the entity operates if the entity is a self-contained unit operating in a foreign country.

   *EXAMPLE: An entity (1) whose operations are not integrated with those of the parent, (2) whose buying and selling activities are primarily local, and (3) whose cash flows are primarily in the foreign currency.*

3. There may be several functional currencies if there are many self-contained entities operating in different countries.
4. The functional currency might be the US dollar if the foreign entity's operations are considered to be a direct and integral part of the US parent's operations.

   *EXAMPLE: An entity (1) whose operations are integrated with those of the parent, (2) whose buying and selling activities are primarily in the parent's country and/or the parent's currency, and (3) whose cash flows are available for remittance to the parent.*

5. Functional currency for a foreign entity, once determined, shall be used consistently unless it is clear that economic facts and circumstances have changed.
   a. If a change is made, do not restate previously issued financial statements
6. If a foreign entity's bookkeeping is not done in the functional currency, the process of converting from the currency used for the books and records to the functional currency is called remeasurement.
   a. Remeasurement is intended to produce the same result (e.g., balances for assets, expenses, liabilities, etc.) as if the functional currency had been used for bookkeeping purposes.
   b. In highly inflationary economies (cumulative inflation over a 3-year period is $\geq 100\%$), the remeasurement of a foreign entity's financial statements shall be done as if the functional currency were the reporting currency (i.e., the US dollar).
7. The functional currency (if not the US dollar) is translated to the reporting currency (assumed to be the US dollar) by using appropriate exchange rates (see item C. below).
   a. If the functional currency is the US dollar, there is no need to translate (if the books and records are maintained in US dollars).

**C.** The translation of foreign currency FS (those incorporated in the FS of a reporting enterprise by consolidation, combination, or the equity method of accounting) should use a current exchange rate if the foreign currency is the functional currency.
1. Assets and liabilities—exchange rate at the balance sheet date is used to translate the functional currency to the reporting currency
2. Revenues (expenses) and gains (losses)—exchange rates when the transactions were recorded shall be used to translate from the functional currency to the reporting currency

    a.   Weighted-averages for exchange rates may be used for items occurring numerous times during the period.

3.   Translation adjustments will result from the translation process if the functional currency is a foreign currency.

    a.   Translation adjustments are not an element of net income of the reporting entity.

    b.   Effects of current translation adjustments are reported in other comprehensive income for the period with the accumulated amount reported as part of the reporting entity's owners' equity and labeled accumulated other comprehensive income.

    c.   Accumulated translation adjustments remain part of the owners' equity until the reporting entity disposes of the foreign entity.

       (1)  In period of disposal, these adjustments are reported as part of the gain (loss) on sale or liquidation.

**D.**  **Foreign currency transactions** are those which are denominated (fixed) in other than the entity's functional currency.

1.   Receivables and/or payables, which are fixed in a currency other than the functional currency, may result in transaction gains (losses) due to changes in exchange rates after the transaction date.

2.   Transaction gains or losses generally are reported on the income statement in the period during which the exchange rates change.

3.   Deferred taxes may have to be provided for transaction gains or losses that are realized for income tax purposes in a time period different than that for financial reporting.

**E.**  **A forward exchange contract** represents an agreement to exchange different currencies at a specified future rate and at a specified future date.  (Accounting and reporting now specified by SFAS 133)

**F.**  FS disclosures required

1.   Aggregate transaction gain (loss) that is included in the entity's net income

2.   Analysis of changes in accumulated translation adjustments which are reported as part of other comprehensive income

3.   Significant rate changes subsequent to the date of the financial statements including effects on unsettled foreign currency transactions

---

**FASB INTERPRETATION NO. 37  ACCOUNTING FOR TRANSLATION ADJUSTMENTS UPON SALE OF PART OF AN INVESTMENT IN A FOREIGN ENTITY**

    If an enterprise sells part of its ownership interest in a foreign entity, a pro rata portion of the accumulated translation adjustment component of equity attributable to that investment shall be recognized in measuring the gain (loss) on the sale.

---

## SFAS 57 (R36) Related-Party Disclosures

**A.**  Definitions

1.   **Affiliate**—Party is controlled by another enterprise that controls, or is under common control with another enterprise, directly or indirectly

2.   **Control**—Power to direct or cause direction of management through ownerships contract, or other means

3.   **Immediate family**—Family members whom principal owners or management might control/influence or be controlled/influenced by

4.   **Management**—Persons responsible for enterprise objectives who have policy-making and decision-making authority

    a.   For example, board of directors, chief executive and operating officers, and vice-presidents

    b.   Includes persons without formal titles

5.   **Principal owners**—Owners of more than 10% of a firm's voting interests

    a.   Includes known beneficial owners

6.   **Related parties**—Affiliates, equity method investees, employee benefit trusts, principal owners, management or any party that can significantly influence a transaction

**B.**  FS shall include disclosures of material transactions between related parties except

1.   Compensation agreements, expense allowances, and other similar items in the ordinary course of business

2.   Transactions which are eliminated in the preparation of consolidated/combined FS

C.  Disclosures of material transactions shall include
    1.  Nature of relationship(s)
    2.  Description of transaction(s), including those assigned zero or nominal amounts
    3.  Dollar amounts of transactions for each income statement period and effect of any change in method of establishing terms
    4.  Amounts due to/from related parties, including terms and manner of settlement
D.  Representations concerning related-party transactions shall not imply that terms were equivalent to those resulting in arm's-length bargaining unless such statement can be substantiated.
E.  When a **control** relationship exists, disclose such relationship even though no transactions have occurred.

## SFAS 66 (Re1, R10) Accounting for Sales of Real Estate
A.  Other than retail land sales
    1.  Use the full accrual method if the following criteria are satisfied:
        a.  Sale is consummated
        b.  Buyer's initial and continuing investments demonstrate a commitment to pay for the property
        c.  Seller's receivable is not subject to future subordination
        d.  Risks and rewards of ownership have been transferred
    2.  When the criteria are not met and dependent upon the particular circumstance, use one of the following methods:
        a.  Installment method
        b.  Cost recovery method
        c.  Deposit method
        d.  Reduced profit method
        e.  Percentage-of-completion
B.  Retail land sales (not outlined due to specialized nature)

## SFAS 78 (B05) Classification of Obligations That Are Callable by the Creditor
(Amends ARB 43, Chapter 3A)
A.  Statement specifies that the current liability classification is also intended to include
    1.  Obligations that, by their terms, are due on demand or will be due on demand within one year (or operating cycle, if longer) from balance sheet date, even though liquidation may not be expected within that period
    2.  Long-term obligations that are or will be callable by creditor either because
        a.  Debtor's violation of debt agreement provision at balance sheet date makes obligation callable **or**
        b.  Violation, if not cured within grace period, will make obligation callable
B.  Callable obligations in A.2. should be classified current unless one of the following conditions is met:
    1.  Creditor has waived or subsequently lost the right to demand repayment for more than one year (or operating cycle, if longer) from balance sheet date
    2.  For long-term obligations containing grace period within which debtor may cure violation, it is probable violation will be cured within that period
        a.  If obligation meets this condition, the circumstances shall be disclosed
C.  This statement does **not** modify SFAS 6 or 47

## SFAS 84 (D10, D14) Induced Conversions of Convertible Debt
(Amends APB 26, para 2)
A.  Establishes accounting and reporting standards for conversion of convertible debt to equity securities when debtor induces conversion of the debt
    1.  Applies only to conversions that both
        a.  Occur pursuant to changed conversion privileges exercisable only for limited period of time
        b.  Include issuance of all of the equity securities issuable pursuant to the original conversion privileges for each instrument that is converted
    2.  Examples of changed terms to induce conversion
        a.  Reduction of original conversion price
        b.  Issuance of warrants or other securities not included in original conversion terms
        c.  Payment of cash or other consideration to debt holders who convert during the specified time period

**B.** Debtor enterprise shall recognize expense equal to excess of fair value of all securities and other consideration transferred in the transaction over fair value of securities issuable pursuant to the original conversion terms.
1. Expense is not an extraordinary item.
2. Fair value of securities/other consideration measured as of inducement date
   a. Typically date converted by debt holder or binding agreement entered into

## SFAS 86 (Co2) Accounting for the Costs of Computer Software to Be Sold, Leased, or Otherwise Marketed

**A.** Establishes standards of financial accounting and reporting for the costs of computer software to be sold, leased, or otherwise marketed as a separate product or as part of a product or process, whether internally developed and produced or purchased.

**B.** Research and development costs consist of all costs to establish technological feasibility.
1. Evidence of technological feasibility
   a. Process of creating the computer software product includes a detailed program design **or**
   b. Process of creating the computer software product includes a product design and a completed working model.

**C.** Capitalization costs include costs incurred subsequent to establishing technological feasibility.
1. Capitalization shall cease when product is available for general release to customers.

**D.** Amortization of capitalized software costs is performed on a product-by-product basis.
1. Annual amortization is the greater of
   a. The amount computed using the ratio current gross product revenues to total current and anticipated future gross product revenues **or**
   b. S-L method using the estimated economic life of the software product
2. Amortization begins when product is available for general release to customers.
3. Unamortized capitalized costs cannot exceed the net realizable value (NRV) of that software product. Any excess shall be written off at the end of the year.

**E.** Inventory costs include costs incurred for duplicating software materials and for physically packaging the product.
1. Costs of maintenance and customer support are charged to expense.

**F.** FS disclosures shall include
1. Unamortized computer software costs
2. Total amount charged to amortization expense and amounts written down to NRV

## SFAS 87 (C59, I67, P16, Re6) Employers' Accounting for Pensions
(Supersedes ARB 8 and SFAS 36, Amended by SFAS 132[R])

Applies to any arrangement that is similar in substance to pension plan regardless of form or means of financing. Applies to written plan and to plan whose existence may be implied from well-defined, although perhaps unwritten, practice of paying postretirement benefits. Does not apply to plan that provides only life insurance benefits or health insurance benefits, or both, to retirees. Does not apply to postemployment health care benefits.

The following terms are given specific definitions for the purposes of SFAS 87:

**Accumulated benefit obligation**—Actuarial present value of benefits (whether vested or nonvested) attributed by the pension benefit formula to employee service rendered before a specified date and based on employee service and compensation (if applicable) prior to that date. The accumulated benefit obligation differs from the projected benefit obligation in that it includes no assumption about future compensation levels. For plans with flat-benefit or non-pay-related pension benefit formulas, the accumulated benefit obligation and the projected benefit obligation are the same.

**Actual return on plan assets component (of net periodic pension cost)**—Difference between fair value of plan assets at the end of the period and the fair value at the beginning of the period, adjusted for contributions and payments of benefits during the period.

**Actuarial present value**—Value, as of a specified date, of an amount or series of amounts payable or receivable thereafter, with each amount adjusted to reflect (a) the time value of money (through discounts for interest) and (b) the probability of payment (by means of decrements for events such as death, disability, withdrawal, or retirement) between the specified date and the expected date of payment.

**Amortization**—Usually refers to the process of reducing a recognized liability systematically by recognizing revenues or reducing a recognized asset systematically by recognizing expenses or costs. In pension accounting, amortization is also used to refer to the systematic recognition in net pension cost over several periods of previously **unrecognized** amounts, including unrecognized prior service cost and unrecognized net gain or loss.

**Defined contribution pension plan**—Plan that provides pension benefits in return for services rendered, provides an individual account for each participant, and specifies how contributions to the individual's account are to be determined instead of specifying the amount of benefits the individual is to receive. Under a defined contribution pension plan, the benefits a participant will receive depend solely on the amount contributed to the participant's account, the returns earned on investments of those contributions, and forfeitures of other participants' benefits that may be allocated to such participant's account.

**Gain or loss**—Change in the value of either the projected benefit obligation or the plan assets resulting from experience different from that assumed or from a change in an actuarial assumption. See also **Unrecognized net gain or loss**.

**Gain or loss component (of net periodic pension cost)**—The gain or loss component is the net effect of delayed recognition of gains and losses (the net change in the unrecognized net gain or loss) except that it does not include changes in the projected benefit obligation occurring during the period and deferred for later recognition.

**Interest cost component (of net periodic pension cost)**—Increase in the projected benefit obligation due to passage of time.

**Market-related value of plan assets**—Balance used to calculate the expected return on plan assets. Market-related value can be either fair market value or a calculated value that recognizes changes in fair value in a systematic and rational manner over not more than five years. Different ways of calculating market-related value may be used for different classes of assets, but the manner of determining market-related value shall be applied consistently from year to year for each asset class.

**Net periodic pension cost**—Amount recognized in an employer's financial statements as the cost of a pension plan for a period. Components of net periodic pension cost are service cost, interest cost, actual return on plan assets, gain or loss, amortization of unrecognized prior service cost, and amortization of the unrecognized net obligation or asset existing at the date of initial application of SFAS 87. SFAS 87 uses the term **net periodic pension cost** instead of **net pension expense** because part of the cost recognized in a period may be capitalized along with other costs as part of an asset such as inventory.

**Prepaid pension cost**—Cumulative employer contributions in excess of accrued net pension cost.

**Prior service cost or credit**—Cost of retroactive benefits or credit granted in a plan amendment.

**Projected benefit obligation**—Actuarial present value as of a date of all benefits attributed by the pension benefit formula to employee service rendered prior to that date. The projected benefit obligation is measured using assumptions as to future compensation levels if the pension benefit formula is based on those future compensation levels (pay-related, final-pay, final-average-pay, or career-average-pay plans).

**Service cost component (of net periodic pension cost)**—Actuarial present value of benefits attributed by the pension benefit formula to services rendered by employees during the period. The service cost component is a portion of the projected benefit obligation and is unaffected by the funded status of the plan.

**Unfunded accrued pension cost**—Cumulative net pension cost accrued in excess of the employer's contributions (usually used without word "unfunded").

**Unfunded accumulated benefit obligation**—Excess of the accumulated benefit obligation over plan assets.

**Unrecognized net gain or loss**—Cumulative net gain (loss) that has not been recognized as a part of net periodic pension cost. See **Gain or loss**.

**Unamortized prior service cost or credit**—Portion of prior service cost or credit that has not been recognized as a part of net periodic pension cost.

A. Single-Employer Defined Benefit Plans
   1. Pension benefits are part of compensation paid to employees for services
      a. Amount of benefits to be paid depends on a number of future events specified in the **plan's benefit formula**.
   2. Any method of pension accounting that recognizes cost before payment of benefits to retirees must deal with two problems
      a. Assumptions must be made concerning future events that will determine amount and timing of benefits

      b. Approach to attributing cost of pension benefits to individual years of service must be selected

**B.** Basic Elements of Pension Accounting

    1. Prior service cost

        a. Except as specified otherwise, prior service cost shall be amortized by assigning an equal amount to each future service period of each employee active at the date of a plan amendment who is expected to receive benefits under plan.

        b. If all/almost all of plan's participants are inactive, cost of retroactive plan benefits should be amortized over remaining life expectancy of those participants.

        c. Consistent use of alternative amortization approach that more rapidly reduces unrecognized cost of retroactive amendments is acceptable.

            (1) Alternative method used should be disclosed.

        d. When period during which employer expects to realize economic benefits from amendment granting retroactive benefits is shorter than entire remaining service period of active employees, amortization of prior service cost should be accelerated.

        e. Plan amendment can reduce, rather than increase, the projected benefit obligation.

            (1) Reduction should be used to reduce any existing unrecognized prior service cost.

            (2) Excess should be amortized on same basis as cost of benefit increases.

    2. Gains and losses

        a. Gains (losses)

            (1) Result from changes in amount of either projected benefit obligation or plan assets due to experience different than assumed and changes in assumptions

            (2) Include both **realized** and **unrealized** amounts

        b. Asset gains (losses) include both changes reflected in the market-related value of assets and changes not yet reflected in the market-related value.

            (1) Asset gains (losses) not yet reflected in market-related value are not required to be amortized as B.2.c. below.

        c. As a minimum, amortization of unrecognized net gain (loss) should be included as a component of net pension cost for a year if, as of the beginning of the year, that unrecognized net gain (loss) $\geq$ .10 of the larger of the projected benefit obligation or the market-related value of plan assets.

            (1) Minimum amortization should be the excess divided by the average remaining service period of active employees expected to receive benefits under the plan.

                (a) Amortization must always reduce beginning-of-the-year balance.

                (b) Amortization of a net unrecognized gain (loss) results in a decrease (increase) in net periodic pension cost.

            (2) If all or almost all of plan's participants are inactive, average remaining life expectancy of inactive participants should be used instead of average remaining service.

        d. Any systematic method of amortization of unrecognized gains (losses) may be used in lieu of the minimum specified above provided that

            (1) Minimum is used in any period in which minimum amortization is greater (reduces the net balance by more)

            (2) Method is applied consistently and disclosed

    3. Recognition of liabilities and assets

        a. Liability (asset) is recognized if net periodic pension cost recognized exceeds (is less than) amounts the employer has contributed to the plan.

**C.** Attribution

    1. Pension benefits should be attributed to periods of employee service based on plan's benefit formula.

    2. When employer has a present commitment to make future amendments, and substance of plan is to provide benefits attributable to prior service that are greater than benefits defined by written terms of the plan.

        a. The substantive commitment should be basis for accounting, and

        b. Existence and nature of the commitment to make future amendments should be disclosed

    3. Assumptions

        a. Assumed discount rates reflect rates at which pension benefits could be effectively settled

            (1) Used in measurements of projected and accumulated benefit obligations and the service and interest cost components of net periodic pension cost

    b.   Assumed compensation levels (when measuring service cost and the projected benefit obligation) should reflect an estimate of the actual future compensation levels of employees involved, including future changes attributed to general price levels, productivity, seniority, promotion, and other factors.

    c.   Accumulated benefit obligation shall be measured based on employees' history of service and compensation without estimate of future compensation levels.

    d.   Automatic benefit increases specified by plan that are expected to occur should be included in measurements of projected and accumulated benefit obligations and the service cost component.

    e.   Retroactive plan amendments should be included in computations of projected and accumulated benefit obligations.

        (1)   Once they have been contractually agreed to

        (2)   Even if some provisions take effect only in future periods

**D.**   Measurement of Plan Assets

   1.   For purposes of determining the funded status of the plan and required disclosures, plan investments, whether equity or debt securities, real estate, or other, should be measured at their fair value as of measurement date.

   2.   Market-related asset value is used for purposes of determining the expected return on plan assets and accounting for asset gains and losses.

**E.**   Acceptable Measurement Dates

   1.   As of date of financial statements, or

   2.   If used consistently from year to year, as of a date $\leq$ 3 months prior to that date

   3.   Measurement date is not intended to require that all procedures be performed after that date.

   4.   Information for items requiring estimates can be prepared as of an earlier date and projected forward to account for subsequent events (e.g., employee service).

   5.   The "assets and liabilities" reported in interim financial statements should be the same "assets and liabilities" recognized in previous year-end balance sheet.

     a.   Adjusted for subsequent accruals and contributions unless measures of both the obligation and plan assets are available as of a current date or a significant event occurs, such as plan amendment, that would call for such measurements

   6.   Measurements of net periodic pension cost for both interim and annual financial statements should be based on assumptions used for previous year-end measurements.

     a.   If more recent measurements are available or a significant event occurs, use these more recent measurements.

   7.   For fiscal years ending after December 15, 2008, the measurement date is the fiscal year-end of firm

**F.**   Disclosures (Amended by SFAS 132[R] and SFAS 158)

## SFAS 88 (P16) Employers' Accounting for Settlements and Curtailments of Defined Benefit Pension Plans and for Termination Benefits (Supersedes SFAS 74, Amended by SFAS 132 Revised)

Statement applies to an employer that sponsors a defined benefit pension plan accounted for under the provisions of SFAS 87 if all or part of the plan's pension benefit obligation is settled or the plan is curtailed. It also applies to an employer that offers benefits to employees in connection with their termination of employment.

The following terms are given specific definitions for the purposes of SFAS 88:

**Settlement**—Transaction that (a) is an irrevocable action, (b) relieves the employer (or the plan) of primary responsibility for a pension benefit obligation, and (c) eliminates significant risks related to the obligation and the assets used to effect the settlement.

**Annuity contract**—Irrevocable contract in which an insurance company[2] unconditionally undertakes a legal obligation to provide specified benefits to specific individuals in return for a fixed consideration or premium. It involves the transfer of significant risk from the employer to the insurance company.

**Curtailment**—Event that significantly reduces the expected years of future service of present employees or eliminates for a significant number of employees the accrual of defined benefits for some or all of their future services.

---

[2]   *If the insurance company is controlled by the employer or there is any reasonable doubt that the insurance company will meet its obligation under the contract, the purchase of the contract does not constitute a settlement for purposes of this statement.*

**A.** Relationship of Settlements and Curtailments to Other Events
  1. Settlement and curtailment may occur separately or together.
**B.** Accounting for Settlement of Pension Obligation
  1. For purposes of this statement, when a pension obligation is settled, the maximum gain or loss subject to recognition is the unrecognized gain or loss defined in SFAS 87 plus any remaining unrecognized net asset existing at the date of initial application of SFAS 87.
  2. If the purchase of a participating annuity contract constitutes a settlement, the maximum gain (but not the maximum loss) should be reduced by the cost of the participation right before determining the amount to be recognized in earnings.
  3. If the cost of all settlements in a year is less than or equal to the sum of the service cost and interest cost components of net periodic pension cost for the plan for the year, gain or loss recognition is permitted but not required for those settlements.
**C.** Accounting for Plan Curtailment
  1. Unrecognized prior service cost is a loss.
  2. The projected benefit obligation may be decreased (a gain) or increased (a loss) by a curtailment.
**D.** Termination Benefits
  1. Employer may provide benefits to employees in connection with their termination of employment.
  2. Termination benefits may take many forms consisting of
     a. Lump-sum payments
     b. Periodic future payments
  3. The cost of termination benefits recognized as a liability and a loss shall include the amount of any lump-sum payments and present value of any expected future payments.

## SFAS 89 (C28) Financial Reporting and Changing Prices

This statement **encourages** but does not require a business enterprise that prepares its financial statements in US dollars and in accordance with US generally accepted accounting principles to disclose supplementary information on changing prices.
**A.** Measurement
  1. Inventory
     a. Current cost is the current cost of purchasing or manufacturing, whichever is applicable
        (1) Or recoverable amount if lower
  2. Property, plant, and equipment
     a. Current cost is current cost of acquiring same service potential (or recoverable amount if lower)
        (1) That is, the same operating costs and output
        (2) Three valuation methods
           (a) Current cost of new asset less depreciation
           (b) Cost of comparable used asset
           (c) Adjusting new asset cost for differences in
              1] Useful life
              2] Output capacity
              3] Nature of service
              4] Operating costs
  3. Recoverable amount
     a. Current worth of net amount of cash expected to be recoverable from the use or sale of an asset
  4. Increase or decrease in current cost amount of inventory and PP&E, net of inflation
     a. Differences between current cost at entry dates and exit dates
        (1) Entry dates are the later of the beginning of the year or date of acquisition
        (2) Exit dates are the earlier of date of use, sale, etc., or year-end

## SFAS 91 (Bt7, D22, Fi4, In6, I89, L10, L20, Mo4) Accounting for Nonrefundable Fees and Costs Associated with Originating or Acquiring Loans and Initial Direct Costs of Leases

(Rescinds SFAS 17, Amends SFAS 13, 60, and 65)

Establishes the accounting for nonrefundable fees and costs associated with lending, committing to lend, or purchasing a loan or group of loans. Applies to all types of loans.
**A.** Loan origination fees shall be recognized over life of related loan as adjustment of yield.

**B.** Certain direct loan origination costs shall be deferred over the life of the related loan as a reduction of the loan's yield.

**C.** All loan commitment fees shall be deferred except for certain retrospectively determined fees.

　1. Those commitment fees meeting specified criteria shall be recognized over the loan commitment period.

　2. All other commitment fees shall be recognized as an adjustment of yield over the related loan's life.

　3. If commitment expires unexercised, then recognize in income upon expiration of the commitment.

**D.** Loan fees, certain direct loan origination costs, and purchase premiums and discounts on loans shall be recognized as an adjustment of yield generally by the interest method based on contractual terms of the loan.

　1. Prepayments by debtors may be anticipated in certain specified circumstances.

## SFAS 94 (C51) Consolidation of All Majority-Owned Subsidiaries (Amends ARB 51 with related amendment of ARB 43, Chapter 12, and APB 18)

**A.** Precludes use of parent company FS prepared for issuance to stockholders as FS of primary reporting entity

**B.** Requires consolidation of all majority-owned (ownerships, directly or indirectly, of more than 50% of outstanding voting shares of another company) subsidiaries

　1. Unless control

　　a. Temporary

　　b. Not held by majority owner (e.g., subsidiary)

　　　(1) Is in legal reorganization or bankruptcy

　　　(2) Operates under foreign exchange restrictions, controls, or other governmentally imposed uncertainties

　2. Even if

　　a. Subsidiary's operations nonhomogeneous

　　b. Large minority interest exists

　　c. Subsidiary located in foreign country

## SFAS 95 (C25) Statement of Cash Flows

**A.** Statement of Cash Flows in General

　1. Required for each period results of operation (income statement) are provided

　2. Objectives

　　a. Provide information about cash receipts and cash payments

　　b. Provide information about operating, investing, and financing activities

　　c. Helps users to assess

　　　(1) Ability to generate future net cash flows

　　　(2) Ability to meet obligations and pay dividends

　　　(3) Reasons for differences between income and associated cash receipts and payments

　　　(4) Both cash and noncash aspects of entity's investing and financing activities

　3. Shall report

　　a. Cash effects during a period from

　　　(1) Operating activities

　　　(2) Investing activities

　　　(3) Financing activities

　　b. Noncash financing and investing activities in supplemental schedule

**B.** Gross and Net Cash Flows

　1. Gross amount of cash receipts and payments is relevant.

　　a. For example, must show issuance of bonds and retirement of bonds separately

　2. Statement should explain change during the period in **cash and cash equivalents**.

　　a. Cash equivalents

　　　(1) Short-term, highly liquid investments that are

　　　　(a) Readily convertible into known amounts of cash

　　　　(b) Near maturity (original maturity of three months or less from **date of purchase** by the enterprise) and present negligible risk of changes in value

    (2) Examples
        (a) Treasury bills
        (b) Commercial paper
        (c) Money market funds

**C.** Classification
  1. Investing activities
    a. Include
      (1) Lending money and collecting on those loans
      (2) Acquiring and selling, or disposing
        (a) Securities that are neither cash equivalents nor held in a trading portfolio
        (b) Productive assets expected to generate revenue over long periods of time
      (3) Cash inflows
        (a) Receipts from loans by
          1] Principal repayments
          2] Sale of loans made by the entity
        (b) Receipts from sale of
          1] Securities of other entities carried in held-to-maturity (debt only) or available-for-sale portfolios (debt or equity)
          2] Property, plant, and equipment
      (4) Cash outflows
        (a) Loans made or purchased by the entity
        (b) Payments to acquire assets
          1] Securities of other entities carried in held-to-maturity (debt only) or available-for-sale portfolios (debt or equity)
          2] Property, plant, and equipment
  2. Financing activities
    a. Include
      (1) Obtaining resources from owners and providing them with a return on, and a return of, their investment
      (2) Obtaining resources from creditors and repaying the amounts borrowed
    b. Cash inflows
      (1) Proceeds from the issuance of
        (a) Equity securities
        (b) Bonds
        (c) Mortgages
        (d) Notes
        (e) Other short- or long-term borrowing
    c. Cash outflows
      (1) Payments of dividends
      (2) Outlays to repurchase entity's shares
      (3) Repayments of amounts borrowed
  3. Operating activities
    a. Include
      (1) All transactions and other events that are not investing and financing
      (2) Delivering or producing goods for sale and providing services
      (3) Cash effects of transactions and other events that enter into the determination of income
    b. Cash inflows
      (1) Cash receipts from sale of goods or services
      (2) Interest and dividends received
      (3) Other operating cash receipts
      (4) Sales of "trading portfolio" securities
    c. Cash outflows
      (1) Payments to employees and other suppliers of goods or services
      (2) Income taxes paid
      (3) Interest paid
      (4) Other operating cash payments

(5) Purchases of "trading portfolio" securities

**D.** Exchange Rate Effects

1. Report the reporting currency equivalent of foreign currency cash flows using exchange rates in effect at time of cash flows
   a. Weighted-average exchange rate may be used, if result substantially same.

**E.** Content and Form

1. Report net cash provided or used by operating, investing, and financing activities
2. At end of statement, reconcile beginning and ending cash and cash equivalents by showing net increase or decrease for period as addition to beginning balance to obtain ending balance
3. Cash flow from operating activities
   a. Direct presentation (encouraged by FASB)
      (1) Report major classes of operating receipts and payments (C.3.b.-c. above)
      (2) Difference between cash receipts and payments—net cash flow from operating activities
      (3) Supplemental schedule using indirect presentation must be presented when direct method used in body of statement
   b. Indirect presentation (acceptable format)
      (1) Shall separately report all major classes of reconciling items
         (a) Deferrals of past operating cash receipts and cash payments such as depreciation and changes during the period in inventory and unearned revenue
         (b) Accruals of expected future operating cash receipts and cash payments such as changes during the period in receivables and payables
      (2) Interest paid (net of amounts capitalized) and income taxes paid must appear in related disclosures
   c. Does not include cash flows from transactions or events whose effects are included in income, but which are not operating activities; for example,
      (1) Gain or loss on extinguishment of debt—financing activities
      (2) Gain or loss on sale of assets or from disposal of discontinued operations—investing activities
4. Inflows and outflows of cash from investing and financing activities
   a. Noncash aspects should be clearly identified in separate schedule; for example,
      (1) Conversion of debt to equity
      (2) Acquisition of assets by assuming liabilities
         (a) Includes capital lease obligations
      (3) Exchanges of assets or of liabilities
5. Enterprise shall disclose policy for determining items included in cash equivalent.
   a. Change in policy is change in accounting principle requiring restatement of comparative FS.

**F.** Cash flow per share shall not be reported.

## SFAS 98 (L10) Accounting for Leases (Amends SFAS 13, 66, and 91. Rescinds SFAS 26 and Technical Bulletin 79-11)

*NOTE: The outline below includes those changes that relate to all leases. The remainder of SFAS 98 deals with real estate leases that are not outlined since they are not expected to be tested on the exam.*

**A.** Lease term, as redefined, includes

1. All periods covered by bargain renewal options
2. All periods for which failure to renew the lease imposes a penalty
3. All periods during which a loan, directly or indirectly related to the leased property, is outstanding
4. All periods covered by ordinary renewal options preceding the exercisable date of a bargain purchase option
5. All periods representing renewals or extensions of the lease at the lessor's option

## SFAS 106 (P40) Employers' Accounting for Postretirement Benefits other than Pensions
(Supersedes SFAS 81; amends APB 12, SFAS 87, APB 16; Amended by SFAS 132)

Standard applies to all forms of postretirement benefits, particularly postretirement health care benefits. Applies to written plan and to a plan whose existence may be implied from well-defined, although perhaps unwritten, practice of paying postretirement benefits (called the substantive plan). Does not apply to pensions.

The following terms are given specific definitions for purposes of SFAS 106:

**Attribution period**—The period of an employee's service to which the expected postretirement benefit obligation for that employee is assigned. The beginning of the attribution period is the employee's date of hire unless the plan's benefit formula grants credit only for service from a later date, in which case the beginning of the attribution period is generally the beginning of that credited service period. The end of the attribution period is the full eligibility date.

**Benefit formula**—The basis for determining benefits to which participants may be entitled under a postretirement benefit plan. A plan's benefit formula specifies the years of service to be rendered, age to be attained while in service, or a combination of both that must be met for an employee to be eligible to receive benefits under the plan.

**Full eligibility date**—The date at which an employee has rendered all of the service necessary to have earned the right to receive all of the benefits expected to be received by that employee (including any beneficiaries and dependents expected to receive benefits).

**Health care cost trend rates**—An assumption about the annual rate(s) of change in the cost of health care benefits currently provided by the postretirement benefit plan, due to factors other than changes in the composition of the plan population by age and dependency status, for each year from the measurement date until the end of the period in which benefits are expected to be paid.

**Incurred claims cost (by age)**—The cost of providing the postretirement health care benefits covered by the plan to a plan participant, after adjusting for reimbursements from Medicare and other providers of health care benefits and for deductibles, coinsurance provisions, and other specific claims costs borne by the retiree.

**Net periodic postretirement benefit cost**—The amount recognized in an employer's financial statements as the cost of a postretirement benefit plan for a period. Components of net periodic postretirement benefit cost include service cost, interest cost, actual return on plan assets, gain or loss, amortization of unrecognized prior service cost, and amortization of the unrecognized transition obligation or asset.

**Plan amendment**—A change in the existing terms of a plan. A plan amendment may increase or decrease benefits, including those attributed to years of service already rendered.

**Transition asset**—The unrecognized amount, as of the date this statement is initially applied, of (a) the fair value of plan assets plus any recognized accrued postretirement benefit cost or less any recognized prepaid postretirement benefit cost in excess of (b) the accumulated postretirement benefit obligation.

**Transition obligation**—The unrecognized amount, as of the date this statement is initially applied, of (a) the accumulated postretirement benefit obligation in excess of (b) the fair value of plan assets plus any recognized accrued postretirement benefit cost or less any recognized prepaid postretirement benefit cost.

**Unrecognized transition asset**—The portion of the transition asset that has not been recognized either immediately as the effect of a change in accounting or on a delayed basis as a part of net periodic postretirement benefit cost, as an offset to certain losses, or as a part of accounting for the effects of a settlement or a curtailment.

**Unrecognized transition obligation**—The portion of the transition obligation that has not been recognized either immediately as the effect of a change in accounting or on a delayed basis as a part of net periodic postretirement benefit cost, as an offset to certain gains, or as a part of accounting for the effects of a settlement or a curtailment.

A.  Single Employer Defined Benefit Plans
   1.  Postretirement benefits are part of compensation paid to employees for services
      a.  Amount of benefits to be paid depends on future events specified in plan's benefit formula
   2.  Postretirement benefits formerly were accounted for on a pay-as-you-go (cash) basis. SFAS 106 changes this practice by requiring accrual, during the years that the employee renders necessary service, of **expected** cost of providing those benefits to an employee. Any method of postretirement benefits accounting that recognizes cost before payment of benefits to retirees must deal with two problems.
      a.  Assumptions must be made concerning future events that will determine amount and timing of benefits.
      b.  Approach to attributing cost of postretirement benefits to individual years of service must be selected.
B.  Basic Elements of Postretirement Benefits Accounting
   1.  Prior service cost

a.   Except as specified otherwise, prior service cost shall be amortized by assigning an equal amount to each future service period of each employee active at the date of a plan amendment who was not yet fully eligible for benefits at that date.
b.   If all or almost all of a plan's participants are fully eligible for benefits, prior service cost shall be amortized over remaining life expectancy of those participants.
c.   Consistent use of alternative amortization approach that more rapidly reduces unrecognized cost of retroactive amendments is acceptable.
  (1)  Alternative method used should be disclosed.
d.   When period during which employer expects to realize economic benefits from amendment granting increased benefits is shorter than entire remaining service period of active employees, amortization of prior service cost shall be accelerated.
e.   Plan amendment can reduce, rather than increase, accumulated postretirement benefit obligation
  (1)  Reduction should be used to reduce any existing unrecognized prior service cost
  (2)  Then to reduce any remaining unrecognized transition obligation
  (3)  Excess, if any, shall be amortized on same basis as specified for prior service cost
2.  Gains and losses
  a.   Gains (losses)
    (1)  Result from changes in amount of either accumulated postretirement benefit obligation or plan assets due to experience different than assumed and changes in assumptions
    (2)  Include both **realized** and **unrealized** amounts
  b.   Asset gains (losses) include both (a) changes reflected in market-related value of assets and (b) changes not yet reflected in market-related value.
    (1)  Asset gains (losses) not yet reflected in market-related value are not required to be amortized as c. below.
  c.   As a minimum, amortization of unrecognized net gain (loss) should be included as a component of net postretirement benefit cost for a year if, as of the beginning of the year, that unrecognized net gain (loss) > .10 of the larger of the accumulated postretirement benefit obligation or the market-related value of plan assets.
    (1)  Minimum amortization should be the excess divided by the average remaining service period of active employees expected to receive benefits under the plan
      (a)  Amortization must always reduce beginning of the year balance
      (b)  Amortization of a net unrecognized gain (loss) results in a decrease (increase) in net periodic pension cost
    (2)  If all or almost all of plan's participants are inactive, average remaining life expectancy of inactive participants should be used instead of average remaining service.
  d.   Any systematic method of amortization of unrecognized gains (losses) may be used in lieu of the minimum specified above provided that
    (1)  Minimum is used in any period in which minimum amortization is greater (reduces the net balance by more)
    (2)  Method is applied consistently and disclosed
3.  Recognition of liabilities and assets
  a.   SFAS 106 requires an employer's obligation for postretirement benefits expected to be provided to an employee be **fully** accrued by the full eligibility date of employee, even if employee is to render additional service beyond that date
  b.   Transition obligations
    (1)  SFAS 106 measures the transition obligation as the unfunded and unrecognized accumulated postretirement benefit obligation for all plan participants. Two options are provided for recognizing that transition obligation.
      (a)  **Immediate** recognition of the transition obligation as the effect of an accounting change (i.e., include all of the obligation as part of the net periodic postretirement benefit cost)
      (b)  Recognize the transition obligation in the balance sheet and income statement on a delayed basis over the plan participants' future service periods, with proper disclosure of the remaining unrecognized amount. Note that delayed recognition **cannot** result in less rapid recognition than accounting for the transition obligation on a pay-as-you-go basis.

C.  Attribution
    1.  The expected postretirement benefit obligation shall be attributed, in equal amounts, to each year of service in the attribution period.
    2.  However, if a benefit plan contains a benefit formula that attributes a disproportionate share of the expected postretirement benefit obligation to employees' early years of service, the postretirement benefits should be attributed based on the plan's benefit formula.
    3.  Assumptions
        a.  Assumed discount rates shall reflect time value of money in determining present value of future cash outflows currently expected to be required to satisfy postretirement benefit obligation
            (1)  Used in measurements of expected and accumulated postretirement benefit obligations and service and interest cost components of net periodic postretirement benefit cost
        b.  Assumed compensation levels (when measuring service cost and expected and accumulated postretirement benefit obligations) shall reflect estimate of actual future compensation levels of employees involved, including future changes attributed to general price levels, productivity, seniority, promotion, and other factors.
        c.  Accumulated postretirement benefit obligation shall be measured based on employees' history of service and compensation without estimate of future compensation levels.
        d.  Automatic benefit changes specified by plan that are expected to occur should be included in measurements of projected and accumulated benefit obligations and the service cost component.
        e.  Plan amendments should be included in computations of projected and accumulated benefit obligations.
            (1)  Once they have been contractually agreed to
            (2)  Even if some provisions take effect only in future periods
D.  Measurement of Plan Assets
    1.  For purposes of required disclosures, plan investments, whether equity or debt securities, real estate, or other, shall be measured at FMV as of measurement date.
    2.  Market-related asset value is used for purposes of determining the expected return on plan assets and accounting for asset gains and losses.
E.  Acceptable Measurement Dates
    1.  As of date of financial statements, or
    2.  If used consistently from year to year, as of a date $\leq$ 3 months prior to that date
    3.  Measurement date is not intended to require that all procedures be performed after that date
    4.  Information for items requiring estimates can be prepared as of an earlier date and projected forward to account for subsequent events (e.g., employee service)
    5.  Measurements of net periodic postretirement benefit cost for both interim and annual financial statements shall be based on assumptions used for previous year-end measurements
        a.  If more recent measurements are available or a significant event occurs, use more recent measurements
F.  Disclosures (amended by SFAS 132)

## SFAS 107 (F25) Disclosures about Fair Value of Financial Instruments

A.  Statement requires entities to disclose the fair value of financial instruments, both assets and liabilities whether recognized or not recognized in the statement of financial position, for which it is practicable to estimate fair value.
    1.  Applies to all entities
    2.  Does not change any recognition, measurement, or classification requirements for financial instruments in financial statements
    3.  Fair value disclosures of financial instruments previously prescribed by GAAP meet the requirements of this statement.
B.  Financial Instruments include
    1.  Cash
    2.  Evidence of ownership interest in an entity, or
    3.  A contract that both
        a.  Imposes contractual obligation on one entity to deliver cash or another financial instrument to second entity or to exchange financial instruments on potentially unfavorable terms with second entity, and

      b.  Conveys contractual right to second entity to receive cash or another financial instrument from first entity or to exchange financial instruments on potentially favorable terms with first entity

**C.** Fair value of a financial instrument is defined by SFAS 157 as "the price that would be received to sell an asset or paid to transfer a liability in an orderly transaction between market participants at the measurement date."

**D.** Standard lists a number of areas for which the disclosure requirements are not applicable, including pensions and other deferred compensation arrangements and leases.

**E.** Disclosure Requirements
1. When practicable (i.e., without incurring excessive costs), an entity must disclose the fair value of financial instruments in either the body of the financial statements or in the accompanying notes.
   a. Disclosure must include the method(s) and significant assumptions used in estimating fair value
      (1) Quoted market price is generally the best estimate of fair value.
      (2) If quoted market price is not available, management must estimate fair value based upon similar financial instruments or valuation techniques.
      (3) No disclosure is required for trade receivables and payables when carrying amount approximates fair value.
   b. Disclosure must distinguish between financial instruments held or issued for
      (1) Trading purposes
      (2) Purposes other than trading
2. If estimation of the fair value of financial instruments is not practicable, entity must disclose
   a. Information pertinent to estimating the fair value (i.e., the carrying amount, effective interest rate, and maturity), and
   b. The reason why estimation of fair value is not practicable.
3. Derivative financial instruments may not be combined, aggregated or netted with nonderivative or other derivative financial instruments.
4. If financial instruments disclosed in more than one area in FS, one note must contain a summary table cross-referencing the location of the other instruments.
5. Disclosure of concentrations of credit risk of all financial instruments
   a. Disclose all significant concentrations of credit risk from **all** financial instruments, whether from an individual counterparty or groups of counterparties.
   b. Group concentrations exist if a number of counterparties are engaged in similar activities and have similar economic characteristics such that they would be similarly affected by changes in conditions.
   c. Disclose for each significant concentration
      (1) Information about the (shared) activity, region, or economic characteristics
      (2) The amount of accounting loss the entity would incur should any party to the financial instrument fail to perform according to the terms of the contract and the collateral or security, if any, is of no value.
      (3) The entity's policy of requiring collateral or security, the entity's access to that collateral or security, and the nature and brief description of the collateral or security.

## SFAS 109 (I27) Accounting for Income Taxes
(Supercedes SFAS 96, 100, 103, and 108)

**A.** Establishes financial accounting and reporting requirements for income taxes resulting from an entity's activities during the current and preceding years.
1. Continues BS oriented asset and liability approach consistent with SFAC 6.
2. Objectives
   a. Recognize taxes payable or refundable for current year.
   b. Recognize deferred tax liabilities and assets for future tax consequences of events previously recognized in financial statements or tax returns.

**B.** Basic principles
1. Recognize current tax liability or asset for estimated taxes payable or refundable on tax returns for current year
2. Measure and recognize deferred tax liability or asset using enacted tax rate(s) expected to apply to taxable income in periods in which the deferred tax assets and liabilities are expected to be realized or settled

3.  Adjust measurement of deferred tax assets so as to not recognize tax benefits not expected to be realized
4.  Deferred tax assets and liabilities are **not** discounted to reflect their present value

**C.  Measurement of Deferred Taxes**

1.  Temporary differences
    a.  Difference between tax basis of asset or liability and its reported amount for financial accounting which results in taxable or deductible amounts in future years
        (1)  Includes all timing differences
        (2)  Includes tax-book differences in asset's bases
    b.  Future effects
        (1)  **Taxable amounts** are from temporary differences that will result in lower amounts of expense or higher amounts of revenue being reported on the tax return than are reported on the books in the future period.
        (2)  **Deductible amounts** are from temporary differences that will result in higher amounts of expense or lower amounts of revenue being reported on the tax return than are reported on the books in the future period.
2.  Deferred tax liability or asset measured each BS date
    a.  Identify types and amounts of existing temporary differences **and** nature of each type of operating loss and tax credit carryforward and the remaining length of the carryforward period
    b.  Measure total deferred tax liability for taxable temporary differences using the enacted applicable tax rate
    c.  Measure total deferred tax asset for deductible temporary differences and operating loss carryforwards using the enacted applicable tax rate
    d.  Measure deferred tax assets for each type of tax credit carryforward
    e.  Reduce deferred tax assets by a valuation allowance, **if more likely than not** (a likelihood of more than 50%) that some or all of deferred tax asset will not be realized
        (1)  All available evidence (positive and negative) should be considered to determine whether valuation allowance is needed.

**D.  Changes in Tax Rates**

1.  Change in rates
    a.  Change previously recorded amounts of deferred tax liabilities or assets
    b.  Net adjustments shall be reflected in tax expense on continuing operations in period that includes enactment date.

**E.  Business Combinations**

1.  Recognize deferred tax asset or liability for differences between assigned values and tax basis of assets and liabilities recognized in a purchase combination

**F.  Intraperiod Tax Allocation**

1.  Allocate income tax expense or benefit for the period among continuing operations, extraordinary items, other comprehensive income, and items charged or credited to stockholders' equity
    a.  In cases where there is only one item after continuing operations, portion of income tax expense (benefit) remaining after allocation to continuing operations is amount allocated to that item.
    b.  In cases where there are two or more items after continuing operations, portion left after allocation to continuing operations is allocated among other items in proportion to their individual effects on income tax expense (benefit).

**G.  Financial Statement Presentation and Disclosure**

1.  Balance sheet
    a.  Report deferred tax liabilities and assets as current or noncurrent based on classification of related asset or liability
    b.  Classify deferred tax liabilities or assets not related to an asset or liability (i.e., one related to a carryforward) according to the expected reversal date of the temporary difference
    c.  For a taxpaying component of an enterprise and within a particular tax jurisdiction
        (1)  All current deferred tax liabilities and assets should be offset and reported as a single amount
        (2)  All noncurrent deferred tax liabilities and assets should be offset and reported as a single amount

2. Must disclose the following components of the net deferred tax liability or asset:
   a. The total of all deferred tax liabilities
   b. The total of all deferred tax assets
   c. The total valuation allowance for deferred tax assets
3. Additional disclosures
   a. Disclose any net change in the total valuation allowance
   b. Disclose the types of temporary differences, carryforwards, and carrybacks
4. Income statement
   a. Components of tax expense attributable to continuing operations shall be disclosed in financial statements or notes. For example
      (1) Current tax expense or benefit
      (2) Deferred tax expense or benefit (exclusive of other components listed below)
      (3) Investment tax credits
      (4) Government grants (to the extent recognized as a reduction of income tax expense)
      (5) Benefits of operating loss carryforwards
      (6) Tax expense resulting from allocation of certain tax benefits either directly to contributed capital or to reduce goodwill or other noncurrent intangible assets of an acquired entity
      (7) Adjustments of a deferred tax liability or asset resulting from enacted changes in tax laws, rates, or status
   b. Variances between statutory and effective tax rates must be disclosed.
      (1) Public entities should disclose reconciliation using percentages or dollar amounts.
      (2) Nonpublic entities must disclose nature of significant reconciling items.
   c. Disclose amounts and expiration dates of operating loss and tax credit carryforwards **and** any portion of the deferred tax asset valuation allowance for which subsequently recognized tax benefits will be allocated to reduce intangible assets or directly reduce accumulated other comprehensive income.

## SFAS 112 (C44) Employers' Accounting for Postemployment Benefits

**A.** Statement sets forth accounting standards for employers providing post**employment** benefits to former/inactive employees, **after employment but before** retirement.
   1. Applies to any postemployment benefits provided to former employers and their beneficiaries and dependents except
      a. Special or contractual termination benefits addressed by SFAS 88 and 106.
      b. Postemployment benefits derived from post**retirement** benefit or pension plans.
      c. Stock compensation plans covered by APB 25.
      d. Deferred compensation plans for individual employees that are covered by APB 12.
   2. Postemployment benefits may
      a. Result from death, disability, layoff, etc.
      b. Be paid in cash or in kind
      c. Be paid upon assumption of inactive status or over a period of time
**B.** Applicable postemployment benefits must be accounted for according to SFAS 43, which states:
   1. Liability for future compensated absences must be accrued if
      a. Obligation relates to services already provided by the employee,
      b. Rights to compensation vest or accumulate,
      c. Payment of obligation is probable, **and**
      d. Amount to be paid is reasonably estimable.
**C.** If conditions listed above are not met but the benefits are within scope of SFAS 43, they are accounted for according to SFAS 5, which states:
   1. Estimated loss contingency accrued if
      a. It is known before FS are issued that it is probable that asset has been impaired or a liability incurred and that future events will probably confirm the loss, **and**
      b. Amount of loss is reasonably estimable.
**D.** Disclosure required if liability for postemployment benefits not accrued solely because amount not reasonably estimable.

**SFAS 114 (D22) Accounting by Creditors for Impairment of a Loan** (Amends SFAS 5 and 15; amended by SFAS 118)
A.  Scope of SFAS 114
1.  Applies to all creditors and to all loans except for those specified in A.3 (a.-d.)
2.  Applies to all loans (including A.3.a.) that are restructured in a troubled debt restructuring involving a modification of terms
3.  Exceptions
a.  Large groups of smaller-balance homogeneous loans collectively evaluated for impairment
b.  Loans that are measured at fair value or at the lower of cost or fair value
c.  Leases
d.  Debt securities
4.  Does not specify how a creditor should identify loans that are to be evaluated for collectibility
B.  Recognition of Impairment
1.  A loan is impaired when it is probable that a creditor will be unable to collect all amounts due according to the contractual terms.
a.  Probable—future event or events are likely to occur
b.  All amounts due according to the contractual terms include both interest and principal payments collected as scheduled in loan agreement.
2.  If a loan qualifies as exception A.3.a., the creditor may not apply the provisions of SFAS 114 until the debt is restructured.
3.  Instances when a loan is not impaired
a.  Insignificant delays or shortfalls
b.  A delay in which creditor expects to collect all amounts due including interest accrued for the period of delay
C.  Measurement of Impairment
1.  Creditor measures impairment based on present value of expected future cash flows discounted at the loan's effective interest rate
a.  Effective interest rate—rate implicit in loan at time of origination
b.  If effective interest rate varies (based on an independent index or rate)
(1)  May be calculated based on the index or rate as it changes over life of loan
(2)  Or may be fixed at rate in effect at date the loan meets impairment criterion
c.  Expected future cash flows determined as creditor's best estimate based on reasonable and supportable assumptions and projections (including estimated costs to sell)
2.  Loans with common risk characteristics may be aggregated and impairment measured using historical statistics and a composite effective interest rate.
3.  Alternative measures of impairment
a.  Loan's observable market price
b.  Fair value of collateral if loan is collateral dependent
(1)  Collateral dependent means repayment provided solely by the underlying collateral
(2)  This method must be used when foreclosure is probable (and loan is collateral dependent)
4.  When measure of impaired loan is less than recorded investment in loan
a.  Create valuation allowance with charge to bad debt expense
b.  Or adjust existing valuation allowance with charge to bad debt expense
5.  Significant changes (increases or decreases) subsequent to initial measure of impairment
a.  Recalculate impairment
b.  Adjust valuation allowance
c.  Net carrying amount of loan may never exceed recorded investment in loan
D.  Income Recognition
1.  The present value of an impaired loan changes over time and also changes because of revised estimates in the amount or timing of cash flows.
2.  Recognition and measurement methods to reflect changes in present value are not specified in this statement as amended.
E.  Disclosures
1.  The recorded investment in impaired loans, total allowance for credit losses related to impaired loans, and amount for which no allowance for credit losses

2. The creditor's income recognition method, including cash receipts
3. For each period presented which relates to the impaired loans
    a. Average recorded investment
    b. Interest revenue recognized
    c. If practicable, interest revenue recognized on a cash basis

## SFAS 115 (I80) Accounting for Certain Investments in Debt and Equity Securities
(Supersedes SFAS 12)

A. Establishes financial accounting and reporting requirements for all investments in debt securities and for small investments in equity securities with readily determinable fair values
   1. "Small" investments are those not accounted for by the equity method or involving consolidated subsidiaries
B. Segregates debt and equity securities into three categories
   1. Held-to-maturity securities
      a. Applies only to debt securities
      b. Requires intent and ability to hold to maturity
         (1) Will **not** sell in response to changes in
             (a) Funding terms and sources
             (b) Interest rates and prepayment risk
             (c) Foreign currency risk
             (d) Attractiveness of alternative investments
             (e) Liquidity needs
         (2) In rare cases, intent may change due to nonrecurring and unforeseeable circumstances.
             (a) Continuing deterioration of issuer's credit
             (b) Elimination of tax-exempt status of interest
             (c) Business combination or disposition that increases interest rate risk or credit risk
             (d) Regulatory change in permissible investments
             (e) Downsizing to meet industry capital requirements
             (f) Increased risk weight of debt securities held as regulatory risk-based capital
         (3) Considered maturity if
             (a) Sale occurs so close to maturity that interest rate risk is virtually eliminated
             (b) Sale occurs after at least 85% of the principal has been collected
      c. Balance sheet
         (1) Report at amortized cost
         (2) Classify as current or noncurrent on an individual basis
      d. Income statement
         (1) Do not report unrealized holding gains and losses
         (2) Include realized G(L) in earnings
         (3) Include interest income and premium/discount amortization in earnings
      e. Statement of cash flows
         (1) Classify cash inflows from sales and outflows from purchases gross (not netted) as investing activities
   2. Trading securities
      a. Applies to debt and equity securities held for current resale
      b. Balance sheet
         (1) Report at fair value (See SFAS 157 for fair value measurements)
         (2) Classify as current assets, generally
      c. Income statement
         (1) Include unrealized holding G(L) in earnings
         (2) Exclude previously recognized realized G(L) from earnings
         (3) Include dividend and interest revenue
      d. Statement of cash flows
         (1) Classify purchases and sales as operating activity
   3. Available-for-sale securities
      a. Applies to debt and equity securities not categorized as held-to-maturity or trading securities
      b. Balance sheet

           (1) Report at fair value (See SFAS 157 for fair value measurements)

           (2) Classify as current or noncurrent on an individual basis

           (3) Report net unrealized holding G(L) in other comprehensive income and accumulated other comprehensive income as separate component of stockholders' equity

      c. Income statement

           (1) Include realized G(L) in earnings

           (2) Include dividend and interest revenue and premium/discount amortization in earnings

      d. Statement of cash flows

           (1) Classify sales and purchases gross (not netted) as investing activity

**C.** Transfers between categories are accounted for at fair value

    1. From trading

      a. Do not reverse recognized unrealized holding G(L) at date of transfer

    2. To trading

      a. Recognize unrealized holding G(L) immediately

    3. To available-for-sale from held-to-maturity

      a. Report unrealized holding G(L) as other comprehensive income

      b. Transfers from held-to-maturity should be rare

    4. To held-to-maturity from available-for-sale

      a. Report unrealized holding G(L) as other comprehensive income

      b. Amortize G(L) over remaining life of security as adjustment to yield

**D.** Impairment of Securities

    1. Applies to held-to-maturity and available-for-sale securities

    2. If permanent decline

      a. Write down to fair value

      b. Include realized loss in earnings

    3. No write-up for subsequent recoveries

**E.** Disclosures

    1. Only held-to-maturity and available-for-sale securities

    2. By major security type

      a. Aggregate fair value

      b. Gross unrealized holding gains and losses

      c. Amortized cost basis

    3. By maturity of debt securities

      a. All enterprises disclose contractual information.

      b. Financial institutions disclose fair value and amortized cost for four or more groups of maturities

          (1) Up to one year

          (2) Over one through five years

          (3) Over five through ten years

          (4) Over ten years

      c. Securities maturing at multiple dates

          (1) May disclose separately

          (2) May allocate over groupings

    4. Available-for-sale securities

      a. Proceeds from sales

      b. Gross realized G(L)

      c. Cost basis for determining G(L)

      d. Change in net unrealized holding G(L) reported as comprehensive income in stockholders' equity

    5. Trading securities

      a. Change in net unrealized holding G(L) reported in earnings

    6. Transfers

      a. Gross G(L) on transfer from available-for-sale to trading

      b. Of held-to-maturity securities

          (1) Amortized cost

          (2) Realized or unrealized G(L)

          (3) Reason for sale

## SFAS 116 (C67) Accounting for Contributions Received and Contributions Made

Establishes accounting standards for contributions received or made for all types of entities, not-for-profit, and business enterprises.

A. Contributions—defined

Contributions can be defined as an unconditional promise to give cash or other assets to an entity. A cancellation of a liability is also considered a contribution.

B. Contributions received (donee accounting)
1. Shall be capitalized by the donee at FMV of the item and recognized as revenue in period received.
2. Contributions with donor imposed restrictions shall be reported as restricted revenues or gains unless the restrictions are met in the same reporting period.
3. Receipts of unconditional promises to give the payments due in the future shall be reported as restricted support unless the donor intends the funds to be used for current operations.
4. Not-for-profit organizations shall recognize the expiration of donor-imposed restrictions as they expire.

C. Contributions made (donor accounting) shall be recognized at FMV as expense in period the item is donated
1. Donation expense should be classified under other expense on the income statement.
2. If difference exists between the FMV and book value of the item, then gain or loss on disposal will be recognized.

## SFAS 117 (No5) Financial Statements of Not-for-Profit Organizations

Establishes the reporting standards for the general-purpose external financial statements of not-for-profit organizations.

A. A complete set of financial statement for a not-for-profit organization shall include
1. A statement of financial position
2. A statement of activities
3. A statement of cash flows
4. Accompanying notes

B. Voluntary health and welfare organizations shall also include a statement of functional expenses

C. The statement of financial position provides relevant information bout liquidity, financial flexibility, and the interrelationship of the organization's assets and liabilities
1. Assets and liabilities should be aggregated in reasonably homogenous groups
2. Cash or other assets received with a donor-imposed restriction that limits their use to long-term purposes should not be classified with cash or other assets that are available for current use
3. Information about liquidity may be provided by one or more of the following
   a. Sequencing assets according to their nearness of conversion to cash and liabilities according to maturity
   b. Classifying assets and liabilities as current and noncurrent
   c. Note disclosure about liquidity and maturity
4. A statement of position shall present
   a. Permanently restricted net assets
   b. Temporarily restricted net assets
   c. Unrestricted net assets

D. The statement of activities is designed to provide information about
1. The effects of transactions and other events that change the amount and nature of net assets
2. The relationships of those transactions and other events and circumstances to each other
3. How the organization's resources are used

E. The statement of activities should show the change in permanently restricted net assets, temporarily restricted net assets, and unrestricted net assets for the period
1. Generally, revenues and expenses shall be reported at gross amounts
2. However, gains and losses may be shown at net amounts if they result from peripheral or incidental or from events and circumstances that are beyond the control of management
3. Expenses should be presented according to their functional classification

F. The statement of cash flows is designed to provide information about cash receipts and payments of the organization during the period

**SFAS 123 Revised (C36) Share-Based Payment**

**A.** Provides a fair value based method of accounting for stock-based payment plans
  1. Supersedes APB 25, amends SFAS 123
  2. Applies to all transactions between an entity and its "suppliers" (whether employees or nonemployees) in which the entity acquires goods or services through issuance of equity instruments or incurrence of liabilities based on fair value of the entity's common stock or other equity instruments
  3. Examples include stock purchase plans, stock options, restricted stock, and stock appreciation rights
  4. Classifies share-based payment as either equity or liability

**B.** Transactions with Nonemployees—Accounted for based on fair value of consideration received or fair value of equity instruments given, whichever is more readily determinable.

**C.** Transactions with Employees—Uses fair value based method

**D.** Measurement Methods
  1. Share-based payments recorded as equity
     a. Measured at fair value at grant date
     b. Stock options are measured at fair value which is based on the observable market price of an option with the same or similar terms and conditions, or via use of an option pricing model which considers, as of grant date, exercise price and expected life of the option, current price of underlying stock and its anticipated volatility, expected dividends on the stock, and risk-free interest rate for expected term of the option.
     c. If fair value cannot be determined as of grant date, final measure shall be based on stock price and any other pertinent factors when it becomes reasonably possible to estimate that value. Current intrinsic value shall be used as a measure until a final determination of fair value can be made.
  2. Share-based payments recorded as liabilities
     Requires the recording of liability based on current stock price at end of each period. Changes in stock price during service period are recognized as compensation cost over service period. A change in stock price subsequent to service period is recognized as compensation cost of that period.

**E.** Recognition of Compensation Cost
  1. Total compensation cost is based on the number of instruments that eventually vest
     a. Vesting is defined as moment when employee's right to receive or retain such instruments or cash is no longer contingent on performance of additional services
     b. No compensation cost shall be recognized for employees that forfeit eligibility due to failure either to achieve service requirement or performance condition
     c. Compensation cost shall not be reversed if vested employee's stock option expires unexercised
     d. Company must estimate forfeitures due to service or performance condition not being met
     e. Total compensation cost is amortized straight-line over the requisite service period
  2. Acceptable accrual methods
     a. As of grant date, base accruals of compensation cost on best available estimate of the number of options or instruments expected to vest, with estimates for forfeitures
     b. As of grant date, accrue compensation cost as if all options or instruments that are subject only to a service requirement will vest

**F.** Tax consequences of stock-based compensation transactions shall be accounted for pursuant to SFAS 109
  1. Excess tax benefits are recognized as additional paid-in capital
  2. Cash retained as a result of excess tax benefits is presented on the statement of cash flows as a cash inflow from financing activities

**G.** Disclosures
  1. The method of estimating the fair value of goods or services received or fair value of the equity instruments granted during the period
  2. The cash flow effects from share-based payments
  3. Vesting requirements, maximum term of options granted, and number of shares authorized for grants of options or other equity instruments
  4. The number and weighted-average exercise prices of each group of options
  5. The weighted-average grant-date fair value of options granted during the year, classified according to whether exercise price equals, exceeds, or is less than fair value of stock at date of grant
  6. A description of methods used and assumptions made in determining fair values of the options
  7. Total compensation cost recognized for the year

**SFAS 128 (E11) Earnings Per Share**

**A.** Presentation on Financial Statements

1. Entities with publicly held common stock and simple capital structures (no potential common shares) need only present basic per share amounts. All other entities must present basic and diluted per share amounts with equal prominence.

2. Must present EPS on face of income statement for
   a. Income from continuing operations
   b. Net income

3. May present on face of income statement or in notes
   a. Discontinued operations
   b. Extraordinary items
   c. Cumulative effect of change in accounting principle

**B.** Basic EPS—Measures entity performance over a period of time

1. Computed as net income minus preferred dividends divided by the weighted-average number of common shares outstanding. The claims of senior securities (nonconvertible preferred dividends) should be deducted from income prior to computing EPS to properly determine net income available to **common** shareholders. Therefore, dividends on cumulative preferred are deducted whether or not declared, while dividends on noncumulative preferred are deducted only if declared.

2. EPS figures should be based upon consolidated income figures after consolidating adjustments and eliminations.

3. To compute the weighted-average of common shares outstanding, treasury shares should be excluded as of date of repurchase.

4. EPS data for all periods presented should be retroactively adjusted for all splits and dividends, even those subsequent to the period being presented.

5. For stock issued in purchase combinations, use weighted-average from date of combination. For pooling combination, shares assumed outstanding the entire period regardless of when issued.

**C.** For Diluted EPS, these additional procedures apply

1. The "if-converted" method is used to adjust EPS on outstanding common shares for dilutive convertible securities.
   a. The convertible securities are considered to have been converted at the beginning of the period (or at issuance if later) increasing the denominator of EPS.
   b. For convertible bonds, the interest savings net of tax is added to the numerator of EPS.
   c. For convertible preferred, the preferred dividends deducted in arriving at EPS are not deducted, thereby increasing the numerator. There is no tax effect because dividends are not an expense.

2. The "treasury stock" method is used to adjust EPS on outstanding common shares for dilutive options and warrants (i.e., those for which the exercise price is below the market price).
   a. The options and warrants are assumed to be exercised at the beginning of the period (or the date the options and warrants were issued if later). The shares assumed issued increase the denominator of EPS.
   b. The hypothetical proceeds are used to purchase treasury stock at the average price over the year.
   c. No retroactive adjustment should be made to EPS figures for options and warrants as a result of market price changes.

3. When convertible securities require payment of cash at conversion, they are considered the equivalent of warrants. The "if-converted" method is used for the conversion and the "treasury stock" method is applied to the cash proceeds.

4. Fixed awards and nonvested stock to be issued to an employee under a stock-based compensation arrangement are considered options and are considered to be outstanding as of the grant date even though their exercise may be contingent upon vesting.

5. Contingently issuable shares are shares whose issuance is contingent upon the satisfaction of certain conditions and shall be considered outstanding and included in the diluted EPS computation as follows:
   a. If all necessary conditions have been satisfied by the end of the period, the shares should be included as of the beginning of the period in which the conditions were satisfied (or as of the date of the contingent stock agreement, if later).

    b.  If all necessary conditions have not been satisfied, the number of contingently issuable shares shall be based on the number of shares (if any) that would be issuable if the end of the reporting period were the end of the contingency period and if the result would be dilutive. These shares shall be included in the diluted EPS denominator as of the beginning of the period (or as of the date of the contingent stock agreement if later).

    6.  Antidilutive securities shall not be included in diluted EPS computations.

**D.**  Additional Disclosure Requirements

    1.  A reconciliation of the numerators and denominators of the basic and diluted per share computations for income from continuing operations, including the individual income and share amount effects of all securities that affect earnings per share.

    2.  The effect that has been given to preferred dividends in arriving at income available to common shareholders in computing basic EPS.

    3.  Securities that are antidilutive for the period(s) presented but could potentially dilute basic EPS in the future.

    4.  A description of any transaction that occurs after the end of the most recent period but before issuance of the financial statements that would materially change the number of shares outstanding at the end of the period if the transaction had occurred before the end of the period.

## SFAS 129 (C24) Disclosure of Information about Capital Structure

**A.**  Information to Be Disclosed about Securities within the Financial Statements

    1.  The rights and privileges of the various securities outstanding; for example

      a.  Dividend and liquidation preferences

      b.  Participation rights

      c.  Call prices and dates

      d.  Conversion/exercise prices/rates and dates

      e.  Sinking fund requirements

      f.  Unusual voting rights

      g.  Significant terms of contracts to issue additional shares

    2.  The number of shares issued upon conversion, exercise, or satisfaction of required conditions during at least the most recent annual fiscal period and any subsequent interim period presented.

**B.**  Disclosure of Liquidation Preference of Preferred Stock within the Financial Statements

    1.  Relationship between the preference in liquidation and the par/stated value of the shares when preferred stock (or other senior stock) has a preference in involuntary liquidation considerably in excess of the par/stated value of the shares. This disclosure should be made in the equity section of the balance sheet in the aggregate, either parenthetically or "in short."

    2.  Aggregate or per share amounts at which preferred stock may be called or is subject to redemption through sinking fund operations or otherwise.

    3.  Aggregate and per share amount of arrearages in cumulative preferred dividends.

**C.**  Disclosure of Redeemable Stock within the Financial Statements

    1.  The amount of redemption requirements, separately by issue or combined, for all issues of capital stock that are redeemable at fixed or determinable prices on fixed or determinable dates in each of the five years following the date of the latest balance sheet presented.

## SFAS 130 (C49) Reporting Comprehensive Income

**A.**  Establishes standards for reporting and display of comprehensive income (net income plus **other comprehensive income**) in a full set of general-purpose FS

**B.**  Items, and changes therein, to be included as part of and separately classified in **other comprehensive income**

    1.  Foreign currency items

    2.  Unrealized gains (losses) on certain investments in debt and equity securities

    3.  The amounts for overfunded or underfunded pension plans

**C.**  Presentation of comprehensive income

    1.  Alternative display options

      a.  At the bottom of IS, continue from net income to arrive at a **comprehensive income** figure (equals net income plus other comprehensive income), or

      b.  In a separate statement that starts with net income, or

    c.  In the statement of changes in stockholders' equity; FASB prefers a. or b.
2. Components of other comprehensive income may be displayed net of related tax effects or before related tax effects with one amount shown for the aggregate income tax effect (with detail shown in notes)
3. Reclassification (recycling) adjustments
    a.  Made to avoid double counting of items included in other comprehensive income in a prior year or current year that are included in net income (earnings) for the period
    b.  Display separately from the balance of each item adjusted (B.1. and B.2. above) (gross display)
      (1) For reclassification adjustments related to the minimum pension liability, a single amount shall be displayed (net display)
**D.** Separate EPS numbers are not required for other comprehensive income or comprehensive income

## SFAS 131 (S30) Disclosures about Segments of an Enterprise and Related Information[3]

**A.** Requires disclosures about
Operating segments of an enterprise, products and services, geographic areas, major customers
1. Disclosures are required for **public** companies in complete annual FS per GAAP and in condensed FS of interim periods including comparative presentations
2. Purpose of disclosures is to better assist statement users in appraising past and future performance of the enterprise and assessing prospects for future net cash flows.
**B.** Definitions
1. **Management approach.** Method chosen by the FASB to determine what information should be reported; it is based on the way that management organizes segments internally for making operating decisions and assessing performance.
2. **Operating segment.** Component of an enterprise that may earn revenues and incur expenses, about which separate financial information is available that is evaluated regularly by the chief operating decision maker in deciding how to allocate resources and in assessing performance.
3. **Chief operating decision maker.** Person whose general function (not specific title) is to allocate resources to, and assess the performance of, the segments of an enterprise.
4. **Segment revenue.** Includes revenue from unaffiliated customers and intersegment sales (use company transfer prices to determine intersegment sales).
5. **Segment operating profit (loss).** Segment revenue less all operating expenses, including any allocated revenues or expenses.
6. **Segment assets.** Tangible and intangible assets directly associable or used by the segment, including any allocated portion of assets used jointly by more than one segment
**C.** To determine reportable segments
1. Identify operating segments under management approach
2. Determine if aggregation of operating segments is appropriate.
3. Perform quantitative threshold tests (10% tests).
**D.** Operating segments may be aggregated by management if they have similar economic characteristics and if segments are similar in each of the following areas:
1. Nature of products and services
2. Nature of production processes
3. Type of customer for their products and services
4. Methods used to distribute their products or provide their services
5. Nature of regulatory environment; for example, banking
**E.** Operating segments that meet any of the three quantitative thresholds (10% tests) are immediately deemed reportable segments.
1. Segment revenue is $\geq$ 10% of combined revenue (revenue includes intersegment revenue).
2. Segment operating profit or loss is $\geq$ 10% of the greater of, in absolute amount
    a.  Combined operating profit of all operating segments with profit, or
    b.  Combined operating loss of all operating segments with loss
3. Segment assets are $\geq$ 10% of combined assets of all segments.

---

[3] *Refer to the flowchart on page 742 you study this outline.*

**F.** Additional considerations when determining reportable segments
   1. Management may combine information about operating segments that do not meet the 10% tests with information on other operating segments that do meet the 10% tests to produce reportable segment only if majority of the aggregation criteria exists.
   2. Segment that was reported previously should continue to be reported if judged to be of continuing significance by management even if it does not meet the 10% tests in current period.
   3. Combined sales to nonaffiliated customers of segments reporting separately must be at least 75% of total consolidated sales
      a. If not, additional segments must be identified as reportable segments
   4. All other operating segments which are not reportable shall be combined with any other business activities (e.g., corporate headquarters) and disclosed in "all other" category.
   5. Number of reportable segments probably should not exceed ten.
      a. Combine closely related segments if number of segments becomes impracticable
**G.** Information is to be presented for each reportable segment and in aggregate for remaining segments not reported separately
   1. General information, including
      a. Explanation of factors used to identify the enterprise's reportable segments
      b. Types of products and services from which revenue is derived
   2. An enterprise shall report a measure of profit or loss and total assets for each reportable segment. To the extent the following is included in the measure of profit or loss or assets it shall also be disclosed:
      a. Revenues from external customers
      b. Revenues from transactions with other operating segments of the same enterprise
      c. Interest revenue
      d. Interest expense
      e. Depreciation, depletion, and amortization expense
      f. Unusual items not qualifying as extraordinary items
      g. Equity in net income of investees accounted for by equity method
      h. Income tax expense or benefit
      i. Extraordinary items
      j. Significant noncash items other than depreciation, depletion, and amortization expense
   3. For segment assets
      a. Total expenditures for additions to long-lived assets
      b. Amount of investment in equity method investees
   4. Enterprise shall provide an explanation of the measurements of segment profit or loss and assets, including
      a. Basis of accounting
      b. Nature of any differences between measurement of profit and loss or assets for the segment and that of the consolidated enterprise
      c. Nature of any changes from prior periods
      d. Nature and effect of asymmetrical allocations (e.g., allocating depreciation, but not related assets to segment)
   5. Enterprise will need to provide reconciliations for the segment amounts disclosed to the corresponding enterprise amounts.
   6. Although not as extensive as in the annual report, certain disclosures are required in the interim reports.
**H.** Previously issued segment information must be restated (unless impractical to do so) if any enterprise changes structure of internal organization that causes composition of reportable segments to change
**I.** Information about products and services
   1. Enterprise-wide disclosure required even if only one and segment disclosures required.
   2. Revenue from external customers for each product and service shall be reported by the enterprise.
**J.** Information about geographic areas (individual countries)
   1. Enterprise-wide disclosure required even if only one and segment disclosures required.
   2. Enterprise shall report revenues from external customers and long-lived assets attributable to its domestic operations and foreign operations.

3. If enterprise functions in two or more foreign geographic areas, to the extent revenues or assets of an individual foreign geographic area are material, then these amounts should be separately disclosed.

**K.** Major customers
1. Enterprise-wide disclosure required even if segment disclosures are not required
2. Disclose amount of revenue to each customer accounting for ≥ 10% of revenue
3. Disclose similarly if ≥ 10% of revenue derived from sales to domestic government agencies or foreign governments
4. Identify segment making sales

## SFAS 132 Revised (P16) Employers' Disclosures about Pensions and Other Postretirement Benefits
(Amends SFAS 87, 88, 106, and 132) (Amended by SFAS 158)

**A.** Disclosures for defined benefit pensions plans and defined benefit postretirement plans
1. A reconciliation of beginning and ending balances of the benefit obligation with the effects of the following shown separately:
   a. Service cost
   b. Interest cost
   c. Contributions by plan participants
   d. Actuarial gains and losses
   e. Foreign currency exchange rate changes
   f. Benefits paid
   g. Plan amendments
   h. Business combinations
   i. Divestitures
   j. Curtailments
   k. Settlements
   l. Special termination benefits
2. A reconciliation of beginning and ending balances of the fair value of plan assets with the effects of the following shown separately:
   a. Actual return on plan assets
   b. Foreign currency exchange rate changes
   c. Contributions by the employer
   d. Contributions by plan participants
   e. Benefits paid
   f. Business combinations
   g. Divestitures
   h. Settlements
3. The funded status of the plans
4. The amounts recognized and the amounts not recognized in the statement of financial position such as
   a. Any unamortized prior service cost or credit
   b. Any unrecognized net gain or loss
   c. Any unamortized net obligation or net asset existing at the initial date of prior SFAS 87 or 106 that are still unrecognized
   d. Prepaid assets or accrued liabilities of the net pension or other postretirement benefits
   e. Any intangible asset
   f. The amount of other comprehensive income recognized
5. Information about plan assets including
   a. For each major category of plan assets, including equity securities, debt securities, real estate, and all other assets, the percentage of the fair value of total plan assets held as of the measurement date
   b. A description of investment policies and strategies, including target allocation percentages or ranges of percentages for each major category of plan assets, and other factors that are pertinent to understanding the investment policies and strategies, (i.e., investment goals, risk management practices, permitted and prohibited investments)
   c. A description of the basis used to determine the overall expected long-term rate-of-return-of assets assumption, the general approach used, the extent to which ROA assumption was based on historical returns, adjustments made to reflect expectations of future returns, and how adjustments were determined.

    d.   Disclosure of additional asset categories and additional information about specific assets is encouraged if the information is useful in understanding risks and long-term rate of return.

6.   For defined benefit pension plans, the accumulated benefit obligation.

7.   The benefits are expected to be paid in each of the next five fiscal years, and in the aggregate for the five fiscal years thereafter.

8.   The employer's best estimate of contributions expected to be paid to the plan during the next fiscal year. The estimated contributions may be presented in the aggregate combining contributions required by funding regulations or laws, discretionary contributions, and noncash contributions.

9.   The recognized amount of the net periodic benefit cost with the components shown separately

10.   The amount caused from a change in the additional minimum pension liability that was included in other comprehensive income

11.   On a weighted-average basis, the rates for
    a.   Assumed discount rate
    b.   Rate of compensation increase
    c.   Expected long-term rate of return on plan assets

12.   The assumptions used to determine the benefit obligation and the net benefit cost

13.   Trend rates assumed for health care cost for the next year and thereafter

14.   The measurement date(s) used to determine pension and other postretirement benefit measurements for plans that make up the majority of assets and benefit obligations

15.   The effects of a one-percentage-point increase or decrease of the trend rates for health care costs on
    a.   The aggregate of the service and interest cost components
    b.   The accumulated postretirement benefit obligation

16.   If applicable
    a.   The amounts and types of securities of the employer or a related party in plan assets
    b.   The amount of future benefits covered by insurance contracts issued by the employer or a related party
    c.   Any significant transactions between the plan and the employer or a related party
    d.   Any substantive commitment used as the basis for accounting for the benefit obligation
    e.   The cost of special or contractual termination benefits recognized during the period with a description of the event

17.   An explanation of significant changes in the benefit obligation or plan assets that is not apparent in the other disclosures required

**B.**  Disclosures for employers with more than one plan

1.   Disclosures required in this statement may be disclosed in aggregate for an employer's defined benefit pension plans and in aggregate for an employer's defined benefit postretirement plans but must still present separately prepaid benefit costs and accrued benefit liabilities recognized in the statement of financial position.

2.   An employer may not combine the disclosures of plans outside the US and plans in the US if the benefit obligation of the plans outside the US represent a significant portion of the total benefit obligation and significant differences exist in the assumptions used.

**C.**  Disclosure requirements for nonpublic entities

1.   Nonpublic entities may choose to disclose the following instead of the disclosures stated in A.:
    a.   Benefit obligation
    b.   Fair value of plan assets
    c.   Funded status of the plan
    d.   Contributions by the employer and the participant
    e.   Amounts recognized in the statement of financial position of
        (1)  Prepaid assets or accrued liabilities
        (2)  Any intangible asset
    f.   Amount of accumulated other comprehensive income recognized and the amount resulting from a change in the minimum pension liability recognized
    g.   Net periodic benefit cost recognized
    h.   Rates for
        (1)  Assumed discount rate
        (2)  Rate of compensation increase
        (3)  Expected long-term rate of return on plan assets

i.  Trend rates assumed for health care cost for the next year and thereafter
j.  If applicable
(1) Amounts and types of securities of the employer or a related party
(2) Future annual benefits covered by insurance contracts issued by the employer or a related party
(3) Any significant transactions between the plan and the employer or a related party
k.  Nature and effect of significant nonroutine events
**D.** Disclosures for defined contribution plans
1.  Amount of cost recognized for pension or postretirement benefit plans must be separate from the cost recognized for defined benefit plans
2.  Nature and effect of any significant changes that affect comparability must be disclosed
**E.** Disclosures for multiemployer plans
1.  Amount of contributions to multiemployer plans
2.  Nature and effect of changes which affect comparability
3.  If withdrawals made by an employer from a multiemployer plan will result in an obligation for a portion of the unfunded benefit obligation or the unfunded accumulated postretirement benefit obligation, follow the provision of SFAS 5, *Accounting for Contingencies*

## SFAS 133 (D50) Accounting for Derivative Instruments and Hedging Activities
(Amended by SFAS 155)
**A.** Foundation principles for SFAS 133
1.  Financial instruments should be measured at fair value (See SFAS 157 for fair value measurements)
2.  Changes in fair value, or gains and losses, should be reported in comprehensive income or in current earnings
3.  Hedging instrument criteria
a.  Fair value hedge
(1) Recognized asset or liability
(2) Unrecognized firm commitment
b.  Cash flow hedge
(1) Recognized asset or liability
(2) Forecasted transaction
c.  Foreign currency hedge
(1) Unrecognized firm commitment
(2) Available-for-sale security
(3) Forecasted transaction
(4) Net investment in foreign operations
**B.** Definition of derivative instrument
1.  Contract must contain one or more underlyings and one or more notional amounts
2.  Contract requires no initial net investment, or a smaller initial net investment than required for contracts with an expected similar response to market changes
3.  Terms that require or permit net settlement, net settlement by means outside the contract, or delivery of an asset that results in a position no substantially different from net settlement
**C.** Embedded derivative instruments
1.  Financial instruments which contain features which separately meet the definition of a derivative instrument
2.  Three criteria used to determine whether the instrument should be separated from the host contract
a.  The embedded derivative instrument meets the definition of a derivative instrument (e.g. strips)
b.  The hybrid instrument is not regularly recorded at fair value
c.  The economic characteristics and risks of the embedded instrument are not clearly and closely related to the economic characteristics of the host contract
3.  An election can be made not to bifurcate the instrument. See outline of SFAS 155.
**D.** Hedging instruments criteria
1.  Sufficient documentation must be provided at the beginning of the process
a.  Identify the objective and strategy of the hedge
b.  Identify the hedging instrument and the hedged item
c.  Identify how the effectiveness of the hedge will be assessed on an ongoing basis

2.  The hedge must be highly effective throughout its life
    a.  Measured every three months and whenever earnings or financial statements are reported
E.  Fair value hedges
    1.  Specific criteria
        a.  Hedged item must be a specific portion of a recognized asset/liability or an unrecognized firm commitment
        b.  An unrecognized firm commitment must be binding on both parties, specific with respect to all significant terms, and contain a nonperformance clause that makes performance probable.
    2.  Gains and losses will be recognized in current earnings
F.  Cash flow hedges
    1.  Specific hedges
        a.  The change in cash flows must be the same, or linked, for the hedge's asset/liability and the hedging instrument
        b.  A forecasted transaction's cash flows must be considered probable
        c.  A forecasted series of transactions must share the same risk exposure
    2.  Accounting for
        a.  Effective portion reported in other comprehensive income
        b.  Ineffective portion reported in earnings
G.  Foreign currency hedge
    1.  Unrecognized firm commitment
        a.  Accounted for as fair value hedge if requirements met
    2.  Available-for-sale securities
        a.  Accounted for as fair value hedge if requirements met and
            (1)  Cannot be traded on exchange denominated in investor's functional currency
            (2)  Dividends must be denominated in same foreign currency as expected sale proceeds
    3.  Foreign currency denominated forecasted transactions
        a.  Accounted for as cash flow hedges
    4.  Net investments in foreign operations
        a.  Must meet hedge effectiveness criterion
        b.  Change in fair value recorded in other comprehensive income
H.  Forward exchange contracts
    1.  Mark to market using the forward exchange rate at each reporting date
    2.  Recognize changes in fair value in current earnings
I.  Disclosures
    1.  Objectives and strategies for achieving financial instruments
    2.  Context to understand the instrument
    3.  Risk management policies
    4.  A list of hedged instruments
    5.  Disclosure of fair value of financial instruments required when practicable to estimate fair value

**SFAS 134 (I80, Mo4) Accounting for Mortgage-Backed Securities Retained after the Securitization of Mortgage Loans Held for Sale by a Mortgage Banking Enterprise**
(The authors believe that this topic is too specialized for the CPA exam.)

**SFAS 135 (P16) Rescission of FASB Statement No. 75 and Technical Corrections**
(The SFAS 75 rescission deals with pension plan requirements that is covered in Module 38. The technical corrections have been made throughout this volume.)

**SFAS 136 (C67, No5) Transfers of Assets to a Not-for-Profit Organization or a Charitable Trust That Raises or Holds Contributions for Others**
(This statement deals with a topic covered on the Accounting and Reporting Examination; it is included in Module 39.)

**SFAS 137 Accounting for Derivative Instruments and Hedging Activities—Deferral of the Effective Date of FASB Statement No. 133.**
In June 1999, the FASB issued this statement which delays the effective date of SFAS 133 for one year.

**SFAS 138 (D50) Accounting Certain Derivative Instruments and Certain Hedging Activities: An Amendment of FASB Statement No. 133**

A. Amended four specific items in SFAS 133
1. Normal purchases and sales exception extended
   a. Applies to contracts that require delivery of nonfinancial assets to be used in the normal operations of an entity
   b. These contracts need not be accounted for as derivative instruments unless the contracts require net settlements of gains or losses
2. Redefined the interest rate risk
   a. Permits a benchmark interest rate to be designated as the hedged risk in a hedge of interest rate risk
   b. This benchmark presents the risk-free rate and is the interest rate on direct Treasury obligations of the US government, or the London Interbank Offered Rate (LIBOR)
   c. A company's actual interest rate above the benchmark interest rate reflects that company's credit risk which is separate from the risk-free rate of interest
3. Hedging recognized foreign currency denominated assets or liabilities
   a. Permits a recognized foreign currency denominated asset or liability, for which a foreign currency transaction gain or loss is recognized in earnings under the provisions of SFAS 52, to be the hedged item in a fair value or cash flow hedge.
   b. The foreign currency denominated asset or liability continues to be remeasured using the spot exchange rates to compute the transaction gain or loss for the period
   c. In the case of cash flow hedges, the transaction gain or loss would be offset by an equal amount of reclassified from other comprehensive income. In the case of fair market value hedges, the hedging instrument would be a hedge of both interest rate risk and foreign exchange rate risk. The foreign currency denominated asset or liability would be adjusted for changes in fair value attributable to changes in foreign interest rates before remeasurement at the spot exchange rate. This eliminates the differences on earnings related to the use of different measurement criteria for the hedged item and the hedging instrument
4. Hedging with intercompany derivatives
   a. Permits derivative instruments entered into with another member of the consolidated group to qualify as hedging instruments in the consolidated financial statements if those internal derivatives are offset by unrelated third-party contracts on a net basis
   b. Previously, the internal derivative had to be offset on an individual derivative contract basis with a third party

**SFAS 140 (F35 and L35) Accounting for Transfers and Servicing of Financial Assets and Extinguishment of Liabilities**
(As amended by SFAS 156)

A. Provides accounting and reporting standards for transfers and servicing of financial assets and extinguishment of liabilities
B. Transfer of Assets
1. Necessary conditions to qualify as a sale
   a. Transferred assets have been isolated from the transferor or its creditors,
   b. Transferee has the unconstrained right to pledge or exchange the transferred assets, and
   c. Transferor does not maintain effective control over the transferred assets through
      (1) An agreement that obligates the transferor to repurchase or redeem them before their maturity, or
      (2) The ability to unilaterally cause the holder to return specific assets
2. Upon any transfer of assets, the transferor shall
   a. Initially recognize and measure at fair value the servicing assets and servicing liabilities that require recognition
   b. Allocate the previous carrying amount between the assets sold and the interests that continue to be held by the transferor based on relative fair values at the date of transfer
   c. Continue to carry in its balance sheet any interest it continues to hold in the transferred assets
3. Upon any completion of a transfer of assets which satisfies the conditions of a sale, the transferor shall
   a. Derecognize all assets sold

    b.  Recognize all assets obtained and liabilities incurred in consideration as sale proceeds

    c.  Initially measure at fair value assets obtained and liabilities incurred in a sale

    d.  Recognize in earnings any gain (loss) on sale

  4.  Upon any completion of a transfer of assets which satisfies the conditions of a sale, the transferee shall

    a.  Recognize all assets obtained and liabilities incurred at fair value

  5.  If transfer of assets does not meet the criteria for a sale, the transfer shall be accounted for as a secured borrowing with pledge of collateral

**C.**  Servicing Assets and Liabilities

  1.  Recognize and initially measure at fair value a servicing asset or servicing liability if enter into a servicing contract in any of the following situations:

    a.  Transfer of the servicer's financial assets that meets the requirements for sale accounting

    b.  Transfer of the servicer's financial assets to a qualifying SPE in a guaranteed mortgage securitization in which transferor retains the securities and classifies them as available for sale or trading securities

    c.  An acquisition or assumption of an obligation that does not relate to the financial assets of the servicer or its consolidated affiliates

  2.  If entity transfers financial assets to a qualified SPE in a guaranteed mortgage securitization and transferor retains all securities and classifies them as held-to-maturity securities, may either recognizing the servicing assets or servicing liabilities separately or report them with the asset being serviced

  3.  Measure servicing assets and servicing liabilities with one of two methods

    a.  Amortization method

      (1)  Initially record at fair value

      (2)  Amortize in proportion to and over the period of estimated net servicing income or net servicing loss

      (3)  Assess for impairment or increased obligation based on fair value.

    b.  Fair value method

      (1)  Initially record at fair value

      (2)  Measure at fair value at each reporting date

      (3)  Report changes in fair value in earnings in the period in which the change occurs

  4.  Election must be made for each class of servicing assets and servicing liabilities

  5.  Once an election is made to use the fair value method, election cannot be reversed

  6.  Report servicing assets and servicing liabilities measured at fair value separately on the balance sheet from amortized assets in one of two ways

    a.  Display separate line items for amounts valued at fair value and amounts measured by amortization method, **or**

    b.  Present aggregate amounts for all servicing assets and liabilities, and disclose parenthetically the amount that is measured in fair value that is included in the aggregate amount

**D.**  Financial Assets Subject to Prepayment

  1.  Shall be measured like investments in debt securities classified as available-for-sale or trading

**E.**  Secured Borrowing and Collateral

  1.  Pledge

    a.  Debtor grants a security interest in certain assets

    b.  Collateral is transferred to the secured party

  2.  Accounting for noncash collateral

    a.  Debtor to separate asset on balance sheet into an encumbered asset section if secured party has right to sell or repledge collateral

    b.  Secured party recognizes the proceeds from sale and obligation to return collateral if it sells collateral pledged to it

    c.  Debtor defaults under terms of agreement and is no longer entitled to redeem the pledged asset

      (1)  Derecognize the pledged asset

      (2)  Secured party recognizes collateral as an asset at fair value

      (3)  If collateral already sold, secured party derecognizes its obligation to return collateral.

**F.** Extinguishment of Liabilities
   1. Debtor shall derecognize a liability when it has been extinguished
      a. Debtor pays the creditor and is relieved of its obligation for the liability
      b. Debtor is legally released from being obligor under the liability, either judicially or by the creditor.
**G.** Required Disclosures
   1. Collateral
      a. Policy for requiring collateral or other security due to repurchase agreements or securities lending transactions
      b. Carrying amount and classification of pledged assets as collateral that are not reclassified and separately reported in the balance sheet
      c. The fair value of collateral that can be sold or repledged and information about the sources and uses of that collateral
   2. Extinguished debt
      a. General description of transaction
      b. Amount of debt that was considered extinguished at end of period
   3. Description of assets set aside for satisfying scheduled payments of a specific obligation
   4. Nonestimable fair value of assets
      a. Description of the assets or liabilities
      b. The reasons why it is not practicable to estimate the assets or liabilities
   5. For all servicing assets and servicing liabilities
      a. Management's basis for determining its classes
      b. Description of risks, the instruments used to mitigate income statement effect of changes in fair value (Quantitative information, including fair value at beginning and end of period is encouraged but not required)
      c. Amount of contractually specified servicing fees, late fees, and ancillary fees for each period on income statement, with description of where each amount is reported in income statement
   6. For servicing assets and servicing liabilities measured at fair value
      a. For each class, the activity including
         (1) Beginning and ending balances
         (2) Additions
         (3) Disposals
         (4) Changes in fair value from changes in valuation inputs or assumptions used, other changes in fair value
         (5) Other changes that affect balance and description of changes
      b. Description of the valuation techniques used to estimate fair value, with qualitative and quantitative information about assumptions used in the model
   7. For servicing assets and servicing liabilities amortized
      a. For each class, the activity including
         (1) Beginning and ending balances
         (2) Additions
         (3) Disposals
         (4) Amortization
         (5) Application of valuation allowance to adjust carrying value
         (6) Other than temporary impairments
         (7) Other changes that affect balance and description of changes
      b. For each class, the fair value at the beginning and end of period if practicable to estimate the value
      c. Description of the valuation techniques used to estimate fair value, with qualitative and quantitative information about assumptions used in the model
      d. The risk characteristics of the underlying financial assets used to stratify servicing assets for measuring impairment
      e. The activity by class in any valuation allowance for impairment of servicing assets, including beginning and ending balances, additions charged, recoveries made, and write-downs charged against the allowance for each period
   8. Transfer of securitized financial assets accounted for as a sale
      a. Accounting policies for measuring the retained interest
      b. Characteristics of securitizations and the gain (loss) from sale

  c. Key assumptions used in measuring the fair value of retained interests at time of securitization

  d. Cash flows between the securitization SPE and the transferor

 9. Retained interests in secured financial assets

  a. Accounting policies for subsequently measuring retained interests

  b. Key assumptions used in subsequently measuring fair value of retained interests

  c. Sensitivity analysis or stress test showing hypothetical effect of unfavorable variations on the retained interest's fair value, including limitations of analysis

  d. Securitized assets

   (1) Total principal outstanding, portion derecognized, and portion that continues to be recognized

   (2) Delinquencies at end of period

   (3) Credit losses, net of recoveries

## SFAS 141 (B51) Business Combinations

The purchase method of accounting is required for all business combinations initiated after June 30, 2001.

**A.** Application of the **purchase method**

 1. Identifying the acquiring entity. In identifying which entity is the acquiring entity that will continue into the future, the following facts and circumstances shall be considered:

  a. The relative voting rights in the combined entity after the combinations

  b. The existence of a large minority voting interest in the combined entity when no other owner or organized group of owners has a significant voting interest

  c. The composition of the governing body of the combined entity

  d. The composition of the senior management of the combined entity

  e. The terms of the exchange of equity securities

 2. The standard historical cost principle is applied in purchase accounting.

  a. Assets and liabilities are recorded using the fair value of the property given or fair value of property received, whichever is more clearly evident

 3. The cost of a company includes direct costs of acquisition but not indirect general expenses

 4. Additional payments to be made, contingent on future earnings and/or security prices, should be disclosed but not recorded as a liability

  a. If contingent payments are made because of attainment of specified earnings levels, the additional payment is considered an increase in the cost of the subsidiary (usually results in an increase in goodwill)

  b. If contingent payments are made due to attainment of specified security price levels, the cost of the acquired company is not affected. Rather the amount originally recorded as consideration in acquisition should be reduced by the contingency payment (usually results in decreasing paid-in capital).

  c. If contingent payments are based on both security prices and earnings, the payments should be separated and accounted for as in a. and b. above

 5. The acquiring entity should allocate the cost of the acquired company to assets and liabilities acquired (determining their revised values). Independent appraisals may be used based on the following principles:

  a. Marketable securities—fair value

  b. Receivables—present value after allowance and collection costs

  c. Finished inventories and work in process inventories—net realizable value less normal profit

  d. Raw materials—replacement cost

  e. Plant and equipment to be used—replacement cost for similar capacity

  f. Plant and equipment to be sold—fair value less costs to sell

  g. Intangible assets that arise from contractual or legal rights or are separable from the entity—fair value

  h. Other assets—appraised value

  i. Payables—present value

  j. Pensions and other postretirement obligations—in accordance with SFAS 87 or SFAS 106

  k. Liabilities and accruals—present value

  l. Preacquisition contingencies—fair value, if determinable

 6. Previously recorded goodwill of the acquired company should not be recorded by the acquiring company

7. A deferred tax liability or asset shall be recognized for differences between the assigned values and the tax bases of the recognized assets and liabilities acquired

8. The value assigned to net assets should not exceed cost
   a. If the cost of the net assets acquired exceeds the net revised asset values, the excess should be recorded as goodwill
   b. If the net revised asset value exceeds cost, the excess should be credited, pro rata, to all noncurrent assets except marketable securities, assets to be disposed of, deferred tax assets, and prepaid assets relating to pension or other postretirements benefit plans
   c. If any excess remains after reducing to zero the amounts that otherwise would have been assigned to those assets, the remaining excess shall be recognized as an extraordinary gain

9. Goodwill should be allocated to individual reporting units which are equivalent to the operating segments or one level below. (See the outline of SFAS 142.)

10. The date of acquisition is the date assets are received and securities issued

11. The notes of the acquiring company in the year of purchase should include
    a. Name and description of acquired company
    b. The primary reasons for the acquisition, including a description of the factors that contributed to the purchase price that results in recognition of goodwill
    c. The periods for which the results of operations of the acquired entity are included in the income statement of the combined entity
    d. The costs of the acquired entity and, if applicable, the number of shares of equity interests issued or issuable
    e. A condensed balance sheet disclosing the amount assigned to each major asset and liability caption on the date of acquisition
    f. Contingent payments, options, or commitments and the related proposed accounting
    g. The amount of purchased research and development costs written off in the period
    h. For any purchase price allocation not finalized, that fact and the reasons therefor

12. If the amounts assigned to goodwill or other intangibles are significant in relation to the total cost, disclosure should include
    a. For intangible assets subject to amortization
       (1) The total amount assigned to each major class of asset
       (2) The amount of any residual value, in total and by major asset category
       (3) The weighted-average amortization period, in total and by major asset category
    b. For intangible assets not subject to amortization, the amount assigned, in total and by major asset category
    c. For goodwill
       (1) The total amount assigned and the amount expected to be tax deductible
       (2) The amount of goodwill by reportable unit

13. Pro forma results of operations of the current and immediate prior period (no other prior periods) of public business enterprises should reflect operations of the combination including
    a. Revenue
    b. Income before extraordinary items
    c. Net income
    d. EPS

14. Accounting for intangible assets, including goodwill—see outline of SFAS 142

## SFAS 142 (G40) Goodwill and Other Intangible Assets

This standard provides guidance on accounting for intangible assets including goodwill.

A. Initial Recognition and Measurement of Intangible Assets
   1. Intangible assets not acquired in a business combination
      a. An intangible asset that is acquired either individually or with a group of other assets shall be initially recognized at its fair value
      b. The cost of assets acquired as a group should be allocated to the individual assets based on their relative fair values and shall not give rise to goodwill
   2. Intangible assets (including goodwill) acquired in a business combination shall be recognized in accordance with SFAS 141

3.  Costs of internally developing, maintaining, or restoring intangible assets that are not specifically identifiable, that have indeterminate lives, or that are inherent in a continuing business and related to an entity as a whole, shall be recognized as an expense when incurred

**B.** Accounting for Intangible Assets

1.  The cost of an intangible asset with a finite useful life is amortized over its estimated useful life
    a.  The useful life of an intangible asset should be estimated by considering factors such as
        (1) Expected use
        (2) Expected useful life of assets related to the intangible asset
        (3) Legal, regulatory, and contractual provisions that may limit or extend the useful life
        (4) The effects of obsolescence, demand, competition, and other economic factors
        (5) The level of expenditures expected to be required to maintain the asset
    b.  The method of amortization shall reflect the pattern in which the economic benefits of the intangible assets are consumed; if the pattern cannot be reliable determined, a straight-line amortization method shall be used
    c.  The residual value of the intangible asset will be presumed to be zero unless there is a commitment from a third party to purchase the asset at the end of its useful life, or the residual value can be determined by reference to an exchange transaction in an existing market
    d.  The remaining useful life of the intangible asset should be reevaluated each reporting period—if it is no longer appropriate the carrying amount should be amortized prospectively over the revised remaining useful life
    e.  Intangible assets with finite useful lives should be reviewed for impairment in accordance with SFAS 144

2.  An intangible asset that is determined to have an indefinite useful life should not be amortized until its useful life is determined to be no longer indefinite
    a.  An intangible asset that is not subject to amortization should be tested for impairment annually, or more frequently if events or changes in circumstances indicate that the asset might be impaired
    b.  The impairment test involves comparison of the carrying amount of the asset to its fair value

3.  Goodwill should not be amortized
    a.  Goodwill should be tested for impairment at the level of reporting referred to as a reporting unit (an operating segment or one level below). See the outline of SFAS 131
    b.  A two-step test for impairment is required
        (1) The first step involves a comparison of the fair value of the reporting unit with its carrying amount. If the carrying amount of the unit exceeds its fair value, the second step is performed. In estimating the fair value of a reporting unit, a valuation technique based on multiples of earnings or revenue or other performance measure may be used.
        (2) The second step involves a comparison of the implied fair value of goodwill of the reporting unit with the carrying amount of that goodwill
        (3) The implied fair value of goodwill is determined in the same manner as the amount of goodwill recognized in a business combination—see outline of SFAS 141. That is, all assets in the segment are valued in accordance with SFAS 141 and the excess of the fair value of the reporting unit as a whole over the amounts assigned to its recorded assets and liabilities is the implied goodwill. If the implied value of goodwill is less than the carrying amount, goodwill is written down to its implied value and an impairment loss is recognized.
    c.  Goodwill should be tested for impairment on an annual basis and between annual dates if one or more of the following events occur:
        (1) A significant adverse change in legal factors or in the business climate
        (2) An adverse action or assessment by a regulator
        (3) Unanticipated competition
        (4) A loss of key personnel
        (5) A more-likely-than-not expectation that a reporting unit or a significant portion of a reporting unit will be sold or otherwise disposed of
        (6) The test for recoverability under SFAS 144 within a reporting unit reveals that a significant group of assets are recorded at amounts above their recoverable values
        (7) Recognition of a goodwill impairment loss in the financial statements of a subsidiary that is a component of a reporting unit

d. A reporting unit may be tested at any time during the fiscal year as long as it is tested at the same time each year. Different reporting units may be tested at different times during the year.

e. Initially goodwill is allocated to reporting units. Then the assets and liabilities of the reporting units are valued individually with goodwill being measured as the difference between the cost assigned to the reporting unit and the fair value of the individual assets and liabilities.

C. Disclosures
1. In the period of acquisition
   a. For intangible assets subject to amortization
      (1) The amount assigned in total and by major intangible asset class
      (2) Significant residual value, in total and by major intangible asset class
      (3) The weighted-average amortization period, in total and by major intangible asset class
   b. For intangible assets not subject to amortization, the amount assigned in total and by major intangible asset class
   c. The amount of research and development assets acquired and written off and in which financial statement line items the amounts are included
2. Continuing disclosures
   a. For intangible assets subject to amortization
      (1) The gross carrying amount and accumulated amortization, in total and by major intangible asset class
      (2) The aggregate amortization expense for the period
      (3) The estimated aggregate amortization expense for each of the five succeeding fiscal years
   b. For intangible assets not subject to amortization, the carrying amount in total and by each major intangible asset class
   c. The changes in the carrying amount of goodwill during the period including
      (1) The aggregate amount of goodwill acquired
      (2) The aggregate amount of impairment losses recognized
      (3) The amount of goodwill included in the gain or loss on disposal of all or a portion of a reporting unit
   d. For each other-than-goodwill impairment loss recognized (other than for goodwill)
      (1) A description of the impaired intangible asset and the facts and circumstances leading to the impairment
      (2) The amount of the impairment loss and the method of determining fair value
      (3) The caption in the income statement or the statement of activities in which the impairment loss is aggregated
      (4) If applicable, the segment in which the impaired intangible asset is reported under SFAS 131
   e. For each goodwill impairment loss recognized
      (1) A description of the facts and circumstances leading to the impairment
      (2) The amount of the impairment loss and the method of determining the fair value of the associated reporting unit
      (3) If a recognized impairment loss is an estimate that has not yet been finalized, the facts and circumstances and the amount of subsequent adjustments

## SFAS 143 (A50) Accounting for Asset Retirement Obligations

This standard provides guidance on accounting for obligations associated with the retirement of tangible long-lived assets.

A. The guidance applies to legal obligations associated with the retirement of long-lived assets that result from the acquisition, construction, development and/or normal operation of a long-lived asset, except for certain obligations of lessees. Examples include
1. Costs to decommission a nuclear utility plant at the end of its useful life
2. Costs to dismantle and remove an offshore oil platform at the end of its useful life

B. Such legal obligation may arise from
1. Existing or enacted law, statute, ordinance
2. Written or oral contract
3. Legal construction of a contract under the doctrine of promissory estoppel (inferred legal obligation)

C. An asset retirement obligation is recognized at its fair value in the period in which it is incurred providing that a reasonable estimate of fair value can be made

**D.** Upon initial recognition of a liability, the entity shall increase the carrying amount of the related long-lived asset by the same amount as that recognized for the liability

**E.** The cost shall be subsequently expensed using a systematic and rational method over periods no longer than that for which the related asset is expected to provide benefits

**F.** Initial measurement of the liability

1. The best source of fair value of the liability would be provided by market-determined values but they will seldom be available
2. In the absence of a market, expected present value of future cash flows should be used. In determining the expected present value, the entity should
   a. Use probability-weighted present values in a range of the expected cash flows
   b. The amounts should be discounted to present value using a credit-adjusted risk-free rate

**G.** Subsequent to the initial measurement of the liability the obligation should be adjusted for

1. The passage of time, and
2. Revisions in estimates of timing or amounts of future cash flows

**H.** Adjustments to the liability for revisions in estimates of timing or amounts of cash flows should also be reflected in the carrying value of the related asset

**I.** Disclosures related to asset retirement obligations should include

1. Description of the obligation and related asset
2. Description of how fair value was determined
3. The funding policy, if any
4. A reconciliation of the beginning and ending aggregate carrying value

## SFAS 144 (D60 and I08) Accounting for the Impairment or Disposal of Long-Lived Assets

**A.** Establishes financial and reporting requirements for the impairment or disposal of long-lived assets. In addition to property, plant, equipment, and intangible assets being amortized, SFAS 144 applies to capital leases of lessees, long-lived assets of lessors subject to operating leases, proved oil and gas properties that are being accounted for using the successful efforts method of accounting, and long-term prepaid assets.

**B.** If a long-lived asset (or assets) is part of a group that includes other assets and liabilities not covered by SFAS 144, the statement applies to the group.

**C.** Assets to be held and used

1. Reviewed for impairment when circumstances indicate that the carrying amount of a long-term asset (or group) is not recoverable and exceeds its fair value. The carrying amount of a long-lived asset (asset group) is not recoverable it if exceeds the sum of the undiscounted cash flows expected to result from its use and eventual disposal.
2. A long-lived asset (asset group) shall be tested for recoverability whenever events or changes in circumstances indicate that its carrying amount may not be recoverable. Examples of such events include
   a. Significant decrease in market value
   b. Change in way asset used or physical change in asset
   c. Legal factors or change in business climate that might affect asset's fair value or adverse action or assessment by regulator
   d. Asset costs incurred greater than planned
   e. Current-period operating or cash flow loss combined with historical or projection of such amounts demonstrates continuing losses from the asset
   f. A current expectation that, more likely than not a long-lived asset will be disposed of significantly before the end of its previously estimated useful life
3. Impaired if the expected total future cash flows are less than the carrying amount of the asset (asset group)
   a. Assets should be grouped at lowest level for which there are identifiable cash flows independent of other groupings
   b. Expected future cash flows are future cash inflows to be generated by the asset (asset group) less the future cash outflows expected to be necessary to obtain those inflows
   c. Expected future cash flows are **not** discounted and do not consider interest charges
   d. If the management has alternative courses of action to recover the carrying amount, or if a range of possible cash flows are associated with a particular course of action, a probability-weighted approach may be useful

4. Written down to fair value and loss recognized upon impairment
   a. Fair value is "the price that would be received to sell an asset or paid to transfer a liability in an orderly transaction between market participants at the measurement date." (SFAS 157)
   b. If quoted market price in active market is not available, the estimate of fair value should be based on best information available
5. An impairment loss for an asset group shall reduce only the carrying amounts of the long-lived assets. Impairment of other assets in the group should be accounted for in accordance with other applicable accounting standards
6. If an impairment loss is recognized, the adjusted carrying amount becomes it new cost basis
7. Fair value increases on assets previously written down for impairment losses may not be recognized
8. Disclosures
   a. Description of impaired asset (asset group) and circumstances which led to impairment
   b. Amount of impairment and manner in which fair value was determined
   c. Caption in income statement in which impairment loss is aggregated, if it is not presented separately thereon
   d. Business segment(s) affected (if applicable)

**D.** Long-lived assets to be disposed of other than by sale
1. Long-lived assets to be abandoned are disposed of when they cease to be used
2. Long-lived assets to be exchanged for similar assets or to be distributed to owners are disposed of when they are exchanged or distributed

**E.** Long-lived assets to be disposed of by sale
1. Long-lived assets to be sold shall be classified as "held-for-sale" in the period in which all of the following criteria are met:
   a. Management commits to a plan of disposal
   b. The assets are available for sale
   c. An active program to locate a buyer has been initiated
   d. The sale is probable
   e. The asset is being actively marketed for sale at a fair price
   f. It is unlikely that the disposal plan will significantly change
2. Reported at lesser of the carrying amount or fair value less cost to sell
   a. Cost to sell includes broker commissions, legal and title transfer fees, and closing costs prior to legal title transfer
3. In future periods, adjusted carrying amount of asset shall be revised down or up to extent of changes in estimate of fair value less cost to sell, provided that the adjusted carrying amount does not exceed the carrying amount of the asset prior to the adjustment reflecting the decision to dispose of the asset
   a. Thus, recoveries may be recognized when assets are to be **disposed of** but not on impaired assets that continue to be used

**F.** Reporting long-lived assets and disposal groups to be disposed of
1. Discontinued operations of a component of an entity
   a. A component of an entity comprises operations and cash flows that can be clearly distinguished, operationally and for financial reporting purposes
   b. The results of a component of an entity that either has been disposed of or is classified as held for sale shall be reported as discontinued operations if both of the following conditions are met:
      (1) The operations and cash flows of the component have been (will be) eliminated from ongoing operations
      (2) The entity will not have any significant continuing involvement in the operations of the component after disposal
   c. In reporting discontinued operations, the income statement should present the results of discontinued operations separately after income from continuing operations and before extraordinary items as shown below

| | | |
|---|---|---|
| Income from continuing operations before income taxes | $xxxxx | |
| Income taxes | xxx | |
| Income from continuing operations | | $xxxx |

Discontinued operations (Note X)
    Loss from operations of discontinued Component Z (including loss
      on disposal of $xxx)                         xxxx
    Income tax benefit                                  xxxx
    Loss on discontinued operations                   xxxx
        Net income                              $xxxx

2. A gain or loss recognized for long-term asset (group) classified for sale that is not a component of an entity shall be included in income from continuing operations before income taxes
3. Disclosures
    a. Description of assets to be disposed of, reasons for disposal, expected disposal date, and carrying amount of those assets
    b. Gain or loss, if any, resulting from changes in carrying amount due to further changes in market value
    c. If applicable, amounts of revenue and pretax profit or loss reported in discontinued operations
    d. If applicable, the segment of the business affected (see outline of SFAS 131)

## SFAS 145 (I17, L10, and L35) Rescission of FASB Statements No. 4, 44, and 64, Amendment of FASB Statement No. 13, and Technical Corrections (Rescinds SFAS 4, 44, and 64 and amends SFAS 13)

A. Rescinds SFAS 4, 44, and 64 to no longer allow treatment of extinguishment of debt as an extraordinary item in the statement of income
B. Amends SFAS 13 to require that when a modification of a capital lease terms gives rise to a new agreement classified as an operating lease, the lessee should account for the new agreement under the sale-leaseback requirements of SFAS 98 (see outline)

## SFAS 146 (L32) Liabilities: Exit or Disposal Costs

A. A liability for cost associated with an exit or disposal shall be recognized and measured initially at its fair value in the period in which the liability is incurred
    1. There is an exception for a liability for one-time termination benefits that involves employees providing future services
    2. When fair value cannot be reasonably estimated, the liability shall be recognized initially in the period in which fair value can be reasonably estimated
B. An exit activity includes but is not limited to restructurings which are programs that are planned and controlled by management, and materially changes either
    1. The scope of a business undertaken by the company, or
    2. The manner in which that business is conducted
    3. Examples include
        a. Sale or termination of line of business
        b. Closure of business activities at a particular location
        c. Relocation of business activities from one location to another
        d. Changes in management structure
        e. Fundamental reorganization of the business
C. Exit or disposal activities covered by this statement do not include those that involve an entity acquired in a business combination, nor do they include disposals covered by SFAS 144. It also does not apply to costs associated with the retirement of a long-lived asset covered by SFAS 143. Examples of exit or disposal activities covered by this statement include
    1. Termination benefits provided to involuntarily terminated employees (other than ongoing arrangements and deferred compensation agreements)
    2. Costs to terminate a contract that is not a capital lease
    3. Costs to consolidate facilities or relocate employees
D. A liability for a cost associated with an exit or disposal activity shall be recognized and measured initially at fair value in the period in which the liability is incurred
    1. This typically is measured by determining the present value of the liability by discounting it using the entity's credit-adjusted risk-free interest rate
E. In the unusual circumstance in which fair value cannot be reasonably estimated, the liability shall be recognized initially in the period in which fair value can be reasonably estimated
F. Subsequent to initial recognition, the liability is adjusted over time by using the discount rate used to initially determine the liability

G. Measurement of onetime termination benefits
    1. A onetime termination agreement exists when the plan of termination meets the following criteria and has been communicated to the employees:
        a. Management commits to the plan
        b. The plan identifies the number of employees to be terminated, their job classifications and locations, and the expected completion date
        c. The plan establishes the terms of the benefit arrangement
        d. It is unlikely that significant changes in the plan will be made
    2. The liability is recognized and measured at the communication date if
        a. The employees are not required to perform additional services to receive termination benefits, or
        b. The employees will not be retained to render services beyond the minimum retention period (not to exceed the legal notification period)
    3. If the employees are required to render service until they are terminated in order to receive termination benefits and will render service beyond the minimum retention period
        a. The liability for termination benefits shall be initially measured at the communication date based on the fair value of the liability as of the termination date, and
        b. The liability shall be recognized ratably over the future service period
H. Measurement of contract termination costs
    1. Costs to terminate the contract before term end
        a. Recognized and measured when the contract is terminated
    2. Costs that will be incurred for the remaining term without benefit to the entity
        a. Recognized and measured when the entity ceases to use the rights conveyed by the contract (e.g., when the entity returns the leased assets)
I. Disclosure
    1. A description of the exit or disposal activity
    2. For each major type of cost associated with the activity
        a. The total amount expected to be incurred
        b. A reconciliation of the beginning and ending liability amounts
    3. The line items in the income statements in which the costs are included
    4. For each reportable segment, the total amount of costs expected to be incurred in connection with the activity
    5. If a liability cannot be reasonably estimated, the reasons therefor

## SFAS 147 (B51, G40, Bt7) Acquisitions of Certain Financial Institutions, an amendment of FASB Statements No. 72 and 144 and FASB Interpretation No. 9
(The authors believe that this topic is too specialized for the CPA exam.)

## SFAS 149 Amendment of Statement 133 on Derivative Instruments and Hedging Activities
A. This statement clarifies under what circumstances a contract with an initial net investment meets the characteristics of a derivatives. It also clarifies when a derivative contains a financing component, and amends the definition of an underlying to conform to language used in FASB Interpretation 45, and amends other existing pronouncements.
B. This statement amended existing pronouncements to clarify that the use of the term "expected cash flows" does not have the same meaning as the term is defined and used in SFAC 7, *Using Cash Flow Information and Present Value in Accounting Measurements*.

## SFAS 150 Accounting for Certain Financial Instruments with Characteristics of both Liabilities and Equity
A. This statement addresses how an issuer classifies and measures certain financial instruments with characteristics of both liabilities and equity. F the financial instrument embodies an obligation to the issuer, then it should be reported as a liability.
B. Terms: An obligation is a conditional or unconditional duty or responsibility to transfer assets or to issue equity shares. The duty may require a physical settlement (repurchasing its equity shares), a net cash settlement (transferring cash), or a net share settlement (issuing shares to settle).
C. This pronouncement applies to three classes of financial instruments: mandatorily redeemable preferred stock, obligations to repurchase the issuer's equity shares by transferring assets, and certain obligations to issue a variable number of shares.

1. Mandatorily redeemable preferred stock is classified as a liability unless the redemption only occurs upon liquidation or termination of the entity.
2. If a financial instrument embodies an obligation to repurchase the issuer's equity shares and requires settlement by transferring assets, then the instrument is classified as a liability.
3. If the financial instrument has an obligation that the issuer must settle by issuing a variable number of its equity shares, then it is classified as a liability if the value of the obligation is based on a fixed monetary amount or an amount tied to variations or inverse variations in something other than the issuer's securities.

**D.** These items are presented in the liabilities section of the statement of financial position. For EPS purposes, mandatorily redeemable preferred and forward contracts to repurchase equity shares are excluded in the calculation of earnings per share. Dividends and participation rights are deducted in computing income available to common shareholders in calculating EPS.

**E.** Disclosure: The following must be disclosed in the notes to financial statements:
1. The amount that would be paid or number of shares that would be issued and their fair value if settlement were to occur at reporting date
2. How changes in fair value of the shares would affect the settlement amounts
3. The maximum number of shares that could be required to be paid for a physical settlement
4. The maximum number of shares that could be required to be issued
5. That a contract does not limit the amount that the issuer could be required to pay or issue shares
6. If the forward contract or option indexed to the issuer's equity shares, the forward price or option strike price, the number of issuer's shares to which the contract is indexed and the settlement date or dates

## SFAS 151 Inventory Costs (amends ARB 43, Chapter 4)

**A.** Requires that abnormal amounts of idle facility expense, freight, handling costs, and wasted material (spoilage) may be treated as current period charges.

**B.** Requires that fixed overhead allocation be based on normal capacity of production facilities.
1. Normal capacity is a range of production levels.
2. Normal capacity is production expected to be achieved over a number of periods or seasons under normal circumstances, taking into account loss of capacity due to planned maintenance.
3. Normal capacity varies on business and industry-specific factors.

**C.** Factors that might cause abnormally low production level include significantly reduced demand, labor and material shortages, unplanned facility or equipment downtime

**D.** Actual level of production may be used if it approximates normal capacity.

**E.** In periods of abnormally high production, amount of fixed overhead allocated to each unit is decreased so inventories are not measured above cost.

**F.** Items treated as period costs include
1. Unallocated overhead costs are recognized as expense in period in which they are incurred.
2. General and administrative expenses (under most circumstances).
3. Selling expense.
4. Abnormal freight, handling costs, amount of wasted materials (spoilage).

## SFAS 152 Accounting for Real Estate Time Sharing Transactions—An Amendment of FASB Statements No. 66 and 67

(Amends SFAS 66 and SFAS 67)

Requires real estate time-sharing transactions to be accounted for as nonretail land sales. AICPA SOP 04-2 provides guidance on accounting for real estate time-sharing transactions. This statement also amends SFAS 67 (*Accounting for Costs and Initial Rental Operations of Real Estate Projects*), so that SFAS 67 does not apply to real estate time-sharing transactions. Restatement of previously issued financial statements is not permitted.

## SFAS 153 Exchanges of Nonmonetary Assets—An Amendment of APB Opinion No. 29

(Amends APB 29)

**A.** Requires that nonmonetary exchanges should be measured based on fair values unless certain conditions are met. It removes the distinction of "similar" and "dissimilar" assets found in APB 29 and outlines exceptions to fair value treatment. The statement also clarifies when APB 29 does not apply. The provisions of the statement are to be applied prospectively.

**B.** A nonmonetary exchange is a reciprocal transfer only if the transferor has no substantial continuing involvement in the asset, and the risks and rewards of ownership are transferred.

**C.** APB 29, *Accounting for Nonmonetary Exchanges,* does **not** apply to
   1. Business combination accounted for under SFAS 141
   2. Transfer of nonmonetary assets between companies under common control
   3. Acquisition of nonmonetary assets or services on the issuance of capital stock
   4. Stock issued or received in stock dividends and stock splits
   5. A transfer of assets in exchange for an equity interest in entity
   6. A pooling of assets in a joint undertaking to find, develop, or produce gas or oil
   7. Exchange of a part of an operating interest owned for a part of another operating interest owned by another party
   8. Transfers of financial assets within the scope of SFAS 140

**D.** Measure exchange based on fair value unless
   1. Fair value is not determinable
   2. It is an exchange transaction to facilitate sales to customers
   3. The transaction lacks commercial substance

**E.** Commercial Substance
   1. A nonmonetary change has commercial substance if the entity's future cash flows are expected to be significantly changed as a result of the exchange of assets.
      a. Configuration (risk, timing, and amount) of future cash flows differs significantly from that of the asset transferred.
      b. Entity-specific value of the asset differs from the entity-specific value of asset transferred, and that difference is significant in relation to fair values exchanged. Entity specific value can be computed per SFAC 7 by using expectations about use
   2. If transaction has commercial substance, the exchange is measured at fair value.
   3. If transaction lacks commercial substance, measure based on recorded amount of nonmonetary asset relinquished.
   4. Cash flows from tax effect are not considered in determining if the transaction has commercial substance.

## SFAS 154 Accounting Changes and Error Corrections
(Supersedes APB 20 and SFAS 3)

**A.** Defines an accounting change as (1) change in principle; (2) change in an estimate; or (3) change in reporting entity. The correction of an error is not an accounting change.

**B.** Once an accounting principle is adopted, it must be used consistently for similar events and transactions. An entity may change an accounting principle only if the change is required by a new accounting pronouncement, or if the entity can justify that the alternative method is preferable.

**C.** Change in accounting principle
   1. Is given retrospective application of the new accounting principle to all prior periods, unless it is impracticable to do so. This includes
      a. Cumulative effects of the change are presented in the carrying amounts of assets and liabilities as of the beginning of the first period presented
      b. Offsetting adjustment is made to opening balance of retained earnings for that period
      c. Financial statements of each period are adjusted to reflect period-specific effects of the new accounting principle
   Only direct effects of change are recognized (i.e., changes in inventory balances, deferred taxes, impairment adjustments). Indirect effects are reported in period in which the accounting change is made.

**D.** If cumulative effect can be determined, but period-specific effects cannot be determined, cumulative effect is applied to the earliest period to which it can be calculated. Offsetting adjustment is made to retained earnings of that period.

**E.** If it is impracticable to determine the cumulative effect of the change in any prior period, treat prospectively.

**F.** Notes to the financial statements must include
   1. The nature and reason for the change with explanation as to why the new method is preferable
   2. The method of applying the change
   3. A description of the prior period information retrospectively adjusted

4.  Effect of change on income from continuing operations, net income, and other affected line items on financial statements, and any per share amounts for current period and all periods adjusted
5.  The cumulative effect of the change on retained earnings and other components of equity or net assets as of the earliest period presented
6.  If retrospective application is impracticable, the reason and a description of how the change was reported
7.  A description of the indirect effects of the change and amounts recognized in the current period and related per share amounts
8.  The amounts of indirect effects of the change and per share amounts

G.  Disclosures for interim periods should disclose the effect of change on income from continuing operations, net income, and related per share amounts for postchange interim periods.

H.  Once the change in method is disclosed, financial statements in subsequent periods do not need to repeat disclosures.

I.  Change in accounting estimate
1.  Treat on prospective basis in current and future periods
2.  If change is effected by change in principle, treat as change in estimate
3.  Change in depreciation method is treated as change in estimate
4.  If change in estimate is caused by change in principle, must show footnote disclosures required by change in accounting principle

J.  Change in reporting entities
1.  Change is retrospectively applied to the financial statements of all periods presented
2.  Previously issued interim statements presented on a retrospective basis
3.  Footnote disclosures include the nature and reason for change, net income, other comprehensive income, and any related per share amounts for all periods presented

K.  Correction of an error
1.  Errors are errors in recognition, measurement, presentation, or disclosure (Change from non-GAAP to GAAP is a correction of error)
2.  Treat as prior period adjustment by restating financial statements
3.  Cumulative effect of error is reflected in carrying value of assets and liabilities at the beginning of the first period presented, with an offsetting adjustment in the opening balance in retained earnings
4.  Restate financial statements to reflect period-specific effects of error
5.  Footnote disclosures must disclose that previously issued statements were restated, along with description of error.
6.  Effects of error and any per share amounts must also be disclosed for each period presented
7.  Cumulative effect of the change on retained earnings or other components of equity should be presented for the earliest period presented.
8.  Gross effects and net effects from income taxes on net income of prior period must be disclosed. Amount of income tax applicable to each prior period must be disclosed.
9.  Once correction of error is disclosed, financial statements of subsequent years do not need to repeat disclosure

## SFAS 155 Accounting for Certain Hybrid Financial Instruments
(Amends SFAS 133 and SFAS 140)

SFAS 155, issued in February 2006, amends SFAS 133. SFAS 155 changes the accounting for hybrid financial instruments that would normally be required to be bifurcated.

A.  An election can be made **not** to bifurcate the instrument
B.  The election is irrevocable and is made on an instrument by instrument basis
C.  Changes in fair value of the hybrid instruments are recognized in earnings each year
D.  Balance sheet disclosure may be presented in one of two ways
1.  As a separate line item for the fair value and non–fair value instruments, **or**
2.  As an aggregate amount of all hybrid instruments with the amount of the hybrid instruments at fair value shown in parentheses
E.  Initial adoption of SFAS 155 requires the difference between the total carrying amount of the components of the bifurcated hybrid instruments and the fair value of the hybrid instruments to be recognized as a cumulative effect adjustment to the beginning balance of retained earnings

**F.** Notes to financial statements should indicate the gross gains and losses of the cumulative effect adjustments. Prior periods are not restated

**G.** SFAS 155 does not apply to hedging instruments

## SFAS 156 Accounting for Servicing of Financial Assets
(Amends SFAS 140)

SFAS 156, issued in March 2006, amends SFAS 140. It provides that an election may be made to use the fair value method to value servicing assets and servicing liabilities. Election must be made for each class of servicing assets and servicing liabilities. Once the election is made, it cannot be reversed. SFAS 156 allows balance sheet disclosure to be presented in one of two ways: either displayed as separate line items for amounts valued at fair value and amounts measured by the amortization method, **or** by presenting aggregate amounts for all servicing assets and liabilities with a parenthetical disclosure for the amount that is measured using fair value. Additional footnote disclosures are required for all servicing assets, with separate disclosures for servicing assets measured at fair value and servicing assets measured by the amortization method.

See the outline of SFAS 140, paragraphs B, C, and G.

## SFAS 157 Fair Value Measurements

**A.** Fair value is the price that would be received to sell an asset or paid to transfer a liability in an orderly transaction between market participants at the measurement date (an exit price).

**B.** Applying the fair value measurement approach involves
1. Identify the asset or liability to be measured
2. Determine the principal or most advantageous market *(highest and best use)*
3. Determine the valuation premise *(in-use or in-exchange)*
4. Determine the appropriate valuation technique *(market, income, or cost approach)*
5. Obtain inputs for valuation *(Level 1, Level 2, or Level 3)*
6. Calculate the fair value of the asset

**C.** Assumes the asset or liability is sold or transferred in either the principal market or most advantageous market
1. Principal market has greatest volume and level of activity
2. Most advantageous market minimizes price received for the asset or minimizes amount paid to transfer liability
3. Market participants have the following characteristics:
   a. Be independent of the reporting entity (not related parties)
   b. Knowledgeable
   c. Able to transact
   d. Willing to transact (motivated, but not compelled to transact)
4. Do not adjust prices for costs to sell
5. If location is attribute of asset or liability, price is adjusted for costs necessary to transport asset or liability to market

**D.** Assumes the highest and best use of the asset
1. Highest and best use maximizes the value of asset or group of assets
2. Highest and best use must be
   a. Physically possible
   b. Legally permissible
   c. Financially feasible at measurement date
3. Highest and best use determines the valuation premise used

**E.** Valuation Premise
1. In use:
   a. Asset provides maximum value by using it with other assets as a group
   b. Valuation based on price to sell asset assuming it is used with other assets
2. In-exchange:
   a. Asset provides maximum value on stand-alone basis
   b. Valuation based on price to sell the asset stand-alone

**F.** Valuation Techniques
1. Market approach
   a. Uses prices and relevant information from market transaction for identical or comparable assets or liabilities
2. Income approach
   a. Uses present value techniques to discount cash flows or earnings to present value amounts
3. Cost approach
   a. Relies on current replacement cost to replace the asset with a comparable asset, adjusted for obsolescence.

**G.** Levels of Input for Valuation
1. Use fair value hierarchy to prioritize inputs to valuation techniques
2. Fair value hierarchy is Level 1, Level 2, and Level 3
3. Inputs should be based on lowest level of input (i.e., highest priority is lowest level)
4. Level 1 inputs—lowest level, highest priority
   a. Uses quoted prices (unadjusted prices) from active markets
   b. Examples are quotes from NYSE, quotations from dealer markets
5. Level 2 inputs
   a. Inputs that are directly or indirectly observable other than quoted prices of Level 1.
   b. Examples are quoted prices for similar assets or liabilities, observable inputs such as yield curves, bank prime rates, interest rates, volatilities, loss severities, credit risks, and default rates.
6. Level 3 inputs
   a. Unobservable inputs
   b. May only be used if observable inputs are not available
   c. May reflect reporting entity's own assumptions about market
   d. Based on best information available

**H.** Change in Valuation Premise or Technique
1. Treat as change in estimate on a prospective basis
2. Requirements of SFAS 154 do not apply

**I.** Disclosures
1. For assets measured at fair value on recurring basis
   a. Valuation techniques used
   b. Identify level of hierarchy or measurements used
   c. If Level 3 used, the effect of measurements on earnings for the period, purchases, sales, issuances, and settlements, and any transfers in or out of Level 3 are disclosed
2. For assets and liabilities measured at fair values on a nonrecurring basis (i.e., impaired assets), identify the following:
   a. The fair value measurements used
   b. The reasons for the measurements
   c. The level within the hierarchy
   d. A description of the inputs used for Level 3 measurements
   e. The valuation techniques used

## SFAS 158—Employers' Accounting for Defined Benefit Pension and Other Postretirement Plans (An Amendment of FASB Statements 87, 88, 106, and 132[R])

*NOTE: SFAS 158 is effectively for publicly traded companies for fiscal years ending after 12/15/06, and for nonpublicly traded companies for fiscal years ending after 12/15/07.*

**A.** Recognize funded status of benefit plans
1. Aggregate status of all overfunded plans and show as noncurrent asset on balance sheet
2. Aggregate status of all underfunded plans, and show as current liability, noncurrent liability, or both on balance sheet.
3. Recognize as other comprehensive income the gain and loss and the prior service costs or credits that arise during the period but are not a part of pension expense.

**B.** Effective for fiscal years ending after December 15, 2008, the measurement date is the employer's fiscal year-end balance sheet date.

**C.** Disclosures
1. Funded status of the plans, and the amounts recognized in the balance sheet, showing separately the noncurrent assets, current liabilities, and noncurrent liabilities recognized.
2. Disclose the net gain or loss, net prior service cost or credit recognized in OCI for the period, and any reclassification adjustments of OCI that are recognized in pension cost.
3. The amounts in accumulated OCI that have not yet been recognized as pension costs. Show separately the following items:
   a. Net gain or loss
   b. Net prior service cost or credit
   c. Net transition asset or obligation
4. The amount and timing of any plan assets expected to be returned to the employer during the next 12-month period after the most recent balance sheet date.

**SFAS 159—The Fair Value Option for Financial Assets and Financial Liabilities—including an amendment of FASB Statement 115**
**A.** Scope
1. Applies to
   a. Financial assets and financial liabilities (includes available-for-sale, held-to-maturity, and equity method investments, and liabilities)
   b. Firm commitments that involve financial instruments
   c. Written loan commitments
   d. Nonfinancial insurance contracts that can be settled by paying third party
   e. Warranties that can be settled by paying third party
   f. Host financial instruments resulting from separation of embedded nonfinancial derivative instrument from a nonfinancial hybrid instrument
2. Does **not** apply to consolidations, pensions, share-based payments, stock options, OPEB, exit or disposal activities, leases, and financial instruments that are component of equity
**B.** Definitions
1. **Fair value**—The price that would be received to sell an asset or paid to transfer a liability in an orderly transaction between market participants at the measurement date
2. **Financial asset**—Cash, evidence of an ownership interest in an entity or a contract that conveys a right to receive cash or another financial instrument or to exchange other financial instruments on potentially favorable items
3. **Financial liability**—A contract that imposes an obligation to deliver cash or another financial instrument to exchange other financial instruments on potentially favorable terms
4. **Firm commitment**—An agreement, usually legally enforceable, that specifies all significant terms, including quantity, fixed price, and timing of transaction. The agreement includes a disincentive for nonperformance that makes performance probable
**C.** Fair Value Option (FVO)
1. Can elect to measure financial asset or financial liability at fair value
2. Must elect to use fair value method on specific items
   a. Can be elected on instrument-by-instrument basis
      (1) If multiple advances to one borrower for single contract, fair value options is applied to larger balance and not each individual advance
      (2) If fair value applied to investment that can use equity method, it must be applied to all interests in same entity (i.e., debt and equity)
      (3) If applied to insurance contracts, must be applied to all claims and obligations for that contract
   b. Is irrevocable
   c. Must apply to entire instrument, not a portion of instrument
3. Report unrealized gains and losses in earnings
4. Classification on statement of cash flows—rules of FAS 95 apply
**D.** Election Dates
1. The date an eligible item is first recognized
2. The date the entity enters into a firm commitment
3. When financial assets cease to qualify for fair value treatment due to specialized accounting rules, can elect to use fair value (i.e. equity method for investments)

   4.  Percentage of ownership change and can no longer consolidate
   5.  Modifications of debt
E.  Financial Statement Disclosure Requirements—two methods permissible
   1.  Present aggregate fair value and non–fair value amounts in same line, with amounts measured at fair value parenthetically disclosed
   2.  Present two separate line items for fair value and non–fair value carrying amounts
F.  Disclosures to Notes to Financial Statements—Balance Sheet
   1.  Management's reasons for electing fair value option for each item or group of items
   2.  If fair value option is elected for some but not all items
      a.  Description of similar items and reason for partial election
      b.  Information to understand how group of similar items relates to individual line items on balance sheet
   3.  Information to understand how line items relate to major categories of assets and liabilities presented in SFAS 157 fair value disclosure requirements
   4.  Aggregate carrying amount of items included in each line item in balance sheet that are not eligible for fair value option
   5.  Difference between aggregate fair value and aggregate unpaid principal balance of
      a.  Loans and long-term receivables using FVO
      b.  Long-term debt instruments using FVO
      c.  Aggregate fair value of loans that are 90 days or more past due
      d.  Aggregate fair value of loans in nonaccraul status if interest is recognized separately from changes in fair value
      e.  Difference between aggregate fair value and aggregate unpaid principal balance for loans 90 days or more past due
   6.  For investments that would have used equity method, the information required by APB 18 for equity method
G.  Required Disclosures for Income Statement Items
   1.  Amounts of gains/losses included in earnings for each line item in balance sheet
   2.  Description of how interest and dividends are measured and reported on the income statement
   3.  For loans and receivables held as assets
      a.  Estimated amount of gains/losses in earnings that is attributed to changes in credit risk
      b.  How the gains/losses were determined
   4.  For liabilities affected by credit risk
      a.  Amount of gains/losses attributable to changes in credit risk
      b.  Qualitative information about reasons for changes
      c.  How gains/losses were determined
   5.  Methods and significant assumptions to estimate fair value
H.  Transition Requirements
   1.  Report as cumulative effect adjustment to opening balance of retained earnings
   2.  Remove balance sheet effects such as
      a.  Amortized deferred costs, fees, premiums, discounts
      b.  Valuation allowances (such as allowance for loan losses)
      c.  Accrued interest

# STATEMENTS OF FINANCIAL ACCOUNTING CONCEPTS (SFAC)

Statements of Financial Accounting Concepts (SFAC) set forth financial accounting and reporting objectives and fundamentals that will be used by the FASB in developing standards. While practitioners may also use SFAC in areas where promulgated GAAP does not exist, it is important to note that the SFAC do not constitute authoritative GAAP.

## SFAC 1 Objectives of Financial Reporting by Business Enterprises
A.  Financial accounting concepts are fundamentals on which standards of financial accounting and reporting are based.
   1.  That is, do not establish GAAP
      a.  And do not come under AICPA Ethics Rule 203

    2.   Defines financial accounting concepts broader than financial statements and other data
- **B.** Environmental context of objectives
  1. Financial reporting provides information for making business and economic decisions.
  2. The United States is a market economy
     - a. Dominated by investor-owned enterprises
     - b. Even though the government generates economic statistics
- **C.** Characteristics and limitations of information
  1. Primarily financial (quantitative) in nature
  2. Limited to individual business enterprises
  3. Based on approximated measures (i.e., estimates)
  4. Largely limited to past transactions (i.e., historically based)
  5. Just one source of users' data base
  6. Must conform to cost-benefit rationale
- **D.** Potential users and their interests
  1. "Owners, lenders, potential investors, suppliers, creditors, employees, management, directors, customers, financial analysts and advisors, brokers, underwriters, stock exchanges, lawyers, economists, taxing authorities, regulatory authorities, legislators, financial press and reporting agencies, labor unions, trade associations, business researchers, teachers and students, and the public."
  2. Users are generally interested in cash flow generation.
     - a. Amounts, timing, and uncertainties
  3. Many external users lack authority to prescribe information.
     - a. For example, absentee owners, customers, etc.
- **E.** General-purpose external financial reporting
  1. To satisfy informational needs of external users who lack authority to prescribe data they desire
  2. Focuses on external users
     - a. Management may prescribe data for their needs
  3. Directed primarily at investors and creditors
     - a. Which results in data of likely usefulness to others
- **F.** Objectives of financial reporting
  1. "Financial reporting should provide information that is useful to present and potential investors and creditors and other users in making rational investment, credit, and similar decisions."
  2. "Financial reporting should provide information to help present and potential investors and creditors and other users in assessing the amounts, timing, and uncertainty of prospective cash receipts from dividends or interest and the proceeds from the sale, redemption, or maturity of securities or loans."
  3. "Financial reporting should provide information about the economic resources of an enterprise, the claims to those resources (obligations of the enterprise to transfer resources to other entities and owner's equity), and the effects of transactions, events, and circumstances that change resources and claims to those resources."
     - a. Economic resource, obligation, and owners' equity data permit assessment of
       - (1) Liquidity and solvency
       - (2) Financial strength
     - b. Funds flow data is important
     - c. Earnings performance data permit assessment of future performance
       - (1) Thus, primary focus of reporting is on earnings
     - d. Management stewardship and performance are reported on
     - e. Management explanation and interpretation are important

## SFAC 2 Qualitative Characteristics of Accounting Information
(Para 4 superseded by SFAC 6)
- **A.** Purpose is to examine the characteristics that make accounting information useful and establish criteria for selecting and evaluating accounting alternatives.
  1. Guidance needed by both FASB and individual accountants
  2. The usefulness of accounting information must be evaluated in relation to decision making.
  3. Based on objectives of financial reporting (SFAC 1)
  4. Applies to financial information reported by business enterprises and not-for-profit organizations

**B.** The hierarchy of accounting qualities
    1.   User-specific qualities (not inherent in information)
        a.   Understandability
        b.   Decision usefulness
    2.   Decision-specific qualities (necessary for usefulness)
        a.   **Relevance**—"capacity" of information to "make a difference" in a decision
            (1)  **Timeliness**—being available while able to influence decisions
            (2)  **Predictive value**—improves decision makers' capacity to predict
            (3)  **Feedback value**—enables users to confirm or correct prior expectations
        b.   **Reliability**—freedom from error and bias and faithful representation of what is claimed to be represented
            (1)  **Verifiability**—secures a high degree of consensus among independent measurers
            (2)  **Representative faithfulness**—agreement between data and resources or events represented (validity)
            (3)  **Neutrality**—freedom from bias toward a predetermined result
    3.   Secondary and interactive qualities
        a.   Comparability between enterprises
        b.   Consistency in application over time
    4.   Constraints
        a.   **Materiality**—information should not be provided if below the user's threshold for recognition
        b.   **Costs and benefits**—benefits derived from disclosure must exceed associated costs

## SFAC 5 Recognition and Measurement in Financial Statements of Business Enterprises

**A.**  Statement addresses principal items that a full set of FS should show and provides fundamental recognition criteria to use in deciding which items to include in FS.
    1.   Recognition criteria presented are not radical change from current practice
    2.   Only applies to business enterprises
**B.**  FS
    1.   A principal means of communicating financial information to those outside an entity
    2.   Some useful information is better provided by other means of financial reporting, such as notes to the statements or supplementary information (SFAC 1).
    3.   Objectives of financial reporting (which encompasses FS) are detailed in SFAC 1.
    4.   Full set of FS should show
        a.   Financial position at end of period
        b.   Earnings for period
        c.   Comprehensive income for period
        d.   Cash flows for period
        e.   Investments by and distributions to owners during period
    5.   Are intended as "general-purpose" statements and, therefore, do not necessarily satisfy all users equally well
    6.   Simplifications, condensations, and aggregations are necessary and useful, but focusing on one figure (i.e., "the bottom line") exclusively should be avoided.
    7.   FS interrelate and complement each other.
    8.   Information detailed in 4. above is provided by the following individual financial statements:
        a.   **Statement of Financial Position**
            (1)  Provides information about entity's assets, liabilities, and equity and their relationships to each other at a particular point in time
            (2)  Does not purport to show the value of an entity
        b.   **Statement of Earnings and Comprehensive Income**
            (1)  Shows how the equity of an entity increased or decreased from all sources (other than from transactions with owners) during period
            (2)  Item "earnings" is similar to present net income term but does not include certain accounting adjustments recognized in current period (i.e., change in accounting principle).
            (3)  Earnings is a performance measure concerned primarily with cash-to-cash cycles.
            (4)  Comprehensive income includes all recognized changes in equity except those from transactions with owners (SFAC 6).

      (5) The terms "gains" and "losses" are used for those items included in earnings.

      (6) The terms "cumulative accounting adjustments" and "other nonowner changes in equity" are used for those items excluded from earnings but included in comprehensive income.

  c. **Statement of Cash Flows**

      (1) Shows entity's cash flows from operating, investing, and financing activities during a period

  d. **Statement of Investments by and Distributions to Owners**

      (1) Shows capital transactions of entity which are increases and decreases in equity from transactions with owners during period

9. FS help users assess entity's liquidity, financial flexibility, profitability, and risk.

10. Full set of FS based on concept of financial capital maintenance—a return is achieved only after capital has been maintained or recovered.

**C.** Recognition criteria

1. Recognition is presentation of item in both words and numbers that is included in the totals of the financial statements (SFAC 6).

2. Item should meet four fundamental recognition criteria to be recognized

  a. **Definitions**—item is element of FS as defined by SFAC 6

  b. **Measurability**—item has a relevant attribute that is measurable with sufficient reliability

      (1) Five measurement attributes are used in current practice

         (a) Historical cost (historical proceeds)

         (b) Current (replacement) cost

         (c) Current market value

         (d) Net realizable (settlement) value

         (e) Present (discounted) value of future cash flows

      (2) Statement suggests that use of different attributes will continue

      (3) The monetary unit of measurement of nominal units of money is expected to continue to be used

  c. **Relevance**—item has capacity to make a difference in users' decisions (SFAC 2)

  d. **Reliability**—item is representationally faithful, verifiable, and neutral (SFAC 2)

      (1) Reliability may affect timing of recognition due to excessive uncertainties

      (2) A trade-off may sometimes be needed between relevance and reliability because waiting for complete reliability may make information untimely

**D.** Guidance in applying recognition criteria

1. Need to identify which cash-to-cash cycles are substantially complete

2. Degree of skepticism is needed (SFAC 2)

3. **Revenues and gains**

  a. Generally not recognized until realizable (SFAC 6)

      (1) Realizable means assets received or held are readily convertible to known amounts of cash or claims to cash

  b. Not recognized until earned (APB 4, SFAC 6)

4. **Expenses and losses**

  a. Generally recognized when economic benefits are consumed or assets lose future benefits

  b. Some expenses are recognized when associated revenues are recognized (e.g., cost of goods sold).

  c. Some expenses are recognized when cash is spent or liability incurred (e.g., selling and administrative salaries).

  d. Some expenses are allocated by systematic and rational procedures to periods benefited (e.g., depreciation and insurance).

**E.** Recognition of changes in assets and liabilities

1. Initial recognition generally based on current exchange prices at date of recognition

2. Changes can result from two types of events

  a. Inflows and outflows

  b. Changes in amounts which can be a change in utility or substance (e.g., depreciation) or changes in price

3. Current price information may only be used if it is reliable, cost justified, and more relevant than alternative information.

## SFAC 6 Elements of Financial Statements
(Replaces SFAC 3)

A. Statement contains definitions of FS elements

    1. Definitions provide a significant first screen in determining content of FS.

        a. Possessing characteristics of a definition of an element is necessary but not sufficient condition for including an item in FS

        b. To qualify for inclusion in FS an item must

            (1) Meet recognition criteria (e.g., revenue recognition tests)

            (2) Possess a relevant attribute which can be measured reliably (e.g., historical cost/historical proceeds)

B. Elements of FS of both business enterprises and not-for-profit organizations

    1. **Assets** are probable future economic benefits controlled by a particular entity as a result of past transactions or events.

        a. Characteristics of assets

            (1) Probable future benefit by contribution to future net cash inflows

            (2) Entity can obtain and control access to benefit

            (3) Transaction or event leading to control has already occurred

        b. Asset continues as an asset until collected, transferred, used, or destroyed.

        c. Valuation accounts are part of related asset.

    2. **Liabilities** are probable future sacrifices of economic benefits, arising from present obligations of a particular entity that result from past transactions or events.

        a. Characteristics of liabilities

            (1) Legal, equitable, or constructive duty to transfer assets in future

            (2) Little or no discretion to avoid future sacrifice

            (3) Transaction or event obligating enterprise has already occurred

        b. Liability remains a liability until settled or discharged.

        c. Valuation accounts are part of related liability.

    3. **Equity** (net assets) is the owner's residual interest in the assets of an entity that remains after deducting liabilities.

        a. Business enterprises

            (1) Characteristics of equity

                (a) The source of distributions by enterprise to its owners

                (b) No unconditional right to receive future transfer of assets; depends on future profitability

                (c) Inevitably affected by enterprise's operations and circumstances affecting enterprise

            (2) Transactions or events that change owners' equity include revenues and expenses; gains and losses; investments by owners; distributions to owners; and changes within owners' equity (does not change total amount)

        b. Not-for-profit organizations

            (1) Characteristics of net assets (equity)

                (a) Absence of ownership interest

                (b) Operating purposes not centered on profit

                (c) Significant receipt of contributions, many involving donor-imposed restrictions

            (2) Classes of net assets

                (a) **Permanently restricted net assets** is the part of net assets of a not-for-profit organization resulting from

                    1] Contributions and other inflows of assets whose use by the organization is limited by donor-imposed stipulations that neither expire by passage of time nor can be fulfilled or otherwise removed by actions of the organization

                    2] Other asset enhancements and diminishments subject to same kinds of stipulations

                    3] Reclassifications from (or to) other classes of net assets as a consequence of donor-imposed stipulations

                (b) **Temporarily restricted net assets** is the part of net assets of a not-for-profit organization resulting from

        1] Contribution and other inflows of assets whose use by the organization is limited by donor-imposed stipulations that either expire by passage of time or can be fulfilled and removed by actions of the organization pursuant to those stipulations

        2] Other asset enhancements and diminishments subject to same kinds of stipulations

        3] Reclassifications to (or from) other classes of net assets as a consequence of donor-imposed stipulations, their expiration by passage of time, or their fulfillment and removal by actions of the organization pursuant to those stipulations

    (c) **Unrestricted net assets** is the part of net assets of a not-for-profit organization that is neither permanently restricted nor temporarily restricted by donor-imposed stipulations. They result from

        1] All revenues, expenses, gains, and losses that are not changes in permanently or temporarily restricted net assets and

        2] Reclassifications from (or to) other classes of net assets as a consequence of donor-imposed stipulations, their expiration by passage of time, or their fulfillment and removal by actions of the organization pursuant to those stipulations

  (3) Transactions and events that change net assets include revenues and expenses, gains and losses, and changes within net assets that do not affect assets or liabilities (including reclassifications between classes of net assets).

  (4) Changes in classes of net assets of not-for-profit organizations may be significant because donor-imposed restrictions may affect the types and levels of services that a not-for-profit organization can provide.

    (a) Characteristics of change in permanently restricted net assets

        1] Most increases in permanently restricted net assets are from accepting contributions of assets that donors stipulate must be maintained in perpetuity. Only assets that are not by their nature used up in carrying out the organization's activities are capable of providing economic benefits indefinitely. Gifts of cash, securities, and nonexhaustible property are examples.

    (b) Characteristics of change in temporarily restricted net assets

        1] Most increases in temporarily restricted net assets are from accepting contributions of assets that donors limit to use after specified future time or for specified purpose. Temporary restrictions pertain to contributions with donor stipulations that expire or can be fulfilled and removed by using assets as specified.

    (c) Characteristics of change in unrestricted net assets

        1] Change in unrestricted net assets for a period indicates whether organization has maintained the part of its net assets that is fully available (free of donor-imposed restrictions) to support the organization's services to beneficiaries in the next period.

4. **Revenues** are increases in assets or decreases in liabilities during a period from delivering goods, rendering services, or other activities constituting the entity's major or central operations.

  a. Characteristics of revenues

    (1) Accomplishments of the earning process

    (2) Actual or expected cash inflows resulting from central operations

    (3) Inflows reported gross

5. **Expenses** are decreases in assets or increases in liabilities during a period from delivery of goods, rendering of services, or other activities constituting the entity's major or central operations.

  a. Characteristics of expenses

    (1) Sacrifices involved in carrying out earnings process

    (2) Actual or expected cash outflows resulting from central operations

    (3) Outflows reported gross

6. **Gains (losses)** are increases (decreases) in equity from peripheral transactions of entity excluding revenues (expenses) and investment by owners (distribution to owners).

  a. Characteristics of gains and losses

    (1) Result from peripheral transactions and circumstances that may be beyond control

    (2) May be classified according to sources or as operating and nonoperating

    (3) Change in equity reported net

7. **Accrual accounting** and **related concepts** include

a. **Transaction**—external event involving transfer of something of value between two or more entities

b. **Event**—a happening of consequence to an entity (internal or external)

c. **Circumstances**—a set of conditions developed from events which may occur imperceptibly and create possibly unanticipated situations

d. **Accrual accounting**—recording "cash consequence" transactions as they occur rather than with movement of cash; deals with process of cash movement instead of beginning or end of process (per SFAC 1)

    (1) Based on cash and credit transactions, exchanges, price changes, changes in form of assets and liabilities

e. **Accrual**—recognizing revenues and related asset increases and expenses and related liability increases as they occur; expected future cash receipt or payment follows recognition of revenue (expense)

f. **Deferral**—recognizing liability for cash receipt with expected future revenue or recognizing asset for cash payment with expected future expense; cash receipt (payment) precedes recognition of revenues (expenses)

g. **Allocation**—process of assigning or distributing an amount according to a plan or formula

    (1) Includes amortization

h. **Amortization**—process of systematically reducing an amount by periodic payments or write-downs

i. **Realization**—process of converting noncash resources and rights into money; refers to sales of assets for cash or claims to cash

    (1) Realized—identifies revenues or gains or losses on assets sold

    (2) Unrealized—identifies revenues or gains or losses on assets unsold

j. **Recognition**—process of formally recording an item in financial statements

    (1) Major differences between accrual and cash basis accounting is timing of recognition of income items

k. **Matching**—simultaneous recognition of revenues with expenses which are related directly or jointly to the same transaction or events

C. Elements of FS exclusive to business enterprises

    1. **Investments by owners** are increases in net assets resulting from transfers by other entities of something of value to obtain ownership.

    2. **Distributions to owners** are decreases in net assets resulting from transferring assets, rendering services, or incurring liabilities by the enterprise to owners.

    3. **Comprehensive income** is the change in equity of an entity during a period from transactions and other events of nonowner sources (i.e., all equity amount changes except investment and distributions).

        a. Term "comprehensive" income is used instead of net earnings (net income) because the board is reserving "earnings" for a component part of comprehensive income yet to be determined.[4]

        b. Concept of capital maintenance or recovery of cost is needed in order to separate return **on** capital from return **of** capital.

        c. Financial capital maintenance concept vs. physical capital maintenance concept

            (1) Financial capital maintenance—objective is to maintain purchasing power

            (2) Physical capital maintenance—objective is to maintain operating capacity

        d. Comprehensive income is return on financial capital.

        e. Characteristics, sources, and components of comprehensive income include

            (1) Cash receipts (excluding owner investments) less cash outlays (excluding distributions to owners) over life of enterprise

                (a) Recognition criteria and choice of attributes to be measured affect timing, not amount.

            (2) Specific sources of income are

                (a) Transactions between enterprise and nonowners

                (b) Enterprise's productive efforts

---

[4] *Although SFAS 130 has defined comprehensive income as including net income plus other comprehensive income, it has not yet changed the components that comprise net income. Additionally, prior period adjustments are still reported in the retained earnings statement, not as comprehensive income.*

(c) Price changes, casualties, and other interactions with environment
(3) **Earnings process** is the production and distribution of goods or services so firm can pay for goods and services it uses and provide return to owners.
(4) Peripheral activities may also provide income.
(5) Components of comprehensive income
  (a) Basic components—revenues, expenses, gains and losses
  (b) Intermediate components result from combining basic components
(6) Display considerations (e.g., items included in operating income) are the subject of another SFAC.

## SFAC 7 Using Cash Flow Information and Present Value in Accounting Measurements

**A.** Statement provides
1. A framework for using future cash flows as the basis for accounting measurements
   a. At initial recognition
   b. In **fresh-start measurements**—measurements in period following initial recognition that establish a new carrying amount unrelated to previous amounts and accounting conventions.
   c. For the **interest method of allocation**—reporting conventions that use present value techniques in the absence of a fresh-start measurement to compute changes in the carrying amount of an asset or liability from one period to the next. Like depreciation and amortization conventions, interest methods are grounded in notion of historical cost.
2. General principles that govern the use of present value
   a. Especially when uncertainties exist in
     (1) The amount of future cash flows
     (2) The timing of future cash flows, or
     (3) Both (1) and (2)
3. Common understanding of objective of present value in accounting measurements
4. **Guidance on measurement issues only—recognition issues are not addressed by SFAS 7.**

**B.** Statement does not specify when fresh-start measurements are appropriate
1. FASB expects to decide whether a particular situation requires a fresh-start measurement (or some other accounting response) on a project-by-project basis.

**C.** Objective of present value in an accounting measurement is to capture, to the extent possible, the economic difference between sets of estimated cash flows
1. Without present value, a $3,000 cash flow due tomorrow and a $3,000 cash flow due in fifteen years appear the same.
2. Because present value distinguishes between cash flows that might otherwise appear similar, a measurement based on the present value of estimated future cash flows provides more relevant information than a measurement based on the undiscounted sum of those cash flows.
3. A present value measurement that fully captures the economic differences between various sets of future cash flows would necessarily include the following elements:
   a. An estimate of the future cash flow (or in more complex cases, series of future cash flows at different times)
   b. Expectations about possible variations in the amount or timing of those cash flows
   c. The time value of money, represented by the risk-free rate of interest.
   d. The price for bearing the uncertainty inherent in the asset or liability.
   e. Other sometimes unidentifiable factors, including liquidity and market imperfections

**D.** To provide relevant information in financial reporting, present value must represent some observable measurement attribute of assets or liabilities.
1. In the absence of observed transaction prices, accounting measurements at initial recognition and fresh-start measurements should attempt to capture the elements that taken together would comprise a market price if one existed, that is, fair value.
   a. The **fair value** of an asset (or liability) is the amount at which that asset or liability could be bought (or incurred) or sold (or settled) in a current transaction between willing parties.
2. While the expectations of an entity's management are often useful and informative, the marketplace is the final arbiter of asset and liability values.
3. The entity must pay the market's price when it acquires an asset or settles a liability in a current transaction, regardless of its intentions or expectations.

4. For some assets and liabilities, management's estimates may be the only available information.
    a. In this case, the objective is to estimate the price likely to exist in the marketplace, if there were a marketplace.

E. The techniques used to estimate future cash flows and interest rates will vary from one situation to another depending on the circumstances surrounding the asset or liability in question. Certain general principles govern any application of present value techniques in measuring assets or liabilities.
    1. To the extent possible, estimated cash flows and interest rates should reflect assumptions about the future events and uncertainties that would be considered in deciding whether to acquire an asset or group of assets in an arm's-length transaction for cash.
    2. Interest rates used to discount cash flows should reflect assumptions that are consistent with those inherent in the estimated cash flows. Otherwise, the effect of some assumptions will be double-counted or ignored. For example, an interest rate of 12% might be applied to contractual cash flows of a loan. That rate reflects expectations about future defaults from loans with particular characteristics. That same 12% rate should not be used to discount expected cash flows because those cash flows already reflect assumptions about future defaults.
    3. Estimated cash flows and interest rates should be free from both bias and factors unrelated to the asset, liability, or group of assets or liabilities in question. For example, deliberately understating estimated net cash flows to enhance the apparent future profitability of an asset introduces bias into the measurement.
    4. Estimated cash flows or interest rates should reflect the range of possible outcomes rather than a single most-likely, minimum, or maximum possible amount.

F. An accounting measurement that uses present value should reflect the uncertainties inherent in the estimated cash flows. Otherwise items with different risks may appear similar.

G. Accounting applications of present value have typically used a single set of estimated cash flows and a single interest rate. SFAC 7 introduces the expected cash flow approach.
    1. The expected cash flow approach focuses on explicit assumptions about the range of possible estimated cash flows and their respective possibilities.
    2. The traditional approach treats those uncertainties implicitly in the selection of an interest rate.
    3. By incorporating a range of possible outcomes, the expected cash flow approach accommodates the use of present value techniques when the timing of cash flows is uncertain.

H. The measurement of liabilities involves different problems from the measurement of assets.
    1. The most relevant measurement of an entity's liabilities at initial recognition and fresh-start measurements should always reflect the credit standing of the entity.

I. Interest method of allocation
    1. Present value techniques are also used in periodic reporting conventions known collectively as **interest methods of allocation**.
    2. Financial statements usually attempt to represent the changes in assets and liabilities from one period to the next. By using current information and assumptions, fresh-start measurements capture all the factors that create change, including
        a. Physical consumption of assets (or reduction of liabilities)
        b. Changes in estimates, and
        c. Holding gains and losses that result from price changes
    3. Accounting allocations are planned approaches designed to represent only consumption or reduction.
    4. Changes in estimates may receive some recognition, but the effects of a change often have been spread over future periods.
    5. Holding gains and losses are generally excluded from allocation systems.
    6. In principle, the purpose of all accounting allocations is to report changes in the value, utility, or substance of assets and liabilities over time.
    7. Accounting allocations attempt to relate the change in an asset or liability to some observable real-world phenomenon.
        a. An interest method of allocation relates changes in the reported amount with changes in present value of a set of future cash flows.
    8. Allocation methods are only representations (not measurements) of an asset or liability.

9. While an interest method could be applied to any asset or liability, it is generally considered more relevant than other methods when applied to assets and liabilities that exhibit one or more of the following characteristics:
   a. The transaction giving rise to the asset or liability is commonly viewed as a borrowing or lending
   b. Period-to-period allocation of similar assets or liabilities employs an interest method
   c. A particular set of estimated future cash flows is closely associated with the asset or liability
   d. The measurement at initial recognition was based on present value

10. Like all allocation systems, the manner in which an interest method of allocation is applied can greatly affect the pattern of income or expense. In particular, the interest method requires a careful description of the following:
    a. The cash flows to be used (promised cash flows, expected cash flows, or some other estimate)
    b. The convention that governs the choice of an interest rate (effective rate or some other rate)
    c. How the rate is applied (constant effective rate or a series of annual rates)
    d. How changes in the amount or timing of estimated cash flows are reported

11. In most situations, the interest is based on contractual cash flows and assumes a constant effective interest rate over the life of those cash flows.
    a. That is, the method uses promised cash flows (rather than expected cash flows) and bases the interest rate on the single rate that equates the present value of the promised cash flows with the initial price of the asset or liability.

12. In reality, actual cash flows often occur sooner or later in greater or lesser amounts than expected. Changes from the original estimate of cash flows, in either timing or amount, can be accommodated in the interest amortization scheme or included in a fresh-start measurement of the asset or liability.
    a. Presently, the FASB doesn't address the conditions that might govern the choice between those two approaches.

13. If a change occurs in the amount or timing of estimated cash flows and the item is not remeasured, the interest amortization scheme must be altered to incorporate the new estimate of cash flows.
    a. The following techniques have been used to address the changes in estimated cash flows:
       (1) A prospective approach computes a new effective interest rate based on the carrying amount and remaining cash flows.
       (2) A catch-up approach adjusts the carrying amount to the present value of the revised estimated cash flows, discounted at the original effective interest rate.
       (3) A retrospective approach computes a new effective interest rate based on the original carrying amount, actual cash flows to date, and remaining estimated cash flows. The new effective interest rate is then used to adjust the carrying amount to the present value of the revised estimated cash flows, discounted at the new effective interest rate.
    b. The FASB considers the catch-up approach to be preferable to other techniques for reporting changes in estimated cash flows because
       (1) It is consistent with the present value relationships portrayed by the interest method, and
       (2) It can be implemented at a reasonable cost
       Under the catch-up approach, the recorded amount of an asset or liability (assuming estimated cash flows do not change) is the present value of the estimated future cash flows discounted at the original effective interest rate. If a change in estimate is effected through the catch-up approach, the measurement basis after the change will be the same as the measurement basis for the same asset or liability before the change in estimate (estimated cash flows discounted at the original effective rate).
    c. The prospective approach obscures the impact of changes in estimated cash flows and, as a result, produces information that is both less useful and less relevant. The interest rate that is derived under the prospective approach is unrelated to the rate at initial recognition or to current market rates for similar assets and liabilities. The amount that remains on the balance sheet can be described as "the unamortized amount," but no more.
    d. In some pronouncements, the retrospective approach has been used. Some consider it the most precise and complete of the three techniques listed above. However, the retrospective approach requires that entities retain a detailed record of all past cash flows. The costs of maintaining these detailed records usually outweigh any advantage provided by this approach.

# FINANCIAL ACCOUNTING AND REPORTING
## TESTLET 1

**Items 1 and 2** are based on the following:

The town of Silverton adopted the provisions of GASB 34, *Basic Financial Statements—and Management's Discussion and Analysis—for State and Local Governments,* for its financial statements issued for 2007. As of December 31, 2007, Silverton compiled the information below for its capital assets, exclusive of infrastructure assets.

| Cost of capital assets financed with general | |
|---|---|
| obligation debt and tax revenues | $5,000,000 |
| Accumulated depreciation on the capital assets | 1,000,000 |
| Outstanding debt related to the capital assets | 2,000,000 |

**1.** On the government-wide statement of net assets at December 31, 2007, under the governmental activities column, what amount should be reported for capital assets?
- a. $5,000,000
- b. $4,000,000
- c. $3,000,000
- d. $2,000,000

**2.** On the government-wide statement of net assets at December 31, 2007, under the governmental activities column, the information related to capital assets should be reported in the net assets section at which of the following amounts?
- a. $5,000,000
- b. $4,000,000
- c. $3,000,000
- d. $2,000,000

**3.** Tree City reported a $1,500 net increase in fund balance for governmental funds. During the year, Tree purchased general capital assets of $9,000 and recorded depreciation expense of $3,000. What amount should Tree report as the change in net assets for governmental activities?
- a. $ (4,500)
- b. $ 1,500
- c. $ 7,500
- d. $10,500

**4.** A not-for-profit voluntary health and welfare organization received a $500,000 permanent endowment. The donor stipulated that the income must be used for a mental health program. The endowment fund reported $60,000 net decrease in market value and $30,000 investment income. The organization spent $45,000 on the mental health program during the year. What amount of change in temporarily restricted net assets should the organization report?
- a. $75,000 decrease.
- b. $15,000 decrease.
- c. $0
- d. $425,000 increase.

**5.** Oz, a nongovernmental not-for-profit organization, received $50,000 from Ame Company to sponsor a play given by Oz at the local theater. Oz gave Ame 25 tickets, which generally cost $100 each. Ame received no other benefits. What amount of ticket sales revenue should Oz record?
- a. $0
- b. $2,500
- c. $47,500
- d. $50,000

**6.** Under Statement of Financial Accounting Concepts 2, the ability through consensus among measurers to ensure that information represents what it purports to represent is an example of the concept of
- a. Relevance.
- b. Verifiability.
- c. Comparability.
- d. Feedback value.

**7.** When a company changes the expected service life of an asset because additional information has been obtained, which of the following should be reported?

| | Pro forma effects of retroactive application | Retrospective application |
|---|---|---|
| a. | Yes | Yes |
| b. | No | Yes |
| c. | Yes | No |
| d. | No | No |

**8.** Gilbert Corporation issued a 40% stock split-up of its common stock that had a par value of $10 before and after the split-up. At what amount should retained earnings be capitalized for the additional shares issued?
- a. There should be no capitalization of retained earnings.
- b. Par value.
- c. Market value on the declaration date.
- d. Market value on the payment date.

**9.** A nonmonetary asset was received by Company Y in a nonreciprocal transfer from Company Z that has commercial substance. The asset should be recorded by Y at
- a. Z's recorded amount.
- b. Z's recorded amount or the fair value of the asset received, whichever is higher.
- c. Z's recorded amount or the fair value of the asset received, whichever is lower.
- d. The fair value of the asset received.

**10.** A development stage enterprise
- a. Does **not** issue an income statement.
- b. Issues an income statement that only shows cumulative amounts from the enterprise's inception.
- c. Issues an income statement that is the same as an established operating enterprise, but does **not** show cumulative amounts from the enterprise's inception as additional information.
- d. Issues an income statement that is the same as an established operating enterprise, and shows cumulative amounts from the enterprise's inception as additional information.

**11.** During a period of inflation, an account balance remains constant. With respect to this account, a purchasing power gain will be recognized if the account is a
- a. Monetary liability.
- b. Monetary asset.
- c. Nonmonetary liability.
- d. Nonmonetary asset.

**12.** The summary of significant accounting policies should disclose the

    a. Pro forma effect of retroactive application of an accounting change.

    b. Basis of profit recognition on long-term construction contracts.

    c. Adequacy of pension plan assets in relation to vested benefits.

    d. Future minimum lease payments in the aggregate and for each of the five succeeding fiscal years.

**13.** The following items relate to the preparation of a statement of cash flows:

| | 2007 | 2006 | | 2007 |
|---|---|---|---|---|
| Cash | $150,000 | $100,000 | Net sales | $3,200,000 |
| AR--net | 420,000 | 290,000 | CGS | (2,500,000) |
| Merchandise | | | | |
| inventory | 330,000 | 210,000 | Expenses | (500,000) |
| AP | 265,000 | 220,000 | Net income | $ 200,000 |

All accounts payable relate to trade merchandise. Accounts payable are recorded net and always are paid to take all of the discount allowed. The direct approach is used for operating activities. Under operating activities, cash payments during 2007 to suppliers amounted to

    a. $2,575,000

    b. $2,500,000

    c. $2,455,000

    d. $2,335,000

**14.** Boa Constructors, Inc. had an operating loss carryforward of $100,000 that arose from ordinary operations in 2007. There is no evidence that indicates the need for a valuation allowance. The income tax rate is 40%. For the year ended December 31, 2007, the tax benefit should be reported in the income statement as

    a. A $40,000 reduction in income tax expense from continuing operations.

    b. An extraordinary item of $40,000.

    c. An operating gain of $40,000.

    d. An extraordinary item of $100,000.

**Items 15 through 17** are based on the following information:

The December 31, 2007 balance sheet of Ratio, Inc. is presented below. These are the only accounts in Ratio's balance sheet. Amounts indicated by a question mark (?) can be calculated from the additional information given.

| *Assets* | |
|---|---|
| Cash | $ 25,000 |
| Accounts receivable (trade) | ? |
| Inventory | ? |
| Property, plant and equipment (net) | 294,000 |
| | $432,000 |
| *Liabilities and stockholders' equity* | |
| Accounts payable (trade) | ? |
| Income taxes payable (current) | 25,000 |
| Long-term debt | 100,000 |
| Common stock | 300,000 |
| Retained earnings | ? |
| | ? |

| *Additional information* | |
|---|---|
| Current ratio (at year-end) | 1.5 to 1 |
| Total liabilities divided by total stockholders' equity | .8 |
| Inventory turnover based on sales and ending inventory | 15 times |
| Inventory turnover based on cost of goods sold and ending inventory | 10.5 times |
| Gross margin for 2007 | $315,000 |

**15.** What was Ratio's December 31, 2007 balance in the inventory account?

    a. $ 21,000

    b. $ 30,000

    c. $ 70,000

    d. $135,000

**16.** What was Ratio's December 31, 2007 balance in trade accounts payable?

    a. $ 67,000

    b. $ 92,000

    c. $182,000

    d. $207,000

**17.** What was Ratio's December 31, 2007 balance in retained earnings?

    a. $ 60,000 deficit.

    b. $ 60,000

    c. $132,000 deficit.

    d. $132,000

**18.** Companies A and B have been operating separately for five years. Each company has a minimal amount of liabilities and a simple capital structure consisting solely of voting common stock. Company A, in exchange for 40% of its voting stock, acquires 80% of the common stock of Company B. This was a "tax free" stock for stock (type B) exchange for tax purposes. Company B assets have a total net fair market value of $800,000 and a total net book value of $580,000. The fair market value of the A stock used in the exchange was $700,000. The goodwill on this acquisition would be

    a. Zero.

    b. $ 60,000

    c. $120,000

    d. $236,000

**19.** Empire Corporation owns an office building and leases the offices under a variety of rental agreements involving rent paid monthly in advance and rent paid annually in advance. Not all tenants make timely payments of their rent. Empire's balance sheets contained the following information:

| | 2007 | 2006 |
|---|---|---|
| Rentals receivable | $3,100 | $2,400 |
| Unearned rentals | 6,000 | 8,000 |

During 2007, Empire received $20,000 cash from tenants. How much rental revenue should Empire record for 2007?

    a. $17,300

    b. $18,700

    c. $21,300

    d. $22,700

**20.** Moore Company carries product A in inventory on December 3, 2007, at its unit cost of $7.50. Because of a sharp decline in demand for the product, the selling price was reduced to $8.00 per unit. Moore's normal profit margin on product A is $1.60, disposal costs are $1.00 per unit, and the replacement cost is $5.30. Under the rule of cost or market, whichever is lower, Moore's December 31, 2007, inventory of product A should be valued at a unit cost of

    a. $5.30

    b. $5.40

    c. $7.00

    d. $7.50

**21.** On January 1, 2007, Richmond, Inc. signed a fixed-price contract to have Builder Associates construct a major plant facility at a cost of $4,000,000. It was estimated that it would take three years to complete the project. Also on January 1, 2007, to finance the construction cost, Richmond borrowed $4,000,000 payable in 10 annual installments of $400,000 plus interest at the rate of 11%. During 2007 Richmond made deposit and progress payments totaling $1,500,000 under the contract; the average amount of accumulated expenditures was $650,000 for the year. The excess borrowed funds were invested in short-term securities, from which Richmond realized investment income of $250,000. What amount should Richmond report as capitalized interest at December 31, 2007?

    a.  $ 71,500
    b.  $165,000
    c.  $190,000
    d.  $440,000

**22.** On May 1, 2007, Lane Corp. bought a parcel of land for $100,000. Seven months later, Lane sold this land to a triple-A rated company for $150,000, under the following terms: 25% at closing, and a first mortgage note (at the market rate of interest) for the balance. The first payment on the note, plus accrued interest, is due December 1, 2008. Lane reported this sale on the installment basis in its 2007 tax return. In its 2007 income statement, how much gain should Lane report from the sale of this land?

    a.  $0
    b.  $12,500
    c.  $37,500
    d.  $50,000

**23.** On January 1, 2007, Derby Company lent $20,000 cash to Elliott Company. The promissory note made by Elliott did not bear interest and was due on December 31, 2008. No other rights or privileges were exchanged. The prevailing interest for a loan of this type was 12%. The present value of $1 for two periods at 12% is 0.797. Derby should recognize interest income in 2007 of

    a.  $0
    b.  $1,913
    c.  $2,030
    d.  $2,400

**24.** Platt Co. has been forced into bankruptcy and liquidated. Unsecured claims will be paid at the rate of $.50 on the dollar. Maga Co. holds a noninterest-bearing note receivable from Platt in the amount of $50,000, collateralized by machinery with a liquidation value of $10,000. The total amount to be realized by Maga on this note receivable is

    a.  $35,000
    b.  $30,000
    c.  $25,000
    d.  $10,000

**25.** Included in W. Cody's assets at December 31, 2007, are the following:

2,000 shares of Dart Corporation common stock purchased in 2005 for $100,000. The market value of the stock was $80 per share at December 31, 2007.

A $500,000 whole life insurance policy having a cash value of $72,000 at December 31, 2007, subject to a $30,000 loan payable to the insurance company.

In Cody's December 31, 2007 personal statement of financial condition, the above assets should be reported at

    a.  $232,000
    b.  $202,000
    c.  $172,000
    d.  $142,000

**26.** Footnotes to the financial statements are beneficial in meeting the disclosure requirements of financial reporting. The footnotes should not be used to

    a.  Describe significant accounting policies.
    b.  Describe depreciation methods employed by the company.
    c.  Describe the principles and methods peculiar to the industry in which the company operates, when these principles and methods are predominantly followed in that industry.
    d.  Correct an improper presentation in the financial statements.

**27.** SFAS 95, *Statements of Cash Flows*, classifies cash receipts and cash payments as arising from operating, investing, and financing activities. All of the following should be classified as investing activities except

    a.  Cash outflows to purchase manufacturing equipment.
    b.  Cash inflows from the sale of bonds of other entities.
    c.  Cash outflows to lenders for interest.
    d.  Cash inflows from the sale of a manufacturing plant.

**28.** Initial direct costs incurred by the lessor under a sales-type lease should be

    a.  Deferred and allocated over the economic life of the leased property.
    b.  Expensed in the period incurred.
    c.  Deferred and allocated over the term of the lease in proportion to the recognition of rental income.
    d.  Added to the gross investment in the lease and amortized over the term of the lease as a yield adjustment.

**29.** An appropriation of retained earnings by the board of directors of a corporation for future plant expansion will result in

    a.  The establishment of a fund to help finance future plant expansion.
    b.  The setting aside of cash to be used for future plant expansions.
    c.  A decrease in cash on the balance sheet with an equal increase in the investments and funds section of the balance sheet.
    d.  The disclosure that management does not intend to distribute, in the form of dividends, assets equal to the amount of the appropriation.

**30.** According to SFAS 131, *Disclosures about Segments of an Enterprise and Related Information*, an industry segment is a reportable segment if it is significant to the enterprise as a whole. An industry segment is considered significant when any of the following conditions are met **except** when the

    a.  Segment revenue is 10% or more of the combined revenue of all of the company's segments.
    b.  Segment identifiable assets are 10% or more of the combined identifiable assets of all segments.

c.  Segment identifiable liabilities are 10% or more of the combined identifiable liabilities of all segments.

d.  Absolute value of a segment's operating profit or operating loss is 10% or more of the combined operating profit of all segments that did not incur an operating loss.

## FINANCIAL ACCOUNTING AND REPORTING

### TESTLET 1 ANSWERS

| | | | | | | | | | | | |
|---|---|---|---|---|---|---|---|---|---|---|---|
| 1. | b | 6. | b | 11. | a | 16. | a | 21. | a | 26. | d |
| 2. | d | 7. | d | 12. | b | 17. | a | 22. | d | 27. | c |
| 3. | c | 8. | b | 13. | a | 18. | b | 23. | a | 28. | b |
| 4. | c | 9. | d | 14. | a | 19. | d | 24. | b | 29. | d |
| 5. | b | 10. | d | 15. | c | 20. | b | 25. | b | 30. | c |

### *Hints for Multiple-Choice Questions*

1. Capital assets are presented net of accumulated depreciation.

2. In the net assets section capital assets are presented net of related debt.

3. Net assets is increased by increase in fund balance and increase in capital assets.

4. Endowment is a permanently restricted amount.

5. Ticket revenue is at fair value.

6. A characteristic of reliability.

7. This is a change in an accounting estimate.

8. This constitutes a large stock dividend.

9. No tricks here.

10. Must follow GAAP

11. Monetary items are fixed in amount.

12. Entity should disclose the accounting principles followed and methods of applying those principles.

13. Cash payments to suppliers is determined by adjusting **CGS** for changes in **inventory** and **AP**.

14. The operating loss reduces income from operations.

15. Calculate inventory algebraically—Sales = (10.5)

$$(INV) + \$315,000 = (15)(INV).$$

16. First calculate total current assets, then use current ratio.

17. Liabilities/SE = 0.8/1.0.

18. Measurement of GW.

19. Review Cash to accrual, Module 7, Section A.4.

20. Floor is NRV less normal profit.

21. Capitalized interest is avoidable interest.

22. Installment method can only be used under GAAP where collection is not reasonably assured.

23. $20,000 is both the PV and FV of this note.

24. Only $40,000 of the note is unsecured.

25. Present estimated current values of assets and current amounts of liabilities.

26. Footnotes provide additional information.

27. Investing activities relate to investments in property, plant, and equipment and securities.

28. Initial direct costs are part of cost of sales.

29. An appropriation simply informs users of the reason that dividends will not be declared.

30. Remember the test for segment reporting.

# FINANCIAL ACCOUNTING AND REPORTING

## TESTLET 2

**1.** For which of the following governmental entities that use proprietary fund accounting should a statement of cash flows be presented?

| | *Swimming pool* | *Government utilities* |
|---|---|---|
| a. | No | No |
| b. | No | Yes |
| c. | Yes | Yes |
| d. | Yes | No |

**2.** The Williamsburg Zoo, a private not-for-profit organization, established a $1,000,000 quasi endowment on July 1, 2007. On the zoo's financial statement of financial position at December 31, 2007, the assets in this quasi endowment should be included in which of the following classifications?

a. Temporarily restricted net assets.
b. Unrestricted net assets.
c. Permanently restricted net assets.
d. Either temporarily or permanently restricted net assets, depending on the expected term of the endowment.

**3.** Chase City imposes a 2% tax on hotel charges. Revenues from this tax will be used to promote tourism in the city. Chase should record this tax as what type of nonexchange transaction?

a. Derived tax revenue.
b. Imposed nonexchange revenue.
c. Government-mandated transaction.
d. Voluntary nonexchange transaction.

**4.** Pica, a nongovernmental not-for-profit organization, received unconditional promises of $100,000 expected to be collected within one year. Pica received $10,000, prior to year-end. Pica anticipates collecting 90% of the contributions and has a June 30 fiscal year-end. What amount should Pica record as contribution revenue as of June 30?

a. $ 10,000
b. $ 80,000
c. $ 90,000
d. $100,000

**5.** Why is a reclassification adjustment used when reporting other comprehensive income?

a. Adjustment made to reclassify an item of comprehensive income as another item of comprehensive income.
b. Adjustment made to avoid double counting of items.
c. Adjustment made to make net income equal to comprehensive income.
d. Adjustment made to adjust for the income tax effect of reporting comprehensive income.

**6.** In a statement of cash flows, interest payments to lenders and other creditors should be classified as cash outflows for

a. Operating activities.
b. Borrowing activities.
c. Lending activities.
d. Financing activities.

**7.** When treasury stock is purchased for cash at more than its par value, what is the effect on total stockholders' equity under each of the following methods?

| | *Cost method* | *Par value method* |
|---|---|---|
| a. | Increase | Increase |
| b. | Decrease | Decrease |
| c. | **No** effect | Decrease |
| d. | **No** effect | **No** effect |

**8.** When the allowance method of recognizing bad debt expense is used, the allowance for doubtful accounts would decrease when a(n)

a. Specified account receivable is collected.
b. Account previously written off is collected.
c. Account previously written off becomes collectible.
d. Specific uncollectible account is written off.

**9.** In computing basic earnings per share, a company would include which of the following?

a. Dividends on nonconvertible cumulative preferred stock.
b. Dividends on common stock.
c. Interest on convertible bonds.
d. Number of shares of nonconvertible cumulative preferred stock.

**10.** On January 2, 2005, a company established a sinking fund in connection with an issue of bonds due in 2014. At December 31, 2007, the independent trustee held cash in the sinking fund account representing the annual deposits to the fund and the interest earned on those deposits. How should the sinking fund be reported in the company's classified balance sheet at December 31, 2007?

a. The entire balance in the sinking fund account should appear as a noncurrent asset.
b. The entire balance in the sinking fund account should appear as a current asset.
c. The cash in the sinking fund should appear as a current asset.
d. The accumulated deposits only should appear as a noncurrent asset.

**11.** For interim financial reporting, an inventory loss from a market decline in the second quarter that is **not** expected to be restored in the fiscal year should be recognized as a loss

a. In the fourth quarter.
b. Proportionately in each of the second, third, and fourth quarters.
c. Proportionately in each of the first, second, third, and fourth quarters.
d. In the second quarter.

**12.** A review of the December 31, 2007 financial statements of Rhur Corporation revealed that under the caption "extraordinary losses," Rhur reported a total of $260,000. Further analysis revealed that the $260,000 in losses was comprised of the following items:

• Rhur recorded a loss of $50,000 incurred in the abandonment of equipment formerly used in the business.

- In an unusual and infrequent occurrence, a loss of $75,000 was sustained as a result of hurricane damage to a warehouse.
- During 2007, several factories were shut down during a major strike by employees. Shutdown expenses totaled $120,000.
- Uncollectible accounts receivable of $15,000 were written off as uncollectible.

Ignoring income taxes, what amount of loss should Rhur report as extraordinary on its 2007 statement of income?

- a. $ 50,000
- b. $ 75,000
- c. $135,000
- d. $260,000

**13.** On December 30, 2006, Future, Incorporated paid $2,000,000 for land. At December 31, 2007, the current value of the land was $2,200,000. In January 2008, the land was sold for $2,250,000. Ignoring income taxes, by what amount should stockholders' equity be increased for 2007 and 2008 as a result of the above facts in current value financial statements?

|   | 2007 | 2008 |
|---|------|------|
| a. | $0 | $ 50,000 |
| b. | $0 | $250,000 |
| c. | $200,000 | $0 |
| d. | $200,000 | $ 50,000 |

**14.** Kenny Company, a publicly traded company, adopted a defined benefit pension plan on January 1, 2006. The following data are available at December 31, 2007:

| | |
|---|---|
| Pension expense 2007 | $103,000 |
| Pension funding 2007 | 90,000 |
| Fair value of plan assets 12/31/07 | 225,000 |
| Accumulated pension obligation 12/31/07 | 208,000 |
| Projected benefit obligation 12/31/07 | 290,000 |

At December 31, 2006, Kenny reported prepaid pension cost of $11,000. Kenny's pension liability to be reported in the December 31, 2007 balance sheet is

- a. $0
- b. $ 2,000
- c. $13,000
- d. $65,000

**15.** On May 1, 2005, the board of directors of Edgewood, Inc. approved a plan to sell its electronic component. The plan met the criteria to classify the component as "held for sale." During 2007 the component had a loss from operations of $500,000. In addition, the carrying value of the component's assets is estimated to be $700,00 greater than their fair value less costs to sell. Edgewood's effective tax rate for 2007 is 40%. For the year ended December 31, 2007, Edgewood should report a total loss (net of taxes) from discontinued operations of

- a. $240,000
- b. $400,000
- c. $480,000
- d. $720,000

**16.** Tapscott, Inc., is indebted to Bush Finance Company under a $600,000, 10%, five-year note dated January 1, 2005. Interest, payable annually on December 31, was paid on the December 31, 2005 and 2006 due dates. However, during 2006 Tapscott experienced severe financial difficulties and is likely to default on the note and interest unless

some concessions are made. On December 31, 2007, Tapscott and Bush signed an agreement restructuring the debt as follows:

> Interest for 2007 was reduced to $30,000 payable March 31, 2008.
> Interest payments each year were reduced to $40,000 per year for 2008 and 2009.
> The principal amount was reduced to $400,000.

What is the amount of gain that Tapscott should report on the debt restructure in its income statement for the year ended December 31, 2007?

- a. $120,000
- b. $150,000
- c. $200,000
- d. $230,000

**17.** Included in Kerr Corporation's liability account balances at December 31, 2007, were the following:

| | |
|---|---|
| 14% note payable issued October 1, 2007, maturing September 30, 2008 | $250,000 |
| 16% note payable issued April 1, 2005, payable in 6 equal annual installments of $100,000 beginning April 1, 2006 | 400,000 |

Kerr's December 31, 2007 financial statements were issued on March 31, 2008. On January 15, 2008, the entire $400,000 balance of the 16% note was refinanced by issuance of a long-term obligation payable in a lump sum. In addition, on March 10, 2008, Kerr consummated a noncancelable agreement with the lender to refinance the 14%, $250,000 note on a long-term basis, on readily determinable terms that have not yet been implemented. Both parties are financially capable of honoring the agreement, and there have been no violations of the agreement's provisions. On the December 31, 2007 balance sheet, the amount of the notes payable that Kerr should classify as short-term obligations is

- a. $0
- b. $100,000
- c. $250,000
- d. $350,000

**18.** On July 1, 2007, Diamond, Inc. paid $1,000,000 for 100,000 shares (40%) of the outstanding common stock of Ashley Corporation. At that date the net assets of Ashley totaled $2,500,000 and the fair values of all of Ashley's identifiable assets and liabilities were equal to their book values. Ashley reported net income of $500,000 for the year ended December 31, 2007, of which $300,000 was for the six months ended December 31, 2007. Ashley paid cash dividends of $250,000 on September 30, 2007. In its income statement for the year ended December 31, 2007, what amount of income should Diamond report from its investments in Ashley?

- a. $ 80,000
- b. $100,000
- c. $120,000
- d. $200,000

**19.** West Company determined that it has an obligation relating to employees' rights to receive compensation for future absences attributable to employees' services already rendered. The obligation relates to rights that vest, and payment of the compensation is probable. The amounts of West's obligations as of December 31, 2007, are reasonably estimated as follows:

| Vacation pay | $110,000 |
| Sick pay | 80,000 |

In its December 31, 2007 balance sheet, what amount should West report as its liability for compensated absences?

a. $0
b. $ 80,000
c. $110,000
d. $190,000

**20.** The balance in Ashwood Company's accounts payable account at December 31, 2007, was $900,000 before any necessary year-end adjustment relating to the following:

- Goods were in transit from a vendor to Ashwood on December 31, 2007. The invoice cost was $50,000, and the goods were shipped FOB shipping point on December 29, 2007. The goods were received on January 4, 2008.
- Goods shipped FOB shipping point on December 20, 2007, from a vendor to Ashwood were lost in transit. The invoice cost was $25,000. On January 5, 2008, Ashwood filed a $25,000 claim against the common carrier.
- Goods shipped FOB destination on December 21, 2007, from a vendor to Ashwood were received on January 6, 2008. The invoice cost was $15,000.

What amount should Ashwood report as accounts payable on its December 31, 2007 balance sheet?

a. $925,000
b. $940,000
c. $950,000
d. $975,000

**21.** At December 31, 2007, Arno Beauticians had 1,000 gift certificates outstanding that had been sold to customers during 2007 for $75 each. Arno operates on a gross margin of 60%. How much revenue pertaining to the 1,000 outstanding gift certificates should be deferred at December 31, 2007?

a. $0
b. $30,000
c. $45,000
d. $75,000

**22.** On January 1, 2004, Green Company purchased a machine for $800,000 and established an annual depreciation charge of $100,000 over an eight-year life. During 2007, after issuance of the 2006 financial statements, Green applied the recoverability test to the machine and concluded that: (1) the machine suffered permanent impairment of its operational value, and (2) $200,000 is a reasonable estimate of the amount expected to be recovered through use of the machine for the period January 1, 2007 to December 31, 2011. The fair value of the machine is $160,000. In Green's December 31, 2007 balance sheet, the machine should be reported at a carrying amount of

a. $0
b. $100,000
c. $160,000
d. $400,000

**23.** On December 1, 2007, Poplar, Inc. purchased for cash at $18 per share all 200,000 shares of the outstanding common stock of Spruce Co. At December 1, 2007, Spruce's balance sheet showed a carrying amount of net assets of $3,200,000. At that date, the fair value of Spruce's

property, plant and equipment exceeded its carrying amount by $150,000. In its December 1, 2007 consolidated balance sheet, what amount should Poplar report as goodwill?

a. $550,000
b. $400,000
c. $250,000
d. $0

**24.** Cicci and Arias are partners who share profits and losses in the ratio of 7:3, respectively. On October 5, 2007, their respective capital accounts were as follows:

| Cicci | $35,000 |
| Arias | 30,000 |
| Total | $65,000 |

On that date they agreed to admit Soto as a partner with a one-third interest in the capital and profits and losses, upon his investment of $25,000. The new partnership will begin with a total capital of $90,000. Immediately after Soto's admission, what are the capital balances of Cicci, Arias, and Soto, respectively?

a. $30,000; $30,000; $30,000
b. $31,500; $28,500; $30,000
c. $31,667; $28,333; $30,000
d. $35,000; $30,000; $25,000

**25.** A not-for-profit organization receives $1,000 from a donor. The donor receives two tickets to dinner with a fair market value of $150. What amount should be recorded as contribution revenue?

a. $0
b. $ 150
c. $ 850
d. $1,000

**26.** SFAS 144, *Accounting for the Impairment or Disposal of Long-Lived Assets*, applies to all of the following **except:**

a. Buildings currently used in the business.
b. Financial instruments.
c. Land.
d. Mini-computers used to run a production process.

**27.** According to SFAS 154, *Accounting Changes and Error Corrections*, a change from the sum-of-the-years' digits depreciation method to the straight-line depreciation method is accounted for as a(n)

a. Accounting estimate change.
b. Accounting principle change.
c. Error correction.
d. Prior period adjustment.

**28.** On December 1, Charles Company's board of directors declared a cash dividend of $1.00 per share on the 50,000 shares of common stock outstanding. The company also has 5,000 shares of treasury stock. Shareholders of record on December 15 are eligible for the dividend, which is to be paid on January 1. On December 1, the company should

a. Make no accounting entry.
b. Debit retained earnings for $45,000.
c. Debit retained earnings for $55,000.
d. Debit retained earnings for $50,000.

**29.** Depreciation of a plant asset is the process of

a. Asset valuation for statement of financial position purposes.
b. Allocating the cost of the asset to the periods of use.

   c.   Accumulating a fund for the replacement of the asset.

   d.   Asset valuation based on current replacement cost data.

**30.** When classifying assets as current and noncurrent for reporting purposes

   a.   The amounts at which current assets are carried and reported must reflect realizable cash values.

   b.   Prepayments for items such as insurance or rent are included in an "other assets" group rather than as current assets as they will ultimately be expensed.

   c.   The time period by which current assets are distinguished from noncurrent assets is determined by the seasonal nature of the business.

   d.   Assets are classified as current if they are reasonably expected to be realized in cash or consumed during the normal operating cycle.

# FINANCIAL ACCOUNTING AND REPORTING

## TESTLET 2 ANSWERS

| | | | | | | | | | |
|---|---|---|---|---|---|---|---|---|---|
| 1. c | 6. a | 11. d | 16. b | 21. d | 26. b |
| 2. b | 7. b | 12. b | 17. a | 22. c | 27. a |
| 3. a | 8. d | 13. d | 18. c | 23. c | 28. d |
| 4. c | 9. a | 14. d | 19. d | 24. b | 29. b |
| 5. b | 10. a | 15. d | 20. d | 25. c | 30. d |

### *Hints for Multiple-Choice Questions*

1. Required for proprietary funds and governmental entities that use proprietary fund accounting.

2. Voluntarily established endowments are still part of unrestricted net assets.

3. Taxes on exchanges are derived tax revenue.

4. Contribution revenue is reported on accrual basis.

5. Reverse amounts that have been recognized.

6. Operating activities section of SCF parallels IS.

7. Cost—subtract from stockholders' equity; par value—subtract from shares issued.

8. Allowance increases when account previously written off becomes collectible.

9. Want to find income available to common stockholders.

10. These funds have been segregated for the company's long-term needs.

11. Defer if temporary.

12. A strike is not considered extraordinary.

13. Current cost accounting discards historical cost.

14. Pension liability = FV plan assets – PBO (SFAS 158).

15. Loss on sale is estimated.

16. Gain = Prerestructure carrying amount (including unpaid interest) – Future cash flows.

17. Account for as short-term obligations expected to be refinanced (SFAS 6).

18. The investment was held only for the last six months of the year.

19. Recall the four conditions for accrual.

20. Under the terms "FOB shipping point," title is transferred when goods are delivered to the common carrier.

21. Review Module 10, Section C.1.h.

22. Depreciate over remaining useful life.

23. Purchase price minus fair market value of identifiable assets. $3,600,000 – $3,350,000 = $250,000.

24. Allocate bonus according to P & L ratio.

25. Contribution is amount above fair market value.

26. FASB 144 applies to fixed assets.

27. Change in method and change in estimate may be related.

28. What entry is required on the day of declaration?

29. How are plant assets valued?

30. What is the definition of a current asset?

## FINANCIAL ACCOUNTING AND REPORTING
### TESTLET 3

1. Wildlife Fund, a private not-for-profit organization, received contributions restricted for research totaling $1,000,000 in 2007. None of the contributions were spent in 2007. In 2008, $650,000 of the contributions were used to support the research activities of the organization. The net effect on the statement of activities for the year ended December 31, 2008, would be a
   a. $350,000 increase in temporarily restricted net assets.
   b. $650,000 decrease in temporarily restricted net assets.
   c. $650,000 increase in unrestricted net assets.
   d. $650,000 decrease in unrestricted net assets.

2. The statement of activities of the government-wide financial statements is designed primarily to provide information to assess which of the following?
   a. Operational accountability.
   b. Financial accountability.
   c. Fiscal accountability.
   d. Functional accountability.

3. According to GASB 34, *Basic Financial Statements—and Management's Discussion and Analysis—for State and Local Governments,* certain budgetary schedules are required supplementary information. What is the minimum budgetary information required to be reported in those schedules?
   a. A schedule of unfavorable variances at the functional level.
   b. A schedule showing the final appropriations budget and actual expenditures on a budgetary basis.
   c. A schedule showing the original budget, the final appropriations budget, and actual inflows, outflows, and balances on a budgetary basis.
   d. A schedule showing the proposed budget, the approved budget, the final amended budget, actual inflows and outflows on a budgetary basis, and variances between budget and actual.

4. Nox City reported a $25,000 net increase in the fund balances for total governmental funds. Nox also reported an increase in net assets for the following funds:

| | |
|---|---|
| Motor pool internal service fund | $ 9,000 |
| Water enterprise fund | 12,000 |
| Employee pension fund | 7,000 |

The motor pool internal service fund provides service to the general fund departments. What amount should Nox report as the change in net assets for governmental activities?
   a. $25,000
   b. $34,000
   c. $41,000
   d. $46,000

5. Forkin Manor, a nongovernmental not-for-profit organization, is interested in having its financial statements reformatted using terminology that is more readily associated with for-profit entities. The director believes that the term "operating profit" and the practice of segregating recurring and nonrecurring items more accurately depict the organization's activities. Under what condition will Forkin be allowed to use "operating profit" and to segregate its recurring

items from it nonrecurring items in its statement of activities?
   a. The organization reports the change in unrestricted net assets for the period.
   b. A parenthetical disclosure in the notes implies that the not-for-profit organization is seeking for-profit entity status.
   c. Forkin receives special authorization from the Internal Revenue Service that this wording is appropriate.
   d. At a minimum, the organizations reports the change in permanently restricted net assets for the period.

6. If inventory levels are stable or increasing, an argument that is not in favor of the LIFO method as compared to FIFO is
   a. Income taxes tend to be reduced in periods of rising prices.
   b. Cost of goods sold tends to be stated at approximately current cost in the income statement.
   c. Cost assignments typically parallel the physical flow of the goods.
   d. Income tends to be smoothed as prices change over time.

7. If financial assets are exchanged for cash or other consideration, but the transfer does not meet the criteria for a sale, the transferor should account for the transaction as a

| | Secured borrowing | Pledge of collateral |
|---|---|---|
| a. | No | Yes |
| b. | Yes | Yes |
| c. | Yes | No |
| d. | No | No |

8. In accounting for a long-term construction contract using the percentage-of-completion method, the amount of income recognized in any year would be added to
   a. Deferred revenues.
   b. Progress billings on contracts.
   c. Construction in progress.
   d. Property, plant, and equipment.

9. In calculating the carrying amount of a loan, the lender deducts from the principal

| | Direct loan origination costs incurred by the lender | Loan origination fees charged to the borrower |
|---|---|---|
| a. | Yes | Yes |
| b. | Yes | No |
| c. | No | Yes |
| d. | No | No |

10. How is compensation expense measured by public entities under SFAS 123(R)?
   a. Use the normal hourly rate of the employees.
   b. Measure the intrinsic value of options difference between market price and exercise price at measurement date.
   c. Measure the fair value of options using an option-pricing model.
   d. Measure the difference between the market price and the fair value of the options.

**11.** A gain on the sale of a marketable equity security from the available-for-sale portfolio should be presented in a statement of cash flows in which the operating section is prepared using the direct method as a(n)

a. Inflow of cash under investing activities only.

b. Deduction from net income under operating activities and as an inflow of cash under investing activities.

c. Inflow of cash under operating activities only.

d. Deduction from net income only.

**12.** Lee Corporation's checkbook balance on December 31, 2007, was $4,000. In addition, Lee held the following items in its safe on December 31:

| | |
|---|---|
| Check payable to Lee Corporation, dated January 2, 2008, not included in December 31 checkbook balance | $1,000 |
| Check payable to Lee Corporation, deposited December 20, and included in December 31 checkbook balance, but returned by bank on December 30, stamped "NSF." The check was redeposited January 2, 2008, and cleared January 7 | 200 |
| Postage stamps received from mail order customers | 75 |
| Check drawn on Lee Corporation's account, payable to a vendor, dated and recorded December 31, but not mailed until January 15, 2008 | 500 |

The proper amount to be shown as Cash on Lee's balance sheet at December 31, 2007, is

a. $3,800

b. $4,000

c. $4,300

d. $4,875

**13.** The books of Curtis Company for the year ended December 31, 2007, showed income of $360,000 before provision for income tax. In computing the taxable income for federal income tax purposes, the following differences were taken into account:

| | |
|---|---|
| Depreciation deducted for tax purposes in excess of depreciation recorded on the books | $16,000 |
| Royalty income reported for tax purposes in excess of royalty income recognized on the books | 12,000 |

Assuming a corporate income tax rate of 40%, what should Curtis record as its current federal income tax liability at December 31, 2007?

a. $137,600

b. $142,400

c. $144,000

d. $145,600

**14.** Walker, Inc., a US corporation, ordered a machine from Pfau Company of Germany on July 15, 2007, for 100,000 marks when the spot rate for marks was $.4955. Pfau shipped the machine on September 1, 2007, and billed Walker for 100,000 marks. The spot rate was $.4875 on this date. Walker bought 100,000 marks and paid the invoice on October 25, 2007, when the spot rate was $.4855. In Walker's income statement for the year ended December 31, 2007, how much should be reported as foreign exchange gain?

a. $0

b. $ 200

c. $ 800

d. $1,000

**15.** On July 1, 2007, Jasmine Corporation borrowed $30,000 from the bank on a 5-year note. On July 5, Jasmine used the money as a down payment to buy equipment cost-

ing $50,000. On the statement of cash flows for the year ending December 31, 2007, how should Jasmine disclose the July transactions?

a. Operating activities $20,000 decrease; investing activities $50,000 increase.

b. Investing activities $50,000 decrease; financing activities $50,000 increase.

c. Investing activities, $30,000 increase; financing activities $50,000 increase.

d. Investing activities $50,000 decrease; financing activities $30,000 increase.

**16.** Howard Co. incurred research and development costs in 2007 as follows:

| | |
|---|---|
| Materials used in research and development projects | $ 400,000 |
| Equipment acquired that will have alternate future uses in future research and development projects | 2,000,000 |
| Depreciation for 2007 on above equipment | 500,000 |
| Personnel costs of persons involved in research and development projects | 1,000,000 |
| Consulting fees paid to outsiders for research and development projects | 100,000 |
| Indirect costs reasonably allocable to research and development projects | 200,000 |
| | $4,200,000 |

The amount of research and development costs charged to Howard's 2007 income statement should be

a. $1,500,000

b. $1,700,000

c. $2,200,000

d. $3,500,000

**17.** Kay Company, a lessor of office machines, purchased a new machine for $600,000 on January 1, 2007, which was leased the same day to Lee. The machine will be depreciated $55,000 per year. The lease is for a four-year period expiring January 1, 2011, and provides for annual rental payments of $100,000 beginning January 1, 2007. Additionally, Lee paid $64,000 to Kay as a lease bonus. In its 2007 income statement, what amount of revenue and expense should Kay report on this leased asset?

| | Revenue | Expense |
|---|---|---|
| a. | $100,000 | $0 |
| b. | $116,000 | $0 |
| c. | $116,000 | $55,000 |
| d. | $164,000 | $55,000 |

**18.** In January 2007 Bell Company exchanged an old machine, with a book value of $39,000 and a fair value of $35,000, and paid $10,000 cash for a similar used machine having a list price of $50,000. The transaction has commercial substance. At what amount should the machine acquired in the exchange be recorded on the books of Bell?

a. $45,000

b. $46,000

c. $49,000

d. $50,000

**19.** During the course of your examination of the financial statements of H Co., a new client, for the year ended December 31, 2007, you discover the following:

• Inventory at January 1, 2007, had been overstated by $3,000.

• Inventory at December 31, 2007, was understated by $5,000.

- An insurance policy covering three years had been purchased on January 2, 2006, for $1,500. The entire amount was charged as an expense in 2006.

During 2007 the company received a $1,000 cash advance from a customer for merchandise to be manufactured and shipped during 2008. The $1,000 had been credited to sales revenues. The company's gross profit on sales is 50%.

Net income reported on the 2007 income statement (before reflecting any adjustments for the above items) is $20,000.

The proper net income for 2007 is
- a.   $26,500
- b.   $23,500
- c.   $16,500
- d.   $20,500

**20.** The following information is available for Cooke Company for 2007:

| | |
|---|---|
| Net sales | $1,800,000 |
| Freight-in | 45,000 |
| Purchase discounts | 25,000 |
| Ending inventory | 120,000 |

The gross margin is 40% of net sales. What is the cost of goods available for sale?
- a.   $  840,000
- b.   $  960,000
- c.   $1,200,000
- d.   $1,220,000

**21.** Warrants exercisable at $20 each to obtain 10,000 shares of common stock were outstanding during a period when the average market price of the common stock was $25. Application of the treasury stock method for the assumed exercise of these warrants in computing diluted earnings per share will increase the weighted-average number of outstanding common stock shares by
- a.   8,000
- b.   8,333
- c.   2,000
- d.   1,667

**22.** Greg Corp. reported revenue of $1,250,000 in its accrual-basis income statement for the year ended June 30, 2007. Additional information was as follows:

| | |
|---|---|
| Accounts receivable June 30, 2005 | $400,000 |
| Accounts receivable June 30, 2006 | 530,000 |
| Uncollectible accounts written off during the fiscal year | 15,000 |

Under the cash basis, Greg should report revenue of
- a.   $  835,000
- b.   $  850,000
- c.   $1,105,000
- d.   $1,135,000

**23.** On January 1, 2007, Mann Company's allowance for doubtful accounts had a credit balance of $30,000. During 2007 Mann charged $64,000 to doubtful accounts expense, wrote off $46,000 of uncollectible accounts receivable, and unexpectedly recovered $12,000 of bad debts written off in the prior year. The allowance for doubtful accounts balance at December 31, 2007, would be
- a.   $48,000
- b.   $60,000
- c.   $64,000
- d.   $94,000

**24.** Greene Company bought a patent from White Company on January 1, 2007, for $102,000. An independent research consultant retained by Greene estimated that the remaining useful life of the patent was four years. Its remaining legal life was six years. Its unamortized cost on White's books at January 1, 2007, was $30,000. How much should be amortized by Greene for the year ended December 31, 2007?
- a.   $  5,000
- b.   $  7,500
- c.   $17,000
- d.   $25,500

**25.** On January 1, 2007, Harry Corporation sold equipment costing $2,000,000 with accumulated depreciation of $500,000 to Anna Corporation, its wholly owned subsidiary, for $1,800,000. Harry was depreciating the equipment on the straight-line method over twenty years with no salvage value, which Anna continued. In consolidation at December 31, 2007, the cost and accumulated depreciation, respectively, should be
- a.   $1,500,000 and $100,000
- b.   $1,800,000 and $100,000
- c.   $2,000,000 and $100,000
- d.   $2,000,000 and $600,000

**26.** A loss that is material, unusual in nature, and infrequent in occurrence should be reported as
- a.   Part of continuing operations.
- b.   Part of discontinued operations.
- c.   An extraordinary item.
- d.   A prior period item.

**27.** According to SFAS 154, *Accounting Changes and Error Corrections*, a change in the liability for warranty costs requires
- a.   Presenting prior period financial statements as previously reported.
- b.   Presenting the effect of pro forma data on income and earnings per share for all prior periods presented.
- c.   Restating the financial statements of all prior periods presented.
- d.   Reporting current and future financial statements on the new basis.

**28.** Items reported as prior period adjustments
- a.   Do not include the effect of a mistake in the application of accounting principles as this is accounted for as a change in accounting principle rather than as a prior period adjustment.
- b.   Do not affect the presentation of prior period comparative financial statements.
- c.   Do not require further disclosure in the body of the financial statements.
- d.   Are reflected as adjustments of the opening balance of the retained earnings of the earliest period presented.

**Questions 29 and 30** are based on the following information. Patterson Company has the following information on one of its vehicles purchased on January 1, 2005:

| Vehicle cost | $50,000 |
|---|---|
| Useful life, years, estimated | 5 |
| Useful life, miles, estimated | 100,000 |
| Salvage value, estimated | $10,000 |
| Actual miles driven, 2005 | 30,000 |
| 2006 | 20,000 |
| 2007 | 15,000 |

No estimates were changed during the life of the asset.

**29.** The 2007 depreciation expense for the vehicle using the sum-of-the-years' digits (SYD) method was

    a.   $ 6,000
    b.   $ 8,000
    c.   $10,000
    d.   $13,333

**30.** The fiscal 2006 year-end accumulated depreciation balance, using the double-declining balance method was

    a.   $12,000
    b.   $16,000
    c.   $25,600
    d.   $32,000

## FINANCIAL ACCOUNTING AND REPORTING

### TESTLET 3  ANSWERS

| | | | | | | | | | | | |
|---|---|---|---|---|---|---|---|---|---|---|---|
| 1. | b | 6. | c | 11. | a | 16. | c | 21. | c | 26. | c |
| 2. | a | 7. | b | 12. | c | 17. | c | 22. | c | 27. | d |
| 3. | c | 8. | c | 13. | b | 18. | a | 23. | b | 28. | d |
| 4. | b | 9. | c | 14. | b | 19. | a | 24. | d | 29. | b |
| 5. | a | 10. | c | 15. | d | 20. | c | 25. | d | 30. | d |

### Hints for Multiple-Choice Questions

1. Spending of funds results in decrease in restricted assets.

2. Statement of activities focuses on operations.

3. Original budget, final budget, and actual inflows, outflows, and balances.

4. Water enterprise and pension fund are excluded.

5. Unrestricted net assets must be shown.

6. Most recent purchases go to CGS first, reducing income and matching current costs to revenues.

7. What is debt?

8. Recall the account to be debited.

9. How is lender's investment affected by these?

10. Recognize compensation in cases where APB 25 does not.

11. The direct method is **not** based on net income, which includes gains and losses.

12. Postdated check should be excluded.

13. Deduct excess tax depreciation from book income.

14. Walker was billed at $.4875, but only had to pay $.4855.

15. Borrowing from the bank increases cash from financing activities by $30,000; purchasing equipment decreases cash by the amount of the purchase $50,000.

16. Only intangibles or fixed assets purchased from others having alternative future uses may be deferred.

17. The bonus is amortized over the lease term.

18. Losses are **always** recognized when FV is determinable.

19. The portion of the cash advance representing income = **unearned** revenues.

20. Freight-in and discounts are already included in cost of sales and ending inventory.

21. Calculate number of shares that could be reacquired with proceeds.

22. The entry to write off bad debts debits the allowance account (not expense).

23. A recovery is charged back to the allowance account.

24. Review Module 9, Sec. J.

25. Intercompany transactions must be eliminated.

26. What are unusual and infrequent items?

27. Warranty liabilities are estimated liabilities.

28. Prior period adjustments result in restatement.

29. Ratio is three-fifteenths.

30. DDB rate is equal to 40%.

**SIMULATION PROBLEM 1** (50 to 55 minutes)

| Situation | | | | |
|---|---|---|---|---|
| | **Property, Plant, and Equipment** | **Depreciation** | **Communication** | **Research** |

At December 31, 2006, Cord Company's plant asset and accumulated depreciation accounts had balances as follows:

| Category | Plant assets | Accumulated depreciation |
|---|---|---|
| Land | $ 175,000 | $ -- |
| Building | 1,500,000 | 328,900 |
| Automobiles and trucks | 172,000 | 100,325 |

### Depreciation methods and useful lives

Buildings—150% declining balance; twenty-five years.
Automobiles and trucks—150% declining balance; five years, all acquired after 2000.
Depreciation is computed to the nearest month.
The salvage values of the depreciable assets are immaterial.

### Transactions during 2007 and other information

On January 6, 2007, a plant facility consisting of land and building was acquired from King Corp. in exchange for 25,000 shares of Cord's common stock. On this date, Cord's stock has a market price of $50 a share. Current assessed values of land and building for property tax purposes are $187,500 and $562,500, respectively.

- On August 30, 2007, Cord purchased a new automobile for $12,500.
- On September 30, 2007, a truck with a cost of $24,000 and a carrying amount of $9,100 on date of sale was sold for $11,500. Depreciation for the nine months ended September 30, 2007, was $2,650.
- On November 4, 2007, Cord purchased for $350,000 a tract of land as a potential future building site.

| | **Property, Plant, and Equipment** | | | |
|---|---|---|---|---|
| Situation | | **Depreciation** | **Communication** | **Research** |

Complete the following spreadsheet analyzing the changes in each of the plant asset accounts during 2007. Show supporting calculations in the space provided below the table.

| | A | B | C | D | E | F | G |
|---|---|---|---|---|---|---|---|
| 1 | Cord Company | | | | | | |
| 2 | ANALYSIS OF CHANGES IN PLANT ASSETS | | | | | | |
| 3 | For the Year Ended December 31, 2007 | | | | | | |
| 4 | | | | | | | |
| 5 | | Beginning | | | | Ending | |
| 6 | Item | Balance | Additions | | Disposals | Balance | |
| 7 | | | | | | | |
| 8 | Land | $175,000 | | [1] | | | |
| 9 | Buildings | $1,500,000 | | [1] | | | |
| 10 | Automobiles & Trucks | $172,000 | | | | | |
| 11 | | $1,847,000 | | | | | |
| 12 | | | | | | | |

**Supporting Calculations:**

| Situation | Property, Plant, and Equipment | Depreciation | Communication | Research |
|---|---|---|---|---|

For each asset category, complete the following spreadsheet showing the amounts as indicated.  **Round computations to the nearest whole dollar.**  Show supporting calculations in the space provided.

|    | A | B | C | D | E | F | G |
|----|---|---|---|---|---|---|---|
| 1  | Cord Company | | | | | | |
| 2  | ANALYSIS OF CHANGES IN PLANT ASSETS & DEPRECIATION | | | | | | |
| 3  | For the Year Ended December 31, 2007 | | | | | | |
| 4  | | | Accumulated | | Accumulated | | |
| 5  | | | Depreciation | Current Year | Depreciation | Book | |
| 6  | Item | Cost | 1/1/2007 | Depreciation | 12/31/2007 | Value | |
| 7  | | | | | | | |
| 8  | Land | | | | | | |
| 9  | Buildings | | | | | | |
| 10 | Automobiles & Trucks | | | | | | |
| 11 | | | | | | | |
| 12 | | | | | | | |

**Supporting Calculations:**

| Situation | Property, Plant, and Equipment | Depreciation | Communication | Research |
|---|---|---|---|---|

Cord Company's controller, Linda Heinz, wants a memorandum prepared providing the theoretical justification for use of accelerated methods of depreciation for presentation to the audit committee of the board of directors.  Prepare the memorandum requested by Ms. Heinz.

To:    Ms. Linda Heinz
         Controller
From: CPA Candidate

| Situation | Property, Plant, and Equipment | Depreciation | Communication | Research |
|---|---|---|---|---|

Research the issue of the capitalization of interest on self-constructed assets.  Input the reference to professional standards that provides guidance on the type of assets that qualify.  Use the current text reference.

**SOLUTION TO SIMULATION PROBLEM 1**

| | Situation | Property, Plant, and Equipment | | Depreciation | Communication | Research |
|---|---|---|---|---|---|---|

| | A | B | C | D | E | F | G |
|---|---|---|---|---|---|---|---|
| 1 | **Cord Company** | | | | | | |
| 2 | **ANALYSIS OF CHANGES IN PLANT ASSETS** | | | | | | |
| 3 | **For the Year Ended December 31, 2007** | | | | | | |
| 4 | | | | | | | |
| 5 | | **Beginning** | | | | **Ending** | |
| 6 | **Item** | **Balance** | **Additions** | | **Disposals** | **Balance** | |
| 7 | | | | | | | |
| 8 | Land | $175,000 | $312,500 | [1] | $-- | $487,500 | |
| 9 | Buildings | 1,500,000 | 937,500 | [1] | -- | 2,437,500 | |
| 10 | Automobiles & Trucks | 172,000 | 12,500 | | 24,000 | 160,500 | |
| 11 | | $1,847,000 | $1,262,500 | | $24,000 | $3,085,500 | |
| 12 | | | | | | | |

## Explanation of amounts

[1]    Plant facility acquired from King 1/6/07—
allocation to Land and Building

     Fair value—25,000 shares of Cord
common stock at $50 market price          $1,250,000

     Allocation in proportion to appraised
values at the exchange date

| | *Amount* | *% to total* |
|---|---|---|
| Land | $187,500 | 25 |
| Building | 562,500 | 75 |
| | $750,000 | 100 |
| Land | ($1,250,000 × 25%) | $ 312,500 |
| Building | ($1,250,000 × 75%) | 937,500 |
| | | $1,250,000 |

| | Situation | Property, Plant, and Equipment | Depreciation | | Communication | Research |
|---|---|---|---|---|---|---|

*Cord Company*
**DEPRECIATION EXPENSE**
*For the Year Ended December 31, 2007*

Building
     Carrying amount         $1,171,100
     Building acquired 1/6/07       937,500

     Total amount subject to depreciation    2,108,600
     150% declining balance rate [(100% ÷ 25) × 1.5]    ×     6%

       Depreciation on buildings for 2007            $126,516

Automobiles and trucks
     Carrying amount, 1/1/07 ($172,000 – $100,325)    $ 71,675
     Deduct carrying amount, 1/1/07 on
     truck sold 9/30/07 ($9,100 + $2,650)      11,750

     Amount subject to depreciation        59,925
     150% declining balance rate [(100% ÷ 5) × 1.5]    ×     30%      17,978

     Automobile purchased 8/30/07        12,500
     Depreciation for 2007 (30% × 4/12)    ×     10%      1,250

     Truck sold 9/30/07—depreciation
     for 2007 (1/1 to 9/30/07)             2,650

       Depreciation on automobiles and trucks for 2007    $ 21,878

     Total depreciation expense for 2007            $148,394

| | A | B | C | D | E | F | G |
|---|---|---|---|---|---|---|---|
| 1 | **Cord Company** | | | | | | |
| 2 | **ANALYSIS OF PLANT ASSETS & DEPRECIATION** | | | | | | |
| 3 | **For the Year Ended December 31, 2007** | | | | | | |
| 4 | | | **Accumulated** | | **Accumulated** | **Book** | |
| 5 | | | **Depreciation** | **Current Year** | **Depreciation** | **Value** | |
| 6 | **Item** | **Cost** | **1/1/2007** | **Depreciation** | **12/31/2007** | **12/31/2007** | |
| 7 | | | | | | | |
| 8 | Land | $487,500 | $0 | $0 | $0 | $487,500 | |
| 9 | Buildings | $2,437,500 | $328,900 | $126,516 | $455,416 | $1,982,084 | |
| 10 | Automobiles & Trucks | $160,500 | $100,325 | $21,878 | $122,203 | $38,297 | |
| 11 | | $3,085,500 | $429,225 | $148,394 | $577,619 | $2,507,881 | |
| 12 | | | | | | | |

| Situation | Property, Plant, and Equipment | Depreciation | Communication | Research |
|---|---|---|---|---|

Ms. Linda Heinz
Controller
Cord Company

January 15, 2008

Dear Ms. Heinz:

This memorandum is in response to your request for a discussion of the theoretical justification for accelerated methods of depreciation. Accelerated methods of depreciation are justified based on the following assumptions:

1. As asset is more efficient in the earlier years of its life. Therefore, larger depreciation charges in the earlier years would be matched with the larger revenues generated from that asset in those years.
2. Repair expenses on an asset increase in the later years of its life. Therefore, smaller depreciation charges in the later years combined with the larger repair expenses in those years would result in a smooth or level pattern of total expenses of operating the asset over its useful life.

If you have any additional questions regarding this issue, please contact me.

| Situation | Property, Plant, and Equipment | Depreciation | Communication | Research |
|---|---|---|---|---|

I67.105-108

**SIMULATION PROBLEM 2**                                    (45 to 50 minutes)

| Situation | | | | |
|---|---|---|---|---|
| | **Financial Statement Amounts** | **Stockholders' Equity** | **Per Share Amounts** | **Research and Communication** |

Moxley Co. is a publicly held company whose shares are traded in the over-the-counter market. The stockholders' equity accounts at December 31, 2006, had the following balances:

| | |
|---|---|
| Preferred stock, $100 par value, 6% cumulative; 5,000 shares authorized; 2,000 issued and outstanding | $    200,00 |
| Common stock, $1 par value, 150,000 shares authorized; 100,000 issued and outstanding | 100,00 |
| Additional paid-in capital | 800,000 |
| Retained earnings | 1,586,000 |
| Total stockholders' equity | $2,686,000 |

Transactions during 2007 and other information relating to the stockholders' equity accounts were as follows:

- February 1, 2007—Issued 13,000 shares of common stock to Ram Co. in exchange for land. On the date issued, the stock had a market price of $11 per share. The land had a carrying value on Ram's books for $135,000, and an assessed value for property taxes of $90,000.

- March 1, 2007—Purchased 5,000 shares of its own commons stock to be held as treasury stock for $14 per share. Moxley uses the cost method to account for treasury stock. Transactions in treasury stock are legal in Moxley's state of incorporation.

- May 10, 2007—Declared a property dividend of marketable securities held by Moxley to common shareholders. The securities had a carrying value of $600,000; fair value on relevant dates were

| | |
|---|---|
| Date of declaration (May 10, 2007) | $720,000 |
| Date of record (May 25, 2007) | 758,000 |
| Date of distribution (June 1, 2007) | 736,000 |

- October 1, 2007—Reissued 2,000 shares of treasury stock for $16 per share.

- November 4, 2007—Declared a cash dividend of $1.50 per share to all common shareholders of record November 15, 2007.

- December 20, 2007—Declared the required annual cash dividend on preferred stock for 2007. The dividend was paid on January 5, 2008.

- January 16, 2008—Before closing the accounting records for 2007, Moxley became aware that no amortization had been recorded for 2006 for a patent purchased on July 1, 2006. Amortization expense was properly recorded in 2007. The patent was properly capitalized at $320,000 and had an estimated useful life of eight year when purchased. Moxley's income tax rate is 30%. The appropriate correcting entry was recorded on the same day.

- Adjusted net income for 2007 was $838,000.

**Items 1 through 8** represent amounts to be reported in Moxley's financial statements. **Items 9 and 10** represent other financial information. For all items, calculate the amounts requested. On the CPA exam, a list of numeric answers would be provided for the candidate to select from.

| | **Financial Statement Amounts** | | | |
|---|---|---|---|---|
| **Situation** | | **Stockholders' Equity** | **Per Share Amounts** | **Research and Communication** |

**Items 1 through 4** represent amounts to be reported on Moxley's 2007 statement of retained earnings.

1. Prior period adjustment.

2. Preferred dividends.

3. Common dividends—cash.

4. Common dividends—property.

| | | **Stockholders' Equity** | | |
|---|---|---|---|---|
| **Situation** | **Financial Statement Amounts** | | **Per Share Amounts** | **Research and Communication** |

**Items 1 through 4** represent amounts to be reported on Moxley's statement of stockholders' equity at December 31, 2007.

1. Number of common shares issued at December 31, 2007.

2. Amount of common stock issued.

3. Additional paid-in capital, including treasury stock transactions.

4. Treasury stock.

| Situation | Financial Statement Amounts | Stockholders' Equity | Per Share Amounts | Research and Communication |
|---|---|---|---|---|

**Items 1 and 2** represent other financial information for 2006 and 2007.

1. Book value per share at December 31, 2006, before prior period adjustment.

2. Numerator used in calculation of 2007 basic earnings per share for the year.

| Situation | Financial Statement Amounts | Stockholders' Equity | Per Share Amounts | Research and Communication |
|---|---|---|---|---|

Research the professional standards and write a memo to the files describing the appropriate accounting for the issuance of a stock dividend.

To:    Client files
From: CPA Candidate

## SOLUTION TO SIMULATION PROBLEM 2

| Situation | | | | |
|---|---|---|---|---|
| | **Financial Statement Amounts** | **Stockholders' Equity** | **Per Share Amounts** | **Research and Communication** |

This problem is a collection of miscellaneous stockholders' equity problems. The candidate should start the problem by scanning the required information to determine the amounts to be calculated. While scanning, the candidate should recognize that some of the required items are related, such as 2 (preferred dividends) and 10 (numerator used in calculating EPS) and 5 (number of common shares issued) and 6 (amount of common stock issued); 7 (additional paid-in capital) and 8 (treasury stock). These relationships require that the candidate label each answer so that it will be possible to quickly find that answer when it is used in a subsequent problem.

Unlike many previous exam problems, the order of the information concerning the transactions does not coincide with the order of the required answers. This arrangement makes it necessary to read the required amount and then hunt for the transaction information needed to calculate that required amount.

| | **Financial Statement Amounts** | | | |
|---|---|---|---|---|
| **Situation** | | **Stockholders' Equity** | **Per Share Amounts** | **Research and Communication** |

**1. ($14,000)** Prior period adjustment is the term generally applied to corrections of errors of prior periods. In this problem no amortization had been recorded in a prior year—an error. Since this is not a self-correcting error, it still existed in 2008. The calculation is cost ($320,000) ÷ useful life (eight years) for 1/2 year (purchased July 1). Prior period adjustments are disclosed net of tax (30%). $320,000/8 × 1/2 × (1 − .3) = $14,000. In accordance with SFAS 154, an adjustment is made to the opening balance of retained earnings in 2008. In addition, the financial statements of the prior period are restated to reflect the correct amounts of assets and liabilities at the beginning of the first period presented. Financial statements for each prior period are adjusted to reflect the correction of the period-specific effects of the error.

**2. ($12,000)** Preferred dividends are 6% and cumulative. They were declared during 2007 and paid in 2008. The declaration is sufficient to record and recognize the dividends legally; they do not have to be paid in the current year to be recognized during that time period. These dividends will be used in the numerator in question 10 when calculating the 2007 EPS. Since these dividends are cumulative, they would be used in the calculation of EPS even if they had not been declared. The amount of preferred dividends is derived by multiplying the par value of the stock by its rate. 6% × $200,000 par = $12,000 dividends.

**3. ($165,000)** Common dividends—cash is calculated by the formula: Common shares outstanding × Dividend per share. In this problem the number of shares outstanding is affected by the beginning shares (100,000), shares issued (13,000), and treasury shares purchased and sold (5,000 purchased, 2,000 sold) prior to the dividend date of November 4. 100,000 + 13,000 − 5,000 + 2,000 = 110,000 shares outstanding × dividend rate $1.50 = $165,000.

**4. ($720,000)** Common dividends—property differ from cash dividends because the property may be carried in the accounts at an amount which does not equal its fair value (cash is always at its fair value). Management intends to distribute the property at its fair value, therefore it is necessary to bring the property to fair value on the date management is legally forced to distribute it (the declaration date). Value fluctuations beyond that date are irrelevant.

| | | **Stockholders' Equity** | | |
|---|---|---|---|---|
| **Situation** | **Financial Statement Amounts** | | **Per Share Amounts** | **Research and Communication** |

**1. (113,000)** The number of shares issued differs from the number of shares outstanding which was used in question 3. Shares issued include those outstanding as well as those held in the treasury. Shares outstanding from question 3, 110,000 plus 3,000 treasury shares = 113,000 shares.

**2. ($113,000)** Amount of common stock issued—This question takes the answer from question 5 (113,000 shares) and multiplies that figure by the par value of each share, $1.

**3. ($934,000)** The additional paid-in capital, including treasury stock transactions, is derived by adding the beginning balance ($800,000) to the excess ($10) of issue price ($11) over par value ($1) for the shares issued (13,000) to acquire land on February 1, 2007. In addition, the sale of the treasury stock (2,000 shares) at an amount ($16) greater than cost ($14) gives rise to a nonoperating gain that cannot be included in net income since it was both not related to operations and is a transaction in the company's own stock. $800,000 + (13,000 × $10) + (2,000 × $16 − $14) = $934,000.

**4. ($42,000)** Treasury stock—Since the Moxley Co. follows the cost method of accounting for treasury stock, this answer is derived by multiplying the shares of treasury stock (3,000) by their cost ($14). 3,000 × $14 = $42,000.

| Situation | Financial Statement Amounts | Stockholders' Equity | Per Share Amounts | Research and Communication |
|---|---|---|---|---|

**1.** **($24.86)** Book value per share is a concept that relates common stockholders' equity to shares of common stock. The "per share" referred to is always the **common** shares unless the problem states some other type of shares. In this case it is to be calculated before the prior period adjustment. It is necessary to subtract preferred stock's total liquidating value ($100 × 2,000 sh = $200,000) from total stockholders' equity ($2,686,000) to obtain common stockholders' equity. In this problem no liquidating value is given, so par value is used. The resulting amount ($2,686,000 – $200,000 = $2,486,000) is divided by the common shares outstanding (100,000) to obtain book value per share ($24.86). ($2,686,000 – $200,000) ÷ 100,000 = $24.86.

**2.** **($826,000)** The formula for calculating earnings per share is (NI – Preferred dividends) ÷ Wtd-avg. shares outstanding. The numerator is income available to common stockholders. The problem states that adjusted net income for 2007 was $838,000. The word "adjusted" tells the candidate that net income includes all information concerning transactions in the problem and need not be changed in any way. Preferred dividends ($12,000) were calculated in question 2. $838,000 – $12,000 = $826,000.

| Situation | Financial Statement Amounts | Stockholders' Equity | Per Share Amounts | Research and Communication |
|---|---|---|---|---|

To:     Client files
From: CPA Candidate

The proper accounting for a stock dividend depends on its size. Small stock dividends of less than 20 to 25% of the shares outstanding involve the capitalization of retained earnings in an amount equal to the fair value of the shares issued. A large stock dividend of more than 20 to 25% of the shares outstanding should involve a capitalization of retained earnings in an amount equal to the par value of the shares issued. (ARB43, Ch7b)

## FINANCIAL ACCOUNTING AND REPORTING TESTLETS RELEASED BY AICPA

**1.** For $50 a month, Rawl Co. visits its customers' premises and performs insect control services. If customers experience problems between regularly scheduled visits, Rawl makes service calls at no additional charge. Instead of paying monthly, customers may pay an annual fee of $540 in advance. For a customer who pays the annual fee in advance, Rawl should recognize the related revenue

    a. Evenly over the contract year as the services are performed.
    b. At the end of the contract year after all of the services have been performed.
    c. When the cash is collected.
    d. At the end of the fiscal year.

**2.** Simm Co. has determined its December 31 inventory on a FIFO basis to be $400,000. Information pertaining to that inventory follows:

| | |
|---|---|
| Estimated selling price | $403,000 |
| Estimated cost of disposal | 20,000 |
| Normal profit margin | 60,000 |
| Current replacement cost | 360,000 |

Simm records losses that result from applying the lower of cost or market rule. At December 31, what should be the amount of Simm's inventory?

    a. $400,000
    b. $388,000
    c. $360,000
    d. $328,000

**3.** A bond issued on June 1, 2002, has interest payment dates of April 1 and October 1. Bond interest expense for the year ended December 31, 2002, is for a period of

    a. Three months.
    b. Four months.
    c. Six months.
    d. Seven months.

**4.** Governmental financial reporting should provide information to assist users in which situation(s)?

  I. Making social and political decisions.
  II. Assessing whether current-year citizens received services but shifted part of the payment burden to future-year citizens.

    a. I only.
    b. II only.
    c. Both I and II.
    d. Neither I nor II.

**1. (a)** Revenue is generally recognized when **realized or realizable** and **earned**. Revenues are considered earned when the entity has substantially accomplished what it must do to be entitled to the benefits represented by the revenues. Therefore, service revenue generally is earned as the work is performed, and it should be recognized evenly over the contract year as the monthly services are performed. Answer (c) is incorrect because accrual basis accounting is preferable; SFAC 6 explains that cash method provides little information about the results of operations. Answer (d) is incorrect because revenue should be recognized when earned. Answer (b) is incorrect because the completed-contract method should only be used when reasonable estimates of contract costs, revenues, and the extent of progress toward completion cannot be reasonably estimated.

**2. (c)** ARB 43 requires the use of lower of cost or market (LCM) for financial reporting of inventories. The market value of inventory is defined as the replacement cost (RC), as long as it is less than the ceiling (net realizable value, or NRV) and more than the floor (NRV less a normal profit, or NRV – NP). In this case, the amounts are

| | |
|---|---|
| Ceiling: NRV = $408,000 est. sell. price – $20,000 dep. cost = | $388,000 |
| Replacement cost | $360,000 |
| Floor: NRV – NP = $388,000 – $60,000 = | $328,000 |

The designated market value is the replacement cost of $360,000 because it falls between the floor and the ceiling. Once market value is designated, LCM can be determined by simply picking the lower of cost ($400,000) or market ($360,000). Thus, the inventory should be reported at market.

**3. (d)** Under the accrual basis of accounting, expenses should be recognized when incurred, regardless of when cash is paid. Therefore, expense from the bond issue date (6/1/02) through year-end (12/31/02) should be recognized in 2003.

The seven months (6/1/02 - 12/31/02) of interest expense would be the net effect of entries prepared on the issuance date, the October 1 interest date, and December 31 (adjusting entry).

**4. (c)** Financial reporting by state and local governments is used in making economic, social, and political decisions and in assessing accountability. Additionally, current year citizens need information concerning when costs of current services are actually paid for. Thus, both items I and II are provided to the users of governmental reporting.

**5.** During the year, Jones Foundation received the following support:

- A cash contribution of $875,000 to be used at the board of directors' discretion;
- A promise to contribute $500,000 in the following year from a supporter who has made similar contributions in prior periods;
- Contributed legal services with a value of $100,000, which Jones would have otherwise purchased.

At what amounts would Jones classify and record these transactions?

|  | Unrestricted revenue | Temporarily restricted revenue |
|---|---|---|
| a. | $ 875,000 | $500,000 |
| b. | $ 975,000 | $500,000 |
| c. | $ 975,000 | $0 |
| d. | $1,375,000 | $0 |

**5.**    **(b)**    Under FASB Statement 116, restricted revenues are recorded only when a restriction has been placed by the donor.  One type of restricted revenue is a pledge that has not been received during the year.  This is considered a time restriction; accordingly, the $500,000 would be considered a temporarily restricted revenue based on a time restriction.  The $875,000 and the $100,000 would be considered unrestricted revenues.  The $100,000 is considered contributed services and carries no restriction.  Contributed services are recognized, according to FASB 116, when the services received (1) create or enhance nonfinancial assets or (2) require specialized skills, are provided by individuals possessing those skills, and would typically need to be purchased if not provided by donation.  The $100,000 contribution meets the second criterion.

**SIMULATION 1**                              (50 to 60 minutes)

| Situation | | | | | | |
|---|---|---|---|---|---|---|
| | Treatments | Cumulative Effect | Journal Entries | Financial Statement | Written Communication | Research |

On January 1, 1999, Charleston Company purchased machinery at a cost of $150,000. The machinery was depreciated under the double-declining balance method, assuming a ten-year life and no salvage value. The company took full-year depreciation in the year of acquisition. During 2002, management decided to change depreciation methods to the straight-line method for financial reporting purposes, but it continued to use the accelerated method for tax purposes. Charleston has a 40% effective income tax rate. (APB 20 is used to report accounting changes in this problem.)

| | Treatments | | | | | |
|---|---|---|---|---|---|---|
| Situation | | Cumulative Effect | Journal Entries | Financial Statement | Written Communication | Research |

In the table below, determine which description applies to each event by double-clicking the shaded box in the Description column and selecting the appropriate description. Then determine the appropriate accounting treatment for each event by double-clicking the shaded box in the Accounting treatment column and selecting the appropriate accounting treatment. Assume that all events are material in amount. A selected item may be used once, more than once, or not at all.

| *Description* | *Accounting treatment* |
|---|---|
| Change in accounting principle | Current income |
| Change in accounting estimate | Cumulative effect in current income |
| Correction of error | Prospective treatment |
| Neither a change nor an error correction | Retroactive adjustment |
| | No impact |

| Event | Description | Accounting treatment |
|---|---|---|
| Change in long-term construction contract from percentage-of-completion method to completed-contract method | | |
| Write-off of uncollectible receivables under the direct write-off method | | |
| Write-off of uncollectible receivables under the reserve method | | |
| Change in salvage value of a depreciable asset | | |
| Change in useful life of a patent | | |

| | | Cumulative Effect | | | | |
|---|---|---|---|---|---|---|
| Situation | Treatments | | Journal Entries | Financial Statement | Written Communication | Research |

Using the spreadsheet below, calculate the amount of the cumulative effect of Charleston's accounting change at December 31, 2001. You may record your entries as numbers or as formulas that produce the correct number. Be sure that the value of the change appears in the shaded cell at the bottom of the spreadsheet.

*NOTE: To use a formula in the spreadsheet, it must be preceded by an equal sign (e.g., = B1 + B2).*

| A | B | C | D |
|---|---|---|---|
| | | Depreciation expense | |
| **Double-declining balance method** | | | |
| | 1999 | $30,000 | |
| | 2000 | $24,000 | |
| | 2001 | $19,200 | |
| **Straight-line method** | | | |
| | 1999 | $15,000 | |
| | 2000 | $15,000 | |
| | 2001 | $15,000 | |
| **Cumulative effect of accounting change (before tax)** | | | |

| | | | Journal Entries | | | |
|---|---|---|---|---|---|---|
| Situation | Treatments | Cumulative Effect | | Financial Statement | Written Communication | Research |

Use the form below to complete the journal entries required to record Charleston's accounting change, to adjust the amount of Charleston's deferred income taxes, and to record Charleston's depreciation expense for 2002 based on the change from the double-declining balance method to the straight-line method. Enter the appropriate account title in column A by clicking the shaded box and then selecting the desired account title from the list provided. Account titles may be used once, more than once, or not at all.

Use columns B and C to record the dollar value corresponding to each journal entry. Be sure your entries appear in the appropriate shaded spaces. Some of the shaded spaces may not be used.

_Column A_

| | |
|---|---|
| Accounts payable | Deferred income taxes |
| Accounts receivable | Depreciation expense |
| Accumulated depreciation | Income tax expense |
| Cash | Prior period adjustment |
| Cumulative effect of change in accounting | Retained earnings |
| Retained earnings | |

| A | B | C |
|---|---|---|
| | Debit | Credit |
| | | |
| | | |
| | | |
| | | |
| | | |
| | | |
| | | |
| | | |
| | | |

| Situation | Treatments | Cumulative Effect | Journal Entries | Financial Statement | Written Communication | Research |
|---|---|---|---|---|---|---|

Use your solutions to other parts of this simulation to complete the following excerpts from Charleston's balance sheet at December 31, 2002, and income statement for the year ending December 31, 2002.  Insert the appropriate values in the shaded cells in column D below.  Indicate in column F whether the net cumulative effect is income or expense by clicking the shaded box in column F and then selecting either "Income" or "Expense."

_NOTE:  To use a formula in the spreadsheet, if must be preceded by an equal sign (e.g., = B1 + B2)._

| A | B | C | D | E | F | H |
|---|---|---|---|---|---|---|
| Charleston Company | | | | | | |
| Balance sheet | | | | | | |
| December 31, 2002 | | | | | | |
| | Machinery | | | | | |
| | Accumulated depreciation | | | | | |
| | Net | | | | | |
| Charleston Company | | | | | | |
| Income statement | | | | | | |
| Year ending December 31, 2002 | | | | | | |
| | Depreciation expense | | | | | |
| | Cumulative effect of change in accounting principle | | | | | Indicate "Income" or "Expense" |

| Situation | Treatments | Cumulative Effect | Journal Entries | Financial Statement | Written Communication | Research |
|---|---|---|---|---|---|---|

A junior staff accountant in your department seems to be confused about what constitutes an accounting change for financial reporting purposes.  In a brief memorandum to the junior accountant, describe the three basic types of accounting changes.  Type your description in the space below using the word processor provided.

_Reminder:  Your responses to this prompt will be graded for both technical content and writing skills.  For writing skills, you should demonstrate the ability to develop your ideas, organize them, and express them clearly.  Do not convey information in the form of a table, bullet point list, or other abbreviated presentation._

To:       Junior Staff Accountant
Subject:  Types of accounting change

| Situation | Treatments | Cumulative Effect | Journal Entries | Financial Statement | Written Communication | Research |
|-----------|-----------|-------------------|-----------------|---------------------|-----------------------|----------|

Use the resource materials available to you by clicking the Standards button to find the answer to the following question in either the Current Text or Original Pronouncements. Highlight and copy the appropriate citation in its entirety from the source you choose. Then click on the gray field below and paste the citation into the space provided below. Use only one source.

What constitutes the cumulative effect of an accounting change and how is it presented in an income statement?

## SOLUTION TO SIMULATION 1

*NOTE:  The solution to this testlet is based upon APB 20, **Accounting Changes** (pre-SFAS 154).  This question and solution is presented in its original form for you to see an actual simulation released by the AICPA.  Alternate solution with SFAS 154 follows.*

| Situation | **Treatments** | Cumulative Effect | Journal Entries | Financial Statement | Written Communication | Research |
|---|---|---|---|---|---|---|

| Event | Description | Accounting treatment |
|---|---|---|
| Change in long-term construction contract from percentage-of-completion method to completed-contract method | Change in accounting principle | Cumulative effect in current income |
| Write-off of uncollectible receivables under the direct write-off method | Change in accounting estimate | Current income |
| Write-off of uncollectible receivables under the reserve method | Neither a change nor an error correction | No impact |
| Change in salvage value of a depreciable asset | Change in accounting estimate | Current income |
| Change in useful life of a patent | Change in accounting estimate | Current income |

| Situation | Treatments | **Cumulative Effect** | Journal Entries | Financial Statement | Written Communication | Research |
|---|---|---|---|---|---|---|

| A | | B | C | D |
|---|---|---|---|---|
| | | | Depreciation expense | |
| **Double-declining balance method** | | | | |
| | | 1999 | $30,000 | |
| | | 2000 | $24,000 | |
| | | 2001 | $19,200 | |
| **Straight-line method** | | | | |
| | | 1999 | $15,000 | |
| | | 2000 | $15,000 | |
| | | 2001 | $15,000 | |
| **Cumulative effect of accounting change (before tax)** | | | | $28,200 |

| Situation | Treatments | Cumulative Effect | **Journal Entries** | Financial Statement | Written Communication | Research |
|---|---|---|---|---|---|---|

| A | B | C |
|---|---|---|
| | Debit | Credit |
| Accumulated depreciation | $28,200 | |
| Deferred income taxes | | $11,280 |
| Cumulative effect of change in accounting | | $16,920 |
| | | |
| Depreciation expense | $15,000 | |
| Accumulated depreciation | | $15,000 |

| Situation | Treatments | Cumulative Effect | Journal Entries | **Financial Statement** | Written Communication | Research |
|---|---|---|---|---|---|---|

| A | B | C | D | E | F | H |
|---|---|---|---|---|---|---|
| Charleston Company | | | | | | |
| Balance sheet | | | | | | |
| December 31, 2002 | | | | | | |
| | Machinery | | $150,000 | | | |
| | Accumulated depreciation | | ($60,000) | | | |
| | Net | | $90,000 | | | |
| Charleston Company | | | | | | |
| Income statement | | | | | | |
| Year ending December 31, 2002 | | | | | | |
| | Depreciation expense | | ($15,000) | | | |
| | Cumulative effect of change in accounting principle | | $16,920 | | Income | Indicate "Income" or "Expense" |

| Situation | Treatments | Cumulative Effect | Journal Entries | Financial Statement | Written Communication | Research |
|---|---|---|---|---|---|---|

To: Junior Staff Accountant
Subject: Types of accounting change

The technical points to be covered in this response should include. The three basic types of accounting change

- Change in accounting principal
- Change in accounting estimate
- Change in accounting entity

| Situation | Treatments | Cumulative Effect | Journal Entries | Financial Statement | Written Communication | Research |
|---|---|---|---|---|---|---|

## CT – A06.116

The amount shown in the income statement for the cumulative effect of changing to a new accounting principle is the difference between (a) the amount of retained earnings at the beginning of the period of a change and (b) the amount of retained earnings that would have been reported at that date if the new accounting principle had been applied retroactively for all prior periods that would have been affected and by recognizing only the direct effects of the change and related income tax effect. The amount of the cumulative effect shall be shown in the income statement between the captions "extraordinary items" and "net income." The cumulative effect is not an extraordinary item but shall be reported in a manner similar to an extraordinary item. [APB20.20] Presentation of per share amounts for the cumulative effect of an accounting change shall be made either on the face of the income statement or in the related notes.

[FAS128, 163(a)]
APB20.20

### ALTERNATE SOLUTION TO SIMULATION 1

*NOTE: This alternate solution is modified to reflect application of FAS 154, issued in May 2005. FAS 154, issued in May 2005, is required for fiscal years beginning after December 15, 2005. These solutions are modified, assuming the problem is changed to reflect acquisition of the asset on January 1, 2003, and change in depreciation method in 2006, so that FAS 154 applies.*

| Situation | Treatments | Change in Depreciation | Journal Entries | Financial Statement | Written Communication | Research |
|---|---|---|---|---|---|---|

| Event | Description | Accounting treatment |
|---|---|---|
| Change in long-term construction contract from percentage-of-completion method to completed-contract method | Change in accounting principle | Retrospective application |
| Write-off of uncollectible receivables under the direct write-off method | Change in accounting estimate | Current income |
| Write-off of uncollectible receivables under the reserve method | Neither a change nor an error correction | No impact |
| Change in salvage value of a depreciable asset | Change in accounting estimate | Current income |
| Change in useful life of a patent | Change in accounting estimate | Current income |

| Situation | Treatments | Change in Depreciation | Journal Entries | Financial Statement | Written Communication | Research |
|---|---|---|---|---|---|---|

As per FAS 154, there is no cumulative effect of change in method on the income statement for a change in depreciation method. The change is treated as a change in estimate effected by a change in accounting method. A change in estimate is accounted for in the period of the change and future periods.

The machinery was depreciated using the double-declining balance method assuming a ten-year life and no salvage. Assume the machinery was acquired on January 1, 2003, and the change in depreciation method to straight-line was made in 2006. To account for the change on a prospective basis, it is necessary to calculate the book value of the machinery as of December 31, 2005, at the end of Year 3.

Double-declining balance method

| | |
|---|---|
| Year 1 (2003) | $30,000 |
| Year 2 (2004) | 24,000 |
| Year 3 (2005) | 19,200 |
| Total depreciation 12/31/05 | $73,200 |

To calculate book value at 12/31/05

| | |
|---|---:|
| Historical cost | $150,000 |
| Less: Accum. depr. | (73,200) |
| Book value | $ 76,800 |

To calculate depreciation expense for 2006, straight-line depreciation is calculated using the book value at the beginning of the year in which the change is made and the remaining useful life of the asset.

($76,800 – $0 salvage) ÷ 7 years remaining life = $10,971

| Situation | Treatments | Change in Depreciation | **Journal Entries** | Financial Statement | Written Communication | Research |
|---|---|---|---|---|---|---|

There is no journal entry for a cumulative effect of change in accounting principle for a change in depreciation method. Since the accounting change is accounted for on a prospective basis, depreciation expense is calculated and recorded for the current year.  The depreciation expense entry for Year 4 (2006) is

| Depreciation expense | 10,971 | |
|---|---|---|
| Accumulated depreciation | | 10,971 |

| Situation | Treatments | Change in Depreciation | Journal Entries | **Financial Statement** | Written Communication | Research |
|---|---|---|---|---|---|---|

| | A | B | C | D | E | F | H |
|---|---|---|---|---|---|---|---|
| | Charleston Company | | | | | | |
| | Balance sheet | | | | | | |
| | December 31, 2006 (End of Year 4) | | | | | | |
| | Machinery | | | $150,000 | | | |
| | Accumulated depreciation | | | $ (84,171) | | | |
| | Net | | | $65,829 | | | |
| | Charleston Company | | | | | | |
| | Income statement | | | | | | |
| | Year ending December 31, 2006 (Year 4) | | | | | | |
| | Depreciation expense | | | $ (10,971) | | | |

| Situation | Treatments | Change in Depreciation | Journal Entries | Financial Statement | **Written Communication** | Research |
|---|---|---|---|---|---|---|

To:      Junior Staff Accountant
Subject:  Types of accounting change

The technical points to be covered in this response should include.  The three basic types of accounting change

- Change in accounting principal
- Change in accounting estimate
- Change in accounting entity

| Situation | Treatments | Change in Depreciation | Journal Entries | Financial Statement | Written Communication | **Research** |
|---|---|---|---|---|---|---|

In accordance with FAS 154, this question would be modified to read

What constitutes a change in accounting principle and how is it presented in the financial statements?

**FAS 154, Para 2(c)**

2.   The following terms are defined as used in this Statement:
   c.   Change in accounting principle—a change from one generally accepted accounting principle to another generally accepted accounting principle when there are two or more generally accepted accounting principles that apply or when the accounting principle formerly used is no longer generally accepted.  A change in the method of applying an accounting principle also is considered a change in accounting principle.

**FAS 154, Para 7**

7.   An entity shall report a change in accounting principle through retrospective application of the new accounting principle to all prior periods, unless it is impracticable to do so.  Retrospective application requires the following:

   a.   The cumulative effect of the change to the new accounting principle on periods prior to those presented shall be reflected in the carrying amounts of assets and liabilities as of the beginning of the first period presented.

    b.   An offsetting adjustment, if any, shall be made to the opening balance of retained earnings (or other appropriate components of equity or net assets in the statement of financial position) for that period.

    c.   Financial statements for each individual prior period presented shall be adjusted to reflect the period-specific effects of applying the new accounting principle.

## Or Current Text A07.403 and A07.106

### A07.403

.403   Change in accounting principle. A change from one generally accepted accounting principle to another generally accepted accounting principle when there are two or more generally accepted accounting principles that apply or when the accounting principle formerly used is no longer generally accepted. A change in method of applying an accounting principle also is considered a change in accounting principle. [FAS154, ¶2(c)]

### A07.106

.106   An entity shall report a change in accounting principle through retrospective application of the new accounting principle to all prior periods, unless it is impracticable to do so. Retrospective application requires the following:

    a.   The cumulative effect of the change to the new accounting principle on periods prior to those presented shall be reflected in the carrying amounts of assets and liabilities as of the beginning of the first period presented.

    b.   An offsetting adjustment, if any, shall be made to the opening balance of retained earnings (or other appropriate components of equity or net assets in the statement of financial position) for that period.

    c.   Financial statements for each individual prior period presented shall be adjusted to reflect the period-specific effects of applying the new accounting principle.

## FINANCIAL ACCOUNTING AND REPORTING

**1.** A material overstatement in ending inventory was discovered after the year-end financial statements of a company were issued to the public. What effect did this error have on the year-end financial statements?

|     | *Current assets* | *Gross profit* |
| --- | --- | --- |
| a. | Understated | Overstated |
| b. | Overstated | Overstated |
| c. | Understated | Understated |
| d. | Overstated | Understated |

**2.** Jen Co. had 200,000 shares of common stock and 20,000 shares of 10%, $100 par value cumulative preferred stock. No dividends on common stock were declared during the year. Net income was $2,000,000. What was Jen's basic earnings per share?

    a.   $ 9.00
    b.   $ 9.09
    c.   $10.00
    d.   $11.11

**3.** On December 31, year 1, Taylor, Inc. signed a binding agreement with a bank for the refinancing of an existing note payable scheduled to mature in February, year 2. The terms of the refinancing included extending the maturity date of the note by three years. On January 15, year 2, the note was refinanced. How should Taylor report the note payable in its December 31, year 1 balance sheet?

    a.   A current liability.
    b.   A long-term liability.
    c.   A long-term note receivable.
    d.   A current note receivable.

**4.** At the end of year 1, Lane Co. held trading securities that cost $86,000 and which had a year-end market value of $92,000. During year 2, all of these securities were sold for $104,500. At the end of year 2, Lane had acquired additional trading securities that cost $73,000 and which had a year-end market value of $71,000. What is the impact of these stock activities on Lane's year 2 income statement?

    a.   Loss of $2,000.
    b.   Gain of $10,500.
    c.   Gain of $16,500.
    d.   Gain of $18,500.

**1.** **(b)** The requirement is to identify the effect of the error on the year-end financial statements. Ending inventory is overstated. Therefore, current assets are overstated on the balance sheet. If ending inventory is overstated, cost of goods sold is understated for the year. Therefore, answer (b) is correct because an understatement of cost of goods sold will result in gross profit being overstated for the year.

**2.** **(a)** The requirement is to compute basic earnings per share. The formula for basic earnings per share is (net income minus preferred dividends) divided by the weighted-average common shares outstanding. Although no dividends were declared during the year, the preferred dividend must be subtracted because the preferred stock is cumulative. The preferred dividend of $200,000 (10% × $2,000,000 par) must be subtracted in determining the numerator for basic earnings per share. Accordingly, answer (a) is correct because basic EPS is ($2,000,000 net income – $200,000 preferred dividends) ÷ 200,000 weighted-average common shares outstanding = $9.00 per share.

**3.** **(b)** The requirement is to identify how the note payable would be presented. A note is normally considered a current liability if it is due and payable in one year. However, if a company has both the intent and ability to refinance the debt on a long-term basis (APB 6), the note can be classified as a long-term liability in the December 31, year 1, balance sheet. Therefore, answer (b) is correct.

**4.** **(b)** The requirement is to determine the effect of the stock activities on Lane's income statement. According to SFAS 115, both realized and unrealized gains and losses on trading securities are recognized in the income statement. At the end of year 1, the trading security with a historical cost of $86,000 was written up to fair value of $92,000, and a $6,000 gain was recognized on the year 1 income statement. During year 2, when this security was sold, the gain recognized on the year 2 income statement would be $12,500 ($104,500 – $92,000). The trading security purchased during year 2 at a cost of $73,000 would be valued at the fair value of $71,000 on the year 2 balance sheet, and an unrealized loss of $2,000 would be recognized on the year 2 income statement. Therefore, answer (b) is correct because the total gain/loss on securities in year 2 would be $10,500 (gain of $12,500 on the first set of securities, and an unrealized loss of $2,000 on the second set of securities).

**5.** Which of the following is true regarding the comparison of managerial to financial accounting?
  a. Managerial accounting is generally more precise.
  b. Managerial accounting has a past focus and financial accounting has a future focus.
  c. The emphasis on managerial accounting is relevance and the emphasis on financial accounting is timeliness.
  d. Managerial accounting need **not** follow generally accepted accounting principles (GAAP) while financial accounting must follow them.

**6.** In the preparation of the statement of activities for a nongovernmental not-for-profit organization, all expenses are reported as decreases in which of the following net asset classes?
  a. Total net assets.
  b. Unrestricted net assets.
  c. Temporarily restricted net assets.
  d. Permanently restricted net assets.

**7.** Oak Co., a newly formed corporation, incurred the following expenditures related to land and building:

| | |
|---|---|
| County assessment for sewer lines | $ 2,500 |
| Title search fees | 625 |
| Cash paid for land with a building to be demolished | 135,000 |
| Excavation for construction of basement | 21,000 |
| Removal of old building $21,000 less salvage of $5,000 | 16,000 |

At what amount should Oak record the land?
  a. $138,125
  b. $153,500
  c. $154,125
  d. $175,625

**8.** Paper Co. had net income of $70,000 during the year. Dividend payment was $10,000. The following information is available:

| | |
|---|---|
| Mortgage repayment | $20,000 |
| Available-for-sale securities purchased | 10,000 increase |
| Bonds payable—issued | 50,000 increase |
| Inventory | 40,000 increase |
| Accounts payable | 30,000 decrease |

What amount should Paper report as net cash provided by operating activities in its statement of cash flows for the year?
  a. $0
  b. $10,000
  c. $20,000
  d. $30,000

**9.** Parker Co. amended its pension plan on January 2 of the current year. It also granted $600,000 of unrecognized prior service costs to its employees. The employees are all active and expect to provide 2,000 service years in the future, with 350 service years this year. What is Parker's unrecognized prior service cost amortization for the year?
  a. $0
  b. $ 2,000
  c. $105,000
  d. $600,000

**5.** **(d)** The requirement is to identify the correct statement regarding the comparison of managerial accounting to financial accounting. Answer (d) is correct because managerial accounting does not have to follow GAAP. Answer (a) is incorrect because both managerial and financial accounting should be precise. Answer (b) is incorrect because financial accounting has a past focus. Answer (c) is incorrect because the emphasis on managerial accounting is timeliness.

**6.** **(b)** The requirement is to identify the section of the statement of activities where all expenses are reported. Answer (b) is correct because expenses are reported as decreases in unrestricted net assets. Answer (a) is incorrect because expenses are reported as decreases in unrestricted net assets, not in total assets. Answer (c) is incorrect because contributions, income, or gains affect temporarily restricted net assets, not expenses. Answer (d) is incorrect because permanently restricted net assets are affected by contributions, income or gains, but not expenses.

**7.** **(c)** The requirement is to determine how much Oak should record for the land. Oak should capitalize all costs to place the land in its intended and useful state. The costs for the sewer lines, title search fee, land, and removal of the old building (less salvage) should all be included in the cost of the land. Therefore, answer (c) is correct because the land should be recorded at $2,500 + $625 + $135,000 + $16,000 = $154,125.

**8.** **(a)** The requirement is to calculate the amount that should be reported as net cash provided by operating activities. Net cash from operating activities is net income plus or minus the changes in inventory and accounts payable. Therefore, answer (a) is correct because the net cash from operating activities is $70,000 − $40,000 − $30,000 = $0. The mortgage repayment is a financing activity. The available-for-sale securities purchased are an investing activity, and the bonds issued are a financing activity.

**9.** **(c)** The requirement is to calculate the amount of unrecognized prior service cost amortization for the year. The amortization per service year is calculated as $300 ($600,000 prior service cost ÷ 2,000 service years). Answer (c) is correct because there are 350 service years in the current year, and 350 × $300 = $105,000 of amortization.

*NOTE: SFAS 158 changed the terminology from unrecognized prior service cost to net prior service cost or credit.*

**10.** Entor Co. sold equipment to Pane Co. for $50,000. The equipment had a net book amount of $30,000. The collections were $20,000 in the first year, $15,000 in the next year, and $15,000 in the last year. What is the amount of gross profit for the third year if Entor used the installment-sales accounting method for the transaction?

    a.   $0
    b.   $ 5,000
    c.   $ 6,000
    d.   $15,000

**11.** Johan Co. has an intangible asset, which it estimates will have a useful life of 10 years, while Abco Co. has goodwill, which has an indefinite life. Which company should report amortization in its financial statements?

|   | Johan | Abco |
|---|---|---|
| a. | Yes | Yes |
| b. | Yes | No |
| c. | No | Yes |
| d. | No | No |

**12.** Envoy Co. manufactures and sells household products. Envoy experienced losses associated with its small appliance group. Operations and cash flows for this group can be clearly distinguished from the rest of Envoy's operations. Envoy plans to sell the small appliance group with its operations. What is the earliest point at which Envoy should report the small appliance group as a discontinued operation?

    a.   When Envoy classifies it as held-for-sale.
    b.   When Envoy receives an offer for the segment.
    c.   When Envoy first sells any of the assets of the segment.
    d.   When Envoy sells the majority of the assets of the segment.

**13.** Which of the following transactions is an expenditure of a governmental unit's general fund?

    a.   Contribution of enterprise fund capital by the general fund.
    b.   Operating subsidy transfer from the general fund to an enterprise fund.
    c.   Routine employer contributions from the general fund to a pension trust fund.
    d.   Transfer from the general fund to a capital projects fund.

**14.** In a not-for-profit organization, which of the following should be included in total expenses?

|   | Grants to other organizations | Depreciation |
|---|---|---|
| a. | Yes | Yes |
| b. | Yes | No |
| c. | No | No |
| d. | No | Yes |

**15.** Which of the following funds of a governmental unit records depreciation?

    a.   Capital projects fund.
    b.   Debt service fund.
    c.   Internal service fund.
    d.   Special revenue fund.

**10. (c)** The requirement is to determine the gross profit for the third year. The total gross profit on the equipment is $50,000 – $30,000 = $20,000. Under the installment-sales method, gross profit is recognized proportionally with the amount of the installment payment each year. The gross profit that should be recognized in year 3 is $15,000/($20,000 + $15,000 + $15,000) = 30% of the total revenue. Therefore, answer (c) is correct because $6,000 (30% × $20,000 total gross profit) of gross profit should be recognized in year 3.

**11. (b)** The requirement is to determine the amount of amortization that should be reported on the financial statements. Answer (b) is correct because, according to SFAS 42, an intangible asset with a definite useful life should be amortized. Goodwill is no longer amortized; it is tested for impairment.

**12. (a)** The requirement is to identify the earliest point at which Envoy may report discontinued operations. Answer (a) is correct because, according to SFAS 144, the earliest point at which Envoy should report the small appliance group as a discontinued operation is when Envoy classifies it as held-for-sale.

**13. (c)** The requirement is to identify the transaction that is an expenditure of the general fund. Answer (c) is correct because a routine employer contribution from the general fund to a pension trust fund is an expenditure from the general fund. Answer (a) is incorrect because a contribution of enterprise fund capital is not an expenditure from the general fund. Answer (b) is incorrect because an operating subsidy transfer is not an expenditure from the general fund. Answer (d) is incorrect because transfers are not expenditures from the general fund.

**14. (a)** The requirement is to identify the items that should be included in total expenses. Answer (a) is correct because both grants to other organizations and depreciation are included in total expenses. Answers (b), (c), and (d) are incorrect because both grants to other organizations and depreciation are included in total expenses.

**15. (c)** The requirement is to identify the fund that records depreciation. Answer (c) is correct because internal service funds are the only ones listed that record depreciation. Answers (a), (b), and (d) are incorrect because these funds do not record depreciation.

**16.** A county's balances in the general fund included the following:

| | |
|---|---|
| Appropriations | $435,000 |
| Encumbrances | 18,000 |
| Expenditures | 164,000 |
| Vouchers payable | 23,000 |

What is the remaining amount available for use by the county?

    a.   $230,000
    b.   $248,000
    c.   $253,000
    d.   $271,000

**17.** Stent Co. had total assets of $760,000, capital stock of $150,000, and retained earnings of $215,000. What was Stent's debt-to-equity ratio?

    a.   2.63
    b.   1.08
    c.   0.52
    d.   0.48

**18.** Belle Co. determined after 4 years that the estimated useful life of its labeling machine should be 10 years rather than 12 years. The machine originally cost $46,000 and had an estimated salvage value of $1,000. Belle uses straight-line depreciation. What amount should Belle report as depreciation expense for the current year?

    a.   $3,200
    b.   $3,750
    c.   $4,500
    d.   $5,000

**19.** Which of the following is a generally accepted accounting principle that illustrates the practice of conservatism during a particular reporting period?

    a.   Capitalization of research and development costs.
    b.   Accrual of a contingency deemed to be reasonably possible.
    c.   Reporting investments with appreciated market values, at market value.
    d.   Reporting inventory at the lower of cost or market value.

**20.** Foley Co. is preparing the electronic spreadsheet below to amortize the discount on its 10-year, 6%, $100,000 bonds payable: Bonds were issued on December 31 to yield 8%. Interest is paid annually. Foley uses the effective interest method to amortize bond discounts.

| | A | B | C | D | E |
|---|---|---|---|---|---|
| | | Cash | Interest | Discount | Carrying |
| 1 | Year | paid | expense | amortization | amount |
| 2 | 1 | | | | $86,580 |
| 3 | 2 | $6,000 | | | |

Which formula should Foley use in cell E3 to calculate the bonds' carrying amount at the end of year 2?

    a.   E2 + D3.
    b.   E2 – D3.
    c.   E2 + C3.
    d.   E2 – C3.

**16. (c)** The requirement is to determine the amount available for use by the county. Answer (c) is correct because the available funds are equal to appropriations minus expenditures and encumbrances, or $253,000 ($435,000 – $164,000 – $18,000).

**17. (b)** The requirement is to calculate the debt to equity ratio. The debt to equity ratio is equal to total liabilities divided by total owners' equity. Total owners' equity is common stock plus retained earnings, or $365,000 ($150,000 + $215,000). Since assets equal liabilities plus owners' equity, liabilities are equal to $395,000 ($760,000 – $365,000). Answer (b) is correct because the debt to equity ratio is equal to 1.08 ($395,000/$365,000).

**18. (d)** The requirement is to determine the amount of depreciation expense for the year. According to SFAS 154, a change in the useful life of an asset should be accounted for on a prospective basis. The depreciation on the equipment the first four years can be calculated as ($46,000 – $1,000)/12 years = $3,750 per year. Accumulated depreciation at the end of year 4 is $3,750 × 4 = $15,000. The book value at the beginning of year 5 is $31,000 ($46,000 – $15,000). If the asset's life is determined to be 10 years, the book value of $31,000 is depreciated over the remaining six-year life of the asset. Therefore, answer (d) is correct because depreciation expense in the year of the change is $5,000 [($31,000 – $1,000)/6 years].

**19. (d)** The requirement is to identify the principle that illustrates the practice of conservatism. Answer (d) is correct because reporting inventory at the lower of cost or market illustrates conservatism since it conservatively states assets and net income. Answer (a) is incorrect because capitalizing research and development costs would increase net income for the period. Answer (b) is incorrect because according to SFAS 5, accrual of a contingency should occur when it is deemed to be probable. Therefore, this practice is not GAAP. Answer (c) is incorrect because reporting investments at market values is not conservative.

**20. (a)** The requirement is to identify the correct formula. The carrying amount of a bond is the previous year carrying amount plus the amortization of the discount for the period. Therefore, E2 + D3 is the appropriate formula and answer (a) is correct.

**21.** During 2002, Fleet Co.'s trademark was licensed to Hitch Corp. for royalties of 10% of net sales of the trademarked items. Returns were estimated to be 1% of gross sales. On signing the licensing agreement, Hitch paid Fleet $75,000 as an advance against future royalty earnings. Gross sales of the trademarked items during the year were $600,000. What amount should Fleet report as royalty income for 2002?

   a.   $54,000
   b.   $59,400
   c.   $60,000
   d.   $75,000

**22.** Red Co. had $3 million in accounts receivable recorded on its books. Red wanted to convert the $3 million in receivables to cash in a more timely manner than waiting the 45 days for payment as indicated on its invoices. Which of the following would alter the timing of Red's cash flows for the $3 million in receivables already recorded on its books?

   a.   Change the due date of the invoice.
   b.   Factor the receivables outstanding.
   c.   Discount the receivables outstanding.
   d.   Demand payment from customers before the due date.

**23.** On January 1, year 1, Frost Co. entered into a two-year lease agreement with Ananz Co. to lease 10 new computers. The lease term begins on January 1, year 1 and ends on December 31, year 2. The lease agreement requires Frost to pay Ananz two annual lease payments of $8,000. The present value of the minimum lease payments is $13,000. Which of the following circumstances would require Frost to classify and account for the arrangement as a capital lease?

   a.   The economic life of the computers is three years.
   b.   The fair value of the computers on January 1, year 1, is $14,000.
   c.   Frost Co. does **not** have the option of purchasing the computers at the end of the lease term.
   d.   Ownership of the computers remains with Ananz Co. throughout the lease term and after the lease ends.

**24.** Which of the following types of entities are required to report on business segments?

   a.   Nonpublic business enterprises.
   b.   Publicly-traded enterprises.
   c.   Not-for-profit enterprises.
   d.   Joint ventures.

**25.** Bain Co. entered into a 10-year lease agreement for a new piece of equipment worth $500,000. At the end of the lease, Bain will have the option to purchase the equipment. Which of the following would require the lease to be accounted for as a capital lease?

   a.   The lease includes an option to purchase stock in the company.
   b.   The estimated useful life of the leased asset is 12 years.
   c.   The present value of the minimum lease payments is $400,000.
   d.   The purchase option at the end of the lease is at fair market value.

**21. (b)** The requirement is to determine the amount of royalty income for the year. Gross sales are $600,000 for Hitch Corp. The estimated 1% returns should be subtracted from gross sales to determine the net sales for the period, or $594,000 ($600,000 – $6,000). Therefore, answer (b) is correct because the royalty amount for the year is equal to $59,400 ($594,000 net sales × 10% royalty rate).

**22. (b)** The requirement is to identify the strategy that would alter the timing of Red's cash flows. Answer (b) is correct because if Red wishes to receive cash for the receivables already recorded on its books, the company should factor the receivables outstanding. Factoring involves the sale of accounts receivable to a third party. Answers (a) and (d) are incorrect because the company cannot change the terms of the sale after the fact. Answer (c) is incorrect because discounting receivables is a term used to describe the pledging of the receivables as collateral for a loan.

**23. (b)** The requirement is to determine the circumstance that would require Frost to classify the lease as a capital lease. SFAS 13 requires that if a lease meets one of four criteria, it must be classified as a capital lease. Answer (b) is correct because the present value of the minimum lease payments ($13,000) is greater than 90% of the fair value of the leased asset. Answer (a) is incorrect because the economic life of the computer must be greater than or equal to 75% of the economic life of the asset to qualify for capital lease treatment. Answer (c) is incorrect because there must be a bargain purchase option to qualify for capital lease treatment. Answer (d) is incorrect because capital lease treatment is required if there is a transfer of title to the lessee at the end of the lease term.

**24. (b)** The requirement is to identify the type of entity that must report business segments. Answer (b) is correct because, according to SFAS 131, segment reporting is required of publicly traded enterprises. Answers (a), (c), and (d) are incorrect because they are not within the scope of SFAS 131.

**25. (b)** The requirement is to identify the condition that would require the lease to be accounted for as a capital lease. According to SFAS 13, if a lease meets one of the four criteria, it must be classified as a capital lease. Answer (b) is correct because the ten-year lease term is greater than or equal to 75% of the life of the leased asset (10/12 = 83%). Answer (a) is incorrect because there are no criteria in SFAS 13 related to the purchase of stock in the company. Answer (c) is incorrect because capital lease treatment is required if the present value of the minimum lease payments is greater than or equal to 90% of the fair value of the leased asset. In this case it is only 80% ($400,000/$500,000). Answer (d) is incorrect because capital lease treatment is required if the purchase option at the end of the lease term is a bargain purchase option.

**26.** Loft Co. reviewed its inventory values for proper pricing at year-end. The following summarizes two inventory items examined for the lower of cost or market:

|  | Inventory item #1 | Inventory item #2 |
|---|---|---|
| Original cost | $210,000 | $400,000 |
| Replacement cost | 150,000 | 370,000 |
| Net realizable value | 240,000 | 410,000 |
| Net realizable value less profit margin | 208,000 | 405,000 |

What amount should Loft include in inventory at year-end, if it uses the total of the inventory to apply the lower of cost or market?

    a.   $520,000
    b.   $610,000
    c.   $613,000
    d.   $650,000

**27.** Baker Co. issued 100,000 shares of common stock in the current year. On October 1, Baker repurchased 20,000 shares of its common stock on the open market for $50.00 per share. At that date, the stock's par value was $1.00 and the average issue price was $40.00 per share. Baker uses the cost method for treasury stock transactions. On December 1, Baker reissued the stock for $60.00 per share. What amount should Baker report as treasury stock gain at December 31?

    a.   $0
    b.   $200,000
    c.   $400,000
    d.   $980,000

**28.** On December 1, 2002, Paxton Co. had a note payable due on August 1, 2003. On January 20, 2003, Paxton signed a financing agreement to borrow the balance of the note payable from a lending institution to refinance the note. The agreement does not expire within one year, and no violation of any provision in the financing agreement exists. On February 1, 2003, Paxton was informed by its financial advisor that the lender is not expected to be financially capable of honoring the agreement. Paxton's financial statements were issued on March 31, 2003. How should Paxton classify the note on its balance sheet at December 31, 2002?

    a.   As a current liability because the financing agreement was signed after the balance sheet date.
    b.   As a current liability because the lender is **not** expected to be financially capable of honoring the agreement.
    c.   As a long-term liability because the agreement does **not** expire within one year.
    d.   As a long-term liability because **no** violation of any provision in the financing agreement exists.

**26. (b)** The requirement is to determine the amount of inventory at year-end. If Loft uses the total of the inventory to apply the lower of cost or market method, it must compare the original cost of $610,000 ($210,000 + $400,000) to the market value of the inventory. The total replacement cost of the inventory is $520,000; the net realizable value is $650,000 (the ceiling), and the net realizable value less normal profit margin is $613,000 (the floor). Market value is the replacement cost, limited by the ceiling and the floor. Therefore, the floor value of $613,000 is used for the market value and compared with the original cost of $610,000. Therefore, answer (b) is correct because the lower of cost or market is the cost of $610,000.

**27. (a)** The requirement is to determine the amount of treasury stock gain at December 31. Answer (a) is correct because gains and losses are never recorded in the income statement for treasury stock transactions.

**28. (b)** The requirement is to identify how Paxton should classify the note on its balance sheet at year-end. According to FAS 6, para 11, three conditions must be met to disclose the short-term obligation as a long-term liability: the agreement does not expire within one year, no violation of any provision in the financing agreement exists at the balance sheet date, and the lender is expected to be financially capable of honoring the agreement. Answer (b) is correct because this item indicates that the lender is not expected to be financially capable of honoring the agreement. Answer (a) is incorrect because if the company has the intent and ability to refinance before the balance sheet is issued, then the liability could be classified as long-term. Answers (c) and (d) are incorrect because although the agreement meets these two criteria, the other provision of FAS 6 is not met.

**29.** Carlson City's fiscal year ends December 31.  On August 1, the city issued a purchase order for new vehicles to be delivered at the rate of two per month beginning October 15.  Twelve vehicles were delivered as scheduled and payments of $264,000 were made upon delivery.  If these were the only transactions made by the city, which of the following balances would appear on the balance sheet as of December 31?

| | | |
|---|---|---|
| a. | Encumbrances | $132,000 |
| | Reserve for encumbrances | 132,000 |
| b. | Fund balance | $132,000 |
| | Reserve for encumbrances | 132,000 |
| c. | Reserve for encumbrances | $264,000 |
| | Fund balance | 264,000 |
| d. | Encumbrances | $264,000 |
| | Reserve for encumbrances | 264,000 |

**30.** RST Charities received equities securities valued at $100,000 as an unrestricted gift.  During the year, RST received $5,000 in dividends from these securities; at year-end, the securities had a fair market value of $110,000.  By what amount did these transactions increase RST's net assets?

a. $100,000
b. $105,000
c. $110,000
d. $115,000

**31.** The Turtle Society, a nongovernmental not-for-profit organization, receives numerous contributed hours from volunteers during its busy season.  Chris, a clerk at the local tax collector's office, volunteered ten hours per week for 24 weeks transferring turtle food from the port to the turtle shelter.  His rate of pay at the tax office is $10 per hour, and the prevailing wage rate for laborers is $6.50 per hour.  What amount of contribution revenue should Turtle Society record for this service?

a. $0
b. $  840
c. $1,560
d. $2,400

**32.** The following information pertains to Ceil Co., a company whose common stock trades in a public market:

| | |
|---|---|
| Shares outstanding at 1/1 | 100,000 |
| Stock dividend at 3/31 | 24,000 |
| Stock issuance at 6/30 | 5,000 |

What is the weighted-average number of shares Ceil should use to calculate its basic earnings per share for the year ended December 31?

a. 120,500
b. 123,000
c. 126,500
d. 129,000

**33.** In financial reporting of segment data, which of the following must be considered in determining if an industry segment is a reportable segment?

| | Sales to unaffiliated customers | Intersegment sales |
|---|---|---|
| a. | Yes | Yes |
| b. | Yes | No |
| c. | No | Yes |
| d. | No | No |

**29.  (b)**   The requirement is to identify the balances that would appear on the balance sheet as of December 31.  Answer (b) is correct because one-half of the vehicles would have been received and paid for by December 31, $132,000.  Therefore, the reserve for encumbrances would equal $132,000 ($264,000 – $132,000).  In addition, the fund balance would include the amount necessary to pay for the remaining vehicles.  Answers (a), (c), and (d) are incorrect because they do not represent appropriate balances.

**30.  (d)**   The requirement is to determine by what amount the transactions increased net assets.  Answer (d) is correct because the net assets at year-end would be increased by the fair value of the stock plus any dividends received, or $115,000.  Answer (a) is incorrect because it only reflects the value of the securities at the time of the gift.  Answer (b) is incorrect because it ignores the increase in fair value of the securities.  Answer (c) is incorrect because it ignores the dividends received.

**31.  (a)**   The requirement is to determine the amount of contribution revenue that should be recorded.  Answer (a) is correct because contributed services are only recognized if they create or enhance nonfinancial assets, or require specialized skills.  The services by Chris do not meet these requirements.

**32.  (c)**   The requirement is to compute the weighted-average number of shares outstanding.  Answer (c) is correct because the weighted-average shares outstanding is calculated as follows:

| | | |
|---|---|---|
| Shares outstanding at 1/1 | 100,000 shares × 12/12 | 100,000 |
| Stock dividend at 3/31 | 24,000 shares × 12/12 | 24,000 |
| Stock issued on 6/30 | 5,000 shares ×  6/12 | 2,500 |
| Total weighted-average common shares outstanding | | 126,500 |

*NOTE:  The stock dividend is treated as if the shares were outstanding for the entire year.  The stock issued during the year is weighted by the number of months outstanding.*

**33.  (a)**   The requirement is to identify the items that must be considered in determining if an industry segment is reportable.  Answer (a) is correct because, according to SFAS 131, intersegment sales are included in segment revenue to determine if the segment revenue is 10% or more of the combined segment revenues.  Sales to unaffiliated customers are used to determine if 75% of unaffiliated revenues have been reported by the segments.

**34.** On December 31, 1999, Key Co. received two $10,000 noninterest-bearing notes from customers in exchange for services rendered. The note from Alpha Co., which is due in nine months, was made under customary trade terms, but the note from Omega Co., which is due in two years, was not. The market interest rate for both notes at the date of issuance is 8%. The present value of $1 due in nine months at 8% is .944. The present value of $1 due in two years at 8% is .857. At what amounts should these two notes receivable be reported in Key's December 31, 1999 balance sheet?

| | | *Alpha* | *Omega* |
|---|---|---|---|
| a. | | $ 9,440 | $ 8,570 |
| b. | | $10,000 | $ 8,570 |
| c. | | $ 9,440 | $10,000 |
| d. | | $10,000 | $10,000 |

**35.** Bake Co.'s trial balance included the following at December 31, 2003:

| | |
|---|---|
| Accounts payable | $ 80,000 |
| Bonds payable, due 2004 | 300,000 |
| Discount on bonds payable | 15,000 |
| Deferred income tax liability | 25,000 |

The deferred income tax liability is not related to an asset for financial accounting purposes and is expected to reverse in 2004. What amount should be included in the current liability section of Bake's December 31, 2003 balance sheet?
- a. $365,000
- b. $390,000
- c. $395,000
- d. $420,000

**36.** Savor Co. had $100,000 in cash-basis pretax income for 1999. At December 31, 1999, accounts receivable had increased by $10,000 and accounts payable had decreased by $6,000 from their December 31, 1998 balances. Compared to the accrual basis method of accounting, Savor's cash pretax income is
- a. Higher by $4,000
- b. Lower by $4,000
- c. Higher by $16,000
- d. Lower by $16,000

**37.** Zest Co. owns 100% of Cinn, Inc. On January 2, 1999, Zest sold equipment with an original cost of $80,000 and a carrying amount of $48,000 to Cinn for $72,000. Zest had been depreciating the equipment over a five-year period using straight-line depreciation with no residual value. Cinn is using straight-line depreciation over three years with no residual value. In Zest's December 31, 1999 consolidating worksheet, by what amount should depreciation expense be decreased?
- a. $0
- b. $ 8,000
- c. $16,000
- d. $24,000

**38.** Which of the following items is an example of imposed nonexchange revenue for a governmental entity?
- a. Personal income taxes.
- b. Retail sales tax.
- c. Federal grant money.
- d. Property taxes.

**34.** **(b)** The requirement is to determine the amounts that should be reported for the two notes receivable. Notes that arise from customers in the normal course of business and are due in one year are classified as current liabilities and recorded at their maturity value. Notes that are due in more than one year are classified as long-term liabilities and are recorded at their present value (APB 21). Answer (b) is correct because the Alpha note should be recorded at $10,000, and the Omega note should be recorded at its present value of $8,570 (.857 × $10,000).

*NOTE: This answer assumes the fair value option of SFAS 159 is not elected.*

**35.** **(b)** The requirement is to determine the amount that should be included in the current liability section of the balance sheet. The accounts payable and the bond payable are classified as current liabilities because they are due within the next 12 months. The bond payable is valued at its carrying value of $285,000 ($300,000 – $15,000 discount). The deferred income tax liability is classified as a current liability because it not related to an asset and it is expected to reverse in the next 12 months. Answer (b) is correct because the amount of current liabilities is equal to $390,000 ($80,000 + $285,000 + $25,000).

**36.** **(d)** The requirement is to determine the difference between cash-basis and accrual-basis income. This question requires the calculation of accrual-based income, as shown below.

| | |
|---|---|
| Cash-basis pre-tax income | $100,000 |
| Increase in accounts receivable | + 10,000 |
| Decrease in accounts payable | +___6,000 |
| Accrual-basis income | $116,000 |

Answer (d) is correct because cash pretax income is $16,000 ($116,000 – $100,000) lower than the accrual-basis income.

**37.** **(b)** The requirement is to determine the amount that depreciation expense should be decreased. Zest, the parent, was depreciating the equipment at $16,000 per year ($80,000 cost/5 years = $16,000). To Cinn the equipment has a historical cost of $72,000 and it will be depreciated over 3 years ($72,000/3 years) for depreciation expense of $24,000 per year. Answer (b) is correct because the elimination entry would decrease depreciation expense by $8,000 ($24,000 – $16,000).

**38.** **(d)** The requirement is to identify the example of imposed nonexchange revenue. Answer (d) is correct because imposed nonexchange revenue is derived from taxes and other assessments by governments that are not derived from underlying transactions. Property taxes are examples of such a revenue source. Answers (a) and (b) are incorrect because they represent examples of derived tax revenues. Answer (c) is incorrect because it is an example of voluntary nonexchange revenue.

**39.** Cash receipts from grants and subsidies to decrease operating deficits should be classified in which of the following sections of the statement of cash flows for governmental, not-for-profit entities?
   a.  Operating.
   b.  Noncapital financing.
   c.  Capital and related financing.
   d.  Investing.

**40.** Baker Co. sells consumer products that are packaged in boxes. Baker offered an unbreakable glass in exchange for two box tops and $1 as a promotion during the current year. The cost of the glass was $2.00. Baker estimated at the end of the year that it would be probable that 50% of the box tops will be redeemed. Baker sold 100,000 boxes of the product during the current year and 40,000 box tops were redeemed during the year for the glasses. What amount should Baker accrue as an estimated liability at the end of the current year, related to the redemption of box tops?
   a.  $0
   b.  $ 5,000
   c.  $20,000
   d.  $25,000

**41.** Which of the following statements is correct concerning start-up costs?
   a.  Costs of start-up activities, including organization costs, should be expensed as incurred.
   b.  Costs of start-up activities, including organization costs, should be capitalized and expensed only if an impairment exists.
   c.  Costs of start-up activities, including organization costs, should be capitalized and amortized on a straight-line basis over the lesser of the estimated economic life of the company, or 60 months.
   d.  Costs of start-up activities should be capitalized and amortized on a straight-line basis over the lesser of the estimated economic life of the company, or 60 months, while organization cost should be expensed as incurred.

**39. (b)** The requirement is to identify the section of the statement of cash flows that includes cash receipts from grants and subsidies to decrease operating deficits. Answer (b) is correct because grants and subsidies to decrease operating deficits should be classified as noncapital financing activities. Answers (a), (c), and (d) are incorrect because grants and subsidies are not included in these sections of the statement of cash flows.

**40. (b)** The requirement is to determine the amount that should be accrued as an estimated liability. The estimated liability at the end of the current year is calculated as follows: boxes sold 100,000 × 50% estimated to be redeemed = 50,000 box tops estimated to be redeemed. Since 40,000 box tops have been redeemed, this leaves an estimated 10,000 box tops to be redeemed. It takes 2 box tops and $1 to receive the unbreakable glass. Therefore, 5,000 (10,000 ÷ 2) unbreakable glasses are estimated to be redeemed. The cost of the glasses is $2.00 each, and 5,000 units × $2.00 = $10,000, which is the estimated cost of the glasses. However, the customer must pay $1.00 per glass, so the estimated liability is $5,000 ($10,000 cost less $5,000 customer payment), and answer (b) is correct.

**41. (a)** The requirement is to identify the correct statement regarding start-up costs. Answer (a) is correct because SOP 98-5 requires start-up costs to be expensed as incurred. Answers (b), (c), and (d) are incorrect.

**42.** Main, a pharmaceutical company, leased office space from Ash. Main took possession and began to use the building on July 1, 2000. Rent was due the first day of each month. Monthly lease payments escalated over the 5-year period of the lease as follows:

| Period | Lease payment |
|---|---|
| | $0 – rent abatement during |
| July 1, 2000 – September 30, 2000 | move-in, construction |
| October, 1, 2000 – June 30, 2001 | 17,500 |
| July 1, 2001 – June 30, 2002 | 19,000 |
| July 1, 2002 – June 30, 2003 | 20,500 |
| July 1, 2003 – June 30, 2004 | 23,000 |
| July 1, 2004 – June 30, 2005 | 24,500 |

What amount would Main show as deferred rent expense at December 31, 2003?

    a.   $50,658
    b.   $52,580
    c.   $68,575
    d.   $71,550

**43.** Goodwill should be tested for value impairment at which of the following levels?
    a.   Each identifiable long-term asset.
    b.   Each reporting unit.
    c.   Each acquisition unit.
    d.   Entire business as a whole.

**44.** An extraordinary gain should be reported as a direct increase to which of the following?
    a.   Net income.
    b.   Comprehensive income.
    c.   Income from continuing operations, net of tax.
    d.   Income from discontinued operations, net of tax.

**45.** On January 1 ten years ago, Andrew Co. created a subsidiary for the purpose of buying an oil tanker depot at a cost of $1,500,000. Andrew expected to operate the depot for ten years, at which time it is legally required to dismantle the depot and remove underground storage tanks. It was estimated that it would cost $150,000 to dismantle the depot and remove the tanks at the end of the depot's useful life. However, the actual cost to demolish and dismantle the depot and remove the tanks in the tenth year is $155,000

What amount of expense should Andrew recognize in its financial statements in year 10?
    a.   None, recognized in prior years.
    b.   $5,000 expense.
    c.   $150,000 expense.
    d.   $155,000 expense.

**42. (d)** The requirement is to determine the amount of deferred rent expense at year-end. This problem involves uneven rent payments, and accounting standards require rent expense to be recognized evenly over the contract period. The rent per month to be paid over the 60-month period can be calculated as follows:

| | | $ |
|---|---|---|
| First 3 months | | 0 |
| Next 9 months | 17,500 × 9 | 157,500 |
| Year 2 | 19,000 × 12 | 228,000 |
| Year 3 | 20,500 × 12 | 246,000 |
| Year 4 | 23,000 × 12 | 276,000 |
| Year 5 | 24,500 × 12 | 294,000 |
| Total rent payments | | $1,201,500 |
| Divided by 60 months | | ÷ 60 months |
| | | $ 20,025 per month |

The amount of rent paid as of December 31, 2003, is

| | |
|---|---|
| July 1, 2000 to June 30, 2001 | $157,500 |
| July 1 2001 to June 30, 2002 | 228,000 |
| July 1, 2002 to June 30, 2003 | 246,000 |
| July 1, 2003 to December 30, 2003 | 138,000 (6 months) |
| Total rent paid | $769,500 |

The amount of rent that should be recognized as total rent expense for the period July 1, 2000, to December 31, 2003, is $841,050 (42 months × $20,025 per month). Answer (d) is correct because the amount of rent that should be recorded as deferred/accrued rent expense is $71,550 ($841,050 – $769,500). Note that the question asks for deferred rent but in this case the rent is actually accrued (payable).

**43. (b)** The requirement is to identify the level at which goodwill should be tested for impairment. Answer (b) is correct because, according to SFAS 142, goodwill should be tested for impairment at the reporting unit level. Answers (a), (c), and (d) are incorrect.

**44. (a)** The requirement is to identify the effect of an extraordinary gain. Answer (a) is correct because an extraordinary gain (net of tax) is included after discontinued operations on the income statement to arrive at net income. Extraordinary gains will increase net income.

**45. (b)** The requirement is to determine the amount of expense that should be recognized in the financial statements in year 10. According to SFAS 143, an asset retirement obligation is recognized when incurred and displayed as a liability. The asset retirement cost is capitalized as part of the asset's carrying value and allocated to expense over the asset's useful life. Because year 10 is the final year of the asset's life and a change in estimate is treated on a prospective basis, the additional $5,000 in expense would be recognized in year 10. Therefore, answer (b) is correct because $5,000 ($155,000 – $150,000) would be recognized in year 10.

**46.** The controller of Peabody, Inc. has been asked to present an analysis of accounts receivable collections at the upcoming staff meeting. The following information is used:

|  | 12/31, year 2 | 12/31, year 1 |
|---|---|---|
| Accounts receivable | $100,000 | $130,000 |
| Allowance, doubtful accounts | (20,000) | (40,000) |
| Sales | 400,000 | 200,000 |
| Cost of goods sold | 350,000 | 170,000 |

What is the receivables turnover ratio as of December 31, year 2?

a. 5.0
b. 4.7
c. 3.5
d. 0.6

**47.** Which of the following is generally associated with the terms of convertible debt securities?

a. An interest rate that is lower than nonconvertible debt.
b. An initial conversion price that is less than the market value of the common stock at time of issuance.
c. A noncallable feature.
d. A feature to subordinate the security to nonconvertible debt.

**48.** During the current year, Ace Co. amortized a bond discount. Ace prepares its statement of cash flows using the indirect method. In which section of the statement should Ace report the amortization of the bond discount?

a. Financing activities.
b. Operating activities.
c. Investing activities.
d. Supplemental disclosures.

**49.** Beach Co. determined that the decline in the fair market value (FMV) of an investment was below the amortized cost and permanent in nature. The investment was classified as available-for-sale on Beach's books. The controller would properly record the decrease in FMV by including it in which of the following?

a. Other comprehensive income section of the income statement only.
b. Earnings section of the income statement and writing down the cost basis to FMV.
c. Extraordinary items section of the income statement and writing down the cost basis to FMV.
d. Other comprehensive income section of the income statement, and writing down the cost basis to FMV.

**50.** During the first quarter of the calendar year, Worth Co. had income before taxes of $100,000, and its effective income tax rate was 15%. Worth's effective annual income tax rate for the previous year was 30%. Worth expects that its effective annual income tax rate for the current year will be 25%. The statutory tax rate for the current year is 35%. In its first quarter interim income statement, what amount of income tax expense should Worth report?

a. $15,000
b. $25,000
c. $30,000
d. $35,000

**46. (b)** The requirement is to compute receivables turnover at December 31, year 2. Accounts receivables turnover is calculated as net credit sales divided by average accounts receivable. Average accounts receivable is calculated as (beginning of year A/R plus end of year A/R) divided by 2. If an allowance for doubtful accounts is used, the net realizable value of accounts receivable should be used to calculate average accounts receivable. Therefore, the accounts receivable turnover is 4.7 [400,000/(80,000 + 90.000)/2].

**47. (a)** The requirement is to identify the condition that is generally associated with the terms of convertible debt securities. Answer (a) is correct because convertible debt generally will have an interest rate that is lower than nonconvertible debt. Answers (b), (c), and (d) are incorrect, because these are not features associated with convertible debt.

**48. (b)** The requirement is to identify the section of the statement of cash flows that should contain amortization of bond discount. According to SFAS 95, the payment of interest is an operating activity. Therefore, the adjustments made for bond amortization to change accrual-basis interest expense to the cash interest paid will be reported in the operating section of the statement of cash flows, and answer (b) is correct.

**49. (b)** The requirement is to determine the proper classification of the decrease in FMV of an investment. According to SFAS 115, an available-for-sale security is valued at fair value at the balance sheet date, and any temporary decline in value is recorded in other comprehensive income for the period. However, because the decline was permanent (not temporary in nature), the available-for-sale security should be written down to fair value, and the amount of the write-down should be recorded in the income statement as a loss. Therefore, answer (b) is correct. The new cost basis would not be changed for subsequent recoveries in fair value; however, subsequent increases in the fair value of the available-for-sale security would be included in other comprehensive income in the year of the increase.

*NOTE: This answer assumes the fair value option of SFAS 159 is not elected.*

**50. (b)** The requirement is to determine the amount of income tax expense that should be reported. Answer (b) is correct because the year-to-date income is multiplied by the effective annual income tax rate of the current year (25%) to calculate income tax expense on the interim income statement. Worth should report income tax expense of $25,000 ($100,000 × 25%).

**SIMULATION 1**                                                          (50 to 60 minutes)

| Directions | | | | |
|---|---|---|---|---|
| | **Situation** | **Accounting Treatment** | **Communication** | **Research** |

In the following simulation, you will be asked various questions regarding accounting and reporting for stockholders' equity. You will use the content in the **Information Tabs** to complete the tasks in the **Work Tabs**. (The following pictures are for illustration only; the actual tabs in your simulation may differ from these.)

**Information Tabs:**

| Directions | Situation | Standards | Resources |
|---|---|---|---|

Beginning with the Directions tab at the left side of the screen, go through each of the **Information Tabs** to familiarize yourself with the simulation content. Note that the **Resources** tab will contain useful information, including formulas and definitions, to help you complete the tasks. You may want to refer to this information while you are working.

**Work Tabs:**

| 𝖎Cost Method | 𝖎Amt to Report | 𝖎COGS | 𝖎Invent Costs | 𝖎Form 1065 | 𝖎Communication | 𝖎Review Letter |
|---|---|---|---|---|---|---|

The **Work Tabs,** on the right side of the screen, contain the tasks for you to complete.

Once you complete any part of a task, the pencil for that tab will be shaded. ▌ Note that a shaded pencil does NOT indicate that you have completed the entire task.

You must complete all of the tasks in the **Work Tabs** to receive full credit.

If you have difficulty answering a **Work Tab,** read the tab directions carefully.

*NOTE: If you believe you have encountered a software malfunction, report it to the test center staff immediately.*

| | Situation | | | |
|---|---|---|---|---|
| **Directions** | | **Accounting Treatment** | **Communication** | **Research** |

Quonset, Inc. is a public company whose shares are actively traded in the over-the-counter market. The company's stockholders' equity account balances at December 31, year 1, were as follows:

| | |
|---|---|
| Common stock: $1 par value; 1,650,000 shares authorized; 850,000 shares issued and outstanding | $ 850,000 |
| Additional paid-in capital | 3,100,000 |
| Retained earnings | 3,700,000 |
| Total stockholders' equity | $7,650,000 |

During the year ended December 31, year 2, transactions and other information relating to Quonset's stockholders' equity were as follows:

- On February 1, year 2, Quonset issued 13,000 shares of common stock to Carson Co. in exchange for land. On the date issued, the stock had a market price of $13 per share. The land had a carrying value on Carson's books of $140,000 and an assessed value for property taxes of $95,000.
- On March 5, year 2, Quonset purchased 21,000 of its shares to hold as treasury stock at $12 per share. The shares were originally issued at $13 per share. Quonset uses the cost method to account for treasury stock. Treasury stock is permitted in Quonset's state of incorporation.
- On March 15, year 2, Quonset purchased a portfolio of marketable securities to be held as available-for-sale securities.
- On June 5, year 2, Quonset declared a property dividend of inventory. The inventory had a $65,000 carrying value and a $55,000 fair market value.
- On July 1, year 2, Quonset declared and issued a 15% stock dividend.
- On December 5, year 2, Quonset declared a cash dividend of $1 per share to all common stockholders of record on December 15, year 2. The dividend was paid on January 5, year 3.
- Net income for year 2 was $1,443,000.
- At December 31, year 2, unrealized gain on the portfolio of marketable securities purchased during the year was $95,000, net of tax.

Assume that Quonset does not elect the fair value option for reporting its financial assets.

| | | Accounting Treatment | | | |
|---|---|---|---|---|---|
| **Directions** | **Situation** | | | **Communication** | **Research** |

Using the stockholders' equity balances as of December 31, year 1, and the transactions and other information relating to Quonset's stockholders' equity during year 2, complete the following worksheet analysis of stockholders' equity for year 2. Ignore the effect of income taxes.

For each item in column A

- Enter in column B the effect (if any) on the number of Quonset shares issued and outstanding.
- Enter in columns C through G the dollar amount effect (if any) on the appropriate equity account(s).

Total stockholders' equity values at column H and ending balance in row 10 will automatically calculate based on your entries.

Enter increases to stockholders' equity as positive numbers and decreases to stockholders' equity as negative numbers. If there is no amount to enter in a particular shaded cell, enter a value of zero (0).

| | A | B | C | D | E | F | G | H |
|---|---|---|---|---|---|---|---|---|
| 1 | Accounts | Number of shares issued and outstanding | Common stock | Additional paid-in capital | Retained earnings | Accumulated other comprehensive income (loss) | Treasury stock | Total stockholders' equity |
| 2 | Beginning balances | | | | | | | |
| 3 | Issuance of shares for property | | | | | | | |
| 4 | Purchase of treasury stock | | | | | | | |
| 5 | Property dividends distributed | | | | | | | |
| 6 | Stock dividend issued | | | | | | | |
| 7 | Cash dividend | | | | | | | |
| 8 | Net income for the year | | | | | | | |
| 9 | Unrealized gain (loss) on marketable securities available-for-sale | | | | | | | |
| 10 | Ending balances | | | | | | | |

| | | | **Communication** | | |
|---|---|---|---|---|---|
| **Directions** | **Situation** | **Accounting Treatment** | | | **Research** |

The management of Quonset, Inc. intends to issue stock options to key employees. Generally accepted accounting principles (GAAP) requires the fair value method of accounting for stock options. As the CFO of the company, write a memo to management discussing the fair value method of measuring and accounting for the cost of stock options. Include in your memo a discussion of when the cost is recognized for book purposes and the financial statement impacts of this recognition.

Type you communication in the response area below the horizontal line using the word processor provided.

*REMINDER: Your response will be graded for both technical content and writing skills. Technical content will be evaluated for information that is helpful to the intended reader and clearly relevant to the issue. Writing skills will be evaluated for development, organization, and the appropriate expression of ideas in professional correspondence. Use a standard business memo or letter format with a clear beginning, middle, and end. Do not convey information in the form of a table, bullet point list, or other abbreviated presentation.*

To:

From:

| | | | | **Research** |
|---|---|---|---|---|
| **Directions** | **Situation** | **Accounting Treatment** | **Communication** | |

The company made open-market purchases of its own common stock with the intent to reissue the shares in the future. It is anticipated that the market price of the stock will be in excess of the purchase price when the stock is reissued. List the proper citation from the authoritative literature that provides guidance as to how the company should account for the excess of the market price at the time of reissuance over the purchase price of the common stock.

Find guidance in the FASB Standards that authoritatively addresses the situation above. To complete this task, first split the screen and choose this tab (the RESEARCH tab) in one window and the STANDARDS tab in the other. Use the search capabilities provided by the STANDARDS tab to find the numbered paragraph in either the Original Pronouncements or Current Text that addresses the issue above. Click (highlight) the appropriate numbered paragraph and then click on the **TRANSFER**

**TO ANSWER** button located in the upper left of the STANDARDS tab. Your selected paragraph will appear in the answer space below.

*NOTE: A paragraph may include one or more subparagraphs; all parts of a paragraph will be considered part of your answer, even if they are not highlighted and transferred to the answer space with the numbered paragraph.*

*If you try to transfer more than one numbered paragraph, the previous one will be replaced by the current selection.*

*If your cursor turns to a ⊘ symbol, the text is not selectable as a response. Correct responses must be chosen from numbered paragraphs and never appear in unselectable text.*

*The Copy and Paste icons on the helm do **not** work with this tab. Use the **TRANSFER TO ANSWER** button on the Standards tab to complete the task.*

**SOLUTION TO SIMULATION 1**

| | Directions | Situation | Accounting Treatment | | | Communication | Research |
|---|---|---|---|---|---|---|---|

| | A | B | C | D | E | F | G | H |
|---|---|---|---|---|---|---|---|---|
| 1 | Accounts | Number of shares issued and outstanding | Common stock | Additional paid-in capital | Retained earnings | Accumulated other comprehensive income (loss) | Treasury stock | Total stockholders' equity |
| 2 | Beginning balances | 850,000 | 850,000 | 3,100,000 | 3,700,000 | | | 7,650,000 |
| 3 | Issuance of shares for property | 13,000 | 13,000 | 156,000 | | | | 169,000 |
| 4 | Purchase of treasury stock | –21,000 | | | | | –252,000 | –252,000 |
| 5 | Property dividends distributed | | | | –55,000 | | | –55,000 |
| 6 | Stock dividend issued | 126,300 | 126,300 | | –126,300 | | | 0 |
| 7 | Cash dividend | | | | –968,000 | | | –968,300 |
| 8 | Net income for the year | | | | 1,443,000 | | | 1,443,000 |
| 9 | Unrealized gain (loss) on marketable securities available-for-sale | | | | | 95,000 | | 95,000 |
| 10 | Ending balances | 968,300 | 989,300 | 3,256,000 | 3,993,400 | 95,000 | –252,000 | 8,081,700 |

## Explanation of Solution

2/1  Issue 13,000 shares of common stock for land.  The fair value of the stock is $13.  The journal entry to record the issue of the stock is

| | | |
|---|---|---|
| Land | 169,000 | |
|     Common stock | | 13,000 |
|     Additional paid-in capital | | 156,000 |

3/5  The journal entry to record the treasury stock is

| | | |
|---|---|---|
| Treasury stock | 252,000 | |
|     Cash | | 252,000 |

    (21,000 shares × $12 = 252,000)

3/15  There is no effect on the stockholders' equity.

6/5  The journal entry to record the property dividend at fair value is

| | | |
|---|---|---|
| Retained earnings | 55,000 | |
|     Inventory | | 55,000 |

    Note that the loss on inventory would be recorded on the income statement, and is already included in the amount given for net income for the year.

7/1  Normally a stock dividend less than 20-25% of the outstanding shares of stock would be valued at fair value.  However, in this problem, no fair value of the stock was indicated.  The AICPA solution indicates the dividend is recorded at the par value.  First, the number of shares outstanding must be calculated as follows:  Original shares outstanding 850,000 + 13,000 new shares issued – 21,000 shares of treasury stock = 842,000 shares outstanding × 15% = 126,300 shares for the stock dividend × $1 par = $126,300.

    The journal entry to record the stock dividend is

| | | |
|---|---|---|
| Retained earnings | 126,300 | |
|     Common stock | | 126,300 |

12/6

| | | |
|---|---|---|
| Retained earnings | 968,300 | |
|     Dividends payable | | 968,300 |

    To calculate the cash dividend, the number of shares of stock is required.  The number of shares before the stock dividend is 842,000 + 126,300 new shares issued for a stock dividend = 968,300 shares of stock × $1 dividend per share = $968,300.

12/31  The journal entry to record net income includes a credit to retained earnings of $1,443,000.

12/31  The journal entry to record the unrealized gain on available-for-sale securities is

| | | |
|---|---|---|
| Investments (available-for-sale) | 95,000 | |
|     Unrealized gain on AFS securities—OCI | | 95,000 |

| Directions | Situation | Accounting Treatment | Communication | Research |
|---|---|---|---|---|

To:      Manager, Quonset, Inc.
From:    CPA Candidate
Re:       Accounting for stock compensation

Accounting for stock compensation to employees is governed by the accounting rules in SFAS 123(R), issued in December 2004. These rules apply to all share-based payments issued in the form of stock shares, share options, or other equity instruments.

Share-based payments to employees are measured at fair value on the grant date or measurement date. The fair value of the option is measured based on the observable market price of an option with the same or similar terms and conditions. Valuing the option can be estimated using an options pricing model such as the Black-Scholes model.

The employee service cost or compensation cost is the fair value of the shares less any amounts the employee is required to pay for the shares. At the measurement date, the compensation cost is recorded by debiting deferred compensation expense (a contra equity account) and crediting stock options outstanding (an equity account) on the balance sheet. The deferred compensation cost is then amortized on a straight-line basis to compensation expense over the requisite service period. The requisite service period is the period in which the employee is required to provide the services in order to receive the stock options.

No compensation cost is recognized if an employee forfeits the shares because a service or performance condition is not met. However, if an employee renders the requisite service and the options expire or are not exercised, previously recognized compensation expense is not reversed.

If you would like additional help or guidance in measuring the fair value of stock options or preparing the required accounting entries, please contact my office.

*[Signature]*

*[Date]*

| Directions | Situation | Accounting Treatment | Communication | Research |
|---|---|---|---|---|

Current text C23.103 or APB 6, par. 12(b).